# DICTIONARY

OF

# NATIONAL BIOGRAPHY

1941–1950

THE

# DICTIONARY

OF

# NATIONAL BIOGRAPHY

---

## 1941–1950

Edited by L. G. Wickham Legg

and

E. T. Williams

---

With an Index covering the years 1901–1950
in one alphabetical series

OXFORD UNIVERSITY PRESS

1959

*Oxford University Press, Amen House, London E.C.4*

GLASGOW NEW YORK TORONTO MELBOURNE WELLINGTON
BOMBAY CALCUTTA MADRAS KARACHI KUALA LUMPUR
CAPE TOWN IBADAN NAIROBI ACCRA

© *Oxford University Press 1959*

PRINTED IN GREAT BRITAIN

# PREFATORY NOTE

THE 725 men and women recorded in this Supplement had this in common: all for a significant period of their lives were British subjects; all died between 1 January 1941 and 31 December 1950. One was born as early as 1845; another remembered seeing Wellington. By contrast, the two youngest were born as late as 1918, in the closing months of one war, to die in another. Some met violent deaths, by accident or by enemy action; a few died by their own hand. Most, however, their labours done, died in their beds. These labours varied exceedingly. Yet, in one way or another, all the men and women to be met here revealed in their several labours qualities which marked them out from among their fellows. To try to write a nation's history from their brief biographies would be to draw one's evidence only from the unusual; moreover, it must be remembered that it is only the decade in which they died which brings them together here. Even so, much of the story of the first half of this century in Great Britain and beyond is necessarily reflected in the thousand pages which follow: the development, for example, of a 'Welfare State' or of a Labour party at home, of the separate but linked nationhoods of the British Commonwealth abroad; significant advances in science and in medicine; distinguished contributions to literature and the arts. Eight Nobel prizewinners are recorded here and (before adding one who died, his appointment to the Order not yet announced) no fewer than eighteen members of the Order of Merit: architects, chemists, doctors, lawyers, painters, philosophers, physicists, sociologists, sailors, soldiers, statesmen. As well as two prime ministers of this country—Lloyd George and Baldwin—here also are Mackenzie King and Bennett of Canada, Smuts and Hertzog of South Africa, with other prime ministers from the British Commonwealth, three from Australia, for example, and three from New Zealand, among them Peter Fraser. One in every seven of the worthies here described had a clergyman for father or was a son of the manse. More than half received a university education; some had no formal schooling at all. Right across the lives of all, whatever their opportunity, whatever their avocation, came the impact of two world wars. Many lost sons, some their own lives. In a volume such as this, recording achievement more obviously than promise, few young men and women may be commemorated in detail. Those who are individually recorded here, Rex Whistler, Robert Byron, Guy Gibson, Amy Johnson, Orde Wingate, or Adrian Warburton, may perhaps be held to represent not just their unique selves but to stand symbol, too, for many others of a generation scythed suddenly and before its time.

Many of those included took part in one or in the other war, some in both. Six of the admirals here remembered saw service in their day

v

at Jutland. Roger Keyes reminds us of Zeebrugge; Bertram Ramsay of Dunkirk; Harwood of the river Plate. Reginald Hall created naval intelligence in the first war; in the second, for three strenuous years Dudley Pound was first sea lord. On the western front Elles took into action at Cambrai the tanks which Tritton had provided; Herbert Lawrence was Haig's chief of the general staff throughout the battles of 1918; Maud McCarthy directed the nursing services from the first day to the last. Ian Hamilton and Braithwaite were at Gallipoli; Milne in Salonika; Cavan at the Piave; Chetwode, Chauvel, and Archibald Murray in Egypt and Palestine. In the second war Gort kept the British Expeditionary Force intact and later Malta; Wavell on a shoestring won those first desert victories, Gott and Campbell among his paladins. With one brief exception, there is record here of every chief of the imperial general staff from Cavan to John Dill; as there is also of every British ambassador in Berlin between the wars and of all but one of those in Paris. The volume commemorates too the rise of the Royal Air Force, its early days marked by men such as Burnett, Gossage, Higgins, Mitchell, and Swann, as well as by Maurice Baring's service as personal staff officer to the R.A.F.'s creator; its leaders in a second war by men like Peter Drummond, Coningham of the Desert Air Force, or Leigh-Mallory, the air commander (alongside Bertram Ramsay) for the invasion of Normandy in 1944. Just as, long before, Narbeth had designed the *Dreadnought,* so for this new dimension Bird built the Spitfires and Roy Chadwick designed the Lancasters which Adrian Warburton and Guy Gibson were to pilot.

War, too, found its artists: in Paul Nash, Francis Dodd, William Rothenstein, Eric Ravilious, or C. R. W. Nevinson whose father H. W. Nevinson shone in a gallery of fine war correspondents, as Cruttwell among war historians. There followed, in commemoration, the Imperial War Graves Commission devised by Fabian Ware; the Imperial War Museum with ffoulkes as its first curator; Hardiman's powerful statue of Haig; Strachan's stained-glass windows at Edinburgh Castle; the moving simplicity of Lutyens's Cenotaph; or the memory of a poem 'For the Fallen' from the heart of Laurence Binyon.

War split a great political party and thus made room for another. The kaleidoscopic and war-winning dynamism of Lloyd George broke the Liberals (as Margot Asquith had sensed) and changed the potential career of men like Walter Runciman or that of Reginald McKenna who joined that banking world of which Montagu Norman was for so long the acknowledged and mysterious head—and J. H. Clapham the chosen historian. Nor would that gifted pre-war administration which silhouetted the welfare state have been so impressive without the aid of great civil servants like Llewellyn Smith, Hopwood, Bradbury, or Warren Fisher then just beginning that vigorous career which took him to the headship of the Civil Service; the help too of medical administrators such as Newman and Newsholme; of industrial arbitrators of the calibre of Askwith; perhaps also of soldiers of the temper of Macready to sustain the civil power. The party which came to take the Liberal place had itself still to come together in organized unity. Among the influences here to be perceived were: the trade-union movement in the lives of Ben Tillett, Will Thorne, or Tom Mann—all prominent, with John Burns, in the great dock strike of 1889—and of J. R. Clynes or J. H. Thomas, both members of the first Labour Cabinet; the Fabian Society with Sidney and Beatrice Webb, George Bernard Shaw, and Sydney Olivier among its moving spirits, and H. G. Wells for a time an impatient member; university teachers like Harold Laski; an older evangelistic Radicalism in Robert Blatchford's *Merrie England*; the Independent Labour Party in James Maxton; the 'distressed areas' which found a champion in Ellen Wilkinson. If there is here no obvious representative of that strong and familiar Labour link with Nonconformity there is by contrast the outstanding and beloved example of William Temple, the first archbishop to have been a member of the Labour Party. Perhaps also not unimportant to Labour's rise was that Conservative prime minister who conceived it his duty to respect the parliamentary Labour party and who, by lowering the temperature of party strife, as also by steering the Commonwealth through the crisis of the royal abdication, may have made his contribution (if few then thought so) to the unity in which this country entered upon a second world war.

For nearly a quarter of the present century two men in their very differing modes dominated our domestic politics and their own restive followers; for Stanley Baldwin's chosen ways were deliberately different from Lloyd George's and fitted more cosily into the Chequers which Lee of Fareham provided and Blomfield restored for our prime ministers. Perhaps nowadays, as his signal contribution to victory ebbs into history, our attention is too readily directed to the defects of Lloyd George's brilliant qualities. The British constitution is scarcely geared to accommodate genius, in peacetime. There were other divisive matters: Ireland and India, for example. Here are recorded the Curragh incident in the life of Seely, the last Irish viceroy in FitzAlan of Derwent, with Crewe among his predecessors (and a link with the first Home Rule bill), the last chief secretary in Hamar Greenwood, the last lord chief justice of all Ireland in Thomas Molony. Here too are Indian viceroys like Hardinge, Willingdon, or Wavell; governors like Lytton, the energetic George Lloyd, or F. S. Jackson, the cricketer; Indian Civil Servants of the stature of Marris; missionaries like Graham or Tyndale-Biscoe; policemen as imperturbable as Tegart; judges with Rankin's grasp of Indian jurisprudence; philologists like George Grierson; or Indian writers such as Rabindranath Tagore. The creators of New Delhi, Herbert Baker and Edwin Lutyens, are here; and with them the creators of new India itself, Gandhi and Patel, as Jinnah of Pakistan.

Hardly less significant to the Commonwealth than growth in nationhood was the progress in this half-century in communications. We find here the development of the motor-car by Lanchester and Austin, of motor-racing by Malcolm Campbell; the construction of the *Queen Mary* and the *Queen Elizabeth* through the confidence of Royden and Bates; Whitten Brown's navigation of that first non-stop aerial crossing of the Atlantic, record-breaking flights by Amy Johnson, the new vocation of test-pilot in the story of Geoffrey de Havilland. We remember too in the career of Wakefield or Cadman the oil which made such haste possible; Elphinstone's invention of the speedometer; the Merlin engine produced by Rolls-Royce under the direction of Sidgreaves; or Hele-Shaw's automatic variable-pitch airscrew. The engineers and scientists were hurrying us all into a new era. The heavens again became of interest to the layman (an interest subsequently reinforced by the need to navigate in a desert) through the writings of Eddington and Jeans: at a time when Plaskett was developing stellar spectroscopy for the initiated, A. N. Whitehead attempting a bridge for the philosopher, and Aston establishing the phenomenon of isotopy. To take but one letter of the alphabet, we may note the pioneer work of Barkla on the polarization of X-rays, in crystallography by William Bragg, or Vernon Boys's accurate instruments, Blackman's work in photosynthesis, Biffen's on plant-breeding, or that of Berkeley (among the last, with Rayleigh, to have his private laboratory) on osmotic pressure. Banting and his colleagues—in this typical of the teamwork and interdependence which modern scientific researches so notably demand—discovered insulin; Gowland Hopkins the vitamin and the lore of biochemistry; Collie took the first X-ray photograph of metal in the human body. It was an age of great advances in medicine and in surgery. No parent but might think with gratitude of the pioneer work in paediatrics of Parsons or Still, or of Almroth Wright in immunology; no cripple but may have received some alleviation of his plight because of the skill in orthopaedics of Girdlestone or Agnes Hunt. The nursing profession owes its debt to Mrs. Fenwick and Rosalind Paget; as the medical profession to the statesmanship of Dawson of Penn. In the art of healing Herbert Barker was a controversial figure; and in Spilsbury and Willcox we may note again that modern interdependence: medicine at the service of the law.

We may remark too the growing application of science to industry: in the work of men like Pickard or by way of Frank Heath's Department of Scientific and Industrial Research, a fruitful outcome of the first war. Notable also are some of the great amalgamations which followed upon that war: the railways, exemplified by Granet and Stamp; London Transport, by Ashfield and Pick; the gas industry, by Milne-Watson; Imperial Chemical Industries, by Bain; or Unilever, by D'Arcy Cooper. The profits of modern industry in their turn made possible great artistic benefactions, as the life and taste of Samuel

Courtauld made evident. And we may well be grateful for the encouragement of art by industry: in Frank Pick's insistence on using the lettering of men like Edward Johnston; in Hornby's influence upon commercial printing; and in the development of the poster with patrons like Luke and practitioners of the quality of William Nicholson and Pryde or the output of John Hassall. In the new movements in art itself we may record the influence of such men as Wilson Steer, Sickert, Pissarro, D. S. MacColl, or Frederick Brown.

In literature as in art it was inevitably an age of unrest and experimentation and we moved a long way from the robust traditionalism of Quiller-Couch, the perky optimism of H. G. Wells, even the fertility of Hugh Walpole, to the essentially private but immensely influential writing of James Joyce and Virginia Woolf. From the romantic 'nineties of Le Gallienne, Symons, and Rhys we have made the long journey to Orwell's *Nineteen Eighty-Four*. Perhaps only the nursery classics of Beatrix Potter remain almost undated. Newspapers too were changing: great editors like J. A. Spender or A. G. Gardiner—both casualties of the Liberal split—yielding place to those like R. D. Blumenfeld or proprietors like Southwood; although Geoffrey Dawson's influence continued in Barrington-Ward, and Crozier would still find room for leader-writers of the calibre of J. L. Hammond; nor, at the week-end, was J. L. Garvin unmindful of the arts.

To the theatre came the stimulus of Shaw's plays and Granville-Barker's productions; matched by actors like Henry Ainley, or by Violet and Irene Vanbrugh leading their graceful way to make the stage an accepted career for women of education. To music the educative talent of Hugh Allen and Walford Davies brought a wider appreciation, as Ambrose Fleming, by his invention of the wireless valve, a new dimension and a permanence to Henry Wood's Promenade Concerts. By wireless, too, in a second wartime, Tommy Handley could make an ebullient contribution, only comparable with that of Harry Lauder, in a more personal medium, in the earlier and, for the British, more cruel slaughter. Oswald Stoll had barely made the music-hall fit for the family before it began to yield place to the cinema, commemorated here in the lives of George Arliss, Leslie Howard, or Dame May Whitty, as well as by Tyrrell, one of the very ablest of our diplomatists, whose countrymen, ironically enough, knew him best perhaps as the censor of their films. And today television, the outcome of J. L. Baird's lonely researches, is in its turn providing the cinema with a rival as, we are told, family life with a new focus.

In the meantime Gordon Selfridge revolutionized our shops and Maynard Keynes our economics; Lugard reconceived our methods of colonial government as Alec Paterson our prisons. A casual choice from among the institutions with which we have grown familiar will reveal the variety of men's tastes and wishes in this first half-century: Baden-Powell's Boy Scouts; the Victoria and Albert Museum of which

Harcourt-Smith became the first director as recently as 1909; Chatham House with which we associate the names of Power and Meston; the Church Army of Prebendary Carlile; P.A.Y.E. devised under Kingsley Wood; Women's Institutes, introduced by Mrs. Alfred Watt; Whipsnade, the achievement of Chalmers Mitchell; Wycombe Abbey, Frances Dove's public school for girls; the London School of Economics, the creation of the Webbs. In this regard we may note too, if not the birth, then the coming of age, of the civic universities of the United Kingdom; reflected here in the careers of Mackinder, Sibly, or de Burgh at Reading, Michael Sadler at Leeds, Grant Robertson and de Selincourt at Birmingham, or the number of those who served together, though not always in unison, in the university of Liverpool: Charles Reilly, Bernard Pares, Oliver Elton, H. C. K. Wyld, and Ramsay Muir. Most notably is it exhibited by those scientists who, in putting their individual departments into a premier place, thereby brought the whole university in which they were so admirably serving into a greater prominence: P. F. Frankland and Norman Haworth at Birmingham, for example, or Kipping at Nottingham. Two administrative devices vitally affecting our universities also make their appearance: for Frank Heath was not only the first secretary of the Department of Scientific and Industrial Research but also helped to establish the University Grants Committee. From the many scholars recorded in this volume, may it suffice to single out, with Arthur Evans or A. F. Pollard, only, in addition, those members of the Order of Merit not yet mentioned here among their fellows: James Frazer, J. W. Mackail, and William Holdsworth.

Many have left their names behind them as a label, an abbreviation—in a discovery or invention, perhaps: 'the Barcroft', 'Barlow's disease', the 'Bulloch jar', or the 'Ryle tube', not to mention 'Hardy's law' in genetics which G. H. Hardy himself apparently set little store by; 'the Lane technique' in surgery, or the mineral Miersite. Others will be remembered by an Act of Parliament—Rowlatt, for example—or, not infrequently, by a street-name; even by having a mountain called after them. Others, however, may more often be commemorated by their chairmanships: the May committee, the Sankey commission, or the Uthwatt report. Or they may be remembered by a memorandum, as in Selborne's case, by a belt (as well as a library) in Lonsdale's, a forage-cap in Brodrick's, in Derby's a scheme, in Portal's a prefabricated house, a race-course in Mildmay's, a green in the case of Reilly, a medical textbook in Hale-White's, or as an adjective like Heath Robinson. Others will always have their name, gladly, associated with a cause, as Ethel Smyth's with women's suffrage, or Eleanor Rathbone's with family allowances. Nor should it be thought, because they are not mentioned by name in this prefatory comment upon a changing world, that we are unmindful of those commemorated in this volume who by their services to religion and to even-handed justice helped to substantiate and enrich those traditions for which this country fought in two world wars.

To live in retrospect among 725 men and women such as these has been a most interesting experience; through them, rewarding too to have met, at least by correspondence, those who have so generously consented to write about them. In yielding here their personal knowledge of a worthy, contributors have more than compensated, it is our belief, for the inevitable loss of objectivity by the freshness of an intimacy not otherwise to be recaptured. In compiling a volume of this kind, hard upon the event, much detail remains not yet available. These notices necessarily represent *interim* judgements, written when possible by those who knew personally the men and women concerned. We have usually chosen, however, to invite to contribute neither a close relative nor the author of the 'official' biography: a practice, it will be remarked, not invariably observed. When usefully relevant publications have come to our attention subsequently to the completion of a notice for printing, in some instances they have been added in brackets, below the contributor's signature. There are many quotations in a volume such as this: all of which we would wish to acknowledge here; and in particular the permission to quote kindly granted by the following authors and publishers: the late Mr. L. S. Amery and Hutchinson & Co. (from *My Political Life*); John Murray (from Henry Page Croft: *Twenty-two Months under Fire*); Sir Lewis Namier and Hamish Hamilton (from *Avenues of History*); Sir Harold Nicolson (from his *Lord Carnock* and his *Peacemaking*); Lady Peck and Faber & Faber (from *A Little Learning*); Sir Osbert Sitwell and Macmillan & Co. (from *Laughter in the Next Room*).

Mr. L. G. Wickham Legg, who edited the previous Supplement, began this volume and had made almost ready for printing many of the notices of those who died before the end of 1945. In this he was greatly assisted by two successive sub-editors, Miss K. E. M. Ross and Miss Helen M. Palmer. The present Editor's responsibility has been to complete the volume. His delay in the task has meant that many contributors have been troubled again as new evidence has become available. He wishes to thank them all for their friendly patience and their invariable helpfulness. Further, he would like especially to acknowledge the valuable advice given to Mr. Wickham Legg or to himself by the following: Dr. H. K. Andrews, Sir Thomas Armstrong, Mr. C. T. Atkinson, Sir Vincent Baddeley, Mr. J. N. L. Baker, Mr. R. P. Bell, Mr. A. M. Binnie, Mr. W. J. Bishop, Sir James Bowker, Sir Denis Boyd, Sir Lawrence Bragg, Lord Brand, Mr. Martin S. Briggs, Sir Alan Burns, Sir Patrick Cadell, Sir Alexander Cadogan, the late Sir Hugh Cairns, Lord David Cecil, Dr. R. W. Chapman, Mr. D. N. Chester, the late Mr. E. Graham Clark, Sir George Clark, Professor G. D. H. Cole, Dr. Alexander Cooke, the late Dr. H. W. Dickinson, Sir George Dyson, Captain John Ellerton,

Sir Robert Ensor, Professor Cyril Falls, Air Vice-Marshal W. F. MacNeece Foster, Sir Ralph Furse, Mrs. E. S. Goodrich, Mr. W. Curtis Green, Sir Percival Griffiths, the late Sir Henry Guy, Lord Hailey, Professor H. G. Hanbury, Sir Keith Hancock, Sir Harold Hartley, Dr. Trevor Heaton, Sir Cyril Hinshelwood, the Rev. Dr. L. Hodgson, Mr. G. T. Hollis, the late Lord Horder, Sir Frederick Hoyer Millar, Lord Hurcomb, Sir Robert Hutchison, Mr. J. F. Kerslake, Professor W. B. R. King, Sir Walter Lamb, the Very Rev. John Lowe, the late Sir Ian MacAlister, the late Very Rev. Dr. Norman Maclean, the late Sir Dougal Malcolm, Dr. D. C. Martin, Colonel Kenneth Mason, Professor P. B. Medawar, the Rev. Dr. Nathaniel Micklem, the late Sir Humphrey Milford, Professor N. F. Mott, the late Professor Gilbert Murray, Mr. J. C. Nerney, Sir Lancelot Oliphant, the late Dr. C. S. Orwin, Dr. K. T. Parker, the late Sir Richard Peck, Sir James Penny, Professor H. H. Plaskett, the late Professor G. V. Portus, Sir Maurice Powicke, Professor M. H. L. Pryce, Sir David Pye, Mr. Michael Richey, Sir David Ross, Sir Paul Sinker, Professor J. A. Steers, Lord Tedder, Rear-Admiral H. G. Thursfield, Professor E. C. Titchmarsh, Miss Margaret Toynbee, Professor J. A. Westrup, Dr. K. C. Wheare, the late Mr. Geoffrey Whitworth, the Right Rev. the Bishop of Winchester, and Professor L. J. Witts. The Editor hopes that nobody who has in any way contributed to this volume in writing or by counsel remains by his negligence unthanked. A few especial gratitudes remain to be conveyed: to Dr. Austin Lane Poole, for example. Nor would this Supplement have ever reached the public as it is even now, were it not for the tenaciously conscientious pursuit of accuracy by Miss Helen Palmer, its Assistant Editor, whose persistent and perceptive industry and whose friendship the Editor here acknowledges most humbly. He is truly thankful. He would wish, also, on her behalf especially, to thank the staff of the Bodleian and its associated Libraries for many ungrudging kindnesses. He is personally most grateful, too, to two successive Secretaries to the Delegates of the Oxford University Press, Mr. A. L. P. Norrington and Mr. C. H. Roberts, together with their staff, for their habit of making it so very pleasant to be one of their editors.

E. T. W.


*Rhodes House, Oxford*

*5 November* 1958

ADAM, Colin Gurdon Forbes:
*Lloyd (G. A.).*
ADCOCK, Sir Frank Ezra:
*Charlesworth.*
†ADDISON, Sir Joseph:
*Vincent (D'Abernon).*
†ALINGTON, Cyril Argentine:
*Lyttelton.*
†ALLEN, Herbert Stanley:
*Barkla.*
ALLEN, Herbert Warner:
*Gwynne.*
†ALNESS, Robert Munro, Baron:
*Aitchison.*
ALTHAM, Harry Surtees:
*MacLaren.*
ANDERSON, Mosa Isabel:
*Noel-Buxton.*
†ANSELL, William Henry:
*Ashbee.*
ARMER, Sir (Isaac) Frederick:
*Gibbon.*
ARMSTRONG, Sir Thomas Henry Wait:
*Gardiner (H. B.); Wood (T.).*
ASHTON-GWATKIN, Frank Trelawny Arthur:
*Tyrrell.*
ASPINALL-OGLANDER, Cecil Faber:
*Beatrice; Hamilton.*
ASTOR OF HEVER, John Jacob Astor, Baron:
*Somers-Cocks (Somers).*
†ATKINS, Sir Ivor Algernon:
*Colles.*
†ATKINS, John Black:
*Brodrick (Midleton).*
ATKINSON, Christopher Thomas:
*Elles; Haking.*
ATKINSON, William Christopher:
*Stevenson.*

BABINGTON, Sir Philip:
*Mitchell (W. G. S.).*
BABINGTON SMITH, Constance:
*Warburton.*
BADDELEY, Sir Vincent Wilberforce:
*Bacon; Browning; Goodenough; Greene; Halsey; Lee.*
†BADELEY, Henry John Fanshawe Badeley, Baron:
*Arthur (Connaught and Strathearn).*
†BAILEY, Cyril:
*Mackail; Walker (E.).*
BAILEY, Frederick Marshman:
*Macartney.*
†BAILLIE, Donald Macpherson:
*Cairns.*
BAILLIE, John:
*Martin.*
BALL, Sir William Valentine:
*Watson (Thankerton).*
BARKER, Sir Ernest:
*Muir.*
†BARNE, George Dunsford:
*Tyndale-Biscoe.*

BARNS, John Wintour Baldwin:
*Gunn.*
BARRINGTON-WARD, Mark:
*Garvin.*
BARSTOW, Sir George Lewis:
*May.*
BARTLETT, Sir Frederic Charles:
*Myers (C. S.).*
†BARTON, Edwin Alfred:
*Barlow.*
†BATES, Frederic Alan:
*Royden.*
BATTISCOMBE, Georgina:
*Orczy.*
BEAGLEHOLE, John Cawte:
*Fraser.*
BEAN, Charles Edwin Woodrow:
*Chauvel; Gellibrand.*
BEAUMAN, Eric Bentley:
*Drummond; Higgins (J. F. A.); Sutton.*
BELGRAVE, Sir Charles Dalrymple:
*Sykes.*
BELL, Sir Harold Idris:
*Crum; Flower.*
BELLASIS, Margaret:
*Dashwood (E. M. Delafield); Hannay (George A. Birmingham); Hichens; Oppenheim.*
†BENIANS, Ernest Alfred:
*Rose.*
†BENNETT, George Macdonald:
*Robertson (R.).*
BENNETT, Henry Stanley:
*Coulton.*
BERRY, Sidney Malcolm:
*Jones (J. D.).*
BEST, Charles Herbert:
*Banting.*
BETJEMAN, John:
*Tyrwhitt-Wilson (Berners).*
BEVERIDGE, William Henry Beveridge, Baron:
*Stamp.*
BINCHY, Daniel Anthony:
*MacNeill.*
BING, Gertrud:
*Saxl.*
BIRCUMSHAW, Louis Leighton:
*Haworth.*
BIRLEY, Robert:
*Marten.*
BISHOP, William John:
*Arkwright; Armstrong-Jones; Buzzard; Gauvain; Oliver (T.); Rolleston; Still; Topley; Walker (N. P.); Wallace; Wheeler; Willcox; Yorke.*
BLACKMAN, Vernon Herbert:
*Farmer.*
†BLAGDEN, Claude Martin:
*Strong (T. B.).*
BLUNDEN, Edmund Charles:
*Bottomley; Nichols.*

BOASE, Thomas Sherrer Ross:
*Courtauld.*
BODKIN, Thomas:
*Lavery.*
†BONE, Stephen:
*Schwabe.*
BOWERMAN, Elsie Edith:
*Dove.*
†BRAILSFORD, Henry Noel:
*Garnett; Nevinson (H. W.).*
†BREBNER, John Bartlet:
*Wrong.*
BREWIS, John Salusbury:
*Palmer (Selborne).*
BRIDGE, Joseph Fenwick:
*Ellis.*
†BRIERLY, James Leslie:
*Williams (J. F.).*
BRIGGS, George Edward:
*Blackman.*
BRIGGS, Martin Shaw:
*Blomfield; Horder; Voysey.*
BRITTAIN, Frederick:
*Manning; Quiller-Couch.*
BROCKINGTON, Colin Fraser:
*Ryle.*
BROCKMAN, Ronald Vernon:
*Pound.*
BROGAN, Denis William:
*Lewis (W. H.).*
†BROOKS, Frederick Tom:
*Buller; Hill (A. W.).*
†BROWN, Sir Frank Herbert:
*Freeman-Thomas (Willingdon); Meston.*
BROWN, Ivor John Carnegie:
*Agate; Lauder.*
BRUNYATE, John Waddingham:
*Uthwatt.*
BRYSON, Alice Stewart Glegg:
*Fenwick.*
BRYSON, John Norman:
*Reid.*
BUCKNILL, Sir Alfred Townsend, Lord Justice Bucknill:
*Langton.*
BULLARD, Sir Reader William:
*Young (H. W.).*
BULLOCK, Sir Ernest:
*Bairstow.*
BURKILL, Isaac Henry:
*Prain.*
BURKILL, John Charles:
*Young (W. H.).*
BURNE, Alfred Higgins:
*Campbell (J. C.).*
BURNETT, Richard George:
*Smith (R.).*
BURNS, Sir Alan Cuthbert:
*Bourdillon; Cameron (D. C.).*
BUTTERWORTH, John Blackstock:
*Atkin.*

CALDER, (Peter) Ritchie:
*Wells.*
CALLAWAY, William Bertram:
*Leigh-Mallory.*
†CALMAN, William Thomas:
*Thompson (D'A. W.).*

CAMERON, Sir Gordon Roy:
*Parsons (L. G.).*
CAMERON, John Cameron, Lord:
*Fleming (D. P.).*
CAMPBELL, John McLeod:
*Azariah.*
CAMPBELL, (John) Maurice (Hardman):
*Hale-White.*
†CAMPION, Gilbert Francis Montriou Campion, Baron:
*FitzRoy; Lowther (Ullswater).*
†CARPENTER, Geoffrey Douglas Hale:
*Poulton.*
CARR, Sir Cecil Thomas:
*Binnie; Graham-Harrison.*
CARTON, Ronald Lewis:
*Higgins (E. J.).*
CASSON, Sir Lewis:
*Granville-Barker; Webster (B. and M. L.).*
CASSWELL, Joshua David:
*Hawke.*
†CAVE, Sydney:
*Garvie.*
CAZALET, Peter Victor Ferdinand:
*Mildmay.*
CECIL, Lord (Edward Christian) David (Gascoyne):
*Woolf.*
CHALLENGER, Frederick:
*Kipping.*
CHALMERS, William Scott:
*Brock.*
CHAPMAN, Robert William:
*Gordon.*
CHAPMAN, Sydney:
*Jeans.*
CHARLES, Fred:
*Nunn.*
CHARLTON, George:
*Brown (F.).*
CHILSTON, Eric Alexander Akers-Douglas, Viscount:
*Akers-Douglas (Chilston).*
CHRISTOPHERSON, Derman Guy:
*Hele-Shaw.*
CLARK, Sir George Norman:
*Clapham (J. H.); Pollard (A. F.).*
CLARKE, Sir (Henry) Ashley:
*Clive.*
†CLAY, Sir Henry:
*Flux; Norman.*
CLEGG, Hugh Anthony:
*Ledingham; Lewis (T.).*
COATMAN, John:
*Paton (J. L. A.).*
COCHRANE, Hon. Sir Ralph Alexander:
*Gibson (G. P.).*
COGHILL, Sir (Marmaduke Nevill) Patrick (Somerville), Bart.:
*Somerville (E. A. Œ.).*
†COLE, George Douglas Howard:
*Burns; Thorne.*
COLEBROOK, Leonard:
*Wright (A. E.).*
COMPTON, Samuel James Moore:
*Cameron (D. Y.).*
COOKE, Arthur Hafford:
*Boys.*

COSTLEY-WHITE, Harold:
*David.*
COWEN, Zelman:
*Isaacs.*
†CRAWFORD, Osbert Guy Stanhope:
*Williams-Freeman.*
CREASY, Sir George Elvey:
*Ramsay.*
†CROMER, Rowland Thomas Baring, Earl of:
*Hardinge.*
CRONE, Gerald Roe:
*Cornish.*
CROSS, Frank Leslie:
*Stone.*
CROWE, Sir Edward Thomas Frederick:
*Barton.*
CRUMP, Norman Easedale:
*Withers.*
CUNNINGHAM, Ebenezer:
*Larmor.*
CUNNINGHAM, Sir George:
*Donald.*
CURLING, Bryan William Richard:
*Donoghue.*
CURTIS, Basil:
*Towse.*

DALE, Sir Henry Hallett:
*Hopkins; Lyons.*
DALEY, Sir (William) Allen:
*Menzies.*
DANBY, Hope:
*Backhouse.*
DARBISHIRE, Helen:
*Penrose; Selincourt.*
DARWIN, Bernard:
*Braid.*
DARWIN, Sir Charles Galton:
*Bragg.*
†DAVISON, Sir Ronald Conway:
*Betterton (Rushcliffe).*
DAWSON, Warren Royal:
*Newberry.*
DAY, James Wentworth:
*Campbell (M.).*
DEARMER, Geoffrey:
*Kennet.*
DE BEER, Sir Gavin Rylands:
*Goodrich.*
†DE MONTMORENCY, Sir Geoffrey Fitzhervey:
*Tiwana.*
DE NORMANN, Sir Eric:
*Earle.*
D'ERLANGER, Leo Frederic Alfred:
*Gibson (J. W.).*
†DOBELL, Clifford:
*Bulloch.*
DOBSON, Sir Roy Hardy:
*Chadwick (R.).*
DON, Alan Campbell:
*Lang of Lambeth.*
†DONNAN, Frederick George:
*Collie.*
DORLING, Henry Taprell:
*Mansfield; Somerville (J. F.).*
†DORWARD, Alan James:
*Hicks (G. D.).*
DUFF, Patrick William:
*Buckland.*

†DUNSANY, Edward John Moreton Drax Plunkett, Baron:
*Villiers (Jersey).*
EADY, Sir Wilfrid Griffin:
*Siepmann.*
ECCLES, Hon. Sybil Frances Dawson Eccles, Lady:
*Dawson of Penn.*
EDGELL, Sir John Augustine:
*Field (A. M.).*
†EDMONDS, Sir James Edward:
*Braithwaite (W. P.); Montgomery-Massingberd; Murray (A. J.).*
EDWARDS, John Goronwy:
*Lloyd (J. E.).*
EGERTON, Sir Alfred Charles Glyn:
*Strutt (Rayleigh).*
EKWALL, Bror Oscar Eilert:
*Mawer.*
ELLIOT, Sir John:
*Pick.*
ELLIOTT, Dorothy Mary:
*Wilkinson.*
ELMHIRST, Sir Thomas Walker:
*Coningham.*
ELMSLIE, William Alexander Leslie:
*McLean.*
ELTON, Godfrey Elton, Baron:
*Guedalla.*
EMMONS, Robert Van Buren:
*Sickert.*
ENGLEDOW, Sir Frank Leonard:
*Biffen.*
†ENSOR, Sir Robert Charles Kirkwood:
*Blatchford; Parker; Thomas (J. H.).*
ERVINE, St. John Greer:
*Shaw (G. B.); Tempest.*
EVANS, Edward Walter:
*Read.*
EVERETT, Dorothy:
*Chambers.*

FALLS, Cyril Bentham:
*Dill; Lambart (Cavan); Vereker (Gort).*
FARRER, Hon. Dame Frances Margaret:
*Watt.*
FEATHER, Norman:
*Aston.*
FEETHAM, Richard:
*Duncan.*
FERGUSSON, Bernard Edward:
*Inskip (Caldecote); Wauchope; Wavell.*
†FERMOR, Sir Lewis Leigh:
*Holland.*
FIELDING, Sean:
*Walls.*
†FIRTH, John D'Ewes Evelyn:
*Rendall.*
FITZHARDINGE, Laurence Frederic:
*Cook (J.).*
FLEURE, Herbert John:
*Peake.*
†FLUGEL, John Carl:
*Spearman.*
FOLEY, Sir (Ernest) Julian:
*Kemball-Cook.*
FOOT, Michael Richard Daniell:
*Croft; Greenwood.*

FORBER, Sir Edward Rodolph:
*Monro.*
FORDHAM, Royston Edward:
*Freeman.*
†FOSS, Hubert James:
*Moeran.*
FREEMAN, William:
*Douglas.*
FULFORD, Roger Thomas Baldwin:
*Lawrence (H. A.); Seely (Mottistone).*

GADD, Cyril John:
*Thompson (R. C.).*
GALBRAITH, Vivian Hunter:
*Tait (J.).*
GALTON, Dorothy:
*Pares.*
GARDINER, Sir Thomas Robert:
*Murray (G. E. P.).*
GARDNER-SMITH, Percival:
*Jackson (F. J. F.).*
GARNER, William Edward:
*Frankland.*
GATHORNE-HARDY, Hon. Robert:
*Smith (L. L. P.).*
†GIBB, Sir Claude Dixon:
*Stoney.*
GIBB, Sir Hamilton Alexander Rosskeen:
*Nicholson (R. A.).*
GIBSON, George Howard:
*Gibson (J. W.).*
GILBERT, Edmund William:
*Mackinder.*
GILBERT, Stuart:
*Joyce.*
GILLESPIE, Dame Helen Shiels:
*McCarthy.*
†GLANCY, Sir Bertrand James:
*Bikaner.*
†GLANVILLE, Stephen Ranulph Kingdon:
*Thompson (H. F. H.).*
GLASS, David Victor:
*Kuczynski.*
GLOVER, James Alison:
*Newman.*
GODFREY, Walter Hindes:
*Nicholson (C. A.).*
†GOGARTY, Oliver St. John:
*Gwynn; Stephens.*
GORDON, John Rutherford:
*Blumenfeld.*
GORE, John Francis:
*George (Kent); Ponsonby.*
†GOULD, Sir Basil John:
*Bell.*
†GRANT, Sir Francis James:
*Bowes-Lyon (Strathmore and Kinghorne).*
GRANT, Frederick Clifton:
*Lake.*
GRANT, William Frank:
*Adamson.*
GRAY, Charles Reginald:
*Bird.*
†GREAVES, William Michael Herbert:
*Plummer.*
GREEN, Margaret Mackeson:
*Ward.*
GREEN, Owen Mortimer:
*Bland.*

GREEN, Roger Lancelyn:
*Mason.*
GREG, Sir Walter Wilson:
*Pollard (A. W.).*
†GRENFELL, Russell:
*Harwood (H. H.).*
GRIER, Lynda:
*Sadler.*
GRIFFITHS, Sir Percival Joseph:
*Jinnah.*
GRIMSDITCH, Herbert Borthwick:
*Askwith; Austin; Clausen; Elias (South-wood); Grenfell (St. Just); Johnston (Luke); Legh (Newton); MacColl; Olsson; Plender; Ravilious; Robinson (W. H.); Selfridge; Snell; Stoll; Wakefield; Walcot; Whistler.*
GUNN, George Sinclair:
*Welch.*
GWYNN, Denis Rolleston:
*Hyde.*
GWYNNE-JONES, Allan:
*Manson; Steer.*

HAARHOFF, Theodore Johannes:
*Hofmeyr.*
†HACKFORTH, Reginald:
*Cornford.*
†HAIG, Sir Harry Graham:
*Marris.*
HAILEY, William Malcolm Hailey, Baron:
*Hartog; Lugard.*
†HALCROW, Sir William Thomson:
*Hindley.*
HALL, Hessel Duncan:
*Purvis.*
HAMILTON, Sir Horace Perkins:
*Fisher.*
HAMILTON, Mary Agnes:
*Webb (M. B. and S. J., Passfield).*
HAMSON, Vincent Everard:
*Mackintosh.*
HANBURY, Harold Greville:
*Hewart; Holdsworth; Sankey; Stallybrass; Walton; Wrottesley.*
†HARDIE, Martin:
*Short.*
HARDY, Sir Alister Clavering:
*Kemp.*
†HARRIS, (Henry) Wilson:
*Spender.*
HART, William Ogden:
*Acton.*
HARTLEY, Sir Harold:
*Berkeley; Granet; Milne-Watson.*
HARTLEY, Leslie Poles:
*Asquith (Oxford and Asquith); Myers (L. H.).*
HAWARD, Edwin:
*Dane.*
HAWKES, Jacquetta (Mrs. J. B. Priestley):
*Turner (W. J. R.).*
HAWTREY, Sir Ralph George:
*Bradbury.*
HENCKEN, Mary Thalassa Alford Cruso:
*Randall-MacIver.*
HENDERSON, Kenneth David Druitt:
*Newbold.*
HENRY, Thomas Anderson:
*Dunstan.*

HERBAGE, Julian Livingston-:
*Wood (H. J.).*
HEUSTON, Robert Francis Vere:
*Romer.*
HIGHAM, Thomas Farrant:
*Blakiston.*
HILL, James William Francis:
*Tritton.*
HINDLE, Edward:
*Mitchell (P. C.).*
HODGSON, Leonard:
*Quick.*
HOLFORD, Sir William Graham:
*Reilly.*
HOLLAND, Sir Henry Tristram:
*McMahon.*
HOOD, (Archibald) Frederic:
*Green.*
HOPKINS, Gerard Walter Sturgis:
*Williams (C. W. S.).*
HORNER, David:
*Sitwell.*
HOWES, Frank Stewart:
*Bantock; Harty; Smyth.*
HUBBLE, Douglas Vernon:
*Langdon-Brown.*
HUDSON, Derek:
*Brodribb; Pryde.*
HUMPHREYS, (Travers) Christmas:
*Spilsbury.*
HURCOMB, Cyril William Hurcomb, Baron:
*Bates.*
HURD, Sir Archibald:
*Runciman.*
HUSSEY, Christopher Edward Clive:
*Lutyens.*
HUTTON, Sir Thomas Jacomb:
*Milne (G. F.).*
HYDE, Harford Montgomery:
*Le Gallienne; Vane-Tempest-Stewart (Londonderry).*

ILSLEY, James Lorimer:
*Ralston.*
†IREMONGER, Frederic Athelwold:
*Temple.*
†IRVINE, Sir James Colquhoun:
*Henderson (G. G.).*
ISHAM, Sir Gyles, Bart.:
*Gott.*

JACOB, Ernest Fraser:
*Jacob; Robertson (C. G.).*
JAMES, Edwin Oliver:
*Frazer.*
JAMES, Ivor Benjamin Hugh:
*Bridge.*
JAMES, Sir William Milburne:
*Hall (W. R.); Keyes.*
JEFFRIES, Sir Charles Joseph:
*Stockdale; Wilson.*
JOHNSON, Charles:
*Hall (H.).*
JOHNSTON, Thomas:
*Maxton.*
JONES, Daniel:
*James.*
†JONES, Thomas:
*Baldwin; Lloyd George.*

JORDAN, Louis Arnold:
*Cullen.*
JOUBERT DE LA FERTE, Sir Philip Bennet:
*Gossage; Swann.*

KEETON, George Williams:
*Lightwood.*
KEMP, Eric Waldram:
*Williams (N. P.).*
KENDREW, Wilfrid George:
*Shaw (W. N.).*
†KENYON, Sir Frederic George:
*Smith (A. H.).*
KENYON, Joseph:
*Pickard.*
KEPPEL-JONES, Arthur Mervyn:
*Smuts.*
KILLICK, John Spencer:
*Maybury.*
KNOWLES, Michael Clive (David):
*Brooke; Previté-Orton.*
KNOX, Edmund George Valpy:
*Partridge; Raven-Hill.*
KNOX, Thomas Malcolm:
*Collingwood; de Burgh.*
KRAMER, Leonie Judith:
*Richardson.*

LAMB, Sir Walter Rangeley Maitland:
*Llewellyn.*
LANDON, Philip Aislabie:
*Bankes; MacKinnon; Scott.*
LANE, Margaret (Countess of Huntingdon):
*Potter.*
LANG, William Dickson:
*Woodward.*
LANG, William Henry:
*Bower.*
LATTER, John Cecil:
*Macready.*
LAVER, James:
*Drury; Eves; Gray; Harcourt-Smith;*
*Pissarro.*
†LAWRENCE, Gerald Leslie:
*Arliss.*
LAYTON, Thomas Bramley:
*Lane.*
LEARMONTH, Sir James Rögnvald:
*Stiles.*
LE FANU, William Richard:
*Power (D'A.).*
LEITH-ROSS, Sir Frederick William:
*Goode.*
†LE QUESNE, Charles Thomas:
*du Parcq; Greer (Fairfield).*
†LESLIE, Robert Walter Dickson:
*Field (F. L.).*
LEWIS, Aubrey Julian:
*Bond.*
LEWIS, Michael Arthur:
*Callender.*
LEY, Henry George:
*Davies (H. W.); Harwood (B.).*
LHOMBREAUD, Roger André:
*Symons.*
LHOYD-OWEN, John Hugh:
*Alexander-Sinclair; Bruce; Fuller; Tait*
*(W. E. C.); Wake-Walker; Walker (F. J.).*

LIDDELL HART, Basil Henry:
*Chetwode.*
LITTLEWOOD, Samuel Robinson:
*Ainley; Hicks (E. S. G.); Lang; Martin-Harvey; Vanbrugh (I.); Vanbrugh (V.).*
LORAINE, Sir Percy Lyham:
*Rodd (Rennell).*
LUKE, Sir Harry Charles:
*Stubbs.*
LUNN, Sir Arnold Henry Moore:
*Smythe.*
†LYON, Kenneth:
*Stanley (Derby).*

MACADAM, Sir Ivison Stevenson:
*Power (J. C.).*
†MACALISTER, Sir Ian:
*Gotch.*
McCLEARY, George Frederick:
*Olivier.*
McCORMICK, Eric Hall:
*Hodgkins.*
McCREA, William Hunter:
*Milne (E. A.).*
†MACDONALD, Margaret:
*Stebbing.*
McEWEN, Sir John Helias Finnie, Bart.:
*Lindley.*
McFADYEAN, Sir Andrew:
*Lever.*
MacGREGOR-MORRIS, John Turner:
*Fleming (J. A.).*
McKENNA, David:
*Stanley (Ashfield).*
McKENNA, Stephen:
*McKenna.*
McKIE, Sir William Neil:
*Nicholson (S. H.).*
MacKINNON, Donald MacKenzie:
*Taylor.*
MACLAGAN, Michael:
*Doubleday; Scott-Ellis (Howard de Walden).*
MacMICHAEL, Sir Harold Alfred:
*Huddleston.*
†MACMILLAN, Hugh Pattison Macmillan, Baron:
*Murray (Dunedin); Younger (Blanesburgh).*
MACMILLAN, William Miller:
*Reitz.*
MacNALTY, Sir Arthur Salusbury:
*Newsholme.*
MACQUEEN-POPE, Walter James:
*Graves.*
†MALCOLM, Sir Dougal Orme:
*Baker; Dawson (G. G.); Hely-Hutchinson (Donoughmore).*
MANN, Sir James Gow:
*ffoulkes.*
MANSERGH, Philip Nicholas Seton:
*Cripps (Parmoor).*
MANSON, William:
*Smith (G. A.).*
MARGOLIOUTH, Herschel Maurice:
*Thompson (E. J.).*
†MARKHAM, Violet Rosa (Mrs. Carruthers):
*Tennant.*
MARSH, Norman Stayner:
*Rowlatt.*

MARSHALL, (Charles) Arthur (Bertram):
*Brazil.*
MARSHALL, Charles William:
*Page.*
MARSHALL-CORNWALL, Sir James Handyside:
*Rumbold.*
MARTIN, (Basil) Kingsley:
*Laski.*
MARTIN, Hugh Gray:
*Deverell.*
†MARTINDALE, Hilda:
*Delevingne.*
MASON, Kenneth:
*Stein; Younghusband.*
MASON, Philip:
*Patel.*
MATHESON, Donald MacLeod:
*Chubb.*
MATTHEWS, Walter Robert:
*Mozley.*
MAVROGORDATO, John Nicolas:
*Marett.*
MAXWELL, Sir Alexander:
*Paterson.*
†MERSEY, Charles Clive Bigham, Viscount:
*Pease (Gainford).*
MICKLEM, Nathaniel:
*Paton (W.); Selbie.*
MIDDLETON, James Smith:
*Clynes; Mann; Turner (B.).*
†MILNE, Edward Arthur:
*Fowler; Newall.*
†MONK, Winston Francis:
*Forbes (G. W.).*
MONNINGTON, Walter Thomas:
*Russell (W. W.).*
MONTEITH, Charles Montgomery:
*Molony.*
MOODY, Theodore William:
*Curtis.*
MORGAN, (Mary) Diana (Mrs. Robert Mac-Dermot Barbour):
*Braithwaite (F. L.).*
MORGAN, Walter Thomas James:
*Robison.*
MORISON, Stanley:
*Barrington-Ward; Hornby.*
MORRELL, William Parker:
*Stewart.*
MORRIS, Sir Charles Richard:
*Ogilvie.*
MORRIS-JONES, Sir (John) Henry:
*Graham-Little.*
MOYNE, Bryan Walter Guinness, Baron:
*Guinness (Moyne).*
MUNRO, Ion Smeaton:
*Graham (R. W.).*
†MURRAY, (George) Gilbert (Aimé):
*Bevan; Hammond.*
MYERS, Walter Harold:
*Julius.*
†MYRES, Sir John Linton:
*Dalton; Evans.*

NEILSON, John Beaumont:
*Wright (W. C.).*
NEWTON, Eric:
*Nicholson (W. N. P.).*

†NEWTON, (Wilfrid) Douglas:
  *Hinsley.*
NORTON, Jane Elizabeth:
  *Lawrence (A. S.).*

†O'DONOVAN, William James:
  *Sequeira.*
OLDHAM, James Basil:
  *Hobson.*
OLIPHANT, Sir Lancelot:
  *Lindsay.*
†O'NEIL, Bryan Hugh St. John:
  *Clapham (A. W.).*
ORTON, Harold:
  *Wyld.*
†ORWIN, Charles Stewart:
  *Hall (A. D.).*
O'SULLIVAN, Richard:
  *Finlay; Russell of Killowen.*
OTWAY-RUTHVEN, Annette Jocelyn:
  *Phillips (W. A.).*

PAGE, Denys Lionel:
  *Denniston.*
PAGE, William Walter Keightley:
  *Rankin.*
†PALAIRET, Sir (Charles) Michael:
  *Akers-Douglas (Chilston).*
PALMER, Helen Maud:
  *Glyn; Hirst; Hopwood (Southborough); Stanley (A.); Tagore; Wood (H. K.).*
PALMER, Russell:
  *Jones (J. S.).*
†PARES, Richard:
  *Williams (A. F. B.).*
†PARKER, John:
  *Howard (L.).*
PARKER, William Mathie:
  *Strachan.*
PAYNE, Ernest Alexander:
  *Robinson (H. W.); Rushbrooke.*
PECK, Arthur Leslie:
  *Rouse.*
PERKINS, George:
  *Barker.*
PETERKIN, Hugh Grant:
  *Elphinstone.*
PETRIE, Sir David:
  *Tegart.*
PHILBY, Harry St. John Bridger:
  *Thomas (B. S.).*
PHILLIPS, Henry:
  *Lloyd (D. J.).*
†PIM, Sir Alan William:
  *Hewett.*
PIPER, (Mary) Myfanwy:
  *Nash.*
POWELL, Roger:
  *Cockerell.*
POWICKE, Sir (Frederick) Maurice:
  *Carlyle; Little.*
PRATT, James Davidson:
  *Bain.*
PRATT, Sir John Thomas:
  *Teichman.*
PYE, Edith Mary:
  *Paget.*

RAMSEY, Stanley Churchill:
  *Adshead.*

RANDALL, Terence George:
  *Salmon.*
RANKEILLOUR, Henry John Hope, Baron:
  *Howard (FitzAlan of Derwent).*
†RATCLIFFE, Samuel Kerkham:
  *Gardiner (A. G.).*
RAWLINSON, Alfred Edward John, Bishop of Derby (John Derby):
  *Parsons (R. G.).*
†RAYLEIGH, Robert John Strutt, Baron:
  *Balfour.*
READ, Herbert Harold:
  *Flett.*
READE, Brian Edmund:
  *Dodd.*
REDMAN, Roderick Oliver:
  *Plaskett.*
REES, Sir Richard Lodowick Edward Montagu, Bart.:
  *Blair (George Orwell).*
REFFOLD, Albert Edward:
  *Carlile.*
REYNOLDS, Ernest Edwin:
  *Baden-Powell.*
REYNOLDS, Graham:
  *Forbes (S. A.).*
RICARDO, Sir Harry Ralph:
  *Lanchester.*
RICHARDSON, Sir Albert Edward:
  *Cooper (T. E.).*
RITCHIE, Sir (John) Douglas:
  *Broodbank.*
†ROBERTS, Paul Ernest:
  *Marriott.*
ROBERTS, Sir Sydney Castle:
  *Child; Glover; Sampson; Whibley.*
ROBERTSON, Muriel:
  *Stephenson.*
ROBINSON, Edward Austin Gossage:
  *Keynes.*
ROBINSON, Edward Stanley Gotch:
  *Hill (G. F.).*
†ROBINSON, (Esmé Stuart) Lennox:
  *Fay.*
ROGERSON, Sidney:
  *Wadsworth.*
ROSKILL, Stephen Wentworth:
  *Troubridge.*
ROSS, Angus:
  *Allen (J.).*
ROSS, Sir (William) David:
  *Prichard.*
ROTH, Cecil:
  *Hertz.*
ROUGHTON, Francis John Worsley:
  *Barcroft.*
ROWLEY, John de la Mare Clarke:
  *Purse.*
ROXBURGH, Sir Ronald Francis:
  *Luxmoore.*
†RUDMOSE BROWN, Robert Neal:
  *Hinks; Ryder.*
RUNCIMAN, Hon. Sir Steven (James Cochran Stevenson):
  *Miller.*

†SADLEIR, Michael:
  *Jacobs; Walpole.*

SADLER, Donald Harry:
*Comrie.*
SALMOND, Sir John Maitland:
*Burnett.*
SALMOND, Hon. Monica Salmond, Lady:
*Grenfell (Desborough).*
SALTER, James Arthur Salter, Baron:
*Smith (H. Ll.).*
SAMUEL, David Sydney:
*Dryland.*
†SANDWELL, Bernard Keble:
*King.*
SANKEY, Avice Edith:
*Hunt.*
SARGENT, Sir Orme Garton:
*Henderson (N. M.); Phipps.*
†SCOTT, Ernest Findlay:
*Moffatt.*
SCOTT-JAMES, Rolfe Arnold:
*Lynd.*
SCOTT THOMSON, Gladys:
*Russell (M. A.).*
SEARLE, Humphrey:
*Dunhill.*
SEDDON, Herbert John:
*Girdlestone.*
SELBORNE, Roundell Cecil Palmer, Earl of:
*Cecil (Salisbury).*
SHARP, Martin:
*de Havilland.*
SHAW, James Byam:
*Dodgson.*
SHEEPSHANKS, Sir Thomas Herbert:
*Robinson (W. A.).*
SHEFFIELD, John Vincent:
*Portal.*
SHEPHERD, Edwin Colston:
*Brackley; Brown (A. W.).*
†SHEPPARD, Samuel Townsend:
*Sastri.*
†SHERA, Frank Henry:
*Coward.*
†SHIELS, Sir (Thomas) Drummond:
*Moody.*
SILLAR, Frederick Cameron:
*Ware.*
†SIMON, John Allsebrook Simon, Viscount:
*Crewe-Milnes (Crewe); Hogg (Hailsham).*
†SIMONSEN, Sir John Lionel:
*Forster.*
†SIMPSON, Thomas Blantyre:
*Clyde.*
†SINGLETON, Sir John Edward, Lord Justice Singleton:
*Stanley (O. F. G.).*
SLINGSBY, Francis Hugh:
*Shaw (W. A.).*
SMITH, David Nichol:
*Elton.*
SMITH, Sir Frank Edward:
*Cadman.*
SMITH, Nowell Charles:
*Binyon.*
SPARROW, John Hanbury Angus:
*Hutchinson.*
SPEAIGHT, Robert William:
*Baring.*
SPRY, Graham:
*Aberhart.*

STABLE, Sir Wintringham Norton:
*Lewis (W. H. P.).*
STANLEY, Carleton Wellesley:
*Falconer; Roy.*
STANTON, Walter Kendall:
*Allen (H. P.).*
STEVENS, Herbert Lawrence:
*Hall (A. H.).*
STEVENSON, John Alexander:
*Beatty; Bennett; Dafoe; Leacock.*
STOCK, Alfred Robert:
*Coker.*
STOCKS, Mary Danvers:
*Rathbone.*
†STORRS, Sir Ronald:
*Gaselee.*
STRUTT, Hon. Guy Robert:
*Balfour.*
STUART, Sir Campbell:
*McLintock.*
STUDD, Bernard:
*Studd.*
†SUMNER, Benedict Humphrey:
*Benson (Charnwood).*
SYKES, Christopher Hugh:
*Byron.*

TALBOYS, Rollo St. Clare:
*Pollock.*
TAYLOR, Joseph John:
*Tillett.*
TELFER, William:
*Chadwick (H. M.).*
TEMPERLEY, Clive Errington:
*Strakosch.*
†THATCHER, Sir Reginald Sparshatt:
*McEwen.*
THICKNESSE, Cuthbert Carroll:
*Winnington-Ingram.*
THOMAS, David Winton:
*Cook (S. A.).*
†THOMAS, Frederick William:
*Keith.*
THOMAS, Herbert Samuel:
*Hassall.*
THOMAS, Hugh Hamshaw:
*Seward.*
THOMAS, Ruth Rees:
*Pinsent.*
THROCKMORTON, Geoffrey William Berkeley:
*Hope (Rankeillour).*
THURSFIELD, Henry George:
*Phillips (T. S. V.); Richmond.*
TILTMAN, Ronald Frank:
*Baird.*
TINDALL, Benjamin Arthur:
*Rose-Innes.*
TITCHMARSH, Edward Charles:
*Hardy.*
TIZARD, Sir Henry Thomas:
*Heath; Miers.*
†TOWNDROW, Kenneth Romney:
*Rothenstein.*
TOYNBEE, Jocelyn Mary Catherine:
*Strong (E.).*
TREVELYAN, George Macaulay:
*Winstanley.*
TREWAVAS, Ethelwynn:
*Regan.*

TURNER, James William Cecil:
*Oliver (D. T.).*
TURNER, Sir Ralph Lilley:
*Grierson.*
TYERMAN, Hugo Nelson:
*Mee.*
TYRRELL-EVANS, Herbert Godfrey:
*Oakley.*

UNDERWOOD, Ernest:
*Johnson.*
URQUHART, William Spence:
*Laird.*

VAISEY, Sir Harry Bevir:
*Clauson.*
VERITY, Conrad Edward Howe:
*Pearce.*
VERNON, Marjorie:
*Underhill.*

†WADSWORTH, Alfred Powell:
*Crozier.*
WALKER, Eric Anderson:
*Hertzog; Malan.*
WARNER, Sir Pelham Francis:
*Jackson (F. S.).*
WATSON-WATT, Sir Robert Alexander:
*Mill.*
WAUGH, Alec:
*Rhys.*
†WAVELL, Archibald Percival Wavell, Earl:
*Wingate.*
†WEBB, Clement Charles Julian:
*Bevan; Joseph.*
WEBB, Geoffrey Fairbank:
*Esdaile.*
WEDGWOOD, Cicely Veronica:
*Wedgwood.*
WEEKLEY, Charles Montague:
*Johnston (E.).*
WHEARE, Kenneth Clinton:
*Curtin; Keith; Watson (J. C.).*
WHEELER, Sir Charles Thomas:
*Hardiman.*
WHELDON, Sir Wynn Powell:
*Davies (D.).*
†WHITTAKER, Sir Edmund Taylor:
*Eddington; Forsyth; Whitehead.*
WIGGLESWORTH, Muriel Helen:
*Fogerty.*

WIGGLESWORTH, Vincent Brian:
*Imms.*
†WILBRAHAM, Sir Philip Wilbraham Baker, Bart.:
*Sargant.*
WILENSKI, Reginald Howard:
*Nevinson (C. R. W.).*
WILLIAMS, Aeneas Francon:
*Graham (J. A.).*
WILLIAMS, Alwyn Terrell Petre, Bishop of Winchester (Alwyn Winton:):
*Cruttwell; Headlam; Henson; Oman.*
WILLIAMS, Edgar Trevor:
*Bonar.*
WILLIAMS, Sir William Emrys:
*Handley.*
WILSON, Charles Henry:
*Cooper (F. D'A.).*
WILSON, Sir Horace John:
*Mackenzie (Amulree).*
WILSON, Sir (James) Steuart:
*Strangways.*
WINSTEDT, Sir Richard Olaf:
*Clementi; Clifford; Swettenham.*
WITTS, Leslie John:
*Hurst.*
WOLTERS, Albert William Phillips:
*Sibly.*
WOOD, Frederick Lloyd Whitfield:
*Coates.*
WOOD, Herbert George:
*Harris.*
WOODALL, Mary:
*Whitley.*
WOODHOUSE, Hon. Christopher Montague:
*Bulwer-Lytton (Lytton).*
WOOLLARD, Lloyd:
*Narbeth.*
WOOLLEY, Sir (Charles) Leonard:
*Petrie.*
WORTHAM, Hugh Evelyn:
*Helena Victoria; Lascelles (Harewood); Lowther (Lonsdale).*
WRIGHT, John Nicholson:
*Stout.*
WYLIE, Sir Francis Verner:
*Gandhi.*
†WYNN, Harold Edward, Bishop of Ely (Edward Ely):
*Knox.*

# DICTIONARY

OF

# NATIONAL BIOGRAPHY

(TWENTIETH CENTURY)

## PERSONS WHO DIED 1941–1950

ABERHART, WILLIAM (1878–1943), Canadian provincial politician and evangelist, was born in the Hibbert township, near Seaforth, Ontario, 30 December 1878, the son of William Aberhart (who as a child had been brought from Germany), by his wife, Louisa Pepper, daughter of an Englishman. He was educated at schools in Ontario and at a business college at Chatham, Ontario, and he graduated from Queen's University, Kingston, as B.A. in 1906. Devoting himself to teaching, he became principal of a school at Brantford. In 1910 he moved to Alberta, then an agricultural region recently established as a province, and in 1915 became principal of Crescent Heights High School, Calgary, a post which he held until he entered the provincial Government in 1935. As an active lay preacher he formed in 1918 an institute for the study of the Bible. He began broadcasting in 1924 and funds from his audience quickly enabled the institute to build premises for its classes in 1927 and to extend its broadcasting. It was known as the Calgary Prophetic Bible Institute.

The universal collapse of wheat prices after 1929 caused profound distress among the wheat farmers, and to them, as to the urban unemployed in the years of depression, Aberhart's vigorous broadcasts at once brought the comforts of evangelical preaching and the hope of economic relief through the issue of a free, popular currency known as Social Credit. His monetary theories, which he began to broadcast after 1932, were adopted from those of Major Clifford Hugh Douglas, of Fearnan, Perthshire, who visited Canada several times and whose views had already been made familiar by the United Farmers Party of Alberta, which had formed the Alberta Government since 1921 and was also represented in the House of Commons at Ottawa. In 1933 Aberhart published a pamphlet, *The Douglas System of Economics*, which found a wide sale.

Aberhart's advocacy of Social Credit drew increasing attention to his broadcasts and led to the formation of listening or study groups throughout Alberta, which were later organized as the Alberta Social Credit League. This league at first had no intention of challenging the provincial Government, but it adopted political tactics in pressing its policies upon the Government by petitions, delegations, and extensive activity by the local study groups, to which the Government replied by appointing Douglas as one of its advisers. In the elections of August 1935, Social Credit candidates, approved by Aberhart and the party leaders, won fifty-six out of the sixty-three seats in the provincial legislature, and Aberhart, who later was returned for Okotoks–High River by acclamation, was called upon to form a Government. He became premier and minister of education.

Aberhart was a man of robust physique, genial in his personal relations and, though at times a bitter controversialist, he won respect for his energy and fervour. In office, as in education, he proved a sound administrator and organizer. His electoral success, in the critical economic situation of the time, flowed from his popular influence as a Bible teacher and an advocate of Social Credit, one of the aspects of which was an election promise to distribute a 'social dividend' of $25 a month to every inhabitant of the province. More significantly, his power with the public was due to his championship of the debtors against their creditors, whom he described as eastern Canadian and international bankers and financiers. Indeed, in its early, more radical years, the Social Credit Party might most aptly be described as the revolt of frontier debtors and, as a movement, not wholly different from earlier farm debtors' movements in western America, such as that for 'free silver'. Provincial legislation to distribute currency or cancel debts, public or private, was, however, found *ultra vires* by the courts and disallowed, and beyond brief experiments with token money in the form of dated stamp script, no application of Social Credit principles was achieved. Attempts to control the press were also ineffective. Aberhart and his Government, indeed, increasingly departed from the principles of Douglas, with whose followers in Alberta and Britain continuing controversy developed. Although the Government was active in social welfare, labour questions, and the field of education, it moved away from radical experimentation, especially after the outbreak of war, turning towards both cautious administration and opposition to the State activity in business advocated by Socialists.

Aberhart died in office, 30 May 1943. He married in 1902 Jessie, daughter of George Flatt, of Galt, Ontario, and there were two daughters of the marriage.

[John A. Irving, 'The Evolution of the Social Credit Movement' in the *Canadian Journal of Economics and Political Science*, vol. xiv, No. 3, August 1948; W. A. Tutte, *Douglas Social Credit for Canada*, Vancouver, 1934; *Canadian Annual Review*, Toronto, 1935–6, 1937–8; private information; personal knowledge.]                    GRAHAM SPRY.

ACTON, SIR EDWARD (1865–1945), judge, was born at Stretford in Lancashire 6 November 1865. He was the son of Henry Morell Acton, one of the editors of the *Manchester Guardian*, by his wife, Anne Shaw, daughter of Nathaniel Williamson, sharebroker, of Manchester. He was educated at Uppingham, where he was an exhibitioner, and Wadham College, Oxford, where he held a classical scholarship and the Hody Greek exhibition. He was at Oxford from 1884 to 1888 and thus was a precursor rather than a member of that remarkable group of Wadham lawyers which included the future Earl of Birkenhead [q.v.], Lord Roche, and Viscount Simon. After being placed in the first class in classical moderations (1886) and in the second class in *literae humaniores* (1888), Acton joined the Inner Temple, where he was awarded a foundation scholarship in 1890 and was called to the bar in 1891, later becoming a bencher of his Inn.

Acton joined the Northern circuit and practised in Manchester and Liverpool. He soon built up an extensive practice, and

in 1913 became a lecturer in the law of evidence and procedure at the university of Manchester. In 1918, when he might have been expected to be thinking of taking silk, he surprised those who knew him by accepting appointment as a County Court judge. For the next two years he worked on Circuit 18 at Nottingham.

In 1920 arrears of work in the King's Bench division made necessary the appointment of two additional judges and Acton was chosen to fill one of these posts by Birkenhead, himself an old member of the Northern circuit. Such a promotion from the County Court to the High Court had never been made before. The experiment was, however, successful and the precedent created in Acton's case has since been followed. In 1934 ill health compelled him to retire and he lived quietly, a semi-invalid, at his home at Churt in Surrey until his death there, 17 November 1945.

At the bar Acton had a large and solid practice; as an advocate he was sound and accurate but not spectacular. These qualities he displayed on the bench. In his judgements he was content to deal closely with the case in hand without feeling it necessary to elaborate on the surrounding legal field or to strive after the distinction of creating precedents for quotation in the books. Although he was so modest, his decisions satisfactorily stood the test of appeal.

Acton received the customary knighthood in 1920. He married in 1903 Edith Nina, daughter of Conrad William Alexander Tulloch, a chartered accountant, of London. Throughout their joint married lives Acton and his wife were devoted to each other; there were no children of the marriage. He was interested in the theatre and music, though as an auditor rather than a performer.

A portrait by John St. Helier Lander is in Wadham College, of which he was elected an honorary fellow in 1923. The artist's attempt to overcome the belittling effect on the face which the wearing of a full-bottomed wig can have has not been entirely successful, and the picture gives the impression that Acton was of larger proportions than was the fact.

[*The Times*, 19 November 1945; private information.]                    W. O. HART.

ADAM SMITH, SIR GEORGE (1856–1942), Old Testament scholar and theologian. [See SMITH.]

ADAMSON, Sɪʀ JOHN ERNEST (1867–1950), educationist, was born at Westgate Common, Wakefield, 11 January 1867, the son of Tom Adamson, engine fitter, and his wife, Eliza Stokoe. In the late 'eighties he entered St. Mark's College, Chelsea, to train as a teacher, and thereafter taught for some years during which he graduated B.A. at London University in 1894; he proceeded D.Lit. in 1920. In 1902, when master of method at the South Wales Training College, Carmarthen, he was appointed principal of the Normal College, Pretoria. Three years later, in 1905, he became director of education for the Transvaal, a post which he occupied until 1924.

In 1907, when the Transvaal had been given responsible government, J. C. Smuts [q.v.] became minister of education. Working in close collaboration, Smuts and Adamson laid the foundations of the Transvaal educational system. Smuts's experience of men and of politics and Adamson's wide knowledge of all aspects of education produced the Transvaal Education Act of 1907. Introducing compulsory European education, the Act provided a system of public education designed to unite the Dutch and English sections of the European population and susceptible of modification and expansion in accordance with the rights of both. It provided non-sectarian religious teaching and, for the children of the Dutch (Afrikaans)-speaking population, it guaranteed home-language instruction up to the third standard, and the use of Dutch thereafter in not more than two subjects. It provided local control of education by school boards and committees and a central council of education to advise the minister on matters of policy and to link the central Government with the local authorities. As chairman of the council Adamson succeeded in reaching agreement with opponents of the government system who had established schools to provide a Christian and national education for children of Dutch parentage. His reports as director of education from 1906 onwards are indispensable to the study of the problem of education in the Transvaal after the South African war.

In his presidential address in 1915 to the education section of the South African Association for the Advancement of Science, Adamson outlined a scheme for the control of education by the Union Government. Many years' experience had convinced him that provincial control was unsatis-factory. He advocated a system by which the central authority would frame an educational policy to be carried out by thirteen regional authorities. The scheme was set forth in detail in a memorandum submitted in 1916 to the provincial administrative commission appointed to consider the question of Union control of education. But his suggestions were not adopted.

In 1924 Adamson retired and the following year became master of Rhodes University College, Grahamstown, and professor of education, retiring in 1930. From 1922 until 1926 he was vice-chancellor of the university of South Africa and for six months during 1935 he was acting professor of education at the Institute of Education in the university of London. For his services to education he was appointed C.M.G. in 1923 and knighted in 1924.

Adamson wrote many articles and several books on education, the most important of which is *The Individual and the Environment* (1921), the sub-title of which is *Some Aspects of the Theory of Education as Adjustment*. Reflecting fifteen years' experience in adjusting the two sections of the European population of the Transvaal to an educational system which synthesized Boer-Republican and British elements, this volume may be regarded as stating the theoretical basis of Adamson's educational practice. Among his other works are *The Teacher's Logic* (1898), *The Theory of Education in Plato's Republic* (1903), and a book of verse *Songs from the South* (1915). Adamson's outstanding characteristic was his sympathetic understanding of the aspirations of the Afrikaans-speaking section of the people. His personal qualities made friendship and co-operation with diverse elements easy and fruitful. With prominent members of the Dutch Church he co-operated closely. His knowledge of Afrikaans enabled him to establish close contact with Afrikaans leaders and teachers. His life was by no means without its lighter side; he was an ardent golfer, a good companion on the course, and a regular player until his eightieth year.

In 1897 he married Gwendolyn Mary, daughter of John Howell Thomas, of Starling Park, Carmarthen, who predeceased him and by whom he had no issue. He died 25 April 1950 at Muizenberg, Cape Province.

[Private information; personal knowledge.]
W. F. Gʀᴀɴᴛ.

ADSHEAD, STANLEY DAVENPORT
(1868–1946), architect and professor of
town planning, was born in Bowdon,
Cheshire, 8 March 1868, the second child
and eldest son of Joseph Adshead, a painter and sometime member of the Manchester Academy, by his wife, Eliza
Davies. After serving his articles to an
architect in Manchester, Adshead went to
London and worked in the offices of
several architects including (Sir) Guy Daw-
ber and (Sir) Ernest George [qq.v.].
Afterwards he was for some four years
with William Flockhart who in addition
to being an able architect was a fine
draughtsman. It was no doubt due to
Flockhart's influence, added to the gift of
pictorial representation which Adshead
had inherited from his father, that he became one of the most notable perspective
artists of his generation. At one time he
had as many as twenty perspectives exhibited in the architectural room of the
Royal Academy.

Towards the end of the century Adshead
set up a London practice of his own. His
first success was winning a competition
for a library at Hawick, although he did
not carry out the actual building. He then
built a pavilion and library for the Ramsgate corporation. His design for the interior of the pavilion was largely influenced
by the Marie Antoinette theatre at Versailles, and was a triumph of refined detail.
Other commissions followed, including the
remodelling of the Bath Assembly Rooms,
and a block of offices in Tooley Street,
London.

In 1909 Adshead accepted an invitation
to become the first lecturer in civic design,
with the title of associate professor, at
Liverpool University, a position which he
occupied until 1912 when he became professor of civic design. The founding of the
lectureship and of this chair, the first of
its kind in this country, was due to the
munificence of W. H. Lever (later Viscount Leverhulme, q.v.). Adshead was
the ideal occupant. To the imaginative
qualities of an artist was added the breadth
of vision necessary to the explorer of a new
field of aesthetics. To Adshead nothing
really counted unless the ultimate realization of a project resulted in an accession
of beauty. To him, civic design, which
embraced all aspects of town and regional
planning, was essentially an art.

It is to his example that town planning
in this country owes so much in the way
of creative enterprise; he blazed the trail.
His influence as an authority on the sub-

ject soon began to extend beyond the
department and the school. He contributed regularly to the *Town Planning
Review* which he had helped to found in
1910, beginning with 'An Introduction to
the Study of Civic Design' in the first
issue.

Although his tenure of the Lever chair
was relatively brief—he resigned in 1914
to accept the appointment as first professor of town planning in the university of
London—he left the department of civic
design at Liverpool firmly established,
with a reputation extending far beyond
this country. He was succeeded by (Sir)
Patrick Abercrombie who had been his
chief assistant. Whilst at Liverpool, Adshead reconstructed an existing theatre for
the Liverpool Repertory Company, making it a model of what such a theatre should
be. In 1925 Liverpool conferred upon him
the honorary degree of M.Arch.

In 1911 Adshead was asked to undertake the reconstruction of the Duchy of
Cornwall estate at Kennington, south
London, a work which occupied some
twenty-one years. It was then that he
entered into partnership with Mr. S. C.
Ramsey, an association which lasted for
thirty years. The years immediately following the war of 1914–18 were exceedingly busy, and the partners were engaged
on innumerable housing schemes for various
local authorities as well as in the building
of Dormanstown—a garden village for the
workers of Dorman, Long & Co. at Middlesbrough—in association with Abercrombie.
Adshead was also consultant to the corporations of Brighton and Norwich; and in
1930, at the invitation of the colonial
secretary, he visited Northern Rhodesia to
choose the site for a new capital. He prepared a report, together with a road plan,
on the selected site at Lusaka.

Adshead's work as a town planner resulted in a great many reports, sometimes
in association with others, on various towns
and regions, including south Tees-side, the
Thames valley, west Essex, Scarborough,
Southampton, Teignmouth, and York. A
feature of the reports with which he was
concerned was the series of charming
drawings from his brush and pencil with
which they were invariably illustrated.
Among his other publications are *Town
Planning and Town Development* (1923), *A
New England* (1941), and *New Towns for
Old* (1943).

In addition to his other work, Adshead
was a very active member of the Royal
Institute of British Architects of which

he was elected a fellow in 1905. He was a vice-president (1919–22), a member of the council, of the town planning committee, and at various times served on twenty-seven other committees. He was a founder-member of the Town Planning Institute and president, 1918–19. He was also a member of the Royal Fine Art Commission from 1927 to 1934. In the following year he retired from his London professorship and he died at Ashley, New Milton, Hampshire, 11 April 1946.

In 1900 he married Mary Annie, daughter of Andrew Blackie, of Strathpeffer; their daughter, Mary (Mrs. Stephen Bone), is the well-known mural painter.

[*The Times*, 13 April 1946; records of the Royal Institute of British Architects; *Journal of the Town Planning Institute*, May–June 1946; personal knowledge.]

S. C. RAMSEY.

AGATE, JAMES EVERSHED (1877–1947), dramatic critic, was born at Pendleton, Lancashire, 9 September 1877, the eldest of the six children of Charles James Agate, cotton manufacturer's agent, and his wife, Eulalie Julia Young. Although generally regarded during his lifetime as the writer from Manchester who had conquered London in the 'man from the provinces' manner of Arnold Bennett [q.v.] and Mr. J. B. Priestley, Agate was not of Lancashire ancestry. His father came originally from Horsham, Sussex, and his mother was a Yorkshirewoman who had been educated in France and Germany and had studied the piano under a pupil of Chopin. The young Agates were taught to speak French fluently and to appreciate the fine points of music and the arts. Their father was chairman of the committee of the Unitarian chapel which the family attended; James in his teens was its secretary. Charles Agate was also a keen theatregoer who had once run away from home to see Macready. He encouraged his children to visit good plays and took James to see Sarah Bernhardt perform; she became for the child the model of theatrical performance ever after; his only sister May later studied under her in Paris.

Agate was educated at Giggleswick and at Manchester Grammar School and there is no record of exceptional precocity. Oxford or Cambridge would have suited him perfectly but he went into his father's business, learned to weave, and sold grey cloth for seventeen years. Although his mind was more concerned with the arts than with the cotton trade, he was no urban aesthete in a city which then had the best of plays and music continually available: he liked to live in Derbyshire, to dress like a sporting farmer, and to own and to exhibit show hackneys.

At the same time he began dramatic criticism with the *Daily Dispatch* in Manchester; after a year, in 1907, he joined the *Manchester Guardian* team of critics which included C. E. Montague [q.v.] and Allan Monkhouse. With them he concluded his 'further education' in letters.

During the war of 1914–18, with his experience of horses, Agate was sent as a captain in the Army Service Corps to buy hay in the south of France. This duty gave some leisure for writing. His first book, in the form of letters, *L. of C.* (*Lines of Communication*), came out in 1917 and was followed by a book of essays of the theatre, *Buzz, Buzz!* (1918). His wartime marriage to a Frenchwoman was soon dissolved.

Back in London Agate bought, with characteristic caprice, a general store in south London. He was also able to write a 'personal novel' called *Responsibility* (1919) which had his abundant vivacity to cover up the absence of a narrative technique. Rapidly failing as a shopkeeper, he no less rapidly succeeded as a critic. In 1921 Filson Young appointed him to the chair of dramatic criticism on the *Saturday Review*, a covetable post once held by G. B. Shaw [q.v.] whose contributions had fired Agate with the ambition to become a dramatic critic. Here he was in his element and on his toes; the brilliance that he displayed won him, in 1923, the theatre critic's post on the *Sunday Times* which he held until his death. He was also dramatic critic for the British Broadcasting Corporation from 1925 to 1932.

Agate published, as well as many volumes of reprinted essays and notices, two more novels, *Blessed are the Rich* (1924) and *Gemel in London* (1928). But fiction about others was less his line than fact about himself. He set out accordingly to be the diarist of his epoch and in twelve years from 1935 wrote nine volumes under the title of *Ego*, the last appearing posthumously. They record chiefly the books, plays, personalities, club talk, and Bohemian life of the time: Agate had no interest in politics or social problems and this limited what might have been a wonderful landscape of London life. Yet, within its limits, the *Ego* series is remarkable for its constancy of wit in causerie and comment, ranging from the pert to the profound.

Agate never lost his sense of himself as a character bestriding his own stage. Unashamedly the egoist, he played the part with a nice mixture of humour and panache. Also he performed with rare energy, for he worked interminably to shape a paragraph to his taste. Beneath his airy mixture of the country sportsman and the *petit maître* of letters, beneath his exhibitionism and his extravagance, was a random scholarship and a burning devotion to the arts, or what he thought best in the arts; he was as much excited by music and painting as by writing for reader or playgoer. When the best was on the table he was omnivorous and insatiable. Because of this he took his place in the great line of English critics. He was a lover of the French classical drama, of Shakespeare, of emotional splendour, of the rattle of wit, and of all that had the flow of soul. For the later feast of reason as set by Shaw and his disciples he had less appetite. Deemed capricious of judgement by authors and actors, he was none the less credited with complete integrity. What he disliked he damned with wit and no mercy: what he liked he fought for with wit and no hesitation. He enjoyed a battle of argument as he enjoyed the beauty of a horse in movement. He was a hedonist in the best sense, seeking pleasure of the senses to the end; but his hedonism was mitigated by discernment. His model was Hazlitt and it may fairly be assumed that Hazlitt would have approved his devotee. He died in London 6 June 1947.

[Personal knowledge.]    IVOR BROWN.

AINLEY, HENRY HINCHLIFFE (1879–1945), actor, was born at Leeds 21 August 1879, the only son and eldest child of Richard Ainley, cloth finisher, by his wife, Ada Hinchliffe. After education at the church school of St. Peter's, Morley, he became clerk in a bank at Sheffield, where he took part in amateur dramatics. When (Sir) George Alexander [q.v.] and his company were on tour in 1899 young Ainley was permitted to 'walk on'. He then joined the company of (Sir) Frank Benson [q.v.], making his first London appearance at the Lyceum Theatre in 1900 when he played Gloucester in *Henry V*. He was still a Bensonian when Alexander saw him as Lorenzo in *The Merchant of Venice* and chose him for Paolo in *Paolo and Francesca* by Stephen Phillips [q.v.]. So perfectly fitted was Ainley, both in looks and voice—from which the north country accent had gone during his training under Benson—that he became famous on the first night (6 March 1902). His manner at that time was gently, though eagerly, romantic—in complete contrast to the masterfulness which he afterwards acquired.

In 1903 Ainley went to the United States and made his first appearance in New York as leading man to Maude Adams, playing, among other parts, the Rev. Gavin Dishart in *The Little Minister*. In the following year he returned to London to appear as Lancelot in *Merely Mary Ann* and in 1905 paid a short visit to Paris, where he was seen as Romeo in the balcony scene at the Opéra Comique. In 1906 he returned to the St. James's Theatre to play Orlando in *As You Like It* to the Rosalind of (Dame) Lilian Braithwaite [q.v.], and later joined the Vedrenne–Barker company at the Royal Court Theatre, appearing as Orestes in Euripides' *Electra* and as Hippolytus. He gave a fine performance as Cassio in the production of *Othello* by Lewis Waller [q.v.] in May 1906. He was for several periods in the company of Sir Herbert Tree [q.v.] at His Majesty's Theatre, where in 1910 he took part in six plays during the Shakespeare festival.

It was in a production by Harley Granville-Barker [q.v.] at the Savoy Theatre in 1912 that Ainley made one of his biggest and most original Shakespearian successes as Malvolio in *Twelfth Night*, giving the character an altogether new power and appeal. He also appeared memorably as Leontes in *The Winter's Tale*. Another remarkable development in the direction of strong character was his creation (1913) of Ilam Carve in *The Great Adventure* which ran for nearly two years at the Kingsway Theatre. Another notable character part which he made his own was Joseph Quinney in *Quinneys'* at the Haymarket Theatre (1915). In 1916 he joined the army with a commission in the Royal Garrison Artillery, serving in France and Italy. He returned in 1919 and went into management at the St. James's Theatre, opening as Fedya in *Reparation*, and playing Mark Antony in a revival of *Julius Caesar* (1920). At His Majesty's Theatre in 1923 he gave a superb performance in the title-part of *Hassan*. At the Prince's Theatre in 1926 he played Macbeth to (Dame) Sybil Thorndike's Lady Macbeth. After two years' illness he returned (July 1929) to play one of the most successful of all his characters as James Fraser in *The First Mrs. Fraser* at the Haymarket Theatre. In 1930 he appeared as Hamlet in a revival which was chosen for a royal command performance in the same year. At the Westminster Theatre in 1931 he did excellent work as Dr. Knox in *The Anatomist* and in 1932 as the Archangel in *Tobias and the Angel.*

After an absence from the stage of six years caused by illness, Ainley gave a single performance in 1938 at the Vaudeville Theatre of a scene from *Hassan.* After 1915 he appeared in a number of films, but made no deep impression in that medium. His broadcasts, on the other hand, have been specially preserved by the British Broadcasting Corporation as examples of fine diction. No other actor of his time was better equipped for greatness than Ainley. In the romantic charm of his early performances and in the forceful but appealing character-creations of his later years he remained unexcelled. His Hamlet and Macbeth were not wholly satisfactory in construction and relation to the other characters; but they had magnificent moments. Whatever the type of play, Ainley's personality gave distinction to every part he took.

Ainley was twice married: first, in 1903 to an American actress, Suzanne (died 1924), daughter of Richard Sheldon, of New York; secondly, in 1917 to Elaine, daughter of J. Willis Titus, of the United States. Both marriages were dissolved. Henry Ainley had four children, two daughters and two sons, the elder of whom, Richard, has also proved himself an actor of high ability. Henry Ainley died in London 31 October 1945.

A chalk drawing by R. G. Eves remained in the possession of the artist's family. A pen-and-ink caricature by Harry Furniss is at the National Portrait Gallery.

[*The Times,* 1 November 1945; *Who's Who in the Theatre*; private information; personal knowledge.]                    S. R. LITTLEWOOD.

AITCHISON, CRAIGIE MASON, LORD AITCHISON (1882–1941), lord justice-clerk of Scotland, was born at the Erskine Manse, Falkirk, 26 January 1882, the second son of the Rev. James Aitchison, minister of the United Presbyterian Church, by his wife, Elizabeth Mason Craigie. Aitchison was educated at Falkirk High School and went with a scholarship to the university of Edinburgh, where he graduated M.A. in 1903. He was a Vans Dunlop scholar in logic and meta-physics, and Muirhead prizeman in civil law. In 1906 he qualified as LL.B. with distinction. He was called to the Scottish bar in 1907 and took silk in 1923. In 1929 he was appointed lord advocate—the first Socialist to hold that great office—and sworn of the Privy Council. In 1929 he entered Parliament as Labour member for the Kilmarnock division of Ayrshire, sitting from 1931 as a National Labour member, and had a distinguished career in the House of Commons. In 1933 the degree of LL.D was conferred upon him by the university of Edinburgh, and in the same year he became lord justice-clerk of Scotland, with the judicial title of Lord Aitchison.

The bare recital of these facts fails to present a true picture of Aitchison's personality and achievements. At the bar he specialized in criminal work. It is not too much to say that he was the greatest criminal advocate in Scotland of his time. He appeared for the defence in many murder trials, and in none of them did the Crown secure a verdict. His forensic eloquence, coupled with a pleasing voice and a gracious personality, was unmatched by any of his contemporaries. The cases of John Donald Merrett (1927), of the Oscar Slater appeal (1928), and of the Scottish Amalgamated Silks, Ltd. (1932)—all well known to Scottish lawyers—were the highlights of his career at the bar. The Merrett case was one of alleged matricide, in which, on that charge, he secured a verdict of not proven. In the Slater appeal he succeeded in quashing a twenty-year-old conviction recorded against the accused man. The Silks case, an alleged long firm fraud, lasted for thirty-three days.

In the office of lord justice-clerk he amply justified the expectations entertained regarding him by his colleagues and friends. He was a just and merciful judge. His opinions were luminous and convincing, and they stood well with the House of Lords. Their literary form was unimpeachable. In his later years Aitchison seemed to become in appearance, manner, and personality the embodiment of the old Scottish judges whom Raeburn loved to paint, with their characteristic combination of massive dignity, kindly good humour, and broad humanity. Of his love of art and good literature, space forbids a full assessment. He was liberally endowed with the gift of friendship, and his friendship was loyal and abiding. A contemporary commentator and friend wrote of him, quoting what Sir Walter Scott said to Lockhart at John Ballantyne's funeral: 'I feel as if there would be less sunshine for me from this day forth.'

In 1919 Aitchison married Charlotte Forbes, daughter of James Jones, J.P., of Torwood Hall, Larbert, Stirlingshire; they had two sons. He died in Edinburgh 2 May 1941. There is a portrait of Aitchison by Stanley Cursiter in the Parliament Hall, Edinburgh.

[Scotsman, 3 May 1941; Scots Law Times, 10 May 1941; personal knowledge.]
ALNESS.

AKERS-DOUGLAS, ARETAS, second VISCOUNT CHILSTON (1876–1947), diplomatist, was born in London 17 February 1876, the elder son of Aretas Akers-Douglas, afterwards first Viscount Chilston [q.v.]. He was educated at Eton, and after serving for a short time in the Royal Scots entered the diplomatic service in 1898. His first post was in the following year in Cairo under Lord Cromer [q.v.] whose esteem he quickly won, not least through his proficiency as a classical scholar—an interest which remained with him throughout his life. Indeed, his skill in modern, as well as ancient, languages greatly enhanced his standing and value as a diplomat at many stages of his career —including his last appointment at Moscow, where he took the pains to learn Russian.

After serving at Madrid and Constantinople, he was promoted to be a second secretary in 1905 whilst serving in Athens. During the following years the growing confidence in his abilities was evinced not only by his appointment to two such front-ranking chancelleries as Rome (1907) and Vienna (1909), but in a perhaps even more striking manner by his being entrusted with British representation as acting agent and consul-general at Sofia (1907) and as chargé d'affaires at the unique court of King Nicholas of Montenegro (on three occasions, in 1911 and 1913–14), as well as at Bucharest (1912) where he returned as first secretary (1914–15). Representation at some of these Balkan posts at that period, whilst leaving the envoy an apparently enviably free hand through the almost complete absence of official directives, for this very reason demanded a high standard of diplomatic acumen and resourcefulness, not to mention a certain degree of physical and mental endurance.

At the end of the war of 1914–18, during most of which he was employed at the Foreign Office, Akers-Douglas was attached to the British delegation to the peace conference at Paris and on his return was appointed diplomatic secretary to the secretary of state for foreign affairs. Here his tact and conscientiousness gained for him the hard-won favour and esteem of that august, but often harsh and capricious, taskmaster, Lord Curzon [q.v.]. He could thus recognize reward when he was appointed in November 1921 to be minister at Vienna, a post which, although it had in certain obvious respects declined in grandeur since pre-war days, was nevertheless of considerable importance in the new Europe then emerging, as well as personally congenial to Akers-Douglas through old associations. Here he remained for nearly seven years, spanning the period of the young republic's quick growth out of post-war chaos and depression into a remarkable but all too short spell of stability and prosperity before the rising mist of Nazism enveloped and blotted it out.

From Vienna Chilston (as he now was) went in 1928 to Budapest where he managed to win universal popularity despite the difficulties of steering a careful course, not only between the supporters of the Regent, Admiral Horthy, and the 'legitimists', who considered the latter to have usurped the throne, but between Hungarians of all shades of opinion who bent every effort to obtain British support for the recovery of the territories lost as a result of the war. Despite these current polemics Budapest was at this time an agreeable post and, in an age of change and economic depression, somehow managed to preserve an air of unbelievable bien-être and even feudal orderliness.

From this 'old-worldliness' Chilston in 1933 was suddenly called upon to take up the toughest ambassadorship in the gift of the Foreign Office. Moreover, on his arrival in Moscow, he inherited the aftermath of one of the tensest passages in Anglo-Soviet relations—the affair of the British engineers—and replaced an ambassador who had, as a result, felt obliged to ask for his recall. Chilston brought his natural patience, tolerance, and zeal to bear upon the sorely strained relations which he found, and in a remarkably short space of time established a new modus vivendi with the Soviet Union. The foreign minister, Litvinoff, soon came to have such a genuine personal regard for Chilston that, despite the immense contrast between the two men and the policies of their respective countries, accord or compromise could often be reached where friction or mistrust might so easily have been engendered. The success of Chilston's mission was attested by its prolongation (in 1936) for a further two years. He retired from the service a month after the Munich agreement, just as the short-lived German–Russian *rapprochement* was beginning to develop, and, with it, automatically the star of Litvinoff was beginning to wane.

Chilston married in 1903 Amy Constance, daughter of Captain John Robert Jennings-Bramly, R.H.A., and had two sons. He succeeded his father as second viscount in 1926, but was only able to live on his much-loved Kentish estate during his last years, after his retirement, and these were of course beclouded by the war of 1939–45, in which characteristically he played his part as a local Home Guard leader. He was appointed C.M.G. in 1918, promoted K.C.M.G. in 1927 and G.C.M.G. in 1935, and was sworn of the Privy Council in 1939. He died at Chilston Park, Maidstone, 25 July 1947, and was succeeded in his titles by his younger son Eric Alexander (born 1910), the elder, Aretas, having died in 1940. A portrait of Chilston, painted by his wife, is at Chilston Park.

[Personal knowledge.]
                    MICHAEL PALAIRET.
                    CHILSTON.

ALEXANDER-SINCLAIR, SIR EDWYN SINCLAIR (1865–1945), admiral, was born in Malta 12 December 1865, the second son of Captain John Hobhouse Inglis Alexander, C.B., R.N., of Southbar and Boghall, Renfrew, by his wife, Isabella Barbara, daughter of Thomas Cochrane Hume, of Halifax, Nova Scotia, and Isabella, daughter and heiress of William Sinclair, of Freswick and Dunbeath in Caithness. He succeeded his elder brother to the Southbar property in 1892, and in 1894, on succeeding as twelfth laird to the estate of Freswick, adopted the additional surname of Sinclair.

Entering the Royal Navy as a cadet in 1879 Alexander served on the China station from early 1881 in the armour-plated iron ship *Iron Duke*, flagship of (Sir) George Willes [q.v.]. He was promoted midshipman in August 1881 and sub-lieutenant in January 1886. After serving in the *Active* and taking a staff course he joined the *Fearless* in the Mediterranean in March 1888, but left her on promotion to lieutenant in January 1890 to become flag

lieutenant to (Sir) Richard Tracey [q.v.] in the Channel squadron. When Tracey became admiral superintendent, Malta, in 1892 Alexander accompanied him and thus gained early insight into dockyard and administrative work.

From 1893 to 1896 he served in the battleship *Ramillies*, flagship of Sir Michael Culme-Seymour, commander-in-chief, Mediterranean, and from 1897 to 1900 was his flag lieutenant when he was commander-in-chief at Portsmouth. After his promotion to commander in 1901, Alexander-Sinclair commanded the destroyer *Albatross* from June 1902 and the dispatch vessel *Surprise* from January 1904. He was promoted captain in June 1905 at the comparatively early age of thirty-nine. His first appointment in his new rank was that of captain of the Royal Naval College, Osborne, where he remained until 1908. From 1909 to 1910 he commanded the second destroyer flotilla in home waters and in 1911 became flag captain to Sir Arthur Moore, the commander-in-chief at Portsmouth. After holding this appointment for over two years he returned to sea in September 1913, as captain of the battleship *Temeraire* in the Home Fleet and was still in command of her at the outbreak of war in 1914.

As a part of the extensive reorganization of the Grand Fleet which followed the battle of the Dogger Bank in January 1915, Alexander-Sinclair became commodore commanding first light cruiser squadron with his broad pennant in the *Galatea*. On 31 May 1916 the *Galatea* was part of the screen of the battle cruiser fleet under Sir David (later Earl) Beatty [q.v.] when she altered course to examine a neutral merchant vessel. As Alexander-Sinclair closed this ship he sighted two enemy destroyers approaching from the opposite direction. His 'enemy in sight' signal brought the battle cruiser fleet, and subsequently the whole Grand Fleet, into the action known as the battle of Jutland.

Alexander-Sinclair was appointed C.B. in 1916. In 1917, when he reached flag rank at the age of fifty-one, he was appointed rear-admiral commanding sixth light cruiser squadron with his flag in the *Cardiff* and in November 1917 played a prominent part in the action with the German second scouting group in the Heligoland Bight. Twelve months later he had the great honour of leading the surrendered German High Sea Fleet into Rosyth with the British Grand Fleet in columns on either beam. For his war services he was appointed K.C.B. In the spring of 1919 the sixth light cruiser squadron was transferred to the Mediterranean under his command and renamed third light cruiser squadron.

In 1920 Alexander-Sinclair was appointed admiral superintendent, Portsmouth dockyard. In 1922 he became vice-admiral commanding first battle squadron with his flag in the *Barham* and for a while, during the illness of the commander-in-chief, Sir John De Robeck [q.v.], was senior admiral in the Atlantic Fleet. Then, in June 1925, he became commander-in-chief, China station, with his flag in the *Hawkins*, and showed great tact, forbearance, and judgement in handling difficult situations during the advance of the Chinese nationalist armies. In October 1926 he was promoted to the full rank of admiral and returned to the United Kingdom in 1927 to become commander-in-chief at the Nore. He relinquished his command in May 1930 and became first and principal aide-de-camp to King George V. At the end of the year he was placed on the retired list on attaining the age of sixty-five. On his retirement he was promoted G.C.B.

During his naval career of more than fifty years he had received several foreign decorations, including the American D.S.M., the French croix de guerre, and had been appointed a commander in the Legion of Honour.

Alexander-Sinclair married twice: first, in 1892 Julia Margaret (died 1930), daughter of Colonel Charles Vereker Hamilton-Campbell, of Netherplace, Ayrshire. By this marriage he had two sons and one daughter. Secondly, in 1933 he married Maud Kathleen, widow of Major William Robinson Campbell, of the 14th Hussars, and younger daughter of Captain Samuel Yates Holt Davenport, the Royal Sussex Regiment, Territorial Army.

He died at his home, Dunbeath Castle, after a short illness, 13 November 1945.

A portrait of Alexander-Sinclair is included in Sir A. S. Cope's group, 'Some Sea Officers of the War of 1914–18', in the National Portrait Gallery; a drawing by Francis Dodd is in the Imperial War Museum.

[*The Times*, 14 November 1945; *Annual Register*, 1945; private information; personal knowledge.]     J. H. LHOYD-OWEN.

ALLEN, SIR HUGH PERCY (1869–1946), musician and musical statesman, was born at Reading 23 December 1869,

the youngest of the seven children of John Herbert Allen, who was in business with Huntley & Palmers of Reading. His mother, Rebecca, was the daughter of Samuel Bevan Stevens, a member of the firm of Huntley, Bourne & Stevens which made the tins for Huntley & Palmers' biscuits.

There is not much evidence that the home was one in which music was seriously cultivated, nor do we hear of any particular success achieved by the boy at Kendrick School, Reading, but the arrival of Dr. Frederick John Read as organist of Christ Church, Reading, when Allen was eight, was a milestone in his life. Determined to have lessons from Read, Allen obtained local organistships—Coley (1880), Tilehurst (1884), Eversley (1886), and in 1887 he combined the latter post with some teaching at Wellington College. In that year he went as assistant to Read who had been appointed organist of Chichester Cathedral. This settled Allen's life-work. Chichester gave him experience in cathedral services, the training of a choir, and the responsibilities of a cathedral organist. As yet, however, he had no paper qualifications. He therefore took his B.Mus. examinations at Oxford in 1892, and in the same year was appointed organ scholar of Christ's College, Cambridge. Here appeared the first signs of his power to influence others musically. Contemporaries speak of his ability to make people do more than they thought possible. The college music society, the college orchestra (a new venture, and a real *ad*venture in 1892), the university musical club, performances of Greek plays —all these gained by his infectious enthusiasm and his drive. He graduated in arts in 1895 and in 1896 took his D.Mus. examinations at Oxford, although he was prevented by regulations from taking the degree until 1898.

In 1897 Allen was appointed organist of St. Asaph Cathedral, and in the one year that he spent there vastly improved the standard of singing and radically altered the repertoire. The next year he went to Ely Cathedral. Here he was not slow to forge musical links with Cambridge. Performances of the St. Matthew Passion, Brahms's Requiem and 'Schicksalslied' must have astonished this quiet cathedral town, and the importation of singers and orchestral players from Cambridge must have created abnormal activity on an otherwise sleepy railway line.

In 1901 the organistship of New College,

Oxford, was vacant. Four distinguished musicians were shown the short list of four names, and their opinions were invited. All of them warned the college not to appoint Allen. If ever serious advice was wisely rejected, it was then, for Allen gave New College unstinted and selfless devotion for eighteen years. As at St. Asaph and Ely, the choir at New College was soon required to sing much difficult music, and the weekly service lists show both progressiveness and catholicity. In 1908 the college showed its appreciation of Allen's work by offering him a fellowship, at that time a most unusual recognition of a mere musician. The crowds at the Christmas carol services were testimony to the regard felt for organist and choir, not only by the university but also by the city. There was, however, a wider sphere awaiting Allen in the amalgamation of two choral societies (of different traditions and understandable rivalry) into the Oxford Bach Choir. Allen then formed an orchestra to accompany the choir in the fine works which he taught them, and music was soon raised to a position in Oxford which it had never before occupied and became an integral part of the life of university and city.

It was not surprising that Allen should be approached by musical authorities outside Oxford. He became director of the Petersfield Festival (1906), conductor of the London Bach Choir (1907–20), director of music at University College, Reading (1908–18), director of music at Cheltenham Ladies' College (1910–18). In 1913, and again in 1922, 1925, and 1928 he was one of the conductors at the Leeds Festival. The stories of his forgetfulness of rehearsals and his refusal to answer letters and telegrams are legion, but all these places bear the marks of Allen's influence.

In 1918 Sir Walter Parratt [q.v.] resigned the professorship of music at Oxford, and there was no doubt about his successor. Oxford was glad to have at last a resident professor. But when Sir Hubert Parry [q.v.] died later in the year Allen was appointed director of the Royal College of Music, and Oxford thought it would lose him. As usual with Allen, nothing of the sort occurred. He retained his professorship, kept his rooms at New College, and for another seven years conducted the Oxford Bach Choir. His activity was ceaseless and it is said that he once went from Oxford to London and back three times in a day.

Allen's arrival at the Royal College of Music coincided with post-war expansion. The number of students rose from 200 to 600 and many of the director's plans for extension of work, which were made quickly and, as it seemed, temporarily, eventually became permanent. For nineteen years he directed the affairs of the College, but in 1937 he felt he ought to retire. Retirement with Allen was a synonym for change of occupation; to the end of his life he retained his Oxford professorship and made Oxford his headquarters, keeping a watchful eye on musical activities, advising, encouraging young people, working (which meant in his case fighting) for the creation of a music faculty, which the university granted in 1944. New premises and the setting up of a Music School occupied him continuously from this time until his death.

Allen's position in the musical world was very distinguished, but most unusual. This was not curious, for most things about him were unusual. From the time of his first appointment his aim was to spread the love of music, and to teach people, both individually and in large numbers, how to make music. In Oxford he galvanized generations of undergraduates of both sexes into musical action, and showed them, with a technique of his own, how to get hold of music and how to get inside it. He was criticized for being content with less than perfect performances, but his critics, while having a modicum of truth on their side, failed to perceive his aim. In Allen's mind rehearsals were more important than performances. At rehearsals he could talk and teach, at performances he could only glower and frown when he was not satisfied. Nevertheless, members of his choir and orchestra have spoken of many occasions when they sang and played far better than they knew how —all because of Allen's inspiring command. Thousands of young people came under his influence in the provinces, and when he went to London thousands more were added. Many of these went out into the world carrying with them the infection of his enthusiasm which they transmitted to others. In this way, Allen probably did more good musically than anyone else of his generation.

Partly because of his twofold offices in London and Oxford, but chiefly because of the man himself, Allen gradually became a focal point for musical employers and potential employees. His advice and help were sought by many musical organizations. The Incorporated Society of Musicians owes its reconstitution and its revivification chiefly to him; Kneller Hall sought his help; he was a member of the council of the corporation of the Royal Albert Hall; the Royal Philharmonic Society needed, and got, his advice; the British Broadcasting Corporation made him chairman of its music advisory committee in 1936. There was a time, just before he retired from the Royal College of Music, when it could be safely said that there were few musical happenings in the country about which Allen had not been consulted.

This pre-eminent musico-political position has tended to obscure the eminence of Allen as a musician. Those who knew him well will remember his executant ability. They will remember, perhaps enviously, his uncanny power of sight-reading, whether of an orchestral score or an eight-part vocal score with clefs now obsolete. His knowledge of actual music was vast. Bach and Brahms were his special favourites, but Beethoven's Mass in D he sometimes felt was the greatest of all. He was an authority on the composers of the earlier German school, especially Heinrich Schütz, but could talk knowledgeably about Schönberg. A lesson with him in score-reading was memorable.

Musical historians of the future will have no easy task in assessing his place. He did not compose; he was not well known as a player: few realized how much actual music he knew, but there will be few accounts of musical events of his time which do not mention him. His work was with human beings. He was a human dynamo; but to state that, and that only, will give but little impression of him either as man or musician.

One might have thought that Allen's only interest was music, but there was a love of the sea in his bones, and this cemented his friendship with Parry. Astronomy intrigued him, and he knew more about it than most amateurs. His mind travelled to vast spaces—the sea, light years, the stars.

It was natural that honours should come to Allen, although he set but little store by them. He was knighted in 1920, appointed C.V.O. in 1926, promoted K.C.V.O. in 1928 and G.C.V.O. in 1935. Besides his Oxford doctorate he was an honorary Mus.D. of Cambridge (1925), D.Litt. of Reading (1938), Litt.D. of Sheffield (1926), and D.Phil. of Berlin. He was also an honorary fellow of Christ's College,

Cambridge (1926); and in 1937 he was master of the Worshipful Company of Musicians.

In 1902 Allen married Edith Winifred, daughter of Oliver Hall, of Dedham, Essex; they had one son and one daughter. On 17 February 1946 Allen was knocked down by a motor-cyclist in Oxford and the severe injuries which he received caused his death three days later on the 20th. A sudden death, with a touch of violence about it, seemed characteristic of the man.

A portrait of Allen by L. Campbell Taylor is at the Royal College of Music and a pencil drawing by J. S. Sargent is at New College, Oxford.

[Cyril Bailey, *Hugh Percy Allen*, 1948; personal knowledge.]    W. K. Stanton.

ALLEN, Sir JAMES (1855–1942), New Zealand statesman, was born 10 February 1855 near Adelaide, South Australia. A year later he was taken by his parents, James Allen and Mary Bax, to Dunedin, New Zealand. At the age of six he was sent to England and later went to Clifton College, and to St. John's College, Cambridge, where he obtained a third class in the natural sciences tripos in 1877. Having been captain of the Lady Margaret Boat Club and a Cambridge Rugby blue, he later captained the Otago provincial Rugby team. On his return to Dunedin in 1877 he managed the considerable estate his father had built up. In 1884–7 he again visited England and attended the Normal School of Science and Royal School of Mines, South Kensington, where he won the Bessemer and Murchison medals.

He began his political apprenticeship in the Dunedin city council, 1880–83. In 1887 he was appointed the last life member of the council of the university of Otago; he was later to be both vice-chancellor (1903–9) and chancellor (1909–12). In 1887, after an exciting contest for Dunedin East in the New Zealand House of Representatives, Allen defeated Sir Robert Stout [q.v.] then premier of New Zealand—a striking opening to a long career in Parliament. Defeated at the 1890 election, he was returned to Parliament at a by-election in 1892 for Bruce, South Otago, a seat which he held until 1920. A lengthy term in the Opposition was ended in July 1912 when the Reform Party, under W. F. Massey [q.v.], took office, with Allen, as second-in-command, taking the ministries of finance, defence, and education. Since 1891 he had commanded various volunteer defence units. In 1912 he retired from the command of the Dunedin division of garrison artillery with the territorial decoration and the honorary rank of colonel.

Although his first budget earned him a reputation for sound finance, and his education bill of 1914 reorganized the administration of education, it is as minister of defence that Allen is remembered in New Zealand. In 1912, *en route* to England, he discussed with the Australian Commonwealth premier and defence minister the formation of a Pacific naval unit financed by the three Pacific Dominions. In London he discussed with the War Office and the Committee of Imperial Defence the type of expeditionary force which New Zealand might supply in the event of war. In opposition to (Sir) Winston Churchill, then first lord of the Admiralty, he advocated the creation of a New Zealand division of the Royal Navy —a naval unit which was established by the Naval Defence Act, 1913. With the outbreak of war in 1914, Allen was able to see many of his plans put into action. Within eleven days the New Zealand Government sent troops to capture German Samoa and, by 14 October 1914, the main body of the New Zealand Expeditionary Force had embarked for Egypt.

In the national coalition Government formed in August 1915, Allen continued as minister of defence. He was mainly responsible for the system of war pensions established in 1915 and improved during the succeeding years. In 1916 he introduced conscription by the Military Service Act for men between the ages of twenty and forty-six. He himself described the resulting system as 'the most just, the most democratic, the most scientific, and the surest way to secure the necessary men, and to win the war'. Although much criticized, it certainly ensured that the New Zealand division in the field was maintained at full strength, and it resulted in over 40 per cent. of the male population within the age-group going overseas in the forces.

When Massey and Sir Joseph Ward [q.v.] went to England in 1917, Allen carried additional burdens as deputy prime minister. In that year he was appointed K.C.B. for his war services. After the war he was responsible for a comprehensive repatriation scheme for discharged servicemen.

On the dissolution of the national Government in August 1919, Allen took over the ministries of defence and finance in addition to administering the departments of land and income-tax, stamp-duties, State advances, and war pensions. He drew up and saw through the House of Representatives the bill empowering New Zealand to undertake the mandate for Western Samoa. Early in 1920 he led the parliamentary delegation to visit Samoa and New Zealand's island territories. In 1920 Allen was appointed high commissioner of New Zealand in the United Kingdom, an office he was to hold with honour to himself and his country for six years. During that period he represented the Dominion on a great variety of committees on imperial defence, economic and other subjects, and at many conferences, including the Imperial Economic Conference and one on State-aided empire settlement. He acted for the Dominion high commissioners on the small executive committee of the British Empire Exhibition of 1924. During the same years, he also represented his country at all meetings of the Assembly of the League of Nations and was prominent on several League committees. In 1926, in recognition of his many services, he was appointed G.C.M.G.

On his return to New Zealand in 1927 he was appointed to the Legislative Council where he moved the address in reply on two occasions and made several notable speeches on imperial and international affairs. He became Dominion president of the Institute of Pacific Relations and a member of its Pacific council. A loyal churchman, he was a keen supporter of the Bible-in-Schools League, of which he was the New Zealand vice-president and Otago chairman. In 1938 he ceased to attend meetings of the Legislative Council and withdrew from public life. He died at Dunedin 28 July 1942.

In 1877 Allen married his cousin, Mary Jane Hill (died 1939), daughter of John Richards, farmer, of Alford, Somersetshire; they had three sons and three daughters.

Portraits of Allen by Archibald F. Nicoll are in the New Zealand National Art Gallery, the Allen hall of the university of Otago, and at New Zealand House, London.

[*Otago Daily Times*, 29 July 1942; *Dunedin Evening Star*, 28 July 1942; L. C. Voller, *Sir James Allen—Statesman*, an unpublished thesis.]

ANGUS ROSS.

AMULREE, first BARON (1860–1942), lawyer and industrial arbitrator. [See MACKENZIE, WILLIAM WARRENDER.]

ARKWRIGHT, SIR JOSEPH ARTHUR (1864–1944), bacteriologist, was born at Thurlaston, Leicestershire, 22 March 1864, the youngest of the five children of Arthur William Arkwright, gentleman farmer, of Broughton Hall, Astley, in the same county, by his wife and second cousin, Emma, daughter of John Wolley, of Beeston, Nottinghamshire. His great-great-grandfather, Sir Richard Arkwright [q.v.], inventor of machinery for textile manufacture, was one of several forebears who had won scientific distinction. Arkwright was educated at Wellington College and at Trinity College, Cambridge, taking the natural sciences tripos in 1884–6 with zoology as his major subject. He completed his medical training at St. Bartholomew's Hospital and qualified in 1889. After holding residential posts there and afterwards at the West London Hospital and the Victoria Hospital for Children, he engaged in general practice chiefly at Halesowen, Worcestershire, from 1893 to 1904. In 1906 he joined the staff of the Lister Institute of Preventive Medicine, first as a voluntary worker and from 1908 onwards as assistant bacteriologist. He retired from active duty in 1927 but continued to work at Chelsea as an honorary member of the staff. From 1932 to 1944 he represented the Royal Society on the governing body of the Institute.

Arkwright's early investigations were concerned with the spread of diphtheria in schools and the differentiation of meningococcus strains. Much of this work was summarized in a book on The Carrier Problem in Infectious Diseases (1912), which he wrote in collaboration with (Sir) J. C. G. Ledingham [q.v.]. In 1915 he studied an epidemic of cerebrospinal meningitis among troops encamped on Salisbury Plain. Later in the year he joined the Royal Army Medical Corps and was posted as pathologist in charge of the laboratory at St. George's Hospital, Malta, where he made interesting observations on convalescent carriers in bacillary dysentery, and on blackwater fever. In 1918 he was appointed a member of the War Office committee on trench fever, and with his colleagues Arthur William Bacot and F. Martin Duncan demonstrated the constant association of the virus of trench fever with Rickettsia quintana in lice. The subject with which his name will always be

associated is, however, that of bacterial variation. His fundamental researches on the variants denoted by him as R and S (rough and smooth) in bacilli of the dysentery and enteric group were reported in the Journal of Pathology and Bacteriology in 1921 and in his Bradshaw lecture to the Royal College of Physicians in 1929. In 1922 he accompanied Bacot to Cairo at the request of the Egyptian Government to investigate the aetiology of typhus fever. After two months' work both contracted the disease, of which Bacot died. Arkwright recovered after a long illness, and on returning to the Lister Institute turned to other matters, among them animal diseases. His investigations into foot-and-mouth disease extended over more than twenty years. From 1925 onwards he was a member of the Ministry of Agriculture's committee on the subject and he became its chairman in 1931. He was a member of the Agricultural Research Council from 1931 until 1940, and chairman of the council's committee on Brucella abortus infection and on Johne's disease. He was also chairman of the joint committee on tuberculosis of the Agricultural and Medical research council.

The most remarkable characteristic of Arkwright was his singular modesty. He was the author of more than fifty papers on bacteriology and immunology and of several important sections in the Medical Research Council's System of Bacteriology (1929–31). He became F.R.C.P. (London) in 1916 and F.R.S. in 1926, and was knighted in 1937. He died in London 22 November 1944. Apart from his special studies he was a man of wide culture and he possessed an exceptional knowledge of field botany and of horticulture. He married in 1893 Ruth (died 1950), daughter of Joseph William Wilson, civil engineer; they had three daughters.

[Sir Charles Martin in Obituary Notices of Fellows of the Royal Society, No. 14, November 1945; Journal of Pathology and Bacteriology, vol. lviii, January 1946; British Medical Journal and Lancet, 9 December 1944; Nature, 30 December 1944.] W. J. BISHOP.

ARLISS, GEORGE (1868–1946), actor, whose real name was AUGUSTUS GEORGE ANDREWS, was born in London 10 April 1868, the third son of William Joseph Arliss Andrews, printer and publisher, and his wife, Rebekah Tomkins. The boy was educated in London and an early friendship with the two sons of the actress Nellie Farren [q.v.] turned his ambitions towards the stage. He made his first appearance in 1886 at the Elephant and Castle Theatre where he obtained a variety of experience under Joseph A. Cave, an actor and manager of the old school. He then toured throughout the provinces for some years, eventually returning to London where his first appearance of note was his performance as Cayley Drummle in *The Second Mrs. Tanqueray* with Mrs. Patrick Campbell [q.v.], whom he accompanied to America in November 1901. He was next engaged by David Belasco to support Blanche Bates at the Belasco Theatre, New York, and in 1902 made an immense success as Zakkuri in *The Darling of the Gods*. Later he passed under the management of Harrison Grey Fiske and appeared with Mrs. Fiske in *Becky Sharp, Leah Kleschna, Hedda Gabler*, and various other plays. In 1911 he played the title-role in *Disraeli*, a play written for him by L. N. Parker [q.v.], which, on stage and screen, served him well and faithfully for many years.

Most of Arliss's best work on the stage was done in America, but in 1923 he returned to London after an absence of twenty-two years and for over a year at the St. James's Theatre gave a memorable performance of the Rajah of Rukh in *The Green Goddess*. This play, by William Archer [q.v.], was an excellent vehicle for Arliss who in 1928 used it for the first of the remarkable series of talking films which brought him fame. It was followed by *Disraeli*, and *Old English* from the play by John Galsworthy [q.v.]. Other notable successes were *Voltaire, The House of Rothschild, The Iron Duke* (his first British film), *Cardinal Richelieu* (from the play by Lord Lytton, q.v.), and *Dr. Syn* from the novel by Mr. Russell Thorndike, set in Arliss's beloved county of Kent.

Had Arliss been a painter he would probably have been a pre-Raphaelite or a miniature painter. Louis Parker used to say of him that he could 'express more with one finger than most actors can express with their entire bodies'. His work was not cast in a heroic mould. His performance of Shylock was the portrait of a Jew in miniature. It was intensely interesting, with a mass of detail, but it lacked the magnificent sweeping breadth of character which the poet gave him. 'I have never been able to rise to those great heights', he said, apropos of Richelieu. But if he could not attain the full stature of some of his characters, his miniature performances were always dignified and thoughtful studies. They could not, however, altogether conceal his very distinctive features, and a charm of voice and personality which was not assumed. It was this, perhaps, rather than his undoubted talents as a character actor, which endeared him to the 'family' audiences for whom his films were made. He received a gold medal for diction from the American Academy of Arts and Letters, the honorary degree of M.A. from Columbia University in 1919; and he was elected a fellow of the Royal Society of Arts in 1934.

As a man Arliss was of a rather shy, retiring, and cautious disposition. He was not to be hurried, and although for long he thought of himself as a stage actor and intended to return to the theatre, he found less nervous strain in making films. Arliss was a vegetarian on principle. He was a first-rate player of contract bridge, but his chief recreation was walking which he loved, especially by the sea. For many years he owned first a cottage and then a house at St. Margaret's Bay to which he and his wife came regularly every year from America. The house was fortunately untenanted when it was completely destroyed in 1942 by a fifteen-inch shell fired from the *Gneisenau* when with the *Scharnhorst* she slipped through the English Channel.

Arliss married in 1899 Florence Kate Montgomery (died 1950) daughter of Douglas Gordon Montgomery Smith. It was a singularly happy marriage. She was herself an actress who frequently played the part of his wife on stage and screen. They had no children. He died in London 5 February 1946.

A portrait by Charles Sneed Williams is in the possession of the artist; the Garrick Club has a pastel of Arliss as Disraeli by Anders Randolf, and a portrait of him as Shylock by V. U. Noyes.

[George Arliss, *On the Stage*, 1928, and *George Arliss by Himself*, 1940; private information; personal knowledge.]

GERALD LAWRENCE.

ARMSTRONG-JONES, SIR ROBERT (1857–1943), alienist, was born at Ynyscynhaiarn, Caernarvonshire, 2 December 1857, the second child and eldest son of the ten children of the Rev. Thomas Jones, Congregational minister, of Eisteddfa, Criccieth, by his wife, Jane Elizabeth, daughter of Robert Jones, also of Eisteddfa. His mother claimed to be the twenty-first in lineal descent from Collyn ap Tangno, lord of Eifionydd. He assumed the additional surname of Armstrong in 1913. He was educated at Portmadoc Grammar School, at the University College of Wales, Aberystwyth, and at Grove Park School, Wrexham. After spending six months in the surgery of a general practitioner he entered St. Bartholomew's Hospital in 1876. He qualified as L.S.A. (1880), M.B. (London, 1880), and M.D. (1883). He was admitted M.R.C.P. (London) in 1900 and F.R.C.P. in 1907. Leaving St. Bartholomew's in 1880 he was for two years junior medical officer at the Royal Earlswood Institution, and then for six years at the Colney Hatch Asylum. He had an early inclination towards surgery and in 1885 took the F.R.C.S. (England), but soon decided that psychiatry was to be his life's work. In 1888 he returned to Earlswood as medical superintendent, and after five years in this capacity he became in 1893 the first medical superintendent of the London County Council's new asylum at Claybury.

Armstrong-Jones remained at Claybury for twenty-three years, resigning in 1916. His medical and administrative ability, and the research work of his colleague (Sir) Frederick Mott [q.v.], spread the renown of Claybury far and wide. It was the first asylum under municipal control to receive paying patients and the first to institute a special course of training for mental nurses. As its directing genius Armstrong-Jones played a great part in introducing the modern treatment of mental diseases. He was also for many years consulting physician in psychological medicine to St. Bartholomew's Hospital, and during the war of 1914–18 he acted as consulting physician in mental diseases to the London and Aldershot commands. From 1921 to 1931 he was one of the three lord chancellor's visitors in lunacy. He was a justice of the peace for Essex and justice of the peace and deputy-lieutenant for the counties of London and Caernarvon, and in 1929 high sheriff of Caernarvonshire. In 1910 he gave evidence before the Royal Commission on divorce and matrimonial causes, and in 1920 he served on the archbishop of Canterbury's special committee on spiritual healing. He was Gresham professor of physic (1917–27); general secretary of the Royal Medico-Psychological Association (1897–1906), and its president (1906–7); president of the section of psychological medicine of the British Medical Association (1903), and of the section of psychiatry of the

Royal Society of Medicine (1929). He was knighted in 1917 and appointed C.B.E. in 1919; he was also a knight of grace of the Order of St. John of Jerusalem. He received the honorary degree of D.Sc. from the university of Wales in 1920. He travelled widely for the purpose of visiting mental hospitals, and was keenly interested in social questions, upon which he wrote vigorous letters to *The Times*. He published a *Text-book of Mental and Sick Nursing* (1907) and contributed many articles to encyclopaedias, treatises, and journals. He died 30 January 1943 at his home at Plâs Dinas, Caernarvon, where there is a portrait by Frederic Whiting. In 1893 he married Margaret Elizabeth (died May 1943), daughter of Sir Owen Roberts who was a justice of the peace and deputy-lieutenant for the counties of London and Caernarvon. They had one son and two daughters.

[*British Medical Journal* and *Lancet*, 6 February 1943; *The Times*, 1 February 1943.]

W. J. BISHOP.

ARTHUR WILLIAM PATRICK ALBERT, DUKE OF CONNAUGHT AND STRATHEARN (1850–1942), the third son and seventh child of Queen Victoria, was born at Buckingham Palace 1 May 1850, the eighty-first birthday of his godfather the Duke of Wellington, after whom he received his first name; his second name was after the Prince of Prussia, later German Emperor, his third in remembrance of Queen Victoria's visit to Ireland in 1849; Albert was after his father. He became the favourite son of the Queen who 'adored our little Arthur from the day of his birth. He has never given us a day's sorrow or trouble, she may truly say, but ever been like a ray of sunshine in the house.' Even in early days he was attracted to things military, and in the gardens at Osborne there still stand miniature earthworks of military formations about which he used to play. When the Prince was not yet nine years old, (Sir) Howard Crawfurd Elphinstone [q.v.] was appointed his governor, and so began a companionship and friendship which was to last for more than thirty years.

Until 1862 Prince Arthur's life had been spent at home, but in that year he took up residence at Ranger's House, Greenwich Park. His life, he said, was a lonely one, 'called at 6.45 a.m. and I worked till about 9 a.m., when I breakfasted, work being resumed at 10 a.m. until 1 p.m. Then I had a short walk and lunched at 2 p.m. In the afternoon I walked and twice a week boys came from various schools to play with me. We played football, hockey, etc. Lessons were again resumed at 5 p.m. until 7.30 p.m. Supper at 8 p.m. and afterwards I prepared lessons until about 10 p.m. for the following day.' In 1864 he began to see more of the world for himself: he stayed at the Rosenau for two months perfecting his German, went on a walking tour in Switzerland and did some climbing; then to improve his French he went to Ouchy near Lausanne, and returned to England after a further short visit to Germany with his great friend Prince Adolphus of Mecklenburg-Strelitz. Next year he made a tour of the Mediterranean in the *Enchantress*, visiting Italy, Greece, Asia Minor, and Palestine. His first public function was performed in 1865, when he unveiled a statue of his father at Tenby; in the next year he 'passed very well' into the Royal Military Academy, Woolwich, where, still living at Ranger's House, he underwent the military training common to all cadets. A visit to the Emperor Napoleon in 1867 and a severe attack of smallpox interrupted his studies, but he passed out in 1868, and at the final inspection he was called out to receive his commission in the Royal Engineers at the hands of the Duke of Cambridge [q.v.], the commander-in-chief, feeling 'very proud at having at last become an officer'.

After a short period at the School of Military Engineering, the Prince visited Switzerland and was then transferred to the Royal Artillery at Woolwich, where he had charge of men, horses, and guns, and acquired 'an idea of responsibility'. In 1869 he was transferred to the 1st battalion of the Rifle Brigade, then stationed at Montreal. His company commander, finding the Prince a keen soldier, went on leave and left him in command. From the political point of view, the posting was opportune. Canada was restless, loyal to the Queen, but exasperated with the home Government. 'The more I visit Canada', wrote Prince Arthur to the Queen, 'the more I like and admire the people. They are a set of fine honest free thinking but loyal Englishmen.' Among the various visits paid was one to the headquarters of the Fenians at Buffalo in the United States: reports were rife that the Prince would be held as a hostage, but the visit was a complete success. After a brief visit to Washington, New York, and Boston, where he thoroughly enjoyed himself, he saw action

in 1870 against a body of Fenians who had invaded Canada. At the end of a 'very happy and interesting year', he rejoined his battalion at Woolwich.

On coming of age in 1871 Prince Arthur, who had been invested as K.G. on the Queen's birthday in 1867, was promoted captain and given the command of 'B' company. He also received the freedom of the City of London and was introduced into the Privy Council. On a visit to his eldest sister Victoria, then the German Crown Princess [q.v.], in 1872 he was admitted to the Order of the Black Eagle, 'a tremendous function'. In 1873 at a visit to his second sister Alice, afterwards Grand Duchess of Hesse-Darmstadt [q.v.], the Prince was introduced to the sport of wild-boar hunting, and next visited Rome where he was received by Pope Pius IX. Later in the year, after a visit to Vienna for the opening of the International Exhibition, Elphinstone was able to allay the anxieties of the Queen about this visit to this gayest of capitals by reporting that it had done a great deal of good, as the Prince became wearied with the constant life of pleasure and the late hours. In January 1874 he was best man at St. Petersburg to his brother Alfred, Duke of Edinburgh [q.v.], at his wedding to the Grand Duchess Marie, daughter of the Emperor Alexander II. When the Emperor and Empress of Russia visited Queen Victoria in May the Prince's troop ('A') of the 7th Hussars (to which he had been transferred in April) was sent as an escort and he was in attendance on various occasions and inspections, during one of which the Duke of Cambridge, the commander-in-chief, ordered the Prince to 'charge the crowd', which he said he did with great reluctance.

In spite of all these special duties, the chief interest and occupation of the Prince, who in 1874 was created Duke of Connaught and Strathearn and Earl of Sussex, were his military duties. In 1873 he had been attached to the staff of an infantry brigade at Aldershot, and during the manœuvres later he was brigade-major. His room in one of the lower huts of his battalion was 'so small that I could lie in bed and open the window and poke the fire', while of his work, his colonel wrote: 'Prince Arthur works like a slave and his General told me that no poor man in the Army working for his advancement could work harder than he does or do his duty better.' In 1875 he attended the German army manœuvres, a significant event for him personally, for he met the 'Red Prince', Prince Frederick Charles Nicholas of Prussia, and in October he took up the duties of assistant adjutant-general at Gibraltar. By nature a good linguist, he took the opportunity of learning Spanish, and in company with the Prince of Wales he visited King Alfonso XII at Madrid in the spring of 1876, rejoining at Gibraltar after visiting Toledo and Seville for the Easter ceremonies. Later he went to Liverpool to take command of a detached squadron, and he was present in August when the Queen unveiled the statue of the Prince Consort at Edinburgh. A change came in September when he went from the 7th Hussars to the command of the 1st battalion of his old regiment, the Rifle Brigade, as lieutenant-colonel, stationed in Dublin. Throughout the next year and until 1878 the Duke was at the Curragh, but in February he went to Berlin to attend the weddings of the Crown Princess's daughter Charlotte to Prince Bernhard of Saxe-Meiningen and of a daughter of the Red Prince to the Grand Duke of Oldenburg. The Duke then fell in love with the Red Prince's third daughter Louise Margaret Alexandra Victoria Agnes and, though the Queen was anxious about the match at first, the visit of the Princess to her in May was the beginning of a deep and lasting affection between mother and daughter-in-law. The marriage took place at St. George's Chapel, Windsor, 13 March 1879 and until the Duchess died thirty-eight years later the union was an ideally happy one. The honeymoon was mainly spent on board the royal yacht *Osborne* in a trip to Lisbon, Gibraltar, Spain, Malta, Sicily, the Aegean, Greece, and the Adriatic to Venice, whence the Duke returned home and resumed the command of his battalion at Aldershot. It was not until after Christmas 1880 that the Duke and Duchess were able to take up residence at Bagshot Park, where the Duke found real joy in the beautiful grounds on which he spent time and care and in the glorious trees of which he had expert knowledge and which he was never tired of inspecting and showing to his friends. For London residence, until the death of Queen Victoria, they lived at Buckingham Palace, but thereafter their London home was Clarence House.

The importance which the Duke attached to thoroughness in his military career is illustrated by a letter which he wrote to the Queen before his marriage. The question of promotion having arisen,

he wrote: 'up to now I have worked my way up through every grade, from Lieutenant to Lieutenant-Colonel, and I should not wish to skip the rank of Colonel' (Royal Archives). In 1880 he was promoted colonel-in-chief of the Rifle Brigade: the Prince of Wales relinquished the post reluctantly, but took up that of colonel-in-chief of the Household Cavalry; the Duke was also promoted major-general in 1880, and appointed to command the 3rd Infantry brigade at Aldershot, but in 1882 he was put in command of the 1st Guards brigade, then serving in the Egyptian war, under (Sir) G. H. S. Willis [q.v.]. From reading his notes it is easy to realize the constant care which the Duke had for his men in conditions in which comfort was very deficient. He had a narrow escape from death in action when a shell burst between himself and another officer. He was thrice mentioned in dispatches, and Sir Garnet (later Viscount) Wolseley [q.v.] writing to the Queen in September 1882 says that he 'takes great interest in his work and is indefatigable in his duties as Brigadier'; and again, after the battle of Tel-el-Kebir, 'On all sides I hear loud praises of the cool courage displayed yesterday, when under an extremely heavy fire, by H.R.H. the Duke of Connaught. . . . He is a first-rate Brigadier-General, and takes more care of his men and is more active in the discharge of his duties than any of the Generals now with me.' The Duke of Cambridge wrote: 'He has won golden opinions from everyone.' On his own share in the action, the Duke characteristically entreated the Queen not to give him any honour greater than an officer commanding a brigade would naturally receive. 'I covet', he wrote, 'a C.B., and if I get that I shall be so proud.' He was appointed C.B. and received the thanks of both Houses of Parliament. Wolseley appointed him commandant of Cairo, and he subsequently went for an extended trip up the Nile, after which he returned home in November and was invested by the German Crown Prince with the Prussian Order *pour le mérite*. In 1883 he was appointed colonel of the Scots Guards.

The Duke next served in Bengal until 1886 when, after some discussion, Lord Salisbury's Cabinet approved his appointment to the Bombay Command. This post he held for four years, managing, in spite of difficulties, to attend the Queen's jubilee in 1887. He was promoted lieutenant-general in 1889. During these years both he and the Duchess devoted their time and their services to India and its peoples of whom he ever after spoke with understanding and affection. They learnt to speak Hindustani fluently. One friendship, which left a permanent mark on the decoration of the billiard-room at Bagshot, was with Rudyard Kipling's father, then curator of the museum at Lahore. On problems even then arising in India, the Duke deprecated 'a tendency . . . to bring forward Indian questions for party purposes at home' lest it should lead to 'serious trouble in India'.

On his return to England in 1890 the Duke was appointed to command the Southern district at Portsmouth, and it was the first of a series of disappointments to him when his desire to be commander-in-chief in India was not realized; nor did he ever become commander-in-chief at home. This project came up repeatedly in the last years of Queen Victoria, who was anxious that the office should be retained and that her son should hold it. Neither of Lord Salisbury's Cabinets, however, nor Lord Rosebery's could meet her wishes. Wolseley indeed urged the Duke's claims to be made adjutant-general as a preparation for succeeding the Duke of Cambridge. In 1895, when the Duke, hitherto in ignorance of what was going on between the Queen and her ministers, was told that he was not to be commander-in-chief, he was greatly vexed, and he had to undergo the same disappointment when Lord Roberts [q.v.] succeeded Lord Wolseley in 1901.

In 1893 the Duke, who had found Portsmouth uncongenial, was promoted general and appointed to the Aldershot Command. The five years' tenure of this office was punctuated by missions abroad: to the coronation of the Emperor Nicholas II, at Moscow, in 1896, to the centenary of the birth of the Emperor William I, at Berlin, in 1897, and, more professionally, to the autumn manœuvres of the French Army in 1898 when he received the grand cordon of the Legion of Honour. In spite of his desire to go on active service in South Africa, consent was not forthcoming and he made no secret of his disappointment. Instead he was appointed commander-in-chief in Ireland (1900), and he was there when his mother made her historic visit to Dublin.

In 1899 the Duke was called to make an important decision about his future life. The hereditary prince of Saxe-Coburg-Gotha died early in the year, leaving the Duke in the direct succession to the duchy, then held by his second brother Alfred,

Duke of Edinburgh. After discussions between the Queen, the Duke, and Lord Salisbury, the Duke and his son Prince Arthur [q.v.] renounced their right to the ducal throne, which consequently devolved on the Duke's nephew, Charles Edward, Duke of Albany.

With the death of the Queen, the Duke reached the summit of his military career. In 1902 his brother King Edward VII appointed him a field-marshal and his representative at the coronation durbar held at Delhi in 1903. In 1904 he was appointed inspector-general of the forces, visiting South Africa in 1906 and making an extended tour in the Far East in 1907. In that year he became high commissioner and commander-in-chief in the Mediterranean, a post which he held until 1909. In 1910 he opened the newly formed Union Parliament of South Africa on behalf of his nephew King George V. The press hailed the visit as 'a great personal triumph' for the Duke who had been 'accessible to British, Dutch, and native alike. What can be done to improve the relations between the white races has been done.'

The visit to South Africa was the prelude to a greater mission. In October 1911 the Duke took up one of the posts in which his personality found vivid expression. As governor-general of Canada, he renewed the affection he had felt for the Canadians ever since he had been quartered among them as a subaltern. Without exacting great deference to himself, he won popularity with all classes of people by his friendliness and affability. No programme of public engagements was too heavy for him. If he kept greater state at Rideau Hall than his predecessors, the presence there of a royal prince was a valuable stimulant to Canadian patriotism during the war of 1914–18. The only unfortunate episode of his term of office which lasted until 1916 was a quarrel with the extremely eccentric Sir Sam Hughes [q.v.], then minister of militia, which arose from the intelligible desire of an experienced professional soldier of the highest rank to play in military affairs a role incompatible with his constitutional position as governor-general. In 1918 the Duke visited Greece, Egypt, and Palestine, going up to Khartoum and returning after three months of travelling, which covered 20,000 miles. In December 1920 he left for an extensive visit to India. In February 1921 at Delhi he opened the new Chamber of Princes, the Imperial Legislative Assembly and the Council of State.

In 1928 he received the congratulations of the Army Council on completing sixty years of service in the army.

The Duke had suffered cruel losses in the previous ten years. The Duchess had died in 1917 and the sorrow cast a shadow over the remainder of his life; in 1920 his elder daughter, the Crown Princess of Sweden, died rather suddenly. In 1928 he ceased, although still physically and mentally active, to take an active part in public life, dividing his time between Bagshot Park and Clarence House and, until his later years, spending a part of every year in the south of France, first at Beaulieu and later at his own villa, 'Les Bruyères', at Cap Ferrat; here his love of horticulture found full scope, and many officers and men of the Royal Navy remembered his garden which he threw open to all ranks when units of the fleet came to Villefranche. He often spoke of his pleasure at the French acknowledgement of his position in the military world in making him honorary 'caporal' in a battalion of the Chasseurs Alpins. When visits to France became inadvisable, winters were spent at Sidmouth or at Bath. The Duke died at Bagshot Park 16 January 1942. He had issue a son, Prince Arthur, who died in 1938, and two daughters, Princess Margaret Victoria Augusta Charlotte Norah, who married in 1905 Prince Gustavus Adolphus, Duke of Scania, later King Gustavus VI of Sweden, and Princess Victoria Patricia Helena Elizabeth, who married in 1919 Captain (subsequently Rear-Admiral Sir) Alexander Robert Maule Ramsay, son of the thirteenth Earl of Dalhousie, taking rank, as Lady Patricia Ramsay, next below duchesses. The Duke was succeeded by his grandson, the Earl of Macduff, and on the latter's death in 1943 the dukedom of Connaught and Strathearn and the earldom of Sussex became extinct.

It was a natural consequence of his birth that the Duke held many of the highest honorary posts in civil life. One of his greatest interests was in freemasonry; he became grand master of the United Grand Lodge in 1901 and kept in close touch with it down to his death. He succeeded King George V as master of Trinity House, presiding regularly at the Trinity Monday courts; he was grand prior and bailiff of the Order of St. John of Jerusalem and on one occasion his intervention during the war of 1914–18 brought the activities of the order into better relation with those of the British Red Cross Society.

But the Duke's overriding interest was in the army, and the constant care which he showed for the welfare of the men under his command, entirely consistent with his personal character, won him a degree of affectionate respect which has been accorded to few. He fully carried out his mother's advice given to him in 1871: 'Continue to be kind and considerate to those below you, and treat those who faithfully serve you as friends'; and again: 'It is by those below us that we are most judged and it is of great value to be beloved' (Royal Archives). Beloved the Duke certainly was both by the army in particular and the people generally, but more particularly by those who knew him personally, and especially by his mother.

The Duke has often, and justly, been spoken of as a great gentleman. Endowed with a great measure of administrative ability, he was naturally impatient of official obstruction. He was invariably courteous and considerate, and if he was quick to notice irregularities, however trivial, in uniform or etiquette, his correction did not hurt. The absolute straightforwardness of his character found no room for pettiness or insincerity in others; he gave his friendship unstintingly, but expected a high standard of loyalty in return.

The Duke received from his mother all the honours which it was in her power to give. After her death he became great master of the Order of the Bath in 1901, and received the Royal Victorian Chain in 1902; in 1917 his nephew appointed him G.B.E. He received honorary degrees from many universities.

Of existing portraits of the Duke, the following may be mentioned. In the royal collections there are three by F. X. Winterhalter: 'The First of May, 1851' in which the Duke of Wellington is presenting a casket to the infant Prince in the presence of the Queen and the Prince Consort; a small portrait at the age of about three years; and another in Scots Guards uniform, at the age of about five; one by (Sir) Hubert von Herkomer (c. 1900) in the full-dress uniform of a general; one by J. S. Sargent (1910) in blue frogged frock-coat of the Grenadier Guards (with a replica at Government House, Ottawa); a large equestrian portrait by Edouard Detaille in the blue frock-coat of a general, with King Edward VII (as Prince of Wales) at an Aldershot review (c. 1898). A small sketch of the Duke's figure in this picture, by Edouard Detaille himself, belongs to

Lady Patricia Ramsay, who also possesses an unfinished head and shoulders, in field-marshal's uniform, by Sir A. S. Cope (1923). A portrait (1878) by H. von Angeli, in Rifle Brigade uniform, belongs to the officers of the Rifle Brigade. Cartoons by 'Spy' appeared in *Vanity Fair* 17 June 1876 and 2 August 1890.

A bronze statue of the Duke in uniform (before 1907) by George Wade was erected on the waterfront at Hong Kong.

[Royal Archives, Windsor Castle, *passim*; M. H. McClintock, *The Queen Thanks Sir Howard*, 1945; *Letters of Queen Victoria*, second and third series, 1926–32; private information; personal knowledge.]

BADELEY.

ASHBEE, CHARLES ROBERT (1863–1942), architect, craftsman, and town planner, was born at Isleworth, Middlesex, 17 May 1863, the only son of Henry Spencer Ashbee, by his wife, Elizabeth Jenny, daughter of Charles Lavy, merchant, of Hamburg. On his father's side, Ashbee came of a Kentish yeoman farmer stock, while the Lavy family was of Jewish extraction, cultured and musical, with a long Hanseatic tradition.

Ashbee was educated at Wellington College and at King's College, Cambridge, where he obtained a second class in the historical tripos of 1886. Having decided to become an architect, he was articled to G. F. Bodley [q.v.]. It was a busy office concerned mainly with church work, including the ancillary building crafts which such work at that time demanded. Ashbee therefore made a particular study of fine handicraft which was profoundly to affect his later career.

On leaving Bodley's office, Ashbee was soon in practice for himself, but his purely architectural work was small in quantity and of relatively minor importance. He built the 'Magpie and Stump' for his mother, a house on Cheyne Walk, Chelsea Embankment, described and illustrated in the *Studio*, May 1895, together with the four adjoining houses, of which the bombing of 1941 has left but little trace. A few pleasant country cottages, a house in Sicily, and the rebuilding and restoration of some old houses comprise the major part of his practice.

Ashbee's main purpose in early days was the revival of the artistic handicrafts. He founded the London Survey Committee and in the editing and compiling of its monographs did some most useful work. In 1897 he was elected a member of the

Art-Workers' Guild, of which he was master in 1929, and he took a prominent part in the masque which it produced at Guildhall in 1899. But his enthusiasm lay in the Guild of Handicraft which, under the influence of John Ruskin and William Morris [qq.v.], he established in 1888 in Commercial Street and in 1891 moved to Essex House, Mile End Road. Here he collected and trained a body of craftsmen who practised furniture-making, metalwork, jewellery, silversmithing, printing, and bookbinding, with the object, as stated in the rules, of doing good work and doing it 'in such a way as shall best conduce to the welfare of the workman'. But in 1902 he moved the Guild, numbering 150 men, women, and children, to Chipping Campden in Gloucestershire. The financial results disappointed his enthusiasm and in 1907 the company was wound up. Its most notable work was its printing. Ashbee bought William Morris's two presses and employed three of his workmen. The King Edward Prayer Book and the Essex House Song Book are examples of really fine printing and binding.

Until the war of 1914–18 Ashbee continued desultory architectural practice combined with successful lecture tours in America. He served with a field ambulance in the Middle East during the war, and in 1918 was teaching in the public instruction department in Egypt when he received an invitation from the military governor of Jerusalem, (Sir) Ronald Storrs, 'to visit Jerusalem and write a report on its possibilities'.

This prospect fired all Ashbee's enthusiasm. He was appointed civic adviser and secretary to the Pro-Jerusalem Society, recently formed for preserving and safeguarding the amenities of the holy city without favour or prejudice to race or creed. Its two volumes of records, edited by Ashbee (vol. i published in 1921, and vol. ii in 1924, after Ashbee's departure from Palestine), prove the value of the Society's work. Supported by the governor's tireless efforts in collecting money, Ashbee was full of enthusiasm and keenly appreciative of the beauty of the city, but not infrequently unpractical. Still, the citadel was cleaned, the city fosse cleared and planted, the rampart walk round the city was re-created and encroachments cleared away. Ashbee's restoration of the Suk el Qattanin, the old cotton market, which had for many years been a public latrine, gave back to Jerusalem one of its finest buildings. A park system was prepared in 1920, regulations were instituted by the governor and Ashbee on the building materials to be used in the city, and on the preservation of open spaces and skylines, while a special effort, which particularly interested Ashbee, was made to revive Arab crafts, such as pottery, tile-making, weaving, glass-blowing, and woodwork.

The development of the modern city of Jerusalem had been the subject of a plan prepared at the request of Sir Edmund (later Viscount) Allenby [q.v.] in 1918; a second plan by (Sir) Patrick Geddes [q.v.] followed in 1919, and in 1921 a central town planning commission was set up. The resultant '1922 plan,' incorporating many of Ashbee's ideas, was based on more accurate surveys and, being more practicable than its two predecessors, laid the foundation of the later more detailed schemes.

Ashbee resigned his post at Jerusalem in 1922, and published, besides several books of essays on the social importance of craftsmanship, a book on *Caricature* (1928) and a delightful book called *Grannie* (1939), a study of his mother's character and upbringing. In 1898 he married Janet Elizabeth, daughter of Francis Augustine Forbes, stockbroker, of Godden Green, Sevenoaks; they had four daughters.

Ashbee was a man of quick enthusiasms and restless mind, apt to disregard mundane restrictions and to be impatient with those who differed from him, but to his friends, and particularly to his old friends, loyal and steadfast. In his work for the preservation of threatened beauty in towns and buildings, the encouragement of the crafts, the provision of parks and open spaces, he was undoubtedly on the side of the angels, who, however, may often have found him a difficult and even exasperating ally. He died at Godden Green 23 May 1942. The Art-Workers' Guild has a bust by the Rev. Allan G. Wyon.

[C. R. Ashbee, *Craftsmanship in Competitive Industry*, 1908, *A Palestine Note-Book, 1918–1923*, 1923, and *Grannie*, 1939; H. J. L. J. Massé, *The Art-Workers' Guild, 1884–1934*, 1935; Henry Kendall, *Jerusalem City Plan*, 1948; private information; personal knowledge.] W. H. ANSELL.

ASHFIELD, BARON (1874–1948), chairman of the London Passenger Transport Board. [See STANLEY, ALBERT HENRY.]

ASKWITH, GEORGE RANKEN, BARON ASKWITH (1861–1942), barrister, arbitrator, and member of many government committees and commissions, was born at Waltham Abbey, Essex, 17 February 1861, son of William Harrison Askwith, then colonel in the Royal Artillery (later general), by his wife, Elizabeth, daughter of George Ranken. Educated at Marlborough and at Brasenose College, Oxford, he took first class honours in modern history in 1884, read law, and was called to the bar by the Inner Temple and the Middle Temple in 1886.

Askwith worked first in the chambers of Sir Henry James (later Lord James of Hereford, q.v.) who in later life specialized as arbitrator in labour disputes; and the young lawyer was able to draw from this association knowledge and experience which in future years stood him in good stead when similar work came his way. James's good offices also brought him the appointment of counsel for H.M. Commissioners of Works and counsel for the Crown in peerage claims. He took silk in 1908, although a year earlier he had abandoned active practice at the bar to take up the post of assistant secretary in the railway branch of the Board of Trade.

Thenceforward Askwith's career was closely bound up with public and official affairs. In 1908 he was government representative at the international copyright conference at Berlin. The following year he became controller-general of the commercial, labour, and statistical department of the Board of Trade, and chairman of the fair wages advisory committee. In 1911 he was appointed chief industrial commissioner, holding this post until 1919.

The years just prior to the war of 1914–18 were clouded with industrial troubles, and it was in judicially working out the rights and wrongs of disputes between masters and men that Askwith acquired a national reputation. There were dangerous potentialities in nation-wide clashes in major industries, and his services as a conciliator in such matters (especially the railway and dock troubles of 1911) were notable.

Among the many posts held by Askwith during an extremely active life were: chairman of the committee on production (1915–17) which acted as a tribunal to deal with disputes on government work; member of the Royal Commission on cattle importation (1921); chairman of the Royal Commission on Malta (1931); chairman of the parliamentary delegation to Bermuda

(1932); member of the panel for commissions of inquiry under article 412 of the Treaty of Versailles (1934). He was chairman of the council of the Royal Society of Arts (1922–4); of the governors of Royal Holloway College; of the council of Cheltenham Ladies' College, and a member of the council of St. Hilda's College, Oxford; he served as president of the British Science Guild, the Institute of Patentees, the National Association of Trade Protection Societies, and the Institute of Arbitrators.

In 1912 Oxford awarded Askwith the honorary degree of D.C.L., and in 1919 he was elected an honorary fellow of Brasenose. He received the honorary degree of LL.D. from Leeds University in 1937. He was appointed C.B. in 1909, promoted K.C.B. in 1911, and in 1919 was created a baron. He died in London 2 June 1942.

In 1908 Askwith married Ellen, daughter of Archibald Peel, and widow of Major Henry Graham of the 20th Hussars. There was one daughter of the marriage, but no son, so that the peerage became extinct.

[*The Times*, 3 June 1942.]

HERBERT B. GRIMSDITCH.

ASQUITH, EMMA ALICE MARGARET (generally known as MARGOT), COUNTESS OF OXFORD AND ASQUITH (1864–1945), was born at The Glen, Peeblesshire, 2 February 1864. She was the sixth daughter and eleventh child of (Sir) Charles Tennant, later first baronet [q.v.], by his first wife, Emma, daughter of Richard Winsloe, of Mount Nebo, Taunton, Somerset. She was educated by governesses and tutors until the age of fifteen, when she attended for a few months Mlle de Mennecy's finishing school in Gloucester Crescent. From there she went to study in Dresden. Throughout her life she was a great reader of serious literature and remembered what she read. Benjamin Jowett [q.v.], master of Balliol, described her as 'the best-educated ill-educated woman that I have ever met'.

The year Margot Tennant 'came out' she started a crèche in Wapping with her sister Laura (died 1886, the first wife of Alfred Lyttelton, q.v.). From 1886 to 1894, whenever she was in London, she made frequent visits to a factory of women workers in Whitechapel. 'I have derived as much interest and more benefit', she wrote, 'from visiting the poor than the rich and I get on better with them.' In 1880 she first took up fox-hunting. She was a fearless rider and for many years hunting, chiefly in Leicestershire, remained an absorbing interest. Her boundless energy, however, had already found an outlet in other fields. 'After fox-hunting', she wrote, 'the greatest pleasure I have had in life has been intellectual and endearing conversation.' She was one of the group known as 'the Souls', men and women in London society whose bond of association was intellectual and aesthetic rather than political. Her close friendship with Jowett lasted from 1887 until his death in 1893. Among her other friends were W. E. Gladstone, Arthur Balfour, the Duke of Devonshire, the Cecil and Lyttelton families, Sir William Harcourt, Lord Milner, Lord Rosebery, Lord Haldane, Lord Midleton, Randall Davidson (archbishop of Canterbury), John Addington Symonds, John Morley, and Virginia Woolf.

In May 1894 she married, as his second wife, Herbert Henry Asquith [q.v.]. If she took her husband with her into the innermost circles of the *beau monde*, this was, some believed, at the cost of his apparent partial withdrawal from those who had hitherto given him unwavering support as a fellow nonconformist. Her own attitude to politics was intensely personal. Of good Liberal stock by birth, as the wife of a Liberal leader she became a fervent party-politician. But if all outside the Liberal fold were automatically political enemies, many Conservatives remained her appreciative personal friends; and even within the Liberal ranks, as in every other walk of life, she discriminated with her own remarkable shrewdness. She was among the first, if not the first, to detect in David Lloyd George a discontented subordinate and to divine that his appointment in 1916 as secretary of state for war presaged her husband's departure from 10 Downing Street.

As her stepdaughter Lady Violet Bonham Carter has truly said, 'To her politics meant men not measures', and it was certainly in the politicians themselves that she was interested, rather than in their problems, of which she had little grasp. Political principles were in fact a blind spot with her, as was bridge, a game she played with ardent incompetence. Her loyalties, and their resulting animosities, were passionately her own, and passionately expressed: for being a woman of unrestrained candour she could never 'bring herself to believe that truth could wound'. From 1908 to 1916—a period of increasing political tension—her very excellences as a human being were therefore politically always a potential liability, the more so in that she was the wife of a premier whom she herself described as possessing 'a modesty amounting to deformity'. She was, said Sir Desmond MacCarthy, 'unteachable and splendid', neither of them qualities likely to appeal to the British public in the wife of a prime minister, especially in wartime. If her husband was accused of intellectual aloofness, she too was criticized for her over-impetuous generosities.

The years which followed the war were a time of discouragement for the Liberal Party. In 1925 Asquith entered the House of Lords with the title of the Earl of Oxford and Asquith, and he gave up the Liberal leadership in the following year. Until his death in 1928 Lady Oxford entertained regularly at The Wharf, Sutton Courtney, their country house in Berkshire, and at their London house in Bedford Square. She also found time for writing. The first volume of her *Autobiography* appeared in 1920; the second in 1922. *Places and Persons*, a record of visits to Egypt, America, Spain, and Italy, followed in 1925; *Lay Sermons*, a collection of essays on a wide range of subjects, in 1927; *Octavia*, a novel based on her early experiences in the hunting field and in political life, in 1928; *More Memories* in 1933, and *Off the Record*, further gleanings from the harvest of her recollections, in 1943.

Lady Oxford's writing is distinguished by directness, force, and wit. She was a master of the *bon mot* and the vivid, startling metaphor. From the Scottish ancestry of which she was always proud she may have inherited her devout, undogmatic Christianity, with its strongly ethical tone. She was fundamentally a puritan and the qualities she most admired in human nature were sincerity and heart. In *More Memories* she writes of 'the "desperate seriousness of the moral choice", and the infinite difference between right and wrong'. Critics who have accused her of frivolity were utterly mistaken. She was a crusader with a serious purpose in nearly everything she wrote and a quixotic, sometimes ill-judged determination to remedy abuses whenever she saw them. 'When I hear nonsense talked', she wrote, 'it makes me physically ill not to contradict.'

Her writings, striking and provocative as they are, do not give the full flavour of her personality or explain how she came to be a legend in her lifetime. They testify to the courage on which she was frequently complimented, to the breadth of reading about which she was unjustifiably modest, and to her capacity for friendship, but not to less easily defined qualities—her instinctive kindness and generosity, the infectious gaiety of her presence, the magnetic originality which made even people who did not know her flock to see her. Her flair for what was beautiful left its mark on taste and fashion for nearly half a century. Owing to the different conditions prevailing now it is a little difficult to estimate or appreciate the influence she had on the social world; but she quotes Lord Balfour as saying that 'no history of society in the nineteenth century can fail to write of the influence which you and your friends have had in the social and political life of this country. Till "the Souls" emerged into London, Tories and Liberals of distinction never met.'

Unperturbed by air raids, Lady Oxford spent the closing years of her life in London and died there 28 July 1945. She had five children, only two of whom—Elizabeth, afterwards Princess Antoine Bibesco (1897–1945), and Anthony (born 1902)—survived infancy. A portrait of Lady Oxford by Sir John Lavery is in the possession of her son.

[Her own writings; *The Times*, 30 July 1945; *Sunday Times*, 29 July 1945; *Listener*, 11 June 1953; private information; personal knowledge.]      L. P. HARTLEY.

ASTON, FRANCIS WILLIAM (1877– 1945), experimental physicist, was born at Harborne, near Birmingham, 1 September 1877, the third of the seven children of William Aston, metal merchant, by his wife, Fanny Charlotte, daughter of Isaac Hollis, founder of the engineering firm which eventually became the Birmingham Small Arms Company.

After attending private schools until he was nearly fourteen, Aston spent two years at Malvern College, then at sixteen he entered Mason College, Birmingham, where his interests turned towards organic chemistry. For many years he had had a workshop and 'laboratory' of his own in his father's house, and when he was awarded the Forster scholarship in 1898 and started research with P. F. Frankland [q.v.] he was already an accomplished, if self-taught, experimenter and a skilled glass-blower. During the tenure of his scholarship he was able also to take a course in fermentation chemistry. With the added qualification so obtained he gained an appointment with a firm of brewers in Wolverhampton. He held this position from 1900 to 1903, continuing his work in his private laboratory in his spare time. Already having considerable experience in high-vacuum technique, he became intensely interested in the construction of X-ray tubes of novel design and in the phenomena of gas discharges at low pressure. This work attracted the attention of J. H. Poynting [q.v.], professor of physics in the then newly established university of Birmingham, and in 1903 Aston returned to academic research to continue his investigations in Poynting's department. After five years of sound, if unhurried, progress, the work was interrupted. Aston spent the next year travelling round the world by way of Ceylon, Malaya, Australia, New Zealand, the Pacific islands, the United States, and Canada. Thus refreshed he held—for one term—the only university teaching post of his creer, a lectureship in physics in the university of Birmingham. But he was not by inclination a teacher, and in January 1910 he accepted the position of research assistant to Sir J. J. Thomson [q.v.] and became a member of Trinity College, Cambridge. This college was to be his home for the rest of his life.

Since 1906 Thomson had been working on the positive rays, and in 1910 he had reached the stage of applying the method of crossed electric and magnetic deflections in order to obtain the characteristic 'parabolas' by means of which the first mass-analysis of the rays was achieved. Aston's immediate contribution to this work was mainly technical. In particular, the large spherical discharge tubes which he designed for Thomson's positive-ray apparatus solved the problem of ensuring steady operation at the low pressures essential for successful working, and his general experience in high-vacuum technique was invaluable. As seen from the standpoint of a later generation the most significant result of the work was the discovery of the second parabola due to neon. We now know that in this observation the isotopic constitution of a stable element was for the first time revealed; Thomson, however, was chary of using the same chemical symbol for the two constituents, of masses 20 and 22, present in the rare gas samples which he analysed. Nevertheless, to his assistant, Aston, he assigned the task of attempting the separation of these constituents by methods which assumed that the most significant differences in their properties would be those depending primarily on mass. In 1913 Aston reported partial separation by the method of repeated diffusion through pipeclay. His success in this endeavour owed much to sheer perseverance, but equally as much to his development of a quartz microbalance by means of which very accurate determination of density could be made with small samples of gas. At this stage Aston's period as Thomson's assistant ended and the distinction of his own work was recognized by the university's electing him as Clerk Maxwell student. He had taken his B.A. degree by research in 1912. Little more was achieved, however, before the outbreak of war in 1914 when Aston moved to Farnborough as technical assistant at the Royal Aircraft Establishment.

At Farnborough neon discharge tubes again became a subject of research, now as sources of light for stroboscopic work, but chemical investigations on dope for aeroplane fabric occupied most of the time.

Aston's first mass-spectrograph was built soon after his return to Cambridge in 1919. By replacing Thomson's arrangement of electric and magnetic fields applied over the same element of path of the positive rays, by fields applied over successive elements and so directed as to produce contrary deflections, Aston was able to achieve velocity focusing of the rays—that is deviation without velocity dispersion—when the field intensities were suitably adjusted. This provided an instrument which was a great advance on Thomson's in sensitivity and in accuracy, for it gave a line spectrum of almost constant mass-dispersion in place of a system of parabolas. With its aid all the elements available in simple gaseous form were analysed within a very short time. The results with neon were confirmed, and the instrument was sufficiently accurate to show that the chemical atomic weight of the element was different from that of either of the isotopes and very likely to represent the average mass of all the atoms in the normal isotopic mixture. Not only elements such as chlorine of which the chemical atomic weight is far from integral on the oxygen scale, but others like bromine with a much more nearly integral atomic weight were shown to be mixtures of two or more species: the phenomenon of isotopy was in fact established as one of the basic phenomena of nature. Significant regularities emerged naturally from these observations—the whole number rule, stating effectively that the masses of all atoms are integral multiples of the mass of the atom of hydrogen to an accuracy of at least 1 per cent., and the rule of odd and even, recording the fact that the mass numbers of the isotopes of odd-numbered elements are almost always odd and those of even-numbered elements predominantly even. These regularities were developed and given further precision as the result of later work, but from the first they contained the germs of significant truth.

Widespread acclamation greeted the publication of Aston's astoundingly simple but entirely revolutionary results, and honours came quickly. In 1920 he was elected first holder of one of the newly created research fellowships at Trinity College and received the Mackenzie Davidson medal of the Röntgen Society; in 1921 he was elected F.R.S.; in 1922 he received the Hughes medal of the Royal Society and the Nobel prize for chemistry; in 1923 the John Scott medal (Philadelphia) and the Italian Paterno medal, as well as being elected fellow of the (Royal) Institute of Chemistry and made an honorary LL.D. of the university of Birmingham.

Having obtained all the information on isotopes which his instrument could give by way of mass-analysis of the positive rays produced in gas discharges, Aston turned his attention for the next few years to the metallic elements. The technique here was more difficult, but he gradually mastered the art of producing 'accelerated anode rays' and by 1925 analyses of fifty-six elements had been made. By this time a further generalization became obvious: odd-numbered elements are either simple elements or are constituted of two isotopes only. The distinction between even- and odd-numbered elements thus became more clearly discerned, for even-numbered elements frequently have many more isotopes than two.

In 1927 Aston was Bakerian lecturer of the Royal Society. He had just completed his second mass-spectrograph and had obtained the first results with its aid. The resolving power of his original instrument had been insufficient for successful work with the heaviest elements and its precision of measurement was about 1 part in 1,000. In the new instrument precision was improved by a factor of 10 and resolution was adequate for all likely requirements. Here was an instrument capable of detecting a difference of mass equal to the electron mass in the mass of an alpha particle (helium nucleus); by its use the whole-number rule was shown to be only approximate and the way lay open for a direct check of the Einstein law of equivalence of mass and energy when the results of experiments on nuclear transmutation were taken into account. The application of the method of photometric comparison of intensities of mass-spectrum lines in 1930 made available for the first time a purely physical method of precision for the determination of chemical atomic weights. In the years 1927 to 1935 a complete resurvey of the elements was made with the new spectrograph and Aston's essential contribution to the subject was complete. In the latter year he further improved his spectrograph, increasing its accuracy of measurement by another large factor, but now many younger men were active in similar work and with the outbreak of war in 1939 he soon abandoned regular experimenting and did not live long enough to resume it again in less violent times.

Aston's whole life was dominated by hobbies. That his research was a hobby is evident from the fact that he worked alone, never taking on a research student for help or training. Travel was a life-long hobby, particularly in order to observe an eclipse. Photography and the care of the Trinity College clock were scientific hobbies, music and the collection of Chinese porcelain cultural hobbies, and at various stages of his life cycling, motoring, tennis, swimming, ski-ing, and golf took him out of doors with enthusiasm—and often with reward. He died, unmarried, at Cambridge, 20 November 1945.

Honours not already mentioned were: foreign membership of the Academy of Sciences of the U.S.S.R. (1925) and the Accademia dei Lincei (1926), the honorary degrees of D.Sc., Dublin (1929), Ph.D., Freiburg (1930), D.Sc., Benares (1937), and D.L., Calcutta (1938), a Royal medal, Royal Society (1938), the Joykissen Mookherjee medal, Indian Association for the Cultivation of Science (1938), and Duddell medal, Physical Society (1944). He was president of the mathematics and physics section of the British Association in 1935.

[G. C. de Hevesy in *Obituary Notices of Fellows of the Royal Society*, No. 16, May 1948; *The Times*, 22 November 1945; *Cambridge Review*, 2 February 1946; private information; personal knowledge.]

N. FEATHER.

ATKIN, JAMES RICHARD, BARON ATKIN (1867–1944), judge, was born at Brisbane, Australia, 28 November 1867, the eldest son of Robert Travers Atkin, of Fernhill, county Cork, who settled in Queensland and became a member of the legislative assembly, by his wife, Mary Elizabeth, daughter of Laurence Ruck, of Newington, Kent. (It is an interesting coincidence that Atkin's ancestors (Atkyn, Atkyns) of four to five hundred years earlier included judges and lawyers.)

After his father died Atkin's mother, who was Welsh, went to live in Merionethshire where Atkin was brought up with his mother's family (who were connected with the Darwins since Amy Ruck had married (Sir) Francis Darwin, q.v.). In consequence Atkin always regarded himself as a Welshman. He was educated at Christ College, Brecon, and became a demy of Magdalen College, Oxford. He was a considerable games player and just missed being chosen to play tennis against Cambridge. He took a second in both classical moderations (1887) and *literae humaniores* (1889), undergoing a severe attack of influenza during his final examination. On leaving Oxford he joined Gray's Inn and was called to the bar in 1891. He read as a pupil in the chambers of (Sir) T. E. Scrutton [q.v.] who was later to be his colleague in the Court of Appeal, and received there a grounding in the common law from one of its acknowledged masters.

During his first ten years at the bar, Atkin had little work, but when his opportunity finally came he was quick to seize it. A period of speculation on the London Stock Exchange after the South African war resulted in a flood of litigation. Juniors familiar with the law and practice of the Stock Exchange were few and Atkin began to find himself briefed in these actions, in which the facts were complicated and the law difficult and frequently unsettled. His conduct of these cases was quickly appreciated and the ability and learning which lay behind Atkin's gentle style of advocacy soon came to be recognized. From 1901 onwards his practice grew rapidly and widened; the knowledge of marine insurance which he had acquired in Scrutton's chambers gave him a footing in the Commercial Court and he even appeared in 'society' litigation. His conduct of proceedings in chambers and before the masters of the King's Bench division has been considered a model.

In 1906 Atkin took silk and thenceforward his practice became more commercial in character although it continued to include common law actions where the issue depended upon difficult questions of law or the unravelling of complicated sets of facts. He appeared rarely in jury actions, his style of advocacy being generally unsuited to that type of work, but he was regularly before the House of Lords and the Privy Council. At that time Lord Macnaghten [q.v.] considered that Atkin and S. O. (later Viscount) Buckmaster [q.v.] were the most brilliant of those who habitually addressed the House.

In 1913 Atkin was raised to the bench as a judge of the King's Bench division, was knighted as is customary, and began a long and outstanding period of thirty-one years as a judge. Gentle, firm, patient, learned in the law, dignified, he was an immediate success as a judge of first instance, not only in the Commercial Court (for he was soon placed on the rota of that court) but also, despite his having little or no experience of criminal work at the bar, as a criminal law judge. In 1919 he was appointed a lord justice of appeal, was sworn of the Privy Council, and was instantly successful as an appellate judge. In 1928 he was appointed a lord of appeal in ordinary, with a life peerage, and in the appellate work of the House of Lords and the Privy Council had the freedom and scope to apply and develop the principles of the law as he conceived them.

For Atkin the law was dynamic and although he recognized the necessity for having settled legal rules, he was prepared whenever possible to develop legal principles to provide a remedy when a proven injury had been suffered. His insistence upon the importance of principles together with a lucid style and the ability frequently to coin an apposite phrase made certain the recognition of his considerable influence upon the common law. Atkin made important contributions in many fields of English law, in the law of contract and quasi-contract, in the law of evidence, in criminal law and in commercial law, in constitutional and administrative law and in the interpretation of statutes, particularly the Workmen's Compensation Acts, in company law, and in the law concerning negligence and defamation.

An indication of Atkin's influence may be seen in the considerable number of his judgements which have become starting-points for further developments. Such was his enunciation of the fundamental rule in the law of negligence in the case of *Donoghue* v. *Stevenson*, [1932] A.C. 562, where a lady, who had consumed ginger beer in a café, was awarded damages in negligence against the manufacturers of the beverage on account of the injury which she had suffered through the presence of the decomposed remains of a snail at the bottom of the opaque ginger-beer bottle. In the law of contract he drew attention to the worst features of the doctrine of frustration (in the *Fibrosa* case, [1943] A.C. 32), and attempted to rationalize the concept of mistake in the formation of contract (in *Bell* v. *Lever Brothers*, [1932] A.C. 161). In *Fender* v. *Mildmay*, [1938] A.C. 1, where the plaintiff was permitted to bring an action for breach of promise to marry against a defendant who made the promise after obtaining a decree nisi but before obtaining a decree absolute, Atkin reviewed the extent to which public policy should be allowed to exert an influence upon the law.

One of the most characteristic features of his judicial work was his concern for the individual, and particularly for the underdog. In workmen's compensation cases he earned a reputation for being a judge who would always give a sympathetic hearing to workmen. But probably the most striking instance of his concern for the rights of the individual was his dissent in *Liversidge* v. *Anderson*, [1942] A.C. 206. In that case the House of Lords decided that the famous regulation 18B did not enable the court to inquire whether the secretary of state had reasonable grounds for believing a person to be of hostile association when ordering his detention. 'In this country, amid the clash of arms, the laws are not silent', Atkin maintained. 'They may be changed, but they speak the same language in war as in peace. It has always been one of the pillars of freedom, one of the principles of liberty for which on recent authority we are now fighting, that the judges are no respecters of persons and stand between the subject and any attempted encroachments on his liberty by the executive, alert to see that any coercive action is justified in law. In this case I have listened to arguments which might have been addressed acceptably to the Court of King's Bench in the time of Charles I. I protest, even if I do it alone, against a strained construction put on words with the effect of giving an uncon-

trolled power of imprisonment to the minister.'

Atkin dissented alone, for his colleagues took a different view of the powers which were conferred upon the executive in a national emergency, but it may well be that Atkin's opinion will be regarded as being nearer to the general rule applicable in normal times.

In addition to his work for the bench, Atkin undertook a considerable amount of public work. During the war of 1914–18 he presided over a number of committees set up to investigate such different topics as aliens, women in industry, munitions, and the termination of the war, and in 1922–3 he presided over the important committee on crime and insanity appointed by the lord chancellor after the *Ronald True* case. It made a number of valuable proposals and recommended the retention of the M'Naghten rules. Atkin was deeply interested in legal education and from 1919 to 1934 was chairman of the Council of Legal Education. He did much to bridge the gap between professional and academic lawyers and to improve the status of law teachers. He was a constant advocate of the desirability of teaching the elements of law in upper forms at school on the grounds that to be properly equipped a citizen must know something of his legal system. Atkin was twice treasurer of Gray's Inn and was president of the Medico-Legal Society (1923–7). He sat on the governing body of the University College of Wales at Aberystwyth, and of other educational institutions.

He was elected to an honorary fellowship at Magdalen in 1924 and F.B.A. in 1938. He received honorary degrees from the universities of Oxford (1931), Cambridge (1936), Reading (1938), and London (1939).

He married in 1893 Lucy Elizabeth (died 1939), daughter of William Hemmant, at one time acting premier of Queensland. Atkin died at Aberdovey 25 June 1944 and was survived by one son and six daughters. A portrait by (Sir) Oswald Birley is at Gray's Inn.

[*Law Quarterly Review*, vol. lx, October 1944; private information.]

J. B. BUTTERWORTH.

AUSTIN, HERBERT, BARON AUSTIN (1866–1941), motor manufacturer, was born at Little Missenden, Buckinghamshire, 8 November 1866, son of Giles Stephen (or Stevens) Austin, farmer, of

Wentworth, Yorkshire, by his wife, Clara Jane, daughter of Willoughby Simpson, officer in H.M. Customs, of Rotherhithe. After education at Rotherham Grammar School and Brampton College he went out with an uncle to Australia in 1884 and served his apprenticeship to engineering at Langlands Foundry, Melbourne. He moved thence to the Wolseley Sheep Shearing Machine Company, where he soon became manager. In 1893 he returned home, serving as production manager to this company in Birmingham, first at a small workshop in Broad Street and later in a bigger works at Alma Street, Aston. As the sale of sheep-shearing machinery was seasonal, the company also made bicycle components and small machine parts. Austin was therefore able to acquire varied experience, and his adaptability and inventiveness were displayed by many patents taken out in his name at this period. He was invited to join the board in 1901, and from 1911 onwards served as chairman.

Austin's early Australian experiences had necessitated long and arduous journeys over very bad roads; and so, having had personal experience of slow and uncomfortable road travel, he was one of the earliest engineers in England to envisage the possibilities of the petrol-driven vehicle. As early as 1895 he produced his first Wolseley car, a three-wheeler. Soon afterwards an improved model was shown at the Crystal Palace. Long hours over the drawing-board and in the workshop brought the reward of a silver medal and first prize in a thousand-mile trial held in 1900.

In the following year Vickers Sons and Maxim were approached by the Wolseley company and took over the machine tool and motor side of the concern, trading as the Wolseley Tool and Motor Car Company, Ltd., with Austin as general manager. In 1905 Austin launched out into business for himself, with a modest capital in the region of £20,000, as the Austin Motor Company, Ltd. His choice of a site at Longbridge, then outside the confines of Birmingham, betokened foresight, in that there was ample room for expansion, and that road and railway communications were excellent. Beginning with 270 hands, the works produced 120 cars in 1906; and by 1914 the firm, capitalized at £250,000, was employing a staff of 2,000 and had an annual output of 1,000 cars. During the war of 1914–18 the plant was turned over to the making of guns, shells, and aero-

planes, and as many as 22,000 workers were employed. Austin's services to war production were recognized in 1917 by appointment as K.B.E. and by admission as commander of the Order of Leopold II in Belgium. From 1918 to 1924 he was Conservative member of Parliament for the King's Norton division of Birmingham, and from 1919 to 1925 served on the government labour resettlement committee.

Meanwhile, with his works restored to their proper purpose, Austin was continuing his inventive career and maintaining his position among the major British car manufacturers. An outstanding production, which gave him world-wide reputation, was the Austin Seven, put on sale in 1922. This little 7-horse-power car, known as the 'Baby Austin', at last brought motoring within the means of people of very modest incomes, and as a vehicle for moving about from place to place (not, perhaps, in the greatest of comfort) carried out its function most efficiently. The Austin Twenty (of 1919) catered for a more opulent public and the Austin Twelve (1921) was another very popular model. Austin was sensible of the need for keeping abreast with motor manufacturing developments in other countries and made sundry journeys to the United States, France, and elsewhere. A stream of new and improved models issued from the works as the years went on; and by 1937 the original factory site of $2\frac{1}{2}$ acres had expanded to 220 acres, staff had risen from 270 to 16,600, and annual production from 120 to 78,000 vehicles. In the war of 1939–45, as in the earlier one, the company's resources were mainly devoted to military needs.

As Austin's wealth increased he devoted large sums to philanthropic causes, notably to the work of the Birmingham hospitals, which he had supported from an early period in his business career. He was nominated chairman of the Birmingham General Hospital in 1932, and in 1940 was president of the Birmingham United Hospital and governor of the Royal Cancer Hospital, London. He equipped many hospitals for deep-ray therapy, and in 1936 gave £250,000 to the university of Cambridge to forward the work of Lord Rutherford [q.v.] at the Cavendish Laboratory.

Austin was created a baron in 1936. He was prominent in the councils of the various engineering and transport associations, served on the Transport Advisory

Council in 1934 and was chairman of the 'shadow' aero engine committee (to provide for possible war needs) from 1937 to 1940. The university of Birmingham conferred upon him the honorary degree of LL.D. in 1937 and elected him a life member of its court of governors in 1940.

Like Henry Ford in the United States and Lord Nuffield in England, Austin was first and foremost a skilled engineer who rose through the workshop, the drawing office, and the sales organization, by originality, foresight, and determination. The foundation of his success was the novelty and excellence of his designs for motor-cars. It was, for example, the 'Twelve' and 'Seven' models which re-established his firm in the difficult post-war period and initiated a new and still more successful phase in its history. His technical skill and the modesty of his bearing made him popular with his employees, for he knew how a piece of work should be done, and would often lend a hand on a difficult task, or suggest the right way out of a technical impasse. An insatiable appetite for work often made him spend part of his week-end alone in the factory, pondering on improvements or planning new models, and by his acumen he realized that no wide expansion of the motor industry could take place so long as the ownership of a car remained a luxury. His temper might be sharp, but an outbreak would be over in a few moments and give way to friendly talk with the person who had provoked it. He never forgot that economic worries, from which he himself was free, fell to the lot of common man, and he would exercise self-denial in order to help the less fortunate.

In 1887 Austin married Helen (died 1942), daughter of James Dron, of Melbourne. They had two daughters, and one son who was killed in action in France in 1915. The peerage therefore became extinct when Austin died at Lickey Grange, near Bromsgrove, 23 May 1941. A portrait by George Harcourt was destroyed by fire during the war of 1939–45.

[*The Times*, 24 May 1941; *Autocar*, 30 May 1941; *Austin Magazine*, June 1941; private information.]   HERBERT B. GRIMSDITCH.

AZARIAH, SAMUEL VEDANAYA-KAM (1874–1945), first Indian bishop of an Anglican diocese, was born at Vellalanvillai 17 August 1874, the son of the Rev. Thomas Vedanayakam, by his second wife, Ellen. The parents were Tamil by race and of peasant ancestry; the father had become a Christian in 1839 and was ordained thirty years later. Azariah was educated at the Church Missionary Society's school at Mengnanapuram, at the Society's college at Tinnevelly, and at the Madras Christian College, which he joined in 1893. In 1896 he became travelling secretary in South India for the Young Men's Christian Association, of which in 1903 he became associate general secretary; he founded (with others) in 1903 the Indian Missionary Society of Tinnevelly, and from being its secretary he was promoted in 1906 to be secretary of the National Missionary Society of India which had been founded in 1905 to evangelize India with Indian men and Indian resources. In 1907 he visited Japan as a delegate of the World Student Christian Federation, of which he became a vice-president in 1909. These secretarial duties were largely given up when he was ordained deacon and priest in 1909. He served as head of the Dornakal Mission in the Telugu country from 1909 to 1912, in which year he was consecrated bishop of Dornakal.

The lifetime of Azariah coincided with the growth of the movement for Indian independence, and this coloured the whole of his ecclesiastical outlook. Believing that the time had passed for the retention of patriarchal missions from outside India, he advocated ardently and with success, not only that the ministry of the Church in India must be indigenous, but also that in its worship Indian postures, Indian poetry, Indian idioms were to be encouraged. Even in the cathedral which he built the plan harmonizes with that of the South Indian temple, nor did it reject Saracenic domes as an attraction to Moslems. Hence he hailed with approval the Act which came into force in 1930 establishing a self-governing province of India, Burma, and Ceylon, dissociated from the State. By the time of his death, the clergy of his diocese had been completely indianized and the total of 50,000 Christians within it at his consecration had been multiplied fivefold.

On Church union, Azariah held strong views. It was to him a matter of life and death; but he did not live to see the formation of the Church of South India which united episcopalians and non-episcopalians in one communion. Nevertheless, his share in the work leading up to this consummation and in the growth of the Oecumenical

Movement beyond India was important, and at the Edinburgh missionary conference of 1910 he immediately came to prominence. He was frequently present at meetings of the International Missionary Council which grew out of it, and from 1929 onwards was chairman of its all-India branch, the National Christian Council. He also took a leading part in the 'Faith and Order' conference at Edinburgh in 1937 which led to the formation of the World Council of Churches.

In secular politics, Azariah supported the cause of Indian independence, but with 'trembling conviction'. He saw two reefs which must be avoided: a communal award which must set up a Christian electorate, and participation in violence against the powers that be. The former would lead to a separation between Church and country, the latter would be a denial of the higher loyalty of Christians. Abjuring political agitation, he accepted the delicate role of reconciler.

Azariah married in 1898 Anbu Mariammal Samuel, of Tinnevelly, by whom he had four sons and two daughters in addition to three children who died in infancy. In 1920 the university of Cambridge conferred upon him the honorary degree of LL.D. He died at Dornakal 1 January 1945. The National Portrait Gallery has a photograph of Azariah.

[Carol Graham, *Azariah of Dornakal*, 1946; personal knowledge.]

J. McLeod Campbell.

BACKHOUSE, Sir EDMUND TRELAWNY, second baronet (1873–1944), historian and authority on China, was born at Middleton Tyas, Yorkshire, 20 October 1873, the eldest son of (Sir) Jonathan Edmund Backhouse, who became first baronet, by his wife, Florence, youngest daughter of Sir John Salusbury Salusbury-Trelawny, ninth baronet. Admiral of the Fleet Sir R. R. C. Backhouse [q.v.] was a younger brother. Backhouse was educated at Winchester where he gained a scholarship, and at Merton College, Oxford, of which he was a postmaster. He was placed in the second class in classical honour moderations in 1894. Owing to ill health he did not proceed to a final school. Before leaving Oxford he had shown signs of an extraordinary ability to learn foreign languages, and eventually he mastered those of most European and Asiatic countries. With these accomplishments he became attached

to the British legation at Peking as a student interpreter, and eventually he was able to read and write Chinese perfectly and even to translate the difficult 'bamboo' characters. The Boxer rising took place in 1900, three years after his arrival in Peking, and he went through the siege of the legations, gaining the China medal and clasp. In 1903 he was appointed a professor at Peking University, a post which he held for ten years, and it was then that he established his reputation as a scholar of Chinese. He made a vast collection of rare Chinese books and manuscripts; these, numbering 27,000, he afterwards presented to the Bodleian Library.

While at Peking University Backhouse collaborated with J. O. P. Bland [q.v.] in an historical work, *China under the Empress Dowager* (1910), and in *Annals & Memoirs of the Court of Peking* (1914). He also collaborated with (Sir) Sidney Barton [q.v.] in the revision of Sir W. C. Hillier's *English–Chinese Dictionary of Peking Colloquial* (1918). In 1913 he was appointed head of the school of Chinese at King's College, London, but the appointment was not taken up.

By his translations of State documents Backhouse rendered valuable service to the British Government. Among them were the secret Russo-Chinese agreement of February 1901, the Anglo-Tibetan treaty of September 1904, and the imperial patent in Manchu and Nepalese conferred on the King of Nepal by the Emperor Ch'ien Lung of China in 1790. Between 1922 and 1926 he assisted with the production of a 'Documentary Course of Chinese for Student Interpreters of the British Legation, Peking', and in 1923 he translated into Chinese the encyclical letter of the Lambeth Conference of 1920. From June 1936 until April 1937 he acted as honorary translator in Japanese to the British embassy in Peking, and he translated many State documents for *The Times*.

Backhouse succeeded his father as second baronet in 1918, later becoming a member of the standing council of the baronetage. He was elected a member of the Académie Diplomatique Internationale, Paris, and was offered distinguished posts in Europe, but China called. He had never married, and now he devoted his whole life to study and writing, becoming a recluse as time went on. In his house in the West City of Peking he lived the life of a Chinese scholar, even wearing the long native robes. Little by little he gave up all social contacts with his European and American friends, and would receive only two or three of them; thus he gained the reputation of being something of a mystery man. But he continued to see his Chinese friends, among whom were scholars, officials, and members of the old imperial family. It was during this period that he worked on an immense English–Chinese dictionary, and he wrote the histories of the private lives of some of the Manchu emperors of the Ta Ch'ing dynasty. When the Japanese invaded Peking in 1937 Backhouse was forced to leave his Chinese home, and he took refuge in the compound of the former Austrian legation, later going to live in a house in the British embassy grounds. The Japanese, deeply suspicious of all written documents, made a bonfire of his papers and manuscripts, among them the dictionary and histories, and so the priceless records and labour of nearly half a century were lost. Turning to religion in his last few years he became a Roman Catholic in 1941. After war was declared between Great Britain and Japan in 1941 and the foreign diplomats were repatriated, his name was on the list of civilians to be sent home, but he refused to leave Peking, the city he loved above all others. The Japanese authorities permitted him to stay, even when most other British residents were sent to a prisoners' internment camp in Shantung. Backhouse died in the French Hospital, Peking, 8 January 1944.

[Personal knowledge.]        HOPE DANBY.

BACON, SIR REGINALD HUGH SPENCER (1863–1947), admiral, was born 6 September 1863 at Wiggonholt rectory, Sussex, the youngest of the eight children of the rector, the Rev. Thomas Bacon, and his wife, Emma Lavinia, daughter of George Shaw, of Teignmouth.

He entered the *Britannia* in January 1877 and was joined there by the Princes Edward and George. Success in the final examinations won him rating as midshipman on leaving, and he was appointed (January 1879) to the *Alexandra*, flagship in the Mediterranean of Sir Geoffrey Hornby and later of Sir Beauchamp Seymour (later Lord Alcester) [qq.v.]. A shooting accident at Corfu in 1882 sent him to hospital, but in 1883 he became acting sub-lieutenant in February and lieutenant in August, after complete success in his examinations at Greenwich.

He next went to sea in the sailing training ship *Cruiser*, and then, having decided to specialize in torpedo, went to the *Vernon* torpedo school. As torpedo lieutenant, in 1888 he joined the *Northumberland*, flagship of the Channel squadron which was relieved by the *Camperdown* next year. He served on the staff of the *Vernon* from August 1891 until May 1893, and with the *Vesuvius*, attached to the *Vernon*, as lieutenant and commander, until in June 1895 he was promoted commander. He was appointed in 1896 to the cruiser *Theseus* of the special service squadron which in January 1897 was suddenly withdrawn from the Mediterranean to join the squadron of Sir Harry Rawson [q.v.] on the west coast of Africa in order to deal with the critical situation in Benin where an English visiting party had been massacred. Bacon accompanied the land expedition from the coast to Benin city as intelligence officer and was mentioned in dispatches and appointed to the D.S.O.

In June 1897, having in the meantime written a spirited account of the expedition, *Benin, The City of Blood* (1897), he was transferred to the *Empress of India* which, after taking part in the jubilee review, joined the Mediterranean Fleet. In October 1898 she was ordered to Crete to take part in the punitive operations conducted by Sir Gerard Henry Uctred Noel after a massacre of Christians including the British vice-consul and his family.

At the end of 1899 Sir John (later Lord) Fisher [q.v.], fresh from the first Hague conference, took command of the Mediterranean Fleet. Bacon was one of the first officers to comply with his request for suggestions for torpedo-boat manœuvres. During his time in the *Vernon* he had in several annual naval manœuvres been in charge of torpedo craft. Fisher was so much pleased with the scheme which Bacon produced that he employed him frequently in strategic problems and on Fisher's recommendation Bacon was promoted captain in June 1900.

As a recognized torpedo and electricity expert he was at once sent to Paris to report on the electrical part of the 1900 Paris Exhibition, and then attended one of the first war courses at Greenwich. Thereafter he was given the duty of superintending the introduction and construction of submarine boats for the navy. Just before G. J. (later Viscount) Goschen [q.v.] had left office as first lord he had decided to order five submarine boats of the American (Holland) type to be built experimentally by Vickers Sons and Maxim. Bacon was placed in charge of this project, with the appointment of inspecting captain of submarines, and retained the post until October 1904. He thus became the father of the submarine service: both in the boats' construction and trial, and in training the crews.

Fisher, on becoming first sea lord in October 1904, asked Bacon to join him for a year as naval assistant. Bacon was chiefly occupied with the work of the famous Designs committee of which he was a member. It produced the designs of the *Dreadnought* and the first battle cruisers In December 1905 he was given command of the *Irresistible* in the Mediterranean. His tenure was short, for in July 1906 he was transferred to be the first captain of the *Dreadnought*, but during it he wrote a private letter to Fisher in which he referred to conversations he had recently had with the King in the Mediterranean and which contained the remark 'Lord Charles and Admiral Lambton have been getting at the King' (on the subject of naval reforms to which they were opposed). The letter was printed by Fisher for private circulation; it was one to which no reasonable exception could be taken as coming from his former naval assistant, but some years later its existence became public; the mention of the King made it impossible for Fisher to publish the text, and Bacon received a good deal of odium which affected his career in the Service on the assumption that as an officer of the fleet he had been sending confidential reports on his superior officers direct to the Admiralty.

When Sir Francis Bridgeman [q.v.] hoisted his flag in the *Dreadnought* as admiral of the Home (Reserve) Fleet, Bacon became his chief of staff. In 1907 he was appointed to succeed Sir John (later Earl) Jellicoe [q.v.] as director of naval ordnance and torpedoes. Bacon was promoted rear-admiral 12 July 1909. Reginald McKenna [q.v.] then invited him to join the Board as controller in succession to Jellicoe after a short period afloat. But at the same time he was offered the post of managing director of the Coventry Ordnance Works, and he decided to obtain leave to retire from the navy in order to accept it, having come to the conclusion that, after serving the usual term of years as controller, he was unlikely, owing to his short sea experience, to obtain any important command afloat.

He was accordingly placed on the retired list in November 1909 and went to Coventry to undertake the new duties for which his experience as director of naval ordnance fully equipped him. On the outbreak of war in 1914 he designed and produced at Coventry some new 15-inch howitzer guns for use in Flanders and was sent in charge of them to France in January 1915 with the temporary rank of colonel 2nd commandant Royal Marines. (Sir) Winston Churchill, however, recalled him in April to become rear-admiral, Dover Patrol, and senior naval officer, Dover, which had become one of the most important war appointments. He was promoted vice-admiral later in the year. On the efficiency of the Dover Patrol depended not only the military sea routes across the Channel, sustaining our armies in France, but also the security of the shipping passing through the Straits, assembling in the Downs, and bringing supplies to the port of London. The forces at Bacon's command, which he set to work with characteristic zeal to organize for the duties involved, were at first meagre in the extreme, and although they were later strengthened, the strategic situation was always such that the enemy was in a position to bring superior force to bear before reinforcement could arrive. The measure of Bacon's success during his period of command is that the patrol stood firm, despite enemy attack, and our shipping moved in safety in this dangerous area both behind the mine barrage and on its way to the Thames estuary. The Dover Patrol took an active part in supporting the sea flank of the armies in France. This support, which Bacon always provided on demand, involved naval operations in waters of great difficulty navigationally, and in face of formidable enemy defences. An outstanding incident amongst many actions with the enemy occurred in April 1917 when the *Swift* and the *Broke* defeated a division of German destroyers in a night action. Throughout his tenure of the command Bacon's work and conduct had the complete approval of his chiefs in Whitehall; and he enjoyed the trust and enthusiastic admiration of the numerous officers under his command, notably of Commander Edward Evans of the *Broke* (later Lord Mountevans) who became his chief of staff. But when Sir Eric Geddes [q.v.] was sent by Lloyd George to take charge of the Admiralty there was a marked change,

and at the end of 1917 Bacon shared the fate of his illustrious friend and leader, Jellicoe, and was abruptly dismissed from his command.

Bacon's public services were, however, far too valuable to be lost, and (Sir) Winston Churchill, then minister of munitions, at once appointed him controller of the department of munitions inventions. His advisory panel included the most distinguished scientists in the country. On 31 March 1919 Bacon finally retired into private life, having been advanced to the rank of admiral in September 1918. He received the official appreciation of the Ministry for 'valuable assistance given while holding his responsible and important post'.

Bacon had from boyhood been devoted to shooting game, and recognizing that his public career was over he retired to his home in Hampshire and during the winter months spent many days shooting with his neighbours and friends. He records that in one season he met 149 different guns. He also became chairman of the Romsey bench. In the summer he lived on a property near Lerici in Italy where he had built a house. Apart from country pursuits he soon found opportunities for showing his merit as a writer. He wrote his autobiography in two volumes, *A Naval Scrap-Book, 1877–1900* (1925) and *From 1900 Onward* (1940); two books on the Dover Patrol; *The Jutland Scandal* (1924), an able and trenchant justification of Jellicoe's conduct of the battle, the title of which was, however, much resented in some naval circles; and the standard biographies of Fisher (1929) and Jellicoe (1936).

King Edward VII had appointed Bacon C.V.O. on his inspection of the Home Fleet in 1907. In 1916 he was appointed K.C.B. in recognition of his work in the Dover Patrol, and also promoted K.C.V.O. He held several foreign decorations. Bacon was a man of brilliant professional attainments with a most original mind. He was perhaps the cleverest of the many able young naval officers of his time, and Fisher picked him out as his principal lieutenant in promoting drastic reforms in naval education, strategy, and ship construction. He won early promotion by sheer merit, and his early work on submarines as well as his command of the Dover Patrol was of inestimable service to his country during the critical years of the war of 1914–18.

Bacon married in 1894 Cicely Isabel (died 1955), daughter of Henry Edward Surtees, M.P., M.F.H., of Redworth Hall, county Durham; they had one daughter and two sons, the elder of whom died on active service in the battle of Loos, and the younger while a naval cadet. Bacon died at his home, Braishfield Lodge, near Romsey, 9 June 1947. A portrait by Lance Calkin is in the possession of the family, and a drawing by Francis Dodd is in the Imperial War Museum.

[Bacon's own writings; Admiralty records; private information; personal knowledge.]

VINCENT W. BADDELEY.

BADEN-POWELL, ROBERT STEPHENSON SMYTH, first BARON BADEN-POWELL (1857–1941), lieutenant-general, and founder of the Boy Scouts and Girl Guides, was born in London 22 February 1857, the sixth son among the ten children of the Rev. Baden Powell [q.v.], Savilian professor of geometry at Oxford, by his third wife, Henrietta Grace, eldest daughter of Admiral William Henry Smyth [q.v.], who claimed collateral descent from John Smith of Virginia [q.v.] and was a great-niece of Nelson. Robert was named after his godfather, Robert Stephenson [q.v.], the engineer. His father died in 1860, and Mrs. Baden-Powell had to bring up a large family on moderate means. She encouraged the children to study natural history, and, when they were old enough, allowed the boys to go camping and boating in their holidays.

In 1870 Baden-Powell went as a gown-boy foundationer to Charterhouse. He owed much to the influence of the head-master, William Haig Brown [q.v.]. Although pre-eminent neither as scholar nor as athlete, Baden-Powell took his share in all activities. His triumphs were gained in theatricals and as a cartoonist. His love of outdoor life led him to break bounds and spend hours in the woods increasing his knowledge of woodcraft. In 1876 he entered for an army examination before going to Oxford where his brothers, George (Sir George Smyth Baden-Powell, q.v.) and Frank, had been at Balliol College; but Benjamin Jowett [q.v.] did not think Robert 'up to Balliol form'. The search for another college ended when the results of the army examination were announced; Robert was placed second on the cavalry list and was thus excused Sandhurst. He was gazetted sub-lieutenant, and sailed for India to join his regiment, the 13th Hussars.

After his general training he specialized in reconnaissance and scouting. His technical knowledge was set down in two books, *Reconnaissance and Scouting* (1884) and *Cavalry Instruction* (1885). He was promoted captain in 1883, and served as adjutant from 1882 to 1886. He was a keen polo player, and in 1883 won the Kadir Cup for pigsticking, a sport on which he wrote a standard book, *Pigsticking or Hoghunting* (1889). Lighter diversions were theatricals and sketching.

In 1884 the 13th Hussars left India, but disembarked in Natal to be in reserve should Sir Charles Warren [q.v.] need support in Bechuanaland. Baden-Powell surveyed the lesser-known passes of the Drakensberg; disguised as a reporter, he gained important information and corrected the maps. When the crisis passed the regiment sailed for England, but he remained for a hunting expedition in East Africa. In 1888 he was appointed aide-de-camp to his uncle, (Sir) H. A. Smyth [q.v.], who had been made G.O.C. in South Africa. Baden-Powell took part in the Zululand campaign of 1888; in 1889 he was secretary to the mixed British and Boer commission on Swaziland, and in 1890 he joined Smyth as his assistant military secretary and aide-de-camp at Malta, where Smyth had been appointed governor. The formal official life was little to Baden-Powell's liking and he welcomed his appointment in 1891 as intelligence officer for the Mediterranean. In the course of his investigations he had some of the experiences afterwards recorded in *My Adventures as a Spy* (1915). He was promoted major in 1892 and in the following year rejoined his regiment in Ireland.

Baden-Powell's next task was to organize and train a native levy for the Ashanti expedition of 1895–6; pioneering the route and scouting for the enemy were his responsibility. For his services he received the brevet of lieutenant-colonel, and he wrote an account of the expedition in *The Downfall of Prempeh* (1896). It was during this bloodless war that he first wore the cowboy hat associated with him; by the natives he was known as 'Kantankye'—'he of the big hat'. Within a few months, in May 1896, he was called again for special duties, this time as chief staff officer in Matabeleland where a native rising necessitated the use of imperial troops. It was mainly through his night scouting that the positions of the natives in the fastnesses of the Matopos were discovered; they called him 'Impeesa' —'the wolf that never sleeps'. After the war

Baden-Powell received the brevet of colonel, and during his leave he wrote *The Matabele Campaign* (1897).

In 1897 at the age of forty Baden-Powell was appointed to the command of the 5th Dragoon Guards, then stationed in India. He now had full opportunity to develop training in scouting as part of a soldier's work; for this he instituted a special badge (the first of its kind) for efficiency. He described the course of instruction in *Aids to Scouting* (1899). Great stress was put on developing the powers of observation and of deduction, and by organizing the men in small units he emphasized the need for initiative.

While home on leave in 1899, Baden-Powell was again gazetted for extra-regimental employ. The tense situation in South Africa made war likely; he was therefore sent out to raise two regiments for the defence of Bechuanaland and Matabeleland. When war broke out he was at Mafeking. General Piet Cronje at once invested the town. The total defence force was 1,251 men; equipment was inadequate and much of it antiquated.

The romance of the siege gave Mafeking an exaggerated value in popular opinion; nevertheless, this small town was of strategic importance, for the defence held 9,000 Boers inactive at a critical period. It was Baden-Powell's own genius for organization and improvisation which sustained the siege for 217 days. The deterioration in food supplies, the constant bombardment, and the series of British defeats might well have disheartened the people in Mafeking, but Baden-Powell was resourceful in schemes to puzzle the besiegers and in devising ways of keeping the besieged busy and cheerful. One improvisation gave some offence at home. Postage stamps were needed; the first design, printed without Baden-Powell's knowledge, bore his head; he had these withdrawn at once and there was substituted a new design showing a boy on a bicycle, recording thus the work of the cadets whose efficiency made a lasting impression on him. Mafeking was relieved 17 May 1900; the news was received in London with such wild rejoicing that a new verb was added to the language ('to maffick'). Baden-Powell was rewarded by promotion to the rank of major-general at the age of forty-three.

After the relief he was in command of a force attempting to capture General Christiaan De Wet [q.v.] until in August 1900 Sir Alfred (later Viscount) Milner [q.v.], having decided to establish a constabulary to police the country after the war, chose Baden-Powell for the task of raising and training the force. This was a congenial duty, for it was without precedent and gave full scope for his special method of training men in small units. The prolongation of war meant that the South African Constabulary took service in the field. After the war their work to which Joseph Chamberlain referred as a 'great civilizing and uniting influence' showed how well they had been trained for a delicate task.

Sick leave at home in 1901 gave this country an opportunity of hero-worshipping Baden-Powell. He took such demonstrations as they came but did not seek them. When, for instance, he was summoned to Balmoral to be invested as C.B. by King Edward VII, he took a circuitous route to avoid the crowds. Early in 1903 he was appointed inspector-general of cavalry. After studying cavalry training in other countries, he established the Cavalry School at Netheravon in 1904, and in the following year founded the *Cavalry Journal*. During 1906 he accompanied the Duke of Connaught [q.v.] to South Africa and afterwards travelled north to Egypt, a tour which gave birth to his book *Sketches in Mafeking and East Africa* (1907); an exhibition in 1907 of the original water-colours and sketches for this book, and the acceptance in the same year of a bust of John Smith by the Royal Academy displayed his considerable talent as an artist. His term of inspector-general ended in 1907, but he was persuaded by R. B. (later Viscount) Haldane [q.v.] to take command in 1908 of the Northumbrian division of the newly formed Territorials. Haldane and he had frequently discussed the Territorial scheme together. Baden-Powell ceased to hold this command in March 1910, and on 7 May he retired from the army, at the age of fifty-three. He had been promoted lieutenant-general in 1907.

Baden-Powell gave up the prospect of higher rank in order that he might devote himself to the interest which came to fill his life—the Boy Scouts. On his return from South Africa in 1903 he had been surprised to learn that his *Aids to Scouting* was being used by teachers. His interest in boys had been roused by the success of the cadets in Mafeking, and by the many letters he received from young hero-worshippers. At an inspection of the Boys' Brigade in 1904 he was greatly impressed by their bearing and efficiency, and he wondered how more boys could be attracted. He discussed the question with (Sir) William Alexander Smith, founder of the Brigade, who suggested that *Aids to Scouting* should be rewritten for boys. Baden-Powell's thoughts turned to his camping days with his band of brothers and his own delight in woodcraft. With these in mind he drew up a preliminary scheme which he discussed with friends and experts. Amongst his sympathizers was (Sir) C. Arthur Pearson [q.v.] who encouraged and initially financed the separate organization of Boy Scouts. A trial camp was held on Brownsea Island in Poole Harbour in July and August 1907, for which Baden-Powell tried the experiment of selecting boys from varied social classes; he found that they mixed happily together and thoroughly enjoyed the outdoor activities of 'backwoodsmen, explorers, and frontiersmen'. The key to success lay in the patrol organization by which the boys were divided into small units of five, each unit having its own leader with responsibility for maintaining keenness and a high standard of behaviour. As an aid to the latter, he framed a scout law setting out in positive terms the code of conduct a scout promises to observe.

*Scouting for Boys* was published in parts in 1908. Boys bought them eagerly and within a few weeks Boy Scout troops sprang up all over the country. The same result came when copies of the book reached the Dominions and Colonies and some foreign countries. A rally at the Crystal Palace in 1909 brought together 11,000 Boy Scouts. Girls demanded that they too should have the same fun, so the parallel scheme of Girl Guides was framed with Baden-Powell's sister, Agnes (died 1945), as first president of their council. It soon became clear that this rapidly spreading movement would need careful guidance, so the founder decided, with the approval of King Edward VII, to leave the army and give all his time to the Boy Scouts and Girl Guides. In 1910 he made the first of many extensive tours of the Empire and other countries to ensure that the main principles of his scheme were observed.

Opposition came from those who saw in the Boy Scouts a subtle attempt to give military training under another name; Baden-Powell replied that the aim of the movement was to develop those qualities of character which serve the country best in peace or in war. On the outbreak of war in 1914 he wrote a small manual, *Quick Training for War*, which had enormous sales. The Boy Scouts were soon familiar figures in public offices, in hospitals, during air raids, and in the harvest fields. Their most sustained effort was undertaken at Kitchener's request: Sea Scouts (started in 1909) replaced coastguardsmen and during the war over 20,000 scouts were so employed. Baden-Powell made many visits to the western front, and took an active part in organizing recreation huts provided by the Young Men's Christian Association and by Boy Scouts. There is no foundation for the popular belief that he was engaged in secret-service work.

In spite of the loss of scoutmasters, the movement expanded; patrol leaders carried on until they too were called up. There was a demand for training for boys below Boy Scout age. After a period of experiment, the Wolf Cubs were started in 1916. Baden-Powell made use of the stories of Mowgli from the *Jungle Books* to give these young boys an imaginative world of their own. The scheme was explained in *The Wolf Cub's Handbook* (1916). To meet the needs of those above Boy Scout age a scheme of Rover Scouts was developed after the war, and for the guidance of these youths Baden-Powell wrote *Rovering to Success* (1922).

A rally of scouts was arranged for 1920. To this Baden-Powell gave the name of 'Jamboree', a word of uncertain origin but now with a new meaning. What at first was planned as a British gathering was expanded to include scouts from many countries. At the final rally, Baden-Powell was acclaimed as Chief Scout of the world. There were four other Jamborees during his lifetime: 1924 in Denmark, 1929 in England, 1933 in Hungary, and 1937 in Holland. On the occasion of the Jamboree of 1929 he was raised to the peerage as Baron Baden-Powell, of Gilwell, in the county of Essex, taking his territorial title from the training camp for scoutmasters which he had established in 1919; this soon became an international centre from which trained men carried Baden-Powell's interpretation of scouting to many lands. He left the detailed conduct of the movement to his headquarters commissioners; he was opposed to too great a centralization of direction, and wished those training the boys to have wide liberty within the scheme. As the years passed, so his interest became more concentrated on the international development of the

scouts and guides; in this he saw a means of furthering friendliness amongst nations. His work for peace was recognized by the award of the Carnegie Wateler peace prize in 1937.

Baden-Powell spent his eightieth birthday in India in a farewell parade with his old regiment of which he had become honorary colonel in 1911. In the same year (1937) he was appointed to the Order of Merit; this was the last of a long series of honours from many countries. Honorary degrees were conferred on him by the universities of Edinburgh (1910), Toronto, McGill, and Oxford (1923), Liverpool (1929), and Cambridge (1931). He had been appointed K.C.V.O. and K.C.B. in 1909, created a baronet in 1922, G.C.V.O. in 1923, and G.C.M.G. in 1927. In 1913 he was master of the Mercers' Company.

In the autumn of 1938 Baden-Powell went to Kenya in the hope of regaining health. To the last he was fertile in ideas and suggestions for the development of scouting. He found his pleasure in sketching and painting. His doctors forbade his return to England when war broke out in 1939 and he died at Nyeri, Kenya, 8 January 1941. A stone to his memory was unveiled in Westminster Abbey in 1947. He was succeeded as second baron by his son (Arthur Robert) Peter (born 1913).

Baden-Powell was of medium height and slender build; he was sandy-haired and freckled. He was a man of simple habits and of the friendliest disposition. He was little affected by the hero-worship to which he had to submit during the greater part of his life. His chief recreation after leaving India was fishing; this gave him the solitude he needed and the joys of river and mountain scenery. His sketchbook was seldom out of reach.

He wrote some thirty books; nearly all were illustrated by himself. In addition to those mentioned above, two should be noted: *Indian Memories* (1915) and *Lessons from the 'varsity of Life* (1933); both are autobiographical. His plain style was lightened by many touches of the humour which characterized his talk and his speeches.

During one of his world tours Baden-Powell met Olave St. Clair, younger daughter of Harold Soames, a retired business man, of Lilliput, Dorsetshire. They were married in 1912, and had one son and two daughters. Lady Baden-Powell showed that she had gifts of her own to bring to the Girl Guide movement, and she was elected Chief Guide in 1918. She was appointed G.B.E. in 1932.

There are painted portraits of Baden-Powell by G. F. Watts (1901) at Charterhouse School; by (Sir) Hubert von Herkomer (1901) at the Cavalry Club; by Harold Speed (1905) in the possession of the family; by David Jagger (1929), two versions, one at the Mercers' Hall, the other at Boy Scout headquarters; by Simon Elwes (1930) at Girl Guide headquarters. The first three show him in the uniform of the South African Constabulary and the last three as Chief Scout.

[E. E. Reynolds, *Baden-Powell*, 1942; records at Boy Scout headquarters; private information; personal knowledge.]

E. E. REYNOLDS.

BAIN, SIR FREDERICK WILLIAM (1889–1950), chemical industrialist, was born 22 March 1889 at Macduff, Banffshire, the son of James Bain, agent for the Macduff Commercial Company, and his wife, Isabella Strachan. Educated at the Banff Academy he was only seventeen when the death of his father put an end to his hopes of a university career. He moved with his mother and younger sister to Aberdeen where he worked for a company distributing fertilizers and in his spare time attended chemistry classes at the university. In 1915 he went to Flanders as company quarter-master sergeant in the 4th (Territorial) battalion of the Gordon Highlanders which he had joined in 1908.

He soon received his commission, was mentioned in dispatches, and awarded the M.C. for gallantry, but on Christmas Day in the same year he was severely wounded and lost his left arm in a bomb accident. Upon his recovery he entered the Ministry of Munitions with a post, which soon became that of deputy director, in the section of the trench warfare supply department which was responsible for the supply of materials for chemical warfare.

When the war ended Bain found himself without a job and handicapped by recent illness. By chance he met (Sir) Christopher Clayton of the United Alkali Company and went with him to Liverpool as his personal assistant. He was soon a director of the company and on the formation of Imperial Chemical Industries in 1926 he entered the new combine with enthusiasm, becoming vice-chairman (1931), and later chairman, of the General Chemicals group. He became an executive manager of I.C.I. in 1939, a director in 1940,

and a deputy chairman in 1945, an appointment which he held until his death.

Between 1941 and 1944 Bain was seconded to the Ministry of Supply as chairman of the chemical control board, and he was also chairman of the chemical planning committee of the Ministry of Production, 1942–4. For these services he was knighted in 1945. After the war, he was one of the most active presidents (1947–9) the Federation of British Industries has ever known. He was a member of innumerable committees and councils, including that of the Society of Chemical Industry, and one of his particular interests was the Association of British Chemical Manufacturers of which he was for several years vice-chairman and of which he was made an honorary member and honorary vice-president shortly before he died.

Although Bain had studied chemistry he made no claim to be a chemist. The knowledge he had acquired was nevertheless invaluable to him in the career which he made for himself. With typical courage, undaunted by his small beginnings and his physical misfortune, he seized his slender opportunity and turned it to success. Hard work and natural ability played their part, but they were informed and vitalized by a tremendous zest for life which enabled him to bring a cheerful enthusiasm to everything he undertook. He played as hard as he worked, for he had many gifts and wide interests. He loved plays, and poetry, and good talk of an evening with his friends, when he could always prove himself the master in any argument over Burns, Milton, or Shakespeare. Those friends were many, for 'Freddy's' gay and generous personality was magnetic. Informal and eminently approachable, he had a remarkable memory for names and a gift for leadership which was never more happily exercised than in his devoted work for Toc H, particularly in Lancashire where he was a pioneer of the movement. Social work, politics (he was always a staunch Liberal), and the repertory theatre also claimed his vigorous attention while he was in Liverpool. In later years he travelled widely on business and at the time of his death he was one of the joint chairmen of the Anglo-American Council of Productivity. He was everywhere welcome and respected, but he received no recognition which he valued more than the honorary LL.D. of the university of Aberdeen (1950).

In 1921 Bain married Isabel, daughter

of J. G. Adami [q.v.], vice-chancellor of the university of Liverpool. They had one son, after whose birth his wife unfortunately suffered almost continuously from ill health until her death in 1945. Bain died five years later, in London, 23 November 1950, as the result of a fall which might have been insignificant had he not been without an arm to save himself. A posthumous sketch by James Gunn is in the possession of the the Federation of British Industries.

[Private information; personal knowledge.]
J. Davidson Pratt.

BAIRD, JOHN LOGIE (1888–1946), television pioneer, was born at Helensburgh, Dumbartonshire, 13 August 1888, the youngest of the four children of the Rev. John Baird, minister of the West Parish church, by his wife, Jessie Morrison Inglis, who came of a shipbuilding family in Glasgow. He took an electrical engineering course at the Royal Technical College, Glasgow, and afterwards went to Glasgow University, where he was in his final B.Sc. year when the war of 1914–18 interrupted his studies. Rejected as unfit for the forces, Baird served as superintendent engineer of the Clyde Valley Electrical Power Company, but at the end of hostilities he had to give up engineering owing to ill health. He then set up in business, marketing successively a patent sock, jam, honey, and soap, but each business venture, whether in Glasgow, the West Indies, or in London, although otherwise successful, was ended by the ill health which was to dog him throughout life.

Following a complete physical and nervous breakdown, he retired to Hastings, Sussex, in 1922. Here he turned to his early love of research and decided to concentrate upon television which had been the dream of scientists for fifty years. Baird occupied an attic at 8 Queen's Arcade, and, having very little capital, assembled his crude, makeshift apparatus on a washstand. The base of his motor was a tea-chest, a biscuit tin housed the projection lamp, scanning discs were cut from cardboard, and fourpenny cycle lenses were utilized. Scrapwood, darning needles, string, and sealing-wax held the apparatus together. In 1924 at Hastings he transmitted the flickering image of a Maltese cross over a distance of feet; in that year he brought his crazy apparatus to London, where he occupied two attic rooms at 22 Frith Street, Soho, and struggled alone under the twin handi-

caps of ill health and poverty. Success came at last, and on 26 January 1926 Baird gave the world's first demonstration of true television in his attic before about fifty scientists. The London County Council blue plaque commemorates this event; the apparatus used is now in the Science Museum, South Kensington.

Later in the same year Baird demonstrated 'Noctovision', or seeing-in-darkness by use of infra-red rays. In 1927 he demonstrated television over 438 miles of telephone line between London and Glasgow. In that year the Baird Television Development Company, Ltd., was formed, the Television Society was founded, and Baird was elected a fellow of this and of the Physical Society. In 1928 came his world's first transatlantic television transmission between London and New York and the world's first transmission to a ship in mid-Atlantic. The same year he gave the world's first demonstrations of television in natural colour, and also stereoscopic television. An experimental television service on the Baird system was inaugurated by the British Broadcasting Corporation in 1929, but sound and vision were sent alternately until 1930 when both were broadcast simultaneously; it was not until 1932 that the Corporation took over responsibility for the programmes which up to then had been provided by Baird's company.

In 1930 Baird showed big-screen television in the London Coliseum programme and afterwards sent his big-screen to Berlin, Paris, and Stockholm. In 1931 he televised the Derby from Epsom and in 1932 he gave the world's first demonstration of ultra-short wave transmission. In 1937 he was the first British subject to receive the gold medal of the International Faculty of Science and in the same year he was elected an honorary fellow of the Royal Society of Edinburgh. In spite of his physical and financial handicaps Baird was the first exponent of every development associated with television. Following the report of a committee of inquiry in January 1935, a rival all-electronic television system, working on 405 lines to Baird's 240, was tried out by the British Broadcasting Corporation side by side with Baird's system, and in 1937 the latter was dropped. Baird continued his colour, stereoscopic, and big-screen experimental work until he died at Bexhill, Sussex, 14 June 1946.

Baird married in 1931 Margaret, daughter of the late Henry Albu, diamond merchant, of Johannesburg, who had come to London to study music and was known as a concert pianist. They had one son and one daughter. A portrait of Baird by James Kerr-Lawson is in the engineering section of Glasgow University, and a pencil drawing by the same artist is in the Scottish National Portrait Gallery; a bust by Donald Gilbert, which was shown at the Royal Academy exhibition in 1943, became the property of the sculptor's mother.

[R. F. Tiltman, *Baird of Television*, 1933; Maurice Gorham, *Broadcasting and Television since 1900*, 1952; personal knowledge.]

R. F. TILTMAN.

BAIRSTOW, SIR EDWARD CUTHBERT (1874–1946), musician, was born at Huddersfield 22 August 1874, the eldest child and only son of James Oates Bairstow, wholesale clothier, and his wife, Elizabeth Adeline Watson. His father had a tenor voice and was a member of the Huddersfield Choral Society. Bairstow was educated at the High School, Nottingham, where his grandparents lived, until in 1889 his father retired and the family removed to London where he attended the Grocers' Company School at Hackney Downs, and later had coaching from a private tutor. In Huddersfield he was taught the organ by Henry Parratt (brother of Sir Walter Parratt, q.v.), and in Nottingham by Arthur Page. Soon after arrival in London he had lessons from John Farmer [q.v.], then organist of Balliol College, Oxford, and later (1892–9) he was a pupil of Sir Frederick Bridge [q.v.], organist of Westminster Abbey. During this time he became organist of All Saints' church, Norfolk Square, Paddington. In 1894 he obtained the degree of B.Mus. at Durham University, proceeding D.Mus. in 1900. In 1899 on Bridge's recommendation he was appointed organist of Wigan parish church and conducted the choral society there and also at Blackburn. In 1906 he was appointed to the more important post at Leeds parish church. In addition to his church duties he had a busy life teaching, lecturing, performing, composing, and travelling each week to Preston and Blackburn to conduct the choral societies. At the Leeds triennial Festival in 1907 he was official organist under the conductorship of Sir Charles Stanford [q.v.].

Another chapter of his life began in 1913 when he became organist and master of the choir at York Minster where he re-mained until his death. The increased duties of his cathedral work made it impossible for him to continue conducting the choral societies in Lancashire but, now that his reputation as a choral trainer was established, he accepted the invitation to conduct the York Musical Society, the Bradford Festival Chorus, and the Leeds Philharmonic Society. At York Minster Bairstow's devoted work with the choir and music generally became well known and widely appreciated and perhaps reached the highest level of excellence during the 1300th celebrations in 1927.

Meanwhile he had become known as a judge at musical competition festivals in this country, and in 1928 he also judged in Canada. His natural ability, teaching experience, and fearless judgements had a stimulating effect on the movement. He was much in demand, although he realized that he was not 'popular'; consequently he often remarked 'I have judged at every competition festival in the country—*once*.'

On the death of Joseph Cox Bridge in 1929 Bairstow accepted the chair of music at Durham University, his alma mater. The professorship at that time was non-resident and he was able to continue his work at York Minster. At Durham he set himself to raise the standard of the degree in music. In 1932 he was knighted, and he received the honorary degree of Litt.D. (1936) from Leeds and D.Mus. (1945) from Oxford. For various periods he held office as president of musical bodies such as the Incorporated Society of Musicians and the Royal College of Organists; of the latter he was for many years an examiner and member of the council.

Probably Bairstow's chief influence was through his many pupils. He was a born teacher. His success was due to his uncanny insight into the problems of teaching, to his sympathy, patience, perseverance, enthusiasm to stimulate the imagination of the pupil, appreciation of honest work done, and above all to his great love of music. His courage, forthright speech, and transparent sincerity made him greatly beloved by many, even though it was sometimes misunderstood by and embarrassing to a few.

He published two textbooks on music, and one on singing written in collaboration with his friend H. Plunket Greene [q.v.]. His published compositions include church and organ music, songs, part-songs, and chamber music. For the coronation of King George VI in 1937 he wrote the introit.

In 1902 he married Edith Harriet, daughter of John Thomas Hobson, a government inspector of alkali works. They had a happy married life, and their home at York became well known for its generous hospitality and good friendship, which was shared by many, especially fellow artists. They had two sons and a daughter. Bairstow died at York 1 May 1946.

[*Musical Times*, August 1944; an unfinished autobiography in manuscript; private information; personal knowledge.]

ERNEST BULLOCK.

BAKER, SIR HERBERT (1862–1946), architect, was born at Owletts, Cobham, Kent, 9 June 1862, the fourth child in a family of eleven. His father was Thomas Henry Baker, J.P., landowner and farmer, of Cobham, and his mother Frances Georgina, daughter of Robert William Davis, of independent means, of Rochester. Throughout his life Baker retained a vivid interest in the English country life in which he had been brought up, and, wherever he might be, in local architecture.

He was educated at Tonbridge School, where he reached the sixth form and distinguished himself at cricket and football. On leaving, he was articled to his cousin, Arthur Baker, an architect in London, and he has recorded that his most valuable experience at that time was that of being resident architect to the church at Llanberis in North Wales. Baker studied at the Royal Academy school of architecture and later worked in the office of (Sir) Ernest George [q.v.] where he was for a time a fellow pupil with (Sir) Edwin Lutyens [q.v.]. In 1890 he became an associate of the Royal Institute of British Architects, having been awarded the Ashpitel prize for heading the examination lists in the previous year.

In 1892 Baker went out to South Africa in the hope of finding there a favourable field for the exercise of his profession; and was at first the guest of his cousin, Admiral Henry Nicholson, then commanding the naval station at Simonstown. Shortly after his arrival Baker was a guest at a dinner party which included Cecil Rhodes [q.v.], but found himself too shy to take any part in the conversation and went away feeling that he had failed to take advantage of his opportunity. Rhodes, however, had noticed 'that silent young man' and inquired who he was. When out riding early one morning he met Baker who was walking and invited him to go to his house next day because he wanted to restore it. In Rhodes Baker found his Maecenas. For all his visions of new worlds to conquer Rhodes was always greatly interested in the beauties and antiquities of Cape Town and its surroundings. Here was a bond of sympathy between him and young Baker, to whom the examples of the best school of Dutch domestic architecture of the eighteenth and early nineteenth centuries, with which the Cape Peninsula abounds, had brought a new revelation of beauty. The work of restoring Groote Schuur was entrusted to Baker and Rhodes was pleased with the result; indeed, so high an opinion did he form of the young architect's promise that, with characteristic munificence, he provided the funds to send him on a protracted tour round all the countries of the Mediterranean, there to study the architectural and artistic traditions of classical times.

With a mind enriched by this experience Baker returned to the Cape where he practised his profession for several years. He built many beautiful dwellings, using in the main the old Dutch houses as his models, although with developments of his own, and with a meticulous care for the details of appropriate internal decoration. In this manner the greatest specimen of his art at the Cape is the new Groote Schuur, built for Rhodes in 1896 after the destruction of the old house by fire. This was Rhodes's home in his later years, and was left by him in his will to be the official residence of the prime minister of South Africa when the country should have become united.

At Cape Town also, Baker built the chancel and the eastern part of the nave of the Anglican cathedral, generally in the decorated Gothic style; and, after Rhodes's death, the memorial to him on the slope of Table Mountain above Groote Schuur, mainly classical in form, although in front of it stands a replica of the impressionistic statue of 'Physical Energy' by G. F. Watts [q.v.] with its great equestrian figure looking forward northward to Rhodes's 'hinterland', the promised land of his wide political vision.

In 1902, after Rhodes's death in March, two months before the end of the South African war, Baker accepted an invitation from Lord Milner [q.v.] to go up to the newly annexed Transvaal to help in the work of reconstruction. There he became closely associated with that remarkable band of young men known as 'Milner's kindergarten'.

In the Transvaal, as in the Orange Free State of that time, the art of architecture may hardly be said to have existed. The hardy 'voortrekkers' of the early nineteenth century and their successors seem to have left all their national art behind them at the Cape; nor in this field did the 'uitlander' immigrants, who came into the country from 1886 onwards in search of mineral wealth, bring with them anything worth having from Europe. Johannesburg, for instance, was mainly a city of corrugated-iron with irrelevant ornament. But Baker brought a new spirit in building. For the wealthier citizens he made many beautiful homes in the northern suburb of Park Town and elsewhere close to the city, along with smaller houses for himself and some of his friends, in the style which he had employed at Cape Town, in which, however, a certain Italian influence began to appear mingling with the original Cape Dutch. This is especially noticeable at 'Arcadia', the house at Johannesburg which he built for Sir Lionel Phillips. Baker did not confine himself to Johannesburg. At Bloemfontein, the capital of the Orange Free State, he added a lofty tower to the cathedral, and, more important, at Pretoria, the capital of the Transvaal, he built, on a site overlooking the town, a stately Government House, first occupied by Lord Selborne in 1907; and in 1909 on a natural shelf farther along the ridge he designed his largest single work in South Africa, the Union Buildings, consisting of two porticoed wings joined by a semicircular colonaded block enclosing a paved amphitheatre with terraced gardens falling away to the valley below. He also built in Pretoria the first portion of an Anglican cathedral in the Gothic manner.

Rhodesia too has fine specimens of Baker's work, notably in the original part of a house which he built for Rhodes on rising ground above Bulawayo on the site of what had been King Lobengula's head kraal; and in the nave of a grey granite cathedral in the Norman style at Salisbury, unfinished, like those at Cape Town and Pretoria. In Kenya, also, Baker built Government House at Nairobi (1925). It may fairly be said that Baker's influence has permeated the whole of the vast territory of South, south Central, and East Africa.

In India, in 1912 and afterwards, Baker collaborated with Lutyens as architect for the new Imperial Delhi. He was himself responsible for the two Secretariat buildings, the Legislative building, and the houses for government officials. In 1913 Baker opened an office in London, and to him, in collaboration with his partner Mr. Alexander Thomson Scott, we are indebted for the new Bank of England (1921) inside the old Soane curtain-wall, for India House (1925) at Aldwych, for South Africa House (1930) at Trafalgar Square, for Church House (1934) at Westminster, and for many other buildings in London. In 1917 Baker was appointed to the Imperial War Graves Commission, designing, amongst others, memorials at Neuve Chapelle and Delville Wood. He was also responsible for war memorials at Harrow, Winchester, King's School, Canterbury, and at Haileybury.

At Oxford Baker built Rhodes House and in 1934 he published *Cecil Rhodes by his Architect*, a short and touching tribute of hero-worship. *Architecture and Personalities* (1944) gives Baker's own theory of his art, and is adorned by many illustrative photographs.

Baker was knighted in 1926, appointed K.C.I.E. in 1930, and elected R.A. in 1932. He received the Royal gold medal for architecture in 1927, the honorary degree of LL.D. from the Witwatersrand University in 1934, and of D.C.L. from Oxford in 1937. He was elected an honorary fellow of Downing College, Cambridge, in 1932.

In his latest years Baker was afflicted by physical disabilities, bravely endured, which crippled his bodily achievements, but not his genius. He was the gentlest, kindest, and most modest of men. He died 4 February 1946 at his home at Owletts, Cobham, which he had presented to the National Trust in 1937, and his ashes were buried in Westminster Abbey. He was survived by his widow, Florence, daughter of Major-General Henry Edmeades, of Nurstead Court, Kent, whom he married in 1904; they had three sons and one daughter.

On leaving South Africa Baker founded an architectural scholarship at the British School at Rome for young South African students and in his will he left money to found a scholarship in London for 'advanced students from Great Britain and Northern Ireland and the Commonwealth for the purpose of fostering inter-collaboration between the three Arts,

Architecture, Sculpture and Painting, and the fourth Art of Poetic Literature'.

A portrait of Baker by A. K. Lawrence hangs in the Bank of England where there is also a marble bust by (Sir) Charles Wheeler; a bronze bust by the same sculptor is in South Africa House and a copy of it is at Owletts.

[Sir Herbert Baker, *Architecture and Personalities*, 1944; private information; personal knowledge.]     DOUGAL O. MALCOLM.

BALDWIN, STANLEY, first EARL BALDWIN OF BEWDLEY (1867–1947), statesman and three times prime minister, was born at Lower Park, Bewdley, 3 August 1867, the only son of Alfred and Louisa Baldwin. His father's folk had been for centuries Shropshire yeomen who had settled as ironmasters within the Worcestershire border. Alfred Baldwin was the head of an old-fashioned business of the patriarchal type, a model employer. Among his ancestors were country parsons and Quaker missionaries to the American colonies. Louisa, Stanley Baldwin's mother, was one of the remarkable children of the Rev. George Browne Macdonald, a Wesleyan minister of Highland stock which settled in Northern Ireland after the 'forty-five' and came under the influence of John Wesley. Macdonald married Hannah Jones, of Manchester, but Welsh from the Vale of Clwyd. They had two sons and five daughters who survived infancy. Louisa's eldest sister Alice was the mother of Rudyard Kipling; Georgiana was the wife of Sir Edward Burne-Jones; Agnes of Sir Edward Poynter [qq.v.].

Stanley, an only child, was left much to himself and found his sustenance in the novels of Scott, the *Morte d'Arthur*, the *Pilgrim's Progress*, and the Lambs' *Tales from Shakespeare*. He was sent to Hawtrey's preparatory school, then in 1881 to Harrow, and in 1885 to Trinity College, Cambridge, where he was placed in the third class in the historical tripos in 1888. He entered the family business and (apart from a visit to the United States, significantly at a time when McKinley was running on the protectionist 'ticket') for four years, until his marriage, he lived at home at Wilden where his father had built a church, a school, and a vicarage. He learnt to know every man in the works, became a parish and county councillor, a magistrate, and a member of the Oddfellows' and the Foresters' friendly societies. A farm was attached to the works and he learnt about pigs and cows. His experience in industry was of a phase which was passing swiftly. 'It was the last survivor of that type of works, and ultimately became swallowed up in one of those great combinations.' In 1892 he married Lucy, the eldest daughter of Edward Lucas Jenks Ridsdale, of Rottingdean, a former assay master of the Mint. Three sons (the first stillborn) and four daughters were born to them.

In 1906 Baldwin unsuccessfully contested Kidderminster and blamed his defeat on the failure of the Conservative Party to help the trade unions by reversing the Taff Vale judgement. His father had been member for the Bewdley, or West, division of Worcestershire from 1892 and on his death in 1908 he was succeeded by his son who was unopposed. Stanley Baldwin held the seat until he went to the Lords in 1937. His maiden speech (June 1908) was in opposition to the coal mines (eight hours) bill. In the years which followed he spoke seldom and attracted little attention. Andrew Bonar Law had known Alfred Baldwin and on the formation of the War Cabinet in 1916 welcomed the son as his parliamentary private secretary. In June 1917 Stanley Baldwin became joint financial secretary to the Treasury with Sir Hardman Lever [q.v.] who was engaged in special duties in America and had no seat in the House. In the 'coupon' election in 1918 Baldwin was unopposed and was reappointed to his post at the Treasury. On 24 June 1919 there appeared in *The Times* a letter signed 'F. S. T.' (long afterwards revealed as an abbreviation for 'Financial Secretary to the Treasury') which appealed to the wealthy classes to tax themselves voluntarily and thus help to reduce the burden of war debt. The writer, having estimated his own estate at £580,000, had decided to realize 20 per cent. and purchase £150,000 of the War Loan for cancellation. The secret of the writer's identity was well kept for some years, even from (Sir) Austen Chamberlain [q.v.] who was chancellor of the Exchequer at the time. It was the first revelation, though veiled, of Stanley Baldwin's unusual character.

In April 1921 Baldwin, who had been made a privy counsellor in the previous year, entered the Lloyd George Cabinet as president of the Board of Trade and piloted through Parliament the safeguarding of industries bill. In a Cabinet of 'first-class brains' he was inarticulate and uncomfortable. He was shocked by what he deemed the levity and cynicism of some of his colleagues and reflecting on his position while on holiday at Aix-les-Bains he wondered whether to resign. He was recalled to London (29 September 1922) at the time of the Chanak crisis. He was convinced that the country had been driven too near to the edge of war; and when he and other Conservatives realized that the party leaders—Austen Chamberlain, Balfour, and Birkenhead [qq.v.]—were prepared to face a general election under Lloyd George, they rebelled. A Carlton Club party meeting (19 October) brought the coalition to an end by the resolution that the Conservatives should fight 'as an independent party, with its own leader and its own programme'. Baldwin's passionate speech revealed an intense distrust of Lloyd George: 'a dynamic force is a very terrible thing; it may crush you, but it is not necessarily right'. The speech not only carried the Carlton Club meeting but, after the general election which followed, brought Baldwin himself to the chancellorship of the Exchequer, 'the limit', he had said, of his ambitions.

His first major task was to arrange for the settlement of the American debt. He went to Washington (January 1923) with the governor of the Bank of England (Montagu, later Lord, Norman, q.v.) and negotiated with Andrew Mellon who exacted terms more severe than were contemplated by Bonar Law, the British prime minister. Ultimately Baldwin agreed to recommend terms which would extinguish the debt in sixty-two years at an interest rate of 3% for the first ten years, $3\frac{1}{2}\%$ thereafter, and $4\frac{1}{2}\%$ for arrears. This was equivalent to an annual payment of £33 million for the first ten years, a tolerable sum in the view of the City. Unguarded words from Baldwin to newspaper reporters on his return home inflamed American opinion and made any reduction of the terms unlikely. On 31 January the Cabinet reluctantly approved them.

In the months which followed Bonar Law was a sick man and in April Baldwin came to lead the House of Commons. He had made a remarkable speech on the Address (16 February) revealing his unexpected recipe for 'salvation for this country . . . Faith, Hope, Love and Work'. The speech left a deep impression on a House unaware of Baldwin's stature and in a country which recognized a new note in its counsels. In April Baldwin introduced a budget which was well received

and on 20 May Bonar Law, a dying man, resigned. To the acute disappointment of Lord Curzon [q.v.] Baldwin, 'a man of the utmost insignificance', became prime minister on 22 May. But a week before Baldwin had been expressing the jocular hope of returning to Worcestershire 'to read the books I want to read, to live a decent life, and to keep pigs'. The premiership was uncovenanted. 'The position of leader came to me when I was inexperienced', Baldwin told Asquith in 1926, 'before I was really fitted for it, by a succession of curious chances that could not have been foreseen. I had never expected it.' 'Presently', wrote a colleague, 'there shaped itself in his mind the idea of what a Prime Minister ought to be. It was, to begin with, to be as unlike Lloyd George as possible—plain instead of brilliant; steady instead of restless; soberly truthful instead of romantic and imaginative; English and not Welsh. . . . Above all he must be patriotic; a lover of all his fellow-countrymen, of his country's history, of its institutions, its ancient monarchy, its great parliamentary tradition, its fairness, its tolerance. All these things were innate in his own disposition. But he steeped himself in them as the part which it was his duty to play as a Prime Minister, and they became more deeply ingrained in consequence.'

The seeming plainness and provincialism of Baldwin's character and his intense love of England were conveyed to the nation in a series of speeches which lodged him deep in its confidence. To an increasingly urban population he echoed a nostalgia for the English countryside from which it rooted, and he did this mainly in monosyllables. 'I speak', he said, 'not as the man in the street even, but as a man in a field-path, a much simpler person steeped in tradition and impervious to new ideas.' The elaborated ordinariness of a pipe-smoking premier matched the unadventurous public mood which welcomed 'a quiet man at the top'. Confidence may have been somewhat shaken when Baldwin returning from Aix met Poincaré in Paris (19 September 1923) and joined in a communiqué of surprising warmth considering the division of view about the occupation of the Ruhr and the payment of reparations. Baldwin never again willingly ventured into foreign affairs. Two months later confidence was certainly shaken when he suddenly plunged the country into a general election. It was a calculated—some thought an impetuous —decision to consolidate the still not re-united Conservative Party by outbidding Lloyd George, and to gain a mandate for protection which Baldwin held to be the essential remedy for unemployment. He felt it dishonourable to introduce a tariff policy without first consulting the elec-torate. 'I think Baldwin has gone mad', Birkenhead had written in August to Austen Chamberlain. 'He simply takes one jump in the dark; looks round; and then takes another.' Now, in their dif-fering phraseology, Balfour and Curzon agreed with Birkenhead's opinion. To Baldwin himself, however, the dissolution was 'deliberate and the result of long re-flection'.

Instead of controlling a majority of 77 over all parties, the Conservatives were returned with 258 seats against Labour's 191 and the Liberals' 159. On Baldwin's defeat in the House, the King sent for Ramsay MacDonald and the first Labour Government took office. Baldwin's priv-ate secretary, Sir Ronald Waterhouse, re-tained the post under MacDonald, both retiring and incoming prime ministers agreeing that their positions would likely be reversed within nine months.

Despite the electoral set-back Baldwin was re-elected to the leadership of the Conservative parliamentary party and with the return of Birkenhead to the fold its formal unity was achieved. The Govern-ment fell on 8 October 1924. The ensuing election in which the 'Zinoviev letter' played its part, sent back the reunited Conservatives, now supported by the Beaverbrook and Rothermere press, with a firm majority: 419 seats to Labour's 151 and the Liberal 40. The Conservative leader became prime minister for the second time (4 November). Again might be noted a 'curious incoherence between Baldwin's political ideas and his actions and ap-pointments'. Sir Arthur Steel-Maitland [q.v.] was appointed minister of labour, and to everyone's surprise, not least his own, (Sir) Winston Churchill went to the Ex-chequer. In his budget (28 April 1925) Churchill announced the crucial decision to return to the gold standard. In the pre-vious month the prime minister had once more revealed his own unusual character, moved the House and impressed the country by closing a speech on the trade union (political fund) bill with the prayer 'Give peace in our time, O Lord': a note which he alone in public life would dare to strike and which put Baldwin once

again in a position of unrivalled ascen-dancy as a national leader. 'There is only one thing', he had said in January, 'which I feel is worth giving one's whole strength to, and that is the binding together of all classes of our people in an effort to make life in this country better in every sense of the word. That is the main end and object of my life in politics.'

The industrial situation was difficult and in many speeches he pleaded for con-ciliation. When in July 1925 the miners were on the eve of forcing a general stop-page Baldwin resorted to a Royal Com-mission and a subsidy. In 1925 'we were not ready'. 'I still think', he wrote two years later, 'we were right in buying off the strike in 1925 though it proved once more the cost of teaching democracy. Democracy has arrived at a gallop in England and I feel all the time it is a race for life. Can we educate them before the crash comes?' The Government set about preparing and improving administrative measures with which to counter a strike on a national scale. The Samuel report on the coal industry was published on 10 March 1926 and while opposed to nationali-zation it advocated some wage reduction on condition that both sides accepted a policy of reorganization. Decisive leader-ship—but that was not in Baldwin's nature—might have secured the immedi-ate adoption of the report. He went no farther than 'we accept the report pro-vided that the other parties do so'. In-determinate negotiations followed. The trade unions issued telegrams on Saturday evening, 1 May, instructing men 'not to take duty after Monday next'. The general strike began on 4 May and was called off on 12 May. The fairmindedness which Baldwin revealed in his broadcasts enor-mously contributed to this result. He was made, it was said, for the microphone, to which his delightful voice and intimate manner were remarkably attuned. He deprecated 'malice or vindictiveness or triumph' and pleaded for patience in re-building the prosperity of the coal in-dustry. Exhausted by the strain of the crisis he had surmounted, Baldwin failed, when his influence was at its maximum, to follow through with an immediate attempt to pacify the industry. 'The Baldwin of 1926 stood on a moral level' to which it has been doubted that 'he ever returned. He might have done anything. He did nothing. And ever after he seemed to be trading on an accumulated fund of confidence which was never replenished.'

1926 he presided at his second Im-
al Conference in London (his first was
1923) and in August 1927 paid with the
rince of Wales a visit to Canada where
he was received with enthusiasm and affection. In a series of speeches he did
much to interpret Great Britain to Canada
and was happy in his references to the historic traditions of her provinces.

In July 1928 the franchise was extended
to women of twenty-one years and upwards on the same terms as men. The
main domestic problem remained the
burden of unemployment especially in the
mining areas where millions were spent
on 'uncovenanted' or 'transitional' benefit
known as 'the dole'. There were demands
for protection, subsidies, and the safeguarding of industry. Baldwin was pledged
to resist any general measure of protection
or taxes on food but encouraged a measure
of safeguarding. His Government—in
slack water—did not escape the deterioration accompanying a safe majority; there
were complaints of his indolence in Cabinet
and even demands for his resignation.
Yet he could point to Locarno abroad, and
at home to a Local Government Act, a
Pensions Act, an Electricity Act, a Franchise Act, a safeguarding policy, and to a
million houses built. Nor could he be
charged with failure to instruct the electorate: he made many political speeches
and many on literary or historical subjects—the Bible, William Booth, the Oxford Dictionary, Mary Webb's novel
Precious Bane, the Boy's Own Paper. In a
political speech at Yarmouth (27 September 1928) he maintained: 'It is not wise in
a democracy to go too far in front of
public opinion. The British people are
slow to make up their minds on a new
question but they are thinking and thinking hard.' They may have been wondering
too at the absence of leadership, as each
member of the Cabinet seemed to go his
own way with apparently nobody at the
helm. The 'torpid, sleepy, barren' Government (as Lloyd George called it) was defeated at the general election of 30 May
1929. The Conservative Party paraded
the uninspiring slogan 'Safety First' before
the eyes of the new young voters, the
Socialists issued a manifesto 'Labour and
the Nation', and Lloyd George, spending
his fund freely, announced that the Liberals
could conquer unemployment. The poll
gave Labour 288 members, Conservatives
260, and Liberals 59. Baldwin who had
fully expected to return to Downing Street
with a small but sufficient majority was
again succeeded by Ramsay MacDonald,
but his personal popularity was undiminished. 'The leader of the outgoing
party', said The Times, 'remains in popular estimation the most generally trusted
and acceptable personality in political
life.' Honours were showered upon him.
He had already been lord rector of the
universities of Edinburgh (1923–6) and
Glasgow (1928–31), and he now accepted
the offices of chancellor of the universities
of St. Andrews (1929) and Cambridge
(1930) and became the first chairman of
the Pilgrim Trust.

Baldwin did not court controversy and
was seldom roused to take notice of it.
In October and November 1929, however,
he had rebuked in the House of Commons
newspaper attacks upon him concerning
his Indian policy. Now two newspaper proprietors, Lords Beaverbrook and Rothermere, were running an Empire Free Trade
campaign. Baldwin was only in partial
agreement. Overtures between November
1929 and March 1930 came to nothing.
Then Rothermere overplayed his hand to
the extent of demanding that he should be
acquainted by Baldwin 'with the names of
at least eight, or ten, of his most prominent colleagues in the next Ministry'.
At a party meeting in the Caxton Hall (24
June 1930) Baldwin replied with unwonted force and passion to this 'prepos-
terous and insolent demand', was given a
vote of confidence with only one dissentient, and a thunderous welcome when he
entered the House of Commons later in
the day. But the campaign of abuse continued and he confronted it again in the
same hall and with the gloves off (30
October) when by 462 votes to 116 he was
confirmed in the leadership. It was a
triumph of character, a character which
appealed to a multitude of moderate citizens: 'the average voter upon whom his
gaze was constantly fixed'.

He had chosen Lord Irwin (subsequently
the Earl of Halifax) as viceroy of India in
1925 and unlike some of his party Baldwin
was in full agreement with the policy
which Irwin pursued and which culminated
in his pledge of Dominion status made at
the end of October 1929. In June 1930 the
Simon statutory commission issued its report. The Round Table conference opened
on 12 November 1930 but in December
Churchill, speaking for the 'Diehards',
dismissed the Indian claims as 'absurd
and dangerous pretensions'. For some
time, on both Empire Free Trade and
India, it seemed that Baldwin was losing

his hold over his party. In March 1931 he struck back and captivated the Conservatives by another speech on India which ranked among his finest parliamentary performances; and at the Queen's Hall (17 March) he replied fiercely to the press lords in phraseology more typical of his cousin Kipling than of his own familiar usages. When his lethargy was most exasperating and the mutiny of his followers most menacing Baldwin could produce—often at his wife's prompting—an energy and quality of speech which never failed to remind his grumbling party that he was its greatest electoral asset.

Meanwhile the Labour Government had its own troubles. The cost of unemployment insurance and the dole was mounting rapidly. The committee appointed with Sir George (later Lord) May [q.v.] as chairman to overhaul public expenditure proposed drastic reductions which divided and broke up the Labour Government. On 25 August 1931 a 'national' Government was formed, MacDonald remaining prime minister. Baldwin became lord president of the Council. At the general election which followed (27 October) the coalition Government secured over 550 seats, 471 of which were held by Conservatives. Had Baldwin wished to press his own claims to be prime minister again, it is now known that he could have done so successfully; he was content to serve as lord president for four years, a position not inconsistent with the exercise of considerable influence in the Cabinet and commanding authority over his party. An import duties bill imposing a general tariff and setting up an Import Duties Advisory Committee (1 March 1932) marked the definite return to the protectionist era for which Baldwin had always yearned. In July and August he presided with patience and good temper at the imperial economic conference at Ottawa. The free trade members of the coalition who had threatened resignation as early as January 1932 could no longer 'agree to differ' and resigned.

Japan's successful aggression in Manchuria revealed, early in 1932, the impotence of the League of Nations in the Far East with two Pacific powers absent, Russia and the United States. In Europe the appointment of Hitler as German chancellor in January 1933 was a prelude to a series of explosions. This country was profoundly pacifist and its obstinate faith in disarmament was demonstrated in the East Fulham by-election (October 1933) by a marked turnover of votes to Labour. Baldwin looked back on this event in a speech to the House on 12 November 1936: 'My position as the leader of a great party was not altogether a comfortable one. I asked myself what chance was there —when that feeling that was given expression to in Fulham was common throughout the country—what chance was there within the next year or two of that feeling being so changed that the country would give a mandate for rearmament? Supposing I had gone to the country and said that Germany was rearming and that we must rearm, does anybody think that this pacific democracy would have rallied to that cry at that moment? I cannot think of anything that would have made the loss of the election from my point of view more certain.' He was to pay dearly for this disclosure in after years: for his 'appalling frankness' was to be quoted against him, not always with much care about its original context. The Putney by-election (November 1934) again saw a marked reduction in Conservative support. Although Baldwin had told the House (30 July 1934) that the air arm had abolished old frontiers—'When you think of the defence of England you no longer think of the chalk cliffs of Dover; you think of the Rhine'—he sounded no urgent alarm, when introducing a measure of rearmament, at the growth of German air power and his advisers were slow to give credence to the reports of this growth which were reaching them. He deprecated panic; he saw 'no risk in the immediate future of peace being broken'. In November he admitted that looking ahead 'there is ground for very grave anxiety' but maintained that 'It is not the case that Germany is rapidly approaching equality with us'. By May 1935 he admitted frankly that his estimate of the future situation in the air had been 'completely wrong'.

Ramsay MacDonald, deserted by his old friends and associates, dependent therefore on reluctant Conservative support and primarily interested in establishing peaceful foreign relations, was betraying increasing signs of declining powers. At last in June 1935 he exchanged places with Baldwin who became prime minister for the third time at the age of nearly sixty-eight. Baldwin took the fruitful course of sending Sir Philip Cunliffe-Lister (subsequently the Earl of Swinton) to take charge of the Air Ministry, and inviting chill—his fiercest critic—to join the .mittee on air defence research. In .arch 1935 the Government had issued a white paper (Cmd. 4827) which not only proposed an expansion of the Air Force but gave the Government power to take preliminary steps in regard to all the forces on which a subsequent policy of rearmament was based. This was eight months before the general election. It was an early step in the educational process which Baldwin believed had to be gradual. Doubtless he remembered his precipitancy in 1923.

Meanwhile Churchill had not been Baldwin's critic on the subject of rearmament only. There was also India. 'He had gone about threatening to smash the Tory party on India', said Baldwin, 'and I did not mean to be smashed.' On 4 December 1934 Baldwin at a Conservative central council meeting made it clear that he accepted the white paper (Cmd. 4268) of 1933 and the report of the joint select committee of both Houses (November 1934). The Government of India bill was published 24 January 1935 and on the second reading (11 February) Baldwin, having been urged to consolidate the party, showed himself once again 'the most powerful man in the House of Commons'. The bill received the royal assent on 2 August 1935.

The League of Nations Union, the chief propagandist body in Britain, conducted a ballot which in June 1935 revealed a vote of 10½ millions (over 90 per cent. of those who voted) in favour of an all-round reduction of armaments by international agreement. At the general election which followed in November, while the Government supported a new defence programme, both parties protested their pacific intentions and placed the support of the League Covenant in the forefront of their platforms. To the Peace Society (31 October) Baldwin, who even when electioneering—and it proved an electoral asset—tended to speak rather as a national than a party leader, managed to have arms and the League in one and the same breath: 'We mean nothing by the League if we are not prepared, in the end, and after grave and careful trial, to take action to enforce its judgement. . . . Do not fear or misunderstand when the Government say that they are looking to our defences. . . . I give you my word that there will be no great armaments.' Baldwin was returned with 430 supporters against an opposition of 184.

On 11 September the foreign secretary (Sir Samuel Hoare, subsequently Viscount Templewood) in a speech at Geneva had conveyed the impression that this country was embarking on a vigorous League policy which might not stop short of war on the Abyssinian issue. There was clamour for sanctions against Italy. Baldwin's view was that 'real sanctions mean war'; so sham sanctions were imposed, futile because they omitted a ban on oil. In December Hoare initialed in Paris an agreement with Pierre Laval, the French prime minister, for a proposed settlement of the Abyssinian war by the cession of Ethiopian territory to Italy. A surprised Baldwin acquiesced, but the country, still in the exalted mood of Hoare's Geneva speech, apparently endorsed by the general election, compelled the prime minister, not for the first time in his experience, to reverse his engines. He disavowed his foreign secretary. Hoare resigned and many thought that Baldwin should have resigned also. He made lame, uncomfortable speeches. His lips, he said, were sealed: a remark which the cartoonists were to remember.

The King died in January 1936 and Baldwin was deprived of a steady source of strength, if George V himself had sometimes (so it would seem from his biographer) been impatient with his prime minister's 'deft quietism'. The months which followed were heavy with trouble: the occupation of the Rhineland, the fall of Abyssinia, rioting in Palestine, civil war in Spain. The Government issued another white paper on 3 March (Cmd. 5107) admitting that conditions in the international field had worsened and that the level of national armaments continued to rise all over the world. It announced that the prime minister had presided over the defence policy and requirements sub-committee and had subjected the armed forces to a prolonged and exhaustive examination. As was to be expected, it stressed the importance of retaining the goodwill of industry. The new policy introduced 'the first real measure of expansion'.

On 7 March Hitler reoccupied the Rhineland. Sir Thomas Inskip (later Viscount Caldecote, q.v.) not Churchill, was appointed minister for the co-ordination of defence. On 6 April, but six months after the election, the prime minister was forced to obtain a vote of confidence: yet 'the honours of the day were with Churchill and Austen Chamberlain'. Even Baldwin's skill in Parliament seemed to be deserting him. There was a budget leakage which distressed him greatly. He seemed overwhelmed by domestic and international problems, and by midsummer he appeared to have reached the end of his tether. He grew more and more depressed and towards the end of July his doctor, Lord Dawson of Penn [q.v.], ordered him to take three months' complete rest. When he returned to Downing Street on 12 October he was able to handle with freshness and vigour what became known as the abdication crisis which arose out of the decision of the new King, Edward VIII, to marry Mrs. Wallis Simpson, an American citizen who had divorced one husband and was on the eve of divorcing a second. Thanks to the voluntary discretion of the British press the matter had only reached a small fraction of the public but it was well known abroad. The prime minister's first interview with the King on the subject was on 20 October when he found his mind irrevocably fixed on marriage. On 2 December the silence of the press unexpectedly ended and an intense emotional release of comment followed. The suggested device of a 'morganatic' marriage was given short shrift by the Cabinet, still shorter by the Dominions, and was not pressed by the King. There was talk for a moment of a 'King's party', but receiving no support from the King himself it swiftly passed. Nor was there deep discord in Parliament or in the country. Baldwin knew his provinces. In announcing to the House of Commons (10 December) that the King had renounced the throne, Baldwin told the story of his conversations with him in a speech simple, direct, dignified, and compelling assent. Baldwin throughout the whole episode had revealed a sureness of judgement which immeasurably enhanced his prestige. It was the second crisis in which he became the incarnation of the national will. Baldwin will go down to history as the prime minister who steered the country successfully through the general strike and the Empire through the royal abdication.

Baldwin was now in his seventieth year and had already indicated Neville Chamberlain as his successor. On 5 May 1937 he delivered his last set speech in the Commons—an appeal for peace in the mining industry, then threatened with stoppage—and on 27 May he announced the Government's proposal to increase from £400 to £600 the salaries of members of Parliament. On 28 May, a fortnight after the coronation of King George VI, he went to the Palace to tender his resignation, fourteen years to the day since he had been elected leader of the Conservative Party in succession to Bonar Law. His Majesty bestowed on him a knighthood of the Garter and on 8 June he became an earl. Baldwin was worn out and suffering from increasing deafness. He resolved to make no political speeches, neither to speak to the man at the wheel nor to spit on the deck. By 1939 he was well enough to visit Toronto and New York where he delivered addresses on his favourite subjects, democracy and citizenship. Then came the war and he withdrew to Astley Hall, his Worcestershire home, where he lived quietly, reading few newspapers, listening regularly to the radio news, delving among family archives, re-reading Scott, Jane Austen, Wordsworth, and Hardy, or scanning a new book sent to him by its author. He was often in pain from arthritis and limped with the aid of a stick. He went rarely to London and refused invitations to broadcast on the war effort lest he should stir up controversy. He was aware that he was widely supposed to be responsible for all that had happened since 1931 'by people who have no historical sense'. On 12 September 1942 he and Lady Baldwin celebrated their golden wedding. She, who shared his faith and was his perfect sympathizer, died in June 1945. He followed on 14 December 1947 and his ashes were laid with his wife's in Worcester Cathedral. He was succeeded by his elder son, Oliver Ridsdale, Viscount Corvedale (1899–1958), author and Labour politician, who became governor and commander-in-chief of the Leeward Islands (1948–50).

In appearance, Baldwin was a sturdy countryman of medium height, broad-shouldered, with mobile countenance, sandy, shaggy eyebrows, and sandy hair parted in the middle and well smoothed down. His eyes were blue, his hands broad and sensitive. He had a shrewd, quizzical expression and a musical voice which carried well. He was a lover of books, the friend of scholars, and an inveterate smoker. During his political life he played neither tennis nor golf but, until crippled in his later years, he was always an enthusiastic walker, with a great affection for the atmosphere and simple fare of old country inns.

For fourteen years (1923–37) Baldwin dominated the British political scene and at the coronation in 1937 he 'almost divided the cheering with the royal pair themselves'. Already in 1922 'probably the best-liked man in the House', from then onwards he revealed an extraordinarily acute sense of the House of Commons over which he was increasingly to exercise his own 'sedative authority'. Whenever possible he avoided the direct debating speech: preferring rather to lower the temperature by a disarming, even 'appalling', frankness; but on occasion—which he made great—he could 'conceive and be delivered of a powerful oration' and 'the ironmaster turned goldsmith'. His speeches usually transcended the bounds of party; many were lay sermons with the emphasis upon the eternal commonplaces. One colleague noted that 'he was not so effective on the platform as in the House of Commons, but there he obtained for several years such ascendancy that, if a member interrupted him, it seemed almost like brawling in church'.

He was happier as prime minister than as a departmental head because he had little capacity for detail or quick decision. Mastering figures, of the unemployed in Great Britain, or of rearmament in Germany, was not his forte and his uneasiness about both problems did not result in active and positive measures to tackle them. He trusted to goodwill in industrial relations which perhaps had changed—like industry itself—more than Baldwin realized. As one Labour member said to him after Baldwin's moving speech in the Macquisten debate (6 March 1925) 'It was true, prime minister, every word was true. But those times have gone.' He had little interest in foreign affairs and was never quite willing to face the growing German problem frontally. His chosen biographer has suggested that 'the nerve, injured in October 1933, the East Fulham nerve, never quite healed: he was afraid of the pacifists: ... And he was not sure of himself. He could never master the logistics ... of defence. All his shortcomings combined to keep him off that ground—his indolence, his lack of scientific interest, his indifference to administrative concerns.' He conceived his function to be that of a non-intervening chairman. He was neither vain nor arrogant nor was he easily impressed and he could escape from high politics with disconcerting suddenness into talk of cricket or clouds or flowers or other irrelevance. He was genuinely modest and never quite got over his surprise at being elevated to the premiership. A political career he regarded as akin to that of a Christian minister: he was a

religious man with a serious view of life. Withal he was (to Churchill) 'the greatest party manager the Conservatives had ever had' and, by a genius for waiting on events, he reformed them as a party and kept them in power for a generation in the knowledge that, however much they might worry about the direction, Conservatives were unlikely to drop a pilot who went too slowly; and after 1923 Baldwin was never again in danger of moving too fast. Nor, in the event, was any party likely to jettison a leader with so singular a capacity to garner the suffrages of the doubting voter. 'My worst enemy', it was Baldwin's pride to maintain, 'could never say that I do not understand the people of England': especially middle-class England.

His lethargy was often a mask to cover impulsive, emotional, and exhausting spurts of nervous energy. The long spells on the front bench sniffing the order paper, contemplating his finger tips or reading Dod's *Parliamentary Companion*, or again, solving crossword puzzles or playing patience in the Long Gallery at Chequers (he claimed not to be able to think in 10 Downing Street), or on holiday at Aix: all were indispensable modes and means of recuperation. He was incapable of prolonged continuous effort. His exasperating indecisions were charmed away by his sweetness of temper, his rapid and pungent conversation, and the unexpected turn of his humour. Reverie to him was not a vacuum but a refreshment. 'There is a cloud round my mind, it takes shape, and then I know what to say' was his own explanation. 'Baldwin', said Lloyd George, 'is one of us. He is a Celt.' If so, he persuaded the English (having early persuaded himself) that he was a typical Englishman. He had no time for foreigners and in a series of farewell speeches reviewing his political career he made no mention whatever of international problems. For intellectuals of all parties he had a profound contempt. 'Use your commonsense: avoid logic: love your fellow men: have faith in your own people, and grow the hide of a rhinoceros' was his advice to the political man. He saw his role as that of a national statesman as much as that of the accomplished if idiosyncratic party leader he evidently was. 'I sometimes think', he said in a broadcast (5 February 1935), 'that, if I were not the leader of the Conservative Party, I should like to be the leader of the people who do not belong to any party'. If he dined with the Tories, he smoked with the trade-unionists. Labour members he treated with marked respect and sympathy. His long hours in the House held the hope that the Labour Party would choose the parliamentary way, to which he was devoted, in the belief that it would fulfil their purposes when their inevitable turn came. He sought to diminish class hatred, to retain national unity and to take the bitterness out of political life. 'The reason for his long, tenacious, successful hold over the electorate', one of his juniors has conjectured, 'is probably to be found in the simple fact that he was, fundamentally, a nice man; and the country knew it.' At the first Trinity Commemoration dinner (13 March 1948) after Baldwin's death, Dr. G. M. Trevelyan, master of his old Cambridge college, made this his epitaph: 'Stanley Baldwin was an Englishman indeed, in whom was much guile, never used for low or selfish purposes. In a world of voluble hates, he plotted to make men like, or at least tolerate, one another. Therein he had much success, within the shores of this island. He remains the most human and lovable of all the Prime Ministers.'

There are busts of Baldwin, by Lady Kennet at Bewdley Town Hall, by Sir Alfred Gilbert at Shirehall, Worcester, by Newbury A. Trent (1927) in the possession of the third Earl Baldwin who has also a small portrait by Seymour Lucas (1910). A portrait by R. G. Eves (1915) is in the possession of Lady Huntington-Whiteley, one by (Sir) Oswald Birley was with the second Earl Baldwin, and a portrait by Thomas Monnington is at Trinity College, Cambridge; another by Francis Dodd is at Rhodes House, Oxford (Baldwin was from 1925 a Rhodes Trustee). The National Portrait Gallery has a portrait by R. G. Eves and a chalk drawing by Sir William Rothenstein.

[*Lord Baldwin, a Memoir*, published by *The Times*, 1947; Nourah Waterhouse, *Private and Official*, 1942; Winston S. Churchill, *The Second World War*, vol. i, 1948; Trinity College, Cambridge, *Annual Record*, 1948; *Cambridge Journal*, November 1948; *Listener*, 15 February 1951 and 1 January 1953; G. M. Young, *Stanley Baldwin*, 1952; Harold Nicolson, *King George V*, 1952; D. C. Somervell, *Stanley Baldwin*, 1953; L. S. Amery, *My Political Life*, vol. ii, 1953; private information; personal knowledge.]

THOMAS JONES.

[Robert Blake, *The Unknown Prime Minister, The Life and Times of Andrew Bonar Law*, 1955; A. W. Baldwin, *My Father: The True Story*, 1955; C. L. Mowat in *Journal*

*of Modern History*, vol. xxvii, Chicago, 1955; Lord Percy of Newcastle, *Some Memories*, 1958; Lord Vansittart, *The Mist Procession*, 1958.]

**BALFOUR, GERALD WILLIAM,** second EARL OF BALFOUR (1853–1945), politician and psychical researcher, was born in Edinburgh, 9 April 1853, the fourth son of James Maitland Balfour, of Whittingehame, East Lothian, by his wife, Lady Blanche Mary Harriet Cecil, daughter of the second Marquess of Salisbury. He was the brother of Arthur James, first Earl of Balfour, and Eleanor Mildred Sidgwick [qq.v.]. He was educated at Eton and at Trinity College, Cambridge, where he was a scholar and gained the fifth place in the classical tripos in 1875. He was elected a fellow in 1878 and he lectured in classics, but finding teaching uncongenial he left Cambridge in 1881 and resided in a villa at Florence for two years, studying metaphysics, but without satisfaction to himself. He therefore turned to politics, and in 1885 he was elected Conservative member for Central Leeds, and acted as private secretary to his brother Arthur who from 1885 to 1886 was president of the Local Government Board. In 1895, strengthened by experience on parliamentary committees in the intervening Parliaments, he was appointed chief secretary for Ireland. In that office he carried in 1898 the Local Government (Ireland) Act, establishing county and district councils, which in no small degree accustomed the Irish to govern themselves. In 1900 he was transferred to the presidency of the Board of Trade, and sworn of the Privy Council. He supported the export-tax of a shilling per ton on coal imposed by the chancellor of the Exchequer, and was responsible for the Sugar Convention Act of 1903. For a few weeks in 1905 he was president of the Local Government Board, but on being defeated at the general election in 1906 he retired from politics. He never approached the political stature of his brother, whose incisiveness in debate he lacked. His talents lay rather in the careful weighing and presentation of evidence, and this fact led to his being depicted by caricaturists as a schoolmaster in cap and gown; he was often described as an 'academic chief secretary'.

Balfour therefore in 1906 turned to other interests. He accepted directorships of public companies, with varying success. His great interest, however, lay in psychical research, in which he was probably inspired by his sister, Mrs. Sidgwick, and as life went on he became more and more absorbed in this study. He had been one of a group at Cambridge which included the Sidgwicks, his brother Frank, and his brother-in-law, J. W. Strutt, third Baron Rayleigh, A. W. Verrall [qq.v.], and others. His approach to the subject was through metaphysics and psychology; he paid little or no attention to the physical phenomena supposed to occur in the presence of spiritualistic mediums. A more promising line, he thought, could be found in the trance utterances of mediums which seemed to reveal knowledge which could not have been acquired by normal means; and in interpreting the utterances or the scripts, many of which contained recondite classical allusions purporting to come from dead scholars, his knowledge of the classics proved useful. In his presidential address to the Society for Psychical Research in 1906 he maintained that if communication with the dead was by word of mouth, gesture, or physical contact, it was not unreasonable to conjecture that telepathy might play a part; he suggested that the impressions which keep streaming through the mind without obvious external impulse might be telepathic in origin and come from one or more extraneous minds, and that telepathy might be a commoner activity than was recognized; and he propounded the idea that the human organism might have many souls which communicate with each other by telepathy.

In 'A Study of the Psychological Aspects of Mrs. Willett's Mediumship, and of the Statements of the Communicators concerning Process' (*Proceedings* of the Society for Psychical Research, part 140, vol. xliii, May 1935) Balfour revealed his complete confidence in the good faith of that medium's scripts, and this confidence was shared by other investigators whose names carried weight in the academic world. He thought that the automatic communications came in some cases from a dissociated self, in others from an external agent, and in others again from both agencies acting in co-operation. His interpretations did not admit independent clairvoyance as a source of knowledge; they depended on assuming communication from one mind to another, without excluding the possibility of one or both of these minds being discarnate. He described his sensations as like listening in to a telephone conversation where it was not always clear who was speaking or whether there was not interference from other speakers owing to

imperfection of the machine at the exchange. Moreover, he felt that some of the speakers might be repeating at second hand what they had imperfectly heard or grasped, or what might be scarcely intelligible without specialist knowledge. In interpreting Mrs. Willett's scripts a knowledge of the classics was essential, for they purported to be communicated by dead classical scholars such as A. W. Verrall, S. H. Butcher, F. W. H. Myers, and Edmund Gurney [qq.v.].

A more definite contribution to psychical research is to be found in his paper entitled 'The Ear of Dionysius' (*Proceedings* of the Society for Psychical Research, part 73, vol. xxix, March 1917) in which he studied four automatic scripts or utterances of Mrs. Willett of four separate dates in 1914 and 1915. His researches made him a convinced believer in survival after physical death, but the evidence on which he rested this belief has never been fully published, for it was in part derived from words in the Willett scripts concerning confidential matters which he was not free to publish or discuss because of their concern with people's private lives. It must always be remembered that the natural bias of his mind was sceptical rather than credulous.

In private life, Balfour was a most kindly and genial companion and the centre of a devoted family circle. In 1887 he married Lady Elizabeth Edith Bulwer-Lytton (died 1942), daughter of the first Earl of Lytton [q.v.] by whom he had a son, Robert Arthur Lytton (born 1902), who succeeded him in the earldom in 1945, and five daughters. He himself succeeded his brother in 1930 under a special remainder. In personal appearance he was gifted with a classical profile of an intellectual cast, which lasted unimpaired, as did his faculties, into extreme old age. He died at Whittingehame 14 January 1945. A portrait by G. Fiddes Watt is in the possession of the family. A cartoon by 'Spy' appeared in *Vanity Fair*, 10 December 1896.

[*The Times*, 15 January 1945; *Proceedings* of the Society for Psychical Research, part 169, vol. xlvii, May 1945, and *passim*; Blanche E. C. Dugdale, *Arthur James Balfour, first Earl of Balfour*, 2 vols., 1936; personal knowledge.]
                                    RAYLEIGH.
                                    GUY STRUTT.

BANKES, SIR JOHN ELDON (1854–1946), judge, was born 17 April 1854 in London, the eldest son of John Scott Bankes, of Soughton Hall, Flint, by his first wife, Annie, daughter of Sir John

Jervis [q.v.], chief justice of the common pleas. He was directly descended from Sir John Bankes [q.v.], chief justice of the common pleas in 1641, who bought Corfe Castle, Dorset, which is still the property of the senior branch of the family. His father's mother was the daughter of the lord chancellor, John Scott, first Earl of Eldon [q.v.]. Heredity thus marked him out for a legal career.

Bankes was educated at Eton and University College, Oxford, where he obtained a second class in jurisprudence in 1876. He was called to the bar by the Inner Temple in 1878 and was a pupil of Richard Webster (later Viscount Alverstone, q.v.). He had a good practice on the common law side and took silk in 1901, having become a bencher of his Inn in 1899. He was Unionist candidate for Flint in 1906 but was not elected. In 1910 Lord Chancellor Loreburn [q.v.] appointed him a puisne judge and he received the customary knighthood; five years later he was promoted to the Court of Appeal and was sworn of the Privy Council.

As judge and lord justice, he won a high reputation as a careful, clear-headed, and able lawyer. It fell to his lot, during his latter years in the Court of Appeal, to act as chairman of one of its branches, and in this capacity, often sitting with Sir T. E. Scrutton and Sir J. R. (later Lord) Atkin [qq.v.] as his colleagues, he gave the first judgement in many important cases. Thus, taking at random a single volume of the Law Reports, [1921] 3 K.B., we find therein no fewer than seven well-known decisions, each illustrating his grasp of common law principles. The prestige of this branch of the Court of Appeal at this time, under his chairmanship, is shown by the fact that in not one of these cases was there an appeal to the House of Lords from its unanimous decision. Bankes retired in 1927 and was made a G.C.B. in 1928.

Throughout his long life he was a devoted churchman; he was at one time treasurer and later chairman of the London Diocesan Fund; and together with (Lord) Sankey [q.v.] and (Lord) Atkin drew up the constitution of the Church in Wales when it was disestablished. For a number of years he was chairman of the representative body of the Church in Wales. At the age of eighty-one he was appointed chairman of the Royal Commission upon traffic in arms. He was chairman of Flintshire quarter-sessions for thirty-three years.

In 1923 Bankes was treasurer of the Inner Temple. He was an honorary LL.D. of Wales (1921) and Manchester (1923), an honorary fellow of University College, Oxford, and a fellow of Eton. As an undergraduate he was president of Vincent's Club, having rowed in the crew in 1875 when, after five successive defeats, Oxford won the boat race against Cambridge by ten lengths.

In 1882 Bankes married Edith (died 1931), daughter of Robert Peel Ethelston, of Hinton Hall, Shropshire, and had two sons and two daughters; his surviving son, Robert Wynne Bankes, was private secretary to successive lord chancellors from 1919 to 1929; his daughter, Margaret Annie, married Sir W. H. P. Lewis [q.v.].

Bankes died aged ninety-two, 31 December 1946, at Soughton Hall, where there is a portrait of him by John St. Helier Lander.

[Family and personal information.]

P. A. LANDON.

BANTING, SIR FREDERICK GRANT (1891–1941), Canadian surgeon and physiologist, was born near the town of Alliston, Ontario, Canada, 14 November 1891, the fourth son and fifth and youngest child of William Thompson Banting, a farmer of Irish extraction, by his wife, Margaret, daughter of Alexander Grant, a millwright, of Alliston, whose ancestry was Scottish. He received his early education in Alliston, and on leaving the high school in 1910 entered Victoria College at the university of Toronto in order to prepare for the ministry of the Methodist Church, but after two years he entered the medical school of that university. In 1915, his medical training uncompleted, he joined the Royal Canadian Army Medical Corps as a private. A short time later he was sent back to the university to complete his course in medicine, and upon graduation in 1916 he was immediately granted a commission. He went overseas, served in England and in France, and for exceptional bravery under fire at Cambrai in September 1918 he was awarded the M.C. He was wounded there and it was feared for a time that he might lose his right arm.

The war over, Banting returned to Canada and received an appointment in surgery at the Hospital for Sick Children, Toronto. He developed a particular interest in orthopaedics and became a highly qualified surgeon. In 1920 he began practice at London, Ontario. Patients were not very numerous, and in order to augment his income he accepted a post in the university of Western Ontario as a part-time demonstrator. During the session of 1920–21 he conducted some research in the department of physiology, but the results were not published until the work on insulin was well advanced.

While preparing a course of lectures on the pancreas, Banting was excited by the idea that the failure of previous workers to obtain the hormone of the pancreas was due to the fact that the enzymes of the external secretion might have destroyed the hypothetical internal secretion during the course of the preparation of the extract. This idea was the turning-point of his life. In 1921 he gave up his work in London and sought an opportunity to test his hypothesis at Toronto where J. J. R. Macleod [q.v.] was able to provide him with the facilities which he needed at the department of physiology of the university.

This year 1921 was one of the most strenuous as well as one of the most productive in Banting's life. In May he was joined by the writer of this notice, then an advanced student in physiology, who had been invited by Macleod to join in the proposed search. It was begun on 16 May and as it became apparent after unremitting labour that an active diabetic principle could be prepared from degenerated or from normal pancreas, the young workers were excited beyond measure and were soon completely convinced of the success of their investigations and looked forward eagerly to the application of their findings to the human diabetic. When in the autumn Macleod returned from Scotland, the work continued under his general direction. On 14 November the first report of the work on the antidiabetic hormone was made by Banting and Best at the Physiological Journal Club: the first report outside Toronto was delivered by Banting, Best, and Macleod before the American Physiological Society at a meeting at New Haven, Connecticut, in December. In February and May 1922 two detailed papers were published by Banting and Best in the *Journal of Laboratory and Clinical Medicine*, describing their work from its inception up to that time. At the same time advances of great importance in methods of purification were begun by Professor James Bertram Collip. In January 1922 the first human being was treated with insulin prepared by Banting and Best. This was a boy of fourteen at the Toronto General Hospital. By all precedents he would have been

dead within a very short space of time, but by means of the insulin injections given to him he was permanently restored to health.

Banting, who in the autumn of 1921 had been appointed lecturer in the department of pharmacology, was appointed during 1922 senior demonstrator in the department of medicine, and he held this post until the Banting and Best Department of Medical Research was created in 1923 by an Act of the Ontario legislature. To the support of this department the Ontario Government made a grant of $10,000 per annum, and funds were obtained from various sources to pay the stipends of the staff. Banting was appointed head of this new department, and in the same year the Parliament of Canada granted him an annuity for life of $7,500.

The discovery of insulin brought to Banting honours from the whole scientific world. The university of Toronto awarded him the Starr gold medal for his M.D. thesis and the George Armstrong Peters prize for his important contributions to surgical science, both in 1922, and in the next year the Reeve prize (with Best) and the Charles Mickle fellowship. In 1923 the Nobel prize in medicine was awarded to Banting and Macleod. Banting immediately divided his share of the money with Best, as did Macleod with Collip. In the next year Banting was awarded the John Scott medal (Philadelphia) and the Rosenberger gold medal (Chicago), in 1927 the Cameron prize (Edinburgh), in 1931 the Flavelle medal of the Royal Society of Canada; in 1934 the Apothecaries' medal (London) and in 1936 the F. N. G. Starr gold medal of the Canadian Medical Association. In 1930 he was elected honorary F.R.C.S. (England), in 1935 F.R.S., and in 1936 honorary F.R.C.P. (London); and he was an honorary fellow or member of many foreign scientific societies. In 1934 he was appointed K.B.E.

Besides achieving his great discovery Banting was greatly interested in work on the adrenal cortex and made strenuous efforts to prolong the life of dogs from which this organ had been removed, by giving extracts of various types. Although these attempts were not successful he did achieve a definite advance in knowledge in this field. He also spent much of his own time in cancer research.

The outbreak of war in 1939 found Banting occupying a leading place in Canadian medical science. He was placed at the head of the central medical research committee of the National Research Council of Canada, and proved tireless in his efforts to stimulate research from one coast of Canada to the other. Even before war was declared he had taken steps in his own department to initiate medical research into the problems raised by aviation.

When in 1940 it was necessary to effect a liaison with medical workers in Great Britain, Banting insisted on going himself. No risks were too great for him. He returned to throw himself into research and organization. When a second journey to England was deemed necessary he welcomed the opportunity, but the bomber in which he was travelling crashed in a forced landing and he died 21 February 1941 in a remote spot in Newfoundland.

Banting was an energetic and forceful character and his scientific curiosity was boundless. He was keenly interested in many branches of medical work and was always ready to advise and assist those who consulted him about their problems. In addition to his scientific achievements he had many other interests. He was a member of the Arts and Letters Club of Toronto and one of Canada's most accomplished amateur painters. He delighted in sketching trips, and his oil-paintings of Arctic life, scenes round Quebec, and in the Canadian Rocky Mountains are excellent examples of his skill. His great interest in Canadiana showed itself in a collection of books and manuscripts concerning the development of medical practice in Canada.

As memorials of his work there have been founded in the university of Toronto: the Banting Institute, the Banting Research Foundation, and the Banting memorial lectureship. His name will ever be remembered by successive generations of diabetics and his brilliant and fearless career will always be an inspiration to young investigators.

Banting was twice married: first, in 1924 to Marion, daughter of William Robertson, physician, of Elora, Ontario; and secondly, in 1939 to Henrietta, daughter of Henry Tenny Ball, a customs official, of Stanstead, Quebec. The first marriage, of which the issue was a son, was dissolved in 1932.

A portrait of Banting in oils, painted in 1925 by Curtis Williamson, hangs in the main entrance hall of the Banting Institute. A bust by Frances Loring is now in the possession of the university of Toronto.

[C. H. Best in *Obituary Notices of Fellows of the Royal Society*, No. 11, November 1942; *Canadian Medical Association Journal*, Banting memorial number, vol. xlvii, November 1942; *British Medical Journal*, 8 March 1941; Seale Harris, *Banting's Miracle*, Philadelphia, 1946; Lloyd Stevenson, *Sir Frederick Banting*, Toronto, 1946; personal knowledge.]

C. H. BEST.

BANTOCK, SIR GRANVILLE RANSOME (1868–1946), composer, was born in London 7 August 1868, the eldest son of George Granville Bantock, a gynaecologist and surgeon of sufficient eminence to challenge Lister's new ideas of antisepsis. Dr. Bantock was born in the north of Scotland, where his father was factor to the Duke of Sutherland, from whom the name Granville is derived. He married Sophia Elizabeth Ransome, who came of a family of East Anglian Quakers.

Bantock was educated at a private school and the Royal Academy of Music, to which, however, he only proceeded after an attempt at a scientific training at the City and Guilds Institute, undertaken at the instance of his father who cherished the ideas first of the Indian Civil Service and then of chemical engineering as a career for his musical son. In September 1889 young Bantock had his way and began the study of composition at the Academy under Frederick Corder. Here he remained for four years, turning his hand to the practice of clarinet, violin, and piano, as well as other instruments in varying measures of assiduity. The experience served him well since his chief distinction as a composer lies in his instrumentation at a time when, with the exception of Sir Edward Elgar [q.v.], his elders and contemporaries among English musicians did not emulate the romantic, virtuoso orchestration of the post-Wagnerians on the continent. He won the Macfarren scholarship at the end of his first term with some wholly untutored music which included Satan's monologues from *Paradise Lost*. The choice was characteristic, for he regarded himself as a rebel against all the established orders and to the end of his life went his own way. The long list of compositions comprised under 146 headings (many of them containing several titles) show more pagan than Christian themes, as many oriental as western titles, exotic sources of inspiration in profusion, and sympathy with the early Socialists. However, his time at the Academy passed smoothly and prolifically and at the end of it he obtained work as conductor of George Edwardes's touring musical comedies, which took him round the world.

Contact with the theatre might, in a country with better operatic conditions than those prevailing in Britain at the end of the nineteenth century, have led to a more profitable employment of Bantock's talents, for seen in retrospect they are rich in descriptive ability and defective in the self-subsistent musical interest required for non-dramatic forms of music. But it was not to be: in 1897 he was appointed director of music at New Brighton in Lancashire. Here he fought battles for the improvement of public taste and for contemporary composers. Sibelius was one of his novelties and in return for his introduction to the English public Sibelius dedicated his third symphony to Bantock. But Bantock was all too successful in outgrowing the conditions of the job and it came to an end in 1900 after giving a fillip to English music.

Not long before he left the north in 1900 to take up the post of principal of the music school attached to the Midland Institute at Birmingham, Bantock married (in 1898) Helen Francesca Maude, daughter of Hermann von Schweitzer, a research chemist; there were three sons and one daughter of the marriage. Other issues of it were the 'Helena Variations' for orchestra and many poems from his wife's pen which became song-texts. In 1901 he was made fellow of the Royal Academy of Music.

Bantock's versatility, product of his wide-ranging curiosity and impressionability, and the facility of his technique prejudiced the development of a personal style: the more he wrote the less did he consolidate a recognizable individuality. In his large output of music in every form the orchestral works, the overture 'The Pierrot of the Minute', the tone-poem 'Fifine at the Fair', and the 'Hebridean' Symphony, show his instrumental mastery; the choral cantata with orchestra and soloists 'Omar Khayyám' is probably his greatest achievement, since it concentrates in one work his partiality for oriental subjects, his powers of musical illustration, and a capacity less frequently manifested for large-scale organization. Another *tour de force* is 'Atalanta in Calydon', a choral symphony for unaccompanied voices in twenty parts which are treated in a semi-orchestral manner. His interest in virtuoso choralism had been aroused by the competition festival movement and he wrote a huge quantity of part-songs for all sorts of vocal combinations with and without accompaniment. His only opera was *The Seal-Woman*, described as a Celtic folk-opera based on Hebridean tunes, but he wrote much incidental music for plays as diverse as *The Bacchae*, *Macbeth*, and Arnold Bennett's *Judith*. Programme music and grandiose orchestration in the manner of Richard Strauss appeared in the first decade of the twentieth century to be the line of advance for English music, but the war of 1914–18 deflected it into less cosmopolitan channels, so that Bantock's music seemed even before his death, and still more subsequently, to be not only outmoded but too rootless to leave a permanent mark on the art. But it represented a phase in the revival and he served his generation well. He remained in Birmingham until 1934, when he retired from the professorship at the university in which, in 1908, he had succeeded Elgar, for whom the chair was created. He was knighted in 1930. The rebel thus became an academic and the recipient of official honours. After his retirement he went to London and interested himself in the work of the Trinity College of Music, undertaking on its behalf another tour round the world. He died in London 16 October 1946.

Burly and bearded, Bantock was a good mixer among men of many sorts and had wide sympathies, as his choice of literary texts, his travels, and his democratic leanings in their different ways amply testify. There is a portrait (1920) by J. B. Munns at the Barber Institute, university of Birmingham.

[H. Orsmond Anderton, *Granville Bantock*, 1915.]                    FRANK HOWES.


BARCROFT, SIR JOSEPH (1872–1947), physiologist, was born 26 July 1872 at The Glen, Newry, county Down, the second of the five children of Henry Barcroft, D.L., a man of many talents—intellectual, inventive, industrial, and philanthropic—and his wife, Anna Richardson, daughter of David Malcolmson, of Melview, county Tipperary, a woman of much kindness and sagacity. Both his parents were active members of the Society of Friends, as was Joseph Barcroft himself for more than half his life. His paternal ancestors, for eight generations back, were North Ireland Quakers of substance, although the Barcrofts came originally of an ancient family which had held lands in Lancashire from the earliest times to which records extend. The Irish branch of the family was founded by an officer in Cromwell's army, William Barcroft, despite the fact that his first wife and five children were drowned when crossing to Ireland to join him. On the maternal side, there were strong connexions with the linen trade, as well as with milling and shipbuilding.

Barcroft was taught at home until at the age of twelve he went to the Friends' School, Bootham, York, and later to the Leys School, Cambridge, from which he precociously passed the London B.Sc. (1891). After a period of rest he entered King's College, Cambridge (1893), and obtained first class honours in the natural sciences tripos (1896, 1897). During the next thirteen years he became famous through his pioneer work on haemoglobin and on the metabolism of isolated organs of the animal body. For his researches he was awarded the second Walsingham medal and a prize fellowship at King's College (1899), shared the Gedge prize of 1900 with (Sir) Henry Dale, and was elected F.R.S. in 1910. During this period he held a series of college and university appointments.

In 1908 Barcroft invented the differential blood gas manometer, an instrument which not only aided his own researches greatly but also passed into world-wide use as 'the Barcroft'. He took a leading part in two mountain expeditions to study the physiology of life at high altitudes and his work on haemoglobin, oxygen metabolism, and high altitudes was summarized in *The Respiratory Function of the Blood* (1914). The appeal of this most inspiring book lay not only in its clear record of new achievements, but also in the humorous, vivid, and sometimes naïve descriptions of the difficulties encountered by the author and his friends. In the preface, which is a particularly fine piece of writing, Barcroft immortalized his love of sailing and likened it to scientific research in evoking the qualities necessary to venture 'beyond the visible horizon'.

In 1915 Barcroft was called to national service in relation to the medical aspects of gas poisoning. After some initial difficulty in reconciling the war with his Quaker faith he had cast his doubts aside and he now entered wholeheartedly upon his work. In 1917 he was appointed chief physiologist at the gas-warfare centre at Porton, near Salisbury. There he became the leader of a brilliant team, which ac-complished much important experimental work and applied it in practical and intrepid fashion to front-line problems. For these services he was awarded the C.B.E. (1918).

In 1919 he returned to Cambridge, first as reader and then, on the death of J. N. Langley [q.v.] in 1925, as professor of physiology. During this period he resumed his fruitful laboratory researches on haemoglobin and oxygen physiology problems, led the third and last of his high-altitude expeditions—to the Peruvian Andes—won a Royal medal of the Royal Society (1922), and held the Fullerian professorship of physiology at the Royal Institution. At Cambridge he supervised a large extension of the physiology laboratory and made many changes in the teaching courses before he retired in 1937.

Between 1923 and 1940 Barcroft opened up two further major fields of scientific research, the study of the spleen, especially as a blood reserve, and the physiology of the developing foetus. This later work, like his earlier, attracted research workers from all over the world, but especially from the United States to which he paid several highly successful scientific visits. He published another fine book, *Features in the Architecture of Physiological Function* (1934), which, as the great Danish physiologist A. S. Krogh said in 1948, 'ought to be read by everyone who is going into experimental work in physiology. It gives the general ideas which cannot be obtained from any other book in existence.' In 1935 Barcroft was knighted and gave the Croonian lecture of the Royal Society.

On the outbreak of war in 1939 Barcroft resumed his old service at Porton, with which he had maintained close contact since 1919. Fortunately gas warfare did not materialize and 1941 saw him back in Cambridge as head of the Agricultural Research Council unit in animal physiology. He was also deeply involved with food problems and became chairman of the Nutrition Society in 1945. In 1943 he received the Copley medal of the Royal Society.

After the war he returned to work on foetal physiology and published in 1946 his last book, *Researches on Pre-Natal Life* (vol. i). In the preface he wrote 'This work partakes very much of the nature of a will —I hope not my last'. During his final eighteen months he also kept up with unabated zest many old interests, especially those concerned with haemoglobin. He never grew old but continued to display in full measure the constant flow of ideas, the simple and direct methods of work, the enthusiasm tempered by patience and imperturbability when things went wrong, the free and unpretentious friendships, the loyalty and sense of fun, in short, all the magnetic attraction and inspiration which had brought him throughout his life hosts of friends, admirers, and pupils from all over the world.

He died suddenly of a heart attack 21 March 1947 whilst hurrying home to lunch from a typically active and happy morning's work in his laboratory. A year later his memory was honoured by a special international conference on haemoglobin in Cambridge. The *Proceedings*, subsequently published in book form, opened with eight vivid biographical sketches by friends who had known him well at different stages of his scientific career, in the course of which, in addition to his major works, he published about 350 papers, many of them in collaboration, and also carried out an immense amount of good committee work for his college, his university, the Government, and many scientific societies. A portrait by R. G. Eves hangs in the Cambridge University Physiological Laboratory which also possesses a coloured cinema film, with sound accompaniment, of Barcroft performing some of his classical experiments on haemoglobin.

In 1952 Mount Barcroft, a peak (13,023 feet) in the White Mountains range in California, was named in his honour. The university of California has established a high-altitude laboratory on this mountain.

In 1903 Barcroft married Mary (Minnie) Agnetta, daughter of the astronomer Sir Robert Ball [q.v.] and sister of Sir W. V. Ball who contributes to this SUPPLEMENT. They had two sons, the elder of whom, Dr. Henry Barcroft, F.R.S., is professor of physiology at St. Thomas's Hospital.

[K. J. Franklin, *Joseph Barcroft 1872–1947*, 1953; F. J. W. Roughton in *Obituary Notices of Fellows of the Royal Society*, No. 18, November 1949; *Haemoglobin* (Barcroft memorial conference), edited by F. J. W. Roughton and J. C. Kendrew, 1949; *Burke's Landed Gentry of Ireland*, 1912; personal knowledge.]          F. J. W. ROUGHTON.

BARING, MAURICE (1874–1945), poet and man of letters, was born in Mayfair, London, 27 April 1874, the fifth son of Edward Charles Baring, who became first Baron Revelstoke, banker, by his wife, Louisa Emily Charlotte, daughter of John Crocker Bulteel, of Flete and Lyneham, Devon, and granddaughter of the second Earl Grey [q.v.]. Evelyn Baring, first Earl of Cromer [q.v.] was his uncle. Baring was educated at Eton and Trinity College, Cambridge, but he left the university without taking a degree. A genius for languages led him (1898) into the diplomatic service, where he served as attaché in Paris, Copenhagen, and Rome and also worked for a year at the Foreign Office in London. He resigned from the service in 1904. During his years spent *en poste* he had formed several of the friendships which were so notably to enrich his life, and many of the tastes, particularly in music and literature, which were afterwards to compose the cultural background of his works. He went abroad again in 1904 as war correspondent for the *Morning Post* in Manchuria, and remained, after the conclusion of the Russo-Japanese war, as special correspondent for the same newspaper in St. Petersburg. During these years he learned Russian and developed an abiding sympathy for the Russian people which no political changes could disturb. In 1909 he went as correspondent to Constantinople and in 1912 he represented *The Times* in the Balkans. All this early period of Baring's life was admirably described in *The Puppet Show of Memory* (1922) which remains a classic of autobiography, personal without ever quite being intimate. The most important event of the period under review—his reception into the Roman Catholic Church—was covered in a single sentence: 'the only action in my life which I am quite certain I have never regretted'.

Baring had already published a number of books when war broke out in 1914. Two plays—*The Black Prince* (1902) and *Gaston de Foix* (1903)—showed his double interest in history and the theatre, and revealed also a talent for the more traditional modes of verse. *Dead Letters* (1910) and *Diminutive Dramas* (1911) revealed a lightly satiric humour playing on historic themes. Baring had also published his war memoirs, *With the Russians in Manchuria* (1905), and an excellent short account of Russian literature, *Landmarks in Russian Literature* (1910). Here he displayed for the first time his remarkable gifts as a translator. During the war of 1914–18 he was attached to the Royal Flying Corps branch of the British Expeditionary Force and for four years from

August 1915 was 'mentor and guide' to Hugh (later Viscount) Trenchard. He became a staff officer of the Royal Air Force in 1918.

Several of Baring's closest friends were killed during the war: Raymond Asquith, Patrick Houston Shaw-Stewart, Auberon Herbert, eighth Baron Lucas [q.v.], and the Grenfell brothers, Julian [q.v.] and Gerald William. The death in action of these men inspired him to some moving verse, which he published in 1919. Meanwhile he was preparing his first novel, *Passing By* (1921). This showed, in miniature, all the characteristics which were to make *C* (1924), *Cat's Cradle* (1925), and *Daphne Adeane* (1926) representative and popular novels of the same decade. An easy and conversational style; a picture of society, neither romantic nor cynical, drawn from the inside; an inflexible scale of moral values allied to intense human sympathies; a rather mischievous sense of humour—all these were at once apparent. In the later and longer novels his immense culture, which he nevertheless carried so lightly, had more chance to display itself. Here Baring combined length with verbal and emotional economy, a lesson he had learned from the Russian masters. Later, in such books as *The Lonely Lady of Dulwich* (1934), he returned to the shorter form of the *nouvelle*; and in *Robert Peckham* (1930) and *In my End is my Beginning* (1931), which is the story of Mary Stuart as it might have been told with slight variations by each of her four ladies-in-waiting, he returned to history for his subject. He also published, in 1933, a short biography of Sarah Bernhardt, whom he had known and ardently admired.

In 1936 Baring was already suffering from paralysis agitans; the last book he was able to write was perhaps his most popular. *Have You Anything to Declare?* (1936), an anthology of favourite quotations in several languages, with translation and comments, showed his character as well as his culture and revealed how intimately the two were allied. In 1940 he left his house and carefully tended garden at Rottingdean, and was looked after thenceforward by friends in Scotland. His house was destroyed by enemy action. Baring died, unmarried, at Beauly, Inverness-shire, 14 December 1945.

In 1918 he was appointed O.B.E.; in 1925 he was given an honorary commission as wing commander in the Reserve of Air Force Officers; and in 1935 he was appointed officer of the Legion of Honour.

He was a fellow of the Royal Society of Literature.

A painting of Baring, G. K. Chesterton, and Hilaire Belloc (1932), by James Gunn, has been lent to the National Portrait Gallery by Mrs. George Balfour and family.

[Maurice Baring, *The Puppet Show of Memory*, 1922, and *R.F.C. H. Q. 1914–1918*, 1920; Dame Ethel Smyth, *Maurice Baring*, 1938; Laura Lovat, *Maurice Baring; a Postscript*, 1947; Leslie Chaundy, *The Writings of Maurice Baring*, 1925; *The Times*, 17 and 18 December 1945; *Times Literary Supplement*, 6 March 1948; personal knowledge.]

ROBERT SPEAIGHT.

BARKER, HARLEY GRANVILLE GRANVILLE- (1877–1946), actor, producer, dramatist, and critic. [See GRANVILLE-BARKER.]

BARKER, SIR HERBERT ATKINSON (1869–1950), manipulative surgeon, was born at Southport 21 April 1869, the only son of Thomas Wildman Barker, a lawyer who became coroner for southwest Lancashire, and his wife, Agnes Atkinson, both of whom died whilst Barker was a schoolboy. After leaving the grammar school at Kirkby Lonsdale, he visited Canada for his health and on his return was apprenticed to his cousin, John Atkinson, the bone-setter of Park Lane, who had been taught by the famous Robert Howard Hutton [q.v.]. Before he was twenty-one Barker set up practice on his own, and was successful in Manchester and Glasgow before he managed, at his second attempt, to establish himself in London.

Barker was a stormy petrel. He soon fell foul of the medical profession which does not look kindly on people who practise the healing art without having received the traditional education of a teaching hospital, an attitude partly excused by the sincere wish to protect the public from quacks professing to cure disease. But—'what is a quack?', *The Times* was asking in 1912, pointing out that Barker did cure patients, many of whom had failed to obtain relief from qualified doctors. The medical profession, however, sets its face against the unqualified person, whether competent or not. Moreover, the ethics of medicine differ from those of commerce, and Barker was a business man who used a business man's methods in his lifelong fight for recognition of the status of bone-setter, or, as he preferred, manipulative surgeon.

This 'hinterland of surgery' as W. T. Stead [q.v.] called it (*Review of Reviews*, October 1910) was soon familiar territory to newspaper readers, for Barker had many journalistic friends, such as R. D. Blumenfeld [q.v.], to press his claims, and many of the patients whom he cured were well known in sporting and public life. The controversy reached its height after 1911 when Dr. F. W. Axham was struck off the register for acting as anaesthetist for Barker. This action ranged the public behind Barker, who gained further sympathy in 1917 when the refusal of his offer to treat soldiers was discussed in Parliament. It was eventually conceded that men might consult an unqualified person on their own responsibility. By this time many eminent people, including leading medical men, were seeking some sort of recognition of Barker's skill. The archbishop of Canterbury in 1920 was asked to exercise his special powers and bestow on Barker the degree of doctor of medicine, although this would not have 'qualified' him since he would still not have been registered by the General Medical Council. Finally, Barker was knighted in 1922. He retired from regular practice soon afterwards and thereafter spent much of his time on the continent and in the Channel Islands.

The animosity of the doctors gradually died down. In 1936 Barker gave a demonstration of his skill before the British Orthopaedic Association at St. Thomas's Hospital which was later reported, with details of the case histories, in the *Lancet*, 27 February 1937. In 1939 a film was made showing the great wizard at work. It lies neglected in a drawer. Nevertheless, Barker did a service to humanity, not only in relieving suffering but also in stimulating doctors to make more use of this form of therapy. In 1941 he was elected as a manipulative surgeon to Noble's Hospital in the Isle of Man.

There had been many bone-setters before Barker, but none attained his eminence. His name became a household word, due in part to the notoriety of his squabble with the doctors whose antagonism, nevertheless, would not have been aroused had he not already acquired a considerable reputation. The secret of Barker's remarkable success was that in spite of being outside the pale he was a true physician. He had the gift of healing. He believed firmly in himself, he exuded confidence, and his personality was striking. He willed his patients back to normal life and he did not leave them alone until they were cured. A long experience taught him which patients were unlikely to benefit at his hands; and his doctor friends (of whom he had many) were inundated with patients, mostly incurable, sent on by Barker.

In 1907 Barker married Jane Ethel, daughter of William Wilson Walker, J.P.; there were no children. He died at Lancaster 21 July 1950. There is a portrait by Augustus John in the Tate Gallery, presented by the Maharaja of Kutch and other grateful patients, and another in the possession of Lady Barker who also has a portrait by Sir John Lavery.

[Sir Herbert Barker, *Leaves from My Life*, 1927.]      GEORGE PERKINS.

BARKLA, CHARLES GLOVER (1877–1944), physicist, was born at Widnes, Lancashire, 7 June 1877, the second son of John Martin Barkla, secretary of the Atlas Chemical Company, who was of Cornish extraction. His mother, Sarah Glover, came from Prescot. Charles was educated at Liverpool Institute, and in 1895 began his undergraduate career at University College, Liverpool. After taking second class honours in mathematics (1898) he specialized in experimental physics under (Sir) Oliver Lodge [q.v.], obtaining first class honours.

In 1899 Barkla went to Cambridge with one of the 1851 Exhibition scholarships as a research student at Trinity College, under (Sir) J. J. Thomson [q.v.]. He was a musician of rare ability, having a magnificent bass voice. In his second year he joined King's College, and became a member of the chapel choir under A. H. Mann [q.v.]. In the Cavendish Laboratory he worked on the velocity of electric waves along wires, using Rutherford's magnetic detector. Later he studied the secondary radiation from gases subject to X-rays, and was awarded the Cambridge B.A. research degree (1903).

In 1902 Barkla accepted the Oliver Lodge fellowship at Liverpool, where Lionel Robert Wilberforce was then professor of physics. With some lecturing, Barkla occupied himself mainly in research, publishing (1903) an account of his X-ray work and obtaining (1904) the D.Sc. degree of the university of Liverpool. It was about this time that the important discovery of the partial polarization of X-radiation was made. Barkla was guided by J. J. Thomson's hypothesis that the rays are electromagnetic pulses. In 1905 he obtained a primary X-radiation which gave rise to a secondary radiation from air and light solids differing in intensity in the two principal directions by about 20 per cent. He adopted Wilberforce's idea 'of producing a plane polarized beam by a secondary radiator, and of testing the polarization by a tertiary radiator'. By using carbon as the radiator and a second mass of carbon in the secondary beam, the relative intensities of the tertiary radiations were observed for different positions of the X-ray bulb. The results indicated almost complete polarization of the secondary beam (1906).

Assisted by Charles A. Sadler who died in early manhood, and Arthur Llewelyn Hughes (afterwards professor in Washington University, St. Louis) Barkla examined the connexion between the atomic weight of the radiator and the absorptiveness of the radiation. A periodic relation connected with the chemical properties of the elements was indicated. About this time the important discovery of 'characteristic' or 'fluorescent' X-rays was made. When primary rays impinge on a substance, the secondary X-radiation consists not only of scattered rays similar in quality to the primary, but also homogeneous rays, the hardness of which is a characteristic property of the atoms of the substance. The penetrating power of the rays was measured by means of their absorption in aluminium plates. The radiation from chemical compounds consisted of the rays of the component elements. Further investigation led Barkla to distinguish (for certain elements) between a harder K-radiation and a softer L-radiation.

The need for a continuous propagation of radiation and the necessity at the same time of a discontinuous character presented a difficult problem. Much discussion took place between Barkla, a strong supporter of the wave theory, and (Sir) W. H. Bragg [q.v.] who at one time held the view that X-rays were corpuscular in nature. Einstein in 1905 suggested the hypothesis of light quanta, or, as we should now say, 'photons'. Physicists now admit that there must be an essential duality in the behaviour of the fundamental physical entities.

Barkla became demonstrator and assistant lecturer in physics in 1905, and in 1907 a lectureship in advanced electricity in the university of Liverpool was created for him. In 1909 he was appointed Wheatstone professor of physics at King's College, London. In 1912 he was elected F.R.S., and commenced experiments with George Herbert Martyn on the diffraction of X-rays by a crystal. Independently H. G. J. Moseley [q.v.] secured photographs showing well-defined lines in the X-ray spectrum of certain elements.

In 1913 Barkla was appointed professor of natural philosophy in the university of Edinburgh, where he became a friend of the musician, (Sir) Donald Tovey [q.v.]. Owing to the war, work on X-rays was continued under great difficulties. Some of the results were described in the Bakerian lecture of 1916, and in 1917 Barkla was awarded the Hughes medal by the Royal Society. The Nobel prize in physics for the same year was awarded to him, and in June 1920 he lectured at Stockholm, suggesting the existence of probable J characteristic radiations. In a private letter of 1926 he wrote: 'Yes! the J-phenomenon is very interesting and is so fundamentally new, but it may take a generation to work it out thoroughly.' The J-phenomenon engaged his attention to the end, but unfortunately he was reluctant to adopt the departure from the classical standpoint demanded by the Compton effect. Dr. Arthur Holly Compton concluded that scattering is a quantum phenomenon.

If the experiments of Professor Robert Taylor Dunbar in Edinburgh, and later in Cardiff, produced results which could be accounted for by Dr. Compton's theory, those of Barkla and Miss Marthe Dallas (1924) on 'corpuscular radiation excited by X-rays' were not directly concerned with J-radiation. But they are of special interest, because these and earlier results foreshadow the discovery of the Auger effect. This may be described as a compound photoelectric effect in which internal conversion takes place in the electronic system of an atom.

Barkla married in 1907 Mary Esther, daughter of John Thomas Cowell, J.P., of the Isle of Man. They had three sons and one daughter, all of whom became graduates of the university of Edinburgh. Barkla was extremely fond of children, and his charming way with them soon won their affection. He was a deeply religious man, and like his ancestors was a faithful adherent of the Methodist Church. The death of his youngest son, Michael, at Carthage in August 1943 as the result of an accident while on service as a surgeon in the Royal Air Force was no doubt largely responsible for the failure of the father's health and his death in Edinburgh 23 October 1944.

[H. S. Allen in *Obituary Notices of Fellows of the Royal Society*, No. 15, May 1947; *Nature*, 23 December 1944; *Proceedings* of the Physical Society, vol. lvii, part 3, May 1945; private information; personal knowledge.]

H. S. ALLEN.

BARLOW, SIR THOMAS, first baronet, of Wimpole Street, London (1845–1945), physician, was born at Edgworth, Lancashire, 4 September 1845, the eldest son of James Barlow, of Greenthorne, Edgworth (who established the cotton mills of Barlow and Jones at Manchester and Bolton), by his wife, Alice, daughter of James Barnes, also of Edgworth. As a young man he worked for a time at his father's business, but his energetic mind turned towards medicine as his career. At that time (Sir) H. E. Roscoe [q.v.] was exerting his great influence over the Owens College, Manchester, and here Barlow studied so successfully that at the age of twenty-two he graduated B.Sc. (London), his honours subjects being geology and palaeontology—an unusual choice for a medical student.

Barlow was brought up as a strict Wesleyan, and University College, London, may have been chosen because this college was recognized as being definitely nonconformist. Here he came into contact with (Sir) R. J. Godlee [q.v.], with whom he made a warm and lifelong friendship. At Barlow's final examination he obtained a second class in surgery and a first class in medicine, but without the coveted gold medal. Both Godlee and Barlow were destined to obtain positions on the staff of University College Hospital, and later both were at the same time presidents respectively of the Royal College of Surgeons and of the Royal College of Physicians.

On becoming qualified, in 1871, Barlow was chosen as house-physician at University College Hospital to Sir William Jenner [q.v.], a man of profound learning and very insistent upon the utmost accuracy in clinical work, and especially in the post-mortem room. Here may be traced the influence of Jenner's teaching in Barlow's life-work in the close similarity of their methods of investigation, concluded by meticulous post-mortem examination.

In 1874 Barlow was appointed medical registrar at the Hospital for Sick Children,

Great Ormond Street, being elected assistant physician the following year. In 1885 he was promoted full physician, retiring in 1899. He was also on the staff of the Charing Cross Hospital (1876–8) and the London Fever Hospital (1884–8) and on that of the London Hospital (1878–80) as assistant physician, finally returning to his old school at University College Hospital in 1880 as assistant physician, being full physician from 1885 to the time of his retirement in 1910, when he became consulting physician. He held the Holme chair of clinical medicine from 1895 to 1907.

Although Barlow was recognized as a brilliant general physician, he is best known for his original researches on scurvy in infants and young children. Until his time scurvy was a common disease amongst sailors and prisoners deprived of fresh food; but scurvy was not recognized in infants and children and was looked upon as a condition of 'acute rickets', and the isolation of scurvy from rickets as a definite and separate disease—although often concomitant in the same child—was a triumph of deductive reasoning. Abroad infantile scurvy still goes by the name of 'Barlow's disease'. All this was long before the discovery of vitamins, and when an infant was unable to be breast-fed the artificial substitutes contained no essential vitamin for the prevention either of scurvy or of rickets, and in consequence infant mortality was very high.

In 1883 Barlow published his first findings in infantile scurvy and their postmortem appearances in three fatal cases in the *Medico-Chirurgical Transactions* (March 1883) in a paper entitled 'Cases described as Acute Rickets ... the Scurvy being an Essential and the Rickets a Variable Element'. This is reprinted in the *Archives of Disease in Childhood* (vol. x, 1935) in a special number in commemoration of Barlow's ninetieth birthday. His Bradshaw lecture in 1894 is entitled 'Infantile Scurvy and its relation to Rickets' and is reported in the *Lancet* of that year (vol. ii). In this lecture he added thirty-three more cases from his own personal experience. In other children's diseases he made important discoveries, notably on the distinction between tuberculous and simple meningitis. An account of the former may be seen in Allbutt's *System of Medicine* (1899, vol. vii) and also in Allbutt and Rolleston's *System of Medicine* (1910, vol. viii). He also published with D. B. Lees 'Simple Meningitis in Children' in Allbutt's *System of Medicine* (1899, vol. vii). In 1878 Barlow in association with S. J. Gee [q.v.] wrote in *St. Bartholomew's Hospital Reports* (vol. xiv, 1878) an article on 'Cervical Opisthotonos of Infants'. With Francis Warner he published, in the *Transactions* of the International Medical Congress (1881), a paper on the subcutaneous tendinous nodules met with in acute rheumatism of childhood. His work on 'Rheumatism and its Allies in Childhood' is printed in the *British Medical Journal* (1883, vol. ii). Barlow's Harveian oration entitled 'Harvey, the Man and the Physician' is reported in the *British Medical Journal* (1916, vol. ii). During the time that he was president of the Royal College of Physicians (1910–15) he was chosen with universal approval to preside over the great International Medical Congress held in London in 1913.

Barlow was physician-extraordinary to Queen Victoria from 1899 to the date of her death in 1901, and continued to hold court appointments under King Edward VII and also under King George V. In 1900 he was created a baronet and he was appointed K.C.V.O. in 1901. He was elected F.R.C.P. (London) in 1880 and F.R.S. in 1909, and he received honorary degrees from eleven universities.

Barlow's Wesleyan upbringing influenced his whole life. Until middle age he was an active Methodist, and at King's Cross chapel was a leader in the weekly Bible class. Later, as the result of his friendship with the Rev. Page Roberts of St. Peter's church, Vere Street, whose teaching he admired, he attended the Church of England services. He never touched alcohol and took a large share in the work of temperance associations. He was president of the Royal Medical Benevolent Fund from 1920 until his death.

In 1880 Barlow married Ada Helen (died 1928), daughter of Patrick Dalmahoy, writer to the signet, of Edinburgh, and sister at the Great Ormond Street Hospital; they had three sons and two daughters, the younger of whom died in infancy. His eldest son, who succeeded his father as second baronet, is Sir (James) Alan (Noel) Barlow (born 1881), joint second secretary to the Treasury, 1938–48; the second is Sir Thomas Dalmahoy Barlow; the third, Patrick Basil, died at Rouen in 1917, while serving in the ranks

of the Grenadier Guards. Barlow himself died in London 12 January 1945 in his hundredth year.

Barlow was of middle height, broad, and strongly built. He had a short and carefully trimmed beard, and always wore spectacles. He possessed the capacity of being able to sleep at any time, night or day—a merciful gift which enabled him to travel all over England without fatigue in his many journeys for consultations, for provincial schools were very few in his active days, and London consultants were in frequent request. Thus he was always able to be fresh and ready after travelling all night to take his work at the hospital or in his consulting room.

Barlow will ever be remembered by all who knew him for his wise and sane humanity. No sentimental views had he, and his patients, poor and rich, were treated exactly the same. The writer, who was his assistant, never saw him angry. Everyone loved him, not only for his consummate knowledge, but for something even higher, for he was an ideal physician. A portrait by (Sir) Oswald Birley hangs in the library of University College Hospital Medical School.

[T. R. Elliott in *Obituary Notices of Fellows of the Royal Society*, No. 14, November 1945; *British Medical Journal*, 20 and 27 January 1945; *Lancet*, 27 January 1945; *University College Hospital Magazine*, March–April 1945; *The Times*, 15 January 1945; private information; personal knowledge.]

E. A. BARTON.

BARRINGTON-WARD, ROBERT McGOWAN (1891–1948), journalist, was born at Worcester 23 February 1891, the fourth son of Mark James Barrington-Ward, inspector of schools, and later rector of Duloe in Cornwall and an honorary canon of Truro, and his wife, Caroline Pearson. He attended Westminster where he was captain of the school and did exceptionally well at classics (he later wrote one epilogue to the Latin play and collaborated on two similar occasions with his younger brother John). While at Balliol College, Oxford, where he was a scholar, he contributed light verse to the university magazines, was for a time editor of the *Blue Book*, and was president of the Union. He was placed in the second class in classical moderations (1911) and the third class in *literae humaniores* (1913), and intending a legal career obtained the Tancred studentship at Lincoln's Inn

(1911). He then decided to combine journalism with legal studies and was introduced to Geoffrey Robinson (later Geoffrey Dawson, q.v.), editor of *The Times*. He was appointed to the staff in 1913 and his ability was such that he was made editorial secretary on 16 February 1914.

On the outbreak of war in August he enlisted and was commissioned in the 6th battalion of the Duke of Cornwall's Light Infantry, of which he became adjutant in 1916. Later he was transferred to the general staff, attached to the 58th division as brigade-major of the 174th Infantry brigade; and in 1918, on the staff of Major-General Sir Ivor Maxse, he wrote *Platoon Training* and other applications of the tactical lessons of recent fighting. His gallantry in action won him three mentions in dispatches, the award of the M.C. (1917) and his appointment to the D.S.O. (1918).

His war experiences permanently impressed him, not only with the sacrifice and heroism of men but with the waste and ineffectiveness of war. Since he had been spared he charged himself with the duty of contending for peace and of furthering a process of social change which, in his opinion, had long been desirable and was made inevitable by the war. Accordingly, on resuming his career, although he was called to the bar in 1919, he decided that, for him, journalism was preferable to law as, in his phrase, 'a way to get things done'. In 1919 he went to the *Observer* as assistant editor. From J. L. Garvin [q.v.], then editor, he supplemented his knowledge of newspaper work and learnt the use of political journalism for the furtherance of his ideas.

During the eight years he spent at Tudor Street he developed the convictions which underlay his later policy. In October 1927 he returned to *The Times* to be an assistant editor and chief leader-writer. The post of foreign editor was abolished in 1928 and thereafter he and the editor were responsible for the treatment of foreign affairs in the paper. Barrington-Ward became deputy editor in 1934 and succeeded Dawson as editor on 1 October 1941.

On Anglo-German relations about which he wrote extensively Barrington-Ward took his own line and longer than many people before he despaired of the possibility of finding a way other than war of dealing with the Nazi régime. His more successful if not more outstanding contri-butions to *The Times* lay, however, in domestic affairs. In 1934 his leading articles and the articles he commissioned on unemployment led to the appointment of a government commission. In 1941 he analysed in a series of leaders the definition of democracy held by the Allies, and appealed for immediate and positive social legislation. He later paid particular attention to planned consumption, unemployment and poverty, educational reform, and social insurance.

Persistent in his industry, relentlessly conscientious, and reserved in public, Barrington-Ward, as a man, was warm-hearted and quick of wit, a faithful and generous friend to an exceptionally wide and diverse range of men and women. In religion he was a loyal Protestant attached to ethics rather than dogma. He was the author of 'The Foreign Office and its Agencies' in the *Oxford Survey of the British Empire* (1914) and in 1924 of a memoir of James Gow, headmaster of Westminster. He sat for many years on the finance committee of the school, becoming chairman in 1946 and, *ex officio*, a governor. He served on the Balliol Holywell Manor appeal committee and the London committee of the Oxford Society, whose journal, *Oxford*, owed much to his experience. In 1947 he was made an honorary fellow of Balliol.

He married in 1926 Margaret Adele, daughter of the late Evasio Hampden Radice, C.I.E. of the Indian Civil Service, and had two sons (the elder of whom is a contributor to this SUPPLEMENT) and one daughter. He died 29 February 1948 while on a sea voyage to South Africa, taken in the hope of restoring his health, and was buried at Dar-es-Salaam.

[*The Times*, 1 March 1948; *The History of 'The Times'*, vol. iv (2 parts), 1952; private information; personal knowledge.]

STANLEY MORISON.

BARTON, SIR SIDNEY (1876–1946), diplomatist, was born at Exeter 26 November 1876, the fourth and youngest son of Captain James Barton, R.A., by his wife, Mary Barbara, daughter of Sir David Barclay, tenth baronet, of Pierston, Ayrshire. During the wave of religious feeling which swept through the country after the Crimean war, Barton's father resigned his commission in the army and became a Plymouth Brother, and from him Barton inherited the religious feeling which dominated his life. He was a foundation scholar of St. Paul's School and in 1895 was appointed a student interpreter in the consular service, going out to Peking immediately upon leaving school. The Boxer rising found him absent on special service, but he contrived, as ever, to reach the centre of things by joining the China Field Force which stormed Tientsin and subsequently took part in the relief of the legations. For his services he was awarded the China medal with clasp and was mentioned in dispatches.

Barton passed with distinction through the various grades in the consular service and in 1910 was called to the bar by the Middle Temple. The following year he was promoted to the responsible post of Chinese secretary in Peking and in 1922 he became consul-general in Shanghai, a post which at that time came next to New York in importance. He was able to render most valuable services to British interests which he defended to the limits of his great vitality and nervous energy. This naturally made him very popular with the British community whilst he was respected but cordially disliked by the Chinese officials with whom he had to deal. Although temperamentally inclined to forceful measures he was by no means a 'gunboat consul'. In a period when central government, indeed any government at all, had broken down, strong measures were frequently necessary for the protection of British interests. Barton was never afraid to advocate such measures or to take them on his own responsibility, but he was careful not to overstep the line between the defensive and the aggressive. His qualities of strength, resourcefulness, and good temper under strain were exactly right in the circumstances of the time and he played a leading part in keeping alive British trade and influence through long years of storms.

In 1929 Barton was promoted to the diplomatic rank of British minister in Addis Ababa. His methods were characteristically blunt and he proved himself, as in China, to be quite fearless and at his best in dangerous situations. He won the confidence of the Emperor to an exceptional degree and was making a great success of his post when the troubles between Italy and Abyssinia came to a head. Barton was deeply upset at the failure of the League of Nations and in particular of his own country to take a strong line. With his usual energy he undertook the

work of organizing security for the British community and he made ready to receive them and other refugees in the British Legation. He remained at his post until after the capture of Addis Ababa by the Italians in May 1936 when he returned to England and retired in the following year. He maintained his keen interest in Abyssinian affairs and was partly instrumental in securing the secret return of the Emperor to his capital.

Barton was appointed C.M.G. in 1913, K.B.E. in 1926, and K.C.V.O. in 1931, and was promoted G.B.E. in 1936. In 1904 he married Mary Ethel Winifred, eldest daughter of Alexander Palmer MacEwen, a director of the Far Eastern firm of Jardine, Matheson & Co. She was appointed O.B.E. in 1928 and advanced to C.B.E. in 1937 for her welfare work in Addis Ababa. She died a few months before Barton's own death in London 20 January 1946. They had two sons and two daughters.

[*The Times*, 22 January 1946; *Burke's Landed Gentry of Ireland*, 1912; personal knowledge.] EDWARD CROWE.

BATES, SIR PERCY ELLY, fourth baronet (1879–1946), merchant and shipowner, was born at Liverpool 12 May 1879, the second son of (Sir) Edward Percy Bates who became second baronet, and his wife, Constance Elisabeth, daughter of Samuel Robert Graves, a former mayor of and member of Parliament for Liverpool.

Educated at Winchester, Bates began his business career as an apprentice with William Johnston & Co., shipowners, of Liverpool, and at the age of twenty-one joined the family business of Edward Bates & Sons, merchants and shipowners, long established in Liverpool and Calcutta, in which he remained a partner until his death. In 1903 he succeeded his brother in the baronetcy and in 1910 began his connexion with the Cunard Steam-Ship Company of which he became deputy chairman in 1922.

In the war of 1914–18 Bates joined the transport department of the Admiralty and, when the Ministry of Shipping was created, continued as director of commercial services, a branch of the Ministry which dealt with the shipment of the country's civilian supplies and largely also with the shipment of supplies to the Allies. Shortage of shipping made it daily imperative to find sources of supply which exerted the least demand upon it. Bates's wide knowledge of the world's trade, of which hardly any aspect save manufacture was unfamiliar to him, often enabled him to suggest such sources and to detect and challenge extravagant demands. He was appointed G.B.E. in 1920, was an officer of the Legion of Honour and held the Order of the Crown of Italy.

By temperament and training Bates disliked government control and its interference in commerce. 'History is against State trading', he would say, and he saw in it an inevitable lack of success because governments insist upon political margins which commerce cannot afford. In later years he tended to over-estimate what might have been achieved without control, although nobody was more decisive than he in exerting executive authority during the war years. In the war of 1939–45 he was a member both of the advisory council and of the liner committee of the Ministry of War Transport. The same problems arose as he had faced in the earlier war, although not always in identical form, and his advice was the more valuable because he was aware of the differences.

Between the wars, in 1924, Bates became a director of the *Morning Post*, often acting as chairman, until the sale of the paper in 1937. His views and influence must be assumed to be reflected in the opinions of that journal. One result of this association was a friendship and correspondence with Rudyard Kipling [q.v.], whom he greatly admired and often quoted.

In 1930 Bates became chairman of the Cunard company and at the end of that year signed the contract for the vessel afterwards known as the *Queen Mary*, as six years later he signed the contract for the *Queen Elizabeth*. He had already explained to the shareholders that for the first time in the history of naval architecture it had become practicable to run a weekly service from Southampton to New York via Cherbourg 'with two steamers which can pay'. Hitherto three had been required. 'The company is projecting a pair of steamers which, though they will be very large and fast, are, in fact, the smallest and slowest which can fulfil properly all the essential economic conditions. To go beyond these conditions would be extravagant; to fall below them would be incompetent.' In spite of all impediments he remained a constant exponent and strong advocate of this policy, but the economic crisis of the following year forced the company to take a painful decision, the responsibility and disappointment of which fell inevitably upon him. At the end of 1931 work on the new ship (then known as Number 534) was suspended. Eventually prolonged negotiations with the Government resulted in the North Atlantic Shipping Act of 1934: the Atlantic assets of the Cunard and the Oceanic companies were incorporated in the new Cunard White Star limited company, of which Bates was chairman, and the Treasury was empowered to advance to the new company sufficient funds to enable them to complete Number 534 and to build a second ship. Work was resumed early in 1934 and the ship was launched by Queen Mary in September. The sister ship, the *Queen Elizabeth*, was launched in September 1938 by Queen Elizabeth and in 1940 on her maiden voyage moved for safety to the other side of the Atlantic. Bates was insistent that she should, like the *Queen Mary*, be used for carrying troops and he liked to think, as was certainly the case, that the service of these two great vessels materially assisted the war effort. The fact that they were built in spite of difficulties so formidable is testimony to Bates's foresight, courage, and energy.

Bates never encumbered his talk with platitudes, or troubled to obscure the directness of his thought. He was terse in speech and trenchant in judgement. These characteristics, with a determined jaw and on occasion an emphatic manner, made him formidable to those who did not know him well. But he was always scrupulous in the use of power, ready for interchange of ideas and considerate and sensitive in personal relationships. He regarded himself as fortunate in having a group of brothers and other colleagues who looked to him for leadership and on whose support he relied. During his career he gave due time to those offices which fall to a leading shipowner; he was a member of the Mersey Docks and Harbour Board (1908–10), chairman of the Liverpool Steamship Owners' Association (1911, 1945), president of the Institute of Marine Engineers (1939) and chairman of the General Council of British Shipping (1945). He was also high sheriff of Cheshire, 1920–21, and a justice of the peace for the county.

He found relaxation in golf and shooting, was enthusiastic about curling, and a keen salmon fisher. From his earliest days he knew the River Erne and in 1939 he fished in Iceland and became interested in the Icelandic sagas, particularly in their descriptions of the topography of the areas where he fished.

In 1907 he married Mary Ann, daughter of William Lefroy [q.v.], dean of Norwich. They had one son, Edward Percy, a pilot officer in the Royal Air Force whose death in action over Germany in 1945, borne by his father with outward stoicism, was a deep wound. Having presided as host on a short preliminary run of the *Queen Elizabeth*, Bates died 16 October 1946 on the very morning when he should have sailed in her on her first voyage as an Atlantic passenger ship. He was succeeded in his title by his nephew, Geoffrey Voltelin Bates (born 1921). There are portraits of Bates by A. T. Nowell at Hinderton Hall, Cheshire, where he lived and died, and by Sir Gerald Kelly at the Midland Bank, 62 Castle Street, Liverpool.

[*The Times*, 25 September 1930; private information; personal knowledge.]

HURCOMB.

BEATRICE MARY VICTORIA FEODORE (1857–1944), princess of Great Britain and Ireland, the fifth daughter and youngest child of Queen Victoria, was born at Buckingham Palace, 14 April 1857. From her earliest days she gave promise of unusual personality and charm, and when two years old was described by a contemporary diarist as 'a delicious child . . . full of wit and fun'. To her, the much-loved 'Baby' of the Prince Consort, the Queen turned for solace at the time of her husband's death, and the young Princess was never long out of her sight. When her elder sisters married she was the daughter who always stayed at home, and she was soon filling, with great discretion and tact, the difficult role of the Queen's constant companion and close confidante. Great pains were taken over her education, and her marked artistic talents were fostered in every possible way. She was a first-rate pianist and a talented musician, several of whose compositions were published. In her younger days she knew most of the great musicians, and was a friend of many of them. For some years she had no thought of marriage, but at the age of twenty-eight she fell in love with Prince Henry Maurice of Battenberg [q.v.] and the Queen consented to their union on the strict understanding that, so long as she lived, they should remain under her roof and make their home with her. The marriage took place in Whippingham church, near Osborne, 23 July 1885. Four children were born of the marriage. The

only daughter, Princess Victoria Eugénie Julia Ena, married King Alfonso XIII of Spain. The three sons were Prince Alexander Albert (subsequently the Marquess of Carisbrooke), Prince Leopold Arthur Louis (later Lord Leopold Mountbatten) who died in 1922, and Prince Maurice Victor Donald, who as a lieutenant in the 60th Rifles was killed in the first battle of Ypres in 1914. Prince Henry of Battenberg volunteered for active service in 1895 and died on the way home from the Ashanti expedition 20 January 1896. After his marriage the Queen had appointed him governor of the Isle of Wight, an ancient office analogous to that of lord lieutenant. Princess Henry was now given this appointment, and continued her close attendance on the Queen, so that it was not until the Queen's death in 1901 that she and her children were to know a home of their own at Osborne Cottage. Later, in 1914, the Princess made the governor's house at Carisbrooke Castle her summer residence, the winters being spent abroad or at Kensington Palace.

Queen Victoria bequeathed to the Princess all her private journals, consisting of many manuscript volumes dating back to before 1837, with the injunction that she was to modify or destroy any portions which appeared to her unsuitable for permanent preservation. This work she carried out with devoted care, every page being transcribed in her own hand, and the original manuscript thereupon destroyed. The task was so vast that it was not completed until 1942, and the transcribed journal is now preserved among the royal archives at Windsor. From an historical point of view it is perhaps to be regretted that Queen Victoria's private opinion of various contemporary personages and events may thus have been lost to posterity, but the Princess acted in accordance with her instructions, and nothing was allowed to remain which, in her opinion, might hurt the feelings of the persons concerned, or even of their relations. Her other literary work included the translation of extracts from the diary of Queen Victoria's maternal grandmother Augusta, Duchess of Saxe-Coburg-Saalfeld, which were published in 1941 under the title of *In Napoleonic Days*.

In 1917 the family name of Battenberg was changed at the request of King George V to Mountbatten, and the Princess resumed her former title of Princess Beatrice. During her long tenure of the governorship of the Isle of Wight, despite an inherited shyness which she was never able to eradicate, the Princess was zealous in the performance of her public duties, and particularly in the support of every movement for the relief of sickness and distress. Her understanding sympathy undoubtedly derived from her own long experience of sorrow. Her whole youth had been darkened by the pall of perpetual mourning which shrouded her life for so many years after her father's death; she herself had been widowed at the age of thirty-eight and had subsequently mourned the loss of two sons. She was ever guided by a deep sense of duty and an unfailing kindness of heart, while those admitted to her friendship could never forget her great loyalty, her sense of humour, and her devoutly religious convictions. She died at Brantridge Park, Balcombe, Sussex, 26 October 1944, and after the war was buried beside her husband in the chapel which she had prepared at Whippingham.

The best portrait of Princess Beatrice was painted by P. A. de László in 1912. There are two others by H. von Angeli (at the ages of eighteen and thirty-five), one by J. Sorolla (1904), and a small head by F. X. Winterhalter. All are in the possession of the Marquess of Carisbrooke.

[Private information; personal knowledge.]
C. F. ASPINALL-OGLANDER.

BEATTY, SIR EDWARD WENT-WORTH (1877–1943), Canadian man of business, was born at Thorold, Ontario, 16 October 1877, the son of Henry Beatty, shipowner, by his wife, Harriett M. Powell. He was educated at Upper Canada College and at the university of Toronto. He was called to the bar of Ontario in 1901, and his ability, after he joined the legal department of the Canadian Pacific Railway, brought him steady promotion: he became general counsel for the railway in 1913 and one of its vice-presidents in 1914. Four years later its directors chose Beatty for its presidency in preference to other high officials with long experience in the practical operation of railways. His lack of such experience was undoubtedly a handicap to him in guiding the fortunes of the railway through a very difficult period, when the consequences of economic depressions which reduced its revenues were aggravated by the keen competition of the newly created Canadian national system which had the resources of the State behind it. Beatty always resented this competition as unfair and laboured to end it through a merger of the two systems,

free from direct State control, and it was a bitter blow to him when a Royal Commission pronounced against him in 1932. But, aided by a revival of Canadian prosperity, his efforts to extricate his railway from its difficulties were meeting with some success when a progressive decline in his health caused his retirement from the presidency in 1942.

While the merits of Beatty as a railway executive are a subject of controversy, no business magnate of his time had an equal fund of public spirit or gave more generously of his time, abilities, and money to good causes. He served as chancellor of Queen's University (1919–23) and of McGill University (1921–43), as chairman of the Rhodes scholarship committee for the province of Quebec, as trustee and president of the Royal Victoria Hospital in Montreal, and as president of the Boy Scout Association of Canada; for many years he was the president and chief financial mainstay of the Boys' Farm and Training School at Shawbridge, Quebec. Since he was also a director of the Bank of Montreal and other large corporations there was no busier man in Canada, but he had a wide range of interests. His personal charm and friendly ways made him very popular with the staff of his great railway and won him many friends in all walks of life. In 1935 he was appointed G.B.E. and made an honorary bencher of the Middle Temple. He became a Dominion K.C. in 1915 and received honorary degrees from twelve universities. He died, unmarried, in Montreal 23 March 1943.

[Gazette, Montreal, and Montreal Star, 24 March 1943; private information; personal knowledge.]
J. A. STEVENSON.

BELL, SIR CHARLES ALFRED (1870–1945), Indian administrator, was born at Calcutta 31 October 1870, the third son of Henry Bell, of the Indian Civil Service and later barrister-at-law practising in the High Court, Calcutta, by his wife, Anne, daughter of George Dumbell, of Douglas, Isle of Man. From Winchester, where he held a scholarship, Bell passed into the Indian Civil Service in 1889, proceeded to New College, Oxford, and was appointed to the province of Bengal in 1891. Nine years' varied work in the plains gave experience which was to prove of great value but taxed a constitution which was never strong, and in 1900 he was posted to the better climate of the Darjeeling district. Here he had frequent contact with Tibetans and with Indian subjects of Tibetan stock. He at once applied himself to learning Tibetan and in 1905 he published a *Manual of Colloquial Tibetan*, of which the first part was a grammar and phrase book and the second an English–Tibetan dictionary. An enlarged version of this work, published in two separate volumes, has continued to hold the field as the best practical guide to the spoken language. In connexion with the mission of (Sir) Francis Younghusband [q.v.] to Lhasa in 1903–4, Bell was in charge of a party which investigated the possibility of making a road from the plains of Bengal through Bhutan to the Chumbi valley, a project abandoned on the score of expense, and a little later he was put in charge of the administration of the Chumbi valley, which had been temporarily ceded by Tibet to Britain under the terms of the treaty of 1904. After twice acting as political officer in Sikkim during the absence of John Claude White, who held the post for nearly twenty years, Bell succeeded him in 1908, and remained in Sikkim, in charge of the relations of the Government of India with Sikkim, Bhutan, and Tibet, until 1918. He then decided to retire from government service but spent most of 1919 and 1920 on leave in Darjeeling, collecting material for his books which were to follow. He was thus on the spot when his services as political officer in Sikkim were again needed in 1920.

The main features of Bell's work in the Sikkim State were the evolution, on simple practical lines, of a system of administration which gradually brought an isolated and backward area into relationship with contemporary progress in India; the restoration of full powers to the ruler of the state; the development of local resources; and the protection of a region of precipitous hills and torrential rainfall from erosion. With Bhutan in 1910 he negotiated a treaty whereby the ruler, while retaining full autonomy in internal affairs, placed the foreign relations of his country in the hands of His Majesty's Government.

The high-lights in Bell's life were the intimate friendship and understanding which he formed with the thirteenth Dalai Lama of Tibet at the time when the latter, in order to escape from Chinese pressure in Lhasa, fled to India in 1910; and the part which Bell played as adviser on Tibetan affairs to the British plenipotentiary, Sir Henry McMahon [q.v.], during the tripartite negotiations which, subsequent to the Chinese revolution of 1911, took place in Simla in 1913–14. A convention was initialed whereby China would assure to Tibet a definite frontier running southwards from the upper waters of the Dichu (Yangtze) and practical autonomy west of that frontier, and Tibet in return would admit Chinese suzerainty; but at the last moment China declined to proceed to full signature of the convention. The Tibetan and British representatives then signed, as bilateral instruments, the convention, a map defining the Tibet–India frontier, and new Anglo-Tibetan trade regulations. It was in large measure the confidence which the Dalai Lama and his plenipotentiary, prime minister Lonchen Shatra, had in Bell which brought about agreement at that time and the good relations which subsequently existed between Tibet on the one hand and the British Government and the Government of India on the other. It was on foundations laid by Bell that after 1936 first British and later Indian representation was established in Lhasa.

The cordiality of these relations was confirmed by Bell's visit to Lhasa in 1920 at the repeated invitation of the Dalai Lama whose last words to Bell when he left in 1921 were: 'We two are men of like mind.' A man of deep religious feeling Bell was the better able to understand the religious outlook of others. With a strong will and steadfastness he combined unfailing courtesy and the grace of humility.

Bell retired from government service in 1921 and devoted the rest of his life to writing books in which he sought to make Tibet intelligible to the world and to vindicate the right of Tibet to independence. These indispensable sources of information include *Tibet Past and Present* (1924), *The People of Tibet* (1928), and *The Religion of Tibet* (1931). His culminating work, *Portrait of the Dalai Lama* (1946), was completed only a few days before his death. It was with this book in view that Bell revisited Tibet and travelled in Mongolia, Siberia, Manchuria, and China (1933–5), and it was in order that he might complete his task that, with war in Europe imminent, he uprooted himself in 1939 from his home in Berkshire, where he lived surrounded by treasures from Tibet, Sikkim, and Bhutan, and went to British Columbia. He died there, at Oak Bay, Victoria, 8 March 1945.

In 1912 Bell married Cashie Kerr (died 1935), daughter of the late David Fernie, shipowner, of Liverpool; they had one son and two daughters. Bell was appointed

C.M.G. in 1915, C.I.E. in 1919, and K.C.I.E. in 1922. He received the Lawrence memorial medal of the Royal Central Asian Society in 1937.

[Personal knowledge.]     B. J. Gould.

BENNETT, RICHARD BEDFORD, Viscount Bennett (1870–1947), Canadian prime minister, was born at Hopewell, New Brunswick, 3 July 1870, the eldest of the three sons of Henry J. Bennett, shipbuilder, and his wife, a former schoolmistress, Henrietta, daughter of Captain Daniel Stiles, of Hopewell. Educated at public and high schools in New Brunswick, Bennett qualified as a teacher; but he was possessed of an ambition to attain riches and the highest possible office in the service of his country. As soon as he had sufficient funds he took his law degree at Dalhousie University (1893) and was called to the bar of New Brunswick. He began practice in Chatham but in 1897 moved west to a partnership in a law firm in Calgary where he was rapidly recognized as a very capable advocate. He took silk (1905) and became western counsel for the Canadian Pacific Railway.

His political career began in 1898 when he was elected a Conservative member of the legislature of the North-West Territories, in which he sat until Alberta was created a separate province in 1905. He failed to secure election to the new provincial legislature until 1909, but in the two years which followed he conducted the opposition to the policies of a very powerful Liberal ministry almost singlehanded, with a skill and vigour which established his reputation as a formidable politician. He had already run for the Canadian House of Commons in 1900 but it was not until 1911 that he was elected, as Conservative member for Calgary. His large law practice and successful investments had by this time brought him financial independence.

At Ottawa Bennett did not take kindly to the role of a back-bencher, and he was frequently at loggerheads with his leaders, notably on railway matters. In 1915 he accompanied the prime minister, Sir Robert Borden [q.v.], on a visit to England and France and in October 1916 became director-general of national service, conducting a vigorous campaign in an effort to avoid conscription. He was not included in, and did not greatly favour, the Unionist Conscriptionist Government formed in the following year and he did not stand at the ensuing general election.

For a time he thought of entering British politics but instead he returned to Calgary and his law practice. He was defeated in 1921 and it was not until the election of 1925 that he was back in the House to become a formidable member of the Conservative Opposition in the stormy session which followed.

When Mr. Arthur Meighen resigned the leadership of the party in 1927 Bennett had no serious competitor at the national convention which met to choose a successor. His only experience in office so far had been in Mr. Meighen's pre-election Cabinets of 1921 and 1926 in which he had held respectively the portfolios of justice and finance. He now proceeded to lead the Opposition with great ability and to build up an efficient party organization before the election of 1930 in which he won an easy victory over W. L. Mackenzie King [q.v.]. The shadow of the depression was lengthening and apprehensive voters were reassured by the confident promises of this notoriously successful business man to end unemployment and blast Canada's way into the markets of the world.

Once in office, retaining until early in 1932 the portfolio of finance, Bennett's remedies turned out to be the narrowly orthodox ones of retrenchment and high tariffs, with public works and camps for the unemployed. He went to the Imperial Conference of 1930 with views on imperial preference, always strongly held, which were not acceptable to the British Labour Government. His proposals revealed a desire to receive rather than to concede which brought down upon them the terse description 'humbug' from the Dominions secretary, J. H. Thomas [q.v.]. Undeterred, Bennett pressed for an imperial economic conference which was held in Ottawa in 1932 in an atmosphere of crisis and resulted in agreements more beneficial to imperial than to world trade. Canada's economic plight was dependent upon world conditions, and her survival and gradual recovery were governed more by these than by Bennett's policy of Canada for the Canadians. Despite his preoccupation with, and faith in, the Empire, Bennett was not unmindful of the importance to Canada of the American market, and in 1933 he discussed with President Roosevelt a trade agreement for which the Liberal Party was to receive the credit since it was not concluded until Mackenzie King was back in office. Meanwhile Bennett dealt with the depression as best he could with decisions which were always bold and vigorous. Much useful work was done and these years saw the establishment of a central bank and a national broadcasting system, as well as a thorough investigation of the railway systems, and a comprehensive reform of the federal budgetary system which strengthened the control of the Treasury over expenditure.

Early in 1935 Bennett startled the country by announcing a New Deal of far-reaching reforms which some thought was inspired by his close contact with American trends through his brother-in-law, W. D. Herridge, Canadian minister in Washington. Others more cynically pointed to the forthcoming election which Bennett already had little chance of winning since he could not be considered to have redeemed his over-confident promises and had, however unfairly, to shoulder the blame for the hardships of the depression. The party had been weakened by the defection of Mr. H. H. Stevens after his damaging revelations of undesirable methods in big business, and the announcement of the New Deal weakened it still further. Bennett went on to represent himself as 'the indispensable man' at a time when the danger of authoritarianism was plain for all to see. It was not perhaps surprising that the country proved unwilling to entrust a programme of reform to a Conservative so traditional as to have restored the granting of titles discontinued since 1919. After leading the Opposition for three years Bennett realized that he had alienated many of the wealthier Conservatives by his last-minute reforms. Most of his social measures had been pronounced unconstitutional by the courts, but they were subsequently adopted in amended form by the Liberal Party, reaping once more where Bennett had sown. He, meanwhile, had retired to England where he purchased a property in Surrey from his old friend Lord Beaverbrook and continued his lifelong advocacy of empire co-ordination.

Despite his high ability, great energy, and very evident honesty, Bennett was never a popular figure. He ruled his Cabinet with a domineering hand, yet he was always a great stickler for the rights of Parliament and the constitutional proprieties. He had a serene confidence, sometimes misplaced, in his own ability to mould public opinion and he employed a vein of sonorous eloquence for the exposition of his policies and ideals. His autocratic temper was not always under perfect control and he was prone to rash impulses, which had sometimes disastrous consequences. In private life, however, he was a man of considerable charm, tall, portly, and elegant, an agreeable companion and an excellent host. He was by upbringing a Methodist, and he never broke an early promise to his mother to observe Sunday as a day of rest and neither to drink nor to smoke.

Bennett inherited from a friend, whose sudden death prevented her marriage to him, a very large fortune, which enabled him to give rein to his philanthropic instincts. At one time he was supporting eleven boys at school or college, and before he died he had distributed a substantial part of his fortune to universities and other institutions, in this country and in Canada.

When he visited Britain in 1930 Bennett received the freedom of London, Edinburgh, and Sheffield and was sworn of the Privy Council. Many other honours came to him, including honorary degrees from sixteen universities. In 1941 he was created a viscount, a title which became extinct when he died, unmarried, at his home at Mickleham 27 June 1947. He was buried close to the grave of Sir James Jeans [q.v.] in the churchyard of the parish church which he had regularly attended.

There is a portrait of Bennett by Lawren Harris, junior, in the university of New Brunswick.

[Private information; personal knowledge.]

J. A. STEVENSON.

**BENSON, GODFREY RATHBONE,** first BARON CHARNWOOD (1864–1945), Liberal politician and man of letters, was born at Alresford, Hampshire, 6 November 1864, the fourth son of William Benson, barrister, by his wife, Elizabeth Soulsby, daughter of Thomas Smith, of Colebrooke Park, Tonbridge. The third son was the actor-manager Sir Frank Benson [q.v.].

Benson was educated at Winchester and Balliol College, Oxford. He obtained a first class in *literae humaniores* (1887) and was appointed lecturer in philosophy at Balliol. He worked in close association with R. L. Nettleship [q.v.], the second volume of whose *Philosophical Lectures and Remains* (containing the well-known lectures on the *Republic* of Plato) he edited in 1897. He also wrote a memoir for the *Essays and Addresses* (1929) of his friend John Burnet [q.v.].

Benson was called to the bar by the Inner Temple in 1898. His active political interests brought him into the House of Commons as Liberal member for the Woodstock division of Oxfordshire (1892–5). He fought several contests for his party, but his public gifts were best suited to the House of Lords to which he was elevated in 1911 as Baron Charnwood, of Castle Donington, Leicestershire. He was initially an ardent supporter of Home Rule and later of imperial federation and national service. He did much social, charitable, and municipal work, serving as chairman of the council of the Charity Organization Society, president of the National Institute for the Deaf, chairman of quarter-sessions, a deputy-lieutenant for Staffordshire, and mayor of Lichfield.

Benson's deepest interests were religious and intellectual, and, partly through his friendship with Randall Davidson and H. M. Burge [qq.v.], he was closely associated with various causes connected with the Church of England. In 1930 he edited a volume of Burge's *Discourses and Letters*. His own personal views on religion were set out in a very candid study of St. John's Gospel, *According to St. John* (1926), and, in revised form, in *A Personal Conviction* (1928). His very widely known biography of Abraham Lincoln (1916) brought him the highest tributes, both in the United States and in this country, and stands as a classic of its kind. He also published *Theodore Roosevelt* (1923).

In 1897 Benson married Dorothea Mary Roby (died 1942), daughter of Roby Thorpe, of Nottingham, and granddaughter of A. J. Mundella [q.v.]; the marriage brought him, through her great gifts and energy, unfailing stimulus and happiness, as well as unexpected fortune and much enlarged political connexions; they had two sons, the younger of whom died in childhood, and two daughters.

Despite the heavy claims of London, Benson gave himself unstintedly to Lichfield, where he played a major part in the inauguration and activities of the Johnson Society. He was a man of broad views, and broad churchmanship, moderate in his outlook yet categorical in statement. Superficially reticent, even austere and abrupt, he was singularly kind, outspokenly honest, and enduring in friendships. He died in London 3 February 1945 and was succeeded by his son, John Roby (1901–55), who, as an ophthalmic surgeon, did valuable research in space perception. Benson's elder daughter, Antonia, married as her second husband (Sir) Cyril John (subsequently Lord) Radcliffe, and the other, (Eleanor) Theodora (Roby) Benson, became a novelist and writer of books on travel. Portraits by Hugh Eastman and Sir Frank Dicksee are in the possession of the family.

[*The Times*, 5 February 1945; private information; personal knowledge.]

HUMPHREY SUMNER.

BERKELEY, RANDAL MOWBRAY THOMAS (RAWDON) eighth EARL OF BERKELEY (1865–1942), scientist, was born at Ixelles, Brussels, 30 January 1865, the only son of George Lennox Rawdon Berkeley, by his wife, Cécile, daughter of Edward Drummond (Viscomte de Melfort, in France) and divorced wife of Sir F. B. R. Pellew [q.v.]. He assumed the courtesy title of Viscount Dursley from 1882 (when his father took the title of seventh Earl of Berkeley) until his father's death in 1888; in 1891 his right to the peerage was established.

Berkeley was educated in France until he came to England to be coached for the Royal Navy, joining the *Britannia* in 1878. As a young officer he showed great promise and was outstanding among his contemporaries, but his high spirits made naval discipline irksome and he was often in trouble. However, it was his interest in science and mathematics and his determination to do research which decided him to resign his commission in 1887. He then worked for a short time at chemistry at South Kensington, but after a serious illness he bought a house at Foxcombe just outside Oxford and began research in the Christ Church and Balliol laboratories on crystal structure and the electrolysis of glass. In 1898 he built a laboratory at Foxcombe and began to plan the researches on osmotic pressure for which his name will always be remembered. His ultimate objective was the application of van der Waal's equation of state of gases to substances in solution and for this a knowledge of osmotic pressure was necessary. It was a difficult field, as semi-permeable membranes had to be made capable of standing pressures up to 150 atmospheres, but Berkeley had an instinct for engineering design, and a genius for devising and perfecting new experimental methods. In 1902 he was joined by Ernald Hartley who was associated with him in most of his osmotic pressure work.

Few osmotic pressures can be measured directly, so Berkeley's first objective was to check the accuracy of the values found by the indirect method based on vapour pressure measurements by measuring directly the osmotic pressures of the same solutions. In spite of improvements in the vapour pressure technique the results of the two methods still showed considerable differences. Berkeley then examined the equation due to Arrhenius on which this indirect method was based, and he introduced into it an important correction. This started his interest in thermodynamics, in which he became a great adept particularly in cyclic processes applied to solutions. Meanwhile, following his lead, Alfred William Porter had derived a more exact form of the Arrhenius equation and in 1907 Berkeley invited Charles Vandeleur Burton, a physicist from the Cambridge Scientific Instrument Company, to join him in work on the compressibilities which were now involved and on other osmotic problems.

With the advent of Burton the theoretical field was extended and a joint paper 'Contribution to the Osmotic Theory of Solutions' (*Philosophical Magazine*, April 1909) broke fresh ground, to be followed by Berkeley's most daring venture, a paper on 'Solubility and Supersolubility from the Osmotic Standpoint' (ibid., August 1912). As the scope of attack widened, the Foxcombe team was enlarged to meet the growing programme of experimental research, which included diffusion and the stratification of centrifuged solutions. From 1910 to 1914 Berkeley had a well-balanced group of young physical chemists working under his stimulating leadership. Those were the great days of the Foxcombe laboratory. Much of the work was left unfinished when the team dispersed to war work and Berkeley was left to gather up the threads of the osmotic pressure work which he had pursued with such tenacity and refinement of method. The table summarizing his final results showed a very close agreement between the values of the osmotic pressures determined by the direct and indirect methods. It established, finally, the validity of the vapour pressure method and was a fine ending to his research in this most exacting field. Berkeley, however, was never satisfied and was always striving more and more for perfection. Work continued at Foxcombe until 1928 on further refinements and on its extension to non-aqueous solvents.

On the death of his kinsman, Lord Fitzhardinge, in 1916, Berkeley succeeded to the Berkeley estates. The castle was in a sad state of disrepair, and he threw himself, as his own architect and clerk of works, into its restoration with the same enthusiasm and energy which had marked his scientific work. One of his ancestral responsibilities was the mastership of the Berkeley hounds, and he took to hunting when over fifty years of age with his usual pluck and dash and was generally up to hounds. But he never lost his interest in osmotic pressure and osmotic phenomena. Long after the Foxcombe laboratory was closed he was constantly seeking new equations with physical significance to express his experimental results.

Berkeley married in 1887 Kate, daughter of William Brand, a landed proprietor, and widow of Arthur Jackson, a composer and teacher of harmony and composition at the Royal Academy of Music. She died in 1898 and in 1924 he married Mary Emlen Lloyd, daughter of John Lowell, of Boston, Massachusetts. He died at Berkeley Castle, 15 January 1942. There were no children by either marriage and the earldom of Berkeley ended with him. A fine portrait by Sir William Orpen is at Berkeley Castle commemorating Berkeley's rare combination of F.R.S. (1908) and M.F.H.

[Sir Harold Hartley in *Obituary Notices of Fellows of the Royal Society*, No. 11, November 1942; personal knowledge.]

HAROLD HARTLEY.

BERNERS, fourteenth BARON (1883–1950), musician, artist, and author. [See TYRWHITT-WILSON, SIR GERALD HUGH.]

BETTERTON, HENRY BUCKNALL, BARON RUSHCLIFFE (1872–1949), politician, was born at Woodville, Blackfordby, Leicestershire, 15 August 1872, the son of Henry Inman Betterton, J.P., brewer, by his wife, Agnes, daughter of Samuel Bucknall. Educated at Rugby and Christ Church, Oxford, he obtained a fourth class in modern history in 1893. He was called to the bar by the Inner Temple at the age of twenty-four and practised, not unsuccessfully, as a lawyer for twenty years. He was appointed O.B.E. in 1918 and C.B.E. in 1920 for services during the war and entered politics as Conservative member for the Rushcliffe division of Nottinghamshire in December 1918. He was parliamentary secretary to the Ministry of Labour during the Conservative administrations of 1923 and 1924–9 and was created a baronet in 1929.

Although fundamentally a Conservative

in politics, he made his mark when he became minister of labour under Ramsay MacDonald's leadership in the 'national' Government of 1931, and was sworn of the Privy Council. He was not a particularly ambitious man and probably never expected or sought to become a minister of the Crown, least of all the minister in charge of labour questions. He was, however, guided by a strong sense of duty, and he found himself sympathetic towards the new trends of social thought which were developing within the Conservative Party. His pleasant and tactful manner made him many friends in all parties and no one was more skilful in handling the difficult problems with which he was confronted.

His major political task was undoubtedly that of piloting the Unemployment Act of 1934 through the House of Commons. This was a highly controversial measure designed to strengthen and expand unemployment insurance financed by contributions of workers and employers and to establish a new basic system of State relief for those normally in the employment field who were in need. The Unemployment Assistance Board was set up as a central organization with local offices. It was this Board which first discovered an acceptable and uniform way of administering cash assistance without invidious conditions, but also without abandoning the principle of a test of needs and means. Betterton, with his wide human sympathy and tactful personality, was largely responsible for this important step forward in Britain's social policy, and it was natural that he should be selected as the first chairman of the Board which he had created. In 1934 he retired from Parliament to join the Board where he remained until 1941. In 1935 he was created Baron Rushcliffe, of Blackfordby, in the county of Leicester, and in 1941 he was promoted G.B.E.

Rushcliffe served on many committees and was chairman of the one which in 1943 determined an improved wage-scale for British nurses which became known as the Rushcliffe scale. He was also active as chairman of the special committee on legal aid and legal advice.

He was twice married: first, in 1912 to Violet (died 1947), widow of Captain Hervey Greathed of the 8th Hussars, and daughter of John Saunders Gilliat, formerly governor of the Bank of England. In 1948 he married Inez Alfreda, Lady Snagge (died 1955), whose first marriage

had been dissolved, and who was the daughter of the late Alfred Lubbock, of Par, Cornwall. There were two daughters by the first wife, but there was no son to inherit the titles which therefore became extinct.

[Private information.]

R. C. DAVISON.

BEVAN, EDWYN ROBERT (1870–1943), scholar, historian, philosopher, and publicist, came of a remarkable family. He was the seventh son of the banker, Robert Cooper Lee Bevan, of Fosbury House, Wiltshire, and Trent Park, and the third by his second wife, Emma Frances, daughter of P. N. Shuttleworth [q.v.], bishop of Chichester. A. A. Bevan [q.v.] was his brother and his father's sister was Mrs. Favell Lee Mortimer [q.v.], the authoress. Bevan was born in London 15 February 1870. While being educated at Monkton Combe School, he insisted on having tuition in Greek, and won an open scholarship at New College, Oxford, of which he was later elected an honorary fellow. After obtaining first classes in classical moderations (1890) and *literae humaniores* (1892) he travelled in India, a visit which led to a permanent interest in Indian problems and personal friendship with many Indians. He next spent a year, partly at the British School of Archaeology in Athens, partly at excavations in Egypt. By inheritance he was a man of ample means, but in 1921 a widespread failure on the Stock Exchange suddenly engulfed all his investments and made him hastily look for paid work. He took the blow with his usual serenity; even his children did not know that anything particular had happened. King's College, London, offered him a post as lecturer in Hellenistic history and literature which he held from 1922 to 1933, when increasing deafness made teaching difficult and a legacy enabled him to retire. After this he devoted himself chiefly to problems of religion and philosophy. His Gifford lectures (Edinburgh), delivered in 1933 and 1934, on *Symbolism and Belief* (published in 1938) are particularly notable.

Brought up in evangelical traditions and a convinced Christian, whose religion inspired all his activities, and who as an undergraduate used to hold meetings for prayer in his college rooms, Bevan, without abandoning the regular practice of a devotional life as unconcealed as it was unobtrusive, early emancipated himself from a belief in the inerrancy of scripture which might have restricted the freedom of his historical investigations. Nothing about any subject interested him so nearly as its bearing upon the Christian religion. Of that religion he found the classical statement in Philippians ii. 5–11. Those nearest to him speak of the serenity of his faith, which was not disturbed by his full appreciation of the difficulties which make many find it impossible to reconcile such a faith with the outlook of a modern educated man. Without denying the possibility of miracles he did not consider Christianity committed to any which differed in principle from the 'familiar miracle' involved in every determination of motion by desire or will. Even in respect of Christ's resurrection our faith was not 'vain', so long as we were convinced that His disciples experienced a personal intercourse with their risen Master.

Like many religiously minded scholars of his generation, Bevan owed much to Baron Friedrich von Hügel [q.v.]. He was a member of the London Society for the Study of Religion, of which that remarkable man was the founder and oracle; and, with him, enjoyed and valued the friendship of the Jewish scholar and theologian, C. J. Goldsmid-Montefiore [q.v.]. Like the latter, he was an active member of the Society of Jews and Christians founded for the frank discussion of their mutual agreements and disagreements. Nor would an account of his life be complete without reference to his interest in the Student Christian Movement and his intimacy with one of its prominent figures, John Leslie Johnston, a young fellow of Magdalen College, Oxford, who fell in the war of 1914–18, a memoir of whom Bevan published in 1921 and to whose memory as his 'friend, ever-living with God' he dedicated his *Christians in a World at War* (1940). It is in this latter book, in the concluding essays of *Hellenism and Christianity* (1921), and in his presidential address of 1927 to the Oxford Society of Historical Theology on 'Some Aspects of the Present Situation in Regard to the Gospel Record' that Bevan's religious position can best be studied. To these should be added the admirable little book, addressed to a wider public, *Christianity*, published in 1932 in the Home University Library.

It was through this deep devotion to the Christian religion that Bevan was drawn to the study of the Hellenistic age. In 1902, after seven years of concentrated study, he published *The House of Seleucus*

(2 vols.), a pioneer work in Hellenistic history. The period fascinated him as the marriage-place of Greek and Hebrew thought and the background of primitive Christianity. This book established him as one of the chief authorities on the Hellenistic age, and was followed in 1904 by *Jerusalem under the High Priests*, the chapter on 'The Jews' in the *Cambridge Ancient History*, vol. ix, and those in the eleventh edition of the *Encyclopaedia Britannica* on Alexander, Lysimachus, Perdiccas, and the Ptolemies. Turning more to the Greek side of the same age, he wrote on 'Deification' in Hastings's *Encyclopaedia of Religion and Ethics*, on 'Mystery Religions' in *The History of Christianity in the Light of Modern Knowledge* (1929), and in 1913 a book on *Stoics and Sceptics*. In the same year he published a small but enlightening volume on *Indian Nationalism*. The war of 1914–18 took him, after a short time in the Artists' Rifles, to the departments of propaganda and information and finally to the political intelligence department of the Foreign Office. For his services he was appointed O.B.E. in 1920. All his war writings show the same fairness of mind and patient understanding; noteworthy are *The Land of the Two Rivers* (1917) on Mesopotamia, and *The Method in the Madness* (1917) on the psychological aberration which then, as twenty years later, seemed to be at work in the German mind. He never forgot the nobler and more liberal elements in Germany, however, and translated Rudolf Olden's book *Is Germany a Hopeless Case?* (1940).

A true historian and a true artist, Bevan was exact and scholarly in his treatment of evidence; he used the resources of a fine imagination to understand past ages and to see contemporary events as processes rooted in the past. He considered the process of history not as a series of different civilizations but as 'a single *élan spirituel* in two efforts'. Behind our modern world is the Hellenic civilization, which he saw as 'the unique beginning of something new in the history of mankind'. It failed and was swamped by primitive barbarians, to recover and get a fresh embodiment in our modern 'western world'. True civilization is now making 'its second try'. There was something Hellenic also in his constant desire for knowledge, shown in his studies of French and German literature, of Dante, and of the Hebrew language. There was something Hellenic too in the beauty of form and finish which marked all his writings, and the sympathetic understanding which made his conversation, even with the drawback of deafness, so unfailingly attractive.

Bevan received the honorary degrees of LL.D., St. Andrews (1922), and D. Litt., Oxford (1923), and was elected F.B.A. in 1942. He married in 1896 Mary Waldegrave (died 1935), youngest daughter of the third Baron Radstock. They had two daughters. Bevan died in London 18 October 1943.

[Gilbert Murray in *Proceedings* of the British Academy, vol. xxix, 1943; *Burke's Landed Gentry*, 1952; private information; personal knowledge.]

GILBERT MURRAY.
CLEMENT C. J. WEBB.

BIFFEN, SIR ROWLAND HARRY (1874–1949), geneticist, plant breeder, and professor of agricultural botany, the eldest of the family of two boys and three girls of Henry John and Mary Biffen, was born 28 May 1874 at Cheltenham where his father was headmaster of the Christ Church higher-grade school. From Cheltenham Grammar School he entered Emmanuel College, Cambridge, as an exhibitioner, and was placed in the first class of both parts of the natural sciences tripos (1895, 1896). In 1896 he became Frank Smart student in botany at Gonville and Caius College. Shortly after graduating he accompanied a small expedition to Brazil, Mexico, and the West Indies to study rubber production. On returning he served as university demonstrator in botany under H. Marshall Ward [q.v.], made investigations on fungi and evolved a new method (British patent 3909/1898) of handling rubber latex. Contact with rubber planting had drawn him, however, to agricultural, in preference to pure, botany, and in 1899 he eagerly took up a lectureship in the School of Agriculture which had just been established in the university of Cambridge.

From its foundation in 1908 until he retired in 1931, Biffen occupied the chair in agricultural botany at Cambridge. His teaching was brilliant, inspiring, yet reluctant, for it taxed his rather meagre constitutional strength and limited his time for research. Imaginative and gifted in experimentation, he was caught up in the enthusiastic study of heredity kindled by the revelation to the scientific world in 1900 of Mendel's laws (the account of which had lain neglected since it appeared in 1865–6). Biffen perceived, with clarity and conviction far beyond contemporary

opinion, the powerful agency offered by this new understanding of heredity to the improvement of cultivated plants by hybridizing. His own essays had confirmed his scientific conclusion that the current, empirical plant breeding owed such successes as it gained mostly to chance. Gradually, despite much prejudice and doubting in biological circles, investigations in several countries firmly established the applicability of Mendel's principles to the mode of inheritance of morphological characters in plants generally. Biffen's own work was important at this stage. His mind, however, was ranging much more boldly. In 1903 he published evidence that the inheritance of a 'constitutional' character in wheat (length-of-life cycle) conformed with Mendelian principles and he predicted that this would prove to be the case even with resistance to specific plant diseases. Proof was furnished in the case of yellow rust disease of wheat by his paper 'Mendel's Laws of Inheritance and Wheat Breeding' (*Journal of Agricultural Science*) in 1905. This discovery, his greatest achievement, quickly expanded into the realization that all characteristics, of constitution as well as of form, in all plants and animals, were hereditarily transmitted in Mendelian fashion. His subsequent genetic researches helped to enlarge and develop knowledge of heredity without fundamentally influencing it.

To produce better varieties, especially of wheat, was always his ultimate purpose, study of heredity being largely a means to this end, although also inspired by his deep biological interest. By theoretical demonstration and practical achievement he, more than any other, transformed plant breeding from empiricism to orderly, scientific method. He opened the way for those further, remarkable advances in breeding which have sprung from the later discovery of the chromosome basis and other genetic phenomena. Yeoman (1916) and Little Joss (1910), the best known of his wheats, and the first-fruits of modern plant breeding, are still well known in England and have been much used as parents by several successful breeders.

A Plant Breeding Institute was founded by government grant for the expansion of his work and he was its director from 1912 to 1936. Other institutes at Cambridge, for vegetable research and for study of plant viruses, developed under him and he was closely connected with the founding and work of the National Institute of

Agricultural Botany. He and John Percival, professor of agricultural botany at Reading, were for many years the leading British agricultural botanists. Government frequently sought his scientific advice and in 1926–7 he made a field study of the wheat-rust problem for the Government of Kenya. He was knighted in 1925. Academic honours included his election as F.R.S. (1914), and the Society's Darwin medal (1920), a professorial fellowship of St. Catharine's (1909), and an honorary fellowship at Emmanuel (1911). He received the honorary degree of D.Sc. from the university of Reading in 1935.

With Mary, eldest daughter of Edmund Hemus, of Holdfast Hall, Upton-on-Severn, whom he married in 1899, he lived in great happiness until her death in 1948. They had no children. Their beautiful garden, whose rarities included many fine specimens, especially of auriculas, bred by himself, gave them unquenchable pleasure. Versatile of gift, he was accomplished in architecture, the study of British wild flora, archaeology, and photography. Although he was entirely untaught, his sketches and water-colours, most of them landscapes, were of high quality.

Biffen was slight in build, although a vigorous walker, and delicate in constitution. He was a confirmed pipe smoker and copious reader. The quiet of garden, countryside, and laboratory suited him best and he shunned routine administration and any but intimate society. Unfailingly calm in mind, in judgement discerning and charitable, he was a high exemplar to his pupils and his friends. A portrait by Kenneth Green (1926) hangs in the School of Agriculture, Cambridge. He died at Cambridge 12 July 1949.

[Sir Frank Engledow in *Obituary Notices of Fellows of the Royal Society*, No. 19, November 1950; personal knowledge.]

F. L. ENGLEDOW.

BIKANER, MAHARAJA SHRI SIR GANGA SINGH BAHADUR, MAHARAJA OF (1880–1943), was born in Bikaner 13 October 1880, the son of Maharaj Lall Singh, and seven years later (August 1887) became the twenty-first ruler of Bikaner, in succession to his half-brother, Maharaja Dungar Singh. The young Maharaja showed early signs of promise and he was fortunate in his tutor, (Sir) Brian Egerton, who was responsible for his education after

he had spent five years at the Mayo College, Ajmer. At the age of eighteen he was invested with ruling powers.

The Maharaja had no easy task in front of him. His state, though it extended over an area of 23,000 square miles, was almost entirely desert. The annual rainfall was only eleven inches and precarious at that. Famine, or at least severe scarcity, was of frequent occurrence. Very soon after the Maharaja's minority ended Bikaner and the surrounding states were visited by the worst famine of modern times. He set to work with great energy and did his utmost to relieve distress. This experience led him to seek more permanent measures of relief, and after persistent efforts he succeeded in securing a share in the waters of the Sutlej, and constructed the Gang Canal (opened in 1927), which ran in a cement-lined channel through ninety miles of Punjab territory and converted a large area of the Bikaner State into a land of plenty.

This was undoubtedly the most striking of all the Maharaja's achievements, but beside it he could place the great extension of the railway system of Bikaner, the provision of hospitals and schools, and the transformation and improvement of the capital of his state.

Another problem which confronted the Maharaja was presented by the virtual independence of his *thakurs*. These semi-feudal barons were intolerant of all interference and, as throughout Rajputana, there were wide areas in which the *Darbar's* authority was only grudgingly acknowledged. This was a position which a man of the Maharaja's strong personality could never accept, and he soon made himself the unquestioned master of his dominions. He was fully alive, however, to the need for constitutional progress. He was one of the first princes to introduce a representative assembly. This institution, created in 1913, was given the power of initiating and passing legislation subject to the right of veto by the ruler; a further advance was made in 1937 when an elected majority was established.

The Maharaja firmly believed that the princes should combine together in promoting the common interests of their order. It was mainly at his instigation that during the war of 1914–18 the viceroy initiated an annual conference of rulers which developed into the Chamber of Princes, officially inaugurated in 1921. The Maharaja of Bikaner was elected the first chancellor and held that office continuously for the next five years.

In a wider field of constitutional development the Maharaja was again in the forefront. In 1930, the year in which he led the Indian delegation to the League of Nations Assembly at Geneva, he attended the Round Table conference in London, and he and the Nawab of Bhopal were the first two princes to support the scheme propounded by Sir Tej Bahadur Sapru for an all-India federation incorporating the states. This materially improved the prospects of reaching a lasting solution of India's problem, and after prolonged discussions something approaching general agreement was secured and the Government of India Act was passed. Provincial autonomy (Part I of the Act) was introduced in 1937. Federation was to follow when the requisite proportion of princes were ready to accede. The agents of the Congress Party, however, which had come into power in the great majority of provinces, set to work to foment unrest and disorder in the adjoining states. The main object of this campaign was to coerce the rulers into forgoing the right of nominating their federal representatives and to substitute popular election, which would increase the hopes of a Congress majority at the centre. The princes were greatly perturbed, and many of them, including the Maharaja, came round, not altogether surprisingly, to the view that, if this were a foretaste of federation, they would do well to hesitate. Federal negotiations were thus sadly protracted and were still incomplete when war supervened in 1939.

If the Maharaja wavered in his support of the federal programme, he never faltered in his devotion to the Crown. Always a keen soldier, his first military campaign was during the Boxer rising of 1900 in China where he commanded his well-known Camel Corps, the Ganga Risala. At the outbreak of the war of 1914–18 he placed all his resources at the disposal of the Crown, and he served personally in France and Egypt. He was a member of the Imperial War Conference of 1917 and a signatory to the Treaty of Versailles. He was appointed honorary major-general in 1917, lieutenant-general in 1930, and general in 1937, the first Indian to be given the rank of general in the British Army. He was for many years an honorary A.D.C. to the King. In the war of 1939–45 he was unable, to his great regret, to play an active part. But he again proffered all his resources, substantially increased his

state forces, supplied many contingents to swell the Indian Army, and in 1941 he paid a welcome visit to the Middle East.

The Maharaja in his early days was an ardent polo-player, but his main recreation was shooting, at which he excelled. Twenty miles from his capital, at Gajner, where his world-famous sand-grouse shoots took place, he had built himself an ideal country residence. Here it was his delight to entertain his many friends, and no one could have been a more perfect host. He was a great organizer, an untiring worker, and a most considerate master to all who served him faithfully.

The Maharaja was appointed K.C.I.E. (1901), K.C.S.I. (1904), G.C.I.E. (1907), G.C.S.I. (1911), K.C.B. (1918), G.C.V.O. (1919), and G.B.E. (1921). Honorary degrees were conferred upon him by the universities of Cambridge, Edinburgh, Oxford, Benares, and by Osmania University, Hyderabad. He was succeeded by his only surviving son, Maharaj Kanwar Sadul Singh (died 1950), on his death at Bombay 2 February 1943.

A portrait of the Maharaja is included in the group 'Some Statesmen of the War of 1914–18', painted by Sir James Guthrie, in the National Portrait Gallery, and in 'The Signing of Peace in the Hall of Mirrors, Versailles', by Sir William Orpen, in the Imperial War Museum.

[*The Times*, 3 February 1943; K. M. Panikkar, *His Highness the Maharaja of Bikaner*, 1937; personal knowledge.]

B. J. GLANCY.

BINNIE, WILLIAM JAMES EAMES (1867–1949), civil engineer, was born at Londonderry 10 October 1867, the eldest son of (Sir) Alexander Richardson Binnie [q.v.]. Educated at Rugby and Trinity College, Cambridge, where he was placed in the second class of part i of the natural sciences tripos in 1888, he completed his studies at the Karlsruhe Polytechnic. His early engineering experience was acquired on railway extension eastwards from Chesterfield, Mansergh's Welsh water scheme for Birmingham, and the construction, under Sir Benjamin Baker [q.v.], of the Central London Railway and the Khedivial graving dock at Alexandria.

In 1902 he joined his father who had just set up in private practice. Opposition frustrated their far-sighted project of bringing pure water to London by gravity from Wales, but the partnership prospered. When G. F. Deacon [q.v.] died in 1909 they took over his important contracts for supplying Birkenhead and Merthyr Tydfil from Welsh rivers. William Binnie's reputation grew steadily. He was president of the Institutions of Sanitary Engineers (1917) and Water Engineers (1921), a member of the Ouse Drainage Commission (1925), and adviser to the Doncaster Area Drainage Commission (1926). Competent and co-operative, he served acceptably on international bodies —as technical adviser to the British representative on the Central Rhine Commission (1922) and as one of the three commissioners for raising the level of the Aswan dam (1928) and for developing electric power from the Nile (1937). He was elected president of the Institution of Civil Engineers in 1938, an honour conferred upon his father in 1905. His presidential address, reflecting his sense of the past, ranged from Archimedes to Leonardo da Vinci, from the physics of Lucretius to the public works of Frontinus, *curator aquarum* in imperial Rome.

A recognized authority on flooding and water conservation, he wrote on 'Reservoir Storage in relation to Stream Flow' with Herbert Lapworth (Institution of Water Engineers, 1913), and 'Floods with special reference to Waste-Weir Capacity' (Institution of Civil Engineers, 1928). He was chairman of the Institution of Civil Engineers' committee on floods which issued a valuable interim report (1933) on 'Floods in relation to Reservoir Practice', and of the British committee of the International Commission on Large Dams (1933–46). Perhaps his most notable work was the boldly designed Gorge Dam at Hong Kong (Institution of Civil Engineers, paper 5188, *Journal*, March 1939, with Mr. H. J. F. Gourley).

Much as a son may owe to a distinguished father, Binnie earned his own success. His lively intelligence showed itself early when, not yet twenty-three, he described to the British Association at Leeds some experiments in measuring the size and intervals of drops, conducted while making an electric self-recording rain-gauge (*Journal* of the Royal Meteorological Society, January 1892). His warm-hearted, generous, and responsive nature brought him happy contacts. He was an honorary member of the American Society of Civil Engineers and of the New England Waterworks Association, and president of the British section of the Société des Ingénieurs civils de France. He was made a chevalier of the Legion of Honour in 1948, yet he received no public recognition in this country.

He travelled extensively—to Coolgardie, Western Australia, to advise on pipeline corrosion, and to Kano, Rangoon, Benares, Hong Kong and Singapore on waterworks. These journeys he enjoyed, however adventurous. While he flew back from Rangoon in June 1940 Italy declared war and France suspended hostilities. His French airliner finally grounded him at Algiers. He reached Gibraltar only by signing on as pantryman to assist the Chinese cook of a small collier whose Turkish crew had mutinied. The duties, no sinecure, were faithfully performed.

He married in 1900 Ethel (died 1947), daughter of Remy Morse, of Lounde Hall, Suffolk; they had three sons. He died at Tilehurst 4 October 1949. His portrait by John St. Helier Lander (1939) is in the Institution of Civil Engineers.

[*Journal* of the Institution of Civil Engineers, December 1949; *Journal* of the Institution of Water Engineers, November 1949; Norman Douglas, *Looking Back*, pp. 227–9, 1933; personal knowledge.]    CECIL CARR.

BINYON, (ROBERT) LAURENCE (1869–1943), poet, art-historian, and critic, was born at Lancaster 10 August 1869, the second son of the Rev. Frederick Binyon, vicar of Burton-in-Lonsdale, by his wife, Mary, daughter of Robert Benson Dockray, resident engineer of the London and Birmingham Railway. Binyon, who was of Quaker stock on both sides, was a scholar of St. Paul's School and of Trinity College, Oxford. He was awarded the Newdigate prize for an English poem on Persephone, a first class in classical moderations (1890) and a second in *literae humaniores* (1892). He entered the department of printed books in the British Museum in 1893, but was transferred to the department of prints and drawings in 1895, becoming assistant keeper in 1909. From the first he united the practice of poetry with that of the care, exhibition, and interpretation of the drawings and prints which were his special charge. As a boy he had hesitated between poetry and painting as means of expression; a self-portrait at the age of about seventeen survived him in the possession of his family. He had contributed as an undergraduate to a slim pamphlet *Primavera: Poems by Four Authors* (1890), the other three being his cousin Stephen Phillips [q.v.], Arthur S. Cripps, and Manmohan Ghose; and he continued to publish small volumes of lyrics and dramas at short intervals through most of his life.

Similarly, he issued at intervals a considerable number of annotated catalogues, of lectures and essays, in many of which the affinity of poetry with the visual arts was felt or actually indicated.

Binyon's first official work was the production in four volumes (1898–1907) of the *Catalogue of Drawings by British Artists and Artists of Foreign Origin working in Great Britain preserved in the Department of Prints and Drawings in the British Museum*; his first independent publications were an essay on the Dutch etchers of the seventeenth century and another on Crome and Cotman (Portfolio Monographs, 1895, 1897). He followed these up with a study of Girtin (1900) and *The Life and Work of J. S. Cotman* (1903). Meanwhile he had been engaged with the Chinese and Japanese paintings and colour-prints, of which the museum had a fine store, greatly enriched in 1910 by the Wegener and in 1913 by the Morrison collections. The art of the East was henceforth Binyon's principal subject, and in 1913 a special sub-department of oriental prints and drawings was put in his charge. By acquisitions for the museum, by exhibitions and catalogues, by lectures and essays, most notably by his *Painting in the Far East*, first published in 1908 and successively enlarged in three further editions, and his lectures as Charles Eliot Norton professor at Harvard on 'The Spirit of Man in Asian Art' (1933–4), he did more than anyone to spread the appreciation of the art not only of China and Japan, but of India and Persia.

At the same time Binyon's devotion to poetry and to Western art was unabated. Indeed his influence upon the appreciation of Blake and the water-colourists Girtin, Cotman, and Francis Towne [qq.v.], the last of whom he practically 'discovered', was no less fruitful than his work on oriental art. He edited Blake's *Woodcuts* (1902), *Drawings and Engravings* (1922), *Engraved Designs* (1926), and published an essay on *The Art of Botticelli* (1913) and an important study of *The Followers of William Blake* (1925). Both Blake and Botticelli made special appeal to him by their 'faculty of communicating the reality of floating movement and rushing light; a faculty which seems especially to belong to artists of poetic nature and of spiritual imagination, to seers of visions'— a faculty which together with his brooding love of the English earth and legends pervades so much of Binyon's own poetry and such prose as *Landscape in English*

*Art and Poetry* (1931) and *English Water-Colours* (1933).

With Binyon the practice of poetry was as much a part of his nature as the study and interpretation of visual art. 'Verse is to me', he wrote, 'a much more natural medium than prose.' But composition was limited by the zealous discharge of his professional duties. In 1929 he wrote to a friend: 'having a seven-hours official day to put in, I rarely have time to write on a first stimulus: I am obliged to keep things in my mind for months, and so they tend to grow and expand of themselves.' He refers here to the two great imaginative odes, *The Sirens* (1924) and *The Idols* (1928). He went on: 'I long in my heart to get away from the Museum and write a magnum opus, cherished for twenty years or more, though not a line of it has been written.' This was a drama about Merlin, of which the first part, still unfinished, was published after his death under the title *The Madness of Merlin* (1947); the other two parts had been scarcely begun. But even after he had retired in 1933, having for the last year served as keeper of his department, he devoted long and intense labour to the translation of Dante's *Divina Commedia* into the *terza rima* of the original. This he found in his own words 'a fascinating labour and discipline'. It exercised his pre-eminent faculty of interpretation and his constant feeling for purity of style.

Binyon's sensitiveness to emotional eloquence in poetry is manifest in his odes, in his poetical dramas, and in his active participation in the movement for the speaking of verse, associated especially with the name of Dr. John Masefield, the poet laureate. Several of his shorter plays were written for this movement. Of the six plays performed in the ordinary theatre, the first was *Attila*, produced by Oscar Asche [q.v.] in 1907, with scenery and dresses by Charles Ricketts and music by Sir Charles Stanford [qq.v.]. The longest, *Arthur: a Tragedy*, written 'for and with' Sir John and Lady Martin-Harvey, although not actually played by them, was produced in 1923 at the Old Vic with music by Sir Edward Elgar [qq.v.].

Closely linked with Binyon's interest in the speaking of verse was that in versification. In this he began experimenting while still at Oxford, after meeting Robert Bridges [q.v.] who introduced him to the as yet unpublished poetry of Gerard Manley Hopkins. He followed Bridges and

Hopkins in giving the natural stress-accent of English speech a far greater dominance than had been the rule since Chaucer. This appears already in one of his most perfect lyrics, 'The Little Dancers' (*London Visions*, 1896), and is constant throughout his subsequent poetry. At the same time he never fell into the fallacy of formless 'free verse'; his speech-rhythms were always woven into an harmonious pattern.

Binyon was neither a mere aesthete nor a mere versifier. His poetry has a rich spiritual content, an alternation, often a blend, of brooding consciousness of the sorrows and frustrations of human life with lofty and imaginative aspiration; and his personal happiness in an ideal marriage is reflected in many genuine and exquisite love-poems. For those capable of appreciating it the fine art of his poetry only enhances the unconscious self-portraiture of a character endeared to his friends by its rare beauty, steadfastness, and integrity. His style was too refined, his thought too swift and subtle for the generality of even the reading public; but once, at the climax of national mourning, the perfect simplicity, dignity, and euphony of his poem 'For the Fallen' (first published in *The Times* 21 September 1914) met with universal acclaim. It has been said or sung at countless memorial services and one of its quatrains is inscribed on countless memorial stones, including the one at the British Museum.

Binyon's *Collected Poems* were published in two volumes in 1931. Later publications included *Brief Candles*, with a valuable preface on the modern drama in verse (1938), *Art and Freedom*, being the Romanes lecture at Oxford (1939), *The North Star and other poems* (1941); and, posthumously, *The Burning of the Leaves* (1944).

Binyon lectured four times in the United States between 1912 and 1934, and in China and Japan in 1929. He enjoyed travel, especially in France and Italy; and in the first year of the war of 1939–45, at the age of seventy, he occupied for some months the Byron chair of English letters at Athens. He was made a C.H. in 1932, and in the following year an honorary D.Litt. of Oxford and an honorary fellow of Trinity College. He was also honorary LL.D. of Glasgow University (1921), and a chevalier of the Legion of Honour —the last in recognition of his service as an orderly of the Red Cross in the war of 1914–18. He was a fellow of the Royal Society of Literature, and president of the English Association for 1933–4. He married in 1904 Cicely Margaret, daughter of Henry Pryor Powell, banker, of Ockley, Surrey. There were three daughters of the marriage, the second of whom married Basil Gray, successor to Binyon in charge of the oriental prints and drawings at the British Museum. Binyon died at Reading 10 March 1943.

The National Portrait Gallery has a pencil drawing of Binyon by William Strang who also executed a drypoint (1898) and an engraving (1918), impressions of both of which are in the department of prints and drawings, British Museum. A lithograph by Sir William Rothenstein is in the Bradford City Art Gallery and one of several drawings is reproduced in *Twenty-Four Portraits* (2nd series, 1923). A pencil drawing by Rothenstein is in the Manchester City Art Gallery. In the possession of the family is an excellent caricature by Edmund Dulac in the style of an actor-print by the Japanese artist Sharaku.

[Private information; personal knowledge.]
NOWELL SMITH.

BIRD, SIR JAMES (1883–1946), naval and aircraft constructor, was born in London 19 March 1883, the second son of Samuel Bird, merchant, of East Cowes, Isle of Wight. He was educated at Marlborough where he was a prefect, played in the hockey eleven, and captained the football fifteen. He next served an apprenticeship with Armstrong Whitworth & Co., Ltd., and practised as a consulting naval architect until the outbreak of war in 1914 when he joined the Royal Navy. He had early taken an interest in flying and had built his first aircraft in 1909 at Wivenhoe, Essex, where he became managing director of the Rennie, Forrestt shipbuilding, engineering, and dry dock company. He obtained his aviator's certificate in 1915, was appointed O.B.E. in 1916, and left the Royal Naval Air Service at the end of the war with the rank of squadron commander.

Joining the Supermarine Aviation Works, Southampton, as a director in 1919, Bird acquired control of the firm in 1923. With R. J. Mitchell [q.v.] as chief engineer and designer the firm went from strength to strength in the production of seaplanes, and in 1927 gained first and second place in the Schneider Trophy race at Venice. In the same year the company provided the flying-boats for the Royal Air Force's Far East formation flight from Plymouth to Singapore, round Australia, and back to Singapore. In the following year Bird sold out to Vickers, becoming a director of Vickers (Aviation), Ltd. On the outbreak of war in 1939 Bird reluctantly agreed with Vickers and the Air Ministry that it was his patriotic duty to emerge from his semi-retirement and return to the works to supervise the production of Mitchell's famous Spitfire. Bird was the right man for a task upon which so much depended. He had great technical and practical knowledge, a gift for organization, and a personal charm and kindliness which made it easy for others to work as his colleagues or subordinates. He faced the subsequent destruction of the works by enemy action with his usual cheerful fortitude and at once set about the immense task of organizing dispersal factories in the south of England. Nearly 19,000 Spitfires had been built before he retired at the end of the war. In 1945 he was knighted for his services.

Bird was for many years a member of the council of the Society of British Aircraft Constructors, and he served as chairman of the Royal Aero Club Schneider Trophy committee and was on the aviation committee of Lloyd's. He was prominent in the business life of Southampton and was for long a member of the Southampton Harbour Board. He was always fond of the sea and spent most of his spare time in the summer racing his yacht. He looked more like a naval officer than a business man, with a 'strong' face, always very bronzed, clear blue eyes, and dark hair. He was well built, with broad shoulders, but the strain of the war impaired his health and he died at Wickham, Hampshire, 13 August 1946.

Bird was thrice married and by his second wife had one son, John Samuel Bird, who became a test pilot.

[Private information; personal knowledge.]
CHARLES R. GRAY.

BIRMINGHAM, GEORGE A. (pseudonym), novelist. [See HANNAY, JAMES OWEN.]

BISCOE, CECIL EARLE TYNDALE-(1863–1949), missionary and educationist in Kashmir. [See TYNDALE-BISCOE.]

BLACKMAN, FREDERICK FROST (1866–1947), plant physiologist, was born at Lambeth 25 July 1866, the eldest son and third child of Frederick Blackman, a doctor, by his wife, Catherine Elizabeth Frost. His interest in plants showed itself at an early stage by his starting a herbarium during his schooldays at Mill Hill. On leaving school in 1883 he entered St. Bartholomew's Hospital to train as a doctor. He graduated B.Sc. (London) in 1885 while still at the hospital. In 1887, despite success in his medical studies, his plans were changed and he went to St. John's College, Cambridge, where he was placed in the first class of both parts of the natural sciences tripos (1889, 1891). This success was repeated by two of his brothers who followed him to St. John's, one of whom, Dr. Vernon Herbert Blackman, who contributes to this SUPPLEMENT, became professor of plant physiology at the Imperial College of Science and Technology.

In 1891 Blackman was appointed to a demonstratorship in the Cambridge Botany School, becoming lecturer in 1897, reader in 1904, and remaining there until his retirement in 1936. His chief published contributions are in two series of papers which include contributions by his students. The first series entitled 'Experimental Researches in Vegetable Assimilation and Respiration' began in 1895; the second, 'Analytical Studies in Plant Respiration', in 1928.

Blackman's first paper described an elaborate apparatus for determining simply and precisely the carbon dioxide in small samples of a gaseous mixture such as air. With this he was able to show conclusively, for the first time, that the bulk of the exchange of carbon dioxide between foliage leaves and the air was via the stomata. In 1904 his student, Miss G. L. C. Matthaei, showed that at high intensities of illumination the rate of photosynthesis is determined by chemical (now called 'Blackman') and not by photochemical reactions. In April 1905 there appeared in *Annals of Botany* his classical paper on 'Optima and Limiting Factors'. In this paper he showed himself a pioneer in the application of physico-chemical ideas to biological problems while still retaining a full awareness of the latter's complexity. This theme was further developed in his presidential address to the botany section at the meeting of the British Association in 1908. Until then, there had been much confused thinking and, as Blackman said, the prevalent view was 'that every change in which protoplasm takes part is a case of *reaction of an irritable living substance to a stimulus*'. From 1918 onwards the work of his many research students was focused on the problems connected with respiration in plants. In 1928 he gave his interpretation of the results of experiments on the effect of change in the partial pressure of oxygen. He advanced the view that the products of glycolysis were used for the reformation of carbohydrates at a rate which was reduced by lowering the supply of oxygen, by a process he called oxidative anabolism. This paper, which has established itself as a classic, shows his powers to organize a complicated set of data and produce 'a plausible interpretation of all the quantitative variations'. He considerably developed his views in papers which were ready for publication at the time of his death.

The two previous holders of the readership in botany, S. H. Vines and Sir Francis Darwin [qq.v.], had made individual contributions to the subject of plant physiology, but under Blackman a vigorous school of research developed, largely due to his leadership. His lucid lectures attracted many to the subject and he was a source of great inspiration to those who had the privilege of working under his guidance. In the design of apparatus he was particularly gifted and in the analysis of the experimental results he was masterly.

Blackman made contributions to other aspects of life in Cambridge. He helped greatly in the administration of the Botany School and in planning the extension in 1933. Among his services to the university was his long membership of the Fitzwilliam Museum syndicate. He was a member of the board of the Cambridge Instrument Company from 1901 to 1936. He gave freely of his time and ability to the service of St. John's College of which he became a fellow in 1895, where he lived as a bachelor until 1917, and served as steward from 1908 to 1914. His contributions to Cambridge owe their value to his breadth of outlook, for he combined a critical and candid intelligence with a wide interest which included the arts as well as the sciences. With knowledge he combined good judgement.

He was elected F.R.S. in 1906, was awarded a Royal medal in 1921, and was Croonian lecturer in 1923. In 1924 his students presented him with a portrait by Miss F. A. de Biden Footner, which is in the possession of the family. After his retirement in 1936 he was presented with his portrait painted by Henry Lamb which he gave to the Botany School.

Blackman married in 1917 Elsie, daughter of Samuel Chick, of Chestergate, Eal-

ing, who survived him when he died in Cambridge 30 January 1947. There was one son.

[Private information ; personal knowledge.]
G. E. BRIGGS.

BLAIR, ERIC ARTHUR (1903–1950), author, known under the pseudonym of GEORGE ORWELL, was born at Motihari, Bengal, 25 June 1903, the only son of Richard Walmesley Blair, of the Bengal Civil Service, and his wife, Ida Mabel Limouzin. On leaving Eton, where he was a King's scholar, in 1921, he went not to a university but to Burma to serve in the Imperial Police, but after five years he returned to Europe and set himself with extraordinary conscientiousness to learn the facts of poverty by experience, as a dish-washer in Paris and as a tramp in England. He described this later in his first book, *Down and Out in Paris and London* (1933). He next worked as a schoolmaster and as a bookseller's assistant and during this period he wrote three novels. The best of these, *Burmese Days* (1935), is an able and bitter analysis of social strains in Burma in the early 'twenties. A later novel, *Coming up for Air* (1939), makes a high-spirited defence of the small man in the toils of big business, standardization, and urbanization.

From 1937 onwards Orwell's political thought, an unorthodox and very individual Socialism, was developed through *The Road to Wigan Pier* (1937), *Homage to Catalonia* (1938), *The Lion and the Unicorn* (1941), and *Animal Farm* (1945) to an apocalyptic vision of doom in *Nineteen Eighty-Four* which was published in 1949. It is on these books and on his literary essays that his reputation chiefly stands. Just as his character combined adventurousness with a love of peaceful country pursuits, so his mind was both libertarian and tradition-loving, but these divergent and sometimes conflicting tendencies were fused together by a passionate generosity and love of justice which illuminate his best work with a flash of genius. Although his books were influential from about 1938 onwards he remained poor until near the end of his life.

Satire was his best medium, although if he had lived longer he might have gone beyond it, for he had also a poetic gift. But the political fable, *Animal Farm*, the form of which was influenced by the *Tale of a Tub*, remains his most technically perfect work. His polemical writing was virile and fearlessly honest, although not without an occasional touch of extravagance and perversity. Among the objects of his attack were capitalism, pacifism, spiritualism, Roman Catholicism, and the servile state, whether Fascist, Socialist, or Communist; and as a result of his experiences in the Spanish civil war, in which he was severely wounded, fighting as a Socialist militiaman, he became one of the most formidable and best-equipped critics of Stalinism. But it is in his literary essays, on Dickens and Kipling for example (*Critical Essays*, 1946), that the more conservative and traditional aspects of his thought are seen at their best.

Orwell was twice married: first, in 1936 to Eileen Maud (died 1945), daughter of the late Laurence O'Shaughnessy, of the Inland Revenue; and secondly, in 1949 to Sonia Mary, daughter of Charles Neville Brownell, a business man in India. He was survived by an adopted son. He died in London, 21 January 1950, after a long struggle against consumption.

[*The Times*, 23 January 1950; Ian Willison, *George Orwell: Some materials for a bibliography*, in the Library of London University; private information; personal knowledge.]

R. REES.

BLAKISTON, HERBERT EDWARD DOUGLAS (1862–1942), president of Trinity College, Oxford, and vice-chancellor (1917–20) of Oxford University, was born at St. Leonards, Sussex, 5 September 1862, the eldest of the six children of Douglas Yeoman Blakiston (1832–1914), by his wife, Sophia Matilda, youngest child of the Rev. William Dent, of Crosby Cote, Yorkshire. In 1881 he entered Trinity from Tonbridge School with an open scholarship in classics and proceeded to first classes in honour moderations (1882) and *literae humaniores* (1885). After visiting Italy as a private tutor and teaching at Clifton College he took holy orders, returning to Trinity in 1887 as fellow, chaplain, and lecturer in classics. There he was destined to reside for the next fifty-one years.

His father, ordained at the age of thirty-seven, had previously been an artist by profession—a fact which helps to explain Blakiston's keen interest in the arts, his willing service as a visitor of the Ashmolean Museum, and the nature of his bequests (mostly for the purchase of works of art) to his own college and university and to University College, Durham. It is also worth recording that difficult family circumstances, further complicated by his

father's vainly protracted fight for the exemption of Easter offerings from income-tax (see *Blakiston* v. *Cooper*, a leading case reported at [1909] A.C. 104), forced upon him from about 1877 the strictest lessons of thrift and caution, tending also to increase his natural shyness and restrict his sociability. These lessons were reinforced in 1908, when his parents' home, The Vicarage, East Grinstead, Sussex—apparently uninsured—was destroyed by fire; and the total extinction by 1916 of his whole family circle (his brothers, all by sudden death, in 1887, 1889, 1896; his mother, who had long relied on his spiritual and material support, in 1912; his father and both sisters in the next four years) not only had profound effects on his inner life but caused him from that date to centre all his interest and affection upon his college.

Blakiston held office as tutor from 1892 and as senior tutor and junior bursar from 1898 until his election as president in 1907. On the death of R. W. Raper [q.v.] in 1915 he took over the duties of estates bursar, which he retained until 1938, when he resigned the presidency, wishing to retire while still active and alert. The college hastened to elect him an honorary fellow and looked forward, as he did, to a long-continued connexion; but on 28 July 1942 he was struck down by a motor-car near his house on Boars Hill and died, without recovering consciousness, next day. Trinity owed an immense debt to his able conduct of both bursarial offices—especially to his prudent finance in difficult times and to his share in promoting and providing the War Memorial library; but it owed still more to his maintenance of good traditions which the war might have broken and to his close watch on vital interests at the time of the Royal Commission on the university.

As vice-chancellor (1917–20) Blakiston brought to his task experience of university affairs gained as junior proctor (1899–1900) and as auditor (1903–17), together with a thorough knowledge of collegiate economy. It was this combination which enabled him to carry through his main work of constructive statesmanship—a financial statute dealing with problems which some years before Lord Curzon [q.v.] as chancellor had handled less acceptably. His appointments as a curator of the University Chest (1922–32) and a delegate of the University Press (1922–37) were a tribute to his business capacity; but critics were not wanting who found him over-suspicious of external influences in fiscal as in other matters and too little aware—for he never married—of the post-war costs of family life.

Between the wars Blakiston attained more fully than before the recognized status of 'a character'. An ocular weakness, a peculiar gait, and old-fashioned habits in dress combined to make him a noticeable figure. Anecdotes reflected also his brusquerie (an effect of shyness), his economies, his firm belief in 'gentry of estate and name', his anti-feminism, his sermons read from his own illegible manuscript, his horsemanship, his motoring, his irrepressible desire to score off pretentious persons—sometimes in the style of his early idol Macaulay—and his schoolboy gusto in recounting their discomfiture. Less widely reported were his shrewdness of judgement, his strong sense of justice, and essential kindness of heart. He lectured well, if somewhat dogmatically, on Cicero and Theocritus; and was a good composer, as shown by his contributions to *Nova Anthologia Oxoniensis* (1899) of which his colleague Robinson Ellis [q.v.] was an editor; by some Latin inscriptions in the college; and by his Latin speeches as vice-chancellor. But his main publications were antiquarian rather than classical, and archaeology, more especially church architecture and organization, was among his keenest interests. His many contributions to this DICTIONARY reveal something of his literary style and much of his environment.

As the sole survivor of his family and a graduate in the school of thrift he amassed considerable means and his bequests were substantial. A portrait (posthumous, from photographs) by Allan Gwynne-Jones hangs in the President's Lodgings at Trinity.

[*The Times*, 30 July 1942; *Oxford Magazine*, 5 November 1942; *Oxford*, Summer 1943; private information; personal knowledge.]
T. F. HIGHAM.

BLAND, JOHN OTWAY PERCY (1863–1945), writer on Chinese affairs, was born 15 November 1863, in county Antrim, the second son of Major-General Edward Loftus Bland, of Whiteabbey, county Antrim, by his wife, Emma Frances, daughter of Robert Fergusson Franks, of Jerpoint, county Kilkenny. He was educated in Switzerland, at Victoria College, Jersey, and at Trinity College, Dublin. In 1883 he entered the Chinese imperial maritime customs and for two years was secretary to Sir Robert Hart [q.v.]. He resigned in 1896 on appointment as secretary to the International Settlement of Shanghai (his nickname as 'the uncrowned king of Shanghai' throws a light on the forcefulness of his character), but resigned in 1906 in order to become agent of the British and Chinese Corporation, Ltd., in which capacity he negotiated four loans to China. He was correspondent of *The Times* (1897–1910), first in Shanghai, then in Peking, his dispatches being noted for their wide incisive surveys. In 1916 he retired from China to Aldeburgh, Suffolk, but continued to write widely. In 1912 he lectured on the Far East at the Lowell Institute, Boston.

Bland's life in China coincided with a period of stirring events in her history—Japan's first war with China; the 'Hundred Days' reforms of the Emperor Kuan Hsü, and the Empress Dowager's *coup d'état* in 1898; the Boxer rising and the siege of the legations in 1900; Japan's war with Russia (1904–5) and annexation of Korea; and the Chinese revolution of 1911 and the downfall of the Manchus. Trenchant and witty in conversation, Bland, as a writer, was a master of a singularly mellifluous and lively style. Of his numerous books, *China under the Empress Dowager* (1910) and *Annals & Memoirs of the Court of Peking* (1914), both in conjunction with (Sir) Edmund Backhouse [q.v.], may well rank as classics. Another brilliant book was the life of *Li Hung-Chang* (1917); and, in another vein, *Houseboat Days in China* (1909) gives a charming picture of an era gone for ever. *Recent Events and Present Policies in China* (1912), *China, Japan and Korea* (1921), the outcome of a return visit to the Far East, and *China: the Pity of It* (1932), urging that the powers should take China under joint tutelage, bear witness to his unalterable disbelief that the westernized Kuomintang had anything permanent to offer China, which later events fully justified. *Men, Manners and Morals in South America* (1920) resulted from several visits there in 1914–18; and *Something Lighter* (1924) is an agreeable collection of Chinese stories. He held the Orders of the Imperial Double Dragon, Pao Hsing (China), and the Rising Sun (Japan).

Bland married in 1889 Louisa, daughter of Captain H. C. Dearborn, of the United States, who predeceased him; they had no children. He died at Ipswich 23 June 1945.

[*The Times*, 25 June 1945; personal knowledge.]
O. M. GREEN.

# Blanesburgh

D.N.B. 1941–1950

BLANESBURGH, Baron (1861–1946), judge. [See Younger, Robert.]

BLATCHFORD, ROBERT PEEL GLANVILLE (1851–1943), journalist, author, and Socialist, was born at Maidstone 17 March 1851 and named after the Conservative statesman who died the previous year. His English father, John Glanville Blatchford, and his half-Italian mother, Georgiana Louisa Corri, granddaughter of Domenico Corri [q.v.], were both provincial actors, and the father died before he was two years old. His mother continued acting for eight years in order to bring up her two children, Montagu, the elder, and Robert; but she hated the stage, determined to keep her sons off it, and had them both apprenticed to trades. Robert at fourteen was indentured for seven years to a brushmaker at Halifax; but when twenty he ran away, tramped from Yarmouth to London, starved there for some weeks, and finally enlisted in the 103rd Regiment, an old 'John Company' corps newly back from India. He did well and in eighteen months was promoted sergeant; he also became a marksman. He finally left the service in 1878, having obtained a situation as a timekeeper at Northwich under the Weaver Navigation Company. His pay was 27s. a week, and in 1880, when it was 30s., he married. His wife, Sarah Crossley, he had met thirteen years before at the Halifax brush shop; and their union, which was a very happy one, did much to shape the rest of his life.

Blatchford soon needed to earn more. His bent was towards art, but at Northwich he had nowhere to learn it. So he turned to writing. He earned his first half-guinea in 1883 with a story in a paper called the *Yorkshireman*. In 1884 he came to know Alexander Mattock Thompson, thenceforward his lifelong friend and ally. Thompson was working at Manchester on the *Sporting Chronicle* owned by the father of (Sir) Edward Hulton [q.v.]; and when in 1885 Hulton bought *Bell's Life in London* and made it a daily, Thompson recommended Blatchford for a post on it. He was engaged at £4 a week, left Northwich for London, and became a professional journalist. In the same year Hulton started the *Sunday Chronicle* in Manchester, and Blatchford wrote its leaders from London. In 1887 he moved to Manchester, and then first became known as an individual writer. He began with soldier stories and sketches; next he went to Ire-

land to write up the land war; then he started writing about the Manchester slums. His experiences made him a Socialist, and his Socialism cost him, in 1891, his post on the *Sunday Chronicle* in which he was earning £1,000 a year. With his friend Thompson, his brother Montagu, and another Hulton journalist, Edward Francis Fay, he started the *Clarion*, as a Socialist weekly. They put up the capital between them; it was only £400. The paper's first sale was 40,000, and then it remained for some years about 34,000. Despite its brilliance and the charm of its writing (not least E. F. Fay's), the paper stuck there. Then a series of articles on Socialism by Blatchford was reprinted as a book, *Merrie England* (1893), and in the next year they issued a penny edition of it. This sold like wildfire; helped to make Socialism really popular in England for the first time; and sent the *Clarion's* circulation up to 60,000. Ultimately in Great Britain, in America, and through translations elsewhere, the book sold over two million copies. It was indeed Blatchford's highest flight as a propagandist; he never surpassed it; and through it mainly he left his mark upon history.

The death of Fay in 1896 hit the *Clarion* hard, but it continued for another three years to be the chief popular organ of English Socialism. It was indeed much else; it popularized a wide range of good literature and poetry; it 'sang to its readers', and with genial tolerance found space for almost any kind of forward-looking movement. Nothing could damp its gay courage and infectious good nature. In all this it mirrored Blatchford himself, who was much more a crusader than a politician. Many attempts were made by his admirers to get him upon platforms or nominate him for Parliament. But he was no speaker, disliked party manœuvring, and was never happy with the leaders of the then dominant Independent Labour Party. On the outbreak of the South African war this division became sharper, because the party became pro-Boer, while Blatchford was pro-war. With the war's ending the *Clarion* entered calmer waters, or would have done, if Blatchford had not stirred up new opposition by entering on a campaign against orthodox religion. This lost him many readers, but added more. As much could not be said of his warnings against Germany before the war of 1914–18; they were seen after the event to have been justified, but at the time alienated most English Socialists, especi-

86

ally when he carried his views into the columns of the *Daily Mail*. This last episode started a connexion between him and the Northcliffe press which lasted until the summer of 1916. Thereafter he wrote for Hulton in the *Sunday Chronicle* until 1924, for the *Sunday News* from 1924 until 1927, and then became a freelance. He kept the *Clarion* going for some years, but had eventually to abandon it. After his wife's death in 1921 he came to believe in spiritualism.

Blatchford published many books, of which *Britain for the British* (1902), *God and my Neighbour* (1903), and *The Sorcery Shop* (1907) were outstanding. Many of them were collections of short articles or stories. His short stories about soldiers were excellent, but his fiction was not otherwise remarkable. His essays in literary criticism showed his feeling for style; his favourite books were neither fiction nor poetry, but prose belles-lettres like those of Sir Thomas Browne. His controversial appeal, it has been said, was in inverse ratio to his reader's education; but he was vigorous and sincere, and at his best he wrote very pure English. His Socialism was that of William Morris [q.v.]; he knew nothing of Marx; and little more, perhaps, of Sidney and Beatrice Webb [qq.v.]. His Utopia, *The Sorcery Shop*, is closely akin to *News from Nowhere*. In 1931 he published a vivid autobiography, *My Eighty Years*.

Blatchford had four sons, three of whom died in infancy, and two daughters; the loving care of the latter made happy his last twenty-two years. He died at Horsham, Sussex, 17 December 1943.

[R. P. G. Blatchford, *My Eighty Years*, 1931; *Manchester Guardian*, 20 December 1943; Laurence Thompson, *Robert Blatchford*, 1951; private information; personal knowledge.]     R. C. K. ENSOR.

BLOMFIELD, SIR REGINALD THEODORE (1856–1942), architect, was born at Bow vicarage, Devon, 20 December 1856, the third son of the Rev. George John Blomfield, who became vicar of Dartford in 1857 and rector of Aldington, Kent, in 1868, and his wife, a distant cousin, Isabella, second daughter of C. J. Blomfield, bishop of London [q.v.]. In 1869 Blomfield entered Haileybury and was awarded a leaving exhibition in 1875 when he also won a Stapledon scholarship at Exeter College, Oxford. He obtained a first class in *literae humaniores* in 1879. On several occasions he played cricket for the university eleven and full-back in the university fifteen, but he never achieved a 'blue'. Although he confessed that he was 'keenly interested in art in a very amateur way' at this stage, he attributed his choice of architecture as a profession to the circumstance that his mother's brother (Sir) A. W. Blomfield [q.v.], whose office he entered in 1881, 'was already a successful architect'. He became an associate of the Royal Institute of British Architects and joined the Royal Academy school of architecture, but left his uncle within two years after a 'misunderstanding', the first of many in his lively career. He then travelled for three months in France and Spain, returning with a crowded sketchbook and the illuminating discovery that he had 'never really cared for Gothic'.

Blomfield began practice on his own account in London in 1884, and courageously married in 1886, but it appears from the long list of buildings executed by him that for about eight years his commissions were limited to a few small houses and restorations of churches. Meanwhile he occupied his spare time by writing articles on historical architecture, beginning with Sussex ironwork and half-timbered houses, followed by a series on English Renaissance architects. In 1901 he joined the committee which assumed the editorial direction of the *Architectural Review*, and contributed many articles to its columns until 1905, when he had a disagreement with its proprietors. His first book, *The Formal Garden in England* (1892), was followed in 1897 by his masterly *History of Renaissance Architecture in England 1500–1800* (2 vols.) and in 1900 by his *Short History* of the same period. These volumes—learned, admirably written, and well illustrated—introduced him to many owners of historic mansions who employed him as architect. Rebuilding at Brocklesby Park was among the first-fruits, and other famous houses altered, enlarged, or restored by him included Apethorpe, Chequers, and Mellerstain near Kelso. By 1910 his practice had become extensive, consisting mainly of houses but also involving the erection of the remarkable warehouse in Greycoat Place, Westminster, for the Army and Navy Stores; yet he managed to continue writing, and his important *History of French Architecture, 1494 to 1774* was completed by 1921 (vols. i and ii, 1911; vols. iii and iv, 1921). Other and later books, besides several volumes of collected articles and lectures, were his

*Memoirs of an Architect* (1932), *Modernismus* (a witty and slashing attack upon new fashions in architecture, 1934), and biographies of *Sebastien Le Prestre de Vauban* (1938) and *Richard Norman Shaw* (1940).

Among many public and commercial buildings which Blomfield designed and carried out were the Usher Art Gallery, public library, and water-tower at Lincoln; Paul's Cross in St. Paul's churchyard; Lady Margaret Hall, Oxford; the United University Club and the refacing of the Carlton Club, in London; additions to several public schools; municipal war memorials at Leeds, Luton, and Torquay; the Royal Air Force and Belgian war memorials on the Victoria Embankment; the 'Headrow' at Leeds; and Lambeth Bridge. His work for the Imperial War Graves Commission from 1918 to 1927 included the design of the 'Cross of Sacrifice', the layout of many cemeteries, and the enormous Menin Gate at Ypres. Another notable commission was the rebuilding of the Regent Street Quadrant together with the County Fire Office and Swan and Edgar's premises in Piccadilly Circus (1910–30). In this work, he attempted to reconcile the massive design by R. Norman Shaw [q.v.] of the Piccadilly Hotel in the Quadrant with insistent demands from shopkeepers for more window-space. So far as one can generalize about so wide a range of buildings, Blomfield's designs recall English and French architecture of the seventeenth and eighteenth centuries. He had a special fondness for bull's-eye windows and carved swags or festoons.

A man of abounding energy, sincerity, downrightness, self-assurance, and pugnacity, as well as scholarship, Blomfield inevitably created some opposition and became embroiled in many controversies which he thoroughly enjoyed. Various 'excellent fights' are fully described in his racy memoirs, such as the battles over the proposed 'destruction' of the London City churches, the demolition of Waterloo Bridge, and the project for a new Charing Cross Bridge. He had come to be regarded as *arbiter elegantiarum* for so many years that a sensation was caused in 1932 when it was announced that he had prepared designs for a tall office building in Carlton Gardens to rise high above the stately skyline of Nash's Carlton House Terrace as seen from St. James's Park. He replied to his critics with gusto, questioned the merits of Nash's architecture, and published a design for rebuilding the whole of the terrace, a project which he had been asked by the Government to bear in mind when preparing his plan for the offices. A defence committee was formed with many influential names among its 400 members, and a debate in Parliament ensued. The fact that Blomfield was a member of the Royal Fine Art Commission which had hastily approved his design aggravated the situation and Blomfield resigned from the Commission.

Such incidents were frequent during Blomfield's career, for he was a fearless critic of many established institutions. In 1891 he resigned from the Royal Institute of British Architects on the question of registration, but became a fellow in 1906 and rendered invaluable services to his profession, notably as chairman of the board of architectural education, and as president of the Institute, 1912–14; he received the Royal gold medal for architecture in 1913. He was on the executive committee of the British School at Rome from its foundation, and first chairman of the faculty of architecture. In 1903 he resigned from the Art-Workers' Guild, to which he had been elected in 1887; he was again a member from 1921 to 1923; in 1915 he resigned his chairmanship of the Arts Club. His extraordinarily frank memoirs also record his chief disappointments in life: in not being appointed surveyor to St. Paul's Cathedral, architect with (Sir) Edwin Lutyens [q.v.] for New Delhi, or president of the Royal Academy. His phenomenal vitality continued to the very end. A big and powerful man, he played most games well and some to a great age. He took up hunting when he was nearly forty and enlisted in the Inns of Court Volunteers in 1900 and again in the war of 1914–18. He was a genial figure in the billiard-room of the Athenaeum up to the last.

Blomfield was elected A.R.A. in 1905 and R.A. in 1914; he was professor of architecture at the Royal Academy from 1906 to 1910; he was elected honorary fellow of Exeter College, Oxford, in 1906, received the honorary degree of Litt.D. from Liverpool University in 1920, and was knighted in 1919. He was also awarded several foreign decorations.

He married in 1886 Frances, daughter of Henry Burra, Indian civil servant, and had two sons, one of whom became an architect, and one daughter. In 1896 he built a pair of houses in Frognal, Hampstead, and lived in one of them until his death 27 December 1942. He also acquired and subsequently extended a cottage at Point Hill, Rye, as a country retreat.

Blomfield's portrait by Sir J. J. Shannon hangs in the building of the Royal Institute of British Architects, 66 Portland Place, London. A bronze bust by (Sir) W. Reid Dick (1927) is in the National Portrait Gallery.

[Sir R. T. Blomfield, *Memoirs of an Architect*, 1932; C. H. Reilly, *Representative British Architects of the Present Day*, 1931; *The Times* and *Manchester Guardian*, 29 December 1942; *Journal* of the Royal Institute of British Architects, January and February (list of works) 1943; *Builder*, 8 January 1943; personal knowledge.]      MARTIN S. BRIGGS.

BLUMENFELD, RALPH DAVID (1864–1948), editor, known in the journalism of his generation as 'R. D. B.', was born 7 April 1864 at Watertown, Wisconsin, in the United States, the fourth son of David Blumenfeld, a former professor of literature and history at Nuremberg who had emigrated to the States with the revolutionaries of 1848 and in Watertown founded *Der Weltbürger*, one of the first German-language newspapers in the midwestern states. His mother, Nancy Levensen, born in the province of Schleswig-Holstein when it belonged to Denmark, was a woman of fine intelligence and ruthless determination, in marriage the mainspring of a family of five sons and two daughters.

A chance remark overheard in his home, that an editor was more powerful than kings or politicians, made Blumenfeld determined to be an editor before he was old enough even to understand what the word meant. That ambition never died. His cultured father guided him very early in wise and wide reading. As a printer's devil he had a sound grounding in the craft of printing in his father's shop. To that he added training as a telegraphist, and moved eastward to New York determined to join the *New York Herald*, then a newspaper of great vigour. His repeated applications were rejected and from 1885 he worked for the United Press who sent him to London in 1887 to report Queen Victoria's jubilee. Shortly after his return, while walking in a New York suburb, he came upon an exciting fire, wrote a dramatic 2,000-word description, and sold it to the *Morning Journal*, then owned by Albert Pulitzer, brother of the more famous Joseph, for ten dollars and an engagement as reporter at thirty dollars a week.

By chance, on the day it was published, James Gordon Bennett the younger, owner of the *Herald*, arrived in New York on one of his infrequent visits. After reading Blumenfeld's account of the fire he gave instructions that he was to be taken on the *Herald* staff. So began an association which was the most powerful influence in shaping Blumenfeld's career in journalism. He achieved some distinction as a special correspondent, edited, for a time, Bennett's *Evening Telegram*, became head of the *Herald* office in London (1890), and eventually, in 1893, superintendent of the *Herald* in New York and one of Bennett's closest associates. In 1894 there was a rift in their relationship and Blumenfeld resigned. He returned to England and for several years went into business selling linotype machines. Although not unsuccessful, he missed the creative satisfaction he had found in journalism.

One day in 1900 on a chance meeting in a barber's shop in Fleet Street, Alfred Harmsworth (later Viscount Northcliffe, q.v.) offered him, and he accepted, the news editorship of the *Daily Mail*, then only four years old, but firmly established in the leadership of the new popular journalism. Blumenfeld found that life in the Harmsworth empire had its disadvantages and two years later he became foreign editor of the *Daily Express*, newly founded by (Sir) C. Arthur Pearson [q.v.] to challenge the *Daily Mail*. In 1904 he became its editor, a position he held with distinction for twenty-eight years, holding the title of editor-in-chief from 1924. In those fruitful years he saw the departure of Pearson due to blindness and the rise of the *Daily Express* to the leadership in popular journalism under Lord Beaverbrook who, having acquired financial control in January 1917, began to take a close personal interest in the paper as the war drew to a close in the following year.

Blumenfeld, who became a British subject in 1907, retired in 1932, and in the following year published *The Press in My Time*, recording the great changes which had taken place in journalism since he entered Fleet Street. After a sudden and physically incapacitating illness in January 1936, his activities were curtailed, but he remained, from its formation in 1915 until his death, the chairman of the London Express Newspaper Company which in time owned also the *Sunday Express*, the London *Evening Standard*, and the Glasgow *Evening Citizen*. He was president of the Institute of Journalists in 1928 and founded the Company of Newspaper Makers, which merged with the ancient Stationers' Company in 1933. In the following year, when the Prince of Wales became the first master of the combined companies, Blumenfeld was chosen as deputy master.

Blumenfeld had a considerable influence in shaping the popular journalism born in his generation. In the front-page presentation of news he outstripped all his competitors. Indeed, more than any other man, he forced front-page news upon British journalism. He was a great reporter, and kept his newspaper alive through most difficult years, and in the face of most intense competition, by the urgency and enterprise of its news gathering. He could display news with a vividness and drama which matched the zest with which he gathered it. But a curiously persistent predilection for punning in headlines, probably an expression of his natural facetiousness, was a weakness he never overcame. Nor had he the same sure touch in feature articles as he had in news. He realized better than most of his contemporaries the value of the sports pages to a popular newspaper and continually stimulated and improved them although he never had a personal interest in any sport except game-shooting at which he was first class.

As an editor he had political flair and understanding. Indeed, as the years passed, politics absorbed him more and more. He declined a knighthood offered by a Conservative Government for political services in support of tariff reform, and, at his request, was elected instead to membership of the Carlton Club. It was an honour he valued highly but it was not wholly beneficial to him because in later years he tended at times to permit fellow members of the club to influence his own more sure and experienced judgement of news.

In 1892 Blumenfeld married his second cousin, Daisie (died 1957), daughter of Louis Blumfeld, of Hampstead. They had two sons (one of whom, Sir John Elliot, chairman of London Transport Executive, contributes to this SUPPLEMENT) and two daughters. Blumenfeld died at Great Easton, Dunmow, Essex, 17 July 1948.

Among other works Blumenfeld wrote R. D. B.'s Diary (1930), All in a Lifetime (1931), in which is his account of the coronation of King George V, probably his finest piece of descriptive reporting, R. D. B.'s Procession (1935), and in 1944 his autobiographical Home Town.

A portrait of Blumenfeld painted by Neville Lewis and presented to him in his fortieth year in Fleet Street is in the possession of the family. Another by Patrick Larking, painted from photographs, is in the board-room of Beaverbrook Newspapers, Ltd. A third, by Mrs. Faith K. Sage, is in the possession of the Stationers' and Newspaper Makers' Company.

[R. D. Blumenfeld, Home Town, 1944; private information; personal knowledge.]

JOHN GORDON.

BONAR, JAMES (1852–1941), political economist, was born in the manse at Collace, near Perth, 27 September 1852, the elder son and second of the six children of the Rev. Andrew Alexander Bonar [q.v.] (after whom Andrew Bonar Law was named), and his wife, Isabella, younger daughter of James Dickson, wholesale stationer, of Edinburgh. Horatius Bonar [q.v.], the hymnologist, was his uncle. His father becoming minister of Finnieston in 1856, James Bonar was educated at Glasgow Academy, the universities of Glasgow (M.A., with first class honours in classics and mental philosophy, 1874), Leipzig, and Tübingen, then with a Snell exhibition at Balliol College, Oxford. He was placed in the second class in classical honour moderations (1875) and in the first class in literae humaniores (1877). Influenced by Arnold Toynbee and by Alfred (later Viscount) Milner, his Balliol contemporary, Bonar was for three years (1877–80) a pioneer as university extension lecturer in political economy in east London where he founded an Adam Smith club mainly from his old pupils. After a year as a private tutor in Oxford, he was appointed in 1881 a junior examiner in the Civil Service Commission and promoted a senior examiner in 1895. In 1885 he formed a bookbinders' co-operative society in Bloomsbury, an early experiment in profit-sharing which continued until within a few years of his death. At the instance of his friend Henry Higgs, at that time a private secretary to the prime minister (Campbell-Bannerman), Bonar left the Civil Service Commission in 1907 to become deputy master of the Ottawa branch of the Royal Mint, a post from which he retired on pension after the war to 13 Redington Road, Hampstead, where he lived from 1919 until he died there in his sleep 18 January 1941.

Bonar's earliest book in the field of political economy (he had published a translation of Beck's Biblical Psychology in 1877) was his sketch of Parson Malthus

(1881), followed four years later by the fuller study of *Malthus and His Work* (2nd ed. 1924) which soon resulted in his becoming recognized as the unrivalled expert on Malthus. In 1887 came his edition of Ricardo's letters to Malthus. 'That definitive biography of Malthus, for which', said J. M. (later Lord) Keynes [q.v.] in his own essay on Malthus (*Essays in Biography*, 1933), 'we have long waited vainly from the pen of Dr. Bonar', remains, however, in manuscript, unpublished. In 1893 Bonar produced his *Philosophy and Political Economy* (3rd ed. 1922), and in the year following there appeared his scholarly *Catalogue of the Library of Adam Smith* (2nd ed. 1932), the first of those contributions which were to make him a leading authority on Adam Smith. Even Professor William Robert Scott (1868–1940), who was to add so greatly to our knowledge of Adam Smith, would, in doubt, refer to Bonar who had *The Wealth of Nations*, it seemed, by heart.

Besides producing, if we include two translations, thirteen books (three of which were substantially enlarged for their second editions) between 1877 and 1931, this wise and kindly Scotsman contributed over eighty learned articles and reviews to the *Economic Journal* and, in addition to his editorial help, no fewer than seventy articles to Palgrave's *Dictionary of Political Economy* (3 vols., 1894–9) of which, in addition to those on Malthus and Adam Smith, that on the Austrian school of political economy (about which he had written a remarkable paper in the *Quarterly Journal of Economics* in October 1888) was particularly noteworthy. One of his own favourite papers was his 'Economics of John Stuart Mill' in the *Journal of Political Economy* (November 1911).

Bonar was a useful public servant and a careful and erudite scholar with a prodigious memory, friendships well tended as they were wide, and austere yet boyish enthusiasms, who delighted in fencing, skating, and ski-ing in his youth, mountains and music all his life (he took up the 'cello at fifty), as well as in books and his fellow men. His club was the Savile. For more than thirty years Bonar was a widower; otherwise time dealt with him lightly and he retained his vigour and perceptiveness almost to the end of his days. It was his habit to go walking in Hampstead with F. Y. Edgeworth [q.v.] until his great friend died in 1926; and,

while his fellow Scot was living there, often with James Ramsay MacDonald. Before the end of his remarkably long career of 'eminent usefulness', Bonar, who was born in the same year as John Neville (the father of John Maynard) Keynes, had come to be regarded as the doyen of British political economists. And 'to the end', as he himself said of Edgeworth, 'his early heroes remained on their pedestals'.

On the recommendation of his revered teacher Edward Caird [q.v.], Bonar received the honorary degree of LL.D. from the university of Glasgow (1887) at the singular age of thirty-four; and that of Litt.D. from the university of Cambridge (1935) in connexion with the centenary celebrations of Malthus, a Cambridge man. Bonar, who was president of the economics section of the British Association in 1898, was one of the founders and subsequently, from 1930, a vice-president of the Royal Economic Society, a vice-president of the Royal Statistical Society (from 1920, as frequently as the rules permitted) and an honorary member of the Political Economy Club. In 1929 he delivered the Newmarch lectures in the Galtonian Laboratory, university of London, which were published, with additions (1931), as *Theories of Population from Raleigh to Arthur Young*. He was elected F.B.A. in 1930 and a foreign member of the Accademia dei Lincei in 1932.

In 1883 he married Mary Mewburn (died 1908), daughter of the late George Spurstow Miller, a Liverpool shipbroker, by his wife, Caroline, daughter of Francis Mewburn, solicitor to the Stockton and Darlington Railway and to George Stephenson [q.v.]. There were four children of the marriage, one son dying in infancy; a son and two daughters survived their father. Bonar's library is now in the university of Glasgow.

[*The Times*, 20, 23 January, and 4 February 1941; *Diary and Letters of Andrew A. Bonar*, edited by Marjory Bonar, 1894; *Balliol College Register, 1833–1933*, 1934; *Economic Journal*, December 1926 and April 1941; G. Findlay Shirras in *Proceedings of the British Academy*, vol. xxvii, 1941, a notice from which this entry is, for the main part, derived and which includes a photograph of Bonar and a list of his principal writings.]     E. T. WILLIAMS.

BOND, SIR (CHARLES) HUBERT (1870–1945), psychiatrist and administrator, was born at Ogbourne St. George, Wiltshire, 6 September 1870, the elder son of the Rev. Alfred Bond, who became chaplain to the Worcester County Asylum, and his wife, Frances Elizabeth, daughter of Charles Smallridge, clerk of peace for Gloucester. Bond's younger brother, Sir Reginald Bond (1872–1955), became medical director-general of the Royal Navy. At Edinburgh University Bond graduated M.B. in 1892 and B.Sc. in public health in 1893. He then entered on his long psychiatric career by taking a junior appointment at Morningside Asylum (Royal Edinburgh Mental Hospital) of which (Sir) Thomas Clouston was the outstanding head. Subsequent posts at Wakefield, Banstead, and Bexley led to his appointment as first medical superintendent of Ewell Colony for Epileptics in 1903; after four years he became medical superintendent of a new London County Council mental hospital at Long Grove. During the next five years he established a reputation as an administrator and gathered round him a group of able young men who were to become leaders of this branch of medicine in the period between the two world wars.

In 1912 Bond was appointed a commissioner in lunacy, and in due course he became senior commissioner of the Board of Control. The duties of this post were exactly suited to his temperament and gifts. He enjoyed the periodic visits to mental hospitals, where his clinical interests, his regard for young men beginning their lives in the specialty, and his humane concern for the patients' wellbeing could all find satisfaction. He did his best to raise the level of medical work in these institutions, and was eager to keep psychological medicine closely linked with other branches of medicine. This led to his giving more support than it merited to the belief that much mental illness was due to focal sepsis and should be treated accordingly.

Bond had far-sighted views about the future of mental hospitals and the legislation needed to give them their due place in the health services of the community. These views he expressed in the lengthy address which he delivered to the Royal Medico-Psychological Association in 1921. Like an earlier commissioner, Samuel Gaskell, he pressed for the voluntary admission of mentally ill patients rather than their certification, as the means of obtaining treatment in a mental hospital. It was not, however, until 1930 that the Mental Treatment Act made this advance possible. In the meantime Bond had had a painful ordeal. A patient whom he had interviewed sued him and another doctor in 1924 for wrongful detention. The jury found for the plaintiff and awarded the very heavy damages of £25,000. The Court of Appeal (later confirmed by the House of Lords) set the verdict aside and ordered a retrial, but this did not take place as the plaintiff accepted £250 paid into court. Bond's undeserved misfortune no doubt had a considerable effect in bringing about the changes in the law which were recommended by the Royal Commission on lunacy in 1926 and embodied in the Act of 1930.

Bond did not contribute original observations to the literature of psychological medicine, but his early papers on the need for systematically collecting accurate data indicate a precise mind. He lectured for twenty years at the Maudsley Hospital to successive classes of young psychiatrists on the legal relationships of mental disorder. In both world wars he gave much help in turning mental hospitals over to meet military and other needs of the time. For many years he was consultant in neurology and mental disorders to the Royal Navy. Although of slight build, Bond was of distinguished appearance and had a somewhat foreign air, largely due to his Vandyke beard. He was appointed C.B.E. in 1920 and advanced to K.B.E. in 1929. He died 18 April 1945 at St. Anne's-on-Sea, less than a month after retiring from his post at the Board of Control. He married in 1900 Janet Constance, daughter of Frederic Robert Laurie, of Worcester, and had one daughter.

[*Lancet*, 5 May 1945; personal knowledge.]

AUBREY LEWIS.

BOTTOMLEY, GORDON (1874–1948), poet and dramatist, was born at Keighley, Yorkshire, 20 February 1874, son of Alfred Bottomley, a cashier at a worsted mill, by his wife, Ann Maria Gordon. Educated at Keighley Grammar School, he became a bank clerk, but was forced by poor health to give up his occupation and live in seclusion at Silverdale, near Carnforth. Of momentous happenings, apart from his literary experiments and some travels, Bottomley's life was uncommonly free. He devoted his hours to the humanities, and even when his name was widely known he remained something of a recluse. Among his distinctions were the Femina Vie Heureuse prize (Paris) in 1923 for the play *Gruach*, and three honorary degrees: LL.D., Aberdeen, 1930; D.Litt., Durham, 1940; and Litt.D., Leeds, 1944.

Bottomley's writings, not all published

when he died, were profuse. 'I have published', he wrote in 1937, 'twenty-three dramatic pieces in verse since 1902.' He had appeared as a poet six years earlier in 1896 with *The Mickle Drede*, published at Kendal. Considered as an elegiac or epic-minded poet, he was most fittingly recognized by his inclusion in the first series of *Georgian Poetry* (1912). The selection was made from his *Chambers of Imagery* (1907, 1912), and the subjects, 'The End of the World' and 'Babel: The Gate of The God', attest the sublimity of his imaginative intention. In 1925 Bottomley gathered his representative choice of his *Poems of Thirty Years*, which made it again apparent that he was in many ways following where Landor had moved in *Gebir* and Shelley in *Alastor*, though he made discoveries of his own in pictorial, rhythmical, and reflective felicity.

The theatre, however, attracted him more strongly than the book; he was one of several poets, from Stephen Phillips to Laurence Binyon [qq.v.], who contended for the revival of a new romantic drama wherein poetry should once more dominate. At first he believed that the Elizabethan kind of play, varied by the new age and the new writer, might capture the general audience; later he was more concerned with finding a special platform for the recital of dramatic poems, and this he described in *A Stage for Poetry* (1948). Among his earlier productions *King Lear's Wife* (1915) and *Gruach* (1921) were nearest to drama. That the author was insufficiently versed in the problems of the theatre was speedily seen, but that he was not essaying Shakespearian levels of heroic theme without strength of imagination and eloquence was also agreed. The best verdict on Bottomley's aspiring poetic plays was that had he been trained as a playwright he might even have been a modern equivalent of John Fletcher.

In personal life Bottomley was liked and admired. He maintained the standards and culture which he knew historically and aesthetically with a generous courtesy. He believed in rural tradition, community, and craftsmanship. His influence on the minority who are sensitive to the power of poetry and especially of poetry heard communally was due to his gift of friendship and direct encouragement as well as his writings.

Bottomley married in 1905 Emily, daughter of Matthew Burton, of Arnside, who fully shared his tastes and whose death in 1947 was an event which he could

not long survive. He died at Oare, near Marlborough, 25 August 1948.

A drawing by (Sir) William Rothenstein was reproduced in *Twenty-Four Portraits* (2nd series, 1923). Two drawings by Paul Nash [q.v.] are reproduced in *Poet and Painter* (1955), the correspondence between Bottomley and Nash; the originals are in the Carlisle Art Gallery.

[*The Times*, 27 August 1948; Gordon Bottomley's writings; private information.]
                    EDMUND BLUNDEN.

BOURDILLON, SIR BERNARD HENRY (1883–1948), colonial governor, was born at Emu Bay, Tasmania, 3 December 1883, the eldest son of the Rev. Bernard Keene Bourdillon, at that time incumbent of the Emu Bay parsonage. His mother was Laura Elizabeth, daughter of Richard Townsend, of county Cork.

Bourdillon was brought to England when he was two years old and then taken for another two years to South Africa; he returned to England while still very young, after his father's death. He won a scholarship to Tonbridge School and another to St. John's College, Oxford, where he was placed in the second class of the honours list in *literae humaniores* in 1906.

He passed into the Indian Civil Service by competitive examination in 1908, and in 1913 was appointed under-secretary to the Government of the United Provinces. In 1915 he became registrar of the High Court of Allahabad. In 1917 he joined the army as a temporary second lieutenant and went to Iraq the following year, rising to the rank of major in 1919. He was mentioned in dispatches for his services during the Iraq rebellion.

At the end of his military service Bourdillon was seconded to the civil administration of Iraq and became political secretary to the high commissioner in 1921, and was counsellor from 1924 to 1929. In 1925–6 he acted as high commissioner with plenipotentiary powers for the negotiations which led to the Anglo-Iraq treaty of 1926.

In 1929 Bourdillon was transferred to the Colonial Civil Service as colonial secretary of Ceylon where he served until 1932, twice acting as governor of the colony. In 1932 he was appointed governor and commander-in-chief of the protectorate of Uganda, and in 1935 he became governor and commander-in-chief of Nigeria. In 1939 he was selected for the post of governor-general of the Anglo-Egyptian

Sudan, but the outbreak of war made a change inexpedient and he remained in Nigeria until his retirement on medical advice in 1943.

In India Bourdillon made a name for himself as a linguist, and his knowledge of the vernacular was of great value in his work. In Uganda he did much to develop the trade and economy of the protectorate. His best work in Nigeria was the encouragement of education, and in this territory he became extremely popular with the inhabitants, a fact which was made obvious by the universal expressions of regret at his departure. Bourdillon was the principal architect of the West African Governors' Conference which at the outbreak of hostilities in 1939 did good service in co-ordinating the war effort of the four West African territories. When France collapsed in 1940 Bourdillon worked untiringly, and in some cases with marked success, to win over the neighbouring French colonies to the cause of the Allies.

After he retired, Bourdillon maintained his interest in the welfare of the colonies and was a member of the Colonial Economic and Development Council. His book, *The Future of the Colonial Empire*, was published in 1945. During his term of office in Nigeria he had initiated a government service to take over and extend much of the anti-leprosy work which had previously been undertaken entirely by missionary societies, and after his retirement he became treasurer, and later chairman, of the British Empire Leprosy Relief Association to which he devoted much of his time. He also became a director of Barclays Bank (Dominion, Colonial and Overseas), and of Barclays Overseas Development Corporation.

Bourdillon was a fine horseman and a keen polo player. Late in life he took a great interest in bird-watching, and at his death he was a member of the council of the Zoological Society. His administrative ability and wise advice were invaluable to this and to those other organizations to which he gave his services.

He was appointed C.M.G. in 1924, K.B.E. in 1931, K.C.M.G. in 1934, and G.C.M.G. in 1937. He became a knight of grace of the Order of St. John of Jerusalem in 1933. In 1943 Bourdillon was elected an honorary fellow of St. John's College, Oxford.

He married in 1909 Violet Grace, daughter of the Rev. Henry Godwin Billinghurst, of Lynch, Sussex, by whom he had three sons, one of whom was killed in 1946 when the King David hotel in Jerusalem was blown up. Bourdillon died at St. Helier, Jersey, 6 February 1948.

[Official publications; *The Times*, 7 February 1948; private information; personal knowledge.]  ALAN BURNS.

BOWER, FREDERICK ORPEN (1855–1948), botanist, was born at Ripon 4 November 1855. His father, Abraham Bower, came of an old Yorkshire family of wool-staplers and clothiers. His mother was Cornelia Morris, sister of the naturalist Francis Orpen Morris [q.v.]. Bower was the youngest of the family and was educated at Repton where, by individual study, he laid the foundation of a knowledge of botany and decided that it should be his work in life. He went to Trinity College, Cambridge, where he graduated with first class honours in the natural sciences tripos in 1877. At first he found nothing of the training he expected, but later S. H. Vines [q.v.] became lecturer at Christ's College and introduced instruction in modern botany. At Würzburg in 1877 Bower had the great experience of learning laboratory methods from Julius Sachs. In 1879 he went to Strasbourg for a year and carried out his first investigations under Heinrich Anton de Bary. Returning to England he settled in London for five fruitful years, in 1882 becoming lecturer in botany in the department of T. H. Huxley [q.v.] at South Kensington. Much of his time was free for research in the Jodrell Laboratory at Kew.

He had decided that London was his best scientific environment. In 1885, however, he was virtually directed by Sir Joseph Hooker [q.v.] and other senior botanists to accept the regius chair of botany in the university of Glasgow. He occupied this for forty years, during which time he built up a well-equipped department, housed in the first botanical institute to be erected in Great Britain. Bower was an all-round botanist, a good organizer, an inspiring teacher in lecture-room, laboratory, and in the field, and a wonderful departmental chief to a succession of young botanists. Above all, he was devoted to original work in morphological botany, in which his department had a world-wide reputation.

Only the main lines of Bower's scientific production in numerous memoirs, addresses, and books may be indicated here. At first he dealt with a variety of plants and problems, but from 1890 he came to concentrate on the evolutionary morphology of the Pteridophyta. Three great books mark phases in his attack on this problem. In *The Origin of a Land Flora, a theory based upon the facts of alternation* (1908), the early stages of the evolution of the sporophyte, because of ignorance at that time of primitive fossils, had to be dealt with by working hypotheses. The valuable accounts of all the groups of Pteridophyta were full of newly ascertained facts. There followed during the next twenty years a comprehensive survey of the Filicales, resulting in *The Ferns (Filicales)* in three volumes (1923–8). This deliberately inductive work carried the classifications framed by the systematists to the higher level of critical evolutionary treatment. After his retirement from Glasgow in 1925, Bower's work continued at Ripon. *Primitive Land Plants, also known as the archegoniatae* (1935) summed up the position at which he had arrived for all the classes of Bryophyta and Pteridophyta. The changes which had come about in his views were partly due to his own investigations on existing plants, but also to the increase of knowledge of early and primitive fossil plants, unknown at the date of the *Land Flora*.

A digression into physiological morphology which greatly interested Bower in his later years was dealt with in *Size and Form in Plants* (1930). His last book, published in 1938, was *Sixty Years of Botany in Britain, 1875–1935*. It was autobiographical and gave an account of the introduction of the 'new botany' in which he had taken part. Although Bower's constructive work had reached its conclusion, the preparation of the fourth edition of *Botany of the Living Plant*, based (in 1919) on his elementary lectures, carried his botanical activity to the last years of his life.

Bower was elected F.R.S. in 1891 and received a Royal medal (1910) and the Darwin medal (1938). He was elected a fellow of the Royal Society of Edinburgh in 1886, was president, 1919–24, and was awarded the Neill prize in 1926. He was president of the British Association meeting at Bristol in 1930 and was thrice president of the botany section. He was an honorary member of many foreign societies, and he received the honorary degrees of D.Sc. from Dublin (1919), Sydney (1914), and Leeds (1927); and of LL.D. from Aberdeen (1919), Glasgow (1925), and Bristol (1930).

Bower had excellent health throughout his life, which with his energetic, sanguine temperament he enjoyed immensely. He was domesticated, and social, but unmarried. He played the 'cello and was devoted to chamber music, but his scientific work and writing was pursued as his greatest and most continuous pleasure; the clear and vivid style conveyed his personal interest to the reader. He made large additions of new facts, but his tendency was always to get farther by the critical use of his scientific imagination. He was recognized as the leading plant-morphologist through a long period of the development of modern botany.

He died at Ripon 11 April 1948 in his ninety-third year. A portrait by his cousin Sir William Orpen [q.v.] was presented to the university of Glasgow in 1927.

[W. H. Lang in *Obituary Notices of Fellows of the Royal Society*, No. 18, November 1949; personal knowledge.]     W. H. LANG.

BOWES-LYON, CLAUDE GEORGE, in the peerage of Scotland fourteenth and in the peerage of the United Kingdom first EARL OF STRATHMORE AND KINGHORNE (1855–1944), was born at Glamis 14 March 1855, the eldest son of Claude Bowes-Lyon, who succeeded his brother as thirteenth Earl of Strathmore and Kinghorne in 1865, by his wife, Frances Dora, daughter of Oswald Smith, of Blendon Hall, Kent. He succeeded his father as fourteenth earl, 16 February 1904, and thereby also became the twenty-second Lord Glamis in the peerage of Scotland, and in the peerage of the United Kingdom the second Baron Bowes, of Streatlam Castle, in the county of Durham, and Lunedale, in Yorkshire. He was educated at Eton and was given a commission in the 2nd Life Guards, which he resigned in 1882 after his marriage in the previous year to Nina Cecilia (G.C.V.O., died 23 June 1938), daughter of the Rev. Charles William Frederick Cavendish-Bentinck, grandson of the third Duke of Portland [q.v.]. Of his six sons the eldest, Patrick (1884–1949), succeeded to the title, the fourth, a captain in the Black Watch, was killed in action, 27 September 1915; and of his four daughters, the second, Mary Frances, married Sidney, sixteenth Baron Elphinstone, the third, Rose Constance, married William Spencer Leveson-Gower, afterwards fourth Earl Granville, and the youngest, Elizabeth Angela Marguerite, married, 26 April 1923, Prince Albert Frederick Arthur George, Duke of York, afterwards King George VI.

Lord Strathmore was decorated with the grand cross of the Royal Victorian Order in 1923, and subsequently he received from King George V the Order of the Thistle in 1928 and the Garter in 1935. In 1937 he was created Earl of Strathmore and Kinghorne in the peerage of the United Kingdom, and, in order to commemorate the fact that a daughter of the house of Strathmore had become Queen-Consort, King George VI, after consulting the Lord Lyon, granted to Lord Strathmore in 1938 the issue of a warrant to add the following royal augmentation to the arms of the earl and his successors in that title, viz. 'An inescutcheon *en surtout* azure, thereon a rose argent, barbed vert, seeded or, ensigned with an imperial crown proper, within a double tressure flory-counter-flory of the second, the latter to indicate the earl's double royal descent from King Robert II through his two daughters (1) Jean, who married Sir John Lyon, first of Glamis, and (2) Euphemia, Countess Palatine of Strathearn, daughter of David, Earl of Strathearn (son of the said King Robert) and her husband, whose daughter married her cousin Sir John Lyon, second of Glamis.'

Lord Strathmore was of a retiring disposition, but was a very popular landlord, taking a strong personal interest in the welfare of his tenantry, and in the management of his estates. On these there were many small-holdings, a form of tenancy which he encouraged, and he probably had more of these than any other proprietor in the district south and east of Aberdeenshire and Argyll. Interest in forestry led him to take an active part in the development of his plantations, especially of larch, and he was one of the first to rear larch from seed brought over by him from Norway. In 1904 he was appointed lord lieutenant of Angus in succession to his father, but he resigned in 1936; he was also president of the Territorial Association of the county. He died at Glamis 7 November 1944.

[Register of Arms, Lyon Office; personal knowledge.]                FRANCIS J. GRANT.

BOYS, SIR CHARLES VERNON (1855-1944), physicist, was born at Wing, Rutlandshire, 15 March 1855, the eighth child of the rector, the Rev. Charles Boys, by his wife, Caroline Goodrich Dobbie. His paternal grandmother was a sister of B. L. Vulliamy and Lewis Vulliamy [qq.v.]. He was educated at Marlborough, where he owed much to G. F. Rodwell, the first science master to be appointed at the school. From Marlborough he went to the Royal School of Mines where he was taught physics by Frederick Guthrie and chemistry by (Sir) Edward Frankland [qq.v.], but he appears to have been entirely self-taught in mathematics. It was while at the Royal School that he showed his remarkable inventiveness in mechanics by designing and constructing an integrating machine, presumably that described in the *Philosophical Magazine* of May 1881. He graduated in mining and metallurgy, and after a short time in a colliery was brought back by Guthrie who later, in 1881, appointed him demonstrator in physics. He became an assistant professor but left in 1897 to take up an appointment as one of the metropolitan gas referees, a body which ultimately operated for the whole country.

Boys was an experimenter and above all an inventor of instruments. His most important contribution to experimental technique was his invention of the fused quartz fibre suspension for galvanometers and other delicate instruments in which the forces on the moving system are measured by the twisting of a fibre from which it is suspended. Seeking a more sensitive and more reliable material than the unspun silk fibres then in use, he discovered that quartz could be fused into a glass and drawn into very fine filaments, the elastic properties of which were ideal for his purpose. They were stronger than steel wires of the same thickness and after being twisted and released they took no permanent set. He devised a machine by which the filaments could be drawn far thinner than any wire. One end of a quartz rod was attached to an arrow which could be shot across the room by a cross-bow. By firing the cross-bow after fusing the quartz in an oxy-hydrogen flame, he could produce long uniform filaments as thin as a hundred-thousandth of an inch.

The first instrument to which he applied this invention was the radiomicrometer, a combined thermocouple and galvanometer for the detection of the radiation emitted by a hot body. The idea of the instrument had occurred independently to others, but Boys brought it to perfection. Using his quartz-fibre suspension he built an instrument capable of detecting the light of a candle at a distance of nearly two miles. Between 1888 and 1890 he made several attempts to measure the heat radiated by stars, working in the garden of his father's rectory at Wing.

Although his apparatus was far more sensitive than that of earlier workers who had claimed success he was unable to detect the radiation of any of the fixed stars, and he concluded correctly that the earlier results were spurious.

He next turned to the experiment which was to prove his masterpiece, a precise determination of the Newtonian constant of gravitation. Henry Cavendish [q.v.], a century earlier, had determined the constant by measuring the gravitational attraction of two large lead spheres upon two smaller spheres attached to the ends of a beam suspended by a fine copper wire. In a remarkable analysis of the experiment, characteristically blending theoretical and practical considerations, Boys showed that the dimensions of the whole apparatus could be reduced without impairing the sensitivity of the measurement, provided that at the same time the suspension was refined so as to leave the time of swing of the beam unaltered. By using his quartz-fibre technique he could make the apparatus as small as he pleased, and could then increase the effect to be observed by making the attracting masses much larger in proportion to the rest of the apparatus. Cavendish had used a beam approximately 6 feet long. Boys decided to use a beam of just under 0·9 inches. It was a bold decision, calling for the highest precision in the construction of the apparatus and technical skill in carrying out the measurements, which occupied him for several years. As the tiny apparatus was affected by earth tremors due to the traffic in London, he made the final observations in a cellar of the Clarendon Laboratory in Oxford, working at nights during the week-ends, when the shunting at the railway station a mile away had ceased. His account of the experiment, which remained for many years the standard determination of the Newtonian constant, was published in 1895 in the *Philosophical Transactions* of the Royal Society, vol. clxxxvi A.

As a gas referee he devoted many years to the design and improvement of an automatic recording calorimeter to measure the calorific value of gas, so that its price might be related to its thermal value and not merely to its volume. His appointment left him considerable leisure in which he built up an extensive practice as an expert witness in patent cases. The stream of his inventions continued until he retired in 1939. Two have proved of lasting importance: the process which he devised in 1892 for the photography of a bullet in flight, and his rotating lens camera for the study of the formation of lightning discharges, invented in 1900.

Boys, who was elected F.R.S. in 1888, was awarded a Royal medal in 1896 and the Rumford medal in 1924. He received the Duddell medal of the Physical Society (1925) and the Elliott Cresson medal of the Franklin Institute, Philadelphia (1939). He was an honorary member of the New York Academy of Sciences and of the Physical Society of Moscow. He received the honorary degree of LL.D. from Edinburgh University (1932) and was elected fellow of the Imperial College of Science and Technology in the first list of elections. He was president of the Physical Society (1916–17), of the Röntgen Society (1906–7), and of the mathematics and physics section of the British Association in 1903. In 1935 he was knighted.

In 1892 Boys married Marion Amelia, daughter of Henry Pollock, master of the Supreme Court of Justice. He divorced her in 1910 and she subsequently married A. R. Forsyth [q.v.]. Boys had one daughter and one son, Geoffrey Vernon Boys, who became secretary of the Institution of Naval Architects and died in 1945. Boys died 30 March 1944 at St. Mary Bourne, Andover, Hampshire.

[Lord Rayleigh in *Obituary Notices of Fellows of the Royal Society*, No. 13, November 1944; *Proceedings* of the Physical Society, vol. lvi, part 6, November 1944; private information.]     A. H. COOKE.

BRACKLEY, HERBERT GEORGE (1894–1948) air transport pioneer, was born in Islington 4 October 1894, the second of the seven children of George Herbert Brackley, a master tailor, and his wife, Lilian Sarah Partridge. The family later removed to Kent and Brackley was educated at Sevenoaks School. In 1912 he entered the employ of Reuters and in 1915 was commissioned in the Royal Naval Air Service and learned to fly at Eastchurch. From that time his life was devoted to flying and particularly to the development of commercial air transport, although he gave distinguished service as an officer in the two wars. The war of 1914–18 introduced him to the big bomber, and for nearly two years he commanded one of the first bomber squadrons to be based in France, taking part in seventy raids. He was appointed to the D.S.O. in 1917 and awarded the D.S.C. After the war ended he was sent to Newfoundland as pilot of the four-engine Handley Page bomber, which had taken no part in the war, to attempt to make the first direct crossing of the Atlantic. Hawker and Grieve got away ahead of him, only to come down in the ocean. Then (Sir) John Alcock and (Sir) Arthur Whitten Brown [qq.v.] also took off before he was ready and were successful. Brackley therefore turned his great aircraft in the other direction and made the first flight from Newfoundland to New York and followed this with a number of pioneer flights in the United States. In 1920 he became chief pilot of the Handley Page Transport Company which was starting air services between London and Paris. In 1921 he accepted an invitation to join the British air mission to Japan which undertook the organization and training of the Japanese naval air service. Early in 1924, when the principal air transport companies were amalgamated to form Imperial Airways, Brackley was appointed superintendent in charge of operations, training, and route development.

Brackley's especial merit, throughout his career, lay in his aptitude for putting big aircraft into service, for arranging the details of their regular operation, and for selecting and preparing bases for their service along new routes. During his fifteen years with Imperial Airways he had a big share in expanding the work of that company, surveying new routes, trying new aircraft, recommending improvements, and setting a standard for the company's air crews which led to a measure of prosperity and established a high tradition in British air transport. When flying-boats were adopted by Imperial Airways for all long-distance services in 1935, he surveyed the whole route between England and Australia and advised flying overland for great distances in Europe, Iraq, and India. That policy, based on his faith in the four-engine Empire flying-boat, was adopted and was fully justified in several years of operation.

When war broke out in 1939, Brackley returned to the Royal Air Force. His wide experience of flying-boats and transport operations was applied first in senior staff posts in Coastal Command and afterwards in the position of senior air staff officer in Transport Command which dealt with paratroops and their gliders, as well as the delivery of supplies to army and Air Force units in the field. He was appointed C.B.E. in 1941 and promoted air commo-

dore in March 1943. While the war was in progress Imperial Airways was taken over by the British Overseas Airways Corporation and Brackley returned at the end of the war to this new government body to be appointed special assistant to the chairman. Among his other duties it was he who arranged the evacuation of 35,000 persons between India and Pakistan during the troubles of 1947. In the following year he became chief executive of the British South American Airways Corporation. He was drowned 15 November 1948 while swimming at Rio de Janeiro during a break in a journey through South America which he had undertaken on behalf of the Corporation with the object of improving the organization of British air services in that area. Soon after his death the Corporation was merged with the British Overseas Airways Corporation.

Brackley married in 1922 Frida Helene, elder daughter of (Sir) Robert Mond [q.v.]; they had two sons and one daughter.

[*The Times*, 16 and 20 November 1948; F. H. Brackley, *Brackles*, 1952; private information; personal knowledge.]

E. COLSTON SHEPHERD.

BRADBURY, JOHN SWANWICK, first BARON BRADBURY (1872–1950), civil servant, was born at Winsford, Cheshire, 23 September 1872, the only surviving son of John Bradbury, oil merchant, and his wife, Sarah, daughter of William Cross, of Winsford. He was educated at Manchester Grammar School and at Brasenose College, Oxford, where he was a scholar and was placed in the first class in *literae humaniores* (1895) and in modern history (1896). In this year he entered the Civil Service where he was to play a great part in its evolution into the new kind of service embracing the great diversity of functions which twentieth-century democracy demands.

After a short time in the Colonial Office he was transferred to the Treasury. His selection at the end of 1905 to be private secretary to Asquith, the chancellor of the Exchequer in the newly appointed Liberal Government, marked him out for advancement, and when Lloyd George succeeded Asquith in April 1908, Bradbury became head (or as it was then principal clerk) of one of the six divisions by which the work of the Treasury was carried on. In that capacity he took a responsible part in the preparation of Lloyd George's famous budget of 1909. He had not long emerged from the strenuous work which this involved, when he became deeply engaged in Lloyd George's health-insurance project. He had to plan the financial fabric of this vast scheme and when the measure became law the Treasury had also to take the initiative in building up a new administrative machine since none existed. The Civil Service was combed for men of ability and energy to man the new department, and Bradbury himself became an insurance commissioner (1911), without relinquishing his post at the Treasury.

In 1913, when Sir Robert (later Lord) Chalmers [q.v.] resigned the permanent secretaryship of the Treasury, it was decided to appoint two joint permanent secretaries, and the choice fell on Bradbury, who had charge of the purely financial functions, in collaboration with Sir Thomas Heath [q.v.] who attended to the administrative side. They were later rejoined by Chalmers.

In the acute crisis which attended the outbreak of war in 1914, Bradbury saw at once that what was needed to keep the financial machine working was an issue of paper money of conveniently small denomination in place of gold. By a combination of sure and prompt decision and ingenious improvisation he was able to provide a new issue of currency notes which actually reached the banks within a week. The notes, which bore a facsimile of his signature, were for long known as 'Bradburys' and made his name familiar in every home.

Throughout the war Bradbury remained the Government's chief financial adviser, rendering services to his country too numerous to mention. It should, however, be recorded that to him more than to anyone is due the credit for devising in the war savings certificate a type of security which has gained a permanent footing in the structure of government finance.

The Treaty of Versailles brought Bradbury a new sphere of work. He left the Treasury in 1919 to become principal British delegate to the Reparation Commission. The five years which followed gave only too ample scope for his gifts of tact, clear judgement, and humour. Whilst the Dawes committee was preparing its report which put an end to illusions never shared by Bradbury he was 'indefatigable behind the scenes with ideas and formulae'. He was raised to the peerage in January 1925 as Baron Bradbury, of Winsford, and retired shortly afterwards. He had been appointed C.B. in 1909, promoted K.C.B. in 1913 and G.C.B. in 1920. He was an

honorary fellow of Brasenose (1926) and an honorary LL.D. of Cambridge and Manchester (1925).

From 1925 to 1929 Bradbury was chairman of the Food Council and he was also for a time a government-appointed director of the Anglo-Persian Oil Company. His financial abilities were much sought after and a variety of business appointments also occupied his time. He was a member of the Treasury (Macmillan) committee on finance and industry (1929–31), but dissented from its report. He was an orthodox economist who had strongly recommended the return to the gold standard in 1925 and who considered the country's financial plight in 1931 to be due to the maintenance of an unjustifiably high standard of living. His dissenting memorandum suggested that 'the best contribution which the State can make to assist industry and promote employment is strict economy in public expenditure and lightening the burden of debt by prudent financial administration'.

Bradbury was tall, but with a slight stoop, his face pale and rather deeply lined, with a jowl, not actually prominent, but indicative of a bull-dog tenacity. Tenacity founded on clear thinking, combined with a lively sense of humour, a wide tolerance, and a capacity for witty comment, went far to account for the important achievements which marked his public career.

In 1911 Bradbury married Hilda Maude (died 1949), daughter of William Arthur Kirby, chartered accountant, of Hampstead. They had one daughter and two sons, the elder of whom, John (born 1914), succeeded him as second baron when he died in London 3 May 1950. A portrait of Bradbury by A. E. Orr is in the possession of the family.

[Sir James Grigg, *Prejudice and Judgment*, 1948 ; personal knowledge.]

R. G. HAWTREY.

BRAGG, SIR WILLIAM HENRY (1862–1942), physicist, was born at Westward, near Wigton, in Cumberland, 2 July 1862, the eldest of the three sons of Robert John Bragg, who after serving as a young officer in the Merchant Navy had set up as a farmer at Stoneraise Place, Westward. His mother, who died when he was barely seven, was Mary, daughter of the Rev. Robert Wood, perpetual curate of Westward. He went to school first at Market Harborough, then at King William's College, Isle of Man ; from there in 1881 he went as a scholar to Trinity College, Cambridge. Here he studied mathematics and in 1884 graduated as third wrangler, after which he continued his studies for another year in Cambridge. He was then appointed to the Elder professorship in Adelaide, South Australia, which had just been vacated by (Sir) Horace Lamb [q.v.]. He took up his duties in 1886. The chair was that of both mathematics and physics, and his whole training had hitherto been only in mathematics, so that it was through this appointment that he was led into the field in which he was later to become famous. In 1889 he married Gwendoline (died 1929), daughter of (Sir) Charles Todd, F.R.S. [q.v.], postmaster-general and government astronomer of South Australia. The family of two sons and one daughter were united by strong ties of affection. The younger son was killed at the Dardanelles in 1915; the elder, Sir (William) Lawrence Bragg, was appointed in 1953 to the same position at the Royal Institution as had earlier been held by his father.

In 1909 Bragg became Cavendish professor of physics in the university of Leeds, and from there he moved in 1915 to the Quain professorship at University College, London. Among those who have achieved high distinction in scientific research Bragg is remarkable in that his success started late in life. During the first part of his period in Australia there is no sign of any intention on his part to do research. His time was filled with organizing his department, and with the many pleasant activities open to a professor in a small university. He did, however, acquire a knowledge of experimental methods and a skill in setting up apparatus, so that, for example, when the discovery of X-rays was announced, he immediately set up an X-ray tube, probably the first in Australia. It was almost as important that during this period he perfected his gifts for clear and simple exposition. The first stimulus to research came to him at the age of forty-two when, in 1904, he was called on to make a presidential address to a scientific society. He took as his subject the particles emitted by radioactive substances, and in the course of reading about it he was led to the conclusion that certain new experiments ought to be tried.

After the discovery of electrons and X-rays and radioactivity, there had been much discussion of the nature of their various radiations. One of the chief methods of investigation was the study of

how they penetrated matter, that is, the extent to which they were absorbed and scattered by gases and solids. For X-rays the absorption was exponential, and so it was, at any rate roughly, for the $\beta$-particles of radium, but Bragg was led to conclude that this should not be so for the much heavier $\alpha$-particles, and that properly designed experiments should show these to possess the very different characteristic of a definite range. He obtained some radium shortly afterwards, and verified this result, finding that the $\alpha$-particle in passing through air produces ionization at a slowly increasing rate until, at the end of its path, ionization suddenly ceases. The work drew much attention and Bragg was at once recognized as one of the leaders in the field of radioactivity.

He next turned his attention to the study of X-rays. The character of these was still something of a mystery; for the most part they were thought to be like light of very short wave length, but there was not very much direct evidence. He studied their ionization in detail and brought out certain characteristics wherein they more closely resembled particles of matter. To explain this he advocated tentatively the view that they were some kind of neutral corpuscle, but the question had to be left open, and the discrepancy, which he fully recognized, was not resolved until twenty years later, when the quantum theory gave the answer. Perhaps the most important outcome of this work for Bragg was that through it he became a complete master of the very difficult technique of studying X-rays by their ionization, so that when the time came he was fully equipped to take the leading part in the work for which most of all he will be remembered.

In 1912 von Laue showed that the X-rays possess one of the basic characteristics of light, in that they are diffracted by the atoms of a crystal in the same manner as light is diffracted by a grating. Laue used a photographic method with the rays going right through the crystal, so that the effects, although unmistakable, were feeble in intensity and rather complicated. Bragg at once made two great improvements, by using ionization, and by studying glancing reflections at the face of the crystal. In all this work he co-operated closely with his son, and between them they founded the modern science of crystallography. They established for the first time how the atoms are arranged in crystals such as rocksalt and diamond, and it is hardly too much to say that the whole science has been nothing but an elaboration of their work. All this early work, together with a full account of the subject, was embodied in 1915 in a book, *X-Rays and Crystal Structure*, written by father and son.

The war interrupted the progress of this work, and for a time Bragg was engaged on underwater acoustics for the Admiralty, being especially concerned with the development of the hydrophone used in detecting submarines. At its end he returned to the X-rays, and studied the arrangement of the atoms in various organic compounds, where the large number of the atoms in each molecule often gives rise to formidable difficulties. It was during this period that he became known as an exceptionally good lecturer. There was never anything at all oratorical about his manner; it was more like that of a man discussing with friends a subject on which he happens to know a little more than they do. The exposition was done with great charm, and he could make simple and clear matters which from others would have appeared subtle and difficult.

In 1923 Bragg was chosen to succeed Sir James Dewar [q.v.] as Fullerian professor of chemistry at the Royal Institution. The holder of this post resides in the building, and is also director of the Davy–Faraday Laboratory. All his qualities eminently suited him for this post. His distinction as a lecturer was exhibited in his Christmas lectures for young people, all most carefully prepared and afterwards published as books, including *The World of Sound* (1920) and *Concerning the Nature of Things* (1925). Nor must mention be omitted of the geniality with which he and his wife presided over the many receptions and ceremonies which take place at the Royal Institution. After the death of his wife his daughter acted as hostess for him.

This new life at the Royal Institution called for activities in a wider field. Scientific work continued, but more through directing the work of others in the Davy–Faraday Laboratory than in his own hands. Work was still mainly on the X-rays, now applied to the study of biological materials, and a number of those who later were to be leaders in this field learnt their craft under him. He had become one of the most prominent scientific figures in the country, and had many calls on his time for giving lectures, attending conferences, presiding over committees, and advising on the country's scientific policy. Among these activities mention may be made of the Riddell memorial lectures delivered in 1941 and published in a book, *Science and Faith*, in which his religious beliefs and sense of reverence are admirably expressed.

Many honours and distinctions came to Bragg who was a corresponding member of many foreign academies, received honorary degrees from nearly twenty universities, and in 1920 elected an honorary fellow of his college. In 1915 he received, jointly with his son, the Nobel prize for physics. In 1917 he was appointed C.B.E., in 1920 K.B.E.; and in 1931 he was admitted to the Order of Merit. He presided over the Glasgow meeting of the British Association in 1928 and from 1930 to 1932 was president of the Physical Society. He received the Rumford (1916) and Copley (1930) medals of the Royal Society, of which he was elected a fellow in 1907, and president in 1935. The presidency, in which he continued until 1940, is always arduous, but in his case was more than usually so, since in 1939 he was called on to serve as chairman of the Cabinet committee on scientific policy and on several other bodies, none of them sinecures. He died in London 12 March 1942.

A portrait of Bragg by Harold Knight hangs in the rooms of the Royal Society. A pencil drawing by Randolph Schwabe (1932) is in the National Portrait Gallery and a drawing by Sir William Rothenstein (1934) is the property of the city of Carlisle.

[*The Times*, 13 March 1942; E. N. da C. Andrade in *Obituary Notices of Fellows of the Royal Society*, No. 12, November 1943; *Proceedings* of the Physical Society, vol. liv, part 6, November 1942; private information; personal knowledge.] C. G. DARWIN.

BRAID, JAMES (1870–1950), golfer, was born at Earlsferry, Fifeshire, 6 February 1870, the son of James Braid, ploughman and later forester, by his wife, Mary Harris. He began very early to play golf, was a caddie, and won boys' competitions. Earlsferry was then a nursery of famous golfers, notably the brothers Jack and Archie Simpson, and Douglas Rolland, a cousin of Braid's, and the boy on leaving school at thirteen was anxious to take up golf professionally. His parents did not approve and he was apprenticed to a joiner in a neighbouring village. His golf was thus confined to Saturday afternoons and summer evenings, but at sixteen he had won the scratch medal of the Earlsferry Thistle Club with a record score. At nineteen he went to work as a joiner in St. Andrews, where he played with Hugh and Andrew Kirkaldy and other leading golfers, and at twenty-one he moved to Edinburgh. There he joined the Edinburgh Thistle Club and won an amateur competition on the Braid hills open to all Edinburgh golfers.

In the autumn of 1893 his boyhood's friend, Charles Ralph Smith, then head clubmaker at the Army and Navy Stores, suggested that Braid should work under him, and, although he had never then made a club, he accepted the offer and went to London. He remained at the Stores for nearly three years, playing week-end golf on London courses. In 1894 he played in his first professional competition at Stanmore, finishing fifth, and soon after was tenth in the open championship at Sandwich. He first became widely known at the end of 1895, through halving an exhibition match with John Henry Taylor, then open champion, at West Drayton. In 1896 he was appointed professional at Romford where he stayed until 1904 when he became the first professional at Walton Heath and remained there for the rest of his life. After his match with Taylor, Braid was generally recognized as one of the best golfers of the day, a very long driver and a magnificent iron player, but his putting was a weak point for several years until he adopted the aluminium club with which he became one of the best putters of his time. He was second in the championship of 1897, beaten by one stroke by Harold Hilton. He won it for the first time at Muirfield in 1901 with a score of 309. About this time Harry Vardon, Braid, and Taylor were generally grouped together as the three leading golfers under the name of the Triumvirate, but Braid did not win the championship again until 1905 at St. Andrews with 318. He won at Muirfield in 1906 with 300, at Prestwick in 1908 with 291, and at St. Andrews in 1910 with 299. He was thus champion four times in six years, a unique achievement. He also won the *News of the World* tournament, now officially recognized as the professional match-play championship, in 1903, 1905, 1907, and 1911, and the French championship in 1910. His eyes, into which lime had been accidentally thrown when he was a boy, had always troubled him to some extent and did so more as he grew older. This may partly account for

his winning no more great events after 1911, although he remained a very fine golfer, and in 1927, at the age of fifty-seven, was runner-up in the *News of the World* tournament.

Braid played no outstanding single challenge match during his career, but several foursomes; in particular that in 1905 in which he and Alexander Herd for Scotland met Vardon and Taylor for England. It was played over four greens, St. Andrews, Troon, St. Anne's, and Deal, the Englishmen winning by 13 up and 12 to play. Braid never ceased to play with a youthful enthusiasm: he could usually be relied upon to go round Walton Heath in a score under the number of his own years, and on his eightieth birthday, a wet, stormy day, he holed the course in 81. In his later years he did much work as a golf architect, and had a share in laying out, among many other courses, Gleneagles and Blairgowrie.

In his best years Braid weighed twelve stone six pounds and he was six feet one and a half inches in height. He was a man of quiet and reserved nature, who never rashly commit himself, and he was possessed of great discretion and common sense. As a player he combined a cool, steady nerve with dash and boldness. He had a natural dignity, a pleasant sense of humour, and a remarkable power of inspiring affection among all who knew him. He was an honorary member of the Walton Heath and Royal and Ancient golf clubs, and in the clubhouse of the former there is a portrait of him by James Gunn.

Braid married in 1893 Minnie Alice, daughter of Henry Wright, labourer, of Upminster, who predeceased him and by whom he had two sons. He died in London, after an operation, 27 November 1950, and was buried at Walton-on-the-Hill.

[James Braid, *Advanced Golf*, 1908; Bernard Darwin, *James Braid*, 1952; *Golfer's Handbook*; private information; personal knowledge.]      BERNARD DARWIN.

BRAITHWAITE, DAME (FLORENCE) LILIAN (1873–1948), actress, was born in Ramsgate 9 March 1873, the daughter of the Rev. John Masterman Braithwaite, then a curate, and later vicar of Croydon, by his wife, Elizabeth Jane, daughter of Colonel Thomas Sidney Powell, C.B., of the 53rd Regiment. She was the eldest of seven children, five of them boys, of whom two achieved distinction in the Services (Colonel Francis

Powell Braithwaite and Vice-Admiral Lawrence Walter Braithwaite). A third became European manager of the *Christian Science Monitor.*

Lilian was educated at Croydon and Hampstead high schools and in Dresden. Starting as an amateur actress, her ambition to become a professional aroused a storm of family protest which, however, she managed to overcome and, joining the Shakespearian company of William Haviland and Gerald Lawrence, she sailed for South Africa and made her first professional appearance at Durban in 1897. Her first appearance in London was in 1900 with Julia Neilson in *As You Like It* at the Opera House, Crouch End; she then played in *Sweet Nell of Old Drury* at the Haymarket Theatre. In 1901 she joined (Sir) Frank Benson [q.v.] and appeared in a Shakespeare season at the Comedy Theatre. Then followed a tour with (Sir) George Alexander [q.v.] and she appeared under his management at the St. James's Theatre, 1901–4.

Her ethereal beauty and undoubted talent brought many offers of engagements, and she now embarked upon a west-end career which was to end only with her death. Among her early parts were Lady Hermione Wynne in *The Flag Lieutenant*, and Mrs. Panmure in *Preserving Mr. Panmure*; in 1912 she appeared as the Madonna in (Sir) C. B. Cochran's production of *The Miracle* at Olympia; in 1913 she was Mrs. Gregory in *Mr. Wu* with Matheson Lang [q.v.], and in 1921 Margaret Fairfield in *A Bill of Divorcement*. Tall, dark, serene, and lovely, she appeared regularly and successfully in play after play, becoming identified in the mind of theatregoers with beautiful suffering heroines and drawing-room dramas at the Haymarket Theatre. In 1924, however, there came a great change in her career when she accepted at short notice the part of Florence Lancaster in Mr. Noël Coward's *The Vortex* at the Everyman Theatre, later transferring to the west end and then appearing in the same part in New York. With the shingled, sinning Florence, Lilian Braithwaite gained recognition as a dramatic actress and said good-bye for ever to suffering heroines. Her parts at this time included the possessive matriarch of *The Silver Cord* and other dramatic roles.

In 1928 her métier changed again. She appeared as a 'ten per cent. lady' in Ivor Novello's *The Truth Game* at the Globe Theatre and made an enormous success as a light comedienne. The public now could not have enough of this actress who made such malicious remarks in such honeyed accents, and a succession of successful comedies followed one another, among them *Flat to Let, Fresh Fields, Family Affairs, Full House, The Lady of La Paz, Bats in the Belfry, Comedienne,* and *Tony Draws a Horse.* Nevertheless, she twice reverted to more dramatic roles with Elizabeth in *Elizabeth, la Femme sans Homme* at the Haymarket Theatre (1938) and Lady Mountstephan in *A House in The Square* (1940) at the St. Martin's Theatre.

In 1940 she went to the Theatre Royal, Drury Lane, to work for the Entertainments National Service Association and in 1943 she was appointed D.B.E. In December 1942, in her seventieth year, she entered upon her greatest success of all with the part of Abby Brewster in *Arsenic and Old Lace* at the Strand Theatre which ran until the beginning of March 1946. She died in London 17 September 1948 confident that her illness was but a passing thing and that soon she would be rehearsing a new play. She rehearsed, said Mr. Noël Coward, 'with a dry, down to earth efficiency which was fascinating to watch'. Her 'popularity' as an actress was inclined to make serious students of the drama underrate her great ability—her grace, her perfect technique, her exquisite timing. She was a wise and witty woman whose *bons mots* have passed into theatrical history; and her work for theatrical charities was never-ending. She also acted for the cinema and appeared in many British productions.

In 1897 Lilian Braithwaite married Gerald Leslie Lawrence, the actor-manager. Their daughter, Joyce Carey, who also became an actress, was born in 1898. The marriage was subsequently dissolved. A portrait of Lilian Braithwaite by Charles Sims is in the possession of her daughter; another by Harold Speed remained the property of the artist.

[*Who's Who in the Theatre*; Noël Coward, *Present Indicative*, 1937; Joseph Foster, *Our Noble and Gentle Families of Royal Descent*, 1885 (*s.v.* Braithwaite of Hookfield Grove, Surrey); personal knowledge.]

DIANA MORGAN.

BRAITHWAITE, SIR WALTER PIPON (1865–1945), general, was born 11 November 1865 at Alne, near Easingwold, Yorkshire, the youngest son and twelfth child of the vicar, the Rev. William

Braithwaite, and his wife, Laura Elizabeth Pipon, daughter of the Seigneur of Noirmont, Jersey. After being educated at Bedford School and the Royal Military College, Sandhurst, he was commissioned in the Somerset Light Infantry in 1886 and joined the 2nd battalion in Burma in time for the later stages of the war in progress, and was mentioned in dispatches. In 1898 he went to the Staff College, but without quite completing the course was sent, with other students, to South Africa on the outbreak of war in 1899 as a special service officer. He served throughout the war as a staff officer, first as a brigade-major and then as deputy assistant adjutant-general, taking part in most of the major actions from the relief of Ladysmith onward. He was thrice mentioned in dispatches, and received a brevet majority (1900). Returning home he was continued on the staff in the Salisbury Command, first under Sir Evelyn Wood and then Sir Ian Hamilton [qq.v.]. His devotion to his duties, good looks, and charming manners, added to his war experience, led in 1906 to his being given a half-pay lieutenant-colonelcy and being appointed to the instructional staff of the Staff College, of which (Sir) Henry Wilson [q.v.] became commandant. In 1909 Braithwaite was promoted colonel and transferred to the directorate of staff duties, War Office, then under Sir Douglas (later Earl) Haig [q.v.]. In 1911 he was appointed commandant of the Staff College, Quetta.

On the closing of the college at the outbreak of war in 1914 Braithwaite returned to the War Office as director of staff duties, and in 1915 was selected to be chief of staff for the Gallipoli campaign. Sir Ian Hamilton reported that he was the best chief of general staff whom he had ever met, and Braithwaite was promoted to be major-general (1915). He accompanied his commander when Hamilton was recalled to England, and was given command of the 62nd (2nd West Riding) division, a second-line Territorial division then in training; under his care it was an exceptionally good formation when it was ordered to France in 1917. In Sir Hubert Gough's Fifth Army the division was engaged in the fighting round Bullecourt in both April and May, a severe test for Braithwaite's young troops; under Sir Julian (later Viscount) Byng [q.v.] it took part in the battle of Cambrai, and in holding the German offensive of March 1918; and during the final German offensive, to

the Marne, in July against the French was one of the divisions sent to their assistance. In August, to the regret of his division, Braithwaite was promoted to command the XXII Corps, but was transferred in September to the IX Corps in the Fourth Army, and this corps he led in the advance to victory.

He remained with the Army of the Rhine, and then held in succession the Western Command, India, the Scottish Command, and the Eastern Command, until in 1927, having been promoted general in the previous year, he was appointed adjutant-general to the forces and a member of the Army Council, acting at the same time as an aide-de-camp general to the King. Appointed C.B. in 1911 he was promoted K.C.B. in 1918 and G.C.B. in 1929. He was appointed to the Legion of Honour, was a grand officer of the Order of the Crown of Belgium, and received the croix de guerre of France and Belgium. He retired in 1931 and became governor of the Royal Military Hospital, Chelsea, until 1938. He was colonel of the Somerset Light Infantry from 1929 until 1938, and in 1933 was appointed Bath King of Arms. On leaving Chelsea Braithwaite destroyed all his military papers, including those on the training and leading of improvised troops, in which matters he had shown himself to be a master. A portrait of Braithwaite was painted by (Sir) Oswald Birley but its whereabouts are unknown.

Braithwaite died suddenly 7 September 1945 at Rotherwick, near Basingstoke. He married in 1895 Jessie Adine (died 1950), daughter of Caldwell Ashworth, banker, of London. They had one son who, after winning the M.C., was killed in 1916 on the first day of the battles of the Somme.

[Sir J. E. Edmonds and others, (Official) *History of the Great War. Military Operations, France and Belgium, 1914–18, 1922–48*; C. F. Aspinall-Oglander, (Official) *History of the Great War. Military Operations, Gallipoli*, 2 vols., 1929–32; private information; personal knowledge.]                    J. E. EDMONDS.

BRAZIL, ANGELA (1868–1947), writer, was born in Preston 30 November 1868, the fourth and youngest child of Clarance Brazil, cotton manufacturer, and his wife, Angelica McKinnell. Angela Brazil has the distinction of having founded a genre: the girls' school story as we know it today is chiefly her work. She was herself an experienced pupil, attending an old-fashioned dame school near Liverpool, the junior department of the Manchester High School, and Ellerslie College, where she was latterly a boarder and of which she became head girl. The college was advanced in educational method but it had no organized games and no prefectorial system. It is possible that these deprivations had their effect on Angela Brazil, for her stories abound in games and authority of all kinds.

She studied art at Heatherley's, where she was a fellow student with Baroness Orczy [q.v.], and was then a governess. After her father's death, she travelled in Europe and the Middle East with her mother and sister, subsequently living in a country cottage in Wales where, at the age of thirty-six, she began to write professionally, although she had been writing stories for her own amusement since the age of nine.

The strength and novelty of her stories lay in the fact that she had no patience with the Victorian girl of fiction, with the simpering goody-goody, all blushes and saccharine sweetness. She preferred fact and she wrote of schoolgirls as she had found them, with their tiffs, jealousies, pettinesses, and their womanly respect for regimentation. Her schools are ruled by humanly tyrannical headmistresses: Mrs. Morrison, of *A Patriotic Schoolgirl* (1918), is a fine example, chosen perhaps to show that educational severity is not necessarily connected with spinsterhood. Angela Brazil's monitors are appointed for their almost morbid devotion to duty, and her schools have rigid systems of rules and punishments, but within these firm limits her schoolgirls, with their dramatic and even sensational lives, are extraordinarily happy.

Her stories, of which she wrote over fifty, had an immediate success, principally with the upper and middle classes. Reviewers praised their realism, and parents could, without an anxious tremor, see their children absorbed in them. Their sale was remarkable and Angela Brazil died a rich woman.

Angela Brazil's choice of Christian names provides an interesting study: in her middle period we find chiefly Marcia, Jessie, Rhoda, Deirdre, Milly, Katie, Rachel, Maisie, Lettice, Bunty, Marion, Edna, and Annie. Her schoolgirl slang is extremely representative of the first twenty years of the century and changes little throughout her books: 'We'd best scoot', 'Squattez ici', 'Good biz!', 'Do you twig?', 'Spiffing'.

Among her best books must be mentioned *A Fourth Form Friendship* (1911), *The Jolliest Term on Record* (1915), *The Madcap of the School* (1917), *Monitress Merle* (1922), *Captain Peggie* (1924), and what is perhaps her masterpiece, *The School by the Sea* (1914).

Angela Brazil (her name should be pronounced to rhyme with 'dazzle') was unmarried and died 13 March 1947 in Coventry where she had long lived and whither she had often banished, for a period, many of her fictional schoolgirls.

[Angela Brazil, *My Own Schooldays*, 1925.]
ARTHUR MARSHALL.

BRIDGE, FRANK (1879–1941), musician, was born at Brighton 26 February 1879, the son of William Henry Bridge, of Brighton, and his wife, Elizabeth Warbrick. The father was a musician, a conductor under whom Frank Bridge played, usually violin, but sometimes other instruments, and even, when required, conducting. This early experience was of inestimable value to the young musician, giving him intimate knowledge of the range and colour of the orchestra, and generally laying the foundation of that skill and knowledge which he came to display. He went to the Royal College of Music as a violin student, and in 1899 won a scholarship for composition, studying under (Sir) Charles Stanford [q.v.]. He transferred from violin to viola without having any tuition on the latter instrument, of which he became a superb player.

So exceptional were his qualities that when Wirth, the viola of the Joachim Quartet, was prevented by illness from coming to England, Bridge was chosen to take his place (1906), and earned from Joachim and his colleagues the most enthusiastic appreciation.

In his earliest days Bridge earned his living by playing in theatre and other orchestras—he was also a member of the Royal Philharmonic Orchestra; in fact he was an expert and versatile musician who rose from quite a humble beginning. A colleague who shared his desk in a performance of the *Messiah* said it had been a revelation to hear what Bridge found in the viola part. He played in the Grimson (second violin), the Motto (viola), and the English (viola) string quartets; but when this last quartet disbanded in 1927, he practically ceased playing and concentrated on composing and conducting.

As a composer Bridge ranged over a wide field; he produced educational solos for piano, for violin, and three sets of miniature trios for young players for piano, violin, and 'cello. He won various important prizes, of which his full-sized string Quartet in E minor won a *mention d'honneur* at an international competition held at Bologna in 1906. His 'Phantasie' string Quartet in F minor won a prize in the first competition organized by Walter Willson Cobbett (1905); the 'Phantasie' Trio in C minor was awarded the first prize in the second competition (1908), the purpose of these competitions being to produce works in which the instruments should have equally interesting parts. Cobbett also commissioned him to write the very beautiful 'Phantasie' Quartet for piano and strings in F sharp minor (1910), and in 1915 his prize for a string quartet in which both violins should have equal interest was awarded to Bridge's second string Quartet, in G minor. Other compositions included a Quintet for piano and strings (1905) and a Sextet for strings (1912). Bridge's chamber music was perhaps the most important of his creative work, and is of real value. He also wrote a Sonata for piano (1921–4), one for piano and 'cello (1913–17), and another for piano and violin (1932). For orchestra his works included a symphonic poem 'Isabella' (1907), a suite 'The Sea' (1910–11, published under the auspices of the Carnegie Trust), a rhapsody 'Enter Spring' (1927), and a 'Lament' for strings (1915) written in memory of a young friend drowned at sea; 'Phantasm' for piano and orchestra (1931), also 'Oration' (1930) for 'cello and orchestra. Besides these he composed solos for organ, piano, violin, viola, 'cello, a number of songs, and a divertimento (1938) for wind instruments.

He had great gifts as a conductor and took the New Symphony Orchestra, shortly after its foundation, in repertory rehearsals; he was in charge of a season at the Savoy Theatre (1910–11) in which Marie Brema produced Gluck's *Orfeo*, and was included in the 1913 autumn season at Covent Garden. He was frequently called on in an emergency to conduct various concerts, including some of the Royal Philharmonic Society, and it is interesting to note that a number of those who played under him said that he was one of the few who really interpreted the works, for so many beat time, but so few interpret. His one permanent position as a conductor was with the Audrey Chapman Orchestra,

formed chiefly of amateurs, with professional strengthening for the concerts. The standard of playing in this orchestra under Bridge's training reached a very high level of musicianship and sensitiveness. Although he possessed these gifts as a conductor, he never attained the position which was his due, owing possibly to his very direct and penetrating criticism of those whom he conducted.

Bridge made four visits to the United States; he conducted several times in Boston, Detroit, Cleveland, and New York, having many works performed in these cities as well as in California. Mrs. Elizabeth Sprague Coolidge commissioned from Bridge the piano Trio No. 2 (1929), and also the string Quartets No. 3 (1926) and No. 4 (1937), both of which were played by the Brosa, Pro Arte, and many other organizations. In composition he had a fine technique and a masterly command of form.

In 1908 Bridge married Ethel Elmore Sinclair, a fellow student from Australia who had won the Clarke scholarship at Melbourne which brought her to the Royal College of Music, London, in 1898. Bridge died at Friston-Field, near Eastbourne, 10 January 1941. There were no children of the marriage.

[Private information; personal knowledge.]
IVOR JAMES.

BROCK, SIR OSMOND DE BEAUVOIR (1869–1947), admiral of the fleet, was born at Plymouth 5 January 1869, the eldest son and second of the six children of Commander Osmond de Beauvoir Brock, R.N., of Guernsey, by his wife, Lucretia Jenkins, daughter of Henry Clark, of Clifton, Bristol. Brock entered the Royal Navy in January 1882, and after leaving the *Britannia* served as a midshipman in masted ships for three and a half years. While in the *Raleigh* he was awarded the Royal Humane Society's certificate on vellum for saving a stoker from drowning in Simon's Bay. In his sub-lieutenant's courses he gained the maximum award of seniority, being promoted to lieutenant in February 1889 at the age of twenty. He specialized in gunnery and served as gunnery officer in the *Cambrian*, and then for five years in the flagship of the commander-in-chief, Mediterranean.

Promoted to commander on 1 January 1900, he became executive officer of the *Repulse* in the Channel, and afterwards of the *Renown*, the flagship in the Mediterranean of Sir John (later Lord) Fisher [q.v.]. In 1903 he commanded the *Alacrity* in China and was promoted to captain on 1 January 1904.

He was flag captain to Lord Charles (later Lord) Beresford in the Mediterranean and later to Sir Berkeley Milne [qq.v.] in the Home Fleet. Between sea appointments he served at the Admiralty as assistant director of naval intelligence and as assistant director of naval mobilization.

In 1913 he commissioned the new battle cruiser *Princess Royal* and joined the flag of David (later Earl) Beatty [q.v.]. He fought his ship successfully at the battles of Heligoland and the Dogger Bank, becoming Beatty's flag captain while the *Lion* was being repaired. He was promoted to rear-admiral on 5 March 1915 and given command of the first battle squadron with his flag in the *Princess Royal*. He followed in the wake of Beatty's flagship throughout the battle of Jutland, and when her wireless was shot away became responsible for passing on all Beatty's signals and reports. He was two years older than Beatty, but they saw eye to eye in all naval matters and were close friends. So when Beatty became commander-in-chief of the Grand Fleet, he naturally selected Brock to be his chief of staff. It was a wise choice. The studious and intellectual Brock was the ideal complement. Beatty said of him in a letter: 'O. de B. has developed a tremendous capacity for work and is perfectly excellent, clear as a bell, and is of the very greatest assistance'. Brock was promoted to vice-admiral in 1919 and accompanied Beatty to the Admiralty as deputy chief of the naval staff. He became commander-in-chief of the Mediterranean Fleet in April 1922, and held the appointment for three years. His firm attitude to the Turks, after they had driven the Greeks out of Anatolia, was commended by the first lord of the Admiralty in the House of Commons in 1923. He was promoted to admiral in July 1924 and in 1926 hoisted his flag as commander-in-chief, Portsmouth. Three years later he was promoted to admiral of the fleet, and was placed on the retired list 31 July 1934. He died at Winchester 14 October 1947.

Brock was appointed C.B. (1915), K.C.B. (1919), G.C.B. (1929), C.M.G. (1916), K.C.M.G. (1918), and K.C.V.O. (1917); he received the honorary degree of D.C.L. from the university of Oxford in 1929; he was a commander of the Legion of Honour and held a number of other foreign decorations. There is a portrait of him in Sir A. S. Cope's group 'Some Sea Officers of the War of 1914–18' in the National Portrait Gallery; and a drawing by Francis Dodd in the Imperial War Museum.

He married in 1917 Irene Catherine Wake (died 1939), daughter of the late Vice-Admiral Sir Baldwin Wake Walker, second baronet, granddaughter of Admiral Sir Baldwin Wake Walker [q.v.], and widow of Captain Philip Francklin who was killed at the battle of Coronel. They had one daughter.

Brock had great tact and charm of manner, and a humility which endeared him to those with whom he was closely associated. He was brilliantly clever and a tremendous reader. His analytical brain was ever active, and his knowledge ranged over a wide field from art to the nuclear theory. He was more interested in things than in people, but he was generous, tolerant, and a great example. Although he paid great attention to detail, he never lost sight of the principles governing a problem, and his judgement was always sound.

[*The Times*, 15 October 1947; Admiralty records; private information; personal knowledge.]    W. S. CHALMERS.

BRODRIBB, CHARLES WILLIAM (1878–1945), journalist, scholar, and poet, was born in London 11 June 1878, the elder son of Arthur Aikin Brodribb, for many years in charge of the parliamentary reporting staff of *The Times*, by his wife, Dinah Alice, daughter of William Crook, a Wiltshire farmer. He was distantly related to Sir Henry Irving [q.v.], the actor, whose original name was Brodribb; and his father's half-brother was W. J. Brodribb [q.v.], translator of Tacitus. Through his paternal great-grandmother, he was a great-great-grandson of Gilbert Wakefield [q.v.], classical scholar, while he was also a collateral descendant of Mrs. A. L. Barbauld [q.v.], *née* Aikin.

Brodribb was a scholar both at St. Paul's School and at Trinity College, Oxford. After taking honours in classical moderations (1899) and a third class in *literae humaniores* (1901), he was appointed a temporary assistant master at St. Paul's. Joining the editorial staff of *The Times* in April 1904 he remained in its service for the rest of his life. Beginning as a sub-editor, he soon became one of the editor's secretaries, and just before the war of 1914–18 he was appointed an assistant editor and a special writer for *The Times* and its *Literary Supplement*. His influence on the paper, and therefore on educated opinion in England, was very considerable. Although his classical scholarship did not bring him the highest academic distinctions, it remained throughout his life his primary interest, which was reflected in the columns of *The Times* and continually cultivated and refreshed. London and its antiquities, especially St. Paul's Cathedral, claimed from him a loving attention. His knowledge of English literature was wide, but he was particularly at home in the periods of Milton, Pope, and Johnson. Brodribb's verse, with its precision and strength in lightness, and its epigrammatic wit, has affinities with the verse of these three, as also with that of Robert Bridges [q.v.]; patriotism and love of scholarship are its abiding themes. During the war of 1939–45 Brodribb was chiefly responsible for the series of daily quotations in *The Times* under the heading 'Old and True' (collected edition 1945), which brought encouragement to many, and for *The Times Broadsheets for the Services* (collected edition 1948). He did not long survive the victory, but died at his brother's home at Bucklebury Common, near Reading, 21 June 1945.

Brodribb was a good churchman and a churchwarden of St. Bride's, Fleet Street. Complete integrity and unselfish generosity governed his personal relations. He married in 1923 Sylvia Corrie, second daughter of Perceval Charles Woolston, M.R.C.V.S., and had one son.

Brodribb published little under his own name, but a pamphlet on Pope (*Pope: his Friendships and his Poetry*, 1925), written for the National Home-Reading Union, and a translation of the *Georgics* of Virgil into English hexameters (1928) may be mentioned. A selection of his poems with an introduction by Mr. Edmund Charles Blunden appeared in 1946. A sketch by Sir Muirhead Bone is at the United University Club.

[*The Times*, 22 June 1945; E. C. Blunden, introduction to *Poems* by C. W. Brodribb, 1946; private information; personal knowledge.]                DEREK HUDSON.

BRODRICK, (WILLIAM) ST. JOHN (FREMANTLE), ninth VISCOUNT MIDLETON and first EARL OF MIDLETON (1856–1942), statesman, was born in London 14 December 1856, the eldest of the three sons of William Brodrick, later eighth Viscount Midleton, by his wife, Augusta Mary, third daughter of Sir Thomas Francis Fremantle, later first Baron Cottesloe [q.v.]. He was a nephew of G. C. Brodrick [q.v.]. Until 1870, when his father succeeded to the title, Brodrick was taught strictly but affectionately to fit himself for hard work. He was, however, a worker by disposition. He was educated at Eton, where his greatest friend was Alfred Lyttelton [q.v.], and at Balliol College, Oxford, where he obtained a second class in modern history and was president of the Union in 1878. After taking his degree he soon made himself financially independent as his father had desired, beginning with journalism and later making a much more profitable and a permanent connexion with telegraphic cable companies.

In 1880 Brodrick entered the House of Commons unopposed as a Conservative member for West Surrey: from 1885 to 1906 he represented the Guildford division. The acute Irish problem at once seized his attention in the House. He disapproved of the neglectful conduct of many Irish landowners; he did not forget that the principal part of the fortune which he was destined to inherit was derived from Midleton in county Cork. But the unusual knowledge of Irish affairs which he acquired, and which was commended by Gladstone, by no means shook his conviction (until the war of 1914–18 brought new conditions) that the well-being of Ireland depended upon kindly and intelligent rule by England. His first office was that of financial secretary to the War Office (1886–92). It was he who in opposition during the Liberal Government of 1892–5 discovered the deficiency of ammunition for the army and inspired the motion which caused Rosebery's fall. In 1895 he became under-secretary of state for war, and in 1898 under-secretary for foreign affairs. He was sworn of the Privy Council in 1897.

Such experience amply prepared Brodrick for his appointment as secretary of state for war after the election of 1900. The South African war had just entered its second year. He introduced valuable administrative reforms at the War Office which made for speed and economy; and the creation of the Committee of Imperial Defence in 1902 was a memorable achievement. To the general public his most notable reform was the introduction of a new forage cap for the Brigade of Guards, which was in no way his work but which came to be known by his name. His real service, however, was dimmed partly by his inability, or disinclination, to impress his personality upon the country, and partly by the general concentration of interest on the Royal Commission (1902) under the chairmanship of Lord Elgin [q.v.] which inquired into the military preparations and other matters connected with the South African war, and on the War Office reconstruction committee (1903) under Lord Esher [q.v.].

From 1903 to 1905 Brodrick was secretary of state for India. The methods of Lord Curzon [q.v.] as viceroy had been agitating Balfour's Cabinet and Brodrick was soon immersed in the most painful controversy of his career, for he and Curzon had been friends from boyhood. Brodrick has stated that the facts of the dispute were generally unknown at the time and that there was consequently much misguided support for Curzon. He acknowledged that this was natural in the circumstances. Not until 1926, at the earnest request of Balfour, did he put 'all the facts on record' in a pamphlet marked 'secret'. This record, which might easily have erred in bias or taste, won Balfour's unreserved praise. It is a frank but obviously reluctant account of Curzon's provocative policy in Tibet and Afghanistan, his persistent indifference to the Government's wishes, and his arrogant rejoinders to protests and advice. As Balfour said, he claimed for the Indian Government a predominance which would raise India to the position of an independent and not always friendly power. Brodrick sadly attributes all these faults to Curzon's notorious habit of overtaxing his strength, his deep anxiety about his wife's health, and Curzon's own almost unceasing physical pain. He insists that it was Curzon's general behaviour, not merely the viceroy's backing of the military member of his council against Lord Kitchener [q.v.], which brought about his enforced resignation in 1905. In that year John (later Viscount) Morley [q.v.] publicly declared that Curzon had acted in the right constitutional spirit when he upheld the importance of maintaining a mediator between a commander-in-chief and the spending departments. But when Morley had taken over the India Office and had read all the correspondence, he said to Brodrick, 'I told the Cabinet to-day that I would not have stood from Curzon for two months what you have stood for two years'.

At the general election of 1906 Brodrick was defeated and in 1907 he succeeded his father and took up his residence at Peper Harow, near Godalming. He now had more time to attend to Ireland and he became leader of the southern unionists. The most important event in this connexion was his part in 1917, when the sympathy and help of Ireland were desperately needed for the war, in trying to arrange through the Irish convention a settlement between north and south. The aim was a united, autonomous Ireland 'within the British Empire' with adequate safeguards for unionist minorities. The first flush of general enthusiasm soon faded into the old suspicions and enmities. It was widely thought that Midleton overestimated the likelihood that Ulstermen would subject their intense loyalty to the Union to conditions under which, as they believed, they could hardly maintain it. After the breakdown of the convention Lloyd George pressed Midleton to accept the lord-lieutenancy of Ireland; but Midleton declined when he learned that he would have to support a double policy of 'autonomy and conscription', in which he profoundly disbelieved. In July 1921, having been invited to Dublin by Mr. de Valera, he was able to persuade Lloyd George to agree to a truce, pending discussions, which he proceeded to negotiate in consultation with Sir Nevil Macready [q.v.]. But Midleton considered the subsequent settlement a 'lamentable conclusion' and thereafter took no further part in Irish affairs.

In politics Midleton was notable for his sincerity; he would join with zest in fair political stratagem, but never in intrigue. His long experience of men and affairs left him with an unexpected simplicity which was very attractive to his friends. As a landowner he was profoundly conscious of his responsibilities.

Midleton was twice married: first, in 1880 to Hilda Charteris (died 1901), daughter of Lord Elcho, later tenth Earl of Wemyss and March [q.v.], and had one son and four daughters; secondly, in 1903 to Madeleine Cecilia Carlyle, elder daughter of Colonel John Constantine Stanley, Grenadier Guards, and had two sons, both of whom were killed in action at Salerno (1943). He was an alderman of the London County Council from 1907 to 1913; was appointed K.P. in 1916; was advanced to an earldom in 1920; and received the honorary degree of LL.D. from Trinity College, Dublin, in 1922. He died at Peper Harow 13 February 1942, and was succeeded in his titles by his eldest son, George St. John (born 1888).

A full-length portrait of Midleton, by William Carter, was a gift from his constituents and is now in the County Hall at Kingston upon Thames. A cartoon by 'Spy' appeared in *Vanity Fair*, 18 July 1901.

[*The Times*, 16 February 1942; the Earl of Midleton, *Ireland—Dupe or Heroine*, 1932, and *Records and Reactions 1856–1939*, 1939; private information; personal knowledge.]

J. B. ATKINS.

BROODBANK, SIR JOSEPH GUINNESS (1857–1944), public servant, was born at Poplar 15 July 1857, the eldest son of Caleb Broodbank, accountant, of Folkestone, by his wife, Sarah, daughter of Captain Thomas Coburn, Merchant Service, of Poplar. He was educated at private schools in London and in 1872 entered the service of the East and West India Dock Company as a junior clerk. In 1875 he was transferred to the secretary's office where he was fitted to take the important part in the affairs of the Port of London which began in 1889 when he was appointed secretary of the East and West India Dock Company; on this company being amalgamated with the London and St. Katharine Docks Company in 1901 he became the secretary of the new London and India Docks Company.

In 1909 when the Port of London Authority was established under the Act of the previous year and took over control of the docks, Broodbank was appointed a Board of Trade member and elected chairman of the dock and warehouse committee, retiring from the Authority's service the following year, but continuing as a member of the Authority until 1920. His wide knowledge of dock undertakings led the Government to call upon his services during the war of 1914–18. He was the only member of the port and transit executive committee to serve throughout its existence (1915–21) and was an original member of the traffic diversion committee appointed by the Board of Trade in 1917, in which year he was knighted. He also served as technical adviser to the committee of transport of the League of Nations and as British commercial adviser to the Central Rhine Commission. From 1920 to 1933 Broodbank was a member of the harbours, docks, and piers sub-committee of the rates advisory committee of the Ministry of Transport. In 1918 he became a member of the food investiga-

tion board of the Department of Scientific and Industrial Research and served as its chairman from 1928 to 1934.

For twenty years Broodbank was responsible for all insurance matters affecting London's docks and in 1916 he became a director of the Employers' Liability Assurance Corporation, and was chairman from 1928 to 1934. He was a founder-member of the Institute of Transport and became its first honorary treasurer in 1919, vice-president in 1921, and president in 1923, and was made an honorary member in 1934. Towards the end of this period Broodbank was gradually losing his sight and eventually became blind. Nevertheless, he continued until his death to be a director of this corporation and also of the Clerical, Medical and General Life Assurance Society, the Merchants' Marine Insurance Company, and the General Reversionary and Investment Company. His disability brought out his fine and endearing character and his remarkable grasp and memory.

Broodbank published a *History of the Port of London* (2 vols., 1921) and many pamphlets and articles on port questions. His connexion with the port enabled him to do much good work for the Poplar Hospital for Accidents and in 1895 he was elected vice-chairman and served as chairman from 1920 to 1923.

Broodbank was twice married: first, in 1883 to Alice (died 1916), daughter of Robert William Reid, wine and fruit importer, of Woodford, Essex; secondly, in 1917 to Maud Mary (died 1948), daughter of Samuel Barfoot, carpet merchant, of Wanstead, Essex. There were no children of either marriage. Broodbank died at Chelmsford 14 July 1944.

There are two portraits of Broodbank, an oil-painting and a water-colour, both by Ralph Peacock, at the head office of the Employers' Liability Assurance Corporation.

[*The Times*, 15 July 1944; Port of London Authority records; private information; personal knowledge.]

J. D. RITCHIE.

BROOKE, ZACHARY NUGENT (1883–1946), historian, was born at Sutton, Surrey, 1 February 1883, the third child and eldest son of George Brooke, a barrister attached to the Inland Revenue Department at Somerset House, and his wife, Alice Elizabeth, daughter of the Rev. Tresillian George Nicholas, vicar of West Molesey. His father's family had long associations with Cambridge, one of his forebears, Zachary Brooke [q.v.], having been Lady Margaret professor of divinity, and on both his father's and his mother's side clerical and scholastic connexions were numerous. His mother died when he was four, and the authoritarian character of his father left its mark on the boy for life.

After a school career at Bradfield, he entered St. John's College, Cambridge, as a classical scholar and was placed in the first class of part i of the classical tripos in 1905, but moved over to history, being placed in the first class of part ii in 1906. He won the Gladstone and Winchester Reading prizes in 1906, and in 1907 was awarded the Lightfoot scholarship in ecclesiastical history; thenceforward the history of the Church in the eleventh and twelfth centuries was the subject of his choice. Elected fellow of Gonville and Caius College in 1908, he remained there for the rest of his life, save for a year's research in Rome in 1911–12, and four years' military service from 1915–19, during which, in 1916, he became a captain.

Already heavily burdened with work, he became in 1921 joint-editor of the *Cambridge Medieval History*, a task which occupied him for the next fifteen years, bringing him into close and harmonious contact with his contemporary and friendly rival, C. W. Previté-Orton [q.v.]. His own literary work and research inevitably suffered, and he produced only two books, *The English Church and the Papacy* (1931), fruit of the Birkbeck lectures (1929–31), and his *A History of Europe, 911–1198* (1938), a standard textbook. He proceeded Litt.D. in 1932, and was elected F.B.A. in 1940. When at last elected to the chair of medieval history early in 1944, he looked forward to leisure for his own research, but less than three years later, 7 October 1946, he died suddenly from a heart attack in his home.

In 1919 Brooke married Rosa Grace, daughter of the Rev. Alfred Herbert Stanton, rector of Hambleden, Henley-on-Thames, who had nursed him when he was invalided home with trench-fever during the war. Then for the first time in his life he enjoyed happiness without restraint in a home of his own. His integrity and simplicity of character, and his sincere piety (he was a devout churchman) were respected by all, but his shy and sensitive nature, concealed under a somewhat brusque exterior, restricted the more intimate manifestations of his personality to his ideally happy home circle, in which his three sons grew up to share his interests, and to a few friends and pupils to whom he was both generous and intensely loyal. As a scholar he took some of his colour from the austere and exacting standards of post-Acton Cambridge; this, added to the circumstances of his career and a meticulous accuracy which rendered composition toilsome, limited his output and prevented the production of what might have been a definitive work on the Gregorian Reform, but his thankless and unseen work as editor and lecturer did much for the well-being of medieval studies at Cambridge which he had so much at heart.

[H. M. Cam in *Proceedings* of the British Academy, vol. xxxii, 1946; the *Eagle* (magazine of St. John's College), April 1948; personal knowledge.]      M. D. Knowles.

BROWN, Sir ARTHUR WHITTEN (1886–1948), air navigator and engineer, was born in Glasgow 23 July 1886, the only child of American parents, Arthur George Brown, an electrical engineer, and his wife, Emma Whitten. Like his father Whitten Brown became an electrical engineer. He served an apprenticeship with the British Westinghouse Electric and Manufacturing Company (later known as the Metropolitan-Vickers Electrical Company, Ltd.) at Trafford Park, Manchester, studying at the university in his spare time; subsequently he went to South Africa on work for the company. He returned to England in the summer of 1914 and joined one of the Universities and Public Schools battalions. Thereafter he held a commission in the Manchester Regiment from which he was transferred to the Royal Flying Corps and trained as an observer. He was shot down over enemy territory, permanently injuring one leg, in November 1915 and remained a prisoner of war until he was repatriated in September 1917. He worked in the aircraft production department of the Ministry of Munitions until the end of the war, and obtained his private pilot's licence in 1918. In 1919 he was in search of employment when (Sir) John Alcock [q.v.] invited him to join him as navigator in an attempt to make the first direct flight across the Atlantic. A prize of £10,000 had been offered in 1913 by the *Daily Mail* for the first non-stop flight across the Atlantic in less than seventy-two hours, and this offer had been renewed in 1918.

A Vickers Vimy two-engine bomber, suitably adapted, was made available and sent to Newfoundland where other aircraft and aspirants had already assembled; and something like a race ensued to get ready first. In the meantime in May 1919 a United States flying-boat made the first crossing of the Atlantic in eleven days, taking the Azores route to Portugal, with an interval between each hop. On the evening of the 14 June 1919 the Vimy, heavily loaded with fuel, just managed to take off from the short grass runway at St. John's at 4.13 p.m. G.M.T. The flight was completed in 16 hours and 27 minutes, the aeroplane landing at 8.40 a.m. G.M.T., the following day, in what looked like a grass field but proved to be a bog at Clifden in Galway. A wing was damaged, but the occupants were unhurt. In the course of their flight they were mostly in or below clouds. For part of the journey the airspeed indicator was out of action, its pitot tube probably blocked by ice, so that the navigator had to make his own estimate of the speed for the purposes of dead reckoning. Only on four occasions (and only once during the hours of darkness) was Whitten Brown able to take his bearings and make a more accurate plot of the aircraft's position. Making a landfall in Galway only sixteen hours out was therefore an excellent piece of navigation on a 1,900 miles journey in an aeroplane which cruised at about ninety miles an hour, even though it was probably helped by an average tailwind of about thirty miles an hour. The achievement was acknowledged as outstanding. Alcock and Whitten Brown were fêted on their arrival in London and appointed K.B.E. a few days later. Eight years were to pass before the next non-stop flight was made across the Atlantic.

For a short time after his ocean flight Whitten Brown worked with Vickers, Ltd., the makers of the Vimy bomber. Then he returned to his original employers, Metropolitan-Vickers. In 1923 he was appointed the company's chief representative at Swansea, a centre from which he covered a wide area. During the war of 1939–45 he returned to the Royal Air Force in order to train pilots in navigation and engineering. He died in Swansea 4 October 1948 from an accidental overdose of veronal. He married in 1919 Marguerite Kathleen, daughter of Major David Henry Kennedy, O.B.E., of the Royal Air Force. There was one son, Arthur, who was killed in action as a flight lieutenant of the Royal Air Force on D-Day 1944 at the age of twenty-two.

A memorial to Alcock and Whitten Brown was erected in 1952, near the field from which they took off at St. John's, by the Historic Sites and Monuments Board of Canada. There is also a memorial by William McMillan at London Airport. A portrait of Whitten Brown by Ambrose McEvoy is at the Royal Aero Club.

[*The Times*, 16 June 1919 and 6 October 1948; *Journal* of the Institution of Electrical Engineers, December 1948; Graham Wallace, *The Flight of Alcock & Brown*, 1955; private information.]      E. Colston Shepherd.

BROWN, FREDERICK (1851–1941) professor of fine art, was born at Chelmsford 14 March 1851, the third child and second son of the seven children of William Brown, an artist, largely self-taught, by his wife, Susan Brewster. He was educated at the grammar school at Chelmsford where he won prizes, but no small part of his education was received from his surroundings in an artist's home. At the age of seventeen he went to study at the National Art Training School (later the Royal College of Art), South Kensington, where not only was he unhappy, but the mechanical methods of teaching and the complete absence of knowledge of the practice of drawing as understood by the great masters evoked from him then and in later years bitter comment. He endured 'about eight years of this' but in 1875 the appointment of (Sir) Edward Poynter [q.v.] as director heralded better things. Although he could make little headway against the South Kensington system, Poynter did introduce Alphonse Legros [q.v.] as visiting teacher of etching, and Brown's contact with him, although not extensive, seems to have been very significant, because, as Brown remarked, 'Legros swept all this aside', and one of his demonstrations of drawing at the Slade School of Fine Art Brown 'found very good as a systematic method'. Another teacher who impressed him favourably was F. W. Moody. Otherwise most advantage was derived from studying the exhibits in the South Kensington Museum.

When, in 1877, Brown took charge of the Westminster School of Art on the recommendation of his predecessor, Owen Gibbons, another pupil of Moody, he entered on his historic role as a reformer of the teaching of art in this country. The school at that time was only a night class for workmen, but it gave Brown a chance and he steadily developed his ideas of what teaching should be. Six months in Paris under Bouguereau and Tony Robert-Fleury enlarged his ideas yet more, and when he left Westminster, it had become 'the largest school in London exclusively devoted to the study of figure-drawing and painting', and he was attracting many keen pupils, among whom was Aubrey Beardsley [q.v.]. J. Havard Thomas was Brown's first teacher of sculpture, and here he first met Henry Tonks [q.v.] who came as a student in the evening when he was free from his medical duties.

In 1893 a wider field of opportunity came to Brown when he succeeded Legros on his retirement from the Slade chair. Continuing and indeed expanding the teaching and liberal outlook of Poynter and Legros, he strove primarily to develop the individuality of his pupils, while encouraging them to study form by means of an analytical rather than a copying attitude to draughtsmanship. He collected a strong staff about him. In 1894 he appointed Tonks as his assistant; and about a year later he added P. Wilson Steer [q.v.]. Later there were to come as teachers (Sir) Walter Russell, Ambrose McEvoy [qq.v.], J. Havard Thomas, and Derwent Lees. Soon after his appointment came two very notable students, Mr. Augustus John and (Sir) William Orpen [q.v.], and throughout his time he produced a succession of distinguished artists of great individuality, who spread his influence far and wide. He retired from the chair in 1917.

Brown was by no means solely concerned with the reform of the teaching of art. As a keen practical artist he was distressed both by the low standard of public taste and by the restrictive attitude of the official societies towards new movements. In the revolt of the new school, Brown played a leading part in the foundation, not without difficulty, of the New English Art Club in 1886, the main concern of which was masterly draughtsmanship and the painting outlook of Constable and the French Impressionists. Brown's own work, vigorous yet sensitive, was based upon these influences, with, in early years, something also of Bastien-Lepage. Three of his works, one of them a self-portrait, are in the Tate Gallery; 'Hard Times', painted in 1886, is in the Walker Art Gallery, Liverpool; a self-portrait is at the Slade School, and another in the Ferens Art Gallery, Hull.

Lean and spare, Brown has been described as rock-like, but beneath a somewhat severe exterior there was a deep sincerity and sympathy. He died, unmarried, at Richmond, Surrey, 8 January 1941. A pencil and pen-and-ink drawing by Aubrey Beardsley is in the Tate Gallery and a portrait in oils by Dame Ethel Walker in the Bradford City Art Gallery. A bronze by Dora Gordine is in the collection of the Hon. Richard Hare.

[Letters by Brown at the Slade School; *Artwork*, Nos. 23 and 24, Autumn and Winter 1930 (two articles by Brown); private information; personal knowledge.]

G. CHARLTON.

BROWN, SIR WALTER LANGDON LANGDON- (1870–1946), physician and regius professor of physic in the university of Cambridge. [See LANGDON-BROWN.]

BROWNING, SIR MONTAGUE EDWARD (1863–1947), admiral, was born 18 January 1863 the eldest child of Captain (later Colonel) Montague Charles Browning, who subsequently became a justice of the peace for Suffolk when living at Manningtree, by his wife, Fanny Allen, daughter of the Rev. Edward Hogg, rector of Fornham St. Martin, Suffolk, where their first child was born.

He entered the *Britannia* as a naval cadet in July 1876 and after two years was appointed midshipman in the *Invincible*, Mediterranean station. In September 1880 he was transferred to the corvette *Carysfort* on special service and served in her as acting-lieutenant during the Egyptian war of 1882, being awarded the war medal and the Khedive's bronze star. Promoted sub-lieutenant in July 1882 he returned home to the *Excellent* gunnery school for examinations and obtained first class certificates in all subjects. He remained in the *Excellent* until November 1884. While doing a year's sea service, he was promoted lieutenant in June 1885, and, except for three years as gunnery lieutenant in the battleship *Dreadnought*, he was employed almost continuously in the *Excellent* until promoted commander in January 1897, and then was specially employed on the preparation of a handbook for quick-firing guns. He served as commander in the *Prince George*, Channel squadron, from January 1898, and then in September 1900 he was chosen to be secretary of the committee which had been appointed by G. J. (later Viscount) Goschen [q.v.], after the acute controversy which had agitated both the engineering profession and Parliament, to report on the respective merits of the cylindrical and water-tube types of boiler and on those of the Belleville and other types of water-tube boilers.

After promotion to captain in January 1902 he remained for six months with the committee until the presentation of its first report, and then joined Sir Archibald Douglas, commander-in-chief, North America and West Indies station, as flag captain in the *Ariadne*. In 1905 he became flag captain to Sir Lewis Beaumont at Devonport. In May 1907 he commissioned the battleship *Commonwealth* in the Channel Fleet and a year later was transferred to the *King Edward VII* as chief of staff to Lord Charles (later Lord) Beresford [q.v.]. In July 1909 he took command of the *Britannia*, and at the end of the next year was given the appointment of inspector of target practice, in recognition of his reputation as a gunnery expert. He continued in this duty after promotion to flag rank (September 1911) until August 1913. He then hoisted his flag in the *Hibernia* as rear-admiral in the third battle squadron of the Grand Fleet. In July 1915 he was appointed to the command of the third cruiser squadron, with his flag in the *Antrim*, which with the third battle squadron had been stationed at Rosyth since the war began. In April 1916 both squadrons were detached from the Grand Fleet and moved to the Swin (Thames estuary), whence they returned north after the battle of Jutland.

In August 1916 he was appointed commander-in-chief of the North America and West Indies station with the acting rank of vice-admiral with his flag in the *Leviathan*. In that capacity he represented his country in discussions with the United States naval authorities on joint action on the conduct of the war at sea. He was promoted vice-admiral in April 1917, and in February 1918 returned to the Grand Fleet to take command of the fourth battle squadron with his flag in the *Hercules*. After the armistice of November 1918 he was appointed president of the allied naval armistice commission, and paid visits in the *Hercules* to the German naval ports to see that the settled terms were duly carried out. Generosity to a fallen foe was not his conception of his role in that capacity and he acted with determination and strict justice. He joined the Board of Admiralty as second sea lord in March 1919 and was promoted admiral on 1 November. He had no previous experience of administrative work in Whitehall and was more happily placed at Devonport where he became commander-in-chief for three years in September 1920. He was appointed first and principal naval aide-de-camp to the King in May 1925 and placed on the retired list in October 1926. He returned to court duty in March 1929 as rear-admiral of the United Kingdom, became vice-admiral of the United Kingdom in February 1939, and finally retired in June 1945.

Browning was appointed M.V.O. (1908), G.C.V.O. (1933), C.B. (1916), K.C.B. (1917), G.C.B. (1924), and G.C.M.G. (1919). He held a number of foreign decorations. In 1889 he had the misfortune to lose his left hand through an accident while visiting the *Inflexible*. Thereafter he wore an iron hook, a crippling disability which Browning endured throughout his life with an uncomplaining fortitude. The reference to it, and indeed the whole passage about Browning by Lord Keynes [q.v.] in one of his posthumously published *Two Memoirs* (1949) seemed most uncalled-for to those who knew Browning himself, for he was a fine type of sea officer, with great natural ability, good brains, and a thorough knowledge of the Service. A stern disciplinarian with a determined character, he was never unfair, and was liked and trusted by his subordinates; in spite of his somewhat grim manner, the great respect which was felt by those who served with him could develop into real affection. He reached well-merited high rank in his profession, to which he was devoted, and no censure ever marred his career.

He married in 1890 Ruth, daughter of Lieutenant-General George Neeld Boldero, by whom he had one daughter. His portrait is included in Sir A. S. Cope's group, 'Some Sea Officers of the War of 1914–18', in the National Portrait Gallery. He died 4 November 1947 at his home at Winchester.

[Admiralty records; private information; personal knowledge.]

VINCENT W. BADDELEY.

BRUCE, SIR HENRY HARVEY (1862–1948), admiral, was born at Stoke Damerel, Devonport, 8 May 1862, the only son of Commander (later Captain Sir) Thomas Cuppage Bruce, who became superintendent of packets, Dover, by his first wife, Elizabeth, daughter of Henry Wise Harvey, of Middle Dealhouse, Kent. Entering the *Britannia* in 1875, Bruce next served in the *Black Prince*, one of the first two ironclads in the Royal Navy, and then went to the Mediterranean in the screw frigate *Raleigh*. In November 1879 he transferred to the iron turret-ship *Monarch*, and in her took part in the bombardment of Alexandria in July 1882, being awarded the Egyptian medal and Khedive's bronze star. He returned home in August 1882 following his promotion to sub-lieutenant in June and spent some months at the Royal Naval College, Greenwich, before joining the gunboat *Swinger* on the Australia station. He was promoted lieutenant in December 1884 and went to the cruiser *Porpoise* on the China station in February 1888 and to the sloop *Beagle* on the south-east coast of America in August 1891. Although not a gunnery specialist, he was appointed for gunnery duties to the cruiser *Marathon* in the East Indies in January 1894, and after a short gunnery course in the *Excellent* in 1897 joined, as gunnery lieutenant, the cruiser *Sirius*, which was employed carrying relief crews out to the Mediterranean.

In July 1898 he took over his first command, the torpedo gunboat *Jason* which, like the *Sirius*, was employed on special duties. After his promotion to commander in June 1901 he commanded successively the store-ship *Tyne* in the Mediterranean and the cruiser *Medea* in home waters. In 1905 he was naval officer in charge and King's harbour master at Bermuda, where he gained the first-hand experience of dockyard administration which was destined to prove so useful to him during the war of 1914–18. Promoted captain at the end of 1905 he commanded the reserve cruiser *Blenheim* which during his term of command was converted into a destroyer depot and repair ship at Chatham. After a course at the Royal Naval War College, Portsmouth, in 1908, he took over command of the cruiser *Arrogant*, and later the battleship *Prince George*, both in the Home Fleet. For two years he commanded the *Defence*, one of the four cruisers to escort the liner *Medina* carrying King George V and Queen Mary to and from India for their coronation durbar in December 1911. For this service Bruce was appointed M.V.O. He was again at the War College in April 1913 but in June became captain of the battleship *Hercules* which he commanded in the Grand Fleet during the opening months of the war. In June 1915 he became the first commodore superintendent of the new Rosyth dockyard and remained there

for five vital years, being promoted rear-admiral and admiral superintendent in April 1917. Rosyth developed into the most up to date of the fleet bases, and the efficiency of its organization under Bruce was invaluable to the fleet, by reason of its geographical position. He was appointed C.B. in 1917 and K.C.B. in 1920. He retired with the rank of vice-admiral in 1922 and was promoted admiral in 1926.

Bruce was a thickset bearded man of fine physique and medium height, a man of great physical energy and strength of character. Although outwardly brusque, beneath the surface he possessed a kindly and considerate personality and was ever solicitous for the welfare of the officers and men under his command. He maintained a lively interest in Service charities and at his death was patron of the metropolitan branch of the British Legion. He was knocked down by a motor-car in London 18 August 1948 and died from his injuries 14 September. In 1913 Bruce married Nina Catherine Marian Broome (died 1915), daughter of the late Frederick Edward Nicholson, solicitor, of Ashfield Balby, and Leicester House, Doncaster. They had one son. There is a drawing by Francis Dodd in the Imperial War Museum.

[*The Times*, 16 September 1948; private information; personal knowledge.]

J. H. Lhoyd-Owen.

BUCKLAND, WILLIAM WARWICK (1859–1946), legal scholar, was born 11 June 1859 at Newton Abbot, the fifth son of Francis Buckland, furniture dealer, and his wife, Sarah Segar. Buckland, whose twin brother did not survive, was one of ten children. His mother died when he was very young and his father married again, moving to Edmonton where he practised as a surveyor. Buckland was educated at Guines, near Calais, at St. John's College, Hurstpierpoint, at the Crystal Palace School of Engineering, and at Gonville and Caius College, Cambridge. He was placed first in the first class of the law tripos in 1884 and awarded the Chancellor's medal for legal studies in 1885. He became a scholar of his college in 1884, a fellow in 1889, the year in which he was called to the bar by the Inner Temple, and a college lecturer in 1895. In 1900 he was attacked by tuberculosis and there followed a long period of precarious health during which he underwent two operations and spent many months in

South Africa and the Canary Islands. Eventually he made a good recovery and, although he was always small and thin, and in his later years somewhat deaf, he was active and alert in body and mind to the end.

In 1903 Buckland became a tutor of his college and from 1912 was senior tutor until his appointment in 1914 as regius professor of civil law. During the war of 1914–18 he served for a time in the Ministry of Munitions. In 1923 he was elected president (vice-master) of his college, and he was at his best in his relations with the younger fellows and in his reception of their guests. He retired from the professorship in September 1945, but lectured for one more term.

Buckland taught all branches of English law before he became professor, and was to the end of his life an excellent lecturer, provided his audience was able and willing to follow the speed of his thought and speech. He might have become an historian of English law had his close friendship and great admiration for F. W. Maitland [q.v.] started sooner. But in fact his enduring monument is what he wrote about Roman law.

His first book was *The Roman Law of Slavery* (1908), a thorough and masterly survey of 'the most characteristic part of the most characteristic intellectual product of Rome'. *Equity in Roman Law* (1911) and *Elementary Principles of the Roman Private Law* (1912) were shorter works, difficult but stimulating. His masterpiece was *A Text-book of Roman Law from Augustus to Justinian* (1921, 2nd ed. 1932), much the most important work on Roman law ever published in English. The broad principles are plainly expounded, but closer study reveals an endless wealth of detail, and countless independent and acute judgements on disputed issues. The chief concern of contemporary Romanists was the 'interpolation problem': Buckland was 'conservative', in that he attributed more of Justinian's *Digest* to the 'classical jurists' before A.D. 250, and less to the compilers, than did most scholars; but his main contention was that the classical age was a time of active growth, that 'the period from A.D. 180 to A.D. 250 was far more constructive, and the "Byzantine" age far less constructive, in private law, than is commonly supposed, that most of what it is now the fashion to call Byzantine is Western, and that much of this is not post-classical, but late classical'. The *Text-*

book was awarded the Ames prize of the Harvard Law School.

Buckland also wrote *A Manual of Roman Private Law* (1925, 2nd ed. 1939) covering the whole subject briefly for beginners; *The Main Institutions of Roman Private Law* (1931), an advanced discussion of selected topics; and *Some Reflections on Jurisprudence* (1945), a short and characteristic book full of common sense and realism; and collaborated with his former pupil (Sir) A. D. (subsequently Lord) McNair (later president of the International Court of Justice) in *Roman Law and Common Law* (1936, 2nd ed. by Professor F. H. Lawson 1952); and with Hermann Kantorowicz in *Studies in the Glossators of the Roman Law* (1938). He published many articles in legal periodicals, English, French, and American. Here he gave freer rein to his pen than he thought appropriate in his books, and showed himself not only a redoubtable but also a witty controversialist. A good example is 'Interpolations in the Digest', *Yale Law Journal*, vol. xxxiii, February 1924.

Buckland received honorary degrees from the universities of Oxford, Edinburgh, Harvard, Lyons, Louvain, and Paris, and was elected F.B.A. in 1920. In 1890 he married Eva (died 1934), daughter of Christopher Mardon Taylor, of Exeter; they had one daughter. He died in Cambridge 16 January 1946. An excellent portrait by James Gunn is in the possession of his college.

[Sir A. D. McNair and P. W. Duff in *Proceedings* of the British Academy, vol. xxxiii, 1947; personal knowledge.]    P. W. DUFF.

BULLER, ARTHUR HENRY REGINALD (1874–1944), botanist and mycologist, was born at Moseley, Birmingham, 19 August 1874, the son of Alban Gardner Buller, J.P., solicitor, by his wife, Mary Jane Huggins. He was educated at a preparatory school at Moseley, then at Queen's College, Taunton. At the age of eighteen he entered Mason College, Birmingham, to study science, including botany, and obtained the B.Sc. (London) in 1896. He was awarded the Heslop memorial gold medal in 1895. In 1897 he went to Leipzig to research under the plant physiologist Wilhelm Pfeffer, and while there he won an 1851 Exhibition scholarship. In 1900 he moved to Munich to work under Robert Hartig and thereby acquired a lifelong interest in the fungi. He returned to Birmingham in 1901 as assistant lecturer in botany, and was awarded the D.Sc. degree of the newly established university in 1903. In 1904 he was appointed the first professor of botany at the university of Manitoba, where he became a potent influence in shaping university policy. He soon built up a successful botanical department in Winnipeg and continued active researches on the fungi. He returned to England every summer to work at Birmingham University or at the Royal Botanic Gardens, Kew.

The results of Buller's investigations chiefly appeared in seven volumes entitled *Researches on Fungi*. The first six were issued in 1909, 1922, 1924, 1931, 1933, and 1934, and the last one was published posthumously, for the Royal Society of Canada, in 1950. In his *Researches on Fungi* he made a most important contribution to knowledge of their general biology and sexuality, especially in the higher groups. No one had as yet done so much to show the adaptation of common fungi to their environment and the intimate relation of the structure of their parts to function. These profusely illustrated *Researches* are written in an exhilarating style and exhibit Buller as an observant field naturalist as well as a most skilful experimentalist.

Buller was an inspiring teacher of botany and was in great demand as a lecturer on fungi in both academic and popular circles; he had just that touch of the showman about him which served to communicate enthusiasm to his audience.

He was much interested in the history of mycology, and his presidential address to the British Mycological Society in 1914 was on 'The Fungus Lore of the Greeks and Romans'. He was largely instrumental in arranging for an English translation, published in 1931, of the mycological classic *Selecta Fungorum Carpologia* written by the brothers Tulasne in Latin.

During his early residence at Winnipeg Buller witnessed the great expansion of wheat cultivation in western Canada, and in 1919 his book, *Essays on Wheat*, gave an interesting account of this development.

Buller took an active part in the general scientific life of Canada, especially in connexion with its Royal Society and National Research Council. The former elected him president for 1927-8 and in 1929 conferred on him the Flavelle medal for distinction in scientific attainment. Many other honours were bestowed on him. He was elected F.R.S. in 1929 and was awarded a Royal medal in 1937. He was honorary LL.D. of the universities of Manitoba (1924), Saskatchewan (1928), and Calcutta (1937), and honorary D.Sc. of the university of Pennsylvania (1933).

Buller was interested in all aspects of country life and was a great bird watcher; having musical talent he could repeat the songs of birds. He had a flair for writing humorous verse about all sorts of topics, including fungi. He composed not a few limericks, one of which about relativity, published in *Punch*, 18 December 1923, became famous.

He retired from the chair of botany at Winnipeg in 1936. He returned to England and resided chiefly at Kew where he regularly worked in the herbarium. Early in 1939 he went for the last time to Winnipeg where he continued his researches until he fell ill. He died there, unmarried, 3 July 1944.

[*Nature*, 5 August 1944; F. T. Brooks in *Obituary Notices of Fellows of the Royal Society*, No. 14, November 1945; private information; personal knowledge.]

F. T. Brooks.

BULLOCH, WILLIAM (1868-1941), bacteriologist, pathologist, and medical historian, was born at Aberdeen 19 August 1868, the younger son of John Bulloch by his wife, Mary, daughter of Andrew Malcolm, schoolmaster, of Leochel-Cushnie. John Malcolm Bulloch (1867-1938), journalist and genealogist of the house of Gordon, was his elder brother. His father, an engraver and later a man of business, who edited *Scottish Notes and Queries* in his spare time, was son of another John Bulloch [q.v.], a working brass-finisher remembered as the author of *Studies of the Text of Shakespeare* (1878). The family name was formerly spelled Balloch ('freckled' in Gaelic) and they were supposedly descended from the Macdonalds of the Isles.

After early education in the grammar schools of Aberdeen, Bulloch entered the university. He first joined the faculty of arts, but soon transferred to medicine and qualified M.B., C.M. with highest honours in 1890, winning the Murray medal. In 1894 he graduated M.D. with equal distinction, and was awarded the Struther gold medal in anatomy. Scholarships and prizes enabled him to study pathology under D. J. Hamilton [q.v.] at Aberdeen and with the best masters abroad: so he worked for a time at Leipzig, Vienna, Paris, and Copenhagen, where he formed lifelong friendships with the famous pathologists and bacteriologists of his day. Birch-Hirschfeld, Roux, and Salomonsen were his teachers, and he also ultimately counted among his friends Ehrlich, Koch, Metchnikoff, Madsen, and Lord Lister [q.v.]. A score of his letters from the last were given to the Lister Institute after his death.

On his return to England he was appointed (1895) bacteriologist to the British (later Lister) Institute of Preventive Medicine and shortly afterwards (1897) bacteriologist to the London Hospital, with which he remained intimately associated for the rest of his life. In 1919 he was elected first Goldsmiths' Company's professor of bacteriology in the university of London, and retired with the title of professor emeritus in 1934, remaining consultant in bacteriology to the hospital. He was elected F.R.S. in 1913, and received the honorary degree of LL.D. from the university of Aberdeen in 1920. He was also an original member (1913) of the Medical Research Committee (later Council) and served actively on other government committees, while he was chairman of the governors of the Lister Institute from 1932 until his death.

Copious writer as he was, Bulloch did much research and teaching, and had even greater influence in his profession than might appear from his signed publications; for he silently edited and supplemented the works of innumerable pupils and colleagues and the reports of the many committees of which he was a member. His publications—alone and in collaboration—number well over a hundred. In addition he contributed hundreds of anonymous reviews and abstracts to medical periodicals. His own researches were mainly in serology and immunology, and in medical history and biography; but he will long be remembered as inventor of the 'Bulloch jar' for cultivating anaerobic bacteria (1900), and for his classical work on 'The Preparation of Catgut for Surgical Use' (Medical Research Council, Special Report, No. 138, 1929, with L. H. Lampitt and J. H. Bushill). He also had an enduring interest in haemophilia, on which he contributed (with (Sir) Paul Fildes) an important monograph to the *Treasury of Human Inheritance* (1912) of Karl Pearson [q.v.]. His unique manuscript record of the incidence of this complaint in the royal family was deposited after his death with the Royal Society of Medicine, of which he was an early fellow and honorary librarian.

His chief publication, however, was *The History of Bacteriology* (1938), incorporating his Heath Clark lectures. This is the only complete treatment of the subject from the beginning, and garners the harvest of a lifetime of patient research. It is a work of prime importance in medicine, based on profound study of sources and personal knowledge of many of the pioneers. Like all his writings it is characterized by clarity in thought, accuracy in data, simplicity in expression, and the exactitude of its references. Two other major historical works on which he spent many years were left incomplete and unpublished—a detailed inquiry into the life and works of Spallanzani, and a biographical *Roll of the Fellows of the Royal Society* from its foundation. The manuscript of the latter was acquired by the Society after his death.

In 1923 Bulloch married Irene Adelaide, daughter of Alexander Peyman, and widow of Alfred Augustus Baker, stockbroker. He had no children. In his last years he was hampered by gradually progressing Parkinson's disease, and he died after an emergency operation in his old hospital 11 February 1941.

In appearance Bulloch was short, thickset, clean-shaven, with dark hair and light-brown eyes. Despite long residence in the capital he never lost his native Doric accent. An informal and helpful man, he had countless appreciative friends in many walks of life all over the world. Lively, humorous, and energetic, he yet took no exercise and played no games; his only hobby was historical research. His portrait, painted in oils by his friend Sir Luke Fildes in 1913, was bequeathed to the university of Aberdeen.

[Sir J. C. G. Ledingham in *Obituary Notices of Fellows of the Royal Society*, No. 10, December 1941; *Journal of Pathology and Bacteriology*, vol. liii, September 1941; *Aberdeen University Review*, vol. xxviii, No. 83, Spring 1941; private information; personal knowledge.]

CLIFFORD DOBELL.

BULWER-LYTTON, VICTOR ALEXANDER GEORGE ROBERT, second EARL OF LYTTON (1876–1947), was born at Simla, in India, 9 August 1876, to a family tradition of equal eminence in public service and the arts. He was the grandson of a famous novelist, Bulwer-Lytton (first Baron Lytton, q.v.), who was also in politics, and the son of a viceroy of India and ambassador to Paris, Edward Robert Bulwer Lytton, first Earl of

Lytton [q.v.], who was also well known as a poet under the pseudonym of Owen Meredith. Lytton was the third, but first surviving, son, and he succeeded in 1891 when still a schoolboy to his father's titles and to the old and lovely estate of Knebworth in Hertfordshire. One of his sisters married the second Earl of Balfour and another Sir Edwin Lutyens [qq.v.].

Although never a wealthy man, his circumstances left him free to choose the life that pleased him best. True to the family tradition, he gave himself impartially to public service and the arts with a devotion that drew no distinction between them as ideals. After finishing his education at Eton and Trinity College, Cambridge, where he obtained a second class in the historical tripos in 1898 and was awarded a Winchester Reading prize, and after a few years of travel in Europe, he began his career in 1901 as assistant private secretary to George Wyndham [q.v.], then chief secretary for Ireland. It seemed a natural beginning to an orthodox career. But Lytton's temperament was highly original, and some of his habits of thought only seem orthodox in retrospect because others, who once scorned them, have since learned to take them for granted. He was at once a passionate and a practical idealist, with a wide and witty sense of humour.

One of his earliest heterodoxies was his belief in free trade which separated him at heart from most of his fellow Conservatives without carrying him across to the Liberal Party. Another was the devotion, which he shared with his sister, Lady Constance Lytton, to the cause of women's suffrage. When the suffragettes published a feminist rival to *Who's Who*, Lytton's was one of the very few masculine names to appear in it. Such intended honours were of small importance compared with the cause that inspired him; so was the temporary isolation from the circle of his political friends. Although he never returned to the orthodox career of success which might have awaited him in the Conservative Party, and remained throughout his life at heart a man without party ties, what really mattered to him was that in the end the cause for which he fought was won.

Other activities filled the years of political frustration. In 1910–11 he was chairman of the Royal Commission for the Brussels, Rome, and Turin exhibitions, and in 1913 he joined the advisory council of the Victoria and Albert Museum.

In the latter year he also published his first literary work, a biography of his grandfather, Bulwer-Lytton, who was also the subject of his last work, a short critical study, published posthumously in 1948. With the outbreak of war in 1914 the political atmosphere changed and enabled Lytton to show his powers in more sympathetic conditions: first as a civil lord of the Admiralty (1916), then as additional parliamentary secretary to the Admiralty (1917) and then in succession as British commissioner for propaganda in France (1918), as civil lord again (1919), and as parliamentary under-secretary to the India Office (1920).

The last appointment began a long association with India, where he had connexions both by birth and by marriage. He was appointed governor of Bengal in 1922 and during his term of office he also served for a short time as viceroy while Lord Reading [q.v.] was absent on leave. His warm sympathy for the Indian people and his high hopes of political progress were met by many disappointments, which included both the non-co-operation of Indian leaders and frustrations from higher authority. There were violent disturbances in Calcutta in 1926; there were bitter criticisms and personal threats against him. But he succeeded in winning respect and affection by his dignity and sense of justice; and this success was shown not only by his many friendships with all classes of Indians, especially with their cultural and spiritual leaders, but also in the invitations to him in 1927 and 1928, after his return to England, to lead the Indian delegation to the League of Nations Assembly at Geneva.

The League of Nations, and its successor, the United Nations, held perhaps the chief place among Lytton's political ideals during the latter part of his life. The best known of his untiring activities on its behalf, apart from his share in founding the League of Nations Union, was his chairmanship of the League of Nations mission to Manchuria, which produced the Lytton report in 1932. This report, which condemned Japan's aggression against China, was widely praised but weakly ignored by the governments to which it was addressed; and this weakness, in contrast to the courage and integrity of Lytton's mission, marked perhaps the first fatal steps in the decline of collective security in the 'thirties towards the outbreak of war at the end of the decade. Apart from the chairmanship of a number of governmental and other committees between 1935 and 1945, Lytton held no further official post. It was characteristic of him that he resigned from one of his last governmental positions, as chairman of the Council of Aliens (1939–41), because he could not approve of the political direction to which he was subjected.

In many ways his later life of service was only the fuller for its lack of official ties. His estates at Knebworth were always a deeply loved preoccupation. So were his services to the arts, through the Old Vic Association, the National Theatre Committee, the Royal Society of Literature, and many other bodies; so were winter sports and all kinds of outdoor activities; so were social services of all kinds, ranging from boys' clubs to town planning; and so above all was the English language, which he both spoke and wrote with an enviable accomplishment. Among a number of books, his most successful and moving, as well as the most original, was *Antony: A Record of Youth* (1935), written in commemoration of his elder son, Viscount Knebworth, who was killed on duty as an Auxiliary Air Force pilot in 1933. This work, which won sympathy and gave inspiration all over the English-speaking world, showed better than anything else in Lytton's life the greatness of his character in rising above tragedy and disappointment. His younger son was killed in action at El Alamein in 1942.

Lytton was sworn of the Privy Council in 1919, appointed G.C.I.E. in 1922, G.C.S.I. in 1925, and K.G. in 1933. He never retired from the innumerable activities of his life of service, and he died in full vigour at the age of seventy-one, 26 October 1947, at his beloved Knebworth. In his last years he was rightly described as one of the last of a vanishing race—in appearance and manner and character a natural aristocrat. There are two portraits of him by his brother, Neville Stephen (1879–1951), who succeeded him in his titles; also a head in bronze by Onslow Whiting, and a bronze plaque by Paul Vincze done for the Royal Society of Literature. All are in the possession of the family.

In 1902 Lytton married Pamela, daughter of Sir Trevor John Chichele-Plowden, K.C.S.I., a distinguished Indian Civil Servant. She survived her husband, together with their two daughters.

[Private information; personal knowledge.]
C. M. WOODHOUSE.

BURNETT, SIR CHARLES STUART (1882–1945), air chief marshal, was born at Brown's Valley, Minnesota, 3 April 1882, the second of the four sons of John Alexander Burnett, of Kemnay, Aberdeenshire, by his wife, Charlotte Susan, daughter of Arthur Forbes Gordon, of Rayne, Aberdeenshire. Educated at Bedford Grammar School he joined the 8th Company, Imperial Yeomanry, at the age of seventeen for service in the South African war and was discharged at his own request in June 1901. Four months later he received a commission as second lieutenant, Highland Light Infantry, and was employed with Imperial Yeomanry until 1903. He was then seconded for three years to the West African Frontier Force. He was twice mentioned in dispatches and in October 1907 was promoted in his regiment to lieutenant, Highland Light Infantry. Two years later he resigned his commission and went to Portuguese Guinea where he served in a French shop. From 1911 to 1913 he was assistant resident in Northern Nigeria at Ilorin.

On the outbreak of war in 1914 Burnett joined the Royal Flying Corps and by 1915 was a flight commander with No. 17 Squadron, Middle East. He next commanded No. 12 Squadron in France (1916–17) where he earned a mention by the secretary of state for war. In 1918 he was promoted to command the Fifth Wing and subsequently the Palestine Brigade. He was appointed to the D.S.O. in 1918, created C.B.E. in 1919, and three times mentioned in dispatches.

Early in 1919 Burnett relinquished his army commission as brigadier general staff, to become a wing commander in the Royal Air Force. He was posted to command headquarters in the Middle East and in 1920 was in command of the Royal Air Force in Iraq where he took part in operations under General Sir J. A. L. Haldane. He returned to England in the following year and after commanding the Royal Air Force base, Leuchars, went to the Air Ministry for three years as deputy director, operations and intelligence. From 1927 he commanded the Central Flying School until January 1929 when, having been promoted air commodore, he went to Iraq as air chief staff officer. In January 1931 he returned to England as deputy chief of the air staff and director of operations and intelligence, as air vice-marshal. In November 1932 he went back to Iraq for two years as A.O.C. and carried out successful operations against tribal incursions near Kuweit during which Burnett himself was wounded. Returning to England at the beginning of 1935 he commanded the Inland Area until in 1936 it became the new Training Command and Burnett, now air marshal, its commander-in-chief, with a heavy burden of responsibility for the expansion of the Royal Air Force in face of the threat of war. In 1939 he became inspector-general of the Royal Air Force but in 1940 he went to Australia on special duty as chief of air staff, Royal Australian Air Force, where he again showed his ability to build up an effective striking force. He always preferred command to work in an office and bore the latter with equanimity and a stoically assumed patience. But his success in both was outstanding and the variety of his employment, in both administration and command, revealed his versatility. He possessed those subtle qualities which make a good commander: his was a rugged personality but essentially human and just, as those under his command quickly realized.

In 1942 Burnett went on the retired list but in 1943 he became commandant, Central Command, Air Training Corps. He died at the Royal Air Force hospital, Halton, 9 April 1945, with the rank of air chief marshal. He had been appointed C.B. in 1927 and advanced to K.C.B. in 1936. He married in 1914 Sybil Maud, daughter of John Bell, of Saltburn, Yorkshire. His wife, a relative of Gertrude Bell [q.v.], survived him. There were four daughters.

[*Burke's Landed Gentry*, 1952; personal knowledge.]     J. M. SALMOND.

BURNS, JOHN ELLIOT (1858–1943), Labour leader and politician, was born in south Lambeth (not in Battersea or at Nottingham as he himself stated on different occasions) 20 October 1858, the second surviving son and sixteenth of the eighteen children of Alexander Burns, an engine-fitter who had migrated from Ayrshire to London, by his wife, Barbara Smith who came from Aberdeen. One of John Burns's brothers, as he liked to tell his audiences, became a pugilist. It has often been said that Burns's mother was left a widow in his infancy, but in fact his father died in 1876; it seems probable that he had deserted his wife and family much earlier. Burns's mother was unable to write, and signed his birth certificate with a cross.

Burns left school at the age of ten, and after a period of service as a page-boy, found employment in Price's candle factory before he was twelve. He was next a rivet-boy in an engineering works in Wandsworth Road, and, at the age of fourteen, managed to become apprenticed to a firm at Millbank, despite his mother's poverty, as a skilled engineer. He assiduously attended night schools, and was also a keen cricketer and handy with his fists, as well as a precocious politician and trade-unionist. He took part in agitations among the apprentices, and also in struggles over the right of public meeting on Clapham Common and in other Radical movements. In connexion with one of his meetings he was arrested and locked up, but not for long.

In the works where he was employed, Burns met and became friendly with an old *Communard*, Victor Delahaye, who had been active in Karl Marx's International Working Men's Association. Delahaye was also prominent in the movement for the eight-hour day and for international labour legislation, and he probably taught Burns a great many of his Socialist and Radical ideas. As soon as Burns had finished his time he took a post as foreman engineer under the Niger Company at Akassa in West Africa, but came back to England after a year's absence and resumed his propagandist activities while working at his trade in south London. In 1881 for six months he drove at the Crystal Palace the first electric tram in England. In 1882 he married Martha Charlotte (Pattie), daughter of John Knight Gale, shipwright, of Battersea: he had been friendly with her before his journey to Africa. For many years they were childless, and Burns often told his audiences that the reason was his inability to afford a family and to serve his fellow workers at the same time. His only child, a son, was born in 1895 and predeceased him; his wife died in 1936.

Soon after his marriage, leaving his wife at home, Burns made a journey on the continent, tramping from place to place and meeting a number of foreign trade-unionists and Socialists, with whose help he made some study of labour conditions in the countries which he visited. These included France, Germany, and Austria, and perhaps others. He once boasted that he had walked from Moscow to Madrid; but this, like many of his autobiographical statements, should be taken with a grain of salt. He seems to have been away for only six months in all. On his return he soon threw himself into the new Socialist movement which H. M. Hyndman [q.v.] had organized in 1881 as the Democratic Federation and which in 1884 became the Social Democratic Federation. Burns joined this body in the latter year. In 1883 he had achieved some prominence in connexion with the renewed struggles with the police over the right of public meeting in London parks and open spaces. In the quarrel which rent the Social Democratic Federation asunder at the end of 1884 he took the side of Hyndman against William Morris [q.v.] and the group which seceded to form the anti-parliamentary Socialist League, and he became an executive member of the Social Democratic Federation immediately after the split. He was also active in his trade union—the Amalgamated Society of Engineers—and claimed to have been the youngest delegate at its conference in 1885. In the same year he made a lively appearance on behalf of the Social Democratic Federation at the industrial remuneration conference presided over by Sir Charles Dilke [q.v.]. He there stated that he had been discharged from his employment on account of his attendance at the conference; and he was certainly out of work for seven weeks at this time, and experienced a touch of personal hardship. He was by now well known as a Socialist speaker in the provinces as well as in London; and in 1885 the Nottingham Socialists (Nottingham was an old Radical stronghold) invited him to become their parliamentary candidate in the west division. He polled 598 votes, against 6,669 for the successful Liberal and 3,797 for the unsuccessful Conservative candidate.

Back in London, Burns took a leading part in the demonstrations by the unemployed of 1886 and in the contest over the right of public meeting in Trafalgar Square. In February he was arrested in connexion with an 'unemployed riot' in the square, after which a section of the demonstrators, driven from the square by the police, broke windows in Pall Mall, in retaliation, it is said, for jeers cast at them from the Carlton Club. Burns, Hyndman, and other leaders were tried for seditious conspiracy, but were acquitted, after Burns had defended himself in a challenging speech, which was reported under the title 'The Man with the Red Flag', for he made a practice of carrying a large red flag at his open-air meetings. This trial did much to spread his fame and he also became well known as the principal orator of the Metropolitan Radical Federation, which was pressing hard for reform in municipal as well as in national politics. In 1887 he was the prime mover in leading unemployed processions to visit the principal London churches on Sundays and, after attending the service, to hold meetings outside. He created a disturbance in St. Paul's Cathedral by singing a Socialist version of 'Dare to be a Daniel' after E. H. Gifford [q.v.] had preached a sermon against Socialism. In November 1887 he was again arrested after an attempt to force his way into Trafalgar Square with R. B. Cunninghame Graham [q.v.] on 'Bloody Sunday' as it came to be called, and was sentenced to six weeks' imprisonment.

In 1889 Burns was elected to represent Battersea on the newly created London County Council, and his supporters founded the John Burns Fund to maintain him, at first at the rate of two guineas a week, but by 1892 at five pounds. At about the same time (1889) he quarrelled with the Social Democratic Federation and left it, being charged with co-operating with the Liberals; and he founded the Battersea Labour League, which thereafter served as the main basis for his political work. Burns's public reputation was immensely enhanced by the part which he played as leader in the great London dock strike of 1889. Burns had no connexion with the beginning of the strike, which was mainly a spontaneous movement; but with Tom Mann [q.v.] and others he went to the help of Ben Tillett [q.v.] and the strikers, who were mostly unorganized, and soon made himself the effective leader of the movement. He not only took the lead in oratory and in avoiding clashes with the police, with whom he managed to keep on excellent terms, but also organized soup-kitchens and distributions of such meagre strike-pay as could be afforded, and took the chief part in the negotiations which, with help from the lord mayor, Cardinal Manning [q.v.], and other notable people, at length procured a settlement including the 'dockers' tanner', that is, a minimum rate of sixpence an hour. This famous strike, out of which sprang the Dockers' Union, was followed in 1890 by Burns's first appearance at the Trades Union Congress, as a delegate of the Amalgamated Society of Engineers. He there opposed both the old unionists associated with the Liberal Party and the new school which advocated independent Labour representation, demanding instead a trade-union party based directly upon the industrial movement, and standing for Socialism, but keeping clear of the support of middle-class intellectuals. By a stroke of luck, although defeated for election to the Trades Union Congress parliamentary committee, he became a member of that body when one of the elected members withdrew; but he did not seek re-election the following year, devoting most of his time to work on the London County Council (he continued to represent Battersea until 1907) and to itinerant speaking. On the Council he secured in 1892 the adoption of a fair-wages clause in public contracts, the predecessor of many similar clauses and of the national fair-wages clause adopted by the House of Commons in 1909.

In 1892 Burns was returned to Parliament for Battersea in a straight fight with a Conservative by 5,616 votes to 4,057. He thus became (with J. Keir Hardie and J. Havelock Wilson, qq.v.) one of the first three independent Labour members; but he refused to join Hardie in an independent Labour group, although Hardie offered to act under his leadership. In the London County Council, Liberals and Socialists were already acting together as 'Progressives'; and Burns, even apart from his personal antagonism to Hardie, was doubtless unwilling to associate himself with a definitely anti-Liberal attitude in Parliament. He refused to join the Independent Labour Party when it was founded under Hardie's leadership in 1893, although in that year he was still advocating Socialism at the Trades Union Congress. He was re-elected to the parliamentary committee of the Congress, and was made chairman. In 1894 he refused minor office in Rosebery's administration. He was re-elected for Battersea in 1895 by 5,019 votes to the Conservative candidate's 4,766, still as a Socialist; but at the Trades Union Congress he took the lead in procuring the expulsion from membership of the trades councils, which were the main strongholds of Independent Labour Party Socialism, and in so amending the Congress rules as to exclude himself from further participation, for the new rules laid down that delegates must either be trade-union officials or be actually working at their trades. He thus dropped out of the trade-union movement, as he had done previously out of the Socialist movement, and was thenceforth in effect a 'progressive' working with the Liberals, mainly in connexion with London municipal politics.

Like many other Radicals, Burns opposed the South African war; and in 1900 he barely held his Battersea seat, by 5,860 votes to 5,606. In that year he attended the inaugural conference of the Labour Representation Committee (later the Labour Party) but played no further part in it, associating instead with Lloyd George and the anti-war Radicals in the Democratic League. During the next few years he wrote and spoke extensively in favour of municipal Socialism and against tariff reform; in December 1905 he was made president of the Local Government Board with a seat in the Cabinet (being the first artisan to reach that rank) in Campbell-Bannerman's administration and consequently was sworn of the Privy Council. He was again returned for Battersea (this time with a substantial majority) in January 1906.

Burns's tenure of office which lasted until 1914 is chiefly notable for two things: the enactment of the Housing, Town Planning, &c., Act of 1909, the first measure which provided for town planning (in a permissive form), and his steady and bitter opposition to the measures of Poor Law reform advocated in the reports of the Royal Commission on the Poor Laws and relief of distress, published in 1909. He was especially hostile to the proposals of Sidney and Beatrice Webb [qq.v.] for the 'break-up' of the Poor Law and for the assumption by the State of responsibility for providing work or maintenance for the unemployed. Professing to stand for Poor Law reform, he believed that the necessary changes could be made mainly by administrative action, and was regarded by most Poor Law reformers as being little better than a puppet in the hands of the permanent officials. He was hated above all because of the part which he played in 1906 in the affair of the Poplar board of guardians, who were accused of corrupt practices. The corruption was there; but the conduct of the inquiry was such as to bring public odium on Will Crooks [q.v.] and other Socialist guardians who were entirely innocent of any share in it.

Despite his unpopularity with the Socialists, Burns was twice re-elected at Battersea in 1910 as a Liberal. Early in 1914 he was made president of the Board of Trade; but he fell foul of his Cabinet colleagues first over the question of Ulster, then over the entry of Great Britain into the war. He wanted a stronger policy of coercion to be applied to Ulster; and in common with Lord Morley [q.v.], he was opposed to the British declaration of war on Germany, and resigned office on that issue. He always refused to give the reasons for his resignation, or to answer charges of being a pro-German; but it seems clear that he had been an opponent of the foreign policy of Asquith and Grey, and believed that war could have been avoided.

From 1914 onwards Burns was out of public life; and he never made any serious attempt to return to it. He retired from Parliament in 1918 and in the following year received an annuity of 5,000 dollars under the will of Andrew Carnegie [q.v.]. The rest of Burns's long life was spent mainly in collecting books about old London and the early history of the Labour movement. He was an enthusiastic student of London history and of London's river. It was he who called the Thames 'liquid history'. His books on London were bought and presented by Lord Southwood [q.v.] to the London County Council in December 1943, and another section of his library was acquired by the Amalgamated Engineering Union. Almost to the end he was a familiar figure at the National Liberal Club, noted as a raconteur of his earlier experiences and for a naïve boastfulness about his own part in them.

In his public life, Burns owed a great deal to his exceptional bodily vigour and to his powerful voice, which stood the strain of an immense amount of outdoor speaking. His oratory was simple and direct, and made a great appeal to the then politically unawakened strata of the working class—dockers, gas-workers, casual labourers, and not least their wives. He had also in his early days something of a genius for organization, as well as for getting personally into the limelight. He displayed both qualities in his conduct of the London dock strike, during which he became, instead of 'the Man with the Red Flag', 'the Man in the White Straw Hat', a headgear adopted in order to draw attention to himself, not only for reasons of personal publicity, but also in order that he might be recognized when he threw himself into the fray to check troubles between strikers and blacklegs, or police. Later, this oratory deserted him, and he made no mark as a speaker in the House of Commons. His great physical vigour he kept almost to the end, until he suffered

serious concussion during a German air raid on London, a shock from which he made no full recovery. He died, 24 January 1943, at Bolingbroke Hospital, Wandsworth Common, having been removed there from his home at Clapham Common where he had been a well-known resident for many years. He was buried in St. Mary's churchyard, Battersea Rise, where are also the graves of his wife and son. He received honorary degrees from the universities of Liverpool (1910), and Aberdeen and Birmingham (1911).

A posthumous portrait of Burns by G. W. Leech hangs in Battersea Town Hall. There are also portraits in the National Portrait Gallery by John Collier (1889) and in the National Liberal Club by Harold Speed. This last was presented to Burns in 1912 and given by him to the club. A painting of Burns speaking in a park about 1897 by A. J. Finberg is in the Battersea Library. The National Portrait Gallery has also a pen-and-ink drawing by H. Furniss, and caricatures by Sir Max Beerbohm and Sir F. Carruthers Gould. A cartoon by 'Spy' appeared in *Vanity Fair*, 15 October 1892.

[G. D. H. Cole, *John Burns* (Fabian Biographical Series), 1943; Joseph Burgess, *John Burns: The Rise and Progress of a Right Honourable*, 1911; G. H. Knott, *Mr. John Burns, M.P.*, 1901; William Kent, *London Worthies*, 1939, and *John Burns, Labour's Lost Leader*, 1950; private information, especially from Mr. William Kent, an old friend of Burns to whom particular thanks are due; Burns's papers, including diaries and letters, are in the British Museum.]

G. D. H. COLE.

BUXTON, NOEL EDWARD NOEL-, first BARON NOEL-BUXTON (1869–1948), politician and philanthropist. [See NOEL-BUXTON.]

BUZZARD, SIR (EDWARD) FARQUHAR, first baronet (1871–1945), physician, was born in London 20 December 1871, the eldest of the four sons of Thomas Buzzard, the eminent neurologist, by his wife, Isabel, daughter of Joseph Wass, of Lea, Derbyshire. He was educated at Charterhouse, where he was awarded a leaving exhibition in science, and at Magdalen College, Oxford. In his early days he was renowned for his prowess at Association football. He played for the university (1893–4) and for the Old Carthusian eleven, winners of the Amateur Cup (1894, 1897), the London Senior Cup (1895–7), and the London Charity Cup

(1896). After obtaining a fourth class in natural science (physiology) in 1894, he completed his medical training at St. Thomas's Hospital, where he won the Mead medal in 1897. From St. Thomas's he went to the National Hospital for Nervous Diseases at Queen Square, which was then in its hey-day as a centre of neurological study and research. After acting as house-physician to J. Hughlings Jackson [q.v.] he held successively the appointments of medical registrar and pathologist and in 1905 was elected assistant physician, a post which he held until 1922. In 1903 he became assistant physician to the Royal Free Hospital, an appointment which was followed later by that of full physician and lecturer in medical pathology. In 1910 he returned to St. Thomas's Hospital as physician to out-patients, and was for eleven years assistant physician to the Belgrave Hospital for Children. He was also physician or consulting physician to the Queen Alexandra Military Hospital, Millbank, the Royal Hospital for Incurables, the Throat Hospital, Golden Square, and the Artists' Annuity and Benevolent funds.

Buzzard was a keen clinical observer and he had in a marked degree the qualities of a good consultant. Although his name is not associated with any important discovery or notable addition to knowledge, he made several valuable contributions to neurology, such as the clinical differentiation and morbid anatomy of sub-acute combined degeneration of the spinal cord, in which he was associated with Frederick Eustace Batten and James Collier. His literary output was considerable but was mostly in the form of contributions to textbooks. During the war of 1914–18 he was consultant to the London Command, with the rank of colonel, and in 1918 he edited the 'Military Medical Manuals' of Athanassio-Benisty on *Clinical Forms of Nerve Lesions* and *Treatment and Repair of Nerve Lesions* and of J. Babinski and J. Froment on *Hysteria or Pithiatism*. With Dr. J. G. Greenfield he wrote a monograph on *The Pathology of the Nervous System* (1921). He was Lettsomian (1926), Maudsley (1932), and Earl Grey memorial (1939) lecturer.

In 1928 when at the height of his career as a consultant Buzzard accepted an invitation to succeed Sir A. E. Garrod [q.v.] as regius professor of medicine at Oxford. He soon became immersed in medical and academic activities of all kinds, and he greatly strengthened the importance and influence of the Oxford medical school.

In his presidential address to the British Medical Association at its Oxford meeting in 1936, Buzzard outlined the ambitious dream of a medical school primarily devoted to clinical research and to the training of men who would pass on to be research workers and teachers. Thanks to the vast benefactions of Lord Nuffield, whose physician, friend, and adviser he was, this dream became a reality. Buzzard took the leading part in the foundation of the Nuffield Institute for Medical Research (1935) and the scheme for enlarging the scope of the Oxford medical school (1937). As the scheme developed he became more and more convinced of the importance of the study of preventive medicine and of environmental conditions and, as the first chairman of the Nuffield Provincial Hospitals Trust, he was largely instrumental in directing its activities into the field of social medicine. He was responsible for the foundation of the chair and institute of social medicine at Oxford to which J. A. Ryle [q.v.] was appointed in 1943.

Buzzard's term of office as regius professor was extended five years beyond the normal age of retirement and he did not become emeritus professor until 1943. At the Royal College of Physicians, of which he was elected a fellow in 1906, he was Goulstonian lecturer (1907), councillor (1922–3), censor (1923–4, 1927), representative on the General Medical Council (1927–9), and Harveian orator (1941). In 1928 he was a member of the team attending King George V in his serious illness; from 1932 to 1936 he was one of the physicians-in-ordinary; and from 1937 physician-extraordinary to King George VI. He was appointed K.C.V.O. in 1927, and in 1929 was created a baronet. In 1937 he stood unsuccessfully as a Conservative candidate for the university of Oxford. He was president of the sections of neurology, psychiatry, and clinical medicine of the Royal Society of Medicine, of the International Society of Medical Hydrology, of the Institute of Hospital Almoners, and of the Association of Physicians of Great Britain and Ireland. In 1940 he was awarded the Osler memorial medal by the university of Oxford, and he was an honorary LL.D. of Queen's University, Belfast, and of the university of Manitoba. He was elected an honorary fellow of Magdalen in 1928 and an honorary student of Christ Church in 1943.

Buzzard retained his love for almost every form of active sport and his other interests included the Turf, sketching, the collection of pictures, and the exploration of old churches. In 1899 he married May, daughter of Edward Bliss, of Edgbaston, and by her he had two sons and three daughters. He died at Oxford 17 December 1945, and was succeeded in the baronetcy by his elder son Anthony Wass (born 1902), a rear-admiral in the Royal Navy, and director of naval intelligence, 1951–4. A portrait by James Gunn is at Christ Church, Oxford.

[*The Times*, 19 December 1945; *British Medical Journal* and *Lancet*, 29 December 1945; *St. Thomas's Hospital Gazette*, February 1946; *Nature*, 23 February 1946.]

W. J. BISHOP.

BYRON, ROBERT (1905–1941), traveller, art critic, and historian, was born at Wembley 26 February 1905, the only son among three children of Eric Byron, civil engineer, by his wife, Margaret, daughter of William Robinson, of Southall Manor, Middlesex. He was educated at Eton and Merton College, Oxford, where he obtained a third class in modern history in 1925. In that year his first travels took him to Greece, a country for which he had a passionate admiration and where, as a member of the family of Lord Byron, he was well received. His first book, *Europe in the Looking-Glass* (1926), was a high-spirited account of this undergraduate jaunt, and it was followed during the next four years by three ambitious studies in late Hellenism of which *The Byzantine Achievement* (1929) is the most satisfying.

In 1929 he travelled to India as special correspondent for the *Daily Express*, and in the next year made a brief journey into Tibet. The first literary result of these experiences was *An Essay on India* (1931) which, in the opinion of the viceroy, Lord Willingdon [q.v.], contained the best brief statement of Indian political problems at that time. His Tibetan journey was recorded two years later in *First Russia, then Tibet*.

A period of journalism in London was followed by a visit to Persia and Afghanistan during 1933 and 1934, an adventure which prompted the best of his books, *The Road to Oxiana* (1937). This may be described as an inquiry into the origins of Islamic art presented in the form of one of the most entertaining travel books of modern times. He wrote it in China dur-ing 1935 and 1936 after making the overland journey to the Far East through Russia.

In 1936 Byron settled in London where shortly after the outbreak of war in 1939 he was engaged as a sub-editor in the overseas news department of the British Broadcasting Corporation. While on his way to Cairo as a special war correspondent for a group of English newspapers he was drowned by enemy action, probably on 24 February 1941. He was unmarried.

Byron's writing showed continuous growth and even his lightest things, such as *How We Celebrate the Coronation* (1937), were written with all his energy and care. His development was very rapid and while still a young man he became, what he remained, the only writer of his time to convey a vivid idea of Byzantine art and civilization to the common reader. His first books sometimes erred on the side of massiveness of expression but his most considered and interesting performance, *The Road to Oxiana*, was written with such charm and gaiety that most contemporary readers did not recognize it as a serious and original contribution to Islamic studies. Paradoxically it was better appreciated by the specialists, for whom he had no liking, than by the unspecialized readers to whom it was addressed. He may be said to have anticipated views which later scholarship has adduced from fuller evidence than was then available.

He was of a polemical disposition and unfortunately he allowed this to leave blemishes on all his books, even his best. There is some disproportion in his work as a result, but the fault is compensated by the delight which goes with intense enthusiasm.

A portrait of Byron by A. M. Daintrey is in the possession of the family.

[Christopher Sykes, *Four Studies in Loyalty*, 1946; Harold Acton, *Memoirs of an Aesthete*, 1948; personal knowledge.]

CHRISTOPHER SYKES.

CADMAN, JOHN, first BARON CADMAN (1877–1941), scientist and public servant, was born 7 September 1877 in the mining village of Silverdale, north Staffordshire, the eldest of the thirteen children of James Cope Cadman and his wife, Betty, daughter of Joseph Keeling. He was educated at the High School, Newcastle under Lyme, and went with a county scholarship to the Durham College of

Science (later Armstrong College), Newcastle upon Tyne, and graduated B.Sc. in the university of Durham in 1899, later proceeding M.Sc. and D.Sc. He was trained as a mining engineer by his father, a civil engineer specializing in mining problems, and his knowledge of engineering, chemistry, and physics was extensive. After serving as assistant manager of the collieries at Silverdale and Trimdon Grange, he was appointed a government inspector of mines in 1902. At first he was stationed in east Scotland where he came in touch with the Scottish shale-oil industry and the work of James Young [q.v.] on the distillation of coal and shale. From that time he took a keen interest in oil. He made great efforts to reduce the loss of life in coal-mines and was always ready to risk his own life in his search for information. He was awarded a gold medal for exceptional bravery in rescue work after a disaster at the Hamstead colliery in 1908, and for other brave actions he was awarded the North Staffordshire Brigade rescue medal with five clasps.

In 1904 Cadman was seconded from the Home Office to the Colonial Office for service in Trinidad as government mining engineer, and on returning to this country undertook special research for the Royal Commission on mines, 1907–8. In the latter year he was appointed professor of mining at Birmingham University where he remained for thirteen years. He organized a school of petroleum technology which was the first of its kind in the world. Until then foreigners had been responsible for the development of all petroleum projects abroad, but Cadman's school turned out fully trained technologists able to take their place in the field. Cadman loved his professorial duties and planned coal and petroleum research on a large scale. His work was interrupted when in 1913 he was appointed to an Admiralty commission to investigate the potentialities of the Persian oilfields. The Royal Navy was by now committed to the adoption of oil as its principal fuel and an assured supply from the newly formed Anglo-Persian Oil Company appeared to be essential. As a result of the work of the commission an agreement was completed between the Admiralty and the company. When the oil position became critical in the course of the war of 1914–18 Cadman became director of the Petroleum Executive and chairman of the Inter-Allied Petroleum Council.

Resigning his professorship in 1920

Cadman became technical adviser to the Anglo-Persian Oil Company in 1921, a director in 1923 and later chairman. He was also chairman of the Iraq Petroleum Company, a director of the Suez Canal Company and of the Great Western Railway Company. In addition he did much public work, serving on the Post Office committee of inquiry, 1932, on the Post Office Advisory Council, 1936–9, on the Advisory Council, Department of Scientific and Industrial Research, 1920–28 and 1934–9, on the Fuel Research Board, 1923–41, on the Economic Advisory Council, 1930–41; he was chairman of the civil aviation inquiry, 1937–8, and of the television advisory committee, 1939.

Many honours, including several foreign decorations, came to Cadman who was appointed C.M.G. in 1916 and promoted K.C.M.G. (1918) and G.C.M.G. (1929) and raised to the peerage as Baron Cadman, of Silverdale, in 1937. He was an honorary LL.D. (1934) of Birmingham, D.C.L. (1937) of Durham, and D.Eng. of Melbourne, and he was elected F.R.S. in 1940. He presided at various times over the Institute of Petroleum, which he helped to found, the Institution of Mining Engineers, the Institute of Fuel, and the Society of Gas Engineers. He combined scientific and technical knowledge with business ability and an unusual understanding of men. The importance of the human factor in industrial efficiency was preached and practised by him. He was a good churchman, of moderate views, and while chairman of the Anglo-Iranian Oil Company he appointed a resident chaplain in Abadan. Later he appointed the Rev. P. T. B. ('Tubby') Clayton, founder of Toc H, to travel to and fro on the various ships of the tanker fleet and subsequently made him chaplain to the company, with an office at London headquarters.

Cadman was staunch and faithful as a friend and was ever ready to help and offer a word of advice. Coal was always his main interest and he often laughingly remarked that he was not an oil man. Coal, he said, was in his blood and always would be. Although he was not in favour of nationalizing the coal-mines, he advocated a federation to control or advise on all operations from the pit to the consumer. He was a friendly critic of the gas industry and put forward proposals for the transmission of gas at pressures up to 600 pounds per square inch, with transforming stations to reduce the pressure to the requirements of the consumer.

On the outbreak of war in 1939, although very unwell, Cadman offered his help to the Government and served as honorary principal adviser on oil; he served also as the first chairman of the Scientific Advisory Council appointed by the minister of supply. The work taxed his strength to the utmost and after a long illness he died 31 May 1941 at his home near Bletchley, Buckinghamshire. He was buried in the churchyard of the parish church at Silverdale. In 1907 he married Lilian, daughter of John Harragin, a stipendiary magistrate, of Trinidad. They had two daughters and two sons, the elder of whom, John Basil Cope (born 1909) succeeded to the title. A portrait by J. A. A. Berrie hangs in the boardroom of the British Petroleum Company at Britannic House, Finsbury Circus, London.

[Sir Frank Smith in *Obituary Notices of Fellows of the Royal Society*, No. 10, December 1941; private information; personal knowledge.]

F. E. Smith.

CAIRNS, DAVID SMITH (1862–1946), Scottish theologian, was born 8 November 1862 at Stichill (or Stitchel) in Roxburghshire, the third of four children of the Rev. David Cairns, minister of the United Presbyterian church there, and his wife, Elisabeth, daughter of the Rev. Dr. David Smith, of Biggar. After his schooling at Ednam and the High School, Kelso, he took his arts degree at Edinburgh University and studied theology at the United Presbyterian College in Edinburgh, of which his uncle, the celebrated John Cairns [q.v.], was principal, spending one semester also at Marburg University, where he was influenced by the Ritschlian theologian Wilhelm Herrmann. He was ordained in 1895 and became minister of the United Presbyterian church at Ayton, Berwickshire. In 1907 he became professor of dogmatics and apologetics in the United Free Church College, Aberdeen. Of this college, known since the Church union of 1929 as Christ's College, he became principal in 1923; and in it he taught until he retired in 1937 and went to live in Edinburgh.

Cairns took an active part in the life of the Church and in many public movements, and made lecture tours both in America and in the Far East. In 1923 he was elected moderator of the General Assembly of the United Free Church of Scotland. He received the honorary degree of D.D. from the universities of Aberdeen (1909), Debrecen (Hungary, 1929), and Edinburgh (1933), and of LL.D. from St. Andrews (1937) and Aberdeen (1938). In 1918 he was appointed O.B.E. in recognition of work done for the troops during the war.

Cairns was above all a Christian apologist, interpreting the Christian faith to his age in the light of modern science and historical criticism. In his undergraduate days he had passed through a profound crisis of religious doubt, under which his health broke down, and he had to interrupt his studies for a period of foreign travel; when his faith was restored he was committed to the lifelong enterprise of thinking it out and giving theological help to other questioners. This he did not only in a succession of theological works, but in many more personal contacts, for which his warm human sympathy well fitted him. His thought was dominated by the conviction, which found its most original expression in his most influential book, *The Faith that Rebels* (1928), that the universe was not a closed system but a purposive universe, in which nothing was impossible to God, and therefore nothing was impossible to a human faith which absolutely trusted Him, as Jesus did. It was along this line that he interpreted the miracles, and closely connected with this was his interpretation of the Kingdom of God and its victory in this world, including the victory over disease and suffering.

In 1901 Cairns married Helen Wilson (died 1910), daughter of Henry Hewat Craw, gentleman farmer, of West Foulden, Berwickshire. They had one daughter and one son, Professor David Cairns, of Christ's College, Aberdeen. Cairns died in Edinburgh 27 July 1946. A portrait of him by Gordon Shields hangs in Christ's College, Aberdeen.

[David Cairns, *An Autobiography*, 1950; private information; personal knowledge.]

D. M. Baillie.

CALDECOTE, first Viscount (1876–1947), lawyer and statesman. [See Inskip, Thomas Walker Hobart.]

CALLENDER, Sir Geoffrey Arthur Romaine (1875–1946), naval historian and first director of the National Maritime Museum, was born at Didsbury, Manchester, 25 November 1875, the only son of Arthur William Callender, cotton-mill owner, and his wife, Agnes Louisa, daughter of the Rev. George Stephen Woodgate, vicar of Pembury, Kent. Educated at St. Edward's School, and at Merton College, Oxford, where he was placed in the second class of the honours list in modern history in 1897, he was appointed in January 1905 to the new Royal Naval College, Osborne, where he embraced the study of naval history with characteristic enthusiasm. Finding no textbook suitable for naval cadets, he instantly set about producing his *Sea Kings of Britain* (3 vols., 1907–11). He became head of the History and English department in January 1913, and there-after the navy and its history were the guiding interests of his life. In 1921 he moved to the Royal Naval College, Dart-mouth, as head of the history department there. But he did not remain long. Experience gleaned from the war of 1914–18 showed that a study of history was essential at all levels of naval education: a chair of history was therefore established at the Royal Naval College, Greenwich, where a Staff College and a War College were also being formed. Callender was appointed first occupant in 1922 and it was there that he published his best-known work, *The Naval Side of British History* (1924).

Meanwhile (1921–4), the Society for Nautical Research was conducting its great campaign to save H.M.S. *Victory*. Callender was already that body's honorary secretary and treasurer—a dual post which he held continuously from 1920 until his death—and he was largely responsible for the successful outcome of the campaign.

He now embarked upon his dearest project: the foundation of a museum which would assemble under one roof the priceless naval and maritime treasures of this country. The co-operation of the Society for Nautical Research and bene-ficent sympathizers like Sir James Caird secured the acquisition of the magnificent Macpherson collection of naval and nautical prints for the nation (1928), to form, with the pictures and models already at the college, the nucleus of the new museum. The ideal site was Inigo Jones's Queen's House, then occupied by the Royal Hospital School; and on the latter migrating to Holbrook, the last difficulty was overcome. The National Maritime Museum Act was passed in 1934 and Callender became, as of right, the first

director. Into the immense task of restoring the Queen's House, preparing the galleries, assembling the exhibits and arranging them he threw his whole energy, and the museum was opened by King George VI, 27 April 1937. Callender was knighted in the following year and spent the rest of his life improving and adding to the collections. He died, suddenly, but fittingly, in the museum 6 November 1946. He was unmarried.

Callender was a man of exceptional personality, a born conversationalist, and a brilliant lecturer, respected and beloved by several generations of naval officers, and possessed of an encyclopaedic know-ledge of nautical antiquities. His portrait by D. S. Ewart hangs in the board-room of the museum.

[Private information; personal knowledge.]
MICHAEL LEWIS.

CAMERON, SIR DAVID YOUNG (1865–1945), painter and etcher, was born in Glasgow 28 June 1865, the third, but eldest surviving, son in a family of nine born to the Rev. Robert Cameron, a scholarly minister of the Scottish Church, by his wife, Margaret Johnson, daughter of Donald Robertson, surgeon, who her-self was greatly gifted as a painter in water-colours. At the age of nine Cameron entered Glasgow Academy, where, as he said, he fell in love with art under the influence and enthusiasm of John Mac-laren, the master of writing, drawing, and music. In 1881 he was put into the office of a Glasgow iron foundry, which he hated. Before and after office hours, he attended classes at the Glasgow School of Art. It was seen that his heart was not in com-merce, and it was likewise with law, which was tried in an uncle's law office in Perth. Here he bought Bristol boards and pen-sketched subjects in Perth, on the Tay, and also in Arran. At length he was allowed to follow his bent and at twenty he entered the Mound School of Art in Edinburgh where he impressed his fellow students by his industry, persistence, and enthusiasm. While still a student he first exhibited in 1886 in the Royal Scottish Academy, and also associated himself with the young rebel artists of the Glasgow school whose work was opposed to the art ideals of the Academy in that they desired to represent nature seen as a whole, and by strength and vigour of handling to bring out the mass and weight of things rather than the superficial realism of trivial detail which was then the vogue.

In 1887 George Stevenson of Glasgow, an expert amateur etcher and a friend of (Sir) F. Seymour Haden [q.v.], was greatly impressed by Cameron's pen-and-ink sketches and suggested he should try etching, in which, under Stevenson's encouragement, tuition, and temporary co-operation, he became remarkably proficient. From then onwards Cameron etched or dry-pointed over 500 prints including book-illustrations and a series of ex-libris. So impressive was his early etching of 'A Perthshire Village' that, while also active as a painter, he was elected, at the age of twenty-four, an associate of the Royal Society of Painter-Etchers. He contributed some 125 works to the exhibitions of this Society, but in 1902 he and William Strang [q.v.], being members of the council, resigned from the Society as a protest against the admission of reproductive engravings for exhibition.

While resident in Glasgow, Cameron travelled in Holland, Italy, France, and Belgium and began to exhibit abroad. In 1893 he was awarded medals from Antwerp and Chicago and two years later the Brussels silver medal, to be followed in 1897 by the Dresden gold medal and in 1900 and 1905 by those of Paris and Munich. After his marriage in 1896 with Jean (died 1931), daughter of Robert MacLaurin, a Glasgow merchant, he went in 1898 to live at Kirkhill, Kippen, Stirlingshire, where was begun the building of Dun Eaglais, his permanent home, from which the view to Ben Ledi and the Grampians was for almost half a century his unfailing inspiration, and, in the early morning light, was to occupy him long in his last painting, 'Dawn'. A visit to Egypt in the winter of 1908-9 made him realize yet more the massive grandeur of the prehistoric region of his own land. Influences such as these stimulated yet more his artistic bent which displayed, along with delicacy and serenity, breadth of vision, originality, and penetration.

A month after he had been elected in 1904 as an associate of the Royal Society of Painters in Water Colours (he became a member in 1906) Cameron, whose name and fame had passed beyond Scotland, was elected an associate of the Royal Scottish Academy. Fourteen years later he became an academician. In 1911 he was elected an associate engraver of the Royal Academy, and in 1916 was once more elected an associate, for his painting, with full privileges and unreserved rights to contribute in either section, a double honour of which Cameron was the only recipient. In 1920 he was elected an academician.

During the war of 1914-18 Cameron was one of a group of artists selected by the Government of Canada to make pictorial records of the war; for this he spent the summer and autumn of 1917 in France on the Canadian front and then in December began his painting of 'The Battlefield of Ypres', out of which came the inexorably desolating 'Garment of War' which he presented to the Scottish Modern Arts Association.

In 1919 Cameron bought a house in London for his annual spring and autumn visits. In that year also he joined the British School at Rome, taking part in the work of the faculties of painting and engraving and in the general administration of the school, which he visited in 1923 and 1924. He was chairman of the faculty of painting from 1925 to 1938 and served on the council and executive committee to the day of his death. In 1925 the Speaker of the House of Commons offered him the position of master painter in a scheme for the decoration of St. Stephen's Hall with eight mural paintings to represent 'the building of Britain'. It was Cameron's close connexion with the British School at Rome which enabled him to choose all but one of the eight artists either from the members of his faculty of painting or from other Rome scholars.

Cameron was knighted in 1924 and in 1933 appointed King's painter and limner in Scotland. He was also a trustee of the National Galleries of Scotland, of the Tate Gallery, an original member of the Royal Fine Art Commission and later of the Commission for Scotland. A member of the National Art-Collections Fund he never rested until Millais's 'Christ in the House of His Parents' was secured for the nation.

Cameron was a man of strong and attractive personality and withal of very deep religious faith which showed itself, especially after his wife's death, in an increasing feeling for design and harmony, and in his unwearied appeals for a greater recognition of the arts by the Church, and especially the Church of Scotland. His own parish church at Kippen he beautified and adorned by colour and symbol, and it was after an impassioned appeal to give the arts their place in worship that he collapsed and died at Perth 16 September 1945. He was an honorary LL.D. of

Glasgow, Manchester, Cambridge, and St. Andrews.

There is a portrait of Cameron in oils by his friend A. K. Lawrence, and a bust in bronze by Percy Portsmouth; the latter is now in the possession of the Scottish Modern Arts Association, the former which is privately owned will go eventually to the Scottish National Portrait Gallery.

[*Glasgow Herald* and *Scotsman*, 17 September 1945; *The Times*, 18 September 1945; David Martin, *The Glasgow School of Painting*, 1897; Frank Rinder, *D. Y. Cameron—An Illustrated Catalogue of his Etchings and Dry-Points, 1887–1932*, 1932; A. M. Hind, *The Etchings of D. Y. Cameron*, 1924; *The Glasgow Academy, 1846–1946*, 1946; private information; personal knowledge.]

S. J. M. COMPTON.

CAMERON, SIR DONALD CHARLES (1872–1948), colonial governor, was born in British Guiana 3 June 1872, the second son of Donald Charles Cameron, sugar planter, of Plantation Blankenberg, and later of Georgetown, Demerara. His mother, Mary Emily, daughter of Richard Brassington, of Dublin, died when he was a boy, and, his father marrying again, Cameron was brought to England and later sent to Rathmines School in Dublin, where he remained until he was eighteen. He returned to British Guiana in 1890 and entered the inland revenue department of the Civil Service. The following year he was transferred to the colonial secretariat in which he served until 1904, rising to the rank of principal clerk by 1901. On several occasions he acted as private secretary to the acting governor, Sir Cavendish Boyle, and as assistant government secretary and clerk of councils. While on leave in 1902–3 he acted as private secretary to Boyle who had been promoted to be governor of Newfoundland.

In 1904 Boyle was appointed governor of Mauritius and Cameron's transfer to that colony as assistant colonial secretary in the same year was probably made at his request. Cameron acted as colonial secretary on various occasions and was serving in that capacity in 1907 when the incident occurred which altered his whole life.

The secretary of state for the Colonies had selected for the post of receiver-general of Mauritius an experienced officer who was not a native of the island, and this was resented by the local politicians who favoured a local candidate. At a meeting of the council of government on 9 July, Cameron, in a speech justifying the action of the secretary of state, made remarks about a certain section of the Mauritian public service which were bitterly resented. At a subsequent meeting, on 23 July, a motion was presented by an elected member regretting that the acting colonial secretary should have cast an undeserved slur on the public officers of the colony; the motion was held to be out of order by the votes of a majority of the council (the official and nominated members) and this resulted in a public demonstration which led the governor to suspend the meeting. A request was later made to the secretary of state by the elected members for Cameron's removal.

There is no doubt that while in Mauritius Cameron did his work capably and conscientiously, and that in the fearless (and perhaps tactless) discharge of his duties he offended some of those whose vested interests suffered as a result. He seems, however, to have received little support from his superiors and the governor agreed with alacrity to Cameron's offer to proceed on leave so as not to embarrass the administration. Before he left the island Cameron was threatened with personal violence and suffered much unpleasantness.

As a way out of the difficulty Cameron was transferred to the Southern Nigerian service in 1908, as assistant secretary in the secretariat. In 1909 he served as secretary to the Southern Nigeria liquor trade inquiry committee. He acted on various occasions as provincial commissioner and in 1912 he twice acted as colonial secretary of Southern Nigeria.

The amalgamation of Northern and Southern Nigeria under Sir Frederick (later Lord) Lugard [q.v.] in January 1914 resulted in the appointment of Cameron to be central secretary, a post of considerable responsibility, but of little real authority, and even less status, in the official hierarchy. Cameron, still smarting under the unfair treatment which he felt he had received in connexion with the Mauritius incident, thought that his services had not been adequately recognized by this appointment, and he never really forgave Lugard. However, when Sir Hugh Clifford [q.v.] went to Nigeria as governor in 1919 he quickly recognized Cameron's ability and, following an administrative reorganization, Cameron was appointed chief secretary to the Government on 1 January 1921. In this post he was Clifford's chief adviser and the close co-operation between these two brilliant men brought the administration of Nigeria to a high level of efficiency. Cameron acted three times as governor during Clifford's absence on leave, and in 1924 was himself appointed governor and commander-in-chief of Tanganyika, assuming duty in the Territory in April 1925.

Tanganyika had been assigned by the League of Nations to Great Britain, under mandate, in 1922, after a period of military rule which followed the conquest of German East Africa during the war of 1914–18. Uncertainty about the future had prevented any real development of this backward country, and Cameron quickly applied himself to the task of reconstruction. He established a legislative council, reorganized the African Civil Service, and devoted much attention to education. He applied to the Territory the principles of native administration which, under Lugard's wise guidance, had proved so successful in Northern Nigeria. Cameron was a believer in the value of 'indirect rule', based on the indigenous institutions of the people themselves, as a means of teaching backward tribes the idea of self-government and efficient administration, but he was no blind worshipper of the fetish of native administration and adapted what he had seen established in Nigeria to the conditions existing in Tanganyika.

During his governorship the question of the union of Tanganyika with the adjoining territories of Kenya and Uganda was actively considered. To such a union Cameron was strongly opposed except on such conditions as would safeguard the interests of the natives of Tanganyika. Failing such safeguards he made it clear to the secretary of state for the Colonies that he would resign his appointment if union were effected. In his book, *My Tanganyika Service—and some Nigeria*, published in 1939, he indicated that in this controversy he counted on the 'strong opposition of the powerful Labour Party', and, in the end, after some four years of discussion, the question of 'closer union' was dropped.

In 1931 Cameron was appointed governor and commander-in-chief of Nigeria, which was at the time suffering from the world depression. The revenue of the country had fallen by one-third and the drastic economies necessary made progress almost impossible. It was unfortunate that these circumstances prevented Cameron's long experience of Nigeria being applied effectively to its development.

In 1935, owing to the illness of his wife, Cameron retired and came to live in England. He continued to take a lively interest in colonial affairs, and served as a member of the Colonial Office advisory committee on education and as vice-chairman of the governing body of the Imperial College of Tropical Agriculture.

Cameron had a remarkable capacity for work, a quick grasp of essentials, an astounding memory for details, and a facility for lucid expression in writing and speech. His manner was often forbidding and his mordant humour made many enemies. In his official life he was ruthlessly efficient and he never learned to suffer fools gladly; his dislikes were often too obvious and sometimes cruel in their results. He was, however, a man of deep sympathies and humanity and he delighted in secret kindnesses to those in need. Never popular with the crowd, he was greatly liked and respected by his intimate friends and by those who worked in close contact with him. He had a genuine sympathy for the people of Africa.

Cameron married in 1903 Gertrude, daughter of Duncan Gittens, a sugar planter, of Oldbury, Barbados. The death of their only child, Geoffrey Valentine Cameron, legal secretary to the Government of Malta, who is presumed to have lost his life in an aircraft which disappeared at sea in May 1941; his wife's long illness; and his own increasing blindness saddened Cameron's last years. He died in London 8 January 1948.

Cameron was appointed C.M.G. in 1918, K.B.E. in 1923, K.C.M.G. in 1926, and G.C.M.G. in 1932. He received the honorary degree of LL.D. from Cambridge University in 1937.

[Official publications; *The Times*, 10 January 1948; private information; personal knowledge.]    ALAN BURNS.

CAMPBELL, JOHN CHARLES (1894–1942), major-general, was born at Thurso, Caithness, 10 January 1894, the second child and only son of Daniel Alexander Campbell, later in business in India, by his wife, Marion, daughter of Donald MacKay, sheep farmer, of Skelpick, Sutherland. He was educated at Sedbergh School, and on the first day of war in 1914 he enlisted in the Honourable Artillery Company, and in July 1915 was commissioned second lieutenant from the

Royal Military Academy, Woolwich. He joined the British Expeditionary Force in August, was wounded in February and May 1916, and in September was sent back to England, but returned to the front in August 1917. At the end of the war he was serving in France as a captain in the Royal Horse Artillery and had been awarded the M.C.

Between the wars Campbell made his mark as an equitation instructor at Woolwich and later at Weedon, with a reputation of being an ideal regimental officer and a first-class horseman. He was fond of all animals and particularly devoted to horses, excelling at polo, being in all three Royal Artillery teams which won the inter-regimental polo cup and for some years he was probably unsurpassed in the shires as a heavyweight rider to hounds. The outbreak of war in 1939 found him a major in command of C battery, 4th Regiment, Royal Horse Artillery, in Egypt. In July 1940 he succeeded to the command of his regiment and when in September the Italian advance began, he soon distinguished himself by the boldness and judgement with which he handled his guns in a series of rearguard actions while commanding alternately the 4th and 3rd Regiments, R.H.A. During this period he organized and led a number of mobile columns, consisting of a few guns and escort, against the Italian communications, and when used against the Germans these were nicknamed, after him, 'Jock columns'. For this service he was appointed to the D.S.O.

During the long advance to Benghazi in which, for his work on 14 December 1940, he received a bar to the D.S.O., Campbell displayed the same dash and enterprise, and during the subsequent retreat to Sollum he rendered marked service.

The climax of his career came in the autumn of 1941 when he was appointed to the command of the 7th support group with the rank of brigadier (3 September). His handling of the group during the two most critical days of the battle of Sidi Rezegh (21 and 22 November) became an epic of the war. When almost surrounded by superior forces, Campbell acted as one inspired; he was the heart and soul of the defences. Thrice he led tank forces against the advancing enemy, guiding his troops from his open car with a blue handkerchief; thrice he helped personally in the service of the guns at critical moments of the battle and though wounded at the height of the battle he refused to be evacuated. For this work he was awarded the Victoria Cross.

In the following February Campbell was appointed to command the 7th Armoured division with the rank of major-general, but on 26 February 1942 he was killed in a motor accident at Halfaya Pass.

Campbell married in 1922 Rosamond Elizabeth, daughter of William Rhodes, J.P., a nephew of Cecil Rhodes [q.v.]; they had two daughters.

[Official records; Roy Farran, *Winged Dagger*, 1948; personal knowledge.]

ALFRED BURNE.

[J. A. I. Agar-Hamilton and L. C. F. Turner, *The Sidi Rezeg Battles, 1941*, 1957.]

CAMPBELL, SIR MALCOLM (1885–1948), racing motorist, was born 11 March 1885 at Chislehurst, Kent, the only son and elder child of William Campbell, watchmaker and jeweller of Cheapside, and his wife, Ada Westerton. Descended from a Campbell who had fought at Culloden, and the heir to a considerable fortune from the family business, Malcolm Campbell was educated at Uppingham and in Germany and France. He next worked for three years on Lloyd's, for the first two without a salary and for the third for less than a pound a week, which he invested in motor-cycles. At the age of twenty-one he became an underwriting member of Lloyd's and shortly afterwards had the brilliant idea of insuring newspapers against libel action which enabled him to build up a good and profitable business.

Campbell's spare time was devoted to buying cars and motor-cycles and racing them. He made his first appearance at Brooklands in 1908. In 1910 he bought the big Darracq which had won the Vanderbilt Cup in America the year before and was capable of 100 m.p.h. Campbell called it the 'Blue Bird' after the play by Maeterlinck which was having a successful run in London and sat up half the night painting the car blue. He won his race at Brooklands the next morning and thereafter named each of his principal racing cars 'Blue Bird'.

The first of Campbell's many escapes from death occurred at Brooklands in the first 'Blue Bird' in 1912 when she suddenly lost her off back and front wheels almost simultaneously. The car, travelling at over a mile and a half a minute on two hubs, slewed sideways. Campbell wrenched the car instantly on to the edge of the track, engaged the two clattering off-side hubs in the sharp edge of the concrete and shot over the finishing line fourth in the race.

On the outbreak of war in 1914 Campbell enlisted as a dispatch rider, was soon commissioned in the Royal West Kent Regiment, and then transferred to the Royal Flying Corps. He had first flown in 1909 when he built his own aeroplane in a disused barn in a strawberry field near Orpington, Kent. At the first attempt it flew, stalled, nose-dived, and crashed. It was repaired and he flew it again for more than a hundred yards, so that he may be counted one of the pioneer fliers of this country. From 1916 until the end of the war he served first as a ferry pilot and then as a flying instructor. On demobilization, with the rank of captain and an M.B.E., Campbell turned to motor-racing as his major interest and during the ensuing years won more than 400 trophies, including the 200-mile race at Brooklands in 1927 and 1928, and the Boulogne grand prix in 1927.

He determined to make world records a hobby and despite endless disappointments, many risks, and numerous hairbreadth escapes from death to which his attitude was fatalistic, he set up a series of world land-speed records which placed him in the front rank of racing motorists. In 1925, at Pendine sands in Wales, driving a 350 h.p. Sunbeam, he was the first man to travel at over 150 m.p.h. In the meantime he was having built at his own expense a Napier–Campbell 'Blue Bird' in which he reached 174·88 m.p.h. in 1927. The car was rebuilt and in the following year at Daytona beach achieved 206·95 m.p.h. A new 'Blue Bird', incorporating as much material as possible from the old, reached 246·09 m.p.h. at Daytona in 1931. On his return home Campbell was given a triumphal progress through London to Westminster Hall and the honour of a knighthood. In 1932 he raised his record to over 250 m.p.h. and finally in 1935, in a Rolls-Royce–Campbell 'Blue Bird', he exceeded 300 m.p.h. at the Bonneville salt flats, Utah, after which he declared himself content. He turned his attention to water-speed records culminating in 141·74 m.p.h. in 1939, for which in the following year he was awarded the trophy founded in memory of his close rival Sir Henry Segrave.

Campbell contributed to the *Field* and the *Daily Mail* and wrote a number of books on motoring. He had no other lasting interest, although he was a keen fisherman, but was subject to sudden impulses which took him, for example, in 1926 to Cocos Island in the Pacific in search of buried treasure and which convinced him that it was his patriotic duty to stand in the Conservative interest for Deptford in 1935. He was not successful. In the early part of the war of 1939–45 he was in command of a motor-cycle unit and served for the remainder on the staff of Combined Operations. He died at Reigate 31 December 1948.

In 1920 Campbell married Dorothy Evelyn, daughter of Major William Whittall, by whom he had one son and one daughter. The marriage was dissolved in 1940. An earlier marriage in 1913 and a later marriage in 1945 were of short duration and were dissolved. His son, Donald, raised the water-speed record to 239·07 m.p.h. in 1957. A bronze head of Campbell by J. A. Stevenson was exhibited at the Royal Academy in 1933.

[Sir Malcolm Campbell, *My Thirty Years of Speed*, 1935, and *Speed on Wheels*, 1949; J. Wentworth Day, *Speed, the Authentic Life of Sir Malcolm Campbell*, 1931; private information; personal knowledge.]

J. WENTWORTH DAY.

CARLILE, WILSON (1847–1942), founder of the Church Army, was born at Brixton 14 January 1847, the eldest of the twelve children of Edward Carlile, a merchant in the City of London, where his father had settled, and whose forebears had for some generations been prominent in the civic and business life of Paisley. Wilson Carlile's mother was Maria Louisa, second daughter of Benjamin Wilson, a Yorkshireman who had come to London as a silk mercer, and became master of the Haberdashers' Company. He was a second cousin of Sir R. W. Carlyle and A. J. Carlyle [qq.v.].

The regular course of Carlile's education was greatly hampered by a spinal weakness from which he suffered throughout his long life and which prevented him from taking an active part in sports or exercises. After attending a private school at Brixton he entered his maternal grandfather's business at the age of thirteen, but shortly afterwards went for a year to school at Lille where he became fluent in French. Of this he made good use during the Franco-Prussian war, when he travelled widely in France in order to take advantage of the unsettled state of the silk market. Later he learnt to speak German with equal facility and he acquired a good knowledge of Italian. When Carlile came of age the business became his property and by 1873 he had laid the foundations of a small fortune when a slump ruined him.

A serious illness supervened and turned Carlile's thoughts to religion in which his interest hitherto had been no more than conventional. His parents who had been devout Congregationalists had recently joined the Church of England in which, on recovery, Carlile was confirmed after a brief attraction to the Plymouth Brethren. He was now in partnership with his father, giving his spare time to mission work in the parish of Holy Trinity, Richmond, where his family had settled. Having great musical ability he also acted as deputy organist to Ira D. Sankey during the great Moody and Sankey missions, and this brought him into touch with the leading missioners of the day.

In 1878 Carlile went out of business in order to be trained for holy orders at St. John's College, Highbury. He was ordained deacon in 1880 and priest in 1881, being appointed in the former year curate at St. Mary Abbots church, Kensington. The happy association of ten or twelve curates of widely different views under Edward Carr Glyn, later bishop of Peterborough, greatly influenced Carlile when he founded the Church Army as a strictly non-party society within the Church of England. He was profoundly impressed by the lack of contact between the Church and the working classes, and by the absence of any facility in the Church for using the efforts of devout working people in active mission work. He began open-air meetings in which the help of working men and women was enlisted and which eventually caused so much obstruction to traffic that he was asked to give them up. Indoor meetings, conducted on very unconventional lines, also attracted the working people.

In 1882 Carlile resigned his curacy and founded the Church Army which (like the Salvation Army begun four years earlier) in its early days in the slums of Westminster met with great violence. Two or three times Carlile was gravely injured; yet not infrequently his roughest opponents came to be his best helpers. Opposition came also from within the Church where many disliked his unconventional methods: but the movement grew and the success which soon came was due in no small degree to Carlile's own humility which led him to devolve responsible duties on his workers to a unique degree. In 1884 a Church Army Training College was established at Oxford, in which working men, without cost to themselves, were trained to be full-time evangelists; and in 1887 a similar college for women workers was opened in west London where for many years they were trained by Carlile's sister, Marie Louise Carlile. Under an order of Convocation made in 1897 the male students were admitted, on the successful conclusion of their training, by the bishop of London to the 'office of Evangelist in the Church of God' and by this specially created office the Church Army workers obtained an official status which was extended to women in 1921. During the war of 1914–18 Carlile's work at the front in France and Belgium led to the spread of the Church Army beyond the British Isles, so that by the time of his death there were autonomous descendants of the original Church Army in many parts of the English-speaking world.

Carlile based his organization upon the parish, in which there was a 'corps' under the guidance of Church Army officers, whose members were required to bear private and public testimony to their faith. During a serious illness in 1926 Carlile conceived the idea that every parish, including those without any trained Church Army officer, should organize its members into 'corps' or 'news teams', and this method has, since his death, received official support.

By building up the largest lay society within the Church of England Carlile not only greatly increased the field in which the ordinary layman could help the work of the Church, but also stimulated similar efforts inside the Church independent of the Church Army. His influence on the evangelistic side of the Church of England was therefore very great. His social work was equally influential. In 1889 he established Church Army homes for ex-prisoners, tramps, and ne'er-do-wells, and two or three times each winter week he would spend the night on the Thames embankment; sometimes 2,000 homeless men and women would gather for Church Army food and shelter. This and other aspects of his social work were criticized on the ground that they were only palliatives; but the fact remains that Carlile's efforts not only alleviated a great amount of misery but did much to rouse the social conscience. By practical help, and not by platform eloquence, he drew public attention, for instance, to the problem of overcrowding in the 'twenties. As a result of his appeals for gifts of money or loans at low interest nearly a thousand houses were built for large families with small incomes, and his example led to the foundation of other similar societies.

In collaboration with his eldest son, Victor, Carlile wrote *The Continental Outcast* (1906), an account of a tour of labour colonies and other establishments in Denmark, Belgium, Holland, and Germany. He also composed a simple choral Communion Service which is widely used. In 1891 he was presented to the rectory of St. Mary-at-Hill, an empty City church which he filled to overflowing until he retired in 1926, retaining a connexion as honorary curate. Meantime the success attending the work of the Church Army brought him honours both in Church and State. In 1906 he was appointed a prebendary of St. Paul's Cathedral; in 1915 he received the honorary degree of D.D. from the university of Oxford and in 1926 from the university of Toronto. In 1926 he was appointed C.H.

In 1870 Carlile married Flora (died 1925), daughter of Thomas Vickers, lawyer, of north Brixton, and had five sons. His grandson, the Rev. E. Wilson Carlile, became chief secretary of the Church Army in 1949. Carlile died at Woking 26 September 1942. A portrait by Sir A. S. Cope is in the possession of the family, and another by L. R. Galesta is at Church Army headquarters.

[Edgar Rowan, *Wilson Carlile and the Church Army*, 5th edition, revised by A. E. Reffold, 1955; A. E. Reffold, *Seven Stars*, 1931, and *The Audacity to Live*, 1938; Sidney Dark, *Wilson Carlile*, 1944; private information; personal knowledge.]

A. E. REFFOLD.

CARLYLE, ALEXANDER JAMES (1861–1943), political philosopher, ecclesiastical historian, and social reformer, was born in Bombay 24 July 1861, the younger son of the Rev. James Edward Carlyle, minister of the Free Church of Scotland in Bombay, by his wife, Jessie Margaret, daughter of James Milne, of Huntly, Aberdeenshire. The elder son was Sir R. W. Carlyle [q.v.]. His father, who returned to Scotland when Alexander was a month old, was compelled for reasons of health to take charge of Presbyterian churches abroad, so that Alexander's boyhood was passed in Rome,

Paris, Berlin, and South Africa. His knowledge of foreign languages and literature, and his enjoyment of foreign travel, were the outcome of this experience.

Carlyle had no regular schooling, and, apart from two years at Glasgow University (1876–8), his systematic studies began when, in 1883, he entered Exeter College, Oxford, as an exhibitioner. He obtained a first class in modern history in 1886 and a second class in theology in 1888, and in the latter year was ordained to a curacy at St. Stephen's church, Westminster, where his sympathies as a social reformer were first aroused. In 1893 he was elected to a fellowship at University College, Oxford; and, although he had to vacate his fellowship in 1895 on his marriage to Rebecca Monteith (died 1941), daughter of the Scottish poet and preacher Walter Chalmers Smith [q.v.], he continued to serve the college as lecturer in politics and economics, and as chaplain. In 1935 he was elected an honorary fellow.

From 1895 to 1919, however, Carlyle's centre in Oxford was the city church of St. Martin and All Saints, of which he was rector. During these years he took a leading part, as a liberal thinker and Christian Socialist, formally attached to no political party, in the social life of the city and in religious movements. His friendship with Sidney and Beatrice Webb [qq.v.] and other reformers, his co-operation with the high-church Anglicans associated with Charles Gore [q.v.]—for whom, although he did not share his ecclesiastical and theological opinions, he had a deep regard —and his close alliance with his old Exeter College friend, John Carter, testify to his breadth of outlook. He was one of the early advocates of planned social reform, the unity of the Churches, and better informed relations between the city and the university of Oxford. He was a mainstay of the Christian Social Union, which was largely sustained by disciples of Gore and Henry Scott Holland [q.v.], a friend and adviser of local trade-unionism, a promoter of inter-denominational 'summer schools' of theology which for a number of years were held in Oxford, and he was in close touch with liberal leaders of religious life and thought abroad, such as Lars Olof Jonathan (Nathan) Söderblom, archbishop of Upsala, as well as with men of such various outlook as Baron Friedrich von Hügel [q.v.] and the leaders in England of the Free Churches.

Carlyle's resignation of the living of the

city church in 1919 enabled him to give more time to his work as writer and teacher. He had never neglected these interests, and had owed much to the inspiration of William Sanday [q.v.], whose seminars he was wont to attend, and to co-operation with Hastings Rashdall [q.v.], whose theological views he largely shared. Before 1919 he had published a life of *Hugh Latimer* (with his wife, 1899), an essay on the Church in the composite volume, *Contentio Veritatis* (1902), short books (1912) on *The Influence of Christianity upon Social and Political Ideas* and on *Wages*, and, with J. V. Bartlet [q.v.], a volume on *Christianity in History* (1917). But ever since 1895 his main preoccupation had been the great *History of Mediaeval Political Theory in the West* which he had then planned with his elder brother. Although Sir Robert Carlyle was able to contribute only to the fifth volume of the book (1928)—the volume on the thirteenth century which represents more or less what in 1895 they had first thought to produce—the two men discussed the work continuously, and the sixth and last volume (1936) was dedicated by Alexander to Robert's memory. As the work proceeded (1903–36) it gradually won the high place in historical literature which it will long hold both on the continent and in the English-speaking world. Written with lucidity and with a simplicity which is apt to be misleading, it is an invaluable guide to an immense series of texts, ranging from the early Roman law books and the writings of the Fathers to the works of Bodin and Althusius. Its main theme is the rule of law, firmly rooted in the nature of things, as the basis of the search for and maintenance of justice and liberty. It was followed in 1941 by a volume on *Political Liberty*, concerned with the seventeenth century. The Political Philosophy and Science Club, which Carlyle founded in 1909, primarily for teachers in the universities of Oxford, Cambridge, and London, was the practical expression of his wide political and social interests.

Apart from four years (1930–34) as a canon of Worcester Cathedral, Carlyle lived continuously in Oxford from 1895 until his death there 27 May 1943. Throughout this period he was an active teacher and lecturer, working for several colleges, including the women's colleges, as a tutor in history, economics, politics, and modern languages. His diversity of interests and his unconventional manner of speech provoked criticism in some quarters, but his inspiration as a teacher and his influence upon many who, in later life, attained distinction are indisputable and confirm the impression which his incisive and provocative table-talk made upon all who knew him. At different times he was the intimate and valued friend of such men as Rashdall, Sidney Ball, J. A. Smith [q.v.], and H. H. Joachim [q.v.]. His home, where his wife and his two daughters supported him with an independent devotion, was a delightful social centre. He was an urbane, cultivated man, who, although he rarely talked about it and was unclerical in demeanour, was, in the words of one of his younger friends, 'dominated by religion'. As a curate in Westminster he was so much impressed by the evil social effects of intemperance that he became a total abstainer; but he never 'preached', although he was a good and forthright preacher, and was a living example to others by his belief that complete frankness and generous tolerance are not incompatible. In a word, he expressed in action his belief in personal liberty.

Carlyle was, in some ways, more successful abroad than in England, whether in lecturing tours in Scandinavia or at juristic conferences in Rome. He gave the Olaus Petri lectures in Upsala (1918) and the Lowell lectures in Boston (1924), as well as the Birkbeck lectures in ecclesiastical history at Trinity College, Cambridge (1925–7). In 1936 he was elected F.B.A. He received the honorary degree of D.D. from Glasgow University (1934) and was a foreign member of the Royal Academy of Naples.

A drawing of Carlyle, by Alistair Sinclair (1919), and a portrait in oils, by the same artist, are in the possession of the family.

[F. M. Powicke in *Proceedings* of the British Academy, vol. xxix, 1943; private information; personal knowledge.]

F. M. POWICKE.

CAVAN, tenth EARL OF (1865–1946), field-marshal. [See LAMBART, FREDERICK RUDOLPH.]

CECIL, JAMES EDWARD HUBERT GASCOYNE-, fourth MARQUESS OF SALISBURY (1861–1947), was born at 21 Fitzroy Square, London, 23 October 1861, the eldest son of Lord Robert Arthur Talbot Gascoyne-Cecil who became the third Marquess of Salisbury [q.v.] in 1868. The eldest of five brilliant brothers, he was in some respects the ablest. Without the eloquence of his youngest brother, Lord Hugh Cecil (later Lord Quickswood), or the magnetism of Lord Robert Cecil (subsequently Viscount Cecil of Chelwood), he was endowed with wisdom, farsightedness, and tact.

Lord Cranborne, as he was by this time, was educated at Eton and at University College, Oxford, where he obtained a third class in mathematical moderations (1882) and a second in modern history (1884). In 1878 he accompanied his father to the Congress of Berlin, and thus began his public association with his father whose teaching was throughout life his guiding star. He was brought up in politics from infancy, listening to the discussions of his parents and the distinguished politicians and ambassadors who were frequent visitors at Hatfield. Throughout his life he endeavoured to give expression to the principles of the art of politics which he learnt there in his early years.

In 1887 Cranborne married Lady Cicely Alice Gore (died 1955), the second daughter of the fifth Earl of Arran, a brilliant hostess and ideal wife who made a major contribution to his life. Without such a wife to encourage and assist him, he might easily have been overshadowed by the eminence of his father and the brilliance of his younger brothers. Her sparkle and charm made their home a social and political centre and brought contacts which his own diffidence might have prevented.

He had already entered Parliament in 1885, at the age of twenty-four, as member for the Darwen division of North-East Lancashire. He was defeated in 1892 but was returned for Rochester in the following year and sat until he succeeded to the peerage in 1903. Until the year before his death his father was either prime minister or leader of the Opposition, and during this time he relied greatly on his son to keep him in touch with the moods and currents of opinion in the House of Commons. Cranborne thus became increasingly his father's confidant and learnt to see political problems from the viewpoint of both the Cabinet and the back bench. In the House he made his own mark as a zealous churchman. He engaged actively in the debates on Welsh disestablishment and tithes, and in the education controversies was a champion of the voluntary schools. From 1893 to 1900 he was chairman of the Church parliamentary committee and in 1896 he introduced a benefices bill to prevent the institution and provide for the disciplining of unworthy incumbents. Some of his measures were subsequently taken up by the Government and enacted in 1898.

Cranborne inherited from his grandfather, the second marquess, a love of soldiering which was the second dominant secular interest in his life. While still an undergraduate he received a commission in his county militia battalion, the 4th Bedfordshire, and commanded it in the South African war, being mentioned in dispatches and awarded the C.B. He was recalled in 1900, however, to become undersecretary for foreign affairs when his father relinquished the office of foreign secretary to Lord Lansdowne [q.v]. Cranborne had the important task of defending his chief's foreign policy in the House of Commons at a time when it came under sharp criticism from the Liberal Party. He did not find it easy to answer supplementary questions when unable to consult his chief, for he had not the art of making ambiguous statements and he was sometimes accused of those 'blazing indiscretions' for which his father had been famous.

In October 1903, by then Lord Salisbury, he was appointed lord privy seal in Balfour's reconstructed Cabinet. The fiscal question had rent the Conservative Party in two, and his own brothers had violently sided with the minority of the party in opposition to the protectionist proposals of Joseph Chamberlain. Salisbury, although also by conviction a free trader, saw that the Conservative Party stood for causes much more important than the question of a moderate tariff on foreign imports. He therefore rallied to support Balfour's unsuccessful endeavour to keep the party together and he was president of the Board of Trade in the last reconstruction before the Government gave way to the Liberals in December 1905.

During the first half of Salisbury's career his party was in power and pursuing a policy in which he ardently believed. For the rest of his life the Conservative Party was swayed by influences which he mistrusted and deplored. Conservatism, as he had learnt it, was a creed which included social reform, but it had nothing in common with Liberalism. He never lost his faith in Conservatism as a militant creed and although he was never in any sense a reactionary he gradually became recognized as the leader of the old Conservatives in the Unionist Party.

He first emerged as a parliamentary

debater of high rank in the controversy over the budget of 1909 and the Parliament bill. Up to that time the House of Lords had powers almost equal to those of the House of Commons, not only legally but also in admitted constitutional practice which nevertheless prescribed that the Lords should pay great respect to the ultimate views of the nation and that the Commons should have the last word in matters of finance. Lloyd George's budget of 1909, however, was regarded, rightly or wrongly, as an attempt to initiate social legislation under cover of supply. Salisbury held that if they allowed it to pass into law without reference to the electors, the Lords would be abdicating their responsibilities. The finance bill was rejected by the Lords on the second reading, but was passed the following year after the general election of January had confirmed the Liberals in office, albeit with a majority so reduced as to make them dependent on the Irish vote. The House of Commons passed resolutions which were then drafted into a Parliament bill intended to deprive the Lords of their power of veto.

In the cooler atmosphere of the new reign a constitutional conference attempted unsuccessfully to resolve the deadlock and a second general election ensued in December 1910. In the following year the Parliament bill passed through the Commons but was returned to them so amended by the Lords as to be unacceptable. The prime minister, Asquith, then revealed that King George V had promised before the dissolution that should this happen he would accept his Government's advice to create sufficient peers to ensure the passage of the bill. Asquith now intimated that if the Lords insisted on their amendments he would so advise. The Conservative Party then became split. Lansdowne and Lord Curzon [q.v.], supported by Balfour, took the view that the House of Lords should submit rather than allow itself to be swamped by the elevation of five hundred nobodies which would bring the whole peerage into contempt. Halsbury, Selborne [qq.v.], Salisbury and others held, on the contrary, that since the Government owed its majority only to the support of the Irish members who saw in the removal of the veto their only hope of Home Rule, it had no mandate from the electors of Great Britain for any such constitutional revolution. Although there was much talk at this time of the reform of the House of

Lords and Asquith declared that it 'brooked no delay', they feared that if the House consented to the emasculation of its powers it would sink into impotence without being reformed. The swamping of the peerage, on the other hand, would make the reform of the House of Lords, and with it some restoration of its powers, inevitable.

This party became known as 'the Diehards', and under the leadership of aged Lord Halsbury they defied their own political leaders, the Government, and the King. On the eve of the crucial debate, a meeting of the Diehards was held in Salisbury's house in Arlington Street, where they resolved to insist on the amendments. On 10 August 1911, however, the Government prevailed by 131 votes to 114. Thirty-seven Conservative peers and thirteen prelates voted with the Government. Lansdowne and his supporters abstained.

The controversy over the second chamber was the turning-point in Salisbury's life. He had seen his party in 1909 ready to fight under the old Conservative banner. In 1911 he saw it falter under social pressure. For the rest of his life he never ceased to agitate for the reform of the House of Lords and some restoration of its previous powers.

In the war of 1914–18 Salisbury's military capacity again emerged. In 1914 he was still in command of the 4th Bedfordshire, now a special reserve battalion, and he served with it in England until he was made a major-general commanding a division of the Home Army in 1917. When conscription was introduced in 1916 Salisbury was appointed chairman of the supreme tribunal to which conscientious objectors and others could appeal for exemption. This was work to which his blend of good sense and tenderness to other people's scruples was particularly suited, and to which he gave infinite pains. He remained in uniform until the armistice although what he considered to be the feeble conduct of the war and the rising chaos in Ireland caused him to make frequent incursions into debates in the House of Lords. He repeatedly demanded firm government in Ireland, the state of which he declared to be a danger to the Empire, always maintained that Home Rule could never work, and strongly opposed the treaty of 1921.

When he returned to civil life Salisbury had found Lloyd George, whom he profoundly mistrusted, prime minister by Conservative support in the Commons, but pursuing an opportunist rather than a Conservative policy. Although the Government had the support of the leading intellects of the Conservative Party, such as Balfour, Birkenhead, and Curzon, Salisbury at once set about recalling the Conservative Party to its principles. He was the first to state publicly (in a letter to the *Morning Post*, 20 June 1921) that 'the Coalition Government no longer possesses the full confidence of the Unionist Party'. He sought to rally Conservative opinion in the country by speaking at meetings and by letters to the newspapers and in July 1922 he was elected leader of 'the Conservative and Unionist Movement', that group within the party which, in his own words (September 1922), stood 'for the spirit of Conservatism and against the spirit of the Coalition'. An important meeting of this group was held at his house in Arlington Street, 17 October 1922, when Salisbury's strenuous demand that the Conservative Party should free itself from the coalition had its effect on the outcome of the famous Carlton Club meeting two days later.

In Bonar Law's Cabinet which followed the break-up of the coalition Salisbury became lord president of the Council and chancellor of the Duchy of Lancaster, retaining the former office under Baldwin. During this period he rendered signal service on the Committee of Imperial Defence. In March 1923 Bonar Law appointed him chairman of a sub-committee to consider the co-ordination of national and imperial defence. In August it recommended, first, the development of the chiefs of staff committee which had existed on a temporary footing since the Chanak crisis of 1922 and was to become the focus of British military organization in the war of 1939–45; secondly, that the prime minister, while retaining the presidency of the Committee of Imperial Defence, should appoint a chairman as deputy to preside in his absence. The chairman, assisted by the chiefs of staff, was to keep the defence situation as a whole constantly under review, advise the Committee on planning and preparation and exercise the 'wider initiative'. Salisbury himself became the first chairman. The policy was confirmed in a full report published in 1924 and was continued by the Labour Government but thereafter lapsed.

When ill health compelled Bonar Law to resign the premiership in 1923 he made it known that he would prefer not to be consulted about his successor. The King,

therefore, caused a number of leading Conservatives to be consulted, among whom was Salisbury who recommended that Lord Curzon be sent for. Other counsels prevailed, however, and Stanley Baldwin became prime minister. In spite of his past sympathies with free trade Salisbury rallied like-minded Conservatives to support Baldwin when he went to the country on protection in the autumn of 1923. In Baldwin's second Government (1924–9) Salisbury was lord privy seal and, after the death of Curzon in 1925, leader of the House of Lords. Nevertheless, his collaboration with Baldwin was never easy, although they were personal friends. The prime minister was by now convinced that he could not govern without a large measure of Liberal or moderate Labour support, to secure which he was prepared to jettison some of the pre-1914 traditional Conservative policy. Although other differences were soon to follow, the first clash between Baldwin and Salisbury was over the House of Lords. Salisbury vainly did everything he could to persuade the prime minister to honour the repeated Conservative pledges to place the constitution on a securely bi-cameral basis. During the second Labour Government Salisbury was a member of the shadow Cabinet and leader of the Opposition in the House of Lords but thenceforward he pursued an increasingly independent line which tended to diverge from that of Baldwin. He called attention to the enforced resignation of Lord Lloyd [q.v.] from Egypt, in contrast with the Conservative leaders in the House of Commons who gave Lord Lloyd no more support than they had done when in office; and later in 1929 Salisbury carried a motion in the House of Lords severely criticizing the precipitation of the Labour Government's policy in seeking a treaty with Egypt, warning them that they were embarking on a course highly prejudicial to the interests of Great Britain. In June 1931 he resigned from the Conservative leadership in the House of Lords 'for reasons of health' and he did not join the 'national' Government formed in August. The fact was that he saw clearly that the coalition was unlikely to pursue a policy which he could support.

Salisbury now lost no time in trying to move Conservative and public opinion to force the Government into activity on the constitutional issue. Even the Liberals had declared the Parliament Act to be provisional and temporary and in the meantime the country had through lethargy slipped into single-chamber government. He persuaded the House of Lords to appoint a committee whose recommendations (with certain alterations as a result of conferences with members of the House of Commons) he embodied in a bill providing for a House consisting of 150 hereditary peers elected by the peers, 150 lords of Parliament chosen in pursuance of a resolution of both Houses of Parliament, together with the royal peers, the law lords, and a small episcopal representation. Money bills were more closely defined and were to continue to enjoy the special procedure provided by the Parliament Act, but any other bill rejected for the third time by an absolute majority of the reformed House of Lords was not to be presented for the royal assent unless the House of Commons in the next Parliament so resolved.

The Conservative Party, however, was by now deeply divided on the issue. Whereas a large section of the party shared Salisbury's apprehensions, many felt with Baldwin that the existing system worked well enough and that public opinion would not favour its reform until it had been shown to have broken down. In May 1934 the second reading was carried by 171 to 82 after a three days' debate rendered academic by the statement of Lord Hailsham [q.v.], leader of the House, on the first day, that the Government would abstain from the division, had reached no conclusion on the problem, and could give no facilities for its discussion in the House of Commons. In a passionate peroration rebuking the Government for its incapacity to act, Salisbury correctly foretold that there would be a Labour majority in the House of Commons in the next Parliament but one. Hailsham's declaration caused alarm to a large section of the Conservative Party and within a few days 163 members of the House of Commons signed a petition to the prime minister declaring the necessity of an alteration in the constitution and powers of the House of Lords in the present Parliament. If a party conference on the subject had then been held Salisbury would probably have received the support of the majority. In 1936 he returned to the attack. He introduced a deputation of some 150 members of both Houses to Baldwin, and followed this up by supporting Lord Lloyd's resolution on the subject which was carried without a vote at the Conservative Party conference. The crisis of the abdication and the rise of

Hitlerism, however, turned the public's attention in other directions.

In the meantime Salisbury found himself in direct opposition to the Government on the question of self-government for India. To his mind India was totally unprepared, if not inherently unsuited, for democratic government. He was deeply distressed that the Conservative Party should lend itself to what he regarded as the betrayal of millions of innocent peasants for whose welfare the British were responsible. Finding, however, that not only the Liberal and Labour parties but also many Conservatives thought some advance in Indian self-government necessary, Salisbury concentrated his endeavours on diminishing the pace at which the experiment was tried. With eight others he dissented from the report of the joint parliamentary select committee on Indian constitutional reform and he himself drafted an amendment, supported by four colleagues, which sought to confine the grant of self-government to the provinces. At a meeting of the central council of the Conservative Party (4 December 1934) he poured scorn on the 'paper safeguards' of the majority report and moved an amendment accepting provincial autonomy but rejecting central responsible government. In this he received the support of (Sir) Winston Churchill but they were defeated by 1,102 to 390 votes. In June 1935 Salisbury took the unusual course of opposing the first reading of the Government of India bill and made his final protest when it came up for third reading but did not divide the House.

Salisbury was also greatly preoccupied by the rising menace of Hitler and by what he felt was the inadequacy of the military preparations of the Government to meet it. On 27 February 1936 he initiated a debate in the House of Lords on national defence, advocated the reappointment of a chairman of the Committee of Imperial Defence on the lines of the report of 1924, a policy which Baldwin had allowed to lapse, and contended that, had it been adhered to, the country would not have been caught asleep. On the same day Baldwin announced that such an appointment would be made. On 28 July 1936 Salisbury was among the eighteen privy counsellors who went on a deputation introduced by Sir Austen Chamberlain [q.v.] and (Sir) Winston Churchill to the prime minister to beg the Government to take a more realistic view of the situation. In 1938 Salisbury declared openly for conscription and after the outbreak of war favoured a national Government from the first.

Salisbury was by now seventy-eight but continued very active. He immediately formed a 'watching committee' consisting of prominent members of both Houses, which met fortnightly throughout the war, acting as a private liaison between Parliament and Downing Street and rendering useful service in many other ways. From 1942 onwards he directed the attention of the committee to post-war problems. A number of questions which came before the committee he ventilated in the House where he always gave strong support to (Sir) Winston Churchill.

From 1942 until 1945 Salisbury was president of the National Union of Conservative and Unionist Associations. After the general election of 1945 he witnessed the situation he had for so many years foreseen, a Socialist House of Commons armed with the Parliament Act and an unreformed House of Lords. His last letter to *The Times* in 1946 was on this subject. But his greatest concern was still with India and almost his last speech in the House of Lords was a vehement protest in February 1947 at the betrayal of fifty million untouchables. And so he continued in harness to the end.

A most regular attendant in both Houses of Parliament in his day, Salisbury spoke authoritatively on a wide variety of subjects of which the principal were ecclesiastical and moral questions (he was an uncompromising opponent of easier divorce), industrial problems, local government, housing, town planning, military and imperial matters, and foreign policy in which he was a consistent supporter of the League of Nations. For the last thirty years of his life he was on many issues in direct conflict with the leaders of his own party and still more so with the Liberal and Labour parties. Yet he enjoyed immense popularity and respect and exercised a unique influence in the House of Lords. Returning there after an illness in 1931 he was greeted with a round of cheers which interrupted a speech by Lord Peel. In the tense debate on the King's abdication in 1936 only the leaders of the three parties and the archbishop of Canterbury spoke, but all eyes then turned to Salisbury who rose and indicated in a short and characteristic speech his support of Baldwin.

When Salisbury died a bust of him by Benno Elkan was placed in the precincts

of the House of Lords 'by peers of all Parties in token of their affection and esteem': an honour paid to few. This esteem was due not only to his unfailing courtesy, his broad and humane outlook on all questions and his transparent integrity, but also to the moderation and cogency of his arguments which made him a formidable force in debate. A Liberal peer, a great industrialist, once remarked as Salisbury passed, 'There goes the wisest man in England!' To the outside world, however, he was little more than a distant figure, the bearer of a great name. He was without those gifts of popular oratory or demagogy by which politicians impress their personalities on the general public. In his own counties, in Hertfordshire and Dorset, and in Liverpool, it was very different. He was vitally interested in his three estates and regularly visited his tenants. At great personal expense he entirely reformed his important Liverpool property and built over 500 cottages in Hertfordshire and Dorsetshire. His speeches in Parliament on housing problems were those of a practical expert. It was extraordinary how much time he found to give to local work, as chairman of quarter-sessions (1896–1911), and as alderman of Hertfordshire County Council. He was a member of the visiting committee of St. Albans prison, and even in the last months of his life he made a special study of remand homes in Hertfordshire. He was president of many county associations, a member of Hatfield parochial church council and of St. Albans diocesan conference where he was a frequent speaker. This activity was accompanied by much generosity. He presented Hertford Castle to the borough; and he gave great sums of money and many sites for the building of churches and church schools. He was a man of the deepest personal religion who believed that personal Christian endeavour was the only way of life; and that it was worth while to take infinite trouble to achieve that end. He was essentially a humble man of a gentle fastidious nature, greatly affected by unhappiness in others which he sought to alleviate by many acts of kindness. He was chairman of the Canterbury House of Laymen (1906–11) and for twenty-five years a member of the Church Assembly. His last public act, a week before he died, was to lead a deputation, against his doctor's advice, to appeal to the archbishop of Canterbury to give a strong and dramatic lead against the prevalent post-war materialism and irreligion which if unchecked would inevitably destroy civilization. He collapsed during this final speech and died in London 4 April 1947. He was buried in the family graveyard of St. Etheldreda's church, Hatfield.

Salisbury was about five feet eight inches in height, clean-shaven with moustache, well proportioned, and handsome in appearance. In London he was always immaculately dressed in the frock coat and top hat which had been *de rigueur* in his youth and which he was one of the last to wear. He was not fond of games, and only moderately of sport. His hobbies were riding and wood-carving to which he was never able to give the time he would have liked. He had a love and knowledge of architecture and made his tenure of Hatfield notable by restoring the early Tudor bishop's palace to its former beauty, and by adding a muniment room for the proper storage of the many State and other documents which had accumulated there over four hundred years.

Salisbury was appointed aide-de-camp to the King in 1903, G.C.V.O. in 1909, and K.G. in 1917. He was high steward of Westminster and of Hertford, and he officiated as lord high steward at the coronation of King George VI when he bore St. Edward's Crown. He was an honorary fellow of University College and an honorary D.C.L. of Oxford (1926). Although after the death of Curzon there was a movement to nominate him for election as chancellor of the university his name did not in the end go forward and Lord Cave [q.v.] was elected.

Portraits of Salisbury are at Hatfield, as a boy with his mother by George Richmond, at his coming of age by Sir William Richmond, and a third full length in robes by Glyn Philpot. There are also portraits of him at University College, Oxford, with three brothers, by F. H. Shepherd, and at Church House by Glyn Philpot.

Salisbury had two sons and two daughters. He was succeeded by his elder son, Robert Arthur James (born 1893), who was called to the Lords as Baron Cecil of Essendon in 1941. His younger son, Lord David Cecil, contributes to this SUPPLEMENT. Lady Beatrice Cecil married the fourth Lord Harlech; Lady Mary Cecil married the tenth Duke of Devonshire and in 1953 became mistress of the robes to Her Majesty Queen Elizabeth II.

[*Hansard, The Times*, and *Annual Register, passim*; private information; personal knowledge.]     SELBORNE.

CHADWICK, HECTOR MUNRO (1870–1947), Anglo-Saxon scholar and historian of early literature, was born 22 October 1870 at the vicarage, Thornhill Lees, Yorkshire, the third son of the vicar, the Rev. Edward Chadwick, and his wife, Sarah Anne Bates, whose father had been in business in Oldham. From Wakefield Grammar School he went, as Cave exhibitioner, to Clare College, Cambridge, in 1889, becoming a scholar the following year. In 1892 he was placed in the third division of the first class of part i of the classical tripos. He had, however, been developing individually. As a dayboy with an eight-mile journey into Wakefield and back each day, he had taught himself German in the train, and his exceptional qualities began to appear when in 1893 he was placed in the first class of part ii of the classical tripos, with distinction in the philology section. In the same year he became a fellow of his college. From 1895 he taught for section B of the medieval and modern languages tripos, the subjects of which ranged over the whole background of Old English.

In 1899 came his first book, *The Cult of Othin*, already exhibiting the highest linguistic and archaeological competence in collecting evidence, together with remarkable ability in discerning the significant patterns which evidence yielded in combination. *Studies on Anglo-Saxon Institutions* followed in 1905, and *The Origin of the English Nation* in 1907. In 1909 the board of medieval and modern languages reported that 'it would be of advantage to the University and a fit recognition of the scholarship and learning of Mr. Chadwick' if a university lectureship in Scandinavian were created for him. Quite exceptional as such a step then was, the advice was taken and the appointment made in 1910. In 1912 Chadwick published *The Heroic Age*. Its main achievement was to bring together early Teutonic with Greek heroic poetry, to the better understanding of both. There were also 'Notes' on Slav and Celtic heroic poetry, indicative of the widening scope of Chadwick's studies. In 1912 he succeeded W. W. Skeat [q.v.] in the Elrington and Bosworth chair of Anglo-Saxon. He loved to recall the founder's wish that the subject should not be Anglo-Saxon only but 'the languages cognate therewith, together with the antiquities and history of the Anglo-Saxons'. The war years which followed gave opportunity to reconsider the studies carried on under the medieval and modern languages board. Modern linguists were declaring that Britain had been a tight little island too long, and needed a living interest in other peoples rather than academic concentration on language. Herein Chadwick saw both reason and opportunity for removing English studies from the school of modern languages, and, at the same time, reshaping the study of the origins and background of English literature, so as to make philological scholarship serve the knowledge of history and civilization. For this far-reaching reform of Cambridge studies, Sir Arthur Quiller-Couch [q.v.] declared, in the Senate House, nine-tenths of the credit was due to Chadwick.

In 1922 Chadwick married Norah, daughter of James Kershaw, a cotton-mill owner of Farnworth, Lancashire, a former pupil. Their marriage established a most remarkable literary partnership, of which their *Growth of Literature* (3 vols., 1932–40) is an abiding monument. Meanwhile the study of modern English literature at Cambridge had greatly developed, and in 1927 Chadwick took the opportunity to transfer his department to the new faculty of archaeology and anthropology where his group of studies might, like the classics, constitute an independent discipline. On reaching the age limit in 1940 he continued as head of the department until 1945.

His last works were *The Study of Anglo-Saxon* (1941), *The Nationalities of Europe and the Growth of National Ideologies* (1945), and *Early Scotland* which was unfinished when he died in Cambridge 2 January 1947, but was published by his widow in 1949. There were no children of the marriage.

Chadwick was elected F.B.A. in 1925; and received the honorary degrees of D.Litt. from Durham University (1914) and Oxford (1944) and of LL.D. from St. Andrews in 1919. His talent as a teacher is reflected in some thirty of his pupils who held university posts.

[J. M. de Navarro in *Proceedings* of the British Academy, vol. xxxiii, 1947 (bibliography); private information; personal knowledge.]     W. TELFER.

CHADWICK, ROY (1893–1947), aeronautical engineer, was born at Farnworth, near Bolton, Lancashire, 30 April 1893, the elder son of Charles Henry Chadwick, a mechanical engineer in Manchester, and his wife, Agnes Bradshaw. Educated at a school in Urmston and at the Manchester College of Technology,

Chadwick was early fascinated with the idea of flying machines, and made model gliders and aeroplanes. Having decided to make aeronautics his career, in 1911 he became associated with (Sir) Alliott Verdon-Roe, a pioneer of British aviation. With R. J. Parrott and (Sir) Roy H. Dobson they dedicated their lives to the design and manufacture of aeroplanes, in the small concern known as A. V. Roe & Co., Ltd., later one of the largest aircraft companies. Chadwick was, therefore, from the beginning closely associated with the design of practical aircraft, including the famous Avro 504. During the war of 1914–18 he worked on the design of several twin-engined biplanes and experimental fighters, and when hostilities ceased he was recognized as one of the youngest and most experienced aircraft designers.

Chadwick next designed several big military aircraft and also several light machines, including the Avro Baby, probably the first real light aeroplane in the world, to be followed later by the Avro Avian, famous for the record-breaking flights from England to Australia by H. J. L. Hinkler (1928) and (Sir) Charles Kingsford Smith [q.v.] in 1930. He also devoted his energies to the development of the all-metal aeroplane.

Much of Chadwick's genius lay in an uncanny understanding of the need for perfect control in aeroplanes. This subtle characteristic was particularly noticeable in his trainer aircraft such as the Tutor which in 1932 replaced the 504, thus perpetuating the Avro tradition of training in the Royal Air Force. Some years later, during the war of 1939–45, another design by Chadwick, the Anson, was used extensively for training purposes. Already in 1935 events compelled him to turn his thoughts to military aviation. He designed the Manchester twin-engined heavy bomber which marked a gigantic step forward in aircraft design, although at first the project was almost abandoned on account of the failure of the engines to produce the power promised. Chadwick eventually proved the rightness of his design, however, and it was out of the Manchester that there emerged his greatest triumph, the four-engined Lancaster, capable of carrying a ten-ton bomb, and extensively used for night attack on Germany. Other war-time designs were the York and the Lincoln, followed after the war by the Lancastrian which, with the York, was used for civil aviation.

Chadwick's first true post-war aircraft,

however, was the Tudor, the first pressurized civil aeroplane in the world. A national controversy arose over the Tudor design, but throughout Chadwick never lost faith in his aeroplane. Although production was greatly curtailed, the Tudor later proved its worth on the Berlin airlift. The Ashton, a Royal Air Force research aircraft, was a direct development of the Tudor. It was a tragic irony that it was in a Tudor that Chadwick was killed during a test flight, 23 August 1947. His death was an incalculable loss to the cause of British aeronautics which he had greatly served, particularly in the two wars. He designed some forty successful aircraft and the benefit of his last thoughts on design are to be seen in the Coastal Command Shackleton, and the Avro Delta plan form aircraft. Chadwick was friendly and good humoured, but untiring in his quest for the better aeroplane. A combination of visionary and practical engineer, he could always see the next step clearly, and before he died he saw the enormous potential of jet propulsion, particularly in conjunction with the Delta plan form.

In 1943 Chadwick was appointed C.B.E and he received the honorary degree of M.Sc. from Manchester University in 1944. He was a fellow of the Royal Aeronautical Society. In 1920 he married Mary, daughter of Hubert Gomersall, head cashier of the English Sewing Cotton Company, Manchester; they had two daughters.

[*Aircraft Development and Production*, 1948; *Aeroplane*, 29 August 1947; private information; personal knowledge.]     ROY DOBSON.

CHAMBERS, RAYMOND WILSON (1874–1942), scholar and writer on English language and literature, was born at Staxton, Yorkshire, 12 November 1874, the only son of Thomas Herbert Chambers, commercial traveller, by his wife, Annie, daughter of William Wilson. He was educated at the Grocers' Company's School and at University College, London, where he graduated in 1894 with a first class in English. After working in various libraries, among them the Guildhall Library, he returned in 1899 as Quain student to University College, which he was never again to leave. There he was in close contact over a period of years with such eminent men as A. E. Housman and W. P. Ker [qq.v.]. His own contribution to the college, both as librarian and as teacher, was outstanding. He became a fellow in 1900, librarian in the next year,

and assistant professor of English in 1904. In 1922 he succeeded Ker as Quain professor of English language and literature, and he held the chair until 1941 when the college made him a special lecturer. He received the degree of D.Lit. of the university of London in 1912, and the honorary degree of D.Litt. from the universities of Durham and Leeds in 1932 and 1936.

Chambers was elected F.B.A. in 1927, and henceforth maintained close relations with the British Academy, lecturing before it on several occasions and becoming a member of its council in 1937. By this time his reputation as a scholar had become widely recognized. He was made an honorary member of the Modern Language Association of America in 1930, and became a corresponding member of the Bavarian Academy in 1937. He gave the Turnbull lectures at Johns Hopkins University in 1933, and the Clark lectures at Trinity College, Cambridge, in 1935. He was president of the Philological Society in 1933 and honorary director of the Early English Text Society from 1938 until his death.

Chambers was unmarried. He lived with his only sister in north London for many years. When in 1939, at the outbreak of war, University College migrated to Wales, Chambers went to Aberystwyth. He was taken ill in the course of a lecture tour to the scattered groups of the college, and died at Swansea 21 April 1942.

Although all Chambers's work came under the general heading of English studies, its range was nevertheless considerable, extending in time from early Germanic legend and history to Shakespeare and Milton, and occasionally beyond, and in kind from textual study to literary criticism and biography. His earliest books were *Widsith: A Study in Old English Heroic Legend* (1912), which remains the most generally illuminating work on the subject, *Beowulf* (1914), a very thorough revision of A. J. Wyatt's edition, and *Beowulf: An Introduction to the Study of the Poem* (1921). These placed Chambers among the foremost Old English scholars. His part in the facsimile edition, *The Exeter Book of Old English Poetry* (1933), was his last publication in this field. Prior to any of this work he had begun his study of *Piers Plowman*. Although the definitive edition, which was his aim, was never completed, he wrote and inspired a number of articles which contributed to the solution of some knotty problems. Another subject which long engaged his attention was the literary and historical significance of Sir Thomas More. The book which resulted, *Thomas More* (1935), made Chambers's name known outside academic circles and called forth the unusual tribute (to a son of the Church of England) of a letter of thanks from Pope Pius XI. It was awarded the James Tait Black memorial prize. Chambers produced several other books well known to students of English and a large number of important essays and articles.

Chambers had great energy and untiring intellectual curiosity; he had, in addition, gifts of imagination, wit, and humour which enabled him to put life into a recondite subject. He often engaged in controversy, but only to vindicate the truth as he saw it, and with consideration for his opponents. Though his opinions have not always stood up to further investigation, much that he wrote is likely to remain of value, particularly as a stimulus to other workers. As he grew older, Chambers's reverence for the great men of the past became ever more prominent in his writings. He admired the courage and strength of mind, grounded in religious faith and submission to discipline, which he found in More. These qualities, in some measure, he himself possessed, as his colleagues and friends discovered during the early years of the war of 1939–45. Beneath his reserve, he was a man of generous affections and strong loyalties. His relations with his invalid father and his sister were the deeper manifestations of this; the public signs were his many friendships and his capacity for successful collaboration with other scholars.

[*The Times*, 24 April 1942; C. J. Sisson in *Proceedings of the British Academy*, vol. xxx, 1944 (bibliography); C. J. Sisson, *R. W. Chambers*, first Chambers memorial lecture, 1951; private information; personal knowledge.]                    D. EVERETT.

CHARLESWORTH, MARTIN PERCIVAL (1895–1950), classical scholar, was born at Eastham, Cheshire, 18 January 1895, son of the Rev. Ambrose Charlesworth, then curate of Eastham, and his wife, Alice Whish. He was educated at Birkenhead School and Jesus College, Cambridge, of which he was a Rustat scholar, and was awarded university scholarships, the Bell (1915), Stewart of Rannoch (1916), and, after service in the war of 1914–18, the Craven (1920). He was first Chancellor's

medallist in 1921. After being placed in the first division of the first class in the classical tripos, part i (1920), and in the first class in part ii in 1921 with distinction in ancient history, he became visiting fellow at Princeton (1921–2). He was a fellow of Jesus College (1921), and became fellow and lecturer at St. John's (1923), and tutor in 1925, an office which he held until, in 1931, he was appointed to the Laurence readership in classics (ancient history) in the university. He had been a university lecturer on the subject since 1926.

Charlesworth first made his name by a Hare prize essay, *The Trade Routes and Commerce of the Roman Empire* (1922, published 1924), which enjoyed a high reputation and was translated into French and Italian. In 1927 he was appointed an editor of the *Cambridge Ancient History*, to which he rendered great services until its completion twelve years later. His contributions to volumes viii, x, and xi displayed notable skill in handling evidence, a sympathetic while penetrating appraisement of individuals, and an easy vigorous style. This was especially apparent in his treatment of Tiberius, Claudius, and the Flavians. In 1935 he delivered the Martin lectures at Oberlin College, Ohio, on notable figures in the Empire, published under the title of *Five Men* (1936). Some of his best work was in the interpretation of the ideas revealed in coins linked with literary evidence. He was keenly interested in Roman-British studies; the last book he lived to publish was the Gregynog lectures of 1948, *The Lost Province; or the Worth of Britain* (1949). While he was well versed in ancient history, his especial field was the Roman Empire, of which his skilful survey in the Home University Library was passed for press during his last illness.

Besides his activity as an historian, both as writer and lecturer, he devoted himself to St. John's, which repaid his services with affection and admiration. This was attested by his election by the fellows as president in 1937, an office in which he revealed high social gifts. He had very many friends throughout the university and among scholars, so that his untimely death at Leeds, 26 October 1950, was widely lamented. In 1940 he had taken holy orders, and although he desired no ecclesiastical preferment, he was a devoted churchman. He was an active president of the Society for the Promotion of Roman Studies (1945–8), fellow of the Society of

Antiquaries and fellow (1940) and member of the council (1948) of the British Academy. In 1947 he received the honorary degrees of D.Litt. from the university of Wales and D.-ès-L. from Bordeaux. He was unmarried.

[*Cambridge Review*, 20 January 1951; *Eagle* (magazine of St. John's College), January 1951; F. E. Adcock in *Proceedings* of the British Academy, vol. xxxvi, 1950 (bibliography).]      F. E. ADCOCK.

CHARNWOOD, first BARON (1864–1945), Liberal politician and man of letters. [See BENSON, GODFREY RATHBONE.]

CHAUVEL, SIR HENRY GEORGE (1865–1945), general, was born 16 April 1865 at Tabulam, Clarence River, New South Wales, the second son of Charles Henry Edward Chauvel by his wife, Fanny Ada Mary, daughter of Henry Kerrison James, of Sydney. His grandfather, Captain Charles G. T. Chauvel of the East India Company's service, had bought a cattle station at Tabulam and his father, who was unable to follow the family tradition by entering the regular army, raised in 1886 the Upper Clarence Light Horse Regiment. Harry Chauvel, reared in a district famous for its riders, dreamed of a career in the British cavalry, and was educated for Sandhurst at Toowoomba and Sydney grammar schools. But at this stage his father's monetary losses through droughts placed that career beyond his means and he became manager of one of his father's stations. At school he had been an enthusiastic cadet, and he joined his father's regiment and spent a European holiday largely in watching the British and foreign armies. In 1894 he became a temporary officer of the Queensland Mounted Police, and two years later eagerly accepted appointment as captain on the Queensland military staff. In 1897, on visiting England with a detachment for Queen Victoria's diamond jubilee, he trained for a year with the British Army. In the South African war Chauvel, now major, saw hard fighting in the Queensland Mounted Infantry during the relief of Kimberley and later; at Vet River he personally captured a mischievous machine-gun. For a time he commanded his regiment and a small independent force, but he was not allowed to extend his one year's war service. However, the Australian colonies having just then federated, he managed to reach South Africa again as commander of a battalion of the newly raised Australian Commonwealth Horse, only to find the war ending.

Back in Australia he was entrusted with training mounted troops (thenceforward known as light horse) for the new Australian forces, and many leaders soon to become noted were exercised in his staff rides. When in 1910 Lord Kitchener [q.v.] went out to advise on the scheme for compulsory service, Chauvel successfully urged that the old militia be retained as the core of the new force. In 1911 he became adjutant-general and second member of the military board, and in July 1914 he was sent to England as Australian representative on the imperial general staff. With wife and family he was on the voyage when war broke out. Seeking, as always, active service he learnt at the War Office that Australia had given him command of the 1st Light Horse brigade due for England in the force under (Sir) W. T. Bridges [q.v.].

It was partly through Chauvel's concern about the condition of camps on Salisbury Plain that Kitchener diverted the Australian contingent to Egypt. There his brigade trained under him as part of the Australian and New Zealand division of the Anzac Corps, but the mounted troops were not at first taken to Gallipoli. When it was presently suggested that they be drawn on for reinforcements for the infantry, Chauvel and his fellow brigadiers, by urging that they should serve as brigades, dismounted, probably averted their merging in the infantry. At Anzac, after commanding in two central sectors, Chauvel was transferred in December 1915 as major-general to the 1st Australian Infantry division at the evacuation. But after returning to Egypt he was soon restored to his favourite arm when the Anzac Mounted division was formed in March 1916 and allotted to the defence of Egypt. A Turkish force then threatened the Suez Canal. The plan of Sir Archibald Murray [q.v.] by which it was allowed to come on and then shattered by mounted troops delivering a flank stroke at Romani (4 August 1916) was partly of Chauvel's devising. In the ensuing thrust to Palestine Chauvel commanded the Desert Column (April 1917) and later, as lieutenant-general (2 August 1917), the Desert Mounted Corps which ultimately included two Anzac and two British-Indian divisions. He was also administrative commander of all Australian troops in that theatre. In the two great thrusts in Palestine

Chauvel was the trusted commander of the mounted arm used by Sir Edmund (later Viscount) Allenby [q.v.]; in each case to play a decisive role. In the first it turned the Gaza line by a daring thrust from the desert through Beersheba (31 October 1917) and thence to the coastal plain; and in the second it dashed through the breach made on 19 September 1918 by the infantry on the coastal flank, and encircled and captured most of two Turkish armies. At Damascus Chauvel met T. E. Lawrence [q.v.] who had entered the city before him, determined to shape the Arab rule there; but the mischievous picture of Chauvel given in *Seven Pillars of Wisdom* may widely mislead readers as to the true quality of this wise, competent, and considerate leader. Allenby ordered Chauvel to march on Aleppo which was reached just before hostilities ended. Returning to Australia Chauvel, as inspector-general and later also, from 1923, chief of the general staff, was mainly responsible for such efficiency as the Australian Army retained during this time of financial semi-starvation. He retired at the age of sixty-five in 1930, but held important business directorships until his death. His military reputation rests not on any brilliance but on his wise and successful handling of by far the most effective cavalry force in the war of 1914–18. His caution was sometimes criticized but was vital in operations in the desert where, if water was not reached, the horses must come back for it or disaster follow.

He married in 1906 Sybil Campbell Keith, daughter of George Keith Jopp, a surveyor, of Karaba, Queensland; they had two sons and two daughters. He was appointed C.B. in 1916, K.C.M.G. in 1917, K.C.B. in 1918, and G.C.M.G. in 1919. He died in Melbourne 4 March 1945. There is a portrait of Chauvel by W. B. McInnes in the Australian War Memorial at Canberra, and he is the chief figure in a group of mounted officers entitled 'Leaders of the Australian Light Horse, 1918' by H. Septimus Power. A portrait by G. W. Lambert is in the possession of the family, and by James McBey in the Imperial War Museum.

[H. S. Gullett, (Official) *History of Australia in the War of 1914–18*, vol. vii, 1923; Chauvel's notes in the Australian War Memorial; private information; personal knowledge.]

C. E. W. BEAN.

CHETWODE, SIR PHILIP WAL-HOUSE, seventh baronet, and first BARON

CHETWODE (1869–1950), field-marshal, was born in London 21 September 1869, the elder son of (Sir) George Chetwode, who became sixth baronet, and his wife, Alice Jane, daughter of Michael Thomas Bass and sister of M. A. Bass, first Baron Burton [qq. v.]. Educated at Eton, Chetwode gained athletic distinction by winning the hundred yards, the quarter mile, and the hurdles in 1887; he also played in the Oppidan Wall and Field elevens. He entered the army through the militia, receiving his first commission in the 3rd battalion the Oxfordshire and Buckinghamshire Light Infantry, and in 1889 a regular commission in the 19th Hussars. This impregnation with two distinct traditions of mobility, of light infantry and of cavalry, was both an influence and an augury.

He was fortunate to have an early chance of active service, in the Chin Hills expedition, Burma, of 1892–3. He was promoted to captain in February 1897 after only seven years' service, when with his regiment in South Africa, and he was there when war broke out two years later. He took part in the defence of Ladysmith, and before the end of the war had been twice mentioned in dispatches and appointed to the D.S.O. Sir John French (later the Earl of Ypres, q.v.), who had been his first commanding officer in the 19th Hussars, was strongly impressed by Chetwode's potentialities and sought his appointment to the staff on receiving the Aldershot Command. Chetwode had not, however, passed through the Staff College and the War Office would not relax the rule. But in 1906 he became French's assistant military secretary. In the previous year he had succeeded his father in the baronetcy. In 1908 he was given command of his regiment in the cavalry brigade commanded by Edmund (later Viscount) Allenby [q.v.] who, like French, was struck by Chetwode's quick grasp of a problem and keen eye for ground.

Soon after completing his four years' term of regimental command Chetwode was given the London Yeomanry brigade in the Territorial Force. During the Curragh incident of March 1914 he was chosen to replace (Sir) Hubert Gough in command of the 3rd Cavalry brigade when Gough and other senior officers tendered their resignations. The issue was settled and the resignations withdrawn, but Chetwode's provisional acceptance caused ill feeling which long persisted in some quarters. He was, however, given command of the 5th Cavalry brigade shortly afterwards and took it to France on the outbreak of war in August 1914. His brigade helped to cover the retreat from the frontier, and at Cérizy inflicted a valuable check on the pursuing Germans. In the subsequent advance from the Marne it joined with the 3rd under Gough's command, the two then being designated the 2nd Cavalry division. During this phase there was some criticism of Chetwode's caution in pursuit, although not of his general capacity as a commander. After the check on the Aisne, he moved up to Flanders with the rest of the cavalry and took part in the defensive battle of Ypres. In July 1915 he was promoted to command the 2nd Cavalry division on French's recommendation, but by that time the trench deadlock had turned the opportunity into a *cul-de-sac*.

More fortunate than most cavalrymen, Chetwode was provided with a wider scope by transfer to the Near East in December 1916 as commander of the Desert Column in the Egyptian Expeditionary Force under Sir Archibald Murray [q.v.]. Here Chetwode showed striking ability in devising and planning bold manœuvres, although in execution these several times fell short of their prospect from a sense of caution fostered by his concern for the water supply of the horses.

In January 1917 Chetwode advanced against the Turkish fortified post at Rafah on the Palestine border. The post was surrounded soon after dawn, following a night approach through the desert, but the attack made such slow progress that in the afternoon Chetwode was instructing Sir Henry Chauvel [q.v.] to prepare to withdraw when the key position was stormed. In March an advance was made on Gaza by a larger force under Sir Charles Dobell, with Chetwode commanding the Desert Column. Gaza was enveloped and the garrison on the verge of surrender when the attack was broken off at nightfall after consultation between Dobell and Chetwode who expected a Turkish countermove and were anxious about water for the horses. A second attack in April failed at heavy cost, the enemy having been reinforced. Dobell was then replaced by Chetwode and in June Allenby took Murray's place. On Allenby's arrival in Egypt he received a plan of manœuvre finely conceived by Chetwode and his staff officer Brigadier-General Guy Payan Dawnay. When applied in the autumn this resulted in levering the Turks out of their defences.

Chetwode was now in command of the newly formed XX Corps which was brought up in the subsequent advance on Jerusalem when the XXI Corps was checked. To him was due both the conception and direction of the stroke which turned the Turks' resistance in the hills and opened the way to the capture of the holy city.

In 1919 Chetwode became military secretary to the secretary of state; he was deputy chief of the imperial general staff, 1920–22, and for a short time adjutant-general: a notable series of appointments for an officer who was not a Staff College graduate. In 1923 he was given the highest command at home, Aldershot. It was a time of retrenchment but he exerted a helpful influence on the remodelling of the army by his constant insistence on the need to break loose from entrenchment and revive manoeuvre in warfare. While he still cherished the horse and was rather sceptical of the tank, his demand for 'a general quickening up all round' of movement and leadership was encouraging to those younger men who were proclaiming the new vision of lightning strokes by armoured forces.

At the end of his four years' tenure Chetwode was only fifty-seven but the two posts senior to him had been filled within the previous two years. In 1928 he accepted a temporary step down and became chief of the general staff in India. The prospect of Chetwode eventually becoming chief of the imperial general staff disappeared when the holder, Sir George (later Lord) Milne [q.v.], obtained an extension, but in 1930 Chetwode became commander-in-chief in India, a five years' appointment. It was a very difficult period: the military need for modernizing the army in India conflicted with the economic and political demands for reducing military costs, while there was growing pressure to indianize the army. Chetwode came through this ordeal with remarkable success, showing the qualities of statesmanship in the way he steered a course amid the rocks and swirling currents of British conservatism and Indian nationalism. His frankness of speech and downright manner both helped and hid his diplomacy. The proportion of entirely Indian-officered units was much increased, an Indian Sandhurst created, and also an Indian Air Force, while the Indian Marine became the Indian Navy. The slight progress made in modernizing the army and its equipment was not surprising. Chetwode had to work in a very conservative military environment, and within a limited military budget—in which he achieved considerable economies and an overall reduction.

Chetwode had greater natural gifts than most of the eminent soldiers of his time. Not intellectual, he was highly intelligent. His shrewd and incisive comments in conference, delivered in a racy 'Newmarket twang', made a lasting impression. He gripped an audience as few generals could —all the more because he looked and spoke like a leader. He was a 'big' man both physically and in personality. His 'military testament' delivered to the Quetta Staff College before leaving India was one of the most penetrating indictments of orthodoxy and of mental atrophy and stimulating calls for imagination ever delivered from the throne of military authority. To an unusual extent he practised what he preached. He shone even more in peace than in war since his unusual capacity for imagination, which may have caused an occasional hesitation in carrying through battle-plans which he had masterfully conceived, became an increasing asset, as did his flexibility, as he rose higher and entered the sphere of statecraft.

Chetwode was promoted to field-marshal in 1933 and on returning from India was appointed to the Order of Merit in 1936 and received the honorary degree of D.C.L., Oxford. Earlier honours were C.B. (1915), K.C.B. (1918), G.C.B. (1929), K.C.M.G. (1917), and G.C.S.I. (1934). He was constable of the Tower of London 1943–8 and rendered valuable service during the war of 1939–45 as chairman of the executive committee of the Red Cross and St. John joint war organization. He was colonel of the Royal Scots Greys, the 15th/19th Hussars, and the 8th Light Cavalry (Indian Army). He was created a baron in 1945 and died in London 6 July 1950.

He married in 1899 Hester Alice Camilla (died 1946), daughter of Colonel the Hon. Richard Southwell George Stapleton-Cotton and great-granddaughter of Sir Stapleton Cotton, first Viscount Combermere [q.v.]. They had one son and one daughter. The son died in 1940 and the titles thus passed to Chetwode's grandson, Philip (born 1937). The daughter married Mr. John Betjeman who contributes to this SUPPLEMENT. A portrait of Chetwode by Flora Lion is at the Ex-Services Victory Club, Seymour Street, London; another by (Sir) Oswald Birley is at the Cavalry Club.

[Cyril Falls, (Official) *History of the Great War. Military Operations, Egypt and Palestine, 1914–18,* 3 vols., 1928–30; private information; personal knowledge.]

B. H. LIDDELL HART.

CHILD, HAROLD HANNYNGTON (1869–1945), author and critic, was born at Gloucester 20 June 1869, the second son of the Rev. Thomas Hannyngton Irving Child, afterwards rector of Stratton, Gloucestershire, by his wife, Florence, daughter of Thomas Crossman, solicitor, of Thornbury, Gloucestershire. He was a scholar both of Winchester and of Brasenose College, Oxford. After being awarded a second class in *literae humaniores* in 1892 he was articled to a firm of solicitors in Thornbury. Later, when he was sent to work in the office of the firm's London agents, he rebelled against the tedium of his apprenticeship and determined to abandon the law. At Oxford he had been intimate with George Bancroft, son of (Sir) Squire and Marie Bancroft [qq.v.] and in 1894 he played a small part in *Slaves of the Ring* by Sydney Grundy, the first play criticized by G. B. Shaw [q.v.] in the *Saturday Review.* For the next two years Child was a member of various companies, playing the 'light juvenile gentleman' in *Niobe* (by Harry and Edward Paulton) and other plays. The story of these two years is told with humorous charm in *A Poor Player* (1939).

Even before he left the stage Child had begun to write. Introduced to the *Star* by Richard Le Gallienne [q.v.], he contributed a series of short stories to that paper and his first book, *Phil of the Heath* (1899), was a romantic novel of the Reform Bill period. Child was by nature a man of letters, but he never disdained the varieties of journalistic experience. Between 1905 and 1910 he was successively assistant editor of the *Academy* and the *Burlington Magazine* and was dramatic critic of the *Observer* from 1912 to 1920. Meanwhile he had joined his old friend (Sir) Bruce Lyttelton Richmond in producing the *Times Literary Supplement,* which was founded in 1902. To this *Supplement* he contributed substantial critical articles over a period of forty years. Good judges noted the quality of these essays at an early stage and Child was invited to write a number of chapters for the *Cambridge History of English Literature.* The range of these chapters was notably wide, for Child could write about Crabbe or about Jane Austen with the same sympathy and scholarship as he devoted to the drama of the Elizabethan or any other age. The theatre retained a special place in his interest; for many years he shared the dramatic criticism of *The Times* with A. B. Walkley [q.v.] and his personal experience of the stage enabled him to appreciate the work of the producer and the actor as well as that of the playwright. Of Shakespearian production, in particular, he gradually established himself as an authoritative historian and up to the time of his death each volume of 'The New Shakespeare', edited by Sir Arthur Quiller-Couch [q.v.] and Professor John Dover Wilson, contained a stage-history written by him. He wrote a number of notices for this DICTIONARY, including those of the Bancrofts, Walkley, Irving, Wyndham, Esmond, and Ellen Terry.

Apart from the theatre, Child had a keen interest in poetry, music, and the arts. He was secretary from 1902 to 1905 of the Royal Society of Painter-Etchers and Engravers and translated Dimier's *French Painting in the Sixteenth Century*; he was the author of a book on Thomas Hardy (1916), of the libretto of Ralph Vaughan Williams's *Hugh the Drover*, and of a small book of love poems, *The Yellow Rock* (1919). But it was to *The Times* that the greater part of his energy was devoted. Apart from literary and dramatic criticism, he was a supremely reliable contributor of special articles and 'light leaders', and a selection of these is preserved in *Essays and Reflections* (1948). In the hurly-burly of the day's writing he never lowered his standards. He could meet the demand of the hour without descending to the cliché. In one series of articles, published as a book entitled *Love and Unlove* (1921), he revealed something of his own approach to life: 'Happiness is not a negative measure of shutting out, but a positive measure of taking in more and more.' A victim of recurrent asthma, Child nevertheless remained a good clubman and a most sensitive companion. Neither his failing health nor the bombing of his London flat destroyed the buoyancy of his faith in spiritual values.

Child married in 1896 Drusilla Mary (died 1918) sister of Kate Cutler (1870–1955), the actress, and daughter of the late Henry Cutler, an artist; secondly in 1934 he married Helen Mary, daughter of H. Spenser Wilkinson [q.v.]. There were no children of either marriage. He died at Littlehampton 8 November 1945.

[S. C. Roberts, a memoir prefaced to Child's *Essays and Reflections*, 1948; *The Times*, 9 and 10 November 1945; personal knowledge.]

S. C. ROBERTS.

CHILD-VILLIERS, MARGARET ELIZABETH, COUNTESS OF JERSEY (1849–1945). [See VILLIERS.]

CHILSTON, second VISCOUNT (1876–1947), diplomatist. [See AKERS-DOUGLAS, ARETAS.]

CHUBB, SIR LAWRENCE WENSLEY (1873–1948), protagonist of open space preservation and other amenities, was born at Lauraville, Victoria, Australia, 21 December 1873, the son of Lawrence Wensley Chubb, J.P., prospector and mine-owner, of Copeland, New South Wales, by his wife, Esther Collins. He came to England in 1887 and completed his education in London at St. Olave's and St. Saviour's Grammar School and the Borough Polytechnic. His chief recreation was exploring the countryside on foot with an alert mind and observant eye. At the Polytechnic debating society he attracted the attention of Octavia Hill [q.v.] and through her he was appointed in 1894 secretary of the Kent and Surrey committee of the Commons Preservation Society. A year later Octavia Hill, Sir Robert Hunter [q.v.], Canon H. D. Rawnsley, and others formed the National Trust for places of historic interest or natural beauty and Chubb became its first secretary. Although so young Chubb was already remarkable for his discretion and tact as well as for his driving power and ability, and in 1896 he resigned from the National Trust to become secretary of the Commons Preservation Society.

For over fifty years he was largely responsible, as secretary, for the work of this body which became the Commons, Open Spaces, and Footpaths Preservation Society; but this was only one of his activities. He was a moving spirit in many individual schemes for preserving open spaces, such as the Hindhead commons, Brockwell Park, Box Hill, and Ken Wood. In 1905 he founded, with others, the Ramblers' Association of which he was first secretary and later a vice-president. He was also from 1916 secretary of the Scapa Society (later the Advisory Council for the Control of Outdoor Advertising); from 1928 secretary of the National Playing Fields Association; and from 1902 until 1929 secretary of the Coal Smoke Abatement Society.

In the course of years Chubb acquired a quite unrivalled legal knowledge of the complex questions related to open spaces, footpaths, and public advertising, and was often consulted by local authorities and government departments. His unfailing tact made him invaluable in negotiation and on deputations to ministers, and he served on many committees concerned with open spaces, with liaison between the Forestry Commission and amenity societies, with the establishment of nature reserves and national parks, with the agricultural use of commons in wartime, and kindred matters. He was knighted in 1930 for his many and varied services to the English countryside which continued almost to the end of his life.

Inevitably there was a section among the rambling clubs which felt Chubb too ready for compromise, and he was criticized for trying to do too many things, but this was not the opinion of those who had seen most of the achievements of his tact, judicial temperament, and wide knowledge in the cause he had so deeply at heart.

In 1905 he married Gertrude Elizabeth, daughter of William Willers Anthony, of Southwark, and had one son and one daughter. He died at his home at Richmond, Surrey, 18 February 1948.

[The Times, 19 February 1948; private information; personal knowledge.]

D. MacLeod Matheson.

CLAPHAM, Sir ALFRED WILLIAM (1883–1950), archaeologist, was born at Dalston, London, 27 May 1883, the son of the Rev. James Ernest Clapham, a Wesleyan minister, and his wife, Lucy Elizabeth Hutchinson. He was educated at Dulwich College and on leaving school was articled to an architect, James Weir. His mind turned to historical studies, and for some years he worked for the *Victoria County History*. In 1912 Clapham became a member of the staff of the Royal Commission on Historical Monuments in England, and thereafter his life's work was done for that body. He became technical editor in 1913. After serving with the Royal Sussex Regiment during the war of 1914–18, he returned to the Royal Commission where he remained technical editor until 1933 when he succeeded Sir George Duckworth as secretary to the commissioners, retiring in 1948.

Clapham was one of the last of the great English medieval archaeologists of the nineteenth-century school, who combined with wide historical learning a sound knowledge of architecture. Others before him had been architects in practice or, like himself, had at least started life in the profession, thus imbibing in the traditional manner that automatic awareness of the significance of detail. Their work, oral and written, Clapham's in particular, seemed so polished and perfect, that little appeared to remain for accomplishment. The architectural profession was, however, turning away from traditional study, whilst the attention of younger archaeologists was diverted to the contemplation of earlier periods of the country's history. Thus it came about that by the time of his death Clapham stood alone without a successor, although there were already those who realized how much could still be learnt by continuing to work upon the lines which he had made so familiar to them. He combined a close attention to detail with a knowledge of certain or likely parallels and sound historical training, and expressed his conclusions in an able and lucid manner which seldom failed to carry conviction.

Although he was at home in any period of the country's history and its architectural illustration, Clapham's predilection was for the architecture and sculpture of the British Isles from the introduction of Christianity by St. Augustine of Canterbury to the end of the Romanesque period, c. A.D. 1200. The results of a lifetime of study in this field and of prolonged travels, especially in France, as well as all parts of the British Isles, were expressed for the general reader in his two volumes entitled *English Romanesque Architecture*, volume i 'Before the Conquest' (1930) and volume ii 'After the Conquest' (1934), as well as in his *Romanesque Architecture in Western Europe* (1936). His earliest studies and publications in learned journals had, however, been concerned rather with the plans and the history of monastic establishments, and to this subject throughout his life he paid particular attention, some of his posthumous works being devoted thereto. Amongst the most useful articles are those on the Premonstratensians in England and on the Order of Grandmont (with Dr. Rose Graham) in *Archaeologia*, volumes lxxiii and lxxv respectively. In later years Clapham also devoted much attention to Irish buildings, writing important papers on the Cistercian Order in Ireland (with Mr. H. G. Leask) and on 'Some Minor Irish Cathedrals'.

The total of Clapham's published books and articles gives but a hint of his work and influence. For over thirty years his scholarship and power of lucid expression can be traced in the Inventories of the Royal Commission which he served. The succinct entries, full of accurate information and observation, yet eminently readable, show the mark of his guiding hand, whilst the prefaces, whether signed or not, are recognizably from his pen. The high standing of the Inventories in the world of scholarship may be largely attributed to him, either directly or through his choice and training of staff.

Clapham also devoted much of his time to the affairs of the Society of Antiquaries of London. Elected a fellow in 1913, he served on the council on several occasions; he became secretary in 1929 and president for the term 1939–44, at the conclusion of which he was knighted; he received the Society's gold medal in 1948. He had been appointed C.B.E. in 1932, was elected F.B.A. in 1935, and in 1944 became a trustee of the London Museum. He gave much assistance as well to the Royal Archaeological Institute and more of his work, written for the benefit of his fellow members, may be read in the programmes and reports of the summer meetings of the Institute between 1928 and 1950. He served on the Institute's council for many years, and was elected president in 1945. He died in London, unmarried, 26 October 1950 and was honoured by a memorial volume (*Archaeological Journal*, vol. cvi, Supplement, 1952), which contains a bibliography of his writings and further details of his life.

[Personal knowledge.]
B. H. St. J. O'Neil.

CLAPHAM, Sir JOHN HAROLD (1873–1946), historian, was born at Broughton, Salford, Lancashire, 13 September 1873, the younger son of John Clapham, jeweller and silversmith, by his second wife, Mary Jane, daughter of John Chambers, accountant, of Manchester. He was educated at the Leys School, Cambridge, where he distinguished himself as an athlete and games player and won a history exhibition to King's College, Cambridge. Going into residence there in 1892, he was elected to a scholarship two years later and took a first class in the historical tripos in 1895. As a young graduate he came under the influence of Lord Acton [q.v.], and, after

winning the Lightfoot scholarship in ecclesiastical history in 1896 and the Prince Consort prize in 1898, he became a fellow of King's in that year. His prize dissertation, published with the title *The Causes of the War of 1792* (1899), and *The Abbé Sieyès; an Essay in the Politics of the French Revolution*, which was published as late as 1912, are good specimens of political history as Acton conceived it; but as early as 1897 Alfred Marshall [q.v.] singled Clapham out as the man who ought to write an 'account of the economic development of England in the last century', and Clapham's mind turned slowly but decisively in this direction. In 1902 he became professor of economics at the Yorkshire College, shortly to become the university of Leeds, and took the opportunity to study the local industries. In 1908 he returned to Cambridge, being once more elected into a fellowship at King's to take part in the historical teaching there. He succeeded W. H. Macaulay as tutor in 1913.

During the war of 1914–18 Clapham served from 1916 in the Board of Trade; he became a member of the Cabinet committee on priorities and was appointed C.B.E. in 1918. Returning to Cambridge after the war he resumed his active part in teaching and in college and university administration, and in 1921 published his book *The Economic Development of France and Germany, 1815–1914*. This was followed in 1926–38 by the three volumes of his most important work, *An Economic History of Modern Britain*, which covers the period from about 1820 to 1914 on a large scale, with an epilogue on the succeeding years. Two years after the publication of the first volume Clapham was elected to the newly created chair of economic history in Cambridge, and so was relieved of much routine work; but he continued his many subsidiary activities. From 1933 to 1943 he was vice-provost of King's, where he retained his fellowship until the end of his life. In 1938 he retired from his chair under the superannuation rule; but, partly in consequence of the outbreak of war in 1939, in the following period he was no less active than before. The death of Eileen Power [q.v.] in 1940 left him in sole charge of the editing of the first volume of the *Cambridge Economic History of Europe* which was published in 1941. He was entrusted with the writing of the *History of the Bank of England*. This appeared in two volumes in 1944 on the two hundred and fiftieth anniversary of the grant of the Bank's charter, carrying the history down to 1914. An unpublished continuation goes down to 1939.

A bibliography of Clapham's writings was published in volume viii, No. 3, of the *Cambridge Historical Journal* (1946). To it should be added the posthumous *Concise Economic History of Britain from the Earliest Times to 1750* (1949), edited by Mr. John Saltmarsh. This gives the substance of a course of lectures which for many years was the mainstay of the Cambridge teaching of the subject. As a lecturer Clapham ranked very high. His complete mastery in delivery and presentation was matched by his tall and massively built figure. The portrait by James Gunn at King's College, Cambridge, is an excellent likeness, but it was painted when Clapham was past his prime. Throughout his life, however, he maintained great physical and intellectual energy. Mountaineering was his chief delight for nearly forty years: late in life he was elected a vice-president of the Alpine Club. As an historian, after his sheer capacity for work, his best quality was a power of reducing large masses of detailed facts to systematic form. His interest in economic history was never entirely dissociated from the interest in contemporary social problems which he inherited from Marshall. He was a supporter of the Liberal Party and the social reforms of the Asquith period, regarding some of which he privately made constructive suggestions; but he looked upon historical writing as a scientific activity detached from practical aims. Although well versed in economic theory, he presented his matter as concretely as possible, aiming rather at providing materials than at analysing their significance. His criticism of his sources was acute and robust; his style racy and vigorous, if impaired in his last years by mannerisms. No other historian has treated any period of British economic history as exhaustively as Clapham did the nineteenth century, nor provided such a large body of well-chosen and well-prepared information.

In 1940 Clapham became president of the British Academy, of which he had been a fellow since 1928, and his tenure of this office was renewed in 1944 and 1945. In 1943 he was knighted. Among many public services of his last years the most noteworthy was the chairmanship of the government committee on the organiza-

tion of social and economic research known as the Clapham committee. He saw the report of this committee in draft. It was published (Cmd. 6868), and its recommendations were adopted, after his death which occurred very suddenly, 29 March 1946, whilst travelling by train from London to Cambridge. Had he survived he would have received the honorary doctorate which Montpellier University had offered to him: he had already been honoured in this way by Harvard and Leeds, and he was a corresponding member of the Royal Swedish Academy.

In 1905 Clapham married Mary Margaret, daughter of William Edward Green, surgeon, of Ross-on-Wye. By her he had one son and three daughters, all of whom survived him.

[*The Times*, 30 March 1946; G. N. Clark in *Proceedings* of the British Academy, vol. xxxii, 1946; M. M. Postan in *Economic History Review*, vol. xvi, No. 1, 1946; G. M. Trevelyan in *Economic Journal*, September 1946, reprinted with other contributions and a reproduction of James Gunn's portrait in *John Harold Clapham, 1873–1946*, printed for King's College, Cambridge, 1949; private information; personal knowledge.]

G. N. Clark.

CLAUSEN, Sir GEORGE (1852–1944), painter, was born in London 18 April 1852, the second son of George Johnsen Clausen, a Danish decorative artist who had arrived in England before 1849, by his wife, Elizabeth Fillan. After attending St. Mark's College, Chelsea, he entered in 1867 the drawing office of Messrs. Trollope, builders and decorators, and attended evening classes at the National Art Training School, South Kensington (later the Royal College of Art), to which he won a national scholarship in 1873. He then carried out pictorial research for the historical painter E. L. Long [q.v.] and concurrently copied pictures by Rembrandt, Titian, and Velazquez at the National Gallery.

Early in 1876 Clausen made a journey to Holland and Belgium, and one picture which he brought back, 'High Mass at a Fishing Village on the Zuyder Zee', was his first accepted contribution to the Royal Academy exhibition, being hung that year. His progress in water-colour painting was also marked in 1876 by his election to an associateship of the Royal Institute of Painters in Water Colours. He was promoted full R.I. in 1886, elected associate of the Royal Society of Painters in Water Colours in 1889, and full R.W.S. in 1898.

At the outset of his painting career Clausen worked under Bouguereau and Tony Robert-Fleury in Paris, and also visited the studios of Jean Léon Gérôme and Carolus Duran, having some idea of working in one or the other. But he abandoned this project and, returning to England, began to paint the life of the agricultural labourer. Strongly influenced at first by Bastien-Lepage (on whom he contributed a study to André Theuriet's memoir of Lepage published in 1892) he worked out of doors and from early days showed a preoccupation with strong lighting effects. His 'Labourers after Dinner', shown at the Academy of 1884, brought him wide repute, and 'The Girl at the Gate' (1889) was the first of his works to be bought out of the Chantrey bequest: it is now in the Tate Gallery. At this period he was spending much time in the Essex countryside making many sketches from direct observation of farm-hands at their daily work. Agricultural life remained his chief subject, but he also painted pure landscape, as well as a number of portraits of grave beauty, some barn interiors which reveal his mastery of tone and colour, and some nudes, town interiors, and still lifes.

From 1904 to 1906 Clausen (who had been elected A.R.A. in 1895) was professor of painting at the Royal Academy. His collected lectures, *Six Lectures on Painting* (1904) and *Aims and Ideals in Art* (1906), are broad and temperate in outlook, show deep study of the methods of the old masters, and are full of wise technical counsel. He held one-man shows at intervals in London as well as exhibiting at Chicago, Paris, Brussels, Vienna, and Munich. He was elected R.A. in 1908 and knighted in 1927.

Although, like the Impressionists, Clausen was preoccupied with the effects of light, unlike them he retained solidity of form. He was especially interested in figures seen against the sun, and produced effects of vibration and glow by skilfully applied small strokes of pure colour. In water-colour (which he practised right on into old age) he had a very delicate touch and a scholarly command of the medium. His versatility was shown by such things as his lunettes at High Royd, Honley, Yorkshire, which are true decorations, far tighter in handling than his easel-pictures, and by the posters which he designed in 1923 for the London Midland and Scottish Railway. He was most open-minded, not only giving sympathetic welcome to newer schools but changing his own style several times. In personal character he was quiet, modest, kindly, and of courtly manners.

In 1881 Clausen married Agnes Mary (died March 1944), daughter of George Webster, newspaper editor, of King's Lynn, and had three sons and two daughters, of whom the younger, Katherine, a painter of mark, predeceased her father, and the elder, Margaret Mary, was the wife of the artist Thomas Derrick. Clausen died at Cold Ash, near Newbury, 22 November 1944.

A self-portrait of Clausen (1918) is in the Fitzwilliam Museum, Cambridge, and another belongs to the Art-Workers' Guild, of which he was master in 1909.

[*The Times*, 24 November 1944; Ulrich Thieme and Felix Becker, *Allgemeines Lexikon der bildenden Künstler*, vol. vii, 1912; D[yneley] H[ussey], *George Clausen* (Contemporary British Artists), 1923; private information.]     HERBERT B. GRIMSDITCH.

CLAUSON, ALBERT CHARLES, BARON CLAUSON (1870–1946), judge, the younger of the two sons of Charles Clauson, merchant, by his wife, Julia Burton, daughter of the Rev. John Wall Buckley, vicar of St. Mary's, Paddington Green, was born in London 14 January 1870. His mother's family was one of considerable note, and several of its members had a recognizable influence upon his career, particularly his uncle H. B. Buckley [q.v.] the eminent lawyer who became the first Baron Wrenbury. From a home of quiet distinction Clauson entered the Merchant Taylors' School in 1881, proceeding as a scholar to St. John's College, Oxford, where he was placed in the first class in both classical moderations (1889) and *literae humaniores* (1891). Later he became a senior scholar of the college (1894) and an honorary fellow (1927).

Clauson was called to the bar in 1891 by Lincoln's Inn, of which he was treasurer in 1937. His association with his uncle, who had taken silk in 1886, enabled him to acquire a large junior practice at an unusually early age. His collaboration in several editions of Buckley's classical treatise on Companies brought him lucrative business in that branch of the law, and when in 1910 he took silk, he was one of the busiest of the Chancery juniors. His success as a leader was soon such that he ceased to be attached to the court of a particular judge, as was then the rule, and joined the select band of 'specials' who accepted briefs only when marked with a special fee. During the war of 1914–18 Clauson took up work at the Admiralty, where he acted as the legal member, unpaid, of the controller's staff. He was appointed C.B.E. for his services in 1920. In 1918–19 he was in India with his brother-in-law, Lord Southborough [q.v.], who was chairman of the Indian franchise committee.

On his return to the bar Clauson resumed his position as one of the leading equity practitioners, and was soon engaged as much in the House of Lords and Privy Council as in the Strand. He was standing counsel to the university of Oxford and to the Royal College of Physicians. The success of Clauson's advocacy was due less to profundity of knowledge than to a clear and logical mind finding felicitous expression in apt and lucid language. He argued his cases with much distinction of style, although his precision of manner appeared on occasions to be pedantic, and he was probably always more at home in legal argument than in the handling of witnesses.

Clauson was appointed to the Chancery bench in 1926 and received the customary knighthood. Many of his qualities appeared to even greater advantage after he became a judge; he was courteous, and he was rapid, although inclined at times to an excess of subtlety and ingenuity. His twelve years' work as a Chancery judge was efficient and unobtrusive. His judgements in every branch of the equity jurisdiction were careful and scholarly, and he did much to elucidate the Law of Property Act, 1925, and the other reforming and consolidating statutes known to lawyers as the Birkenhead Acts which came into force in the year of his appointment.

He was made a lord justice of appeal and sworn of the Privy Council in 1938, and displayed in the higher tribunal the same judicial aptitudes. But his time there was comparatively brief. He retired at the beginning of 1942 and was created a baron. Thereafter, until shortly before his death, he occasionally sat at the hearing of appeals both in the House of Lords and in the Privy Council.

Clauson's intellectual gifts found ample and congenial scope in the administration and practice of the law, and his ambitions were, no doubt, fully satisfied by the success which he achieved therein. By a kindliness of heart imperfectly concealed by a somewhat austere manner he won the affection of a large circle of friends both in his profession and beyond it. He maintained throughout his life a close interest in the Merchant Taylors' Company of which he was twice master. His portrait painted by L. Campbell Taylor in 1939 fortunately survived the destruction of the Company's Hall.

In 1902 Clauson married Kate, daughter of James Thomas Hopwood, barrister, of Lincoln's Inn, widow of Lucas Thomasson, and sister of Sir Francis Hopwood (later Lord Southborough). They made their home at Hawkshead House, near Hatfield, where he died 15 March 1946, a few weeks after the death of his wife. There was no issue of their marriage, and the peerage became extinct.

[*The Times*, 16 March 1946; private information; personal knowledge.]

H. B. VAISEY.

CLEMENTI, SIR CECIL (1875–1947), colonial administrator and traveller, was born 1 September 1875 at Cawnpore, the eldest son of Captain Montagu Clementi of the 1st Bengal Cavalry, later colonel and judge advocate-general in India, by his wife, Isabel Collard. Clementi was educated at St. Paul's School and was elected a demy of Magdalen College, Oxford, where he obtained a first class in classical moderations (1896) and a second class in *literae humaniores* (1898). In 1897 he was awarded the Boden Sanskrit scholarship and he was *proxime accessit* for the Gaisford prize for Greek prose (1897) and for the Chancellor's Latin essay prize (1899). His interest in the classics led him later to publish an edition of the *Pervigilium Veneris* (1911, reprinted 1928, 1936). He was elected an honorary fellow of Magdalen in 1938.

Although fourth in the Home and Indian Civil Service lists of 1899, Clementi, following his uncle and godfather, Sir Cecil Clementi Smith, preferred an Eastern cadetship and was posted to Hong Kong. He passed his examinations in Cantonese in 1900 and in Pekingese in 1906. In 1904 he published a Chinese text with notes and translations of some *Cantonese Love-songs* to interest students in vernacular poetry and assist them to understand Chinese.

Clementi was seconded for special service under the Government of India in 1902 and for famine relief work in

Kwang-si in 1903. As land officer and police magistrate in the then newly leased territories on the mainland (1903–6) he had the task of recognizing the land-titles. There were 300,000 claims. Every ingenious device was used to establish baseless titles, but there was not a single appeal against his decisions, and the country people remained his firm friends for life, a fact which was to be of great assistance to him when he returned as governor of Hong Kong in more troubled times. He travelled widely in all eighteen provinces and mastered several local languages. In 1907–8 he walked and rode from Andijan in Central Asia to Kowloon, publishing in 1911 a *Summary of Geographical Observations*. His maps were subsequently incorporated in the Survey of India's map of 'Tibet and adjacent countries', and he received the Cuthbert Peek award of the Royal Geographical Society in 1912.

In 1913 Clementi was appointed colonial secretary of British Guiana where he administered the government in 1916–17, 1919, and 1921. He travelled extensively in the practically unknown hinterland establishing a trail to bring cattle from the Brazilian border to the coast. He mapped from a prismatic compass traverse a route which he and his wife discovered from the Kaieteur Falls on the Potaro river to the summit of Mount Roraima where the colony's unsurveyed frontier touches Brazil and Venezuela (*Geographical Journal*, vol. xlviii, 1916; an account of the journey was published by his wife in 1920). He was greatly concerned with problems of health, drainage, immigration, and development, and his 'Report on the conditions of the Colony and the chief problems awaiting solution' (1919) remains a notable document. He published a short book on *The Chinese in British Guiana* (1915) and, after retirement, a *Constitutional History of British Guiana* (1937).

In 1922 Clementi became colonial secretary in Ceylon where he administered the government in 1922–3 and 1925. In that year he became governor of Hong Kong where he found life paralysed by general strikes, caused by intimidation from Canton, where a Russian mission had engineered a boycott of its trade. His primary task was to restore confidence in Hong Kong itself, to restore friendly relations with Canton, and to check the piracy and violence which had brought trade to a standstill and caused a series

of frontier incidents. The geographical situation of Hong Kong caused a governor so far-sighted as Clementi to be pre-occupied with British relations not only with China but also with the Japanese whose good will he saw to be essential to peace in the Far East. The university of Hong Kong, of which he was chancellor and from which he received the honorary degree of LL.D. in 1926, was close to his heart. He strove to assure adequate funds for its maintenance and development and established a school of Chinese classical literature and philosophy.

In 1930 Clementi became governor of the Straits Settlements and high commissioner for the Malay States. Here his policy was to achieve federation of all nine Malay states. To prepare for self-government and fulfil the promises of many years to the Malay Rulers, he enlarged the responsibilities of the councils of the four Federated Malay States, at the same time offering opportunities to the other states to make use of federal departments, such as public works, civil aviation, health, and education, believing that with a customs and postal union a true federation would come into being. He sought to bring home to the Malays the necessity of taking a more active part in the life of their country. The raising of the first battalion of the Malay Regiment was inspired by him. His knowledge of Chinese affairs enabled Clementi to understand and check the secret schemes of the Kuomintang by which the nationalist Government of China was obtaining control of the Chinese population of Malaya and also the Moscow-inspired plan for 'colonial revolution' throughout South-East Asia. His support and encouragement of the police enabled subversive activities to be controlled and ensured the peace of Malaya at least for the decade.

In 1934 Clementi retired on account of ill health. He had been appointed C.M.G. in 1916 and promoted K.C.M.G. (1926), and G.C.M.G. (1931). He was a knight of grace of the Order of St. John of Jerusalem; and he served on the court of the Mercers' Company from 1935 to 1941, was master 1940–41, and on the court of assistants until 1945.

In 1912 he married Marie Penelope Rose, daughter of Captain (later Admiral) Cresswell John Eyres, by whom he had one son and three daughters. He died 5 April 1947 at his home, Holmer Court, High Wycombe. The university of Hong

Kong possesses a portrait of Clementi by A. Schuster.

[Official records and reports; private information; personal knowledge.]

R. O. WINSTEDT.

CLIFFORD, SIR HUGH CHARLES (1866–1941), colonial administrator, was born in London 5 March 1866, the eldest son of Colonel (later Major-General Sir) Henry Hugh Clifford [q.v.] and grandson of the seventh Baron Clifford of Chudleigh [q.v.]. His mother was Josephine Elizabeth, only child of Joseph Anstice [q.v.], of Madeley Wood, Shropshire, a professor of classics at King's College, London. He was educated at Woburn Park under Mgr. William Joseph (later the thirteenth Baron) Petre, and, although he passed for Sandhurst, in 1883 he joined the Civil Service of the Malay States during the governorship of his father's cousin, Sir F. A. Weld [q.v.]. From 1887 he served in Pahang, inducing the Sultan to accept first a British agent and then in 1888 a British resident, displaying courage and tact in suppressing a rising by a rebel chief (1892–4). He was British resident, Pahang, from 1896 to 1899 and was then nominated governor of North Borneo and Labuan under the Chartered Company, but in 1901 he resigned and returned to his post at Pahang. In 1903 he was appointed colonial secretary for Trinidad and Tobago and in 1907 for Ceylon, a post which he held until 1912. In that year he was transferred to the Gold Coast as governor, in 1919 to Nigeria, afterwards again to Ceylon (1925), and to the Straits Settlements in 1927 with the office of high commissioner for the Malay States and British agent in Borneo. He resigned owing to his wife's illness in 1929.

Clifford's charming, forceful, but never dictatorial personality won him the respect and confidence of all races, even when the onset of cyclical insanity led to eccentricities of behaviour. Neither by education nor by temperament was he tempted to political innovations. His administration and literary hobbies owed much to the example of his senior, Sir Frank Swettenham [q.v.]. Much light is thrown on his life and career in Malaya by *In Court and Kampong* (1897) and many other books. A review of *Studies in Brown Humanity* (1898) by his friend Joseph Conrad [q.v.] in his *Notes on Life and Letters* criticized them for being only the truth, whereas 'art veils part of the truth of life'. Besides his tales he was the author of a translation into Malay of the penal code and with Swettenham the joint author of part of a dictionary of the Malay language. For his public services he was appointed C.M.G. in 1900 and promoted to K.C.M.G. in 1909 and G.C.M.G. in 1921. In 1925 he was appointed G.B.E.

Clifford was twice married: first, in 1896 to Minna (died 1907), daughter of Gilbert à Beckett by whom he had one son (killed in action in 1916) and two daughters; and secondly, in 1910 to Elizabeth Lydia Rosabelle (died 1945), daughter of Edward Bonham, of Bramling, Kent, and widow of Henry Philip Ducarel de la Pasture. As Mrs. Henry de la Pasture she was well known as a novelist and she had among her forebears a former governor of the Straits Settlements, Sir S. G. Bonham [q.v.]. Clifford died at Roehampton 18 December 1941.

[Sir R. O. Winstedt, *A History of Malaya*, 1935 (vol. xiii, part 1 of the *Journal* of the Royal Asiatic Society, Malayan Branch); W. Linehan, *A History of Pahang*, 1936 (ibid., vol. xiv, part 2); Clifford's own works; private information; personal knowledge.]

R. O. WINSTEDT.

CLIVE, SIR ROBERT HENRY (1877–1948), diplomatist, was born in London 27 December 1877, the third son of Charles Meysey Bolton Clive, J.P., of Whitfield, Herefordshire, and a first cousin four times removed of Clive of India. His mother was Lady Katherine Elizabeth Mary Julia Feilding, daughter of the seventh Earl of Denbigh.

Educated at Haileybury and Magdalen College, Oxford, where he graduated B.A. in 1899, Clive entered the diplomatic service in 1902 and spent the early years of his career at Rome, Tokyo, Cairo, and Berne. In 1913 he was appointed to Stockholm, becoming a first secretary in 1915 and acting on several occasions as chargé d'affaires. In 1919 he was transferred to the Foreign Office, appointed C.M.G., and in the following year became counsellor in Peking.

In 1923, as consul-general at Munich, Clive was sent to inquire into the separatist movement which had succeeded in establishing itself in the Bavarian palatinate, then under French occupation. His tact and perspicacity in discharging this mission were an important contributory factor in the eventual restoration of order. It was a tribute to his skill that the French authorities raised no objection when, in the following year, he was appointed consul-general at Tangier. As the first British representative on the committee of control, he helped substantially to launch the new international régime set up by the convention of 1923 and to harmonize the interests of the signatory powers.

Clive's five years as minister in Teheran (1926–31) covered a period of increasing Persian nationalism and xenophobia and his efforts to conclude a commercial and a general treaty were frustrated. His patience and the objectivity of his judgement were nevertheless of great value during this difficult, although not uncharacteristic, period in Anglo-Persian relations. He was promoted K.C.M.G. in 1927. After a short time as minister to the Holy See, Clive was appointed ambassador in Tokyo in 1934 and was sworn of the Privy Council. Japan was no longer the country he had known in the hey-day of the Anglo-Japanese alliance. The termination of the alliance in 1922, naval rivalry, Japan's conquest of Manchuria and her withdrawal from the League of Nations had estranged the two countries, while Japanese military ambitions were beginning to threaten British interests in China and the Far East generally. Clive's task was in the circumstances a difficult one, but he set himself to it with his usual determination. He was successful in reducing tension, but he had few illusions about the dangerous potentialities of the situation and his reports to his Government were models of clarity and good sense. He was advanced to G.C.M.G. in 1936. It was not until after Clive's departure that Japan took the irrevocable step of war with China.

When he arrived in Brussels as ambassador in the summer of 1937, Great Britain had lately renewed her guarantee to Belgium. That little progress was made towards the more specific understandings desired by his Government was not for want of pertinacity on Clive's part for he again displayed those diplomatic gifts which were pre-eminently his: patience and clear-headedness. But he was unable to prevail against the Belgian King's 'policy of independence' and reliance on German undertakings to respect Belgium's neutrality. He retired at the end of 1939.

Clive was characteristic of the best in the diplomatic service, reliable, modest, sensitive but dispassionate. An utterly devoted public servant he was undeterred by the succession of difficult and frustrating posts to which he was assigned. He had many outside interests, had a gift for both drawing and poetry and was a connoisseur of furniture, oriental porcelain, and rugs, of which he was a keen collector. In appearance he almost outdid literary tradition with his blue eyes, white hair, invariably faultless attire, and his air of distinction. But he lacked entirely the vanity which often mars these attributes. His abounding interest in his fellow human beings made him a stimulating companion and inspired affection in all those who served with him.

Clive was particularly happy in his family life. In 1905 he married Magdalen, daughter of Sir Kenneth Augustus (later Lord) Muir-Mackenzie, permanent principal secretary to the lord chancellor and clerk of the Crown in Chancery. Her support throughout Clive's career was a constant source of strength to him. She survived him when he died at his home near Forest Row, Sussex, 13 May 1948. They had two sons and one daughter.

[*The Times*, 14 May 1948; private information; personal knowledge.]

ASHLEY CLARKE.

CLYDE, JAMES AVON, LORD CLYDE (1863–1944), lord justice-general of Scotland, was born at Dollar 14 November 1863, the second son of James Clyde, LL.D., by his wife, Elizabeth Rigg, of Whitehaven, Cumberland. His father was a distinguished teacher of the classics, first at Dollar Academy and later for many years at the Edinburgh Academy. Young Clyde himself entered the latter school and after being dux of all his classes and of the school proceeded to the university of Edinburgh, where his career was equally brilliant. He graduated with first class honours in classics in 1884, winning the Gray scholarship in that year, and became LL.B. in 1888. During his university days he was a prime mover in the establishment of a students' representative council and a students' union; he learned to debate at the Speculative Society, training-ground of many famous lawyers, and was successively librarian and president of that body, becoming an honorary member in 1921. In 1910 he was made honorary LL.D. of Edinburgh, and in 1923 received the same distinction at St. Andrews.

Clyde passed advocate in 1887. He had no influence, but his contemporaries at the 'Spec' and elsewhere were convinced that he would go straight to the top. And this, after one or two lean years, he proceeded to do. In addition to great natural ability he was a tireless worker, and once he had secured a hearing the easy maturity of his style made such a strong impression that work flowed in. Well armed at every point as an advocate, he had established the heaviest junior practice at the bar by 1901, when he became a K.C. Thereafter he carried all before him, and the House of Lords reports attest the almost universal sweep of his activities as counsel. He became solicitor-general in 1905 during the closing months of the Unionist Government, and later returned to office as lord advocate from 1916 (when he was sworn of the Privy Council) to 1920. He had become dean of the Faculty of Advocates in 1915, and on his appointment as lord advocate his brethren paid him the unique distinction of asking him to continue in office as dean in spite of his new duties. He resigned the deanship in 1919; he was elected honorary bencher of Gray's Inn in the same year. Of all the many celebrated cases in which Clyde appeared perhaps the most noteworthy was that heard in 1918 by the Judicial Committee of the Privy Council regarding the ownership of the unalieneted lands of Southern Rhodesia. Clyde led for the British South Africa Company, and in a galaxy of counsel which included many of the leaders of the English bar, among them Sir F. E. Smith (later the Earl of Birkenhead, q.v.), there was general agreement that Clyde's performance was easily the finest.

A lifelong Unionist in politics, Clyde became member for West (subsequently North) Edinburgh in 1909, and retained his seat until his elevation to the bench in 1920. With one noteworthy exception, his contributions to the work of the House of Commons were almost wholly those of an efficient law officer. The exception occurred in August 1919, when he replied to strictures on the lord advocate and his department for failing to prosecute in a case of fraud at Renfrew aerodrome. A member present wrote that 'Clyde's answer did not contain a violent or a bitter word; but throughout it there ran an undercurrent of mockery, which was gentle and playful—and deadly'. Hopes that he would thereafter take a more prominent part in the business of the House were ended in 1920 by his appointment, with the judicial title of Lord Clyde, as lord justice-general of Scotland

and lord president of the Court of Session in succession to Lord Strathclyde [q.v.].

Clyde's fifteen years as head of the court in Scotland constitute the most important chapter in the story of his life. A sound lawyer, he was never afraid to enunciate general principles, and his judgements, ranging over every department of Scots law, increasingly provide material to writers, advocates, and judges in their work. The burden of the court fell heavily on Clyde's shoulders during his period of office, since with some noteworthy exceptions his immediate colleagues were not distinguished for ability or teamwork. His extempore judgements were always impressive, assisted as they were by his fine presence, good voice, and easy flow of English. They were as finished and well expressed as the written judgements of others. In his reserved judgements there was a tendency to over-elaboration, but all were written out first in his own hand, and were therefore free from the verbosity born of dictation. He once deprecated 'unreceptive judicial silence', and certainly did not indulge in it himself. But his interventions made for a high standard of pleading, and he had a stimulating influence on all who appeared before him. He loved battle, and like a good fighter he was always prepared to take as good as he gave. Throughout his career, and into old age, he was always the dominant figure in any gathering. His appearance, his manner, even his walk, suggested, as was the fact, that he was endowed with an immense store of vitality and power.

No account of Clyde's presidency would be complete without reference to two heavy outside tasks undertaken by him during its currency. In 1926 he became chairman of the Royal Commission appointed to report on the Court of Session and the office of sheriff principal. The labour involved was immense, and the report, an exhaustive one, advised drastic reforms in procedure, which were partly carried out by statute in 1933. Clyde deplored the transfer of the advocates' library to the nation in 1925, but as an *ex officio* member of the new board of trustees he played an indefatigable part in seeing the new institution through its teething troubles. From 1936 he was chairman of the board and its main driving force.

Always a lover of the country, Clyde retired in 1935 to his home at Briglands, Kinross-shire, literally 'to cultivate his garden', for he was a great rose-grower. He became lord lieutenant of Kinross-shire and when the war came took an active part in organizing the war savings of the county, with results remarkable for an agricultural community. When still lord president, he had found time to publish, in two volumes, his own translation of Craig's *Jus Feudale* (1934). He followed this up in his retirement by the publication, in two volumes (1937–8) for the Stair Society, of Hope's *Major Practicks 1608–1633*. Finally, again for the Stair Society, he published (1943) an edition of the *Acta Dominorum Concilii 1501–1503*. It may be regretted that to these works of scholarship he did not add his personal reminiscences, for he had, in informal talk, a great gift of vivid and racy characterization.

In 1895 Clyde married Anna Margaret McDiarmid (died 1956), daughter of Peter Wallwork Latham, Downing professor of medicine at Cambridge; they had two sons, of whom the elder, James Latham McDiarmid Clyde, became lord justice-general of Scotland and lord president of the Court of Session in 1954. Clyde died in Edinburgh after a short illness 16 June 1944. A water-colour portrait by R. S. Forrest hangs in the entrance to the National Library of Scotland.

[*The Times* and *Scotsman*, 17 June 1944; personal knowledge.]          T. B. SIMPSON.

CLYNES, JOHN ROBERT (1869–1949), Labour leader, was born at Oldham 27 March 1869, the elder son of Patrick Clynes, an Irish farmworker who, evicted in 1851, emigrated to Lancashire. Unable to read or write, he worked as a corporation gravedigger for 24s. a week, upon which he and his wife Bridget Scanlan reared two sons and five daughters. John attended elementary school which he detested, and at the age of ten began work as a 'little piecer' in a textile mill, working from six in the morning until noon for half-a-crown a week and continuing at school in the afternoon. At twelve he became a 'full timer' at 10s. a week and from his early wages bought a tattered dictionary for 6d. and Cobbett's *Grammar* for 8d. He received 3d. a week for reading regularly to three blind men, whose political discussions aroused his interest in what he read to them from the local press. He paid 8d. for tuition on two nights a week from an ex-schoolmaster. By 1883 he was a 'big piecer' earning

17s. 6d. a week and gathering ideas from Carlyle, Ruskin, Mill, Emerson, and Renan. Attracted to debate, Clynes practised oratory with a workmate in a disused quarry outside the town. Learning the meaning and value of words, he contributed to the local press under the pen-name 'Piecer', describing the conditions of child life in the mill, and writing on trade-unionism, Socialism, and labour representation. He successfully rebelled against having to clean and oil machinery without pay, and organized a Piecers' Union, for piecers had no direct representation in the Spinners' Union. In 1891, at the invitation of Will Thorne [q.v.], he left the mill to serve as a district organizer at 30s. a week for one of the first organizations for unskilled workers, the National Union of Gasworkers and General Labourers, which Thorne had inaugurated in 1889. He described Clynes at this time as 'a mere slip of a lad, hardly more than a boy', and throughout his life Clynes carried the effect of his early factory hardships. Yet for all the unobtrusiveness of his seemingly insignificant personality, he gained the confidence of organized Labour by the very moderation with which he steadfastly promoted its cause. It was said of him in 1901 that he was a man of peace who thought that what was mostly wanted was a sense of humour. His was a 'sweet reasonableness' which was often to prevail when the more aggressive tactics of some of his colleagues had failed.

He was president of the Oldham trades council in 1892 and its secretary from 1894 to 1912. In Lancashire towns, as elsewhere in the 'nineties, William Morris, H. M. Hyndman, J. Keir Hardie [qq.v.], and many lesser lights preached the Socialist gospel and Clynes became a devotee. He attended the foundation conference of the Independent Labour Party at Bradford in 1893, and in the same year was a delegate to the international Socialist congress at Zürich. The *Clarion* had an important share in evoking his interest in life and literature, for Clynes was the typical 'John Smith of Oldham' to whom Robert Blatchford [q.v.] addressed himself in *Merrie England*. A twenty weeks' lock-out in the cotton trade about the same time emphasized in his mind the need for working-class organization. Representing his union at the Belfast Trades Union Congress in 1893, he supported nationalization as a principle. He was appointed secretary for the

Lancashire district of his union in 1896. His union was foremost in the advanced political movement and Clynes represented it at the Plymouth Trades Union Congress in 1899 when it was decided to form the Labour Representation Committee, known from 1906 as the Labour Party. At the inaugural conference in London in February 1900, he again attended for his union, and in 1904 was elected to represent the affiliated trades councils upon the national executive; from 1909 to 1939 he was consistently elected to the trades union section. He was chairman of the party organization in 1908, presiding over the Portsmouth conference in 1909.

Clynes's parliamentary career began in 1906 when he was returned for the North-Eastern (later Platting) division of Manchester as a member of the first parliamentary Labour Party, and he lived to be its last survivor. With the exception of 1931 he was re-elected at all subsequent elections until his retirement in 1945. Among various journeys abroad he attended the 1909 Toronto convention of the American Federation of Labor as fraternal delegate from the British Trades Union Congress.

In 1915 Clynes opposed the entry of Labour into the Asquith coalition in which three of his colleagues had appointments; but after the formation of the Lloyd George coalition he served on the Food Commission in 1917 and in the same year joined Lord Rhondda [q.v.], minister of food, as parliamentary secretary. A system of rationing was gradually introduced and a consumers' council set up, of which Clynes was chairman. He was sworn of the Privy Council in 1918 and succeeded Rhondda as minister when the latter died in that year. When the war ended Clynes opposed the withdrawal of the Labour Party from the Government, sharing the view of his colleague, G. N. Barnes [q.v.], that Labour should assist in the formulation of the peace treaties; but when the party decided against that policy, Clynes, unlike Barnes, conformed, and resigned his office. Returned unopposed at the general election in 1918, Clynes was elected vice-chairman of the parliamentary party, becoming chairman in 1921 after the resignation of William Adamson, and leading the party in the general election of 1922. In the election for chairman of the parliamentary party which followed he was defeated by Ramsay MacDonald by five votes, and accepted

the vice-chairmanship. In January 1924 he moved the successful vote of no confidence which brought about the defeat of the Baldwin Government and led to MacDonald's first Labour administration in which Clynes himself was lord privy seal and deputy leader of the House of Commons.

Opposed to the principle of a general strike, Clynes and his parliamentary friends in 1926 strove to adjust the differences between the Miners' Federation, the mine-owners, and the Government. Nevertheless, when the strike took place he stood by the miners throughout the dispute which cost his union £200,000 in strike pay. In MacDonald's second Government of 1929, Clynes as home secretary gave much attention to prison reform and was also actively interested in the cotton-trade inquiry. It also fell to him to decide to refuse Trotsky permission to settle in England. In 1931 he introduced an electoral reform bill providing for the alternative vote, and also abolishing university representation, a clause which was deleted by four votes in the committee stage in the House of Commons. The bill was drastically amended in the House of Lords and soon afterwards the economic situation brought the Labour Government to an end.

On the formation of Ramsay MacDonald's 'national' Government, Clynes refused the party leadership which went to Arthur Henderson [q.v.]. In the ensuing general election Clynes lost his seat and devoted himself to the work of his union of which he had been president since 1912. The union, which was by then known as the National Union of General and Municipal Workers, had become one of the largest in the country and when Clynes retired from the presidency in 1937 catered for nearly half a million members in a great many industries.

In 1935 Clynes returned to Parliament and was content to be counted an elder statesman of the Labour movement generally, wise in counsel, sincere and loyal in all his relationships. Quiet and unobtrusive, he possessed sound judgement, the result of serious reading and steady thought. He had no tricks of oratory, but in measured and unadorned English he carried conviction throughout his life both in Parliament, on the platform, in council, and in personal converse. None of all the Labour members among his contemporaries commanded higher regard. In 1945 he retired upon reaching the parliamentary age limit set by his union and lived quietly and frugally, upon the pension which it gave him, in his Putney home. In 1947 Clynes wrote to *The Times* and other journals relating his straitened circumstances owing to the insufficiency of his union pension, and a fund was raised by his parliamentary colleagues and friends. Those closest to him felt that his complaints were a reflection of his war-time and other trials and were hardly justified, a view which was somewhat confirmed when his will came to be published. He married in 1893 a cardroom hand, Mary Elizabeth, daughter of the late Owen Harper, watchmaker, of Oldham. She sustained serious air-raid injuries in the war of 1939–45 and was thereafter a confirmed invalid. Clynes died in London, 23 October 1949, leaving his widow who died soon afterwards, and two sons; a daughter had died earlier.

Clynes received the honorary degree of D.C.L. from the universities of Oxford and Durham in 1919. A portrait by Margaretta Hicks is in the possession of the National Union of General and Municipal Workers.

[J. R. Clynes, *Memoirs*, 2 vols., 1937; Anon., *Sixty Years of the National Union of General and Municipal Workers, 1889–1949*, 1949; *The Times* and *Manchester Guardian*, 25 October 1949; personal knowledge.]

J. S. MIDDLETON.

COATES, JOSEPH GORDON (1878–1943), prime minister of New Zealand, was born at Pahi, New Zealand, 3 February 1878, the eldest son of Edward Coates, farmer, and his wife, Eleanor, daughter of Thomas Aickin, surgeon, of Auckland. Educated at Matakohe public school, Coates followed his father as a farmer and served his political apprenticeship in local affairs: in farmers' organizations, in the Territorial Force, and in the Otamatea County Council. In 1911 he entered national politics. As member for Kaipara, he was at first an independent, and was most interested in factors governing economic development: land policy, roads, and the provision of railways. He joined the New Zealand Expeditionary Force in 1916; his service was distinguished, and at the armistice he was a major in command of a company, holding the M.C. with bar. Back in New Zealand he entered the post-war Cabinet of W. F. Massey [q.v.] in September 1919 as minister of justice and postmaster-general, and went on to hold a group of portfolios charged with opportunities, notably those of public works (1920–26), railways (1923–8), and

native affairs (1921–8). Shortly after Massey's death in May 1925 he became prime minister. He was regarded not as a skilled professional politician, but as a man of vigorous personality who got things done: 'the farmer, the soldier, the administrator, the man slow of speech and quick of action'.

Coates's first period of office coincided with post-war reconstruction, disillusionment, and economic slackness. He was in poor propagandist and was roundly defeated by the United Party in 1928. Yet he was a good and far-sighted administrator. He understood the future importance of mechanization in public works, of motor transport, and of cheap power; hence the Main Highways Act (1922) which linked central and local authorities, and a courageous acceleration in hydro-electric development. He knew the Maori people, and won their warm personal affection. When minister for native affairs he characteristically picked a man of vision for his adviser and stood by him. Good feeling between New Zealand's two races owes much to the long, informal alliance between Coates and Sir Apirana Ngata, and the land legislation of 1926 and the Royal Commission of 1927 broke new ground. In 1926 Coates came to England for the Imperial Conference which produced the Balfour statement on Dominion status. He gave an excellent impression of balance and good sense. He was sworn of the Privy Council, received honorary degrees from Cambridge, Edinburgh, and Dublin, and the freedom of London and several other cities.

Coates's defeat in 1928 meant that the first impact of the great depression was handled by the 'United' Government which from 1930 was led by G. W. Forbes [q.v.]; yet there was, as there long had been, little essential difference between the policies of the two main parties. The crisis accordingly brought in September 1931 a coalition Government which at first accepted the need for sharp retrenchment, and at a time of great suffering was blamed bitterly. Coates's personal influence grew, however, and he became known among Conservatives as a dangerous meddler with accepted principles. As minister of public works and in charge of employment (1931–3) and minister of transport (1931–5) and more especially as minister of finance and customs (1933–5), in place of W. Downie Stewart [q.v.] he insisted increasingly on attacking the causes of depression and trying the new if old methods failed. His least controversial action was keen advocacy of self-help within the Empire. His battle to keep the vital British market open to New Zealand on favourable terms was bravely and skilfully fought and he took a leading part in the Ottawa conference of 1932. Within New Zealand he made increasing use of the State's great powers to guide economic development, to an extent which brought structural changes of far-reaching importance. The Agricultural Emergency Powers Act was a near-revolutionary measure, and to the alarm of many he was responsible for the further depreciation of the exchange rate from £N.Z.110 to £N.Z.125 to £100 sterling. He established a powerful Reserve Bank partially under State control, and forced down mortgage indebtedness and interest rates. He was no economist but was bold in choice of expert advisers, supported them loyally and was served with devotion.

The Government's recovery programme, although soundly conceived, was scarcely popular, and the Labour Party won resounding victories in November 1935 and October 1938. With increasing international tension, however, party asperities softened, and on the outbreak of war Coates, while retaining the right of criticism, went far towards shelving domestic controversy in face of external crisis. He was a vigorous advocate of his own country's economic interest and of her right to form an independent judgement on foreign affairs. Yet he was always conscious and proud of New Zealand's close dependence on Britain and saw that in the last resort British leadership must prevail.

The Labour Party rejected the idea of war-time coalition. Although Coates's personality and experience commanded respect it was not until after the military crisis of mid-1940 that he entered a two-party War Cabinet under the premiership of Peter Fraser [q.v.] in which he served until his sudden death in Wellington 27 May 1943. In this last phase he worked fruitfully with erstwhile political opponents in war-time administration and policy-making at the cost of a breach with his party affiliations. By some he could never be trusted after his depression-time unorthodoxies, and some thought he went too far in subordinating party to national interest in wartime. In November 1940 a strong party man became leader of the Opposition. Just before Coates's death it was announced that at the next election

he would stand as an independent, as he had when first he entered Parliament.

Coates was a big man, physically and by temperament. He was honest, careless of criticism, jaunty of manner—one whom the Maoris recognized with affection as a warrior and on whom political opponents concentrated their fire without personal animosity. He was disconcertingly direct and energetic, young in spirit and with an eye for new ideas. As a young native-born prime minister in 1925 he was perhaps over-confident and certainly too much was expected of him. He learnt wisdom in defeat but he was, on the whole, an unsuccessful politician. He was perhaps too busy, too preoccupied with his objectives, to pay much attention to political machinery. Yet his influence powerfully aided New Zealand's adjustment to the economic and political tensions of twenty-four uneasy years.

In 1914 Coates married Marjorie Grace, daughter of Walter Coles, a doctor. They had five daughters.

[*New Zealand Parliamentary Debates*; *Round Table, passim*; W. B. Sutch, *Recent Economic Changes in New Zealand*, 1936; H. Belshaw, *Recovery Measures in New Zealand*, 1936; New Zealand Institute of International Affairs, *Contemporary New Zealand*, 1938; private information.]                    F. L. W. WOOD.

COCKERELL, DOUGLAS BENNETT (1870–1945), bookbinder, the third of four sons of Sydney John Cockerell, coal merchant, of London, by his wife, Alice Elizabeth, elder daughter of (Sir) John Bennett [q.v.], was born at Clifton Cottage, Sydenham Hill, 5 August 1870. He was seven when his father died. At fifteen he had left St. Paul's School to go to Canada with £5 in his pocket. During three years as a farm-hand, and a short period as a wool-carder he came in contact with Indian woodwork and watermanship. A junior clerkship in a Toronto bank followed and three years later charge of a branch in the Far West with a loaded revolver to hand. He liked the cowboys, and earning his living educated him where orthodox schooling had made little impression. But he did not return to Canada after coming home on leave.

After two years of uncertainty as a handyman he made two trial bindings for William Morris [q.v.] to whom his brother (Sir) Sydney Cockerell was already private secretary, and by 1893 he was binding in earnest under T. J. Cobden-Sanderson [q.v.] at the Doves Bindery in Hammersmith.

In 1896 W. R. Lethaby [q.v.] appointed him to teach bookbinding at the newly created London County Council Central School of Arts and Crafts where he continued, except for the break of the war years, until 1935; thereafter he lectured at the Royal College of Art almost until his death.

By 1898 he had his own workshop near the British Museum, moving to Ewell in 1902. In 1905 he merged with W. H. Smith & Son's bindery of which he was controller until the war of 1914–18 during which he worked in the Ministry of Munitions, although advice to Smiths continued. Later he advised the Imperial War Graves Commission on printing and it was not until 1924 that he started a bindery of his own again, in partnership with his son Sydney, at Letchworth.

His *Bookbinding and the Care of Books* was published in 1901; the first of the series on the crafts edited by W. R. Lethaby. It set a new standard of painstaking honesty in craftsmanship and of a freshness in well-designed decoration. Translated in many countries it has remained a standard textbook for students of binding for fifty years. This book, his activity in the (Royal) Society of Arts' investigation of decay in leather for bookbinding, and his successful binding of many important and valuable volumes put him in undisputed lead of the binders of his day; a fact reflected later in the flourishing Letchworth bindery. And it was to him that the trustees of the British Museum turned for the binding of the *Codex Sinaiticus*.

There can be few English binders who are not indebted to the teaching of Douglas Cockerell; even trade binderies, although antagonistic to an implied criticism, responded to his lead. Circumstances and his own native ability brought it about that he had probably more influence on bookbinding practice and design than any one man has had before. It is significant that he thought of a book as a whole in its functional capacity; decoration did not take priority over structure.

A keen gardener who gave flowers away with a lavish hand, much of his book decoration was based on growing forms. Few bookbinders can have had such happy, if unusual, conditions in which to bind as those who were privileged to work and learn with him looking out on his Letchworth garden. He was appointed M.B.E. in 1920 in recognition of his war work and was one of the twelve original recipients of the Royal Society of Arts' R.D.I. in 1937.

He married twice: first, in 1898 Florence Margaret Drew (died 1912), daughter of Samuel Drew Arundel, box-maker, of London, by whom he had two sons and one daughter; and secondly, in 1914 Bessie Marion, daughter of William Gilford, dealer in real estate at Redhill. He died at Letchworth 25 November 1945.

A portrait drawing by William Strang (1902), a bust by Onslow Whiting (1928), and a portrait etching by Malcolm Osborne are in the possession of his family.

[*The Times*, 26 November 1945, amplified in the *Journal* of the Royal Society of Arts, 21 December 1945; private information; personal knowledge.]     ROGER POWELL.

COCKS, ARTHUR HERBERT TENNYSON SOMERS-, sixth BARON SOMERS (1887–1944), chief scout for Great Britain and the British Commonwealth and Empire, and governor of Victoria. [See SOMERS-COCKS.]

COKER, ERNEST GEORGE (1869–1946), engineer, was born at Wolverton, Buckinghamshire, 26 April 1869, the son of George Coker, an engine-fitter, and his wife, Sarah Tompkins. Educated at a private school, from 1883 until 1887 he was an apprentice and then draughtsman in the London and North Western Railway carriage works at Wolverton. Evening study enabled him to enter the Normal School (later the Royal College) of Science, London, where he gained a first class associateship in mechanics. A Whitworth scholarship in 1890 took him to Edinburgh University where he graduated B.Sc. in engineering in 1892. The following year he entered Peterhouse, Cambridge, where he graduated B.A. in 1896 with a first class in part i of the mechanical sciences tripos. In 1897 he took part ii with a double distinction in the first class.

During college vacations he spent periods in the railway works at Wolverton and at Crewe where in the testing house he carried out experiments which probably aroused his interest in the stress and strain in materials in which he was later to specialize. In 1892 he became an assistant examiner in the Patent Office and retained this post whilst he was at Cambridge, but in 1898 he resigned to enter upon his career as an engineering educationist. Although only twenty-nine years old he became assistant professor in civil engineering at McGill University. Later he became an associate professor, and during the whole of the period worked as principal assistant to Henry Taylor Bovey, both at the university and in his private practice, testing materials of various kinds and doing experimental work on Canadian water-power schemes.

In 1905 Coker returned to England to become professor of mechanical engineering and head of the department of civil engineering at the City and Guilds of London Technical College, Finsbury, where he built a new engineering laboratory described in his paper before the British Association in 1907. Here he began the experiments, for which his name became known, on the use of photo-elastic methods for the determination of stress distribution in metals, machines, and structures, devising apparatus and models for this work, and communicating results to the engineering profession through the medium of papers read before the Institution of Mechanical Engineers and other technical and scientific bodies. Public demonstrations of his photo-elastic methods were given as early as 1910. All this work continued, including consulting engineering, when in 1914 he became professor of civil and mechanical engineering at University College, London. He later became dean of the faculty of engineering and director of the engineering laboratories, and retired in 1934 as professor emeritus.

Coker's chief work, *A Treatise on Photo-Elasticity*, was written jointly with L. N. G. Filon [q.v.] and published in 1931. He delivered the thirteenth Thomas Hawksley lecture to the Institution of Mechanical Engineers in 1926 on 'Elasticity and Plasticity', and a lecture given to the Junior Institution of Engineers in 1935 on 'The Design and Equipment of Photo-Elastic Laboratories' summed up much of his life's work: which had an international reputation in its rather limited field. He was elected F.R.S. in 1915, was also F.R.S.E., and a member of the leading engineering societies from which he received many medals, including the Thomas Hawksley medal (1922) from the Institution of Mechanical Engineers, the Telford medal (1921) from the Institution of Civil Engineers, and the gold medal of the Institution of Naval Architects (1911). The Royal Society awarded him the Rumford medal in 1936, and from the Franklin Institute, Philadelphia, he received the Howard N. Potts (1922) and Louis E. Levy (1926) medals. He was also an honorary

D.Sc. of the universities of Sydney and Louvain.

In person Coker was rather modest and retiring, and he was happiest when in his laboratory. He married in 1899 Alice Mary (died 1941), daughter of Robert King, an engineer, of Wolverton. He died at Ayr 9 April 1946.

[*Engineer* and *Engineering*, 19 April 1946; *Proceedings* of the Institution of Mechanical Engineers, vol. clvi, 1947; personal knowledge.]

ALFRED R. STOCK.

COLLES, HENRY COPE (1879–1943), musical historian and critic, was born at Bridgnorth, Shropshire, 20 April 1879, the third child and elder son of Abraham Colles, M.D., F.R.C.S. (and great-grandson of Abraham Colles, q.v.), by his wife, Emily Agnes Georgiana, daughter of Major Alexander R. Dallas, and granddaughter of A. R. C. Dallas [q.v.]. He was educated privately and at the Royal College of Music (1895–9), where his interest in musical history was early aroused by Sir Hubert Parry whose notice he contributed to this DICTIONARY. In 1899 he became organ scholar at Worcester College, Oxford, where he attracted the attention of (Sir) Henry Hadow [q.v.], then dean of the college, whose lectures doubtless helped in shaping Colles's future career.

At Oxford he obtained the degree of B.A. in 1903 and the additional degree of B.Mus. in 1904, and in 1932 the university conferred upon him the honorary degree of D.Mus.; he was elected honorary fellow of Worcester in 1936. After leaving Oxford he studied at the Temple Church (1903–5) with (Sir) Walford Davies [q.v.], a lifelong friend whose biography he wrote in 1942.

In 1905, at the instigation of Hadow, Colles began his career as a writer, contributing a weekly article on music to the *Academy* at the request of H. H. Child [q.v.]. He also began work at *The Times* in 1905 and became an assistant to J. A. Fuller-Maitland [q.v.], whom he succeeded as musical editor in 1911, and he retained this post until his death. On his appointment as editor he at once inaugurated and maintained the weekly articles on musical affairs, for the most part written by himself, which attracted wide attention both in England and abroad and by their scholarship and research soon acquired considerable importance.

During the war of 1914–18 Colles served in Macedonia as a captain in the Royal

Artillery, receiving the Greek Cross in 1918. On his return he was invited, in 1919, by (Sir) Hugh Allen [q.v.] to join the staff of the Royal College of Music as lecturer in musical history, analysis, and appreciation. In 1923 he accepted an invitation from the *New York Times* to act as 'guest music critic', remaining in America for some months. In 1927 he was Cramb lecturer at Glasgow University, taking for his subject the interdependence of the English language and the English musical genius—especially as exemplified in Purcell. The substance of these lectures was reproduced in his *Voice and Verse* (1928). He lectured also at Liverpool University, the Royal Institution, and elsewhere.

In 1927 appeared the third and revised edition of *Grove's Dictionary of Music and Musicians*, the editorship of which had been entrusted to him some years before. It was a task for which his ripe scholarship eminently qualified him. He was also responsible for a further revision and a supplementary volume in 1940.

In private life Colles was a staunch friend and a man of deep loyalties, none perhaps being more marked than that to the English Church. To her he gave steadfast service in many ways. As a writer he constantly stressed the value and importance of her great musical traditions, and the need of their continued maintenance; as a practical musician he gave strong support to the School of English Church Music founded by his friend Sir Sydney Nicholson [q.v.], the Church Music Society, and St. Michael's College, Tenbury Wells. His wide knowledge on musical matters also placed at the service of the British Council.

Colles's attitude to contemporary music may have been regarded as conservative, yet in the main he was not unsympathetic and, at any rate, he had unusual sanity of judgement. His daily criticisms were valuable in being helpful and constructive, yet where condemnation was called for he was fearless.

Colles's published works show ease, clearness, and accuracy. They include *Brahms* (1908); *The Growth of Music* (1912–16), a much-used textbook of musical history; *Oxford History of Music*, volume vii *Symphony and Drama, 1850–1900* (1934), a critical and well-proportioned survey of an interesting period in music; a collection of Colles's shorter writings was edited by his wife, with a short memoir, and published as *Essays and Lectures* in 1945,

In 1906 Colles married Hester Janet (died 1952), daughter of Thomas Matheson, a member of Lloyd's. Colles died in London 4 March 1943. A chalk drawing by Mrs. Campbell Dodgson was in the possession of his widow.

[*The Times*, 6 March 1943; *Times Literary Supplement*, 13 March 1943; *Music Review*, vol. iv, 1943; H. J. Colles, 'H. C. C.—a Memoir' in *Essays and Lectures*, 1945; personal knowledge.]     IVOR ATKINS.

COLLIE, JOHN NORMAN (1859–1942), chemist and mountaineer, was born at Alderley Edge, Cheshire, 10 September 1859, the second son of John Collie, man of business, by his wife, Selina Mary, daughter of Henry Winkworth, a silk merchant, and sister of Catherine and Susanna Winkworth [qq.v.]. Collie was educated at Charterhouse and Clifton College. He studied chemistry under Edmund Albert Letts at University College, Bristol, where he obtained a chemical scholarship, and later under Wislicenus at Würzburg University, obtaining the degree of Ph.D. in 1884. Adopting a career of teaching and research in chemistry, he was assistant to Letts at Queen's College, Belfast, 1880–83; on his return from Germany he became science lecturer at the Ladies' College, Cheltenham, 1885–7; he was assistant to (Sir) William Ramsay [q.v.] at University College, London, 1887–96; professor of chemistry at the College of the Pharmaceutical Society, London, 1896–1902; professor of organic chemistry in the university of London at University College, 1902–28. After his retirement he was elected an honorary fellow and continued scientific work at University College until 1933.

Collie was a skilful experimenter who could construct his own apparatus, including 'vacuum' tubes in which gases could be exposed to electrical discharges. He collaborated with Ramsay in much work on argon and helium, and he made what was really the first neon lamp. Independently of each other, Collie and Hubert Sutton Patterson detected the presence of neon in hydrogen after the passage of the electrical discharge through the latter at low pressure. This apparent 'transmutation' could not be repeated by other skilled investigators, and must have been due to the leakage of minute quantities of air. Collie was responsible for the first photograph taken by means of X-rays of a metal object in the human body. His great scientific work was in the field of organic chemistry. The subjects are so technical that only a brief reference to some of them may here be made: phosphonium compounds and phosphines; dehydracetic acid, its constitution, reactions, salts and derivatives; pyrones and derivatives; salts of dimethylpyrone and the 'quadrivalence' of oxygen; oxonium hydroxide, $H_3O$ (OH), and oxonium compounds; the keten group —$CH_2.CO$—and derivatives of the multiple keten group; derivation in practice and theory of many natural systems from the polyacetic acids, and the construction of a possible general relation between all these systems and the carbohydrates, via the polyketides; space formula for benzene.

Collie was elected F.R.S. in 1896 and received the honorary degrees of LL.D. from the universities of Glasgow and St. Andrews, and D.Sc. from Belfast and Liverpool. Besides his eminence as a scientist, he acquired great fame as a climber and explorer of mountains. Beginning with the Coolin peaks in Skye, where he discovered many new climbs, he climbed with notable success in the Alps, and went in 1895 with A. F. Mummery [q.v.] to the Himalaya, where they attempted the ascent of Nanga Parbat. Collie also climbed in the Lofoten Islands, but his greatest work was done in his pioneering climbing, mapping, and surveying in the Canadian Rockies. His books, *Climbing on the Himalaya and other Mountain Ranges* (1902), and (with Hugh E. M. Stutfield) *Climbs and Exploration in the Canadian Rockies* (1903) are famous records. But Collie did not disdain our own hills. He climbed some eighty separate peaks of over 3,000 feet and did many rock climbs on Snowdon and in the Lake District. He was elected president of the Alpine Club in 1920 and was an honorary member of many other climbing clubs.

Collie was also a connoisseur of many fine things and a great collector. In his earlier years he collected minerals, and later books and pictures. His great collection, however, consisted of antique objects of Japanese and Chinese art—Japanese lacquer and metal work, and Chinese porcelain, bronzes, and jade. He made an investigation of certain coloured glazes on Chinese porcelain, published in the *Transactions* of the Oriental Ceramic Society, 1921–2.

Whether at Glen Brittle House or the Sligachan Inn, Skye became Collie's beloved summer home. There he could fish and shoot, as well as climb. There he died, unmarried, at Sligachan 1 November 1942.

To those who knew him he was a great host and a faithful friend. A portrait in oils by A. T. Nowell was exhibited at the Academy in 1927 and is in the possession of Collie's niece, Mrs. Holmes, Featherston, Wellington, New Zealand.

[E. C. C. Baly in *Obituary Notices of Fellows of the Royal Society*, No. 12, November 1943; *Alpine Journal*, May 1943; private information; personal knowledge.]    F. G. Donnan.

COLLINGWOOD, ROBIN GEORGE (1889–1943), philosopher and historian, was born at Cartmel Fell, Lancashire, 22 February 1889, the only son of William Gershom Collingwood by his wife, Edith Mary, daughter of Thomas Isaac, corn merchant, of Notting Hill. His mother was an accomplished pianist; his father was a painter and archaeologist who was Ruskin's secretary and biographer and became professor of fine art at University College, Reading. His parents were poor and indifferent to money; even food was not always plentiful: and at first their son was perforce educated at home. He early learnt the frugality which often showed itself in later life as when in travelling he seemed to prefer conditions of maximum discomfort or when he wrote books and lectures on the back of scholarship examination papers. He became deft-fingered, adept at making paper boats or cardboard boxes, and this manual dexterity was in evidence throughout his maturity in, for example, his firm and regular handwriting, his carpentry, and his bookbinding. From his parents he absorbed the love of art which never left him, and he learnt to play the violin and the piano, as well as to draw and paint. But he also received from his father more formal instruction, especially in Greek and Latin, and it is to his father that he refers in the dedication of *Speculum Mentis* (1924) as his 'first and best teacher'.

A friend's generosity enabled his father to send him at thirteen to a preparatory school and a year later to Rugby. More studious, more widely read, more intellectually alert than most boys of his age, he was perhaps out of place in a public school, and his unhappiness there is reflected in his remarks on education in *The New Leviathan* (1942). When he went up to University College, Oxford, with a classical scholarship in 1908, he breathed more congenial air. Here he could drink his fill of learning without shame or constraint; perhaps he drank too deep, for he may have sown the seeds of his later ill health, and it was certainly then that he first made the acquaintance of his life-long enemy, insomnia. When he came to read *literae humaniores*, after obtaining a first class in classical moderations in 1910, he was unwilling to specialize in either the philosophical or the historical side of the school; he mastered both, but then, as always, he gave to philosophy a certain primacy, and it was to a philosophical fellowship that he was elected at Pembroke College in 1912 shortly before his first class in *literae humaniores* was announced.

In the war of 1914–18 Collingwood worked in the intelligence department of the Admiralty. In the autumn of 1918 he vacated his fellowship for a few months on his marriage to Ethel Winifred, third daughter of Robert Chelles Graham, land-owner, of Skipness; they had a son and a daughter. From 1921 to 1928 he under-took the philosophical teaching for Lincoln College in addition to his work at Pem-broke, and from 1927 to 1935 he was university lecturer in philosophy and Roman history. In 1935 he left Pembroke for Magdalen on his appointment as Waynflete professor of metaphysical philo-sophy.

During his years at Pembroke Colling-wood had acquired international repute as an authority on Roman Britain in virtue of his numerous publications in that field, and his first care was to wind up his his-torical work by fulfilling his promise to write the first volume of the *Oxford History of England* (*Roman Britain and the English Settlements*, 1936, with Mr. J. N. L. Myres), and by placing in other hands for publication in the corpus of Roman inscriptions the drawings which he had made of all the important Roman inscrip-tions in Britain. This left him free to de-vote all his energies to preparing for the press a series of volumes on philosophy; but these energies were already seriously impaired. In 1932 he had been granted a term's leave of absence for ill health, but it was not then realized that he had begun to suffer from a process which led in 1938 to the first of a series of strokes which eventually reduced him to helplessness. In 1941 he resigned his chair and even-tually retired to Coniston, where he died from pneumonia 9 January 1943. In 1942 his marriage was dissolved on his wife's petition, and in the same year he married Kathleen Frances, daughter of Francis Edgcumbe Edwardes, mathematical master at Fettes and later at Harrow. A daughter was born of his second marriage. He was

elected F.B.A. in 1934 and he received the honorary degree of LL.D. from the uni-versity of St. Andrews in 1938.

In breadth of interest and knowledge, Collingwood invites comparison, amongst modern philosophers, with Hegel. He was in fact one of the most learned men of his generation, and he had his learning con-stantly at command. But he also posses-sed an originality of mind which enabled him in history to pose new questions and in philosophy to take a promising line of his own. In this very strength, however, lay his weakness; he had critical gifts of a high order, but his imagination outranked them. Alike in history and archaeology he sometimes saw more than the evidence warranted and even overlooked what evi-dence there was; and in philosophy he had visions the validity of which he did not succeed in justifying to others by argument. In later years, ill health clouded his judge-ment, and the books of his last quinquen-nium, despite their wealth of fructifying ideas, are marred by febrility and a sense of strain. In history he made it his obliga-tion to strengthen the school of Romano-British studies founded by F. J. Haverfield [q.v.]; his work on Roman inscriptions is a permanent monument to his memory; and his earlier papers on Roman Britain are milestones in the progressive study of the subject. In philosophy, especially in his philosophical masterpiece, *An Essay on Philosophical Method* (1933), he carried forward the tradition of the English ideal-ists by modifying and developing their doctrine through meeting the criticisms levelled against it by his contemporaries, but he also brought about a *rapprochement* between philosophy and history by showing how a modern philosophy must become through and through historical and so orien-tate itself to history just as the philosophy of the last three centuries had orientated itself to natural science. His whole work gains its individuality from the fact that he was at once a philosophical historian and an historically minded philosopher; in the crucible of his powerful mind history and philosophy were fused.

In his family circle and with a few in-timate friends Collingwood was kindly and affectionate. But he was too much con-centrated on his original work not to be something of a recluse. He had a fondness for the society of young women, but he had little time for attending discussion clubs or fulfilling social engagements. He gave up the violin before his first marriage; at one time he composed songs and much instrumental music, and even thought of devoting his life to composition, but this too he abandoned before he was thirty; he played the piano or painted a picture occasionally until his health broke down; he was always fond of sailing a yacht, but archaeology, which he described as his hobby, was the only recreation to which he devoted himself with any continuity during his maturity, unless there could be included in that category his work as a delegate of the University Press from 1928 to 1941. All his life he was deeply interested in religion. The influence of Dr. Albert Schweitzer early made him a liberal in theology but partly through talks with intimate friends, partly by a study of the scholastics, he gradually worked his way to the more positive and even dogmatic attitude which underlies his *Essay on Metaphysics* (1940). In politics, and in college business, he was on the conservative side for most of his life, but his views turned sharply to the Left when the attitude of the British Government to the European dictatorships seemed to him to be too supine. As a lecturer in Oxford he attracted large audiences of undergraduates; his voice was high-pitched and clear; the spoken word was as polished as his written prose. He wrote remarkable letters to his friends, but he did not wish them to be published, and he directed that no attempt should be made to write his biography. There is a bibliography of his publications in the *Proceedings* of the British Academy, volume xxix, corrected and supplemented in the preface to his *Idea of History* (1946).

[R. G. Collingwood, *An Autobiography*, 1939; R. B. McCallum in *Proceedings* of the British Academy, vol. xxix, 1943, with supplementary notices by T. M. Knox and I. A. Richmond; *Times Literary Supplement*, 16 January 1943; *Oxford Magazine*, 4 February 1943; private information; personal knowledge.]      T. M. KNOX.

COMRIE, LESLIE JOHN (1893–1950), astronomer and computer, was born 15 August 1893 at Pukekohe, New Zealand, the son of John Alexander Comrie and his wife, Helen Lois Smith. His father was a farmer, and both the Comrie and Smith families originally came from Scotland. Although his early environment played little part in his later life, he never forgot the country of his birth; his hospitality to any New Zealander, particularly a serving member of the forces, was renowned.

He was trained as a chemist at Auckland University College, taking his M.A. degree in 1916 with honours in chemistry. In spite of deafness, which became increasingly acute in later years, he served with the New Zealand Expeditionary Force in the war of 1914–18 and was wounded, losing a leg. After the war he forsook chemistry for astronomy and computation, subjects in which he had become interested in Auckland. He went as a research student to St. John's College, Cambridge, was elected to an Isaac Newton studentship in 1921, and was awarded his Ph.D. degree in 1924 for a thesis on the occultation of stars by planets.

From Cambridge, Comrie proceeded to the United States, where he taught astronomy and computing, first at Swarthmore College, Pennsylvania, and then at Northwestern University, Illinois. He returned to England in 1925 to enter the Nautical Almanac Office, where the following year he became deputy superintendent with a virtual certainty of early promotion, since the superintendent, Philip Herbert Cowell, had only a few years longer to serve. Comrie duly became superintendent in 1930, but left the Office in 1936 to found the Scientific Computing Service, Ltd., a professional organization catering for large-scale numerical computation, particularly in the scientific and mathematical fields. He rapidly built up a powerful team of experienced computers, whose resources were soon to be fully stretched by the demands of government departments during the war of 1939–45. During and after the war he worked for extremely long hours, and after a strenuous tour of Australia and New Zealand he was afflicted by a stroke, which impaired his speech but left him with an active mind. After a second stroke two years later he died 11 December 1950 at his home in Blackheath.

In the short space of ten years Comrie revolutionized the work of the Nautical Almanac Office. His greatest achievement was the complete revision, almost single-handed, of the *Nautical Almanac* for 1931; it had been essentially unchanged since 1834. In a paper presented to the Royal Astronomical Society, he proposed the use of a fixed frame of reference for the computation of orbits of comets and minor planets and later provided the necessary data in the Office publications; this may well be his most lasting contribution to astronomy. He introduced new methods, computing techniques, and calculating machines, and transformed the Office into the most efficient computing organization of its time; he widened its international responsibilities, and laid the foundation for its expansion to fulfil them.

Comrie was the foremost computer and table-maker of his day. He entered the field when the large majority of computing was done by the aid of logarithms and he lived long enough to see in operation the first of the automatic digital computing machines. Although he played no direct part in the design of these machines, his influence, precept, and example over a period of thirty years prepared the way for this sensational advance. During this period he was the acknowledged leader in all aspects of computing, table-making, and the application of commercial calculating machines to scientific work. He set new standards of precision, of numerical accuracy, and of presentation which are incorporated in a series of mathematical tables of unsurpassed merit. The greatest of these, in which Comrie compressed a lifetime's experience, is *Chambers's Six-Figure Mathematical Tables* (2 vols., 1948-9). He had previously edited 'Barlow's Tables' (1930), produced, with Professor Louis Melville Milne-Thomson, the *Standard Four-Figure Mathematical Tables* (1931), collaborated with J. Peters of Berlin in the compilation of comprehensive tables of natural trigonometrical functions for every second of arc, which led to the publication in Germany of the justly famous *Achtstellige Tafeln*, and, as secretary of the British Association mathematical tables committee, had been largely responsible for the splendid series of B.A. Mathematical Tables. He also compiled *Hughes' Tables for Sea and Air Navigation* (1938), the finest navigational tables of their type ever produced, together with many other minor tables and descriptions of computational techniques. It was only fitting that his work in these fields should be recognized by his election in 1950 as F.R.S.

Comrie was a wholehearted individualist, passionately devoted to his twin loves of astronomy and computation. He worshipped precision and competence in all matters and would himself spare no effort to attain them. Proud, sensitive, and inclined to be intolerant and critical of others, he could not understand, or forgive, lack of appreciation of his work by those not possessing his energy, application, or thoroughness. Such a personality was incompatible with a civil service career,

and, after constant friction with administrative authority, led to his break with the Admiralty in 1936. It was this same unduly critical attitude which led to some difficult personal relationships. But this was only one aspect; thorough in everything, he was extremely generous, particularly in giving his own time and energy to helping others; he endured severe physical handicaps with patience; and he gave his friendship wholeheartedly.

He was twice married: first, in 1920 to Noeline Dagger, of New Zealand; the marriage was dissolved in 1933 and in the same year he married Phyllis Betty, daughter of H. D. Kitto, of Stroud, Gloucestershire. There was one surviving son of the first marriage and one of the second.

[Private information; personal knowledge.]
D. H. SADLER.

CONINGHAM, SIR ARTHUR (1895–1948), air marshal, was born at Brisbane, Australia, 19 January 1895, the elder son of Arthur Coningham, chemist and Australian cricketer, by his wife, Alice Stanford. His parents moved to New Zealand where he was educated at Wellington College. On the outbreak of war in 1914 he enlisted as a trooper in the Canterbury Mounted Rifles in which he served first in Samoa and later in the Gallipoli campaign. From this service in a New Zealand regiment came his nickname of 'Maori' (which was distorted through usage to become 'Mary') by which he was thereafter generally known. Coningham transferred to the Royal Flying Corps in August 1916 and in December went to France as a second lieutenant in No. 32 Squadron, in which he served for the first seven months of 1917 until he was wounded. In this short period he was appointed to the D.S.O., awarded the M.C., and promoted to captain for his gallantry as a fighter pilot. The citation for these two decorations mentions his dash and fine offensive spirit, his splendid example of pluck and determination, qualities which were to mark him throughout his career.

After a year in England he returned to France in July 1918 as major commanding No. 92 Squadron with which he remained until war ended. He was awarded the D.F.C. for his services during this period. Early in 1919 he reverted from major to captain and in August was granted a permanent commission in the Royal Air Force as a flight lieutenant.

Between the two wars he commanded

No. 55 Squadron in Iraq and, among other appointments, served as a flying instructor at the Royal Air Force College, Cranwell, and as a staff officer at Middle East headquarters in Cairo and likewise at the headquarters of Coastal Area. As a wing commander he commanded the Royal Air Force detachment in the Sudan and as a group captain the flying-boat base at Calshot. When a staff officer at Cairo he was selected in 1925 to command and lead a 'trail-blazing' flight across Central Africa from Cairo to Kano and, after the successful conclusion of the flight, was awarded the A.F.C.

Just before the outbreak of hostilities in 1939 Coningham was promoted to air commodore and given command of No. 4 Group which consisted of the long-range night bombers based in Yorkshire. His group was actively engaged in operations over Germany during the two years he was in command, and in 1941 he was appointed C.B. for his services. In that year he was selected to command the Desert Air Force supporting the Eighth Army in the North African campaign, as part of Air Marshal A. W. (subsequently Lord) Tedder's Middle East Air Force. Coningham remained in command of this force in support of the Eighth Army under its successive commanders throughout the ebb and flow of the desert campaigns of 1941 and 1942, including the El Alamein battle, after which he was promoted K.C.B. After the capture of Tripoli in January 1943 he was switched to the Algerian front to form the 1st Allied (North African) Tactical Air Force. His new command controlled the British and American air forces supporting their respective armies in the campaign for the capture of Tunisia. He set up his headquarters on 17 February 1943 along-side those of the newly formed 18th Army Group under Sir Harold Alexander (subsequently Earl Alexander of Tunis). After Tunis fell Coningham was responsible for command of the Allied Tactical Air Forces employed in the capture of Pantelleria and Sicily and thereafter in support of the British and American armies in southern Italy. In January 1944 he returned to England to take command of the 2nd Tactical Air Force then preparing to go to Europe alongside the 21st Army Group. Coningham moved to Normandy with his force in July 1944 and remained in command until the conclusion of the war in Europe. His appointment for the last year of the war was that of a commander-in-chief, and his force, commanded finally from his headquarters in Germany, consisted of some 1,800 first-line aircraft and 100,000 men, spread from Copenhagen and Bremen in the north to Marseilles in the south, and comprising British, Canadian, Belgian, French, Dutch, Polish, and Norwegian air forces.

Coningham, as air vice-marshal and air marshal, was commanding air forces operating against the Germans from the first day of the war until the last. Although he was highly strung he seemed to have no nerves, and his youthful and gay spirit inspired his whole force and in particular young pilots with whom he was at his best. In command of a force in which he knew the strength and weakness of every subordinate commander he was outstanding, but as his sphere of operations necessarily expanded his personal touch could then be felt less keenly. His most remarkable contribution therefore was made, perhaps, from his small, neat caravan in the Western Desert, a part of North Africa he came to know in exceptional detail even at a time when many claimed to know every ridge and wadi. Coningham was a very handsome man whose fine head had silvered early. He held himself well and his young, springy step gave that impression of alertness which was reinforced by the swift eagerness of his mind and interest. He was exceptionally quick in the uptake; moreover, he talked well, with a fluent and vivid vocabulary which held his hearers, to whom he exhibited a singular capacity to transfer his excitement in being alive and 'on the job'. He was always intensely loyal to his superior commander and he seldom made a mistake in his choice of commanders to serve under him. He took no leave between 1939 and 1945 and concentrated his entire and most remarkable energies on defeating the enemy air force in front of him. Where commendation was due he commended with a singular directness, but he was ruthless where there was inefficiency. A clear thinker and an exciting strategist, he seemed the very personification of the offensive spirit. His directions when commanding Tactical Air Forces had the sole purpose of destroying the enemy air forces opposed to him, on the ground or in the air, and thereafter putting the whole weight of his force onto targets which would assist the advance of the army he was supporting. He was quite clear about his purposes and priorities. Although his air forces in the field were, of course, always independent of the army, he invariably set himself the task of assisting the land forces to the fullest extent, and from the day of his arrival in the desert in 1941 until the end of the war he always set up his headquarters alongside those of the army in order to ensure the closest co-operation. A pioneer in this, he was also the original architect of Tactical Air Forces and the way in which he used them was a model for all who came or may come after him.

For his services in the final 'Liberation' campaign he was appointed K.B.E. in 1946 and awarded a number of foreign decorations. He returned from Germany after the war to take up the appointment of commander-in-chief of the Royal Air Force Flying Training Command but retired at his own request in 1947. He was an active pilot himself throughout his Air Force career but it was as a passenger that he lost his life as a result of an accident to the aeroplane 'Star Tiger' between the Azores and Bermuda 30 January 1948.

Coningham married in 1932 Nancy Muriel, daughter of John Brooks, and widow of Sir Howard George Frank, first baronet, and had one daughter. A portrait of him painted by Raeburn Dobson is in the possession of the family. A drawing by H. A. Freeth is reproduced in Philip Guedalla's *Middle East, 1940–1942* (1944); a drawing was also made by Sir William Rothenstein.

[Private information; personal knowledge.]
T. W. ELMHIRST.

CONNAUGHT AND STRATHEARN, DUKE OF (1850–1942). [See ARTHUR WILLIAM PATRICK ALBERT.]

COOK, SIR BASIL ALFRED KEMBALL- (1876–1949), civil servant. [See KEMBALL-COOK.]

COOK, SIR JOSEPH (1860–1947), Australian politician, was born at Silverdale, Staffordshire, 7 December 1860, the son of William Cooke, coal-miner, and his wife, Margaret Fletcher. He began work as a pit-boy at the age of nine, and three years later, on the death of his father, became the main support of his family. In 1885 he emigrated with his wife to New South Wales, finding employment as a coal-miner at Lithgow. He studied for a time for admission to the Methodist ministry, but, although he continued an active lay preacher, he was increasingly drawn to public affairs. In 1887 he became secretary of the Lithgow Miners' Association, and during the maritime strike of 1890 he was a member of the Labour defence committee. Always an advocate of moderation, he was one of the first to turn, after the failure of the strike, to political action, and in 1891 he entered the Parliament of New South Wales as a member of the first Labour Party. When some of this party joined the Protectionists, Cook became leader of the remainder, but refusing to take the 'solidarity' pledge in 1894 he was expelled from the party and re-elected to Parliament as an independent. Cook had already been drawn by way of the land-tax movement into the free-trade camp, and it was natural that (Sir) George Reid [q.v.], seeking working-class support for his Government, should turn to him. He became postmaster-general in 1894 and was later (1898–9) minister for mines and agriculture, building a reputation as an honest and dependable administrator.

On the formation of the Commonwealth in 1901 Cook followed Reid into the Federal Parliament. A long period in opposition developed his talents as a dour fighter with a bitter and somewhat cynical tongue, no orator, but with a bluntness and rough sarcasm which made him increasingly formidable in debate. When, after the fall of the Reid–McLean coalition of 1904–5, the Free Trade Party assumed a stronger role against Labour, Cook became deputy leader and, on Reid's resignation in 1908, succeeded him to the leadership. He was active in the negotiations which led to the 'fusion' of the anti-Labour forces in 1909 and took second place under Alfred Deakin [q.v.] in the resulting party. In Deakin's third ministry (1909–10) Cook held the defence portfolio, and in spite of the short life of the Government this was perhaps the period of his greatest achievement, since it fell to him both to lay the foundations of the scheme of compulsory military training, on which he obtained the advice of Lord Kitchener [q.v.] and which was put into operation by his successor, and to conclude with Britain the agreement which established the Royal Australian Navy.

On Deakin's retirement in 1913 Cook was elected leader by a margin of one vote over Sir John (later Lord) Forrest [q.v.] and following the elections of that year he became prime minister. Lacking a majority in the Senate, and dependent in the House of Representatives on the Speaker's casting vote, he could achieve nothing positive, and as soon as the constitutional requirements could be filled he asked for and was granted a dissolution of both Houses. In the ensuing elections his party was swept out of office, and meanwhile Australia found herself at war. On 3 August Cook had cabled an offer of 20,000 men to Britain and undertaken to place the Royal Australian Navy at the disposal of the Admiralty. As leader of the Opposition he supported the war effort of the Labour Governments of Andrew Fisher [q.v.] and William Morris Hughes, while criticizing their administration on detail. After the split in the Labour Party over conscription in 1917, and the resulting expulsion of Hughes and his followers, Cook again found himself second-in-command of a coalition in which the great majority consisted of his former followers. Galling though this situation must have been, he gave loyal support to Hughes, and the respect and confidence which his administration as navy minister commanded from both sides of the House often served to blunt the effect of his more controversial leader. In 1918 Cook accompanied Hughes to England and sat with him as a member of the Imperial War Cabinet. In 1919 he was a delegate to the peace conference where he sat on the committee on Czechoslovakia and impressed it by the downrightness and common sense of his remarks, if not by his knowledge of the subject. 'Old Cook is all right', wrote (Sir) Harold Nicolson (*Peacemaking 1919*, 1933). 'He has sense. The French the other day started an endless argument about the Delbrück nationality laws. When the whole thing had been translated into English, old Cook was asked to record his views. "Damn Delbrück" was what he said.'

In 1920 Cook became Commonwealth treasurer but resigned in 1921 on succeeding Fisher as high commissioner in London where he prepared the ground for the Australian delegation to two Imperial Conferences, and devoted himself to the post-war problems of immigration and trade. He also represented Australia at the Assembly of the League of Nations at every meeting from 1922 to 1926. After his return to Australia in 1927 he lived in retirement in Sydney where he died 30 July 1947. He was not an original or creative statesman, but he had administrative ability and tenacity and developed considerable skill in parliamentary tactics and in the cut and thrust of debate. He was politically shrewd, and his mind generally reflected that of the ordinary voter. His early belligerence mellowed somewhat as he began to play the part of an elder statesman, but his best work was done in administration. He was sworn of the Privy Council in 1914 and appointed G.C.M.G. in 1918.

In 1885 Cook married Mary, daughter of George Turner, of Chesterton, Staffordshire, who was appointed D.B.E. in 1925. They had six sons and three daughters. There is a portrait of Cook in Parliament House, Canberra, by Norman Carter; he is also included in the group by Sir James Guthrie 'Some Statesmen of the War of 1914–18' in the National Portrait Gallery, and an oil sketch for his portrait in this group is in the Scottish National Portrait Gallery.

[*Daily Telegraph*, Sydney, 3 August 1894; H. G. Turner, *The First Decade of the Australian Commonwealth*, 1911; *Commonwealth Parliamentary Handbook 1901–30*, 1930; Ernest Scott, (Official) *History of Australia in the War of 1914–18*, vol. xi, 1936; *Sydney Morning Herald* and *The Times*, 31 July 1947; private information.]

L. F. FITZHARDINGE.

COOK, STANLEY ARTHUR (1873–1949), Semitist, biblical scholar, archaeologist, and student of religion, was born 12 April 1873 at King's Lynn. He was the son of John Thomas Cook, coal merchant, by his wife, Frances Sarah Else. He was educated at Wyggeston School, Leicester, and at Gonville and Caius College, Cambridge, where he was a scholar. He was placed in the first class of the Semitic languages tripos in 1894, was Tyrwhitt Hebrew scholar and Mason Hebrew prizeman in 1895, and in 1896 gained the Jeremie Septuagint prize. From 1904 until 1932 he was lecturer in Hebrew at his old college of which he became a fellow in 1900, and from 1912 until 1920 was lecturer also in comparative religion. In 1931 he was appointed university lecturer in Aramaic, and in 1932 he was elected to the regius professorship of Hebrew, which he held until his retirement in 1938. He was the first layman to be elected to this chair.

Cook grew up in the days of William Robertson Smith, T. K. Cheyne, A. B. Davidson, S. R. Driver [qq.v.], and other pioneers in Old Testament research, and he belongs with them to the history of biblical scholarship. His association as a young man, from 1896 until 1903, with the *Encyclopaedia Biblica* was the beginning of a long period of editorial work, which included the editorship for thirty years, 1902–32, of the *Quarterly Statement* of the Palestine Exploration Fund. He was on the editorial staff of the eleventh and fourteenth editions of the *Encyclopaedia Britannica*. For more than fifty years he produced original work which in extent and variety is astonishing. Up to 1910 his interest was centred on Semitic languages, inscriptions, history, Old Testament analysis, and archaeology. After 1910 he was drawn to the study of psychology, philosophy, sociology, and religion in all its aspects. The publication of *The Study of Religions* (1914) marks the transition from his earlier to his later interests. Henceforward his life's work was directed towards the relating of his vast knowledge of Semitic antiquity to all problems of human existence. In the views he held he was bold, but not rash, and his writings, although difficult to read, are always stimulating and often challenging. Some of his earlier work has been superseded, but his more solid contributions, such as his fine chapters in the *Cambridge Ancient History*, of which he was a joint editor, and his monumental Schweich lectures (1925, published 1930) will long retain their value.

Cook married in 1898 Annette (died 1942), daughter of the late William Thomas Bell, lithographic printer's manager. There were no children of the marriage. Cook was elected president of the Society for Old Testament Study in 1925; an honorary member of the Society of Biblical Literature and Exegesis (U.S.A.) in 1931; and F.B.A. in 1933. He received the honorary degrees of D.D. from the university of Aberdeen (1937) and D.Litt. from Oxford in 1938. He took the degree of Litt.D. at Cambridge in 1920. On the occasion of his seventy-fifth birthday a volume of *Essays and Studies*, which contains a select bibliography of his writings, was presented to him. He died after a short illness in Cambridge 26 September 1949.

[*The Times*, 28 September and 4 October 1949; *Cambridge Review*, 28 January 1950; D. Winton Thomas in *Proceedings* of the British Academy, vol. xxxvi, 1950; personal knowledge.]     D. WINTON THOMAS.

COOPER, SIR (FRANCIS) D'ARCY, baronet (1882–1941), industrialist, was born in London 17 November 1882, the only son of Francis Cooper, chartered accountant, and his wife, Ada Frances, daughter of Henry Power, surgeon. Educated at Wellington College and on the continent, he was articled in the family firm, Cooper Brothers & Co., becoming a partner in 1910. He enlisted in the army in 1915, received a commission in the Royal Field Artillery, and was badly wounded on the Somme. Later he served at the War Office before returning to his firm where he rapidly established a reputation as one of the ablest members of his profession.

For many years Cooper Brothers & Co. had been auditors for Lever Brothers, which by 1920 was the largest company manufacturing oils and fats in the British Empire, with extensive interests in many parts of the world. During the post-war boom, Lord Leverhulme [q.v.] had enormously expanded his business, not least by the purchase of other concerns, notably the Niger Company, and the slump of 1920 brought serious financial difficulties. Finding himself in 1921 under pressure from the banks, who were his principal creditors, Leverhulme called in Cooper who was able to retrieve a desperate situation. Thenceforward Cooper's prestige in the Lever business steadily increased: in 1923 he became a director and joint vice-chairman, and within a week of Leverhulme's death in 1925 he was appointed chairman.

He shirked no measures, however unpopular, which he deemed necessary to restore stability and confidence, and by 1929 he had achieved a large measure of success. In that year he completed the complicated negotiations with the Margarine Union, the largest continental manufacturers of oils and fats. The concern which emerged, under the name of Unilever, was one of the largest businesses in the world. Not a little of the credit for its creation must go to Cooper's patient and resolute diplomacy. No less remarkable was his success in reorganizing new concern and guiding it through the economic troubles of the 'thirties. To weld into a unity a number of former competitors of several different nationalities was an arduous process, but he would allow no personal considerations or old affiliations to stand in the way of complete unification. Beginning with little technical knowledge he showed a swift mastery of detail and a genius for shaping and executing policy which earned him the respect of his new colleagues.

Had it not been for Cooper, the Lever business might well have shared a fate which has often befallen the creations of dynamic personalities who have failed to provide against their own decline or economic changes. Cooper's qualities, notably of judgement and foresight, became increasingly indispensable to business enterprise during the 'twenties.

By substituting an orderly system of management for personal autocracy, Cooper proved himself a leading member of the rising class of professional managers of large-scale business.

Tall and powerfully built, Cooper possessed a natural habit of command which compelled respect. But he had also an unaffected humanity and a simple hatred of anything savouring of dishonesty which endeared him to those who worked with him. He was, said Leverhulme, one of those men who 'most resemble a warm fire and people naturally come up to him for warmth', and he had a gift for developing a sense of responsibility in subordinates. As Cooper overcame his natural shyness, his humour and a sense of style, derived from a love of good literature, made him an effective and engaging speaker. Believing that the conduct of modern business called for the best talent available, he gave valuable service as a member of the Cambridge University appointments board (1929–40) and did much to strengthen ties between the universities and industry. In the years immediately before the war his services were increasingly in demand in connexion with government economic policy and from 1940 he was principally occupied as chairman of the executive committee of the export council of the Board of Trade. He paid a useful visit to the United States in the autumn and was created a baronet in 1941. He received honours from Norway and Belgium, countries with which Levers had important connexions, and also from Bulgaria.

In 1913 Cooper married Evelyn Hilda Mary, daughter of Arthur Locke Radford, of Bovey House, Beer, Devon. There were no children and the baronetcy became extinct when Cooper died at Reigate 18 December 1941. A portrait by George Harcourt is at Unilever House, Blackfriars.

[Charles Wilson, *The History of Unilever*, 2 vols., 1954; *Port Sunlight News*, October 1936 and May 1938; private information.]

CHARLES WILSON.

COOPER, SIR (THOMAS) EDWIN (1874–1942), architect, was born at Scarborough 21 October 1874, the eldest child of Samuel Cooper, carriage proprietor, by his wife, Ann, daughter of Thomas Pickering, an agricultural labourer. He was educated locally. His father died in his childhood and it was left to his mother to recognize his talent for drawing and to arrange for his career in architecture.

Living at a time when training for this profession was limited to evening schools, he became an articled pupil, studying independently and travelling each year, as opportunity offered, in Italy and France.

The last decade of the nineteenth century witnessed a revival of Renaissance and classical architecture in France and America which caused similar reactions in England. This period of transition coincided with the erection of a vast number of town halls and public buildings, the designs for which were the outcome of open competition. The reputations of many young architects were gained in this way, and that of Cooper was no exception. His earlier years of practice were in partnership first with J. Hall and Herbert Davis and later, until 1910, with Samuel Bridgeman Russell. For the later years of his life he practised independently.

From the first Cooper was an untiring worker, sketching and measuring historical buildings, making water-colour drawings, and through observation extending his knowledge of architectural composition. Then came the testing time when he assisted several leading architects before venturing upon the uncertainties of architectural competition. He strove and he achieved by his unflagging energy. It was in fact his ability to find the most logical solution to a problem of planning which placed him in the forefront of competitive architects. Eventually there came a time when his advice was sought for buildings of civic importance. He was elected to the fellowship of the Royal Institute of British Architects in 1903, serving for some years on various committees and on the council for three periods. Elected A.R.A. in 1930 he became R.A. seven years later and was treasurer for the last few years of his life. In 1931 he received the Royal gold medal for architecture. He was knighted in 1923 for his work as the designer of the Port of London Authority building (1912–22) dominating Tower Hill, a Piranesian *tour de force*.

The forty years which separate the close of the Victorian era from the war of 1939–45 must be regarded as a period of uncertainty in the sphere of the arts. It was not a fortunate period for English architecture; the influences from France and America were both strong at the beginning, while towards the end disruption of taste became general in Europe. For an individual architect practising in England at this period the task of expressing contemporary needs in terms of competitive design was almost impossible. Cooper very rightly devoted his skill to planning; he was never content with an easy solution but pursued every possible variation until he had achieved a perfect pattern. He built up his experience stage by stage and by sheer force modelled his conceptions to fit the intricate sites with which he had to deal. For his treatment of elevations and internal decoration he remained loyal to the classical tradition which contemporary fashion demanded. In one sense he viewed architectural design through American spectacles, in another sense he aimed at precise detail and the correct assembling of authentic classic motifs. This latter method which had proved successful in the eighteenth century both in France and England, was indeterminate in face of the modern complexity of needs. Had the Edwardian period been truly receptive of the classic point of view, it is possible that a return to the qualities of eighteenth-century architecture would have followed. Scholarship, grace, and general culture, however, were lacking, and no individual architect, however earnest, could hope to make up for these deficiencies in his own work. An architect employs the forms and symbols which are current in his own day to complement certain basic principles. Cooper realized this truism but could not escape mannerisms which were universal. The Neo-Georgian movement, which succeeded the Edwardian, had many cultured exponents. The aim was to bring reticence to elevations and finesse to detail. Between the wars of 1914–18 and 1939–45 many fine buildings were achieved which are notable for proportion and beauty. Cooper's earlier works epitomize the various tendencies which were current at that time, the most pronounced being the set 'competition manner'. His later works, the outcome of study and experience, show greater sincerity of purpose and desire for perfection.

Marylebone Town Hall is a representative example of a long series of Edwardian civic buildings, and was won in competition in 1911. In the City Cooper found more scope for his ingenuity. Lloyd's Registry of Shipping (1929) both internally and externally attains the distinction of being superior to style or fashion. This might also be said of many buildings of similar character in Paris or New York. The National Provincial Bank (1931–2) is an example of compressing too many departments on a site far too cramped. This is a condition which no architect can hope to overcome, for the initial difficulties are reflected in the elevational treatments.

Cooper's activities extended into many specialized spheres. He was called upon to extend St. Mary's Hospital and to design the Medical School at Paddington. He designed the Devonport School of Pathology and Nurses' Home, Greenwich; Riddell House, St. Thomas's Hospital; the College of Nursing; the Star and Garter Home at Richmond; the Cowdray Club, Cavendish Square; and the South London Hospital for Women. He was called upon to design the Customs House and police housing at Tilbury, a convincing treatment in brick. In the provinces he designed the Guildhall and the Law Courts at Hull, and the new chapel for Bryanston School. At Oxford he designed the library of St. Hilda's College, and at Cambridge the School of Biochemistry.

For some years Cooper was president of the Institute of Registered Architects, and towards the end of his life he devoted much time to the furtherance of the Royal Academy plan for London. His devotion to his work led to corresponding loyalty among his many assistants, for the vast buildings he erected and supervised called for unending care in the preparation of drawings. From the three-dimensional standpoint Cooper's buildings are models of ingenuity. Everything seems to be combined within a small compass: both deep below ground and soaring skywards. The aim was to produce comprehensive perspective effects internally and rigid academic symmetry externally. The architectural and sculptural enrichments, however, were dictated by the taste of a prosperous period which demanded an expression of opulence.

Cooper married in 1898 Mary Emily (died 1957), daughter of Henry Wellburn, merchant, of Scarborough; they had a son and a daughter. He died in London 24 June 1942.

[*Journal* of the Royal Institute of British Architects, July 1942.]

A. E. RICHARDSON.

CORNFORD, FRANCIS MACDONALD (1874–1943), classical scholar, was born at Eastbourne 27 February 1874, the second son of the Rev. James Cornford, by his wife, Mary Emma Macdonald. He was educated at St. Paul's School under F. W. Walker [q.v.] and at Trinity College, Cambridge. After obtaining a first class in both parts of the classical tripos (1895,

1897) and being bracketed equal for the Chancellor's classical medal (1897) he was elected a fellow of Trinity in 1899, and was appointed assistant lecturer in classics in 1902 and lecturer in 1904. Except for the period of the war of 1914–18 almost the whole of his adult life was spent in Cambridge, where he became Brereton–Laurence reader in classics in 1927 (with special direction to instruct in ancient philosophy) and the first holder of the Laurence professorship of ancient philosophy in 1931. He received the honorary degree of D.Litt. from Birmingham University in 1937 and was elected F.B.A. in the same year.

As a lecturer Cornford was from the first dissatisfied with the somewhat narrow nineteenth-century ideal of 'pure scholarship', and in an early pamphlet (*The Cambridge Classical Course*, 1903) advocated a more humane, less philological type of instruction, as well as a better co-ordinated inter-collegiate lecture system in place of the semi-chaotic conditions then prevailing. The wit and light satire which mark this pamphlet found fuller scope in *Microcosmographia Academica* (1908), a skit on university politics, 'one of the few university satires', it has been said, 'which have outlived their occasion'; it was reissued in 1922, 1933, 1949, and 1953.

Recognizing that lectures ought not to repeat what can better be got from books, Cornford always aimed at stimulating his classes by an original treatment of his subject; the better men appreciated this, but his methods were perhaps less well suited to the mediocre minds which formed the majority of his audiences. Concurrently with lecturing he had a considerable amount of individual college teaching; but although he never scamped this work his heart was from early days elsewhere, namely in the writing of books, and apart from the professorial lectures of his last years it is as a writer rather than as a teacher that he will chiefly be remembered.

Before his first book, *Thucydides Mythistoricus* (1907), appeared Cornford had come under the influence of Jane Harrison (whose notice he later contributed to this DICTIONARY), a pioneer in the study of Greek religion, and in this and his other works of the years before the war of 1914–18 the bent of his mind was largely determined by her, also by Gilbert Murray, and to some extent by A. W. Verrall and W. G. Headlam [qq.v.]. What primarily interested him in this period

was the study of those primitive modes of thought and feeling which provided the background, largely unrealized, of the writers—poets, historians, and philosophers—of the classical age of Greece, and the investigation of the ritual forms in which those thoughts and feelings found outward expression. *Thucydides*, although highly original and stimulating, is probably the least convincing of the three books of this period; it was strong meat for the historians, who were not slow to challenge some of its arguments. *From Religion to Philosophy* (1912) is notable for its penetrating interpretation of the pre-Socratic thinkers, and *The Origin of Attic Comedy* (1914) for its analysis of the structure of Aristophanes' plays and the detection of a ritual sequence lying behind them. After a break of some nine years appeared *Greek Religious Thought from Homer to Alexander* (1923), consisting of translated extracts with a valuable introduction.

From this time onwards Cornford's work became more strictly concerned with ancient philosophy. Important papers on 'Mysticism and Science in the Pythagorean Tradition' (*Classical Quarterly*, vol. xvi, 1922), and on 'Anaxagoras' Theory of Matter' (ibid., vol. xxiv, 1930) were followed by an edition of Aristotle's *Physics* in the Loeb Classical Library (2 vols., 1929–34); this was in collaboration with Philip Henry Wicksteed, whose rather free translation was in many passages supplemented by Cornford's alternative rendering and masterly annotation. In 1935 came the first of the three great commentaries on Plato's later dialogues, which crown Cornford's achievement and place him in the forefront of modern Platonic scholars: *Plato's Theory of Knowledge* (a translation of the *Theaetetus* and *Sophist* with introduction and interspersed commentary); *Plato's Cosmology* (1937, a similar treatment of the *Timaeus*); and *Plato and Parmenides* (1939). In his last years he produced an excellent translation of the *Republic* (1941), with interpretative summary, section by section, and a judicious pruning of the encumbrances of dialogue-form. He also published two papers in which certain misguided contemporary theories were powerfully challenged, the first entitled 'Was the Ionian Philosophy Scientific?' (*Journal of Hellenic Studies*, vol. lxii, 1942), the second 'The Marxist View of Ancient Philosophy' (summary in *Proceedings* of the Classical Association, vol. xxxix, May 1942) which was reprinted in *The Unwritten Philosophy and Other Essays*, edited with a memoir by Professor W. K. C. Guthrie in 1950. Another posthumous work, issued under the same editorship, was *Principium Sapientiae* (1952), which contained his latest speculations on the origins of Greek philosophical thought.

Outside his professional work Cornford had many interests: one of these was in the Working Men's College in London, members of which he brought up for an annual visit to Cambridge during many years, enlisting the help of his pupils in their entertainment. He was deeply appreciative of classical music. In his early days he edited the *Cambridge Review*, the pages of which he sometimes enlivened with witty verse of his own. He retired from his chair in 1939 and died at Cambridge 3 January 1943.

Cornford married in 1909 Frances Crofts, only daughter of (Sir) Francis Darwin [q.v.], the botanist, and had three sons and two daughters. Mrs. Cornford became well known as a poet. The eldest son was killed in 1936 while fighting against the forces of General Franco in the Spanish civil war. A drawing of Cornford by Eric Gill (1929) is in the library of Trinity College, Cambridge.

[*The Times*, 5 January 1943; Gilbert Murray in *Proceedings* of the British Academy, vol. xxix, 1943; *Cambridge Review*, 30 January 1943; personal knowledge.]

REGINALD HACKFORTH.

CORNISH, VAUGHAN (1862–1948), geographer, was born 22 December 1862 at Debenham, Suffolk, the third and youngest son of the Rev. Charles John Cornish, a cousin of F. W. Warre-Cornish [q.v.], and his wife, Anne Charlotte Western. His father was then vicar of Debenham, but the family had long been established in the Sidmouth district of Devon, where they had lived from the fifteenth century as 'squireens, members of the lesser county gentry, farming their own lands'. Cornish was proud of this connexion, which he maintained throughout his life. He was sent unusually late to St. Paul's School where his eldest brother, C. J. Cornish (whose notice he wrote for this DICTIONARY), was later to become assistant classical master. Cornish owed much of his early education to his mother, who, although accepting the inspiration of the Bible, encouraged his bent for original research and developed in him an appreciation of nature. At school his interests were chiefly in the natural sciences and he went on to the Owens College, Manchester, partly on account of the facilities it offered for chemical research. He graduated B.Sc. with honours in 1888 and proceeded D.Sc. in 1901.

For some years Cornish was director of technical education to the Hampshire County Council, but in 1895 he resigned to devote himself to private research. In this decision he was encouraged and supported by his wife, Ellen Agnes, daughter of Alfred Provis, artist, of Kingston Lisle, Berkshire, whom he had married in 1891 and who had private means. Sharing mutual interests in travel, they gave up a permanent home to further his inquiries. His first subject was the study of surface waves of all types, and to observe them he journeyed extensively, studying dunes in the Libyan desert, the action of wind on snow in Canada, the length and speed of waves on voyages across the Atlantic, and the tidal bores of the Severn and Trent. For many years little interest was taken by physicists in the theory of the subject, but Cornish persisted and amassed 'a larger quantity of observational material than any other worker'. In 1900 he was awarded the Gill memorial of the Royal Geographical Society for his work. His results were finally published in *Ocean Waves and Kindred Geophysical Phenomena* (1934) with theoretical explanations and extensions by (Sir) Harold Jeffreys. Cornish was an expert photographer and used many of his own photographs to illustrate his books. He also, in 1901, directed the making of a cinematograph film of the Severn bore.

The Cornishes were in Kingston, Jamaica, at the time of the earthquake of 1907 and had a narrow escape with minor injuries. His wife died in 1911 and two years later he married Mary Louisa, widow of his second cousin the explorer E. A. Floyer (whose notice he also contributed to this DICTIONARY). Cornish's extensive travels and study of physical phenomena had equipped him as a geographer so that, having also a grounding in history, he came to an interest in historical and strategical geography, first aroused by studies of the effects of the Panama Canal. He had begun before 1914 to write on aspects of imperial strategy, and after the outbreak of war he gave courses of lectures to naval and military officers. These continued throughout the war, during

179

which he visited Scapa Flow and the western front. Some of them were later published. His exposition was based on a sound appreciation of global position, lines of communication, and national resources, and on a careful study of the map, leading up to the key principle of the concentration of resources. In historical geography his most considerable work, *The Great Capitals* (1923), might be described as the strategical geography of the past. In it he sought to establish a single generalization—the forward position of capital cities, 'not at the centre of internal communications, but at a common focus of internal and foreign communications with the principal neighbours'.

In the later years of his life Cornish turned his attention to the study of natural beauty, in response to an address by Sir Francis Younghusband [q.v.] to the Royal Geographical Society in 1920. For this he could draw upon his knowledge of many countries and his habit of accurate observation and careful recording. Believing as he did that satisfaction of the sense of beauty is one of the chief contributions to human happiness, it was natural that he should have become identified with efforts to preserve the English countryside from spoliation. He worked and wrote vigorously on behalf of the Council for the Preservation of Rural England. He gave evidence in 1929 for the Council before the National Parks Committee, speaking with authority on scenic amenity and on the areas most worthy of preservation from a geographical and aesthetic point of view. His insistence in particular on the necessity of protecting the coastline has been amply justified. When he inherited the farm of South Combe, near Sidmouth, within the bounds of which is the great red Salcombe cliff, the third highest on the south coast, he gave practical expression to his views, for he entered on behalf of himself and his heirs into an agreement with the local authority to preserve the amenities of the estate in perpetuity.

Cornish was of a somewhat austere bearing, aloof and reserved but courteous. His reserve would easily thaw when he discussed his lifelong interests; he had too a warm sympathy with the young and there were many who benefited from his encouragement and advice. These qualities were displayed as president of the geography section of the British Association at Liverpool in 1923, and of the Geographical Association in 1928. He

died at Camberley 1 May 1948. There were no children of either marriage.

[V. Cornish, *The Travels of Ellen Cornish*, 1913, *A Family of Devon*, 1942, and *Kestell, Clapp and Cornish*, 1947; *Geographical Journal*, vol. cxi, 1948.]     G. R. CRONE.

COUCH, SIR ARTHUR THOMAS QUILLER-, ('Q') (1863–1944), Cornishman, man of letters, and professor of English literature. [See QUILLER-COUCH.]

COULTON, GEORGE GORDON (1858–1947), historian and controversialist, was born at King's Lynn 15 October 1858, the third son and sixth child of John James Coulton, a well-known solicitor of that town, and his wife, Sarah Radley. After some early schooling in Lynn and at the lycée at St. Omer, he was sent to Felsted School, and in 1877 went to St. Catharine's College, Cambridge, where he was a scholar. He went down with an *aegrotat* degree, and, after a brief period as a preparatory schoolmaster, read with C. J. Vaughan [q.v.] for holy orders, and was ordained deacon in 1883 and priest in 1884. The following year, however, he felt himself unable to continue, and he later accepted posts in various public schools, with a happy interval of sixteen months in a private school in Heidelberg. Overwork while at Dulwich in 1895 brought on a breakdown, and on his recovery he joined a friend who ran a coaching establishment at Eastbourne, where for the next thirteen years he worked happily in conditions which gave him freedom to pursue his own studies.

By this time Coulton had determined to devote his energies to the serious study of medieval life and thought, and in particular to the working of the ecclesiastical system. His marriage eight years later forced him to pay more attention to 'bread-work', and he began to put out books such as *From St. Francis to Dante* (1906) and *Chaucer and his England* (1908) into which he poured some of the considerable knowledge he had already acquired. His growing reputation was enhanced by the appointment as Birkbeck lecturer in ecclesiastical history conferred on him by Trinity College, Cambridge, in 1910, and as a result of this he decided to migrate to Cambridge to set up as a free-lance lecturer and coach the following year. This he did; but the war of 1914–18 hit him hard, and it was not until the autumn of 1918, when he began to lecture for the newly founded English tripos, as well as for the historical tripos, that things became easier for him. In 1919 he was elected into what was then the sole university lectureship in English, and a little later in the same year he was made a fellow of St. John's College, Cambridge, so that at sixty-one, for the first time in his career, he could look forward to an assured income and work suitable to his talents.

From then onwards, save for the years 1940–44, when he was guest lecturer at Toronto, his life was spent in Cambridge, where he produced an unending flow of works, and enjoyed a growing reputation both as scholar and as an ever-ready adviser to those who sought his aid in matters historical. Coulton's reputation rested upon his very wide knowledge of many sides of medieval life and thought. Although ecclesiastical history was his first concern, he had a remarkable knowledge of the art, architecture, and everyday life of the Middle Ages. His outstanding works were *Five Centuries of Religion* (4 vols., 1923–50), *The Medieval Village* (1925), *Art and the Reformation* (1928), and *Medieval Panorama* (1938). In modern affairs he was a lifelong advocate of compulsory national service, and in this and in the championship of what he termed the 'moderate Protestant position' he took up an uncompromising attitude, unwelcome to many, but central to his own convictions, which reading and thinking had made overwhelmingly imperative. In the cause of national service he investigated personally conditions in France and Switzerland, and was at the side of Lord Roberts [q.v.] throughout his campaign for that cause. He spoke and wrote continuously against pacifist views, publishing a number of books and pamphlets, the best known being *The Case for Compulsory Military Service* (1917). His strongly expressed religious views entangled him in a number of prolonged and stormy contests with Roman Catholic historians and divines and in the opinion of many raised more dust and heat than light. He was an eager and resourceful conversationalist and speaker, whose tall, emaciated form and piercing blue eyes first attracted attention, and whose personal friendliness and courtesy impressed all who came into close contact with him.

Coulton received the honorary degree of D.Litt. from Durham University (1920), and of LL.D. from Edinburgh (1931) and Queen's University, Kingston, Ontario

(1942). He was elected F.B.A. in 1929 and an honorary fellow of St. Catharine's College in 1922. He married in 1904 Rose Dorothy, daughter of Owen Ilbert, of Thurlestone, Devon, and niece of Sir C. P. Ilbert [q.v.]; they had two daughters. He died at Cambridge 4 March 1947. A portrait by Mrs. A. Shore is in the possession of the family, and will ultimately pass to St. John's College.

[G. G. Coulton, *Fourscore Years*, 1943; Sarah Campion (M. R. Coulton), *Father*, 1948; H. S. Bennett in *Proceedings* of the British Academy, vol. xxxiii, 1947; personal knowledge.]      H. S. BENNETT.

COURTAULD, SAMUEL (1876–1947), industrialist and art patron, was born at Bocking Place, Braintree, Essex, 7 May 1876, the second son of Sydney Courtauld by his wife, Sarah Lucy, daughter of William Sharpe, and great-granddaughter of Sutton Sharpe, father of Daniel and Samuel Sharpe [qq.v.]. His grandfather, George Courtauld, was one of the original members of the family silk-weaving business founded at Bocking in 1816. They were members of an old Huguenot family, famous as silversmiths, who had come to England after the revocation of the Edict of Nantes. He was educated at Rugby and at the age of twenty went to Krefeld to study silk weaving. In 1904 a decisive step was taken in the family business, when it was registered as a public company and bought the British rights to manufacture rayon yarn by the viscose process: a rapid expansion took place and in 1909 a branch of the business was opened in America. Samuel Courtauld became general manager of the textile mills in 1908, joined the board of directors in 1915, and became chairman in 1921. During his twenty-five years' tenure the growth of the firm's interests continued: there were more than twenty factories in the United Kingdom and very numerous commitments abroad.

As an industrialist, he was known not only as a man of great foresight and practical sense, but also as one deeply interested in problems of management and of industrial relationships. Some of his speeches on this subject were collected after his death in a volume called *Ideals and Industry* (1949), but his contribution was made not through speeches or articles, though his speeches as chairman often had wide implications, but through personal contacts with a wide and varied circle of men holding key positions in many branches of life. Not a ready talker, nor anxious to thrust forward his own views, he had a compelling sincerity which arrested attention and made those with him eager to elicit his opinions. His insistence on the individuality of the worker, the need to break away from many outworn business theories, and the power of 'spiritual values' in all human affairs, coming from one so versed in the practice of industry, was a factor of some moment in the thought of his time. He was a visiting fellow and trustee of Nuffield College, Oxford, a trustee of the Houblon–Norman Fund created by the Bank of England in 1944 for research in economic and social science, and a member of many committees dealing with managerial and other problems.

Meanwhile his name was gaining international fame in a quite different context, that of art patronage. In 1901 he had married Elizabeth Theresa Frances, daughter of Edward Kelsey, whose understanding for music and the visual arts matched and stimulated his own. Their home at 20 Portman Square, a fine Adam house, became a centre for the artistic life of London. From 1925 to 1927 they were associated with the direction of the Covent Garden Opera seasons, and in 1929 Mrs. Courtauld started the Courtauld–Sargent Concert Club, the main achievement of which was to raise the standard of orchestral playing by abolishing the deputy system which prevailed at rehearsals. It also provided an opportunity for organized parties of workers or students to hear performances of the highest order at reasonable prices.

In 1923 the Courtaulds gave £50,000 for the purchase of French paintings by a selected list of artists for the Tate Gallery. This fund much enriched the representation of Impressionist and Post-Impressionist art and the pictures purchased by it included Seurat's great masterpiece 'Une Baignade' and Van Gogh's 'Sunflowers'. Courtauld's own collection contained such world-famous pictures as Manet's 'Bar aux Folies-Bergère', Cézanne's 'Montagne Sainte Victoire', 'Lac d'Annecy', and one of the finest versions of 'The Card Players', Van Gogh's self-portrait, and Renoir's 'La Loge'. On his wife's death in December 1931 many of these paintings were presented to London University, along with the leasehold of 20 Portman Square and a capital sum to provide an annual endowment and a building fund for the foundation of the Courtauld Institute of Art, the first institute in England where students might take a full honours course in the history of art. It was a project in which Courtauld took great personal interest and later he was largely responsible for bringing the Warburg Institute, displaced from Hamburg, to London, where eventually it also was incorporated in the university. His services to art and learning were recognized by the honorary degree of D.Lit. from London University in 1931, and his particular devotion to French painting by his becoming an officer of the Legion of Honour (1933). He was twice chairman of the National Gallery board of trustees and was a trustee of the Tate Gallery. In the art world of England he was a much respected figure, in whose judgement and integrity all had confidence.

His art patronage was strongly individualist: his preference for French Impressionist painting was based on his own response to it, although he also felt that its lack of adequate representation was a great defect in our national collections. The memorial exhibition held after his death of pictures owned by him or purchased by the Courtauld Trust was one of the most remarkable displays of the work of this school which has been held in any country. His taste, however, was not rigidly limited and some of his favourite pictures belonged to quite other periods. In everything, it was the response to beauty which mattered, and the implications of that response. Art was to him, in his own phrase, 'religion's next-of-kin'.

During the war of 1939–45 the wide-flung commitments of his firm brought new and difficult problems, many of them of national importance. Throughout the raids he spent most nights at his office to be with his staff, many of whom used it as a refuge. He had a serious illness in 1946 and died in London 1 December 1947. He had one daughter, who married Mr. Richard Austen Butler; she died in 1954. Two portraits of Courtauld were painted in 1947 by Roy de Maistre. One is in the possession of the family, and the other is in the offices of Courtaulds, Ltd., 16 St. Martin's-Le-Grand, London, E.C. 1.

[*The Times*, 3 December 1947; *Burlington Magazine*, January 1948; S. Courtauld, *Ideals and Industry*, with a preface by Charles Morgan, 1949; C. H. Ward-Jackson, *A History of Courtaulds*, 1941; Memoir by Anthony Blunt in D. Cooper, *The Courtauld Collection*, 1954; personal knowledge.]

T. S. R. BOASE.

COWARD, Sir HENRY (1849–1944), musician, was born at Liverpool 26 November 1849, the only son of Henry Coward, a Sheffield-born cutler who became an innkeeper and nigger-minstrel, by his wife, Harriet Carr. A hard and penurious youth as a cutler's apprentice in Sheffield was followed from 1870 by seventeen years of school-teaching, of which sixteen were spent as headmaster of various elementary schools, a remarkable performance by one who at the age of twenty-one could hardly write or spell. In 1876 he founded the Sheffield Tonic Sol-fa Association, later named the Sheffield Musical Union, and directed it for nearly sixty years (1876–1933).

In 1887 music became Coward's life-work. He obtained at Oxford the degrees of B.Mus. in 1889 and D.Mus. in 1894. From 1896 to 1908 he was chorus master of the Sheffield Musical Festival which quickly achieved world-wide fame by setting up and maintaining a new standard of choral excellence. In 1906 and 1910 he took a Yorkshire chorus to Germany. In 1908 he was training and conducting choral societies in Sheffield, Leeds, Huddersfield, Newcastle, and Glasgow. In that year he and his singers toured Canada and in 1911 they made a round-the-world tour of the Empire. These years were the zenith of his career, but his vitality and enterprise were undiminished for many years to come. In later years his effects were criticized as mere tricks, and it must be admitted that the scope of his musicianship was always limited by his inability to handle an orchestra. A valuable exposition of his methods is given in his *Choral Technique and Interpretation* (1914) and its supplement '*C.T.I.*', the *Secret* (1938).

Coward's manner was brusque and his utterance awkward, for his mind moved too speedily for his power of self-expression. He was somewhat formidable at a first encounter, but those who came to know him soon learnt to admire his intense industry, his high sense of duty, whether religious, artistic, or civic, and to value his generous humanity. He lived simply, and enjoyed a game of bowls or, still more, a walk in Derbyshire.

Coward was knighted in 1926, and was made an honorary freeman of the city of Sheffield and of the Cutlers' Company of Hallamshire. In 1933 he received the honorary degree of D.Mus. from the university of Sheffield. He was a lifelong advocate of the Tonic Sol-fa system of sight-singing and was president of the Tonic Sol-fa College, London, 1929-43.

Coward was three times married: first, in 1875 to Mary Eliza, daughter of Charles Best, silversmith, of Sheffield; secondly, in 1894, abroad, to Louisa Hannah Best, sister of his first wife who had died; and thirdly, after the death of his second wife, in 1911 to Semima Alice, daughter of Simeon Dewsnap, cabinet-case manufacturer of Sheffield. There were four sons and four daughters of the first marriage. Coward died at Sheffield, at the age of ninety-four, 10 June 1944.

A portrait by James Moore is at the Tonic Sol-fa College, London.

[Henry Coward, *Reminiscences*, 1919; J. A. Rodgers, *Dr. Henry Coward*, 1911; *Musical Times*, July 1944; private information; personal knowledge.]      F. H. SHERA.

CREWE-MILNES, ROBERT OFFLEY ASHBURTON, second Baron Houghton, and Marquess of Crewe (1858–1945), statesman, was born in London 12 January 1858, the only son of Richard Monckton Milnes, later first Baron Houghton [q.v.]. His mother was Annabella Hungerford, daughter of the second Baron Crewe. He was educated at Harrow, where he won the prize poem on the subject of 'Gustavus Adolphus', never telling his father that he was competing until the announcement of his success. Lord Houghton, in expressing his paternal pride, shrewdly commented: 'It was very discreet of you to keep your own counsel so completely as to the poem. Nobody can now say that I wrote it.'

He received his university education, like his father and grandfather before him, at Trinity College, Cambridge, where he graduated in 1880, having developed the scholarly and literary tastes which remained with him throughout his life. In London, Houghton delighted to make the young man known to friends like Carlyle and other celebrities in the wide circle of cultivated and distinguished people where he was a leading and welcome figure. From the beginning, 'Bobby' Milnes shared the Liberal view which his father had espoused in the latter part of his political career, but, unlike his father, he was never a member of the House of Commons. He was five years old when Monckton Milnes was made a peer, at the instance of Palmerston, and when Houghton died in 1885, the son, then twenty-seven years of age, succeeded to the barony and took his place in the House of Lords, where he was destined to exercise his talents and acquire an increasing and impressive authority over a span of sixty years.

His apprenticeship to politics had already begun, for in 1883 Lord Granville [q.v.], the secretary of state for foreign affairs, had appointed him to be an assistant private secretary. Three years later he became a lord-in-waiting to Queen Victoria in Gladstone's third administration, which ended in July 1886. He thus had a ministerial connexion with the first Home Rule bill, and throughout his life remained firmly attached to the Gladstonian treatment of the Irish problem.

After six years of Conservative government under Lord Salisbury, Gladstone became prime minister for the fourth time in 1892. John (later Viscount) Morley [q.v.] returned to his post in the Cabinet as chief secretary for Ireland, and Houghton was appointed viceroy and was sworn of the Privy Council. He discharged his duties with unfailing dignity and discretion. Morley, in his *Recollections* (vol. i, 1917), has described the lord-lieutenancy at that time as 'the most thankless office that any human being in any imaginable community could undertake'; but he goes on, 'No appointment could have been better justified, nor was any chief secretary more fortunate in a colleague. He speedily divined the spirit and difficulties of Irish administration; from first to last he showed himself assiduous, acute, uncommonly clear-headed, invariably cool, considerate, loyal.' In 1894 his uncle, the third Lord Crewe, died, and Houghton succeeded to the Crewe estates and by royal licence took the name of Crewe as a prefix to that of Milnes. He was continued in the post of viceroy of Ireland when Rosebery succeeded Gladstone until the Liberal Government collapsed in 1895. On giving up office, he was created Earl of Crewe.

There followed ten years during which he sat on the front Opposition bench in the House of Lords, taking part in many debates with a quiet reasonableness which earned the respectful attention of the Conservative majority. In 1894 he became president of the Royal Literary Fund and held this office until 1903, when, like his father before him, he was elected a vice-president. Both father and son were generous benefactors to the Fund over a long period. Crewe's political gifts, combining calm judgement with strong conviction, made him a valuable addition to the inner councils of his party. When differences of opinion arose among Liberal leaders at the time of the South African war, he discouraged extreme views on either side, and, as always, exercised a healing influence among his colleagues. The long Conservative domination in British politics ended when Balfour resigned the premiership in December 1905, and on Campbell-Bannerman succeeding him, the new prime minister chose Crewe to be lord president of the Council. For the next eleven years Crewe continued to hold one or other of the main Cabinet portfolios, and on the resignation, 14 April 1908, of Lord Ripon [q.v.], who was his senior by thirty years, the leadership of the House of Lords devolved upon him. His firm but conciliatory approach to political questions, and the mingled moderation and courage with which he presented the government case when most of the House differed from him, was exactly in tune with the traditions of place and secured for the view of the minority a considerate hearing in that assembly. When the House of Lords, at the instance of Lord Lansdowne [q.v.], insisted upon drastic amendments to the education bill of 1906 which the Liberal majority in the Commons would not accept, Crewe made a spirited speech in which he declared that the responsibility for wrecking the bill rested wholly upon the Opposition. In March 1908 Campbell-Bannerman recommended Crewe for the Garter. It was almost the last act of the dying premier: Asquith became prime minister in April and Crewe was appointed secretary of state for the Colonies in succession to Lord Elgin [q.v.]. The principal event during his tenure of this office was the union of South Africa, effected after the convention of delegates from each of the four South African Parliaments had drawn up a scheme. The bill, which embodied the agreement thus arrived at, was passed by the imperial Parliament in the autumn of 1909, Crewe moving the second reading in the House of Lords, with (Sir) L. S. Jameson and Louis Botha [qq.v.] on the steps of the throne and Lord Milner [q.v.] on the cross-benches. From October 1908 to October 1911 and in 1912–15 Crewe also held the office of lord privy seal.

From 1910 to 1915 Crewe was secretary of state for India. While holding this office he was concerned with planning the Delhi durbar which he attended, and had the responsibility of transferring the capital of British India from Calcutta to Delhi and of cancelling the partition of Bengal. Crewe was one of the four members of the Liberal Government who took part, with four Conservative leaders, in the unfruitful constitutional conference which met at Downing Street in the summer of 1910, shortly after the accession of King George V. In 1911, in the list of honours at the coronation, Crewe was made a marquess, with the additional title of Earl of Madeley, which became the courtesy title of his son (who died in 1922). In 1912 Crewe received the Royal Victorian Chain.

At the beginning of the war of 1914–18 he placed his London residence, Crewe House, in Curzon Street, at the disposal of the Government, which used it as a centre for British propaganda. In the coalition formed by Asquith in May 1915 he was lord president of the Council and in 1916 president of the Board of Education. He left office with his leader when Lloyd George succeeded Asquith in December 1916. Crewe's position in his years of ministerial office was one of high and exceptional authority: Asquith placed much confidence in his counsel and was heard to declare that he regarded him as the wisest of his advisers.

After Asquith's resignation, Crewe never held political office again, except for a few months in Ramsay MacDonald's 'national' Government before the general election of 1931, when he was secretary of state for war. But he continued to render a series of public services in other fields. In 1917 he was elected chairman of the London County Council, thus accepting the municipal post which his father-in-law had been the first to discharge. From 1922 to 1928 he was British ambassador in Paris in succession to Lord Hardinge of Penshurst [q.v.], representing this country there in the period which witnessed the French and Belgian occupation of the Ruhr, the Dawes plan, and the discussions which led up to the Locarno conference. His long experience of affairs, his highly cultivated mind and attractive personality, together with the social graces by which he and his wife surrounded their tenure of the Paris embassy, showed how well a politician of his distinction could exercise the art of diplomacy.

On ceasing to be ambassador, Crewe resumed his political activities in the House of Lords. From 1936 to the end of 1944 he was assiduous as leader of the Independent Liberals in the upper House.

Crewe could not be described as a born orator: the occasional pauses in his delivery were due partly to his fastidious feeling after the most appropriate word and partly to his desire to express his thought with exactly the shade of meaning that was in his mind. This quiet, and sometimes hesitating, mode of discourse, with his hands firmly clenched before him, made plain to his audience that what he was saying was the result of reflection, based on real conviction. It was noticeable that the report in *Hansard* next day read as a polished performance. He had the Gladstonian quality of finding complete relaxation from political work by turning aside to discharge a different duty with equal energy.

Crewe was a striking example of a type of politician more commonly met in an earlier generation—a man of wealth and classical culture and long descent who devoted himself assiduously to parliamentary business, but whose interests were at the same time deeply engaged in country pursuits, in racing, in the breeding of shorthorn cattle, and in his library, which included a fine collection of autograph letters. He published a volume under the title of *Stray Verse, 1889–90* (1891), and in 1915 wrote the touching poem 'A Harrow Grave in Flanders' which finds a place in several anthologies. He was the author of the biography of Lord Rosebery, his father-in-law, which appeared in 1931.

It was written of Crewe after his death that the story of his life showed how in this country it is possible for a man of high cultivation and scrupulous honour to play a sturdy part in acute political and party controversy without ever suffering a stain on his escutcheon, and without losing the deep respect of friend and foe alike.

Crewe married as his first wife, in 1880, Sibyl Marcia, daughter of Sir Frederick Ulric Graham, third baronet. She died in 1887, leaving him with a son, who died when seven years old, and three daughters. Secondly, in 1899, he married Lady Margaret Primrose, daughter of the fifth Earl of Rosebery. The well-known portrait of her as a child by Millais—'Lady Peggy Primrose'—hangs at West Horsley Place, near Leatherhead, a residence which he acquired in 1931. They had two children, a son who died at the age of eleven, and a daughter.

He received the honorary degrees of

D.C.L., Oxford (1912) and Durham (1919), and of LL.D., Liverpool (1909), Leeds (1910), and Cambridge (1911). He was lord lieutenant of the county of London (1912–44), an elder brother of Trinity House, and chancellor of Sheffield University (1918–44). Crewe died at West Horsley Place, Leatherhead, 20 June 1945, after serenely bearing a long and painful illness. His peerages became extinct.

The best portrait of Crewe is one by Walter Osborne in the National Portrait Gallery. There are drawings by Bakst and Sir William Rothenstein at West Horsley Place.

[*The Times*, 21 June 1945; personal knowledge.]                                        SIMON.

[James Pope-Hennessy, *Lord Crewe*, 1955.]

CRIPPS, CHARLES ALFRED, first BARON PARMOOR (1852–1941), lawyer and politician, was born at West Ilsley, Berkshire, 3 October 1852, the third son and sixth of the eleven children of Henry William Cripps, a well-known ecclesiastical lawyer who was for many years chancellor of the diocese of Oxford, by his wife and cousin, Julia, daughter of Charles Lawrence [q.v.]. Cripps went as a scholar to Winchester and to New College, Oxford, where his academic career was brilliant. He obtained four first classes: in mathematical moderations (1872), in history (1874), in jurisprudence (1875), and in civil law (1876); he played for the university at Association football. He was elected in 1876 to an open fellowship at St. John's College which he resigned on his marriage in 1881. He was elected an honorary fellow of New College in 1919.

Cripps, not greatly attracted by academic life, had decided before his marriage to pursue a legal career. In 1876 he had obtained the senior studentship at the Inns of Court and was called to the bar in 1877 by the Middle Temple. In 1890, with Asquith and Haldane both his juniors, he took silk. With his outstanding abilities and his family connexion he quickly acquired a large and lucrative junior practice, having at one time a number of general retainers for the great railway companies before the Railway Commission and parliamentary committees. The famous Manchester Ship Canal case established his reputation as a leading parliamentary junior. In 1881 he had published *A Treatise on the Principles of the Law of Compensation*. He became a bencher of his Inn in 1893 and treasurer

in 1917. Between 1895 and 1914 he was attorney-general to three successive Princes of Wales and in 1908 he was appointed K.C.V.O. In 1904 he was elected a fellow of Winchester College.

In politics Cripps was first regarded as a left-wing Liberal but when the Home Rule split came, much influenced by his brother-in-law L. H. Courtney (later Lord Courtney of Penwith, q.v.), he supported the Liberal Unionists. He was elected Conservative member for the Stroud division of Gloucestershire in 1895 but he lost his seat in 1900. He re-entered Parliament the following year for the Stretford division of Lancashire, but was defeated in 1906. In January 1910 he was returned for his home constituency, the Wycombe division of Buckinghamshire. In his first parliamentary term Cripps was a member of the select committee on the Jameson raid but his main concern throughout his period in Parliament was the championship of Church interests, particularly in education, from the standpoint of an advanced high churchman. On other questions his influence was a moderating one. He supported A. J. Balfour and Lord Lansdowne in the constitutional crisis of 1911 and on two occasions his chairmanship of meetings of Unionist members helped to strengthen their position against the party extremists. Early in 1914 he was raised to the peerage, on Asquith's recommendation, as Baron Parmoor, of Frieth, in the county of Buckingham, and sworn of the Privy Council, being appointed an unpaid member of the Judicial Committee. During the war he did a considerable amount of work as a member and at times as president of the Judicial Committee which then constituted the court of appeal in Admiralty prize cases.

The turning-point in Parmoor's career came in 1914 when from the outset he was opposed to British participation in the war and a principal champion of the conscientious objector. He concerned himself greatly with plans for a future world order and in 1917 publicly supported Lansdowne's peace letter. In March 1918 he opened a very important debate in the House of Lords on the desirability of constituting a League of Nations. After the armistice he became chairman of the 'Fight the Famine Council', the honorary secretary of which he married as his second wife in 1919.

In 1924, in his seventy-second year, Parmoor accepted Ramsay MacDonald's invitation to serve in the first Labour Government as lord president of the Council. It was characteristic that he should have indicated in his letter of acceptance that his principal concern was that the Labour Party should pursue 'a new foreign policy on new lines, substituting friendliness and goodwill for the war spirit'.

Parmoor shared with Lord Haldane the Labour spokesmanship in the House of Lords and he was in addition made specially responsible for League of Nations affairs, being in 1924 chief British representative at the Council and Assembly of the League. He was thus very directly concerned with the negotiations about the Geneva protocol, the possible contribution of which to the cause of peace he rated very highly. But the breaking down of responsibility for foreign policy did not work out smoothly in practice, and Parmoor's relations with the Foreign Office were neither intimate nor uniformly easy. In opposition, Parmoor continued, so far as his health allowed, to act as Labour spokesman in the Lords, and with the formation of the second Labour Government in 1929 he returned to his office as lord president, declining, however, to resume his former responsibility for League affairs. He was contemplating early retirement on grounds of health when the crisis of August 1931 broke upon the Government. He dissented strongly from the policy of Ramsay MacDonald which he condemned as both wrong in itself and based on a misunderstanding of constitutional convention. He then finally withdrew from politics.

In a long and busy life Parmoor maintained an active interest in the running of his farm and in local affairs. He served, like his father before him, as chairman of the Buckinghamshire County Council and of quarter-sessions. Nor did he ever fail to devote much of his time to Church affairs. He was for many years vicar-general of Canterbury (1902–24) and chancellor and vicar-general of York (1900–14). He played a prominent part in the appointment of the Archbishops' Committee on Church and State, and was unanimously chosen first chairman (1920–24) of the House of Laity when the Church Assembly was instituted.

Parmoor was twice married: first, in 1881 to Theresa (died 1893), sixth of the nine gifted daughters of Richard Potter, sometime chairman of the Great Western Railway, of Standish, Gloucestershire, and sister of Beatrice Webb [q.v.]; and secondly, in 1919 to Marian Emily (died 1952), daughter of John Edward Ellis, member of a well-known Quaker family and a former Liberal junior minister. By the first marriage he had four sons and one daughter, the youngest son being Sir (Richard) Stafford Cripps, chancellor of the Exchequer from 1947 to 1950.

A great lawyer and an eminent churchman, Parmoor achieved high office in politics but not the full measure of success which his gifts might have commanded. Never a strong party man, he had neither aptitude nor liking for the arts which win popularity. He was indeed a man of high seriousness of mind and of the highest integrity, who never, least of all in his old age, lost the vision of a more just and a more Christian world. He died at Parmoor, Henley-on-Thames, 30 June 1941, and was succeeded as second baron by his eldest son, Alfred Henry Seddon (born 1882), fellow and sometime bursar of Queen's College, Oxford.

A portrait of Parmoor by Sir John Lavery hangs in the Church House at Westminster. A cartoon by 'Spy' appeared in *Vanity Fair*, 10 April 1902.

[Lord Parmoor, *A Retrospect*, 1936; *The Times* and *Manchester Guardian*, 2 July 1941; personal knowledge.]          N. MANSERGH.

CROFT, HENRY PAGE, first BARON CROFT (1881–1947), politician, was born 22 June 1881 at Fanhams Hall, Ware. He was the second son and youngest of the eight children of Richard Benyon Croft who had resigned a commission in the Royal Navy and joined the business of Henry Page, maltster, of Ware, upon his marriage to Page's only child, Anne Elizabeth. Croft, who was a great-grandson of Sir Richard Croft [q.v.], was educated at Eton, Shrewsbury, and, as a rowing man, at Trinity Hall, Cambridge, which he left without taking a degree in 1902 to go into the family business. He was captivated by Joseph Chamberlain's policy for imperial preference and organized a tariff reform league in Hertfordshire. With a number of friends he formed a secret protectionist 'confederacy' to which—because it was secret—more importance was attached than the inexperience of its members warranted. He contested Lincoln as a protectionist in January 1906, coming bottom of the poll, but splitting his party's vote, so that a free-trade Conservative was unseated. For three years he campaigned vigorously in the Christchurch division of Hampshire, where he was elected by a narrow majority in January 1910. Two years later he published *The Path of Empire*, a brief plea for imperial unity. He remained in the House of Commons for thirty years, carrying the Bournemouth half of his constituency when it was divided in 1918 and retaining the seat thereafter, once (in 1931) by a majority of 29,916.

He had joined the 1st Hertfordshire Volunteer battalion of the Bedfordshire Regiment while an undergraduate. It became the 1st Territorial battalion of the Hertfordshire Regiment; he went to France with it in November 1914, and commanded it in 1915. In 1916 he commanded the 68th Infantry brigade and saw fighting on the Somme. He was appointed C.M.G. in 1915 and was twice mentioned in dispatches. It had, however, been suggested to him by Sir Henry Wilson [q.v.] and others that his duty lay as an advocate of the manpower measures before the House of Commons and in August 1916 he returned home to resume his career as an extreme Conservative back-bencher.

In September 1917 Croft formed, with a few friends, a 'National Party' with a programme of xenophobic imperialism; it ran twenty-three candidates in the general election of 1918, but only Croft and Sir Richard Cooper were successful. They protested with special vigour at the practice of selling honours to provide party funds, and against the Irish settlement. Croft returned to the Conservative fold when Lloyd George fell, and his forceful and absolutely honest personality earned him a baronetcy in the resignation honours in 1924. He was made an honorary brigadier-general in the same year. He now took a leading part in the agitation for tariffs. When in 1926 he became chairman of the Empire Industries Association he made its policy more uncompromisingly protectionist, and turned it into an efficient propaganda organization. He was also chancellor of the Primrose League in 1928–9 and in 1946 grand prior. By 1931 the whole Conservative Party had come to accept a tariff programme which was enacted in 1932.

Croft now became convinced that India was unsuitable for self-government; in October 1934 he came near to persuading his party's annual conference to adopt his view, and he spoke nearly 300 times in Parliament against the Government of India bill, 1935. This brought him into close association with (Sir) Winston Churchill and he was one of the small group of Churchill's friends who discussed defence and foreign policy in the years before the war, although he found himself temporarily estranged from them when he supported the Munich agreement in 1938. He was also a prominent advocate of General Franco throughout the Spanish civil war. In May 1940, on Churchill's recommendation, he was created Baron Croft, of Bournemouth, and became joint parliamentary under-secretary for war, answering for the War Office in the House of Lords. A speech on 4 February 1942 in which he supported, among other weapons, the use of 'pikes' (bayonets fixed to staves) by the Home Guard attracted attention; otherwise he supervised army administration and welfare unobtrusively. He was sworn of the Privy Council in 1945 and resigned with the rest of the Conservative administration in July that year, dying in London 7 December 1947.

He married in 1907 Nancy Beatrice (died 1949), daughter of Sir Robert Hudson (later first Baron) Borwick, and had three daughters and a son, Michael Henry Glendower Page (born 1916), who succeeded him.

[H. P. Croft, *Twenty-Two Months under Fire*, 1917, and (Lord Croft), *My Life of Strife* (in which is reproduced a portrait by P. A. de László), published posthumously, 1949; *The Times*, 9, 10, and 29 December 1947.]

M. R. D. Foot.

CROZIER, WILLIAM PERCIVAL (1879–1944), journalist, was born at Stanhope, Durham, 1 August 1879, the youngest son of the Rev. Richard Crozier, a miner's son who became a Wesleyan Methodist minister, by his wife, Elizabeth Hallimond. He was educated at Manchester Grammar School, was a scholar of Trinity College, Oxford, and obtained first classes in classical moderations (1900) and *literae humaniores* (1902). After a year as a schoolmaster (at Knaresborough) and some months on *The Times* he joined the *Manchester Guardian* under C. P. Scott [q.v.] in 1903. He soon became Scott's right-hand man in charge of the news-gathering and the make-up of the paper. Under his guidance an old-fashioned paper modernized itself to meet the challenge of the 'new journalism'. In 1918 he succeeded Herbert Sidebotham [q.v.] as military critic. In 1919 he declined the editorship of the *Daily News*; in 1921 he became a director of the Manchester Guardian, Ltd. On the death of E. T. Scott (C. P. Scott's son) in April 1932, Crozier succeeded to the editorship which he held until his death.

Crozier, like Sidebotham and J. A. Spender [q.v.], was an instance of the scholar-journalist. He kept up his classical studies; in his scanty leisure he wrote *Letters of Pontius Pilate* (1928), a delicately ironical essay in reconstruction, in imaginary letters to Seneca, of the procuratorship of Judaea, and *The Fates are Laughing* (1945), a novel of Tiberian Rome, completed just before his death. He brought to his journalistic work a remarkable range of exact knowledge, from sport to foreign affairs. He had a flair for new trends and the paper was ahead of most in treating films and broadcasting as seriously as the theatre and music.

As an editor Crozier was distinguished for his close oversight of the paper and for his studied restraint and fairness in comment. He wrote more himself than do most modern editors; his own style was vigorous and concise, strongly tinged by Bunyan and the Bible; and by admonitory notes to his staff he kept up a daily struggle against jargon and verbiage. His outward manner was rather reserved and sceptical; he maintained, but with more detachment, the Liberal policies of C. P. Scott, a brilliant character-sketch of whom he contributed to J. L. Hammond's *C. P. Scott* (1934). He was warmest when his hatred of cruelty was stirred, as by the Nazi persecutions, when he risked his readers' favour by the persistence of his exposures. He was the leading supporter in the daily press of the Jewish national home. Almost his only public associations outside his paper were with the Liberal Party and the university of Manchester.

Crozier married in 1906 Gladys Florence, daughter of George Frederick Baker, draper and furnisher, of Maidstone; they had one son and two daughters. He died in Manchester 16 April 1944.

[*Manchester Guardian*, 17 and 18 April 1944; *The Times*, 17 April 1944; *C. P. Scott, 1846–1932. The Making of the 'Manchester Guardian'*, 1946; personal knowledge.]

A. P. WADSWORTH.

CRUM, WALTER EWING (1865–1944), Coptic scholar, was born at Capelrig, Renfrewshire, 22 July 1865, the eldest son of Alexander Crum, manufacturer, then of Capelrig, later of Thornliebank,

near Glasgow, and Liberal member of Parliament for Renfrewshire from 1880 to 1885, by his wife, Nina, daughter of Alexander Ewing, bishop of Argyll and the Isles. Walter Crum was educated at Eton and at Balliol College, Oxford, where he obtained a second class in modern history in 1888. Failure to obtain a first class was due to his devotion to music; he was a fine violinist and spent in playing hours which should have been given to study. He lamented this in later life, but at the time had some idea of taking up music as a profession.

At Oxford Crum developed an interest in Egyptology, and on leaving proceeded to Paris, where he studied under William Groff and (Sir) Gaston Maspero. In 1890 he went on to Berlin, where he spent nearly three years. He began his studies there under Johann Peter Adolf Erman (whose close friend he became), but on the suggestion of Georg Steindorff decided to specialize on Coptic, which soon became his main preoccupation. As a candidate in 1892 for a post in the department of Egyptian and Assyrian antiquities at the British Museum he was placed first on the list but was rejected on medical grounds. Having sufficient means, Crum made no attempt to obtain any other post but devoted his life and much of his income to Coptic studies. He began early to contribute articles to learned periodicals, and from 1892 to 1909 prepared the annual bibliography of Coptic studies and Christian Egypt for the *Archaeological Report* of the Egypt Exploration Fund (later Society). His first independent volume was *Coptic Ostraca* (1902), published by the Fund. Larger works were the monumental *Catalogue of the Coptic Manuscripts in the British Museum* (1905) and the *Catalogue of the Coptic Manuscripts in the Collection of the John Rylands Library, Manchester* (1909). To *The Monastery of Epiphanius at Thebes*, published by the Metropolitan Museum, New York, in 1926, he contributed the section on the literary material (part 1) and edited the Coptic ostraca and papyri (part 2). He was responsible for the Coptic texts in volume iv of the catalogue of *Greek Papyri in the British Museum* (1910), for the Coptic portion of *Wadi Sarga* (1922), for many texts in the Berlin Museum's *Koptische Urkunden* (1904), and for volume i (1912) of *Koptische Rechtsurkunden des achten Jahrhunderts aus Djême*, a work undertaken in collaboration with Steindorff. He published articles in

German and French, which he wrote with ease, as well as in English.

All this activity was, however, subsidiary to Crum's main purpose, the preparation of a comprehensive Coptic dictionary. He had early realized the need for such a work, and to it for thirty-five years he devoted the major part of his time and much of his resources. It appeared in six parts (1929–39) and at once took rank as the definitive dictionary of the Coptic language. It was completed at Bath where Crum settled in 1927; in its later stages invaluable help was given by Crum's close friend Sir Herbert Thompson [q.v.], who moved to Bath for that purpose.

Remarkably handsome (some Cambridge friends called him 'our Coptic Apollo'), of great nervous force, and abrupt in his movements, Crum was a striking figure in any company. He was naturally shy, and his exceptional ability was matched by great modesty. His interests were many-sided, his reading wide. He was generous of his help, and his high sense of duty, his loyalty, and the thoroughness with which he tackled every problem of scholarship made him the most helpful of colleagues.

Crum received honorary degrees from the universities of Berlin (1910) and Oxford (1937). He was elected F.B.A. in 1931 and was an honorary member of the American Oriental Society and of the American Philosophical Society. He married in 1896 Ella, daughter of the physician Sir Edward Henry Sieveking [q.v.]. They had no children. Crum died suddenly at Bath 18 May 1944.

[*The Times*, 22 May 1944; *Year Book* of the American Philosophical Society, 1944; *Chronique d'Égypte*, vol. xx, 1945; *Journal of Egyptian Archaeology*, vols. xxv and xxx, 1939 and 1944; private information; personal knowledge.]       H. I. BELL.

CRUTTWELL, CHARLES ROBERT MOWBRAY FRASER (1887–1941), historian, was born at Denton, near Harleston, Norfolk, 23 May 1887, the eldest of the three sons of the Rev. Charles Thomas Cruttwell, historian of Roman literature [q.v.], by his wife, Annie Maud, elder daughter of Sir John Robert Mowbray, first baronet [q.v.]. He was educated at Rugby whence he proceeded with an open scholarship in classics and history to the Queen's College, Oxford. After obtaining first classes in classical moderations (1908), *literae humaniores*

(1910), and modern history (1911), he was elected to a fellowship at All Souls (1911) and while in residence there began to teach history as a lecturer at Hertford College (1912). He served from August 1914 as a second lieutenant in the Royal Berkshire Regiment, fighting in France and Belgium during 1915 and 1916 until he was invalided home. In 1918–19 he worked in the military intelligence department of the War Office, and was then (1919) elected to an official fellowship at Hertford College. He soon became one of the busiest members of the university. As statutory commissioner for the university (1923), university lecturer (1926–30), delegate of the University Press, member of the hebdomadal council, and the holder of many other offices, he gave full proof of a decisive, wide-ranging mind and of forcible judgement based upon knowledge both extensive and exact, upon a ready memory, and upon quick insight. In 1930 he was elected principal of Hertford. He unsuccessfully contested Oxford University as a Conservative in 1935.

Although he gave much time to university business and to writing, Cruttwell's strongest interest lay in his college. No questions of critical importance for its policy arose during his time, and he was able to devote himself to the normal concerns of college life. His hospitality to undergraduates was unceasing: he concerned himself with their work, their games, and their future careers: during term at Oxford and in vacation at his little country-house, Vinnicks, near Highclere, Hampshire, he made many close friends among them. The combination of quick but weighty judgement with genuine friendliness and a characteristic half-humorous ferocity of speech won a deep, amused affection from those who came to know him well. He had his prejudices (although misogyny, of which some suspected him, was not among them), and no one had a more vigorous command of picturesque invective; but fairness of mind in decisions of importance was no less characteristic of him than vehement expression of his opinion on persons or affairs. Both in life and in literature he saw clearly and loved the best. Perhaps the warmth of his nature appeared most attractively in his passion for flowers and for country life: he was never happier than at Vinnicks with a friend and a gun.

No doubt Cruttwell will be longest remembered for his *History of the Great War, 1914–1918* (1934, 2nd ed. 1936). It has justly been called a great book, for it has that kind of truth and power which springs from the working of an informed, distinguished mind upon a vast and tragic subject. A short biography of Wellington (1936), a model of critical appreciation, well illustrates Cruttwell's perception of greatness and his refusal to ignore its limitations. A wide and judicious knowledge of modern history appears in all his writings, which include *The Role of British Strategy in the Great War* (Lees Knowles lectures, 1936) and *A History of Peaceful Change in the Modern World* (1937).

In his youth Cruttwell had been a man of strong although rather clumsy physique, but a breakdown of health damaged by war service and further strained by his labours on the *History of the Great War*, led to his resignation of the principalship in 1939. He died at Bristol, after a long and distressing illness, 14 March 1941. He was unmarried.

There is a good portrait of Cruttwell, by his cousin, Grace Cruttwell, at Hertford College.

[*Oxford*, Summer 1941; *Oxford Magazine*, 8 May 1941; private information; personal knowledge.]

ALWYN WINTON: (A. T. P. WILLIAMS.)

CULLEN, WILLIAM (1867–1948), chemist and metallurgist, was born at Shettleston, Glasgow, 18 May 1867, the son of William Cullen and his wife, Margaret Johnston, of Uddingston, Glasgow. He came of a thrifty hard-working family engaged in the woollen industry and was educated at Hutcheson's Grammar School, Glasgow, and the Andersonian (later the Royal Technical) College, Glasgow. There he studied chemistry under William Dittmar and remained as his assistant for five years. Finally, he took a course in metallurgy and mining at the School of Mines in Freiberg, Saxony.

In 1890 he joined Nobel's Explosives Company, Ltd., Glasgow, a connexion which was preserved throughout his active life. For a time he worked with Kynoch's, then a rival explosives firm, and spent over two years at their Arklow factory. He returned to Nobel's in 1900 and was appointed almost immediately manager at the Modderfontein factory of the firm which in 1902 became the British South African Explosives Company. The factory was then the largest explosives works in the world and in this environment Cullen was extremely successful. He became general manager in 1901 and later a director, an office he retained until its successor company, African Explosives and Chemical Industries, Ltd., was formed in 1924. Technically, his work was mainly concerned with the development of smokeless powders and the design of plant for the convenient manipulation of the plastic mixtures which become the explosive. As Colonel Cullen he returned to England in 1915 and after a short time joined the department of explosives supply of the Ministry of Munitions where he served with his friend, Kenneth Bingham Quinan, C.H., until 1919. Thereafter Cullen found ample interest and activity in consulting work, mainly connected with explosives and gold-mining, in serving as director of several public companies, and in the work of the various scientific societies which commanded his attention.

Cullen's arrival in the Transvaal in the middle of the South African war gave him opportunities for service which he did not fail to render, and there is little doubt that he played a part, if only a modest one, in the settlement of the South African provinces into the Union and the Empire. He liked to think of himself as something of a pioneer in the Rhodes tradition, as indeed he was, and he was extremely proud of his lifelong friendship with J. C. Smuts [q.v.] whom he greatly admired. He knew every public personage in South Africa over many years. Gold to him meant the Witwatersrand. In his day mining conditions were bad and silicosis was a scourge. Cullen did great work in promoting good health conditions underground. This activity aroused in him an interest in education for which he worked assiduously through organizations which ultimately developed into the university of the Witwatersrand from which he received the honorary degree of LL.D. in 1924. In England he was a British representative of the university to which he gave distinguished service, not least in organizing a successful appeal for books for the university library to replace those lost in the disastrous fire on Christmas Eve 1931.

In South Africa he was active in the then newly formed scientific societies and was president for two years (1905–6) of the Chemical, Metallurgical and Mining Society. He was also secretary of the South African Association for the Advancement of Science, and the first chairman of the South African Red Cross Society with the foundation of which his name is closely identified. His first wife became head of the South African Red Cross Society in Britain and was awarded the O.B.E. for her services. Cullen also served in the Johannesburg Mounted Rifles of which he was for two years second-in-command; and for eight years he commanded the regiment of Imperial Light Horse; at one time he was invited to command all the mounted troops in the Transvaal.

In England he rendered distinguished service in various capacities to the professional bodies of which he was a member, notably the Institution of Mining and Metallurgy of which he was president (1929-30), the Royal Institute of Chemistry, the Institution of Chemical Engineers (president, 1937-9), and the Society of Chemical Industry (president, 1941-3, and later an honorary member), with its chemical engineering group. For some years he was honorary treasurer of the Universities Bureau of the British Empire; member of the advisory council on mineral resources and chairman of the consultative committee on base metals, both at the Imperial Institute. Anything touching the Empire claimed his instant attention and he wrote many papers and gave many addresses on Empire matters. His interest in education never flagged and took varied forms: for many years, up to a few months before his death, he was a member of Surrey Education Committee and particularly concerned himself with 'further education'. He was president of the Science Masters' Association in 1944.

Cullen was twice married: first, in 1897 to Jean Crichton Maclachlan (died 1945), by whom he had three sons and one daughter; secondly, in 1946 to Agnes Campbell Macmillan, who survived him when he died in Edinburgh 14 August 1948.

[Private information; personal knowledge.]
L. A. JORDAN.

CURTIN, JOHN (1885-1945), prime minister of Australia, was born 8 January 1885 at Creswick, Victoria, the son of John Curtin, a policeman, and his wife, Katherine, daughter of John Bourke, a farmer who was born in county Cork, Ireland, and later emigrated to Australia.

Curtin received his early education at State schools and thereafter began work as a printer's devil on a small country newspaper. Later he was employed in potteries and in a canister factory. From early youth he was interested in Labour politics,

and he served from 1911 to 1915 as secretary of the Victorian branch of the Timber Workers' Union in Melbourne. During the war of 1914-18 he opposed conscription, relinquishing his office in the Timber Workers' Union to become secretary of the Anti-Conscription League. His activities led to his serving a sentence of imprisonment. In 1917 he turned to journalism and became editor of the *Westralian Worker*, a Labour weekly paper, at Perth until in 1928 he was elected to the House of Representatives of the Commonwealth as Labour member for Fremantle, a seat which he held continuously, except for a period from 1931 to 1934, until his death in 1945.

Although the Labour Party was in office under the prime-ministership of James Henry Scullin from 1929 to 1931, Curtin had no place in the ministry, but he was a respected back-bencher. It was something of a surprise, therefore, when in 1935 he was elected, in preference to Mr. Francis Michael Forde, to succeed Scullin as leader of his party, then in opposition in the Commonwealth Parliament. It fell to his lot, on the outbreak of war in 1939, to declare his party's position, and he did not hesitate to pledge its full support in the fight against Germany, although he refused, in accordance with the rules of his party, to join in a coalition Government. When on 3 October 1941 (Sir) Arthur William Fadden's ministry was defeated in the House on a vote of censure, Curtin was called upon to take office and had scarcely had time to organize his ministry before Japan entered the war on 7 December 1941. Curtin realized Australia's serious plight, with British forces already heavily engaged in the Middle East, and he did not hesitate to say in a New Year message that he looked to the United States for aid 'free of any pangs as to our traditional links or kinship with the United Kingdom'. The statement came as a shock to some people in Australia and in the other nations of the British Commonwealth, the more especially as Australia had chosen to make a separate declaration of war upon Japan in 1941, instead of entering, as she had in 1939 against Germany, by virtue of the British declaration. Curtin was misunderstood. He believed fully in the value of the British Commonwealth, but he knew also that it alone could not save Australia in those terrible weeks when the Japanese forces moved steadily southward. He recognized and stated a fact when he declared Australia's dependence on the United States.

In the years that followed Curtin proved himself a great leader of the Australian people. He did not hesitate, in spite of his previous history, to introduce a measure of conscription in Australia, although he and his party did not go so far as some would have wished. In the years from 1941 to 1943 he was confronted with certain parliamentary difficulties. His Cabinet was inexperienced—only four of them had held office in Scullin's Government. His party lacked a majority in the Senate and was sometimes in trouble in the House where he was dependent upon the votes of the independent members and where in June 1943 his ministry escaped defeat on a motion of censure by one vote only. At the general election in August 1943, however, he obtained a great victory, and for the first time since 1914 the Labour Party had a majority in both Houses. Curtin visited London in 1944 to attend the conference of prime ministers of the British Commonwealth. In November, while travelling home from Canberra to Perth, he became ill at Melbourne, and, although he recovered and was able to resume his duties, he developed congestion of the lungs in March 1945, and, after a serious set-back in June, died at the prime minister's lodge in Canberra, 5 July 1945, just about a month before Japan sued for peace. Although Curtin was of Roman Catholic parentage, he joined the Rationalist Association in later life, but at his funeral at Karrakatta cemetery, Perth, the Presbyterian minister of Canberra participated in the service.

Curtin was a man of frail physique, and a defect of vision impaired the impressiveness of his appearance. He was, however, a man of great sincerity and force of character, and his leadership of Australia in the most critical years of her history won the respect of all parties in the country. He asserted strongly the right of Australia to be consulted in the decisions which were taken about the conduct of the war in the Pacific and, although grateful for American help, he did not hesitate to affirm that Australia must be treated as a partner and not as a satellite. With many thousands of American troops on Australian soil and the flamboyant personality of General Douglas MacArthur in command, Curtin had many problems of political and social adjustment to deal with. He urged that there should be closer association and consultation between the members of the British Commonwealth; and at a speech in Adelaide early in 1944 before he came to Britain he spoke in favour of a Commonwealth secretariat or council which could make co-operation and consultation more of a reality. Curtin advocated this policy because he believed that it would give Australia greater rather than less opportunity to express her views and make her equality of status effective in practice. His proposals were not acceptable to other members of the Commonwealth and he had, in particular, to agree to differ, as he said, with W. L. Mackenzie King [q.v.], the prime minister of Canada.

Curtin was nominated to the Privy Council in 1942. He had visited Europe in 1924 when he attended the conference of the International Labour Organization at Geneva as a nominee of the Australian Labour Party. He married in 1917 Elsie, daughter of Abraham Needham, a trade-union official and Labour politician in Western Australia. They had one son and one daughter. A portrait of Curtin by Dattilo Rubo hangs in Parliament House, Canberra.

[*The Times*, 5 July 1945; *Sydney Morning Herald*, 6 July 1945.]    K. C. WHEARE.

CURTIS, EDMUND (1881–1943), historian, the fifth child of Francis Curtis, of Rathmullen, county Donegal, by his wife, Elizabeth Elliott, of Belfast was born 25 March 1881 at Bury, Lancashire, whither his parents had emigrated. At fifteen years of age he was working, much against the grain, in a rubber factory at Silvertown, east London, and voicing his melancholy in verses of which a selection found their way into the weekly press. The resulting publicity brought him two benefactors, through whose generosity he was sent to Allhallows School, Honiton, where one of them, the Rev. Cecil Grant, was an assistant master. Curtis proved a rewarding pupil, and when Grant, in 1898, became headmaster of a new co-educational boarding-school at Keswick, he took Curtis with him as head boy. In 1900 Curtis went to Keble College, Oxford, as a commoner, and gained a first class in modern history four years later.

As history lecturer at Sheffield (1905–14) Curtis published *Roger of Sicily* (1912) and became recognized as a medieval scholar. He had frequently visited Ireland, and had acquired a working knowledge of Irish, when in 1914 he was appointed professor of modern history at Trinity College, Dublin. Here his genius found full scope, and in his twenty-nine remaining years (the last four as Lecky professor), he made an outstanding contribution to Irish history. Combining erudition with independence of judgement, appreciative alike of Gaelic and of Anglo-Norman civilization and familiar with the historical sources for both, Gaelic-nationalist in sympathy but none the less proud of his Protestant and 'planter' ancestry, and a warm admirer of English character and institutions, he had an unusual blend of qualities for an Irish historian. It is true that he worked too much in isolation, taking too little cognizance of current research, and that he neglected social and institutional history; his writing is structurally weak and not always accurate in detail; his editing of documents has serious technical deficiencies. But he had the merits of a pioneer. His *History of Medieval Ireland* (1923, 2nd, enlarged, ed. 1938) is an achievement of bold and original scholarship in a peculiarly complex field. His outline *History of Ireland* (1936), the most successful survey of the kind which has appeared, is illuminated by his judgements on the leading personalities and issues of Irish history. His *Calendar of Ormond Deeds* (6 vols., 1932–43) has unlocked the treasures of the greatest collection of medieval manuscripts in Ireland. These and numerous lesser works entitle Curtis to be ranked among the foremost modern historians of Ireland.

Curtis married in 1918 Margaret Louise, daughter of Richard Barrington, of the Royal Irish Constabulary. The marriage was dissolved. There were no children.

Although pensive and solitary, Curtis was well endowed with social gifts, was a memorable talker, and had a large circle of acquaintances. He died in Dublin 25 March 1943, and is buried in the Protestant churchyard at Malahide.

[*Hermathena*, May 1944; *Irish Historical Studies*, September 1943 (bibliography); *Analecta Hibernica*, March 1946; personal knowledge.]      T. W. MOODY.

D'ABERNON, VISCOUNT (1857–1941), financier and diplomatist. [See VINCENT, SIR EDGAR.]

DAFOE, JOHN WESLEY (1866–1944), Canadian journalist, was born near Combermere in the Ottawa valley, Ontario, 8 March 1866, the eldest son of a pioneer farmer, Calvin Dafoe, by his wife, Mary Ann, daughter of John Elcome, farmer, of Bangor, Ontario. He was educated at local schools and was a country teacher from the age of fifteen until in 1883 he secured employment as a reporter on the *Montreal Star*, whose editor, Hugh Graham (later Lord Atholstan, q.v.), gave him a sound training in his craft. It was as parliamentary correspondent of the *Star* that he made his reputation as a competent journalist and, after a brief but unsuccessful interlude as the first editor of the *Ottawa Journal*, he broadened his experience by six years' work on the staff of the Winnipeg *Free Press*. From 1892 to 1895 he was editor of the *Montreal Herald* and in the latter year he rejoined the editorial staff of the *Montreal Star*.

Meanwhile Dafoe had abandoned the Conservative faith in which he had been reared for an ardent Liberalism and his abilities had impressed (Sir) Clifford Sifton (whose notice he later contributed to this DICTIONARY) so much that when that prominent Liberal politician acquired control of the Winnipeg *Free Press* in 1901 he provided Dafoe with his real life-work by appointing him its editor. His wide knowledge of politics and economics, his immense powers of industry, and his large funds of courage and imagination were an admirable equipment for this post and, when he developed in it a lucid and vigorous style of writing and enlisted as his assistants a group of able writers, he made his editorial page the best in Canada. The progressive development of western Canada made the *Free Press* a prosperous paper but he took more pride in its attaining a position comparable to that enjoyed by the *Manchester Guardian* in Britain as an exponent of Liberal ideas and doctrines.

A crisis in Dafoe's fortunes occurred in 1911, when he refused to conform to the wishes of the owner of the *Free Press*, who wanted it to support his own opposition to the Taft–Fielding reciprocity treaty, but he emerged from it with full control of the editorial policy of his paper. The loyalty thus displayed to Sir Wilfrid Laurier [q.v.] ended, however, in 1917, when the latter opposed military conscription. Dafoe's attitude was a decisive factor in securing Liberal support for the coalition ministry formed by Sir Robert Borden [q.v.] which enforced conscription.

In the years between the two wars, after the Liberal Party was rejuvenated under the leadership of W. L. Mackenzie

King [q.v.], Dafoe gave it independent support, tempered by severe criticisms of its foreign policy. In this period his two dominant interests, for which he conducted persistent crusades, lay in the achievement of full nationhood for Canada and in the firm establishment of collective security through the League of Nations. The failure of the second of these causes to prosper made him a violent critic of the policies of British ministries from 1930 onwards and he was freely, but unfairly, accused of being anti-British. But, when war broke out in 1939, he ranged his paper enthusiastically behind the national war effort and no editor did more to sustain the morale of the Canadian people during the darkest days of the struggle. When the attack on the United States in 1941 assured the eventual defeat of the Axis, he relaxed his editorial labours, but he rejected all suggestions about retirement on a pension and worked until he died at Winnipeg after a short illness 9 January 1944.

Dafoe, a large, powerfully built man with shaggy red hair, was a notable personality in any company, and no Canadian public figure of his day had a more powerful intellect. He was greatly beloved by his staff and he was at his best socially when he shed his normal editorial austerity in a gathering of old friends and gave free play to his keen sense of humour. His determination to live and die a journalist caused him to reject offers of Cabinet office and a high diplomatic post and he refused a knighthood, proffered in 1919 as reward for his services as Canada's chief press representative at the peace conference. From 1937 to 1939 he rendered useful public service as a member of a Royal Commission on dominion-provincial relations and he was chancellor of the university of Manitoba from 1934 until his death.

Most of Dafoe's writing is buried in the files of the Winnipeg *Free Press* but he also wrote a number of interesting books— *Over the Canadian Battlefields* (1919), *Laurier: a study in Canadian Politics* (1922), *Clifford Sifton in Relation to his Times* (1931), *Canada, an American Nation* (1935), and edited *Canada Fights* (1941). He was elected a fellow of the Royal Society of Canada in 1926 and the universities of Manitoba, Queen's, Alberta, and British Columbia conferred honorary degrees upon him.

In 1890 Dafoe married Alice, daughter of William G. Parmelee, of Ottawa, deputy minister of customs and excise. They had three sons and four daughters. A portrait of Dafoe by Sir E. Wyly Grier hangs in the office of the *Free Press* at Winnipeg.

[G. V. Ferguson, *Life of Dafoe*, Toronto, 1948; *Proceedings* of the Royal Society of Canada, 1944; private information; personal knowledge.]     J. A. STEVENSON.

DALTON, ORMONDE MADDOCK (1866–1945), classical scholar and medieval archaeologist, was born at Cardiff 3 January 1866, the second of the three sons of Thomas Masters Dalton, solicitor, by his wife, Emily Mansford. From Harrow he won an exhibition at New College, Oxford, where he obtained a first class in classical moderations (1886) and in *literae humaniores* (1888). He then travelled in France and Germany, visited a brother's coffee plantation at North Coorg in India, and in 1894 taught at Abbotsholme School in Derbyshire. In 1895 he entered the department of British and medieval antiquities at the British Museum under Sir A. W. Franks [q.v.] and was promoted first class assistant in 1901 and assistant (later called deputy) keeper in 1909. In 1921 Dalton became keeper of British and medieval antiquities when that very heterogeneous collection was separated from ceramics, ethnography, and oriental antiquities.

In the British Museum Dalton's first duties were ethnographical. He collaborated with (Sir) C. H. Read [q.v.] in *Antiquities from the City of Benin* (1899) and with Thomas Athol Joyce in the *Handbook to the Ethnographical Collections* (1910). He became a fellow of the Royal Anthropological Institute in 1895, was honorary secretary and editor of its *Journal* from 1896 to 1897, and contributed to its publications. He was elected a fellow of the Society of Antiquaries in 1899, served four times on its council, and contributed important articles to *Archaeologia*; he was elected F.B.A. in 1922. But Dalton's interest changed from ethnology to archaeology with his *Catalogue of Early Christian Antiquities and Objects from the Christian East . . . in the British Museum* (1901), the official *Guide to the Early Christian and Byzantine Antiquities* (1903, 2nd ed. 1921), and his account of the *Treasure of the Oxus* (1905, 2nd ed. 1926) which had been acquired through Franks. He was one of the secretaries (with Robert Weir Schultz) of the Byzantine Research and Publication Fund which produced *The Church of the*

*Nativity at Bethlehem* (1910), *The Church of Saint Eirene at Constantinople* (1913), and the *Church of Our Lady of the Hundred Gates* (1920), by various authors, and collected much still unpublished material. Dalton's *Guide to the Mediaeval Room* (1907, which in 1924 appeared in a revised form as the *Guide to the Mediaeval Antiquities and Objects of Later Date*), the *Catalogue of the Ivory Carvings of the Christian Era* (1909), papers on the great Cyprus treasure of silver plate (*Archaeologia*, vol. lvii, part 1, 1900, and vol. lx, part 1, 1906; *Burlington Magazine*, March 1907), and the catalogue of the McClean Bequest in the Fitzwilliam Museum (1912), were followed by the *Catalogue of the Engraved Gems of the Post-Classical Periods . . . in the British Museum* (1915). But his most distinguished work is *Byzantine Art and Archaeology* (1911), an encyclopaedic survey of all fields of craftsmanship except architecture. This omission was repaired in his translation (with Mr. Hermann Justus Braunholtz) of Strzygowski's *Origin of Christian Church Art* (1923), and in *East Christian Art. A Survey* (1925). Other interests are represented by a translation (with introduction) of the *Letters of Sidonius* (2 vols., 1915), a translation (with long introduction) of the *History of the Franks* by Gregory of Tours (2 vols., 1927), and an uncompleted version of the Dialogues and Letters of Sulpicius Severus.

Inveterate shyness limited Dalton's activities outside the British Museum, but at Bath, where he retired in 1928, he was an assiduous host. Glimpses of his inner life are afforded by three books published under the pseudonym of W. Compton Leith (*Apologia Diffidentis*, 1908, *Sirenica*, 1913, and *Domus Doloris*, 1919), certainly his, although never fully acknowledged. The third resulted from a painful accident which ended his war work for the Admiralty. In official life, however, he was courteous and kindly, a skilful collector and critic, of boundless industry and learning.

In 1940 Dalton moved to his cottage at Holford in the Quantocks, where he acquired unspoiled land and transferred it to the National Trust. There he died, unmarried, 2 February 1945, leaving his estate to New College to found a research scholarship.

[Sir George Hill in *Proceedings* of the British Academy, vol. xxxi, 1945; personal knowledge.]                                   JOHN L. MYRES.

DANE, SIR LOUIS WILLIAM (1856–1946), Indian civil servant, was born 21 March 1856 at Chichester where his father, Richard Martin Dane, was an army staff surgeon; he later became an inspector-general of hospitals. Dane's mother was Sophia Eliza, daughter of Colonel Charles Griffiths who served in the 'army of the Indus' under Sir John (later Lord) Keane [q.v.] in the first Afghan war, and granddaughter of Henry Griffiths, a close friend in India of Warren Hastings. The Dane family had long dwelt in Fermanagh and, although Dr. Dane moved to England, he nevertheless sent Louis, who was his fifth son, and an elder brother, (Sir) Richard Morris Dane, to Kingstown School, Dublin, whence in turn they entered the Indian Civil Service. Louis passed the examination in 1874 and in 1876 was posted to the Punjab. As assistant commissioner in Dera Ghazi Khan he ensured supplies for the Pishin Column in the second Afghan war (1878–80). In 1879 he became private secretary to Sir Robert Egerton, lieutenant-governor of the Punjab. After good work as settlement officer, Gurdaspur, a post which his brother held before him, he was appointed chief secretary to the Punjab Government in 1898. In 1900 he went on leave and seemed to have ended his Indian career, for he became resident magistrate of Tralee, county Kerry.

In November 1901, however, he was recalled to India by Lord Curzon [q.v.] to become resident of Kashmir, and in March 1903 foreign secretary in the Government of India. Curzon was especially concerned over Afghan affairs. In 1901 Amir Habibullah had succeeded his father, Abdur Rahman, whose reign of twenty years had been marked by friendship with India, although at its end certain issues were unsettled. In October 1904 Dane headed a mission to Kabul where his fine personality, unshakeable good humour, and fluency in Persian gained the young Amir's respect. But negotiations were too protracted for the forceful viceroy who wanted to withdraw the mission. Dane, boldly dissenting, held that the Amir's renewal of his father's engagements should be accepted as sufficient. The Cabinet in London supported Dane and the treaty was signed in March 1905. Dane, who had been appointed C.S.I. in 1904, was now made a K.C.I.E. The value of his achievement was more clearly appreciated in the war of 1914–18 when, despite persistent German pressure, Habibullah maintained his country's neutrality in the face of domestic dangers which were tragically underlined by his assassination in 1919.

In 1908 Dane became lieutenant-governor of the Punjab. Facing the rising nationalism of the time, he combined firmness with understanding, laid the foundations of the province's industrial development, and specially encouraged the growth of the canal colonies. His tireless energy in touring his province set a high example to his officers. His linguistic gifts, handsome presence, and charm of manner which was not allowed to overlook the need for forcefulness when occasion demanded, won for him general respect and public confidence. In December 1911 he was called upon to arrange the memorable people's fair at the royal durbar. He was promoted G.C.I.E. and, exactly a year later, had to hand over to the Government of India the Delhi district as part of the enclave of the new capital. The viceroy, Lord Hardinge of Penshurst [q.v.], was seriously wounded on his way to the ceremony which took place nevertheless. In this emergency, Dane, after his formal speech, 'laid aside the typescript', wrote Sir Henry Sharp, 'and began to talk [in Urdu] . . . It swept through the audience like a strong wind. Formality melted in emotion.' In May 1913 Dane's successful rule of the Punjab ended and he retired to London. In 1914 his portrait, painted by John St. Helier Lander, was hung in the Lawrence Hall, Lahore.

After his retirement Dane continued to take an active interest in Indian affairs and was for many years on the board of the Attock Oil Company. On 13 March 1940, at a joint meeting of the East India Association and Royal Central Asian Society, he was badly wounded in the arm by the assassin who killed Sir Michael O'Dwyer [q.v.]. He was then nearly eighty-four, and lived to be almost ninety, dying in London 22 February 1946.

In 1882 Dane married Edith (died 1948), daughter of (Sir) Francis Booth Norman [q.v.]. They had four daughters and three sons, the youngest of whom, Henry, died in captivity in Japan in 1942 and was posthumously appointed to the D.S.O. in 1946.

[Burke's Landed Gentry of Ireland, 1912; private information; personal knowledge.]
EDWIN HAWARD.

DASHWOOD, EDMÉE ELIZABETH MONICA (1890–1943), authoress, better known by her pen-name of E. M. DELA-

FIELD, was born 9 June 1890 at Steyning, Sussex, the elder daughter of Count Henry Philip Ducarel de la Pasture, of Llandogo Priory, Monmouthshire, a member of a noble family which settled in England after the French revolution, by his wife, Elizabeth Lydia Rosabelle, daughter of Edward William Bonham, who, as Mrs. Henry de la Pasture, became known as a novelist. The girlhood of E. M. Delafield was spent in the last days of the Edwardian era, and that formal sheltered society is reproduced with dry fidelity in many of her books. At the outbreak of war in 1914 she became a member of a voluntary aid detachment in Exeter, and there, in snatched moments, wrote her first novel, *Zella Sees Herself*, which was published in 1917. At the end of the war she was working for the south-western region of the Ministry of National Service, at Bristol; and after two years in the Malay States she and her husband, Major A. P. Dashwood, settled at Cullompton in Devonshire, where Mrs. Dashwood became a magistrate, and a great worker for Women's Institutes.

Meanwhile, no year in the 'twenties or 'thirties passed without the publication of one of her books, often several. These were chiefly fiction, but she also wrote three plays, and was probably most widely and popularly known for her humorous sketches. Had her output been less, her literary reputation would have been higher, as it deserved to be; but even her least-considered work is unfailingly readable. Romance and beauty were outside her deliberately narrowed range; what interested her was the mechanism of human behaviour, particularly the phenomena of vanity and self-deception. Her mood suited the decades when the word 'debunking' gained currency, and her plain style fitted the unsparing common sense and somewhat feline wit of her fiction in general. Perhaps her best novel was *Thank Heaven Fasting* (1932). Typical of her more serious work was *Nothing is Safe* (1937), an indictment of the harm caused to children by easy divorce; and her interest in criminology inspired the earlier *Messalina of the Suburbs* (1923), a reconstruction of a well-known crime. Another hobby, the study of the lesser Victorian novelists, resulted in a book not seen in her list of published works, *The Bazalgettes* (1935), a pastiche of Rhoda Broughton [q.v.] so exact as to deceive many critics. Her gift for mimicry was also evident in her series for *Punch* 'As

Others Hear Us': and pre-eminently in the books which gave her the greatest popularity, *The Diary of A Provincial Lady* (1930) and its sequels. The Provincial Lady appeared originally in *Time and Tide*, of which E. M. Delafield was a director; and this lovable creation, always ready to laugh at herself, presents, in the opinion of friends, a better clue to the gentle and generous personality of the writer than does her more satirical work.

In 1919 she married Major Arthur Paul Dashwood, second surviving son of Sir George Dashwood, sixth baronet. They had one son and one daughter. E. M. Delafield died at Cullompton, Devonshire, 2 December 1943. A portrait painted in 1909 by D. A. Wehrschmidt (later Veresmith) is in the possession of the family.

[*The Times*, 3 December 1943; *Time and Tide*, 11 December 1943.] M. BELLASIS.

DAVID, ALBERT AUGUSTUS (1867–1950), headmaster and bishop, was born in Exeter 19 May 1867, the second son of the Rev. William David, then principal of the Exeter Diocesan Training College for Schoolmasters and later priest-vicar of the cathedral, and his wife, Antonia Altgelt. From Exeter School he was elected to an open classical scholarship at the Queen's College, Oxford, where he was placed in the first class in both classical moderations (1887) and *literae humaniores* (1889). He felt called to the teaching profession and for the next fifteen years gained a wide and varied experience, first as a lecturer at his college, then as assistant master at Bradfield and Rugby, eventually as a fellow and assistant tutor of his college. By 1905 his name in the scholastic field stood so high that he was appointed headmaster of Clifton College. He was well equipped for the task, and the more so since he had already been in holy orders for a number of years, having been ordained deacon in 1894 and priest in 1895. The four years spent at Clifton in surroundings entirely congenial to his temperament and outlook were among the smoothest and most successful of his life. The school flourished, and his keen interest in the activities and government of the great city at its gates—an interest which he also communicated to his boys as a live element in their education—gave him a position of weight in Bristol. The reputation of the school was growing with

that of its headmaster when at the end of 1909 he was selected for the headmastership of Rugby, where the return of an old colleague was welcomed by the staff.

David's aims as a headmaster are set out in a book which he wrote in 1932, *Life and the Public Schools*. He held that the teacher should study boys rather than subjects; and that hitherto too much attention had been concentrated on the clever boys. He maintained that few, if any, boys were stupid, and that there should be a larger measure of controlled freedom in work and a wider choice of occupations for the benefit of the majority. Critics of his ideas and methods there were, of course; but they were conciliated by his patient temper and the sincerity of his beliefs.

By the end of the war in 1918 David, who had proceeded D.D. in 1910, was marked out in popular opinion for high preferment. His capacity as an administrator was proved; he had long been participating in the larger affairs of the Church; his counsel was sought by clerics and laity up and down the country. It was understood that he had declined a bishopric more than once when in 1921 he was consecrated bishop of St. Edmundsbury and Ipswich. In this extensive rural diocese he had barely time to get to know his clergy or to visit more than a proportion of the parishes before he was translated in 1923 to a sphere of a different character to become third bishop of Liverpool.

Here he immediately held out the right hand of fellowship to people of all kinds and all parties in this vast and complex community. The great new cathedral, still unfinished, was consecrated, and he set himself both to draw up its constitution and to devise financial schemes whereby it should eventually be completed. When troubles arose, whether over the extravagant practices of some few of his own clergy, or with the Roman Catholics, he showed patience, moderation, and dignity in resolving them. His personal relations with the Roman Catholic archbishop remained unimpaired. In his practical devotion to the cause of reunion he was wont to give permission, as a bishop is entitled to do, for Free Church ministers to speak in Anglican churches. When, however, on one occasion, through some misunderstanding, a prominent Unitarian preached in the cathedral at a statutory service, extensive protests were raised, and the bishop, accepting responsibility, submitted with characteristic grace to reproof from the archbishop in provincial synod. In 1935, his health being impaired by the burdens and anxieties of his office, he made a voyage to Australia, whence he returned refreshed and with a wider vision of the opportunities of the Church in the Empire. After raising a sum of £85,000 for the diocese, he retired in 1944. He was elected an honorary fellow of the Queen's College, Oxford, in 1920, and received the honorary degree of D.D. from Glasgow University in 1937.

A tall, impressive figure, lucid and concise in speech, he was a courageous bishop and a humble man of heart. There are portraits of him by H. G. Riviere at Clifton and by Sir Walter Russell at Rugby, and a bronze by Lady Kennet at Diocesan House, Liverpool.

In 1909 David married Edith Mary, daughter of the late Thomas William Miles, of the Public Works Department, India. She, and the three sons and one daughter of the marriage, survived him when he died at Trebetherick, Cornwall, 24 December 1950.

[*The Times*, 27 December 1950; personal knowledge.]      H. COSTLEY-WHITE.

DAVIES, DAVID, first BARON DAVIES (1880–1944), public benefactor, was born 11 May 1880 at Llwynderw, Llandinam, the only son of Edward Davies and his wife, Mary, daughter of the Rev. Evan Jones, of Llandinam. He was educated at Merchiston Castle, Edinburgh, and King's College, Cambridge, where he was placed in the third and second classes respectively of parts i and ii of the historical tripos (1901, 1903). Rooted in the puritanism of rural Wales, and endowed with a vigorous mind and body, Davies inherited many of the qualities as well as the wealth of his grandfather, David Davies, who had amassed a large fortune by railway construction, coal-mining in the Rhondda, and building docks at Barry. Edward Davies died in 1898 after some years of failing health, and his son early acquired a firm grasp of his industrial responsibilities to which later in life he added directorships of the Great Western Railway Company and the Midland Bank.

Davies was soon drawn into a life of public service which centred mainly upon Wales. He was a member of the councils of the university colleges and of the university court, and from 1926 president and chairman of the council of the University College at Aberystwyth. He was from the beginning closely involved in the project of founding a National Library of Wales at Aberystwyth, and he was its president from 1927. In 1911, breaking new ground, he founded with an initial gift of £150,000 the King Edward VII Welsh National Memorial Association to combat the ravages of tuberculosis in Wales, and as its president until his death he succeeded in uniting all the public bodies in Wales in its support. He endowed research centres at Cardiff and in 1921 the David Davies chair of tuberculosis at the Welsh National School of Medicine. Before his death the mortality rate from tuberculosis in Wales had been more than halved. The Presbyterian Church in Wales was also well aided, especially by the foundation of a theological college at Aberystwyth. New housing estates in various centres in Wales were another valuable interest. Much of this munificence was quietly carried out by Davies in partnership with his stepmother and sisters. He also in 1922 resuscitated the Royal Welsh Agricultural Society and was its chairman until his death. He received the honorary degree of LL.D. from the university of Wales in 1913 and the freedom of Cardiff in 1931.

In 1906 Davies became Liberal member of Parliament for Montgomeryshire, but he was never closely bound by party ties. He intervened rarely in debate and never attained ease in public speaking. Appointed to command the 14th Royal Welsh Fusiliers in 1914 he proved himself a strenuous officer, but was recalled from France in June 1916 to become parliamentary private secretary to Lloyd George, and in January 1917 he accompanied Lord Milner [q.v.] on his mission to Russia. Although Davies supported Lloyd George against Asquith in the conduct of the war, he was faithfully unsparing in comment and criticism; this proved unwelcome and Lloyd George dismissed him abruptly in June 1917. To Davies party politics were of less importance than the need for an effort on a world basis to make war impossible again, and towards the end of the war he interested himself in the possibility of a League of Nations, becoming later a founder and trustee of the League of Nations Union and permanent chairman of its Welsh council. He endowed at Aberystwyth the Wilson chair of international politics, and in 1929 he gave up his seat in the House in order to devote more time to international affairs, being raised to the peerage as Baron Davies, of Llandinam, in 1932. He had come to the conclusion that there could be no prospect of permanent peace without an international police force, and to that end he founded the New Commonwealth movement in 1932. His ideals for peace were pursued relentlessly in speech and writing. He acquired control of the National Press Agency, the *Review of Reviews*, *Everyman*, and some local newspapers. In addition to numerous articles and popular booklets he published in 1930 *The Problem of the Twentieth Century* and in 1934 *Force*.

Davies did not, however, forget earlier commitments. In 1938 at a cost of £65,000 he provided the Temple of Peace and Health at Cardiff as an administrative centre for the Welsh League of Nations Union and the King Edward VII Welsh National Memorial Association. A retentive memory, developed, in his view, by learning verse, including hymns and the poetry of Adam Lindsay Gordon [q.v.], helped him at any time to pick up old threads. He was pre-eminently the public-spirited Welshman of his age, gifted with a considerable capacity to take a distant view. But he was prone to rely on his wealth to achieve results and did not always realize that there are problems which admit of no short cuts. In much that he set out to do he could be imperious and impatient and he was perhaps (as Elizabeth Barrett Browning once described an acquaintance) 'notable for kindness and terribleness'. From early youth Davies pursued all field sports; in his younger days he travelled widely, frequently on big-game hunting expeditions, and he kept hounds at Llandinam.

In 1910 Davies married Amy (died 1918), daughter of L. T. Penman, of Broadwood Park, Lanchester, by whom he had one daughter who died in infancy and one son David, known as Michael (born 1915), who succeeded him as second baron and was killed shortly afterwards in Holland in September 1944. In 1922 Davies married Henrietta Margaret (died 1948), daughter of James Grant Fergusson, of Baledmund, Pitlochry. They had two sons and two daughters. Davies died at Llandinam 16 June 1944. The National Library of Wales has a bust by Sir W. Goscombe John and a portrait by Murray Urquhart; the National Museum of Wales has a portrait by S. Morse Brown. A portrait by Augustus John is at Berthddu, Llandinam.

[Personal knowledge.]
WYNN P. WHELDON.

DAVIES, SIR (HENRY) WALFORD (1869–1941), musician, was born at Oswestry 6 September 1869, the seventh child and fourth surviving son of John Whitridge Davies, who founded and conducted a choral society there, and was choirmaster of the Congregational church. His wife, Susan, was the daughter of Thomas Gregory, jeweller, of Oswestry. In 1882 Walford Davies was admitted a chorister at St. George's chapel, Windsor, by the organist, Sir George Elvey [q.v.]. When his voice broke, he became organist of the royal chapel of All Saints, Windsor Great Park, pupil assistant to (Sir) Walter Parratt (Elvey's successor), and secretary to Dean (afterwards Archbishop) Randall Davidson [qq.v.]. In 1890 he was awarded an open scholarship for composition at the Royal College of Music, (Sir) Hubert Parry [q.v.] becoming his teacher for that subject. During this period he was organist of St. George's church, Campden Hill, for three months, and St. Anne's church, Soho, for one year, resigning the latter appointment owing to illness. In the following year he became organist of Christ Church, Hampstead, and in 1895 was appointed teacher of counterpoint at the Royal College of Music, a post which he held until 1903, returning again as superintendent of the choir training class from 1910 to 1916. He proceeded Mus.D. (Cambridge) in 1898.

In the same year Davies succeeded E. J. Hopkins [q.v.] as organist of the Temple Church. For the next twenty-one years the music of this church was his chief concern and its services, already famous for their music, attracted a large congregation. His principal innovation was the monthly 'cantata service', which included Bach's cantatas, the Passion music, and the Christmas Oratorio at their appropriate seasons. He conducted the London Bach Choir from 1902 to 1907, and the London Church Choirs' Association annual festivals in St. Paul's Cathedral from 1901 to 1913. In 1915 he organized concerts for troops, and compiled and edited the *Fellowship Song Book*. Three years later he became musical director to the Royal Air Force with the rank of major and in 1919 he was appointed O.B.E. In the same year he accepted the professorship of music at University

College, Aberystwyth, and with it the post of director of music and chairman of the National Council of Music for the university of Wales. Here he laboured unceasingly for the musical enlightenment of the principality, and in 1922, on Lloyd George's retirement from office, he was knighted. He finally ended his connexion with the Temple in 1923. In 1924 he gave the Cramb lectures at Glasgow, broadcast for the first time from Savoy Hill, and was appointed Gresham professor of music in the university of London. He resigned his professorship at Aberystwyth in 1926, but retained his chairmanship of the National Council of Music until his death. He was organist and director of the choir of St. George's chapel, Windsor, from 1927 to 1932, and in the latter year was appointed C.V.O. On the death of Sir Edward Elgar [q.v.] in 1934, he was appointed master of the King's musick. In the following year he organized the remarkable jubilee concert in the Royal Albert Hall, which brought singers from all over the United Kingdom to sing British music in the presence of King George V and Queen Mary. He took a prominent part in arranging the music for the coronation of King George VI, and was promoted K.C.V.O. in 1937. At the outbreak of hostilities in 1939 he removed to Bristol with the British Broadcasting Corporation to which he had been a musical adviser since 1926. He was a member of C.E.M.A. which later became the Arts Council. He died at Wrington, near Bristol, 11 March 1941, and was buried in the graveyard of Bristol Cathedral. His elder brother, Edward Harold Davies, who had for many years been professor of music in the university of Adelaide and director of music at the Elder Conservatorium, died in 1947.

Davies's creative work had made its mark while he was still a student at the Royal College of Music. From 1902 to 1912 he contributed important works for solo voices, chorus, and orchestra for several of the principal festivals, including a cantata (Leeds, 1904) founded upon the old morality play *Everyman*, which remains his most important and best-known work on a large scale, and the 'Song of St. Francis' (Birmingham, 1912). Of his smaller works, the songs and the 'Six Pastorals' for vocal quartet, strings, and piano (1897) have a delicacy and charm all their own. His love of children is well illustrated in the 'Four Songs of Innocence' (1900), in the 'Nursery Rhymes' for vocal quartet (1905 and 1909), the 'Sacred

Lullabies' (1909), and the 'Peter Pan' Suite for string quartet (1909). The well-known and popular 'Solemn Melody' for organ and strings, originally written for the Milton tercentenary celebrations, was produced at a Promenade concert in 1908.

As organist, choirmaster, and composer Davies's influence on the church music of his generation was conspicuous. Of his many compositions, the anthems 'God created man' (1899), the 'Walk to Emmaus' (1899), and the well-known introit 'God be in my head' (1908) all display his individual style. He was one of the first members of the Church Music Society, for which he lectured, wrote pamphlets, and edited works.

A remarkable power of getting into touch with every kind of audience made Davies one of the most effective judges at competition festivals. This gift was developed further through the advent of broadcasting, an art in which he proved himself a master. His courses of lectures to schools, and to adult listeners, became widely popular by reason of his exceptional power of thinking aloud, and thinking with his listeners, who thus felt drawn into his confidence.

Davies married in 1924 Constance Margaret, daughter of William Evans, canon of St. David's, and rector of Narberth. Honorary degrees were conferred upon him by the universities of Leeds (LL.D., 1904), Glasgow (LL.D., 1926), Dublin (Mus.D., 1930), and Oxford (D.Mus., 1935). He also held the honorary diplomas of F.R.C.O. (1904), F.R.A.M. (1923), and F.R.C.M. (1926).

A charcoal drawing by Evan Walters is in the National Museum of Wales.

[*The Times*, 12 March 1941; H. C. Colles, *Walford Davies*, 1942; *Grove's Dictionary of Music and Musicians*; personal knowledge.]

HENRY G. LEY.

DAWSON, BERTRAND EDWARD, VISCOUNT DAWSON OF PENN (1864–1945), physician, was born at Croydon 9 March 1864, the fourth son and fifth child of Henry Dawson, architect, by his wife, Frances, daughter of Obadiah Wheeler, of Perivale. He was educated at St. Paul's School and University College, London, where he lived at the Hall when Henry Morley [q.v.] was principal. As an undergraduate he was influenced by the work of Charles Bradlaugh and T. H. Huxley [qq.v.] and began to show that interest in social and political problems which persisted throughout his life.

In 1884 Dawson entered the London Hospital as a medical student and, after some early failures in the examination hall, obtained the degree of B.Sc. in 1888 and qualified in 1890, becoming M.R.C.S. (England) in the same year, M.D. and M.R.C.P. (London) in 1893, and F.R.C.P. in 1903. In these early days he earned his living through hospital appointments and as a lecturer. In 1896, when he became assistant physician at the London Hospital, he launched himself as a private consultant. Remembering these years of struggle, with few opportunities for research, in later life he took an active part in the foundation of a postgraduate medical school at London University.

By the close of the century Dawson's advice was being sought on diseases of the lymphatic gland, diabetes, rheumatoid arthritis, and gastro-intestinal diseases. Extending his work in this field, he produced a paper on 'The Microbic Factor in Gastro-Intestinal Disease and its Treatment' (*Lancet*, 29 April 1911), and in 1912 gave an address before the British Medical Association on 'Pathogenesis, Diagnosis, and Medical Treatment of Gastric Ulcer'. He became full physician at the London Hospital in 1906. In the next year he was appointed physician-extraordinary to King Edward VII, a post which he retained with King George V until 1914 when he became physician-in-ordinary. In 1911 he was appointed K.C.V.O.

Upon the outbreak of war in 1914, Dawson, who had become commandant of the 2nd London General Hospital in the Territorial Army in 1908, went to France as consulting physician with the acting rank of major-general. He attended the King at the time of his accident at Hesdigneul in 1915 and remained in France until 1919. Although his time was largely occupied with hospital organization he made use of the medical experience of war to write on paratyphoid, trench-fever, infective gastro-enteritis, and influenza. In co-operation with (Sir) William Errington Hume and (Sir) Samuel Phillips Bedson he engaged in a study of infective jaundice and Weil's disease which culminated in a paper with W. E. Hume in the *Quarterly Journal of Medicine* (vol. x, 1916-17), another with W. E. Hume and S. P. Bedson in the *British Medical Journal* (15 September 1917), and an address on 'Spirochaetosis Icterohaemor-rhagica' before the section of medicine of the Royal Society of Medicine (*Lancet*, 2 November 1918).

The years in France convinced Dawson that while the 'diseases of invasion' were receding before the advance of medical knowledge the 'diseases of stress' would multiply with the quickening pace of life. Among the fighting men cases of shock were frequent and he experimented with their treatment in clinics established at Wimereux, Étaples, Rouen, and Étretat. This early attempt at rehabilitation was imperfectly understood and at times vigorously criticized. But the results were promising.

The war revealed also that the British standard of physical fitness was low. In Dawson's opinion it was going to become as much the duty of the medical profession to promote national health as to cure sickness in the individual. In 1918 he developed this idea in the Cavendish lectures before the West London Medico-Chirurgical Society on 'The Nation's Welfare: the Future of the Medical Profession'. As a result he was drawn into the government consultations concerning the formation of a Ministry of Health and in 1919 he was made chairman of the consultative council on medical and allied services set up by Christopher (later Viscount) Addison, the first minister of health.

This committee produced in 1920 the Dawson report which foreshadowed a national health service. Subsequently the proposals of this report were modified and developed but Dawson held fast to its basic assumption: that any health service must be centred on the medical profession and the hospital services with the teaching hospitals at the head. Dawson was opposed to a full-time salaried service, believing that doctors should work in conditions of freedom. But he was equally anxious that the new needs of the century should be recognized by the profession assuming its share of responsibility for future developments. He held that success depended upon the steady growth of co-operation between the doctor in practice and the officers of the new public service. He would have liked the Ministry of Health to be released from the numerous cares of the Local Government Board, but to his lasting disappointment this was held to be administratively impossible. In any case, retrenchment was in the air; the report was pigeon-holed.

In 1920 Dawson was created a baron, taking the title of Lord Dawson of Penn, of Penn, in the county of Buckingham. His elevation to the House of Lords marked the opening of a period of legislation which touched increasingly upon the interests and responsibilities of the medical profession whose spokesman he became. When in 1921 the report of the Cave committee on the position of the voluntary hospitals was debated in the House of Lords, Dawson asked for the special functions of the teaching hospitals to be considered when the new government grant was distributed. In 1929, during the passage of the local government bill, he again championed the cause of the voluntary teaching hospitals and obtained from the Government an amendment which obliged a local authority when providing new hospital accommodation to consult the representatives of the appropriate voluntary hospitals.

To the measure for the reform of the Prayer Book Dawson gave his support. A man of profound though undogmatic religious conviction he was disturbed by the waning strength of Christian belief and teaching, and saw in the Prayer Book reform one means of reconciling old ideas with new. In 1936 he successfully opposed the voluntary euthanasia (legalization) bill in a characteristic speech: 'We do not lay down edicts for these things. It is a gradual growth of thought and feeling that entwines itself into the texture of our thoughts. . . . This is something which belongs to the wisdom and conscience of the medical profession and not to the realm of law.' In 1937 he supported the matrimonial causes bill and a year later was mainly responsible for the infanticide bill.

Although after 1920 public work made growing demands upon his time, Dawson continued in practice and hospital teaching and with his work as examiner for the London Hospital and Royal College of Physicians. In these years he held many hospital appointments, served from 1929 on the advisory committee to the Ministry of Health and the council of King Edward's Hospital Fund, on the Medical Research Council (1931–5), and in 1936 became chairman of the Army Medical Advisory Board. He found time to read papers on 'The Colon and Colitis' (*British Medical Journal*, 9 July 1921), and 'Dyspepsia and the conditions underlying it' (ibid., 3 June 1922). In 1921 he addressed the Church Congress on 'Sexual Relationships' (published as *Love—Marriage—Birth-Control*, 1922) and found himself plunged in controversy. He addressed the Medico-Legal Society on 'Professional

Secrecy' (*Lancet*, 1 April 1922) when the privileges of the medical profession had been assailed in two actions for divorce. Again, in 1926 he upheld the refusal of the General Medical Council to register unqualified osteopaths—notably Sir Herbert Barker [q.v.]—and defended his views before a meeting of members of both houses of Parliament.

From 1928 to 1930 Dawson was president of the Royal Society of Medicine and did much to improve the management of the Society's finances. In 1932 he was elected president of the British Medical Association for its centenary year. From 1931 to 1938 he was president of the Royal College of Physicians and promoted research in rheumatoid arthritis, anaemia, pneumococcal and lobar pneumonia, the surgical treatment of cardiac ischaemia, and the uses of radium. He drew the College out of its learned seclusion into active participation in the problems which lay before the medical profession, and widened its representation by encouraging the election of medical men who were members of the salaried government service. Dawson hoped that eventually the three Royal Colleges would unite to form an academy of medicine capable of exercising a far-reaching influence upon public affairs.

During the grave illness of King George V in 1928 Dawson did signal service in saving His Majesty's life, and in 1929 he was sworn of the Privy Council. The death of the King in 1936 brought to an end many years of watchful care by Dawson who himself drafted the bulletin which informed the nation that 'The King's life is moving peacefully towards its close'. He was promoted to a viscountcy (1936) and remained on the household of both King Edward VIII and King George VI.

When war broke out in 1939 Dawson was engaged in the organization of the Emergency Medical Service and his common sense contributed to the reconciliation of civilian with military needs. He was also a member of the medical planning commission set up by the British Medical Association to consider a health service for the nation, and the white paper of 1944 was based to some extent upon its work. In the meantime Dawson had been re-elected president of the British Medical Association in September 1943 and in the period of negotiation which followed the publication of the white paper his main endeavour was to reconcile the legitimate claims of the profession with those of the public interest. While he was anxious for the doctors to give their support to the principle of a national health service he was keenly aware that dangers might accrue from a hasty search for political advantage, and that without sympathetic handling the union which might fruitfully be made between State medicine and private practice would never come to pass.

Before this work was completed Dawson died in London 7 March 1945. His reputation rests not so much upon contributions to medical science or literature, though these were distinguished, but upon his qualities as a doctor and medical statesman. He was noted for his sensitive power of diagnosis which was aided by a remarkable clinical memory and a profound understanding of men and women. He was a firm and consistent leader, sometimes impatient but invariably generous. Outside his profession his capacity for inspiring implicit trust in men of most diverse temperaments and occupations was no less remarkable. Ecclesiastics, like Archbishop Lang, statesmen, like Lloyd George with whom he paid a visit to Hitler at Berchtesgaden in 1936, showed their appreciation of this characteristic. As a host he was genial and entertaining and nothing delighted him more than the company of youth.

Dawson married in 1900 Ethel, daughter of (Sir) Alfred Fernandez Yarrow [q.v.]. They had three daughters but no son and the peerage became extinct when Dawson died. In addition to those already mentioned Dawson's many honours included appointment as C.B. (1916), G.C.V.O. (1917), K.C.M.G. (1919), and K.C.B. (1926). In 1925 during a visit to Canada and the United States he received honorary degrees from McGill University and the university of Pennsylvania, and was elected an honorary fellow of the American College of Surgeons. He received also honorary degrees from the universities of Oxford (1926), Edinburgh (1927), Bristol (1933), Padua and Athens, and was elected an honorary F.R.C.S. (1932).

Portraits by (Sir) Oswald Birley and James Gunn are in the possession of the family. Another by P. A. de László was presented to the Royal College of Physicians by Viscountess Dawson.

[*The Times*, 8 March 1945; *British Medical Journal* and *Lancet*, 17 March 1945; Francis Watson, *Dawson of Penn*, 1950; private information; personal knowledge.]

SYBIL D. ECCLES.

DAWSON, (GEORGE) GEOFFREY (1874–1944), twice editor of *The Times*, was born at Skipton-in-Craven, Yorkshire, 25 October 1874, the eldest child of George Robinson, banker, by his wife, Mary, fourth daughter of William Mosley Perfect, and assumed in 1917 by royal licence the name and arms of Dawson on succeeding his mother's eldest sister, Margaret Jane Dawson, and a long line of squires in the estate of Langcliffe Hall, Settle.

Geoffrey Robinson went in 1887 as a King's scholar to Eton; his time there was uniformly happy and creditable to him; and in his later years he served as a fellow of the college. In 1893 he went as a demy to Magdalen College, Oxford, obtaining first classes in classical moderations (1895) and *literae humaniores* (1897). He then entered the Civil Service by open competitive examination in 1898 and was first employed in the Post Office, whence he was transferred in the next year to the Colonial Office, under Joseph Chamberlain, who was then at the height of his power and influence. In 1898 he was elected to a fellowship at All Souls College, Oxford, and, in different capacities, retained it throughout his life.

When the South African war broke out in 1899, Robinson was working as a junior clerk in the South African department of the Colonial Office; and that accidental circumstance was destined to determine the whole course of his career. In 1901 he was promoted to be assistant private secretary to Chamberlain; and later in that year, Lord Milner [q.v.], then high commissioner for South Africa, asked for Robinson's services in the same capacity. Although the war was still far from its end Milner had exchanged his governorship of the Cape Colony for the administratorship of the newly annexed colonies of Transvaal and Orange Free State and had set up his seat of government at Johannesburg. There Robinson went, and until Milner's retirement in 1905 served him, as a member of his famous 'kindergarten', with a filial devotion, imbibing from him lessons in the art of government and a faith in the high mission of the British Empire which were to guide him throughout his life.

When Milner went home he left several of his young men in key positions in the Transvaal to help in carrying through, under his successor, Lord Selborne [q.v.], his work of reconstruction of a country ravaged by war. Among them was Robinson, who resigned from the Civil

Service on being appointed, largely through Milner's influence, editor of the Johannesburg *Star*. This post he held for five years (1905–10) which coincided with Selborne's term of office. From 1906 onwards he was also South African correspondent of *The Times*. South African politics were frankly racial, and the *Star*, the leading newspaper of the Transvaal, was also the chief organ of the British party, but Robinson's level judgement forbade extreme partisanship. He gave steady but never uncritical support to the crown colony government until responsible government, granted in 1906, was established in 1907, and was a strong supporter of the movement which led, in 1910, to the inauguration of the Union of South Africa under Louis Botha [q.v.] as its first prime minister.

In that year Robinson returned to England and in 1911 took service with *The Times*, of which Lord Northcliffe (whose notice he was later to contribute to this DICTIONARY) was then the chief proprietor. In August 1912, before he had reached the age of thirty-eight, Robinson was appointed editor on the retirement of G. E. Buckle [q.v.], and held that important and arduous post throughout the war of 1914–18 until February 1919. His personal relations with Northcliffe were cordial, but with the return of peace in 1918 the insistence of the great newspaper proprietor on his own views on the conduct of the paper were felt by Dawson (as Robinson had now become) to be inconsistent with what he held to be due to *The Times* tradition of editorial independence; and his resignation became inevitable.

Dawson returned to Oxford as estates bursar of All Souls, and went into business as a director of the Consolidated Gold Fields of South Africa, Ltd. He was secretary to the Rhodes Trust from 1921 to 1922, and was elected a trustee in 1925. Always an active member of the group, for a time he edited the *Round Table*.

On 1 January 1923 Dawson, now forty-eight years of age, returned to *The Times* for a second term of editorship. Northcliffe had died in August 1922: the chief proprietorship of the paper had passed to Colonel John Jacob Astor (subsequently Lord Astor of Hever) and Mr. John Walter; and no recurrence of earlier difficulties was to be apprehended. This second term lasted until Dawson, in failing health, retired on 30 September 1941, and was succeeded by his deputy, R. M.

Barrington-Ward [q.v.]. Thus it covered the last sixteen and a half years of uneasy peace between the two wars and the first two years of the second war. Throughout that long and stormy period Dawson upheld the great tradition of *The Times* of giving general support to the Government of the day, while maintaining a position of independence and never refraining from criticism when criticism seemed called for.

Like J. T. Delane [q.v.], Dawson was a great figure in the political and social worlds of his day; indeed, behind the scenes he probably wielded more power and influence than most Cabinet ministers. He was especially intimate with Stanley Baldwin and more intimate than most people with Neville Chamberlain. He gave steady support to successive Governments in the Indian policy which resulted in the Act of 1935; and, as the German menace grew in intensity, to Chamberlain's policy of exhausting the possibilities of reasonable and peaceful settlement until the German invasion of Czechoslovakia in March 1939 made war clearly inevitable.

The strain of the first two years of that war was almost too much for Dawson's physical strength, although his sane common sense, his steady, level judgement, and his sense of humour never failed him. After his resignation he again edited the *Round Table* and busied himself with local affairs in Yorkshire until he died in London 7 November 1944, dear to a host of friends whom it had been his joy to gather round him to share the sport of the hills surrounding his exceptionally happy home.

Dawson was elected an honorary fellow of Magdalen College, Oxford, in 1926, and received the honorary degree of D.C.L. from the university of Oxford in 1934. He married in 1919 Margaret Cecilia, younger daughter of Sir Arthur Lawley (later sixth Baron Wenlock), lieutenant-governor of the Transvaal from 1902 to 1905; they had one son and two daughters.

There are portraits of Dawson by (Sir) Oswald Birley, at Langcliffe Hall; by Francis Dodd, at Rhodes House; and by James Gunn, in the possession of the family. A fourth portrait of him is included in the conversation piece, by Birley, at the offices of *The Times* in Printing House Square.

[*The Times*, 8, 10, and 11 November 1944; *Burke's Landed Gentry*, 1952 (*s.v.* Dawson of Langcliffe Hall); *The History of 'The Times'*,

vol. iii, 1947, and vol. iv (2 parts), 1952; private information; personal knowledge.]
                                    DOUGAL O. MALCOLM.
[Sir Evelyn Wrench, *Geoffrey Dawson and our Times*, 1955.]

DE BURGH, WILLIAM GEORGE (1866–1943), philosopher, was born at Wandsworth 24 October 1866, the son of William de Burgh, barrister and civil servant, who died when de Burgh was twelve, by his wife, Hannah Jane, daughter of Captain Thomas Monck Mason, R.N. He went to Winchester, thence as a postmaster to Merton College, Oxford, where he was awarded a second class in classical moderations (1887) and a first class in *literae humaniores* (1889). Some difficult years followed in which he tried schoolmastering and, living at Toynbee Hall, was censor of studies at Balliol House. In 1896 he found his life-work on appointment as lecturer in Greek and Latin in the University Extension College at Reading, where he remained until 1934. For many years his teaching burden was excessive; he soon added philosophy to his curriculum and became professor of the subject in 1907; he taught classics until 1910. His administrative cares were hardly less absorbing: from the first he had faith in the future of Reading and he had the satisfaction of guiding the development of the college into a university. The credit for this achievement is generally ascribed to W. M. Childs [q.v.], and de Burgh was willing that this should be so; but while the acquisition of the necessary funds was Childs's work, the academic statesmanship was de Burgh's.

The enforced leisure of 1914–18 was used by de Burgh to prepare work for publication, and *The Legacy of the Ancient World* (1924, revised ed. 1947) proved the most successful of his books. Although his intellectual gifts were highly regarded by his pupils and by the Oxford philosophers who were his contemporaries and friends, their wider recognition was belated: he was Gifford lecturer at St. Andrews (1937–8) and Riddell memorial lecturer at Newcastle (1938); not until 1938 was he elected F.B.A. The reason for this may have lain in his disinterestedness; for himself he sought neither fame nor reward. He had a strong sense of duty as a categorical imperative, and in fulfilling his obligations the only standard he failed to satisfy was his own. Inflexible when any matter of principle was at stake, he was nevertheless warm-hearted and genial,

an unfailing tonic to his friends. His sympathy with the young, his forensic gifts, and his vitality were the secret of his success as a teacher. Tall, slim, and erect, he made walking his only physical recreation; his other diversions lay in art, literature, light verse, and the complexities of the railway system. His radiance of personality had its roots in the religious faith expressed in his motto, *A Cruce Salus*, the keynote of his life. A student of scholasticism, yet much influenced by modern idealism, he endeavoured to construct a distinctively Christian philosophy by developing a philosophical argument to the truth of the Gospel. His project was unfashionable at a time when Protestant theologians were disparaging reason and when few philosophers were interested in religion, but his argument, based on the experience of a lifetime and elaborated by the resources of his vigorous mind, has been found impressive by those in sympathy with his views.

In 1897 de Burgh married Edith Mary, daughter of William Francis Grace, vice-consul at Mogador, by whom he had two daughters and one son. He died at Toller Porcorum, Dorset, 27 August 1943. His portrait, drawn by Mrs. Campbell Dodgson, is in the possession of the family.

[A. E. Taylor in *Proceedings* of the British Academy, vol. xxix, 1943; private information; personal knowledge.]     T. M. KNOX.

DE HAVILLAND, GEOFFREY RAOUL (1910–1946), test pilot, was born 18 February 1910 at Crux Easton, Hampshire, the son of (Sir) Geoffrey de Havilland and his wife, Louise, daughter of Richard Thomas, of Chepstow. His father in 1920 founded the de Havilland Aircraft Company, Ltd., which became a world-wide enterprise under his technical leadership. The eldest of three sons, Geoffrey Raoul was born near to the site of his father's first flying experiments, which attained the success of full controlled flight in the summer of 1910, a few months later. He was educated at Stowe School and in 1928 entered the de Havilland company at Stag Lane, Edgware, as an apprentice. While serving his three years in the engineering departments of the company, he learned to fly at the Royal Air Force Reserve School on Stag Lane aerodrome, then spent about a year in South Africa, where he gained useful flying experience. Returning to England in 1932 he became a flying instructor at the de Havilland

Aeronautical Technical School and later at the London Aeroplane Club, which had by then removed to the company's new aerodrome at Hatfield, Hertfordshire. From the first he had shown exceptional ability as a pilot, and a desire to follow this calling in its most exacting branch led him to turn, at the age of twenty-five, from flying instruction to test piloting on the staff of the parent de Havilland company.

The first aircraft which he tested was an economical twin-engined transport called the Dragon, which was being manufactured for world use. Aircraft of this class, including Dragonflies, Dragon Rapides, and four-engined D.H. 86's, occupied him for a couple of years until the company produced a clean, high-performance 22-passenger monoplane airliner, the Albatross, for Imperial Airways. The later development trials of this were conducted by Geoffrey de Havilland when he became chief test pilot in succession to Robert John Waight who was killed in a flying accident 1 October 1937.

Taking Waight's place was a considerable step for one who had not up to that time flown a wide variety of aircraft. Fifteen months later he undertook the first flight of a twin-engined metal transport aircraft, the Flamingo, and conducted its whole flight development. For the next seven years he made the first flight, and did the tests, of every de Havilland prototype. They were the years of the war when the de Havilland company entered in all seriousness the field of military aviation, and the aircraft concerned were high-performance combat machines, the fastest in their categories. Notable among them were the Mosquito twin-engined two-seat multi-purpose aircraft, first flown 25 November 1940; the Vampire jet fighter with de Havilland Goblin engine, 20 September 1943; and the Hornet long-range twin-propeller fighter, 28 July 1944. He visited Canada in 1942 to test the Canadian-built Mosquito and to demonstrate it in Canada and the United States. In recognition of his services de Havilland was appointed O.B.E. in 1945.

He was a keen sporting pilot and took part in a great many races and contests. He shone in the low turns of pylon racing and was one of the finest exhibition pilots British aviation has known. His favourite personal racer was a clean little monoplane, the T.K. 2, designed and built by students of the de Havilland Aero-

nautical Technical School. With a love of the sport he combined a serious attitude to his work. His upbringing helped him to become a practical and analytical test pilot of the calibre most valuable to the aerodynamicist and the designer.

Geoffrey de Havilland met his death above the Thames estuary 27 September 1946, when testing an experimental tailless high-speed jet aircraft, the D.H. 108, on the eve of an essay which was expected to raise the world's speed record by a considerable margin. It is probable that he was flying this aircraft at a speed greater than had previously been attained by man. His youngest brother, John, had been killed 23 August 1943 while testing a Mosquito.

In 1933 Geoffrey de Havilland married Gwendoline Maud Alexander. The marriage was dissolved in 1942 and he married in 1943 Pipette Marion Scott Bruford. There were no children of either marriage. A portrait by (Sir) Oswald Birley is in the possession of the family and a bronze memorial in bas-relief by Eric Kennington is at the de Havilland company headquarters at Hatfield.

[Private information; personal knowledge.]
MARTIN SHARP.

DELAFIELD, E. M. (pseudonym), authoress. [See DASHWOOD, EDMÉE ELIZABETH MONICA.]

DELEVINGNE, SIR MALCOLM (1868–1950), civil servant and reformer, was born in London 11 October 1868, the second son of Ernest Thomas Shaw Delevingne, city merchant, of Sutherland Road, Ealing, by his wife, Hannah, daughter of Richard Gresswell. He was educated at the City of London School and Trinity College, Oxford, where he was a scholar and showed that he had unusual intellectual gifts. He was placed in the first class of the honours lists in classical moderations (1889) and *literae humaniores* (1891). In 1892 he passed into the Civil Service and after serving for a short time at the Local Government Board was transferred to the Home Office where he remained for the whole of his official career. From being private secretary to the secretary of state he rose by successive stages to the position of deputy under-secretary of state in 1922 which he retained until he retired in 1932.

Although he was brought into touch with many sides of the work of the Home Office, it was with the development of measures for promoting the safety, health, and welfare of the industrial worker that Delevingne became especially associated. In 1905, 1906, and 1913 he was sent as British delegate to the international conferences on labour regulations at Berne, and in 1919 he was the British representative on the labour commission of the peace conference in Paris, and later at the International Labour Conferences at Washington and Geneva. His wide knowledge of the subject and his administrative ability and influence enabled him to take a large part in the establishment of the International Labour Office on sound lines.

It was under his guidance and by means of his hard work that much of the industrial legislation in the shape of Factory Acts and regulations was passed during the first quarter of the century, while the factory department at the Home Office was so reformed and developed that it was held in high esteem, not only in the Civil Service but in the industrial world generally. The establishment of the Industrial Museum as a permanent exhibition of methods for promoting safety, health, and welfare in factories, was largely the result of his power to initiate, and it was his good fortune to see the conditions of employment for the industrial worker revolutionized, and to have the satisfaction of knowing that he had done much to bring this about. Safety in coal-mines was also a subject to which he gave close consideration and the Act of 1911 was largely due to his preliminary work. He served on the Royal Commission on the subject in 1936 and was chairman of the Safety in Mines Research Board, 1939–47. Allied to these questions is the rehabilitation of persons injured by accidents, and in 1936 he was chairman of an inter-departmental committee on the subject which issued a report resulting in far-reaching reforms.

The limitation of the manufacture of and trade in dangerous drugs such as opium engaged a great deal of his attention and took him repeatedly to Geneva and even as far as Bangkok as a British delegate at the international opium conferences. He represented not only the Home Office but also the Foreign and Colonial offices in this matter and soon gained world-wide recognition for his knowledge of the subject. He was chairman of the supervisory body under the international convention of 1931 for the limitation of manufacture of dangerous drugs, member of the permanent central board under the international convention of 1925 relating to dangerous drugs, and representative of Great Britain on the League of Nations' opium committee, 1921–34. Even after his retirement he represented the British Government at the international conferences on opium, and in 1932 was nominated by the Privy Council a member of the council of the Pharmaceutical Society. In recognition of his services he was appointed C.B. in 1911, K.C.B. in 1919, and K.C.V.O. in 1932.

His chief recreation during his official career was travelling. After his retirement, and until his health gave way, he devoted himself to social administrative work of various kinds, notably on the council of Dr. Barnardo's Homes of which he became chairman in 1939. His unobtrusive manner concealed great determination and a quick penetration; he improved and vitalized any work he undertook and his loyalty to his colleagues and to his department never failed. Above all, although seldom mentioned, he held a strong religious faith which was the mainspring of his life and the guiding force in all he did. He died, unmarried, 1 December 1950, at his home in London.

[*The Times* 1 and 8 December 1950; Hilda Martindale, *Some Victorian Portraits and Others*, 1948; private information; personal knowledge.]      HILDA MARTINDALE.

DENNISTON, JOHN DEWAR (1887–1949), classical scholar, was born 4 March 1887, at Bareilly, India, the younger surviving son of James Lawson Denniston, of the Bengal Civil Service, and his wife, Laura Mary Davies. He was a scholar of Winchester and of New College, Oxford, where he gained a first class in classical moderations in 1908 and a second class in *literae humaniores* in 1910. He was Craven scholar in 1909 and in 1913 was elected a fellow of Hertford College, where he remained for the rest of his life with the exception of the war years. In 1914 he was commissioned in the King's Own Scottish Borderers, served in France and was twice wounded. He later transferred to the War Office and was appointed O.B.E. for his services; and he returned to the War Office again for the duration of the war of 1939–45.

Denniston ranks among the most gifted and distinguished classical scholars of his time. His principal publications include *Greek Literary Criticism* (1924), Cicero's *Philippics I and II* (1926), *The Greek*

*Particles* (1934, 2nd, revised, ed. 1954); and Euripides' *Electra* (1939), one of the best extant editions of a Greek tragedy. The quality of all his work is very high; but his greatest contribution to knowledge is his monumental book on the Greek particles. This is a work which bears comparison with the achievements of the great scholars of the past. It represents the exercise of an original and penetrating mind in a field of vast extent. The whole of classical Greek literature is explored; the examples (which number over 20,000) depend on his own reading and judgement; their complexity is reduced to system by a lucid, accurate, and vivacious intellect, the myriad interpretations are each the result of fresh and fine meditation. The style is vigorous, and the ideal humane: Denniston was concerned much less with linguistic schematism than with niceties of meaning; the Greek particles are keys to the undertones of meaning, and Denniston was the first to detect and interpret the undertones in thousands of passages of Greek prose and poetry. The book is indispensable in all fields of Greek literature, and it is difficult to see how it can ever be superseded.

Denniston was a joint editor of the *Oxford Classical Dictionary* (1949) to which he contributed a masterly survey of Greek metre, a subject of which his knowledge was unsurpassed among his contemporaries. For posthumous publication he left a draft of an edition of Aeschylus' *Agamemnon* and a completed work on Greek prose style.

Denniston was among the most successful classical tutors of his time at Oxford. He required of his pupils keenness and honesty in their work: it then seemed no effort to him to treat them on terms of equality; to regard the tutorial hour as a matter of importance, almost of urgency; to be outspoken in praise or blame; and to impart something of his own love and understanding of the ancient world, and of his high ideals of scholarship. A considerable part of the work which he did with his pupils is published in *Some Oxford Compositions* (1949) of which he was a joint editor and a principal contributor. He has probably never been surpassed in the art of rendering English prose into classical Greek.

From his schooldays Denniston was devoted to music, but his chief delight was in good conversation and in the happy and frequented home which was for many years a centre of lively entertainment in

Oxford. For him, conversation meant argument on a stated theme. Through smaller talk he would growl absently; then a phrase would attract him, and with much brushing of the coat-lapel and lightening of the eyes he would attack. His mind was singularly clear and quick, his speech candid and forceful, almost violent. No quarter was given, nor yet offence. Ironical but not sarcastic, subtle but not sophistical, he left in the mind of the listener the impression of a powerful intellect controlled by good humour, a warm heart, and a profound inner modesty. He was a lifelong Liberal.

Denniston was elected F.B.A. in 1937 and proceeded D.Litt. at Oxford in 1949, shortly before his death which took place at Church Stretton 2 May 1949. He married in 1919 Mary Grace, daughter of Joseph John Morgan, solicitor, of London; there were no children.

[C. M. Bowra in *Proceedings* of the British Academy, vol. xxxv, 1949; private information; personal knowledge.]    D. L. PAGE.

DERBY, seventeenth EARL OF (1865–1948). [See STANLEY, EDWARD GEORGE VILLIERS.]

DESBOROUGH, BARON (1855–1945), athlete, sportsman, and public servant. [See GRENFELL, WILLIAM HENRY.]

DE SELINCOURT, ERNEST (1870–1943), scholar and literary critic. [See SELINCOURT.]

DEVERELL, SIR CYRIL JOHN (1874–1947), field-marshal, was born in St. Peter Port, Guernsey, 9 November 1874, the son of Lieutenant (later Major) John Baines Seddon Deverell and his wife, Harriet Strappini Roberts. He was educated at Bedford School and in 1895 was gazetted a second lieutenant in the 2nd battalion, the West Yorkshire Regiment. In the autumn of the same year he accompanied his battalion to West Africa to take part in the bloodless Ashanti campaign. Shortly afterwards he transferred to the 1st battalion in India, and thereby lost his chance to see service in South Africa. In 1902 he married Hilda, daughter of Lieutenant-Colonel Gerald Grant-Dalton, who was then his commanding officer. In the army of those days to marry so young was unusual, and was regarded as something of a handicap. Even at this early stage, however, Deverell contrived to make his mark. In 1906 he received a special nomination to the Staff College at Quetta and afterwards held several junior staff appointments in India with marked success.

When war broke out in 1914 Deverell was in England and in the autumn he was at Winchester where the 28th division, a K-1 division, was assembling. He went out to France as one of its brigade-majors early in the new year. Abrupt in manner and somewhat retiring, Deverell was at his best in the field. There, by his force of character and obvious gift of command, this tall, well-built man inspired confidence in all around him. In two years of war he rose from captain to major-general; in four years he received three brevets and seven mentions in dispatches.

After gaining invaluable experience as a brigade-major throughout the second battle of Ypres in the spring of 1915, Deverell was given command of the 4th battalion of the East Yorkshire Regiment. There followed four strenuous months as a battalion commander in the trenches which fitted him for the command of the 20th brigade of the 7th division. He led his brigade successfully in two of the opening operations of the battle of the Somme and was promoted once more— this time to command the 3rd division. Throughout the later fighting in 1916 on the Somme and Ancre, in 1917 at the battles of Arras, Ypres, and Cambrai, and in 1918 throughout the German offensives in Picardy and Flanders and the victorious allied advance, he commanded his division with the greatest distinction.

In 1919 Deverell was back in England commanding the Welsh division (Territorial Army). Two years later he went to India to command the United Provinces district for four years. In 1927 he was appointed quarter-master-general in India. After three years in this exacting post, during which he was promoted lieutenant-general, he became chief of the general staff in Delhi. His long record of distinguished staff work, particularly in these two principal appointments at Army Headquarters, India, showed that he was no less gifted as an organizer and administrator than as a commander in the field.

In 1931 Deverell came home once more, to take over the Western Command. Two years later he was promoted general and transferred to the Eastern Command. In the army manœuvres of 1935 he commanded one of the two opposing corps. The appointment of chief of the imperial general staff was about to fall vacant.

Deverell was an obvious candidate, and so, too, was the opposing commander, who was the only rival then visible in the military firmament. To both commanders, therefore, and to the army generally, these manœuvres assumed a particular significance. In the outcome it was Deverell who won a sweeping victory by a remarkably subtle manœuvre. No surprise was felt, therefore, when in October 1935 he was named successor to Sir Archibald Montgomery-Massingberd [q.v.].

In 1936 Deverell was promoted field-marshal and took up his new appointment as chief of the imperial general staff. At that time the British Army, through long neglect and financial starvation, had reached its nadir. Both Regular and Territorial armies were so short of men that they were little more than shadows. As for equipment, much of it was obsolete and much more wholly lacking. Deverell set himself to do whatever man could do to improve this situation. To recover the years which the locusts had eaten, however, proved a long business and Deverell himself was vouchsafed small part in it. In 1937 there came a new secretary of state who, convinced of the imminence of war with Germany, was bent on building a new army in the shortest possible time. He felt that, to further his reforms, he needed a younger Army Council and at the end of the year Deverell, who was sixty-three, was summarily replaced.

In retirement at Lymington, where he was greatly respected, Deverell took a leading part in local affairs. He was on the borough council and chairman of the defence committee during the war. He died at Court Lodge, Lymington, 12 May 1947. His widow and a son and daughter survived him. For thirteen years before his death he had been colonel of his old regiment, the West Yorkshire. He was appointed C.B. in 1918, K.B.E. in 1926, K.C.B. in 1929, and G.C.B. in 1935. He was an officer of the Legion of Honour and held the croix de guerre with palm. Portraits by Richard Marientreu and A. D. Wales Smith are in the possession of the family.

[*The Times*, 13 May 1947; *Ça Ira*, vol. xii, No. 2, June 1947; regimental records.]

H. G. MARTIN.

DILL, SIR JOHN GREER (1881–1944), field-marshal, only son and second child of John Dill, by his wife, Jane, daughter of George Greer, of Woodville, near Lurgan, county Armagh, was born

25 December 1881 at Lurgan, where his father was then manager of the local branch of the Ulster Bank. He was educated at Cheltenham College and the Royal Military College, Sandhurst. Having been gazetted to the Leinster Regiment, he left England in May 1901 to join its 1st battalion, then on active service in South Africa. The war had then only a year to run. Dill served in the field until the conclusion of peace.

In 1907 Dill married Ada Maud, daughter of Colonel William Albert Le Mottée, late of the 18th Regiment of Foot. He was promoted to the rank of captain in 1911, and was a student at the Staff College, Camberley, at the outbreak of war with Germany in August 1914. At this early stage of his career several of those who knew him well marked him out as destined for a distinguished future—one prophesied in that year that he would eventually become chief of the imperial general staff. He was not what is commonly called an intellectual, but his talent for military affairs, sense of duty, and strength of mind were strongly marked. They were combined with a purity of character which made it impossible to conceive that he would ever be involved in or even contemplate an unworthy action. Good looks and personal charm contributed to his prospects.

In October 1914 Dill was appointed brigade-major of the 25th brigade (8th division), with which he went to France in the following month. He was present at the battles of Neuve Chapelle and Aubers Ridge and the action of Bois Grenier. In 1916 he was appointed G.S.O.2 to the Canadian Corps and promoted to the rank of major. Early in 1917 he became G.S.O.1 to the 37th division, which was heavily engaged that Easter at Arras and in the summer at Ypres. It was already apparent that he was a staff officer of exceptional ability and possessed a wide vision. These qualities were recognized when he was transferred to G.H.Q. as G.S.O.1 in the operations branch. In March 1918, the month of the first great German offensive, he was appointed chief of that branch, with the temporary rank of brigadier-general. In the course of the war he was wounded and awarded the D.S.O. (1915), the C.M.G. (1918), as well as French and Belgian decorations, and was eight times mentioned in dispatches. His reputation in the army was assured. He was, it is believed, the only officer of the British Army who held a post as high as that which he reached in the war of 1914–18 and also held the highest military appointments almost to the end of that of 1939–45.

In 1919 Dill's first post-war appointment was as chief assistant to the commandant of the Staff College, on its reopening. Next year he was promoted colonel. In 1922, after a brief period on half-pay, he took over command of the Welsh Border brigade, Territorial Army. In November 1923 he was transferred to the command of the 2nd, a regular brigade, at Aldershot. His training methods were thorough and effective, so that the esteem in which he was held continued to grow. Late in 1926 he was appointed army instructor—the first commandant being a naval officer, Sir Herbert Richmond [q.v.]—at the new Imperial Defence College. In 1929 he went to India as chief general staff officer to the Western Command, where he remained two years. He was given accelerated promotion to the rank of major-general (1930), and in January 1931 became commandant of the Staff College, where he was thus stationed for the third time. As a consequence he acquired an almost unexampled knowledge of the officers of the army destined to reach high command or to hold senior staff appointments. He proved a successful and popular commandant, practical, painstaking, and inspiring. In January 1934 he became director of military operations and intelligence at the War Office, again adding to his reputation. He remained at the War Office until 1936, in which year he was promoted lieutenant-general and took part in the important Anglo-French staff talks in April.

That September Dill was sent to the Middle East in command of the forces in Palestine and Trans-Jordan. An Arab campaign of violence was then in progress, and to combat it the decision had been taken to end the system of Royal Air Force control and place an army officer in command. Dill acted with a combination of determination and patience, but he was not allowed to remain long enough in the country to bring about the restoration of law and order. A year later, in October 1937, he was transferred to the Aldershot Command. Aldershot was at that time on the down-grade as a training-centre and about to yield pride of place to the Southern Command, with its more extensive facilities on Salisbury Plain, but when Dill arrived there it was still the principal command in the United Kingdom. His immediate predecessors had been farther advanced in seniority than he, who had been promoted to the rank of lieutenant-general only the year before. He returned to the task of training troops enriched with experience and observation. Always carefully watching the character and talents of subordinates, he now noted a number who subsequently distinguished themselves, the senior of whom was the commander of the 3rd division, Major-General Henry Maitland (subsequently Lord) Wilson, a man a few months older than himself, to whom promotion had come more slowly.

Hitherto Dill had climbed the ladder steadily and without a check, and all his ambitions had been fulfilled. Now, however, he suffered a set-back. He had looked forward with every justification to becoming the next chief of the imperial general staff, an appointment which might be expected to involve the reversion of the command of the expeditionary force, if one should be sent to the continent in the event of war. However, when Leslie (later Lord) Hore-Belisha, the secretary of state for war, decided to rejuvenate the general staff at the War Office, his choice for chief of the imperial general staff fell upon Major-General Lord Gort [q.v.], Dill's junior in seniority and in rank. When war broke out in 1939 and Gort was in fact appointed to command the Expeditionary Force, Sir Edmund (subsequently Lord) Ironside was chosen as his successor. Dill was appointed to command the I Corps, which was transported to France with all possible speed. There can be no doubt that he experienced deep disappointment, although he took pains to conceal it.

Dill's corps was stationed on the frontier of Belgium, then neutral, and its commander had no major tasks other than those of supervising its training and improving the skeleton frontier defences. In training he was in his element. The troops were kept fully occupied lest the period of waiting, out of contact with the enemy, should exercise an adverse moral effect. On 1 October Dill was promoted to the rank of general, with seniority from December 1937. He was not destined to see active service in command in this war. It was decided to create a new appointment at the War Office, that of vice-chief of the imperial general staff, to relieve the chief of some of his burdens. Dill came back to England to assume this post in

April 1940, thus missing the great German offensive, although his visits across the Channel at the height of the crisis between 20 and 25 May served the Government well by affording it a clearer view of the desperate situation. On 27 May he succeeded General Ironside as chief of the imperial general staff.

It was an ideal appointment, since the holder held the confidence of the army as a whole and was well and favourably known to the chiefs of the sister Services. The legacy was, however, a sorry one. The fall of France appeared to have brought about the collapse of the whole military structure, in view of the German possession of the west coast of Europe from Trondheim to Bayonne, the strengthening of Axis prospects in the Middle East, and the terrible strategic effects of the footing which Japan speedily demanded and obtained in French Indo-China. There was little enough that Dill could effect positively at this period. More often than not, indeed, he felt himself compelled to advocate restraint and even inaction rather than accept risks which he considered might involve ruin. To throw cold water upon schemes for the offensive is never a welcome task for a soldier in a position such as Dill's, and when the head of the Government is at once as ardent, courageous, inventive, impetuous, and impatient of warning as was (Sir) Winston Churchill, the role may become very difficult and ungrateful. This happened in Dill's case, although his taste for the offensive was shown by his support of the Commandos, if indeed they did not originate with him.

One difference with the prime minister and minister of defence followed another. Churchill gradually came to believe that Dill was over-cautious, obstructive, and unimaginative. Dill became haunted by anxiety lest the nation should be rushed into undertakings which in his view would not only fail in themselves but which would at best heavily discount future prospects (by using up resources he believed ought to be husbanded for more favourable occasions), and which at worst would bring about irretrievable disaster. In matters of high strategy the main weight fell upon him. His colleagues on the chiefs of staff committee were able heads of their own Services, but tended to confine themselves to problems which affected these. Under this strain, increased by intolerably long hours of work and conferences which often lasted into the small hours of the day, Dill's health weakened. The long illness of his wife depressed him. She died in 1940, leaving a son, an officer in the Royal Artillery.

Between February and April 1941, Dill visited the eastern Mediterranean. Affairs in that quarter had become complex. The winter offensive had resulted in brilliant successes against the Italians, a great part of whose forces in North Africa had been destroyed. Meanwhile the Greeks also had inflicted heavy defeat on the Italians, who had wantonly attacked them at the end of October 1940. Germany at first regarded this conflict as a minor episode, but early in 1941 the likelihood of her intervention increased. It was hoped, although with little confidence, that Yugoslavia and Turkey would intervene in favour of Greece. Britain had already assisted Greece against the Italians, chiefly in the air. Now it had to be decided whether British land forces should be sent to the Greek mainland.

The general staff, including Dill, had opposed this course, and he had held that forces sent to Greece would be lost. It was argued that such strength as could be assembled, mostly from the Middle East, would not provide equality with the Germans if they attacked, and that withdrawal of forces from Cyrenaica would ruin the prospects of success there. If all available resources were employed in the task it seemed possible that the North African coast up to the Tunisian frontier might be occupied, which would be of incalculable benefit. Ironically enough, the Greeks at first advocated this course as the correct British strategy, whereas they considered that the landing of small British forces in Greece would bring the Germans down upon that country in overwhelming force. The earlier argument in favour of reinforcing Greece was mainly moral, but it may fairly be said that in the end it was decided to do so on military considerations even though these may have been mistaken. Dill was much occupied in negotiations with the Turks and Yugoslavs—he visited both Ankara and Belgrade—but the Greek problem also engaged him. He changed his mind in favour of the landing of British troops in Greece, but was bitterly disappointed in the extent and efficacy of aid from allies on the spot. The affair ended in a disaster, on the mainland mercifully mitigated by courage and good fortune, and in a more complete disaster in Crete. Another consequence was the heavy defeat of the depleted British forces in North Africa.

In October 1941 Dill married again. His second wife was Nancy, daughter of Henry Charrington, brewer, of London, and widow of Brigadier Dennis Walter Furlong. Dill became manifestly a happier man, but he did not recover his full powers. Churchill therefore decided to make a change. On 18 November it was announced that, on attaining the age of sixty on Christmas Day, Dill would relinquish his appointment as chief of the imperial general staff and would be succeeded by Sir Alan Francis Brooke (subsequently Viscount Alanbrooke). It was also stated that the King had conferred the rank of field-marshal upon Dill and approved of his appointment as governor-designate of Bombay. Dill was saddened by the prospect of leaving the army, but it is probable that he could not in any case have continued at his post much longer.

Feeling that his influence must necessarily be weakened during the next five weeks, he prevailed upon General Brooke to assume the heavy responsibilities at the War Office as quickly as possible and did not continue his work there until the nominal end of his appointment. After the entry of Japan into the war he accompanied the prime minister to the United States, and there he stayed. The decision was taken to set up in Washington a body of representatives of the British chiefs of staff who would form with the American counterpart a joint staff. Dill was the senior member of this body and in a special position, since under him there was a British representative of the Army as well as representatives of the Royal Navy and Royal Air Force. He was thus concerned mainly with matters of high moment and was commonly called in only when difficulties in the way of agreement about plans or about the performance of those upon which agreement had been reached threatened to become insuperable. Freed of the burden of unending office work at high pressure, he appeared to make a great improvement in health. In May 1942 the tenure of the office of the governor of Bombay was extended for six months and at the end of the year a new governor was appointed, with the announcement that Dill's post in the United States was no longer to be considered as temporary.

In January 1943 he attended the Casablanca conference, where his tact and persuasiveness proved invaluable in reconciling conflicting opinions, and afterwards he flew to India and China to confer with Sir Archibald (later Earl) Wavell [q.v.] and General Chiang Kai-shek. That year he did a great deal more travelling, visiting Brazil, returning in July to England, attending the Quebec conference in August, visiting Canada again in October, and attending the Teheran conference at the end of November.

In the United States Dill won the trust and even the affection of the President and became the personal friend of the chief of staff of the army and the commander-in-chief of the fleet, General Marshall and Admiral King. His prestige became extraordinarily high. Few Britons have established themselves more firmly in the confidence of the official and military world of the United States, although he was little known to the public, at least outside Washington. However, in 1944 he received the exceptional honour of the Howland memorial prize from Yale University and an honorary doctorate of laws from the College of William and Mary at Williamsburg. He also received honorary degrees from Princeton and Toronto. Late in 1944 his health again broke down, and on 4 November he died in hospital in Washington. He was buried in Arlington cemetery.

The supreme American honour accorded to him was posthumous, that of the D.S.M., conferred by President Roosevelt, who spoke of him as 'the most important figure in the remarkable accord which has been developed in the combined operations of our two countries'. If his appointment as chief of the imperial general staff had ended unhappily, that as senior British representative on the combined chiefs of staff committee in Washington had been completely successful and fulfilled his highest promise. From his own country, apart from the field-marshal's baton, the only honour bestowed on him took the form of promotion in the Order of the Bath. He had been appointed C.B. in 1928 and promoted to K.C.B. in 1937; in 1942 he was advanced to G.C.B. The Leinster Regiment having been disbanded, he became colonel of the East Lancashire Regiment in 1932 and colonel commandant of the Parachute Regiment, Army Air Corps, in 1942.

Dill was not a genius, but he will rank as one of the most capable of a generation of able soldiers. He was thorough in mental processes and in action. Mental and physical fatigue were the only weaknesses he showed as chief of the imperial general staff. Although even-tempered, he could not contrive to the same extent as his successor strong defences against assaults on his energy and patience. In personality he was most attractive, kindly and considerate, with a pleasant sense of humour. All who came in contact with him were left with the impression of a charming as well as of a high-minded man.

A portrait painted in Washington by the American artist Edward Murray is on long loan from Dill's son to Cheltenham College. There is a copy in the Imperial War Museum in London. A statue has been erected to his memory in Washington.

[L. F. Ellis, (Official) *History of the Second World War. France and Flanders, 1939–40*, 1953; I. S. O. Playfair and others, (Official) *History of the Second World War. The Mediterranean and Middle East*, vols. i and ii, 1954–6; official announcements; private information; personal knowledge.]                    CYRIL FALLS.

[Sir Arthur Bryant, *The Turn of the Tide, 1939–1943; a study based on the diaries and autobiographical notes of Field Marshal the Viscount Alanbrooke*, 1957; Sir John Kennedy, *The Business of War*, edited by Bernard Fergusson, 1957.]

DODD, FRANCIS (1874–1949), painter and etcher, was born at Holyhead 29 November 1874, the third son of the Rev. Benjamin Dodd, a Wesleyan minister who had once been a blacksmith, by his wife, Jane, daughter of Jonathan Shaw, cotton broker, of Liverpool. After the removal of his family to Glasgow Dodd attended Garnett Hill School, where in 1889 he began to learn painting. Here also he met his future brother-in-law and lifelong friend (Sir) Muirhead Bone. For a short time during 1890 he was employed by the National Telephone Company and afterwards became a china decorator in the Glasgow firm of Messrs. MacDougal. Meanwhile he began to study at the Glasgow School of Art, winning the Haldane travelling scholarship there in 1893. With the money thus available he went to Aman-Jean's academy in Paris; but on the advice of J. A. McN. Whistler [q.v.] he spent some time at Venice, studying Tintoretto, and he also visited Florence, Milan, and Antwerp.

In 1895 Dodd settled with his family at Manchester. His circle of acquaintances there included C. P. Scott, L. T. Hobhouse, Oliver Elton [qq.v.], and the artist,

Isabel Dacre, who posed for his painting 'Signora Lotto' now in the Manchester City Art Gallery. Dodd's nature was reserved and critical, his work vividly circumstantial and thoroughly wrought. He had absorbed something of the Glasgow school Impressionism and something of the style of Alfred Stevens, the Belgian artist; but it was at Manchester that he began to explore the possibilities of suburban scenes. Works in various media were exhibited by him in the Manchester Academy, and in 1898 Bernhard Sickert invited him to exhibit with the New English Art Club. He became an active member of both institutions, the latter owing much to his skilful handling of its finances.

In 1901 Dodd went on the first of three visits to Spain, and in 1904 he settled in London, his friends at this period including Charles March Gere, Mr. Henry Lamb, and Mr. Henry Rushbury, all ultimately royal academicians. Dodd began to exhibit at the Royal Academy in 1923, was elected A.R.A. in 1927, and R.A. in 1935. He was also a member of the Royal Society of Painters in Water Colours and of the Royal Society of Portrait Painters, and a trustee of the Tate Gallery, 1929–35.

As official artist to the Ministry of Information during the war of 1914–18, Dodd made portraits of the British naval and military commanders, and was afterwards attached to the Admiralty to carry out drawings of submarines. All these are now in the Imperial War Museum. Portraits by him are in the National Portrait Gallery and at Oxford and Cambridge; while his work in etching and drypoint is represented in the print rooms of the British Museum, the Victoria and Albert Museum, and the Metropolitan Museum, New York. His painting 'A Smiling Woman' was purchased for the Tate Gallery in 1924 out of the Chantrey bequest. A self-portrait is in the Fitzwilliam Museum at Cambridge, and a portrait by Stephen Bone is in the Manchester City Art Gallery.

In 1911 Dodd married Mary Arabella (died 1948), daughter of John Brouncker Ingle, solicitor, of London. In 1949 he married as his second wife Ellen Margaret, daughter of Charles Tanner, builder, of London, who had posed for so many of his pictures. There were no children of either marriage. Dodd died 7 March 1949 at his home in Blackheath.

[*The Times*, 10 March 1949; Sir Muirhead Bone, MS. reminiscences of Dodd in the Victoria and Albert Museum; Randolph Schwabe, 'Francis Dodd' in the *Print Collector's Quarterly*, October 1926.]

BRIAN READE.

**DODGSON, CAMPBELL** (1867–1948), critic and historian of art, was born at Crayford, Kent, 13 August 1867, the youngest of the eight children of William Oliver Dodgson, stockbroker, and his wife, Lucy Elizabeth Smith. He was a scholar of Winchester and of New College, Oxford, where he took a first in classics in 1890 and a second in theology in 1891. He abandoned the idea of ordination, and in 1893 was appointed to the department of prints and drawings at the British Museum, where he succeeded Sir Sidney Colvin [q.v.] as keeper in 1912 and remained in that post until his retirement in 1932. He soon established an international reputation as the leading authority on early German prints, writing German without difficulty, and making many contributions to the learned German periodicals; and the two volumes of his *Catalogue of Early German and Flemish Woodcuts in the British Museum* (1903 and 1911) were accepted, in Germany as elsewhere, as the standard work on the subject. He was co-editor of the Dürer Society publications (1898–1911); and he produced a short but valuable catalogue of the engravings, etchings, and drypoints of Dürer (1926).

Dodgson's interest in prints was not confined to one school or period; the *Print Collector's Quarterly*, which appeared under his editorship from 1921 to 1936, provides evidence of the variety of his interests in this field. Other publications include *Old French Colour-Prints* (1924), the Roxburghe Club catalogue of the proof states of Goya's *Desastres de la Guerra* (1933), and catalogues of the work of several contemporary British etchers, including Sir Muirhead Bone and Mr. Augustus John. A short essay called *The Classics* (New York, 1938) is a good statement of faith in the collecting of prints, to which he devoted so much of his life. On his own account he collected chiefly prints, British and French, of the nineteenth and twentieth centuries, which were little represented in the museum; but also drawings, of the early German and other schools, and some rare illustrated books; and he let it be known that he intended to leave his collection to the British Museum, so that there could be no conflict of interest with his official activities in that respect. Altogether the museum benefited by more than 5,000 items from his bequest; and he himself contributed £2,000 towards the price of an important drawing by Dürer, which was acquired for the museum in 1930.

During the war of 1914–18, although he continued to work part of his time in the British Museum, his knowledge of German proved of value to the intelligence department of the War Office, and in 1918 he was appointed C.B.E. for his services. He received honorary degrees from both Oxford (D.Litt., 1934) and Cambridge (Litt.D., 1936), and decorations from France and Belgium; he was also awarded the Goethe medal by the German Government for his services to the history of German art; and he was elected F.B.A. in 1939.

In manner Dodgson was reserved, and some thought him austere; but he was invariably helpful and generous to colleagues and students, both in this country and abroad, and more than one British etcher owed much to his encouragement. Of several existing portraits, the best likenesses are the etching by H. A. Freeth (1938), and the pen drawing, now in the British Museum, from which this was made. Dodgson married in 1913 Frances Catharine (died 1954), daughter of William Archibald Spooner [q.v.], warden of New College, Oxford. She was herself a talented artist. There were no children. He died in London 11 July 1948.

[Private information; personal knowledge.]
J. BYAM SHAW.

DONALD, SIR JOHN STEWART (1861–1948), Indian civil servant, was born at Ferozepore, Punjab, 8 September 1861, the son of Alexander John Stewart Donald, of the Punjab Provincial Service, by his wife, Susan Britten Hilliard. He was educated at Bishop Cotton School, Simla, and in 1882 entered the Punjab Provincial Service. For the next seven years he was employed on ordinary magisterial and executive duties and in 1889 was appointed assistant to Sir Robert Sandeman [q.v.] who was at that time occupied in opening communications between Baluchistan, Waziristan, and the Punjab. Donald's intimate knowledge of the border and its peoples contributed in no small measure to Sandeman's great achievement. He was promoted to the Imperial Service in 1890 and spent almost the whole of the rest of his career on the North-West Frontier.

In 1893 Donald accompanied Sir H. Mortimer Durand [q.v.] on his mission to Kabul for negotiations with the Amir of Afghanistan on the Indo-Afghan frontier and other matters, and next year he was chosen as British commissioner to demarcate the southern section of the agreed frontier. This commission became largely a trial of patience between Donald and a procrastinating Afghan commissioner, a trial in which Donald, with his good-humoured unconcern, was an easy victor. He was appointed C.I.E. in 1894 and was also awarded the Afghan decoration, Izzat-i-Afghani. Ten years later he was again employed in negotiations with the Afghans, when (Sir) Louis Dane [q.v.] headed a mission to Kabul.

In 1908 the new post of resident in Waziristan was created to co-ordinate the civil administration of the whole of Waziristan and the adjoining districts. Donald was selected for it and was indeed the obvious choice. He had an unrivalled knowledge of Wazir and Mahsud tribal law and customs; he could talk Waziri Pushtu almost with the fluency of a Wazir and could join without effort in the chatter of a tribal gathering; he had the simple straightforward nature which appeals to a Pathan. These qualities bore their fruit. For, except for some months in 1917, the Waziristan border gave no serious trouble while 'Dollan'—as all tribesmen called him—was resident. In 1911 he was appointed C.S.I. and in 1915 K.C.I.E. He had then for eighteen months been acting chief commissioner of the North-West Frontier Province. In 1916 he was appointed an additional member of the imperial legislative council of India, combining this duty for a time with the post of resident in Waziristan. In 1920 he retired, living first in Jersey and then in Cyprus where he died 30 July 1948.

In 1905 Donald married Henrietta Mary (died 1955), daughter of Colonel Edward Lacon Ommanney of the Indian Political Service and a nephew of Sir Erasmus and G. D. W. Ommanney [qq.v.]. There were two sons and two daughters of the marriage.

[Private information; personal knowledge.]
GEORGE CUNNINGHAM.

DONOGHUE, STEPHEN (1884–1945), jockey and trainer, was born 8 November 1884 at Warrington, Lancashire, the eldest son of an ironworker, Patrick Donoghue, of Irish blood, and his wife, Mary Mitchell. Steve's father earned good money but lost most of it in unsuccessful betting on race-horses so that the boy was obliged to seek half-time employment in his father's works at an early age. He was, however, determined to become a jockey and when he was fourteen played truant, walking from Warrington to Chester race-course to see John Porter, then perhaps the most famous trainer of his time, to ask for employment in his stable at Kings-clere. He was told to come back with his father the next day, when it was arranged that Donoghue should go to Porter on trial. Thus he started in a famous stable, but after less than a year he became home-sick and returned to Warrington where for a time he was in a wire-works. One day he was attacked by a bully and in defending himself knocked down his opponent who struck his head on the kerbstone. Fearing that he had killed him, Donoghue ran away from home with his younger brother and took employ-ment with the leading northern trainer, Dobson Peacock, of Middleham, York-shire. Under him Donoghue first learnt to ride well, but he had given an assumed name and when officials arrived to take a census he and his brother abruptly left. They made their way to Newmarket where Donoghue joined the stables of Alfred Sadler junior. Soon afterwards he went to France where he had his first experience of race-riding and won a race for the first time at Hyères in 1905. It was on the sharp twisting courses of the Midi that Donoghue learnt the importance of balance, dash, and quick judgement, all of which were to stand him in good stead at his spiritual home, Epsom, in the years ahead.

In 1907 Donoghue went to Ireland to ride for P. Behan's stable, and in 1910 had his first ride in the Derby, finishing third on Charles O'Malley. He became leading jockey in Ireland and soon afterwards he began to ride for his first English stable, that of H. S. Persse, at Stockbridge, Hampshire. In 1913, for Persse, Donoghue rode Major Dermot McCalmont's The Tetrarch, one of the fastest horses of all time, and it was this horse, unbeaten on the race-course, which made Donoghue's reputation in this country.

Success now flowed fast to Donoghue. He won two war-time Derbys on Pom-mern (1915) and Gay Crusader (1917), and then four more at Epsom in five years:

on Humorist (1921), Captain Cuttle (1922), Papyrus (1923), and Manna (1925): to become the only rider in the history of the Derby to win the race six times. Later he had a wonderful partnership with Brown Jack, owned by Sir Harold Wernher, on which he won the Queen Alexandra Stakes at Ascot in six succes-sive years (1929–34). In 1937, at the age of fifty-two, he won his last classic victory, in the Oaks on Exhibitionnist, and retired from race-riding that year in order to become a trainer. On 23 March 1945 he died suddenly in London.

Donoghue was champion jockey for ten years in succession from 1914 to 1923. He was immensely popular, having charm and a great way with a horse, beautiful hands, perfect balance, great dash, and the ability to get the best out of a horse without punishing it. At Epsom no jockey has ever been his equal. He had no idea of money: as soon as he made any he gave it away or spent it. He was twice married: first, in 1908 to Bridget, daughter of the Irish trainer, P. Behan; this mar-riage was dissolved. Secondly, in 1929 he married a music-hall artiste, Ethel, daughter of the late Michael Finn, an American barrister. He had two sons and one daughter by the first marriage.

There are portraits of Donoghue by Sir John Lavery in the Royal Scottish Academy, Edinburgh, by Sir Alfred Munnings in the United States, and by Lynwood Palmer (of Donoghue on Captain Cuttle) at Cottesbrooke Hall, Northamp-ton, with a copy in the Jockey Club rooms at Newmarket.

[Steve Donoghue, *Just My Story*, 1923, and *Donoghue Up!*, 1938; R. C. Lyle, *Brown Jack*, 1934; private information; personal know-ledge.]     B. W. R. CURLING.

DONOUGHMORE, sixth EARL OF (1875–1948), chairman of committees of the House of Lords. [See HELY-HUTCHIN-SON, RICHARD WALTER JOHN.]

DOUBLEDAY, HERBERT ARTHUR (1867–1941), publisher and genealogist, was born at Hamburg 23 November 1867, the son of William Bennett Doubleday, a City merchant, by his first wife, Agnes Hannah Newman Fenn, of Beccles. Doubleday was educated at Dulwich College and London University, and served with various booksellers and publishers in London. In 1891 he founded the firm of Archibald Constable & Co. with his stepmother's brother of that name, a grandson of Scott's publisher. Among other books they published works by Meredith and Conan Doyle, but their most important single project was the *Victoria History of the Counties of England*, conceived and launched mainly by Doubleday himself. From 1901 to 1903 he was chief editor, and was then succeeded by William Page [q.v.]. Ten volumes of the *Victoria County History* appeared under his sole editorship or in collaboration with Page. Doubleday possessed a keen appreciation of the qualities of good paper and type; both the *History* and later *The Complete Peerage* owed much to his skill and taste.

In 1903 he left Constable & Co. and for a time lived in Bruges, where he published books in English and French. With Mr. Cuthbert Wilkinson he founded in 1908 the St. Catherine Press, a combination of two earlier enterprises, one in Bruges and one in London, of which the latter, Arthur Doubleday & Co., had already produced some notable fine books including a reprint of Evelyn's *Sylva*. It was to the St. Catherine Press that Vicary Gibbs [q.v.] entrusted his new edition of *The Complete Peerage* and Doubleday chose the Caslon type for it. Almost from the first Doubleday's share was more than that of an ordinary publisher, and in volumes iii and iv his assistance was recognized by Gibbs on the title-page. In 1916 he formally became assistant editor and in 1920 editor. Under his direction and with various colleagues volumes v to x and xiii were issued; this was almost entirely due to Doubleday's unflagging energy in organization and in the more irksome task of raising the necessary funds. He himself contributed an important appendix on 'Earldoms and Baronies' to volume iv, and in 1920 replied in print to a hostile review of this by J. H. Round [q.v.]. Doubleday's wide view of the scope of the work and his ardent desire for authoritative reference to original sources make the later volumes (especially in their medieval matter) even more valuable to scholars than the earlier ones, which he hoped one day to re-edit.

He married in 1896 Katherine Alice Lucile, daughter of Thomas Lawrence, of Desford, Leicestershire; they had two daughters. He died at Barnes after a long illness 27 March 1941.

[F. M. Powicke and others, *H. A. Doubleday*, 1942; private information.]

MICHAEL MACLAGAN.

DOUGLAS, LORD ALFRED BRUCE (1870–1945), poet, the third son of John Sholto Douglas, eighth (or ninth) Marquess of Queensberry [q.v.], by his wife, Sybil, daughter of Alfred Montgomery, a commissioner of inland revenue, was born at Ham Hill, near Worcester, 22 October 1870. After private education he was sent in his fourteenth year to Winchester, where in addition to being extraordinarily good-looking he proved to be a very fair runner, winning the school steeplechase in 1887. He edited an ephemeral school magazine, the *Pentagram*, and at Magdalen College, Oxford, he contributed to the *Oxford Magazine* and also edited the *Spirit Lamp*.

In 1891 Douglas was introduced by Lionel Johnson, the poet, to Oscar Wilde [qq.v.]. The two men were extraordinarily complementary to one another; on the one hand was Wilde's literary and aesthetic prestige; on the other Douglas's youth, physical charm, and aristocratic background. In the course of the four following years their intimacy so exasperated Lord Queensberry that he cut off Douglas's allowance and left him dependent on such resources as were allowed him by his mother who had by now divorced her husband. She persuaded her son to take a holiday in Florence, but Wilde followed him there. Douglas went on to Cairo as the guest of Lord Cromer [q.v.], and it was arranged that he should be appointed honorary attaché to Sir P. H. W. (later Lord) Currie [q.v.] at Constantinople; but Douglas returned to London without informing Currie who was furious, and the appointment never took place. On the growth of more rumours, Queensberry took the action which led to the conviction of Wilde. Douglas was not legally involved, but the connexion with Wilde was not broken. On Wilde's release they spent a few weeks together in a villa at Naples where Douglas wrote some of the sonnets on which his reputation as a poet rests; and they met at intervals in Paris until Wilde's death in 1900.

In 1902 Douglas made a runaway match with Olive Eleanor (died 1944), daughter of Colonel Frederic Hambledon Custance, a retired Guards officer, of Weston Hall, Norwich. Douglas had already dissipated his share of his father's fortune and the insistent problem of obtaining a settled income was solved in 1907 by Sir Edward Tennant (later Lord Glenconner) who offered him the editorship of the *Academy* which he had recently purchased. After a brilliant beginning, ignorance of journalism, grossly unbusinesslike methods, and erratic temperament led to a series of violent quarrels with Thomas William Hodgson Crosland, the assistant editor, and also with Tennant, and in 1910 the paper passed into other hands. Legal actions occupied the following years, as well as the publication of volumes concerning his relations with Wilde. His vendettas extended to his wife's family and in 1913 he was bound over for libelling his father-in-law. In 1923 he was defendant on the charge of accusing (Sir) Winston Churchill of falsifying the facts of the battle of Jutland. For this Douglas was sentenced to six months' imprisonment.

In verse Douglas reached his highest level in his sonnets, of which *A Triad of the Moon* and *To Olive* are examples; but his longer serious poems are second-rate, and his books of humorous verse are easily forgotten. In prose, *Oscar Wilde and Myself* (1914), is a virulent attack on Wilde, written, as he later alleged, with the assistance of Crosland. In *Oscar Wilde —a Summing-Up* (1940) he repudiated much of the earlier volume. His *Autobiography* (1929) is an extraordinary specimen of self-revelation. In his last years he was in receipt of a small Civil List pension. He died at Lancing 20 March 1945, having become a Roman Catholic in 1911. There was one son of his marriage. A cartoon of Douglas by H. G. Bzeska is in the possession of Mr. A. L. M. Cary.

[William Freeman, *The Life of Lord Alfred Douglas*, 1948; The Marquess of Queensberry and Percy Colson, *Oscar Wilde and the Black Douglas*, 1949.]     WILLIAM FREEMAN.

DOVE, DAME (JANE) FRANCES (1847–1942), founder of Wycombe Abbey School, was born at Bordeaux 27 June 1847, the daughter of the Rev. John Thomas Dove, curate of Swaton, Lincolnshire, and later for forty-four years vicar of Cowbit, Spalding, by his wife, Jane Ding, daughter of Thomas Lawrance, of Dunsby, Lincolnshire. As the eldest of ten, she had many home duties, including the teaching of three younger sisters, two of whom subsequently entered Girton College. Her own education included lessons from her father with her brothers, a period at Queen's College, Harley Street, and later a year at a most unsatisfactory boarding-school. This last experience gave her the idea of obtaining for girls educational opportunities similar to those enjoyed by their brothers.

In 1869 she entered the college for women just opened at Hitchin by Emily Davies [q.v.]. When this was transferred to Girton, Frances Dove was the first student to cross the threshold and in 1874 she attained to the standard of the ordinary degree in the Cambridge natural sciences tripos. In 1905 she took the *quasi ad eundum* degree of M.A. at Dublin University shortly after it had been made available to suitably qualified women who could not at that time obtain degrees at Oxford or Cambridge. Before leaving Girton she was appointed an assistant mistress at Cheltenham Ladies' College. In 1877 under Louisa Lumsden she joined the staff of the newly founded school at St. Andrews later to be known as St. Leonards School. In 1882 Miss Lumsden retired through ill health and Frances Dove succeeded her. During the next fourteen years the school expanded rapidly and under her guidance its reputation and traditions were established.

In 1896 she left St. Leonards to found a similar boarding-school in England. She formed the Girls' Education Company to provide the necessary capital and the school opened at Wycombe Abbey in September 1896 with 40 girls. When she retired in 1910 there were 230 girls and over 50 mistresses. In 1923 another school in the same tradition was founded in Kent at Benenden.

Always prominent in the civic and religious life of the places in which she lived, Frances Dove was the first woman town councillor of High Wycombe and a justice of the peace of Buckinghamshire. She was a staunch churchwoman and Wycombe Abbey is a Church of England school. It was also one of the first schools to join the Union of Girls Schools for Social Service, of which Frances Dove was an early and generous benefactor.

Her main principles of education were the development of character and a sense of responsibility. Discipline was maintained by the girls themselves with little staff supervision. Believing that all sides of a girl's life should receive their due attention, she was one of the first headmistresses to advocate physical culture and outdoor games for girls as well as lessons in handicrafts and gardening. She was not primarily a scholar or a teacher in the direct sense of the word (although her gift of clear exposition was remarkable), but by her vision and faith, her disregard of all obstacles and her powers of administration she made a contribution to girls' education which was recognized when she was appointed D.B.E. in 1928.

A vivid account of life in the school by one of her first pupils may be found in *A Little Learning* (1952) by Lady Peck who describes how 'her flashing dark eyes, in an oval, finely moulded face, crowned by prematurely white hair, her full tall commanding figure, all revealed her personality. At once you felt yourself in the presence of intense vitality, fierce driving power, originality, indomitable will and courage: she would obviously charm and bully by turns. But hardly enough credit has been given to her amazing sense and keen instincts; in the educational world, one might put it, she had a flair, a genius for seizing on the opportunity presented by the market.' There is a portrait by Sir William Richmond at Wycombe Abbey. It hangs in the library which was given to the school as a memorial to their founder by the association of former pupils known as 'Seniors', a group owing its origin to the initiative of Dame Frances herself. She died, unmarried, at High Wycombe 21 June 1942.

[*The Times*, 23 June 1942; *Bucks Free Press*, 27 June and 3 July 1942; private information; personal knowledge.]

E. E. Bowerman.

DRUMMOND, Sir PETER ROY MAXWELL (1894–1945), air marshal, was born at Perth, Western Australia, 2 June 1894, the eldest son of John Maxwell Drummond, a company director, and his wife, Caroline Lockhart. He was educated at the Scotch College, and at the Perth Technical School where he studied medicine. Soon after the outbreak of war in 1914 he enlisted in Australia as a medical orderly, and early in 1915 took part in the Gallipoli campaign. In the autumn of the same year he was invalided to England.

On leaving hospital Drummond succeeded in obtaining a commission in the Royal Flying Corps by the original and resolute method of walking straight into the office of the general officer commanding the area and asking to be transferred immediately to the Royal Flying Corps. The general was so struck with the initiative, keenness, and bearing of this young Australian private that Drummond was gazetted as a second lieutenant in the Corps in April 1916. He soon justified his

selection, for he served with great gallantry and distinction in the Palestine campaign, receiving the M.C. in August 1917, and being appointed in March 1918 to the D.S.O. to which a bar was added in July. He finished the war as an acting major, Royal Air Force, and the following year he was given a permanent commission as a flight lieutenant.

One of his first duties in peacetime was to carry out a survey of air routes in the Middle East. He was then placed in command of a small unit which operated successfully against the Garjak Nuer tribe in the Sudan. For this 'most excellent work' he was appointed O.B.E. in 1921. After graduating in 1923 at the new Royal Air Force Staff College, where he was contemporary with the future Viscount Portal of Hungerford, and the future Lord Douglas of Kirtleside, he served two years as a squadron leader at the Air Ministry, for much of the time directly under Sir Hugh (later Viscount) Trenchard, the 'father' of the Royal Air Force.

The next four years (1925–9) were spent with the Royal Australian Air Force, where as deputy chief Drummond was able to foster a close spirit of co-operation between Australia and this country, a policy which he always warmly advocated. On his return to England he attended a course at the Imperial Defence College and soon afterwards was promoted wing commander. Towards the end of 1931 he was appointed to command an important unit of the air defence of Great Britain, the fighter station at Tangmere, where he spent eighteen busy months. Once more back at the Air Ministry he held various staff appointments for a period of more than three years, one of which included research work into fighter tactics, and later he had command of a fighter experimental unit at Northolt, where he was promoted group captain in January 1937.

In November 1937 Drummond returned to the Middle East as senior air staff officer. In that theatre he spent over five most eventful and profitable years during which he served under five different commanders, rose to the rank of air marshal, and for the last two years acted as deputy A.O.C.-in-C. to Sir A. W. (subsequently Lord) Tedder in one of the most critical phases of the war. Lord Tedder, when receiving the freedom of the City of London in 1946, referred to Drummond as his right-hand man whose ability and loyalty had made his job possible. It was not only in the hard-fought campaign, but also in the difficult and arduous years of preparation beforehand that Drummond's foresight, hard work and knowledge of the country were so valuable. To him, as much as to anyone, was due the smooth and efficient working of the Middle East Air Force when the test came.

In the spring of 1943 Drummond returned to England and was appointed to the Air Council as air member for training. For nearly two years he directed all Air Force training, and in addition planned the post-war Royal Air Force. On the morning of 27 March 1945, while on his way to Canada, with other officials, to thank the Canadian Government on behalf of the Air Council for Canada's great assistance to the war effort through the Empire Air Training Scheme, the Liberator in which he was flying was lost near the Azores. Apart from his exceptional personal bravery, Drummond possessed high qualities which would have carried him to the very top. His vision and judgement were remarkable, and the many who sought his advice seldom went unrewarded. His pleasant unaffected manner made him popular with officers and men. He always treated his duties very seriously, but once away from his work he had the knack of relaxing completely, either in his happy family life or in the energetic pursuit of golf, ski-ing and mountaineering. He was appointed C.B. in 1941 and promoted K.C.B. in 1943 when he took his nickname Peter as an additional Christian name.

In 1929 Drummond married Isabel Rachael Mary, only daughter of the late Paris Frederick Drake-Brockman, barrister of the Inner Temple. They had one son and two daughters. There is a pastel of Drummond by Eric Kennington and a drawing by H. A. Freeth in the Imperial War Museum; an oil-painting by Cuthbert Orde is at present at the Air Ministry.

[*The Times*, 13 April 1945; private information; personal knowledge.]

E. BENTLEY BEAUMAN.

DRURY, (EDWARD) ALFRED (BRISCOE) (1856–1944), sculptor, was born in London 11 November 1856, the son of Richard Drury, tailor, of London, and later of Oxford, by his wife, Emma Rachel Tombs. He received his general education at New College Choir School, Oxford, and his earliest specialist instruction at the Oxford School of Art. He next moved to the National Art Training School (later the Royal College of Art), where he studied drawing under F. W. Moody, a follower of Alfred Stevens [q.v.]; at about this time the French sculptor Aimé Jules Dalou came to London, and Drury soon fell strongly under his influence. When Dalou returned to Paris, Drury followed him and from 1881 until 1885 he worked in his studio as an assistant. In 1885 his first exhibit was accepted by the Royal Academy; this was a terra-cotta group, entitled 'The Triumph of Silenus'; in the same year he returned to London, where he became for a time an assistant of (Sir) J. E. Boehm [q.v.]. Drury's work during the next ten years mostly took the form of portrait busts; in 1896 his 'Griselda' was bought out of the Chantrey bequest; it is now in the Tate Gallery. Two years later he was at work on his first important public commission, the decorative sculpture for the city square, Leeds; models for this work, which included a statue of Joseph Priestley, were exhibited at the Academy in 1898 and 1899.

From this time Drury was kept busy with a long series of public commissions for decorative and memorial sculpture; such works he often exhibited, either in their finished form, or as sketch models, at the Academy. Chief among them were eight groups of sculpture for the War Office (1905), sculptures for the main entrance of the Victoria and Albert Museum (1908), four bronze figures for Vauxhall Bridge (1909), and sculpture for the gate pillars of the Victoria Memorial (1911). Drury also made some notable portrait-sculptures; among these are the statues of Queen Victoria (1903) at Portsmouth and Bradford, the bust of King Edward VII (1903) at Warrington, and also portraits of (Sir) Arthur Schuster (1902), Sir Robert (later Lord) Baden-Powell (1915), and (Sir) Frank Brangwyn (1919).

Perhaps Drury's best-known single work is the statue of Sir Joshua Reynolds, which stands in the courtyard of Burlington House. This was the result of a competition; after several false starts, Drury completed it in 1931. For this work he was awarded the silver medal of the Royal Society of British Sculptors in 1932. Thereafter until his death Drury did little sculpture. He died at Wimbledon 24 December 1944.

Drury became A.R.A. in 1900 and R.A. in 1913. He was a good all-round sculptor, but his particular excellence lay in his ability to relate his decorative sculptures to their architectural settings, and it is probably for this rather than for other qualities that his work will be remembered.

He married in 1900 Phebe Maud (died 1928), daughter of the Rev. George Lyon Turner, a Congregational minister and professor at Hackney College; by her he had two sons, one of whom, (Alfred) Paul Dalou Drury, is also an artist whose portrait drawing of his father is in the British Museum.

[*The Times*, 27 December 1944; *Studio*, February 1906; private information.]

JAMES LAVER.

DRYLAND, ALFRED (1865–1946), chartered civil engineer, was born at Aldington, Kent, 2 March 1865, the son of William and Sarah Dryland. His father was a farmer. He was educated at Farnham Grammar School and served his articles of pupilage as a civil engineer under the borough engineer of Folkestone. Dryland became borough surveyor of Deal in 1883 and after the establishment of county councils he became in 1890 assistant county surveyor of Kent.

In 1898 Dryland was appointed county surveyor and architect for Herefordshire and in 1906 county surveyor of Wiltshire, with the duties of architect to the education and asylum committees. He was responsible for the reorganization of the system of highways in the region of Salisbury Plain made necessary by the formation of large permanent military establishments in that area.

In 1908 Dryland became county surveyor of Surrey where he supervised the modernization of the system of highway maintenance and introduced a variety of new methods for the surface treatment of roads in tarred macadam and asphalt. He was chairman of a committee set up to investigate routes for a number of arterial roads in the London area, and many of the existing radial and circular routes are largely due to his foresight and energetic planning.

Dryland in 1920 became county engineer of Middlesex where in addition to his duties as chief of the highways department he was in charge of the departments dealing with river regulation and licensing. He was responsible for the construction of several new arterial roads including the Great West, New Cambridge, North Circular roads, the Barnet and Watford by-pass roads, and the Western Avenue.

The construction of the Great West Road from Chiswick to East Bedfont, which was formally opened by King George V in 1925, was a triumph of modern engineering skill in the face of formidable problems. In this field Dryland was considered the greatest expert of his day and he was a pioneer in the planning and construction of motorways in this country. He studied highway problems and traffic conditions in Canada, the United States, and on the continent and wrote many articles for professional societies and technical journals on road questions. In road planning he played a prominent part as chairman of a technical committee for three regional schemes in Middlesex and also for a similar committee dealing with the large area within the jurisdiction of the London Traffic Advisory Committee. He was also engineer to the joint committee of Middlesex and Surrey for new bridges over the Thames at Chiswick and Twickenham, and a member of the engineering advisory committee of the Road Board until its dissolution.

Dryland was appointed C.B.E. in 1930 and retired in 1932. In that year he was elected a member of the council of the royal borough of Kingston upon Thames and in 1935–6–7 served as mayor. His wide experience as an engineer and administrator, together with his wise counsel, enabled him to give unique service to the community and also to the professional associations of which he was a member. He was for many years honorary secretary and treasurer of the County Surveyors' Society and its president in 1908. Witty, urbane, a delightful conversationalist, he was a man of dignified presence, well liked and respected by all his colleagues. He found his relaxation in golf and shooting.

In 1885 Dryland married Edith Rose Constance, daughter of H. R. Clarke, magistrate and collector in the Indian Civil Service; they had two sons and one daughter. He died at Kingston upon Thames 26 November 1946. A portrait by A. E. Wragge is in the possession of the family.

[*Journal* of the Institution of Municipal and County Engineers, 3 December 1946; *Journal* of the Institution of Civil Engineers, February 1947; personal knowledge.]

D. S. SAMUEL.

DUNCAN, SIR PATRICK (1870–1943), South African statesman and governor-general, was born at Fortrie, King Edward parish, Banffshire, 21 December 1870, the second son of John Duncan, a tenant farmer (the third John Duncan to hold Fortrie, a farm on the Fife estate), by his wife, Janet, granddaughter of Alexander Taylor, schoolmaster at Belhelvie, Aberdeenshire, who succeeded his father as laird of Balmand in King Edward parish. At the age of five Patrick Duncan began to attend King Edward parish school, walking a distance of two and a half miles there and back every day. By the time he had reached the age of eleven, he had made such progress, particularly in Latin, Greek, and French, that the headmaster of the school, Dr. John Milne, drew the attention of the inspector of schools to the boy's promise, and the inspector, happening to be a brother of George Ogilvie the headmaster of George Watson's College, Edinburgh, suggested that the boy should try for a scholarship there. He won it, and at the age of twelve entered the school. Three years later he passed out as 'dux' and gold medallist with a bursary at Edinburgh University, where he came under the influence of W. Y. Sellar and S. H. Butcher [qq.v.]. In 1888 he entered for a classical scholarship at Balliol College, Oxford, and headed the list of scholars for that year. When he left Edinburgh for Oxford in 1889, he had not only won a degree with first class honours in classics, but he had also been elected to a Warner exhibition at Balliol, open only to men, or the sons of men, born in Scotland. In 1890 he won a Craven scholarship, and he obtained first classes in classical moderations (1891) and *literae humaniores* (1893).

After a short time at the Toynbee Hall settlement and some study of Aristotle in London, Duncan entered the Department of Inland Revenue in 1894 and became secretary to Alfred (later Viscount) Milner [q.v.] then chairman of the Board, and held the same post under Milner's successor, (Sir) G. H. Murray [q.v.], rising to be principal clerk.

Having been offered the post of colonial treasurer of the Transvaal at Milner's request, Duncan assumed his new duties in March 1901. He continued to serve as colonial treasurer until the latter part of 1903, when he became colonial secretary. He retained this post until responsible government was introduced in February 1907, but for the last few months of his tenure of office he was required to serve as acting lieutenant-governor. He had served as a member of the inter-colonial council for the Transvaal and the Orange River Colony, and he was chairman of its railway committee which administered and developed the railways of those two colonies, then unified as the Central South African Railways.

Thus, throughout the critical period from 1901 to 1907, Duncan had been called upon to play a very important part in the re-establishment of civil government. Like most of the members of Milner's 'kindergarten' he continued to serve under Milner's successor, Lord Selborne [q.v.], and he shared with them in the discussions which produced the Selborne memorandum of 1907 and eventually led to the National Convention of 1908-9 and the South Africa Act of 1909. He had indicated what was his definite choice for life when, at a St. Andrew's Day banquet at Johannesburg in 1906, he had made an important speech on South African affairs. He diagnosed 'disunion' as the root of all the various troubles which beset the four colonies, and prescribed 'union' as the cure. 'I do not', he said, 'come forward as a doctor prescribing a bitter draught and then going away and leaving the unfortunate patient to swallow it. I intend, so far as we can make plans in this world, to remain to drink my share of that draught.' Therefore early in 1907 he resumed his legal studies in London in the chambers of J. A. (later Viscount) Simon and, having been called to the bar by the Inner Temple, he returned to the Transvaal in 1908, in order to practise as an advocate in Johannesburg. Shortly afterwards he indicated his intention to take an active part in politics by joining the Progressive Party under Sir George Herbert Farrar; by the end of the year the question of union had become dominant in South African politics, and he had been appointed one of the two legal advisers to the Transvaal delegation to the National Convention. It was characteristic of him that in 1909 he gave up a pension of £450 to which he was entitled as colonial secretary on the ground that a man of his age, and capable of further work, ought not to receive a pension.

In the first general election (1910) after the passing of the South Africa Act, Duncan stood as Unionist candidate for Fordsburg, a district where working-class voters of various races predominated, and in a three-cornered contest won the seat by a small majority, This was the beginning of a parliamentary career which, save for a break of one year in 1920–21, was to last for twenty-six years, and severely restricted his opportunities for practice at the bar. Nevertheless, except in the years when he held office, he continued to practise and he took silk in 1924. For various periods between 1916 and 1933 he acted as legal adviser to the high commissioner for South Africa, and from 1929 to 1933 he was judicial commissioner for the high commission territories.

In Parliament, Duncan's wide experience of public affairs and his critical powers in debate made him a valuable asset to his party, but he was much more than a party politician. Fairmindedness and freedom from racial prejudice, exemplified by his early acquisition of a good working knowledge of Afrikaans, often enabled him to exert a moderating influence on such controversial questions as the national flag and the language which tended to arouse bitter racial feeling. He gradually won for himself in an exceptional degree the respect and confidence of members of all parties. There were even occasions when he went so far as to vote against his own party, the most conspicuous being when he persisted in voting with the small group of Labour members against those clauses of the indemnity bill of 1914 which sanctioned and condoned the deportation of the British leaders of the strike of that year to the United Kingdom. In social welfare and education he took a deep interest. The children's protection bill of 1913 owed much to his vigilance, and his bill of 1917 to regulate the wages of women and young persons in specified trades led to an inquiry by a select committee and to a subsequent passing in 1918 of a minimum wages bill and a factories bill. Moreover, the lead which he gave to Transvaal members in debates on the university legislation of 1916 secured amendments which enabled the South African School of Mines and Technology to develop into a university college and eventually, in 1921, to obtain full status as the university of the Witwatersrand, Johannesburg.

In the general election of 1920 Duncan was defeated at Fordsburg but returned to Parliament as member for the Yeoville district of Johannesburg after the general election of 1921. He then joined the Cabinet of J. C. Smuts [q.v.] as minister of the interior, health and education, but the victory of the Nationalists in 1924 under J. B. M. Hertzog [q.v.] aided by the Labour Party under Colonel Frederic

Hugh Page Creswell, put him into opposition as Smuts's chief lieutenant in the South African Party until 1933, when the alliance of Hertzog and Smuts was followed in 1934 by the fusion of their parties into the 'United Party'. In May 1933 this coalition under Hertzog as prime minister gained a substantial overall majority and Duncan for the rest of his parliamentary career served in Hertzog's Cabinet as minister of mines.

Service in Hertzog's ministry did not mean that Duncan had abandoned the views on the native question which he had propounded in 1912 in his *Suggestions for a Native Policy*. In this pamphlet, he had severely criticized the policy of racial 'segregation' propounded by Hertzog, who was then minister of justice in Botha's Cabinet, and had urged that it would be impossible to maintain in South Africa two completely separate types of civilization, a native and a European, that it was necessary to recognize the inevitable effects of the impact of the more advanced type upon the less advanced, and that it was the duty of Europeans to enable natives to share to a steadily increasing degree in the benefits of European culture, which would open the way to their fuller development and to their attainment of higher standards of life. Any policy which denied to natives their share in such benefits would, he held, be 'fatal' to the future prospects of European civilization in South Africa, by reason of its inevitable reflex effects on the Europeans themselves. While adhering in general to his liberal views of 1912, Duncan supported the restriction on the rights of native voters in the Cape Province contained in Hertzog's native legislation of 1936 mainly on the ground that in view of the great prospective increase in the number of such voters it was necessary to impose a definite limit on the extent of the representation to which they were to be entitled, if 'a dangerous conflict of racial feeling', with results similar to those reported from the southern states in America, was to be avoided.

When in November 1936 it was announced that Hertzog had advised the King to appoint Duncan to the vacant post of governor-general of South Africa, it was widely agreed that, setting aside the controversial question whether the governor-general should be a South African, Duncan was the best possible choice. The reputation for fairness which he had won overrode all objections to the appointment of a party politician and a member of the Cabinet. After a visit to England during which he was appointed G.C.M.G., he was sworn in, 5 April 1937. At the coronation in May he was nominated a privy counsellor, but owing to absence from Britain he was never sworn. Duncan had required much persuasion before he reluctantly acquiesced in the view that on public grounds it was his duty to accept the office of governor-general; nevertheless, until life became overshadowed by war-time anxieties and loss of health, he seemed on the whole to be happy in a position which brought him welcome relief from parliamentary and ministerial routine, and allowed him time for his favourite studies. But the revival of racial feeling consequent on the celebration of the centenary of the Great Trek was a deep disappointment, and the bitter controversy about the war defeated his hope that, as governor-general, he might meet with a friendly response from all sections of the European population.

Less than two days after the outbreak of war, Duncan was called on to make a momentous decision. On 2 September the Union Parliament had assembled in Cape Town for a special session not directly connected with the threatened outbreak of war. A deep cleavage of opinion immediately showed itself in the Cabinet. On 4 September Hertzog moved in the House of Assembly a resolution committing the Union to neutrality. An amendment by Smuts against neutrality and in favour of an immediate severance of relations between the Union and Germany was carried by a majority of thirteen votes. Hertzog then advised Duncan to dissolve Parliament, but Duncan rejected this advice on the ground that the circumstances of the Union were such as to render a general election undesirable. Hertzog had indeed frequently stated that in the event of an outbreak of war between Great Britain and a European power it would be for the Union Parliament to decide the question of participation in such a war, and this statement itself afforded, apart from all other considerations, a strong prima facie argument in favour of Duncan's action, which subsequent events fully justified. Hertzog resigned and Smuts accepted the governor-general's invitation to form a new Government and became prime minister of a coalition Cabinet containing representatives of the Labour and Dominion parties. A declaration of war on Germany followed

almost immediately; volunteer forces were raised and equipped and, when Italy entered the war on the side of Germany, South African forces could take the initiative by invading the Italian colonies in North Africa.

In April 1942 Duncan's appointment as governor-general was renewed for a second term, but in October his health had so far given way that he had to accept relief from his official duties, which were carried out by the chief justice, Mr. Nicolaas Jacobus de Wet. Duncan had already in October 1941 undergone a severe operation, and although as a result of a later operation his health had shown some improvement and he resumed the burdens of his office in May 1943, the improvement was not long maintained, and he died at Government House, Pretoria, 17 July 1943. At the State funeral in Pretoria Cathedral, Smuts spoke of Duncan in terms the truth of which none of his intimate friends could fail to recognize: 'In him there was a happy blend of high culture and the public man, the man of affairs, which gave him a place of his own in our public life. He brought to practical affairs a mind and an outlook which went much deeper than affairs. As has been so finely expressed by one of the master spirits of the race, he was in the world but not of it. And this background gave a colouring, a tone, a subtle flavour to his practical activities which can only come from the inner spirit. Behind the practical politician was the scholar, the philosopher, the man who was deeply imbued with the ultimate religious values of life. In that spirit he did his work as a public man— trusted and respected as few men in our public life have been. . . . He was much too big to push against others, and in his single-mindedness and modesty he was content to be himself and to give of his best to his fellows. If he was not of the stuff which makes popular leaders, he had in him the stuff which leads the leaders.... We all trusted him and we had implicit confidence in his character, ability and judgement.'

Duncan retained throughout his life his deep interest in Greek philosophy. In 1928 he published a translation of the *Phaedo*, and in November 1942 he contributed an essay on the 'Immortality of the Soul in the Platonic Dialogues and Aristotle' to the *Journal* of the British (later Royal) Institute of Philosophy. The honorary degree of LL.D. was conferred upon him by the university of

Edinburgh in 1931, and by the university of Cape Town in 1939. In the latter year he was also elected an honorary fellow of Balliol College.

Duncan married in 1916 Alice Dora Amanda (died 1948), daughter of Victor Dold, a trader at Kokstad, East Griqualand; there were three sons and one daughter. The loss of the second son, Major Andrew Duncan, D.F.C., in an air patrol over North Africa in 1942 came as a heavy blow when Duncan's health was already seriously impaired. Lady Duncan was Sir Patrick's devoted helpmate; as hostess at Government House and a tireless patroness and supporter of social welfare work for the benefit of all races, her energy and ability found full scope. A bust of Duncan by M. Kottler stands on a pedestal near the entrance to the Queen's Hall in the Houses of Parliament at Cape Town. The great dock there, completed during the war and formally opened early in 1943, was named the Duncan Dock, and in 1945 Duncan's ashes were deposited within the stone structure on which the name of the dock is inscribed.

[*Cape Times* and *Rand Daily Mail,* 19 July 1943; *Johannesburg Star,* 17 July 1943; private information; personal knowledge.]

RICHARD FEETHAM.

DUNEDIN, VISCOUNT (1849–1942), judge. [See MURRAY, ANDREW GRAHAM.]

DUNHILL, THOMAS FREDERICK (1877–1946), composer, was born 1 February 1877 in Hampstead, the third son and fourth child of Henry Dunhill, a manufacturer of sacks, ropes, and tarpaulin, in the Euston Road, and his wife, Jane Styles. His mother kept a music shop in Hampstead and was herself musical. Dunhill was educated at a private school in Hampstead and later at Kent College, Canterbury, his family having removed to Harbledown near by. At the age of sixteen he entered the Royal College of Music, studying with (Sir) Charles Stanford, whose notice he contributed to this DICTIONARY, and Franklin Taylor; he won an open scholarship in 1897, and two years later he was appointed piano professor at Eton College. He remained there until 1908 and returned in 1942. In 1905 he joined the staff of the Royal College of Music and also became an examiner for the Associated Board of the Royal Schools of Music, visiting Australasia in this capacity in 1906 and 1908. In 1907 he founded the Thomas Dunhill Concerts in London, with the particular object of

giving second performances of works by young British composers. He continued to work as a teacher, lecturer, and adjudicator for the remainder of his life; he was awarded an honorary doctorate of music by Durham University (1940), a fellowship of the Royal College of Music, and an honorary fellowship of the Royal Academy of Music. In 1938 he was president of the Oxford and Cambridge Musical Club.

Dunhill wrote a large number of compositions of all kinds. Many of his earlier works were for chamber combinations; these include a Quintet for wind, string, and piano (1898), a piano Quartet (1903), a 'Phantasy' string Quartet (1906) and a 'Phantasy' Trio (1911), and two violin Sonatas, of which the second, in F (1916–17), is his most mature chamber work. In 1924 Dunhill was the first recipient of the Cobbett chamber music medal. Other works include 'Comrades' for baritone and orchestra (1905); 'Capricious Variations' for 'cello and orchestra (1911); a Symphony in A minor, which was performed in Belgrade and at the Bournemouth Festival of 1923; 'Elegiac Variations' for orchestra, in memory of Sir Hubert Parry [q.v.], performed at the Gloucester Festival of 1922; a one-act opera *The Enchanted Garden,* which won a Carnegie award in 1925; and a pageant play, *The Town of the Ford,* written in the same year for Guildford.

The work which chiefly made Dunhill's name known to the general public was the light opera, *Tantivy Towers* (1931), with a libretto by (Sir) A. P. Herbert, which showed an individual gift for comic invention. This was followed by a children's opera, *Happy Families* (1933), with a libretto by Rose Fyleman, and by two ballets, 'Dick Whittington' and 'Gallimaufry', of which the latter was produced at the Hamburg State Opera House in 1937. His later works included 'Triptych' for viola and orchestra (1942) and an overture 'Maytime' (1945). Dunhill also wrote numerous songs, of which 'The Cloths of Heaven' and 'The Fiddler of Dooney' (from the song cycle 'The Wind among the Reeds') have become well known, and a number of children's cantatas, operettas, and songs. All these works showed him to be a thoroughly professional composer who could write with fluency and distinction in all forms; in particular he had a real talent for composing original music in lighter vein. He was also the author of *Chamber Music, a Treatise for Students* (1913), *Mozart's*

*String Quartets* (1927), *Sullivan's Comic Operas* (1928), and *Sir Edward Elgar* (1938).

Although professing no specific religious belief, Dunhill believed that any gift brought great obligations to its possessor, and that it was his duty to write as much music as he was capable of producing. His musical standards were high, and he never compromised for the sake of popularity or immediate effect; he also distrusted innovation for its own sake. When adjudicating at musical festivals he always told competitors exactly what he thought; he had a great fund of humour, and was loved for his entertaining remarks on these occasions. He was always willing to help and advise young composers and performers and to undertake unpaid committee work. His tastes were simple, and he had a great love of the country.

In 1914 Dunhill married Mary Penrose (died 1929), daughter of Edward Arnold, of Pook Hill, near Godalming, and great-granddaughter of Thomas Arnold [q.v.], headmaster of Rugby. There were two sons and one daughter of this marriage. In 1942 he married Isabella Simpson, daughter of the late John Featonby, of Scunthorpe. Dunhill died at Scunthorpe 13 March 1946.

[*Grove's Dictionary of Music and Musicians*; *Cobbett's Cyclopedic Survey of Chamber Music*; private information.]

HUMPHREY SEARLE.

DUNSTAN, SIR WYNDHAM ROWLAND (1861–1949), chemist and director of the Imperial Institute, was born at Chester 24 May 1861, the elder son of John Dunstan and his wife, Catherine, daughter of Philip Cipriani Hambl(e)y Potter [q.v.], principal of the Royal Academy of Music. John Dunstan was constable and governor of Chester Castle.

Wyndham Dunstan was educated at Bedford School and abroad. In 1879 he was appointed assistant to Theophilus Redwood, professor of chemistry in the Pharmaceutical Society's School of Pharmacy, and later was demonstrator in the chemical laboratories; he succeeded Redwood in 1886. Meantime he had acquired a connexion with the university of Oxford by being made a demonstrator in the university chemical laboratories in 1884 and a year later university lecturer on chemistry in relation to medicine. From 1892 to 1900 he was lecturer on chemistry in St. Thomas's Hospital medical school. In 1896 he became director of the scientific and technical department of the Imperial Institute and succeeded Sir F. A. Abel [q.v.] as director of the Institute in 1903, retaining this appointment until he retired in 1924.

Dunstan was an excellent teacher and his lectures were attractive in diction and style. At the Imperial Institute his driving power, clear foresight, and organizing ability were all operative in developing the functions of that organization to the greatest extent possible with the rather meagre financial resources available.

During his period at the School of Pharmacy Dunstan's research work naturally lay in the domain of pharmaceutical chemistry and dealt with such matters as the quality of chemical compounds used in medicine and with the development of methods for the standardization of preparations of such potent drugs as nux vomica and belladonna. In 1887 the Pharmaceutical Society's research laboratory was inaugurated with Dunstan as director, and there important work was done on various drugs including the alkyl nitrites, and an investigation was started on the alkaloids of monkshood (*Aconitum Napellus*) which was later extended to a series of Indian aconites when Dunstan moved to the Imperial Institute. The Institute had been founded to investigate new or little-known mineral and vegetable resources of the countries of the Empire, to collect and disseminate commercial and technical information about these resources, and to form and maintain a permanent exhibition illustrating the nature and chief resources of overseas countries of the Empire. Dunstan set to work to fulfil this programme which required a considerable increase of trained staff; thanks to the receipt of grants from various public bodies and other donors this was achieved. After 1900, when the building was taken over by the Government, development of the Institute's work became a matter of gradually increasing official interest. A detailed report was published in 1923, which illustrates the remarkable volume and range of the work done and is a tribute to the success of the Institute under Dunstan's direction in investigating and adding to our knowledge of the resources of the Empire in useful raw materials.

The results of these investigations were published in official reports, such as those on the mineral surveys which Dunstan was instrumental in establishing in Ceylon, Nigeria, and Nyasaland. Cotton cultivation in British possessions was also the subject of several reports. From 1903 current reports were published in the quarterly *Bulletin* of the Imperial Institute, which also contained special articles contributed by the staff on the industrial utilization of raw materials and on progress in tropical agriculture and production.

Dunstan was also interested in the teaching of science and in philosophy; the first led to his service as secretary with the British Association committee on this subject, and the second to his connexion with the foundation of the Aristotelian Society of which he was a vice-president and for some time edited the *Proceedings*. He was elected F.R.S. in 1893 and was a member of the council, 1905–7. As president of the International Association of Tropical Agriculture, he presided over the third international congress held in London in 1914; and he was president of the chemistry section of the British Association meeting at York in 1906. He was successively member of council, secretary, and a vice-president of the Chemical Society, served on the council of the Royal Geographical Society (1916), and was a corresponding member of the Institut Égyptien. He received the honorary degrees of M.A. from Oxford in 1888 and of LL.D. from Aberdeen in 1904. He was also a commander of the Order of Leopold of Belgium, and was appointed C.M.G. in 1913 and promoted K.C.M.G. in 1924.

In 1886 Dunstan married Emilie Fordyce, daughter of George Francis Maclean. She died in 1893, leaving a son and a daughter, and in 1900 Dunstan married Violet Mary Claudia, daughter of Frederick Stephen Archibald Hanbury-Tracy, member of Parliament, and son of the second Baron Sudeley. She survived her husband with a second daughter. He died at East Burnham End, near Slough, 20 April 1949.

A portrait of Dunstan painted in 1906 by Colin Forbes hangs in the rooms of the Chemical Society at Burlington House.

[T. A. Henry in *Obituary Notices of Fellows of the Royal Society*, No. 19, November 1950; *Journal* of the Chemical Society, 1950, part 1; Report on the operations of the Imperial Institute, in the *Bulletin* of the Imperial Institute, vol. xxi, 1923; private information; personal knowledge.]     T. A. HENRY.

DU PARCQ, HERBERT, BARON DU PARCQ (1880–1949), judge, was born in St. Helier, Jersey, 5 August 1880. His father, Clement Pixley du Parcq, was a bookseller, stationer, and printer in St. Helier and came of a family which had long been established in the island. His mother, Sophia Thoreau, belonged to the same family as the American author and naturalist, Henry David Thoreau. Du Parcq, who was the only child, was educated at Victoria College, Jersey, and, having been elected to an open scholarship in classics at Exeter College, Oxford, was placed in the first class in classical moderations in 1901 and the second class in *literae humaniores* in 1903. He was elected to a King Charles I senior scholarship at Jesus College in 1904 and took the further degree of B.C.L. in 1908. He became secretary and treasurer of the Union and was president in the Michaelmas term of 1902.

Du Parcq was called to the bar by the Middle Temple in 1906 and was admitted to the Jersey bar by the Royal Court of Jersey in the same year. He joined the Western circuit. In 1928 he became recorder of Portsmouth and in 1929 recorder of Bristol and judge of the Bristol Tolzey Court. In 1926 he took silk and in 1931 became a bencher of his Inn. He was a member of the General Council of the Bar, 1928–32. He was a member of the Council of Legal Education from 1933 and he was chairman of the Council from December 1947 until his death. At the bar he acquired a large and varied practice and in 1931 he was sent as commissioner on the spring assize of the Northern circuit. On 24 January 1932 there were disturbances in Dartmoor prison, which aroused some anxiety about its administration. The home secretary appointed du Parcq to inquire into the disturbances, and his report, published 7 February 1932, added to his reputation. He was appointed a judge of the King's Bench division, and knighted, in 1932, and displayed upon that ampler stage the judicial quality of which he had already given clear proof in his two recorderships. His subsequent promotion was not long delayed. He became a member of the Court of Appeal in 1938, being sworn of the Privy Council, and was advanced to the House of Lords as a lord of appeal in ordinary in 1946, with the title of Baron du Parcq, of Grouville, the parish in Jersey with which his paternal ancestors had been connected. In addition to his work as a law lord he undertook the duties of chairman of the Royal

Commission on justices of the peace which issued its report in 1948. He became an honorary fellow of both Exeter and Jesus colleges in 1935 and an honorary LL.D. of the university of Birmingham in 1947. He was a member of the Permanent Court of Arbitration at The Hague from 1945. He died in London 27 April 1949.

Du Parcq was uniformly patient and courteous towards counsel and litigants alike, but none the less he exercised a firm control over the proceedings in his court, and, whilst he allowed no waste of time, he was free from any defect of hastiness. He paid due regard to established principles and previous decisions without becoming over-rigid. His fellow judges have borne testimony to his excellent qualities as a colleague in the appeal tribunals to which he was promoted. He solved successfully the problem of reconciling a proper regard for the opinions of his colleagues with the legitimate exercise of his own independent judgement. In *Fox* v. *Newcastle-upon-Tyne Corporation*, [1941] 2 K.B. 120, a cyclist sued a municipal authority for damages which he had suffered through coming into collision with a shelter during the blackout period, and he alleged that the authority had been negligent in that they had failed either to erect a light on the shelter or to mark it by white paint. The other two lords justices dismissed the claim, but du Parcq dissented from them on a question of principle, and their judgement was afterwards disapproved by the Court of Appeal in *Fisher* v. *Ruislip–Northwood Urban District Council and Middlesex County Council*, [1945] 1 K.B. 584. His judgements are admirably expressed and are brightened by touches of vivacity and also by a kindly humour and a gentle irony, as for instance in *Bowater* v. *Rowley Regis Corporation*, [1944] K.B. at pp. 482–3. He was a fine and accomplished speaker with a pleasant voice and delivery, uniting charm of manner with grace and neatness of diction. After becoming a member of the House of Lords, he took part with much effect on more than one occasion in debates when legal matters were being discussed.

When the Germans occupied the Channel Islands in 1940 he acted as chairman of the Channel Islands refugees committee until its work was completed some five years later. He spared no trouble in his efforts to help and, when travelling was far from comfortable, he went repeatedly to towns at a considerable distance from London in order to speak a word of greeting to the refugees. He took an active part in the negotiations for the dispatch of a Red Cross vessel to the islands, and made three impressive and successful appeals for funds in the broadcast of the Week's Good Cause.

He married in 1911 Lucy, daughter of John Renouf, of St. Helier; they had one son and two daughters.

[Private information; personal knowledge.]
C. T. LE QUESNE.

EARLE, SIR LIONEL (1866–1948), civil servant, was born in London 1 February 1866, the second son of Captain Charles William Earle, Rifle Brigade, by his wife, Maria Theresa, daughter of Edward Ernest Villiers, younger brother of the fourth Earl of Clarendon [q.v.]. Her sister married the first Earl of Lytton [q.v.].

Educated at Marlborough and then sent abroad to learn languages, Earle studied at Göttingen and the Sorbonne at which time he seems to have contemplated medicine as his future career. He went up to Merton College, Oxford, but did not take a degree and, after attempting unsuccessfully to enter the diplomatic service, he accepted in 1898 a post as assistant secretary to the Royal Commission on the Paris Exhibition. In 1902–3 he was private secretary to Lord Dudley [q.v.], lord lieutenant of Ireland, and in 1907 private secretary to the lord president of the Council, Lord Crewe [q.v.], whom he followed to the Colonial Office shortly afterwards as principal private secretary. When Lewis (later Viscount) Harcourt [q.v.] succeeded Crewe in 1910, Earle continued to serve in the same capacity for the next two years. In 1912 Asquith appointed him permanent secretary to the Office of Works where he remained until his retirement in 1933.

Earle held this post with success. Affable, although somewhat distant in manner, handsome and well connected, he had many social contacts and was able to give valuable assistance to successive Governments, particularly in artistic matters where his cultured mind and good taste found adequate scope. In his day the Office was small and the staff few, and Earle's experience as a man of the world supplemented happily the departmental knowledge of his officials. It was especially due to his efforts that the Royal Fine Art Commission was established in 1924, and he gave that body active support.

Government hospitality, until then some-what haphazard, he helped to develop on liberal and dignified lines. Earle took great interest in the royal parks, and his tenure of office was notable for improve-ments in layout and the display of rare and beautiful plants. In the field of public memorials and statues he did valuable work. No statue may be erected in London in any public place without the authority of the department, and in the spate of memorials and statues which followed the war of 1914–18 Earle's influence was invariably exerted to bring about the selection of suitable sculptors and the allocation of appropriate sites.

In the more humdrum work of providing accommodation for government staffs Earle was less interested; and he was inclined to chafe at the restrictions of esti-mates procedure and public accounting; but his tact and common sense, together with the gift of knowing where to go for advice, remedied a somewhat impulsive judgement. He was popular with his staff and respected by them.

He was appointed C.M.G. (1901), C.B. (1911), K.C.B. (1916), K.C.V.O. (1921), and G.C.V.O. (1933). In 1926 he married Betty Strachey, daughter of William Edward Marriott and granddaughter of Sir John Strachey [q.v.]. The marriage was dissolved in 1937 and there was no issue. He died in London 10 March 1948. His recollections under the title *Turn Over the Page* appeared in 1935. A chalk and pastel drawing by Sir William Rothen-stein is in the possession of the family.

[Private information; personal knowledge.]
E. DE NORMANN.

EDDINGTON, SIR ARTHUR STAN-LEY (1882–1944), mathematician and astrophysicist, was born at Kendal, Westmorland, 28 December 1882, the second child and only son of Arthur Henry Eddington, a Somersetshire man who was headmaster of the Friends' School in Kendal, by his wife, Sarah Ann Shout, of Darlington, whose family was originally Dutch.

When Eddington was not yet two years old, his father died of typhoid, leaving the widow and two young children with very straitened means. They removed to Weston-super-Mare, where they lived from 1884 to 1913, and where the boy attended a small private school. From this he gained in 1898 a Somerset county scholar-ship which enabled him at the age of fifteen to enter the Owens College, Man-

chester. Here he had the good fortune to have as professors (Sir) Arthur Schuster in physics and (Sir) Horace Lamb in mathematics [qq.v.], both men of the highest eminence, under whose influence his intellectual power rapidly developed: he graduated B.Sc. with first class honours in physics in 1902, then entered Trinity College, Cambridge, which had awarded him an entrance scholarship in the previous December. At Cambridge he read mathe-matics, being senior wrangler in part i of the tripos of 1904. The following year he was placed in the first division of the first class in part ii.

In 1906 the chief assistant to the astronomer royal at Greenwich Observa-tory, (Sir) F. W. Dyson [q.v.], was ap-pointed astronomer royal for Scotland, and Eddington was chosen to succeed him. Concurrently with a certain amount of observational work, mostly with the meridian circle, he undertook a theoretical investigation, making a study of stellar proper-motions and star-drifts. The Dutch astronomer Jacobus Cornelis Kapteyn had discovered in 1904 that the distribu-tion of the peculiar motions of the stars is not random, but is preferential in two opposite directions in space; that, in fact, there are two 'star streams'. Eddington devised a powerful mathematical method for analysing these motions, and greatly extended Kapteyn's results. This in-vestigation formed the subject of a Smith's prize essay and a Trinity fellowship dis-sertation (both successful) in 1907.

In 1913 he was elected to the Plumian professorship of astronomy at Cambridge in succession to Sir G. H. Darwin [q.v.]. At that time the chair was not associated with the observational work, which was under the control of the Lowndean pro-fessor, Sir R. S. Ball [q.v.]; but after Ball's death, the directorship of the observatory was conjoined in 1914 with the Plumian professorship, and Eddington took up his residence there with his mother and sister. His first book, *Stellar Movements and the Structure of the Universe*, was published in the same year; its greatest significance was in the last chapter, which created a new subject, stellar dynamics.

In 1916 Eddington, who was now secre-tary of the Royal Astronomical Society, in that capacity received from Professor Willem de Sitter the manuscript of a paper on the new theory of gravitation which had been published by Einstein in the preceding year, and which is known as 'general relativity'. He became deeply interested, and in 1918 prepared for the Physical Society a report on it, which was ultimately expanded into a treatise, *The Mathematical Theory of Relativity*, in 1923. Among his original contributions must be mentioned specially a masterly analysis of the nature and propagation of gravitational waves, and a method of bringing electromagnetic phenomena into the scheme, which involved the creation of a new type of connexion between neighbouring portions of space-time. This latter, which was published in 1921, has proved of capital importance in the subsequent development of differential geometry, and has given Eddington a place of high honour among pure mathematicians.

Eddington himself attached great importance to an interpretation of general relativity which he set forth in two short papers in the *Philosophical Magazine* in 1921–2. Starting from the principle that there is no such thing as absolute length (so that to say a length is constant merely means that its ratio to some other length is constant), he inferred that what we call a metre at any place and in any direction is always a constant fraction of the radius of curvature of space-time associated with that place and direction. Hence the Riemann curvature at a point of space-time must be the same for all orientations, and must be the same for all points of space-time. But the conditions for this are precisely the Einstein equations for the gravitational field in empty space. Thus Einstein's law asserts the homogeneity and isotropy of space-time as regards Riemann curvature; but the mystery of the homogeneity and isotropy disappear when we realize that it is not intrinsic in the external world, but in the measurements we make of the world: the law simply expresses the fact that our survey of the world is made by instruments which are themselves part of the world. With this new insight came the conviction, which dominated the rest of his life, that the true foundation of natural philosophy must be in epistemology—the theory of knowledge.

The year 1916 saw also the beginning of Eddington's researches on the internal constitution of the stars. He introduced the principle that the chief agent in the transport of heat from the inner to the outer regions of a star is not (as had been generally supposed hitherto) convection, but radiation, and moreover that radiation-pressure plays an important part in supporting the weight of superincumbent material. His discussion led to the discovery of the mass-luminosity relation (viz. that the luminosity of a star depends chiefly on its mass). This was proved in the first place for 'giant' stars, within which the laws of perfect gases are obeyed: later, finding that his results were true also for the sun and stars in general, he inferred that they too must obey the gas-laws, and that this could be explained by their high state of ionization. These discoveries were the foundation for all subsequent developments, and made possible the modern theory of stellar evolution.

One of the observational facts which were for the first time understood in the light of this work was the very limited range of stellar masses. This was explained when it was calculated that for masses between one-tenth and a hundred times the sun's mass, the radiation-pressure and gas-pressure are of the same order of magnitude, but for greater masses the radiation-pressure would be so much in excess as to cause instability.

Another problem now solved was that of the nature of the stars known as 'white dwarfs'. These do not obey the mass-luminosity relation, and indeed the usual methods of computing the density of a component of a binary star gave for the best-known example (the companion of Sirius) a density over 50,000 times that of water. Eddington remarked that this enormous value could be accepted if the nuclei of the atoms were supposed to be stripped of their surrounding electrons, and pressed close together: and that an observational test was possible, since if the star's density were really so high, its spectral lines would show a marked Einstein shift. This was actually observed in 1925 by Walter Sydney Adams at Mount Wilson.

The results of the astrophysical investigations were collected in a book *The Internal Constitution of the Stars*, published in 1926, which was at once accepted as the most important work ever written on the subject.

The last sixteen years of Eddington's life were occupied chiefly with the discovery and development of certain new principles in physics, which he used in the first place in order to calculate theoretically the 'constants of nature' (such as the ratio of the mass of a proton to the mass of an electron, or the ratio of the electrostatic force to the gravitational force between an electron and a proton): he did in fact succeed in deriving exactly the values of all those constants of nature which are pure numbers. Later he showed that his ideas could be presented as a coherent system, to which he gave the name 'fundamental theory'.

The chief aim of physical theory, as it was conceived by all physicists before Eddington, was the prediction of events: being informed of the state of a system at some instant of time, it was desired to know what its state would be at some subsequent instant. In the new Eddington physics, the aim is not to predict events, but to determine by theoretical methods the structure of nature, that is, the values of the fundamental numbers (such as the two constants above-mentioned) which had previously been known only from observational or experimental measurements.

The position may be illustrated by reference to the history of an older problem. The ancient Egyptians were acquainted with the fact that the ratio of the area of a circle to the square on its radius is independent of the size of the circle; and for this number, which we denote by $\pi$, they found by actual measurement the value $\frac{256}{81} (= 3 \cdot 16...)$. In the third century before Christ, Archimedes showed that the number can be found to any desired degree of accuracy by pure theory, without the necessity for making measurements. For this purpose he assumed the axioms and propositions of geometry as they had been set forth in the preceding generation by Euclid; so that what Archimedes did was to assume the qualitative part of geometry and to deduce a quantitative aspect of it, namely the number $\pi$.

Now Eddington was simply the modern Archimedes. He regarded himself as at liberty to borrow anything in qualitative physics—he did in fact assume many propositions of the most advanced physical theory—but he did not assume any number determined empirically: and he deduced the quantitative propositions of physics, i.e. the exact values of the pure numbers that are constants of science—the numbers that are analogous to the number $\pi$ in geometry.

The investigation of the constants of nature may be regarded as, in some sense, a continuation of Eddington's researches in the theory of relativity. But the impetus which led to the new development came with the publication, in February 1928, of a celebrated paper by (Professor) P. A. M. Dirac on the wave-equation of the electron, in which it was shown that the power of the quantum theory to explain atomic spectra could be greatly increased by introducing relativistic ideas. Both quantum-mechanics and relativity were now well-developed mathematical theories, each remarkably successful in its own domain: and as they represented complementary aspects of the world (relativity finding most of its applications in the astronomical field, while quantum-mechanics was of use chiefly in connexion with atomic physics), Eddington felt that the time had come to construct a comprehensive doctrine combining and transcending both. He realized that while each theory separately had attained remarkable power as regards predicting the future, it would be necessary to look to some combination of the two in order to determine the ultimate structure of things.

The first stage was to find a common meeting-point of relativity and quantum theory—to consider a problem which could be solved rigorously by both methods. Such a problem is the state of equilibrium of a radiationless self-contained system of a very large number of particles. In molar relativity this problem was first solved by Einstein. The presence of the matter produces a curvature of space, depending on the total number of particles: so we obtain a closed curved space, in which the mutual gravitational attraction of the particles is exactly balanced by their mutual repulsion due to the cosmical term in general relativity. Such a system is called an Einstein universe.

We pass now to the other aspect; in quantum-mechanics a radiationless steady system is said to be in its ground state. We have therefore to determine the conditions to be satisfied by a system of particles treated (a) as an Einstein universe, (b) as a quantized system in its ground state. The two answers must agree; and a comparison of them yields relations between the constants of nature.

The most fundamental of these constants is the 'cosmical number' $N$, defined as the number of particles in an Einstein universe which is composed of hydrogen and which satisfies the requirements of quantum theory; its value is

$$N = \tfrac{3}{2} \cdot 136 \cdot 2^{256}.$$

It had already been recognized that the constants of nature fall into three groups, namely, (1) numbers between 1 and 2,000, (2) numbers of the order of $10^{39}$, (3) numbers of the order of $10^{79}$. It was now clear that these groups are simply (1) the numbers that do not involve $N$, (2) those that involve $\sqrt{N}$ as a factor, (3) those that involve $N$ as a factor.

Eddington's first contribution to the theory appeared in December 1928; in it he asserted that the 'fine-structure constant' of spectroscopy must be the reciprocal of a whole number, which was determined in a second paper (February 1930) to be 137. The cosmical number was found not long afterwards. The final systematic presentation was given in his book *Fundamental Theory*, published posthumously in 1946.

Eddington was elected a fellow of the Royal Society in 1914, was awarded a Royal medal in 1928, was knighted in 1930, and was appointed to the Order of Merit in 1938; he was president of the Royal Astronomical Society in 1921–3, of the Physical Society in 1930–32, and of the International Astronomical Union from 1938 to the end of his life. He received medals, prizes, and foreign associateships from many foreign academies and societies, and honorary doctorates from thirteen universities in the British Isles, South Africa, India, and the United States.

Eddington was a member of the Society of Friends, and the Quaker outlook influenced his views on many questions. He wrote excellent English, and was the author of many semi-popular works which had a great circulation, amongst which must be mentioned his Gifford lectures delivered at Edinburgh in 1927 on *The Nature of the Physical World* (published in 1928); but he was not a good extempore speaker, and was a shy man socially. He died, unmarried, at Cambridge 22 November 1944.

[*The Times*, 23 November 1944; H. C. Plummer in *Obituary Notices of Fellows of the Royal Society*, No. 14, November 1945; *Monthly Notices* of the Royal Astronomical Society, vol. cv, No. 2, 1945; *Observatory*, February 1945; *Proceedings* of the Physical Society, vol. lvii, part 3, May 1945; personal knowledge.]      E. T. WHITTAKER.

ELIAS, JULIUS SALTER, VISCOUNT SOUTHWOOD (1873–1946), newspaper proprietor, was born in Birmingham 5 January 1873, the youngest of the seven children of David Elias, Whitby jet merchant, by his wife, Esther Jones. His father failed in business and moved to London, settling as a newsagent and con-

fectioner at Hammersmith. Julius delivered morning papers before school, but this business also failed and the family moved to north London where he attended a private school for 4*d*. a week. At thirteen he left, to become successively shop-boy to a jeweller in Houndsditch and office-boy in several printing works. He was unemployed when, in 1894, a former colleague introduced him to William James Baird Odhams, partner in the small printing firm of Odhams Brothers.

Starting at 25*s*. a week, Elias soon won advancement by his keen business ability and devotion to duty. He was quickly promoted manager, and thereafter it was mainly his brain and energy which built up one of the largest publishing businesses in England. He saw that expansion lay first in the printing, then in the ownership, of journals. In 1896 a beginning was made with *Table Talk*, formerly house-journal of the Hotel Cecil, which made little mark or money. But in 1898 Odhams Brothers became Odhams, Ltd. (a private limited liability company until 1912, and thereafter a public company, finally merged with John Bull, Ltd., in 1920 as Odhams Press, Ltd.). Elias was a director from 1898 and by 1906 resources were such that the firm hoped to print *Tribune* (a national daily) and in 1907–8 even *The Times*.

Neither project eventuated, but in 1906 Odhams, Ltd., printed the first issue of *John Bull*, a combative popular weekly launched by Horatio Bottomley [q.v.]. Its main function was then the castigation of abuses and the unmasking of alleged rogues. The frequent libel actions which ensued (in which Odhams, Ltd., were joined with Bottomley as defendants) caused considerable anxiety, which was not lessened by Bottomley's financial vagaries. Nevertheless *John Bull* prospered, reaching its financial apogee in 1919. In 1920 Bottomley sold out of ownership, but remained editor. In 1921, deeply suspicious of Bottomley's 'Victory Bonds' scheme, Odhams parted company with him, and in May 1922 Bottomley was sent to penal servitude. An undiscriminating public now withdrew its support, and circulation fell from 1,700,000 copies to about 200,000. Even this crushing blow did not daunt Elias, who had become managing director of his firm in 1920, for he raised new capital, and with skilled editorial aid rehabilitated *John Bull* in a new guise as a respectable family journal. *John Bull* continued a mainstay; but meanwhile great rotary printing presses lay partially unemployed. Elias's solution was a Sunday paper, and in 1925 Odhams bought the *People* from Colonel Grant Morden. It was losing money and circulating at roughly 300,000; within three years (partly by free insurances for readers and other adventitious aids) Elias had multiplied this figure by ten.

Once again the existence of partially-unoccupied machines presented a challenge and an opportunity. The production of a daily newspaper was the answer, and in 1929 Odhams, Ltd., took over the Labour Party's *Daily Herald* (with a 51% holding against the Trades Union Congress's 49%). A separate company, Daily Herald (1929), Ltd., was formed, to put Labour's paper into real competition with its political rivals. Elias had a hard task, between the Charybdis of an expanding capitalistic concern and the Scylla of a militant organization with a strong socialistic bias. Years later he told Lord Camrose that 'he was near despair on more than one occasion and that he had walked round Covent Garden market, quite close to his offices in Long Acre, late at night wondering if he could get through or whether he had better admit defeat'. But the task was accomplished; and from some 300,000 the *Daily Herald* rose in circulation in ten years to over two million. A Manchester office was opened, and these premises were used also for the *People*.

From 1934 Elias was chairman of a group which, as time went on, controlled such remunerative periodicals as *Illustrated*, *News Review*, *Sporting Life*, *Woman*, and a miscellaneous brood ranging from Debrett's *Peerage* to Dean's rag-books. In 1936 there was opened a huge printing works at Watford, which worked not only for the parent company, but for such large concerns as Illustrated Newspapers, Ltd., of which Elias became chairman, and which controlled the *Sphere*, the *Tatler*, and other highly popular sheets. By 1947 the market value of the main company stood at over £7 million.

In 1937 Elias was raised to the peerage as Baron Southwood, of Fernhurst, in the county of Surrey, and was advanced to a viscountcy in 1946. Disposing of an ample income in his later years, he lived unostentatiously and contributed lavishly to hospitals and to bodies concerned with the welfare of printers and newsvendors. He was also highly successful in raising charitable funds. In politics he was a

Tory democrat, but he voted with the Labour Party in the House of Lords and for some time acted as one of its whips. He spoke with most zest on what he called 'a Southwood subject', that is, a humanitarian cause. Childless himself, he was deeply interested in children and their welfare. His relationships with his own staff were of the happiest, for he never forgot his own early experiences, and he loved to know that he was affectionately called (from his slight and spare build) 'the little man'. Southwood had a deep-seated and fundamental kindness of heart which manifested itself not only in multifarious philanthropic activities but in his dealings with his fellow men, and even in his dislike of seeing personal abuse in any of his papers. Born of Jewish parents, he was not a practising Jew, and would chuckle at quips about the race which came to his ears in the works. His religious feeling, in the broadest sense of the term, was strong, but consisted of a vague and unclassifiable theism. He was not a lettered man, but he became a connoisseur of typography and took the greatest interest in the layout of all his papers. He died at Southwood Court, Highgate, 10 April 1946.

In 1906 Elias married Alice Louise (died 1951), daughter of Charles Stone Collard, chartered accountant, of London. A portrait of Elias by T. C. Dugdale was presented in 1949 by Odhams Press to the Printers' Pensions Almshouse and Orphan Asylum Corporation, and hangs in their Lord Southwood Homes of Rest, Wood Green, London. Another, by James Gunn, is at Odhams Press.

The ashes of Southwood and his wife are buried in a small garden in the churchyard of St. James's, Piccadilly, which has as its central feature a fountain designed by A. F. Hardiman [q.v.]. The garden was given by Southwood to commemorate the courage of the people of London throughout the war of 1939–45.

[*The Times*, 11 April 1946; W. J. B. Odhams, *The Business and I*, 1935; Bernard Falk, *Five Years Dead*, 1937; Viscount Camrose, *British Newspapers and their Controllers*, 1947; *Report* of the Royal Commission on the Press, 1949; R. J. Minney, *Viscount Southwood*, 1954; private information.]

HERBERT B. GRIMSDITCH.

ELLES, SIR HUGH JAMIESON (1880–1945), general, was the third son of Captain (later Lieutenant-General Sir) Edmond Roche Elles who saw much service on the North-West Frontier of India and was military member of the viceroy's council. His mother, Clare Gertrude, was the daughter of a Mutiny veteran, Brigadier-General Octavius Edward Rothney, of the 4th Sikhs. Born in India 27 April 1880, Hugh Elles followed his brothers to Clifton and passed high into the Royal Military Academy, Woolwich, in 1897, again following his eldest brother who passed in first and out second, but lost his life in a gallant attempt to rescue a drowning soldier. Passing out second, Hugh Elles was commissioned in the Royal Engineers in June 1899 and saw active service in the later stages of the South African war. Promoted to lieutenant in 1901 and captain in 1908, he served as adjutant, Royal Engineers, at Aldershot before going to the Staff College in 1913. On mobilization he was appointed deputy assistant quarter-master-general, 4th division, and was present at Le Cateau, on the Aisne, and in the fighting of 1914 round Armentières. Appointed brigade-major, 10th brigade, in March 1915, he was wounded 25 April 1915 in the brigade's great counter-attack near St. Julien. He went to G.H.Q. in August 1915 as G.S.O.2 in the operations section, being promoted to major in November 1915. Early in 1916 he was sent home by Sir Douglas (later Earl) Haig [q.v.] to report on the progress of the tanks, and after their rather disappointing first appearance in September 1916 he was appointed to command them, becoming temporary colonel. He did great work in improving the tactical training and handling in action of the new arm, factors of no less importance than the improvements in design which the first experiment had shown to be needed. An inspiring leader, imaginative and resourceful, but level-headed, Elles saw the reward of his work at Cambrai (November 1917) where on ground better suited to them than they had met at Ypres they scored under his personal command their first substantial success.

Promoted to brigadier-general in 1917 and to (temporary) major-general in 1918, Elles retained command of the Tank Corps in France until the end of hostilities, being appointed to the D.S.O. in 1916, and C.B. in 1918. On returning home in 1919 as a colonel, having received two brevets, he was given command of the Tank Corps training centre at Wool, transferring to the War Office as inspector, Tank Corps, in May 1923. He then commanded the 9th brigade from October 1923 to August 1926, was chief general staff officer, Eastern Command, until May 1930, being promoted to major-general in November 1928. From May 1930 until October 1933 he was director of military training, and after commanding the 42nd (East Lancashire Territorial) division returned to London as master-general of the ordnance in May 1934, having become a lieutenant-general in March. It was a time of great difficulty; even when the needs of the situation came to be appreciated, much leeway had to be made up; but under Elles much was achieved. Promoted to general in 1938 he was made colonel of the Royal Tank Corps in 1934 and of the Royal Engineers in 1935. He was appointed K.C.M.G. in 1919, K.C.V.O. in 1929, and promoted K.C.B. in 1935. He was a commander of the Legion of Honour and received the French and Belgian croix de guerre and the American D.S.M.

Retiring in 1938 he found an outlet for his energies in industry where his contribution was much valued by those with whom he worked. In 1939 his services were soon required for civil defence, and as regional commissioner for the south west he did great work. His headquarters were at Bristol, a heavily bombed centre, where he made himself trusted and liked, helping and encouraging all under him. The strain was heavy, particularly in dealing with the influx of American troops and the civil side of the preparation for the landing in Normandy. He survived until the surrender of Germany, dying in London 11 July 1945. He had not only a fine brain and great capacities as an administrator but he could get the best out of those under him; tactful and cheerful, if he could be critical, he was just and appreciative and a real leader. A fine tactician and a most inspiring commander, his work for the development of the tanks was of great importance. If he was not one of those who made them he showed how to use them.

Elles married first, in 1912, Geraldine Ada (died 1922), daughter of the late Lieutenant-General Sir Gerald de Courcy Morton, K.C.I.E., by whom he had two daughters; secondly, in 1923 he married May (died 1937), widow of Lieutenant-Colonel George Despard Franks, C.M.G., of the 19th Hussars; and thirdly, in 1939 Blanche, daughter of John Peter Hornung, of West Grinstead Park, and widow of Lieutenant-Colonel Arthur Houssemayne du Boulay. There is a portrait in the Imperial War Museum by Sir William Orpen.

[*Cliftonian*, December 1945; Sir J. E. Edmonds and others, (Official) *History of the Great War. Military Operations, France and Belgium, 1914–18*, 1922–48; *The Times*, 13 July 1945.]                    C. T. ATKINSON.

ELLIS, THOMAS EVELYN SCOTT-, eighth BARON HOWARD DE WALDEN and fourth BARON SEAFORD (1880–1946), writer, sportsman, and patron and lover of the arts. [See SCOTT-ELLIS.]

ELLIS, SIR WILLIAM HENRY (1860–1945), civil engineer, was born at Thurnscoe Hall, near Rotherham, 20 August 1860, the fourth son of John Devonshire Ellis [q.v.], one of the original three partners of John Brown & Co., manufacturers of armour plate and steel at Sheffield.

William Ellis was educated at Uppingham and in November 1878 entered the works of Tannett, Walker & Co. of Leeds, passing through their various shops and drawing office. In 1882 he had charge on their behalf of the erection of a vertical blowing engine at some copper smelting works in Serbia, and afterwards he was, for two years, a foreman in their erecting shop in Leeds. In October 1885 he went to Sheffield to take charge of the construction at John Brown's of a 4,000-ton hydraulic forging press, a pair of hydraulic pumping engines, and two overhead travelling cranes in connexion with the press. After this work had been completed in October 1887 he entered the employment of John Brown & Co. as under-manager of their forge department. He was appointed a director of the company in 1906, and became managing director in 1919.

Ellis, who throughout his career displayed marked ability in technical, commercial, and administrative work, found time to render public service also in various ways. He was master cutler of Sheffield from 1914 to 1918. The high value set on his services to metallurgical science and industry was shown by his election as president of the Institution of Civil Engineers (1925–6), and of the engineering section of the British Association at its meeting in Glasgow in 1928. In a wider sphere he became a member of bodies such as the council of the university of Sheffield, the executive board of the National Physical Laboratory, the govern-

ing body of the Imperial College of Science and Technology, and the appointments board of the university of Cambridge. For his services he was appointed G.B.E. in 1918 and a commander of the Order of the Crown of Italy. He received the honorary degree of D.Eng. from Sheffield University in 1918.

Apart from business activities, what may well have been nearest to Ellis's heart were mountains and hills. A keen and intrepid mountaineer, he climbed the Matterhorn on his seventieth, and the Jungfrau on his seventy-fifth, birthday, and preserved his memory in Switzerland by endowing in 1938 the 'Sir William Ellis Trust for Guides of Swiss Nationality' with a sum of £4,000, the income of which was to be used to help Swiss guides and their dependants in cases of necessity. The Derbyshire moorlands were an open book to him; he looked forward to his week-ends, when walks of sixteen to twenty miles over the wild heather-clad moors and fells of the Pennines were his delight and afforded him mental rest in invigorating air, and equipped him for the work of the ensuing week. Besides this, he was an accomplished organist, who enjoyed entertaining friends of an evening with selections from famous composers.

Ellis married in 1889 Lucy Rimington (died 1938), daughter of Francis William Tetley, director of the firm of Joshua Tetley & Son, brewers and maltsters, of Leeds, by whom he had two sons and two daughters. He died in Sheffield 4 July 1945. A portrait by Arthur Hacker hangs in the Sheffield Royal Infirmary, and a copy is at the Institution of Civil Engineers.

[*Engineer* and *Engineering*, 13 July 1945; *Journal* of the Institution of Civil Engineers, October 1945; *Alpine Journal*, November 1945; private information; personal knowledge.]                    J. F. BRIDGE.

ELPHINSTONE, SIR (GEORGE) KEITH (BULLER) (1865–1941), engineer, was born at Musselburgh 11 May 1865, the second son of Captain Edward Charles Buller Elphinstone, 92nd Highlanders, brother of the fifteenth Lord Elphinstone. His mother was Elizabeth Harriette, daughter of Sir George Clerk, sixth baronet, of Penicuik [q.v.].

He was educated at Charterhouse, and on leaving school entered the firm of M. Theiler & Sons, of Canonbury, which he had purchased. His earliest work was the installation of some of the first privately owned electric lighting and telephone equipment in London. In 1893 he became a partner in the firm of Elliott Brothers, electrical and mechanical engineers, with which he remained associated until his death, having been chairman of the company for some years.

Between 1893 and 1914 Elphinstone was connected with the invention and development of many electrical and mechanical devices and with the manufacture of the first micrometers in this country. He designed the first continuous-roll chart recorder, installed the original electric speed-recording apparatus used at Brooklands, and invented speedometers in motor-cars. With the outbreak of war in 1914 he became closely associated with the design and manufacture of gunfire-control apparatus for use in ships of the Royal Navy. He collaborated with Prince Louis of Battenberg (later the Marquess of Milford Haven, q.v.), with Captain (later Rear-Admiral) John Saumarez Dumaresq, and with (Sir) Frederic Charles Dreyer in the development of fire-control tables. This confidential work remained his chief interest for the rest of his life, and led to many close friendships with senior naval officers. In spite of great technical advances in this field of engineering, he kept himself fully conversant with all the details of the latest designs. His services to the Admiralty were recognized by his appointment in 1917 as O.B.E., and in 1920 he was promoted K.B.E.

Elphinstone died at his home in London 6 July 1941 after a life of personal courage and endurance in overcoming a severe physical handicap, for an illness in childhood left him with partially paralysed legs and prevented him from entering the navy. He was a man of great charm and integrity, respected by all who knew him. The artist in him found expression in various ways: water-colour painting, woodcuts, and the construction of many pieces of furniture and clocks, including a fine hand-made calendar clock.

He married twice: first, in 1899 Katherine Amy (died 1925), daughter of Colonel Alfred James Wake, R.A., of Blackheath, by whom he had one daughter; secondly, in 1926 Isobel Penrose (died 1953), daughter of Sir Theodore Fry, first baronet. A portrait of Elphinstone by Edward I. Halliday is in the possession of the writer.

[Private information; personal knowledge.]
H. GRANT PETERKIN.

ELTON, OLIVER (1861–1945), scholar and critic, was born at Gresham Grammar School, Holt, Norfolk, 3 June 1861, the only child of the Rev. Charles Allen Elton, headmaster of the school, by his wife, Sarah Amelia, daughter of John Ransom, solicitor, of Holt. Educated by his father until he went to Marlborough College in 1873, he entered Corpus Christi College, Oxford, as a classical scholar in 1880, and was awarded a second class in classical moderations in 1881 and a first in *literae humaniores* in 1884. He was closely associated with the newly founded *Oxford Magazine*, and contributed to it his first verse translations. On leaving Oxford he engaged in private tutoring in London, gave extension lectures, began reviewing, edited for schools two of Shakespeare's plays (*I Henry IV*, 1889, *King John*, 1890) and the early poems of Milton (1890–93), and translated from the Icelandic, on the suggestion of F. York Powell [q.v.], *The Life of Laurence Bishop of Hólar in Iceland* (1890). His first university appointment came in 1890, when he was made independent lecturer in English literature at the Owens College, Manchester. His friendship with C. E. Montague [q.v.] brought him into connexion with the *Manchester Guardian* for which he wrote reviews and dramatic criticisms—six of which (one on Forbes-Robertson's Hamlet) were reprinted in *The Manchester Stage, 1880–1900* (1900). During his ten years in Manchester he published three books— his translation of the first nine books of the *Danish History* of Saxo Grammaticus with an introduction by York Powell to which he contributed a large part (1894); his *Introduction to Michael Drayton* (Spenser Society, 1895, largely rewritten as *Michael Drayton, a critical study*, 1905); and *The Augustan Ages* in Saintsbury's 'Periods of European Literature'. With the publication in 1899 of this last volume, which covers the period roughly from 1650 to 1730 and contains his fullest treatment of French literature, he won his place among the academic critics.

Elton was invited to Liverpool to be King Alfred professor of English literature, in succession to (Sir) Walter Raleigh [q.v.], and entered on his new duties in January 1901. When the college at Liverpool (hitherto in the federal Victoria University) was raised to the status of an independent university in 1903, he played a tireless part in the problems connected with its development. His colleagues might make friendly comments on his scrupulous rectitude, but he could be counted on all his life not to express a prejudiced opinion.

The first book which Elton published while at Liverpool was *Frederick York Powell, a life, and a selection from his letters and occasional writings* (2 vols., 1906), a tribute to the encourager of his early days. In *Modern Studies* (1907) he included four articles contributed to the *Quarterly Review* ('Giordano Bruno in England', 'The Meaning of Literary History', 'Recent Shakespeare Criticism', 'The Novels of Mr. Henry James') and, among other pieces, his inaugural lecture at Liverpool, on Tennyson, in which he had surprised his audience by his qualifications of the then accepted verdict. But by this time he was beginning to think of what was to prove his main work, his 'surveys' of our literature during three periods of fifty years. *A Survey of English Literature 1780–1830* (2 vols.) appeared in 1912; *Survey 1830–1880* (2 vols.) followed in 1920, and *Survey 1730–1780* (2 vols.) in 1928. Each, as he said in the preface to the first, was not so much a history as 'a direct criticism of everything I can find in the literature of fifty years that speaks to me with any sound of living voice'. Together they form the fullest account that any single writer has attempted of any 150 years of our literature, and while their value lies chiefly in the sanity and freshness of the estimates of individual authors or works, the ordinary matter of professed histories is not neglected. His gift of concise yet clear expression is nowhere seen better than in his *Surveys*. He was careful of every sentence that he wrote, and it was not his habit to waste a word.

In 1908 Elton was asked by the English Association to give its centenary address on Milton and took as his subject 'Milton and Party'; and in 1932, as its president, he spoke on 'Robert Bridges and *The Testament of Beauty*'. Between these two dates he contributed three essays ('English Prose Numbers', 'Reason and Enthusiasm in the Eighteenth Century', 'The Poet's Dictionary') to the Association's *Essays and Studies*, and edited two volumes in the series (1914, 1925). He gave two lectures to the British Academy —the Warton lecture in 1914 on 'Poetic Romancers after 1850' and the Shakespeare lecture in 1936 on 'Style in Shakespeare'. He gave the Taylorian lecture at Oxford in 1929 on Chekhov. The earlier of these are included in *A Sheaf of Papers*

(1922), the last collection of his lectures or essays which he published while at Liverpool.

On retiring from his professorship in 1925 Elton made his home in Oxford. He had paid his first visit to America in 1892 when he lectured at Johns Hopkins University, and he had been in India at the Punjab University in 1917–18. He now began his retirement by spending several months in America in 1926 as visiting professor at Harvard and as Lowell lecturer. He gave courses at Bedford College, London, in 1927–8 and Gresham College, London, in 1929–30. He was again visiting professor at Harvard in 1930–31. Thereafter he was to remain at home.

At Oxford he completed his third *Survey*, and then wrote another tribute to a great friendship, *C. E. Montague, a memoir* (1929). But the chief work of his later years was *The English Muse, a Sketch* (1933), an account of English poetry in its whole range from Anglo-Saxon times to the war of 1914–18. He described it as 'a companion to an imaginary, and most imperfect, anthology'. Though independent of the *Surveys* even when it covers the same ground, it is like them in the vigour and sureness of its criticism and the lucid conciseness of its style. In the same year he edited as literary executor a collection of Saintsbury's *Prefaces and Essays* (1933) and wrote the obituary of Saintsbury for the British Academy. *Essays and Addresses* (1939), largely composed of pieces mentioned above, was his last collection of his own writings. It included 'The Nature of Literary Criticism', his Ludwig Mond lecture at Manchester in 1935, and 'Alexander Pushkin', delivered at the Royal Institution in 1938.

Elton had a wide command of languages. In his early days he had translated from Icelandic and from Anglo-Saxon ('Judith 1–121' in the *English Miscellany presented to Dr. Furnivall*, 1901). During the war of 1914–18 he learned Russian, and in the leisure of his retirement he found happy occupation in making verse renderings of poems in Russian, Polish, and Serbo-Croat. They were contributed to the *Slavonic Review* and *Year-book*, and formed two independent volumes, *Verse from Pushkin and Others* (1935) and *Evgeny Onegin* (1937). On the latter, his reputation as a translator rests securely.

Among the last things which Elton published were the obituary of Lascelles

Abercrombie for the British Academy (1939), translations from Mickiewicz's *Pan Tadeusz* (1940), and the preface to J. B. Yeats's *Letters to his son W. B. Yeats and Others* (1944). He died in Oxford, 4 June 1945, the day after he completed his eighty-fourth year. He had hurt his heart by cycling against a head wind in 1933, and latterly his handsome frame—he was well over six feet—had put an increasing strain on it. Since the death of Saintsbury he had been held in honour as the doyen of English studies.

Elton received honorary degrees from the universities of Durham (1912), Manchester (1919), Edinburgh (1922), Oxford (1925), Liverpool (1928), and Reading (1935). He was elected F.B.A. (1924), and honorary fellow of Corpus Christi College, Oxford (1930).

In 1888 he married Letitia Maynard (died 1947), daughter of the Rev. Dugald MacColl, of Glasgow, and sister of D. S. MacColl [q.v.]. They had two sons.

On leaving Liverpool Elton was presented with his portrait painted by Augustus John; it now hangs in the University Club, Liverpool. An etched portrait by Francis Dodd is reproduced in *Proceedings* of the British Academy, volume xxxi. Elton is also one of a group painted by Albert Lipczinski (1915) of some of the staff of the university of Liverpool which hangs in the common-room of the faculty of arts.

[L. C. Martin in *Proceedings* of the British Academy, vol. xxxi, 1945; *Manchester Guardian*, 6 June 1945; *The Times*, 7 June 1945; Anne Treneer, *Cornish Years*, 1949; private information; personal knowledge.]

D. NICHOL SMITH.

ESDAILE, KATHARINE ADA (1881–1950), art historian, was born in London 23 April 1881, the daughter of Andrew McDowall, secretary to the Girls' Public Day School Trust, by his wife, Ada Benson, sister of E. W. Benson [q.v.], archbishop of Canterbury, and first headmistress in turn of Norwich, Oxford, and Bedford high schools. The daughter was educated at Notting Hill High School and was a scholar of Lady Margaret Hall, Oxford. She read classics, obtaining a third class in honour moderations in 1903, and the direction of her future studies was foreshadowed by her special interest in antique sculpture. This interest she pursued, after leaving Oxford, at the British School at Rome. In 1907 she married

A. J. K. Esdaile (died 1956), from 1926 to 1940 secretary of the British Museum. It was not until 1919, after the birth of her third child, that she was able to devote herself to the intensive study of post-medieval sculpture in England, the subject which she made peculiarly her own. The foundations of her knowledge were laid equally in visiting churches and in the British Museum, more particularly by her work on the manuscript notebooks of George Vertue [q.v.]; and when the first volumes of these manuscripts were published by the Walpole Society in 1930 (vol. xviii) and subsequent years Mrs. Esdaile was acknowledged as having prepared the material for press. In the meantime a number of articles by her, mainly on sculpture of the later seventeenth and eighteenth centuries, had appeared in the *Architect*, the *Burlington Magazine*, *The Times*, and the publications of the Walpole Society, and in 1924 she produced a short illustrated book on the work at Trinity College, Cambridge, of L. F. Roubiliac [q.v.].

In 1927 Mrs. Esdaile published *English Monumental Sculpture since the Renaissance* and in 1928 *The Life and Works of Louis François Roubiliac*, two works which were complementary to each other, for the latter being concerned with every aspect of the sculptor's work included a large body of portrait sculpture necessarily excluded or at the most treated shortly in the earlier book. These two books may reasonably be considered the solid core of her achievement and the first of them shows her at her best as an art historian. The chapters on 'Symbolism', on 'Costume', and that called 'The Need of Understanding' in particular show the breadth of her knowledge of the social, religious, and literary background of her subject, a quality which distinguishes her work from that of scholars who have been strongly influenced by the self-contained art historical world of Central Europe. *English Monumental Sculpture since the Renaissance* also shows that these qualities are hardly less perceptible in her handling of the early seventeenth-century or late sixteenth-century material than in the later periods. This implies that her preoccupation with studies at least closely related to her later specialization dated from long before her work on the manuscript material in the British Museum and elsewhere. In this connexion it is perhaps worth noting that in the latter part of the war of 1914–18 she worked for Messrs. Batsford, the architectural publishers.

In her work on the earlier post-medieval sculpture Mrs. Esdaile built on the foundation laid by Lady Victoria Manners who had published the documents concerning the memorable series of Manners tombs in Bottesford church, Leicestershire, in 1903, and the publication of the Nicholas Stone notebooks and account book by the Walpole Society in 1919 (vol. vii). With her remarkable knowledge of the documentary and literary sources and her vast first-hand experience of the monuments themselves she was able to carry the study of Elizabethan and early seventeenth-century sculpture far beyond these modest though important beginnings.

Mrs. Esdaile's later works included the *Temple Church Monuments* (1933) and a short history of St. Martin-in-the-Fields (1944), and a last volume, *English Church Monuments* (1946), which embodies much of the material published in short articles elsewhere, especially in learned journals. Of these shorter articles, the most remarkable are that on Epiphanius Evesham in *The Times* in 1932, and that on the Stantons of Holborn, a family of three generations of London sculptors whose activities covered the centuries from Charles I's time to George II's, published in the *Archaeological Journal* for 1928.

In 1928 Mrs. Esdaile received a medal for her work from the Royal Society of Arts and in 1937 she was awarded a Leverhulme fellowship. She was a much valued member of the Society for the Protection of Ancient Buildings and other kindred bodies. In her later years she lived at West Hoathly in Sussex, where she died 31 August 1950.

[Private information.]
       Geoffrey Webb.

EVANS, Sir ARTHUR JOHN (1851–1941), archaeologist, was born at Nash Mills, Hemel Hempstead, 8 July 1851, the eldest of the three sons of the distinguished archaeologist and numismatist (Sir) John Evans [q.v.], by his first wife, Harriet Ann, younger daughter of his maternal uncle John Dickinson, paper-maker. Arthur resembled his father in features and tastes, and as early as 1866 accompanied him on his first visit to the Somme gravels, and himself found a 'palaeolith' *in situ*. He became a collector, a draughtsman, and a linguist; unusual short sight did not debar him from enjoyment of country life, and enabled him to detect minute details such as artists' signatures on Greek coins and gems.

From the preparatory school of C. A. Johns [q.v.], a naturalist, at Chipperfield, Hertfordshire, he entered Harrow, reached the sixth form in 1867, and was placed fourth in the examination for leaving scholarships in April 1870, distinguishing himself in English literature, Greek and Latin verse, modern languages, and natural science, and by editing the *Harrovian* and a satirical *Pen-Viper* which was suppressed. He was already an ardent Liberal, and a keen Slav partisan in Balkan politics. In October 1870 he entered Brasenose College, Oxford, and was placed in the first class in modern history in 1874.

A year's study at Göttingen was preceded and followed by adventures in Bosnia (1871), Herzegovina, Finland, and Lapland (1873–4), and in 1875 he sent to the *Manchester Guardian* letters republished in 1876 as *Through Bosnia and the Herzegovina on Foot, during the Insurrection, August and September 1875*; this was followed by *Illyrian Letters* (1878). In 1878 he married Margaret, eldest daughter of the historian Edward Augustus Freeman [q.v.], an accomplished and devoted comrade until her death in 1893. At Ragusa he had found in the Casa San Lazzaro a convenient centre for the study of language, antiquities, and customs, and spent six years there in all. During the Crivoscian insurrection of 1882 he was arrested and condemned to death by the Austrians, but was reprieved and expelled. His political ideal was a 'South Slavonic monarchy built out of Austria and the Balkans'; to this he recurred vigorously in 1914–16 and later he saw it temporarily realized. His archaeological studies in these years were published in *Archaeologia*, volumes xlviii and xlix (1884, 1885), and summarized in his unpublished Ilchester lectures delivered at Oxford in 1884, and in his Rhind lectures given at Edinburgh in 1895. In Italy and Sicily he collected vases and coins, and wrote on 'The "Horsemen" of Tarentum' (*Numismatic Chronicle*, vol. ix, 1889) and 'Syracusan "Medallions" and their Engravers' (ibid., vol. xi, 1891).

With this wide experience and equipment Evans was in 1884 appointed keeper of the Ashmolean Museum at Oxford which had fallen into neglect and was overlapped by the classical sculpture and vases of the Randolph Gallery in

Beaumont Street, where (Sir) W. M. Ramsay [q.v.], the first occupant of the Lincoln and Merton chair of classical archaeology and art, was provided with a small space for a library and a cast-collection. With the munificent help of C. D. E. Fortnum [q.v.] and Greville Chester the collections were removed in 1894 to a new building behind the Randolph, repeatedly enlarged and always overflowing, and in 1908, after many years of controversy and negotiation, the combined institutions were supplied with a single board of visitors. After temporary occupancies, Ashmole's original building in Broad Street was assigned to the Museum of the History of Science, inaugurated by the collections of Evans's brother Lewis.

The conditions of Ashmole's keepership prescribe travel and lectures, and Evans took full advantage of both. In 1890 he gave a summer course on British prehistoric antiquities, but he was not a popular lecturer, and most of his later discoveries were announced at meetings of the British Association. Meanwhile he excavated a Roman villa at Frilford, near Oxford, and in 1891 the late Celtic urnfield at Aylesford in Kent. In 1893 he acquired an estate called Youlbury, near Oxford, and created there an earthly paradise and a second home to three generations of friends.

In his Rhind lectures, Evans had to study the highly controversial question of the influence of ancient oriental cultures on those of early Europe. As a young man he had been influenced by the work of Heinrich Schliemann at 'Troy' and Mycenae and Tiryns, by Wolfgang Helbig's Das homerische Epos (1884) with its Italian archaeology, and by Arthur Milchhoefer's Die Anfänge der Kunst in Griechenland (1883) inferring from the geographical distribution of certain engraved seal-stones that Crete had been a principal centre of 'Mycenaean' culture. In 1889 the Ashmolean acquired such a seal-stone from Greville Chester; Evans found others in Athens (1893) and in the Berlin Antiquarium. Such surface-finds could be explored even in a malcontent province of Turkey. In 1893 came news of painted pottery in the Candia Museum from the Kamárais cave on Mount Ida, identical with 'Aegean imports' announced by (Sir) Flinders Petrie [q.v.] from Kahun, a twelfth-dynasty site in the Fayyûm. The same year Evans announced his clue to the existence of picture-writing in Greek lands; and in

March 1894 he travelled in Crete, collecting from the peasant women many prehistoric seal-stones inscribed with pictorial signs; he copied a clay tablet (afterwards destroyed) with a linear inscription; and noted masons' marks on pre-Hellenic walls. These finds were announced to the British Association in August (Journal of Hellenic Studies, vol. xiv, 1894) and extended in subsequent years (ibid., vol. xvii, 1897). The general bearing of these discoveries was communicated to the British Association in 1896 (The Eastern Question in Anthropology) and their significance for Greek religion in 'Mycenaean Tree and Pillar Cult' (Proceedings of the British Association, 1896; Journal of Hellenic Studies, vol. xxi, 1901). In 1897, when war was imminent between Greece and Turkey, he explored the 'megalithic' structures of Tripolitania—actually Roman oil-presses; and the survivals of a linear script among the caravan traders from Ghadames.

In 1894 Evans had acquired a share, under Ottoman law, of the estate at Kephála, near Candia, the classical Knossos, where 'Mycenaean' remains had been found in 1878; so when the Turks evacuated Crete in 1899 he was able at once to gain full possession, and excavate in association with the British School of Archaeology at Athens and its director D. G. Hogarth [q.v.]. There was no overload of later remains, and some of the best finds were close to the surface. The first season (1899–1900) revealed an elaborate palace, of the late Bronze Age (c. 1700–1400) with many clay tablets inscribed in the 'linear' script already detected, superimposed upon earlier buildings with 'Kamárais' pottery (c. 2000), brilliant frescoes, and imported Egyptian and Babylonian objects. Work continued for eight seasons, followed by intermittent enterprises in the 'palace', its suburbs, and cemeteries. The principal works of art were exhibited in London in 1903, and more fully in 1936. The first volume of Scripta Minoa was published in 1909, the second in 1952, and The Palace of Minos at Knossos in four volumes, in 1921–35 (index, 1936). Concurrent excavations by Italians at Phaestos and Hagia Triada, by Frenchmen at Mállia, by Americans at Gourniá, Mochlos, and other sites, and by the British School at Praesos, Palaikastro, and Zakro, supplemented the record of Knossos, and made it necessary to present the new prehistoric culture as a whole. Evans proposed in advance a ninefold classification into 'early', 'middle', and 'late', each subdivided into periods I, II, and III, recalling the 'nine seasons' of the legendary Cretan ruler Minos, but actually corresponding with major phases of civilization both in Crete and in Egypt and at Knossos with extensive demolitions and reconstructions. Below the early Minoan lay a deep Neolithic deposit, and above the latest Minoan a rapid replacement of Bronze-Age by early-Iron-Age occupancy. Less symmetrical crises were the great earthquakes which ended Middle Minoan II (c. 1700) and Late Minoan II (the specifically 'palace' style, c. 1400). In Late Minoan III a growing divergence between the culture of Crete and that of the 'Mycenaean' or 'Helladic' mainland led to the predominance of the latter over a wide colonial region, from Cyprus to Sicily. This preliminary scheme for classification was published in Athens in 1904, London in 1906, and Rome in 1912. The reclassification of the later mainland phases as 'Helladic' was never accepted by Evans.

The deep substructures of the palace of Knossos having become choked with hillwash before they collapsed, staircases and even floors could be reconstructed to an unusual extent, to the third story and even above it; wall frescoes, shattered or insecure, were removed to the museum and replaced by copies; courtyards were paved, and much skilful restoration—the only alternative to reburial—made the complex structure vividly intelligible as the abode of a vigorous and original mode of life. A modern villa overlooking the site serves as an abode for a curator and for visiting archaeologists, and a considerable estate contributes to the endowment. In 1926, being no longer able to supervise it personally, as hitherto, Evans agreed with the Greek Government to convey the whole property in trust to the British School of Archaeology at Athens, but he returned to excavate the 'royal tomb' hard by in 1931. *A Handbook to the Palace of Minos at Knossos* by John Devitt Stringfellow Pendlebury, the curator, was published in 1933. Both palace and museum were undamaged in the German invasion of 1941.

Resigning the keepership of the Ashmolean in 1908, and completing *Scripta Minoa I*, Evans gained time for other interests. Always a strong Liberal, in 1909 he was induced to offer himself as Tariff Reform candidate for the university of Oxford; but there were cross-currents,

and he was persuaded by Lord Lansdowne to withdraw. Balkan affairs were becoming urgent; Lord Curzon was pressing university reforms upon Oxford; and Evans was of an age and eminence to preside over many learned societies. He was a founder of the British School at Athens (1886) and of the British Academy (1902). In 1909 he received the Royal gold medal of the Royal Institute of British Architects, an honour rarely conferred upon a layman; in 1911 he was knighted. He was the fourth generation of his family to be elected (1901) a fellow of the Royal Society and in 1936 he received its Copley medal, to add to the gold medals of the Swedish Academy and the Society of Antiquaries, and many other academic and scientific distinctions. Honorary degrees were conferred upon him by the universities of Edinburgh, Dublin, and Berlin, and he was an honorary fellow of his own college, Brasenose.

During the war years Evans was president of the Society of Antiquaries (1914-19) and of the British Association (1916-19), and as a trustee of the British Museum helped, in 1918, to rescue that institution from the Air Board, and hasten its rehabilitation. He took an active part in South Slav politics—Italy now replacing Austria as the oppressor of nationalities—and promoted on geographical and historical grounds the 'Simplon route' for through traffic to the Near East.

Although his health was normally excellent, and his physical energy inexhaustible—'he never worked when he was tired, and was seldom too tired to work'—a severe operation in 1938 restricted Evans's movements to local explorations round his home, but in 1939 he went by air to Geneva, returning along the Rhine. Until the summer of 1941 he went frequently to the Ashmolean Museum, and another operation did not prevent him from receiving on his ninetieth birthday the congratulations of the Hellenic Society and the British School at Athens, and showing with pride his account of a newly traced Roman road from Oxford to the south coast. Three days later he died at Youlbury, 11 July 1941.

In a very long career Evans made generous use of great gifts, wide experience, and ample means, for he inherited two fortunes in middle life, when Cretan work was most costly. His knowledge was wide and profound, his judgement and flair unerring, and his encouragement of others unfailing. He had a genius for friendship, and was most at home among simple people. He loved children and guests, outdoor life, and his woods and gardens at Youlbury, which he intended as a 'private open space' in concert with the Oxford Preservation Trust, together with the 'Jarn' mound raised on the crest of Boars Hill, and its wild garden. He was a generous patron of the Boy Scouts, who were given a training station at Youlbury and an interest in his long study of beacons, and of craftsmanship of all kinds. In his greater enterprises he enlisted the loyal help of many different allies, learned and simple, and in Crete he was a popular hero after the liberation. In archaeology, although his historical knowledge was wide, and his political views emphatic, his strength, like his father's, was as a critic of craftsmanship and style. Here his judgements were seldom challenged, and always supported by strictly archaeological evidence, often of his own discovery: as he put it 'omne ignotum pro falso is a dangerous motto in the Minoan field' and more widely.

In person Evans was small-built, thickset, of great strength and endurance, with dark complexion and aquiline features. A portrait by Sir William Richmond (1907) is in the Ashmolean Museum, which also owns a fine crayon drawing by Robin Guthrie (1937). The marble bust, by David Evans (1936), in the Ashmolean, and the bronze bust, by a Greek sculptor, at Knossos, are less happy. A pencil drawing (1935) by Francis Dodd is in the National Portrait Gallery.

[J. L. Myres in Proceedings of the British Academy, vol. xxvii, 1941, and in Obituary Notices of Fellows of the Royal Society, No. 10, December 1941; Joan Evans, Time and Chance: The Story of Arthur Evans and his Forebears, 1943; Slavonic Review, January 1946; personal knowledge.]    J. L. MYRES.

EVES, REGINALD GRENVILLE (1876–1941), painter, was born in London 24 May 1876, the son of William Henry Eves, J.P., by his second wife, Anne Grenville. As a child he showed a talent for painting and drawing, and while at University College School, where he was educated, he won the Trevelyan Goodall scholarship in art, which took him to the Slade School of Fine Art. Working there under Alphonse Legros, Frederick Brown, and Henry Tonks [qq.v.], he won the Slade scholarship.

Eves left the Slade School in 1895 and spent the next five years living on a farm in Yorkshire, where he devoted his time to painting landscape, animals, and portraits. In 1901 he returned to London and took a studio in Fitzroy Street; the same year he exhibited for the first time at the Royal Academy. Official success did not come quickly to him, and it was not until 1912, when his portrait of Sir H. H. (later Lord) Cozens-Hardy excited considerable praise, that he became a regular exhibitor. From then until his death he showed every year (with the exception of 1931) never fewer than two paintings at the Academy. He also exhibited at the Royal Institute of Oil Painters, the Paris Salon, and elsewhere. His sitters were for the most part men, but he showed in a number of telling works, such as his portraits of the Queen of Spain (1921) and of Miss Kyra Nijinsky (1935), that he could be equally successful in painting women. During his career he painted many of the most prominent men in British public and artistic life. His portraits of Sir Ernest Shackleton (1921), Thomas Hardy (1923), Sir Frank Benson (1924), Stanley Baldwin (1933), Lord Jellicoe (1935), Leslie Howard, Sir Frederick Pollock, Sir William Watson, and Sir Charles Scott Sherrington are in the National Portrait Gallery; another portrait of Hardy (1924) and one of (Sir) Max Beerbohm (1936) are in the Tate Gallery.

In 1931 there was a controversy concerning some architectural paintings which Eves had sent to the Academy and which were rejected on the ground that a photographic process had been used at one stage in their production. Eves submitted that he had been unaware of the regulation forbidding such a practice. This slight conflict with the authorities at Burlington House did not, however, hold up his advancement, for in 1933 he became an associate, and in 1939 a full academician.

In 1940 Eves was appointed an official war artist, and in 1941, at the time of his death, eight portraits by him of war leaders were on exhibition at the National Gallery.

In his style Eves steered a middle course between the quick study and the formal portrait. He had a remarkable gift for catching and fixing a characteristic expression, and the quality of his paint was excellent. Although portraiture was his major preoccupation, he also painted landscapes in oil and water-colour, in a style which owed something to J. A. McN. Whistler and P. Wilson Steer [qq.v.].

In 1903 Eves married Bertha Sybil, younger daughter of Philip Oxenden Papillon, J.P., D.L., of Crowhurst Park, Battle, Sussex, and Lexden Manor, Colchester; they had one son. Eves died at Middleton-in-Teesdale, county Durham, 13 June 1941. A memorial exhibition of his work was held at the R.B.A. Gallery in 1947. There is a self-portrait in the National Portrait Gallery.

[*The Times*, 16 June 1941; Adrian Bury, *The Art of R. G. Eves*, 1940.]

JAMES LAVER.

FAIRFIELD, BARON (1863–1945), judge. [See GREER, (FREDERICK) ARTHUR.]

FALCONER, SIR ROBERT ALEXANDER (1867–1943), Canadian educationist, was born at Charlottetown, Prince Edward Island, 10 February 1867, the eldest son of the Rev. Alexander Falconer, Presbyterian minister, by his wife, Susan, fourth daughter of the Rev. Robert Douglas. He was educated at the Queen's Royal College School, Trinidad, and with a West Indian Gilchrist scholarship went to the universities of London (B.A. 1888) and Edinburgh (M.A. 1889, B.D. 1892, and D.Litt. 1902). After study at Leipzig, Berlin, and Marburg, he was appointed lecturer (1892) and professor of New Testament Greek (1895) at Pine Hill Presbyterian Theological College, Halifax, Nova Scotia, of which he was principal during the last three years of his residence. In 1907 he was appointed president of the university of Toronto and retired in 1932.

Falconer's chief interest in life was the study of New Testament criticism, in which he was considered an authority before he was thirty years of age, but he was also keenly interested in the subject of education, in international affairs, and Canadian history. The fact that his native province had not been absorbed in the Dominion of Canada until 1871, and the circumstance that eight years of his youth had been spent in Trinidad meant that he approached the problem of the position of Canada from a different angle from that of most Canadians, for the Caribbean sea meant to him the base of British fleets in former days, while Edinburgh and the German universities awoke him to the new stirrings in scholarship, science, and divinity. When, therefore, he returned to Canada he grasped its peculiar position in regard to the Empire and the United States. He came to regard Western civilization as one great web, of which Canada might become an important thread. In his presidential address to the Royal Society of Canada in 1932 he concluded: 'If we are to be a really cultured people we must take our share in pondering the universal problems of civilization and human thought.' A cool judge, he caught the adventurous spirit of Canadian life and paid warm tribute to the Canadians of genius such as Sir J. W. Dawson the geologist, L. H. Fréchette the poet [qq.v.], and Simon Newcomb the astronomer.

When Falconer went to the university of Toronto the secondary schools for decades had had scholarly and scientific teachers, themselves the product and the feeders of the honours courses of the university. The early political and religious feuds in higher education had been healed in no small degree by a federation of institutions. A governing board on which there sat such remarkable men as Goldwin Smith and Sir B. Edmund Walker [qq.v.] had the support of the unusually enlightened Government of Sir James Pliny Whitney, and the combination offered Falconer a great opportunity for the advancement of education which he was not slow to take. He never ceased to urge eloquently the aspirations and the principles which alone could make a university great, and appeal in their defence to the conscience of the community against powerful tendencies of which he disapproved. He had a lofty conception of scholarship, the humanities, and of the Christian religion, and a strong love of freedom and integrity. He stood aloof from public debate, and although outwardly serene he would express his indignation at slippery arguments and horror at dubious appointments in public life. Yet he once warned an undergraduate audience that they should not assume complacently that politics were cleaner in Canada than in the United States, and twice at least he did open battle for academic freedom.

Falconer received many honours: he was appointed C.M.G. in 1911 and K.C.M.G. in 1917. He was awarded honorary degrees by the universities of Edinburgh (D.D.), Oxford (D.C.L.), Glasgow, Dublin, Toronto, McGill, Harvard, Princeton, Yale, and other United States universities (LL.D.) and Manchester and Laval (D.Litt.); in 1916 he was elected a fellow of the Royal Society of Canada and was president for 1931–2. He married in 1897 Sophie, elder daughter of the Rev. Joseph Gandier, of Ontario, and had two sons. He died in Toronto 4 November 1943. A portrait by Maurice Greiffenhagen is in the possession of the university of Toronto.

[*University of Toronto Quarterly*, January 1944; *Proceedings* of the Royal Society of Canada, 1944; private information; personal knowledge.]     CARLETON STANLEY.

FARMER, SIR JOHN BRETLAND (1865–1944), botanist, was born at Atherstone, Warwickshire, 5 April 1865, the only son of John Henry Farmer, of independent means, by his wife, Elizabeth Corbett, daughter of John Bretland, of Nottingham, who came of a family of small landed proprietors. He was for five years educated at the Queen Elizabeth Grammar School, Atherstone, and afterwards privately. He matriculated from Magdalen College, Oxford, with a demyship in natural science, in 1883, obtaining a first class in the honour school of natural science in 1887. Owing much to (Sir) I. B. Balfour [q.v.], then Sherardian professor of botany, he was appointed university demonstrator in botany in 1887 and in 1889 was elected at his college to a fellowship which he held until 1897. In 1892 he was appointed assistant professor of botany in the Royal College of Science at South Kensington (later merged in the Imperial College of Science and Technology). This post in 1895 was raised to the status of a full professorship, and Farmer retained it until his retirement in 1929; to the professorship was added in 1913 the directorship of the biological laboratories of the College.

A visit to India and Ceylon in the winter of 1892–3 proved to be an experience which, combined with his rural upbringing, developed Farmer's idea of the type of university department of biology which the times demanded; for in Ceylon he realized how many were the agricultural problems which the biologist would be called upon to solve in the rubber plantations (then in their infancy) and in other similar industries. He therefore returned to England determined to develop a department where students would receive a training which would fit them to be workers in applied botany abroad as well as teachers and investigators in academic botany at home. How fully he achieved his aim is shown by the growth of the department from a staff of two working in two rooms in 1892 to a staff of twenty-one working in two large buildings in 1929; and when he retired his students were to be found working in applied botany throughout the Empire.

Between 1888 and 1915 Farmer published over sixty papers in pure botany, his favourite field being plant cytology. He was responsible, with John Edmond Salvin-Moore, for the valuable and universally used cytological terms *meiosis* and *meiotic*. In December 1902 he read before the Royal Society, of which he had been elected a fellow in 1900, a paper with the thesis that the cells of malignant growths in man were similar to normal reproductive cells in that they showed a reduction in the number of chromosomes to onehalf. The view propounded in this paper (in which J. E. Salvin-Moore and Charles Edward Walker collaborated) was not fully supported by later research, but the observations were of value because they drew attention to the cytological peculiarities of malignant cells. In his work on centrospheres, structures appearing during cell-division, Farmer recognized them as transitory phenomena, and not, as had been held by others, derived from permanent parts of the cell. In his Croonian lecture to the Royal Society in 1907, 'On the structural constituents of the nucleus, and their relation to the organization of the individual', he exhibited fully his biological insight, for although the part played by the nucleus in the mechanism of heredity was then largely a closed book, there is to be found in the lecture a groping towards the idea, now almost universally accepted, of the gene and its interaction with the environment. He was awarded a Royal medal by the Royal Society in 1919, and was president of the botany section of the British Association in 1907.

With his knowledge of affairs, wide experience, balanced judgement, and administrative capacity, Farmer did most valuable service on many advisory and administrative bodies; and when the Imperial College was constituted he played an important part in directing its policy. But his most lasting monument will be his service to colonial agriculture. He was a member of the committee appointed in 1924 to report on the organization and administration of the agricultural departments of the non-self-governing dependencies. Other bodies on which he sat were the Empire Cotton-Growing Corporation, the Advisory Council of the

Department of Scientific and Industrial Research, the Agricultural Research Council, the Royal Commission for the Exhibition of 1851, and the Lawes Agricultural Trust Committee. He was knighted in 1926.

Farmer was a keen climber—a member of the Alpine Club and president of the Climbers Club for 1910–12. He married in 1892 Edith May Gertrude, daughter of the Rev. Charles Pritchard [q.v.], Savilian professor of astronomy at Oxford. Her sister married Sir Peter Chalmers Mitchell [q.v.]. Farmer had one daughter. He died at Exmouth 26 January 1944. A portrait by Miss F. A. de Biden Footner hangs in the botany department of the Imperial College at South Kensington.

[V. H. Blackman in *Obituary Notices of Fellows of the Royal Society*, No. 14, November 1945; *Nature*, 1 April 1944; private information; personal knowledge.]

V. H. BLACKMAN.

FAY, WILLIAM GEORGE (1872–1947), actor and producer, was born in Dublin 12 November 1872, the second son of William Patrick Fay, a civil servant, and his wife, Martha Dowling. Fay was educated at Belvedere College, Dublin. He and his elder brother Frank started life with united aims and affections. They loved the theatre with a deep-rooted love and set themselves with concentrated energy and dogged persistence to train themselves and others for a theatrical career. By 1902 Fay had his own company playing in small halls in Dublin and in the country. In 1903 he joined forces with AE (G. W. Russell, q.v.), and a year later he joined W. B. Yeats and Lady Gregory [qq.v.], a combination which led to the creation of the Abbey Theatre with the help of Miss A. E. F. Horniman [q.v.]. Fay was a man of the theatre through and through and the importance of the work he did for the Irish theatre from 1904 until January 1908 cannot be too greatly emphasized. His brother Frank was a beautiful verse-speaker; William was more interested in character and comedy, and the brothers made a perfect combination. When differences of opinion with the directors of the Abbey Theatre led Fay to resign in 1908 Yeats wrote: 'We are about to lose our principal actor. William Fay has had enough of it, and we don't wonder, and is going to some other country where his exquisite gift of comedy and his brain teeming with fancy will bring him an audience, fame, and a little money.'

At the Abbey Theatre he created such great parts as Martin Doul in *The Well of the Saints* by J. M. Synge [q.v.]; Shan Grogan in William Boyle's *The Building Fund*; Jeremiah Dempsey in Boyle's *The Eloquent Dempsey*, which is said to have been his favourite part although from another source we learn that he preferred his creation of Christy Mahon in Synge's *The Playboy of the Western World*.

After he left the Abbey Theatre Fay had a distinguished career on the English stage, beginning with *What the Public Wants, John Bull's Other Island*, and *The O'Flynn* with Sir Herbert Tree [q.v.]. During the latter part of the war he produced plays for the Navy and Army Canteen Board, and he was afterwards producer for the repertory theatres in Nottingham (1920–21) and Birmingham (1925–7). Although he never retired from the stage or from production, in later years he appeared more often in films, notably in *The Blarney Stone, General John Regan, Oliver Twist, London Town, Spring Meeting*, and, very late in life, perhaps his best screen part as Father Tom in *Odd Man Out*. He touched no part which he did not adorn, for although he had not a striking stage personality he had a genius for character and comedy, and he excelled in Lady Gregory's one-act comedies. In 1935 he published his reminiscences in collaboration with Catherine Carswell under the title *The Fays of the Abbey Theatre*. A fine portrait of him painted by J. B. Yeats is at the Abbey Theatre, and another by the same artist is in the Municipal Gallery of Modern Art, Dublin.

Fay married in 1906 Anna Bridget (died 1952), daughter of Thomas Joseph O'Dempsey, lawyer, of Enniscorthy, county Wexford; they had one son. Fay died in London 27 October 1947.

[Private information; personal knowledge.]

LENNOX ROBINSON.

FENWICK, ETHEL GORDON (1857–1947), pioneer of nursing reform, whose maiden surname was MANSON, was born 26 January 1857 at Spynie House, Morayshire, the younger daughter of David Davidson Manson, farmer, of Spynie House. Her mother, Harriette, was a Palmer of Thurnscoe Hall, Yorkshire. Educated privately, at the age of twenty-one Ethel Manson entered the Children's Hospital, Nottingham, as a paying probationer. She continued her training at the Royal Infirmary, Manchester (1878–9), and then became a sister at the London Hospital. In 1881, at the early age of twenty-four, her recognized ability secured for her the post of matron and superintendent of nursing at St. Bartholomew's Hospital, London. She resigned this post in 1887 upon her marriage with Bedford Fenwick (died 1939), a doctor, by whom she had one son, Christian Bedford Fenwick, a county court judge.

Mrs. Fenwick now entered upon a wider sphere of public service. As her rapid advance to a post of great responsibility had shown, she was possessed of a remarkable intellect combined with a very considerable talent for organization. She had the ability to inspire others with her own enthusiasms which were now directed towards the proper organization of the nursing profession in this country. She founded in 1887 the (Royal) British Nurses' Association, the first organization of professional women to receive a royal charter (1893); the Matrons' Council of Great Britain; the National Council of Nurses of Great Britain (and Northern Ireland); and, somewhat later, in 1926, the British College of Nurses. She also acquired the *Nursing Record* which became the *British Journal of Nursing* and which she edited almost until her death.

Her most important work, however, lay in her leadership of the movement for the State registration of nurses, a movement which met with the strong and active opposition of Florence Nightingale, and which lasted for thirty-four years before the passing of the Nurses Registration Act in 1919, when Mrs. Fenwick became a member of the first General Nursing Council. Nevertheless, she was actively associated with the educational memorial to Florence Nightingale which was later incorporated in the Florence Nightingale International Foundation of which she was the honorary president in 1934.

Mrs. Fenwick was also the founder and president of the International Council of Nurses which held its first congress at Buffalo in 1901. She 'was known in every land where organized nursing is established', and her work received recognition from the Governments of France and Belgium, whilst in America she was an honorary member of the Nurses' Association and the National League for Nursing Education. She had a striking and dominant appearance, and being exceedingly fond of bright colours dressed richly. Pungent and witty in her speech she re-

vealed herself as a woman of remarkable foresight. She had a strong sense of justice and indomitable courage which made her a formidable and not infrequently a merciless adversary. It was mainly due to her efforts that the status of the nursing profession in this country had long been assured when she died at London Colney vicarage 13 March 1947, at the age of ninety.

[*The Times*, 17 March 1947; *British Journal of Nursing*, March and April 1947; personal knowledge.]        A. STEWART BRYSON.

FFOULKES, CHARLES JOHN (1868–1947), first curator of the Imperial War Museum and master of the armouries of the Tower of London, was born in London 26 June 1868, the younger son of Edmund Salusbury ffoulkes who had been an Anglican clergyman and fellow and tutor of Jesus College, Oxford, until he had followed his friend Newman into the Roman Catholic Church. Eventually he returned to the Church of England and became vicar of St. Mary the Virgin, Oxford. ffoulkes's mother was Anne, daughter of Sir Thomas A. L. Strange [q.v.], and he was thus a great-grandson of Sir Robert Strange [q.v.], the well-known engraver.

ffoulkes was educated at the Dragon School, Oxford, at Radley and Shrewsbury and at St. John's College, Oxford. On leaving the university without taking a degree he studied at the Académie Julian in Paris, exhibited at the Royal Academy in London, and was represented in the Paris Exhibition of 1900. Soon, however, he abandoned painting for metalwork and the difficulties presented by this medium aroused in him something more than a romantic interest in armour and weapons. He had the good fortune at this time to meet the seventeenth Viscount Dillon, a notice of whom he was subsequently to contribute to this DICTIONARY. A close friendship developed and Dillon, who was then curator of the Tower armouries, and a former president of the Society of Antiquaries, was glad to impart to the younger man his accumulated store of wisdom and scholarship. ffoulkes began his new career by publishing a number of papers and gave a series of lectures on arms and armour at Oxford where he obtained the degree of B.Litt. in 1911. *The Armourer and his Craft* (1912) embodied his thesis and was his most original work.

When Dillon gave up his post at the Tower at the end of 1912 his mantle devolved on ffoulkes, who never failed to acknowledge the debt he owed to his master in arms. On assuming charge of the armouries, ffoulkes undertook a complete rearrangement of the contents of the White Tower and published the official *Inventory and Survey of the Armouries of the Tower of London* (2 vols., 1916).

In 1917 the Government decided to set up a War Museum and ffoulkes, from whom the suggestion had come, was appointed its first secretary and curator. He left the Royal Naval Volunteer Reserve in which he had been serving in the anti-aircraft defences of London and became a major of the Royal Marines (unattached) in order to be able to work closely with the armed forces without belonging to either of the major Services. An immense amount of hard work, in all branches, and on all fronts, resulted in what is now the Imperial War Museum. It was opened by King George V at the Crystal Palace, 9 June 1920. ffoulkes had spread his net wide. Besides collecting representative weapons and equipment of both sides, he had established a picture gallery which made the reputation of many young artists of the modern school who had served in the forces and whose work was hitherto unknown. The museum also included a large reference library, documents, and a collection of thousands of photographs taken by official photographers during the war which were to prove invaluable to future historians.

The museum was later moved to the Imperial Institute in South Kensington on a reduced scale, many bulky and redundant exhibits being jettisoned, and in 1936 went to its final home at Bethlem Hospital, S.E. At first there had been some criticism of the cost of maintaining a big organization which it was thought would inevitably lose in public interest as the generation which had served in the war died out, but a second world war twenty years later confirmed its permanence. In this war ffoulkes served as a sergeant of pioneers in the Home Guard. He retired from the War Museum on reaching the age limit in 1933 and was made a trustee. He continued at the Tower armouries, where the ancient title of 'master' was revived for him, until the end of 1938 when he went to live in Oxford. In his later years his interests turned from the Middle Ages to the regimental arms and equipment of more

modern times, and his last act at the Tower was to accumulate from official sources a large collection of firearms of the nineteenth century. He published *The Gun-founders of England* (1937), *Sword, Lance, and Bayonet* (with E. C. Hopkinson, 1938), and after his retirement a volume of reminiscences, *Arms and the Tower* (1939), and *Arms and Armament* (1945). He also compiled a catalogue of the armour belonging to the Armourers' and Brasiers' Company of which he was an honorary freeman. He was a fellow of the Society of Antiquaries, was appointed O.B.E. in 1925 and C.B. in 1934, and received the honorary degree of D.Litt. from the university of Oxford in 1936.

ffoulkes was twice married: first, in 1894 to Maude Mary Chester, daughter of the late William Craven, of Brighton; secondly, in 1942 to Dorothy Agnes, daughter of the late Rev. Charles Foster Garratt, for many years vicar of Little Tew. ffoulkes died in Oxford 22 April 1947. His portrait by Maurice Codner hangs in the board-room of the Imperial War Museum.

[C. J. ffoulkes, *Arms and the Tower*, 1939; personal knowledge.]    JAMES MANN.

FIELD, Sir (ARTHUR) MOSTYN (1855–1950), admiral, was born at Braybrooke, near Market Harborough, 27 June 1855, the youngest of the three children of Lieutenant (later Captain) John Bousquet Field, R.N., and his wife, Cecilia, daughter of Thomas Mostyn, Army Medical Department. Educated at the Royal Naval School, New Cross, he entered the *Britannia* in January 1869, became chief cadet captain and headed the list of forty cadets when the final examinations were held two years later, winning prizes for navigation and seamanship. Having served the necessary time as a midshipman he again excelled in his examinations, obtaining full marks for his navigation papers and receiving the Beaufort testimonial for 1875. He was promoted to lieutenant in October of that year and in the following June began his close association with the hydrographic department of the Admiralty when he joined the surveying ship *Fawn* commanded by (Sir) William Wharton [q.v.] for service in the Red Sea, east coast of Africa, Mediterranean, and Sea of Marmora. For a few months in 1881 he was given his first independent piece of work as a surveyor when he charted the approaches to the Oil Rivers on the west coast of Africa. He then joined the *Sylvia*, until early in 1884 under Wharton, for service on the east coast of South America and in the Magellan Straits, and later on the east coast of Africa north of Natal.

Towards the end of 1884 Field returned to England and was appointed in command of the *Dart* and in charge of surveys and investigations to be made in collaboration with the Royal Society on the coasts of Australia, with particular reference to the Barrier Reefs. Returning to this country in 1889 Field was highly commended for his work and promoted to commander in June. In July of the following year he was given command of the *Egeria* on the China station and during the next three years executed surveys in British North Borneo, Hong Kong, Singapore, and the Anambas Islands. He then went to the Royal Naval College, Greenwich, for a course, and in June 1895 was promoted captain. Appointed next to the *Penguin* on the Australia station, Field was employed from 1896 to 1899 in making surveys of numerous groups of islands in the South Pacific; these included the Friendly, New Hebrides, and Phoenix islands, and in collaboration with the Royal Society he carried out investigations of coral reefs, including a boring to a depth of 700 feet at Funafuti Island. His last sea-going command was the *Research*, and from 1900 to 1904 he was engaged in making surveys of lochs and harbours in Scotland and Ireland.

In 1904 Field was appointed hydrographer of the navy in succession to Wharton and in the following year he was elected F.R.S. In 1906 he was promoted to rear-admiral. During his time at the Admiralty he was able to replace four of the very old surveying ships by much more modern vessels and the total of eight ships so employed were continuously in service in the Mediterranean, China, Indian Ocean, Australia, Africa, and the British Isles where many valuable surveys, including Scapa Flow, were completed. Retiring from his post in 1909 Field was promoted vice-admiral in 1910, his elder brother reaching the same rank, on the retired list, at the same time. Field was Admiralty representative on the newly formed Port of London Authority (1909–25), was a nautical assessor to the House of Lords, and acting conservator of the Mersey (1910–30). He was a British

Government delegate at a scientific congress at Buenos Aires in 1910 and was appointed K.C.B. in the following year, being promoted to admiral on the retired list in 1913. He was a fellow of the Royal Astronomical and Geographical societies and, in addition to a number of articles and papers on professional subjects, he revised two editions (1909, 1920) of Wharton's *Hydrographical Surveying*.

Of average height, sturdily built and bearded, Field was a very active man and an indefatigable worker. He was deeply religious and although on occasion he was something of a tartar he mellowed with advancing years. He suffered much in later life from loss of memory but he retained his interest in naval matters and only a year before his death he visited his old department at the Admiralty and evinced great interest in such recent innovations as echo sounding, radar, and modern methods of printing and reproduction by photography. He died at his home at Woodgreen, Hampshire, 3 July 1950, having outlived all his contemporaries but having also inspired both affection and respect in the younger generation of naval officers who had specialized in the same work.

Field married in 1894 Laura Mary (died 1956), daughter of Captain George Herbert Hale, of the Bengal Army. There were two daughters of the marriage and an only son who was killed at the battle of Jutland whilst serving as a midshipman in the *Queen Mary*.

[Sir John Edgell in *Obituary Notices of Fellows of the Royal Society*, No. 20, November 1951; personal knowledge.]

J. A. EDGELL.

FIELD, SIR FREDERICK LAURENCE (1871–1945), admiral of the fleet, was the second son of Colonel Spencer Field, 6th Royal Warwickshire Regiment, by his wife, Catherine, daughter of Colonel Charles Darrall, 97th Regiment. He was born in Killarney 19 April 1871, the fifth child of a family of ten. Educated privately, he joined the *Britannia* in 1884, and went to sea in 1886. In the Boxer rising (1900) Field, who was then torpedo lieutenant of the *Barfleur*, had his first experience of active service. Landing at Tientsin he was given the task of repairing damaged armoured trains and earned a special mention in dispatches for carrying out very strenuous work under continuous heavy fire. Later during the capture of

Tientsin native city he was wounded in the head by a bullet which, although it left a permanent scar, fortunately did no serious damage.

Field was promoted to the rank of commander in 1902 and served in the *Albion* until 1904, when he was appointed to the *Vernon*, the principal torpedo school, at Portsmouth. Here he soon made his mark in a sphere in which he had already shown a particular aptitude, and was commended by the Admiralty for his ingenuity in designing a submersible target. In 1907 he left the *Vernon* and was given command of the *Defiance*, the branch torpedo school at Devonport, and promoted to the rank of captain. He went to the Mediterranean in 1910 as flag captain to (Sir) Martyn Jerram [q.v.] in the *Duncan*, returning home two years later to be appointed superintendent of signal schools. He held this appointment until September 1914, when he returned to the *Vernon*, this time in command, and earned further commendation from the Admiralty for the design and production of special wireless signalling apparatus for torpedo craft.

As flag captain to Jerram, Field commanded the *King George V*, in the Grand Fleet, at the battle of Jutland 31 May 1916, and was mentioned in dispatches for 'the great skill with which he handled the *King George V*, as leader of the line, under very difficult conditions'. He was also appointed C.B. From November 1916 to April 1918 he was chief of staff to Sir Charles Madden [q.v.], commanding first battle squadron, first in the *Marlborough* and later in the *Revenge*, and for his 'valuable services' he was appointed C.M.G. in 1919. He had established his reputation as a torpedo and mining expert while in the *Vernon* and *Defiance*, and this was followed in June 1918 by his appointment as director of torpedoes and mines at the Admiralty; while there he was promoted rear-admiral in February 1919. He joined the Board of Admiralty as third sea lord and controller in March 1920, and, during the three years in which he served in this exacting appointment, his great administrative ability and sound judgement undoubtedly marked him for the highest command. He was advanced to K.C.B. in January 1923, and went to sea again, in the same year, in command of the battle cruiser squadron with the *Hood* as his flagship.

In 1923 it was decided to send a special service squadron round the world to 'show the flag', and Field, with the acting rank of vice-admiral, was given command of the squadron, which consisted of the battle cruisers *Hood*—the largest warship then afloat—and *Repulse*, together with the light cruisers, *Delhi* (wearing the flag of Rear-Admiral the Hon. Sir Hubert George Brand), *Dauntless*, *Danae*, *Dragon*, and *Dunedin*. Later the Australian light cruiser *Adelaide* replaced the *Dunedin*.

The cruise, which lasted from November 1923 to September 1924, did much to enhance the navy's prestige, and the ships received a great welcome at every port of call. The success of the tour was largely due to Field's striking personality and leadership. On his return he was appointed K.C.M.G. At each of the many places visited Field was called upon to make a long and very carefully prepared speech. Fortunately he was a most gifted speaker and this, added to his great natural charm, made him extremely popular wherever he went, and he received many personal tributes from all parts of the Empire. Perhaps one incident during the cruise best exemplified his amazing thoroughness and retentive memory. At each port visited it was the custom for all the principal officials to be presented to him when he first landed. At one place, where the introductions were being made by the A.D.C. to the governor, on the chief of police coming forward the A.D.C. said: 'I am sorry sir, but this officer only arrived last week, and his name has escaped my memory.' Without a moment's hesitation Field said with his charming smile: 'I am delighted to meet you, Colonel . . . [mentioning the correct name]. I hope you had an enjoyable passage out.' The names and appointments of all officials to be introduced—sometimes as many as forty or fifty—were sent to the flagship on arrival, and Field apparently just glanced through them; not even his own staff knew, until this incident occurred, that he invariably memorized the list.

After giving up command of the battle cruiser squadron in 1924, Field became in 1925 deputy chief of the naval staff and a lord commissioner of the Admiralty, a post which he held until June 1928, when he was appointed commander-in-chief in the Mediterranean. There he earned the appreciation of the lords of the Admiralty for the great success of the visit of the fleet to Turkish waters, which was mainly due to his personal participation. While on this visit he was entertained by Kemal Ataturk, who impressed him very much by his forceful character and progressive outlook. Field was promoted admiral in April 1928. After two years in the Mediterranean he returned to the Admiralty as first sea lord and chief of the naval staff, thus achieving the zenith of a naval officer's career.

His last term of office was a particularly trying one. The restrictions imposed by the London naval conference of 1930 were followed by the financial crisis of 1931. An internal complaint from which Field had suffered for many years was beginning to take its toll and he was on leave and seriously unwell when he learnt that naval economies were envisaged. He returned at once to the Admiralty and caused the Government to be warned in writing that the Board would not be held responsible for the consequences if restorations were made in the proposed cuts for other Services which would result in those which the Board had accepted for naval personnel becoming proportionately greater. The gravity of the financial crisis and the immediate steps the Government considered essential were the direct causes of the trouble which ensued at Invergordon. The lower scales of pay were notified to the British Broadcasting Corporation and appeared in the Sunday newspapers before the Admiralty had an opportunity of explaining to the fleet the reason for the severe hardships imposed. The Board took the risk of ordering the Atlantic Fleet to proceed to home ports so that cases of hardship might be investigated; but, before inquiries could take place, the Government decided that in no case should reductions in pay exceed 10 per cent.

Field relinquished his appointment 20 January 1933, and was promoted admiral of the fleet. In June 1933 he was appointed G.C.B. Among his foreign decorations he held the American D.S.M. (gold) and was an officer of the Legion of Honour.

Field had great moral and physical courage and was supremely calm in an emergency. Known to his contemporaries as 'Tam Field', this highly gifted officer was a leader who was very popular with officers and men. He was chairman of the committee of the Royal Navy Club (1765 and 1785) for the years 1935–7. Possessed of the highest principles Field allowed nothing to come before his duty to the navy, of which he was intensely proud.

A man of simple tastes, he hated ostentation and was modest to a degree, but he had a keen sense of humour. He was always ready to give a helping hand to a shipmate in trouble. His favourite relaxation was golf and he was seldom happier than when on the links. He was also an expert conjurer and a member of the Magic Circle.

Field married in 1902 Annie Norrington, daughter of John Harris, civil servant, and widow of Roundell Palmer Jackson, barrister, of Plymouth. There were no children. He died 24 October 1945 and was buried in Escrick, Yorkshire. A drawing by Francis Dodd is in the Imperial War Museum.

[Admiralty records; personal knowledge.]
R. W. D. LESLIE.

FINLAY, WILLIAM, second VISCOUNT FINLAY (1875–1945), judge, was born in London 15 October 1875, the only child of Robert Bannatyne (afterwards first Viscount) Finlay [q.v.] who became lord chancellor in 1916. Educated at Eton and at Trinity College, Cambridge, William Finlay was placed in the third division of the third class in part i of the classical tripos in 1897, but gained distinction by serving as president of the Union in the Easter term of 1898. He was called to the bar by the Middle Temple in 1901 and joined the Northern circuit. In 1905, just before the fall of the Conservative Government, his father, then attorney-general, appointed him junior counsel to the Board of Inland Revenue where he gave every satisfaction. He took silk in 1914. In 1916 he became chairman of the contraband committee and, from 1917 to 1919, was vice-chairman of the allied blockade committee. He was also a temporary legal adviser to the Foreign Office during the peace conference, and for these services he was appointed K.B.E. in 1920 and made a member of the Legion of Honour and the Italian Order of St. Maurice and St. Lazarus.

Returning to practice at the bar Finlay was retained in a series of important appeals before the Judicial Committee of the Privy Council. In 1921 he was appointed commissioner of assize for the Northern circuit and did so well that his promotion to the bench in the near future was taken for granted. He continued to serve as a commissioner of assize until in 1924, Parliament having authorized the appointment of two new judges, Finlay was made a judge of the King's Bench division. He won an immediate reputation for dignity and courtesy, scrupulous fairness and balanced judgement: a combination of natural charm and legal efficiency which was appreciated in the profession. In 1925 he was appointed chairman of the committee on legal aid for the poor which issued two reports (1926, 1928) and pointed the way to later schemes of legal aid.

When Finlay became a judge his father was himself still performing judicial duties, but he died in 1929, when Finlay succeeded to his titles. The strength and ability of the second Viscount Finlay as a judge were shown in his handling of the trial at Princetown in April and May 1932 of thirty-one convicts on charges arising out of the Dartmoor mutiny in the previous January and one convict who had wounded a warder two days before the mutiny. The trial, which was probably the most notable over which he presided, lasted for sixteen days, and the sentences on twenty-three men, ranging from six months to twelve years, all to follow the sentences then being served, took three hours to pronounce.

In 1933 Finlay was elected Lent reader by the Middle Temple and gave in Hall a reading on 'Law in Literature' which showed him as something of a scholar with a vein of old-world culture. A citation which he made from Sir Walter Scott's *Guy Mannering* was perhaps especially revealing. Pleydell shows to Mannering his library of 'the best editions of the best authors', and says, 'These are my tools of trade. A lawyer without history or literature is a mechanic—a mere working mason; if he possesses some knowledge of these he may venture to call himself an architect.'

In 1937 Finlay was appointed to be *ex officio* commissioner for England under the Railway and Canal Traffic Act, 1888. In 1938, on the constitution for the first time of a third court of appeal, he was appointed a lord justice of appeal and sworn of the Privy Council. Soon afterwards he became knight president of the Knights of the Round Table and in due course he succeeded Sir Cecil Hurst as chairman of the Grotius Society. During the war of 1939–45 Finlay was seconded from the Court of Appeal to act as chairman of the contraband committee. Its work being virtually at an end, in January 1945 he was promoted G.B.E. and appointed United Kingdom representative on the United Nations War Crimes Com-

mission, of which he was an assiduous and zealous member. A visit of inspection to certain German prison camps took toll of his health and to an intimate friend he confessed that he never felt really well again. His appointment as the British member of the International Court of Justice was widely anticipated, but he died at Redhill, Surrey, 30 June 1945. There is at the Middle Temple a portrait of him in pastel by Mrs. Blakeney Ward, a gift to the Inn by his daughter.

Finlay married in 1903 Beatrice Marion (died 1942), daughter of Edward Kirkpatrick Hall, of Hollybush, Staffordshire. There was one daughter of the marriage and the titles became extinct.

[*The Times*, 2 and 3 July 1945; *Law Journal* and *Solicitors' Journal*, 7 July 1945; private information; personal knowledge.]

RICHARD O'SULLIVAN.

FISCHER WILLIAMS, SIR JOHN (1870–1947), international lawyer. [See WILLIAMS.]

FISHER, SIR (NORMAN FENWICK) WARREN (1879–1948), civil servant, was born in London 22 September 1879. He came of Cumberland stock, the only son of Henry Warren Fisher, of independent means, by his wife, Caroline, daughter of Colonel Charles Wilford, East India Company, of Boston, Lincolnshire. Fisher was educated at the Dragon School, Oxford, and was a scholar both of Winchester College and of Hertford College, Oxford. He was placed in the first class in classical moderations in 1900 and the second class in *literae humaniores* in 1902. In 1903 he entered the Civil Service and was posted to the Inland Revenue department. There he attracted the attention of Robert (later Lord) Chalmers [q.v.], who became chairman of the Board of Inland Revenue in 1907. After two years as Chalmers's private secretary Fisher was sent to deal with the work connected with the introduction of the super-tax, a new field in which he showed unusual drive and initiative in the organization and use of staff. Moreover, it led to his being noticed by Lloyd George who, according to Fisher, was partly responsible for his being seconded in May 1912 to the newly appointed National Health Insurance Commission for England under Sir Robert Morant [q.v.] where, again, Fisher showed his capacity to strengthen and develop a new organization.

In May 1913 he returned to Somerset House as a commissioner of inland revenue. He was appointed deputy chairman of the Board in October 1914 and chairman in August 1918. He was the driving force behind the Inland Revenue Department during the war of 1914–18 when he built up and maintained an efficient war-time organization. He fought for the status of the department in relation to the Treasury and to Whitehall generally, and, within the department, effected radical and salutary alterations in the composition of the Board and in the organization of the secretariat and the inspectorate. His personal contact whilst at Somerset House with all classes of civil servants was to prove invaluable. He also gained much by his membership of the committee on staffs which sat in 1918–19 under the chairmanship of Sir John (later Lord) Bradbury [q.v.] to inquire into the organization and staffing of government departments. Here Fisher was able to apply his ideas on staff management to the Civil Service as a whole, and to acquire a detailed knowledge of other departments. The committee made a number of recommendations designed to improve the status and efficiency of establishment work and it insisted on genuine co-operation between the Treasury and other departments, a point of view Fisher emphasized throughout his career, in his opposition to Civil Service departmentalism.

On 1 October 1919 Fisher went to the Treasury as permanent secretary where he remained until his retirement in 1939. His immediate problems, all inter-related, were the organization of the Treasury, the situation in the Civil Service, and control of expenditure. Fisher found awaiting him at the Treasury a new scheme of organization (which had been announced in *The Times* on 27 August 1919 at the time of his appointment) by which the Treasury was split into three departments, each under a controller with direct responsibility to ministers. The permanent secretary had certain powers of co-ordination and supervision, but he was clearly not expected to concern himself with the work of the three departments, save in a very general sense.

This reorganization, as *The Times* reported before Fisher took office, had been 'carried out by the Chancellor of the Exchequer and the Finance Committee of the Cabinet, presided over by the Prime Minister'. The scheme was not of Fisher's authorship, although it has often been attributed to him. Before the Public Accounts Committee in 1936 Fisher described it as having proved extremely unwieldy. The permanent secretary, he said, had been left 'deliciously vague, floating somewhere rather Olympian'. The arrangement had lasted in a modified form until four years previously when the Treasury reverted to the traditional form of organization: the three departments disappeared and from 1932 there remained but one department, the Treasury as a whole, with the permanent secretary in full charge.

It was laid down in 1919 as part of the new organization that the permanent secretary should act as permanent head of the Civil Service and advise the first lord in regard to Civil Service appointments and decorations, a decision which Fisher viewed more favourably. In the following year the Government decided that certain senior appointments in the Civil Service, notably those of heads of departments, should, while continuing to be made by the departmental ministers, require the consent of the prime minister. Under the new arrangements the prime minister in giving or withholding consent was to be advised by the permanent head of the Treasury. Fisher held strongly that in the interests of both efficiency and economy the first need was to have the right men in charge of departments, and that to get them the manpower resources of the Civil Service should be pooled. These arrangements gave rise to much controversy and were the subject of several debates in both Houses of Parliament. Discussion centred round the advisory function of the permanent secretary: with Fisher's own strong personality as a background. The arguments took many forms, but all were directed to the possible effects of the arrangements upon the constitutional position of ministers and the outlook of senior members of the Civil Service. In exercising these advisory functions, Fisher's one criterion was fitness for the job and, in his search for the right man, he covered the whole Service and persons of varied origins and experience. Some criticism might perhaps have been avoided had the work been in the hands of an official with less 'temperament', but there is no doubt about the fearlessness, knowledge, and resource which Fisher brought to bear on these most important duties.

In the matter of Treasury organization

Fisher broke with tradition in two important respects. He brought about a substantial increase in the Treasury establishment which in his view had been consistently undermanned and hopelessly overworked. He also ceased to recruit the administrative staff of the Treasury direct from the open competition. Instead, selected officers were taken after a few years' experience in other departments, men likely, therefore, in Fisher's view, to be more constructive than recruits direct from the universities.

In the Civil Service as a whole, Fisher found that, as a result of war conditions, departments to a great extent had lost their sense of corporate responsibility. It had become vitally important, therefore, to inculcate the doctrine of team-work which had been stressed by the committee on staffs. Fisher applied the same principle to the control of expenditure and rejected the conception of a stern Treasury forcing economy upon reluctant departments. Treasury officials were not to regard themselves, he said, as 'the single-handed champions of solvency'. Team-work between the Treasury and the departments was the right way to secure economy; and they were to enjoy a 'conjoint and co-operative responsibility'.

To emphasize the responsibility of departments for economy, Fisher advised that the permanent secretary of a department, and not the principal finance officer, should have, under ministers, the chief responsibility for economy. Policy and finance were not to be kept in watertight compartments, and those responsible for advising ministers on policy were equally responsible for its financial implications. The Government in 1920 approved Fisher's proposal, but the further suggestion that permanent secretaries should in all cases be accounting officers did not find immediate favour with the Public Accounts Committee which did not accept Fisher's proposals in full until 1925. They were then approved by the Government. The committee examined Fisher again on this arrangement in 1936 and endorsed his conclusion that it had worked satisfactorily.

Again in order to foster the idea of team-work Fisher set his face against formal methods of doing business, encouraging instead personal discussion and semi-official correspondence rather than the exchange of formal official letters. For himself he relied on the spoken word to get his ideas across to his fellow officials and through them his views on team-work became known throughout the Service.

Fisher strove in particular to bring about more friendly and informal relations between the Treasury and the Service departments and himself led the way by securing the goodwill of senior members of the fighting Services, notably the chiefs of staff. He used to think of the fighting Services and the Civil Service as equal partners: 'the four Crown Services'. He was a warm supporter of the Imperial Defence College in bringing together members of all four Services in the study of common problems. For similar reasons he welcomed the friendly rivalry of members of the Services in the field of sport. It was indeed the ideal of team-work which was largely responsible for Fisher's enduring interest in Civil Service sport and its organization on a Service basis. It appealed to him also as a movement making for the greater welfare of all ranks.

Another feature of Fisher's career at the Treasury was his emphasis on the supreme importance of the highest possible standard of conduct in the Civil Service. He was swift to take action, for instance in seeking prompt approval for setting up a board of inquiry, whenever that standard was called in question. Fisher also played an active part in 1937 when the question of the acceptance of business appointments by Crown servants came up for consideration. The Government eventually made rules requiring departmental concurrence in certain cases, although making it clear, as Fisher had advised, that there was nothing intrinsically improper or undesirable in an officer accepting such an appointment at the end of his Service career.

Fisher regarded as equally important the principles which should govern the attitude of senior civil servants to their ministers. The relations between ministers and their official advisers should, he told the Royal Commission on the Civil Service in 1930, be marked by 'integrity, fearlessness and independence of thought and utterance' so that ministers might be 'assured that their decisions are reached only after the relevant facts and the various considerations have, so far as the machinery of government can secure, been definitely brought before their minds'.

Successive Governments made extensive use of Fisher's services as chairman of inter-departmental committees and, with the growing threat of war in the 'thirties, he presided over many such committees concerned with the possible emergency. During that period the need for rearmament became his main preoccupation, so much so, it has been suggested, that he took less and less interest in his proper Treasury functions. This, however, was not the view of those who worked most closely with him in that period. No doubt Fisher did not cease to express himself strongly in the highest quarters on defence policy. But no one who knew Fisher would have expected him to act otherwise if he felt that the country was in grave danger. And the work which he did on matters connected with organization in the event of war, for instance the planning of the regional organization for civil defence, was very much the proper work of the permanent secretary to the Treasury.

Fisher retired formally from the Civil Service on 30 September 1939, but some time before this, in anticipation of war, he had been designated as regional commissioner for the north-western region with headquarters in Manchester, a post which he held until May 1940. In September of that year he was appointed a special commissioner in the London region to co-ordinate the work of restoring roads and public utility services and to organize the clearance and salvage of debris. In this his drive and capacity for rapid improvisation were as much in evidence as in his early days and proved invaluable in producing order out of confusion. This appointment came to an abrupt conclusion in 1942 when Fisher wrote to the press protesting against what he considered to be the unjust treatment by the home secretary of a former colleague in the north-western region. This action was held to be incompatible with Fisher's position as a special commissioner and his public service came to an end.

Fisher's remarkable personality was always in evidence whatever he might be doing. His actions were governed by instinct and intuition rather than by logical reasoning and he had a temperament which he himself described as unruly. He had qualities of drive, determination, and courage possessed by few; these, added to unusual distinction of appearance and manner, made a formidable combination. He inspired devotion in some and hostility in others; there seemed no limit to what he would do for his friends, as the final episode of his public career notably revealed. At the Treasury Fisher made no claim to be a financial expert, but he took the lead in all matters concerning the standing, efficiency, and welfare of the Civil Service. Above all, he strove for the conception of the Service as a unity instead of a series of quasi-independent departments, and it is the measure of his achievement that this is now accepted as a commonplace of administration.

In 1916 Fisher was appointed C.B., promoted K.C.B. in 1919, G.C.B. in 1923, and appointed G.C.V.O. in 1928. He rendered good service to the university of Oxford in 1930 by presiding over an external committee on college contributions to the university. Three years later he was made an honorary D.C.L. and elected to an honorary fellowship of Hertford College. He received the honorary degree of D.Sc. from the university of Reading in 1937. After he retired from the Civil Service he held directorships in banking, insurance, and commercial companies, and acted as honorary treasurer of the Royal College of Music.

Fisher married in 1906 Mary Ann Lucy, daughter of Major Edward Charles Thomas, sometime commandant of the Duke of York's School, Chelsea; she survived him when he died in London 25 September 1948. There were two sons of the marriage.

[Public and departmental records; Sir H. P. Hamilton, 'Sir Warren Fisher and the Public Service', in *Public Administration*, vol. xxix, 1951; private information; personal knowledge.]      H. P. HAMILTON.

**FITZALAN OF DERWENT**, first VISCOUNT (1855–1947). [See HOWARD, EDMUND BERNARD FITZALAN-.]

**FITZROY, EDWARD ALGERNON** (1869–1943), Speaker of the House of Commons, was born in London 24 July 1869, the younger son of Charles FitzRoy, third Baron Southampton, by his second wife, Ismania Katherine, daughter of Walter Nugent, a baron of the Austrian Empire. He was descended through the second Duke of Grafton from Charles II. His mother was for twenty-three years a lady of the bedchamber in ordinary to Queen Victoria to whom Edward FitzRoy was himself a page of honour. He was educated at Eton and the Royal Military College, Sandhurst, and was gazetted to the 1st Life Guards in 1889, but on his marriage two years later his preference for the life of a country gentleman led him to retire to Northamptonshire, where he became a noted breeder of dairy shorthorns and for twenty-five years served on the county council. His interest in local affairs soon led him to turn his attention to politics, and in 1900 he entered the House of Commons as Conservative member for South Northamptonshire. At the general election of 1906 he did not stand and the seat was won by the Liberals, but he stood again successfully in January 1910 and thereafter held the seat (which in 1918 became the Daventry division) until his death. On the outbreak of war in 1914 he rejoined his regiment with the rank of lieutenant, and in November of that year was wounded in the first battle of Ypres. He returned to France in 1915, and until 1916 was in command of the mounted troops of the Guards division.

On his return to political life in 1918 FitzRoy played an unassuming though valuable part which led to his appointment in 1922 as deputy chairman of ways and means under James Fitzalan Hope (later Lord Rankeillour, q.v.). This post he held until 1928, except during the short-lived Labour administration of 1924, and when in 1928 J. H. Whitley [q.v.] resigned the speakership, FitzRoy was unanimously elected to succeed him.

FitzRoy's speakership covered fifteen years and, although it was during his occupation of the chair that, in July 1930, Mr. John Beckett, the Labour member for Peckham—in almost the last scene of disorder which the chamber witnessed—made his eccentric attempt to carry off the mace, the period was more memorable for external events than for the domestic problems of Parliament. This was perhaps fortunate, for FitzRoy had not the legal training which so many of his predecessors could call to their aid. He was, indeed, the first soldier Speaker of recent times, and it was by good sense and good 'hands', rather than by any store of parliamentary book-learning, that this ex-cavalryman, with his tall and commanding figure, proved his worth in the chair. The financial crisis of 1931, the abdication of King Edward VIII in 1936, the outbreak of war in 1939, and the destruction of the Commons' chamber in 1941, although they profoundly stirred the nation, left little permanent mark on the institution of Parliament. But the war and the air raids on London put a heavy strain upon

FitzRoy as head of the administration of the House; as did also his constant watch on the debates and conduct of the House itself, lest the free expression of opinion might inadvertently give secret information to the enemy. These duties he performed with success, but the burden proved seriously to have impaired his strength, and he succumbed to a sudden attack of pneumonia at his official residence in the Palace of Westminster 3 March 1943. He was buried in the chancel of St. Margaret's, the church traditionally associated with the House of Commons.

As a private member FitzRoy made no attempt to shine in debate. After he became Speaker opportunities of hearing him were necessarily few, but when he was called upon to speak as 'mouth' of the House, notably at the ceremonial meetings of Parliament in Westminster Hall on the occasions of King George V's silver jubilee in 1935 and the visit of M. Lebrun, President of the French Republic, in March 1939, he showed that he had the gift of combining grace with formal oratory. He carried his office with great dignity. When at the general election of 1935 the Labour Party in his constituency chose to disregard the old-established convention under which the Speaker, once elected, could rely upon being returned to Parliament unopposed, FitzRoy refused to allow the speakership to be dragged into party politics and, taking no active part in the contest, was rewarded by an increased majority. Throughout the vicissitudes and the emergencies of the period of his speakership he retained the confidence of members of all parties, and the tributes which were paid to him on the occasion of his golden wedding in 1941 showed that he had won the esteem and affection of the whole House.

FitzRoy married in 1891 Muriel, elder daughter of Colonel Archibald Charles Henry Douglas-Pennant, younger son of the first Baron Penrhyn, and had three sons, the second of whom was killed in action in 1915, and one daughter. He received honorary degrees from the universities of Cambridge (1931) and Oxford (1934), was a J.P. and D.L. for Northamptonshire, and was sworn of the Privy Council in 1924. In recognition of his services his widow, who had been appointed C.B.E. in 1918, was raised to the peerage in 1943 with the title, in her own right, of the Viscountess Daventry.

A portrait of FitzRoy by (Sir) Oswald Birley hangs in the Speaker's House in the Palace of Westminster.

[*The Times*, 4 March 1943; personal knowledge.]      CAMPION.

FLEMING, DAVID PINKERTON, LORD FLEMING (1877–1944), Scottish judge, was born at Rutherglen, near Glasgow, 11 February 1877, the fourth son of John Fleming, writer (*anglice* solicitor), and his wife, Isabella Wark Pinkerton. He was educated at Glasgow High School and the universities of Glasgow (M.A., 1895, LL.B., 1896), and Edinburgh where he took classes in evidence and procedure. He also studied technical subjects in electricity, engineering, and accountancy at the Heriot-Watt College, Edinburgh, and the knowledge there obtained stood him in good stead in his later forensic career. Determined by family tradition and personal inclination upon the law he was admitted to the Faculty of Advocates in 1902. Unlike many who later achieve distinction Fleming did not have long to wait before practice came his way and he early showed that he was competent to undertake it. He soon acquired by merit one of the best junior practices at the bar. Within six months of the outbreak of war in 1914 Fleming was commissioned in the Scottish Rifles (Cameronians). With them and later with the 13th Royal Inniskilling Fusiliers he saw much hard active service in France, was awarded the M.C. and the Belgian croix de guerre, and was mentioned in dispatches. He was seriously wounded at Tournai in October 1918 and returned to the bar in 1919. He rapidly regained his practice in the 'boom' years of litigation which followed and there were few commercial or Admiralty cases of any substance or importance in which David Fleming was not briefed on one side or the other. It is a characteristic of the Scottish bar that its members do not specialize as in England; consequently the range of practice of busy pleaders tends to be substantially wider than at the English bar.

In 1919 Fleming was appointed advocate depute by Lord Advocate (afterwards Lord President) Clyde [q.v.], and thus gained a wide experience in criminal matters as a responsible Crown prosecutor. In 1921 he took silk and in the following year he was appointed solicitorgeneral for Scotland in Bonar Law's administration. He had no seat in the House of Commons and was unsuccessful in contesting Dumbartonshire in December 1923, but gained the seat at the general election of 1924 when Baldwin renewed his appointment as solicitorgeneral for Scotland. He was no stranger to party politics, for prior to 1914 he had been adopted as prospective Conservative candidate for Kilmarnock Burghs. Fleming's political career, however, was brief, for in December 1925 came the announcement of his elevation to the Scottish bench, with the judicial title of Lord Fleming. Throughout his career as a pleader he had been distinguished by a breadth of outlook and moderation in argument which testified to his humanity and liberality of mind. In addition, he possessed the invaluable gift of common sense. These qualities, allied to a high measure of professional capacity and legal knowledge, were admirably combined with a natural patience and courtesy and excellently equipped him for the successful discharge of his high judicial office. He was brisk in expression, patient and receptive in argument, and possessed not only a firm grasp of legal principles but a determination to achieve a just decision. In every sense he was a wise and upright judge whose judgements, owing nothing to external graces or picturesque phrases, are of increasing value for their plain lucid and accurate statements of apposite legal principle.

Fleming's personal activities and interests went outside the boundaries of his profession: his interest in youth showed itself in his presidency of the Boys' Brigade in Edinburgh and in his chairmanship of the departmental committee set up in June 1942 to consider means whereby the association between the English public schools and the general educational system of the country might be developed and extended. This committee, over which he presided with painstaking zeal and care, in its unanimous report outlined a plan for opening the doors of English public schools to children from all local authority schools. The Fleming report owed much to Fleming himself and bore the marks of his common sense and realistic outlook and remains as a notable contribution to educational thought and policy in this country. Fleming also served from May 1940, until appointed chairman of the public schools committee, as chairman of the London appellate tribunal for conscientious objectors, while his patriotic zeal took him on its formation into the Home Guard as a private. He was an honorary LL.D. of his own university of Glasgow (1938) and an honorary bencher of the Middle Temple (1940). As a member of an old Rutherglen family (his father, grandfather, and great-grandfather all having been provosts of the burgh) he received the freedom of that ancient and royal burgh on the celebration of its octocentenary in 1926. He died in Edinburgh without issue after a very brief illness 20 October 1944, survived by his wife, whom he married in 1913, Beatrice Joan, daughter of James Swan, a well-known Scottish livestock dealer. Genial and kindly in manner, in personal appearance Fleming was of middle height and good physique, and greatly attached to open-air life. Fishing, shooting, golf, and (in his earlier years) mountaineering all claimed his active pursuit in his leisure.

[Personal knowledge.]     JOHN CAMERON.

FLEMING, SIR (JOHN) AMBROSE (1849–1945), electrical engineer and inventor of the wireless valve, was born at Lancaster 29 November 1849, the eldest child of the Rev. James Fleming, D.D., a Congregational minister, by his wife, Mary Ann, daughter of John Bazley White, of Swanscombe, Kent, a pioneer in the manufacture of Portland cement. His mother's eldest sister, Ellen Henrietta Ranyard [q.v.], founded the female Bible mission known later as the Ranyard Mission. In 1853 James Fleming and his family moved to London where he continued his ministry at Kentish Town, living in or near Tufnell Park until his death in 1879.

Ambrose Fleming was educated at University College School and University College, London. He obtained his B.Sc. in 1870, being placed, with only one other candidate, in the first division, despite the fact that for the last two years he had been working as a clerk with a firm of stockbrokers and was able to study only in his spare time. Subsequently (1872–4) he studied at South Kensington, first under (Sir) Edward Frankland and later under Frederick Guthrie [qq.v.]. This time was sandwiched between two periods as a science master, the one at Rossall School and the other at Cheltenham College. In 1877 he entered St. John's College, Cambridge, having won an entrance exhibition and saved £400 to pay the fees. Later, he was awarded a foundation scholarship and won several prizes.

His object in going up was to attend the lectures of J. Clerk Maxwell [q.v.] and to work in the Cavendish Laboratory. He had previously studied Clerk Maxwell's famous *Treatise on Electricity and Magnetism* (2 vols., 1873), and was an ardent admirer of Clerk Maxwell, even though the lecturer's 'paradoxical and allusive way of speaking' made him difficult to follow. In the laboratory, Fleming's main research was on the development and use of a special resistance bridge for the accurate comparison of standards of resistance, and the bridge which he devised, nicknamed 'Fleming's banjo', was subsequently used for several years in the Cavendish Laboratory. In 1880, having in the previous year obtained the degree of D.Sc. (London), he was placed in the first class, in chemistry, physics, and mineralogy, in the natural sciences tripos with distinction in physics.

After serving as demonstrator in mechanism and applied mechanics at Cambridge, Fleming was appointed in 1881 to the newly created chair of mathematics and physics at University College, Nottingham, but resigned this post in the following year to take up consulting work in London with the Edison Electric Light Company. In 1883 he was elected into a fellowship at St. John's. In the next year he gave a few lectures on electrical technology at University College, London, and in 1885 was appointed professor. His forty-one years of service to electrical engineering in this chair coincided with a rapid growth in the subject, and he was one of the small number of English scientists who contributed greatly to its progress. Fleming used to say (but this was exaggeration) that on his appointment he found the equipment to consist of a blackboard and a piece of chalk. An electrical laboratory was founded and new laboratories were opened in 1893 by the Duke of Connaught. During the early years of his professorship, Fleming, besides his teaching, was engaged on practical problems dealing with alternating-current transformers and high-voltage transmission. He read important papers on these subjects to the Institution of Electrical Engineers and in 1889 and 1892 he published his two volumes on *The Alternate Current Transformer* which for many years was a standard treatise. In pure science he collaborated with (Sir) James Dewar [q.v.] at the Royal Institution, and during the six years 1892–8 there were published from the results of their work seventeen joint papers on the electrical and magnetic properties of materials at the temperature of liquid air.

In the early days of electric lighting, Fleming was impressed by the need for an authoritative body to which questions of electrical standards might be referred. He read a paper on the subject in 1885 before the Society of Telegraph-Engineers and Electricians (later the Institution of Electrical Engineers). The negotiations which followed led to the establishment of the Board of Trade laboratory and Fleming's paper also marked a step forward towards the foundation of the National Physical Laboratory.

Fleming's attention had been drawn to photometry while he was working for the Edison Electric Light Company, and he became one of the leading expositors of the subject in this country. On the opening of the new electrical laboratory at University College the photometric gallery was one of its notable features. The paper which he read at the meeting of the British Association at Cambridge in 1904, 'On Large Bulb Incandescent Electric Lamps as Secondary Standards of Light', marks an important stage in the advance of photometry. Fleming was also known as 'the great apostle of the potentiometer', both for the contribution which he made to its development by introducing a continuously adjustable resistance and thereby making it direct-reading, and for his vision of the great possibilities inherent in the instrument, for it was he who induced R. E. B. Crompton [q.v.] to put it on the market in a practical form.

Fleming's name, however, will best be remembered in the field of wireless telegraphy. At University College he carried out almost unending experiments on wireless transmitters and receivers, and he gave special courses of experimental lectures on Hertzian or wireless waves at University College, the Royal Institution, and the Royal Society of Arts. He had unwittingly prepared himself in a remarkably thorough way for his most famous invention by his early work with Guthrie and his careful study of the Edison effect in carbon filament lamps in 1890 and 1896. This study led to his close connexion with Marconi and Marconi's Wireless Telegraphy Company, and so later to his work on the generating plant for the Atlantic transmission from Cornwall to Newfoundland, culminating in Marconi's successful reception of Morse signals across the Atlantic in December 1901.

In 1904 another great step forward was made with Fleming's experimental proof that the known rectifying property of a thermionic valve operating at power frequencies (say, 50 cycles/sec.) was still operative at wireless frequencies (say, 1,000,000 cycles/sec.). This is a root principle in the operation of the wireless valve in the radio set of the present time. His paper read before the Royal Society, 'On the Conversion of Electric Oscillations into Continuous Currents by means of a Vacuum Valve' (1905), gives the earliest scientific account of the 'Fleming' valve. In the same year he described his electric wave measurer, or cymometer as he called it, and demonstrated it to the Royal Society.

During his distinguished career, Fleming contributed more than a hundred important papers to the Proceedings of learned societies; more than one-third of them appeared in those of the Physical Society. His association with this society was indeed remarkable. He read the very first paper read to it on its foundation in 1874, and no less than sixty-five years later he read his last paper before it in 1939 and illustrated it with experiments. He was an active president of the Television Society of London from 1930 to the time of his death, and strongly supported J. L. Baird [q.v.] in his pioneering work. He was one of the leading teachers of his time. His flair for linking together the mathematical bases of little-understood phenomena with their practical effects was a factor which drew many distinguished engineers to his special lectures at University College, as well as to his Cantor lectures at the Royal Society of Arts. He also ranked highly as a popular scientific lecturer. Few men of his time could hold an audience so thoroughly as he did, for example, in his four courses of Christmas lectures at the Royal Institution in 1894, 1901, 1917, and 1921. His success was due alike to his care in selecting suitable experimental illustrations and to his unremitting attention to their effective demonstration. His crisp articulation was also a great advantage.

Besides those already mentioned, Fleming's valuable written works include The Principles of Electric Wave Telegraphy (1906) and The Propagation of Electric Currents in Telephone and Telegraph Conductors (1911). A collection of his scientific and allied papers, 149 in number, in five volumes, was presented to University College, London, in 1948 by Lady Fleming. His services were recognized by a knighthood in 1929, and he was the recipient of many honours. From the Royal Society, of which he was elected a fellow in 1892, he received the Hughes medal in 1910; he also received the Albert medal of the Royal Society of Arts (1921), the Faraday medal of the Institution of Electrical Engineers (1928), the Duddell medal of the Physical Society (1931), the gold medal of the Institute of Radio Engineers, U.S.A. (1933), the Franklin medal of the Franklin Institute, U.S.A. (1935), and the Kelvin medal of the engineering institutions of Great Britain (1935). He was elected an honorary fellow of his college at Cambridge in 1927 and in 1928 received the honorary degree of D.Eng. from Liverpool University. On his retirement in 1926 he became professor emeritus. He went to live at Sidmouth where he died, aged ninety-five, 18 April 1945.

In person, Fleming was remarkable for his mental alertness, forthrightness, power of concentration (increased perhaps by his deafness), and his ability to express himself clearly; but this very keenness at times made it difficult for him to suffer fools gladly. His main recreations were photography and sketching in water-colour. The photographs which he took by the wet-plate process of his younger days during his travels in Switzerland, and later in Italy and Egypt, have considerable artistic merit. A Congregationalist by upbringing, he inclined as years went on more to the Church of England on its evangelical side. That he held strong opinions on the relation of evolution to religion was shown by his presidency of the Victoria Institute from 1927 to 1942. His deep conviction of the truth of the Christian faith was manifested in later years by both his writings and his public utterances.

Fleming was twice married: first, in 1887 to Clara Ripley (died 1917), daughter of Walter Freak Pratt, solicitor, of Bath; secondly, in 1933 to Olive May, daughter of George Franks, business proprietor, of Cardiff. There were no children.

A portrait of Fleming by Sir William Orpen is at University College, London; the Institution of Electrical Engineers possesses a replica given to it by Fleming. A bust by G. H. Paulin (1932) is in the electrical engineering department of University College, London.

[Sir J. A. Fleming, *Memories of a Scientific Life*, 1934; W. H. Eccles in *Obituary Notices of Fellows of the Royal Society*, No. 14, November 1945; *Proceedings* of the Physical Society, November 1945; J. T. MacGregor-Morris, *The Inventor of the Valve*, 1954, and *Sir Ambrose Fleming* (*Jubilee of the Valve*) in *Notes and Records of the Royal Society*, March 1955; private information; personal knowledge.]    J. T. MacGregor-Morris.

FLETT, Sir JOHN SMITH (1869–1947), geologist, was born at Kirkwall, Orkney, 26 June 1869, the second son of James Ferguson Flett, merchant and bailie, and his wife, Mary Ann Copland. He was educated at Kirkwall Burgh School and George Watson's College, Edinburgh, and in 1886 passed to the university of Edinburgh where, after a brilliant academic career, he graduated in arts and science (1892) and medicine (1894). After a short spell in medical practice, he joined the staff of the geological department of his university, then under the direction of his beloved teacher James Geikie. Soon after he became lecturer in petrology and during the next half-dozen years he laid, by study and research, the foundations of his distinguished career in that branch of his science. Among his earliest researches, noteworthy are his investigations into the stratigraphy of the Old Red Sandstone of Orkney and into the petrography of the remarkable suite of alkaline dykes found in this formation; on this Orkney work he was in 1900 awarded the D.Sc. of his university.

In 1901 Flett succeeded (Sir) Jethro Teall [q.v.] as petrographer to the Geological Survey of Great Britain. During his ten years' tenure of this post, he made petrological contributions to some thirty Survey memoirs ranging over the whole country, and thus acquired a comprehensive knowledge of British rocks which was to be of inestimable value in his later work. He was part-author of two important memoirs dealing with Land's End and the Lizard, and in these he studied in particular the relationships between intrusion and stress-action in igneous complexes. During this period he described the rocks of the Lewisian Inliers of the Northern Highlands and shared in the demonstration of polymetamorphism around the Inchbae Granite in Ross-shire. In another field, he proposed, with Henry Dewey, that the pillow-lavas and spilites formed an independent igneous suite indicative of a special geological environment.

Whilst Survey petrographer, Flett collaborated with Tempest Anderson, under the auspices of the Royal Society, in studying the vulcanicity of the Soufrière and Mont Pelée in the West Indies. Especially important were his contributions to the knowledge of the special kind of eruption known as *nuées ardentes*.

In 1911 Flett was promoted assistant to the director of the Geological Survey in Scotland. During the war of 1914–18 he was responsible for the supply of geological information required, and afterwards reorganized the Scottish branch of the Survey and superintended its transfer to new offices.

The last stage of Flett's career began in 1920 when he succeeded Sir Aubrey Strahan as director of the Geological Survey. He reorganized and enlarged the Survey to meet the growing demand for geological information. To this end he established district offices in the principal British coalfields. Fundamental research was not, however, neglected; under his direction the classic tertiary igneous complexes of the Hebrides, the Sutherland migmatites, the geology of Anglesey and of Orkney were described. Two months before his retirement, Flett's dearest ambition was fulfilled—the transfer of the Survey in 1935 from the cramped quarters in Jermyn Street to the new magnificent Geological Museum at South Kensington.

In addition to his scientific papers and memoirs, Flett published in 1937 *The First Hundred Years of the Geological Survey of Great Britain*. Twenty years before, he had written, with Marion I. Newbigin, a charming biography of his old teacher, James Geikie.

Flett was a man of strong character, forceful in debate, seemingly blunt at times, but genuinely interested in the scientific development of his staff. Possibly much of his bluntness arose from the deafness which afflicted him for most of his life. He had an immense knowledge of geological literature, travelled widely, and was known to geologists all over the world. But he never lost his early love for the classics and the best of ¦English literature.

Many honours came to him: he was elected F.R.S. in 1913 and fellow of the Royal Society of Edinburgh in 1900, being awarded the Neill prize in 1901; he had the Bigsby (1909) and Wollaston (1935) medals of the Geological Society; the Bolitho medal of the Royal Geological Society of Cornwall; and he was a foreign member of many overseas societies and academies. He served as president of the Edinburgh Geological Society, the Mineralogical Society, and many kindred bodies; and was president of the geology section of the British Association meeting in Edinburgh in 1921. He received the honorary degree of LL.D. from Edinburgh University in 1912. In 1918 he was appointed O.B.E. and in 1925 he was promoted K.B.E.

In 1897 he married Mary Jane, daughter of David Meason, of Kirkwall; there were two sons and two daughters of the marriage. He died at Ashdon, Essex, 26 January 1947.

[H. H. Read in *Obituary Notices of Fellows of the Royal Society*, No. 16, May 1948; *Quarterly Journal* of the Geological Society of London, vol. ciii, 1947; *Year Book of the Royal Society of Edinburgh, 1948 and 1949, 1950*; an autobiographical fragment appeared in the *University of Edinburgh Journal*, Autumn 1950; private information; personal knowledge.]     H. H. READ.

FLOWER, ROBIN ERNEST WILLIAM (1881–1946), scholar and poet, was born at Meanwood, Leeds, 16 October 1881, the son of Marmaduke Clement William Flower (son of the Rev. William Balmbro' Flower, a writer and patristic scholar) and his wife, Jane Lynch. Both parents had Irish blood; the Flowers had been English settlers in Ireland, and Jane Lynch came of a Galway family. Marmaduke Flower became a landscape and portrait painter, a pupil of (Sir) Hubert von Herkomer [q.v.], whom he assisted in his school at Bushey. Robin Flower was educated at Leeds Grammar School and Pembroke College, Oxford, which he entered as a classical scholar in 1900. He was placed in the first class of the honours list in classical moderations in 1902 and in *literae humaniores* in 1904. A breakdown in health during the examination for the Civil Service necessitated a prolonged rest, in the Orkneys and later at Cologne. After trying unsuccessfully for a post in the Victoria and Albert Museum he was appointed an assistant in the department of manuscripts, British Museum, where he began duty in 1906.

After joining the British Museum, Flower began to learn Irish, and was commissioned to complete the catalogue of Irish manuscripts begun by Standish Hayes O'Grady. He went to Dublin for a few weeks in 1910 to study Irish under Professor Carl J. S. Marstrander, the Norwegian philologist, and during repeated visits to the Great Blasket steeped himself in the spoken language and traditions of the island; the result is seen in his admirable translation of Tomás Ó Crohan's autobiography, *The Islandman* (1934), and his original work *The Western Island* (1944). The *Catalogue of Irish Manuscripts in the British Museum* appeared in 1926, volume i by O'Grady, and volume ii by Flower, and was acclaimed as a work of the first importance. Flower did not live to complete the third volume (introduction and indexes). He became deputy keeper of manuscripts in 1929, and from 1939 he was in charge of the British Museum manuscripts sent to the National Library of Wales, Aberystwyth. He was taken ill in October 1943, resigned from the British Museum in 1944, and was appointed C.B.E. in 1945. He was an honorary lecturer in Celtic at University College, London, and in 1935 lectured at Yale and other American universities. He was elected F.B.A. in 1934 and was also a member of the Royal Irish Academy, a corresponding fellow of the Mediaeval Academy of America, and a leading member of various societies, including the Irish Texts Society, of which he was chairman of the council, and the Early English Text Society of which he became honorary acting director in 1940. He received the honorary degrees of D.Litt. Celt. from the National University of Ireland (1927), and D.Litt. from Dublin (1937).

Endowed with manifold gifts and a power of intense concentration, an accomplished poet and inspired translator, master of a lively and attractive prose style, a good linguist, a scholar equally at home in Celtic and in medieval studies, and possessing a wide acquaintance with English literature and some knowledge of Anglo-Saxon, Flower had capacities which his comparatively early death and the very range of his interests prevented him from using to the full. The projected history of Irish literature which he was uniquely qualified to write got no farther than the studies posthumously printed as *The Irish Tradition* (1947), and his published work is but a small part of what he planned. He was a forceful and arresting personality, a brilliant talker, and a man of great kindness. He published several volumes of poems, a selection from which appears in *Poems and Translations* (1931).

In 1911 Flower married Ida Mary, daughter of John Soper Streeter, solicitor,

of Croydon, and the youngest sister of Canon B. H. Streeter [q.v.]. They had one son and three daughters, the eldest of whom, Barbara, a gifted scholar, died in 1955. Flower died in London 16 January 1946. A pencil drawing by David Bell and a water-colour portrait by W. Bennett are in the possession of the family.

[Sir H. I. Bell in *Proceedings* of the British Academy, vol. xxxii, 1946; *Nineteenth Century and After*, March 1946; private information; personal knowledge.]                    H. I. BELL.

FLUX, SIR ALFRED WILLIAM (1867–1942), economist, statistician, and civil servant, was born in Portsmouth 8 April 1867, the only son of John Flux, a journeyman cement-maker, by his wife, Emily, daughter of Alfred Prince, dairy farmer, of Newport, Isle of Wight. He was educated at Portsmouth Grammar School and entering St. John's College, Cambridge, as a minor scholar, he was bracketed senior wrangler in 1887, and was elected a fellow of his college in 1889; he won the Marshall prize in the same year. His interests had turned to economics after graduating, and he left Cambridge in 1893 to join the Owens College, Manchester, as Cobden lecturer in political economy, becoming Stanley Jevons professor of the same subject in 1898. Three years later he accepted an invitation to McGill University, where he stayed as William Dow professor of political economy until 1908. In that year the Board of Trade was organizing the first census of production; Flux was brought in as statistical adviser to the controller-general of the commercial, labour, and statistical department, and, although not given the titular position of director until 1911, was responsible for the final report. In 1918 he became an assistant secretary of the Board in charge of the statistical department. He retired in 1932.

The early years of the century had seen a great widening and deepening of interest in economic statistics. The Board of Trade, thanks to the inspiration and organizing ability of Sir Robert Giffen and later Sir Hubert Llewellyn Smith [qq.v.], had done much to stimulate this interest. But official statistics were still in the main a by-product of administration. Flux arrived at a time when the scientific collection of economic data with no immediate and specific administrative object had become politically possible. He had not the dynamic qualities of Giffen and

Llewellyn Smith; but his technical competence and academic prestige, added to his personal qualities of candour, devotion to his subject, and complete freedom from party feeling, admirably fitted him to take advantage of the opportunity they had created. He played a chief part in a revolution in official statistics. The census of production made possible the quantitative study of the structure and interrelations of British industry. This was followed by an adequate index of prices (1921), indexes of industrial activity (1927), and an estimate of national income on the basis of product, to supplement earlier estimates made by aggregating individual incomes (1929).

Flux also influenced other official statistics, as Board of Trade representative on inter-departmental committees, and international comparisons, as British representative on many inter-governmental committees and conferences. After his retirement he served, often as chairman, on a series of committees through which the League of Nations was working out uniform classifications and common standards for economic statistics. His knowledge of languages and wide experience made him an admirable agent in this work, which he enjoyed. He was appreciated, receiving the rare distinction of honorary membership of the International Institute of Statistics in 1929.

Flux's official position nevertheless allowed him to participate fully in scientific discussion. He was an honorary secretary of the Royal Statistical Society from 1910 to 1928, when he became president. He was awarded the Society's gold Guy medal in 1930. The new developments in his official work were presented to the world in papers to the Society; and the meetings provided an outlet, denied to him as a civil servant, for rather lengthy and formal oratory, in which he delighted. No member of the Society was more respected or held in greater affection.

As an economist Flux was sound rather than original. His *Economic Principles* (1904, revised ed. 1923), a clear and independent restatement of classical theory, was widely read. His account of *The Foreign Exchanges* (1924) had the same qualities. His chief service to economics was, however, to inculcate and assist a quantitative approach to its problems. His services were recognized by appointment as C.B. in 1920 and by a knighthood on the occasion of the Royal Statistical Society's centenary in 1934. In this year

the university of Manchester conferred upon him the honorary degree of LL.D. He was a member of many foreign statistical societies. He married in 1895 Emilie, daughter of Wilhelm Hansen, man of business, of Copenhagen, and died at Ladeplatts, Denmark, 16 July 1942. There were no children.

[*Journal* of the Royal Statistical Society, vol. cv, 1942; private information; personal knowledge.]      HENRY CLAY.

FOAKES JACKSON, FREDERICK JOHN (1855–1941), divine. [See JACKSON.]

FOGERTY, ELSIE (1865–1945), founder and principal of the Central School of Speech Training and Dramatic Art, was born at Sydenham, London, 16 December 1865, the daughter of Joseph Fogerty, engineer and architect, of Dublin, by his wife, Hannah Cochrane, of Limerick. An only child, she travelled widely with her parents and was educated privately at Sydenham. Languages were easily absorbed, and she was well read and had an exceedingly retentive memory. She studied for some time at the Paris Conservatoire under Coquelin *aîné* and Delaunay, and with Hermann Vezin [q.v.] in London.

In 1889 she was appointed lecturer in English and speech at the Crystal Palace School of Art and Literature and for many years taught in schools in and about London and on the south coast, including Roedean (1908–37). From the beginning she opposed wholeheartedly the artificialities of 'elocution' as it was then taught. In 1898 she began to hold classes at the Royal Albert Hall, and, with the assistance of other experts, she worked out a three years' training course for teachers of speech and drama. No other school attached so much importance to the speaking of verse and for many years her students distinguished themselves at the Oxford recitations. For nearly twenty years she worked to secure university recognition for her school, and when in 1923 her efforts were rewarded by the establishment at London University of a diploma in dramatic art her school was one of the three with an approved course of training.

Elsie Fogerty was a dynamic personality, short, but of a commanding presence. She had a remarkable understanding of character and her pupils owed much to her efforts to fit them for their careers.

Her one aim was to improve the standard of speech in all classes of the community and her influence was far-reaching. In 1912 she was allowed to open a speech clinic at St. Thomas's Hospital, and thus became a pioneer of speech therapy. She gave university extension lectures at the Royal Albert Hall and for many years took evening classes for London County Council teachers. A wide circle of actors and actresses consulted her about their voices, and students from the United States and the Dominions attended her summer schools. She served on the council of the British Drama League from its foundation until her death and was a keen supporter of the projected national theatre. In 1934 she was appointed C.B.E. She never married, but devoted her entire life to her work.

In 1944 her flat was destroyed and thereafter she lived in a South Kensington hotel. She died 4 July 1945 in a nursinghome at Leamington. A portrait by R. G. Eves is in the possession of the Central School.

[Private information; personal knowledge.]
MURIEL H. WIGGLESWORTH.

FORBES, GEORGE WILLIAM (1869–1947), prime minister of New Zealand, was born at Norwich Quay, Lyttelton, New Zealand, 12 March 1869, the third son of Robert Forbes, ship chandler, and his wife, Annie Adamson. He attended the borough school and the Christchurch Boys' High School (1882–3) and after three years with a firm of Christchurch merchants spent the next seven working with his father in Lyttelton. As a young man he showed athletic ability and in 1892 captained a famous Canterbury Rugby touring side. These were depression years and in them, by his association with George Laurenson, subsequently Liberal member for Lyttelton, Forbes absorbed Radical convictions, particularly relating to land settlement, which endured throughout his life.

In 1894 he began a new life as a farmer on the Cheviot estate recently subdivided for settlement on perpetual Crown lease. There he farmed progressively, was active in local politics, and in 1905 was appointed to the McKerrow Land Commission. In 1908 he entered Parliament as Liberal member for Hurunui, a seat which he had unsuccessfully contested in 1902 and was now to hold for thirty-five years. His transition to national politics curiously epitomized the arrival there of the farmer

class whose characteristic, described by Pember Reeves, was 'to see clearly but not far, and walk steadily because it never looked aloft'.

When in 1912 the Liberal Government gave way to the Reform administration of W. F. Massey [q.v.], with its lure to farmers of freehold tenure, Forbes became Liberal whip. The retirement of (Sir) Thomas Mason Wilford in 1925 left him, aged fifty-six and publicly little known, leader of the party. On the eve of the 1928 elections, however, Sir Joseph Ward [q.v.], ailing but still dynamic, resumed the leadership and raised the party's appeal sufficiently for it (now under the name of United) to come back into power with Labour support. Ward's health declining, the responsibility of government devolved increasingly on Forbes who, both as deputy for the prime minister and as minister of agriculture, bore the burden of forcing through Parliament against determined opposition the Government's programme for closer settlement. This included penal taxation of great estates and provision, through a lands development board, for financial assistance in land development.

On 28 May 1930, on Ward's retirement, Forbes formed an administration, still dependent on Labour support, which was obliged to face the social and financial problems arising out of the world depression. He took office, as minister of finance and external affairs as well as prime minister, in an atmosphere of goodwill, due to his reputation for courage and hard work and his agreeable and modest bearing. But his reliance on orthodox methods for dealing with the slump—all-round retrenchment, increased taxation, and uneconomic relief works—proved unpopular and ineffective. A 10 per cent. cut in wages, announced in March 1931, brought the informal alliance with Labour to an end; but it was not until 18 September that Forbes's appeal for a coalition with Reform was accepted by J. G. Coates [q.v.]. In the Government formed on 22 September 1931 Forbes remained prime minister and took the portfolios of railways and external affairs, to which he later added those of attorney-general (28 January 1933) and native affairs (1 November 1934).

An unsatisfactory period followed. Expert committees had recommended a recovery programme, out of which Forbes first enacted those measures which pressed hardest on the working class—wage cuts, social-service retrenchment, and emasculation of the arbitration procedure. Major reflationary measures, such as exchange depreciation, debt conversion, and the reduction of bank overdraft rates, had to await the supersession of W. Downie Stewart [q.v.] as finance minister on 28 January 1933 by the bolder and more imaginative Coates. Forbes's own position at this time may be understood from his remark that he 'considered it his duty to remain on deck and if necessary go down with the ship'. The new trend in public policy towards economic planning which produced a Reserve Bank, co-ordination of marketing, and facilitation and adjustment of mortgage finance in 1934, and gave effect to the Ottawa trade agreements of 1932, although it was endorsed by Forbes, was due primarily to the drive of Coates.

Forbes attended two major overseas conferences, the 1930 Imperial Conference and the 1933 world economic conference, to which he contributed faith in imperial preference, acquiescence in 'quotas' and satisfaction with the *status quo* in imperial relations. In his disapproval of the Statute of Westminster, he accurately represented New Zealand opinion at the time but to preserve Commonwealth unanimity he gave it formal support on condition that the Dominion should be exempted from its provisions save through specific enactment by its own legislature. Forbes also took part in the meeting of Dominion prime ministers in May 1935, when he accepted the principle of cautious conciliation of Germany. His earlier suspension of compulsory military training (1930) while continuing to contribute to the Singapore base reflected this pacific disposition as well as the need for economy. 'It is difficult to understand', he said, 'the logic of those who argue that preparedness for war promotes peace.' A similar generosity lay behind his support of Sir Apirana Ngata in his policy of Maori regeneration.

On 10 May 1935 the United and Reform parties 'federated'; but this did not stave off their electoral defeat, and on 4 December 1935 Forbes resigned office. He remained leader of the Opposition until 31 October 1936 when the new National Party found it expedient to give up the leaders with whom 'depression policies' had been associated. He took no further active part in politics and retired from Parliament in 1943.

Slightly under medium height and stockily built, Forbes bore the appearance of a prosperous yeoman farmer. Simple in his tastes, entirely unaffected, with a gift of quiet anecdote, he combined singleness of purpose with a conciliatory approach which won him objectives which escaped abler men. In 1930 he was sworn of the Privy Council, received the freedom of the cities of London and Edinburgh, and was given honorary doctorates of law by the universities of Edinburgh and Belfast. In 1898 he married Emma Serena, daughter of Thomas James Gee, a Christchurch builder, by whom he had a son and two daughters, all of whom survived him when he died at his home, Crystal Brook, Cheviot, 17 May 1947.

[*New Zealand Parliamentary Record, 1840–1949*, edited by G. H. Scholefield, 1950; *The Times*, 19 May 1947; *Round Table*, London, and Christchurch *Press* and *Star Sun, passim*; *New Zealand Parliamentary Debates*; private information.]     W. F. MONK.

FORBES, STANHOPE ALEXANDER (1857–1947), painter, was born in Dublin 18 November 1857, the younger son of William Forbes, at that time manager of the Midland Great Western Railway of Ireland, by his wife, Juliette de Guise. William Alexander Forbes and James Staats Forbes [qq.v.] were his cousin and uncle respectively. His elder brother, Sir William Forbes, followed his father's career and became general manager of the London, Brighton, and South Coast Railway. Stanhope Forbes, however, showed an early propensity for sketching which was encouraged by John Sparkes the art master of Dulwich College where Forbes was educated. Later, when Sparkes was master at the Lambeth School of Art, he prepared Forbes there for the Royal Academy Schools which he entered in 1874. In 1878 he went for two years' further training in the studio of Léon Bonnat at Clichy; but more important influences at this time were the open-air paintings of peasant life by Bastien-Lepage and Forbes's sketching trips in Brittany in company with his school friend H. H. La Thangue.

In 1884 Forbes visited Cornwall and first saw Newlyn which was soon to become his permanent home and to supply the label by which his art was to be classified. The year 1885 in which he exhibited at the Royal Academy his first large-scale painting of a Newlyn scene, 'A Fish Sale on a Cornish Beach', virtually marks the birth of the movement known

# Forbes, S. A.

as the 'Newlyn School'; for earlier in that year Walter Langley, who had been painting at Newlyn since 1882, exhibited with equal acclaim his 'Waiting for the Boats' at the Royal Institute of Painters in Water Colours. Other painters associated with the group, which had come somewhat fortuitously together, were Frank Bramley, Chevallier Tayler, Fred Hall, and T. C. Gotch. Forbes was from the beginning recognized as one of the strongest, and remained one of the most faithful, exponents of its tenets. The characteristics of his art were an uncompromising realism in his treatment of the life of fisherman or countryman exactly as it presented itself to his eye; his insistence that so far as possible the painting should be completed in the surroundings and under the lighting which it portrayed; and a broad manner which eliminated inessential detail. With many of his young contemporaries who were enthusiastic for this aspect of recent French painting, Forbes was included in the first exhibition of the New English Art Club in 1886, but he did not long maintain his membership. His progress towards popularity and success was marked by his exhibition at the Royal Academy of paintings which found their way into public collections, such as 'Off to the Fishing Ground' (1886, Walker Art Gallery, Liverpool); 'The Village Philharmonic' (1888, Birmingham); 'The Health of the Bride' (1889, Tate Gallery); 'Christmas Eve' (1897, Brighton); 'The 22nd of January, 1901' (a family reading the news of Queen Victoria's death; Exeter). In 1897 he was commissioned to paint one of the frescoes in the Royal Exchange, his subject being the great fire of London.

Stanhope Forbes was elected A.R.A. in 1892 and R.A. in 1910. In 1904 he was appointed correspondent to the Institut de France in succession to G. F. Watts [q.v.]. He exhibited for the last time at the Royal Academy in 1945 and died at Newlyn 2 March 1947. He married in 1889 Elizabeth Adela (died 1912), daughter of William Armstrong, of the Civil Service, Ottawa. She was also a successful painter and with her Forbes founded a school of art in Newlyn in 1899. They had one son. In 1915 he married Maude Clayton, daughter of Edward Hume Palmer, of Bexhill. A self-portrait painted by Forbes in 1891 is in the Aberdeen Art Gallery.

[*The Times*, 3 March 1947; Ulrich Thieme and Felix Becker, *Allgemeines Lexikon der bildenden Künstler*, vol. xii, 1916; C. Lewis Hind, 'Stanhope A. Forbes R.A.' in the *Art Journal*, Christmas Number, 1911; Mrs. Lionel Birch, *Stanhope A. Forbes, A.R.A., and Elizabeth Stanhope Forbes, A.R.W.S.*, 1906.]

GRAHAM REYNOLDS.

FORSTER, SIR MARTIN ONSLOW (1872–1945), chemist, was born in south London 8 November 1872, the fourth and youngest child of Martin Forster, a clerk in the Bank of England, and his wife, Ann Hope Limby. Educated at Dane Hill House, known as Boulden's, Margate, he showed a leaning towards chemistry and in October 1888 entered Finsbury Technical College intending to train for the chemical industry. He obtained his certificate after only two years, being bracketed first. Then followed a year's research under Raphael Meldola and a further year under Emil Fischer at Würzburg where in 1892 he obtained his Ph.D. *summa cum laude*. On returning to England he was appointed research assistant to (Sir) William Augustus Tilden at Mason College, Birmingham. Two years later he decided upon a career as a university teacher and, recognizing the necessity for a British university degree, went as a research student to the laboratory of H. E. Armstrong [q.v.] at the Central Technical College where he was soon awarded the first Salters' Company research fellowship. Although he spent only one year in the laboratory this period profoundly influenced the whole of his future research. Armstrong suggested to Forster that he should investigate the action of fuming nitric acid on camphor and Forster's main contributions to chemistry were to deal with the reactions of camphor and its derivatives.

In 1895 Tilden, who had migrated from Birmingham to the Royal College of Science, offered Forster the post of demonstrator in chemistry which he accepted. Forster obtained his D.Sc., and with it the Granville scholarship, from the university of London in 1899. In 1902 he became assistant professor of chemistry, a post which was virtually a professorship of organic chemistry. Forster took full advantage of the opportunities which it offered. He gathered round him an enthusiastic band of research students including a number from Switzerland among whom the most distinguished was H. E. Fierz, later to hold a chair in Zürich. Whilst the main publications from the laboratory dealt with the chemistry of camphor, an important series of papers was devoted to triazo-compounds.

After Tilden's retirement from the Royal College of Science in 1909 his successors had little sympathy with organic chemistry. Forster therefore retired in 1913, intending to enter politics. The outbreak of war altered his plans: in 1915 he became chairman of the technical committee of British Dyes, Ltd., and in 1916 director. In 1918 he was appointed first director of the Salters' Institute of Industrial Chemistry, a post which left him sufficient leisure to return to experimental work in the Davy–Faraday Laboratory.

Forster was essentially an experimentalist and had little interest in theory. The value of his original work was recognized by his election as F.R.S. in 1905 and by the award in 1915 of the Longstaff medal of the Chemical Society. Nearly all Forster's papers were published by the Chemical Society of which he was elected a fellow in 1892. He served on the council, 1901–4, was honorary secretary, 1904–10, vice-president, 1910–13, and treasurer, 1915–22. He was twice vice-president of the (Royal) Institute of Chemistry and from 1914 to 1922 he was convocation member of the senate of London University. He was prime warden of the Dyers' Company 1919–20, president of the chemistry section of the British Association meeting at Edinburgh, 1921, and president of the Indian Science Congress in 1925.

Despite his influential position in the Chemical Society and elsewhere, his fine presence, and his impressiveness as a public speaker, Forster was not remarkable as a leader. He seemed to hold himself aloof, with an air of superiority which did not make for popularity, and, except in his own research, he tended to avoid difficulties. He was more successful in India where he went in 1922, on the recommendation of Sir W. J. Pope [q.v.], as director of the Indian Institute of Science, Bangalore. There his relations with both staff and students were most cordial. Although unable to continue his own experimental work, his social and administrative activities made a valuable contribution to the advancement of science in India. He was due to retire in 1927 but remained until 1933, and was knighted on his retirement. He did not return to England, but settled in Mysore, where he died 24 May 1945.

Forster married in 1907 Madeleine,

daughter of William Henry Nichols, manufacturing chemist, of New York. The marriage was dissolved in 1916. In 1925 he married Elena Josefina (died 1941), daughter of William Hall Haynes, of Cadiz, and widow of Horace P. Parodi, a barrister, of Gibraltar. There were no children of either marriage.

[E. F. Armstrong and J. L. Simonsen in *Obituary Notices of Fellows of the Royal Society*, No. 14, November 1945 ; personal knowledge.]

J. L. SIMONSEN.

FORSYTH, ANDREW RUSSELL (1858–1942), mathematician, was born in Glasgow 18 June 1858, the only child of John Forsyth, whose family had come from Campbeltown, by his wife, Christina Glen, of Paisley. When Andrew was in his sixth year, his mother died: and his father, who was now engaged as a marine engineer in a Liverpool boat trading with the Mediterranean, entered him at Liverpool Collegiate Institution (later Liverpool College), where he remained for eight years. In March 1875 his father died, and it was only by overcoming great financial difficulties that he was able in April 1877 to compete for the entrance scholarships at Trinity College, Cambridge: he was successful, and entered the college in the following October. The Cambridge professors at the time were of unsurpassed eminence—Cayley in pure mathematics, Stokes and Clerk Maxwell in mathematical physics, and Adams (the discoverer of Neptune) in celestial mechanics: but they did not teach undergraduates, and Forsyth obtained most of his instruction from his coach, E. J. Routh [q.v.]. However, he had the audacity to attend a course by Cayley, where he was the only auditor under the standing of M.A.

Forsyth graduated as senior wrangler and first Smith's prizeman in 1881, and in October of the same year won a Trinity fellowship with a dissertation on the theory of the double theta functions. This subject is almost incredibly rich in identities of all kinds, great numbers of which were already known: what Forsyth did was to show that practically all of them can be obtained by specialization from a single theorem of immense generality, which includes 4,096 particular cases. On the basis of this theorem he developed the whole subject systematically. In October 1882 he left Cambridge to become the first professor of mathematics in the newly established University

College at Liverpool; in January 1884 Trinity called him back as a college lecturer and at the end of 1885 appeared his well-known *Treatise on Differential Equations*. A number of original papers followed: and in 1886, at the age of twenty-seven, he was elected a fellow of the Royal Society. By 1890 he had come to be recognized generally as the most brilliant pure mathematician in the British Empire.

He had for some time realized, as no one else did, the most serious deficiency in the Cambridge school, namely its ignorance of what had been and was being done on the continent of Europe. He determined to reform this state of things, and with this aim published in 1893 his *Theory of Functions*, a book which had a greater influence on British mathematics than any work since Newton's *Principia*. From the day of its publication, the face of Cambridge was changed: most of the pure mathematicians who took their degrees in the next twenty years became function-theorists.

The extraordinary and tragic part of the story is that not long after this great triumph, which secures for Forsyth a place of outstanding honour in the record of British university studies, his own reputation as a mathematician began to decline. The fact was that, although he was the initiator of the new developments, he himself belonged essentially to the old order. His special gift was a wonderful dexterity and generalship in operations involving a great number of symbols. In discovering formulae expressive of relations and identities, or structural forms invariant under transformations, he was supreme; but he arrived at his results by a combination of manipulative skill and intuition rather than by conscious logical processes, and he was not fitted by nature to excel in the types of problem which now came into fashion, such as those concerning the range of validity of equalities involving limit-processes.

In 1895 Forsyth was elected to succeed Cayley in the Sadleirian chair of pure mathematics. As head of the Cambridge school he was conspicuously successful, and many of the wranglers of the period 1894–1910 became original workers of distinction. British mathematicians were already indebted to him for the first introduction of many theories which had originated on the continent, and the importation of novelties continued to occupy his attention. A great traveller

and a good linguist, he loved to meet eminent foreigners and invite them to enjoy Trinity hospitality.

In 1910 Forsyth married Marion Amelia (died 1920), daughter of Henry Pollock, master of the Supreme Court of Justice, and up to this time the wife of (Sir) C. V. Boys [q.v.]. He then resigned his chair and his fellowship and left Cambridge for ever. In April 1913 he was appointed to a chair in the Imperial College of Science and Technology, South Kensington, at that time an institution of comparatively recent origin, where his organizing ability did great service. He retired under the age limit in 1923, and died in London 2 June 1942.

Honorary degrees were conferred upon Forsyth by the universities of Dublin, Manchester, Oxford, Liverpool, Calcutta, Wales, Glasgow, Aberdeen, and Christiania. He was president of the mathematics and physics section of the British Association in 1897 and 1905, of the Mathematical Association, 1903–4 and 1936, and of the London Mathematical Society in 1904–6, and a member of many scientific societies at home and abroad. He was awarded a Royal medal by the Royal Society in 1897.

[E. T. Whittaker in *Obituary Notices of Fellows of the Royal Society*, No. 11, November 1942; personal knowledge.]

E. T. WHITTAKER.

FOWLER, SIR RALPH HOWARD (1889–1944), mathematician and mathematical physicist, was born at Fedsden, Roydon, Essex, 17 January 1889, the elder son of Howard Fowler, by his wife, Frances Eva, daughter of George Dewhurst, cotton merchant, of Manchester. From his father, who had represented England at Rugby football, and Oxford at Rugby and cricket as well, Ralph inherited his general athletic ability. His sister Dorothy became an even more distinguished golfer than Ralph himself, winning the English Ladies' Close Championship for golf in 1925 and playing for England, 1921–8.

Fowler was elected in 1902 to a scholarship at Winchester of which he was to become a fellow in 1933. During this period the Fowler family moved from Essex to Norfolk, a county for which Ralph subsequently played cricket. From Winchester he won an entrance scholarship at Trinity College, Cambridge, where he obtained a first class in part i of the mathematical tripos in 1909, and became a wrangler in part ii in 1911 with special credit in schedule B. He was awarded a Rayleigh prize for mathematics in 1913, and the Adams prize in 1924. He represented Cambridge at golf in 1912.

After taking his degree he began research in pure mathematics, working on the behaviour of solutions of second-order differential equations, and for this work was elected into a prize fellowship at Trinity in 1914. The war, however, was completely to change Fowler's mathematical interest, as it led to his forsaking pure mathematics (at which he was exhaustive rather than brilliant) for applied mathematics and theoretical physics, which gave him full scope both for his true mathematical powers and for his strong practical common sense. The maturity of judgement and vision which Fowler subsequently developed in his researches in mathematical physics surprised and delighted those who had known him in his younger years.

On the outbreak of war Fowler obtained a commission in the Royal Marines; he was severely wounded in the Gallipoli campaign. Whilst convalescing in England he began a notable collaboration with (Professor) Archibald Vivian Hill, the first great influence in his career. With him he organized the anti-aircraft experimental section of the munitions inventions department of the Ministry of Munitions. Later he became its assistant director, was promoted captain, and appointed O.B.E. in 1918. Some of his joint researches in other members of the section in anti-aircraft gunnery afterwards became classical, an account of 'The Aerodynamics of a Spinning Shell' being subsequently published in the *Philosophical Transactions* of the Royal Society (A, vols. ccxxi, 1920–21, and ccxxii, 1921–2). This memoir had a considerable influence on ballistics in the war of 1939–45.

In 1919 Fowler returned to Cambridge and in 1920 he was appointed lecturer in mathematics at Trinity, and came under the second great influence in his life, Sir Ernest (later Lord) Rutherford [q.v.], whose daughter, Eileen Mary, he married in 1921. She died in 1930, leaving two sons and two daughters. Fowler became a prolific researcher in the domains of statistical mechanics and atomic physics. His early collaboration with (Sir) Charles Galton Darwin resulted in the publication of his Adams prize essay in the form of *Statistical Mechanics* (1929, 2nd ed.

1936), which exhibits Fowler's professional competence and complete mastery of detail. He was elected F.R.S. in 1925, and he was awarded a Royal medal by the Society in 1936. He delivered the Bakerian lecture in 1935. He was elected first Plummer professor of mathematical physics at Cambridge in 1932. In 1938 he was appointed director of the National Physical Laboratory, but an attack of the illness to which he eventually succumbed prevented his taking up the appointment and he retained the Plummer chair.

On the outbreak of war in 1939 Fowler resumed his associations with the fighting departments. He was soon sent to Canada to co-ordinate war research there with war research in this country; he later extended these activities to the United States. For the success of this mission he was knighted in 1942. In spite of failing health he became a full-time member of a research section at the Admiralty, but he was prematurely worn out and died at Cambridge 28 July 1944.

Fowler, who was a man of great personal charm, will be remembered as a mathematical physicist of amazing quickness and versatility of mind. His most original work was his paper 'Dense Matter', published in the *Monthly Notices* of the Royal Astronomical Society (vol. lxxxvii, 1927), wherein he showed that the material in a 'white dwarf' star must consist of gas in the degenerate state in the sense of the statistics of Enrico Fermi and (Professor) P. A. M. Dirac. A return to earlier interests, again arising from an astronomical context, was shown in his work on Emden's differential equation (published in *Monthly Notices* of the Royal Astronomical Society, vol. xci, 1931). But he was at his best as a collaborator: he radiated an infectious enthusiasm which made collaboration with him an exciting and memorable experience. He could enter into other people's minds and ideas with celerity and facility; he had a lightning-like power of grasping and summing up the essentials of a scientific situation at very short notice. He was not usually a pioneer of ideas; but he brought to bear on any problem submitted to him impressive powers of insight and argument.

[E. A. Milne in *Obituary Notices of Fellows of the Royal Society*, No. 14, November 1945; *Nature*, 19 August 1944; *Cambridge Review*, 14 October 1944; personal knowledge.]

E. A. MILNE.

FOX STRANGWAYS, ARTHUR HENRY (1859–1948), schoolmaster, music critic, and founder-editor of *Music and Letters*. [See STRANGWAYS.]

FRANKLAND, PERCY FARADAY (1858–1946), chemist, was born in London 3 October 1858, the second son of (Sir) Edward Frankland [q.v.] and his first wife, Sophie Fick. His father's contributions to chemical thought in the nineteenth century established his reputation as one of the leading scientists of the period, and the son was thus given the opportunity of meeting many of the famous scientific personalities of the day.

Frankland was educated at University College School and in 1875 became a student in the Royal School of Mines. His choice of a career would have been medicine and he secured a Brackenbury scholarship at St. Bartholomew's Hospital but his father persuaded him to embark on chemistry. He spent two years at the university of Würzburg on organic chemistry research under the influence of Wislicenus and took his Ph.D. On his return to England in 1880 he was appointed a demonstrator at South Kensington under his father, with whom he made investigations on water analysis, and he graduated B.Sc. at London University in 1881. He also carried out independent bacteriological researches in his private laboratory. He married in 1882 Grace Coleridge, youngest daughter of Joseph Toynbee [q.v.], the celebrated aurist.

In 1888 Frankland left London to become professor of chemistry at University College, Dundee, where he continued his work on bacteriology and commenced his researches on stereochemistry, which were ultimately to form his main scientific interest. He was a great friend of Thomas Purdie of St. Andrews, who had been a student with him under Wislicenus and whose scientific interests were very similar to his own. He was also a friend of (Sir) D'Arcy Thompson [q.v.]. In his investigations on the culture of bacilli he was much helped by his wife, and they published jointly a volume on *Micro-organisms in Water* in 1894 and a life of Pasteur in 1898. He also published in 1893 a book entitled *Our Secret Friends and Foes*. His researches on the chemical reactions occurring during fermentation and on the chemistry of optically active compounds were recognized by his election as F.R.S. in 1891.

In 1894 Frankland became professor of chemistry at Mason College, later the university of Birmingham, where over the years he developed a very strong school of chemistry which supplied many notable men to industry and the universities. The university of Birmingham owes much to Frankland's strong personality and to his organizing ability as dean of the faculty of science from 1913. His influence was felt in the establishment in this country of science degrees for postgraduate research. He took a keen interest in chemistry as a profession and as a part of national life. He was president of the (Royal) Institute of Chemistry from 1906 to 1909, and in that office he was very largely responsible for the solution of many problems confronting the chemical profession at that time. He was able to weld the consultants, the academic, and the industrial, chemists into a coherent profession. He served as censor of the Institute from 1906 to 1921, and initiated the Institute examination on biological chemistry. He was president of the Chemical Society, 1911–13.

In the war of 1914–18 he carried out much research for the chemical warfare committee on synthetic drugs, on explosives intermediates, and on mustard gas, and he was responsible with (Sir) W. J. Pope [q.v.] for the adoption of Guthrie's method for the manufacture of mustard gas. He was a member of the Admiralty inventions board and of missions sent to France and Italy. In 1919 he was made an officer of the Order of St. Maurice and St. Lazarus of Italy and appointed C.B.E. in 1920. He received honorary doctorates from the universities of St. Andrews (LL.D., 1902), Dublin (Sc.D., 1912), Birmingham (LL.D., 1924), and Sheffield (D.Sc., 1926), and was awarded the Davy medal of the Royal Society in 1919.

Frankland was fond of wild country and spent his vacations on his sheep farm in Westmorland and in travelling throughout Europe. He retired in 1919 to the House of Letterawe on Loch Awe where he remained until his death, a few weeks after that of his wife, 28 October 1946. There was one son of the marriage. Frankland was keenly interested in antiquities, history, and music, but did not appreciate modern music and art. Sir D'Arcy Thompson said of him that he was 'a man of singularly high principle, of unusual integrity and simple goodness'. He was an impetuous, generous, warm-hearted man eager to combat injustice of any kind.

Under a superficial irascibility there lay a kindly disposition and a keen interest in his students. He was considered by those who knew him in Dundee and in Birmingham to be one of the great teachers of his time. He expected a very high standard of teaching from his staff, and he was very critical of carelessness of experiment, speech, or thought in his students.

His early bacteriological investigations and those on the purification of water were of vital importance to this country in securing that the water supplies to large towns were kept free from contamination. He discovered new bacteria and studied the variation in their activity on changing the media in which they grew. He was the first after Pasteur to isolate pure optically active compounds from fermentation processes. The isolation of these substances led naturally to his stereochemical researches. In these he was mainly interested in the effects of substitution by different groups on the optical activity of molecules. He says himself about this work, 'Although these ... researches have not led to comprehensive generalizations, they have revealed a number of interesting regularities'. These regularities have long since secured an important place in the framework of structural organic chemistry.

[W. E. Garner in *Obituary Notices of Fellows of the Royal Society*, No. 16, May 1948; private information; personal knowledge.]

W. E. GARNER.

FRASER, PETER (1884–1950), prime minister of New Zealand, was born 28 August 1884 at Fearn, Ross-shire, the son of Donald Fraser, the village shoemaker, and his wife, Isabella McLeod. Both were natives of Fearn who had emigrated to Canada where they married but eventually decided to return home. After leaving his Board-school Fraser was apprenticed to a carpenter, educating himself by reading economics and the current Socialist journals and in farm-workers' agitation for the Small-holders Act. At the age of sixteen he was secretary of the local branch of the Liberal Party. Later, making his way to London, in 1908 he joined the Independent Labour Party, and in 1910, attracted by the reputation of New Zealand for social advancement, he emigrated.

In New Zealand at that moment the Liberal hegemony was almost over, and Labour, although not politically organized, was restive. To its small but active group of leaders Fraser allied himself. He found employment first as a labourer and on the wharves in Auckland, where he became president of the General Labourers' Union; then worked his way through the country; and finally settled in Wellington as a watersider. Here he rapidly made his abilities felt, both as a Sunday orator on the waterfront with a proper respect for the class-struggle, and as a negotiator with more interest in politics than in strikes. In 1912 while still in Auckland and already on the executive of the Federation of Labour, he took part in the settlement of the bitter Waihi strike. At the important 'Unity Conference' of 1913, which closed the ranks after this disaster, he became secretary-treasurer of a short-lived Social Democratic Party—in which capacity he had a large share, at a further conference of 1916, in the organization of the New Zealand Labour Party, with political action as its aim. He remained a member of the party's national executive to the end. In 1916–17, also, strongly opposing conscription of men without conscription of wealth, he spent some months in jail; and emerging, found his role as a journalist (he acted as editor of the *Maoriland Worker* in 1918 when that paper was adopted as the party's official organ) and election organizer.

The year 1918 was important for Fraser. He first, with immense energy and ability, ensured the return to Parliament of Harry Holland, the party leader; then, with equal energy and ability, helped to fight the influenza epidemic in Wellington, adding thereby greatly to his reputation; and on 3 October, at a by-election, won the seat for Wellington Central which he held until his death. Until he achieved Cabinet rank he was prominent also in Wellington municipal politics. In 1919 he married Janet Henderson, daughter of William Munro, a Glasgow storeman, and formerly wife of Frederick George Kemp; she was another very able person who added to his influence in the Labour movement as well as to his domestic happiness. Fraser was secretary of the parliamentary Labour Party, 1919–35, becoming in addition in 1933, when Holland died, deputy to the new leader, Michael Joseph Savage. Through all this period he had a considerable part in shaping Labour policy; and in 1935, when disaster overwhelmed the coalition Government, he inevitably took what Labour regarded as key portfolios. He was a superb minister of education; under his impetus not merely was ground lost in the depression regained, but striking reforms were instituted in every branch of the system. In health his work was remarkable, and it was he who prepared the groundwork for the National Health Service and the great Social Security Act of 1938.

When war broke out Savage was already a dying man, and Fraser, then acting prime minister, left on a visit to England for the arrangement of supplies and military equipment; in discussions on general war policy he made a considerable impression. In April 1940, after Savage's death, he became prime minister; and, throwing his entire mind, force of character, and physical powers into the struggle, exerted an influence which at critical moments ranged far beyond New Zealand. He flew to London frequently, and at prime ministers' conferences and in America made a reputation for sound sense and statesmanship which New Zealanders were slower to admit. He displayed these qualities again in the negotiation of the Australian–New Zealand Agreement of 1944; while at the San Francisco conference of 1945 and at the meetings of the United Nations General Assembly in 1946 and 1948 he assumed international stature as a leader of the 'small nations' against the 'veto' provision of the Charter as well as in social and trusteeship matters. In the late 'forties also he was a much-valued adviser in the settlement of Irish and Indian relations to the Commonwealth. The postwar years in New Zealand were marked both by highly useful work in Maori affairs, and by a not very effective struggle against the growing exhaustion of the party, a struggle in which bitter attacks from dissident elements in its industrial wing, together with over-reliance on the party machine on Fraser's own part, weakened his power in the country. To carry Labour into support of conscription when the international horizon again darkened needed courage, and was a great personal triumph, but could not keep it in power; and in December 1949 Fraser, then senior prime minister of the Commonwealth, became leader of the Opposition. Totally exhausted by his labours in office, he had no bodily resistance against a complication of diseases that fell on him in the ensuing months, and he died in Wellington 12 December 1950. His wife had died in 1945; he had no children. He was sworn of the Privy Council in 1940 and appointed

C.H. in 1946. He received the freedom of a number of cities, including London, and several honorary degrees.

Fraser's character was not a simple one. A most adroit politician, he was first-rate in a crisis, or in any situation where his gifts as a negotiator, or for seeing all that was implied in a particular course of action, could have full play; his judgement indeed was quite extraordinarily acute and penetrating. In day-to-day administration he was less good; dilatory in decision, he was apt to act on sudden impulse. Never learning to husband his own strength, or to order his time, he was, in this respect, as inconsiderate with others as he was with himself. Yet he could inspire as well as exasperate. Generally affable, and sometimes magnanimous, he had a long memory for enmities as well as for affections. Interested in things of the mind, he was often difficult to advise and tenacious of his own amateur opinion; and devoted though he was to education, he had a very complete mistrust of the professionally academic person. As a speaker he was powerful in agitation, in opposition, or in debate; on a purely formal occasion he plumbed the gulfs. In conversation, one of his chief delights, he displayed an enormous and perpetually surprising range of knowledge. Although his eyesight had begun to fail in his sixteenth year, all his life he read widely, peering through the thick spectacles which came to seem an almost inseparable part of New Zealand. While he never had a general hold on the country's affections comparable to Savage's, he did, by sheer weight of ability and accumulated wisdom in some departments of statesmanship, in the end win its admiration and respect.

[James Thorn, *Peter Fraser*, 1952; private information; personal knowledge.]

J. C. BEAGLEHOLE.

FRAZER, SIR JAMES GEORGE (1854–1941), social anthropologist, was born at Glasgow 1 January 1854, the elder son of Daniel F. Frazer, leading partner in a long-established firm of chemists, by his wife, Katherine, daughter of John Brown, merchant. He was educated at Springfield Academy and Larchfield Academy at Helensburgh, and in 1874 he graduated M.A. at the university of Glasgow. He obtained a minor scholarship at Trinity College, Cambridge, and during his first year of residence he was awarded a foundation scholarship. He was placed second in the first class of the classical tripos of 1878. In 1879 he was elected by the college into a fellowship which he held for the rest of his life. In 1882 he was called to the bar by the Middle Temple, but he never practised.

Frazer's interest in anthropology was first aroused by reading the great book, *Primitive Culture*, by (Sir) E. B. Tylor [q.v.], published in 1871, but it was the influence of his most intimate friend, William Robertson Smith [q.v.], which determined his career. Although he never realized the full significance of the sociological principles which lay at the root of Robertson Smith's *Lectures on the Religion of the Semites* (1889), this remarkable volume marked for Frazer 'a new departure in the historical study of religion'. Moreover, it was at Robertson Smith's suggestion that in 1888 Frazer contributed the articles on 'Taboo' and 'Totemism' to the ninth edition of the *Encyclopaedia Britannica*. 'The researches I made for these articles', he explained, 'were the beginning of a systematic application to anthropology, and especially to a study of the backward races of men whom we call savages and barbarians.' It was not, however, until *The Golden Bough* (1st ed. 1890; 2nd ed. 1900; 3rd ed. completed 1915) appeared in its three editions that the full significance of his indefatigable labours was recognized, and his position became assured.

Since Frazer was born five years before the publication of *The Origin of Species*, the formative period of his life was lived in an age permeated with evolutionary thought in which the progressive development of mankind from savagery to civilization was axiomatic. For him and his contemporaries it seemed that the ideas and institutions of men were as distinctly stratified as the rocks of the earth on which they dwelt, and that the course of social and religious evolution had been substantially similar among all races. Therefore, the beliefs and practices of mankind could be arranged in a chronological sequence by the adoption of the comparative method. To this end he collected and classified similar phenomena from all parts of the world, and from his vast stores of data he worked out by induction a continuous development in human institutions based upon the concept of survival as a link between the various stages.

Thus, in *The Golden Bough*, in attempting to find an answer to the riddle of the King of the Wood in the Arician grove of Diana on the sylvan shores of Lake Nemi, he embarked on a voyage of the magnitude of which he had no conception when he first set out to explain the rule of an ancient Italian priesthood. Insensibly he was led on step by step to 'far-spreading fields of primitive thought which had been but little explored' by his predecessors. In attempting to settle one question he soon found that he had raised many more, until, as the book grew in his hands, the slender thread of connexion with his original subject threatened to snap under the weight of each successive edition of the work. When the ponderous treatise at length became a series of separate dissertations Frazer wisely followed the hint of a friendly critic and decided to publish them in several volumes under the general title of *The Golden Bough*. To these he added a supplement in 1936 to bring the inquiry up to date.

The cycle of *The Golden Bough*, as he pointed out, 'depicts, in its sinuous outline, in its play of alternate light and shadow, the long evolution by which the thoughts and efforts of man have passed through the successive stages of Magic, Religion and Science'. Starting from his theory of an age of magic centred in a misapplication of the principles of association of ideas, preceding an age of religion and finally attaining to the present scientific era, he assumed that the direct control of natural events by an appropriate spell or rite was psychologically simpler than the propitiation and conciliation of personal powers superior to man believed to direct the course of nature and of human life, or than the interpretation of natural processes by the scientific method. Although in the light of more recent anthropological knowledge the theory is untenable, it served the purpose of the investigation of the principles of magic, and the evolution of the sacred kingship in general, with which the first two volumes (*The Magic Art*, 1911) of the third edition of *The Golden Bough* were mainly concerned. He traced the rise of the magician to the exalted position of chief or king, whereafter, by the influence of religion, the king was transformed into a divine being who controlled the forces of nature. It was one of these sacred monarchs who in due course became the *rex nemorensis* of Aricia and was espoused to Diana, the sylvan queen. As the representative of the god of the sky he controlled the processes of vegetation, and therefore upon the union of the King of the Wood with Diana the fecundity of man, beast, and the crops depended.

Since the Arician priest was 'the point

of support on which hangs the balance of the world', he was surrounded with an intricate system of ritual prohibitions. Consequently, the next volume was devoted to *Taboo and the Perils of the Soul* (1911), and set forth innumerable examples, drawn from all over the world, of persons, words, and objects set apart from profane usages on account of their sacred character. In this way, it was argued, a complex fabric of society had been built up and consolidated under the restraining influence of supernatural sanctions. But notwithstanding the sanctity of the King of the Wood, sooner or later he was destined to pay the supreme penalty of his office. Thus, in a brilliant conjecture in *The Dying God* (1911), based upon what he believed to be the Arician rule, Frazer maintained that the man-god was slain before he lost his virility lest with the enfeeblement of his ageing body his sacred spirit should suffer a corresponding decline, which might weaken the cosmic energies under his control. Since he first made this suggestion, the custom of putting to death divine kings as soon as they reveal symptoms of infirmity or old age, has been recorded among the Shilluk of the Upper Nile, and in certain Nigerian tribes, thereby confirming the deduction from his data.

If the growth and decay of vegetation were directly dependent upon the waxing and waning strength of divine kings, the alternations of summer and winter, spring and autumn, were interpreted also in terms of gods and goddesses who were born and died. This belief found classical expression in the great seasonal dramas associated with the names of Attis, Adonis, and Osiris, and their female counterparts, Cybele, Aphrodite, and Isis. Therefore, it was to the oriental mystery cults that Frazer next turned his attention in the two massive volumes bearing the title of the three dying and reviving vegetation gods of western Asia and Egypt, *Adonis, Attis, Osiris* (1st ed. 1906; 3rd ed. as part 4 of *The Golden Bough*, 1914). This inquiry was followed by an investigation of the same theme in other religions and areas (published in 1912 as *Spirits of the Corn and of the Wild*), beginning with the Thracian worship of Dionysus as the vine-god, and then passing on to that of Demeter and Persephone as the corn-mother and the corn-maiden respectively.

The remarkable similarity between the dying and reviving deities in the oriental religions of classical antiquity and the 'spirits of the corn and of the wild' in ancient Greece and the West, was explained by Frazer in accordance with his conviction that the less-developed human mind among all races reacts in precisely the same way to identical circumstances, corresponding 'to the essential similarity in their bodily frame revealed by comparative anatomy'. Nevertheless, although he always maintained the theory of the independent origin of customs and beliefs produced under like conditions as a general principle against that of culture contact, he realized that 'we must always be on our guard against tracing it to a multitude of particular resemblances which may be and often are due to simple diffusion, since nothing is more certain than that the various races of men have borrowed from each other many of their arts and crafts, their ideas, customs and institutions'. But his adoption of the universalist form of the comparative method was based upon the assumption that the human mind everywhere and at all times operates according to specific laws of thought and action, and so it was a continuity of mental process rather than cultural connexion that he sought to establish. In following this line of approach he often confused priority in type with priority in time, and brought together phenomena which showed superficial resemblances regardless of the non-comparability of the actual occurrences.

Next, Frazer passed to an examination of the scapegoat, as a means of removing evil. He thought that this practice arose with the idea of the transference of pollution from men to animals or some inanimate object, by means of which it was either carried away or actually destroyed (*The Scapegoat*, 1913). In following the practice through many by-paths all over the world he was led on to a discussion of a great variety of topics, such as the calendrical sacrificial system in Mexico, which hardly fall within the scope of the term 'scapegoat'. Similarly, in the concluding volumes (*Balder the Beautiful*, 1913) the parallel between the Norse god Balder and the King of the Wood at Nemi was used more as a pretext for an examination of the external soul in popular belief and the fire-festivals of Europe than to prove the identity of the Italian priest and the Scandinavian deity. Balder the Beautiful, in fact, as Frazer admits, became 'little more than a stalking-horse to carry two heavy pack-loads of facts'; and he was prepared to grant that 'what is true of Balder applies equally to the priest of Nemi himself'. Around both these figures he had gathered 'the long tragedy of human folly and suffering which has unrolled itself before the readers of these volumes, and on which the curtain is now about to fall'.

Whatever may be the ultimate explanation of the strange rule of the Arician priesthood, in this vast survey and mighty synthesis of customs and beliefs of primitive man Frazer has placed on record an array of facts, collected with infinite pains and accuracy, which is of unique value as a permanent contribution to knowledge. Often he showed himself capable of brilliant and far-reaching hypotheses in his use of the comparative method. His knowledge was purely theoretical; in all probability he had never seen a savage in the flesh. Despite his strong prejudices and fixed ideas, he attached singularly little importance to his theories, and was ever ready to change his opinions in the light of new evidence. He failed, however, really to understand the cultural, sociological, and psychological implications of his data. Just as he refused to read adverse criticisms and reviews of his books, so he was content completely to ignore Freud and the findings of the psycho-analytical school, and was out of touch with current sociological theory. For him it sufficed to describe in vivid and graceful language exotic ideas and practices without attempting to discover their deeper meaning and significance, or the function which they fulfil in an organized society and established tradition. So, although he was forced to recognize that magic and religion have developed round the primary wants of man, he was mainly impressed by what seemed to him to be the utter futility of the world which he surveyed. Nevertheless, fascinated by the quest, as soon as the first edition of *The Golden Bough* was published in 1890, Frazer, with a view to the production of a full-scale edition in twelve volumes, continued to follow 'the ghastly priest' of the Arician grove through many lands.

In the meantime he had also returned to his earlier classical studies in the preparation of an edition of Pausanias's *Description of Greece*, in the preface of which in 1898 he paid eloquent tribute to the foundation which had thrice renewed his fellowship. It was in his rooms at Trinity that in 1879 the *Cambridge Review* was founded. There in his library, seldom for less than twelve hours each day, for half a century he wrote volume after volume 'without the aid of a secretary', as he tells us, 'or of any mechanical appliance other than a common steel pen'. It was his custom to begin his work at eight o'clock every morning, irrespective of the day of the week or the season of the year, and sometimes to continue his labours well into the night. The fruits of his gleanings were copied in a series of quarto notebooks, and arranged in two sets; the one of which he described as 'unclassified', the other 'classified'. In the first of these he entered extracts from his original authorities and sources of information. In the second the material was arranged in the order of the subject, such as birth, initiation, marriage, burial customs, hunting, fishing, agriculture, war, and disease. These served the purposes of indexes, and so the matter was usually given in a much abbreviated form, although care was taken to supply the exact reference to the authority quoted.

In 1938 and 1939 the contents of the 'unclassified notebooks' were published under the title *Anthologia Anthropologica* in four large volumes as a selection of passages referring to customs and beliefs among the native races of Africa and Madagascar (1938), and Australasia, Asia, Europe, and America (1939). This constitutes the last contribution of one of the most prolific writers of any generation. Indeed, as H. N. Brailsford said, 'when posterity comes to estimate the work of our age, the record of Sir James Frazer would suffice, almost of itself, to redeem it of a charge of sterility. . . . The mere bulk which this man has produced, since *The Golden Bough* grew from its two to its twelve volumes, would compel respect, but when one analyses a page of his writing, with its closely-packed material drawn from a dozen sources in five or six languages, one asks by what miracle he fitted twenty-four months into his year.'

In 1905 Frazer delivered a course of lectures at Trinity College on 'The Sacred Character and Magical Functions of Kings in Early Society' in which he developed in greater detail the evolution of the kingship which he had sketched in outline in two earlier lectures at the Royal Institution. Substantially they consisted of extracts from the third edition of *The Golden Bough* which he was then preparing, but he printed the manuscript as a separate volume called *Lectures on the Early History of the Kingship* (1905). In 1907 a chair of social anthropology was created for him at the university of Liverpool, but he could not adapt himself to the conditions of an academic institution in a great city. Therefore, although retaining his chair until 1922, at the end of his first session he returned to Cambridge to resume his literary activities in the seclusion of his rooms at Trinity, unmolested by the claims and distractions of professorial duties and the bustle of a busy port.

In the following year Frazer published his inaugural lecture on *The Scope of Social Anthropology*, and in 1913 reprinted it in the second edition of *Psyche's Task*, first published in 1909. This small volume (reissued in 1928 under the title *The Devil's Advocate*) was perhaps the most original of all his works. In it he examined the part played by 'superstitions' in some of the fundamental social institutions—government, private property, marriage, and respect for human life. But although, as in the four volumes on *Totemism and Exogamy* (1910), he considered ritual and belief within the context of society, he failed to realize their true function, notwithstanding his vivid descriptions of the setting of the institution of totemism.

In 1911 and 1912 Frazer delivered his Gifford lectures at St. Andrews, and seized the opportunity to examine *The Belief in Immortality and the Worship of the Dead*, among the aborigines of Australia, the Torres Straits Islands, New Guinea, and Melanesia; these were published in 1913. He returned to the same theme in 1922 and 1924, extending his field to Polynesia and Micronesia respectively. In 1924 and 1925 he delivered a second course of Gifford lectures, this time at Edinburgh, and selected *The Worship of Nature* as his topic; these were published in 1926. Reflection on the nature of things caused primitive man, he thought, to people 'with a multitude of individual spirits every rock and hill, every tree and flower, every brook and river, every breeze that blew, and every cloud that flecked with silvery white the blue expanse of heaven'. From this unlimited number of indwelling beings a limited pantheon of deities emerged, believed to control the various departments of nature. 'Instead of a separate spirit for every individual tree, they came to conceive of a god of the woods in general, a Silvanus or what not; instead of personifying all the winds as gods, each with his distinct character and features, they imagined a single god of the winds, an Aeolus, for example, who kept them shut up in bags and could let them out at pleasure to lash the sea into fury.'

By a further generalization, 'the instinctive craving of the mind after simplification and unification of its ideas', as polytheism had evolved out of animism, so the many gods were deposed in favour of one supreme deity, the maker and controller of all things, when polytheism passed into monotheism.

This typical Frazerian evolutionary scheme was illustrated in the customary manner by examples of the worship of the sky among Vedic Indians, Greeks, Romans, ancient Babylonians, Egyptians, Chinese, and native African tribes. And the earth and the sun were dealt with in similar fashion, although Frazer never extended the survey to other aspects of nature as apparently he intended at the time. Instead he turned his attention to *The Fear of the Dead in Primitive Religion* in a course of William Wyse lectures given at his own college and published in three volumes between 1933 and 1936. Finally, in 1936 he supplemented *The Golden Bough* with an *Aftermath* to round off the study with which his name will always be associated. To the last he maintained the solution he offered to the riddle of King of the Wood in the Arician grove of Diana, but he registered the opinion that should his writings survive, it would be 'less for the sake of the theories which they propound than for the sake of the facts which they record'. With this conclusion most anthropologists will agree.

If social anthropology was Frazer's principal interest and the field in which he made his greatest contribution, his classical learning was also immense. His edition of Pausanias was the product of nine years of exhaustive study involving several visits to Greece, and such were its merits that the maps, plans, and a modicum of the text to explain the sites were reissued in 1930 under the editorship of Professor Albert William Van Buren, as 'a portable atlas for travellers' entitled *Graecia Antiqua*. In 1929 he produced an edition of the *Fasti* of Ovid in which he threw new light on many obscure customs and beliefs in Rome and its lore at the zenith of its power and glory. Again, in the sphere of biblical studies, in his *Folk-lore in the Old Testament* (1918), for which he learned Hebrew by way of preparation, he proved himself an able pupil of Robertson Smith, enriched with his own inimitable gift of descriptive narrative. Nowhere is this better illustrated than in his delightful account of the meeting of David and Abigail, which leads up to a discussion of the reference to 'the bundle of life'. The patriarchal narratives in the book of Genesis afforded opportunities for excursions into such untrodden paths as those of ultimogeniture, or the rights of the youngest son, the *jus primae noctis*, the observance of 'Tobias nights', cross-cousin marriage, and the cult of the mandrake. The period of the judges and the kings was prefaced with an examination of the birth of Moses and followed by character studies of Samson and Delilah, and an essay on Saul and his encounter with the witch of Endor. Among Jewish customs, the prohibition against seething a kid in its mother's milk and the adorning of the priest's robes with golden bells were selected for consideration. In dwelling on the lower side of Hebrew life, however, he was careful to point out that he was far from disparaging 'the spiritual religion and pure morality of which the Old Testament is the imperishable monument', but that these baser elements serve rather 'as a foil to enhance by contrast the glory of a people which from such dark depths of ignorance and cruelty could rise to such bright heights of wisdom and virtue'.

Frazer himself had been nurtured in the pious environment of a devout Presbyterian household where the reading of the Scriptures was a prominent feature of the daily routine. His father, he records, read a portion of the Bible without comment every day at family prayers, and throughout the whole of his life the sublime beauty of the sacred literature never ceased to make a strong appeal. Thus, in the preface to the second edition (1909) of a volume of passages of the Bible chosen for their literary beauty and interest, he said: 'Though many of us can no longer, like our fathers, find in its pages the solution of the dark, the inscrutable riddle of human existence, yet the volume must still be held sacred by all who reverence the high aspirations to which it gives utterance, and the pathetic associations with which the faith and piety of so many generations have invested the familiar words. The reading of it breaks into the dull round of common life like a shaft of sunlight on a cloudy day, or a strain of solemn music heard in a mean street. It seems to lift us for a while out of ourselves, our little cares and little sorrows, into communion with those higher powers, whatever they are, which existed before man began to be, and which will exist when the whole human race, as we are daily reminded by the cataclysms and convulsions of Nature, shall be swept out of existence for ever. It strengthens in us the blind conviction, or the trembling hope, that somewhere, beyond these earthly shadows, there is a world of light eternal, where the obstinate questionings of the mind will be answered and the heart find rest.' In these words Frazer gives a glimpse of his own spiritual perceptions, and if he did not adhere to the faith in which he had been reared, he never ceased to respect and to be profoundly interested in it, alike as a storehouse of anthropological material and for its higher moral and spiritual content.

Frazer was not a controversialist, nor a brilliant conversationalist, nor an inspiring lecturer, but emphatically he was the writer of fine prose based upon the best eighteenth-century models which hitherto had never been surpassed. His delightful biographical sketch prefaced to his edition of *The Letters of William Cowper* (1912), his favourite poet, and his description of an imaginary visit to Coverley Hall (which served as a preface to his selection of Addison's essays, 1915, and is reprinted in *The Gorgon's Head*, 1927), are worthy to rank with the noblest examples of English prose. How successfully he had mastered the style of Addison is revealed in his essay, 'Sir Roger de Coverley in Cambridge', while his ability to write excellent Ciceronian Latin was also displayed in *The Gorgon's Head*, a volume which took its name from an introductory fantasia from his own pen. His style showed more Latinity than Addison's and was closer to that of Gibbon. But, as Mr. (Henry Fitz) Gerald Heard has pointed out, 'Gibbon only made ordered and more amusing for the polished world what was known to every contemporary scholar about the ancient world. But Frazer revealed a completely strange world, and strove to interpret, not to mock, its strangeness. . . . Moreover, Frazer adds to man of letters and historian also the title of scientist. Almost as much as his history is his own, is the philosophy with which he interprets that history.'

While he hated the limelight, avoided public discussion, and steadfastly refused any appointment or honour which was calculated to interfere with his self-chosen vocation, Frazer's learning, industry, and unique abilities in so many fields did not pass without due recognition. In 1914 he was knighted and in 1925 he was appointed to the Order of Merit. Honorary degrees were conferred upon him by the universities of Oxford, Cambridge, St. Andrews, Glasgow, Durham, Manchester, Paris, Strasbourg, and Athens. In 1920 he was elected F.R.S. and he was an original member of the British Academy. He was elected an honorary fellow of the Royal Society of Edinburgh in 1910, and in 1932 he received the freedom of his native city, Glasgow. In 1921 a lectureship of social anthropology was founded in his name, to be held in turn at the universities of Oxford, Cambridge, Glasgow, and Liverpool. He was elected (1931) an honorary bencher of the Middle Temple, where for some time he resided. His marriage in 1896 with Elisabeth (Lilly) Johanna, widow of Charles Baylee Groves, master mariner, and daughter of Sigismund Adelsdorfer, merchant, helped to establish his French connexions and made him hardly less widely known and respected in France than in his own country. He was an associate member of the Institut de France and a commander of the Legion of Honour. A special medal was given to him and his wife by the university of Nancy in 1923. Although he felt compelled to decline an invitation to succeed to the lectureship in the history of religion at the Sorbonne, previously held by Renan, he delivered an address before the President of the Republic on the occasion of the Renan centenary in 1923. He was a corresponding member of the Prussian Academy of Sciences, an extraordinary member of the Royal Netherlands Academy of Sciences, and commander of the Order of Leopold.

Lady Frazer was herself endowed with no small literary talent, and had written a number of books still considered among the best for the teaching of French, as well as the volume on *Dancing* in the Badminton Library. She produced admirable translations and abridgements of her husband's works and gave herself wholly to assisting him. In his last days when he was almost totally blind she read to him incessantly. Frazer died at Cambridge 7 May 1941; a few hours later Lady Frazer followed him. There were no children of the marriage. If his death marks the end of an epoch in anthropology, Frazer's work and memory will survive for all time by reason of the irrefutable evidence which he assembled with such outstanding literary merit and skill, and the inspiration which he has given to other workers in the field in which he toiled so long and arduously, leaving for future generations an imperishable monument of his learning

and industry. There is a drawing by Lucien Monod (1907) in the Fitzwilliam Museum, Cambridge, and another by the same artist in the Scottish National Portrait Gallery.

[Sir J. G. Frazer, *Creation and Evolution in Primitive Cosmogonies*, 1935; R. A. Downie, *James George Frazer*, 1940; Theodore Besterman, *A Bibliography of Sir James George Frazer*, 1934; B. K. Malinowski, *Sir James George Frazer: a Biographical Appreciation* in *A Scientific Theory of Culture* (University of North Carolina Press), 1944; R. R. Marett in *Proceedings of the British Academy*, vol. xxvii, 1941; H. J. Fleure in *Obituary Notices of Fellows of the Royal Society*, No. 10, December 1941; *Cambridge Review*, 23 May 1941; private information; personal knowledge.]

E. O. JAMES.

FREEMAN, JOHN PEERE WILLIAMS- (1858–1943), archaeologist. [See WILLIAMS-FREEMAN.]

FREEMAN, SIR RALPH (1880–1950), civil engineer, born 27 November 1880 at Hoxton, London, was the third child of George James Freeman, cigar manufacturer, by his wife, Edith Henderson. He was educated at the Haberdashers' School and won a Siemens scholarship to the Central Technical College of the City and Guilds of London Institute. He was an outstanding student and on leaving in 1900 was awarded the Siemens medal in civil and mechanical engineering. The following year he joined the staff of Sir Douglas Fox & Partners, consulting engineers, London. He was made a partner in 1912 and remained with the firm throughout his life, becoming senior partner in 1921. In 1938 the name of the firm changed to Freeman, Fox & Partners and he was in active control up to the day of his death.

Although he was responsible for a wide range of engineering work such as railways and irrigation works in Africa, hydro-electric works in North Wales, and explosives works for the Admiralty, his talents found their fullest expression in the design of steel bridges. In 1903 he assisted G. A. Hobson in the design of the arch bridge over the Zambezi at the Victoria Falls. As consulting engineer to the Beit Trust he designed five important highway bridges in the Rhodesias. His most notable work was in connexion with the Sydney Harbour bridge, New South Wales. Dorman, Long & Co. submitted alternative tenders based on a number of designs prepared by Freeman, and in 1924 one of these was accepted. He was then appointed consulting engineer to the builders and was alone responsible for the design of the bridge. It is of the two-hinged spandrel braced arch type with a clear span of 1,650 feet and a deck to accommodate 4 railway tracks, a roadway 57 feet wide, and two footways each 10 feet wide.

A series of papers describing this great work was presented to the Institution of Civil Engineers in 1934. Freeman's paper dealt with the design of the structure and foundations of the bridge. The Institution awarded him a Telford gold medal for this paper and the first Baker gold medal in recognition of the development in engineering practice made by him as described in the paper. In conjunction with Lawrence Ennis he contributed a paper on the manufacture of the structural steelwork and erection of the bridge for which the authors received a Telford premium. At the time of his death, Freeman was engaged on designs for the River Severn suspension bridge with a span of 3,300 feet and a bridge across the harbour at Auckland, New Zealand.

He was transferred to membership of the Institution of Civil Engineers in 1917 and served on the council from 1937 to 1942. He was elected a fellow of the City and Guilds Institute in 1932, and in the same year became one of the first nine fellows of the Imperial College of Science and Technology. He was president of the Institute of Welding from 1942 to 1944 and a member of the Royal Fine Art Commission from 1939 to 1948.

Freeman had a brilliant intellect which, combined with his mastery of fundamentals and a supreme self-confidence, enabled him to achieve the boldness of conception and simplicity of design exemplified in most of his work. He was alive to the importance of technical education and from 1920 to 1925 he lectured to fourth-year students at the City and Guilds College. In 1933 he delivered four lectures on the design of long span bridges at the university of London. His qualities made him an able chairman of a number of committees dealing with structural engineering design and research. His contribution to civil engineering was recognized by a knighthood in 1947. He died at his home in Finchley 11 March 1950. He married in 1908 Mary, daughter of Joseph Lines, toy manufacturer, of

Stoke Newington, and had three sons and one daughter.

[Private information; personal knowledge.]
R. E. FORDHAM.

FREEMAN-THOMAS, FREEMAN, first MARQUESS OF WILLINGDON (1866–1941), governor-general of Canada and viceroy of India, was born at Ratton, Sussex, 12 September 1866, the only son of Frederick Freeman Thomas, Rifle Brigade, of Ratton and Yapton, by his wife, Mabel, third daughter of Henry Bouverie William Brand, later first Viscount Hampden [q.v.]. In 1892 he assumed the additional surname of Freeman by deed poll. At Eton he played in the cricket eleven for three years, the last of them as captain; he was also president of the Eton Society. At Trinity College, Cambridge, he played for four years (1886–9) in the university eleven, being captain in the last year, and also for Sussex and I Zingari. He never lost his love of sport, and many good judges regarded him as the most attractive of contemporary cricketers. Like his father he was for some years master of the Eastbourne foxhounds. He was sometime major in the Sussex Yeomanry, and was for fifteen years in the Sussex Artillery Militia. In 1936 he was appointed honorary colonel of the 5th battalion, Royal Sussex Regiment.

In 1892 Freeman-Thomas married Marie Adelaide, fourth daughter of the first Baron (later Earl) Brassey [q.v.]. Her charm, zest, and dynamic personality contributed in a marked degree to his great success as an agent of the Crown in many lands. A remarkably handsome pair, they were inseparable in aim and outlook. His first post abroad was that of aide-de-camp to his father-in-law whilst governor of Victoria. At the general election of 1900 Freeman-Thomas was returned as Liberal member of Parliament for Hastings. When his party took office at the end of 1905 he was made a junior lord of the Treasury, but lost his seat in the general election in 1906. In July of that year, however, he won a by-election in the Bodmin division of Cornwall. For a time in the House he did secretarial work for Asquith, the prime minister. In 1910 he was raised to the peerage as Baron Willingdon, of Ratton, and in 1911 was appointed a lord-in-waiting to King George V; he was the King's favourite partner at tennis.

In April 1913 Willingdon was appointed

governor of Bombay and the war became the first of many severe tests to which the fine qualities of the Willingdons were subjected. They met it magnificently in promoting enthusiasm for the allied cause, in welcoming the many troops passing through the Bombay base, and in caring for the sick and wounded sent there, especially from the ill-starred earlier Mesopotamian operations. Then and subsequently perhaps their most signal service to India was that of breaking down, by both example and precept, the old tradition of British social exclusiveness. The Willingdon Sports Club in Bombay and the Willingdon Club in Madras were happily established by them for British and Indian fellowship in hours of relaxation.

Willingdon's quinquennial term was extended for eight months to December 1918. In the following April he was again in India as governor of Madras. He had scant liking for the provincial dyarchical system of the Montagu–Chelmsford reforms introduced in 1921, but under his genial guidance it came nearer to success in Madras than in any other province. He arranged for the two sides of his Government, responsible respectively for the 'reserved' and the 'transferred' subjects, to confer as a single team. The success of the non-Brahmin party at the polls helped to bring the system nearer to the parliamentary model which the governor knew so well.

On returning home in the spring of 1924 Willingdon was promoted to a viscountcy. In the autumn of 1925 he led the Indian delegation to the League of Nations Assembly at Geneva. In 1926 he went to China as chairman of an Anglo-Chinese mission to devise the best methods of spending for the benefit of the Chinese the balance of the British share of the Boxer indemnity fund. While still on this mission, he accepted the governor-generalship of Canada. He was the first holder of that high office under the 'equal status' system, with a high commissioner for Great Britain transacting the normal business of intermediary between the Dominion and Whitehall. Willingdon's influence as the personal representative in Canada of the King was both great and constructive. The people were delighted by the zest with which he and his wife took to the national sports and by their most friendly leadership in social life.

At the end of 1930 Willingdon was called from Ottawa to succeed Lord Irwin (subsequently the Earl of Halifax) as vice-roy of India. He was raised to an earldom and sworn of the Privy Council (1931). It was in fulfilment of a long-cherished ambition that he took oath as viceroy in April 1931. Although now sixty-five he was fully equal to the great burden of responsibility which fell on him at a time of political turmoil and during the further elaboration of the federal plan eventually authorized under the Government of India Act of 1935. The civil disobedience campaign, in abeyance under the Irwin–Gandhi pact of March 1931, was revived on the return of Gandhi from the second Round Table conference. Applying his straightforward logic to the situation the viceroy refused to have discussions with law-breakers, so long as the challenge to duly constituted authority continued. Under the persistent pressure of the law the subversive movement petered out and was ultimately abandoned. Of Willingdon's loyalty to the policy of far-reaching political reform there was constant evidence. The serious effect on India of the world trade slump of the early 'thirties and the occurrence of two devastating earthquakes were among the stresses of the time. Willingdon always showed faith and courage in adversity, and his firmness in administration was mellowed by such social graces as friendly candour and a keen sense of humour.

On returning home in May 1936 Willingdon was raised to a marquessate, and made constable of Dover Castle and lord warden of the Cinque Ports. He had been appointed G.C.I.E. (1913), G.B.E. (1917), G.C.S.I. (1918), and G.C.M.G. (1926), being now made chancellor of the last order. He was awarded a number of honorary degrees and the freedom (amongst others) of Canada (1927) and Edinburgh (1934). In 1937 he was chairman of a committee on the supply of army officers. In the following year he headed a successful 'goodwill' mission to South America on behalf of the Ibero-American Institute. He represented the home Government in 1940 at the centennial celebrations of New Zealand. Later in the year he headed an important trade mission to the South American republics. To the end of his life he was an indefatigable traveller by air. He occupied many positions of a non-official character, and was on several boards, including that of the Westminster Bank. Lady Willingdon was appointed a lady of the Imperial Order of the Crown of India (1917) and G.B.E. (1924).

Willingdon had scarcely known a day's

illness when he was stricken by pneumonia and died at his London home, Lygon Place, 12 August 1941. His ashes were interred in Westminster Abbey. His elder son was killed in France in September 1914 and he was succeeded as second marquess by his younger son, Inigo Brassey (born 1899).

Statues of Willingdon, raised by public subscription, were at New Delhi, by Sir W. Reid Dick, and at Madras by a local sculptor, M. Nagappa. A portrait by P. A. de László, at Government House, Bombay, was the gift of survivors of the Mesopotamian campaign. A portrait by (Sir) Oswald Birley, was at New Delhi.

[*The Times*, 13 August 1941; private information; personal knowledge.]

F. H. Brown.

FULLER, Sir CYRIL THOMAS MOULDEN (1874–1942), admiral, was the son of Thomas Fuller, late captain in the 18th Hussars, by his wife, Mary Ada, daughter of Frederick William Fryer, of Clarence House, West Cowes, where the child was born 22 May 1874.

Entering the Royal Navy in 1887 Fuller served in the Mediterranean as a cadet and later as midshipman in the battleship *Collingwood* from November 1889 and as a midshipman in the battleship *Trafalgar* from May 1890. He was promoted sub-lieutenant in October 1893 and, after passing first class in all his examinations and winning the Goodenough medal for gunnery, was promoted lieutenant in April 1894, a few weeks before his twentieth birthday. After serving on the China station as a watchkeeper in the cruiser *Rainbow* he returned to the United Kingdom to specialize in gunnery and was appointed gunnery officer of the battleship *Canopus* in the Mediterranean Fleet in December 1899. He joined the senior staff of the gunnery school at Portsmouth in January 1902 and was promoted commander in December 1903 at the early age of twenty-nine. For a short time he served as executive officer of the battleship *Majestic* but in February 1905 he joined the battleship *King Edward VII* as flag commander to Sir William May [q.v.], the commander-in-chief, Atlantic Fleet. Then, from 1908 to 1910 he commanded the dispatch vessel *Alacrity* in China. After his early promotion to captain in December 1910 he served for nearly three years on the staff of the inspector of target practice.

In May 1914 he returned to sea in command of the cadet training cruiser *Cumberland*. After the outbreak of war in August 1914 the *Cumberland* was employed in the operations against German territory in the Cameroons, where Fuller was senior naval officer. In November he transferred to the light cruiser *Challenger* and in March 1915 to the light cruiser *Astraea*. He had been appointed C.M.G. in January and in 1916 was appointed to the D.S.O. in recognition of the ability and success with which he had organized the Cameroon naval operations.

On returning home he was appointed, in August 1916, to the command of the new battle cruiser *Repulse* in the Grand Fleet, but in October 1917, after serving for a month in the intelligence division, became with (Sir) Dudley Pound [q.v.] an assistant director of the newly formed plans division of the naval staff of the Admiralty. He succeeded Roger (later Lord) Keyes [q.v.] as director in January 1918 and in this capacity headed the naval section of the peace conference in Paris in 1919. In October 1919 he was gazetted C.B.

His next appointment was that of chief of staff to Sir Charles Madden [q.v.], the commander-in-chief, Atlantic Fleet, in the battleship *Queen Elizabeth*. In June 1921 he was promoted rear-admiral and on 1 December 1922 became a lord commissioner of the Admiralty and assistant chief of the naval staff, but in May 1923 was appointed third sea lord and controller of the navy. Then, in April 1925, he returned to sea in command of the battle cruiser squadron with his flag in the *Hood*. He reached vice-admiral's rank in July 1926 and was appointed K.C.B. in 1928.

In the spring of 1928 he became commander-in-chief, North America and West Indies, and on his promotion to admiral two years later, in May 1930, was appointed second sea lord and chief of naval personnel. His term of office proved to be one of exceptional difficulty. It was a period of severe retrenchment following the conclusion of the London naval conference in April 1930. He was still in office when the financial crisis of 1931 led to the naval mutiny at Invergordon. Although his connexion with the incident was perhaps only nominal, as a member of the Board of Admiralty his career, like those of his brother members, suffered. When he left the Admiralty in August 1932 he was not again employed and was placed on the retired list in 1935. During his long naval career he had received several foreign decorations; he was a commander of the Legion of Honour and of the Order of the Crown of Italy and a member of the Order of the Rising Sun of Japan; he held the French croix de guerre, the United States D.S.M., and the Board of Trade medal for life saving.

In 1902 Fuller married Edith Margaret (died 1947), daughter of Charles Connell, shipbuilder, of Rozelle, Glasgow. They had two sons and two daughters. He died at Whilton Lodge, Long Buckby, Northamptonshire, 1 February 1942. There is a black chalk and water-colour portrait by Sir Muirhead Bone in the Imperial War Museum.

[*The Times*, 3 February 1942; private information; personal knowledge.]

J. H. LHOYD-OWEN.

GAINFORD, first BARON (1860–1943), politician and man of business. [See PEASE, JOSEPH ALBERT.]

GANDHI, MOHANDAS KARAM-CHAND (1869–1948), Indian political leader and social reformer, was born in Porbandar 2 October 1869, the third son and youngest child by his fourth wife of Karamchand Uttamchand Gandhi, chief minister in Porbandar, a small territory situated in the peninsula of Kathiawar, the modern Saurashtra. His family were Vaisyas by caste, and belonged to the sub-caste of banias or merchants, the name Gandhi meaning grocer. His mother-tongue was Gujerati. There are in Gujerat many Jains, a sect which insists on absolute non-violence. Gujerat is also the home of a race of hard-headed business men. Whereas his father seems to have been a man of some independence of character, the principal formative influence in Gandhi's childhood was undoubtedly his mother, Putlibai, a woman of intense piety, much given to fasting and to the meticulous performance of this and other religious observances undertaken by vow. As Hindu social custom then ordained, Gandhi was married at the age of thirteen to Kasturbai, the daughter of a Porbandar merchant. He was educated at Porbandar, and at Rajkot where his father was transferred. At the age of nineteen he went to England to study law and entering at the Inner Temple was called in 1891. His mother was reluctant for him to go and made him vow to avoid wine, women, and meat. His caste leaders refused consent to his departure and declared him outcaste. In England he dressed fashionably and at first took dancing and elocution lessons

and generally tried to conform to European, and particularly English, standards and ways. This he soon gave up, however, and presently set himself to lead a life of extreme frugality, spending, he claimed, not more than 1s. 3d. a day. The friends he made in London were mostly vegetarians like himself. His interest in religion, all religions, had quickened by this time. He studied religious books, chief among them the *Bhagavad Gita* from which he was to draw inspiration throughout the rest of his life. The New Testament, and in particular the Sermon on the Mount, also influenced him deeply.

Immediately after his call to the bar, Gandhi returned to India. He tried legal practice first in Bombay and then in Rajkot, but with no great success in either place. He was nervous and lacked confidence as a speaker. He probably found the atmosphere of the Indian law courts uncongenial as well. Presently, therefore, he accepted an offer from a Moslem business man of Porbandar, who had interests in South Africa, to go there for a year as the firm's legal adviser. In May 1893 he arrived in Natal. There he came in contact for the first time with racial antagonisms in acute form. Gandhi felt humiliated and distressed by the conditions in which his countrymen were living. He decided that they must be encouraged to claim at any rate their legal rights as British subjects. He was twenty-four and now quickly put off the uncertainty which had hampered his early forensic efforts. Before many months were out he stood forth as the champion of Indian rights in Natal. It is significant that almost his first advice to his countrymen was to look to their own shortcomings: they should tell the truth whether there was profit in it or not; they should abandon insanitary habits; and they should remember that they were all Indians, irrespective of creed or caste. At the end of the year for which he had originally gone to South Africa he was persuaded to stay on to serve his countrymen. He took up legal practice and was soon a prosperous lawyer. At the same time he campaigned indefatigably for equal rights for Indians.

All this time Gandhi was searching for a way of life which would satisfy his own inner needs. He ate sparingly, making continual experiments with his diet. He learned to make his own clothes and those of his family, while he not only performed the most menial household tasks himself but insisted that his wife and children did likewise. He recalled his mother's habit of fasting and disciplined his body to the same practice. Among other books, chiefly on religion and morals, he read Tolstoy's *The Kingdom of God is within You*. In the South African war he formed an ambulance unit in aid of the British forces, holding that if Indians sought the advantages of their status as British subjects they must also accept its obligations. Gandhi led his men on to the battlefield to remove the wounded; the corps was mentioned in dispatches and Gandhi received the war medal.

At the end of 1901 he returned with his family to Bombay where he intended to settle, but he was soon recalled to Durban to head a delegation of Indians to Joseph Chamberlain. He began to practise law in Johannesburg and became the recognized leader of the Indians in South Africa. In 1904 a friend lent him Ruskin's *Unto This Last*. With Gandhi, believing was doing: Phoenix Farm near Durban was the result. There, manual labour was compulsory, while smoking tobacco and drinking alcohol were absolutely forbidden. In 1906 he again formed an Indian ambulance unit, for service in the operations against the Zulus, and received another medal. During this campaign he decided that the habits of self-discipline to which he was schooling himself required that he should take the Brahmachari's vow of complete sexual abstinence.

The Transvaal legislative council passed a law, re-enacted by the Transvaal Parliament in 1907, requiring all Asiatics to take out registration cards. Summoned urgently to the Transvaal to advise the Indian community about this new threat to their self-respect, Gandhi first conceived of and, after a visit to England, led 'passive resistance' to the Act. Indians in large numbers sought imprisonment in the Transvaal jails where Gandhi himself spent on various occasions no fewer than 249 days. As the name 'passive resistance' was considered to be inadequate, he coined the name 'Satyagraha' (truth-force) for this new revolutionary technique. It was only later that he read Thoreau's 'Essay on Civil Disobedience'. On the eve of South African union Gandhi again visited England on behalf of Indian interests. In 1910 Tolstoy Farm was established near Johannesburg for the benefit of those taking part in Satyagraha, a movement which finally ended with the Smuts–Gandhi compromise signed in

1914. This agreement, while it represented less than complete victory for the Indian cause, nevertheless demonstrated the efficacy of the new political weapon which Gandhi had forged.

In England, at the outbreak of war in 1914, Gandhi raised an Indian ambulance unit. The following year he returned to India and received the Kaisar-i-Hind gold medal from the viceroy for his services to the Empire. For a time he took no prominent part in politics. In 1918 he spoke in favour of Indians enlisting in the British Indian Army and even conducted a recruiting campaign. He had intervened, however, in a dispute between Bihar tenants and their landlords (1917) and again (1918) on behalf of the textile workers who were on strike for more pay and better living conditions at Ahmedabad where, across the river at Sabarmati, he had established his *ashram*. In the latter dispute he used for the first time the weapon of the fast, to compel the textile workers to stand firm. In the long struggle with the British Government in India which was now to follow, the fast was the principal addition which he made to the revolutionary technique he had invented in South Africa.

With the end of the war, as was to be expected, Indian national aspirations took on an added urgency. Under Gandhi's guidance the Indian National Congress, until then largely an urban middle-class organization, extended its activities to the villages of India. The emancipation of the Indian peasant, Hindu–Moslem unity, and the abolition of untouchability, these, with hand-spinning, became, as they remained, the principal planks in his social and political programme. The actual forms of government were to him of secondary interest. He had, indeed, something of a distaste for organized governments, foreign or indigenous. What seemed to him to matter was how people lived their personal rather than their collective lives.

His first head-on clash with the British Government came in 1919 over the so-called Rowlatt Act. For the first time he then introduced the *hartal*, a strike during which the people devoted themselves to prayer and fasting. The ensuing disturbances caused Gandhi to call off this first attempt at passive resistance and Sir Rabindranath Tagore [q.v.] wrote to warn him that 'power in all its forms is irrational. . . . Passive resistance is a force which is not necessarily moral in itself.' Nevertheless, widespread resentment

# Gandhi

D.N.B. 1941–1950

had been aroused by the action of General R. E. H. Dyer [q.v.] in the face of disturbances in the Punjab and in 1920 Gandhi returned his medals to the viceroy, stating 'my life is dedicated to the service of India through the religion of non-violence which I believe to be the root of Hinduism'. The Indian National Congress accepted his 'non-co-operation' technique as its policy. Gandhi forecast that if properly supported the movement would achieve self-government within a year. The Moslems at this time were in opposition to the British over the Khilafat question and it seemed for a while that Hindu and Moslem differences might be forgotten in the common struggle. The sole dissentient to Gandhi's policy at this meeting of Congress was M. A. Jinnah [q.v.].

A campaign against the use of foreign cloth provided Gandhi with the opportunity to develop the mystique of the spinning-wheel. From now onwards hand-spinning became a cardinal tenet in his doctrine and something of an obsession. Spinning was to be at the same time a form of manual training, a spiritual exercise, and the means of freeing India from 'the strangle-hold of foreign capitalist exploitation'. The visit of the Prince of Wales in 1921 was boycotted, but a programme of mass civil disobedience was abandoned by Gandhi in 1922 when he saw that it would end in violence. Shortly afterwards he was arrested, for the first time in India, on a charge of sedition, and was sentenced to six years' imprisonment. He was now disbarred by the Inner Temple. Released in 1924, following an operation for appendicitis, he undertook his first major fast a few months later—for Hindu–Moslem unity, in the house of a Moslem. There followed a period of withdrawal from politics during which he travelled all over India preaching Hindu–Moslem unity, the abolition of untouchability, which he maintained was not an essential part of the Hindu religion, and hand-spinning. He was now known throughout the country as the Mahatma—the great soul. He was later to be known even more widely by the affectionate-respectful appellation of 'Gandhiji'. He had adopted by this time a very personal style of dress: white loin-cloth, white shawl, and sandals. This, with his long stick and his beaming toothless smile, presently made his appearance, in caricature and photograph, familiar to newspaper readers all over the world. Publicity was not unwelcome to

him. On the contrary, he had a shrewd sense of its value.

The year 1928 was memorable for the visit of the Simon commission and 1929 for Lord Irwin's pronouncement on Dominion status for India. At the end of that year the Indian National Congress declined to be represented at the proposed Round Table conference, declared for complete independence, and authorized the resumption of civil disobedience. In the course of this major challenge to the established Government Gandhi in 1930 undertook his much-publicized march to the sea to break the salt law. He was imprisoned with the approval of the British Cabinet, but was released in 1931 to discuss the proposals of the Round Table conference and had a series of talks with Lord Irwin (subsequently the Earl of Halifax) which resulted in the Delhi Pact. Civil disobedience was 'discontinued'. Gandhi went to London as plenipotentiary on behalf of the Indian National Congress to attend the second Round Table conference. He chose to stay in the east end; spun daily, and observed Monday as usual as his day of silence; visited Eton, Oxford, Cambridge, and Lancashire; went, in his usual attire, to a reception at Buckingham Palace; broadcast to America, addressed members of Parliament, and met a great many notabilities. He was less successful in conference than outside. He had little understanding of the compromises and balances in which political settlements consist. The art of statesmanship, the skilful management of public affairs, was not in his way of thinking. The discussions proved abortive and Gandhi returned to India where he threatened a resumption of civil disobedience and was arrested. Some months later he entered upon a fast unto death to prevent the establishment of separate electorates for the depressed classes. Alternative suggestions were made, resulting in the Poona Pact, and accepted by the British Cabinet. In 1933 he undertook a twenty-one-day self-purification fast, at the beginning of which he was released from prison. Arrested again shortly afterwards, he undertook another fast and was released when his life became endangered. He now removed his *ashram* to Wardha near Nagpur. In 1934 civil disobedience was discontinued and in that year Gandhi resigned from Congress. Not all his doctrines were acceptable to its members, but he remained until his death its oracle

284

and mentor. In 1937 when Congress swept the polls under the new constitutional structure, he prevailed upon it to accept office after much discussion and with the intention of working towards independence. Meanwhile his work for untouchables occupied most of his attention and he apparently failed to realize the gradual deterioration in Hindu–Moslem relations which resulted from the claims of Congress to represent all India and the growing importance of the Moslem League, although he had one unfruitful meeting with Jinnah in 1938. In these years his health several times broke down.

The outbreak of war in 1939 confronted Gandhi with an intolerable dilemma. He was by now a convinced pacifist and, although his sympathies were with the democracies, he was not prepared to countenance the use of force even for the defence of India. Congress was quick to demand independence as a condition of co-operation and, failing to receive satisfaction from the British, the provincial ministries resigned. In 1940 Gandhi assumed the leadership of Congress but relinquished it the following year when it became clear that to Congress non-violence was an expedient, not a creed. In 1942 the proposals of Sir Stafford Cripps were rejected. Gandhi was now maintaining that Japan would not attack a free India but that, if she did, she must be met with non-co-operation even at the risk of losing several million lives. Congress, guided by Gandhi, adopted the famous 'Quit India' motion, which meant civil disobedience, and Gandhi was again in jail. He was held responsible for the rebellion which ensued and in self-vindication in 1943 undertook a three-weeks' fast which he survived, much to the relief of the Government which, nevertheless, with (Sir) Winston Churchill at its head, stood firm. In 1944 Gandhi's wife died; his health deteriorated and he was released.

Gandhi and Jinnah now sought to find a solution of the Hindu–Moslem problem but failed to reach agreement, perhaps because Gandhi had no real conviction that the problem existed. Once the British had gone, he said, a new nation would be born to which partition would be vivisection. Jinnah, the realist, was determined that partition must take place before the British withdrew leaving the Hindus in a majority. There followed the Cabinet mission's negotiations with the Indian leaders (1946) in the course of which Gandhi threw the whole weight of his immense influence against the partition of the country. But it was not enough. Partition came, with the accompanying tragedies of mass migrations, wholesale murders, and almost unbelievable suffering. To Gandhi partition was an unmitigated evil. Yet it argued a strange lack of political understanding on his part that he either could not or would not see that, when a complete transfer of power was at last to take place, Moslem fears and Moslem pride constituted political facts of such capital importance that they could no longer be ignored. He could not find it in his heart to join at Delhi in the celebration of Independence Day, 15 August 1947. Instead, in Calcutta he fasted the whole day and prayed. He fasted again in September and peace was restored in Calcutta. He then went to Delhi where in January 1948 he undertook a fast unto death for peace and goodwill between the two warring communities, a fast which was only broken when all the principal Indian leaders at Delhi took oath by his bedside to work for communal harmony. But his pleadings for co-operation had provoked the hostility of that militant section among the Hindus which was ready to undo partition by force. On 30 January 1948 one of these, Nathuram Godse, shot the Mahatma dead as he approached the dais in a garden in Delhi where he was accustomed each day to lead the people in prayer.

Widely divergent views have been held both about Gandhi's personality and about his methods. What he was is perhaps less important to history than what people thought he was; and by the majority of Indians, even in his lifetime, he was regarded as a saint. To his opponents, and these included some sections of his own countrymen, he appeared primarily as a shrewd and even artful politician. Judging by the influence which he wielded over many millions of men and women, however, he was the greatest Indian of his time and perhaps among the greatest Indians of any time. His power lay in his influence over the masses to whom he brought a new vitality and self-respect. All his life he held to a few, comparatively simple, truths. He was neither a great writer—although he wrote voluminously— nor a great orator. He gained adherents first by his example: he practised what he preached; then by precept. He had a genius for the mass propagation of ideas. In journeyings, in prayer meetings, in pamphlets, newspapers, and books he hammered away at his few simple, some of them deceptively simple, themes. Their very simplicity, perhaps, caused some to think Gandhi hypocritical. He may have deceived himself but he was undoubtedly sincere. On all with whom he came in personal contact he exercised what seems to have been a particular charm. Influence radiated from him. He was at his best perhaps with children and young people, although with his own children he was an exacting father. His first child died at birth but thereafter he had four sons to whom he did not accord the educational advantages he had himself enjoyed. His eldest son turned bitterly against him and became a Moslem.

Gandhi was patient in argument but little receptive of other people's views: 'My mind is narrow, I have not read much literature, I have not seen much of the world. I have concentrated upon certain things in life and beyond that I have no other interest.' He was not a profound but rather a muddled and wishful thinker, with a tendency to ignore the facts when they failed to agree with his theories. Nothing which touched his central faith was changeable, although on what he regarded as secondary issues he was ready publicly to avow his mistakes. Intensely religious, and a pious Hindu, he disliked proselytizing and had little use for dogma. He opposed untouchability and child marriage but was prepared to give his life for the cow which he called 'a poem on pity' and 'the mother to millions of Indians'. He relied essentially upon his private judgement and judged from the humanitarian, even sentimental, point of view. Much of his asceticism was adopted for reasons more social or political than religious, although he acknowledged and later sought its spiritual benefits. Problems of diet and health fascinated him and his own wish, in which he did not however persist against family opposition, was to study medicine. He was not a statesman, nor even a politician, in any accepted sense of the word. He was interested primarily in the individual life of men and women. Similarly he concerned himself little with consciously selected ends. If the means were good the ends could look after themselves. Let the people only be good and good government would follow. He was no Socialist, of the Marxist variety or otherwise. Class war to him suggested violence which he abhorred. He would have raised the standard of living of the ordinary people, but not above a certain

modest competence. He had no particular quarrel with the rich—indeed they had their uses. A rich man who followed his teaching would presently, however, have little need for his wealth. He disliked machinery because it undermined the worker's individuality. He looked forward not to the industrialization of India but to the regeneration of the Indian village. One of his reasons for wanting Britain out of India was his distrust and dislike of the impact of Western civilization upon his country and his religion; but he came too late to put back the clock.

Gandhi's compulsive fasts have been called political blackmail. That he chose the occasions for these with shrewd psychological skill, particularly when he fasted in jail, need not be denied. He had a strong sense of drama. A particular merit of the fast weapon was that it could be brought to bear on the opponent from jail. Yet the appeal to the opponent through suffering touches deep springs in human nature. Non-violent pressure through suffering is, too, an old tradition in India. In other hands the inevitable movement for British withdrawal might have been more violent yet less quickly successful. By making the British feel morally uncomfortable, he achieved what force alone could not perhaps so soon have accomplished. The last months of his life, however, were clouded with sorrow and disappointment, for paradoxically the violence which he abhorred and had largely averted from the British fell upon his countrymen, and finally upon himself. In those last months much that had been so certain must have seemed no longer sure. Perhaps Satyagraha, non-violent resistance to evil, had after all its limitations. Nevertheless in the first half of the twentieth century Gandhi did as much to change the course of history as any other single man, not excluding Lenin.

A portrait by V. R. Rao is at India House, London.

[M. K. Gandhi, *An Autobiography, or the Story of my Experiments with Truth*, 1949, and *Satyagraha in South Africa*, 1928; J. Nehru, *The Discovery of India*, 1946, and *Autobiography*, new edition, 1942; Romain Rolland, *Mahatma Gandhi*, 1924; *Gandhiji, His Life and Work*, published on his 75th birthday, 1944; *Mahatma Gandhi, Essays and Reflections on His Life and Work*, edited by S. Radhakrishnan, memorial edition, 1949; Louis Fischer, *The Life of Mahatma Gandhi*, 1951; *Gandhi's Letters to a Disciple*, 1951; H. S. L. Polack, H. N. Brailsford, and Lord

Pethick-Lawrence, *Mahatma Gandhi*, 1949; D. G. Tendulkar, *Mahatma*, 8 vols., Bombay, 1951–4.]     FRANCIS WYLIE.

[V. P. Menon, *The Transfer of Power in India*, 1957; S. Gopal, *The Viceroyalty of Lord Irwin*, 1957.]

GARDINER, ALFRED GEORGE (1865–1946), author and journalist, was born at Chelmsford 2 June 1865. He was of Essex stock. His father, Henry James Gardiner, a cabinet-maker, was unambitious and irresponsible, so that the care of a family of five devolved upon the mother (whose maiden name was Carter), a woman of competence and fine character from whom her youngest son inherited vitality and moral passion. Educated privately, he read widely and eagerly, resolved to be a writer, and followed three older brothers into newspaper work. In his late teens he was a reporter in Bournemouth, and in 1886 joined the *Northern Daily Telegraph*, a new Liberal paper published in Blackburn. There the training was thorough. He showed exceptional ability in both political and descriptive work, and rose to be leader-writer and editor of the weekly edition. He was clearly marked out for a metropolitan career.

The London press was under heavy strain during the South African war. The *Daily News*, the chief Liberal organ, suffered with its fellows and underwent a change of ownership, George Cadbury [q.v.] becoming governing proprietor. Gardiner was chosen for the editorship at the age of thirty-six. The appointment, a surprise to Fleet Street, was made at the instance of the managing director, T. P. Ritzema, who at the time was chief proprietor of the northern papers. Gardiner took charge in February 1902, three months before the end of the war. Circulation and revenue had fallen to a low level. The position was most difficult for an editor without London experience. The Liberal tide, however, was running strongly, and the electoral triumph of 1906 made a decisive change in the paper's standing. Gardiner was ardent and resourceful in support of the Campbell-Bannerman ministry, and of the Asquith–Lloyd George reforms, political and social, from 1908. He was brilliantly served by a succession of leader-writers among whom were: H. W. Massingham, H. W. Paul, C. F. G. Masterman, H. W. Nevinson [qq.v.], (Sir) R. C. K. Ensor, and H. N. Brailsford; with Robert Lynd [q.v.]

as literary editor and G. K. Chesterton [q.v.] a much-admired contributor.

Gardiner had no doubts concerning the rightness of the decision for war with Germany in 1914. Two years later, when the rift occurred between the prime minister and Lloyd George, he stood firmly by Asquith as leader of the nation, and in the later months of the war was in sharp disagreement with Lloyd George. He was thus out of accord with the line adopted by the British delegation at the peace conference and took his stand with the severest critics of the Treaty of Versailles. A powerful article from his pen in May 1919 began a period of tension between the owners of the paper and himself. He retired from the *Daily News* in September, after a noteworthy editorship of eighteen years.

Gardiner was then fifty-four, in the enjoyment of a high reputation as a Liberal publicist. He did not seek another editorial post, but turned to authorship and independent journalism, being assured of a large public and ample rewards. His influence in the country had been greatly enhanced by his regular signed articles, and especially by the portrait sketches which over many years were the leading Saturday feature of his paper. His vivid style and large personal acquaintance made him admirably suited to this mode of writing. They were combined with a talent for incisive personal judgement and a generous temper to which, save now and again in the case of a political opponent, he gave full rein. Of these studies he wrote in all about 150. A first selection, in 1908, appeared as *Prophets, Priests, and Kings*. It was followed by three more volumes: *Pillars of Society* (1913), *The War Lords* (1915), and *Certain People of Importance* (1926). After leaving the *Daily News* Gardiner's major task was his life of Sir William Harcourt (2 vols., 1923), a standard work. He wrote also lives of George Cadbury and Sir John Williams Benn. Further, he had a gift for the light occasional essay. It was happily displayed in a large number of short papers contributed to the *Star* and signed 'Alpha of the Plough'. They were collected in four popular volumes beginning with *Pebbles on the Shore* (1916).

In 1888 Gardiner married Ada (died 1948), daughter of Peter Claydon, of Witham, Essex; there were two sons and four daughters. He died at Princes Risborough 3 March 1946.

[Personal knowledge.] S. K. RATCLIFFE.

GARDINER, HENRY BALFOUR (1877–1950), composer, was born in London 7 November 1877, the son of Henry John Gardiner, merchant, and his wife, Clara Elizabeth Honey. Gardiner showed from the first a notable talent for music, which was encouraged by his family as part of a normal education at Charterhouse and New College, Oxford, where he obtained a second class in honour moderations (1898) and a fourth in *literae humaniores* (1900). His musical training in the more advanced stages was completed by two periods of study at Frankfurt under Ivan Knorr, at that time a busy and successful teacher. There Gardiner was the centre of a group of young musicians who afterwards did much for English music, among them Mr. Cyril Scott, Mr. Percy Grainger, Roger Quilter, and Norman O'Neill. Although he was never in a full sense one of the 'Frankfurt Group', Frederick Delius [q.v.] was much associated in later years with these artists. From his studies with Knorr, Gardiner returned, as Grainger has said, 'a magnificent pianist, a resourceful conductor . . . a thoroughly practical music-maker, and . . . one of the most inspired composers of his generation.'

From 1900 onwards Gardiner produced a steady output of music, including a Symphony (1908), an Overture, and many smaller pieces. Important among these early works are a Quartet and a Quintet for strings, and a ballad for chorus and orchestra called 'News from Whydah' (1912) which secured wide popularity. Other works for chorus and orchestra are the specially beautiful 'April' (1912) and 'Philomena'(1923). A projected opera on the subject of Thomas Hardy's story 'The Three Strangers' was never completed, despite the fact that a great deal of work was done upon it. An extract from the music, however, entitled 'Shepherd Fennel's Dance', became very popular and has proved to be Gardiner's most frequently played, although by no means his most characteristic, composition. Some of his most personal music is to be found among his songs and the shorter pieces for pianoforte.

Gardiner's music is firm in design, masterly in effectiveness, warm in colour, and impassioned in feeling. He had learnt in Frankfurt how to use the full resources of the post-Wagnerian orchestra, and if he was to some extent, like Grainger and Delius, influenced by Grieg, he was also much affected by the English folk-songs, of which in the early days of the revival he was an active collector.

At the outbreak of war in 1914 Gardiner's career was at its height, and he returned from the army five years later in the full intention of resuming it. He found, however, that in the intervening years the musical climate had changed. The warm romanticism of pre-war days had given way to the more austere and intellectual atmosphere that is found in the later works of Gustav Holst [q.v.] and in the period of Ralph Vaughan Williams's Mass in G minor. This mood was foreign to Gardiner's temperament: and the realization of this, coupled with his naturally self-critical character, led him to renounce music with almost dramatic suddenness. He devoted himself exclusively to the country pursuits in which he was always interested and had the means to enjoy, and after 1924 he wrote no more music.

Gardiner influenced the music of his generation by his ready appreciation of other men's work as well as by the quality of his own. His enterprising spirit and his wealth enabled him to initiate and support some influential musical activities, including many large-scale London orchestral concerts at which important works by his contemporaries were produced. The full story of his beneficent activities cannot be told, but these were great, and many distinguished artists, including Holst and Delius, were helped by them. This generosity, like Gardiner's energy of action and utterance, was the expression of a rich and abundant nature. In everything Gardiner was a character. His judgements and reactions were decided, individual, and totally uninfluenced by the opinions of the majority or by academic considerations. He was loved by many friends. He died, unmarried, at Salisbury 28 June 1950.

[Private information; personal knowledge.]
THOMAS ARMSTRONG.

GARNETT, CONSTANCE CLARA (1861–1946), translator of the Russian classics, was born in Brighton 19 (registered as 20) December 1861, the daughter of David Black, coroner, and his wife, Clara Patten. One grandfather, a Scotch sea-captain, served as naval architect to Tsar Nicholas I, the other was George Patten, the portrait painter [q.v.]. The novelist Clementina Black was her sister. One of eight children, Constance was a cripple until the age of six. At seventeen she went from Brighton High School with a scholarship to Newnham College, Cambridge, where she was placed in the second class of part i and in the first class of part ii of the classical tripos in 1882 and 1883. After serving as librarian at the People's Palace, she married in 1889 Edward Garnett, the author, who died in 1937, and who was a son of Richard Garnett [q.v.]. Her husband's friends among Russian exiles, notably Peter Kropotkin and Felix Volkhowsky, awakened her interest in their country's literature, and she began to learn its language to occupy the time before the birth of her only child, David, in 1892. In the winter of that year she went to Russia, travelling long distances by post sledge. The bearer of money for famine relief, she visited the stricken areas around Nizhniy Novgorod, carried papers for her Socialist friends, Stepniak and N. V. Tchaikowsky, and visited Tolstoy at Yasnaya Polyana. In 1904 came a second journey to Russia.

On her return to England early in 1893, with the encouragement of Stepniak, she began the translations which were to be her life-work. These fill seventy volumes and include all the more important works of Russian prose literature—the whole of Turgenev, Dostoevski, and Gogol, and virtually all of Chekhov. She also translated the two great novels of Tolstoy, Herzen's memoirs, a novel by Goncharov, a play by Ostrovsky, and a story by Gorky. This immense achievement was possible only because she worked rapidly, with unflagging concentration. Into it she put more than a scrupulous literary conscience and a scientific respect for both the languages in which she worked; she felt for the Russia of the last century a warm affection. In her translations she gave a people she loved a new incarnation. Her style is clear, simple, and direct; rarely in this immense output is there a questionable rendering and never a lapse of taste. She is happiest in reproducing the styles of Tolstoy and Chekhov. To innumerable readers she revealed a new world and thanks chiefly to her translations the Russian classics exerted in the first half of the twentieth century a deep influence on English literature and thought.

In spite of her shyness she had a circle of friends who valued her original personality. A decided rationalist, the

credulity of mankind baffled her. Her sympathies went rather to the Russian social revolutionaries than to the Marxists, and she detested the Bolshevik tyranny. In her old age she became a strong Conservative. She spent most of her life in her country home near Edenbridge in Kent. Her eyesight was always bad and in her later years she had to dictate her translations after hearing the Russian read aloud. She died at Edenbridge 17 December 1946.

[Private information; personal knowledge.]
H. N. BRAILSFORD.

[David Garnett, *The Golden Echo*, 1953.]


GARVIE, ALFRED ERNEST (1861–1945), theologian and Church leader, was born 29 August 1861 at Zyrardow, in a part of Poland under Russian rule, the second surviving son and fifth surviving child of Peter Garvie by his wife, Jane, daughter of Alexander Kedslie, manager of a flour mill in Warsaw. His parents belonged to Scottish families who had settled in Poland in the eighteen-twenties, his father being a linen manufacturer. Garvie was at George Watson's College in Edinburgh (1874–8), then studied for a year at the university there, but gave up his course because of his defective sight and was in business in a wholesale drapery warehouse in Glasgow for four years, spending much of his time in mission work. His sense of call to the ministry became too strong to be resisted, and he entered the university of Glasgow in 1885, and graduated in 1889 with first class honours in philosophy, receiving the Logan gold medal as the most distinguished arts graduate of his year. He had belonged to the United Presbyterian Church, but, as he was unwilling to sign the Westminster Confession, he went to Mansfield College, Oxford, to train for the Congregational ministry. Here he took first class honours in theology in 1892. In the following year he began his ministry at Macduff, two years later moving to Montrose. In 1902 he became chairman of the Scottish Congregational Union. In the following year he was given the honorary degree of D.D. by Glasgow University and became professor of the philosophy of theism, comparative religion, and Christian ethics at Hackney College and New College, Hampstead. In 1907 he became principal of New College and in 1922 of Hackney College. In 1924 the two colleges were legally united and he became the principal of what was then called Hackney and New College and later New College, London. He resigned his principalship in 1933, but continued in his retirement to serve the many movements with which he was associated. Garvie wrote very many books. One of the earliest of these, *The Ritschlian Theology* (1899), is not likely to be superseded. Two of his books had a very large circulation: *A Guide to Preachers* (1906) and *Studies in the Inner Life of Jesus* (1907). As he approached the time of his retirement, he summed up the results of his thought and study in three massive volumes: *The Christian Doctrine of the Godhead* (1925), *The Christian Ideal for Human Society* (1930), and *The Christian Belief in God* (1932).

In his later years Garvie regarded his literary work as less important than his public activity. In 1920 he was chairman of the Congregational Union of England and Wales; in 1924 president of the National Free Church Council and vice-chairman of the inter-denominational Conference on Politics, Economics, and Citizenship ('Copec'); in 1927 he was deputy chairman of the Lausanne conference on 'Faith and Order', and in 1928 moderator of the Free Church Federal Council.

Garvie was not a 'pacifist' but he was supremely a peacemaker and, aided by his fluent use of German and French, did much to bring together the Church leaders of lands estranged by the war of 1914–18; in 1930 Berlin University conferred on him its D.Th. degree in recognition not only of his theological learning but of his 'devotion in evangelical love and faith to the unity of the Church of Christ'. On his retirement from New College, London University conferred on him its honorary D.D. (1934), a distinction which is very seldom given. The university orator introduced him in words which well express the impression he made on his many friends and pupils: 'a great divine and a much loved leader, scholar, philosopher and theologian; rich in manifold learning and endowed with a rare and beautiful personality'. Great as were his gifts and wide as was his learning, those who knew him best think first of his infectious faith and his cheerful goodness.

In 1893 Garvie married Agnes (died 1914), daughter of William Gordon, of Glasgow; they had two daughters. He died in Hendon 7 March 1945.

[A. E. Garvie, *Memories and Meanings of*

*My Life*, 1938; 'Selbstdarstellung', giving a full account of his writings, in *Die Religionswissenschaft der Gegenwart in Selbstdarstellungen*, edited by E. Stange, Bd. iv, 1928; *Christian World*, 15 March 1945; personal knowledge.]      SYDNEY CAVE.

GARVIN, JAMES LOUIS (1868–1947), editor of the *Observer*, was born at Birkenhead 12 April 1868, the younger son of an Irish immigrant, Michael Garvin, who was lost at sea when Garvin was two, and his wife, Catherine Fahy. Garvin, who was brought up as a Roman Catholic but moved to a Christian mysticism outside any Church, took the name Louis at confirmation. Until he was twelve and a half he attended the school attached to the church of St. Laurence in Park Street. In his spare time he helped his mother by delivering newspapers and medicines. The family moved to Hull (1884) and to Newcastle upon Tyne (1889) where Garvin worked as a clerk in corn, starch, electrical, and coal businesses. As a boy he is remembered as pale and reserved. Yet, quietly bubbling with ideas, he devoured books and taught himself French and German, and, to fit himself for a better job, Spanish. He began writing regularly at Hull, sending to the *Eastern Morning News* letters defending Irish Home Rule. Following the lead of his elder brother, a schoolmaster, Garvin took part in organizing local Irish opinion in defence of Parnell. In the summer of 1891 he contributed regularly to *United Ireland* and, when the branch of the business in which he was working closed, settled his destiny by becoming a proof reader on the *Newcastle Chronicle* of Joseph Cowen [q.v.] with permission to contribute for nothing. After six weeks he was writing full time and his reporting of Parnell's funeral put his future beyond doubt.

Garvin, who had resolved not to go to London until he was thirty, now began a close study of the foreign press and a systematic reading in European literature, in history and travel, later expressed in a fine library. A review of Francis Thompson's poems, which began his enthusiastic championship of them, brought him into touch with Wilfrid and Alice Meynell [q.v.] in London. In 1895 he began making his mark in the influential reviews by sending to W. L. Courtney [q.v.] for the *Fortnightly Review* a contribution on the future of Irish politics which was, as he had asked, used at once and placed first.

Through this connexion he went in 1899 to London to the *Daily Telegraph* as a leader and special writer.

Until the war of 1914–18 his thought was directed by two related themes, developed at Newcastle, which brought him into the Unionist camp. Most notably as 'Calchas' in the *Fortnightly Review* he pressed for awareness of the German peril and for an alliance with Russia. From 1905 he worked with Sir John (later Lord) Fisher and Lord Roberts [qq.v.] in the cause of military preparedness. Secondly, originally like Cowen a Liberal imperialist, he threw himself into Joseph Chamberlain's campaign for tariff reform with articles which soon attracted attention. In 1905–6 he edited the *Outlook* in opposition to the Unionist but free-trading *Spectator* but after a change of ownership he left. In January 1908 Lord Northcliffe [q.v.] secured him as editor and manager with a fifth share of the old but languishing Sunday paper, the *Observer*. In just over two years he made it both a paying proposition and a fiery force in the Unionist Party. He took the lead in encouraging the Lords to throw out Lloyd George's budget, presenting the alternatives in *Tariff or Budget* (1909). On the death of King Edward VII, proclaiming a 'truce of God', he strongly advocated the constitutional conference between Government and Opposition; and when it failed he urged the Lords to reject the Parliament bill in order to force a reconstruction of the second chamber. On Ireland, adding his vision of imperial union and a realization that Ulster would not join an all-Ireland Parliament to the understanding of Home Rule born in him, he proposed a federation of the British Isles.

In 1911 a difference of opinion with Northcliffe over food taxes, in which Garvin publicly attacked the views of the *Daily Mail*, resulted in an ultimatum that Garvin should buy Northcliffe out or himself sell. Garvin brought in W. W. (later Viscount) Astor, who in April, on the initiative of his elder son, Waldorf, acquired the sole ownership of the *Observer*. Garvin also edited the evening paper, the *Pall Mall Gazette*, much improving its position, from 1912 to 1915 when Astor sold it.

The war and the peace greatly increased Garvin's reputation, not least abroad. His policies won him an audience among many formerly opposed to him while the seal was set on the business success of the *Observer*. His search for a resolute national war policy made him a strong supporter of Lloyd George and of Lord Milner [q.v.]. He pressed for a true War Cabinet, for national service and ministries of munitions and shipping. This resolution, and his attitude to Germany before the war, underlined the force of his criticism of the Treaty of Versailles as 'peace and dragon's teeth'. In *The Economic Foundations of Peace* (1919) he asked for the reshaping of the war-time instruments of economic co-operation to create a new world partnership under the League of Nations, and a peace system which Germany could enter as an equal. He became a critic of Poincaré as 'the Kaiser of the peace' and the rise of Hitler found him still determined to miss no reasonable chance of avoiding by negotiation another world war, which he expected to be yet more tragic than the last. But, unlike others, he always insisted that the foundation of peace must be British strength, especially in the air. He hammered for rearmament and felt deeply the humiliation of British impotence as the real limitation on policy.

In 1935 he took a controversial stand. Information given him about Amharic rule shaped the expression of his view that Britain should not interfere with the Italian invasion of Abyssinia; but behind it was the belief, borne out by events, that, once Mussolini had been allowed to embark on the venture, the half-measures proposed would not help Abyssinia but would throw Italy into the arms of Germany and end the independence of Austria. Subsequently he argued that Britain should reserve her attitude on the unsolved questions of East and Central Europe. He opposed making commitments which could lead to a war, for which Britain was unprepared, to keep German-speaking peoples who might wish to enter the Reich outside it. But two weeks after the Munich agreement there was a sharp change when German comment convinced him that there was no limit to Hitler's ambitions, and he insisted that this must be the last concession.

Between the wars Garvin moderated his belief in tariffs in favour of a conscious policy of national economic and social development. He was strongly in favour of the formation of a national Government in 1931, in line with his lifelong advocacy of coalitions in emergency. His social philosophy is given in his phrase, coined in 1909, 'for every child a chance'.

In February 1942 Garvin's thirty-four

years' editorship ended. There had been differences before between editor and proprietor. Garvin essentially believed in the editor as captain of his ship, Waldorf Astor in government by committee. In 1918, at the suggestion of Lord Milner, a permanent tribunal had been appointed to mediate in case of need. By 1942 there was on one side an editor who had given his life to the paper and from its own resources rescued it from near-extinction, on the other a proprietor who desired to make a change. A prospective compromise by which Garvin was to have remained as editor until the end of the war with an associate in London was upset when Garvin, contrary to Lord Astor's known views, in commenting on ministerial changes, in particular defended (Sir) Winston Churchill's retention of the post of minister of defence and said that Lord Beaverbrook should return soon to the War Cabinet. For nearly three years Garvin wrote in the *Sunday Express* and then returned in March 1945 to the *Daily Telegraph* in which his last article appeared a week before he died.

As an editor Garvin said that he set out 'to give the public what they don't want' by which he meant giving them something better than they knew. He communicated his vitality to the paper as a whole and his contributors found his encouragement bracing. Not only did he make the *Observer* a political force through his own comment, with which it was particularly identified, but, helped by a change in social habits, he pioneered a new pattern of Sunday journal which was to be both a first-class newspaper and a companion for the week-end with especially full treatment of the arts.

As a writer he established a remarkable personal influence. The source of his authority, which made him appear at times inconsistent, was an intense capacity to enter into the life of events and yet to be outside them. In his long weekly article, which became an institution, he gathered the audience with drumming headlines and the colourful thrust of a very individual style. His writing could be ponderous and too repetitive, but at its best, in these articles and in his quieter literary appreciations, there was a flow of feeling, imaginative and moral insight, wit and range of reference which found expression in bold and compelling phrases.

Garvin's achievement derived from an overflowing fullness of mind and character.

There was a gusto and breadth which stamped his writing and his superb conversation. He had an immense memory, storing long passages from his favourite writers, and an acute geographical sense. These were facets of the outstanding 'visualizing' power through which he could evoke characters in a book or places which he had never visited. His combination of mental vigour and imaginative force made him seem somehow larger than life. His physical appearance matched his powers. The most striking feature was his eyes, deep-set and yet seeming to leap out of the face. His frame was massive but beautifully built.

Garvin edited the supplementary volumes which made up the thirteenth edition of the *Encyclopaedia Britannica*. He then undertook the herculean task of editing the fourteenth edition (1929) which he modernized for a new public on both sides of the Atlantic without debasing essential standards. He wrote three volumes of the *Life of Joseph Chamberlain* (1932–4); this work, which pressure of international events prevented him from finishing, remains a vivid and notable portrait of a man and an age, although the interpretation of some episodes has been criticized. He was president of the Institute of Journalists (1917 and 1918), chairman of the council of the Empire Press Union (1924–6), and president of the Newspaper Press Fund (1932–3). He received the honorary degrees of D.Litt. from Durham (1921) and LL.D. from Edinburgh (1935). He declined a knighthood from Lloyd George but in 1941 was happy to become a Companion of Honour.

In 1894 Garvin married Christina Ellen (died 1918), daughter of Robert Wilson, superintendent of police, of Newcastle upon Tyne, by whom he had one son, Roland Gerard, who was killed in the war of 1914–18, and four daughters. His eldest daughter, Viola, was literary editor of the *Observer* (1926–42). Another daughter, Mrs. Una Ledingham, became consultant physician at the Royal Free Hospital and the Hampstead General Hospital. Garvin married secondly, in 1921 Mrs. Viola Woods, daughter of Harry Ashworth Taylor, King's messenger, and granddaughter of Sir Henry Taylor [q.v.]. Garvin died 23 January 1947 at his home, Gregories, Beaconsfield, once the bailiff's house on Edmund Burke's estate.

There is a portrait of Garvin by P. Ivanovitch in the possession of Mrs. Ledingham, and a bust by Jo Davidson at

Beaconsfield; a drawing, made for *Punch* by Sir Bernard Partridge, is in the National Portrait Gallery.

[Katharine Garvin, *J. L. Garvin*, 1948; private information; personal knowledge.]

M. Barrington-Ward.

GASELEE, Sir STEPHEN (1882–1943), librarian, scholar, and connoisseur, was born in London 9 November 1882, the elder son of Henry Gaselee, a distinguished equity draughtsman and conveyancer, by his wife, Alice Esther, daughter of the Rev. George Frost, second master of Kensington Grammar School. His great-grandfather was Sir Stephen Gaselee [q.v.], justice of the court of common pleas. Having been grounded at Temple Grove, East Sheen, he was elected (second in the list) a King's scholar at Eton, where he edited the *Eton College Chronicle*, won prizes for Latin verse, was awarded the Newcastle medal, and elected a scholar of King's. At Cambridge he obtained a first class in part i of the classical tripos (1904) and a second class in part ii (1905). He left Cambridge in that year and, as tutor to Prince Leopold of Battenberg (later Lord Leopold Mountbatten), travelled widely, attaining that experience of foreign countries and courts which was to stand him in good stead for his later duties. In 1907 he returned to Cambridge and after failing, to the surprise of his friends, to win (by his dissertation on Petronius) a fellowship at King's in the following year, accepted two months later the Pepysian librarianship at Magdalene, which he held until 1919. Moving there in the autumn he was elected in 1909 into a fellowship which he held for thirty-four years. He mastered his Pepysian duties and concentrated awhile on Coptic studies, cataloguing the Coptic manuscripts in the University Library, lecturing on Coptic dialects, and publishing a series of texts, edited with a Latin translation and commentary, entitled *Parerga Coptica*. From 1903 he had steadily pursued his study of Petronius, adding to his original fellowship dissertation a handlist, and a preface and Latin text of the *Satyricon* to face the translation by William Burnaby of 1694 which was privately printed by Ralph Straus in 1910. For the Loeb Classical Library he reprinted an amended version of William Adlington's Apuleius (1915), Parthenius (1916), and Achilles Tatius (1917). He contributed a brief preface to the anonymous 1588 translation, *Sixe Idillia*, of

Theocritus (1922); edited (with H. F. B. Brett-Smith) Caxton's translation of books x–xv of Ovid's *Metamorphoses* from a manuscript in the Pepys Library (1924); and wrote for the Tudor Translation series an introduction to John Frampton's *Joyfull Newes out of the Newe Founde Worlde*, a translation of 1577 from the Spanish of Nicolas Monardes (2 vols., 1925). In 1925 he published an *Anthology of Medieval Latin*, in 1928 *The Oxford Book of Medieval Latin Verse*, and in 1938 he edited for the Roxburghe Club, of which he was a member, the 'Costerian' *Doctrinale* of Alexander de Villa Dei.

In 1916 Gaselee entered the Foreign Office and was rewarded for his services in 1918 by appointment as C.B.E. By Michaelmas term 1919 he was back in Cambridge, lecturing on Coptic, but his outstanding qualities had not been lost upon the Foreign Office and on 1 January 1920 he was made librarian and keeper of the papers. He was appointed K.C.M.G. in 1935, and served the Crown until his death.

Stephen Gaselee was strikingly more than his career or his literary output. The value of his department was enhanced, partly by the extent and profundity of his knowledge and experience, and partly by his conception of its duties. He improved and enlarged the Foreign Office library from insignificance to 80,000 books, missing no single publication, in whatever language, which bore usefully upon foreign affairs; he also ensured that diplomatic missions abroad were likewise appropriately provided, not infrequently at his own expense. He compiled a list of 'Libraries and Sources of Information in Government Departments' (*Proceedings of the Twelfth Conference of the Association of Special Libraries and Information Bureaux*, 1935). He was widely and constantly consulted not only by his colleagues at home and abroad, but also by foreign scholars, diplomatists, and public institutions. Irreplaceable in personality, he was succeeded after many months by the director of research, with whose responsibilities those of the librarian were henceforth merged.

At Cambridge, Gaselee had been both as undergraduate and don a noteworthy figure, with a remarkable variety of unusually combined interests. To his eminence as Latinist, Coptologist, medievalist, palaeographer, liturgiologist, and hagiographer he added later that of president of the Bibliographical Society (1932) and honorary librarian of the Athenaeum from 1928. In 1934 he presented to the Cambridge University Library his own collection of 300 early printed books, the largest gift of the kind ever received by the university; to which he added in 1940 his rare and large collection of early sixteenth-century books. He was an ardent high churchman, his convictions strengthened by the width and profundity of his knowledge; striving for restoration of the unsupplemented Anglican use, together with an ultimate union—of unity without uniformity—with the Roman as with the Orthodox Church.

As Gaselee's punctual, methodical intellect had infused a State department with the spirit of exact scholarship, so in return his cultured interest in the exchange of international courtesies seemed to extend the frontiers of Cambridge. The personality of this dignified traditionalist, 'proud to be by hereditary right a Cloth-worker', was enhanced by his gentle serene manner, his clear tenor voice, and by the archaic originality of his broadcloth cutaway tailcoat, his spats, red socks, and Old Etonian bow tie. As a sopra-dilettante in the best sense of the word he dispensed a distinguished hospitality, in which luxurious and often experimental dining was set off not only by wines chosen (and whimsically explained) with the discrimination of a connoisseur, but also by discourse of unusual information imparted with curious felicity. With like generosity he gave his wise counsel, his exhilarating company, and his practical friendship to both sexes and all ages.

In addition to those already mentioned Gaselee's honours included the honorary degree of Litt.D. from the university of Liverpool (1933), the honorary fellowship of King's College (1935), the Sandars readership in bibliography at Cambridge (1935), the presidency of the Classical Association (1939) and the Egypt Exploration Society (1941), and the fellowship of the British Academy (1939).

In 1917 Gaselee married May Evelyn, daughter of E. Wyndham Hulme, librarian of the Patent Office; they had three daughters. He died in London 16 June 1943.

[A. S. F. Gow in *Proceedings* of the British Academy, vol. xxix, 1943; *Cambridge Review*, 23 October 1943; Sir Ronald Storrs, *Orientations*, 1937; personal knowledge.]

RONALD STORRS.

GAUVAIN, SIR HENRY JOHN (1878–1945), surgeon and specialist in tuberculosis, was born in Alderney 28 November 1878, the second son of William Gauvain, receiver-general for the island, by his wife, Catherine Margaret, daughter of Peter Le Ber, jurat of Alderney. He was educated at Tonbridge High School, King's College, London, and St. John's College, Cambridge, where he was a scholar. After being placed in the first class of the honours list in part i of the natural sciences tripos in 1902 he went to St. Bartholomew's Hospital as senior science scholar. He qualified in 1906 and proceeded to the M.D. and M.Ch. degrees (Cambridge) in 1918. In 1908 Sir William Treloar [q.v.] founded the Lord Mayor Treloar Cripples' Home at Alton, Hampshire, for children suffering from surgical tuberculosis, and offered Gauvain the post of resident medical officer. He accepted the appointment and after paying a brief visit to Berck-sur-Mer, where the treatment for these cases by conservative methods had been carried out for about thirty years, he began treatment at Alton on the same lines. Gauvain's work and the results obtained were such that the institution rapidly acquired both a national and an international reputation; its name was changed to the Lord Mayor Treloar Cripples' (later Orthopaedic) Hospital and Gauvain was appointed medical superintendent.

Gauvain was a great believer in the value of fresh air, sunlight, and sea-bathing. In 1919 a marine branch of the hospital was opened at Sandy Point, Hayling Island, where Gauvain was able to demonstrate the remarkable benefits of sea-bathing in conjunction with helio-therapy in suitable cases. His was the first country hospital to have a properly equipped light department (*Lancet*, 4 July 1925). Gauvain recognized the need for children at Alton to have some form of education. At first this was given by nurses chosen for the purpose, but following a visit from Lloyd George the matter was brought before Parliament, and Alton (1912) became the first of the hospital schools in this country (*Lancet*, 13 April 1929). In 1925 Gauvain opened the Morland Hall Clinics for private patients, and some five years later the hospital at Alton was rebuilt. He wrote numerous papers on surgical tuberculosis, hospital design, and heliotherapy, and in 1918 described a useful sign of pathological activity in tuberculous disease of the hip-joint (*Lancet*, 16 November 1918).

Gauvain was consulting surgeon to the King Edward VII Welsh National Memorial Association for the treatment of tuberculosis, to the London, Essex, and Hampshire county councils, and to King George's Sanatorium for Sailors, Bramshott. He was president of the electrotherapeutic and diseases of children sections of the Royal Society of Medicine and vice-president of the National Association for the Prevention of Tuberculosis. In 1920 he was knighted for his services to crippled children, and in 1927 he was elected F.R.C.S. (England). In 1926 he went on a lecture tour of the United States and Canada, and in 1936 he was awarded the distinguished service gold key of the American Congress of Physical Therapy. On the occasion of the British Medical Association's meeting in Australia in 1935 he was president of the section of public medicine and received the honorary degree of M.D. from Melbourne University.

Gauvain's experience in surgical tuberculosis was second to none and his professional skill was matched by his humanity and abundant kindness. He was a man of remarkable personality and charm and was beloved by his patients and his staff. He died at Morland Hall, Hampshire, 19 January 1945. He married in 1913 Louise Laura (died March 1945), daughter of Surgeon-Major William Butler, formerly of the Indian Medical Service. He had one son who predeceased him and a daughter who entered the medical profession.

A posthumous portrait by Frank O. Salisbury is at the Lord Mayor Treloar Orthopaedic Hospital; a bust in bronze by Charles Pibworth is in the possession of the family.

[*British Medical Journal* and *Lancet*, 3 February 1945; *The Times*, 20 January and 13 February 1945; *Journal of Bone and Joint Surgery*, April 1945.]     W. J. Bishop.

GELLIBRAND, Sir JOHN (1872–1945), major-general, was born at Ouse, Tasmania, 5 December 1872, third son and sixth child of Thomas Lloyd Gellibrand, a sheep-farmer, and grandson of Joseph Tice Gellibrand, the first attorney-general of Tasmania and one of the founders of Melbourne. John Gellibrand was sent to Europe for his education, at King's School, Canterbury, and at Frankfurt and elsewhere in Germany. He entered the Royal Military College, Sandhurst, gaining the first place in passing both in and out, and received a commission in 1893 in the 1st South Lancashire Regiment, with which

he went in 1900 to South Africa. He fought in the relief of Ladysmith and at Pieter's Hill. In May 1900 he transferred to the Manchester Regiment, and was afterwards selected for a staff college course at Camberley. After ten years of service with his regiment, and with militia and volunteers, and several years on the staff (as deputy assistant adjutant and quarter-master-general, Ceylon, 1908–12) he retired when still a captain on finding that he must lose seniority when his battalion was disbanded in the course of War Office economies.

Gellibrand then took up an orchard at Risdon in Tasmania, but on the outbreak of war in 1914 volunteered for service in the Australian Imperial Force, was appointed to the staff of the 1st Australian division, sailed with it to Egypt and Gallipoli, and was wounded at the Anzac landing. After serving on the staffs of the 1st and 2nd divisions during that campaign he was appointed to command first the 12th battalion, and then, in the reorganization which followed the evacuation of the peninsula, the 6th Infantry brigade. He was wounded again on several occasions, and became known as a commander of devoted courage, sardonic but kindly humour, and supreme ability in training, especially of young officers. Dressing and living with the simplicity of his men, he turned his brigade into a most formidable fighting instrument. The Australian official history, referring to the second tense struggle at Bullecourt, 3–4 May 1917, when, on the 16-mile front before Arras, little except the ground attacked by his brigade was permanently held, records that, 'if ever a fight was won by a single brain and character', this battle 'was won by John Gellibrand'. After a prominent part in many battles as commander of the 6th and later 12th brigades and a term as director of training at the Australian Imperial Force depots, he commanded the 3rd Australian division through the victories of 1918. For his services in the field he was appointed D.S.O. (1916), with bar (1917), C.B. (1917), and promoted to K.C.B. in 1919; in the same year he was appointed officer of the Legion of Honour, received the French croix de guerre, and the United States D.S.M.

On returning to Australia Gellibrand became successively public service commissioner of Tasmania (1920) and commissioner of police in Victoria (1920–22), and then (1925–8) Nationalist member for Denison (Tasmania) in the Federal

Parliament. His independent spirit, however, found it difficult to brook either political or official life and he returned to his 'recreation', farming, first on his Tasmanian orchard but eventually on a sheep-station near Yea in Victoria. In Tasmania he founded the Remembrance Club—the forerunner of the important Legacy Clubs of Australia—to continue the war-time comradeship of all ranks and undertake the guidance and sponsorship of children of fallen comrades. In the war of 1939–45 he had just been appointed commander of the Volunteer Defence Corps in Victoria when he was struck down by illness from which he never really recovered. He died at Murrundindi, Victoria, 3 June 1945.

With standards which seemed at times impossibly high, Gellibrand was a great leader but a sensitive and often difficult subordinate. He was fortunate in serving under a commander and chief of staff who were aware of his rare qualities of mind and moral courage. He married in 1894 Elizabeth Helena (died 1949), daughter of Charles Frederick Alexander du Breul, shipping merchant, of Shortlands, Kent, and had one son and two daughters. His portrait by James Quinn is in the Australian War Memorial, Canberra.

[C. E. W. Bean, (Official) *History of Australia in the War of 1914–18*, vols. i–vi, 1921–42; private information; personal knowledge.]    C. E. W. BEAN.

GEORGE EDWARD ALEXANDER EDMUND, DUKE OF KENT (1902–1942), the fourth son of King George V and Queen Mary, was born at York Cottage, Sandringham, 20 December 1902. He passed through Dartmouth into the Royal Navy, in which he served until 1929, visiting many parts of the Empire, and he accompanied his brother the Prince of Wales on visits to Canada in 1927 and to South America in 1931. After working at the Foreign Office in 1929 he was attached to the Home Office. In 1934 at the invitation of the Government of the Union he made an extensive tour of South Africa and also visited the territory of Basutoland, the protectorate of Bechuanaland, and Rhodesia, the Belgian Congo, and Portuguese West Africa. Shortly before his marriage in November 1934 to Princess Marina, daughter of Prince Nicholas of Greece, he was created Duke of Kent, Earl of St. Andrews, and Baron Downpatrick. His happy marriage was a

turning-point in his life, strengthening his character, and making his purpose in life more definite. In 1935 he was appointed lord high commissioner to the General Assembly of the Church of Scotland, and in 1938 was designated governor-general of Australia, but the outbreak of war prevented his taking up the post. He remained in this country, attached in 1939 to the naval intelligence division of the Admiralty with the rank of captain (later rear-admiral), visiting naval establishments. In April 1940 he was appointed staff officer in the Training Command of the Royal Air Force in which he held the rank of group captain (later air commodore). His duties, the supervision of welfare work for the members of the Royal Air Force, took him not only to stations in Britain but also overseas, including Canada and the United States, which he visited in the summer of 1941. On 25 August 1942 the Duke set out to inspect establishments in Iceland, but was killed when his aircraft crashed at the Eagle's Rock, near Dunbeath in Caithness. He was buried at Windsor. He was survived by his widow and three children, Prince Edward George Nicholas Paul Patrick (born 1935) who succeeded to his titles; Princess Alexandra Helen Elizabeth Olga Christabel (born 1936); and Prince Michael George Charles Franklin (born July 1942).

The Duke was endowed with more than ordinary charm, his wavy brown hair and bright blue eyes contributing to a notably handsome appearance; in maturity he rather exceeded the average height and build of his family. A cheerful and amusing companion, there was no meanness in his nature, and he had many friends; he was fond of sport, hunted in the shires and was a fair game shot, but being devoted to walking, he was perhaps happiest when stalking or playing golf. He shared with his mother an informed interest in furniture and works of art, of which he built up a notable collection. He appreciated music and played the piano with enjoyment; he read intelligently and even widely and would have been accounted a cultured man in any society. He made his home at Coppins, Iver, Buckinghamshire, which he inherited from his aunt, Princess Victoria.

[Private information.]    JOHN GORE.

GEORGE, DAVID LLOYD, first EARL LLOYD-GEORGE OF DWYFOR (1863–1945), statesman. [See LLOYD GEORGE.]

GIBBON, SIR (IOAN) GWILYM (1874–1948), civil servant, was born at Ystrad y fodwg, Glamorganshire, 26 November 1874, the son of David Gibbon, colliery overman, by his wife, Ann Williams. He was educated at Oswestry High School and later as an external student of the London School of Economics and Political Science. He graduated B.A. in 1898 with a first class in mental and moral science, and proceeded D.Sc. (Econ.) in 1911. Thrown upon his own resources at sixteen, he entered the Civil Service as a boy clerk, and accomplished the rare feat of passing by open competition, while in the service, first into the second division and later, in 1903, into the first division, when he was posted to the Local Government Board. He was promoted first class clerk in 1914, and during the war of 1914–18 was given charge of the department set up to create and administer machinery for obtaining men for the armed forces; he was also secretary of the central tribunal under the Military Service Acts which involved the supervision of some 2,000 local tribunals. For his work on these tasks, to which he brought great energy and fertility of mind, he was appointed C.B.E. in 1918. When the Ministry of Health was formed in 1919, Gibbon was made an assistant secretary in the new department. He advanced to principal assistant secretary in 1925 and to director of the local government division in 1934, retiring at the end of the following year. In recognition of his services in the Ministry he was appointed C.B. in 1931 and knighted in 1936.

From 1921 until he retired Gibbon had the main responsibility for administering the functions of the Ministry of Health in relation to town planning, then within the Ministry's jurisdiction, and to local government, other than housing and the personal health services of local authorities, and he played a leading part in the framing of a number of Acts of Parliament, including those landmarks in local government law, the Rating and Valuation Act, 1925, and the Local Government Act, 1929. He fostered and supported the policy of expansion in health and other social services which was so significant a feature of this period. This policy threw a heavy burden and many new functions on local authorities, and the success with which they faced their difficulties owed much to Gibbon's stimulating encouragement and help.

In the town planning field, too, his influence was marked. He was a strong advocate of comprehensive planning powers extending to built as well as unbuilt areas. When this service first came within his purview, the position was governed by the Housing, Town Planning, &c., Acts of 1909 and 1919 which conferred planning powers only for land in course of development, or appearing likely to be used for building purposes. Conceived as little more than facilities for site planning in connexion with housing development, the powers of the Acts proved capable of a much wider interpretation, and, under Gibbon's vigorous encouragement, were used by local authorities to lay the foundation for effective correlated planning control over wide areas. He was also the chief architect of the Town and Country Planning Act of 1932 extending planning powers to built as well as to all unbuilt areas. He published amongst other works two books on town and country planning, and a *History of the L.C.C. 1889–1939* (with R. W. Bell, 1939).

Gibbon, who was unmarried, died at Twickenham, Middlesex, 4 February 1948. He left about £50,000 to Nuffield College, Oxford, the income to be used for the study of problems of government, especially by co-operation between academic and non-academic persons.

[Private information; personal knowledge.]

I. F. ARMER.

GIBSON, GUY PENROSE (1918–1944), airman, was born in Simla 12 August 1918, the younger son of Mr. Alexander James Gibson, of the Indian Forest Service, and his wife, Nora Mary Strike. He was educated at St. Edward's School, Oxford, where his housemaster, Mr. A. F. Yorke, describes him as 'strong-minded without obstinacy, disarmingly frank and of great charm'. As a prefect, he exerted his authority without apparent effort, whilst at games, although he had no special aptitude, he forced himself into good teams by sheer determination, showing signs of that physical stamina which was later to stand him in such good stead.

Gibson left school somewhat early to join the Royal Air Force. He was granted a short-service commission in November 1936 and ten months later joined No. 83 (Bomber) Squadron as a trained pilot. He took part in the first attack—on the Kiel canal—of the war of 1939–45. In July 1940 he was awarded the D.F.C. and shortly afterwards completed his first full operational tour. This would normally have earned him a rest at a training unit, but within two months his persistence had gained him access to Fighter Command where he carried out a further operational tour on night fighters, shooting down at least four enemy aircraft and gaining a bar to his D.F.C.

In April 1942, at the early age of twenty-three, he was promoted wing commander and returned to Bomber Command in command of No. 106 Squadron. At this time he had reached operational maturity and the quiet forcefulness of his character permeated the whole squadron, although it must be admitted that his relations with his aircrews had a special intimacy which he was never quite able to achieve with the groundcrews. He held command of the squadron for eleven months, an unusually long period and one covering the intensive fighting associated with the early attacks on the Ruhr, culminating in the first 1,000-bomber raid, and the difficult period in the winter of 1942–3. One who knew him well during this period said that he was the best captain he ever flew with and that it would have had to be a very smart night-fighter pilot to catch him out. It was during this period that he was appointed to the D.S.O. and later awarded a bar, a recognition of the pre-eminence which the squadron had attained under his leadership, and his own exceptional contribution of 172 sorties.

By ordinary standards, Gibson should have been more than usually ready for a spell away from operations, but his rest proved short-lived, and after only a week at headquarters No. 5 (Bomber) Group, setting down his thoughts on bomber tactics, he was offered the command of No. 617 Squadron, which was then about to be formed for a special attack on the Möhne and Eder dams. He accepted with alacrity and thus entered a period which was to show the full measure of his leadership, in the intensive, and at times highly dangerous, preliminary training, and in the meticulous planning which alone made the subsequent operations possible. During the attack on the Möhne dam on the night of 16–17 May 1943 Gibson himself released the first weapon at low level in the face of heavy fire, and then flew so as to draw the fire of the defences from each crew as they went into attack. For this gallant act, and for his leadership throughout this highly successful action, he was awarded the Victoria Cross.

During the next twelve months Gibson undertook a variety of staff appointments, including a lecture tour in America, where his modesty, his straightforward approach to all problems, and the aura of operational success, made him a notable figure; but in June 1944 he was back once more in No. 5 (Bomber) Group where he took up the appointment of operations officer in No. 55 Base which included his old squadron, No. 617.

For some weeks Gibson strove hard for permission to fly on operations but met with a firm refusal. However, on the night of 19–20 September 1944, when the main Lancaster force of No. 5 Group was attacking a target involving only slight penetration into enemy-held territory, it was agreed that he should fly in a Mosquito and act as 'master bomber'. Gibson successfully directed the attack, wished the Lancaster force 'good-night' and turned for home in the normal manner. He did not reach base and it was subsequently learned that through some unknown cause his aircraft crashed in Holland. He was buried in the small cemetery at Steenbergen, Bergen-op-Zoom, Holland.

Thus ended a career which has few equals in the history of air warfare—a career of action, of which the mainspring was a wholly phenomenal faith. Given this faith, all things were possible, for if the devil ever temptingly suggested that a project was beyond him, he would unceremoniously order him where he belonged. In this attitude, there was nothing that was foolhardy, for every action which he took was planned in detail and he knew precisely what he would do in every emergency. Throughout, he had the loyal support of all who flew with him.

In 1940 Gibson married Evelyn Mary Moore; there were no children. A portrait by Cuthbert Orde hangs in the R.A.F. officers' mess at Scampton, Lincolnshire. A drawing by Sir William Rothenstein is reproduced in his *Men of the R.A.F.* (1942).

[Guy Gibson, *Enemy Coast Ahead*, 1946; Air Ministry records; private information; personal knowledge.]

RALPH A. COCHRANE.

GIBSON, SIR JOHN WATSON (1885–1947), contracting engineer, was born 9 August 1885 at Middlesbrough, the second son of Robert Elwin Gibson, accountant, and his wife, Ruth Eleanor Hugill. Educated at Middlesbrough High School, he began his career as a civil engineering contractor under (Sir) John Scott on the Middlesbrough dock contract and one of the Huddersfield corporation reservoirs; and later, for another contractor, he was in charge of the construction of reinforced-concrete jetties at Southampton and near Tralee in Ireland. He next joined the organization of Lord Cowdray [q.v.] on the construction of one of the Hull docks and a reservoir for the Metropolitan Water Board, subsequently going out to take charge of the huge project in the Sudan comprising the construction of the Sennar dam and some hundreds of miles of large irrigation canals.

During the war of 1914–18 Gibson was loaned to the Ministry of Munitions. He worked on the production of small arms and went in 1916 to the United States with a small party of British officials dealing with munitions. In 1917 he accompanied Sir Frederick William Black on a mission to India as his technical assistant, and in June of that year became director of aeronautical requirements and statistics. He was appointed O.B.E. for his services in 1918. At the close of hostilities he joined the firm of Lord Weir under whom he had been working, but shortly afterwards Cowdray secured his services once more and on the completion of the Sennar dam and irrigation works he was requested by the Sudan Government to carry out further schemes on his own. Commencing on these with a large excavation contract for the extension of the canalization, he was joined by his brother, Howard, and together over the next few years they constructed the Sennar dam aprons, some considerable canalization extensions in the Gezira, and the salt works at Port Sudan. His next important contract was for the construction of the 3⅛-mile-long Gebel Aulia dam for the Egyptian Government. To carry out this work the Gibsons linked up with the old-established firm of Pauling & Co., Ltd., forming Gibson and Pauling (Foreign), Ltd., of which Gibson was chairman. On the completion of this work he joined the board of Pauling & Co., Ltd.

During the war of 1939–45 Gibson was controller of building construction at the Ministry of Supply (1940–41) in which capacity he was responsible for the construction of royal ordnance factories. Subsequently he was engaged on the provision and layout of storage sites for colliery-produced coal and on initiating the open-cast coal workings. Shortly afterwards the Mulberry artificial harbours were planned for the invasion of Normandy, and he undertook the direction at headquarters of much of their construction. The work was carried out by many of the main contracting firms of this country with help from America. In recognition of this work Gibson was knighted in 1945.

After the war, in collaboration with the British Iron and Steel Federation, he formed a group of contractors who with their associates erected over 30,000 houses. His last task was in connexion with the ground-nuts scheme in Tanganyika, but almost immediately his fatal illness developed and he died in London 19 March 1947. One of Gibson's greatest gifts was an unfailing ability to get on with others and to encourage them to give of their best. He had a clear-thinking brain, and his capacity for hard work, combined with this ability always to see and evoke the best in his associates, largely contributed to the success which attended every stage of his career.

He married in 1911 Lily, daughter of John Armstrong, blacksmith, of Middlesbrough; there were two sons and three daughters of the marriage.

[Private information; personal knowledge.]
HOWARD GIBSON.
LEO D'ERLANGER.

GIRDLESTONE, GATHORNE ROBERT (1881–1950), orthopaedic surgeon, was born 8 October 1881 at Wycliffe Hall, Oxford, the only son of the principal, the Rev. Robert Baker Girdlestone, who became an honorary canon of Christ Church, by his second wife, Mary Matilda, daughter of John Wood, of Thedden Grange. He was the grandson of Charles Girdlestone [q.v.]. He was educated at Charterhouse and at New College, Oxford, where he obtained a second class in natural science (physiology) in 1904. He entered St. Thomas's Hospital as a university scholar and qualified in 1908. After holding resident appointments at St. Thomas's he settled in 1911 at Oswestry in Shropshire as a general practitioner-surgeon. He became attracted to (Sir) Robert Jones (whose notice he later contributed to this DICTIONARY) and his work at the orthopaedic hospital at Baschurch which had been founded by (Dame) Agnes Hunt [q.v.]. From being a spectator he became an assistant—and quickly grasped the significance of their endeavours to make the hospital the centre of a group of orthopaedic after-care clinics in the surrounding counties.

Between 1915 and 1919 Girdlestone

served in the Royal Army Medical Corps and was in charge of a military orthopaedic centre established at the Wingfield convalescent home in Headington, Oxford. When, in 1919, the hospital came under the Ministry of Pensions Girdlestone remained in charge of it. Later, beds were reserved for crippled children, and as the work for pensioners diminished so, in 1922, the Wingfield Orthopaedic Hospital emerged. After the war Robert Jones and Girdlestone embarked on their national campaign for the relief of cripples and in 1920 the Central Council for the Care of Cripples was formed. Together they worked out a plan on the Oswestry model to serve as a guide for developments elsewhere. Girdlestone's own scheme was based on the Wingfield and served Oxfordshire, Buckinghamshire, and Berkshire.

During the following decade Sir William Morris (subsequently Viscount Nuffield) became aware of Girdlestone's pioneer work and his ambition to rebuild the Wingfield. He provided the money and in 1933 the new Wingfield-Morris Orthopaedic Hospital was opened. (It was later renamed the Nuffield Orthopaedic Centre.) Girdlestone, now a close friend of Lord Nuffield, was also concerned in the negotiations which led up to his gift of £2 million to the university of Oxford for the establishment of professorial clinical departments. Again with Lord Nuffield's generous aid he established orthopaedic schemes for Northern Ireland and for the Union of South Africa which he visited in 1937. From 1937 to 1939 Girdlestone was professor of orthopaedic surgery in Oxford, the first to hold such a chair in this country; he was not, however, a scientist and was disturbed by the intrusion into medicine of experimental investigation.

The war called for an extension of the Wingfield, but as regional orthopaedic consultant in the Emergency Medical Service Girdlestone wisely persuaded the Ministry of Health to erect a separate hospital; its design, far better than that of the standard emergency hospital, was largely his own work. It was named the Churchill Hospital and, at Girdlestone's suggestion, was first occupied by an orthopaedic unit from the United States called the American Hospital in Britain. The hospital ultimately became a valuable part of the United Oxford Hospitals. Thus Girdlestone helped to give Oxford two of its three premier hospitals. In 1940 he became consulting orthopaedic surgeon to the Ministry of Pensions, honorary consultant to the army, and in 1942-3 president of the British Orthopaedic Association.

Girdlestone wrote with clarity and elegance; a number of his papers have an abiding value, so also has his book on *Tuberculosis of Bone and Joint* (1940). He was a handsome man; his portrait by Sir William Rothenstein, in the possession of the family, does him scant justice. Another by Frank Eastman is at the Nuffield Orthopaedic Centre. He gave and inspired great affection and his life was governed by deeply religious feelings. It was his passionate belief in the importance of his mission rather than cool statesmanship which accounted for the success of his enterprises and for his great influence. Essentially an autocrat, he was uncompromising and, in consequence, sometimes came into conflict with those whose ideas differed from his own.

He died in London 30 December 1950. In 1909 he married Ina Mabel (died 1956), daughter of George Chatterton, J.P., of Wimbledon, a consulting civil engineer; there were no children.

[*British Medical Journal* and *Lancet*, 13 January 1951; private information; personal knowledge.]          H. J. SEDDON.

GLOVER, TERROT REAVELEY (1869-1943), classical scholar and historian, was born at Bristol 23 July 1869, the eldest child and only son of the Rev. Richard Glover, Baptist minister, by his wife, Anna Finlay. Educated at Bristol Grammar School, he was admitted to St. John's College, Cambridge, as a scholar in 1888. In *Cambridge Retrospect* (1943), published just before his death, Glover recalled some characteristics of the teaching and the teachers, Leonard Whibley, (Sir) J. E. Sandys [qq.v.], William Emerton Heitland, and others, of his undergraduate years. After gaining the Browne medal twice, the Chancellor's medal, and the Porson prize as well as first classes in both parts of the classical tripos (1891, 1892), Glover was elected into a fellowship of his college in 1892. Four years later he left to become professor of Latin at Queen's University, Kingston, Ontario. In 1901 he returned to his own college as a teaching fellow; in 1911 he was appointed university lecturer in ancient history, and Cambridge was his home for the rest of his life.

Thus, on the face of it, Glover's life might seem to have been just that of a college don and in many of his writings he displays much of the humour and whimsicality which are commonly associated with donnishness. He was, for instance, an extremely facile writer of light verse; as an undergraduate he was a frequent contributor to the *Granta*, and in later years he produced a felicitous Latin version of Stevenson's *A Child's Garden of Verses* (1922). When he became orator of the university in 1920 he was able to display his epigrammatic ingenuity to full advantage: *Dat vitam vitaminando* was one of his phrases in presenting Sir Frederick Gowland Hopkins [q.v.] for an honorary degree. But, in fact, Glover was much more than an academic figure. 'I modestly claimed', he once wrote, 'to understand irrelevance', and in his university lectures, as elsewhere, he covered a wide range of digression. 'It's a poor subject', he said, 'that cannot be brought into an ancient history lecture.' Meanwhile a restless mind and a fluent pen quickly led him to authorship. His first substantial work was *Life and Letters in the Fourth Century* (1901); this was followed by *Studies in Virgil* (1904) and *The Conflict of Religions in the Early Roman Empire* (1909); and to the end of his life Glover was a prolific author of books and essays on classical themes. Among them were *Herodotus* (1924), *Democracy in the Ancient World* (1927), and *Greek Byways* (1932), and in all of them he showed first, an abiding faith in the value of a classical education; secondly, an intense delight in the byways as well as in the highways of literature; and thirdly, a rebellious protest against philology, textual criticism, and the stricter canons of classical scholarship. Indeed, he combined with his deep love of Cambridge a scornfully sceptical attitude towards the Cambridge tradition of accurate learning. His own books, he said, were too readable to win the approval of the purists. In dedicating *Greek Byways* to F. J. Foakes Jackson [q.v.] he wrote: 'I send you my *Byways*, to be sure of one reader who is not a candidate for a Tripos and who will realize that they were written for people bred like you and me on the Classics, and fond of them, and in no great hurry to do something else. What a world the others miss!' But Glover could not rest content with purely classical subjects. Puritan as he was by training and conviction, his literary taste was truly catholic. The romantics, the adventurers, the buccaneers made an immediate appeal to him;

he loved Horace as well as Virgil, Don Quixote as well as Bunyan, Erasmus as well as Luther; in his *Poets and Puritans* (1915) he contrived to include an essay on James Boswell.

Apart from his literary and academic work, Glover was a man of fervent religious activity. From his father he inherited a loyalty to the Baptist Church which never faltered and he became president of the Baptist Union in 1924. Furthermore, his influence as a preacher extended beyond his own denomination. He preached in the chapel of his own college from time to time and also in St. Edward's church, Cambridge. For him, the central point in the history of the ancient world was the life of Jesus Christ, and his aim both as historian and as Christian was 'to see the Founder of the Christian movement and some of his followers as they appeared among their contemporaries'. *The Jesus of History* (1917), which grew out of lectures delivered in various Indian cities in 1915–16, was the most popular exposition of this theme and made Glover's name known to thousands who had never heard of his classical studies.

Another vital characteristic of Glover was his restless passion for travel. His five years in Ontario imbued him with a deep love of Canada which he frequently revisited. This affection for the Dominion sprang in part, perhaps, from his Highland descent of which he was inordinately proud and Heitland once told him that he had taken to Canada 'as a duck to green peas'. Canada was for Glover a land of high romance and in *A Corner of Empire* (1937), written in collaboration with his friend D. D. Calvin, he demonstrated his vital interest in Canadian history. He crossed the Atlantic forty times; he preached and lectured in many American as well as Canadian universities, was Lowell lecturer at Boston in 1922 and Sather professor in classics in the university of California in 1923. Both at home and abroad other universities honoured him with degrees: he was LL.D. of Queen's (1910), McMaster (1917), and Glasgow (1930); D.D. of St. Andrews (1921); and Litt.D. of Trinity College, Dublin (1936). He was also president of the Classical Association in 1938. In his own university he twice held the office of proctor which brought him many adventures in theatres and public houses which were normally unfamiliar to him. He liked to recall that he had once fined

Prince Albert (afterwards King George VI) for smoking in academical dress; similarly, he was proud, as orator, to have presented for degrees six prime ministers, two kings, and one god (the Crown Prince of Japan). He retired in 1939, becoming orator emeritus, and died at Cambridge 26 May 1943.

In 1897 Glover married Alice, second daughter of Harry Gleaves Few, corn merchant, of Cambridge, and had two sons and four daughters. A portrait of Glover by H. Wilkinson belongs to his family; another by Mrs. Lipscomb hangs in Christ's College Lodge.

[T. R. Glover, *Cambridge Retrospect*, 1943; *Times Literary Supplement*, 13 October 1945; H. G. Wood, *Terrot Reaveley Glover*, 1953; personal knowledge.]                S. C. ROBERTS.

GLYN, ELINOR (1864–1943), novelist, was born in Jersey 17 October 1864, the younger daughter of Douglas Sutherland, a Scottish civil engineer, and his wife, Elinor, daughter of Thomas Saunders (the son of an English father and an aristocratic French mother) who had emigrated to Ontario with his Irish wife. Three months after the birth of his second child Douglas Sutherland died, his ambition to prove himself heir to the seventh Lord Duffus unfulfilled. The young widow returned to Canada where for some years the children were trained by their grandmother in a code of manners modelled on the French aristocracy of the eighteenth century. Elinor never forgot these lessons on the duties and privileges, and the self-discipline required, of those born to high estate. In 1871 Mrs. Sutherland married David Kennedy, an elderly and parsimonious Scot who tyrannized over her but failed to subdue his stepchildren who heartily disliked him. Returning to Europe the family settled in St. Helier where a succession of governesses abandoned the attempt to instruct two rebellious and lonely little girls. Elinor, however, became bilingual in French, read voraciously and precociously in a large library, and lived in a dream-world of her own. Kingsley's *The Heroes* became and remained her favourite work. In later years she profited by her friendships with men such as Lord Curzon, Lord Milner, and F. H. Bradley [qq.v.] to fill in some of the gaps in her education. Orthodox Christianity she rejected at an early age, but it was not until later in life that she came increasingly to believe in reincarnation.

Red-headed and green-eyed, Elinor had been brought up to believe that she was ugly, but her first essays into society in Paris and in England soon made her aware that this was untrue. There were some extravagant scenes: four rivals for her attentions at a house party in mid-winter threw each other into the lake and then bathed in champagne to ward off chills. Marriage, however, was long delayed by reason of the conflict between her innate romanticism and a streak of practicality and even cynicism traceable to her French ancestry: she sought romance, but there must be money too. In the event, her marriage to Clayton Glyn (died 1915), a personable landowner, into which she entered with high hopes in 1892, brought neither. Her husband's affection waned as he became reimmersed in country interests which Elinor did not share; and he was profoundly disappointed that she bore him two daughters but no son. Nevertheless, marriage gave her an assured position in society and her life with its round of country-house parties interspersed with foreign travel was not unhappy.

That she was a detached and acute observer of her milieu was revealed when during a period of convalescence she embarked on her first book. *The Visits of Elizabeth*, the letters of a young girl to her mother, ingenuously exposing the foibles and philandering of society, was first serialized in the *World*, and then published in book form in 1900. Its success encouraged her to write several more 'society' novels before turning to a passionate romanticism in which her heroines were haughty, her heroes masterful, her settings luxurious, and her plots improbable. Judged by later standards her novels are only rescued from absurdity by her genuine ability to tell a story. In her own time they were much admired. *Three Weeks* (1907), an extra-marital interlude between a Balkan queen and an Englishman, ending in death for the one and regeneration for the other, created something of a sensation, being widely condemned and still more widely read. Curzon and Milner both presented her with a tiger skin, a much-publicized feature of the story. For Milner, with whom she discussed the Greek philosophers, she had no more than 'a gentle admiration'; but there was a mutual attraction between herself and Curzon. He was for her the great romantic figure, 'the sun, moon and stars to the end of time'; the announcement of his engagement in 1916 without a word to her before or afterwards was a bitter blow.

It was not the first which she had faced with courage: in 1908 Clayton Glyn had revealed that for years he had been living on capital and was now deeply in debt. Henceforth Elinor Glyn wrote of necessity, and many of her novels were designed merely to entertain her wide public in England and America. The winter of 1909–10 was spent by invitation at the court of St. Petersburg which provided a brilliant and well-observed background for *His Hour* (1910), one of her ablest romances. Of her more serious character studies may be mentioned *Halcyone* (1912), with its recognizable portraits of Bradley and Curzon, *The Career of Katherine Bush* (1917), in which her heroine for once was not well-born, *Man and Maid* (1922), and *It* (1927). The last, a short novel in an American setting, made the word 'It' for many years synonymous with personal magnetism. A new career as a script writer began in 1920 in Hollywood where a number of her own novels were filmed, including *Three Weeks* and *It*. Her personal success in America would have been more rewarding had she not been totally incapable of managing her finances. In 1929 she returned to England and after an unsuccessful attempt at film production resumed her novels. Her autobiography, *Romantic Adventure*, appeared in 1936. She was by now a legendary figure, thriving on admiration, and almost to the end she remained beautiful and vital. 'I am enjoying it all', she wrote from London at the height of the air raids. She died there 23 September 1943.

A portrait by P. A. de László belongs to her younger daughter, Lady Rhys-Williams; another by Henrietta Cotton to her elder daughter, Lady Davson. A portrait by J.-E. Blanche and a sketch by P. A. de László were destroyed by enemy action during the war of 1939–45 and exist only in reproduction.

[Elinor Glyn, *Romantic Adventure*, 1936; Anthony Glyn, *Elinor Glyn*, 1955; private information.]     HELEN M. PALMER.

GOODE, SIR WILLIAM ATHEL-STANE MEREDITH (1875–1944), journalist and financial adviser, was born at Channel in Newfoundland 10 June 1875, the younger son of the Rev. Thomas Allmond Goode, a missionary of the Society for the Propagation of the Gospel, by his wife, Jane Harriet, daughter of the

Rev. Richard Meredith, for many years vicar of Hagbourne, Berkshire. He was educated at Doncaster Grammar School and at Foyle College, Londonderry, Ireland. At an early age he showed a taste for adventure by going to sea in 1889 and enlisting in the United States cavalry in 1892. After discharge, he took up journalism, and attaching himself to the Associated Press of America was their representative on board Admiral Sampson's flagship throughout the Spanish–American war, of which he wrote an account (*With Sampson through the War*, 1899). From 1898 to 1904 he was their special correspondent in London, but in the latter year he joined the *Standard* as managing editor until 1910, and in 1911 he became joint news editor of the *Daily Mail*. The lucid and forceful style of writing which he acquired during these years were to stand him in good stead in his more public life.

Goode's first introduction to public affairs was in 1913–14, when he acted as honorary secretary of the British committee for the Panama Pacific Exposition. During the war of 1914–18 he was honorary secretary and organizer of the national committee for relief in Belgium (1915), member of the Newfoundland and West Indian military contingents committees (1916), and from 1917 to 1919 director of the cables department of the Ministry of Food and its liaison officer with the United States and Canadian food administrations. In 1919 he became British director of relief missions, serving as a member of the British delegation at the peace conference, and of the Supreme Economic Council from 1919 to 1920. Goode came into prominence through his classic report on economic conditions in Central Europe (presented to Parliament as Cmd. 521, 1920) which gave a vivid account both of the work accomplished by the relief missions and of their short-comings. He was next appointed British delegate and president of the Austrian section of the Reparation Commission, and so reached a position of dignity and authority. But within a few weeks he was convinced that the reparation clauses were unworkable, and in November 1920 he reported that so far from being able to collect reparations from Austria, the allied Governments would have to organize and finance a comprehensive programme of reconstruction, which he outlined. Although his report was endorsed by the Austrian section, it was most unpalatable to the allied Governments, which rejected it. But the facts could not be belied and in March 1921 they agreed to postpone their claims for reparation, whereupon Goode arranged for the Austrian section to be dissolved. The Austrian Government invited Goode to remain as financial adviser, but the financial committee of the League of Nations, which was now preparing plans for Austrian reconstruction, discouraged this proposal. The League protocols, however, which were signed in October 1922, followed in all essentials Goode's original recommendations.

Unable to serve Austria, Goode turned to Hungary and became its unofficial financial adviser and acted as its financial agent in London until after the outbreak of war in 1939. He then joined the new Ministry of Food as chief security officer and director of communications, which he organized both at home and abroad so as to secure secrecy and smooth working between the various departments of the Ministry. His arrangements were successful and endured until the end of the war. He returned, despite ill health, to his old task of organizing relief and became chairman of the Council of British Societies for Relief Abroad in 1942. In 1944 he underwent a severe operation which gave him temporary recovery but he died in London 14 December of that year.

Goode was a versatile man whose complex character was compounded of courage, imagination, tact, shrewdness, buoyancy of temperament and wit, all of which contributed to his success. He never professed much technical knowledge, but his social gifts not only earned him countless friends but gave him access to sources from which he could obtain the best advice possible. His sound administrative sense, coupled with diplomatic skill and judicious use of publicity, enabled him in his international work to get difficulties settled and constructive action taken with the minimum friction. Into the organization of relief he threw himself wholeheartedly and disinterestedly. He was appointed K.B.E. in 1918, and was a commander of the Order of the Crown of Belgium and of that of Isabella the Catholic.

Goode married in 1899 Cecilia (died 1938), daughter of Dr. Charles Augustus Sippi, of London, Ontario, and had a daughter. A portrait of Goode by Augustus John is in the possession of the artist.

[Sisley Huddleston, Those Europeans, 1924; private information; personal knowledge.]
F. W. LEITH-ROSS.

GOODENOUGH, SIR WILLIAM EDMUND (1867–1945), admiral, was born 2 June 1867 in lodgings on the Hard, Portsmouth, the second son of Captain James Graham Goodenough [q.v.] who became commodore and senior officer of the Australia station and was killed by natives in the island of Santa Cruz in 1875. His mother was Victoria Henrietta, whose brother became tenth Baron Belhaven and Stenton and whose father was William John Hamilton [q.v.]. F. C. Goodenough [q.v.] was a first cousin. Goodenough went to the Britannia as a naval cadet in January 1880, and in December 1881 joined the Northampton on the North America and West Indies station, being promoted midshipman in October 1882. He remained in her for over four years, and then joined the Calypso (training squadron). After promotion to sub-lieutenant in October 1886 he went to the Excellent gunnery school for the usual examinations.

From March 1888 to May 1889 he served in the Raleigh, Cape of Good Hope station, with a short period as acting lieutenant in the Brisk. He was then sent home to take up appointment as sub-lieutenant in the Victoria and Albert which brought him promotion to lieutenant in August 1889. Of his eleven years as lieutenant, three were spent in the Trafalgar and three in the Surprise (commander-in-chief's yacht), both in the Mediterranean, and over two in the Hermione, China station. His ship being in south China waters, he had no opportunity of active service during the Boxer rising. In June 1900 he was promoted commander and returned home.

After a few weeks on half-pay, he was appointed commander in the Resolution, Channel Fleet. In October 1901 her whole crew was turned over to the newly built Formidable which was commissioned at Portsmouth for duty on the Mediterranean station. There he remained for three years and was promoted captain 1 January 1905.

The new scheme of naval education promulgated by Lord Selborne [q.v.] at Christmas 1902 reduced the age of entry of cadets from 14½–15½ to 12–13, and required a period of four years' training on shore. A new college was built at Osborne in the grounds of Queen Victoria's residence and opened in September 1903 with R. E. Wemyss (later Lord Wester Wemyss, q.v.) as captain and (Sir) Cyril Ashford as headmaster and a joint staff of naval officers and civilian masters. By 1904 Osborne was full and so the new college at Dartmouth, built by Sir Aston Webb to replace the old *Britannia* training ship, was used to complete the second half of the new cadets' training. Ashford and some of his staff were then transferred to Dartmouth and Goodenough was selected to be captain of the new college; after spending six weeks at Osborne to learn the work he took up the appointment at Dartmouth in May 1905. Wemyss and Ashford had established a happy concordat at Osborne, and Goodenough took a little time to accommodate himself to the novel situation. But experience and goodwill soon resolved any chance of friction. He remained at Dartmouth until August 1907 when he joined the *Albemarle* as flag captain to Sir John (later Earl) Jellicoe [q.v.] in the Atlantic Fleet for a year and then went to the *Duncan* as flag captain to Sir George Callaghan [q.v.], second-in-command of the Mediterranean Fleet, until August 1910.

After short periods in command of the *Cochrane*, in which he escorted King George V to the Indian durbar, and was appointed M.V.O., and of the *Colossus*, second battle squadron of the Grand Fleet, in July 1913 he was appointed to the *Southampton* as commodore second class of the first light cruiser squadron. After a year's strenuous training his squadron was ready when war broke out.

In the action in the Heligoland Bight of 28 August 1914, Goodenough with six light cruisers under him took a large part in the fighting including sinking the light cruiser *Mainz* which had previously been in action with our battle cruisers. He was next in action during the German raid on Scarborough in December 1914, when in low visibility he got to within 3,000 yards of a German light cruiser and opened fire, at the same time informing Sir David (later Earl) Beatty [q.v.]. A persistent order from Beatty to recall light cruisers (intended only for the *Nottingham* which he required for look-out duties on his other bow, but made in error also to the *Birmingham* and *Southampton*) caused Goodenough reluctantly to abandon his contact. The enemy profited by the misunderstanding and vanished in the mist. Things went somewhat better six weeks later, when in attempting a similar undertaking the German battle cruisers were caught off the Dogger Bank, 24 January 1915, and only escaped at the cost of severe damage and the loss of the *Blücher*. In the following May, on the advent of

some new light cruisers to the Grand Fleet, Goodenough's squadron was renamed the second light cruiser squadron. In command of it and with his broad pennant still in the *Southampton*, he took part in the battle of Jutland, and was commended in dispatches for his tenacity in maintaining touch with and reporting the movements of enemy heavy ships. It was from the *Southampton* that the presence of the German battle fleet, coming up to support action begun an hour earlier, was first reported to Jellicoe and Beatty. The squadron became heavily engaged in a night action with German light forces, in the course of which the *Southampton* sustained very heavy damage and casualties but sank the German light cruiser *Frauenlob*.

He was promoted to flag rank soon after Jutland, appointed C.B. in 1916, and in December of that year transferred to the *Orion* as rear-admiral of the second battle squadron until the end of the war. Promoted K.C.B. at the new year, 1919, in May he became admiral superintendent of Chatham dockyard, and a year later was made commander-in-chief, Africa station, being promoted to vice-admiral in July 1920.

In August 1922 he returned home and enjoyed twelve months' half-pay for the first time in his life. Then after a short period in command of the Reserve Fleet, in March 1924 he was appointed commander-in-chief at the Nore for a term of three years, being promoted admiral in May 1925. For seven months before his retirement in May 1930 he served as first and principal naval aide-de-camp to the King, being advanced to G.C.B. at the new year.

For his war service he had been awarded the Order of St. Vladimir, third class with swords, the Order of the Rising Sun of Japan, second class, and the French croix de guerre (bronze palm). After retirement he revived the great interest he had taken in the Royal Geographical Society and was its president (1930–33). His maternal grandfather had several times been president and his great-grandfather, William Richard Hamilton [q.v.] was one of the founders. He was also chairman of the British Sailors' Society on whose behalf he addressed letters to *The Times*, urging the need for improving the conditions of the Merchant Service, and he represented the corporation of London on the Port of London Authority.

Goodenough was throughout his career

a highly competent and distinguished seaman who always received devoted service from both officers and men in his ship. His appointment as commodore of a light cruiser squadron at a time when the duties of these vessels were entering a new phase, gave him his opportunity. He fully appreciated the role that would be his in war and took pains to train his captains to read his mind and know what he would do in a variety of circumstances and so be ready to act without instructions. He had thus the complete confidence of his officers and men, and in battle his handling of his squadron was faultless.

In his later years his zeal for the Service led him to criticize the administration of the Admiralty, of which he had, however, no personal experience. But when in 1925, on the death of the second sea lord, Sir Michael Culme-Seymour, he was invited by W. C. (later Viscount) Bridgeman to take his place on the Board, Goodenough declined the offer, the acceptance of which would have given him the opportunity of redressing the faults in the matter of personnel of which he had complained.

Goodenough married in 1901 Henrietta Margaret (died 1956), daughter of Edward Lyulph Stanley [q.v.] who became fourth Baron Sheffield and fourth Baron Stanley of Alderley. There were two daughters of the marriage. His portrait is included in Sir A. S. Cope's group 'Some Sea Officers of the War of 1914–18' in the National Portrait Gallery. A drawing by Francis Dodd is in the Imperial War Museum, and one by P. A. de László belongs to the family. Goodenough published *A Rough Record*, a volume of reminiscences, in 1943. He died at his home, Parson's Pightle, Coulsdon, 30 January 1945.

[Admiralty records; private information; personal knowledge.]

VINCENT W. BADDELEY.

GOODRICH, EDWIN STEPHEN (1868–1946), zoologist, was born 21 June 1868 at Weston-super-Mare, the youngest of the three children of the Rev. Octavius Pitt Goodrich, rector of Humber, Herefordshire, by his wife, Frances Lucinda Parker. His father who, like Thomas Goodrich, bishop of Ely, and John Goodricke, the astronomer [qq.v.], was descended from Edward Goodrich of West Kirby, died when he was two weeks old, and his mother took the family to live with her mother at Pau. Goodrich went to a French school and to a local English

one, and his experiences of early childhood at a time when France suffered the Prussian invasion were responsible for his deep affection for France and aversion from Germany in after life. In 1888 Goodrich was entered as a student of the Slade School of Fine Art where he came into contact with (Sir) E. R. Lankester [q.v.], then professor of zoology, and switched his studies towards zoology with a view to entering the British Museum (Natural History). But in 1891 Lankester was appointed to the Linacre chair of comparative anatomy at Oxford and he offered Goodrich a post as his assistant. Goodrich accepted, and entered Merton College as a commoner in 1892. While much of his time was taken up with demonstrating and teaching, Goodrich was responsible for reorganizing the exhibition cases of the University Museum; but his major activities were bound up in the researches which he had already started. In 1894 he was awarded the Rolleston memorial prize, and in the following year he obtained a first class in the final honour school of natural science (morphology). Also in 1895 he was awarded the Naples biological scholarship and spent some time researching at the Stazione Zoologica. In 1898 he obtained the Radcliffe travelling fellowship, with the help of which he visited India and Ceylon to study their marine fauna. In the same year he succeeded William Blaxland Benham as Aldrichian demonstrator in comparative anatomy, and in 1900 he was elected a fellow of Merton.

In 1921 Goodrich succeeded G. C. Bourne [q.v.] as Linacre professor of zoology and comparative anatomy at Oxford, a chair associated with Merton College, from which Goodrich was therefore never parted throughout his long career at Oxford. He resigned from the chair in 1945, within a few months of his death, and was elected an honorary fellow.

Goodrich's first paper was published in 1892, and in the dozen years which followed his researches raised him to a position of such eminence that in 1905, at the age of thirty-six, he was elected F.R.S. For over half a century he worked without intermission on nearly all the groups of the animal kingdom, in every case making contributions to knowledge of the first importance. To obtain his material he went all over the world; in addition to the zoological stations at Plymouth and at Naples, he visited Tatihou, Roscoff, and Banyuls in France, Munich and

Heligoland, the United States, Canada, Bermuda, Ceylon, Malaya, Java, Madeira, the Canary Isles, Morocco, Tunisia, the Balearic Islands, and Egypt.

One of his first and greatest contributions to knowledge was the demonstration of the difference between the nephridium or primitive kidney and the coelomoduct or primitive reproductive duct. These two sets of ducts had been confused and wrongly described. Basing himself on the view that they were originally distinct and separate, Goodrich proceeded to show that they could be recognized and distinguished from each other in all the groups of the animal kingdom, and thereby he produced order out of a chaos from which no textbook before his day was free.

It was characteristic of Goodrich's researches that he started from the hypothesis that, however complex a problem might appear, its solution must rest on a simple basis, and he planned his researches in consequence. With a remarkable flair for the facts of significance, he was able to unravel such tangles as the segmental structure of the head, both in invertebrates and in vertebrates. He enabled a sound classification of fishes to be built on his recognition of the true nature of the differences between the various types of fish-scales. He analysed the evidence on which Gegenbaur had produced his theory that the limb-girdles of vertebrates were of the same nature as the gill-arches, and he showed that it was completely untenable. On the other hand, in his study of the evolutionary history of the ossicles of the mammalian ear, he found irrefutable new evidence to prove that Reichert's theory of their derivation from the jaws and hyoid arches of lower vertebrates was perfectly correct.

While the major part of Goodrich's publications consisted of the papers, beautifully illustrated by himself, in which he described the results of his researches, he also wrote a number of books which have had a vast influence on the teaching of zoology in all countries. But they, too, really fall under the category of research, because he undertook personal investigations of all the more important points on which there had been uncertainty. This applies particularly to his textbook on *Cyclostomes and Fishes* (1909) and to his *Studies on the Structure and Development of Vertebrates* (1930). At the same time he never lost sight of the subject of zoology as a whole, and his book, *Living Organisms: An Account of Their Origin and Evolution* (1924), is a masterpiece of critical analysis and careful exposition.

The effect of his teaching, both in the class-room and in the research laboratory, has been widespread, and has resulted in the recognition that detailed studies in the comparative anatomy of related animals are capable of giving results of great importance from the point of view of general principles, such as evolution and homology, and in the field of taxonomy, embryology, and neurology.

Goodrich's early leanings towards art never deserted him and may even be said to have formed part of his training in research and in teaching. His studies of landscapes in water-colours were frequently exhibited by him in London.

He received a Royal medal of the Royal Society in 1936, and he was vice-president in 1930–31 ; he was awarded the gold medal of the Linnean Society in 1932. He was an honorary or foreign member of the New York Academy of Sciences, the Academy of Sciences of the U.S.S.R., the Royal Swedish Academy of Sciences, the Académie Royale de Belgique, and the Société de Biologie de Paris.

In 1913 Goodrich married Helen Lucia Mary, the protozoologist, daughter of the Rev. Charles Henry Vincent Pixell, vicar of St. Faith's, Stoke Newington, London. She collaborated with him in some of his researches, and assisted him with teaching. There were no children. Goodrich died in Oxford 6 January 1946.

[*Quarterly Journal of Microscopical Science*, No. 348, vol. lxxxvii, 1946; G. R. de Beer in *Obituary Notices of Fellows of the Royal Society*, No. 15, May 1947; private information; personal knowledge.]

G. R. DE BEER.

GORDON, GEORGE STUART (1881–1942), president of Magdalen College, Oxford, and professor of poetry, was born 1 February 1881 at Falkirk, of an Aberdeenshire family. He was the eldest son and second child of William Gordon by his wife, Mary, daughter of Andrew Napier, farmer, of Netherley, Kincardineshire. His father was procurator fiscal of Falkirk. As a boy Gordon was short-sighted, and this prevented the due enjoyment of outdoor life. Later he learned to ride and to play golf; but his enjoyment of scenery was always limited, his ignorance of the commonest plants a joke. He was a precocious child and an omnivorous reader, acquiring early the habit, which he never quite cured, of reading to the end regardless of the clock. At Glasgow University he took honours in classics, and became a favourite pupil of J. S. Phillimore and of (Sir) Walter Raleigh [qq.v.], then professors of Greek and English literature. In 1902 he won a Bible-clerkship at Oriel College, Oxford, where he took firsts in classical moderations (1904) and *literae humaniores* (1906), and won the Stanhope prize in 1905 with an essay on the Fronde. His contemporaries at Oriel included Mr. Wilfrid Guild (subsequently Lord) Normand (who became lord justice-general of Scotland and later a lord of appeal in ordinary) and (Dr.) R. W. Chapman, later secretary of the Clarendon Press. Gordon and Normand spent a year together in Paris studying modern history and politics.

In 1907 Magdalen College, of which Raleigh was a fellow, offered a prize fellowship in English literature, and Gordon was elected, although it was obvious that he was only an amateur of that study. This determined the directions of his studies, and in 1913 he became professor at Leeds. He there became a member of the Officers' Training Corps, and so was ready for a commission in a Yorkshire regiment when war broke out. He became a competent officer, serving in France, where he was wounded, and reaching the rank of captain.

At Oxford Gordon had done work for the Clarendon Press, notably editions for schools of some of Shakespeare's plays. These had less success than their sound judgement, enlivened by wit, was seen by Shakespearian scholars to deserve. His other main literary activity was in the service of the *Times Literary Supplement*. His front-page articles were remarked and remembered by many to whom the writer was unknown. They were the chief ground of his election in 1922 to succeed Raleigh as Merton professor of English literature at Oxford.

Gordon presided over the English school, and maintained a high standard of both learning and elegance, until in 1928 he was elected president of Magdalen College. Nature had intended him for a scholar and writer, and it was by sheer force of character that he became an efficient administrator. The habit of punctuality in the dispatch of business came to him by painful self-discipline. He was never content to do anything unless he did it as well as he could do it. A memorandum, a speech, a lecture, he learned to produce on time, but with far

more labour than most men of his nimble intelligence would have found necessary.

Literature did not profit by this austerity. He continued indeed to write, and in 1933 allowed himself to become professor of poetry. His writing, if it lost some of the *bravura* of his earlier style, gained in weight and suppleness. But where he could be fastidious, he would. It was hard to persuade him that even a lecture was fit to be printed; if he parted with the manuscript, he clung to the proof. Of anything much more than a lecture his friends learned to despair. The sum of his occasional publications is none the less substantial, and they are some index of the range of his knowledge and the scope of his thinking. They show his intimacy with English literature of all ages, with a core of classical learning and a peripheral acquaintance with European letters both medieval and modern. The strength of his writing, apart from its technical accomplishment and a style both nervous and graceful, arose from that sympathy with all sorts and conditions of men which alone made the tasks of administration tolerable. In letters as in life he was a liberal conservative: rooted in tradition, political and moral, yet prepared to face the facts of innovation, as they confronted him in his children, his pupils, and his younger colleagues, in a catholic and tolerant spirit. He had a foot in both camps, for he was never a diehard. He was able, when over fifty, to see where the young poets were aiming, and even that they had in some sense got there. He was brought up as a Presbyterian, but lost touch with that community, and ultimately became a member of the Church of England.

Gordon was vice-chancellor in 1938-41 and fulfilled the ceremonial duties of the office with conspicuous dignity. At the close of an arduous and successful term the university—*auctore ipso Cancellario*—gave him its highest honour, the degree of D.C.L. He received many other honours: he was honorary LL.D. of his old university of Glasgow (1930) and D.Litt. of Leeds (1937), a fellow of Eton (1934), an honorary fellow of Merton and Oriel colleges, and a member of that augustly anonymous sodality 'the' Club. He had a host of friends in many walks of life.

Gordon married in 1909 Mary Campbell, daughter of John Wilson Biggar, schoolmaster, of Polmont, a lady who had early shared his interests and tastes and who survived him. They had three sons and one daughter. After his death in Oxford 12 March 1942, following a short illness, his widow and his friends did their best with manuscripts which, often revised, were not ready for publication. *Anglo-American Literary Relations* appeared in 1942, *Shakespearian Comedy* (pulled together by the master-hand of Sir Edmund Kerchever Chambers) in 1944. 'M.C.G.' published in 1943 a selection from his letters, and in 1945 a short *Life*. Not the least engaging of his books is *Lives of Authors* (1950).

A portrait of Gordon by (Sir) William Coldstream is at Magdalen College; a drawing by Christopher Ellis is in the possession of the family.

[*The Times*, 13 and 16 March 1942; private information; personal knowledge.]

R. W. Chapman.

GORT, sixth Viscount (1886–1946), field-marshal. [See Vereker, John Standish Surtees Prendergast.]

GOSSAGE, Sir (ERNEST) LESLIE (1891–1949), air marshal, was born 3 February 1891 at Toxteth Park, Liverpool, the elder son of Ernest Frederick Gossage, soap manufacturer, and his wife, Emily Lewis Jackson. He was educated at Rugby and at Trinity College, Cambridge, where he took his B.A. in 1912, and was then commissioned in the Royal Artillery. In 1914 he went to France with his battery with which he was in action at Mons, the Marne, the Aisne, and in the first battle of Ypres. At this time volunteers to join the Royal Flying Corps were called for and Gossage was accepted for training. He qualified for his wings in March 1915 and subsequently saw over three years' service with the Corps in France, an unusually long period, during which he was four times mentioned in dispatches, received the M.C. (1916) and was appointed to the D.S.O. (1919). In 1919 he transferred to the Royal Air Force as a squadron leader.

Gossage's clear and analytical brain predestined him for a career on the staff and in the following years he held a number of appointments, at the Army Staff College, at the Air Ministry, and at command headquarters. He specialized at first in army co-operation duties, but in 1930 he carried out a tour as air attaché in Berlin. Here his kindly manner and ready sympathy stood him in good stead. Further posts abroad followed: Iraq as a senior staff officer, and Aden as A.O.C. In 1936 he was posted to the newly formed No. 11 (Fighter) Group which was to bear the full brunt of withstanding German bomber raids in 1940. In February of that year, however, he was appointed inspector-general and saw others benefit from the good work he had put into training his group to such a high pitch of efficiency. Two months later he was made the member of the Air Council in charge of personnel; a few months later he was appointed A.O.C., Balloon Command, a position of great importance which he held until 1944. In February of that year he was put in charge of the Air Training Corps, a post in which his personal charm and high organizing ability had full scope. In 1946 he retired and his premature death at Abbotswood, Buxted, 8 July 1949, was a profound loss to his many friends.

In 1917 he married Eileen Gladys, daughter of Brigadier-General Edmund Donough John O'Brien, of Buxted, Sussex, and had two sons, one of whom was killed on active service. Gossage was appointed C.B. and C.V.O. in 1937 and advanced to K.C.B. in 1941. A crayon drawing by Henry Lamb is in the Imperial War Museum.

[*The Times*, 9 July 1949; personal knowledge.]

P. B. Joubert.

GOTCH, JOHN ALFRED (1852–1942), architect and author, was born at Kettering 28 September 1852, the third son of Thomas Henry Gotch by his wife, Mary Anne, daughter of John Gale. For more than 150 years the Gotch family was intimately associated with the town of his birth. His great-grandfather, Thomas Gotch, was the first to open in Kettering, about 1786, a factory for the manufacture of boots and shoes which in time became the town's staple trade. Gotch went to Kettering Grammar School and later studied at the university of Zürich and at King's College, London. He was articled in to Robert Winter Johnson, architect and surveyor, of Melton Mowbray, and on Johnson's death his practice at Kettering was taken over by Alfred Gotch and Charles Saunders; their partnership endured for fifty-five years. The buildings for which they were responsible included Corby House, Clopton Manor House, Thornby Grange, Quenby Hall, The Gables (Peterborough), the Irthlingborough viaduct over the Nene valley, the Alfred East Art Gallery and the grammar school at Kettering. They built a number of branch buildings for the Midland Bank and the firm was associated with Sir Edwin

Lutyens [q.v.] in building the head office in Poultry. They also designed secondary and elementary schools at Kettering and in Northamptonshire and Bedfordshire, as well as many war memorials for Kettering and the county. In 1882 Gotch became surveyor to the Kettering urban district council.

Gotch was not only a successful practising architect, but also one of the prominent names of his time as an architectural historian. He was a tireless student and voluminous writer and several of his works, based on years of patient research, remain standard authorities for the period which particularly interested him. These include *The Buildings of Sir Thomas Tresham* (1883), *Kirby Hall* and *Haddon Hall* (1889), *Architecture of the Renaissance in England* (2 vols., 1891), *Early Renaissance Architecture in England* (1901), *The Growth of the English House* (1909), *The Original Drawings for the Palace at Whitehall* (1912), *The English Home from Charles I to George IV* (1918), *Old English Houses* (1925), *Inigo Jones* (1928), *The Old Halls and Manor-Houses of Northamptonshire* (1936), *Squires' Homes and other Old Buildings of Northamptonshire* (1939), together with a vast number of papers and lectures on kindred subjects. So thoroughly has Gotch covered the whole field that it is unlikely that his work will be rivalled or outdated by any other scholar.

All Gotch's writings bear the imprint of his character which was one of extreme simplicity and solidity. He had no affectations of any sort. He was direct, almost blunt, in speech, courteous in manner, and with a dignity which was quite unforced. He had a keen though quiet sense of humour and a perfectly balanced temper. As an architect he belonged to a generation and school of thought which had quite passed away by the time of his death. His knowledge of and admiration for the work of the periods to which he devoted his life were so deeply engrained that he had no sympathy with any modern trends in design. He made no attempt to understand them and was content to go on working in the styles which he had admired all through life. He was almost happier in faithful restoration of old buildings than in designing new ones, although to the latter he gave the best of his knowledge and skill. He loved the building crafts of old days and if he could reproduce some of their fine qualities he was entirely satisfied.

Many professional distinctions came to him. In 1886–7 he was president of the Architectural Association of London and for nearly forty years he was a member of the council of the Royal Institute of British Architects of which, in 1923–5, he was the first architect from outside London to serve as president. He received the honorary degree of M.A. from the university of Oxford in 1924 and in 1934 he edited the Institute's centenary history. He was a member for some years of the Royal Fine Art Commission, an honorary corresponding member of the American Institute of Architects, and he was the first president of the Northamptonshire Association of Architects.

For many years Gotch was the leading citizen of Northamptonshire. He was a member of the county council, served as chairman of the Kettering bench as far back as 1893, was chairman of the Northamptonshire quarter-sessions, of the records committee, and of the Kettering Liberal Association. He was president of Northamptonshire Men in London and in 1938 he was elected the first charter mayor of the borough of Kettering after its incorporation. After his death at Weekley Rise, near Kettering, 17 January 1942, the *Kettering Leader and Guardian* wrote that 'with his death passes the last of the distinguished Gotch family who have left an indelible mark not only upon every phase of life in their native town but throughout the county and far beyond'.

Gotch married in 1886 Annie (died 1924), daughter of John Maddock Perry, lace manufacturer, of Nottingham. He had one son, who was killed in action in 1916, and one daughter. His portrait as president of the Royal Institute of British Architects was painted by his brother, T. C. Gotch, and hangs in the Institute buildings, 66 Portland Place, London.

[*Journal* of the Royal Institute of British Architects, February 1942; *Architect*, 30 January 1942; *Builder*, 23 January 1942; private information.]    IAN MACALISTER.

GOTT, WILLIAM HENRY EWART (1897–1942), lieutenant-general, born at Scarborough 13 August 1897, was the elder son of William Henry Gott, of Armley House, Leeds, by his wife, Anne Rosamond (Rosa), third daughter of the Rev. William Collins, of Knaresborough. A direct ancestor, Benjamin Gott (mayor of Leeds, 1799), was one of the founders of the modern Yorkshire woollen industry, whose son William married a sister of

William Ewart, the Liberal politician [q.v.]. Other kinsmen of Gott's were John Gott [q.v.], vicar of Leeds and later bishop of Truro, and A. J. Ewart [q.v.].

Gott was educated at Harrow and the Royal Military College, Sandhurst. In 1915 he was gazetted to a commission in the King's Royal Rifle Corps, and was soon nicknamed 'Strafer' after the German execration. He served with the 2nd battalion in France, where he was wounded in the action at Nieuport in July 1917, which later won him the M.C. At the time, however, he was captured by the enemy, while awaiting evacuation at the field dressing-station, and remained a prisoner until the end of the war, despite several attempts at escape, in one of which he got as far as the Dutch frontier. After the war much of his service was spent in India, but he was adjutant of the 13th London Regiment, Territorial Army, from 1925 to 1928, an appointment he found very congenial, and later he entered the Staff College, from which he graduated in 1931. From 1934 to 1938 he held various staff appointments in India as a major, and after a brief period as second-in-command of the 2nd battalion, King's Royal Rifle Corps, in 1938 he was appointed to command the 1st battalion, which had just arrived in Egypt from Burma.

Gott told his officers that the battalion must now prepare for war, and with great energy supervised its transformation from an infantry into a motor battalion, as part of the newly formed armoured division in Egypt. He learnt, and trained his men, to know the desert exceptionally well, a knowledge which proved invaluable when war came. He became G.S.O. 1 of the 7th Armoured division, and just before Italy entered the war was made commander of the support group, comprising the artillery and the rifle (motor) battalions of the Armoured division. In war conditions in the Western Desert, the support group seldom functioned in the way envisaged, and, more often than not, Gott had tanks and armoured cars under his command as well as infantry and artillery. He conducted a very skilful withdrawal before Graziani's advance in September 1940, inflicting considerable damage on the Italians, with negligible casualties to his own force of 3,000, which was the sole guard on the frontier; and he played an equally important part in the campaign which began with the battle of Sidi Barrani in December 1940, and resulted in the virtual destruction of the Italian armies in Libya in the spring of 1941: a campaign remarkable in that the British forces were outnumbered by nearly ten to one. The need to send help to Greece, however, brought an end to the advance, and the 7th Armoured division was withdrawn to Cairo for refitting.

The appearance in Libya of the German Africa Corps under General Rommel, and the subsequent defeat of the British holding forces brought Gott back to the desert. With a small force he kept the Egyptian frontier in the summer of 1941, while the Australians in Tobruk contained sufficient Germans to prevent a large-scale invasion of Egypt. When the Eighth Army was formed Gott was appointed to command the 7th Armoured division, the left wing in the resumed offensive of the autumn of 1941. In February 1942 he took over, as of right, the command of the XIII Corps. Despite a stubborn defence, the Eighth Army was defeated in the battle of Gazala (May–June 1942) and after the fall of Tobruk Gott's corps took part in the retreat to the Alamein position.

In July the prime minister decided on a personal visit to reorganize the British command in the Middle East. For the command of the Eighth Army itself, as (Sir) Winston Churchill later wrote, 'General Gott seemed in every way to meet the need. The troops were devoted to him, and he had not earned the title "Strafer" by nothing.' To make certain, however, that Gott was still physically fit for the post despite his long, hard desert service, the prime minister contrived what proved to be a 'first and last meeting' with him on 5 August. Reassured, he next day recommended his appointment to the command and Gott was sent back to the Delta on leave before taking over. Before he left Gott completed the broad plan of defence against the next German attack, discerning the importance of the Alam Halfa ridge which a month later proved to be the essential barrier to the last offensive effort of the Germans in the Western Desert. But 'Strafer' himself was not there to put the plan into effect since the slow transport aircraft in which he was travelling to Cairo on 7 August 1942 was shot down by a German fighter, and Gott was killed. Lieutenant-General B. L. Montgomery (later Viscount Montgomery of Alamein) was then appointed to the vacant command, with which his name will always be associated.

Gott was a man of six feet two inches, with searching blue eyes, early silvered hair, and the appearance, some said, of a bishop. He had a marked, because unsought, capacity of gaining the confidence of the troops and, in those private days before Alamein, that 'Strafer has a plan' seemed sufficient. More than any British commander he stood out as a desert leader in the years between Graziani's advance and the retreat to Alamein, the epitome—and the legend—of the individuality of the warfare in the Western Desert of that day. There was an exceptional breadth and patience in his judgement, uninfluenced by reverses or local opinion, a serenity which held at once knowledge and humility. Modest and reserved by nature, with a very individual sense of humour, and essentially a peace-loving man (although he could be ruthless when occasion required), he gave himself wholly to the task in hand, and no man knew the desert better. 'To him who knows it,' he said, 'it can be a fortress: to him who does not, it can be a death trap.' He commanded devotion because men believed, what they attributed to few in that period, that he 'knew his stuff'.

In 1934 Gott married Pamela Frances Mary, younger daughter of Brigadier-General Walpole Swinton Kays, King's Royal Rifle Corps. There were two daughters of the marriage but Gott never saw the younger. During the desert campaigns he was awarded the D.S.O. and bar (1941) and was appointed C.B.E. (1941) and C.B. (1942). In 1943 a memorial tablet was unveiled in the Anglican cathedral in Cairo to his memory, and to that of his close associate J. C. Campbell [q.v.].

There are two posthumous portraits of Gott, one by Joseph Oppenheimer in the possession of the family, and the other, by Patrick Phillips, at the Green Jackets' Depot at Winchester.

[*The Times*, 11 and 14 August 1942; Winston S. Churchill, *The Second World War*, vol. iv, 1951; Sir Evelyn Barker in *The King's Royal Rifle Corps Chronicle*, 1942; Alexander Clifford, *Three Against Rommel*, 1943; unpublished letters in the possession of the family; personal knowledge.]

GYLES ISHAM.

GRAHAM, JOHN ANDERSON (1861–1942), missionary, was born in London 8 September 1861, the second of the four sons of David Graham, a civil servant in H.M. Customs, by his wife, Bridget Nolan, who was of Irish parentage. David Graham having retired in 1863 to Auchen-

sale, Cardross, Dumbartonshire, John was educated at Cardross parish school and at Glasgow High School, on leaving which he worked in a law office in Glasgow, becoming eventually a civil servant in Edinburgh (1877–82). There he came under the influence of the religious movement which had taken its rise under A. H. Charteris and later was carried on by W. P. Paterson [qq.v.], and he abandoned the law to become a student at the university of Edinburgh and at the Divinity Hall, where he graduated. Charteris, who had founded the Church of Scotland Young Men's Guild, of which Graham became a secretary, conceived the idea of a mission under the Guild. In 1889 Graham was licensed by the presbytery of Edinburgh, ordained, and appointed the first Guild missionary.

Together with his wife, whom he married in that year, Graham sailed for India, and went to Kalimpong, then a tiny hamlet occupied by the Scots mission from Darjeeling, placed at a focal point on a ridge among the hill tribes of the Himalayas in north-eastern Bengal. It was not long before Kalimpong, with government help in the construction of roads, telegraphic communications, and eventually the building of a railway (1916), became a centre of educational advance and religious life, and an example of practical application of the Christian ethic. Maternity care, child-welfare, and work among lepers were centred in the Charteris Hospital; the Scottish Universities Mission situated in Sikkim developed in Bengal its education (including the training of teachers) up to university standard, and the combined efforts of these agencies resulted in the formation of an indigenous church.

In this advance the influence of Graham and his wife was paramount, all the more so because it was to a great extent unseen. It penetrated the area in a manner not to be explained merely by the statesmanlike contacts which they and their family made, for it lay in the deep sympathy they showed to their fellow men and which was rewarded by the deep affection felt for the Grahams by their people.

Nevertheless, the name of Graham and his wife will be remembered even more for one of the finest examples of philanthropic work. In 1900 there was founded at Kalimpong the St. Andrew's Colonial Homes, later known as Dr. Graham's Homes. It became the model of an institution for needy children, of pure or mixed blood, who require a home atmosphere and a Christian background. On a beautiful estate granted by the Government of India, there grew up a little township, the building up of which was in itself a life's work; but Graham and his wife were the joint founders and builders of this 'children's city', and this they did over and above their work in the Kalimpong mission. It was their crowning achievement.

Mrs. Graham died at Kalimpong 15 May 1919. She was Catharine (Kate), daughter of John McConachie, a wine merchant who came of respected forebears in the farming region of Morayshire. She was warmhearted, kindly, and exceptionally gifted, and her insight and foresight were of the utmost value to her husband in his work; her name will always be coupled with his. In 1916 she was awarded the gold Kaisar-i-Hind medal, and a chapel was built at Kalimpong in her memory.

Honours came freely to Graham himself from the Government of India; in 1903 he received the gold Kaisar-i-Hind medal, to which by a very rare and signal honour there was added a bar in 1935, and in 1911 he was appointed C.I.E. In Scotland he was elected moderator of the General Assembly of the Church of Scotland 1931, being the first missionary to be so elected, and he received the honorary degree of D.D. from the university of Edinburgh in 1904 and of LL.D. from the university of Aberdeen in 1932. He died in 1942 at Kalimpong on the anniversary of his wife's death and was buried beside her. They had two sons and four daughters.

A portrait of Graham, by John Dobbie, is in the possession of the family; another, by the same artist, hangs in the Church Offices in Edinburgh.

[A. Francon Williams, *Eastern Himalayas* (Church of Scotland Publications), 1945; J. A. Graham, *On the Threshold of Three Closed Lands*, 1926; private information; personal knowledge.]

ÆNEAS FRANCON WILLIAMS.

GRAHAM, SIR RONALD WILLIAM (1870–1949), diplomatist, was born in London 24 July 1870, the elder son of (Sir) Henry John Lowndes Graham, who became clerk of Parliaments, by his first wife, Edith Elizabeth, daughter of Gathorne Hardy who became the first Earl of Cranbrook [q.v.]. Graham was educated at Eton, where he won the Prince Consort's prize for French, and then studied abroad for two years. Nominated

attaché in the diplomatic service early in 1892, he passed a competitive examination three months later and in the following year was posted for duty to Paris. In 1894 he was promoted third secretary and passed an examination in public law. He transferred to Teheran in 1897 as second secretary, and to St. Petersburg two years later. He then spent four years in the Eastern department of the Foreign Office, during which he served as British agent before the Muscat arbitration tribunal at The Hague (1905) and went on special service to Crete in 1906. In April 1904 he was one of seven old Etonians to attain the rank of first secretary.

Graham was appointed to Cairo in 1907 with the rank in the diplomatic service of counsellor of embassy. For the following seven years he helped to pilot British interests through a complicated period in Anglo-Egyptian relations, and for several periods acted as British agent and consul-general. After the political crisis marked by the assassination of the Coptic prime minister, Boutros Pasha, in 1910 he was seconded as adviser to the Ministry of the Interior in the Egyptian Government. He was faced with new problems on the outbreak of war in 1914 when Egypt was still nominally under the suzerainty of Turkey but occupied by the British. In November 1914 Graham was appointed by Sir John Maxwell [q.v.], the general officer commanding troops in Egypt, to act for him with the Egyptian administrative authorities with the rank of a chief staff officer. Graham continued in these duties until the safety of the Suez Canal had been assured. He was mentioned in dispatches and received the grand cordon of the Order of the Nile.

In 1912 Graham married Sybil Brodrick (died 1934), daughter of Viscount (later the first Earl of) Midleton [q.v.] and the first four years of their happily married life was spent in Egypt where his wife began social services which were to play an important part in Graham's diplomatic missions throughout his career. He returned to London in 1916 to take up duties at the Foreign Office as assistant under-secretary of state. He was a member of the Empire cotton-growing committee (1917–19) and was acting permanent under-secretary of state whilst Lord Hardinge of Penshurst [q.v.] attended the Paris peace conference in 1919. Later that year he was sent as minister plenipotentiary to The Hague, serving also as minister to the Duchy of Luxembourg.

In November 1921 Graham was sworn of the Privy Council and went as ambassador to Rome where he remained until he retired from the diplomatic service in 1933. During this unusually long tenure of office he was confronted by problems arising out of one of the more turbulent periods in the history of the kingdom of Italy. He found a nation bitterly disillusioned with the interpretation of the Treaty of Versailles so far as Italy's share of the spoils of war was concerned; a people distracted by a succession of governments unable to curb sanguinary conflicts between Communists and Fascists; while Fiume was still defiantly occupied by partisans of the militant poet d'Annunzio. When the King of Italy as a desperate resolve called Mussolini to the premiership after the Fascist 'March on Rome' in 1922, Graham had the delicate task of seeking a renewal of Italian confidence in her war-time allies, Britain and France. Mussolini was persuaded to visit London at the end of 1922 for allied talks on reparations when he informed the other premiers that Italy would consider reparations and war debts as one inseparable problem. Graham saw Anglo-Italian friendship popularly confirmed in the following year by the visit to Italy of King George V and Queen Mary, when he was invested with the G.C.V.O. and received the Order of St. Maurice and St. Lazarus from the King of Italy. But the progressively dictatorial methods of Mussolini in both home and foreign affairs made Graham's mandate to maintain and safeguard friendship with Italy increasingly difficult and, as far as foreign alliances were concerned, more essential. The strain of these relationships was deftly concealed in the social life which he and Lady Sybil developed at the embassy, where Mussolini was several times guest in the earlier years of his régime.

Graham was active in negotiations which led to a pact of entente and collaboration between the four western powers of Britain, Italy, France, and Germany. The proposal for such a four-power pact was formally put forward by Mussolini in March 1933. Four months later a text acceptable to all the powers concerned was successfully negotiated. One of Graham's last acts was to sign on behalf of his country on 15 July, for he retired in November of the same year. Six months after leaving Rome he was left a widower. There were no children. He was British Government director of the Suez Canal

Company from 1939 to 1945; chairman of the Lincolnshire and Central Electricity Supply Company (1939-48), and he was a trustee of the British Museum from 1937 and on its standing committee until his death in London 26 January 1949. In addition to his other honours he was appointed C.B. (1910), G.C.B. (1932), K.C.M.G. (1915), and G.C.M.G. (1926).

[Foreign Office records; *The Times*, 27 January 1949; personal knowledge.]

I. S. MUNRO.

GRAHAM-HARRISON, SIR WILLIAM MONTAGU (1871-1949), parliamentary draftsman, was born at Charlton, Kent, 4 February 1871, the youngest child of Captain Thomas Arthur John Harrison, R.A., then stationed at Woolwich, and his wife, Mary Elizabeth Thompson. Educated at Wellington College and Magdalen College, Oxford, he was placed in the first class in classical moderations in 1892 and in jurisprudence in 1894. In 1895 he gained a fellowship at All Souls and the Vinerian law scholarship, and after two years as pupil of (Sir) Charles Sargant [q.v.], the future lord justice, he was called to the bar by Lincoln's Inn. The next year or two he spent in the busy chambers of R. J. (later Lord) Parker [q.v.], but soon he was invited back to 'devil' for Sargant. In 1900 he married Violet Evelyn Cecilia, daughter of the late Sir Cyril Clerke Graham, fifth baronet, of Kirkstall, thereupon changing his name to Graham-Harrison. He had been elected in that year to the London School Board, but resigned his membership when in 1903 he left the bar and entered the Parliamentary Counsel Office to assist (Sir) Arthur Thring and (Sir) Frederick Liddell, an All Souls colleague also previously in Sargant's chambers, and a lifelong friend. Temporarily assigned by Lloyd George to be legal adviser to the nascent National Insurance Commission in 1912, he was appointed solicitor for H.M. Customs and Excise a year later. In the latter capacity, when war came, he devised and helped to operate the drastic Trading with the Enemy Act of 1914.

These contacts with practical administration proved useful when in 1917, Thring having become clerk of the Parliaments, Graham-Harrison was brought back as second parliamentary counsel under Liddell whom he ultimately succeeded as head of the office in 1928. He was not the first of his family to draft

314

government bills. His accidental discovery of a book-plate in Lincoln's Inn library displaying the name and arms of Harrison enabled him to establish to his satisfaction kinship with one William Harrison who, a hundred years earlier, had borne the same title of parliamentary counsel to the Treasury, and discharged much the same functions as himself. This William was elder brother to Sir George Harrison [q.v.], an eminent Treasury official, Graham-Harrison's own great-grandfather.

Graham-Harrison's drafting was distinguished by orderliness, and the style and fastidiousness of a scholar. A major bill, he maintained, needed three months for its proper preparation. Time sufficed in the early Edwardian era when there was no autumn session. During his own thirty years' official experience the legislative tempo was progressively quickened by the enactment of new social policies, by a war, its improvisations and sequelae, and by recurrent emergencies. When sessions began in the autumn, the draftsmen got no respite. Only exemplary competence and devotion could have met these incessant and abnormal demands without disaster.

He rejected in mid-career the chance of the Chichele professorship of international law and diplomacy at Oxford for which indeed he would have been well qualified. Although he had withdrawn his candidature, he was chosen by the electors who supposed his withdrawal to be a gesture of modesty which could be ignored. But Graham-Harrison decided to remain in Whitehall. Two essays which he found time to write showed his gifts of lively and authoritative exposition. One, his thesis for the D.C.L. which he took in 1932, dealt with subordinate law-making, its form, operation, publication, and parliamentary control. It reaffirmed his conclusion, already stated to the committee on ministers' powers, that delegated legislation was indispensable, and it gave his reasons. The other, his address to the Society of Public Teachers of Law in 1935, was a reply to popular and judicial criticisms of the statute book. It made apt reference to evidence and opinions recorded by a House of Commons committee on the same subject sixty years before.

He retired from the Parliamentary Counsel Office in 1933, needing relaxation but not idleness. His name went up again on the door of chambers in Lincoln's Inn. He undertook some private drafting of government bills. His accidental discovery of a book-plate in Lincoln's Inn library displaying the name and arms of Harrison enabled him to establish to his satisfaction kinship with one William Harrison who, a hundred years earlier, had borne the same title of parliamentary counsel to the Treasury, and discharged much the same functions as himself. This William was elder brother to Sir George Harrison [q.v.], an eminent Treasury official, Graham-Harrison's own great-grandfather.

bills as well as working on the consolidation of the enactments relating to the Customs. In 1936 he held an important brief (his first for over thirty years) in the Belfast Corporation case before the Judicial Committee when the validity of a Northern Ireland Finance Act was disputed. He presided over departmental committees on national marks, coal-mines investigations, and the Northern Ireland Civil Service. He was British member of the Institut International pour l'Unification du Droit Privé at Rome. He gave valued help to the Church Assembly as a member of its legal board and of its three commissions which led to amendment of the law of faculties in 1938. He was chancellor of the diocese of Durham, Gloucester, Truro, and Portsmouth. At Truro it fell to him in 1938 to decide the St. Hilary case, afterwards reviewed in the Court of Arches, on the placing and removal of ornaments.

The outbreak of war in 1939 interrupted his activities. He and his wife were in Switzerland and there they remained, their health deteriorating, for ten years of increasingly tedious exile. Brought home at last to London, Graham-Harrison died there suddenly, 29 October 1949, only two days after his return. There were two sons and one daughter of his marriage.

Graham-Harrison was appointed C.B. in 1920 and promoted K.C.B. in 1926. He became a K.C. in 1930 and was elected an honorary fellow of Magdalen College in 1938. A portrait by Harry Collison is in the possession of the family.

[Private information; personal knowledge.]

CECIL CARR.

**GRAHAM-LITTLE, SIR ERNEST GORDON GRAHAM** (1867–1950), physician, and member of Parliament for London University, was born at Monghyr, Bengal, 8 February 1867, the only child of Michael Little, of the Indian Civil Service, by his wife, Anna, daughter of Alexander English, of Cape Town. His mother died when he was four years old and he was taken to South Africa where his uncle, F. A. English, a friend of Rhodes, became his guardian. He was educated at the South African College and in 1887 graduated B.A. in the university of the Cape of Good Hope, heading the honours list in literature and philosophy, thereby becoming a university scholar. In the same year he was awarded the Porter studentship which took him to London University where he studied medicine, his hospitals being Guy's and St. George's. He graduated with honours in 1893 and later went to the Rotunda Hospital, Dublin, and the university of Paris. He stated in after years that throughout his student career he maintained himself by scholarships and prizes.

In 1895 he was appointed physician to the East London Hospital for Children where in 1925 he was to become consulting physician. In 1902 he decided to make skin diseases his speciality, when he was appointed physician to the skin department of St. Mary's Hospital and lecturer in dermatology in its medical school. In 1934 he became consulting physician and maintained his connexion with the hospital until he died. He established a world-wide reputation as a dermatologist, contributing voluminously to publications and treatises dealing with skin diseases, and became a corresponding or honorary member of many learned societies at home and abroad. He was honorary president of the International Dermatological Congress held in Budapest in 1935. He was a pioneer in the use of carbon dioxide in the treatment of skin conditions, and one of the first to use crude coal-tar preparations. In 1923 he was the first to describe fully a disorder which became known as 'Benign Superficial Epithelioma of Graham-Little'.

In 1906 Little was elected to the senate of the university of London and he remained a member until the year in which he died. He was chairman of the external council (1922-46), a member of the court from its inception, and for long served on fifteen of the university committees. He regarded the university as a great Commonwealth link, and never wavered from the fundamental principle upon which it was founded: equality of opportunity, independent of race, sex, or class. He was mainly instrumental in securing recognition of the West London Hospital as an institution for the admission of women medical students to the university, and successfully resisted an effort to impose on the university official co-operation with the conjoint board in its final M.B. examinations which, in his judgement, would have lowered the standard of the London medical degree.

The general election of 1924 by chance coincided with an important issue for London University. The Haldane scheme of reform was thought by many to jeopardize the external side of the university. The Graduates' Association opposed the plan, and Little was adopted by them as an independent candidate (originally for a by-election in the university which was cancelled when the general election supervened) in opposition to the candidates for the three main parties all of whom supported the scheme. His election by a majority of 389 had a decisive influence on the Act of 1926 under which representation of both graduates and teachers on the senate was retained intact. Thereafter he continued to hold the seat, usually with large majorities, until the university franchise was abolished in 1950. He was knighted in 1931 when he assumed the surname of Graham-Little.

In Parliament he was a convincing although not a fluent speaker. He never addressed the House or asked a question except on subjects he knew thoroughly and on some of which he was an authority. He was the founder and first chairman of the university members' committee, which only functioned under his leadership. He resisted any concession to unqualified medical practitioners, fought for professional secrecy for doctors' evidence in law courts, and opposed the compulsory notification of venereal disease. From the first he was an implacable opponent of the National Health Service which he maintained would ruin the art of medicine. He was one of the few members of Parliament who voted against the Yalta agreement. Although a strong anti-Socialist he was in many respects progressive. He pleaded unceasingly for equality of opportunity for the sexes, for pure food, pasteurized milk, and wholewheat bread. School buildings, teachers' pay, and milk in schools were matters of great interest to him. He was the first member to press for tests for driving licences for motorists. A sturdy individualist and a strong supporter of the Society of Individualists, he was a persistent controversialist, a formidable pamphleteer, a scholar, a linguist, an enthusiastic player of chess— and a kind and gentle friend.

In 1911 he married Sarah Helen, daughter of Maurice Kendall. She was a constant support to him throughout his life which was not without its sorrows, for their only daughter was drowned while bathing in 1932 and their only son killed whilst flying on active service in 1942. In this war also their house in Wimpole Street which contained priceless art treasures was destroyed by enemy action.

He removed to Epsom where he died 6 October 1950.

[*The Times*, 10 October 1950; *British Medical Journal*, 14 October 1950; *Lancet*, 11 November 1950; private information; personal knowledge.]

HENRY MORRIS-JONES.

GRANET, SIR (WILLIAM) GUY (1867–1943), barrister, railway administrator, and chairman, was born at Genoa 13 October 1867, the second son of William Augustus Granet, a banker living at Genoa, by his wife, Adelaide Julia, daughter of E. Le Mesurier. He was educated at Rugby and at Balliol College, Oxford, where he obtained a second class in modern history (1889) and was captain of the boat club. After four years in business in Genoa he was called to the bar by Lincoln's Inn in 1893 and practised on the Northern circuit. In 1900 he left the bar to become secretary of the Railway Companies' Association, and there he soon showed the qualities which were to make him one of the central figures in the railway world of his generation. In 1905 he joined the Midland Railway Company as assistant general manager with the reversion of the general managership a year later. He found the Midland Railway inclined to live on its reputation, but under his vigorous leadership that was quickly changed. Granet brought to railway problems a keen analytical brain which refused to accept established practice as the last word. He soon saw the possibilities of a scientific study of train movements and he appointed as general superintendent (Sir) Cecil Walter Paget, who with Granet's wholehearted support completely reorganized operating methods on the Midland and made it outstanding in the economy of its traffic operation.

Granet's mercurial temperament was not always easy for his staff, but he won their loyal support by his readiness to listen, his shrewd judgement, and his human qualities. It was a period of much railway legislation, and here Granet's legal training stood him in good stead. He was said to be one of the most persuasive expert witnesses who ever gave evidence before a parliamentary committee. He had a weight and deliberation of utterance and a massive demeanour which inspired confidence.

Granet took a special interest in labour problems, and he did much to improve conditions of service. In 1907 he took a leading part in the negotiations which led to the establishment of conciliation boards and again in 1911 in the settlement of the railway strike at the time of the Agadir crisis.

In 1912 Granet was appointed a member of the Royal Commission on the Civil Service and he signed a minority report in 1914. When war came in that year his energy and organizing ability were in constant demand by the Government. In 1915 he was appointed controller of import restrictions and in 1916 deputy director-general of military railways at the War Office under Sir Eric Geddes [q.v.]; he was largely responsible for introducing train ferries to carry traffic across the Channel, at the suggestion of (Sir) Follett Holt. In 1917 he became director-general of movements and railways and a member of the Army Council, and in 1918 chairman of the British and Allied provisions commission and representative of the Ministry of Food in the United States and Canada. He was a member of the Geddes committee on national expenditure in 1921–2.

He resigned the general-managership of the Midland Railway in 1918 and was elected to a seat on the board, becoming chairman in 1922. On the amalgamation of the railways he became deputy chairman of the London, Midland, and Scottish Railway, succeeding Lord Lawrence of Kingsgate as chairman in 1924. Realizing that some radical changes were needed he persuaded Sir Josiah (later Lord) Stamp [q.v.] to come in 1926 as chief executive with the title of president, to devise a new organization. It was a bold step as Stamp knew nothing of railway problems, but Granet's judgement was justified by the result. In 1927, recognizing the success achieved by Stamp with his executive committee, Granet resigned the chairmanship to him so as to give him wider scope. But Stamp always relied greatly on Granet's experience, and as chairman of the traffic committee of the board Granet continued to exert much influence on the railway company's policy. He was chairman of the South African railways commission in 1933.

Granet in 1919 became a member of the firm of Higginson & Co., merchant bankers, and he was a director of a number of companies, including Lloyds Bank and The Times Publishing Company. When financial reverses came to him towards the end of his life he bore them with the same courage and equanimity with which he fought the five years of his final illness, continuing in active work to the end. He died at Burleigh Court, near Stroud, Gloucestershire, 11 October 1943.

In 1892 Granet married Florence Julia (died 1949), daughter of William Court Gully (later Viscount Selby, q.v.), and had a daughter (died 1949), who married Mr. Denis George Mackail, the novelist son of J. W. Mackail [q.v.]. Granet was knighted in 1911 and appointed G.B.E. in 1923.

Granet had a masterful personality, holding strong views to which he gave vigorous expression. Beneath his rather formidable manner there was a warmhearted affection and loyalty to individuals and institutions and unfailing generosity and kindness. The only portrait of him is a charcoal drawing by J. S. Sargent belonging to the family.

[*The Times*, 12 and 14 October 1943; *Railway Gazette*, 22 October 1943; private information; personal knowledge.]

HAROLD HARTLEY.

GRANVILLE-BARKER, HARLEY GRANVILLE (1877–1946), actor, producer, dramatist, and critic, was born in Kensington 25 November 1877, the only son and elder child of Albert James Barker, who came of an old Warwickshire and Hereford family. He is spoken of as an architect, but the family was largely dependent on his wife, Mary Elisabeth Bozzi Granville, who was a well-known elocutionist and reciter of the Victorian type. She was the granddaughter of Augustus Bozzi Granville [q.v.], the son of Dr. Carlo Bozzi, who in 1806 took the name Granville to commemorate his Cornish grandmother who had married an Italian, Rapazzini. There were therefore two strains of Italian blood in Harley, both on the maternal side.

There is no record of his schooling, but he grew up in an atmosphere of good speech and drama and at an early age had a thorough knowledge of Dickens and Shakespeare. A precocious child, he frequently assisted at his mother's recitals, and even deputized for her. He began his professional career in 1891 at Harrogate and in Sarah Thorne's famous stock company at Margate; his first London appearance was at the Comedy Theatre in 1892. A tour with (Sir) Phillip Ben Greet in 1895 brought him to the notice of William Poel [qq.v.] for whom he played Richard II in 1899. An introduction to the Fabian set, with which the founders of the Stage Society were closely allied, led to his great friendship with

G. B. Shaw [q.v.] which had a profound influence on his career and lasted until his second marriage in 1918. For the Stage Society he produced or acted in a number of first performances of plays such as *Candida*, and *Mrs. Warren's Profession*, and his own *Weather Hen* and *The Marrying of Ann Leete*. His position once established, he devoted himself to the task of raising the standard of English acting and drama, and accustoming the English actor and audience to the permanent repertory company: with the idea of a national theatre in view. With William Archer [q.v.] in 1904 he drew up in great detail *A Scheme and Estimates for a National Theatre* which was not made public until 1907. Meanwhile his own first great chance came when, at Archer's suggestion, he was invited to produce *Two Gentlemen of Verona* at the Royal Court Theatre in 1904. He accepted on condition that during the run he might present a set of matinées of *Candida*. These were so successful that in partnership with John E. Vedrenne, the manager of the Court Theatre, and in close association with Shaw, he embarked upon the famous Vedrenne–Barker season which lasted until 1907, made Barker's name as a director and Shaw's as a dramatist, and became a landmark in the history of the British theatre. A new standard of intelligence and social criticism was brought into the theatre and in both plays and acting there was an intense regard for truth to life rather than for meretricious theatrical effect. Some 950 performances were given of 32 plays by 17 authors, including 11 of Shaw's, first plays of Galsworthy, St. John Hankin [qq.v.], and Mr. John Masefield, and works by Euripides (in Gilbert Murray's translations), Ibsen, Maeterlinck, and Barker. Expenses, including the actors' salaries, were kept very low but the financial stability of the enterprise was largely dependent on the success of Shaw's plays, especially *You Never Can Tell, John Bull's Other Island*, and *Man and Superman*. For the two latter Miss Lillah McCarthy joined the company in 1905 and in 1906 she and Barker were married.

The growing success of the Vedrenne–Barker partnership prompted a move in the autumn of 1907 to a larger theatre, the Savoy, but expenses increased more than receipts, Barker's new play, *Waste*, was forbidden by the censor, there were internal disputes over casting, and something of the joyful pioneering spirit had gone. The season petered out at Christmas and the new plays in preparation, Masefield's *Nan* and Galsworthy's *Strife* and others, were produced by Barker with all his care and skill but for Sunday societies or short runs under other managements. He was offered but declined control of the Millionaires' Theatre (later the Century), just completed in New York, which he found too vast for his style of work. In 1910, at the instigation of (Sir) James Barrie [q.v.], Charles Frohman mounted a season of real repertory at the Duke of York's Theatre, with Barker and Dion Boucicault [q.v.] sharing the productions. Galsworthy's *Justice* in Barker's hands made a great sensation, and among other plays was Barker's own *The Madras House*. Although business was quite good the theatre was unsuitable for repertory, the expenses enormous, and the venture failed in three months. Barker had increased his reputation but not his finances and to recoup them he appeared for a season at the Palace Variety Theatre in a series of Schnitzler's *Anatol* duologues translated and produced by himself. In 1911 his wife, with the help of Lord Howard de Walden [q.v.], raised a small syndicate to take the Little Theatre where they produced *The Master Builder* and Shaw's *Fanny's First Play*. The latter was a great success and, transferred to the Kingsway Theatre, ran until 1912.

Plans were now maturing for building a national theatre in time for the Shakespeare tercentenary in 1916, and in preparation for this, with the backing of Lord Howard de Walden and others, Barker in 1912 mounted at the Savoy two plays by Shakespeare which set a completely new standard of production never since surpassed. Continuity of action, an apron stage, the full text spoken with great beauty and a new swiftness, an entirely new approach to the plays in intelligence, truth, and taste, a brilliant company headed by Henry Ainley [q.v.] and Miss Lillah McCarthy, and exquisite simple settings by Albert Rothenstein (afterwards Rutherston) and Norman Wilkinson [q.v.], all contributed to Barker's achievement. He was perhaps too far in advance of his time; even the critics were startled by the violent changes from the accepted traditions, and the first play, *The Winter's Tale*, was a comparative failure. *Twelfth Night*, although almost as revolutionary, was a more familiar play and ran for a hundred nights.

These two productions, with *A Midsummer Night's Dream* in 1914, have had a profound and permanent effect on the approach to Shakespeare in the theatre. Further productions proved impracticable but meanwhile in 1913 Barker achieved a great comedy success at the Kingsway Theatre with Ainley in *The Great Adventure* by Arnold Bennett [q.v.] which ran until after the outbreak of war. The same year (1913) saw the opening of a season at the St. James's Theatre with Shaw's *Androcles and the Lion*, followed by revivals of *Nan*, *The Doctor's Dilemma*, and plays of Ibsen and Maeterlinck. Barker was now at the height of his powers, and his productions, although costly to his backers, greatly enhanced his European reputation and marked him as the future director of the national theatre.

The war demolished all his hopes. Barker presented Hardy's *Dynasts* in an adaptation of his own with outstanding artistic success, but the theatre had turned to frivolity and the production failed completely. In 1915 he produced *Androcles and the Lion*, *The Doctor's Dilemma*, and *A Midsummer Night's Dream* in New York for an American syndicate of millionaires. A mutual attraction between Barker and the wife of Archer Huntington (one of the backers) broke his marriage, and as neither of their partners wished a divorce there ensued a period of great strain during which Barker worked first for the Red Cross in France and then enlisted, later undertaking military intelligence work. Eventually the divorces went through and in 1918 Barker married Helen Huntington (died 1950) who as Helen Gates was a poet and novelist of some distinction. Archer Huntington settled a large sum on her and Barker was able to live henceforth in luxury. His wife insisted on almost complete severance from his work in the theatre and all his friends, however old and intimate, connected with it, and above all from Shaw.

Potentially perhaps the most remarkable theatre personality of this century Barker's career thus proved on the whole a disappointment and his influence on the theatre of this country fell far short of the hopes inspired by his brilliant start. His remaining work for the theatre was mainly professorial and literary, although almost surreptitiously he did a certain amount of directing of his own plays and translations. His last acknowledged stage production was Maeterlinck's *The Betrothal* at the Gaiety Theatre in 1921. In 1919 he took up with enthusiasm the work of the British Drama League recently founded by Geoffrey Whitworth, and was its valuable chairman for thirteen years. In 1920 he made a rather pathetic attempt to live as a country gentleman in south Devon and during this period wrote his last two plays and the first of his series of translations from the Spanish (with his wife) which introduced the Quintero brothers and Sierra to the British public. As a dramatist Barker was too meticulous a writer to be very prolific. He experimented in a number of styles and probably his best work is found in the high comedy of *The Voysey Inheritance* and *The Madras House* and in the tragedy of *Waste*. Although slow moving, the characterization is vivid and as social criticism of their time they have a cutting edge. The two plays written in retirement, *His Majesty* and *The Secret Life*, seem never to have been publicly performed and have the rarefied atmosphere of one who has detached himself from the task of satisfying an audience which has paid for its seats. His *Exemplary Theatre* (1922) shows how far his mind had travelled even then from the contemporary theatre.

In 1923 Barker undertook the part editorship of 'The Players' Shakespeare', and although the series was abandoned he continued until his death to write the prefaces he had begun for it. They will probably outlive all his other written work, for they are most valuable interpretations of the plays from the director's point of view, and as a director Barker may be regarded as the first and greatest of the moderns. As an actor he had too much critical intelligence to be really successful for, with a certain lack of common humanity, it showed vividly through his impersonations. This was valuable in detached parts such as Marchbanks and Keegan, or even John Tanner, but it marred his performance of more ordinary characters. His face lacked the true flexibility of the actor's mask and his expressive voice, probably from being overworked as a boy, had too little ground tone to carry its strong higher harmonics. Yet he was an actor to his finger-tips, and with this he combined a first-class analytical and administrative brain and an outstanding gift for leadership. As a producer he used all his varied gifts completely selflessly in the service of the dramatist to bring out and express the full emotional and intellectual content of the play. His mastery of the play before starting rehearsals inspired confidence in his actors and he had the power to stimulate and use their own imaginative ideas, blending and moulding them within the framework of the play as he saw it. His intuitive grasp, as a dramatist, of human motives, thought, and emotions, and his technical knowledge of how to express them were continually at the service of his cast with every device of witty metaphor and amusing illustration. He was a perfectionist but no dictator, criticizing to the last inch and the last rehearsal, always with good humour, every tiniest movement or vocal inflexion, until the whole play became a symphony in which every phrase, rhythm, melody, and movement reached as near perfection as he could make it.

In 1930 Barker was appointed to the Clark lectureship at Trinity College, Cambridge, and in 1937 he was Romanes lecturer at Oxford. He received honorary degrees from Edinburgh (1930), and from Oxford and Reading in 1937, in which year he became director of the British Institute in Paris where he had been living for some time. He continued to take some interest in the British theatre and in 1940 came over to take a major share of the direction of (Sir) John Gielgud's *King Lear* at the Old Vic, on condition that his name did not appear. He resigned from the British Institute in 1939 and when Paris fell he went to America where he was a visiting professor at Yale and Harvard. He returned to England in failing health in 1945 and to Paris in 1946 where he died 31 August and was buried in the cemetery of Père Lachaise. He had no children.

Of slight, wiry build, almost five feet eleven in height, until well past middle age Barker still gave an extraordinary impression of youth both in face and figure. He had a sensitive face, strong and masculine with humorous warm brown eyes, and a mouth always harder than the eyes, tending even to grimness in his later days. His thick red-brown hair was parted in the middle and thrown back. A curious feature was his very flabby handshake. The British Drama League has a bust in bronze by Clara Billing and a posthumous bust by David McFall; the National Portrait Gallery has a painting by J.-E. Blanche; a bronze by Lady Kennet is at the Shakespeare Memorial Theatre, Stratford on Avon, and a portrait statuette by the same artist is at the Garrick Club.

[Desmond MacCarthy, *The Court Theatre, 1904–7*, 1907; C. B. Purdom, *Harley Granville Barker*, with a complete catalogue of his known writings, 1955; *Who's Who in the Theatre*; private information; personal knowledge.]     LEWIS CASSON.

GRAVES, GEORGE WINDSOR (1873?–1949), comedian, was born in London, by his own account in 1876 but more probably 1 January 1873, the youngest child of Thomas Graves, a publican, and his second wife, Martha Alice, daughter of John Mulvey, a compositor. From early childhood it was his desire to be an actor although he had no theatrical ancestry. He left Margate College at the age of ten when his father died, and at fourteen entered a solicitor's office, but found it little to his liking. There followed a series of dead-end jobs, most of which he lost through practical joking. In 1896 he got his first professional engagement on the stage and toured the country—he did more, he toured the world, and he actually appeared in Russia in 1899 in the George Edwardes productions of *A Runaway Girl*, *The Shop Girl*, and *The Geisha*. His first appearance in pantomime—and he became a great pantomime comedian—was at the Prince's Theatre, Manchester, in 1900, as the Emperor of China in *Aladdin*. His first London success was at the Prince of Wales's Theatre, on 9 May 1903, as General Marchmont in *The School Girl*, a musical comedy. He had then been on the stage for only seven years, but he presented something quite new in the way of comic elderly men. From that success he never looked back. He had a clear-cut, incisive style, a number of curious mannerisms, and a most distinctive voice. He developed a wonderful propensity for 'gagging'—he was in that respect second only to Arthur Roberts, and would convulse not only the audience but his fellow players by jokes invented on the spur of the moment. He had a long and distinguished career as a comedian in the very front rank of musical comedy. He played comedy lead in no fewer than seven Drury Lane pantomimes between 1909 and 1915. He was also well known on the music-halls, where he appeared in sketches, notably 'Koffo of Bond Street' and 'The Key of the Flat'. He was just as popular in revue. Perhaps his greatest success was as Baron Popoff in *The Merry Widow* at Daly's Theatre in 1907. His amazing

discourses on the adventures of 'Hetty the Hen' were never forgotten by those who heard them. Nor had his performance of General Des Ifs in *The Little Michus* at the same theatre in 1905 been far behind in brilliance. In that he invented a strange little creature called 'The Gazeka' which became 'all the rage'.

However much Graves clowned and gagged, he always remained in character and in the general picture, for he was an excellent actor apart from his amazing gifts of comedy, and he possessed a fine stage sense. One of his last big successes was in the long-running musical show *Me and My Girl*, first produced at the Victoria Palace in 1937, in which he gave a memorable performance of a rich and fruity county gentleman of title. He had success on the films as well and was one of the best-known men of his time, almost a household word. His dressing-room was full of surprising gadgets, such as chairs which collapsed when sat upon, glasses which dripped all over their users, cigars which blew up. He could never resist a joke, practical or otherwise. This did not always endear him to his colleagues. He was a member of the Savage Club, he was a follower of sport, a regular attendant at race meetings and big fights, and a keen card player. One of the last great gagsters and individualists of the actor-manager period, he died in London 2 April 1949, active to the very last.

In 1901 Graves married Lillian Josephine, daughter of an actor, Thomas Finnellan Doyle; this marriage was dissolved and in 1918 he married the actress Madge Compton, daughter of George Mussared; this marriage was also dissolved and in 1927 Graves married Flora Emily Sarah, daughter of the late Foster Richard Courtenay, an actor. There was one daughter of the first marriage.

[George Graves, *Gaieties and Gravities*, 1931; personal knowledge.]     W. MACQUEEN-POPE.

GRAY, GEORGE EDWARD KRUGER (1880–1943), designer, was born 25 December 1880 in Kensington, the son of Edwin Charles Kruger, merchant, of St. Helier, Jersey, by his wife, Frances Hester, daughter of John Dafter Harris, of Bath. He did not add the surname Gray until his marriage in 1918 to Audrey Gordon, daughter of the Rev. John Henry Gray, who was at one time archdeacon of Hong Kong.

He was educated at the Merchant Taylors' School, Great Crosby, and afterwards at the Bath School of Art. While studying there he won a scholarship at the Royal College of Art, where he worked under W. R. Lethaby [q.v.] and took his diploma in design. He exhibited water-colours at the Royal Academy from 1905; the earliest of these were landscapes, flower-studies, and portraits, and it was not until after the war of 1914–18 in which he served with the Artists' Rifles and the camouflage section of the Royal Engineers that he began to achieve positive success in the types of designing for which he became known. In 1923 a group exhibit of coin-age at the Royal Academy included casts from original models of the half-crown, florin, and farthing pieces which Kruger Gray executed for the Union of South Africa; thereafter he was much employed is a designer of coinage, being later re-jponsible for the King George V and King George VI silver coinage, and for the King George V jubilee crown piece. He also designed the Great Seal of King George VI, the reverse of the Great Seal of Ulster, the Great Seal of the Dominion of Canada (1939), and many other seals and medals.

Kruger Gray also designed and executed a large number of stained-glass windows. His series of windows for Eltham Palace (1936) and for the chapel of King's School, Canterbury (1939–40), are among his most important figure-subjects; he was equally prominent for his heraldic designs, which he executed for Sheffield City Hall (1930), for Exeter University College (1936), and also for public buildings in Manchester, Leeds, Taunton, and Chelmsford. In much of this public work Kruger Gray was associated with Mr. (Emanuel) Vin-cent Harris, the architect.

Among his more miscellaneous tasks, Kruger Gray designed two maces for the Ulster Parliament, and one of his last works before he died was the design for the Dean's mace for Westminster Abbey. He also designed and painted a series of panels in memory of distinguished Harro-vians for Harrow School, and his further versatility is shown by his work on the historical costumes for the Aldershot military tattoo between 1935 and 1939. He was appointed C.B.E. in 1938.

Kruger Gray's success as a designer was securely based on his knowledge of heraldry and of the materials for which he worked. He seldom gave his designs to others to execute, but normally carried them through to their final form himself. The result was that he was able to maintain a high standard of excellence throughout,

and during the last twenty years of his life his work was much in demand.

Kruger Gray died at Chichester 2 May 1943, survived by his wife and the one son of his marriage.

[*The Times*, 4 May 1943; private informa-tion.]                                JAMES LAVER.

GREEN,    CHARLES    ALFRED HOWELL (1864–1944), archbishop, the eldest son of the Rev. Alfred John Morgan Green, then curate of Llanelly, and his wife, Elizabeth Bond, daughter of Richard Thomas Howell, also of Llanelly, was born in that place, 19 August 1864. He was educated by his father until he won scholarships successively at Charterhouse and Keble College, Oxford. He became librarian and afterwards president of the Union and was already noted at that time for his eloquence. He was placed in the second class of the honours list in *literae humaniores* in 1887, was ordained deacon in 1888 and priest in 1889. The first twenty-six years of his ministry were spent at Aberdare, where he was curate for five years and vicar for twenty-one. In this parish he made an indelible mark as scholar, pastor, teacher, administrator, and strict disciplinarian. His many col-leagues during those years have lived to thank him for the training given them at Aberdare. From 1914 until 1921 he was archdeacon of Monmouth and canon residentiary of Llandaff Cathedral. As a learned canonist, Green took an im-portant, although unobtrusive, part in the drawing up of the constitution of the Church in Wales, which was framed after disestablishment. When the new diocese of Monmouth was formed, Green was the obvious choice for its first bishop, and he was duly consecrated in 1921. Here he maintained a high standard in those whom he ordained. If a priest was ill or in trouble, he would often go himself and take Sunday duty. No one was more exact than Green in his adherence to the Book of Common Prayer; but in 1922 he had occasion to defend himself against the charge made by Hensley Henson [q.v.] that the ceremonial which had been used at an ordination did not comply with the constitution of the Church in Wales.

In 1928 Green was elected to the see of Bangor, and a characteristic sense of duty led him to accept, and thus to leave his familiar South Wales. In 1934 he was elected archbishop of Wales. He retained the bishopric of Bangor until his death there, 7 May 1944, having resigned the archbishopric a month before. The universal respect in which he was held maintained and enhanced the prestige of the Church in Wales. He was elected a proctor in Convocation (1913), a member of the court of governors of the University College of South Wales (1914), a member of the theological board of the university of Wales (1915), a member of the council and court of governors of the University College of North Wales (1933), of the National Museum of Wales (1935), and the National Library of Wales (1936). He took his B.D. in 1907 and D.D. in 1911, and proceeded to B.C.L. and D.C.L. when he was seventy-four years old, his book *The Setting of the Constitution of the Church in Wales* (1937) being accepted as a thesis for these degrees. He was a select preacher at Cambridge (1923) and Oxford (1927–9), and was elected an honorary fellow of Keble College in 1935.

In 1899 Green married Katharine Mary, daughter of Sir William Thomas Lewis [q.v.] who was subsequently created Baron Merthyr, of Senghenydd. There were no children.

Green was shy and retiring, sometimes considered unapproachable, but in reality warm-hearted. He was exact in every detail, and kept up his scholarship throughout his life. In churchmanship he was deeply imbued with the spirit of the Tractarians, not least with their austerity. Although fearless in defence of what he believed to be the truth, he was eirenic in argument, and tolerant of those who differed from him. He is buried in the cemetery of Llandaff Cathedral.

[*The Times*, 8 May 1944; private information; personal knowledge.]

FREDERIC HOOD.

GREENE, SIR (WILLIAM) GRAHAM (1857–1950), civil servant, was born at Takeley, Essex, 16 January 1857, the eldest son of William Greene who later resided at East Lodge, Bedford, and his wife, Charlotte, daughter of William Smith, of Wrawby, Lincolnshire. He was educated at Cheltenham College and in Germany. Between 1875 and 1879 he worked for some time in a brewery at Bury St. Edmunds which belonged to his family, and then trained in engineering at Bedford; but having given this up through ill health, he studied for the Civil Service examination for the higher division, and in July 1879 was appointed assistant surveyor of taxes under the Board of Inland Revenue. From the outset his wish was for work at the Admiralty and in June 1881 he was transferred to the department of the accountant-general of the navy and in April 1884 moved to the Admiralty secretariat as a junior clerk. Here he was soon selected for special duty in the military, political, and secret branch and was chosen to be secretary of the foreign intelligence committee (the forerunner of the naval intelligence department). In January 1887 Lord George Hamilton [q.v.] appointed him his assistant private secretary. This post he retained for fifteen years under successive first lords, Hamilton, Spencer, Goschen, and Selborne [qq.v.].

From very early days the title of private secretary was held by the succession of distinguished seamen who advised the first lord on the appointment to ships and commands of those ranks in the Service which were in the absolute control of the minister. As assistant private secretary and head of the first lord's private office, Greene gradually built up a position which was unique in the public service. On behalf of the first lord and subject to his approval he controlled the nomination and entry of naval cadets and assistant clerks (the junior rank of the paymaster branch); the arrangements for all ceremonial functions such as official dinners and receptions and visits of the Board of Admiralty to the naval ports, and the voyages of the Admiralty yacht; the presentation of officers and Admiralty civilians at levées, correspondence with the court on matters requiring the Sovereign's approval, submissions to the Sovereign for sanction to chief appointments and commands and to the award of decorations and orders. He also advised the first lord on all official business which did not require the professional view of the naval private secretary.

In 1899 Greene was appointed C.B. and in December 1902 was promoted principal clerk and placed in charge of the personnel branch of the secretariat and thus was mainly responsible for carrying into effect the scheme of educational reform promoted by Sir John (later Lord) Fisher [q.v.] and promulgated by Lord Selborne at Christmas in that year. In 1907 he became assistant secretary of the Admiralty and in 1911 was promoted K.C.B. and appointed permanent secretary. On the outbreak of war in 1914 (Sir) Winston Churchill made him one of the inner council at which all important matters were settled. He enjoyed the complete confidence of Churchill's successors, Balfour and Carson. In July 1917, when Sir Edward (later Lord) Carson was replaced by Sir Eric Geddes [qq.v.], Lloyd George, who had never seen Greene, insisted upon his immediate retirement. Churchill, however, who at the same time became minister of munitions, welcomed the opportunity of securing his services as secretary of the Ministry, an office which he held until the Ministry was disbanded after the end of the war. Carson related afterwards: 'I met Churchill in the prime minister's room and congratulated him on his knowledge of men. "What do you mean?", said Lloyd George. "Well", I said, "Winston has the wisdom to choose for a much bigger job the man whom you dismissed from the Admiralty".'

In 1920 Greene began work not requiring continuous attendance in London, which he continued for twenty years, on a number of sub-committees of the Committee of Imperial Defence, dealing with statistics and such subjects as the history of the Ministry of Munitions, and the use of national manpower. In retirement he lived mainly at his home at Harston near Cambridge and soon became fully engaged in local activities. He was a justice of the peace of London and Cambridgeshire and of the latter also county councillor and, in 1942, alderman. He was until 1948 treasurer of the Navy Records Society which he had helped to found in 1893. He was a commander of the Legion of Honour and the Order of Leopold of Belgium, and had the Japanese Order of the Rising Sun, first class.

Greene was an active man all his life, fond of hunting and shooting in younger days, and a keen gardener at his country home until the end. He was one of the ablest civil servants of his generation. Although of slight physique he was a tireless worker with a single-minded devotion to his official duty, part of which he conceived to be the maintenance of the authority of the minister at the head of the department in which he served. His portrait by R. E. Fuller-Maitland, subscribed for by his official associates, was presented by Balfour and forms part of the collection of secretaries of the Admiralty in Admiralty House. He died, unmarried, at Harston, 10 September 1950.

[Admiralty records; Morning Post, 24 September 1934; private information; personal knowledge.]          VINCENT W. BADDELEY.

GREENWOOD, HAMAR, first VIS-COUNT GREENWOOD (1870–1948), politician, was born 7 February 1870 at Whitby, near Toronto, the eldest son of John Hamar Greenwood, a lawyer who had left Wales for Canada as a boy, and his wife, Charlotte Churchill Hubbard, descendant of a loyalist emigrant from the American revolution. At his birth, his Christian names were registered as Thomas Hubbard. He went to Whitby High School and Toronto University, worked in the provincial department of agriculture, and served for seven years as an officer in the Canadian militia; he did not take his arts degree until 1895. In that year he moved to England to seek his fortune. He never drank alcohol, and his views on the drink question attracted him at once to the English Liberals, for whom he spoke and wrote fluently. He was called to the bar by Gray's Inn in 1906, became a bencher in 1917, and took silk in 1919, but left no mark as a lawyer. He helped in 1902 to raise the King's Colonials (afterwards King Edward's Horse), a yeomanry regiment of British subjects from overseas. He refused the offer of a parliamentary candidacy in 1900, but in 1906 became senior Liberal member for York, and acted as (Sir) Winston Churchill's parliamentary private secretary for four years. He made some stir in the Commons with speeches on imperial defence, more welcome to Conservatives than Liberals; lost his seat in January 1910; and returned to Parliament in December as Liberal member for Sunderland. In 1913 he published a small book, *Canada as an Imperial Factor*, a description of his mother country more enthusiastic than critical.

In August 1914 his sister's husband, L. S. Amery, brought him into the recruiting department of the War Office where he developed his gifts for quick decisions in emergency. Greenwood himself raised the 10th battalion, South Wales Borderers, and commanded it at the front in France; in February 1915 he was created a baronet. A year later Lord Derby [q.v.] brought him back to London for more work on recruiting; and in August 1916 he returned to politics, becoming the personal adherent of Lloyd George. In January 1919 he became under-secretary for home affairs; was moved in July to take charge of overseas trade; and in April 1920 was advanced to the Cabinet as the (last) chief secretary for Ireland.

Ireland was already in a state of undeclared war. Greenwood shared Lloyd George's view that the Irish people were terrorized by a 'murder gang', and was determined to re-establish the authority of Dublin Castle by force. The army, under Sir Nevil Macready [q.v.], was reinforced, but since the Cabinet was not yet prepared to declare a state of martial law, the main burden fell upon the Royal Irish Constabulary, now seriously depleted in numbers. An extra 5,800 men, most of them lately demobilized, were hastily recruited in Britain; their improvised uniforms earned them the nickname 'Black and Tans', from a famous pack of Limerick hounds. (The nickname was sometimes also given to 1,500 auxiliary police, mainly former officers.) The Black and Tans were undisciplined—some of them it turned out were ex-convicts—and inappropriately trained, and their ignorance of the country and its people often left them at the mercy of the Irish Republican Army, whose violent methods they soon adopted in reprisal for the attacks made upon them. In Parliament the chief secretary took it upon himself to defend all that they did; his stonewalling statements there were not unfairly caricatured as 'there is no such thing as reprisals, but they have done a great deal of good'.

As the 'competition in murder' increased, the actions of the Black and Tans defeated their own object, for the British conscience was awakened to the unhappy state of affairs in Ireland. Moreover, Irish opinion became more devoted in favour of the insurgents, making a prolonged guerrilla possible, despite the fact that the Irish volunteers, according to Michael Collins [q.v.], never numbered as many as 3,000 armed men at any given moment. That the Irish hated the British, and would suffer anything to see them go, was the main cause of Greenwood's failure. Lloyd George realized this before Greenwood did himself. By April 1921, while Greenwood was assuring the King's secretary that 'the Republic exists no longer', Lloyd George was already feeling out the chances of negotiation with the Irish republican leaders. Immediately after King George V's visit to Belfast (22 June 1921) Lloyd George entered into direct communication with Mr. de Valera, and the truce of 11 July was arranged over Greenwood's head. Greenwood attended the Anglo-Irish conference in Downing Street in October, and signed the treaty of 6 December 1921 (a day late), but he took little active part in the discussions which preceded it. When the Irish Free State was set up in the following month he maintained his narrowly chivalrous view that his only duty was to his subordinates, and kept the post of chief secretary in order to do his best for the pension rights of the Royal Irish Constabulary, a body which the Free State at once disbanded. When Lloyd George fell in October 1922 Greenwood resigned also; and in the general election of November he lost his seat.

He failed again to carry Sunderland in the general election of 1923, and eventually returned to Parliament, bearing the label 'anti-Socialist', for East Walthamstow in that of 1924. No office was offered him; but in 1929 he was granted the barony of Greenwood, of Llanbister, his father's original home in Radnorshire, in the resignation honours. From 1933 to 1938 he served as honorary treasurer of the Conservative Party, bullying, in a jovial way, substantial cheques out of his many acquaintances in the business world. In 1937 he was advanced to a viscountcy.

His talents for conducting meetings briskly were valuable to him in business; at one time he was chairman of eight out of sixteen companies on the boards of which he sat. These included Dorman, Long & Co. (he was president of the Iron and Steel Federation in 1938), and the Aerated Bread Company. His boyhood talent as an actor flowered into an incomparable gift for after-dinner speaking, which carried him, in the last year of his life, to the presidency of the Pilgrims Society; in that post he arranged the placing of the Roosevelt statue in Grosvenor Square. He died in London 10 September 1948.

In 1911 Greenwood married Margery, daughter of Walter Spencer, a Herefordshire gentleman; she was appointed C.B.E. in 1920 and advanced to D.B.E. in 1922 for her services in Ireland. They had two sons and two daughters; the elder son, David Henry Hamar (born 30 October 1914), succeeded to the titles.

[W. A. Phillips, The Revolution in Ireland, 2nd ed., 1926; Frank Pakenham, Peace by Ordeal, 1935; The Times, 11 and 21 September 1948; Harold Nicolson, King George V, 1952; L. S. Amery, My Political Life, vol. ii, 1953; private information.]

M. R. D. FOOT.

GREER, (FREDERICK) ARTHUR, BARON FAIRFIELD (1863–1945), judge, was born in Liverpool 6 October 1863, the eldest of the fourteen children of Arthur Greer, a Manxman, by his wife, Mary Hatfield Moore. The father was a metal merchant who lived mostly in the Isle of Man. He bought the famous steamboat *Great Eastern* when she was due for breaking up. After some preliminary education Greer was sent to the Old Aberdeen Grammar School, and he went on to the university of Aberdeen, where after a brilliant academic career he graduated with first class honours in mental philosophy and won the Fullerton scholarship (1883). Family circumstances no doubt compelled him to start work in his profession without delay and he proceeded to London and was called to the bar by Gray's Inn in 1886 after winning there the Bacon and Arden scholarships. He joined the Northern circuit, but success did not come quickly, and for some years he had to supplement his income by writing for the *Liverpool Daily Post* and the *Liverpool Courier*. At one moment hope almost failed and he decided to abandon the bar and take to journalism. He applied to Sir Edward Richard (later Lord) Russell, the famous editor of the *Liverpool Daily Post*, for a place on the staff of the paper. Russell advised him to reconsider his decision, and Greer continued his struggle at the bar and his writing for the newspapers.

In 1902 the turn of the tide came in a civil action at the Liverpool assizes which aroused much local interest. Greer appeared for the plaintiff. His conduct of the case attracted the attention of solicitors in Liverpool and his practice on the circuit grew steadily. He also lectured on law in the university of Liverpool for three years. In 1907, twenty years after his call, and while still a junior, he moved to London and practised both there and at the Liverpool assizes. Work at those assizes together with appeals to courts in London made up the largest part of his substantial practice. In 1910 the persuasion of his friends at length overcame his modesty and he applied for silk which was immediately granted. In 1911 he appeared for the defendants in the famous case of *Lloyd* v. *Grace, Smith & Co.*, [1911] 2 K.B. 489 and [1912] A.C. 716, a case of the liability of a principal for the fraudulent act of a servant, where the decision of Sir T. E. Scrutton [q.v.] at Liverpool in favour of the plaintiff was reversed in the Court of Appeal and restored in the

House of Lords. Greer's work continued for some time after he took silk to be mainly on the Northern circuit, but he eventually established an excellent practice in London, mainly in the Commercial Court and in the higher courts. In the war of 1914–18 he was engaged in several of the more important cases in the Prize Court. Those who knew him about that time will remember the tall figure, the piercing blue eyes, the bent shoulders, the keen, intellectual face, and also the lines of pain which chronic attacks of arthritis had already begun to trace upon his features.

In 1919 Greer was appointed a judge of the King's Bench division, receiving the customary knighthood, and he sat frequently in the Commercial Court. The most famous criminal case over which he presided was the trial of Frederick Rothwell Holt for the murder of Mrs. Breaks, which aroused great excitement at the Manchester assizes in 1920. His discharge of his judicial duties created a general expectation that he would be promoted and in 1927 he was appointed a lord justice of appeal and sworn of the Privy Council. He sat in the Court of Appeal until his retirement in 1938.

Greer was admirably equipped both in mind and temper for the work of a judge. He was patient and free from any tendency to rush to a conclusion. He had a wide knowledge of the principles of law and especially of the common law. When a number of decisions bearing on a principle of law had to be scrutinized and assessed he accomplished the task with equal niceness and accuracy of discrimination. He had a marked aversion from any obscurity in thought or in expression. One of his most notable characteristics was a strong independence of mind, and, despite his modesty, if he was unable to agree with his colleagues in the Court of Appeal he never shrank from the responsibility of expressing his dissent. On several occasions his dissenting judgements were afterwards approved in the House of Lords. His judgements were well arranged, and free from digression and from obscurity or artifice in language. They reveal admirably the vigour and the lucidity of his mind. If need arose he was always ready to ease and smooth the path of forensic controversy. He was courteous to all who appeared before him in any capacity and beneath a shy and reserved demeanour he hid a real kindliness of heart.

Greer received the honorary degree of

LL.D. from the university of Aberdeen in 1926 and from Liverpool in 1930. He became a member of the Council of Legal Education in 1917 and served as chairman from 1934 to 1936. He collaborated with his son-in-law, Ronw Moelwyn Hughes, K.C., in the article on bills of exchange, promissory notes, and negotiable instruments which appeared in the second edition of Halsbury's *Laws of England.*

Greer was twice married: first, in 1901 to Katherine (died 1937), daughter of Emanuel van Noorden, of Orangeburg, South Carolina, and had as issue one daughter; and secondly, in 1939 to Mabel, daughter of William John Fraser, civil engineer, of London, and widow of Charles Woodward Neele, chief electrical engineer of the Great Central Railway. In 1939 Greer was raised to the peerage as Baron Fairfield, of Caldy, in the county palatine of Cheshire. He died at Caldy 4 February 1945, and his peerage became extinct. There is a portrait of him in the robes of a lord justice at Gray's Inn, of which he was treasurer in 1921; another in judge's robes is in the possession of the family.

[Private information; personal knowledge.]
C. T. LE QUESNE.

GRENFELL, EDWARD CHARLES, first BARON ST. JUST (1870–1941), banker and politician, was born in London 29 May 1870, the only son of Henry Riversdale Grenfell, banker and member of Parliament, by his wife, Alethea Louisa, daughter of Henry John Adeane, landowner and member of Parliament, of Babraham, Cambridge. Lord Desborough, a notice of whom appears below, was his cousin. Grenfell was educated at Harrow and Trinity College, Cambridge, where he won the Greaves essay prize in 1891 and obtained a second class in history in 1892. Electing to follow his father's profession of banking, he went first to Brown, Shipley & Co., and, after two years, moved in 1894 to Smith, Ellison's Bank at Lincoln, eventually becoming manager of the Grimsby branch.

Meanwhile Grenfell had made the acquaintance of Walter Hayes Burns, partner in the Anglo-American banking firm of J. S. Morgan & Co. in London, who, forming a high opinion of his abilities, appointed him manager of that house in 1900. He was given a partnership in 1904; and in 1909, when the house style had to be changed under the provisions of J. S. Morgan's will, it was renamed Morgan,

Grenfell & Co. Grenfell quickly made his mark in the City and acquired other interests. He was a director of the Bank of England from 1905 till 1940 and served on the board of the Sun Assurance group. He was also a director of the White Star Line, and was closely concerned with the purchase of that steamship company by the American corporation, International Mercantile Marine, Inc., on the London committee of which he sat.

During the war of 1914–18 it was decided that all British and allied purchases of American war materials should pass through the Morgan firm in New York; and Grenfell with his fellow partners was closely concerned with the great task of organization involved in this immense series of transactions.

Grenfell's reputation in the City of London was such that, when he aspired to Parliament in 1922, he was adopted as Conservative candidate for that constituency. At a by-election in May 1922 he was returned with a majority of 3,936; and in the general elections of 1922 and 1923 both he and Sir Frederick Banbury (later Lord Banbury of Southam, q.v.) were returned unopposed. He remained in the House of Commons until 1935, when he was raised to the peerage as Baron St. Just, of St. Just in Penwith, in the county of Cornwall.

Grenfell continued throughout his life to take a lively interest in the affairs of Harrow School, and served as governor from 1922 until his death, which took place at Bacres, Henley-on-Thames, 26 November 1941.

Grenfell's life was bound up with the City and with Parliament, but both in business and in politics he moved with great caution and circumspection. He held definite views on finance, which he made known behind the political scenes rather than in the House, feeling that many of his constituents would not concur with them. In a period of changing manners and values he was jealous to preserve at all costs the solid reputation of his firm. His standing derived mainly from his great loyalty and integrity, which inspired trust and confidence in those with whom he had dealings. Always formally and correctly well dressed, he appeared to superficial acquaintances a conventional and reserved man; but to those who knew him well there was revealed a fund of affectionate friendship.

In 1913 Grenfell married Florence Emily, elder daughter of George William

Henderson, merchant importer, of London. He was succeeded in the barony by his only child, Peter George (born 1922). A portrait of Grenfell by (Sir) Oswald Birley is in the possession of the family.

[*The Times*, 28 November 1941; private information.]    HERBERT B. GRIMSDITCH.

GRENFELL, WILLIAM HENRY, BARON DESBOROUGH (1855–1945), athlete, sportsman, and public servant, was born in London 30 October 1855, the eldest son of Charles William Grenfell, M.P., of Taplow Court, Buckinghamshire, by his wife, Georgiana Caroline, daughter of William Saunders Sebright Lascelles, son of the second Earl of Harewood [q.v.]. His great-grandfather, Pascoe Grenfell [q.v.], was at one time member of Parliament for Great Marlow, a constituency which 'Willy' Grenfell was himself to represent a hundred years later. At Harrow he was, as a redoubtable bowler, in the cricket eleven (1873–4), and he also excelled in the school sports. In due time he went up to Balliol College, Oxford, of which in 1928 he was elected an honorary fellow; he graduated in 1879 and in 1938 he received the honorary degree of D.C.L. from the university.

When Grenfell left Oxford he was invited to stand for Parliament as a member for Salisbury. He came of Liberal stock with a long Whig tradition behind him and he was elected in 1880. In 1882 he was appointed a parliamentary groom-in-waiting; but this involved a by-election and by a narrow margin he was defeated. He was returned, however, at the next general election in 1885 and was private secretary to the chancellor of the Exchequer, Sir William Harcourt [q.v.]; but on the defeat of Gladstone over the first Home Rule bill in 1886 Grenfell lost his seat again and, although he was candidate for Windsor at a by-election in 1890, it was not until 1892 that he was returned as a Gladstonian Liberal for Hereford City. But he was unable to accept Gladstone's second Home Rule bill and he preferred to resign rather than support it. He did not stand again until he won the Wycombe division of Buckinghamshire as a Conservative in 1900. In 1905 he was raised to the peerage as Baron Desborough, of Taplow, a title which he took from the old hundred of Desborough in Buckinghamshire.

On the surface such an outcome seems to be a great disappointment to what was

acclaimed as a promising parliamentary career. But the bare recital of Desborough's activities and achievements is extremely impressive. He filled almost all the offices in local government and local justice which were open to him in Berkshire and Buckinghamshire, and it has been calculated that at one time he was actually serving on no fewer than 115 committees, where his services were recognized as of real value. His appointments show his true bent for public duty, including as they did the chairmanship of the Thames Conservancy Board for thirty-two years; of the special committee of the London Chamber of Commerce which successfully opposed the Declaration of London in 1911; the presidency of the London Chamber of Commerce and of the British Imperial Council of Commerce. His duties took him to Toronto in 1920 to attend the ninth congress of the Chambers of Commerce of the British Empire and this may have inspired the offer made in 1921, but declined for family reasons, to become governor-general of Canada. He was also chairman of the Home Office committee on the police of England, Scotland, and Wales; in 1923 president of the international navigation congress in London, and in 1925 president of the Royal Agricultural Society. During the war of 1914–18 he was president of the Central Association of Volunteer Training Corps which passed more than a million men into the regular army and was eventually taken over by the War Office. In 1915 he represented the minister of munitions in France, selecting and recalling workmen for key positions in the war effort; in addition he administered a naval hospital at Southend and turned his own house at Taplow into a rest home for nurses.

To most of his countrymen Desborough's name was known as that of a man with an extraordinarily wide range of activities. Without his genial and friendly manner and without his example no one could have handled men as he did. He could speak in public with ease, and his unprepared speeches were both good and amusing. He looked, in his young days, the ideal athlete, and in the field of sport and athletics, by land and by water, he held a place unrivalled by any of his contemporaries. Only a happy and resolute nature could have made so much out of the hours of each day. Whilst at Oxford he rowed in the dead-heat race against Cambridge of 1877, and in the following year, when he was president of the University Boat Club, he was in the crew which won by ten lengths. He was also president of the Oxford University Athletic Club, and it is believed that no other man has been president of both clubs. Further, he combined these exertions with the mastership of the university draghounds. Outside Oxford he won the Thames punting championship for three successive years (1888–90) and then retired unbeaten; he stroked an eight across the Channel; with two others he sculled the London–Oxford stretch of the Thames in twenty-two consecutive hours, and when he was a member of the House of Commons he rowed for the Grand Challenge Cup. Small wonder that he was for many years a steward of Henley regatta. He twice swam Niagara, crossing the pool just below the falls in the supposedly calm water between the thundering falls and the undertow. In the Alps he had remarkable success: he ascended the Matterhorn by three different routes, and, in one long vacation, within eight days climbed the little Matterhorn, the Matterhorn, Monte Rosa, the Rothorn, and the Weisshorn. On one occasion in the Rocky Mountains he was lost when his companion strayed from the camp and perished. Although not a regular soldier he saw active service as a special correspondent of the *Daily Telegraph* in the Suakin campaign of 1888, when not only was he under fire but at one time found himself confronted by the advancing enemy, alone, and with no better weapon in his hand than an umbrella.

At Taplow he kept his own harriers which had formerly been King Edward VII's, and, point-to-points played a great part in his life. He loved 'the hill' and stalking in Scotland, fishing in many countries, big-game hunting in the Rockies, in India, and in Africa, and he caught a hundred tarpon off the coast of Florida. He greatly encouraged fencing in this country and was president of the Amateur Fencing Association from its foundation until 1926. In 1908 he was president of the Olympic games held in London. An excellent whip, he was president of both the Coaching Club and the Four-in-Hand Club, being proud of his team of bays. He was also in his time president of the Marylebone Cricket Club and the Lawn Tennis Association, president and chairman of the Bath Club from its foundation in 1894 until 1942, and chairman of the Pilgrims of Great Britain from 1919 to 1929.

While still a young man Desborough was known and loved by many, and his strong literary and artistic sense made a wide appeal. Many distinguished friends relied upon the wisdom of his judgement. To friendship and good sense he added executive capacity. 'Willy' Grenfell was a man who was able 'to get things done'.

He married in 1887 Ethel Anne Priscilla (died 1952), daughter of Julian Henry Charles Fane [q.v.]. They had three sons and two daughters. The two eldest sons (the eldest was Julian Grenfell, q.v.) were killed in action in 1915 and the third son who was unmarried died in 1926 as the result of a motor-car accident. The peerage therefore became extinct when he died at Panshanger, Hertford, 9 January 1945. His elder daughter is the wife of Marshal of the Royal Air Force Sir John Salmond, and the younger is the Viscountess Gage.

Desborough was appointed C.V.O. in 1907 and advanced to K.C.V.O. in 1908 and G.C.V.O. in 1925; and in 1928 he was admitted as a knight of the Order of the Garter. From 1924 to 1929 he was captain of the Yeomen of the Guard. In the possession of the family there are portraits of him by Ellis Roberts and Sir A. S. Cope, and a drawing by J. S. Sargent.

[Private information; personal knowledge.]
MONICA SALMOND.

GRIERSON, SIR GEORGE ABRAHAM (1851–1941), Indian civil servant and philologist, was born at Glenageary, county Dublin, 7 January 1851, the eldest son of George Abraham Grierson, LL.D., printer to the Queen in Dublin, by his wife, Isabella, daughter of Henry Ruxton, Royal Navy, of Ardee, county Louth. Educated at St. Bees and Shrewsbury schools and at Trinity College, Dublin, where he read mathematics, he passed (twenty-eighth in the list) into the Indian Civil Service in 1871. In the two further probationary years at Trinity College, during which he won university prizes in Sanskrit and Hindustani and was placed twelfth in the final examination, he fell deeply under the influence of Robert Atkinson [q.v.] who inspired him with his own linguistic interests and before Grierson sailed for the East in 1873 proposed to him a life-task in the form of a linguistic survey of India.

Appointed to the Bengal presidency, Grierson fulfilled for the next twenty-three years the active duties of a member of the Civil Service. In 1881 he was assistant and for a time officiating magistrate and collector at Patna, where in 1884 he became joint magistrate and collector. After special duty at Howra he spent five years at Gaya (1887–92), becoming magistrate and collector in 1890. After two further years at Howra he was appointed additional commissioner at Patna in 1895. His last normal appointment (1896) was as opium agent for Bihar. In 1898 he was designated superintendent of the newly sanctioned *Linguistic Survey of India*.

In 1877, four years after Grierson's arrival in India, appeared the first of the long succession of articles, reviews, and books on the languages and folk-lore of India which flowed from his pen in an unbroken stream year by year for nearly sixty years. The mere list of his writings between 1877 and 1933 occupies twenty-one large octavo pages in the volume of *Indian and Iranian Studies* presented to him on his eighty-fifth birthday (*Bulletin* of the School of Oriental Studies, vol. viii, parts 2 and 3, 1936), and even on this occasion he offered to the deputation waiting on him his own latest volume, *Puruṣaparīkṣā*, published a few weeks earlier.

During the decade following his first publications Grierson's attention was mainly focused on the languages and dialects of Bihar. Although the independence of this important group of Indo-Aryan languages was clearly demonstrated by A. F. R. Hoernlé in his *Comparative Grammar of the Gaudian Languages* (1880), it is to Grierson that we owe detailed knowledge of both their structure and their content. Two works of major importance belong to this period: *Seven Grammars of the Dialects and Subdialects of the Bihārī Language* (in 8 parts, 1883–7) and *Bihār Peasant Life, being a Discursive Catalogue of the Surroundings of the People of that Province* (1885). This latter, a volume of 592 pages, reprinted in 1926, contained an exhaustive account of the life of an agricultural population and of the implements they used, in which the comparative vocabularies are illustrated by drawings, photographs, and descriptions.

From Bihar Grierson's interest spread out into the languages of Hindustan proper. He wrote extensively on both their modern forms and their medieval literature, studying especially the two great epics, the *Rāmāyaṇ* of Tulsīdās, and

the *Padumāvatī* of Jaisī, an edition and translation of the first thirty-five cantos of which he published in 1896 in collaboration with Sudhākara Dvivedī. As early as 1889 *The Modern Vernacular Literature of Hindustan* had appeared as a special number of the *Journal* of the Asiatic Society of Bengal. In the previous year his translation of Émile Senart's *The Inscriptions of Piyadāsī* had been published in the *Indian Antiquary*. Doubtless this work intensified an interest already aroused in the history and comparative philology of the whole Indo-Aryan group of languages, an interest which resulted not only in numerous articles on individual languages but also in a conspectus of the main lines of their development described in his articles in the *Zeitschrift der Deutschen morgenländischen Gesellschaft* in 1895, 'On the Phonology of the Modern Indo-Aryan Vernaculars'.

In the same year appeared the first of a long series of articles and books on Kashmiri, culminating in *A Dictionary of the Kashmīrī Language*, a quarto volume of 1,252 pages of which the first part appeared in 1916 and the last in 1932. Kashmiri is one of the Dardic languages; to these Grierson attributed, although perhaps wrongly, the gipsy dialects of Europe and Asia, on the affinities of which he wrote a number of articles from 1888 onwards. The other members of the Dardic group, spoken in the remote and inaccessible valleys of the upper Indus and its tributaries among the mountains of the Hindu Kush, were after the Muhammadan invasion of north-west India largely cut off from the main stream of Indo-Aryan linguistic development and show both many archaic features and striking innovations. These languages were little known and in some cases quite unknown and undocumented. To such knowledge as was available from notes and word lists compiled mainly by soldiers and political officers was now added further information which began to be collected in connexion with the *Linguistic Survey of India*. All this Grierson utilized in studying the Dardic, or, as he named them, the Piśāca languages in numerous articles beginning in 1898, and in two books: *The Piśāca Languages of North-Western India* (1906) and *Torwālī* (1929). Affinities which he traced in certain Iranian languages to the Dardic group led to the publication of two monographs *Ōrmuṛī* (1918) and *Ishkashmī, Zebakī and Yazghulāmī* (1920). Any attempt to follow the history of the Indo-Aryan languages necessarily involves study of the Prakrit dialects which stand as intermediaries between Sanskrit and the modern languages. In this direction also Grierson made notable contributions, especially by his studies of the eastern school of Prakrit grammarians. The collection of material for the *Linguistic Survey* further brought Grierson into contact with language families outside the Indo-Aryan, and he published papers on Ahom, an old language of Assam, and, in conjunction with Professor Sten Konow, on the Kuki-Chin languages.

Grierson's output of scientific work over the whole field was thus actively continued throughout the time he was engaged in the compilation of the *Linguistic Survey of India*, namely from its inception in 1898 to its completion in 1928. In fulfilment of the injunction of his old teacher Atkinson, Grierson introduced the project of a general linguistic survey of India before the Oriental Congress held in Vienna in 1886. The congress recommended it to the Government of India and the scope and general lines of procedure as adopted by the superintendent had been under discussion for the four years preceding his appointment. The materials were to include as far as possible for every language, dialect, and subdialect, which in many districts varied from village to village or as between classes or sexes, a version of the parable of the prodigal son, an orally elicited narrative or statement, and a scheduled vocabulary of words and phrases. For this purpose Grierson had a multitude of correspondents, official and non-official. After the critical examination and selection of texts and translations, the final entry contained in each case geographical and census particulars, bibliography, discussion of group relations, and a grammatical sketch, based on the materials, with reference to any prior knowledge, and comprising phonology, morphology, syntax, and script. The immensity of this task may be judged by the fact that the nineteen folio volumes containing nearly 8,000 pages provide descriptions of 179 separate languages (of which the test is mutual unintelligibility) and 544 dialects belonging to five separate and distinct families, the Mon-Khmer and Tai, the Tibeto-Burman, the Munda, the Dravidian, the Indo-Aryan and Iranian. For some years Grierson was assisted by the Norwegian scholar, Sten Konow, but he himself compiled at least two-thirds of the total. This monumental work is not only an inexhaustible mine for all those who study the languages of India, but beyond any other stimulated in Indians a pride in their own vernaculars and a deep interest in the long history which lies behind them. In 1903 Grierson retired from India and continued his work on the *Survey* at Camberley where he built his house Rathfarnham (named after his grandfather's castle in county Dublin) which was to become during nearly forty years a place of pilgrimage to a long succession of orientalists and other, especially Indian, visitors.

Grierson was appointed C.I.E. in 1894, K.C.I.E. in 1912, and appointed to the Order of Merit in 1928. He received honorary degrees from the universities of Halle, Dublin, Cambridge, Oxford, and Bihar, and he was an honorary member of numerous learned societies. He was a fellow of the British Academy from 1917 to 1939.

No attempt to assess Grierson's work could be complete without reference to his broad humanity, his delightful humour, his love and practice of music, his never-failing kindness. He was big in body, mind, and soul. He had a boundless energy and enthusiasm and a firmness of spirit which, held undeviating on the path he had chosen, triumphed over every difficulty of circumstance. Neither age nor sickness diminished that enthusiasm or dimmed that spirit. He died at Camberley 9 March 1941.

Grierson married in 1880 Lucy Elizabeth Jean (died 1943), daughter of Maurice Henry Fitzgerald Collis, M.D., a famous Dublin surgeon. There were no children.

[F. W. Thomas and R. L. Turner in *Proceedings* of the British Academy, vol. xxviii, 1942; *Journal* of the Royal Asiatic Society, 1941; *The Times*, 10 March 1941; personal knowledge.]     R. L. TURNER.

GUEDALLA, PHILIP (1889–1944), historian and essayist, was born 12 March 1889 in Elgin Avenue, Maida Vale, the only son of David Guedalla, an almond broker in Mincing Lane, who came of a Spanish-Jewish family, and his wife, Louise Soman. Guedalla's talents developed early, and at Rugby, where he became head of the school, the epigrammatic irreverence of his editorials in the school magazine, the *Meteor*, was a startling and popular innovation. This was a vein which he exploited with zest to the end of his life and never more successfully than during his brilliant career at Balliol College, Oxford. His *bons mots* as president of the Union went the rounds of the university; he figured as a much discussed Mark Antony in the O.U.D.S. production of *Julius Caesar*, and despite these distractions obtained first classes in classical moderations (1910) and modern history (1912). Before he left Oxford he had published two collections of light verse, *Ignes Fatui* and *Metri Gratia*, but at this time his ambitions were not primarily literary; he confidently hoped to enter politics by way of the bar, to which he was called by the Inner Temple in 1913, and to become a Liberal Cabinet minister, preferably as secretary of state for war. During the war of 1914–18 he served as legal adviser to the contracts department of the War Office and Ministry of Munitions, and from 1917 to 1920 organized and acted as secretary to the flax control board. He stood for Parliament five times between 1922 and 1931, but he was always defeated; and unlike so many of his Liberal contemporaries he steadily refused to transfer his allegiance to the rising star of Socialism. Working-class audiences, moreover, were sometimes mystified by speeches which retained all the epigrammatic glitter of his Oxford Union days.

Since his first ambitious work, *Supers and Supermen* (1920), was marked by both verbal fireworks and lack of reverence for established reputations, it was inevitable that he should be hailed as a disciple of Lytton Strachey [q.v.], whose *Eminent Victorians* had appeared in 1918. But although the new fashion of denigration was doubtless not uncongenial to him, Guedalla had set his literary course, and indeed formed the essentials of his literary style, before he left Oxford. And although as a writer he lacked Strachey's urbane subtlety, he was a more conscientious historical scholar. An historical work, he believed, should be good entertainment, but it should be based upon sound research, and he sometimes complained that critics of his writings were too apt to be distracted from the research by the entertainment. He was always more interested in men than movements, and *The Second Empire* (1922) was a study of the Emperor rather than of the Empire. In *A Gallery* (1924) and *Independence Day* (1926) he presented further collections of historical sketches in lighter vein, but in *Palmerston* (1926) he first displayed his full powers.

Here, as in *Gladstone and Palmerston* (1928), *The Queen and Mr. Gladstone* (2 vols., 1933), and most conspicuously perhaps in *The Duke* (1931), a full-length study of Wellington, was depth as well as brilliance; Guedalla was now not only entertaining a considerable audience, but making solid contributions to knowledge. *The Hundred Days* (1934) was followed by *The Hundred Years* (1936) which anticipated the centenary of Queen Victoria's accession. In this last work, and notably in his study of (Sir) Winston Churchill (1941) and in *The Two Marshals* (1943), a comparison of Bazaine and Pétain, his interest in the contemporary scene began to transfer itself, now that he had abandoned politics himself, to his writings. He died in London 16 December 1944, of an illness contracted during the journeys which, as a temporary squadron leader in the Royal Air Force, he had devoted to preparing his last work, *Middle East 1940–1942, A Study in Air Power* (1944).

Despite the cynical note which he occasionally sounded, Guedalla was a man of simple and kindly nature; and the persistence of his taste for epigram was itself evidence that he had remained young at heart. He married in 1919 Nellie Maude, daughter of Albert Reitlinger, banker, of 192 Queen's Gate, S.W. 7, who survived him. There were no children.

An early portrait by John Collier and two cartoons by Sir Max Beerbohm (of whose work Guedalla was an eager collector) are in the possession of the family.

[*The Times*, 18 December 1944; private information; personal knowledge.] ELTON.

GUINNESS, WALTER EDWARD, first BARON MOYNE (1880–1944), statesman and traveller, was born in Dublin 29 March 1880 in the house, 80 St. Stephen's Green, which was afterwards presented to the Irish nation by his brother in 1939 and now contains the Irish Department of External Affairs. He was the third son of Edward Cecil Guinness, later the first Earl of Iveagh [q.v.], and like his brothers was educated at Eton where he rowed for three years in the eight and in due course became captain of the boats. Under him as president, the Eton Society was reformed so as to admit intellectual as well as athletic representatives, and its debates were revived. Moreover, at Eton he developed a particular and enduring interest in biology, but instead of pursuing this bent at Oxford, as he had intended, he volunteered for service in the South African war with the Suffolk Yeomanry (Loyal Suffolk Hussars). He was wounded, mentioned in dispatches, and awarded the Queen's medal with four clasps.

While Walter Guinness was growing up, the family spent an increasing amount of time in England, and in the early 'nineties his father bought a famous sporting estate at Elveden in Suffolk, a circumstance which made it appropriate that Walter Guinness should stand as Conservative candidate for the Stowmarket division. Although defeated at the general election of 1906, he was returned at a by-election in 1907 for Bury St. Edmunds which, as a division of Suffolk, he continued to represent until 1931. He was a member of the London County Council from 1907 to 1910. From the war of 1914–18 Guinness retired as lieutenant-colonel, having served first in Gallipoli and Egypt as a major with the Suffolk Yeomanry and afterwards with the 10th battalion of the London Regiment. He had been three times mentioned in dispatches, and was awarded the D.S.O. in 1917 and a bar in 1918.

Guinness's high public spirit and wide interests led him to pursue an extremely full life in which politics, scientific travel, and a share in the direction of his father's benefactions in England and Ireland, as well as of the Guinness breweries, were intertwined. His service as a statesman opened with his appointment as under-secretary of state for war in 1922, followed by the financial secretaryship of the Treasury in 1923, and again in 1924–5 under (Sir) Winston Churchill as chancellor of the Exchequer. He was sworn of the Privy Council in 1924 and entered the Cabinet in November 1925 as minister of agriculture. During his tenure of the office, he introduced the system of the national mark for eggs, and it was largely owing to his efforts that the sugar-beet industry was built up. With the defeat of the Conservatives in 1929 he retired from office, and in 1932 he was raised to the peerage as Baron Moyne, of Bury St. Edmunds, in the county of Suffolk.

Out of office Moyne was able increasingly to combine his public service with that eagerness for travel which he had always displayed. As early as 1902 he had gone on the first of many big-game hunting expeditions—later in life he grew less inclined towards shooting except as neces-

sary for food—and before 1914 he had travelled extensively on map-making expeditions in Asia Minor and become conversant with the plight of the Armenians and other minorities, for whom he then saw hope in Turkish reform rather than in foreign intervention. (It was during one of his absences in Asia Minor that the *Outlook*, of which he had become the proprietor, published without his knowledge a series of articles on the Marconi affair in 1912. On his return home he gave evidence in support of the editor before the select committee of inquiry.) After being raised to the peerage he not only acted as chairman of the departmental committee on housing in 1933, of the Royal Commission on the university of Durham in 1934, and of the departmental committee on British films in 1936, but he was also financial commissioner to Kenya in 1932 and chairman of the West India Royal Commission in 1938 and 1939, placing his yacht *Rosaura* at the disposal of the members for residence and for transport. This yacht was a sister-ship to another named *Roussalka* which was wrecked in 1933 off the west coast of Ireland, and both were used by Moyne to enable him to travel to distant places in search of biological specimens and archaeological material. In 1934 he travelled to the island of Komodo, near New Guinea, and brought back living specimens of Komodo dragons for the gardens of the London Zoological Society. His subsequent journey to New Guinea in 1935 he described in his book *Walkabout* (1936), and a later journey to Greenland and to the little-known Bay Islands off the coast of Honduras in *Atlantic Circle* (1938).

On the outbreak of war in 1939 Moyne undertook to act as chairman of the Polish Relief Fund and lent for its offices part of his London house at 10 and 11 Grosvenor Place. Although he had served as minister of agriculture, he agreed to serve as joint parliamentary secretary to the minister on the formation of the Churchill Government in 1940. The next year Moyne succeeded Lord Lloyd [q.v.] as secretary of state for the Colonies and leader of the House of Lords. In August 1942 he was appointed deputy minister of state in Cairo, and in January 1944 he succeeded Mr. Richard Gardiner Casey as minister resident in the Middle East; but on 6 November following he was assassinated in Cairo by terrorists from the Stern gang in Palestine.

Guinness married in 1903 Lady Evelyn

Hilda Stuart Erskine, daughter of the fourteenth Earl of Buchan, a talented lady of great beauty and unusual sensibility; she died in 1939, leaving two sons, of whom the elder, Bryan Walter (born 1905), succeeded his father as second baron, and one daughter who married in 1951 the fourth Marquess of Normanby. A portrait by P. A. de László, painted during the war of 1914–18, is in the possession of the family.

[*The Times*, 7 November 1944; private information; personal knowledge.]    MOYNE.

GUNN, BATTISCOMBE GEORGE (1883–1950), Egyptologist, was born in London 30 June 1883, the elder son of George Gunn, of the London Stock Exchange, by his wife, Julia Alice, daughter of John Moore Philp, journalist, of London. After being educated at Bedales, Westminster, and finally at Allhallows School, Honiton, he went to a tutor in Wiesbaden until, when he was eighteen, a financial crisis overtook his family and he had to return to England. His interest in Egyptology, which had begun very early, had never been encouraged, and the family difficulties did nothing to improve his prospect of pursuing a study which seemed unpractical; temporary employment was found for him in a bank, while further plans were made for a business career; but none of these attracted Gunn, whose tastes and talents were literary and artistic. In these years of discouragement his love of Egyptology never weakened; it bore fruit in the production of *The Instruction of Ptah-hotep* (1906), a book of translations of ancient Egyptian wisdom literature. When in 1908 he became private secretary to (Sir) Arthur Pinero [q.v.] and when in 1911 he went to Paris, where he was for a short time sub-editor of the *Continental Daily Mail*, he never lost sight of it in the pursuit of general literary and artistic interests.

Gunn had by now won the attention of such leading Egyptologists as (Sir) Flinders Petrie [q.v.] and (Sir) Alan Gardiner; and it was with the encouragement of the former that he first visited Egypt in 1913, working at Harageh with Reginald Engelbach (see *Harageh*, British School of Archaeology in Egypt Memoir No. 28, 1923) until the outbreak of war in 1914 when he volunteered, but was soon invalided out of the army. He then returned to London to work under the direction of Dr. Gardiner, passing gradually from the position of a pupil to that

of a highly valued collaborator; the product of several years' independent work was *Studies in Egyptian Syntax* (1924), Gunn's great contribution to the science of Egyptian language. He went back to Egypt to take part, with (Sir) Leonard Woolley and T. E. Peet [q.v.] in the excavation of El-Amarna, 1921–2 (see *The City of Akhenaten*, part 1, Egypt Exploration Society Memoir No. 38, 1923), and was shortly afterwards given a post in the Service des Antiquités de l'Égypte, in which capacity he excavated with Cecil Mallaby Firth at Saqqara, 1924–7 (see *Teti Pyramid Cemeteries*, 1926).

In 1928 Gunn was made assistant keeper in the Egyptian Museum, Cairo, where he remained until his appointment, in 1931, as curator of the Egyptian section of the University Museum, Philadelphia. In 1934 he succeeded Peet as professor of Egyptology and fellow of the Queen's College, Oxford; and in September 1935 he undertook the editorship of the *Journal of Egyptian Archaeology*, which he retained until December 1939. He was elected F.B.A. in 1943. As a professor much of his time was spent in teaching, although he was a frequent contributor to Egyptological journals. He died at Oxford 27 February 1950. Gunn was twice married: first to Lillian Florence Hughes, daughter of Charles Stephen Meacham, director, of Godstone Green, Surrey, by whom he had a son; the marriage was dissolved and in 1948 he married Constance Anna, daughter of Peter Rogers, civil servant, of Edinburgh.

Although experienced in the archaeological field, Gunn's chief interest lay in the written word; in the universality of his knowledge of Egyptian literature, writing, and grammar he was perhaps unrivalled. This in itself would have been enough to put him in demand as a teacher; a genius for instruction and selfless patience with pupils made this doubly sure; and many fellow scholars benefited from his ungrudging help. It was inevitable that his own original work should suffer, quantitatively, from these commitments, and it will be long before the publications of unfinished writing, and the testimony of successful pupils, will make the extent of his services to Egyptology fully known. Gunn was a charming and diversely brilliant man who, mistrustful of his own versatility, imposed first upon himself and then upon others an almost excessive discipline of accuracy. But the severity of the scholar never overcame or disguised the sympathetic nature of the man.

A drawing of Gunn by David Morris is in the possession of Mr. Clifford Bax.

[Warren R. Dawson in *Proceedings* of the British Academy, vol. xxxvi, 1950 (bibliography); *Annales* du Service des Antiquités de l'Égypte, vol. i, 1951; *Journal of Egyptian Archaeology*, vol. xxxvi, 1950; *Oxford Magazine*, 27 April 1950; *The Times*, 2 March 1950; Clifford Bax, *Inland Far*, 1925; private information; personal knowledge.]

J. W. B. BARNS.

GWYNN, STEPHEN LUCIUS (1864–1950), author and Irish nationalist, was born 13 February 1864 at St. Columba's College, near Dublin, the eldest child of John Gwynn [q.v.], then warden of the college, and his wife, Lucy Josephine, daughter of William Smith O'Brien [q.v.]. John Gwynn later became regius professor of divinity at Trinity College, Dublin, of which one of his sons, Edward John Gwynn (1868–1941), was to become provost, and another, the Rev. Robert Malcolm Gwynn, vice-provost, senior tutor, and senior dean. Stephen Gwynn, however, on leaving St. Columba's, went to Brasenose College, Oxford, where he was a scholar and was placed in the first class in classical moderations (1884) and *literae humaniores* (1886). It was apparently whilst he was at Oxford that his philosophy, a kindly stoicism, was formed.

After some years of schoolmastering, Gwynn in 1896 went to London to seek his living as a journalist; but in 1904 he settled in Ireland. From 1906 to 1918 he represented Galway City as a Nationalist member of Parliament, under the leadership of John Redmond [q.v.]. Although over fifty, he enlisted as a private in 1915, was commissioned in the Connaught Rangers, became a captain in that year, and served in France with the 16th Irish division until 1917 in which year he was made a chevalier of the Legion of Honour. In the same year he was appointed a member of the Irish convention, but this was to mark the end of his political career.

Gwynn had derived an immense patriotism from his mother who had seen her father's revolt against the slow because legal tactics of Daniel O'Connell [q.v.]. But his own patriotism took a form almost unique in Ireland; it had little in common with ephemeral politics; rather was it concerned with the natural beauty and

traditions of the land, particularly those of the eighteenth century. Not only was he an authority on that century, but he became a student of Irish history, topography, sport, legend, and poetry. He was himself a considerable poet who may be compared with another Oxford man, Robert Bridges [q.v.], for the precision of his technique, although the subjects of his verse have a more emotional appeal. 'Verses', he wrote to a friend, 'are the only things that are really fun to write.' To him poetry came easily. His humour and his metrical skill are well shown in his 'Lay of Ossian and Patrick' (1903) which reveals the conflict between paganism and Christianity upon which the old story-tellers of Ireland loved to linger. His first collection of verse, *The Queen's Chronicler and Other Poems*, appeared in 1901 when he had already published a novel, a number of essays, and a biography of James Northcote. He was later to publish the lives of such writers as Thomas Moore (1905), Sir Walter Scott (1930), Dean Swift (1933), Oliver Goldsmith (1935), whose influence is noticeable in Gwynn's prose, and Robert Louis Stevenson (1939). By far the greater number of his books, however, have the beauty of Ireland as their theme. Yet he did not become prominent as a leader of the Irish renaissance. It may be noted that writers such as Yeats, Shaw, and Synge [qq.v.] owed their reputation in two hemispheres to their association with the drama. In spite of his book *Irish Literature and Drama* (1936) and some early association with the Irish Players in London, Gwynn himself had little to do with drama, and stood apart from the fame and influence of the Abbey Theatre. Those who had identified themselves with 'the national being' as they called it, cared as little for *Tennyson: a critical study*, or for essays and sketches on *The Decay of Sensibility* (both 1899) as they did for his book *In Praise of France* (1927). But shortly before his death Gwynn received the medal of the Irish Academy of Letters founded by Yeats and Shaw; and he was an honorary D.Litt. of the National University of Ireland (1940) and of Dublin University (1945).

Gwynn's long life witnessed many changes both slow and abrupt: three major wars, a rebellion, and a civil war. None of these affected his imperturbability. He was stationary but not a recluse. Unobtrusively he lived and died, but for patriotism, scholarship, and integrity he was the greatest figure in the

Ireland of his time. In stature he was about the middle size or somewhat over. He was lean but not thin. His complexion was very fair as the name Gwynn in Cymric means. A portrait of him by Sir William Rothenstein hangs in the Municipal Gallery of Modern Art, Dublin. There are portraits of him by other artists in the galleries of Galway and Cork. They show a fair, blue-eyed man with forehead bent in a scrutinizing look, or a look that is open and far away. This was his most habitual appearance. He kept fit and active all his life, as his soldiering at fifty indicates; but he lost an eye through an accident when he was swinging an axe some years before his death which took place in Dublin 11 June 1950.

In 1889 Gwynn married his cousin Mary Louisa (died 1941), daughter of the Rev. James Gwynn. They had four sons and two daughters. One son, Denis Rolleston Gwynn, who contributes to this SUPPLEMENT, became research professor of modern Irish history at University College, Cork; another, Aubrey Gwynn, a Jesuit priest and professor of medieval history at University College, Dublin.

[S. L. Gwynn, *Experiences of a Literary Man*, 1926; private information; personal knowledge.]

OLIVER ST. JOHN GOGARTY.

GWYNNE, HOWELL ARTHUR (1865–1950), journalist, was born 3 September 1865 in the district of Kilvey near Swansea, the son of Richard Gwynne, schoolmaster, by his wife, Charlotte Lloyd. He was educated at Swansea Grammar School and abroad. A friendship struck up on holiday with the King of Romania laid the foundation of his career and in 1893, after a short spell as Balkan correspondent of *The Times*, Gwynne was appointed Reuter's correspondent in Romania. He remained in the service of that news agency until 1904, acting as special and war correspondent. In 1895 he went to Ashanti, in 1896 accompanied Kitchener to Dongola, in 1897 followed the Greco-Turkish war, and was in Peking in 1898–9. In 1899 he organized Reuter's South African war service, giving Edgar Wallace [q.v.] his first employment as a journalist, and himself reported Methuen's campaign, being present at the battle of Magersfontein; later he covered the operations directed by Lord Roberts [q.v.] who became his lifelong friend. In 1902 he returned to England, but immediately went back to South Africa with Joseph Chamberlain on the tour which was to be followed by the split of the Conservative Party over tariff reform. The murder of the King and Queen of Serbia took him to Belgrade, and in 1904 he was appointed foreign director of Reuter's agency. In the same year he accepted the editorship of the *Standard*, a post which he held until 1911 when he became editor of the *Morning Post*, remaining until it was merged in the *Daily Telegraph* in 1937. He was appointed C.H. in the following year.

The visit to South Africa with Chamberlain was the decisive factor in Gwynne's career. His close friendship with Cecil Rhodes, Lord Milner [qq.v.], and Chamberlain himself, and his wholehearted acceptance of tariff reform as a bond of empire marked him out for the editorship of the *Standard*, when the paper was bought by (Sir) C. Arthur Pearson [q.v.] to support that policy. The task which Gwynne undertook was formidable, since it demanded the conversion of Conservative readers of moderate and old-fashioned views to a policy with which they had no sympathy at all. The cry of 'dear food' filled them with an alarm which no doctrines of imperial union could allay. The circulation of the *Standard* rapidly dwindled, but by an extraordinary chance Gwynne was able to transfer to another equally famous paper. The outer world knew nothing of the troubles behind the calm and dignified façade of the *Morning Post*. The morale of its staff had been badly shaken through want of wise direction since the death of Lord Glenesk [q.v.], its second founder, and Gwynne, whose friends believed that he had done his best in an impossible task, had only to step into an editorial vacancy where his tact and good humour restored confidence in a surprisingly short time.

The readers of the *Morning Post* were of sterner stuff than those of the *Standard* and had long been nourished on protectionist dogma, but politics were changing, and it used to be said that each day the paper's circulation decreased by the number of deaths announced in its columns. Possibly a very great editor might have found new readers, but Gwynne lacked imagination and the breadth of view and elasticity of mind which might have enabled him to reconcile the policy he believed in with the spirit of the times. Yet there were few important political events of his time which he did not influence. He had a remarkable gift for making and keeping friends. People who mattered consulted 'Taffy', knowing that he never betrayed a confidence, and they often followed the advice of one whose strength it was to be very much shrewder than he looked. Intimacy with Kitchener, Carson, Haig, Kipling, and indeed every person of note who shared his convictions gave to the paper he edited an influence out of proportion to its circulation, all the more because he never swerved in his respect for the highest principles and dignity of journalism. But a newspaper cannot live on prestige alone and even the brilliant leaders of Ian Colvin [q.v.], backed by Gwynne's knowledge of the secret springs of political action, failed to attract new readers, and journalism was the poorer when the *Morning Post* followed the *Standard* out of independent existence.

In 1907 Gwynne married Edith Douglas, daughter of Thomas Ash Lane, who had at one time owned property in Shanghai; they had no children. He died 26 June 1950 at Little Easton, Dunmow, Essex. A portrait of Gwynne by Sir Bernard Partridge is in the possession of the family.

[Wilfrid Hindle, *The Morning Post 1772–1937*, 1937; private information; personal knowledge.] H. WARNER ALLEN.

HAILSHAM, first VISCOUNT (1872–1950), statesman and lord chancellor. [See HOGG, DOUGLAS McGAREL.]

HAKING, SIR RICHARD CYRIL BYRNE (1862–1945), general, was born 24 January 1862, probably in Halifax where he was baptized and where his father, the Rev. Richard Haking (otherwise Hacking), was curate in the parish of King Cross. His mother was Mary Elizabeth, daughter of Henry Byrne, card manufacturer, of Brighouse. He was educated at the Royal Military College, Sandhurst, and was the last subaltern appointed to the 67th Foot, 22 January 1881, shortly before it became the 2nd battalion, Hampshire Regiment. With the 2nd Hampshire he saw active service in the Burma campaigns of 1885–7, doing good work in command of a detachment and being mentioned in dispatches. From 1886 to 1891 he was adjutant of the 2nd battalion, being promoted to captain in 1889, and after passing through the Staff College, where he made a great impression on his contemporaries for ability, he served on the staff in South Africa, where he was

again mentioned in dispatches. He had obtained his majority in 1899 but was promoted out of the regiment in 1903, having since 1901 been an instructor at the Staff College, where he remained until 1906. His work there as a teacher of tactics and strategy was of great value and his contribution to the preparation of the army for war was substantial: he was a clear thinker and expositor and taught on sound lines. His *Company Training* (1913) was a most useful and helpful work.

After leaving the Staff College with a brevet as colonel, he was first G.S.O. 1, 3rd division (1906–8), then B.G.G.S., Southern Command (1908–11), and in 1911 received command of the 5th brigade at Aldershot which he took to France in August 1914. The brigade was engaged at Mons, had a big share in forcing the passage of the Petit Morin (8 September) and at the passage of the Aisne it established itself on the ridge of the Chemin des Dames, but, being unsupported, had to come back. Haking was wounded next day (15 September) but returned to France in December, having meanwhile been promoted to major-general for distinguished conduct in the field, to take command of the 1st division which had sharp fighting on the Givenchy–Cuinchy front early in 1915 and was heavily engaged on 9 May 1915 at Rue du Bois. On the formation in August 1915 of the XI Corps Haking was given command, but at Loos he had little chance of handling it, the divisions being taken from him and thrown into the battle piecemeal. Subsequently the corps took over the left of the First Army's front, roughly from Vermelles to Laventie, with headquarters at Hinges, and this line it was to hold almost unchanged until the autumn of 1917. The corps was not called upon to undertake any major operations and Haking was thus denied the opportunities he might have been relied upon to turn to good account. After the Italian defeat at Caporetto Haking was sent with the XI Corps to the assistance of the Italians, but was brought back to France in March 1918 when his corps took over its old frontage. In resisting the German attack of April 1918 it had very heavy fighting, and did much to check the German exploitation of their original success, holding on in front of Nieppe Forest and Hazebrouck. Subsequently it carried out in June a very successful local recovery of ground. In the final advance the XI Corps was on the left of the Fifth Army and advanced past

Lille to Tournai, overcoming at times quite stiff resistance.

After the armistice, Haking, who had been mentioned in dispatches eight times, was chief British representative on the allied armistice commission and then later in 1919 chief of the British military commission to Russia and the Baltic provinces. He commanded the allied troops in the East Prussia plebiscite area in 1920 and from 1921 to 1923 was high commissioner for the League of Nations at Danzig. He commanded the British troops in Egypt from 1923 to 1927, being promoted to general in 1925. He retired in 1927 and died at Bulford 9 June 1945, having become in 1924 colonel of his old regiment, the Hampshire, a connexion which he and the regiment valued highly.

A man of practical capacity and high intellectual ability with an equable and well-balanced mind, Haking did admirable work, as a teacher before the war, in command of troops during the war, and in the diplomatic and political duties entrusted to him after it. 'Whatever Haking did', a contemporary has said, 'was well thought out and well carried out.'

Haking married in 1891 Rachel Violette (died 1939), daughter of Sir Henry James Burford Hancock, sometime chief justice of Gibraltar. There were no children. A drawing by Francis Dodd is in the Imperial War Museum.

[*The Times*, 11 June 1945; Sir J. E. Edmonds and others, (Official) *History of the Great War. Military Operations, France and Belgium, 1914-18*, 1922-48.]

C. T. ATKINSON.

HALE-WHITE, SIR WILLIAM (1857-1949), physician, was born in London 7 November 1857, the eldest son of William Hale White [q.v.] better known as the novelist Mark Rutherford. Educated at the City of London School and Framlingham College, he entered Guy's Hospital as a medical student in 1875. Here he made many friends and seems to have been exceptionally happy from the start. In 1879 he obtained his final M.B. (London). After holding various house appointments he became demonstrator of anatomy in 1881 and assistant physician to Guy's Hospital in 1885. It was not long before his practice grew and in 1890 he was appointed full physician at the unusually early age of thirty-three.

Hale-White (the hyphen was adopted at about the time of his father's death) was always a consistent worker and a prolific writer, at first mainly of case reports in the *Transactions* of the Pathological Society, covering almost all branches of medicine. In addition he was working hard in the laboratory, particularly on the methods by which the heat of the body is maintained, and this led to work on hibernating animals. The textbook which made his name familiar to generations of students was his *Materia Medica, Pharmacology and Therapeutics* (1892) which by the time of his death had reached its twenty-eighth edition and is affectionately known as 'Hale-White'.

By 1896 he seemed successful and well established but in this year he was found to have tuberculosis of the lungs. He spent the winter in Switzerland but was not much better; he was advised to give up work completely but family responsibilities made this impossible and he worked for most of each year, taking two months' holiday in the winter in the Channel Isles or Cornwall. Throughout this difficult time he continued his hospital work and practice and gradually as his health recovered resumed his full activity. He developed a large consulting practice, was fond of speaking at medical societies and in later years often found himself their president, and held many examinerships in materia medica and in medicine.

Hale-White had been one of the editors of the *Guy's Hospital Reports* from 1886 to 1893 and had contributed many of its papers. A list of these is given in the number for July-October 1932 (vol. lxxxii) which, in honour of his seventy-fifth birthday, contains articles by eleven of his former house-physicians. He was associated with (Sir) William Osler, (Sir) A. E. Garrod [qq.v.], and others in 1907 in founding the Association of Physicians of Great Britain and Ireland of which he became treasurer, and he was for twenty years an editor of its *Quarterly Journal of Medicine*.

In the war of 1914-18 he acted as consulting physician to various war hospitals with the rank of colonel and served as chairman of Queen Mary's Royal Naval Hospital, Southend. He was due to retire from Guy's in 1917 but was asked to stay on until the war ended. In 1919 he was appointed K.B.E. He received honorary degrees of M.D. from Dublin (1909) and LL.D. from Edinburgh (1927). Although he was soon back at his consulting and other work he had more leisure: he lost his worn-out look and his old buoyancy and enthusiasm returned.

He finally gave up his practice in 1927 and devoted more of his time to the study of medical history. As a Guy's man he had a great affection for Keats. In 1925 he published in the *Guy's Hospital Reports* an account of Keats as a medical student, and in the same year distributed to various institutions photographic copies of Keats's student anatomical and physiological notebook, which was eventually edited by Maurice Buxton Forman and published in 1934. The final result of his interest in the apothecary-poet was a book *Keats as Doctor and Patient* (1938). In addition he wrote many medical biographies, most of which were published in *Guy's Hospital Reports*. These combine accuracy with a scholarly method of writing which makes them charming and easy to read, as might be expected of Mark Rutherford's son. Some of the best are those on Richard Bright and his discovery of the disease bearing his name (1921, 1928), on Thomas Hodgkin (1924), and on Golding Bird and Addison (1926). In 1935 Hale-White published *Great Doctors of the Nineteenth Century* in which he was happy to be able to include many Guy's men. During the war of 1939–45, although he was over eighty, he acted as chairman of the Queen's Institute of District Nursing and became chairman of the council of Bedford College of which he was elected fellow in 1947.

Hale-White was probably one of the last physicians to cover such a wide range of medicine. There were few branches on which he had not written, and his knowledge was based on a wide experience of clinical medicine and pathology. If nothing that he wrote had the fundamental importance of the papers of his great predecessors, his work was sound and accurate and helped to mould the medical opinion of the day. He was a great teacher by both the spoken and printed word, and doctors and students found him readily approachable, partly because he treated everyone as an equal and at once put them at their ease. His simplicity and kindliness were the basis of his very real influence. That he enjoyed his writing is evident from the time which he devoted to it after he retired. He was fond of travelling and liked to go off the beaten track in many parts of the world: Palestine, Syria, Greece, Spain, and India. He was a delight to talk to, for he had many interests including golf, bridge, and photography. He drove his own car fast and badly until the age of seventy-five and even as he grew older always found it easy to fill his

time. He was a small dapper figure and for most of his life had a large black beard, although he did not grow it again after his war service. To the end of his days he retained an amazing interest in life, his smile, and his sense of humour.

In 1886 Hale-White married Edith Jane Spencer (died 1945), the sister of his friend and future colleague (Sir) Alfred Downing Fripp, daughter of Alfred Downing Fripp, the painter in water-colours, and niece of G. A. Fripp [q.v.]. For nearly sixty years she made their home a happy centre for many friends, but there were sad family losses, for their second son was drowned at sea in the *Natal* in 1915 and their eldest son died in 1939 after a distinguished career as a civil engineer in India. Their third son, a doctor, survived him when he died at Oxford 26 February 1949.

[*Guy's Hospital Reports*, vol. xcviii, Nos. 1 and 2, 1949; unpublished notes left by Sir William Hale-White; private information; personal knowledge.] MAURICE CAMPBELL.

HALL, SIR (ALFRED) DANIEL (1864–1942), educationist, administrator, and scientific research worker, was born at Rochdale 22 June 1864, the elder son of Edwin Hall, flannel manufacturer, by his wife, Mary Ann Billett, daughter of Alfred Birks, warehouseman, of Manchester. He was educated at Manchester Grammar School, of which he was a scholar, and at Balliol College, Oxford, where he was elected to a Brackenbury scholarship in natural science at the age of seventeen. There he stroked the college eight, debated in the Union, and took a first class in natural science (chemistry) in 1884.

Going down from Oxford, Hall took up teaching; he was senior science master at King Edward's School, Birmingham, in 1888, amongst his initiates being Ernest William Barnes, later bishop of Birmingham. In 1891 he became lecturer under the Oxford university extension delegacy in Sussex, Surrey, and Kent. Here began the principal work of his life, when he introduced the teaching of agricultural chemistry into his courses of lectures on fundamental science to country classes. In 1894 he was installed as first principal of the South Eastern Agricultural College at Wye, Kent. He collected a small staff of well-qualified and enthusiastic university graduates, and together they evolved a system of agricultural education upon which have been based all the departments of agriculture of the universities and the agricultural colleges founded since that time. Simultaneously, he attacked the problem of agricultural research. There were then no public advisory services available to farmers and by the organization of winter lectures to farmers and of experimental work on their farms the educational work of the College was extended.

In 1902 Hall, the obvious selection, succeeded to the directorship of the agricultural experimental station at Rothamsted, in Hertfordshire. During the previous half-century the place had become world famous by the work of its founder Sir J. B. Lawes and his friend and colleague Sir J. H. Gilbert [qq.v.], and the time had come for a complete review of its organization, its scope, and its achievements. This was the task to which Hall applied himself, and in the following years he supplied the agricultural student and the more educated farmer with a series of publications illuminating the fundamental problems of soil science and food production. The first was his classic on *The Soil* (1903), and this was followed by *The Book of the Rothamsted Experiments* (1905) summarizing the life-work of Lawes and Gilbert. *Fertilisers and Manures* (1909) and *The Feeding of Crops and Stock* (1911) were students' textbooks and in the latter year was published also *The Agriculture and Soils of Kent, Surrey and Sussex*, embodying the results of a long-term investigation and survey undertaken in his Wye College days in collaboration with (Sir) E. John Russell. There followed *A Pilgrimage of British Farming* (1913), the record of surveys made by Hall in the three previous summers in the company of T. B. Wood, professor of agriculture at Cambridge, and E. S. Beaven, barley expert to Arthur Guinness & Co.

In 1910 Lloyd George invited Hall to become a member of the Development Commission. This appointment was part-time and unpaid, but two years later, the Rothamsted Experimental Station being by that time satisfactorily reorganized, he resigned from it to devote himself wholly to the work of the Commission. This consisted, for the most part, in supplementing the work of the Board of Agriculture and Fisheries in organizing agricultural education and research, particularly by grants in aid and establishing centres for specialist research, and by advising farmers through the county councils. Other activities falling within the Commission's scope were the promotion of agricultural co-operation; the reclamation of sub-marginal land; and the examination

of the economics of new crops, such as sugar-beet and tobacco.

The outbreak of war in 1914 found Hall in Australia, as president of the agriculture section of the British Association. Hurrying back to England, he was soon involved in the problem of feeding the nation at war. He was a member of the committee, over which Lord Milner [q.v.] presided, to advise upon measures for the increase of production. This recommended guaranteed prices for wheat, but these were not introduced until 1917. In 1916 R. E. Prothero (later Lord Ernle, q.v.) was appointed president of the Board of Agriculture, and at his request Hall left the Development Commission in 1917, to become secretary of the Board. In this capacity he was largely concerned with the president's war-time measures for stimulating food production in the face of the submarine menace, and for the post-war efforts of the Government to carry through a policy for stabilizing the position of the agricultural industry. Considerable success attended the former, but the latter broke down with the return of peace and plenty.

From 1920 to 1927 Hall continued at the Ministry of Agriculture (as it had now become) as chief scientific adviser. His field of work was a wide one, extending from the completion of the chain of research stations covering all branches of agricultural science to the representation of the Government at international gatherings.

Hall had long been a member of the governing body of the John Innes Horticultural Institution, at Merton, and in 1927 he succeeded William Bateson [q.v.] as director. He remained at Merton for twelve years, retiring in 1939 just before the outbreak of war, and the position which he established for the Institution was another proof of his versatility as a scientist and administrator. He was not a geneticist by training, but his capacity to appreciate the nature of the work enabled him to select and encourage a team of young botanists who made the John Innes Institution famous throughout the world. During this time Hall produced two notable books, one, on *The Apple* (1933) in collaboration with his colleague, Mr. M. B. Crane; the other, a monograph on *The Genus Tulipa* (1940). Other books written by him were *Agriculture after the War* (1916), *Digressions of a Man of Science* (1932), and a book for children, *Our Daily Bread* (1938). Shortly before his death, he produced *Reconstruction and the Land* (1941) in which he formulated a national agricultural policy for the future, based on a lifetime's experience of agricultural practice, administration, and research.

Many public honours and distinctions were bestowed upon him. He was elected a fellow of the Royal Society in 1909, but refused an offer of nomination for its presidency some years later. He was appointed K.C.B. in 1918, and honorary doctorates were conferred upon him by the universities of Oxford, Cambridge, and Aberdeen. He was Rede lecturer at Cambridge and Heath Clark lecturer in London in 1935. He was chairman of the Kenya agricultural commission in 1929, and a member of the Agricultural Research Council and of the Economic Advisory Council. In 1939 he was elected to an honorary fellowship at Balliol, and in the same year, on the occasion of his seventy-fifth birthday, a group of his friends presented him with a book of essays entitled *Agriculture in the Twentieth Century*.

Hall was a man of extraordinary versatility, who touched life at many points. Music, painting, and literature were constant pleasures to him, and he was a collector of early Chinese pottery, upon which he was a recognized authority. A discriminating palate for French wines and a devotion to fly-fishing rounded off a personality unusually complete and well balanced.

Hall was twice married: first, in 1892 to Mary Louisa (died 1921), daughter of John Brooks, director of companies, of Edgbaston; and secondly, in 1922 to Ida Scott Audsley, daughter of Alfred Beaver, author and journalist, of London. By his first marriage he had two sons, of whom the elder was killed on the western front in 1917, and the younger died in 1949. Hall died in London 5 July 1942. A portrait of Hall by his son, Christopher, hangs in the Hall at the Lord Wandsworth College, Long Sutton, Hampshire.

[*The Times*, 7 July 1942; Sir John Russell in *Obituary Notices of Fellows of the Royal Society*, No. 11, November 1942; H. V. Taylor in *Journal* of the Royal Horticultural Society, vol. lxvii, 1942; H. E. Dale, *Daniel Hall*, 1956; lifelong personal friendship.]

C. S. ORWIN.

HALL, ARTHUR HENRY (1876–1949), engineer, was born at Clifton 17 August 1876, the eldest son and second of the eight children of Henry Sinclair Hall by his wife, Anne Leigh Keturah, daughter of Matthew Knapp, of Little Linford Hall, Buckinghamshire. His father, an old Cliftonian, had returned to the college as a mathematical master and was in charge of its military side from its inception. He was co-author of the well-known textbooks *Hall and Knight's Algebra*, *Hall and Stevens's Geometry*, and other works. Arthur entered Trinity Hall, Cambridge, with a scholarship in 1895 after his early education as an exhibitioner of Clifton College. He read engineering and was placed in the first class of part i of the mechanical sciences tripos in 1898.

He next served his five years' engineering apprenticeship with W. Denny Brothers, of Dumbarton, and in 1905 became an assistant mechanical engineer at Woolwich Arsenal. He became an assistant superintendent in 1914 and from the outbreak of war until 1917 he supervised the purchase and installation of the additional plant needed by the Arsenal for war-time production. For the next two years he was at the Admiralty directing the production of torpedoes, mines, and other anti-submarine devices. It was during this period that he exhibited a particular talent for arranging the supply in quantities of urgently required stores in periods of time which up to then had been regarded as impossibly short. From 1919 he was in control of the disposal of various surplus stores and showed a similar talent for disposing of equipment as rapidly as he had collected it.

With the decision to intensify experiment and research on large rigid airships, Hall was next appointed in 1926 to the post of superintendent of production at Cardington where the ill-fated R 101 was built. He had much to do with obtaining the high dimensional accuracy required in the long girders used where the tolerances demanded on the overall lengths between the end fittings were of an order not previously realized in such light construction. In view of the tragic disaster which overtook the R 101 on her maiden flight to India in 1930 (by which time Hall was already in his next post), it should be recorded that in his opinion she was not sufficiently tested to be allowed to undertake this flight so early in her career. In 1928 Hall had been appointed chief superintendent of the Royal Aircraft Establishment at Farnborough, with a mandate to enforce economy and increase efficiency by centralizing such common services as transport, workshops, and drawing-office staffs. It says much for his personality that a policy necessarily unwelcome to the technical departments was carried out in reasonable harmony. By the middle of his term of office the policy had changed to one of expansion in the air and the Royal Aircraft Establishment entered upon a period of intensive growth which continued unchecked throughout the subsequent war. Hall's knowledge of men and ability to direct them were here invaluable, for he was able to attract the right types and to select for promotion those best equipped to carry additional responsibility. He knew, and conversed intimately with, every man and woman in the Establishment and he was to them a stimulating personality, for he had a keenly analytical mind and a visual memory of remarkable range and character.

On his retirement in 1941 Hall continued for some five years as consultant to the Ministry of Aircraft Production and the English Electric Company. He was appointed C.B.E. in 1918, C.B. in 1937, and he was an honorary fellow of the Institute of Aero Sciences of the United States, a distinction rarely accorded outside that country.

With his parentage and qualifications, it is surprising that Hall wrote little of a technical nature. His publications were confined to articles on photography and fly-fishing which, in conjunction with ornithology, were his hobbies. Some of his photographs of gulls on the Embankment were exhibited and he was a keen and polished exponent of colour photography, delighting in reproducing the type of scenery encountered in his favourite fishing haunts. He married in 1910 Maud Henrietta (died 1953), daughter of Lieutenant-Colonel G. H. Webster, by whom he had three sons, only to lose them all in the most tragic circumstances, the eldest at the age of seven, and the other two in their twenties. He died at Farnham, Surrey, 10 September 1949.

[The Times, 12 September 1949; Clifton College Register, 1862 to 1947, 1948; private information; personal knowledge.]

H. L. STEVENS.


HALL, HUBERT (1857–1944) archivist, was born at Hesley Hall, near Doncaster, 27 July 1857, the younger son of Richard Foljambe Hall by his wife, Elizabeth Breese Orridge. Educated at Shrewsbury, where his main (and indeed lifelong) interest was in natural history and fishing, he obtained a place in the Civil Service in 1879 and entered the Public Record Office as a junior clerk. He was promoted senior clerk in 1892 and assistant keeper in 1912; he acted as resident officer from 1891 and as an inspecting officer from 1905, retiring in 1921.

Hall's official work lay in modern departmental records, but he spent his leisure more and more in research on medieval history. His Introduction to the Study of the Pipe Rolls appeared in 1884 in the series published by the Pipe Roll Society, of which his colleague W. D. Selby [q.v.] was treasurer; it was followed by The Antiquities and Curiosities of the Exchequer (1891), The Receipt Roll of the Exchequer for Michaelmas Term xxxi. Henry II, A.D.1185 (1899), and The Pipe Roll of the Bishopric of Winchester . . . 1208–9 (1903). He succeeded Selby as editor of the 'Rolls Series' edition of The Red Book of the Exchequer (3 vols., 1896). It was viciously criticized by J. H. Round [q.v.], but its undeniable faults were mainly due to the original plan, and beyond Hall's power to amend. More popular were Society in the Elizabethan Age (1886) and Court Life under the Plantagenets (1890), both based upon documents in the Public Record Office.

Hall served the Royal Historical Society as literary director (1891–1938), honorary secretary (1894–1903), and vice-president (1923–7), adding considerably to its reputation, and actively promoting its succession to the work of the defunct Camden Society (1897). He also took an active part in the work of the Selden Society, of which he was vice-president from 1939 to 1942. He was closely associated with Sidney and Beatrice Webb [qq.v.] in their history of English Local Government (1906–29) and in the foundation in 1895 of the London School of Economics and Political Science. There from 1896 to 1919, and at King's College from 1919 to 1926, as a reader in London University, he taught palaeography, diplomatic and economic history, and trained many of the contributors to the Victoria County History. His Studies in English Official Historical Documents (1908), with the valuable Formula Book (1908–9), and his Select Bibliography for the Study, Sources and Literature of English Mediaeval Economic History (1914) sprang from this work. This varied experience made his appointment as secretary (1910–18) of the Royal Commission on public records an obvious choice, and the valuable appendixes to its three reports (1912–19) are mainly his work. In 1931 and 1932 he was invited to the United States, where he supervised the arrangement of British family manuscripts in the Huntington Library. Cambridge University conferred upon him the honorary degree of Litt.D. in 1920.

Hall was twice married: first, in 1882 to Edith (died 1889), daughter of James Robinson, and had a son and a daughter, both of whom predeceased their father; secondly, in 1895 to Jane Winifred, daughter of Robert Robert Evans, who was in business, and had a son. He died at Rochester, on his birthday, 27 July 1944, from shock after his house at Walderslade, near Chatham, had been partly destroyed by a German bomb.

Hall's learning was extensive rather than precise, but his patience, good-nature, and unselfishness were as valuable in maintaining contact with American and continental scholars as in training historical workers.

[*Transactions* of the Royal Historical Society, 4th series, vol. xxviii, 1946; private information; personal knowledge.]

CHARLES JOHNSON.

HALL, SIR (WILLIAM) REGINALD (1870–1943), admiral, was born at The Close, Salisbury, 28 June 1870, the elder son and second child of Lieutenant (later Captain) William Henry Hall, R.N., of Ross, Herefordshire, the first director of naval intelligence and later captain superintendent of Pembroke dockyard, by his wife, Caroline Elizabeth, daughter of the Rev. Henry Thomas Armfield, vicar of the cathedral and the close of Salisbury.

Hall's first sea trip was in his father's ship, the *Flamingo*, gun-vessel, at the age of ten. He entered the *Britannia* as a cadet in 1884 and became a lieutenant in January 1890. Of the two specialist branches (gunnery and torpedo) then open to lieutenants who had passed their examinations with credit, Hall chose the gunnery branch. His forceful personality and driving power were already in evidence and, after serving a commission at sea as gunnery lieutenant, he was appointed a senior staff officer on the books of the *Excellent*, then one of the most coveted appointments in the navy. He was promoted to commander in 1901 and, as executive officer of a battleship, achieved distinction by his methods of enforcing discipline. On one occasion the depot sent all the men of bad character to his ship, confident that he would either reform them or rid the Service of them. But, although a terror to malefactors, he was already implementing views on the welfare of the ship's company and on brightening their lives when afloat which were far in advance of the times. He was promoted to captain in 1905 and, after serving as inspecting captain of the new mechanical training establishments, in 1907 assumed command of the cadet training cruiser, the *Cornwall*. His next ship was the *Natal*, cruiser, where his keen interest in gunnery was reflected by the ship retaining the first place in the navy at the annual gunnery tests. From 1911 to 1913 he was naval assistant to the controller of the navy.

In 1913 Hall assumed command of the new battle cruiser, the *Queen Mary*. He now had the opportunity of introducing a wide range of reforms to which he had given much thought. Convinced of the importance of raising the prestige of the petty officers, in his view the most important link in the chain of command, he had all their messes reconstructed in order to give them greater comfort. At the Admiralty's suggestion he accepted the responsibility of commissioning without the customary staff of ship's police and trusting to the petty officers to undertake police duties. He broke with tradition by introducing a three-watch system for the organization of the ship's company instead of the two-watch system, because he was convinced that a three-watch system was more suitable for wartime. When war broke out, all the larger units followed this lead. The first cinematograph, the first laundry, the first bookstall, the first adequate hot-water system on board were other fruits of his imagination and devoted interest in the welfare of his men. A deeply religious man, he built into the ship the first chapel in a man-of-war; a few years later all big ships were fitted with chapels. In a conservative Service, these reforms inevitably aroused a storm of adverse criticism, but this never deflected Hall from his crusade to improve life on board ship. His monument is to be found in every ship which flies the white ensign.

Hall was in command of the *Queen Mary* at the battle of Heligoland Bight (28 August 1914), but before the end of the year he was invited to become director of the intelligence division of the Admiralty. He had, in abundant measure, all the qualities for his new post. Officer prisoners from German submarines who had stubbornly refused to respond to ordinary interrogation often became as putty in his hands. There was a hypnotic power about his glance which broke their resistance. On occasions his manner became explosive, and the facial twitch, which gave him his nickname of 'Blinker', became exaggerated; at other times his disarming smile and twinkling eyes looking out from bushy eyebrows overcame opposition to a new scheme for gaining intelligence.

The main source of intelligence of the German fleet was through intercepted signals. On the outbreak of war Sir Alfred Ewing [q.v.], then director of naval education, formed a small department to study German naval signals. When the German cruiser *Magdeburg* was sunk in the Baltic, a drowned signalman was picked up clasping a signal book in his arms, and as soon as this book reached the Admiralty the deciphering of German signals began to exercise a profound influence on the movements of the British fleet. Wireless stations for the interception of German naval signals on all waves were rapidly erected, and the staff of cryptographers was augmented to deal with the increasing number of signals arriving at the Admiralty. The department could no longer remain a private enterprise under Ewing; naval officers were needed to interpret the deciphered signals; someone vested with authority was required to enrol additional staff and order the erection of new wireless stations. The work was properly a function of the naval intelligence division, and so it was transferred into that division and Hall took control. Under his driving power the new section (called Room 40 O.B.) extended its work until there were over a hundred men and women deciphering signals and issuing intelligence reports to the Admiralty and commanders-in-chief afloat, and fifty wireless stations in direct landline communication with Room 40. Hall spread his net far and wide to draw into Room 40 a staff who were German scholars and gifted with the type of brain which can unravel ciphers. There came a time when the movements of the British fleets and squadrons were entirely governed by this intelligence, and it was a principal factor in winning the long-drawn-out battle against the German submarines.

Hall also developed the interception of messages between Germany and Spain for onward transmission by cable to Mexico and the United States, and between Germany and Turkey. These messages which frequently contained information of vital importance were properly the concern of the Foreign Office, but the Cabinet trusted Hall implicitly and left to him the responsibility of deciding when the purport of a signal should be shown to ministers. From these messages the trend of German foreign policy and the activities of German diplomatic officials and of German-paid saboteurs could be followed. Hall was able to forewarn the British authorities of a German conspiracy in Persia and Afghanistan, and of plans to destroy the Siberian railway. He was able to follow closely the activities of the Indian revolutionaries in the United States whose efforts to foment a rising in India continued unabated until the end of the war. These messages also enabled him to get on the track of Sir Roger Casement [q.v.] who in the early months of the war was assisting saboteurs in America, and to follow him to Germany where he sought the support of German armed forces for a rebellion in Ireland, and finally to come up with him when he landed from a submarine on the west coast of Ireland.

The most important message handled by Hall was the famous Zimmermann telegram, in which the German foreign minister instructed the German minister in Mexico to propose an offensive alliance with that country should America enter the war on the side of the Allies. Relations between America and Mexico were severely strained and Germany hoped that by offering financial support and an undertaking that Mexico should reconquer her lost territories in Texas, New Mexico, and Arizona, the Mexicans would declare war and strain America's war potential, as yet undeveloped, to such an extent that no military help could be given to the Allies. Hall handled this message most skilfully. He had to convince President Wilson that it was genuine, yet, in order to safeguard Room 40, to arouse no suspicion that it had been deciphered by the British intelligence service. When the Zimmermann telegram was published, and the credit given to the American intelligence service, it did much to influence the American decision to declare war on Germany. At a later stage of the war Hall employed the same safeguards when his staff deciphered a series of messages to Berlin from the German minister in the Argentine in which he recommended that merchant shipping should be sunk without trace. The publication of these messages in America severely strained relations between the South American republics and Germany which had hitherto been friendly.

Throughout the war Hall worked in close accord with (Sir) Basil Thomson [q.v.], assistant commissioner of the metropolitan police. Information in the intercepted messages considerably helped their joint efforts to counter the activities of spies and agents. Hall employed his own agents in Spain, Morocco, and Mexico to counteract the attempts of German agents to refuel and reprovision their submarines. Among the most successful of these agents was A. E. W. Mason [q.v.]. Hall also devised many ruses to deceive the German high command, such as planting false code-books on German agents in Holland and passing false information to Germany by the same means.

Few men made a greater contribution to winning the war than did Hall. He not only exploited to the full every field of intelligence but made the best use of everything that came to hand. His work was recognized by his appointment as C.B. in 1915 and as K.C.M.G. in 1918. He was promoted rear-admiral in 1917, vice-admiral (retired) in 1922, and admiral in 1926. The university of Oxford conferred upon him the honorary degree of D.C.L. in 1919 and Cambridge that of LL.D. in 1920.

At the end of the war Hall retired and entered the House of Commons as Conservative member for the West Derby division of Liverpool. Ill health hampered his political career, but on the few occasions on which he addressed the House on naval subjects he commanded a respectful hearing through his obvious sincerity and his detailed and inside knowledge of international and imperial affairs. In March 1923 Hall became principal agent of the Conservative Party, an office which he held until after the Conservative losses at the general election of December. The qualities which had stood him in such good stead as director of naval intelligence were other than those required in a principal political agent when his party's fortunes were on the wane, and he was not well suited for the post. He lost his seat at the election but re-entered Parliament in 1925 as member for Eastbourne. Ill health caused his retirement from politics at the general election of 1929. He died in London 22 October 1943.

Hall married in 1894 Ethel Wootton (died 1932), daughter of (Sir) William de Wiveleslie Abney [q.v.]. They had one daughter and two sons, both of whom became naval officers, the elder dying in 1942.

A drawing of Hall by Francis Dodd is in the Imperial War Museum. A crayon drawing by Louis Raemaekers is in the possession of the family. A bust by Lady Kennet is at the Royal Naval College, Dartmouth.

[*The Times*, 23 and 29 October 1943; Sir William James, *The Eyes of the Navy*, 1955; private information; personal knowledge.]

W. M. JAMES.

HALSEY, SIR LIONEL (1872–1949), admiral, was born 26 February 1872 in London, the fourth son of (Sir) T. Frederick Halsey, who became first baronet, of Gaddesden, Hertfordshire, by his wife, Mary Julia, daughter of Frederick Octavius Wells, of the Bengal Civil Service. He joined the *Britannia* as a naval cadet in January 1885, and after serving on various stations was sent to the royal yacht in July 1893 and promoted lieutenant in August. He then served in the Mediterranean and on the North America and West Indies station, afterwards joining the *Powerful*. He was landed with his captain, Hedworth Lambton (later Sir Hedworth Meux, q.v.), and took part in the defence of Ladysmith in charge of a battery of naval 4·7-inch guns. For this service he was mentioned in dispatches, awarded the South Africa medal with Ladysmith clasp, and specially promoted commander, 1 January 1901. He served as commander in the cruiser *Diana* in the Mediterranean until June 1902 and then from November 1902 for two years in the *Good Hope*, Sir Wilmot Fawkes's flagship in the first cruiser squadron which took Joseph Chamberlain and his wife on their memorable visit to South Africa. In January 1905 he was appointed naval member of the Admiralty committee which administered the new Royal Navy Volunteer Reserve force; after being promoted captain in June he rejoined his old ship *Powerful* in August as flag captain to Sir Wilmot Fawkes, commander-in-chief, Australia, and in 1908 returned with him to Devonport to remain as flag captain there until April 1911, having served with Fawkes for nearly nine years.

Halsey then commanded the *Donegal*, fourth cruiser squadron, until September 1912 when he was selected to command the new battle cruiser *New Zealand*, built at the charge of the New Zealand Government, on her cruise round the world to 'show the flag'. Halsey's speeches at the ports visited and the smartness and obvious efficiency of the ship and her crew did much to stimulate pride in and affection for the mother country, and in 1913 he was appointed C.M.G.

In January 1915 he was mentioned in dispatches for services in the Dogger Bank action. In June he left the *New Zealand* for the *Iron Duke* on joining the staff of Sir John (later Earl) Jellicoe [q.v.] as captain of the fleet with the rank of commodore first class. Jellicoe's Jutland dispatch of 18 June 1916 states: 'My special thanks are due also to Commodore Lionel Halsey, C.M.G., the Captain of the Fleet, who also renders me much assistance in the working of the Fleet at sea, and to whose good organization is largely due the rapidity with which the Fleet was fuelled and replenished with ammunition on return to its bases.' Halsey was appointed C.B. in 1916.

On 4 December 1916 when Jellicoe joined the Board of Admiralty as first sea lord he brought Halsey with him as fourth sea lord. In May 1917, when Sir Eric Geddes [q.v.] at Lloyd George's instance was appointed to the Admiralty Board with the revived title of controller, Halsey was made third sea lord. Geddes, having himself become first lord in July, assigned responsibility for the administration of the business relating to the *matériel* of the navy to the controller for 'design and production' and to the third sea lord for 'requirements of design'. Halsey, who had been promoted rear-admiral in April 1917 (having until then retained the rank of commodore first class), remained on the Board until June 1918. The Australian Government had placed its naval ships at the disposal of the Admiralty and in September 1918 Halsey was lent to that Government to take command of the second battle cruiser squadron of the Grand Fleet in the battle cruiser *Australia* as his flagship. In this capacity he was present at the surrender of the German Fleet at Scapa Flow. He came on shore in March 1919 and was employed as president of Admiralty committees on officers' pay and on the position of accountant officers, with an interval from August to the end of December during which he commanded the *Renown* as chief of staff to the Prince of Wales for his tour of Canada and the United States. From February until November 1920 he

resumed his duties in the *Renown* as chief of staff to the Prince on visits to Australia, New Zealand, and the West Indies and other colonies.

At the end of this cruise he was appointed comptroller and treasurer to the Prince of Wales, a member of the council of the Duchy of Cornwall, and in 1921 extra equerry to the Prince. He thus began a long period of service on his personal staff which lasted until the new reign in 1936. In 1937 he was appointed extra equerry to King George VI. He was placed on the retired list of the navy, 1 November 1922, having been promoted vice-admiral 5 July 1921. He was promoted admiral on the retired list in October 1926. He was appointed K.C.M.G. (1918), G.C.M.G. (1925), K.C.V.O. (1919), G.C.V.O. (1920), and K.C.I.E. (1922). He also received several foreign decorations.

In his naval service he was universally popular; an able seaman and a zealous and enthusiastic officer, whose charm of manner and open character won him the affection and admiration of all ranks; his were all 'happy ships' and no one grudged him the advantage which his early promotion after Ladysmith gave him. His appointment as comptroller to the Prince of Wales was unusual, for, unlike the regular courtier, he came straight from the sea with little previous knowledge of political affairs and few previous contacts in the intellectual or social worlds; but Halsey's vitality, transparent honesty, friendliness, and keen interest in his new associations made him a valuable counsellor for the Prince, who would readily accept sometimes unpalatable advice from a mentor with such an obviously high sense of duty. He had acquired at sea a knowledge of the Dominions and Colonies which proved of great value during the Prince's overseas tours. After 1932, however, there was a change in their relations.

Halsey married in 1905 Morwenna, younger daughter of Major Bevil Granville, of Wellesbourne Hall, Warwickshire; they had two daughters. He was a prominent freemason and his portrait, painted by (Sir) Oswald Birley, belongs to the Hertfordshire freemasons. There are two small drawings by Francis Dodd in the Imperial War Museum.

He died at his home near Biggleswade 26 October 1949.

[Admiralty records; private information; personal knowledge.]

VINCENT W. BADDELEY.

HAMILTON, SIR IAN STANDISH MONTEITH (1853–1947), general, was born at Corfu 16 January 1853, the elder son of Captain (later Lieutenant-Colonel) Christian Monteith Hamilton of the 92nd Highland Regiment of Foot (2nd battalion Gordon Highlanders), by his wife, Maria Corinna, daughter of John Prendergast Vereker, third Viscount Gort, and granddaughter of Standish O'Grady, first Viscount Guillamore [q.v.], an Irish judge famous for his wit. Owing to his mother's death when he was three years old Hamilton was brought up at Hafton, the Argyllshire home of his paternal grandparents. There he learnt to shoot with gun and rifle, and developed an eye for country.

Destined for the army, he was sent to R. S. Tabor's school at Cheam, and thence to Wellington College, but neither at work nor play did he show much promise. Nevertheless, in 1870, after six months with a crammer, he made light of the examination for a commission, and was seventy-sixth in a list of 392 successful candidates. He then spent a year in Dresden, receiving tuition from a retired German general, and returned to England in 1871 to attend a special twelve months' course at the Royal Military College, Sandhurst, where, too, his record was disappointing.

Posted to the 12th Foot (Suffolk Regiment) in April 1872, Hamilton served with them in Ireland for eighteen months, and was then transferred to the 92nd Highlanders in India. There he found himself at home, for his father had only recently given up command of the regiment, and his character developed rapidly. Quick, intelligent, and blessed with abundance of charm, 'Johnny' Hamilton had much to recommend him. Intellectually he was far ahead of the majority of his companions. Ambitious to excel, he worked hard at everything he undertook, and he wrote with a fluent and picturesque pen. He was a good sportsman and an unusually fine shot, and, combined with these tastes, he had a flair for painting and a keen appreciation of music and poetry. He loved crowds, but was equally content with solitude. Emergency found him at his best, and he courted the thrill and excitement of personal danger. The drab routine of regimental life could not satisfy his restless spirit for long, and he soon set himself to study Hindustani, with the idea of obtaining early staff employment. Meanwhile, his military interest lay in improving the musketry efficiency of his company, and whenever leave could be had his delight was to spend it alone on a Himalayan hillside, in search of a bigger 'head' than had ever been shot before. This ambition was achieved in 1876 when he bagged the largest markhor head on record. In 1877, while on furlough in England, he attended a course at the Musketry School at Hythe and exhibited marked proficiency. Later he became musketry instructor to his battalion, and made it the best-shooting battalion in India.

Hamilton's first experience of active service was with the Gordons in Afghanistan in 1879. There, in an outpost affair, his plucky initiative changed the course of his life. His general, Sir Frederick (later Earl) Roberts [q.v.], asking him to describe the incident in detail, was so struck by his personality that he determined to have him as aide-de-camp when opportunity offered. Meanwhile he sent him as orderly officer to W. G. D. Massy [q.v.] commanding the Cavalry brigade. In this, his first campaign, Hamilton was twice mentioned in dispatches.

Early in 1881 the Gordons were ordered to Natal and on 27 February Hamilton was present, with a small detachment of the regiment, at the disastrous engagement of Majuba Hill. There he received a wound which crippled his left arm for life, and he was specially mentioned in dispatches for conspicuous gallantry. Invalided home, he was invited to Osborne by Queen Victoria to tell her his story of the battle. Early in 1882, while studying for the Staff College examination, he was offered and accepted the post of aide-de-camp to Roberts, then serving as commander-in-chief, Madras. Thus began an association and close friendship which lasted twenty years and saw Hamilton rise from captain to lieutenant-general. In the autumn of 1884 he obtained leave from India in the secret hope of getting himself employed with the Gordon relief expedition. When his ship reached Suez he dashed up to Cairo, left for the front next day with the 1st battalion of his regiment, and was present at the action of Kirbekan. He was again mentioned in dispatches and was promoted brevet major. Early in 1886 he returned as aide-de-camp to Roberts, now commander-in-chief in India, and at the end of the year he accompanied him to Burma for three months, in connexion with the final pacification of that country after its annexation. He was again mentioned in dispatches and became brevet lieutenant-colonel in 1887.

In 1890 Hamilton was appointed assistant adjutant-general for musketry, Bengal, and in two and a half years he improved the musketry efficiency of the Indian Army beyond recognition. He became full colonel in 1891, and when Roberts left India in 1893 and was succeeded by Sir George White [q.v.], Hamilton was brought back to Simla as White's military secretary. In 1895, during the operations in Chitral, he was on the staff of the lines of communication, and six months later, after another mention in dispatches and the appointment of C.B., he returned to Simla as deputy quarter-master-general. In 1897 he was given command of the 3rd brigade of the Tirah Expeditionary Force but broke his leg before the campaign began, and only rejoined his command when the fighting was over.

After twenty-five years of almost continuous service in India, he sailed for England in April 1898, on his appointment to command the Musketry School at Hythe. In September 1899, in view of the threat of war, he was ordered to Natal as assistant adjutant-general to White. A month later he was commanding a column with the temporary rank of major-general. At the battle of Elandslaagte he showed such conspicuous gallantry at a critical moment that he was recommended for the Victoria Cross, but, as it had never previously been awarded to an officer commanding a brigade, the Duke of Cambridge refused to establish a precedent. During the siege of Ladysmith Hamilton again exhibited resolution and valour; after the relief he was called to Bloemfontein by Roberts, who had meanwhile assumed the chief command in South Africa, and given charge of a mounted infantry division, with the rank of lieutenant-general, for the final advance on Pretoria. For this Hamilton was appointed K.C.B., and when Roberts returned to England as commander-in-chief at the War Office, he went with him as military secretary. Some months later, when Lord Kitchener [q.v.] was finding himself increasingly tied to his office, Roberts offered him Hamilton as chief of staff. The offer was accepted and Hamilton returned to Pretoria. But Kitchener was ever inclined to decide everything himself. Hamilton was little more than 'so-called' chief of staff, and four months after his arrival he was sent to the Western

Transvaal to take command of four columns whose action was hanging fire for lack of central direction. Thus he suddenly found himself in command of 17,000 men and in charge of the final great 'drive' which brought the war to an end. Promoted substantive lieutenant-general, and with a record surpassed by none of his contemporaries, he returned to England with Kitchener to resume his duties as military secretary at the War Office. Nine months later, in 1903, he became quarter-master-general.

Hamilton, however, could not be long content with any sedentary post, and early in 1904, on the outbreak of the Russo-Japanese war, he was appointed chief of a military mission with the Japanese armies in the field. Although the movements of foreign attachés in the war area were severely restricted, he made the most of his opportunities, and his trenchant diary, *A Staff Officer's Scrap Book* (2 vols., 1905-7), was widely read in England and on the continent. In 1905 he was recalled to the Southern Command and held the appointment for four memorable years. Tidworth House, then the official residence, was admirably suited to the requirements of a commander and his wife who, with no financial cares, had a genius for entertaining. The Government found that the most popular way of entertaining foreign royalties and other distinguished visitors was to send them to Salisbury Plain to see the army at work and enjoy the hospitality of the Hamiltons.

Promoted general in 1907, Hamilton became adjutant-general in 1909. A year later, after being promoted G.C.B. (1910), he was given the Mediterranean Command, recently vacated by the Duke of Connaught, with headquarters at Malta; the importance of the appointment was increased by making him in addition inspector-general of oversea forces. Before leaving England, however, he was asked by R. B. (later Viscount) Haldane [q.v.], then secretary of state for war, to assist him by writing, for his private information, a memorandum on the highly controversial subject of compulsory service which was being advocated by the National Service League under the powerful leadership of Roberts. The Government was unconvinced of its necessity and Hamilton, despite his long association with Roberts, pointed out in his memorandum that his old chief's proposals were far less suited to British needs than was the existing system of voluntary enlistment. It was decided that the memorandum should be published. Signed by Hamilton, with an introduction by Haldane, and entitled *Compulsory Service*, its publication in the autumn of 1910 caused considerable surprise in military circles; and a few months later its arguments were indignantly answered by Roberts himself in *Fallacies and Facts* (1911). The controversy lasted for years. Roberts was not to live to see the end of it; and it was not until the war of 1914–18 had been raging for two years that conscription was introduced into the British Army.

After four years at Malta, Hamilton returned to England in 1914, and was appointed aide-de-camp general to the King. When war broke out and Kitchener assumed charge at the War Office, one of his first acts was to give Hamilton command of the Central Force, responsible for the defence of England in the event of enemy invasion.

The supreme opportunity of Hamilton's career, and the highest test of his capacity, began on 12 March 1915, when Kitchener summoned him and told him to start next day to assume command of an Anglo-French army which, Kitchener disclosed, was already assembling at Mudros in connexion with the allied resolve to force the Dardanelles. His formal instructions, written on one sheet of paper, were necessarily vague, for no military plans had been made. The navy had undertaken to force the Straits, and apart, perhaps, from some minor military enterprises to occupy areas where hidden guns might be impeding progress, it was expected that the fleet would get through unaided. In this case the army would not be wanted until Constantinople was approached, and it was even hoped that Turkish resistance would collapse with the arrival of allied transports in the Marmora. Yet if the navy failed—and on this point Kitchener's instructions were precise—Hamilton was to throw in his whole force to open the way for the fleet. 'Having entered on the project of forcing the Straits', Kitchener said, 'there can be no idea of abandoning the scheme.'

Hamilton accepted his uncertain task with equanimity. 'Are not the best moments in life', he had written in his *Scrap Book*, 'those in which it is borne in to a poor mortal that some immortal has clearly designated the field of action, wherein he has only to be true to his convictions and himself, and advance

confidently by word of command to the accomplishment of some predestined end?' Kitchener's demeanour had fixed Hamilton's attention more firmly on the gleaming minarets of Constantinople than on the rugged precipices of the Peninsula, and when he left London, 13 March, with his hastily collected staff, Hamilton's sanguine temperament was already painting pictures of easy victory. 'If the fleet gets through, Constantinople will fall of itself', Kitchener had told him that morning, 'and you will have won, not a battle, but the war!' But on 18 March, from the deck of a light cruiser, Hamilton was an eye-witness of the fleet's losses in the unsuccessful attempt to force the Dardanelles. Later, when the admiral reported that he could not renew the attack until the army had captured the Peninsula, Hamilton concurred, and on 27 March, after a fruitless effort by (Sir) Winston Churchill to persuade the Government to insist upon a further unaided attack by the navy, the dreaded alternative of military operations was decided upon. Not until after the war did it become clear that Churchill's hopes had perhaps been well founded. The losses which the admiral had attributed to floating mines or shore torpedo-tubes had been due to a small and unsuspected minefield. The Turks on the night of the 18th were weighed down by a premonition of defeat. Most of their ammunition had been shot away, and they expected a renewed attack next morning. In Constantinople a British victory was thought to be inevitable, and the Germans feared a revolt in the capital.

It would be hard to exaggerate the difficulties of Hamilton's problem. His knowledge of the situation on shore was nil, and his maps were out of date. His army, mostly still on the high seas, had been shipped without regard to possible tactical requirements on arrival. There were no quays in the wind-swept harbour of Mudros; the whole force would have to be unpacked and repacked in the glare of publicity at Alexandria; and at least a month must elapse before it could be ready to undertake that most difficult of military tasks—a landing from ships' boats on an open beach, in face of opposition. All chances of secrecy and surprise had gone, and the Turks were digging for their lives. But Hamilton remained confident and infected his command with his own spirit. When the landing took place on 25 April it was within an ace of succeeding. Three times in the next six weeks, with unexampled courage, his troops renewed the battle, and on each occasion it was mainly the want of another fresh brigade, or of more ammunition, which cheated them of victory. But Hamilton himself cannot be absolved of all responsibility for these checks. The enthusiasm, self-confidence, and personal courage demanded of the military commander-in-chief, he possessed in full measure. But he lacked the iron will and dominating personality of a truly great commander. Although the force originally allotted to him bore no relation to his possible requirements, but consisted merely of such numbers as Kitchener had felt able to provide without embarrassment in France, he refused to risk Kitchener's displeasure by asking for one man more than his sanguine temperament hoped would just suffice. When Kitchener learnt, from the Admiralty not from Hamilton, of the crying need for more troops, he immediately ordered them from Egypt, but they arrived just too late. Hamilton's optimism, too, inclined him to over-confidence in battle. He left too much to his subordinates and hesitated to override their plans, even when in his opinion they were missing opportunities.

Later in the summer, when for a short time, in their anxiety to force a decision, the Government made Gallipoli the main British theatre, Hamilton was allotted lavish reinforcements for a new offensive in August. The kernel of the whole plan, which consisted of three independent attacks on three separate fronts, was a surprise landing at Suvla, to be followed by a turning movement. When battle was joined on the night of 6 August, the weak Turkish detachments at Suvla, completely surprised, began to retire. But disastrous delays occurred on the Suvla beaches, and the whole British plan eventually fell to bits. After the initial success on the 6th, Hamilton's habitual optimism and his confidence in an untried leader had allowed him to dismiss the Suvla front from his mind and concentrate his attention elsewhere. Only on the afternoon of the 8th were his suspicions at last aroused, and he hurried to intervene in the Suvla battle, but by then the chance of victory had gone.

Hamilton had now lost the confidence of the Government. In view of the difficulties of sparing him further men, and the vanishing chances of success, the feasibility of evacuating the Peninsula was considered. When, in October, he replied to Kitchener that, at best, an evacuation might cost him half his force, and, at worst, might end in catastrophe, it was decided to replace him by a general who would view the situation with a fresh and unbiased mind.

No further command was offered to Hamilton; he became lieutenant of the Tower in 1918 and in 1919 he was appointed G.C.M.G. He was for many years colonel of his old regiment, the Gordon Highlanders, of which he was ever the firm friend and supporter. After his retirement in 1920 he published *Gallipoli Diary* (2 vols., 1920), a faithful record of his experiences and a revealing self-portrait. He took an active interest in the British Legion and in all organizations for the benefit of servicemen, as also in the Gordon Boys' Home and in Wellington College, of which he became a governor. From 1932 to 1935 he was lord rector of Edinburgh University, and in 1947 he was given the freedom of Inverness. He was a grand officer of the Legion of Honour and received decorations from Germany, Japan, and Spain.

Hamilton married in 1887 Jean Miller (died 1941) the beautiful and gifted daughter of Sir John Muir, first baronet, of Deanston, Perthshire. There were no children of the marriage, but after the war Lady Hamilton adopted a baby boy, Harry, who had been abandoned in the Paddington crèche of which she was president, and who died of wounds received in action in 1941. Hamilton died in London 12 October 1947, and was buried beside his wife at Doune, Perthshire. A portrait of Hamilton by J. S. Sargent is in the Tate Gallery and another in the Scottish National Portrait Gallery. A pencil drawing by Sir William Rothenstein is in the National Portrait Gallery.

[Sir Ian Hamilton, *When I Was a Boy*, 1939, *Jean*, 1942, and *Listening for the Drums*, 1944; C. F. Aspinall-Oglander, (Official) *History of the Great War. Military Operations, Gallipoli*, 2 vols., 1929-32; personal knowledge.]                    C. F. ASPINALL-OGLANDER.

HAMMOND, JOHN LAWRENCE LE BRETON (1872-1949), journalist and historian, was born at Drighlington, Yorkshire, 16 July 1872, the second son of the rector, the Rev. Vavasor Fitzhammond Hammond, who came of an old Jersey family, by his wife, Caroline Annie

Webb. Educated at Bradford Grammar School and St. John's College, Oxford, he was an accomplished classical scholar and made his mark as a Liberal in the Union debates. He became the centre of the group containing J. A. (later Viscount) Simon, Francis W. Hirst, Hilaire Belloc, (Sir) P. J. Macdonell [q.v.], and J. S. Phillimore [q.v.], with whom he produced *Essays in Liberalism* by 'Six Oxford Men' in 1897, after being placed in the second class in *literae humaniores* in 1895.

Hammond began journalism while secretary to Sir John Brunner, as leader-writer for the *Leeds Mercury* and the *Liverpool Post*. Two years later, in 1899, he undertook the editorship of the *Speaker*, a new Liberal weekly, started after the Home Rule split in opposition to the *Spectator* and to what he regarded as a rising tide of 'Jingoism' or imperialism, which took shape eventually in the South African war. He worked closely with the 'pro-Boer' group of Liberal statesmen, such as Morley, Campbell-Bannerman, Courtney, and Bryce [qq.v.], was leader-writer in the *Tribune* and the *Daily News*, and joined with Hirst and Gilbert Murray in *Liberalism and the Empire* (1900). In 1907 the *Speaker* for financial reasons had a change in management and became the *Nation* with H. W. Massingham [q.v.] as editor and Hammond as a regular leader-writer and member of the board.

In 1907 Hammond left journalism to become secretary of the Civil Service Commission, a post which he held for six years. In 1914, although over forty, he joined the Field Artillery, where he served for a year; subsequently he was drafted into the Ministry of Reconstruction. He returned to journalism as special correspondent of the *Manchester Guardian* at the peace conference, and remained continuously associated with that paper for the rest of his life. In 1939, at the outbreak of war, he went to Manchester as a permanent member of the staff, but in 1945 retired for reasons of health to Hemel Hempstead.

Hammond married in 1901 his Oxford contemporary, Lucy Barbara, daughter of the Rev. Edward Henry Bradby, formerly master of Haileybury. She was one of the most brilliant students of her time and as ardent as Hammond himself for Liberal causes. His first historical work was a life of *Charles James Fox* (1903), but after his marriage, and especially when his Civil Service appointment gave him more regular leisure, he joined with his wife in a series of books based on an intensive study of the social history of the period reaching from the latter part of the eighteenth century to the middle of the nineteenth. *The Village Labourer, 1760–1832*, published in 1911, had on its readers almost the effect of a revelation. Most of the essential facts were, of course, already known to historians; but much knowledge had been added by patient research and the whole story was illuminated by a remarkable power of historic imagination and human sympathy. The Hammonds were accused of neglecting the great general value, indeed the economic necessity, of the enclosures which inflicted such suffering on the village population, but that point, which they quite recognized, was not after all their subject, which was the effect produced on the village labourer. *The Town Labourer, 1760–1832*, was finished by 1914, but, owing to the war, not published until 1917. In 1919 the trilogy was completed by *The Skilled Labourer, 1760–1832*. These studies led naturally to a life of *Lord Shaftesbury* (1923) and *The Age of the Chartists* (1930); and *The Bleak Age* (1934) carried the story down to what has been called 'the next great watershed' of 1850. Much of the same material was treated from another standpoint in *The Rise of Modern Industry* (1925), which compared the industrial capitalism of the nineteenth century with the economic structure of earlier civilizations.

Hammond returned to biography in his *James Stansfeld* in 1932, again in collaboration with his wife, and *C. P. Scott* in 1934; still more remarkable was his *Gladstone and the Irish Nation* (1938). In each of these biographies the man selected represented a cause, but a cause expressed through a personality. In Fox, Hammond saw, beneath the loose, pleasure-loving aristocrat, the idealist ready to sacrifice for the principle of freedom everything, 'even my darling popularity'; in Shaftesbury, the wonderful courage and compassion which transfigured that somewhat narrow-minded peer; in Stansfeld, the curious foresight which made a second-rank politician almost a prophet in advocating causes, such as women's suffrage and international co-operation, which only rose to importance after his death; in Scott, the remarkable combination of journalist and philosopher which made the *Manchester Guardian* a leader of thought to a degree not paralleled by any previous newspaper. In *Gladstone and the Irish Nation* Hammond produced not only a masterly survey of Anglo-Irish relations but also the finest interpretation of a great leader who had at the time gone somewhat out of fashion. Hammond appreciated the unworldly sincerity, the unswerving appeal to high motives, which gave that 'old parliamentary hand' such unique hold over the British people. He considered that the great issue in British politics towards the end of the century was between the Gladstonian principle of 'public right as the common law of Europe' and both the *civis Romanus sum* of Palmerston and the expansionism of Chamberlain.

Hammond was both an historian and a journalist, a most valuable combination. As a journalist he dealt with present issues steadily, understandingly, in the light of history; as an historian, dealing with the past, he saw it vividly as something alive and present. It has been said of him that he worked for eternal causes in the form which they happened to assume in his day. He fought from the beginning against that lust of power and expansionist imperialism which were to have but a brief reign in England, as was shown by the immense reaction of public feeling after the South African war, but which in other nations have proved a menace to civilization. But Hammond will be even more remembered for his work on another ever-recurring social danger. He revealed to his generation a blind spot of the sort which, taking different forms in different civilizations, makes those in the fashion unaware of the truths which are not in fashion, and the strong or dominant classes or nations apathetic to the wrongs or sufferings which are not forced upon their notice. The Hammonds uncovered this phenomenon in the first half of nineteenth-century England by showing, amid all the material success and imaginative idealism of the age, the suffering and degradation which the onset of the industrial revolution brought to the dispossessed labouring classes, not through the callousness of wicked or hard-hearted men, but through the blindness of the good. Their great trilogy received what was perhaps the unexampled honour from the university of Oxford when husband and wife were awarded the honorary degree of D.Litt. on the same day, in 1933. In 1937 Hammond was made an honorary fellow of his college, in 1942 he was elected F.B.A., and in 1944 he received the honorary degree of D.Litt. from Manchester. He was appointed an officer of the Legion of Honour in 1948.

The co-operation of the Hammonds is comparable to that of Sidney and Beatrice Webb [qq.v.], but while the work of the Webbs was more massive and more immediately related to contemporary politics, that of the Hammonds had a quality of style and historical imagination which was all their own. It was in part a classical sense of form which is not common in books of social research, in part a power of sympathy and understanding towards the objects of their severest criticism. It was said of Hammond himself that, although constantly a leader in vehement political controversies, he never made a personal enemy or lost a friend.

Hammond died at his home near Hemel Hempstead 7 April 1949, survived by his widow; there were no children. A drawing by Sir William Rothenstein is in the possession of the family.

[Private information; personal knowledge.]
GILBERT MURRAY.

HANDLEY, THOMAS REGINALD (1892–1949), radio comedian, was born in Liverpool 17 January 1892, the son of John Handley, a cowkeeper, and his wife, Sarah Ann Pearson. On leaving school he worked as a salesman but he had a good singing voice and was determined to go on the stage. He toured for a short time in *The Maid of the Mountains* and in 1917 joined the Royal Naval Air Service where he soon found himself a member of a concert party. After the war he went on tour and became well known on the halls in the sketch 'The Disorderly Room', a skit on army life which reached the London Coliseum and a royal command variety performance (1924). It was the British Broadcasting Company, however, which lifted him out of the rut of variety, and as early as 1925, when broadcasting was still a primitive medium, Tommy Handley was producing and acting in his own radio revues. Broadcasting, touring, and an occasional film kept him fully occupied until in 1939 he found the opportunity which made him the greatest British radio comedian of his generation.

When Handley died in 1949, for nearly ten years he had delighted a faithful audience of millions with his versatility and prowess in a weekly wireless extravaganza called ITMA. This household word, as it soon became, was an abbreviation, in the current fashion, of 'It's That Man Again!', a phrase first coined in veiled reference to Hitler, the bogey-man of that summer of 1939 when the show was first put on. ITMA was a radio cartoon of daily life in the war years and, week by week, relieved the tension of the times by the fun which it poked at the common hazards and endurances of the British public. In the Office of Twerps, war-time bureaucrats were ridiculed for their pomposity and mismanagement. As the strain of the war increased Handley, in a much-needed holiday mood, became mayor of the seaside resort, 'Foaming-at-the-Mouth', with its famous corporation cleanser, 'Mrs. Mopp'. Another very popular figure was Funf the German spy. Handley later turned his attention to factory work, then to post-war planning, and after the war, taking a fresh leaf from the book of traditional satire, ITMA put on the map the Island of Tomtopia, where the austerities and vanished hopes of a brave new world were genially depicted. Such comic fictions as these—and there were scores of them—were sustained by Handley and his fellow clowns in a brand of vocal impersonation which brought the characters of these lampoons most vividly to life without benefit of vision. For this reason, ITMA was pure sound radio, so faithful to its subtle medium as to be incapable of translation into the terms of television. On 21 April 1942 ITMA made history by being chosen as the first royal command performance of a radio programme.

Tommy Handley was the leader of these weekly revels, but he was sustained in them by ten or a dozen other actors and actresses who learned from him the new alphabet of wireless comedy. They employed verbal mannerisms which were a kind of audio-shorthand; they exploited dialects, foreign accents, and sheer mumbo-jumbo in a wonderland of words where any absurdity was feasible. Tommy Handley was not only the keystone and inspiration of the actual performance of ITMA; he was one of the three men who invented it week after week. The script-writer was Ted Kavanagh, an old and shrewd hand at radio comedy; the producer was Francis Worsley; but it was Handley who fused the talents of this accomplished pair into a creative comic team. So much of his vital personality and quicksilver wit went into ITMA

that the show perished on the day he died. For him there was no substitute, in either invention or performance.

Tommy Handley was as unique in radio as Charlie Chaplin was in the silent film. If, indeed, all the world spoke the same language, Tommy Handley would have been an international favourite. For he, too, in his own medium, had the power to identify and delineate those humours and absurdities which are common to mankind. There were differences, of course. Chaplin was best when he was in trouble; Handley when he was nimbly getting out of trouble. But their respective arts were different sides of the same medal: in their separate ways both of them personified the common man.

In 1929 Handley married a singer, Rosalind Jean (died 1958), daughter of Robert Allistone, a jeweller, and formerly wife of William Henshall; there were no children. He died suddenly in London 9 January 1949. A memorial service was held at St. Paul's Cathedral. A bust by E. Whitney-Smith was in the possession of his widow.

[Ted Kavanagh, *Tommy Handley*, 1949; private information; personal knowledge.]
　　　　　　　　　　　W. E. WILLIAMS.

HANNAY, JAMES OWEN (1865–1950), novelist under the pseudonym of GEORGE A. BIRMINGHAM, was born in Belfast 16 July 1865, the son of the Rev. Robert Hannay, a clergyman who became vicar of the parish church of St. Anne's, Belfast, by his wife, Emily, daughter of the Rev. William Wynne. He was educated at Haileybury and Trinity College, Dublin, where he graduated in 1887 as a junior moderator in modern literature. He was ordained deacon in 1888, obtaining a curacy at Delgany, county Wicklow; and priest the following year. In 1892 he was appointed to the rectory of Westport, county Mayo, where he remained until 1913'. He chose the name of 'Birmingham', which is very common in Mayo, when planning some novels with an Irish background. He had been writing under his own name since 1890: magazine stories, newspaper articles, and scholarly works upon *The Spirit and Origin of Christian Monasticism* (1903) and *The Wisdom of the Desert* (1904). His first five novels, beginning with *The Seething Pot* (1905) and *Hyacinth* (1906), have been termed disguised political tracts; a contemporary authority observed that to read them was to understand 'the Irish problem'; also to understand its insolubility. Hannay himself said that he had no solution to offer, in his *An Irishman Looks at His World* (1919), where he confessed that he was 'more interested in Ireland than in anything else'.

In 1908 Hannay struck a vein of humour which he worked, in response to the demands of a faithful public, to the end of his long life. *Spanish Gold*, published in that year, had for its central character the Reverend J. J. Meldon, a red-haired curate of undaunted audacity and unceasing loquacity. Similar characters, such as the doctor in *Send for Dr. O'Grady* (1923), enlivened many later novels; and in 1913 *General John Regan*, which concerns the erection in a small Irish town of a statue to a totally imaginary Irish hero, was very successful as a play in London with (Sir) Charles Hawtrey [q.v.]. When performed in Westport, however, it led to a riot. Hannay's parishioners relished neither his astringent humour nor his political bias; when his pseudonym was penetrated, they boycotted him. After this stormy ending to his pastorate in Mayo, he departed for a lecture tour of the United States, and afterwards wrote *Connaught to Chicago* (1914).

From 1916 to 1917 he served as a chaplain to the forces in France, describing his experiences in *A Padre in France* (1918). From 1918 to 1921 he was rector of the small parish of Carnalway, county Kildare, and chaplain to the lord lieutenant of Ireland. Upon his resignation he also gave up, in 1922, the canonry in St. Patrick's Cathedral which he had held since 1912. After a couple of years abroad, during which he served as chaplain to the British legation in Budapest (*A Wayfarer in Hungary* was published in 1925), he was offered the living of Mells in Somerset where he settled happily in 1924. In 1929, however, his rectory was burnt down, with heavy loss; and in 1933 his wife died. He was glad therefore to change the scene in 1934 for the small, quiet London parish of Holy Trinity, Prince Consort Road. Here his preaching was appreciated; and his friends at the Athenaeum and Garrick clubs could take pleasure in his company. With curling grey hair, and blue eyes which twinkled behind spectacles, he remained tall and robust in person at past seventy. Every year he produced at least one 'George A. Birmingham' novel; the last was completed only just before his death in London 2 February 1950.

Although known to the general public as a novelist, Hannay always thought of himself as a priest first and a novelist second. His own faith was expressed in *Can I be a Christian?* (1923), letters addressed to those who, although out of touch with the Church, yet desired to be Christians. In later life he wrote biographies of Isaiah (1937) and Jeremiah (1939). In 1946 Trinity College, Dublin, conferred upon him the honorary degree of Litt.D.

In 1889 Hannay married Adelaide Susan, daughter of his mother's second cousin, Canon Frederick Richards Wynne, afterwards bishop of Killaloe, whose biography he wrote in 1897. Another kinsman was W. R. C. Wynne [q.v.]. There were two sons and two daughters of the marriage.

[*The Times*, 3 February 1950; *Burke's Landed Gentry of Ireland*, 1912 (*s.v.* Wynne of Hazlewood).]                    M. BELLASIS.

HARCOURT-SMITH, SIR CECIL (1859–1944), archaeologist and director of the Victoria and Albert Museum, was born at Staines, Middlesex, 11 September 1859, the second son of William Smith, solicitor, and his wife, Harriet, daughter of Frederic Harcourt, of Ipswich. He was a scholar of Winchester and in 1879 joined the department of Greek and Roman antiquities in the British Museum. He soon became known for his archaeological interests, and as quite a young man he was one of the founders of the *Classical Review*, which for some time he also edited. In 1887 he was attached to a diplomatic mission to Persia, and from 1895 to 1897 was granted special leave in order to fill the post of director of the British School at Athens. The School had just received a subvention from the Treasury and was able to extend its activities. Harcourt-Smith instituted the *Annual*, and began the School's excavations in the island of Melos, which contributed much to knowledge of Aegean civilizations.

While in Athens he had been promoted assistant keeper of his department in the British Museum and in 1904 he succeeded A. S. Murray [q.v.] as keeper. He was soon, however, to transfer his activities to another sphere. The collections of applied art at South Kensington, which had accumulated round the nucleus of the objects purchased by the Government after the Great Exhibition of 1851, were badly in need of reorganization. In 1908 Harcourt-Smith became chairman of the commission appointed to consider the matter, and his report was so highly approved that he was offered the post of director and secretary of what was henceforward to be known as the Victoria and Albert Museum. He took up his duties in 1909 when the new building had just been completed, and remained director until his retirement in 1924.

In the following year he was appointed adviser for the Royal Art Collections and in 1928 surveyor of the Royal Works of Art. This post he held until the death of King George V. Among his varied public activities, Harcourt-Smith played a leading part in the foundation of the Central Committee for the Care of Churches; he was chairman of the committee of the Incorporated Church Building Society, vice-chairman of the British Institute of Industrial Art, and of the British Society of Master Glass-Painters. He was also vice-president of the Hellenic Society, president of the Society of Civil Servants, and British representative on the International Office of Museums. He was an honorary member of the British Drama League and an honorary associate of the Royal Institute of British Architects. In addition to writing for the art journals he wrote a number of monographs: on 'The J. P. Morgan Antiquities', 'The Art Treasures of the Nation', and, as its honorary secretary, on 'The Society of Dilettanti, its Regalia and Pictures'.

It is, however, for his work at the Victoria and Albert Museum that Harcourt-Smith is best remembered. He raised the status of the technical staff and obtained for them the same pay and conditions as the officials of the British Museum had already. He established students' rooms in all departments and encouraged the issue of guides and catalogues. He instituted official guide-lecturers, and sponsored such special displays as the Franco-British exhibition of 1921. It was under his directorship that the museum was enriched by the acquisition of the Salting collection, the Talbot Hughes collection of costumes, the Pierpont Morgan stained glass, and the Rodin sculptures (although these were afterwards transferred to the Tate Gallery). His arrangement of the contents of the museum according to their material was hailed as an innovation, and was, no doubt, of great assistance to the specialist and scholar. It lasted until after the evacuation of 1939 when it was aban-

doned in favour of a chronological sequence more likely to be understood by the general public.

Harcourt-Smith was a man of striking appearance, tall, slender, and erect. In his youth he was known to some of his friends as 'the light dragoon'; in his age, with his white hair and moustache, his immaculate clothes and his ambassadorial manners, he was an impressive figure on all occasions. He was knighted in 1909, appointed C.V.O. in 1917, and advanced to K.C.V.O. in 1934. He also held a number of foreign decorations. He received honorary degrees from the universities of Aberdeen (LL.D., 1895) and Oxford (D.Litt., 1928).

He married in 1892 Alice Edith, daughter of H. W. Watson, of Burnopfield, county Durham, by whom he had two sons. He died at Stoatley, Bramley, Surrey, 27 March 1944. A portrait bust by Lady Welby stands in the library of the Victoria and Albert Museum.

[*The Times*, 29 March 1944; private information; personal knowledge.]
　　　　　　　　　　　　JAMES LAVER.

HARDIMAN, ALFRED FRANK (1891–1949), sculptor, was born in London 21 May 1891, the son of Alfred William Hardiman, silversmith, of Holborn, and his wife, Ada Myhill. Hardiman studied sculpture at the London County Council Central School of Arts and Crafts, the Royal College of Art, and the Royal Academy Schools. In 1920 he gained the Rome scholarship and spent two years at the British School there. It was then that Hardiman developed his style. This was based on Roman, early fifth-century Greek, and Etruscan work. It was on the borderline between archaism and naturalism in sculpture, it would seem, that he found his happy hunting-ground among the classical masters. Etruscan terracottas, and pre-Phidian Greek sculpture, especially the bronze charioteer from Delphi, had marked influence on his designs which were characterized by a strong decorative sense, tending at times to hardness. Thorough in all his hand attempted, he would spare no pains to attain perfection in his craft as a sculptor and in his two hobbies, fishing and gardening, at both of which he excelled.

Hardiman's best-known work is the equestrian statue of Earl Haig, erected by

Parliament in Whitehall in 1937. This bronze aroused considerable controversy, the conformation, anatomy, and stance of the horse being harshly criticized. There was also opposition to the Field-Marshal's being represented hatless. Through all the storm Hardiman stood firm and silent; he allowed his work to speak for itself, as indeed it does in its nobility of design, for it has sculpturesque qualities which are missing in many other equestrian statues in London. Very generally admired are his heraldic lions flanking the main entrance to the Norwich Town Hall; and this work perhaps exhibits most fully the attributes peculiar to his style. On the same building he also made some stone figures, although more familiar statues in stone are those which he carved on the eastern half of County Hall, London, where he successfully solved the problem of continuing the architectural figure decoration begun by another hand on the western half. In these sculptures of Hardiman there is the hardening of the muscular forms, even in the female figures, which resulted from his bias towards the archaic. Other works in London may be seen on the memorial to Lord Southwood in the churchyard of St. James's, Piccadilly. Hardiman could also make fine busts: a notable example of his power is that of Cecil Rhodes at Rhodes House, Oxford.

It is, of course, difficult to assess what influence Hardiman will have on future sculpture. But assuredly students will find his work interesting, if not inspiring, and those who aspire to excellence in craftsmanship, especially in the surface finish of bronze, will do well to study his example.

Hardiman was elected A.R.A. in 1936 and R.A. in 1944. He became a fellow of the Royal Society of British Sculptors in 1938 and the following year received their silver medal for his statue of Haig. In 1946 he received a gold medal for his bronze fountain figure for the New Council House, College Green, Bristol, which however was never erected.

In 1918 he married Violet, daughter of Herbert Clifton White, of London, and had two daughters. He died at Stoke Poges 17 April 1949.

[Private information; personal knowledge.]
CHARLES WHEELER.

HARDINGE, CHARLES, BARON HARDINGE OF PENSHURST (1858–1944), statesman, was born in London 20 June 1858, the second son of Charles Stewart Hardinge, second Viscount Hardinge, by his wife, Lady Lavinia Bingham, daughter of the third Earl of Lucan, field-marshal [qq.v.]. The first Viscount Hardinge [q.v.], field-marshal and governor-general of India, was his grandfather. After a spartan childhood spent at home and at Cheam, he went to Harrow, where he played cricket for the school at Lord's. Failing on medical grounds to qualify for entrance to the Royal Navy, he entered as a commoner at Trinity College, Cambridge, whence he graduated in the mathematical tripos in 1880, and in the same year joined the Foreign Office, being attached to the German department. From this 'extraordinary department', after passing an examination in public law, he began an extensive service at foreign courts. He was attaché at Constantinople under G. J. (later Viscount) Goschen and Lord Dufferin [qq.v.] (1881–4), 'the most interesting, most profitable and most happy years' of his career; at Berlin (1884) as third secretary; and as second secretary at Washington (1885–6). After six months at Whitehall, at two days' notice he went as chargé d'affaires at Sofia (1887–9), thence to Constantinople as second secretary under Sir William Arthur White [q.v.], returning to Sofia in 1890–91, and transferring to Bucharest as chargé d'affaires in 1892–3. There, besides negotiating the marriage of the Crown Prince of Romania with Princess Marie of Saxe-Coburg and Gotha, granddaughter of Queen Victoria, he was able to secure the removal of the prohibition on the entry of British cotton goods into Romania, and negotiated an extradition treaty between Great Britain and Romania. That mission fulfilled, he was appointed head of chancery in the embassy at Paris in 1893, serving once more (until 1896) under his old chief Lord Dufferin. The next two years were spent as first secretary to the legation at Teheran and in 1898 he was appointed secretary of embassy at St. Petersburg.

Hardinge made good use of the ten years which he had spent mainly in the Middle East, but with shorter terms at Berlin, Washington, and Paris, for he built up a wide acquaintance with the more prominent personages who were on the public stage at the end of Queen Victoria's reign, and had been marked at Downing Street as a well-informed man. But it was not until he came to be closely associated with King Edward VII that he became a figure of European importance. In 1903 he returned from St. Petersburg to be assistant under-secretary of state, and accompanied the King on his tour to the capitals of western Europe; the visit to Paris in May facilitated the conclusion of the Anglo-French agreement of 1904. In that year Hardinge was sworn of the Privy Council, appointed K.C.M.G. and K.C.V.O., and returned to St. Petersburg as ambassador. Relations between Britain and Russia were far from easy, but at the time of the Dogger Bank affair (October 1904) Hardinge helped materially to secure the reference of the matter to arbitration. The Emperor later referred to the great service Hardinge had rendered 'at a most critical time to his own country and to me'. On his return from St. Petersburg in 1906, Hardinge became permanent under-secretary of state for foreign affairs: his knowledge of the Middle East was of the greatest value in negotiating the Russian agreement of 1907, and, under a secretary of state who had no wide acquaintance with foreign statesmen, he became almost an indispensable attendant to King Edward VII on his visits to the German Emperor, to the Kings of Spain and Italy in 1907, and to the Emperor of Russia in 1908. This last visit showed what fruits Hardinge's policy had borne in Anglo-Russian relations; with the German visits, however, it was otherwise, and no more success attended these attempts to lay the foundations of an Anglo-German understanding than attended the mission of Lord Haldane [q.v.] in 1912.

The year 1910 was to see a very great change in Hardinge's life. Even before the death of King Edward VII (an event which was a great blow to Hardinge) the problem of Indian sedition had caused serious anxiety at home, and Hardinge's name had been canvassed as a possible successor to Lord Minto [q.v.]. After the accession of the new King, Hardinge was appointed viceroy, and raised to the peerage as Baron Hardinge of Penshurst, in the county of Kent. He landed in India in November 1910.

It was Hardinge's policy as viceroy to attempt to promote what may be called the legitimate aspirations of the literate classes of India, cultivating at the same time the goodwill of the princes of India, and if such a policy could achieve success Hardinge with his long experience of delicate negotiation and the prestige of

his name was the man to do it. Unfortunately in 1912 a bomb thrown from a window in Delhi into the viceroy's howdah as he was making a state entry on the first anniversary of the imperial durbar seriously incapacitated him, and although he kept without swerving to his policy of conciliation, the stern measures taken both in private and in public to protect his person did not increase the prestige of his office. Now that war with Russia was highly improbable, he hoped to be able to save expenditure on armaments in India and devote the savings to social services such as public works, sanitation, and education. In the last department the Moslem university at Aligarh and the Hindu university at Benares may long stand as the chief monument of his viceroyalty. In foreign affairs his diplomatic skill was used with success in establishing friendly relations of much value with the Amir of Afghanistan; and the controversy over the status of Indians in South Africa and the question of opium in China were handled with firmness by the viceroy.

The outbreak of war checked Hardinge's scheme for the social betterment of the peoples of India. Hardinge was not slow to insist that the Indian Army should have its share in the honour of fighting on the western front, and that the prohibition of the use of Indian troops against Europeans, which had been imposed in the South African war, should not be renewed. Therefore in the winter of 1914 Indian troops served on the western front; but the entry of Turkey into the war brought the Persian Gulf into the forefront of the strategic problem. Hence the ill-starred expedition to Mesopotamia ending in the surrender of Kut-el-Amara in 1916, for which Hardinge and (Sir) Austen Chamberlain [q.v.] both received censure from the commission of inquiry which reported in 1917. (The Government at first proposed but later decided not to proceed with the judicial inquiry for which Hardinge pressed. He was by this time permanent under-secretary of state for foreign affairs and his resignation, three times proffered, was refused since 'it would be detrimental to the public interest if the Foreign Office should be deprived at the present juncture of the services of Lord Hardinge'.) Nor did another expedition dispatched against German East Africa throw any great credit on the staff of the Indian Army. It must, however, be remembered, against these military failures, that Hardinge was a heavily stricken man. Although the bomb outrage at Delhi had left Lady Hardinge uninjured, she never recovered from the shock, and the support which she had unfailingly given was removed when she died shortly before the outbreak of war in 1914; nearly six months later his elder son, who had been appointed to the D.S.O. in 1914, died of wounds received in action.

In April 1916 Hardinge's term of office came to an end, and he was appointed K.G. He entered on public life at once, as chairman of the Royal Commission on the rebellion in Ireland, and also returned to his old post at the Foreign Office. At the peace conference of Paris in 1919 he was overshadowed by the more dynamic personality of the prime minister, but he realized one of his chief ambitions when in 1920 he was appointed ambassador in Paris, where he remained until the end of 1922. His retirement was something of a surprise, but Anglo-French relations were deteriorating in a manner which could not have been other than distressing to the architect of the French entente. That he found Lloyd George and Lord Curzon [q.v.] difficult to work with may have been in some degree due to the reserve of his manner, which gave to strangers and acquaintances an impression of austerity, but concealed an innate sense of the humorous which ever lurked near the surface; to this he gave vent with greater freedom with advancing years. Staunchness in friendship, courage, and optimism, with undaunted determination, were ever dominant in his character.

After 1922 Hardinge adapted himself to a life of retirement, living mostly at Oakfield near Penshurst, where he died 2 August 1944. He spoke occasionally in debates in the House of Lords but generally he took but little part in public life. He had married in 1890 his first cousin, Winifred Selina Sturt, daughter of the first Baron Alington, of Crichel [q.v.], a friend of King Edward VII. By her he had two sons and one daughter. He was succeeded by his younger son, Sir Alexander Henry Louis Hardinge (born 1894), who was private secretary to King Edward VIII, and to King George VI until 1943.

In addition to the honours already mentioned and numerous foreign decorations Hardinge was appointed C.B. (1895), C.V.O. (1903), G.C.M.G. and G.C.V.O. (1905), G.C.B., G.C.S.I., and G.C.I.E. (1910), and received the Royal Victorian

Chain in 1912. From Cambridge he received the honorary degree of LL.D. in 1929. After his death his letters and papers (1880–1922) were acquired by the university library. Portraits by Sir William Nicholson and P. A. de László are in India and a sketch for the latter is in the possession of the family.

[*The Times*, 3, 7, and 8 August 1944; Lord Hardinge of Penshurst, *Old Diplomacy*, 1947, and *My Indian Years*, 1948; private information; personal knowledge.]                    CROMER.

HARDY, GODFREY HAROLD (1877–1947), mathematician, was born at Cranleigh, Surrey, 7 February 1877, the only son of Isaac Hardy, a master at Cranleigh School, by his wife, Sophia Hall. In childhood he already showed great interest in numbers, and by the age of twelve had reached the top of Cranleigh School. He went on to Winchester, and from there obtained an entrance scholarship to Trinity College, Cambridge, in 1896. In Cambridge he came under the influence of A. E. H. Love [q.v.], who introduced him to Camille Jordan's *Cours d'Analyse de l'École Polytechnique*, and this he considered as the beginning of his career as a 'real mathematician'. He was fourth wrangler in 1898, and in 1900 was elected into a prize fellowship at Trinity.

He now flung himself eagerly into mathematical research, and at once published the first of more than 350 original papers, which were to be the main work of his life. His success in this field was soon recognized: he was elected F.R.S. in 1910 and the title of Cayley lecturer in mathematics was conferred on him by Cambridge University in 1914. To this period belongs his well-known book *A Course of Pure Mathematics* (1908), which has since gone through numerous editions and been translated into several languages. The standard of mathematical rigour in England at that time was not high, and Hardy set himself to give the ordinary student a course in which elementary analysis was for the first time done properly.

In 1908 Hardy made a contribution to genetics which has found its way into textbooks as 'Hardy's law'. There had been some debate about the proportions in which dominant and recessive Mendelian characters would be transmitted in a large mixed population. The point was settled by Hardy in a letter to *Science* (vol. xxviii, new series). It involves only some simple algebra, and no doubt he attached little weight to it. As it happens, the law is of central importance in the study of Rh-blood groups and the treatment of haemolytic disease of the newborn. In a book *A Mathematician's Apology* (1940) in which he reviewed his career, Hardy wrote 'I have never done anything "useful". No discovery of mine has made, or is likely to make, directly or indirectly, for good or ill, the least difference to the amenity of the world.' It seems that there was at least one exception to this statement.

In 1912 began his long series of papers published in collaboration with (Professor) J. E. Littlewood. Hardy liked collaboration, and much of his best work was done in this way. The two authors made fundamental contributions to the theory of Diophantine approximation, or the approximate solution of given equations by means of integers; the theory of the summation of divergent series; the theory of Fourier series; the theory of the Riemann zeta-function and the distribution of prime numbers; the solution of Waring's problem concerning the expression of a number as a sum of cubes, fourth powers, and so on; and attempted to prove the hypothesis of Goldbach, that every even number can be expressed as the sum of two prime numbers. Later still they worked together on the theory of inequalities, and in 1934 published, with Profesor George Pólya, their book *Inequalities*.

In 1914 began Hardy's equally successful collaboration with the Indian mathematician Srinivasa Ramanujan, although this was cut short six years later by Ramanujan's early death. An account of this association is given in the introductions to Ramanujan's collected works, which Hardy edited, and to Hardy's book *Ramanujan* (1940). In a letter to Hardy in 1913, Ramanujan sent specimens of his work, which showed that he was a mathematician of the first rank. He came to England in 1914 and remained until 1919. He was largely self-taught, with no knowledge of modern rigour, but his 'profound and invincible originality' called out Hardy's equal but quite different powers. Hardy said 'I owe more to him than to anyone else in the world with one exception, and my association with him is the one romantic incident in my life'.

Hardy was a disciple of Mr. Bertrand (subsequently Earl) Russell, not only in his interest in mathematical philosophy, but in his political views. He sympathized with Russell's opposition to the war of 1914–18, although he did not go to the lengths which brought Russell into collision with the authorities. Hardy described the Russell case in a little book entitled *Bertrand Russell and Trinity*, which he had printed for private circulation in 1942.

In 1920 Hardy was elected to the Savilian professorship of geometry at Oxford, with a fellowship at New College. His inaugural lecture at Oxford, 'Some famous problems in the theory of numbers and in particular Waring's problem', was published in that year.

Hardy liked lecturing, and was an admirable lecturer. His matter and delivery, like his handwriting (a specimen of which appears on the dust-cover of *A Mathematician's Apology*), were fascinating. Although no original geometer, he fulfilled the conditions of his Oxford chair by lecturing on geometry as well as on his own subjects. He also lectured occasionally on 'mathematics for philosophers', and drew large audiences of Oxford philosophers to whom ordinary mathematics made no appeal. He gave the Rouse Ball lecture, entitled 'Mathematical Proof', at Cambridge in 1928.

Hardy had singularly little appreciation of science, and claimed that real mathematics is useless. Nevertheless, he was a fellow of the Royal Astronomical Society, which he joined in 1918 in order that he might attend the meetings at which the theory of relativity was debated by (Sir) Arthur Eddington and (Sir) James Jeans [qq.v.].

The London Mathematical Society occupied a leading place in his affections. He served on its council from 1905 to 1945 with some short gaps, was for a long time secretary, and was twice president. In his presidential address (1928) he boasted that he had been at every meeting both of the council and of the Society, and sat through every word of every paper, since he became secretary in 1917. He was awarded the Society's De Morgan medal in 1929. He was also awarded many honours by other scientific societies, including a Royal (1920), the Sylvester (1940), and Copley (1947) medals of the Royal Society, and he held honorary degrees from a number of universities.

In 1928–9 he went to the United States as visiting professor at Princeton University and at the California Institute of Technology, Dr. Oswald Veblen coming to Oxford in his place.

In 1931 Hardy was elected to the Sadleirian chair of pure mathematics at Cambridge in succession to E. W. Hobson [q.v.], and became again a fellow of Trinity. He held this position until his retirement in 1942. He died at Cambridge 1 December 1947, the day on which the Copley medal was due to be presented to him.

In addition to the books already mentioned, Hardy published four volumes in the series of Cambridge Mathematical Tracts, *An Introduction to the Theory of Numbers* (1938, with Professor E. M. Wright), and *Divergent Series* (1949).

Hardy's researches in pure mathematics, covering almost every kind of analysis, are very copious as well as highly original. He described himself as a problem-solver, and did not claim to have introduced any new system of ideas. Nevertheless, if we may judge by the references to his work in the writings of others, he had a profound influence on modern mathematics. The influence of his personality in England was just as striking. He started his career at a time when the theory of functions, the creation of the great European mathematicians, was only just beginning to be known in England. He made this one of the chief mathematical studies in English universities. He communicated his own enthusiasm for this subject to his many pupils and colleagues, and made the audiences at his classes feel that nothing else but the proofs of his theorems really mattered. At the same time he took a most sympathetic interest in all those whose researches he supervised, and himself quietly put a good deal into their dissertations. The most memorable feature of his later period at Cambridge was the Littlewood–Hardy seminar or 'conversation class'. Here mathematicians of all nationalities and ages were encouraged to hold forth on their own work, and ample scope was given for free discussion after each paper. The topics dealt with were very varied, and the audience was always amazed by the sure instinct with which Hardy put his finger on the central point and started the discussion with some illuminating comment, even when the subject seemed remote from his own interests.

He was an entertaining talker on a great variety of subjects, and one sometimes noticed everyone in the room waiting to see what he was going to talk about. Conversation was one of the games which he loved to play, and it was not always easy to make out what his real opinions were. He played several games well, particularly real tennis, but his great passion was for cricket. He would read anything on this subject, and talk about it endlessly. One of his annual amusements was captaining a New College senior common-room cricket team against the Choir School and other opponents. In a paper entitled 'A Maximal Theorem with Function-theoretic Applications', published in the Scandinavian journal *Acta Mathematica* (1930), and presumably addressed to European mathematicians in general, he said 'The problem is most easily grasped when stated in the language of cricket. . . . Suppose that a batsman plays, in a given season, a given "stock" of innings. . . '.

Hardy was unmarried. He was meticulously orderly in everything but dress. His college rooms were crowded with books and papers, but he knew what everything was and where to find it. He would never use a watch or fountain-pen, the telephone only under compulsion, and corresponded chiefly by pre-paid telegrams and postcards. He was a violent anti-clerical who had many clerical friends. He came to be generally recognized as the leading English mathematician of his time.

[E. C. Titchmarsh in *Obituary Notices of Fellows of the Royal Society*, No. 18, November 1949; *Journal of the London Mathematical Society*, vol. xxv, part 2, April 1950; C. P. Snow, 'A Mathematician and Cricket' in the *Saturday Book*, 8th Year, 1948; private information; personal knowledge.]

E. C. Titchmarsh.

HAREWOOD, sixth Earl of (1882–1947). [See Lascelles, Henry George Charles.]

HARRIS, JAMES RENDEL (1852–1941), biblical scholar, archaeologist, and orientalist, was born in Plymouth 27 January 1852, the second son of Henry Marmaduke Harris, a house decorator, and his wife, Elizabeth Carter Budd. He was a cousin of H. Austin Dobson, A. M. Rendel, and G. W. Rendel [qq.v.]. Educated at Plymouth Grammar School and at Clare College, Cambridge, where he was a scholar, he was third wrangler in 1874. Elected a fellow of Clare in 1875 he stayed on as mathematical lecturer until 1882 when he went to the United

States and was appointed to teach New Testament Greek in Johns Hopkins University. When his denunciation of vivisection created difficulties, he accepted an invitation to the Quaker Haverford College, Pennsylvania, where he was professor of biblical languages and literature from 1885 to 1892. He had long been interested in such studies. In Cambridge he had studied under F. J. A. Hort [q.v.] whom he always regarded as his master. His first publication, *The Teaching of the Apostles and the Sibylline Books*, appeared in 1885 and was followed in 1887 by his essay on *The Origin of the Leicester Codex*.

During his first visit to the monastery of St. Catherine on Mount Sinai in 1889, he found the Syriac version of the lost *Apology of Aristides*. This was published in 1891 and in the same year appeared his study of the *Codex Bezae*. He called for a revaluation of the western text, asserting that 'the textual critics of modern times have in certain directions overbuilt their foundations'. Hort was impressed but not convinced, and wrote, 'it is a pity that (Harris) does not allow himself time to think of more than one theoretical possibility at once'.

In 1893 Harris returned to Cambridge as lecturer in palaeography. Specialist studies followed in quick succession, among them *The Origin of the Ferrar Group* (1893), *Stichometry* (1893), and *Hermas in Arcadia* (1896). In 1893 he again visited Mount Sinai to assist Agnes Lewis [q.v.] and her sister in deciphering the *Sinai Palimpsest*. In 1896 he and his wife spent six months organizing relief for the Armenians in Asia Minor and recorded their experiences in *Letters from the Scenes of the Recent Massacres in Armenia* (1897). A lifelong friend of the Armenians, in 1912 he journeyed to Constantinople on their behalf during the Balkan war.

In 1903 Harris was invited to fill the chair of early Christian literature and New Testament exegesis at Leyden, but in the same year went instead as first director of studies to Woodbrooke, the Quaker settlement for religious and social study in Selly Oak, Birmingham. Originally a Congregationalist, he had joined the Society of Friends in 1880. Religiously he had been influenced by the second evangelical revival and by contact with Robert and Hannah Pearsall Smith, the parents of Logan Pearsall Smith [q.v.]. He was also attracted to the mystics, particularly Madame Guyon. He shared the conviction of George Fox [q.v.] that the Christian life is to be a joyous overcoming life. His devotional writings have a singular charm. Addresses belonging to his early Cambridge period were published as *Memoranda Sacra* in 1892; some delivered after his return appeared in *Union with God* (1895); and many addresses given at Woodbrooke were published in *The Guiding Hand of God* (1905) and later volumes.

In 1909 Harris discovered in a manuscript in his own possession a Syriac version of the lost *Odes of Solomon*, a find which rivalled in interest that of the *Apology of Aristides*. A last visit to the Middle East and Mount Sinai in 1922–3 produced no great discovery, but he acquired some papyri in Egypt of which a selection was edited by Mr. J. Enoch Powell and published as *The Rendel Harris Papyri* (1936).

Setting out to join J. H. Moulton [q.v.] in India in 1916, he did not get beyond Egypt, since he was torpedoed in the Mediterranean. The return voyage in the following year was the more distressing, for he was torpedoed again, spent four days in an open boat, and lost his friend Moulton who died from exposure.

In 1918 he was appointed curator of eastern manuscripts in the John Rylands Library, Manchester, where he pursued his studies in folk-lore. Before leaving Cambridge in 1903 he had lectured on the Dioscuri in Christian legend. He had become interested in twin-lore and pushed his speculations to daring lengths. At Woodbrooke he had written *Boanerges* (1913), discovering more than one pair of twins among the apostles. At Rylands he also produced many studies of the origins of Greek gods. His researches into the early Christian use of passages from the Old Testament in controversy with Jews resulted in two books of *Testimonies* (1916 and 1920) in which Vacher Burch collaborated. The tercentenary in 1920 of the sailing of the *Mayflower* also led him to advance the theory that the barn at Jordans Friends' Meeting-House was built of the timbers of the *Mayflower*.

In 1925 he retired to Birmingham, sadly handicapped by failing eyesight. He now became intensely interested in tracing the spread of Egyptian culture in the millennia before Christ. Egypt bulks large in the series of essays which poured from his pen. The ingenuity of his suggestions, the play of his humour, and the charm of his writing were undiminished but Hort's criticism seemed more pertinent than ever. He died in Birmingham 1 March 1941.

Harris received the honorary degrees of Litt.D. from Dublin (1892), of LL.D. from Haverford (1900), and Birmingham (1909), of D.Theol. from Leyden (1909), and D.D. from Glasgow (1914). He was an honorary fellow of Clare from 1909 and was elected F.B.A. in 1927. He was a leader among Free Churchmen, and was president of the National Free Church Council in 1907-8.

He married in 1880 Helen Balkwill (died 1914), a Quaker, also of Plymouth; there were no children. A portrait by Percy Bigland is at Woodbrooke.

[*Friend,* 7 March 1941; personal knowledge.]                           H. G. Wood.

HARRISON, Sir WILLIAM MONTAGU GRAHAM- (1871-1949), parliamentary draftsman. [See GRAHAM-HARRISON.]

HARTOG, Sir PHILIP(PE) JOSEPH (1864-1947), educationist, was born in London 2 March 1864, the son of Alphonse Hartog who belonged to a Jewish family which had left Holland and settled in Paris late in the eighteenth century. The father came to London at the age of twenty-two as a teacher of French and in 1845 married Marion, the daughter of Joseph Moss, of Portsmouth. He had a hard struggle to maintain himself, but all his five surviving children earned distinction in different ways. Philippe Joseph, as he was named at birth, was the youngest, and was only seven when his eldest brother, Numa Edward Hartog [q.v.], died at the age of twenty-five.

Hartog entered University College School, London, in 1875, and in 1880 went to the Owens College, Manchester, where his brother Marcus was assistant lecturer in biology. In 1882 he graduated B.Sc. at the Victoria University and then pursued his chemical studies in laboratories in France and Germany. While in France he was closely associated with the cultured circle of friends of his sister Helena who had married the philologist Arsène Darmesteter.

In 1885 Hartog obtained his B.Sc., London, with second class honours in chemistry, and continued to study abroad until, in 1889, he was awarded a Bishop Berkeley fellowship in chemical physics at the Owens College, where he became assistant lecturer in chemistry in 1891.

He wrote on scientific matters for the *Manchester Guardian* and through his friend T. F. Tout [q.v.] began to contribute to this DICTIONARY, writing the lives of nearly forty chemists and physicists. His contributions to chemical research, however, received little recognition, and his subsequent distinction he owed to his activity in the part-time appointment of secretary to the Victoria University extension scheme, of which Tout was chairman. This earned for him in 1903 the appointment of academic registrar of the university of London.

In the course of the seventeen years during which Hartog held this post, the university, originally mainly an examining body, developed into an institution which took its full share in teaching and research. In this development he took a much more formative part than the title of his post would suggest, but he found time to complete in 1907 a work, *The Writing of English*, which was widely acclaimed as providing a new outlook on the teaching of English composition. To the movement which sought to promote the establishment in London of a School of Oriental Studies he devoted an enthusiasm which went far to justify the School in saluting him as its founder when, thirty years afterwards, it awarded him its honorary fellowship. The School received its charter in 1916, when Hartog became a Crown representative on its governing body. He was appointed C.I.E. in 1917.

His work as academic registrar of the university of London had now given him an established position in the educational world and in 1917 he was appointed a member of the Calcutta University commission under the chairmanship of his friend (Sir) Michael Sadler [q.v.]. He was a strong advocate of an advanced policy of education in India, and when, as one result of the report of the commission, the university of Dacca was established in 1920, he was appointed its first vice-chancellor. He held this post for five years during which he greatly increased his reputation as an educational administrator in spite of financial obstacles and of difficulties due to communal tension. He received the honorary degree of LL.D. from the university in 1925; was knighted in 1926; and soon after became a member of the newly created Indian Public Service Commission. His work was interrupted for some months in 1928 and 1929 when he acted as chairman of the committee on Indian education, appointed as part of the inquiries undertaken by the Indian statutory commission on constitutional advance in India. He resigned his appointment on the Public Service Commission in 1930 and was appointed K.B.E.

He returned to England at the age of sixty-six to devote the rest of his life to a great variety of activities connected with the study of educational problems. He was for seven years director of the English committee of an international body created to inquire into the reliability of examinations, a subject to which he had long given much consideration. He was joint author, with Dr. E. C. Rhodes, of two works, *An Examination of Examinations* (1935) and *The Marks of Examiners* (1936), which helped him to secure general recognition of the distinction between examinations designed to test utilizable skills and those which are designed merely to test educational progress. The work of this committee led to the establishment in 1945 of the National Foundation for Educational Research in England and Wales.

Hartog had identified himself from its inception with the Liberal Jewish movement led by C. J. Goldsmid-Montefiore [q.v.] and was a member of the council of the Liberal Jewish Synagogue in London. Always ready to help his community, in 1933 he visited Palestine to report on the organization of the Hebrew University of Jerusalem, and after the advent of Hitler he was active on behalf of refugees.

In 1939 he became chairman of a government committee to select linguists for war work. In 1946 he was still engaged in finishing his last published work, *Words in Action* (1947), a more extended treatment of the subject of his earlier work, *The Writing of English*, when his health broke down. He died in London 27 June 1947.

Apart from Hartog's academic activities, his studies on educational systems had a marked influence on contemporary thought and practice. He had an engaging personality, which combined an exceptional capacity for work and tenacity of purpose with a wide culture and great personal courtesy. He married in 1915 Mabel Hélène, daughter of Henry Joseph Kisch, of London, who, besides three works dealing with India, published in 1949 a biography of her late husband. She was killed in a mountaineering accident in 1954. There were three sons of the marriage.

The School of Oriental and African Studies possesses a portrait of Hartog painted by his sister Helena.

[Lady Hartog, *P. J. Hartog*, 1949; *Bulletin* of the School of Oriental and African Studies, vol. xii, 1948; *Journal* of the Chemical Society, June 1948; personal knowledge.]

HAILEY.

HARTY, Sir (HERBERT) HAMILTON (1879–1941), musician, was born at Hillsborough, county Down, 4 December 1879, the third son of William Michael Harty, organist of Hillsborough church, by his wife, Annie Elizabeth, daughter of Joseph Hamilton Richards, soldier, of Bray, county Dublin. It was from his father that the more famous son had his earliest instruction in piano, viola, and theory. At the age of eight he could deputize for his father at the organ, and by the time he was twelve he had an organist's post of his own at Magheragall, county Antrim. Thence he went in succession to Belfast and Dublin to fill organ appointments. He was helped in his studies by Michael Esposito, the Neapolitan musician who for forty years was prominent in the musical life of Dublin. Harty made his mark in Dublin as an exceptionally sensitive accompanist, and on going to London in 1900 he quickly established himself as one of the best of the day. His association with singers in this capacity led naturally to the composition of songs and to the writing of piano accompaniments for Irish folk-songs. In 1901 he won a prize at the Feis Ceoil (Dublin) for a piano Trio, and a Lewis Hill prize in 1904 for a piano Quintet; but the orchestra, which was to dominate the last thirty years of his life, began to attract him. He wrote a successful 'Comedy' Overture in 1907 and the 'Ode to a Nightingale' for soprano solo with orchestra which was produced at the Cardiff Festival of that year, with his wife as soloist. He began about this time to appear as a conductor with the London Symphony and other orchestras.

Musicians who combine in themselves great abilities in three cognate but nevertheless competing activities of piano-playing, conducting, and composing—von Bülow, Busoni, and Rachmaninov were eminent continental instances—inevitably gravitate towards one at the expense of the other two. Harty never looked like becoming a great composer, even of the stature of Busoni or Rachmaninov, and his name is kept alive in concert programmes more by the brilliantly apt arrangements for full modern orchestra which he made of Handel's 'Water Music', of the same composer's 'Music for the Royal Fireworks', and of some pieces by John Field [q.v.] which he made into a suite in 1939. The feeling for orchestral colour and effect, which makes these transcriptions into an expression of Harty's musical personality without trespass upon the original composers', he had learned as an interpreter of Berlioz. As a conductor his personal predilections were for the romantics, although his taste was securely grounded in the classics, and he had no sympathy with the more eccentric brands of modernism of his day. Yet he had an open mind to what he regarded as legitimate developments: he performed Sibelius's symphonies, and gave the first performances of Constant Lambert's 'The Rio Grande' (in which he played the piano part, 1929), and of (Sir) William Walton's Symphony (1935).

As a composer, Harty wrote wholly within the romantic tradition and by historical accident he came just at the moment when the vein was showing signs of exhaustion. The change in the mental climate between the years before and after the war of 1914–18 made music composed in the decade before the war, to which belong Harty's tone-poem 'With the Wild Geese' (1910) and his cantata 'The Mystic Trumpeter' (1913), seem outmoded. In the last resort they were derivative from an expiring German romanticism, however much other elements, such as Harty's own Irish characteristics, succeeded in giving them a temporary independence. The violin Concerto which he wrote in 1909 made a great impression at the time, whereas the 'Irish' Symphony of 1924, which contains much fine music derived from Irish folksong, was seen from the very fact of its romantic euphony to be speaking a dead language. Its scherzo, which reconciled the conflict of symphonic form with folkmusic more satisfactorily than the other movements written more or less round a programme, may well survive as an independent piece. His songs, which evoke Celtic atmosphere with their close-knit union of the vocal and piano writing, keep a place in the long and honourable tradition of English song.

Thus, in an age of increasing specialization, Harty still followed the older continental tradition of versatility. Beginning his career as an organist, he subsequently won distinction in three other fields, piano accompanying, composition, and orchestral conducting. His thirteen years (1920–33) as conductor of the Hallé Orchestra brought him widespread fame far beyond Manchester, taking him as a conductor of international repute several times to the United States, and in 1934 to Australia. His manner with an orchestra was quiet, and his unquestioned authority was derived in part from his sterling musicianship and in part from the warmth and lively humour of his personality.

Harty was knighted in 1925; he received the honorary degree of D.Mus. from Trinity College, Dublin, in the same year, from Manchester in 1926 and from the De Paul University, Chicago, in 1936, and of LL.D. in 1933 from the Queen's University, Belfast, where the Hamilton Harty chair of music was founded in 1951. He was elected a fellow of the Royal College of Music in 1924, and received the gold medal of the Royal Philharmonic Society in 1934, after he had relinquished the conductorship of the Hallé Orchestra, which he had restored to its former distinction.

Harty married in 1904 Agnes Helen, daughter of Albert Chapman Nicholls, managing director of Cavendish House, Cheltenham. She was a well-known singer under her maiden name and was appointed C.B.E. in 1923. Harty's last years were chequered by ill health, but he still took conducting engagements. He died at Hove 19 February 1941. There were no children. A sketch drawing by William Weatherby is in the Manchester City Art Gallery; Harty was also painted by Harold Speed.

[*The Times* and *Manchester Guardian*, 21 February 1941; *Musical Times*, March 1941; P. A. Scholes, *Oxford Companion to Music*; *Grove's Dictionary of Music and Musicians*; private information; personal knowledge.]                    FRANK HOWES.

HARVEY, SIR JOHN MARTIN MARTIN- (1863–1944), actor-manager. [See MARTIN-HARVEY.]

HARWOOD, BASIL (1859–1949), musician and composer, was born of Quaker stock at Woodhouse, Olveston, Gloucestershire, 11 April 1859, the eighth son and youngest of the nine children of Edward Harwood, banker, and justice of the peace, and his first wife, Mary, daughter of Young Sturge, of Bristol. He was educated at Charterhouse and Trinity College, Oxford, where he obtained a second class in classical moderations (1879) and a third in modern history (1881). After a brief period of study at Leipzig under Reinecke and Jadassohn, he became a pupil of George Riseley, organist of Bristol Cathedral. He began his musical career in 1883 as organist of St. Barnabas' church, Pimlico, where the use of plainsong had a formative influence on his composition. In 1887 he succeeded E. T. Chipp [q.v.] as organist of Ely Cathedral, and in 1892 was appointed organist of Christ Church, Oxford, as successor to Harford Lloyd. In addition to his work at the cathedral, he was for some time precentor of Keble College, conductor of the Oxford Orchestral Association, choragus of the university, and the first conductor of the Oxford Bach Choir, which he helped to found in 1896. He retired from professional life in 1909, and returned to his birthplace to manage the estates which he inherited from his father. He took an active part in the musical life of Bristol and was for some time president of the Madrigal Society and the Musical Club.

Apart from five works for chorus and orchestra (written for festivals at Gloucester, Leeds, Oxford, and St. Paul's Cathedral), some part-songs, and solo songs, Harwood's compositions consist chiefly of church and organ music. His best-known liturgical work is the Service in A flat, although the later Service in E minor is more mature, and forms an interesting link with the Service in E major of S. S. Wesley [q.v.]. Of the various anthems written for the seasons of the Church, 'O how glorious is the Kingdom', and 'When the Son of Man shall come' are conspicuous for both their original treatment and their craftsmanship, and contain some of his finest music. His chief editorial work is The Oxford Hymn Book, displaying both scholarship and fastidious taste. It contains several of his own tunes, two of which, 'St. Audrey' and 'Thornbury', have become widely used. His accompaniments to the plainsong hymns are models of their kind and his editions of Merbecke and the 'Missa de Angelis' are noteworthy.

Appearing at a time when English organ music was at a low ebb, Harwood's works for that instrument form an important addition to its literature. The Sonata in C sharp minor (1886), for which he received one shilling, was hailed as 'the finest organ sonata written by an Englishman', and such works as 'Dithyramb', 'Paean', 'Requiem aeternam', and the organ Concerto, all from the 'Twenty-four original compositions for the organ' which he completed in 1931, reveal his marked individual style.

Relying on a firm diatonic basis reinforced with a lavish use of strong discords, he imposed a scheme of decoration which renders any page of his organ writing recognizable at a glance. For their performance the true setting for his works is a cathedral, with an instrument of ample resources, and a performer technically equipped to meet their sometimes formidable demands.

Harwood was a retiring, humble, very reserved, and deeply religious man. His strict Quaker upbringing probably accounts for a certain austerity in his music, especially his later works. He married in 1899 Mabel Ada, daughter of Josiah George Jennings, of Castle Eve, Parkstone, Dorset, and Ferndale, Clapham, by whom he had two sons. He died in London 3 April 1949; his ashes were buried beneath a memorial tablet in the chancel of St. Barnabas' church, Pimlico, where he held his first appointment.

[Musical Times, May 1949; Grove's Dictionary of Music and Musicians; English Church Music, July 1949; Musical Compositions by Basil Harwood, 1950; Burke's Landed Gentry, 1952.]　　HENRY G. LEY.

HARWOOD, SIR HENRY HARWOOD (1888–1950), admiral, was born in London 19 January 1888, the son of Surtees Harwood Harwood, barrister, of Ashman's Hall, Beccles, Suffolk, and his wife, Mary Cecilia Ullathorne, a distant relative of Archbishop Ullathorne [q.v.]. Choosing the Royal Navy as a career, Harwood joined the Britannia in 1903 and soon displayed high intellectual capacity by gaining first class certificates in all subjects in his examinations for lieutenant. In 1911 he specialized in torpedo and thereafter served as torpedo officer in a number of ships. He did not, however, get the chance of seeing action in the war of 1914–18, although his service in the Grand Fleet was recognized by the award of the O.B.E. in 1919.

Harwood's first post-war service was a two-year commission in the South American squadron, during which he took the trouble to gain a working knowledge of Spanish which was to stand him in good stead twenty years later. His subsequent peace-time service was notable for its high proportion of staff posts and included periods at the Naval Staff College, the Admiralty plans division, the Imperial Defence College, on the staff of the senior officers' war course, and as fleet torpedo officer in the Mediterranean. He was promoted to commander in 1921 and to captain in 1928.

In 1936 Harwood received the appointment of commodore in command of the South American division of the America and West Indies station, which he was still holding when war came in 1939. The outbreak brought him reinforcements and, after some weeks, the news that the German pocket battleship the *Admiral Graf Spee*, with heavier guns and thicker armour than any of his own ships possessed, was operating in the South Atlantic. Mentally prepared for just such a contingency, Harwood went in search with the three cruisers *Ajax* (broad pennant), *Exeter*, and *Achilles*, and by skilful estimation sighted the enemy off the River Plate early on 13 December. Harwood's captains being already aware of his battle plan, there ensued an immediate British offensive by the novel method of an attack from widely different angles which was highly successful. Disconcerted by the British onslaught and confused by Harwood's original tactics, the German captain stood his ground for about twenty minutes and then made for the land. Harwood followed: but although the action was pressed for more than another hour, with much damage on both sides, the *Admiral Graf Spee* had not been crippled before shortage of ammunition compelled Harwood to break off the fight and resort to shadowing. The German ship was thus able to reach Montevideo about midnight. There she remained until 17 December, when she emerged only to blow herself up, her captain later committing suicide.

This British success could not have been more timely or welcome, for it gave Hitler his first rebuff. Honours poured in. Harwood himself was promoted to rear-admiral and appointed K.C.B. by wireless, the accolade being waived, and he reached international fame overnight.

A year later Harwood was brought home to be an assistant chief of the naval staff at the Admiralty where his work so impressed the prime minister that in 1942 the latter appointed him commander-in-chief, Mediterranean, in succession to Sir Andrew Cunningham (subsequently Viscount Cunningham of Hyndhope). For a rear-admiral to receive such a post was almost unknown in modern times. In this important command, with forces gravely attenuated by recent fleet casualties, Harwood found one of his main tasks to be the flank support and seaborne supply of the Eighth Army. This duty, on which the speed of the military advance from El Alamein largely depended, was so energetically pursued that the navy was several times the first to occupy a port after the Germans had evacuated it. Unhappily ill health made Harwood unequal to the task. He was compelled to relinquish his appointment (by then entitled the Levant Command) early in 1943, and although he held the less exacting Orkneys and Shetlands Command for some months he was finally invalided from the navy in 1945 with the rank of admiral. He retired to his house at Goring-on-Thames where he died 9 June 1950.

Harwood's services received recognition from many quarters. He was awarded the Chilean Order of Merit for earthquake rescue work and the Greek war cross. He received in 1940 the freedom of Exeter; the Gosport council gave his name to a road on its Bridgemary estate, and an avenue was called after him in the new town of Ajax, Ontario, whilst in South America two streets were named after him, one in Punta del Este and one near Carrasco, Montevideo.

A keen sportsman, Harwood was an excellent shot, a fine fisherman, and had a golf handicap of seven at Sandwich. His personality played no small part in his success. A natural geniality and charm of manner brought out the best in his subordinates and smoothed his relations with others, notably in the South American countries where these qualities, reinforced by his command of Spanish, had already earned him much goodwill among influential civilians when his victory off the Plate made him the most popular British figure for generations. At his death public requiem Masses were said for him—for he was a Roman Catholic—in the cathedral at Montevideo and in the basilica at Buenos Aires.

In 1924 Harwood married Joan, daughter of Selway Chard, of West Tarring, Sussex; they had two sons, both of whom entered the Royal Navy. Four portraits were painted of Harwood: by (Sir) Oswald Birley for the Greenwich Collection at the Royal Naval College, Greenwich (of which a copy is in the

*Vernon*); by T. C. Dugdale (subsequently lost at sea); by A. D. Wales Smith; and by Neville Lewes, in South Africa.

[*The Battle of the River Plate*, published by H.M.S.O., 1940.]     RUSSELL GRENFELL.

[Dudley Pope, *The Battle of the River Plate*, 1956; S. W. Roskill, (Official) *History of the Second World War. The War at Sea*, vols. i and ii, 1954–6.]

HASSALL, JOHN (1868–1948), poster artist, was born at Walmer 21 May 1868, the eldest son of Lieutenant Christopher Clark Hassall, R.N., of a Cheshire family of wine merchants, and his wife, Louisa, daughter of the Rev. Joseph Butterworth Owen, incumbent of St. Jude's, Chelsea, and son of the architect Jacob Owen [q.v.]. Hassall's father, who had served in the fleet at the siege of Sevastopol, was paralysed as the result of an accident on board ship and died at the age of thirty-eight. His mother married again, to an officer in the Royal Marines at Chatham who later became General Sir William Purvis Wright, K.C.B. John Hassall, who was educated at Newton Abbot College and Neuenheim College, Heidelberg, was intended by his stepfather for the army, but he twice failed to pass the appropriate examination. Accordingly in 1888 he and his brother Owen were sent on a cattle-boat to a ranch in Minnedosa, Canada, to study farming. The two years which he spent there were vital to the development of his imagination and personality. For a time he acted as path-finder to a tribe of Sioux Indians and in spirit he remained so all his life.

Hassall occupied his spare time with sketching, and his efforts were so much admired that he sent some pen drawings depicting a Manitoba 'surprise' party to the *Daily Graphic* which published them 26 February 1890. This decided him; he determined to make a living as a draughtsman. He returned home and was sent by his mother to the art school at Antwerp under Charles van Havermaet. He studied for two years, spending six months in Paris at the Académie Julian, and then returned to London where he made his one and only appearance at the Royal Academy exhibition with two large paintings which were hung 'on the line'. Meanwhile his drawings were appearing in the *Sketch*, *Pick-Me-Up*, and other papers. In 1895, in answer to an advertisement issued by David Allen & Sons, the printers, he entered upon a career which lasted for fifty years and earned

him the title of 'the poster king' and in 1939 the grant of a Civil List pension for his services to poster art. When Hassall began, poster advertising as an art was in its infancy and his designs were a cheerful addition to the street scene. His work was humorous, robust, and simple, with a direct advertising message which nevertheless attained a high standard of decorative art. The fisherman prancing along the sands with the caption 'Skegness is so bracing' was typical of his work and was still in use after his death. He advertised many commodities and also designed the posters for many of the Drury Lane pantomimes and the series for *Peter Pan*. In 1901 he was elected a member of the Royal Institute of Painters in Water Colours and at about that time began work as an illustrator of children's books which were the delight of generations of youngsters. He also helped Baden-Powell to design the uniform for the Boy Scouts. In the war of 1914–18 he was a special constable in London, and frequently appeared at charity shows where over 3,000 of his drawings were auctioned. During his holidays at Walton-on-the-Naze Hassall accumulated one of the largest private collections of prehistoric flint implements which substantially contributed to the archaeological history of East Anglia. He was a man of strong personality whose great friendliness and charm made him a much-loved member of the Savage Club where there is a portrait of him by James Gunn. Hassall died in London 8 March 1948.

In 1893 while studying abroad Hassall married a fellow student, Isabel Dingwell (died 1900), by whom he had one son and two daughters. In 1903 he married Constance Maud (died 1950), daughter of the Rev. Albert Brooke Webb, rector of Dallinghoe, Wickham Market, Suffolk. They had a son, Christopher Vernon Hassall, the author, and a daughter, Joan Hassall, the painter.

[*Studio*, December 1905; A. E. Johnson, *John Hassall R.I.*, 1907; private information; personal knowledge.]     BERT THOMAS.

HAWKE, SIR (JOHN) ANTHONY (1869–1941) judge, was born at Tolgulla, near Redruth, Cornwall, 7 June 1869, the second son of Edward Henry Hawke, merchant, by his wife, Emily Catherine, daughter of Captain Henry Wooldridge, R.N. He was educated at Merchant Taylors' School and at St. John's College, Oxford, of which he was a scholar and subsequently, from 1931, an honorary fellow. He was placed in the first class of the honour school of jurisprudence in 1891, and was called to the bar by the Middle Temple in 1892. Both in London and on the Western circuit, where he was marked as a future judge and became a keen and deservedly popular figure, he showed himself a vigorous and forceful advocate who, although a doughty opponent, never violated the good traditions of his profession. He took silk in 1913. Although his all-round practice did not involve him in many *causes célèbres*—perhaps the most notable was that inquiry in which he defended the cause of Miss Violet Douglas-Pennant in 1919—it was with universal approbation, both from the bar and from his fellow Cornishmen, that he was appointed a justice of the King's Bench division, with a knighthood, in 1928.

Before this, the closeness of Hawke's ties to his native county had appeared in his appointment as recorder of Plymouth in 1912, and, in 1923, as attorney-general to the Prince of Wales. That his affection for Cornwall was reciprocated was amply proved by his being returned twice to Parliament: in 1922 and, after a defeat in 1923, in 1924 as a Conservative member for the traditionally Liberal constituency of St. Ives. Even if it is true that he only addressed the House occasionally, he appealed to his fellow Cornishmen not only by his frank and candid approach to local and national problems, but also by his diligence to the constituency to which he devoted all his vacations. He was president of the London Cornish Association for many years, and he saw the Association grow from a comparatively small body to what is among the largest and most active of the county associations.

On the bench, Hawke showed himself industrious, conscientious, and essentially kindly, and he invariably maintained its dignity. In criminal trials he never overstrained the case against the prisoner, and his sentences were tempered with understanding and mercy. In the case of *Fender* v. *Mildmay*, [1935] 2 K.B. 334, he was called upon to decide whether a promise of marriage made between the decree *nisi* and absolute was void; he decided that it was. The decision was upheld in the Court of Appeal, but reversed by three to two in the Lords. On more than one occasion, however, after reversal in the Court of Appeal, his judgements were restored by the House of Lords. He was elected treasurer of the Middle Temple in 1937.

Hawke married in 1894 Winifred Edith Laura, daughter of Nicholas Henry Stevens, surgeon, of London. They had one son, Sir (Edward) Anthony Hawke, who became common serjeant of the City of London in 1954, and one daughter. On 30 October 1941 Hawke was found dead in his bed at the Judges' Lodgings at Chelmsford. A portrait of Hawke by R. G. Eves is in the possession of the family.

[*The Times*, 31 October 1941; private information; personal knowledge.]

J. D. Casswell.

HAWORTH, Sir (WALTER) NORMAN (1883–1950), chemist, was born at Chorley, Lancashire, 19 March 1883. He was the second son and fourth child of Thomas and Hannah Haworth and came of a family distinguished in both business and professional men. He attended the local school and at fourteen entered the linoleum factory of which his father was manager. The young Haworth had decided, however, to be a chemist and in spite of complete lack of encouragement from his family, with the aid of a private tutor he managed to pass the entrance examination to the Victoria University. He took the honours course in chemistry at Manchester and graduated with a first in 1906. At Manchester he came under the influence of W. H. Perkin [q.v.], under whom he began research on the synthesis of the terpenes. After three years' work on this subject, he was awarded an 1851 Exhibition scholarship and proceeded to Göttingen to work under Wallach. A year later he returned to Manchester as a research fellow and continued to work on the chemistry of the terpenes.

In 1911 he was appointed to the chemistry staff of the Imperial College of Science and Technology, but the next year obtained a lectureship in the university of St. Andrews. This was a most important step. Haworth came into contact with that vigorous research school, under Thomas Purdie and (Sir) James Colquhoun Irvine, engaged in investigating the structural chemistry of the sugars. This field Haworth was subsequently to make very much his own. After the break necessitated by the war of 1914–18, he continued his work on the carbohydrates and in 1920 was elected to the chair of organic chemistry at Armstrong (later King's) College, Newcastle upon Tyne, in the university of Durham.

In 1925 Haworth was called upon to

succeed (Sir) G. T. Morgan [q.v.] as Mason professor of chemistry at Birmingham University. He brought with him from Newcastle a large nucleus of research students and soon made the chemistry department of the university of Birmingham what was probably the most important school of carbohydrate chemistry in the world. About 1928 Szent-Gyorgyi isolated from orange juice a substance which he called hexuronic acid. This substance, important in the oxidations and reductions which occur in the animal body, was afterwards identified with vitamin C. Haworth, early in 1932, with a well-trained team of research workers, attacked the chemistry of this substance with his usual vigour and he was shortly afterwards able to announce the synthesis of ascorbic acid (vitamin C) thus effecting the first chemical synthesis of a vitamin. Although Haworth had many duties inside the university—he was for several years dean of the faculty of science—his extra-mural activities were many and varied. For a number of years he was chairman of the chemical research board of the Department of Scientific and Industrial Research. He played a large part in building up the Rubber Producers' Research Association and the Colonial Products Research Council. Early in the war of 1939–45 he was appointed chairman of the British chemical panel for atomic energy, and directed research in the preparation of highly pure uranium and the search for a volatile compound of that metal other than the hexafluoride.

Naturally he received many honours from many parts of the world. He was elected F.R.S. in 1928. He was awarded the Longstaff medal of the Chemical Society, jointly with Irvine, in 1933, and the Davy (1934) and the Royal (1942) medals of the Royal Society. At the meeting of the British Association at Norwich in 1935 he presided over the chemistry section, and in 1937 he was the first British organic chemist to be awarded a Nobel prize (shared with Professor Paul Karrer). He received the honorary degree of D.Sc. from the Queen's University, Belfast, Oslo, and Zürich, and that of Sc.D. from Cambridge (1939) and LL.D. from Manchester (1947). He was president of the Chemical Society, 1944–6, and vice-president of the Royal Society in 1947, in which year he was knighted.

In 1948 Haworth retired from the Mason chair which he had held with such distinction for twenty-three years. He was asked to represent the Royal Society at the seventh Pacific Science Congress which was held in New Zealand in 1949. He took the opportunity to visit and lecture at a number of universities in Australia and New Zealand. He had been home less than a year when he died suddenly at his home in Barnt Green, Birmingham, 19 March 1950.

He gave the impression of being austere and somewhat aloof, but underneath resided a kindliness and solicitude which perhaps only his intimate friends and colleagues perceived. He will always be remembered as a great man of science—particularly as a great organizer of research.

Haworth married in 1922 Violet Chilton, daughter of Sir James Johnston Dobbie, F.R.S. She, with her two sons, survived him.

[E. L. Hirst in *Obituary Notices of Fellows of the Royal Society*, No. 20, November 1951.]

L. L. BIRCUMSHAW.

HEADLAM, ARTHUR CAYLEY (1862–1947), bishop of Gloucester, was born at Whorlton Hall, county Durham, 2 August 1862, the eldest of the four sons and five children of the Rev. Arthur William Headlam by his first wife, Agnes Sarah, daughter of James Favell, of Normanton, Yorkshire. A younger brother was Sir James Wycliffe Headlam-Morley [q.v.]. His father held successively three Durham incumbencies, Whorlton, St. Oswald's, Durham, and Gainford, and became an honorary canon of Durham Cathedral. On his mother's side, through the Caley family, Headlam had a link of descent from Oliver Cromwell. In 1876 he won a scholarship at Winchester, where his vigorous ways won him the nickname of 'the General'. In 1881 he went with a scholarship to New College, Oxford, obtaining a second class in classical moderations in 1883, a first in *literae humaniores* in 1885, and a fellowship of All Souls in the same year. He was ordained deacon in 1888 and priest in 1889, taught theology in Oxford, travelled and explored in the Near East with (Sir) W. M. Ramsay [q.v.], and in 1895 with William Sanday [q.v.] produced a standard commentary on the Epistle to the Romans. From 1896 he held the rectory of Welwyn, Hertfordshire, until in 1903 he was appointed principal of King's College, London. He proceeded D.D. in the same year.

At King's College Headlam found

abundant scope for his energy, for his powers of organization, and for a determination which did not easily brook opposition. He was successful in dividing the college, hitherto a unitary medley of faculties and educational bodies, into two separate parts, the larger of them consisting of the secular faculties, and being incorporated in the university of London. The smaller part, King's College Theological Department, kept its independence under its own council as a denominational body of teachers and students. The system of collegiate life and government thus established may seem, as indeed it was, complicated. But in fact King's College retained a real unity of spirit and the 'dualist' plan has been called by one of Headlam's successors 'a remarkable piece of statesmanship'. It was not achieved without hard fighting, and Headlam's resignation after ten years' work was due to his desire for more leisure to read and write and to differences of opinion both with the senate and with the Board of Education.

Throughout his life, indeed, despite administrative cares, he was a prolific and vigorous author on biblical and theological subjects, while his editorship of the *Church Quarterly Review* (1901–21) gave him opportunities which he used to the full, especially during the war of 1914–18, of expressing with unvarying clarity his opinions on contemporary affairs. In 1918 he was appointed regius professor of divinity at Oxford. He was a strong head of the faculty, convinced that its primary purpose was to train ministers of religion and in particular clergy of the Church of England, convinced also of the need to promote the advanced study of theology: for this latter purpose he created a seminar. The Bampton lectures of 1920 on 'The Doctrine of the Church and Christian Reunion', his most notable achievement during his professorship, expressed with characteristic independence and confidence some much-controverted judgements on subjects which deeply engaged his thought. Headlam had by this time won a well-deserved reputation as a scholar, an administrator, and a churchman of vigour and decision. He had for long been closely concerned with the problems of Christian reunion at home and abroad, combining strong adherence to historic episcopacy with equally strong conviction of the validity of the ministries and sacraments of the great nonconformist communities, and with the desire to move towards reunion by recognizing that validity. His familiarity with the Orthodox Churches of Eastern Europe, with the Old Catholics and with the Lutherans was founded not only on his historical knowledge but upon close acquaintance with contemporary conditions gained through much travel and correspondence: he showed generous hospitality during the war of 1914–18 and later to members of many foreign Churches. He was appointed C.H. in 1921. His consecration as bishop of Gloucester in 1923 increased his influence in œcumenical affairs and throughout his episcopate he devoted much time to them. From 1933 to 1945 he was chairman of the Church of England Council on Foreign Relations.

In his work as a bishop, as in many other relations of life, Headlam often appeared brusque and insensitive, even hard and unsympathetic. He always knew his own mind and expressed himself with uncompromising clearness: a characteristic reserve and unsentimentality combined with a quick temper and a disregard of criticism often made him seem difficult and unapproachable. Certainly he could be bluntly impervious to the effect of his words. But he respected and welcomed forthrightness in others: differences of opinion did not damage old friendships, and there was a strong sense of justice and kindness in his dealings with those in trouble. Solidity and directness attracted him both in learning and in life. The cares of his diocese did not put an end to his long series of books on theology and the interpretation of the New Testament. In these fields he was an enlightened conservative, keeping in touch with new knowledge and new theories but strongly critical of views which seemed to strain the evidence or to move far from the positions which his own studies had tested and to his mind established. These central positions changed little throughout his life, and a big book on *Christian Theology* (1934) was not very closely relevant to the particular theological interests of that time. But in liturgical matters the Prayer Book controversy deeply engaged him: he became a stout supporter of the revision and urged the need for fresh and continuous study of the whole subject. And at the end of his life he was busy in reconsideration of the problems of the Fourth Gospel.

Headlam was elected an honorary fellow of New College in 1936. After resigning his see in 1945 he lived at

Whorlton Hall, his home in county Durham. He had many interests: his books, his coin collection, above all his garden to which he had often returned with delight. Deafness had long troubled him, but until near the end of his life he was a man of strong and massive frame. He died at Whorlton Hall 17 January 1947. His wife, Evelyn Persis, daughter of the late Rev. George Wingfield, whom he married in 1900, died in 1924. There was no issue of the marriage. A portrait of Headlam by George Hall Neale is at Gloucester, and a drawing by Francis Dodd is at Whorlton Hall.

[Biographical essay by Agnes Headlam-Morley, prefixed to *The Fourth Gospel as History*, 1948; *The Times*, 18 January 1947; F. J. C. Hearnshaw, *Centenary History of King's College, London*, 1929; *Burke's Landed Gentry*, 1952 (*s.v.* Headlam and Parry-Wingfield of Tickencote); personal knowledge.]

ALWYN WINTON: (A. T. P. WILLIAMS.)

HEATH, SIR (HENRY) FRANK (1863–1946), academic and scientific administrator, was born in London 11 December 1863, the eldest son of Henry Charles Heath, miniature painter to Queen Victoria, and his wife, Georgina Woodcock. He was grandson and great-grandson of the engravers Charles Heath (1785–1848) and James Heath (1757–1834) [qq.v.].

Heath was educated at Westminster School and University College, London, where he won the college prize and an exhibition in English and was placed in the second class in mental and moral science in 1886 and later became a fellow. He studied for three years at the university of Strasbourg and from 1890 until 1896 was professor of English literature and language at Bedford College, and also for some years lecturer in English language at King's College. In 1895 he became assistant registrar and librarian of London University and in 1901 was promoted to be academic registrar and acting treasurer. The university had just begun to exercise the enlarged powers granted to it under the new constitution of 1900 and Heath's post was of special importance. He held it for two years and in that time did much to strengthen the administration of the largest and most complex of English universities.

In 1903 Heath joined the Board of Education as director of special inquiries and reports in succession to (Sir) Michael Sadler [q.v.]. It was a period when great changes were taking place at the Board; Heath became deeply interested in the general problems of the universities and made a special study of scientific and technical education. Until 1910 the Treasury gave direct grants to the newer universities and university colleges for the promotion of arts and science; the Board of Education gave grants in aid of engineering; and medical schools received no State aid. Heath served as joint secretary to the Royal Commission on university education in London from 1909 to 1913 and was a member of the Treasury advisory committee on grants to university colleges from 1909 to 1911. In this year the committee was transferred to the Board of Education which had in 1910 set up a branch controlling all financial assistance to the universities. Heath became principal assistant secretary in administrative charge of the new branch, whilst retaining his directorship of special inquiries and reports. He soon simplified and improved the conditions for the support of engineering, and then proposed a similar scheme for grants to medical schools. This progress was not achieved without a struggle between Sir Robert Morant [q.v.], secretary of the Board until 1911, and the Treasury. Finally the administrative skill of Heath and the leadership of Sir William McCormick [q.v.] led to the establishment in 1919 of the Treasury University Grants Committee, independent of the Board of Education, through which the State made steadily increasing grants to universities without affecting their autonomy.

From 1904 to 1916 Heath was also education correspondent to the Government of India. In the meantime the outbreak of war in 1914 had revealed the commanding position of Germany in the application of science to industry. (Even the khaki dye needed for British uniforms was a German monopoly.) Before the end of the year Heath was ready with suggestions for dealing with the situation. His memorandum was submitted to a secret committee under McCormick; and plans were completed for the creation of a permanent government organization for scientific and industrial research, by the appointment of a standing scientific Advisory Council responsible to a committee of the Privy Council. The first Advisory Council was appointed in July 1915, consisting of seven distinguished scientists and McCormick as chairman, with Heath as secretary. In 1916 an executive Department of Scientific and Industrial Research was created, and Heath, resigning from his other posts, became its first permanent secretary.

In the remaining years of the war the Council was mainly engaged on plans for the future, which could not bear fruit until 1918. The National Physical Laboratory was then attached to the new department and soon grew in strength and influence. A Fuel Research Station was established in 1918 and was the forerunner of similar research stations for the benefit of industries of special national importance. The initiative in such cases rested with the Advisory Council: Heath was the administrator rather than the originator. But he made his own distinctive contribution to policy in the formation of self-governing industrial research associations, mainly designed to promote the application of science to the older scattered industries but not confined to these. With the strong backing of the Advisory Council, and the irresistible advocacy of McCormick, a grant of one million sterling was obtained from the Treasury to help finance the associations in the early years of their existence. Unfortunately the hope that the associations would soon become self-supporting was not fulfilled; but the value of the scheme has been widely recognized and similar schemes, with modifications, have been adopted by other countries. In 1925–6 Heath visited Australia and New Zealand to assist in the development of research departments on similar lines to his own. Canada, India, and South Africa also have organizations which are the direct result of Heath's foresight in 1914.

In 1927 Heath retired, and in that year was appointed G.B.E., having been appointed C.B. in 1911 and K.C.B. in 1917. He was elected a governor of the Imperial College of Science and Technology in 1931 and attended his last meeting of the governing body on the day before his death. He took a prominent part in the cultural work of the League of Nations; was a member of the research committee of the Colonial Office, 1924–33, of the Royal Commission for the Exhibition of 1851 from 1924, and of the Universities China Committee from 1932; he was secretary of the Universities Bureau of the British Empire, 1929–30, and honorary director, 1930–34. In 1946 he published with Mr. A. L. Hetherington a book on *Industrial Research and Development in the United Kingdom.*

Heath had a remarkable vitality throughout his long life. He took an immense interest in the details of everything he undertook. His skill as an administrator was enhanced by an exceptional gift of imaginative foresight. His upbringing and experience gave him a wide outlook on life and letters. He edited the *Modern Language Quarterly* from 1897 to 1903 and with A. W. Pollard [q.v.] and others had edited the 'Globe Chaucer' (1898). But he was never a scholar in the accepted sense and rightly abandoned an academic for an administrative career, entering into that close association with McCormick, also a former professor of English, which was to have so profound an influence on the development of scientific and industrial research in Great Britain.

Heath's appointment as secretary of the Department of Scientific and Industrial Research did not pass without criticism, for many scientists felt that it was wrong for a layman to be in a position to exert such a powerful influence on scientific developments. And although he soon gained the confidence of the strong individualists who formed the first Advisory Council, the criticism from outside never quite ceased. There was little justification for it. His work was of signal benefit to the nation and all the institutions which he helped to found and encouraged during their early years became permanent institutions. The consequences of his work have spread far and wide.

In person Heath was of middle height, sturdy, and physically robust. His work absorbed all his interests; his sole recreation was walking. He wrote easily and clearly, but without great distinction. A portrait in oils, by his brother Dudley Heath, is an excellent likeness and hangs in the Department of Scientific and Industrial Research.

Heath married twice: first, in 1892 Antonia Johanna Sophie Theresa (died 1893), daughter of Friedrich Gottlieb Eckenstein, merchant, of Canonbury; secondly, in 1898 Frances Elaine (died 1939), daughter of James Hawkins Sayer, linen-draper, of High Barnet and Hastings. There were two sons of this marriage. He died in London 5 October 1946.

[*The Times*, 7 October 1946; *Nature*, 7 December 1946; Ministry of Education; private information; personal knowledge.]

H. T. TIZARD.

HEATH ROBINSON, WILLIAM (1872–1944), cartoonist and book-illustrator. [See ROBINSON.]

HELE-SHAW, HENRY SELBY (1854–1941), engineer, was born at Billericay, Essex, 29 July 1854, the eldest of the thirteen children of Henry Shaw, a solicitor, by his wife, Marion, daughter of the Rev. Henry Selby Hele, vicar of Grays, Essex. His scientific genius and inventiveness seem not to have appeared before in the family, although his younger brother, Philip Egerton Shaw, became professor of physics at Nottingham. Shaw added his mother's maiden name to his own surname in his early twenties.

Shaw was privately educated, and at the age of seventeen was apprenticed at the Mardyke engineering works of Rouch and Leaker in Bristol. Ten hours' practical work a day was then required of an apprentice, and this had to be supplemented by long evening classes. In 1876 he obtained the first of a number of Whitworth prizes, enabling him to become a student at University College, Bristol. He repeated and improved on this performance in each of his three years as a student. When the time came for the final and most important examination he was found to be suffering from congestion of the lungs. In spite of medical advice he attended the examination wrapped up in blankets, and was placed first on the list. In addition he was in 1880 awarded the Miller scholarship from the Institution of Civil Engineers for a paper on 'Small Motive Power'.

On obtaining his degree in 1880, Hele-Shaw was appointed lecturer in mathematics and engineering in his own college at Bristol, and in 1881 he became the first professor of engineering there. He was then only twenty-seven. In 1885 he became the first occupant of the chair of engineering at the University College of Liverpool, which he held until 1904. In that year he accepted an invitation to initiate yet another college of engineering, this time at the Transvaal Technical Institute, of which he became principal within a year. This was, of course, at a time when the importance of engineering science as a university subject was becoming recognized and a number of new colleges were coming into existence, but even so, Hele-Shaw's record in founding three such departments—all of which have from the first held a high place—is probably unique.

He remained in South Africa for only two years, and after his return to England in 1906 he never again held an academic appointment, although he retained his interest in education to the end of his life. As a teacher he had no difficulty in holding the attention and interest of his students. On his own subject of kinematics he was a fine lecturer, making use of frequent demonstrations which his inventiveness suggested to him. His geniality and his undoubted pre-eminence as a practical engineer never failed to earn him the affection and respect of his students.

It is, however, mainly as an inventor and research worker that Hele-Shaw will be remembered. His inventions cover a wide range, beginning in 1881 with several instruments for the measurement and recording of wind velocities, and proceeding next by a logical development to the field of integrating machines. For his paper to the Institution of Civil Engineers on 'Mechanical Integrators' in 1885 he received the Watt gold medal and Telford premium. Similarly, his main contributions to science arose from the facility with which he designed new apparatus for experiment. A good example of this may be found in his demonstration of the nature of streamline flow of which a theoretical exposition was provided at the time by Sir G. G. Stokes [q.v.]. The scientific significance of this work was great, since not only were the hydrodynamic equations involved considered to be insoluble, except in a few cases, but hydrodynamics as a whole was regarded as a purely mathematical subject with little application to real fluids. His work drew severe criticism from Osborne Reynolds [q.v.], who, in *Nature*, 15 September 1898, both disputed the conclusions reached and implied that he himself had anticipated many of the results in earlier work of his own. Hele-Shaw defended himself stoutly against his great antagonist, and his election as F.R.S. the next year (1899) in recognition of this work shows that even at the time it was clear that Reynolds had underestimated both the value of the investigation and the extent of Hele-Shaw's contribution. In his whole career Hele-Shaw contributed more than a hundred papers, many of them of great importance, to various learned societies. He was awarded honorary degrees by the universities of St. Andrews (LL.D., 1897), Bristol (D.Sc. in engineering, 1912), and Liverpool (D.Eng., 1931).

Even in the years in which he was most absorbed in research Hele-Shaw found time to take an immediate interest in practical engineering progress. In 1896 the Locomotives on Highways Act opened an entirely new field to British engineering, and in the first years while the industry was acquiring experience he was in touch with every problem which arose. He acted as judge in almost every trial, and the famous Liverpool trials on commercial motor vehicles in 1897 were organized by him. He invented a number of important devices, including a friction clutch which at one time was fitted to the majority of all motor vehicles. In his enthusiasm for motoring and its future, he would, before the Act of 1896, demonstrate the working of a car on the public roads with someone walking before, carrying the statutory red flag.

A number of Hele-Shaw's inventions are in the field of hydraulics; among these are his 'streamline' filter, his hydraulic transmission gear—the first of a type which has since become very important—and his hydraulic steering gear for ships, together with several pumps and hydraulic motors.

For the last thirty years of his life he was engaged entirely as a consulting engineer, in invention, and in the exploitation of previous inventions. Unlike many research workers he had a flair for the commercial exploitation of his discoveries. Some of these, of course, were unsuccessful, but a number are still widely employed. With Mr. T. E. Beacham he introduced in 1924 the first practical automatic variable-pitch airscrew. At that time little advantage was obtainable from this device, but twenty years later it was essential for almost all fast aircraft.

In later life Hele-Shaw took an increasing interest in the professional engineering institutions. He was president of the Institution of Automobile Engineers in 1909 and of the Institution of Mechanical Engineers in 1922. It may well be that his most important service to British engineering was his influence in introducing the national certificate scheme in 1920, which was organized jointly by the Board of Education and the Institution of Mechanical Engineers, through which a very large number of engineers have since received their training.

Except during his years of self-denial as apprentice and student Hele-Shaw was a keen sportsman, a first-class player at golf and lacrosse, and a good mountaineer and yachtsman. He was a lively and humorous conversationalist, and an excellent speaker. He grew up in an age of robust scientific controversy, and he enjoyed it. In his old age he was sometimes thought to be intolerant of opinions which differed from his own, but he never failed in kindliness towards his juniors.

Hele-Shaw married in 1890 Ella Marion (died 1947), daughter of Samuel Greg Rathbone, of the famous Liverpool family. They had one son who was killed in the war of 1914–18 and one daughter. Hele-Shaw retired to Ross-on-Wye in Herefordshire at the age of eighty-five and died there 30 January 1941.

A portrait by Harold Speed is at the Institution of Mechanical Engineers.

[H. L. Guy in *Obituary Notices of Fellows of the Royal Society*, No. 10, December 1941; *Proceedings* of the Institution of Mechanical Engineers, vol. cxlv, 1941; *Engineer* and *Engineering*, 7 February 1941; private information.]                    D. G. CHRISTOPHERSON.

HELENA VICTORIA, PRINCESS, whose full names were VICTORIA LOUISE SOPHIA AUGUSTA AMELIA HELENA (1870–1948), was born at Frogmore, Windsor Park, 3 May 1870, the third child and elder daughter of Prince Christian of Schleswig-Holstein and Princess Christian, Queen Victoria's third daughter, Princess Helena Augusta Victoria. Her early life was spent at Windsor where her parents had a house in the Park of which her father was Ranger. She naturally saw a great deal of her grandmother who in her letters always referred to her as 'Thora', a childhood contraction of her first name.

As a public figure Princess Helena Victoria grew up to follow the example of her mother and supported many and various philanthropic and benevolent causes, among them the Princess Christian Nursing Home at Windsor of which she succeeded her mother as president. She particularly identified herself with the Young Men's Christian Association and took the closest interest in every branch of its work, visiting France on its behalf during the war of 1914–18. It was she who obtained from Lord Kitchener [q.v.] permission to send musical and theatrical entertainments to the troops at the front. In 1917 King George V accorded her the style of Highness and the territorial name of Schleswig-Holstein was dropped.

In contemporary social life the Princess made for herself a definite place: she played lawn tennis, and also golf at a time when few women had become its votaries; and she maintained a lifelong zest for ballroom dancing. She had inherited the musical tastes of both her maternal grandparents and in the period between the two wars she and her sister, Princess Marie Louise, made their home, the last house in Pall Mall to be used as a private residence, into a musical centre. She died in London 13 March 1948 after some years of failing health.

A portrait by Harrington Mann was in the possession of Princess Marie Louise.

[Contemporary newsprints; private information.]     H. E. WORTHAM.

[H.H. Princess Marie Louise, *My Memories of Six Reigns*, 1956.]

HELY-HUTCHINSON, RICHARD WALTER JOHN, sixth EARL OF DONOUGHMORE (1875–1948), chairman of committees of the House of Lords, was born in London 2 March 1875, the only son of John Luke George Hely-Hutchinson, fifth Earl of Donoughmore, and his wife, Frances Isabella, of the Tasmanian family of Stephens. Donoughmore, who until the death of his father in 1900 bore the courtesy title of Viscount Suirdale, was educated at Eton and at New College, Oxford, where he obtained a second class in modern history in 1897 and was elected an honorary fellow in 1931. A Conservative in politics, he was appointed under-secretary of state for war in 1903 and held office until the fall of Balfour's Government at the end of 1905. He was always assiduous in his attention to his duties in the House of Lords, and in 1911 was made chairman of committees. He was appointed K.P. in 1916 and sworn of the Privy Council in 1918. Deeply interested in his office and always adroit and conciliatory in the conduct of its business, he held it for twenty years until he was obliged by ill health to resign in 1931. At the same time he was forced to relinquish his work in the important committee on ministers' powers over which he had presided since 1929. He had earlier (1927–8) served as chairman of a special commission on the constitution of Ceylon.

Donoughmore was endowed with a genial presence, with a kindly and humorous disposition and with a wide range of sympathy with philanthropic objects. From 1933 until his death he was chairman of the National Radium Commission, and he rose to high eminence in the craft of freemasonry both in England and Ireland. While his health allowed of it he was a good player of golf and lawn tennis, and remained afterwards a keen patron of those games; but severe arthritis which fell upon him in middle life forbade him all further physical activity. He retained throughout life a scientific interest in music and in horticulture; and built up at his residence, Chelwood Beacon, Sussex, a very remarkable collection of all species of rhododendron. There and at his Irish home at Knocklofty he delighted in hospitality. His social contacts with all sorts and conditions of people alike in England and in Ireland were extensive and he was a deservedly popular figure, whose premature retirement from public life was a considerable loss.

In 1901 he married Elena Maria (died 1944), daughter of Michael Paul Grace, of New York, one of the founders of the firm of W. R. Grace & Co. which has extensive business interests in South America and owns the Grace Line of steamships. There were two sons and one daughter of the marriage and Donoughmore loved to surround himself with his children's young friends among whom he and his wife were generally known by the affectionate nickname of 'Mr. and Mrs. D.' Donoughmore endured his physical disability with exemplary courage and fortitude, but a severe motor accident hastened his death which took place at Knocklofty 19 October 1948. He was succeeded by his elder son, John Michael Henry (born 1902).

[Personal knowledge.]
DOUGAL O. MALCOLM.

HENDERSON, GEORGE GERALD (1862–1942), chemist, was born in Glasgow 30 January 1862, the second son of George Henderson, merchant, by his wife, Alexandrina Kerr. He was descended from a long line of Scottish country lairds but there is no evidence of any ancestral scientific interests. Nevertheless, when he matriculated in the university of Glasgow at the early age of fifteen and a half he broke away violently from school and home influences and read science in preference to the liberal arts. Before he reached his twentieth birthday he graduated with first class honours in chemistry and had published a meritorious original paper. Thereafter, reversing the usual order of study, he read for an arts degree, acquiring scholarly tastes which never forsook him—there were few professors in his generation who were university prizemen in both chemistry and Greek.

Having definitely pledged himself to chemistry, he spent the winters as a lecturer in Glasgow and the summer semesters as a research pupil of Wislicenus in Leipzig. The fruits of this strenuous programme were soon apparent and in 1889 Henderson was appointed head of the chemistry department in Queen Margaret College, Glasgow. Here his attractive teaching technique was perfected, and he was an obvious choice when in 1892 the Freeland chair became vacant at the Glasgow and West of Scotland (later the Royal) Technical College. In this new environment his personality, his skill as a lecturer, and his appearance (tall, slim, athletic, and well tailored) commanded respect. Most of his students were preparing to become works chemists and their intellectual quality varied greatly, but each man felt he was the professor's special care.

Although his researches had now focused on the constitution of terpenes he built up close relationships with the manufacturing interests of the west of Scotland and took a leading part in providing the Technical College with appropriate buildings. Soon after occupying his new laboratories, however, he was recalled in 1919 to his university as regius professor and became involved for the second time in the creation of a new chemistry institute. It was a long struggle but once more Henderson 'found Rome brick and left it marble'. He acted as dean of the faculty of science and as an assessor on the university court, was elected president of the Society of Chemical Industry (1914), the (Royal) Institute of Chemistry (1924–7), and the Chemical Society (1931). Other honours included the fellowship of the Royal Society (1916), and honorary degrees from St. Andrews (LL.D., 1912), Belfast (D.Sc., 1934), and Glasgow (LL.D., 1938).

In 1895 Henderson married his cousin, Agnes Mackenzie, daughter of John Crawfurd Kerr, and although they had no children she made his life glad for more than forty years. Her sudden death coincided with Henderson's resignation from his chair in 1937 and it was a weary, broken-hearted man who retired to the Isle of Harris to seek consolation in scenes hallowed by precious memories. He died 28 September 1942 at Tarbert, Isle of Harris, closing a record of achievement which, taken in the aggregate, is not exceeded by any chemist of his generation. He was probably the last of the professors of chemistry in this country expected to represent all branches of a subject which was developing rapidly as the nineteenth merged into the twentieth century. Within these few decades inorganic chemistry was reborn, organic chemistry attained its highest flights, physical chemistry sprang into first importance, and above all the relationship between chemistry and industry was placed on a new footing. In these developments Henderson played a prominent part, greatly to the advantage of chemistry and of Great Britain. His life's work was centred in Glasgow, but this statement, which implies a narrow range of activity, can give no idea of the profound influence he wielded over succeeding generations of students, or of the value of the contributions he made to science and to industry.

[Sir James Irvine and J. L. Simonsen in *Obituary Notices of Fellows of the Royal Society*, No. 13, November 1944.]

J. C. IRVINE.

HENDERSON, SIR NEVILE MEYRICK (1882–1942), diplomatist, was born 10 June 1882, the second son and third child of Robert Henderson by his wife, Emma Caroline, daughter of John Hargreaves, of Cuffnells, Lyndhurst, Hampshire. The family hailed from Leuchars in Fife, and Nevile Henderson's grandfather had founded a prosperous merchant business in Glasgow, trading to the Far East under the name of R. & I. Henderson. The father, who had managed the family business, became a director of the Bank of England, having settled in Sussex at Sedgwick Park, Horsham, where Nevile Henderson was born and brought up. As his father died when he was yet a child, it fell to the mother, a woman of strong character, to decide that he should enter the diplomatic service, although his natural bent was towards a military career and he did actually pass the entrance examination to the Royal Military College. He grew up to be a tall, slim, good-looking man with fine features. He never married but affection for his mother played a large part in his life, as did also certain close female friendships.

After leaving Eton, Henderson studied abroad for four years and entered the diplomatic service in 1905. He served successively as secretary in the Foreign Office, at St. Petersburg (1905), Tokyo (1909), again at St. Petersburg (1912),

Rome (1914), Nish (1914), in the Foreign Office (1915), at Paris (1916), and Constantinople (1920), where, under Sir Horace Rumbold [q.v.], he spent a particularly interesting and difficult period. He was in charge during Rumbold's absences at the Lausanne conference and, later, pending the arrival of (Sir) Ronald Lindsay [q.v.]. He was promoted counsellor in 1922. In 1924 he was transferred to Cairo with the rank of minister plenipotentiary. He arrived immediately after the murder of Sir Lee Stack [q.v.], and on the departure of Lord Allenby [q.v.] he stayed on under the new high commissioner Lord Lloyd [q.v.], with whose views he disagreed, being himself in favour of a policy of timely concessions to be embodied in a new treaty. In 1928 he was appointed counsellor-minister at Paris.

In 1929 Henderson was given the first of the three posts in which he was head of a mission, Belgrade. This mission may be considered as the turning-point in his career, for during the five years of its duration he formed a close friendship with King Alexander of Yugoslavia, who by that time had established himself as dictator, and whom Henderson greatly admired. In 1935 he was transferred to Buenos Aires on a short, uneventful, and not particularly congenial mission before entering upon his historic embassy at Berlin in 1937.

It was always a matter of regret to Henderson that he had only served for two short periods in the Foreign Office, for it meant that in later life, after his mother's death and the sale of Sedgwick Park, he had but few roots in Britain, although always essentially British in appearance and outlook. He had become a reserved man, not easy of approach outside his own circle, with fixed ideas based on the belief that Great Britain could set a limit to her European commitments and still play the part of independent arbitrator in continental politics. This rigidity of opinion in a rapidly changing world made Henderson very critical of the ineffectual efforts which the French were making, in the interests of the balance of power, to contain Germany after the war of 1914–18, and led him to accept in large measure the German claims upon which Hitler based his treaty-breaking and subsequent acts of aggression.

At the same time Henderson was fatalistic, and when he was appointed to Berlin a strain of mysticism showed itself

in his statement that he felt himself to be the preordained instrument for helping to end the growing antagonism between Nazi Germany and Great Britain. Unlike any of his predecessors, he attended the Nuremberg party rallies in 1937 and 1938 as a friendly gesture to the régime. He had no preconceived dislike of authoritarian government as such, and was therefore ready to believe that Great Britain and Germany could be reconciled even if this meant tacit acquiescence by Britain in the adoption by Germany of the Nazi philosophy of life and system of government, as well as in the aggrandizement of Germany in Central Europe. Presumably he did not believe that Hitler was planning to dominate the whole of Europe. He did not therefore find himself out of sympathy with the policy of the British Government at that time, and his reports were such as to encourage ministers to persevere in their efforts to find reasons for acquiescing in Hitler's ever-increasing demands rather than to persuade them to organize means for resisting them. Nor did the invasion and annexation of Austria in March 1938 and the Czechoslovak crisis which almost immediately followed lead him to revise his views or change his outlook, and he strongly supported the Munich settlement. Only by the occupation of Czechoslovakia on 15 March 1939 was he finally and completely disillusioned.

In order to mark their disapproval of Hitler's outrage, the British Government recalled Henderson to London, but he was sent back to his post in April after only five weeks' absence. During the summer of 1939 he was actively engaged in what he then realized was the hopeless task of trying to dissuade Hitler from precipitating a war with Great Britain and France by an attack on Poland. On the outbreak of war on 3 September he returned to England; his offer to serve in any junior post was declined, and increasing ill health prevented him from undertaking any further public employment.

Henderson wrote an account of his ambassadorship at Berlin under the title of *Failure of a Mission* (1940) in which he defended his own action and the policy of the British Government. If he is a controversial figure it is not because when ambassador at Berlin he was the author of any particular policy or followed any line of his own. It is merely because he sincerely believed in and laboured on behalf of that policy of 'appeasement' which was that of the British Government at the time, but which both then and subsequently gave rise to bitter personal recriminations and heated political argument.

After a lingering illness, borne with great fortitude, Henderson died in London 30 December 1942. During his last days he occupied himself in recording his reminiscences in a short volume entitled *Water under the Bridges* (1945). He was appointed C.M.G. in 1923, promoted K.C.M.G. in 1932 and G.C.M.G. in 1939, and sworn of the Privy Council in 1937. A portrait by A. R. Thomson is in the possession of the family.

[Sir Nevile Henderson, *Failure of a Mission*, 1940, and *Water under the Bridges*, 1945; *The Times*, 31 December 1942; private information; personal knowledge.]

O. G. SARGENT.

HENSON, HERBERT HENSLEY (1863–1947), bishop successively of Hereford and Durham, was born in London 8 November 1863, the fifth son of Thomas Henson, a man of business, by his wife, Martha Fear. Broadstairs was his home as a boy and there he attended a private school of which he was later a boarder and head boy. His mother had died before he was seven years old: his father shortly married again, and it was chiefly to his German stepmother that Henson owed his early love of reading. She too urged that he should go to Oxford, after a difference of opinion with his headmaster had led him to leave school abruptly and to teach for a time in the grammar school at Brigg. It had been 'an unhappy and ill-ordered boyhood'; family means were narrow; his father's interests were absorbed by a bigoted type of nonconformity; but he allowed his son to enter the university as a non-collegiate student in 1881. He won a first class in modern history in 1884 and, prompted by W. H. Hutton [q.v.], a fellowship at All Souls in the same year. This election was a turning-point in his life: it brought him a wider outlook, financial independence, many warm friends, and boundless scope for a most lively critical incisive mind and tongue.

After many 'doubts and questionings' Henson was ordained deacon in 1887, becoming head of Oxford House, Bethnal Green, in the same year. In 1888 he was ordained priest and appointed by his college to the living of Barking, where he spent seven vigorous and not uncontroversial years. Already he was moving away from his earlier Anglo-Catholic opinions, and when he accepted in 1895 Lord Salisbury's offer of the chaplaincy of Ilford Hospital he was ready to carry out the bishop of St. Albans' wish that 'Roman' tendencies there should be checked. His health, severely strained by the work of his Barking parish, grew stronger: there was more leisure and opportunity for reading and for the development of his great gifts as a preacher; writing, speaking, and a strenuous share in ecclesiastical conflicts made him widely known. In 1900 his nomination to a canonry of Westminster Abbey carrying with it the rectorship of St. Margaret's gave him a position and an opportunity uniquely suited to his peculiar gifts. His eloquence and independence of mind attracted and held great congregations: his increasingly liberal churchmanship commended him to the prevailing temper of a large and influential body of thought: his courage, his wit, and the personal friendliness which mellowed the sharpness of his speech won deep affection even from those who disliked his opinions. He was ever a 'stormy petrel', a doughty fighter in many fields of strife. As a proctor in Convocation (1903–12), generally in the minority, but personally popular, he was a lively critic of the episcopate, a strong upholder of the Establishment, and a determined advocate of closer relations with the Free Churches. When his old friend but ecclesiastical adversary Bishop Gore [q.v.] forbade him to preach in the institute of Carr's Lane Congregational church in Birmingham in 1909 Henson defied the bishop's authority; and he lost no opportunity of denouncing Anglo-Catholicism. His just condemnation in 1912 of the conduct of the rubber industry in the Putumayo district of Peru on which Roger Casement [q.v.] had reported won general support.

In this year he was appointed to the deanery of Durham. Departure from London imposed no check on his activity in public affairs: he was quickly involved in the Kikuyu controversy, and strongly opposed the Life and Liberty Movement as a threat to the Establishment. But his work as dean was never allowed to suffer: he was deeply concerned in the work of the university of Durham: his preaching in the cathedral and in the churches of the diocese, his devotion to the interests of the city, and his generosity of spirit won him a great position in the north. He had become one of the best known of English churchmen. In 1917 he was nominated to the see of Hereford. Strong opposition was aroused: his orthodoxy was suspect to many Anglo-Catholics, for he had been a protagonist in the cause of liberty of interpretation. He himself afterwards admitted that he had said much 'crudely and hastily', and his critics were not slow to exaggerate the significance of such utterances. But he also strongly maintained that he had published nothing which he wished to recall. He was able to convince Archbishop Davidson [q.v.] that he had been misunderstood, and he was duly consecrated on 2 February 1918. The agitation had distressed and angered him. But neither he nor his diocese allowed it to mar the course of his episcopate. His justice and sympathy met affectionate response: although the Herefordshire climate did not suit him he enjoyed his work in the country parishes, and when in 1920 he was translated to the very different see of Durham his departure was as widely regretted in Hereford as his return to the north was welcomed there.

On his resignation of the bishopric of Durham in 1939 all his clergy expressed their 'affectionate gratitude for a great and generous episcopate'. It was a just tribute, and all the more significant because he bated none of his controversial ardour, and on at least one great issue, when he became an ardent advocate of disestablishment after the rejection of the revised Prayer Book by Parliament, found himself unable to convert his diocese from a cause which he had long championed and now regarded as no longer defensible. His courageous sincerity, his kindness in personal relations, his eloquence and distinction prevailed over differences of opinion. The economic depression caused wide and long-lasting unemployment in the county: Henson's outspoken opposition to Socialist remedies often aroused irritation and even hostility among the miners, but he was active in efforts to relieve distress, his sympathy was deeply stirred, and even those who violently disagreed with him admired a man who so plainly had the courage of his convictions. His strenuous and successful efforts for the preservation of Durham Castle were not the least of his achievements. He found time to take a full share in the debates of Convocation, of the Church Assembly, and—as far as distance from London allowed—the House of Lords. Without question he was among the best speakers

of his time, delighting even if he did not convince. In 1935–6 he delivered the Gifford lectures on 'Christian Morality'. But perhaps the best of his writing, always admirable in force and clarity, is to be found in his charges *Ad Clerum* (1937) and in *Bishoprick Papers* (1946).

Hintlesham near Ipswich was his home from 1939 until his death. In 1940 he was again appointed to a canonry of Westminster and again preached with vigour. The state of his eyes compelled him to resign in 1941. During his last years he wrote his autobiography, *Retrospect of an Unimportant Life*, a work of peculiar interest and vivacity containing a mass of extracts from the journal he had begun to keep in 1885 and had steadily continued throughout his life: many volumes of this journal survive, written in a beautifully clear uncial hand in notebooks of many sizes and shapes. Henson published numerous collections of his sermons and addresses. All were marked by a rounded and lucid dignity. He was a great master of the art of conversation, witty and epigrammatic: his letters were delightful in both form and content, and, barbed though they often are, they do him fuller justice than his *Retrospect*, the first two volumes of which are overweighted with the record of controversy: the last is more mellow in temper.

He died at Hintlesham 27 September 1947, survived by his wife, Isabella Caroline (died 1949), only daughter of James Wallis Dennistoun of Dennistoun, nephew of James Dennistoun [q.v.]. They were married in 1902. She brought him many Scottish friends and interests. There were no children. There is a portrait of Henson at Auckland Castle by Harold Speed.

[H. H. Henson, *Retrospect of an Unimportant Life*, 3 vols., *Letters*, edited by E. F. Braley, 2 vols., 1950–54, and *Bishoprick Papers*, 1946; G. K. A. Bell, *Life of Archbishop Davidson*, 2 vols., 1935; *The Times*, 29 September 1947; personal knowledge.]

ALWYN WINTON: (A. T. P. WILLIAMS.)

HERTZ, JOSEPH HERMAN (1872–1946), chief rabbi of the United Hebrew Congregations of the British Empire, was born 25 September 1872 at Rebrin, Slovakia, the son of a Hebrew teacher, Simon Hertz, and his wife, Esther Fanny Moskowitz. In 1884 the family migrated to America. Here he received his education at New York City College (B.A., 1891) and Columbia University (Ph.D., 1894). Meanwhile he had entered the newly founded Jewish Theological Seminary of America in New York, and was its earliest graduate as rabbi (1894). In that year he received his first appointment at Syracuse, New York, and in 1898 was appointed rabbi of the principal synagogue of Johannesburg, South Africa. As a result of his 'uitlander' sympathies and his vigorous condemnation of religious discrimination, he was expelled from the Transvaal Republic shortly after the outbreak of the South African war, but in 1901 he returned to his pulpit. He served as a member of the high commissioner's consultative committee, and in 1906-8 was professor of philosophy in the Transvaal University College.

In 1911 he went back to America as rabbi of the Orach Chayim congregation in New York. In 1913, partly through the strong recommendation of Lord Milner [q.v.] whom he had known in South Africa, Hertz was elected chief rabbi of the United Hebrew Congregations of the British Empire in succession to Hermann Adler [q.v.] who had died in 1911. He threw himself into his duties with an explosive energy which almost scandalized the conservative elements of his flock. In contrast to his gentle, highly anglicized predecessor he adopted the standpoint and interests of the Eastern European immigrants who in the past generation had become a majority in the Anglo-Jewish community; denounced the Russian persecution of the Jews and the 'yellow ticket' system at a Mansion House meeting in the presence of the Russian ambassador; adopted a militant attitude towards the newly founded Liberal Jewish movement, and carried on a perpetual polemic with its advocates in his sermons and publications. His very strong Zionist sympathies proved decisive when he was consulted by the Government in 1917 before the publication of the 'Balfour declaration', the policy of which was opposed by some of the most distinguished English Jews. In 1920-21 he carried out the first pastoral tour of the Jewish communities of the Empire. In his last years his attention was absorbed by the problems created by the triumph of anti-semitism in Germany and the subsequent extermination of continental Jewry at Nazi hands. His unflagging attempts to rouse public opinion and to demonstrate the urgent necessity of providing a haven for the refugees—in his view, inevitably in Palestine—earned him a position in the Jewish world at large equalled perhaps by no other rabbi of the age.

His prodigiously wide reading and retentive memory were turned to advantage in his writings—particularly in his remarkable anthology, *A Book of Jewish Thoughts*, which, originally issued in 1917 for distribution to Jewish members of the forces, in the end appeared (partly indeed owing to his own sedulous efforts) in several languages, and more than twenty editions. His other major works include commentaries, homiletic rather than expositional, on the Pentateuch (1929-36) and the Jewish liturgy (1941-5), and a volume of sermons embodying his criticism of Liberal Judaism, *Affirmations of Judaism* (1927). As a writer his genius was eclectic rather than original, and perhaps restricted by his combative conservatism.

Hertz was appointed C.H. in 1943; was a commander of the Order of Leopold II; and received the honorary degree of LL.D. from London University in 1938. He married in 1904 Rose Freed (died 1930) of New York, and had three sons and three daughters. He died in London 14 January 1946.

Bursting with energy; stocky; with a square-cut black beard, ultimately grizzled, and a somewhat rasping voice; full of himself, but at the same time overflowing with native kindliness; somewhat bellicose—it was once said of him that he never failed to seek a peaceful solution of a problem when all other possibilities had failed; constantly swayed by an overwhelming compassion for his suffering co-religionists, which would impel him to display on occasion a lion-like courage; Hertz was certainly the most remarkable character who has filled the English chief rabbinate since its inception. There is a portrait in oils by Joseph Oppenheimer in the council-room of Jews' College, London.

[Biographical contributions in *Essays in honour of J. H. Hertz on the occasion of his seventieth birthday, 25 September 1942*; *Joseph Herman Hertz: In Memoriam*, 1947 (bibliography); P. Paneth, *Guardian of the Law*, 1943; *The Times*, 15 January 1946; *Jewish Chronicle*, 18 January 1946; personal knowledge.]                CECIL ROTH.

HERTZOG, JAMES BARRY MUNNIK (1866-1942), prime minister of South Africa, was born at his father's farm, Zoetendal, Groenberg, near Wellington, Cape Colony, 3 April 1866, the fifth son and eighth of the twelve children of Johannes Albertus Munnik Hertzog by his wife, Susanna Maria, daughter of Pieter Hamman, a farmer, of Stellenbosch, Cape Colony. The family moved north to the diamond fields at Kimberley in 1872 and Jagersfontein, Orange Free State, in 1879. Having taken degrees at Victoria College, Stellenbosch (1888), and Amsterdam University (1892), Hertzog practised as an attorney and official reporter in the High Court of the South African Republic (1892–5). In 1894 he married Wilhelmina Jacoba, daughter of Charles Marais Neethling, a retired farmer, of Stellenbosch, by whom he had three sons. He was a judge of the High Court of the Orange Free State from 1895 to 1899, fought throughout the South African war, became chief commandant of the Free State Southern Commandos and head of the artillery, making a notable raid into the Cape Colony (December 1900–February 1901). At the last, he was a signatory of the peace of Vereeniging in May 1902.

Rather than retire to a proffered Cape peninsular farm or the chair of South African law at Leyden, Holland, Hertzog took to politics. He challenged Milner's policy of anglicization, encouraging private schools which put Dutch on an equal footing with English, and taking the lead in organizing the Orangia Unie Party. In 1907 he became attorney-general and minister of education in the Orange River Colony, and began his long rivalry with J. C. Smuts [q.v.], whose Transvaal Education Act made far less provision for Dutch than the Act which he himself finally passed in 1910, and enforced by dismissing several British education officers. In the National Convention (October 1908–May 1909) that made the Union, Hertzog helped powerfully to ensure the equality of Dutch and English as the official languages of South Africa.

Hertzog knew that Louis Botha [q.v.] had been most reluctant to include him in the first Union Cabinet (1910) as minister of justice (and in 1912 also as minister of native affairs). Without being anti-British, but holding that Botha was subordinating South African to imperial interests, he opposed to Botha's vague talk of 'conciliation' his own 'two-stream' policy, which insisted that the Dutch- and English-speaking white peoples could not yet be treated as one people, but also that such of them as put 'South Africa first', and no mere 'foreign fortune-seekers', were alone entitled to rule the Union. At

last, after having failed to induce Hertzog to resign, Botha, himself resigned and re-constituted his ministry without him (December 1912).

Hertzog then formed the National Party in 1913. On the outbreak of the war of 1914–18, he opposed the invasion of neighbouring German South-West Africa, but neither condemned publicly nor encouraged the ensuing rebellion. In spite of marked Nationalist electoral gains and his own long-term desire, he urged, against the widespread demand for an immediate republic, that the recovery of freedom from outside control was more important at the moment than forms of government. He did, however, half-heartedly lead a deputation to the Paris peace conference to ask that the Union, or at the least the Free State, should be a republic. The Nationalists emerged from the next general election (1920) as the largest party in the House of Assembly but failed to reunite with Smuts's predominantly Afrikaans-speaking South African Party, mainly because Tielman Johannes de Villiers Roos and many other of their own Transvaal members claimed the right of secession from the Empire. Smuts's followers fused with the 'British' Unionists and won the next elections (1921). Their majority dwindled steadily. Colonel Frederic Hugh Page Creswell's Labour Party came to terms with the Nationalists in common hostility to the so-called subservience of Smuts to the gold-mining magnates and the Empire, and these two 'pact parties' presently gained for Hertzog a majority big enough to make him prime minister and minister for native affairs (1924).

Favoured by better times, the pact ministry protected home industries and white labour, founded a State iron and steel corporation, sought non-British markets, gave the Union its own flag, citizenship, and ministers plenipotentiary, and substituted Afrikaans for Dutch as one of the official languages. It failed, indeed, to carry most of Hertzog's measures for segregating non-Europeans; on the other hand, it welcomed the Prince of Wales to southern Africa (1925), while the Nationalist Party formally acknowledged the definition of Dominion status in the Balfour statement, which its leader had helped to word at the Imperial Conference, as the 'attainment of sovereign independence' (1926).

Harassed by a split in the Labour Party (1928) and the republican intrigues of his lieutenants, Tielman Roos in the Transvaal and Dr. Daniel François Malan in the Cape, Hertzog could only win the next general election by having recourse to the 'Black Manifesto', which falsely accused Smuts of proposing to swamp white civilization in a great 'Kaffir' State extending far into Central Africa and endowed with equal rights for all (1929). Having relegated Roos to the appeal bench, Hertzog remained in office as premier and minister for external affairs. At the Imperial Conference of 1930, he helped to draft the Statute of Westminster which provided for the clearing away of all legal checks on Dominion sovereignty, and saw the imperial office of high commissioner separated from that of governor-general (April 1931). He had just instituted white adult suffrage when the return of Roos to politics (1932) drove the Union off the gold standard and himself into a coalition with Smuts. The coalition won the elections (1933), and then decreed in the Status Act that no British legislation should be applied to the Union save by an act of its own Parliament (1934). It transformed itself into a 'United Party' at the price of seeing Dr. Malan's isolationist and secessionist 'purified' Nationalists become His Majesty's Opposition.

At this juncture, Roos died. Despite strong resistance from people of all races, Hertzog at last carried most of his segregation programme, above all the virtual disfranchisement of the Cape Bantu, who, alone of the vast native majority of the Union's population, had hitherto possessed the vote (1936). Not unnaturally, the imperial authorities declined to hand over to the Union the governance of Basutoland, Bechuanaland, and Swaziland, although they made no objection to the appointment of a South African citizen, Sir Patrick Duncan [q.v.], as governor-general (April 1937). Meanwhile, Hertzog was showing himself ready to enforce sanctions against Mussolini in Abyssinia, but to appease Hitler by restoring colonial territory to Germany; then, as the League of Nations wilted and he realized that masses of English-speaking South Africans had indeed become good 'Afrikaners', he spoke up for the once suspect Empire and navy as safeguards of South Africa's freedom.

Thereafter, Hertzog lost hold steadily. Soon after the United Party's electoral triumph (1938), two ministers resigned in protest against his appointment to the Senate of a man, notoriously incapable of speaking for the non-Europeans, whom he was determined to have in his Cabinet. Worse still, 'purified nationalism', worked up to fever-heat during the centenary celebrations of the Great Trek (1938), began to breed Nazi-minded associations intent on reviving a 'Kruger' republic in which those of their own faith should monopolize power. Hertzog would have none of it; but that did not save him. Defeated in the Cabinet and in both Houses on his proposal to maintain neutrality during the war, he made way for Smuts as premier (5 September 1939). A year later, he lost his hold on the Nationalist rank and file, who were counting on a German victory, rather than deny to English-speaking folk that equality which was 'the very foundation of Union'. He resigned the Smithfield seat which he had held since 1910, and retired to Waterval, his farm, near Witbank, Transvaal, where he convinced himself that Germany must win and that National Socialism accorded with the Afrikaner way of life. Seven months after the death of his wife, he died at Waterkloof, Pretoria, 21 November 1942, and was buried at Waterval by her side, deserted by all the people for whom he had done so much, save only those few who had rallied to carry on his work.

A bust of Hertzog by M. Kottler and a portrait by Edward Roworth are in the Houses of Parliament, Cape Town. Another portrait by Roworth is in the possession of the family.

[L. E. Neame, General Hertzog, 1930.]

ERIC A. WALKER.

[Oswald Pirow, James Barry Munnik Hertzog, 1958.]

HEWART, GORDON, first VISCOUNT HEWART (1870–1943), lord chief justice of England, was born at Bury, Lancashire, 7 January 1870, the eldest son of Giles Hewart, draper, by his wife, Annie Elizabeth Jones. He was educated at Bury and Manchester grammar schools, and University College, Oxford, where he won an open classical scholarship. He obtained a second class in classical moderations (1889) and again in literae humaniores (1891).

Hewart early fixed on the law as his career, but in order to supplement a too-meagre income he joined the parliamentary reporting staff of the Manchester Guardian and subsequently became principal leader-writer on the Morning Leader. Pressure of journalistic work delayed his call to the bar by the Inner Temple until

1902. Then, however, he joined the Northern circuit, where his name was known, and his rise was rapid. In 1912 he took silk, and in 1913 was elected Liberal member of Parliament for Leicester (sitting for the East division of Leicester from 1918 to 1922). He became solicitor-general and was knighted in 1916, was sworn of the Privy Council in 1918, became attorney-general in 1919, with a seat in the Cabinet from 1921, and in 1922 succeeded Lord Trevethin [q.v.] as lord chief justice. He was raised to the peerage as Baron Hewart, of Bury, in the county of Lancaster, and advanced to a viscountcy on laying down his office in 1940.

Hewart was a really brilliant advocate. The case which perhaps springs most readily to the mind in connexion with his name is *E. Hulton & Co.* v. *Jones*, [1910] A.C. 20, where the House of Lords laid down that it is no defence to an action for libel that the defendant did not intend to defame the plaintiff; the test of liability is the probable effect of the publication on the minds of reasonable people. Hewart's conduct of criminal prosecutions was a model of what such conduct should be; the exacting sense of justice and of professional rectitude, which rendered it utterly impossible for him unduly to press a case against a prisoner, was supported by a knowledge of the rules of evidence which seemed to be an integral part of his very system. As a law officer of the Crown he proved to be among the most effective holders of his office, and an excellent speaker in the House of Commons.

As a judge, Hewart was perhaps not quite so successful as he had been as an advocate; it was said of him that he did not always remember that he was no longer an advocate. But it is certain that he never consciously took sides, for no man had more reverence for the high traditions of his great office, or was more tenacious of its dignity. Of the nature of law he had the loftiest views. In his mind, law was no mere mundane collection of statutes and precedents, but a mighty engine for the vindication of the fundamental rights of man. He could be terrible in anger, and stern in punishment towards those convicted of mean and atrocious crimes; blackmailers in particular, for whose foulness he often expressed extreme abhorrence, would look in vain to him for mercy. But his gentleness on the bench was unfailing towards innocent persons and those whom he had reason to believe the victims of persecution by police or other officials who had taken advantage of ignorance or inexperience to transgress their proper functions. He always showed the utmost courtesy to learned counsel, especially to young counsel. He exhibited a fund of dry judicial humour which never palled on his hearers and could not offend them. His description of a familiar variety of common law actions as 'collisions between two stationary motor-cars' has become classic. *Jutson* v. *Barrow*, [1936] 1 K.B. 236, was a case arising out of an information preferred against the respondent for advertising himself as a 'manipulative surgeon', when unregistered under the Medical Act, 1858. The respondent sought to show that the adjective qualified the noun in such a way as to make it clear that he was not a surgeon within the meaning of the Act. This argument was disposed of by Hewart with the comment: 'If the respondent is . . . sincere, there are many ways open to him of telling the public that he is not a surgeon other than the way of telling the public that he is a surgeon.'

Hewart had great faith in the jury system and would even go so far as to express the opinion that a jury never goes wrong, at any rate in criminal cases, but he was forced to abandon this opinion in the famous Wallace case (1931, 23 Cr. App. R. 32), where he delivered the judgement of the Court of Criminal Appeal quashing the prisoner's conviction for murder on the express ground that the verdict was against the weight of evidence. In *R.* v. *Armstrong*, [1922] 2 K.B. 555, he uttered a grave animadversion on a jury-man who had communicated to the press certain incidents in their deliberation tending to make public the method whereby he and his fellows had reached their verdict.

A staunch Liberal, he looked askance at the growth of bureaucracy and the habit of delegated legislation. His book, *The New Despotism*, which appeared in 1929 is far more than a mere essay; it is a learned and well-reasoned restatement of the fundamental postulates of the British constitution.

Throughout his life he loved the classics and all good literature. He was president of the Classical Association in 1926 and of the English Association in 1929. He loved the theatre and Sir Henry Irving was a figure whom he never ceased to regard with veneration. Most of all he enjoyed the company of his friends, for he had the priceless gift of winning and keeping the affection of many. He died at Totteridge, Hertfordshire, 5 May 1943.

Honorary degrees were conferred upon Hewart by the universities of Manchester (1922), Oxford (1926), Toronto, Sheffield (1927), Birmingham (1928), and the Witwatersrand (1936). He was elected an honorary fellow of his college in 1922. He became a bencher of the Inner Temple in 1917 and was treasurer in 1938.

Hewart was twice married: first, in 1892 to Sara Wood (died 1933), daughter of Joseph Hacking Riley, engineer and machinist, of Bury; and secondly, in 1934, to Jean, daughter of James Reid Stewart, of Wanganui, New Zealand. By his first wife he had two sons and one daughter. The elder son was killed in the war of 1914–18; the second, Hugh Vaughan (born 1896), succeeded him as second viscount. There is a portrait of Hewart by (Sir) Oswald Birley at the Inner Temple and another by John St. Helier Lander at University College, Oxford.

[*The Times*, 6 May 1943; *Law Times*, 15 May 1943.]                    H. G. HANBURY.

HEWETT, SIR JOHN PRESCOTT (1854–1941), Indian civil servant, was born at Barham, Kent, 25 August 1854, the eldest son of the Rev. John Hewett, vicar of Babbacombe, Torquay, by his wife, Anna Louisa Lyster, daughter of Captain William Hammon of the Honourable East India Company's navy. Educated at Winchester, where he was a scholar and in the cricket eleven, and at Balliol College, Oxford, he passed the Indian Civil Service examination in 1875, and two years later went out to the North-Western Provinces and Oudh (later the United Provinces of Agra and Oudh). In 1886 he was appointed under-secretary to the home department of the Government of India and in 1890 he became deputy secretary. He acted as private secretary to the viceroy in 1888 and 1892. In 1893 after a period as magistrate and collector in the North-Western Provinces, he was appointed secretary of the Royal Commission on opium. Their report on that very controversial question largely pacified the critics of the Government of India, and was much relied on at various international conferences on opium and narcotic drugs.

In 1895 Hewett returned to the home department as secretary, and, with an interval as member of the plague commission in 1898–9, he held that post until Lord Curzon [q.v.] sent him to the Central Provinces as chief commissioner in 1902. He was there for eighteen months and had to deal with a famine in the eastern districts of those provinces, and with the difficulties connected with the annexation of Berar under the treaty with the Nizam, 1903. His famine administration won the special commendation of the Government of India. When in 1904 Curzon persuaded the secretary of state to approve the formation of a department of commerce and industry, Hewett was selected as the first holder of the portfolio in the viceroy's executive council. He there won the esteem of the business community by the energy and drive which he put into industrial and commercial questions. His most important contribution to Indian industrial advance was the encouragement which he gave to (Sir) Thomas Holland [q.v.], director of the Geological Survey, to press forward the economic activities of that department, and his support of the great project which, initiated earlier by Jamsetji Tata [q.v.], led in 1911 to the establishment of the key steel industry at Jamshedpur in Orissa by his son (Sir D. J. Tata, q.v.) and successors.

In January 1907 Hewett, then appointed K.C.S.I., succeeded Sir James La Touche as lieutenant-governor of the United Provinces. He at once started a preliminary survey of the industrial position and possibilities of the provinces. This was followed by the Naini Tal industrial conference, perhaps the most comprehensive which had yet been held in India. The conference put forward a balanced scheme for industrial and educational advance, but the main proposals for active governmental participation in industrial development were vetoed by the secretary of state, Lord Morley [q.v.], much to Hewett's disappointment.

The financial resources of the United Provinces were, however, gravely affected by the failure of the monsoon in 1907, causing serious distress in Eastern Oudh and in Bundelkhand in 1907–8. The famine was not on the scale of that which had been dealt with by Sir Antony (later Lord) MacDonnell [q.v.] ten years earlier, and relief was more easily organized on the experience then gained. Vigorous and successful action was taken, and the lessons learned were applied in the revision of the famine code and in the promotion of projects for the construction of protective canals in the more precarious areas.

In general administration Hewett's

energy left its mark on many branches both of the central and of local government. He took special interest in the establishment of an agricultural college at Cawnpore, and in the development of local industries. An example of his organizing power was the great exhibition at Allahabad at the close of 1910, designed (like Wembley in later years) to advance agriculture, trade, and industry. The reclaiming of the criminal tribes was an old and baffling problem. Hewett gave the task to the Salvation Army, notwithstanding strong opposition. The experiment was a great success.

When King George V and Queen Mary decided to visit India in 1911 for a coronation durbar Hewett was selected to preside over the durbar committee. His success in the immense task of organizing this last great pageant of the old British India was recognized by his promotion to G.C.S.I. in the durbar honours.

After a nine months' extension of his period of office in the United Provinces, Hewett returned to England at the close of 1912 and took up work in the City. He joined the boards of a number of companies, being chairman of some of them. He was also active in public work, and in the war of 1914–18 he was chairman of the Indian Soldiers' Fund committee, and also presided over Lady Lansdowne's Officers' Families Fund. For these services he was appointed K.B.E. in 1917. At the close of the war, he went to Mesopotamia to investigate the financial and economic problems connected with the occupation and the transfer of authority from military to civil control. In hospital work he played an important part as knight of justice and chancellor, and later as bailiff of Egle, in the Order of St. John of Jerusalem.

He was the first chairman of the governing body of the School of Oriental Studies. He was also one of the British members of the international commission set up by the League of Nations in 1921 to enable Nansen to give aid to famine-stricken areas in Russia.

In the general election of 1922 Hewett was the successful Conservative candidate for Luton in a three-cornered contest, but he made no impression in the House of Commons, and lost the seat a year later.

In the sphere of Indian constitutional advance he was one of the opponents of the Montagu–Chelmsford scheme who formed the Indo-British Association under the chairmanship of Lord Sydenham of Combe [q.v.]. When, however, the Government of India Act of 1919 had been passed, he carefully avoided doing or saying anything which might stand in the way of the great experiment. He paid repeated visits to India, and, in a letter to *The Times*, 8 March 1930, wrote that he had been astounded at the changes which had taken place in the period between his visits, and appealed for trust in Lord Irwin (subsequently the Earl of Halifax). Hence, while critical of some features of the white paper on which the Act of 1935 was based, he refused to join the India Defence League, but favoured federation as a prerequisite to the grant of responsibility at the centre.

Essentially an administrator and man of business, with great driving force, Hewett had an extraordinary power of disentangling the vital points of any problem from a mass of details, and of reaching rapid and clear decisions in the light of existing conditions and of the requirements of the moment. He was less interested in the historical aspects of any question. To the assistants most closely associated with him in his official work, whom he always called his 'colleagues', he was considerate and appreciative, even if exacting. In general official relations his judgements often seemed severe, if just, and were controlled by a usually equable temper. Socially he extended a wide and generous hospitality. His manner of life, including the sometimes disconcerting practice of starting work at four o'clock in the morning, enabled him to find time for sport and social pleasure. His main source of enjoyment was the shooting of big game, and his reminiscences, mainly of shoots on the grand scale, are gathered up in *Jungle Trails in Northern India* (1938).

In 1879 Hewett married Ethel Charlotte (died 1945), daughter of Henry Binny Webster, of the Bengal Civil Service; they had one son and two daughters. Hewett died 27 September 1941 at his home at Chipping Warden, Banbury.

[*The Times*, 30 September 1941; Sir John Hewett, *Jungle Trails in Northern India*, 1938; private information; personal knowledge.]                          A. W. PIM.

HICHENS, ROBERT SMYTHE (1864–1950), novelist, was born 14 November 1864 at Speldhurst, Kent, the eldest son of the Rev. Frederick Harrison Hichens, then a curate, and his wife, Abigail Elizabeth Smythe. Educated at a private school and at Clifton College, his heart was set upon becoming a musician, and he studied for several years in Clifton before proceeding to the Royal College of Music. A parallel talent for writing, however, presently proved the stronger. After achieving a number of lyrics—one of which was sung by Patti—he began to write stories and at twenty-four determined to make a career as an author. He took a year's course at a school of journalism, and contributed industriously to many newspapers. His juvenile novel, *The Coastguard's Secret*, written when he was seventeen, had been published in 1886 and well reviewed; but he was alarmed at the proposal to reprint this crude effort after he scored his first great success in 1894. This was *The Green Carnation*, published anonymously after a holiday, enforced by illness, in Egypt, a place which was always to prove fortunate and inspiring for him. London was delighted with the novel, a sparkling sophisticated satire on Oscar Wilde [q.v.] and his followers.

Hichens became music critic on the *World* in succession to G. B. Shaw [q.v.], but eventually gave up regular journalism in order to travel abroad and write his books which had a rapidly increasing public. Edwardian society was alternately shocked, thrilled, intrigued, and dissolved in laughter. The jests of one generation seldom amuse the next; but *The Londoners* (1898) is still a very funny piece of pure fooling. Hichens kept his humour in its place, however, and did not allow it to interfere with the dramatic tension of his romances, or the horror of his essays in the macabre. Of these latter, the short story 'How Love Came to Professor Guildea' (in *Tongues of Conscience*, 1900) is acknowledged a small classic. His greatest success and best-known novel was *The Garden of Allah* (1904) which he later dramatized. So popular was this romance of passion and conflict in the desert that he wrote from time to time other stories with a similar setting. Egypt and North Africa were familiar ground to him; he spent much of his time there, riding in the desert; and otherwise preferred the Riviera or Switzerland to any permanent residence in England. He belonged to a generation of writers eminent for good workmanlike story-telling; and to the very end his hand never faltered, although naturally there must be some loss of power and freshness in the course of half a century. He also wrote several plays, including *Becky Sharp* written for (Dame) Marie Tempest [q.v.]

in collaboration with Cosmo Gordon-Lennox.

In 1947 Hichens published his memoirs, *Yesterday*, which illustrate his confession: 'The Edwardian age through which I lived was certainly very attractive to me.' He never married. He died in hospital at Zürich 20 July 1950.

[R. S. Hichens, *Yesterday*, 1947; *The Times*, 22 July 1950.]          M. BELLASIS.

HICKS, SIR (EDWARD) SEYMOUR (GEORGE) (1871–1949), actor-manager and author, was born at St. Helier Jersey, 30 January 1871, the son of Lieutenant (later Major) Edward Percy Hicks of the 42nd Highlanders, and his wife, Grace Seymour. Hicks had no ancestral call to the theatre, although his younger brother, Stanley Brett, followed his example. Educated at Prior Park College, near Bath, and at Victoria College, Jersey, he was only sixteen when he 'walked on' in *In the Ranks* at the Grand Theatre, Islington. It was the two years he then spent with W. H. and (Dame) Madge Kendal [qq.v.], in both England and America, taking parts in early plays by (Sir) Arthur Pinero [q.v.] like *The Money Spinner* and *The Squire* and other classics of the period—all before he was twenty-one—that gave him an invaluable grounding. On his return, thanks to a recommendation from (Dame) Irene Vanbrugh [q.v.] and adopting a Scottish accent, he went to (Sir) James Barrie [q.v.], who immediately gave him the part of Andrew McPhail, the young Scottish medical student, in *Walker, London*, at Toole's Theatre, 1892, in which he made a great hit, the play running for over a year. Then in 1893, whilst at the Court Theatre, he engaged in and wrote with Charles H. E. Brookfield and Edward Jones what was really the first London revue, *Under the Clock*. It contained burlesques of current plays and was called a 'musical extravaganza'. Another visit to the United States, in *Cinderella*, was followed by his first appearance under George Edwardes's banner at the Gaiety Theatre as Jonathan Wild in *Little Jack Sheppard* in 1894, and afterwards, until 1897, in *The Shop Girl* and *The Circus Girl*. In 1899 he was the Duc de Richelieu—quite a new type of part for him—in *A Court Scandal* at the Court, paid another visit to America, and on his return registered another success as the Mad Hatter in *Alice in Wonderland* at the Vaudeville (1900). At the same theatre in 1901 he gave a performance of the utmost tenderness and charm in Basil Hood's *Sweet and Twenty*. Here also he appeared as Scrooge in John Baldwin Buckstone's play of that name and as Dicky in his own *Bluebell in Fairyland* with Walter Slaughter's music. His Valentine Brown in Barrie's *Quality Street* came at the Vaudeville in the next year, succeeded by an astonishing portrait of Edmund Kean in Gladys Buchanan Unger's one-act play of that title, and Moonshine and Happy Joe in his own *The Cherry Girl* to Ivan Caryll's music in December 1903. In September 1904 came his great Vaudeville success, *The Catch of the Season*, written by himself with Cosmo Hamilton, which ran until 1906.

Hicks now went in for the building of new west-end theatres. He built the Aldwych which he opened in December 1905 with *Bluebell in Fairyland*, playing there the following year in his own and Cosmo Hamilton's *The Beauty of Bath*. With this he also opened the Hicks—later the Globe—in Shaftesbury Avenue, built for Charles Frohman. His next adventures, alike as actor and author, were *The Gay Gordons* at the Aldwych in 1907 with music by Guy Jones, followed by *The Dashing Little Duke* with music by Frank E. Tours at the Hicks in 1909, in which he appeared as his old friend, the Duc de Richelieu, a part also played by his wife. Finding himself in financial difficulties he went next to the Coliseum at the invitation of (Sir) Oswald Stoll [q.v.]. In 1914 he organized a concert party and gave a series of performances to the British forces at the front in France. In 1922 he had a memorable season at the Garrick Theatre, which he opened with himself as *The Man in Dress Clothes* which he had adapted from the French. He was afterwards seen in *Vintage Wine*, adapted from the Hungarian by himself and Mr. Ashley Dukes, and presented, with himself as Charles Popinot, at Daly's Theatre in 1934. In 1938 he appeared as Captain Hook in *Peter Pan* at the Palladium, and at the Coliseum in 1939 appeared in *You're Telling Me*, an adroit Franco-British sketch, with Sacha Guitry as his companion. Though his ready laugh and blinking eyes made comedy his natural vehicle, his flashes of tragic expression when called for—as in *Edmund Kean*—were unforgettable. Hicks was, needless to say, extremely popular in films.

Hicks was knighted in 1935 and was made a chevalier of the Legion of Honour in 1931, largely for his services to French drama in London. He was elected president of Denville Hall in 1935. He published *Twenty-Four Years of an Actor's Life* in 1910 and many volumes, mostly anecdotal, in his later career, and *Me and My Missus—Fifty Years on the Stage*, in 1939.

Throughout his entire career Hicks owed an incalculable deal to the inspiration of his beautiful, talented, and devoted wife, the charming actress Ellaline Terriss (Mary Ellaline Lewin, daughter of William Terriss, q.v.). They married in 1893. He died at his home at Fleet, Hampshire, 6 April 1949, survived by his widow and one daughter. A son died at birth. Hicks was the most versatile and brilliant comedian of his time, and a delightfully intelligent and imaginative personality. A portrait of him as Lucien in *The Man in Dress Clothes* painted by Maurice Codner has hung on loan from the artist at the Garrick Club, of which Hicks was a leading member.

[His own writings; Ellaline Terriss, *Just a Little Bit of String*, 1955; private information; personal knowledge.]      S. R. LITTLEWOOD.

HICKS, GEORGE DAWES (1862–1941), philosopher, was born at Shrewsbury 14 September 1862, the eldest child of Christopher Hicks, solicitor, by his wife, Victoria, daughter of John Samuel Dawes, of Smethwick Hall, near Birmingham. In 1866 the family moved to Guildford where Hicks was educated at the Royal Grammar School. During his boyhood he was keenly interested in natural science, but he soon formed a desire to enter the Unitarian ministry, and went to the Owens College, Manchester, in 1883. Graduating in philosophy with first class honours in 1888, he continued the study of the subject at Manchester College, Oxford, and then at Leipzig, which he left in 1896 with the degree of Ph.D. From 1897 to 1903 he was minister at Unity Church, Islington.

In the following year (1904) Dawes Hicks was appointed to the chair of moral philosophy at University College, London. Thereafter he lived in Cambridge, travelling to London several times weekly, and he also gave some lectures in Cambridge. He obtained the degree of B.A., Cambridge, by research in 1909, and that of Litt.D., Manchester, in 1904. He retired from his chair in 1928. In 1927 he was elected F.B.A. He was president of the

Aristotelian Society in 1913 and Hibbert lecturer in 1931.

As a philosopher, Dawes Hicks united two very different qualities—immense learning and real independence of mind. Combined with his remarkable command of the German language (his first published work was written in German) these made him a leading authority on Kant, as well as on Berkeley, and he was a complete master of the history of philosophy. The range and breadth of his learning are well exhibited in the surveys of recent philosophical literature which, over a long period, he contributed twice in each year to the *Hibbert Journal*, of which he was sub-editor.

Dawes Hicks's reputation as an original thinker will rest on his theory of knowledge. His starting-point was Kant, and to the end of his life he always looked back to Kant; but after a short period of neo-Hegelianism, he tended steadily towards the realistic theory of his final years. In this development he was much influenced by the arguments of James Ward [q.v.] and of Professor G. E. Moore; and perhaps by the example of his first teacher Robert Adamson [q.v.], who in his later period began to work out a realistic theory.

Dawes Hicks's final views are set out in the collection of essays called *Critical Realism* (1938), a name which he claimed to be the first to use, although it later became the description applied by some American epistemologists to their own theory. His theory rests essentially on a distinction between the act of knowing and the object known; this position is, of course, common to all realists. But while insisting that it is always the object that we know, he distinguishes further between the content of the object and the apprehended content. There are many difficulties in this theory, of all of which he was well aware, and he attempted in his essay 'On the Nature of Images' to meet one of the most serious. Whatever the difficulties, the whole theory is a strikingly original and penetrating piece of work.

Dawes Hicks was twice married: first, in 1902 to Lucy Katherine (died 1908), daughter of William Henry Garrett, of independent means, of Highbury, London; and secondly, in 1923 to Frances Jane Bovill (died 1935), daughter of John Langley Whitty, schoolmaster, and widow of Edward Corrado Aguggia. He had no children. He was on the whole of a retiring disposition, and most of his energies were given to thinking and teaching. In spite of his apparently frail physique he had a passion for mountaineering, although at the age of sixty-nine he complained to a friend that his climbing days were almost over. Domestic unhappiness, ill health, and disappointment arising from his belief that his fellow countrymen had not accorded to him the recognition which was his due, overcast his later years. He died at Cambridge 16 February 1941.

[W. G. de Burgh in *Proceedings* of the British Academy, vol. xxvii, 1941; *Mind*, July 1941; private information; personal knowledge.]　　　ALAN DORWARD.

HIGGINS, EDWARD JOHN (1864-1947), third general of the Salvation Army, was born 26 November 1864 at Highbridge, Somerset, the son of Edward Higgins, saddler and harness maker, and his wife, Martha Deacon. His father became a commissioner in the Salvation Army; in fact, father and son joined the organization within a year of each other. Both were men of vision, devotion, and piety, and well equipped to undertake the duties appropriate to the high office they attained. The younger Higgins was a fluent, forceful, and persuasive speaker. He also had much business acumen, and a gift for organization which secured for him the rapid promotion which may have startled some of his less energetic colleagues.

In 1896 Higgins, who had already done useful work in the training of young officers, was sent to the United States, with the rank of colonel, as chief secretary to Booth-Tucker, and did much to establish the Salvation Army there on a firm footing. This appointment was followed by one in which he was directly concerned with the Army's foreign affairs, and was consequently called upon to handle a multiplicity of problems arising from the peculiar difficulties which beset those of his colleagues who were carrying out the Salvation Army's mission abroad. There its intentions were often doubted, its aims often misunderstood or misinterpreted. But Higgins's tact, his skill in negotiation, and patience in counsel stood the Army in good stead and contributed much to its success in maintaining its evangelizing campaign in many lands. Such work, however, was not all done from a desk in London. He travelled widely with both General Booth and his son William Bramwell Booth [qq.v.]. In 1911 he became British commissioner, and as such was responsible for the Army's evangelical work at home. For his services during the war of 1914–18 he was appointed C.B.E. in 1920. In December 1918 he became chief of staff, a position in which he was, as all earlier holders of the office had been, the leader's right-hand man and confidential agent.

In 1928 there developed a crisis within the Salvation Army. The high council, an authoritative group of senior officers, some of whom had long felt that, for many reasons, a change in command was desirable, and that the system whereby a retiring general was able to nominate his successor was outmoded in a changing world, met in London to consider what they should do, within the fairly wide limits of their powers. Discussion was protracted. Bramwell Booth offered to surrender the right to nominate his successor, but declined to resign his own office. Eventually on 13 February 1929 the high council, by a very large majority, and after hearing a mass of evidence and speeches by counsel, declared Bramwell Booth 'unfit for the office of General of the Salvation Army', removed him therefrom and recorded that their resolution was based upon the state of his health. These events, while they did not lack some of the essential qualities of drama, had also their pathos. In all of them Higgins took a leading part. It is for this principally that he will be remembered within and without the ranks of the Salvation Army. Having deposed the leader and destroyed the dynastic principle at a stroke, the high council immediately elected Higgins to the generalship by a majority of twenty-five over the other candidate, Commander Evangeline Booth, herself prominent in the move to depose her brother.

Higgins took office knowing that the problems he must now face dwarfed any with which he had been called upon to grapple earlier. The drastic action in which he had very actively shared so recently did not gain the immediate or unanimous support of all senior officers or of the whole of the rank and file. It had, however, been taken only after profound and prayerful thought, and after the co-operation of Bramwell Booth and his supporters had been vigorously sought. For a time it seemed as if the Salvation Army might falter in its march. Higgins and his staff, however, initiated further reforms which were concerned with the powers of the general, the status and duties of officers, and the fundamental constitution of the organization, to introduce into it a more democratic spirit. The Salvation Army Act was passed in 1931.

Higgins's retirement in 1934 was marked by a demonstration in the Royal Albert Hall at which their Royal Highnesses the Duke and Duchess of York were present. Subsequently Higgins went to live in the United States, and died in New York 14 December 1947. In 1888 he married Catherine Price (died 1952), of Penarth, herself a Salvationist, by whom he had four sons and three daughters. A portrait of Higgins by Frank O. Salisbury was presented to the Salvation Army by the artist in 1934.

[Personal knowledge.]

RONALD CARTON.

HIGGINS, SIR JOHN FREDERICK ANDREWS (1875–1948), air marshal, was born at Farnham, Surrey, 1 September 1875, the son of William Higgins, chemist, and his wife, Catherine Harriette Andrews. He was educated at Charterhouse and then attended the Royal Military Academy, Woolwich, from which he passed out third. In 1895 he was commissioned in the Royal Artillery; he saw his first active service in the South African war when he was severely wounded; he was mentioned in dispatches, awarded the Queen's medal, four clasps, the King's medal, two clasps, and appointed to the D.S.O. He then became one of the pioneers of flying among army officers, and having qualified as a pilot in 1912 he was seconded for four years to the Royal Flying Corps (military wing) as a flight commander. At that time no one in the Corps had fired any sort of gun from the air, and he took part in some interesting if unauthorized experiments with (Sir) Robert Brooke-Popham, his commanding officer in No. 3 Squadron. In 1913 Higgins was given command of the newly formed No. 5 Squadron, and when war was declared in 1914 his was one of the four squadrons to go overseas with the first Expeditionary Force. For his gallantry in these early months, when he was wounded in the air above Bailleul, he was made an officer of the Legion of Honour. In December 1914 he was posted to Netheravon, with the rank of wing commander, to form the Fourth Wing.

In France again in June 1915 to command the Third Wing, he returned to England in August to form No. II Brigade as brigade commander, Royal

Flying Corps, and temporary brigadier-general. In January 1916 he was given command of No. III Brigade in France and commanded it throughout the battles of the Somme, when he contributed much to the solution of Royal Flying Corps co-operation with the artillery which was then in a rather sketchy state. He again proved his ability in the spring of 1917 when the Royal Flying Corps was faced with the danger of losing local air superiority before and during the battle of Arras; for the enemy were by then producing more efficient fighters and using them to good purpose by copying our methods, whereas our best fighter, the Nieuport, had developed a tendency to break up in the air. By his powers of leadership and his driving energy to get technical defects corrected Higgins undoubtedly helped to save the air situation at a critical time. He was promoted to major-general in the Royal Air Force on its formation in 1918.

At the end of the war Higgins was made a C.B., awarded the A.F.C., and given command of the air force attached to the Rhine Army. On being granted a permanent commission in the Royal Air Force in 1919 as major-general, which was later converted into air vice-marshal, he resigned his army commission. In 1924 he went East as A.O.C., Iraq Command, and while there he was instrumental by his initiative, prompt action, and characteristic calm in resolving what was potentially a highly explosive situation on the northern frontier. Official appreciation of his conduct was followed by the K.B.E. in 1925. Higgins probably did his most valuable work two years later, during his appointment as air member for supply and research of the Air Council. He was a realist with a fund of common sense, a great deal of experience, and a good working technical grasp of aircraft types and their equipment. He was promoted K.C.B. in 1928 and appointed air marshal in 1929. He retired in September 1930 and worked in India for some years on the board of an aircraft company in Bangalore, but was recalled in 1939 and served until September 1940 as A.O.C.-in-C., India. He finally retired in November 1940 and died at his home at Leamington Spa 1 June 1948.

Higgins married in 1919 Ethel Beatrice, daughter of Edward Newport Singleton, of Quinville Abbey, county Clare; there were no children.

[*The Times*, 4 June 1948; private information; personal knowledge.]

E. BENTLEY BEAUMAN.

HILL, SIR ARTHUR WILLIAM (1875–1941), botanist, was born at Watford 11 October 1875, the son of Daniel Hill, estate agent, by his wife, Annie Weall. He went to Marlborough College in 1890 and there acquired an interest in field botany which persisted throughout life. He entered King's College, Cambridge, as an exhibitioner in 1894 and studied science, especially botany, subsequently becoming a foundation scholar. He was placed in the first class of both parts of the natural sciences tripos (1897, 1898) and was elected a fellow of his college in 1901 and an honorary fellow in 1932. After graduation he remained at Cambridge to pursue botanical research, at first with Walter Gardiner on the finer details of plant histology. He was appointed university demonstrator in 1899 and lecturer in 1904, soon after his return from a botanical expedition to the Andes of Bolivia and Peru. In 1907 he became assistant director of the Royal Botanic Gardens, Kew, and thereafter his life was centred on Kew, for he became director on the retirement of Sir David Prain [q.v.] in 1922.

Notwithstanding heavy administrative duties Hill continued to carry out botanical research, some aspects of which were facilitated by the wealth of plants grown in the Gardens. He had collected much valuable material during his travels in the Andes and for some years his investigations were concentrated on its elucidation. He had a profound knowledge of ornamental garden and glasshouse plants and was much interested in the amazing development of some of them since introduction from the wild. Natural plant hybrids also fascinated him, and he wrote several intriguing papers on peculiar methods of seed germination.

The herbarium at Kew is perhaps the largest and most important in the world, and Hill played a full part in maintaining its reputation. Floras of many parts of the Commonwealth and Empire are compiled at Kew, and Hill himself made valuable contributions to *The Flora Capensis*, *The Flora of Tropical Africa*, and *The Flora of Trinidad and Tobago*. He was instrumental in initiating a new *Flora of West Tropical Africa*. Kew is also wholly or partly responsible for several other important botanical publications, notably the *Index Kewensis*, *Hooker's Icones Plantarum*, and *Curtis's Botanical Magazine*, all of which Hill edited while he was director.

Hill was most successful in obtaining additional funds to increase the multifarious activities and amenities of the Royal Botanic Gardens. During his régime a new wing was added to the herbarium, laboratory facilities were extended, land was made available for experiments, and a new banana house was erected in which old-world species of bananas could be kept under observation in quarantine before transmission to the West Indies for breeding new varieties resistant to disease. Notable gifts during this period were the Sherman Hoyt cactus house (presented by Mrs. Sherman Hoyt of Pasadena, California) and the South African succulent house, provided by private donors to commemorate the silver jubilee of King George V. Hill was much concerned about the deleterious effect of the smoky atmosphere of London on the conifers at Kew, and with the co-operation of the Forestry Commission he was largely instrumental in establishing a new national pinetum at Bedgebury, Kent.

As director of Kew, Hill was botanical adviser to the secretary of state for the Colonies. He rendered much valuable service to the Dominions and Colonies in connexion with botanical and agricultural matters, and at one time or another he visited most of these territories. His visits were always welcome, for he had great knowledge of the economic utilization of plants.

Hill was a keen practical gardener and the Royal Horticultural Society often sought his assistance. The Society awarded him its Victoria medal of honour and also a Veitch memorial medal for his services to horticulture. He was the chief horticultural adviser to the Imperial War Graves Commission. He was elected F.R.S. in 1920 and was appointed C.M.G. in 1926 and K.C.M.G. in 1931.

Hill died as a result of a riding accident on the mid-Surrey golf course 3 November 1941. He was unmarried.

[F. T. Brooks in *Obituary Notices of Fellows of the Royal Society*, No. 11, November 1942; private information; personal knowledge.]

                    F. T. Brooks.

HILL, Sir GEORGE FRANCIS (1867–1948), numismatist, was born 22 December 1867, at Berhampore, Bengal, the youngest of five children all of notable ability, one of whom, Micaiah John Muller Hill, became a distinguished mathematician and F.R.S. His father, the Rev. Samuel John Hill, was a missionary of rigid and exemplary character who felt it his duty to live continuously in, and for, India; and it fell to his mother, Leonora Josephine Müller, although of mixed Danish and Portuguese stock rooted in India, to bring the children to England for education. Family means were straitened and the divided home left a deep mark on their youngest child.

After an unhappy period at the School for the Sons of Missionaries, later Eltham College, Hill passed into University College School, thence with a scholarship to University College, London, where his abilities were quickly recognized, and so in 1888 on to Oxford, as an exhibitioner of Merton College. After an easy double first in classics (1889, 1891), it was his intention to stay on as a teacher in the university. He failed, however, to obtain a fellowship, and when in 1893 a vacancy occurred in the department of coins and medals in the British Museum he applied for the post and was selected. Already in his last year at Oxford he had been increasingly attracted by Greek art and archaeology and had been studying Greek coins under Percy Gardner [q.v.].

He entered the museum at a moment of great activity in Greek numismatics, when, largely through the work of the keeper, Barclay V. Head [q.v.], scholars had begun to realize how great a contribution this science could make to the study of the ancient world. He was at once set to work on the Greek catalogue, to which he contributed successive and exemplary volumes on Lycia, Cyprus, Cilicia, Phoenicia, Palestine, and Arabia, &c.

Meanwhile his leisure produced several widely used manuals of more general scope: on Greek and Roman coins (including the revision in part of Head's *Historia Numorum*), on Greek historical inscriptions, and on sources for Greek history between the Persian and Peloponnesian wars. Parallel with his classical interests, and at least equal to them in his eyes, ran his interest in the history and culture of medieval and Renaissance Italy, fostered by frequent visits to Rome and elsewhere. His work in this field was no less impressive, including, besides his careful studies of the medals and drawings of Pisanello, the monumental *Corpus of Italian Medals before Cellini* (2 vols., 1930), and the unique collections of material for Italian heraldry and iconography which he bequeathed to the British Museum and the Warburg Institute. Characteristically his last years were devoted to producing the four volumes of what has now become the standard *History of Cyprus* (1940–52) from the earliest times to the present day.

In 1912 Hill became keeper of his department, and in 1931 director and principal librarian of the British Museum (the first archaeologist to hold an office hitherto reserved for librarians), receiving a K.C.B. in 1933, having been appointed C.B. in 1929. Outstanding events of his directorship were the launching of a successful national campaign to acquire the *Codex Sinaiticus*, and the purchase, in conjunction with the Victoria and Albert Museum, of the magnificent Eumorfopoulos collection of oriental antiquities. He retired in 1936.

His departmental experience had given him a deep interest in the subject of treasure trove (characteristically while director he found time to write the standard work on the subject) and he was able to effect a revolutionary change in its administration which now goes far to prevent concealment and clandestine disposal of finds. Indeed, in addition to his scholarship, Hill had a strongly practical side. He was secretary of the Archaeological Joint Committee from its inception, and was thus instrumental in drafting antiquities laws for Iraq, Palestine, and Cyprus. There can be few journals touching his special interests of which he was not, at some time, editor; he was a founder of the Vasari Society, an active fellow of the British Academy to which he was elected in 1917, and of the Society of Antiquaries, of which he was vice-president, as he was also of the Royal Numismatic, the Hellenic, and the Roman societies. He was a fellow of University College, London, and an honorary fellow of Merton College; he also received a number of honorary degrees, including the D.C.L. of Oxford and Litt.D. of Cambridge.

In 1897 Hill married Mary (died 1924), daughter of John Dennis Paul, F.G.S., J.P., of Leicester; there were no children. He died in London 18 October 1948. A portrait by James Gunn and a drawing by Mrs. Campbell Dodgson are in the possession of the trustees of the British Museum. Merton College has a portrait by H. G. Riviere.

[*A Tribute to Sir George Hill on his eightieth birthday*, with a complete bibliography, prepared by the Royal Numismatic Society, 1948; E. S. G. Robinson in *Proceedings* of the British Academy, vol. xxxvi, 1950.]

E. S. G. ROBINSON.

HILL, LEONARD RAVEN- (1867–1942), artist, illustrator, and cartoonist. [See RAVEN-HILL.]

HINDLEY, SIR CLEMENT DANIEL MAGGS (1874–1944), railway engineer and public servant, was born in Dulwich 19 December 1874, the son of Charles Hugh Hindley, carpet warehouseman, and his wife, Mary Ann Miller. He was educated at Dulwich College and at Trinity College, Cambridge, where he was placed in the second class of part i of the mechanical sciences tripos in 1896. In the following year he was appointed assistant engineer on the East Indian Railway. After a visit in 1904 to America and Canada as member of an official delegation from the Institution of Civil Engineers, he returned to India to become in 1905 personal assistant to the chief engineer of the East Indian Railway. He took charge in 1906 of the technical section of the agent's office, with responsibility for the scrutiny of all plans and estimates for engineering works. Later he assumed charge of the Delhi district and the completion of the works for the Agra direct access project. In 1909 he was appointed resident engineer of the works for the completion of the Gya–Khatrasgarh railway. He became secretary of the East Indian Railway in 1914, deputy general manager in 1918, and general manager in 1920.

In 1921 Hindley was appointed chairman of the commissioners of the Port of Calcutta, and in the following year became the first chief commissioner of railways for India, with responsibility for decisions on technical matters. He was the sole adviser to the Government of India on railway policy and during his tenure of office many important changes were introduced, including the reorganization of the railway department, the separation of railway finance from the general budget, the transfer of the East Indian and Great Indian Peninsula railways to State management, and the opening of the first railway staff college. He did much to restore the Indian railways to a state of efficiency after the effects of the war of 1914–18 and initiated a programme of new construction which added 4,000 miles to the railways. He was knighted in 1925 and, retiring in 1928, was appointed K.C.I.E. in 1929. He was also a commander of the Belgian Order of Leopold.

On his return to England Hindley was appointed first chairman of the Racecourse Betting Control Board and although his task was difficult, and entirely new to him, his wisdom, tact, and great administrative ability soon made themselves felt. He was much in demand for committee work, for he was a master of procedure and his memoranda were remarkable for their clarity: his attention was thus turned to matters which included the Channel tunnel, forest products, inland water, building research, and fuel efficiency. He was a member of the Advisory Council for Scientific and Industrial Research, of the board of the National Physical Laboratory, and chairman of the Steel Structures Research Committee. From 1939 to 1942 he was regional works adviser for the London civil defence region. At the time of his death he was chairman of the codes of practice committee for civil engineering and building under the minister of works, and of the building and civil engineering industries 'holidays with pay' scheme. He was a valued member of the Institution of Civil Engineers of which he was president, 1939–40, and had much to do with the initiation of its *Journal* and its research committee.

Hindley married in 1899 Anne, daughter of Henry Rait, of Murshidabad, Bengal, and had three sons. He died at Hampton Court 3 May 1944. Hindley was a man of imposing personality and great charm of manner. There is a portrait (1940) by Anthony Devas at the Institution of Civil Engineers.

[*The Times*, 6 May 1944; personal knowledge.]      W. T. HALCROW.

HINKS, ARTHUR ROBERT (1873–1945), astronomer and geographer, was born in London 26 May 1873, the eldest son of Robert Hinks, civil servant, of Croydon, Surrey, by his wife, Mary Hayward. In 1892 he went from Whitgift Grammar School, Croydon, to Trinity College, Cambridge, where he read for the mathematical tripos. In 1895 he was placed among the senior optimes and was appointed second assistant at the Cambridge observatory under Sir Robert Ball [q.v.] and also demonstrator in practical astronomy in the university. He was chief assistant from 1903 to 1913. He was actively concerned in the design and the installation of the Sheepshanks telescope and in the new science of photographic astrometry. He spent much time in the determination of the solar parallax and of the mass of the moon from observations of Eros; for this he was awarded the gold medal of the Royal Astronomical Society in 1912 and elected F.R.S. in 1913. He was secretary of the Royal Astronomical Society from 1909 to 1912 and a vice-president from 1912 to 1913.

In 1908 Hinks was appointed lecturer in surveying and cartography in the Cambridge school of geography and so began an association with the Royal Geographical Society which had cooperated with the university in the establishment of the school. In 1913 he was appointed assistant secretary of the Society and his interests then turned more and more to geography although from 1913 to 1941 he gave the annual Gresham lectures in astronomy at the university of London. He was one of the four British delegates to the international map conference at Rome in 1913 which standardized the style and the characteristic sheets for the international one-to-a-million map. In 1915 he succeeded (Sir) J. S. Keltie [q.v.] as secretary of the Royal Geographical Society and editor of the *Geographical Journal*, posts which he retained until the end of his life.

It was a period of change in the fortunes of the Society, apart from the difficulties of maintenance in the years of war. The Society's move from Savile Row to Lowther Lodge, Kensington Gore, entailed adaptation of the latter to its new function and the reorganization of the staff. Hinks took a great interest in these changes, and found further scope in the planning of the new building, opened at the centenary in 1930. He also widened the scope of the *Journal* by including many cartographical papers and even papers on the newer aspects of human geography, a subject, however, which, with his precise mind, he seemed to regard with a little misgiving. During the war of 1914–18 he directed the compilation of a hundred sheets of a provisional edition of the one-to-a-million map of Europe and Asia for the General Staff. A beginning was also made on a one-to-two-million map of Africa. During the war of 1939–45 the Society's drawing office under his guidance compiled a map of Europe and the Middle East, including an Arabic edition, for the British Council. His interest in cartography and map projections found expression also in various papers as well as in his *Map Projections* (1912) and *Maps and Survey* (1913) both of which went into several editions. One important aspect of his study of projections was his calculation of several oblique Mercators which simplified the drawing of great circles. Hinks was also deeply interested in the value of survey by oblique air photographs and he brought stereophotogrammetry within the range of the Society's work. His interest in maps was not limited to their scientific accuracy: he wanted his maps to be things of beauty in colour and lettering, besides being precise documents, as may be seen from his presidential address to the geography section of the British Association in 1925, 'The Science and Art of Map-Making'. Among his other works was the eleventh edition of *Hints to Travellers* and his recasting, in collaboration with many explorers, of the second volume (1938) of that work. He was also a leading figure of the Mount Everest committee of the Alpine Club and the Royal Geographical Society.

In 1920 Hinks was appointed C.B.E. and chevalier of the Belgian Order of the Crown; in 1938 he received the Victoria medal of the Royal Geographical Society and in 1943 the Cullum medal of the American Geographical Society. He married in 1899 Lily Mary (died 1928), daughter of Jonathan Packman, civil engineer, of Croydon; they had two sons of whom the elder, Roger, became an art critic, and the younger, David (died 1948), junior bursar of Trinity College, Cambridge. Hinks died at Royston, Hertfordshire, 18 April 1945.

[*The Times*, 19 April 1945; *Geographical Journal*, vol. cv, 1945; Sir H. Spencer Jones and H. J. Fleure in *Obituary Notices of Fellows of the Royal Society*, No. 16, May 1948; private information.] R. N. RUDMOSE BROWN.

HINSLEY, ARTHUR (1865-1943), cardinal, was born at Carlton, near Selby, Yorkshire, 25 August 1865, the second son of Thomas Hinsley, carpenter, by his wife, Bridget, daughter of John Ryan, farmer, of Cloonascragh, Tuam. He passed from a local Roman Catholic school to St. Cuthbert's College, Ushaw, Durham, at the age of eleven in order to study for the priesthood, and after obtaining the degree of B.A. at the university of London (1889) he went to the English College, Rome, in 1890, where he graduated D.D. at the Gregorian University and obtained a diploma in philosophy at the Academy of St. Thomas.

After ordination as priest 23 December 1893, Hinsley returned to teach at Ushaw until 1897, when he became assistant priest at Keighley, Yorkshire. In 1899 he founded the Roman Catholic Grammar School of St. Bede, Bradford, acting as its headmaster until 1904, when he was transferred to the diocese of Southwark. Here he lectured on the sacred scriptures at the diocesan seminary at Wonersh while acting as pastor at Sutton Park (1904-11) and Sydenham (1911-17) where he worked indefatigably on behalf of Belgian refugees after the outbreak of war. He was also during this time confidential adviser to the bishop of Southwark and deepened his friendship with Cardinal Gasquet [q.v.], the protector of the English College, Rome, a fact which led to his being chosen rector of that college in 1917. His energy and administrative ability in reorganization left a definite mark on that historic foundation, which he was also instrumental in saving when Mussolini's grandiose road-making plans threatened to sweep it away. Made a domestic prelate in 1917, he was consecrated titular bishop of Sebastopolis by Cardinal Merry del Val [q.v.] in November 1926.

In December 1927 Hinsley took up his appointment as visitor apostolic to Africa with a view to reorientating the missionary schools along the lines of the Phelps-Stokes reports. He was then sixty-three years of age, but his splendid physique enabled him to surmount tropical conditions, while his zest and practical acumen made his mission so fruitful that it was made permanent, and he became the first delegate apostolic in Africa in 1930, with the title of archbishop of Sardis and a seat at Mombasa. His work in Africa was regarded both in Rome and in British colonial circles as an achievement of the highest order. His belief in personal contact, his sympathy and tact, no less than his administrative ability, won a happy co-operation among the various nationalities making up the missionary body, as well as with colonial officials, and proved of inestimable value both to native education and to the Roman Catholic missions generally.

An attack of paratyphoid forced Hinsley to leave Africa in 1934 and he accepted what he regarded as virtual retirement, a canonry of the archbasilica of St. Peter's, Rome. It was therefore with real trepidation that he learnt that he had been chosen by Pope Pius XI to be archbishop of Westminster after the death of Cardinal

Bourne [q.v.]. Although he pleaded age and his disabilities, he obeyed, and received the pallium from the hands of the Pope himself in April 1935. He was created cardinal priest of the title of St. Susanna in December 1937.

In his rule at Westminster he inaugurated a number of boards to advise him, including a diocesan council, a finance board, and a schools commission, on which laymen sat as well as priests. Always deeply interested in education, he championed the cause of voluntary schools no less than his predecessors. With the coming of war he at once bent all his energies by pen, sermon, and broadcast to the spiritual service of the Allies. Not only did he readily join his name to that of the archbishop of Canterbury and the leaders of the other Churches in public appeals, but in 1940 he launched the 'Sword of the Spirit' movement, which sought to enlist all denominations in a unified effort for 'the restoration in Europe of a Christian basis for both public and private life, by a return to the principles of international order and Christian freedom'. Not even increasing ill health was allowed to interfere with his tireless efforts for the spiritual and material welfare of the men and women in the Services, among whom he distributed more than 50,000 special 'cardinal's crosses'.

Hinsley's genuine sincerity, expressed with a frank and homely force, made a deep impression in Britain and overseas. The university of Oxford recognized him as 'a great Englishman' in bestowing upon him the honorary degree of D.C.L. in 1942. He had received the honorary degree of D.Lit. from London University in 1936.

A tall man of imposing physique, Hinsley mingled dignity and gentleness with impulsiveness and a native shrewdness. In his faith and friendship he was the humblest of men, yet on principles he was unyielding. He hid a deep spirituality and sound learning under a fatherly simplicity; he was fond of children and sympathetic with the oppressed; he enjoyed cricket and the friendship of his fellow men. His intense faith enabled him to bear with great fortitude the suffering which came to him before he died of angina pectoris at Buntingford, Hertfordshire, 17 March 1943. He was buried in Westminster Cathedral.

A portrait of Hinsley (1942) by Neville (later the Earl of) Lytton is at St. Edmund's College, Ware. Another portrait (1940) by Simon Elwes is at Archbishop's House, Westminster.

[*The Times*, 18 March 1943; *Tablet*, 20 March 1943; *Catholic Who's Who*; J. C. Heenan, *Cardinal Hinsley*, 1944; private information; personal knowledge.]

DOUGLAS NEWTON.

HIRST, HUGO, BARON HIRST (1863–1943), chairman of the General Electric Company, was born in Munich 26 November 1863, the son of Emanuel Hirsch. Educated in Munich he at first studied chemistry, intending to go into his father's business, but instead came to this country and entered the electrical industry. He took the name Hirst on naturalization in 1883 and three years later joined Gustav Byng who had founded a firm for the sale of electrical appliances. Hirst had the vision to see the possibilities which lay in the manufacture of such goods and the determination necessary to carry the project through to success. In 1889 the firm was transformed into the General Electric Company of which Hirst became managing director in 1900 and chairman in 1910, holding both appointments until his death. By that time the company had some forty factories in Great Britain as well as subsidiary organizations in Commonwealth and other countries and 'G.E.C.' was known the world over for the manufacture and supply of every kind of electric equipment.

The leading position which the company attained was due in no small measure to the creative energy with which Hirst matched the opportunities offered by a new and expanding industry. He was among the first to realize the importance of research and before long the company had its own laboratories doing valuable work at Wembley. He had, moreover, the wisdom—and humility—to rely upon his staff, giving them responsibility, a full share of credit, and his unfailing support. He believed strongly in the advantages of attracting university and public-school men into industry and himself employed them wherever possible. In staff relations the company was ahead of its time, for Hirst, a sincere and kindly man, of simple and unaffected manner, never forgot that, however vast it might become, his organization was comprised of human beings. He himself enjoyed a game of billiards or golf, kept a good racing stable, was one of the earliest motorists, and took a keen personal interest in providing for the welfare and recreation of his employees.

Hirst was generous in his benefactions which included a gift of £20,000 to the benevolent fund of the Institution of Electrical Engineers of which he became an associate in 1888, a member ten years later, and an honorary member in 1935. Prominent, as was natural, in all that concerned his own industry, he was active also in a wider field, for he always felt himself deeply indebted to the country which had given him his chance and he rarely missed an opportunity to forward the cause of British industry or empire. From the days of Joseph Chamberlain he was a convinced protectionist and for nearly twenty years was treasurer of the Empire Industries Association. He was also chairman of the empire committee of the Federation of British Industries, and over the Federation itself he presided in 1936 and 1937. He came to be recognized by the Government as an expert in international trading and he served at various times as a member of the advisory council of the Board of Trade, as economic adviser to the Cabinet Research Committee, as a member of the Cabinet Trade and Employment Panel, and on the Committee on Industrial Research. He was also a member of the Blanesburgh committee of inquiry into unemployment insurance (1925–7) and of the committee of inquiry into the possibilities of co-operative selling in the coal industry (1926). He took part in the Mond–Turner discussions in 1928 and later in the year went with three others on a prolonged economic mission to Australia which would have proved more fruitful had not the world economic crisis supervened.

For his services Hirst was created a baronet in 1925 and in 1934 was raised to the peerage as Baron Hirst, of Witton, Warwickshire. He married in 1892 his cousin Leontine (died 1938). They had two daughters and one son, Harold, who died in 1919 of an illness resulting from four years' active service on various fronts. Four months after the latter's death a son, Hugh, was born who was killed on operational duties as a pilot officer in 1941. The peerage therefore became extinct when Hirst died at his home, Foxhill, near Reading, 22 January 1943.

[*The Times*, 25 and 26 January 1943; *Electrician*, 29 January 1943; *Nature*, 20 February 1943; *Journal* of the Institution of Electrical Engineers, vol. xc, 1943.]

HELEN M. PALMER.

HOBSON, GEOFFREY DUDLEY (1882–1949), historian of bookbindings, was born 17 March 1882, at Bromborough, Cheshire, the fourth son of Richard Hobson, D.L., of The Marfords, Bromborough, cotton broker and company director, by his wife, Mary Eleanor, daughter of John Chadwick, D.L., of Stockport.

He was educated at Harrow and University College, Oxford, where he was placed in the first class of the honours list in modern history in 1903. He passed the Foreign Office examination and was called to the bar, but, owing to his loss of hearing which occurred about this time, he never practised. After travelling on the continent, in 1909 he bought, in conjunction with others, the old-established auctioneering firm of Sotheby, Wilkinson and Hodge. Here, too, his deafness handicapped him, and he never conducted sales in the rostrum. But this did not debar him from exercising his shrewd business talents, while the work at Sotheby's gave scope to his critical taste as applied to the *objets d'art* of many kinds which came his way. In regard to these, however, he did not profess to be a specialized expert; his interest turned to early books, and particularly bookbindings, and on the latter he became the greatest authority of the day. For, while most writers on bindings in all countries had specialized in the work of their own lands, and usually in that of a single period, Hobson developed a wide knowledge of western European bindings, although it was strongest on the Romanesque period, on English sixteenth-century panel-stamps, and on the gold-tooled bindings of France in the sixteenth century and of England in the seventeenth and eighteenth centuries. His unique collection of photographs and rubbings provided a comprehensive basis for his study of individual binders' tools, but he somewhat underestimated the importance of evidence on the technical side of the craft.

In *Maioli, Canevari and Others* (1926), Hobson first showed his critical powers by destroying convincingly long-accepted myths which had hitherto been treated too unscientifically. As Sandars reader at Cambridge in 1927 he produced an elaborate study of Romanesque work in *English Binding before 1500* (1929), although he subsequently modified his views as to the nationality of much of it. At the same time he took up the rewriting of a book projected by two other scholars and produced a monumental work, *Bindings in Cambridge Libraries* (1929). This involved him in a study of bindings of all kinds, and the same may be said of his catalogue of the *English Bindings 1490–1940 in the Library of J. R. Abbey* (1940), except that in the latter case they were limited to one country. To his painstaking methods Hobson added a free imagination and a remarkable flair for reaching, by an uncanny instinct, conclusions which subsequent research proved to be justified. It is no disparagement of the pioneer work of earlier writers to say that, by the number and range of his books and articles, by his scientific approach, scholarship, and industry, by the way in which he illuminated his discussions of bindings by parallels, particularly in iconography, drawn from other forms of art, and by the inspiring encouragement which he gave to beginners in the subject, Hobson did more than any-one else to promote the serious study of bindings which has been a recent feature in bibliography.

Although he could at times be autocratic in his relations with his staff, and occasion-ally even in academic discussion, Hobson's great charm as a conversationalist, and his discriminating taste as a connoisseur of wine and food made him a welcome companion in private life and an out-standing host.

He married in 1920 Gertrude Adelaide (died 1938), daughter of the Rev. Thomas Walter Vaughan, and widow of Henry Dyson Taylor. There was one son. In 1922 Hobson was appointed M.V.O. He died in London 5 January 1949.

[*Times Literary Supplement*, 22 January 1949; Ernst Kyriss in *Gutenberg Jahrbuch*, 1950; private information; personal knowledge.]      J. B. OLDHAM.

HODGKINS, FRANCES MARY (1869–1947), painter, was born 28 April 1869 at Dunedin, New Zealand, the third child and second daughter of William Mathew Hodgkins, solicitor and amateur landscape painter, who had emigrated from England in 1859. Through her mother, Rachel Owen Parker, she was descended from a family settled in New South Wales since 1822. She was educated at private schools in Dunedin, received casual instruction in painting from both her father and G. P. Nerli, an Italian artist, and attended classes at the Dunedin School of Art. From 1890 onwards she exhibited regularly with the New Zealand art societies, acquiring local reputation as a figure painter in water-colour. Her work, although conventional, was vigorous in treatment and already revealed the artist's strong colour sense. In 1896 she formed her first sketching class and continued teaching until in February 1901 she left New Zea-land for a visit to Europe.

Setting out with the intention of re-turning to New Zealand in twelve months, she remained in Europe almost three years. She attended classes held by Borough John-son and Norman Garstin, but most of her time was spent in sketching tours in France, Italy, Morocco, and Holland, interspersed with visits to England. Before returning to New Zealand in November 1903, she had exhibited at commercial galleries in London, and in May 1903 at the Royal Academy. She attempted to re-establish herself in New Zealand, but was irresistibly drawn back to Europe, embark-ing in January 1906 on what was again in-tended as a brief visit. This time she remained for seven years. Once more she travelled widely until November 1908 when she settled in Paris. Her chief object in visiting Paris was to gain experience in oil-painting, but her skill in water-colour was so greatly admired that she continued working in her old medium and won modest success both as painter and as teacher. She exhibited at the Salon and with the leading water-colour societies, taught at the old-established Académie Colarossi, and later formed her own class. Only in October 1911, as a result of this success, did she decide to remain per-manently in Europe. The following year she again left for New Zealand to visit her relatives and exhibit her work. The Impressionist style she had developed in Paris created great interest in the art circles of Australia and New Zealand and, after a highly successful tour of the chief cities, she returned to Europe at the close of 1913.

On the outbreak of war Frances Hodg-kins transferred her headquarters from Paris to St. Ives, Cornwall, where she re-mained until she moved to London and later to Burford. While at St. Ives she began to work seriously in oils and, encour-aged by her younger friends, broke away from her Impressionist manner. She ex-hibited with the Royal Academy for the last time in 1916, after which the distance be-tween her own outlook and that of the more academic English painters gradually increased. In the post-war years she managed to exist only with difficulty on the proceeds of rare sales and the fees from classes held each year in such resorts as Tréboul and St. Valéry-sur-Somme. More than once, discouraged by poverty and lack of recognition, she thought of returning to New Zealand. In April 1925 she had booked a passage and was staying in Manchester with two of her pupils when she met the chairman of the Calico Printers' Association, through whom she was offered a post as designer to the Association. With the death of her mother in 1926 the strongest link with New Zealand was broken and she did not again seriously consider leaving Europe.

The venture as a commercial designer proving unsuccessful, Frances Hodgkins left Manchester in 1927 to make a further bid for recognition in London. In that year she met the art dealer Mr. Arthur R. Howell with whom she later concluded an agreement which led in 1932 to a contract with the firm of Alex. Reid and Lefevre. Freed from the necessity of teaching, she now devoted herself wholly to painting and, in the search for congenial surroundings and subjects, made many expeditions abroad, travelling as far afield as the Balearic Islands (1932–3) and Tossa de Mar, Spain (1935–6). In this period she allied herself with the more experimental younger artists in such groups as the 'Seven and Five' Society, and 'Unit One' founded by Paul Nash [q.v.]. Her reputation as one of the exponents of modern English painting steadily grew, but it was not until the war years that she received widespread recognition. In 1940 she was one of the five painters who were to have represented Great Britain at the Venice Biennale, and in April 1942 she was awarded a Civil List pension. The climax of this period, indeed of her whole career, was a retrospective exhibition held at the Lefevre Gallery in November 1946. Although ill at the time, Frances Hodgkins was able to travel from Corfe Castle, Dorset, her home during the war years, to visit the exhibition. She died six months later, 13 May 1947, at Herrison, Dorchester.

Frances Hodgkins is generally acknowledged to have been one of the leading members of the modern movement in English art in the nineteen-thirties. Any further appraisal of her place in the history of English painting is made difficult by the bulk of her work, its varying quality, and its dispersal in two hemispheres. It seems likely, however, that she will rank as one of the notable colourists of the English school and as one of the most gifted and

original of women painters. In May 1952 a memorial exhibition was held in the Tate Gallery which has several of her works in its permanent collection. She is also represented in the Victoria and Albert Museum, in many public galleries in Great Britain, and in the principal galleries of Australia and New Zealand. A portrait by her friend Sir Cedric Morris is in the City Art Gallery, Auckland.

[*The Times*, 16 May 1947; Myfanwy Evans, *Frances Hodgkins*, 1948; A. R. Howell, *Frances Hodgkins: Four Vital Years*, 1951; E. H. McCormick, *Works of Frances Hodgkins in New Zealand*, 1954, and *The Expatriate*, 1954.]

E. H. McCormick.

HOFMEYR, JAN HENDRIK (1894–1948), South African statesman, was born in Cape Town 20 March 1894, the younger son of Andries Brink Hofmeyr, a newspaperman, and his wife, Deborah Catherina Beyers. Hofmeyr was a delicate child but when eventually he went to the South African College School near his Cape Town home he had a meteoric career, moving up the school in record time and winning every scholarship and prize which came his way. He took an honours degree in classics at the university of the Cape of Good Hope in 1909 at an age when other boys matriculate; a year later he obtained an honours degree in mathematics and was placed above a particularly brilliant student who had taken the normal time for the degree. He was awarded a Rhodes scholarship in 1910, but, too young to go at once to Oxford, he beguiled himself by writing a massive book on his uncle, the famous Cape politician Jan Hendrik Hofmeyr [q.v.], whom he greatly admired. By the time this was published in 1914 he was at Balliol College where he obtained a double first: in classical honour moderations (1914) and *literae humaniores* (1916). He was a member of the Union and took an interest in the Oxford and Bermondsey Mission and the Student Christian Movement.

Returning to South Africa with his widowed mother who had accompanied him to Oxford, Hofmeyr lectured in classics for a short time at his alma mater, the South African College, which was soon to become the university of Cape Town. He showed his versatility by gaining the Ebden prize (1916) for an essay on national debts. In 1917 he went to Johannesburg as professor of classics in what was then the South African School of Mines and Technology. He became principal in 1919 at the early age of twenty-five and before he retired in 1924 the school had become the university of the Witwatersrand. During this time he published (with Professor T. J. Haarhoff) *Two Studies in Ancient Imperialism* (1920). In 1924 J. C. Smuts [q.v.], whose wife was related to Hofmeyr's mother, made Hofmeyr administrator of the province of the Transvaal, a position which he held with distinction until 1929. In the work of organization and administration his phenomenal memory stood him in good stead and those who came to him with petitions generally found that he knew more than they did about the case. This was perhaps the happiest period of his life.

In 1929 he entered party politics as member for Johannesburg North, a constituency which he continued to represent until his death. He joined the South African Party, but was often distressed by the impossibility of applying his Liberal principles to practical life and by the demands of the party machinery. However, he retained his sense of humour, and his witty after-dinner speeches were famous. On the coalition of Smuts and Hertzog which he helped to bring about in 1933, Hofmeyr became minister of the interior, public health, and education. From 1936 to 1938 he was minister of mines, education, and labour and social welfare; in 1939 when the split between Smuts and Hertzog took place he supported South Africa's declaration of war and returned to the Cabinet as minister of finance and education.

Hofmeyr, like Smuts, believed in South Africa as a whole; in South Africa first, but not South Africa alone. He favoured the practice of preserving what was good in local tradition while at the same time adapting, not merely adopting, what could be fruitfully learned from other traditions. Because of this, he always supported and promoted the positive values in Afrikaans culture, appreciated the work that had been done for the language and saw its value as an instrument of creative co-operation. Those who worked under his chairmanship on the *Forum*, a Liberal paper which he began, realized that he would only countenance views which were fair and balanced and that he deprecated all sentimentality or partisanship. More than once he met with criticism because he would appoint members of the Opposition to the councils of important public bodies.

On the native question, Hofmeyr upheld the old Cape Liberal tradition. But he believed in advancing step by step and in hastening slowly, notwithstanding the more extreme attitudes, such as support of miscegenation, which were attributed to him in the political arena. He based his policy on a deep sense of Christian values, as he made clear in his Hoernlé memorial lecture (1945). Whereas he opposed racial tyranny or prejudice, Hofmeyr recognized that in his own lifetime some racial discrimination in political and social matters was perhaps inevitable. His views on the native question governed the whole of his political career and were far from popular. He vigorously opposed the native bills in 1936 and in 1938 resigned from the Cabinet in protest at an action which he called 'a prostitution of the Constitution': the nomination of a senator to represent native interests, not because he was qualified to do so, but because it was the only way to retain him in the Cabinet. In 1939 he resigned from the United Party caucus over the Asiatics bill and in 1943 offered his resignation from the Cabinet to Smuts over the 'pegging bill', but was persuaded to withdraw it in the interests of the war effort. Nor was his popularity enhanced by the budgets which he introduced to finance that effort, since increased taxation will always arouse hostility even when (and this was not always so in Hofmeyr's case) it is seen to be necessary. Nevertheless, Hofmeyr was generally looked upon as the likely successor to Smuts. He acted as prime minister whenever Smuts was out of the country and in January 1948, when he exchanged the portfolio of finance for that of mines, he was officially named deputy prime minister and leader of the House in which he had always been a brilliant speaker. The evident intention that Smuts should be succeeded by someone far less given to compromise may have contributed to the defeat of the party at the general election in that year. Not long afterwards Hofmeyr died in Pretoria 3 December 1948, two years before Smuts himself. Although so many years Hofmeyr's senior Smuts had by no means overshadowed him in the South African scene. Indeed, some felt that Smuts, by his preoccupation with world events, had left Hofmeyr to bear too great a burden of the nation's affairs and so hastened his death. A visitor to the Government Buildings in Pretoria one Christmas found all the junior ministers on vacation; only two people in that vast edifice were at work—Smuts and Hofmeyr. Hofmeyr was undoubtedly a hard and rapid worker, yet he loved his game of cricket and, undaunted by his lack of prowess, was proud to place his short stocky figure at the head of the Witwatersrand university staff eleven or later the parliamentary team. He insisted on being bowled out by a Test cricketer.

After he had abandoned an academic career Hofmeyr continued to take an interest in classical studies and believed in their application in the modern world. He tried throughout his political career to apply Roman wisdom and Christian principle to South African affairs. Consequently he was often misunderstood; yet this effort, when the alarums and excursions of the party fight have faded away, will be his main title to remembrance. In 1931 he published a volume on South Africa in 'The Modern World' series which is crammed with interesting facts and is marked by his sense of balance. He always admired this quality in the Emperor Augustus and at times seemed to show something of his coldness and hardness, but he mellowed in later life. He lived simply and deprecated wastefulness. He lost his father when he was very young. He never married and lived the whole of his life with his mother whom he predeceased despite her possessive care. The household from his earliest days always included several cats which he liked because he found them intelligent. They would go back and forth with him between Pretoria and Cape Town.

Many honours fell to him: he was president of the Classical Association of South Africa and a vice-president of the Classical Association of Great Britain. He was also president of the South African Association for the Advancement of Science, 1928–9, and of the national council of the Young Men's Christian Association of South Africa from 1939. He was an honorary D.Sc. of Cape Town (1929), from 1926 to 1930 vice-chancellor and from 1938 chancellor of the university of the Witwatersrand. On a brief visit to England in 1945 he was sworn of the Privy Council and received the honorary degree of D.C.L. from the university of Oxford. The following year he was elected an honorary fellow of Balliol and an honorary bencher of Gray's Inn.

There is a portrait by Percival Small in the Senate room of the university of the Witwatersrand; and a posthumous portrait by Katharine Lloyd is at Rhodes House, Oxford.

[Private information; personal knowledge.]

T. J. HAARHOFF.

HOGG, DOUGLAS McGAREL, first VISCOUNT HAILSHAM (1872–1950), statesman and lord chancellor, was born in London 28 February 1872, the eldest of the three sons of the philanthropist Quintin Hogg [q.v.]. He was educated at Eton, where he became captain of Oppidans, and then entered his father's firm of sugar merchants, Hogg, Curtis, Campbell & Co. The experience he there gained in sugar-growing in the West Indies and British Guiana gave him a practical knowledge of commerce which stood him in good stead in his subsequent career. In the South African war he served as a trooper with the Lothian and Berwick Yeomanry, when a bullet which would have killed him was diverted by a silver flask in his pocket. On his father's death in January 1903 he threw himself into work of the Polytechnic Institution which Quintin Hogg had founded and developed. This remained one of Douglas Hogg's main interests throughout his life. He had already been called to the bar by Lincoln's Inn in January 1902. Starting in the profession of his choice when nearly thirty years of age, he made rapid progress in the best class of commercial and common law business and built up one of the most substantial junior practices of his time. He took silk in 1917 and met with instant success in the front row. He was made a bencher of Lincoln's Inn in 1920 and in the same year was appointed attorney-general to the Prince of Wales.

Hogg had all the qualities which go to make a leader at the bar: an accurate grasp of complicated facts, a clear view of the principles of law which had to be applied to them, a sturdy attitude in face of the situation with which he had to deal, and a manner which was genial and conciliatory with a persuasive force behind it well calculated to win assent from the tribunal he was addressing. He was never at a loss, and no counsel was more adept at preparing the way to meet the difficulties in his case.

Hogg's political opinions were Conservative. He had been approached with the invitation to be the prospective candidate in that interest in St. Marylebone, but had stood down to promote party unity in that constituency. But when the coalition Government of Lloyd George collapsed in

1922 and Bonar Law became prime minister, the latter invited Hogg to become attorney-general in his Government, although he was not as yet a member of the House of Commons. He was, however, immediately returned without a contest for St. Marylebone. He thus had the unusual experience (as was also the case with Sir Richard Webster, later Viscount Alverstone, q.v.) of beginning his parliamentary career on the front bench as attorney-general. Within three days he was making a persuasive speech in support of the Irish Free State constitution bill, and he continued to show the parliamentary aptitude which usually proceeds from a long apprenticeship. He was sworn of the Privy Council in November, and knighted in December, 1922.

When in 1923 Baldwin succeeded Bonar Law, the new prime minister retained Hogg as attorney-general. After Labour came into office in the following year Hogg took an active part from the front Opposition bench and his speech on the Campbell case, presenting the Conservative view, helped to secure the overthrow of the Labour Government. He now became attorney-general for the second time, with a seat in the Cabinet, and, on the resignation of Lord Chancellor Cave [q.v.] a few days before his death in March 1928, attained the Woolsack with the title of Baron Hailsham, of Hailsham, county Sussex. He was advanced to a viscountcy in the following year and after the Socialist victory at the general election of 1929 led the Conservative Opposition in the House of Lords through the years 1930 and 1931.

When the 'national' Government was formed in the November after the general election of 1931, Hailsham was appointed secretary of state for war and acted as leader of the House of Lords throughout that administration. His service at the War Office was distinguished. The times were not easy for a Service minister, for during the long years of peace and disarmament grave deficiencies had accumulated both in the army and in the other fighting Services. Hailsham soon won the confidence of the Army Council, the general staff, and the whole of the department by his shrewd guidance and administration and his powerful advocacy of their claims in the higher counsels of the Government. By the time he handed over to his successor, co-ordinated plans for the rearmament of the Services had been approved, and the War Office had become a centre of activity and team-work which will be long remembered.

In January 1932 Hailsham suggested that the Cabinet should depart from its usual practice of collective responsibility and agree to differ, accepting a majority decision, on the matter of protection. This kept the free-traders within the Cabinet until after the Ottawa conference at which Hailsham was a British delegate. He also attended the world economic conference in 1933. When Baldwin formed his third administration in 1935, Hailsham again became lord chancellor, presiding with dignity over the deliberations of the Upper House, and in his judicial capacity delivering many judgements which illustrated his power of lucid reasoning and his command of appropriate language. Good examples of Hailsham's quality in these respects will be found in the reports of the Appeal Cases—for instance in *Addie* v. *Dumbreck* (injury to child trespasser, 1929); *Tolley* v. *Fry* (defamation, 1931); and *Swadling* v. *Cooper* (contributory negligence, 1931).

Hailsham presided in 1935 at the trial for manslaughter of Lord de Clifford by his peers, being appointed lord high steward for the purposes of the trial, and ruled that there was no case to answer, at the same time admitting that there was something to be said in favour of the view that this ancient institution for investigating a charge of felony against a peer had outlived its usefulness. It was, in fact, the last instance of the trial of a peer by his peers, for the ordinary jurisdiction of judge and jury was substituted by a clause of the Criminal Justice Act, 1948.

In March 1938 Hailsham succeeded Lord Halifax as lord president of the Council, his place on the Woolsack being taken by Lord Maugham. On 31 October of that year he resigned the presidency on account of illness. His health had been declining since 1936, when he had a severe set-back, but he struggled on manfully with his Cabinet work while a minister, and after his resignation made an effort to take part as a private member in debates in the House of Lords. His head remained clear and his judgement good, but he was no longer the vigorous expounder of his views which he had been. His many friends and admirers grieved to note the failing powers of a man who had once been thought of as the future leader of the Conservative Party. He died at his dearly loved Sussex home, Carter's Corner Place, 16 August 1950.

Hailsham was twice married: first, in 1905 to Elizabeth (died 1925), the widow of the Hon. Archibald John Marjoribanks; secondly, in 1929 to Mildred Margaret, widow of the Hon. Alfred Clive Lawrence. The succession to his title passed to the elder son of the first marriage, Quintin McGarel (born 1907), a barrister who had entered the House of Commons as member for Oxford City about the time of his father's retirement. Hailsham was president of the Marylebone Cricket Club in 1933. Honorary doctorates were conferred on him by Oxford, Cambridge, Birmingham, Belfast, and Reading. There is a portrait of Hailsham by Sir William Nicholson at Lincoln's Inn, and another, by J. A. A. Berrie, in the offices of the Abbey National Building Society. A bust by Lady Kennet is in the possession of the family.

[The Times, 17 August 1950; long personal knowledge.]                    SIMON.

HOLDSWORTH, SIR WILLIAM SEARLE (1871–1944), lawyer, was born at Beckenham, Kent, 7 May 1871, the eldest son of Charles Joseph Holdsworth, solicitor, by his wife, Ellen Caroline Searle. He was educated at Dulwich College and at New College, Oxford, where he was a history exhibitioner. He gained a first class in history in 1893 and another in jurisprudence in 1894, and a second class in the B.C.L. examination in 1896. He won the Barstow scholarship at the Inns of Court in 1895, and read for a short time in chambers, being called to the bar by Lincoln's Inn in 1896. But his heart was set on the academic life and he was elected in 1897 to a fellowship at St. John's College, Oxford. Here he was not only an indefatigable teacher of every branch of law, but filled many college offices. By 1909 he had already completed three volumes of his monumental History of English Law, and his claims to succeed A. V. Dicey [q.v.], who in that year resigned the Vinerian professorship of English law, were strong. The choice of the electors, however, fell on William Martin Geldart, Holdsworth being appointed in 1910 to the All Souls' readership in English law vacated by Geldart's elevation. In 1922 Geldart died, and Holdsworth's succession, long a foregone conclusion, became a fact.

That Holdsworth's name, among Oxford jurists, ranks second only to that of Sir William Blackstone [q.v.] is an opinion which has received support from the learned. He was best known as a writer, but he had the qualities of a great teacher, and his pupils always received a generous portion of his best. His activities were not confined to Oxford, for he always felt strongly that it was the duty of an academic lawyer to keep in touch not only with his academic but also with his professional colleagues. For many years he was reader at the Inns of Court, successively in equity and in constitutional law, and he played a very prominent part in the Society of Public Teachers of Law. He was professor of constitutional law at University College, London, 1903–8. His advice was in great request by the Government, and he was a very valuable member of the Indian States inquiry committee in 1928, and of the committee on ministers' powers (1929–32). Invitations to lecture abroad came thick and fast upon him. In 1927 he made an extended lecture tour of the United States, and in 1938 he revisited India, as Tagore professor at Calcutta.

Holdsworth's energy was extraordinary. Not only did he add nine more volumes to his great history, but he rewrote the first three, and left sufficient material for the posthumous publication of two final volumes. His expressed aim was that the range of his work should extend from the earliest times to the Judicature Act of 1873, but several topics, notably that of conspiracy as a crime and as a tort, are brought down to a much later date. His work lacks Maitland's perfection and attractiveness of style, but his enthusiasm for the wealth of his material saves his treatment from lapsing into dullness; the work may be read by students with pleasure as well as with great profit.

Legal history, in Holdsworth's view, was largely a matter of biography; no man was farther than he from the determinist viewpoint. His lectures on legal history at Oxford often took the form of studies of the lives and influence of the great jurists of the past who lived again in Holdsworth's phrases. The same habit of thought persists in his written work, and a great deal of its subject-matter is devoted to the study of the professional development of the law by judges, whether common law, equity, or civilian, and to the appreciation of legal literature.

Like Blackstone before him, Holdsworth by no means confined himself to one book. His output was colossal. He contributed much to the publications of the Selden Society, for which he worked almost until the time of his death, for volume xxii of the Year Books series (*11 Edward II, 1317–1318*, 1942), which he compiled jointly with Mr. J. P. Collas, contains a graceful obituary notice by Professor Theodore Plucknett. His preoccupation with the biographical aspect of legal history impelled him to write his *Sources and Literature of English Law* (1925), a mine of information and a model of lucid expression. Another book which, even had it been his only publication, would have marked him out as a jurist of the highest mark, is *Some Lessons from our Legal History* (1928). Although law was the absorbing interest of his life, he found time for much general reading. His *Charles Dickens as a Legal Historian* (1928) not only serves as one further demonstration of his mastery of the intricacies of legal procedure, but shows also that he had a knowledge of the works of the great novelist which even professors of English literature might envy.

Holdsworth was the most affectionate and convivial of men. From 1924 he was a bencher of Lincoln's Inn and took a great delight in the society of his fellow benchers. In Oxford he was much loved, alike by colleagues, by pupils, and by the college staff at All Souls and St. John's. No trouble was too great for him to take for the assistance of a young legal writer.

Holdsworth was knighted in 1929 and appointed to the Order of Merit in 1943. Honorary degrees were conferred upon him by the university of Cambridge (1926), the Northwestern University, Chicago, and the universities of Southern California (1927), Birmingham (1928), Edinburgh (1931), Upsala (1933), Calcutta (1938), and Leeds (1939). He was elected F.B.A. in 1922 and an honorary fellow of St. John's College in 1926. He died at Oxford 2 January 1944.

In 1903 Holdsworth married Jessie Annie Amelia Gilbert, daughter of Gilbert Wood, of Bickley, Kent. The only child of the marriage, Richard William Gilbert Holdsworth, had a meteoric career. He gained a first class in law, rowed in the Oxford boat three times against Cambridge (twice as stroke), and became Stowell civil law fellow of University College. He was killed on active service as a flight lieutenant in the Royal Air Force in 1942. An unsigned portrait of Holdsworth by a Belgian artist hangs in the rooms of the Vinerian professor at All Souls. There is a painting of the son by A. M. Campbell at University College.

[*The Times*, 3 January 1944; *Law Quarterly Review*, vol. lx, April 1944; private information; personal knowledge.]

H. G. HANBURY.

HOLLAND, SIR THOMAS HENRY (1868–1947), geologist and educational administrator, was born at Helston 22 November 1868, the son of John Holland and his wife, Grace Treloar, daughter of William Roberts, both of Cornish farming stock. Winning a national scholarship to the Normal School of Science and Royal School of Mines, South Kensington, he came under the influence of T. H. Huxley [q.v.] as also of J. W. Judd. He took the associateship in geology in 1888 having won the Murchison medal and prize in the previous year. After a short period as Berkeley fellow (1889) at the Owens College, Manchester, Holland joined the Geological Survey of India as assistant superintendent in October 1890. He became director of the Survey in February 1903; and on retiring from the service in 1910 he returned to Manchester to become professor of geology at the Victoria University.

During his earlier service in India, Holland devoted his attention mainly to mineralogy and petrology, and as curator of the Geological Museum and Laboratory in Calcutta he rearranged the rock collections in the mineral gallery. The geological work for which Holland is best known is his discovery of a suite of Archaean hypersthene-bearing rocks in southern India, which he termed the charnockite series after Job Charnock [q.v.], the founder of Calcutta, whose tomb in St. John's churchyard there is made of one of these rocks (hypersthene-granite). Similar suites have since been found in Antarctica, Africa, and elsewhere, and they continue to excite the interest of geologists because their origin is still a matter of controversy. Holland also wrote on the elaeolite-syenites of Sivamalai, the mica deposits of India, and the mica-apatite-peridotites of the coalfields of Bihar and Bengal. He recognized too the essential identity of bauxite and laterite. In addition Holland studied landslips in the Himalaya, and early attracted attention to himself by a successful prediction of the date of rupture of the dam of a lake caused by the Gohna landslip. He was elected F.R.S. in 1904 at the age of thirty-five.

After becoming director, Holland reorganized the Geological Survey of India, obtained increases of staff and emoluments, inaugurated surveys of the principal minerals of economic value in India, and secured for the department control of the assemblage, analysis, and publication of the statistics of mineral production in India. He also arranged the transfer to the Survey of the duty of advising the Government of India on the grant of mineral concessions. He initiated experiments into the relative durability of the marbles of India and Europe, the results of which caused Lord Curzon [q.v.], the viceroy, to agree that the Victoria Memorial Hall in Calcutta should be built of Indian marble similar to that used for the Taj Mahal. Holland also organized a diamond-drilling campaign in Singhbhum which led to the revival of the copper industry of that district. As a result of Holland's initiative as director, the Geological Survey—to use a geological metaphor—was faulted up into a position of esteem and importance in India greater than it had ever occupied before. For this work Holland was appointed K.C.I.E. in 1908.

Holland was one of the principal organizers and directors of India's military efforts in the war of 1914–18. He returned to India in 1916 as president of the Indian Industrial Commission; and in 1917 he became president of the newly formed Indian munitions board. He was appointed K.C.S.I. in 1918 and in the same year resigned his Manchester professorship. When the war ended the Indian munitions board eventually became the department of munitions and industries of the Government of India and in July 1920 Holland became a member of the viceroy's executive council. At the end of 1921 a difference with the viceroy (Lord Reading, q.v.) led to Holland's resignation; but both the secretary of state for India and the viceroy bore public testimony to the great services which Holland had rendered to India. This check in his career was of brief duration, for in 1922 he became rector of the Imperial College of Science and Technology, and thus began a career as an educational administrator. In that office his great achievement was the conclusion, in 1925, of the agreement with the university of London which led to the institution of the internal (special) B.Sc. degree for students of the College.

In 1929 Holland accepted appointment as principal and vice-chancellor of the university of Edinburgh, an office which he retained until he retired on reaching the age limit in 1944. During these fifteen years Holland's administrative experience and gifts enabled him to guide the university's policies with conspicuous success. He negotiated successfully the fusion of the university faculty of divinity with the New College of the Church of Scotland, and he also effected the affiliation of the Heriot-Watt College and the Royal (Dick) Veterinary College. In recognition of his services to the city Holland was a deputy-lieutenant for the county of the city, and he was also an honorary member of the Edinburgh Merchant Company.

Although Holland was almost continuously in harness for fifty-four years his energy and organizing ability also led him to take a leading part in the administration of various societies and institutions. In 1906, with William Henry Pickering, chief inspector of mines in India, he founded the Mining and Geological Institute of India, of which he became the first president. In England he was president of the Institutions of Mining Engineers (1915–16), of Mining and Metallurgy (1925–7, gold medal 1930), and of Petroleum Technologists (1925–7); of the Geological Society of London (1933–4, Bigsby medal 1913), and of the Mineralogical Society of London (1933–6); he was chairman of the Royal Society of Arts (1925–7, Albert medal 1939), and vice-president of the Royal Society (1924–5); elected a fellow of the Royal Society of Edinburgh in 1930 he was vice-president, 1932–5; he was chairman of the Empire Council of Mining and Metallurgical Institutions (1927–30); he served the British Association as sectional president in geology in 1914 and in education in 1926, and was president of the Association at its meeting in South Africa in 1929. At the time of his death he was president-designate of the eighteenth session of the International Geological Congress to be held in Great Britain in 1948. He received the honorary degrees of D.Sc. from Calcutta, Melbourne, and the Witwatersrand, and of LL.D. from Manchester, Glasgow, Edinburgh, Aberdeen, St. Andrews, and Queen's (Ontario) universities. He was an honorary fellow of the Asiatic Society of Bengal of which he was president in 1909.

Holland married in 1896 Frances Maud (died 1942), daughter of Charles Chapman, deputy commissioner in Oudh; they had one son and one daughter. In 1946 he married Helen Ethleen, daughter of Frank Verrall, of Bramley, near Guildford, who survived him.

A portrait by John Collier hangs in the rooms of the Asiatic Society of Bengal, Calcutta; and one by Stanley Cursiter at the university of Edinburgh.

[Sir Lewis Fermor in Obituary Notices of Fellows of the Royal Society, No. 17, November 1948; *Year Book of the Royal Society of Edinburgh, 1948 and 1949*, 1950; personal knowledge.]       L. L. FERMOR.

HOPE, JAMES FITZALAN, first BARON RANKEILLOUR (1870–1949), parliamentarian, was born in London 11 December 1870, the only surviving son of James Robert Hope-Scott, Q.C. [q.v.]. His mother, who died at his birth, was Lady Victoria Alexandrina FitzAlan-Howard, daughter of the fourteenth Duke of Norfolk [q.v.], and was his father's second wife.

His father died in 1873 and the boy with his three sisters went to live at Arundel with his grandmother the Dowager Duchess of Norfolk (Duchess Minna). Her son, the fifteenth Duke of Norfolk [q.v.], after his marriage, bought for her the estate of Heron's Ghyll at Uckfield which had been created by Coventry Patmore [q.v.]. There the children, who later reverted to their father's original name of Hope, grew up. One of Hope's sisters married Sir Nicholas O'Conor and another Wilfrid Ward [qq.v.]; the third became a nun. Hope himself became so attached to Heron's Ghyll that after the death of his grandmother he persuaded his uncle to keep the property so that he might purchase it when he came of age. In the meantime he was educated at the Oratory School, Birmingham, and went to Christ Church, Oxford. He then served as private secretary to his uncle when postmaster-general. After unsuccessfully contesting the Elland division of Yorkshire in 1892 and Pontefract in 1895, Hope entered Parliament in 1900 as Conservative member for the Brightside division of Sheffield, and held various parliamentary private secretaryships to Conservative ministers until the political landslide of 1906 when he lost his seat. He was returned unopposed, however, for the Central division of Sheffield at a by-election in 1908. On the formation of the coalition Government in 1915 he was one of the Conservative whips; from 1916 until 1919 he was a junior lord of the Treasury, and in 1919 he was appointed parliamentary and financial secretary to the Ministry of Munitions.

Whatever political aspirations Hope may have cherished—and he certainly cherished some—were put on one side in 1921, when, at the request of the prime minister, Lloyd George, he accepted the post of chairman of ways and means and deputy Speaker, and in that office he remained, except during the first Labour Government in 1924, until 1929. He was sworn of the Privy Council in 1922.

Although a fair but firm chairman, very well versed in the rules of parliamentary procedure, his tenure of office was marked by occasional clashes with members of the Labour Party new to the rules of the House, especially those led by James Maxton [q.v.]. In 1926 several Labour members put down a motion of censure criticizing his conduct in the chair, this being promptly countered from the Conservative side by a motion of confidence.

In 1928 J. H. Whitley [q.v.] resigned the speakership but Hope did not present himself for election for he had 'conceived the strongest repugnance to the life involved' with its isolation from fellow members of the House. He continued to act as chairman until the general election of 1929 when, having given up his Sheffield constituency, he stood for a Walthamstow division and was defeated.

Raised to the peerage as Baron Rankeillour, of Buxted, Sussex, in 1932, he served on the joint select committee on India, and with Lord Salisbury [q.v.] and others advocated a more gradual approach to the question of Indian reform. He took an active share in putting forward amendments during the passage of the bill in 1935, and was generally a regular contributor to the House of Lords debates, especially on the education bill of 1944 when he was an able representative of the Roman Catholic attitude.

Apart from his political life, he was a prominent layman in the Roman Catholic world with a membership of various Catholic associations. A strong sense of duty combined with deep religious conviction to make him 'the finest example of what used to be called the "*Garden of the Soul* Catholic"'. In appearance Hope markedly recalled his Howard ancestry but his mental make-up derived more perhaps from his Scots father. Although ill health prevented his taking a degree at Oxford, he was a man of intellect with a considerable knowledge of the classics.

Quotations from Horace and Juvenal came easily to his lips and to the end of his life he read the Epistles and Gospels in Greek. He had an astonishing memory and could quote whole sentences from books which he had not read for years. He delighted in ironic humour but save for literature he had no use for the arts, for he was not an imaginative man. The minor troubles of those around him passed unobserved but in more serious matters he was capable of deep perception, great kindliness, and much tactful charity. He disliked emotion or demonstrativeness of any kind and his reserved shy manner made him seem somewhat diffident to strangers and acquaintances. In fact, he was most determined and in his own spheres self-confident, although in a quite unaggressive way, for he was always equable in temper. He was, *au fond*, a solitary man, yet much beloved by his family circle and intimate friends.

Hope was a keen, indeed solemn, cricketer, and a reasonable though not enthusiastic shot, who cared little for his appearance and was amused to be mistaken for a Sussex farmer. On a winter evening he would return home after hunting, with mud on his cheeks and yet another dent in his 'topper', ready to argue about anyone from Socrates to 'Ranji'. His prejudices were many but his interests were wide. He travelled extensively in Europe, particularly in the Balkans about which he was very knowledgeable.

In 1892 Hope married Mabel Ellen (died 1938), daughter of Francis Henry Riddell, of Cheeseburn Grange, Northumberland, by whom he had three sons and one daughter. In 1941 he married Lady Beatrice Minny Ponsonby Kerr-Clark, daughter of the ninth Earl of Drogheda, and widow of Captain Struan Robertson Kerr-Clark, of the Seaforth Highlanders. He died in London 14 February 1949, was buried at Heron's Ghyll, and was succeeded by his eldest son, Sir Arthur Oswald James Hope (1897-1958).

[*Southwark Record*, April 1949; private information; personal knowledge.]

GEOFFREY THROCKMORTON.

HOPKINS, SIR FREDERICK GOWLAND (1861-1947), biochemist, was born 20 June 1861 at Eastbourne, whither his parents had moved on their marriage. They had both been born and brought up in the City of London, their fathers being engaged there in the bookselling and jewellery trades and living, as was then not uncommon, at their places of business. While Hopkins was still an infant his father, Frederick Hopkins, died, so that he had no memory of him; but the papers and instruments which he left were found to give evidence of a strong interest in natural science in which, indeed, he seems to have been a recognized leader of a group of City amateurs. Hopkins's father was a first cousin to Gerard Manley Hopkins, the Jesuit poet, and to Sir F. A. Abel [q.v.] who became a well-known expert on the chemistry of explosives.

The education of Hopkins, as arranged by his widowed mother, Elizabeth, and her brother, James Gowland, a City merchant, did not follow a conventional pattern. He was, for successive periods of a few years, at a dame's school at Eastbourne, at the City of London School, and then at an indifferent private school. After six months in an insurance office he was articled for three years to a consulting analyst in the City, where he was conscious of learning only something of an analyst's technique and dexterity, although these he may have undervalued. With a small legacy he entered himself at twenty for a course in chemistry at South Kensington under (Sir) Edward Frankland, and then, after a spell of analytical practice with the son P. F. Frankland [qq.v.], studied at University College, London, for the associateship of the Institute of Chemistry. His performance in this examination brought him to the notice of (Sir) Thomas Stevenson [q.v.], Home Office analyst and lecturer at Guy's Hospital on forensic medicine. Stevenson offered Hopkins a post as his assistant which he eagerly accepted. During his engagement in this more interesting and responsible analytical work, Hopkins began to read for his B.Sc. (London), cramming himself for matriculation and the subsequent examinations by private study, largely on daily journeys between Enfield and Guy's. He graduated in 1890, having in 1888 entered Guy's Hospital as a medical student, being immediately awarded the Gull research studentship. In 1891 he published in *Guy's Hospital Reports* a method for determining uric acid in urine, which remained standard practice for many years. And, meanwhile, the work on uric acid probably drew his attention to the scale-pigments in the wings of the Pieridae, a large family of common white and yellow butterflies.

Years before, when he was seventeen, he had published in the *Entomologist* some boyish observations on the purple vapour ejected by the bombardier beetle, which, as he later claimed, had made him already 'a biochemist at heart'. A preliminary note on the pigments of the Pieridae and their suggested relation to uric acid was published in 1889, and the full paper was communicated by (Sir) E. R. Lankester [q.v.] to the Royal Society and published in their *Philosophical Transactions* of 1895. Work in more recent years by Dr. Heinrich Wieland and others did not substantiate Hopkins's early suggestions concerning the relation of these pigments to uric acid; but towards the end of his life he returned to the subject, more than fifty years after his first note, and left a number of suggestive points which merit further inquiry.

After medical qualification, in 1894, Hopkins became an assistant in the department of physiology at Guy's, making contacts and friendships for life with E. H. Starling, (Sir) W. M. Bayliss [qq.v.], and others. To make ends meet he undertook a number of other part-time duties, including one which contributed to the formation of the Clinical Research Association. He found time, however, for important researches on halogen derivatives of proteins and on the crystallization of the albumins of blood serum and egg white—the latter published later, after his removal to Cambridge. This decisive step in his career was taken in 1898 when (Sir) Michael Foster [q.v.] invited Hopkins to become lecturer at Cambridge on chemical physiology—an aspect of the subject which had then fallen into neglect. The lectureship, however, carried but a meagre stipend for a married man and a prospective father, and Hopkins found it necessary to supplement his income by tutorial work at Emmanuel College, which later expanded into a full tutorship. This work, with the primary obligation of building, on scant foundations, a vigorous and inspiring course of advanced study on chemical physiology, left but a small margin of time for research. What little there was, however, was used by Hopkins to such purpose that there followed, in logical succession from an initial chance observation in his practical class, discoveries of the nature of the reagent in the Adamkiewicz colour-test for proteins, of the amino-acid tryptophane responsible for the reaction, and then of the nature of the amino-acids necessary

in a mammalian diet for maintenance and growth. Thus he was led to a clear apprehension that a diet containing only purified proteins, fats, carbohydrates, and salts, in whatever proportions and abundance, will not suffice for complete animal nutrition, but that traces, too small to contribute to energy value, of then unknown substances present in natural, fresh foods—now so widely known as vitamins—were also essential. It was later recognized that observations in this direction had been made earlier by others, but generally overlooked and forgotten; and Hopkins's own work on the matter suffered interruption for a year, at a critical period, through a temporary failure of health. It was generally recognized, however, that the paper which he published in 1912 in the *Journal of Physiology* was of primary importance, in giving precision and focus to ideas in this field and to methods of exploring them. The award of a Nobel prize in 1929, jointly to Hopkins and Eijkman of Holland, was widely applauded.

Hopkins's lectureship had been raised to a readership in 1902, but the growing needs of his family had made the tutorial post at Emmanuel College a necessary addition. During his year of illness in 1910, due to overwork, relief from this position came with the offer from Trinity College of a praelectorship, with no formal obligation but his own researches. Hopkins was thus enabled to embark on the studies in which during the rest of his life he endeavoured to unravel successive strands in the skein of intermediary metabolism—the complex of linked chemical reactions, catalysed by intracellular enzymes, which provides the physical and energetic basis for the process of life in general and of cellular respiration in particular. As marking successive stages in the development of this line of Hopkins's researches, we may note his work with (Sir) W. M. Fletcher [q.v.] on the contractile metabolism of voluntary muscle, on which they gave a Croonian lecture to the Royal Society in 1915; his isolation and characterization in 1921 of glutathione, a substance later identified as a tripeptide with a reversibly oxidizable SH group, enabling it to function as a carrier of oxygen; and the discovery of a widely distributed enzyme, xanthin-oxidase, catalysing the oxidation of the purine bases, xanthine and hypoxanthine, to uric acid. These, however, only typify successive phases, as it were, of a life's work and interest which, continuous in Hopkins himself, exercised a most remarkable stimulating influence on the group of eager investigators of a younger generation who gathered round him in later years. This growth of a 'school', with a far-reaching effect on the development of biochemistry in this country, began to be possible when in 1914 the removal of Cambridge physiology to a fine new building enabled Hopkins, who now became professor of biochemistry, to expand into its former quarters, from the almost incredibly restricted and unsuitable ones to which his work had until then been confined. A much wider opportunity came in 1921 when the trustees of the late Sir William Dunn furnished money to Cambridge for a new institute of biochemistry and the endowment of a chair in that subject, which Hopkins was to hold until 1943 within a few years of his death.

Except in the one year already mentioned, Hopkins, although small and very light in physique, enjoyed unusually good health for most of his long life. During his last few years, however, he was crippled by several increasing disabilities, including the loss of eyesight. He continued, however, until it was no longer physically possible, to go to his laboratory and there to pursue his researches with the help of others. If he had been asked to define the central aim of his life's work, he would have named the exploration of the chemistry of intermediary metabolism, and the establishment of biochemistry as a separate discipline concerned with this active chemistry of the life process, and not merely with its fuels and end-products. He lived to see the acceptance of this aim by a great army of investigators in all countries, and the identification of the parts played even by many of the vitamins in different cycles of this dynamic biochemistry.

Hopkins was a member of the first Medical Research Committee, appointed in 1913; he was knighted in 1925 and appointed to the Order of Merit in 1935. He was elected F.R.S. in 1905, was awarded a Royal medal in 1918, the Copley medal in 1926, and was president (1930–35). He was president of the British Association in 1933, and received many honorary degrees, including the D.Sc., Oxford (1922), and Sc.D., Cambridge (1933). In 1898 he married Jessie Anne (died 1956), daughter of the late Edward William Stevens, of Ramsgate. There were three children of the marriage: a son

who entered the medical profession and two daughters, one of whom, Jacquetta Hawkes (Mrs. J. B. Priestley), is well known as a writer on the archaeology of Great Britain and contributes to this SUPPLEMENT.

A portrait of Hopkins was painted by Meredith Frampton for the Royal Society; another by George Henry is in the Sir William Dunn Institute of Biochemistry at Cambridge, and a charcoal drawing by E. X. Kapp is in the Fitzwilliam Museum. Hopkins died in Cambridge 16 May 1947.

[Sir Henry Dale in *Obituary Notices of Fellows of the Royal Society*, No. 17, November 1948; typescript autobiography in the possession of the Royal Society; private information; personal knowledge.]

H. H. DALE.

HOPWOOD, FRANCIS JOHN STEPHENS, first BARON SOUTHBOROUGH (1860–1947), civil servant, was born in London 2 December 1860, the eldest son of James Thomas Hopwood, a barrister and brother of Charles Henry Hopwood [q.v.], by his wife, Anne Ellen, daughter of John Stone, D.L., of the Prebendal, Thame, Oxfordshire, and Long Crendon, Buckinghamshire. He was educated at King Edward VI School, Louth, of which his uncle, Canon Walter William Hopwood, was headmaster, and was admitted a solicitor in 1882. He became an assistant law clerk to the Board of Trade in 1885, assistant solicitor in 1888, and private secretary to the president of the Board in 1892. During these years his work took him several times to Canada, Newfoundland, and the United States, and it was on his return from Newfoundland in 1891 that he pointed out the opportunities for service in those parts to the Royal National Mission to Deep-Sea Fishermen on the board of which he sat. As a result (Sir) W. T. Grenfell [q.v.] went out to Labrador to found his medical mission. In 1893 Hopwood was appointed secretary to the railway department of the Board of Trade, and as British delegate attended the international railway congresses in London (1895) and Paris (1900). In 1901 he became permanent secretary to the Board where, as the Association of Chambers of Commerce was later to record, he rendered 'very valuable and distinguished services to the manufacturing and commercial interests of this country'. He also represented the Board at several colonial conferences, and served on the London traffic commission (1903), the canals and waterways commission (1906), and the commission on ocean freights and shipping 'rings' (1906).

In 1897 Hopwood, who had attracted the attention of Joseph Chamberlain, had acted as secretary to the chairman of the select committee of the House of Commons on the Jameson raid. It was by now apparent that he had special talents for working in committee and for undertaking individual tasks requiring tact and skill in negotiation. He was accordingly sent in 1906 to South Africa as a member of the committee under Sir J. West Ridgeway [q.v.] to consider the constitutions to be given to the Transvaal and the Orange River Colony. On his return, declining the offer of a railway commissionership, he became, in 1907, permanent under-secretary of state for the Colonies. In this capacity he accompanied the Prince of Wales to Canada in 1908 and the Duke of Connaught to South Africa in 1910 for the opening of the Union Parliament. He found time in 1909 to serve on the Royal Commission on electoral reform and to undertake railway arbitration; but he resigned from the Colonial Office at the end of 1910 on being pressed, against his inclination, to become vice-chairman of the Development Commission. He was far from unwilling to return to the Colonial Office temporarily in 1911 for the period of the Imperial Conference, for he preferred to be in the main stream of events and found the Commission something of a backwater. He left it the following year when he was sworn of the Privy Council and made an additional civil lord of the Admiralty, the first lord being his close acquaintance (Sir) Winston Churchill. At the Admiralty he concerned himself especially with contracts. The outbreak of war in 1914 brought additional duties with the chairmanship of the Board of Trade arbitration court, the grand committee on war trade dealing with contraband and blockade, and, from 1916, the war trade advisory committee. He was also from 1914 a member of the committee of the National Physical Laboratory.

An unusual and secret mission was entrusted to Hopwood in February 1917 when he visited Scandinavia to investigate rumours of Austrian peace proposals, but it proved impossible for him to make direct contact with responsible Austrian diplomats. A few months later he was elected secretary to the Irish convention, a post in which his somewhat similar experience in South Africa and his 'detached impartiality' were of value. He did not, however, share the optimistic views of his chairman, Sir Horace Plunkett [q.v.], and very rightly foresaw that 'there must be another episode of blood & tears & sorrow & shame before we can settle this difficult business'. Later, in a letter to The Times, 30 October 1919, he offered his services as an intermediary between the Sinn Fein leaders and the Government of this country. As The Times remarked, there 'was no one who could more ably and would more impartially play such a part', but the proposal, 'frankly and honestly made', was rejected by the Irish.

Meanwhile, in the autumn of 1917 Hopwood was raised to the peerage as Baron Southborough, of Southborough, Kent, and in the next year undertook the chairmanship of the committee which went to India to report on questions of franchise in the light of the proposed Montagu–Chelmsford reforms. In the years which followed Southborough, turning his attention to business, accepted a number of directorships, notably, in 1926, at a difficult time for armament firms, the chairmanship of Sir W. G. Armstrong, Whitworth & Co. He continued for some time to give his services on public matters, acting as chairman of committees of inquiry into the position of ex-servicemen in the Civil Service (1923), and economic and social development in East Africa (1924), as well as of committees on disinterested public-house management (1925) and British trade in China (1926). He was also at different times chairman of the British Empire League, the China Association, the National Council of Mental Hygiene, a governor and treasurer of Wellington College, and an honorary member of the Institution of Electrical Engineers.

In the House of Lords Southborough took no part in politics, but spoke occasionally on matters which aroused his concern, such as the effect of shell-shock, on which he also contributed two articles to The Times (2 and 5 September 1922) when the War Office committee of inquiry, over which he presided, issued its report. It was seldom, however, that he brought himself before the public eye, for he was correctly and essentially a civil servant, and, in his time, one of the most popular. Extremely capable himself, he was quick to appreciate the diversity of talent in others, and this made him an excellent chairman of committees. He had a fine presence and a quiet, dignified, yet friendly manner, behind which lay deep resources of knowledge, wisdom, and strength of character. He was not easy to know well for his temperament was cool and he never 'gave himself away'. A most successful career in business lay open to him, but he preferred to offer his abilities to the public service and to those of his friends, such as Lord Stamfordham [q.v.], who sought and valued his advice. He liked to feel that, although unseen, he was close to the centre of events, and that he was not without influence on the great.

In 1885 Hopwood married Alice, daughter of Captain William James Smith-Neill, R.A., and granddaughter of James George Smith Neill [q.v.]. They had one son and one daughter. His wife died in 1889 and in 1892 he married Florence Emily (died 1940), daughter of Lieutenant-General Samuel Black, C.S.I., C.I.E. They had one son and two daughters.

Hopwood was appointed C.M.G. (1893), C.B. (1895), K.C.B. (1901), K.C.M.G. (1906), G.C.M.G. (1908), G.C.B. (1916), G.C.V.O. (1917), and K.C.S.I. (1920). He died in London 17 January 1947 and was succeeded in his title by his elder son, James Spencer Neill (born 1889). Portraits by Sir William Llewellyn and Frank O. Salisbury are in the possession of the family. Another by Salisbury belongs to the Tilbury Dredging Company of which Southborough was chairman.

[Harold Nicolson, *King George V*, 1952; *The Times*, 18 January 1947; private information.]                    HELEN M. PALMER.

HORDER, PERCY (RICHARD) MORLEY (1870-1944), architect, was born at Torquay 18 November 1870, the eldest son of the Rev. William Garrett Horder, Congregational minister and hymnologist, by his wife, Mary Annie Morley. He was educated at the City of London School, and was then articled in the office of George Devey [q.v.].

About 1902 Horder's first designs for houses began to appear in the professional press. His work for the following ten years was mainly confined to houses; thereafter educational and commercial buildings appear among his commissions. From 1919 to 1925 he worked in partnership with Mr. Briant Poulter. He was elected F.R.I.B.A. in 1904, resigned in 1926, and resumed his membership from 1936 until his death. He became a member of the Art-Workers' Guild in 1916, but resigned in 1930.

Horder's numerous country-houses were erected chiefly in the home counties, the Cotswolds, and Dorset, but also farther afield. They were carefully planned, with due regard to practical needs, and often with considerable originality. The relation of house and garden was always borne in mind. His handling of building materials was extremely sensitive. For most of his houses he favoured the 'traditional' treatment fashionable in his day, with gables, dormers, prominent chimneys, mullioned windows, leaded lights, inglenooks, brick fireplaces, and panelling; but he seldom used half-timber. Among his best brick houses were a group built at Walton Heath (including one for Lloyd George), and others at Bexhill and at Hartfield in Sussex. At 'Greystoke', Warwick, and in several other cases he adopted rough-cast for exteriors; for houses at Charminster and Dorchester he used stone dressings with rough-casted walls; and at the Thatched House near Guildford he introduced elm weather-boarding and a thatch roof in conjunction with rough-cast. His domestic buildings in traditional stonework included houses at Stinchcombe, Stroud, Dursley, and Pitchford, and the Gyde Orphanage near Painswick, all in the Cotswolds; at Hawes in Yorkshire, at Arnside in Westmorland, and at Minehead in Somerset. Among his successful restorations were Nettlestead Place in Kent and Brimshot Farm on Chobham Common, Surrey. He also designed attractive groups of housing for officers' families at Morden, Surrey, and near Cambridge.

Horder's first educational building was Cheshunt College at Cambridge (1913), a college for training Congregational ministers, formerly located at Cheshunt in Hertfordshire. It is a charming 'traditional' design carried out in local sand-coloured bricks with stone dressings. The interior treatment is as tasteful as the exterior. Later work at Cambridge included Westcott House, extensions to Jesus College, and the large National Institute of Agricultural Botany (1919), where Horder adopted the style of Wren, with steep roofs and bold chimneys. This is one of his best works. At Oxford his new buildings for Somerville College (1934) complied very skilfully with the local tradition in stone; and in his little Institute for Research in Agricultural Economics he ingeniously incorporated Regency houses in a simple design.

About 1917 Horder began building shops for Boots, the chemists, the chief examples being at Bristol, Lincoln, Windsor, Brighton, and Regent Street (London). His friendship with Sir Jesse Boot (later Lord Trent, q.v.) led to the important commission for Nottingham University College, where in 1925–8 he produced a great group of stone buildings in Italian Renaissance style, with a campanile. Much of the credit for the dignified design of the London School of Hygiene and Tropical Medicine in Blooms-bury (1926–9) must be ascribed to his collaborator, Mr. Verner Owen Rees. Horder also built St. Christopher's School at Letchworth, showrooms for the Totten-ham District Power Company, and a village hall at Turnham Green. Among Congregational churches designed by him are those at Brondesbury Park (1913) of brick in Italian Romanesque style; at Penge (1911) of stone in an original variant of late Gothic; and at Mill Hill (1913), a very cheap but most attractive little building, now demolished. In 1925 he added a really beautiful 'Little Church' to his late father's Victorian-Gothic chapel on Ealing Green in a quasi-Byzantine style. In these last two instances, as in the chapel of Cheshunt College, he displayed a combination of perfect taste in form and colour with stark simplicity.

Horder possessed the artistic tempera-ment in excess, cultivated a Bohemian appearance, and exasperated his clients and contractors by his erratic, wayward, and unbusinesslike habits. Yet he managed to retain the goodwill of his patrons, and most of those who employed him pro-fessionally continued to entrust him with commissions and to recommend him to their friends.

Horder married in 1897 Rosa Catherine, daughter of Ebenezer Apperley, dental surgeon, of Stroud, Gloucestershire; they had two daughters. From about 1909 onwards he intermittently hyphened his name as Morley-Horder. He died at East Meon, Hampshire, 7 October 1944. His portrait by Clive Gardiner is at the National Institute of Agricultural Botany, Cambridge.

[*The Times*, 12 October 1944; *Builder*, 20 October 1944; *Architect*, 20 October 1944; *Journal* of the Royal Institute of British Architects, November 1944; private informa-tion.]     Martin S. Briggs.

HORNBY, CHARLES HARRY ST. JOHN (1867–1946), printer and connois-seur, was born at Much Dewchurch, Herefordshire, 25 June 1867, the eldest son of the Rev. Charles Edward Hornby, then a curate, by his wife, Harriet Catherine, daughter of the Rev. Henry Turton, vicar of Betley, Staffordshire. He was educated at Harrow, where he was second in the school, and New College, Oxford. A six-footer, he rowed for the university in 1890, the year Oxford won by a length. He gained a first class in classical moderations in 1888 and a third class in *literae humaniores* in 1890.

Called to the bar in 1892, Hornby gave up law that year to enter, at the invitation of W. F. D. Smith (later Viscount Hamble-den, q.v.), the firm of W. H. Smith & Son. He became a partner in 1894. The firm's revenues were at this period principally derived from railway bookstalls and advertising. With Hornby's support the chain of distinctive shops was established after 1905 and the wholesale trade expanded. Other developments included the extension of the firm's London printing business and the purchase in 1908 of the Arden Press which Hornby trans-ferred to Letchworth, where he also initiated a bookbinding department. These undertakings gave scope to his taste and judgement as a printer, and under his inspiration the reorganized press became the first large commercial business success-fully to incorporate the principles of the English private press movement into mechanical typographical production. Throughout the advance of the firm's interests, which rapidly ranked Smiths with the country's leading multiple stores, Hornby succeeded in main-taining the highest standards of design and workmanship, and in preserving the loyalties which mark a family business.

In his spare time Hornby indulged his interest in printing as an art. At the age of twenty-seven he installed a hand press at Ashendene, Hertfordshire, where his father was then living. His love of books and a desire to use his hands were quickened by a visit in 1895 to William Morris [q.v.], when he saw the Kelmscott Press at work on its folio Chaucer. Hornby's first production (1895) was the *Journal of Joseph Hornby*, his grandfather. The Ashendene Press enjoyed a longer life than any other English private press, and earned a reputation hardly less illustrious than that of the Kelmscott Press. During forty years, until it closed in 1935, it produced forty major works and a number of minor pieces.

Hornby used first the Fell types of the Oxford University Press, but, like Morris, he sought to have his private type. Through an introduction from (Sir) Sydney Cockerell he met (Sir) Emery Walker [q.v.] and their combined knowledge enabled Hornby to gratify his ambition. 'Subiaco', his first personal typographical possession, was the result. Based on the type of Sweynheym and Pannartz (Subiaco, 1465), it was first used for a text of Dante's *Inferno* printed according to the recension of the original by Edward Moore [q.v.]; it was characteristic of Hornby to pay attention to the critical value of a selected text. The whole edition of 135 copies on paper and 14 on vellum was worked solely by Hornby and issued in 1902 from Shelley House, Chelsea, to which the Ashendene Press had been removed in 1899. There were fifteen illustrations cut on wood, a craft to which the Press was faithful throughout its career. In 1927 Hornby had cut for his *Don Quixote* another type, the 'Ptolemy', based on the face used by F. Holle for his Ptolemy (Ulm, 1482).

Hornby began in 1903 to collect medieval and Renaissance manuscripts and printed books (his vigorous script antedated his taste for Renaissance calligraphy). He was an active member of the Roxburghe Club after 1911, and was appointed a trustee of the Wallace Collection in 1933 and of the British Museum in 1936. In 1934 he was prime warden of the Goldsmiths' Company.

He married in 1898 Cicely, daughter of Charles Barclay, of Bayford, Hertfordshire, a director of the National Provincial Bank; they had three sons and two daughters. He died at his home, Chantmarle, Dorchester, 26 April 1946. There is a portrait at Strand House by (Sir) William Coldstream, and a chalk drawing by Sir William Rothenstein is in the National Portrait Gallery.

[*The Times*, 27 April 1946; published by W. H. Smith & Son for private circulation: *C. H. St. J. Hornby, Jubilee Celebrations*, 1943, *C. H. St. J. Hornby, an Anthology of Appreciations*, 1946, and *The Story of W. H. Smith & Son*, 1949; *A Descriptive Bibliography of the Books Printed at the Ashendene Press, 1895-1935*, written, printed, and published by C. H. St. J. Hornby, 1935; private information; personal knowledge.]

STANLEY MORISON.

HOWARD, EDMUND BERNARD FITZALAN-, first VISCOUNT FITZALAN OF DERWENT (1855-1947), was born in London 1 June 1855, the third, and second surviving, son of Henry Granville Fitz-Alan-Howard, Earl of Arundel, who became fourteenth Duke of Norfolk [q.v.] in the following year. He was educated at the Oratory School, Birmingham, where he gained a lifelong reverence for its founder Cardinal Newman [q.v.]. In 1876 he assumed the surname of Talbot under the terms of the will of the seventeenth Earl of Shrewsbury, and until his elevation to the peerage in 1921 was known as Lord Edmund Talbot. His early career and way of life was that of a regular officer in the 11th Hussars, and in those days he hunted and shot, although in later years his interest in sport waned. Even as a young man he had political aspirations, and after three unsuccessful attempts to enter Parliament, he was returned unopposed at a by-election in 1894 as Conservative member for Chichester, a constituency he continued to represent until 1921.

He returned to the army to take part in the South African war, served on the staff of Lord Roberts [q.v.], and was appointed to the D.S.O. After the war he devoted himself once more to politics and resumed his work as private secretary to St. John Brodrick (later the Earl of Midleton, q.v.). In 1905 he was a junior lord of the Treasury and in 1915 became joint parliamentary secretary. From 1913 to 1921 he was chief Conservative whip, first in opposition and then under the two coalition Governments. His manifest integrity, and his ability to combine tact with firmness, made him a notable success in this post. Before the outbreak of war in 1914 he played a leading part in the conversations which led to the Conservative leaders assuring Asquith of their support if the Government were compelled to declare war on Germany.

The Government of Ireland Act, 1920, made it possible, for the first time since the Reformation, for a Roman Catholic to be viceroy of Ireland, and in 1921, on the advice of Lloyd George, whose respect and affection he had won, Talbot was appointed to that post and raised to the peerage as Viscount FitzAlan of Derwent. At the same time he resumed his paternal surname of FitzAlan-Howard. In the words of (Sir) Winston Churchill, 'Devotion to public duty alone inspired him to undertake so melancholy a task' as that of viceroy. Few of his predecessors could have been faced with comparable problems, but he met them with courage and firmness. A Catholic viceroy, as an Irishman remarked, was 'no more welcome than a new Catholic hangman', and his difficulties would seem to have been increased rather than lessened by his religion. The 'Black and Tan' policy which FitzAlan detested, had already been discarded as unacceptable to British public opinion, but military action had to be taken to stem the tide of disorder and assassination. *Malgré lui* FitzAlan found himself at the head of a military Government. He soon came to see that order in Ireland could be restored only by military action on an enormous and continuing scale or by coming to some terms with the Sinn Fein leaders. In spite of his strong unionist convictions, he reluctantly advocated the latter course, which also became the view of the Government in the summer of 1921. The rest of the year was spent in long-drawn-out negotiations. On the establishment of the Irish Free State FitzAlan retired in 1922 in favour of T. M. Healy [q.v.], a political opponent but a personal friend.

FitzAlan was then a man of sixty-seven, and he never again sought office. Punctilious in his attendance in the House of Lords, he frequently intervened in debate, notably in 1930 on the occasion of the dispute between Lord Strickland [q.v.] and the Church authorities in Malta, and again in 1935 when he vigorously opposed the Government of India bill. He was always keenly concerned about the defence of the country and in July 1936 was one of the Conservative representatives of the House of Lords on a deputation to the prime minister, Baldwin, to urge the necessity of rearmament under the threat of Nazi Germany. His interest in politics never abated and through his wide circle of friends he wielded considerable influence. He was on intimate terms with King George V, with whom he had many characteristics in common. Among his particular friends were Baldwin, the fourth Marquess of Salisbury, and Lord Craigavon [qq.v.]. Most of the Conservative leaders—and many other notable figures—might be found at his week-end parties at Cumberland Lodge, in Windsor Great Park, which the King had placed at his disposal in 1924, FitzAlan's own residence in Derbyshire, Derwent Hall, having been acquired under a water scheme.

It is not only, and perhaps not primarily, as a politician that FitzAlan should be remembered. He was a profoundly religious man, holding his Catholic faith with robust simplicity. Two of his eight sisters entered religion, one as a Carmelite and the other as a Sister of Charity; a third was the mother of Lord Rankeillour [q.v.], himself a prominent Roman Catholic. After the death in 1917 of his brother, the fifteenth Duke of Norfolk [q.v.], Talbot acted as deputy earl marshal during the minority of his nephew and became the leading Roman Catholic layman in the country. Innumerable duties fell to him which he discharged with unfailing conscientiousness. For many years he was president of the Catholic Union of Great Britain. He was an intimate personal friend of Cardinal Vaughan [q.v.] and it is known that in later days Cardinal Hinsley [q.v.] relied on his judgement. Successive Governments sought his advice where Catholic interests and sentiments were concerned. His good-humoured yet clear statement of his point of view did much to remove prejudice against Catholics in public life, and he himself received signal honours. He was sworn of the Privy Council in 1918, appointed M.V.O. in 1902 and G.C.V.O. in 1919, and K.G. in 1925. An Englishman to the core, he was nevertheless sympathetic to his Irish co-religionists, and there can be little doubt that his influence with his friend, Lord Craigavon, was to the benefit of the Catholic minority in Northern Ireland.

Although his powers of mind were much above the ordinary, FitzAlan was not an intellectual man. The arts meant little to him, and, being eminently sociable, he preferred conversation to reading. He had, however, a wide experience of men and matters, and was a shrewd and charitable judge of human nature. His personal charm, somehow enhanced by a certain brusquerie of manner, had its roots in his extraordinary integrity and sense of duty, allied to kindliness and a homely sense of humour. Short, stocky, and erect, he remained a soldier to the last. Although not well known to the general public, his influence with the Catholic community was very considerable, and his name was held by them in great affection and respect. Few men have left a more endearing memory to those who knew them.

In 1879 he married Mary Caroline (died 1938), daughter of Montagu Arthur

Bertie, Lord Norreys, who became seventh Earl of Abingdon. They had one son, Henry Edmund (born 1883), who succeeded to the title, and one daughter. FitzAlan lived to the great age of nearly ninety-two and it was only in the last year or two of his life that his sight and hearing began to fail. He died 18 May 1947 at Cumberland Lodge, and was buried at Arundel, where there is a portrait of him by (Sir) Oswald Birley.

[Private information; personal knowledge.]
RANKEILLOUR.

HOWARD, LESLIE (1893-1943), actor, producer, and film director, whose original name was LESLIE HOWARD STEINER, was born at 31 Westbourne Road, Forest Hill, London, 3 April 1893. He was the eldest son of Ferdinand Steiner, a stockbroker's clerk, by his wife, Lilian Blumberg. He was educated locally in Dulwich and then became a bank clerk. On the outbreak of war in 1914 he enlisted and was a second lieutenant in the Northamptonshire Yeomanry from March 1915 until May 1916 when he resigned his commission. During his army service an early interest in theatricals increased, and on returning to civilian life he sought a professional engagement, adopted the name by which he was known henceforth, and made his first appearance as a professional actor in 1917, touring the provinces in the part of Jerry in Peg o' My Heart. He made his first appearance in London at the New Theatre, 14 February 1918, in the small part of Ronald Herrick, in the 'idyll of suburbia', The Freaks by Sir Arthur Pinero [q.v.].

Howard continued to act in London until the summer of 1920, appearing notably in Our Mr. Hepplewhite, Mr. Pim Passes By, and The Young Person in Pink. He then went to the United States, first appearing in New York at the Henry Miller Theatre in November 1920 in Just Suppose. He continued to act in America until 1926, appearing successfully in a variety of plays, notably as Henry in Outward Bound, and as Napier Harpenden in The Green Hat. He returned to London for a short engagement in 1926, but went back to New York to play in Her Cardboard Lover, and in Escape by John Galsworthy [q.v.]. Subsequently he divided his time between New York and London. He played Peter Standish in Berkeley Square in both cities. His only other performance of note in London was at the Lyric Theatre in October 1933 when he appeared as Shakespeare in This Side Idolatry. He played the leading part, Alan Squier, in The Petrified Forest which he presented with Gilbert Miller in 1935 at the Broadhurst Theatre, New York, and in November 1936 appeared as Hamlet at the Imperial Theatre, New York, in his own production which, however, proved somewhat of a disappointment.

Thereafter Howard devoted his talents to films, both as actor and director, and it was in this medium (in which he first appeared in 1930) that he gained full recognition. As a film actor he made notable successes in Outward Bound, Smilin' Through, Berkeley Square, The Scarlet Pimpernel, The Petrified Forest, Pygmalion, of which he was co-director, Gone with the Wind, 49th Parallel (a war film), and many others. After the outbreak of war in 1939 he took to production and was part-producer of some of the best British war films: in Pimpernel Smith and The First of the Few he also played the leading part, and he was raconteur in The Gentle Sex, a story of the A.T.S. A film of the nursing profession, The Lamp Still Burns, was released after his death. The unescorted passenger aeroplane in which he was returning from a visit to Spain and Portugal under the auspices of the British Council was shot down by the enemy on 1 June 1943.

Leslie Howard was a polished actor, quiet in his method, with a certain wistfulness which added to his natural charm of manner and intelligence. His voice was charming, gracious, and beautifully modulated. In private life he was of a rather shy and retiring nature, but he was extremely popular. He married in 1916 Ruth Evelyn, daughter of Henry William Martin, laundry manager, of Colchester; they had one son and one daughter. A portrait of Leslie Howard by R. G. Eves is in the National Portrait Gallery, and another by the same artist in the Huddersfield Art Gallery.

[Who's Who in the Theatre; private information; personal knowledge.] JOHN PARKER.

HOWARD DE WALDEN, eighth BARON, and fourth BARON SEAFORD (1880-1946), writer, sportsman, and patron and lover of the arts. [See SCOTT-ELLIS, THOMAS EVELYN.]

HUDDLESTON, Sir HUBERT JERVOISE (1880–1950), soldier and administrator, was born at Thurston, Suffolk, 20 January 1880, the second son of Thomas Jervoise Huddleston, of Little Haugh, Norton, Suffolk, who had a distinguished career at Eton and Christ Church, Oxford, and died in 1885. His mother, Laura Josselyn, was a sister of Colonel F. Josselyn, chief constable of Bedford.

Huddleston was educated at Bedford and Felsted schools. Determined by any means to join the army, he enlisted in the Coldstream Guards in 1898 and in 1900 was drafted to the 2nd battalion and sent to South Africa. In May 1900 he was commissioned in the Dorsetshire Regiment of which he eventually became colonel in 1933. From 1903 to 1908 he served with the West African Frontier Force, and in 1909, with the rank of captain, went to the Sudan, with which his name will always be associated. At first he was employed in administrative work in the turbulent district of the Nuba mountains, but at his own desire he joined the 10th Sudanese battalion of the Egyptian Army and took part, in 1910 and again in 1914, in punitive expeditions in the same area. He was awarded the M.C. in 1914.

After the outbreak of war Huddleston remained in the Egyptian Army in command of the Camel Corps, one of its finest units, and played a leading part in the expedition sent in 1916 to subdue the rebellious Sultan of Darfur, Ali Dinar. After the occupation of El Fasher, it was Huddleston who, sent to establish a post at Dibbis, ignored the risk of exceeding his orders and taking the initiative ran the Sultan to earth in the far south. This ended the rebellion and Huddleston was appointed to the D.S.O. in 1917. At the close of 1916 he temporarily severed his connexion with the Egyptian Army and commanded a brigade during the campaign of Sir Edmund (later Viscount) Allenby [q.v.] in Palestine, and he was appointed C.M.G. in 1918. Subsequently he held staff appointments in Iraq and Persia, but in 1922 he found himself back in Egypt where disturbances had broken out. He rejoined the Egyptian Army in 1923 as chief staff officer and adjutant-general under Sir Lee Stack [q.v.]. When Stack was murdered in 1924 it fell to Huddleston to enforce the evacuation of the Sudan by Egyptian troops and to suppress the mutiny which they had engineered in a Sudanese battalion. In 1925 the Sudanese and Arab units were reorganized as the Sudan Defence Force with Huddleston, who was appointed C.B., as its first commandant ('Kaid el 'Amm') with the local rank of major-general. He held this post, and that of commanding officer in the Sudan, until 1930. As a member of the governor-general's council during this period he became familiar with the political and administrative problems which were, a decade later, to become his own responsibility.

Towards the end of 1930 Huddleston again left the Sudan, to take command of the 14th Infantry brigade. In 1933 he was promoted major-general and from 1934 until 1938 commanded districts in India. He was then placed on retired pay and appointed lieutenant-governor of the Royal Hospital, Chelsea, but was recalled to active service in 1940 and became commanding officer in Northern Ireland. Towards the end of the year, however, he was appointed governor-general of the Sudan, which was threatened with an Italian invasion from Eritrea. No better appointment could have been made, for his name was honoured and respected throughout the whole vast country. For seven years he held this post, fearlessly countering Egyptian claims and intrigues, and maintaining with determination the rights of the Sudanese to eventual self-government.

Huddleston was promoted K.C.M.G. in 1940 and G.C.M.G. in 1947, and was appointed G.B.E. in 1946. In 1947 he retired, but he did not live long to enjoy the rest he had earned, for he died in London 2 October 1950.

Huddleston's main characteristics were his absolute straightness and simplicity. His strength of character and courage earned him respect and admiration; his modesty and kindness of heart, combined with a whimsical sense of humour, brought affection. He was a great reader and had the most variegated store of knowledge.

In 1928 he married Constance Eila, daughter of the late Frederick Hugh Mackenzie Corbet, advocate-general of Madras; there was one daughter of the marriage.

[War Office records; Cyril Falls, (Official) *History of the Great War. Military Operations, Egypt and Palestine, 1914–18*, 3 vols., 1928–30; private information; personal knowledge.]

H. A. MacMichael.

HUNT, DAME AGNES GWENDO-
LINE (1866–1948), pioneer in work
amongst cripples, was born in London
31 December 1866, the seventh child of
Rowland Hunt, of Boreatton Park,
Baschurch, Shropshire, and his wife,
Florence Marianne, daughter of R. B.
Humfrey, of Kibworth Hall, Leicester-
shire, and Stoke Albany House, North-
amptonshire. Her father was a cousin of
G. W. Hunt [q.v.].

Her early childhood was spent at home
in a large country house. The stern
régime of Victorian parents was partially
mitigated by the companionship of ten
brothers and sisters, and many horses,
dogs, and other pets. At the age of ten
she developed osteomyelitis, which left
her severely crippled for the rest of
her life. Afterwards she looked back with
gratitude to the spartan attitude of her
family and especially of her mother towards
her as a cripple. She was never allowed
to consider herself an invalid, and had to
share in every way possible in the normal
life of her brothers and sisters, so learning
early the self-reliance and independence
which she was later to instil into so many
of her fellow cripples. Her mother was
a woman of indomitable spirit and considerable eccentricity. After the death of
her husband she departed to Australia
with several of her children, including
Agnes, with the intention of buying an
island and rearing Angora goats. Fortunately for Agnes, who bore the brunt of most
of her mother's enterprises, the goats did
not materialize, and the family gradually
drifted back to England, the elder sisters
all to be married, one to (Sir) Frederic
Kenyon, an old friend and neighbour.
Agnes, after an absence of some years, the
last spent with a brother in Tasmania,
returned to embark upon a long-cherished
ambition to become a nurse. Hospital
after hospital refused to take her on
account of her lameness. The one year's
course of a 'lady-pupil' took her three
years to accomplish owing to repeated
breakdowns in health, but at last she
succeeded in obtaining her certificate.
She went on to qualify as a Queen's nurse
and also in midwifery and spent several
years as a district nurse during which she
had experience of epidemics of smallpox
and typhoid.

After a visit with Agnes to America,
her mother announced that she intended
henceforth to live with her daughter and
suggested that she should open a convalescent home for children in Baschurch.

This she did in 1900 with her friend Emily
Selina Goodford. From the first the
Baschurch Home exerted a magnetic
attraction for cripples, for whom it was in
no way suited by reason of its stairs. To
get over this difficulty three-sided wooden
sheds were erected in the garden, and thus
Agnes Hunt founded the first open-air
hospital for cripples in the world.

Four years later (Sir) Robert Jones
[q.v.], who had recently operated on
Agnes, became consulting surgeon to the
Home. Together they revolutionized the
treatment and mentality of cripples and
the attitude of the general public towards
them. On his visits to Baschurch Jones
brought with him distinguished surgeons
from all over the world and the remarkable
results which were being achieved caused
similar hospitals to spring up abroad.
During the war of 1914–18 soldiers were
also housed in open sheds and tents and
in 1918 Agnes Hunt was awarded the
Royal Red Cross in recognition of her
services. She was appointed D.B.E. in
1926.

In 1921, with the help of a Red Cross
grant, the hospital was moved to Oswestry
where it became known as the Robert
Jones and Agnes Hunt Orthopaedic
Hospital. Gradually during the last years
of the war she had started a network of
after-care clinics which were held in the
small market towns of Shropshire and the
surrounding counties. These clinics were
originally intended to obviate the difficulty of taking cripples long distances by
train for out-patient supervision; soon they
also became centres for preventive treatment. In them, too, Agnes Hunt recognized an opportunity for bringing the
problem of cripples to the public notice,
and around each clinic she formed a
committee of local people working for the
social welfare of cripples as distinct from
their treatment. Before very long most
other orthopaedic hospitals adopted
similar systems.

Agnes Hunt early realized that treatment was not enough. Cripples must be
given independence and made to feel the
equal of their more fortunate fellows.
This could only be achieved by training
them to become self-supporting in competition with their able-bodied rivals.
To this end, in 1927 she founded the
Derwen Cripples' Training College, near
Oswestry, where boys and girls were
taught a variety of trades, best suited to
their disability. Before she died Agnes
Hunt was able to see many of her trainees

successfully employed in the open market, and supporting not only themselves but a wife and family.

A woman of outstanding personality and great vision, Agnes Hunt devoted her life to the cause of cripples with an absolute singleness of purpose, great determination, and a dauntless courage in meeting not only her own physical handicaps and incessant pain, but also the difficulties and set-backs which beset the path of every pioneer. Her autobiography, *This is My Life* (1938), reveals her rollicking humour and tremendous sense of fun and joy of life, with which she had the power to imbue almost everyone with whom she came in contact. She was also keenly interested in all social problems, in politics, world affairs, and natural history. Owing to frequent illness she had little regular education, but she had read widely and had a great love of English verse—much of which she would quote at great length. She had a serene and childlike religious faith—the outcome of some years of doubt and struggle—and an unfaltering conviction that the God whom she tried to serve in service to others would never fail her. She died, unmarried, at Baschurch 24 July 1948.

[*Burke's Landed Gentry*, 1952; Dame Agnes Hunt, *This is My Life*, 1938; private information; personal knowledge.]

AVICE E. SANKEY.

HURST, SIR ARTHUR FREDERICK (1879–1944), physician, was born at Bradford 23 July 1879, the third son of William Martin Hertz, wool merchant, by his wife, Fanny May, daughter of Julius Baruch Hallé, merchant, of Clapham Park, London. Sir Gerald Hurst was his elder brother. He was educated at Bradford and Manchester grammar schools and at Magdalen College, Oxford, where he was awarded a demyship and placed in the first class in the final honour school of physiology (1901). From Oxford he went to Guy's Hospital with a university science scholarship and qualified B.M. (Oxon.) in 1904, winning gold medals in medicine and surgery, and D.M. in 1907. He was awarded the Radcliffe travelling fellowship in 1905 which sent him to study in Munich, Paris, and the United States, and in 1909 the Radcliffe prize. He was appointed assistant physician to Guy's Hospital, in charge of the neurological department, at the age of twenty-seven and remained on the staff,

as physician from 1918, until his retirement as senior physician in 1939, when he became consulting physician to the hospital, and a member of the board of governors.

Together with (Sir) James Mackenzie and (Sir) Thomas Lewis [qq.v.], Hurst was largely responsible for starting the disinterested study of clinical phenomena by the methods of exact physiology, which was later to become known as clinical science. His first major piece of work was on the sensibility of the alimentary tract (Goulstonian lectures, 1911); in it he showed that the common stimulus for the production of pain is muscular tension. During the war of 1914–18 he was consulting physician at Salonika and later in charge, from 1916 to 1918, of the neurological section at Netley, and, 1918–19, of the Seale Hayne Military Hospital for war neuroses, where he achieved remarkable results in the treatment of shell-shock by suggestion. In 1916 he changed his name to Hurst by deed poll. After the war he continued his studies on the alimentary tract with particular reference to the new method of radiological examination, and established the basis for the rational treatment of peptic ulcer and constipation. He introduced the conception of achalasia, or absence of relaxation, to explain troublesome dilatations of the oesophagus, the bowel, and the ureters, and devised special methods for their treatment. He maintained that pernicious anaemia and sub-acute combined degeneration of the cord were primarily diseases of the alimentary tract and was naturally delighted when his ideas were confirmed after the introduction of liver treatment.

Hurst soon became dissatisfied with the conditions of a single-handed consulting practice in London and he concentrated his work at New Lodge Clinic, Windsor Forest, where he built up a team of colleagues for the investigation of disease by modern methods. Another of his great interests was the *Guy's Hospital Reports*, which he edited from 1921 to 1939 and increased greatly in size and scope. Deafness spared him from committee work and examining, but he was an enthusiastic member of the Association of Physicians of Great Britain and Ireland, of which he was made an honorary member, and he was founder of the Medical Pilgrims Club, with which he made many visits abroad. He was elected

F.R.C.P. (London) in 1910, and was Goulstonian (1911) and Croonian (1920) lecturer, Harveian orator (1937), and Moxon medallist (1939) of the College. He was president of the medical section of the Royal Society of Medicine (1927–9), and of the International Society of Gastro-Enterology, and an honorary member of many foreign medical societies. In 1935 he was awarded the Osler memorial medal, and in 1937 he was knighted. His retirement from Guy's Hospital in 1939 coincided with the beginning of the war. New Lodge Clinic was disbanded and Hurst went to live at Oxford, where he taught in the newly established clinical school. He was a master of the art of clinical demonstration and drew large audiences to his ward rounds at Guy's Hospital and the Radcliffe Infirmary. His ideas were ready at his finger tips and he was prepared to talk on any subject within his specialty at short notice and without notes.

Throughout his life Hurst had intractable asthma, which he bore with great courage, and he died suddenly from this disease at Birmingham 17 August 1944.

Hurst married in 1912 Cushla, daughter of Frederick Riddiford, of Hawera, New Zealand; one son and two daughters were born of the marriage. A portrait in oils by Sir Hubert von Herkomer (1912) and another in crayon by (Sir) William Rothenstein (1927) are in the possession of the family.

[Sir Arthur Hurst, *A Twentieth Century Physician*, 1949; *Guy's Hospital Reports*, vol. lxxxix, No. 4, 1939 (bibliography), and vol. xciv, Nos. 1 and 2, 1945; personal knowledge.]                         L. J. WITTS.

HUTCHINSON, FRANCIS ERNEST (1871–1947), scholar and canon of Worcester, was born at Forton, near Gosport, Hampshire, 17 September 1871, the third son of the vicar, the Rev. Charles Pierrepont Hutchinson (who was descended from the father of John Hutchinson, the regicide, q.v.), by his wife, Louisa, daughter of the Rev. Alleyne Higgs Barker, vicar of Rickmansworth. Hutchinson was educated at Lancing and Trinity College, Oxford, where he read modern history, graduating with a second class in 1894. He was ordained deacon in 1896 and priest in 1897. After some years of schoolmastering at Radley (1895–1900) and Cooper's Hill College (1900–3) he was

appointed, in 1904, chaplain of King's College, Cambridge, where he remained until 1912, when he became vicar of Leyland, Lancashire. He spent eight years in this industrial parish before returning to Oxford as secretary to the university's delegacy for extra-mural studies, a post which he held with great success from 1920 to 1934. In 1934 Hutchinson accepted a canonry of Worcester, thus severing for a time his association with Oxford, to which he had become bound more closely by his appointment in 1928 to be chaplain, and, in March 1934, to be a fellow, of All Souls. At Worcester Hutchinson was a universally popular member of the chapter, and his influence extended beyond the close: his home was described as 'a centre of pilgrimage to all lovers of art, music, and good causes in Worcester and beyond'. In 1943 he resigned his canonry and returned to Oxford, where he devoted himself to literary work, maintaining none the less his old associations, notably with Lady Margaret Hall (he was a member of its council for more than twenty-three years) and All Souls, where he again enjoyed and enriched the society of the common-room as a quondam fellow. He was still mentally and physically active when he died suddenly at Oxford of heart failure 21 December 1947.

Hutchinson was an Anglican of the old school, who felt his affinity with the Caroline divines he studied; but he was tolerant in outlook and liberal in his activities, and he worked indefatigably for the cause of adult education in the Workers' Educational Association. Diminutive in person, bright-eyed, and in later years white-haired, with an engagingly naïve vivacity of manner, he made many friends by his charm and was successful as a lecturer alike with learned and with simple audiences. But it is as a student of Caroline poetry that Hutchinson claims remembrance; he was a modest, careful, sensitive scholar in that field, as is shown by his contributions to the Cambridge *Bibliography* and *History of English Literature*; his edition of the works of George Herbert (1941) was definitive; and his life of Henry Vaughan (1947) was a model of its kind. He published also *Christian Freedom* (1920, the Hulsean lectures of 1918–19) and *Milton and the English Mind* (1946), and at his death was at work on a life of John Donne. After his death appeared a brief study of *Cranmer and the English Reformation* (1951) and an account of *Medieval Glass at All Souls College* (1949) based by Hutchinson on the notes of G. M. Rushforth.

Hutchinson was made a D.Litt. of Oxford in 1942 and elected F.B.A. in 1944. In 1904 he married Julia Margaret, daughter of Colonel George Adam Crawford, R.A., by whom he had one son and one daughter: all survived him.

[*The Times*, 23 and 30 December 1947; private information; personal knowledge.]

JOHN SPARROW.

HUTCHINSON, RICHARD WALTER JOHN HELY-, sixth EARL OF DONOUGHMORE (1875–1948), chairman of committees of the House of Lords. [See HELY-HUTCHINSON.]

HYDE, DOUGLAS (1860–1949), Gaelic revivalist, poet, and first president of Eire, was born at Frenchpark, county Roscommon, 17 January 1860, the third son and fourth child of the Rev. Arthur Hyde, later rector of Tibohine and canon of Elphin, by his wife, Elizabeth, daughter of the Ven. John Orson Oldfield, archdeacon of Elphin. Hyde's family, of Berkshire stock, had received a grant of land in county Cork from Queen Elizabeth, and later produced a succession of clergymen in counties Cork, Kerry, Leitrim, and Roscommon. Douglas Hyde spent his boyhood at his father's rectory; and with a keen taste for reading and languages was largely self-taught. Irish, although rapidly dying out, was still spoken among the rough hillsides and lakes of Roscommon; Hyde learnt it orally from old native speakers and recorded a wealth of folk-lore and lyric poetry which they taught him. He entered Trinity College, Dublin, in 1880 and the following year won the Bedell scholarship intended to encourage future preachers in Irish. He graduated with a large gold medal in modern literature in 1884; obtained a first class in the final divinity examination in 1885; won a special theology prize in 1886; but then transferred to the law school and took his LL.D. in 1888. He won the Vice-Chancellor's prize for English verse in 1885, for prose in 1886, and both prizes in 1887. Besides his command of Latin, Greek, and Hebrew, he was fluent in French and German as well as Irish. In 1891 he went for a year to Canada as interim professor of modern languages in the university of New Brunswick.

Returning to Ireland he made his home at Ratra Park in Roscommon, and devoted himself to literary studies and the preservation of the Irish language. He had published his first collection of folk-tales, gathered in the west, in 1889. His *Love Songs of Connacht*, with verse translations by himself, followed in 1893. That year saw the foundation of the Gaelic League by a group of Gaelic scholars who elected Hyde as president at their first meeting in Dublin. Thereafter he undertook a propaganda campaign all over Ireland to arouse interest in the language. His verse translations, which showed a real lyric gift and often diverged widely from the originals, have been included in many anthologies of English verse. His folk-tales aroused the interest of contemporary Irish writers including W. B. Yeats, Lady Gregory, George Russell, and George Moore [qq.v.]. He also displayed a surprising power of popular leadership, with remarkable gifts of oratory and wit and a shrewd insight into Irish character. The signature An Craoibhin Aoibhinn (the delightful little branch), which he had borrowed from a poem he translated, became his popular name all over Ireland, as president of the Gaelic League. Its many local branches organized lessons in Irish speaking and encouraged Irish dances and games, and became a vital force in the movement for a self-reliant Irish Ireland. By 1905 the League had over 550 branches, and Hyde went to America to collect funds for wider propaganda and had a highly successful tour. Soon after, he was leading the agitation which made the Irish language a compulsory subject for entrance into the new National University of Ireland, founded in 1908. Hyde then accepted the professorship of modern Irish in the newly constituted University College, Dublin. He retired in 1932.

Hyde had always insisted that the Gaelic League should avoid any sort of political or sectarian commitments. But his revival of the Irish language and its traditions had helped to galvanize the separatist movement during the bitter controversy over Home Rule. Hyde's repudiation of any political aim aroused impatience among his younger followers, and in 1915 he resigned his presidency of the League. Confining himself to academic work in Dublin, he kept out of politics during the Anglo-Irish conflict and the transition to national government. He was nominated for a seat in the Senate in 1925 but was not re-elected. When the Senate was reconstructed under the revised constitution of 1937, Hyde was again appointed a senator; but a few months later, when all parties were searching for a candidate 'above and apart from politics', Hyde was invited by unanimous request to become the first president of Eire, after the office of governor-general had been abolished. Although advanced age and ill health left him incapable of serious activity, he continued in office until his term expired in June 1945. He was then provided with an official residence in Phoenix Park, Dublin, where he spent his last years until his death there 12 July 1949.

Hyde received the honorary degree of D.Litt. from the Royal University of Ireland (1906), the university of Wales (1927), and Dublin University (1933). He was awarded the Gregory medal by the Irish Academy of Letters (1937). His principal publications were *Beside the Fire* (1890), *Love Songs of Connacht* (1893), *Religious Songs of Connacht* (1906), *The Story of Early Gaelic Literature* (1895), *Literary History of Ireland* (1899), and *Medieval Tales from the Irish* (1899). His Irish plays, which had been produced publicly since 1901, were collected in book form in 1905. His personal part in the Gaelic League is described by him in *Mise agus an Connradh* (1937). Hyde had great charm of manner at all stages of his life, whether with poor or rich, young or old; and he was remarkably free from malice, or even resentment, when he was discarded by the younger generation. But his habit of flattery and picturesque speech sometimes suggested the stage Irishman of fiction. His appearance was very striking, with a tall graceful figure and well-poised round head, with mischievous blue eyes and large black moustaches which made him conspicuous anywhere. Early portraits of him by Sarah Purser and J. B. Yeats are in the National Gallery of Ireland. Later portraits were painted, while he was president of Eire, by Sean O'Sullivan (now in Trinity College, Dublin), and William Conor (University College, Dublin). There is a bust by Seumas Murphy and a portrait by Leo Whelan in the President's Lodge, Dublin.

In 1893 Hyde married Lucy (died 1939), daughter of Charles Kurtz, a distinguished German research chemist and art-collector, who had left Russia and settled in England. They had two daughters.

[*Irish Times* and *Irish Press*, 13 July 1949; Diarmid Coffey, *Douglas Hyde*, 1938; Desmond Ryan, *The Sword of Light*, 1939; *Studies*, Dublin, September 1949; P. S. O'Hegarty, *A Bibliography of Dr. Douglas Hyde*, Dublin, 1939.]        DENIS GWYNN.

IMMS, AUGUSTUS DANIEL (1880–1949), entomologist, was born 24 August 1880 at Moseley, Worcestershire, now in the city of Birmingham, the only son and elder child of Walter Imms, a member of the staff of Lloyds Bank. His mother, Mary Jane Daniel, was born in the United States, of British parents who returned to England a few years later. None of his relatives appears to have been noteworthy in science.

He was educated at St. Edmund's College, Birmingham; but his schooldays and indeed his whole working life were constantly interrupted by attacks of asthma. Debarred from many of the activities of his fellows, he early became intensely interested in the collecting of insects and when, on leaving school, he joined the science classes at Mason College, Birmingham, the attraction of biology was such that he abandoned his father's intention that he should become an industrial chemist and in 1903 graduated with second class honours in zoology in the university of London. After spending two years in research on the anatomy of fishes under T. W. Bridge [q.v.] at Birmingham, he was awarded an 1851 Exhibition science scholarship and in 1905 entered Christ's College, Cambridge.

From that time onwards Imms devoted himself entirely to entomology. After carrying out a fine piece of work on the anatomy of the larva of the *Anopheles* mosquito under G. H. F. Nuttall [q.v.] for which he was awarded the Darwin prize of Christ's College (1907), and having obtained his B.A., Cambridge, and D.Sc., Birmingham, in the same year, he accepted appointment to the newly established professorship of biology at the university of Allahabad. Here, in the face of great material difficulties, he had to build up his new department from the foundations. In 1911 he was appointed forest entomologist to the Government of India with headquarters at Dehra Dun, where again he had to design new laboratories.

In 1913 Imms left India for reasons of

health and was appointed reader in agricultural entomology at the Victoria University, Manchester, and during the war of 1914–18, being excluded by ill health from military service, he acted as an additional crop pest inspector and reporter for the Board of Agriculture. In 1918, largely as the result of Imms's representations to Sir A. D. Hall [q.v.], an entomological department was founded at Rothamsted and Imms was given the post of chief entomologist at the experimental station. Once more he had to plan and equip extensive laboratories, occupying the whole upper floor of the new Institute of Plant Pathology. During his period of tenure from 1918 to 1931 much good work came out of this department, but his own efforts were largely put into the writing of his famous textbook of entomology. In 1931 when the Rockefeller Foundation made possible the establishment of a readership in entomology at Cambridge, Imms was appointed to the new post. As from Manchester, so from Cambridge, many of Imms's pupils came to hold important posts in entomology in all parts of the world. He retired in 1945, becoming an honorary fellow of Downing College, of which he was elected a fellow in 1940.

The published researches of Imms, nearly all of which deal with insect morphology, although of a high quality, are limited in number. His main contribution to entomology has been in his books. The most important of these was his *General Textbook of Entomology*, first published in 1925, which passed through seven editions in his lifetime. This became at once the standard treatise in the English language. Its influence upon the science of entomology has been profound, introducing as it did a more scientific outlook into the subject. Other books, including *Recent Advances in Entomology* (1931), *Outlines of Entomology* (1942), and *Insect Natural History* added to the 'New Naturalist' series in 1947, all helped to spread Imms's influence among a wide circle of entomologists.

Personally Imms was reserved, and probably few people knew him intimately. But he was an excellent judge of promise in young research workers and the real investigator could count on him for unswerving support and friendship. He was elected F.R.S. in 1929, was president of the Royal Entomological Society of London (1936–8), and (1930–31) of the Association of Economic (later Applied)

Biologists, of which he was a co-founder. He was a corresponding member of the Agricultural Academy of France, an honorary member of the Entomological Societies of Holland, Finland, and India, and in 1947 he was elected a foreign member of the American Academy of Arts and Sciences.

In 1913 Imms married Georgiana Mary, daughter of T. W. French, resident magistrate of county Tyrone, and a cousin of Sir John French, later the Earl of Ypres [q.v.]. There were two daughters of the marriage who with their mother survived Imms when he died at his home at Tipton St. John, Sidmouth, 3 April 1949.

A portrait in pencil by Paul Drury is in the Department of Zoology, Cambridge.

[V. B. Wigglesworth in *Obituary Notices of Fellows of the Royal Society*, No. 18, November 1949; *Nature*, 7 May 1949; personal knowledge.]                    V. B. WIGGLESWORTH.

INGRAM, ARTHUR FOLEY WINNINGTON- (1858–1946), bishop of London. [See WINNINGTON-INGRAM.]

INNES, SIR JAMES ROSE- (1855–1942), chief justice of South Africa. [See ROSE-INNES.]

INSKIP, THOMAS WALKER HOBART, first VISCOUNT CALDECOTE (1876–1947), lawyer and statesman, was born in Bristol 5 March 1876, the second son of James Inskip, a leading solicitor in that city, and the first son of his second wife, Constance, daughter of John Hampden. Inskip was educated at Clifton and at King's College, Cambridge, where he obtained a third class in part i of the classical tripos in 1897. He had been brought up in a deeply religious evangelical environment; and while at Cambridge he addressed religious meetings in the town and had serious thoughts of becoming a missionary. Eventually, however, he was called to the bar by the Inner Temple in 1899, and began to practise on the Western circuit where, with his strong local connexions, his natural endowments and his commanding presence—he was six feet four inches tall—he rapidly built up a considerable practice.

In 1906 and January 1910 he stood unsuccessfully as a Unionist against Sir Edward Grey (later Viscount Grey of Fallodon, q.v.) at Berwick-on-Tweed; in 1914 he took silk. He served in naval intelligence in London throughout the war of 1914–18, became head of the naval law branch in 1918, and represented the Admiralty on the war crimes committee (1918–19). Entering the House of Commons as Conservative member for the Central division of Bristol in 1918, he became solicitor-general in the Bonar Law administration in 1922 and, with two short interludes while Labour was in power, remained a law officer of the Crown until 1936. He first became attorney-general in March 1928 when Sir Douglas Hogg [q.v.] went to the Woolsack as Lord Hailsham; but in the 1929 election Inskip lost his Bristol seat, and was out of the House for two years before being returned as member for Fareham. In the 'national' Government which was re-formed after the election, he reverted, with characteristic self-effacement, to the junior office to enable the Labour attorney-general, Sir William (later Earl) Jowitt, who was supporting the Government, to retain the senior. He replaced Jowitt as attorney-general in the course of the following year.

During his fourteen years as a law officer, Inskip appeared for the Crown in many important cases, criminal and civil. There was in his advocacy neither drama nor rhetoric. His approach was straightforward rather than subtle, but points, whether of law or of fact, were unlikely to escape him. He penetrated to the core of the problem. This gift stood him in good stead in the House of Commons. When the Government of India bill of 1935 was in preparation and before the House, assisted by the solicitor-general, Sir Donald Somervell (subsequently Lord Somervell of Harrow), Inskip dealt with great ability with the many legal and constitutional issues involved.

At this time Inskip was best known to the public for the part he had played in the rejection of the revised Prayer Book in 1927 and 1928. To him, a lifelong evangelical, the proposed revisions not only offered the prospect of dangerous licence to the Anglo-Catholics but threatened the very foundations of the Church of England as established by the Reformation. He was generally recognized both by his associates and by his adversaries as the main instrument in defeating the revisions, Archbishop Lang [q.v.] recording in his diary, 'When Inskip spoke with great force I saw that the chances of the measure were gone'.

Inskip had declined to be proposed for the speakership in 1928 and declined the mastership of the Rolls in 1935. In 1936, when it was decided to appoint a minister for the co-ordination of defence, Baldwin and Chamberlain agreed in selecting Inskip for the task. The appointment came as a great surprise to the country and to Inskip whose strong sense of duty nevertheless impelled him to accept. His powers were ill defined, since the three Service departments retained their full autonomy and independence. The work of co-ordination could be accomplished only by persuasion and argument leading to consent. The control of aircraft in naval operations was a problem which faced him at the outset. As the power and significance of carrier-borne aircraft increased, the Admiralty was correspondingly anxious to control this weapon. It was largely as a result of Inskip's work that the Air Ministry eventually agreed to relinquish control of what became the Fleet Air Arm.

In the wide and varied field of supply Inskip's talents and energy were of the greatest public service. Each of the Services had its own supply department, and although some progress had been made with the single purchase of stores common to all three, the system was by no means adequate to the vast expansion of forces contemplated. While any hope of peace remained, the Government was anxious to avoid giving publicity to preparations which might be construed as provocative. There could be no coercive powers to procure supplies or to order production. Everything had to be done voluntarily as the result of explanation and persuasion in an endless series of committees. In these, Inskip's manifest integrity and absence of glitter gained him first the confidence and then the co-operation of both Service officers and industrialists. Despite the difficulties much was done in these days from which the nation afterwards gained.

The need for secrecy, however, imposed on ministers, and particularly on Inskip, a style of speech which could not satisfy those who were pressing for rearmament. In January 1939 Inskip was transferred to the Dominions Office. His successor, Admiral of the Fleet Lord Chatfield, went out of his way in the House of Lords to tell the country that it was deeply indebted to Inskip; and others since then have paid tribute to the results he achieved in what was then a thankless and secret task. In September 1939 on the outbreak of war he was appointed lord chancellor in place of Lord Maugham and created Viscount Caldecote, of Bristol. In May 1940 he returned to the Dominions Office and was leader of the House of Lords, but in October 1940 he was appointed lord chief justice in succession to Lord Hewart [q.v.], whose relations with the bar had sometimes been strained. The advent of Inskip began a new chapter. He was reckoned to be a good judge, sound in his conclusions, courteous and patient in his conduct of a case. He enjoyed the respect and affection of his colleagues on the bench and of members of the bar. But as the war progressed his health declined; by the time he resigned in January 1946 he had greatly aged; and he died at Enton Green, near Godalming, 11 October 1947. Inskip was a man who attained to the highest offices, not by brilliance, influence, or luck, but by character and sound judgement. Apart from his aptitude for hard work he was chiefly characterized by his integrity and his deep religious convictions. Although a strict sabbatarian and almost a teetotaller and non-smoker, he was far from being a gloomy companion; a successful athlete in his youth, he made his home in Scotland for the last thirty years of his life and spent most of his leisure out of doors, shooting or playing golf, until ill health overtook him and he settled down near Godalming. He engaged deeply in good works, playing a prominent part in several charitable organizations, and as lord chief justice was closely associated with the Discharged Prisoners' Aid Society. Although he had earned large sums through his legal career, he died a comparatively poor man, his fortune dispersed in anonymous benefactions.

He was a privy counsellor (1932), a C.B.E. (1920), a bencher of the Inner Temple, and an honorary LL.D. of Bristol University; at different times he was chancellor of Truro diocese, recorder and also high steward of Kingston upon Thames, vice-president of the Classical Association, and chairman of the Council of Legal Education. He married in 1914 Lady Augusta Helen Elizabeth Orr Ewing, eldest daughter of the seventh Earl of Glasgow, and widow of Charles Lindsay Orr Ewing, Unionist member for Ayr Burghs. He left one son, who succeeded him in his title, Robert Andrew (born 1917), who served in the Royal Navy during the war of 1939–45 and became a fellow of King's College, Cambridge. A portrait by Augustus John

hangs in the benchers' rooms in the Inner Temple, and another by Frederick Brill is in the possession of the family.

[*The Times*, 13 October 1947; private papers and information; personal knowledge.]

BERNARD FERGUSSON.

ISAACS, SIR ISAAC ALFRED (1855–1948), chief justice and governor-general of Australia, was born at Melbourne 6 August 1855. He was the eldest of the three children of Alfred Isaacs, a tailor, of Auburn, Victoria, by his wife, Rebecca, daughter of Abraham Abrahams, of London. Isaacs was educated at a Victorian elementary state school, Beechworth Grammar School, and at the university of Melbourne where he graduated in law with distinction in 1880.

Isaacs was called to the Victorian bar in the same year, and rapidly acquired a good practice, particularly before appellate tribunals. His work was distinguished by great care in the preparation of his cases, and he enjoyed a reputation as a pertinacious advocate. He took silk in 1899. In 1892 he entered politics as a member of the Victorian state legislative assembly. In the following year he joined the Government as solicitor-general. In 1894 he was appointed attorney-general and held this office until 1899, and again from 1900 to 1901.

In 1897 Isaacs was elected a member of the Australian Federal Convention. To this body was entrusted the task of drafting the Commonwealth Constitution, which was subsequently enacted as a statute by the Parliament at Westminster. Isaacs resigned from the Victorian Parliament in 1901 to enter federal politics, and in the same year was elected a member of the first Federal House of Representatives. In 1905 he was appointed attorney-general of the Commonwealth and held this office until the following year when he was appointed to the High Court bench. In 1930 he was appointed chief justice upon the retirement of Sir Adrian Knox.

During his long period of service in the High Court, Isaacs established a great and lasting reputation as a judge. His judgements on Australian constitutional law are of especial importance. In this field, he laid great emphasis on what he regarded as the predominant place of the Commonwealth (as opposed to the States) in the federal compact. For many years he and Mr. Justice (Henry Bournes) Higgins, who was Isaacs's exact contemporary on the bench, found themselves in a position of lone dissent on points of great importance. The majority in the court held that the Constitution must be read subject to implied prohibitions which denied to Commonwealth legislation a power to bind the States and their instrumentalities and vice versa. After the retirement of Chief Justice (Sir Samuel Walker) Griffith in 1919, the view propounded by Isaacs prevailed, and in the *Engineers' Case* (1920) the majority in the court held Commonwealth legislation effective to bind States and their instrumentalities. Since Isaacs's retirement from the bench, certain limitations on the scope of the *Engineers'* doctrine have been propounded in the High Court, but that decision represented a monumental victory for the position which Isaacs had consistently maintained for so long in dissent. His interpretations of the Commonwealth power to legislate with respect to industrial disputes also promoted the extension of central authority. He opposed the limitation of Commonwealth power to situations arising out of existing industrial disputes, and gave a broad interpretation to the notion of industrial matters. The result was to vest in the Commonwealth Arbitration Court a wide power of control over industrial conditions in Australia.

Isaacs's interpretation of the supremacy clause in the Constitution, under which inconsistent State legislation gives way to Commonwealth laws, characteristically favoured the Commonwealth. Again, in *Farey* v. *Burvett* (1916), where the High Court held that the Commonwealth defence power authorized the regulation of the price of bread in wartime, Isaacs took the most extreme position in the court in support of Commonwealth power. He was also called upon to interpret section 92 of the Constitution which provides that 'trade, commerce and intercourse among the States . . . shall be absolutely free'. Isaacs held that this provision invalidated all manner of State control over inter-state trade, but that it did not bind the Commonwealth. On both points relating to section 92 Isaacs's view has been rejected in subsequent decisions.

The fact that the High Court of Australia enjoys a general appellate jurisdiction gave Isaacs wide scope in the non-constitutional field. He left his mark in many and varied branches of the law. Brief reference may be made to his famous dissenting judgement in *Wright* v. *Cedzich* (1929–30). In opposition to the majority of the court, he held that a wife was entitled to sue for damages for the enticement of her husband. In a powerful judgement he attacked the majority position which, in his view, was founded on outmoded historical considerations, and which disregarded the modern developments towards equality of the spouses. His judgement is replete with apposite quotations from *The Taming of the Shrew* and *Macbeth*. It may be remarked that the position taken here by Isaacs accords with the modern decisions of the English courts.

Isaacs's career was crowned by his appointment as the first Australian governor-general of the Commonwealth. There was some opposition to the appointment of an Australian, but the Government insisted and Isaacs assumed office in 1931. He discharged the duties of this high office in full accordance with its traditions until his retirement in 1936.

Isaacs was sworn of the Privy Council in 1921. He was appointed K.C.M.G. in 1928, promoted G.C.M.G. in 1932, and appointed G.C.B. in 1937. In 1888 he married Daisy, daughter of Isaac Jacobs, of Melbourne, and had two daughters. Isaacs died at Melbourne 11 February 1948 at the age of ninety-two.

There are portraits of Isaacs in the King's Hall, Parliament House, Canberra, by Sir John Longstaff, and at Monash House, Melbourne, by Percy White.

[*Australian Law Journal*, 17 June 1948; private information.] ZELMAN COWEN.

JACKSON, SIR (FRANCIS) STANLEY (1870–1947), cricketer and administrator, was born at Chapel Allerton, near Leeds, 21 November 1870, the younger son and seventh child of William Lawies Jackson, later first Baron Allerton [q.v.]. Jackson was educated at Harrow, where it was soon apparent that he was a cricketer of great natural gifts. He was three years in the eleven, captain in 1889, and showed himself a boy of high character with evident powers of leadership. In the Eton and Harrow match of 1888 he scored 21 and 59 and took 11 wickets for 68 runs, and from then onwards his cricketing career was a sequence of success on great occasions. Going up to Trinity College, Cambridge, where he graduated in 1892, he gained his blue as a freshman, and played for four years in the eleven, which he captained in 1892 and 1893. In this last year he was selected to play for England against Australia and made 91 at Lord's and 103 at the Oval. Thenceforward he was indispensable to any representative England eleven, and he played for the great Yorkshire elevens built up by Lord Hawke [q.v.]. His appearances were not, however, always regular, for business claims intervened. Jackson was never able to visit Australia and this led to A. C. MacLaren [q.v.] being accepted as England's regular captain. MacLaren was a great tactician in the middle, but in what might be called the wider field of strategy he lacked both the composure and the balanced judgement of Jackson.

The latter was appointed captain, with MacLaren as his 'chief of staff', in 1905 for all five test matches against Australia, and enjoyed a great personal triumph. He won the toss in every match, headed the batting averages by scoring 492 runs for an average of 70 and the bowling with 13 wickets, average 15, and England won the rubber. At Leeds he scored 144 not out, an innings marked by splendid cutting and powerful driving on a rather slow wicket, while at Nottingham he bowled one of the historic overs in test cricket. M. A. Noble [q.v.] and C. Hill were firmly set when off Jackson's first ball Noble was caught at the wicket, the fourth bowled Hill, and the last ball had J. Darling caught at slip. This was the pinnacle of Jackson's cricketing career and the following season he retired. As a batsman he was a great driver on both sides of the wicket and a superb cutter. No batsman in a crisis inspired greater confidence. As a bowler he had a graceful action with a marked rhythmic swing of the arm and could turn the ball sharply from the off.

In 1915 Jackson was elected Conservative member for the Howdenshire division of Yorkshire and from 1922 to 1923 he was parliamentary and financial secretary to the War Office. He had served in the South African war; and he raised, and from 1914 to 1917 commanded, the 2nd/7th West Yorkshire Regiment. In 1923 he succeeded Lord Younger of Leckie [q.v.] as chairman of the Conservative Party organization and was among those who confidently advised his Harrovian contemporary Stanley Baldwin, the new prime minister, to go to the country on the tariff issue, a venture which proved, in the first instance, unsuccessful. Jackson's own political career was cut short by his appointment in 1927 as governor of Bengal. The province was in a very disturbed state and his prede-

cessor had been forced to apply for enactment of the measure known as the Bengal Ordinance. The spirit of the Montagu–Chelmsford reforms was essentially liberal, but to infuse it into a very troubled atmosphere was no easy task. Matters became acute when the provincial legislature sought to overrule the ministers. Jackson dissolved it in April 1929, took over control of the transferred departments, and formed a new ministry. Many schemes were held up by financial stringency which largely handicapped his efforts; yet he felt able to claim that the new ministry had rendered 'most creditable service to the people'. Jackson's work in Bengal may be summed up in his own words: 'I have tried my best to keep the scales even.' This he undoubtedly did, at the risk of being accused of indecision and in the face of much mixed criticism. It is not insignificant that all the members of the ministry he had formed remained with him to the end of his term of office. Shortly before he left Calcutta in 1932, an attempt was made to assassinate him in the Senate hall of Calcutta University, of which he was chancellor, by a girl graduate who fired five shots from a revolver at close range. He and Lady Jackson who was near him behaved with great courage and coolness, and he resumed his address as soon as his assailant had been removed. Jackson was always at his best against fast bowling.

On leaving for India Jackson had been appointed G.C.I.E. (1927), and on retirement was appointed G.C.S.I. (1932). He was sworn of the Privy Council in 1926. He received the honorary degrees of D.Litt. from the universities of Calcutta and Dacca, and of LL.D. from Sheffield (1936).

Jackson was a man of great personal charm and wide interests. He was a governor of Harrow School, 1923–7 and 1939–47, and chairman of the governors from 1942. He was a director of the Great Northern Railway and of the *Yorkshire Post*, and in 1921 president of the Marylebone Cricket Club. After his retirement from public life he was a frequent visitor at Lord's where a portrait of him by Gerald Reynell hangs in the pavilion.

In 1902 Jackson married Julia Henrietta (died 1958), daughter of Henry Broadley Harrison-Broadley, M.P., of Welton House, Brough, East Yorkshire, and had one son. In the last year of his life Jackson was knocked down by a taxi-cab, an accident from which he never fully recovered, and he died in London 9 March 1947.

[*Wisden's Cricketers' Almanack*, 1948; *Bengal Administration Reports*, 1927-32; private information; personal knowledge.]

P. F. WARNER.

JACKSON, FREDERICK JOHN FOAKES (1855-1941), divine, was born at Ipswich 10 August 1855, the posthumous son of the Rev. Stephen Jackson, proprietor of the *Ipswich Journal* and the fifth of his family to conduct the journal since 1739, and his wife, Catharine, daughter of Frederick Cobbold, of the 1st Dragoon Guards, a member of a distinguished Suffolk family. In 1858 his mother married Thomas Eyre Foakes, barrister, and when she sent her son to school at Brighton she entered him as Frederick John Jackson Foakes, by which name he was known later at Eton. He subsequently changed it to Foakes Jackson, and when, many years later, he consulted an American lawyer about legalizing the name in that form he was told that 'he had already made it legal by making it famous'.

Foakes Jackson went up to Trinity College, Cambridge, and in 1879 was placed in the first class of the theological tripos. He won the Jeremie Septuagint and Scholefield prizes, the Crosse scholarship and the Lightfoot scholarship. This last distinction indicated his predominating interest, which was in the field of ecclesiastical history. Ordained deacon in 1879 and priest in 1880, he served as curate at Ottershaw in Surrey, and at the churches of St. Giles and St. Botolph in Cambridge. In 1882 he was appointed chaplain and lecturer in divinity and Hebrew at Jesus College, Cambridge. Four years later he was elected into a fellowship which he held for fifty-five years and from 1895 to 1916 he was dean of the college. He proceeded B.D. in 1903 and D.D. in 1905.

Soon after Foakes Jackson settled in Cambridge his family became involved in an unfortunate lawsuit, and only after some years of exacting work was he able to discharge the debt incurred. In spite of much teaching he early began to write, and in 1891 appeared the first edition of his well-known *History of the Christian Church*. At first it dealt only with the period up to the death of Constantine, but it was soon continued and brought down to the year 461. The book gave theological students what they needed and has remained a standard textbook.

Foakes Jackson contributed to the *Cambridge Medieval History*, the *Cambridge Theological Essays*, and the *Cambridge History of English Literature*. In 1912 he edited *The Parting of the Roads*, a volume of essays on theological subjects by some of his former pupils. But his chief literary output belongs to his later years when, relieved of the burden of Cambridge teaching and removed from the allurement of Cambridge society, he published a number of books in rapid succession. His most considerable work was *The Beginnings of Christianity*, planned in co-operation with Kirsopp Lake [q.v.]. Five volumes appeared between 1920 and 1933, but the partnership was not entirely successful and for the last two volumes Lake was alone responsible. Foakes Jackson's last work, published in 1939, was entitled *A History of Church History*, and he described it as offered to Bishop Lightfoot's memory by one of his grateful scholars.

Foakes Jackson's range was wide, but he never specialized enough to win fame as an original scholar. His real claim to distinction was as a teacher, and he was justly proud of the number of his pupils who rose to eminence in the field of theological and historical learning. He claimed that over a considerable period Jesus men won more first classes in the theological tripos than all the other candidates put together. He had a flair for penetrating a mass of detail to point out the essential facts, and he could make any subject interesting. This was mainly due to his extraordinary personality. He has been aptly described as the last eighteenth-century wit. His conversation was characterized by an astonishing flow of shrewd humour which, combined with his personal eccentricities and his unfailing kindness, made him immensely popular. For many years he was one of the best-known and best-loved figures in Cambridge, and the interest he took in the success of his pupils was rewarded by their unfailing gratitude and devotion. The stories which circulated about 'Foakey'—his doings and sayings—would fill a volume, and most of them were true.

In 1916 at the age of sixty-one he crossed the Atlantic to deliver the Lowell lectures at Boston, and during his visit he was offered and accepted the Briggs graduate professorship of Christian institutions at the Union Theological Seminary,

New York. In America he built up another great reputation. He retired in 1934, but remained active almost to the end of his life. He had innumerable interests: in his younger days he was a prominent oarsman and was for many years treasurer of the Cambridge University Boat Club. He was also fond of fishing and shooting. He held high office among the freemasons, being at one time grand chaplain of England. His scholarship brought him into touch with Jewish leaders and from 1924 to 1927 he held a lectureship at the Jewish Institute of Religion, New York. He received honorary degrees from the university of Strasbourg (D.Th., 1933) and the university of the South, Sewanee, Tennessee (D.Litt., 1935). He was an honorary canon of Peterborough (1901–26), a fellow of the Royal Historical Society, honorary correspondent of the Institut Historique et Héraldique de France, and fellow of the American Academy of Arts and Sciences.

Foakes Jackson was twice married: first, in 1895 to Anna Maria (died 1931), daughter of the late George Grimwade Everett, of Hadleigh, Suffolk; secondly, in 1932 to Clara Fawcett, widow of Arthur Jackson Tomlinson, of New York. There were no children. Foakes Jackson died at Englewood, New Jersey, 1 December 1941. There is a portrait by Francis Lutyens at Jesus College.

[Personal knowledge.]

P. GARDNER-SMITH.

JACOB, SIR CLAUD WILLIAM (1863–1948), field-marshal, was born at Mehidpore, Bombay, 21 November 1863, the son of Lieutenant (later Major-General) William Jacob, Indian Army, nephew of Sir George Le Grand Jacob [q.v.], and his wife, Eliza, daughter of the Rev. George Andrew Jacob, headmaster of Christ's Hospital, London. He was educated at Sherborne School and the Royal Military College, Sandhurst, and was commissioned in the Worcestershire Regiment in 1882. In 1884, when stationed at Quetta, he was transferred to the Indian Army. He took part in the Zhob Valley expedition (1890) and soon afterwards was selected to command the Zhob Levy Corps which kept the peace along the Waziristan and southern Afghanistan border. At the end of 1901 he took part in the campaign against the Mahsuds, and in 1904 formed the 106th Hazara Pioneers for work on frontier communications. He commanded them for seven years until his appointment in 1912 as G.S.O.1 to the Meerut division. The first thirty years of his service he therefore spent as a regimental officer, almost entirely on the frontier.

The Meerut division he accompanied to France in time to see the closing stages of the battle of La Bassée in the autumn of 1914. His gallantry and coolness in a critical situation which arose on the front of the Indian Corps just before Christmas marked him out for promotion; at the beginning of 1915 he was appointed to command the Dehra Dun brigade which he led in March at Neuve Chapelle and in May at Aubers Ridge. On 6 September 1915 he was given the Meerut division and fought with it in the costly action of Pietre at the time of the battle of Loos. When the Indian Corps was preparing to leave for Mesopotamia Jacob was retained, through the intervention of Sir Douglas (later Earl) Haig [q.v.], to take over (18 November 1915) the 21st division of the New Armies. He was the only Indian Army senior officer of the corps to remain in France and receive high promotion. By his example and thoroughness he brought his new command to an efficient fighting pitch. Early in March 1916 he was wounded by a shell which fell on his headquarters and killed his chief of staff. In May he was back with his division, but he did not command it during the opening stages of the battle of the Somme for he had been transferred to a reserve corps held at the disposal of the commander-in-chief from which it was Jacob's duty to familiarize himself with the dispositions and course of the battle along the whole Somme front.

In September 1916 Jacob was appointed to command the II Corps in the Fifth Army. On 26 September his corps carried Thiepval which the Germans claimed to be impregnable, and in the subsequent fighting secured the Zollern, Stuff, and Schwaben redoubts. On 13 November, attacking in a fog at 5.45 a.m., he captured St. Pierre Divion at comparatively light cost, thus greatly facilitating the operations of the V Corps north of the River Ancre. When the Germans were conducting a hard-fought retreat towards the Hindenburg line, he took the corps past Achiet-le-Grand and beyond St. Leger which he reached 19 March 1917. Later, as part of the Second Army under Sir Herbert (later Viscount) Plumer [q.v.], Jacob's corps took a prominent part in the Passchendaele fighting, discharging a particularly stiff assignment on the Gheluvelt plateau. In 1918 he was in the Flanders fighting during the final German onslaught, and led his corps during the allied advance which broke the German opposition and brought hostilities to an end in November 1918. His corps then formed part of the Army of the Rhine and Jacob was stationed at Cologne. He had been appointed C.B. in 1915 and promoted K.C.B. in 1917 for his services on the Ancre and made lieutenant-general 3 June 1917.

In January 1920 Jacob returned to India as chief of the general staff and was promoted general in May. In 1924–5 he held the Northern Command, India, and after the death of Lord Rawlinson [q.v.] in 1925 served temporarily as commander-in-chief; but the appointment was not made permanent and he returned to England as secretary of the military department, India Office, 1926–30. He was aide-de-camp general to the King, 1920–24, and field-marshal, 1926. He was constable of the Tower of London, 1938–43, and in his last years was colonel commandant of the Church Lads' Brigade, a force in which he took a great interest. He was appointed K.C.M.G. (1919), G.C.B. (1926), K.C.S.I. (1924), and G.C.S.I. (1930). His decorations included the grand cross of the Legion of Honour; the Belgian Order of the Crown (grand officer) with croix de guerre, and the Order of Leopold (grand officer); the American D.S.M.; and the Russian Order of St. Vladimir, 4th class, with swords. He was colonel of the Worcestershire Regiment, 1927–38, and of the 2nd/10th Baluch Regiment from 1928.

Jacob was a practical soldier with a high degree of common sense, great thoroughness in method, and the ability to learn from experience. Straightforward in character, he never sought publicity, and his modesty may have kept him from even higher positions. He had an unrivalled knowledge of regimental soldiering, and when in high command possessed the continuous and undiminished confidence of all ranks. He married in 1894 Clara Pauline, daughter of the Rev. Joseph Light Wyatt, a missionary in Trinchinopoli, who survived him when he died in London 2 June 1948. They had one son, Lieutenant-General Sir Ian Jacob, assistant military secretary of the War Cabinet (1939–46) and from December 1952 director-general of the British Broadcasting Corporation. A drawing of Jacob by Francis Dodd is in the Imperial War Museum.

[Sir J. E. Edmonds and others, (Official) *History of the Great War. Military Operations, France and Belgium, 1914–18*, 1922–48; *The Times*, 3 June 1948; private correspondence (unpublished); personal knowledge.]

E. F. JACOB.

JACOBS, WILLIAM WYMARK (1863–1943), writer, was born in Wapping, 8 September 1863, the eldest child of William Gage Jacobs by his first wife, Sophia Wymark. The boy's father was a wharfinger; and in his teens young Jacobs spent much time on Thames-side, growing familiar with the life of the neighbourhood, the habitués resident and transient, and the comings and goings of ships. The family was a large one, living on narrow and precarious means, so that W.W. (as he came to be known to his friends) regarded the times when with his brothers and sisters he ran wild in Wapping as happy interludes in a life of nagging discomfort. Almost the only other alleviations of a dreary and restricted childhood were sojourns at a cottage near Sevenoaks and visits to relations in rural East Anglia. Those fleeting delights permanently endeared country-village life to him, and produced the 'Claybury' stories which, although less popular than the vernacular reminiscences of the Night Watchman, are no less beautifully wrought, no less perfect in timing and in unobtrusive compression.

Jacobs was educated at a private school in the City, and later at Birkbeck College, where he made friends with Pett Ridge. In 1879, at the age of sixteen, he became a boy clerk in the Civil Service, formally joined as a second division clerk in the Savings Bank department in 1883, and there remained until 1899. His work became increasingly a drudgery; but memories of a boyhood of poverty caused him to cling to the safety of a dull and subordinate job until he could feel reasonably sure of earning a living by his pen.

Already in 1885 he had contributed anonymous and tentative sketches to *Blackfriars*, but not until in the early 'nineties Jerome K. Jerome [q.v.] accepted a number of his stories for the *Idler* and for *To-day*, not until about 1895, when he was admitted to the well-paid preserves of the *Strand Magazine*, was there any foreshadowing of the Jacobs to come. These tales—artless, almost naïve—had individuality and gave promise, although as yet experimental, of the humour and mastery of his medium which, in its matured form, was to ensure both livelihood and international repute. In 1896 appeared his first collection of stories, *Many Cargoes*, followed in 1897 by a novelette, *The Skipper's Wooing*, with, appended, a moderately successful horror story, and in 1898 by *Sea Urchins*. The next year he resigned the Civil Service and became an author by profession.

On account of his shy, low-voiced address and gentle melancholy of manner, Jacobs—slight, pale-complexioned, and of almost albino fairness—seemed a smaller man than he really was. In a crowded room he withdrew into self-effacement; but enjoying casual conversation with one or two of his own kind, he talked (as he looked) with a twinkle, and gained stature in proportion as his diffidence fell away. To listen to Jacobs chatting with Will Owen, his inspired illustrator, and with Pett Ridge, was to savour the essence of a wholly distinctive epoch of English humour which, for the time being at any rate, has ceased to exist. Pett Ridge, plump and genial, would recall the latest cockney absurdity, overheard or encountered on the top of an omnibus; Owen, ridiculously like one of the sturdy little seafarers whom he created for his friend's stories, would chuckle rosily; while W.W., hardly raising his eyes and speaking out of the corner of his mouth, would throw in a simple but deft aside, whose fun was implied and at one remove.

Jacobs wrote short stories of three kinds—describing the misadventures of sailor-men ashore; celebrating the unscrupulous ingenuities of the artful dodger of a slow-witted country village; and tales of the macabre. He also wrote half a dozen novels (they are really series of short stories woven together) of which the two best (*At Sunwich Port*, 1902, and *Dialstone Lane*, 1904) display his genius for re-rendering personalities, comic episodes, and characteristic talk without repeating them or himself. Popularity as a humorist obscured, even in his hey-dey, Jacobs's superb technique as a writer of stories. His economy of language, his perpetual understatement, his refusal himself to be the joker but the suggestion in a rapid exchange of conversation by his characters of the ludicrous catastrophes which have overtaken or are about to overtake them—these are qualities in a writer granted only to a master of his craft.

It is instructive to compare his first collection of stories with one of those published at the zenith of his powers. *Many Cargoes* contains several of the principal personages and types who were to make Jacobs famous. The Night Watchman is there; also the quick-witted beauty, sparring with, scoring off, and finally succumbing to, an unabashed and persistent lover; also rival ladies exchanging barbed civilities; also embarrassed skippers baited by their mates with allusions to redundant feminine entanglements. Yet, although the patterns of stories are dimly conceived, construction is lacking. The tales are mere anecdotes, whereas, by the time we reach *Light Freights* (1901), every moment, from the nonchalant opening to the gentle click of the closing door, is deliberately planned and faultlessly controlled.

Uncritical public favour apart, the period of Jacobs's supremacy as an artist in story-writing lasted for less than fifteen years. In *Light Freights* not only Ginger Dick, Peter Russet, and old Sam Small, but also Bob Pretty, Henery Walker, the bibulous ancient on the bench outside the 'Cauliflower', and other notabilities of Claybury made their bow. In 1902 came *The Lady of the Barge* which contained the author's master-tales of horror —*The Monkey's Paw*, *The Well*, and *In the Library*—deftly mixed with seafaring and bucolic absurdities. *The Monkey's Paw* was dramatized by L. N. Parker [q.v.] with whom Jacobs collaborated in writing *Beauty and the Barge* (1904). He wrote a number of other plays, and published several collections of stories, all on the highest level, ending with *Night Watches* (1914).

One cannot read the books which appeared after 1914 without feeling that Jacobs had begun to tire of what readers still tirelessly demanded. He never published slipshod work, and did his best to devise new variations on old themes; but the heart had gone out of him. He allowed nothing to be issued in volume form in the seventeen years before he died in London 1 September 1943. In 1900 he married Agnes Eleanor, daughter of Richard Owen Williams, bank accountant, of Leytonstone, Essex. They had two sons and three daughters. A portrait of Jacobs (1910) by C. Moore-Park was presented in 1944 by Jacobs's executors to the National Portrait Gallery where there is also a pen-and-ink drawing by H. Furniss.

[Personal knowledge.]

MICHAEL SADLEIR.

JAMES, ARTHUR LLOYD (1884-1943), phonetician, was born at Pentre, Glamorganshire, 21 June 1884, the son of William James, colliery manager, and his wife, Rachel Clark. He was educated at Llanelly, the Pontypridd Pupil Teachers' Centre, and University College, Cardiff, where he graduated with third class honours in French in 1905. After a year or two of teaching he went as an advanced student to Trinity College, Cambridge, and in 1910 graduated in medieval and modern languages, specializing in Old French and Provençal. He then taught French and phonetics at the Islington Training College until the war of 1914-18 during which he served with the Royal Engineers.

In 1920 Lloyd James accepted a lectureship in phonetics at University College, London, and entered upon a career of much distinction, concentrating at first upon the phonetics of English and French, but soon branching out into such fields as the phonetics of Hausa, Yoruba, and other languages of West Africa which he studied with native speakers who happened to be in London. In 1925 he took a prominent part in work for the proposed International Institute for African Languages and Cultures (later the International African Institute) and he had some share in its decision to work especially upon the unification of the orthographies of African languages on a phonetic basis.

In 1927 Lloyd James became the first head of the department of phonetics set up by the School of Oriental Studies, later the School of Oriental and African Studies, in the university of London. This appointment, which began as a lectureship, was raised to a readership in 1930 and a professorship in 1933. It gave Lloyd James much scope for the exercise of his linguistic talents, and the department, which was greatly strengthened by the addition of Ida Ward [q.v.] in 1932, soon became a large and important adjunct to the language departments. A great many students were given an insight into modern methods of acquiring proficiency in exotic spoken languages, and much valuable research into the phonetics of Asian and African languages was carried out.

Lloyd James published a number of works on phonetics including a very scholarly *Historical Introduction to French Phonetics* (1929). He contributed the article on pronunciation to the fourteenth edition of the *Encyclopaedia Britannica* and he was a frequent broadcaster on speech and language. He also lectured at the Royal Academy of Dramatic Art (1924-33) and acted as adviser on phonetics to the Linguaphone Institute. His wide interests led him amongst other things to undertake some pioneer investigations into the intelligibility of recorded speech, and to devise some phonetic tests for telephone operators. His main work outside the university, however, was done for the British Broadcasting Corporation. He was, for the term of its existence (1926-40), honorary secretary of the Corporation's advisory committee on spoken English which considered and reported upon words and proper names of difficult or disputed pronunciation. He assembled the evidence, with the assistance of some of the Corporation's regular staff, and edited the committee's findings in a series of remarkable booklets. His success in this task led to his appointment in 1929 to train announcers and to act generally as an adviser to the Corporation on points of pronunciation not dealt with by the committee. He showed particular ingenuity in devising suitable anglicizations for those foreign personal and place names with which announcers are apt to be confronted at short notice. In 1938 his position was accorded the official title of linguistic adviser to the B.B.C. On the outbreak of war he became adviser on radio-telephonic speech to the Royal Air Force and investigated problems involved in transmitting speech between air and ground.

In 1914 Lloyd James married Elsie, daughter of Luther Owen, a professional musician, of Llanelly. She was a fellow of the Royal Academy of Music and well known as a violinist. Their only child, David Owen Lloyd James, joined the staff of the B.B.C. The marriage was a particularly happy one until during the stress and anxieties of war Lloyd James fell a victim to depressive insanity. Fearing separation from, and hardship to, his wife, he took her life in 1941 and his own, in Broadmoor, 24 March 1943. He had been a man of much sociability and high-mindedness, with a passion for punctuality and a scrupulous regard for truth. A pencil drawing by D. N. Ingles is in the possession of his son.

[Personal knowledge.]                    DANIEL JONES.

JEANS, SIR JAMES HOPWOOD (1877-1946), mathematician, theoretical physicist, astronomer, and popular expositor of physical science and astronomy, was born 11 September 1877 at Birkdale, Southport, the only son of William Tulloch Jeans, parliamentary journalist, by his wife, Martha Ann Hopwood. He had two younger sisters. His grandfather, who was town clerk of Elgin, Scotland, and his great-grandfather were newspaper proprietors, and his father wrote two books of lives of scientists.

Precocious, Jeans's chief childish interest was in clocks; he could tell the time at the age of three, and early read leading articles from *The Times* to his parents, the pious atmosphere of whose home was not, however, very congenial to him. Living at Tulse Hill, London, he attended Merchant Taylors' School, and proceeded as mathematical entrance scholar to Trinity College, Cambridge, where in 1898 he was bracketed second wrangler. He studied also practical physics for one year at the Cavendish Laboratory, and in 1900 gained a first class in part ii of the mathematical tripos, an Isaac Newton studentship in astronomy and optics, and in 1901 a Smith's prize. In that year he became a fellow of his college.

He had to leave Cambridge in 1902 to enter sanatoria for treatment of tuberculosis of the joints which was completely cured. While there he wrote his *Dynamical Theory of Gases* (1904) on original lines. This important work embodied much research of his own on the theory of statistical equilibrium and equipartition, the persistence of molecular velocities after collision, and the escape of gas from planetary atmospheres. Later editions included some quantum theory; in 1940 he rewrote and reissued it as *An Introduction to the Kinetic Theory of Gases*.

His period of active mathematical research in physics and astronomy lasted from 1900 to 1928; he soon achieved a deservedly great reputation, and was elected F.R.S. in 1906 at the age of twenty-eight. He taught mathematics from 1904 to 1912: as university lecturer at Cambridge (1904–5), and later as Stokes lecturer there (1910–12), after a period (1905–9) at Princeton as professor of applied mathematics.

At Princeton he published two university textbooks, which included examples to be worked out: *Theoretical Mechanics* (1906) and *The Mathematical Theory of Electricity and Magnetism* (1908). There also he married in 1907 Charlotte Tiffany (died 1934), daughter of Alfred Mitchell, explorer and traveller, of New London, Connecticut. By her he had one daughter.

In 1912 he resigned the Stokes lectureship, and thereafter held no university or other regular office; his wife was well-to-do, and in later life he wrote many lucrative books. They lived in London from 1912 to 1918. He gave the Bakerian lecture before the Royal Society in 1917, on 'The configurations of rotating compressible masses'; he was awarded the Adams prize of the university of Cambridge, also in 1917, for a remarkable essay, *Problems of Cosmogony and Stellar Dynamics*, which set out his own and others' contributions to the subject; it was published as a book in 1919. He had become a fellow of the Royal Astronomical Society in 1909, and while in London played an active part in its life, and in that of the dining club which forms its inner circle. He took little part in the scientific effort involved during the two wars.

From 1919 to 1929 he was one of the two (honorary) secretaries of the Royal Society; as such he wielded (with great self-confidence and success) considerable power and influence in the British scientific world; this period coincided with the presidencies of Sir Charles Scott Sherrington and Sir Ernest (later Lord) Rutherford [q.v.].

During these years, and later, he received many honours: in 1919 a Royal medal of the Royal Society; in 1922 the gold medal of the Royal Astronomical Society for his cosmogonic work; the Hopkins prize of the Cambridge Philosophical Society for 1921–4, for his work on gas-theory, radiation, and the evolution of stellar systems. He gave the Halley lecture (Oxford, 1922) on the nebular hypothesis and modern cosmogony, and the Guthrie lecture (Physical Society, 1923), and the Rouse Ball lecture (Cambridge, 1925). He was president of the Royal Astronomical Society (1925–7), to which in 1926 he gave £1,000 to endow an annual 'George Darwin' lecture. He was knighted in 1928. He became research associate of the Mount Wilson Observatory, California, in 1923, and visited it more than once. He was a foreign member of the National Academy of Sciences, Washington; and received the Franklin (1931), Joykissen Mookherjee (1937), and Calcutta (1938) medals, and many honorary degrees.

The release from his secretarial work for the Royal Society in 1929 marked also the end of his mathematical researches, and the beginning of a highly successful new career as a popularizer of science. His books, *Eos or the Wider Aspects of Cosmogony* (1928), *The Universe Around Us* (1929), *The Mysterious Universe* (1930; the Rede lecture, Cambridge), *The Stars in their Courses* (1931), *The New Background of Science* (1933), *Through Space and Time* (1934), followed in quick succession and won immediate widespread fame. They were fluent and persuasive, full of apt and striking similes. They were also somewhat over-positive. This was hardly a fault in the eyes of the general reader, but that and his deistic inferences were criticized by some of his colleagues. One of his most famous passages (in *The Mysterious Universe*), discussing the nature of God, concludes that God is a pure mathematician.

After science, music was one of Jeans's greatest interests; he played the organ from the age of twelve, and the piano still earlier. At Cleveland Lodge, Dorking, where he lived from 1918, he had an organ built, and often played for three or four hours a day, but never to other people, even friends. Bach was one of his favourite composers. In 1935 he married as his second wife the concert organist Susanne (Susi), daughter of Oskar Hock, of Vienna, originally of Prague; she survived him and by her he had two sons and one daughter. Music was a great common interest between them, and he installed at Cleveland Lodge a second organ for her use, designing sound insulation so that both could play without disturbance. He became a director of the Royal Academy of Music in 1937, and in the same year (at his wife's suggestion) he produced his admirable semi-popular book *Science and Music* dedicated to her. This deals with the human ear, the theory of pure tones and harmonics, different musical scales and instruments, the acoustics of concert rooms, and the acoustic properties of materials.

In 1934 Jeans was president of the British Association meeting at Aberdeen. In 1935 the Royal Institution established a chair of astronomy, and he was annually elected its professor until he resigned owing to ill health in 1946. In 1939 he was appointed to the Order of Merit, and in 1941 became honorary fellow of his old college. In 1937–8 he took the presidency of the jubilee meeting of the Indian Science Congress, vacant owing to Rutherford's death. He received the freedom of the Merchant Taylors and so became a freeman of the City of London.

In January 1945 Jeans had an attack of coronary thrombosis; recovering, he reduced his activities, but succumbed, after six hours of suffering, to a second attack, 16 September 1946, at his Dorking home, to which he had been able to return after the war (when it had been requisitioned and he had lived in Somerset). In his book *Physics and Philosophy* (1942) he showed that in his last years he felt the need to survey the universe as a whole; according to E. A. Milne [q.v.], who traversed the same road from mathematics, physics, and astronomy to philosophy, it 'affords little pleasure to either physicists or philosophers'.

Jeans's scientifically productive period, twenty-eight years long, began with a series of brilliant attacks on problems of gases, equipartition of energy, radiation, which established the necessity for some form of quantum theory. Then he directed his main efforts to cosmogony, mainly dealing with the forms of equilibrium of rotating gravitating masses, but also with kinetic theories of aggregates of stars. This was perhaps the greatest and most enduring part of his work. The last decade was devoted to stellar structure and evolution; it included his important recognition of radiative viscosity in stars. For a few years around 1917 the meetings of the Royal Astronomical Society were enlivened by scientific controversy between Jeans and (Sir) Arthur Eddington [q.v.] on the subject of stellar structure.

Jeans's bearing was somewhat aloof, and he occasionally gave offence by remarks which seemed supercilious. He was immensely hard-working, not only in his researches and authorship, but also in scientific business, in which at times he acted with rather ruthless decision. His manner was partly a shield for a shy and sensitive spirit; only a few knew him in simple unconstrained friendship. Working always alone, he had no personal disciples and created no school of research.

There is a portrait of Jeans by P. A. de László at Cleveland Lodge, Dorking.

[E. A. Milne in *Obituary Notices of Fellows of the Royal Society*, No. 15, May 1947; E. A. Milne, *Sir James Jeans*, 1952; personal knowledge.]                    SYDNEY CHAPMAN.


JERSEY, COUNTESS OF (1849–1945). [See VILLIERS, MARGARET ELIZABETH CHILD-.]

JINNAH, MAHOMED ALI (1876–1948), creator of Pakistan, was born in Karachi 25 December 1876, into a family belonging to the Moslem sect of Khojas and coming originally from Rajkot, at one time the home of M. K. Gandhi [q.v.]. Jinnah's father, Jinnah Punja, was a merchant in Karachi, where he became the main proprietor of the Valji Punja Company. Of Mahomed Ali Jinnah's mother little is known save her name, Mithi Bai. After an elementary education in his mother tongue, Gujerati, and an English secondary education in Karachi and Bombay, Jinnah entered Lincoln's Inn and was called to the bar in 1896. Returning to India, he read in the chambers of the advocate-general and then acted for six months as a presidency magistrate in Bombay. Thereafter he rapidly built up a lucrative practice at the Bombay bar where he acquired a great reputation for his ability to destroy an opponent's case.

He had already been influenced by the nationalist movement, particularly by such moderate nationalists as Gokhale, Pheroze Shah Mehta, and Dadabhai Naoroji, and for a short time he was private secretary to the last when president of the Indian National Congress. Jinnah's rising reputation as a barrister and his enthusiasm for the nationalist movement led to his election in 1909 as the Bombay Moslems' representative on the imperial legislative council. He soon won a reputation as a debater and in 1913 introduced the Waqf validating bill—the first private member's bill ever to reach the statute book. In 1913 he joined the All India Moslem League, although still remaining a loyal member of the Indian National Congress. The League was as truly inspired by nationalist sentiment as the Congress, but considered that, as a minority, the Moslems required safeguards. Jinnah was strongly averse from any kind of separatism and it was after he had become president of the Moslem League that the Congress and the League in 1916 made the Lucknow Pact, under which a united demand for self-government was presented, while the Congress accepted separate electorates and weightage for minorities in the various legislative bodies.

In 1919 Jinnah resigned from the imperial legislative council as a protest against the so-called Rowlatt Act. Nevertheless, he bitterly opposed the non-co-operation movement started by the Congress in 1920 and resigned from that body on this issue. There was a widening gulf between himself and Gandhi, whom he accused of being a perpetual cause of disunity. In 1923 Jinnah was elected to the central Legislative Assembly where he led an independent party. He was, however, still a powerful figure in the Moslem League, presiding over its Lahore session in 1924 and the Calcutta session in 1928. During this period he took the leading Moslem part in all attempts to establish unity with the Hindus. He participated in the Round Table conferences of 1930–31 and 1931 and it was there, he said later, that 'I received the shock of my life . . . the Hindu attitude led me to the conclusion that there was no hope of unity'. For four years he remained in England to practise law. He visited India in 1934 to preside over the council of the All India Moslem League and once again pressed for Hindu–Moslem unity, although never abandoning the demand for separate electorates and safeguards for Moslems. Later in 1934 he was elected by the Bombay Moslems to represent them in the new Legislative Assembly, and returning to India devoted himself thenceforth wholly to political activities.

When the Government of India Act, 1935, transferred substantial powers to the hands of Indian ministers, the Moslems hoped for seats in the Cabinets in those provinces where they were in a minority. The Congress decided, however, that such Cabinet posts could be given only to Moslems prepared to join the Congress Party. Relations between Hindus and Moslems deteriorated, and minority communities felt insecure. In October 1937 Jinnah stated, perhaps for the first time, that Moslems could expect neither justice nor fair play from the Congress Government. During the next year or so, the Moslems complained bitterly of their position in the Hindu majority provinces, and by 1939 the breach between the Congress and the Moslem League, as well as between Gandhi and Jinnah, was complete. When the Congress ministers in the provinces resigned after the outbreak of war in 1939 the Moslem League, at the insistence of Jinnah, observed a 'day of deliverance and thanksgiving as a mark of relief that the Congress régime has at last ceased to function'. In March 1940 Jinnah presided over the Moslem League session at Lahore and inspired the passage of the resolution demanding the formation of Pakistan. From then onwards the ascendancy of Jinnah over the Molsem League was complete and he never once wavered over the principle of the partition of India, with which his name will always be associated. He had striven sincerely for Indian independence on the basis of Hindu–Moslem co-operation, but ultimately convinced that this was impracticable he applied the whole force of his dynamic personality to the achievement of Pakistan.

Jinnah combined, to a remarkable degree, inflexibility, incorruptibility, and an uncanny sense of tactics which stood him in good stead in his dealings both with the British Government and with the Congress—between the devil and the deep sea, as he put it. Far more important than his tactical ability, however, were his complete sincerity and his capacity to take long-term views. Although the Moslem League, for tactical reasons, refrained from officially supporting Britain in the war, in practice the Moslem community responded well to all appeals for recruits and other help, and stood entirely aloof from the Congress revolt in 1942. In that year, however, Jinnah rejected Sir Stafford Cripps's constitutional proposals for India since they did not explicitly accept the principle of Pakistan. Conversations between Jinnah and Gandhi in 1944 showed how unlikely it was that they would compose their differences. The two men were indeed poles apart. Gandhi was above all a mystic, guided by instinct rather than reason; a man with his head in the clouds and worshipped therefore by the common people as a god. Jinnah, on the other hand, was a man of the world—elegant in appearance, practical-minded and approaching every problem in a coldly analytical spirit. It was indeed inherently improbable that two such men could ever agree.

In 1945 at the conference of political leaders called by Lord Wavell [q.v.] at Simla, Jinnah insisted that the Moslem League should have the sole right to nominate the Moslem members of the executive council. His general position was greatly strengthened at the elections in 1946 when the League captured all the Moslem seats in the central Assembly, and 446 out of 495 of the Moslem seats in the provincial assemblies. Thus reinforced, Jinnah, although accepting the Cabinet mission's constitutional proposals in 1946, expressed grave dissatisfaction with the viceroy's handling of the plans for an interim Government and embarked on direct action to achieve Pakistan. Bitter communal fighting broke out in many parts of the country, and in 1947, in despair of any other solution, the British Government accepted the principle of Pakistan. In August Jinnah became the first governor-general of the new Dominion. His moral authority was supreme—he was known as Qaid-i-Azam or 'the Great Leader'—and on him fell the burden not only of restoring stability in Pakistan after the appalling communal massacres in the Punjab, but of laying the foundations of its policy and administration. Without Jinnah, Pakistan might have been created, but it is doubtful whether it would have survived the shocks of the days immediately after partition. On 11 September 1948 Jinnah died in Karachi, after two months spent in Ziarat for reasons of health. The shock of his death to Pakistan was severe, but he had already accomplished his task of building Pakistan on sure foundations and Liaquat Ali Khan, his trusted lieutenant for many years, naturally assumed the mantle of his authority, until he was assassinated in 1951.

Before proceeding to England as a student Jinnah married Amrit Bai; after her early death, in about 1918 he married a Parsee, Ratan Bai (died 1929), great-granddaughter of Sir Dinshaw Petit [q.v.]. They had one daughter.

[M. Hasan Saiyid, *M. A. Jinnah*, Lahore, 1945; R. Symonds, *The Making of Pakistan*, 1950; private information; personal knowledge.]      P. J. GRIFFITHS.

[V. P. Menon, *The Transfer of Power in India*, 1957.]

JOHNSON, AMY, otherwise AMY MOLLISON (1903–1941), airwoman, was born at Kingston-upon-Hull 1 July 1903, the eldest daughter of John William Johnson, herring importer, by his wife, Amy, granddaughter of William Hodge, sometime mayor of Hull. The paternal grandfather was a Dane, named Anders Jörgensen, who sailed to Hull at the age of sixteen, settled down in England, changed his name to Johnson, and married a Devonshire woman named Mary Holmes.

Amy Johnson attended the Boulevard Secondary School at Hull and, intending to be a teacher, went to the university of Sheffield where she graduated B.A. in 1925; but she changed her mind and took a secretarial post in a firm of London solicitors. In the London Aeroplane Club at Stag Lane, Edgware, her interest in aviation was aroused, for she was fascinated by anything mechanical, and she spent nearly all her spare time there. She was the first woman in the country to be granted an Air Ministry's ground-engineer's licence, and she received the full navigation certificate. It was with no wider experience of flying than from London to Hull that on 5 May 1930 she started on her spectacular attempt to break the light aeroplane record in a solo flight to Australia in a tiny Moth with a Gipsy engine, purchased with the assistance of Lord Wakefield [q.v.] and named *Jason*, after the trademark of her father's firm. She arrived at Karachi in six days, breaking the record for that distance, but she failed to break the record to Port Darwin since she did not arrive there until 24 May. However, she flew on to Brisbane, but, either from weariness or inexperience, or both, she overshot the aerodrome and wrecked the machine. If her inexperience be borne in mind, the flight was an astonishing one; it aroused universal enthusiasm. She was appointed C.B.E., the *Daily Mail* made her a gift of £10,000, the children of Sydney raised a sum of money with which she bought a gold cup, now offered annually at Hull for the most courageous juvenile deed of the year, and when she returned to England she was met on arrival by the secretary of state for air, Lord Thomson [q.v.].

Her very striking feat was the forerunner of other remarkable long-distance flights: in July 1931 across Siberia to Tokyo where she arrived in ten days, also a record, even as was the return journey; in 1932 she broke the record then held by her husband (Mr. J. A. Mollison) for a solo flight to Cape Town; and her return journey was also a record; a non-stop flight in 1933 with her husband from England to New York via Newfoundland and Canada only failed for lack of petrol when within sixty miles of their destination. In 1934 they made a record flight to Karachi, and in May 1936 in a solo flight to the Cape and back she beat the records for both flights and for the double journey. This was the last of her long flights, but such a career fully bore out the opinion of aeronautical circles that she was a woman of unusual intrepidity and presence of mind. No diminution was apparent when in 1939 she joined the Air Transport Auxiliary. She was lost over the Thames estuary 5 January 1941 when ferrying a 'plane with material for the Air Ministry. Her death was presumed in the Probate Court in December 1943.

So remarkable a career fully justified the many honours which Amy Johnson received. Besides those already mentioned she received the president's gold medal of the Society of Engineers (1931), the Egyptian gold medal for valour (1930), the women's trophy of the International League of Aviators (1930), the Segrave trophy (1933), the gold medal of honour of the League of Youth (1933), and the gold medal of the Royal Aero Club (1936).

When Amy Johnson wrecked her machine at Brisbane in 1930, she was piloted to Sydney by James Allan, son of Hector Alexander Mollison, a consultant engineer, of Glasgow. She married him in 1932; there were no children of the marriage which was dissolved in 1938 when she resumed her maiden name. An oil portrait of her by J. A. A. Berrie is in the possession of her family; another, by Charles Gerrard, presented by Lord Wakefield, hangs in the Ferens Art Gallery at Hull, and a memorial bust by Siegfried Charoux is on loan from the Gallery for an indefinite period to the Kingston High School, Hull.

[*The Times*, 8 January 1941; private information.]      E. UNDERWOOD.

JOHNSTON, EDWARD (1872–1944), calligrapher and designer of lettering, was born in Uruguay 11 February 1872, the second son of Captain Fowell Buxton Johnston, 3rd Dragoon Guards, whose family was of Rennyhill, Fife, by his wife, Alice, daughter of Adam Thomson Douglas, settled in Uruguay, formerly of Moneylaws, near Berwick-on-Tweed. Through his paternal grandmother Edward Johnston was descended from the philanthropist Sir T. F. Buxton [q.v.] and from the Gurneys of Earlham; Elizabeth Fry [q.v.] was his great-great-aunt.

Johnston was brought as a child to England, where weak health, which dogged him throughout life, caused him to be educated at home. As a little boy he exhibited an innate delight in the forms of letters on the texts which he wrote out on Sundays. At the age of seventeen he bought *Lessons in the Art of Illuminating* (1885) by W. J. Loftie [q.v.] and worked from it for some months. After spending two years as a youth in an uncle's office in the city, Johnston studied medicine at Edinburgh (1896–7), but his health broke down.

A magnanimous uncle, who was a successful business man, encouraged Johnston in his artistic ambition. W. R. Lethaby [q.v.], to whom Johnston was introduced, advised him to study manuscripts at the British Museum. With the aid of these inanimate teachers and a modest private income, Johnston achieved his wonderful mastery of the craft which he had embraced, and in all he owed much to the discerning encouragement of (Sir) Sydney Cockerell.

From 1899 to 1912 Johnston taught writing and lettering at the London County Council Central School of Arts and Crafts of which Lethaby was principal. From 1901 onwards he also taught at the Royal College of Art. Among his pupils were Eric Gill, T. J. Cobden-Sanderson [qq.v.], and William Graily Hewitt. In 1906 was published Johnston's *Writing and Illuminating, and Lettering*, a manual almost beyond praise, which has since gone through very many editions. This was followed by *Manuscript and Inscription Letters* (1909).

Apart from work as a scribe and illuminator, Johnston designed for typography. The splendid block letters which he designed between 1916 and 1931 at the request of Frank Pick [q.v.] for the London electric railways and later for the London omnibuses afford a widespread monument to the craftsmanship of a frail recluse. Johnston also worked for the Doves Press and for Count Kessler's Cranach Press. His influence, especially in Germany, was immense. To the practice of a single craft he probably brought as much genius as any craftsman who ever lived. There are some works by him in the Victoria and Albert Museum, where a commemorative exhibition was held from October 1945 to January 1946.

Johnston was appointed C.B.E. in 1939. In 1903 he married Greta Kathleen, daughter of James Booth Greig, bank manager, of Laurencekirk, Kincardine, and had three daughters. He died at Ditchling, Sussex, 26 November 1944.

A drawing of Johnston by Sir William Rothenstein is in the possession of the family, and another by E. X. Kapp is in the National Portrait Gallery.

[*The Times*, 28 November 1944; *Artwork*, No. 27, Autumn 1931; *Times Literary Supplement*, 3 November 1945; *Tributes to Edward Johnston*, privately printed by permission of the Society of Scribes and Illuminators, 1948; private information; personal knowledge.]
MONTAGUE WEEKLEY.

JOHNSTON, GEORGE LAWSON, first BARON LUKE (1873–1943), man of business and philanthropist, was born in Edinburgh 9 September 1873, the second son of John Lawson Johnston, of Kingswood, Kent, by his wife, Elizabeth, daughter of George Lawson, biscuit manufacturer, of Edinburgh. He was educated privately in Canada, at Dulwich College, and at Blair Lodge, Polmont (a Scottish public school now closed). His father had founded the firm of Bovril, Ltd., producers of meat extract, and into this firm George Johnston went directly from school. For some years he worked in Canada, Australia, Africa, and Argentina, laying the foundations of an expert knowledge of raw materials and imperial trade.

In 1896 Johnston returned from Argentina to join the board of Bovril, Ltd. He was made vice-chairman in 1900 on the death of his father, chairman in 1916, and managing director in 1931. Other business interests were directorships of the *Daily Express* (from its foundation in 1900 until 1917), of Lloyds Bank, of the Australian Mercantile, Land and Finance Company, and the vice-chairmanship of the Ashanti Goldfields Corporation. He served on the council of the London Chamber of Commerce, and as chairman of the national committee of the International Chamber of Commerce. During the war of 1914–18 he was a member of the leather control board under the surveyor-general of supply at the War Office. In 1920 he was appointed K.B.E.

In 1901 Johnston began a lifelong association with King Edward's Hospital Fund for London as a committee member. He was one of its honorary secretaries from 1929 until his death, and was honorary secretary of the thank-offering fund for King George V's recovery from illness. In 1922 he was chairman of the organizing committee of the hospitals of London combined appeal. He was honorary treasurer of the Royal Northern Hospital, London (1909–23), chairman of the British Charities Association, treasurer of the County of London Red Cross, chairman of the Ministry of Health committee on nutrition, and a vice-president of the British and Foreign Bible Society. He was raised to the peerage in 1929 as Baron Luke, of Pavenham, in the county of Bedford. He chose his title partly from St. Luke's patronage of hospitals, partly from his long association with the parish of St. Luke, Old Street, E.C. 1, and partly for its brevity. In 1935 he introduced in the House of Lords the voluntary hospitals (paying patients) bill which was enacted the following year.

As a business man Luke was distinguished by his deep knowledge of international trade, and was welcomed abroad as a worthy representative of British commercial life. He understood the principles of good advertising, and gave the closest supervision to the successful Bovril campaigns. His powers of concentration were highly developed; he was calm, quiet, and modest, and a man of deep religious conviction which expressed itself in the doing of good works.

Luke became high sheriff in 1924 and lord lieutenant of Bedfordshire from 1936. A portrait by William Brealey is at Shire Hall, Bedford. In 1902 he married Edith Laura (died 1941), daughter of the sixteenth Baron St. John of Bletso. There were two sons and four daughters of the marriage. Luke died in London 23 February 1943, and was succeeded as second baron by his elder son, Ian St. John Lawson (born 1905).

[*The Times*, 24 February 1943; private information.]     HERBERT B. GRIMSDITCH.

JONES, (JAMES) SIDNEY (1861–1946), composer, was born at Islington 17 June 1861, the second of the six children of James Sidney Jones, bandmaster of the 5th Dragoon Guards, by his wife, Anne Eycott. All the children possessed musical talent and Sidney Jones showed his capabilities early; at the age of fourteen he was already playing solo clarinet in his father's band. By this time the family had settled in Leeds where his father was appointed musical director of the Grand Theatre. With growing experience the boy took to conducting theatre orchestras, and thereafter spent some time as the conductor of travelling opera companies in England, Australia, indeed all over the world.

In 1892 Jones first began to make a name, with the song 'Linger Longer Loo', and the following year there appeared at the Prince of Wales's Theatre, where he was musical director, *A Gaiety Girl*, the first of the operettas which were to make him famous as a popular and successful composer for the theatre. In 1895 *An Artist's Model* began a successful series at Daly's Theatre with (Dame) Marie Tempest [q.v.] which included *The Geisha* (1896), *A Greek Slave* (1898), and *San Toy* (1899). Later productions were *My Lady Molly* at Terry's Theatre (1903), *The*

*Medal and the Maid* at the Lyric Theatre (1903), *See-See* and *The King of Cadonia* at the Prince of Wales's Theatre (1906 and 1908), and *A Persian Princess* at the Queen's Theatre (1909).

The operetta upon which Jones's fame chiefly rests, *The Geisha*, with words and lyrics by Owen Hall and Harry Greenbank, was, as *The Times* recorded after the opening night, 'a distinct and emphatic success.... Musically Mr. Jones has never previously reached so lofty a standard.' The similarity of the subject drew favourable comparisons with *The Mikado*. *The Geisha* had an inexhaustible fund of melody. Moreover, the quality of Jones's melody was always beautifully clean and refreshing, exactly suited to the situation, and his orchestration most attractive, particularly in the use of pure string tone. He never clogged his scores with heavy, theatrical brass, although he could use it with splendid effect when necessary. *The Geisha* has been successfully revived on several occasions and excerpts from the score are popular in programmes of light music. Perhaps one of the reasons why his works were rarely performed during the last thirty years of his life was his extreme modesty. He was never a man to reveal himself and much preferred a fishing trip to a much-publicized first night. Nevertheless, he will be remembered as the writer of some of the most charming and expressive music of the English theatre.

In 1885 Jones married an actress Kate (died 1948), daughter of Imos Linley, an artist, and had one daughter and four sons, none of whom was professionally interested in music. He died at Kew 29 January 1946.

[*The Times*, 27 April 1896; private information.]     RUSSELL PALMER.

JONES, JOHN DANIEL (1865–1942), Congregational minister, born 13 April 1865 at Ruthin, Denbighshire, was the third of the four surviving sons of Joseph David Jones [q.v.], schoolmaster and musical composer, by his wife, Catherine, daughter of Owen Daniel, a farmer of Penllyn, Towyn, Merionethshire. His father died in 1870 and in 1877 his mother married the Rev. David Morgan Bynner, Congregational minister at Chorley. After schooldays spent at Towyn Academy and Chorley Grammar School, Jones proceeded to the Owens College, Manchester, with a Hulme exhibition supplemented by other scholarships and prizes. He graduated

B.A. of the Victoria University with honours in classics in 1886, then trained for the Congregational ministry at Lancashire College of which later in life he was invited to become principal; an invitation which after much thought he declined. He proceeded M.A. in 1889 and in the same year took his B.D. at St. Andrews and was ordained to the ministry at Newland church, Lincoln, where he remained until 1898. In that year he accepted the invitation to become minister of Richmond Hill church, Bournemouth. Under his leadership this church became known to a far wider circle than his own town, denomination, or even his own country. It was crowded Sunday by Sunday, not only by his own people but by the many visitors to Bournemouth from all parts of the world. They were attracted by the personality of the preacher, his appearance, the beauty of his voice, and his simple and eloquent expositions of Scripture. He was pre-eminently an expository preacher with a gift of telling application to the problems and needs of practical life. During the long period of his ministry which ended in 1937 the town extended its borders and the church became the centre of a group of Congregational churches founded by his statesmanlike vision and by the generosity of his people. It was fitting that in 1938 Bournemouth should recognize the great part he had played in its life by making him an honorary freeman.

Jones's work for the denomination may not easily be summarized. He gave himself unsparingly to the Congregational churches throughout the country and loved nothing better than to serve the village churches at their anniversaries. It was his sympathy for the village minister which led him to the campaign for the Central Fund of £250,000 for bringing ministerial stipends up to a minimum figure, while later he was the prime mover in raising the Forward Movement Fund of £500,000; one of the objects of which was to make better provision for pensions for retired ministers and ministers' widows.

The denomination in its turn gave Jones all the honours within its power to bestow. He was elected chairman of the Congregational Union of England and Wales in 1909–10, and again in 1925–6, while in 1919 he was elected an honorary secretary of the Union, a position which he held for the rest of his life. During his ministry he paid several visits to the churches in the United States and in the British Common-wealth as well as in the mission field. It was therefore natural that in 1930 he should be chosen as moderator of the International Congregational Council, an office which he still held at the time of his death. The Free Churches of the country also called him to high offices and in 1921–3 he was moderator of the Free Church Federal Council, and in 1938–9 president of the National Free Church Council. He played a leading part in discussions on Church unity following the Lambeth appeal of 1920, although he thought it unlikely that any specific act of union would result. He welcomed the increased understanding which these conversations afforded and himself preached from time to time from Anglican pulpits. Through his preaching and through the many books of sermons and addresses which he published he made a vital impression on the whole religious life of his age which was recognized by his appointment as C.H. in 1927. In the course of his ministry he received the honorary degree of D.D. from the universities of St. Andrews, Manchester, and Wales. But his renown as one of the outstanding Free Church leaders rested not so much upon the high offices which he filled or the honours which came to him as upon the simplicity and strength of his faith and the devotedness of his service of his Church.

Jones married in 1889 Emily (died 1917), daughter of Joseph Cunliffe, a calico-printer, of Chorley, by whom he had one son and one daughter. In 1933 he married a member of his congregation, Edith Margery, daughter of the late William Wilberforce Thompson. He died at Bala 19 April 1942, and was buried in Bournemouth. An elder brother, Sir Henry Haydn Jones, Liberal member of Parliament for Merionethshire, 1910–45, died in 1950. His younger brother, the Rev. Daniel Lincoln Jones, was one of the first moderators of the Congregational Church, an innovation for which J. D. Jones was largely responsible. There is a portrait of Jones by Ernest Moore in the Memorial Hall, London.

[J. D. Jones, *Three Score Years and Ten*, 1940; Arthur Porritt, *J. D. Jones of Bournemouth*, 1942; personal knowledge.]

SIDNEY M. BERRY.

JONES, SIR ROBERT ARMSTRONG- (1857–1943), alienist. [See ARMSTRONG-JONES.]

JORDAN LLOYD, DOROTHY (1889–1946), biochemist. [See LLOYD.]

JOSEPH, HORACE WILLIAM BRINDLEY (1867–1943), philosopher, was born at Chatham 28 September 1867, the second of the three sons of Alexander Joseph, rector of St. John's church, Chatham, and honorary canon of Rochester Cathedral, who, although brought up a Christian, was on both sides of Jewish descent, by his wife, Janet Eleanor, daughter of George Acworth, solicitor, a member of his congregation. She was a first cousin of Sir W. M. Acworth [q.v.], the railway economist, and was lineally descended from a half-brother of 'Mr. Ackworth', the Woolwich storekeeper often mentioned by Pepys. Horace Joseph's home, after ill health had compelled his father to give up parochial work, was successively at Croydon, Wimborne (where he attended the grammar school as a day boy), Malvern, and Clevedon. In 1877 he was sent, by the advice of E. C. Wickham [q.v.], as a boarder to Allhallows School, Honiton, and in 1880 was elected, first on the roll, to a scholarship at Winchester, where he became and remained to his life's end a devotedly attached son of Wykeham's foundation. He was elected a fellow of Winchester in 1942. After a distinguished career at school, winning three gold medals (an unprecedented honour) and becoming prefect of hall, Joseph passed in 1886 to New College, Oxford, with the first Winchester scholarship of the year, the second falling to the poet Lionel Johnson [q.v.]. At Oxford he obtained first classes in classical moderations (1888) and *literae humaniores* (1890), the junior Greek Testament prize (1889), and the Arnold historical essay prize (1891). In 1891 he was elected a fellow of New College.

Joseph's father had died in 1890, and, in view of new family responsibilities (his elder brother had not survived childhood), he accepted with his fellowship, but not without characteristic diffidence and with some hankering after a career in the outside world, a lectureship in philosophy, which W. L. Courtney [q.v.] had recently resigned. On the death of Alfred Robinson in 1895 he became the senior philosophical tutor of the college and also junior bursar. The former position he occupied for thirty-seven years, during twenty-one of which Hastings Rashdall [q.v.] was his colleague; the latter office he held until 1919. The academic successes of his pupils soon reconciled him to a profession for which his gifts peculiarly fitted him. He always preferred private work with his pupils to public lecturing, but spared no pains with the latter, and was long the principal lecturer in the university on Plato's *Republic.* In 1932 he exchanged his official fellowship as tutor for a 'supernumerary' fellowship which he retained until his death. His retirement did not bring leisure: while still pursuing his philosophical studies, continuing to teach, and taking a full share in the affairs of his college he became a member of the city council and the active chairman of its education committee. He was elected F.B.A. in 1930.

Until her death in 1917 his home in vacations (to which he would often welcome his pupils as guests) was with his mother, first at Holford in Somerset and from 1912 at Dinder near Wells. In the summer he frequently went abroad with a sister or a friend; in 1901, by medical advice, he took a year's holiday, and visited India (where his younger brother was a civil servant) and the Far East. In 1919 he married Margaret, younger daughter of the poet laureate Robert Bridges [q.v.], and enjoyed seven years of great happiness with her. There were no children of the marriage. She died in 1926, and he founded in her memory—she was an accomplished musician—a scholarship in music at New College. He made the college his residuary legatee. He died at Oxford 13 November 1943. A tablet to himself and his wife was placed in the cloisters of New College by the warden and fellows.

Upon many generations of his pupils Joseph made a profound impression of intellectual integrity. He was, they felt, a man 'to whom truth and right meant all the world'. In his teaching, to use words quoted by himself of J. Cook Wilson [q.v.], he 'was always pricking some bubble of language or thought'. To some he recalled Socrates 'in the determination to clear up confusion, in his ruthless exposure of half-knowledge and pretentious verbiage, in his humility and courtesy and wit, most of all in his absolute consecration to his duty, and his utter disregard of comfort and convenience'. 'All his qualities seemed to be expressed in his powerful head, and his short, square, strongly built and rapidly moving body.' He was singularly free from self-consciousness and conventional inhibitions. *Bene vixit qui bene latuit* was his chosen motto.

Joseph left no systematic account of his philosophy. He owed much to Cook Wilson, whom he followed in leaving the epistemological idealism which had been dominant at Oxford in his undergraduate days for a realism to which spirit is as real as matter, and which is nearer than any epistemological idealism to the position of Plato, who was above all others his master in philosophy. In *An Introduction to Logic* (1906, 2nd ed. 1916), which had a large circulation on both sides of the Atlantic, he combined an exposition of the traditional logic with a serious philosophical criticism of its doctrines. In 1923 appeared his only published work on economics, a subject always of much interest to him. This was an able discussion of *The Labour Theory of Value in Karl Marx*. In *Some Problems in Ethics* (1931) he intervened in a discussion begun by his friend H. A. Prichard [q.v.] and attempted to mediate between a rigid discrimination of the 'right' from the 'good' and a utilitarianism which would reduce 'right' conduct to a choice of means to an end 'good' only in the sense of satisfying desire, by the Platonic doctrine of 'a good absolute, the form of which would determine what the lives of all in the common world should be'. The *Essays in Ancient and Modern Philosophy* (1935) had most of them appeared before; among them the Herbert Spencer lecture of 1924 on *The Concept of Evolution*, perhaps the most important of his philosophical writings. *Knowledge and the Good in Plato's Republic* was published posthumously in 1948. To *Mind* he contributed several remarkable papers on our perception of things in space.

No small part of his attention in later years was given to an examination of the view, propounded by the school of 'analysis' associated with the name of Bertrand (Earl) Russell, that the methods employed in mathematics are not merely those appropriate to that science in consequence of the nature of its subject-matter but are equally applicable to all reasoning. Without denying the right of mathematicians to determine their own procedure, Joseph claimed for philosophy the right to question the assumptions, which seemed to him to underlie it, that 'what is genuinely one is in no sense many' and that 'logic studies not our thought about things but our statements of our thoughts or our thoughts about those statements'. In philosophical debate Joseph displayed an extraordinary grasp of the points at issue, an unfailing memory for the course taken by the argument, and a readiness in meeting opponents which excited the admiring astonishment of those who heard him for the first time.

Joseph was of a deeply religious disposition, and *pietas* towards the religious traditions of his home and his school inspired his character and conduct to the end, leading him to take all opportunities permitted him by his sensitive intellectual conscience to join in worship with his family and his college. Familiarity with the Bible was obvious in his writings and conversation, while his constant reference in both to the thought of God, although used only by way of illustration or as, in Kantian phrase, a 'regulative idea', imparted to his representation of the world a theistic colouring. In the hymn 'Immortal, invisible, God only wise' he found a congenial expression of his personal sentiments. Joseph's possession of a true poetic gift is evidenced in the verses addressed to his wife which were included in a small collection privately printed after his death.

A drawing of Joseph, by Kenneth Knowles, is in the possession of New College, Oxford.

[*The Times*, 15 November 1943; A. H. Smith in *Proceedings* of the British Academy, vol. xxxi, 1945 (bibliography), and *Address in New College Chapel*, 20 November 1943 (privately printed); *Oxford Magazine*, 2 December 1943; *Wykehamist*, 16 December 1943; *Mind*, April 1944; private information; personal knowledge.]

CLEMENT C. J. WEBB.

JOYCE, JAMES AUGUSTINE (1882–1941), poet, novelist, and playwright, was born in Dublin 2 February 1882, the eldest son of John Stanislaus Joyce, a member of an old Cork family and a well-known Dublin figure. A fine singer, a wit, and a jovial companion, he figures prominently in Joyce's first novel and also in certain episodes of *Ulysses*. His personality made a deep impression on young Joyce and the verbal audacity of *Ulysses* no less than the boisterous humour of *Finnegans Wake* certainly owes much to this early influence. 'Hundreds of pages and scores of characters in my books', wrote Joyce in a private letter, 'come from him.' Joyce's mother, a brilliant pianist, was Mary Jane, daughter of John Murray, an agent for wines, of Longford. In 1893 Joyce entered Belvedere College, Dublin, a Jesuit school, where his natural taste for literature was fostered by an exceptionally able English master and he was also given a good grounding in French and Italian. He went on to University College, Dublin, where, while specializing in languages, he sharpened his wits on the works of St. Thomas Aquinas and Aristotle, the influence of both of whom is apparent throughout his work. Joyce's first work was published in the *Fortnightly Review* in April 1900. It was an essay entitled 'Ibsen's New Drama'—a remarkable achievement for an eighteen-year-old undergraduate.

After graduating in 1902 Joyce left Dublin. Following a brief stay in London where he had a friendly reception from W. B. Yeats and Arthur Symons [qq.v.], he crossed to Paris, devoting himself to enlarging his knowledge of life and literature. He lived on loans and small sums of money sent by his family and friends and came near to destitution. The next year the illness and death of his mother caused him to return to Dublin where in 1904 he met Nora Joseph Barnacle. Together they left Ireland, and after a short stay in Zürich Joyce taught English for a time in the Berlitz school, first in Pola and then in Trieste. He found great difficulty in supporting himself and his family (he had one son and one daughter), and tried many methods of increasing his income, including writing articles in Italian for the *Piccolo della Sera*, and starting the Volta cinema theatre in Dublin. In 1912 he paid his last visit to Dublin with a view to securing the publication of his book of short stories, *Dubliners*. Failing in this, he returned to Trieste.

Joyce spent the greater part of the war of 1914–18 in Zürich, where he soon found himself in financial straits. His literary abilities were beginning to be recognized and the prime minister, Asquith (at the suggestion of (Sir) Edmund Gosse, W. B. Yeats, George Moore, qq.v., and (Sir) Edward Marsh), granted Joyce £100 from the privy purse. In 1918 Mrs. Harold McCormick (daughter of J. D. Rockefeller) provided him with a monthly allowance of a thousand Swiss francs which continued until the autumn of 1919. Meanwhile in 1917 Miss Harriet Shaw Weaver (editor of the *Egoist* magazine) added an allowance of half this amount. Subsequently on two occasions she settled on Joyce substantial capital sums, the income from which ensured his monetary independence.

In 1920 Joyce moved to Paris, his home for the next nineteen years. Throughout his life he had trouble with his eyes and during his later years he underwent many operations for cataract. His method of literary composition, which entailed the fitting together mosaic-wise of thousands of brief entries jotted down in the big notebooks he always carried in his pockets, put a great strain on his sight, but he could count on the aid of his many friends for the deciphering of these sometimes almost illegible notes, and his powerful memory enabled him always to indicate the page and often even the line where each fragment was to be inserted.

Joyce's first published book, *Chamber Music* (1907), was a set of lyrical poems composed in early youth. They have a delicate precision which owes something to the French poets of the late nineteenth century, and much to the Elizabethans. His next published work was *Dubliners* (1914), a collection of *nouvelles* somewhat in the manner of Flaubert, whose style and methods Joyce most admired. In 1916 Joyce's first full-length work, *A Portrait of the Artist as a Young Man*, was published in the United States and sheets were imported into England for publication in the following year. An autobiographical novel (the condensed version of a much longer work, *Stephen Hero*, a fragment of which was published after Joyce's death, in 1944), the *Portrait* described with exactitude the formative years of the writer's life and the theory of aesthetics he had built up from his wide reading. It served as a prelude to *Ulysses* (1922), the major work on which Joyce spent seven years and which brought him world-wide fame. Owing to the strong language used in certain passages, *Ulysses* could not be published in Great Britain or the United States and it was produced by Miss Sylvia Beach, owner of a well-known Anglo-American bookshop, Shakespeare and Company, in Paris. A growing understanding of the true nature of *Ulysses* (in no sense a pornographic work) gradually paved the way to a removal of the ban. A New York publishing firm instigated a test case and after a long and careful hearing it was decided that *Ulysses* might be published in the United States. It appeared in 1934 and in Great Britain two years later.

It is easy to understand the influence which *Ulysses* exercised on writers of the period between the wars. This influence was chiefly concerned with problems of style and technique, notably in the use as a means of narrative of the so-called *monologue intérieur*, which purports to be an exact transcript of the 'stream of consciousness' in the mind of a character. The structure of *Ulysses* (which is a modern approximation to the Odyssey) is highly elaborate; each of its eighteen interlocking episodes has its own style, symbol, Homeric references, associated colour and technique, and the whole action takes place within twenty-four hours. Thus, despite its air of romantic turbulence, *Ulysses*, the record of a Dublin day (16 June 1904), has an internal logic, structural harmony, and almost scientific precision of language entitling it to be regarded as, in a sense, a 'classic' of its age.

During the next seventeen years Joyce was engaged on what he himself regarded as his magnum opus, *Finnegans Wake* (1939). The strangeness of the language, recalling the 'portmanteau words' invented by Lewis Carroll, and the extreme complexity of its structure gained for it a mixed reception, and no final verdict on this work, despite many expository articles, had been pronounced ten years after its appearance. It has been aptly described as a *divertissement philologique*. But it is also a mine of rich, earthy humour, interspersed with passages of much verbal beauty. The central idea, as in *Ulysses*, is that of recurrence; the history of the world, the rise and fall of civilizations, is condensed into a Dublin Night's Dream. For his purposes Joyce created a language of his own, compounded of a vast number of languages dead and living, and based less on philological affinities than on sounds. None of the new terms used is a 'nonsense word'; each is tightly packed with allusions, the greater part being basically English. Joyce also wrote one play, *Exiles* (1918), somewhat in the Ibsen manner, and a second volume of poems, *Pomes Penyeach* (Paris, 1927).

Joyce had an agreeable presence and a quiet distinction which came as a surprise to some of those visiting the author of *Ulysses* for the first time. In conversation he used none of those ribald turns of speech which gave offence to many readers of that work, and he tacitly discouraged such remarks in his entourage.

He was very fond of music and himself possessed a fine tenor voice. His mind was at once encyclopaedic and synthetic and he rejected no scrap of knowledge on the score of its triviality. While it seems unlikely that *Finnegans Wake* will have the influence of *Ulysses*, it may well hold its place as the most remarkable book of its period, a treasury of curious scholarship and word-lore.

In 1940 Joyce migrated to Zürich where he died 13 January 1941. His wife (they were married in 1931) died in 1951. There are two portraits of Joyce by J.-E. Blanche, in the National Portrait Galleries of London and Dublin; another by Patrick Tuohy is owned by the family and one by Frank Budgen is privately owned. There are also drawings by Augustus John, Wyndham Lewis, Sean O'Sullivan, Brancusi, and others.

[Herbert Gorman, *James Joyce*, 1941; L. A. G. Strong, *The Sacred River*, 1949; Alan Parker, *James Joyce: A Bibliography*, Boston, 1948; J. J. Slocum and Herbert Cahoon, *A Bibliography of James Joyce, 1882–1941*, 1953; *Letters of James Joyce*, edited by Stuart Gilbert, 1957; personal knowledge.]

STUART GILBERT.

[Stanislaus Joyce, *My Brother's Keeper*, edited by Richard Ellmann, 1958.]

JULIUS, Sir GEORGE ALFRED (1873–1946), consulting engineer, was born 29 April 1873 in Norwich, where his father the Rev. Churchill Julius, who became archbishop and primate of New Zealand, was then a curate. His mother was Alice Frances, daughter of Colonel Michael John Rowlandson. Julius was educated at the Church of England Grammar School, Melbourne, and at Canterbury College where, inheriting a taste for engineering from his father, he graduated B.Sc. in engineering in the university of New Zealand in 1896. For a time he worked on the engineering staff of the Western Australian government railways and during this period made an investigation into the properties of West Australian hardwoods. His reports on this subject, and on Australian hardwoods generally, remain most comprehensive and accurate.

In 1907 Julius set up a consulting practice in Sydney, founding the firm of Julius, Poole and Gibson to which came a variety of work from many public and private bodies. His extraordinarily versatile intellect was brought to bear on many engineering problems and he found the frequent laudatory references to himself as the inventor of the automatic totalizator for race-course betting an amusing commentary on the public lack of appreciation of his other services to the community. In addition to his consulting practice, he sacrificed much, in time, money, and health, in giving the best that was in him to furthering the development of the Australian Commonwealth. In 1926 he became chairman of the Commonwealth Council for Scientific and Industrial Research, an appointment which he held until 1945. Although his training and experience had been in engineering subjects, he at once appreciated that the most urgent problems facing the Council at that time related to the primary production industries in Australia, such as food supplies, wool, timber, and the investigation of diseases affecting them. He and his colleagues, in particular the chief executive officer (Sir) David Rivett, so rapidly produced practical results that, before a decade had passed, the Council readily obtained from the Commonwealth administration greatly increased capital sums and annual monetary grants which enabled the growing activities of the Council to be put on a substantial and permanent footing. These grants were voluntarily increased by considerable financial aid from farmers and graziers.

Some years before the outbreak of war in 1939 Julius turned his attention towards the requirements of secondary and manufacturing industries, and with his colleagues was again successful in persuading the Commonwealth authorities to assist in providing for physical testing, engineering and chemical investigations, and the standardization of fundamental measurements, in conformity with those established in Great Britain. He was president of the Australian National Research Council from 1932 to 1937, and chairman of the Standards Association of Australia from 1926 to 1940. An Industrial Chemical Laboratory was built in Melbourne, a National Standards Laboratory in Sydney, and Julius gave his personal attention to the details of an Aeronautical Research Laboratory which came into service by the outbreak of war. During most of the war years he was the chairman of the Australian Council of Aeronautics.

Julius held very strong opinions which he did not hesitate to express, but he seldom failed to gain his point when facing an audience, large or small. He had a very engaging personality, and although hardly

an orator of the conventional kind, his clear and precise diction, together with the persuasive logic of his views and his obvious earnestness had their effect, enhanced no doubt by his rather gaunt face, his crop of curly brown hair, and his very luminous blue eyes. Many honours came to Julius who was knighted in 1929. He was president of the Institution of Engineers, Australia, in 1925, and received its Peter Nicol Russell memorial medal in 1927. He was also awarded the William Charles Kernot memorial medal by the university of Melbourne in 1938 and in 1940 he received the honorary degree of D.Sc. from his old university of New Zealand.

In 1898 Julius married Eva Dronghsia Odierna, daughter of Charles Yelverton O'Connor [q.v.], then engineer-in-chief for Western Australia. She survived him when he died in Sydney 28 June 1946. They had four sons, the eldest of whom became a partner in his father's firm.

A portrait of Julius by Norman Carter is in the possession of the Council for Scientific and Industrial Research at Melbourne.

[Private information; personal knowledge.]
W. H. MYERS.

KEITH, ARTHUR BERRIEDALE (1879–1944), Sanskrit scholar and constitutional lawyer, was born at Portobello, Edinburgh, 5 April 1879, one of the four gifted sons of Davidson Keith, an advertising agent in Edinburgh, by his wife, Margaret Stobie Drysdale. Sir W. J. Keith [q.v.] was his brother. After early education at the Royal High School, Edinburgh, he graduated at the university in 1897 with first class honours in classics and won the Guthrie fellowship in 1899. In the meantime he had also won the Vans Dunlop (Edinburgh, 1896), Ferguson (Glasgow, 1897), and Boden Sanskrit (Oxford, 1898) scholarships. Entering Balliol College, Oxford, as a scholar, he was placed in the first class in classical moderations (1899), the school of oriental languages (1900), and literae humaniores (1901). In the Home and Indian Civil Service examination in 1901 he outdistanced all his competitors, and, it was said, any previous candidate, by more than a thousand marks. In 1904 he was called to the bar by the Inner Temple, again with first class honours in the examination. In 1907–8 he was acting as deputy to the Boden professor of Sanskrit at Oxford, and in 1914 he was appointed regius professor of Sanskrit and comparative philology at the university of Edinburgh.

This interest in oriental studies which appeared thus early in Keith's life was no passing whim. His most important contributions to oriental studies were predominantly on the Vedic period, and began with an edition, with a masterly introduction, of the *Aitareya Āraṇyaka* (Anecdota Oxoniensia, Aryan Series, part 9, 1909) which was preceded by his *Śāṅkhāyana Āraṇyaka* (published in 1908). In 1914 came a translation of 'The Veda of the Black Yajus School' (*Taittiriya Samhita*, Harvard Oriental Series, vols. xviii and xix), and in 1920 'Rigveda Brāhmaṇas' (*Aitareya* and *Kauṣītaki*, vol. xxv of the same series). The two volumes (xxxi and xxxii of the same), entitled *The Religion and Philosophy of the Veda and Upanishads* (1925), may be regarded as the rounding off of Keith's Vedic studies, which had rendered accessible some large tracts of the literature until then hardly more than surveyed. Even in 1912 he had produced the bulk of the matter contained in the *Vedic Index of Names and Subjects*, now indispensable, which had been planned by his old teacher, A. A. Macdonell [q.v.] who had become his collaborator.

The year 1916 may be taken as the terminus of Keith's Vedic studies, but there was no interruption in his labours on general (as apart from merely Vedic) Sanskrit linguistics and philosophy. Almost in his student days he had attained the competence in literature and scripts requisite for the completion of M. Winternitz's second volume (1905) of the *Catalogue of Sanskrit Manuscripts in the Bodleian Library*. He now more systematically entered the less recondite field of the classical Sanskrit, and published his compact manuals, by no means devoid of original observations and independent judgements, on the Samkhya (1918), Nyāya-Vaiśesika (*Indian Logic and Atomism*, 1921), and Buddhist (1923) philosophies. Two substantial volumes surveyed with full documentation and critical appreciation the history of the Sanskrit drama (1924) and that of the classical literature at large (1928). At the same time he was engaged in completing the India Office Library catalogue of Sanskrit and Prakrit manuscripts, a monumental work which, considering the

mass and range of subjects and the variety of scripts, he accomplished with marvellous speed and concinnity (2 parts, 1935). One of Keith's special interests was tracing religious origins, an idea derived possibly from L. R. Farnell [q.v.] which bore fruit in a treatise on *Indian Mythology* (1917); and it would not be just to omit a reference to his occasional, and sometimes exhaustive, contributions in the form of prefaces to books, and articles to periodicals.

That this output of learned work should come from a professor of Sanskrit is by itself no great cause for wonder, but when it is considered that from 1901 to 1914 Keith was engaged as a civil servant in the Colonial Office, as secretary to the Crown Agents for the Colonies (1903–5) and in numerous other ways, and that even after his acceptance of the chair at Edinburgh it was many years before he became free from government work, his achievement fully bears out the reputation as a prodigy which he had won at Oxford. It was during the period at the Colonial Office, and in particular in its Dominions department, that Keith began that systematic study of the constitutional law of the British Empire which made him within a decade the leading authority upon that subject, a position which he held without a rival until his death. His greatest book, *Responsible Government in the Dominions*, had its beginning when it appeared in 1909 as a relatively small work of 300 pages. In 1912 it was published, greatly expanded, and rewritten, in three volumes—probably its most valuable version—and a revised edition in two volumes appeared in 1928. No later edition of this authoritative work was to appear, but Keith published a long series of other books on the subject, and brought them up to date as each year, especially after 1920, made revisions necessary. The most valuable were probably *Imperial Unity and the Dominions* (1916), *The Sovereignty of the British Dominions* (1929), *The Constitutional Law of the British Dominions* (1933), *The Governments of the British Empire* (1935), and *The Dominions as Sovereign States* (1938). Nor were Keith's interests confined narrowly to the law or to the Dominions. He wrote a lucid and useful history of the colonial empire from its origins to the loss of the American colonies, entitled *Constitutional History of the First British Empire* (1930); he expounded the constitutional development of India in *A Constitutional History of*

*India, 1600–1935* (1936); and in his later years he became interested in the constitutional history of the home country itself, publishing *The King and the Imperial Crown* (1936), *The British Cabinet System, 1830–1938* (1939), and *The Constitution of England from Queen Victoria to George VI* (2 vols., 1940); he edited the fourth edition of Anson's *The Law and Custom of the Constitution, vol. ii, The Crown* (1935). He had entered the field of the conflict of laws in 1922 when in collaboration with A. V. Dicey [q.v.] he produced the third edition of the latter's treatise on that subject.

With prodigious learning and inexhaustible energy Keith combined celerity and exactness in acquisition and an extraordinary memory for citation of relevant materials. His Sanskrit work is praised for the promptness and soundness of its judgement, as well as for his moral background shown in a self-command not dismayed by the formidableness of any task, nor elated by its completion. In his other field, where he was more exposed to emotion, his judgements on legal matters were apt to be sharp and summary, and his pugnacity aroused great controversy. In his letters to *The Times* and the *Scotsman* he naturally displayed his talent for hard hitting and his touch of prejudice. His books, many of which were variations on a previous theme under a new name, show signs of hurry, and the corrections made in attempts to bring the books up to date were not always well thought out. The style is not usually attractive: its excessive legalism and crabbed obscurity prevented him from ever attaining the influence exercised on legal thought by Dicey. Nevertheless, his works are authoritative and are quoted on both sides in any constitutional crisis within the Commonwealth. In his nature there was a kindness and generosity which was not apparent at first acquaintance, and younger men beginning their labours in the field where he was master soon became aware of the openhandedness of his assistance.

Keith married in 1912 Margaret Balfour (died 1934), daughter of Charles Allan, town clerk of Bathgate, West Lothian. She assisted him greatly in his work and in particular in the composition of his letters to the press. They had no children. After his wife's death, which was a great blow to him, he became more and more of a recluse, and he died in Edinburgh 6 October 1944. He obtained the degrees of D.C.L. (Oxford, 1911) and D.Litt. (Edinburgh, 1914), and he received the honorary degree of LL.D. from the university of Leeds in 1936. He was elected F.B.A. in 1935, resigning in 1939.

[Personal knowledge.]

F. W. Thomas.
K. C. Wheare.

KEMBALL-COOK, Sir Basil Alfred (1876–1949), civil servant, was born at Brighton 21 May 1876, the second son of Herbert Kemball Cook, headmaster of a preparatory school at Stanmore, and his wife, Marion, daughter of Henry Davies. He was a nephew of Sir Edward Tyas Cook [q.v.]; two other uncles were distinguished schoolmasters, at Winchester and St. Paul's, while another became chief charity commissioner.

Kemball-Cook was educated at Temple Grove, where he won scholarships for Westminster and Eton, choosing the latter. He went to Cambridge in 1895, having been elected into a scholarship at King's College, and in 1898 was placed in the first division of the second class of part i of the classical tripos. He did not distinguish himself on the playing fields— he had a severe illness when about thirteen —but he rowed in the King's College trial eights in 1895, was a keen cyclist and hill walker in his earlier years, and later became and remained an enthusiastic motorist. He was always a skilful photographer. At Cambridge he belonged to a little society which included men of the calibre of (Sir) John Evelyn Shuckburgh and Mr. Hugh Fletcher Moulton, an association which continued after they came down.

Kemball-Cook passed into the first class of the Civil Service by open competition and was appointed to the transport department of the Admiralty in 1900. This department was responsible for providing the merchant shipping required for the sea conveyance of naval, military and, later, air personnel, *matériel*, munitions, coal, oil, and all other requirements of the fighting forces of the Empire which had to be moved overseas. This work required close and daily contact and negotiation with the British shipping industry. The outbreak of war with Germany in 1914 threw great responsibilities on the department and led to rapid increases in staff. Kemball-Cook had been promoted to principal and when the department became part of the newly created Ministry of Shipping and, in effect, took control of all British shipping, he became director of naval sea transport (1917). He distinguished himself in this post and in 1918 was appointed C.B. To ability and energy he joined the capacity for working harmoniously with the representatives of the United States, France, and other countries whose shipping interests were large, and whose goodwill, and help were necessary. This led in 1920 to his being seconded for service with the Reparation Commission in Paris where he became chairman of the managing board of the Maritime Service. In 1921 he was appointed assistant British delegate on the Reparation Commission, a post which he held until 1926, and which necessitated long residence in Paris. In 1925 he was appointed K.C.M.G. When his work with the Reparation Commission ended he retired from the Civil Service.

In 1927 Kemball-Cook became managing director of the British Tanker Company, Ltd., a post in which he was responsible for the efficiency of the shipping fleet of the Anglo-Persian Oil Company. This post he held until 1935. From 1936 to 1938 he was director of the British Guiana Consolidated Goldfields, Ltd. During the war of 1939–45 he served as an air-raid warden and from 1942 to 1948 he acted first as deputy and then as divisional food officer for London.

A man of high intellectual qualities, quick in comprehension, lucid, crisp, and orderly in discussion, ready to accept a new or different point of view and quick to assess its validity; firm in maintaining his position if not convinced by arguments, he was a first-rate organizer and a rapid worker. His personality was pleasant and friendly, his manner cheerful and easy. These qualities made him acceptable to foreigners, who soon learned to have confidence in his fairness and good faith. He received a number of foreign decorations. He had a keen sense of humour; read much, and in his Admiralty days was a great admirer of Pepys whom he quoted to good purpose.

He was twice married: first, in 1906 to Nancy Annie, daughter of Henry Pavitt, superintendent of a sugar works, by whom he had four sons and one daughter. The marriage was dissolved in 1931 and he then married in that year Cécile Protopopesco, a widow, and daughter of Paul Olenitch, a former general in the Imperial Russian Army. He died in London 28 November 1949.

[*The Times*, 29 November 1949; private information; personal knowledge.]

E. JULIAN FOLEY.

KEMP, STANLEY WELLS (1882–1945), zoologist and oceanographer, was born in London 14 June 1882, the second of the three sons of Stephen Benjamin Kemp, professor of pianoforte at the Royal Academy of Music and the Royal College of Music, by his first wife, Clara Wells, daughter of Frederick Beasley, of London, of independent means. He was educated at St. Paul's School and at Trinity College, Dublin, where he graduated in 1903 with a first senior moderatorship (gold medal) in natural science, with zoology as his special subject. He obtained the degree of Sc.D. in 1919. While he retained a lifelong interest in entomology which began in his earliest schooldays, his first appointment gave him a love of marine biology which determined the whole course of his career. As soon as he had graduated he was appointed assistant naturalist in the fisheries branch of the Department of Agriculture of Ireland and came under the influence of Ernest W. L. Holt who was then its scientific adviser and one of the early pioneers in fisheries research; with Holt he took part in a series of cruises to explore the life of the continental slope to the west and southwest of Ireland from depths of 300 to 1,000 fathoms. He wrote many papers on the results of these dredgings and trawlings, and became an authority on the decapod Crustacea.

In 1910 he was appointed senior assistant superintendent of the zoological and anthropological section of the Indian Museum, which was later, in 1916, reconstituted as the Zoological Survey of India. He continued to work on the Crustacea and between 1910 and 1925 published thirty-three papers on the group in addition to a larger monograph on 'The Crustacea Stomatopoda of the Indo-Pacific region' and several other zoological papers. During his period in India he took part in many expeditions. In 1911 he visited the Kumaon Lakes in the Western Himalayas and in the following year, while accompanying the Abor expedition to the north-east of India, discovered the first onychophoran (Peripatus-like animal) to be found in Asia. In 1913 and 1914 he made marine collections at the extreme south of India and also investigated the Chilka Lake in Orissa; in the following year he collected on the coral reefs of the Andaman Islands and visited the Sundarbans to explore the life of the Gangetic delta where he discovered some remarkable new fish and crustacea with a striking resemblance to deep-water forms. He became superintendent of the reconstituted Zoological Survey in 1916 and carried out extensive war-time researches to see if any of the freshwater snails of India might be possible second hosts for the dreaded human parasite *Schistosoma* (*Bilhartzia*); he was able to dispel the fear that this disease might be introduced by troops returning from Mesopotamia. He visited the Andaman Islands once more in 1921, and in 1922 made an outstanding exploration of the Siju cave in the Garo Hills of Assam.

Kemp left India in 1924 to become the first director of the *Discovery* investigations set up by the Colonial Office to study all the physical and biological conditions of the Antarctic seas; the main object was to gain the necessary knowledge to enable the stocks of whales to be conserved by regulating according to scientific findings the rapidly developing 'fishery'. Kemp planned in the broadest possible manner and led the first two major expeditions; these were the voyage in 1925–7 of the *Discovery*—Captain Scott's famous ship re-equipped for oceano-graphical work—and the voyage in 1929–31 of the *Discovery II*, which was specially built to Kemp's design to incorporate all the improvements based upon the experience gained on the former expedition. The many volumes of the *Discovery Reports* recording the results of these expeditions are a monument to Kemp's vision and energetic leadership. As was truly stated in *The Times*: 'No finer leader and no better companion for a long and lonely voyage in sub-Antarctic waters could be imagined.' In 1931 Kemp was elected F.R.S. and in 1938 he was president of the zoology section of the British Association. He received the Victoria medal of the Royal Geographical Society in 1936. Having the *Discovery* investigations thoroughly well organized and feeling he should now leave the leadership of expeditions to a younger man, he resigned in 1936 and became secretary of the Marine Biological Association and director of their laboratory at Plymouth. Those who were present with him at the aerial bombardment of Plymouth in March 1941 make it clear that he saved the laboratory from destruction by fire, when he directed all efforts to that end while leaving his own adjoining house, with all his personal possessions, to perish.

Kemp married in 1913 Agnes, daughter of the Rev. William Spotswood Green, C.B., world traveller, author, mountaineer, and government inspector of Irish fisheries; they had a daughter. Kemp was tall and well proportioned; he combined modesty and a dislike for publicity with a powerful personality; he had also a sense of humour and a gift of genuine friendship. He died at Plymouth 16 May 1945.

[*The Times*, 18 May 1945; W. T. Calman in *Obituary Notices of Fellows of The Royal Society*, No. 15, May 1947; *Proceedings* of the Linnean Society of London, Session 157 (1944–5), part 2, 1946; *Journal* of the Marine Biological Association of the United Kingdom, vol. xxvi, No. 3, July 1946; private information; personal knowledge.]

A. C. HARDY.

KENNET, (EDITH AGNES) KATHLEEN, LADY KENNET (1878–1947), sculptor, who exhibited as KATHLEEN SCOTT, was born at Carlton-in-Lindrick, Nottinghamshire, 27 March 1878, in the rectory of her father, Canon Lloyd Stewart Bruce. Her mother was Jane, daughter of James H. Skene, and granddaughter of James Skene of Rubislaw [q.v.], the friend of Sir Walter Scott. Kathleen was Canon Bruce's seventh daughter and the youngest child of eleven, by his first marriage. Orphaned at an early age—her mother went blind when she was born and died shortly afterwards—she spent a secluded childhood. Her father married again and died in 1886, and Kathleen, with most of her brothers and sisters, was brought up by her grand-uncle, W. F. Skene [q.v.], in Edinburgh, where decorum was of the strictest. Not less strict, but very different in religious influence, was the convent school to which she was sent in 1892, where she remained until her eighteenth year. In her twenty-first year she studied under Henry Tonks [q.v.] at the Slade School of Fine Art for a few months, and in 1901 went to Paris as a student at the Académie Colarossi.

Her life in Paris was eventful, happy, frugal, and by no means unexciting, as she herself revealed in her *Self-Portrait of an Artist* (1949). It was a formative period. She continued to paint, and, although she felt that she would not go far in this medium, the experience was undoubtedly valuable to her, for she became a sound critic of painting. Her enthusiasm for the work of Mr. Augustus John, for instance, was unbounded. A chance visit to the sculpture class, an impulse to grasp and mould the wet clay, made her aware that this was her medium. The *jeune Anglaise toute seule* became a familiar figure in Chartres where 'the magical and columned saints of the twelfth century' began to exert an influence as great as that of Rodin. To Rodin, her friend, she was at first a *chère élève*, but a never-to-be-forgotten day came when he addressed her as *chère collègue*. By this time she had carried off Colarossi's highest honours, and within three months of her initiation as a sculptor had a group accepted by the Salon, where she was often to exhibit, as later at the Royal Academy.

Art for life's sake, never art for art's sake, was her motive. She would abandon her work to help a friend in need, an acquaintance in trouble, or a cause however dangerous and unpleasant. In 1903, at the entreaty of N. E. (later Lord) Noel-Buxton [q.v.], she joined the Macedonian relief expedition, and no pages of her autobiography are more vivid than her modest description of the privations she endured in Macedonia until illness put an end to them.

In Robert Falcon Scott [q.v.] she saw the ideal father of her children—and that she would have sons, not daughters, she never doubted. She married him in 1908. Their home was in London until the Scott Antarctic expedition sailed in 1910. On board ship on her return voyage to New Zealand to meet him in 1913, she learnt of her husband's death the previous year. It was characteristic of her that she faced this terrible deprivation in gratitude for what she had possessed of her husband, and in a refusal to be daunted, still less defeated, by grief. She was granted by royal warrant the rank of a K.C.B.'s widow. Their son, Peter Markham Scott, the well-known artist and leading authority on birds, was barely four years old at the time.

Lady Scott now turned to her work in earnest. She laboured with cheerful intensity at her first masterpiece, the Scott memorial in Waterloo Place. During the war of 1914–18 she undertook with unfailing zest and success tasks to her as uncongenial as they seemed necessary. For though to help in establishing an ambulance service in France could not have been uncongenial, to enlist in 1915 as a factory hand in an armament works had few compensations but those of human relationships for which she was especially gifted. Her last war work was as private secretary to the permanent secretary of the Ministry of Pensions. In friendship, her greatest gift, her range could be said to be unlimited. She had a passionate and lifelong preoccupation with babies, nor were they in her eyes less remarkable than the Cabinet ministers (including three prime ministers) who became her close personal friends.

In 1922 she married Lieutenant-Commander Edward Hilton Young, who in 1935 was created Baron Kennet, of the Dene, by whom she had a second son, Wayland Hilton-Young. For the rest of her life she became of increasing value to her husband in his political career. She took to speech-making with reluctance and, after determined application, with ever-increasing success in 1931 and during the next four years, when her husband was minister of health and in the Cabinet. Her work as a sculptor meanwhile went on as actively as before, particularly in commissioned portrait busts and statues. A number of her sitters are noticed in this SUPPLEMENT. She became an associate and later a fellow of the Royal Society of British Sculptors and took a warm interest in the society. Her modelling possesses a mastery which only talent and training can achieve. It is both vital and controlled. In her portrait sculpture she achieves to a remarkable degree a profound appreciation of her subject's personality. In her full-length portraits even the pose of the figure expresses the predominant characteristics of the subject. Her symbolic work possesses a classic economy relieved of austerity by a touch of romanticism. Examples of her work are to be seen at the Tate Gallery (Asquith), the Imperial War Museum (Lloyd George), Westminster Abbey (Adam Lindsay Gordon), the National Portrait Gallery (Lord Reading and W. B. Yeats), and the Birmingham City Art Gallery (Neville Chamberlain). These, and other works, are illustrated in *Homage, A Book of Sculptures by K. Scott*, with a commentary by Stephen Gwynn [q.v.] (1938).

Lady Kennet died in London 25 July 1947 in her seventieth year. 'No happier woman', she claimed with justice, 'ever lived.' In appearance she was of medium height, with clear-cut and regular features. Her vivid blue eyes and clear skin, never tarnished by cosmetics, reflected the warmth and gaiety of her disposition.

There is a portrait of her (1908) by Charles Shannon in the Johannesburg Municipal Gallery.

[*Self-Portrait of an Artist*, from the diaries and memoirs of Lady Kennet, 1949; private information.]          GEOFFREY DEARMER.

KENT, DUKE OF (1902–1942). [See GEORGE EDWARD ALEXANDER EDMUND.]

KEYES, ROGER JOHN BROWN-LOW, first BARON KEYES (1872–1945), admiral of the fleet, was born 4 October 1872 at Tundiani on the North-West Frontier of India, the second of the nine children of Colonel (afterwards General Sir) Charles Patton Keyes by his wife, Katherine Jessie, daughter of James Norman, man of business, of Havana and Calcutta, and sister of Field-Marshal Sir H. W. Norman [q.v.]. The family is directly descended from the Norman house of Guiz or Gyse. The chevalier Robert de Guiz entered the service of King John in 1203; his grandson, Sir Anselm de Gyse, was constable of the Tower of London in 1275. Sir Anselm's great-great-grandson, Richard Keyes, was serjeant-at-arms to Richard II, Henry IV, and Henry V; Richard's grandson, Roger Keyes (or Keys) [q.v.], was summoned by Archbishop Chichele to be the architect of All Souls College, Oxford, and became its warden; in 1528 a Richard Keyes was serjeant-at-arms to Henry VIII; his son Thomas Keyes was deputy master of the horse to Queen Elizabeth, and his grandson Thomas settled in Derry where he became sheriff in 1623. For the next two hundred years the Irish estate which he acquired passed from father to son.

Roger Keyes entered the *Britannia* as a naval cadet in July 1885, and two years later was appointed to the *Raleigh*, flagship on the Cape of Good Hope station. In January 1890 he was transferred to the *Turquoise* and saw service boat-cruising for slavers. He was promoted lieutenant in August 1893, and in January 1899 appointed in command of the *Fame*, destroyer, on the China station. For his services during the Boxer rising he was specially promoted to commander in November 1900, and he served next in destroyers and in the intelligence division of the Admiralty. From January 1905 he was for three years naval attaché, Rome, being promoted captain in June 1905, and was then for two years in command of the cruiser *Venus*. In November 1910 he was appointed inspecting captain of sub-marines, and, in August 1912, commodore in charge of the submarine service.

For the first six months of the war of 1914–18 Keyes was responsible for operating submarines in the North Sea and adjacent waters, being frequently afloat, and flying his broad pennant in a destroyer. On 28 August 1914, when conducting an operation in the Heligoland Bight in conjunction with the Harwich Force under (Sir) Reginald Tyrwhitt, he found himself in the presence of greatly superior enemy forces. The position was restored on the arrival of Sir David (later Earl) Beatty [q.v.] commanding the battle cruiser squadron. For his part in this action, known as the battle of the Heligoland Bight, Keyes, who rescued 220 of the crew of the German cruiser *Mainz*, was mentioned in dispatches. He also in December 1914 received from the Admiralty an appreciation of his services during a seaplane attack on Cuxhaven.

During his six months in command of submarines Keyes had earned the reputation of being a fearless and inspired leader who never missed an opportunity of striking at the enemy. In February 1915 he became chief of staff to (Sir) Sackville Carden [q.v.] in command of the squadron operating off the Dardanelles, and a month later chief of staff to (Sir) John De Robeck [q.v.] when, owing to Carden's ill health, De Robeck assumed command of the Dardanelles operations. In the planning of the naval operations and for the army landings Keyes took a prominent part. The great attempt to force the Narrows on 18 March ended in a severe defeat. By October it was evident that the army could make no headway against the stubborn Turkish defence and General Sir Charles Monro [q.v.] advised evacuation, but Keyes pressed De Robeck to make another attempt to force the Narrows. De Robeck considered the risks involved out of all proportion to the gain even if it attained the highest degree of success which could be expected, but the matter was of such capital importance that he sent Keyes home to lay the plan before the Admiralty. The Government then requested Lord Kitchener [q.v.] to go out in person and report on the situation. As a result of Kitchener's report the operations were abandoned and the army was evacuated. For his services during the campaign Keyes was twice mentioned in dispatches, appointed to the D.S.O., and made a C.M.G. and commander of the French Legion of Honour.

From June 1916 to June 1917 Keyes was in command of the *Centurion*, battleship in the Grand Fleet, and on promotion to rear-admiral was appointed to the fourth battle squadron with his flag in the battle-ship *Colossus*. In October 1917 he became director of plans at the Admiralty. At this period of the war the German Admiralty was concentrating all its efforts on the submarine campaign, which was showing promise of gaining the victory at sea as the British counter-measures were failing to stem the heavy losses on the trade routes. If the passage of the Straits of Dover and the use of Ostend and Zee-brugge could be denied to the submarines the German campaign would be seriously hampered; and it was to these projects that Keyes turned his attention as soon as he arrived at the Admiralty. By December he had prepared plans for a barrage across the Straits and for blocking the two bases. In January 1918 he was appointed vice-admiral, Dover Patrol, in succession to Sir Reginald Bacon [q.v.] to implement the plans which he had pre-pared; thus began the most notable period of his naval service.

Keyes now proved himself a master of narrow-seas warfare; the officers and men of the patrol were soon aware that a leader had appeared who would make great demands on them, but would never spare himself and would be afloat whenever there was a chance of meeting the enemy. After strengthening the barrage across the Straits and introducing many devices for deterring the German submarines from attempting the passage, Keyes turned his attention to his most cherished project: of blockading Ostend and Zeebrugge. For the defence of the entrances to these ports the Germans had mounted powerful batteries, and unless these batteries were silenced it would not be possible to sink blockships in accurate positions. For Zeebrugge, Keyes's plan may be sum-marized as follows: under cover of smoke, the old cruiser *Vindictive* and the Mersey ferry-boats, *Daffodil* and *Iris*, were to proceed alongside the mole and land a storming party of marines and blue-jackets who would put the German batteries out of action; an old submarine, loaded with explosives, was to be blown up under the viaduct leading to the mole, so as to prevent reinforcements being sent. Meanwhile three old cruisers were to pass down the other side of the mole and sink themselves in the canal entrance, the crews being taken off by coastal craft. At Ostend, where there was no mole, two old cruisers were to be sunk under cover of smoke screens.

This operation, perhaps the most elaborate ever undertaken by the British navy up to that time, demanded the finest seamanship and fighting qualities, and all vessels taking part were manned by volunteers. On 22 April Keyes led his force to sea, and by midnight the *Vindic-tive* was approaching the mole. Despite heavy casualties, the plan for Zeebrugge was carried out in its entirety, but at Ostend, owing to a buoy having been moved, the blockships did not reach their positions. A second attempt at Ostend, using the *Vindictive* as blockship, also failed.

The Germans cleared the Zeebrugge channel in a few hours, but the audacity of the operation, and the superb courage of all who took part in it, attracted world-wide attention and admiration. Keyes was promoted to K.C.B. on the day after the attack, and he also received the French croix de guerre, and was appointed grand officer of the Legion of Honour and grand cross of the Order of Leopold. Until the end of the war Keyes conducted an unremitting offensive with monitors, destroyers, and coastal craft against the enemy established on the Belgian coast. He was mentioned in dispatches and re-ceived the American D.S.M. In December he was appointed K.C.V.O. and in the list of peace awards he was created a baronet and received a grant of £10,000.

In March 1919 Keyes was appointed to command the battle cruiser squadron and after hauling down his flag in 1921 he was transferred to the Admiralty as deputy chief of the naval staff, having been promoted to vice-admiral in May. One of the chief tasks before him was to arrive at an agreement with the Air Ministry on the administration of the Naval Air Service. It was placed under the dual control of the two departments and the compromise agreement on their respective tasks reached in 1924 remained in force until 1937. In May 1925 Keyes became commander-in-chief, Mediterranean Fleet, a year later being promoted to admiral. He held this appointment for the custom-ary three years and in April 1929 he was appointed commander-in-chief, Ports-mouth. In May 1930 he was promoted to admiral of the fleet, and in June to G.C.B. A year later he relinquished his command and in May 1935 he was placed on the retired list.

Even before his retirement Keyes had turned his attention to politics and at a by-election in 1934 he was elected Conservative member of Parliament for North Portsmouth. He had no oratorical gifts, but when he spoke on naval affairs his sincerity, knowledge, and experience won the attention of the House.

When war broke out again in 1939, Keyes was nearly sixty-seven, but he was still young in heart and physique, and he at once sought active service. In the debate of 7 May 1940 in the House of Commons which led to the resignation of Neville Chamberlain he took a prominent part, strongly criticizing the naval staff for mishandling the Norwegian campaign. Three days later he joined King Leopold III of Belgium, whose army was deployed to stem the German westward advance. As liaison officer he was with the King during all the fierce fighting which ended on 27 May when the King asked the Germans for an armistice. When in Parliament and in the press the Belgian King's conduct was sharply criticized Keyes constantly championed his cause.

In June 1940 (Sir) Winston Churchill proposed that units of officers and men should be selected from existing units to be trained as storm troops or 'leopards'. Eventually they emerged as the famous 'Commandos'. Keyes, in July, was made the first director of a new and separate Combined Operations Command for the study of these operations, for which his experience of inshore operations fitted him well. The chief object of study was raids on the enemy coast by bodies of between five and ten thousand men, and also the supervision of the training of the personnel needed for these raids. Keyes thus became the officer responsible for the training and equipment of the first Commandos, but in October 1941 his appointment was terminated. In the months which followed he attacked the Government in the House of Commons for failing to use the Commandos to the best advantage, criticized the workers in the dockyards and shipyards, and pressed for industrial conscription.

In January 1943 Keyes was raised to the peerage as Baron Keyes, of Zeebrugge and of Dover, and in the summer of 1944 he set out on a lecture tour of Canada, the United States, Australia, and New Zealand, under the auspices of the minister of information; at the invitation of the commander-in-chief of the American Pacific Fleet, he was present at the battle of the Philippines in October 1944.

Thus almost to the very end of his life (if only as a spectator) Keyes was in the midst of a hot fight. He died at Buckingham 26 December 1945, and was buried in the Zeebrugge corner of St. James's cemetery at Dover. A plaque, set in the wall of the Nelson chamber of the crypt of St. Paul's Cathedral, commemorates him and his elder son.

Keyes married in 1906 Eva Mary Salvin, daughter of Edward Salvin Bowlby, of Gilston Park, Hertfordshire, and Knoydart, Inverness-shire, by whom he had two sons and three daughters. His elder son, Lieutenant-Colonel Geoffrey Charles Tasker Keyes, Scots Greys, was killed while leading a Commando raid on General Rommel's headquarters in Libya on 18 November 1941, and was posthumously awarded the Victoria Cross. The title passed to Roger George Bowlby (born 1919), Keyes's younger son, then a lieutenant, Royal Navy.

In *Naval Memoirs* (2 vols., 1934–5), *Adventures Ashore and Afloat* (1939), *The Fight for Gallipoli* (1941), and *Amphibious Warfare and Combined Operations* (1943) Keyes put on record his experiences and his conclusions. He received the honorary degrees of D.C.L. from the university of Oxford and LL.D. from Cambridge, Aberdeen, St. Andrews, and Bristol. From 1932 to 1943 he was honorary colonel commandant of the Portsmouth division of the Royal Marines, in whose officers' mess at Eastney there hangs his portrait by P. A. de László. Another portrait by the same artist is in the possession of the family; one by Glyn Philpot is in the Imperial War Museum, where there is also a drawing by Francis Dodd. Keyes is also included in Sir A. S. Cope's group 'Some Sea Officers of the War of 1914–18' in the National Portrait Gallery.

It was Keyes's complete lack of fear and his gift for drawing wholehearted service from his officers and men which fitted him so well for the inshore operations and narrow-seas warfare with which his name will always be associated. His eagerness to strike at the enemy was not always tempered with good judgement; his plan for a second attempt to force the Dardanelles and some of his plans for utilizing the Commandos, although bold and imaginative, may have held little promise of success or of making a definite contribution to final victory; but had the plans been approved, he would have been in the forefront of the battle. A place in history is assured for him not only for the planning and execution of the raids on Zeebrugge and Ostend, but also for his conduct of the Dover Command during a critical period of the war of 1914–18.

[Keyes's own writings; *The Times*, 27 December 1945; C. F. Aspinall-Oglander, *Roger Keyes*, 1951; private information; personal knowledge.]          W. M. JAMES.

KEYNES, JOHN MAYNARD, BARON KEYNES (1883–1946), economist, was born in Cambridge 5 June 1883, the elder son of John Neville Keynes (1852–1949), for twenty-seven years lecturer in moral science and from 1910 to 1925 registrary in the university. Whereas Neville Keynes's most important work was his *Formal Logic* (1884), he was well known to economists of his generation for his *Scope and Method of Political Economy* (1891). He was a close friend of Alfred Marshall, as well as of Henry Sidgwick and Henry Fawcett [qq.v.]. Economics then lay within the moral sciences tripos and Neville Keynes until 1919 was chairman of the special board which governed its teaching and examination. Through his father, Maynard Keynes thus grew up in close association with the Cambridge economists of the older generation, whilst through his mother he learned something of the social problems of the day. She was Florence Ada (died 1958), daughter of the Rev. John Brown, long minister of Bunyan's chapel at Bedford, and author of a well-known study of Bunyan. A sister of Sir Walter Langdon-Brown [q.v.], she had been an early student of Newnham College, and in addition to a wide interest in public and social work became justice of the peace, alderman, and mayor of Cambridge. Keynes's younger brother, Sir Geoffrey Langdon Keynes, achieved distinction as a surgeon and bibliophile; his sister, Margaret Neville, married Professor A. V. Hill, C.H., secretary (1935–45) of the Royal Society.

Maynard Keynes went as a scholar to Eton where he was eventually elected to the Society. Educated in the classical tradition—he was in the Newcastle Select —he made his mark principally as a mathematician and the winner of the Tomline prize. An Eton scholarship in mathematics and classics took him to King's College, Cambridge. He was no more than twelfth wrangler in 1905. But

at Cambridge, as at Eton and throughout his life, his interests were much wider than his formal studies. He won the Members' prize for an English essay on the political doctrines of Edmund Burke (1904), was president of the Liberal Club, and in 1905 president of the Union. His athletic activities at Cambridge were never strenuous. At Eton he had played the Wall game with enthusiasm and some skill and had rowed with energy rather than distinction; now, abandoning rowing after his first term, he engaged in a little occasional golf and riding and rather more strenuous bridge. The natural centre of attraction for this uncompromising pursuer of truth, companionable and argumentative by nature, rationalist and iconoclastic by conviction, was undoubtedly the group of brilliant undergraduate friends whose efforts to identify good states of mind, with the aid of (Professor) G. E. Moore's *Principia Ethica*, have been described by Keynes in 'My Early Beliefs' (*Two Memoirs*, 1949). They included Lytton Strachey [q.v.] and Mr. Leonard Woolf—through whom he became a member of a small, select, and intimate society known as 'the Apostles' —James Strachey, Adrian and Thoby Stephen, and others who later, with Keynes, became identified as the Bloomsbury group. 'We were the forerunners of a new dispensation, we were not afraid of anything . . . water spiders gracefully skimming . . . the surface of the stream without any contact at all with the eddies and currents underneath.'

Within mathematics, Keynes's chief interest was in the borderland between that subject and philosophy; he continued for many years to work in this field, and his fellowship dissertation at King's was on the theory of probability. After taking the tripos, however, he turned to the study of economics and first came into working contact with Alfred Marshall and the teaching of Cambridge economics. Marshall, greatly impressed by Keynes's ability, expressed hopes that he might become a professional economist; although Keynes found economics 'increasingly satisfactory' he decided to sit for the Civil Service into which he passed second in 1906. Posted to the India Office at a time when it was still small and intimate, he found an interest in Indian currency and finance which later formed the theme of his first book (1913) in the field of economics. Meanwhile he was working on his fellowship dissertation, but to his great disappointment when he submitted this in 1908 he was not elected. At this moment Alfred Marshall offered him a lectureship in economics with a salary of £100 a year and Keynes decided to abandon the Civil Service and return to Cambridge. His revised dissertation was accepted in the following year, when he also won the Adam Smith prize for an essay on index numbers.

Until 1915 Keynes remained teaching in Cambridge; but wider claims upon him soon developed. In 1912 he became editor of the *Economic Journal* in succession to F. Y. Edgeworth whose notice, together with that of Marshall, Keynes was later to contribute to this DICTIONARY. Through the journal, which he edited to within a year of his death, he exercised great influence over a younger generation of economists. In 1913 he became secretary of the Royal Economic Society, and in the same year he was a member of the Royal Commission on Indian finance and currency. The great impression which he made upon the chairman (Sir) Austen Chamberlain and others such as Sir Robert (later Lord) Chalmers, permanent secretary of the Treasury, [qq.v.] was later to serve him well.

Through (Sir) Basil Blackett [q.v.] who had been secretary of the commission, Keynes advised successfully against the suspension of specie payments on the outbreak of war in 1914, and in January the following year he was invited to join the Treasury. By 1917 he had reached a position of considerable responsibility as head of the department dealing with external finance, and was appointed C.B. for his services. Despite these preoccupations and a widening circle of friendships which included the McKennas and the Asquiths, Bloomsbury was still the centre of his life in London. Prompted by his friend Mr. Duncan Grant, he obtained permission to help the French balance of payments by the purchase of paintings for the National Gallery from the Degas collection. By purchases on his own account made at the same time he laid the foundations of his own collection.

Early in 1919 Keynes went to Paris as principal representative of the Treasury at the peace conference. He was present at the meetings of the Council of Four and acted as deputy for the chancellor of the Exchequer on the Supreme Economic Council. He was not himself a member of the Reparation Commission, to which Lloyd George had appointed W. M. Hughes

(prime minister of Australia), Lord Cunliffe, and Lord Sumner [q.v.], but no representative of either the Treasury or the Board of Trade, and thus Keynes could not directly influence the work of that body. He found himself in vigorous disagreement with much that was being advocated in respect both of frontiers and of reparations, and was convinced that the proposals were unjust and inexpedient and would jeopardize recovery from the war. He resigned in June and returned to England to write, with the encouragement of J. C. Smuts [q.v.], *The Economic Consequences of the Peace* (1919), embodying his criticisms of the draft treaty. The book, outspoken and brilliantly written like all his work, provoked violent controversy in the United States and Europe as well as in England. It has more recently been suggested (for instance by Étienne Mantoux in *The Carthaginian Peace or the Economic Consequences of Mr. Keynes*, 1946), that his denigration of the peacemakers was the source of subsequent disaster in Europe. This view will not in fact bear investigation. In the United States, rejection of the treaty was certain before the book was published. But its influence on the economic negotiations of the next few years was beyond doubt.

Henceforth Keynes was in the centre of all controversy about the economic reconstruction of Europe. In a series of books and pamphlets, in articles and letters in the press, and at the Liberal summer schools, he brought his remarkable powers of lucid analysis and exposition to bear upon the urgent problems of the moment: reparations, exchange rates, the return to the gold standard, unemployment and effective demand. In 1923 he became chairman of the Liberal *Nation and Athenaeum* in which he wrote regularly until it merged with the *New Statesman* when he found himself increasingly out of sympathy with the policy of the joint venture. A 'real' rather than a 'true' Liberal, as he put it, his association with the Liberal Party was closer in these years than at any other time. He contributed much that was important to the 'Liberal Yellow Book', *Britain's Industrial Future* (1928); in the following year his conviction that unemployment could be cured if there was the will to cure it was apparent in Lloyd George's election claims, supported by Keynes in a pamphlet (with (Sir) Hubert Henderson), *Can Lloyd George do it?*

This conviction, and a more academic interest in work begun by (Sir) D. H. Robertson on the nature of saving and investment, and their relation to rising and falling prices, resulted in Keynes's most original contributions to economic thought, and those which have since been most closely identified with his name. Keynes's thought was developed, first in *A Treatise on Money* (2 vols., 1930) and later in the much more revolutionary *General Theory of Employment, Interest and Money* (1936) on which his fame as the outstanding economist of his generation must rest. This caused a furore almost equal to that of *The Economic Consequences of the Peace*. For Keynes was determined that his readers should face the full implications of his new ideas, and in particular the likelihood that the economic system had not an automatic tendency to full employment, as they had been taught by many generations of economists to believe. He expounded a new theory of the rate of interest and of the forms of short-period equilibrium. Almost equally important were his emphasis and development of a method of thought in which he had numerous predecessors: the study of flows of income and expenditure and the factors which determined their magnitude. For a time economists all over the world were divided into two violently opposed camps. In the following twenty years, while controversy on detail has persisted (particularly as concerns his theory of the rate of interest) and minor improvements have been formulated, his general approach to the effects of saving and investment has won wide acceptance.

The influences of Keynesian economics were not confined to a stimulus of academic discussion. As a member of the Macmillan committee on finance and industry (1929–31) which reported on Keynesian lines, and as chairman of a committee of the Economic Advisory Council, of which he was also a member, 'to review the present economic condition of Great Britain . . . and to indicate conditions of recovery', he found himself in controversy with 'the Treasury view' that measures to cure unemployment were likely to be ineffectual. The acceptance of some of his ideas for a planned economy by the Roosevelt 'New Deal' administration in the United States equally involved him in controversy, which made his name antipathetic to many who have unconsciously accepted the essentials of the policies he advocated. The fact that he wrote in the depression years of the 'thirties in terms of the stimulation of effective demand by low interest rates and public investment left a general impression that his ideas were essentially inflationary. Such a view will disappear when it is possible to publish some of the war-time official memoranda, in which he himself used the same concepts and techniques to handle the problems of inflation.

In the years between the two wars the stimulus of Keynes's rapid intelligence and financial skill were felt in many spheres. He had a remarkable ability not only to switch his complete attention from one subject to another, but also to bring each part of his varied activities to bear on the rest of his life. He was chairman from 1921 of the National Mutual Life Assurance Society and director of other companies. By investment and bold speculation he was amassing a very considerable fortune which owed its beginnings in no small part to the profits of his writings. This enabled him to pursue with increasing enthusiasm the discriminating collection of books, which he had begun whilst still at Eton; he acquired a valuable library, later bequeathed to his college, which included a comprehensive collection on the history of thought. He was always in close and intimate touch with the Bloomsbury group and a wider circle of writers and painters and proved himself a generous patron of the arts. He shared many interests with his friend Samuel Courtauld [q.v.] and with him founded the London Artists' Association. In 1925 he married Lydia Lopokova, famous in her own right as a dancer in the Imperial Ballet at St. Petersburg and later in the remarkable company organized by Diaghilev. With her he several times visited Russia and through her he interested himself in the ballet. To Keynes's restless mind, interest meant constructive action and it was largely due to his efforts as well as hers that the Vic–Wells ballet became firmly established.

After his marriage Keynes acquired the lease of Tilton, Sussex, a property which had once belonged to his recusant forebears some of whom, such as George and John Keynes [qq.v.], had become Jesuits. There he spent his vacations, and began to take a knowledgeable interest in farming. In term-time he spent the middle of the week in London and went at the week-ends to Cambridge where he had cut down his teaching commitments after 1919. In that year he had become second, and in 1924 first, bursar of King's College. To the problems of college finance, as to all else, Keynes brought a fresh and reforming mind. He challenged all the basic assumptions as to how a college should invest its funds and, with money at the free disposal of the college, adopted policies which to the bursars of the older tradition seemed dangerously unorthodox. In his hands these methods were successful in raising very greatly the income of King's College and endowing it with the resources for bold new ventures in building and expansion. It was characteristic that he should insist that the greater income was the means to greater expenditure and that he should be contemptuous of the colleges which hoarded reserves upon reserves. It was equally characteristic that his unorthodoxy had in a generation become orthodoxy which enabled those colleges which imitated his policies to weather the dangers of war and post-war inflation.

He was responsible too for the conception, building, and financing of the Arts Theatre in Cambridge (1935) which he designed to provide a home in Cambridge for the drama, cinema, opera, ballet, and music, under management which would maintain standards worthy of the town. He built the theatre almost wholly at his own expense, and then, after a brief period of trial, handed over his shares as a gift to trustees with funds to see the venture through its early years. This generous gift, designed in some sense as a memorial to the services of his parents to the town and university, provided Cambridge with a lively centre of experiment in those arts for which Keynes had a special affection.

In 1937 Keynes fell seriously ill with heart trouble and, forced to lighten his work, resigned most of his financial activities. When war broke out in 1939 he was still a sick man with severe limits on his activities. But when invited in 1940 by Sir Kingsley Wood [q.v.], then chancellor of the Exchequer, to join the Treasury as one of his advisers, he accepted. At first he was primarily concerned with war finance, and was chiefly responsible for a new concept of budgetary policy, instituted in the budget of 1941, which aimed to estimate the flows of personal income and of goods for consumption, and to prevent inflation by framing taxation to equate expenditure with the goods available. In 1942, in recognition of these and other services, he was raised to the peerage as Baron Keynes, of Tilton, with the very appropriate heraldic motto *Me tutore tutus eris.*

Later, Keynes was more directly concerned with the problems of the transition from war to peace. In 1943, a British scheme for an international clearing union was published almost simultaneously with an American variation on the same theme. Both were intended to secure a satisfactory compromise between rigid exchange fixity and uncontrolled fluctuations. Both embodied ideas which Keynes had been advocating since the early 'twenties. An agreed scheme, which owed more to the original American concept than to the British, was referred to an international conference at Bretton Woods (1944) in which Keynes played a leading part. There emerged the International Monetary Fund and the International Bank for Reconstruction and Development which became the main instruments for the regulation of exchanges and foreign lending after the war. Although his swift sarcasm and pointed witticisms occasionally caused offence, they did much also to relieve tension and formality in the series of long and arduous meetings. His domination of the conference was acknowledged when he had moved the acceptance of the Final Act and the delegates rose to pay spontaneous tribute to him.

In May 1944 the coalition Government published a white paper on employment policy. This raised to the level of orthodoxy the ideas for which Keynes had been fighting almost single-handed in the early 'thirties. The final version owed little, if anything, to his pen, but served to show how much of his thinking had won acceptance, even among those who earlier had been his critics.

In the autumn of 1944 Keynes was engaged in negotiating the terms of 'lend-lease' aid from the United States in the event of the war with Japan continuing after hostilities with Germany had ceased. The complexities of Britain's post-war economic problems were for the first time revealed to the American authorities, but that they were not sufficiently appreciated became apparent when lend-lease was abruptly cancelled on the sudden termination of the Japanese war. In August 1945 Keynes was sent to the United States to join Lord Halifax and Mr. R. H. (subsequently Lord) Brand in seeking financial arrangements to meet the emergency. Ever optimistic, Keynes set out with high hopes of convincing America that, in terms of sacrifice, Britain had borne more than her share and that an outright gift was justifiable. He developed the British case at length, but although his arguments were sympathetically received, the negotiations resulted only in a loan, coupled with the cancellation of the greater part of the lend-lease account. This offer, immensely generous as it was, fell far short of hopes entertained in London and negotiations were tortuous and protracted, the more so since the loan was conditional on the early establishment of the convertibility of the sterling earnings of other countries. Keynes came home to face widespread criticism. In the House of Lords, in one of the most effective speeches of his life, he was able to convince his hearers of the impossibility of much that was being demanded. The loan gave Britain a very essential breathing space. But the subsequent crisis of 1947, when convertibility was momentarily established, justified the fears of some of his critics.

Keynes returned exhausted. Ever since 1940, sustained only through his wife's unceasing care and vigilance, he had carried more than a fit man's load of work and responsibility despite constantly recurring heart trouble. Nevertheless in the spring of 1946 he went back to America for the sixth time in as many years to pilot the last stages of the Bretton Woods negotiations through the inaugural meetings of the Fund and the Bank, on both of which he had been made Britain's governor. Strong differences of opinion emerged; the moment was a delicate one, for the loan agreement was still before Congress. Keynes returned to England once more very near to collapse. Within a few days, on Easter Sunday, 21 April 1946, he had a sharp heart attack at his home at Tilton and died within a couple of hours, his death undoubtedly accelerated by the arduous labours of the past few years.

Ill health and great responsibilities had not narrowed his interests. In these last years he had become a fellow of Eton College, a trustee of the National Gallery, a director of the Bank of England, and high steward of the borough of Cambridge. He was chairman and leading spirit of the Committee for the Encouragement of Music and the Arts, and of the Arts Council into which it grew, and of the new trust which reopened the Royal Opera House at Covent Garden. He had been elected F.B.A. in 1929, and among the honours conferred upon him none gave him greater pleasure than the degree of D.Sc. from Cambridge (1946). He died before his appointment to the O.M. could be announced. His wife survived him, but there were no children of the marriage and the title therefore became extinct.

The qualities in Keynes which most impressed themselves on his contemporaries were his immense vitality and activity, and his unfailing optimism and conviction that problems were soluble. Around Keynes, something was always happening. With him, to see a problem was to do something about it. And to do something involved almost always three stages: first, the intellectual solution; second, an administrative technique to achieve it; third, to persuade others of the need to accept his solution. He had a gift, particularly in the economic field, of seeing an emerging problem when it was still obscured to others. He had a still more remarkable gift for dissecting a problem and seeing in analytical terms the underlying issues which required intellectual solution before the problem could be handled administratively; his power to break down a problem and to stimulate thought on the basic issues is evident, both in the earlier discussions on reparations and the problem of transfer and in the later problems of unemployment and the determination of effective demand.

But Keynes was no hermit. He never thought in isolation. The intellectual solution was often reached, after he had posed the question, in discussion with his Cambridge and other friends. His stimulus to thought about the urgent problems of the world was seminal. What passed to the world as the product of Keynes's thinking was often that of himself and others in proportions which neither he nor they could possibly determine. It remains that without Keynes something of the essential vitality and urgency of earlier argument disappeared. It was remarkable, indeed, that his intellectual vitality seemed little if at all diminished by ill health. The body was tired, but the brain was indefatigable, even in the years after 1937.

The intellectual solution once discovered, there came the task of finding a practicable administrative technique of applying it. Keynes took pleasure always in the game of inventing technical solutions of his problems; for almost every major economic issue between the wars there was a Keynes plan. But these seldom represented the unique possible technical solution to the fundamental underlying problem, and Keynes often disconcerted his less discerning friends by switching from one possible technique of achieving his main objective to another. He acquired thereby a not wholly justified reputation for changing his mind—a quality which he himself regarded as more often worthy of praise than of blame.

And finally came the task of persuasion. While he had a great gift for persuading by word of mouth, which showed itself during the years of the two wars in meetings and conferences, and at a critical moment in the House of Lords, it was his pen which to Keynes was the main instrument. He enjoyed writing and took infinite trouble to get the effect he wanted from his words. While he wrote rapidly, as he did most other things in his life, he was the master of a concise, lucid English with an exquisite choice of words and an enchanting irony, which lent to all that he wrote an animation and a lively persuasiveness rivalled by few of his age. 'In one art, certainly', wrote Mr. T. S. Eliot of him after his death, 'he had no reason to defer to any opinion: in expository prose he had the essential style of the clear mind which thinks structurally and respects the meanings of words.' In *Essays in Biography* (1933) Keynes's creative powers as an artist had freer rein than in his strictly economic writings; the delineation both of those whom, like Marshall and Edgeworth (or Dr. Melchior in *Two Memoirs*, 1949), he loved and admired, and of those who were temporarily his antagonists, was superbly sharp and economical. The success of his advocacy, illustrated in *Essays in Persuasion* (1931), owed much to the beauty of the prose in which he argued his case.

It is almost a paradox to say of Keynes that his second great quality was his optimism. He had a reputation, and enjoyed it, of being a Cassandra. He was as quick as the most pessimistic to foresee trouble and to warn of the dangers ahead. But, unlike the pessimists, he was active to defeat trouble. He always assumed that a problem was soluble if the intelligence and the determination existed to solve it. He hated stupidity and defeatism because they were obstacles to the solution of the world's problems. And it was largely through this quality of optimism that Keynes created enthusiasm in

his pupils and colleagues to fight for the solution of all the economic problems that confronted the world during the troubled years from 1914 to 1946. He could easily have retreated after Versailles, with his King's and Bloomsbury friends, into cynicism, or the discussion of states of mind, or have buried himself in mathematical philosophy. He remained determined to grapple with the problems of the world. And it is arguable that it was his optimism and determination, more than anything else, that has permanently changed the world's attitude to unemployment and has removed it from the list of inescapable disasters, to be fatalistically accepted, into the realm of the things which are under the control of human thought and action.

There is no major portrait of Keynes. A bust by Benno Elkan is in the library at King's College, Cambridge.

[R. F. Harrod, *The Life of John Maynard Keynes*, 1951; *Times Literary Supplement*, 23 February 1951; A. C. Pigou in *Proceedings of the British Academy*, vol. xxxii, 1946; *Economic Journal*, March 1947; *American Economic Review*, September 1946; *John Maynard Keynes, 1883–1946*, a memoir printed for King's College, Cambridge, 1949; F. A. Keynes, *Gathering Up the Threads*, 1950; personal knowledge.]

E. A. G. ROBINSON.

[Clive Bell, *Old Friends*, 1956.]

KING, WILLIAM LYON MACKENZIE (1874–1950), Canadian statesman, was born in Berlin (renamed Kitchener during the war of 1914–18), Ontario, 17 December 1874, the son of John King, Q.C., an able lawyer, and his wife, Isabel Grace, daughter of William Lyon Mackenzie [q.v.], the leader of the rebels of 1837 against whom John King's father had served as an officer of the Royal Horse Artillery. King, who was the second child and elder son, was baptized with the full name of his maternal grandfather, and was brought up to regard him as the champion of the popular will against irresponsible authority, and himself as destined to carry on the same struggle. Responsibility in his mind meant responsibility to the elected House of Commons, and in later life it did not greatly disturb him that he had built up a concentration of power in the office of prime minister, and a habit of submissiveness in the Canadian House of Commons which considerably diminished the real responsibility of that office.

King studied political science at the

university of Toronto, graduating in 1895 and taking his LL.B. in the following year. His family had now moved to Toronto where his father lectured in the law school. They were intimate with Goldwin Smith [q.v.], a near neighbour, and with (Sir) William Mulock, and moved freely in the more liberal intellectual circles. King became interested in social welfare work of the settlement house kind, and when he went to Chicago for graduate study in political economy he lived at Hull House and worked with Jane Addams. Returning to Toronto in the vacation he wrote for a local paper on social questions and was soon uncovering sweatshop conditions, almost as bad as those of Chicago, in work done under contracts for the Post Office which was then in the charge of Mulock, a Liberal Government having come into power in 1896. The young reformer was promptly given authority to make an investigation for the Government, and his report led to the first fair-wage legislation in Canada. Between 1897 and 1900 King was a fellow in political science of Harvard University where he took his A.M. in 1898 and his Ph.D. in 1909 with a thesis on oriental immigration to Canada. He was travelling in Europe in 1900 when the Canadian Government decided to set up a Labour department and offered King the civil service post of deputy minister. After some hesitation, in favour of a teaching post at Harvard, King accepted and returned to Canada.

In December 1901 he was greatly shaken by the tragic death of his most intimate friend, Henry Albert Harper, a fellow student and co-worker in the Labour department, who was drowned attempting to save the life of a woman skater. In 1906 King published a small book, The Secret of Heroism, as a tribute to Harper's memory, and thereafter he seems never again to have allowed himself the satisfaction of a deeply shared friendship.

King was highly successful both in labour conciliation work and in international negotiations such as the 'gentleman's agreement' with Japan on immigration to Canada. He was appointed C.M.G. in 1906 and both Sir Wilfrid Laurier [q.v.] and Mulock soon looked on him as Cabinet material. In 1908 he ran for Parliament successfully in the constituency containing his native city, and became minister of labour the following year. The defeat of Laurier in 1911 put an end to this stage of King's career in

office. He lost his seat and was defeated again in the election of 1917 when he ran as a Laurier Liberal against a Unionist Conscriptionist candidate. His absence from Parliament throughout the war was to have the advantage that he was not over-much involved in his party's schism over conscription. In the spring of 1914 he was offered the post of director of industrial research by the Rockefeller Foundation. Accordingly, much of the war was spent in the United States, where he resolved many labour conflicts, but he retained his residence in Ottawa and his political interests in Canada where he still spent a considerable part of his time. In 1918 he published Industry and Humanity, a study in the principles underlying industrial reconstruction.

After Laurier's death in 1919 King was considered by many to be the late leader's candidate for the succession and at the party convention in August he became the party leader on the third ballot. Thanks largely to his tact and determination the breach over conscription was soon healed. King returned to Parliament as member for the Prince constituency of Prince Edward Island and leader of the Opposition until the election of 1921 when, with the support of Ernest Lapointe, a powerful influence in Quebec, the Liberals returned as the largest single party. King himself was elected for North York, Ontario (where he had suffered defeat in 1917), and became prime minister in December. The balance of power lay, however, in the hands of the Progressive Party which, although willing to give general support to most Liberal measures, was not, of course, amenable to Liberal discipline, a factor which greatly hampered King in the development of his policies.

For almost the whole of his career as prime minister King retained the portfolio of external affairs, and with the mantle of his grandfather upon him he proceeded to set himself steadfastly towards the development of Canadian autonomy upon which he considered the unity of the country to depend. He rebuffed Lloyd George's request for Canadian troops in anticipation of war with Turkey in 1922, stating that Parliament must be consulted. At the Imperial Conference in London next year he steadily maintained his view that concerted action must be by free decision after consultation and not by previous commitment. Despite all the efforts of J. C. Smuts [q.v.], already a statesman of long standing, King, the newcomer, would not agree that the Commonwealth should act as a single unit in world politics or economics. Already a treaty made between Canada and the United States on halibut fisheries had been signed by the Canadian minister concerned without a British endorsement. This was Canada's affair. Lausanne and Locarno, on the contrary, were not.

The general election of 1925 returned the Conservatives as the largest single party with 116 seats. The Liberals had 101 seats, the balance of power again going to the Progressives, now only 25 in number. King himself was defeated and had to seek another seat. Moreover, his leadership of the party was threatened by a movement aimed at replacing him by Charles Avery Dunning, a brilliant prairie Liberal from Saskatchewan. Nevertheless, King decided to govern with the support of the Progressive Party, apparently giving the governor-general, Lord Byng [q.v.], an undertaking to make way for Mr. Arthur Meighen, the Conservative leader, should he be defeated. He was able to maintain himself with narrow majorities until June, when the report of a committee of inquiry into customs scandals was laid before the House. King took the unprecedented step of asking for a dissolution in order to avoid the motion of censure which was evidently going to succeed. Byng refused his request. King maintained that, having held office for several months, his undertaking to the governor-general was now a thing of the past, and insisted that the Conservatives would not be able to govern. He suggested that Byng should consult with London, but the governor-general declined to enter a somewhat obvious trap. King then resigned without waiting for the Crown to seek other advisers. Mr. Meighen had little alternative but to take office from a sense of public duty and loyalty to the Crown. He appointed acting ministers only, in order to maintain the tenuous majority likely to be jeopardized had ministers sought re-election in the by-elections then customary on taking office. King, having failed to defeat the Government on a question of confidence, then attacked the constitutionality of the Government itself. On this motion Mr. Meighen was defeated by the chance of a broken pair and was granted the dissolution which had been refused to King. The constitutional issues involved in the events between 26 June and 2 July have been bitterly disputed.

What is not in dispute is that King was thereby enabled to present himself to the country simultaneously as the champion of Canadian independence whose advice as an undefeated prime minister had been refused by the unwarranted interference in Canadian politics of the British governor-general; and as the saviour of the British constitutional method endangered by an illegal Government. Thus enjoying the best of both Canadian political worlds, with the customs scandal relegated to the background, the Liberal Party returned to power with a working majority and with King, who had so artfully manœuvred to snatch victory from defeat, now undoubtedly its master.

At the Imperial Conference of 1926 Smuts had given way to J. B. M. Hertzog [q.v.] and King's position, a middle course between Hertzog's views and those of the prime ministers of Australia and New Zealand, gained the agreement which was enshrined in the Balfour statement, leading later to the Statute of Westminster. The governor-general became the representative of the sovereign in Canada, a high commissioner acting for the British Government. In the meantime Canada had already appointed her first diplomatic representative abroad by sending Mr. Vincent Massey to Washington. King did not live to see him become the first Canadian-born governor-general.

Meanwhile the advent of the depression in 1929 soon obliged the provinces, which bore the whole responsibility of relief, to call for federal help. King, in one of his rare indiscretions, stated in Parliament that, with respect to the provincial Governments 'with policies diametrically opposed to those of this Government, I would not give them a five-cent piece'. This caused the Liberals their only defeat under King's leadership but it had the unintentional advantage of relieving them of further responsibility for dealing with the depression.

Despite the Liberal Party's sojourn 'in the valley of humiliation' over the Beauharnois affair, when it appeared that there had been a disreputable exchange of concessions and contributions to party funds, it was returned at the 1935 election with an overwhelming majority. The Conservative leader, R. B. (later Viscount) Bennett [q.v.], had broken up his party by issuing a last-minute ultra-reformist programme for which it was unprepared and which, coming from that flank, was viewed with suspicion by the voters. The Progressive Party had now given place to other new parties with more durability and more definite platforms. These were the Co-operative Commonwealth Federation, an attempt to combine Labour Socialism and Agrarianism, and the Social Credit Party with a currency reform platform, both greatly strengthened during the Conservative administration by the continuing depression. King, however, albeit with a more restrained offer of reform, shifted his policy nimbly to the Left, in particular accepting the principle of State control of money, and by playing both ends against the middle left his opponents little room. His future difficulties were to arise not from the Opposition in the House but from resistance by the provinces to Ottawa policies, and eventually from threatened revolts in his own following.

King took office when the League of Nations was discussing sanctions against Italy following her attack on Ethiopia. The Canadian representative, Dr. W. A. Riddell, proposed that sanctions should be extended to certain vital war materials including oil, and this was agreed at Geneva, but the Canadian Government repudiated the 'personal opinion' of its representative. For this, King has been charged with a large responsibility for the breakdown of the League of Nations, but it is doubtful whether any stronger pro-League policy would have been supported by the Canadian people, certainly not by the French Canadians upon whom King was always dependent. Moreover, it was soon evident that Canada's fear of precipitating war was amply shared by Britain and France.

Having made it clear that Canada was not prepared to go crusading in Europe, King contented himself, after attending the coronation, with visiting Hitler in 1937, when he told the Führer that Canada would fight along with Britain should Germany provoke a war. He would seem, however, to have come away with the impression that Hitler was no danger to world peace. Nevertheless, Canada's military appropriations were increasing year by year, and the subject of joint defence was raised with Roosevelt, King now entering upon what was to be his most important role in international affairs as negotiator, and when necessary conciliator, between Britain and the United States. In 1935 King had at last concluded a reciprocal trade agreement with Canada's southern neighbour, and in 1938 Britain joined in to bring about a three-way agreement, Canada having renewed Bennett's Ottawa agreements the previous year.

At home the depression was lifting and the sense of urgency in reform had passed. Nevertheless, the promise to nationalize the Bank of Canada was fulfilled; an important commission was appointed to overhaul the federal system, and the first steps were taken towards unemployment insurance. In 1939 the first visit of a British sovereign to one of his Dominions brought King some of his proudest moments and made it evident that history, not geography, would determine Canada's part in the conflict ahead. The seven days which elapsed between Britain's declaration of war and that of Canada sufficed to emphasize Canada's independence and to enable Roosevelt to rush supplies to a technically neutral country. Virtually unanimous support in the Commons for Canadian participation in the war was obtained, but only by both major parties pledging themselves against conscription for overseas service.

A little later Mr. Mitchell F. Hepburn, Liberal premier of Ontario and a former Liberal member at Ottawa, where he had not found favour with King, moved a resolution which was passed in the Ontario legislature regretting that Ottawa had 'made so little effort to prosecute Canada's duty in the war'. This was a move in an operation designed to replace the King administration with a 'National Government' favourable to conscription for overseas service. King promptly turned this into account by securing a dissolution on the ground that he could not fight a war and this sort of sniping at the same time without a clear mandate from the people. The movement to dethrone him was premature and many voters feared the effect of a Government formed without French participation. He secured a record majority at the election in 1940, with Quebec solidly behind him.

Meanwhile King was still jealous for Canada's independence. The British Government in 1938 had sought to train air crews in Canada and this now developed into the vital Empire Air Training Scheme. King insisted upon Canadian administration on Canadian territory. He also strongly opposed the suggestion of an Imperial War Cabinet.

Dunkirk brought a reassessment of Canada's contribution to the war and the country underwent an industrial revolution almost overnight. Turning herself into a vast arsenal she made war supplies of every kind available to the United Nations, under mutual aid, for the remainder of the war. Conscription, except for overseas service, and the bold venture of a wages and prices freeze were among the necessary measures taken. Roosevelt's confidence in King meantime bore fruit in the Ogdensburg agreement on joint defence (1940), followed in 1941 by the Hyde Park declaration integrating the economies of the two nations; in agreements on the St. Lawrence waterway and the highway to Alaska; and in the removal of misunderstandings between Roosevelt and (Sir) Winston Churchill. The most potent outcome of co-operation between all three countries was the atom bomb.

At home, King had still to hold off the growing demand for conscription for overseas service. A plebiscite in 1942 on whether the Government should be released from its pledge resulted in an overwhelming 'yes' in eight provinces and an overwhelming 'no' in Quebec. This convinced King that conscription would split the nation. Although a bill was passed to make conscription unlimited King had no intention of using his powers without further reference to Parliament. J. L. Ralston [q.v.], minister of defence, knew this but was determined that if necessary conscription should come. He offered his resignation; whereupon King compromised, promising that if conscription became necessary it would not again be debated in Parliament but would be imposed by order in council, Parliament being asked merely for a vote of confidence. Much turned upon the interpretation of the word 'necessary'. After the landing in Europe in 1944 the attrition on the Canadian troops became heavy. Ralston deemed conscription necessary, not indeed for the general outcome of the war but for the maintenance of Canada's accepted role. A prolonged Cabinet crisis ended in King's requiring Ralston's resignation. Three weeks later, 22 November 1944, voluntary service was abandoned. It was recommended that 16,000 men of the forces conscripted for home defence be sent overseas. This apparent compromise proved acceptable and, through Ralston's patriotic unselfishness, the party held together with few defections. The collapse of Germany removed the issue from practical politics and in June 1945 King was able to win his last election on a programme of reconstruction already initiated in the previous year with the decision for family allowances and the establishment of departments to deal with veterans' affairs, reconstruction, and social welfare. Nevertheless, his majority was reduced and he himself defeated and forced to find another seat. He had little time for electioneering for, intent upon seeing that Canada played her due part in international affairs, he was busy in London, in San Francisco at meetings of the United Nations, and in Washington for consultations on atomic energy. Soon the uncovering of the Soviet spy ring revealed new international dangers, particularly for Canada as a principal source of uranium. King's health was now declining and he relinquished the portfolio of external affairs in the autumn of 1946 after attending the Paris peace conference.

The Canadian Citizenship Act of 1946, and in 1949 the power of constitutional amendment assumed by the Canadian Parliament in matters not affecting provincial rights, gave King the satisfaction of knowing that his work for Canadian autonomy was completed. In 1947 he was in London for the marriage of the Princess Elizabeth, when the distinction of the O.M. was added to the many honours which came to him throughout his life from many sources. In August 1948 he resigned as leader of the Liberal Party, but remained in office as prime minister until 15 November, having then exceeded Walpole's record for length of service as prime minister in a Parliament under the British system. Before he died, 22 July 1950, at his country place, Kingsmere, near Ottawa, his own party had once more returned to office, and Newfoundland had become the tenth province of Canada, a union which he had long been striving to encompass.

King never married and until her death in 1917 he continued in the closest association with his mother. Her portrait by J. W. L. Forster still dominates, as it did throughout King's later life, the library in Laurier House (bequeathed to King by Lady Laurier and by him to the nation) where from 1922 most of his work was done. King was till the end of his days a practising Presbyterian, but his strong sense of the personal survival of those near to him developed during and after his term of freedom from office in 1930–35 into a spiritualistic belief in communication which was especially strong in connexion with his mother. Mediums whom he consulted agree, however, that he never sought other-world advice on questions of State, and his interest was kept very strictly secret.

King came to be respected as an elder statesman of international stature who had skilfully conducted Canada to full nationhood with an assured position in North America as well as in the Commonwealth; and who had taken a united country into and beyond a world war to which she had made a tremendous contribution. He had for long been admired as a superb party leader, despite his studiously commonplace appearance, his inability to kindle affection, and his ponderous speeches. These he made carefully monotonous lest a more brilliant passage might be inconveniently remembered; and in content they were so laboriously concerned to convey his exact shade of meaning and to cover every possible eventuality that they seemed more inconclusive than perhaps they were. He was always careful to leave himself a way of retreat, if only by the breadth of a hair for subsequent splitting. Infinitely patient, and a trained conciliator, he sought always the middle course which he conceived to be necessary for Canadian unity, even if it took his own party away from orthodox Liberalism and almost extinguished the Opposition. Keeping to the crown of the road and leaving little room for any to pass, he steered the Liberal Party at his own pace along his chosen, if sometimes devious, path. That he reached his destination cannot be denied, but there were casualties by the wayside. He had a good deal of luck, which he knew how to use, and his genius for political manœuvre embittered his opponents and sometimes his colleagues. He enjoyed good living, had an iron constitution, and was careful to conserve his own energies. Colleagues and subordinates were notoriously overworked. The most durable, certainly the most successful, if not the most lovable of Canadian statesmen, Mackenzie King was the rock upon which many broke but upon which modern Canada was built.

There are two portraits of King by J. W. L. Forster at Laurier House and another by Sir William Orpen which will go eventually to the National Gallery in Ottawa. A fourth, done in 1945 by Frank O. Salisbury, is in the Parliament Buildings.

[*The Times*, 24 July 1950; Bruce Hutchison, *The Incredible Canadian*, 1952; H. Reginald Hardy, *Mackenzie King of Canada*, 1949; Eugene A. Forsey, *The Royal Power of Dissolution of Parliament*, 1943; J. A. Gibson, 'Mr. Mackenzie King and Canadian Autonomy' in the *Annual Report* of the Canadian Historical Association, 1951; E. K. Brown, 'Mackenzie King of Canada' in *Harper's Magazine*, 1943; J. W. Pickersgill, 'Mackenzie King's Speeches' in *Queen's Quarterly*, Autumn 1950; Nicholas Mansergh, *Survey of British Commonwealth Affairs*, 1952; D. M. LeBourdais, *Nation of the North*, 1953; personal knowledge.]

B. K. SANDWELL.

[H. S. Ferns and B. Ostry, *The Age of Mackenzie King*, 1955; R. MacGregor Dawson, *William Lyon Mackenzie King*, vol. i, 1958.]

KIPPING, FREDERIC STANLEY (1863–1949), chemist, was born at Higher Broughton, Manchester, 16 August 1863, the eldest son of James Stanley Kipping, an official in the Manchester branch of the Bank of England, and his wife, Julia, daughter of the painter Charles Allen Duval [q.v.]. Educated at Manchester Grammar School, he was already interested in chemistry through the public analyst for Cheshire, who was a friend of his family. After a year at the lycée at Caen, he matriculated at the university of London and entered the Owens College, Manchester, where he studied mathematics, physics, botany, chemistry, and zoology. He then became chemist to the Manchester Gas Department, but in 1886 entered von Baeyer's laboratory in the university of Munich, where he met W. H. Perkin [q.v.]. His first research, on the synthesis of closed carbon chains, commenced under Perkin's guidance. Thus began an association which continued until Perkin died in 1929.

Kipping received the Ph.D. degree *summa cum laude*, obtained the D.Sc. of London University in 1887, and was appointed demonstrator in chemistry under Perkin at the Heriot-Watt College, Edinburgh, later becoming assistant professor of chemistry and lecturer in agricultural chemistry. He continued his research on cyclic compounds during this time, and three years later became chief demonstrator in the chemistry department of the Central Technical College, where he was associated with H. E. Armstrong, (Sir) W. J. Pope, (Sir) M. O. Forster [qq.v.], and Arthur Lapworth. During this period he published several joint papers with Pope and Lapworth, chiefly on derivatives of camphor. His collaboration with Pope continued for many years, and together they introduced *d*-bromocamphorsulphonic acid as an aid to stereochemical research.

In 1897 Kipping was elected F.R.S. and appointed to the chair of chemistry at University College, Nottingham, which he held until 1936. Here, at first unaided, then in collaboration with his staff and students, he initiated various lines of research. After 1901 he was mainly concerned with organic compounds of silicon, on which he published over fifty papers. He showed that the asymmetric silicon atom can give rise to optical activity and resolved three compounds containing such atoms into their enantiomorphs. For this work he was awarded the Longstaff medal of the Chemical Society in 1909. With Robert Robison [q.v.] he studied the structure of the polymerization products of the dialkyl- and diaryl-silicanediols. This work involved detailed examination of many intractable oils, several of which finally crystallized. Those which did not were of the types which have since found numerous technical applications in America, the 'silicone' polymers. He also published many papers on the stereochemistry of nitrogen, and during the war of 1914–18 collaborated in the scheme for the preparation of some very scarce synthetic drugs. He received the Davy medal of the Royal Society in 1918.

Kipping was one of the foremost among those professors of chemistry who, in the early years of the twentieth century, with few students and very slender resources, upheld the high standard of British chemical research. Through his work the department of chemistry at Nottingham became known throughout the world. His severe standard of scientific accuracy was at once the despair and the inspiration of research students. His dry, humorous remarks, his caustic comments and rather gruff encouragements, long remained in the memories of his pupils. To those who gave of their best his friendly interest and readiness to help throughout the years knew no bounds. He was an athlete and a sportsman, and it was said that he owed his perennial youth to an expert manipulation of cyclic compounds on the golf course, the tennis court, and the billiard table.

In 1921 Sir Jesse Boot (later Lord Trent, q.v.) gave the site now known as University Park, defraying the cost of the building and equipment of a new University College, and endowed the chair of chemistry. Kipping entered into occupa-

tion of his new department in 1928. Eight years later he retired, but continued to work in his old laboratory and to direct a few research students. In 1936 he received the honorary degree of D.Sc. from the university of Leeds, and delivered the Bakerian lecture of the Royal Society on 'Organic derivatives of silicon'.

In September 1939 he removed to Criccieth where he and his younger son rewrote the well-known *Organic Chemistry* begun in collaboration with Perkin and first published in 1894–5. He died at Criccieth 30 April 1949, shortly after his old college at Nottingham had acquired university status. Kipping married in 1888 his cousin, Lily, daughter of William Thomas Holland, J.P., of Bridgwater. Her sister married Perkin. There were two sons and two daughters of Kipping's marriage.

[Frederick Challenger in *Obituary Notices of Fellows of the Royal Society*, No. 19, November 1950; personal knowledge.]

FREDERICK CHALLENGER.

KNOX, WILFRED LAWRENCE (1886–1950), biblical scholar and divine, was born 21 May 1886 in Kibworth Beauchamp, Leicestershire, the third son of the Rev. Edmund Arbuthnott Knox, later bishop of Manchester [q.v.], and his first wife, Ellen Penelope French. From Rugby he entered Trinity College, Oxford, as a scholar, and after being placed in the first class in classical moderations (1907) and in *literae humaniores* (1909), was appointed to the Board of Education. Under the influence of William Temple [q.v.] he came into contact with the Workers' Educational Association, and, while at the Board of Education, lived at the Trinity College Mission in Stratford, of which he was for a short time warden. The interest in social problems and deep sympathy for the poor, which he gained in east London, remained with him for the rest of his life.

In 1913 he resigned from the Civil Service and was ordained deacon by the bishop of London in 1914 to the church of St. Mary, Graham Street. He was ordained priest the following year and in 1920 moved to Cambridge as a member of the Oratory of the Good Shepherd until 1922. After two years in Hoxton, north London, he became warden of the Oratory House, Cambridge, until 1940. In 1933 he was made an honorary canon of Ely. He incorporated as a member of Pembroke College, Cambridge, in 1935 and proceeded to the degree of B.D. in 1937 and D.D. in 1943. In 1940 he was appointed chaplain, and in 1946 elected a fellow, of Pembroke College. He was elected F.B.A. in 1948 and died, unmarried, in Cambridge 9 February 1950.

His published work falls into three classes: most of his earlier writings were 'apologetic' and aimed at providing a reasoned case for the Anglican school of Liberal Catholics. Secondly, he published some instructions on the Christian way of life. These, of which *Meditation and Mental Prayer* (1927) is the best known, give simple and direct teaching on prayer, penitence, and the love of God. Thirdly, there were the works of pure scholarship. Shortly after his ordination, he began intensive study of the New Testament writings. *St. Paul and the Church of Jerusalem* was published in 1925; *St. Paul and the Church of the Gentiles* in 1939; and in 1944 *Some Hellenistic Elements in Primitive Christianity* (the Schweich lectures of 1942). He wrote many articles in the *Journal of Theological Studies*, and had almost finished *The Sources of the Synoptic Gospels* when he died: the first of its two volumes was published posthumously in 1953.

His biblical work was concerned mainly with the influence of Hellenism on the language and thought of the New Testament writers. A careful and exact classical scholar, with a wide knowledge of Hellenistic and early patristic literature, Knox was regarded in both Europe and America as a leading authority in the biblical field. He was an able and sympathetic teacher, and in Cambridge exercised a deep influence.

[Personal knowledge.]

EDWARD ELY. (H. E. WYNN.)

KRUGER GRAY, GEORGE EDWARD (1880–1943), designer. [See GRAY.]

KUCZYNSKI, ROBERT RENE (1876–1947), demographer, was born in Berlin 12 August 1876, the son of Wilhelm Kuczynski, a banker, and his wife, Lucy Brandeis. He attended the French Gymnasium in Berlin and later the universities of Freiburg, Strasbourg, Berlin, and Munich. He was a student of Lujo Brentano, the historian, with whom he later collaborated, but a more important intellectual stimulus came from Richard Boeckh, a distinguished statistician and demographer who was director of the Berlin Statistical Office which Kuczynski joined in 1898. Between 1900 and 1902 he worked in the Census Office, Washington, and then became director, first of the Statistical Office of Elberfeld (1904–5), and subsequently of that of Berlin-Schoeneberg (1906–21).

Kuczynski's interests showed a range remarkable even for his generation. In addition to his work as an administrative statistician he produced pioneer studies on the history of wages, on German economic and financial problems, on food production and on labour problems. He edited two weekly economic news letters and published, during the inflation years, his own weekly cost-of-living index. He took an active part in politics, and was perhaps best known for his association, after the war, with the plebiscite for expropriating the Kaiser and the princes who were receiving substantial pensions from the Weimar Republic. He had already made important contributions to demography when in 1926 he became a member of council of the Brookings Institution of Washington and began to concentrate on the population studies which marked the second main phase in his career: *The Balance of Births and Deaths* (1928, 1931), *Birth Registration and Birth Statistics in Canada* (1930), and *Fertility and Reproduction* (1932).

In 1933 Kuczynski left Germany and made England his home, joining the staff of the London School of Economics and Political Science, initially as research fellow and later (1938) as reader in demography, the first such university appointment to be created in Britain. He continued to contribute to the methodological side of his subject—*The Measurement of Population Growth* (1935) is ample evidence —but he also focused increasingly on British colonial territories. After the appearance of *Colonial Population* (1937) and *The Cameroons and Togoland* (1939), and his retirement from the readership in 1941, he became demographic adviser to the Colonial Office (1944). He became a British subject in 1946. Age did not affect his productivity. Until a few weeks before his death he was actively engaged with promoting new and more accurate censuses, especially in the West Indies. He also found time to undertake a massive *Demographic Survey of the British Colonial Empire*, completed with the assistance of his daughter Brigitte and published in three volumes (1948–53) after his death. He was in addition a most active member of the statistics committee of the Royal Commission on population.

Kuczynski's influence on demography did not derive primarily from his theoretical contributions, although the gross reproduction rate which he devised is a fertility index of considerable importance. His systematic analysis of population and vital statistics was an even more significant contribution, and one to which he brought a unique combination of insight, vast common sense, and impeccable scholarship. He was a man of great personality and charm, stimulating others by his own example and by his help and advice. No one who met him could fail to be impressed by his warmth and generosity. He died in London 25 November 1947, a few months after the death of his wife, Berta Gradenwitz, whom he married in 1903. They had one son and five daughters. A charcoal drawing by his wife is in the possession of his family.

[Bibliography of the demographic studies of Dr. R. R. Kuczynski in *Population Studies*, vol. ii, No. 1, June 1948; private information; personal knowledge.]                    D. V. GLASS.

LAIRD, JOHN (1887–1946), regius professor of moral philosophy in the university of Aberdeen, was born at Durris, Kincardineshire, 17 May 1887, the eldest son of the Rev. D. M. W. Laird by his wife, Margaret, daughter of John Stewart, schoolmaster. His father was the third in succession to enter the ministry of the Scottish Church, and this hereditary connexion was not without its influence on young Laird. The place of his birth was symbolic of his character. His home was set just where the Dee valley becomes smoother as it approaches the sea, but in the distance there are glimpses of lofty mountains; and in Laird's nature there was an unusual mingling of rugged strength with tenderness and kindliness. The locality was also suggestive of his philosophical work, for in the adjacent parish was born Thomas Reid [q.v.], the Scottish philosopher whose metaphysical realism Laird afterwards discovered that he shared.

His education at the village school of Durris was simple but effective and the headmaster had an awakening influence. Two years at the grammar school of Aberdeen followed, and then the family moved to Edinburgh where Laird entered the university. Although in the eyes of his fellow students he soon established himself as one of the most brilliant of their number, he himself was not enthusiastic about his Edinburgh days. He admired A. S. Pringle-Pattison [q.v.], the best-known member of the philosophical faculty, but thought his lectures 'smelled of lavender'. He graduated M.A. with a first class in philosophy in 1908 and in that year was awarded the Shaw fellowship, the blue riband of Scottish philosophical scholarship.

Laird's philosophical awakening came at Cambridge, where he himself said that he 'began all over again'. Beginning again was an abiding characteristic; his lifelong attitude is suggested in the opening paragraph of his first book: 'a complete or final answer . . . is of course unattainable until the day when all speculative problems have found their solution'. He was a senior scholar of Trinity College and was placed in the first class in both parts of the moral sciences tripos (1910, 1911). After a year as assistant in St. Andrews University and another short period as professor of philosophy at Dalhousie University, Nova Scotia, he went in 1913 to Queen's University, Belfast, as professor of logic and metaphysics. His wish to be a Scots professor was fulfilled in 1924 by his appointment as regius professor of moral philosophy in Aberdeen, where he remained for the rest of his days, resisting temptations to move to any wider sphere to which his growing reputation would have given him entrance. He accepted, however, several invitations to give special lectures in other universities—the Gifford lectures in Glasgow (1939), the Herbert Spencer lecture in Oxford (1944), the Forwood lectures in Liverpool (1945), and others. In Aberdeen he made his influence forcibly felt, not only in the work of his chair but in the wider administration of the university, and he left behind him a reputation for penetrative insight and fair dealing.

From his special subject of moral philosophy he frequently escaped in the direction of metaphysics, which he alleged were 'always breaking in'. His first book, *Problems of the Self* (1917), an expansion of his Shaw lectures, was a manifesto of his philosophical intention, and his *Study in Realism* (1920) defines further his prevailing epistemological and metaphysical position. The particular type of realism which he adopted is stated with great clearness in his brilliant contribution to *Contemporary British Philosophy* (1924). One or two more purely ethical books followed, and then he turned his attention for a while to the history of philosophy, and produced three valuable short studies —on Hume, Hobbes, and *Recent Philosophy*. He returned to more strictly ethical writing in his *An Enquiry into Moral Notions* (1935), but its somewhat critical reception slightly disappointed him, as he thought the importance of the subject (the relation between the 'right' and the 'good') called for more sympathetic attention. He therefore very willingly accepted the opportunity, which the Gifford lectures gave him, of turning his attention once more to metaphysics, and these lectures provided the substance of his two greatest books, *Theism and Cosmology* (1940) and *Mind and Deity* (1941). He was a slightly repressive guardian in respect of all theological speculation, but seemed to think that theologians might be justified if they did not overreach themselves and were careful about the solidity of their foundations. Perhaps he himself was excessively nervous about his foundations, but in the latter book he raises a more conspicuous superstructure, and reaches securely the firm conviction that theism, which in his earlier days he had described as 'a decrepit metaphysical vehicle harnessed to poetry', could carry arguments of considerable weight. *The Device of Government* (1944), war-time lectures to the troops, attracted considerable attention. Several smaller books appeared shortly after his death, which took place at Aberdeen 5 August 1946. One of these, *Philosophical Incursions into English Literature* (1946), is in lighter vein than the rest of his works, and shows his abiding literary interests. He received the honorary degrees of LL.D. from the university of Edinburgh (1935), and of D.Lit. (1945) from Belfast, and was elected F.B.A. in 1933.

He married in 1919 Helen Ritchie, daughter of John Forbes, linen manufacturer, of Belfast; they had one son who died in childhood.

[*Aberdeen University Review*, vol. xxxii, 1947–8; W. S. Urquhart in *Proceedings* of the British Academy, vol. xxxii, 1946; private information; personal knowledge.]

W. S. Urquhart.

LAKE, KIRSOPP (1872–1946), biblical scholar, was born in Southampton 7 April 1872, the son of a physician and surgeon, George Anthony Kirsopp Lake, and his wife, Isabel Oke Clark. He was educated at St. Paul's School and Lincoln College,

Oxford, where he was placed in the second class of the honours list in theology in 1895, and was Arnold essay prizeman in 1902. He was curate of Lumley, Durham, from 1895 until 1896 when he was ordained priest. From 1897 to 1904 he was curate of St. Mary the Virgin, Oxford. Here one of his most important works was written, *The Text of the New Testament* (1900, 6th, revised, ed. by Silva New, 1928). He also edited *Codex 1 of the Gospels and its Allies* (1902) the group of manuscripts now known as 'Fam. 1' or the 'Lake Group', and also various texts from Mount Athos.

From 1904 to 1914 he was professor ordinarius of early Christian literature and New Testament exegesis at the university of Leyden, where in addition to further research and writings in the field of textual criticism he produced two major works, *The Historical Evidence for the Resurrection of Jesus Christ* (1907) and *The Earlier Epistles of St. Paul* (1911). The latter, characterized alike by wide learning and careful judgement, was a kind of prolegomenon to his work, undertaken with F. J. Foakes Jackson [q.v.], *The Beginnings of Christianity* (5 vols., 1920–33), as an immense introduction to the Book of Acts. Lake gave to many readers of the *Earlier Epistles* a sense of their relation to the contemporary world of the first century, a realization of the importance of Koine Greek and of the ubiquitous and all-pervasive influence of the Jewish and Hellenistic religions in the world of St. Paul and his earliest converts. All later New Testament study has been influenced by this book. In 1911 he published, with his wife, his photographic facsimile of the *Codex Sinaiticus Petropolitanus: the New Testament, the Epistle of Barnabas, and the Shepherd of Hermas*.

In 1914 Lake removed to the United States and became professor of early Christian literature at Harvard; in 1919 he became Winn professor of ecclesiastical history and in 1932 professor of history. In 1934–9 he published in ten fascicles a series of examples of *Dated Greek Minuscule Manuscripts to the Year 1200*. In 1938 he retired as emeritus, and died at South Pasadena, California, 10 November 1946.

As an archaeologist and palaeographer he made many summer visits to Mount Athos and other libraries; during his Harvard days he headed the archaeological expeditions (1930, 1935) to Serabit in the Sinai Peninsula, to Samaria (1932, 1934), and to Lake Van in Turkey (1938,

1939). He was elected an honorary fellow of Lincoln College, Oxford, in 1941, was a fellow of the American Academy of Arts and Sciences, a corresponding member of the Preussische Akademie der Wissenschaften, and in 1936 was awarded the British Academy medal for biblical studies. He received the honorary degrees of D.D., St. Andrews (1911), Th.D., Leyden (1922), Litt.D., Michigan (1926), and Ph.D., Heidelberg (1936). His chief contributions to scholarship have been in the historical field, especially the study of St. Paul and the Acts of the Apostles, and in textual criticism, where he not only popularized the study and introduced it to many students, but made marked, permanent progress in such new areas as the identification of the Lake Group of manuscripts and of the so-called Caesarean text, the type of text associated with the ancient library of Pamphilus at Caesarea.

Lake was twice married: first, in 1904 to Helen Courthope, daughter of Sidney Mills Forman, a business man of Newcastle upon Tyne. They had one son and one daughter. The marriage was dissolved in 1932 and in that year Lake married Silva Tipple New, daughter of Bertrand Tipple, who survived him. There was one son of the second marriage.

A drawing of Lake by J. S. Sargent is at Lincoln College, Oxford.

[Private information; personal knowledge.]
F. C. GRANT.

LAMBART, FREDERICK RUDOLPH, tenth EARL OF CAVAN (1865–1946), field-marshal, was born 16 October 1865 at the rectory of Ayot St. Lawrence, Hertfordshire, the benefice held by the Rev. John Olive, his maternal grandfather. He was the eldest son of Frederick Edward Gould Lambart, Viscount Kilcoursie, later the ninth Earl of Cavan, and his wife, Mary Sneade Olive. The founder of the family fortunes was a well-known Elizabethan soldier, Sir Oliver Lambart, first Baron Lambart of Cavan [q.v.]. The boy was educated at Eton where, as he recalled many years later, 'a villain with a black beard' (the sergeant major) rejected him as too small, at sixteen, for the cadet corps, and he had to wait another half before reaching the height of five feet four inches. On 29 August 1885 he was gazetted to the Grenadier Guards from the Royal Military College, Sandhurst. In 1887, on his father's accession to the

earldom, he assumed the courtesy title of Viscount Kilcoursie.

His military career began on the lines then normal for a young officer of the Brigade of Guards. Between 1891 and 1893 he was aide-de-camp to the governor-general of Canada, Lord Stanley, later sixteenth Earl of Derby [q.v.]. In August 1897 he became regimental adjutant, being promoted captain two months later. In March 1900 he reverted to command of a company in order to serve in the South African war. He took part in the actions of Biddulphsberg and Wittebergen, and was mentioned in dispatches. He succeeded to the peerage in 1900 while on active service. In February 1908 he became a lieutenant-colonel and took over command of the 1st Grenadier Guards. In 1912 he went on half-pay as a colonel. He was temporarily recalled next year to command a Guards brigade in manœuvres, proof that someone in authority appreciated his ability; and this incident may well have affected his future. He felt, however, little zest for military service in time of peace; he had an estate, Wheathampstead, near St. Albans, to look after; and, as a keen foxhunter, he was attracted by the offer of the mastership of the Hertfordshire Hunt. He therefore retired.

Recalled on the outbreak of war, Cavan took command of a Territorial brigade, but a casualty at the front resulted in his transfer to that of the 4th (Guards) brigade, 11 September 1914. He was in his forty-ninth year, strong, fit, and active in body; cool, self-possessed, and confident in mind. Beyond that, however, he had hidden and perhaps unsuspected qualities. First came the indefinable gift of leadership, unusually indefinable in his case because, although he did not lack power of self-expression, he was inclined to mistrust it and to make little use of it. In brigade, division, army corps, and army, the confidence which officers and rank and file felt in him added to the quality of the formation. He was not a brilliant man, but he excelled in the clear common sense which he applied to all problems. He was the same in adversity, of which he had a full share, as in success: determined, bold, but at the same time prudent, and inexhaustible. His personality expanded as he rose in rank and in the last phase he was certainly a great army commander.

Soon after Cavan's arrival, the British Expeditionary Force was transferred from the Aisne to Flanders. In the Ypres fighting, which was as hard as any in the war, he played a great part when things were blackest and established firmly his reputation as a fighting commander. In May 1915 he was engaged in the hopeless and muddled battle of Festubert. Here he showed strength of mind by breaking off the attack when he saw that it was becoming a useless sacrifice. In June he was appointed to the command of the 50th division, but two months later was transferred to that of the newly formed Guards division. The battle of Loos in September was rendered notorious by a breakdown in traffic control which caused calamitous congestion and delay, and in this the Guards division was involved. Its advance south of the Hulluch road on 27 September was carried out with great gallantry, but the chances, which had seemed propitious at the outset, had slipped away, and the attack failed after a good start.

In January 1916 Cavan took over command of the XIV Corps. The Guards division keenly regretted his departure, but found a measure of compensation in the fact that it was later allotted to his corps over a long period. His introduction to the battle of the Somme came in August 1916 when his headquarters was summoned to take over opposite Guillemont. During the next two months the XIV Corps was engaged in a dogged advance against stiff opposition. Then the weather broke, so that by the end the battlefield had become a sea of mud and it took a dozen horses to move a field-gun. On 25 September, when the Guards division had come in and the objectives included Morval, 'the battalions of the XIV Corps, admirably served by their artillery, advanced steadily and methodically, with no delay and few serious checks, to their final objective'. In October the attacks of the Fourth Army in general brought small profit, but most ground was gained by the XIV Corps on the right. Cavan's last experience of the western front was at 'third Ypres' in the summer of 1917 when his troops fought on the British left, next to the small French army engaged in this battle. He was not, however, to see it out to the end.

Cavan was now generally regarded as the best British corps commander on the western front. In consequence he was selected to take a reconstituted XIV Corps to Italy after the disaster at Caporetto in late October. He left France 2 November, with the Prince of Wales as one of his aides-de-camp. The situation looked desperate. One Italian army had dissolved. At a conference which discussed the next stage of the retreat Cavan said in a homespun phrase that he did not intend to retreat anywhere. However, the enemy halted on the Piave and the German divisions went to France. In March 1918 Cavan took over command of all the British troops in Italy. All was fairly quiet until June, when the Austrians launched a double offensive. One wing struck mainly British and French divisions in the mountains and was defeated after a day's hard fighting. The other, on the Piave, achieved a passage against the Italians and looked dangerous, but the rise of the river compelled the attackers to withdraw.

It is no exaggeration to say that Cavan was the soul of the final offensive. He urged it constantly on the Italian command, but on a visit to England in September he also pressed for British cooperation and succeeded in preventing the dispatch of three tired divisions from France to replace the three fine British divisions which remained with him. He was given command of a small army, containing two of these and two Italian divisions, on the Piave. The river was in roaring flood, but expert Italian boatmen —whom he never failed to praise in after years—ferried his British troops over, to fan out on the far bank and clear a way for Italian troops who had been unable to get across. The Austrian armies shortly broke up and submitted to an armistice. When Cavan was leaving Italy, the best Italian army commander, the Duke of Aosta, said to him: 'Without the presence of you and your troops there would have been no Vittorio Veneto.'

Cavan ended the war with the appointments of K.C.B. (1918) and G.C.M.G. (1919). He had also received, in 1916, an honour not usually associated with military awards, knighthood of the Order of St. Patrick. Within the next few years he had been awarded the grand cross of the chief orders (G.C.V.O. 1922, G.C.B. 1926, G.B.E. 1927), together with several foreign decorations. He was also an honorary LL.D. of Cambridge (1919) and an honorary D.C.L. of Oxford (1926). He became colonel of the Irish Guards in 1925 and of the Bedfordshire and Hertfordshire Regiment in 1928. His peerages were all Irish and did not entitle him to a seat in the House of Lords, but in 1915 he had been elected a representative peer for Ireland.

In November 1920 Cavan was given the Aldershot Command, then still the chief army home station. In 1921 he was head of the War Office section of the British delegation to the Washington conference. In February 1922 he was appointed chief of the imperial general staff. In recent times few officers of his seniority had had so little staff experience. Virtually all Cavan's career, from subaltern to general officer, had been in command of troops. Some of the secondary wars which succeeded the great war were over, but he had to deal with the Turkish advance on Constantinople, when it was almost as hard to find battalions as it would have been to find divisions four years earlier. For the rest, the period was one of retrenchment, during which the army hardly began to take a new shape. After four years in office Cavan retired for the second time. A few more military duties fell to him. In 1927 he accompanied the Duke of York, afterwards King George VI, on his Australian and New Zealand tour, as chief of staff. In 1932, after his reserve service had come to an end, he was created field-marshal. In 1937 he commanded the troops at the coronation.

In 1893 he married Caroline Inez (died 1920), daughter of George Baden Crawley. In 1922 Cavan married Lady Hester Joan Mulholland, daughter of the fifth Earl of Strafford, and widow of Captain the Hon. Andrew E. S. Mulholland, who had been killed in the first year of the war. Cavan kept his health and a measure of vigour well into old age, and died in London 28 August 1946. He had two daughters by his second marriage and the titles passed to his brother, the Venerable Horace Edward Samuel Sneade Lambart (1878–1950), archdeacon of Salop.

Cavan's name did not attract as much public attention as did those of several of his contemporaries, but the army recognized and remembered him as the pattern of a good soldier, and in his own shire his fame was deeply established. He was rather below middle height, broad-shouldered and deep-chested, altogether powerfully built. His face matched his temperament. His features were good and regular, but not commonly marked by much change of expression. They expressed his dependability and imperturbability, but did not reveal the qualities which often inspired those whom he led. In 1917 H. P. (later Lord) Croft [q.v.] described him as 'one of those exceptional personalities who give confidence from the first moment you meet them, but, unlike most famous generals and admirals, he makes you feel his friendship at once, and you realise that you are dealing with a very human man. Short in stature, very strongly built, with a somewhat large head, he meets you with a merry twinkle in his eyes, and you find a rather unusual type of soldier, master of hounds, statesman, leader, and friend all rolled into one.' (*Twenty-Two Months under Fire.*)

A portrait by P. A. de László is in the possession of the family; another by Sir William Orpen is in the Guards Club; and a drawing by Francis Dodd is in the Imperial War Museum. Cavan is also included in J. S. Sargent's group 'Some General Officers of the War of 1914–18' in the National Portrait Gallery.

[Sir J. E. Edmonds and others, (Official) *History of the Great War. Military Operations, France and Belgium, 1914–18*, 1922–48, *Italy, 1915–19*, 1949; private information.]

CYRIL FALLS.

LANCHESTER, FREDERICK WILLIAM (1868–1946), engineer, was born in Lewisham 23 October 1868, the son of Henry Jones Lanchester, architect, by his wife, Octavia Ward. Lanchester was educated at the Hartley College, Southampton, and went in 1886 to the Normal School (later the Royal College) of Science where he became a devoted disciple of Thomas Minchin Goodeve, and finally studied workshop practice at the Finsbury Technical College.

In 1889 he joined T. B. Barker & Co., of Birmingham, makers of the Forward gas-engine and soon became their works manager and designer. At once he set himself to overhaul their designs and manufacturing technique, greatly improving the performance of their engines and reducing production costs. At the same time, he devised and developed the pendulum governor, a simple and ingenious device for controlling the speed of gas-engines, and the famous Lanchester gas-starter. Both these inventions were applied almost universally to all gas-engines within the next twenty years.

About 1894 Lanchester decided to start out on his own account to develop a motor-car, and for this purpose he formed a small private syndicate. His first car, a purely experimental model, was completed in 1895, and his second, which won a gold medal and is now at South Kensington, was completed in 1897. But Lanchester sought to produce a genuine motor-car as distinct from the so-called horseless carriages of that date. He realized that to do this he must break away from the existing conceptions of design which were based on the horse-drawn vehicle. To this end he designed an entirely novel form of engine which was completely vibrationless and almost completely noiseless, a transmission gear which was also noiseless, and a system of springing and of steering adapted to the much higher speeds of a power-driven vehicle. His first car embodying all these features was introduced in 1901 and created a great sensation. In contrast to the excessive noise, vibration, and bumping of contemporary vehicles, the new Lanchester car travelled with a smooth, noiseless glide. The year 1899 saw the formation of the Lanchester Engine Company, of which Lanchester himself was general manager, works manager, and designer. He introduced many new techniques of manufacture, for which he had to design and himself produce the tools. To him we owe, among many other developments, the centreless grinder, the short roller bearing and the splined shaft, now universal, the high efficiency worm drive, the torsional vibration damper, and the conception of a dynamically balanced engine for road vehicles.

Although the Lanchester car was a remarkable success from the point of view of technique and performance, and could justly be described as the first real motor-car, the Lanchester company soon fell into financial difficulties, and in 1903 a receiver was appointed. Lanchester still carried on as before, but with diminishing interest. In 1905 a new company was formed under the name of the Lanchester Motor Company, Ltd., but owing to disagreements with the management he himself virtually ceased to take any active part. In 1910 he was appointed consulting engineer to the Daimler Motor Company, but it seems that this appointment gave him too little scope for his ingenuity, although he remained with them until 1930.

In the meantime Lanchester had become deeply interested in the science of aeronautics and had devoted such spare time as he had to its study and to carrying out experiments, mostly with paper models. As early as 1895 he read a paper before the Birmingham Natural History and Philosophical Society in which he laid down the fundamental conditions for sustained flight and outlined for the first time the conception of the vortex theory of sustentation in flight. Subsequently this paper was amplified to form two volumes, *Aerial Flight*, published in 1907 (*Aerodynamics*) and 1908 (*Aerodonetics*), which for several decades were the text-books of aircraft designers. In this early paper and these two volumes, Lanchester laid the foundations of aircraft design, and his conclusions, arrived at by sheer intuitive genius, and long before any power-driven aeroplane had left the ground, hold good to this day.

In 1909 Lanchester became a member of the newly formed Advisory Committee on Aeronautics, in which he took a very active part until 1920. His many lectures and papers extended over a very wide range of subjects from thermodynamics to industrial economics. Although from then onwards his main interests were in aeronautics, he became deeply interested also in wireless and in musical instruments, and it was characteristic of the man that he produced a loud-speaker greatly superior to any that had hitherto been evolved.

Although Lanchester's work received international recognition, probably few realize to the full how much he accomplished, always working alone, and usually with very few resources. In 1922 he was elected F.R.S. He received the honorary degree of LL.D. from Birmingham University (1919), was an honorary member of the Institutions of Mechanical and Automobile Engineers and was awarded (1926) the gold medal of the Royal Aeronautical Society of which he was an honorary fellow. He received also the Daniel Guggenheim gold medal (U.S.A.) in 1931, the Alfred Ewing gold medal of the Institution of Civil Engineers in 1941, and in 1945 the James Watt international medal, the highest award which the Institution of Mechanical Engineers can bestow.

Lanchester married in 1919 Dorothea, daughter of the Rev. Thomas Cooper, vicar of Field Broughton, Grange-over-Sands; there were no children. He died in Birmingham 8 March 1946.

[Sir Harry R. Ricardo in *Obituary Notices of Fellows of the Royal Society*, No. 16, May 1948; *Engineer* and *Engineering*, 15 March 1946; private information; personal knowledge.]

HARRY R. RICARDO.

LANE, SIR (WILLIAM) ARBUTHNOT, first baronet (1856–1943), surgeon, was born at Fort George, Inverness-shire,

4 July 1856, the eldest child of Benjamin Lane, surgeon to the 80th Foot, by his wife, Caroline Arbuthnot, daughter of Joseph Ewing, a retired inspector-general of hospitals, an Ulsterman. On his father's side the family of Lane had been settled since the plantation of Ulster at Limavady near Lough Foyle. When he was a fortnight old the regiment was moved to South Africa to take part in the first Kaffir war and his mother insisted on accompanying her husband with her child. For the first twelve years of his life they were constantly on the move between England and Ceylon, India, the Ionian Islands, Malta, Nova Scotia, and Ireland. The extraordinary number and variety of impressions which Lane had received before the age of twelve may have been the cause of the remarkable independence of mind which he showed throughout life. He then spent four years at school in Scotland, first with a Mr. Braidwood and afterwards at Stanley House, Bridge-of-Allan, founded by Braidwood's two sons.

In 1872 Benjamin Lane was stationed at Woolwich and the only seven years in which he led a settled life corresponded with those spent by his two sons at Guy's Hospital. William entered in 1872. Being educated in Scotland he had twice to go back and take other examinations in classics and general knowledge, once for his F.R.C.S. (England) and again for the London degree of M.B. (1881). He took his M.R.C.S. in 1877 and then added to his experience of the world by spending a year in the Caribbean as a ship's surgeon. After this he was house-physician to W. Moxon and C. H. Fagge [qq.v.], both of whom, especially the former, influenced him profoundly. He wished to take up medicine and it was Moxon who tactfully persuaded him to turn to surgery instead. He then became house-surgeon at the Victoria Hospital for Children, Chelsea, where he took his F.R.C.S. in May 1882 and remained until he was appointed demonstrator of anatomy to Guy's Hospital in October of that year. On the strength of a paper which he then wrote on empyema he has been wrongly credited with being the first person to resect a rib for empyema, but the incident is typical of his work. Original in outlook rather than in conception, he was criticized by his seniors but accepted, at least for a time, by his juniors and most of his contemporaries.

Having finished his examinations by taking his M.S. (London) in 1883, Lane started on work which can be traced throughout his whole career. He had three characteristics: wonderful manual dexterity, absolute independence of thought, and the experiencing nature. The first was unrivalled, and approached by but a few; in the story of Guy's only by C. A. Key [q.v.] and by Arthur Durham. The second forbade him to accept traditional ideas as true if the evidence which he had before him said otherwise. It was accompanied by an insufficiency of self-criticism, which was magnified by the vituperative abuse with which each of his ideas was met. The third could change a paper-knife into a surgical instrument or adapt the glass lining of a restaurant in Grenoble to an operating theatre. He began by studying the bones of working men in the dissecting room and described changes which took place in the skeleton of the coal-trimmer, the cobbler, and the brewer's drayman which enabled them to perform their tasks with the minimum of expenditure of muscular energy. Evolution was still new and he was a keen evolutionist and a physiologist of the mechanistic school. He believed that he was exposing in these bones evidence of evolution occurring in a single lifetime, and he formulated certain principles to which he adhered throughout life. In the fourth edition of his book on *The Operative Treatment of Chronic Intestinal Stasis* (1918) he states them thus: 'The skeleton represents the crystallization of lines of force which when exerted in a single direction are laid down as compact tissue; when in varying directions are laid down as cancellous tissue' (p. 1), and 'every change in the anatomy of the individual which develops during life-time to enable him to accommodate himself more efficiently to his surroundings tends to shorten his life' (p. vi, preface). Anyone who wishes to try to understand Lane must bear these in mind whether he agrees with them or understands them or not. He repeated them in notes written another thirty years later, when eighty years of age. Although revolutionary with regard to other men's thoughts, he was singularly conservative with regard to his own.

In 1888 Lane was appointed to the staff of Guy's Hospital. His marvellous manual dexterity at once brought him to the fore in abdominal surgery which was then developing at a great rate. For many years a person whose abdomen was opened by Lane had a greater hope of survival than if this were done by anyone else. This soon removed Lane from all financial anxiety.

Lane had what Bertrand (Earl) Russell has called 'the impulse of humanity' and the desire to relieve suffering spurred him on in each of those three surgical procedures which may be called his great subjects. The first was cleft palate, in which he extended the flap operation of J. N. C. Davies-Colley, his senior colleague at Guy's, and reduced the age at which the operation was done to one day. It was the same with the treatment of simple fractures. Dockers with fractures which were supposed to have been set well insisted that they could not do their work. He went down to the docks to watch them and came to the conclusion that every broken bone must be put back into exactly the position which the pieces had held before. He could only do this by applying an internal splint directly to the bone after replacement by open operation. To enable himself to do this with safety he devised an aseptical surgical excellence which as 'the Lane technique' has influenced the whole world, and remains his most enduring work. The third of his great subjects was 'chronic intestinal stasis'. He tried to free the costive woman from the thrall of her purgative pills and to give her a more abounding life. This he tried to do by giving her cream, subsequently replaced by the use of liquid paraffin, and then by operation, putting the end of the small intestine into the lower part of the large gut to short-circuit it. He subsequently removed the whole of the large gut. It was then that he met Metchnikoff who had a great influence on him as he held very similar views on the uselessness of the large gut and on the poisoning of the body which resulted from decomposition in this cess-pit. This was no new idea, being held by the men of the front rank in Lane's youth, such as Sir James Paget [q.v.]. It was developed into the 'focus of sepsis' theory to which most diseases were subsequently attributed. Lane took this up very enthusiastically, believing that it acted not only directly in rheumatoid arthritis, but also by lowering resistance in tuberculosis, and in cancer which he believed to be infective in origin.

During the war of 1914–18 Lane was consulting surgeon to the Aldershot Command, in addition to his work at Guy's

and at the Hospital for Sick Children, Great Ormond Street (1883–1916). He went on a lecture tour with Sir James Mackenzie [q.v.] and others through the United States, and he was asked to organize and to open Queen Mary's Hospital at Sidcup, which became the nursery of all modern plastic work. At the end of the war he retired from Guy's; and shortly afterwards extended his views on health from the individual to the nation and the world. In 1925 he founded the New Health Society which was the first organized body to deal with what later became known as social medicine. In order to free himself for this work, which involved writing in the public press and publishing a journal, he removed his name from the register of medical practitioners in 1933.

Lane was created a baronet in 1913. Having been known to all his students and friends as 'Willie' for over twenty years, he took his second name, Arbuthnot, to use with this honour. He was appointed C.B. in 1917 and was also a chevalier of the Legion of Honour. He died in London 16 January 1943.

Lane was twice married: first, in 1884 to Charlotte (died 1935), daughter of John Briscoe, an army officer, of Tinvane, county Tipperary, the sister-in-law of his old teacher, Hilton Fagge. By her he had three daughters and one son, William Arbuthnot (born 1897), who succeeded him as second baronet. Of the daughters, Rhona, the eldest, became headmistress of Wycombe Abbey School (1925–7). In 1935 he married his son-in-law's sister, Jane, daughter of Nathan Mutch, building contractor, of Rochdale.

He wrote enormously, producing in all 313 papers for the medical press and a number of short books. A bibliography of his works was prepared by Mr. G. A. R. Winston, the Wills' librarian to Guy's Hospital. This was rearranged under anatomical and surgical headings by Mr. W. E. Tanner and is added as an appendix to his life of Lane. Lane's great versatility and kindliness appeared in his fondness for animals, his connoisseurship in porcelain and, in later years, in bronzes, and in his skill in fishing; nor should mention be omitted of his superb dancing which he carried on until old age. His affection for the Hospital for Sick Children was second only to his love for Guy's.

A portrait of Lane by Edward Newling, presented to the governors by his past house-surgeons, belongs to Guy's Hospital.

[W. E. Tanner, *Sir W. Arbuthnot Lane, Bart., C.B., M.S., F.R.C.S., His Life and Work*, 1946; *Guy's Hospital Reports*, vol. xciv, Nos. 3 and 4, 1945; *Lancet*, 30 January 1943; *British Medical Journal*, 23 January 1943; *The Times*, 18 January 1943; private information; personal knowledge.]

T. B. LAYTON.

LANG, (ALEXANDER) MATHESON (1877–1948), actor-manager and dramatist, was born in Montreal, Canada, 15 May 1877, a cousin of Cosmo Gordon Lang, archbishop of Canterbury, a notice of whom appears below, and youngest of the seven children of the Rev. Gavin Lang, minister of the Scottish Presbyterian church of St. Andrew's, Montreal, and his wife, Frances Mary Corbett.

Educated at Inverness College and St. Andrews University, Lang, after watching Sir Henry Irving [q.v.], finally decided to go on the stage. He made his first appearance with Louis Calvert in 1897, and afterwards joined the company of (Sir) Frank Benson [q.v.]. In 1902 he played with Mrs. Langtry at the Imperial Theatre in a royal command performance, and toured with her through America. At the Imperial, too, in 1903, he played Benedick to the Beatrice of (Dame) Ellen Terry [q.v.]. He later toured with her in repertory. In 1907, after an excellent Othello at Manchester, he was with (Sir) George Alexander [q.v.] in *John Glayde's Honour* at the St. James's Theatre, and with John E. Vedrenne and Harley Granville-Barker [q.v.] at the Savoy Theatre in the same year, when he played Dick Dudgeon in *The Devil's Disciple*. Also in 1907 he took part in a great adventure of popular drama with Ernest Carpenter, the manager of the Lyceum Theatre. He played John Storm in *The Christian*, and Romeo in 1908. At this time he took great interest in the promotion of a national theatre. In March 1909, still at the Lyceum, he played Hamlet; but unfortunately with the death of Carpenter in that year the Lyceum organization broke up.

Lang next toured in Australia and in 1911 started his own management, taking an extensive repertory, largely Shakespearian, to South Africa and the Far East. On his return, Sir Herbert Tree [q.v.] asked him to play Charles Surface in *The School for Scandal*. Lang's next personal success was as Wu Li Chang in *Mr. Wu* by Harry M. Vernon and Harold Owen, at the Strand Theatre, 1913, and in 1914 he played Hotspur in *King Henry IV, Part I*. At the New Theatre, 1920, he presented *Carnival*, which he had adapted from the Italian with H. C. M. Hardinge, and he was remarkable as Matathias in E. Temple Thurston's drama, *The Wandering Jew*, which ran for twelve months. At the New he presented matinées as Othello—an extremely fine and memorable performance—to the Iago of Arthur Bourchier [q.v.]. In 1926–7 Lang toured Canada with a repertory company and in 1928 played his favourite part of Count Pahlen in *Such Men are Dangerous*, adapted by Mr. Ashley Dukes from the German play by Alfred Neumann and presented at the Duke of York's Theatre. He next produced *The Chinese Bungalow* by Marion Wallace Osmond and James Corbett—a *nom de plume* of his own. Then, at the Duke of York's, he produced *Jew Süss* (1929) adapted by Mr. Ashley Dukes from the book by Dr. Lion Feuchtwanger. This play, which included a charming little ballet by Marie Rambert (Mrs. Ashley Dukes), for which music was arranged and conducted by Constant Lambert, made a unique attraction.

In 1916 Lang began his screen career, which included nearly all his stage successes, with a remarkable performance of Shylock in a film of *The Merchant of Venice*. Although he never claimed the credit which was his due, he was one of the chief helpers of Lilian Baylis [q.v.] in her early efforts at the Old Vic. He made Shakespearian production possible, as a member of her first committee, by granting her for nothing a loan of any scenery or costumes she required.

Lang was helped all his life by a personality of marked dignity, thanks to his tall figure and commanding features. The grand manner came naturally to him, without any need for affectation. Owing to illness he was not seen in London for the last eleven years of his life, and it was only ill health which prevented him from achieving the supreme position to which he was in so many ways entitled. He married in 1903 Nellie Hutin Britton, who was with him as a member of the Benson company and with Ellen Terry and played many principal parts in his productions. She was keenly interested in the Old Vic and was a member of the governing body for many years. Lang wrote an autobiography, *Mr. Wu Looks Back* (1940), and died at Bridgetown, Barbados, 11 April 1948. There were no children of the marriage.

473

A portrait of Lang as Hamlet, by Somerled Macdonald, is in the possession of the family.

[Private information; personal knowledge.]
S. R. LITTLEWOOD.

LANG, (WILLIAM) COSMO GORDON, BARON LANG OF LAMBETH (1864–1945), archbishop of Canterbury, was born 31 October 1864 at Fyvie Manse, Aberdeenshire, the third son of the Rev. John Marshall Lang [q.v.] then minister of the parish, by his wife, Hannah Agnes, daughter of the Rev. Peter Hay Keith, minister of Hamilton. His childhood was spent partly in Glasgow and partly at Morningside, Edinburgh, and on the appointment of his father to the Barony church, the family settled in Glasgow.

Cosmo Lang attended the Park School until, at the age of fourteen, he entered the university of Glasgow. There he came under the influence of Edward Caird [q.v.] to whose inspiration he attributed his intellectual and spiritual awakening. Soon after qualifying for the degree of M.A. he crossed the Border and visited Cambridge. Captivated by the beauty of King's College chapel, he applied for membership of the college, and in January 1882 he passed the entrance examination. His essay was pronounced to be very good, his mathematics shaky, and his handwriting almost illegible. On second thoughts he decided to go to Oxford. Having entered Balliol College as a commoner in October 1882, he won the Brackenbury scholarship during his first term, and decided to read for *literae humaniores*. As a freshman he rapidly gained prominence as a debater at the Union, of which he was elected president, unopposed, in 1884. He was also secretary of the Canning Club, was one of the founders of the Oxford University Dramatic Society, and with (Sir) Michael Sadler [q.v.] undergraduate-secretary of Toynbee Hall. This activity led Benjamin Jowett [q.v.] to remind him: 'your business here is not to reform the east end of London, but to get a first class in the school of *literae humaniores*'. In the event he was placed in the second class, but he made up for it by a first in the school of modern history a year later (1886).

On leaving Oxford, Lang entered the chambers of W. S. (later Lord) Robson [q.v.] paying his way by delivering Oxford university extension lectures and by journalism. The summer of 1887 found him in Germany, attending lectures at Göttingen, and in 1888 he successfully renewed his candidature of 1886 for a fellowship of All Souls. This gave him an assured income for seven years, but at the back of his mind he was disturbed by the persistent question: 'Why should you not be ordained?' A vivid spiritual experience in Cuddesdon church, henceforth to be called his 'Mecca', settled the matter, and on the eve of being called to the bar he withdrew his name and announced his intention of seeking holy orders in the Church of England. This step roused severe comment among his Presbyterian compatriots.

After being confirmed by the bishop of Lincoln, Edward King [q.v.], Lang went to Cuddesdon College and was ordained deacon by the bishop of Oxford, William Stubbs [q.v.], in 1890 and priest in 1891. He served as curate of Leeds parish church under E. S. Talbot [q.v.] and in 1893 he was elected fellow of Magdalen College, Oxford, with the office of dean of divinity. A year later he was also appointed vicar of the university church of St. Mary the Virgin, but his stay in Oxford was not long, for in 1896 he was presented to the vicarage of Portsea, where, with a large staff of curates, he ministered for five years to a population of 40,000 people, and preached in a church which was filled to overflowing. In these eight years he was at his hey-day as a preacher, and no disapproval was expressed when in 1901 he succeeded A. F. Winnington-Ingram [q.v.] in a canonry at St. Paul's with the suffragan bishopric of Stepney.

During the next eight years Lang travelled all over the country pleading for the East London Church Fund and addressing meetings of the Church of England Men's Society, of which he was chairman. This peripatetic ministry, added to his care of the Church in east London and his canonical duties at St. Paul's, brought into full play all his varied powers, and clearly marked him out for preferment. He made a deep impression at the Lambeth Conference of 1908. It was none the less a surprise when, shortly after he had declined the bishopric of Montreal, he was nominated by Asquith to the archbishopric of York.

Lang was enthroned on 25 January 1909. The bishops of the northern province were all much older than himself, and, with one exception, definitely low churchmen. The rapidity with which the high church archbishop won their trust was evidence of his tact in handling men; as also was the success with which he carried through, with the minimum of dissension, the partition of his unwieldy diocese by the formation of that of Sheffield in 1914, and subsequently by the transfer in 1927 of the rural deanery of Pontefract to the bishopric of Wakefield. As a member of the Royal Commission on divorce and matrimonial causes (1909–12), presided over by Lord Gorell [q.v.], he signed, together with Sir William Anson and Sir Lewis Dibdin [qq.v.], the minority report which attracted much attention in 1912; and in his maiden speech in the Lords on 30 November 1909, he supported Lloyd George's budget. In 1911 he voted for the Parliament bill, thereby incurring the anger of many Conservatives.

This criticism was nothing compared with the clamour, as uncharitable as the words which provoked it were ill timed, when in the early months of the war of 1914–18 he spoke of his 'sacred memory' of the German Emperor. War fever was at its height, and a flood of abuse in certain sections of the press undermined his influence for a time, and deeply wounded a lonely and sensitive man. An onset of alopecia which followed this trouble, and may have been caused by it, changed a young-looking dark-haired man into an elderly-looking man completely bald but for a fringe of white hair above his ears. More happy activities during the war were his visit to the Grand Fleet in 1915, and to the western front in 1917. He took a leading part in the National Mission of Repentance and Hope in 1916, and early in 1918, at the invitation of the Episcopal Church in America, he toured the United States and Canada, preaching and speaking no fewer than eighty-one times in the course of forty days. While in New York he stayed with John Pierpont Morgan, thus starting a friendship which lasted until Morgan's death in 1943.

After the war Lang felt isolated and lonely: he sorely missed the companionship of his dearly loved chaplain, killed in action, and in 1921 he lost his mother to whom he was deeply attached. None the less, during the remainder of his time at York he devoted himself with his usual tireless energy to his episcopal duties, and had the satisfaction of completing his visitation of every parish in the diocese. Moreover, his intimate association with the archbishop of Canterbury, Randall Davidson [q.v.], involved constant journeys to Lambeth, where he had a suite of rooms in Cranmer Tower. This partnership between the two archbishops, so diverse in age and temperament, was both a novel and a notable achievement, for to it may be attributed the general continuity of policy which, for better or for worse, marked the period covered by the leadership of the two men. Lang acted as chairman of the Commission on the Ecclesiastical Courts and of the Cathedrals Commission: in the lengthy discussions on the revision of the Book of Common Prayer he took a full share. He advocated the adoption of the Communion Office of the Prayer Book of 1549 as an alternative rite, but he was overruled, and loyally accepted, although without enthusiasm, the decision of the majority. When the revised Prayer Book was brought before Parliament in 1927 he wound up the debate in the House of Lords which resulted in a surprisingly large majority in favour of the Book. The second rejection of the Prayer Book by the House of Commons in 1928 was closely followed by the resignation of Davidson. The prime minister, Stanley Baldwin, lost no time in recommending Lang as successor, and the King most readily agreed.

Lang was enthroned 4 December 1928, but on 23 December he was stricken by sudden illness, caused, no doubt, by persistent overwork. For the next three years the man who had often boasted that he had never spent a day in bed was dogged by ill health. In 1930, just before the Lambeth Conference, duodenal trouble developed, followed in succession by fifth-nerve neuralgia, acute fibrositis, and shingles. Thanks to his physicians and his own invincible determination, he managed to struggle through this bad period, but his patience was grievously tried. Having at length reached the throne of St. Augustine, he seemed doomed to frustration. Suddenly in 1932 he recovered his health and his serenity, and for ten more years he sustained the almost intolerable burden of the primacy without any relapse.

These years of ill health brought their compensations. Chief among them was the opportunity afforded by convalescence of accepting an invitation to a Mediterranean cruise in Pierpont Morgan's yacht *Corsair*. In April 1929 and March 1931, sunshine and sea-breezes, combined with congenial company, brought refreshment to body and soul. Looking back, Lang used to say that these cruises brought him more happiness than any other events in his life. They also offered him an opportunity of visiting leading ecclesiastics of the Orthodox Church, and thereby of fostering the growth of friendly relations between the Church of England and the Churches of the East. On two occasions he was received by the archbishop of Athens; in 1931 he visited Jerusalem; and finally in 1939, during a third cruise, he had the unique experience of exchanging courtesies with the œcumenical patriarch of Constantinople at the Phanar itself. This last event was the crown of his lifelong efforts to promote Christian unity. From his ordination onwards, he had never ceased to work to that end. His most notable contribution was the 'Appeal to All Christian People' issued by the Lambeth Conference of 1920. It was stamped with the impress of his mind, he conceived it and largely gave it expression; he expounded it at meetings throughout the country and by it gave an impetus to the whole movement for reunion.

As archbishop of York, Lang had presided over the joint conference with the English Free Churches, and had followed with cautious and understanding sympathy the informal conversations between Anglicans and Roman Catholics at Malines under the presidency of Cardinal Mercier. He had scrutinized with anxious care the scheme of reunion taking shape in South India. As archbishop of Canterbury, he addressed the General Assembly of the Church of Scotland in May 1932, and thereby initiated conversations which, although short lived, did something to clarify the issues. At the Lambeth Conference of 1930 he welcomed a delegation of Old Catholics, which a year later issued in the establishment of full communion between the Church of England and the Old Catholic Church. He also received a powerful delegation of Orthodox ecclesiastics, headed by the Patriarch Meletios, which led to a joint theological commission assembling at Lambeth in 1931. In 1933 he brought into being the Church of England Council on Foreign Relations, an advisory body of specialists with the bishop of Gloucester, A. C. Headlam [q.v.], as chairman. In the next year, a commission under Headlam held conversations with Lutherans of the Church of Finland, and in 1938 with those of Latvia and Estonia. In 1935 he commissioned a delegation under the bishop of Lincoln, F. C. N. Hicks, to visit the Romanian Church, which led to Romania

joining with Jerusalem, Constantinople, Cyprus, and Alexandria in an acknowledgement by 'Economy' of Anglican orders and ministrations. A year later, the patriarch of Romania, Miron Cristea, visited Lambeth; further conversations took place in Sofia, Belgrade, and Athens with such happy results that it looked as though the Lambeth Conference of 1940 would set the seal on the work of twenty years. But the outbreak of war shattered all his hopes, and there was no conference in 1940.

Of the lesser eastern Churches, the Assyrian, with its young patriarch, the Mar Shimun, was that for which he felt a special responsibility. The massacre of the Assyrians by the Iraqi army in 1933 and the subsequent transportation of the patriarch to Cyprus involved Lang and his staff in long-drawn-out correspondence which led to no satisfactory conclusion, while the 'enosis' movement in Cyprus also caused him much anxiety.

In home affairs Lang attended the House of Lords whenever matters in which he was specially concerned came up for debate. His utterances on politics were as a rule cautious. In 1936 he agreed to the total 'extinguishment' of tithe; in 1937 he incurred some criticism by abstaining from voting on the matrimonial causes bill. He was a member of the joint committee on Indian constitutional reform set up in 1933. As principal trustee of the British Museum he was instrumental in purchasing in 1934 the Codex Sinaiticus. As chairman of the governors of the Charterhouse he took a leading part in the formation of the Governing Bodies Association in 1939.

These outside activities, while they consumed time, were a welcome relief from the specifically ecclesiastical affairs which continually pressed upon him day by day. He was at work seven days in the week, and found little or no time for recreation: as he used to say, his life was 'incredible, indefensible and inevitable'.

When war came in 1939, Lang resided at first at Lambeth, going to Canterbury as usual for the week-ends. Even after 20 September 1940, when the palace received a direct hit, he continued, when in London, to sleep in Lollards' Tower or the basement. He was in residence on the night of 10 May 1941 when the blast of one of the four bombs which fell in the courtyard threw him to the ground. The palace was rendered uninhabitable. That summer, at a house near Benenden in

Kent, he wrestled with the question of his resignation. He came to the conclusion that he ought to give way to a younger man, and hoped that the choice would fall on the archbishop of York, William Temple [q.v.]. He announced his decision to a joint meeting of the Convocation of Canterbury held in College Hall, Westminster Abbey, on 21 January 1942, and the resignation took effect on 31 March. He retired to the King's Cottage, Kew Green, which was put at his disposal by a gracious act of the King, while his financial worries were dissipated by the generosity of Pierpont Morgan who made over to him a sum of £15,000. A peerage (as Baron Lang of Lambeth, 1942) gave him the satisfaction of retaining his membership of the House of Lords, where he spoke only two days before his death. Co-option as a trustee continued his connexion with the British Museum and he remained one of the governors of the Charterhouse. For three years his retirement was passed in the peaceful neighbourhood of Kew Gardens before the end came suddenly on 5 December 1945. While hurrying to the railway station at Kew, he collapsed in the street and died almost immediately. After his cremation the ashes were placed in St. Stephen's chapel at Canterbury Cathedral, near the tomb of his predecessor, Henry Chichele, the founder of All Souls College, where so many of the happiest days of his life had been spent.

Lang's association with the royal family began when, as vicar of Portsea, he used to preach at Osborne before Queen Victoria, and was appointed one of her chaplains. In that capacity he conducted a service on board the *Alberta* when the coffin containing her remains was taken ashore at Portsmouth: King Edward VII and the Kaiser were present. Lang, as recorded above, recalled in an unguarded moment the 'sacred memory' of the two monarchs kneeling in prayer by the side of the bier.

With King Edward VII Lang was not on terms of intimacy: but it was otherwise with King George V, at whose coronation in 1911 he preached a sermon masterly in its brevity and its content. Year after year he was the King's guest at Balmoral and elsewhere, and the King and Queen came increasingly to rely on his judgement and to value his companionship, while he in his turn conceived a genuine affection for them both. He ministered in prayer to the King on his death-bed and officiated at his funeral. He has been freely accused of being a courtier, but his association with the royal family was rather that of a valued counsellor and friend who, if he received much, had also much to give.

With King Edward VIII his relations were naturally difficult, but the idea, widespread at the time and long afterwards repeated, that he conspired with the prime minister to bring about the King's abdication is quite untrue. He was, however, consulted by the prime minister on the subject of ecclesiastical difficulties which might arise in the event of the marriage of the King to Mrs. Simpson. His broadcast after the abdication was widely criticized, as he had indeed anticipated, and this did not increase his popularity. But he had done what he conceived to be his duty and had spoken, as Baldwin said, 'for Christian England'. With the accession of King George VI his happy relation with the throne was resumed.

Lang was a man of complex character. It may be that he was inhibited by native caution, excessive work, or circumstance from being a daring reformer, but he was one of the most interesting and gifted men who ever presided over the Church of England. With a powerful mind and a mastery of the spoken word he combined good looks, a voice of singular beauty, and a keen dramatic sense, which sometimes betrayed him in public life to standing too much upon his dignity. Throughout his ministry he was driven forward by a compelling sense of duty and by an exceptional capacity for sustained effort. The clergy recognized in him a true father in God, awe-inspiring perhaps, but just and wise and lovable. In his private life he was a lonely man (he never married), self-conscious and reserved, with few intimates, and to the outward observer often formidable and distant. But in reality he was one of the most human of men, with a keen sense of humour, tolerant in his judgements, and with an understanding sympathy which endeared him to a host of friends. Young people of both sexes were at ease with him, and many conceived for him a deep trust and abiding affection. In fact, he was a humble Christian, struggling, in the face of human frailty and the pressure of an overcrowded life, to maintain the exacting standards of the ministerial calling. He could very easily have become the proud prelate cruelly depicted in Orpen's portrait, but year after year in Cuddesdon church and in his 'cell' at Ballure in Kintyre, the home of John Ronald Moreton Macdonald of Largie, his friend from Magdalen days, he replenished the springs of piety and devotion. The distinction with which he discharged the manifold responsibilities of his office entitles him to rank high in the long line of archbishops of Canterbury.

Lang received many honours: he held twelve doctorates, including the Oxford D.C.L. (1913). He was an honorary fellow of Magdalen (1909), Balliol (1928), and All Souls (1942, after resigning his visitorship). He was an honorary bencher of the Inner Temple (1931). He received the Royal Victorian Chain in 1923, and was appointed G.C.V.O. in 1937. In 1933 he was appointed lord high almoner.

Portraits of the archbishop hang at All Souls College, by G. Fiddes Watt; at Bishopthorpe, by Sir William Orpen; at Balliol College by P. A. de László; another by the same artist at the Church House and a third at Lambeth Palace; also at Lambeth is one by Sir William Llewellyn. A cartoon by Spy appeared in *Vanity Fair*, 19 April 1906.

[J. G. Lockhart, *Cosmo Gordon Lang*, 1949; Charles Herbert, *Twenty Years as Archbishop of York*, 1928; private information; personal knowledge.]          ALAN C. DON.

LANGDON-BROWN, SIR WALTER LANGDON (1870–1946), physician and regius professor of physic in the university of Cambridge, was born at Bedford 13 August 1870, the eldest son of the Rev. Dr. John Brown, pastor of Bunyan Meeting and the biographer of John Bunyan, by his wife, Ada Haydon, daughter of the Rev. David Everard Ford, a Congregational minister of Lymington and later Manchester. A sister of Langdon-Brown was the mother of Lord Keynes [q.v]. Brown was educated at Bedford School and after a term at University College, London, obtained a sizarship at St. John's College, Cambridge. He spent the two intervening terms at the Owens College, Manchester, where an enthusiasm for biology, which was to be lifelong, was first awakened by Arthur Milnes Marshall [q.v.]. At Cambridge he responded eagerly to the companionship of many brilliant contemporaries and also to the stimulus of great teachers such as (Sir) Michael Foster and W. H. Gaskell [qq.v.] his indebtedness to whom he was always delighted to acknowledge. He was elected a scholar and was

placed in the first class in both parts of the natural sciences tripos (1892, 1893).

Brown won an open scholarship in science at St. Bartholomew's Hospital which he entered in 1894. In 1897 he qualified and became house-physician to S. J. Gee [q.v.] who also greatly influenced him. In 1900 Brown went to Pretoria as senior physician in charge of the Imperial Yeomanry Hospital; at that time this was a rare and valuable experience by which he greatly profited. He returned at the end of the year to his post as casualty physician at St. Bartholomew's Hospital and in the next year won the Raymond Horton-Smith prize for his Cambridge M.D. thesis on pylephlebitis. He became medical registrar to the hospital in 1906, but he was forty-three before he was appointed assistant physician in 1913 and he did not become full physician until 1924.

Meanwhile his reputation had extended far beyond the walls of St. Bartholomew's. In 1908 he published *Physiological Principles in Treatment*, a timely book which inspired and informed his generation. (Sir) William Osler [q.v.], in his great textbook of medicine, had destroyed the remedies of a dying pharmacy; the chamber of the sick man was swept and garnished and little of therapeutic value remained beyond the patient's faith in his physician. Brown now showed that the new and powerful resources of physiology and pharmacology were ready to be used in the treatment of disease. His was the first textbook of applied physiology and the forerunner of many others.

Brown was elected F.R.C.P. (London) in 1908 and thereafter was a devoted and distinguished servant of the College. He gave the Croonian lectures in 1918 on 'The Sympathetic Nervous System in Disease' in which he emphasized that it was by the autonomic pathways that emotional disturbances produced disorders of bodily function. He was the first English physician to relate the work of psychologists such as Freud, Jung, and Adler to the practice of clinical medicine, and he showed some courage, in a mechanistic age, in defending concepts of disease which did not admit of quantitative assessment. Scientific humanism is a just description of his medical philosophy, and his explanations of the personality disorders were the more readily accepted since he spoke with unimpeachable scientific authority. He became senior censor to the College in 1934 and in 1936 delivered the Harveian oration on 'The Background to Harvey'. This lecture was reprinted in *Thus We Are Men* (1938), a volume of beautifully written essays which revealed the range of Brown's interests and the quality of his intellect.

His retirement in 1930 from the staff of St. Bartholomew's seemed likely to sever his association with undergraduates and young doctors. He was a good teacher, and understood young minds. The sympathy and humanity which made him a great physician was as much in evidence in the hospital wards as in the consulting room, so that he taught by example as well as precept. He continued his busy consulting practice and this, with examining, lecturing, and travelling, for a time filled his days. In 1932 he was appointed regius professor of physic at Cambridge and was elected a professorial fellow of Corpus Christi College. He retired from his chair in 1935 under the age limit, but in this short time made a permanent impression on the medical life of the university. It was a period of great happiness for him, and stimulated by the academic life he loved, his intellectual powers reached their zenith. He was the true 'scholar-physician', widely read in the classics, and in English literature, in poetry and history, and, having a fine memory, could quote where he loved. He was himself a maker of memorable phrases and his description of the pituitary gland as 'the leader of the endocrine orchestra' has been frequently used by other writers. He was also interested in painting and had a remarkable knowledge of Italian art. A large and somewhat formidable figure with bushy eyebrows, Brown had a host of friends whom he entertained with good conversation, food and wine, and endless anecdote.

Brown was knighted in 1935 when he changed his name to Langdon-Brown. Many academic honours were conferred upon him, including the honorary degrees of LL.D. of Dalhousie University and the National University of Ireland in 1938, and the D.Sc. of Oxford (1936). He was an honorary fellow of the Royal College of Physicians of Ireland and of the Royal Society of Medicine, over four sections of which he had presided. He was president of the Medical Society of Individual Psychology, and chairman of the Langdon-Brown committee on postgraduate training in psychological medicine which reported in 1943. After the outbreak of war in 1939 he returned to live in Cambridge where he delivered the Linacre lecture in 1941. In the last year of his life he wrote *Some Chapters in Cambridge Medical History* (1946) much of which was dictated to his second wife, who had been his secretary, on account of his increasing incapacity in a long and difficult illness. He died in Cambridge 3 October 1946.

In 1902 Brown married Eileen Presland (died 1931), a sister at the Metropolitan Hospital where Brown had been assistant physician since 1900 and was physician from 1906 to 1922. The mental disorder from which his first wife suffered caused them both great unhappiness and denied to him for many years the social life which he enjoyed. This period of frustration came to an end in 1931 when he married Winifred Marion (died 1953), daughter of Henry Bishop Hurry, of Eye, Northamptonshire, and there followed fifteen happy years in which his personality expanded and all bitter memories were effaced. In 1951 his widow founded a lectureship in his memory at the Royal College of Physicians, and at her death she bequeathed £2,500 to Corpus Christi College, Cambridge, to endow a Langdon-Brown scholarship and £1,000 to the Royal College of Physicians for the formation of a hospitality fund. There were no children of either marriage. A pencil drawing of Langdon-Brown by Walter Stoye remained the property of the artist.

[*Lancet*, 12 October 1946; *British Medical Journal*, 12 October 1946 and 26 January 1952; *St. Bartholomew's Hospital Journal*, November 1946; *Eagle* (magazine of St. John's College, Cambridge), April 1948; *Cambridge Review*, 12 October 1946; personal knowledge.]                D. V. HUBBLE.

LANGTON, SIR GEORGE PHILIP (1881–1942), judge, was born in London 22 April 1881, the youngest of the six sons of Francis Albert Romuald Langton, of Danganmore, Kilkenny, civil servant, by his wife, Margaret Cecilia, daughter of John Tobin, shipowner, of Montreal. He was educated at Beaumont College, and in 1899 went as a commoner to New College, Oxford, where he was placed in the second class in the school of modern history in 1902.

By way of preparation for the bar, and having been admitted to the Inner Temple, Langton went into a stockbroker's firm in London and then into a solicitor's office. In 1905 he was called to the bar by the Inner Temple and became a pupil of Alfred Henry Chaytor; afterwards he went into the chambers of (Sir) Maurice Hill [q.v.]

and of Daniel Stephens. These chambers dealt mainly with maritime cases, of which the Admiralty work was heard in the Admiralty Court, while the commercial work went to the Commercial Court. Langton also joined the South-Eastern circuit, and was for a time its junior, but the difficulty of combining a practice in the courts of common law and crime with one in the Admiralty and Commercial courts proved insuperable, and he gradually became a specialist in maritime law. This may be regrettable, for Langton's eloquence, humour, personal charm, and dramatic sense (he had been a highly successful president of the O.U.D.S.), combined with great mental and physical vigour, would without doubt have made him a very successful advocate before a jury.

When Langton had begun to do well in his profession, war broke out and before the end of 1914 he had obtained a commission in the Royal Garrison Artillery and was posted at Queenstown, of which he soon became garrison adjutant with the rank of captain. His extreme short sight preventing him from going overseas on active service, he was transferred in 1915 to the intelligence branch of the War Office, then to the Ministry of Munitions in 1916. There, in the capacity of director of the labour department and commissioner of labour disputes, he worked with (Sir) Alan Barlow and used his remarkable powers of persuasion and his witty friendliness with real effect. In 1918 he was made controller of the demobilization department of the Ministry of Labour, until his own demobilization in 1919. He was appointed O.B.E. in 1917.

Langton returned to the bar at a time when several leading juniors in the Admiralty and Commercial courts were taking silk, and at the same time the work in those courts was greatly increased on account of the war. Langton soon acquired a large junior practice, especially in the Admiralty Court under Sir Maurice Hill. From 1922 until his elevation to the bench in 1930 he acted as secretary and adviser to the British Maritime Law Committee. His interest in the Comité Maritime International led to his being appointed its joint general secretary and his presence at all their conferences; his fluent French and light-hearted humour made him a general favourite at these somewhat solemn meetings.

In order to relieve the heavy pressure of work in the Admiralty Court, Sir A. D.

Bateson [q.v.] was appointed an additional judge in 1925. Langton was obviously the man to take his place in the front row, and very shortly afterwards he took silk. At once he became one of the leaders of the Admiralty Court and during the next five years he was employed in a very large proportion of the cases tried there, as well as in many other maritime cases. He also gradually acquired work in other courts, but the question whether he would have become a prominent leader of the common law bar was to remain unanswered, for in October 1930 Hill retired from the bench and Langton was appointed in his place, receiving the customary knighthood. Shortly afterwards he was elected a bencher of the Inner Temple.

During the twelve years in which Langton sat as a judge in the Probate, Divorce, and Admiralty division, he performed his judicial duties with ability and unflagging attention to the task. He thoroughly understood the Admiralty work, and his decisions, from which there was very seldom an appeal (and still less a successful one), were always well thought out and clearly expressed. In divorce cases he took great pains to master the law applicable to matrimonial disputes, and from time to time he found an outlet there for his humour and immense energy, which made it difficult for him to keep silent.

This exuberant energy also showed itself in physical exercise, especially lawn tennis and golf, in both of which Langton became a skilful player with a complete mastery of style. One of his qualities was an immense capacity for taking pains, and this showed itself both in his work and in his recreations. In 1939 he was elected chairman of the executive committee of the All England Lawn Tennis and Croquet Club and he held that position until his death, which took place suddenly at Burnham in Somerset 9 August 1942.

In 1919 he married Alice Mary Katherine, daughter of Daniel Francis Arthur Leahy, justice of the peace and deputy-lieutenant, of Shanakiel, county Cork. He was survived by his wife and a daughter. His portrait, by J. M. Crealock, is in the possession of the family.

[*The Times*, 15 August 1942; private information; personal knowledge.]

A. T. BUCKNILL.

LARMOR, SIR JOSEPH (1857–1942), physicist, was born at Magheragall, county Antrim, 11 July 1857, the eldest son of

Hugh Larmor, trader, by his wife, Anna, elder daughter of Joseph Wright, of Stoneyford, county Antrim. He was educated at the Royal Belfast Academical Institution, from which he went on to Queen's College, Belfast. After graduating there he became a scholar of St. John's College, Cambridge, and took the mathematical tripos in 1880, being placed senior wrangler and first Smith's prizeman. The second wrangler was (Sir) J. J. Thomson [q.v.], who with Larmor laid the foundations of the electromagnetic theory of matter. In 1880 Larmor was elected a fellow of St. John's and in the same year went back to Ireland as professor of natural philosophy at Queen's College, Galway. He returned to St. John's in 1885 on his appointment to a university lectureship in mathematics. This post he held until 1903 when he was appointed to the Lucasian professorship of mathematics in the university of Cambridge in succession to Sir G. G. Stokes, whose notice Larmor contributed to this DICTIONARY.

Larmor's scientific papers were gathered together by himself in two volumes (1929). Of the contents of the first volume he says in the preface: 'About half . . . is of electrical character, the other half being mainly General Dynamics and Thermodynamics including the dynamical history of the Earth, Formal Optics, and Geometry.' We may trace the history of the times in the gradual disappearance of interest in geometrical optics and the emergence of physical optics in the second volume. But general dynamics and particularly the principle of least action is an abiding interest, from the time of the first paper on 'Least Action as the Fundamental Formulation in Dynamics and Physics' (*Proceedings* of the London Mathematical Society, vol. xv, 1884).

The work for which Larmor will be remembered and which marks an epoch in the history of physical science is contained in three large papers in the *Philosophical Transactions* of the Royal Society (1894–7) on 'A Dynamical Theory of the Electric and Luminiferous Medium'. The work of James Clerk Maxwell [q.v.] had shown that the light-bearing medium is the seat of electromagnetic action. Larmor's predecessors had endeavoured to think out models of this aether on a mechanical basis. In particular his fellow countryman James McCullagh [q.v.] had proposed a medium with a peculiar kind of elasticity which he called 'rotational'. Larmor seized on McCullagh's aether and de-

veloped it by his favourite principle of least action, but in doing so he left aside all attempt to construct a model working on mechanical lines. In fact, far from thinking of the aether as a special kind of matter, he set about building up a conception of matter as consisting entirely of an array of electric particles, 'electrons', moving about in the aether according to electromagnetic laws. And the electrons themselves were not material particles, for he wrote, 'an electric point-charge is a nucleus of intrinsic strain in the aether. It is not at present necessary to determine what kind of permanent configuration of strain in the aether this can be, if only we are willing to admit that it can move or slip freely about through that medium much in the way that a knot slips along a rope: we thus in fact treat an electron . . . as a freely mobile singular point in the specification of the aethereal strain. . . .' Thus the roles of matter and aether were completely reversed.

The main conclusions to which Larmor came in these papers were revised and extended and incorporated in an essay which gained the Adams prize in the university of Cambridge. It was published as a book entitled *Aether and Matter: a Development of the Dynamical Relations of the Aether to Material Systems on the Basis of the Atomic Constitution of Matter, including a Discussion of the Influence of the Earth's Motion on Optical Phenomena* (1900). So radical was the analysis of matter into a complex of aether and electrons that (Sir) Horace Lamb [q.v.] remarked in 1904 to the British Association that the book would better have been entitled 'Aether and *no* Matter'. Larmor's ideas were strikingly parallel to those which were published almost simultaneously by Hendrik Antoon Lorentz in Holland. In their main features they were accepted and are still retained fifty years after.

Apart from the general theory, two particular results will always be associated with Larmor's name. He was the first to give the formula for the rate of radiation of energy from an accelerated electron, and also to give an explanation of the effect of a magnetic field in splitting the lines of the spectrum into multiple lines, as discovered by Pieter Zeeman. A natural development from the latter came into prominence later in connexion with radiowaves, when in 1924 Larmor gave considerable stimulus to the theory of the propagation of such waves in the upper atmosphere. His suggestions were quickly taken up by (Sir) Edward Victor Appleton and led to great advances.

Seen in its place in the history of physics, Larmor's work marks the end of the attempt to express everything in terms of the Newtonian mechanics of matter and the beginning of the electromagnetic theory of matter. But it led on immediately to the more revolutionary theory of relativity. For one of the main problems which Larmor attacked was the failure to find definite evidence of motion of the earth through the aether. Of this he was able to give a partial and approximate explanation, again on lines exactly parallel with the work of Lorentz. This explanation led up directly to the more radical outlook of Einstein which, while completing the discussion, shook the rigid framework of Newtonian conceptions of absolute time and space. Not only so, but it can scarcely be doubted that this loosening of classical concepts which for so long had been unquestionably held paved the way for the further new concepts of the quantum theory to be accepted. Thus Larmor stood between the old and the new physics, always conscious of his debt to the past, always labouring to free science from the shackles of the past, building the foundations of the new physics, yet always critical of rash enthusiasm for new paths. A deeply honest thinker, with wide interest in the world at large, never craving for publicity and winning respect from all for his judgement and his probity, he was one of the great band of men who have well deserved the title of professor of natural philosophy.

To his labours in the electromagnetic theory of matter Larmor added a deep concern for thermodynamic principles and was in no small measure responsible for bringing their importance to the fore. He was much interested in the work of Josiah Willard Gibbs to whom he paid tribute in a very instructive obituary notice in the *Proceedings* of the Royal Society (1905). In his memoir in the same journal (1908) on the life of Lord Kelvin [q.v.] he gave a survey of the development of thermodynamics which merits preservation for its own sake. Later he made a very substantial contribution to scientific literature by revising Clerk Maxwell's edition of the papers of Henry Cavendish (1921), and editing the collected works of James Thomson (1912), the fourth and fifth volumes (1904–5) of the works of Sir G. G. Stokes, and the fourth, fifth, and sixth volumes (1910–11) of those of Lord Kelvin [qq.v.].

Apart from his scientific work, Larmor always showed a wide interest and shrewd judgement in the counsels of his college, his university, and the nation. He was for many years a member of the council of St. John's. Here he was often critical, but he never failed to see when an important point was in danger of being overlooked. Although radical in his natural philosophy he was conservative in temperament, questioning modern trends even in such matters as the installation of baths in the college (1920). 'We have done without them for 400 years, why begin now?', he once said in a college meeting. Yet once the innovation was made he was a regular user. Morning by morning in a mackintosh and cap, in which he was not seen at other times, he found his way across the bridge to the New Court baths.

Larmor was always looking for the general principles behind phenomena. This interested him much more than spinning webs of thought out of the mind. He had not much sympathy for the pure mathematician, the geometer, or the analyst. Minute attention to logic or playing with geometrical constructions just for the joy of it were not his way. He was not always willing to give patient attention to details and so at times failed to be convincing. The same generality of view characterized his lectures. To the average student they appeared slow and inconclusive. But to those who were prepared to follow with attention they were full of stimulus, sometimes by their very incompleteness provoking the mind to wrestling and questioning. His outlook was very far removed from that of the famous nineteenth-century coaches for the mathematical tripos, masters of manipulation and of method, solvers of special and artificial problems. For such things he had no use. As his creative powers declined he turned more and more to matters of wide national and cultural interest. Those who knew him in his later years remember him as one of Cambridge's greater men, somewhat remote, impatient of unreality, independent in judgement, doubtful of what the new age was bringing with it.

Elected a member of the London Mathematical Society in 1884, Larmor served on the council of the Society from 1887 to 1912 and was a vice-president in 1890 and 1891. He became treasurer in 1892 and held that office for twenty years. In 1914 he was elected president and in the same year he received the De Morgan medal of the Society.

Of the Royal Society Larmor was elected a fellow in 1892, and in 1901 became one of the secretaries, continuing until 1912. The Society honoured him with a Royal medal in 1915 and with the Copley medal in 1921. During his service as secretary, in 1909, he was knighted. From 1911 to 1922 he represented the university of Cambridge in Parliament as a Unionist. He retired from the Lucasian professorship in 1932 and shortly after, owing to ill health, returned to Northern Ireland and lived there until his death at Holywood, county Down, 19 May 1942. He was unmarried. Something of the kindness of his heart, to which many could bear witness, was shown in the bequests which he made to provide medical and surgical assistance and sick nursing to junior members of the university of Cambridge and for the benefit of the University and College Servants' Association. Another bequest provided prizes to be awarded annually to men of St. John's College who were adjudged to be the most outstanding on general grounds, not purely scholastic, by a committee composed of both junior and senior members of the college.

Honours conferred upon Larmor in recognition of his services to science included honorary degrees from the universities of Dublin, Oxford, Belfast, Glasgow, Aberdeen, Birmingham, St. Andrews, Durham, and Cambridge. He was an honorary freeman of the city of Belfast, an honorary member of the Royal Irish Academy, of the American Academy of Arts and Sciences, of the Accademia dei Lincei, and of a number of other bodies at home and abroad.

[Sir Arthur Eddington in *Obituary Notices of Fellows of the Royal Society*, No. 11, November 1942; *Journal* of the London Mathematical Society, vol. xviii, part 1, January 1943; private information; personal knowledge.]     E. CUNNINGHAM.

LASCELLES, HENRY GEORGE CHARLES, sixth EARL OF HAREWOOD (1882–1947), was born in London at 43 Belgrave Square, the house of his maternal grandfather, 9 September 1882, the elder son of Henry Ulick, Viscount Lascelles, later fifth Earl of Harewood, and his wife, Lady Florence Katharine Bridgeman, daughter of the third Earl of Bradford. From Eton and the Royal Military College, Sandhurst, Lascelles joined the Grenadier Guards. He did not, however, intend to make the army his profession and from 1905 to 1907 he was an honorary attaché in Rome where he was able to cultivate his taste for art. He spent the next four years (1907–11) as aide-de-camp to Earl Grey [q.v.], governor-general of Canada.

In 1913 Lascelles stood for Keighley, a constituency in his native Yorkshire. His ill success may have first given him the distaste for politics which his subsequent experiences confirmed. Later in life he used to declare that every war in which Britain had been involved had been due to the inefficiency of politicians, and that they began what soldiers had to end. From 1914 he was himself thus occupied, having joined his yeomanry unit, the Yorkshire Hussars, on mobilization. But after Neuve Chapelle, when the Guards suffered very severely, he rejoined his old regiment. Wounded in the head a fortnight later, at Givenchy, he was back again in October for the battle of Loos. The end of the war saw him in Belgium commanding the unit in which he had first served, the 3rd battalion of the Grenadier Guards. He had been three times wounded and once gassed, and had received the D.S.O. and bar and the croix de guerre. Subsequently his interest in military affairs was concentrated on the Territorial Army in particular and the welfare of ex-servicemen in general.

During the war his great-uncle, the second and last Marquess of Clanricarde [q.v.], died and left practically his whole fortune of £2½ million to Lascelles with whom he shared a taste for the arts. These, and country pursuits in Yorkshire, were not, however, to be Lascelles's main occupations, for he became a public figure on his marriage in February 1922 to the only daughter of King George V, Princess (Victoria Alexandra Alice) Mary, known from 1932 as the Princess Royal. Besides helping his young wife in her many engagements Lascelles soon acquired a reputation of his own as a business-like chairman and an after-dinner speaker with a dry wit. Although he had, and sometimes showed, a typical dislike for the press, his *obiter dicta* found a ready currency in the newspapers. On the eve of his wedding Lascelles was appointed K.G. He succeeded his father as sixth earl in 1929 and was made a G.C.V.O. in 1934. He was lord lieutenant of the West Riding of Yorkshire from 1927, chancellor of Sheffield University from 1944, and president of the Royal Agricultural Society in 1929 when its show was held at Harrogate. His connoisseurship—he was versed in the classical European schools of painting and English furniture of the eighteenth century—was suitably recognized when he was made royal trustee of the British Museum in 1930. He was also an exponent of the art of *petit point*.

Much of Harewood's time and interest was given to racing and freemasonry. Already in 1926 senior grand warden of England he became in that year provincial grand master in West Yorkshire. In 1943 he became grand master of the United Grand Lodge. In horse-racing of all kinds —flat, national hunt, and pony—he was expertly versed, and he acted as co-editor of *Flat Racing* (1940) for the Lonsdale Library. He appeared before the Royal Commission on lotteries and betting in 1932 when, as a steward of the Jockey Club, he cogently expressed its views on the dangers to racing of large sweepstakes. He died at Harewood House, 24 May 1947, after some years of declining health.

Harewood had two sons, the elder of whom, George Henry Hubert (born 1923), succeeded him as seventh earl.

There are portraits of Harewood in the Harewood collection by Sir William Nicholson, S. J. Solomon, John St. Helier Lander, and (on horseback) with the Princess Royal, by Sir Alfred Munnings; also a drawing by J. S. Sargent. Another portrait by Nicholson is in the Freemasons' Hall, London.

[Tancred Borenius, *The Harewood Collection*, 1936; private information.]

H. E. WORTHAM.

LASKI, HAROLD JOSEPH (1893–1950), political theorist and university teacher, was born at Cheetham Hill, Manchester, 30 June 1893, the second son of Nathan Laski, a cotton shipping merchant, a Liberal and a leader of Manchester Jewry, by his wife, Sarah Frankenstein. Laski, who was extremely precocious, was educated at Manchester Grammar School in the days of the great J. L. Paton [q.v.] and studied eugenics under Karl Pearson [q.v.] at University College, London, in the first half of 1911. In the same year the aged Sir Francis Galton [q.v.] wrote congratulating him upon an article on heredity in the *Westminster Review*. Laski entered New College, Oxford (1911), with a history exhibition, and in 1914 he was placed in the first class of the honours list in modern history and was awarded the Beit memorial prize.

After working for a few months with George Lansbury [q.v.] on the then strug-gling *Daily Herald*, and having been rejected from the army on medical grounds, Laski in the autumn of 1914 accepted a lectureship at McGill University, Montreal, where he remained until 1916. He then joined the staff of Harvard University where he was associated with a distinguished group of Harvard lawyers, and formed specially close friendships with two famous justices of the Supreme Court, Oliver Wendell Holmes (a volume of whose legal papers he edited in 1920) and Louis Dembitz Brandeis, and with Professor Felix Frankfurter who was later also to be appointed to the Supreme Court. In 1919 Laski was bitterly attacked for his sympathetic attitude to the Boston police strikers, and although supported on grounds of academic freedom by the president of Harvard, Abbott Lawrence Lowell, he was warned not to expect further promotion. In 1920 he was appointed to a lectureship at the London School of Economics and Political Science where he became professor of political science in 1926, a post which he retained until his death. His early experience of America had an important effect on his career and the development of his ideas. He visited America frequently, and was a friend of President Franklin Delano Roosevelt. His two principal books on America were *The American Presidency* (1940) and *The American Democracy* (1948). The latter, which was his last large work, aroused much controversy in the United States, mainly on account of its Marxist approach to American history and institutions.

Laski's work during thirty years at the London School of Economics may be classified under three headings. He was a teacher, a political philosopher, and a Labour Party leader. As to his success and influence as a teacher, there is no dispute. His lectures, brilliantly delivered and based on great erudition and a memory of extraordinary power, were always crowded, and his personal popularity with students from Britain, the Empire and Commonwealth countries, from Asia, and from Europe was unparalleled. After his death hundreds of letters from ex-students in various parts of the world testified to his influence and also to his generosity; some later revealed that they owed their chance of education to his personal and secret payment of their fees.

As a political theorist, Laski's numerous books, both historical and topical, were mainly concerned with sovereignty, the nature of the State, and the problem of social change. In his early books, for instance *Studies in the Problem of Sovereignty* (1917), *Authority in the Modern State* (1919), and in his articles in the *Harvard Law Review*, he expounded the pluralist doctrine that the State should be no more than the most powerful of many voluntary associations within a given society. This he argued on the basis of church history, acknowledging his debt to F. W. Maitland and J. N. Figgis [qq.v.], and in *A Grammar of Politics* (1925) he applied a modified pluralism to the entire range of political institutions. In a long preface which he contributed to the 1938 edition, he gave his reasons for jettisoning the pluralist theory of the State. In 1927 he had explained the objections to the Marxist creed in a small volume on *Communism*; these objections, based on his passion for individual liberty and his belief that revolution on the Russian model was not inevitable or desirable in a Western democracy, he maintained until the end of his life. But experience undermined his optimism, and after the downfall of the second Labour Government in 1931 and the slump in Britain and America, he accepted in general the Marxist interpretation of history, and, in innumerable letters, lectures, articles, and books which had wide influence in many countries, he argued that a social revolution in some form was inevitable, but that whether it came peacefully or violently depended on the readiness of the ruling class to yield its power and privilege. In *The Crisis and the Constitution, 1931 and After* (1932), *Democracy in Crisis* (1933), *Parliamentary Government in England* (1938), and other works, he discussed the position of the monarchy and the House of Lords as bulwarks of property, and analysed the functions of British institutions to discover whether they would serve the purposes of the working-class democracy which he believed to be inevitable and what reforms would make them more serviceable. Shortly before his death he delivered the more optimistic Simon lectures in Manchester University which were posthumously published in 1951 under the title *Reflections on the Constitution*.

As a practical politician Laski was on the executive committee of the Fabian Society from 1921 to 1936, and of the Labour Party from 1936 to 1949. His object was to adapt Marxism to British conditions, and thereby to create a political philosophy for the Labour Party. A close friend of Léon Blum, he was an ardent advocate of the Popular Front, and associated with Mr. Victor Gollancz and Mr. John Strachey in the Left Book Club. In 1939 he denounced the Soviet-German Pact and the Communist change of front (see his pamphlet *Is This an Imperialist War?*, 1940, and his preface to *The Betrayal of the Left*, 1941). During the war the central theme of his books, articles, and speeches was that out of the war should come working-class unity and a unique opportunity for revolution by consent (*Where Do We Go From Here?*, 1940, and *Reflections on the Revolution of Our Time*, 1943). In 1945 he was chairman of the Labour Party and during the election was chosen by his opponents as a figure on which to hang the thesis that victory for Labour would mean violent revolution in England. He himself commented on this campaign, which made his name headline news throughout the world's press, in a characteristic article 'On Being Suddenly Infamous' (*New Statesman and Nation*, 14 July 1945). After the election he toured Europe advocating the thesis that social democrats should as far as possible co-operate with Communists, but on no account accept fusion with them, a view he later developed, with much criticism of Communist tactics, in a pamphlet, *The Secret Battalion* (1946).

Laski was a brilliant talker and raconteur, and was known throughout the Labour movement for his platform oratory. Those who most detested his political views and public activities appreciated his lack of personal ambition, his disinterestedness, and his really extraordinary generosity. His personal friendships were numerous and lifelong. Probably the most remarkable was his deeply affectionate, almost filial relationship with Oliver Wendell Holmes, who was fifty-two years his senior. Their voluminous correspondence covered a period of almost twenty years and deals with an immense range of literary and political topics. Its publication, after Laski's death, had the incidental result of confirming before the world—a fact which was already well known to Laski's intimates—that his innumerable anecdotes, though usually founded on fact, were not to be relied upon as historical evidence. Laski received the honorary degree of LL.D. from the university of Athens in 1937; he was a member of the

Industrial Court from 1926, a member of the lord chancellor's committee on ministers' powers (1929-32), the departmental committee on local government officers (1930-34), and the lord chancellor's committee on legal education (1932-4). His single hobby was the collection of a remarkable library, mainly of books on political theory of all periods.

In 1911 Laski married Frida, daughter of Francis John Kerry, farmer and landowner, of Acton Hall, Suffolk, by whom he had one daughter. This early marriage, which was without the consent of his parents, led to a breach of relations with his family which was not healed until 1920. He died in London 24 March 1950.

[Kingsley Martin, *Harold Laski*, 1953; *Holmes–Laski Letters*, edited by Mark DeWolfe Howe; 2 vols., 1953; private information; personal knowledge.]

KINGSLEY MARTIN.

LAUDER, SIR HARRY (1870-1950), comedian, was born in Portobello, near Edinburgh, 4 August 1870, the eldest of the seven children of John Lauder, potter, of Musselburgh, by his wife, Isobella Urquhart Macleod, daughter of Henry MacLennan, of the Black Isle, Ross-shire. Lauder's assumption for stage purposes of Highland dress of a fanciful order was not therefore without ancestral justification. Before Lauder was twelve his father died, and the boy had to take what jobs he could, including work in a flax-mill in Arbroath as a half-timer (one day at work, the next at school), and in a pit-head in Hamilton. He subsequently became a miner, but his voice and his skilful, genial use of it were obviously his fortune. He was soon well known in his area through local concerts, and in a short time became a professional entertainer, at first travelling in concert-parties, and later appearing in the smaller music-halls. He was thirty before he reached London, but once there his conquest of the capital was immediate, rewarding, and unbroken. He began his London triumphs at a hall called Gatti's-in-the-Road, but soon he was the acknowledged 'bill-topper' of the central halls, including the Tivoli, Oxford, and London Pavilion. Such favourite ditties as 'Tobermory' and 'The Lass of Killiecrankie' were already in his repertory.

Lauder's vehicle was the song with an interlude of patter. With his growing popularity his turn became longer and would include four or five 'numbers'. He usually wrote the words and music himself, drawing with instructive shrewdness on traditional airs for the simple, ear-catching lilts which were so easily and widely remembered and so joyously re-sung—and not by Scotsmen only. As time went on, he developed a serious, almost a religious note. He liked to end his performance with 'Rocked in the Cradle of the Deep' or 'The End of the Road', and it was a sign of his genius that he could carry his music-hall audience easily from such frivolities as 'Stop your tickling, Jock' to the more serious ballad of his finale and even into listening patiently while he gave them what was almost a sermon.

At the height of his popularity Lauder was often 'working' four houses a night at an extremely high salary, and he was canny in his handling of the immense sums which he earned. He publicized his own thrift with good humour and some of the Harry Lauder stories were generally supposed to have been invented by himself.

Lauder gave a command performance before King Edward VII in 1908 and came increasingly to be the first citizen, as well as the first favourite, of the vaudeville stage. From 1907 he made nearly every year an immensely successful tour of the Empire and the United States. In the war of 1914-18, in which his only son was killed in action in 1916, he was an ardent recruiter, in speech and song, and a tireless contributor to troop concerts, at home and on the western front; he energetically renewed these efforts in 1939. He was knighted for his services in 1919, and in 1927 received the freedom of the city of Edinburgh. He published several volumes of memoirs.

In later years the serious youth of Scotland began to resent what was deemed to be Lauder's exploitation of a quaint, old Caledonia wherein a laughing wee man, in fantastic tartans and carrying a crinkly cromach, indulged in the sentimentalities and humours of the 'Kailyard School' which was in growing disrepute. Lauder's antics and equipment had indeed little to do with the real Scotland, but they were enormously pleasing to the expatriate Scots all over the world who richly enjoyed a nostalgic heart-glow at the thought of 'Roamin' in the Gloamin'', and would happily fill a glass to the strain of 'A Wee Deoch-an-Doris'. The Scots are not notably a musical nation, but even those who were almost tone-deaf could appreciate, and even share without disgrace, a Harry Lauder chorus.

'Star-quality' on the stage is indefinable; roughly it means that its possessor has a magnetic, even a mesmeric, power which holds the audience immediately and maintains that grasp whatever the performer may be saying or doing. Lauder had that quality to the full. His patter, like his songs, had an elemental nature: he was never bawdy (at a time when the music-hall often was), never subtle, and never ingenious in the smart, 'wisecracking' way which was to come. He wore his heart on his sleeve, and it seemed to be a heart of gigantic size. He sometimes executed part of his turn in the plain clothes of a trousered working-man; there was, for example, the unforgettable loon who lay in his bed crooning 'It's nice to get up in the morning' while his brother Jock the baker rose soon after midnight and was stumbling off to his ovens. In these features he struck a veracity absent from his gurgling, rollicking, absurdly kilted Highlanders. But the latter were the darlings of his public.

Lauder's strutting figure, short, broad, and tough, was that most common in the Lowland industrial districts, but his accent was more of Scotland in general than of any particular area. It was broad enough to give character, but not so broad as to puzzle any southern ear, a valuable factor in his music-hall victories.

Lauder married in 1890 Annie (died 1927), daughter of James Vallance, underground manager of a mine in Hamilton. When not working Lauder lived for a long while near Dunoon and later at Strathaven, nearer the scene of his pit-work and of his first successes as an amateur. He had a bad fall at the age of sixty-eight, but overcame a fractured thigh; he was taken very seriously ill in the autumn of 1949, but lived on beyond expectation until his death at Strathaven 26 February 1950. He had willed to 'keep right on to the end of the road', as he had so often counselled others in song. His friends in all ranks of life were countless; he had built up the reputation, in a half-humorous way, of never 'banging a saxpence' without much careful cogitation, but his kindnesses were quiet, many, and 'known to his own'. A portrait by James McBey is in the Glasgow City Art Gallery.

[*The Times*, 27 February 1950; Harry Lauder, *Harry Lauder at Home and on Tour*, 1907, *A Minstrel in France*, 1918, and *Roamin' in the Gloamin'*, 1928.]

IVOR BROWN.

LAVERY, SIR JOHN (1856–1941), painter, was born in Belfast, the second son of Henry Lavery by his wife, Mary Donnelly. The date of his birth has not been definitely established. In his autobiography he writes, 'to save explanations when asked, I chose St. Patrick's Day as being, for an Irishman, easy to remember'. He was baptized in the Roman Catholic church of St. Patrick, Donegal Street, Belfast, 26 March 1856.

Nothing could have been less propitious than Lavery's childhood. His father, who kept a small and unprofitable public-house, was drowned in 1859 in the wreck of the emigrant ship *Pomona*, while on his way to seek a better occupation in America. His mother died of grief soon afterwards. John, then aged three, was taken by his father's brother to live on a small farm where he was severely but ineffectively disciplined by his harsh aunt. He was given a little schooling in the neighbourhood until in his eleventh year he was sent to Saltcoats in Ayrshire to another relative who owned a pawnshop. Later he returned to Ireland for a time, and at the age of seventeen he found employment in Glasgow as an apprentice to a painter-photographer for three years. During this time he apparently managed to pay his fees as a student at the Glasgow School of Art.

In 1876, when he was twenty, Lavery sold for a few pounds by raffle in a public-house his first painting, done in water-colours from an engraving. In 1879 he showed his first oil-painting at the Glasgow Institute. He then set up as an independent artist. A fortunate fire in his studio enabled him to collect £300 from an insurance company, with which he went to London to study at Heatherley's School of Art, and then to the Académie Julian in Paris where he had some tuition from Bouguereau. He exhibited in the Salon and lived for a while in the artists' colony at Grès-sur-Loing near Fontainebleau before returning to London to show his 'Tennis Party' at the Royal Academy in 1886, where it was much admired and bought for the Neue Pinakothek in Munich. In 1926 it was presented to the Aberdeen Art Gallery by Sir James Murray.

Thereafter Lavery's career was an uninterrupted progression of success. A commission to paint the State visit of Queen Victoria to the Glasgow Exhibition of 1888, on a canvas eight feet by ten, enabled him to establish social connexions through which he continued to procure other commissions for the next half-century. He became friendly with R. B. Cunninghame Graham [q.v.], visited Morocco with him, and bought a house in Tangier where he wintered for many seasons. His headquarters during the last forty years of his life were at 5 Cromwell Place, London, where he and his second wife, Hazel, entertained most hospitably a great variety of people from all grades of society.

The Royal Academy gave Lavery little encouragement at the outset of his career, so he welcomed the establishment of the International Society of Sculptors, Painters, and Gravers in 1897 under the presidency of J. A. McN. Whistler [q.v.] and accepted the office of vice-president. Whistler's influence is very perceptible in his early work, particularly in those full-length portraits of women such as 'Miss Mary Burrell' (Glasgow City Art Gallery), and the 'Printemps' in the Musée National d'Art Moderne, and the 'Été' in the Musée Rodin, in Paris. But his own personality eventually asserted itself fully and the 'Mrs. Lavery Sketching' now in the Municipal Gallery of Modern Art, Dublin, is a highly individual picture. He took lasting and justifiable pride in an early portrait, done about 1900, of the Baroness von Höllrigl, exhibited as 'La Dame aux Perles', of which he made two versions. Austrian charm, elegance, and dignity can seldom have been more delightfully depicted.

In general, Lavery's portraits of men were much less successful than those of women: but the interest he showed during his later life in political movements, particularly in those which culminated in the establishment of the Irish Free State, led him to paint many portraits of contemporary statesmen which have real historical value. He presented notable collections of these to the public galleries of both Dublin and Belfast.

His ambitious nature may well have hindered Lavery from making the best use of his gifts: for his remarkable ability as a visual recorder was less apparent in his paintings of ceremonial occasions than in those of scenes which had a more personal appeal for him. His 'High Treason Trial, 1916', with Sir Roger Casement in the dock and Serjeant Sullivan addressing the five judges, is a most dramatic representation. 'The Jockeys' Room at Epsom' (1924) and the 'St. Patrick's Purgatory' (1930) are, in their own way, as memor-

able. Some of his conversation pieces, such as those of Lady Cunard in her drawing-room with George Moore, or Ramsay MacDonald in his living-room at Lossiemouth, are more attractive than his formal portraits.

The quality and measure of Lavery's success is reflected in his official distinctions. He was knighted in 1918 and was a member of the orders of the Crown of Italy and of Leopold of Belgium. In 1921 he became a full member of the Royal Academy. He was also a member of the Royal Scottish (1896) and Royal Hibernian (1906) academics and of those of Rome, Antwerp, Milan, Brussels, and Stockholm. He received honorary doctorates from the Queen's University of Belfast and Trinity College, Dublin, and was a freeman of both cities. His art is represented, often copiously, in public galleries all over the world. Soon after his death his reputation began to wane: but the sale of three of his largest later works by Christies in June 1949 for prices ranging from four to fourteen guineas is very far from affording a fair index of their aesthetic worth.

Lavery was married twice: first, in 1890 to Kathleen MacDermott who died after giving birth to a daughter, Eileen Marion, who married the Master of (subsequently the nineteenth Baron) Sempill. In 1910 Lavery married Hazel, daughter of Edward Jenner Martyn, of Chicago, and widow of Dr. Edward Livingstone Trudeau, of New York; with her he lived happily until her death in 1935. He died at Rossenarra House, Kilkenny, 10 January 1941.

Lavery often introduced himself into his interiors with figures. Among the best self-portraits may be reckoned 'Père et Fille', which was painted in 1896–7 and is now in the Musée National d'Art Moderne, Paris; a portrait for the Uffizi Gallery at Florence, finished in 1911; and one of himself with Shirley Temple (1936) of which the present whereabouts are uncertain. A portrait of him by Lady Lavery is in the Municipal Gallery of Modern Art, Dublin. A pencil drawing by James Kerr-Lawson is in the Scottish National Portrait Gallery, and a portrait in oils by the same artist at the Ferens Art Gallery, Hull. The Glasgow City Art Gallery has a portrait by Harrington Mann, a red chalk drawing by James Gunn, and a bronze head by G. H. Paulin. A painting of Lavery by (Sir) Winston Churchill is reproduced in Lavery's autobiography, *The Life of a Painter* (1940), written with astonishing verve and frankness in the author's eighty-fourth year.

[W. Shaw-Sparrow, *John Lavery and his Work*, 1912; personal knowledge.]

THOMAS BODKIN.

LAWRENCE, (ARABELLA) SUSAN (1871–1947), politician, was born in London 12 August 1871, the daughter of Nathaniel Tertius Lawrence, a London solicitor and descendant of Philip Henry [q.v.], and his wife, Laura, daughter of Sir James Bacon [q.v.]. She was educated at home, at the Francis Holland School, Baker Street, and at University College, London, where in 1893 she was awarded the Rothschild exhibition for pure mathematics. Her marked mathematical ability induced her parents to continue her education at Newnham College, Cambridge, where she went in 1895, taking part i of the mathematical tripos in 1898. On leaving Cambridge, she interested herself in education, particularly in the welfare of the church schools, became a member of the London School Board in 1900 and in 1904 was co-opted to the education committee of the London County Council. In politics she was a Conservative and it was as a member of the Municipal Reform Party that she was elected to the London County Council for West Marylebone in 1910. Her practical experience here, however, combined with new trains of philosophical and political thought to convince her that she must break with the traditions in which she had been brought up and had hitherto lived. In 1912 she resigned her seat and soon afterwards joined the Labour Party.

During the next ten years she worked with Mary Macarthur [q.v.] for the National Federation of Women Workers and sat on a number of trade boards. She returned to the London County Council in 1913 as Labour member for Poplar, where for a time she made her home. In 1919 she was elected to the Poplar borough council and later made an alderman. In 1921 she and her colleagues were committed to prison for their refusal to collect the poor rate, which they believed was too heavy for the borough to bear alone. Their protest bore fruit later when the burden of London poor relief was partly centralized. In 1923 she was returned to Parliament as Labour member for East Ham North and in the first Labour Government of 1924 she was appointed parliamentary private secretary to the president of the

Board of Education. She was defeated at the election in October of that year, but was returned for East Ham North at a by-election in 1926 and at the general election in 1929. In the session of 1928–9 she distinguished herself by the force and knowledge of her attack on Neville Chamberlain's local government bill and, on the accession of her party to power in 1929, she was appointed parliamentary secretary to what had been Chamberlain's department, the Ministry of Health. In the financial crisis of 1931, the proposal to reduce unemployment benefit and expenditure on the social services led her, with the bulk of the Labour Party, into opposition, and in the ensuing general election she lost her seat.

Susan Lawrence remained a member of the London County Council until 1928, being deputy chairman in 1925. She was on the executive of the Fabian Society from 1913 to 1945. As a member of the Labour Party national executive, 1918–41, and chairman in 1929–30, she played no small part in shaping the policy of her party. Her speeches were remarkable for clarity combined sometimes with a fierceness and biting humour which terrified her opponents. Whether as a disciple of Lord Shaftesbury, or as a follower of Graham Wallas and Sidney Webb [qq.v.], she fought with disinterested passion and all her exceptional mental gifts for those whom she believed to suffer from social injustice.

She died at her home in London 24 October 1947.

[Labour Party annual reports; Fabian Society reports; private information.]

J. E. NORTON.

LAWRENCE, SIR HERBERT ALEXANDER (1861–1943), soldier and banker, was born at Southgate, near London, 8 August 1861, the fourth son of Sir John (later first Baron) Lawrence, of the Punjaub [q.v.] by his wife, Harriette Catherine, daughter of the Rev. Richard Hamilton, a clergyman in Donegal. In 1863 when Lawrence was appointed viceroy of India, Herbert Lawrence was left with family friends in England. In 1869 his father returned and London—26 Queen's Gate—became his principal home. In 1875 he went to Harrow then enjoying the great headmastership of Henry Montagu Butler [q.v.] who was always anxious to encourage members of prominent Indian governing families at Harrow. On leaving school in 1879 Lawrence went to the Royal Military College, Sandhurst, and, desiring to follow the family tradition of service in India, was gazetted to a lieutenancy in the 17th Lancers in 1882. In the India of *Departmental Ditties* there was no great occasion for military gifts to declare themselves and Lawrence enjoyed himself steeplechasing and playing polo, racquets, and cricket. If he was largely remembered by his brother officers as an accomplished sportsman he was likewise recalled, under his nickname of 'Lorenzo', as a popular senior subaltern. He was for some time adjutant, and the comprehensive nature of his position enable him to say that he knew every detail of regimental duty from commanding officer to lance-corporal.

In 1891 Lawrence returned to England and in the following year he married Isabel Mary Mills (died 1941), daughter of the first Baron Hillingdon, then senior partner in Glyn, Mills, Currie & Co. Passing out of the Staff College, Camberley, in 1896, a year ahead of the future field-marshals Haig and Allenby [qq.v.], and having been master of the college drag, Lawrence was selected for employment in the intelligence division, War Office, and posted to the German section. Promoted D.A.A.G. in 1898, on the outbreak of war in the following year he went out to South Africa where he and Haig served as senior staff officers of the Cavalry division under Sir John French (later the Earl of Ypres, q.v.). Haig's business was 'operations', and Lawrence's 'intelligence'. In this period of their lives these two strong characters did not prove a good combination. Lawrence finished the war in command of the 16th Lancers, and received a brevet lieutenant-colonelcy. Gifted with exceptional neatness of expression both in speech and in writing, he contributed a chapter to C. S. Goldmann's *With General French and the Cavalry in South Africa* (1902), a valuable and authentic account. Despite his auspicious start, Lawrence retired from the army in 1903, possibly disappointed that Haig had been preferred to him for the command of the 17th Lancers, and certainly anxious to provide a more stable background for his growing family than was possible for a serving soldier. He entered the City where his own and his wife's connexions were of help to him, although he did not join Glyn's bank until 1907. He was elected a member of the committee of the Ottoman Bank in 1906 and became a director of the Midland Railway in 1913. At the request of King Edward VII he joined King Edward's Horse (King's Colonials) in order to train it on the right lines and from 1904 to 1909 commanded the regiment.

On the outbreak of war in 1914 Lawrence was almost at once appointed G.S.O. 1 to the 2nd Yeomanry division with which he afterwards went to Egypt. In the summer of 1915 Sir Ian Hamilton [q.v.], not without opposition, gave him command of the 127th (Manchester) brigade in the Dardanelles campaign. Although much broken by the death of his elder son, Oliver John, in action in May of that year, Lawrence made a great impression by his coolness in leadership. In July he was sent as deputy inspector-general of communications to Mudros where he successfully averted the breakdown which seemed imminent. He was promoted next month to the command of the 53rd division and transferred the following month to the 52nd (Lowland) division. During the evacuation from the Dardanelles in December and January he was in charge at Cape Helles and was one of the last to leave the beach.

In the following summer Lawrence was in command of the equivalent of a corps and was responsible for the considerable victory at Romani over a mixed German-Turkish force which delivered the Sinai desert into allied hands. In the autumn he returned to England for personal reasons (since he doubted the advisability of invading Palestine) to command the 71st division, Home Forces, until February 1917 when he was transferred to the 66th, a newly raised second-line Territorial formation which he took out to France. The division was engaged with success in October in the fighting at Poelcappelle in the Passchendaele campaign. Towards the end of the year he took over the intelligence branch at G.H.Q. He was appointed C.B. in 1916 and promoted K.C.B. in 1917.

At the beginning of 1918 Lawrence was appointed chief of the general staff to Haig. Lloyd George in a characteristic passage in his *War Memoirs* suggests that Haig gave this vital post to Lawrence because he was a personal friend and a fellow cavalry officer. In fact, Haig and Lawrence were in many ways antipathetic and they were never on terms of close friendship, and it is far from certain that Lawrence was Haig's own choice. Nevertheless, under the compulsion of events and because both were good soldiers they worked together not only harmoniously but as a single force. Their particular achievement was to evolve a clear plan of what they wanted, convey it to the troops and convince them that it would bring victory and peace. In all the delicate negotiations directed to bringing the French into activity during the German attacks of March 1918 Lawrence gave Haig invaluable support, especially at the conference at Doullens (26 March). On more than one occasion Lawrence was able to do much to smooth inter-allied friction, notably in August 1918 when Haig would not accede to Foch's request to persist in the battle on the Fourth Army front. When Haig was in London for meetings of the War Cabinet Lawrence took charge at G.H.Q. and several times—especially when the French were hard pressed in July and asking for British help—he had to make important decisions on his own account. That Lawrence deserved a considerable share of credit for the great British victories in August did not escape the notice of C. R. M. F. Cruttwell [q.v.] in his *History of the Great War* (1934). In his dispatch of 21 October 1918 Haig aptly paid tribute to Lawrence's 'cool judgement, equable temperament and unfailing military insight' which were 'of the utmost value in circumstances demanding the exercise of such qualities in a peculiarly high degree'.

With the end of the war Lawrence, who had been promoted general, returned to the City, but it was still in the balance whether the State might not make further claims on his services. In November 1920 his name was brought forward as a possible successor to Lord Chelmsford [q.v.] as viceroy of India, and eighteen months later his name was again canvassed as a possible successor to Sir Henry Wilson [q.v.] as chief of the imperial general staff. In neither event was he chosen—just as in 1932 he was narrowly to miss promotion to field-marshal—but that his name was raised was indicative of the reputation of one who was, to quote *The Times*, 'for a space one of our greatest soldiers', albeit 'almost unknown to the multitude'.

In the City, Glyn's, of which Lawrence had been made a managing partner and of which he was to be chairman from 1934 until his death, strengthened its position by amalgamations with Holt's in 1923 and with Child's the following year. Lawrence joined the board of Vickers in 1921 and became chairman five years later—a position which was to draw on him some strictures from the Left, but his work in reanimating this company was to bear

fruit in the timely production of the Spitfire. He was on the boards of several international banks and in international affairs—but more significantly in matters domestic—he was an important influence with Montagu (later Lord) Norman [q.v.] to whom he was bound by ties of closest friendship. In Parliament, in Fleet Street, and in official circles, he was recognized as one of the first men in the City, whose sagacity behind the scenes was in constant demand. Sir Ian Hamilton remarked in his *Gallipoli Diary* (vol. i, 1920) that Lawrence combined the thrust of a lancer with the circumspection of a banker. To understand him fully it is necessary to add that he possessed a strength of character and a degree of rectitude which were the secret of his exceptional authority with his fellow men. He was a man whose opinion counted. It was significant that he was one of the four members of the Royal Commission on the coal industry (the Samuel commission) in 1925, after which he was appointed G.C.B. He was a governor of Wellington College, received the honorary degrees of LL.D. from the university of St. Andrews (1922), and D.C.L. from Oxford (1929), was a commander of the Legion of Honour and held many other foreign decorations. He died at Woodcock, Hertford, 17 January 1943, and was buried at Seal near Sevenoaks. A service was held in his memory at St. Michael's, Cornhill.

Of Lawrence's three children, both sons were killed in France during the war of 1914–18. He was survived by his daughter who married Major Desmond Abel Smith. A portrait by (Sir) Oswald Birley is at Glyn's Bank and an earlier portrait by the same artist is at the Cavalry Club.

[*The Times*, 8 November 1920 and 18 January 1943; Sir John Davidson, *Haig: Master of the Field*, 1953; private information.] ROGER FULFORD.

LEACOCK, STEPHEN BUTLER (1869–1944), professor and humorist, was born at Swanmore, near Bishop's Waltham, Hampshire, 30 December 1869, the third son of Walter Peter Leacock, asphalt contractor, who after his marriage went first to South Africa, and then to Canada, where he settled on a farm near Lake Simcoe in Ontario. His wife, Agnes Emma, daughter of the Rev. Stephen Butler, joined him with their children in 1876. Leacock was educated at Upper Canada

College and returned there as assistant master in 1889 whilst attending the university of Toronto. He took his degree in modern languages in 1891 and was appointed modern languages master at Upper Canada College where he remained until 1899. In that year he went to Chicago to do graduate work in political economy and in 1903 he took his degree in philosophy. He was then appointed a lecturer in political science and history at McGill University, Montreal, where he had already been a special lecturer since 1901. In 1905 he became an associate professor in the same subjects, and in 1908 he was appointed William Dow professor of political economy and head of the department of economics and political science, a position which he held until his retirement in 1936.

Leacock proved a more competent teacher of political science than of economics and his *Elements of Political Science*, published in 1906 as his first book, is still considered an excellent textbook. He cultivated the friendship of his pupils, with whom he was very popular, and he exercised a valuable influence upon the general policies of the university for the improvement of its standards of teaching. Leacock's humour was well known to his students. He had begun writing humorous articles whilst teaching at Upper Canada College and many of them were published in North American journals such as *Truth* and *Life*. In 1910 a collection of these was printed privately under the title *Literary Lapses*. The book caught the attention of an English publisher who arranged for its publication in Great Britain in the same year, and in New York in 1911. It was followed by *Nonsense Novels*, and in 1912 *Sunshine Sketches of a Little Town* established Leacock's international reputation as a humorous writer of marked originality.

In his prime Leacock's industry was immense and it was always a mystery how he found time, while he was in charge of an important department of a great university, to produce a book almost every year. In all, he had to his credit more than fifty books, and, while most of them are of a humorous nature, some of his serious works, like his *Baldwin, Lafontaine and Hincks*, in the 'Makers of Canada' series (Toronto, 1907), his biographies of Mark Twain (1932) and of Dickens (1933), and his *Our British Empire* (1940), *Montreal: Seaport and City* (Garden City, 1942), and *Canada: The Foundations of Its Future* (Montreal, privately printed, 1941), are admirable contributions to historical literature.

In his humorous writings Leacock's style was loose and racy with irony and satire given free play, and he employed with great skill an effective blend of American exaggeration and British understatement. Royalties from the wide sale of his books and his large fees as a lecturer whose wit and wisdom could always attract large audiences, particularly in the United States, gave him a big annual income for many years, but heavy losses in the stock market crash of 1929 compelled him to work until the end of his life.

In politics Leacock was a radical Tory, who wanted reforms without revolutions and he crusaded continually against time-serving politicians, ignorant Labour agitators, and ill-educated plutocrats who aspired through their wealth to control the life of universities. But his chief political interests lay in maintaining and strengthening the ties of Canada with Great Britain and the rest of the Commonwealth, and in the encouragement of immigration from Britain, and he intervened frequently and with great effect in controversies concerning these causes. In 1907–8 he made a tour of the Empire for the Rhodes Trust, lecturing on imperial organization. In 1937 Leacock was awarded the Lorne Pierce medal for literature by the Royal Society of Canada. He received the honorary degree of Litt.D. from Brown University, Rhode Island, in 1917, and from Dartmouth College, New Hampshire, in 1920, and of LL.D. from Queen's University, Kingston, Ontario, in 1919.

In private life Leacock was a charming and very companionable man whose superlative gifts as a talker and raconteur made him shine in any company, and in his later years he was regarded as the chief 'character' of Montreal, where he had a wide circle of friends among all classes. After his retirement from McGill University he spent most of each year at his country home near Orillia, Ontario, where his Canadian life had begun, and there he found diversion from his literary labours in gardening, fishing, and dispensing generous hospitality to his friends, until he died in a hospital in Toronto 28 March 1944. Leacock married in 1900, Beatrix (died 1925), daughter of Colonel Robert B. Hamilton, of Toronto. They had one son. There is a portrait of Leacock by Richard Jack at the University Club at Montreal.

[*The Times*, 30 March 1944; Peter McArthur, *Stephen Leacock*, Toronto, 1923; H. A. Innis, lecture on Stephen Leacock as a founder of social studies delivered in the university of Toronto in 1938, reprinted in the *Canadian Journal of Economics and Political Science*, vol. x, No. 2, May 1944, with a tribute by Professor J. P. Day; Stephen Leacock, *The Boy I Left Behind Me*, 1947; private information; personal knowledge.]

J. A. STEVENSON.

LEDINGHAM, SIR JOHN CHARLES GRANT (1875–1944), bacteriologist and director of the Lister Institute, was born 19 May 1875 at Boyndie, Banffshire, the sixth child of the Rev. James Ledingham, minister of Boyndie, by his wife, Isabella, daughter of the Rev. James Gardiner, minister of Rathven. His paternal grandfather was the village blacksmith of Auchleven. He was educated at Boyndie public school, Banff Academy, and the university of Aberdeen, where he distinguished himself in both classics and science. In 1895 he graduated M.A. with first class honours in mathematics and natural philosophy, winning the Simpson mathematics prize, and sharing the Neil Arnott prize in natural philosophy. His ambition was to enter the Indian Civil Service, but he failed to pass the examination.

In 1900 Ledingham took the B.Sc. and in 1910 the D.Sc. He graduated M.B., Ch.B., with honours in 1902 and with the Anderson travelling scholarship went to Leipzig in the same year to study pathology under Marchand. After a year in the pathology department at Aberdeen University he went in 1904 to continue his bacteriological and immunological studies at the London Hospital. In 1905 began his long association with the Lister Institute when he was appointed assistant bacteriologist in the serum department at Elstree. In 1906 he transferred to the main Institute in London, becoming chief bacteriologist in 1909. He retained this post when he became director of the Institute in January 1931.

During the war of 1914–18 Ledingham was for a time in charge of the bacteriological department of King George Hospital, Waterloo; he was next appointed a member of the medical advisory committee in the Mediterranean area in 1915, and in 1917 he became consulting bacteriologist to the forces in Mesopotamia. He was appointed C.M.G. for his services in the following year.

In 1920 Ledingham took part in establishing the National Collection of Type Cultures, acting as its secretary for the next ten years. Much of his time was spent in the work of expert committees, in particular those appointed by the Medical Research Council, the Local Government Board, the Ministry of Health, the London County Council, the National Radium Commission, the British Empire Cancer Campaign, and the Bureau of Hygiene. He was chairman of the tropical diseases committee of the Royal Society, and of the tropical committee of the Medical Research Council (1936). After the outbreak of war in 1939 he served on several committees concerned with problems such as war wounds.

In addition to a steady output of scientific papers, Ledingham wrote a number of useful reviews of subjects within his special knowledge. He was one of the team of contributors to the treatise on diphtheria published by the Medical Research Council in 1923. With (Sir) Paul Fildes he was an associate editor of the Council's *System of Bacteriology* (1929–31) to which he contributed the chapters on natural immunity, tularaemia, and production of active immunity; he also collaborated with William Ewart Gye in an introductory survey to the volume on viruses and virus diseases. He delivered the Harben lectures before the Royal Institute of Public Health in 1924 and the Herter lectures at Johns Hopkins University in 1934. He was a member of the Medical Research Council (1934–8) and president of the second International Congress of Microbiology in London in 1936.

Ledingham was elected F.R.S. in 1921, F.R.C.P. (London) in 1924, and was knighted in 1937 for his contributions to science. In 1920 he was given the title of professor of bacteriology in the university of London and that of emeritus professor in 1942. After retiring from the Lister Institute in 1943 he continued his researches in the laboratories of the Imperial Cancer Research Fund at Mill Hill until he died in London 4 October 1944.

Ledingham's contributions to science show evidence of wide interests, for they include studies in bacteriology, pathology, haematology, immunology, and research on the viruses. In all, he wrote some 130 papers, alone or in collaboration. His first important contribution was an account, with Marchand, of a case of kala-azar which proved the existence (hitherto unsuspected) of that disease in China.

His important studies on phagocytosis appeared between 1908 and 1912. Before the outbreak of war in 1914 he had made a thorough study of the role of the carrier in the spread of typhoid fever, and in 1912 joined with (Sir) J. A. Arkwright [q.v.] in writing a monograph on *The Carrier Problem in Infectious Diseases*. The pathogenesis of blood diseases was a field of inquiry which always attracted Ledingham and one which he felt had for too long been dominated by morphological studies; he was convinced of the need for experimental research into these obscure conditions, giving proof of his conviction by the publication of several papers.

During the last twenty years of his life his chief interest was in the virus diseases. His work on the elementary bodies of vaccinia and fowl-pox supported the belief that the elementary body was the infecting agent. In 1923 he published his observations on the histology of the experimental lesions of tularaemia and of its serological diagnosis in man. In 1935 he collaborated with Gye in research on the nature of the filterable tumour-exciting agent in fowl sarcoma.

Ledingham also took an interest in the practical aspects of preventive medicine, especially vaccination and methods of prophylactic immunization against measles, scarlet fever, diphtheria, whooping-cough, and influenza, being impatient of the tardy adoption of well-tried methods. He was a man of wide international outlook, great industry, and tenacity of purpose. His success as an administrator was due to his ability to isolate the essential from the non-essential.

He was a competent gardener, with a real love of country life, and he liked to play Scottish tunes on his violin or on the piano. He married in 1913 Barbara, daughter of David Fowler, superintendent of the Banffshire Mental Hospital at Boyndie; they had one son and one daughter. A portrait of Ledingham by Alexander Christie was presented to him on his retirement from the Lister Institute and is in the possession of the family.

[*Journal of Pathology and Bacteriology*, vol. lviii, January 1946; S. P. Bedson in *Obituary Notices of Fellows of the Royal Society*, No. 15, May 1947; *British Medical Journal*, 14 October 1944; *Lancet*, 21 October 1944; *Nature*, 18 November 1944.] HUGH CLEGG.

LEE, ARTHUR HAMILTON, VISCOUNT LEE OF FAREHAM (1868–1947), statesman, benefactor, and patron of the

arts, was born 8 November 1868 at Bridport, the youngest child of the rector, the Rev. Melville Lauriston Lee (the son of Sir J. Theophilus Lee, G.C.H., who as midshipman had served at the battles of St. Vincent and the Nile), by his wife, Emily Winter, daughter of Thomas Dicker, banker, of Lewes, Sussex.

Lee was educated at Cheltenham College (he became a life member of the council in 1911 and was president 1917–39), and the Royal Military Academy, Woolwich. In 1888 he joined the Royal Artillery and in 1889 volunteered for service in China where a brilliant feat of intelligence work earned high commendation from the War Office. In 1893 he went to Canada as professor of military history, strategy, and tactics at the Royal Military College, Kingston, until in 1898 he was appointed military attaché with the United States Army in Cuba during the Spanish-American war. He was made an honorary member of the 'Rough Riders' and became an intimate friend of Theodore Roosevelt, who was shortly to become president of the United States. In 1899 Lee was appointed military attaché at the British Embassy in Washington with the rank of lieutenant-colonel.

In that year he married Ruth, daughter of John Godfrey Moore, one of the leading bankers in New York, and on his return to England in 1900 he retired from the army and was elected Conservative member for the Fareham division of Hampshire. Balfour soon selected him for office and he joined the Board of Admiralty as civil lord in October 1903, resigning with the Conservative Government in December 1905. From 1906 until 1914 he was the Opposition spokesman on naval affairs in the House of Commons and took a leading part in the opposition to the Declaration of London. In 1912 he promoted the criminal law amendment (white slave traffic) bill as a private, non-party, measure. He introduced it in an eloquent speech on the second reading and steered it through committee and report with persistence and skill, in spite of considerable opposition, but with support from Reginald McKenna [q.v.] the home secretary. On the outbreak of war he rejoined the army as colonel on the staff and was detailed for special service with the Expeditionary Force. For his able work at the front he was thanked by Kitchener and twice mentioned in dispatches by French [qq.v.]. In October 1915 his former political opponent

Lloyd George invited him to join him at the Ministry of Munitions as parliamentary military secretary and later, in his *War Memoirs*, expressed high praise of Lee's untiring industry, great resource, and practical capacity. In July 1916 he was appointed K.C.B. for these services and on Lloyd George's transfer to the War Office Lee became his personal military secretary.

In February 1917 Lloyd George, as prime minister, made Lee director-general of food production. Up to this time nothing had been done to increase the home production of food. Lloyd George in his first Cabinet had included a minister of food control, whose function was to organize and regulate distribution. Two months later he took the first effective step to stimulate home production by the appointment of Lee as director-general, nominally under R. E. Prothero (later Lord Ernle, q.v.) president of the Board of Agriculture and Fisheries, but with direct instructions from himself to make a success of his important task. Lee conducted this new office with vigour and enthusiasm and Prothero recorded that 'his organizing gift amounted to genius'. But the corn production (amendment) bill which Lee promoted in 1918 to enable him to carry out a further extensive conversion of grass land to arable met with serious opposition as had the Corn Production Act in the previous year. It was severely amended in the Lords, and, failing to agree with Prothero on this and other matters of policy, Lee resigned at the end of July 1918. The end of hostilities was, however, approaching and Lee had made a big personal contribution to safeguarding the nation from acute food shortage. Without his energy and determination it would have been impossible to obtain the labour and machinery necessary for the large addition to the tillage area which he achieved. In January 1918 he had been appointed G.B.E. and just before he resigned his work was recognized by his elevation to the peerage as Baron Lee of Fareham. In August 1919 Lloyd George included him in his Cabinet as president of the Board of Agriculture and Fisheries, and he was sworn of the Privy Council. He successfully carried the Act which converted his Board into a Ministry, but his Agriculture Act of 1920, to amend and continue the Corn Production Act of 1917 and making permanent a guaranteed price for home-grown wheat and oats, was found to be unworkable and both Acts were repealed in the following year.

In February 1921, when Lee was transferred to the Admiralty as first lord, the shadow of the coming Washington conference on reduction and limitation of armaments was already discernible. In the preliminary discussions on the Defence Committee, in the Cabinet, and at the Imperial Conference, Lee, supported by the weighty authority of the first sea lord (Lord Beatty, q.v.) and his assistant, Sir A. E. M. (subsequently Lord) Chatfield, had an important part which he played with such success that he was selected to go to Washington as second British delegate with Balfour. His many American connexions (Theodore Roosevelt's son was assistant secretary to the navy) made him a welcome guest and he acquired a great reputation as the exponent of British views, although, through the opposition of France and the failure of American support, he did not succeed in his attempt to secure the abolition of submarine warfare. The only result of this issue was the ineffective Root 'humanizing' resolution. The service which Lee rendered to Balfour and his country at this conference was rewarded with promotion to a viscountcy in 1922. He had resigned office with Lloyd George's Cabinet in that year and never again took part in politics. But he was ever ready for public service in other ways. An admirable chairman, he presided over three Royal Commissions: on the Civil Service in India (1923–4; he was appointed G.C.S.I. in 1925), London cross river traffic (1926) and police powers and procedure (1928), as well as over the Radium Commission for four years. He was also chairman of the committee on police pay and pensions (1925). He was promoted G.C.B. in 1929.

In 1917 the Chequers Estate Act was passed by which Lee and his wife presented to a trust, for the use of successive prime ministers for ever, the mansion and estate of over a thousand acres in Buckinghamshire which they had acquired in 1909 and entirely restored and equipped with appropriate furniture, works of art, and historical relics. In January 1921 the trust was brought into operation and Lord and Lady Lee finally left the house with its entire contents. They provided an endowment of £100,000 for its upkeep. Lee had acquired a remarkable knowledge of painting and the fine arts generally before and during his years of furnishing

Chequers, and he now began a second collection with zest and a rare flair for finding and acquiring masterpieces of all schools and dates, in which he revealed his real love and understanding of craftsmanship. He bequeathed the whole to the Courtauld Institute of Art, the original conception of which was due to his imagination and energy. With the financial help of Samuel Courtauld [q.v.] it was founded in London University and opened to students in October 1932. Again with Courtauld he persuaded the university to accept the transfer from Hamburg of the famous Warburg Institute and library for the study of the humanities. He personally arranged for its removal and housing in London as a loan to himself until it was refounded in 1944. In 1940 he presented his extensive and valuable collection of early silver and other objects of art to Hart House, Toronto, in memory of his early associations with Canada. In 1924 he was appointed a trustee of the Wallace Collection and in 1926 of the National Gallery, being chairman in 1931-2. He was also for some time chairman of the Royal Fine Art Commission; in fact, his great knowledge of art in all its phases, his resolute character, and his ability in administration made his name the first to be thought of for any such public appointment. He received the honorary degree of LL.D. from the university of Cambridge in 1931.

Lee died 21 July 1947 at Old Quarries, Avening, his Gloucestershire home. There were no children of the marriage and the peerage therefore became extinct. There are portraits and sketches of Lee by P. A. de László at Old Quarries and also at Chequers. There is a portrait by James Gunn at Cheltenham College.

[The Times, 22 July 1947; Sir T. H. Middleton, Food Production in War, 1923; private information; personal knowledge.]

VINCENT W. BADDELEY.

LE GALLIENNE, RICHARD THOMAS (1866-1947), poet and essayist, was born in Liverpool 20 January 1866, the eldest son of John Gallienne, who became manager and secretary of the Birkenhead Brewery, by his wife, Jane, daughter of Richard Smith, of Liverpool. He came of an old seafaring family in the Channel Islands and the prefix 'Le' which he added to his surname on the title-page of his first published poems was in the style of his forebears. He grew up to share with his mother an interest in literature, especially poetry, and as a schoolboy at Liverpool College spent his spare time in the city bookshops. His father apprenticed him to a firm of chartered accountants but he found the drudgery distasteful and perhaps harmful since he suffered from asthma, and he failed his examinations. Instead he began to write verse and, encouraged by Oliver Wendell Holmes, decided upon a literary career.

His first book of poems, My Ladies' Sonnets, was privately printed in 1887 with the financial help of his office friends. Migrating to London the following year he was for a time secretary to the actor-manager Wilson Barrett [q.v.] and met such literary figures as Swinburne, Meredith, and Wilde. Eventually he got regular work in 1891 reviewing books for the Star in which he had a column over the pseudonym 'Log-roller'. With W. B. Yeats, Ernest Rhys, Lionel Johnson [qq.v.], and others he was one of the original members of the Rhymers' Club, meeting in the Cheshire Cheese 'for discreet conviviality, conversation on literary matters, and the reading of their own newborn lyrics'.

In 1889 the London publishing firm newly formed by Elkin Mathews and John Lane [q.v.] published, as the first work to issue from the Bodley Head, a collection of Le Gallienne's verse, Volumes in Folio, in the romantic mood of the period. Shortly afterwards Le Gallienne became the firm's reader and he was able to recommend such writers as Francis Thompson, John Davidson, Laurence Binyon, Lionel Johnson, and Kenneth Grahame [qq.v.]; he also helped in the publication of the Yellow Book, to which he was himself a contributor.

Throughout the 'nineties Le Gallienne turned out a stream of verse and literary criticisms which were widely read, whilst his romantic novel, The Quest of the Golden Girl (1896), had an immediate success. In 1901, however, he decided to settle in the United States which he had already twice visited with Lane. His decision was precipitated partly by the break-up of his second marriage, and partly by the disintegration of the English literary movement of the 'nineties with which he had been so prominently associated and of which he wrote in The Romantic '90s (1925). He made many friends in America and wrote much, particularly for newspapers and magazines, but he never achieved the literary reputation he had made in England. Later he removed to

France where he continued to write for the American press, mainly about life in Paris. Some of these essays were published in book form, in *From a Paris Garret* (New York, 1936; London, 1943) and *From a Paris Scrapbook* (New York, 1938), the latter being awarded a prize by the French Government for the best book of the year written about France by a foreigner. Le Gallienne had a genuine and deep-rooted love of letters which made him do much to bring forward young writers to public attention. He was always a versatile critic and essayist, was less successful as a novelist, and is chiefly remembered for the melodious verses of his earlier period.

Le Gallienne was thrice married: first, in 1891 to Mildred, daughter of Alfred Lee, of Liverpool, with whom he was blissfully happy. She had been a waitress in a Liverpool café, where he took his meals as a young man, and she later inspired the character of 'Angel' in his autobiographical novel *Young Lives* (1899). She died in 1894 leaving one daughter. In 1897 he married Julie, daughter of Peter Norregard, railway director, of Copenhagen. They had one daughter, Eva, who became known as an actress and producer. This marriage was dissolved and in 1911 he married Irma, formerly wife of the American sculptor Roland Hinton Perry. Their daughter, Gwen, achieved a reputation as a painter of portraits. Le Gallienne died at Mentone, where he had eventually settled, 14 September 1947. He is buried in the cemetery above the town, not far from the grave of Aubrey Beardsley [q.v.], his collaborator on the *Yellow Book*. A litho-portrait by P. Wilson Steer is reproduced in the first series of *Prose Fancies* (1894) and another by W. R. Sickert in the *Yellow Book*, vol. iv (1895); a portrait by his third wife is reproduced in *The Lonely Dancer* (1914), and a cartoon by (Sir) Max Beerbohm in *The Romantic '90s* (1925); there are two pastels by Sir William Rothenstein; and a crayon drawing by Miss Gwen Le Gallienne, done in the year of his death, is in her possession.

[*The Times*, 16 September 1947; *Liverpool Echo*, 17 September 1947; *New York Herald Tribune*, 16 September 1947; *Listener*, 16 October 1947; J. Lewis May, *John Lane and the Nineties*, 1936; H. Montgomery Hyde, introduction to the second edition of *The Romantic '90s*, 1951; R. J. C. Lingel, *A Bibliographical Checklist of the Writings of Richard Le Gallienne* (New Jersey, 1926); private information; personal knowledge.]

H. MONTGOMERY HYDE.

LEGH, THOMAS WODEHOUSE, second BARON NEWTON (1857–1942), diplomat and politician, was born at Hillington, King's Lynn, 18 March 1857, the eldest son of William John Legh, later first Baron Newton, by his wife, Emily Jane, daughter of the Ven. Charles Nourse Wodehouse, archdeacon of Norwich. He went to Eton where, in his own words, he 'did as little work as possible', and leaving after a few years, he spent some time abroad with a tutor, visiting most of the European capitals but chiefly living at Dresden and in Austria. In 1876 he entered Christ Church, Oxford, graduating in 1879 with a fourth class in modern history; in the same year he was nominated an attaché by the Foreign Office.

In 1881 Legh was appointed to Paris, under Lord Lyons [q.v.], where he served until the summer of 1886, when he stood for Parliament as Conservative candidate in the Newton division of Lancashire. He was duly elected, and retained the seat until 1898 when he succeeded to the peerage on the death of his father, who had been ennobled in 1892. The climate of the House of Lords seemed to suit his temperament better than that of the Commons and he became active in its work. In 1902 he made an unsuccessful attempt to amend the Vaccination Act by abolishing the option of conscientious objection; and he served on the House of Lords betting committee. In this year, also, convinced that the many set-backs encountered in the South African war were due to the voluntary system of enlistment, he combined with Sir Clinton Dawkins and others to found the National Service League.

The political journalist A. A. Baumann wrote of Newton in *Vanity Fair* in 1908: 'His success has astonished all but the few who knew his quite rare qualities. A rather sleepy appearance is a foil to a clear and alert intelligence which takes nothing on trust and has a humorous contempt for the solemnities of the world. Lord Newton . . . has drafted a Bill for reforming the House of Lords by a process of selection. Wit and humour are powerful aids to the critical faculty and Lord Newton's directness and simplicity of style are irresistible. . . .' The attempt to secure the Lords reform was unsuccessful, as were measures for smoke abatement, for the amendment of the laws on betting, and for the introduction of the 24-hour clock.

In June 1915 Newton was appointed paymaster-general in the first coalition ministry, with the duty of representing the War Office in Parliament whenever the secretary of state was unable to attend. He was sworn of the Privy Council. In March 1916 Sir Edward Grey (later Viscount Grey of Fallodon, q.v.) appointed him an assistant under-secretary at the Foreign Office, in charge of two departments, one concerned with foreign propaganda and the other with prisoners of war. In October 1916 he became controller of a new prisoner of war department and remained in that post until August 1919. He was a very success-ful negotiator, and made arrangements with the Germans and Turks which re-sulted in the liberation of thousands of British prisoners by exchange. In 1919 he moved an amendment to the aliens bill and, in the face of much opposition, obtained its acceptance by both Houses. By this amendment former enemy aliens (who had not been interned during the war) were only to be deported if a satis-factory reason for so doing was produced to the advisory committee; whereas the original bill would have obliged them to seek exemption from deportation by providing reasons why they should stay in this country.

Newton began his travels in adoles-cence; continued them during his diplo-matic career, covering the whole of Europe, the Near and Middle East, and India; and between the two world wars he extended his range to China, Japan, South Africa, and South America. His greatest political interest was the field of foreign politics. He spoke French and German fluently.

The Legh family had been wealthy country gentlemen in Cheshire since the time of Agincourt, and Lyme, their seat in the Peak country, is one of England's great country houses. But despite this opulence, Newton detested ostentation, and was most simple and frugal in his habits. A Labour M.P., hearing him speak in the Lords, said: Who is this chap? He talks like anyone else: the other chaps all talk as if they were addressing their tenants.' Reserved and kind, he was possessed of great physical courage, and was quiet and modest in his ways.

Newton wrote biographies of Lord Lyons (1913) and of the fifth Marquess of Lansdowne (1929), and in 1941 pub-lished his reminiscences under the title of *Retrospection*. He married in 1880 Evelyn Caroline (died 1931), daughter of a Cheshire landowner, William Bromley-

Davenport. There were three daughters and two sons, the elder of whom, Richard William Davenport (born 1888), suc-ceeded him as third baron when he died at Eaton Square, London, 21 March 1942. The younger son, Sir Piers Legh, was master of the household of King George VI, 1941–52, and of Queen Elizabeth II, 1952–3, and died in 1955. A portrait of Newton by A. T. Nowell is at Lyme, which has been since 1947 a property adminis-tered by the National Trust.

[*The Times*, 23 March 1942; Lord Newton, *Retrospection*, 1941; private information.]

HERBERT B. GRIMSDITCH.

LEIGH-MALLORY, SIR TRAFFORD LEIGH (1892–1944), air chief marshal, was born at Mobberley, Cheshire, 11 July 1892, the younger son of the rector, the Rev. Herbert Leigh Mallory, later canon of Chester Cathedral, by his wife, Annie Beridge, daughter of the Rev. John Beridge Jebb, of Walton Lodge, Chester-field, and rector of Brampton. His elder brother, G. L. Mallory [q.v.], was lost in the Mount Everest expedition of 1924. Leigh-Mallory was educated at Hailey-bury and Magdalene College, Cambridge, where he took third class honours in history (1913) and law (1914). In 1914 he was commissioned in the 4th battalion, Lancashire Fusiliers, with which he went to France. In 1916 he was seconded to the Royal Flying Corps. He served in France in Nos. 5 and 15 Squadrons and in command of No. 8 Squadron until the end of the war, being mentioned in dis-patches in 1918 and appointed to the D.S.O. in 1919. In the same year he was granted a permanent commission as major, 'aeroplanes', and resigned from the army.

Between the wars Leigh-Mallory under-went courses at the Royal Air Force College and the Imperial Defence College and was an instructor in air subjects at the Army Staff College. He commanded the School of Army Co-operation, served at the Air Ministry as deputy director of staff duties and was senior air staff officer in Iraq. He was promoted air commodore in 1936 and air vice-marshal in 1938. In 1937 he was appointed to command No. 12 (Fighter) Group, a post which he still held on the outbreak of war in 1939. The main responsibility of the group in 1940 was the defence against air attack of the industrial Midlands and the im-portant east-coast shipping route. It took its full share in the Battle of Britain.

Leigh-Mallory was mentioned in dispatches and appointed C.B. In December 1940 he was transferred to the command of No. 11 (Fighter) Group, which was then recovering from the Battle of Britain and very much on the defensive. With his usual vigour he proceeded to train it for the offensive—a bold and far-seeing step at that stage of the war. Always quick to appreciate the need for changed tactics, he applied them unhesitatingly. The offensive spirit was manifested in the doctrine of the Fighter Wings, offensive sweeps over enemy territory by large fighter formations in mutual support, intruder sorties into Europe by single day or night fighter aircraft making use of cloud cover for surprise attacks on ground or air targets, and support of light bombers in daylight raids and of amphibious raids against the French coast. His knowledge of the needs of the other Services was invaluable when he directed the air part of the Dieppe operation. Time after time he was able to anticipate the requests for air support which came from the land and sea forces. 'Air co-operation faultless' was one of the messages he received from the Dieppe beaches in August 1942.

In July of that year Leigh-Mallory was promoted to acting air marshal and in November 1942 appointed A.O.C.-in-C., Fighter Command. In the new year he was promoted K.C.B. In his new command his whole effort was again directed to the offensive, anticipating the day when the continent could be invaded. He was early appointed air commander-in-chief designate for the invasion of Europe, and, in conjunction with the naval and army commanders designate, entered wholeheartedly into the planning for this great undertaking, in spite of the weighty preoccupations of his active command. By the time he was confirmed as air commander-in-chief, Allied Expeditionary Air Force, in December 1943, with the rank of air chief marshal, the air offensive had succeeded beyond all expectation and hardly an enemy aircraft dared show itself near our coast. Despite the widespread military activities on the south coast, not a single enemy reconnaissance aircraft penetrated the defences to discover the preparations for the invasion. Leigh-Mallory was again mentioned in dispatches.

In his new appointment he exercised full command of the Tactical Air Forces of Britain and operational command of those of the United States which were supporting the invasion in western Europe from the United Kingdom. Some idea of the magnitude of his responsibilities may be gauged from the fact that on D-Day he was in operational command of some 9,000 aircraft. The success of this force is historical. The German air force was virtually swept from the skies, and the German armies were practically immobilized by the destruction of their rail and road communications. His handling of a force of unprecedented size, despite the difficulties inherent in such an inter-allied command, was masterly.

Leigh-Mallory's command ceased on 15 October 1944 when the war in Europe seemed as good as won and there was no longer need for detailed co-ordination of the two Allied Tactical Air Forces. On 14 November 1944 he left London by air to take up his new appointment as allied air commander-in-chief, South East Asia Command, at a time when the offensive against Japan was in full swing. The aircraft in which he and his wife were travelling did not arrive at its destination and in June 1945 documents in the wreckage of an aircraft found in the mountains thirty miles west of Grenoble left no doubt that the aircraft was that in which they had been travelling. His untimely death deprived him of the honours which he had so well earned.

He was a great air commander and a born leader: a man of unbounded energy who seemed never to be off duty. He never spared himself or others, was determined to the point of ruthlessness, never losing sight of his objective, and possessed of great self-confidence which sometimes appeared to be self-conceit to those who did not know him well. But beneath this was a genuine solicitude for those working under him and specially for the fighting man. As a group commander he made a point, perhaps after an exhausting spell of duty, of meeting pilots as they came in from patrol, to learn at first hand of their impressions. Then in the mess over a drink he would listen to their suggestions. He inspired loyalty and trust and was particularly popular with the pilots of Fighter Command. His honours included appointment as a chief commander of the American Legion of Merit and to the first class of the Soviet Order of Ushakov, both in 1944.

In 1915 Leigh-Mallory married Doris Jean, daughter of Edmund Stratton Sawyer, by whom he had a son and a daughter. His wife's great natural charm endeared her to all, and Leigh-Mallory himself would have been the first to acknowledge the deep debt which he owed to her in contributing to his success.

The best portrait of Leigh-Mallory is a pastel by William Dring which hangs at Fighter Command headquarters, Bentley Priory, Stanmore. Another by Eric Kennington is in the Imperial War Museum.

[*Burke's Landed Gentry*, 1952; official records; private information; personal knowledge.]          W. B. CALLAWAY.

LEVER, SIR (SAMUEL) HARDMAN, baronet, of Allerton (1869–1947), chartered accountant, was born at Bootle 18 April 1869, the son of Samuel Lever, cotton dealer, and his wife, Elizabeth Cain. His father had married at an early age and died when only twenty-one, leaving two sons, of whom Hardman was the younger and only an infant. He was educated at the Merchant Taylors' School, Great Crosby, and took his accountancy examinations in London with honours. After a short time with a Liverpool firm he went to New York and joined the firm of Barrow, Wade, Guthrie & Co. Some years later he became a partner, and also set up an office in London under the name of Lever, Anyon, and Spence.

In 1915 the minister of munitions, Lloyd George, then engaged on a large programme of national factory construction, was much exercised about their production costs and the control in general of profits arising from munitions contracts. He was advised to seek the services of the best obtainable expert in cost accountancy, a science then more developed in the United States than in this country. Lever was recommended and came from New York at very short notice in August 1915. Officially he became assistant financial secretary with a wide range of duties, but he was forced to concentrate more and more on the institution of costing systems in the national factories, thus forging a tool which tested relative efficiencies in those factories, and the reasonableness of the prices and profits of outside munition firms.

When at the end of 1916 Lloyd George became prime minister his appointments included several personalities with little or no parliamentary experience and no particular interest in politics. Lever's appointment as financial secretary to the Treasury was a questionable one, for his ambitions did not lie in that direction and his past experience did not demonstrably fit him for an office which demands at once a knowledge of national finance and of parliamentary procedure. He was never, in fact, called upon to carry out the normal duties of his post, for within two months of his appointment he was transferred to another sphere of activity for which he was eminently fitted. The British Government had virtually exhausted all the dollar resources it could command to cover the large commitments into which it had entered for American supplies. In the course of January 1917 it became clear that someone enjoying the confidence of the Government must go to New York to be in intimate contact with J. P. Morgan & Co. who acted as agents for the Government in placing orders and finding funds to pay for them. Lever, who was appointed K.C.B. in February, was the obvious choice since he had lived for many years in New York, and was in touch with and had the confidence of America's industrial and financial leaders. He arrived in America in February 1917 and became the official Treasury representative after the United States entered the war in April. He was also in close touch with the Canadian Government on all financial relations with Great Britain. He did not return to England until the war was over, when he received a baronetcy (1920). He was also a commander of the Legion of Honour and of the Order of the Crown of Italy.

After the war he was a director of several leading industrial companies. He was also called upon from time to time for further public services. He was Treasury representative at the Ministry of Transport from 1919 to 1921, a member of the Weir committee on electricity which recommended the construction of the 'grid', chairman of a committee set up in 1927 to inquire into the inland telegraph service, headed in 1938 an air mission to Canada which led to the construction in that country and the United States of aircraft which were to prove invaluable, and six months later took a similar mission to Australia and New Zealand.

Lever, never thought of as anything but 'Sammie' in his wide circle of friends on both sides of the Atlantic, was essentially a sturdy figure. Once described in New York as 'a Britisher who made American noises', he was, apart from the noises, essentially British and liberal minded.

He took a love of cricket with him to the United States, and even managed in his youth to play it there. In later life he was a keen golfer and an ardent angler.

Outside his profession his main interest was a singularly happy married life, and the exercise of his gift for making and retaining friends. He married in 1900 Mary Edythe, daughter of Matthew Hamilton Gault, of Montreal. There were no children of the marriage and the baronetcy therefore became extinct when he died 1 July 1947 at his home near Winchester.

[Private information; personal knowledge.]
ANDREW McFADYEAN.

LEWIS, SIR THOMAS (1881–1945), physician, was born at Teigil House, Roath, Cardiff, 26 December 1881, the third of the five children of Henry Lewis, a mining engineer, by his wife, Catherine Hannah, daughter of Owen Davies, of Cardiff. At the age of ten he entered Clifton College but owing to poor health left after two years, his education being continued first by his mother and later by a tutor. Joining University College, Cardiff, he was awarded a scholarship and exhibitions and, in 1902, obtained his B.Sc. with first class honours in anatomy and physiology. In the same year he entered University College Hospital, London, with an exhibition, and there he worked for the greater part of his life, despite several offers of posts elsewhere, including (in 1932) the regius professorship of physic at Cambridge. After winning a scholarship and five medals he passed the final M.B., B.S. in 1905 with triple distinction and the university gold medal. He was house-surgeon to Sir V. A. H. Horsley and house-physician to Sir Thomas Barlow [qq.v.]. After a short period in Berlin, where he learnt German, he was appointed in 1907 medical registrar and later assistant physician at the Seamen's Hospital, and out-patient physician at the City of London Hospital. In 1907 he was elected fellow of University College, London, and proceeded M.D.; he was elected F.R.C.P. (London) in 1913.

Lewis worked in the laboratory of E. H. Starling [q.v.] at University College during 1907–8, and in 1909 put up his plate in Wimpole Street. His first outstanding research was on the pulse and respiration and in 1909 he contributed a chapter on the pulse for *Further Advances in Physiology* edited by (Sir) Leonard Erskine Hill. In 1908 Lewis first met (Sir) James Mackenzie (whose notice he later contributed to this DICTIONARY) and became his friend. Mackenzie encouraged him to make a study of the irregularities of the heart's action, a study which had a profound influence on the understanding and control of disease of the heart. During 1908 Lewis worked with (Sir) Arthur Salusbury MacNalty on 'heart-block', the first investigation on a human subject in which the electrocardiograph he had installed in his department was used. He showed auricular fibrillation to be a common form of disordered rhythm of the heart (*British Medical Journal*, 27 November 1909). With the help of Mackenzie, Lewis founded and edited in 1909 a new journal, *Heart*. He was the mainstay of its scientific reputation, being author, or co-author, of about one-quarter of the papers published in it until 1933, when he altered its scope and changed its title to *Clinical Science*.

Lewis divided his time between hospital work and private practice until, in 1910, he was awarded the first of the newly established Beit memorial fellowships. In 1911 he was appointed lecturer in cardiac pathology at University College Hospital, and assistant physician in 1913. He resigned from the Seamen's Hospital and from the City of London Hospital, to which he became consulting physician. He became full physician to University College Hospital in 1919.

Lewis's next important work was to prove the origin and map the course of the excitation wave and he named the sinoauricular node the 'pacemaker of the heart'. His work was published during 1914–15 as a series of papers in *Philosophical Transactions* remarkable both for clarity of presentation and for the beauty of the illustrations, all of which he prepared himself. It was again outlined in his Croonian lecture before the Royal Society in 1917 and led to his election as F.R.S. in 1918. During this period Lewis pursued his investigations into the mechanism of the heart beat. *The Mechanism of the Heart Beat* (1911) became the standard work and was followed by *Clinical Disorders of the Heart Beat* (1912) and *Clinical Electrocardiography* (1913).

In 1916 Lewis was appointed physician on the staff of the Medical Research Committee (afterwards Council) in order to investigate the disordered action of the heart known as 'soldier's heart' which he renamed the 'effort syndrome'. His observations and those of his colleagues were published as a special report in 1917, supplemented by further papers in the *British Medical Journal* and the *Lancet*, and appeared in book form in 1918 (2nd ed. 1940). Lewis was appointed C.B.E. in 1920 and knighted in 1921.

In 1917 Lewis published an important paper on dermatographism, in which he demonstrated the independent contractility of the capillaries. After the war he went back to the study of cardiac irregularities, especially the mechanism underlying auricular flutter and fibrillation, but about 1924 he returned to the study of the vascular reactions of the skin. He obtained evidence that in response to all forms of injury a substance, 'H-substance', was liberated, indistinguishable from histamine, but he refrained from calling it histamine in the absence of conclusive proof. He gave an account of this work in his *Blood Vessels of the Human Skin* (1927). His work on obstructive vascular disease, and his first attack of coronary thrombosis in 1927, led Lewis to his final interest, pain. Work on skin tenderness led him to postulate the existence of a new system of nerves which he named 'nocifensor nerves'. He summarized his researches in *Pain* (1942).

Lewis knew that if his work was to continue after him he must foster a movement to apply the methods of science to the study of human disease. In 1930 he changed the name of his department to 'department of clinical research', and established, and was the first chairman of, the Medical Research Society. The control of *Clinical Science* was passed into the hands of this Society in 1939, although Lewis remained its editor until 1944. Shortly before his death he approached the Nuffield Foundation for a grant whereby the journal could be purchased from the publishers and become the property of the Society. His Harveian oration (1933) was entitled 'Clinical Science' and a book of the same name appeared in 1934. In 1935 he delivered the Huxley lecture on 'Clinical Science within the University'. This and other work was republished in his *Research in Medicine and other Addresses* (1938).

Lewis received a Royal medal from the Royal Society in 1927, its Copley medal in 1941, and the Conway Evans prize of the Royal Society and the Royal

College of Physicians in 1945; he was honoured by many universities and foreign learned societies. He died 17 March 1945 at his home at Loudwater, near Rickmansworth, Hertfordshire. He was buried at Llangorse church, Brecon.

Lewis was of medium height and spare in build. He was intolerant of slipshod thinking and writing, and had an amazing power of concentration on the work in hand, any interference with which by holidays or even meals he resented. 'The pace was terrific, and he left his coworkers panting.' Medical research in Britain owes much to his example, his work, and his advocacy of 'clinical science'. He asserted that 'knowledge requisite to the practice of medicine rests upon a tripod: studies of living men in health and disease; studies of dead men; and correlated studies upon the lower animals. Clinical science in its work embraces all three, but its central and unique province, most fundamental of all work pertaining to the practice of medicine, is that which concerns living men.' He collected round him and inspired young men who, wrote Sir Henry Dale, 'lived in the gleam of an eye—the eye of an eagle—which was always magnificent, indeed, but mild only on occasions when the mission was momentarily out of his mind'. Outside his work Lewis's chief interest lay in natural history. He was an authority on birds and made one of the finest collections of photographs of them in Britain. He left among his papers the manuscript of a small book on birds and their ways.

Lewis married in 1916 Lorna, daughter of Frank Treharne James, of Merthyr Tydfil, and had one son and two daughters. There is a portrait by Evan Walters in the National Museum of Wales, and a copy in the library of University College Hospital Medical School, London.

[*The Times*, 19 March 1945; A. N. Drury and R. T. Grant in *Obituary Notices of Fellows of the Royal Society*, No. 14, November 1945; *Clinical Science*, vol. vi, Nos. 1 and 2, 1946; *British Medical Journal* and *Lancet*, 31 March 1945; *American Heart Journal*, April 1945; *British Heart Journal*, January 1946.]

HUGH CLEGG.

LEWIS, SIR WILFRID HUBERT POYER (1881-1950), judge, was born in London 9 February 1881, the eldest son of Arthur Griffith Poyer Lewis, a practising barrister and recorder of Carmarthen, of Henllan, Narberth, Pembrokeshire, by his wife, Annie Wilhelmine, daughter of James Ellison, M.D., surgeon to the household of Queen Victoria. His paternal grandfather was bishop of Llandaff.

Tall, good-looking, and sociable, Lewis was educated at Eton where he was a dry bob and played cricket, football, and fives, and from an early age was well endowed with those social graces which he preserved throughout his life. At University College, Oxford, he was placed in the third class of the honours list in modern history in 1903.

From heredity and temperament the Church and the law provided the alternatives for his life's work. Lewis chose the law and read in the chambers of J. A. (later Viscount) Simon, and John (later Viscount) Sankey [q.v.]. In 1908 he was called to the bar by the Inner Temple, and began practice in Cardiff where family connexions gave him a start and his own ability a rapidly expanding practice. He maintained his interest in Church affairs throughout his life as a member of the provincial and special provincial courts of the Church in Wales, and of the joint and choir committees of the Temple Church, besides serving as chancellor of the dioceses of Llandaff, Monmouth, Manchester, Blackburn, and Worcester. In 1914 when war broke out, although he was thirty-three and the father of a young family, Lewis applied for and obtained a commission in the Glamorgan Yeomanry. He served in France as aide-de-camp to Sir Charles Fergusson who commanded the 5th division and subsequently the II and XVII corps. Lewis was older and more mature than the usual run of aides-de-camp, and the relationship between the corps commander and himself was one of close friendship. He was twice mentioned in dispatches and was awarded a military O.B.E.

After the war Lewis had to decide whether to resume his local practice at Cardiff or to accept an invitation to join T. W. H. Inskip (later Viscount Caldecote, q.v.) in the old chambers of Sir J. E. Bankes [q.v.] at 3 Hare Court. His choice of London brought rapid success. He was regularly briefed for a leading London newspaper in actions for libel (then more numerous than now) and for the Great Western Railway in their multifarious common law litigation. The variety of his practice was remarkable and took him far outside the ordinary range of a common law junior. His old clients in South Wales and elsewhere briefed him in commercial and Admiralty cases, and he had almost a monopoly of the specialized prize money cases arising from the war. He was an acknowledged authority on ecclesiastical law. Within seven years from the end of the war he had one of the largest and most varied practices in the Temple. In 1930, when the post of junior (common law) counsel to the Treasury fell vacant, his appointment was a foregone conclusion. A bencher in 1929 his appointment as a judge of the King's Bench division, with a knighthood, followed in 1935.

Lewis brought to the bench, besides great natural dignity and a fine presence, a wide experience of life and, although he was never an academic lawyer, a profound knowledge of the law and its practical application. The direct contact between judge and citizen he regarded as the highest judicial duty, and in this his inclinations tallied with his qualifications, pre-eminently those of a judge of first instance. On the bench he was courteous, patient, and detached. He never sought the limelight or to attract attention to himself. He was essentially a shy man, which in some quarters gave rise to the impression that he was unsympathetic towards the Welsh view of life. This was not the case. While a separation between Wales and England was abhorrent to him, he was intensely proud of his long Welsh descent and valued the Welsh way of life which he did much to cherish and preserve.

Although his work occupied the greater part of his life, it was not his main object or interest. Lewis had inherited an estate in Pembrokeshire which had been in his family for many centuries. He was at heart a countryman, and his tastes were those of a Welsh squire. Although he gave ungrudgingly to the service of the law, this was a means to the end of keeping up his property and preserving it from passing into the hands of strangers. It was in Pembrokeshire during his short periods of leisure that he was happiest, managing his estates, visiting his farms, discharging the duties and enjoying the activities of a country gentleman. He was a deputy-lieutenant for the county, chairman of quarter-sessions, a trustee of Llandovery College, besides giving much time to the affairs of the Welsh Church. He was a fellow of Eton (1940) and became an honorary fellow of his college (1943), two honours which afforded him great pleasure. The business of life did not leave much time to play, but he was a keen shot, a fisherman, enjoyed a game of golf, and in particular gained much pleasure from deer stalking. He appreciated fine painting, a good play, but not the cinema, and was well read. He was a most hospitable man, a charming host, and attracted and held the warm affection of his many friends.

In 1950 Lewis would have completed fifteen years on the bench and might well have considered retiring and devoting the remainder of his life to his many interests and activities in South Wales, but the strain of the war of 1939–45, during which he had served in the Home Guard, and the burdens and anxieties it brought in its train had left their mark. In January he was taken ill in the middle of a trial at the Central Criminal Court and he died in London 15 March 1950.

Lewis was a fine judge, of the mettle which has created and maintained confidence in the judicial body. In private life he concealed great warmth of feeling beneath an unemotional exterior. He had an exacting sense of duty, and one who knew him well has said that his chief characteristic was humility. He was twice married: first, in 1908 to Margaret Annie (died 1932), daughter of (Sir) J. E. Bankes; and secondly, in 1934 to Elizabeth Barty, daughter of David Barty King, M.D., of London. There were one son and four daughters of the first, and two sons of the second, marriage.

[*The Times*, 16 March 1950; *Law Times*, 24 March 1950; *Burke's Landed Gentry*, 1952; private information; personal knowledge.]

WINTRINGHAM N. STABLE.

LEWIS, SIR WILLMOTT HARSANT (1877–1950), journalist, was born in Cardiff 18 June 1877, the son of James Oliver Lewis, coal shipper, and his wife, Marion Harsant Butler. He was educated at Eastbourne and at Heidelberg and the Sorbonne. After unavailing attempts to find a niche in journalism he went on the stage and drifted to the Far East where he got to know both Japan and China. He edited the *North China Daily News*, and as correspondent for the *New York Herald* was in China during the Boxer rising and in Korea during the Russo-Japanese war. Later he edited the *Manila Times* (1911–17) where he acquired a very wide range of knowledge of the problems of the region and began to be well known to important Americans. At the request of General Pershing he went to France where he worked under George

Creel in the American information and propaganda services and attended the peace conference as representative of the *New York Tribune*. For his services in France he was made a chevalier of the Legion of Honour.

The turning-point in his career came when Lord Northcliffe [q.v.] engaged him as Washington correspondent of *The Times* in place of Sir Arthur Willert who was returning home. After a brief period of probation Lewis was appointed in 1920. It was a bold move to send him to Washington, for all his journalistic experience had been gained in the Far East; he knew nothing of the methods or spirit of *The Times*; and not a great deal about his native country. The experiment was a great, although not an unqualified, success. Lewis liked the Americans and they liked him. He was very far from being the standard British correspondent and was fond of saying that he owed his popularity and understanding of American ways to the fact that he was not English but a 'Celt'. Tall and handsome, Lewis preserved some of the manners of the stage on which he had served his apprenticeship. He was an admirable after-dinner speaker and a celebrated raconteur. In his office, in the Press Club, at scores of Washington dinner tables he became a great social figure and this served him well in his professional work. He was soon a master of the complicated social and political life of Washington, especially well informed about the inner life of the Senate, and he was recognized as a figure whom it was well worth informing and even consulting.

Lewis began his service in Washington at a difficult time in the history of Anglo-American relations. The rejection of the League of Nations by the Senate ended all hope of open collaboration between Britain and the United States. But the Washington naval disarmament conference of 1921 was followed by the Dawes plan of 1924 and, however much the Republican administrations proclaimed their isolation from European quarrels, they could not and did not stand aloof. Still less did they stand aloof from Asiatic quarrels and Lewis was an excellent interpreter of the American view of 'the Orient'. Other difficulties arose from the change in control of *The Times* and from the return to the editorial chair of Geoffrey Dawson [q.v.]. Although it is unlikely that Dawson would have appointed Lewis, nevertheless he kept him in Washington. As a correspondent Lewis had his weaknesses; not all important news interested him, and his interest in and admiration for his own style sometimes impaired his value as a reporter. But he was one of the leading members of the Washington press corps and his services were justly recognized when he was appointed K.B.E. in 1931. The coming of the Roosevelt administration in 1933 weakened Lewis's position. He did not know the new-comers who flooded Washington and had little sympathy with their enthusiasm or social and political aims. Indeed, the tepidity with which the 'New Deal' was reported caused serious irritation in very high quarters in Washington and some discomfort in the offices of *The Times*.

With the shadow of a second war changing the face of Washington, Lewis was again in his element but he was not as important a reporter as he had been in the days of Presidents Harding, Coolidge, and Hoover. A great deal of the work of his office was now left to assistants and Lewis cast himself with great success in the role of the grand old man of the foreign correspondents in Washington. He retired in 1948 but continued to live in Washington where he died suddenly 4 January 1950.

Lewis married three times: first, to Lina Jessie Ringer; secondly, in 1926 to Ethel Stoddard, daughter of Frank Brett Noyes, president of the Associated Press, by whom he had one son and two daughters; thirdly, in 1939 to Norma, daughter of Colonel T. F. Bowler, of Okemah, Oklahoma. A portrait of Lewis by Bjorn Egeli is reproduced in *The History of 'The Times'*, vol. iv, part 2, 1952.

[*The Times*, 5 January 1950; *New York Times*, 5 and 6 January 1950; *New York Herald Tribune*, 5 January 1950; private information; personal knowledge.]

D. W. BROGAN.

LIGHTWOOD, JOHN MASON (1852–1947), conveyancing counsel and legal writer, was born 6 July 1852 at King's Norton, Birmingham, the second son of the Rev. Edward Lightwood, a Methodist minister, and his wife, Elizabeth, daughter of William Wild, of Milford Haven. He was educated at Kingswood School, Bath, and entering Trinity Hall, Cambridge, was elected a scholar in 1871. He was bracketed eighth wrangler in 1874. In the same year he became a fellow of his college and obtained a first class in mathematics at London University. Until 1878 he was an assistant master at Mill Hill School and the following year was called to the bar by Lincoln's Inn. From then onwards he practised continuously as a conveyancer and draftsman, and in 1932 he was appointed conveyancing counsel to the Court. At the time of his death he was senior conveyancing counsel.

Lightwood combined great learning in the field of real property law with sound historical insight and an exceptional gift of lucid exposition. These qualities are well illustrated in his legal writings, an article which he contributed to the *Cambridge Law Journal* in 1927 on 'Trusts for Sale' providing an extremely good example. His initial contribution to legal literature, however, was in the field of jurisprudence, and his essay upon *The Nature of Positive Law* (1883), a work in the Austinian tradition, temporarily directed his attention to law teaching; he was runner-up to (Sir) Frederick Pollock [q.v.] when the latter was appointed to the chair of jurisprudence at University College, London, in 1882. Thereafter he did not apply for any university appointment, and it is perhaps unfortunate that law teaching never had the benefit of Lightwood's exceptional gifts. In common with other eminent conveyancers, Lightwood's appearances in court were relatively infrequent, but his abilities were held in the highest esteem by the profession, and his practice was very wide. This made the extent and quality of his legal writing the more remarkable. He published substantial works upon *Possession of Land* (1894) and *The Time Limit on Actions* (1909), and he edited Fawcett's *Law of Landlord and Tenant* (1900). Later in his professional career, he revised and largely rewrote Fisher's well-known textbook on the *Law of Mortgage*, and he was joint editor with the author of the fourth edition of Williams on *Vendor and Purchaser* (1936). He was one of the small band of eminent conveyancers whose experience and learning were placed unreservedly at the disposal of Lord Birkenhead and Sir Leslie Scott [qq.v.] at the time when the property legislation of 1922–4 was in preparation. He had advocated for a long time many of the more important changes then achieved.

Lightwood's first contribution to periodical literature was made in 1887, when he began to write for the *Solicitors' Journal*. This was a fortunate experiment, for Lightwood's remarkable capacity for unravelling complicated problems of real property law in the simplest terms was immediately apparent, and was widely welcomed by solicitors. From then onwards he produced, apparently without effort, a stream of articles for various legal journals, and in addition he reviewed many of the most important works of contemporaries in the field of property law. In 1925, when already over seventy, he became legal editor of the *Law Journal*, a position which he retained until after the outbreak of war in 1939. From 1925 onwards, until shortly before his death over twenty years later, few weeks passed without an article, under the general title 'A Conveyancer's Letter', appearing over the initials J. M. L.

Many of the most important titles on real property and conveyancing were contributed by Lightwood to Halsbury's *Laws of England*, and he was one of the editors of the second edition of the *Encyclopaedia of Forms and Precedents* which was prepared to incorporate the great changes introduced by the property statutes of 1925. Of the third edition he was editor-in-chief.

Although much of Lightwood's work might seem to be of temporary importance only, he conferred lasting benefits upon the legal profession, and especially upon the solicitors' side of it, by enabling them to become familiar with the scope and purpose of the new property law which changing social conditions had made necessary. Writing of his contributions to the *Law Journal*, one eminent practitioner has said that 'by their lucidity, their liveliness, and their epigrammatic accuracy' they 'did for practical conveyancing what Maitland's "Lectures" had done for Equity, namely, contributed to the rescue of a subject which had for long been relegated to the category of the dull and dreary, and made the hitherto often regarded dry bones to live and become endowed with vital humanity'.

In 1884 Lightwood married Gertrude, daughter of Henry Clench, who worked for a London firm of silk merchants; they had three sons and three daughters. He died at Sanderstead 4 April 1947.

[*The Times*, 16 April 1947; *Law Journal*, 11 and 18 April 1947; private information; personal knowledge.]    G. W. KEETON.

LINDLEY, SIR FRANCIS OSWALD (1872–1950), diplomatist, was born 12 June 1872 at The Lodge, East Carleton, Norwich. He was the fourth surviving son and youngest child of Nathaniel (later Baron) Lindley [q.v.], who became a lord of appeal in ordinary. He was educated at Winchester, where he imbibed a love of the Hampshire countryside and trout streams which he cherished to the end of his life, and at Magdalen College, Oxford, where his great friend was Lord Lovat [q.v.], the fourteenth baron, whose brother-in-law and biographer he later became. He obtained a third class in jurisprudence in 1893 but, choosing the career which his father had rejected, he entered the diplomatic service as an attaché in 1896, passing a competitive examination the following year when he was promoted to Foreign Office clerk. From 1899 to 1901 he was a third secretary in Vienna and Teheran. The year 1902 saw him in Cairo, first as an official under the Egyptian Government, and then as second secretary under Lord Cromer [q.v.]. From Cairo in 1906 he went for two years to Tokyo, then back to the Foreign Office for a year, and then, as first secretary, to Sofia. After two years there he went to Norway until in 1915 he became counsellor of embassy in Petrograd. He was appointed C.B.E. in 1917. After the withdrawal of the ambassador, Sir George William Buchanan [q.v.], in January 1918 he was left in charge of the mission. In May he was transferred to Archangel as commissioner, and in June became consul-general in Russia. He was appointed C.B. in 1919 and transferred to Vienna as high commissioner, becoming envoy extraordinary and minister plenipotentiary in the following year. In 1921 he went to Athens in a similar capacity. He had only been there twelve months when the revolution broke out which resulted in the second banishment of King Constantine and the judicial murder of the royalist ministers, whose lives, had Lindley's advice been taken in time, might have been saved. Diplomatic relations with Greece were broken off and he was recalled home whence, after some months *en disponibilité*, he was sent as minister to Norway. Here he remained for five years, being appointed K.C.M.G. in 1926, until his promotion in 1929 as ambassador at Lisbon, when he was sworn of the Privy Council. In Portugal he spent two highly successful years until in 1931 he was promoted G.C.M.G. and went to the Far East as ambassador to Japan. In 1934 he was retired having then reached the age of sixty-two.

From first to last Lindley was the embodiment of British common sense, and in this lay the secret of his success as a representative of his country abroad. He never attempted to conceal the fact that he considered his own country to be the finest on earth and the British Empire the greatest instrument for good in the world, and he took it for granted that foreigners were equally patriotic. This attitude, added to an invariably friendly and welcoming manner to high and low, enabled him on many occasions to gain his ends without any rancour left behind, where subtler and more calculated methods would in all probability have failed. He was fond of quoting the remark that the only thing worse than a military defeat was a diplomatic victory.

Lindley sought his relaxation out of doors and his book *A Diplomat Off Duty*, first published in 1928, ranges from ski-running in Norway to tiger-hunting in Korea; further, he was once golf champion of Portugal. He was a keen and untiring sportsman, with both rod and gun, and after his retirement he bought a small property at Alresford in Hampshire where he was able to continue these pursuits. He was chairman of the Test and Itchen Fishing Association, a member of the council and honorary treasurer of the Zoological Society, and from 1943 an official verderer of the New Forest. Local and business interests also occupied his time, for he was a county alderman and held a number of directorships; and in addition to his biography of Lord Lovat published in 1935 he was a frequent correspondent to *The Times*. He was also chairman of the council of the Japan Society of London and of the executive committee of the Anglo-Portuguese Society. In 1937 he stood as Conservative candidate for the combined English Universities at a by-election, but was defeated.

In 1903 Lindley married Etheldreda Mary Fraser, sister of Lord Lovat. She had predeceased Lindley by ten months when he died at his home at Alresford 17 August 1950. There were four daughters. He was buried in Old Alresford churchyard. A portrait by H. von Angeli is in the possession of the family.

[Personal knowledge.]

         J. H. F. McEWEN.

LINDSAY, SIR RONALD CHARLES (1877–1945), diplomatist, was born in London 3 May 1877, the fifth of the six sons of James Ludovic, Lord Lindsay, later the twenty-sixth Earl of Crawford and ninth Earl of Balcarres [q.v.]. His eldest brother was D. A. E. Lindsay, twenty-seventh Earl of Crawford [q.v.]. He was educated at Winchester and after studying foreign languages abroad passed a competitive examination for the diplomatic service in January 1899. After a few months as attaché in the Foreign Office, he spent the first nine years of his service at St. Petersburg, Teheran, Washington, and Paris, until recalled in 1908 for three years in the Foreign Office. At his next post, The Hague, he assisted the British representatives at the international opium conference of 1911.

Early in 1913 an important development occurred in Lindsay's career, when he was seconded for service under the Egyptian Government as under-secretary in the Ministry of Finance at Cairo. Here his duties were not so much diplomatic as administrative, especially during the war of 1914–18 when his patience and gift of complete detachment and impartial study of complicated details combined to assist him in dealing with countless difficult problems arising out of the presence on Egyptian territory of vast numbers of British troops, and the establishment of the British protectorate.

In 1919 Lindsay was transferred as counsellor of embassy to Washington, and then in 1920 to Paris. In 1921 he was moved to London as assistant under-secretary of state in charge of Near Eastern affairs, in which Lord Curzon [q.v.] himself took the keenest interest. Crisis followed crisis. The British protectorate over Egypt was terminated in February 1922; towards the end of the same year the Sultan fled from Constantinople, and within a few months Turkey was declared a republic; in Persia the situation became disquieting after the signature of the Soviet-Persian treaty of 1921. All these incidents required most careful handling, and Lindsay's conduct of affairs won the full approval of Curzon, and earned him a C.B. (1922), to be followed in 1924 by his appointment as His Majesty's 'representative' at Constantinople where his strong personality and correct though friendly bearing enabled him to secure smooth relations. In 1925 his title was changed to ambassador. In that year a critical situation arose over Mosul: and had he not been able, thanks to his exceptional influence, to dissuade the Turks from becoming intransigent, a conflict would unquestionably have broken out. When the dispute was settled by the Treaty of Angora in 1926 the Government congratulated him on the skill with which he had brought the difficult negotiations to such a satisfactory issue, while the secretary of state expressed his personal thanks to Lindsay for his untiring energy and help throughout. The King of Iraq and his prime minister were equally appreciative.

Shortly afterwards Lindsay was sent as ambassador to Berlin, where he had the difficult task of succeeding Lord D'Abernon [q.v.]. Within two years he was appointed permanent under-secretary of state in London. But his stay there was short. In 1930 he was transferred as ambassador to Washington, where he found himself immediately immersed in many important questions of great complexity—disarmament; economic interdependence of all parts of the world; President Hoover's proposal for the postponement for a year of all payments connected with inter-allied debts and the British war debt. When this last question was arranged satisfactorily the secretary of state conveyed to him the warm thanks of His Majesty's Government for his skilful handling of this anxious matter.

The remaining six years of Lindsay's time in Washington, after the election of President Roosevelt and his advocacy of the 'New Deal', were no less strenuous. The role of British ambassador in the United States calls at all times for consummate tact, patience, and a capacity of interpreting conflicting opinions to two kindred but in many respects dissimilar nations. Lindsay possessed these qualities to an exceptional degree, and in consequence enjoyed the confidence and respect of the American public, more perhaps than was sometimes realized at home. The generally satisfactory state of Anglo-American relations during the critical years before the outbreak of war was in fact a notable tribute to the excellence of his work while occupying the post, the closing months of which were distinguished by the visit of the King and Queen to America. On that occasion His Majesty invested Lindsay with the insignia of the G.C.B. in the train while travelling to Washington. Lindsay retired four months later (October 1939).

Among British diplomatists of the period after the war of 1914–18 Lindsay held a high place. Trained in an earlier

and more dignified era, he maintained the best traditions of British diplomacy; and his magnificent physique and distinguished bearing made him a notable figure in any assembly. Few men had more friends. His shy charm, his tolerance and sympathetic understanding of opinions that were not his own, his sense of humour, and his imperturbable nature endeared him to all who knew him, whether in official circles or in general society.

Lindsay married twice: first, in 1909 Martha (died 1918), daughter of James Donald Cameron, senator, of Pennsylvania; and secondly, in 1924 Elizabeth Sherman (died 1954), daughter of Colgate Hoyt, banker, of New York. He had no children.

The honorary degree of LL.D. was conferred upon Lindsay by Harvard University in 1933; in 1935 he was elected honorary member of the State Society of The Cincinnati. He had been appointed grand officer of the Order of the Nile in 1915. Besides those orders already mentioned, he was appointed M.V.O. (1908), C.V.O. (1919), K.C.M.G. (1925), G.C.M.G. (1926), and K.C.B. (1929). He was sworn of the Privy Council in 1925.

Lindsay died at Bournemouth 21 August 1945. There is a portrait by J. S. Sargent in the possession of the family.

[*The Times*, 23 August 1945; Foreign Office papers; personal knowledge.]

LANCELOT OLIPHANT.

LITTLE, ANDREW GEORGE (1863–1945), historian, was born at Marsh Gibbon, Buckinghamshire, 28 September 1863, the second of the three sons of the Rev. Thomas Little, curate, who in 1864 became rector of Princes Risborough, by his wife, Ann Wright, of Chalfont St. Giles. Thomas Little, who was of Scottish birth, was the eldest of eleven children. One of these, David Little, a distinguished ophthalmic surgeon in Manchester, provided a home for Andrew and his brothers after the death of their father and mother in 1876, until his own death in 1902. Andrew owed much to his parents and uncle and to the latter's young wife, all of whom were generally loved and respected.

Little was educated at a preparatory school at Folkestone and at Clifton College, where he went in 1878. At Clifton he was deeply influenced by Charles Edwyn Vaughan who became a lifelong friend and whose fine *Studies in the History of Political Philosophy: before and after Rousseau* he edited in two volumes in

1925, three years after Vaughan's death. In 1882 Little entered Balliol College, Oxford, and there formed another permanent friendship, with his tutor, A. L. Smith [q.v.]. After obtaining a first class in modern history in 1886 he studied in Dresden and Göttingen until the spring of 1888. At Göttingen, although he failed to make much headway with the problems of Domesday Book, upon which he had embarked, he was introduced by Ludwig Weiland to 'the principles and practices of the critical examination of original historical documents', a discipline for which he remained grateful throughout his life. He deserted Domesday Book for ecclesiastical and academic history, making the Franciscans or Grey Friars the centre of his studies.

After four years of private investigation in London and Oxford, in 1892 Little was appointed the first independent lecturer in history in the University College of South Wales at Cardiff. Vaughan, who since 1889 had been professor of English and history, relinquished the teaching of history to his former pupil. In 1898 Little was given a professorial chair, which he resigned in 1901 on account of the poor health of his wife, Alice Jane, daughter of William Hart, of Fingrith Hall, Blackmore, Essex, whom he had married in 1893. In 1902 he settled at Sevenoaks, where he lived until his death there 22 October 1945. He had been a successful professor and had done much for the new university of Wales, but apart from a visiting lectureship (from 1920 a readership) in palaeography in the university of Manchester (1903–28), an engagement most fruitful in results, he undertook no regular teaching work and devoted himself to the writing of history and to the promotion, in every way open to him, of educational and learned enterprises.

Although Little did not write the big book which he planned on the history of the Grey Friars in England, he wrote much. A bibliography may be found in a little volume presented to him on 14 June 1938 by more than two hundred friends, and, for the years 1938–45, in the memoir published in the *Proceedings* of the British Academy. His first book, *The Grey Friars in Oxford* (1892), is still of the first importance, not only for Little's thorough treatment of his subject, but also because he gave a fresh and influential impetus to the study of academic history in England. Moreover, it led to wider investigations and friendly co-operation with foreign scholars. Paul Sabatier's famous book on St. Francis happened to follow close on Little's volume, and the two scholars became friends and allies. In July 1901 Sabatier established a society of Franciscan studies: in September 1902 Little founded a British branch of this society. In order to emphasize the need for the publication of texts the British branch in 1907 was reconstituted on an independent basis as the British Society of Franciscan Studies. Little was chairman and honorary general editor of the new society but Sabatier was retained as honorary president until his death in 1928. While its publications were mainly texts and studies relating to the English friars, the Society never took a narrow view of its opportunities and one of Little's most important publications, a new edition (based on Sabatier's papers, but containing a great deal of his own original work) of Sabatier's *Speculum Perfectionis* (2 vols., 1928–31) was issued by the Society. Before it was dissolved in 1936–7, the Society published twenty-two volumes.

Little's own works express his twofold interest in local history and medieval life and thought as a whole. On the one hand is the long series of studies, many of them contributed to the volumes of the *Victoria County History*, on Franciscan and other houses of friars in the British Isles, culminating in his Ford's lectures, *Studies in English Franciscan History* (1917), which he had delivered at Oxford in 1916; on the other hand are the *Initia Operum Latinorum quae saeculis xiii., xiv., xv. attribuuntur* (1904), his edition of Eccleston's *Tractatus de adventu fratrum minorum in Angliam* (Paris, 1909), his various papers on Roger Bacon, his important paper on the Franciscan school at Oxford (*Archivum Franciscanum Historicum*, vol. xix, 1926), his contributions to the *Proceedings* of the British Academy, and, most notable of all, the volume prepared in co-operation with his friend Father Franz Pelster, S.J., *Oxford Theology and Theologians c. A.D. 1282–1302* (1934). Little, with a profound knowledge of manuscripts at home and abroad, and in close touch with colleagues in England, France, Belgium, and Italy, illuminated, in his numerous writings, nearly every side of medieval life and thought.

Little was anything but a recluse. He welcomed every opportunity to assist historical movements and to guide the studies of younger scholars. At Cardiff he prepared popular lectures on Welsh history, which grew into a little book on *Mediaeval Wales* (1902). From Sevenoaks he exerted a quiet and continuous influence which penetrated far. His physique was not robust, but he rode regularly until 1918, and in his youth rode to hounds. He did much to encourage the study of local history and to maintain a knowledge of current historical literature among the members of the Historical Association, over which he presided from 1926 to 1929. He was chairman of a committee which prepared for the Institute of Historical Research a report on the way to edit documents. In Pelster's words, 'he maintained with vigour the old principle that history is to be founded in facts and not on reveries. . . . He will remain in my mind as a sincere, upright and gifted man of unselfish kindness' (from a letter of 9 December 1946). Many who knew him well observed in him something of the spirit of St. Francis.

Little was elected F.B.A. in 1922. He received honorary degrees from the universities of Oxford (1928) and Manchester (1935). He gave his collection of manuscripts to the Bodleian Library and left his interleaved and annotated copy of his *Initia Operum* to the Institute of Historical Research.

[F. M. Powicke, in *Proceedings* of the British Academy, vol. xxxi, 1945; *Church Quarterly Review*, April–June 1947; *An Address Presented to Andrew George Little, with a Bibliography of his Writings*, 1938; private information; personal knowledge.]

F. M. POWICKE.

LITTLE, SIR ERNEST GORDON GRAHAM GRAHAM- (1867–1950), physician, and member of Parliament for London University. [See GRAHAM-LITTLE.]

LLEWELLYN, SIR (SAMUEL HENRY) WILLIAM (1858–1941), artist and president of the Royal Academy of Arts, was born at Alma Place, Cirencester, 1 December 1858, the son of Samuel Llewellyn, a moulder, by his wife, Alice Jane Jennings. Deciding at an early age to become an artist, he left his home after a bitter quarrel with his parents, who objected to his taking up painting as a profession, and he set out to make his own livelihood independently as an artist, without other means than his own ambition, energy, and ability. For this adventure, indeed, he was well equipped by nature, being tall and handsome in person, with a pleasant, lively manner, and the valuable gifts of quick observation, social tact, frank speech, and sense of humour, all of which stood him in good stead when he came to occupy the high positions which were to be his. Owing to the circumstances of his youth very little can be recalled of his early years. He was trained for some years at the National Art Training School (later the Royal College of Art), South Kensington, under (Sir) Edward Poynter [q.v.], and afterwards at Paris in the studio of Ferdinand Cormon as well as in an atelier visited by Lefebvre and Ferrier. He began exhibiting at the Royal Academy in 1884, at first with etchings as well as paintings (the latter including some landscapes), and continued to do so, under the first names successively of Samuel Henry William and Samuel, until 1889; after that year he used only the name of William, and showed mainly portraits. He became a member of the New English Art Club, the Royal Society of British Artists, and the Royal Society of Portrait Painters, with all of which he exhibited occasionally.

In the year 1912 Llewellyn exhibited at the Royal Academy the State portrait of Queen Mary, and was elected an associate in May. In the painting school he served as visitor in 1913 and some following years, and also on committees of reorganization after the war of 1914–18. In 1920 he was elected an academician, and appointed to the council in 1922 and 1923, the exhibition committee in 1922, and the finance committee in 1923–5. The 'diploma work' deposited by him in the Academy on his election was a portrait of Sir Aston Webb. After serving again on the council in 1927 he was elected president in December 1928 in succession to Sir Frank Dicksee, having as his competitor at the final ballot Sir William Orpen [qq.v.].

Those gifts which had already been noticed as markedly his were displayed to the greatest advantage when he was president; in particular, he showed an easy skill in negotiating and supervising the arrangements for the exhibitions of Dutch, Italian, Persian, French, British, Chinese, and Scottish art which were held at the Academy before the threat of war caused the abandonment of other exhibitions which were under consideration. The combination of these gifts with his steady adherence to fair and orderly dealing, his practical sense and grasp of essentials made him an excellent chairman or vice-chairman of mixed committees, either of British and foreign connoisseurs or of the artists and manufacturers who met to organize what was an entirely new departure, namely the use of the galleries of the Academy for an exhibition in 1935 for the promotion of more regular co-operation between artists and manufacturers. This scheme, originally suggested by Prince George (later the Duke of Kent) and Llewellyn at the Academy dinner in 1932, was energetically promoted by the Royal Society of Arts, and by its mere appearance at the Academy and the novel nature of its exhibits showed to the public with enhanced effect how important a factor was the skill of trained artists for the design of many products of British industry.

In 1938 having, as it was believed, reached the statutory retiring age of seventy-five—for the date of his birth had always been recorded as 1863—Llewellyn could not stand again for the annual election of president. It has since been discovered, however, that he was born in 1858. His retirement was much regretted both inside and outside the Academy. The work which he had accomplished in the winter exhibitions had come to be very widely appreciated, and had won a general respect for himself and for his office.

Besides the State portrait of Queen Mary, the following exhibits at the Royal Academy may be mentioned: Sir George White (1893), Mr. Justice Gorell Barnes (later Lord Gorell, 1896), Sir William (later Lord) Plender (1913 and 1929), the seventeenth Earl of Derby (1934), and the archbishop of Canterbury (later Lord Lang of Lambeth, 1936). These works, refined in colour and skilful in the rendering of surfaces, were sincere and graceful rather than searching or emphatic presentations of character. His occasional landscapes—one of which, 'Sailing at Blakeney', was purchased in 1938 out of the Chantrey bequest and is now in the Tate Gallery—show a delicate sense of light and atmosphere.

Llewellyn received many honours. In 1918 he was appointed K.C.V.O., and in 1931 promoted G.C.V.O. In 1929 he was appointed grand officer of the Order of Orange-Nassau, in 1930 he received the grand cross of the Order of the Crown of Italy, and in 1933 he was appointed commander of the Legion of Honour. In 1933 he received the Albert medal of the Royal Society of Arts for his encouragement of art in industry. In the same year he became a trustee of the National Gallery, and he was an honorary member or fellow of numerous learned societies and academies.

In 1893 Llewellyn married Marion (died 1926), daughter of Thomas William Meates, of Portman Street, London, and the exhibitor of a number of miniatures at the Academy. Their only son, David, a flying officer who made a record flight from the Cape to England in 1935, was killed in a flying accident in 1938, leaving a son Michael who possesses a self-portrait by Llewellyn; they had also a daughter, Gwynedd, widow of the late Louis Meinertzhagen, and another who died at the age of seven. The Royal Academy possesses a bronze bust of Llewellyn by Sir W. Goscombe John presented by the artist in 1933; another by G. H. Paulin belongs to Mr. Luke Meinertzhagen, and a painted portrait by R. G. Eves to Mrs. Meinertzhagen.

In 1940 Llewellyn's health began to fail, and he died in London 28 January 1941. After a funeral service at Westminster Abbey his ashes were deposited in the crypt of St. Paul's Cathedral, alongside the remains of other artists. A memorial tablet was unveiled there later by his successor, Sir Edwin Lutyens [q.v.].

[Records of the Royal Academy of Arts; private information; personal knowledge.]
W. R. M. LAMB.

LLOYD, DOROTHY JORDAN (1889–1946), biochemist, was born in Birmingham 1 May 1889, the daughter of George Jordan Lloyd, surgeon and later professor of surgery in the university of Birmingham, and his wife, Marian Hampson Simpson. One of four children, her schooldays were spent at the King Edward VI High School, Birmingham, and in 1908 she entered Newnham College, Cambridge. She was placed in the first class in part i of the natural sciences tripos in 1910 and in part ii (zoology) in 1912, was a Bathurst student, and became the third Newnham fellow (1914–21). She worked for a time at Cambridge on problems of regeneration and osmotic phenomena in muscle, and this led her to a study of osmotic phenomena in simpler non-living colloidal systems. Her researches were interrupted by the war of 1914–18 when she investigated —for the Medical Research Committee (later Council)—substitute culture media for bacteriology, and the causes and prevention of ropiness in bread.

Dorothy Jordan Lloyd felt keenly that women could do valuable work as scientists, and she was well aware of the need for the application of science to industry which had been revealed by the war. She therefore accepted an invitation from (Sir) R. H. Pickard [q.v.] to join the newly formed British Leather Manufacturers' Research Association (1920). Whilst maintaining her interest in fundamental research, she rapidly acquired an insight into the art of leather manufacture, and introduced many methods of control which have since become normal tannery practice. In 1927 she succeeded Pickard as director, and was, until her death, the only woman leading such an association for industrial research. In spite of many set-backs, including the destruction of new laboratories in an air raid in 1940, support for the Association increased under her directorship, and it was recognized as an integral part of the industry. Dorothy Jordan Lloyd herself served on the councils and committees of many societies, including the executive committee of the International Society of Leather Trades' Chemists. In 1939 she was awarded the Fraser Muir Moffat medal by the Tanners' Council of America for her contributions to leather chemistry. She was also vice-president of the Royal Institute of Chemistry (1943-6) and a member of the Chemical Council.

Besides many contributions to scientific journals, she was the author of *The Chemistry of the Proteins* (1926; 2nd ed., with Miss Agnes Shore, 1938), and planned and contributed to *Progress in Leather Science, 1920-45* (3 vols., 1946-8) which has become one of the world's foremost textbooks on leather technology.

A keen mountaineer, in 1928 Dorothy Jordan Lloyd achieved the distinction of making the first ascent and descent in one day of the Mittellegi ridge of the Eiger. Her other recreation was riding and she competed at the Richmond Royal and the International horse shows.

Like her father and her grandfather, who was also a doctor, Dorothy Jordan Lloyd willingly spent her life seeking knowledge for the benefit of mankind. Her contemporaries also gained much from her stimulating personality and her gift for friendship. She died, unmarried, at Great Bookham, Surrey, 21 November 1946.

[Records of the British Leather Manufacturers' Research Association; personal knowledge.]          HENRY PHILLIPS.

LLOYD, GEORGE AMBROSE, first BARON LLOYD (1879-1941), statesman, was born at Olton Hall, near Solihull, Warwickshire, 19 September 1879, the youngest son of Sampson Samuel Lloyd, man of business, later of Budbrooke, Warwickshire, by his wife, Jane Emelia, daughter of Thomas Lloyd, director of Lloyds Bank, of The Priory, Warwick. The family was of Welsh origin, but early conversion to the tenets of the Society of Friends had led them to sell their land in Wales and to move to Birmingham where the family became famous in commerce and industry. In the nineteenth century they came under the influence of the Tractarian movement, and Lloyd himself was of that school of thought.

Lloyd was educated at Eton (where he was a member of the Society) and Trinity College, Cambridge. In 1899 and 1900 he coxed the winning Cambridge boat; but he left Cambridge without taking a degree, a decision influenced without doubt by the death of his parents in 1899 within a few weeks of one another, and he went to travel in the East. On his return he entered the firm of Lloyd and Lloyd, manufacturers of steel tubes, which his father had founded; but in 1905, after having travelled in the interests of the firm in Australia and the United States, he left it and entered on a career in the public service. For this his experience in business methods was to fit him well and was to prove of value later on when his career as an administrator was interrupted.

In 1905 Lloyd was appointed honorary attaché at Constantinople and in 1907 special commissioner to inquire into the future of British trade in Turkey, Mesopotamia, and the Persian Gulf, on which he wrote a report which enhanced his reputation in the departments concerned. In January 1910 he entered Parliament as Conservative member for the West Staffordshire division, spending the parliamentary recesses in European travel as well as in Africa and the Middle East. He had, however, little taste for debate and was pre-eminently a man of action. This showed itself especially in the days immediately preceding the outbreak of war in 1914, when he played a role remarkable for so young a man, acting energetically with L. S. Amery to ensure that his party should be uncompromising in support of the country's pledges, direct and implied, and particularly those made to France. On 6 August he was mobilized with the Warwickshire Yeomanry, but the years of war he spent mainly in staff posts and on special missions in the Near East. As intelligence officer on the general staff of the Mediterranean Expeditionary Force he landed with the Australians in the Dardanelles on 25 April 1915, but in September he was given a special mission to the Russian high command. In 1916 he was sent to Basra to assist Sir Percy Cox [q.v.] and later in the year to the Hejaz. Subsequently he was attached to the Arab Bureau for special duties in connexion with the Arab revolt and the activities of T. E. Lawrence in Arabia, and he was present with the army of Sir Edmund (later Viscount) Allenby [qq.v.] before Gaza. For these varied services he was appointed C.I.E. and to the D.S.O. in 1917. The relations with the Arab leaders and the sympathy with their cause then engendered remained close and active for the remainder of his life, and made him zealous to defend Arab interests whenever he thought they were unduly threatened.

In January 1918 Lloyd took up new duties as secretary of the British delegation to the Inter-Allied Council at Versailles but in August he was invited by E. S. Montagu [q.v.], then secretary of state for India, to become governor of the Bombay presidency. In this post he was at once faced with serious problems, the legacy in great degree of the war. In the economic field the housing conditions of the city of Bombay, and the general poverty, especially in Sind, were the most pressing problems; in the political field the agitation for self-government had to be guided and if possible controlled. When, five years later, Lloyd left India he had to his credit two achievements which gave him a claim to stand with the greatest of his predecessors: the Bombay development scheme, and the Lloyd barrage across the Indus, which irrigated an area far greater than the cultivated land of Egypt. At the same time the imprisonment of Gandhi had maintained the rule of law; Lloyd had guided the inauguration of the Montagu-Chelmsford constitution and had seen considerable recession in the tide of political agitation and economic discontent. His reputation was now established: in 1924 he received the G.C.S.I. in addition to the G.C.I.E. which had been conferred on him in 1918, and he was sworn of the Privy Council.

On his return to England, Lloyd showed his intention of resuming parliamentary life by standing for the Eastbourne division with success in 1924; but in 1925 he was offered and accepted the office of high commissioner in Egypt in succession to Allenby. In consequence he was raised to the peerage as Baron Lloyd, of Dolobran, in the county of Montgomery. He began his work in Egypt with the same combination of patience and determination which had marked his tenure of office in Bombay, and there was soon ground for thinking that he would once again succeed in bringing a difficult situation under control. But before long the Foreign Office began to take an unfavourable view of his methods, and to address him in critical and even reproving terms. Finally in 1927 negotiations for a treaty were initiated with the Egyptian prime minister, Sarwat Pasha, over the head of the high commissioner and without his knowledge. From that time Lloyd's relations with the Foreign Office and with the secretary of state, Sir Austen Chamberlain [q.v.], became uneasy, Lloyd's methods being apparently too resolute for the home statesman and his views too outspoken for the department. Lloyd felt himself under a burden of disapproval for which he could not account. Under the second Labour Government in 1929, Arthur Henderson [q.v.] very soon addressed to Lloyd a dispatch which left him little option but to resign. In the parliamentary debates which followed, he was roundly accused by Henderson of having shown a restless and turbulent dissatisfaction towards the policy of the Baldwin Government and Chamberlain; and although the case did not seem to be fully proved, no word in his defence was spoken either then or later by Chamberlain. Lloyd's own case is to be found in his book *Egypt since Cromer* (vol. ii, 1934).

There now began for Lloyd a long period of official disfavour during which he continued to do a great amount of public work while earning a living on boards of well-known companies such as the British South Africa Company. He spoke and wrote frequently in support of imperial causes and was president of the Navy League, chairman of the Empire Economic Union, of the governors of the Seamen's Hospital Society, and finally (1937) of the British Council which owed its later worldwide position and influence in large measure to his early inspiration and organizing ability. Perhaps the most remarkable features of this period were his unofficial missions to several European countries. His early travels and his work in the Middle East had made him well known in influential circles and his reputation was high for sound judgement and a wide knowledge of international affairs. He did nothing, however, to diminish official disfavour by his outspoken opposition, in alliance with Lord Salisbury [q.v.] and (Sir) Winston Churchill, to the Government's Indian policy, its attitude to armaments, and the foreign policy of Neville Chamberlain—advocating ceaselessly rearmament, conscription, and the strengthening of European friendships.

Although in 1934 Lloyd had secured a pilot's certificate and in 1937 was gazetted air commodore of No. 600 (City of London) (Fighter) Squadron, when war did come he could spare little time from his work for the British Council which now became of greater importance and carried him to almost every neutral capital in Europe. But in (Sir) Winston Churchill's national Government of 1940 Lloyd became secretary of state for the Colonies; almost at once he undertook the critical task of flying to Bordeaux in order to persuade the French Government, then retiring before the German onset, to remain in being and by all means to continue to fight. He returned thinking to report success, only to find that during his return flight the decision which he thought he had secured had been reversed.

In the Colonial Office Lloyd began at once to display those qualities by which he had made his reputation, and in January 1941 he became leader of the House of Lords; but after a short illness, a career which seemed once again to have the highest promise was suddenly cut short by death in London close on midnight, 4–5 February 1941. He was succeeded in his peerage by his only child, Alexander David Frederick (born 1912). He had married in 1911 Blanche Isabella Lascelles, a maid of honour to Queen Alexandra, daughter of Frederick Canning Lascelles, commander in the Royal Navy, and cousin of the sixth Earl of Harewood [q.v.].

Lloyd's imaginative idealism and resolution, with all their potentialities for high achievement, may have been the qualities which caused final success to elude him, as in Egypt, with the resulting long break in his political career. His vision of his country's imperial destiny was not compatible with prevailing sentiment and led him upon occasions to wide divergence from official policy. Upon the question whether his view should have prevailed no decisive opinion may yet be formed. The reputation he gained as governor of Bombay and later as chairman of the British Council rests upon a solid foundation of achievement. A portrait by (Sir) Oswald Birley is in the possession of the family.

[Lord Lloyd, *Egypt since Cromer*, 2 vols., 1933–4; C. Forbes Adam, *Life of Lord Lloyd*, 1948; *The Times*, 6 and 7 February 1941; private information; personal knowledge.]

C. Forbes Adam.

LLOYD, Sir JOHN EDWARD (1861–1947), Welsh historian, was born in Liverpool 5 May 1861, the son of Edward Lloyd, J.P., draper, by his wife, Margaret Jones. Both parents came from Montgomeryshire, and the ancestral connexions with that region, as also the Welsh nonconformist traditions of the family, were much cherished by their son. Lloyd was educated at the University College of Wales, Aberystwyth, and at Lincoln College, Oxford, where he gained first classes in classical moderations (1883) and modern history (1885). After seven years at Aberystwyth as lecturer in Welsh and history, he became in 1892 registrar and lecturer in Welsh history in the University College of North Wales, and remained in Bangor for the rest of his life, receiving the freedom of the city in 1941. He continued as registrar until 1919, was professor of history from 1899 until his retirement in 1930, and was very influential in developing and shaping the new college. He was prominent in many other national institutions of Wales: thus he served on the councils of the National Library and of the National Museum; he was twice president of the Cambrian Archaeological Association; he was a member of the Royal Commission on Ancient Monuments in Wales; he was also a lay preacher, and was proud to become chairman of the Union of Welsh Independents in 1934–5.

His study of Welsh history was lifelong. Although impelled to it by a robust national feeling, he performed it with a cool mind which instinctively preferred light to heat. Like some of his contemporaries, he had the salutary historical discipline of writing for this Dictionary, to which he was a regular contributor on Welsh subjects between 1893 and 1912. Much of his other work appeared in periodicals (a full list is in the *Bulletin* of the Board of Celtic Studies, vol. xii, part 4, May 1948), but his masterpiece was his *History of Wales to the Edwardian Conquest* (2 vols., 1911): this was, in its own field, a synthesis such as had never previously been achieved, and the greater part of it is likely to stand as a basic survey of lasting value.

Lloyd enjoyed seventeen years of active life in retirement. His output of published work remained constant and varied, the most considerable single item being his *Owen Glendower* (1931). He laboured fruitfully to encourage and organize Welsh historical and literary studies, particularly in connexion with the board of Celtic studies of the university: he prepared the draft constitution of the board in 1919, and as its first chairman (1919–40) was most actively concerned in launching the *Bulletin* and numerous other publications sponsored by the board. He made an excellent chairman: he was clear-headed and systematic; and his genial manner had a touch of Victorian formality which could be very effective in a committee.

He was an honorary D.Litt. of the universities of Wales and Manchester, a fellow of the British Academy (1930), and was knighted in 1934. He died at Bangor 20 June 1947.

He married in 1893 Clementina (died 1951), daughter of John Clunes Millar, of Aberdeen; they were survived by their son and their daughter, the widow of William Garmon Jones, librarian of the university of Liverpool. A portrait by Raeburn Dobson (1931) is in the possession of Mrs. Garmon Jones, and another by Evan Walters (1937) is in the National Museum of Wales.

[*The Times*, 21 June 1947; T. Richards and R. T. Jenkins in *Y Llenor*, vol. xxvi, 1947; J. G. Edwards in *Proceedings* of the British Academy, vol. xli, 1955; private information; personal knowledge.]      J. G. Edwards.

LLOYD GEORGE, DAVID, first Earl Lloyd-George of Dwyfor (1863–1945), statesman, was born in Manchester 17 January 1863, the second child and elder son of William George, a schoolmaster, by his wife, Elizabeth, daughter of David Lloyd, of Llanystumdwy, Caernarvonshire. Failing health led the father to return to his hereditary occupation of farming in Pembrokeshire; here he died in 1864. His widow's brother, Richard Lloyd, like his father a master-shoemaker, immediately welcomed her with her infant daughter and son back into the old home where a third child (William) was born posthumously. Richard Lloyd was a dissenter in whose heart still burned the evangelical and puritanical fervour of the religious revival which had transformed the life of Wales in the eighteenth century; who was versed in the thousand-year-old Welsh literary tradition, and was openly Radical in politics even before the secrecy of the ballot shielded Liberal voters from persecution by the anglicized Tory landowners.

From the daily example of this remarkable man Lloyd George absorbed the Welsh social ideal of the time. He attended the church school, the only one available in his predominantly nonconformist village, where the pupils had to recite the formulas of the established Church of England. Hostility to privilege and to English domination was early sown in his arrogant and sensitive nature alongside an intense pride in a national heritage ignored by the local ruling caste. Thus was nurtured the champion of the underdog and of small nations. Lloyd George was, and remained, a countryman, a child of the village spanning the river Dwyfor near the sea, set in the midst of trees and farmlands, with the heights of Snowdonia in the background.

Poverty was not allowed to interfere with the career of the two boys: both became lawyers. Lloyd George passed the final examination of the Law Society with honours in 1884. By this time the family had moved to Criccieth, which was more convenient for Portmadoc, where the boy had been articled to Breese, Jones, and Casson, solicitors. After qualifying, Lloyd George set up for himself and soon established a high reputation as a wise counsellor and fearless advocate, especially when the interests of landowners or the established Church clashed with those of Welsh peasants and nonconformists.

Endowed with unusual gifts and inspired by the superb eloquence of the preachers of that time, Lloyd George early made his mark as a speaker. Although his personal creed may not have been orthodox, he was always a staunch supporter of organized Christianity and, as one of the Disciples of Christ, a sect of Baptist origin, he delighted his uncle, one of its unpaid ministers, by his addresses. He also spoke in the district on temperance and foreign missions and his political speaking attracted attention by its incisive, graphic quality. He took an active part in parliamentary elections and in the first county council elections of 1889 which resulted in a sweeping victory for Liberals throughout Wales. It was then imagined that the county councils would, by acting together, achieve self-government for Wales. Lloyd George also in his own area organized a farmers' union and as secretary of the Anti-Tithe League for South Caernarvonshire encouraged farmers to defy the law by refusing to pay tithes. His political ambition was early kindled and these activities advanced his prospects. In January of 1889 he was chosen Liberal candidate for Caernarvon Boroughs and, in 1890, he was returned at a by-election, by eighteen votes on a recount, against Ellis Nanney, the squire of Llanystumdwy. He took his seat on 17 April as a member of the Liberal Opposition under Gladstone and on 13 June delivered his maiden speech on a temperance issue. In the House, among the supporters of Lord Salisbury's administration, he found Joseph Chamberlain, once in his eyes a hero, but now a renegade, whom he never forgave or missed an opportunity to attack. He soon impressed the wider audiences provided by London and the provinces, but it was the cause of Wales which was nearest to his heart. Nor was his enthusiasm at all abated by the supercilious denial of nationhood to Wales shown by certain members of the House, and he studied parliamentary procedure and the tactics of the Irish party until he became as adept in advancing, and hindering, business in the House. Among the Welsh members was Thomas Edward Ellis, a pioneer of the Cymru Fydd (Wales of the future) movement with which Lloyd George later sought (in vain as it proved) to identify the North and South Wales Liberal Federations in order to strengthen the advance of Welsh home rule. At the end of 1890 he became the political correspondent of *Y Genedl Cymreig* (The Welsh Nation), and a little later he promoted a company for the purchase of a group of North Wales newspapers.

In the general election of 1892 Lloyd George defeated Sir John Puleston in the same constituency. Under the premierships of Gladstone (1892) and Rosebery (1894), when the Government was in difficulties owing to the rejection of the second Home Rule bill by the Lords and the drastic amendments made by them to two other government measures, Lloyd George himself contributed to those difficulties not a little. Together with (Sir)

Francis Edwards, D. A. Thomas (later Viscount Rhondda, q.v.), and (Sir) Herbert Lewis, he led a revolt after Gladstone's resignation of the premiership to obtain precedence for the Welsh disestablishment bill. Although this bill passed its second reading in the Commons in 1895, it made no further progress owing to Rosebery's resignation. In the Conservative victory in 1895, Lloyd George retained his seat against his squire, Ellis Nanney.

Soon after entering Parliament Lloyd George had settled with his family in London and started practice as a solicitor. His attendance at the House was constant and now, during this eclipse of Liberalism, the persistence, energy, and skill with which he and his Welsh colleagues assailed the Government reanimated the dejected Opposition. His chief attacks were made on measures designed in his view to entrench privilege, such as the agricultural rates bill (1896) and the voluntary schools bill (1897) with its proposals to aid Anglican schools. During a debate on the former bill he and four others were suspended by the Speaker.

In April 1899 occurred the untimely death of the young Welsh leader, Tom Ellis, and in the autumn the South African war broke out. The one tragedy elevated Lloyd George to the chief place in the political life of Wales, the other brought him notoriety and fame throughout the British Isles. Fully realizing the consequences, he plunged into a course of bitter opposition to the war which to him was a crime against a small nation and unworthy of the British Empire. This nearly cost him both life and livelihood and might have ended his parliamentary career. At a meeting in Birmingham in 1901 he only escaped from the mob by disguising himself as a policeman. Nevertheless, although his life had been threatened in his own constituency, he had been returned at the 'khaki' election of 1900. The peace of Vereeniging of 31 May 1902 found him, therefore, still in the House and ready to attack the Government from a new angle.

A. J. Balfour on 24 March had introduced an education bill which received the royal assent in December 1902. Lloyd George, ever zealous in the cause of popular education, did not quarrel with the admirable systematization now applied to it. But the proposal to grant rate-aid to voluntary schools not under complete public control he fought fiercely in and out of Parliament, but without success,

In Wales his plan for the closure of church schools by the county councils was checkmated by the ingenuity of the Government's one-clause Act of 1904 permitting the Treasury to aid these schools directly and repay itself from moneys due to the local authority. Lloyd George countered this by urging the county councils, where the so-called Welsh Coercion Act was applied, to refuse to concern themselves with elementary education; this would be provided by revolt schools to which nonconformists would send their children. Funds were collected and a few schools were actually started but the movement ended with the advent to power of the Liberals in 1905. The agitation had greatly strengthened Lloyd George's position. The campaign had also reconciled the Liberals, divided on the issue of the South African war, and their new unity was cemented by opposition to Joseph Chamberlain's advocacy of protection, which had brought about the collapse of Balfour's Government.

Lloyd George's popularity among his fellow countrymen on the eve of his elevation to Cabinet office led a friend to comment: 'Wales is indeed a one-man show at the present time.' Never again could this be said: his devotion to Welsh causes became suspect as they took their place with other matters in the hierarchy of the new minister's preoccupations. He had in his early days at Westminster complained that Welsh members lacked the single-mindedness of the Irish; he himself proved to be no Parnell but a Welsh leader who took office. On his side it may be urged that Welsh failure to combine through the county councils or under the banner of Cymru Fydd discouraged him from further attempts to unite Wales, except within a scheme of federal home rule in which he always believed. He never wanted Wales to be separated from and independent of the United Kingdom and in his later considered utterances, while expressing his joy in the revival of the Welsh language, he dissociated himself from the view that a nation dies with its ancient tongue, and appeared as a cultural rather than a political nationalist.

Liberal efforts at removing the obnoxious clauses of the Education Act failed for reasons understood in Wales— the might of the Church of England fortified by the veto of the Lords. Moreover, although the Lords had in November 1906 rejected a clause in the education bill setting up a Welsh National Council, Lloyd George had secured a separate Welsh department, with its own permanent secretary, in the Board of Education. The postponement of disestablishment of the Church in Wales was not so well received, and the appointment and conduct of a Royal Commission to look into an issue long since decided proved a further irritant. Welsh nonconformist attempts to embarrass the Government incensed Lloyd George, who faced and won over the trouble-makers at a convention at Cardiff in October 1907. A Welsh Church bill was introduced in April 1909, but the controversies over the budget and the House of Lords put it into cold storage until April 1912. It was bitterly opposed and some of Lloyd George's most vituperative speeches were made in reply to the contention of its opponents, expressed with equal virulence, that the disendowment clauses entailed downright robbery of the Church. In Wales the fight waxed fast and furious, with Lloyd George in the thick of it. The bill, by the operation of the Parliament Act, became law on 18 September 1914. But war had begun and its operation was postponed 'for a year or until the end of the war'. Within a few months Lloyd George, entirely absorbed in the struggle, again vexed his Welsh friends by condoning an attempt at further postponement which, however, was checkmated by the firm stand of the Welsh members. After the election of 1918 had supplied him with an overwhelming majority of Conservative supporters he stood firm against those Church interests which would have sought a repeal or a drastic revision of the Act, but he readily met by a Treasury grant unforeseen financial difficulties created by the war, and on 1 June 1920 Lloyd George, as prime minister, attended the installation of A. G. Edwards [q.v.], bishop of St. Asaph, as first archbishop of Wales.

In Campbell-Bannerman's Liberal ministry of December 1905 Lloyd George was appointed president of the Board of Trade and sworn of the Privy Council, and he and his colleagues initiated a series of measures which were destined during the next forty years profoundly to affect the structure of British industrial society and the distribution of the national income. The period was one when public opinion had been stirred by the London dock strike, the Taff Vale decision, the investigations of Charles Booth [q.v.], and

Joseph Chamberlain's tariff reform campaign. Lloyd George promoted the Merchant Shipping Act, 1906, the Patents and Designs Act, 1907, the Port of London Act, 1908, and in the process he added to his fame as an adroit debater the reputation of a patient negotiator in settling strikes. In 1908 Asquith became prime minister and was succeeded as chancellor of the Exchequer by Lloyd George. This intensified the struggle with the House of Lords which during 1906-8 had blocked Liberal measures of education, land reform, and temperance.

In his first ('the People's') budget (1909) Lloyd George declared war on poverty and unfolded new methods of taxation which provided an expanding mechanism for the future provision of funds for social services. He set up a Road Fund, and a Development Fund for the improvement of transport and agriculture and for the endowment of research, and levied taxes on unearned increment in land values which were the chief bone of contention, but eventually proved unremunerative and were abolished in 1920. In provocative speeches in Limehouse and elsewhere he roused the passions of the electorate against 'the Dukes', and in the House of Commons the bitter fight over the 'revolutionary' finance bill went on for many months. The rejection of the budget by the Lords led to the general election of January 1910. Opinion was evenly divided, so that Asquith had to rely for a working majority on the Irish nationalists and the Labour members. The budget of the previous April now passed both Houses materially unchanged. As-quith in the meantime tabled the resolutions defining the powers of the Lords which subsequently formed the basis of the Parliament Act of 1911, passed after a second appeal to the country in December 1910.

King Edward VII had died on 6 May 1910. At a conference which met in June to resolve the conflict between Lords and Commons, Lloyd George sought to reach agreement with the Opposition leaders on other controversial measures also—Home Rule, tariffs, conscription—but without success. In 1911 on the appearance of the German gunboat, the *Panther*, at Agadir, he surprised all Europe by warning Germany that Britain would actively resist interference with her international interests and obligations. But his main preoccupation at this time was his first, and epoch-making, contributory scheme of insurance covering health and unemployment. It made his name a household word long before the war. In spite of bitter opposition from all classes it passed after many compromises and was followed by further measures dealing with health, education, wages, and employment. These fell short of theoretical Socialism but involved considerable central organization.

Lloyd George was engaged in launching a campaign for the reform of the land system when he was halted by the results of an ill-judged investment suggested to him by his friend Sir Rufus Isaacs (later the Marquess of Reading, q.v.) then attorney-general. In April 1912 he had bought a thousand shares in the American Marconi Company at a moment when the postmaster-general, (Sir) Herbert (subsequently Viscount) Samuel, was concluding a contract with the British Marconi Company. This transaction led to much public criticism and to an investigation by a select committee of the House of Commons. Ultimately in June 1913 a vote of censure on the ministers concerned was defeated, and a motion was adopted accepting the expression of regret on their purchase of the shares and their failure to disclose it earlier, but clearing their honour.

At the end of July 1914 war with Germany was imminent and the crisis found the Cabinet divided. Lloyd George stood with the non-intervention group until it was clear that the Germans had violated the Belgian frontier. At this attack by a powerful state on a small nation his vacillation ceased and with his mind made up he waged war with a will to achieve victory which was not equalled by any of his colleagues.

As chancellor of the Exchequer he sought the advice of experts and handled the immediate crisis with courage and skill. Public credit was put at the disposal of the banks, suspension of specie payments was avoided, new one-pound and ten-shilling notes were issued by the Treasury as legal tender, banks were guaranteed against bad debts made on pre-war bills of exchange, and a moratorium was proclaimed on 3 August which lasted until November.

On 17 November Lloyd George introduced his first war budget, in which he partially suspended the sinking fund, doubled the income-tax, and increased the tea and beer duties. He made repeated attempts, now and later, to check the loss of output due to excessive drinking by reducing hours of sale, by diluting the strength of beer and spirits, and by steep taxation. He very nearly brought off nationalization of 'the trade' but was overborne by the united opposition of temperance extremists and Conservative diehards.

Months passed before the public grasped the vast scale of preparations in men and material and money which would be required to defeat the enemy. 'Absolute war', as waged by Germany, was outside the experience of British soldiers and, indeed, outside their vision. By January 1915 Lloyd George had convinced himself that the higher conduct of the war by the Allies was seriously at fault, and in the first of his many memoranda he advocated the policy of 'side-shows'. The British general staff, on the other hand, favoured concentration in the West so as to give France the maximum support while protecting the Channel ports and the home front. This division of opinion between Easterners and Westerners persisted to the end of the war and was exemplified in the conflict between Lloyd George on the one hand and Sir Douglas (later Earl) Haig and Sir William Robertson [qq.v.] on the other. Some operations in the East could not be avoided once Turkey had thrown in her lot with the Central powers, but it was agreed to regard France and Flanders as the main and decisive theatre of war for the British Empire, a view with which Lloyd George was never really content.

In this area, stretching from the English Channel to the Swiss border, the enemies were locked in almost static trench warfare for nearly four years. Lloyd George was soon obsessed with the costly expenditure of guns and munitions involved and he was also very conscious of the needs of the Allies. When therefore the coalition Government was formed in May 1915, Asquith set up a Ministry of Munitions, with Lloyd George at its head. Here he put forth inexhaustible and ubiquitous energy, issuing orders to existing factories, erecting scores of new ones, mobilizing the engineering and chemical industries of the entire kingdom with the help of big business men of 'push and go'. It was a gigantic task. He early encountered serious difficulties with labour, but succeeded, while still at the Treasury, in concluding an agreement with the trade unions which permitted the relaxation of restrictions on output in return for the limitation of profits. A further result was the extension of the employment of women and of welfare agencies in war industries. Widespread suspicion among the rank and file hindered the enforcement of the Treasury agreement, and compulsory legislation followed. By eloquent speeches Lloyd George sought to rouse the workers to a sense of the gravity of the struggle. In Glasgow on Christmas Day 1915 he was refused a hearing for three-quarters of an hour, but he was undaunted: production was pressed to such a pitch that for the battle of the Somme supplies proved reasonably adequate, and when, on 6 July 1916, he left the ministry to become secretary of state for war, what had taken a year to produce in 1914–15 could be obtained in two or three weeks. Good judges have claimed that by its boldness, its vastness, and its speed his work as minister of munitions was the supreme contribution made by Lloyd George to the winning of the war.

During these months Lloyd George drew nearer to his Tory colleagues; and on the conscription issue he was closer to Curzon and Carson than to the Liberals, Runciman and McKenna [qq.v.]. The first military service bill received the royal assent on 27 January 1916. On 5 June Kitchener was lost in the *Hampshire*. Lloyd George was to have travelled with him to Russia but had been detained to deal with the troubles arising out of the Easter rebellion in Ireland. He apparently reached agreement with Carson and with John Redmond [q.v.] on the question of the six counties, but misunderstandings which followed and opposition from some Cabinet colleagues destroyed all hope of a settlement.

Lloyd George spent five months at the War Office, where Robertson, as chief of the imperial general staff, wielded great power and where the secretary of state chafed and fretted at his inability to change the major strategy of the war. In two directions, however, he left his mark: he persuaded Haig to invite Sir Eric Geddes [q.v.] to report upon and then to reorganize the transport services of the armies in France, and secondly he chose Sir John Cowans [q.v.], quarter-master-general throughout the war, to reorganize the transport system in Mesopotamia which had been mishandled by the Indian Army authorities.

The summer and autumn of 1916 saw a series of offensives: by the Russians in Poland, the British on the Somme, and by the Italians. In August Romania declared war on Austria-Hungary and

Italy on Germany. The results were disappointing. On the Somme casualties were terribly heavy, Romania was quickly overrun and her oilfields secured by Germany. At sea, sinkings increased rapidly. In September Lloyd George told an American journalist, in what was known as the 'knock-out blow' interview, that the British would fight to a finish; but, behind the scenes, there was much uneasiness and departmental friction. He had appealed in vain for some effort to save Romania. The urgent need of equipping the Russian armies weighed so much upon him at this time that he proposed to visit them and examine the position for himself, but he was again prevented.

In November Lord Lansdowne [q.v.] submitted a secret memorandum to the Cabinet in which, in a spirit of pessimism, he examined proposals for a negotiated peace. Throughout these autumn months Lloyd George was deeply agitated by the general situation and by his own impotence to improve it. He talked of exchanging the War Office for a minor post, of resigning from the Government and 'telling the country the truth'; in the press he was being both flattered as the man of destiny and attacked as disloyal. His capricious moods and unguarded rebellious conversations did not prevent his Conservative friends, Bonar Law, Sir William Maxwell Aitken (subsequently Lord Beaverbrook), and Carson, from helping him to reach the summit of power, although he avowed that he had no wish to supplant Asquith. He had a sincere admiration for his great qualities of mind and speech and temper, but believed that Asquith was losing the war and that he himself could do better if given executive control as chairman of a small War Cabinet with Asquith occupying a presidential position in the background but free, at his own discretion, to attend its meetings. This was the proposal which in substance Asquith first accepted, then rejected. The change was mainly wrought by a leading article in *The Times*, 4 December 1916, written by Geoffrey Dawson [q.v.], which the prime minister wrongly thought to have been inspired by Lloyd George. Lloyd George resigned on 5 December and precipitated a crisis, the outcome of which was that Asquith resigned on the same day and was succeeded by Lloyd George on 7 December. The new prime minister secured the support of Conservatives, Labour, and

about one-half of the Liberal members of the House of Commons. To Asquith's surprise, Bonar Law and Balfour agreed to serve under Lloyd George.

Lloyd George was now fifty-four years old and had spent half his life in Parliament. He was at once the most widely known, the most dynamic, and the most eloquent figure in British politics. His primacy in 10 Downing Street was immediately felt. The Cabinet of twenty-three was replaced by a War Cabinet of five provided, for the first time, with a secretary, Sir Maurice (subsequently Lord) Hankey, and numerous assistant secretaries who attended meetings and recorded minutes and conclusions. It met daily and only one of its members was occupied with a department. This was Bonar Law, who became chancellor of the Exchequer, the next-door-neighbour and the closest counsellor of the prime minister. Curzon was lord president of the Council, Milner and Arthur Henderson [qq.v.] were ministers without portfolio. The new foreign secretary was Balfour, who usually attended the War Cabinet. Ministries of Labour, Food, and Shipping were at once set up.

Throughout his first year as prime minister Lloyd George displayed the extraordinary energy, application, and (except at the time of Passchendaele) buoyancy which were characteristic of him. The first four months saw the opening of the unrestricted German submarine campaign on 1 February which entailed the entry of the United States into the war on 6 April, whereas the Russian revolution of 12 March heralded the collapse of that power in the East. The most intractable problem (and one never yet solved) was that of submarine attacks on shipping. In April the losses amounted to an average of ten merchantmen a day. The Board of Admiralty had shown itself resolutely opposed to the convoy system, but shortly before Lloyd George became prime minister Sir John (later Earl) Jellicoe [q.v.] became first sea lord, and with his trained staff had begun to tackle the problem of the protection of shipping. However, he approached its solution by convoys with a caution which exasperated the anxious and impatient prime minister who persisted in urging them. With their adoption, the accession of the American navy, and Lloyd George himself acting as a constant spur to the Admiralty, the losses began slowly to fall after April 1917, and the most grievous danger passed. This was the chief consolation of a year full of military disappointments abroad.

In the land campaign the three ruling strategical ideas of Lloyd George were that allied resources should be pooled, that the allied front from Flanders to Mesopotamia should be regarded as one, the enemy being attacked at their weakest points in the line, and that unity of command on the western front was essential. He succeeded but slowly and very partially in applying these ideas, not only because he was opposed by British and French generals, but also because the heavy responsibilities borne by the British navy and the shortage of shipping made the full execution of the 'side-show' policy impracticable.

In accordance with these ideas, at a conference of the Allies held in Rome 5–7 January 1917, Lloyd George proposed a Franco-British-Italian offensive through the Julian Alps to Laibach and Vienna, but at a conference in London on 15 and 16 January final agreement was reached instead on what came to be known as the Nivelle offensive. Delayed until April, it caused the Germans no surprise, and failed. Simultaneously Haig fought the battle of Arras with some success until it declined into a stalemate in the middle of May. Nivelle's failure spread dejection and mutiny in the French armies, and in May he was superseded by General Pétain, who informed Haig of the situation under pledge of secrecy. From 7 to 14 June Haig fought the battle of Messines, and on 20 July, with grave misgivings, Lloyd George, in the War Cabinet, gave his consent to a heavy offensive with a view to clearing the Germans from their submarine bases on the coast, as was being advocated by Jellicoe. His misgivings arose from lack of confidence in Jellicoe's opinion, and from his preference for Pétain's policy of limited objectives which were constantly to surprise the enemy, as against the long-prepared and elaborately staged offensives favoured by Haig. Accordingly Haig launched his attack on 31 July on the understanding that if progress were not satisfactory the offensive should be called off. It developed into the third battle of Ypres which ended in November at Passchendaele, having entailed terrible casualties, having gained no strategic advantage, yet having provided Pétain with the respite needed to restore the morale of the French Army. On 20 November, ten days after the close of Passchendaele, Haig renewed the attack at Cambrai. The surprise use of tanks without any artillery preparation made such progress that the claim has been made that had not five British divisions been taken away by Lloyd George to relieve the Italians after Caporetto, Haig might have 'consummated a great victory'. However that may be, Lloyd George was profoundly depressed by Passchendaele and would have removed Haig could he have found an acceptable successor.

The military events of 1917 increased Lloyd George's dislike of offensives in the West. His mind was turning towards a policy of delay on that front pending the arrival of American reinforcements. Since Austria was showing signs of exhaustion, and was rumoured to be seeking for peace, he renewed his advocacy of 'knocking away the props' in the East: Austria, Bulgaria, Turkey. The idea was encouraged by the capture of Jerusalem in December. But still more was his desire accentuated for his third principle, unity of command. Some temporary progress had been made in this direction when, much impressed by Nivelle, Lloyd George had given him wholehearted support, even to the extent of temporarily subordinating Haig to Nivelle at the time of his offensive.

One of the first acts of Lloyd George's Government was to summon Dominion ministers to an Imperial War Conference and War Cabinet, and these bodies did much to co-ordinate the war effort of the Empire. Lloyd George found J. C. Smuts [q.v.] so valuable that he offered him a seat in the War Cabinet and Smuts remained a member until December 1918. Peace overtures from Germany and Austria were repelled after consultations with France. A mission under Milner was sent to Petrograd to arrange about munitions and supplies and returned to this country on the eve of the revolution, which the mission did not foresee. In October 1917 Lloyd George propounded his views on a central co-ordinating council to Lord French (later the Earl of Ypres) and Sir Henry Wilson [qq.v.], and also to the French. The proposals were then submitted to Italy and the United States. On 2 November Lloyd George obtained Cabinet approval for an inter-allied council consisting of prime ministers and a member of the Government of each of the great powers fighting on the western front. Each power was to appoint a military representative to serve as a technical adviser to the council. The British representative was Sir Henry Wilson. At a conference at Rapallo Lloyd George used (7 November) the Caporetto disaster to advance the cause of unity of command, and he defended his action when challenged in the House of Commons, a challenge which he had deliberately provoked on his way home by a sensational speech in Paris, deploring lack of allied unity (12 November). The lesson was illustrated by what followed from the overthrow of Kerensky by Lenin, and enforced by military disaster in March 1918.

On the home front the prime minister comprehensively directed the national effort and dealt specially with shipbuilding, food rationing, wages and prices, recruiting, women's suffrage, and postwar reconstruction. The future of Ireland was handed over to a convention of Irishmen who failed to agree. A Cabinet pronouncement in August forecast 'the progressive realization of responsible government in India as an integral part of the British Empire'. A committee under Milner was appointed to study terms of peace, and the publication in the *Daily Telegraph* in November of a letter from Lansdowne, advocating a negotiated peace, led to a demand for a restatement of the Government's war aims. Lloyd George complied on 5 January 1918 in a speech to trade-union delegates in which he placed the restoration of the independence of Belgium in the forefront of a series of conditions which were later to be embodied in the peace treaties. The publication of President Wilson's Fourteen Points three days later showed the two statesmen to be substantially agreed. The Balfour declaration on a national home for the Jews, issued in November 1917, had Lloyd George's enthusiastic support.

The Supreme War Council, born at Rapallo, met at Versailles in December and again at the end of January. In framing plans for 1918 it had to reckon with the transfer of German divisions from Russia, with the slow arrival of reinforcements from America, with warweariness in France, and with the terrific strain on the limited productive manpower of Great Britain. All these pointed to a defensive policy on the western front to which at this stage Haig and Robertson did not object. But several major and minor disputes agitated the Council in the opening weeks of this fateful year. Lloyd George still hankered after bigger efforts against Turkey, and the technical advisers of the Council, to whom the problem was referred, went so far as to agree (21 January) that it would 'be worth any effort that can be made compatibly with the security of our defence in the Western theatres'—a vital qualification. The comparative length of line assigned to the French and British armies caused much soreness in French circles. Haig attributed his failure to extend the British line, as he had promised to do, to the aforementioned dispatch of five divisions to Italy at the bidding of Lloyd George. But Haig had in fact taken over the French line as far as Barisis and Lloyd George (2 February) strongly supported his refusal to yield to further French pressure. When a compromise was reached it was left to Haig and Pétain to arrange when and how a change should be effected.

A third main question before the Council was the formation of a mobile general reserve. This task was placed under an executive War Board of which Lloyd George proposed that Foch should be president, thus paving the way for his appointment (14 April) as général-en-chef des armées alliées in France. Robertson objected to this device and on 18 February he was transferred to a home command and replaced as C.I.G.S. by Wilson.

On 21 March 1918 the Germans launched their great offensive, the blow falling mainly on the British Fifth Army, which covered Amiens. Within less than a week the situation became extremely critical. Pétain, anxious for the safety of Paris, seemed prepared to risk the separation of the French Army from the British. A telegram from Haig brought Milner and Wilson post-haste to a conference with Clemenceau and the British and French generals at Doullens (26 March) where, with Haig's full support, Foch was given powers to co-ordinate the efforts of the British and French armies on the western front, a decision of crucial importance. On 3 April at a similar conference at Beauvais, but with Lloyd George and the American generals, Pershing and Bliss, present, Foch was 'entrusted with' the 'strategic direction of military operations'. Thus, at last, the plan for which Lloyd George, more than any other statesman or general, had so long laboured in public and in private was adopted: only just in time to make its supreme contribution to victory.

(Sir) Winston Churchill, who saw Lloyd George during the anxious opening days of the German offensive, records: 'The resolution of the prime minister was unshaken under his truly awful responsibilities.' Lloyd George took extreme measures. Men were combed out of essential industries and partly trained lads were sent to France. Reinforcements were summoned from Italy, Egypt, and Salonika. Appeal for help was sent to President Wilson. There were hot debates on the training and use of American troops in response, Lloyd George supporting Foch's plea that they should be shipped as infantry units and merged with allied divisions in France.

On 7 May Major-General Sir Frederick Maurice in a letter to *The Times* charged Lloyd George and Bonar Law with making inaccurate and misleading statements in Parliament on military matters. Public opinion at the moment was extremely sensitive owing to losses in France and to the tightening pressure of conscription at home. Asquith proposed an inquiry by select committee but Lloyd George forced an immediate debate in the Commons, persuaded the House at the time that the charges were unfounded, and scored a parliamentary triumph. The importance of the incident was seen later at the general election when those who voted against the Government in this division were refused the coalition 'coupon' and only thirty-three independent Liberals were returned to Westminster.

During the anxious months of this summer and autumn Lloyd George resided at a country house, Danny Park, in Sussex, but was frequently called away to conferences in London and in France. In July he was still contending for an autumn offensive in Palestine and considering the supersession of Haig as British commander-in-chief. But his own disquiet was not allowed to interfere with the task of sustaining the war-will of the people. His incomparable gifts of popular appeal were used to brace the public to hold fast and endure the military casualties, the sinking of naval and merchant crews on the seas, the air raids and food queues at home. To mark the fourth anniversary of the outbreak of war a rousing message from him was read in every theatre and cinema in the country and on 7 August he spoke to a crowded House of Commons in the same confident and resolute spirit. According to his annual custom in Bank Holiday week he

attended the national Eisteddfod in Wales, and it was there he heard of the opening of the battle of Amiens (8 August), in which Haig commanded and with the aid of Canadian and Anzac troops began a movement which was to force back the whole German line. This victorious operation ended all thought of removing Haig, who now, at the request of Foch and with the Cabinet's hesitating approval, proceeded to attack and to pierce the 'impregnable' Hindenburg line. The next few weeks saw the collapse of German resistance at an astonishing rate and the falling of 'the props' which had been held up by Germany. In September Lloyd George supported the attack of Franchet d'Esperey on Bulgaria and of Allenby in Palestine, and he was at Versailles urging on Orlando the importance of an Italian offensive when he learnt (5 October) that the German chancellor, Prince Max of Baden, had requested President Wilson 'to take steps for the restoration of peace'. On 3 November at the residence of Colonel House in Paris he had the satisfaction of hearing that Austria had signed an armistice; but it was hard to realize that fighting was over, and there was a natural suspicion that the German generals might use the armistice to strengthen their position.

On 11 November Lloyd George announced from 10 Downing Street:

'The Armistice was signed at 5 a.m. this morning, and hostilities are to cease on all fronts at 11 a.m. to-day.'

That afternoon the greatest war minister this country had known since the elder Pitt received a great ovation in the House of Commons, and after he had moved its adjournment, with Asquith beside him, he led the House, behind the Speaker, to St. Margaret's, Westminster, to render thanks for the world's deliverance from its great peril. Honours flowed upon him with the same profusion which had 'rained gold boxes' on Pitt. The King in 1919 appointed him to the Order of Merit; from France came the grand cordon of the Legion of Honour, from other countries the highest orders which it was in their power to bestow; universities showered upon him their honorary degrees, and municipalities their freedoms.

The peace terms presented to the Germans by President Wilson had been debated in Paris in the week before the armistice. Two modifications in the Fourteen Points were made at the instance of Lloyd George: the one was concerned with 'the freedom of the seas', the other with the restoration of the invaded territories and compensation for damage done. Colonel House, acting as Wilson's intermediary, objected to the former modification and went so far as to hint at a separate American peace if this were not agreed. But Lloyd George was adamant and had Clemenceau's support when he declared that Britain and France would go on fighting. The changes were accepted and transmitted by Wilson to the German Government on 5 November.

Since the return of the Liberals in December 1910 there had been no general election. In the meantime there had been profound changes in the size and composition of the electorate, notably the extension of the suffrage to women. Lloyd George and Bonar Law decided to appeal to the country as a coalition and obtain a mandate to negotiate the peace and carry out a post-war policy of reconstruction. The Labour Party and the Asquith Liberals decided to go their own way. The coalition programme included 'trial of the Kaiser', payment of indemnities by the Central powers up to the limit of their capacity, and domestic reforms in all spheres.

Lloyd George was justified in consulting the country, but his demagogic conduct of the election did his reputation permanent harm. The Government obtained 526 seats out of 707, an immense majority, but one in which, as Lloyd George found to his cost, Unionists largely predominated, his Liberal supporters numbering only 133.

The country was impatient to bring the soldiers home and to resume 'business as usual', but the peacemakers had been caught unprepared and two months passed before the conference opened in Paris (18 January 1919) and two more months before it brought matters to a head with the reduction of its unwieldy executive, the Council of Ten, to a Council of Four, largely on the initiative of Lloyd George who was used to a small inner Cabinet. The German treaty was signed on 28 June. For most of these five months Lloyd George was in Paris, with Balfour as his colleague, and Sir Maurice Hankey and P. H. Kerr (later the Marquess of Lothian, q.v.) as his secretaries. He at once secured the effective participation of the Dominions and India in the proceedings.

Wilson, idealist as he was, was preoccupied with promoting self-determination and the creation of a League of Nations; Clemenceau, the realist, sought ways of keeping Germany weak and preventing a recurrence of her attack on France; Lloyd George, a blend of idealist and realist, moving between the two, was firm on a few and flexible on many matters but mainly desirous that the wheels of European industry and trade should be made to revolve again. On the day of the armistice he had asked the British food controller 'to pour food into Germany' and in Paris at the Council of Ten he repeatedly urged that Germany should be revictualled, if only to prevent the spread of Bolshevism in Europe. In a memorandum, dated 25 March and written at Fontainebleau, he considered, belatedly, the treaty as a whole and outlined the principles of a settlement with a moderation which infuriated the French and alarmed the 'hard-faced' members of the House of Commons, who telegraphed their protest to Paris. He returned to Westminster and defended his policy with brilliant debating power and audacity.

Back in Paris he fought to place Danzig under the League of Nations and for plebiscites in Upper Silesia and in the Saar basin. In dealing with Italy he and Clemenceau were bound by the Treaty of London of 1915. Wrangling over Italian claims, over Fiume in particular, went on for months and was only ended by the Treaty of Rapallo on 12 November 1920. To meet Clemenceau's demand for occupation of the left bank of the Rhine and the bridgeheads on the right bank, Lloyd George and Wilson offered France a guarantee of military aid against unprovoked aggression, an offer which Wilson was unable to confirm and which therefore lapsed. A similar fate befell the Reparation Commission, which was Lloyd George's device for fixing the amounts and methods of Germany's payments. The decision of the United States not to ratify the treaty involved their withdrawal from the Reparation Commission. In future conferences Lloyd George had to struggle with the French for the reduction of Germany's payments to realistic proportions, and in March 1932 he published *The Truth about Reparations and War-Debts* in which he pleaded for their total abolition.

When Lloyd George left Paris on 29 June 1919 a council of heads of delegations was charged with unfinished business which included treaties with Austria,

Bulgaria, and other states. On 25 June Lloyd George had tried in vain to arrange 'a short sharp peace' which would 'put Turkey out of her misery', a failure which was later to have calamitous results.

The Treaty of Versailles was ratified on 10 January 1920, and at this period Lloyd George was at the summit of his authority and fame. Henceforward he was to be much occupied in a series of conferences aiming at the pacification and economic revival of Europe. 'Diplomacy by conference' provided him with opportunities for the exercise of his gifts of persuasion, and the publicity inseparable from his perambulations introduced the newly enfranchised millions to the discussion of foreign affairs. The climax of the series was the Genoa conference (April, May 1922), his supreme effort to unite the nations of Europe. It was handicapped by Poincaré's refusal to attend and maimed in the first week by Germany and Russia agreeing to resume diplomatic relations and to cancel their mutual claims to compensation. A face-saving adjournment to The Hague for a conference of experts brought no settlement of the Russian debts owed under the Tsarist régime but repudiated by the Soviet Government. From the revolution onwards Lloyd George had sought to maintain friendly relations with the new rulers of Russia; he had been in favour of meeting them in Paris or Prinkipo in 1919 and in March 1921 he welcomed the conclusion in London of a trade agreement with their delegate, Krassin.

During these attempts at peacemaking abroad Lloyd George was haunted by the spectre of a mutinous Ireland. He himself had been a consistent devolutionist and a supporter of all home-rule measures from the day he entered Parliament. Now, repudiating Westminster, the Sinn Fein members were setting up their own Government. In the fighting which followed Lloyd George defended the use of British forces nicknamed 'Black and Tans', who replied in kind to the outrages of Irish republicans. These reprisals shocked British public opinion, which would not support a policy of 'Thorough'. An appeal by King George V for all Irishmen 'to forgive and forget' led to negotiations in London. The Irish 'treaty' which finally resulted was signed on 6 December 1921 and was achieved mainly by Lloyd George's patience and negotiating skill.

The demobilization of four million men and their absorption into industry was bound to create grave social and political difficulties. The lop-sided expansion of war industries had to be adjusted and the housing industry expanded to 'provide homes for heroes'. Lloyd George devised measures to meet this situation and set up new ministries of Health and Transport, an Electricity Commission, and a commission under the chairmanship of Sir John (later Viscount) Sankey [q.v.] to examine the coal-mining industry. All these matters Lloyd George handled very much as a constitutional dictator. The majority of his supporters were Tories; the Liberals were split into coalitionists, Asquithians, and those partial to the Labour Party. There were moments when Lloyd George seemed about to form a centre party, his rooted Liberalism making desertion to the Unionists unthinkable. On 27 February 1922 he wrote to (Sir) Austen Chamberlain [q.v.] offering to give up the premiership and to support a homogeneous Government which undertook 'to carry through the Treaty with Ireland' and would devote itself 'to the work of the pacification of the world'. Chamberlain declined the invitation but in the autumn Lloyd George's resignation was precipitated from another and unexpected quarter.

The fate of Turkey had not been settled at Versailles. The delay was mainly due to uncertainty whether President Wilson could induce America to accept the proposed mandate for Constantinople and Armenia. The Treaty of Sèvres which was signed in August 1920 reserved Constantinople to the Turks but gave to the Greeks, *inter alia*, Smyrna and a large slice of Asia Minor. This was the policy of Venizelos, who had Lloyd George's enthusiastic support. It was successfully resisted by Mustapha Kemal who had gradually gained control of Turkey. He had been no party to the Treaty of Sèvres and he now had the backing of France and Italy. In the dangerous situation created by Kemal's attempt to invade the neutral zone at Chanak, war was finally averted by the firmness of Lloyd George and the tact of Sir Charles Harington [q.v.], but the fear that Lloyd George was about to plunge the country into a new war rallied his opponents and provided a pretext for ending his dominion. Most of the Tory ministers stood by him, but at a Carlton Club meeting (19 October 1922) a majority of the Conservatives were against continuing the coalition. Lloyd George resigned, Bonar Law became prime minister on 23 October, and at the subsequent appeal to the country the Conservatives headed the poll.

Lloyd George was returned at the head of fifty-five National Liberals. They were buttressed by a strong party fund believed to have been acquired largely by traffic in honours. This was later swollen to considerable dimensions by highly remunerated journalism at home and abroad, judicious investment in the *Daily Chronicle* and other periodicals, and their successful management by Lloyd George himself. His personal possession and control of the fund was a matter of much controversy and some scandal for many years. Much of it was put to admirable use in promoting expert investigations into social problems—coal, land, roads, unemployment—into which Lloyd George now threw his reforming energies. A series of able reports followed, the recommendations of which anticipated the planning programmes of later years. He was neither a Socialist nor a rigid doctrinaire Liberal; in the main a free trader and friendly to big business, he encouraged the creating of buffer bodies between the State and the consumer for the provision of public utilities and social services.

In September 1923 Lloyd George left for New York, returning in November. He addressed many meetings in Canada and the United States and was everywhere given a tumultuous welcome. He sought the co-operation of America in the settlement of a desperate Europe and pleaded in the words of his hero Lincoln for 'clemency in the hour of triumph'.

In November the two wings of the Liberal Party were reunited when Stanley Baldwin, seeking to cure unemployment by means of protection, launched a general election. The Conservatives were returned in December with only 258 seats and were defeated in January. Labour with 191 held office for nine months by arrangement with the Liberals who had 159 seats, until after the 'Zinoviev election'. Differences between Asquith and Lloyd George, partly over the personal fund and partly over the line taken by Lloyd George in the general strike of 1926, finally separated them. Lloyd George was in favour of negotiating with the strikers while the strike was on and ridiculed the notion that they had revolutionary aims. In October 1926 Asquith, now Lord Oxford, resigned the leadership of the

party. Lloyd George who was chairman of the parliamentary party worked hard for the next two years to restore the strength and influence of Liberalism.

The dominant domestic problem continued to be unemployment, which reflected a world-wide fall in trade. Lloyd George denounced (Sir) Winston Churchill's return to the gold standard in 1925, and more and more insistently in the next decade he turned to expansionist remedies, then, and for some years to come, considered heterodox. In September 1925 he proclaimed a scheme whereby the State should buy out all landlords and thus give security to the tenants, and in February 1926 his proposals were generally endorsed at a Liberal convention in London.

The fullest exposition of his ideas of reconstruction appeared in January 1928 in *Britain's Industrial Future*, the fruit of the labours of a group of progressive economists. It provided a Liberal policy for the general election of May 1929, and was popularized in a booklet *We Can Conquer Unemployment* (March 1929) which had a large circulation. Money was lavishly spent on helping Liberal candidates and Lloyd George expounded his policies to crowded meetings everywhere. He had discussed privately with (Sir) Winston Churchill (February 1929) the situation which might arise if no party obtained a clear majority. He would have preferred in that event that Liberals should support Conservatives rather than Socialists. Labour led with 288 members, Tories took second place with 260, and after his superhuman efforts Lloyd George's followers numbered only 59. Baldwin did not invite Liberal co-operation, but resigned and made way for a Labour Government. It soon found itself in difficulties, which were accentuated by the slump in the United States. Unemployment continued to increase. In the spring of 1931 Ramsay MacDonald was privately exploring some possible coalition with Lloyd George and his followers. In July Lloyd George had to undergo a major operation which removed him from the arena during the financial crisis which overtook the Labour Cabinet and led to the formation of a 'national' Government with Ramsay MacDonald as prime minister. Lloyd George strongly opposed the general election, upon which the Tories insisted, in October and from which emerged a House of Commons composed of 471 Conservatives, 52 Labour members, and 72 Liberals, divided between 'Simonites' and 'Samuelites' and a family party of four: Lloyd George, his son Gwilym, his daughter Megan, and his son's brother-in-law Goronwy Owen. On 3 November he wrote to Sir Herbert (subsequently Viscount) Samuel declining to stand again for the party leadership and on 19 November he set out for a holiday voyage to Ceylon.

In the field of foreign affairs in this period (1923–31) the Locarno treaties and the Kellogg Pact were signed; but Lloyd George was more concerned that the allied policy of disarmament to which he had pledged himself at Versailles should be carried out. The failure of the British–American guarantee had renewed the determination of France to put security before disarmament. Lloyd George had collaborated with Wilson in Paris in setting up the League but he had never given it his wholehearted support and later was very critical of its delays when dealing with disarmament.

The attempt to disarm Germany in accordance with the treaty had been foiled by many deliberate evasions. As the years passed, open and secret breaches became common and were discounted or justified by Lloyd George, who had misgivings about the treatment meted out to Germany in the peace settlement. In September 1933 he summed up his views plainly on one of its aspects, saying that all the trouble that had arisen in Europe and in Germany in particular had come from a flagrant breach of the undertaking to disarm by all the victor nations except one (Britain), and that the failure of the League of Nations to enforce that pledge had destroyed its moral influence. His hostility to France and partiality to Germany became increasingly marked and in the autumn of 1936 he visited Hitler at Berchtesgaden. He was much impressed by the Führer, who had abolished unemployment in Germany partly by measures similar to those which he himself had vainly advocated at home. It was only slowly that he was brought to recognize that full employment in Germany was mainly due to rearmament and that by treacherous diplomacy Hitler was bent on becoming the master of Europe.

Shortly before leaving office Lloyd George built himself a house at Churt in Surrey, and here, with further purchases of land, he developed an agricultural estate of some 600 acres and learnt farming and fruit-growing. Here also he accumulated his books and papers, and

in the summer of 1932 he settled down to the more onerous task of writing his *War Memoirs* (1933–6) and *The Truth about the Peace Treaties* (1938). Every page of these volumes displays the forensic skill with which the combative author marshals the vast documentary evidence to confound his critics and to justify his own actions and policies. Portraits of the great figures of the war and the peace are drawn with a broad brush, not seldom dipped in venom. He concedes nothing to those who believed that the decisive theatre of war would be in the West and rarely pleads guilty to any mistake of his own.

On 17 January 1935, his seventy-second birthday, at Bangor, amidst a blaze of press publicity, Lloyd George launched a programme for a 'new deal', a revival in essentials of the bold economic remedies he had prescribed in 1929. The Cabinet was compelled to take notice, since not a few young Conservatives were attracted by the 'wizard', and Baldwin even went so far as to consider an invitation to him to join the Government. The ex-prime minister agreed to submit himself to cross-examination. But Ramsay MacDonald was hostile to co-operation with him and the chancellor of the Exchequer (Neville Chamberlain) had not only his own programme (cheap money, tariffs), but had also the strongest personal antipathy to the 'new dealer'. The only result of ten meetings was *A Better Way to Better Times*, issued by the Government by way of reply to Lloyd George's *Organizing Prosperity*.

Rebuffed but undaunted, Lloyd George now attempted to associate his domestic programme with that of the League of Nations in a non-party 'Council of Action for Peace and Reconstruction' at a time when the peace ballot revealed wide support for a policy of disarmament and collective security. The council exercised little influence on the general election which followed, but it continued for a year or two to maintain a staff which assisted candidates pledged to its views to fight by-elections. Lloyd George returned to his farm in Surrey to experiment with stock poultry and fruit and to the task of completing his war memoirs.

Little remains to be said of the last ten years of his life when again war clouds gathered and broke over Europe. At the time of the proposed marriage of King Edward VIII to Mrs. Wallis Simpson Lloyd George was in the West Indies, and he may not have realized the difficulties attendant on the policy which he favoured of a 'morganatic' marriage.

As it became plain that Hitler would not stop short of war to gain his ends Lloyd George advocated closer co-operation with Russia. He seldom spoke in the House of Commons but when he did it was to denounce the cowardice of the 'national' Government in face of Mussolini's Fascist activities in Spain and his rape of Abyssinia, and to chastise Neville Chamberlain in merciless terms for his appeasement policy and demand his resignation. He had no electoral power with which to enforce his appeal but his voice was not without influence in shaping opinion.

Britain declared war on Germany on 3 September 1939 and Churchill became prime minister in May 1940. He formed a coalition of the three parties and in June 1940 he invited Lloyd George to join it. Lloyd George refused the offer: he would have had Chamberlain as one of his colleagues and probably differences with the prime minister in the conduct of the war; besides, he was no longer equal to the strain of a Cabinet post. The same lack of physical resilience prevented his acceptance of the ambassadorship at Washington rendered vacant by the death of Lord Lothian in December.

Five weeks later (20 January 1941) Dame Margaret Lloyd George died at Criccieth. She was the daughter of Richard Owen, a substantial farmer of Mynydd Ednyfed, Criccieth, and Lloyd George had married her in 1888. Delayed on his way to her from Churt by a blizzard in the Welsh mountains he did not reach Criccieth in time to see her. For fifty-three years she had been his loyal comrade, his meteoric career and world fame only serving to bring into relief her serenity, natural dignity, and steadfastness. She was appointed G.B.E. in 1920. There were born to them two sons and three daughters: Richard (born 1889), who succeeded his father as second earl; Mair Eiluned who died in 1907 aged seventeen; Olwen Elizabeth, now Lady Olwen Carey Evans; Gwilym, home secretary from 1954 until 1957, when he became Viscount Tenby; and Megan, from 1929 to 1951 Liberal member of Parliament for Anglesey and from 1957 Labour member for Carmarthen. On 23 October 1943 Lloyd George married Frances Louise, daughter of John Stevenson, of Wallington, Surrey. She had been for thirty years his personal secretary. In September 1944 he left Churt with her

for Ty Newydd, a small farming property he had bought in 1939 near his early home at Llanystumdwy and had transformed into an attractive residence. His powers were now failing and the question of the future representation of the Boroughs had to be faced. The party associations were not agreed on his unopposed return and he was not equal to a contest. In these circumstances the prime minister's offer to submit his name to the King for an earldom was accepted and on New Year's Day 1945 his elevation to the peerage was announced. He took the titles of Earl Lloyd-George of Dwyfor and Viscount Gwynedd of Dwyfor, in the county of Caernarvon. On 26 March he died and on the 30th he was buried in a solitary spot chosen by himself on the bank of the river by which he had played as a boy and from which he had taken his title. It was a strange exit: the deliberate choice of a grave among but not alongside the rude forefathers, the boast of heraldry for the village Hampden but not the Abbey. This assertion of complete separateness was in character.

Lloyd George was not hewn out of one solid block: he was built not of one but of many pieces. His outstanding and varied gifts launched him on a brilliant political career and kept him on a triumphant course for twenty years. By then he had split his own party, and he was now discarded by the Tories. The emergence of the Labour Party and the distrust and hostility of the two older parties combined to exclude him from office for the rest of his life. Possessed of great ability, shrewdness, and nimbleness, neither an echo nor a borrower, he always displayed innate independence and immense courage. He had abounding energy, lived intensely and positively, and was more resourceful and subtle than any of his ministerial colleagues. Neither metaphysician nor mystic, he was artist and actor with nothing prosaic or pedestrian about him; in the daily traffic of life his charm was irresistible and his good temper unfailing. His instinctive adaptability to every sort of audience was uncanny and on high occasions his eloquence was overpowering. He secured innumerable successes in parliamentary debate by his harmonious command of voice and gesture, imagery and humour. Endowed with an exceptional sense of the realities of political power, he did not disdain the popular arts of the demagogue, and there were moments when he stooped to low artifice.

Although without the magnanimity of the finest characters, he commanded the allegiance of statesmen as distinguished and diverse as Balfour and Smuts, Milner and Austen Chamberlain. His hatred of oppression and his genuine human sympathy were revealed most persistently in his radical measures of social reform and in the programmes he provided for his successors of all parties. His genius for leadership found its supreme expression in war, when his indomitable will and buoyant spirit steered the nation to victory in 1918. At Versailles and indeed for the rest of his life he laboured consistently to raise the living conditions of the peoples, to restore Germany, to pacify Europe, and so avert what he desperately feared, and lived to endure, a second world war.

There are portraits of Lloyd George by Sir William Orpen (oils, 1927), Sir Max Beerbohm (pencil and wash), and R. Guthrie (chalk) in the National Portrait Gallery; by Sir John Lavery (1935) and by Christopher D. Williams (1917) in the National Museum of Wales; by Christopher D. Williams in the National Liberal Club; by Sir Luke Fildes, presented to the Incorporated Law Society in 1909; by Augustus John in the Aberdeen Art Gallery. In sculpture, there is a statue in the square in Caernarvon, also a bronze bust (1921) in the National Museum of Wales, a bust and bas-relief in the Ceiriog Memorial Institute, by Sir W. Goscombe John; busts by Lady Kennet in the Imperial War Museum and the National Museum of Wales; a bas-relief by Dora Ohlfsen in the National Library of Wales, Aberystwyth. A cartoon by 'Spy' appeared in *Vanity Fair* in 1907 entitled 'A Nonconformist Genius'. Decorations, caskets, deeds of freedom, and other personal mementoes are preserved in the Lloyd George Museum, Llanystumdwy, North Wales.

[*The Times*, 27 March 1945; W. Watkin Davies, *Lloyd George 1863–1914*, 1939; Herbert du Parcq, *Life of David Lloyd George*, 4 vols., 1912; E. T. Raymond, *Mr. Lloyd George*, 1922; A. J. Sylvester, *The Real Lloyd George*, 1947; Malcolm Thomson, with the collaboration of Frances, Countess Lloyd-George of Dwyfor, *David Lloyd George, the Official Biography*, 1948; Thomas Jones, *Lloyd George*, 1951; David Lloyd George, *The Great Crusade*, 1918, *The Truth about Reparations and War-Debts*, 1932, *Some Considerations for the Peace Conference before they finally draft their Terms*, 25 March 1919 (Cmd. 1614, 1922), *Is it Peace?*, 1923, *Slings and Arrows* (extracts edited by Philip Guedalla), 1929, *War Memoirs*, 6 vols., 1933–6, and *The Truth about the Peace Treaties*, 2 vols., 1938; personal knowledge.]     THOMAS JONES.

[Frank Owen, *Tempestuous Journey*, 1954; Robert Blake, *The Unknown Prime Minister, The Life and Times of Andrew Bonar Law*, 1955; Lord Beaverbrook, *Men and Power, 1917–1918*, 1956; William George, *My Brother and I*, 1958.]

LLOYD JAMES, ARTHUR (1884–1943), phonetician. [See JAMES.]

LONDONDERRY, seventh MARQUESS OF (1878–1949), politician. [See VANE-TEMPEST-STEWART, CHARLES STEWART HENRY.]

LONSDALE, fifth EARL OF (1857–1944), sportsman. [See LOWTHER, HUGH CECIL.]

LOWTHER, HUGH CECIL, fifth EARL OF LONSDALE (1857–1944), sportsman, was born in London 25 January 1857, the second son of Henry Lowther, later third Earl of Lonsdale, and his wife, Emily Susan, daughter of St. George Francis Caulfeild, of Donamon, Roscommon. J. W. Lowther, Viscount Ullswater (a notice of whom appears below), was his cousin. He was educated at Eton, and already at the age of nine had shown his prowess in the shires as a rider to hounds by being in at the death when the field had been reduced to four. Under his father he learnt personally to fulfil every detail of a huntsman's duties. Later he became master in turn of the Woodland Pytchley, Blankney, Quorn, and Cottesmore hounds; the Quorn he raised to an eminence which made it proverbial. There was no more authoritative M.F.H.: one of the many stories relates how he gave personal chastisement to a countryman who had run over and killed a hound. A five-pound note every Christmas always reminded the ill-doer of his offence and his pardon.

In his teens Hugh Lowther toured with a circus in Switzerland, and ever afterwards he loved circus folk, particularly the four-footed. In his early thirties he spent an adventurous year in the Arctic and had the distinction of confirming the presence of gold in the Klondike. A stranger in the House of Lords (he succeeded his brother as fifth earl in 1882), in all sporting circles he was perfectly at ease, genial, forthright, and very knowledgeable. As a judge of a horse or a dog he was all his life recognized as a leading authority; but he had little luck on the turf and the only classic race he ever won was the St. Leger in 1922. Although he showed promise as a steeplechase rider his weight soon extinguished any hope of becoming an amateur jockey. This was no disadvantage, however, in the ring, where his prowess was so remarkable that many judges considered him a potential world champion; a view to which the champion, John L. Sullivan, inclined when Hugh Lowther gave him rough treatment in some sparring bouts in New York and actually brought him down. The Lonsdale Belts of the National Sporting Club remain to associate his name with the sport which he helped so much.

Another of his sports was yacht racing. In 1896 he raced Kaiser Wilhelm's crack cutter *Meteor* and won seventeen prizes in twenty-two races. When the Kaiser, who was a close friend, went to shoot grouse on Wemmergill moor, Lonsdale entertained him in his palatial but uncomely Lowther Castle with its 3,000 acres of park and 90 acres of gardens. No post-war high-level conference ever had a more exuberant press, although later when the war of 1914–18 exacerbated national dislikes Lonsdale was criticized by the envious and the busybodies for not denouncing his friendship with the Kaiser. He ignored such attacks and the bust of his friend remained in its place of honour in the castle. With the same steadfastness Lonsdale kept to the end of his life a resolve made at the age of twenty-one never again to play cards for money or to bet on a horse.

It was the individualist in Lonsdale which made him the idol of the Victorian and Edwardian populace. With his side-whiskers, his nine-inch cigars, his gardenia buttonhole, he was to the crowds the perfect specimen of the sporting grandee. As Lord Birkenhead wrote, 'almost alone, he preserves an atmosphere which, to our grandchildren alas! will be nothing but an historic dream'. The populace looked to him, as it did also to Lord Derby [q.v.], for the same sort of grandeur that their posterity only see at secondhand on the films. When he drove to the royal enclosure from the house at Ascot which he rented for the royal meeting, the crowds watched with wonder the perfect turn-out, the yellow and black wagonette with its exactly matched chestnuts, the grooms and postilions in yellow livery with every buckle and button shining.

In addition to various civic offices in Cumberland and Westmorland, Lonsdale was lord lieutenant of Cumberland from 1917 to 1944. Whether he was the Rutland squire at Barley Thorpe or the chieftain of the Westmorland dales living in princely style at Lowther Castle, the popularity of the 'yellow Earl' (as his friends the costers knew him) was enhanced by his readiness to live up to his role. His establishments were splendid. In his hey-day there would never have been fewer than fifty horses in the stables at both these great places. His clothes came from the wool of his own sheep on the fells. There were two Lonsdale tweeds, one of light grey for the members of his family, another darker for the household. Lonsdale came to his meals with the sportsman's hearty appetite. He drank white burgundy for breakfast. In the mid-morning he liked to relax with his guests over a glass of champagne. His regimen clearly suited him, for he was active until his death at the age of eighty-seven. Throughout his life, until the last decade when his means were straitened, his background favoured him. With an income well into six figures, all the world of sport, racing, hunting, coursing (he won the Waterloo cup), shooting, fishing, yachting, was open to him. His view of dog racing was 'fun, but not sport'.

Except that he had no children, Lonsdale's married life was of the happiest. His wife, Lady Grace Cecilie Gordon (died 1941), daughter of the tenth Marquess of Huntly, whom he married in 1878, was hardly less devoted to sport than was her husband. They celebrated their diamond wedding in 1938 amid congratulations from every class of society, from the royal family to the London 'pearlies', whose lifelong patron Lonsdale was. King George V showed his high opinion of him in 1925 when he appointed him G.C.V.O. In 1928 he became a K.G. There appeared in the following year the first three of the many volumes of 'The Lonsdale Library of Sports, Games & Pastimes' which he edited with Eric Parker; there could be no more fitting memorial to his name. He died at Stud House, Barley Thorpe, 13 April 1944, and was succeeded by his brother, Lancelot Edward (1867–1953).

There is a portrait of Lonsdale by Sir John Lavery at the Mansion House, Doncaster; of Lord and Lady Lonsdale with the Cottesmore hounds by Lynwood Palmer, and of Lord Lonsdale on Mullach leaping the double at Great Dalby by

Basil Nightingale, both in the possession of the family.

[Lionel Dawson, *Lonsdale*, the authorized life, 1946; private information; personal knowledge.]                    H. E. WORTHAM.

LOWTHER, JAMES WILLIAM, first VISCOUNT ULLSWATER (1855–1949), Speaker of the House of Commons, was born in London 1 April 1855, the son of William Lowther, at that time secretary at the British legation in Naples, and later member of Parliament for Westmorland, and his wife, Charlotte Alice, daughter of the famous judge, Sir James Parke (later Lord Wensleydale, q.v.). On his father's side he was great-grandson of the first, and nephew of the third, Earl of Lonsdale [qq.v.] and on his mother's side he was cousin to the ninth Earl of Carlisle, and to the first Viscount Ridley [qq.v.]. His wife, Mary Frances (died 1944), daughter of Alexander James Beresford Beresford-Hope, of Bedgebury Park, Kent, whom he married in 1886, was niece to the great Marquess of Salisbury. If it is true that Lowther owed something at the start of his career to his family connexions, the chief factor in his success was the remarkable fitness for that career of his own character and abilities.

Lowther was at Eton (1868–70) and at Trinity College, Cambridge, from 1874 until 1878 in which year he was placed in the third class of the law tripos. Between those dates he enjoyed a less conventional period at King's College, London, a period to which he looked back with gratitude for the instruction which 'in the absence of competing attractions' he had there absorbed. At Cambridge he entered fully into the social life of college and university, being particularly prominent in the Amateur Dramatic Club, for which he retained a lifelong affection.

After being called to the bar by the Inner Temple in 1879, Lowther devoted himself for a few years to the serious practice of his profession. But his election as Conservative member for Rutland in 1883 and, after a short interval in the wilderness, for the Penrith (later Penrith and Cockermouth) division of Cumberland in 1886 turned his energies to a parliamentary career. In 1887 he was made a charity commissioner; from 1891 until the dissolution in 1892 he served as parliamentary under-secretary of state for foreign affairs—an office in which he was succeeded by Sir Edward Grey (later Viscount Grey of Fallodon, q.v.). On the return of the Conservatives to power in 1895 Lowther was appointed chairman of ways and means and deputy Speaker. In 1898 he was sworn of the Privy Council and in 1905 he was elected to the speakership and held that office, through sixteen of the most critical years of parliamentary history, until 1921.

For some years before his election Lowther's fitness for the speakership had been generally recognized. He had profited by his ten years in the junior chair to familiarize himself with the technicalities of parliamentary procedure. Although he had held minor office in a Conservative Government, he had never been regarded as a strong partisan. His judicial cast of mind (inherited perhaps from his maternal grandfather), imperturbable temper, lively wit, and friendly manners; his air of vigour and distinction; and in the background his well-trained and powerful intelligence, had given him wide popularity and also made him a little formidable.

Lowther's speakership fell during an unprecedentedly cantankerous and uncomfortable period. The split in the Conservative Party, which had resulted in 1905 in leaving the House practically without government leadership; the long-drawn-out quarrel between the large and truculent Liberal majority of 1906 and the House of Lords, culminating in the rejection of the finance bill of 1909 and the passing of the Parliament Act, 1911; the not unconnected re-emergence of Home Rule legislation which inflamed party spirit in Parliament and brought the nation to the verge of civil war in 1914; the strain caused by the repeated scenes between the parties in the House and by the incursions of the suffragettes; the parliamentary problems created by four years of war and the abnormal conditions which followed the peace—it is only necessary to recapitulate these successive experiences in order to realize in how many ways the conditions of the period diverged from those of the nineteenth-century Parliaments in which Lowther had served his apprenticeship, and to what an extent he had to rely on his own resources, his rapid and tolerant judgement, his firm but flexible enforcement of discipline.

Among Lowther's assets as a Speaker were his willing acceptance of responsibility, his power of inspiring confidence in all parties, and his sense of humour.

As a young temporary chairman in 1890 he had 'pulled up' G. J. (later Viscount) Goschen [q.v.], the veteran statesman and Conservative chancellor of the Exchequer, for irrelevance—an invidious duty which he might easily have shirked. So, too, as Speaker, he did not shrink from taking responsibility by a procedural ruling for the destruction of the Balfour scheme of redistribution, the principal item of the session of 1905, and again in 1913 for the withdrawal of the Liberal Government's franchise bill on account of an attempt by amendment to turn it into a female suffrage bill. To his tact and fairness was due the success—the 'almost miraculous' success, as Lloyd George called it—of the daring experiment of submitting the vexed question of electoral reform to a conference of party members presided over by the Speaker. Lowther's sense of humour far exceeded the conventional equipment of the chair. Homely and unforced, it was invaluable in clearing overcharged atmospheres; it also had an astringent quality which was useful for deflating self-assertive opinions.

Upon retiring from the chair in 1921 he was appointed G.C.B. and raised to the peerage as Viscount Ullswater, of Campsea Ashe, in the county of Suffolk. He continued his active public service till a great age, declining flattering invitations from more than one prime minister, but freely giving his services to Royal Commissions and other public bodies. He remained an alderman of the East Suffolk County Council until 1946, attended quarter-sessions regularly, was president of many local societies, and discharged the duties of a large landowner on his estate. He continued until within a few years of his death to ride his sturdy white cob and to shoot. He died at Campsea Ashe 27 March 1949 near his ninety-fourth birthday, having outlived his two immediate successors in the Speaker's chair. There were two sons and one daughter of his marriage and he was succeeded as second viscount by his great-grandson, Nicholas James Christopher (born 1942), whose father, Lieutenant John Arthur Lowther, was private secretary to the Duke of Kent and lost his life with him in the aircraft accident in 1942.

Lowther received the honorary degrees of D.C.L. from the university of Oxford in 1907 and LL.D. from Cambridge and Leeds in 1910. A portrait by P. A. de László is at the Inner Temple of which he was a bencher from 1906, and another by the same artist hangs in the Grand Jury room of the Courts in Carlisle. In the Speaker's House there is a portrait by G. Fiddes Watt who also painted the portrait which is in the County Hall, Ipswich.

[Viscount Ullswater, *A Speaker's Commentaries*, 2 vols., 1925; private information; personal knowledge.]     CAMPION.

LUGARD, FREDERICK JOHN DEALTRY, BARON LUGARD (1858–1945), soldier, administrator, and author, was born at Fort St. George, Madras, 22 January 1858, the eldest son of the Rev. Frederick Grueber Lugard, a senior chaplain on the Madras establishment, by his third wife, a missionary, Mary Jane, daughter of the Rev. John Garton Howard, vicar of Stanton-by-Dale, Derbyshire. The family returned to England in 1863 and in the next year settled in Worcester where Lugard's father had obtained a living. In 1865 his mother died. He was educated at Rossall School whence he passed into the Royal Military College, Sandhurst, his choice of career being influenced by the fact that his uncle, General Sir Edward Lugard, who had earned distinction in the Sikh wars and the Indian mutiny, was permanent under-secretary to the War Office from 1861 to 1871.

Lugard received his commission in the 9th Foot (the Norfolk Regiment) in 1878 after only two months at Sandhurst and joined the second battalion in India towards the end of the year. In 1879–80 he was with Sir H. H. Gough [q.v.] in Afghanistan but saw little action on account of illness which resulted in a year's sick leave in England. On his return to India he devoted much of his leave to sport and became known as a skilled big game hunter. Slight but wiry in build, he had great powers of endurance; but his private means were small; he had indeed paid for his favourite rifle by shooting a man-eating tiger with a reward on its head; and it was this lack of funds which led him to secure secondment in 1884 to the Military Transport Service. He was rewarded for this decision by being dispatched in February 1885 to accompany the Indian contingent which was sent to Suakin in support of the Sudan campaign for the relief of Khartoum, and in March of that year under the command of Sir J. C. McNeill [q.v.] he was engaged in the severe fighting at 'McNeill's zeriba' near Suakin. In 1886 he took part, also as a transport officer, in the troublesome operations in Burma which followed the overthrow of King Thibaw. For these services he received the newly established decoration of the D.S.O. (1887) and was four times mentioned in dispatches.

At the end of 1887, after leave in England, Lugard exchanged to the 1st battalion of his regiment, then proceeding to Gibraltar, but the Burma campaign had left him in very poor health and he was placed on medical leave. It was characteristic that he should have sought to restore his health (in his own words) by 'active hard work', and he tried to obtain permission to join the Italian forces then preparing to meet an attack by the Abyssinians on the protectorate which Italy had assumed over the port of Massawa. Refused permission at Rome he embarked as deck passenger in a tramp steamer from Suez to Massawa, and without passport or other credentials succeeded in making his way up country to the camp of General Baldisera. Here he failed once more to gain leave to join the Italian forces, and, returning to Massawa, he went on to Zanzibar, and Mozambique, still searching for something to do.

His funds were nearly exhausted when Lugard was pressed by the British consul at Mozambique to join a small force which the African Lakes Company was preparing for the defence of a trading station it had established at Karongwa, on the northeast shore of Lake Nyasa. He had by now been deeply impressed by what he had seen of the results of the raiding for slaves by Arabs and Swahilis in East Africa, and had already formed the conviction that it could only be suppressed by taking direct action against the raiders in the hinterland in which they were operating. Nyasaland was then one of the chief centres of their activity and a body of slavers had not only raided widely along the shores of the lake but by attacking the station at Karongwa had threatened the communications with missions established at Blantyre. Satisfied of the purpose which the expedition would serve, Lugard accepted its command and reached Karongwa in May 1888. His force was small and ill-equipped, but the safety of the station was secured, though he himself was severely wounded in an attack on the slavers' stockade, for some time losing the use of his left arm.

In the summer of 1889 he returned to England. His work had attracted the attention of Cecil Rhodes and also of Sir William Mackinnon [qq.v.], the latter of whom had in the previous year founded the Imperial British East Africa Company. Circumstances compelled Rhodes to withdraw the proposal that Lugard should administer the interests of the British South Africa Company in part of Nyasaland, and Lugard accepted Mackinnon's offer of employment in opening up a new route from Mombasa to the interior by the Sabaki river. This had been completed as far as Machakos when Lugard received orders from the Company to proceed to Uganda. After a march of unprecedented rapidity, partly through hostile Masai country, he crossed the Nile in December 1890.

Affairs in Uganda were then in a state of chaos. Anglican missions had been established there in 1877 and French Catholic missions in 1879, but in 1882 a wave of Moslem propaganda had gained temporary ascendancy. Mwanga, the Kabaka of Buganda, was vicious and vacillating. Foiled in a treacherous attack on both Christians and Moslems, he had been deposed, and in 1888 the Moslems had occupied his capital, Mengo, from which, however, they were driven out by the Christians late in 1889. Mwanga, who had now come under the influence of French White Fathers, was restored. In February 1890 Dr. Karl Peters secured from Mwanga a treaty which favoured German intervention, and although this was nullified later in the year when the Anglo-German agreement assigned Uganda to Great Britain, it increased Lugard's difficulty in dealing with the situation at Mengo. His first task was to obtain from Mwanga a treaty giving him, as agent of the Company, the right to intervene in the affairs of Buganda. He had with him a force of only fifty Sudanese soldiers, but by maintaining a resolute front he secured the treaty. Reinforced by a small detachment sent by the Company, Lugard spent the next six months in establishing some kind of order in Buganda and in the Bunyoro, Toro, and Ankoli chiefdoms, crushing opposition when he encountered it. An adventurous journey, passing by way of the Ruwenzori mountains, took him to Kavalli at the south of the Albert Nyanza, where he enlisted some 600 Sudanese soldiers who had been left behind by Emin Pasha and Stanley, and brought back their numerous dependants to settle in Uganda.

Lugard returned to Mengo early in 1892, to find that fighting had broken out between the two Christian factions, and before long the Catholics attacked his headquarters at Kampala. They were repulsed, but the trouble was only suppressed after fighting at Buddu and the Sese Islands. A new treaty between the Company and the king and the chiefs of both Christian parties was signed in April. Meanwhile Lugard had received from the Company orders to evacuate Uganda, as it could not afford to maintain its position there. Although a short respite was secured through the collection of funds by the missionary societies in England, Lugard decided to return home in order to appeal against a decision which he regarded as involving a tragedy for Uganda. Finding that the Government had decided not to interfere with the evacuation of Uganda by the Company, and although he was averse, then as always, from personal publicity, Lugard felt compelled to take a part in the efforts made by the missionary and anti-slavery societies to persuade Gladstone's Government to undertake responsibility for the administration of Uganda. The matter became a political and international issue, in the course of which Lugard's own conduct in Uganda was attacked on the strength of allegations made by the French missions. But it is generally agreed that the personal efforts made by him had a large share in influencing the decision of the Government to dispatch Sir Gerald Portal [q.v.] to Uganda, as the result of which the country was declared a British protectorate in 1894.

Deeply concerned with the problem of the development of East Africa and anxious to make known the truth about his own operations in Uganda, Lugard now devoted himself to the writing of his first book, *The Rise of Our East African Empire*, which was published in 1893 (2 vols.). Written under great pressure of time, it was somewhat discursive in form, but contained much valuable material on the conditions then prevailing in East Africa and on the problems to be solved in dealing with the slave trade.

Lugard's connexion with the British East Africa Company had ended with the completion of his work in Uganda, but the reputation he had now acquired brought an offer of service from Sir George Goldie [q.v.] who had secured a charter for the Royal Niger Company in 1886. Goldie was in 1894 still engaged in concluding treaties with local chiefs which would enable the Company to meet the encroachments of the French in Nigeria. They were known to be preparing an expedition to Borgu on its western border, and Goldie urged Lugard to proceed to Nikki, the chief town of Borgu, in order to obtain a treaty from the ruler before the arrival of the French or Germans. The last part of this journey lay through unexplored country, for no European had as yet visited Nikki, but Lugard, moving with even more than his accustomed speed, won what the French described as the 'steeplechase to Nikki', and in November 1894 secured the treaty with Borgu.

In April of the next year he left the Niger for England where he still hoped that the Government would ask for his services in Uganda. The Government appointed him C.B. in July 1895 but did not engage his services, and he accepted an offer from a newly formed body, the British West Charterland Company, to explore a mineral concession near Lake Ngami in Bechuanaland. Here the chief problem was one of transport, as the journey to Ngamiland involved a trek of some 700 miles through the Kalahari desert, and the epidemic of rinderpest which had swept southwards from East and Central Africa had emptied the country of trek-cattle. The journey was, however, accomplished by September 1896, but in August of the following year Lugard's work in Ngamiland was cut short by an urgent message from the secretary of state, Joseph Chamberlain, calling him to take up work in West Africa. He left at once, leaving the affairs of the Company in the charge of his brother, Lieutenant Edward James Lugard, D.S.O.

The cause for this demand for Lugard's services was basically the same as that which had taken him to Borgu, but French encroachments had in the interval created a dangerous state of tension in Nigeria, and Chamberlain had decided to strengthen the hands of the Niger Company by the creation of the force which afterwards became famous as the West African Frontier Force. Appointed in 1897 as Her Majesty's commissioner for the hinterland of Nigeria, with the temporary rank of colonel, Lugard raised the new force, and continued in command until 1899. His task when he arrived in Nigeria in the spring of 1898 was a delicate one, and that peace was preserved with the French was largely due to the firmness he displayed and the friendly relations he succeeded in maintaining with the commandants of the local French forces. He was promoted major in 1896 and lieutenant-colonel in 1899.

In 1900 the Government terminated the charter of the Niger Company and declared a protectorate over Northern and Southern Nigeria. Lugard's record made him an obvious choice for the first charge of the northern provinces, for although the Niger Company had made treaties with a number of the chiefs, nothing had been done to bring this part of the country under any form of control. Some of the Hausaland emirates were powerful states, proud of their independence, and with a military tradition dating from the Fulani 'holy war' in the early years of the century, but they had also a tradition of slave raiding and internecine warfare. Lugard assumed office as high commissioner of Northern Nigeria in January 1900 and was appointed K.C.M.G. in the following year. He held the temporary rank of brigadier-general from 1900 to 1907.

The six years for which Lugard was high commissioner were for him a period of intense activity. The staff placed at his disposal was small and his finances severely restricted, but the rapidity with which the area was brought under administrative control was remarkable. It was, however, effected with the minimum use of force, for though action had to be taken between 1900 and 1902 in Kontagora, Nupe, Yola, Bauchi, and Bornu, the operations were on a minor scale. Lugard's success was largely due to the fact that his previous experiences had given him a realistic and statesmanlike conception of the relations which should exist between his administration and the chiefs. He regarded them as dependent rulers, to be guided in the conduct of their rule, but to be definitely controlled so far as was needed to abolish slave raiding, and to ensure the administration of justice and moderation in the levy of tax.

Over a large part of the new protectorate the conditions imposed by him were accepted, but towards the end of 1902 it became clear that a trial of strength was inevitable with the four large emirates of Sokoto, Kano, Gando, and Katsina, the traditional strongholds of Fulani supremacy. Although the Colonial Office was opposed to armed intervention, Lugard himself did not hesitate. By a rapid and courageous use of the small force available to him, Kano, a fortified city, was taken by assault in February 1903, and Sokoto submitted after a battle fought in May. Gando and Katsina yielded without the further use of force, and all four states were forthwith brought within the régime now established, with a continuous improvement in administrative standards, throughout the rest of the protectorate.

Lugard resigned his post in September 1906. He had been dissatisfied with the restraints imposed on him by the Colonial Office, and also resented the refusal of the new colonial secretary, Lord Elgin [q.v.], to continue the arrangement by which he had been allowed to carry on the administration of the protectorate from England during part of the summer of each year. In 1907, however, he accepted the governorship of Hong Kong, although the routine duties of the post and the ceremonial functions it involved made no appeal to him. But he found some outlet for his energy in the impulse he gave to educational effort, and he was largely responsible for the creation of the university of Hong Kong in 1911. He was appointed G.C.M.G. in the same year.

Hong Kong, however, proved to be only an interlude in Lugard's service to Nigeria. In 1912 the Government was considering the amalgamation of the colony and the northern and southern protectorates of Nigeria, but informed him that it considered his services essential for carrying this out. Considerations of his wife's health made him hesitate, but he felt that the measure would set the seal on his own work for Nigeria, and he undertook the task. In September 1912 he became governor of the two protectorates, and in January 1914, after his arrangements for the amalgamation were completed, he was appointed, with the personal title of governor-general, to the charge of the united territories, the largest and most populous unit in the British colonial empire. He held this office until his retirement in 1919.

The period of Lugard's tenure thus coincided with that of the war of 1914–18. There was no question of the loyalty of Nigeria, and under his superintendence contingents were dispatched which served with credit in the Cameroons and East Africa. But for the rest, his energies were absorbed in the exacting task of civil administration during a period in which Nigeria was making an almost dramatic advance in its domestic and export economy. If he showed himself prone to keep the direction of administration largely in his own hands he did not shirk the labour this involved; his industry was indomitable, and his abnormal hours of work became a legend in Africa. He nevertheless made time to rewrite, in the form of political memoranda, the instructions originally issued by him in Northern Nigeria, embodying the system of indirect rule which has become associated with his name. His contribution to the development of this system was conspicuous; it lay not so much in the originality of the procedure adopted as in his advocacy of the principle that the traditional institutions of the native peoples provided the surest foundation on which to build up their progress, and that the use of these institutions as an agency of local government was essential to prevent the disintegration of native society and to educate it in the capacity for self-rule. Other governments of British African colonies had hitherto adopted a variety of procedure in dealing with native affairs, determined rather by the circumstances of the native communities they controlled than by any definite principles of policy. But in the course of the next quarter of a century, the majority of these governments had reorganized their system of native administration in accordance with the principles set out in Lugard's instructions and the political memoranda of 1916.

After he retired Lugard spent some months in Ethiopia on behalf of the Abyssinian Corporation. He was sworn of the Privy Council in 1920. He then devoted himself to the preparation of a work, *The Dual Mandate in British Tropical Africa*, which on its issue in 1922 earned him a position of outstanding authority, not only in England but abroad, as an exponent of the principles which should regulate the policy of a colonial power in dealing with backward peoples. The immediate recognition given to this work was not due merely to the fact that it embodied the result, most conscientiously documented, of his own varied experiences of Africa. As one of the results of the war of 1914–18 international opinion had become increasingly critical of the fact that five among the sovereign powers of the world had control of so considerable a part of Asia and Africa, and Lugard's book provided for the first time a generally acceptable standard by which the merits of their stewardship could be judged. He maintained that the justification for the control exercised over backward peoples lay in its capacity to produce a reciprocal benefit to the peoples concerned and to the world at large, and he held that it should be the aim of every colonial administration to fulfil this dual mandate.

From 1922 to 1936 Lugard was a member of the Permanent Mandates Commission of the League of Nations, and if he was at times irked by its absorption in legalistic issues, he won the respect of his colleagues by his courtesy and patience, and by his conscientious examination of the policies of the mandatory administrations, even though this might involve a criticism of his own Government. But he maintained firmly the principle of the undivided responsibility of each state for its own colonies, against any form of international control. His work with the commission, however, was only one of the many duties he undertook in his years of retirement, which became hardly less laborious than those of his active service. He was a member of the international slavery committees of 1924–5 and 1932; he served on the colonial advisory committee on education from 1923 to 1936; and from 1926 onwards he was chairman of the International Institute of African Languages and Cultures, for the promotion of which he was largely responsible.

In 1928 he was raised to the peerage as Baron Lugard, of Abinger, in the county of Surrey, where he had made his home. In 1930 and 1931 he was an active member of the joint select committee of Parliament on closer union in East Africa. Advancing age brought no relaxation in the time and labour he devoted to colonial affairs, partly in making contributions to the press on current issues (of which the German claim to the return of their colonies was most typical), but largely in preparing for a revised edition of his *Dual Mandate*. It is unfortunate that the material thus accumulated became so voluminous that it had finally to be laid aside. He died at Abinger Common, Surrey, working indefatigably to the last, 11 April 1945.

In 1902 Lugard had married Flora Louise (died 1929), daughter of Major-General George Shaw, C.B.; she was a gifted lady who had become widely known as the head of the colonial department of *The Times*. Lady Lugard identified herself closely with her husband's work and in 1905 published, under the title of *A Tropical Dependency*, a history of Northern Nigeria. She was appointed D.B.E. in 1918. They had no children.

Lugard's life spanned almost the whole history of British rule in tropical Africa, but it comprised two periods of special significance: the operations in Uganda in 1890–92, and the administration of Northern Nigeria from 1900 to 1906. The exceptional qualities of initiative and resolution which he had shown in Uganda were largely responsible for its subsequent incorporation in the colonial Empire, but his administration of Northern Nigeria was the more important, both in its immediate results, and in the far-reaching influence which the principles adopted by him came to exercise over the development of colonial policy. In neither case had his own ambition been primarily that of a builder of empire, for his initial concern was for suppression of abuses, such as slave raiding, and for the introduction of order; his ultimate objective was to prepare the African people for self-rule under a tutelage which would assist them to develop their own characteristic institutions without premature modernization by European influences. All his own experiences, however, left him with the profound conviction that this result could best be achieved under British rule.

At the same time his own conception of rule reflected the personal characteristics which had made his success as an administrator. Given the acceptance of the principles he had evolved for guidance in the ruling of backward peoples, he believed that the best results were to be achieved by allowing the greatest measure of responsibility to those in charge of local administration, with a minimum of intervention from Whitehall. This feeling made him at times intolerant of superior authority; he was tenacious of his own views, and he did not readily share his responsibilities with others. But he won the confidence of the African people by his sincerity, and the affection of his colleagues and subordinates by his loyalty to their interests and by the unassuming simplicity of his manner. Although his record of administration and the influence exercised by his writings gave him a unique position in the colonial world, he was the most modest of the great proconsuls of empire. In private life his gentleness and kindness greatly endeared him to his friends.

In addition to the distinctions already recorded, Lugard was commander of the Legion of Honour (1917) and had the grand cross of the Order of Leopold II of Belgium (1936). He received the honorary degree of D.C.L. from the universities of Oxford (1912) and Durham (1913) and that of LL.D. from Hong Kong (1916), Cambridge (1928), and Glasgow (1929). He was gold medallist of the Royal Geographical Society (1902), the Royal African Society (1925), and the Royal Empire Society (1926), and a silver medallist of the Royal Scottish Geographical Society (1892).

The university of Hong Kong has a portrait of Lugard by André Cluysenaar (1915), and there is a portrait by W. J. Carrow (1936) and a miniature (1893) by Eleanor Howard (Mrs. E. J. Lugard) in the National Portrait Gallery. A statuette in bronze by H. H. Cawood was placed in 1938 in the Nigerian Court of the Imperial Institute. A cartoon by 'Spy' appeared in *Vanity Fair*, 19 December 1895.

[*The Times*, 12 April 1945; *Frederick Lugard (1858–1945)*, No. 8, Series A, British Commonwealth Leaflets, 1946; *Africa*, July 1945; Margery Perham, *Lugard, the Years of Adventure, 1858–1898*, 1956; private information; personal knowledge.]     HAILEY.

LUKE, first BARON (1873–1943), man of business and philanthropist. [See JOHNSTON, GEORGE LAWSON.]

LUTYENS, SIR EDWIN LANDSEER (1869–1944), architect, was born in London 29 March 1869, the eleventh of the fourteen children of Captain Charles Henry Augustus Lutyens of the 20th Foot, a great-grandson of Barthold Lutyens of Schleswig-Holstein who came to England and in 1745 acquired British nationality. Captain Lutyens, who had contributed inventions to musketry and was then well known as a painter of horses, lived at 16 Onslow Square, London, and at Thursley, Surrey. His wife, Mary Gallway, who came of an Irish Roman Catholic family, had adopted her husband's Protestantism. She declined Sir Edwin Landseer's offer to adopt her eleventh child but consented to his bearing his names.

'Ned' inherited originality from both parents and early showed a bent for drawing. A delicate child, he received an imperfect education at home. In after life he regretted his lack of public-schooling, which accentuated a natural shyness and sense of difference, but he acknowledged that it had given him leisure to teach himself the elements of building and how to use his eyes. In boyhood the drawings of Randolph Caldecott [q.v.], a family friend, inspired him, and a local builder in Godalming helped him to study the shapes and craftsmanship of traditional buildings in Surrey. In 1885 at the age of sixteen he was sent to what was later to become the Royal College of Art, South Kensington. Whilst there he made designs (unexecuted) for the restoration of the church at Thursley and won a small prize for architecture. Before completing the course he was placed in 1887 as pupil with (Sir) Ernest George [q.v.]. There he learnt little, but formed a long-enduring friendship with (Sir) Herbert Baker [q.v.], and an admiration which increased for R. Norman Shaw [q.v.]. In 1888 he was responsible for alterations to the village shop at Thursley, and when a family friend commissioned designs for a small country-house (Crooksbury, Farnham, exhibited at the Academy, 1890), he set up in practice at 6 Gray's Inn Square, before his twentieth birthday.

Lutyens now became acquainted with the buildings of Philip Webb [q.v.] and with Gertrude Jekyll. The former's integrity and freshness, the rural lore and practical wisdom of the latter, were important formative influences; and through Miss Jekyll he obtained various commissions in Surrey. In 1896 he built for her Munstead Wood, where he moulded traditional materials to his client's wishes with an imaginative sympathy and technical assurance which now began to set his work in a category by itself. He gained the reputation of a young man of genius, to which his unconventional manner and humour, concealing shy but intense seriousness, gave colour and charm.

Through Miss Jekyll's brother, (Sir) Herbert Jekyll, came the commission for the British pavilion at the Paris Exhibition of 1900; and the reputation of Munstead Wood led to a brilliant series of romantic country-houses. Of these, Orchards, Godalming; Goddards, Abinger; Grey Walls, Gullane, for Alfred Lyttelton; Deanery Garden, Sonning, for Edward Hudson, proprietor of *Country Life*; and Marsh Court, Stockbridge, a *tour de force* in chalk, are most characteristic. His skill and invention were also displayed in the restoration of Lindisfarne Castle, Holy Island, for Edward Hudson; Ashby St. Ledgers for Lord Wimborne; and on

Lambay Island, county Dublin, for Mr. Cecil Baring. Miss Jekyll collaborated in his garden designs, among which Hestercombe, Somerset (1904), is notable.

Inarticulate in words and intensely critical, never sketching but memorizing all that interested him, Lutyens had been chiefly animated until 1900 by the ideals of Webb and William Morris [q.v.]. But thenceforward, following Shaw, those of the English Renaissance inspired him increasingly. Determined since boyhood, and of necessity since his marriage, to be 'a successful architect', he saw that to secure 'big work' he must master classicism. He needed the discipline of the Orders, no less than the prizes offered by the grand manner, and resolved to prepare himself for the highest demands. Limited essays in 1902–4 preceded distinguished exercises in the style of Wren, such as the *Country Life* offices (1904), and led to his characteristic middle-period style—a simplified version of Queen Anne, relying on fine proportions and mouldings, with dominant roofs, chimneys, and fenestration-pattern—exemplified in Middlefield, Cambridgeshire (1908), and in additions to Temple Dinsley, Hertfordshire (1908).

In 1906, however, in seeming complete contrast, his original rendering of a high-Renaissance *palazzo* in the Roman Doric key at Heathcote, Ilkley, revealed the analytical mastery of the Orders on which his characteristic simplifications were based. In a letter to Baker he wrote: 'When right they [the Orders] are curiously lovely and unalterable like a plant-form . . . the perfection of the Order is far nearer nature than anything produced on impulse and accident-wise'. In an earlier letter he described the intense mental assimilation of every component which was necessary in order to handle them creatively. Heathcote established Lutyens as an architect of great distinction, able to restate first principles through the media of his own personality and local conditions. The Salutation, Sandwich (1911), and Ednaston Manor, Derby (1912), represent his middle style at its best; the latter is possibly his perfect country-house.

In 1908–9 as consulting architect to Hampstead Garden Suburb, Lutyens designed the churches and houses in the Square and its approaches, the whole presenting the most homogeneous contribution to social architecture and planning of the Edwardian period. Between 1909 and 1911 he was in Rome designing the British pavilion (indifferently adapted later as the British School at Rome) for the international exhibition, and in South Africa, designing the Rand war memorial and the Johannesburg Art Gallery. Italian baroque only confirmed his loyalty to Wren, and colonial lack of tradition convinced him that classicism outside Europe called for more careful, not looser, designing. In addition, several unexecuted works (London County Hall competition, the Edward VII memorial, and Dublin Art Gallery projects for Sir Hugh Lane, q.v.) helped to exercise him in the grand manner expressive of Edwardian imperialism. Designs for Castle Drogo, Drewsteignton, in granite on a specified hill-top site, were interjected on his main development. In this romantic conception (completed to a much reduced scheme in 1929) he successfully embodied the simplifications, optical refinements, and integrated planning of which he was becoming a master.

The great work for which he had been preparing for a decade came in 1912 with his recommendation by the Royal Institute of British Architects as architect to the New Delhi planning commission. He accepted the appointment on condition of his designing the central buildings, and was thus able to ensure that a magnificent city plan and the European classic style should be adopted. His appointment was confirmed in January 1913 with that of Baker (at his suggestion) as joint architect with equal status. Lord Hardinge of Penshurst [q.v.] selected Raisina Hill as the site for Viceroy's House, in preference to the level site first recommended by the commission, and later, on Baker's suggestion, the Secretariats were promoted to this eminence, whilst Viceroy's House with its ancillaries, which constituted Lutyens's main sphere, was moved back 1,100 feet. The architects co-operated closely in the joint design, of which the sketches were exhibited at the Academy in 1914. The ultimate result is the grandest modern expression of British architecture in the Renaissance style. But the intractable problem of the approach gradient, created by the change of site, could not be solved satisfactorily to both groups of buildings, and the compromise adopted constituted, in Lutyens's opinion, a grave aesthetic fault in the joint plan. It was the cause of intense bitterness between the two collaborators.

In Viceroy's House and its adjuncts,

however, Lutyens created one of the finest palaces in architectural history. Larger in area than Versailles, it covers 210,430 square feet, although much of this area is occupied by courts and colonnades —his classical restatement of Indian compounds and verandahs; and it is low in relation to the frontages (630 feet wide, 530 feet deep). This rectangle, designed to be seen from all sides, culminates in the dome of the Durbar Hall. The conception and proportions are classical, but of an order creatively assimilating Indian elements suited to the climate and light; for instance the polychrome Moslem tradition, expressed in the contrast of the red sandstone base with white above, and the shadow-casting Indian cornice (*chujja*) are integrated with the classic formula in a synthesis of East and West which is of original beauty. The intricate yet lucid plan, which combined the functions of an imperial palace and the viceroy's residence with extensive staff and service quarters, is at once closely knit and magnificent. Lutyens experienced prolonged agonies of labour in sustaining his aesthetic conception in the face of conflicting demands for accommodation and economy, and, in the decade of 1916–26, of indifference, criticism, and reduced budgets. Construction, begun in 1913, was intended to take four years, but, being delayed by the war, was not completed until 1930, at a cost of under a million pounds. The interior, for which he also designed the furniture, ranges from the majesty of the Durbar Hall to the country-house comfort of the viceroy's residence. In the remarkable garden he ingeniously blended Persian and European conceptions. The whole is characterized by extraordinary fertility of invention and aristocratic restraint. The supreme quality of this great building may perhaps be expressed as perfect proportioning, both in the technical sense and as implying 'balance between common sense and the urge of continuous invention'.

In 1917 Lutyens was appointed to the Imperial War Graves Commission, designing the 'War Stone' and one of the two variants of cross placed in all cemeteries. On 19 July 1919 Lloyd George invited him to design a temporary 'catafalque' to be erected in Whitehall for the peace procession at the end of that month. Lutyens designated it a 'Cenotaph' and produced a sketch the same evening. Although criticized for its undenominational character, this simple monument, to which his subtle use of Greek curvatures imparts mysterious vitality (there is not a straight line in it), was immediately acclaimed and was re-erected in Portland stone. During the 'twenties Lutyens designed upwards of fifty war memorials, including the cemetery at Étaples, the Australian memorial at Villers-Bretonneux, memorial arches at Leicester and New Delhi, the memorial to 'the Missing of the Somme' at Thiepval, and the Mercantile Marine memorial on Tower Hill.

In the 'War Stone' and Cenotaph Lutyens had begun to dispense with classical notation, whilst retaining its elements and introducing refinements of entasis, curvature, and set-back. Ratios of circles largely determine the proportions of his memorial arches. In this respect his final, 'elemental', phase of design carried the art of architecture to a plane on which few practitioners have worked since Hellenic times. Its most complete manifestation is the Thiepval monument which consists in series of proportionately related arches intersecting within cubic blocks which rise into a stepped pyramidal form: romantic in inspiration, classic in discipline, yet 'abstract' in design. Similar subtleties distinguish the monumental Britannic House, Finsbury Circus (1920–22), and Midland Bank, Poultry (1924–37), in association with the bank's official architects, J. A. Gotch [q.v.], and Charles Saunders. In the latter, his most learned building, the vertical diminution of its parts and its surface subtleties carry Renaissance design to unprecedented refinement. The interior arrangement of both these 'palaces of finance' is based on a very high degree of taste and ingenious planning. He was not interested in the steel framework except in so far as it enabled him to clothe it exquisitely. In his Westminster housing scheme, Page Street (1928–30), multiple blocks of small flats are rendered spectacular by his chequer-board surface treatment but are none the less efficiently planned. The British Embassy in Washington (1926–9), in his country-house style, is fitted effectively to an awkward and restricted site but has been criticized as inconveniently arranged. Gledstone Hall, Skipton (1923, with Mr. Richard Jaques), and Middleton Park, Bicester (1934, in partnership with his son, Robert), are important late country-houses. In Campion Hall, Oxford (1934), he admirably applied his technique of working in local material and tradition to the design of a modern college. From 1926 he collaborated on many large blocks of flats, such as Grosvenor House, Park Lane, seeking to relate their character and scale to Georgian tradition whilst imparting some distinction to their elevations. Between 1919 and 1930 some ninety works emanated from Lutyens's office at 17 Queen Anne's Gate, and he had personally worked on or approved every drawing; the 'record' for the office was the set of sixty-eight sheets for the British Embassy in Washington.

Lutyens's supreme work of the 'thirties was the designs, begun in 1929, for Liverpool Roman Catholic Cathedral, of which the foundation stone was laid in 1933. The crypt alone was finished when work was halted in 1941, but a model was made in 1934 and full detail drawings were completed in 1943. The domed cruciform church in brick and granite was designed to be second in size only to St. Peter's in Rome, which it exceeded in the diameter (168 feet) and total height of the dome (510 feet). The design, developing the principle of progression enunciated in the Thiepval monument, has been termed by A. S. G. Butler 'an epitome of all cathedrals ... it has adapted the features of several great types to a modern requirement and embodied them in a synthesis which touches sublimity'. Unfortunately in 1955 it was decided to adopt a simpler and reduced version of the design, which could, however, be completed in the foreseeable future.

When president of the Royal Academy Lutyens intended to direct scientific study to the aesthetic principles and intuitions of design for application to functional architecture, insisting, however, that art not science must have the last word in building. But the war of 1939–45 and infirmity diverted this aim into the Royal Academy plan for London which he initiated. His largely unexpressed ideal can be understood from papers printed in his *Life* written by Christopher Hussey (1950, *capp*. 16, 18, 19). Lutyens died in London, of bronchial sarcoma, 1 January, and his ashes were placed in St. Paul's Cathedral, 6 January, 1944. He had lived in London continuously, from 1897 until 1913 above his office at 29 Bloomsbury Square, and from 1919 until his death at 13 Mansfield Street. Lutyens married in 1897 Lady Emily, third daughter of the first Earl of Lytton [q.v.], after some family opposition. Although they were temperamentally disparate the marriage was for many years romantically happy. They had one son and four daughters.

It is claimed by Butler that Lutyens was one of the greatest masters of visible proportion and perhaps the greatest artist in building who has practised architecture. Apart from the high artistic integrity exemplified by his whole œuvre and life, his principal legacy to architecture may prove to be the method, demonstrated particularly in his cathedral designs, of applying mathematical ratios to functional designs. By nature kindly and sensitive, he was celebrated for a puckish humour. His wit, early cultivated as a defensive mannerism, was often penetrating, although sometimes censured as levity. Architecturally it saved his least inventive work from dullness, whilst contributing to the conviction of genius produced by his major achievements. In these his refusal to allow material considerations to coarsen, still less to control, his fine conceptions is justified by their perfect performance, which should probably be assessed as the last great efflorescence of the Renaissance spirit.

Lutyens was knighted in 1918, appointed K.C.I.E. in 1930, and received the O.M. in 1942. He became a fellow of the Royal Institute of British Architects in 1906, received the Royal gold medal for architecture in 1921, and was vice-president in 1924–5. He was awarded the gold medal of the American Institute of Architects in 1924 and in the same year he became a member of the Royal Fine Art Commission. He was elected A.R.A. in 1913, R.A. in 1920, and president in 1938. He was appointed an officer of the Legion of Honour in 1932, received the honorary degree of LL.D. from the university of Liverpool in 1928, and that of D.C.L. from the university of Oxford in 1934.

A portrait of Lutyens, by Meredith Frampton, belongs to the Art-Workers' Guild, of which he was master in 1933; another, by Augustus John, to Lord Ridley. Copies of Sir W. Reid Dick's bust in Government House, New Delhi, are at the Royal Institute of British Architects and the Royal Academy; a drawing by Sir William Rothenstein and a copy of the death mask are in the National Portrait Gallery. A portrait sketch by Edmund Dulac is in the possession of the family; other sketches and caricatures are reproduced in the *Life*.

[Lawrence Weaver, *Houses and Gardens of E. L. Lutyens*, 1913; Robert Lutyens, *Sir Edwin Lutyens, an Appreciation in Perspective*, 1942; Christopher Hussey, *The Life of Sir Edwin Lutyens*, and A. S. G. Butler, *The Architecture of Sir Edwin Lutyens* (composing in 4 volumes *The Lutyens Memorial Volumes*, 1950); C. H. Reilly, *Representative British Architects of the Present Day*, 1931; Sir Osbert Sitwell, *Great Morning*, 1948; *Journal* of the Royal Institute of British Architects, January 1944; *Builder*, 7 January 1944; personal knowledge.]　　　CHRISTOPHER HUSSEY.

LUXMOORE, SIR (ARTHUR) FAIRFAX (CHARLES CORYNDON) (1876–1944), judge, was born at Kilburn 27 February 1876, the eldest son of Arthur Coryndon Hansler Luxmoore, artist, of Danescliffe, St. Lawrence in the Isle of Thanet, and of his wife, Katherine Frances Jane, daughter of Richard Martin, of the Irish bar. Although related to an ancient Devon family, he was, as Archbishop Lang described him, 'in every fibre of his being a man of Kent'. His school was the King's School, Canterbury, in the shadow of the cathedral. In 1894 he entered Jesus College, Cambridge, and represented it in almost every sport. He was a good wicket-keeper, but in Rugby football he excelled, as a hard-working, thrusting forward, and he played against Oxford in 1896 and 1897. But as he often ruefully admitted, his studies were neglected and he passed his examinations without distinction. Called to the bar by Lincoln's Inn in 1899, he had the good fortune to become a pupil in the busy chambers of George (later Viscount) Cave [q.v.]. But his athletic career had still not reached its climax. He played for England against Scotland in 1900 and in the following year against Wales. Then he turned to learn his profession. His practice at the bar grew rapidly and he shared to the full the prosperity at 4 New Square. Early to bed and up again at dawn, he thrusted forward through the day. The unwieldy glazed doors of the fine set of Chippendale bookcases which still adorn his chambers were always flung open, and reports piled upon textbooks lay about the floor. Somehow he would steer a course between them as he paced up and down dictating drafts and opinions.

Soon after the end of hostilities—in 1919—he applied for silk, and quickly won a commanding position in the court of Sir J. M. Astbury [q.v.] to which he attached himself. His mature style of advocacy seemed to have been modelled on his forward play: restless, eager, forceful, but never unfair; and the secret of his success lay perhaps in complete mastery of his brief. In 1922 he became a bencher of Lincoln's Inn. Four years later he captained the Bar Golfing Society and revived the match between the English and Scottish bench and bar which had fallen into abeyance.

Luxmoore was appointed a judge of the Chancery division with the honour of knighthood in February 1929. As a judge he had an instinct for the point, and an astonishing memory for cases which guided him to wider principles. He did not plumb the depths of equity or explore the foundations of the legal system. But by careful analysis, clear exposition, and shrewd judgement, he embellished the mosaic which is English law. Of the earlier actions which he tried, *Vanderpant* v. *Mayfair Hotel Company, Limited*, [1930] 1 Ch. 138, which related to nuisance by noise, was of more than local interest; *In re Ross*, [1930] 1 Ch. 377, was an important decision upon the elusive doctrine of 'renvoi'; and *Spyer* v. *Phillipson*, [1931] 2 Ch. 183, clarified the law of tenant's fixtures. In 1934 in *Re Caus*, [1934] Ch. 162, he upheld the validity of a bequest for Masses—a decision still under debate. His promotion to the Court of Appeal in 1938, with the rank of privy counsellor, was in accordance with expectation.

There he participated in many important decisions, and dissenting judgements of his, in several instances, paved the way for successful appeals. One illustration of this arose out of rivalry between two trademarks for stockings, 'Rysta' and 'Aristoc'. In the House of Lords, [1945] A.C. 68, tribute was paid to his formulation of the problem. Indeed, he had an unrivalled knowledge of trademark and patent law. Another illustration is the case of *In re Grosvenor*, [1944] Ch. 138, which related to 'commorientes'; there his minority judgement was converted into a majority decision in the House of Lords of three to two. A third illustration may be found in the case of the '*Liteblue*' diary (*G. A. Cramp & Sons, Ltd.* v. *Frank Smythson, Ltd.*, [1944] A.C. 329). As he did not normally preside in the Court of Appeal or deliver the leading judgement, his extended dissenting judgements are apt to attract notice. But more often he was the powerful ally of the majority, and he played a very full part in the deliberations of the court.

But he was still a man of Kent, where he had bought Bilsington Priory for his home. In 1924 he stood as a Liberal for the Thanet division, but without success. He was mayor of New Romney (1920–26) and speaker of the Cinque Ports. From 1931 to 1940 he was chairman of the East Kent quarter-sessions and from 1929 to 1940 of the East Kent rating appeal committee. He was chairman of a committee which reported in 1943 on post-war agricultural education; and he was president of the Kent County Cricket Club. He loved Kent. 'He loved his home within it', wrote Archbishop Lang, 'its history, its fields, its sport, especially its cricket, and its people. . . . Friendliness, kindness of heart, goodwill to all— these things seemed to flow out of his personality as from a perpetual inward spring.'

But the war, the death of his two sons Charles and Coryndon on active service in November 1939 and June 1940, and the delayed reaction of overwork finally broke his health. In March 1944 he was taken ill in court. He returned to work, with vigour but without illusion. On 25 September 1944 he sat for the last time, and died in London after a heart attack the same evening. He was buried at Bilsington. He was survived by his wife, Dorothea Tunder, daughter of Thomas Popplewell Royle, of Chester, whom he had married in 1907, and by three daughters.

Death cut Luxmoore off from the law's highest honours. But few judges have won such distinction in so many fields. To his love of Kent, his school, and the cathedral must be added his devotion to Jesus College, of which he was elected an honorary fellow in 1938, to Lincoln's Inn, which he served as treasurer in the difficult days of 1943, and to every phase of the administration of justice. His energy was inexhaustible and his capacity for friendship infinite and enduring.

A posthumous portrait by James Bateman is in the possession of King's School, Canterbury.

[*The Times*, 26 September 1944; *Canterbury Cathedral Chronicle*, October 1944; *Cantuarian*, December 1944; Jesus College *Annual Report*, 1945; private information; personal knowledge.] RONALD F. ROXBURGH.

LYND, ROBERT WILSON (1879–1949), journalist and essayist, was born in Belfast 20 April 1879, the son of a distinguished Presbyterian minister, the

Rev. Robert John Lynd, D.D., and his wife, Sarah Rentoul. There were Presbyterian ministers among his ancestors on both sides, one of these, a great-grandfather, having emigrated from Scotland to Ireland. Robert, the second of seven children, was educated at the Royal Academical Institution, Belfast, and at Queen's College (later the Queen's University) where he graduated in 1899 and from which he received the honorary degree of D.Lit. in 1946. In 1901 in the romantic belief that England was an El Dorado for promising littérateurs, he set out to make his fortune, and lived precariously on scanty earnings for seven years. For a few months he worked at Manchester on the *Daily Dispatch*, and then moved to the London of his dreams. Sharing a studio in Kensington with an Ulster artist, Paul Henry, he lived hungrily on free-lance journalism and the conversation of his friends. His first regular job was on the staff of the twopenny weekly *To-day*, where he was paid thirty shillings a week for writing essays, dramatic criticism, book reviews, and gossip, a salary which was raised to two guineas when he also contributed short stories. A little later he added to his earnings by writing book reviews for *Black and White*.

It was in 1908 that Lynd joined the *Daily News*, at first as assistant literary editor under Mr. R. A. Scott-James. He became literary editor towards the end of 1912, and remained on that paper (which became the *News Chronicle* in 1930) until near the end of his life. Although the space allotted to reviews dwindled, he added distinction to his paper with signed essays and characteristic descriptive accounts of football and cricket matches, and other public events. But the best of his journalistic work appeared in weekly papers, first in the *Nation*, and then, from 1913 until the end of the war of 1939–45, in the *New Statesman*. For more than three decades many thousands of readers turned to this journal to read his genial, witty essays, signed 'Y. Y.'. Collected volumes of his essays appeared at frequent intervals, and occasionally other books, such as *Home Life in Ireland* (1909), *Ireland a Nation* (1919), *The Art of Letters* (1920), and *Dr. Johnson and Company* (1927).

Lynd was a romantic personality and a romanticist in temperament. His broad brow and waving hair, his lustrous dark eyes and regular nose and chin made up a face which was arresting and genial.

Devotion to Ireland and Irish nationalism gave a background to his interests, which in the main were humanistic and literary. He was not a scholar, but he wrote with sincerity, common sense, and good taste about authors and books, and with real insight when discussing authors whom he loved, like Johnson or Boswell. He was at his best as a light essayist. In this field he was unique. He went on week after week, year after year, with little effort turning out essays on trifling everyday topics, half-serious, half-whimsical, witty, gracious, engaging—delightful because they are the quintessence of a delightful personality. Enjoying conviviality in all its forms, a good talker and a good listener, generous, gentle, humorous, modest, Lynd had a host of friends and some whom he kept throughout his life.

In 1909 Lynd married Sylvia (died 1952), daughter of Albert Robert Dryhurst, assistant secretary at the British Museum. She herself became novelist, poet, and a leading member of the Book Society committee. Their home in Hampstead was the resort of poets, novelists, publishers, and editors. They had two daughters. In 1942 he was knocked down by a motor-cycle, and had several ribs broken. In consequence he suffered much pain, but went on writing. He died in Hampstead 6 October 1949. A drawing by Henry Lamb is in the National Portrait Gallery, and a bust in bronze by Lady Kennet is at the Queen's University, Belfast.

[*The Times*, 7 October 1949; *John O'London's Weekly*, 1 April 1949; Introduction by Sir Desmond MacCarthy to Robert Lynd's *Essays on Life and Literature*, 1951; private information; personal knowledge.]

R. A. SCOTT-JAMES.

LYON, CLAUDE GEORGE BOWES-, fourteenth EARL OF STRATHMORE AND KINGHORNE (1855–1944). [See BOWES-LYON.]

LYONS, SIR HENRY GEORGE (1864–1944), geographer and scientist, was born in London 11 October 1864, the son of Thomas Casey Lyons, who retired from the army with the rank of general after being governor of Bermuda, by his wife, Helen, daughter of George Young, of Apsley Towers, Ryde, Isle of Wight. Lyons was educated at Wellington College where he was a scholar and showed such aptitude for geology, under encouragement from the science master, that he was elected to the Geological Society in his nineteenth year. From the Royal Military Academy, Woolwich (1882-4), he proceeded as lieutenant, Royal Engineers, to Chatham for a course of military engineering (1884-6). Posted to Gibraltar he used the opportunity to explore its caves. A report, made at the age of twenty-three while he was at Aldershot, on the water supply from the Bagshot Sand was his first scientific publication.

The first major phase of Lyons's scientific career began with his posting, in 1890, to a company of the Royal Engineers at Cairo. He soon found opportunities in spare time and duty travel for researches in geology and Egyptology. In 1895-6 he was sent to Aswan to report on the stability and provide for the strengthening of the temples on the islet of Philae, then in prospect of being submerged for most of each year on the completion of the Aswan dam; his report to the Public Works Ministry on *The Island and Temples of Philae* established his reputation, and he was transferred in 1896, still with active rank in the Royal Engineers, to organize a Geological Survey of Egypt under the Egyptian Ministry of Public Works.

In 1898 Lord Cromer [q.v.], then building a sound basis for Egyptian economy, recognized Lyons as the man to carry out the Cadastral Survey which was needed. Lyons saw, however, that the conduct of two major surveys in succession, while serving as a British officer seconded for special duty, would occupy and compromise his whole career. If he were made director of a combined survey department, charged with the duties relevant to both projects, he offered to retire from the British Army and take permanent service under the Egyptian Government. This offer being accepted in 1901 Lyons was able to build up an organization of great efficiency. His Geological Survey spread widely into the contributory sciences of geodesy, meteorology, and hydrology, and his work on *The Physiography of the River Nile* (Cairo, 1906) was described, on high authority, as recently as 1944, as 'still the most important scientific work on the Nile'. He was able, on the other hand, to complete in eight years a task which most men would have found baffling in its difficulties—his *Cadastral Survey of Egypt* (Cairo, 1908). Meanwhile he had originated and developed, from his combined department, an observatory and a meteorological office. He appears to

have been the first to explore the upper atmosphere by use of instrument-carrying kites. He made the arrangements for British, American, and Russian expeditions to observe a solar eclipse at Aswan in 1905, and for a wider visit to Egypt by members of the British Association. In 1906 he was elected F.R.S. Retiring from Egypt in 1909 he received the grand cordon of the Medjidieh Order.

After two years as university lecturer in geography at Glasgow, Lyons became secretary to the advisory council and assistant to the director of the Science Museum, South Kensington, in 1912, and began the second main phase of his career. He became the keeper of a department in the museum in 1914, but, when war broke out, he was recalled to organize recruiting for the Royal Engineers, and later, as commandant in London, to create a special meteorological service for the Royal Engineers. He then became successively administrator and director of the Meteorological Office where he relieved Sir Napier Shaw [q.v.] until the end of the war.

In 1919, with the retiring rank of colonel, Lyons returned to the Science Museum, where he succeeded Sir Francis Grant Ogilvie as director in 1920. A new building, begun in 1922 and opened in 1928, enabled him completely to reorganize the museum on progressive educational lines. He was knighted in 1926 and retired in 1933.

Meanwhile recognition and opportunity had come to Lyons in a wider scientific community. In 1919 he had become secretary-general of the International Union of Geodesy and Geophysics, and in 1928 succeeded Sir Arthur Schuster [q.v.] as general secretary of the International Research Council, later the International Council of Scientific Unions. He became foreign secretary of the Royal Society in 1928 and a year later its treasurer, holding that office, to the great benefit of the Society's funds, of its business methods, and of the amenities of its quarters, until 1939. As chairman of the committee charged with the matter, he was largely responsible for the edition of the Royal Society's *Record* published in 1940, and the issue of the Society's periodical *Notes and Records* was due to his initiative. In 1940, although displaced from his house and library by bombing, and increasingly crippled by arthritis, Lyons began, and completed in the following years, his book, *The Royal Society, 1660-*

*1940; A History of its Administration under its Charters*, which was not published until after his death which took place at Great Missenden 10 August 1944.

Henry Lyons served his fellow scientists in a number of other directions, as honorary secretary of the Royal Geographical Society, president of the Royal Meteorological Society, and member of the councils of the Geological and the Royal Astronomical societies; while his effective work for the Athenaeum, as chairman of its executive committee, earned the gratitude of all its members. He acted as chairman of a committee appointed in 1935 by the Ministry of Health and the secretary of state for Scotland to advise on the Inland Water Survey of Great Britain. He received the Victoria medal of the Royal Geographical Society (1911), the Symons gold medal of the Royal Meteorological Society (1922), and the honorary degrees of D.Sc. (Oxford, 1906), and Sc.D. (Dublin, 1908).

In 1896 he married Helen Julia, daughter of Philip Charles Hardwick, architect, of London, granddaughter of Philip Hardwick [q.v.]. They had one son and one daughter.

[Sir Henry Dale in *Obituary Notices of Fellows of the Royal Society*, No. 13, November 1944; *Nature*, 9 September 1944; private information; personal knowledge.]

H. H. Dale.

LYTTELTON, EDWARD (1855–1942), schoolmaster, divine, and cricketer, was born at Hagley, Worcestershire, 23 July 1855, the seventh of the eight sons of George William Lyttelton, fourth Baron Lyttelton [q.v.], by his first wife, Mary, daughter of Sir Stephen Richard Glynne, eighth baronet, and sister of Mrs. W. E. Gladstone. He was a brother of Arthur Temple Lyttelton, Alfred Lyttelton, and Sir Neville Gerald Lyttelton [qq.v.].

At Eton, as at Cambridge, Lyttelton was more distinguished as an athlete than as a scholar, although he became a foundation scholar at Trinity College in April 1877, and was placed in the second class of the classical tripos in 1878. He was captain of the Eton eleven in 1874 and also of that famous Cambridge eleven of 1878 which won all its matches, including a defeat of the Australians. He was the only English batsman to make a century against the Australians in that year, and for five years he was one of the outstanding batsmen in the country. His skill at cricket (and at fives) remained with him until he finally left Eton in 1916, and he never lost his enthusiasm for the game.

After two years as an assistant master at Wellington College, he joined the staff at Eton in 1882. For eight years he was one of the most stimulating and beloved of tutors, and after his ordination (deacon 1884, priest 1886) a most effective preacher; it was to his early training at Cuddesdon that he attributed the real awakening of his religious instincts. In 1890 he was appointed master of Haileybury, and fifteen years later he returned to Eton as headmaster in succession to Edmond Warre [q.v.]. At both schools he won the gratitude and affection of countless boys, and even those of his colleagues who criticized some of his actions and were suspicious of his educational policy never failed to regard him as one of the most lovable of men. But organization was to him 'a nightmare', and indeed a 'dull' one, and he did not attempt to dissemble his lack of interest in financial questions. It was not without relief that he resigned in 1916, although a lesser man might have resented some wholly unjustified criticism of his attitude towards the Germans arising from a sermon which he preached at St. Margaret's, Westminster, in March 1915.

The freedom which Lyttelton now gained enabled him to show the true greatness of his character, and the spiritual crisis through which he then passed released unexpected powers. After a brief curacy at St. Martin-in-the-Fields, and the temporary charge of Sidestrand, a small Norfolk parish (1918–20), he became dean of Whitelands Training College, Chelsea, in 1920, for which he did invaluable work until 1929 when he retired after a serious operation. As an honorary canon of Norwich from 1931, he was indefatigable in his work in Norfolk, where he was in constant demand as preacher and speaker. The remarkable affection and esteem which he won there were his also at Lincoln, where the last year and a half of his life was spent.

Lyttelton was brilliant both in talk and as a letter-writer; full of humour and pungency, qualities which are somewhat inadequately represented in his published works. His love of music and his passion for fresh air were tastes which never failed him; no one was ever readier to accept new ideas and to present them in arresting phrases; and if his enthusiasm was sometimes indiscriminate it served to reveal the youthfulness of his temperament and the saintliness of his nature. He married in 1888 Caroline Amy (died 1919), daughter of the Very Rev. John West, dean of St. Patrick's, Dublin; they had two daughters. He died at the Old Palace, Lincoln, 26 January 1942.

A drawing by Sir William Rothenstein is at Eton College and a portrait by J. Harris-Brown at Haileybury.

[E. Lyttelton, *Memories and Hopes*, 1925; private information; personal knowledge.]

C. A. ALINGTON.

LYTTON, second EARL OF (1876–1947). [See BULWER-LYTTON, VICTOR ALEXANDER GEORGE ROBERT.]

MACARTNEY, SIR GEORGE (1867–1945), consul-general at Kashgar, was born at Nankin 19 January 1867, the eldest son of (Sir) Samuel Halliday Macartney [q.v.] and his first wife, a Chinese lady of princely family. George passed his early years in China and spoke the language perfectly. He was educated at Dulwich College and in France where he obtained his *B. ès L.* in 1886. At the end of 1888 he entered the foreign department of the Government of India and as assistant political officer and Chinese interpreter accompanied the British troops which were sent to drive the Tibetans out of Sikkim.

The qualities displayed by Macartney on this occasion led to his being sent in 1890 with (Sir) Francis Younghusband [q.v.] to Chinese Turkestan. When Younghusband returned to India in the following year Macartney remained in Kashgar. The whole of his successful career of twenty-eight years was spent in this isolated and inaccessible post. At first he had no official standing and his position in the eyes both of the Chinese administrators and of the Russian consul-general was extremely difficult. In spite of this he was able to maintain British interests and to thwart Russian pretensions in the days when these two powers were active rivals in Central Asia. In 1908 his position was regularized and he was appointed the first British consul in Chinese Turkestan. His difficulties were not over, however, for the Chinese Government at first refused to recognize his appointment, claiming that consuls could only be sent to treaty ports. Two years later the assent of the Chinese Government was obtained

and the post was raised to that of consul-general. Even then he did not receive the measure of support and encouragement which the Russians accorded to their representative. Nevertheless his influence, immense with the Mohammedan population of Kashgar, spread far beyond its environs. Supported by the British aksakals (as the leaders of the British subjects in the different districts were called), he helped and protected his fellow subjects and took care as well of the interests of the Afghans who at that time had no representation in Chinese Turkestan. The abolition of slavery in that country was largely due to Macartney.

When in 1918 the final time for retirement came, Macartney travelled the fourteen days' journey through the mountains to the Russian railway and reached Tashkent where a British mission was endeavouring to establish friendly contact with the Bolshevik government. Macartney's valuable assistance to the mission showed how his influence had spread from China to the capital of Russian Turkestan. The prospect of reaching England through the warring fronts of 1918 seemed so remote that Macartney turned round and undertook the long and wearisome journey back to India, over the Alai mountains, the Pamirs, the gorges of Gilgit and Kashmir, to the distant railhead of Rawalpindi —a fitting end to a career already filled with so much travel and adventure.

In 1896 Macartney received the thanks of Her Majesty's Government for his work on the Anglo-Russian Pamir boundary commission. He was appointed C.I.E. in 1900 and K.C.I.E. in 1913. In his retirement he settled in Jersey where he lived throughout the German occupation. He died 19 May 1945 just after the Channel Islands had been freed from the enemy.

In 1898 Macartney married Catherina Theodora, daughter of James Borland, of Castle Douglas, Kirkcudbrightshire. She lived for many years in Kashgar where the rare visitors were always assured of the ever open hospitality of the Macartneys. They had two sons and one daughter.

[Lady Macartney, *An English Lady in Chinese Turkestan*, 1931; private information; personal knowledge.] F. M. BAILEY.

McCARTHY, DAME (EMMA) MAUD (1858–1949), Army matron-in-chief, was born 22 September 1858 at Sydney, New South Wales, Australia, the eldest daughter of William Frederick McCarthy, solicitor, and his wife, Emma Mary à

Beckett. She was educated privately and after spending three years in England decided to enter the London Hospital to train as a nurse (1891–3), thereby following a strong philanthropic tendency towards medicine and nursing which had been evinced in her family for generations; one of her ancestors was William Harvey [q.v.].

On the outbreak of war in South Africa Maud McCarthy, then a sister in Sophia women's ward, was one of the six nurses selected from the London Hospital by Queen Alexandra (then Princess of Wales) to go to South Africa as her own special nursing sisters. The day she left the London Hospital, one of the medical staff wrote with a diamond on the window of her ward sitting-room 'Ichabod'. She served with distinction throughout the war, receiving the Queen's and King's medals, the Royal Red Cross (to which in 1918 she was awarded a bar), and a special decoration from Queen Alexandra on her return to England in 1902. Thereupon she became closely concerned with the formation of Queen Alexandra's Imperial Military Nursing Service (later Queen Alexandra's Royal Army Nursing Corps) in which she served as a matron until 1910 when she became principal matron at the War Office.

On the outbreak of war in 1914 she went to France in the first ship to leave England with members of the British Expeditionary Force. In 1915 she was installed at Abbeville as matron-in-chief of the British armies in France, in charge of the whole area from the Channel to the Mediterranean wherever British, imperial, and American nurses were working. In August 1914 the numbers in her charge were 516; by the time of the armistice they had increased to 5,440 on the lines of communication and a further 954 in casualty clearing stations. They came from Canada, Australia, New Zealand, South Africa, Portugal, and the United States as well as from the United Kingdom; not all were trained nurses, for some 1,729 were from voluntary aid detachments. To keep this vast body working harmoniously and efficiently called for administrative talent of the highest order. In 1917 and 1918 there were casualties from air raids and in the latter year the influenza epidemic also took its toll. The constant shortage of trained nurses, the continual movements of position, the personal requirements of individuals: all these raised problems which Maud McCarthy solved with tact

and skill. It is believed that she was the only head of a department in the British Expeditionary Force who remained in her original post throughout the war—a great tribute to her strength of body, mind, and spirit. She was appointed G.B.E. in 1918 and awarded the Florence Nightingale medal and several foreign decorations. When in August 1919 she sailed for England from Boulogne, whither she had transferred her headquarters the previous year, representatives of the French Government and Medical Service were among those who assembled to do her honour.

In 1920 she was appointed matron-in-chief, Territorial Army Nursing Service, and although she retired five years later the advancement of nursing remained her great interest until she died. She had the highest ideals in her profession and an unselfish, modest character. Her devotion to duty and self-sacrifice were an inspiration to all who worked with her. To her own family she was a tower of strength and in every circumstance they turned for advice and comfort to her home in Chelsea where she died, unmarried, at the age of ninety, 1 April 1949. A pastel by Austin O. Spare is in the Imperial War Museum.

[Sir W. G. Macpherson, (Official) *History of the Great War. Medical Services, General History*, vol. ii, 1923; *The Times*, 8 April 1949; private information.]

HELEN S. GILLESPIE.

MacCOLL, DUGALD SUTHERLAND (1859–1948), painter, critic, and art gallery director, was born in Glasgow 10 March 1859, the eldest child and only son of the Rev. Dugald MacColl, a Presbyterian minister, by his wife, Janet Mathieson, daughter of a banker. His schooling began at Glasgow Academy, and from 1873, when his father became minister of the Kensington Presbyterian Church, he spent three years at University College School, Hampstead. He then entered University College, London, graduated M.A. and won the Gerstenberg memorial prize in 1881, and was made a fellow of his college in 1882. In 1881 he proceeded to Lincoln College, Oxford, where he was a scholar. He won the Newdigate prize in 1882 and was placed in the second class of the honours list in *literae humaniores* in 1884. The years 1887–9 were occupied with travel in Italy and Greece, with a visit to Constantinople and a glance at Germany, Holland, and Belgium.

MacColl's travels were undertaken primarily to acquire knowledge of great works of art, and, once back in England, he took instruction from Frederick Brown [q.v.] at the Westminster School of Art. Between 1890 and 1896 he was art critic to the *Spectator*, then, after a short interval, until 1906 on the *Saturday Review*. Possessed of a small private income left to him by his mother, he was very active as a painter, critic, editor, and lecturer. In December 1893 the new Goupil Galleries opened with an exhibition of his water-colours; and he was a regular exhibitor at the New English Art Club from 1892, becoming a member in 1896. In 1902 he published a large and authoritative work on *Nineteenth Century Art*, which was one of the earliest books to rate the French Impressionists at their true worth. In 1900, at the Glasgow Exhibition, he had organized the first British exhibition devoted to the painters of this school.

He edited the *Architectural Review* from 1901 until 1905 as representative of the committee for literary direction. During 1903, in the *Saturday Review*, he engaged in the first of the big controversies which were to stir his Highland blood throughout a long life. Examining the will of Sir F. L. Chantrey [q.v.], he said in forthright fashion that the administrators were departing from its terms, and broadly hinted that they had long been buying mediocre work. *The Administration of the Chantrey Bequest* was published as a book in 1904, and thereafter a government committee initiated reforms. It was the year 1903 also which saw the foundation of the National Art-Collections Fund, largely through the instrumentality of MacColl. He fought hard for the new men emerging in the artistic field, among them P. Wilson Steer [q.v.] and (Sir) Muirhead Bone.

In 1906 MacColl was appointed keeper of the Tate Gallery, where he carried out an energetic and forward-looking programme, which included the showing of many Turners unearthed from store, and the opening of an Alfred Stevens room. In 1911 he was considered to be under threat of tuberculosis, so he resigned and went to Fiesole. Yet before the year was out the fears had proved groundless and MacColl was installed as keeper of the Wallace Collection where he remained until 1924. Here again he acted with characteristic energy, rehanging and re-cataloguing the whole collection and carrying out useful researches. He was also a trustee of the Tate Gallery (1917–27) and a member of the Royal Fine Art Commission (1925–9).

In 1921 MacColl revived his connexion with the *Saturday Review*, and when (Sir) Gerald Barry, the editor, parted company with his proprietor and founded the *Week-end Review* in 1930, MacColl went over with the rest of the staff. During the late 'twenties he was engaged in the most violent, and the only unsuccessful, of all his artistic campaigns. John Rennie's Waterloo Bridge had begun to collapse, and for several years MacColl advocated its repair and preservation against Mr. Herbert Morrison and the massed cohorts of the London County Council, who at length had their way in securing its demolition and replacement.

MacColl suffered no abatement of energy and enthusiasm as he progressed towards old age, but continued painting, authorship, and controversy. His *Confessions of a Keeper* appeared in 1931; in 1940 he collected the *Poems* written over a period of sixty years, which had a quietly original, lyrical vein; in 1945, at the age of eighty-six, he won the James Tait Black memorial prize with his *Life Work and Setting of Philip Wilson Steer*, one of the more notable artistic biographies of the period. Lecturer, connoisseur, critic, poet, curator, and a water-colourist of sensitive technique and fine feeling for colour, he was highly versatile, volcanically energetic, utterly honest and self-confident. Good friends, and what he deemed to be good causes, claimed his undivided loyalty. He was generous-minded, and had a keen business sense which perhaps owed something to the banking line to which his mother's family belonged. His marriage, in 1897, to Andrée Adèle Désirée Jeanne (died 1945), daughter of Dr. Emile Zabé, of Neuilly (Seine), gave a new zest and colour to his life. Elegant, witty, skilled in all the social graces, Mrs. MacColl was a noted beauty, whose portrait by Wilson Steer (in the possession of the family) was one of that artist's more successful figure pieces. There were two sons of the marriage. MacColl died at Hampstead 21 December 1948.

He received the honorary degrees of LL.D. from Glasgow (1907) and D.Litt. from Oxford (1925). He was a council member (1925) of the British School at Rome, and a founder-member of the Contemporary Art Society. He was an honorary associate of the Royal Institute of British Architects and an honorary member of the English and Scottish Royal Societies of Painters in Water Colours. A portrait by D. G. MacLaren is in the Tate Gallery and a pencil drawing in the Scottish National Portrait Gallery. Some excellent caricatures by Henry Tonks appear in Joseph Hone's *Life of Henry Tonks* (1939). A bronze by Dora Gordine is in the collection of the Hon. Richard Hare, and a drawing by Wilson Steer is owned by Professor Thomas Bodkin. MacColl also appears in Sir William Orpen's 'Hommage à Manet' in the Manchester City Art Gallery.

[*The Times*, 22 December 1948; *Journal of the Royal Institute of British Architects*, January 1949; D. S. MacColl, 'A Batch of Memories', *Week-end Review*, 20 December 1930 et seq.; private information.]

HERBERT B. GRIMSDITCH.

McEWEN, SIR JOHN BLACKWOOD (1868–1948), principal of the Royal Academy of Music, was born at Hawick 13 April 1868, the son of the Rev. James McEwen and his wife, Jane Blackwood. His early life was spent in Glasgow where his father was minister of Sydney Place church. He graduated M.A. at the university in 1888 and studied music in Glasgow until 1891, holding successive choirmaster appointments at St. James's Free Church and Lanark parish church. In 1893 he entered the Royal Academy of Music, studying with Ebenezer Prout [q.v.], Frederick Corder, and Tobias Matthay. He returned to Glasgow in 1895 as a teacher of pianoforte and composition at the Athenaeum School of Music (later the Royal Scottish Academy of Music) and was appointed choirmaster of Greenock South parish church. In 1898 he went to London as professor of harmony and composition at the Royal Academy of Music of which in 1924 he became principal in succession to Sir Alexander Mackenzie [q.v.].

McEwen had a wide diversity of gifts as scholar, teacher, composer, and administrator. In spite of the considerable volume, range, and importance of his compositions, his influence will chiefly be felt on account of his distinguished services to the Royal Academy of Music. Both as a teacher and as an administrator his attitude was progressive. His pupils found him sympathetic to the new ideas which were then fermenting in all creative forms of art, while he saw the claims of the traditional and the academic in balanced perspective. As one of the founders of the Society of British Composers and of the Anglo-French Music Publishing Company he displayed an energetic interest in the development of British music and in its wider recognition. He was responsible for important reforms in Academy activities; chief among these were his appointment of Sir Henry Wood [q.v.] to train and conduct the orchestra, and the intensified importance and greater scope given to training in opera and chamber music.

For one so occupied with teaching and administration the volume of McEwen's compositions and of his writings on musical theory and aesthetic is impressive. Although a considerable number of his compositions remain unpublished, his output covers a wide range and includes an opera, choral works, symphonies, and smaller works for orchestra, numerous string quartets, songs, and pieces for piano. His best orchestral works, particularly the 'Solway' Symphony and the Border ballad entitled 'Grey Galloway', deserve a more secure place in the concert repertoire. His craftsmanship and musical invention in writing for string quartet is impressive, and he can with truth be called a pioneer of the renascence of British chamber music composition which took place during the first quarter of the century. Although there was no immediate and easy charm in his strong musical personality, a closer intimacy with his work reveals the strength and virility of his musical thoughts and arouses respect for the economy with which he expresses them.

In 1931 McEwen was knighted, and in 1936 he retired from the Academy where hangs his portrait painted by R. G. Eves. He received the honorary degree of D.Mus. from Oxford University in 1926 and of LL.D. from Glasgow in 1933.

McEwen married in 1902 Hedwig Ethel (died November 1948), daughter of H. A. B. Cole; there were no children. He died at his home in London 14 June 1948.

[*Grove's Dictionary of Music and Musicians*; *Cobbett's Cyclopedic Survey of Chamber Music*; *Musical Times*, July 1948.]

R. S. THATCHER.

MacIVER, DAVID RANDALL- (1873–1945), archaeologist and anthropologist. [See RANDALL-MACIVER.]

MACKAIL, JOHN WILLIAM (1859–1945), classical scholar, literary critic, and poet, was born at Ascog in the parish of

Kingarth, Isle of Bute, 26 August 1859, the only son and second child of the Rev. John Mackail, a Free Church minister who, after service in Malta and Calcutta, had retired in 1852 owing to ill health, by his wife, Louisa Irving, youngest daughter of Aglionby Ross Carson [q.v.], rector of Edinburgh High School. He was educated at Ayr Academy, the rector of which was James Macdonald, father of (Sir) George Macdonald [q.v.] with whom Mackail formed a close friendship. In 1874 he entered Edinburgh University and was greatly influenced by W. Y. Sellar [q.v.], then professor of humanity, by whose advice he sat for a scholarship at Balliol College, Oxford. He was elected to the Warner exhibition (1877) with the rank of honorary scholar.

Benjamin Jowett [q.v.] was then master of Balliol and Mackail's tutors were Evelyn Abbott, R. L. Nettleship, and J. L. Strachan-Davidson [qq.v.], with whom he maintained a lasting friendship. Among the brilliant group of his contemporaries were Samuel Alexander, George Curzon (later Marquess Curzon of Kedleston), (Sir) Sidney Lee, and H. C. Beeching [qq.v.]. Mackail obtained first classes in classical moderations (1879) and literae humaniores (1881), won the Hertford (1880), Ireland (1880), Craven (1882), and Derby (1884) university scholarships, and was without question the most brilliant undergraduate scholar of his time. He was also awarded the Newdigate prize in 1881 for a poem on Thermopylae. He joined with Beeching and Bowyer Nichols in producing three volumes of verse entitled Mensae Secundae (1879), Love in Idleness (1883), and Love's Looking-glass (1891), and contributed to the series of college epigrams known as The Masque of B-ll--l (1881), on which he wrote an article in The Times in 1939.

In 1882 Mackail was elected to a fellowship at Balliol, but instead of pursuing the academic career which lay open to him, he accepted, in 1884, a place in the Education Department of the Privy Council, which later became the Board of Education. Appointed assistant secretary in 1903, he took a prominent part in the establishment of a system of secondary education under the Act of 1902, and in organizing the inspection voluntarily sought by many of the public schools. When in 1919 he resigned from the Board his official life was over.

Meanwhile side by side with his work in the office Mackail was developing the life of a writer and critic, in which he was destined to reach high distinction, if not a wide popular appeal. His writings fall naturally into three main classes: those on classical poetry, those on general literature, and biographies. At first, as was natural, Greek and Latin literature claimed his attention and that interest was never lost. In 1885 he published a translation in prose of Virgil's Aeneid; its manner was traditional and, apart from an occasional brilliant phrase, it was not striking. Virgil (he insisted that this was the correct English spelling of the name) remained always his main interest among Latin poets. He completed his prose translation by versions of the Eclogues and Georgics, published together in 1889, wrote brilliantly of him in his Latin Literature (1895) and in articles included in subsequent books, and in 1923 contributed a volume on Virgil and his Meaning to the World of To-day to the American series of 'Our Debt to Greece and Rome'. The culmination of his work in this field was reached in 1930, when he published an edition of the Aeneid; in this he purposely excluded detailed comment on text, grammar, and metre, and treated it as a great work of poetry, noting points of diction and expression passed over by previous editors, often suggesting the exact English equivalent, and insisting upon the structure of the whole poem and its individual books.

Mackail's best-known contribution to the study of Latin in general is the volume on Latin Literature. This book has been a guide and an inspiration to many generations of students not only for the brilliance of its expression, but for its insight and freshness; it covers the whole range of Latin from the earliest poets to the first Christian writers. His works on Greek, if not so numerous, are substantial and important. In 1890, at the age of thirty, he published a remarkable edition of Select Epigrams from the Greek Anthology. The poems are accompanied by neat prose translations and the notes treat them as living expressions of vital experience. In 1903, 1905, and 1910 appeared three volumes of a translation of the Odyssey, this time not in prose but in a rhyming quatrain; the verse runs smoothly, but most readers have probably felt that the vehicle does not aptly reproduce Homer. In 1910 Mackail also published a volume of Lectures on Greek Poetry; he treats it as a continuous whole, regarding Homer as 'medieval', Sophocles as fully classical, and the Alexandrians as the Romantics in the first stages of decline.

In 1906 Mackail was elected professor of poetry at Oxford, and in the five years of his tenure of the chair attracted large audiences and covered a wide field. Three volumes resulted: the *Lectures on Greek Poetry* have already been noticed, but in the other two he passed outside the classics into his second field and revealed his knowledge of the poetry of other languages and in particular of English. *The Springs of Helicon* (1909) is devoted to studies of Chaucer, Spenser, and Milton; he sets each in his own background and regards them as constituting a progressive development. In the *Lectures on Poetry* (1911), a more miscellaneous collection, Mackail included not only Dante, but Arabic poetry, regarded as the precursor of French ballad-epics. There are also two lectures on Shakespeare, who held for Mackail in English poetry the place occupied in Latin by Virgil, and to him he returned in 1930 in his *Approach to Shakespeare*, which includes an enlightening analysis of each of the plays. *Studies of English Poets* (1926) and *Studies in Humanism* (1938) are collections of essays and lectures written at different times.

This large output was from first to last instinct with the author's view that poetry is at once the interpretation and the pattern of life. Behind all the volumes lies a wealth of learning often concealed in order to expound a broad interpretation, and a deep love of poetry, which it was his life's work to awaken in others.

The third field of Mackail's activity was that of biography. *The Life and Letters of George Wyndham*, which he published with Guy Wyndham in two volumes in 1925, and the memoir of his old tutor Strachan-Davidson (1926), are both sympathetic studies, but the *Life of William Morris* (1899) is something more, for it has appealed to a wide public as a faithful portrait of a great man and his times. It is among the best of modern biographies.

Many honours came to Mackail. He was president of the Classical Association, which he had helped to found, in 1922–3; he was also president of the English Association in 1929–30 and of the newly formed Virgil Society in 1945. In 1914 he was elected F.B.A. and served as president from 1932 to 1936. In 1924 he was appointed professor of ancient literature in the Royal Academy. He received honorary degrees from the universities of Edinburgh, St. Andrews, Oxford, Cambridge, London, Belfast, and Adelaide. He was elected an honorary fellow of Balliol in 1922. In 1935 he was appointed O.M.

Mackail was a tall man and always good-looking; in later life his white hair added a dignity and beauty to his face. He had a fine voice and a meticulously clear enunciation, enhanced by a trace of Scottish intonation. He was suave and courteous and always an interesting talker, but reticent as to his own beliefs and feelings. In 1888 he married Margaret, only daughter of the painter (Sir) Edward Burne-Jones [q.v.], and had one son and two daughters. The son, Denis Mackail, and the elder daughter, Angela Thirkell, made reputations as novelists. J. W. Mackail died in London 13 December 1945.

[Cyril Bailey in *Proceedings* of the British Academy, vol. xxxi, 1945; private information; personal knowledge.]

CYRIL BAILEY.

McKENNA, REGINALD (1863–1943), statesman and banker, was born in London 6 July 1863, the fifth son and youngest child of William Columban McKenna, a civil servant, by his wife, Emma, daughter of Charles Hanby. The family came from county Monaghan and were Roman Catholic, but the father, who had obtained his appointment through the influence of Daniel O'Connell [q.v.], changed his religion and the children were all brought up as Protestants. McKenna was educated at St. Malo and at Ebersdorf, and then, after a short time at King's College School, London, he went to Trinity Hall, Cambridge, as a scholar. He took his degree among the senior optimes in the mathematical tripos of 1885 and rowed bow in the winning university crew of 1887, in which year he was called to the bar by the Inner Temple. In 1916 he became an honorary fellow of Trinity Hall.

In 1892 McKenna stood unsuccessfully as Liberal candidate for Clapham, but in 1895 he was returned for North Monmouthshire, which he continued to represent until 1918. While still at Cambridge he had attracted the notice of Sir Charles Dilke [q.v.], and during the period of Liberal eclipse they worked closely together. McKenna joined in the fray over the Education Act of 1902 and was prominent in organizing the Free Trade Union in opposition to tariff or fiscal reform. He attracted notice by his prompt attack on the distinction made by (Sir) Austen Chamberlain [q.v.] between stripped and unstripped tobacco in the budget debates and was rewarded in 1905 by appointment as financial secretary to the Treasury on the formation of Campbell-Bannerman's administration.

After only one year, McKenna was called up to the Cabinet as president of the Board of Education in January 1907 and was sworn of the Privy Council. He so far established a reputation for administrative skill that Asquith, on becoming prime minister in April 1908, recommended him for appointment as first lord of the Admiralty, a few weeks before McKenna's marriage to Pamela (died 1943), younger daughter of Sir Herbert Jekyll, of Munstead Park, Godalming, by whom he had two sons.

McKenna arrived at the Admiralty at a time when opinion, both professional and lay, was sharply divided on naval matters. The first sea lord, Sir John (later Lord) Fisher, had initiated the construction of *Dreadnoughts* against opinion led by Sir Reginald Custance [qq.v.], and in the Cabinet there was a struggle between the economy school led by the chancellor of the Exchequer, Lloyd George, and the president of the Board of Trade, (Sir) Winston Churchill, on one hand, and those who, on the other hand, like McKenna, believed in the necessity of making provision against the German danger. McKenna had to decide whether the safety of the country was to be jeopardized for the sake of a full programme of social reform, or the reverse. His education abroad had forced on him the conviction that war between France and Germany was an ever-present danger, and he believed that the Lansdowne convention of 1904 had entangled Great Britain in continental affairs without hope of isolation. He requested that six *Dreadnoughts* should be sanctioned in 1909 and six in each of the two following years. The economy school considered four enough, but a threat of resignation by McKenna, who was supported by Sir Edward Grey (later Viscount Grey of Fallodon, q.v.), brought a compromise. Four were to be sanctioned at once, and four later in the year if need were shown. In July McKenna announced that the contingent four were to be built; in each of the two following years five were laid down; and to his determination was due the numerical superiority of the Grand Fleet over the High Seas Fleet in 1914.

The constitutional crisis created by the rejection of the finance bill of 1909 in the House of Lords masked from the public another grave difference within the Cabinet, between the 'admirals' and the 'generals' on strategy, which came to a head in 1911 when the dispatch of the German gunboat *Panther* to Agadir brought an immediate risk of war. Lord Haldane and (Sir) Henry Wilson [qq.v.] envisaged active intervention on the continent and required the Admiralty to be prepared to provide transport for the British divisions. McKenna and Sir Arthur Wilson [q.v.] maintained that the enemy's fleet must first be disposed of. Haldane threatened to resign unless the Admiralty would work in harmony with the War Office, but McKenna refused to give way, and the deadlock was only resolved in October when Asquith offered the Admiralty to (Sir) Winston Churchill and the Home Office to McKenna. In the Cabinet deliberations before war was declared in August 1914 McKenna was one of the 'moderating intermediate body', and later Asquith testified to the very sensible and loyal support which he had received from him.

In the four years which he spent at the Home Office McKenna passed two well-needed Acts, one dealing with mental deficiency (1913) and the other with the administration of criminal justice (1914). But his main tasks were to pilot to the statute book, under the provisions of the Parliament Act, a measure for the disestablishment of the Welsh Church, from which the more indefensible provisions were removed by subsequent legislation, and to solve the problem of suffragette violence. He had here to decide between forcible feeding of the prisoners or allowing them to starve themselves to death. His solution (if such it can be called) was the passing of the Prisoners (Temporary Discharge for Ill-Health) Act, 1913, commonly known as the 'Cat and Mouse Act'; but war broke out before it could be asserted that a permanent solution to the problem had thereby been found.

For the first nine months of the war McKenna remained at the Home Office. His main concern was internal security, and his policy was vigorously attacked for leniency towards enemy aliens by people who overlooked, or forgot, Kitchener's remark that he could not spare troops to guard the home secretary's prisoners. But he also served with Kitchener, Haldane, Lloyd George, Walter Runciman (later Viscount Runciman of Doxford), Lord Lucas [qq.v.], and (Sir) Winston Churchill on a munitions committee of the

Cabinet set up in October, and Asquith asserted that by the time the armies in the field had been multiplied between four- and fivefold, the output of munitions had been multiplied nineteenfold. But nothing could disguise the failures at Festubert and at the Dardanelles, and Asquith was compelled to accept a coalition in which McKenna succeeded Lloyd George as chancellor of the Exchequer in May 1915.

McKenna stayed at the Treasury for eighteen months, a period during which Britain was financially alone, and which was the most critical in all the years of the war. His first budget, in September 1915, was the first serious attempt to put the finances of the country in a state to meet the cost of the war, and to make proper provision to maintain British credit abroad so as to finance the purchase of arms, food, and raw materials. In April 1917 the entry of the United States into the war solved the immediate problems of his successor, Bonar Law, but meanwhile McKenna had to maintain the solvency of a grand alliance, in which the credit of the other Allies could no longer be accepted without collateral security. The City recognized his resourcefulness and audacity when in the summer of 1915 J. P. Morgan & Co. refused to sign new contracts for £52 million unless the British Government made an immediate payment of 25% on account. McKenna obtained from the Prudential Assurance Company, of which the secretary was G. E. (later Lord) May [q.v.], $40 million worth of securities which, with the addition of £5 million in gold from the Bank of England, was handed to the London house of Morgan's, and the contracts were signed.

McKenna delivered two budget speeches: in September 1915 and April 1916. In the former he estimated for expenditure the sum of £1,590 million to be met by an addition of 40% on the existing income-tax rates, with super-tax rising to 3s. 6d. in the pound; a 50% excess profits tax, and an *ad valorem* tax of $33\frac{1}{3}\%$ on certain imports, in order to save shipping and check spending abroad. Although these so-called 'McKenna duties' were criticized as protective and the excess profits tax aroused misgivings, the budget was not seriously opposed. The second budget revealed McKenna looking forward beyond the end of the war. He estimated the total revenue at £509 million of which £86 million was attributable to the excess profits tax and must be regarded as tem-

porary. The total indebtedness at the end of the year would be £3,440 million of which £800 million represented advances to the Allies and the Dominions. The debt charge, allowing for a very substantial sinking fund, would be £145 million. In the last full year of peace the national expenditure, excluding the debt charge, had been £173 million. With the ordinary services on the same scale, and the new charge for debt service, McKenna anticipated that the country's total expenditure after another year of war, and allowing £20 million for pensions, would be £338 million. The existing scale of taxation was therefore providing amply for the war and securing a considerable margin for the remission of taxation on the return of peace. But he increased the maximum rate of income-tax to 5s. and introduced a new tax on amusements.

This budget was open to the criticism that it was a banker's budget which did not sufficiently weigh the danger of military defeat against financial stability. In September 1915 a Cabinet committee had favoured the formation of an army of a hundred divisions. McKenna believed the country could not even afford one of seventy divisions, and when Asquith decided to introduce conscription he tendered his resignation. McKenna (and he was supported by Runciman) believed that the military demands were 'inconsistent with other and not inferior obligations into which we have already entered . . . the maintenance of our full naval superiority, the assistance of our Allies . . . and the preservation of the indispensable part of our commerce and mercantile navigation'. Grey made it known that if McKenna and Runciman went he would go too, but Asquith managed to prevail upon them to remain and McKenna continued in office until Lloyd George became prime minister a year later.

Service under Lloyd George was impossible to McKenna in view of the temperamental difference between the two men. A mind that saw everything in pictures clashed with one that saw everything in figures; emotion was brought daily to earth by calculation; to Lloyd George, McKenna seemed devoid of imagination, to McKenna, Lloyd George was without balance or stability; dislike on Lloyd George's part was matched by distrust on McKenna's. On being defeated in the general election of 1918 McKenna retired from political life. In 1922 he was offered the chancellorship of the

Exchequer by Bonar Law; although willing publicly to support a Conservative Government, he believed that to take office in it would estrange those Liberals who were prepared to give their votes to the new administration, and he accordingly declined. When the invitation was renewed a few months later, McKenna felt that time enough had elapsed for him to accept it, just as Kitchener had accepted the secretaryship of state for war, without wearing a party label; and he underlined his contemplated position as a financial expert by stipulating for an uncontested election to a City of London seat. When, however, Sir Frederick Banbury (later Lord Banbury of Southam, q.v.) refused to make way, the proposal lapsed, and with it any chance there might have been of McKenna's succession to the premiership.

In 1924 McKenna was chairman of a committee on the export of German capital which reported at the same time as the Dawes committee. In 1917 he had accepted a seat on the board of the Midland Bank and in 1919 he succeeded Sir Edward Holden as chairman. His work in the City was the most congenial that he had ever undertaken, and the last twenty-five years of his life, although not without such sorrows as the death of his elder son, were almost certainly his happiest. Holden had expanded his annual address to the shareholders into a consideration of banking theory and kindred subjects of an academic kind, and he had been moved to choose McKenna as his successor so that the practice might be continued. In a discourse of this kind McKenna had no equal and his speech to the Midland Bank's shareholders became an event in the life of the City and was copied by other chairmen of banks. Both in the House of Commons and at a dinner, he made his hearers feel that there was no mystery about the function of money and that at the end they knew as much as he about 'reflation' or the gold standard or a 'managed' currency. A selection of his addresses was published in 1928 under the title *Post-War Banking Policy*, but he resisted all efforts to make him write a treatise on economics or his political memoirs.

For a prompt fighter, whose critics occasionally detected almost too perfect a confidence in his own judgement, McKenna was indeed surprisingly little given to recalling his successes or lamenting his failures. When the race was rowed, the speech delivered, or the rubber ended, he cared almost nothing what his efforts had been or who received the credit; and after going to the City, he could hardly be induced to speak of his life at Westminster. This impersonal absorption in work for its own sake gained him the devotion of his permanent officials, just as his unfailing championship of the services which he controlled won their unstinting loyalty. Those who had seen him taking his political life in his hand knew him to be ignorant of fear and innocent of self-seeking; in the Cabinet his fidelity to his friends was as unshakeable as his hostility to those who intrigued against them; but to the House of Commons he ever remained a puzzle and a source of irritation. Precise in statement and somewhat pedagogic in manner, he too often gave the impression of speaking to a departmental brief, and although he was recognized as a great administrator, members of both sides sometimes asked if he was anything more. His cold businesslike approach to questions about which his audience felt with passion brought him no following in the country and made him more respected than liked in his party. Only those who knew him best were aware of the geniality and high spirits which he reserved for private life, or suspected that under a somewhat aggressive self-confidence he was sensitive, emotional, and shy.

After leaving the Admiralty, McKenna lived in the house built for him by his friend (Sir) Edwin Lutyens [q.v.] in Smith Square, Westminster, until he moved to the official residence of the chairman of the Midland Bank in Pall Mall. He built, with Lutyens again as architect, a new house in Mells Park, Somerset, to replace that burnt down during the war, and after that, another at Halnaker near Goodwood. Throughout his life he preserved the erect carriage and spare figure of an athlete in training. One of the most redoubtable chess players in the House of Commons, he later became one of the best bridge players in London. Rowing and swimming were succeeded by golf and walking, and although advancing age brought increasing deafness, he enjoyed good health until his last weeks. He died in London 6 September 1943, and his ashes were taken to Mells.

McKenna's portrait was painted by James Gunn for the Midland Bank, with a replica for Halnaker Park. A cartoon by 'Spy' appeared in *Vanity Fair* in 1906, and a caricature by (Sir) Max Beerbohm is reproduced in his *Fifty Caricatures* (1913).

[Stephen McKenna, *Reginald McKenna, 1863–1943, a Memoir*, 1948; *The Times*, 7 September 1943; official records; private information; personal knowledge.]

STEPHEN MCKENNA.

MACKENZIE, WILLIAM WARRENDER, first BARON AMULREE (1860–1942), lawyer and industrial arbitrator, was born at Scone, Perthshire, 19 August 1860, the fourth son of Robert Mackenzie, farmer, by his wife, Jean Campbell, daughter of Basil Menzies, farmer. He was educated at Perth Academy and at Edinburgh University: he graduated in 1885 and in 1936 received the honorary degree of LL.D. He was called to the bar by Lincoln's Inn in 1886 and joined the Northern circuit. As a barrister he established a reputation as a knowledgeable adviser and advocate in matters affecting local authorities: those authorities were his principal clients and he specialized in the law relating to their rights, duties, and responsibilities. He was not a great advocate but the judges before whom he appeared respected him for his abilities and for his most thorough knowledge of the law. He edited several editions of Pratt's *Law of Highways*, was one of the editors of Halsbury's *Laws of England* and was responsible for other legal works, including many editions of the *Overseers' Handbook* and Paterson's *Licensing Acts*. Mackenzie's course seemed thus to have been clearly set: he took silk in 1914 and might well have looked forward to becoming a judge of the High Court.

Soon after the outbreak of war in 1914, however, when a considerable degree of labour unrest developed, Mackenzie was appointed arbitrator in a number of wages disputes and for the next eleven years he devoted himself almost exclusively to industrial arbitration. From the outset it was apparent that he possessed in a marked degree the qualities and personality demanded of the independent arbitrator and there was unquestioning acceptance of his awards, whether as an individual arbitrator or as a chairman sitting with others. In 1917 he was appointed one of the chairmen of the Committee on Production—the principal arbitration tribunal operating under the Munitions of War Act, composed of panels of employers' representatives, trade-union representatives, and neutral chairmen. In this capacity Mackenzie helped to find solutions of the many problems brought before the committee, the chief of which was to establish for the various trades a reasonable relativity between the advances in wages awarded from time to time to meet the abnormal conditions of war. After the close of the war he was appointed the first president of the Industrial Court, created under the Act of 1919. He remained in that office until 1926. In 1929 he published *Industrial Arbitration in Great Britain*.

Like the Committee on Production, on which it was modelled, the Industrial Court was formed of panels composed respectively of independent persons, and representatives of employers and workers. The Court played an important part in the readjustment of wages necessitated by the changing circumstances of industry in the post-war years. Reference of disputes to the Court was voluntary and it is a tribute to the wisdom and impartiality of the Court that the employers and employed in many trades accepted its decisions throughout so disturbed a period. Mackenzie's part as president was all-important: downward adjustments of wages were inevitable and it was essential that the arbitrating body should possess the unquestioning confidence of the trade unions.

Mackenzie was also referee under the Electricity (Supply) Acts of 1919 and 1922; and from 1920 to 1926 he was chairman of the Railway National Wages Board and from 1924 of the Tramway Tribunal for Great Britain. These bodies were established by agreement between the railway companies and the tramway undertakings, respectively, and the trade unions representing their employees; under Mackenzie's skilled guidance they solved many of the problems connected with wages and other questions of industrial relations which confronted the transport undertakings in those years.

After leaving the Industrial Court, Mackenzie (who was appointed K.B.E. in 1918 and G.B.E. in 1926 and raised to the peerage as Baron Amulree, of Strathbraan, Perthshire, in 1929) became chairman of many commissions and committees. These included the Royal Commissions on licensing (1929–31) and on Newfoundland (1933). Among the many chairmanships which Amulree accepted were those of an official committee on industrial holidays, an unofficial committee on housing, and a building industry committee representative of all the various elements in that industry. In 1937 and 1938 he was chairman of the council of the Royal Society of

Arts and took an active part in the work of the Society.

In October 1930 Amulree was invited by Ramsay MacDonald to join the Government as secretary of state for air, and was sworn of the Privy Council. His term of office was brief (it ended after the general election of 1931) and undistinguished. Any considerable development of the Royal Air Force at that time would not have been consistent with the views of his colleagues, whose policy was concentrated on disarmament. As a private member of the House of Lords, Amulree took part in numerous debates on subjects with which he had been familiar, such as local government, housing, and licensing.

He married in 1897 Lilian (died 1916), elder daughter of William Hardwick Bradbury, publisher and printer, of Whitefriars, and had one son and one daughter. He died at Winterbourne Stoke 5 May 1942 and was succeeded as second baron by his son, Basil William Sholto (born 1900). There is a portrait of Amulree by P. F. S. Spence in the possession of the family.

[*The Times*, 6 May 1942; *Journal* of the Royal Society of Arts, 18 January 1946; personal knowledge.]     Horace Wilson.

MACKENZIE KING, WILLIAM LYON (1874–1950), Canadian statesman. [See King.]

MACKINDER, Sir HALFORD JOHN (1861–1947), geographer and politician, was born at Gainsborough, Lincolnshire, 15 February 1861, the eldest son of Draper Mackinder, M.D., F.R.C.S. (Edin.), by his wife, Fanny Anne, daughter of Halford Wotton Hewitt, twice mayor of Lichfield. Educated first at Queen Elizabeth's Grammar School, Gainsborough, and then at Epsom College, Mackinder proceeded to Christ Church, Oxford, in 1880 with a junior studentship in physical science. He obtained a first class in natural science in 1883; in the same year he was president of the Union. In 1884 he was awarded a second class in modern history and was elected Burdett-Coutts science scholar. He read for the bar and was called by the Inner Temple in 1886.

In 1885 Mackinder began to serve the Oxford university extension movement and lectured up and down the country on what he called 'the new geography'. Accounts of these lectures reached the Royal Geographical Society, and in

January 1887 he addressed the Society on 'The scope and methods of geography'. Only a few weeks later the university of Oxford decided to establish a readership in geography with financial assistance from the Royal Geographical Society; in July 1887 Mackinder was appointed to the newly created post which he held until 1905. He used to say that Richard Hakluyt, the Elizabethan [q.v.], was the first Oxford reader in geography, and that he himself was only the second. He played the leading part in the revival of British geographical learning at the end of the nineteenth century and laid the foundations upon which British academic geography has been built. His *Britain and the British Seas* (1902) is a classic of modern geographical literature. As a result of his efforts, and with considerable support from the Royal Geographical Society, the school of geography was established at Oxford in 1899. Mackinder became the first director of this, the first British university school of geography.

The Oxford university extension movement had been particularly successful at Reading and in 1892 Christ Church elected Mackinder to a studentship and offered his services to Reading. A college was opened at Reading in the same year and Mackinder was its principal until 1903. He spent eleven years of pioneer work in developing this college which was later to receive its charter as a university. Mackinder was, in his own words, 'a pluralist'; from 1895, simultaneously with his Oxford and Reading appointments, he held a post at the London School of Economics and Political Science, which eventually became a readership in economic geography. Mackinder did not finally retire from teaching in the university of London until 1925; two years earlier he had received the personal title of professor. He was director of the London School of Economics from December 1903 to 1908. While he devoted much time and energy to establishing geography as a university subject, his own geographical work was not wholly academic, for in the summer of 1899 he made the first ascent of Mount Kenya.

Just as Mackinder's academic geographical studies led him to be an explorer in the field, so his interest in politics led him to become a practising politician. After two vain attempts to enter Parliament, for Warwick and Leamington in 1900 as a Liberal, and for Hawick Burghs in 1909 as a Unionist, he was elected for the Camlachie division of Glasgow in

January 1910 by the small majority of 434. He held his seat at the general election in December 1910 by the even narrower margin of 26, and continued to represent Camlachie until he was defeated in 1922 by a Labour candidate. As a lecturer Mackinder was outstanding; Sir Charles Grant Robertson [q.v.] coupled Mackinder and Sir Oliver Lodge [q.v.] as the two best lecturers he ever heard. In spite of this great ability in lecturing, or perhaps because of it, Mackinder was not very successful in the House of Commons. During the war of 1914–18 he organized the recruiting in Scotland of volunteers for the army and he also played a large part in the foundation of the National Savings Movement. He was British high commissioner for south Russia in 1919–20 and was knighted on his return. He served as a member of the Royal Commissions on income-tax and on awards to inventors, both in 1919, and on food prices in 1924–5. He became chairman of the Imperial Shipping Committee in 1920 and held that office until 1945. In 1925 he became chairman of the Imperial Economic Committee, a post which he held until 1931, and in 1926 he was sworn of the Privy Council.

In 1904 he gave a lecture to the Royal Geographical Society on 'the geographical pivot of history' and described a part of Eurasia as the pivot area and later as the heartland. Although these views were expanded in his *Democratic Ideals and Reality* (1919) they received little attention in Great Britain and America until the war of 1939–45. But Mackinder's theory of the heartland as a natural seat of power was closely examined in Germany between the two wars by students of Geopolitik, of whom General Karl Haushofer was the leading figure. In 1944 Mackinder received the Charles P. Daly medal for 1943 from the American Geographical Society at the hands of John G. Winant, then American ambassador in London, who said that Mackinder had 'enlisted geography as an aid to statecraft and strategy'. In 1945 the Royal Geographical Society awarded him its highest honour, the Patron's medal. Mackinder had a masterful personality but he made his colleagues his partners and helped many younger geographers by his encouragement and inspiration. In the words of W. M. Childs [q.v.], his successor at Reading, 'he had a way of blending dreams and hard sense, subtlety and simplicity, and he never seemed to know when he passed from the one to the other'.

Mackinder married in 1889 Emilie Catherine, daughter of Christian David Ginsburg [q.v.], the Old Testament scholar; their only child died in infancy. Mackinder died at his home in Parkstone, Dorset, 6 March 1947. A drawing of him made by Sir William Rothenstein in 1933 is in the possession of the London School of Economics.

[W. M. Childs, *Making a University*, 1933; *The Times*, 8 March 1947; *Geographical Journal*, vol. cx, 1947; *Nature*, 19 April 1947; J. F. Unstead, 'H. J. Mackinder and the New Geography' in the *Geographical Journal*, vol. cxiii, 1949; E. W. Gilbert, 'Seven Lamps of Geography' (bibliography) in *Geography*, vol. xxxvi, 1951; private information; personal knowledge.]                    E. W. GILBERT.

MacKINNON, SIR FRANK DOUGLAS (1871–1946), judge and author, was born in London 11 February 1871, the eldest son of Benjamin Thomas MacKinnon, of Lingfield, Surrey, an underwriting member of Lloyd's for nearly fifty years, by his wife, Katherine, daughter of Joseph Edwards, mahogany broker, of London. He was educated at Highgate School and won an open exhibition at Trinity College, Oxford, where he obtained a first class in classical moderations in 1892 and a second in *literae humaniores* in 1894. Three years later he was called to the bar by the Inner Temple, and along with (Sir) R. A. (subsequently Lord) Wright became a pupil of (Sir) T. E. Scrutton [q.v.], with whom he was intimately associated until Scrutton's death in 1934 and whose life he wrote for this DICTIONARY. Scrutton took silk in 1901, and MacKinnon quickly succeeded to a large part of his junior practice at the commercial bar, where he was helped by the connexion with Lloyd's of his father and his brother, (Sir) Percy Graham MacKinnon. He himself became K.C. in 1914, and was one of the regular leaders in commercial cases throughout the war of 1914–18. He successfully argued the well-known case of *In re Polemis and Furness, Withy & Co.* in 1921.

In 1924, Lord Haldane [q.v.] being lord chancellor, MacKinnon became a judge of the King's Bench division of the High Court on the death of Sir C. M. Bailhache [q.v.] and thereafter frequently sat in the Commercial Court, though he also regularly went on circuit. He received the customary knighthood the same year. He was promoted to the Court of Appeal (and sworn of the Privy Council) in 1937. MacKinnon was a very good lawyer, though his outside interests and a tendency to mental indolence prevented him from emulating either the industry or the erudition of his master, Scrutton. He aided Scrutton in later editions of the famous work on *Charterparties and Bills of Lading*, and eventually for a time became its sole editor. In 1917 he published a pamphlet on *The Effect of War on Contract*, a careful analysis of the development up to that date of the doctrine of frustration; in 1926 a lecture by him on *Some Aspects of Commercial Law* was printed; and in an article 'Origins of Commercial Law', in the *Law Quarterly Review*, vol. lii, January 1936 (his presidential address to the Association of Average Adjusters), he emphasized the initiative of Lord Mansfield. These contributions to legal literature, slight as they are in their content, are enough to prove that he had a genuine interest in academic legal questions.

As a judge of first instance, in the High Court, MacKinnon was quick to see the point in the case before him, and his judgements were always scholarly; but it must be admitted that his intense and almost perverse dislike of reserving judgement prevented him from making any noteworthy addition to our jurisprudence. Dealing with juries in criminal cases, he was on the whole successful, considering that he himself had never been on circuit (he never even joined a circuit) and, on his own testimony, had not addressed a jury 'more than half a dozen times' while he was at the bar. In the Court of Appeal his colleagues appreciated his learning and his sane outlook. His pronouncements were often marked by his dry humour: on one well-known occasion, speaking of the House of Lords' decision in *Jorden* v. *Money* (1854), he said that 'the voices of infallibility, by a narrow majority, held' a doctrine which has been universally disliked (see *Salisbury* (*Marquess*) v. *Gilmore*, [1942] 2 K.B. at p. 51). He also introduced 'the officious bystander'—a mythical personage trying to assist the contracting parties (*Shirlaw* v. *Southern Foundries, Ltd.*, [1939] 2 All E. R. at p. 124). Again, in a workmen's compensation case, 'If by some happy catastrophe the vast mass of reported cases had been wholly destroyed . . . I should be of opinion that this appeal should succeed' (*Noble* v. *Southern Railway Co.*, ibid. at p. 821). The House of Lords took the hint and overruled the authorities in question. Felicities of this sort abound in his judgements. And he had the gift of expressing his argument in pithy and accurate terms, so that his views have since often been cited, if only because of their simplicity and freedom from verbosity.

As time went on, Mackinnon became more and more interested in antiquarianism, especially in the eighteenth century, and he produced a series of charmingly written books, starting with annotations of Lamb's essay, 'The Old Benchers of the Inner Temple'. This, published in 1927, was followed by a learned and scholarly edition of *Evelina* in 1930, and *The Murder in the Temple and other Holiday Tasks* in 1935, and *Grand Larceny* (an account of the trial of Jane Austen's aunt at Taunton assizes) in 1937. After his death, some of these essays, together with certain ephemera, were collected under the title *Inner Temple Papers* (1948). But his largest and most important work was the delightful *On Circuit* (1940), which has preserved for all time the atmosphere surrounding our English assize system. Quite apart from the lively account which is given, in diary form, of the day-to-day life of an itinerant judge, the volume contains a mass of unique and valuable information, legal, historical, literary, and architectural, which entitles it to rank with the best travel books of any era.

Of MacKinnon's other literary work, we may mention the chapter on 'The Law and the Lawyers' in *Johnson's England* (1933); an article on 'The Happy State of the Modern Law Student' in the *Cambridge Law Journal*, vol. iii, No. 1, 1927; an address on 'The Statute Book', delivered when he was president of the Holdsworth Club of Birmingham University; and a series of notes published from time to time in the *Law Quarterly Review*. In this DICTIONARY, besides the life of Scrutton, he wrote notices of Lord Alverstone (held by many to be too censorious in its faint praise), of Lord Sterndale, of Mr. Justice Talbot (possibly too laudatory), of Lord Sumner (where the magnetism of Sumner's personality was perhaps allowed to obscure his undoubted claim to rank amongst the greatest English lawyers), of Sir Mackenzie Chalmers, and of Arthur Cohen.

No account of MacKinnon's life would be complete without a reference to his great devotion to the two old foundations with which he was connected—Trinity College, Oxford, and the Inner Temple. He was made an honorary fellow of his college in 1931, and he enjoyed giving to it various small benefactions: he was particularly proud of a piece of silver which he presented with the inscription: 'Behold how good and joyful a thing it is, brethren, to dwell together in Trinity.' At the Inner Temple he became a bencher in 1923, and was treasurer in the year before his death (1945): he prepared an elaborate memorandum, *The Ravages of the War in the Inner Temple* (1945), with plans and photographs, and he zealously supported, in the last years of his life, the project of restoring and renovating the Inn so that, freed from what he called Victorian vandalism, its buildings might once again become (in Lamb's words, which he quoted) 'the most elegant spot in the metropolis'.

MacKinnon manifestly was not interested in public life, but he was ready to hold positions that appealed to him either as lawyer or as antiquary. At different times, he was chairman of the Average Adjusters' Association (1935), president of the Johnson Society of Lichfield (1933), president of the Buckinghamshire Archaeological Society, chairman of Buckinghamshire quarter-sessions, and a member of the Historical Manuscripts Commission. He was a fellow of the Society of Antiquaries.

It is unnecessary to mention MacKinnon's personal characteristics, for *On Circuit* is a self-revealing document on every page. He was a great pedestrian, and successive marshals who attended him testify to the enormous distances which they were expected to cover. In 1931—his sixtieth year—he climbed Snowdon on two consecutive icy days in January. He always walked to the Law Courts, and it was while he was engaged in this daily exercise that he was seized with the heart attack of which he died almost at once in a London hospital, 23 January 1946.

MacKinnon married in 1906 Frances, daughter of William Henry Massey, of Twyford, Berkshire; she survived him, with one son who became bursar of Eton College. MacKinnon's last years were saddened by the loss in 1941 of his daughter, her husband, and their infant child, in the *Almeda Star* which was torpedoed in the Atlantic.

Shortly before his death his portrait was drawn in pencil by Sir Gerald Kelly: the original is the property of the Holdsworth Club of the university of Birmingham. A duplicate is in the possession of the artist.

[Sir F. D. MacKinnon, *On Circuit*, 1940; private information; personal knowledge.]

P. A. Landon.

MACKINTOSH, Sir ALEXANDER (1858–1948), parliamentary correspondent, was born at Turriff, Aberdeenshire, 3 February 1858, the son of William Mackintosh, station agent, by his wife, Catherine McGrigor. He was educated at Macduff and Aberdeen University, and entered journalism when he was nineteen as a reporter on the *Banffshire Journal*. In 1879 he began his career with the *Aberdeen Free Press* which lasted until 1922. In 1881 he was sent to London to join his paper's parliamentary staff when the Press Gallery was for the first time thrown open to the provincial press. He thus arrived at Westminster in time to hear and report Beaconsfield's last speech in the Lords, and to see Gladstone and Bright side by side on the Treasury bench in the Commons, and Lord Randolph Churchill and Arthur Balfour on the Opposition side.

His parliamentary work soon attracted notice, and in 1887 he became London editor of his paper. In his daily writings, first as sketch writer and later, for the longer period, as lobbyist, he displayed a lively sense of political history and was notably fair in his interpretation of parliamentary events and the policies and activities of statesmen. Notwithstanding that he was a shy and modest man, who found it congenial to lose himself in the anonymity of journalism, he became the personal friend and confidant of most of the leading political figures of his time. Even Asquith, who disliked journalists, was attracted to him and availed himself of Mackintosh's assistance in the compilation of his memoirs and paid tribute in that book to his 'wide and accurate knowledge of our political history'.

In 1923 Mackintosh became the political correspondent of the *Liverpool Daily Post*, and during his fifteen years of service in that position he was the honoured doyen of parliamentary journalists, whom he had already served as chairman of the Lobby Committee (1894) and of the Gallery Committee (1927). He was knighted in 1932 during the premiership of Ramsay MacDonald, who was a close personal friend.

Mackintosh severed his active connexion with the Press Gallery in 1938, but maintained his interest in parliamentary affairs and listened to all the big debates until just before he died. His familiar stocky figure was present in the Gallery for every budget speech between 1881 and 1947. For over forty years he contributed regular political notes to the *British Weekly*. He died in London 15 April 1948, in his ninety-first year.

During his retirement Mackintosh drew on his rich memory to compile his reminiscences under the title *Echoes of Big Ben* (1945). He had in 1906 written *Joseph Chamberlain: An Honest Biography*, a work of deep research and literary charm, for which he claimed that his qualifications were those of an observer from the Press Gallery for twenty-five years. *From Gladstone to Lloyd George*, which he wrote in 1921, was a gossipy essay based on personal observation and knowledge of his subjects.

Mackintosh married in 1884 Annie, daughter of Andrew Bannerman, of Bendigo, Victoria, and had one son and one daughter.

[Parliamentary Press Gallery records; personal knowledge.]          VINCENT HAMSON.

MacLAREN, ARCHIBALD CAMPBELL (1871–1944), cricketer, was born at Moss Side, Manchester, 1 December 1871, the second son of James MacLaren, cotton merchant, by his wife, Emily Carver. By his father's position as treasurer of the Lancashire County Cricket Club the boy was familiarized with first-class cricket from a very early age, and he distinguished himself both at Elstree (then renowned among the preparatory schools for its standard of cricket) and at Harrow. In his first match against Eton in 1887, at the age of fifteen and a half, he batted splendidly for scores of 55 and 67. In his next two matches at Lord's he met with no success, but in his last year, 1890, in which he was captain, his 76 out of 133 on a wet wicket made a profound impression, and in the following August he signalized his first appearance in first-class cricket by making 108 for Lancashire against Sussex. He was now giving every promise of attaining the position which, alike in personality and technique, he was later to hold as one of the foremost figures in what is often referred to as the Augustan age of cricket; but it was not until 1894 that his stature as a batsman was finally recognized by his selection as a member of the team which A. E. Stoddart [q.v.] took to Australia. The fast wickets suited him well, and he scored 228 against Victoria and 120 in the splendidly fought fifth test match which decided the rubber in favour of England. He paid two more visits to Australia, in 1897–8 and 1901–2,

captaining the team in the latter year, and although both sides were defeated in the test matches, he batted so brilliantly as to be ranked by Australians as the best English batsman they had seen since W. G. Grace [q.v.]. On the 1897–8 tour he and Ranjitsinhji [q.v.] were the first England team batsmen ever to make a thousand runs in Australia; at Sydney especially he could do nothing wrong, scoring on the first tour 142 and 100, 109 and 50 not out, 61 and 140, and 65, in consecutive innings, and in the second having a similar sequence of 145 and 73, 116, 167, and 92.

By playing an innings of 424 for Lancashire against Somerset at Taunton on his return to England in 1895, MacLaren not only set the seal on the enhanced reputation which he had gained in Australia, but also established a record for an individual score in first-class cricket which stood for twenty-seven years. Nevertheless, his experience in test matches in this country is a good example of the ironies of cricket history. Although the resources at the disposal of the selectors constituted something of an *embarras de richesses*, when MacLaren captained his country's side in fourteen matches in 1899, 1902, and 1909, he was only twice on the winning side. Nor was his batting in them comparable with his true gifts, with the exception of two innings—the one in the second test match of 1899 when, without any first-class practice whatever, he played a superb if unavailing innings of 88 not out on a crumbled wicket; the other at Nottingham in 1905, when his 140 was acclaimed as masterly.

When captaining England, MacLaren sometimes seemed to lack something of buoyancy and optimism, and on occasion was at no pains to conceal his disagreement with the policy of the selectors and with the material which they provided for him; but his Lancashire elevens swore by his leadership, and no one excelled him in knowledge of the game and tactical acumen. As in captaincy, so in batting; two of his greatest triumphs were deferred until long after he had given up regular participation in the game. In 1921 he made good his claim that he would select and lead eleven amateurs who could defeat W. W. Armstrong's unbeaten Australian side; and in the winter of 1922–3, at the age of fifty-one, he played an innings of 200 not out when captaining an M.C.C. touring side in New Zealand.

Uncertain health, however, and the claims of business made it impossible for MacLaren to play cricket with the regularity of many of his amateur contemporaries, and in a first-class career extending from 1890 to 1909 he achieved an overall aggregate and average which to a later generation may seem modest enough. But no one lucky enough to see him play a typical innings could have any doubt about his batting stature. He adopted a distinct secondary position at the wicket, standing up to his full height with bat lifted head high: from this he would move with grace and confident decision into a wide repertoire of strokes. A natural timer of the ball, he was a splendid driver on both sides of the wicket, especially over and wide of mid-on; he was also a fine cutter, whilst his attack was based on the foundation of a watchful and classically correct defence. Above all, there was about his batting a sense of mastery which impressed itself upon bowler and spectator alike: whatever the prowess of the attack and the difficulty of the pitch, he set himself to dictate and not to be dictated to. As with his famous contemporary in the Harrow and England teams, (Sir) Stanley Jackson [q.v.], an athletic body, good looks, and a certain ease and confidence of bearing made MacLaren an arresting figure on any cricket ground.

In 1898 MacLaren married Kathleen Maud, daughter of Robert Power, amateur steeplechase rider and chairman of the Victoria Racing Club, Melbourne, and had two sons. In December 1914 he received a commission in the Royal Army Service Corps, but was invalided out in October 1917. He died at Bracknell, Berkshire, 17 November 1944. A posthumous portrait painted under the direction of Gerald Reynell hangs in the pavilion at Old Trafford.

[Private information; personal knowledge.]
H. S. ALTHAM.

McLEAN, NORMAN (1865–1947), orientalist, was born at Lanark 2 October 1865, the eldest son of the Rev. Daniel McLean, a minister of the United Presbyterian Church of Scotland, and his wife, Grace Millar. McLean was educated in Edinburgh at the high school, and at the university where he took his degree in 1885 with first class honours in classics and philosophy. In 1887 he entered Christ's College, Cambridge, where he was a scholar. He obtained first class honours

in part i of the classical tripos (1888) and in the Semitic languages tripos (1890), gained various university scholarships and prizes, and in 1893 was elected into a fellowship at Christ's. At that period William Robertson Smith [q.v.] was also a fellow of Christ's, and McLean as his pupil became heir to the highest traditions in Semitic learning. He was appointed lecturer in Hebrew at Christ's, and in 1903 university lecturer in Aramaic, an office which he held until 1931. After the death in 1889 of William Wright [q.v.] McLean completed his unfinished edition of *The Ecclesiastical History of Eusebius in Syriac* (1898), and he was solely responsible for the excellent survey of Syriac literature in the eleventh edition of the *Encyclopaedia Britannica*. But he found his life-work in collaborating with A. E. Brooke [q.v.] in the preparation of the larger Cambridge edition of the Septuagint, which made available the variant readings in all extant manuscripts of any importance, in the ancient versions and in patristic quotations. To this immense task he devoted forty years, continuing the work to within a few years of his death, despite the death of Brooke in 1939 and his own grave illnesses in 1930 and 1933.

In 1911 McLean was made a tutor of Christ's, and from 1927 until his retirement in 1936 he was master of the college. His influence alike in the college and in wider university affairs won him not only respect for his wisdom but a wealth of affection. McLean had deep religious belief, although he rarely talked about it, and his friendship was quiet and unvarying. Although he was a man of strong personality, his mind was not self-centred but directed outwards by interest in and regard for others. As a teacher he was most stimulating, because he was so eager to share his knowledge, and so concerned for his students individually. McLean sought honours for his pupils, but not for himself. It was therefore all the more gratifying to him when he was elected to the mastership at Christ's, and when the university of Edinburgh in 1930 conferred upon him the honorary degree of LL.D., and when he was elected F.B.A. in 1934.

McLean married in 1896 Mary Grace (died 1905), daughter of Colonel Charles R. Luce, J.P., of Malmesbury; there were no children. He died in Cambridge 20 August 1947.

[Private information; personal knowledge.]
W. A. L. ELMSLIE.

McLINTOCK, SIR WILLIAM, first baronet (1873–1947), chartered accountant, was born in Glasgow 26 September 1873, the eldest son of Thomson McLintock, chartered accountant, by his wife, Jeannie, daughter of William Marshall, merchant seaman. McLintock was educated at Dumfries Academy and Glasgow High School, and served his apprenticeship in accountancy in his father's office, being admitted a member of the Institute of Accountants and Actuaries in Glasgow in 1896. He then became a partner in his father's firm, Thomson McLintock & Co., and in due course was senior partner, a position he held until his death. When McLintock entered the firm accountancy was assuming an ever-increasing importance, for not only were the big industrial firms expanding and amalgamating, but the Government was beginning to exercise a stricter control over their affairs, demanding official returns in greater detail for income-tax and other purposes. McLintocks, like other Scottish firms of chartered accountants, set up offices in London and other English towns in order to deal with this work, and after the London office was opened by William McLintock in 1912 the firm became one of the most influential in the country.

During the war of 1914–18 McLintock was very busily engaged on work for his firm in both the Glasgow and London offices. He was by then already recognized as one of the leading authorities on taxation. When coal-mines were taken under government administration as a war-time measure his services were in great demand. He soon found himself primarily engaged with coal control and with the many and intricate problems which that involved. In fact, throughout the whole of the war he was engaged on work which brought him into close touch with the Inland Revenue and other government departments. Another important task having its origin in war-time conditions, and in which McLintock took a prominent part, was the amalgamation of the individual companies comprising practically the whole of the explosives industry of the country.

Shortly after the war McLintock was called in to overhaul the finances of the royal household. He carried out a lengthy and most meticulous investigation as a result of which a number of changes were recommended in the interests of economy and simplicity of administration. He was appointed C.V.O. in 1922 in recognition of his work and in the same year K.B.E., being advanced to G.B.E. in 1929. In 1934 he was created a baronet.

McLintock acted as financial adviser in London in connexion with the agreement with what was then the Anglo-Persian Oil Company, and he was also responsible for seeing that the terms of that agreement were properly implemented after the document had been signed. It was in recognition of these services that in 1921 he received the Order of the Lion and the Sun from the Shah of Persia.

McLintock's personal prestige stood so high that his services were frequently sought by the Government of the day. He was a member of the committees of inquiry on the national debt and taxation (1924–7) and on broadcasting (1935), of the Economic Advisory Council, of the Racecourse Betting Control Board (1928–33), of the Board of Referees, and of the Industrial Arbitration Court. He acted as financial adviser to the Government in connexion with the creation of the London Passenger Transport Board, and one of his most important public activities was his appointment by all the Governments of the Empire to act with Sir Otto Niemeyer as their adviser at the imperial wireless and cables conference of 1928. Chiefly as a result of his counsel there ensued the merger which was subsequently known as Cable and Wireless, Ltd. He served also on the Royal Commission on income-tax and on committees on many other subjects, including company law amendment, unemployment insurance, the electrification of the railway systems of Great Britain, cement production, and financial risks.

In 1934 he was invited by the South African Government to serve as chairman of a commission to inquire into and report upon the financial position and the working of the South African harbours, but he was unable to accept owing to the condition of his health at that time. Four year later he accepted an invitation by the Government of Northern Ireland to be chairman of a commission to inquire into the working of the Northern Ireland Road Transport Board.

A man of remarkable character and ability, McLintock had great, almost relentless, tenacity of purpose. When presented with any problem it was his particular genius to be able to select what he judged to be the central element in it and to concentrate upon it to the exclusion of all minor issues. His energy was prodigious and his enthusiasm for everything he undertook was transmitted to all who worked with him. In this lay one of the secrets of his success. He was able, too, to throw himself into his client's case as if it were his own. He did not suffer fools gladly, but he was possessed of much charm of manner and his kindly humour was never slow to reveal itself. One of his most notable characteristics was his ability to promote happiness in others. No trouble was too much for him, and as a host he excelled in putting his guests at ease; his natural Scots humour—generous and ever kindly—and his unfailing tact and courtesy were always evident.

In 1901 McLintock married Margaret Jane Fanny, daughter of Henry Lyons, of Sligo. They had three daughters and one son, Thomson (1905–53), who succeeded him as second baronet when he died at Bournemouth 8 May 1947. There is a painting by J. A. A. Berrie in the possession of the family.

[*The Times*, 9 May 1947; personal knowledge.]      CAMPBELL STUART.

McMAHON, SIR (ARTHUR) HENRY (1862–1949), military political officer, was born at Simla 28 November 1862, the eldest surviving son of Charles Alexander McMahon [q.v.], the general and geologist, who was for many years a commissioner in the Punjab. Educated at Haileybury and the Royal Military College, Sandhurst, where he passed out first with the sword of honour (1882), he joined the Punjab Commission via the Punjab Frontier Force in 1887 two years after his father had retired. In 1890 he transferred to the Indian Political Department where he served for twenty-four years, the whole of the early period being spent on the North-West Frontier of India.

Honours and promotion came quickly, with the C.I.E. (1894) after accompanying the Durand mission to Kabul, the C.S.I. in 1897 for demarcating the frontier between Baluchistan and Afghanistan, the K.C.I.E. (1906) as a result of the successful Seistan mission, the G.C.V.O. in 1911 during the visit of King George V and Queen Mary to India, and the G.C.M.G. (1916) for his work as high commissioner for Egypt (1914–16). He was agent to the governor-general in Baluchistan, 1905–11, and was appointed foreign secretary to the Government of India in 1911.

As British commissioner to demarcate the boundary between Baluchistan and Afghanistan McMahon first gave proof of an unusual capacity to win the trust and affection of the leading personalities on both sides and to secure agreed conclusions. It was this gift, combined with an infinite patience, contrary to his natural inclinations, which led to the successful conclusion of this and other similar assignments, such as arbitration in Seistan on the boundary between Persia and Afghanistan. During these negotiations a lifelong friendship with the Amir of Afghanistan was established. This friendship was extended to the Amir's two successors and helped greatly to stabilize the difficult relationship between Afghanistan and India. The incident of his career which he remembered with the greatest satisfaction was the time when the Bugti Sardar from Baluchistan and his relations acted as a bodyguard. So loyal and friendly were the chief and his followers that, throughout the three years spent in demarcating the Persian frontier, they never missed a night on guard in the open outside his tent.

Although McMahon's experience had hitherto been confined to the North-West Frontier, Lord Hardinge of Penshurst [q.v.] had little hesitation in selecting him for the post of foreign secretary, where his friendly contacts with every branch of the service were of the greatest value in helping to co-ordinate policy. This gift of friendliness made him the obvious choice as master of ceremonies for the royal visit, after which his diplomatic ability was fully tested as British plenipotentiary in negotiations with China and Tibet (1913–14) for a treaty which stood the strain of nearly forty years.

McMahon was in England on leave when war broke out in 1914 and his appointment as first high commissioner in Egypt under the British protectorate came as no surprise to those who knew his qualifications. (Sir) Ronald Storrs described him at this time as 'slight, fair, very young for 52, quiet, friendly, agreeable, considerate and cautious'. With courage, determination, and patience he conducted negotiations with the Arabs, but at the end of 1916 he was abruptly recalled. Twenty years later McMahon's undertakings came under dispute and in 1939 an Anglo-Arab inquiry failed to reach agreement upon an interpretation of the 'McMahon–Husain correspondence'.

After his retirement McMahon was able to pursue a number of other interests and was active in the Royal Society of Arts, the Society of Antiquaries, and the Zoological Society. He was a fellow of the Royal Geographical and the Geological societies and in addition to a number of business interests was president of the national council of the Young Men's Christian Association and chairman of the Fellowship of the British Empire. Perhaps his keenest interest was reserved, as throughout his career, for freemasonry. In addition to founding several lodges in India, of which distinguished Indians were welcome members, he pursued the craft until he rose to be grand senior warden of the Grand Lodge of England, grand commander of the Temple, and sovereign grand commander of the Supreme Council 33°. In spite of his busy life McMahon delighted in outdoor pursuits, especially fishing and yachting. As a great conversationalist he was apt to keep late hours and was not always the easiest man to approach early in the day, but throughout his life neither young nor old failed to receive every possible help from a generous heart. His name is still remembered with affection and gratitude on the frontiers of India.

He married in 1886 Mary Evelyn (died 1957), daughter of Francis Christopher Bland, of Derryquin Castle, county Kerry, whose comradeship and singular charm were his constant support. He died in London 29 December 1949, survived by two daughters. A portrait by Sir William Orpen was hung in the Freemasons' Hall, Quetta.

[Sir Ronald Storrs, *Orientations*, 1943 edition; private information; personal knowledge.] HENRY HOLLAND.

MacNEILL, JOHN (otherwise EOIN) (1867–1945), Irish scholar and politician, was born at Glenarm, county Antrim, 15 May 1867, the third son of Archibald MacNeill, baker and farmer, and his wife, Rosetta Macauley. James McNeill [q.v.] was his youngest brother. He was educated at St. Malachy's College, Belfast, where he fulfilled his early promise, passing first in all Ireland in the senior grade of the intermediate examination. He graduated at the Royal University in 1888 with second class honours in history, political economy, and jurisprudence. A year previously he had obtained by examination a junior clerkship in the Dublin Law Courts.

MacNeill's interest in the Irish language dated from this period. In 1890 he first

went to the Aran Islands to learn the living dialect and afterwards spent prolonged periods there, his last visit being as late as 1944. In his spare time he also studied Old and Middle Irish under the direction of Edmund Hogan, S.J., in whose scholarly publications he was soon able to collaborate. It was Hogan who first directed his attention to the need for a scientific investigation of the sources of early Irish history. Meanwhile MacNeill had become a fervent supporter of the language revival movement. Together with Douglas Hyde [q.v.] and a few other enthusiasts he founded, in 1893, the Gaelic League. As its first secretary, MacNeill spent much of his spare time organizing branches throughout the country and editing its official organ, the *Gaelic Journal*, with a very characteristic mixture of sound scholarship and romantic nationalism. In 1908 he took a leading part in the successful agitation to make Irish a compulsory subject for matriculation in the new National University.

His growing reputation as a scholar, which had been established by a series of lectures delivered in 1904 (some of them published later as chapters of his *Celtic Ireland*), led to MacNeill being appointed first professor of early Irish history in University College, Dublin. Paradoxically enough, his concern with political affairs increased steadily from this date and made corresponding inroads on his time for research. Always a strong nationalist, he had through his work for the Gaelic League been brought into closer contact with the political extremists, who welcomed the accession of such a distinguished scholar to their ranks. As a counterblast to the Ulster Volunteers, MacNeill advocated and co-operated in the formation of the Irish Volunteers, nominally for the purpose of meeting the threatened resistance to Home Rule. On the outbreak of war in 1914 he assumed the leadership of the extreme section who dissociated themselves from John Redmond's pledge of active support for the Allies. Although nominally 'commander-in-chief' of this section, he was kept in ignorance of the plans for a rising on Easter Monday 1916, and after discovering them at the eleventh hour he issued orders countermanding the general mobilization, a step which caused him to be denounced by the 'gunmen' as a traitor.

Sentenced to penal servitude for life on the collapse of the rebellion, MacNeill was released next year under a general amnesty, and threw himself into the task of organizing the Sinn Fein movement. As member for the National University returned at the general election of 1918, he was Speaker of the Dail when the treaty of 1921, which he warmly supported, was ratified by a small majority. Next year he became minister of education in the Free State Government and was thus prominently associated with the beginnings of the policy of 'compulsory' Irish in the schools.

In 1924 he was appointed Free State representative on the Ulster boundary commission, but after the publication of a 'special forecast' of the contents of the award in the *Morning Post* on 7 November 1925, MacNeill's resignation was announced on 21 November. These events caused intense excitement: the award was sent to London, and by agreement between the three premiers concerned it has never been published. No final judgement on MacNeill's part in the work of the commission can therefore be passed as yet. He was much criticized at the time for his supine attitude on the commission; in the resulting political crisis he was forced to resign his ministry and at the next general election he lost his seat in the Dail. It was the end of a political career which had brought him little but disappointment and for which he was in many ways temperamentally unsuited. The Government made him chairman of the newly instituted Irish MSS. Commission in 1927, and during the last years of his life academic honours were showered on him, including the presidency of the Royal Irish Academy, from which he had been formally expelled as a 'felon' in 1916.

It is as a scholar rather than a politician that MacNeill will be remembered. His critical investigation of the native records dealing with ancient Irish history showed that much which had been accepted as historical by previous writers consisted of fables invented by the medieval Irish literati. At the same time he segregated from this mass of fiction what he considered to be the kernel of fact. Some important points in his reconstruction of the course of early Irish history have since been challenged; a few have been actually disproved. Yet the fact remains that MacNeill provided the first treatment of this difficult subject which deserves to be called scientific. He had small liking for the drudgery of collecting and collating unpublished material; hence his conclu-

sions were too often based on insufficient evidence, yet more than once they have been strikingly reinforced by subsequent evidence. It was said of him that he had 'an old mind' which enabled him to feel curiously at home in the dim past mirrored in the annals and sagas. But this quasi-intuitive approach which served him well in his study of ancient Irish society was much less successful in dealing with linguistic problems. His range of interests was extremely wide: he wrote papers and articles on the Ogam inscriptions, the Gaulish calendar of Coligny, the problem of St. Patrick, the Pictish question, Irish law tracts, annals, glossaries, &c., besides two major works dealing with his own special subject: *Phases of Irish History* (1919) and *Celtic Ireland* (1921). In lectures and conversation he invariably held and stimulated the interest of his hearers.

The most serious criticism of MacNeill's work is that his scholarship was deeply (though doubtless unconsciously) coloured by his political views. The sharpness of his polemic against Mr. Christopher Dawson, who had written of his 'patriotic protests', showed that this shaft was very well aimed; MacNeill had in fact the defects of the patriotic historian as found in Germany. Even his brilliant reconstruction of ancient Irish society tends to become an *apologia* for the Gaelic civilization against its 'enemies' among modern historians. A reference to the 'primitive' customs of the Irish in the works of such sober and objective scholars as Goddard Henry Orpen or Sir Paul Vinogradoff [q.v.] invariably stung him to anger, and in controversy he was not always accurate or even fair. But no breath of controversy was ever allowed to mar his personal relations even with those who differed from him most widely; his kindness, charm, and courtesy made him universally beloved.

In 1898 MacNeill married Agnes, daughter of James Moore, solicitor, of Ballymena; they had four sons and three daughters. He died in Dublin, 15 October 1945. A portrait by Séamas O'Sullivan is at University College, Dublin.

[*Irish Times*, 16 October 1945; *Round Table*, No. 62, March 1926; *Studies*, Dublin, December 1945; *The Bell*, Dublin, December 1945; *Irish Historical Studies*, vol. vi, No. 21, March 1948 (bibliography); *Essays and Studies* presented to Professor Eoin MacNeill on the occasion of his seventieth birthday, edited by John Ryan, S.J., Dublin, 1940; personal knowledge.]      D. A. BINCHY.

MACREADY, Sir (CECIL FREDERICK) NEVIL, first baronet (1862–1946), general, was born in Cheltenham 7 May 1862, youngest son of William Charles Macready [q.v.], the actor, by his second wife, a granddaughter of Sir William Beechey [q.v.], the painter. Educated at Tavistock Grammar School and Marlborough and Cheltenham colleges, he went on to the Royal Military College, Sandhurst. He joined the Gordon Highlanders in 1881 and took part in the Egyptian campaign of 1882, including the battle of Tel-el-Kebir. In 1884 he was appointed staff lieutenant of military police and garrison adjutant at Alexandria. Rejoining his regiment in 1890 he was appointed adjutant of its 2nd Volunteer battalion in 1894. He saw much active service with his regiment in the South African war, including the defence of Ladysmith. Promoted brevet lieutenant-colonel in 1900, he was selected in 1901 to be chairman of a commission to investigate allegations of cattle-driving by Zulus led by a colonial officer. His next appointments were as assistant provost-marshal at Port Elizabeth, chief staff officer to the district west of Johannesburg, and assistant adjutant-general and chief staff officer of Cape Colony. For his work in South Africa he was twice mentioned in dispatches; he was promoted colonel in 1903.

In 1907 he became assistant adjutant-general at the War Office; two years later he was given command of the 2nd Infantry brigade at Aldershot but returned to the War Office in 1910 as director of personal services, whose responsibilities included the use of troops in aid of the civil power. This aspect of his duties loomed largest in his work in the next four years and decisively influenced the rest of his career. In November 1910, soon after his promotion to major-general, he was sent to South Wales to command troops detailed to support strong bodies of police in dealing with possible disorders arising from a miners' strike. Although some rioting occurred, especially in the Tonypandy valley, Macready's firmness and tact in dealing impartially with owners and strikers prevented serious disturbances.

In November 1913 he was sent by the secretary of state for war, Colonel J. E. B. Seely (later Lord Mottistone, q.v.) to Dublin and Belfast to report on the civil and military administration in face of disturbances. After the Curragh incident in March 1914 he went to Belfast as general officer commanding the district,

being also a resident magistrate, whilst still retaining his War Office appointment. On the outbreak of war in August 1914, he joined the British Expeditionary Force as adjutant-general. As such he was responsible for three innovations of lasting importance: the establishment under (Sir) Fabian Ware [q.v.] of the Graves Registration and Inquiries organization; the introduction of the suspended court-martial sentence; and the inauguration of plastic facial surgery in base hospitals. In February 1916 he was recalled to the War Office to become adjutant-general to the forces, with a seat on the Army Council. For the next two and a half years he was faced with the ever-increasing difficulty of maintaining the strength of the armies in the field, and on his advice a minister of national service was appointed; one of the palliatives which Macready initiated was the formation of the Women's Army Auxiliary Corps to replace fit men by women in suitable rearward duties. On the lighter side, he procured the abolition of the regulation that army officers might not be clean-shaven and he removed his own moustache.

On 30 August 1918 the Metropolitan Police went on strike over pay and the recognition of a police union. The strike was quickly settled, but on terms which were ambiguous regarding the union. On 4 September Macready reluctantly took up the post of commissioner of Metropolitan Police. He modernized the organization of the force, introduced women police, and installed a press room at Scotland Yard. He removed existing grievances and provided machinery for discussion in the future. The organizers of the strike, however, persistently tried to force him to recognize a union. He made it clear that he would not do so and would dismiss any member of the force who joined any future strike. In June 1919 he addressed a representative meeting of 3,000 police in the Queen's Hall and won such support for his policy that when, in August 1919, the agitators called another strike, only 5 per cent. of the force came out. They were dismissed and no further trouble occurred.

In April 1920 Macready was appointed G.O.C.-in-C. in Ireland. His first task, not made easier by the weakness of his units and the alternation of government policy between repression and conciliation, was to try to suppress the Sinn Fein rebellion. After the truce of July 1921, which he helped to bring about by going unannounced and unescorted to a conference with the rebel leaders, his role was to secure the observance of the truce terms, to safeguard his troops in the face of much provocation from extremists, and finally to supervise the withdrawal of British military forces and stores from Southern Ireland. He retired in February 1923 on the completion of this work and in the following year published his autobiography in two volumes entitled *Annals of an Active Life*.

He was appointed C.B. (military) in 1906 and C.B. (civil) in 1911, being promoted K.C.B. in 1912. He was appointed K.C.M.G. in 1915, promoted to G.C.M.G. in 1918, and created a baronet on his retirement. During the war of 1914–18 he received a number of foreign decorations; he was promoted lieutenant-general in 1916 and general in 1918. He was appointed J.P. for the county of London in 1918 and sworn of the Privy Council of Ireland in 1920. In 1931 he received the honorary degree of LL.D. from the university of Aberdeen.

Possessing outstanding administrative ability, a distinguished appearance, and a great capacity for work, Macready had an unusual power of adapting himself to unfamiliar situations and successfully undertaking, without regard to his own interests or preferences, any work, military or civilian, to which he was called. A shrewd judge of men, he knew how to get the best out of them; and although his choice of subordinates was not always popular it could never be criticized as inadequate to the task in hand. If a man justified his selection, he could rely on Macready's loyal support against all critics, however highly placed. Although he was a stern disciplinarian, he was very human, possessed a keen sense of humour, and would often deflate pretension with apt wit. 'Completely fearless and completely selfless' was (Sir) Winston Churchill's assessment of him. A talented singer and amateur actor, Macready could no doubt have made an equally successful career on the stage, but such a choice, he said, would have been anathema to his father.

In 1886 Macready married Sophie Geraldine (died 1931), daughter of Maurice Uniacke Atkin, of Ledington, county Cork. They had two daughters and one son, Gordon Nevil (1891–1956), who had a distinguished military career and who succeeded his father as second baronet when he died in London 9 June 1946.

There is a portrait of Macready by Percival Anderson in the royal collection at Windsor Castle, and a drawing by Francis Dodd in the Imperial War Museum.

[Sir Nevil Macready, *Annals of an Active Life*, 2 vols., 1924; private information; personal knowledge.]                J. C. LATTER.

MALAN, FRANÇOIS STEPHANUS (1871–1941), South African statesman, was born at Bovlei, Wellington, Cape Colony, 12 March 1871, the eldest son and second of the fourteen children of Daniel Gerhardus Malan by his wife, Elizabeth Johanna, daughter of David Johannes Malan, of the farm Bovenvallei (Bovlei), Wellington, Cape Colony.

Malan was educated at Paarl High School, Victoria College, Stellenbosch (B.A., 1892), and at Cambridge University (LL.B., 1894). After visits to France, Holland, Germany, and the United States, he was called to the Cape bar, and became editor of *Ons Land*, a Dutch Cape Town paper which supported the Afrikaner Bond (1895–1908).

During the South African war Malan sympathized with the Boer republics. Soon after his unopposed return to the Cape House of Assembly for Malmesbury, he was imprisoned (April 1901–April 1902) because his paper had contained a letter from a concentration camp, mentioning names. After his release, he pressed in vain as leader of the Opposition for the fuller use of Dutch in the public service, and that steps be taken towards the closer union of all the British territories south of the Zambezi (July 1907). As minister for agriculture and education in the Cabinet of John X. Merriman [q.v.] (1908–10) and member of the National Convention (October 1908–May 1909) which framed the South Africa bill, he advocated legislative union rather than federation, and the maintenance of the long-established Cape 'civilization' tests for the parliamentary franchise. He also helped to form a National Union to promote further unification.

Kindly, competent, and a staunch upholder of the best parliamentary traditions, Malan was minister for education (1910–21), agriculture (1919–21), mines and industries (1912–24), acting minister of native affairs (1915–21), and more than once acting prime minister. He was a representative of the newly formed Union at the coronation of King George V and at the Imperial Conference in 1911. He founded the Middelburg and Glen agricultural colleges, the Industrial Advisory Board, and the Electricity Supply Commission, consolidated the South African school system, and recognized the Fort Hare Native University College and the independent universities of Cape Town and Stellenbosch. In 1920 he was sworn of the Privy Council and received the honorary degree of LL.D. from the federal university of South Africa.

Election to the Senate in 1927 gave Malan some compensation for his loss of the Malmesbury seat and of office in 1924. He resisted Hertzog's reduction of the powers of the Upper House (1927–9), and made a great stand against virtual abolition of the Cape Bantu franchise in 1936. He was president of the Senate from 1940 to 1941.

Malan did much for the public and cultural advancement of his country. Before the Union of 1910, he had been elected a member of the Leyden Maatschappij der Nederlandsche Letterkunde and, at home, had helped to found the Suid-Afrikaanse Akademie vir Taal, Lettere en Kuns. After the Union, he served as chairman of the South Africa National Society (1923–41) and the Huguenot University College council, and on the council of the university of Cape Town (1927–41). In later life he received an honorary Stellenbosch doctorate (1931) and was a member of the Voortrekker Monument Commission, and chairman of the South African Akademie, the Historical Monuments Commission, and the Huguenot Memorial Committee. A truly religious man, he was a delegate to numerous Dutch Reformed Church synods and, for many years, an elder of the Groote Kerk, Cape Town. Of his writings *The University South Africa Needs* (1912), *Marie Koopmans-de Wet* (1925), and *Louis Botha* (1931) are noteworthy, and, as part of his defence of a liberal Afrikaner theologian, *Ons Kerk en Professor du Plessis* (1933). He was one of the Union's representatives at the first unofficial British Commonwealth Relations conference at Toronto (1933), the Melbourne centenary celebrations (1934), and the Empire Parliamentary Association conference and the coronation of King George VI (1937).

Malan was twice married: first, in 1897 to Johanna (died 1926), daughter of Barend Brummer, farmer, of Lady Grey, Cape Colony, and was survived by two sons and two daughters; secondly, in 1928 to her sister, Mrs. Anna Elizabeth Attwell. There were no children of this marriage. He himself died at Cape Town 31 December 1941.

A portrait of Malan by Hugo Naude is in the possession of the family.

[*The Times*, 2 January 1942; private information.]      Eric A. Walker.

MALLORY, Sir TRAFFORD LEIGH LEIGH- (1892–1944), air chief marshal. [See LEIGH-MALLORY.]

MANN, THOMAS (1856–1941), trade-unionist and Communist, known as Tom Mann, was born at Foleshill, near Coventry, 15 April 1856, the son of Thomas Mann, a book-keeper at the Victoria Colliery, by his wife, Mary Ann Grant. When Mann's mother died he was but two years old. He had only three years' schooling. At nine he worked on the colliery farm, at ten he became a pit-worker dragging boxes of coal removed to keep clear the air-courses. He crawled on all fours harnessed to the box by a belt and chain. Four years later his father moved to Birmingham, and after a short spell as printer's devil, Mann was apprenticed to engineering in a toolmaker's. By a five months' strike in 1872 the hours (from 6 a.m. to 8 p.m., including two hours' overtime) were reduced to nine; but the fact that this success was initiated by the Tyneside Nine Hours' League and not by the Amalgamated Society of Engineers (which he joined in 1881) turned Mann to the view that trade unions should fight and not confine themselves to the advocacy of their causes.

Shorter hours enabled Mann to attend general and technical courses three evenings a week, a Bible class and the meetings of a temperance society once a week, and a religious service on Sunday evenings. He had been brought up an Anglican, but learned much from the Quakers, and he became a Sunday-school teacher. Politically he was influenced by Joseph Chamberlain in his Radical days, but he owed much also to G. J. Holyoake and Bradlaugh, John Bright, and Mrs. Annie Besant [qq.v.]. In 1877 he moved to London and was employed in various engineering works, and for a few months in New York, until 1886.

Mann's economic opinions developed rapidly. In 1881 he read Henry George's *Progress and Poverty*, but later rejected the single-tax theory. At different times he held and discarded Malthusianism, vegetarianism, and teetotalism as remedies for poverty. More lasting impressions came from personal friendship with Engels, and Marx's daughter Eleanor; and from reading Hyndman's *England for All*, Ruskin's *Fors Clavigera*, and the works of William Morris [qq.v.] which led him to join the Battersea branch of the Social Democratic Federation in 1885 and so brought him into touch with John Burns [q.v.]. His constant demand for shorter working hours was inspired by *Six Centuries of Work and Wages* by J. E. Thorold Rogers [q.v.] and it was in Battersea that he first raised the issue of the eight-hour day as a means of social improvement. In 1886 he published a pamphlet: *What a Compulsory Eight-Hour Day Means*. The notoriety gained by these activities prevented regular employment; he parted with his books, violin, and telescope, and for two years roamed over Tyneside and Lancashire on behalf of the Social Democratic Federation; but he returned to London in 1889 and was enlisted by Ben Tillett [q.v.] in the London dock strike of that year, becoming until 1893 first president of the Dockers' Union.

Mann was now in the front rank, in high demand as a speaker for his wide vocabulary and burning enthusiasm. In 1891 he was one of the seven Labour members of the Royal Commission on Labour and with three others signed a minority report (1894) drafted by Sidney Webb [q.v.] which advocated, amongst other things, the municipalization of the four dock companies and over 150 facility enterprises of the Port of London. He became the first secretary of the London Reform Union which promoted the policy of simplifying the administration of London.

In 1893, after discussions with Archbishop E. W. Benson [q.v.], Mann was invited by the Rev. Thory Gage Gardiner, rector of the church of St. George the Martyr, Southwark, to take orders in the Church of England. Nothing came of this, and in February 1894 Mann became secretary of the Independent Labour Party. He unsuccessfully contested the Colne Valley division of Yorkshire in 1895, North Aberdeen in 1896, and Halifax in 1897. In January of that year he relinquished his work as secretary of the I.L.P. owing to the claims made upon his time by the International Federation

of Ship, Dock and River Workers which he had helped to found in the previous year and of which he was first president. He agitated among dockside workers in France, Holland, Belgium, Norway, and Spain, but on arrival at Hamburg was arrested and deported. In 1898 Mann was largely responsible for launching the Workers' Union for those for whom no proper union already existed. Its history was chequered and in 1929 it was absorbed into the Transport and General Workers' Union. Other activities were his membership of the organizing committee for the international Socialist congress held in London in 1896 and taking charge of the 'Enterprise' tavern in Long Acre, a familiar 'house of call' for earlier trade-unionists and the meeting-place for various revolutionary, Radical, and reform groups.

At the end of 1901 Mann, whose fame had spread to the Dominions, left for New Zealand, moving on to Australia in the following year. He became organizer of the Labour Party of Victoria and delegate for the Amalgamated Society of Engineers to the Melbourne trades council, and toured Western Australia in 1904 and Queensland in 1905. On the formation of the Socialist Party of Victoria in 1906 he edited his first periodical, the *Socialist*, and after participating in a campaign for free speech he was imprisoned at Melbourne, the city where he first advanced the six-hour working day as a practical proposal. Following a visit to South Africa in 1910 at the invitation of the Johannesburg miners, he returned to London after an absence of nine years.

Conditions in Australia had convinced Mann that by revolutionary methods alone could industrial emancipation be secured. Syndicalism, as exemplified by the Confédération Générale du Travail and the Industrial Workers of the World, now became his gospel. From July 1910 to May 1911 he edited the *Industrial Syndicalist* advocating 'industrial solidarity' and 'direct action'. His agitation gained support in South Wales among unofficial trade-unionists, and led to the publication of *The Miners' Next Step* (1912) which repudiated State ownership of the mines and demanded ownership by the miners. At the request of J. Havelock Wilson [q.v.] Mann helped to resuscitate the fortunes of the National Amalgamated Sailors' and Firemen's Union, one of the unions in the National Transport Workers' Federation formed in 1910 on the initiative of the Dockers' Union. By organizing the delay of the steamship *Olympic* in 1911 and declaring strikes at most of the chief ports of Britain considerable concessions were gained, but in Liverpool an authorized mass demonstration led to a conflict in which the Riot Act was read and the military called in.

A 'Don't Shoot' appeal to soldiers, originally written for the *Irish Worker*, was reprinted in 1912 in the first issue of the *Syndicalist*, the editor and printer of which were consequently sent to prison. During the first national miners' strike Mann read the appeal at several meetings, was arrested on a charge of inciting to mutiny, and sentenced to six months' imprisonment. Released at the end of seven weeks as a result of parliamentary and public pressure, Mann renewed agitation, but within legal limits. He revisited the United States in 1913, and when the Union Government in 1914 deported ten Labour leaders without trial he was invited by trade-unionists and Socialists to revisit South Africa. In 1919 he was elected general secretary of the Amalgamated Society of Engineers, and held the same office in the Amalgamated Engineering Union when it was formed in the following year. He retired in 1921.

In 1916 Mann joined the British Socialist Party which became the nucleus of the British Communist Party of which he was a founder-member (1920). In 1921 he attended the first congress of the Red International of Labour Unions in Moscow, declaring his adhesion to the Communist International. At the general election of 1924 he stood unsuccessfully as a Communist for East Nottingham. From that year until 1932 he was chairman of the National Minority Movement which under Communist direction sought to use the trade-union organization to achieve the workers' control of industry. In December 1932 he was sentenced to two months' imprisonment on refusing to be bound over to keep the peace after agitating among the unemployed in London; but when charged in 1934 at the Glamorgan assizes, together with Mr. Harry Pollitt, with uttering seditious speeches, he was acquitted.

On his eightieth birthday Mann was fêted by all sections of the British Labour movement, and he was invited to attend the May Day celebrations that year in Canada. He paid his fourth and last visit to Russia in 1937, and in 1938 he assisted the Swedish Communist Party in its municipal campaigns. After a slight seizure in 1939 he gradually declined until he died at Grassington, Yorkshire, 13 March 1941.

[*Tom Mann's Memoirs*, 1923; Dona Torr, *Tom Mann*, 1936 (reprinted 1944); *The Times*, 14 March 1941.]                    J. S. MIDDLETON.

MANNING, BERNARD LORD (1892–1941), scholar, was born at Caistor, Lincolnshire, 31 December 1892, the only son of George Manning by his wife, Mary Ann, daughter of William Short Lord, man of business, of Caistor. In 1898 George Manning became a minister of the Congregational Church, with the result that his son's home during his schooldays was first at Ravenstonedale (Westmorland) and then at Lincoln.

Bernard Manning was never robust, and a severe illness in boyhood left him a semi-invalid for the rest of his life, with only one effective lung. In 1912, however, he won an open scholarship at Jesus College, Cambridge, from Caistor Grammar School. He obtained a double first in the history tripos (1914, 1915), won the Lightfoot scholarship in 1915, a Thirlwall prize in 1917, and from 1916 to 1918 was a bye-fellow of Magdalene College and editor of the *Cambridge Review*. A short period of national service at the Ministry of Munitions in 1918 was brought to an end by an attack of tuberculosis, but he made a rapid recovery and in 1919 was elected a fellow of Jesus College. He was bursar from 1920 to 1933, senior tutor from 1933 until his death, and a university lecturer in medieval history from 1930. He died, unmarried, at Cambridge 8 December 1941 and was buried at Ravenstonedale.

Bernard Manning was both soundly practical and deeply spiritual. As bursar of his college he proved himself a shrewd business man and a wise administrator. As tutor he showed a remarkable gift for administering discipline while treating his pupils as friends and equals. He was a staunch Congregationalist but possessed the œcumenical mind to a pre-eminent degree; for he absorbed, as few have done, the spirit of the Christian Church throughout the centuries—of the early Church and the medieval Church no less than the fragmented Christianity of post-Reformation times.

Everything that Manning wrote is conspicuous for scholarship, style, wit, and humour, as he shows in *The People's Faith in the Time of Wyclif* (1919, his Thirlwall prize essay), *The Making of Modern English*

*Religion* (1929), *Essays in Orthodox Dissent* (1939), *The Hymns of Wesley and Watts* (1942), two chapters (on 'Edward III and Richard II' and 'Wyclif') in vol. vii of the *Cambridge Medieval History*, and two posthumous volumes of sermons.

[F. Brittain, *Bernard Lord Manning*, 1942; personal knowledge.]      F. BRITTAIN.

MANSFIELD, SIR JOHN MAURICE (1893–1949), vice-admiral, was a son of Edward Dillon Mansfield and his wife, Muriel Edith Campbell-Ross, of Lambrook, Bracknell, Berkshire, where he was born 22 December 1893. He entered the Royal Navy in 1906 and after passing through the colleges at Osborne and Dartmouth went to sea in 1911. The outbreak of war in 1914 found him a sub-lieutenant in the cruiser *Warrior* until, in 1915, he joined the submarine service where he remained for the next six years, being awarded the D.S.C. in 1917. He later served in battleships, as flag lieutenant-commander to the admiral commanding the coast of Scotland, and as executive officer of the cruiser *Cairo*, on the America and West Indies station. Promoted to commander 30 June 1929, he commanded a destroyer division in the Mediterranean, and in 1931–2 attended the courses at the Royal Naval Staff College at Greenwich and the Royal Air Force Staff College at Andover, after which he was appointed executive officer of the aircraft carrier *Courageous*. All this varied experience during his early career was invaluable to an officer of Mansfield's great promise, ability, and personality, and he was promoted to captain 30 June 1934, the junior of his batch, at the age of forty.

There followed two years on the directing staff of the Royal Naval War College, Greenwich, until, in October 1937, he became flag captain and chief staff officer to the commander-in-chief, East Indies, in the cruiser *Norfolk*. The outbreak of war in 1939 found him serving in the same capacity to the flag officer commanding the first cruiser squadron, in the *Devonshire*. In this ship he saw much arduous service in the Mediterranean, on the Northern Patrol, in the Arctic, Norway, Equatorial Africa, and the south Atlantic.

In February 1941, when the U-boat war in the Atlantic had become very serious and Sir Percy Noble became commander-in-chief, Western Approaches, Mansfield became his chief of staff, and played a large part in setting up the new combined sea-air organization. No better choice could have been made. All those at sea in the escort forces, or ashore at headquarters, testified to his great drive and energy, and the unfailing tact and sympathetic understanding with which Mansfield carried out his responsible task during two most difficult years.

Promoted to rear-admiral in 1943, he commanded a cruiser squadron in the Mediterranean with his flag in the *Orion*, where he again rendered conspicuous service during the landing at Anzio in January 1944; in support of the seaward flank of the Fifth (United States) Army during the advance towards Rome; and during the landing in southern France in the following August, for which he was appointed to the D.S.O. in 1945. In October 1944 he commanded the British naval forces employed in the liberation of Greece, where his plans and their execution were invariably successful. After a short period at the Admiralty in 1945, in which year he was appointed C.B., he became flag officer, Ceylon, until in October 1946, as vice-admiral, he became head of his old service as admiral (submarines), where he had the difficult task of demobilization. Forced to relinquish that command in 1948 because of ill health, he was appointed K.C.B. in June of the same year.

Mansfield was known throughout the Service as a fine seaman and brilliant officer whose qualities and record must have raised him to the highest rank. A man of great charm of character and personality he was a loyal colleague with many devoted friends.

He married in 1916, Alice Talbot, daughter of the late Commander Gerard Talbot Napier, R.N., and had one daughter and one son who also entered the navy. Mansfield died at his home at Woodford, near Salisbury, 4 February 1949.

[Private information; personal knowledge.] TAPRELL DORLING.

MANSON, JAMES BOLIVAR (1879–1945), painter and director of the Tate Gallery, was born in London 26 June 1879, the eldest of the four sons of James Alexander Manson, author and editor, by his wife, Margaret Emily, daughter of Charles Deering. He was educated at Alleyn's School, Dulwich, and since his father was unwilling for him to become an artist he was compelled at the outset of his career to work in a bank until he had saved sufficient money to enable him to devote his whole time to the study of painting. He went first to Heatherley's

School of Art in London and later to the Académie Julian in Paris. Manson's talent although small was a very real one; its general direction declared itself from the first and remained unaffected by the fluctuations of fashion. He was a staunch and convinced admirer of the Impressionist painters; although in no sense an imitator, his natural outlook was closest to that of Monet and Pissarro. His work lacked the hard core of drawing with which Monet is sometimes insufficiently credited, but he shared his openness of mind and lack of prejudice in the choice of subject-matter.

Exhibitions of Manson's work were held at the Leicester and Wildenstein galleries in London, in Glasgow and in Paris. He was generally thought to be most successful in his paintings of landscape and still-life, and one of his best flower-paintings 'Michaelmas Daisies' (acquired in 1923) may be seen in the Tate Gallery, where there is also a self-portrait. He exhibited his pictures at both the New English Art Club and the Royal Academy, but in neither did he feel quite at home. When in 1911 a small group of friends, among them W. R. Sickert [q.v.], Harold Gilman, and Spencer Frederick Gore, broke away from the New English Art Club to form the Camden Town Group, Manson joined them and, under the presidency of Gore, became their first secretary, a post which he continued to fill when the movement enlarged in 1913 and became the London Group. In 1912 he was appointed assistant and in 1917 assistant keeper in the Tate Gallery under Charles Aitken whom he succeeded as director in 1930. At that time the funds at the disposal of the Tate were very slender and additions to the gallery were more dependent on private generosity than on extensive government support. Manson, himself a sensitive artist of unconventional outlook, was a good judge of painting and during his directorship the collection was much strengthened, particularly in Impressionist pictures.

As a writer Manson's best-known publications in book form are his short monographs on Rembrandt (1923) and on Degas (1927) which, although intended for the general reader, show a breadth of view and a penetration which is not always found in lengthier volumes. He contributed occasional articles to various art periodicals and was for a time art critic to the *Daily Herald*.

Manson was a largish thickset man, and in later life his exceptionally thick white hair and very bright light-blue eyes together gave a surprising effect of youthfulness. He was an amusing companion, spontaneous and without affectation and was often, not always on the most wisely chosen occasions, extremely funny. His jokes were always spontaneous and always made to the victim's face: he never indulged in the carefully considered malicious witticism 'privately' circulated. But his inability to resist a joke, on the occasion of the official luncheon held in Paris to mark the opening of the 1937 French Exhibition, had the most unfortunate consequences. At an over-solemn moment Manson enlivened the company by crowing like a cock, and later, when the guests were dispersing, he lifted the beard of one of the most distinguished Frenchmen present in order to see 'whether he had a tie on underneath'. The French were tolerant, even amused, by these indiscretions, but a less lenient view was taken by the British authorities and led to Manson's resignation being required. The suggestion, which has often been made, that on occasions he drank much is quite untrue; he drank far less than many of those around him. But it was his misfortune that he had no head for wine: at one moment he would be entirely unaffected, while an additional glass would over-stimulate him. His resignation had the unhappiest consequences. He felt it deeply and, in trying to retrieve his fortunes, ventured his small capital with results which were financially disastrous.

In 1903 Manson married Lilian Laugher; they had two daughters. He died in London 3 July 1945. A bronze by Andrew O'Connor is in the Municipal Gallery of Modern Art, Dublin.

[*The Times*, 4 July 1945; private information; personal knowledge.]

ALLAN GWYNNE-JONES.

MARETT, ROBERT RANULPH (1866–1943), philosopher and anthropologist, was born in Jersey 13 June 1866, the only son and eldest of the four children of (Sir) Robert Pipon Marett [q.v.], attorney-general and later (1880) bailiff and president of the legislative assembly of the island, by his wife, and distant cousin, Julia Anne, youngest daughter of Philip Marett, of La Haule Manor, St. Brelade's. From Victoria College he won a senior exhibition at Balliol College, Oxford, in November 1884. Entering college in Hilary term 1885, he won the Chancellor's prize for Latin verse in 1887, became secretary of the Union in the same year, and took a first class in classical moderations (1886) and, in spite of an attack of meningitis which kept him idle for six months, in *literae humaniores* (1888). In the autumn he entered the university of Berlin and studied German philosophy; and in the following year he was tutor to Lord Basil Blackwood, son of the British ambassador in Rome. He was undecided about a profession. He became a member of the Inner Temple, and was admitted (1891) to the Jersey bar, but in the meantime he returned to Oxford in 1890 and did general coaching for Balliol until he was elected to a fellowship at Exeter College in 1891. When Ingram Bywater [q.v.] left in 1893 on becoming regius professor of Greek he succeeded him as tutor in philosophy. He soon discovered that he loved teaching. His lectures on Plato's *Republic* filled the hall for many years; he never gave the same set of lectures twice; and reviewing for the *Economic Review* (1891–8), the *Athenaeum* (1903–14), and the *Times Literary Supplement* kept him abreast of new publications. As tutor he made the undergraduates feel that philosophical questions were real problems of conduct or belief in their own lives; and he started the Dialectical society, a college discussion group which still flourishes.

In 1893 he succeeded L. R. Farnell [q.v.] as sub-rector, and retained the office until he moved out of college in 1898 on his marriage. In 1918 he served as junior proctor. Meanwhile, in the train of Andrew Lang, (Sir) E. B. Tylor, and (Sir) J. G. Frazer [qq.v.], Marett had begun a course of reading which enabled him to win the Green moral philosophy prize in 1893 with an essay on the ethics of savage races; and (Sir) John Linton Myres induced him to write for the British Association meeting at Dover in 1899 a paper on 'Preanimistic Religion' (reprinted in *The Threshold of Religion*, 1909) which established him as an anthropolgist. When the diploma in anthropology was founded in 1905 he was a member of the first committee; he succeeded Myres as secretary in 1907, and held the post for twenty years. In 1909 he was the principal founder of the Oxford University Anthropological Society, and remained all his life a pillar of inspiration and debate. Appointed reader in social anthropology in 1910, he held the post until 1936, and in the absence of the first holder of the new chair served another year as acting professor, the university then rewarding his services—he was already a D.Sc. (1913)—with an honorary D.Litt. The work of

Émile Cartailhac and Henri Breuil in France and W. J. Sollas [q.v.] at Oxford had attracted him to prehistoric archaeology as early as 1910. He visited the painted caves of France and Spain, and from his home in Jersey conducted successful excavations (1912–15) at La Cotte de St. Brelade. In Australia with the British Association in 1914 he had time to see some tribesmen with his own eyes before the war recalled him across the Pacific to Oxford.

As in games he was once said to succeed by personality rather than by skill, so in anthropology Marett opposed to the rational categories of Tylor and Frazer the 'primitive logic of the heart'. From Tylor's 'animism' he distinguished an impersonal religion, or 'animatism', based on 'awe'—a feeling of 'submissiveness tempered with admiration, hopefulness, and even love'—in the presence of 'any supernormal power', such as that denoted by the Melanesian term *mana*; *mana* in a negative aspect is *tabu*, that is, 'not to be lightly approached'; 'the genuine *tabu* feeling is not paralytic but pregnant'; magic is only to be discriminated from religion as 'wonder-working of a completely noxious kind'—noxious, presumably, for the community. His Gifford lectures (published as *Faith, Hope and Charity in Primitive Religion*, 1932, and *Sacraments of Simple Folk*, 1933) which he regarded as the most complete account of his views 'about primitive religion in both its psychological and its institutional aspects', implied that this theology without a god, a system of activity, puritanism, and confidence, was very much like his own; and in his last work he claimed that as 'possibly a flying-buttress rather than a pillar of the Anglican Establishment', he could read into its ritual forms the meaning that suited him. The conception of 'Präanimismus' was received with interest in Germany by Wilhelm Max Wundt, Konrad Theodor Preuss, and others. He applied and developed it in many of the addresses with which he continued for forty years to stimulate congresses, universities, and learned societies. All his books were in fact made up of such lectures, except the very successful manual in the Home University Library on *Anthropology* (1912), the short life of Tylor (1936), and his *Jerseyman at Oxford* (1941). His services to anthropology in general were thus as notable as they were at Oxford, where the present school owes much of its vigour and sanity to his original enthusiasm and classical background; his many distinguished pupils have helped to change the whole attitude of the Overseas service to native races.

In 1928 on the resignation of Farnell, Marett was elected rector of Exeter College, and thus relieved of his tutorial work. He was given the honorary degree of LL.D. by the university of St. Andrews in 1929 and elected F.B.A. in 1931. As rector he was quick in college affairs and impatient of formalities, although enjoying ceremony and hospitality. He restored the carved ceiling of the lodge, formerly hidden in plaster, and in 1931 persuaded the city council to sell the corner site of Turl and Broad streets. In 1936 the college extended his rectorship for a further term of five years; his portrait by Henry Lamb was hung in the hall; and anthropologists celebrated his seventieth birthday with a volume of essays, *Custom is King*. In October 1940, the war having cut him off from his home in Jersey, he was invited to stay on for another year from June 1941, renewable if necessary, this extension beyond the age of seventy-five being made possible by war-emergency statute. His elder son had been lost in the *Glorious* in June 1940. He carried on, 'temperamentally incapable of harbouring sorrow', nursing the college and various learned societies through war-time difficulties, and in the winter wrote an autobiography only less racy than his conversation. The winter of 1942 brought some weakness of the heart; on 18 February 1943 he was unable to attend, for the second time running, a meeting of the Anthropological Society, and he died awaiting a meeting of the curators of the Indian Institute later in the same afternoon.

Marett was an expert ornithologist and devoted to any form of activity in the open air such as golf or rough shooting. In 1883 he was gazetted a lieutenant in the Jersey militia and at the time of the South African war he joined the 4th Volunteer battalion of the Oxfordshire Light Infantry and as a lance-corporal enjoyed the annual camp at Aldershot. In 1898 he married Nora (died 1954), daughter of Sir John Kirk (1832–1922, q.v.). There were two sons and two daughters of the marriage. The elder son, John Ranulph de la Haule Marett, produced work of substance and originality in genetics (*Race, Sex and Environment*, 1936); the younger, Robert, is known for two books on Mexico, and in 1955 was appointed consul-general in Boston.

[R. R. Marett, *A Jerseyman at Oxford*, 1941; H. J. Rose in *Proceedings* of the British

Academy, vol. xxix, 1943 (bibliography); L. H. D. Buxton in *Custom is King* (bibliography), 1936; *Oxford Magazine*, 11 March 1943; personal knowledge.]

J. N. MAVROGORDATO.

**MARRIOTT**, SIR **JOHN ARTHUR RANSOME** (1859–1945), historian, educationist, and politician, was born at Bowdon, Cheshire, 17 August 1859, the eldest son of Francis Marriott, solicitor, of Bowdon, and Hayfield, Derbyshire, by his wife, Elizabeth, daughter of Joseph Atkinson Ransome, surgeon, of Manchester. Educated at Repton and New College, Oxford, he became lecturer in modern history at his own college (1884–7) and at Worcester College (1885–1920) and was later elected fellow (1914–19) and honorary fellow (1921) of the latter. From 1895 to 1920 he was secretary to the Oxford university extension delegacy for which he had lectured since 1887, and did more than any other man to build up and extend the work of that body. He was one of the most popular of its lecturers, for he was lucid, forcible —with a certain dramatic method of delivery—and careful not to soar too far above the heads of his audience. He had always looked forward to a political career and was member of Parliament for Oxford City (1917–22), and for York (1923–9). He was an enlightened Conservative with special interest in economic and imperial questions. Although he never to any great extent won the ear of the House as a debater, he served on many important committees, such as the select committees on national expenditure and on estimates, and was elected chairman of the latter (1924 and 1925). On 14 April 1921, when the triple alliance of miners, railway men, and transport workers threatened a general strike, Marriott performed his most notable service by presiding, in a committee-room of the House of Commons, over several meetings of members of the House, coal-owners, and miners, by whom he was commissioned to interview the prime minister late at night. The next day the strike was called off.

Marriott was a voluminous writer pouring forth books on history, biography, and politics, articles in the chief quarterly and monthly reviews, besides contributions to the press. A popularizer (in the best sense) rather than a researcher (a title which he frankly disclaimed) he had a real gift of exposition and an effective style. Some of his works reached a high standard of merit, notably *The Life and Times of Lucius Cary, Viscount Falkland* (1907), *Second*

*Chambers* (1910), and *The Eastern Question* (1917), but a few of his later books written in old age and under great difficulties when he was living in Wales separated from his library and manuscripts in his bombed London house fell rather below his former high level of achievement.

Marriott was a bluff, hearty man of untiring industry; the work which he accomplished in lecturing, writing, organizing, and public speaking, would have been beyond the capacity of most men. In addition he was an excellent man of business. He never compromised his very definite opinions, but in spite of this, or perhaps because of it, he had many friends in more than one political camp.

Marriott married in 1891 Henrietta, daughter of the Rev. William Percy Robinson, D.D., warden of Trinity College, Glenalmond, and had a daughter. He was knighted in 1924. He died at Llandrindod Wells 6 June 1945.

[Sir John Marriott, *Memories of Four Score Years*, 1946; *The Times*, 8 June 1945; *Oxford Magazine*, 21 June 1945; personal knowledge.] P. E. ROBERTS.

MARRIS, SIR WILLIAM SINCLAIR (1873–1945), Indian civil servant, was born at Cookley, Worcestershire, 9 October 1873, the eldest son of Charles Marris, chartered accountant, of Birmingham, by his wife, Jessie, daughter of Donald Sinclair, M.D., of London. He came of old Lincolnshire stock, but his grandfather had migrated to Birmingham. When William Marris was eleven years old his father's health made it necessary for the family to leave England and they went to Wanganui in New Zealand. There he was educated under an inspiring headmaster, and afterwards at Canterbury College. His exceptional abilities being recognized it was decided that he should return to England with a view to entering the Indian Civil Service, and after a year's preparation in London he took the first place by a very large margin in the examination of 1895. He spent his probationary year at Christ Church, Oxford, where he was awarded a scholarship, and in 1896 went out to the North-Western Provinces and Oudh, later the United Provinces of Agra and Oudh.

He soon made his mark, and in 1901 was appointed under-secretary to the Government of India, home department. He joined this post when the Government of India secretariat was at the height of its reputation under Lord Curzon [q.v.], and in this stimulating atmosphere his unusual powers of thought and exact expression soon brought him to the front. In 1904 he became deputy secretary in the home department, and two years later was lent to the Government of the Transvaal (1906–8). There he came into the most intimate association with Milner's 'kindergarten', young men who were applying their minds with fervour and imagination to devising a constitutional solution for the South African problems. Marris took a full part in the gradual evolution of these ideas, and returned to India a convinced and valued member of the *Round Table* group. In this formative period he had made lasting friendships, and with Lionel Curtis in particular he was to find himself in close touch again when a new constitution for India was being framed.

There followed some years of district work as collector of Aligarh (1910–14) and a short period as inspector-general of police in the United Provinces. Towards the end of 1917 Marris went back once more to the home department of the Government of India, this time as joint secretary, to assist in the discussions on constitutional reform.

E. S. Montagu [q.v.], the secretary of state, arrived in India in November 1917, and the Montagu–Chelmsford report was signed at Simla 22 April 1918. During that period of little more than five months it was necessary to obtain opinion from many interests and different parts of India, to discuss a great variety of proposals, and to take crucial decisions. The drafting of the report had to proceed while inquiries were still being made and ideas were fluid. Marris was soon asked to undertake the task of drafting, and this he did against a background of crushing pressure on time and in a general atmosphere of considerable nervous strain. This formidable task brought out many of his chief characteristics. His grasp of principle and power of exposition contributed not a little to winning for the report immediate recognition as a great state paper. But he felt his personal responsibility as draftsman acutely. Although he did not himself think the time ripe for such fundamental changes, yet, if a break was to be made with the past, he was eager that the scheme should be the best that was practicable, and that the conditions and facts should be stated with scrupulous fairness. He thus came to exercise a marked influence on the proposals themselves, as well as on the method of their presentation.

Marris returned with Montagu to London

for six months, and then after a rest became reforms commissioner with the Government of India, having been appointed K.C.I.E. in January 1919. In January 1921 he was appointed K.C.S.I. and in March he was made governor of Assam. In December 1922 he succeeded Sir Harcourt Butler [q.v.] as governor of the United Provinces, a post which he held for five years. In strong contrast to his predecessor he was one of the least political of the governors under the new constitution. He had not the experience of having rubbed shoulders with the Indian politicians in the legislatures, and the tone of his mind inclined him to prefer the written to the spoken approach. Early in his period of office he had a disagreement with his ministers, drawn from the Liberal party, who represented the moderate nationalist point of view, and though no broad question of policy was involved, they resigned, thus making it necessary for him to rely largely on the influence of the landlords, who constituted the more conservative element in the legislature. The province, however, was on the whole during his time in a state of political tranquillity, which gave opportunity for carrying through some valuable administrative measures.

On completion of his governorship Marris came home and was appointed a member of the secretary of state's Council. A post more of dignity than of responsibility made little appeal to him, and in 1929 he was glad to accept the principalship of Armstrong (later King's) College, Newcastle upon Tyne, in succession to his friend Sir Theodore Morison [q.v.]. He took a special interest in the departments of classics and fine art, and in general kept a strong and impartial control over finance in days of stringency. He played his full part in the life of Durham University, of which he was for two years vice-chancellor. A Royal Commission dealing in 1934 with issues which had been raised over the termination of the appointment of a professor by the College of Medicine recommended the control of professorial appointments by the university, and the union of the two Newcastle colleges, proposals which Marris had advocated. When these recommendations came into force in 1937, Marris retired, but the principles for which he had striven assisted the rapid development of the united King's College under Lord Eustace Percy (later Lord Percy of Newcastle).

During an exacting official life Marris found time to make translations of con-siderable merit from Horace (1912), Catullus (1924), and Homer (*Odyssey*, 1925, *Iliad*, 1934) into English verse. He also contributed to the *Oxford Book of Greek Verse in Translation*. The love of the classics acquired at Wanganui never left him, and the exercise in exact thought and felicitous expression appealed to his talents and his nature. In the delicate balance between poetry and accuracy, he may at times have inclined a little to the latter, but he knew how to get the general feel of a poem, and his translations of Catullus in particular show a versatility and a lyrical gaiety of their own.

Marris was a man whose great intellectual powers were always directed by an unswerving integrity. In his administration the intellectual side predominated. He grasped with great speed and certainty the essentials of a problem, but the impetus in matters of detail was of less interest to him. In the normal interchange of society a little aloof, his outward reserve covered an unusual depth of feeling, and to his friends he was one of those who inspire a real love.

In 1905 Marris married Eleanor Mary, daughter of James Fergusson, F.R.C.S.E., of Richmond, Surrey. Her death after just one year, when his only son was born, cast a profound shadow over his life. His second marriage in 1934 to Elizabeth Wilford, daughter of Robert Charles Earle, of Wanganui, and widow of Harry Edward Good, also of Wanganui, brought him great happiness. He died at his home at Cirencester 12 December 1945. His son, Adam Denzil Marris, served as counsellor in the British Embassy at Washington during the war of 1939–45, and afterwards became a managing director of Lazard Brothers.

The honours conferred upon Marris included honorary degrees from the universities of Durham (D.Litt., 1929) and New Zealand (Litt.D., 1941). He was a grand officer of the Order of Leopold (1926).

[*The Times*, 14 December 1945 and 11 January 1946; E. S. Montagu, *An Indian Diary*, edited by Venetia Montagu, 1930; private information; personal knowledge.]

HARRY HAIG.

MARTEN, SIR (CLARENCE) HENRY (KENNETT) (1872–1948), provost of Eton, was born in Kensington 28 October 1872, the younger son of (Sir) Alfred George Marten who in 1874 became member of Parliament for Cambridge borough and a Q.C., by his wife, Patricia Barrington, daughter of Captain Vincent Frederick Kennett of the Manor House, Dorchester-on-Thames. Marten was educated at Eton where he was in the house of Miss Evans, the last of the Eton 'dames'. He entered Balliol College, Oxford, in 1891 where A. L. Smith [q.v.] was his tutor. After gaining a first class in modern history in 1895, he was invited by Edmond Warre [q.v.], the headmaster, to return to Eton as an assistant master to teach history. At that time the study of modern history played only a very small part in the curriculum of the school; and only in 1906 did the reform of the curriculum introduced by Edward Lyttelton [q.v.], who had become headmaster in the previous year, make possible the establishment of modern history as one of the main subjects of education. Marten was the leading figure in a development which had a profound effect on the education provided in the public schools and grammar schools of the country. From 1907 to 1927 he was a house master, and from 1926 to 1929 lower master. In 1929 he was appointed vice-provost and in 1945 provost of Eton.

Marten was a remarkable teacher. He combined a great knowledge of history, which he constantly kept up to date, with immense enthusiasm and the ability to transmit this enthusiasm to his pupils. He would always be persuading them to read the great works of historical literature, and he made them free of his splendid library, which he bequeathed to Eton where it now constitutes the Marten library. At the same time, he insisted on clear thinking and an orderly treatment of the subject. His influence was great in wider circles than Eton, especially in the Historical Association, of which he was president from 1929 to 1931.

With G. Townsend Warner, an assistant master at Harrow, he was the author of one of the most used school textbooks of the first half of the twentieth century, *The Groundwork of British History* (1912). He collaborated in other textbooks, and in *The Teaching of History* (1938) he drew on his long experience as a schoolmaster.

In 1938 Marten was entrusted by King George VI with the historical education of the Princess Elizabeth. His teaching of English history, especially that of the constitution of this kingdom and of the British Dominions, was always placed in the framework of the history of Europe, and he paid special attention to the political and constitutional history of the United States. In recognition of his ser-

vices he was appointed K.C.V.O. and he was knighted by the King on the steps of College Chapel in the presence of the school 4 March 1945. A picture of this unique ceremony by R. E. Eurlich is in the gallery of the Memorial Hall at Eton. A portrait by Sir Gerald Kelly is in the Marten library.

Marten, who was unmarried, died at Eton 11 December 1948.

[Personal knowledge.]      R. BIRLEY.

MARTIN, ALEXANDER (1857–1946), Presbyterian theologian and Church leader, was the son of the Rev. Hugh Martin [q.v.], a well-known Scottish minister and author in his day, and his wife, Elizabeth Jane Robertson. Born at Panbride, Angus, 25 November 1857, he was educated at George Watson's College, the University, and New College, Edinburgh. His student career was exceptionally distinguished: he was awarded the Rhind (1879), Bruce of Grangehill and Falkland's (1880), and Ferguson (1881) scholarships (the last in open competition with candidates from all four Scottish universities), and the Hamilton fellowship (1881). Having graduated M.A. with first class honours in philosophy in 1880, he acted as assistant to Henry Calderwood [q.v.] in the department of moral philosophy, while at the same time pursuing his studies in theology at New College where he was Cunningham fellow in 1883. From 1886 to 1888 he was external examiner in philosophy to the university. In 1884 he was called to the ministry of Morningside Free Church in Edinburgh and after thirteen years there he was appointed professor of apologetics and practical theology in New College in 1897, remaining until 1927. Meanwhile, however, in 1918 he had been appointed principal of the college and continued in this office until 1935. In 1900 he spent five months in Australia, ministering to a church in Melbourne.

Martin was twice moderator of the General Assembly of his Church (1920 and 1929)—a very rare distinction; the second occasion included the first sederunt of the enlarged Assembly after the union of the Church of Scotland and the United Free Church, in the negotiations for which he had played a leading part. Perhaps more than any other single individual on the side of the United Free Church he was responsible for their success. In 1929 also he was appointed a royal chaplain, was made a freeman of the city of Edinburgh, and given the honorary degree of

LL.D. in the university (he had already received the honorary degree of D.D. in 1898). He died in Edinburgh 14 June 1946.

Martin attained equal eminence as a teacher and as an ecclesiastic. As the years passed, he became ever more deeply involved in the administrative work of the Church and was always listened to with the greatest respect in the meetings of the General Assembly. He was a man of wise and mature judgement, of fatherly presence, and gracious personality, whose advice was eagerly sought by his former students and others in times and situations of perplexity. To his class-work also he gave a full share of his thought and energy, his theological outlook being of a mediating kind, and deeply evangelical. His published work, however, was limited in quantity—much more limited than he himself had at one time hoped. Apart from pamphlets, mostly dealing with critical stages in the union negotiations, only two published volumes came from his pen— *Winning the Soul* (1897), a volume of notable and scholarly sermons, and his 1928 Cunningham lectures, *The Finality of Jesus for Faith* (1933).

In 1887 Martin married Jane Thorburn (died 1948), daughter of the Rev. Dr. Thomas Addis whom he had succeeded at the Morningside Free Church. They had two sons and two daughters. There are two portraits in oils of Martin, both by Henry W. Kerr, one at New College, and the other in the possession of the family.

[Hugh Watt, *New College, Edinburgh: A Centenary History*, 1946; *Scottish Biographies*, 1938; private information; personal knowledge.]                    JOHN BAILLIE.

MARTIN-HARVEY, SIR JOHN MARTIN (1863–1944), actor-manager, was born at Wivenhoe, Essex, 22 June 1863, the eldest son to survive infancy and fourth of the seven children of John Harvey, a noted builder of yachts and other craft, whose family had been connected with the town for generations. Martin-Harvey's mother was Margaret Diana Mary, daughter of the Rev. David George Goyder, Swedenborgian minister, of the Carmarthenshire family of Gwydyr. Martin-Harvey was brought up as a Swedenborgian, but while still a boy joined the Church of England. He was educated at a succession of schools ending with King's College School, London. The one subject he was good at was drawing. In later years he drew many excellent sketches and believed that he would have

succeeded as a professional artist. Instead, he became an apprentice to his father at Wivenhoe.

His decision to go on the stage was due to a chance remark of his father after a performance of *H.M.S. Pinafore* by children. It was on the advice of (Sir) W. S. Gilbert [q.v.], for whom Harvey was building a yacht, that his son became the pupil of John Ryder [q.v.], Macready's former leading man. Martin-Harvey appeared in 1881 as a boy in *To Parents and Guardians* at the Royal Court Theatre, afterwards touring in *Betsy* and then in 1882 joining the company of (Sir) Henry Irving [q.v.] at the Lyceum Theatre, walking on in *Romeo and Juliet*. He remained with Irving for fourteen years, playing small parts, but doing so with peculiar charm, particularly as the Dauphin in *Louis XI* and as Lorenzo in *The Merchant of Venice*. He went with Irving four times to the United States, and each summer from 1888 to 1894 toured with a repertory company in conjunction with William Haviland and Louis Calvert.

On leaving the Lyceum in 1896 Harvey appeared in several plays at the Royal Court Theatre, including *The Children of the King*. At the Prince of Wales's Theatre his Pelléas in Maeterlinck's *Pelléas and Mélisande* moved the author to declare: 'Il a volé mon âme, ce M. Harvey.' It was in the following year (1899) that 'little Jack Harvey' as (Dame) Ellen Terry [q.v.] still called him, astonished the playgoing world by presenting *The Only Way* at the Lyceum with complete success. This simple and frankly sentimental adaptation of Dickens's *Tale of Two Cities*, made by two Irish clergymen, Freeman Crofts Wills and Frederick Langbridge, was destined to become a stage classic. Much of its appeal was due to the insight and initiative of Martin-Harvey's wife, whom he married in 1889, when both were junior members of the Lyceum company. She was Angelita Helena Margarita (died 1949), daughter of Don Ramón de Silva Ferro, and her name suggests her distinguished Spanish parentage; but she also had Stewart blood through the Earls of Seaforth. She suggested, planned for years, and finally named *The Only Way*. The perfect fitness of the parts of Sydney Carton and Mimi to the Martin-Harveys made its arrival one of the most memorable theatrical events of its time. Martin-Harvey was to present many other productions in the course of a subsequent career of half a century. To the end *The*

*Only Way* remained a never-failing attraction throughout the English-speaking world.

Martin-Harvey's productions of *Hamlet* (1904), *Richard III* (1910), and *The Taming of the Shrew* (1913) were full of original touches and fine work. His Lieutenant Reresby, 'The Rat', in *The Breed of the Treshams* (1903) had a rakish vigour in conscious contrast to sensitive and beautiful studies like his Count Skariatine in *A Cigarette Maker's Romance* (1901) and the natural dignity of his performance in Maeterlinck's *The Burgomaster of Stilemonde* (1918). His *Œdipus Rex* (1912) at Covent Garden was a profoundly impressive performance and an epoch-making production.

Martin-Harvey, who was one of the early supporters of the scheme for the establishment of a national theatre, was knighted in 1921, and received the honorary degree of LL.D. from the university of Glasgow in 1938. He died at East Sheen 14 May 1944. His *Autobiography* (1933) is a delightful record of all that went to the making of an abundantly fruitful life. In it he made no secret of his ungrudged homage to Irving and of his debt to his wife's faith and vision. His sister May (Mrs. Helmsley), who died in 1930, was leading lady to Sir John Hare [q.v.]. He had one son, and a daughter, Muriel, who went on the stage.

There are portraits of Martin-Harvey by Frank O. Salisbury as Richard III, by Harrington Mann as Sydney Carton, and by Arthur Hacker as Hamlet, all reproduced in the autobiography; a number of other portraits and drawings are in the possession of the family and a bust by Sir George Frampton is at Stratford on Avon.

[Sir John Martin-Harvey, *Autobiography*, 1933; *The Book of Martin Harvey*, compiled by R. N. Green-Armytage, 1932; *The Times*, 15 May 1944; *Who's Who in the Theatre*; private information; personal knowledge.]

S. R. LITTLEWOOD.

MASON, ALFRED EDWARD WOODLEY (1865–1948), novelist, was the youngest son of William Woodley Mason, chartered accountant, by his wife, Elizabeth Hobill, daughter of Joseph Gaines, a plumber and glazier of Leicestershire. He was born 7 May 1865 in Camberwell, whence his parents soon moved, settling in Dulwich in 1878. In that year Mason entered Dulwich College, going on in 1884 to Trinity College, Oxford, where he won an exhibition in classics in 1887, being placed in the second class of the honours list in classical moderations (1886) and in the third class in *literae humaniores* (1888). He was a notable speaker in the Union, but after playing Heracles in the O.U.D.S. *Alcestis* in May 1887 turned his attention to acting, and for some years toured the provinces, usually with Edward Compton or Isabel Bateman. In 1894, although appearing in the first production of Shaw's *Arms and the Man*, he failed to find further west-end work and, encouraged by Oscar Wilde and (Sir) Arthur Quiller-Couch [qq.v.], produced his first novel, *A Romance of Wastdale* (1895). Next year *The Courtship of Morrice Buckler* placed him in the front rank of the 'cloak-and-dagger' story-tellers, although *Miranda of the Balcony* (1899) won him fame as a contemporary novelist. *Parson Kelly* (1900), written in collaboration with Andrew Lang [q.v.], and *Clementina* (1901) both showed an advance in historical fiction, but the success of *The Four Feathers* (1902) turned Mason to the novel of contemporary adventure for the next thirty years. This, his most famous book, combining excitement with careful character analysis, represents a new development in his and indeed most other popular fiction which had hitherto so often been content with simple characterization, the whole interest being focused on the action. Mason followed up his success by applying the same method to the detective story with the first of the Inspector Hanaud series, *At the Villa Rose* (1910).

Not content with writing adventurously, Mason sought adventure exploring in Morocco, sailing, and alpine climbing. Of these experiences he made good use in fiction, as of his five years (1906–10) as Liberal member of Parliament for Coventry, and his adventures in the war of 1914–18 in which he was a major in the Royal Marine Light Infantry and performed notable secret service work in Spain, Morocco, and Mexico.

Returning to literature, he achieved increased success with the next three Hanaud stories, *The House of the Arrow* (1924), *The Prisoner in the Opal* (1928), and *They Wouldn't be Chessmen* (1935), his thriller *No Other Tiger* (1927), and the last historical novels which show deeper insight and more subtle understanding of character in action. Of these, *Fire Over England* (1936) and *Königsmark* (1938) represent both popular and artistic success, but with *Musk and Amber* (1942) he touched the fringes of greater literature: as a novelist he will be remembered for this book, as a story-teller for *The Four Feathers* and his detective series.

Mason was less successful as a dramatist, his best play being *The Witness for the Defence* (St. James's, 1911), but he wrote a notable volume of stage history, *Sir George Alexander and the St. James's Theatre* (1935). He wrote the notice of Sir James Barrie for this DICTIONARY and also that of 'Anthony Hope'. He was elected an honorary fellow of Trinity in 1943 where his portrait, painted by (Sir) Oswald Birley in 1946, now hangs.

Mason was tall, broad, with pronounced features, wore an eye-glass, was a member of many famous clubs, a guest much sought in society and at country-houses, a brilliant raconteur, a generous listener whose laugh, said E. V. Lucas, was 'famous in both hemispheres', a good friend, and a man who enjoyed every moment to the full. His books were 'best sellers' for fifty years, and the films made from them, notably *The Drum* (1938) for which he wrote his own scenario, and *The Four Feathers* (1939), among the most popular in their time. He never married, refused a knighthood since 'such honours mean nothing to a childless man', and died still young in spirit in London 22 November 1948.

[*The Times*, 23 November 1948; R. L. Green, *A. E. W. Mason*, 1952; private information; personal knowledge.]
ROGER LANCELYN GREEN.

MASSINGBERD, SIR ARCHIBALD ARMAR MONTGOMERY- (1871–1947), field-marshal. [See MONTGOMERY-MASSINGBERD.]

MAWER, SIR ALLEN (1879–1942), scholar, was born at Bow in London 8 May 1879, the elder son of George Henry Mawer, secretary to the Country Towns Mission, and his wife, Clara Isabella Allen. He was educated by his parents and at the Coopers' Company Grammar School. In 1897 he obtained a first class as an external candidate for the honours degree in English of London University, entered University College as a graduate in 1898 and was a Morley medallist there, but in 1901 went to Cambridge as a foundation scholar of Gonville and Caius College and in 1904 took a first class with double distinction in the English sections of the medieval and modern languages tripos, an unprece-

dented honour. After a year as a research student he was elected in 1905 into a fellowship of Gonville and Caius, which he held until 1911. He was lecturer in English at Sheffield (1905–8), Joseph Cowen professor of English language and literature at Armstrong College, Newcastle upon Tyne (1908–21), and Baines professor of English language at Liverpool (1921–9). In 1930 he returned to University College as its provost and devoted his remaining years to the university where he had begun his brilliant academic career.

Mawer's scholarly interests at first centred round the Scandinavian settlements in England and were historical rather than philological, as seen especially in his admirable *The Vikings* (1913). They were soon transferred to place-names, a field to which he remained ever faithful. In 1920 appeared his *Place-Names of Northumberland and Durham*, which gave him rank as one of the leading scholars in the field of name-study. He next took the initiative for a systematic survey of English place-names, the need for which had long been felt. Thanks to his inspiration and untiring efforts the English Place-Name Society was founded in 1923 in order to finance the survey, and he became its honorary director. He drew up the plan of the work and had the chief responsibility for the publications. Two introductory volumes (one, *Chief Elements used in English Place-Names*, written by Mawer) appeared in 1924, and from 1925 to 1943 one volume came out regularly each year with the exception of 1941. The magnificent series, which deals with sixteen counties, is an honour to English scholarship. The high standard of the volumes is mainly due to Mawer who did the lion's share of the work, and they testify not only to his scholarship and sound method, but also to his skill as an organizer and his faculty of co-operation with fellow workers. Among his numerous publications by the side of the survey his *Problems of Place-Name Study* (1929) deserves special mention.

Mawer's provostship fell in a critical period in the history of University College. His responsibilities and duties must have been specially heavy in the war years when the college was evacuated, and the strain involved may have been a contributory cause of his premature death; he died suddenly, 22 July 1942, in a train at Broxbourne when on his way up to London for a university meeting. His colleagues have borne witness to his signal services to the college, to his administrative skill, his power of initiative, his selfless devotion to duty. 'He was one of the best and most lovable of men, gifted with a wide humanity, a sympathy as ready as it was understanding, a constant cheerfulness, and a delight in the company of his fellow-men, which made the College a better and a happier place.' There is a large crayon portrait of Mawer by P. A. de László at the college.

The British Academy in 1929 awarded him its biennial prize for English studies and in the following year elected him a fellow. He was elected an honorary fellow of Gonville and Caius College in 1935, and held the honorary degrees of Litt.D., Cambridge (1930), and D.C.L., Durham (1937). He was knighted in 1937.

He married in 1909 Lettice Mona Kathleen, daughter of the Rev. Christopher Heath, for many years vicar of Hucclecote, Gloucestershire. She survived him with four daughters. A son died in infancy.

[*The Times*, 23 July 1942; F. M. Stenton in *Proceedings* of the British Academy, vol. xxix, 1943; *English Studies*, vol. xxiv, 1942; University College *Annual Report*, 1943; private information; personal knowledge.]

E. EKWALL.

MAXTON, JAMES (1885–1946), politician, was born in the small burgh of Pollokshaws near Glasgow 22 June 1885, the son of James Maxton, schoolteacher, by his wife, Melvina Purdon, who had also been a schoolteacher before her marriage. Maxton himself started life in the same profession, as did his three sisters; he also married a schoolteacher, so that teaching might be said to have been in his blood. His younger brother, John Purdon Maxton, was director of the Institute of Agrarian Affairs at Oxford from 1941 until his death ten years later.

When Maxton was five years old the family, upon the appointment of his father as headmaster in a Barrhead school, removed there. After some years under his father's tuition, Maxton went with a county bursary to Hutcheson's Grammar School in Glasgow, then trained as a teacher, and leaving the university before taking his degree taught in elementary schools at Pollokshaws and then in Bridgeton, Glasgow. While so engaged he completed his degree course at the university and graduated M.A. in 1909. His university career was not of any exceptional note, but it is interesting to record that the

future leader of the Independent Labour Party gave his first political vote to George Wyndham [q.v.] as Conservative candidate for the lord-rectorship; that he joined the Conservative Club and the 1st Lanarkshire Rifle Volunteers, and is remembered at Gilmorehill as an athlete and for his performances in running the half-mile. In 1904, however, after attending a meeting addressed by Philip (later Viscount) Snowden [q.v.], he joined the Independent Labour Party at Barrhead, became an omnivorous student of Socialist literature, and devoted all his spare time to public expositions of Socialism. He rapidly acquired an all-Scottish reputation as an orator, witty and sentimental, and, eschewing altogether the heavy Marxian dogmas and phrasemongering then so much in vogue, he attracted large audiences of the common folk.

When war broke out in 1914 he was soon in conflict with the authorities and in 1916, after a speech at Glasgow denouncing the deportation of some engineers who had opposed dilution of labour schemes, and calling for a general strike on the Clyde as a protest, he was arrested and sentenced to twelve months' imprisonment for sedition. Upon his release from prison Maxton obtained work as a labourer in a shipyard not engaged upon war work. His dog was stoned to death for his master's anti-war opinions. At the general election of 1918 he stood for the Bridgeton division of Glasgow, and although beaten by 3,027 he polled 7,860 votes and succeeded later in persuading his successful opponent, Alexander MacCallum Scott, to join the Independent Labour Party. He himself became an organizer for the party, and in 1919 was elected to the Glasgow education authority. In that year he married Sarah Whitehead, daughter of John McCallum, master wright, and the next three years of his life, he said, were his happiest. When his wife died in 1922, having exhausted herself in nursing their infant son, the shock nearly broke Maxton and it took him years to recover.

At the general election in 1922 he was elected member for Bridgeton by a majority of 7,692. During the debate in the House of Commons upon the Scottish estimates in 1923 he severely criticized cuts in public health expenditure, and was suspended for describing some members as murderers. He succeeded Reginald Clifford Allen (later Lord Allen of Hurtwood, q.v.) as chairman of the Independent Labour Party in 1926, a post he held until 1931 (and again 1934–9), but administrative responsibility rather irked him; the party drifted into antagonism to the official Labour Party from which it disaffiliated in 1932; and in a few years it sank out of sight as an effective propaganda instrument.

Maxton's personal charm was irresistible; his hold upon the Bridgeton constituency in every general election between 1922 and 1945 unshakeable: his political opponents, both inside and outside the House of Commons, classed him not only as a persuasive propagandist but as a great gentleman, and his wit, his humour, and his burning eloquence contributed greatly from a thousand platforms to the upsurge of the Labour and Socialist movement in Great Britain. He did not enjoy good health, and, taking little exercise, was spendthrift in what he had of it. In 1935 he married again, this time his secretary, Madeline Grace, daughter of the late George Henry Brougham Glasier, estate agent. After a lingering illness, he died at Largs, Ayrshire, 23 July 1946. In 1932 he published *Lenin* and in 1935 *If I were Dictator*. He was, however, happiest on the platform; there he was master. A portrait by Sir John Lavery is in the Scottish National Portrait Gallery, and a portrait head sculpture by Lady Kennet is in the Glasgow City Art Gallery.

[Gilbert McAllister, *James Maxton, the Portrait of a Rebel*, 1935; John McNair, *James Maxton, the Beloved Rebel*, 1955; *Daily Express*, Scottish edition, 23 April 1935 et seq.; private information; personal knowledge.]

THOMAS JOHNSTON.


MAY, GEORGE ERNEST, first BARON MAY (1871–1946), financial expert, was born 20 June 1871 at Cheshunt, the younger son of William May, grocer and wine merchant, by his wife, Julia Ann Mole. He was educated at Cranleigh and entered the service of the Prudential Assurance Company as a junior clerk at the age of sixteen and was in the service of the company until he retired at the age of sixty. His financial gifts quickly made themselves felt; he became a fellow of the Institute of Actuaries in 1897, and was promoted secretary to the Prudential in 1915. In this capacity and in charge of investment policy he gained a reputation in the City for his quickness of apprehension, his energy, and resourcefulness.

The first occasion when May came into public notice outside his immediate City interests was during the war of 1914–18. Some months prior to July 1915 the Prudential had offered to sell or to lend their American securities to the Exchequer in order to support the exchange, and Reginald McKenna [q.v.], then chancellor of the Exchequer, had taken grateful notice of the offer. In July 1915 it transpired that certain munition contracts could be signed only if further funds were made immediately available in the United States. When McKenna recalled this offer and asked for the co-operation of the company, the large dollar investment holdings of the Prudential, amounting to over $40 million, were speedily placed at the disposal of the Treasury. May became manager of the American dollar securities committee which was set up to organize the collection of similar securities held by other companies and individuals. For this work, by common consent admirably performed, May was appointed K.B.E. in 1918. The report of the committee was published in 1919.

During the same war years May, with the rank of deputy quarter-master-general (canteens), was in charge of the administration of canteens, garrisons, and regimental institutes in the United Kingdom and abroad through the Navy and Army Canteen Board, and of the administration of official canteens in France and other theatres of war through the Expeditionary Force canteen committee.

May was created a baronet in 1931 in further recognition of his public services, and retired from the Prudential shortly afterwards. In view of his age and of the grave impairment of his eyesight during his last few years at the Prudential—he had lost the sight of one eye and had had a cataract operation on the other—he might well have felt justified in taking life easily. But he immediately accepted the invitation of Philip (later Viscount) Snowden [q.v.], chancellor of the Exchequer in the Labour Government, to preside over a committee on national expenditure 'to make recommendations . . . for effecting forthwith all possible reductions in the national expenditure on supply services . . .'. The appointment of this committee had been forced on the Government by the other two political parties, but after the repeated reviews of expenditure by various economy committees during the period since the war few people—and certainly not Snowden—imagined that there was scope for further substantial reductions.

May's task was made the harder by the fact that his team was constituted on a political basis with two representatives from each of the three main parties. He threw himself into his difficult task with all the energy and persuasive urbanity of his forceful character, and by the end of July 1931 he had produced a report which was entirely accepted by his Conservative and Liberal colleagues and endorsed in many points in the minority report submitted by the two Labour representatives. Towards meeting an estimated deficiency in the national accounts for the coming financial year of £120 million, the majority submitted recommendations estimated to save over £96½ million, and they coupled these recommendations with severe criticisms of the general attitude and proceedings of recent Governments and members of Parliament in regard to national finance. Not all students of the financial history of those days are in agreement with the committee's estimate of the economies required. Yet it must be remembered that those were still the days when budget deficits were taken seriously. The economies suggested in the social services (£66½ million came under the heading unemployment insurance and £1 million under national health insurance) were the prime cause of the bitter dissensions in the Labour movement of subsequent years.

The report appeared at a grave moment: the financial crisis in the United States following the Wall Street slump of 1929 and political events in Europe had upset the international money market. London was experiencing a heavy drain on its gold reserves, and this was intensified by the revelations and criticisms in the May report. A political crisis supervened and within a month the Labour Government had given place to a 'national' ministry, with Ramsay MacDonald still as prime minister. But this could not save the pound and within another month Britain was forced to abandon the gold standard.

Substantially the same 'national' Government was returned at the ensuing general election in October, pledged not only to drastic retrenchment but also to the reintroduction of a general tariff, and one of the first acts of the new Parliament was to set up machinery to give effect to this revolution in British trading policy. A small independent advisory committee was to be appointed to investigate applications for protection and to make recommendations to the Treasury which was empowered to submit statutory orders accordingly for approval by simple resolution of the House of Commons. Once more the chancellor of the Exchequer of the day (Neville Chamberlain) turned to May to undertake a novel and difficult task. He became chairman of the Import Duties Advisory Committee early in 1932 (the other members being Sir Sydney Chapman and Sir Allan Powell, q.v.) and in the course of the next three years the general lines of a comprehensive tariff had been drawn up and put into operation, to be revised and elaborated in subsequent recommendations of the committee.

May was entirely in accord with Chamberlain's declared policy of using the grant of protection, not as a cloak for inefficiency and high prices, but as a shield behind which British industry could reorganize and re-equip itself to face competition both abroad and at home; his wide knowledge of industry and finance and his acquaintance with leaders in both fields was of inestimable value in the pursuit of this policy. The iron and steel industry provided a crucial test. It had been a source of anxiety to successive Governments ever since the slump of 1920 and May made this industry his special responsibility on the committee. The war of 1939–45 came before its reorganization was complete, but there can be little doubt that the great part it was able to play during the war derived much of its strength from the reforms set in train under the stimulus of the Import Duties Committee.

With the outbreak of war, the committee's activities were practically suspended, and both members and staff were drafted into more urgent tasks. May, who had been raised to the peerage in 1935 as Baron May, of Weybridge, remained as chairman until the completion of his last term of office in 1941. He died in London 10 April 1946 and was succeeded in his titles by his elder son, John Lawrence (1904–50).

In appearance May was tall, slim, and erect, with an air of aloof distinction, emphasized in later life by his poor eyesight and the wearing of a monocle. He was a great believer in personal contact rather than the written word, and his charm, his remarkable memory, his ability to concentrate on essentials and to pursue his objectives with single-minded purpose —these qualities, coupled with his swift and shrewd judgement of men and situations, admirably fitted him for this method of conducting affairs.

In 1903 May married Lily Julia (died 1955), daughter of Gustavus Strauss, merchant, of London; they had two sons and a daughter. His portrait, painted by A. K. Lawrence, belongs to the family.

[Report of the Committee on National Expenditure, Cmd. 3920, 1931; Viscount Snowden, *An Autobiography*, vol. ii, 1934; private information; personal knowledge.]

GEORGE L. BARSTOW.

MAYBURY, SIR HENRY PERCY (1864–1943), civil engineer, the fourth son of Charles Maybury, agriculturalist, by his wife, Jane Matthews, was born 17 November 1864 at Uffington, near Shrewsbury. He passed from Upton Magna School into the office of Robert E. Johnston, chief engineer of the Great Western and London and North Western joint railways at Shrewsbury station and in 1884 was employed by the firm of Johnson Bros. and Slay, contractors, of Wrexham, and later became manager. After having been successively engineer and surveyor to the Festiniog local board (1892) and the Malvern urban district council (1895), he was appointed county engineer and surveyor of Kent in 1904, where he gained his reputation from the work he did in the trial sections of road at Sidcup. In 1910 he joined the Road Board, becoming chief engineer in 1913 and eventually manager and secretary. From the outbreak of war in 1914 he was responsible for the road work undertaken for the War Department and in 1917 was sent to France as director of roads with the rank of brigadier-general. In 1919 he was appointed director-general of roads under the Ministry of Transport from which he retired in 1928, holding the position of consulting engineer and adviser to the minister on road traffic problems until 1932. Concurrently with these posts, Maybury also acted as chairman of the London Traffic Advisory Committee from 1924 to 1933, the year in which he was appointed a member of the newly formed London Passenger Transport Board, and he was also chairman of several departmental committees dealing with the economics and regulation of road vehicles and the development of civil aviation in the United Kingdom.

Honours came freely to a man of such constant activity and proved merit. His services in the war were rewarded by five mentions in dispatches, by the C.B. (1917),

the C.M.G. and K.C.M.G. (1919), and the Legion of Honour (1917). On his retirement he was appointed G.B.E. (1928). In the professional world he was no less honoured. He was president of the Institution of Civil Engineers (1933–4), of the Institute of Transport (1921–2), and of the Institute of Quarrying in 1919. At the time of his death he was president of the Society of Engineers and of the Smeatonian Society; the borough of Shrewsbury in 1928 elected as honorary freeman one who might almost be called one of its sons. At the university of London the Paviors' Company (to which he had been elected in 1918) founded in 1928 a chair of highway engineering which was named after him.

Maybury was twice married: first, in 1885 to Elizabeth (died 1929), daughter of Thomas Sheldon, of Ludlow, by whom he had two sons and two daughters; secondly, in 1942 to Katharine Mary, daughter of Samuel William Pring, company director, of Winchester and Newport, Isle of Wight. A portrait of Maybury by (Sir) Oswald Birley hangs in the Institution of Civil Engineers. He will be remembered for his work in remodelling the roads and the traffic system of Great Britain, and, during the war, in France also. Apart from his professional skill, he possessed qualities which secured for him the confidence of successive ministers of transport, and the wholehearted support, loyalty, and devotion, not only of the staff, but of highway engineers throughout the country. His skill in negotiation enabled him to perform invaluable service for the Government between the two wars in promoting vast road schemes for the relief of unemployment. His vitality was remarkable and he was indefatigable. After his retirement from the public service he entered the commercial world and held a number of directorships until he died at Shrewsbury 7 January 1943.

[*The Times*, 9 January 1943; *Engineering*, 15 January 1943; *Journal* of the Institution of Civil Engineers, March 1943; *Highways and Bridges*, 13 and 27 January 1943; personal knowledge.]                    J. S. KILLICK.

MEE, ARTHUR HENRY (1875–1943), journalist, was born 21 July 1875 at Stapleford, Nottinghamshire, the eldest son and second of the ten children of Henry Mee, railway fireman, and his wife, Mary Fletcher, both pious Baptists. The village schoolmaster, George Byford, encouraged his zest for knowledge, enhanced his inborn capacity for wonder, and trained his prodigious memory. John Derry, editor of the *Nottingham Daily Express*, to which Arthur was apprenticed as reporter at sixteen, taught him so efficiently that he became editor of its subsidiary, the *Nottingham Evening News*, at twenty.

In 1896 Mee, who had been contributing articles to *Tit-Bits*, joined the staff of Sir George Newnes [q.v.] and removed to London. Later he turned to free-lance journalism, then edited *Black and White* for two years, and finally joined the staff of the *Daily Mail* at the request of Alfred Harmsworth (later Viscount Northcliffe, q.v.) who had heard, and appreciated the significance, of the system of 250,000 cross-indexed press-cuttings which Mee had built up. He was soon deputed to produce a *Self-Educator* (1905–7), a vast work which established Mee as an able organizer of popular instruction and a master of both graceful phrase and forceful slogan. Henceforward Mee wrote the advertisements for all his own productions. Among these, between 1907 and 1913, were the Harmsworth serials, *History of the World*, *Natural History*, and *Popular Science*, and finally *I See All* (1928–30), claimed to be the world's first picture encyclopedia, and *Arthur Mee's Thousand Heroes* (1933–4).

It was the *Children's Encyclopedia* which he began to issue in fortnightly parts in 1908 that proved Arthur Mee's most successful enterprise, originating, he declared, in the spate of questions from Marjorie, his only child. This *Book of Knowledge*, as the American editions were called, appealed to children and parents alike by its readable style and apt pictures. Mee was not, in the strict sense, a scholar, but he had an inquiring mind, a fluent pen, and a flair for compressing information. Writing to make plain to himself 'the story of all ages, peoples, and things', he thereby shared this knowledge with each reader. He continued this method in his monthly *My Magazine* until 1933, and from 1919 in his weekly *Children's Newspaper* which 'told the story of the world today for the men and women of tomorrow with an unconquerable faith in goodness and progress'. The *Children's Encyclopedia* was translated into French, Italian, Spanish, Portuguese, Arabic, and Chinese. Frequently revised, both during Mee's lifetime and since his death, it has won high esteem among educationists.

During the war of 1914–18 Mee used his talent in publicity to organize a patriotic temperance crusade called 'The Strength of Britain Movement'. This crusading spirit pervades his *Who Giveth Us the Victory* (1918), a clear, concise confession of that faith which shines through all his books, especially those which he compiled each year from his own articles in *My Magazine* and the *Children's Newspaper*.

A very keen love for Kent, his adopted county, led Arthur Mee to the main task of his last twelve years. This was *The King's England*, a record of what to see in England, which he organized county by county into forty-one volumes, personally visiting and vividly describing hundreds of places. Furthermore, he drastically revised the work of his carefully trained helpers without respite until he died suddenly in London, after an operation, 27 May 1943, leaving the task to be completed by one of his colleagues, Mr. Sydney Warner.

Short, spare, and trim, Arthur Mee was in all things methodical. He had a natural grace and a merry, spontaneous laugh. His success undoubtedly surprised him, for he remained humble and unpretentious. His eager personality has been preserved by his friend, Frank O. Salisbury, in a portrait in oils in the possession of his family. Mee married in 1897 Amelia, daughter of Charles Fratson, of East Cottingwith, Yorkshire.

[Sir John Hammerton, *Child of Wonder*, 1946; personal knowledge.]

HUGO TYERMAN.

MENZIES, SIR FREDERICK NORTON KAY (1875–1949), medical officer of health, was born at Caernarvon 2 November 1875, the second son of John Menzies, civil engineer, by his wife, Edith Madeline, daughter of Robert Kay, of Burnley, Lancashire. He was educated at Llandovery College and the university of Edinburgh where he graduated M.B. in 1899 and in 1903 gained his M.D. He spent some time in postgraduate study in Vienna and Berlin and held resident posts at the Edinburgh Royal Infirmary, and in London at the Hospital for Sick Children, Great Ormond Street, the Brompton Hospital, and the Western Fever Hospital of the Metropolitan Asylums Board.

In 1905 Menzies obtained the diploma in public health and in 1907 was appointed demonstrator and lecturer in public health at University College, London, under Henry Richard Kenwood. In the same year he became deputy medical officer of health of the metropolitan borough of

Stoke Newington and in 1909 joined the staff of the London County Council as a part-time officer. Two years later he was appointed a whole-time assistant medical officer and inaugurated school medical work in the east end of London. His next important duty was to prepare and implement schemes for the control of tuberculosis and venereal diseases in London. This task brought him into close contact with the managements and staffs of the then voluntary hospitals, a happy association which broadened with the years.

In 1923 he inherited Thorpe Abbotts Place, Diss, Norfolk, from his cousin, the daughter of Sir Edward Ebenezer Kay [q.v.]. For many years prior to her death he had managed the estate for her. He was so greatly attached to it that he gave up his London house and went to live there. In 1924 he resigned his full-time post with the London County Council to become director of hospitals and medical services for the British Red Cross Society and the Order of St. John of Jerusalem, but he was persuaded to remain on the Council's part-time staff to act in a consultative capacity for the tuberculosis and venereal diseases schemes.

In 1926 he returned to full-time work for the Council as county medical officer of health. A few years later, torn between his own wish to settle down on his Norfolk estate and the increasing demands made upon him by his official duties, he took the decision to devote all his energies to London and sold the estate.

After 1926, although his responsibilities as county medical officer of health covered a very wide field, his main preoccupation was hospital administration. In 1930 seventy-two general and special hospitals of the Metropolitan Asylums Board and of the twenty-five Metropolitan Boards of Guardians were, on the abolition of those bodies, transferred to the control of the County Council with Menzies as their chief medical adviser. It was an immense task to weld them into an integrated hospital service and was possible only because of his unique knowledge of hospitals of all classes. So successful was he that he received the most unusual distinction of mention in the published report of a government department. The annual report of the Ministry of Health for 1934–5 stated that 'the London County Council . . . were, indeed, fortunate in having a county medical officer whose personality and experience have been so largely responsible for the successful results which

have been achieved'. On his retirement from office in 1939, the London County Council recorded in its minutes the outstanding value of Menzies's services to London.

Menzies then returned to his native Caernarvonshire where he acted as inspector of hospitals and convalescent homes in North Wales for the British Red Cross Society and the Order of St. John of Jerusalem. In 1945 he went back to London and was much in demand for committee work of which he had had so much previous experience. He had been a member of government committees on venereal diseases, the training and employment of midwives, the scientific investigation of crime, and on nursing. He was for many years a Ministry of Health representative on the Central Midwives Board and the General Nursing Council. He also played an active part in the establishment of the Postgraduate Medical School of London at Hammersmith Hospital. A great upholder of voluntary effort, he was a member of the council of King Edward's Hospital Fund for London, the Nuffield Provincial Hospitals Trust and of the boards of St. Thomas's Hospital, the London Hospital, and Queen Mary's Hospital, Roehampton. He was a member of the council of the National Association for the Prevention of Tuberculosis and of the appeals committee of the British Broadcasting Corporation.

Menzies, who was of commanding stature, possessed good judgement, the gift of exposition, and a persuasive tongue. He studied every problem thoroughly and when he had found the solution he refused to compromise with expediency. In 1932 he was appointed K.B.E. and in 1937 was made honorary physician to the King. In 1907 he was elected F.R.C.P. (Edinburgh, Cullen prize, 1934), and in 1932 F.R.C.P. (London, Bisset-Hawkins gold medal, 1941). In 1927 he was elected a fellow of the Royal Society of Edinburgh and in 1933 he received the honorary degree of LL.D. from the university of Edinburgh. He was a knight of grace of the Order of St. John of Jerusalem.

During the later years of his life his health was not good. In February 1949, in his capacity as chairman of the London committee, he went to Port Said to inspect the British hospital there. He was taken ill on the return voyage but was able to reach London where he died, somewhat suddenly, at his home 14 May 1949.

Menzies married in 1916 Harriet May,

daughter of Edward Honoratus Lloyd, K.C., a leader of the parliamentary bar; they had two sons and one daughter; the elder son, a regular soldier, was killed in action in Normandy in 1944.

[*The Times*, 16 May 1949; *British Medical Journal* and *Lancet*, 21 May 1949; Annual address by the president (Lord Moran) to the Royal College of Physicians, London, 3 April 1950; personal knowledge.]

ALLEN DALEY.

MESTON, JAMES SCORGIE, first BARON MESTON (1865–1943), Indian civil servant, and man of affairs, was born at Aberdeen 12 June 1865, the eldest son of James Meston, registrar for the parish of Old Machar, Aberdeen, by his wife, Jane Greig, daughter of James Scorgie, of Aberdeen. At the Aberdeen Grammar School he was dux and gold medallist. From the university of Aberdeen he passed the Indian Civil Service examination of 1883, and then went to Balliol College, Oxford, for his probation. At the close of 1885 he was posted to the North-Western Provinces and Oudh (later renamed the United Provinces of Agra and Oudh). In 1897 he was made director of land records and agriculture. He was financial secretary to government from 1899 to 1905—an anxious period on account of defective monsoons and consequent famine conditions. From 1905 to 1906 his services were loaned to the Cape Colony and Transvaal governments to advise on Civil Service reform.

In the middle of 1906 Meston officiated as secretary to the Government of India in the finance department and was confirmed in the post in the following year. He quickly mastered the intricacies of Indian finance and made them more intelligible to his colleagues by minutes and drafts invariably well couched and in beautiful calligraphy. In the viceroy's legislature he was able to disarm critics by his lucid and persuasive speeches.

In the autumn of 1912 Meston returned to Lucknow to be lieutenant-governor of the United Provinces. The heavy labours inseparable from unshared responsibility for the governance of some 48 million people, with liability to occasional Hindu–Moslem strife, were enhanced in 1914 by the outbreak of war, with its demands on manpower and supplies. His kindly reluctance to refuse any reasonable request, irrespective of the labour it might entail, added to his burdens, but did not lessen his zeal in promoting local self-government, industrial expansion, and education.

In these years also Meston did much to prepare the way for Indian political advance. On his invitation Lionel Curtis, whom he had met in South Africa, went to India in the autumn of 1916 for discussions on the subject. Although Meston could take no public part in the unofficial moves which followed, he gave much help behind the scenes in preparing the way for the substantial reforms of 1919. In 1917 with Sir S. P. (later Lord) Sinha and the Maharaja Ganga Singh of Bikaner [qq.v.], he assisted the secretary of state in representing India in the Imperial War Cabinet and Conference.

In 1918 Meston was called to the viceroy's executive council as finance member. His effective tenure was very short. He was in London again in the summer of 1919 giving evidence for his Government before the joint select committee of Parliament on Indian reform which had for a textbook the Montagu–Chelmsford report. Later in the year the state of his eyesight compelled him under medical advice to relinquish his finance membership and to decline the invitation of E. S. Montagu [q.v.] to be permanent under-secretary at the India Office. In recognition of his services and with the idea of his assisting Lord Sinha, the parliamentary under-secretary for India, he was created in November 1919 Baron Meston, of Agra and of Dunottar, county Kincardine. An ancestor, William Meston [q.v.], had been governor of Dunottar Castle in the eighteenth century.

The Government of India Act, 1919, was now on the statute book, and the provincial dyarchical system, due to come into force in January 1921, involved entirely new financial relations between the provinces and the centre. Meston was made chairman of a small expert committee to recommend adjustments and to work out an equitable plan of provincial contributions to the central exchequer varying according to circumstances. His gift for conciliation amounted to genius, but the resulting 'Meston settlement' gave rise to much inter-provincial argumentation. The Indian statutory (Simon) commission, reporting in 1930, regarded these long-drawn controversies as inherent from the terms of reference rather than as due to any error of judgement by the Meston committee. Later the idea in Whitehall of utilizing Meston's experience for presiding over parliamentary inquiries was chilled by some years of delay in reporting the conclusions of a committee set up under his chairmanship in 1922 by the chancellor of the Exchequer to investigate the system of percentage grants in aid of local administration, especially for educational purposes. The issue was one, however, not wholly free from party differences.

Another reason for delay was the variety of activities engaged in by one of whom Lionel Curtis wrote: 'Few men in our time have contributed more to the public service in so many countries and over so wide a range of institutions.' Meston and Curtis in combination were the main designers of the (Royal) Institute of International Affairs, at Chatham House, St. James's Square, which in turn provided the model for other institutions of the kind, especially in Commonwealth countries. Meston was chairman of the first governing body (1920–26). He was also for many years chairman of the publications committee and of the editorial board of *International Affairs* and he served on the council to the end. Here as elsewhere he won the affectionate loyalty of the staff. The library at Chatham House bears his name. As vice-chairman of the supervisory commission of the League of Nations, he achieved remarkable success in bringing about adjustments of the finances of the League.

To the general public at home Meston was best known for his steadfast fidelity to the Liberal political school at a time of adversity in its fortunes. As president of the Liberal Party organization from 1936 he made frequent speeches in various parts of the country and they often attracted attention in the press. He was for many years to his death chairman of the National Liberal Club. A presentation portrait by M. F. de Montmorency is in the club where a spacious room for committees and private dinner parties is named after him. He was also prominent in freemasonry, being installed at the end of 1926 grand superintendent of the provincial grand chapter of Royal Arch Masons of Berkshire. With his manifold honorary labours he combined much work in the City. He was chairman of the Galloway Hydro-Electric Power Company, the Calcutta Electric Supply Corporation, and of three other limited companies, and was on the boards of nine others. Nor should his short but eminently readable contributions to the literature of Indian reform, *India at the Crossways*, being the Rede lecture at Cambridge in 1920, and *Nationhood for India* (1931) be forgotten.

Meston was appointed C.S.I. in 1908 and K.C.S.I. in 1911 and received the volunteer decoration in 1914. He was a knight of grace of the Order of St. John of Jerusalem, and received honorary degrees from the universities of Aberdeen, Edinburgh, and Zürich, and he was an honorary fellow of University College, London. He received the freedom of the cities of London and Manchester in 1917 and of his native city in 1935. What gave him particular pleasure was his chancellorship of his alma mater, Aberdeen University, from 1928 to his death.

Meston married in 1891 Jeanie (died 1946), only daughter of James McDonald, banker, of Mossat, Aberdeenshire; they had two sons, of whom the elder died in boyhood. The younger, Dougall (born 1894), succeeded as second baron on his father's death at Maidenhead, 7 October 1943. Meston was interred at Allenvale cemetery, Aberdeen.

[*India Office List*; *The Times*, 8 October 1943; *Annual Report* of the council of the Royal Institute of International Affairs, 1943–4; personal knowledge.]

F. H. BROWN.

MIDLETON, ninth VISCOUNT and first EARL OF (1856–1942), statesman. [See BRODRICK, (WILLIAM) ST. JOHN (FREMANTLE).]

MIERS, SIR HENRY ALEXANDER (1858–1942), mineralogist, administrator, and scholar, was born in Rio de Janeiro 25 May 1858, the third son and fifth of the eight children (three of whom died in infancy) of Francis Charles Miers, civil engineer, by his wife, Susan Mary, daughter of Edward Wynn Fry, general merchant, of Handsworth, Staffordshire. John Miers [q.v.], the engineer and botanist, was his grandfather, and Francis Place [q.v.] his great-grandfather. In 1860 his father retired and settled at Beckenham, Kent.

Miers was educated at Eton having gained a scholarship there in classics in 1872. In 1876 he won the public schools gold medal of the Royal Geographical Society and in 1877 he was elected a scholar in classics at Trinity College, Oxford, where he formed a lifelong friendship with the musician Basil Harwood [q.v.]. At Oxford he studied classics, science, and mathematics, being placed in the second class of the honour school of mathematics in 1881.

Miers's life falls into three distinct

phases: the student, the professor, and the administrator. On taking his degree he turned to crystallography and mineralogy, and after studying for three months under Paul Heinrich Groth at Strasbourg, he was appointed in 1882 first class assistant in the department of mineralogy of the British Museum at South Kensington where he remained until 1895. He was also instructor in crystallography at the Central Technical College from 1886 to 1895. Although largely occupied at the museum with routine duties and revising the mineral collections, he found time for special study of the crystal forms of different minerals and for many original papers.

The second phase opened with his election in 1895 to the Waynflete chair of mineralogy at Oxford with a fellowship at Magdalen College. His activity was intensified, somewhat handicapped though he was at first by the need to organize a laboratory for teaching and research, and later by demands upon him to serve on committees which increased as his versatility and practical ability came to be realized. His early published papers were largely descriptive of the materials in the collections, but he was able later to return to his studies of the growth of crystals and to devise new methods. His book, *Mineralogy: an Introduction to the Scientific Study of Minerals* (1902, 2nd ed. 1929), was a masterly survey of the state of knowledge at the time, made many years before modern developments in physics, especially the discoveries of Sir Lawrence Bragg, had made clear the arrangement of atoms in crystals.

The third phase opened with his appointment to the principalship of the university of London in 1908. It was his proved administrative ability rather than his eminence in the scientific world which earned him the position. It ushered in the least happy and productive time of his life. Immersed as he was in routine affairs, and constantly confronted with the difficulties caused by conflicts of interests in the university, he had little time for scientific work. Nevertheless, from the point of view of the university, no better appointment could then have been made. Scrupulously fair in all his dealings with his colleagues, always conciliatory and anxious to extract the best from the views of opposing parties, he held the university together at a time when it was threatening to fall apart. When the outbreak of war showed him that he could not carry out the reforms recommended by the Haldane commission it was some relief to him to accept in 1915 the offer of the vice-chancellorship of the university of Manchester, in that not only was the intellectual climate far more to his liking, but the offer was made still more attractive by the creation for him of a special chair of crystallography, giving him thereby a welcome opportunity to return to his scientific and educational interests. But he published few original papers after 1908. His influence on science was mainly indirect, through his pupils, in his constant readiness to help others and in his interest in their work. The best-known example of his indirect influence is his suggestion to (Sir) William Ramsay [q.v.] that he should investigate the gas evolved when the mineral cleveite was heated, which led in 1895 to the discovery that the rare element helium exists on the earth.

After his retirement from Manchester in 1926 he devoted much of his time to museums, as a member of the Royal Commission which reported in 1929–30, of the standing commission, and as president for five years of the Museums Association. He was also a member of the Royal Commission on the universities of Oxford and Cambridge (1919–22).

In administration Miers showed himself to be almost the ideal chairman of committees. He could gently guide discussion into relevant channels, and was then content to let it follow its course. He had none of the fiery zeal of his great-grandfather, and did not go out of his way to lead or fight any issue. If this may be called a fault, it was one which brought him trust and affection wherever he went. Side by side with these qualities went a keenly adventurous spirit which led him in 1888 to volunteer to go as a passenger in a balloon flight from Olympia to the continent. The aeronaut, Joseph Simmons, when over Essex, decided to descend for the night and put out the grappling iron which caught in a tall tree. In a high wind the balloon burst and the wire cage fell sixty feet to the ground. Simmons was killed, but Miers, although unconscious when he was picked up, recovered completely. Afterwards his adventures took the form of travel, and congenially his work took him often abroad so that between 1892 and 1931 he acquired, by visits to Scandinavia, Finland, Russia, Germany, Canada, and South and East Africa, a knowledge of the museums of other countries which was second to none.

In 1901 he visited the Klondike at the invitation of the Canadian minister of the interior; in 1903 he went to South Africa at the invitation of the Rhodes Trustees to report on educational problems; and in 1918 he was in the United States as chairman of an educational mission representing the British universities.

Of the many honours bestowed upon Miers perhaps the most singular was that, after he had left Oxford, he was continued as an active fellow of Magdalen until the end of his life. He was elected an honorary fellow of Trinity in 1931. He was elected F.R.S. in 1896, and knighted in 1912. Honorary degrees were conferred upon him by the universities of Oxford, Manchester, Sheffield, Christiania, Liverpool, and Michigan. He was an honorary member of many scientific societies at home and abroad, and a Wollaston medallist of the Geological Society of London. He was president of the geological section of the British Association in 1905 and the educational section in 1910, and of the Mineralogical Society, 1904–9. He was also a fellow of Eton College.

In person, Miers was short and wiry, and preserved a boyish appearance until an advanced age. The only portrait of him which exists is a drawing executed after his death by Helen Campbell from a photograph. It is an excellent likeness and hangs in the Senate House of the university of London. His sleeping hours were few: he could not remember a time when he slept more than four hours a night. He was seldom ill, and always cheerful, even when failing eyesight handicapped him severely in the closing years of his life. He was the most modest of men, and a delightful companion of young and old. He died, unmarried, in London 10 December 1942. His name is commemorated in the mineral miersite.

[Sir Thomas Holland in *Obituary Notices of Fellows of the Royal Society*, No. 12, November 1943; *The Times*, 12 December 1942; C. C. J. W[ebb] in the *Oxford Magazine*, 18 February 1943; private information; personal knowledge.]                    H. T. TIZARD.

MILDMAY, ANTHONY BINGHAM, second BARON MILDMAY OF FLETE (1909–1950), gentleman rider, was born in London 14 April 1909, the only son and younger of the two children of Francis Bingham Mildmay, later first Baron Mildmay of Flete, by his wife, Alice Lilian, daughter of Charles Seymour Grenfell, of Elibank, Taplow, a kinsman of Lord Desborough

[q.v.]. Mildmay was educated at Eton and Trinity College, Cambridge, where he took his degree. Like his father, while an undergraduate he hunted, and played polo for the university. He also rode in point-to-point races but showed surprisingly little of the promise which might have been expected from one who was later to hold his own with the best amateur and professional riders of his day.

His father entered Parliament in 1885 as Liberal member for the Totnes division of Devonshire, but, opposing Home Rule, subsequently sat as a Unionist until in 1922 he retired and was raised to the peerage. He served with distinction in the South African war and the war of 1914–18; was sworn of the Privy Council in 1916 and was lord lieutenant of Devonshire (1928–36). He took an active part in public life and his many interests ranged from matters of public health to the breeding of light horses and hunters and of South Devon cattle. Mildmay did not share his father's interest in politics and in 1930 joined Baring Brothers, the banking firm of which his uncle, Alfred Mildmay, was the senior partner. Work at the bank allowed him no time for hunting, so he decided to keep some steeplechase horses at Fairlawne, Mr. Peter Cazalet's home near Tonbridge. He rode in exercise gallops every morning before leaving for the City, and used his free days from the bank to ride in races under National Hunt rules. Thus began his remarkable career as an amateur rider, a career made all the more remarkable by his build which was hardly that of a jockey; he was six feet two inches in height and very long of limb. His weight, on the other hand, was under ten stone.

As steeplechasing had now become the ruling passion of his life, Mildmay decided, during the summer of 1933, to give up his City career. This undoubtedly would have been distinguished, for his intelligence, conscientiousness, and charm of manner would have ensured his success in any walk of life. But he had realized that he could only become a successful jockey by devoting most of his time to riding. Accordingly, in the autumn he started a market garden and farm on his father's estate at Shoreham, continued to live for most of the year at Fairlawne, only a few miles away, and settled down to the life of an amateur steeplechase jockey, riding both his own horses and the mounts of other owners.

Mildmay's first winner was Good Shot

at Wye in the spring of 1933, the year of his first ride in the Grand National. By 1935 he was riding regularly and also taking the falls inevitable in a steeplechase jockey's life, including a particularly serious one in the Foxhunters' Chase at Liverpool when he broke a vertebra, three ribs and an arm, and cracked his skull. Despite this he was back in the saddle a few months later, and in the Grand National of 1936 rode his father's tubed and entire horse Davy Jones. Carrying ten stone and starting at 100–1, he led from the first jump and would undoubtedly have won had not the breaking of the buckle of his reins at the penultimate fence caused him to lose control and run out at the last. However, he took this disaster with his usual sang-froid and by riding twenty-one winners in the season of 1937–8 tied with Captain R. Petre as leading amateur.

On the outbreak of war in 1939 Mildmay served in the Royal Artillery until he joined the Commandos in 1940. In 1941 he transferred to the Welsh Guards, and later served as a captain in the Guards Armoured division from the invasion of Normandy until the end of the war. He was wounded and mentioned in dispatches. On returning to race-riding, stronger in physique and more determined than ever to make himself into a first-class jockey, he was soon, as an amateur, in a class by himself, and could hold his own with the best professionals, particularly in long-distance steeplechases. Thus during the 1946–7 season he finished fourth in the list of winning jockeys with thirty-two winners, and in the Grand National (1948) rode Cromwell into third place and might well have won if the recurrence of an old neck injury had not made him powerless to assist his horse for the last half-mile. On Cromwell again in 1949 he finished fourth after starting favourite. If this was a disappointment there were compensations from his wins in other famous races. Among these were the Grand Sefton Chase at Liverpool (on his own horse), the National Hunt Chase at Cheltenham, and on one memorable afternoon both the Household Brigade Cup and the Royal Artillery Past and Present Steeplechase. In 1947 he succeeded his father as second baron and had by that time become such a favourite with the racing crowd that 'Come on, Lordy' was soon a familiar cry on any race-course.

Throughout his career on the turf Mildmay was known and loved by the humblest to the greatest in the land. The race-course crowd, and many who had only read of his exploits, looked on him as a hero and almost legendary figure. This was not only due to his skill in the saddle, but to his courage and strength of character which refused to be daunted by misfortune or spoilt by success. By his example and work he helped to raise National Hunt sport to a position which it had never held before. He was elected a member of the National Hunt Committee in 1942 and appointed a steward (1944–7 and 1949–50). He was elected a member of the Jockey Club in 1949, the year in which he became manager to the Queen and Princess Elizabeth when, very largely as a result of his suggestion, they began to own steeplechase horses.

Unhappily, his career by this time was almost over. When not riding he spent as much time as possible in Devonshire where he devoted his energies to the Flete estate and the welfare of his tenants and employees. He lived at Mothecombe, a beautiful Queen Anne house on the estate near the sea, and it was while bathing from there that he was drowned in the early morning of 12 May 1950. He was unmarried, and the title became extinct. Memorial races were named after him at Cheltenham, Sandown Park, Plumpton, and Newton Abbot, and a new steeplechase course at Aintree has been called the Mildmay course.

Sir Alfred Munnings painted a portrait of Mildmay on Davy Jones which is in the possession of his sister Mrs. John White, who also owns another portrait, by the same artist, of the first Lord Mildmay, with Lady Mildmay and their two children.

[Private information; personal knowledge.]
P. V. F. CAZALET.


MILL, HUGH ROBERT (1861–1950), geographer and meteorologist, was born in Thurso, Caithness, 28 May 1861, the tenth of the eleven children of James Mill, physician and farmer, and his wife, Harriet Gordon, daughter of the Rev. George Davidson, of Latheron. His father, who shared a great-grandfather with John Stuart Mill [q.v.], had served as a surgeon in a Dundee whaler sailing to Greenland, and as chief magistrate of Thurso was the recipient of the first telegram 'from Land's End to John o'Groat's' dispatched by the mayor of Truro in 1869. His mother, whose French ancestors had long been resident in the

West Indies, was fascinated above all by geography, and was in the chain of causation towards the conclusion of Hugh Miller [q.v.] that the Old Red Sandstone was a freshwater formation. The house of his birth was scarcely less symbolic of his interests and career than was his ancestry. It stood within sound of the cruel Pentland Firth, a short half-mile from the northern shore of Scotland, with no human habitation between it and the North Pole.

Of no little significance in Mill's formation were the tubercular illnesses which, from his tenth to his seventeenth year, deflected him from a formal educational path but enabled him to say that he had read most of the eighth edition of the *Encyclopaedia Britannica*. His mother taught him the use of the globes and passed on to him a taste for literature in general and for poetry in particular without which he might not have found the bonds of interest which held him in lifelong friendship with Sir Ernest Shackleton [q.v.] whose biography he wrote in 1923.

Moving with his widowed mother to Edinburgh in 1877, Mill enrolled for evening study in the Watt Institution and School of Art (later the Heriot-Watt College). He matriculated in the university of Edinburgh in 1880 with distinctions in five out of seven subjects. Medallist in chemistry and natural philosophy, Mill graduated as 'the most distinguished bachelor of science of 1883', and was next year awarded one of the three elective fellowships at the newly founded Scottish Marine Station at Granton. He participated, under (Sir) John Murray (1841–1914, q.v.), in the preparation of the *Challenger* reports to which he contributed an unsigned introduction on the history of oceanography. He was elected F.R.S., Edinburgh, in 1885, and in the following year was awarded his D.Sc.

For the next five years Mill lectured in geography and physiography at the Heriot-Watt College and also for the university extension scheme. Always an ardent worker and campaigner for the adequate teaching of geography, he himself published a number of textbooks and considered his book of physiography, *The Realm of Nature* (1892, 3rd ed. 1924), 'the best thing I have ever done'. He regarded his editorship of the geographical material for the eleventh edition of the *Encyclopaedia Britannica* as an occasion for expressing his own views fully for the first time, and later, in 1933, defined geography as 'the descrip-

tion of the earth's surface, with special regard to the forms of vertical relief and to the influence which these forms exercise on all mobile distributions'.

In 1892 Mill removed to London as librarian of the Royal Geographical Society, where he remained until the end of 1900. During these years he acted as recorder of the geography section of the British Association, and edited *The International Geography* (1899, reissued 1907). He was a university extension lecturer in London and Oxford, and was invited by (Sir) H. J. Mackinder [q.v.] to join in forming the Geographical Association. He also joined the Royal Meteorological Society and after the death of its president, G. J. Symons [q.v.], he left the Geographical Society to become, from the beginning of 1901, joint director of the British Rainfall Organization. After a short interval he became sole director and proceeded to place the organization on a firm and strictly scientific basis, transforming meteorology from a gentlemanly and dilettante pastime into an increasingly exact science. He mitigated the continuing danger of meteorological information becoming an unmanageable mass of disparate, uncoordinated, and uninterpreted numerals. He improved the collection, discussion, and orderly presentation of rainfall data and elaborated the cartometric study of the distribution of rainfall, and the accurate estimation of the average rainfall on any given area, and of its temporal variations. At this time, he said, he could have been set down on any spot in the British Isles and found himself within walking distance of a house where he was known, either personally or by correspondence. He provided a radically improved basis for the economically important estimation of water resources and was rainfall expert to the Metropolitan Water Board (1903–19). He collected the records of rainfall in the British Isles since 1677 and presented them to the trust into which he converted his organization in 1910; nine years later failing eyesight compelled him to abandon his work and the organization passed to the Meteorological Office.

Mill was proud of the adoption of two suggestions which he had made. In 1895 the sixth International Geographical Congress adopted a resolution which he had drafted: 'that the exploration of the Antarctic regions is the greatest piece of geographical exploration still to be undertaken'. And in 1912 the *Titanic* disaster led the Government to ask Shackleton for advice on ice dangers. He recommended consultation with Mill who made the proposal which resulted in the inception of the international ice patrol of the north Atlantic. Mill's position in relation to polar exploration was unique. He was never nearer to direct participation in a polar expedition than when, having refused appointment as scientific leader of the expedition because of his lifelong poor health, he sailed in the *Discovery* to Madeira to instruct, *en voyage*, the scientific staff of the national Antarctic expedition of 1901–4. Yet he was the confidant and inspirer of Scott, Shackleton, Mawson, and others under their leadership. Few polar expeditions started out without consulting him, and returning explorers customarily visited him at East Grinstead to add their verbal contributions to this living storehouse of knowledge on polar exploration. No other man knew as much about the experiences and personal qualities of polar explorers as did this quiet man who had never crossed latitude $66\frac{1}{2}°$. It was characteristic that in preparing *The Siege of the South Pole* (1905), a serious and accurate history which was to form one of a series of lives of the explorers, he accumulated a library which was the basis of a unique collection of more than 500 works on the Antarctic which passed to the Scott Polar Research Institute on the committee of management of which he sat for many years.

Mill served as president of the geography section of the British Association (1901), of the Royal Meteorological Society (1907–9), and the Geographical Association (1932–3). He prepared a *Record of the Royal Geographical Society, 1830–1930* (1930) whilst serving as the Society's vice-president, but declined the presidency in 1933 on account of failing eyesight. He received the honorary degree of LL.D. from the university of St. Andrews in 1900, was an honorary member of many foreign societies and the recipient of many medals, including in 1950 the first Hugh Robert Mill medal and prize founded in his honour by the Royal Meteorological Society.

Despite miserable health in youth and recurrent illnesses throughout a life which ended in a long battle against the approach of blindness, Mill was a warmly human personality. He was an entertaining and instructive conversationalist, with an unbounded range of interest in the world and its events, a remarkable memory, and a pleasing dry humour tempered by measured sentiment.

In 1889 Mill married his second cousin, Frances (died 1929), daughter of Dr. Francis Robertson MacDonald. In 1937 he married Alfreda, daughter of Frederick Dransfield, of Darton, Yorkshire, who had for six years been his secretary and who survived him. There were no children of either marriage. He died at East Grinstead 5 April 1950.

[H. R. Mill, *An Autobiography*, 1951; *Geographical Journal*, vol. cxv, 1950; *Quarterly Journal* of the Royal Meteorological Society, vol. lxxvi, Nos. 329 and 330, July and October 1950; personal knowledge.]

R. Watson-Watt.

MILLER, WILLIAM (1864–1945), historian and journalist, was born at Wigton, Cumberland, 8 December 1864, the eldest son of William Miller, a mine-owner, by his wife, Fanny Perry. He was educated at Rugby and, as a scholar, at Hertford College, Oxford, where he was awarded a first class in classical moderations (1884) and in *literae humaniores* (1887). On leaving Oxford he read for the bar and was called by the Inner Temple in 1889; he never practised but turned instead to journalism. From 1890 onwards he made frequent journeys to the Balkan peninsula, particularly to Serbia, Bosnia, and Montenegro, and soon became known as an authority on Balkan affairs, on which he contributed a number of articles to the leading political reviews. At the same time he began to interest himself in the medieval history of the Near East. His first signed historical article, a review of recent books on Montenegrin history, appeared in the *English Historical Review* in July 1896; and thenceforward he was one of its regular contributors and reviewers. During the next forty years articles and reviews of his appeared in all the important historical journals in Britain; and up to the year of his death he contributed regularly to the *American Historical Review* and to several learned periodicals in Greece. His most important medieval work, *The Latins in the Levant*, was published in 1908, and his most important work on modern history, *The Ottoman Empire, 1801–1913*, was first published in 1913, and reissued in a fourth edition with supplementary chapters in 1934 as *The Ottoman Empire and its Successors, 1801–1934*. From 1903 to 1937 he was correspondent of the *Morning Post* for Italy and the Balkans, and for the first twenty years established himself at Rome. But in 1923, disliking the atmosphere there after Mussolini's attainment of power, he moved his headquarters to Athens; there he remained until the German invasion of 1941 forced him at short notice to leave his flat and almost all his possessions. He retired to South Africa and spent the remainder of his life at Durban.

As a journalist Miller was very well informed, reliable, and objective. Unlike his contemporary J. D. Bourchier [q.v.], he made no attempt to direct international politics; but he was frequently consulted by Balkan statesmen and his opinion was particularly valued by Eleutherios Venizelos. His sympathies were always with the liberal movements in the countries with which he dealt, but they never clouded his judgement. In international politics he became strongly but not uncritically philhellene. The same qualities are apparent in his works on nineteenth- and twentieth-century history, such as his *Ottoman Empire* and his *Greece* (1928), which are admirable and clearly written accounts by one who knew intimately the lands which he described. But his main interest and his chief contribution to historical studies lay in the medieval field. He first concentrated on the history of the Slavs in the Balkans; and his chapters on Serbia and Bulgaria, published in volume iv of the *Cambridge Medieval History*, were derived from his earlier researches. They show wide erudition and a remarkable ability to bring together a vast assembly of facts into a coherent story. Later he turned his attention to Byzantine history and in particular to the period of the Frankish and Italian establishments in the East after the fourth crusade. It was a period which delighted him for its romance and for which his knowledge of Greece and Italy especially suited him. He brought to it still greater detailed scholarship than he showed in his Balkan work and an enthusiasm and sympathy which are reflected in such books as *The Latins in the Levant* (1908) and *Essays on the Latin Orient* (1921). He was not an historian on the grand scale; but his power to present detailed and accurate scholarship in a clear and significant manner, the charm of his style, and the humanity of his outlook make him one of the most readable and most valuable writers on Near Eastern history.

Miller married in 1895 Ada Mary, daughter of Colonel Thomas Parker Wright. She shared in his interests and in the hospitality which he showed to all scholars and students who visited Rome and Athens during his residence there. There were no children of the marriage. He died at Durban 23 October 1945.

Miller was elected F.B.A. in 1932. He received the honorary degree of LL.D. from the National University of Athens, and was an honorary student of the British School at Athens and a corresponding member of the Historical and Ethnological Society of Greece and of the Academy of Athens.

Among Miller's other main works are: *The Balkans* (1896), *Travel and Politics in the Near East* (1898), *Mediaeval Rome* (1901), *Greek Life in Town and Country* (1905), *History of the Greek People, 1821–1921* (1922), and *Trebizond* (1926).

[Private information; personal knowledge.]
STEVEN RUNCIMAN.

MILNE, EDWARD ARTHUR (1896–1950), mathematician and natural philosopher, was born at Hull 14 February 1896, the eldest son of Sidney Arthur Milne, headmaster of a Church of England school there, by his wife, Edith Cockcroft, of Pontefract. He was educated at elementary schools, Hymers College, Hull, and Trinity College, Cambridge. In 1916, when still an undergraduate, he joined the anti-aircraft experimental section of the munitions inventions department of the Ministry of Munitions where he made essential contributions, practical and mathematical, to the achievements of the section. This work had much formative influence in his scientific career; he collaborated and formed lasting friendships with leading mathematicians and scientists; his director, (Professor) Archibald Vivian Hill, and assistant director, (Sir) R. H. Fowler [q.v.], gave him unrivalled training in research; Milne had been recommended to Hill by G. H. Hardy [q.v.] for exceptional promise in pure mathematics, and this experience diverted him to mathematical physics. He played a distinguished part in similar work for the Ordnance Board from 1939 to 1944.

Returning to Cambridge in 1919 Milne was elected a fellow of Trinity College in the following year. This was partly in recognition of theoretical work with (Professor) Sydney Chapman on the earth's upper atmosphere, which helped to lead onwards to his classical investigation of the escape of molecules from stellar and planetary atmospheres. Moreover, it led H. F. Newall [q.v.], in offering Milne the assistant-directorship of the Solar Physics Observatory, to make the highly fruitful suggestion that he should devote himself to the theory of stellar atmospheres. At the time astrophysicists had little exact knowledge of conditions in a stellar atmosphere; ten years later they had reliable quantitative knowledge of the chief properties and had available the theoretical tools the subsequent development of which has yielded solutions of many further problems. This was due primarily to Milne's work, and also to other work which he inspired; it gives him a permanent place in the front rank of astrophysical theorists. The papers in which Milne and Fowler developed M. N. Saha's pioneering work on atomic ionization so as to fix a temperature scale for the stellar spectral sequence make the greatest single modern advance in knowledge of the surface conditions of stars. Milne's Bakerian lecture to the Royal Society (1929) pointed the way to many fresh advances. For these achievements he was awarded the gold medal of the Royal Astronomical Society in 1935.

Most of this work was done at Cambridge, where Milne retained the observatory post until 1924, when he became lecturer in mathematics at Trinity College; he was university lecturer in astrophysics, 1922–5, and was Smith's prizeman in 1922. He continued and largely completed it during 1925–8 when he was at Manchester as Beyer professor of applied mathematics. There he zestfully entered into the teaching, administrative, and scientific life of the university, and was honorary secretary of the Manchester Literary and Philosophical Society, 1927–8.

In 1929 Milne went to Oxford as Rouse Ball professor of mathematics and fellow of Wadham College. For the rest of his life he served the university and his college with unsparing devotion. He revivified applied mathematics at Oxford; a series of brilliant pupils and other young collaborators gained distinction in all the fields of Milne's scientific interests.

Following an individual view of mathematical physics advocated in his inaugural lecture, Milne expended immense labour for the next few years on the theory of stellar structure. He was mistaken in much of the interpretation of this work, particularly when he joined issue with Sir Arthur Eddington [q.v.]. Nevertheless, he stimulated others to achieve a generally agreed theory, and in doing so they employed much of his mathematical procedure. Milne recounted some of the early controversies in this subject in his posthumously published life of Sir James Jeans [q.v.] with whom he had found himself in some degree of sympathy.

What Milne regarded as his main life's work, on which he increasingly concentrated from 1932, was the development of kinematic relativity. This provided an alternative to Einstein's theory of general relativity; it included new systems of cosmology, dynamics, and electrodynamics, and a new basis for atomic physics, all entailing extensive re-examination of the foundations of natural philosophy. As a creation of a single mind, it is remarkable in its wide scope and fullness of development. Its overall value must long remain debatable, but it has certainly yielded invaluable insight into fundamental concepts, particularly (in work partly done jointly with Dr. Gerald James Whitrow) the time-concept.

The conception and presentation of all Milne's work bore the hall-mark of genius. Another notable characteristic was his courage in pursuing and defending his ideas; and also in facing personal ill health and the tragic loss of two wives. In 1928 he married Margaret Scott (died 1938), daughter of Hugh Fraser Campbell, advocate, of Dornoch; in 1940 he married Beatrice Brevoort (died 1945), daughter of William Whetten Renwick, architect, of New York. There were two daughters and one son of the first marriage and one daughter of the second. His courage was supported by a religious faith regained, although in no orthodox form, in his later years. His generous nature won him a host of friends, who counted for much in his life. In 1923 he suffered an attack of epidemic encephalitis and the after-effects made him a sick man in his last years. He died on a visit to Dublin 21 September 1950.

Milne was elected F.R.S. in 1926 and awarded a Royal medal in 1941. He was president of the London Mathematical Society, 1937–9, and of the Royal Astronomical Society, 1943–5. He received numerous honours from other leading scientific societies at home and abroad.

[*The Times*, 23 September 1950; W. H. McCrea in *Obituary Notices of Fellows of the Royal Society*, No. 20, November 1951; personal knowledge.]

W. H. McCrea.

MILNE, GEORGE FRANCIS, first BARON MILNE (1866–1948), field-marshal, was born in Aberdeen 5 November 1866, the only son and youngest child of George Milne, manager of the Commercial Bank of Scotland in that city, by his wife, Williamina, daughter of John Panton, of Knockiemill, Aberdeenshire.

He was educated at the Gymnasium, Old Aberdeen, passed into the Royal Military Academy, Woolwich, and was gazetted to the Royal Artillery in 1885. In 1897, after a period of regimental duty, he passed into the Staff College, but was released to join his battery to proceed up the Nile with Sir H. H. (later Earl) Kitchener [q.v.], directing the battery's fire at Omdurman when a chance hit is said to have struck the tomb of the Mahdi and brought Milne to Kitchener's notice. Rejoining the Staff College he was again released to go to the South African war where he served on Kitchener's intelligence staff. At the end of the war he returned home with the brevet of lieutenant-colonel to join the newly organized intelligence department. After a period of regimental duties in command of a battery, he became successively G.S.O.2 with the 46th North Midland division, Territorial Army, G.S.O.1 with the 6th division in Ireland, and then brigadier-general, R.A., of the 4th division at Woolwich.

Proceeding to France with the division in 1914, he took part in the battles of Le Cateau, Marne, Aisne, and in Flanders, and rapidly made an impression both on his seniors and on those under his command. Rapid promotion followed, first to brigadier-general, general staff, III Corps, then to major-general, general staff, Second Army. Shortly afterwards he was appointed to command the 27th division which was ordered to Salonika. In January 1916 he was given command of the XVI Corps with the temporary rank of lieutenant-general.

In 1916 he assumed command of the British forces in Salonika from Sir Bryan Mahon [q.v.], under the supreme direction of General Sarrail. His difficulties in this role were mitigated by his close friendship with General Guillaumat who for a time succeeded Sarrail, and the respect and affection in which he was always held by the Serbian and Greek forces. The succeeding French commander, General Franchet d'Esperey, although difficult in official relationships, earned his respect and eventually his enduring friendship.

The story of the Salonika campaign is largely one of frustration, due to the nature of the country, the high toll of disease, insufficient troops, and difficulties with both the Allies on the spot and politicians at home. In the final operations Milne's forces had the well-nigh impossible task of carrying out a heavy attack on the Vardar–Dojran front which although not in itself successful was executed with such resolution that it enabled the Serbian and French troops to break through the mountain chain farther west and turn the enemy's position. The British forces then drove forward, forced a pass through the Belasitza mountains, and were the first of the Allies to set foot in Bulgaria. The Bulgarians surrendered and the advance continued to the frontiers of Turkey. Almost immediately the Turks collapsed, and the army occupied Constantinople where Milne remained in command until November 1920. His experiences there were perhaps even more disheartening than in Salonika; the half-hearted support given to the White Russians, the divergent policies of the Allies, and the interminable delays in making peace with the Turks presented him with innumerable problems. He returned home, however, before the Chanak crisis.

He had been promoted to general in 1920 and after over two years on half-pay he was appointed to the Eastern Command, and in February 1926 chief of the imperial general staff. During his time in this post he had to face the repercussions of the peace movement on the army and the accompanying discussions on disarmament, the retrenchment of defence expenditure, and the expansion of the Royal Air Force. The last was perhaps Milne's most difficult problem, for the senior officers of the Air Force judged that the necessities of their case demanded reductions in the army and the handing over of vast areas of potential operations to so-called air control. At the same time Milne was fully convinced of the necessity of modernizing the army and was faced with the impossibility of finding the funds required for extensive mechanization. As chief of the imperial general staff he won the confidence and respect of the governments of the day which included the second Labour and the 'national' governments of Ramsay MacDonald. It was at the insistent request of the Government that his tenure of office was extended from five to seven years. He also placed the relations of the military and civil sides of the War Office on an entirely new footing of mutual understanding and confidence.

Milne was promoted to field-marshal in 1928; on retiring in 1933 he was created Baron Milne, of Salonika and Rubislaw, county of Aberdeen, and performed useful service in the House of Lords. He was appointed colonel commandant, Royal Artillery, in 1918, lieutenant of the Tower of London in 1920, and governor and constable of the Tower in 1933, the only soldier to hold all three appointments. He became the first colonel commandant of the Pioneer Corps in 1940 and was also the founder and head of the Old Contemptibles, an organization of old comrades from the war of 1914–18, and of the Salonika Reunion Association. His last years were clouded by feelings of frustration and his inability to contribute directly to the war effort after 1939 except in the Home Guard and civil defence. As master gunner, St. James's Park, from 1929 to 1946, however, he performed valuable services to his regiment.

Milne was appointed to the D.S.O. in 1902, C.B. (1912), K.C.B. (1918), G.C.B. (1927), and K.C.M.G. and G.C.M.G. (1919), and was aide-de-camp general to the King from 1923 to 1927. He held many foreign decorations and received the honorary degree of LL.D. from the university of Aberdeen in 1921, being also accorded the freedom of that city. The university of Oxford gave him the honorary degree of D.C.L. in 1928 and Cambridge that of LL.D. in 1934.

Possessed of a penetrating intellect, immense energy, a keen wit, and a lovable nature, Milne could always find time to help those who came to him for advice; and these were many. He was, in the opinion of all who served with him, a great commander. But he had no real chance to show his ability. A strong disciplinarian, his high sense of duty and simple, unaffected manner won him the respect and the affection of both officers and men under his command. He wrote no account of his military experiences and destroyed most of his personal diaries.

In 1905 Milne married Claire Marjoribanks, daughter of Sir John Nisbet Maitland, fifth baronet, by whom he had one son and one daughter, the former, George Douglass (born 1909), succeeding him in the title. Milne died in London 23 March 1948.

A presentation portrait of Milne was painted by (Sir) Oswald Birley for the School of Gunnery, Larkhill; a portrait by Maurice Codner was in the possession of the artist; and Milne is included in the group of 'Some General Officers of the War of 1914–18' by J. S. Sargent in the National Portrait Gallery.

[Cyril Falls, (Official) *History of the Great War. Military Operations, Macedonia*, 2 vols., 1933–5; *Royal Artillery Commemoration Book*, 1939–45 war; private information; personal knowledge.]                    THOMAS HUTTON.

MILNE-WATSON, SIR DAVID MILNE, first baronet (1869–1945), man of business, was born in Edinburgh 10 March 1869, the only son and elder child of David Watson by his wife, Anne Carnegie Milne. His father, who was engaged in the iron industry and died while his children were in infancy, was born in 1809; thus the lives of father and son covered the remarkable span of 136 years. David Milne-Watson was educated at Merchiston Castle and Edinburgh University, where he graduated M.A. and LL.B., and then entered the office of a writer to the signet to gain some legal experience. From 1894 to 1896 he was at Balliol College, Oxford, and after contesting the South Eastern division of Essex (Tilbury) as a Liberal in 1895, he went to Marburg University. In the next year he was called to the bar by the Middle Temple, but he decided to forsake the law for industry, and in 1897 he made the decisive step in his career by joining the Gas Light and Coke Company as assistant to the general manager, becoming general manager in 1903, managing director in 1916, and governor and managing director in 1918, holding this position until his retirement in April 1945.

In 1897 the gas industry consisted of some 1,500 separate units, many of them parochial in outlook and traditional in practice. Milne-Watson foresaw that with the possible loss of the lighting load to electricity the future of the gas industry lay in the distribution of heat and in the better commercial use of coke and other by-products. In order to meet the growing competition of its younger rival he saw the need for reorganization in his own company and for co-operation and unity in the gas industry. Largely on his initiative the British Commercial Gas Association was formed in 1911 and in 1916 the National Gas Council, of which he was president from 1919 to 1943, to represent the industry on a national basis.

By the time he became governor Milne-Watson had an intimate knowledge of every aspect of his company's business. Since its original charter in 1812 its area had grown by a series of amalgamations to 125 square miles in 1918. Milne-Watson followed the policy of his predecessors and by 1933 the company had an area of 546 square miles, stretching from Windsor to Southend. He then decided that it had reached the limit of size for the personal management of which he was so skilful an exponent, and further co-operation with neighbouring companies was secured by means of a holding company, the South Eastern Gas Corporation.

Reconstruction after the war gave Milne-Watson the opportunity to reorganize the works by introducing modern mechanized plant and concentrate gas-making as far as possible at the most efficient stations. His foresight and courage, and his confidence in the future of the industry were shown by his readiness to back his staff in new developments like the coke-ovens at Beckton and the ring main connecting the works. Although he had no scientific training, he realized the need for scientific research in industry and he established three laboratories to deal with the manufacture and utilization of gas and its by-products. At the same time the commercial and service departments were reorganized. In his relations with his men, many of whom he knew through frequent visits to the works, he was particularly happy. Like a true Scot who had himself been a wandering scholar, he had a great belief in education, and he gave every encouragement to the staff to take courses of instruction. He was chairman of the co-partnership committee, at which the men's representatives could raise any question of interest to the company. He refused to serve on any boards except those directly connected with the Gas Light and Coke Company, so that he could devote his undivided attention to it, and in talking to the men he could say that, like them, he had only one interest—the company. The value of these good relations was shown by the absence of any labour trouble for many years.

Thus there was no side of the activities of the company in which Milne-Watson did not take a keen and active interest, and in all of them he was a driving force

for many years, placing his company abreast of modern competition. Under him it grew to be the biggest gas company in the world, and it was his single-minded devotion to its interests and his shrewd Scottish wisdom which contributed so much to its success. So often when things were hanging in the balance, it was Milne-Watson's flash of intuition which decided future policy, and his judgement was rarely at fault.

Milne-Watson's interest in the well-being of the gas industry as a whole was second only to that in his company. He did much to foster the unity of the industry by a series of national associations over which he presided as chairman and through which its collective voice was heard in Parliament and elsewhere. As its acknowledged leader he was for twenty-five years a most effective and fearless champion of the interests of the industry. As chairman of the Joint Industrial Council for the Gas Industry from 1919 to 1944 he did much to maintain good feeling between employers and the trade-union leaders. He was a member of the employers' committee during the Mond–Turner conference of 1928 to consider industrial relations and industrial reorganization. He was president of the British Employers' Confederation and on three occasions he represented the employers at the International Labour Conference at Geneva.

Milne-Watson (he assumed the additional surname of Milne- in 1927) was knighted in that year and created a baronet in 1937. In 1899 he married Olga Cecily (died 1952), daughter of the Rev. George Herbert, vicar of St. Peter's, Vauxhall, by whom he had two sons and a daughter. He died at Ashley Chase, Abbotsbury, Dorset, 3 October 1945, and was succeeded in the baronetcy by his elder son, David Ronald (born 1904). His second son, Michael, became governor of the Gas Light and Coke Company in 1947 and chairman of the North Thames Gas Board in 1949.

Of the portraits of Milne-Watson, one, by Harold Knight, is at Gas Industry House; another, by Sir William Orpen, is at the North Thames Gas Board; a third, by James Gunn, belongs to the family. There is a bust by Eric Schilsky at Watson House, Fulham.

[Stirling Everard, *The History of the Gas Light and Coke Company, 1812–1949*, 1949; *The Times*, 4 October 1945; personal knowledge.]          HAROLD HARTLEY.

MILNES, ROBERT OFFLEY ASH-BURTON CREWE-, second BARON HOUGHTON, and MARQUESS OF CREWE (1858–1945), statesman. [See CREWE-MILNES.]

MITCHELL, SIR PETER CHALMERS (1864–1945), zoologist, was born at Dunfermline 23 November 1864, the eldest son and third of the eleven children of the Rev. Alexander Mitchell, D.D., minister of the North Parish, by his wife, Marion Hay, daughter of the Rev. Peter Chalmers, D.D., also of Dunfermline. After education at Dunfermline High School and Aberdeen Grammar School, he was admitted to King's College, Aberdeen, before the end of his sixteenth year, and graduated M.A. in 1884, gaining the university gold medal in English literature. The same year he became an exhibitioner of Christ Church, Oxford, and after obtaining a first class in natural science (1888), was appointed university demonstrator in comparative anatomy and assistant to the Linacre professor, a post which he held for three years. He spent a further two years in Oxford as organizing secretary under the Oxfordshire County Council in connexion with the attempts then being made to provide technical instruction in towns and rural areas. He had previously given a course of university extension lectures in Devonshire and had little difficulty in developing a scheme of technical instruction in Oxfordshire. This position left him more time for work in the University Museum and he also extended his literary activities and in addition to scientific reviews contributed articles to the Daily Chronicle; indeed, throughout his life he wrote articles for the daily press as well as his contributions to scientific journals. In 1892 he became lecturer in biology at the Charing Cross Hospital medical school and in 1894 lecturer at the London Hospital medical college; at the same time he began his long association with the Zoological Society of London, by working under Frank Evers Beddard on the anatomy of the mammals and birds brought to the prosectorium.

Fully engaged though he was in these posts, scientific and general writing occupied much of Mitchell's time, and he continued research work at the prosectorium of the London Zoo. He made frequent visits to France and Germany and came in contact not only with many distinguished foreign zoologists, but also with members of the artistic and literary world, especially in Paris. During this period he translated a number of German and French books including O. Hertwig's *The Biological Problem of To-day: Preformation or Epigenesis?* (1896), Weininger's *Sex and Character* (1906), and Metchnikoff's *The Prolongation of Life* (1907) and *The Nature of Man* (1908). Many years later he translated and adapted for performance by the Stage Society a work of a very different kind, *La Femme et le pantin*, a play by Pierre Louÿs.

Mitchell will be remembered mainly for the great services which he rendered as secretary of the Zoological Society of London from 1903 to 1935. During this period it became the leading institution of its kind in the world and a model for many similar zoological societies which sprang up in the early part of the twentieth century. During his term of office the number of fellows more than doubled and the annual number of visitors to the gardens increased from about 690,000 to more than two million. The animal houses in Regent's Park were largely rebuilt, and in addition he was mainly responsible for the creation of Whipsnade Zoological Park, which he regarded as his crowning achievement.

Soon after coming to London, Mitchell was elected to the Savile Club, which in his own words 'became not only one of the most pleasant things in my life but also the most useful'. To the end of his life, when in town he was nearly always to be found there either at lunch or dinner, the centre of a group of friends who enjoyed his witty conversation, rather sardonic humour, and fund of good stories. After his retirement he went to live in Málaga, but the Spanish civil war forced him to return to London. During this period he published an entertaining biography *My Fill of Days* (1937), and a detailed account of his experiences in Spain, *My House in Málaga* (1938). During the subsequent war he was honorary treasurer of the joint committee for Soviet aid. He died in London 2 July 1945, as the result of a street accident.

Mitchell's scientific work was mainly confined to the early part of his career when he published a series of papers on the anatomy of birds and mammals. Among his books the most notable is a biography of T. H. Huxley (1900) which more than any other of his works reveals his literary gifts. He was also biological editor of the eleventh edition of the

*Encyclopaedia Britannica*, and was for many years scientific correspondent of *The Times*.

Mitchell was elected a fellow of the Royal Society in 1906 and served on its council and many of its committees. He was president of the zoology section of the British Association in 1912, and took a keen interest in the Society for the Preservation of the Fauna of the Empire, acting as president from 1923 to 1927.

During the war of 1914–18 Mitchell was attached to the department of military intelligence in the War Office and was mainly responsible for the distribution of propaganda on the German fronts. He planned the famous *Le Courrier de l'Air*, which was distributed in occupied countries, and, in German, over Germany. These messages were delivered by means of air balloons, and it was apparently the first instance of pamphlets being distributed by air. For his services, he was appointed C.B.E. and mentioned in dispatches. He was knighted in 1929 and received various foreign and academic distinctions, including the honorary degree of LL.D. from his old university, Aberdeen, in 1914; he was elected an honorary student of Christ Church in 1935.

Mitchell's last few years were largely devoted to political activities, in which his sympathies were with the extreme Left. He stood as parliamentary candidate in 1938 for the Scottish Universities as an independent, but was not elected. He was generally regarded as a Communist, and certainly advocated many of their views, but he never joined the party and on one occasion when referred to as a Communist he indignantly denied the label and said he was an anarchist. He was opposed to organized religion and any form of capitalism, and looked forward to a civilization in which 'neither the whip of necessity nor the spur of gaining greater spending power' was a necessary stimulus to work.

In 1893 Mitchell married Lilian Bessie, daughter of the Rev. Charles Pritchard [q.v.], Savilian professor of astronomy at Oxford. Her sister married Sir John Farmer [q.v.]. Mitchell had no children. A portrait by Sir William Nicholson hangs in the council-room of the Zoological Society of London.

[Sir P. C. Mitchell, *My Fill of Days*, 1937; *The Times*, 3 July 1945; E. Hindle in *Obituary Notices of Fellows of the Royal Society*, No. 15, May 1947; personal knowledge.]

EDWARD HINDLE.

MITCHELL, SIR WILLIAM GORE SUTHERLAND (1888–1944), air chief marshal, was born at Cumberland, New South Wales, 8 March 1888, the son of William Broadfoot Mitchell, owner of a brewery, of Sydney, and his wife, Edith Gore. He was educated in England at Wellington College and was commissioned as a second lieutenant, Special Reserve, joining the 3rd battalion, Devonshire Regiment, in 1906. He transferred to the regular army in 1909, joining the Highland Light Infantry. In common with other enterprising and adventurous officers of that period he was seized with a desire to fly and having obtained his pilot's certificate he was accepted for secondment to the Royal Flying Corps after a course at Upavon in December 1913.

On the outbreak of war in 1914 Mitchell went to France with No. 4 Squadron on 13 August and was appointed a flight commander in January 1915. After a spell in England he returned to France where he served on the Somme and in the spring of 1917 commanded the Twelfth Wing at Arras. For his war services he was four times mentioned in dispatches, awarded the M.C. and the A.F.C. and appointed to the D.S.O. In 1918 he took over No. 20 Group, North West Africa, and in the following year he was granted a permanent commission in the Royal Air Force as a wing commander. At the end of 1919 he went to India and for his services in operations in Waziristan he was twice mentioned in dispatches and appointed C.B.E. (1924).

On returning from India in 1924 he first commanded a flying training school and later went to Halton as second-in-command. In March 1928 he went to Aden to command that station when the Royal Air Force first took over responsibility for the protectorate from the army. In October 1929 he was made director of training at the Air Ministry where he served until early in 1933 when he took command of the Royal Air Force College, Cranwell. He was promoted air vice-marshal in that year. His wide experience, energy, interest, and participation in all active work and sports made him perhaps particularly successful in these training appointments. Although he had a bluff and sometimes caustic manner he had a great sense of humour, sympathy, and understanding of men of all ages who quickly had a strong respect for 'Ginger Mitch's' obvious good qualities, keenness, and straightforwardness.

In December 1934 Mitchell went to Iraq as A.O.C., and in 1935 he was appointed C.B. He returned to England in 1937 being made air member for personnel on the Air Council and promoted to air marshal. In 1938 he was advanced to K.C.B. Early in 1939 he was sent to the Middle East as A.O.C.-in-C. with the acting rank of air chief marshal. In 1940 he was appointed inspector-general of the Royal Air Force and in 1941 he passed to the retired list. Later he was posted to work in connexion with the organization of the Air Training Corps which he continued until his death in London 15 August 1944. He was also, in 1941, the first officer of the Royal Air Force to become gentleman usher of the black rod.

In 1919 Mitchell married Essy, daughter of Lieutenant-Colonel William Plant, Indian Army; their only child died in infancy.

[Private information; personal knowledge.]
P. BABINGTON.

MOERAN, ERNEST JOHN (1894–1950), composer, was born at Osterley, Middlesex, 31 December 1894, the second son of the Rev. Joseph William Wright Moeran, vicar of St. Mary's church, Spring Grove, Heston, and his wife, Ada Esther Smeed Whall, of King's Lynn. His father was of partly Irish descent and his paternal grandfather was vicar of Bacton, Norfolk. He was educated at Uppingham and the Royal College of Music; after active service in the army, he studied composition privately for a time with Dr. John Ireland. He was a sufficient pianist to play publicly in his own chamber works and also studied the violin, but his life was devoted to composition. His father's induction as vicar of Salhouse, Norfolk, had a deep effect, for Moeran early became acquainted with the Norfolk peasants and their folk-music, in which he took much interest, becoming a field-collector and arranger.

Moeran's first phase was prolific; his string Quartet (1923) survives in performances, and there were also a Trio for piano, violin, and 'cello (1920), two orchestral rhapsodies (1922 and 1924), and a symphonic impression 'In the Mountain Country' (1921). The piano pieces, like 'Stalham River' (1921), somewhat influenced by Dr. John Ireland, are attractive, and there are a number of excellent songs, especially ''Tis time, I think, by Wenlock town' and the *Shrop-*

*shire Lad* cycle, 'Ludlow Town' (1920). Already Moeran was showing how strongly affected he was not only by folk-song but by the countryside around him. Settings of actual folk-songs were less arrangements for voice and piano than re-creations of the originals' mood.

After a creative lull Moeran returned, around 1930, to chamber music of a more austere kind with his Sonata for two violins alone and his string Trio. He also turned to choral music, writing a suite of six part-songs in the English style to Elizabethan poems, entitled 'Songs of Springtime' (1933); between 1933 and 1939 he wrote six more, published as 'Phyllida and Corydon' (1939), where the style was nearer that of the madrigal, and the influence of Bernard van Dieren was evident. Southern Ireland had long attracted Moeran, and from 1934 he made his home for many months of the year at Kenmare, county Kerry. His last publication was a collection of Irish folk-songs, taken down aurally.

In 1926 Sir Hamilton Harty [q.v.] suggested that Moeran should write a symphony; after abandoning first attempts, he embarked on new ideas and, closely consulting Harty all the time, completed his G minor Symphony in 1937. It is a work redolent of the Atlantic coast of Eire. A later 'Sinfonietta' (1945), however, derives its inspiration from the Radnorshire hills, his family by then having moved to Kington, Herefordshire. The broader, more jovial side of his character is seen in his 'Overture for a Masque', written in the war of 1939–45 for the Entertainments National Service Association. The violin Concerto of 1942 is the most important of Moeran's later works—perhaps of them all. Sensitive, lyrical, it reflects the Southern Irish coast in full summer, with a scherzo representing a Kerry fair. In 1945 Moeran married Kathleen Peers Coetmore, 'cellist, daughter of Stanley Coetmore Jones, estate agent, of Lincolnshire. For her he wrote a 'cello Concerto (1945) which showed a new dramatic power, and a 'cello Sonata (1947) of even greater intensity and sense of struggle.

Physically Moeran was largely built and rubicund, his pale dreaming eyes contrasting with his peasant-like exterior. Lonely by nature, he had nevertheless a great gift for friendship and was happiest when among country folk in a village inn. There his shy talent for mimicry could develop, and also his broad laughter.

Moeran's compositions are essentially musical in quality, expressive more of song than of dance, and despite certain roughnesses often touchingly emotional. He died at Kenmare 1 December 1950. There were no children.

[Private information; personal knowledge.]
HUBERT FOSS.

MOFFATT, JAMES (1870–1944), divine, was born at Glasgow 4 July 1870, the eldest son of George Moffatt, chartered accountant, by his wife, Isabella Simpson, daughter of Robert Starret Morton, general merchant, of Edinburgh. He was educated at Glasgow Academy and Glasgow University where he graduated with honours in classics in 1890. He studied theology in the Glasgow College of the Free Church of Scotland, and became deeply interested in New Testament criticism under the influence of Alexander Balmain Bruce [q.v.]. In 1896 he was ordained minister of the Free Church in Dundonald, Ayrshire, and in the same year married Mary, daughter of Archibald Reith, M.D., of Aberdeen. In 1901 he published *The Historical New Testament*, a work of remarkable learning, in which the New Testament writings were examined in the light of their chronology and mutual relations. The book was so obviously important that in 1902 he received the degree of D.D. from the university of St. Andrews, although it had never previously in Scotland been conferred upon so young a man. From 1907 to 1911 he was minister of the United Free Church at Broughty Ferry, and while there published his *Introduction to the Literature of the New Testament* (1911) which has remained a standard work. In this period, too, he was Jowett lecturer in London, wrote numerous articles on theological and literary subjects, and began his quarterly survey in the *Hibbert Journal* of current religious books, which he continued for the next thirty years.

From 1911 to 1915 he held the professorship of Greek and New Testament exegesis at Mansfield College, Oxford, and in 1913 published his translation of the New Testament, which was followed in 1924 by a translation of the Old Testament on similar lines. This is the work by which he is most widely known, and by means of which he placed the results of biblical scholarship in the hands of the general public throughout the English-speaking world. In 1915 he returned as professor of church history to his college at Glasgow,

receiving the degree of D.D. from the university of Oxford on his departure.

The twelve years during which he now worked in Glasgow were filled with incessant literary production and also with preaching, lecturing, and varied activities on behalf of the great Church in which all the main branches of Scottish Presbyterianism had recently been united. In 1927 he accepted the Washburn chair of church history in the Union Theological Seminary, New York. He was feeling at this time that he had made his contribution to New Testament study, and was anxious to carry his inquiries into later phases of Christian development. With this purpose he wished to make a new start, in different surroundings. He occupied this chair until his retirement in 1939. His plan of devoting himself entirely to his new subject was not fulfilled, for he was now so much identified with New Testament criticism that he was not allowed to break away from it. His published work in church history was confined to a masterly sketch, *The First Five Centuries of the Church* (1938); a book on Tertullian, for which he had gathered much material, was never finished. He quickly adapted himself to American conditions, and made himself a force in the cultural and religious life of the country. Most notably he took the leading part in the American revision of the Bible. In the last year or two of his life his health broke down, but he held resolutely to his work almost to the day of his death which took place in New York 27 June 1944. He was survived by his wife (who died two years later) and by two sons and one daughter. His eldest son had died in boyhood.

James Moffatt was a man of simple and beautiful character, who endeared himself to a multitude of friends. Although a tireless student he had a great variety of interests. In his youth he had been an athlete, and he never lost his enthusiasm for football and golf. He was a musician and at least one tune of his composition, 'Ultima', has found its way into hymnbooks. He was not only a theological writer but a man of letters in the widest sense. He wrote the introductions for an edition of Shakespeare, and his book on George Meredith is valuable. He was the author of a detective novel, *A Tangled Web* (1929), fully as ingenious and exciting as many others of its class. His theological books are nearly forty in number and every one of them was the outcome of very wide reading and intensive study. The most notable are his *Introduction to the Literature of the New Testament* and his single-handed translation of the whole of the Bible, but hardly less noteworthy are the commentaries which he wrote for the series entitled 'The Moffatt New Testament Commentary' which he edited. His significance for the religious life of his time cannot be doubted. A new attitude to the Bible had become imperative, and he showed that nothing essential was lost when it was frankly adopted. To his interpretation of the ancient writings he brought a profound scholarship, a rare power of judgement, and a genuine religious sympathy. He rendered them in a language which enabled the common reader to study them intelligently, in the best light of modern knowledge.

[Private information; personal knowledge.]
E. F. SCOTT.

MOLLISON, AMY (1903–1941), airwoman. [See JOHNSON.]

MOLONY, SIR THOMAS FRANCIS, first baronet (1865–1949), lord chief justice of Ireland, was born in Dublin 31 January 1865. He was the youngest son of James Molony, a Dublin hotel proprietor, by his wife, Jane, daughter of Nicholas Sweetman, of Newbawn, county Wexford. Having received his early education at a Christian Brothers' school, he went on to Trinity College, Dublin, where his academic career was exceptionally brilliant; three times a law prizeman, he graduated in history and political science as gold medallist and senior moderator in 1886. An exhibition at King's Inns was followed by call to the Irish bar in 1887, where he quickly built up a substantial practice. In 1899 he took silk and in 1900 was called to the English bar by the Middle Temple; appointed crown counsel for county Carlow in 1906 and for the county and city of Dublin in 1907, he became in 1911 His Majesty's second serjeant-at-law. His only serious attempt at a political career was made in December 1910, when he unsuccessfully contested the West Toxteth division of Liverpool as a Liberal.

Appointed solicitor-general for Ireland in 1912, he became attorney-general in the following year and, after holding that office for a month, was elevated to the bench. Promotion to the Court of Appeal followed in 1915, and he became, in 1918, lord chief justice of Ireland. He was the last holder of that office. In 1924, when the Irish Free State judicature was established, he resigned, left Ireland, and settled in Wimbledon. He was created a baronet of the United Kingdom in 1925.

The long years of retirement were filled with activity. In 1925 he was co-opted to a directorship of the National Bank and in the same year became chairman of the Home Office committee on the treatment of juvenile offenders, a position which he held until 1927. His time and help were given without stint to many social and philanthropic organizations, especially to those under the auspices of the Roman Catholic Church, of which he was a devout and faithful son. Many honours were bestowed on him; the Inn of Court of Northern Ireland made him an honorary bencher in 1926, and the Middle Temple in 1933. But of all his honours the one he valued most was the vice-chancellorship of his university, to which he succeeded in 1931. Any service to Trinity was a delight to him, and time and again he revisited Dublin for Commencements and other college occasions.

He married in 1899 Pauline Mary (died 1951), daughter of Bernard Rispin, livestock salesmaster, of Eccles Street, Dublin, and had three sons and three daughters. On 3 September 1949 he died at Wimbledon.

Molony's judicial career was set against a background of insurrection and civil war; armed guards accompanied him on assize and often the courts in which he sat were fenced with barbed wire and patrolled by sentries. By temperament a man of peace, by conviction a Roman Catholic Liberal deeply attached to the British connexion, the circumstances of his time and the politics of the majority of his countrymen were abhorrent to him. But both as a man and as a judge he acted throughout with serene, unostentatious courage and upheld to the end the finest traditions of British justice. Unflinching in the punishment of violence, he was equally vigilant to protect the law of the land from those who sought to push too far the extraordinary powers vested in them to suppress disorder. In times less poisoned by hatred and outrage he might have built up over the years a legal reputation equal to that of his greatest predecessors on the Irish bench. As it was, he is chiefly remembered for a series of judgements—notably in *The King* v. *Allen*, [1921] 2 I.R. 241, and *The King* v. *Strickland*, [1921] 2 I.R. 317—which are classic statements on the nature of martial law and its relation to the common law. One remark, extant in the unemotional pages of the *Irish Reports*, vividly illustrates his character, and the character of his times. Counsel suggested to him that he had only been able to take the Cork assizes by permission of the general officer commanding; 'I did not', Molony retorted, 'sit in Cork by permission of any general. I sat in Cork by virtue of His Majesty's command, which no general could dispute.'

By nature Molony was a wise, generous, kindly man, who won the respect and deep affection of innumerable men and women who came into contact with him both in the country of his birth and in the country of his adoption. A portrait by Sir William Orpen, showing him robed as lord chief justice of Ireland, became the property of his eldest son, Hugh Francis (born 1900), who succeeded him as second baronet; a pastel portrait of Molony robed as vice-chancellor of Dublin University, by John Mansbridge, is owned by Molony's daughter, Mrs. F. W. Hunt.

[*The Times*, 5, 8, and 15 September 1949; *Irish Times*, 5 September 1949; private information.]    CHARLES MONTEITH.

MONRO, SIR HORACE CECIL (1861–1949), civil servant, was born 14 May 1861 at Highmore, Henley-on-Thames, the eldest son of the vicar, the Rev. Horace George Monro, and his wife, Margaret Isabella, daughter of the Rev. Archibald Hamilton Duthie, rector of Deal. He was educated at Repton and at Clare College, Cambridge, where he was a scholar. He was placed in the second class in the classical tripos in 1883.

He entered the Civil Service by open competition in 1884 and was appointed to the Local Government Board. He was early chosen to be private secretary to the permanent secretary, Sir Hugh Owen, and was subsequently for some years private secretary to successive presidents of the Board. In 1897 he became an assistant secretary to the Board, and in 1910 permanent secretary.

Monro was a notable administrator, courageous, practical, and patient, ready to listen to suggestions and criticisms, and always concerned to avoid friction and unnecessary expenditure. He was, perhaps, old-fashioned in his distrust of propaganda and in his view that publicity was not the business of a civil servant. His courtesy, unselfishness, and complete disinterestedness earned him the absolute devotion of all who worked with him and he enjoyed at all times the full confidence of his political chiefs.

A wholehearted believer in local government, he was opposed to undue centralization and took pains to establish good relations with local authorities and their associations. This policy did much to ensure smooth administration and bore fruit in the contribution made by local authorities to the solution of many problems arising out of the war of 1914–18. Monro's own activities during the war were many and varied, for in the change from peace to war-time conditions his immense knowledge of local government proved invaluable. He did considerable work in the preparation of the military service bill; and he was made a commander of the Order of Leopold in recognition of his services on behalf of Belgian refugees. He personally took in hand the arrangements made for dealing with them when war broke out and was later, with Lord Gladstone [q.v.], primarily responsible for the organization concerned with their welfare.

In 1919 the Local Government Board was abolished and Monro retired. In his day the work of the Board had embraced many subjects which were now transferred to other ministries. He had, for instance, a large part in devising the machinery of the first Old Age Pensions Act, 1908, and in the earliest arrangements for the regulation of motor traffic. After his retirement he continued to do much valuable work as chairman of government committees on many and various subjects, such as the use of preservatives in food, and land drainage, in particular the commission on Ouse drainage. Under his skilful direction these committees did a great deal of pioneer work, much of which forms the basis of existing law and practice.

Monro had many interests outside his official work. He was a member of the 'Corner' at the National Club about which Austin Dobson [q.v.] wrote 'A Whitehall Eclogue'. Sir Owen Seaman [q.v.], who had been a scholar of Monro's year at Cambridge, was his lifelong friend and Monro for many years attended the weekly dinners of *Punch* to which from time to time he contributed charming light verse. He had a very attractive sense of humour. A man of middle height with the carriage of a tireless walker, Monro was of fair complexion with a pronounced aquiline nose; quite late in his long life there were still a few who continued to refer to him affectionately as 'Beaker Monro of Clare'. For the great part of his days he was a keen ornithologist and botanist, and when failing eyesight and hearing made identification of birds difficult, he continued almost to the end an ardent collector of plants in England and the Pyrenees.

Monro was called to the bar by the Middle Temple in 1900, appointed C.B. in 1902 and promoted K.C.B. in 1911. He died, unmarried, 23 April 1949, at Crowborough, Sussex.

[Private information; personal knowledge.]
E. R. Forber.

MONTGOMERY-MASSINGBERD, Sir ARCHIBALD ARMAR (1871–1947), field-marshal, was born in London 6 December 1871, the second son of Hugh de Fellenberg Montgomery, of Blessingbourne, Fivemiletown, county Tyrone, by his wife, Mary Sophia Juliana, daughter of the Rev. John Charles Maude, rector of Enniskillen and son of the first Viscount Hawarden. His paternal grandmother came of the Swiss military family of de Fellenberg; he was also a cousin of Lieutenant-General Sir (Frederick) Stanley Maude [q.v.]. He added the name of Massingberd to his own in 1926 when his wife, Diana, daughter of Edmund Langton, whom he married in 1896, inherited through her mother the Massingberd estates.

Educated at Charterhouse and at the Royal Military Academy, Woolwich, Montgomery did not excel at any particular branch of knowledge or sport, except in horsemanship. He was commissioned into the Royal Artillery in November 1891. Tall and very good looking, he was gifted with charming manners and a persuasive tongue—characteristics which he retained until the end of his life. His advancement was a matter of course when he added to these an early experience in warfare, fertility in devising expedients, proficiency in managing senior officers of all grades and tempers, and resolution in disaster when those above him were failing. Yet, although he held the highest staff appointments, he never received a command in the field.

He served with the Field Artillery in the South African war almost from beginning to end, being on the staff at Cape Town for the last few months. He was present at the disaster at Magersfontein and the Dutch surrender at Paardeberg, and was slightly wounded at the Caledon River. In January 1905 he entered the Staff College where the commandant was Sir Henry (later Lord) Rawlinson [q.v.], with whom he was later to be long associated. Rawlinson reported so favourably of him that after leaving the college he was selected for a series of staff appointments. In August 1914, being then an instructor —and local lieutenant-colonel—at the Staff College, he was detailed to be the G.S.O.2 of the 4th division. When at the battle of the Marne its commander was injured, Rawlinson was sent to take his place and found Montgomery acting as G.S.O.1. This turned out to be an ideal combination. Montgomery proved a perfect complement to his sometimes impetuous chief. When Rawlinson was promoted to command the IV Corps he managed to have Montgomery appointed his chief of staff, a post which carried the rank of brigadier-general; and when in February 1916 Rawlinson received command of the newly formed Fourth Army, he insisted on taking his chief of staff with him as temporary major-general, general staff. This rank was made substantive to Montgomery in January 1917. Thus he had risen from the rank of major to major-general in two and a half years. Throughout the existence of the Fourth Army Rawlinson and he remained at its head, from the battles of the Somme to the end of 'the advance to victory' of which Montgomery wrote an account, *The Story of the Fourth Army in the Battles of the Hundred Days* (1919).

After the armistice Montgomery held the important appointments of chief of staff with the Army of the Rhine, and deputy chief of the staff to Rawlinson who was commander-in-chief in India. Then he commanded in succession the Welsh Territorial division, the 1st division at Aldershot, and, as lieutenant-general, the Southern Command on Salisbury Plain. A full general in 1930, in March 1931 he became adjutant-general to the forces and member of the Army Council. Finally, in February 1933 he was appointed chief of the imperial general staff, and in 1935 was promoted to field-marshal. It was a period of peace, appeasement, and retrenchment, and he could get very little done, particularly in the province of armoured warfare; so in 1936, in order to facilitate promotion—his predecessor, Lord Milne [q.v.], having occupied the post for seven years—he resigned his appointment and retired to his home, Gunby Hall, Spilsby, Lincolnshire, where he died 13 October 1947. He left no children.

Montgomery was appointed K.C.M.G. (1919), C.B. (1918), K.C.B. (1925), and G.C.B. (1934). Portraits of him were painted by F. E. Hodge and (Sir) Oswald Birley; both are at Gunby Hall, the former owned by his family, the latter by the National Trust to which Gunby Hall was presented in 1944.

[*Journal* of the Royal Artillery, vol. lxxv, No. 1, January 1948; private information; personal knowledge.]     J. E. EDMONDS.

MOODY, HAROLD ARUNDEL (1882–1947), medical practitioner and founder of the League of Coloured Peoples, was born at Kingston, Jamaica, 8 October 1882, the son of Charles Ernest and Christina Elice Moody. His parents were negroes of humble birth but of considerable natural gifts which they imparted to their children, all of whom entered the professions. Moody was educated at Wolmer's Free School in Kingston and at the week-ends assisted at his father's drug-store. A keen student, he was the first boy at Wolmer's to win a distinction in mathematics in the Cambridge senior school certificate. In 1904 he proceeded to King's College, London, to begin his medical studies. He had a very successful course, winning various prizes and medals, and in 1912 qualified M.B., B.S., proceeding M.D. in 1919. Eventually he set up in practice in Peckham where he built up a large connexion and remained for the rest of his life.

Moody early showed his religious bent, and while at the university was president of his college Christian Union. After graduation he did much speaking and lecturing to improve the status and prestige of his own negro people. In 1931 he founded the League of Coloured Peoples to work for all the coloured races. He twice visited Jamaica, and in 1946 and 1947 also made an intensive lecturing tour of the other islands of the West Indies, as well as of the United States. This was very successful, but ended with exhaustion and illness, from which he did not recover, and he died in London 24 April 1947, shortly after his return.

An active Congregationalist, Moody was the first coloured man to hold a number of distinguished positions: he was chairman of the Colonial Missionary

Society (1921), president of the Christian Endeavour Union (1936), and chairman of the London Missionary Society (1943). Deeply sincere, he faced opposition, even sometimes from his own people, with splendid courage. He was a fine public speaker of compelling personality, and his sense of humour and tolerance were great assets.

In 1913 Moody married an English nurse, Olive Mabel, daughter of the late Richard Tranter, traveller, of Henley-on-Thames; the marriage was a very happy one. There were four sons and two daughters, all of whom had successful professional careers, two in medicine. A bust in bronze by Ronald Moody is at Livingstone Hall, Westminster.

[*Newsletter* of the League of Coloured Peoples, May 1947; private information; personal knowledge.]

DRUMMOND SHIELS.

MORLEY HORDER, PERCY (RICHARD) (1870–1944), architect. [See HORDER.]

MOTTISTONE, first BARON (1868–1947), politician and soldier. [See SEELY, JOHN EDWARD BERNARD.]

MOYNE, first BARON (1880–1944), statesman and traveller. [See GUINNESS, WALTER EDWARD.]

MOZLEY, JOHN KENNETH (1883–1946), divine, was born 8 January 1883 at Horsforth, Leeds, the third son of John Rickards Mozley, former fellow of King's College, Cambridge, and an inspector of workhouse schools under the Local Government Board, by his wife, Edith Merivale, daughter of Bonamy Price [q.v.]. Mozley obtained a scholarship at Malvern College but after a serious illness was moved to Leeds Grammar School. He proceeded to Pembroke College, Cambridge, where he was a scholar. His career in the university was distinguished. He was president of the Union, and was placed in the second division of the first class in part i of the classical tripos (1905) and the first class of part ii of the theological tripos (1906). He gained George Williams (1906) and Norrisian (1909) prizes and the Crosse (1906) and Allen (1907) scholarships. He was ordained deacon in 1909 and priest in 1910 and from 1907 until 1919 was occupied in academic work in Cambridge as fellow of Pembroke College of which he became dean in 1909.

In 1920 Mozley left Cambridge to take

up the office of principal of Leeds Clergy School where he remained until 1925 when, to his lasting grief, the school was brought to an end for lack of funds. He found congenial work of a similar kind, however, in his next post as warden of St. Augustine's House, Reading, where he had the opportunity of influencing the undergraduates. From 1920 until 1930 he was lecturer of Leeds parish church, a position which he valued highly and to which he returned in the last year of his life.

Mozley was a Liberal in politics, but, on the whole, a conservative in ecclesiastical affairs. He represented an intelligent and well-informed Anglican orthodoxy, but at the same time he was deeply influenced by the writings of the Rev. Dr. Peter Taylor Forsyth, the Congregationalist. Although perhaps he never produced the *magnum opus* which, with better health, he might have written, Mozley was one of the leading figures in the theological world of his generation. He was an important member of the Archbishops' Commission on Christian Doctrine and one of his most learned books, *The Impassibility of God* (1926), was the outcome of research undertaken for that commission. Among his writings his first published work, *Ritschlianism* (1909), deserves to be remembered as a useful and penetrating account of an influential theological movement. *The Doctrine of the Atonement* (1915) is perhaps the best example of Mozley's power of exposition and the clearest statement of his fundamental convictions. He was able to write for the general reader in an interesting style. A good example of his more 'popular' work is *The Beginnings of Christian Theology* (1931). Up to the time of his death Mozley was engaged on a survey of recent British theology. Unfortunately he did not live to complete it, but the greater part was finished and was published posthumously under the title *Some Tendencies in British Theology* (1951). Even in its imperfect state this book is among his best performances and impresses the reader by the width of the author's reading and by his ability to expound with sympathy systems of the most diverse character.

Mozley's writings had attracted much favourable notice and it was no surprise when he was made a canon of St. Paul's in 1930 and chancellor of the cathedral in 1931. He took a full share in the government of the cathedral and paid much attention to the preparation of his sermons which were both theological and evangelistic in tone. From 1937 to 1944 he was preacher of Lincoln's Inn. In 1941 Mozley felt compelled to resign his canonry. His health had deteriorated, largely, no doubt, as a result of the hardships of life in St. Paul's during the night bombing of the City, and also of the shock of the sudden and tragic death of his wife in that year, which was a consequence of the strain of continuous air raids. He had married in 1910 Mary Geraldine, daughter of the Rev. John William Nutt, sometime fellow of All Souls College, Oxford, and rector of Harpsden, Henley-on-Thames. There were no children of the marriage. From his retirement until his death at Headingley, Leeds, 23 November 1946, Mozley was active in promoting theological study, particularly among women who were reading for the Lambeth diploma.

[Private information; personal knowledge.]
W. R. MATTHEWS.

MUIR, (JOHN) RAMSAY (BRYCE) (1872–1941), historian and politician, was born at Otterburn, Northumberland, 30 September 1872, the eldest child of the Rev. Alexander Bryce Muir, Presbyterian minister (first at Otterburn, and from 1873 at Birkenhead), by his wife, Jane, daughter of Thomas Rowatt, of Edinburgh, of which city he was a bailie. Ramsay Muir was educated at a private school in Birkenhead; from 1889 he was a student of University College, Liverpool (then part of the federal Victoria University), where he was placed in the first class of the honours list in history in 1893; from January 1894 until the summer of 1898 he was a Brackenbury scholar of Balliol College, Oxford, where he took a first class both in *literae humaniores* (1897) and in modern history (1898). He then became an assistant lecturer in history at the Owens College, Manchester, under T. F. Tout [q.v.]; but returning to Liverpool in 1899 he served there first as a lecturer and then, from 1906 to 1913, as professor of modern history. During this period he was active in the foundation of a students representative council, and he took a part in securing a charter for the new university of Liverpool (1903) and in general university politics. He also published works, in 1906 and 1907, on the local history of Liverpool.

Resigning his chair in 1913 Muir took a year's holiday, first in India, where he gave a number of lectures and studied the methods of Indian universities, and afterwards (in the spring and early summer of 1914) in Germany. His visit to India led to his serving on the Calcutta University commission of 1917–19. Meanwhile, he had accepted an invitation from the university of Manchester to be the first holder of a newly created chair of modern history, and he held that post for seven years (1914–21). During these years he published a number of works, largely stimulated by the war of 1914–18, in the field of general modern history. Some of them, such as *Nationalism and Internationalism* (1916) and *National Self-Government* (1918), dealt with current European problems; but one of the most considerable, the two volumes of *A Short History of the British Commonwealth* (1920–22), was concerned with the expansion of Britain, a theme which always engaged his interest and his feelings, and on which he afterwards published an admirable short study (*The British Empire: How it Grew and How it Works*) in 1940.

He had always been interested in politics even in his undergraduate days: one of his early books, published while he was teaching at Liverpool, had been a work on *Peers and Bureaucrats* (1910) stimulated by the political crisis of the budget of 1909 and its rejection by the House of Lords; and the many works which he published during the tenure of his Manchester chair were mainly on themes and problems of contemporary politics. The tradition of Gladstone, a great son of Liverpool, was strong in his mind; and in 1921 he turned from the career of historian and teacher which he had followed for over twenty years, and embraced the political career which filled the remaining twenty years of his life. The Liberal summer school, founded in 1921, found in him its director and chief inspiration. He became a candidate for the constituency of Rochdale in east Lancashire: defeated in one election (1922), he was successful in the next (1923), but was again defeated in 1924. He afterwards stood, without success, at a number of other elections, down to the year 1935. But if he could not serve his party in Parliament, he served it abundantly and faithfully outside, and he played a leading part in the making of Liberal programmes and the conduct of Liberal propaganda as long as he lived. Apart from his work for the Liberal

summer school, he served as chairman of the organization committee of the Liberal Party, 1930–31, and as chairman (1931–3) and president (1933–6) of the National Liberal Federation; and when the Federation was merged into the Liberal Party Organization in 1936, he became a vice-president of the Organization, and the chairman of its education and propaganda committee, and held those offices until his death.

Perhaps he never attained the position which the quality of his mind and the force of his character deserved to command. This was largely due to his double career. If he had continued the career of professor, which he abandoned at the age of fifty, he might have added to the many popular works on history which he produced some more fundamental historical work. If he had flung himself into politics in his youth, say in the year 1905, he might have had a distinguished political career. As it was, he left his career as an historical writer unfinished, and began his political career at a time when he was past his own middle age and when the fortunes of the Liberal Party were becoming increasingly clouded. In the event, he became the scholar-prophet of Liberalism in a time of troubles. It is as such that he will be mainly remembered. Prophecy was in his blood and ancestry: a resonant voice and impressive manner added to its force: he dealt in fine generalities, but he was perhaps deficient in the saving ballast of particulars and details. He received the honorary degree of Litt.D. from the university of Liverpool in 1931. He died unmarried at Pinner, Middlesex, 4 May 1941.

[Ramsay Muir, *An Autobiography*, edited by Stuart Hodgson, 1943, and containing in part 2, 'As Others Saw Him', sketches and appreciations by a number of his friends; private information; personal knowledge.]

ERNEST BARKER.

MURRAY, ANDREW GRAHAM, VIS-COUNT DUNEDIN (1849–1942), judge, was born in Edinburgh 21 November 1849, the only child of Thomas Graham Murray, of Stenton, Perthshire, writer to the signet and crown agent for Scotland from 1866 to 1868. His mother was Caroline Jane, daughter of John Tod, of Kirkhill, Midlothian, writer to the signet, one of the founders of the firm of Tods, Murray, and Jamieson of which his father was a partner. His paternal grandfather, Andrew Murray, of Murrayshall, Perthshire, was a member of the Scottish bar and sheriff of Aberdeen. Educated at Harrow, at Trinity College, Cambridge, of which he was a scholar and where he graduated with a second class in the classical tripos of 1872, and at Edinburgh University, Graham Murray was admitted a member of the Faculty of Advocates in 1874.

Young Graham Murray's ambition cannot have failed to be stirred by the brilliant distinction and ability of the Scottish bench and bar of those days. Lord President (John) Inglis and Lord Justice-Clerk (James) Moncreiff [qq.v.] presided over the two divisions of the Inner House; E. S. Gordon and William Watson [qq.v.], both destined for the House of Lords as lords of appeal in ordinary, were respectively lord advocate and solicitor-general; J. B. Balfour (later Lord Kinross), Alexander Asher, A. S. (later Lord) Kinnear, J. P. B. (later Lord) Robertson [qq.v.], and other well-known advocates paced the floor of the Parliament House. With his influential family connexions in the law and his own outstanding gifts Graham Murray was well equipped for making his way even in so formidable an arena, and before long he was in the enjoyment of a large practice of the best class. In 1888 he was appointed senior advocate depute in the Crown Office and in 1890 entered on the path of promotion as sheriff of Perthshire, for it is traditional that the sheriff of Perthshire never dies. Next year he became solicitor-general for Scotland and took silk. There was at that time and until 1897 no separate roll of Queen's counsel for Scotland and the honour was conferred only upon law officers of the Crown and the dean of faculty whose names were entered in the English roll. In 1892 he went out of office, but was again solicitor-general from 1895 to 1896 when he was appointed lord advocate, which office he held until 1903. Meantime he did not neglect politics, although he had neither inclination nor aptitude for this side of public life. In 1885 he stood unsuccessfully as Conservative candidate for East Perthshire, but he was returned for Buteshire at a by-election in October 1891 and held the seat until 1905. In 1903 he was appointed secretary for Scotland with a seat in the Cabinet.

On the death, in 1905, of Lord Kinross, Graham Murray succeeded him as lord justice-general of Scotland and lord president of the Court of Session, and was raised to the peerage as Baron Dunedin,

of Stenton, Perthshire. In 1913 he left Scotland to become one of the two new additional lords of appeal in ordinary under the Appellate Jurisdiction Act passed in that year, and he held this office for nineteen years until his retirement in 1932.

Graham Murray was sworn of the Privy Council in 1896, and was appointed K.C.V.O. in 1908 and G.C.V.O. in 1923. In 1926 he was advanced to a viscountcy. He was elected an honorary bencher of the Middle Temple in 1910 and received the honorary degree of D.C.L. from the university of Oxford and that of LL.D. from the universities of Edinburgh, Glasgow, and Aberdeen. When along with many other representatives of the bench and bar he visited Canada and the United States in 1930 as a guest of the Canadian and American Bar Associations, Toronto, Chicago, and Columbia universities conferred upon him the honorary degree of LL.D., and at Chicago he delivered an interesting address in which he claimed kinship with Lord Mansfield, as the great-great-grandson of a cousin of that most eminent judge (*Proceedings* of the American Bar Association, vol. lv, pp. 116 et seq.).

The sequence of appointments, promotions, and honours thus briefly catalogued might of itself do no more than betoken a career of conventional success. But Graham Murray was much more than this represents. He was a man of outstanding personality, and combined in himself qualities and gifts not commonly associated. He was indeed a great lawyer—and the epithet is sparingly conceded by a critical profession—and it is as this that he would wish to be remembered. But the cloistered life of the legal devotee had no attraction for him. He liked to be regarded as a man of the world. His prowess at rackets as a boy at Harrow, and in later life his proficiency in shooting and golf—he was captain of the Honourable Company of Edinburgh Golfers and also of the Royal and Ancient Golf Club of St. Andrews—combined with his friendships in high social circles gave to one side of his character as much satisfaction as his pre-eminence in law gave to the other. He was fond of travelling and enjoyed exhibiting his knowledge of French and other languages. Cycling in the early days, photography, and dancing were among his varied hobbies. Yet with all this it is true to say that the dominant interest of his life was his devotion to the law, and first and foremost to the law of Scotland. He was no legal pedant and his scholarship made no pretension to black-letter learning. He enjoyed the working out of legal problems as an intellectual exercise, and what he cared for was the sound administration of the law as a practical system for the governance of human affairs. No legal topics were alien to his mind, but for two he had a special predilection, patent law and feudal law, an incongruous pair, typical of his versatility. He may fairly be said to have been the last of the great Scottish feudalists. In elucidating and liberalizing the interpretation of the Workmen's Compensation Acts he took a prominent part.

The eight years during which Dunedin occupied the president's chair in the Court of Session showed him at his best. The court had suffered a measure of eclipse on the death of Lord President Inglis, whose successor, Lord Robertson, made no secret of his preference for politics, while Lord President Kinross, the next in succession, was a tired man in failing health. From the moment of his taking command of the court Dunedin infused a spirit of animation and efficiency into every branch of its activities. A master was on the bridge of the ship and the whole crew knew it. For the bar it was an education in advocacy to practise before him. Rightly impatient of irrelevancy in argument, he was never obstructive to debate but always appreciative of sound reasoning. He possessed in a high degree the not too common judicial gift of open-mindedness and suspension of judgement, and until the last word was said in a case he remained ready to accept a new point of view and to admit that his first impressions were mistaken. He was much more concerned that the decision of the court should be right than that he himself should be shown to have been right. But when he reached conviction he was tenacious of his opinion and keen that it should prevail. He never lacked courage and always sought to cut through technicalities to the real question at issue.

When he sat in the House of Lords and the Privy Council Dunedin was no longer in command of his court but one of a team. From the outset he fell into step without difficulty and soon acquired a high reputation as a formidable but helpful colleague. His contributions to the law were always characterized by forthrightness and clarity. Without pretension to literary style, his judgements are concerned with substance rather than with form and, true to the Scottish tradition of preferring principle

to precedent, he was an admirable exponent of legal doctrine. His judgements have in consequence acquired an authoritative place in the evolution of the law and are frequently cited, always with respect.

A few of the leading cases in which he took part in the House of Lords may be cited as affording examples of his judicial characteristics and method. One of the earliest is *Sinclair* v. *Brougham*, [1914] A.C. 398, where he dealt exhaustively with what is known to lawyers as the problem of 'unjust enrichment'. He there discussed 'rather on principle than on authority', as he himself said, the whole doctrine of equitable restitution, with illustrations from the Roman and other systems of law. 'Is English equity', he asked, 'to retire defeated from the task which other systems of equity have conquered?' His answer was an emphatic negative. In *Rex* v. *Halliday*, [1917] A.C. 260, a case which concerned the validity of an Order in Council authorizing the internment of a British subject in wartime, Dunedin was one of the majority in favour of upholding the order and was unmoved by Lord Shaw's emotional invocation of the liberty of the subject. Similarly, in *Bowman* v. *Secular Society* in the same year, [1917] A.C. 406, in which the question whether Christianity is part of the law of the land was mooted, he was with the majority in declaring the legality of a bequest to a rationalist society, despite Lord Chancellor Finlay's strenuous dissent. In 1920 he presided at the hearing of the famous case of *Attorney-General* v. *De Keyser's Royal Hotel*, [1920] A.C. 508, and delivered the leading judgement vindicating the right of the owner of property requisitioned by the Crown for the defence of the realm to receive compensation. In *Lord Advocate* v. *Marquess of Zetland*, 1920 S.C. (H.L.) 1, in which the House of Lords was called upon, probably for the last time, to explore the arcana of the feudal law of Scotland, Dunedin was in his element and by his learning greatly assisted the House in solving the recondite question at issue. In *Cantiare San Rocco* v. *Clyde Shipbuilding and Engineering Co.*, [1924] A.C. 226, he did not conceal his preference for the Scottish law of restitution as contrasted with the law of England as it then stood.

It may truly be said that the law reports contain the record of Dunedin's life-work; he made little noteworthy contribution otherwise to legal literature. In his early days at the Scots bar he produced in 1877 a *Digest of Registration Cases* of which a revised edition was published in 1891 together with a treatise on *Qualification of Voters* by R. F. L. (later Lord) Blackburn. In 1892 he compiled an historical pamphlet giving *A Short Account of the Principality of Scotland and the Title of Prince and Steward of Scotland*, and his tenure of the office of keeper of the Great Seal of the Principality from 1900 to 1936 was to him a source of much pride. In 1935 there was printed a lecture which he delivered in that year in the university of Glasgow under the auspices of the David Murray foundation in which he dealt illuminatingly with *The Divergencies and Convergencies of English and Scottish Law*. He was an occasional contributor to the correspondence columns of *The Times* and in a letter published on 20 April 1927 he epigrammatically declared that 'the fundamental difference between the common law of England and that of Scotland lies in this: that in England you have to find the remedy in order to discover the right, whereas in Scotland you have to find the right in order to discover the remedy'. To *The Times* of 18 February 1932 he contributed an article in which he reviewed, in a reminiscent and reflective vein, 'Fifty Years of the Bench and the Bar'. He there recorded that in the course of his professional life he had pleaded before four lord chancellors and sat as a colleague with nine. Contrasting the older with the younger generation of lawyers he noted a decline in erudition, compensated by a greater tendency to practicality. In the modern judiciary he missed the strong flavour of individuality exemplified in Scotland by Lord Deas and in England by Lord Blackburn [qq.v.]. The latter he placed in 'quite the first rank of judges' but in Lord Wensleydale [q.v.] he found his 'absolute ideal'. He recounted his experience of an incursion into the parliamentary bar, then in its hey-day, where he 'was greatly amused and slightly shocked by the turbulence of the proceedings'. After appearing there on two occasions he decided that he was not suited for that class of practice.

Dunedin was twice married: first, in 1874 to Mary Clementina (died 1922), seventh daughter of Admiral Sir William Edmonstone, fourth baronet, of Duntreath, Stirlingshire, and had one son, who predeceased his father without issue, and three daughters, the eldest of whom also died before him; secondly, in 1923 to Jean Elmslie Henderson, C.B.E. (died 1944),

daughter of George Findlay, of Aberdeen. Dunedin died in Edinburgh 21 August 1942. There is a portrait of him in the uniform of a privy counsellor, by Sir James Guthrie, in the Parliament House in Edinburgh. An ink and chalk drawing by Robin Guthrie is in the National Portrait Gallery.

[*Scotsman*, 22 August 1942; *The Times*, 24 August 1942; *Scottish Law Review*, September 1942; *Law Journal*, 3 October 1942; personal knowledge.]     MACMILLAN.

MURRAY, Sir ARCHIBALD JAMES (1860–1945), general, was born 21 April 1860 at Woodhouse, near Kingsclere, Hampshire, the second son and third child of Charles Murray, landed proprietor, by his wife, Anne, daughter of Captain John Baker Graves, of the 19th Regiment, and later judge at Kurunegala, Ceylon. Educated at Cheltenham College, Murray entered the army through the Royal Military College, Sandhurst, and in 1879 was gazetted to the 27th Regiment which, two years later, was given the territorial title of the Royal Inniskilling Fusiliers. His early service was abroad, at Hong Kong, Singapore, and the Cape, where in 1888, as a captain, he took part in the suppression of a Zulu rising.

In 1897 Murray gained entrance to the Staff College, Camberley ; among his fellow students were the future field-marshals Robertson, Haig, and Allenby [qq.v.]. Thoughtful and reserved in manner, Murray seemed old for his years, and was generally spoken of at the college as 'Old Archie'.

At the end of the two-year course, Murray rejoined his battalion, but on the outbreak of the South African war he was appointed intelligence officer on the staff of Sir William Penn Symons [q.v.], commanding in Natal, and was with him when he was mortally wounded, and his senior staff officer killed, in the opening frontier fight at Talana. The next-in-command was out of health, and Murray, appointed chief of staff by him, managed skilfully to extricate the British force from its advanced position and bring it back to Ladysmith. His reputation as a field soldier was made; he received a brevet lieutenant-colonelcy in 1900 and henceforward generals competed for his services. He was on the staff of Sir George White [q.v.] during the siege of Ladysmith; and during 1900 was senior staff officer to Sir Archibald Hunter [q.v.] of the 10th division. In October 1901 Murray

611

was promoted to command the 2nd battalion of his regiment in India, soon to be warned for service in South Africa, where it arrived in February 1902. In leading his men in an attack at Pilskop, in the northern Transvaal, for which he was appointed to the D.S.O., he was dangerously wounded in the abdomen.

Between the South African war and August 1914, Murray held a series of important staff appointments: senior general staff officer of the 1st division (Aldershot); director of military training, general staff, at the War Office, 1907–12 (Haig being one of the other two directors); and inspector of infantry (1912–14). He was promoted major-general in 1910.

Murray had held the command of the 2nd division for six months when war was declared in 1914, but he was appointed chief of the general staff of the British Expeditionary Force, at the express wish of Sir John French (later the Earl of Ypres, q.v.), under whose command he was serving at Aldershot. The early days of the campaign, the battles of Mons and Le Cateau, the retreat on Paris, the advance to the Marne and the Aisne, the transfer of the British Expeditionary Force to Flanders, and the first battle of Ypres, were more than strenuous. According to French's reminiscences, *1914*, at the end of the year Murray was a sick man, and was obliged in January 1915 to go to England for rest, and Robertson (then quarter-master-general) took his place. In February 1915 Murray was appointed by Lord Kitchener [q.v.] to be deputy chief of the imperial general staff for the special purpose of superintending the training of the New Army, and in September he was promoted to be chief of the imperial general staff. In December, however, French resigned and was replaced by Haig; other changes were made, Robertson became chief of the imperial general staff and Murray was appointed to a command in Egypt, where he arrived in January 1916, with instructions to secure the defence of the Suez Canal, instructions which in March were enlarged so as to include the defence of all Egypt and the reorganization of the troops evacuated from Gallipoli. In August, however, after an invading Turkish force had been defeated at Romani (twenty miles from the canal), it was decided to advance to the Palestine frontier, a hundred miles farther on. By December, in spite of opposition and physical difficulties, this had been achieved by laying a railway line and a 12-inch water main. As Allenby said: 'Murray's brilliant campaign in Sinai had removed the danger to Egypt, and had forced the enemy back across his own frontier.'

In March 1917, when Baghdad had just been occupied and the Nivelle offensive in France was imminent, Murray was instructed to advance into Palestine, as part of the general offensive, and on 26 March an attempt was made to capture its gateway at Gaza. This was successful, but, owing to a misunderstanding on the part of a subordinate and absence of water for the horses, the troops were withdrawn. The desperate state of the Turkish troops from sickness and lack of equipment being known, Murray was directed to renew the operations and occupy Jerusalem. He protested that the operations required five instead of his three infantry divisions (New Army troops, who had served in Gallipoli), in addition to his two mounted divisions, in order to widen the front of attack. His request was refused; yet being, as one of his friends subsequently wrote, 'super-disciplined and super-obedient', Murray obeyed his instructions and attacked Gaza again; but this time, the Turks being warned and prepared (and notoriously fighting well on the defensive in entrenchments), Murray suffered a serious defeat. He was superseded by Allenby, who took over on 29 June. Allenby himself would not move until he received the two extra divisions.

The supersession was not justified: Allenby in his final dispatch acknowledged his indebtedness to his predecessor 'who by his bridging of the desert between Egypt and Palestine laid the foundations for the subsequent advances of the Egyptian Expeditionary Force'. Murray by his foresight and strategic imagination 'brought the waters of the Nile to the borders of Palestine, planned the skilful military operations by which the Turks were driven from strong positions in the desert over the frontier of Egypt, and carried a standard gauge railway to the gates of Gaza. The organization he created, both in Sinai and in Egypt, stood all tests and formed the corner-stone of my successes.'

On his return home Murray was appointed to the Aldershot Command which he held until November 1919, having been promoted general in August of that year. He retired from the army in 1922 and died at Makepeace, Reigate, 23 January 1945.

He was appointed K.C.B. (1911), K.C.M.G. (1915), G.C.M.G. (1917), and G.C.B. (1928). He was a grand officer of the Legion of Honour and a member of various other foreign orders.

Murray was twice married: first, in 1890 to Caroline Helen (died 1910), daughter of Lieutenant-Colonel Henry Baker Sweet, of Hillersdon, Tiverton; and secondly, in 1912 to Mildred Georgina, daughter of his former colonel, William Toke Dooner, of Maidstone. There was one son of the first marriage. A portrait of Murray by Arthur Fuller is in the possession of the family and will go eventually to Murray's regiment.

[*The Royal Inniskilling Fusiliers December 1688 to July 1914*, 1934; Viscount French, *1914*, 1919; Sir J. F. Maurice and M. H. Grant, (Official) *History of the War in South Africa 1899–1902*, 1906–10; Sir J. E. Edmonds and others, (Official) *History of the Great War. Military Operations, France and Belgium, 1914–15*, 1922–8; Cyril Falls, (Official) *History of the Great War. Military Operations, Egypt and Palestine, 1914–18*, 3 vols., 1928–30; private information; personal knowledge.]
J. E. EDMONDS.

MURRAY, SIR (GEORGE) EVELYN (PEMBERTON) (1880–1947), civil servant, was born in London 25 July 1880, the only son of (Sir) George Herbert Murray [q.v.] who became secretary to the Treasury. He was a kinsman of the Duke of Atholl and later became heir presumptive to the dukedom.

Murray, who was educated at Eton and Christ Church, Oxford, entered the Civil Service in 1903 and was private secretary to three successive presidents of the Board of Education. In 1912 he was appointed a commissioner of Customs and Excise and in 1914, when only thirty-four years of age, secretary to the Post Office. He held that post until 1934 when he returned to his old department of Customs and Excise as chairman of the Board. He retired in 1940, having been appointed C.B. in 1916 and promoted K.C.B. in 1919.

Murray went to the Post Office within a few days of the outbreak of war, and at a time when there were few of mature experience to assist him, and those few were, in general, past their best. His task was an exceptionally formidable one but he tackled it with ability, energy, and courage. The period of reconstruction which followed the war years proved no less exacting. There was a growing need for mechanization in all phases of Post Office work. War-time experience, and difficulties arising from the rapid expansion of Post Office activities, led to a demand for greater freedom from central control. These facts were but slowly recognized by many in the Post Office, and it was mainly through Murray's early appreciation of them that the Post Office made so great a stride forward in the course of the twenty years during which he was responsible for its management. Milestones in that tale of progress were the conversion of the national telephone system from manual to automatic working; the institution of trans-continental and inter-continental telephony; the establishment of air services as a regular means of conveying mail; and the development of motor transport for the distribution and delivery of letters and parcels.

There were few in the Post Office whose personal association with Murray was sufficiently intimate to permit of their ranking themselves amongst his friends, but those few held his friendship dear. To the many others with whom he had dealings his intellectual qualities made instant appeal. His almost uncanny power of penetration in regard to men and affairs, his flair for finance, and his remarkable capacity for constructive criticism entitled him to a position of pre-eminence amongst the long line of distinguished men who preceded him as secretary to the Post Office. He died in London 30 March 1947.

Murray married in 1906 Muriel Mildred Elizabeth, daughter of Philip Beresford Beresford-Hope, J.P., of Bedgebury Park, Kent. They had one son who was killed in Italy in 1945 while in command of the 80th Medium Regiment, Royal Artillery, leaving a son, George Iain, who succeeded as tenth Duke of Atholl in 1957.

[Private information; personal knowledge.]
T. R. GARDINER.

MYERS, CHARLES SAMUEL (1873–1946), psychologist, was born in London 13 March 1873, the eldest son of Wolf Myers, merchant, by his wife, Esther Eugenie Moses. His earlier ancestors on his father's side were principally interested in commerce. From his mother and her family came powerful social, artistic—especially musical—and philosophical influences. As a boy at the City of London School Myers turned definitely to the fields of science, and later at Gonville and Caius College, Cambridge, he was placed in the first class of the honours list in both parts of the natural sciences tripos (1893,

1895) and was Arnold Gerstenberg student in 1896. He proceeded to his M.B. in 1898, but he was not much inclined towards medical practice, and in that year he went with the Cambridge anthropological expedition to the Torres Straits. He joined W. H. R. Rivers and William McDougall [q.v.] in experimental studies of the sensory reactions of the natives of that area, and he became profoundly interested in primitive music.

In 1902 Myers returned to Cambridge to assist Rivers in teaching the physiology of the special senses, and he remained in Cambridge to become, in succession, demonstrator, lecturer, and, in 1921, reader in experimental psychology. During this period, for three years (1906–9) he also held a professorship in the same subject at King's College in the university of London. During the years preceding and immediately following the war of 1914–18 he did more than any other person to develop and foster the interests of scientific psychology in Great Britain. It was by his influence that the first English experimental laboratory especially designed for psychology was opened at Cambridge in 1912.

In 1915 Myers was given a commission in the Royal Army Medical Corps and in 1916 was appointed consultant psychologist to the British armies in France. The work he did at this time had a great influence on the psychological treatment of what was generally then called 'shell-shock'. When the war ended he returned to his Cambridge position. But he was deeply dissatisfied. He wanted wider opportunities for the development of his more practical interests. It seemed to him that official and academic circles showed little genuine interest in psychology. In 1922 he left Cambridge for London and thereafter to the end of his life devoted himself to the establishment and development of the National Institute of Industrial Psychology which, with Mr. Henry John Welch, he had founded in 1921. He also played a great part in the early activities of what later became the Industrial Health Research Board; he was the principal architect of the fortunes of the British Psychological Society, and he was the foremost representative of British psychology in its international relationships.

Myers's famous *Text-Book of Experimental Psychology* (1909) was for long by far the best work of its kind in any language. His *Introduction to Experimental Psychology* (1911) went through several editions. *Mind and Work* (1920), *Industrial Psychology in Great Britain* (1926), and *Ten Years of Industrial Psychology* (with H. J. Welch, 1932) all dealt with the later interests of his life. He also published two volumes of essays: *A Psychologist's Point of View* (1933) and *In the Realm of Mind* (1937), and his many contributions to problems of primitive music won him an international reputation in the anthropological field.

In 1915 Myers was elected F.R.S.; he was appointed C.B.E. in 1919, and received honorary degrees from the universities of Manchester (D.Sc., 1927), Calcutta (LL.D.), and Pennsylvania (D.Sc.). He was a fellow (1919) and later (1935) an honorary fellow of Gonville and Caius College, Cambridge, a foreign associate of the French Société de Psychologie twice president of the psychology section of the British Association (1922, 1931), president of the International Congress of Psychology in 1923; and editor of the *British Journal of Psychology* (1911–24).

Myers was a man of rather above medium height, well built, with a most mobile countenance, and a rare and famous smile. He made friends all over the world, for he travelled widely; and also, to his own way of thinking, a few persistent enemies. To those who knew him well he was a wonderful and loyal companion and friend, and a very wise counsellor. In his younger years he was fond of mountain climbing, and was quite a good lawn-tennis player. He devoted much of his spare time to music and was himself a very fine violinist. He became a most ardent freemason; and was deeply and practically interested in many philanthropic enterprises for the Jewish community.

In 1904 Myers married Edith Babette, daughter of Isaac Seligman, merchant, of London; they had three daughters and two sons. Their homes, first at Cambridge, then in London, and finally at Winsford in Somerset, became places of abounding hospitality and of friendship for large numbers of students and for visitors from every part of the world. Myers died at Winsford 12 October 1946. A portrait by R. Swan is at the National Institute of Industrial Psychology.

[F. C. Bartlett in *Obituary Notices of Fellows of the Royal Society*, No. 16, May 1948; *A History of Psychology in Autobiography*, edited by Carl Murchison, vol. iii, 1936; private information; personal knowledge.]

FREDERIC C. BARTLETT.

MYERS, LEOPOLD HAMILTON (1881–1944), novelist, was born at Cambridge 6 September 1881, the elder son of F. W. H. Myers [q.v.]. He was educated first at Eton (1894–9), for a year in Germany, and then at Trinity College, Cambridge, which he left in 1901 when his father died. During the war of 1914–18 he held a post at the Board of Trade. In 1925 he visited Ceylon. Having delicate health and sufficient means he followed no profession, and his life in the main was leisured and uneventful.

Myers was a novelist who developed late. In 1908 he published *Arvat*, a play in verse. Fifteen years later appeared his first novel, *The Orissers*, which was at once acclaimed as a work of unusual originality, depth, and power. It was followed in 1925 by *The Clio*, a novel in a much lighter vein but also with a philosophic background. In 1929 he published *The Near and the Far*, the first volume of a series which had India in the reign of Akbar for its setting, and for its hero a young man who discards one mode of life after another in the effort to satisfy his spiritual aspirations. Myers was at this time much interested in oriental religions, in mysticism, and in the relationship of the soul with God; but the book is also a general criticism of a decadent society in which he saw many parallels to his own times. *Prince Jali* (1931) carried on the narrative and developed the ideas. In 1935 he published *The Root and the Flower*, a volume containing the two foregoing novels and a third, *Rajah Amar*, for which he was awarded the James Tait Black memorial and Femina Vie Heureuse prizes. About this time his thought, in common with that of many other men of letters, took on a strongly political cast. His sympathy with Russian Communism, long felt, left its mark on *Strange Glory*, a short, romantic novel published in 1936, and on *The Pool of Vishnu* (1940), the concluding volume of the 'Indian' series, in which the problems already raised found a solution reflecting the recent trends of his thought. Republished in 1943 under the collective title of *The Near and the Far*, these four books established his reputation as one of the outstanding novelists of his time.

Myers was a man of distinguished appearance and fastidious mind. Contemplative, highly strung, and given to melancholy and hypochondria, he did not care greatly for society and belonged to no literary group or movement; but he had an altogether unusual capacity for friendship and the understanding of other people's problems. In later life he came to believe, with almost fanatical intensity, that the condition of humanity could only be improved by a radical change in the structure of society. Of his last book, which was to have embodied these ideas, only a sketch remains.

In 1908 he married Elsie (died 1955), daughter of General William Jackson Palmer, founder of the city of Colorado Springs, United States, by whom he had two daughters. He died by his own hand at Marlow-on-Thames 8 April 1944. There is a portrait bust by Frank Dobson in the hands of the Contemporary Art Society.

[G. H. Bantock, *L. H. Myers*, 1956; personal knowledge.]      L. P. HARTLEY.

NARBETH, JOHN HARPER (1863–1944), naval architect, was born at Pembroke Dock 26 May 1863, the son of John Harper Narbeth who, after serving at Pembroke dockyard as a shipwright apprentice and writer, became a timber merchant. His mother was Anne Griffiths. Harper, the fourth of a family of eight, was from boyhood interested in the sea, and his pastimes of boating and yachting led him to study the behaviour and designs of ships and small craft. He was indentured as shipwright apprentice at the dockyard in 1877, and in 1882, after a competitive examination, took a course of higher training at the Royal Naval College, Greenwich. Three years later he was appointed to the Royal Corps of Naval Constructors, and became an assistant constructor at Portsmouth dockyard.

In 1887 he was transferred to the staff of (Sir) William H. White [q.v.], director of naval construction at the Admiralty. On showing aptitude for design work he was eventually entrusted with the preparation of warship designs of gradually increasing size and importance. These culminated in those of three battleships: *King Edward VII* class (of which eight ships were built), *Lord Nelson* class, and the *Dreadnought*. These ships were described by him in a paper read in 1922 before the Institution of Naval Architects. All were larger and more powerful than their forerunners. The *Dreadnought* also embodied revolutionary changes recommended by a powerful committee over which Sir John (later Lord) Fisher [q.v.] had presided. They included an armament of all big guns, higher speed, turbine propulsion, and underwater protection.

Sir Philip Watts [q.v.], who had succeeded White at the Admiralty and was a member of the committee, prepared, with Narbeth's assistance, a number of alternative designs; the Board of Admiralty selected one which became the *Dreadnought*. Working out the detailed design, Narbeth applied himself with zeal, enthusiasm, and success to the solution of the novel problems encountered.

On promotion in 1912 to be a chief constructor, Narbeth was made directly responsible to the director for the design and construction of minor war vessels; these included high-speed motor-boats, oil-carrying ships, minesweepers, and sloops. Characteristically, he effected noteworthy improvements in each of these widely differing types of vessel. He became joint secretary to the Royal Commission on fuel and engines under the chairmanship of Fisher. During the war of 1914–18 Narbeth designed the *Flower*-class sloops, and by special measures and the elimination of red-tape he arranged for these vessels and minesweepers to be built in large numbers in small shipyards in record time.

Improvements in aircraft during and after the war and their widening use in warfare led to demands from the navy for special ships to carry them. Sir Eustace Tennyson-D'Eyncourt, who had succeeded Watts as director, arranged for Narbeth, who from 1919 was assistant director, to deal with the new designs involved. A few seaplane carriers were first obtained by modifying merchant ships: then, by converting warships, notably the fast battle cruisers of *Courageous* class, carriers were produced with a deck suitable for landing or launching aircraft. These developments demanded boldness, ingenuity, and experience in design, qualities with which Narbeth was well endowed. He was guided by the meetings of a joint Admiralty and Air Ministry technical committee over which he presided (1918–23), and as a result the ships when completed were satisfactory to pilots and naval officers alike.

Narbeth retired in 1923. His services were recognized by his appointment as M.V.O. (1906), C.B.E. (1920), and C.B. (1923). He maintained his technical interests and was also active in social, temperance, and religious work; during his retirement he qualified as a Methodist local preacher. He died at Gloucester 19 May 1944. He married in 1888 Aquila Elizabeth (died 1931), daughter of W. J.

Anstey, foreman shipwright, of Portsmouth. His two sons survived him, one of whom, John Harper Narbeth, also became a chief constructor at the Admiralty.

[Personal knowledge.]   L. WOOLLARD.

NASH, PAUL (1889–1946), artist, was born in London 11 May 1889, the elder son of William Harry Nash, barrister-at-law, recorder of Abingdon, and his first wife, Caroline Maude, daughter of Captain John Milbourne Jackson, R.N. His father's family were comfortable Buckinghamshire yeomen, his mother's belonged to the navy, for which he was at first intended. But with the ingenious capacity of any artist to fail where his heart is not engaged he did not pass the entrance examination and so returned to finish his schooling at St. Paul's, which he left at seventeen. He evaded the alternative careers of architecture and banking and with the consent and support of his father pursued his interest in black-and-white illustration. After a short time at the Chelsea Polytechnic and then at night school in Bolt Court (the London County Council School of Photo-Engraving and Lithography), he went, with the encouragement of (Sir) William Rothenstein [q.v.] to the Slade School of Fine Art from 1910 to 1911. His earliest work was spun out of his own head and illustrated his own boyish visions and poems which were nourished by his reading of the romantic poets, of Dante Gabriel Rossetti and Blake, and of Gordon Bottomley [q.v.] who encouraged him and became his friend.

Unlike some of his contemporaries at the Slade School—Mark Gertler, C. R. W. Nevinson, and Edward Wadsworth [qq.v.], Mr. Stanley Spencer, Mr. Ben Nicholson, and Mr. William Roberts—Nash remained uninfluenced by the Post-Impressionist exhibition organized by Roger Fry [q.v.] in 1910. But one day Sir William Richmond [q.v.] said to him, 'My boy, you should go in for Nature'. He did, looking at it more directly, and drawing it on the spot. The 'nature' that he went in for, although usually without human beings, was always peopled, if not by the 'star-inwrought' visions of his youth, then by what Nash himself many years afterwards called the *genius loci*: a something which was not at first formal, but evanescent, a quality of light and imagination, and which later developed a fantastic, tangible personality expressed most fully by the monoliths and monster trees of his later work.

He had his first one-man exhibition (of water-colours) at the Carfax Gallery in 1912, and in 1913 shared an exhibition at the Dorien Leigh Gallery with his brother, John Northcote Nash. At the outbreak of war he enlisted in the Artists' Rifles; in 1916 he was commissioned in the Hampshire Regiment and in February 1917 he went to the Ypres salient. After four months he was invalided home as the result of an accident, but during those months he had spent all his spare time making drawings which were shown at the Goupil Gallery. John Buchan (later Lord Tweedsmuir, q.v.), then director of information, decided to send him back to the front as an official war artist. Nash held a second exhibition of war drawings at the Leicester Galleries in 1918 and from April of that year until early in 1919 was next engaged on paintings commissioned by the Government, the most famous of which is 'The Menin Road', now, with many others, in the Imperial War Museum. His poetic imagination, instead of being crushed by the terrible circumstances of war, had expanded to produce terrible images— terrible because of their combination of detached, almost abstract, appreciation and absolute truth to appearance.

Nash's first note for his autobiography for the years following 1918 was 'Struggles of a war artist without a war'; but by 1928 he was able to say that a show at the Leicester Galleries was 'a great success'. During these years he illustrated books, designed scenery for Madame Karsavina in Sir James Barrie's *The Truth About the Russian Dancers*, was for a short time an instructor in design at the Royal College of Art, and became established as an English water-colourist of great individuality, still clearly belonging to the English tradition. In 1921, after a severe illness, he had begun the well-known series of pictures of Dymchurch beach, two at least of which, 'Winter Sea' (privately owned) and 'Dymchurch Steps' (National Gallery of Canada) he worked on many years later. These, with their wide angles and dramatic changes of level, have a flavour of the theatrical practice of Mr. Edward Gordon Craig who had become a friend. Elsewhere, however, he began to develop the light palette and flower-like forms which distinguish his later pictures, and also his studies of trees, especially beechwoods, whose sun-crossed verticals often inspired the structure of his near-abstract work, then just begun but in the next decade to be explored further.

During the next ten years he expanded in the new freedom brought by confidence; travelled on the continent and in America (as British representative on the jury of the Carnegie Institute exhibition, 1931), founded (1933) the 'group of imaginative painters and designers' known as 'Unit One', held exhibitions at the Redfern and the Leicester galleries, was on the committee of the first international surrealist exhibition (1936), and showed at the Venice Biennale (1938). During all this time he designed fabrics, posters (notably for Shell-Mex, for which firm he also wrote a guide to Dorset in the Shell Guide series), book-jackets, end-papers, and so on, the execution of which he always supervised with scrupulous care. During this time too he struggled with increasingly serious ill health due to asthma, for which he tried living at Rye, Ballard Down near Swanage in Dorset, and in Hampstead, where he stayed until the outbreak of war. In 1930 he had begun his illustrations for Sir Thomas Browne's *Urne Buriall* and *The Garden of Cyrus*. Sir Herbert Read has stressed how much Browne and Nash were akin in spirit. It was Nash's metaphysical wit combined with his odd, rather bookish sense of visual incongruities which led him to adopt his highly personal attitude to surrealism. For him, surrealism was less an international movement than a licence to paint as he chose within the terms of modern practice. Because he was neither mordant nor rebellious his work had none of the shock-tactics of continental surrealism but retained the sweetness of the English landscape, the uncertainties of the English weather, and the whimsicalities of a cultivated English mind. His excursions into abstract painting had the same personal characteristics.

Nash was fascinated by evidences of prehistory, stones and mounds in fields, and in the personalities of natural stones and flowers and twisted tree-roots, and dwelt upon them both in his painting and in his writing. He wrote with elegance and heart. His fragment of autobiography is shrewd, humorous, observant, and self-searching. He was not only a witty man, but often inspired wit in others since his rapturous reception of remarks sharpened people's intelligence when talking to him. No nuance was ever lost.

When war broke out in 1939 Nash was already a very sick man. He moved to Oxford, opened a bureau to help artists to find the least wasteful job for their capabilities, and became a war artist to the

Air Ministry, later transferring to the Ministry of Information. Although disturbed and worried by the war, as an artist he did not change. His style and his habits were formed, and in the new war he treated his new subjects as he had treated those which he had been thinking about for so long. His palette remained light and brilliant and his touch tender. Only one or two of his paintings bore any resemblance to the desolate wastes of 1917, among them 'Totes Meer' (Tate Gallery), a sea of broken, twisted German aeroplanes on a dump at Oxford. This disparity was partly due to the different nature of the wars, but due much more to the fact that in 1917 the whole of his outraged inexperience was at the service of the war, whereas in 1940 the war was made to serve his experience. Aeroplanes were domesticated to his canvas as tree-trunks or stones had been between the wars. Such an attitude was, by then, an artist's only remedy, his only chance of survival. On the whole, his official patrons were disappointed by his poetical aeroplanes. His last works were of flowers, in particular sunflowers, and landscapes, and giant flowers dominating landscapes.

Nash had a noteworthy sense of order and of the niceties of presentation; his pictures were always beautifully framed, drawings mounted, his studio precisely and decoratively tidy, and oddments which he collected were worked up into compositions (found objects). In his life his sense of fitness extended, even on the most ordinary occasions, to his clothes. His scarf and dressing-gown in the morning would be fit for a play; his suits and his ties, matched, brushed, and pressed as though by a valet. All this, with his black hair, brilliant blue eyes, and fine profile made him seem a very exquisite person. But his features never stayed put, to be admired; they were mobile, sensitive to atmosphere and, this was his saving grace, ironical.

In 1914 Nash married Margaret Theodosia, daughter of the Rev. Naser Odeh, formerly priest in charge of St. Mary's Mission and the Pro-Cathedral, Cairo; there were no children. Nash died at Boscombe 11 July 1946.

A wood-engraving of Paul Nash by himself and a drawing by Rupert Lee are in the possession of Mrs. Paul Nash.

[Paul Nash, *Outline*, 1949; a bibliography, a list of exhibitions, and a complete list of pictures in public galleries may be found in the memorial volume, *Paul Nash*, edited by Margot Eates, 1948; *Poet and Painter* (correspondence between Gordon Bottomley and Paul Nash, 1910–1946), edited by C. C. Abbott and Anthony Bertram, 1955; Anthony Bertram, *Paul Nash: The Portrait of an Artist*, 1955; private information; personal knowledge.]                          MYFANWY PIPER.

NEVINSON, CHRISTOPHER RICHARD WYNNE (1889–1946), artist, was born in Hampstead 13 August 1889, the only son of Henry Woodd Nevinson, a notice of whom appears below. Educated at Uppingham, he studied painting at the St. John's Wood School of Art and, in 1909, at the Slade School of Fine Art where Henry Tonks [q.v.] advised him to abandon art as a career. Undeterred, between 1910 and 1913 Nevinson had contacts with the Camden Town Group (W. R. Sickert, q.v., Harold Gilman, Spencer Frederick Gore, and Percy Wyndham Lewis), and he spent some time in Paris. He also sponsored the Italian futurist, F. T. Marinetti, in London, and signed a manifesto with him.

Throughout his life Nevinson suffered from frequent and serious ill health. Unfit for active military service, in 1914 he nevertheless served with the Friends' Ambulance Unit in France and Flanders, and later with the Royal Army Medical Corps. A second attack of rheumatic fever caused his discharge in 1916, and in that year he aroused much interest with war pictures which were shown at the London Group, the Allied Artists' Association, and the Leicester Galleries. These were grimly felt works, in which semi-Cubist formulas suggested the suffering of the wounded in improvised dressing-stations and showed gunners and infantry as semi-robot cogs in the modern war machine. The success of these pictures, which depicted war without glory, caused the nomination of certain painters as official war artists, and Nevinson returned to France as the first of these in 1917. A second exhibition at the Leicester Galleries in 1918 included views from balloons and aeroplanes, and landscapes of the devastated regions. After the war Nevinson etched, lithographed, and painted town and river scenes from windows in London, Paris, and New York (which he visited in 1919 and 1920), and landscapes, genre and flower pieces, portrait heads, and satirical allegories mainly in naturalistic technique, but stiffened, for some subjects, by semi-Cubist angles. In the war of 1939–45 his works included scenes of bombing in London and, once more, views from aeroplanes, one of which, 'Battlefields of Britain', was presented by (Sir) Winston Churchill to the Air Ministry. Nevinson accompanied the troops on the Dieppe raid in August 1942 but a paralytic stroke immediately afterwards and another in 1943 cut short his career.

Nevinson was a member of the London Group, the New English Art Club, the Royal Society of British Artists, the Royal Institute of Oil Painters, and the National Society. His early dressing-station picture, 'La Patrie', which is privately owned, was shown in Paris in 1937, and in 1938 he was appointed a chevalier of the Legion of Honour. In 1939 he was elected A.R.A.

Nevinson belonged to no artistic coterie. Although at bottom a sensitive neurotic, he addressed himself boldly to the general public and wrote truculently in the newspapers, in the catalogues of his exhibitions, and in his autobiography *Paint and Prejudice* (1937). Although regarded with disfavour by 'ivory tower' artists and purist devotees of Post-Impressionism and abstract painting, his pictures were bought by intelligent people in many walks of life who admired his lively interest in all around him and the lyrical feeling which he sometimes revealed. Sir Michael Sadler, Arnold Bennett, and Sir Osbert Sitwell were among the first to recognize his talent, and H. G. Wells presented Nevinson's 'A Studio in Montparnasse' to the Tate Gallery (1927). There also may be seen his self-portrait, painted when he was twenty-one; 'La Mitrailleuse', presented by the Contemporary Art Society and the subject of considerable controversy; and 'Fitzroy Square', presented by an anonymous donor in 1939. Other of his works are in the Imperial War Museum, the British Museum, the London Museum, the National Gallery of Canada, the Metropolitan Museum, New York, the National Museum of Wales, the National Gallery of Ireland, the Fitzwilliam Museum, Cambridge, and in many provincial galleries.

In 1915 Nevinson married Kathleen Mary, daughter of Christopher Collier Knowlman, a business man, of Highgate. She survived him when he died in Hampstead 7 October 1946, but their only child, a son, died at birth. A portrait of Nevinson painted by R. O. Dunlop is privately owned.

[P. G. Konody, *Modern War Paintings by C. R. W. Nevinson*, 1917; J. E. C. Flitch, *The Great War: Fourth Year. Paintings by C. R. W. Nevinson*, 1918; O[sbert] S[itwell], *C. R. W. Nevinson* (Contemporary British Artists), 1925; M. C. Salaman, *C. R. W. Nevinson* (Modern Masters of Etching), 1932; C. R. W. Nevinson, *Paint and Prejudice*, 1937; *The Times*, 8 October 1946; catalogues of the Leicester Galleries exhibitions, 1916–47; private information; personal knowledge.]
R. H. WILENSKI.

NEVINSON, HENRY WOODD (1856–1941), essayist, philanthropist, and journalist, was born at Leicester 11 October 1856, the second son of George Nevinson, solicitor, by his wife, Mary Basil Woodd, and was brought up in a strictly evangelical atmosphere. He gained a scholarship at Shrewsbury School and a junior studentship at Christ Church, Oxford. A poor examinee, he was placed in the second class in both classical moderations (1877) and *literae humaniores* (1879). For the classics, especially the Greek dramatists, he had an abiding love.

After taking his degree, and spending a short time at Westminster School teaching Greek, Nevinson studied German literature during two sojourns in Germany, mainly at Jena. His first book, *Herder and his Times* (1884), was followed by a volume on Schiller (1889) and, many years afterwards, by another on Goethe (1931). More significant for one phase of his later life was his early passion for soldiering which led him to study the German Army, to advocate conscription and, after thorough training, to command a company of cadets in the east end of London. Experience was to lead him to hate war, but he never lost his scientific interest in military history. At Oxford he had come under the influence of the Christian Socialists and of Ruskin, so that on his return from Germany he settled in Whitechapel and worked at Toynbee Hall. He also lectured on history at Bedford College, and acted as secretary to the London Playing Fields Committee. His opinions gradually developed and by 1889 he had joined the Social Democratic Federation of H. M. Hyndman [q.v.]. Marxism, however, was never congenial to him. As an agnostic who disliked all dogmatic systems, he came near to his friends Peter Kropotkin and Edward Carpenter [q.v.] in his ethical and political outlook. He came to know intimately and affectionately the labouring people among whom he lived, and whose ways he depicted, sometimes in a vein of romance, sometimes with rollicking humour, in *Neighbours of Ours* (1895) a volume written in cockney dialect. In later years he joined the Labour Party. The life of adventure which Nevinson's temperament demanded began in 1897 when H. W. Massingham (whose notice Nevinson later contributed to this DIC-TIONARY), then editor of the *Daily Chron-icle*, made him its correspondent in the Greco-Turkish war. During the next thirty years he was the eyewitness and chronicler of most of the wars and unrest of his generation. He was reporter to the *Daily Chronicle* for the South African war; he visited Russia during the abortive revolutionary movement of 1905–6; he went to India for the *Manchester Guardian* in 1907–8, and he saw the first Balkan war from among the Bulgarians. In the war of 1914–18 he was a correspondent on the western front and at the Dardanelles, where he was wounded. *The Dardanelles Campaign*, which he published in 1918, ranks as a standard book. In 1926, at the age of seventy, he went to Palestine, Syria, and Iraq on behalf of the *Manchester Guardian*.

As a war correspondent, Nevinson was always scrupulously careful in gathering his facts, and he was at his best when his writing could help a people struggling towards freedom. Writing was not his only form of service. He helped to organ-ize relief for the Macedonians (1903) and the Albanians (1911), and to found the Friends' Ambulance Unit in Flanders (1914). When his indignation was deeply aroused, as it was when he witnessed the outrages of the 'Black and Tans' in Ireland, he used the platform as well as the printed page in order to rouse humane opinion. The most difficult, however, of all his crusades was that which he con-ducted, single-handed, against what was slavery in all but name in Portuguese Angola. Penetrating far into the interior in 1904–5, over paths littered with the bones of shackled slaves who had perished on the way to the coast, he retraced the journey to the pestilential plantations of San Thomé and Principe. He made his countrymen understand at what price in human suffering they drank cocoa. Even-tually the leading cocoa firms boycotted the produce of those islands; some of the slaves were repatriated; and, after pro-longed controversy, the accusations which he had made in *A Modern Slavery* (1906) were confirmed by the white paper pub-lished in 1914. The achievement cost Nevinson dear, for he suffered for many years from a painful tropical disease which he had contracted on this journey.

In 1909 he threw up a congenial post on the staff of the *Daily News* as a protest against its policy on women's suffrage, and no man did more than Nevinson in helping women to obtain the vote.

As a man of letters, Nevinson was a master of humane and gracious prose. His *Plea of Pan* (1901) was perhaps the most accomplished thing he wrote. From 1907 to 1923, while Massingham was editing the *Nation*, Nevinson, whenever he was in England, contributed 'middle' articles. Of these essays, written to order and to a prescribed space, the best rank among the classics. He was at home in an astonishing variety of topics, ranging from sheer fun to grave commentary on history and life. In warfare against stupidity and cruelty, he used irony with deadly skill. He stamped his own personality even on a brief essay, and into it he could pack the gleanings from his travels in time and space. These articles were collected in several volumes of which the most notable are *Essays in Freedom* (1909), *Essays in Rebellion* (1913), *Between the Wars* (1936), and *Running Accompaniments* (1936). His poems are few and of uneven quality, but some deserve to be treasured. The best and most enduring of his literary work, selected after his death, is contained in *Essays, Poems and Tales of Henry W. Nevinson* (1948). His manifold experi-ences were retold in three autobiographical volumes (*Changes and Chances*, 1923, and its sequels), skilfully abridged by Ellis Roberts in *Fire of Life* (1935), of which Mr. John Masefield wrote in his preface, 'no better autobiography has been written in English in the last hundred years'.

Nevinson was a singularly handsome man who carried himself with such dis-tinction that his friends nicknamed him 'The Grand Duke'. In his early life pain-fully shy, he was always the most modest of men. If he hated tyrants, of no one else had he an ill word to say. He was not a Don Quixote who tilted at windmills, for all the flags under which he served were carried to victory. Few men have com-bined as he did a romantic zest in adven-ture and a passion for freedom with a discipline so exact and a feeling for form so sensitive. It would be difficult to dis-cover an error of fact in his writings, a clumsy sentence, or a limping rhythm. His blend of humanity and daring made him in his later years one of the most popular figures of his time, and twice in his old age his friends arranged a banquet in his honour and made him a presentation. In 1938 he was president of the London P.E.N. Club; he received the honorary degree of LL.D. from the university of Liverpool in 1935, and that of Litt.D. from the university of Dublin in 1936. In 1939 he was elected an honorary student of Christ Church.

Nevinson was twice married: first, in 1884 to Margaret Wynne (died 1932), daughter of the Rev. Timothy Jones, vicar of St. Margaret's, Leicester; and secondly, in 1933 to the gifted authoress and suffragette, Evelyn (died 1955), daughter of John James Sharp, slate merchant, and sister of C. J. Sharp [q.v.]. By the first marriage he had a son, C. R. W. Nevinson, whose notice precedes this, and a daughter. Nevinson died at Chipping Campden, Gloucestershire, 9 November 1941.

Of three drawings of Nevinson by Sir William Rothenstein one is in the National Portrait Gallery. There is a painting by Joseph Southall in Christ Church, Oxford.

[H. W. Nevinson, *Changes and Chances*, 1923, *More Changes, More Chances*, 1925, and *Last Changes, Last Chances*, 1928; private information; personal knowledge.]

H. N. BRAILSFORD.

NEWALL, HUGH FRANK (1857–1944), astrophysicist, was born at Ferndene, Gateshead, 21 June 1857, the youngest of the six children of Robert Stirling Newall [q.v.], engineer and astronomer, by his wife, Mary, daughter of H. L. Pattinson [q.v.], the inventor of the process of desilverizing lead. At the Exhibition of 1862, R. S. Newall saw and acquired two rough discs of crown and flint glass, and had them figured to make an astronomical objective. By 1871 a dome and mounting had been constructed, and the 'Newall telescope', a 25-inch refractor, the largest then existing, was erected at Ferndene. This telescope (named after the father, not the son) was a dominating influence in H. F. Newall's life and work.

Newall was educated at Rugby and at Trinity College, Cambridge, of which he was elected a fellow in 1909. In the mathematical tripos of 1880 he was a junior optime, and in the same year he was placed in the second class in the natural sciences tripos. From 1881 to 1885 he was an assistant master at Wellington College, but had to give up the post owing to ill health. After declining various offers he accepted an invitation from (Sir) J. J. Thomson [q.v.] to become his personal assistant at the Cavendish

Laboratory at Cambridge, where in 1886 he was appointed a demonstrator in experimental physics. His interests were in physics in the broad sense, and it was as a physicist that he was planning his career when in March 1889 his father offered the Newall telescope to the university of Cambridge. There were difficulties in financing the move and in finding staff, and on 21 April the father died. The son then offered a sum towards initial expenses, together with his own services as observer for five years without stipend. This generous offer (several times renewed) involved the sacrifice of his own scientific predilections, as well as his promising career at the Cavendish Laboratory. The telescope was transported to a site near the old Cambridge observatory, and by 1891 Newall had built himself a house near by, Madingley Rise, where for nearly half a century the Newalls dispensed hospitality to astronomers and scientists of many countries. They also farmed some of the surrounding land.

Newall soon designed spectrographs for the big telescope, and began the study of the spectrum of Capella, the binary nature of which he established simultaneously with W. W. Campbell of Lick Observatory. Newall's definitive paper on the subject was published in 1900. He took part in, or led, eclipse expeditions in 1898, 1900, 1901, 1905, 1914, and 1927, his main object being to study the spectrum and polarization of the solar corona. His scientific responsibilities soon began to increase. The bequest by Frank McClean [q.v.] of £5,000 came to the Newall observatory in 1905, and in 1908 the Royal Society presented the telescopes and spectroscopes used by Sir William Huggins [q.v.] and Lady Huggins in their pioneer work in astrophysics at Tulse Hill. In 1909 Newall was appointed to the newly created chair of astrophysics, which he occupied without stipend until his retirement in 1928. On the retirement of Sir Norman Lockyer [q.v.], the Solar Physics Observatory of South Kensington was transferred to Cambridge, and in 1913 Newall became first director of the newly constituted Solar Physics Observatory, Cambridge, of which he remained director until his retirement from his chair.

Newall was elected F.R.S. in 1902; he was president of the Royal Astronomical Society in 1907–9, and received in 1910 the honorary degree of D.Sc. from the university of Durham. He was a foreign member of the Spettroscopisti Italiani, and a vice-president of the International Astronomical Union for its Cambridge meeting in 1925. He had much to do with its predecessor, the Solar Union, and attended its Mount Wilson meeting in 1910. He was a member of the editorial board of the *Astrophysical Journal*, and had the honour of a paper in the first volume of that periodical.

Newall was a great lover of science, nature, and art—a true amateur of the nineteenth-century type, now disappearing; but he was more remarkable as a man than as a professional scientist. To the distinction of his personal appearance he added the distinction of a way of life and attitude to science which is now rarely met. He hated mechanical music, mechanical modes of transport or of writing or of speech. His brougham and pair made a stir in Cambridge streets long after all his contemporaries were using motor-cars. He loved the mysteries at the heart of things, but did not like to have difficulties removed by modern theories. At the same time he was himself mechanically skilful, an adept at fine instrumental adjustments. His devotion to solar physics (he made contributions to the study of the solar rotation and of solar prominences) and to astrophysics attracted many younger men to those fields, and it may be claimed for him (for he would never have made the claim for himself) that he was the father of astrophysics at Cambridge.

In 1881 Newall married (Susanna) Margaret, daughter of the Rev. Charles Thomas Arnold, master of his old house at Rugby. There were no children of the marriage. Mrs. Newall was a pianist of distinction, who gave her own concerts at Cambridge. She took a considerable part in Newall's frequent eclipse expeditions, coping with difficulties of language and acting as a 'public relations officer'. All their friends thought of the Newalls as an ideal pair. She died in January 1930; in June 1931 Newall married Dame Bertha Surtees Phillpotts [q.v.], who died in January 1932. Newall himself died at Cambridge 22 February 1944. His portrait in oils by G. Fiddes Watt hangs in the director's room at the Observatory.

[E. A. Milne in *Obituary Notices of Fellows of the Royal Society*, No. 13, November 1944; *Nature*, 15 April 1944; *Cambridge Review*, 22 April 1944; *Monthly Notices* of the Royal Astronomical Society, vol. cv, No. 2, 1945; private information; personal knowledge.]

E. A. MILNE.

NEWBERRY, PERCY EDWARD (1869–1949), Egyptologist, was born in Islington 23 April 1869, the younger son of Henry James Newberry, woollen warehouseman, of Lewisham, and his wife, Caroline Wyatt. He was educated at King's College School. As a boy, Newberry was keenly interested in botany and studied the subject in London and at Kew. While still a youth, he was introduced to R. S. Poole [q.v.] who enlisted his assistance in the secretarial work of the Egypt Exploration Fund (later Society) which had been founded in 1882. For several years Newberry worked in Poole's official residence at the British Museum, and there he met Amelia Edwards, (Sir) Flinders Petrie, and F. Ll. Griffith [qq.v.], an association which led him to make Egyptology the principal pursuit of his life, and he studied it with avidity. His knowledge of botany was immediately useful to Petrie who had discovered many ancient floral remains during his excavations in the Fayyûm and Newberry undertook the determination of the species on which he made a communication to the British Association in 1888.

In 1889 Griffith had formulated his scheme for an Archaeological Survey of Egypt, a scheme which was adopted the next year by the Egypt Exploration Fund, and Newberry, young as he was, was placed in charge of the expedition which began work on the famous tombs of Beni Hasan, and afterwards on other sites. After working for the Fund for five seasons, Newberry, as a free-lance, carried out a survey of the Theban Necropolis (1895–1901), and later superintended a number of excavations, and advised on many others including those of Howard Carter [q.v.].

In 1906 Newberry was appointed the first Brunner professor of Egyptology at the university of Liverpool where he proceeded M.A. in 1909. After his resignation in 1919 he was nominated university reader in Egyptian art. In 1908 he had been elected a fellow of King's College, London, and in 1923 was president of the section on anthropology of the British Association. He accepted in 1929 the chair of ancient Egyptian history and archaeology in the university of Egypt at Cairo, and held the post for four years. He was appointed O.B.E. in 1919; was vice-president of the Royal Anthropological Institute in 1926 and of the Egypt Exploration Society shortly before he died.

Newberry's published works, in addition to numerous contributions to scientific journals and to various excavation reports and memoirs, include: the Archaeological Survey volumes *Beni Hasan* (1893, 1894) and *El Bersheh* (2 parts, 1895), *The Life of Rekhmara* (1900), *The Amherst Papyri* (1900), *Scarabs* (1906), *A Short History of Ancient Egypt* (1904, with John Garstang); and three volumes of the great *Catalogue Général* of the Cairo Museum. He left much unfinished material for other works, and his notebooks and papers, together with his scientific correspondence, were presented by his widow to the Griffith Institute at Oxford.

In 1907 he married Essie Winifred (died 1953), daughter of William Johnston, shipowner, of Liverpool and Bromborough, Cheshire; there were no children. Newberry died at his home near Godalming 7 August 1949. He is one of a group painted by Albert Lipczinski (1915) of some of the staff (e.g. (Sir) Charles Reilly, (Sir) Bernard Pares, John Sampson, Oliver Elton, qq.v.) of the university of Liverpool, where the painting hangs in the common-room of the faculty of arts.

[*Journal of Egyptian Archaeology*, vol. xxxvi, 1950; personal knowledge.]

WARREN R. DAWSON.

NEWBOLD, SIR DOUGLAS (1894–1945), civil secretary to the Sudan Government, was born at Tunbridge Wells 13 August 1894, the seventh son of William Newbold, whose business interests took him frequently to the United States and Mexico, and his wife, Eleanor Isabel, daughter of Colonel David Fergusson, of the United States Army, who had emigrated from Blair Atholl in the 1840's. Eleanor Newbold's grandmother, Eleanor Adams, came of a family which gave the United States two presidents. Douglas Newbold never married and his mother, who died in 1942, was the major domestic influence in a life which was marked by close ties with a large family of brothers and sisters. He was a scholar and exhibitioner of Uppingham and a classical scholar of Oriel College, Oxford. His university career was interrupted by the war of 1914–18 in which he was commissioned in the Dorset Yeomanry and the Cavalry Machine Gun Corps. He served in Mudros, Egypt, and Palestine, took part in the cavalry charges of Agagia (February 1916) and Mughar (November 1917), and was wounded at Zeitun after the fall of Gaza in November 1917.

After another year at Oxford Newbold joined the Sudan Political Service, and served in the provinces of Kordofan and Kassala and in the secretariat. In 1932 he was appointed governor of Kordofan and in 1939 he became civil secretary to the Sudan Government. His choice of a career was influenced by an early interest in archaeology, strengthened by a classical education, and his service in Libya and Palestine which had led him to renewed study of the medieval and classical geographers and of the Bible from an historical angle. These interests, combined with a romantic temperament, gave him the taste for desert exploration which took him on three expeditions by camel and car into the Libyan desert in 1923, 1927, and 1930. They might well have led him to abandon his career, for he was impatient of bureaucracy, had he not developed while serving in the Eastern Sudan what was to prove the paramount interest of his life: the effort to make the fullest possible use of what he described as 'a golden chance to use all our powers, moral, intellectual and physical, for the benefit of some of the finest people in the world'.

His protective interests were first aroused on behalf of the Sudanese by what he regarded as an attempt to exploit some of them commercially. This gave birth to a crusading zeal to devise and develop for the Sudanese, and later for Africans in general, institutions which might satisfy their political aspirations as they became progressively more articulate, without sacrificing the social benefits and individual liberties which they had learned to enjoy under a benevolent but autocratic colonial rule. In furthering this purpose he enjoyed the advantage of receiving from Sudanese of all classes the affection and trust which he gave to them, and of early promotion to a position of responsibility. He 'carried the civilizing qualities of the ideal district commissioner with him to the headquarters of government'. The coincidence of the outbreak of war with his assumption of office as civil secretary delayed the realization of his policy. As chief executive officer of the Government during the Italian invasion and the subsequent campaigns in Ethiopia and Libya he had to organize the civilian war effort and arrange for the maintenance of normal administration by a depleted staff before he could devote himself to reform and innovation. Nor did he reach the conviction that Western representative institutions in central and local government were the best solution without long and anxious study of expert opinion to the contrary. It took time to reach a decision, and although once it was made he acted with vigour, it was not until the last year of his life that the advisory council for the Northern Sudan met in Khartoum to prepare the way for full self-government.

Newbold never lost sight of the need for educational advance as a condition of popular government and a responsible Civil Service, and he was the prime mover in the foundation of the Khartoum University College. At the end of his life he was deeply interested in the need for professionalizing colonial administration which had, he felt, been too long in the hands of empiricists. His death at Khartoum 23 March 1945 was due to a fall from his horse affecting an old injury at a time when he was worn out by overwork. He was appointed O.B.E. in 1933, C.B.E. in 1938, and K.B.E. in 1944.

Newbold was an insatiable but discriminating reader and a particularly gifted and prolific letter writer. A selection of his letters, papers, and lectures was published in 1953 under the title *The Making of the Modern Sudan*. He contributed articles on exploration and archaeology to *Antiquity*, the *Geographical Journal*, and *Sudan Notes and Records*.

A posthumous portrait by a Greek artist hangs in the Newbold memorial library of University College, Khartoum.

[K. D. D. Henderson, *The Making of the Modern Sudan*, 1953; private information; personal knowledge.]

K. D. D. HENDERSON.

NEWMAN, SIR GEORGE (1870–1948), pioneer in public and child health, was born at Leominster 23 October 1870, the second son of Henry Stanley Newman, a Quaker and for many years editor of the *Friend*, by his wife, Mary Anna Pumphrey. He was educated at Bootham School, King's College, London, and Edinburgh University, qualifying in 1892 and taking the M.D. in 1895. In the same year he qualified as D.P.H., Cambridge. In 1896 he became demonstrator of comparative pathology and bacteriology at King's College, and lecturer in public health in St. Bartholomew's Hospital medical college. In 1903 he was joint author with Harold Swithinbank of *The Bacteriology of Milk* and in 1905 collaborated with (Sir) Benjamin Arthur Whitelegge in the tenth edition of his *Hygiene and Public Health*.

In 1897 Newman was appointed county medical officer for Bedfordshire, and in 1900 he took the additional post of medical officer of health for Finsbury, then one of the poorest and most overcrowded of the metropolitan boroughs. In the five years 1896–1900 the infant mortality rate in this country had reached 165 per 1,000 births. In 1906 Newman published his memorable report on *Infant Mortality*. The great reduction in infant and maternal mortality rates of the next four decades is due to many causes and to the work of many people, but Newman, by this report and his subsequent work in maternity and child-welfare, had a founder's share in these achievements.

In 1907 the Board of Education set up a school medical service and Newman became chief medical officer, entering the Civil Service at the age of thirty-seven. With the powerful support of Sir Robert Morant [q.v.] Newman drew up a scheme of medical inspection of schoolchildren, to be administered by local education authorities and to be followed by schemes of treatment, although at first the latter were optional. Many authorities were hesitant in their new duties and Newman, by his remarkable annual reports and persuasive tongue, laboured perhaps more abundantly than any other to convince nation and authorities alike of the need for the better care of children. He especially promoted open-air schools for the delicate and the long-stay hospital school for rheumatic children. He was also keenly interested in physical education and was for many years an active chairman of the trustees of the Dartford Physical Training College.

During the war of 1914–18 Newman served on many important committees, such as those on tuberculosis and medical research. He was the first chairman of the health of munition workers committee, which eventually became the Industrial Health Research Board; and he was the medical member of the Central Control Board (Liquor Traffic).

In 1919 Newman went as chief medical officer to the new Ministry of Health which, with Morant as secretary, had taken over the work of the Local Government Board and the National Health Insurance Commission. He had the status of secretary, which no medical officer had previously enjoyed, and which gave him direct access to the minister. He still remained chief medical officer of the Board of Education, a combination of offices intended to correlate the school medical with the other health services.

Newman was now at the height of his power, indefatigable in rousing the public interest by his apt phrasing and by his ability to lay bare the heart of his subject, and at the same time to touch the heart of his reader. He frequently lectured, and gave the Hunterian Society oration in 1926 and the Harveian in 1932; he gave the Dodge lectures at Yale, 1926–7, on 'Citizenship and the Survival of Civilization'; and was Halley Stewart lecturer in 1930 and Heath Clark lecturer (London) in 1931. He also wrote many delightful monographs on medical men, among them Keats, Sydenham, and Osler. These, with Morant, Pasteur, and Florence Nightingale, were some of his heroes, along with his ideal general practitioner: 'the foundation of a medical service—its pivot, its anchor, its instrument.'

Medical education was one of the main interests of his life. In addition to his own reports on the subject (1919, 1923) he was largely responsible for the report of the postgraduate medical committee (1921) which inspired the foundation of the Postgraduate Medical School of London and, with the generous help of the Rockefeller Foundation which Newman helped to secure, the creation of the London School of Hygiene and Tropical Medicine. But his most lasting memorial will be the brilliant series of annual reports, fifteen to the minister of health, twenty-six to the minister of education, which have been an inspiration to many and have had an enduring influence on public health. He retired in 1935 and in 1939 published *The Building of a Nation's Health* which will be the more valued as time goes on.

Newman was also active in the Quaker interests. He was from 1914 to 1919 chairman of the Friends' Ambulance Unit, and for forty years he edited anonymously the *Friends' Quarterly Examiner*, contributing a lively leader from 'The House of the Four Winds' to each number.

In person he was rather short, with a fine head and in later life a mane of white hair; quick in movement, vivacious and dramatic in manner, talking with zest, humour, and charm. As an administrator he had his weak points; despite these, no man of his generation did more in this country for public health, medical education, and the child.

He was knighted in 1911, appointed K.C.B. in 1918, and G.B.E. in 1935. From 1919 to 1939 he was crown nominee on the General Medical Council, and latterly its senior treasurer. He received the Bisset-Hawkins gold medal from the Royal College of Physicians (1935) and the Fothergill gold medal from the Medical Society of London in the same year. He received honorary degrees from Durham (D.C.L., 1919), Oxford (D.Sc., 1936), and of LL.D. from London, Edinburgh, McGill, Toronto, Glasgow, and Leeds universities; and he was an honorary fellow of the Royal College of Surgeons (1928) and of the New York Academy of Medicine.

Newman married in 1898 Adelaide Constance (died 1946), daughter of Samuel Thorp, of Alderley Edge, a lady of great charm and public spirit and an accomplished artist. There were no children. He died at York 26 May 1948, and is buried in the historic Quaker burial ground at Jordans. A portrait by Margaret Lindsay Williams is at the London School of Hygiene and Tropical Medicine.

[*British Medical Journal* and *Lancet*, 5 June 1948; *Friend*, 4 June 1948; personal knowledge.]                    J. A. GLOVE

NEWSHOLME, SIR ARTHUR (1857–1943), expert in public health, was born at Haworth, Yorkshire, 10 February 1857, the fourth son of Robert Newsholme, wool-stapler, by his second wife, Phoebe, daughter of John Binns, wool-comber, of Townend Farm, Haworth. His father, who had been churchwarden to Patrick Brontë [q.v.], and belonged to an old-established family of farmers, died when Newsholme was four years old, and he owed much to his mother's vigorous character. He was educated at the local free grammar school and at a science school in Keighley. After a year of apprenticeship to a Bradford practitioner, he entered St. Thomas's Hospital in 1875, taking the degree of M.B. (London) in 1880 with the gold medal in medicine and a university scholarship. In 1881 he proceeded to the degree of M.D., being qualified for the gold medal. He held resident appointments at St. Thomas's and other hospitals, and then started in general practice at Clapham. His interest was early directed towards public health, for in 1884 he was appointed part-time medical officer of health for the parish of Clapham. His reports here show that he was already making a special study of local and national statistics. He published manuals on *Hygiene* (1884) and *School Hygiene* (1887).

Newsholme was appointed whole-time medical officer of health of Brighton in 1888. Here he worked indefatigably and enhanced his reputation as an administrator and investigator. *The Elements of Vital Statistics* (1889), a standard textbook, and *The Prevention of Tuberculosis* (1908) and his investigations of the epidemiology of tuberculosis, scarlet fever, and diphtheria added to knowledge. In 1895 he gave the Milroy lectures at the Royal College of Physicians on 'The Natural History and Affinities of Rheumatic Fever'. In these four lectures Newsholme showed that rheumatic fever is an infectious disease, that 'explosive' and 'protracted' epidemics occur, that there is evidence of cyclical prevalence, that epidemics can occur in years of minimum rainfall, and that the disease varies greatly in extent in different countries. The statistical approach to this and other problems of disease revealed facts of fundamental importance. A statistical study of 'The Alleged Increase of Cancer' (with G. King), contributed to the *Proceedings* of the Royal Society (1893), also broke fresh ground. Newsholme became F.R.C.P. (London) in 1898.

In 1908 John Burns [q.v.] appointed Newsholme medical officer of the Local Government Board. The Government was beginning to realize that national health was not solely a matter of environmental hygiene. The school medical service had been set up in 1907 and national health insurance was already foreshadowed. In his ten years' tenure of office Newsholme laid the medical foundations of the national health services dealing with tuberculosis, maternity and child-welfare, and venereal diseases, as well as serving during the war of 1914–18 on the army sanitary committee with the rank of lieutenant-colonel, Army Medical Service. He was appointed C.B. in 1912 and advanced to K.C.B. in 1917. He was president of the section of epidemiology and State medicine of the Royal Society of Medicine, president of the Society of Medical Officers of Health (1900), and as member nominated by the Crown served on the General Medical Council from 1910 to 1919.

With the advent of the Ministry of Health, Newsholme retired in 1919, and accepted an invitation to lecture at Johns Hopkins University in 1920 and 1921. During his travels in the United States he made many friends and undertook a large programme of public speaking. In the years of retirement Newsholme's facile

pen was seldom idle, and he visited many countries, including the Soviet Union in 1933, to study their health conditions and to discuss their problems. This work he recorded in a series of *International Studies on the Relation between the Private and Official Practice of Medicine* (3 vols., 1931), and in *Red Medicine*, with J. A. Kingsbury (1934). His last two books, *Fifty Years in Public Health* (1935) and *The Last Thirty Years in Public Health* (1936), are not only autobiographical, but possess scientific and historical value.

Tall, handsome, and bearded, with many social gifts, Newsholme was a popular figure in Great Britain and the United States. He was a kind and sympathetic chief, who worked hard himself and expected his staff to work with equal energy and enthusiasm. His work as administrator and epidemiologist takes high place in the story of British public health.

Newsholme died at Worthing 17 May 1943. He married in 1881 Sara (died 1933), daughter of William Mansford, farmer, of Marlborough, Lincolnshire; they had no children.

[Sir Arthur Newsholme, *Fifty Years in Public Health*, 1935, and *The Last Thirty Years in Public Health*, 1936; *British Medical Journal* and *Lancet*, 29 May 1943; *Nature*, 5 June 1943; private information; personal knowledge.]      ARTHUR S. MACNALTY.

NEWTON, second BARON (1857–1942), diplomat and politician. [See LEGH, THOMAS WODEHOUSE.]

NICHOLS, ROBERT MALISE BOWYER (1893–1944), poet, was born at Shanklin 6 September 1893, the elder son of John Bowyer Buchanan Nichols (1859–1939), of Lawford Hall, Essex, who also wrote poems, and a descendant of John Nichols [q.v.], the eighteenth-century antiquary. His mother was Catherine Louisa, daughter of Captain Edward Bouverie Pusey, R.N., a nephew of Dr. E. B. Pusey [q.v.]. Sir P. B. B. Nichols, ambassador to the Netherlands, 1948–51, is Nichols's younger brother; his sisters married (Sir) George Gater and Mr. H. G. Strauss (subsequently Lord Conesford). Educated at Winchester and at Trinity College, Oxford, Robert Nichols asserted that he owed most to his own unmethodical private reading. The outbreak of war cut short his university career; in October 1914 he became a second lieutenant in the

Royal Field Artillery and served in France in 1915. Several months in hospital followed. In 1917 he was attached to the Foreign Office and in the following year went with the British mission (Ministry of Information) to New York.

Having begun to write verse at school, Nichols became one of the soldier-poets of 1914–18; his *Invocation* (1915) and *Ardours and Endurances* (1917) were widely read and quoted. He was regarded as a sort of new Rupert Brooke [q.v.], and in E. B. Osborn's noted collection *The Muse in Arms* (1917) he was represented more copiously than any other writer. Sometimes he competed with his friends Mr. Siegfried Sassoon and Mr. Robert Graves in graphic records of the battlefield, but he was better qualified for idealizations.

In 1921, after haunting Oxford for a time as a poetical personality, Nichols accepted the chair of English in Tokyo Imperial University. The opportunity of a near view of Japanese art and culture suited his aesthetic habits. As a professor he sought to train new men of letters rather than competent academics. Illness disturbed his programme, but his lectures were amusing and invigorating. He became a busy and zealous essayist in the *Japan Advertiser*, with an abundance of subjects; among his papers there a series of articles on contemporary English novelists was the most considerable. In 1924 he resigned his professorship and went to Hollywood where he found some scope as adviser to Douglas Fairbanks, senior, in his film-making.

Nichols, like Robert Browning, regarded himself as a writer of plays; he wrote other things—prose fiction in *Fantastica* (1923) and *Under the Yew* (1928), and metrical satire in *Fisbo* (1934)—but the drama *Guilty Souls* (1922), stirring but unconvincing, announced his principal object. *Twenty Below* (with Jim Tully, 1927) and *Wings Over Europe* (with Maurice Browne, 1932), although striking, had little success in the theatre; and his vast project *Don Juan*, about which he constantly talked, was never completed. Meanwhile Nichols had seemed to desert the region of lyrical poetry in which his promise had been first recognized; the volume *Aurelia* (1920), containing among other things a 'Shakespearian' sonnet series, was the last of its kind from him. After 1926 he lived in England, at first at Winchelsea, finding his pleasures in music, the fine arts, conversation, and letter-writing. When war came he published an *Anthology of War Poetry*,

*1914–1918* (1943) containing a characteristic discourse in which he generously recalled the soldier-poets of his earlier years.

Nichols was tall, thin, and impulsive in movement, with a face in which the wit and the poet found expression by turns. His talk was rapid and humorous, but tending towards the defence of the lofty Romantic attitude of which he saw himself as a protagonist. His long list of heroes, often recommended to his listeners and correspondents, included Goethe and Berlioz. He wished to be a *vie de Bohème* character in modern life. Confident of his powers, he was nevertheless an example of unselfish activity on behalf of the work of other authors, new or old. The discovery of Vachel Lindsay was one of his great events. One of the latest of his enthusiasms was for a forgotten pastoral *Amarynthus the Nympholept* by Shelley's friend Horace Smith [q.v.] which he found on a stall in Cambridge market. As a poet Nichols was probably hindered rather than helped by his preoccupation with world literature; at all events he did not fulfil his ambitious or visionary schemes, from some defect of solid materials. His 'grim' war poems perhaps damaged his poetical reputation, but on occasion when he was on familiar ground Nichols attained poetry of the high beauty he believed in, willingly admitting detailed resemblances to existing classics, as in his 'Night Rhapsody' included in *Georgian Poetry* (1922). In 1942, as though he were uttering an adieu, he published a selection of his poems entitled *Such was my Singing*. He died at Cambridge 17 December 1944.

Nichols married in 1922 Norah, daughter of Frederick Anthony Denny, of Horwood House, Winslow, Buckinghamshire, and niece of the composer Roger Quilter. There were no children. A sketch of Nichols is reproduced in (Sir) William Rothenstein's *Twenty-Four Portraits* (2nd series, 1923); a chalk drawing by Augustus John is in the National Portrait Gallery.

[*Burke's Landed Gentry*, 1952; private information; personal knowledge.]

EDMUND BLUNDEN.

NICHOLSON, SIR CHARLES ARCHIBALD, second baronet, of Luddenham (1867–1949), architect, was born at 26 Devonshire Place, London, 27 April 1867, the eldest son of Sir Charles Nicholson [q.v.]. Sir S. H. Nicholson, a notice of whom appears below, was a younger brother.

Charles was educated at Rugby and at New College, Oxford, where he graduated in 1889 with a third class in modern history. He entered the architectural profession as a pupil in the office of J. D. Sedding [q.v.] and to his training under this brilliant master of the Victorian interpretation of the Gothic style he owed much of his skill and enthusiasm for church design in structure as well as fittings and adornment. Subsequently he worked with Henry Wilson, another of Sedding's pupils, and in 1893 set up in practice for himself. In that year he won the Tite prize given for architectural design by the Royal Institute of British Architects of which he was elected a fellow in 1905.

From 1895 until 1916 Nicholson was in partnership with Major Hubert Christian Corlette. In 1927, when the see of Portsmouth was founded, Mr. Thomas Johnson Rushton joined him in the adaptation and enlargement of the parish church of St. Thomas à Becket, to form the new cathedral. This association continued until Nicholson's death. In the course of his career Nicholson was appointed consulting architect to seven cathedrals: Lincoln, Wells, Lichfield, Llandaff, Sheffield, Portsmouth, and Belfast, and diocesan architect to the sees of Wakefield, Winchester, Portsmouth, and Chelmsford.

Nicholson's skill and ingenuity are nowhere better shown than in the very large number of new parish churches which he designed and built. Besides these he refashioned, augmented, or furnished a much larger number of existing churches. The close of the war of 1914–18 brought him memorial work from many quarters, and one of the first memorial chapels was that built for his own school at Rugby. Another school chapel, at Clifton College, is much admired for its handling of the hexagonal lantern.

Nicholson's cathedral work included the new east chapel at Norwich, the west front of Belfast (with memorial western porches, a new chapel of the Holy Spirit and baptistry), various additions to Chelmsford, and the reconstruction of Portsmouth. Internal work and restoration were carried out at Brecon, Carlisle, Exeter, Leicester, Lichfield, Lincoln, Llandaff, Manchester, Salisbury, Wakefield, Wells, and Winchester. Nicholson used the English Gothic style with complete freedom, conceiving, in common with his contemporaries, that his work was not the less original in employing its idiom. He was

resourceful and creative and delighted in the constructional problems which each task offered. Practical and realistic, he was always an artist: a finished, indeed a brilliant, draughtsman, he had a delight in colour and used it frequently and with great effect in his decorative design.

Outside his church work, he laid aside the Gothic manner in not a few notable buildings. Burton Manor, in the Wirral, is a distinguished house in the classic style, and, at Kingston, Jamaica, he produced a striking design for the government buildings in reinforced concrete, anticipating the later development of this material. Both these undertakings were carried out in partnership with Major Corlette (died 1956).

Nicholson, who succeeded to the baronetcy in 1903, shunned publicity and found his chief recreation in travel. He was twice married: first, in 1895 to Evelyn Louise (died 1927), daughter of the Rev. Henry Arnold Olivier, and sister of S. H. (later Lord) Olivier [q.v.]. They had one son, John Charles (born 1904), who succeeded his father as third baronet, and two daughters. Nicholson married secondly, in 1931 Catherine Maud, daughter of Luckham Warren, of Winchfield, Hampshire. He died 4 March 1949 at Headington, Oxford, and was buried at South Benfleet, Essex.

[The library and *Journal* (April 1949) of the Royal Institute of British Architects; private information.]

WALTER H. GODFREY.

NICHOLSON, REYNOLD ALLEYNE (1868–1945), orientalist, was born at Keighley, Yorkshire, 19 August 1868, the eldest of the five children of Henry Alleyne Nicholson [q.v.], by his wife, Isabella Hutchison, from Kirkcaldy in Fife. His father, then a practising surgeon, later became professor of natural history at the universities of St. Andrews and Aberdeen. Nicholson went to school in these two cities and from Aberdeen University entered Trinity College, Cambridge, as a pensioner in 1887. After being awarded the Porson prize for Greek verse in his first year he became a scholar of his college and in 1890 obtained a first class in part i of the classical tripos and again won the Porson prize. Although he dropped to a third class in part ii (1891) he gained a first in the Indian languages tripos in 1892. His interest in oriental languages was first stimulated in the library of his grandfather, the biblical scholar John

Nicholson, from whom he inherited a collection of Arabic and Persian manuscripts, but it was more amply fostered by E. G. Browne [q.v.], with whom he read Persian, and by short periods of study at Leyden and Strasbourg, where he read Arabic with Michael Jan de Goeje and Theodor Nöldeke. His election into a fellowship (1893) at Trinity opened the partnership with Browne which lasted down to the latter's death in 1926. Except for one year's tenure of the chair of Persian at University College, London, in 1901–2, the whole of Nicholson's active life was spent in Cambridge. He returned there to succeed Browne first as lecturer in Persian (1902–26), then in 1926 (when he was also re-elected fellow of Trinity) as Sir Thomas Adams's professor of Arabic. After his retirement under the age limit in 1933 he continued to take an interest in the oriental school until in 1940 failing health and eyesight forced him into retreat in North Wales. He died at Chester 27 August 1945. He was an honorary LL.D. of Aberdeen (1913), a fellow of the British Academy (1922), gold medallist of the Royal Asiatic Society (1938), and an associate member of the Persian Academy.

From the first Nicholson was strongly attracted to the literature of Súfism. For his fellowship thesis he made a selection from the mystical odes of Rúmí called Díváni Shamsi Tabríz, the publication of which, with translation and annotation, in 1898 placed him at once in the front rank of oriental scholarship. Between 1905 and 1914 he published editions or translations of four major works on Súfism, two Persian ('Attar's Tadhkiratu 'l-Awliyá, 2 vols., 1905–7, and Kashf al-Mahjúb of Hujwírí, 1911) and two in Arabic (Ibn al-'Arabí's odes called Tarjumán al-Ashwáq, 1911, and Kitáb al-Luma' of Sarráj, 1914), besides collaborating with Browne in various works, and in 1914 summed up his studies in a manual for the general reader, The Mystics of Islam. Meanwhile he had written his Literary History of the Arabs (1907), a personal appreciation of Arabic literature, graced by many of his own verse translations, and issued an annotated series of Arabic readers (1907–11).

Nicholson's work of interpretation was resumed after the war with two important volumes, Studies in Islamic Poetry and Studies in Islamic Mysticism (1921), supplemented in 1923 by a small but luminous work on The Idea of Personality in Súfism. But already he had set to work on a project, long premeditated and for which his studies had given him an unequalled equipment, a complete critical edition with translation and annotation of the Mathnawi of Rúmí, the greatest literary achievement of Persian mysticism. Eighteen years of sustained industry enabled him to issue between 1925 and 1940 the eight volumes he had planned; a final volume, which was to sum up Rúmí's life and work and his place in the history of Súfism, remained unwritten.

Nicholson's work on Súfism was the greatest single contribution made by a European scholar to the subject. Few men have so thoroughly opened up one of the major developments of human thought for both specialists and the lay reader, or so transformed the understanding of it by presenting its highest products with rare imagination and literary taste, as well as with impeccable scholarship. The credit for this must go not only to his industry but also to the poetic sensibility and talent with which he was gifted. In earlier years he wrote light verse, some of which he reprinted in The Don and the Dervish (1911), and in 1922 he published a volume of Translations of Eastern Poetry and Prose. In outward manner he was reserved and in public speech he was diffident, but as a teacher he was greatly beloved. His chief recreation was golf, and as an undergraduate he played in the Cambridge team against Oxford. In 1903 he married his first cousin, Cecilia, daughter of Thomas Varty, of Penrith; there were no children.

[The Times, 31 August 1945; R. Levy in Proceedings of the British Academy, vol. xxxi, 1945; private information; personal knowledge.]      H. A. R. GIBB.

NICHOLSON, SIR SYDNEY HUGO (1875–1947), organist, church musician, and founder of the Royal School of Church Music, was born in London 9 February 1875, the youngest son of Sir Charles Nicholson, first baronet, of Luddenham [q.v.]. He was a brother of Sir C. A. Nicholson (a notice of whom appears above) and of Archibald Keightley Nicholson, the artist in stained glass.

Sydney Nicholson was educated at Rugby, at New College, Oxford, where he obtained a third class in English language and literature in 1897, and at the Royal College of Music. He also studied for a short time in Frankfurt. His first appointment as an organist was at Barnet parish church (1897). He took his B.Mus. at

Oxford in 1902. In 1903 he went to Eton as organist of Lower Chapel, and in 1904 he became acting organist of Carlisle Cathedral where he made a great impression. In 1908 he was offered and accepted the organistship of Canterbury Cathedral; but before he could take up the appointment, the organistship of Manchester Cathedral fell vacant, and under strong pressure Nicholson withdrew his acceptance of the post at Canterbury and went to Manchester instead. Here he found congenial conditions to work in. There was splendid choir material and he brought the cathedral services to a very high standard. He interested himself in the church music of the diocese, and made his influence felt in the musical life of Manchester. His reputation grew steadily, and when Sir Frederick Bridge [q.v.] resigned the post of organist and master of the choristers at Westminster Abbey in 1918, it seemed natural and proper for Nicholson to succeed him.

At the abbey Nicholson showed conspicuous administrative ability. He reorganized the musical foundation; he planned and directed the music at many important special services, chief among which was the marriage of Princess Mary in 1922. He founded and conducted the Westminster Abbey Special Choir, and established a yearly performance of Bach's St. Matthew Passion. His services were much in demand outside the abbey; he was a member of the Cathedrals Commission, and became chairman of the Church Music Society. This brought him in close touch with the problems of music in parish churches, where he had long felt some organization was needed to guide and raise the standard. After much preliminary work he outlined his proposals for a School of English Church Music at a meeting held in the Jerusalem Chamber, Westminster Abbey, on St. Nicolas's Day, 6 December 1927. His scheme was enthusiastically received, and in 1928 he left the abbey to launch the School, and entered upon the last and most important phase of his life's work.

The School began as an affiliation of church choirs desiring to improve their standard of performance; by the end of 1928 there were 105 choirs, by 1939, 1,500, and by 1951, 2,645. In 1929 the College of St. Nicolas was opened at Chislehurst as a teaching institution for a limited number of whole-time students of church music. Nicholson divided his time between directing the College, visit-

ing the choirs, and conducting festivals throughout the country. His work bore fruit in the great festivals of church music which he organized and conducted, in the Royal Albert Hall in 1930 and 1939 with 1,000 singers, and in 1933 and 1936 at the Crystal Palace with 4,000 singers. In 1926 he had been appointed M.V.O. and in 1938 he was knighted for his services to church music. He also received the honorary degree of D.Mus. from the archbishop of Canterbury in 1928. Although resigning the wardenship of the College which reopened at Canterbury after the war of 1939–45, Nicholson continued as director of the School which received a royal charter in 1945 and became the Royal School of Church Music. He died at Ashford, Kent, 30 May 1947, and on 6 June was buried in the cloisters of Westminster Abbey.

Nicholson never married. He was a man of strong physique and character whose appearance changed little during the last thirty years of his life. He was deeply religious and had real humility; but he never hesitated to take a firm line when his sense of purpose deemed it necessary. He rarely provoked opposition or made enemies, for he had great personal charm and a wonderful gift for winning the affection and loyalty of those who served under him. He delighted in the society of his friends, and valued especially the countless friendships he made among organists, choirmen, and choirboys in his travels all over the country.

As a young man he was an able organist; later in life his playing suffered on account of the executive and administrative work which took so much of his time, but he never lost his remarkable skill in extemporization, in which he had no superior. In more favourable conditions he might have achieved real eminence as a composer; he had ideas, technique, and fluency, but always worked at high speed, generally for some particular occasion, and rarely revised or rewrote. Some of his church music will survive; among other secular music he composed some charming operas for boys which have real distinction, of which the best known is *The Children of the Chapel* (1934). He was musical editor of the revised edition of *Hymns Ancient and Modern* (1904), edited the shortened music edition (1939), and was largely responsible for the new and completely revised edition published in 1950. His book *Quires and Places Where They Sing* (1932) is accepted as a standard work.

He had gifts as a painter in water-colour; for many years he did printing as a hobby; he loved mechanical things, and had the curious passion for railways which affects so many organists.

[Unpublished autobiography; private information; personal knowledge.]

WILLIAM McKIE.

NICHOLSON, SIR WILLIAM NEWZAM PRIOR (1872–1949), artist, was born at Newark-upon-Trent 5 February 1872, the youngest child of William Newzam Nicholson, engineer, of the Trent Ironworks, and later M.P. for Newark, and his second wife, Ann Elizabeth Prior, of Woodstock, Oxfordshire. Nicholson's disinclination, at an early age, for the normal routine of studies at Magnus Grammar School, Newark, where he was at first a boarder, and the lively interest which he took in the drawing lessons of the school's art master, W. H. Cubley, finally convinced his parents that it would be foolish to oppose his determination to become an artist.

At the age of sixteen he passed the entrance examination to the school of art at Bushey run by (Sir) Hubert von Herkomer [q.v.]. Here he began to discover in what direction his talents were leading him and to realize that the academic and unadventurous atmosphere of the school was not what he needed for the full development of his art. His period of study at the school ended in his second year and was, on the whole, profitless, yet it was here that he made the acquaintance of James Pryde [q.v.], brother of a fellow student who was to become his first wife.

Nicholson's first taste of a congenial atmosphere came when, shortly after leaving Bushey, he persuaded his parents to allow him to study at the Académie Julian in Paris. He not only worked hard but came to know and love a city in which the attitude to the arts was very different from that of Newark or Bushey. It was here that, without being directly influenced by the teaching at Julian's, his style began to mature. He returned to England full of enthusiasm, married in 1893, and settled, although not for long, in a small house in Denham where he and his wife were almost immediately joined by her brother, James Pryde.

During the next two years Pryde and Nicholson, as the 'Beggarstaff Brothers', began to collaborate in a series of posters which were revolutionary in style with their boldness of outline, simplicity of treatment and striking silhouettes, and their economical handling of black, white, and one colour. The most familiar of them was the large design for Rowntree's cocoa; the best were the two done for Sir Henry Irving [q.v.] for his *Don Quixote* and *Robespierre*, although neither appeared on the hoardings. All three designs may be seen in the Victoria and Albert Museum.

The Beggarstaff partnership was short-lived, but important to poster art and to Nicholson. In the years which followed he evolved out of the posters a personal style which he began to exploit through the medium of the woodcut. In this venture he had the good fortune to be encouraged by J. A. McN. Whistler [q.v.] who recommended him to the publisher William Heinemann [q.v.]. There followed in 1898 the well-known *Alphabet*, the *Almanac of Twelve Sports*, with verses by Rudyard Kipling [q.v.], and *London Types*, with verses by W. E. Henley [q.v.]; the Heinemann windmill colophon designed by Nicholson made its first appearance. For Henley, who was editing the *New Review*, Nicholson had begun a series of portrait woodcuts, the first of which was his unconventional jubilee portrait of Queen Victoria (June 1897). Despite Heinemann's misgivings it was an immediate success.

Other publications followed and Nicholson began to be well known. In 1904 (Sir) James Barrie [q.v.] invited him to design the costumes for the first production of *Peter Pan*. Nicholson was always interested in the art of the theatre and later in life he made a number of excursions into stage design. His drawings for the dresses in *Polly* are in the Victoria and Albert Museum. In 1925 he designed the décor for Massine's ballets in *On With the Dance* produced by his old friend (Sir) C. B. Cochran. Two years later he was responsible for the stage sets and costumes of *The Marquise* at the Criterion Theatre in which the lead was played by (Dame) Marie Tempest [q.v.] whose portrait he painted on several occasions.

Had Nicholson produced nothing but the posters of his early youth and the woodcuts which followed he would have earned a reputation as a stylistic revolutionary on a small scale. It was later that he began to be known as a painter of still-life, of landscape, and finally of portraits for which, as his reputation increased, he became more and more in demand. His woodcuts, partly because of the undoubted influence of James Pryde, but also because of Nicholson's natural understanding of the demands of whatever medium he was using, had been bold and mainly dependent on the striking disposition of masses. In his paintings, as he advanced to maturity, the influence of Pryde weakened and the boldness gave way to an exquisite refinement of subdued tone, pale, clear colour, and firm confident handling of paint for which it would be hard to find a parallel in English painting. His style has affinities with that of Whistler. One might almost describe him as the dandy of English art were it not that in the best of his portraits there is a certain depth of human understanding which goes far beyond the limitations of dandyism and refined taste. Among these may be numbered his portraits of Miss Jekyll in the National Portrait Gallery, of his friend Walter Greaves in the Manchester City Art Gallery, of George Saintsbury at Merton College, Oxford, and the conversation piece of Sidney and Beatrice Webb in the London School of Economics and Political Science. Nicholson never exhibited at the Royal Academy, to which he refused election, and very rarely elsewhere, but a notable retrospective exhibition was held at the National Gallery in 1942.

In that exhibition his powers and his limitations as an artist became clear. On the one hand, a delicacy of perception which excluded all suggestion of drama or pictorial over-emphasis and a sensitivity to the possibilities of pure, pale colour which could achieve anything except richness or exuberance: on the other, an almost uncanny power to extract an elegant, aristocratic beauty from the most commonplace objects, whether still-life, landscape, or portrait. The subjects he chose rarely had the appeal of the obvious, yet he endowed them with a rarefied charm which is unique in the history of British painting.

In figure Nicholson was slight and graceful with clear-cut nervous features. He dressed with the meticulous but unconventional fastidiousness which is characteristic of his paintings. His wardrobe was famous for its delicately spotted shirts, canary-yellow waistcoats, and pale gloves. He had a genius for the kind of friendship which, for all its warmth and generosity, was neither intimate nor hearty. He detested Bohemianism. Something of the preciousness of the 'nineties is contained in his paintings, and the same spirit was apparent in his character and his appearance.

There is a portrait of Nicholson by Augustus John in the Fitzwilliam Museum, Cambridge, and a self-portrait is owned by Mrs. E. Q. Nicholson. Sir William Orpen's 'A Bloomsbury Family' (Scottish Modern Arts Association) was painted when the Nicholsons were living in Mecklenburgh Square. In 1893 Nicholson married Mabel, daughter of David Pryde, formerly headmaster of Edinburgh Ladies' College. They had three sons, the eldest of whom is the artist Ben Nicholson; and one daughter. The second son died on active service in 1918 a few months after the death of his mother in the same year. The following year Nicholson married Edith (died 1958), daughter of Sir Lionel Phillips, first baronet, and widow of Lieutenant-Colonel John Stuart-Wortley. They had one daughter, for whom Nicholson produced the two children's books, *Clever Bill* (1927) and *The Pirate Twins* (1929), also *The Book of Blokes* (1929). Nicholson was knighted in 1936 and died at Blewbury, Berkshire, 16 May 1949.

[Marguerite Steen, *William Nicholson*, 1943; Lillian Browse, *William Nicholson* (with a *catalogue raisonné*), 1956; private information.]                    ERIC NEWTON.

NOEL-BUXTON, NOEL EDWARD, first BARON NOEL-BUXTON (1869–1948), politician and philanthropist, was born in London 9 January 1869, the second son of Sir Thomas Fowell Buxton, third baronet [q.v.], and his wife, Lady Victoria Noel, daughter of the first Earl of Gainsborough. One of a family of ten brothers and sisters, he was brought up at Warlies, in Essex, in the tradition of public service. Educated at Harrow and Trinity College, Cambridge, where he obtained a third class in the historical tripos in 1889, he entered the family brewery at Spitalfields that autumn. The years there were broken by a visit to Japan and, in 1896, by a period in South Australia as aide-de-camp to his father, the governor, and by travel in the Balkan countries, which captured his enduring interest. Stirred by the misery of conditions at Spitalfields, he associated himself with the Christian Social Union and with churchmen of vision such as Talbot, Gore, and Barnett [qq.v.]. Adopting politics as the medium for promoting his social ideals, he joined with Charles Masterman [q.v.] in the Radical *Heart of the Empire* group. After unsuccessfully contesting as a Liberal an election at Ipswich in 1900, he was successful in a by-election at Whitby in 1905.

This seat he lost in the general election of 1906. In 1910 he was victorious in North Norfolk.

As a Liberal, Buxton supported Lloyd George's social legislation but, particularly through the Liberal foreign affairs group, of which he was chairman, he criticized the foreign policy of Sir Edward Grey (later Viscount Grey of Fallodon, q.v.), seeing in the resultant German fears of encirclement a danger to peace. When the war came in 1914, fearing that calm judgement would be an early casualty, Buxton strove for speedy victory and an equitable peace. He accepted an unofficial mission, initiated by (Sir) Winston Churchill and Lloyd George, to the Balkans, with his brother, Charles Roden Buxton, in order to secure Bulgaria's co-operation or, at least, neutrality, and thus check the spread of the war. Grey, who had other plans, was cold and Asquith non-committal. After obtaining Serbian, Greek, and Bulgarian approval for pro-posed lines of readjustment, Buxton failed through lack of government backing. Enemy reactions had been shown in October 1914, when a Young Turk shot and seriously wounded the brothers at Bucharest; thereafter Buxton wore a beard to conceal an injury to his cheek. While visiting the United States in June 1916, in connexion with the Armenian massacres, Buxton discussed with Colonel House, President Wilson's adviser, possi-bilities of American mediation. Through-out the war Buxton maintained that peace terms should be based on justice, unaffected by the vagaries of war. The harshness of the Paris peace treaties was the culminating point in a disillusionment with the Liberal Party which led to his resignation. He had been defeated at the election of 1918 but was returned for North Norfolk in 1922 as a member of the Labour Party which he had joined in 1919.

In January 1924 Buxton, who had always championed the cause of the farm worker, was appointed minister of agri-culture. Legislation in this short-lived Labour Government was difficult, but by perseverance and skilful tactics, Buxton piloted his agricultural wages bill to the statute book. He held the same office in the Labour Government of 1929 but in June 1930 resigned on grounds of health and accepted a peerage as Baron Noel-Buxton, of Aylsham, Norfolk. His wife was elected member for North Norfolk in his place.

Regarding Hitler's advent in 1933 as having some roots in allied policies, Noel-Buxton steadily urged efforts, through international agreements and colonial concessions, to achieve an equitable solu-tion which would meet the reasonable claims of the German people. To see conditions and consult with statesmen, he visited Russia, Germany, Czecho-slovakia, and the Balkans, and supported Chamberlain's efforts to avert war. When it came he advocated a negotiated peace, or at least in victory a due regard for the needs of all nations.

Among Noel-Buxton's enduring inter-ests were the Balkan Committee which he founded with James (later Viscount) Bryce [q.v.] in 1903, with the object of liberating the peoples under the Turkish yoke and promoting Balkan unity, and the Anti-Slavery Society, continuing the concerns of his great-grandfather, 'the Liberator'. In later years his philan-thropic zeal found expression in the Save the Children Fund, of which he was president (1930–48), and in the establish-ment and endowment of the Noel Buxton Trust for public and charitable purposes. He wrote many books, including accounts of his adventurous travels.

Gifted with a subtle and sympathetic understanding which enriched his contact with kings and statesmen as well as more humble people, Noel-Buxton was at his best as a diplomatist. With courage and singleness of purpose and unfailing energy he exerted all his influence on behalf of the welfare of people and of peoples.

In 1914 he married Lucy Edith, daughter of Major Henry Pelham Burn. They had three sons, one of whom died in a riding accident while on active service in 1940, and three daughters. He died in London 12 September 1948, and was succeeded in his title by his eldest son, Rufus Alexander (born 1917). A portrait by Sir William Rothenstein is in the possession of the family.

[T. P. Conwell-Evans, *Foreign Policy from a Back Bench, 1904–1918*, a study based on the papers of Lord Noel-Buxton, 1932; Mosa Anderson, *Noel Buxton: A Life*, 1952; private information; personal knowledge.]

MOSA ANDERSON.

NORMAN, MONTAGU COLLET, BARON NORMAN (1871–1950), governor of the Bank of England, was born in London 6 September 1871, the elder son of Fred-erick Henry Norman, a partner in Martins Bank and son of George Warde Norman [q.v.], a director of the Bank of England.

His mother was Lina Susan Penelope, daughter of (Sir) Mark Wilks Collet, sometime governor of the Bank of England, who was created a baronet for services in connexion with the conversion of the National Debt in 1888. Norman went to Eton but was prevented by ill health from following the family tradition of athletic distinction. He left King's College, Cambridge, after a year, to learn German in Leipzig, where he cultivated his taste for music and discovered an interest in philosophic discussions, and French in Switzerland. Returning to England in 1892 he was for a time in Martins Bank, and then in 1894 joined his maternal grandfather's firm of merchant bankers, Brown, Shipley & Co. After a year and a half in the London office he was sent to the New York house. He found American society congenial, travelled widely, and thereafter made a practice of spending part of each year in the United States.

His banking career was interrupted by service in the South African war. He enjoyed his two years there, which brought him experience of authority and for a time exuberant health. He was appointed to the D.S.O. and was eventually invalided home. After a slow recovery he resumed private banking, occupying his leisure in reconstructing his London house, Thorpe Lodge. But the disabling headaches which had troubled him as a boy recurred; he was out of sympathy with his partners on business policy; the resulting nervous breakdown kept him away from business throughout most of 1913 and 1914. He had been elected to the Court of the Bank of England in 1907. In January 1915 he went to the Bank, resigning from his own firm, to give whole-time assistance to the governors, except that he kept on his work for the War Office as adviser on financial questions arising in the censorship. In 1918 he was appointed deputy governor and in 1920 governor.

It had been expected that after the war the Bank would revert to its traditional practice of two-year governorships, but Norman's term was extended until 1925, subject to formal annual re-election. Thereafter it was understood that he would remain until 1929; and after 1931 there was no arrangement for a time limit. The term of his governorship was bound up with a wider recognition of the duties peculiar to central banks and with a reorganization of the Bank which he sought and secured—a full-time governor, severed from his own business, a full-time deputy, a group of high officials drawn from outside as well as inside the Bank, and an element in the Court of such officials as salaried executive directors.

Norman found himself faced in 1920 with a dangerous inflationary boom, disordered exchanges, unsettled war debts, and the threat of economic collapse in Central Europe. The boom was breaking under its own excesses; the other problems, all interconnected, occupied the next five years. Norman's policy was to separate economic from political issues by working with and through the financial committee of the League of Nations, and subsequently through the independent Dawes and Young committees; to cut down external liabilities to the capacity of the country to bear them; to stop inflation by balancing budgets and, on this condition, to provide foreign loans to finance the restoration of currencies and stabilization of exchanges. The establishment of new central banks became part of this policy. His influence was due partly to force of personality, partly to position; it was indispensable to the restoration of Central Europe and later to a settlement of reparations.

He had hoped that America would cancel war debts; his friend Benjamin Strong, governor of the Federal Reserve Bank of New York, convinced him that this was a political impossibility, whereas an agreed settlement would secure American co-operation in refinancing Europe; Norman accompanied Stanley Baldwin to Washington at the end of 1922 to negotiate the settlement. The return to the gold standard, at the old parity, was the consistent policy of successive Governments from the publication of the Cunliffe report in 1919. Until 1924 Norman had felt it necessary to wait, but a visit to New York in January 1925 decided him that the opportunity had come, and he so advised the Government. Subsequent criticism did not shake his opinion. To have reversed the policy so long affirmed would have checked recovery; devaluation would have lessened the effect of return; the risk that other countries would subsequently adopt parities giving them a competitive advantage was unavoidable—there would have been no return if Britain had not given a lead, and they would have undervalued their currencies whatever parity Britain had adopted: the issue was not *what* parity to adopt, but whether to return to and defend *any* fixed parity. Norman's point of view was the traditional one that the United Kingdom's chief interest lay in cheap imports and an expanding volume of world trade.

The drain of funds to Paris and New York threatened the restored gold standard in 1929; world depression in 1931, influenced by the growing crisis in America, revealed the insecurity of European finance and led to flight of capital from Austria, then from Germany, and finally from the United Kingdom. Norman organized help for Austria and Germany, and was organizing the defence of sterling when, at the end of July, he broke down and was ordered abroad. On his return he set about devising means of controlling the exchanges. He was able to restore confidence in sterling; but he resisted any proposal to hold it at any predetermined level. He was engaged at the same time in assisting the reorganization of industry, partly by his own initiative, with the co-operation of the other banks, in the Bankers' Industrial Development Company, partly at the Government's request; faced with the immediate liquidation of more than one company of national importance, the Government appealed to Norman, and the Bank was able to save them.

In his work in Europe and elsewhere, Norman developed his conception of the central bank as the confidential adviser and agent of the Government in the financial and monetary field, but also as possessing in that field an autonomy which the Government must respect. In the process of reconstruction he did much to fortify or create central banks, free from political interference in their own sphere, which in his view had a duty of international co-operation, parallel with but in technical matters independent of co-operation in the political sphere. A noteworthy example was his work for the development of central banks in the self-governing Dominions.

Norman differed from his predecessors in accepting consciously and continuously the responsibilities of 'lender of last resort'. He completed the transition of the Bank from commercial to central banking, reorganized it, and established its authority; London, although affected by every economic dislocation in the world, was never shaken by a bank failure. He widened the conception of his responsibilities—from the money market to industry, from the United Kingdom to Europe and the Empire; if no one else would take a credit risk necessary to save a Government from collapse or a firm of national importance from bankruptcy he would take it. His approach to his problems was empirical, seldom doctrinaire. He resisted the extension of government intervention in business affairs, because he feared that economic issues would be settled on irrelevant political grounds, or that government action would be too slow. In this respect he clung to the ideas of the liberal economy of his youth which were being superseded; similarly, although always supporting the authority of his own Government and the interests of the Empire, his outlook was international. A great patriot, he was also a good European.

It was Norman's intention to retire in 1939; the approach of war held him back. The planning of war finance, provision for external purchases, exchange control, recalled his experience in the first war and involved him in four more years of strenuous work. He was turning his mind to post-war problems when he was struck down by illness early in 1944. He recovered, but was forbidden by his doctors to accept re-election. A peerage was conferred on him in the same year on the occasion of the 250th anniversary of the Bank's foundation; he had refused one in 1923. He took no further part in public affairs, and died in London 4 February 1950. He was sworn of the Privy Council in 1923; received the honorary degree of LL.D. from Cambridge in the same year and that of D.C.L. from Oxford in 1930. He was also a grand officer of the Belgian Order of the Crown.

In person Norman was tall and moved with easy grace: in later years his broad forehead, striking eyes, and pointed grey beard made him a notable figure. In conversation he was capable of getting on terms with a wide variety of visitors; always courteous, he could be severe. He was farsighted and showed an uncanny capacity not only in his perception of the essentials of a problem but often in his grasp of its detail. Norman was less skilled in exposition and was least impressive on his rare public appearances.

In 1933 Norman married Priscilla Cecilia Maria Worsthorne, daughter of Major Robert Reyntiens of the Belgian Artillery and Lady Alice Reyntiens, daughter of the seventh Earl of Abingdon. Norman's wife survived him, but there were no children and the peerage became extinct. A portrait by Augustus John and a bronze by Lady Kennet are the property of the Bank of England.

[Sir Henry Clay, *Lord Norman*, 1957; private information; personal knowledge.]
                                HENRY CLAY.

NUNN, SIR (THOMAS) PERCY (1870–1944), educationist, the second son of Edward Smith Nunn by his wife, Harriette, daughter of Thomas Luff, accountant, was born 28 December 1870 at Bristol, where his father and his grandfather kept a school which in 1873 was transferred to Weston-super-Mare. There Percy Nunn and his brothers were educated, and at the early age of sixteen he was helping in the teaching, and producing school plays, some of which he had written, and in some of which he acted. He owed much to the precept and example of a local teacher, who inculcated in him the value of hard work and wide interests, a training which bore ample fruit in later years. He continued to help in the school even after matriculation at Bristol University College, but in 1890 his father died, and he inherited the whole responsibility for the management of the school. Feeling that he was too young to gain the confidence of the parents, he resigned the headmastership and taught in Halifax and then at grammar schools in London. During these years he formed the conviction, which was to be perhaps his most notable contribution to the theory and practice of education, that individuality is the ideal of life, and that the prime duty of the teacher is to evoke and develop the capabilities of the pupil. These views he propounded throughout his life from his first book on *The Aim and Achievements of Scientific Method* (1907) to *Education, its Data and First Principles* (1920), which is probably his most widely read work.

In the meantime Nunn had taken his London B.Sc. (1890) and B.A. (1895). His opportunity came in 1905 when, after two years as science master and lecturer at Shoreditch Technical Institute, he was appointed vice-principal of the London Day Training College, a post which after 1913 he combined with the chair of education in London University. In 1922 he was appointed director. Under him the college rapidly developed its activities. A new course in art (1924) was followed in 1927 by the establishment of a department of colonial education. This in turn led to the creation of a division of over-seas students in 1932, when it was clear that the college had grown beyond its status of a municipal school, and it was transformed into the Institute of Education of London University with Nunn as its director. He retired from all his academic posts four years later.

Nunn's abilities were widely recognized outside his university, of the senate of which he was a member from 1929 to 1936. His counsel was sought by the Board of Education and as a member of the advisory committee of the Colonial Office on education, and he served as a statutory commissioner under the University of London Act, 1926. He was knighted in 1930, having been president of the Mathematical Association in 1917, of section L of the British Association in 1923, and of the Aristotelian Society in the same year. This versatility is reflected in a lecture on 'Relativity and Gravitation' (1923), and another before the British Academy on 'Anthropomorphism and Physics' (*Proceedings*, vol. xiii, 1927). After his retirement his philosophical and educational interests met in 'Education and Reality', the tenth Haldane memorial lecture (1939). He was visiting professor at Columbia University in 1925 and he received honorary degrees from the universities of Liverpool and St. Andrews and from Trinity College, Dublin.

Nunn married in 1894 Eliza Alice (Ethel), daughter of Edmund John Hart, carter, and had a daughter who became principal of the Diocesan Training College at Fishponds, Bristol. In his later years he suffered much from bronchitis and emphysema, and this led him to retire to Madeira where he died 12 December 1944.

Nunn was a man of great personal charm with a remarkable gift for expounding complex problems in a manner at once simple and precise. He never quite lost his penchant towards play-writing and he also had some poetical talent. His whimsical sense of humour endeared him to many friends both at home and over-seas, with whom he kept in touch until the end of his life.

A portrait of Nunn by Henry Lamb is at the Institute of Education.

[Official papers of the London County Council; private information; personal knowledge.]                      FRED CHARLES.

OAKLEY, SIR JOHN HUBERT (1867–1946), surveyor, was born in London 11 October 1867, the eldest son of Christopher Percival Oakley, surveyor, of Chislehurst, by his wife, Kate, daughter of Charles Kingsford, of Lewisham Hill, Kent. He was a nephew of John Oakley [q.v.], dean of Manchester, and the grandson of John Oakley, surveyor, a founder in 1868 of the Surveyors' Institution, later the Royal Institution of Chartered Surveyors. Educated at Uppingham, Oakley entered the Royal Agricultural College, Cirencester, in 1885, where he quickly made his mark as a student and athlete. A tall man of powerful physique, at Rugby football he was captain of the college fifteen, was capped for Gloucestershire, and tried for England. He was splendid to watch when high jumping, for he would scorn the usual oblique approach and carry the jump after a straight run like a hurdler.

Having passed out of Cirencester with honours at Christmas 1887, Oakley joined the family firm of Daniel Smith, Son and Oakley, surveyors, land agents, and auctioneers, of London, which had been founded in 1780. He remained with them all his life, first as an articled pupil, subsequently as partner (1892), and senior partner (from 1898).

Handsome in presence and by nature a modest and kindly man, Oakley was held in respect and affection throughout his profession, in which, as in his athletics, he was a great all-rounder. His experience, founded upon an early training in agriculture, took him, as it took many of the older generation of surveyors, over the whole field, urban and rural, of successful general practice. His reputation as a surveyor and valuer of real property was unexcelled; and his professional knowledge was reinforced with wisdom and judgement of a high order. His services as an arbitrator were in frequent demand; it once fell to him to make what amounted to a valuation of the whole city of Hong Kong in order to resolve differences between two government departments. On another occasion he was appointed by the London County Council and the landowners concerned to assess the betterment rate, then one of the first of its kind, to be levied upon lands benefited by, but surplus to, the Kingsway improvement scheme between Aldwych and Holborn. He followed his father as land agent for the St. Germans estates at Blackheath and was responsible for their development.

Oakley was elected to the council of the Surveyors' Institution in 1907 and remained a member until his death. Like his father and father-in-law before him, and his brother-in-law after him, he became president of the Institution, and held office in 1918, the year of its golden jubilee. In 1925 he was elected president of the College of Estate Management, founded six years earlier by his predecessor, Sir William Wells, as a centre of education for surveyors and allied professions.

Oakley's record of public service was notable. He was a member of the Royal Commission on the universities of Oxford and Cambridge which reported in 1922; the committee on crown and government lands (1921–2); the Royal Commission on compensation for suffering and damage by enemy action (1922–4); the River Ouse drainage commission (1925–6); the Irish grants committee (1926–30); and of the advisory committee on crown lands (1933–9). He was knighted in 1919 and appointed G.B.E. in 1928.

Oakley married in 1891 Ida, daughter of Daniel Watney, surveyor, and had one daughter. He died 5 December 1946 in London.

A three-quarter length portrait of Oakley by R. G. Eves hangs in the lecture hall of the Royal Institution of Chartered Surveyors in Westminster.

[*The Times*, 7 December 1946; *Transactions* (1918–19) and *Journal* (January 1947) of the Royal Institution of Chartered Surveyors; private information; personal knowledge.]

H. G. TYRRELL-EVANS.

OGILVIE, SIR FREDERICK WOLFF (1893–1949), economist and university vice-chancellor, was born at Valparaiso, Chile, 7 February 1893, the youngest son of William Maxwell Ogilvie, an engineer, and his wife, Mary Ann Wolff. The Ogilvies were Scots from Dundee. Ogilvie was educated at Clifton and at Balliol College, Oxford, where he had a quiet university career, taking a first in classical moderations in 1913. His reading for *literae humaniores* was interrupted by the outbreak of war in 1914 and within two days he was in the forces as a second lieutenant, 4th Bedfordshire Regiment. He quickly found himself in France. In April 1915 he was seriously wounded at Hill 60, and lost his left arm; he remained in the army, however, until the end of the war, and was demobilized in 1919 with the rank of captain.

He returned at once to Balliol and in the autumn of the same year became lecturer in economics at Trinity College, Oxford, being elected to a fellowship in 1920. In 1926 he was appointed to the chair of political economy in Edinburgh. The interest in the study of economics which he had shown from his early undergraduate days was due partly to a growing social sense, and he showed himself in Oxford and Edinburgh a sympathetic teacher of the subject. At all times his quality as a teacher and friend of the young was enriched by his knowledge of music and his unrestrained enjoyment of the outdoor life. He was also invited to act as guide and mentor in economic matters to a group of younger, and later most distinguished, Conservative members of Parliament. During these years his main interests within his subject proved to be the tourist industry of Great Britain and the economic problems of Scotland. His only book, *The Tourist Movement*, was published in 1933, and he later contributed on the subject to the new edition of *Chambers's Encyclopaedia*. He was a member of the Edinburgh Chamber of Commerce and of trade boards, and also concerned himself with adult education and juvenile employment in Scotland.

In the autumn of 1934 Ogilvie left Edinburgh for Belfast, where he became president and vice-chancellor of the Queen's University. There he remained for four years, and left his mark in his own way. The university found in him a strength, integrity, and courtesy rarely combined in one person. He believed strongly in the value to a university of a wide social and cultural life, and he used his great personal charm and the persuasive impact of his own inner enjoyment of learning and the arts to very good purpose. He might well have been one of the great vice-chancellors, but in the summer of 1938 he was drawn away from the academic world to become the second director-general of the British Broadcasting Corporation in succession to Sir John (subsequently Lord) Reith, who had guided its growth from the beginning and whose masterful single-mindedness had largely made it what it was.

Immediately broadcasting became the absorbing interest of Ogilvie's life. He saw in it a very great power for good, and looked to it especially and characteristically to safeguard and fortify the moral force in man and foster a world-wide fellowship and peace. The most insistent problems of Broadcasting House in wartime, however, must inevitably have seemed to its governors to be organizational and administrative. The Corporation emerged from the war in most remarkable esteem for its unremitting care for truth and for human sympathy throughout a remorseless struggle for the very survival of nations. But in order to play its part at all, triumphs of technical and administrative adjustment had to be achieved almost daily. This was not a sphere in which Ogilvie could by tradition and training easily show his greatest strength, and early in 1942 he resigned. He must have been deeply disappointed in an issue of events which deprived him of an opportunity to achieve what he had close to his heart; but he never complained. He next devoted himself, with his usual application of mind, and notable personal success, to special war duties for the British Council (1943–5).

At this time he thought seriously of taking up editorial work in the national press; but in 1944 he was offered and accepted the position of principal of Jesus College, Oxford. He was now fifty-one, and as it proved he had fewer than five more years to live; but in that short time he showed, as in Belfast, his great gifts for educational work in a university. His wide contacts with the cultural life of the country and his record of public service enabled him to give what he wanted to give to the college. By quietly infusing his own enjoyments and convictions into its way of life he made it a more friendly community, more enlightened and more civilized. In 1948 he was grievously stricken by the death of his eldest son, James William Ogilvie, in a climbing accident on the Matterhorn, and in the last months of his fatal illness Ogilvie must have suffered some loss of the personal force which was his strength. But he left his own mark on the college and will go down in its history, despite his brief tenure, as a remarkable principal in the humane tradition.

In person he was tall and fair, with grey eyes. His expression was serious and thoughtful, but a smile was never far away, for he was easily moved by friendship and his sense of humour was readily aroused. He married in 1922 Mary Helen, eldest daughter of Alexander Beith Macaulay, professor of apologetics and systematic theology at Trinity College, Glasgow, and had three sons. He was knighted in 1942 and died in Oxford 10 June 1949. Lady Ogilvie became in 1953 the principal of St. Anne's College,

Oxford. Their son Robert Maxwell Ogilvie became a fellow of Balliol in 1957.

[*The Times*, 11 June 1949; private information; personal knowledge.]

C. R. MORRIS.

OLIVER, DAVID THOMAS (1863–1947), lawyer, was born at Pontypridd 8 February 1863, the fifth of twelve children of the Rev. Henry Oliver, a Congregational minister, by his wife, Catharine, daughter of the Rev. Joshua Thomas, Congregational minister, of Aberdare. Educated at Caterham School he first entered the Civil Service, from which he resigned after being called to the bar by the Middle Temple in 1888. In the meantime he had served in Ireland and had graduated B.A. at the Royal University of Ireland, proceeding M.A. (1886), LL.B. (1888), and LL.D. (1898). In 1898 he also took the LL.B. degree of the university of London with first class honours. In 1900 he entered Trinity Hall, Cambridge, as an advanced student, taking the degrees of LL.B. in 1902 and LL.M. in 1908.

By this time Oliver had found that his heart was in academic work and he became lecturer in law in his own college and supervisor of legal studies for several other colleges, gradually relinquishing his practice in the Temple. In 1920 he became a fellow of Trinity Hall, a position which he retained until his death. His particular interest in Roman law led him to the study of Roman-Dutch law, in which subject he was appointed to the Monro lectureship which was founded for him by the master and fellows of Gonville and Caius College at the end of 1920 to provide for the needs of the students from South Africa who came to read law in Cambridge. This successful enterprise was eventually taken over by the university and thereafter Oliver carried on the course as university lecturer; and although he was compelled to retire officially from this post in 1928 on reaching the statutory age limit he continued to conduct the teaching of the subject for a number of years until a successor could be found. He was a just and discriminating examiner, adept in setting questions which would give to the candidate of modest attainments a fair chance to display such knowledge as he might possess while at the same time containing some subtle points on which the first class man could reveal his true quality.

As a teacher of those students who were in personal contact with him Oliver had an unrivalled reputation; his remarkable success was due not merely to his encyclopaedic knowledge but even more to his intense sympathy with his pupils and an uncanny power of detecting and disposing of their difficulties. His entirely unselfish devotion to those whom he taught was rewarded by the deep and lasting affection of the men of all kinds who had come under his influence; in all parts of the world to which they might go it was of him they always thought and asked whenever Cambridge was mentioned. He for his part took the greatest pleasure in hearing of the success and well-being of those whom he had known as undergraduates. Although slow of speech he was quick in thought and his penetrating mind could appraise character and detect deceit immediately; but he was incapable of malice or rancour and so great was his charity of heart that he sought always for the best even in the least meritorious of men.

Unremitting industry and an excellent memory enabled Oliver to acquire a wide and deep knowledge of law in all its branches. This range gave him a balanced approach to any legal problem and an instinct for selecting the lines on which its solution could be found, a faculty which he was ever ready to exercise for the benefit of anyone who sought his help. Generous to a fault, with no thought of self-interest he sacrificed so much of his energy and time in the service of others that he had little left for the production of adequate demonstrations of his own learning and acumen in permanent form. His claim to remembrance, however, rests upon the firm foundation of the notable part he took in helping his university to discharge its main purpose, the higher education of its members. By his example and his teaching Oliver inspired generations of his pupils to appreciate scholarship and to strive for a true understanding and application of principle.

His writings included reviews and articles such as 'Roman Law in Aulus Gellius' and 'Roman Law as illustrated in Pliny's Letters', in the *Cambridge Law Journal*, and 'Roman Law in Modern Cases in English Courts' in the volume *Cambridge Legal Essays* (1926). He also published a translation, with commentary, of portions of books XII and XIII of Justinian's *Digest* (*de Condictionibus*), the seventh edition of Goodeve's *Personal Property*, and editions of Willis and

Oliver's *Roman Law Examination Guide*, and Wise and Winfield's *Outlines of Jurisprudence*.

In 1891 Oliver married Lavinia Mary Harrison, who died in 1917, there being no children of the marriage. In 1918 he married Alice Maud, daughter of George Kirby, of Watford, by whom he had two sons, both of whom studied law at Trinity Hall. He died in Cambridge 18 January 1947. A portrait by E. O. D. Hoole is in the possession of the family.

[Private information; personal knowledge.]
J. W. C. TURNER.

OLIVER, SIR THOMAS (1853–1942), physician and authority on industrial hygiene, was born at St. Quivox, Ayrshire, 2 March 1853, the second son of James Oliver, of Ayr, by his wife, Margaret, daughter of Thomas McMurtrie. He was educated at Ayr Academy and at Glasgow University, where he graduated M.B., C.M. with commendation (1874), and M.D. with honours (1880). He visited Paris for postgraduate study and worked under Jean Martin Charcot, whose lectures on disseminated sclerosis he edited and translated for publication in the *Edinburgh Medical Journal* in 1876. He acted for a short period as assistant pathologist at the Glasgow Royal Infirmary, but in 1875 set up in practice at Preston, Lancashire. Here he remained until 1879 when he moved to Newcastle upon Tyne. He was elected physician to the Royal Victoria Infirmary and to the Princess Mary Maternity Hospital. In 1880 he was appointed lecturer in physiology in the medical school at Newcastle attached to the university of Durham. His lectureship was raised to a chair in 1889, and he held it until 1911 when he became professor of medicine.

At Newcastle Oliver came into practical contact with industrial disease and developed an abiding interest in this department of medicine. He was elected F.R.C.P. (London) in 1890 and his Goulstonian lectures in the following year were devoted to the subject of lead poisoning. He served on the white lead commission in 1892–3, and it was largely on his recommendation that the Home Office by regulation abolished female labour in the dangerous manufacture of white lead. In 1898 he was appointed with (Sir) T. E. Thorpe [q.v.] to inquire into the extensive poisoning from the glazes used in various industries in the Potteries, an inquiry which necessitated visits to similar industries in France and Germany. Here again as a result of their recommendations, and in spite of much opposition, changes were introduced which materially reduced the danger to the operative. During the same year he represented the Home Office at the Madrid International Congress on Hygiene. He was the medical expert during the Home Office inquiry on lucifer matches and was a member of the dangerous trades committee.

Oliver's most important publications were *Lead Poisoning in its Acute and Chronic Forms* (Goulstonian lectures, 1891); a translation of Charles Jacques Bouchard's *Lectures on Auto-Intoxication in Disease*, 1894; *Dangerous Trades*, a valuable survey which he edited in 1902; *The Miners' Worm Disease as seen in Westphalian and Hungarian Collieries* (1904); *Diseases of Occupation from the Legislative, Social, and Medical Points of View* (1908); *Occupations from the Social, Hygienic and Medical Points of View* (1916); *The Health of the Workers* (1925); and *The Health of the Child of School Age* which he edited in 1927.

His work for the improvement of industrial conditions took him to the United States, where he received the freedom of the city of Boston (1923); to France, where he was made a chevalier of the Legion of Honour (1929) and was given the gold medal of the Assistance Publique (1924); and to Belgium, where he was given a medal of honour by the university of Brussels (1920). In 1921 he was a delegate of the Australian Commonwealth to the International Labour Conference at Geneva. He was president of the Durham College of Medicine (1926–34) and vice-chancellor of the university of Durham (1928–30). In 1931 at Geneva he was honorary president of the International Congress of Accidents and Industrial Diseases. He was president of the Royal Institute of Public Health and Hygiene (1937–42). He was knighted in 1908, was a deputy-lieutenant for Northumberland, and held the honorary degrees of LL.D., Glasgow (1903), D.Sc., Sheffield (1908), and D.C.L., Durham (1921).

He retired from the chair of medicine in 1927 and died at his home in Newcastle upon Tyne 15 May 1942. He married first, in 1881 Edith Rosina (died 1888), daughter of William Jenkins, of Consett Hall, county Durham; secondly, in 1893 Emma Octavia (died 1912), daughter of John Anthony Woods, of Benton Hall,

Newcastle upon Tyne. There were three daughters and a son by the first marriage and a daughter and a son by the second marriage. A portrait of Oliver by T. B. Garvie hangs in the council-room of the Durham College of Medicine.

[*British Medical Journal* and *Lancet*, 30 May 1942; *The Times*, 18 May 1942; *Journal* of the Royal Institute of Public Health and Hygiene, June 1942.]

W. J. BISHOP.

OLIVIER, SYDNEY HALDANE, BARON OLIVIER (1859–1943), civil servant and statesman, was born at Colchester 16 April 1859, the second son and sixth of the ten children of the Rev. Henry Arnold Olivier, then curate of All Saints, Colchester, by his wife, Anne Elizabeth Hardcastle, daughter of Joseph Arnould, M.D., of Whitecross, Wallingford, Berkshire, and sister of Sir Joseph Arnould [q.v.]. He came of a family of French Huguenots, who after the revocation of the Edict of Nantes in 1685 were deprived of their wealth and the title 'Sieur d'Olivier', and fled first to Holland, then to England.

Olivier was educated at Tonbridge School and at Corpus Christi College, Oxford, where he was an exhibitioner and was awarded a second class in *literae humaniores* in 1881. There he became an intimate friend of Graham Wallas [q.v.]. With another undergraduate friend, Hubert Campion, he wrote a volume of light verse, *Poems and Parodies*, published in 1880. After leaving Oxford he read for the Civil Service competitive examination, and in 1882, having headed the list of successful competitors, he entered the Colonial Office.

In 1885 Olivier joined the Fabian Society and was honorary secretary from 1886 to 1889. Sidney Webb, then a colleague in the Colonial Office, G. B. Shaw [qq.v.], and Graham Wallas joined about the same time; and it was mainly under the influence of the four friends that the Society made its distinctive contribution to the development of modern Socialism. In *Fabian Essays in Socialism* (1889), perhaps the most important of the Society's publications, Olivier wrote on the moral basis of Socialism. He came to. Socialism through Auguste Comte, and remained a Socialist during the rest of his life.

He was colonial secretary of British Honduras in 1890–91, auditor-general of the Leeward Islands in 1895–6, and

secretary to the Royal Commission on the West Indies in 1896–7. In 1898 he was appointed C.M.G. and spent five months in Washington assisting on behalf of the West Indian colonies in reciprocity negotiations with the United States. From 1900 to 1904 he was colonial secretary of Jamaica, on three occasions acting as governor. In 1907 he was appointed captain-general and governor-in-chief of Jamaica and advanced to K.C.M.G. His most urgent task was to repair the havoc caused by earthquake and fire a few months earlier, the work including the reconstruction of Kingston on a new plan, in which he obtained the services of his brother-in-law, Sir Charles Nicholson [q.v.]. He was a highly popular governor. His six years of office formed a memorable period of development in the island's history, one of his many reforms being the introduction of Jamaica's first comprehensive sanitary code. Having returned to England in 1913 as permanent secretary to the Board of Agriculture and Fisheries, he entered the Treasury in 1917 as assistant comptroller and auditor of the Exchequer, and was appointed C.B. the same year. He retired from the Civil Service in 1920. In 1924 he joined Ramsay MacDonald's first Labour Government as secretary of state for India, was sworn of the Privy Council, and created a baron. Ten months later his tenure of office was ended by the resignation of the Government, the prime minister having, so Olivier told him, needlessly thrown up the sponge. In 1929–30, as chairman of the West Indian sugar commission, Olivier paid his last official visit to Jamaica.

Olivier's deep interest in racial colour problems found expression chiefly in two books of international repute: *The Anatomy of African Misery* (1927) and *White Capital and Coloured Labour* (2nd ed. 1929); he discussed such questions also in contributions to periodicals and in two later books: *The Myth of Governor Eyre* (1933) and *Jamaica: The Blessed Island* (1936). His studies led him to reject what he called 'the short-sighted theory that the dividing habits of race are permanently stronger than the unifying power of humanity'.

Tall and handsome, Olivier was a striking figure in any assembly, 'looking', wrote Shaw, 'like a Spanish grandee in any sort of clothes, however unconventional'. He was a man of commanding intellect, and he could, and did, 'labour terribly', exacting a high standard of performance from himself and those who worked with him. He had a remarkable literary endowment, and was a frequent contributor to periodical literature. His philosophical articles and his short story, *The Empire Builder*, won the admiration of William James, whose guest he was on one of his visits to America. His prose style was distinguished and individual, and he had a felicitous turn for light verse. His writings include three plays, one of which, *Mrs. Maxwell's Marriage*, was performed by the Stage Society in January 1900. In 1911 the honorary degree of LL.D. was conferred upon him by the university of Edinburgh.

In 1885 Olivier married Margaret (died 1953), eldest daughter of Homersham Cox, a county court judge, and sister of Harold Cox [q.v.]. They had four daughters but no son, and when he died at Bognor Regis 15 February 1943 the peerage became extinct. One of his younger brothers was Herbert Arnould Olivier, the painter; another brother, the Rev. Gerard Kerr Olivier, was the father of Sir Laurence Olivier, the actor. Two portraits of Olivier were painted by his brother Herbert, and another by Miss Nellie Heath.

[*Sydney Olivier: Letters and Selected Writings*, edited with a memoir by Margaret Olivier with some impressions by Bernard Shaw, 1948; private information; personal knowledge.]                    G. F. McCLEARY.

OLSSON, JULIUS (1864–1942), painter, was born in Islington 1 February 1864, the third son of Martin Olsson, a Swedish timber agent, by his English wife, Elizabeth Henrietta Tucker. Self-trained as a painter, he first exhibited at the Royal Academy in 1890 and the same year settled at St. Ives where he remained for some twenty years, becoming an honoured member of the artists' colony and president of the St. Ives Arts Club. He was a respected local figure as a justice of the peace, a prominent golfer and tennis player, and a reckless yachtsman.

Olsson soon began to take pupils, but eschewed formal teaching, believing rather in acting as adviser to a sketching group. He encouraged his students to look for colour rather than form, deprecating 'over-drawing'. Meanwhile his professional stature grew and he won reputation, chiefly by his moonlit seascapes and renderings of the Cornish coast in stormy weather. He knew and loved the sea in all its moods, from the serenity of 'Moonlit Shore' (bought out of the Chantrey bequest for the Tate Gallery in 1911) to the creaming breakers he often painted. He was romantic in temperament, and a naturalist rather than a decorator. He had such a feeling for the weight of water that sometimes he obscured its fluidity.

Olsson's admission in 1897 to the (Royal) Institute of Oil Painters (of which he was president from 1919 until his death) was followed by his election as A.R.A. in 1914 and R.A. in 1920. The Paris Salon awarded him two gold medals and ruled him *hors concours*; he twice acted on the international jury of the Carnegie Institute, Pittsburgh. During the war of 1914–18, after which he settled in London, he served as lieutenant, Royal Naval Volunteer Reserve, being one of those who urged the desirability of ship camouflage and one of the chief advisers to the Admiralty thereon.

A big, blond, blue-eyed man, Olsson revelled in the large canvas, worked rapidly, and painted in a studio so big that it later became the St. Ives Art Gallery. To the charm of his personality there are many witnesses, who testify to his hospitality, loyalty, integrity, and openheartedness.

Olsson died at Dalkey, county Dublin, 8 September 1942. He was twice married: first, in 1885 to Catherine Mary (died 1923), daughter of Charles Butt, timber merchant, of Hull; secondly, in 1925 to Edith Mary, daughter of Charles Luke Ellison, a country gentleman of Castlereagh who bred horses. There were no children of either marriage.

[*The Times*, 10 September 1942; *St. Ives Times*, 18 September 1942; *Western Echo*, 19 September 1942; private information.]
                    HERBERT B. GRIMSDITCH.

OMAN, SIR CHARLES WILLIAM CHADWICK (1860–1946), historian, was born at Mozufferpore, India, 12 January 1860, the only child of Charles Philip Austin Oman, indigo planter, by his wife, Anne, daughter of William Chadwick, railway constructor. He had, however, no memories of India, for the family was settled in London by 1861 and removed to Cheltenham five years later. He was elected scholar of Winchester and of New College, Oxford, winning the first place on each occasion. His early years at Winchester were not particularly happy; at first he was bullied and miserable; but from 1876 he was thoroughly contented, delighted in his work under W. A. Fearon and George Ridding [q.v.], and made life-long friends. Pure scholarship was never his forte; his successes at Winchester and New College were the fruit of a most lively mind, a wonderful memory, and a passion for reading. A first in *literae humaniores* (1882) and in modern history (1883) was followed by a fellowship at All Souls (1883). Oman had hoped for a New College fellowship, and was convinced that his strong Conservatism and old-fashioned churchmanship prejudiced the college against him. But he was in his element at All Souls and recognized that his election there was 'the greatest piece of good fortune' that ever fell to his lot. In 1884 he won the Lothian prize for an essay on 'The Art of War in the Middle Ages'; already he had laid in a great store of knowledge in many fields of history; he was, too, a numismatist, an archaeologist, a ready writer, a keen politician both in university and in wider affairs. Although for many years he taught both ancient and modern history to undergraduates of New College, his main interests were gradually drawing him to modern history. Yet it would be hard indeed to define the boundaries of his knowledge of men and things in many ages, and since it was his strong conviction that men who know should write, and that they learn as well as teach by writing, he was a prolific author on many subjects and periods. Two textbooks on the history of Greece and of England long held their ground in schools: he had the gift of narrative, an eye for interesting detail, and no lack of vigorous prejudice. For abstractions and movements of thought he had no concern: his strength lay in the realm of fact: no man of learning was ever less of a philo-sopher. But the width of his interests is well illustrated by the publication in successive years of a study of *Warwick the Kingmaker* (1891) and a useful summary of Byzantine history (1892). Meanwhile he was extending the study of military history of which his Lothian essay had been an early evidence. *A History of the Art of War in the Middle Ages* (1898, 2nd, enlarged, ed., 2 vols., 1924) has received and no doubt deserved much criticism and correction, but like several other of Oman's books it had the great merit of setting out a large body of material in clear and orderly fashion.

In 1902 there appeared the first instal-ment of the great *History of the Peninsular War* upon which he was to labour for nearly thirty years. Its seven massive volumes were based upon minute know-ledge of many hitherto unexplored sources, not least upon the Vaughan papers at All Souls. Oman travelled widely in Spain and Portugal to acquaint himself with the detailed topography of the campaigns and battlefields: at home and abroad his work won full recognition and upon it his reputation most securely rests. His election to the Chichele chair of modern history in 1905 gave him more leisure for his long task and bound him still more closely to All Souls. But the Peninsular war was far from absorbing all his time and interest. He wrote con-siderable books on *The Great Revolt of 1381* (1906) and upon *England before the Norman Conquest* (1910). His diligence as a librarian did valuable service to the Codrington library at All Souls over many years, and to the library of the Imperial War Museum. During the war of 1914–18 his military knowledge was wisely used at the Press Bureau and in the Foreign Office and his work was recognized by a knighthood (K.B.E.) in 1920.

From 1919 to 1935 Oman sat in the House of Commons as burgess for the university of Oxford: there as elsewhere he showed himself a convinced Conserva-tive, and there too he delighted his friends by his ready omniscience on all manner of concrete and recondite fact. He retained his professorship, despite an often ex-pressed disappointment at the unreadiness of college tutors to send their men to professorial lectures. Doubtless he would have been wise to give place eventually to a younger man; yet until very near the end of his life he wrote with sustained liveliness on a wide variety of subjects—his memories of travel, of *Things I have Seen* (1933), of Victorian Oxford, of strange or forgotten personalities. Every kind of oddity attracted him; he talked with equal ease about castles or coins or Domes-day Book or the study of the occult or the men and events made real to him by read-ing and experience. He was in no sense a thinker: but his astonishing memory equally hospitable to things trivial and important, his friendliness and simplicity of character made his company fascinating. Physically he was tall, burly, bright-eyed and, from an early age, white haired. He was elected F.B.A. in 1905, served as president of the Royal Historical and Numismatic societies and of the Royal Archaeological Institute; he became an honorary fellow of New College in 1936 and received the honorary degrees of D.C.L. (Oxford, 1926) and LL.D. (Edinburgh, 1911, and Cambridge, 1927).

He died at Oxford 23 June 1946. In 1892 he married a childhood friend, Mary Mabel, daughter of General Robert Maclagan. No marriage could have been happier and Oman repeatedly acknowledged his wife's help and encouragement in all his tasks. She survived him, with a son (C. C. Oman), who has won distinction as an antiquary, and two daughters, one of whom, Carola, has written several remarkable biographies.

There is a drawing of Oman at All Souls College by Francis Dodd.

[Sir Charles Oman, *Memories of Victorian Oxford*, 1941; Sir C. G. Robertson in *Proceedings* of the British Academy, vol. xxxii, 1946; *The Times*, 25 June 1946; personal knowledge.]

ALWYN WINTON: (A. T. P. WILLIAMS.)

OPPENHEIM, EDWARD PHILLIPS (1866–1946), novelist, was born in London 22 October 1866, the son of Edward John Oppenheim, a leather merchant who later moved to Leicester, and his wife, Henrietta Susannah Budd. He was educated at Wyggeston Grammar School, Leicester, where he won a history prize, but invariably had 'shocking reports' for mathematics. He left school in December 1882 in order to help his father, who was at the time in some financial difficulty. Although he was not without inherited business talent, and retained his connexion with the leather trade until middle life, Oppenheim's real ambition was to succeed as a writer. His parents helped him to publish an early first novel, *Expiation* (1887); and on the strength of this appearance in print he presently secured a contract to write six more-or-less sensational serial stories for the Sheffield *Weekly Telegraph*.

Now practised in the story-teller's art, he conceived the idea, during his first Atlantic crossing, of a novel in the genre which he was to make peculiarly his own. The result, *The Mysterious Mr. Sabin* (1898), created a demand; and Oppenheim was launched on a long career of pleasing the public with thrilling romances of intrigue in high places. 'I'm just a yarn-spinner', he said once to an interviewer. 'I'm not what you fellows call a literary man. . . . Yet sometimes I feel that one of my stories, if it's well done, may be remembered after I'm gone.' It was not an unreasonable expectation; his

stories were very well done, in spite of the rapidity with which he wrote. His method of working was mostly by oral dictation: thus, it might be said, continuing in the true tradition of the Eastern story-teller who spreads his mat and holds his audience spellbound. His characters—beautiful adventuresses, cosmopolitan men of mystery, high-class criminals and detectives, politicians, gamblers, spies—acted out their vivid dramas against a setting of the world's great cities, or of the Riviera. His work soon became associated especially with Monte Carlo which entered into the title of several of his most popular novels, such as *Mr. Grex of Monte Carlo* (1915). His novels became well known in the United States and in Europe, but he lost his popularity with the Germans when, in the years before 1914, he published several stories especially devoted to warning his country of the designs of Germany. When the war which he had foreseen finally came, he was employed in escorting neutral journalists on tours of the battle front in France, and at this time he wrote perhaps his best novel of espionage, *The Kingdom of the Blind* (1917). Another to gain an appreciative public was *The Great Impersonation* (1920).

Between the two wars Oppenheim maintained a steady output of several books a year. In 1940 he had to leave his Riviera home; moreover, when the Germans seized the Channel Islands they used his house at Guernsey, Le Vauquiédor, as Luftwaffe headquarters. In 1941 he published his autobiography, *The Pool of Memory*, a pleasant book, but containing far too little about himself and his work. He also wrote several more novels before returning to Guernsey in the autumn of 1945. There he died 3 February 1946. He married in 1891 Elsie Clara (died November 1946), daughter of Alfred and Mary Hopkins, of Easthampton, Massachusetts, both of whom had been born in Leicester. Oppenheim had one daughter.

[*The Times*, 4 February 1946; E. P. Oppenheim, *The Pool of Memory*, 1941.]

M. BELLASIS.

ORCZY, EMMA MAGDALENA ROSALIA MARIE JOSEPHA BARBARA, BARONESS ORCZY (1865–1947), novelist, was born 23 September 1865 at Tarna-Örs, Hungary. She was named Emma (or Emmuska) after her mother, Countess Wass. Her father, Baron Felix

Orczy, a talented amateur musician, came of an ancient landowning family. On taking over the property of Tisza-Abád he attempted to introduce modern farming methods, but when the peasants, distrustful of innovation, burnt his crops and buildings, he abandoned agriculture for a musical career. The family moved first to Budapest, then to Brussels, where Emma was a pupil at the Visitation convent, afterwards attending another convent school in Paris. When she was fifteen the family settled in London where she met many musical celebrities. Having no musical talent herself she studied painting at the West London School of Art and at Heatherley's, and whilst still a student had three pictures hung in the Academy. At Heatherley's she met (Henry George) Montague (Maclean) Barstow, a black-and-white artist and illustrator, son of a clergyman, the late Rev. Michael William Barstow. Their marriage took place in 1894 and their only child, a son, was born in 1899.

With her husband, Baroness Orczy wrote and illustrated some volumes of children's stories, but her career as a writer really began with a short story, 'Juliette', published in August 1899 in the *Royal Magazine*. Her first novel, *The Emperor's Candlesticks*, appeared the same year. It was a failure, but she had considerable success with a series of crime stories in the *Royal Magazine*, entitled 'The Old Man in the Corner'. In 1902 she wrote *The Scarlet Pimpernel*, a novel of the French revolution. The manuscript was rejected by at least twelve publishers, but a dramatic version, written in collaboration with her husband, was accepted for production with Fred Terry [q.v.] and Julia Neilson in the leading parts. Produced in Nottingham in the autumn of 1903, the play did not appear in London until 1905, when, after an unpromising start, it achieved phenomenal popularity. Until Terry's death in 1933 it was regularly revived in London and the provinces, whilst translations appeared abroad in French, German, Spanish, and Italian. The first London production coincided with the publication of the novel, which proved an immense and immediate success. Its hero, Sir Percy Blakeney, the indolent British aristocrat who, as the mysterious Scarlet Pimpernel, rescued victims from the guillotine, quickly became and remained to successive generations one of the best-known characters in popular fiction.

Baroness Orczy was henceforth a prolific writer, producing two and sometimes three books in a year. Several of them were filmed, including *The Scarlet Pimpernel*, played by Leslie Howard [q.v.]. With the exception of an autobiography, a biography of the Duchesse de Berri, and the early crime stories, all are historical romances. The emphasis is definitely on romance rather than history, but a real gift for narrative and for simple characterization distinguish the unsophisticated, swift-moving stories with which she delighted a huge public.

In 1906 Baroness Orczy inherited the property of Tarna-Örs, but she continued to live in England until the end of the war of 1914–18, when she and her husband settled in Monte Carlo. There they were obliged to remain throughout the war of 1939–45, Montague Barstow dying in 1943. Baroness Orczy herself died in London 12 November 1947.

[Baroness Orczy, *Links in the Chain of Life*, 1947; *The Times*, 13 November 1947; private information.] GEORGINA BATTISCOMBE.

**ORTON, CHARLES WILLIAM PREVITÉ-** (1877–1947), historian and editor. [See PREVITÉ-ORTON.]

**ORWELL, GEORGE** (pseudonym), author. [See BLAIR, ERIC ARTHUR.]

**OXFORD AND ASQUITH, COUNTESS OF** (1864–1945). [See ASQUITH, EMMA ALICE MARGARET.]

**PAGE, SIR ARCHIBALD** (1875–1949), engineer and administrator in electricity supply, was born at Alloa, Scotland, 5 September 1875, the only son of John Page, wool merchant, by his second wife, Helen Ann McKillop. His general education was gained at Alloa School and Dollar Academy. After two years of technical training at the Heriot-Watt College, Edinburgh, he served a full apprenticeship in mechanical engineering and supplemented it by a period of electrical engineering with Mavor and Coulson, of Glasgow, who were among the British pioneers in the construction of electrical plant. Meanwhile he added to his theoretical knowledge by studies at the Glasgow and West of Scotland (later Royal) Technical College.

Recognizing the potentialities of electricity supply, he obtained, in 1899, a position as a mechanic in the Port Dundas generating station of the Glasgow corporation electricity department, and ultimately became deputy city electrical engineer. This early progress was due entirely to his sterling qualities as a man and as a practical engineer. He improved the efficiency of the existing generating stations and interconnected them; he installed new plant of, for those times, great capacity; and he planned the first major municipal power-station at Dalmarnock. At about this time he became fully imbued with the principles of electricity supply development advocated by C. H. Merz [q.v.] and he was thereafter invariably guided by them. He examined with meticulous care every plan for which he became responsible and almost invariably suggested improvements. This faculty for constructive criticism had been developed in his purely engineering days when he had to discuss details of plant with the most eminent manufacturing designers.

In 1917 Page joined the Clyde Valley Electric Power Company as deputy manager. Subsequently he became general manager. In that capacity he continued his policy of development on the basis of interconnexion, and acquired a wider experience, in a more difficult territory, of the problems of transmission and distribution. When the Electricity (Supply) Act, 1919, was passed he was an obvious choice as an electricity commissioner, but in 1925 he was called from this administrative appointment to the more specifically constructive post of general manager of the County of London Electric Supply Corporation. His period of office was marked by the construction of the Barking generating station (now one of the largest thermo-electric stations in Europe) and of the associated high-voltage transmission system.

The formation of the Central Electricity Board in 1927 brought Page the final opportunity of his career. With Sir Andrew Rae Duncan as chairman, Page, as general manager, directed the construction of the 'grid' and the standardization of frequency of the national system. The enterprise was conducted with great expedition and spartan economy, both in construction and in operation. This was largely due to the personal example of Page who was knighted in 1930 for his share in the work. In 1935 he succeeded Duncan as chairman of the Board and retired in 1944, although he continued to take a close interest in the industry and its personnel until he died, worn out by excessive toil, 7 March 1949, at Sanderstead, Surrey.

Page's career was planned from first to last and he accomplished, so far as any individual can, all that he set out to do. He read omnivorously documents and publications essential to his duties and relating to electrical engineering, but his general reading was mainly in the book of life. International and foreign electrical developments interested him in a minor degree, mainly to enable him to assess the relative efficiency of Britain and other countries. He was very British in his outlook, and his main business characteristics were objectivity, reliability, thoroughness, and an untiring energy. He was kind, helpful, and had an ironical sense of humour which he exercised on rare occasions to great effect. Almost his only recreations were gardening and an occasional visit to a Rugby international. He loved Scotland and spent each of his annual holidays in the Highlands.

In 1943 he was awarded the Faraday medal of the Institution of Electrical Engineers of which he became a member in 1909 and an honorary member in 1939, serving as president in 1927.

In 1906 Page married Anne, daughter of John Forsyth, a merchant, of Clackmannan; there were one son and three daughters of the marriage. A portrait of Page by James Gunn is in the possession of the family.

[Private information; personal knowledge.]
C. W. MARSHALL.

PAGET, DAME (MARY) ROSALIND (1855–1948), social reformer, nurse, and midwife, was born 4 January 1855 at Greenbank, Liverpool, in the home of her grandfather, William Rathbone (1787–1868, q.v.), whose daughter Elizabeth married John Paget [q.v.]. Her father, who became a London police magistrate, was an ardent Whig who had joined the Reform Club on its foundation, whilst on her mother's side she came of a long line of social reformers, of whom the most recent to be noticed in this DICTIONARY is her cousin, Eleanor Rathbone. Like her, Rosalind Paget seems to have imbibed this atmosphere of public and social service with enthusiasm, oblivious to the attractions of ordinary society. Florence Nightingale was then at the height of her fame and Rosalind Paget, turning her thoughts to the relief of suffering, sought such training in nursing as was then obtainable. At the age of twenty she entered the Westminster Hospital, and went later to the London Hospital (1882–4) and the British Lying-In Hospital at Endell Street. In the course of her work she came to realize the need to protect the infant life of this country through the better education of the mid-wives who brought it into the world. At that time the word midwife was not mentioned in polite society. Although the attendants upon childbirth were often devoted and capable women, they received very little, if any, instruction, and there was much need for reform.

Rosalind Paget returned to the London Hospital where she remained for some years, but she was by this time closely in touch with midwifery questions, for in 1881 she and a small group of women also deeply interested had founded the Mid-wives' Institute, later the Royal College of Midwives. Her object was to obtain better education and training for mid-wives, and to encourage in them that public spirit which has for so long been a marked feature of the profession. A bill for the registration of midwives was introduced into the House of Commons in 1890, but although England in this respect lagged behind most European countries, the measure was continually rejected, mainly because it was considered an unnecessary restriction of individual liberty. In some quarters the advent of trained midwives was felt to be an encroachment not only upon the friendly services of neighbours but also upon the medical profession. Rosalind Paget knew that poor women could not in any case afford medical attention and insisted that it was wholly advantageous for the midwife to be trained and supervised. Finally in 1902 the Midwives Act provided for the regis-tration of midwives, made it an offence for anyone not properly certificated to describe herself or practise as a midwife, and established the Central Midwives Board. Rosalind Paget remained for many years a member of the Board as repre-sentative of the Queen's Institute which had been founded for district nursing by Queen Victoria who had enrolled her as the first Queen's nurse in 1891.

Rosalind Paget was also one of the founders of what later became the Char-tered Society of Physiotherapy, and in 1887 she founded *Nursing Notes* (which became the *Midwives Chronicle*) which she edited for many years. She never married and throughout the whole of her professional life she devoted herself

entirely to the work she took in hand; no detail of a midwife's life or work was too trivial for her interest and she was the friend of all. She refused all recognition of her services until in 1935 she was appointed D.B.E. She found relaxation in music and art, tastes inherited from her father, and died at the age of ninety-three, 19 August 1948, at Bolney, Sussex. There is a portrait by Stella Canzini at the Royal College of Midwives.

[Private information; personal knowledge.]
E. M. PYE.

PALMER, WILLIAM WALDE-GRAVE, second EARL OF SELBORNE (1859–1942), statesman, only son and youngest of the five children of Roundell Palmer [q.v.], created Earl of Selborne in 1882, was born at 30 Portland Place, London, 17 October 1859. He was edu-cated at Temple Grove, East Sheen, and Winchester. His Winchester days were happy and not undistinguished; although unlike his father he never rose to heights of classical scholarship, he won the English silver medal. Edward Grey (later Viscount Grey of Fallodon, q.v.) was his fag. He went up to University College, Oxford, in 1878, and in 1881 appeared with one other candidate in the first class in the recently created honour school of modern history. He showed then as subsequently very good ability without literary brilliance or strictly scholarly qualities, keen insight into practical issues, and a great capacity for concentration. He had a strong desire to make the army his career, but this was overridden by his father who persuaded him to choose politics.

He therefore became private secretary, first to his father as lord chancellor, then to H. C. E. Childers [q.v.] at the War Office and later at the Treasury, thus rapidly acquiring an insight into the work of three great departments of State. On his father's elevation to an earldom, Palmer obtained the courtesy title of Viscount Wolmer. He was elected Liberal member for the Petersfield division of Hampshire after a keen fight in 1885, and a year later, rejecting Gladstone's Home Rule policy, he contested the same seat with equal success as a Liberal Unionist. For ten years until his father's death in 1895 he sat in the House of Commons, during much of this time serving as a popular and energetic Liberal Unionist whip responsible for the organization of the party in the country as well as in the

House. His exact forecast during the election of 1892 that there would be a Home Rule majority of forty reveals his political acumen. He decided for that election not to stand again at Petersfield and became candidate for West Edinburgh where he won the seat from the Liberals by five hundred votes: of this victory he was justly proud since few Englishmen have ever sat for Edinburgh.

On his father's death he decided to test the constitutional issue whether succession to a peerage of the United Kingdom necessarily involved relinquishing a seat in the House of Commons, and attempted to continue to sit as member for West Edinburgh. After a lively debate a select committee was appointed which found against him, and West Edinburgh was declared vacant. Within a few months the general election brought in Salisbury's third Government, the Liberal Unionist leaders supporting the Conservatives. Selborne was appointed under-secretary of state for the Colonies with Joseph Chamberlain as his chief. The five years in which he held this office covered the Jameson raid, the West Africa settlement with France, the first Imperial Conference, the South African war, and the passing of the Commonwealth of Australia Constitution Act. He had to defend his chief's policy in the upper House and from time to time, when Chamberlain was abroad, he was in a highly responsible position.

In the autumn of 1900 Selborne succeeded G. J. (later Viscount) Goschen [q.v.] as first lord of the Admiralty and was sworn of the Privy Council. The next five years were epoch-making in the history of the navy. The technical knowledge, driving force, and dynamic personality of Sir John (later Lord) Fisher [q.v.] were behind most of these changes, but the promotion of Fisher from the Mediterranean command to the Admiralty as second sea lord in 1902 was due to Selborne's personal foresight and courage. The step was deliberately taken in order to promote the educational changes which Selborne had himself independently resolved to pursue. These took shape in the establishment of the naval colleges at Osborne and Dartmouth, the Royal Naval War College, and the system of common entry and training for all naval officers, executive and engineer alike, whereby the field of selection was greatly widened and an invidious social distinction modified. The new method of selection after interview and examination fully justified itself. In 1903 he gave Fisher the Portsmouth command to see the new scheme carried out, and then called him back to the Admiralty when the post of first sea lord fell vacant in 1904. While he was first lord he had great difficulty in resisting the pressure of the Treasury to reduce expenditure at a time when the menace of the new German navy forced upon the Admiralty both construction and strategic reorganization. The wholesale scrapping of out-of-date vessels helped to solve the problem. The establishment of the Committee of Imperial Defence owed much to Selborne's personal initiative and pressure on the Cabinet. The introduction of wireless telegraphy, of submarines, of water-tube boilers, steam turbines, fuel oil, and the establishment of the naval base at Rosyth were among the decisions of the boards over which he presided. When he left the Admiralty the design for the *Dreadnought* had been accepted, the navy in all its branches had been brought to the highest level of efficiency, notably in gunnery, the defences of Gibraltar and Malta had been strengthened, and the system for manning the fleet had been overhauled. He had set up the committee on naval reserves which led to the formation of the Royal Naval Volunteer Reserve and the creation of the Royal Fleet Reserve of short-service men ('Selborne's Light Horse').

In 1904 Selborne accepted the prime minister's suggestion that he should succeed Lord Curzon [q.v.] as viceroy of India, but the decision that Curzon should return to India for a further period nullified the proposal. The suggestion was renewed in 1905 but by that time Selborne was already fully engaged and highly interested in his work in South Africa and thought it his duty to refuse.

In 1905 Selborne was appointed high commissioner for South Africa and governor of the two newly annexed colonies of the Transvaal and Orange River. The brilliant constructive work of Lord Milner [q.v.] had left problems behind it. The introduction of Chinese labour into the Transvaal mines in 1904, although economically necessary as a temporary measure, became politically untenable on the advent of a Liberal Government. Selborne had been only a few months in South Africa when Balfour resigned, and he never had the full support of Lord Elgin [q.v.] who then went to the Colonial Office. Selborne considered Elgin's determination to prevent Witwatersrand control at the risk of a Boer majority in the new Transvaal constitution unwise, and unfair to British interests; and he incurred the censure of the Cabinet when they misunderstood the way in which he used his influence at the time of the West Ridgeway committee. More than once in 1906 he was near to resignation, but he believed it was to the interest of South Africa and the Empire that he should remain, and bore in silence the rejection of his advice by the colonial secretary. Elgin, however, gave him better support in his work of achieving the settlement of Swaziland in 1908–9 for which he made use of the services of George Grey, the brother of the foreign secretary.

Selborne was, however, remarkably successful in winning the confidence of the old Boer population. Without this the Union of South Africa, which was largely the achievement of his personal statesmanship, could not have been effected. After careful preparation and at the request of all the colonies concerned he issued in January 1907 the famous Selborne memorandum recommending a central national Government. This was published in a Cape blue book and in a paper presented in July to the imperial Parliament. In May 1908 it was resolved to hold a National Convention to draft a constitution for South Africa. The convention met in Durban in October and again in Cape Town and Bloemfontein. Selborne's personal part in the work of the convention, of which he was not a member but with which he was in daily touch, consisted chiefly in furthering its progress by work behind the scenes. He also strove with considerable success to protect the interests of the natives of Basutoland, Swaziland, and Bechuanaland. He accompanied the delegates to London and helped the British Government in seeing the South Africa Act of 1909 through the imperial Parliament. In July he was rewarded with the Order of the Garter in recognition of 'the strong and grateful sense on the part of H.M. present Government of his loyal and efficient co-operation during the last four years in a peculiarly difficult situation'. He returned to South Africa in September, but it was decided that the first governor-general of the new Union of South Africa must be a party appointment. His last act in South Africa was to persuade his successor (Lord Gladstone, q.v.) that the first prime minister of the Union should be Louis

Botha [q.v.]. He left South Africa amid universal regret. He carried the standard of South Africa at the coronation of King George V.

In the next five years of Liberal government Selborne was free from the burdens of office, but was prominent during the political crisis which led to the Parliament Act of 1911 and was among those to whom the term 'Diehard' was originally applied. He refused to believe that the interests of the House of Lords or of the country could be served by voting under pressure against his convictions. He was active in promoting the Halsbury Club and ardently advocated reform of the upper House.

In May 1915 he joined the first coalition ministry as president of the Board of Agriculture and Fisheries. Foreseeing the gravity of the submarine menace he worked hard to increase production of home-grown food, but failed to convince the Cabinet of the necessity of the measures which he advocated, among which was a guaranteed minimum price for wheat. In 1915 he appointed the Acland advisory committee on home-grown timber which led to the establishment of the Forestry Commission. In June 1916 he resigned office on the Government's Irish policy. He had a rooted distrust of Lloyd George and subsequently refused offers from him of the viceroyalty of India, the viceroyalty of Ireland, and a marquessate.

He was made chairman of the agricultural policy sub-committee of the Reconstruction Committee which in 1917 supported his views on wheat prices, advocated a minimum wage for farm labourers fixed by wages boards, and State powers to enforce good cultivation. These were embodied in the Corn Production Act of 1917. The final report of this sub-committee remains of permanent value as a survey of British agricultural conditions.

In 1919 he was elected chairman of the joint committee of both Houses of Parliament on the bill to carry out the recommendations of the Montagu–Chelmsford report on India, but the bill which it produced was little to his liking.

In his later years his political activities grew less, but he worked hard for women's suffrage, for the reform of the House of Lords and the revision of the Parliament Act. His concern for a wise agricultural policy never left him. His views as an elder statesman found frequent expression in letters to The Times, notable for their brevity and directness. His wide interests and balanced judgement, backed by a strong, fearless, and lovable nature and deep religious convictions, made his influence considerable. During these years he undertook much work in Hampshire. An original alderman of the Hampshire County Council in 1886, he filled the ancient office of lord high steward of Winchester from 1929 until his death. He was warden of Winchester College from 1920 to 1925. In 1905 he was appointed G.C.M.G.; he was an elder brother of Trinity House from 1904; and he received the honorary degrees of LL.D. from Cambridge (1910) and D.C.L. from Oxford (1911).

Selborne's father had been one of the great ecclesiastical statesmen of the Victorian era, and throughout his life Selborne carried on this work. He was chairman of the commission appointed by the archbishops in 1913 whose recommendations were effected by the constitution of the Church Assembly and the Enabling Act of 1919. He was the first chairman of the central board of finance, and from 1924 until his death he was chairman of the House of Laity in the Church Assembly. He took a chief part in winning the approval of the House of Lords for the Prayer Book measure of 1927. After its rejection by the Commons he became a member of the Archbishops' Commission on the Relations between Church and State which made its report in 1935. His last official act was to assist as chairman of the House of Laity in welcoming the King at the opening of the new Church House in 1940.

In 1883 Selborne married Lady Beatrix Maud Cecil (died 1950), daughter of the third Marquess of Salisbury [q.v.], then leader of the Opposition. They had three sons and one daughter. The second son was killed in action in Mesopotamia in 1916. Selborne died at his home in London 26 February 1942, and was succeeded by his eldest son, Roundell Cecil (born 1887), who had just been appointed minister of economic warfare in (Sir) Winston Churchill's Government, and who contributes to this SUPPLEMENT. Portraits by P. A. de László hang in Church House, and Mercers' Hall, London, and Blackmoor House, Liss.

[Public and private papers; personal knowledge.]                    J. S. BREWIS.

PARES, SIR BERNARD (1867–1949), historian of Russia, was born at Albury, Surrey, 1 March 1867, the third son and seventh of the ten children of John Pares, of independent means, who later lived in Portsmouth. His mother was Katharine, daughter of John Back, J.P., of Byfleet, Surrey, and niece of Sir George Back [q.v.]. From Harrow, Pares went as a foundation scholar to Trinity College, Cambridge, where he read classics, being placed in the second class in part i of the tripos (1887) and in the third class in part ii (1889). After spending some years as a schoolmaster, he decided to turn to history, and studied in France, Italy, and Germany with an especial interest in Napoleon's battlefields which may have led, in 1898, to his first journey to Russia. Thereafter he made Russia his principal study and, after a spell as a Cambridge extension lecturer during which he married, he was appointed reader in Russian history in the university of Liverpool (1906–8), then professor of Russian history, language, and literature in the same university (1908–17). From 1914 until 1917 he was attached to the Russian Army and in 1917 to the British ambassador in Petrograd. He was appointed K.B.E. in 1919 for his services. From 1919 until 1936 he was professor of Russian language, literature, and history in the university of London. In 1922 he became, in addition, director of the School of Slavonic and East European Studies at King's College which, under his guidance, expanded to become, in 1932, a 'central activity' of the university. He retired in 1939.

Pares's whole life was spent in interpreting Russia to the English-speaking world, a task which he undertook with missionary zeal and many-sided enthusiasm. On the one hand, he was a pioneer for the recognition of Russian studies in the universities, by which he meant not only the study of Russian language and literature but also, through a knowledge of the language, of Russian history and society. On the other hand, he was tireless in his efforts, by lecturing and writing, to bring a knowledge of Russian affairs to a circle much wider than that touched by the universities. Before the war of 1914–18, too, he worked to develop friendly relations between Englishmen and Russians, and, as secretary of the Anglo-Russian Committee in London (1909–14), arranged visits of distinguished British representatives to Russia and of representatives of the Russian Duma to England. This side of his work was brought to an end by the revolution of

1917, and although in the 'thirties he made visits to Russia once more, he was frustrated in his ardent desire to establish effective cultural contacts between the two countries.

By the historical student Pares will be remembered for his *History of Russia* (1926) and *The Fall of the Russian Monarchy* (1939); and by the wider public for his *Russia* (1940) which had an immense popularity. The discriminating will perhaps remember best his translations of Krylov's *Fables* (1926), in which he made the Russian originals live anew in English. Apart from his books, however, there were many newspaper articles (particularly in the *Daily Telegraph* and *Manchester Guardian*) in which at various times he published his enlightened comments on Russian affairs; and his editorship (with R. W. Seton-Watson and others) of the *Slavonic Review*, founded in 1922 as the organ of the School of Slavonic Studies, was notable for the collection of articles by many experts on different aspects of Russian and Slavonic affairs.

Although Pares was a very friendly man with a great love of people, his personal life was not happy. Possibly because of this he found great consolation in his love of Russia, and he succeeded in identifying himself with her people as perhaps no other Englishman has done. The revolution of 1917 was a great grief to him, for it destroyed his hopes of a liberalizing movement in Russian government and sent many of his acquaintances to death or exile. The Russia which he loved remained therefore for the rest of his life very much the Russia he had known in the early years of the twentieth century, when he had lived among Russians of every degree. When he talked of this period he was as a man possessed and would recount his varied experiences as if reliving them.

He was one of the first Englishmen to see the threat to the Soviet Union implicit in the Nazi triumph in 1933 and quick to resume his never-forgotten purpose of bringing Englishmen and Russians closer together. On his first visit to the Soviet Union in 1935–6 he was delighted to find that the revolution had not greatly changed the Russian people and that he still felt at home among them. This discovery renewed the fervour with which he pursued his task which culminated, after a brief period in 1939 when he was attached to the Foreign Office, in his nation-wide war-time lecturing tours of

Britain in 1941–2 and of North America after 1942. The last years of his life were clouded over again by the collapse of the alliance between the Soviet Union and the English-speaking democracies of the West, but he refused to lose heart, and was urging up to the end of his life the need for serious study of Russia. His enthusiasm for his subject transcended political barriers, and for fifty years he worked with a singleness of purpose which cared little for the opinion of others.

Pares married in 1901 Margaret Ellis, daughter of Edward Austin Dixon, of Colchester. They had three sons (one of whom has contributed to this SUPPLEMENT) and two daughters. Pares died in New York 17 April 1949. A bronze plaque by Paul Vincze commemorates him in the university of London School of Slavonic and East European Studies. He is also one of a group painted by Albert Lipczinski (1915) of some of the staff (e.g. (Sir) Charles Reilly, John Sampson, Oliver Elton, qq.v.) of the university of Liverpool where the painting hangs in the common-room of the faculty of arts.

[Sir Bernard Pares, *My Russian Memoirs*, 1931, and *A Wandering Student*, New York, 1948; *Slavonic Review*, November 1949; personal knowledge.]   DOROTHY GALTON.

[Preface by Richard Pares to the 1955 edition of the *History of Russia*.]

PARKER, LOUIS NAPOLEON (1852–1944), musician, playwright, and inventor of 'pageants', was born at Luc-sur-Mer in Normandy 21 October 1852, the only son of an American, Charles Albert Parker, by his wife, Elizabeth Moray, an Englishwoman. His grandfather, Isaac Parker (1768–1830), had been chief justice of the Supreme Judicial Court of Massachusetts; but his father at the age of thirty-nine abandoned the law, and began a wandering life in Europe, seldom caring to remain more than a year in any one place. He was temporarily absent when his son was born, and as the child was thought to be dying and the mother could then speak no French, the Frenchman who christened him named him after the then ruler of France, Louis Napoleon. In his eventual English career these names, together with the dark hair and skin which he inherited from his mother, gave him an exotic stamp, despite his intense pro-English feeling.

Parker's first fourteen years were spent with his parents wandering in Italy, Germany, Switzerland, Belgium, France—

chiefly the first two. Not the least striking feature in his charming autobiography, *Several of My Lives* (1928), is the vivid descriptions of those countries before 1866—Rome under Pius IX (who blessed the child), Venice under the Austrians, southern Italy with its brigands, but above all pre-Bismarckian romantic Germany with so many capitals and semi-capitals, each with palace and opera house complete. The boy's first language was Italian, to which he soon added German and French; English was a later acquisition. His regular education was inevitably haphazard; but from his earliest years he was taken constantly to operas and plays, and so obtained an intimate sense of the stage and an everyday familiarity with music, which together shaped his later careers. In 1866 his parents brought him to England, but still kept wandering; and his first settled education began at seventeen, when he was sent to the Royal Academy of Music, of which the principal was then (Sir) William Sterndale Bennett [q.v.].

So the first of Parker's three main careers was music. At the Academy he quickly came to the fore as singer, pianist, and organist. In 1873 Bennett, whose son James was director of music at Sherborne School, asked Parker to go there for six weeks as locum tenens for the piano master. He went, and stayed nineteen years, succeeding Bennett in 1877. They were eventful years, for he not only raised the school's music to a higher level than any public school had till then attained, but he made the town a musical centre with influence radiating far over Somerset and Dorset. He was one of the first English Wagnerians, an early member of the original Wagner Society and, after it ended, president of its successor. He was also a composer with a distinct vein of his own; he equipped Sherborne School with a remarkable set of school songs; and of his three cantatas two, *Silvia* and *Young Tamlane*, show his gift for melody in a most favourable light. But two things ended this career—a temporary but disastrous decline of Sherborne School and, more serious, the onset of deafness. The last left him no future in teaching, conducting, or choir-training. Fortunately another career lay ready for him. For some years his dramatic bent had impelled him to attempt plays; and before he left Sherborne for London (1892) he had had three successes with short pieces and two long ones accepted.

Yet his new career was very uphill. Only dauntless tenacity and fertility carried him through. In November 1893 with *Gudgeons* (in collaboration with Murray Carson) he first attained big box-office success both in London and in America. In 1896 *Rosemary* (again with Murray Carson) much more than repeated it; and thenceforward for twenty years he was one of the best-known playwrights, alternating failures and successes. His most famous plays were *The Cardinal* (1903), *Disraeli* (1911), *Drake* (1912), *Joseph and his Brethren* (1913), and (with W. W. Jacobs, q.v.) *Beauty and the Barge* (1904); to which may be added *Pomander Walk* (1910), which for years broke records in America, though (through bad casting) it failed in London. Parker was also an admirable translator (*L'Aiglon* and *Rosmersholm*) and adaptor (*David Copperfield*, and *The Monkey's Paw* by Jacobs—these two perhaps his most sensitive pieces). Many of his London triumphs were obtained at His Majesty's Theatre under Sir Herbert Tree [q.v.], but they were often anticipated by great successes in America. In Italy *The Cardinal* is a classic played regularly.

Parker's third career—pageant-making—overlapped the second. It began in 1905 with the pageant at Sherborne. He had never ceased to love that beautiful town, and the precincts of its ruined Norman castle gave him a perfect arena. The success of his invention—which with 900 performers achieved seven performances—was quite outstanding; and requests poured in from elsewhere. He organized five more pageants on the great scale—at Warwick, Bury St. Edmunds, Colchester, York, and Dover—besides a few smaller ones. Both his aims and his technique are well summarized in *Several of My Lives.* Unfortunately his many imitators seldom grasped them; they commercialized and vulgarized. But Parker's own standards were extremely high. Few who saw one of his pageants, and still fewer of the thousands who performed in them, but had a memorable experience. On the artistic side, all his sense of stage colour and movement, as developed from his earliest childhood, found here its full scope. His handling of crowds was masterly. On the cultural side, his pageants essentially expressed the settled prosperous life of the historic England as it was before the world wars. Parker himself became a British subject two months before the outbreak of war in 1914. From 1907 until that war he organized and greatly improved the historical section of the Lord Mayor's Show.

Parker suffered by comparison with contemporary dramatists like Shaw, Galsworthy, and Barrie in that he was too polyglot to be a verbal stylist. Nor was he much concerned, as they were, with social problems. But he was no philistine. Great authors and great composers were his daily bread; and just as he was one of the earliest men in England to appreciate in their turn Wagner, Ibsen, and Maeterlinck, so till a late stage his mind remained open to new things. He was extremely generous, not only in giving away fees to causes and charities, but in writing masques, &c., for them. The last two decades of his very long life were spent chiefly at Bishopsteignton in Devon. In 1936, when he was eighty-four, two things pleased him much—the very successful filming of his play *Disraeli*, written for George Arliss [q.v.], and the choice of his *Lily of France* (Joan of Arc) by the city of Nancy for annual production, which, though interrupted by the war of 1939–45, was afterwards resumed. His last published work was a poem 'Fathers and Sons', in *The Times* of 21 September 1939. He died at Bishopsteignton 21 September 1944.

In 1878 Parker married Georgiana Bessie (died 1919), eldest daughter of Charles Calder, of Sherborne. Parker and his wife were both accomplished figure-skaters in the English style. Of their two daughters the younger, Dorothy, attained some distinction on the stage. An oil-painting of Parker by Sir Philip Burne-Jones is in the possession of the Garrick Club, and a life-size pencil portrait by Cyril Roberts belongs to the family.

[L. N. Parker, *Several of My Lives*, 1928; *The Times*, 22 September 1944; private information; personal knowledge.]

R. C. K. Ensor.

PARMOOR, first Baron (1852–1941), lawyer and politician. [See Cripps, Charles Alfred.]

PARSONS, Sir LEONARD GREGORY (1879–1950), paediatrician, was born at Kidderminster 25 November 1879, the son of Theophilus Lessie Parsons and his wife, Sarah, daughter of Timothy Sharpe, a farmer who migrated to the United States. Parsons came of Worcestershire stock long engaged in farming and

devoted to Wesleyan Methodism. He grew up in a home at Aston in which devout living was inculcated through parental example, education was liberal, and hospitality generous. He attended the King Edward VI Grammar School for five years, where his natural bent for chemistry and his lifelong interest in Rugby football were encouraged. In 1896 he entered Mason College, Birmingham, to study zoology; later he turned to medicine, winning many scholarships and acting for a time as a prosector of anatomy. He qualified M.B., B.S. (London) in 1905. During his university years he found time for the affairs of the Student Christian Movement and missionary activities, as well as for developing his talent as a shot and a sprinter and playing tennis and Rugby with great enthusiasm.

Parsons next held junior hospital appointments at Birmingham and London and practised for a few years at Bromsgrove. His habit of self-criticism and inquiry, and an unusual skill with children diverted him to paediatrics. Postgraduate training at the Hospital for Sick Children, Great Ormond Street, London, followed by his election to the staff of the Birmingham Children's Hospital as physician to out-patients in 1910, culminated in an active term of service as lecturer in diseases of children and paediatrics at the university of Birmingham. The war of 1914–18 saw some interruption of Parsons's career, but his service in Greece and Serbia—he was appointed consulting physician to the Serbian Army and in 1917 received the Order of St. Sava—brought new experience and developed his bent for fruitful criticism.

During the post-war years Parsons established himself as a kindly, diligent doctor, surrounded by keen young investigators who shared his love of children. He was greatly in demand as a consultant and personal attendant to doctors throughout the Midlands and his appointment in 1928 as first professor of child health in the university of Birmingham occasioned no surprise. The following year he was elected sub-dean of the medical faculty. New buildings and equipment were added to the Children's Hospital as Parsons's fame grew and research workers flocked to his busy clinic. So great was his personal influence in Birmingham that by 1930 he was able to gather together representatives from various hospitals, the university, and the city council in an active campaign for the prevention of children's diseases; despite serious interruption with the outbreak of war in 1939 this great project resulted in the opening of the Leonard Parsons infants' block at the Children's Hospital in October 1945 and the establishment of the Institute of Child Health in that year. All through these years, too, Parsons served his university and medical school in many capacities with just and balanced enthusiasm. He supported the hospitals centre plan from which came the fine medical centre at Edgbaston; no less care was given to the humdrum matters of university and medical endeavour, which increased almost beyond human capacity when Parsons was appointed dean of the medical faculty in 1941. Yet he found time for all who sought his advice on medical education, child-welfare, the practice or the problems of post-war medicine. Such demands came his way because he was known to be kind of heart, with a deep appreciation of the individual, quick to grasp the essentials of a problem, and conscientious in his attention to his duty. He retired from his professorship in 1946.

Parsons received many honours. Elected F.R.C.P. (London) in 1923, he was knighted in 1946 for his work for children during the war, and in 1948 he was elected F.R.S. for investigations into child health and the wasting disorders of children. He gave many lectures to noted societies and universities, served as president of many conferences and scientific associations, and received the honorary fellowship of numerous societies for the study of children's diseases. He belonged to the small number of physicians who combine great clinical acumen and original talent for scientific investigation with an eminently practical outlook on everyday affairs. Such gifts mark them out for leadership, and chance often determines whether they excel in public life or in the laboratory. Parsons left his mark on medical affairs in Birmingham, and at the same time the medical research conducted in his laboratory brought it an international reputation. By means of painstaking chemical and clinical studies of the blood of children, Parsons's team tracked down the origin of a serious type of jaundice in the new-born infant, which he proved to result from excessive destruction of the red corpuscles and the consequent stimulation of production of new blood cells in various regions of the body. A serious wasting disease of infants was

shown to set up complicated symptoms because fats and vitamin D are absorbed with difficulty from the intestines. Parsons also added significantly to our knowledge of rickets and through the emphasis he placed upon environment and diet did much to prevent and cure this scourge. Finally, he brought clarity to paediatrics by stressing the importance of ante-natal factors. He saw clearly that deficient diet for, or infection of, the mother might well result in serious disability of the child. By his insistence on the need for quantitative chemical investigation of problems often enough dismissed as peculiar to the child, Parsons greatly helped to raise paediatrics to a high scientific level and opened up hitherto unrealized fields of investigation.

A simple, rather shy man, Parsons had a quick sense of humour and delighted in the company of a wide circle of friends. He was respected as a devout and practising Methodist who read his Bible morning and evening and attended chapel with great regularity. It was shortly after returning from the morning service at the Four Oaks Methodist chapel that he died suddenly from cerebral haemorrhage 17 December 1950.

In 1908 Parsons married Ethel May (died 1955), daughter of the Rev. Dr. John Gregory Mantle, a Wesleyan Methodist minister. He had known her since childhood. They had one son who also became a paediatrician, and one daughter.

[G. R. Cameron in *Obituary Notices of Fellows of the Royal Society*, No. 20, November 1951; private information; personal knowledge.]                    G. R. CAMERON.

PARSONS, RICHARD GODFREY (1882–1948), bishop, was born at Pendleton, Lancashire, 12 November 1882, the only son of William Parsons, merchant, of Calcutta, who became secretary of the Bengal Chamber of Commerce, and his wife, Bertha Best, of Thetford. Educated at Durham School, he became in 1901 a demy of Magdalen College, Oxford, obtaining in 1903 a second class in honour moderations and in 1905 and 1906 first class honours in *literae humaniores* and theology, and being elected to a Liddon studentship. Postgraduate work in Germany was followed by residence at the Deanery, Westminster, as the pupil of J. Armitage Robinson [q.v.], and at Cuddesdon. Ordained deacon and priest at London in 1907, with a curacy at Hampstead parish church, Parsons returned to Oxford the same year as fellow, praelector, and chaplain of University College. He quickly began to make his mark. He combined gravity of manner and maturity of character with wide knowledge, sympathy, and humour, and as a theologian became known as the possessor at once of a constructive outlook and of an honest and fearless mind. In 1911 he was made principal of the Theological College at Wells, and in 1912 was associated with B. H. Streeter, William Temple [qq.v.], and others in the publication of *Foundations*, a book which at the time made a considerable stir, and in which Parsons was one of the joint authors of an essay on 'The Interpretation of the Christ in the New Testament'.

The war had by 1916 practically emptied the college at Wells, and in 1916–17 its principal served as a temporary chaplain to the forces in London. In 1916 he became vicar of Poynton, and in 1919 rector of Birch-in-Rusholme, near Manchester. He combined with his parish activities teaching and organizing work for the university of Manchester, in which in 1929 he became dean of the faculty of theology. He had in 1924 taken the degree of D.D. at Oxford. In collaboration with A. S. Peake [q.v.] he prepared for publication and saw through the press the English edition of *An Outline of Christianity* (1926), a work in five volumes originally planned and produced in America. Consecrated in 1927 as bishop of Middleton, he combined until 1931 work as a suffragan bishop with his other already too numerous commitments, but in 1931 he was enabled to shed the cares of his parish by becoming residentiary canon and sub-dean of Manchester. In 1932 Parsons became bishop of Southwark, one of the heaviest and most arduous dioceses in England. Four years later he held a visitation of his diocese, and published a charge bearing the title *The Sacrament of Sacrifice*. But he was much more than a theologian. His deep interest in social problems, together with his wide knowledge and experience, enabled him to enter with insight as well as with sympathy into the lives of his people, who in south London included large numbers of poor working folk.

In the winter of 1940 the diocese suffered heavy bombardment from the air. The bishop shared in the strain, suffering, and perils of his people. Morning by morning the details reached him of parishes devastated, casualties mounting, churches and vicarages destroyed.

His own courage, fortitude, faith, and devotion to duty were an inspiration to those about him, but the strain told on his health. Translation to Hereford in 1941 brought relief and refreshment of spirit and, for a time, renewed health. He loved his new diocese and was able to live and work there and to make his contribution to the wider life of the Church over a period of years. He paid visits to Romania and Yugoslavia: he acted as chairman in 1947 of an inter-Church conference between theologians of the Anglican Church and theologians from Denmark and Iceland. But his health failed again, and he died in Hereford 26 December 1948. He had been since 1942 an honorary fellow of University College, Oxford, and in 1946 he became an honorary D.D. of the John Hus faculty at Prague.

Parsons was a man of mellow wisdom, who made a considerable impact upon the religious and ecclesiastical life of his generation. He had a wide outlook upon Christendom, and a wide circle of friends. He was a wise, charitable, learned, and lovable man. In 1912 he married Dorothy (died 1953), only daughter of Francis Gales Streeter, of Littlehampton and Dunsfold. They had two sons, the elder of whom died of wounds in Egypt in 1942. There is a portrait of Parsons by T. Binney Gibbs at The Palace, Hereford.

[Personal knowledge.]

JOHN DERBY. (A. E. J. RAWLINSON.)

PARTRIDGE, SIR BERNARD (1861–1945), *Punch* artist and cartoonist, was born in London 11 October 1861, the sixth child and third son of Richard Partridge, F.R.S. [q.v.], by his wife, Fanny Turner. His father was professor of anatomy at the Royal Academy and later president of the Royal College of Surgeons, and an uncle, John Partridge [q.v.], was portrait painter extraordinary to Queen Victoria. Bernard Partridge himself was educated at Stonyhurst. Beginning as a stained-glass designer, he was for some time on the stage under the name of Bernard Gould, acted under (Sir) Henry Irving and (Sir) Johnston Forbes-Robertson [qq.v.] and played the part of Sergius Saranoff in the first performance of *Arms and the Man* by G. B. Shaw [q.v.] in 1894. He joined the staff of *Punch* in 1891, and served as junior cartoonist under E. Linley Sambourne [q.v.], succeeding him as second cartoonist in 1901 and as principal cartoonist in 1909. His first political picture appeared in *Punch* of 1899, and his last on 18 April 1945, so that his career in this work was nearly as long as that of Sir John Tenniel [q.v.] and his years of service to *Punch* longer. Ninety-four years of *Punch* cartoons were covered by these two men.

The influence of the theatre was evident in the drawings of Bernard Partridge and he seemed to make his cartoons a stage on which he mounted any scene and setting of tragedy or comedy, faultlessly delineated, and correctly costumed. He was not so vivacious as Tenniel, but a better draughtsman, and his knowledge of historical periods and their proper setting made almost any subject safe in his hands. He seldom burlesqued his characters, although he could do so with considerable power when the occasion served; his general fidelity to truth saved him from the difficulty experienced by cartoonists when called upon to deal with tragic events, or to administer encouragement rather than rebuke. His likenesses were excellent, and he greatly helped to establish all those stock figures of the political cartoon at home and abroad, human or animal, which are recognized by the world.

He was probably at his best in heroic or grandiose scenes, and many of his cartoons during the wars of 1914–18 and 1939–45 were as effective as they were powerful and dignified. Very handsome and courteous, he was often spoken of by his colleagues as one of the last of the Victorians. He occasionally painted in oil, water-colour, and pastel, and exhibited at the Royal Academy and the New English Art Club. He received a knighthood in 1925. In 1897 he married Lydia Faith, daughter of Edward Harvey, of independent means; there were no children. He died in London 9 August 1945. A collection of his drawings, 'Mr. Punch's Personalities, 1926–1929', is at the National Portrait Gallery where there is also a drawing of himself in chalk and wash on paper.

[*The Times*, 11 August 1945; private information; personal knowledge.]

E. V. KNOX.

PASSFIELD, BARON (1859–1947), social reformer and historian. [See WEBB, SIDNEY JAMES.]

PATEL, VALLABHBHAI JAVERABHAI (1875–1950), deputy prime minister of India, was born 31 October 1875 at Karamsad near Anand in Gujerat, the son of Javerabhai Patel, a *patidar*, or peasant proprietor holding a share in the village, and his wife, Shrimati Ladbai. Javerabhai is said to have taken some part against the British Government in 1857. Vallabhbhai, the younger brother of Vithalbai Patel [q.v.], studied at the Nadiad and Baroda high schools, passed the district pleaders' examination, and set up practice first at Godhra and later at Borsad, preferring criminal to civil law. He entered the Middle Temple and was called to the bar in 1913, receiving a certificate of honour. Returning to India he resumed practice at Ahmedabad, acquiring a reputation as a fearless and outspoken defence counsel. In 1916 he first met M. K. Gandhi [q.v.] who was then in Ahmedabad, but at first Patel 'kept himself cynically and sarcastically aloof'. It was not surprising. He was then 'a smart young man dressed in tiptop English Style', and superficially nothing would seem less likely to appeal to his hard-headed realism than Gandhi's Franciscan idealism. But, having been elected to the Ahmedabad municipality, Patel became chairman of the sanitary committee and stood to his post throughout an epidemic of plague, thus first revealing his passionate sense of public duty. It was Gandhi's refusal to obey the order of a magistrate in Champaran in 1917 which first showed Patel a means for nationalists to assert their will. There followed vigorous action in the campaign of civil disobedience, notably his organization of the Kaira no-tax campaign in 1918, in which he was Gandhi's lieutenant for Gujerat; his defence of persons accused under martial law in 1919; and his leadership of the Nagpur flag campaign in 1923. By the mid-twenties he was a national as well as a Gujerati leader. He was president of the Gujerat provincial Congress committee (1921) and for four years (1924–8) president of the Ahmedabad municipality.

In 1928 Patel led civil disobedience in Bardoli, a sub-district of Surat, and was given by general consent the title 'Sardar' or 'leader'. The peasants claimed that a recent enhancement of land revenue did not take sufficient account of improvements they had made themselves; Patel organized a general refusal to pay taxes and eventually secured a reduction. He also helped to organize the civil disobedience movement of 1930 and was imprisoned just before Gandhi's march to the sea. The following year he became president of the Congress, only to return to jail in January 1932 after the failure of the second Round Table conference. He was released in 1934 on medical grounds. In the following year, with Maulana Kalam Azad and Rajendra Prasad, he formed the parliamentary sub-committee which later guided the Congress ministries when they took office in seven provinces. This control attracted criticism at the time; less defensible in terms of parliamentary democracy was the claim now made by Congress to represent all shades of nationalist opinion. The consequent refusal to share office with non-Congress Moslems was perhaps the most serious mistake which Congress made during the period before partition.

The Congress ministries resigned after the outbreak of war in 1939. Patel was imprisoned in the autumn of 1940 and released the following year. In August 1942 Congress launched the 'Quit India' campaign, a move in which so shrewd a calculator as Patel could hardly have acquiesced had he not believed it possible to make a better settlement with Japan than with Great Britain. Patel and other leaders were imprisoned until June 1945 when Lord Wavell [q.v.] began the negotiations which ended in the transfer of power in August 1947. In these negotiations Patel played a leading part and he took office as home member in 1946 when the interim Government was set up with Mr. Nehru as vice-president. In July 1947 Patel assumed the important portfolio of the States and on the transfer of power became deputy prime minister, retaining the three portfolios of home, information and broadcasting, and the States.

In the years which followed, Patel was mainly responsible for two great achievements, the maintenance of order and the integration of the former princely states into one unitary system. The transfer of power was accompanied by much disorder and a loss of life never accurately estimated. The unity, the organization, and the discipline of the Congress Party were largely due to Patel; he had to maintain in office a discipline created in opposition —almost in revolution—to restore order and to meet the twofold threat of the Communists on the left and on the right the militant Hindus who were bitterly disappointed by partition. Patel dealt firmly and courageously with both. The unification of the princely states was a

more spectacular though not more valuable achievement. From the anarchy of the early eighteenth century had emerged nearly 600 jurisdictions bound by treaty to the paramount power. While since 1919 British India had received regular and increasing injections of democratic responsibility, the states had been allotted no more than their rulers could be persuaded to concede. Since the consulate of Lord Dalhousie, the rights of the princes and the autonomy of the states had been respected, perhaps over-scrupulously. The British Government was committed to the doctrine, legally unassailable but hardly realistic, that paramountcy could not be transferred. The states were therefore left to make their own terms with the new Dominions. In what followed, Patel directed: swiftly, yet quite ruthlessly, the smaller states were merged in the normal provincial administration, while larger blocks were formed into unitary systems with rights similar to those of the former provinces. In Junagadh, armed intervention was considered necessary; in Hyderabad there was 'police action' by the military, and a military occupation. Within two years, the princes were either pensioned off or re-employed as presidents of the new blocks.

Patel has been compared to Bismarck, but the parallel cannot be carried far; Patel was courageous, honest, and realistic, but far from cynical. The Congress Party, founded by an English Liberal, never forgot its Gladstonian sources even when its ways led among big business; the shrewd politician and man of affairs who spent his life in the service of the Congress was fundamentally a man of ideals and his understanding of the use of idealists suggests Cavour rather than Bismarck. His natural temper was authoritative but he never allowed himself to be persuaded by love of his own way into seeing things as they were not; he accepted the discipline he imposed and gave up personal views not acceptable to the party. Hindu though he was, he accepted partition as the price of independence and was loyal to the ideal of a secular State. He believed it to be essential to find a *modus vivendi* with a neighbour and there is some reason to believe that in the later stages of the Kashmir dispute his emphasis was more on a peaceful settlement than on prestige. While the first qualities he contributed were courage, discipline, a sturdy individualism, a tough stability, and a sense of the practical, his private life revealed a humorous kindliness, and in spite of nearly thirty years' strife with Britain and some years in jail, he retained a friendship for many individual Britons and a notable courtesy for those who continued in the service of India after partition. He married Javerben Patel and had one son and one daughter; he died in Bombay 15 December 1950.

[P. D. Saggi, *Life and Work of Sardar Vallabhbhai Patel*, Bombay, 1953; private information; personal knowledge.]

PHILIP MASON.

[V. P. Menon, *The Transfer of Power in India*, 1957.]

PATERSON, SIR ALEXANDER HENRY (1884–1947), prison reformer, was born at Bowdon, Cheshire, 20 November 1884, the youngest child of Alexander Edgar Paterson, a solicitor practising in Manchester, and his wife, Katharine Esther Dixon. He was educated at Bowdon College and at University College, Oxford, where he obtained a third class in *literae humaniores* in 1906, and was secretary of the Union. Inspired perhaps by his mother who seems to have worked amongst the poor, Paterson while at Oxford was an habitual visitor at a common lodging-house where he talked companionably with tramps and outcasts. In his first term he heard a talk by John Stedwell Stansfeld, whose work in the poorest part of Bermondsey was the origin of the social centre known as the Oxford Medical Mission and later as the Oxford and Bermondsey Club. Alec Paterson, while still an undergraduate, volunteered to help during vacations, and on coming down from Oxford went to Bermondsey and lived there for the next twenty years. He quickly became Stansfeld's right-hand man, and took a leading part in developing the many activities of the club. For some years he lived in one of the worst tenements on the riverside, and by sharing the life of the people around him became the friend and confidant of his many neighbours. His interest in club work for boys and in the problem of how to lift the ideals of the coming generation led him to take a post for a year as an unpaid teacher in an elementary school, where he made himself a true 'housemaster' to his pupils, visiting their homes and interesting himself in their out-of-door activities. In Bermondsey he wrote *Across the Bridges* (1911)—a short and

vivid book into which he distilled his knowledge and understanding of those who were reared and lived under the severe handicaps of the poverty which then gripped Bermondsey. 'The most urgent need', he said, 'in all social questions is for knowledge and sympathy. There can be no great change that is safe and useful before this understanding between man and man has come.' Deeply religious, his sympathy sprang from a faith which looked upon religion as 'the whole of every day', and as the greatest influence in the redemption of the individual. A Unitarian by upbringing, he became a member of the Church of England whilst he was at Oxford and remained one all his life.

Paterson's social work in Bermondsey inevitably brought him into touch with crime; and in 1908 he undertook the after-care and supervision of youths released on licence from Borstal institutions. In 1911 when the Central Association for the Aid of Discharged Prisoners was formed at the instigation of (Sir) Winston Churchill, then home secretary, Paterson became the assistant director, and made monthly visits to each of the convict prisons to interview men due for discharge and find out how they could best be helped to make a new start.

In the war of 1914–18 he served in France first as a private and later as captain in the Bermondsey battalion in which he was accompanied by many of the young men from his club who for many a long day recalled his prodigious energy, his fearlessness and daring, his high spirits and humour, and his gifts as a spiritual physician from whom men of all types sought help in suffering and distress. He was badly wounded and was awarded the M.C. He became a foundation member of Toc H; and when in 1922 it received its charter, he was the first chairman of its central executive. He served the movement actively until the end of his life.

After working for a time in the Ministry of Labour, Paterson in 1922 accepted an appointment as a member of the Prison Commission. He judged prison conditions by the same standard as he judged social conditions: by their effect on the human soul. His earlier work had shown him what grievous harm imprisonment could do to a man's character by starving his social instincts, cramping his interests and blunting his faculties, depriving him of opportunities for initiative and responsibility, and souring his spirit. The central purpose of Paterson's work as a prison administrator was to counter the mental and moral deterioration which captivity induces in human beings and to make the treatment of prisoners more likely to foster than to destroy their better qualities. He repudiated the established view that prisoners ought to suffer hardships additional to those which the loss of liberty necessarily entails. 'Men', he said, 'come to prison as a punishment, not for punishment.' He maintained that 'the business of prison officers is to keep a man in prison during his sentence and out of it for the rest of his life', and that this could be done only by making prisons as much like training centres for the rehabilitation of offenders as the requirements of safe custody permitted. He recognized that it was as hard to make men better by prison treatment as it was easy to make them worse, but he held that educational treatment must be accorded to all prisoners, whether hopeful subjects or not, lest imprisonment should make the bad man still worse and a greater trouble to the society to which he would eventually return. To make the prisoner's life more strenuous and stimulating was one of the main objects of his policy. Despite these remedies he believed that to the average man imprisonment for longer than ten years must inevitably cause deterioration, and he told the select committee of 1930 on capital punishment that in those capital cases in which 'the choice is between a penalty that destroys the physical life and one that will in the vast majority of cases permanently impair something more precious than the life of the physical body', the second alternative was in his view worse than the first.

The far-reaching reforms chronicled in the annual reports of the Prison Commission from the year 1922 onwards were the work of the commissioners as a team, but they sprang from Paterson's constructive imagination; and it was through his influence on the prison staffs that the new methods were carried out with understanding. He spent a large part of his time in the prisons and Borstal institutions, acquainting himself with all that was going on by day and by night, establishing personal relations with officers of all grades and vitalizing the whole service by his buoyant energy and by the inspiring ideals which governed his attitude to all the practical details of prison management. Among the many changes in prison methods were the abolition of practices which destroyed self-respect, such as marking the prisoners' clothes with broad arrows and cropping their hair; the introduction of opportunities for human intercourse by allowing selected prisoners to associate for meals and recreation; the provision of evening classes and lectures; and the recruitment of a body of voluntary prison visitors to pay social calls on prisoners in their cells. The first step also was taken towards the policy of open prisons by the establishment as an adjunct of Wakefield Prison of a camp where men engaged in agricultural work lived and slept in unlocked quarters. Almost all the main provisions of the Criminal Justice Act of 1948 originated from ideas propounded or experiments started by Paterson.

In the Borstal institutions for the training of young offenders Paterson brought about a transformation of spirit and methods. In place of a discipline which enforced obedience by close control and supervision and had little, if any, effect on character, he substituted an educational method designed to open the eyes of the pupil to new standards of judgement and conduct, and—in words used by Paterson in his handbook on *The Principles of the Borstal System* (1932)— 'stimulate some power within to make him want to live his life aright'. He organized these institutions on the 'house' system, recruiting a picked team of housemasters whose work it was to know each youth as an individual, and so to discover the methods most likely to win his cooperation. 'If a lad's mother is dying 200 miles away, can you send him home to see her and be sure that he will of his own accord be back within the walls on Monday morning as promised? That', he wrote, 'is the measure of our discipline. . . .' Paterson's own youthfulness contributed to his success in dealing with young offenders, for he had a boyish relish for fun and enjoyment.

In the first three years after his appointment as a prison commissioner he spent his annual holidays in touring prisons in Germany, Italy, Holland, and Belgium. For the information of his colleagues he wrote notes containing vivid word pictures of the establishments he visited, and many comments which portray the writer. After recording the good points of a women's prison 'staffed by a splendid body of nuns' and conducted on the 'silent system', he adds:

'It is said that the women are saved from any adverse mental effect by the conversation of the sisters, and that the strict order of silence saves them from being contaminated by other prisoners. But long periods of silence are sometimes more hardening to a woman than conversation with the most abandoned; nor is it good for a woman to speak only with the good.'

In 1925 he visited Burma and Ceylon to advise on penal administration. In Burma, to demonstrate that it was not necessary to keep young offenders cooped behind high walls, even if they were guilty of serious crimes, he took sixteen of them out to a camp for a week, and at the appointed time led 'sixteen smiling lads' back to the jail 'to face some years of imprisonment'. In 1931 he spent four months visiting penal and reformatory institutions in the United States and two articles by him were published in *The Times*, 10 and 11 July 1931, on the 'U.S. Way with Crime'. His advice on penal methods was sought by the Colonial Office, and at the request of that department he visited the West Indies in 1937, the East African dependencies in 1939, the West African colonies in 1943, and Malta and Gibraltar in 1944. In 1937 he obtained permission to visit the French penal settlement on Cayenne. The moving letter which he sent after this visit to the director of penal administration contributed to the decision taken some years later to discontinue the transportation of convicts to Guiana. All Paterson's reports were written with a characteristic clarity and vitality of style which made the good sense and humanity of the views which he expressed the more compelling.

Paterson was an active member of the International Penal and Penitentiary Commission, of which he was a vice-president in 1938 and acting president in 1943. At the congress held in Berlin in 1935 when concentration camps were described as 'educational institutions', and under Nazi influence a resolution was proposed which countenanced reactionary penal doctrines, Paterson headed the opposition. An amendment declaring that 'the object in view in carrying out a prison sentence is the protection of society by the social readaptation of the prisoners' was proposed by him and supported by the delegates of ten nations, including the United States, Belgium, Holland, and the Scandinavian countries. In other ways Paterson's influence spread far and wide beyond this country. Many of the younger men, who as housemasters in Borstal institutions had learnt Paterson's methods, subsequently took posts overseas and adapted those methods to offenders of many races.

During the war of 1939–45 Paterson in addition to his other work acted as director of the Czech Refugee Trust Fund from 1941, interesting himself specially in the welfare of the children and young persons, many of whom were orphans or were separated from parents who had been unable to escape from Czechoslovakia. At the request of the Government at the end of December 1940 he also undertook a mission to Canada where many aliens of enemy nationality from Great Britain had been sent for internment. It was recognized that efforts ought to be made to sort out those whose sympathies were genuinely with this country and Paterson was chosen to do this, as a man who would combine human sympathy with a realistic appreciation of the claims of national security. 'He came among us like an angel from heaven', said one of them. Even when Paterson could not hold out hope of an early release they drew comfort from his courteous patience and evident interest in their affairs.

In addition to his public work Paterson was always busy with personal work on behalf of individuals. Many ex-prisoners kept in touch with him. They wrote to him about their difficulties and their successes; they invited him to weddings and christenings; they called on him at his house and at his office. With every correspondent or caller he maintained that 'understanding between man and man' which was the text of *Across the Bridges*.

Paterson was a man of powerful physique, broad shouldered and deep chested, with the head of a thinker and the contemplative face of one who sees beyond the horizons of this world. In his dynamic saintliness were combined an earnest devotion and driving force, a great capacity for enjoyment, a puckish humour, and an indifference to many conventional values. His war wound was always a burden to him, although few would have guessed it, for he never allowed the pace of his activities in the service of his fellow men to slacken. He had a stroke in 1945 from which he made a temporary recovery but died in London 7 November 1947. He was elected an honorary fellow of his old college at

Oxford in 1944 and was knighted in 1947. He married in 1927 Frances Margaret, daughter of J. Bernard Baker, of Oxford. They had one daughter. A drawing of Paterson by Edward I. Halliday is at University College, Oxford.

[*Paterson on Prisons*, edited by S. K. Ruck, 1950; *Toc H Journal*, January 1948; Barclay Baron, *The Doctor*, 1952; private information; personal knowledge.]      A. MAXWELL.

PATON, JOHN LEWIS (ALEXANDER) (1863–1946), schoolmaster, was born at Brightside, Sheffield, 13 August 1863, the second son of the Rev. John Brown Paton [q.v.], a Congregational minister who moved to Nottingham in that year. After early education in Germany and Nottingham Paton went to Shrewsbury where he became head of the school. Proceeding to St. John's College, Cambridge, where he was a scholar, he was placed in the first division of the first class in part i of the classical tripos in 1886 and in the first class of part ii with special distinctions in the following year when he was also second Chancellor's medallist. Elected a fellow of St. John's in the same year he immediately entered upon his life vocation by joining the staff of the Leys School. In 1888 he became Lower Bench master at Rugby where his most famous pupil was William Temple [q.v.]. Paton's friendly informality won the affection of his pupils at Rugby and later at University College School, Manchester Grammar School, and in St. John's, Newfoundland. Indeed, wherever he went, his interests and labours embraced the entire community. At Rugby he organized classes for working men and met them in their homes. In London he helped the Working Boys' Club and strove to open public schools to working-class children. At Manchester his name became a household word and his influence over working-class boys, exercised largely through the Hugh Oldham Lads' Club, was immense.

His headmastership of University College School (1898–1903) gave his genius for personal influence over his boys full scope. He never forgot a name or a face. Intolerant of insincerity or slackness, he inspired his boys with his own high standards of achievement and public service. Ruthlessly opposed to mere obscurantism he incurred some opposition, but it was usually dispelled by his obvious sincerity and abundant generosity of labour and money.

In 1903 Paton was appointed high master of Manchester Grammar School. Every activity in the school felt the impact of his personality, as did every boy. He started holiday camps and treks in foreign lands ranging from Norway to the Alps. Under his inspiration the boys undertook such jobs as levelling a large patch of ground to extend their playing field. He helped to found the Old Mancunians Association, and, in short, was the *primum mobile* of the school's life. He brought distinguished men from home and abroad to lecture at the school and spent his money freely in helping the poorer boys and young masters. Often after morning prayers he would give short talks on domestic and foreign affairs; and his general-knowledge papers, which every boy had to take at the beginning of the school year, became famous. He revitalized the famous school and made it the exemplar of its kind.

Retiring from Manchester in 1924 he lectured for the Canadian National Council of Education and in 1925 became the first president of the Memorial University College (since 1949 the Memorial University) in St. John's, Newfoundland, where he steadily improved the teaching until he retired in 1933. He studied Newfoundland's economic conditions, made friends with its people, and pressed their cause in Newfoundland and England. During the war of 1939–45 Paton worked in a preparatory school in England in which he continued almost to the day of his death.

Potentially one of the finest classical scholars of Europe, he gave himself entirely to his teaching, and his publications, apart from his life of his father, published in 1914, consist of no more than a number of papers on educational topics. His real memorials, resulting from his strenuous and selfless labours, lie in the modern conception of the scope and influence of the grammar school, and in the achievements, in many spheres of national life, of those boys whose good fortune it was to come under his influence. The most unassuming of men, he would not sit for his portrait, and destroyed his personal papers to ensure the fulfilment of his wish that no memoir of him should be written. It is said that he declined offers both of a knighthood and of the C.H. He died, unmarried, at Beckenham 28 April 1946.

[*Manchester Guardian* and *The Times*, 29 April 1946; private information; personal knowledge.]      J. COATMAN.

PATON, WILLIAM (1886–1943), Presbyterian minister and secretary of the International Missionary Council, was born at Brixton 13 November 1886, the eldest child and only son of James Paton, sales manager in the Singer Sewing Machine Company, by his wife, Elizabeth, daughter of William Dunlop, clerk, of Calder. He was an exhibitioner at Whitgift School and a scholar at Pembroke College, Oxford, where he obtained a second class in *literae humaniores* (1908). From 1908 to 1911 he studied theology at Westminster College in Cambridge, where he was profoundly influenced by John Skinner. From 1911 to 1921 he was on the staff of the British Student Christian Movement, although he spent one of these years (1917–18) in India at the invitation of the Indian Young Men's Christian Association.

In 1917 Paton was ordained a minister of the Presbyterian Church of England. In 1921 he returned to India as a secretary of the Indian Young Men's Christian Association, but within a few months was appointed first secretary of the National Christian Council of India, Burma, and Ceylon. In 1927 he returned to England to act as a secretary of the International Missionary Council. He held this office until his death. From 1927 onwards he also edited the *International Review of Missions*. On behalf of the International Missionary Council he took a large part in the preparation for the Jerusalem meeting in 1928 and the Tambaram (Madras) meeting in 1938. In connexion with the latter he went on a world tour (1935–6) for consultation with the National Christian Councils of countries to be represented at the meeting. In 1938 he was made joint general secretary of the provisional committee of the World Council of Churches. He made many visits to India, to the United States, and to the continent and was the author of a number of books. He received from the university of Edinburgh the honorary degree of D.D. in 1939.

Such a catalogue of events gives some idea of Paton's abounding vitality, but little of the extraordinary place he held in the life of the Church at home and overseas. Amongst his many activities the following may receive particular mention: the lead which he gave to the provincial Christian Councils of India in gathering for the use of the League of Nations a careful statement of the use of opium in India; his work for the return of German missionaries to India after the war of 1914–18; his honorary secretaryship of the Indian Colleges Appeal Fund to follow up and implement the findings of the Lindsay commission which went to India in 1930; his active part in bringing into being the British Council of Churches; his concern for various Anglo-European fellowships during the war of 1939–45 and his labours on behalf of refugees, prisoners of war, and those interned—he had a pass from the War Office for all the civilian camps; his negotiations with the Treasury to secure the transmission of funds to the European foreign missions which were cut off from their home support by conditions of war; his drafting of the Paton memorandum on missionary policy in India.

These immense labours were only possible for a man of astonishing physique. But neither his physical strength nor his remarkable ability would have given him the place he held in the service and regard of all the Churches but for his personal quality. His was a singularly massive and rock-like character; firm, even exuberant in his own clear Christian faith, he was also supremely tolerant and understanding; he could appreciate the persons and the position of Christians of all types, and he was singularly trusted by all. When he died no man in the country had his wide and profound knowledge of the Christian Church in all its branches throughout the world. With knowledge he had judgement. At the memorial service which was held for him (although a Presbyterian minister) in St. Paul's Cathedral, Archbishop William Temple [q.v.], speaking with more authority than any other could have done, said of him: 'I have never known his advice to be at fault', and added, 'if any man in these last days could be called indispensable for doing what seemed to many of us as the most important tasks entrusted to Christian people, it was he.' He had, however, no sense of himself as an important person, never lost his sense of humour nor his serenity; it is significant that he was almost universally known by his Christian name.

In 1912 Paton married Grace Mackenzie, eldest daughter of the Rev. David Macdonald, Presbyterian minister at Bexhill; there were four sons and two daughters of this most happy marriage. Paton died while on holiday at Kendal 21 August 1943.

[*International Review of Missions*, January 1944; *The Church in the World*, new series, No. 4, November 1943; Margaret Sinclair, *William Paton*, 1949; personal knowledge.]

NATHANIEL MICKLEM.

PEAKE, HAROLD JOHN EDWARD (1867–1946), archaeologist, was born 27 September 1867 at Ellesmere, Shropshire, the son of the vicar, the Rev. John Peake, and his wife, Matilda Ann Marshall. Early training in estate management at Leicester gave him insight into changes of land-tenure and land-use considered historically. In 1897, after his marriage, he and his wife went round the world, spending some time on a ranch in British Columbia, whence Peake gained understanding of prehistoric pastoralism. They also studied art and ceramics in Japan and China. Their home at Boxford, Berkshire, from 1899, was a centre of leadership in archaeological and artistic efforts, the latter especially resulting in the organization of the Boxford Masquers who earned a wide reputation. Peake, as the honorary curator of Newbury Museum, developed a selected series of implements, pots, potsherds, and maps, in exhibiting which each century from 3000 B.C. was allocated equal space. The Newbury Museum became well known for its pottery and the series of exhibits were the basis of a published chronological work by Peake, issued soon after 1920.

In addition to serving on a number of local committees, Peake was the motive power of the Newbury District Field Club and superintended its archaeological investigations. In a wider field he served as a member of council and from 1926 to 1928 as president of the Royal Anthropological Institute which gave him its Huxley memorial medal in 1940. He presided over the section on anthropology of the British Association in 1922, and served for a time as member of the council of the Society of Antiquaries of London.

Peake studied deeply the distribution of evidences of the human past, always in relation with the environment of the place and the time, and with the peoples concerned. His catalogue of British prehistoric bronze implements, now including 17,000 entries, with measured drawings and data of location and so on, is in the care of the British Museum. His Gregynog lectures, published in 1922 as *The Bronze Age and the Celtic World*, attempted to relate archaeology and linguistics. In the same year he published *The English Village*, a stimulating study of social evolution. With Professor H. J. Fleure he collaborated, as senior partner, in a series of books (1927–36, tenth and final volume, 1956) entitled *The Corridors of Time*, an attempt towards the interpretation of archaeological data in terms of life. In this study Peake pioneered in research concerning the beginnings of cereal cultivation which, he held, occurred in Syria-Palestine and northern Mesopotamia. He also inquired, with Mr. Herbert Henry Coghlan, into the beginnings of metallurgy. His papers in the *Journal* of the Royal Anthropological Institute have lasting value.

In 1897 Peake married Charlotte Mary Augusta (died 1934), daughter of Captain Richard Lane Bayliff, of the Royal Marine Light Infantry. There were no children. A portrait of Peake as a young man was painted by Agnes Walker.

[Private information; personal knowledge.]

H. J. FLEURE.

PEARCE, SIR (STANDEN) LEONARD (1873–1947), electrical engineer, was born at Crewkerne, Somerset, 28 September 1873, the only child of the Rev. Standen Pearce, a Baptist minister, and his wife, Sarah Young. He was educated at Bishop's Stortford College and the Finsbury Technical College, subsequently serving his apprenticeship with the Electrical Engineering Corporation, of West Drayton, and with Thomas Richardson & Sons, of Hartlepool. After a year as an engineer at sea he returned to work for the Metropolitan Electric Supply Company. Two years later, in 1899, he joined the British Thomson-Houston Company, and took part in the construction of electrical equipment for the Central London Railway. In the following year he became assistant, then shortly afterwards superintendent, engineer of the railway's Shepherds Bush power-station. In 1901 he returned to the electricity supply industry as deputy chief electrical engineer to the Manchester corporation. Three years later he became chief electrical engineer, and then general manager of the electricity department and consulting electrical engineer to the corporation, a post which he held until 1925. During this period he was engaged in much development and constructional work which culminated in the design and erection of Barton power-station. In 1916, at the request of the Board of Trade, he formed a committee to consider the electrical supply resources of Lancashire and Cheshire, and in 1920 he played a leading part in the inception of the south-east Lancashire electricity scheme. The advisory board, of which he was chairman, was the first to function in any of the districts into which the country was divided under the Electricity (Supply) Act of 1919.

In 1924 Pearce spent six months in Australia at the invitation of the municipality of Sydney to advise on various matters in connexion with the electrical developments in that country. In the following year he was appointed an electricity commissioner, but in 1926 he became, and remained until his death, engineer-in-chief of the London Power Company formed to co-ordinate and develop the generation of electricity in the metropolis. Of his valuable work in this capacity the most notable was the design and construction of the Deptford West and Battersea power-stations. His association with Sir Giles Gilbert Scott in designing the latter marked the beginning of a close collaboration between engineers and architects in the building of power-stations. At Battersea, Pearce also initiated and successfully carried through the design and construction of a flue-washing plant to eliminate fumes. For many years power-stations of his design headed the list for efficiency, and his leadership in this field may be attributed not only to his own high standards but to his emphasis on the importance of avoiding fixed ideas and of maintaining a breadth of view able to take account of progress in other spheres of knowledge.

Pearce was a valued member, in some cases an honorary member, of the institutions connected with his profession which he served in various capacities. He was awarded the Constantine gold medal of the Manchester Association, the Watt gold medal of the Institution of Civil Engineers, and finally in 1947 the Faraday medal of the Institution of Electrical Engineers. He was an honorary D.Sc. of Manchester University (1926); was appointed C.B.E. in 1919 and knighted in 1935. These honours he received with his customary reserved and modest attitude towards his own achievements and a generous acknowledgement of the work of colleagues.

To his recreations as to his profession Pearce brought the same unassuming sincerity of purpose. He was a keen musician and when living in Manchester played the organ at the Baptist chapel which he attended. He was an enthusiastic mountain climber, in summer and winter, with more than 150 first-class ascents in the Alps to his credit. He planned methodically, was very safe, and always considerate of his guides. He regarded ski-ing as an aid to winter mountaineering, and he was also an expert skater. In his home and office were pictures of the mountains which he loved and greatly missed during the war years of 1939-45 when he added the work of an electricity commissioner to his other tasks. In 1935 he had accompanied Sir William Ellis [q.v.] when he ascended the Jungfrau in celebration of his seventy-fifth birthday, but Pearce did not live, as he had hoped, to do the same, for he died 20 October 1947 at Bickley, Kent. In 1901 he married Susie Kate (died 1938), daughter of George R. Cockhead, of Crouch End, a dealer in rare books; they had one daughter.

[*Journal* of the Institution of Mechanical Engineers, September 1948; *Engineer*, 24 October 1947; *Alpine Journal*, May 1948; private information; personal knowledge.]

C. E. H. VERITY.

PEARSALL SMITH (LLOYD) LOGAN (1865-1946), writer. [See SMITH.]

PEASE, JOSEPH ALBERT, first BARON GAINFORD (1860-1943), politician and man of business, was born at Woodlands, Darlington, 17 January 1860, the younger son of (Sir) Joseph Whitwell Pease [q.v.]. He was educated at Tottenham Grove House, a Quakers' school, and at Trinity College, Cambridge, where he was captain of the football team, played polo against Oxford, was twelfth man for the university cricket eleven, and master of the university draghounds. He always remained a genuine sportsman. He was a first-class shot, a keen fisherman and rider to hounds; very few could show him the way across country and he twice won the parliamentary point-to-point.

After an early entry into the family iron and coal business with which he was associated all his life, Pease served in 1889 as mayor of Darlington, the youngest mayor in England, and in 1892 he won as a Liberal the Tyneside division of Northumberland which he represented until 1900.

An active and popular member of Parliament, he was private secretary (1893–5) to John (later Viscount) Morley [q.v.], chief secretary for Ireland, and in 1897 he became a junior whip for his party while it was in opposition.

From 1901 to January 1910, when he was defeated, Pease sat for the Saffron Walden division of Essex and thereafter for the Rotherham division of the West Riding of Yorkshire. His speeches on finance, opium, and African slavery attracted attention; on the formation of the Campbell-Bannerman Government in 1905 he was made a junior lord of the Treasury, and under Asquith (1908) was promoted to be chief whip and was sworn of the Privy Council.

In 1910 Pease was appointed chancellor of the Duchy of Lancaster with a seat in the Cabinet, and in the following year president of the Board of Education, a post which he retained until the coalition Government was formed in 1915. His love of children fitted him to do much good work in this office, helping the new health service in schools, improving the training of teachers, and laying the foundations of the Department of Scientific and Industrial Research.

During and after the war of 1914–18 he served as a member of the Claims Commissions in France and Italy, and he was postmaster-general from January to December 1916. In the following year he was raised to the peerage as Baron Gainford, of Headlam, county Durham, after having sat for twenty-four years in the House of Commons; he was to sit for twenty-six in the House of Lords.

During all these years Jack Pease, as he was affectionately known to his friends, had maintained his association with industry; and his advice and knowledge were of wide and practical value. In 1922 he was chosen as a disinterested chairman of the British Broadcasting Company and was vice-chairman (1926–32) after it became a public corporation. In 1927 he was president of the Federation of British Industries and in 1932 of the National Confederation of Employers' Organisations. In the House of Lords he spoke on the Post Office, education, the coal and iron industries, and broadcasting.

Pease was a sound Liberal, a loyal colleague, an experienced negotiator, and a fine sportsman. He had a frank, courteous manner, and his speeches were straightforward and honest. Everyone liked him.

In character he was modest and fairminded, adhering to his Quaker principles, a kind-hearted and competent man of affairs. In his fine Adam house in Mansfield Street he entertained his many friends, and he kept up his country interests to the end.

In 1886 Pease married Ethel (died 1941), daughter of Sir Henry Marshman Havelock-Allan [q.v.]; they had one son and two daughters. He died at Headlam Hall 15 February 1943 and was succeeded as second baron by his son, Joseph (born 1889). A portrait by P. A. de László is in the possession of the family.

[*The Times*, 16 February 1943; private information; personal knowledge.]

                       MERSEY.

PENROSE, DAME EMILY (1858–1942), college principal, was born in London 18 September 1858, the eldest daughter of Francis Cranmer Penrose [q.v.], architect and archaeologist. She was educated at a private school at Wimbledon, studied languages and archaeology in Versailles, Paris, Dresden, and Berlin, and resided in Athens with her father when he was director of the British School. She entered Somerville College, Oxford, in 1889 with fluent knowledge of modern Greek, and close familiarity with classical archaeology but only elementary knowledge of the ancient languages. After three years she was placed in the first class in the school of *literae humaniores*, the first woman to win that distinction. In 1893 she became principal of Bedford College, London, in the next year professor of ancient history, and in 1898 principal of the Royal Holloway College. Her wise conduct of affairs at both colleges led to their constitution as schools of the university of London in 1900. She became chairman of the classical board and was a valued member of the senate until her return to Oxford as principal of Somerville College in 1907. Her exceptional gifts for administration and finance were recognized in her appointments to the advisory committee on university grants (1911); to the Royal Commission on university education in Wales (1916); to that on the universities of Oxford and Cambridge (1919); and as a statutory commissioner for Oxford (1923). She was appointed O.B.E. in 1918 and D.B.E. in 1927. The university of Oxford conferred the honorary degree of D.C.L. upon her in 1926, and the university of Sheffield that of LL.D. in the same year.

The two decades of her headship of Somerville (1907–26), saw important changes in the position of women in the university of Oxford. In 1907 the women's societies were already advancing towards independent standing as colleges with their own teaching staffs; in 1910 their direct relation to the university was recognized by the institution of a delegacy; and in 1920 a statute of the university admitted women to degrees and gave them full membership. In all this movement Emily Penrose, forceful yet unaggressive, played an important part. She had statesmanlike vision, fairness of judgement, devotion to learning, and imperturbable faith in the ends for which she worked. Her own distinguished abilities, as scholar, teacher, and administrator, increased respect for the women's societies in the university. As in London, so in Oxford, she decisively moulded the character of her college. Deeply religious, reserved in all personal matters, scrupulously careful in expressing opinion, she was difficult to know, and formidable to those who did not know her; but she was unfailingly generous to those in want or trouble, and was highly valued by her family and friends. She had unusual artistic gifts in water-colour and embroidery, elegance as a skater, prowess as mountain climber, and delightful humour as raconteuse. She died at Bournemouth 26 January 1942. A portrait by P. A. de László is at the Royal Holloway College and another by Francis Helps is at Somerville.

[*Oxford*, Summer 1942; M. J. Tuke, *A History of Bedford College for Women, 1849–1937*, 1939; private information; personal knowledge.]                    HELEN DARBISHIRE.

PETRIE, SIR (WILLIAM MATTHEW) FLINDERS (1853–1942), Egyptologist, was born at Charlton, Kent, 3 June 1853, the only child of William Petrie by his wife, Anne, daughter of Captain Matthew Flinders, R.N. [q.v.]. Too delicate a child to be sent to school, he owed his education to what he could pick up for himself and what he could learn from his parents. In them he was fortunate. His father, chemist, civil engineer, and surveyor, was an admirable teacher; his mother was a geologist and collector of ancient coins. By the time he was sixteen the boy knew the galleries of the British Museum familiarly—the coins, the minerals, and the Egyptian collections—and was 'jackalling' for the coin room with late Greek and Byzantine coins picked up in suburban shops. With his father's encouragement he started practical surveying by measuring earthworks in southern England, and this whetted his interest in standards of measurement; his first publication, entitled *Inductive Metrology* (1877), was followed in 1880 by an excellent field survey of Stonehenge. In part, this work was a deliberate preparation for Egypt, for his father had been fired by the theories advanced by Charles Piazzi Smyth [q.v.] of prophecies enshrined in the Pyramids to go out and make accurate measurements of the Great Pyramid, and his son was to go with him. In the end, young Petrie went alone.

Two winter seasons of single-handed, strenuous, and often dangerous labour resulted in an authoritative publication sponsored by the Royal Society, whose grant was Petrie's first official recognition. Incidentally, *The Pyramids and Temples of Gizeh* (1883) disproved once and for all the eschatological theories which had prompted the expedition. At Gizeh, Petrie observed and deplored the methods then employed by excavators—'a radical change is required in the way of doing all such things' he declared to his lifelong friend, Flaxman Spurrel, doctor and anthropologist, to whose views on archaeological stratification he owed not a little; and when in 1883 he became joint secretary (unpaid) of the recently formed Egypt Exploration Fund (later Society) he defined explicitly the beliefs which separated him from the old school of excavators. 'The true line', he wrote, 'lies as much in the careful noting and comparison of small details as in more wholesale and off-hand clearances.' His first work for the Fund was at Tanis in the Delta; in the course of it a prospecting tour led to the discovery of the early Greek trading-station of Naucratis, which he excavated in 1884 and 1885 with F. Ll. Griffith and E. A. Gardner [qq.v.]. At Naucratis no buildings survived, and there were to be found none of the sculptures and inscriptions which Egyptologists had learnt to expect from excavations, little, in fact, but broken pottery; but for its contribution to history the excavation was of prime importance, and it more than justified his profession of faith.

After 1885 a quarrel with the staff of the Egypt Exploration Fund (with which he was to collaborate again from 1896 to 1906) threw Petrie back on his own very small resources, but help was soon forthcoming and the discovery at Hawara of encaustic portrait-paintings of the Roman period was a triumphant introduction to his long career of independence. For fifty years his excavations were financed by popular subscriptions to a fund administered by himself under the title (eventually) of 'The British School of Archaeology in Egypt'. His energy and industry —he was a quick worker—were unlimited; while lecturing and teaching in England he organized his school, personally conducted his excavations every year, and every year published the results of his field-work so as to put his material without delay at the disposal of scholars. It is an astonishing record.

Petrie's discoveries included those of the early royal tombs at Abydos, of the Pre-Dynastic cultures, of the Merenptah inscription mentioning the Hebrews in Palestine, of the Hyksos, of early Greek contacts with Egypt at Tell El Amarna, and of the Sinaitic monuments. No less important than the discoveries were the methods which he introduced, amongst them the sequence-dating for Egyptian pottery, an ingenious classification which supplied a chronological framework for the antiquities of prehistoric periods for which there could be no dating in terms of years, an invaluable instrument for all workers in the same field.

In 1891 Petrie had visited Palestine and in a single season at Lachish established the broad lines of that country's archaeological history. In 1926, dissatisfied with conditions in Egypt, he returned to Palestine and spent the rest of his life there. Although he continued digging, his real contribution to field archaeology had been made in Egypt; in these later years increasing ill health allowed of only nominal supervision and his publication of results obtained by other men's work had not the value of his own personal records.

From 1892 until 1933 Petrie was professor of Egyptology in the university of London. The Edwards library, in which he housed his own remarkable and ever-growing Egyptological collection, became a unique centre for the teaching of all branches of Egyptology. Of the numerous assistants employed by him in field-work many became well-known archaeologists, but the teaching given in London and his own publications (beginning with *Methods and Aims in Archaeology*, 1904) were not less effective. Directly or indirectly, every field-worker of the next generation was a disciple of Petrie.

Petrie's output was prodigious and,

naturally, not all of it was of equal value. His factual reports will always be indispensable to the student of Egyptology; his theories were not always well founded. Essentially a free-lance, impatient of all authority, but himself an authoritarian with a dogmatic assurance of his own rightness which he may well have owed to his fundamentalist father, he had little interest in others' work and small respect for others' opinions; typical of him was the way in which he clung to the 'long' Egyptian chronology of his own devising, quite unconcerned by the general agreement of scholars on a shorter date. He was a field-worker, not a scholar, and his mistakes were made when he went outside the sphere in which he was pre-eminent; but they were very small compared with the services which he rendered to a science which was really his creation.

Petrie married in 1897 Hilda Mary Isabel (died 1956), daughter of Richard Denny Urlin, of Rustington Grange, Worthing, and had a son and a daughter. His wife assisted him in his excavations and in the management of the British School of Archaeology in Egypt. He was knighted in 1923 and was elected F.R.S. in 1902 and F.B.A. in 1904. He received honorary degrees from the universities of Oxford (1892), Edinburgh (1896), Strasbourg (1897), and Cambridge (1900). He was a member of the Royal Irish Academy, of the American Philosophical Society, and of many other foreign learned societies. He died in Jerusalem 28 July 1942.

There is a portrait of Petrie by P. A. de László in the common-room, and a watercolour by Mrs. Brunton in the Edwards library, of University College, London. There is an interesting picture in private possession by Henry Willis portraying Petrie at work in the Pyramid field. Portraits by G. F. Watts and P. A. de László are in the National Portrait Gallery.

[Sir Flinders Petrie, *Seventy Years in Archaeology*, 1931; Sidney Smith in *Proceedings* of the British Academy, vol. xxviii, 1942; *Journal of Egyptian Archaeology*, vol. xxix, 1943; *Proceedings* of the Royal Institution, November 1942; *Year Book* of the American Philosophical Society, 1942; *The Times*, 30 July 1942; *Times Literary Supplement*, 8 August 1942; personal knowledge.]

LEONARD WOOLLEY.

PHILLIPS, SIR TOM SPENCER VAUGHAN (1888–1941), admiral, the son of Captain (later Colonel) T. V. W. Phillips, R.A., and his wife, Louisa May

Adeline, daughter of Admiral (Sir) Algernon F. R. de Horsey, was born at Pendennis Castle, Falmouth, 19 February 1888. He became a naval cadet in 1903, midshipman in 1904, sub-lieutenant in 1907, gaining first class certificates in all examinations, and lieutenant in July 1908. He joined the navigating branch and in the war of 1914–18 was navigator first of the cruiser *Bacchante* at the Dardanelles and later of the newer cruiser *Lancaster* in the Far East, and was thus far removed—much to his chagrin—from further active participation in the war. He made his mark, however, for he was granted the acting rank of commander in an unexpected vacancy and was executive officer of his ship from April 1917 onwards. In 1918 he was made acting captain and commanded the *Lancaster* for three months, transferring, still as acting captain, in 1919 to the cruiser *Euryalus* and bringing her home. In June 1919 he joined the Staff College, and after qualifying served for three years under the British naval representative at the headquarters of the League of Nations, being promoted commander in June 1921; and for two years in the plans division of the Admiralty naval staff. In July 1925, after eight months in command of the sloop *Verbena* on the Africa station, he was appointed to the operational staff, Mediterranean, the chief of staff being (Sir) Dudley Pound [q.v.]. Phillips served in that capacity until May 1928, being promoted captain in June 1927.

From September 1928 he commanded the sixth destroyer flotilla until April 1930, when he returned to the plans division as assistant director for over two years. He commanded the *Hawkins*, flagship of the East Indies squadron, from September 1932 to January 1935. In August 1935 he became director of plans, Admiralty, and held that important post, throughout the international naval conference of 1935–6, until April 1938. He was then appointed to command the Home Fleet destroyer flotillas as commodore and, from January 1939, as rear-admiral. In May 1939 Pound, when nominated first sea lord and chief of the naval staff, knowing Phillips's personality and abilities, chose him for the post (hitherto invariably held by a much more senior admiral) of deputy chief—later styled vice-chief—of the naval staff. The choice proved well justified, and Phillips, clear-headed and indefatigable as ever, quickly won the full confidence not only of his brother officers of the staff but also of (Sir) Winston Churchill, who took office as first lord on the outbreak of war; on Churchill's recommendation, he was granted the acting rank of vice-admiral on 7 February 1940. Churchill in the third volume of his history of *The Second World War* (1950) styled Phillips 'our trusted vice-chief of the naval staff'; but the accord between the two men had dwindled. Phillips found himself on more than one occasion a convinced opponent of the policy, or action, upon which the prime minister was set; and he would make no compromise on matters of strategy. Churchill records in his second volume (1949) that in September 1940 Phillips demurred to the suggestion of retaliatory bombing of German cities. Early in 1941 he expressed and maintained the view that to divert forces from Cyrenaica to Greece would be unsound and probably disastrous. That diversion took place in March, and from that time, according to his own statement to an intimate, Phillips's personal contact with the prime minister practically ceased.

In May 1941 he was given the 'dormant' appointment of commander-in-chief of the Eastern Fleet—the formation of which in substantial strength he had himself first suggested when the high probability that Hitler would attack Russia was realized—but continued in the onerous post of vice-chief of the naval staff. He was relieved in that capacity in October 1941 and at once took up his new command, with the acting rank of admiral—thus receiving for the second time acting promotion through two ranks. He sailed for the Far East in the battleship *Prince of Wales*, picking up on the way the only other capital ship of his so-called 'fleet', the old battle cruiser *Repulse*. The aircraft carrier *Indomitable* was to have been of his force, but she had been delayed by an accident and was not available, while commitments elsewhere had prevented the defences of Malaya from being brought up to adequate strength, a measure which he had strongly urged while in office at the Admiralty.

The ships arrived at Singapore on 2 December, and on 8 December, without declaration of war, the Japanese attacks on Malaya began with an amphibious assault at the northern frontier. The admiral was thus faced with a problem as difficult as any that occur in war. The air fighter force in Malaya was small and it was by no means certain that its support could be made available to his ships in need. He was faced with the tragic dilemma of either having to take his ships to the scene of invasion in the face of strong land-based enemy air forces, despite the uncertainty of his own air support, or the apparently pusillanimous course of remaining inactive while an enemy army was landing on British soil only 400 miles away. He did not hesitate. He decided that, given the fighter support for which he asked, and provided he could achieve surprise, he should be able to cut the enemy's supply-line by sea and destroy their reinforcements; and he sailed the same evening. The next morning, 9 December, he learned that fighter support could not be provided, and that strong Japanese bomber forces were believed to be already based in Indo-China. He decided to carry on, however, provided his ships were not sighted by enemy reconnaissance; but later in the day the weather cleared, and when Japanese aircraft were sighted from his flagship so that the chance of surprise had gone, it became clear that to carry out his original plan would not only be ineffective but would expose his ships, the only substantial allied naval force left in the Pacific, to certain disablement if not destruction. At 8.15 p.m. he altered course to return to Singapore. From that intention he was diverted by a report—which afterwards proved to be unfounded—that the enemy was landing at Kuantan, only 140 miles north of Singapore. His detour thither actually had the effect of evading the Japanese striking force which was seeking his ships the next morning, but by pure chance it sighted them on its return flight to its Indo-Chinese base. The *Prince of Wales* and *Repulse* were then attacked with bombs and torpedoes by large numbers of Japanese aircraft and were both sunk less than two hours after the first attack. Phillips was not amongst the 1,285 officers and men who were saved from his flagship.

Phillips was appointed C.B. in 1937 and promoted K.C.B. in 1941. He married in 1919 Gladys Metcalfe, daughter of Captain F. G. Griffith-Griffin, D.C.L.I., and widow of J. H. Brownrigg. There was one son of the marriage who also entered the Royal Navy.

[Admiralty records; S. W. Roskill, (Official) *History of the Second World War. The War at Sea*, vol. i, 1954; Russell Grenfell, *Main Fleet to Singapore*, 1951; private information; personal knowledge.]

H. G. THURSFIELD.

PHILLIPS, WALTER ALISON (1864–1950), historian, was born 21 October 1864 at Lewisham, the youngest son of John Phillips, commission merchant, by his wife, Jane, daughter of John Atkins, solicitor. In 1871, after the death of Phillips's father, the family moved to Weimar, where his mother had a friend in Ottilie von Goethe, the daughter-in-law of the poet; her eldest son, Walther, was Phillips's godfather. They occupied rooms in the Goethehaus until 1875, when he was sent to a private school in Margate. He went to Merchant Taylors' School in 1877, and then to Merton College, Oxford, where he was an exhibitioner. He graduated with first class honours in modern history in 1885 and in 1886 was elected a Merchant Taylors' scholar of St. John's College, Oxford. He was president of the Union in 1886. Originally he had intended to take holy orders, but in 1888 he returned to Weimar, where he studied music and painting until 1891, and its cosmopolitan and liberal society had a profound and lasting influence upon him. For a time he sang professionally in England; then he returned to scholarship, lecturing for the university extension movement. This led to an invitation from Rivingtons to write his *Modern Europe, 1815–1899* (1901) which became a standard textbook. In 1903 he became chief assistant editor of the eleventh edition of the *Encyclopaedia Britannica*, and wrote many of the more important historical articles. He had long been an occasional leader-writer for *The Times* and a regular contributor to the *Times Literary Supplement*, and in 1912–13 he acted as special correspondent in South America and editor of the *South American Supplement*. In 1914 he was appointed to the newly established Lecky chair of modern history at Trinity College, Dublin, and held it until his retirement in 1939. He was elected an honorary fellow of Merton in 1938.

Phillips was never, perhaps, altogether at home in Dublin, to which he came too late in life to adapt himself fully to a society so superficially similar and so fundamentally dissimilar to the English scene, while his whole training and experience put him out of sympathy with such revolutions as he witnessed in Ireland. But he gave real distinction to the new chair. As a lecturer he was always interesting and often brilliant. His cosmopolitan outlook, striking personality, wide interests, and mere length of experience (in the 'thirties he was accustomed to startle his classes by relating how he had watched the troops march out to the Franco-Prussian war) made a profound impression on undergraduates. To his colleagues he was a good friend and a charming and stimulating companion.

Much of his best historical writing was published in encyclopaedias and composite histories. Of his independently published works the most important were *The Confederation of Europe* (1914) and *The Revolution in Ireland, 1906–1923* (1923); he undertook the editorship of an official *History of the Church of Ireland*, published (1933–4) in three volumes.

He married in 1905 Catherine Beatrice, daughter of George Frederick Sennett, accountant's clerk, of Dale, Pembrokeshire; there were no children. He died in London 28 October 1950.

[*The Times*, 31 October 1950; private information; personal knowledge.]

J. OTWAY-RUTHVEN.

PHIPPS, SIR ERIC CLARE EDMUND (1875–1945), diplomatist, was born in Madrid 27 October 1875, the only son of (Sir) (Edmund) Constantine (Henry) Phipps who was later minister at Brussels, by his first wife, Maria Jane, daughter of Alfred Miller Mundy. He sprang from a family distinguished throughout the eighteenth and nineteenth centuries in the navy, diplomacy, and the colonies. The first Earl of Mulgrave was his great-grandfather, and the first Marquess of Normanby [qq.v.] his great-uncle. As a child, he accompanied his parents to their various diplomatic posts, and instead of being sent to school in England, he was educated privately in Dresden, Vienna, and Paris. He spent a year at King's College, Cambridge, and subsequently took his *B. ès L.* in Paris. This education gave a foreign, and especially a French, tinge to his character and tastes, which showed itself in the profound knowledge which he acquired of French politics and culture, and in the sympathy which he felt for France throughout his life.

With such an upbringing and family background it was natural that Phipps should enter the diplomatic service, for which he was nominated as attaché in 1898, and which he entered in 1899. He served as secretary in Paris (three times) and also in Constantinople, the Foreign Office, Rome, St. Petersburg, and Madrid. He was promoted counsellor in 1919, and after a few months in the Foreign Office was appointed (1920) to Brussels under

Sir George Grahame, and to Paris under Lord Crewe [q.v.] in 1922, in which year he was raised to the rank of minister plenipotentiary.

Phipps's first independent post was as minister in Vienna in 1928. His time there coincided with the brief period between the wars when Austria was comparatively peaceful and prosperous. In 1933 he was sworn of the Privy Council and went as ambassador to Berlin in succession to Sir Horace Rumbold [q.v.]. He took up his post at the very outset of Hitler's power. The military reoccupation of the Rhineland in 1936, the completion of German rearmament, and the creation of the German–Italian 'axis' all occurred while he was in Berlin. He soon realized the ruthless character of Hitler's foreign policy, and, although he did not perhaps appreciate how imminent the danger was, he warned the British Government, but in vain, that concessions would only increase Hitler's appetite, and that nothing except British material strength, combined with close alliance with France and friendship with the United States, could curb the Führer's growing territorial ambitions.

In the spring of 1937 Phipps was transferred to Paris as successor to Sir George Clerk. This post he had always desired, and for it he seemed pre-eminently qualified. But by the time he reached Paris a serious demoralization was showing itself in what was still the governing class in France. Phipps saw clearly the implications of this moral breakdown and warned the British Government of it, only to earn the unjust stigma of being 'defeatist'. Where he failed, however, was in not appreciating that the demoralization he saw so clearly was confined to a special section of French life, and that there were other healthier elements which could assert themselves only after the collapse of 1940.

Feeling perhaps that he was not best qualified to be a war-time ambassador, Phipps, having served forty years, retired at his own request in the autumn of 1939, and thus escaped the grief of witnessing the French catastrophe on the spot. He settled in Wiltshire and took no further part in public life, except as a director of the Midland Bank. He died suddenly in London after an operation 13 August 1945.

Phipps was twice married: first, in 1907 to Yvonne (died 1909), youngest daughter of the Comte de Louvencourt; secondly, in 1911 to Frances, daughter of Herbert

Ward, a British explorer and sculptor who had settled in France. There were no children of the first marriage; by the second there were four sons, one of whom was killed in action in 1943, and two daughters. Phipps was in person short and thickset and perhaps Latin rather than English in appearance, a man of great charm and wit, shrewd and somewhat cynical. In normal times there would probably have been greater scope for his special qualities than was possible when Hitler's rise to power made all compromise futile and even dangerous.

Phipps was appointed K.C.M.G. in 1927, G.C.M.G. in 1934, G.C.V.O. in 1939, and G.C.B. in 1941. He also held the grand cross of the Legion of Honour (1938) and was commander of the Belgian Order of Leopold (1922).

[Private information; personal knowledge.]
O. G. SARGENT.

PICK, FRANK (1878–1941), vice-chairman of the London Passenger Transport Board, was born at Spalding, Lincolnshire, 23 November 1878, the eldest child of Francis Pick, draper, of Stamford, and his wife, Fanny Clark, of South Ferraby. His early years were spent at York where he held a scholarship at St. Peter's School and was then articled to a solicitor. Having qualified in 1902 he took his LL.B. (London) with first class honours in the following year. Meanwhile, in 1902, he had entered the service of the North Eastern Railway Company, and after working in various departments joined the staff of the general manager, Sir George Gibb. In 1906 Gibb went to London to take over the management of the Metropolitan District and London Underground Electric railways and took Pick with him. In the following year Gibb retired from his direct managerial responsibility and Pick was transferred to the staff of his successor, A. H. Stanley (later Lord Ashfield, q.v.).

Henceforward Pick was closely associated with Stanley in the management of the Underground railways of London and of the associated company, taken over in 1912, the London General Omnibus Company. As traffic development officer (1909) and commercial manager (1912) he was responsible, in particular, for building up the system of bus routes in London and also for advertising. In 1917 Pick was appointed by his chief, then president of the Board of Trade in Lloyd George's wartime Government, to take charge of the household fuel and lighting branch of the coal-mines control department, under (Sir) Guy Calthrop. Returning to the Underground group of companies after the war, Pick became a joint assistant managing director in 1921 and three years later assumed full administrative control under Ashfield. He became managing director in 1928 and, when the London Passenger Transport Board was formed in 1933 with Ashfield as chairman, Pick was the natural choice for vice-chairman and chief executive officer.

It was the combination of Pick and Ashfield, rather than the work of either as an individual, which brought about the remarkable development of public passenger transport in London in the thirty years prior to the outbreak of war in 1939. The two men were essentially complementary. Ashfield was at his best in dealing with politicians, shareholders, and the public. Pick, on the other hand, was a very shy man, but he had great qualities as an administrator. He was primarily responsible for the day-to-day efficiency of a system which technically was generally acknowledged to be without equal anywhere in the world. He had a very quick mind and an exceptional grasp of operating and engineering principles and techniques. There was no part of the transport undertaking of which he did not have a thorough understanding; and the power of decision came easily to him. Furthermore, he had a wide interest in the visual arts and fervently believed in the importance of good design in everyday things. London's transport system gave him a unique opportunity to encourage modern art. He commissioned Edward Johnston [q.v.] to design an alphabet for display purposes, and London Transport lettering on direction signs and posters became celebrated for its clarity. In the period between the two world wars Pick raised the whole standard of poster design by the example which he set; he sought out artists of quality, both young and old, including such masters of the art of the poster as Mr. Fred Taylor and McKnight Kauffer. Station design, ranging from the overall architecture to details such as waste-paper baskets, was subject to Pick's personal scrutiny to ensure that the fundamental principle of good design, fitness for purpose, was properly observed. The many examples of excellent contemporary architecture in the buildings erected by London Transport in Pick's time are lasting monuments to his ideals. He was president of the Design and Industries Association from 1932 to 1934 and when the Council for Art and Industry was set up by the Board of Trade in 1934, with the object of improving standards of design in the products of industry, he was selected to be its first chairman.

Pick retired from the Transport Board in 1940 and was for a short time director-general of the Ministry of Information. In 1941 he undertook special duties for the minister of transport in connexion with the development of traffic on canals and inland waterways. He died in London 7 November 1941. In 1904 he married Mabel Mary Caroline, daughter of Charles Simeon Woodhouse, solicitor, of York. There were no children.

[Personal knowledge.]      JOHN ELLIOT.

PICKARD, SIR ROBERT HOWSON (1874–1949), chemist, was born at Balsall Heath, Birmingham, 27 September 1874, the elder of the two sons of Joseph Henry Pickard, a tool manufacturer, by his wife, Alice, daughter of Robert Howson, of Birmingham. From King Edward's Grammar School, Camp Hill, he passed to the chemistry department of Mason College, Birmingham, which from 1894 came under the direction of P. F. Frankland [q.v.]. In 1895 he graduated B.Sc. (London) with a first class in chemistry and in January 1896, as an 1851 Exhibitioner, he proceeded to the university of Munich where he obtained the degree of Ph.D. in 1898, *summa cum laude*.

In 1899 Pickard became head of the chemistry department of Blackburn Technical School and from 1908 to 1920 combined the duties of this post with those of principal of the school. During this period of twenty years Pickard published, with others, some thirty-five original papers in the *Journal* of the Chemical Society, dealing mainly with the relation between chemical constitution and optical activity.

During his stay in Blackburn Pickard was consulted from time to time by cotton manufacturers, and he came to realize that the substitution of more scientific methods for empirical and rule-of-thumb procedures would result in great improvements to this complex industry. This experience undoubtedly laid the foundation of the lively interest which he developed and the extensive technical knowledge he gradually acquired, both of which he later put to such effective use.

In 1920 Pickard became principal of Battersea Polytechnic and during his seven years' tenure of this post did much to foster the educational facilities provided by this institution. During the same period he was director of the British Leather Manufacturers' Research Association; but of his many activities the one with which his name is most closely associated is that of his directorship of the British Cotton Industry Research Association, a post to which he was appointed in 1927 and in which he remained until 1943.

He soon realized that the time was opportune for an intensive application of the scientific knowledge which had been accumulated by the Association during the eight years of its existence, and for the introduction of active measures to link the scientists more closely and effectively with the practical men from the mills; in 1928 a liaison department was formed. At the same time investigations, both fundamental and technological, were pursued on a steadily expanding scale; large extensions of both laboratory and work-room accommodation were formally opened in 1936.

Pickard tackled with understanding the peculiar difficulties inherent in a research association connected with an industry divided into several distinct sections (for example, spinning, weaving, bleaching, and finishing), and came to realize that one important function of such an association is to envisage the industry as a whole rather than as a collection of component groups of firms with sectional interests and needs. The success of his policy of co-ordination, taken in combination with the life and vigour which he infused in the Shirley Institute community, may be gauged from the fact that when he retired after seventeen strenuous years, the Research Association was recognized on all sides as an integral part of the textile industry. Pickard regarded his stay at the Shirley Institute as the most congenial and productive period of his career, and it certainly provided an opportunity for his unusual combination of qualities to be exercised to the full.

In the activities of British scientific bodies and educational institutions, Pickard took a prominent part. Elected F.R.S. in 1917, he served as a member of the council, 1936–8. He was president of the Society of Chemical Industry, 1932–3, and its medallist in 1941; vice-president of the (Royal) Institute of Chemistry for many years, and its president, 1936–9; vice-president of the Chemical Society for six years, and chairman of the Chemical

Council, 1935–8; and for several years chairman of the committee of directors of research associations.

He was a member of the senate of the university of London for twenty-two years, a member of the court, 1937–48, vice-chancellor, 1937–9, chairman of convocation in 1948, and for several years chairman of the external council. He was a member of the Surrey education committee and of the consultative committee of the Board of Education, and for eight years chairman of the governing body of Roedean School. He was knighted in 1937.

Pickard married in 1901 Ethel Marian (died 1944), daughter of Henry Wood, provision merchant, of Edgbaston, and had one son and one daughter. He died at Headley, Surrey, 18 October 1949.

[*The Times*, 19 and 27 October 1949; *Nature*, 3 December 1949; J. Kenyon in *Obituary Notices of Fellows of the Royal Society*, No. 19, November 1950; *Journal* of the Chemical Society, 1950, part 3; personal knowledge.] J. KENYON.

PINSENT, DAME ELLEN FRANCES (1866–1949), pioneer worker in the mental health services, was born at Claxby, Lincolnshire, 25 March 1866. Her father, the Rev. Richard Parker, rector there, had thirteen children; Ellen Frances was the youngest of the eight born to him by his second wife, Elizabeth Coffin; Robert John, Baron Parker [q.v.] was a brother.

In 1888 Ellen married Hume Chancellor Pinsent, a solicitor who became a prominent figure in the university and civic affairs of Birmingham. There she became acquainted with the work of local government and was the first woman to be elected to the city council. Particularly interested in the mentally unfit, she was chairman of the special schools sub-committee, and from 1904 until 1908 she sat on the Royal Commission on the feeble-minded. After the consequent passing of the Mental Deficiency Act of 1913 she was appointed an honorary commissioner of the Board of Control. In that year she and her husband moved to Oxford where the latter died in 1920. In 1921 Ellen Pinsent became a commissioner and in 1931 a senior commissioner of the Board. In 1932 she retired but continued to take an active part in questions of mental health. In 1925 she was appointed C.B.E. and in 1937 D.B.E., and she received the honorary degree of M.A. from Birmingham University in 1919.

Dame Ellen was a pioneer in promoting legislation and furthering all measures for the welfare of the mentally unfit. Her experience in Birmingham had left her with the conviction that the care and training of defectives were public obligations, both for their own good and for the protection of society. Henceforward her whole energy and exceptional mind were dedicated to this end. At home and in her work her charm, gaiety, and warmth of heart secured for her a wide circle of friends. There were three children of her marriage: a daughter who married Dr. Edgar Douglas (subsequently Lord) Adrian, who became master of Trinity College, Cambridge; and two sons, one of whom was killed whilst flying for purposes of aeronautical research in 1918 and the other on active service in 1915. She died at her home at Boars Hill, Oxford, 10 October 1949. Two drawings by Miss L. Wren and an unfinished portrait by Christopher Pinsent are in the possession of the family.

[Private information; personal knowledge.] RUTH REES THOMAS.

PISSARRO, LUCIEN (1863–1944), painter, wood-engraver, and printer of books, was born in Paris 20 February 1863, the eldest son of Camille Jacob Pissarro, the Impressionist painter, by his wife, Julie Vellay. His mother was French and his father of Spanish-Jewish stock. Lucien Pissarro passed his childhood in France, with the exception of the greater part of the year 1870 which he spent with his family in England. On growing up, he was employed for short periods with two commercial firms in Paris. He had already shown considerable promise in drawing and painting, and he devoted much of his leisure time to sketching from the life in cafés. In January 1883 Pissarro paid his second visit to London, where his father sent him to learn English. He stayed at the home of his uncle, finding employment with a music-publisher. At the same time he continued to spend his spare moments in drawing, and as soon as the weather permitted he took to painting seriously out of doors. He gave up his employment and planned to join the classes given by Alphonse Legros [q.v.] at the Slade School of Fine Art, but the advice of his father and of Degas prevailed to dissuade him from this step. Instead he studied in the museums, and his letters contain references to the impression made upon him by the water-colours of Turner and the Egyptian sculptures at the British Museum. He was also struck by the art of J. A. McN. Whistler [q.v.] and dismayed by the summer exhibition at the Royal Academy.

In the spring of 1884 Pissarro returned to France, where the state of his family's finances forced him to take employment with an art-publishing firm in Paris. When matters improved, he rejoined his family at the Norman village of Eragny where they had recently settled. During the next six years he worked with his father and laid a solid foundation for the painting of the rest of his life. He became acquainted with many of the important artists of his time, including Van Gogh and Gauguin, and more particularly with Seurat, whose technique of *pointillisme* influenced him profoundly, and through him influenced his father also. He showed paintings in this style at the last Impressionist exhibition in 1886 and at the Salon des Indépendants.

Lucien Pissarro had evinced an early interest in wood-engraving, which had been to some extent fostered by association with the well-known engraver, Auguste Lepère; he did not, however, receive any systematic instruction from him. Much more important for his stylistic beginnings in wood-engraving was the influence of Charles Keene [q.v.], which may be clearly seen in his illustrations to Octave Mirbeau's story 'Maît' Liziard', published in 1886 in the *Revue Illustrée*. During the next few years he experimented further with engraving, and in particular with the technique of the colour-woodcut. In 1890 he returned to London and shortly afterwards made the acquaintance of John Gray, and of C. de S. Ricketts and C. H. Shannon [qq.v.]. His work appealed to these men, with the result that he was invited to contribute woodcuts to the *Dial*, the periodical which Ricketts had founded in 1889. He also issued two portfolios of woodcuts, one set from his own designs, and the other, entitled *Travaux des Champs*, after drawings by his father. He was later to engrave other designs of his father. His interest in fine book-production had been aroused by the associations which he formed in London, and in 1894, with the assistance of his wife, he established his own press, which he named the Eragny Press, after his parents' home. Pissarro had by this time taken up permanent residence in this country, although he was to pay regular visits to France during the remainder of his life. His first book,

which he printed in 1894, was a fairy-story by Margaret Rust, entitled *The Queen of the Fishes*, with illustrations by himself and a hand-written text which was reproduced from line-blocks. In the preparation of the woodcuts for this, as for many others, his wife was his helper. In 1896 he borrowed Ricketts's 'Vale type' for his second book, which he followed with thirteen others printed in the same fount. In 1902 he designed a type of his own, which he called the 'Brook type', and he used this for a further sixteen volumes printed between 1903 and 1914. During his twenty years as a printer of fine editions, Pissarro took his place as one of the most attractive and original designers of his time. Most of his books were illustrated with his own woodcuts which he executed in a variety of styles, ranging from monochrome to colour by way of an intermediate style which can best be described as a revival of the classic chiaroscuro woodcut of the sixteenth century.

Although the greater part of his energies was taken up in this way during the period in question, Lucien Pissarro never ceased to paint. In most years he spent a holiday in his native country, and at these times he was able to devote himself entirely to landscape. Among his English friends were W. R. Sickert and P. Wilson Steer [qq.v.], both of whom he had met in 1891, and in the early years of the twentieth century he was closely associated with Sickert's Fitzroy Street studio. When Sickert's following crystallized into the Camden Town Group, in 1911, Pissarro was an important member. In 1906 he had joined the New English Art Club, with which he continued to exhibit for the rest of his life. Thus during the four or five years preceding the war of 1914–18 he was already becoming well known to the English public as a painter. He held his first one-man show at the Carfax Gallery in 1913, in which year his painting of 'The Railway Cutting, Acton' was acquired by the Leeds Art Gallery. Thereafter he was to hold regular exhibitions in London, first at the Goupil Gallery and from 1922 onwards at the Leicester Galleries. In 1916 he was naturalized a British subject.

In 1920 Pissarro was instrumental in founding the Monarro Group, an international society whose professed aim was to 'concentrate on those artists who have derived inspiration more or less directly from the leaders of the French Impressionist movement, Claude Monet and Camille

Pissarro'. The group held two exhibitions in London, at which Lucien Pissarro and members of his family exhibited. In the winter of 1922 the state of his mother's health necessitated a visit to the south of France, and thereafter he was to spend most winters in this part of Europe. Some of his most satisfying paintings were of the Provençal landscape. If the remainder of his life lacked any striking incident, that is not to suggest that his art stood still or deteriorated. He continued to paint landscapes of a very high standard until his last years.

Lucien Pissarro's painting was the main stream through which the authentic spirit of Impressionism was carried into England. Although his work as a wood-engraver and book-designer was influenced to some extent by English models, his painting remained to the end a pure product of France, which would make it dishonest to claim him for the English school. His technique, however, which was based on a modified form of Seurat's *pointillisme*, had a considerable influence in this country.

Pissarro died at Southchard, Chard, Somerset, 10 July 1944. He was survived by his wife, Esther, daughter of Jacob Samuel Levi Bensusan, merchant, of London, whom he had married in 1892 and who died in 1951. They had one daughter, Orovida, also a painter.

A portrait of Pissarro as a young man by his father was in the possession of his widow, a woman of great artistic talent who presented her valuable collection to the Ashmolean Museum, as well as to the National Gallery, the Tate Gallery, the Fitzwilliam Museum, and other galleries. A portrait of Pissarro in later life by his daughter was also in the possession of his widow, and another by J. B. Manson is in the Manchester City Art Gallery.

Important retrospective exhibitions of Pissarro's work were held at the Manchester City Art Gallery in 1935, and in London at the Leicester Galleries in 1946. Works by Pissarro are in the Tate Gallery and the more important provincial museums and galleries. An oil-painting, 'La Cathédrale de Gisors', is in the Musée National d'Art Moderne in Paris.

[Camille Pissarro, *Letters to his son Lucien*, 1943; John Rewald, 'Lucien Pissarro: Letters from London, 1883–1891' in the *Burlington Magazine*, July 1949; *The Times*, 12 July 1944; T. Sturge Moore, *A Brief Account of the Origin of the Eragny Press*, 1903; Will Ransom, *Private Presses and their Books* (New York, 1929) contains a complete bibliography of books printed at the Eragny Press; private information.]     JAMES LAVER.

PLASKETT, JOHN STANLEY (1865–1941), astronomer, was born at Hickson, near Woodstock, Ontario, 17 November 1865, the eldest son of Joseph Plaskett, farmer, by his wife, Annie Stanley. He was educated at the local village school, and at the high school in Woodstock. He was about sixteen when his father died, leaving him to help bring up a family of younger children; this strengthened the tradition of hard work and self-reliance in which he had been reared. His first employment was with a Woodstock engineering firm, but in 1885 he moved to Schenectady, New York, where he spent four years with the Edison Electric Company. In 1889 he returned to Canada, and obtained a post in the Canadian Edison Company at Sherbrook, Quebec; in 1890 he became foreman of the workshop and lecturer's assistant at Toronto University, where, his interest in science aroused, he enrolled as a student in 1895, finally graduating in 1899 with first class honours in mathematics and physics at the unusually late age of thirty-three.

Meanwhile, in 1892, Plaskett had married Rebecca Hope, daughter of Alexander Hemley, and in his subsequent success paid frequent tribute to her staunch assistance through the hard struggles of his earlier years. Two sons were born of the marriage, of whom the elder, Harry Hemley Plaskett, became Savilian professor of astronomy at Oxford in 1932.

While at Toronto Plaskett became a skilful photographer and it was partly on this account that he was appointed in 1903 to the staff of the small, but rapidly growing, Ottawa Observatory. Few observatories have been so fortunate. In the seven or eight years after his joining the staff he created the astrophysical department of the observatory, designed and installed several new instruments, including two stellar spectrographs, and initiated several programmes of research, including work on solar rotation and a very active programme of measurement of stellar radial velocities. This work was carried on with a 15-inch refractor, which naturally did not satisfy Plaskett for long. Inspired by the success of the then new 60-inch reflector at Mount Wilson, California, he pressed for the construction in Canada of a still larger instrument, and thus was started his biggest achievement, the building of the Dominion Astrophysical Observatory at Victoria, British Columbia, and its 72-inch reflector.

The task of persuading the Canadian Government to give its consent and support to the scheme was considered by some of Plaskett's astronomical colleagues to be a political feat in its way as remarkable as the engineering achievement of building the telescope itself. The necessary approval was, however, obtained in 1913, and, despite the war, the new instrument was finished in 1918, being for a short time the largest telescope in operation. Several of its features, novel at the time of construction, have since become standard practice, and there is little doubt that the completion of this large project, with so little serious trouble and so much ultimate success, was largely due to Plaskett's genius.

The new observatory concentrated on stellar spectroscopy, especially the determination of radial velocities, carrying on at a high standard essentially the same work which had been so ably begun in Ottawa. Leading a small but energetic staff, Plaskett made the observatory known throughout the world as a centre for his chosen line of work, producing during his directorship a large volume of first-class observational material. He retired in 1935, but the observatory has continued its successes, while he himself in retirement was still sought out for advice with regard to the construction of new large telescopes elsewhere. He died at Esquimalt, near Victoria, British Columbia, 17 October 1941.

Plaskett had the good fortune to be endowed with a strong constitution, a great capacity for hard work, indomitable determination and optimism, and very great skill in the construction and use of scientific instruments. Those who worked with him remember also a most attractive personality, kindly, happy, young in mind even into old age, with a keen sense of humour, which frequently expressed itself in a delightful chuckle, or a very characteristic and hearty laugh. He knew how to enjoy life, and a close associate has remarked that he never knew a man who extracted more genuine satisfaction from his later years. He had a host of friends, by no means confined to scientific circles, and for many years was a popular and familiar figure at astronomical gatherings in both America and Europe.

Plaskett was the recipient of many honours, among them the gold medal of the Royal Astronomical Society (1930), the Bruce medal of the Astronomical Society of the Pacific (1932), the Rumford premium of the American Academy of Arts and Sciences (1930), the Flavelle medal of the Royal Society of Canada (1932), and the Draper medal of the National Academy of Sciences, Washington (1935). He received honorary degrees from the universities of Pittsburgh, Toronto, British Columbia, McGill, and Queen's. He was George Darwin lecturer of the Royal Astronomical Society in 1930 and Halley lecturer at Oxford in 1935. He was elected F.R.S. in 1923 and appointed C.B.E. in 1935.

[*Astrophysical Journal*, vol. xcviii, No. 2, September 1943; private information; personal knowledge.]          R. O. REDMAN.

PLENDER, WILLIAM, BARON PLENDER (1861–1946), accountant, was born at Low Felling, Gateshead, 20 August 1861, the eldest of the nine children of William Plender, grocer and draper, by his wife, Elizabeth Agnes Smallpiece, daughter of John Edward Smallpiece Vardy. After education at the Royal Grammar School, Newcastle upon Tyne, he served articles with the local firm of chartered accountants, John G. Benson & Sons, and on qualifying he joined the London house of Deloitte & Co. He was admitted to a partnership in 1897 becoming senior partner in 1904; the house style of the firm, which prospered and expanded in the ensuing half-century, became Deloitte, Plender, Griffiths & Co., with branches in the United States, Canada, South America, Mexico, and South Africa.

By the turn of the century it had become evident that Plender had financial and administrative ability far transcending the limits of a chartered accountant's practice; and as time went on various big public corporations and governmental commissions and committees made increasing use of his services. In 1903 he was active on behalf of the Metropolitan Water Board in the taking over of the London water companies, and in 1908 he was closely concerned in the establishment of the Port of London Authority. In 1911 he officially investigated conditions of medical work and remuneration under the National Insurance Act, and he was knighted in the same year. He served on the Royal Commission on railways in 1913.

The war period of 1914–18 immensely increased the volume of Plender's public commitments. His activities during these four years included service on the metropolitan munitions committee, and on committees upon military service, enemy debts, and demobilization. He was Treasury controller of German, Austrian, and Turkish banks (1914–18), and acted as chairman of the advisory committee of the Enemy Debts Clearing Office (1920). He was appointed G.B.E. in 1918 and created a baronet in 1923. In 1918 he became honorary financial adviser to the Board of Trade. In 1921 he was a member of the tribunal on the Ministry of Munitions, of the lord chancellor's committee on the remuneration of solicitors, and of the railways amalgamation tribunal. The same year he was chairman of the advisory committee on the Trade Facilities Act. The first independent chairmanship of the National Board for the coal industry took up much of his time between 1921 and 1925; and thenceforward for twelve years, up to the age of seventy-six, he was concerned with such varied subjects as coal royalties, London cross-river traffic, Church of England finance, national expenditure, export credits, iron and steel, the Post Office, and German debts.

Interwoven with these affairs of State and municipality was an abiding interest in the profession of accountancy, of which Plender became the acknowledged doyen. He was president of the Institute of Chartered Accountants, 1910–12, and again, 1929–30, and of the fourth international congress on accounting, held in London in 1933.

Plender was created a baron in 1931. He was high sheriff of Kent, 1928–9, and of the county of London, 1927–8, and he was lieutenant of the City of London and deputy-lieutenant of the county of London. He received the honorary degree of LL.D. from Birmingham University in 1927. He was a knight of justice of the Order of St. John of Jerusalem, a governor of St. Thomas's Hospital and of the King's School, Canterbury, and chairman of the governors of the City of London College, 1935–41.

His multifarious public activities marked Plender out as a man of exceptional character and personality, and his mature and balanced judgement was sought by many business clients and private acquaintances. He had a very wide and diverse circle of friends, and was noted for his calm demeanour, his great courtesy, and his far-reaching sympathies. His relaxations were shooting and golf; but perhaps his most absorbing outside interest was the collection of pictures and antique furniture, which he disposed with great taste in his town and country houses. He died at Tunbridge Wells 19 January 1946.

Plender married first, in 1891 Marian Elizabeth, daughter of John Channon, of Woodford Green, Essex. She died in 1930, and he married as his second wife, in 1932 Mabel Agnes, daughter of Peter George Laurie, stockbroker, and widow of George Norton Stevens, publisher, of London. There were no children of either marriage and his titles became extinct. A portrait by Sir William Llewellyn belongs to the Institute of Chartered Accountants.

[*The Times*, 21 January 1946; *Accountant*, 26 January and 16 February 1946; private information.] HERBERT B. GRIMSDITCH.

PLUMMER, HENRY CROZIER KEATING (1875–1946), astronomer and mathematician, was born at Oxford 24 October 1875, the eldest son of William Edward Plummer, then senior assistant at the Oxford University Observatory, and later director of the observatory of the Mersey Docks and Harbour Board and reader in astronomy at the university of Liverpool. His mother was Sarah Crozier. Plummer was educated at St. Edward's School and Hertford College, Oxford, where he was a scholar. He obtained a first class in mathematical moderations (1895) and finals (1897), and a second class in the final honour school of natural science (physics, 1898). After a year as assistant lecturer in mathematics at the Owens College, Manchester, and another year as assistant demonstrator in the Clarendon Laboratory, he was in 1901 appointed second assistant in the Oxford University Observatory. He held this post until 1912 when he was appointed Andrews professor of astronomy in the university of Dublin and royal astronomer for Ireland, in which capacity he was director of the Dunsink Observatory. His career as a professional astronomer ended in 1921 when he accepted the chair in mathematics at the Artillery College, Woolwich (subsequently the Military College of Science). He had been elected F.R.S. the previous year and remained at Woolwich until 1940 when he retired and settled in Oxford, where he was Halley lecturer in 1942.

During his twenty years as a professional astronomer, Plummer published a very large number of original papers. In Oxford he was concerned with the participation of the observatory in the Astrographic Chart and Catalogue and some of his papers dealt with matters relevant to this work. But his activities covered a wider field, and he produced, *inter alia*, papers dealing with dynamical astronomy, the theory of correlation, globular clusters, and stellar motions. In his papers on correlation he effectively demolished the conclusions reached by the redoubtable Karl Pearson [q.v.] who had applied correlation theory to the photometric observations of variable stars. Plummer pointed out the danger of using correlation analysis without due regard to the physical nature of the quantities involved. In 1905 and 1906 he published two papers dealing with the motion of Encke's comet. He showed that the observed anomalous acceleration of this comet could not be ascribed, as had been suggested, to the pressure of solar radiation, but he applied his results to comet 1886 I and found that the observed effective diminution of solar gravitation was consistent with the hypothesis that the cometary nucleus consisted of a swarm of meteoric bodies. He found that the diameters of these bodies must be of the order of three millimetres.

His career at Oxford was temporarily interrupted in 1907 when he went for a year to the Lick Observatory in California on a travelling fellowship. In Ireland Plummer found himself hampered by the wretchedly poor equipment of the Dunsink Observatory, and although he obtained valuable results with the equipment at his disposal, his actual achievement was a sorry contrast with what might have been. The Dunsink programme of photometric observations of variable stars was about the only contribution to astronomy the observatory could make and this was continued under the directorship of Plummer who applied himself with zeal to an analysis of the results. He revealed some curious relationships between the phases of the harmonics of the light curves of certain variables which constitute a challenge to all working on the theory of pulsating stars. The hypothesis that certain variable stars are variable because they are pulsating is now commonplace, but the hypothesis had not been propounded when Plummer went to Ireland. His own researches constituted an important step towards its formulation and justification. In 1913 he combined his interests in dynamical astronomy and variable stars and carried through an important research on the Cepheid variable $\zeta$ Geminorum. The observed Doppler displacements were inconsistent with the idea that this star was a binary, and Plummer showed that the discrepancies could not be attributed to the gravitational action of a third body. He was led to suggest that the Doppler displacements were due, at any rate in part, to radial displacements of the matter forming the stellar atmosphere. Two years later, in an analysis of the observations of another variable,' RR Lyrae, he gave the first attempt at a theoretical investigation of pulsation. But it was left to Sir Arthur Eddington [q.v.] to develop the theory.

It must have been a hard decision for a man who was above all an astronomer for Plummer to accept the Woolwich chair of mathematics in 1921. But he had not been happy in Ireland. The country life at Dunsink did not suit the temperament of one who was a townsman and at that time a bachelor. Moreover, the poor equipment at Dunsink was frustrating, although it brought its compensations in leaving him time to write a valuable *Introductory Treatise on Dynamical Astronomy* (1918).

With his appointment to Woolwich Plummer's prolific output of astronomical research papers came to an end. He did contribute about a dozen papers to the Royal Astronomical Society of which he eventually became president (1939-41), but he was much too conscientious to neglect his new responsibilities. He produced two textbooks during this period, *Principles of Mechanics* (1929) and *Probability and Frequency* (1940). Towards the end of his life he was chiefly occupied in preparing a complete edition of the works of Newton. Unfortunately he did not live to complete this task, which was undertaken at the request of the Royal Society.

Plummer was personally a rather quiet man, modest and self-effacing, but not falsely so, and possessed of the dignity which accompanies true and deep scholarship. As a mathematician he was competent; as an astronomer he was both competent and devoted to his true vocation. In 1924 he married an old friend, Beatrice Howard, daughter of the late Henry Howard Hayward, a Harley Street surgeon. She predeceased him by a few months and this blow probably hastened his own death which took place at Oxford 30 September 1946. There were no children.

[W. M. H. Greaves in *Obituary Notices of Fellows of the Royal Society*, No. 16, May 1948; *Monthly Notices* of the Royal Astronomical Society, vol. cvii, No. 1, 1947; private information; personal knowledge.]

W. M. H. GREAVES.

POLLARD, ALBERT FREDERICK (1869–1948), historian, was born in Ryde, Isle of Wight, 16 December 1869, the second son of Henry Hindes Pollard, a pharmaceutical chemist, by his wife, Emily May Cave. His elder brother, Henry Bargman Pollard, of Christ Church, Oxford, a biologist of much promise, was accidentally drowned at the age of twenty-six. From Felsted School, where he had the good fortune to be taught by John Sargeaunt [q.v.], Pollard went up to Jesus College, Oxford, in 1887 as an exhibitioner. Here, although short of money and not enjoying social 'occasions', he took a full part in college life and was captain of the boats, at a time, however, when the position of the college eight on the river was very humble. In honour moderations (1889) he was placed in the second class, but before that he had decided to read for the final school of modern history, having no inclination for the philosophical part of *literae humaniores*. In 1940 he wrote to his daughter that he was 'always glad to have continued classics up to honour mods., instead of going to Oxford on a history scholarship', and that he doubted the wisdom of letting boys 'specialize' on history at school. He was one of the early Jesus pupils of R. L. Poole [q.v.], who gave him 'endless help' and brought out his aptitude for close work in chronology and in the critical handling of authorities. He won his first class in modern history (1891), but was advised not to stand for a prize fellowship.

Supporting himself by coaching in London, he won the Lothian prize in 1892, and the Arnold prize in 1898. In 1893 he was appointed an assistant editor of this DICTIONARY, on which he worked until the completion of the first Supplement in 1901. He contributed altogether some 500 lives (the equivalent of one whole volume of the original edition), and in so doing he completed his training as an historian. His work lay mainly in the Tudor period, and before the DICTIONARY was finished he wrote two biographical volumes as vigorous as they were original, *England Under Protector Somerset* (1900) and *Henry VIII* (1902).

In 1903 Pollard was elected to a new part-time chair of constitutional history in University College, London, which he held, for most of his tenure as a full-time appointment, until 1931. When he was first appointed there was scarcely even the nucleus of an historical school in London, although in the other English universities historical studies were gaining ground in consequence both of a growing interest among the educated public and of a widening of the area from which university students were recruited. Pollard identified himself with this movement and left his impress on it. In his inaugural lecture he announced a programme which he carried out at the cost of thirty-five years of strenuous activity. He was influential in devising the curricula and regulations for London degree courses and also (partly by a skilful use of public lectures) in attracting students from the schools. In 1906 he founded the Historical Association, a link between teachers of history in schools and universities, of which he was president from 1912 to 1915. In 1916 he persuaded the Association to acquire a derelict periodical, *History*, which he edited for the next six years, raising it to a high level of quality, circulation, and influence. As the London history school grew and prospered, his own position became more important and better rewarded. In 1920 he brought about the foundation of the university's Institute of Historical Research. He hacked his way to this through the tangle of London academic politics virtually single-handed. The necessary financial support, to the tune of £20,000, was supplied by (Sir) John Cecil Power [q.v.], afterwards created a baronet, who was Pollard's neighbour at Putney and who, although no scholar, caught the infection of his enthusiasm. The Institute was admirably conceived. It was inter-collegiate, and, by means of a system of co-operation with the British universities, it soon became a national centre for supervised research in subjects suitable for study in the libraries and archives of London. It was opened in 1921 on the occasion of the first of a useful series of Anglo-American historical conferences. In 1923 it began to publish its own *Bulletin*. Pollard was its head until he retired from his chair in 1931, remaining honorary director until 1939. Under his guidance the work of the Institute steadily expanded. It rescued some historical enterprises, notably the *Victoria County History*, from their embarrassments, and even offered help to some which were not conscious of debility.

Being in London and being so much at home in committee work, Pollard was drawn into public activities connected with history, like the committee on parliamentary records of 1929, and also into some of wider scope. In 1918 he was a member of the government committee on a League of Nations, and in 1924–6 of that on the university of London. In the parliamentary elections of 1922 and the two following years he stood as Liberal candidate for the university of London, but unsuccessfully.

In 1908 he was elected to a research fellowship at All Souls College, Oxford, where he consequently spent many weekends. In All Souls his part was useful but restrained. An excellent 'assistant examiner' for fellowships, he steadily upheld good academic standards in college business, but he did not press for any important changes. He entered good-naturedly into the social life of the college, and it was in 'cock-fighting' in the revels of the bursar's dinner in 1913 that he broke his leg. The result was that, as he soon had to leave for America, he corrected the proofs of two volumes while he was unable to leave his house and work in libraries. Consequently these two (the second and third volumes of *The Reign of Henry VII from Contemporary Sources*, 1914) are the only ones he ever published with a considerable number of textual errors. Except for one special course of lectures and the Ford's lectures of 1927–8, Pollard took no part in the work of the Oxford history faculty. His fellowship gave him new opportunities of informal acquaintance with men in public life. In particular, through his colleague Geoffrey Dawson [q.v.] he formed a close connexion with *The Times* in which he published anonymous articles and many letters on historical and political subjects, besides being a constant contributor to the autonomous *Literary Supplement*. After successive renewals of his research fellowship he was elected a fellow of All Souls in the category of 'distinguished persons'; but he did not visit Oxford after 1935.

Pollard's creative work in administration never checked the flow of his historical writing. The complimentary volume of essays presented to him in 1924 to commemorate his twelve years' chairmanship of the London University board of historical studies bears the appropriate title *Tudor Studies*. This was his main field, although he wrote much, usually on a more popular level, about earlier, later, and even contemporary history. No bibliography of his writings exists, and this is regrettable, since some of his best work was in short contributions to periodicals, and even to their correspondence columns. His major works all related to English history. The volume on Edward VI, Mary, and Elizabeth (1910) in the *Political History of England* edited by R. L. Poole and William Hunt [q.v.] was one of the best of that excellent series. *The Evolution of Parliament* (1920), rather unguardedly positive and ranging outside the limits of his own period, was not well received by specialists on the fourteenth and fifteenth centuries, but it was a work of bold sweep and challenging ideas. In his *Wolsey* (1929), based on his Oxford Ford's lectures, Pollard wrote as a specialist. He was the leading authority on the Tudor period in his generation. It is due to him that so much of the historical work in London University has lain in this field, and his was also one of the earliest and strongest influences in promoting the modern study of parliamentary history. His point of view was Protestant, English, and liberal. His literary style was equally correct and brilliant, the expression of a sharp, swift, and ingenious mind. He delighted in the minute analysis of words. Not reflective or philosophical, he thought in terms of times, places, and personal action; but he handled political ideas easily and well. He had great knowledge, and he also understood how to avail himself of the assistance of others. In early life his first wife, and in later life their friend, Miss Eliza Jeffries Davis, relieved him of much detailed work. He himself did little work on manuscripts, but he excelled in squeezing the last drop from printed evidence.

He was a shortish man, sturdily built, clean-shaven, and wearing pince-nez. A portrait drawing by (Sir) William Rothenstein made in 1926 (in the possession of the family) is not considered so good a likeness as the photograph prefixed to *Tudor Studies*. He talked incisively and quickly, delighting in argument. His physical energy and endurance were almost as remarkable as his capacity for literary and organizing work: he walked, swam, and bicycled vigorously until his old age. Brought up as a Wesleyan Methodist, he went through a phase of religious unsettlement as an undergraduate; in later life he was not hostile to organized religion. He read French and German but did not speak them well. Except for half a dozen holidays in Switzerland he scarcely visited the continent; but he travelled in America twice and found the academic world there very much to his liking. As a teacher he relied rather on force than on sympathy, and as a reviewer he was sometimes unduly severe, mercilessly exposing errors without always recognizing such merits as went along with them. He received many academic honours, including honorary doctorates from Manchester, London, and Oxford, and an honorary fellowship at Jesus; he was elected F.B.A. in 1920 and became a corresponding member of the Académie des Inscriptions et Belles-Lettres in 1930. He was not, however, covetous of public distinctions, and when a knighthood was offered him about the time of his retirement, he declined it.

In 1894 he married Catherine Susanna (died 1934), daughter of William Lucy, of the Eagle Ironworks, Oxford (another of whose daughters married A. H. J. Greenidge, q.v.). By her he had two children, a son, Mr. Graham Pollard the bibliographer, and a daughter who became the wife of Harold Edgeworth Butler, professor of Latin at University College, London. In 1942 Pollard married Marjorie, daughter of the late Thomas Orchardson, a silk merchant, of Bingley, Yorkshire. Pollard died 3 August 1948 at the home in Milford-on-Sea to which he had retired seventeen years before.

[The Times, 5 August 1948; J. E. Neale in English Historical Review, vol. lxiv, April 1949; C. H. Williams in Bulletin of the Institute of Historical Research, vol. xxii, May 1949; V. H. Galbraith in Proceedings of the British Academy, vol. xxxv, 1949; private information; personal knowledge.]

G. N. CLARK.

POLLARD, ALFRED WILLIAM (1859–1944), librarian, bibliographer, and English scholar, was born in London 14 August 1859, the youngest son of a physician, Edward William Pollard, by his second wife, Emma Louisa, daughter of George Edward Thompson, a shipowner, of Woodbridge, Suffolk. It was from John Wesley Hales at King's College School, which he attended for seven years, that he acquired his interest in Chaucer and Shakespeare. In 1877 he went with an open scholarship to St. John's College, Oxford, obtaining first classes in classical moderations (1879) and *literae humaniores* (1881) and, more important, the intimate friendship of A. E. Housman [q.v.]. Debarred by a stammer from teaching, Pollard entered the printed books department of the British Museum in 1883, where, attracted by the artistic quality of early printing, he grew interested in this side of librarianship, and in a few years

became a recognized authority able to take charge of the antiquarian work of the department. In 1893 he was joined by R. G. C. Proctor [q.v.] who already had an established reputation as an incunabulist.

A venturesome but very happy marriage in 1887 made it necessary to supplement a modest salary by literary work and led to his long association with the *Guardian* under Daniel Conner Lathbury. Pollard had already edited several of Chaucer's *Canterbury Tales* (1886–7); in 1893 he produced his *Chaucer* primer; in 1898 he edited the 'Globe Chaucer' in collaboration with (Sir) H. F. Heath, (Sir) W. S. McCormick [qq.v.], and M. H. Liddell, himself undertaking the *Canterbury Tales*. His selection of *English Miracle Plays, Moralities, and Interludes*, a pioneer work often revised, first appeared in 1890; it was followed by editions of the *Towneley Plays* with George England (1897) and of the *Macro Plays* with F. J. Furnivall [q.v.] (1904).

In 1889 (Sir) J. Y. W. MacAlister founded the *Library*, and Pollard, at first a contributor, was acknowledged as co-editor in January 1904. The partnership lasted until in 1920 the *Library* became the organ of the Bibliographical Society under Pollard's control. MacAlister was also largely responsible for the founding in 1892 of the Bibliographical Society, which Pollard joined the next year as honorary secretary, and as such directed its work for over forty years. He also edited a series of 'Books about Books', himself writing that on *Early Illustrated Books* (1893), and the handsome and scholarly quarterly *Bibliographica* (1895–7).

Proctor's peculiar genius prompted the trustees to undertake a *Catalogue of Books printed in the XVth Century now in the British Museum*, designed by him and Pollard; after Proctor's death in 1903, loyalty to his friend and to the trustees induced Pollard to shoulder a task for which he had no innate taste or aptitude. It was this rigorous discipline, however, which turned a gifted amateur into a bibliographer of high technical attainment. The first volume appeared in 1908, and Pollard carried on the work until administrative duties forced him to hand it over to his principal lieutenant, Dr. J. V. Scholderer.

It was in the bibliography and textual criticism of Shakespeare that Pollard made his chief contribution to scholarship. His attention seems to have been accidentally turned in this direction about 1902; the outcome, in 1909, was his *Shakespeare Folios and Quartos: a Study in the Bibliography of Shakespeare's Plays, 1594–1685*, which will remain a milestone in Shakespearian criticism. In it he controverted the views on the transmission of the text which had prevailed since Edmund Malone [q.v.] condemned all quartos as surreptitious, arguing on the contrary that some may even have been printed from autographs. Another dogma of orthodoxy established by Malone, that Shakespeare served an apprenticeship revising the plays of other men, was challenged twenty years later in (Professor) Peter Alexander's *Shakespeare's Henry VI and Richard III*, an investigation inspired and sponsored by Pollard. These two books laid the foundation of most modern textual criticisms of Shakespeare. In line with them are Pollard's lectures as Sandars reader in bibliography in the university of Cambridge (1915), *Shakespeare's Fight with the Pirates and the Problems of the Transmission of his Text* (1917, revised ed. 1920), his detailed analysis of the text of *Richard II* (1916), his British Academy lecture on *The Foundations of Shakespeare's Text* (1923), and his article on 'Shakespeare's Text' in *A Companion to Shakespeare Studies* (1934). Significant too is the volume of studies he promoted and edited on the question of *Shakespeare's Hand in the Play of Sir Thomas More* (1923), claiming that three pages of Shakespeare's autograph survive in MS. Harley 7368. From 1919 to 1932 Pollard was honorary professor of bibliography in the university of London and piloted the students of King's College, of which he had been a fellow since 1907, through some of the most disputed fields of Shakespearian criticism.

To the Oxford facsimile of the authorized version of the Bible, issued for the tercentenary of 1911, Pollard contributed an historical introduction and a collection of documents relating to the translation of the Bible into English, which are of permanent value for biblical studies.

Pollard became keeper of printed books in 1919 at a time of great administrative difficulty, and in five years of strenuous work left his impress on the organization of the department. He retired in 1924. In 1919 the Bibliographical Society had laid plans for *A Short-Title Catalogue of Books Printed in England, Scotland, and Ireland, and of English Books Printed Abroad, 1475–1640*, and much preliminary work

had been done by Gilbert Richard Redgrave. In 1924 Pollard took charge, and two years later appeared a work invaluable to historical students. Other interests too engrossed him, and after the death of Sir Israel Gollancz [q.v.] in 1930 he took an active part in the work of the Shakespeare Association and became director of the Early English Text Society, until 1937. He also took part in the founding of the Central Library for Students, later the National Central Library.

In 1934 Pollard resigned the secretaryship of the Bibliographical Society and the editorship of the *Library*. His work had won him many academic honours; he became an honorary fellow of St. John's in 1923, and received honorary degrees from the universities of Durham (1921) and Cambridge (1934). He was elected F.B.A. and appointed C.B. in 1922. In 1935 he met with an accident while gardening which incapacitated him for serious work, but he lived another nine years, dying at Wimbledon 8 March 1944.

A man of the widest human sympathies and a sincere churchman, Alfred Pollard was deeply religious in a mode peculiarly his own. In 1911 he published anonymously a small book of practical morality, *Life, Love and Light*. He married in 1887 Alice (died 1926), daughter of George England, of Crediton, Devon, and had two sons, both of whom distinguished themselves, and were killed, in the war of 1914–18, and one daughter who survived him. A portrait of Pollard, painted by Frank Brooks, is in the possession of the National Central Library.

[A. W. Pollard and Henry Thomas in *A Select Bibliography of the Writings of Alfred W. Pollard*, 1938; J. Dover Wilson in *Proceedings* of the British Academy, vol. xxxi, 1945, in which is reproduced a drawing (1927) by (Sir) William Rothenstein; personal knowledge.]                    W. W. GREG.

POLLOCK, BERTRAM (1863–1943), headmaster, and bishop of Norwich, was born at Hanworth 6 December 1863, the youngest of the six sons of George Frederick Pollock, senior master of the Supreme Court and later Queen's remembrancer, and his wife, Frances Diana, daughter of the Rev. Henry Herbert, rector of Rathdowney, Queen's County. He was a younger brother of E. M. Pollock, Viscount Hanworth, and a first cousin of Sir Frederick Pollock [qq.v.]. He was a scholar of Charterhouse and of Trinity College, Cambridge, and in 1885 was placed in the first class of part i of the classical tripos. In 1891 he was ordained priest at Salisbury and he proceeded D.D. in 1903. He was an assistant master at Marlborough from 1886 to 1893 when he was appointed master of Wellington College.

The nomination of so young a man to the mastership proved to be justified by the event. The fortunes of the school were at the time precarious, but in the first seven years of his rule he refashioned its structure and revised its destinies. As master he displayed four superlative gifts: a passionate addiction to hard work, swift and inflexible judgement, an astonishing zest for detail, and an unruffled tranquillity of temperament. He reached the zenith of his headmastership at the jubilee of the college in 1909.

In the year following he was consecrated bishop of Norwich. He was an untried man in the work of the Church. He quickly disclosed a remarkable ability in diocesan affairs; he developed a scheme for the endowment of poor benefices, and declared himself in favour of a well-constituted plan for the division of the diocese. In Church politics he remained frigidly aloof, but during the struggle over the revision of the Book of Common Prayer he bore the chief part on the negative side, and as a resolute champion of the old Prayer Book he separated himself for a time from the Lambeth discussions in order to assure his complete independence. Although acclaimed at public meetings, in parliamentary debates he was less effective. In 1939 he was chairman of the Canterbury Convocation committee for the revision of the Lectionary, an office which he retained until his resignation of the bishopric in 1942.

Pollock's appointment as bishop of Norwich made closer his connexion with the Court upon which he personally set much value, and his regard for the royal family was warmly reciprocated. In wider circles, however, he was a sequestered and even secretive figure, but he had singular charm for those who responded to his whimsical humour. To those who knew him best he was an ideal host, a wise counsellor, a generous friend. King Edward VII appointed him C.V.O. in 1909 and one of his chaplains-in-ordinary (1904–10); and King George V promoted him K.C.V.O. in 1921.

In 1928 Pollock married Joan Florence Helena, daughter of the Rev. Algernon Charles Dudley Ryder, grandson of the first Earl of Harrowby [q.v.] and rector of Maresfield, Sussex, by whom he had one daughter. He died at Gissing, Norfolk, 17 October 1943. There are two portraits of him by E. Brock, one of which hangs at Wellington College.

[*The Times*, 19 October 1943; Harold Nicolson, *Some People*, 1927; Bertram Pollock, *A Twentieth Century Bishop*, 1944; personal knowledge.]

R. St. C. Talboys.

PONSONBY, ARTHUR AUGUSTUS WILLIAM HARRY, first Baron Ponsonby of Shulbrede (1871–1946), politician and author, was born at Windsor Castle 16 February 1871, the third son of (Sir) Henry Frederick Ponsonby [q.v.], private secretary to Queen Victoria. His mother was Mary Elizabeth, daughter of John Crocker Bulteel, M.P., and granddaughter of Lord Grey [q.v.] of the Reform Bill. His elder brothers were General Sir John Ponsonby and the first Baron Sysonby. From both parents he inherited strong Whig traditions. At the age of eleven he was made page of honour to Queen Victoria and so remained for five years. In 1884 he went to Eton to Warre Cornish's house of which he became captain; he was a member of the Eton Society and secretary of the Musical Society. He went in 1890 to Balliol College, Oxford, and passed into the diplomatic service in 1894, serving until 1897 in Turkey. Next year he was posted to Copenhagen and from 1900 to 1902 was at the Foreign Office, during which time he made up his mind to enter politics. He resigned from the service after pressing in vain for reforms and shortly afterwards was given a post in the Liberal Central Association. At the general election of 1906 he was narrowly defeated for Taunton soon after Campbell-Bannerman, then premier, whom Ponsonby greatly admired, had appointed him his principal private secretary—a conspicuous honour. In that office he became increasingly oppressed by the glaring contrasts between luxury and misery which marked the age, and gave graceful expression to this in *The Camel and the Needle's Eye* (1909), now a period piece. As early as 1907 he had virtually decided to 'accept the truth of Socialism as an ideal'. Such views were not then inconsistent with membership of the Liberal Party.

When Campbell-Bannerman died, Ponsonby succeeded him at Stirling Burghs. He was quickly out of step with the official leadership of the party and voted against the Government on the question of the King's proposed visit to the Tsar. This brought him a reprimand from the chief whip and cost him the favour of the Court. His name, with those of two others, one of them J. Keir Hardie [q.v.], was deleted from the King's list of garden-party guests and he felt it a duty to his constituents to protest to the King's private secretary. He found himself for a time treated half as a traitor, half as a martyr, and 'did not know which he hated more'. With some of the old pioneers of Socialism he got on well, admiring Keir Hardie and, in early days, John Burns [q.v.]. He criticized the foreign policy of Sir Edward Grey (later Viscount Grey of Fallodon, q.v.), moved for a reduction in armaments, and in 1909 became convinced that the House of Lords was a major obstacle to progress and that the Liberal imperialism of Asquith and Grey was unacceptable to a strong Radical and would destroy the Liberal Party. In 1913 he refused an appointment as junior whip. On 3 August 1914 he courageously spoke in a hostile House against the decision to fight and, with Keir Hardie, commanded attention and respect.

Throughout the war he followed his independent, pacifist line, urging a negotiated peace and enduring, at bodily risk, public and private misunderstanding and obloquy. At the coupon election of 1918, when he contested Dunfermline as an independent democrat, he was inevitably and soundly beaten. Shortly afterwards he joined the Independent Labour Party, where he found himself in more congenial company with other friends like C. R. Buxton and his brother (who became Lord Noel-Buxton, q.v.), E. D. Morel, and (Sir) Charles Trevelyan. For four years he remained out of Parliament during which time he joined the Labour Party and at the general election of 1922 he fought on an advanced programme the Brightside division of Sheffield, a district which in part depended on armaments. He won handsomely. On the formation of the Labour Government in 1924 he was made under-secretary at the Foreign Office—Ramsay MacDonald being both prime minister and foreign secretary. In these circumstances the office was of great consequence and Ponsonby in the few months available made his mark; in the tortuous negotiations over the Russian commercial and general treaties his patience and tact were widely acknowledged, although their conclusion immediately before the summer recess and the provision for a Russian loan

aroused the anger of the Opposition. The treaties were repudiated later in the year when the Conservatives took office. In the interval between the two Labour administrations, he worked ceaselessly for the elimination of war, inaugurating the 'Peace Letter' and writing books and pamphlets condemning the folly and barbarity of war. In the administration of 1929 he was in turn under-secretary for Dominion affairs and parliamentary secretary at the Ministry of Transport (1929–31).

In 1930 he took his seat, as Baron Ponsonby of Shulbrede, in the House of Lords where the Government was under-represented. In both Houses he was well liked for his personal charm and respected for his moral courage, single-mindedness, and lack of pretension. For a short time in 1931 he was chancellor of the Duchy of Lancaster until the formation of the 'national' Government when he became leader of the Labour Party opposition in the Lords. In 1935 he resigned the leadership over the question of sanctions and other matters of foreign policy, restating in a letter to George Lansbury [q.v.] his lifelong belief that force of arms could never secure world peace. By now indeed his differences with the party were unsurmountable. Thereafter he gradually and thankfully retired into private life, emerging only on pacifist occasions, such as the Peace Pledge Union rallies, which kept him busy and travelling. In the Munich period his short-term prophecies were not infallible, yet his vigorous denunciations of rearmament brought him at the time more general support than at any other juncture in his political life. He believed in Neville Chamberlain and, to all intents and purposes, in peace at any price. On 15 May 1940 he resigned from the Labour Party after the formation of the national coalition Government. But a Socialist and a pacifist he remained until his death.

In his public career he had held tenaciously and courageously to the causes he embraced. He chose his time for his political decisions, but he never made them from self-interest. His lifelong friend, J. L. Hammond [q.v.], who disagreed with Ponsonby's pacifism at all times, strongly testified to his integrity. His own unpublished diaries, which cover the whole of his political life to his death, frankly set down the evolution of his political creed; nor would he revise them in the light of after events—an honest and revealing document. He retired to west

Sussex where (as far back as 1902) he had bought and restored an ancient and small priory near Haslemere, and here his books, garden, and cultural interests and the company of his friends filled his days busily and, apart from politics, happily. He wrote a number of books and anthologies, some designed as political propaganda, many more dealing with social and economic problems and history in which he was deeply interested. He was an authority on English diaries, publishing a series of anthologies, and he wrote on Pepys, Evelyn, and Queen Victoria. His *Henry Ponsonby—his life from his letters* (1942) won him the James Tait Black memorial prize and is a book of great charm and humour and of importance for the light it throws on the Court and the office of private secretary. A talent for acting stood him in good stead when he took to broadcasting. He was a pioneer in 'fireside' talks and quickly mastered the technique. In private life he was a delightful companion, a lover and creator of good talk, with a keen sense of humour and a good store of knowledge on literary and antiquarian subjects. Simple in his habits, wholesome in his tastes, he was totally lacking in pretension and pomposity. He derived intense pleasure from painting, skill in which he inherited from his mother, from natural beauty, and from works of art, and he was a member of council of the Royal College of Music. All these interests he closely shared with his wife, Dorothea, daughter of Sir Hubert Parry [q.v.]. Their marriage took place in 1898 and they had a son, Matthew Henry Hubert (born 1904), who succeeded him in his title, and a daughter. Ponsonby died at Hindhead 23 March 1946.

He was a subject for cartoonists in *Punch* and elsewhere, and (Sir) Max Beerbohm chose him for his 'The Old and the Young Self' series (*Observations*, 1926), but in likeness and wit the result falls below that master's high standard.

[Lord Ponsonby's books and unpublished diaries; private information; personal knowledge.]                                JOHN GORE.

PORTAL, SIR WYNDHAM RAYMOND, third baronet, and VISCOUNT PORTAL (1885–1949), industrialist and public servant, was born at Southington House, Overton, Hampshire, 9 April 1885, the elder son of (Sir) William Wyndham Portal, who became second baronet, and his wife, Florence Elizabeth Mary, daughter of St. Leger Richard Glyn, second son

of the first Baron Wolverton. Melville Portal [q.v.] was his great-uncle. Educated at Eton and Christ Church, Oxford, Wyndham Portal was commissioned in the 9th Lancers, later transferred to the 1st Life Guards and resigned in 1911. On the outbreak of war in 1914 he returned to the Life Guards, became a lieutenant-colonel in 1915, and commanded the Household battalion in France. He was appointed to the D.S.O. in November 1917, M.V.O. in 1918, and four times mentioned in dispatches.

Returning to the family business of Portals, Ltd., Portal became managing director in 1919 and chairman in 1931 on the death of his father whom he succeeded in the baronetcy. Portals had manufactured watermarked bank-note paper for the Bank of England since that privilege had been granted in 1724 to Henri Portal, a young Huguenot refugee. The advent of paper money during the war of 1914–18 in place of gold coinage increased enormously the demand for high-quality bank-note paper. Portal was determined that his firm should become the leading manufacturers in the world, and through his immense energy and resource this position was achieved in less than twenty years. In 1919 Portals introduced the cylinder mould made process for the manufacture of the one-pound and ten-shilling notes, and by the time of Portal's death the firm made watermarked bank-note paper for more than eighty different countries and banks of issue. In 1930 Portal became chairman of Wiggins, Teape & Co. (1919), Ltd., paper manufacturers, a position which he held until 1940. He was also a director of the Great Western Railway Company and of the Commercial Union Assurance Company.

In 1932 Portal was made a member of a commission on the pig industry; in the following year he was chairman of a committee set up in connexion with the Pigs and Bacon marketing boards; and in 1935 he became chairman of the Bacon Development Board. Meanwhile the Government had called upon him in 1934 to report upon the distressed areas in South Wales, and in 1936, as an industrial adviser to the Government on distressed areas, he was made chairman of the Special Areas Reconstruction Association, and of the Nuffield trust and the Treasury fund to finance the establishment of industries in these areas. His efforts were greatly appreciated, particularly in Wales where he was given the freedom of both Cardiff and Merthyr Tydfil and received the honorary degree of LL.D. from the university of Wales (1937). He had been created a baron in 1935.

In April 1939 Portal was nominated regional commissioner for civil defence in Wales. He resigned in December and in 1940 became chairman of the Coal Production Council. In the autumn of that year he became an additional parliamentary secretary to the Ministry of Supply, with responsibility for the control of all raw materials. In 1942 he became minister of works and buildings (later works and planning) and first commissioner of works and public buildings, and was sworn of the Privy Council. In this capacity he initiated the programme of prefabricated houses which became known as 'Portal houses'. 'He was one of the ablest of the business men who joined the Government', wrote Mr. C. R. (subsequently Earl) Attlee (*As It Happened*, 1954). 'Extremely generous and public spirited, he won the hearts of Labour by his work for the distressed areas before the war.' Towards the end of 1944, however, it was felt that the minister of works must be in the House of Commons and Portal left the Government. Raised to a viscountcy (1945) he returned to industry, and, rejoining the board of the Great Western Railway, became its chairman in 1945. At the end of 1947 he succeeded Lord Mottistone [q.v.] as lord lieutenant of Hampshire.

Portal was a very keen sportsman, and a particularly good partridge shot. The shoot at Laverstoke became famous under his organization, and the standard which he required of his guests was exacting. He remained to his last day a first-rate shot, and for a man of his bulk was still amazingly quick. There were few finer dry-fly fishermen. Many of Portal's happiest hours were spent on the banks of the Test, which he knew intimately. Moreover, he kept an excellent stud. His association with the Jockey Club towards the end of his life was most active, for he took part in the activities of the club both financial and otherwise which affected racing throughout the country. He was also a keen yachtsman.

As vice-chairman of King George's Jubilee Trust from 1936 until his death Portal did much for the welfare of the younger generation, and the benefit of his sound advice was always available to those concerned with youth organizations. He had an instinct and genius for success, and was sure to know everything that was going on; he had countless sources of information, and his mind was never at rest. He delighted also in surmounting difficult obstacles and persuading difficult people. His generosity was lavish and usually anonymous. He was a 'big' man in every sense of the word. In 1935 he accepted the chairmanship of the British Olympic Association and it was largely due to his munificence that so large and representative a British team was able to attend the Olympic games held in Berlin the following year. He presided over the XIV Olympiad held in London in 1948 and was appointed G.C.M.G. in 1949.

Portal married in 1909 Lady Louise Rosemary Kathleen Virginia Cairns, only child of the second Earl Cairns. There were no children and the peerage became extinct when Portal died 6 May 1949 at his home at Laverstoke where there is an admirable portrait of him by (Sir) Oswald Birley. He was succeeded in the baronetcy by his uncle, Sir Spencer John Portal (1864–1955).

[Personal knowledge.] J. V. Sheffield.

POTTER, (HELEN) BEATRIX, afterwards Mrs. Heelis (1866–1943), writer and illustrator of children's books, was born in South Kensington 6 July 1866, the elder child and only daughter of Rupert Potter, a well-to-do barrister who had never practised, by his wife, Helen, daughter of John Leech, of Dukinfield, Cheshire. Sir H. E. Roscoe [q.v.] was her uncle. Both her parents, who came of north-country dissenting stock, had inherited Lancashire cotton fortunes. Beatrix did not go to school, and had no friends. Excessively reserved and shy, she became much attached to one of her governesses, Miss Hammond, who encouraged her childish talent for drawing and introduced her to the study of natural history in the near-by museum. The happiest periods in a childhood singularly dull, repressed, and conventional, were the summer holidays, when the Potters rented large furnished houses, first in Scotland and later in the Lakes. It was here that Beatrix had her first experience of the countryside, and she responded to it with passion. She studied and drew hedgerow flowers and animals, and when she found them dissected dead mice, birds, hedgehogs, squirrels, and foxes.

Beatrix Potter's sturdy nature, which had had so little human contact or encouragement, turned towards animals with a feeling which was as strong as it was unsentimental. Pet rabbits were smuggled into the London nursery where they passed long, sophisticated lives. She kept mice, bats, frogs, snails, and a tame hedgehog, and pursued her quiet occupation of studying and drawing them.

This amusement was a purely private one until she was twenty-seven (still living in South Kensington with her authoritative parents) when she began writing letters to beguile the convalescence of the child of a former governess. In these and in other letters, illustrated with little drawings of great humour and spirit, she told anecdotes of her pets, Peter Rabbit and Benjamin Bunny, and made up adventures for her tame hedgehog, Mrs. Tiggy-Winkle. They gave such pleasure that Beatrix Potter decided to turn the story of Peter Rabbit into a book; but she failed to find a publisher, and in 1900 had it privately printed, following it in 1902 with another private publication, *The Tailor of Gloucester*. In the meantime there had begun an association, both professional and personal, with Frederick Warne & Co. which was to last her lifetime. During the next thirty years they published no fewer than twenty-four of her highly original little books for young children. Nineteen of them had appeared by 1913, including the tales of Peter Rabbit, Jemima Puddle-Duck, Mrs. Tiggy-Winkle, Squirrel Nutkin and Mr. Jeremy Fisher, which are perhaps the best known.

Against her parents' strenuous opposition Beatrix Potter became engaged, at the age of thirty-nine, to Norman Warne, son of the publisher; but he died a few months later, and she made this the occasion of a partial and tacit escape from her parents. With the earnings from her books she had bought a small mixed farm at Sawrey in the Lancashire corner of the Lake District, and from this time spent an increasing proportion of her time there, producing books for her own pleasure and learning to be a farmer. The books of this period are full of exquisite water-colour paintings of Sawrey and Hawkshead, and of that north-country farming life of her ancestors to which she reverted with satisfaction in middle-age.

In 1913, at the age of forty-seven, again acting against the wishes of her parents, she married William Heelis, solicitor, of Ambleside, and in the thirty years of happy married life which followed developed the shrewd, caustic north-country side of her character. Her creative period was finished, and she put her full energies into hill-sheep farming, becoming a successful breeder and landowner; at the time of her death at Sawrey, 22 December 1943, she was president-elect of the Herdwick Association. Her books, unique in the humour and poetic truth of their stories and in the beauty of their water-colour illustrations, were soon established as nursery classics and were translated into many languages. American enthusiasm for her work persuaded her, in old age, to attempt to revive her unique creative gift and to produce one or two stories for the American public. These attempts, however, were not successful; the stories were unexpectedly prolix, and her eyesight was no longer equal to good drawing. *The Fairy Caravan*, a collection of tales put together for American readers in 1929, was eventually published in England in 1952, but could add nothing to her reputation.

Beatrix Potter's extensive farm property in the Lake District was bequeathed to the National Trust, which still maintains her first little farmhouse, Hill Top, Sawrey, in the same condition as when she lived in it. Twenty-two of her illustrations for *The Tailor of Gloucester* may be seen in the Tate Gallery. A portrait of Beatrix Potter by Delmar Banner is in the National Portrait Gallery.

[Margaret Lane, *The Tale of Beatrix Potter*, 1946; L. Linder and W. A. Herring, *The Art of Beatrix Potter*, 1955; private information.]

MARGARET LANE.

POULTON, SIR EDWARD BAGNALL (1856–1943), zoologist, was born at Reading 27 January 1856, the second child and only son of William Ford Poulton, architect, by his wife, Georgina Selina Bagnall. From his youth he showed a keen enjoyment of natural history, especially of entomology, which became his life's work. But it was not at first encouraged at Oakley House, Reading, and school was 'a long dreary interval in a happy life'. His father wished Edward to follow in his footsteps, but eventually allowed him to study science, and in 1873 Poulton won a scholarship at Jesus College, Oxford, and in 1879 was president of the Union.

Having been placed in the first class in natural science (zoology) in 1876 Poulton became a demonstrator in comparative anatomy under George Rolleston [q.v.], whose brilliant lectures had greatly inspired him, but the emoluments being inadequate he worked for, and gained in

1878, the Burdett-Coutts scholarship in geology, and for a time worked under (Sir) Joseph Prestwich [q.v.]. Thus it came about that his first published researches, in 1880, were on tertiary remains in a Yorkshire cave. Fortunately for zoology, he was able to return to it when appointed in the same year a lecturer at Jesus and Keble colleges and he early attracted attention by morphological studies on the tongues of marsupials and by discovering in the embryos of *Ornithorhynchus* the rudiments of teeth. His last work on vertebrate zoology, in 1894, was a paper on the bill and hairs of *Ornithorhynchus*, with a discussion of the homologies and origin of mammalian hair.

Poulton's contributions to entomology began in 1884, with a paper on his favourite subject, the colours, markings, and protective attitudes of caterpillars. His interest in this was stimulated by finding that some observations he had made as a boy were in accord with the studies of August Weismann. Throughout his life he emphasized the need for observation of the living insect, especially in its behaviour. A series of papers from his pen threw much light on the power possessed by many insects of altering their coloration to harmonize with the environment. Essays by A. R. Wallace [q.v.] turned his attention to the importance of protective colouring in all its forms, concealing, warning, and mimetic, and this is the subject of which he became the foremost exponent.

Much interested in heredity, Poulton was in sympathy with Weismann's theories, and organized an English translation of his work, but when the Mendelian theory was developed he was antagonized by the stress at first laid upon the large, sudden variations then known as 'mutations'. Strongly opposed to the mutation theory he consistently urged the Darwinian principle of evolution through small variations; it is as a stalwart Darwinian that he will always be remembered. As the science of genetics developed he did not enter into it and he never followed its rapid growth. There was, however, enough to occupy him in his own field and he was a prolific writer. In 1890 he produced *The Colours of Animals*, a book remarkable for its concise, simple explanation by natural selection of the many forms of coloration which he ingeniously summarized in a comparative table introducing terms which are now the standard nomenclature.

The Royal Society elected Poulton a fellow in 1889, and in 1893 he was appointed Hope professor of zoology at Oxford. He held the chair until he resigned in 1933. During those forty years he corresponded with many naturalists who, stimulated by his enthusiasm, sent to Oxford the large collections by which the study of warning colours and mimicry, especially in tropical Africa, has been materially advanced. The frequent contributions made by Poulton and his followers to knowledge of these subjects demonstrate that the known facts, as a whole, are better explained by the agency of natural selection than by other causes which, individually, might apply to particular cases.

While Poulton always emphasized the need for observation and experiment in the field, he often found it possible to make important deductions from museum specimens. His explanation of the extraordinary differences, found in African *Precis* butterflies, between the forms occurring in wet or dry seasons, was a good example of his careful work. He showed that the form appearing in the dry season, which is the period of greatest paucity of insect life and therefore of greatest danger to the individual, while better concealed than the wet-season form, could be seen to be derived from it if the minute details of pattern were carefully traced. Such seasonal forms had hitherto been classed as distinct species, until (Sir) Guy Anstruther Knox Marshall, in 1898, bred one from the other. Poulton's self-revealing comment on this was: 'Under the shock of Mr. Marshall's discovery . . . the systematist may well feel doubts about the foundations upon which his science has been erected. In these distracting circumstances a firm belief in natural selection will be found to exercise a wonderfully calming and steadying influence.'

Poulton became deeply interested also in the study of the wide variations of African mimetic butterflies collected in localities where the species usually serving as models were in greatly inferior numbers, and put forward the suggestion that natural selection was here in abeyance. Mimicry is not maintained in the absence of the models because there is no greater selective pressure upon one variant than upon another. There was hardly any bionomic discovery that gave Poulton so much pleasure. As a true Darwinian he was greatly interested in sexual selection, and under his influence much knowledge was gained of the courtship of insects and of the special structures used for that purpose.

Wide recognition came to Poulton as a leader. He was a vice-president of the Royal Society for 1909–10, and its Darwin medallist in 1914. He presided over the Linnean Society of London from 1912 to 1916 and was awarded the Linnean medal in 1922. The Entomological Society of London received from him a lifetime's devotion, and made him president three times, finally electing him honorary life president in 1933 when the title 'Royal' was conferred upon it. The second International Congress of Entomology met under his guidance in 1912, as did the Association of Economic (later Applied) Biologists in 1922–3. An almost lifelong membership of the British Association gave him the social intercourse which he so much enjoyed, and he presided over it in 1937, having been president of the zoology section in 1931. He was a commander of the Swedish Order of the Pole Star, and an honorary member of many foreign learned societies. The universities of Reading, Durham, Dublin, and Princeton conferred honorary degrees upon him. He was knighted in 1935, and died at Oxford 20 November 1943.

Poulton married in 1881 Emily (died 1939), eldest daughter of George Palmer [q.v.], biscuit manufacturer and Liberal member of Parliament for Reading, by whom he had two sons and three daughters. The only child to survive him was his second daughter. The elder son, Edward Palmer Poulton, a distinguished physician, was on the staff of Guy's Hospital. The younger son, Ronald, who took the name Poulton-Palmer, was a famous Rugby football blue and international; he was killed at the front in 1915.

A portrait of Poulton by Miss F. A. de Biden Footner is in the possession of the family, and a drawing by Sir William Rothenstein is at Jesus College, Oxford.

[G. D. Hale Carpenter in *Obituary Notices of Fellows of the Royal Society*, No. 13, November 1944; E. B. Poulton, *John Viriamu Jones and other Oxford Memories*, 1911; personal knowledge.]                G. D. HALE CARPENTER.

POUND, SIR (ALFRED) DUDLEY (PICKMAN ROGERS) (1877–1943), admiral of the fleet, was born at Park View, Wroxall, Isle of Wight, 29 August 1877, the eldest child of Alfred John Pound, barrister, by his wife, Elizabeth Pickman, daughter of Richard Saltonstall Rogers, of Boston, Massachusetts. As a boy, being fond of riding, he wished to join the cavalry, but the sight of a cutter coming under full sail alongside the pier at Stokes Bay in charge of a midshipman turned his thoughts to the Royal Navy, and he entered the *Britannia* as a cadet in January 1891. He therefore refused the offer made by an uncle to find him an opening in the firm of Pierpont Morgan.

From his early days Pound was marked out as likely to go far; he passed his sub-lieutenant's courses with distinction after serving as midshipman in the Channel squadron, in China, and in the old training squadron under sail. The next twelve years were occupied with the ordinary career of a promising naval officer: he commanded torpedo boat 58 at the diamond jubilee naval review, served in the *Opossum* under Roger (later Lord) Keyes [q.v.] with whom then began a close association and friendship lasting for more than forty years; after eighteen months in the *Magnificent* (1898–9), Pound qualified as a specialist torpedo officer, and early in 1902 he was appointed torpedo lieutenant in the *Grafton*. Hopes of leave at the end of this appointment were dashed by an order to begin a course in wireless telegraphy prior to joining (1905) the *King Edward VII*, flagship of Sir William May [q.v.], and the first big ship to have a considerable amount of electric gear. Although this was a source of great anxiety to Pound, he nevertheless demonstrated that it was possible to go through a battle-practice without any misfires. What perhaps was of greater importance in Pound's career was that he was then ship-mates with (Sir) William Fisher [q.v.], for on Fisher being promoted to commander in the summer of 1906, Pound became first lieutenant, and, although not yet qualified in length of service, was ordered to ship the additional 'half stripe' at once.

An uneventful commission as first lieutenant of the *Queen* in the Mediterranean (1907–8), was followed by a term of service at the Admiralty on the torpedo side of the naval ordnance department, and in June 1909 Pound was promoted commander. Two years later he was appointed to the *Superb* (1911–13) whence he went to the new Naval Staff College as instructor, but after being there a year, he accepted, against the advice of the admiral in charge of the college, an offer from Fisher to go as his commander in the *St. Vincent*. He was therefore at sea when war broke out; in December he was promoted captain, and after a few months at the Admiralty as second naval assistant to the first sea lord, he went again to sea as flag captain in the *Colossus*. In that ship he took part in the battle of Jutland and was commended for his services.

Two years' service in the *Colossus* was ended by a recall to the Admiralty which gave to Pound's career a direction towards high politics. The first lord realized that in the pressure of work at the Admiralty there was no officer whose duty it was to foresee and think out problems, and Pound was selected to form a staff. These few men, known as section 15 of the operations division, starting with no office save the bedroom in the Admiralty of the director of operations, founded a branch which eventually expanded into the plans division under an admiral. At the end of 1917 Pound was transferred to be director of operations (home), whence in the autumn of 1920 he was appointed to command the *Repulse* in the battle cruiser squadron. It was a short interval at sea, for in 1922 he returned to his own plans division as director, and as Admiralty representative he attended the Lausanne conference on the Graeco-Turkish crisis, where he was introduced to the manifold international and political issues with which he was to be so closely connected in the future. Three years later he went to the Mediterranean as chief of staff to Keyes, now commander-in-chief, and in March 1926 he was promoted to flag rank; after two years in the Admiralty as assistant chief of naval staff he was appointed in May 1929 to command the battle cruiser squadron. Having been present at the conference on disarmament in 1932 for six months he became second sea lord in August.

In September 1935 Pound was nominated as commander-in-chief, Mediterranean, in succession to Fisher. Fisher not only knew the Mediterranean like the palm of his hand, but he was deeply versed in international affairs and problems of strategy and supply. Pound was therefore not at all surprised when he was informed that the Admiralty did not think it desirable to make a change at the height of the Abyssinian crisis. The sequel illustrates the generosity in Pound's character. Hearing that a relief was required for Fisher's chief of staff, Pound, although now a full admiral, volunteered for the post. The offer was accepted and he remained chief of staff until in March 1936 the situation had eased sufficiently to allow Fisher to return home and Pound to succeed him.

During the three years in which Pound held the command in chief in the Mediterranean, he set himself to perfect the training of the fleet for war. As flag captain in the *Colossus* he had evolved a series of tactical drills and exercises in order to make the most of the short time that each ship had available for exercises at Scapa Flow. He had enlarged these as chief of staff to Keyes, and now, as commander-in-chief, he perfected them. It was a labour of love, for never was Pound so happy as when he was on the bridge training the fleet to meet every emergency, insisting on captains handling their ships boldly, demanding instantaneous action by a squadron or ship ordered to take up a new station, and training officers to use their initiative and not to wait for orders. Towards the end of his command, he was offered the alternative of going as commander-in-chief, Portsmouth, which would probably be a three-year appointment, or of staying on for an additional command of the Mediterranean Fleet with nothing to follow. Without hesitation he chose the latter, and was looking to another year afloat when the resignation of the first sea lord, Sir Roger Backhouse [q.v.], brought Pound home to England in his place. He entered into office in June 1939 and on 31 July he was promoted admiral of the fleet.

Of Pound's fitness for this most responsible work the only ground for doubt was his age. He was now sixty-two. Nevertheless he displayed a toughness of body and a fortitude of mind which rose superior to the intense and dreadful strain which fell upon him for four years. He came to office single-handed, for his predecessor died in July, and the deputy chief of the naval staff, Sir Andrew Cunningham (subsequently Viscount Cunningham of Hyndhope), had been sent to take Pound's place in the Mediterranean, so that the help he might have received from their experience was withdrawn from him. The imminence of hostilities doubled the claims of committees on his time, and consultation with other members of departments and boards rose in a similar measure of frequency. The situation had been foreseen, and it had been decided that, immediately upon the outbreak of war, a deputy should be appointed so that the first sea lord should be free to concentrate entirely on plans and operations; but it was not until the summer of 1942 that the makeshift arrangement which had superseded this wise decision was set aside, and a deputy first sea lord appointed. The change came too late to give Pound's health the relief which it needed.

The history of Pound's achievements as first sea lord is the history of the war at sea, together with that on land and in the air, during these four years. It was not a period of unchequered success; that is a favour of fortune which comes to few in operations of such magnitude. It fell to him to organize the naval strategy which brought about, in the Mediterranean, the victory of Cape Matapan, the evacuation of the British forces from Greece and Crete, the retention of Malta as a base, the unheralded landing in North Africa in November 1942, the recovery of control of the sea in the Mediterranean, and the final landing of the allied forces in Sicily. In the Atlantic his strategy led to the scuttling of the *Admiral Graf Spee* and the sinking of the *Bismarck*, while the defeat of the submarine menace, the creation of the Western Approaches Command under Sir Percy Noble, and the establishment of the naval and air headquarters at Liverpool, contributed in no small degree to turning the battle of the Atlantic in favour of the Allies.

In view of the success of these operations, criticism could only fasten itself on three points. The campaign in Norway in the spring of 1940 is held to have shown Pound and the Admiralty as lacking in offensive spirit. The plan of campaign centred on the capture of Trondheim which Pound, with considerable hesitation, agreed should be effected by a direct fleet attack. As a prelude to this assault, landings were made at Namsos and Aandalsnes, which were initially so successful that Pound considered the risks involved in subjecting the fleet to air attack were no longer justified. The plan of campaign was therefore changed by the chiefs of staff and its success entrusted to the land forces only. When heavy air attack brought about an early collapse of the campaign, there was strong criticism of this lack of naval action. Pound took the unpopular but correct view that the security of sea communications was more important than the hazarding of valuable ships in what could not become a major theatre of war.

Eighteen months later another disaster befell British naval arms. It was a principle firmly held by the Admiralty that the naval resources of the country would not permit the dispersion of the navy in three separate areas at once; for that reason the Far East station had been weakened in order to maintain due strength in the Atlantic and the Mediterranean. But political considerations decided, notwithstanding a warning from Pound, that the *Prince of Wales*, fast battleship, should join the *Repulse*, battle cruiser, and proceed to the Far East, in the hope that this strength, added to the United States fleet in the Pacific, would deter the Japanese from declaring war. The hope was not fulfilled, and when the ships were lost by air attack off the coast of Malaya, criticism, based on various familiar principles of strategy, made itself widely heard.

More noisy, but as the event proved, less substantial, was the outcry which followed the escape of the German cruisers *Scharnhorst* and *Gneisenau* from Brest, where they had remained after the sinking of the *Bismarck*. The upshot showed the critics to be no less hasty than those Englishmen who burnt Lord Hawke in effigy on the day when he destroyed the French fleet in Quiberon Bay.

In January 1943 Pound stated confidently at Casablanca that the worst of the war was over, for the Allies had found the measure of the submarine menace. But he was destined to have no share in the final victory which he foresaw. The death of his wife in July was a heavy blow, and it was only will power which carried him, in company with the prime minister, to the conference at Quebec. Early in September he told (Sir) Winston Churchill at Washington that he must resign, and he returned to England, bade farewell to the Admiralty and to the Fleet, and on Trafalgar Day (21 October) he died in a London hospital. After a funeral service in Westminster Abbey, his ashes were scattered at sea.

Not being well-to-do, Pound declined the peerage which was offered to him early in 1943; but on the fourth anniversary of the outbreak of war he was appointed to the Order of Merit. In 1911 he had received the bronze medal of the Royal Humane Society for great courage in attempting to rescue men who had been overcome by poisonous fumes in the hold of the *Superb*. He was appointed C.B. in 1919, K.C.B. in 1933, G.C.V.O. in 1937, and G.C.B. in 1939. His death prevented him from receiving the high honours which would undoubtedly have been conferred upon him on the cessation of hostilities.

As a personality, Pound had the reputation of being reserved and rather unbending.

On duty, much of this arose from his expectation that others would set themselves the extremely high standard which he set himself. He picked his senior officers on the naval staff with skill and gave them his complete confidence: his personal staff served him at all times with devotion and affection. Off duty he had a keen sense of humour and in a wide circle of friends showed himself an excellent raconteur. His love of sport in all forms, but especially shooting, was most marked, and his verve as a driver of motor-cars led occasionally to remonstrances addressed to the first sea lord from the chief commissioner of police.

In 1908 Pound married Bessie Caroline, daughter of John Livesay Whitehead, physician, of Ventnor, Isle of Wight, whose help to him was constant, and who did much for the wives and families of the men under his command. He was survived by two sons, the elder a naval officer of distinction, the younger an officer in the Royal Marines, and one daughter.

A portrait of Pound by (Sir) Oswald Birley is in the Greenwich Collection at the Royal Naval College, Greenwich.

[Admiralty records; Winston S. Churchill, *The Second World War*, vols. i–v, 1948–52; T. K. Derry, (Official) *History of the Second World War. The Campaign in Norway*, 1952; S. W. Roskill, (Official) *History of the Second World War. The War at Sea*, vols. i and ii, 1954–6; private information; personal knowledge.]    R. V. BROCKMAN.

POWELL, SIR (GEORGE) ALLAN (1876–1948), public servant, was born in Mile End 1 February 1876, the son of Richard Powell, labourer, later caretaker at a Board-school in Stepney, and his wife, Mary Ann Clouter. Educated at Bancroft's School and King's College, London, Powell was called to the bar by Gray's Inn in 1907. He entered the service of the Metropolitan Asylums Board in 1894, later became chief administrator of the fever hospitals, and by the outbreak of war in 1914 was assistant clerk to the Board. He equipped, organized, and managed, throughout the war, as resident officer in charge, the government war refugees' camp at Earl's Court which had 4,000 beds and through which nearly 100,000 refugees passed. He received several foreign decorations and in 1920 was appointed C.B.E. for his services. In 1924 he produced a short account of the work of the camp. In 1922 he became the third and last clerk to the Metropolitan

Asylums Board, the duties and responsibilities of which passed to the London County Council on 1 April 1930. During the last weeks of its existence Powell wrote a brief history of the Board and then transferred to the London County Council where he organized a new department of public assistance.

In the meantime Powell had become known to a wider public by his membership in 1924 of the Royal Commission on food prices and his appointment in the following year as vice-chairman of the Food Council and chairman of its executive committee. In 1927 he was knighted for his services and in 1929 he succeeded Lord Bradbury [q.v.] as chairman. In 1932, however, he resigned from this position and from the London County Council on his appointment as a member of the Import Duties Advisory Committee with Sir George (later Lord) May [q.v.] and Sir Sydney Chapman, his main task being to act as a liaison between them and the consumer. In 1935 he served also on the committee on key industries duties. He maintained his interest in public health and local government by attending the public health congresses of the Royal Sanitary Institute of which he became a vice-president in 1939; and he was an honorary fellow of the American Public Health Association. In Kensington he was elected to the royal borough council in 1932, became an alderman in 1941, and was twice mayor (1937–8–9). He was a member of many of the council's committees and chairman of three: the law and general purposes, public health, and emergency committees.

In the spring of 1939 Powell resigned from the Import Duties Advisory Committee on being appointed chairman of the British Broadcasting Corporation. It was remarked in Parliament that he brought to this new task not only a long experience of public life and extreme efficiency in administration, but also the reputation of being 'a most human being'. A large, genial, and energetic man, his sense of justice, patient kindly consideration, and generous appreciation brought out the best in others and inspired confidence and affection. He was a born chairman of committees with a real flair for business, giving each member a run but keeping them strictly to the point. There was at first some difference between the governors and the director-general (Sir) Frederick Ogilvie [q.v.] who resigned in 1942, but Powell's wise serenity played no small part in helping the Corporation to meet the increasing demands made upon it by the war. His term of office was extended in 1944, in which year he was appointed G.B.E., and he finally retired at the end of December 1946. He died at his home at Gerrard's Cross 24 January 1948, survived by his widow, Jeannie Jack, daughter of John Marshall, physician and surgeon, of Stepney, whom he married in 1904. They had one son.

[*The Times*, 26 January 1948; *Listener*, 29 January 1948; *Journal* of the Royal Sanitary Institute, March 1948; *Public Health*, March 1948; private information.]

POWELL, ROBERT STEPHENSON SMYTH BADEN-, first BARON BADEN-POWELL (1857–1941), lieutenant-general, and founder of the Boy Scouts and Girl Guides. [See BADEN-POWELL.]

POWER, SIR D'ARCY (1855–1941), surgeon and historian, was born in London 11 November 1855, the eldest child of Henry Power, surgeon, by his wife and first cousin, Ann, daughter of Thomas Simpson, banker, of Whitby, Yorkshire. He was educated at Merchant Taylors' School, and after having entered New College, Oxford, as a commoner in 1874, he migrated, on gaining an exhibition in 1876, to Exeter College whence he took his degree in 1878 with first class honours in natural science (physiology). He qualified in 1882 from St. Bartholomew's Hospital, where he held several posts in the medical college, and was ophthalmic house-surgeon to his father, and house-surgeon to (Sir) W. S. Savory [q.v.]. He was the last assistant surgeon appointed by public election (1898), was surgeon from 1904, and on retirement in 1920 was elected consulting surgeon and governor. Late in life, as honorary archivist, he began to calendar the hospital's medieval muniments. He became F.R.C.S. (England) in 1883, served on the council (1912–28), was a vice-president (1921–2), and Hunterian orator (1925); he was appointed honorary librarian in 1929 and a trustee of the Hunterian museum in 1930.

Power was a rapid operator of the old school, and among the first to practise gastric operations in this country. His writings include *Surgical Diseases of Children* (1895), *Some Points in the Anatomy, Pathology, and Surgery of Intussusception* (Hunterian lectures, 1897), *Wounds in War* (1915), and *On Cancer of the Tongue* (Bradshaw lecture, 1919); he

edited *A System of Syphilis* (6 vols., 1908–10; 2nd ed. 1914). During the war of 1914–18 he commanded the first London General Hospital at Camberwell, with the rank of lieutenant-colonel, and was appointed K.B.E. in 1919. He took a leading part in professional and learned societies; was elected fellow of the Society of Antiquaries in 1897, and president of the Medical Society of London in 1916. He was a prominent freemason. Power was widely beloved and trusted for his integrity and shrewd friendliness, which especially showed themselves in his gift of acute yet encouraging criticism and his skill as an unofficial arbiter of private disputes.

Power's best work was literary and historical. He edited *Memorials of the Craft of Surgery in England* (1886), collected by J. F. South [q.v.], and thereafter regularly contributed historical articles to the *British Medical Journal* and the *British Journal of Surgery*. He wrote the lives of surgeons from the letter 'L' for the main work of this DICTIONARY and also contributed to the Supplements. He edited the *Lives of the Fellows of the Royal College of Surgeons of England* (2 vols., 1930) left unfinished by V. G. Plarr, and he wrote the lives between 1930 and October 1940 for the subsequent (1930–51) volume published in 1953. His *William Harvey* (1897) is still the best short account of the discoverer of the circulation. Power edited from the manuscripts the English works of the fourteenth-century surgeon John Arderne [q.v.] (Early English Text Society, 1910) and translated his Latin treatises (1922). He transcribed the manuscript diary of John Ward (1629–81), rector of Stratford on Avon, then belonging to the Medical Society of London. His paper 'Why Samuel Pepys discontinued his diary' (1911) aroused much interest. As president of the Bibliographical Society (1926–8) he surveyed the editions of the Tudor *Birth of Mankind* (1927). He was part author of a tabulated history of medicine, *Chronologia Medica* (1923) and of *A Short History of St. Bartholomew's Hospital, 1123–1923* (1923), and wrote a sketch of *Medicine in the British Isles* (New York, 1930). He visited the United States in 1924 and 1930, lecturing on 'Foundations of Medical History', and went to Australia in 1935; his *Mirror for Surgeons*, an anthology, was published in Boston in 1939. Although never rich he collected a good library.

Power married in 1883 Eleanor (died

1923), younger daughter of George Haynes Fosbroke, M.R.C.S., of Bidford, Warwickshire. He had two sons, the younger of whom died of wounds received in action on the western front in 1915, and one daughter who died in infancy. His elder son became an air vice-marshal in the Royal Air Force medical service. Power died at Northwood, Middlesex, 18 May 1941. He was of middle height, small-featured with keen blue eyes, and wore a moustache. A portrait by Sir Matthew William Thompson is at the Royal College of Surgeons; there is a photograph in Power's *Selected Writings* (1931), with a bibliography of 609 items.

[*British Medical Journal*, 31 May, 7 and 14 June 1941; *The Times*, 19 May 1941; private information; personal knowledge.]

W. R. Le Fanu.

POWER, Sir JOHN CECIL, first baronet, of Newlands Manor, Milford, Hampshire (1870–1950), company director and public benefactor, was born at Eldon, county Down, 21 December 1870, the younger son of William Taylor Power, and his wife, Cecilia, daughter of Colonel John Burgoyne. At ten, Power went to London where, with his brother, he was later to enter the firm of Power, Power & Co., export merchants with considerable business in the East.

As a young man he was delicate and had to spend three years in Italy, a sojourn which implanted in him a love of other countries and of travel which he was later to indulge whenever possible. After his marriage he bought a villa in the south of France to which he would go as often as business and, subsequently, parliamentary duties allowed. He paid a series of visits to the United States and went to Canada, India, and South Africa, afterwards lecturing and writing on his experiences. He served for many years as a member of the executive of the Travel and Industrial Development Association.

Real estate soon tempted him away from the family business; he had an unerring flair for property together with considerable financial talent. His name is associated particularly with Kingsway, a London thoroughfare which opened up what had hitherto been slum property between Holborn and Aldwych. A number of its imposing buildings were of Power's provenance: such as Adastral House.

Power's success in real estate made him a wealthy man and enabled him to become

a generous benefactor. His first great gift was in 1920, an anonymous benefaction prompted by A. F. Pollard [q.v.] of £20,000 towards the founding of an Institute of Historical Research in London. Next, in 1923, came a gift of £10,000 to the British (later Royal) Institute of International Affairs, for the erection of a lecture-hall at the rear of the mansion (given by Colonel and Mrs. R. W. Leonard) in St. James's Square, London, which became known as Chatham House. Power was honorary treasurer of the Institute from 1921 to 1943 and during his long association made many other gifts to the organization which included, in 1938, the leasehold premises of his own house in Chesham Place. This house he had hitherto made available to the British Council (before it moved to larger premises) of which he was honorary treasurer from 1934 to 1950. On the outbreak of war in 1939 the house in Belgrave Square, in which he was then living, was lent to the Government for its use as offices.

Power was for many years associated with the League of Nations Union, serving on the executive committee from 1929 to 1936 and, at various times, on its appeals, finance, and parliamentary committees. In addition, he was a member of the committee of the Royal Humane Society and, from 1934 to 1949, a director of the Royal Insurance Company.

Politics early claimed his attention and in 1924, the year in which he became a baronet, he was elected Conservative member for Wimbledon, a seat which he held until 1945 when, his health beginning to fail, he withdrew to his country home in Hampshire.

Power's friends came from all walks of life; he enjoyed good company and was a generous host. The personal tastes of this tenacious and indomitable Irishman were simple; apart from golf and cricket, he had few hobbies save music. He had fallen under the spell of the opera as a young man and would talk nostalgically of the days when he had frequented the gallery of La Scala. Opera remained his abiding delight, and Power was regularly to be seen at Covent Garden in the London season.

He married in 1902 Mabel Katherine Louisa, daughter of John Hartley Perks, J.P., of London and Wolverhampton; they had two sons and three daughters. Power never fully recovered from the shock of his wife's death in 1945, for they were ideally happy. He continued, however, to make occasional visits to his villa at Grasse, where he died 5 June 1950. He was succeeded, as second baronet, by his elder son, Ivan McLannahan Cecil (1903–1954).

A portrait of Power by (Sir) Oswald Birley and a bronze bust by Siegfried Charoux are in Chatham House.

[*The Times*, 9 June 1950; private information; personal knowledge.]

IVISON S. MACADAM.

PRAIN, SIR DAVID (1857–1944), botanist and administrator, was born at Fettercairn, Kincardineshire, 11 July 1857, the elder child of David Prain, a native of Inchture near Dundee, by his wife, Mary, daughter of George Thomson, farmer and miller, of the Vale of Alford, Aberdeenshire. For at least two hundred years Prain's ancestry on both sides had been country folk. He was educated until the age of fifteen at the Fettercairn parish school; then for one year at the Aberdeen Grammar School and, after that, at the university of Aberdeen where he obtained in 1878 the degree of M.A., with honours in natural science, botany being his strongest subject. A bursary had made it possible for him to enter the university and in vacations he added to his means by teaching. Two years of teaching at Ramsgate College enabled him to return to the university in 1880 to study medicine. He qualified M.B. and C.M. in 1883 with the highest honours; he also qualified L.R.C.S. (Edinburgh) the same year.

The final stage of this long apprenticeship was admission to the Indian Medical Service at the head of the list. Then followed two and a half years of army duties in India, interrupted in 1885 by a few months at the Royal Botanic Garden, Calcutta, during which he acted as curator of the herbarium under (Sir) George King [q.v.]. In 1887 he was recalled to the same position at the Garden, and served there for the next twenty years. Within a year King went on leave and Prain acted for him in the posts of superintendent of the Garden, government quinologist, and professor of botany at the Medical College, Calcutta. He held these positions temporarily again in 1891–2 and succeeded to them (the chair of botany from 1895) when King retired in 1898, and also to that of director of the Botanical Survey of India. He was forthwith made a trustee of the Indian Museum, placed on the committee of management of the Zoological Garden,

Alipur, and on the board of visitors of the Engineering College, Shibpur; and the viceroy nominated him fellow of the university of Calcutta in order that its senate might have the benefit of his knowledge. He showed great wisdom, guiding the cinchona department, for instance, through a general depression with an aptitude for business which was acknowledged gratefully by the Governments of Bengal and India and by the India Office. Over his years at Calcutta he maintained by long hours of work a considerable output of botanical publications, including a flora of Bengal (*Bengal Plants*, 1903). He also collected in Tibet at the time of the expedition under (Sir) Francis Younghusband [q.v.]. He preferred to study plants which in one way or another serve man. He was promoted major in 1896, and lieutenant-colonel in 1904. In 1905 he was elected F.R.S. and at the end of the year was appointed director of the Royal Botanic Gardens, Kew. He was appointed C.I.E. in June 1906.

Prain's life in this new setting was essentially the same as in Calcutta; his output of botanical papers was still maintained by labour expended when the official day was done. The problems raised by the war of 1914–18 took those spare hours from him; and if he is rightly classed as 'botanist and administrator' for his earlier life, the war reversed the order of the appellations. This was due, not so much to the depletion of staff, although this was severe, as to the calls on him to direct on behalf of the Government botanical problems to proper places and proficient minds. He was member or chairman of many committees and by 1919 held most trusted positions. For this work of planning he was singularly fitted and he continued in it until, in his seventies, deafness made committee work difficult. He was editor of the *Botanical Magazine* from 1907 to 1920.

Prain was retired in 1922; and thereafter served as chairman of the advisory council of the Imperial Institute on plant and animal products. During all his time at Kew and to the end of his life he gave a fatherly care to the John Innes Horticultural Institution, being chairman of its council from 1909. He did not much less for the Imperial College of Tropical Agriculture, Trinidad. He was president (1916–19) of the Linnean Society from which he received the Linnean medal; vice-president from 1919 of the Royal Horticultural Society which awarded him the Victoria medal of honour and a Veitch memorial medal; treasurer of the Royal Society, 1919–29; a trustee of the British Museum, 1924–36; president of the Imperial Botanical Conference in 1924; a member of the council of the British Association (1907–14), vice-president (1931), and president of the botany section in 1909. His many honours included appointment as C.M.G. in January 1912 and knighthood in June of the same year; he was a knight of the royal Swedish Order of the Pole Star (1908) and a commander of the Belgian Order of Leopold II (1919). The honorary degree of LL.D. was conferred upon him by the universities of Aberdeen (1900) and St. Andrews (1911); he received the Albert medal of the Royal Society of Arts, and was an honorary member of many foreign learned societies.

The words 'wisdom and friendship', used of Prain by one who knew him well, in the dedication of a book, are excellently descriptive. He married in 1887 Margaret Caird (died 1942), daughter of the Rev. William Thomson, minister of Belhelvie, Aberdeen. They had a son, who was killed in the war of 1914–18. Prain died at Whyteleafe, Surrey, 16 March 1944. There is a portrait of him at Kew by Miss F. A. de Biden Footner.

[I. H. Burkill in *Obituary Notices of Fellows of the Royal Society*, No. 13, November 1944; *Proceedings* of the Linnean Society of London, Session 156 (1943–4), part 3, 1945; personal knowledge.]                    I. HENRY BURKILL.

PREVITÉ-ORTON, CHARLES WILLIAM (1877–1947), historian and editor, was born at Arnesby, Leicestershire, 16 January 1877, the younger son of the vicar, the Rev. William Previté Orton, and his wife, Eliza, whose maiden surname Orton was assumed by her husband when they married. His paternal grandfather was a native of Sicily, but Charles showed little trace of Italian ancestry in either appearance or character.

Shy and diffident by nature, he ended his career at school in Leicester at fourteen owing to eye trouble which resulted in the removal of his left eye, and on account of constant ill health he did not enter St. John's College, Cambridge, until he was twenty-eight, but his university career was both happy and distinguished. He was placed in the first class in both parts of the historical tripos (1907, 1908) and was awarded the Gladstone (1907) and Members' (1908) prizes. In 1911 he was elected a fellow of St. John's, shortly before the appearance of his first book, *The Early History of the House of Savoy* (1912).

College and university work soon came to fill his time. Physically unfit for military service in the war of 1914–18, he completed his *Outlines of Medieval History* (1916) and shortly after joined the editorial board of the *Cambridge Medieval History*, remaining with that undertaking until it was completed. His wide erudition and editorial ability received further recognition when in 1925 he was invited to become joint-editor, and from January 1927 sole editor, of the *English Historical Review*. In the years that followed, the sum total of his teaching and editorial work was very large, but he managed in addition to prepare a critical edition of the *Defensor Pacis* of Marsilius of Padua (1928) and a textbook *A History of Europe, 1198–1378* (1937). He proceeded Litt.D. in 1928 and was elected F.B.A. in 1929, and when in 1937 a chair in medieval history was founded, he became the first holder. Most unfortunately for his work, a haemorrhage in his eye at Christmas of that year caused temporary blindness, and he was obliged to resign the editorship of the *English Historical Review* and to contract all his activities. In 1942 he reached the retiring age and he died suddenly of heart failure at his home in Cambridge 11 March 1947. His *Cambridge Shorter Medieval History* appeared posthumously in 1952.

All who knew 'Previté' admired his scholarship and felt an instinctive affection for his gentle personality, but his devotion to his family, his college, and his books restricted the circle of his intimate friendships. Happiest at home, and in the company of children, he was devoted to his only child, a daughter, and later to his grandsons, and spent hours at his only recreation, bird-watching. He was throughout his life a sincere and observant churchman. As a scholar he was lucid, accurate, and passionless rather than original. As an editor, he was in his element, critical, shrewd, painstaking, and generous, and his work in this field was a notable contribution to medieval studies in this country.

In 1913 Previté-Orton married his first cousin, Ellery Swaffield, daughter of the Rev. John Swaffield Orton.

[M. D. Knowles in *Proceedings* of the British Academy, vol. xxxiii, 1947; *Eagle* (magazine of St. John's College), April 1948; private information.]                    M. D. KNOWLES.

PRICHARD, HAROLD ARTHUR (1871–1947), philosopher, was born in Willesden, London, 30 October 1871, the eldest child of Walter Stennett Prichard, solicitor in Bedford Row, by his wife, Lucy Withers. He was educated at Clifton, and at New College, Oxford, of which he was a mathematical scholar. He was placed in the first class in mathematical moderations (1891) and in *literae humaniores* (1894) and was university mathematical exhibitioner in 1892. He was a fellow of Hertford College from 1895 to 1898, and of Trinity College from 1898 to 1924. After many years of devoted service to Trinity he retired by reason of temporary ill health. In 1928 he was elected to White's professorship of moral philosophy, which carried with it a fellowship of Corpus Christi College; he retired on reaching the age limit in 1937 and was made an honorary fellow of the college. He was elected F.B.A. in 1932 and received the honorary degree of LL.D. from Aberdeen University in 1934.

Prichard wrote very little for publication, but much in order to clear his own mind, to elicit the opinions of his friends, and to help them in their own philosophical problems. The only book he published was *Kant's Theory of Knowledge* (1909). He had accepted from J. Cook Wilson [q.v.], for whom he had the greatest admiration, the realistic view which had begun, in Oxford as elsewhere, to prevail over the Kantian and Hegelian views hitherto in the ascendant. He combined with a great respect for Kant the conviction that at bottom Kant's view is an unsuccessful attempt to mediate between realism and idealism. Prichard's book contains, therefore, both a clear and detailed analysis of Kant's view and a vigorous argument against it. Knowledge, he maintained, is an activity entirely *sui generis* and incapable of being interpreted in terms of anything else. Having expressed this view in his book, he did not return to the theory of knowledge in later writings except in his lectures, published in the posthumous volume *Knowledge and Perception* (1950), on the theories of Descartes, Locke, Berkeley, and Hume. With regard to perception, he expressed in his book on Kant the view that the appearing of bodies to minds is, like knowledge, an unanalysable fact, both when it corresponds to reality and when it does not. But his mind remained open on the subject; he dealt with it in four papers published in the posthumous

volume, and in the last of them, 'The Sense-datum Fallacy' (1938), he expressed the view that the unanalysable fact is best stated as 'some - one - seeing - a - colour', 'some - one - hearing - a - sound', &c., the colour or sound having no separate existence.

In 1912 he published in *Mind* a paper which has had much influence on ethical thought—'Does Moral Philosophy Rest on a Mistake?' As in his book on Kant he had argued in general that there can be no theory of knowledge which supplies an answer to the question 'Is what we have hitherto thought to be knowledge really knowledge?', so he argued that there is no theory which will prove that what we have thought to be obligations really are so; to attain this certainty we have simply to think harder about the facts. To this he added the thesis that while the rightness of an act depends on the nature of the situation in which we are and on the change the act will originate, the goodness of an act depends on its motive. To this view he supplied an important addendum in a British Academy lecture on 'Duty and Ignorance of Fact' (1932), by arguing that since being obliged is an attribute of a person, what makes an action right or wrong for the individual is not the objective situation but the agent's opinion about the situation, and, further, that what he is obliged to do is not to produce a certain change, but to set himself to produce it. Prichard was much pressed to state his view at full length, and he made considerable progress with the negative part of the task, the refutation of the most important existing theories; the result is to be found in the long paper called 'Moral Obligation' included in the posthumous book of the same name (1949), which includes also several shorter papers dealing with important ethical problems.

Prichard was a great teacher, and he had great influence among his fellow teachers at Oxford and elsewhere. He combined unhesitating conviction of what he considered the fundamentals in philosophy with great readiness to examine over and over again detailed problems both about perception and about obligation. Severe on what he regarded as obvious error in others, he was at least equally critical of himself, modest about his own work in philosophy, and never satisfied with what he had done. In controversy he was formidable, in social intercourse friendly and interested in the interests of his friends. In his work as a tutor, as a professor, and in the war of 1939–45 as an air-raid warden, he was conscientious almost to a fault. Physically he was short and slight, but vigorous; as an undergraduate he played lawn tennis for Oxford against Cambridge, and he remained until near the end devoted to golf.

In 1899 Prichard married Mabel Henrietta, daughter of Surgeon-Major Charles Grant Ross, of the Bombay Army. She was herself a graduate with first class honours in *literae humaniores* (1898) who later played an active and able part in the affairs of the city of Oxford and in those of the women students of the university; by her he had two sons and one daughter. He died in Oxford, after a short illness, 29 December 1947.

[H. H. Price in *Proceedings* of the British Academy, vol. xxxiii, 1947; personal knowledge.]                         DAVID ROSS.

PRYDE, JAMES FERRIER (1866–1941), artist, was born in Edinburgh 30 March 1866, the only son among the six children of David Pryde, headmaster of Edinburgh Ladies' College (1870–91), by his wife, Barbara, daughter of William Lauder, niece of the painters R. S. and J. E. Lauder [qq.v.]. Pryde's mother was descended on the maternal side from the French family of Bugeaud, and one of their number, John Beugo (1759–1841), became a celebrated Edinburgh engraver.

From 1872 until the end of Dr. Pryde's headmastership the family lived at 10 Fettes Row, and it was there that Pryde's formative years were spent. He was educated at George Watson's College and at the Royal Scottish Academy School. Deriving his artistic sense from his mother's family, Pryde inherited from his father a feeling for history and especially for the grim romantic spirit of old Edinburgh. From both parents he acquired a lasting interest in the theatre, Sir Henry Irving and J. L. Toole [qq.v.] being intimate friends of his father.

It seems probable that Pryde's early Edinburgh memories—the high-ceilinged dimly-lit interior of the house in Fettes Row, the four-poster bed in Mary Queen of Scots' bedroom at Holyrood, the strings of washing outside the upper windows of the tall tenement buildings off the High Street—all influenced his later imagination. When he was twenty-one he was occupying a studio at 4 Charlotte Place, Edinburgh. His early work included a number of interesting portraits of his family and friends. He received timely encouragement from two members of the young Glasgow school, (Sir) James Guthrie [q.v.] and E. A. Walton, and for three months he studied in Paris under Bouguereau, although his experience seems to have had little effect on his painting. Pryde did not remain long in Edinburgh after his return from Paris but soon made his way south. A pastel drawing, 'Little Girl in Black', exhibited at the Grosvenor Gallery in 1890, first brought him to the notice of the London critics. The little girl was the daughter of his landlady at Bushey, where he was then sharing lodgings with his sister Mabel, a student at the school of (Sir) Hubert von Herkomer [q.v.]. Another student at Bushey, six years younger than Pryde, was (Sir) William Nicholson [q.v.] who in 1893 married Mabel Pryde.

The art of the poster was then just beginning to attract serious attention in England, for Frenchmen like Chéret and de Toulouse-Lautrec had demonstrated the possibilities of the medium. Among those who were drawn to it were Pryde and Nicholson, who set to work in Nicholson's home at Denham to prepare several designs for an exhibition at the Westminster Aquarium in 1894. The 'Beggarstaff Brothers' (as they called themselves) employed a new technique of using cut-out paper to build up a striking silhouette. There was an almost primitive simplicity about the Beggarstaff posters which recalled early Chinese stone reliefs and Japanese prints. Among the most successful which appeared on the hoardings were those for Rowntree's cocoa and for *Cinderella*, but other designs which were never used, such as that for Irving's *Don Quixote*, have been just as influential in reproduction. In fact, the work of the Beggarstaffs between 1894 and 1896, although not very lucrative to the artists, has been a continuing inspiration for poster artists all over the world, particularly in Germany.

In the years which followed the break-up of the Beggarstaff partnership Pryde was compelled to supplement his artistic earnings by occasional appearances on the stage. He had little ability as an actor, although the theatre exerted a considerable influence on his painting. In 1899 he married Marian (died 1945), daughter of George Symons, of Silverton, near Exeter, a partner in a firm of estate valuers and auctioneers. They had a daughter, Betty, talented as a dancer, who was born in 1903 and died in 1932. Pryde separated from his wife about 1914, but clearly the marriage in its early phases had a stimulating influence on his work.

A number of studies of 'Celebrated Criminals', six of which were lithographed and issued in a rare portfolio, were followed in 1906 by a gouache of Irving as Dubosc in *The Lyons Mail*, which was published as a two-colour plate and received high praise from (Dame) Ellen Terry, (Sir) Max Beerbohm, and many others. Meanwhile, he had begun to paint those romantic imaginative landscapes, usually architectural in subject and often, though not always, melancholy in feeling, for which he is best known. The purchase of his 'Guildhall with Figures' (1905) by J. S. Sargent [q.v.] was a landmark in Pryde's career, and henceforth he exhibited regularly at the International Society, of which he eventually became vice-president, and at the Goupil Gallery. In 1909 he exhibited 'The Doctor' (later acquired by the Tate Gallery out of the Chantrey bequest), the first of a series of paintings in which a four-poster bed was the dominant feature. 'The Slum' (1910) is in the Musée National d'Art Moderne, Paris. From 1912 onwards Pryde found a generous patron in Viscountess Cowdray, for whose library at Dunecht House, Aberdeenshire, he painted a series of large decorative canvases. His output, never large, declined both in quantity and in quality after he reached his sixtieth year, although in 1930 he designed effective scenery for a London production of *Othello*. In 1937 he was awarded a Civil List pension of £110 a year. His home in his later years was at Lansdowne House, Holland Park, and he died in London 24 February 1941.

In person Pryde was tall and handsome, a witty and engaging companion. At the same time he was dilatory, extravagant, unproductive for long periods, and he often taxed the patience of his friends. A retrospective exhibition of his work at the Leicester Galleries, London, in 1933 was much praised. In 1949 a comprehensive memorial exhibition organized by the Arts Council was well received in Edinburgh but when brought to London in a reduced form encountered some adverse criticism. Whatever his final place, it is a matter of historical fact that Pryde, with his intensely individual vision, was a powerful influence on many artists and designers of his time, among them Sir William Nicholson, Mr. Edward Gordon Craig, and Sir William Orpen [q.v.]. His work is represented in the Tate Gallery, the Victoria and Albert Museum, and in many municipal collections.

There are three portraits of Pryde by James Gunn (one in the possession of the Scottish Modern Arts Association), a bronze head by Jo Davidson at the Savage Club, and etchings of him by Joseph Simpson and George Belcher. A charcoal drawing by (Sir) W. O. Hutchison is in the Scottish National Portrait Gallery. A miniature by J. W. Brooke (water-colours on ivory) is at the National Portrait Gallery.

[Derek Hudson, *James Pryde, 1866–1941*, 1949; private information; personal knowledge.]　　　　DEREK HUDSON.

PURSE, BENJAMIN ORMOND (1874–1950), blind social worker and expert on blind welfare, was born 29 August 1874 at Salford, Lancashire, the son of Edward Purse, general labourer, and his wife, Matilda Clavering. His sight became defective in early life, but it was not until he was thirteen, when his sight was nearly gone, that he was sent to school at Henshaw's Institution for the Blind, Manchester. He was trained later as a piano-tuner, took the certificate, and struggled for over two years to build up a tuning connexion, but his inclinations were towards a career of professional or public service and to prepare himself he devoured every book he could lay hands on. His first step in this direction was taken when he became the first paid secretary (at eight shillings a week) of the National League of the Blind, a small body which voiced the unsatisfactory conditions prevalent in the blind community. He used a legacy of £60 left to him in 1898 to launch a journal, the *Blind Advocate*, as the organ of the League, and in 1901 he devoted full time to the organization at a weekly salary of twenty-three shillings. In 1902 the League was affiliated to the Trades Union Congress.

The next few years were crowded with activity—writing, lecturing, expending all his efforts for the blind. In 1905 he was a delegate at an international conference of blind welfare workers; between 1904 and 1910 he visited forty-eight municipal authorities and secured travel concession from thirty-seven of them; in 1907 he was the only witness to give evidence concerning the blind before the Royal Commission on the Poor Laws, and he took an active part in the movement which led in 1914 to the compulsory notification of ophthalmia neonatorum, a foremost measure in sight-saving. He was responsible for preparing the preliminary matter and subsequently helped to frame the recommendations which resulted in the setting up in 1917 of the Government's Advisory Committee for the Welfare of the Blind, of which he was a member until 1942.

In 1916 he was induced by Sir C. Arthur Pearson [q.v.] to join the staff of the National Institute for the Blind, but although by so doing he signified his approval of voluntary organizations, he by no means relinquished his efforts to secure a degree of State aid to the blind, and no blind man contributed more than he to the movement which led to the passing of the Blind Persons' Act in 1920.

From 1920 until 1943 he superintended the administration of relief, training, and general employment at the National Institute. In 1921 he took a prominent part in forming what later became the National Association of Blind Workers, and edited its official organ, the *Tribune*, until 1942. In that year he was elected a vice-president of his old school, Henshaw's Institution, an honour no blind person had ever received before; and in 1944 his work for the blind was recognized by his appointment as O.B.E.

Ben Purse's massive intelligence, amazing statistical memory, power of debate, and grim courage left their mark for all time on the British blind community. His published works included *The Blind in Industry* (1925), *The British Blind* (1928), and a book of verse, *Moods and Melodies* (1931).

He married in 1899 Mary Elizabeth, daughter of John Alcock, a collier, of Oldham. She and their two children had predeceased him when he died at Wembdon, Bridgwater, 31 March 1950.

[*Beacon*, August 1925; *New Beacon*, April 1950; personal knowledge.]

J. DE LA MARE ROWLEY.

PURVIS, ARTHUR BLAIKIE (1890–1941), industrialist and buyer of war supplies, was born in London 31 March 1890, the son of William Blaikie Purvis, of Perth, Scotland, and his wife, Annie Marie Baker. He was educated at Tottenham Grammar School and won a scholarship but owing to the death of his father began work at thirteen. In 1905 he joined the firm of Lynch Brothers in London, and in 1910 went to Glasgow to the Nobel Explosives Company, Ltd., where his ability

was quickly recognized by (Sir) Harry Duncan (subsequently Lord) McGowan. He represented the firm in South America and South Africa and despite his youth by 1914 was in charge of the New York office. On the outbreak of war he made one of the largest war purchases: $25 million of acetone which was in acute shortage in the United Kingdom; he remained responsible for the purchase in America of materials for explosives throughout the war. The strain of his task resulted in a prolonged breakdown in health from which, however, by sheer will power, he made a recovery in the Adirondacks so complete that in 1925 he was able to go to Canada as president of Canadian Explosives, Ltd., which he reorganized into Canadian Industries, Ltd. He was eager to encourage chemical research in its application to Canada's natural resources and urged manufacturers to take risks in the adoption of scientific ideas. By 1939 he had become one of the foremost figures in Canadian industry and director of eleven important Canadian concerns. During these years he also devoted much time to community work especially in Montreal where he was a governor of McGill University and, as the remarkably successful chairman of the National Employment Commission (1936–8), to services of a national character.

'A man of the highest integrity with no enemies and, indeed, no critics', as the governor-general of Canada, Lord Tweedsmuir [q.v.], described him, Purvis became director-general of British purchasing in the United States in November 1939, and in the following January chairman of the Anglo-French Purchasing Board 'with a high degree of effective authority' which on the British side did not, however, at first extend beyond making contracts for the Ministry of Supply. Purvis soon found his work hampered by the 'uncontrolled' purchases of other missions which, as he pointed out, 'destroyed his background' with American industry and the United States Government. Even so, not till mid-1940 did he succeed in extending his own direct responsibility for purchase to machine tools, iron and steel, or in receiving, as of right, complete and detailed information from all other purchasing bodies. From the outset, however, all doors in Washington were thrown open to him. He conceived his task as far wider than the mere purchase of American supplies. He entered at once with President Roosevelt and Henry Morgenthau, secretary of the United States Treasury, into the economic planning of the war and the denial of supplies, especially of strategic metals, to the enemy. 'From the first', said Morgenthau, 'Purvis impressed me tremendously.' It was essential, he counselled Purvis, to have a complete statement of all allied requirements lest they be swept aside when a still neutral America turned to war expansion on its own account. Purvis, in his persuasive turn, pressed this lesson upon a British Government not yet imaginatively ready, as Purvis was himself, to 'talk big': or, to Purvis, big enough.

It was Purvis who took immediate action in Washington during the fall of France, first in negotiating the swift transfer of American arms to replace in part those lost by the British at Dunkirk. In one week he signed both the $37½ million contract for this transaction and (on 17 June 1940) the document committing the British Government to the payment of $600 million for the French contracts in America. 'Never', said Lord Woolton in the House of Lords a month later, 'have wider powers to commit this country been delegated to any mission.'

In the next six months Purvis played the leading part in carrying through the decision to empty the British war chest by both financing massive British war contracts in the United States and, by a series of British capital investments, laying the foundations of the American munitions industry. In July 1940 he was joined in Washington by M. Jean Monnet, who like himself recognized the vital importance of the British striking a proper balance between their own competing claims. Without explicit authority Purvis set about the necessary co-ordination at a time when there were a number of separate British missions in the United States, some *ad hoc* and some representing different departments in Whitehall; of these the Air Commission was especially independent. Until December 1940 Purvis achieved such co-ordination as was attained by his personal efforts and persuasion and the especial confidence of Morgenthau. After visiting the United Kingdom in the closing weeks of 1940 for discussions on the strategy of British supply in the States, Purvis was given explicit status on his return in mid-December by his appointment as chairman of the British Supply Council in North America and thus, on the civilian side, director of the entire

British war organization there. If his authority was now assured, to Purvis the basic issue remained unchanged: 'it was a cardinal feature of the Purvis–Monnet programme to get the Americans to raise their sights all round'. The President resumed with Purvis the discussions which had already borne fruit in the idea of the Lend-Lease bill and were now shaping the range and scope of the Act. Purvis now went into action with 'a well-tried weapon from Monnet's armoury': the balance-sheet technique. Largely on his own initiative in January 1941 he boldly translated into dollars the British requirements which he had gathered from departments in Whitehall, produced his estimate of British production and of the resultant deficiency which American production could alone make good. The President took his estimate of fifteen billion dollars, Purvis reported, in his stride. It was held in official circles at the time that Purvis's balance-sheet powerfully influenced the first appropriation under the Lend-Lease Act. British policy in Washington at this period 'formulated in large measure by Monnet's planning mind and propagated by the persistence and persuasiveness of Purvis' was making demands on American industry greatly in advance of contemporary American opinion. Purvis himself was by now the most powerful British influence in the United States. To Morgenthau he was not only 'the ablest British representative in Washington but one of the rarest persons I have ever known'. At the time of his death Purvis was planning to secure from President Roosevelt the greatest directive yet issued, to place all American production on a full war basis. He was killed when the aircraft in which he was returning to Washington crashed on taking off from Prestwick on 14 August 1941. 'Purvis was a grievous loss', wrote (Sir) Winston Churchill (*The Second World War*, vol. iii, 1950), 'as he held so many British, American and Canadian threads in his hands, and had hitherto been the directing mind in their harmonious combination.' The Anglo-American consolidated statement that month represented the climax of Purvis's work and the effective beginning of that Victory programme which thereafter took the central place in the war-time economic planning of the western Allies. Purvis saw—was perhaps the first to see—the size of the problem.

He was nominated to the Privy Council in December 1940 but did not live to be sworn. He married in 1918 Margaret, daughter of Cyrus Emory Jones, of Jamestown, New York; they had one son.

[H. Duncan Hall, (Official) *History of the Second World War. North American Supply*, 1955; W. K. Hancock and M. M. Gowing, (Official) *History of the Second World War. British War Economy*, 1949; E. R. Stettinius, Jr., *Lend-Lease*, 1944; Henry Morgenthau in *Collier's* Magazine, October 1947; *New York Times*, 24 January 1940; *Toronto Star Weekly*, 10 February 1940; *Fortune*, April 1940; *The Times*, 16 and 18 August 1941.]

H. DUNCAN HALL.

QUICK, OLIVER CHASE (1885–1944), divine, the only son of the Rev. Robert Hebert Quick [q.v.], was born 21 June 1885 at Sedbergh vicarage, Yorkshire. He was educated at Harrow and was head of the school at which his father had been a master some years before becoming vicar of Sedbergh. He was elected to an open scholarship at Corpus Christi College, Oxford, in 1904. He obtained a first class in classical moderations in 1906, a third class in *literae humaniores* in 1908, and in 1911 was awarded the Ellerton prize for a theological essay on the value of mysticism in religious faith and practice. After a year at Bishop's Hostel, Farnham, he was ordained deacon in 1911 and priest in 1912.

Quick served for two years as assistant curate in parishes at Beckenham and Wolverhampton. In 1913 he became vice-principal of Leeds Clergy School, but in the following year the outbreak of war led to the closing of the school, and in 1914–15 he spent a year as assistant curate to H. R. L. Sheppard [q.v.] at St. Martin-in-the-Fields. From 1915 to 1917 he was resident chaplain to the archbishop of Canterbury (Randall Davidson, q.v.), in 1917–18 served in France as temporary chaplain to the forces, and was vicar of Kenley, Surrey, from 1918 to 1920. During the rest of his life he held canonries successively at Newcastle (1920–23), Carlisle (1923–30), St. Paul's (1930–34), Durham (1934–9), and Christ Church, Oxford (1939–43). At Durham he was professor of divinity and ecclesiastical history in the university and received the honorary degree of D.D. in 1941; at Oxford, where he received the degree of D.D. in 1939, he was regius professor of divinity.

Quick's contribution to thought in the field of philosophical and doctrinal theology was recognized by the award of the honorary degree of D.D. at St. Andrews in 1928, and marked him out for appointment to his two professorships at Durham and Oxford. To those who only knew him in later life it was a surprise to hear of his low class in 'Greats'. This may partly have been due to an absence of intellectual sympathy between his mind and that of his tutor, F. C. S. Schiller [q.v.]. More important, probably, was the quite devastating sincerity which remained one of his chief characteristics until the end of his days. He had a mind which could not be content until it had got to the bottom of things. Such men mature slowly, and the time allowed to prepare for the examination was not enough to enable him to feel he had anything to say about questions raised in first beginning the study of philosophy.

The publication of *Essays in Orthodoxy* in 1916 expressed the dissatisfaction of his penetrating mind with facile restatements of Christian dogma. That and his later books, of which the most important are *The Christian Sacraments* (1927), *Doctrines of the Creed* (1938), and *The Gospel of the New World* (1944), show him continuing to explore in its depths whatever question he approached. He belonged to no school or party: he was always impatient of any formula which might conceal unexamined confusion of thought. This made him a valuable member of the Archbishops' Commission on Christian Doctrine, a stimulating teacher, and a lovable, candid friend.

In 1917 Quick married Frances Winifred, daughter of Hugh William Pearson, solicitor, of Malton, Yorkshire; they had two sons and two daughters. He died at Larch Hill, Longborough, Moreton-in-Marsh, 21 January 1944. A portrait by David Rolt is in the possession of the family.

[Memoir by Archbishop William Temple prefaced to *The Gospel of the New World*, 1944; private information; personal knowledge.]          LEONARD HODGSON.

QUILLER-COUCH, SIR ARTHUR THOMAS ('Q') (1863–1944), Cornishman, man of letters, and professor of English literature, was born at Bodmin 21 November 1863, the eldest child of Thomas Quiller Couch, a medical practitioner, by his wife, Mary, daughter of Elias Ford, yeoman, of Abbots Kerswell, near Newton Abbot, Devon, and a grandson of Jonathan Couch, the doctor-naturalist [q.v.], and Jane Quiller, both of Polperro, where the Quillers and the Couches had been settled for generations.

After attending Newton Abbot and Clifton colleges Quiller-Couch entered the university of Oxford as a classical scholar of Trinity College in 1882. While there, he wrote for the *Oxford Magazine*, his best contributions being parodies of English poets. It was in the *Magazine* that he first used the pseudonym 'Q', by which he came to be well known. He obtained a first class in classical moderations (1884) and a second class in *literae humaniores* (1886). He stayed a fifth year at Trinity as lecturer in classics and in 1887 left Oxford to take up journalism in London. His first novel—*Dead Man's Rock*, a romance in the style of Robert Louis Stevenson [q.v.]—was published in the same year and was followed by *The Astonishing History of Troy Town* (1888).

In London Quiller-Couch worked partly as a free-lance but chiefly for the firm of Cassell, of whose Liberal weekly, the *Speaker*, he became assistant editor at its foundation in 1890. He contributed literary causeries to it frequently and a short story every week. He was also contributing to other periodicals and writing novels, working very long hours to support his widowed mother and his two brothers and to pay off some family debts for which he was not responsible. Moreover, he married in 1889 Louisa Amelia (died 1948), second daughter of John Hicks, of Fowey, the small Cornish port which had won his affection in boyhood; they had one son, who survived the war but died on active service in 1919, and one daughter. Overwork led to ill health; and this, coupled with an atavistic desire to live by the sea, brought Q's journalistic career to an end in 1892, when he left London and settled at Fowey in a house called The Haven on the harbour-side. Here he was able to gratify a lifelong passion for the sea and yachting and encourage a similar one among his friends of the younger generation.

Except that he continued to write for the *Speaker* until 1899, Q earned his living entirely as a free-lance writer throughout his first twenty years at Fowey. It was during this period that most of his fiction was written, but he produced numerous other works, including several anthologies. The most important of these was *The Oxford Book of English Verse* (1900), of which nearly half a million copies were sold in his lifetime. His services to literature, to the Cornwall education committee, and to Liberalism in the county brought him a knighthood in 1910, and in 1912 the

Liberal Government appointed him King Edward VII professor of English literature in the university of Cambridge. He was also elected a fellow of Jesus College, where he spent the rest of his life during term, returning to Fowey as soon as he could for each vacation.

Q was already so well known when he arrived at Cambridge that the audience at his inaugural lecture overflowed the largest lecture-room available. He proved to be a first-class lecturer, and his lectures were prepared and delivered with the thoroughness that characterized everything which he did. They were works of art, so stimulating and entertaining that attendance at them was long a fashionable pursuit. They presented literature 'with convincing enthusiasm and creative understanding, as something for hearty, rational, disciplined enjoyment by normal human beings' (George Sampson, q.v.). When they appeared in print, under such titles as *On the Art of Writing* (1916) and *On the Art of Reading* (1920), they were as attractive as when they were delivered, for everything that Q wrote was stamped with his charming and courtly personality. He knew nothing about the history of the language, and for him the Middle Ages hardly existed; but, even if he went too far, he freed English studies at Cambridge from over-emphasis on the philological side and from the domination of such terms as 'tendencies', 'influences', 'revivals', and 'revolts'. Above all, he brought to his chair the skill of a practised writer who encouraged his pupils to write. 'Literature', he insisted, 'is not a mere science, to be studied; but an art, to be practised.' Aided by his colleagues, particularly H. M. Chadwick [q.v.] and Dr. Hugh Fraser Stewart, he succeeded in getting an independent honours school of English literature firmly established in the university (1917), and long before he died he had the satisfaction of seeing large numbers of undergraduates reading for the English tripos.

Q was as popular a figure in the university as in Cornwall, and was celebrated for his hospitality, his conversation, his humour, his kindness of heart, and the care he took in choosing and wearing his picturesque clothing. During his later years many honours came to him: he was elected an honorary fellow of Trinity College, Oxford (1926), received honorary degrees from the universities of Bristol (1912), Aberdeen (1927), and Edinburgh (1930), was made a freeman of Bodmin,

Fowey, and Truro, and in 1937–8 was mayor of Fowey, which, disguised as 'Troy', had been the scene of many of his novels and short stories. On his eightieth birthday in 1943 he was saluted as the doyen of English men of letters. He died at Fowey 12 May 1944 and was buried there. There are two portraits of him, by Sir William Nicholson at Jesus College, and by Henry Lamb in the art gallery at Truro. A granite monolith was erected at Fowey as a memorial to him, and a mural tablet placed in Truro Cathedral.

Q was essentially a romantic writer and was as versatile as he was prolific. He produced over sixty substantial volumes and numerous shorter works. He was a successful writer of novels, short stories, literary criticism, serious verse, light verse, and children's books, and conspicuous as an anthologist and a stylist. His chief contribution to letters was his style— neat, colourful, apparently effortless, accurate without being pedantic, and distinguished by a clarity and conciseness that were natural to him and were re-inforced by his early classical training.

[Q, *Memories and Opinions*, 1944; F. Brittain, *Arthur Quiller-Couch*, 1947 (bibliography); *The Times*, 13 May 1944; personal knowledge.]     F. BRITTAIN.

RALSTON, JAMES LAYTON (1881– 1948), statesman, lawyer, and soldier, was born at Amherst, Cumberland County, Nova Scotia, Canada, 27 September 1881, the eldest son of Burnett William Ralston, postmaster, and his wife, Bessie Chipman Layton. His father was of Scottish, his mother of United Empire Loyalist, descent. He was educated at the County Academy at Amherst and at Dalhousie Law School, Halifax. In 1908, when a young practising barrister, Ralston ran as Federal Liberal candidate for Cumberland County and was defeated, but was elected to the legislative assembly of Nova Scotia in 1911 and again in 1916. Before 1916 he had rapidly attained eminence in his profession, first in Amherst and later in Halifax, and was in much demand as counsel. He was made a K.C. in 1914. He had marked energy and physical stamina as well as a fine mind and was noted for the thoroughness with which he prepared his cases and the forcefulness with which he presented them.

In 1915 he enlisted as a lieutenant and in 1916 went overseas with the 85th Canadian Infantry battalion as a major. He reached France early in 1917, served con-tinuously until the armistice, and in 1919 returned to England and then to Canada having commanded the 85th from April 1918 to demobilization in June 1919. He was gazetted lieutenant-colonel in 1918, and colonel in 1924. He was wounded four times, mentioned twice in dispatches, and awarded the C.M.G. and D.S.O. with bar. He was recommended for the Victoria Cross, which was refused him on the ground that a commanding officer should not expose himself to such risks as he ran. The officers and men under his command were devoted to him to an unusual degree, a devotion which was not lessened by the exacting nature of his demands upon them and was enhanced by his well-earned reputation for personal bravery.

Ralston was defeated in provincial elections in 1920 and 1925 and in the federal election of 1926 at a time when the fortunes of his party were low in his province. In 1926 he was taken into the Dominion Cabinet as minister of national defence and never thereafter suffered a personal electoral defeat. In 1922 he had acted as chairman of a Royal Commission on pensions and re-establishment appointed by the Dominion Government and in later years his sensitive sympathy for members of the forces who risked their lives was conspicuous. This had important results in 1944 when the measures known as the Veterans' Charter were under considera-tion by the Government in which he was then minister of defence. From 1930 to 1935 he was in opposition and acted as financial critic of the Conservative Govern-ment then in power. He retired from the House of Commons in 1935, having in 1931 obtained admission to the Quebec bar and entered a law firm in Montreal.

When the war broke out in September 1939 Ralston offered his services in any capacity to the prime minister, W. L. Mackenzie King [q.v.], and entered the Cabinet as minister of finance. He gave his usual exhaustive—probably excessive —attention to detail, but he did not neglect broader considerations and in short order he mastered the underlying principles of war finance. In July 1940 he became minister of defence and in this capacity made his really monumental contribution to Canada's war effort. His labours were prodigious, his determination irresistible —Canada's effort in mobilization of man-power met with striking success. In a sense he became the personification of Canada militant. The winning of the war became the one purpose to which all his thoughts and energies were directed, and with a fire and drive which few could attain. This purpose, along with his determination to keep faith with the man in the firing-line, caused him to demand conscription for overseas service in October 1944. Canada already had conscription for service at home and the Government had the statutory power to send overseas those conscripted. In the early autumn of 1944 Ralston went to Europe. He became satisfied that the stream of reinforcements to those at the front was diminishing and had become inadequate and he demanded that the Government exercise their statutory power. Mackenzie King differed from Ralston on the necessity and advisability of such a step, a crisis in the Government ensued, and Ralston left office, 1 November 1944. His successor, who believed that the reinforcement stream could be adequately replenished by volunteers, found that it was impossible, and about three weeks after Ralston's resignation an Order in Council was passed substantially carrying out the policy advocated by Ralston.

Upon his retirement from the Government Ralston returned to his law practice in Montreal, pursuing his heavy and important work with all his accustomed energy until stricken by a heart attack which resulted in his death in Montreal 22 May 1948.

While mention should be made of the large number of his directorships, indicating among other things the eminence he attained as a corporation lawyer, his prominence as a Baptist layman, his positions as a governor of two universities, and his honorary degrees from seven, Ralston's friends thought of him primarily as a simple, direct, devout man, generous and considerate, of striking soldierly appearance and bearing, and of the highest honour in all relationships. As a soldier, a Cabinet minister, and head of a law firm, his relations with subordinates were always the same. He worked them, as he worked himself, to the limit of their capacity, but their attitude towards him was one of loyal devotion. The esteem in which he was held throughout Canada was exemplified in the offices of his firm where, after his death, his picture remained in every office and his old associates and subordinates continued to refer with deepest respect and affection to 'the Colonel'.

Ralston married in 1907 Nettie Winnifred, daughter of John McLeod, foreman iron moulder, of Amherst. There was one son of the marriage, Stuart Bowman Ralston, who became a justice of the Superior Court of the Province of Quebec for the district of Montreal.

[Private information ; personal knowledge.]
J. L. ILSLEY.

RAMSAY, SIR BERTRAM HOME (1883–1945), admiral, of the Ramsays of Balmain, was born at Hampton Court Palace 20 January 1883, the third son of Captain (later Brigadier-General) William Alexander Ramsay, 4th (Queen's Own) Hussars, by his wife, Susan, daughter of William Minchiner, of Clontarf, county Dublin. He joined the Britannia in 1898. His parents were in India, and the boy spent his holidays with relatives and friends, but from the age of twelve he practically managed his own life, and after he had become midshipman in 1899, with the help of a small allowance from his father, he supported himself, thus gaining independence and self-confidence. He was not physically a big boy, nor did he grow to be a big man, but he showed a natural bent for games and sport, was a keen athlete and a good runner, devoted to horses and later in life became a keen polo player and a bold rider to hounds. He was also a keen fisherman, an average good shot, and an enthusiastic golfer.

Passing out of the Britannia in 1899 Ramsay joined the Crescent, flagship of the North America and West Indies station, in which he spent the whole of his time as a midshipman. Later in life, Ramsay often remarked on his good fortune in starting his sea service in such a happy gunroom on such a pleasant station. In his seamanship examination he gained the coveted first class certificate in 1902 and was promoted sub-lieutenant ; in his next courses he gained first class certificates in gunnery and torpedo, third class in navigation, and second class in pilotage. After spending a few weeks on manœuvres in the Greyhound, he was appointed to the Hyacinth, flagship on the East Indies station.

This commission was memorable in that it brought to Ramsay his first experience of both active service, in the Somaliland expedition of 1903–4, and combined operations, for a detachment of 125 men of the 1st battalion of the Hampshire Regiment fought alongside the navy. He landed with the naval brigade and took part in the battle of Illig ; and for his services he was mentioned in dispatches. Promoted to lieutenant in December 1904, he returned home and spent eighteen months as watchkeeper in the *Terrible*, *Good Hope*, and *Renown*. In September 1906 he was appointed to the *Dreadnought*, and thus served in the first commission of that historic ship. He served in her as watchkeeper for over two years, and then joined the signal school at the Royal Naval Barracks at Portsmouth, in order to qualify as a signal officer. He was next successively flag lieutenant to Sir Colin Keppel, commanding the Atlantic Fleet battle squadron (flag in the *Albemarle*) from 1909 to 1910, and to Sir Douglas Gamble, commanding the sixth cruiser squadron, Mediterranean Fleet (flag in the *Bacchante* and *Good Hope*). He then joined the staff of the signal school from 1912 to 1913 with a short spell at sea in the manœuvres of 1912.

Until this time Ramsay's career had been typical of any promising young officer specializing in signals, but with his appointment in February 1913 to the War College at Portsmouth, came a change which was to affect his career. His was the second course to qualify as staff officers, and thus he was one of the earliest naval officers to gain experience of the newly established staff system. Save for a short spell of sea service in the *Euryalus* for the 1913 manœuvres, he served at the War College until January 1914, when having qualified as a 'war staff officer' he joined the *Orion* on the staff of Sir Robert Arbuthnot [q.v.], rear-admiral of the second battle squadron. Being now a 'senior lieutenant', he became lieutenant-commander when that rank was instituted in March 1914. In July he rejoined Gamble, now commanding the fourth battle squadron in the *Dreadnought*, and thus on the outbreak of war found himself in the Grand Fleet. In February 1915, however, he came ashore to join the new signal section of the Admiralty war staff.

In August 1915 Ramsay received his first command, the *M. 25*, a small monitor. Thus began his association with the Dover Patrol, and for the next two years he spent most of his time off the Belgian coast, supporting the left flank of the armies, a fresh experience of combined operations, expanded by contact with the wing of the Royal Naval Air Service then operating from Dunkirk. He was promoted commander in June 1916 and reappointed to his ship, but in October 1917 he transferred to command the famous fighting destroyer *Broke*, also in the Dover Patrol. In this ship he took part in the Ostend operations, for which service he was mentioned in dispatches, and in December 1918 he was appointed M.V.O., after having had the honour of conveying King George V to his visit to the armies in France after the armistice. For war services he was also made an officer of the Order of the Crown of Italy (1917), chevalier of the Legion of Honour (1918), and he received the Belgian croix de guerre (1919).

In February 1919 Ramsay joined the *New Zealand* as flag commander on the staff of Lord Jellicoe [q.v.] on his tour to the Dominions. On his return he was appointed commander of the *Emperor of India* in 1920, and of the *Benbow* in 1921, both in the Mediterranean Fleet, and in June 1923 he was promoted captain.

After passing the senior officers' war and tactical courses, Ramsay was appointed to command the *Weymouth*, carrying out a trooping trip to China in 1924. Next year he assumed command of the *Danae* in the first cruiser squadron, Mediterranean Fleet, and in the two years before going on to serve on the instructional staff of the Royal Naval War College, he brought his ship to a remarkable state of efficiency. He resumed sea service in 1929 as flag captain and chief of staff to Sir Arthur Waistell, vice-admiral commanding the China station (flag in the *Kent*, which Ramsay commanded for two years), and then returned to instructional duty as the naval officer on the staff of the Imperial Defence College. His military colleague was the future Viscount Alanbrooke and his air colleague the future Lord Douglas of Kirtleside. In November 1933 he assumed command of the *Royal Sovereign* in the Mediterranean Fleet and was still serving in her when he was promoted to flag rank in May 1935.

It was no matter for surprise that the first appointment which Ramsay received as rear-admiral was as chief of staff to the commander-in-chief of the Home Fleet, for he was known as a thoroughly efficient executive officer and a staff officer of great brilliance and wide experience. The commander-in-chief in this appointment, one of the two most important sea-going commands, was to be Sir Roger Backhouse [q.v.]. Those who knew both men had misgivings. Backhouse was of the old school of naval officers, a strong individualist with an infinite capacity for hard work, and a profound believer in centralization, who practised what he believed. Ramsay, one of the leading exponents of the modern school, believed heart and soul in the staff system with its decentralization of detail and control from the top of essentials only. He was under no illusions over difficulties ahead, but he relied on his old friendship with Backhouse (they had been shipmates in the *Dreadnought*), and on his conviction that with a commander-in-chief's responsibilities on his shoulders, Backhouse would be forced to decentralize on his chief of staff.

Ramsay joined the *Nelson* in August 1935. For a time all went well, but unhappily this did not last, and within a few months the situation was becoming intolerable. Backhouse thought that his chief of staff was trying to run the fleet for him; Ramsay believed that his commander-in-chief deliberately excluded him from all responsibility and would neither ask nor brook advice or assistance. In such a clash of personalities, Ramsay was not the man to sit back and accept the situation philosophically. Moreover, he believed that his commander-in-chief was overworking to the point of danger in trying to do everything single-handed, and that it was his clear duty to make way for some other officer with whom Backhouse could work more easily. Accordingly he asked to be relieved, and he left the *Nelson* in December 1935, and twelve days later he was placed on half-pay. He was not again employed, although he carried out two senior officers' courses and was in fact offered an appointment afloat on foreign service. Believing that this was but a prelude to retirement he refused it. He was appointed C.B. in 1936, was placed on the retired list in 1938 on reaching the top of the rear-admirals' list, and promoted vice-admiral in January 1939.

Ramsay's naval career seemed to have come to an end. In many ways a reserved man he never allowed anyone, not even his wife, to know how heavily he felt his retirement, and it was not until after his death that his papers showed how deeply he had been hurt by what he believed to have been an injustice. Meanwhile life ashore had some compensations. In 1929 he had married Helen Margaret, daughter of Colonel Charles Thomson Menzies, of Kames, Duns, Berwickshire, and two sons were born to them. In the close society of his wife and young family he found much happiness and in 1938 they bought Bughtrig, Coldstream, Berwickshire, and there they settled down to country pursuits. This peaceful life, however, was not to last for long. As the shadows of war lengthened, so did naval preparations increase. With his experience in the Dover Patrol in 1914–18, Ramsay was an obvious choice for the post of flag officer-in-charge, Dover, whenever that command should be established. At the Munich crisis in 1938 he did a period of duty on the staff of the commander-in-chief, the Nore, and he made all preparations for the naval headquarters and establishments at Dover. He hoisted his vice-admiral's flag, as flag officer-in-charge, Dover, on 24 August 1939. So the outbreak of war found him at his post and commanding waters very familiar to him. Familiar too must have been the early tasks which came his way: the denial of passage through the Straits of Dover to submarines; defence against possible destroyer raids; protection of cross-Channel military traffic, and other repetitions of 1914–18. A new development which caused him anxiety was the aircraft-carried magnetic mine, but time brought a counter to that weapon.

With the German assault on France and the Low Countries, Dover at once became a centre of great activity, but the climax came when, with the collapse of France, Ramsay was ordered to bring the British soldiers home from Dunkirk. This operation will doubtless remain a classic of improvisation, and may well go down in naval history under its original code name 'Dynamo'. With his forces increased by every destroyer which could be spared and every small craft and every ship which could be found to reach Dover, Ramsay, with a staff multiplied for the occasion, turned to his task. The Luftwaffe attacked in strength to intercept and prevent the work of embarkation and transport. Despite the splendid efforts of the limited numbers of Royal Air Force fighters, inevitable losses and casualties took place. Nevertheless, night and day the work went forward, and the numbers of soldiers coming out of the port of Dunkirk and off the adjacent beaches rose steadily. Operation Dynamo lasted from 6.57 p.m. 26 May until 2.23 p.m. 4 June. Between these dates 338,226 officers and men of the British and allied armies had been lifted from the continent and brought to England. On the completion of this great achievement, Ramsay reported on the operation to the King in person, and was rewarded by the honour of the K.C.B. at His Majesty's hands.

Ramsay returned to a Dover where his problems were multiplied tenfold by an enemy in possession of the French coastline.

For nearly two more years he strove to maintain control of the waters under his command in the face of air attack, the assaults of hostile small craft, and cross-Channel bombardment. Throughout the autumn months of 1940 Dover was in the forefront of our precautions against invasion. Those were anxious days, but Ramsay started with the great advantage of four years' rest and refreshment behind him, and he remained fresh, fit, and imperturbable. Despite losses, our coastwise traffic was kept going. At the end of 1940 he was mentioned in dispatches for his services.

Ramsay left Dover 29 April 1942 to take up an appointment as flag officer, Expeditionary Force, working with General Eisenhower, who had arrived in London to become commanding general, European theatre of operations. The possibility of invading France in 1943 was under active consideration, and Ramsay began to plan for it; but in process of time the project was postponed in favour of an early landing on the coast of North Africa with subsequent operations in the Mediterranean. Under the command of General Eisenhower, now allied commander-in-chief, Ramsay began the detailed planning of this new operation as naval commander-in-chief, Expeditionary Force. It soon became evident that considerable naval forces, with several flag officers commanding the various units, were going to be involved. Objections were raised to so great a force being put under an acting admiral on the retired list who had never actually flown his flag in command at sea. It was therefore decided to bring Sir Andrew Cunningham (subsequently Viscount Cunningham of Hyndhope) back from the United States to take over the naval command, whilst Ramsay was to serve under him as his deputy. This was in accordance with Ramsay's own personal views and wishes, and he did valuable service during the operation as the rear link between the expedition and the British and United States authorities. In connexion with the North African landings he was again mentioned in dispatches in April 1943.

Victory having been achieved in North Africa, it was decided to invade Sicily. Ramsay became the naval commander, Eastern Task Force, in command of the British landing operations, whilst Vice-Admiral Hewitt, United States Navy, commanded the Western Task Force, both under the command of Sir Andrew Cun-

ningham, and the supreme command of General Eisenhower. This was the first large-scale landing on hostile beaches with the enemy present in strength. On both British and American fronts the assault was entirely successful and the subsequent 'build-up' equally effective, in spite of the weather, which deteriorated rapidly and, for the Mediterranean in high summer, unexpectedly. Nevertheless, the stout-hearted decision was taken by the supreme commander to continue the attack, and keen anxiety must it have cost; but the bold decision was justified by steady improvement in the weather. For his success in these operations in the Mediterranean Ramsay was appointed K.B.E. at the end of 1943.

Ramsay returned to London and in December 1943 was appointed allied naval commander-in-chief of the Expeditionary Force. A combined naval, military, and air staff had been working at full pressure on the proposed invasion of France in the spring of 1944. Ramsay's experience in the Mediterranean stood him in good stead during the working out of the campaign; before it came to maturity, to his deep satisfaction he was restored to the active list as vice-admiral and on the following day promoted admiral. His headquarters were originally at Norfolk House, St. James's Square, but in April he moved to battle headquarters at Southwick Park, near Portsmouth, while supreme headquarters were in a near-by wood, as were also those of the 21st Army Group with Sir Bernard Montgomery (later Viscount Montgomery of Alamein) as commander-in-chief. The air commander-in-chief, Sir Trafford Leigh-Mallory [q.v.], had his headquarters at Stanmore; but he maintained a strong liaison link at naval headquarters. It was at Southwick Park that General Eisenhower made his historic decisions, first to postpone the invasion for twenty-four hours, and later, in spite of unfavourable weather reports but on the strength of a prophesied improvement, to launch the assault for dawn, 6 June 1944; and it was at Southwick Park that Ramsay came gradually to realize that this, the greatest of all combined operations, had achieved success at a mere fraction of the cost in casualties which had been anticipated. However, he knew all too well that the future of the allied military operations hinged on the establishment of their 'build-up', and he brought all his powers to bear on the task of moving the vast quantities of men and material across the

Channel with speed and safety. The millionth soldier landed in France twenty-eight days after D-Day, a month over four years since Ramsay had brought the last allied soldier to England from Dunkirk.

During the operation Ramsay spent every day that he could spare from headquarters off the British and American beaches, dealing direct with his task force and assault force commanders. He never spared himself but remained fit and cheerful both in good conditions and in bad. With the advance of the allied armies he transferred his headquarters first to Granville, opposite Jersey, then to St. Germain-en-Laye outside Paris. The most spectacular part of Ramsay's work was now over, but much remained to be done, of which the most eventful was the assault on Walcheren Island, the prelude to the opening of Antwerp. In addition there was the constant work of protecting the cross-Channel traffic against submarines, small craft, and mines, and the opening up of ports as they fell into the hands of the Allies.

On 2 January 1945 Ramsay left his headquarters on a flight to Brussels in order to attend a conference at 21st Army Group headquarters. He took off from the airfield at Toussus-le-Noble in an aircraft allocated to his personal use. It crashed on taking off and Ramsay was killed instantaneously. He was buried at St. Germain-en-Laye. Although he was not to see the day of victory, he died knowing that victory could not be long delayed, and he must have been aware of his considerable contribution to that end; but he doubtless would have had greater pleasure had he known of the measure of affection and admiration in which his memory is held by all who served under his command.

In November 1944 Ramsay was awarded the Russian Order of Ushakov (first class), a rare distinction, and he was posthumously admitted to the American Legion of Merit with the degree of chief commander; he was promoted grand officer of the Legion of Honour, the insignia of this rank being given to his widow in Paris in June 1945.

A lifelike portrait of Ramsay was posthumously painted by (Sir) Oswald Birley for the Greenwich Collection at the Royal Naval College, Greenwich.

[Private information; personal knowledge.]
G. E. CREASY.

RANDALL-MacIVER, DAVID (1873–1945), archaeologist and anthropologist, was born in London 31 October 1873, the only son of John MacIver, shipowner, by his wife, Eliza Mary Rutherford. His father died a young man and his mother later married Richard Randall, barrister-at-law, whose name MacIver added to his own. He was educated at Radley and the Queen's College, Oxford, where he obtained a first class in *literae humaniores* in 1896.

While at Oxford MacIver also found time to investigate the subject of anthropology, and his first ambition was to follow up this interest by work in Yucatan. This project, however, came to nothing and instead he went to Egypt. From 1899 to 1901 he excavated at Abydos for the Egypt Exploration Fund (later Society), and from 1900 to 1906 he was Laycock student of Egyptology at Worcester College, Oxford. Subsequently (1907–11) he directed an archaeological expedition in Nubia for the University Museum in Philadelphia and also served as their curator of Egyptology.

In Egypt MacIver included measuring skulls among the other duties of an excavator and thus added a new and highly important item to the essential data to be compiled by a field-worker. His many excavations during these years, and his able and prompt publication of reports on these early works, have been of invaluable use to his successors in the field. Many of the major names in Egyptology in the first half of the twentieth century owe much to the pioneering work of Randall-MacIver.

In 1905 he went to Rhodesia at the invitation of the British Association and the Rhodes Trustees to excavate at Zimbabwe and other sites. Although much had been written about the immense antiquity of these ruins, MacIver was able to demonstrate in his book *Mediaeval Rhodesia* (1906) that they dated from A.D. 1200 to 1500.

Between 1911 and 1914 MacIver served as librarian of the American Geographical Society, but on the outbreak of war in Europe he returned immediately to England and served on the intelligence staff in both France and Macedonia. After the war he settled in Rome and this period was perhaps the most fruitful in his long and varied career. His publication on the *Villanovans and Early Etruscans* (1924), which was produced during these years and which was perhaps his main achievement, still remains an essential source for any student on the subject. To this period also belong other well-known books on Italian archaeology including *The Iron Age in Italy* (1927), *Italy Before the Romans* (1928), and *Greek Cities in Italy and Sicily* (1931).

In 1907 Randall-MacIver had been elected a fellow of the Society of Antiquaries of London and in 1938 he was elected F.B.A., an honour which greatly pleased him. He was in the United States on the outbreak of war in 1939 and although unable to take an active part in the war he nevertheless found activities of a quieter kind to employ his wide experience. Among these was his invaluable assistance to those charged by the United States War Department with listing Italian monuments to be protected from destruction.

In the archaeological world MacIver was a much beloved and fascinating figure. His appearance throughout his life was extremely striking for he was very tall with bright blue eyes and wavy fair hair; to this was added a smiling sparkling charm of speech which gave a peculiar interest to everything he said and served to kindle in others his own unfailing enthusiasm and optimism. He was a worker with very high standards and he expected others to hold equal standards. Although he was intolerant of slipshod work or thought in any form, and never hesitated to denounce such weaknesses when he found them, he was also full of encouragement and interest in the efforts of others, and always ready to do anything within his power to help young students on the threshold of their own careers.

Randall-MacIver was always exceedingly proud of his Highland origin. He was a complete stranger to any form of narrow nationalism and spent his life with equal serenity in England, Italy, or America. He died 30 April 1945 at his residence in New York. He was twice married: first, in 1911 to Joanna (died 1931), daughter of W. H. Davidge, of New York; and secondly, in 1936 to Mabel, daughter of Edward S. Holden, of St. Louis, U.S.A., and widow of George Tuttle, of New York. His second wife survived him, but both marriages were childless.

[Private information; personal knowledge.]
T. C. HENCKEN.

RANKEILLOUR, first BARON (1870–1949), parliamentarian. [See HOPE, JAMES FITZALAN.]

RANKIN, SIR GEORGE CLAUS (1877–1946), judge, was born 12 August 1877 at Lamington in Lanarkshire, the second son of the Rev. Robert Rankin, minister of Lamington, by his wife, Theresa Margaret, daughter of George John Claus, shipowner, of Liverpool. He was educated at George Watson's College and the university, Edinburgh, where he graduated in 1897 with first class honours in philosophy. He was awarded the Bruce of Grangehill and Falkland prize and won the Vans Dunlop (1897) and Ferguson (1899) scholarships. In October 1897 he entered Trinity College, Cambridge, as a sizar, becoming a scholar the following year, and was placed in the first class of both parts of the moral sciences tripos (1899, 1900). He twice won a Hooper declamation prize and in 1901 was awarded a Whewell scholarship to which he was re-elected in 1903. In 1901 he was also president of the Union. In 1904 he was called to the bar by Lincoln's Inn and entered the chambers of William Pickford (later Lord Sterndale, q.v.) where he became acquainted with (Sir) Lancelot Sanderson. He practised mainly in bankruptcy and commercial cases.

In 1916 Rankin received a commission in the Royal Garrison Artillery and served until 1918. On returning to the bar he found his practice dispersed and was faced with the uncertainty of regaining it, without the advantage of private means and with the anxieties of family responsibilities. In these circumstances, at the suggestion of Sanderson, then chief justice of Bengal, he accepted appointment as a puisne judge of the High Court of Calcutta. In 1919 he served as a member of the Hunter commission appointed to report on the disturbances at Amritsar and the action taken by General R. E. H. Dyer [q.v.]. In 1924 he served as chairman of the civil justice committee appointed to make recommendations for the reform of legal procedure in British India, particularly with reference to the law's delays. In recognition of these services he was knighted in 1925, and a year later, on the retirement of Sanderson, he was appointed chief justice of Bengal, the first puisne judge of the Calcutta High Court to be so promoted. Early in 1934 his health failed; he returned to England on long leave and eventually resigned his office.

In the following year his health was sufficiently restored for him to be able to resume work. He was appointed to inquire into the disorders at Barlinnie prison, Glasgow, was sworn of the Privy Council, and later in 1935 succeeded Sanderson in one of the two paid posts on the Judicial Committee of that body created by the Appellate Jurisdiction Act, 1929. He was elected a bencher of his Inn and in 1937 received the honorary degree of LL.D. from Edinburgh University. In 1944 his health again broke down and he was forced to retire.

In both his private and professional life Rankin was remarkable for his unassuming modesty and natural courtesy. The latter quality in particular endeared him to his colleagues and to the bar, both in India and in Downing Street. It was a friendly courtesy, recognized by practitioners as no mere conventional politeness. But it did not permit the abuse of the time of the court: persistence too prolix in an unacceptable argument met with observations containing more than a touch of acerbity.

Early in his tenure of office in India, Rankin applied himself to an exhaustive study of Hindu and Mohammedan law in both of which systems he attained a profound knowledge. His judgements delivered in India in cases governed by these laws were acknowledged to be of the greatest assistance to the Judicial Committee of the Privy Council in dealing with appeals from Indian courts. He also became thoroughly versed in all the complexities of the Bengal Tenancy Act, probably the most intricate code of law relating to land tenure ever devised by human wit. In dealing with cases which came before him, of whatever nature, Rankin excelled in quickly sifting out the essential questions of fact or law involved. His judgements were distinguished by great clarity of expression: only in rare instances did subtlety of thought find expression in a passage of some seeming obscurity.

When he became a member of the Judicial Committee, it was soon apparent that Rankin was a real addition of strength. However modestly he expressed his views, however seldom he intervened during argument, he proved himself capable of great tenacity in upholding his own opinion. Lord Maugham, on the occasion of his death, wrote of him: 'there has been no judge of my time who more greatly impressed me in a sphere he may be said to have made his own'. He was probably the greatest judicial authority on Indian jurisprudence of his time.

Rankin married in 1910 Alice Maud Amy (died 1924), daughter of Geoffrey Sayer, of Bromley, Kent, by whom he had two daughters. He died at Elie, Fifeshire, 8 April 1946.

[*The Times*, 9 and 12 April 1946; private information; personal knowledge.]

W. W. K. PAGE.

RATHBONE, ELEANOR FLORENCE (1872–1946), social reformer, was born in London 12 May 1872, the daughter of William Rathbone (1819–1902, q.v.), the sixth of a notable dynasty of Liverpool social reformers to bear that name, by his second wife, Emily Acheson Lyle. Eleanor was the youngest but one in a family of ten children. With a childhood spent under the alternating stimuli of Liverpool philanthropy and Westminster politics—since her father was for many years a member of Parliament—Eleanor was nurtured in an atmosphere of strenuous endeavour and social responsibility. Her early education was disrupted by migrations between Liverpool and London, where she went to Kensington High School. It provided an insufficient background of textual scholarship for the school of *literae humaniores* at Oxford in which she achieved second class honours after three years at Somerville College (1893–6). Those who taught her diagnosed a first-class philosophic brain. She herself envisaged a subsequent preoccupation with the problems of pure philosophy which did not long survive her return to Liverpool. An acute awareness of the sufferings of distressed or frustrated human beings precipitated her into contemporary administrative, political, and economic problems.

Among Eleanor Rathbone's many activities after leaving Oxford was a factual inquiry into the position of widows under the Poor Law. This proved to be the starting-point of a penetrating analysis of the economic position of the family which led to her formulation of the case for family allowances—a case for which her first-hand experience in the administration of Service separation allowances during the war of 1914–18 offered practical illustration. She became the leading advocate of family allowances and her book *The Disinherited Family*, published in 1924, may be regarded as the first English textbook on the subject. She published *The Case for Family Allowances* in 1940. Although the initiation and persistent advocacy of this particular reform, which reached the statute book in 1945, was perhaps her greatest achievement, Eleanor Rathbone's career covered a surprising multiplicity of activities. She played a leading part in the women's suffrage agitation before the enactment of a limited measure in 1918. In the following year she succeeded (Dame) Millicent Fawcett [q.v.] as president of the constitutional wing of the women's suffrage movement which under her leadership pressed for a number of legislative reforms affecting the economic and legal position of women. At the same time, as independent member of the Liverpool city council, to which she was elected in 1909, she concerned herself with the inter-war housing campaign, and achieved a rare mastery of its complexities.

Although her interests had never been confined to problems relating to feminism and social administration, her active participation in world affairs dated from about 1928, the year in which women achieved equal voting rights with men. A sudden awareness of the distressing conditions in which very many Indian women were living led to a concern with the position of women both in India and in other parts of the British Commonwealth. This was, she averred, her principal reason for seeking election to Parliament, although she had in fact as an independent candidate unsuccessfully contested a Liverpool constituency in 1922. In 1929 she was elected as independent member for the Combined English Universities, a seat which she retained until her death, being returned unopposed in 1935, but having to fight again for her seat in 1945. She held strong views on the importance of university representation and on the desirability of dissociating this type of constituency from party allegiance. Yet, apart from a continuous concern with the special problems of her graduate constituents, her political interests centred to an increasing extent on overseas affairs. She fought a prolonged battle on behalf of a wider franchise for Indian women during the discussions leading to the passage of the Government of India Act. The publication in 1934 of her book, *Child Marriage: The Indian Minotaur*, was one incident in a campaign which achieved a measure of success in the stiffening of the Sarda Act for the restraint of this evil. In the sphere of foreign affairs she had always been an ardent advocate of collective security, and the trend of British foreign policy from 1931 to 1939 brought her into continuous conflict with the Government. She spoke and wrote with considerable violence in opposition to successive phases of 'appeasement'; her views on the Italian invasion of Abyssinia, 'non-intervention' in Spain, and the isolation of Russia are expounded in a book, *War Can Be Averted*, written at white-heat in the summer of 1937. This polemical phase of her concern with foreign affairs was accompanied by untiring efforts on behalf of refugees, both before and during the war of 1939-45. Her time became increasingly occupied by the organization of relief schemes as well as by tireless personal efforts on behalf of individuals—activities which brought her many Jewish contacts and roused her sympathy with Zionism. Apart from active participation in the agitation for post-war European relief, her last preoccupation was the future of Palestine. She was immersed in its problems when she died suddenly in London 2 January 1946.

Honorary degrees were conferred upon Eleanor Rathbone by the universities of Liverpool (LL.D., 1931) and Oxford (D.C.L., 1938). She was a fellow of the Royal Statistical Society. A portrait of her, painted by James Gunn, is at Somerville College.

Throughout her life Eleanor Rathbone remained free of party affiliation. Against a background of philosophic Liberalism she stood for a generous development of the social services, but Socialism as such did not interest her. Before 1918 Liverpool was her home and the principal field of her activity. Later she divided her time between London and Liverpool, but with the addition of Parliament to her other duties the pull of London increased and the small Westminster house which she shared with a lifelong friend became her main headquarters until its destruction by bombs in 1940. She continued, however, to live in London. Apart from her achievement in converting Great Britain to family allowances, she will be remembered as a human being of outstanding intellectual calibre and tireless energy, with an abnormal sensitivity to human suffering, which her contemplation of the post-war scene did little to assuage. Her enjoyment of good literature, country holidays, and warm friendships, however, provided continual solace. And the obstinate belief, inherited from her father, that 'whatever ought to be done can be done' saved her from despair.

[*The Times*, 3, 4, and 8 January 1946; *Observer*, 21 February 1943; Mary D. Stocks, *Eleanor Rathbone, a biography*, 1949; private information; personal knowledge.]

MARY D. STOCKS.

RAVEN-HILL, LEONARD (1867–1942), artist, illustrator, and cartoonist, was born at Bath 10 March 1867, the son of William Hill, a law stationer, and his wife, Anne Scott. He was educated as a day-boy at the old Bristol Grammar School and, when the site was changed, claimed to be the first boy to be caned in the new school—his only scholastic distinction. He afterwards went to the Devon County School. In spite of some family opposition, he proceeded to study at the City and Guilds of London Art School, Kennington, and later in Paris, exhibiting paintings at the Salon in 1886, and in several subsequent years. In London he was a friend and fellow student of C. de S. Ricketts and C. H. Shannon [qq.v.], but his own inclination led him towards pen-and-ink work. Rapidity of execution and reproduction fascinated him. Outdoor life and adventure were his ideals; he was an enthusiastic Volunteer, and like Rudyard Kipling [q.v.], an early acquaintance and the object of his greatest admiration, he considered the calling of a journalist supreme. He was the art editor of *Pick-Me-Up*, and a founder of the *Butterfly*, light papers of the 'nineties. His first drawing in *Punch* appeared 28 December 1895.

Raven-Hill joined the *Punch* round table in 1901 on the same evening that Sir John Tenniel [q.v.] appeared at it for the last time, and he became a political cartoonist on the death of E. Linley Sambourne [q.v.] in 1910. He excelled in vitality and energy of line, and was never so pleased as when called upon to represent a scene of violent action at the shortest possible notice. In his *Pick-Me-Up* days he had executed a pamphlet of twenty-one drawings within twenty-six hours, and if, as sometimes happened, his design for a *Punch* cartoon proved unsatisfactory, he was willing, and even pleased, to draw an entirely different one on the same morning. He illustrated *Stalky and Co.* for Kipling, and *Kipps* for H. G. Wells to the complete satisfaction of both authors, but his opinions were violently and obstinately conservative, and his last picture in *Punch* was a cartoon, in colour, of Kipling as the Empire's laureate. He was convivial, irascible, and often as inarticulate in speech as he was eloquent with his pen. Failing eyesight made his later work so far inferior to his best that his talent has sometimes been misjudged.

He was twice married: first, in 1889 to Annie (died 1922), daughter of Mark Rogers, wood-carver; and secondly, in 1923 to Marion Jean Lyon (died 1940), for a number of years the able advertisement editor of *Punch*; he was survived by a daughter of his first wife. He died at Ryde, Isle of Wight, 31 March 1942. A portrait by Maurice Greiffenhagen is in the Glasgow City Art Gallery.

[*The Times*, 1 April 1942; an unpublished autobiography by the artist; personal knowledge.]

E. V. KNOX.

RAVILIOUS, ERIC WILLIAM (1903–1942), artist, was born at Acton, London, 22 August 1903, the third surviving son of Frank Ravilious, coach-builder, by his wife, Emma, daughter of William Ford, farmer, of Kingsbridge, Devon. He was educated at the Grammar School and the School of Art, Eastbourne, proceeding thence in September 1922 to the Royal College of Art, where he drew special benefit from the teaching of Alec Buckels and Paul Nash [q.v.]. A far stronger and more lasting influence was derived from Mr. Douglas Percy Bliss (later to become director of the Glasgow School of Art). He struck up a keen friendship, which proved lifelong, with Mr. Edward Bawden, and work by both youths was reproduced in the *Studio* of October 1924. In July 1925 Ravilious left the College with a travelling scholarship, but was not influenced in his practice by the visit to Italy which it provided. He was instructor in design at the College from 1929 to 1938.

Water-colour painting was Ravilious's preferred medium, and he was deeply and precociously learned in the works of the English masters, but his professional life started with book illustration by wood-engravings—a set of cuts for Mr. Martin (Donisthorpe) Armstrong's novel, *Desert* (1926). In the same year began a connexion with Robert John Gibbings's Golden Cockerel Press, which proved one of the *points de repère* in the English typographical revival which followed the war of 1914–18. In that florescence of book production Ravilious played a distinguished part, carrying out all functions of a book-decorator except type-design—dust wrappers, illustrations, end-papers, head-pieces, tail-pieces, all showing a fine sense of congruence with type and layout. His first big commission was a set of signs of the zodiac for the Lanston Monotype Corporation (1929). For the Golden Cockerel he did, among other things, illustrations for Nicholas Breton's *The Twelve Moneths* (1927) and for *Twelfth Night* (1932); for the Nonesuch Press he illustrated a selection in two volumes from the works of Gilbert White of Selborne (1938). The Curwen and Cresset presses and Dent's 'Everyman's Library' were other users of his work. Ravilious also carried out purely commercial tasks for concerns such as the British Broadcasting Corporation, Austin Reed & Co., and the London Passenger Transport Board, imparting a rare taste and distinction to these advertising commissions.

Concurrently with all these exercises in wood-engraving Ravilious was working steadily out of doors at water-colour landscapes, from the start handling the medium freely and without fuss, discovering delightful and unexpected patterns in unlikely places, and evincing a chaste and well-controlled colour-sense and a probity in design cognate with that displayed in his wood-engravings, but, of course, differing according to the feeling and technical demands of the more resilient medium. He held one-man shows at the Zwemmer Gallery (1934 and 1937) and at Arthur Tooth's gallery (1939). Two notable excursions in mural painting have been lost to posterity. One, at Morley College, London, was destroyed by German bombing; the other, at Morecambe, disappeared with the disintegration of a bad surface.

Embarking on yet another medium, Ravilious produced in 1935 lithographs which caused the pottery firm of Wedgwood to commission a number of appliqué decorations which proved highly successful. He also designed for engraving on glass. In 1939 Ravilious joined the Royal Observer Corps, and in 1940 he was gazetted captain in the Royal Marines and employed by the Admiralty as an official war artist. Early in September 1942 he was a passenger in a Coastal Command aeroplane from Iceland which disappeared, and in the following spring he was officially presumed dead.

Ravilious was an artist of most varied talent. His wood-engravings, giving a twentieth-century twist to the Bewick tradition, yet often harked back to an earlier age in their frequent archaism and naïve humour. Technically they were highly accomplished, as were the water-colours he made, not in the English style of swirling, misty washes, but in a delicate and precise system of design which elicited interesting compositions from the most unpromising data. His commercial work was in noteworthy contrast with the cheapness of much contemporary production. Singularly free from artistic snobbery, he threw himself into commercial art with the same sense of purpose that controlled his other activities. His decorative faculty never failed him.

In 1930 Ravilious married Eileen Lucy, daughter of Lieutenant-Colonel Frederick Scott Garwood, Royal Engineers; they had two sons and one daughter. His widow, who married Mr. H. V. L. Swanzy, owns a portrait in oils by Phyllis Dodd (Mrs. D. P. Bliss) and a water-colour portrait by Edward Bawden.

[*Signature*, No. 1, 1935; *Architectural Review*, December 1943; *Graphis*, No. 16, 1946 (Zürich); Robert Harling, *Notes on the Wood-Engravings of Eric Ravilious*, 1946; Introduction by J. M. Richards to the catalogue of the memorial exhibition, Arts Council, 1948; private information.]

HERBERT B. GRIMSDITCH.

RAYLEIGH, fourth BARON (1875–1947), experimental physicist. [See STRUTT, ROBERT JOHN.]

READ, SIR HERBERT JAMES (1863–1949), civil servant, was born at Honiton, Devon, 17 March 1863, the second son of Charles Read, proprietor of a drapery store, and his wife, Mary Ann Avery. Read was one of a gifted family. His elder brother, who died young, was senior classical scholar at Winchester College and a younger brother became professor of metallurgy at Cardiff. Read was educated at Allhallows School, Honiton, and at Brasenose College, Oxford, where he was a scholar and was placed in the first class in both mathematical moderations (1882) and the final honour school of mathematics (1884). He was also a good classical scholar, and his knowledge of the history of London in recent times was encyclopaedic. His career reveals a remarkable range of interests in which appreciation of the value of the sciences was combined with love of the humanities.

Read entered the Civil Service as a higher division clerk at the War Office in

1887. In 1889 he was transferred to the Colonial Office where he remained for nearly forty years. Thenceforward his work was mainly concerned with tropical Africa, beginning at a time when national responsibilities in Africa were quickly expanding and including Joseph Chamberlain's tenure of office as colonial secretary. In Chamberlain, who selected him as his assistant private secretary (1896–8), Read found an appreciative and congenial chief. Read was exceptional amongst his official colleagues, most of whom were graduates in arts from the older universities, in his quick recognition of the importance of scientific research in the future administration and development of tropical dependencies. He was largely instrumental in stimulating official interest in organizations concerned with tropical medicine and agriculture and in establishing contacts between his department and scientific institutions, some of which, such as the London School of Hygiene and Tropical Medicine and the Commonwealth Institutes of Entomology and Mycology, owe their inception largely to him. The early investigation of trypanosomiasis in Uganda was directly due to his influence. Read was also quick to take advantage of opportunities for international collaboration in scientific and technical matters as well as in attacking the abuses which arose from closer commercial contacts between Europeans and Africans and which offended his strong humanitarian instincts.

Read rose to be head, in turn, of both the East and West African departments of the Colonial Office. In 1911–12 he visited East Africa at a time when overseas visits by Colonial Office officials were rare. In 1916 he was appointed an assistant under-secretary of state with supervision over the two African departments. He became a prominent member of several committees which were greatly indebted to him for their achievements. To him a committee was a means of solving, not shelving, a difficult problem, and his capacity to understand and interpret the opinions of experts was invaluable. He was chairman of the colonial survey committee, of the colonial advisory medical and sanitary committee, and of the Bureau of Hygiene and Tropical Diseases. He served as British delegate to several international conferences, including the sleeping sickness conference, London, 1907, and the African arms traffic conference, Brussels, 1908. He was senior member of the Colonial Office delegacy to the Paris peace conference in 1919.

Read went overseas as governor of Mauritius (1924–30) for the final phase of his official career. In retirement he resumed the activities in keeping with his aptitudes, serving on a large number of committees concerned not only with scientific research but with social welfare, an interest to which he was now able to devote more time. He was an active member of the Reform Club, a fellow of the Royal Astronomical Society, and an honorary fellow of the Society for the Preservation of the Fauna of the Empire.

Read was appointed C.M.G. in 1907, promoted K.C.M.G. in 1918 and G.C.M.G. in 1935, and appointed C.B. in 1914; he became a commander of the Order of the Crown of Belgium in 1919. He married in 1905 Violet Kate (died 1951), daughter of the late Major Duncan Maclachlan, 90th Regiment; they had one son and one daughter. Read died at Tunbridge Wells 16 October 1949.

[Private information; personal knowledge.]
E. W. EVANS.

REGAN, CHARLES TATE (1878–1943), zoologist and director of the British Museum (Natural History), was born at Sherborne, Dorset, 1 February 1878, the only son of Charles James Regan, music master at Sherborne School, and his wife, Maria, daughter of William Tate, author of *The Modern Cambist*, first published in 1829. He was educated at Derby School and Queens' College, Cambridge, where he studied zoology under Adam Sedgwick [q.v.] and was awarded a first class in part i (1900) and a second in part ii (1901) of the natural sciences tripos.

In 1901 he was appointed assistant (later known as assistant keeper) in the British Museum (Natural History) and was posted to assist George Albert Boulenger in curating the collection of fishes. At the museum he made his career, soon taking sole charge of the fishes and later becoming keeper of the department of zoology (1921) and in 1927 director of the museum, a post which he held until his retirement in 1938.

Regan's publications number 260 titles. Among these *The Freshwater Fishes of the British Isles* (1911) embodies the results of his observations as an angler and of his museum researches in a way which makes it an authentic and readable reference book for anglers and naturalists. He edited a *Natural History* (1936), in which he wrote the section on fishes. Most of his works, however, were specialist contributions to the zoology of fishes. His anatomical studies were mainly on the skeleton and had as their aim the elucidation of relationships and evolutionary trends. Modifying and amplifying earlier classifications, he defined and surveyed some forty orders of fishes, producing a comprehensive classification which has been accepted as a basis by ichthyologists of the world. This was summarized in his articles on Fishes and Selachians in the fourteenth edition of the *Encyclopaedia Britannica*. His work on the fish collections of the *Scotia* and *Terra Nova* Antarctic expeditions and on Central American fishes, among others, were productive of illuminating zoogeographical generalizations.

He described the nature and fine structure of the complicated copulatory organs of the tiny East Indian Phallostethid fishes ; and in the viviparous fishes of the Cyprinodont family Poeciliidae it was he who first showed that the clue to their classification lay in the detailed structure of the anal fin, or gonopodium, of the male. It was Regan who, in 1925, first recognized for what they were the parasitic dwarf males in certain deep-sea Angler-fishes, and he later published two monographs, the second in collaboration, on the *Dana* collections of this remarkable group. To him the Danes also entrusted the description of the Stomiatoid fishes of their Atlantic and Mediterranean expeditions.

In 1925 Regan was president of the zoology section of the British Association meeting at Southampton and delivered his address on 'Organic Evolution'. It was his interest in evolution which led him to study and to inspire others to study the species flocks of Cichlid fishes in the African lakes, but the completion of this work was left to his successors. He was also attracted to the history of the Primates and did a considerable amount of research on them and their relationship to the Insectivores. Of this only a preliminary summary was published (1930).

In addition to this great volume of scientific research, Regan's administrative duties occupied much of his time, interest, and energy. One of his first duties as director was to report to the Royal Commission on museums. He was thus enabled to enter on his directorial period in

an optimistic atmosphere with a practical plan for the reorganization of the museum according to modern ideas. The financial slump of 1929–31, however, so delayed the building programme that the greater part of the plan remained unrealized when the outbreak of war in 1939 suspended work.

Among the honours by which his contemporaries acknowledged the value of his scientific work were his election as F.R.S. in 1917, the honorary fellowship of his old college (1928), the honorary degree of D.Sc. from Durham University (1929), the foreign membership of the American Academy of Arts and Sciences and of the Royal Danish Academy, and the Geoffroy de Saint-Hilaire medal (1929) of the Société Nationale d'Acclimatation de France.

Regan married in 1904 Elsie, daughter of George Marlow, of Arlington, Berkshire, and had two sons and two daughters. He died at Feltham, Middlesex, 12 January 1943.

[R. H. Burne and J. R. Norman in *Obituary Notices of Fellows of the Royal Society*, No. 12, November 1943; private information; personal knowledge.]          E. TREWAVAS.

REID, FORREST (1875–1947), novelist and critic, was the sixth and youngest son of Robert Reid, who came of a well-established upper middle-class Ulster family, by his second wife, Frances Matilda Parr, a collateral descendant of the sixth wife of Henry VIII. James Seaton Reid [q.v.] was his great-uncle. He was born in Belfast 24 June 1875, and educated at the Royal Academical Institution. After spending some trial years as apprentice in the tea trade he proceeded to Christ's College, Cambridge, where he took his degree in 1908 with a second class in the medieval and modern languages tripos. He then settled down to write in Belfast, which, apart from periods of travel, remained his home for the rest of his life.

Reid's first novel, *The Kingdom of Twilight*, appeared in 1904; *The Garden God*, an idyll of romantic friendship dedicated to Henry James [q.v.], of whom Reid was an early and lifelong admirer, followed in 1905. These are immature in manner and owe much to Walter Pater. With *The Bracknels* (1911) and *Following Darkness* (1912)—both of which he revised and reshaped late in life—he began to find an individual theme and style. *The Spring Song* (1916) and *Pirates of the*

*Spring* (1919)—his most completely happy and objective study of boyhood—are further steps towards the full maturity he reached in *Uncle Stephen* (1931). The sequels to that book, *The Retreat* (1936) and *Young Tom* (1944), adopt the original course of extending the story into the past and take the hero back to early childhood. In *Brian Westby* (1934), perhaps his finest novel, the writer reveals much of his own personality and outlook. *Demophon* (1927) is a re-creation of the ancient Greek world which had for Reid a special attraction: he approached it again in his versions of poems from the Greek Anthology.

Boyhood and adolescence seen through the understanding eyes of an older man supply the subject of most of Reid's work. He endows his study of youth with a moral freshness and poetic nostalgic quality, but his humour and quiet irony make it entirely convincing and save it from sentimentality. His novels are finely shaped in the James tradition; he writes a lucid rhythmic prose and is a master of dialogue. Though not in the narrow sense a regional writer, Reid sets his stories in the Ulster landscape he knew and loved, and he paints it in the light and shade of its varying moods. His mind was sensitive and profound, but there were limits to its range; he knew these well and did not try to write beyond them.

Reid reviewed regularly for the *Spectator* and other papers: *Retrospective Adventures* (1941) contains a selection of his periodical essays. He wrote studies of W. B. Yeats (1915) and Walter de la Mare (1929), writers who appealed to his own taste for music and suggestion in poetry. *Illustrators of the Sixties* (1928), a study of the Victorian artists in woodcut whose drawings he collected, remains an authoritative and original work in a little-explored field.

Reid was unmarried. He led a retired and outwardly lonely life but his interests were many. He was an expert croquet player, a lover of animals and the country, an enthusiast for opera, a discriminating collector, a wide reader, and a stimulating clear-minded talker. He was intimate with many writers of his own generation and to young authors he was generous with help and advice. Most of all he valued his friendships and his spiritual adventures in a supernatural dream-world of his own. Of these he has told in *Apostate* (1926), an autobiography unique in its kind which first brought him to the notice of a wider public.

He was one of the founder-members of the Irish Academy of Letters and received the honorary degree of D.Litt. from the Queen's University of Belfast in 1933. He was awarded the James Tait Black memorial prize for his last novel, *Young Tom*. A portrait in oils by J. S. Sleator is in the Belfast City Art Gallery, and another by Arthur Greeves is in the library of the Royal Academical Institution, Belfast. Reid died at Warrenpoint, County Down, 4 January 1947.

[*The Times*, *Northern Whig*, and *Belfast News Letter*, 7 January 1947; *Burke's Landed Gentry of Ireland*, 1912; Russell Burlingham, *Forrest Reid*, 1953; private information; personal knowledge.] JOHN BRYSON.

REILLY, SIR CHARLES HERBERT (1874–1948), professor of architecture, was born in north London 4 March 1874, the eldest son of Charles Reilly, architect, who for forty years was surveyor to the Drapers' Company in the City of London, and whose wife was Annie Michael, daughter of Charles Mee, gentleman, of Brook Street, London, W. 1. From the Merchant Taylors' School, Charterhouse Square, young Reilly obtained a mathematical scholarship at Queens' College, Cambridge, and took a first in part i of the mechanical sciences tripos in 1896. As an undergraduate he was one of the founders of the Cambridge Fabian Club and remained theoretically a Socialist thereafter. He trained for two years in his father's office and was then articled, as an unpaid improver, to John Belcher, architect [q.v.]. In 1900 he began his teaching career as a part-time lecturer in architectural design at King's College in the Strand and shortly afterwards joined Charles Stanley Peach in an architectural partnership. As one of a number of commissions for power-stations he designed the chimney, shaped like a campanile, which overlooks Lord's cricket ground. The design which he entered in 1902 in the Liverpool Cathedral competition was the only classical scheme commended by the assessors. Classical also and just as exuberant was the design, which he later executed, for the Students' Union in Liverpool. In 1933 he extended this building, much more plainly, in collaboration with his successor, L. B. Budden.

It was not mainly as architect or scholar, but as an architectural teacher and publicist that Reilly made his mark. The opportunity came with his appointment in 1904 to the Roscoe chair of architecture at Liverpool University. His department at first had only twelve part-time students; but the young university had its share of talent, a number of generous benefactors, and almost unlimited scope for educational initiative. Of these assets Reilly took full advantage. He enthusiastically supported all sorts of progressive movements, the 'New Testament' group in the university, and the Liverpool Playgoers Club, from which stemmed the repertory theatre later known as the Playhouse, of which he was elected first chairman in 1911. He persuaded W. H. Lever (later Viscount Leverhulme, q.v.), creator of Port Sunlight, to endow a lectureship in civic design and to found the *Town Planning Review*, and suggested his friend S. D. Adshead [q.v.] as first lecturer and later first holder of the Lever chair. In 1909, the year of the first Town Planning Act in this country, Lever sent Reilly to the United States, the first of many visits which established a link, valuable to a whole generation of students, between American architects and the Liverpool school. In Britain he was, in many different ways, a pioneer of architectural education. His small department grew in numbers, importance, and range. In 1906 he was invited to join the board of architectural education of the Royal Institute of British Architects, of which he had been elected an associate in 1902. In 1909 he was first elected to the Institute's council; he became a fellow in 1912 and was vice-president (1931–3). Reilly, himself an articled pupil, gradually became the champion of university training for architects. One of his early students, H. C. Bradshaw, won the first Rome scholarship in architecture in 1913; and in 1920 the Royal Institute of British Architects granted exemption from their final professional examinations to graduates of the Liverpool school.

Reilly soon added journalism to his other teaching activities. He became a regular contributor to the *Manchester Guardian* and the *Liverpool Post*. For a time he was architectural editor of *Country Life*, and every year reviewed buildings and books for the *Architects' Journal*, the *Architectural Review*, and the *Banker*. His essays on architecture aroused most interest in the quarters where Reilly intended they should do most good, namely among the general public, and among patrons of the art. Of his descriptive writing *Some Manchester Streets and their Buildings* (1924) and articles written during his visit to New Delhi with Sir Edwin Lutyens [q.v.] in 1927–8 are good examples. His architectural ideas are best illustrated in *The Theory and Practice of Architecture* (1932) and in his *Outline Plan for Birkenhead* (published by the corporation in 1947), in which he suggested the grouping of small houses around a series of urban greens. Perhaps of his many ideas for town improvement that of the so-called 'Reilly greens' may endure longest. It was the basis of actual layouts at Bilston and Dudley, and has found its way into the planning textbooks.

Reilly was from 1925 onwards a corresponding member of the American Institute of Architects. He received the honorary degree of LL.D. from the university of Liverpool, with the title of emeritus professor, in 1934, having relinquished his chair in the previous year. He was awarded the Royal gold medal for architecture in 1943 and was knighted in 1944. The pleasure these honours gave him was mainly because of their recognition of his qualities as a teacher. It was for his students that he lived, not only during his thirty years at Liverpool, but after his resignation (for it could not be called retirement) at Brighton and Twickenham. Wearing his big black hat and his check scarf he would knock with his ivory-headed cane on the doors of peers and poets and the poor. Loving publicity he would nevertheless make himself thoroughly unpopular in a good architectural cause; nor was he ever afraid to drop bricks if by so doing he could give one of his students a chance to build with them. He was incorrigible, lovable, and energetic; and on the occasions when these qualities were combined, even his colleagues found him invincible.

Of his own buildings he preferred the church of St. Barnabas, Dalston; but perhaps more important was his influence in 1923 on the design of Devonshire House, Piccadilly, on the location of the Liverpool entrance to the Mersey Tunnel in the early 'thirties, and on the contemporary character of the Peter Jones department store in Sloane Square, Chelsea, in 1936. His own tastes changed with the times, and he was usually a step ahead of his students, even the liveliest, when embarking on architectural adventures.

Reilly married in 1904 Dorothy Gladys (died 1939), second daughter of James Jerram Pratt, of Highgate, a city merchant, and had four children of whom a son and a daughter survived. Reilly died in London 2 February 1948, a few months before the death of a younger brother, Sir (Henry) D'Arcy Cornelius Reilly, formerly chief justice of Mysore. The best portrait of Reilly, as a painting, is that by Augustus John in the Liverpool School of Architecture. The best likeness is by Marjorie Brooks (Lady Holford) in the University Club, Liverpool. He is also one of the 'New Testament' group painted by Albert Lipczinski which hangs in the common-room of the faculty of arts.

[*The Times* and *Manchester Guardian*, 3 February 1948; *Listener*, 15 July 1948; C. H. Reilly, *Scaffolding in the Sky*, 1938; Lawrence Wolfe, *The Reilly Plan*, 1945; private information; personal knowledge.]

W. G. HOLFORD.

REITZ, DENEYS (1882–1944), South African soldier, author, and politician, was born at Bloemfontein 2 April 1882, the third of the five sons of Francis William Reitz by his first wife, Blanca Thesen, the daughter of a shipowner of Stavanger, who, when his ship was wrecked on the coast of South Africa, settled at Knysna, Cape Province. Reitz's was an old and cultured family; his grandfather was sent from Cape Town to school in Edinburgh, and according to family tradition once dined with Sir Walter Scott. His father, who was educated in Edinburgh, and made lively Afrikaans renderings of Burns, served as chief justice and later president of the Orange Free State; in 1898 he became secretary of state to President Kruger and in that capacity presented the ultimatum which precipitated the South African war; after the Union he became first president of the Senate, retiring in 1918; his sister married W. P. Schreiner [q.v.]. At home Deneys Reitz grew to be familiar with the English classics; he saw many leading figures in South African public life, and at twelve years of age joined his father on a tour in Europe. He early learnt to ride and shoot, but formal education ended when at the age of seventeen he joined the Boer forces in the South African war.

After serving in the fighting round Ladysmith, Reitz ranged widely for two years, especially with J. C. Smuts [q.v.] through Cape Colony. Space forbids any account of 'the hairbreadth escapes, the dare-devilry' (to use the words of Smuts); a full account is given with characteristic charm and generosity in Reitz's book, *Commando* (1929), which is an invaluable document on the history of the war from the Boer side. After the peace of Vereeniging (1902) he stood by his father in refusing the oath of allegiance and went into exile. Three years in Madagascar brought him hard work, little pay, and much fever, but even thus early he made the first draft of *Commando*. In 1905 Mrs. Smuts persuaded him to return and he arrived ill and penniless, but life in the Smuts family restored him to health in three years and he was able to begin law practice at Heilbron, Orange Free State, in 1908. In 1914, when he rallied to the party of Louis Botha [q.v.] and Smuts, he had to flee on the outbreak of the rebellion in that year, but only twenty-four hours later he returned as commandant of the Heilbron district. After helping to suppress the rebellion he served with Botha in South-West Africa against the Germans and, later, in East Africa under Smuts. In 1917 this seasoned ex-enemy came to London to enlist and went as a major to the western front where he was twice wounded and in the closing stages of the war was colonel commanding the 1st Royal Scots Fusiliers.

On his return to the Union, Reitz was elected member of Parliament for Port Elizabeth. He proved an effective and skilful debater and was appointed minister of lands. Support from such a strong Afrikaner was invaluable to Smuts; but office life naturally irked Reitz, even though 'lands' at least warranted much local examination of the possibilities of undeveloped districts. Inspired by East African memories of the 'bush' he now acquired a Low Veld farm and took to studying its life; his work prepared the way for his Nationalist successor's inauguration of the Kruger National Park, of which he became an enthusiastic supporter and a devoted trustee. He was out of office from 1924 until 1933, and joined a firm of Johannesburg solicitors who made use of his experience by sending him on business to the Rhodesias. He also found opportunity to visit the Belgian Congo and Angola, and penetrated on one occasion into the wild Kaokoveld of South-West Africa. Comparative leisure helped him in 1929 to complete *Commando*, which gained an immediate success. In the general election of that year, his victory at Barberton, the Low Veld constituency, was the solitary gain made by his party. In the joint Hertzog–Smuts ('fusion') ministry of 1933 he was once again minister of lands, advancing irrigation schemes, notably the Vaaldam.

In 1935 he was appointed minister of agriculture, but his health broke down under the heavy work; in 1938 he transferred to the department of mines, and in 1939 to that of native affairs, also becoming deputy to Smuts. In 1943 he came as South African high commissioner to London, where he died suddenly 19 October 1944.

Reitz's life was a triumph of character. The years he must have expected to spend at a university were wholly swallowed up by guerrilla warfare and rough-riding. We might not otherwise have had a classic like *Commando*, but academic limitations were a handicap in politics where sheer personality carried him through, and a ready-witted skill in debate which his opponents dreaded. His wide, good-humoured tolerance were outstanding in South African public life.

In 1919 Reitz married Leila, daughter of Dr. Claude Wright, of Wynberg, near Cape Town; she was the first woman in South Africa to be elected a member of Parliament. They had two sons, who both served in the South African forces during the war of 1939–45.

[Deneys Reitz, *Commando*, 1929, *Trekking On*, 1933, and *No Outspan*, 1943; private information; personal knowledge.]

W. M. MACMILLAN.

RENDALL, MONTAGUE JOHN (1862–1950), headmaster of Winchester College, the fourth son of the Rev. Henry Rendall and his wife, Ellen Harriette, daughter of Peter Davey and sister of Horace, later Baron, Davey [q.v.], was born 6 May 1862 at Great Rollright, Oxfordshire, where his father was rector. There were in all nine sons of the marriage, closely united in strongly felt devotion to their parents and exceptionally influenced by the standards and values of their early upbringing. From Elstree he won the first entrance scholarship to Harrow in 1876. During his last year at Harrow he was head of the school and first in classics and mathematics. Proceeding to Trinity College, Cambridge, in 1881, he was a Bell scholar (1882) and foundation scholar (1883) and was placed in the first division of the first class in part i of the classical tripos in 1884 and in the first class of part ii in 1885. During his last two years at Cambridge he represented the university at Association football as goalkeeper. In 1887 he made the first of many journeys abroad to study the masterpieces of continental art, and laid the founda-

tions of his lifelong enthusiasm for medieval Italian painting. In the same year he was appointed to the staff of Winchester College.

His immediate and striking success as a teacher, especially of classical composition, to 'Senior Div.', and his enthusiastic and inspiring participation in the life of the school, especially of College, strongly suggested him for appointment as second master in 1899. For the next twelve years his régime in College was of great brilliance and originality, and marked him out for the succession to the headmastership in 1911. Not primarily an administrator, and not much concerned with educational policy or innovation in the large, he yet impressed all those who served under him as a great headmaster. By his vivid and dominating personality he communicated to the school the inspiration derived from his own clear and intense vision of the noblest aims in life and the highest values in literature and art.

The war of 1914–18, through which he carried the school with buoyant courage, made the profoundest impression upon him. To his conception and determination the war memorial cloister at Winchester is primarily due; furthermore, he had become convinced that the public schools had a duty and a mission to make their best gifts available to a wider public in the post-war world. These views were reinforced by his visit in 1919 to some leading independent schools in the United States. He gladly accepted, therefore, after his resignation of the headmastership in 1924, an invitation from the Rhodes Trustees to visit many of the principal schools in the self-governing Dominions; and for the same reason he accepted high office in the Overseas League, the League of the Empire, and the Royal Empire Society, and the chairmanship of the Public Schools Empire Tours Committee. He received the honorary degree of LL.D. from the university of Toronto in 1921 and was appointed C.M.G. in 1931.

In 1926 Rendall began what was a new life rather than a retirement. He acquired the freehold of Butley Priory, near Woodbridge, a medieval religious foundation of which only the gatehouse remained standing; this he restored and transformed with imagination and scholarly care. During his twenty-four years of residence in this Suffolk home he was an active and influential figure in the public life of the county. He was a justice of the peace; served on many educational and church committees; and was on the governing body of several schools and chairman of the governors of Framlingham College. A lifelong churchman of simple and earnest faith, he exercised a considerable Christian influence in his parish. He retained to the end his passionate interest in his garden and in the countryside, together with his love of strenuous physical exercise; he would take a long walk or bicycle ride until he was past eighty-five.

From 1927 until the end of 1932 Rendall was a governor of the British Broadcasting Corporation; and to the end of his life he maintained frequent contacts with London. The Athenaeum was always his London headquarters. Unmarried himself, he delighted in the marriages and the children of his old pupils, and was a frequent and welcome visitor to their homes, as also to his friends in Winchester. He was himself a princely host, being generous almost to the point of improvidence. It was only during his last year of life that his splendid vitality was first seen to be failing; he died suddenly in his sleep, 5 October 1950, at Oxenwood, Bushey Heath, and was buried in the churchyard of Great Rollright, where are the graves also of his parents.

Rendall published but little. He edited *The Schools of Hellas*, by his friend and pupil K. J. Freeman, in 1907; a visit to the Near East in 1908 inspired a short book *Sinai in Spring* (1911). In 1947 he issued for private circulation *The Bells of Great Rollright*, a rhyming chronicle of his personal and family history and experience. An accomplished composer in both classical languages, he was a master of the art of the Greek or Latin monumental inscription.

His portrait, by Glyn Philpot, hangs in 'School' at Winchester College.

[J. D'E. Firth, *Rendall of Winchester*, 1954; private information; personal knowledge.]

J. D'E. FIRTH.


RENNELL, first BARON (1858–1941), diplomatist and scholar. [See RODD, JAMES RENNELL.]


RHYS, ERNEST PERCIVAL (1859–1946), author and editor, was born in Islington 17 July 1859, the second child of John Rhys and his wife, Emma, daughter of Robert Percival, a breeder and doctor of horses, of Hockerill, Hert-

fordshire. John Rhys had been a divinity student who gave up his studies on his marriage and at this time worked in a bookshop in London. He later became a wine merchant and Ernest Rhys spent most of his early years in Carmarthen and Newcastle upon Tyne. After two years at Bishop's Stortford he went to a private school in Newcastle, and refused to go to Oxford, for he was 'tempted by the open-air life and the chance of horses to ride' that was offered by mining engineering. He passed his examinations, but in January 1886 he returned to London, to earn his living as a writer.

He soon became a familiar figure in literary London. Although he never enjoyed a popular success, and was too painstaking and too slow a writer to earn a substantial income as a journalist, editors were always glad to have his reviews and 'middles', and his poems were appreciated by readers of discernment. He was a member of the Rhymers' Club, a group of young poets—W. B. Yeats, Richard Le Gallienne, Lionel Johnson, Arthur Symons [qq.v.], Ernest Dowson, and some half-dozen others—who met in an upper room at the Cheshire Cheese, 'where long clay pipes lay in slim heaps on the wooden tables between tankards of ale', to recite their verses. The Rhymers published two collections of their poems (1892, 1894) to each of which Rhys contributed. 'The Leaf Burners', written during the war of 1914–18, has been included in several anthologies, but his best poem is generally agreed to be the quatrain 'autobiography' with its opening line 'Wales England wed, so I was bred'. He quoted this poem at the luncheon given in his honour on his seventy-fifth birthday.

Writers are, however, often remembered by posterity for work by which they themselves set little store, and Rhys is likely to be remembered less as a poet and a critic than as the editor of 'Everyman's Library'. Sponsored financially by J. M. Dent [q.v.] this Library was planned, in Rhys's words, as 'a collection of the great literatures, beginning with the English, so co-ordinated that if its readers began with one creative book, they would want another and another till the great public had the world literature within its grasp'. Its title was taken from the old mystery play, and the quotation:

'Everyman, I will go with thee, and be thy guide,
    In thy most need to go by thy side'

appears on every title-page. The Library was designed as a collection of a thousand volumes. Beginning in 1906 with Boswell's life of Johnson, 153 volumes were published in the first twelve months; and when Rhys died 983 volumes had appeared. In editing this Library in face of many difficulties, some of which he has described in his autobiography *Everyman Remembers* (1931), Rhys performed a genuine service to literature. But he regarded this task as the necessary hackwork which would buy him the leisure in which to write poems and essays.

Rhys married in 1891 Grace (died 1929), daughter of Bennett Little, J.P., of county Roscommon, a lady of great charm and culture who published amongst other works two or three delicate volumes of belles-lettres. They worked and lived together as a team. They had three children, one son and two daughters, and three homes, all of them in Hampstead. They were as hospitable as their means allowed, perhaps more hospitable than prudence warranted, and 'Sunday afternoon at the Rhys's' was for many years an opportunity for poets, novelists, and critics to meet and discuss their problems. As his autobiography shows, Rhys knew on terms of intimacy practically every important personality in the literary scene, but he was never too busy to provide kindness, encouragement, and help to the young and struggling. He was a much loved man. He died in London 25 May 1946. A portrait drawing by W. H. Caffyn is reproduced in *Everyman Remembers*. A pencil drawing by David Bell has been lent by the artist to the National Museum of Wales.

[Ernest Rhys, *Everyman Remembers*, 1931, and *Wales England Wed*, 1940; private information; personal knowledge.]

ALEC WAUGH.

RICHARDSON, ETHEL FLORENCE LINDESAY (1870–1946), novelist under the name of HENRY HANDEL RICHARDSON, was born 3 January 1870 in Melbourne, Australia, the elder daughter of Walter Lindesay Richardson and his wife, Mary Bailey, of Leicester. Her father, a native of Dublin and a medical practitioner, emigrated to Australia in the 1850's and began his life in the colony on the goldfields of Ballarat at the height of the gold rush. He died in 1879 and her actual memories of him were few, but the story of his career in Australia, recorded in

diaries and letters, furnished her with the material for the trilogy, *The Fortunes of Richard Mahony*, 1930 (*Australia Felix*, 1917, *The Way Home*, 1925, and *Ultima Thule*, 1929). The greater part of H. H. Richardson's early life was spent in various country towns in Victoria as the family fortunes declined with the illness and death of her father and slowly recovered with her mother's advancement in the Civil Service as a postmistress. The two little girls were much alone and the elder read widely and diverted herself with story-making. In 1882 she was sent from Maldon to Melbourne to attend the Presbyterian Ladies' College. This period of her life is described in the autobiographical novel *The Getting of Wisdom* (1910). At school she showed some talent for music, and in 1887 her mother, anxious that she should follow a musical career, took her two daughters to Europe.

After a short visit to England, H. H. Richardson was entered at the Leipzig Conservatorium, where she studied pianoforte for the next three years. She felt herself temperamentally unfitted for the life of an executant musician, and her studies were in any case brought to an end by her engagement to a young Scottish student of German literature, John George Robertson, whom she married in Dublin in 1895. The intervening years were spent in Cambridge, London, and Munich, and during this time of waiting her interest turned to writing. From 1896 until 1904 she lived in Strasbourg, where her husband was first lecturer and then professor of English literature in the university. This was an active and formative period in her career as a writer. She travelled widely and acquired an understanding and appreciation of continental life. She wrote several critical articles, and in 1897 began work on her first novel, *Maurice Guest* (1908), which was based on her experiences in Leipzig. She read widely in French, Russian, German, and Scandinavian literature, and was stimulated by literary discussions with her circle of friends, and by the musical life of the city. In 1904, after her husband's appointment in the previous year to a new chair of German literature in London University, she moved to London, which remained her home until his death in 1933. During this period she made two journeys in connexion with her literary work. In 1907 she revisited Leipzig to refresh her memories before completing *Maurice Guest*; and in 1912 she made a two months' tour of Australia to collect material for *The Fortunes of Richard Mahony*. After her husband's death she moved to Fairlight in Sussex where she remained until her death there 20 March 1946.

The years spent on the continent were undoubtedly the most influential. Although the greater part of H. H. Richardson's writing was done in England, her ideas were formed by her contact with continental life and literature, and her removal to London was in the nature of a retirement. She withdrew from the outside world, and her husband records that when she was deprived of the musical and literary life of Strasbourg, she became progressively more solitary and secluded. Reticence about both herself and her work characterized the years after 1904, and it was not until shortly before her death that she began to write an account of her early life, *Myself When Young* (1948). As a writer she attached the greatest importance to factual accuracy, and for both *The Fortunes of Richard Mahony* and her last novel, *The Young Cosima* (1939), made a careful study of historical sources. Meticulous attention to details of background and character was the legacy of her study, during the Strasbourg period, of the realistic movement in fiction. She made a substantial contribution to Australian literature by her reconstruction of early colonial society in *The Fortunes of Richard Mahony*, but she wrote as an expatriate, and her sympathies, both personal and literary, were with the continent. The peculiar quality of her novels might be summed up in the words she used to describe J. P. Jacobsen's *Niels Lyhne*, which she translated in 1896—'a romanticism imbued with the scientific spirit and essentially based on realism'. To the impartial accuracy of the historian she brought the impassioned insight of the romantic writer, and these contrasting elements are reflected in her style. The clarity, austerity, and economy of her descriptions of setting and historical background are a foil for the highly coloured and sometimes undisciplined language in which she interprets the lives and emotions of her characters.

Those who knew H. H. Richardson describe her as a slight, somewhat austere figure, with striking heavy-lidded eyes, and a manner at once friendly and yet detached, on guard against too intimate probing into her personal history. A sketch portrait by R. G. Eves was presented by H. H. Richardson to the National Gallery of Victoria in 1934.

[H. H. Richardson, *Myself When Young*, 1948; Nettie Palmer, *Henry Handel Richardson*, 1950; manuscript material in the National Library, Canberra.]

LEONIE J. KRAMER.

RICHARDSON, HENRY HANDEL (1870–1946), novelist. [See RICHARDSON, ETHEL FLORENCE LINDESAY.]

RICHMOND, SIR HERBERT WILLIAM (1871–1946), admiral, and master of Downing College, Cambridge, was born at Beavor Lodge, Hammersmith, 15 September 1871, the third child and second son of the artist (Sir) William Blake Richmond [q.v.]. He passed into the *Britannia* in 1885; two years later he went to sea as a midshipman in the *Nelson*, flagship of the commander-in-chief on the Australia station, a twin-screw battleship which nevertheless frequently made long cruises under sail alone. In 1894 he was one of the few lieutenants selected to qualify as torpedo officers, and he later served in that capacity in several battleships, including two years in the *Majestic*, flagship of the Channel squadron, whence he was promoted commander in 1903 and appointed to the naval ordnance department at the Admiralty—a record of service which shows that, as a technical officer, he was in the first rank.

After a year in that department he became executive officer of the *Crescent*, flagship of the commander-in-chief on the Cape of Good Hope station, for nearly three years before returning to the Admiralty where he became naval assistant to the second sea lord. He was promoted captain in 1908 and in 1909 appointed to command for nearly two years the most famous ship in the navy of that day, the *Dreadnought*, then flagship of Sir William May [q.v.], commander-in-chief of the Home Fleet. These appointments left him little leisure for any intensive prosecution of the historical and strategical studies to which his attention had been increasingly given for some years; but in his next command—that of the cruiser attached to the torpedo school—he found time to edit the Navy Records Society's volume on *The Loss of the Minorca* (1913), to deliver a series of lectures on naval history at the Naval War College, and to complete a book, begun in 1907, on *The Navy in the War of 1739–48*, which, however, was not published until 1920. When the naval war staff was created in 1912, Richmond was one of the officers named as original members of it, and the following year he became assistant director of the operations division of the war staff at the Admiralty.

On the outbreak of war in 1914, however, Richmond, in common with the rest of the staff, was denied participation in anything but the clerical and mechanical part of its work, and he chafed at his exclusion from any of the useful tasks for which he felt himself—and indeed was—well qualified. It was a relief to him when he left the Admiralty in May 1915 to become liaison officer with the Italian naval command, a post which he held for four months before returning home to command the old battleship *Commonwealth* in the third battle squadron. In April 1917 he was appointed to command the battleship *Conqueror* in the Grand Fleet, where he was warmly welcomed by Sir David (later Earl) Beatty [q.v.], the commander-in-chief. But in April 1918, he was selected, with the latter's strong approval, as director of the newly formed training and staff duties division of the naval staff at the Admiralty. Richmond's ideas were in advance of his time, however, and practically all of his recommendations were vetoed; he was glad after a few months of frustration to return to the Grand Fleet, in command of the battleship *Erin*.

In 1920 he was promoted to flag rank, and appointed to command the re-established Naval War College to which flag officers and captains were sent to study the higher direction of war; in the conduct of its studies he was at last given a free hand. He profited by the long vacations between war courses to resume work for the Navy Records Society, editing volumes iii and iv of the *Spencer Papers* which Sir Julian Corbett [q.v.] had had to relinquish when he undertook the naval history of the war of 1914–18.

In 1923 Richmond was appointed commander-in-chief of the East Indies station. On his return to England at the end of 1925, he would have welcomed active employment at sea or responsible work at the Admiralty; but he found himself in strong disagreement with the views of those in office at the Admiralty

on the principles which ought to guide British policy in the negotiations which, from 1921 to 1936, were carried on at several international conferences designed to secure limitation of naval expenditure. Richmond complied with a request that he should not make the task of the Admiralty more difficult by public denunciation of the policy to which it was committed; nevertheless he was excluded from all higher commands, by reason of what were regarded as his heterodox views.

In 1926, however, the Imperial Defence College was founded, and he was so obviously the officer best fitted to inaugurate it that not even the Admiralty disapproval which he had drawn upon himself could exclude him. All problems of national and imperial defence and strategy came under investigation by the college, and it is noteworthy that his views on naval limitation, which had been the cause earlier of the Admiralty refusal to employ him, and were to be so again, were there freely expressed without any objection to them being raised. His term as commandant was brought to an end only by the standing rule which prescribed two years as its duration.

Having been chosen to guide the best brains of all three Services, it was not unreasonable in him to hope that he might then expect high command in his own. He had been promoted vice-admiral in 1925 and admiral in 1929. But the disapproval of the Admiralty had not been relaxed. It was reinforced when, on the eve of the naval conference of 1930, Richmond contributed two articles to *The Times* (21 and 22 November 1929) on the subject of naval reduction, which, although designed to assist the Admiralty in attaining the object at which it was aiming, brought him a formal letter of reprimand from their lordships; and he was refused further employment in terms which aroused his keen, but very justifiable, resentment. In April 1931, twelve months before the date on which he would have been subject to compulsory retirement under the standing regulations, he retired at his own request, and thereafter devoted himself to the task of awakening his countrymen to the importance, for a right understanding of the country's needs, of the study of naval history.

'And so it came about', wrote Dr. G. M. Trevelyan, 'that Richmond's greatest service to this country was his work as a naval historian, in which he was not impeded.' In 1931 he published *The Navy* in India, 1763–83, the fruit of researches in the archives of Ceylon and Pondicherry eight years earlier, and a reasoned argument on the theme of naval limitation under the title *Economy and Naval Security*. He also delivered a series of lectures at University College, London, and the Lees Knowles lectures at Trinity College, Cambridge, for that year, published in 1932 in book form under the title *Imperial Defence and Capture at Sea in War*. In 1933 he published a treatise on *Naval Training*, and the following year a more important work on *Sea Power in the Modern World*. In that year he was elected to the Vere Harmsworth chair of imperial and naval history at Cambridge in succession to J. Holland Rose [q.v.]—a great compliment to his eminence as a historian, for under the statutory age limit he could hold it for no more than two years—and he was made a professorial fellow of Jesus College. The academic world proved to be completely congenial to him, and in its turn took him to its heart. At the close of his two years' tenure of the chair, he was elected to the mastership of Downing College, which had just fallen vacant.

He had thus ten more years of happy and valuable academic activity, not confined to Cambridge alone. He was always ready to lecture or write in support of logic and clear thought in defence policy, and he delivered lectures in Paris—where he was made an associate member of the Académie de la Marine—as well as in his own country. On the outbreak of war in 1939 he became chairman of the university joint recruiting board; he welcomed the establishment in his own college of the Cambridge naval division, and he started a series of lectures on foreign affairs and the progress of the war for the junior combination room, afterwards continued and extended as the 'Richmond lectures'. But still his chief enthusiasm was to impress on his countrymen the importance, deduced from every phase of British history, of sea power and of a British strategy based on it. In 1941 he published, in the Cambridge 'Current Problems' series, a booklet surveying British strategy from the days of Queen Elizabeth I; in 1943 he took the same theme for the Ford's lectures which he delivered at Oxford, and these he afterwards expanded into his greatest book, *Statesmen and Sea Power*, published in 1946 only a few weeks before his death. A volume left in manuscript was edited by E. A. Hughes

and published in 1953 under the title *The Navy as an Instrument of Policy, 1558–1727*.

Richmond was appointed C.B. in 1921 and promoted K.C.B. in 1926. He was elected F.B.A. in 1937 and was a fellow of the Royal Historical Society. On the establishment in 1934 of the National Maritime Museum at Greenwich he was appointed one of the trustees. He received the honorary degree of D.C.L. from Oxford in 1939.

He married in 1907 Florence Elsa, second daughter of Sir (Thomas) Hugh Bell, second baronet, of Rounton Grange, and had one son and four daughters. He had a serious illness in 1940, which compelled him thereafter to give up all strenuous physical activity. He died suddenly at the Master's Lodge, Downing College, 15 December 1946. There are two portraits of Richmond at Downing College, one in full-dress admiral's uniform by W. G. de Glehn, and the other, in his academic dress, by R. F. Lamb.

[G. M. Trevelyan in *Proceedings* of the British Academy, vol. xxxii, 1946; Richmond's own papers and journals (now in the National Maritime Museum), and published works; personal knowledge.]

H. G. THURSFIELD.

ROBERTSON, SIR CHARLES GRANT (1869–1948), historian and academic administrator, was born at Naini Tal, India, 22 June 1869, the younger son of John Grant Robertson, Bengal Civil Service, and his wife, Isabel Jane Grant, daughter of a minister in the Western Highlands. Educated at Highgate School and Hertford College, Oxford, of which he was a scholar and became an honorary fellow in 1921, Robertson won the Stanhope prize (1891), took first classes in *literae humaniores* (1892) and modern history (1893), and was elected in 1893 a fellow of All Souls College, a position he retained for the rest of his life, serving as domestic bursar (1897–1920) and during the war of 1939–45 as acting domestic bursar. In 1899 he published a history of the college to which he was ever deeply attached. He was tutor in modern history at Exeter College (1895–9) and at Magdalen College (1905–20). An expert teacher of undergraduates, Robertson acted as history tutor to Edward, Prince of Wales, at Magdalen (1912–14), and for his services was appointed C.V.O. in 1914. At Oxford, his lecturing was noted for its breadth and vigour, wealth of illustration, and geographical knowledge (he published with J. G. Bartholomew [q.v.] an *Historical and Modern Atlas of the British Empire*, 1905, and an *Historical Atlas of Modern Europe*, 1915), while his interest in the arts, not excluding the cinema, lent variety to his celebrated powers of conversation and reminiscence. Junior proctor in 1905-6, and a member of the hebdomadal council (1911-20), he was in close contact with university affairs.

In 1920 Robertson succeeded Sir Oliver Lodge [q.v.] as principal of Birmingham University and served as its vice-chancellor from 1927 until his retirement in 1938. From this position he made himself largely responsible for organizing the (as yet) unofficial Committee of Vice-Chancellors and Principals, over which for a time he presided. At Birmingham he drew city and university more closely together, and left his mark as a public-spirited academic administrator. He was a leading figure in the establishment of the Barber Trust and the foundation of the Barber chair and Institute of Fine Art: and he was chairman of the executive committee which brought into existence the new Birmingham Hospitals Centre adjoining the university buildings at Edgbaston. In the university he was concerned to make the humanities balance in distinction the work done in the scientific and medical faculties, and he gave special attention to library development. In *The British Universities*, first published in 1930 and revised in 1944, he surveyed the growth of the modern university system. He received the honorary degree of LL.D. from the universities of Edinburgh (1925), Glasgow (1930), Bristol (1935), and Birmingham (1939), and of Litt.D. from Sheffield (1936). He was knighted in 1928.

Robertson's historical writings, notable for their sane judgement and grasp of essentials, are mainly on the political and constitutional history of the eighteenth and nineteenth centuries. His textbook of English history, *England under the Hanoverians* (1st ed. 1911), and his book of constitutional documents, *Select Statutes, Cases and Documents to illustrate English Constitutional History, 1660-1832* (1904, new issue 1935), quickly became standard works; at the end of his life he returned to the period in his *Chatham and the British Empire* (1946) and *Bolingbroke* (1947). His particular interest in modern Germany was displayed in *The Evolution*

of *Prussia* (with (Sir) J. A. R. Marriott [q.v.] 1915; revised ed. 1946) and in his *Bismarck* (1918), probably his best book. Later, in a number of historical pamphlets, especially *Religion and the Totalitarian State* (1937) and *The Edict of Nantes and Freedom in the World of Today* (1939), his Liberal views were voiced against the prevailing tendencies in Central Europe. The historian's duty to the public he emphasized in his Creighton lecture, *History and Citizenship* (1928), and the same large spirit animated his presidency (1938-42 and 1945) of the Historical Association.

Robertson, who was unmarried, died at Ringwood 28 February 1948. If the austerity of his last years, when ailments increased, veiled the sprightly author of *Voces Academicae* (1898) or the romantic novelist who had written as 'Wymond Carey', nothing could obscure his 'wise and selfless judgement' (as a biographer put it) or his helpfulness to younger scholars and teachers. At All Souls he made lifelong friendships with Bishop Henson and Archbishop Lang [qq.v.]. A moderate Anglican, Robertson served as a member of the Archbishops' Commission on the Relations of Church and State which reported in 1935. There are two portraits of Robertson: one by Meredith Frampton is in the Scottish National Portrait Gallery, and the other by his sister, Mrs. Nevill, is in her possession at Ringwood.

[J. A. Hawgood, 'Charles Grant Robertson (1869-1948)' in the *University of Birmingham Historical Journal*, vol. i, No. 2, 1948; archives of All Souls College; personal knowledge.]

E. F. JACOB.

ROBERTSON, SIR ROBERT (1869-1949), explosives expert and government chemist, was born 17 April 1869 at Cupar, Fife, the eldest child and only son of John Alexander Robertson, doctor of dental surgery, by his wife, Euphemia, daughter of Andrew Russell, a farmer of Balmerino, Fife.

Educated at Madras Academy (the Bell-Baxter School), Cupar, and St. Andrews University where he graduated in both arts and science, Robertson was for a short time an assistant in the laboratory of the city analyst at Glasgow. In 1892 he was appointed to the staff of the Royal Gunpowder Factory at Waltham Abbey. Here he had practical experience of the processes used, and he also made a study of the chemistry of nitrocellulose and ethylene glycol dinitrate.

As chemist in charge of the laboratory of the factory from 1900, Robertson, in addition to his general analytical work, studied the purification of gun cotton and the stability and rates of decomposition of gun cotton and cordite. He became an acknowledged expert on the stability of explosives and in 1906 he accompanied Sir Frederic Lewis Nathan on a mission to investigate explosions which had occurred in magazines in India.

Robertson was appointed in 1907 as superintending chemist of the research department in Woolwich and during the following years he organized very wide investigations of old and new explosives, their stability, power, and sensitiveness, including particularly tetryl and trinitrotoluene (T.N.T.). In the war of 1914–18 he was responsible for the development of the manufacture and use of T.N.T., and of the explosive mixture 'amatol' which made possible a much larger and cheaper supply of high explosive. Another vital development was his introduction of an alcohol-ether mixture in place of acetone, which was scarce, in the production of propellents.

In 1921 Robertson was appointed government chemist. The work of his department, which provided chemical advice and services to other departments, and particularly to the Board of Customs and Excise, was considerably increased between 1921 and 1936 by the introduction of various new import duties, and by legislation involving chemical control. He also served on numerous government committees.

During this period Robertson undertook some important fundamental research. In collaboration with (Sir) John Jacob Fox who succeeded him as government chemist, he made a detailed study of the infra-red absorption of the gases ammonia, phosphine, and arsine and interpreted the main features of their spectra. This was pioneering work which greatly stimulated the growth of infra-red spectroscopy both in Britain and abroad. Subsequently he made a detailed examination of the infra-red and Raman spectra of diamonds of which a certain proportion showed abnormal physical properties in a number of respects.

After his retirement from the Government Laboratory in 1936, Robertson continued his experimental work at the Royal Institution of which he was treasurer. He also undertook the directorship of the Salters' Institute of Industrial Chemistry.

At the outbreak of war in 1939 Robertson offered his services to the armament research department and was placed in charge of a major branch at University College, Swansea, where he directed general chemical work on explosives and was at the same time chairman of several government committees.

Robertson was a man of great personal vigour. He was an able administrator, working hard himself and expecting his staff to do the same, but his domineering temperament did not make him an easy man to serve. He was not therefore a popular chief. He had a wide range of interests, and was an active supporter of scientific societies both national and international. He held office twice as vice-president of the Chemical Society, was president of the Faraday Society (1922–4), and vice-president of the (Royal) Institute of Chemistry. He also presided over the chemistry section of the British Association at Toronto in 1924.

He received many honours and distinctions. In 1894 he was presented with a gold watch by the secretary of state for war in recognition of gallant behaviour after a factory explosion. He was elected F.R.S. in 1917 and received the Society's Davy medal in 1944. He was appointed K.B.E. in 1918, and received the honorary degree of LL.D. from St. Andrews University in 1923.

Robertson married in 1903 Kathleen (died 1938), daughter of Hugh Hutton Stannus, F.R.I.B.A., lecturer in applied art at South Kensington and Manchester. He died in London 28 April 1949, survived by one son and one daughter.

[R. C. Farmer in *Obituary Notices of Fellows of the Royal Society*, No. 18, November 1949; private information; personal knowledge.]

G. M. BENNETT.

ROBINSON, (GEORGE) GEOFFREY (1874–1944), twice editor of *The Times*. [See DAWSON.]

ROBINSON, HENRY WHEELER (1872–1945), Baptist divine and Old Testament scholar, was born in Northampton 7 February 1872. His father, George Robinson, an artisan, went to South America before the boy's birth, maintaining little or no contact with his wife and child. Robinson's boyhood was a somewhat restricted and shadowed one, but in the home of his mother's uncle, where he lived with his mother, Helen Robinson, the foundations of his strength of character and concentration of purpose were laid. Leaving school at the age of fifteen he entered the counting-house of a wholesale leather merchant and was soon carrying considerable business responsibilities and spending much time in evening classes. Association with College Street Baptist church, one of the strongest nonconformist causes in the Midlands, introduced him to a wider world. He was baptized on profession of faith, 28 March 1888, and began to direct his thoughts towards the Christian ministry. On reaching college his progress was swift and sure. After a year at Regent's Park College, London, as a lay student, he entered Edinburgh University, graduating in 1895. He came to know J. S. Blackie [q.v.], and Andrew Seth (A. S. Pringle-Pattison, q.v.) was among his teachers. He was also influenced by Alexander Whyte and Henry Drummond [qq.v.]. In 1895 he went up to Mansfield College, Oxford. Robinson owed much to the encouragement of A. M. Fairbairn [q.v.], then at the height of his powers, and to the teaching of George Buchanan Gray [q.v.]. He had already determined to concentrate on Old Testament studies. He was placed in the second class of the school of oriental studies (1898), and was awarded the Hall–Houghton Syriac prize (1900), the junior and senior Septuagint prizes (1899 and 1901), and the junior and senior Kennicott Hebrew scholarships (1898 and 1901).

For six years Robinson served as a Baptist minister, first at Pitlochry (1900–3), then in Coventry (1903–6), discharging his duties with characteristic conscientiousness and intensity, and at the same time carrying forward studies in Hebrew psychology and preparing for future literary work. From 1906 to 1920 he was tutor at Rawdon Baptist College. His gifts as a teacher, although he was exacting, were soon evident, and his first three books—a commentary on *Deuteronomy and Joshua* (1907), *The Christian Doctrine of Man* (1911), and *The Religious Ideas of the Old Testament* (1913)—established his reputation among competent critics. A serious illness in 1913 directed his thinking towards the doctrine of the Holy Spirit and the problem of suffering.

Robinson's appointment in 1920 as principal of Regent's Park College,

London, gave him wider scope as a teacher and led to the greatest achievement of his life, the transfer of the college to Oxford. His patient and persistent advocacy of the move overcame the hesitations felt by many of his fellow Baptists. A site off St. Giles' was secured in 1927, but the stone-laying of the new buildings was not possible until 1938 and a formal opening had to be abandoned owing to the outbreak of war. While in London Robinson had become a valued member of the London Society for the Study of Religion and a leading figure in the Society for Old Testament Study. With Dr. Walter Robert Matthews he planned and edited the 'Library of Constructive Theology', an important series of volumes taking religious experience as its starting-point. Robinson himself contributed *The Christian Experience of the Holy Spirit* (1928) and *Redemption and Revelation* (1942). He also published many smaller books and essays on the Old Testament, including a notable study of the Hebrew conception of corporate personality.

In Oxford Robinson quickly became one of the best-known theological lecturers, in frequent demand as examiner and supervisor. In 1934 he was appointed reader in biblical criticism and in 1937–9 was the first Free Churchman to be chairman of the board of the faculty of theology. On his retirement from the principalship of Regent's Park College in 1942, he was elected Speaker's lecturer in biblical studies and planned to give himself to the writing of a major work on Old Testament theology. The posthumously published lectures *Inspiration and Revelation in the Old Testament* (1946) were intended as prolegomena. His health, however, failed shortly after his retirement and he died in Oxford 12 May 1945. Robinson was for many years president of the Baptist Historical Society, and his *Baptist Principles before the Rise of Baptist Churches* (1911) and *The Life and Faith of the Baptists* (1927) had a wide circulation. He received the honorary degree of D.D. from the universities of Edinburgh (1926) and Manchester (1943). The wide range of his intellectual interests and influence and the volume of work he accomplished were possible only by rigid self-discipline, but under a somewhat austere manner lay a simple kindliness, a deep interest in human beings, and unusual spiritual understanding and power. His personal faith was most clearly and simply set forth in *The Veil of*

*God* (1936) and *Suffering, Human and Divine* (1940).

In 1900 Robinson married Alice Laura, daughter of Evan Charles Ashford, chemist, of Northampton, by whom he had a son and two daughters. A portrait by James Gunn is at Regent's Park College.

[E. A. Payne, *Henry Wheeler Robinson*, 1946; a bibliography of his writings to 1942 is in *Studies in History and Religion*, 1942, edited by E. A. Payne.]

E. A. PAYNE.

ROBINSON, SIR (WILLIAM) ARTHUR (1874–1950), civil servant, was born at Long Marton, near Appleby, Westmorland, 9 September 1874. He was the only son of William Robinson, who had a tailor and draper's business there, and his wife, Hannah Kidd. Robinson was educated at Appleby Grammar School and the Queen's College, Oxford, where he obtained a first class in both classical moderations (1893) and *literae humaniores* (1895), and a second class in modern history in 1896. In 1897 he was placed first in the Civil Service examination and entered the Colonial Office. At the Imperial Conferences of 1907 and 1911 he was the assistant secretary.

In 1912 he was appointed assistant secretary in the Office of Works on the representation of (Sir) Lionel Earle [q.v.] who had just become permanent secretary of that Office and had pressed that Robinson, of whom he had a high opinion, should accompany him. Robinson enhanced his reputation in his new post, and in January 1918 was selected as the first permanent secretary of the new Air Ministry.

His contribution there was a material one, but in 1920 he was translated to succeed Sir Robert Morant [q.v.] as permanent secretary of the Ministry of Health. Morant was not an easy man to follow, but Robinson proved fully equal to the task and his claim to be regarded as one of the great civil servants of his day rests principally on his achievements there. One of his private secretaries once asked him what he regarded as his main qualifications for the post and he replied, with that naïve awareness of his own abilities which always intrigued his friends, 'A first-class brain, the constitution of an ox, and some ideals, but not too many'. Certainly the work done at the Ministry in his time called for these qualities in full measure. Its range and scope were remarkable: there was major

legislation on housing; the introduction of the contributory pensions scheme; the Mental Treatment Act of 1930 which by its extension of voluntary treatment to the rate-aided class of patient altered the whole complexion of the approach to mental health; and the great measures of local government and poor law reform embodied in the Local Government Act of 1929. Robinson also took an active part in implementing the recommendations of the postgraduate medical committee for the establishment of the London School of Hygiene and Tropical Medicine and the Postgraduate Medical School of London.

Robinson's reserved temperament made it difficult for his colleagues to get to know him well, and he was not at his best in establishment work. But he was in advance of his time in campaigning for plain English in official correspondence.

In 1935, somewhat reluctantly, he became chairman of the Supply Board in deference to the wishes of Neville Chamberlain, then chancellor of the Exchequer, who as minister of health had formed the highest opinion of Robinson's ability and was anxious to secure his services for rearmament work. In the spring of 1939 when the Ministry of Supply was established he became permanent secretary of the Ministry. In 1940 he retired from the public service after forty-three years of strenuous and fruitful work. He was appointed C.B. (1915), K.C.B. (1919), G.C.B. (1929), C.B.E. (1918), and G.B.E. (1941).

In 1910 he married Jean Pasley, daughter of Robert Mitchell, of North Kensington, London, by whom he had one son. He died 23 April 1950 at Rodmell Hill Cottage, near Lewes.

[Private information; personal knowledge.]
THOMAS SHEEPSHANKS.

ROBINSON, WILLIAM HEATH (1872–1944), cartoonist and book-illustrator, was born at Hornsey Rise, London, 31 May 1872, third son of Thomas Robinson, then principal illustrator on the *Penny Illustrated Paper*, by his wife, Eliza Ann, daughter of William Heath, publican, of London. Educated at schools in Islington, he, like his elder brothers, Thomas and Charles, planned his career in the graphic arts. In 1887 he went to the Islington School of Art, and thence, in 1890, for a brief period, to the Royal Academy Schools. After an initial failure in landscape painting Will began work in his father's studio in the Strand. His first commission came from *Good Words*; but his real beginnings were in book-illustration, early works of note being a *Don Quixote* and a Hans Andersen (both 1897), an *Arabian Nights* (1899), *Poems* of Edgar Allan Poe (1900), and another *Don Quixote* (1902). Although Robinson's fame rests chiefly on his humorous drawings, he continued to work on serious book-illustration, displaying a nervous and sensitive line and a deep sympathy with his text, later books of mark being a *Twelfth Night* (1908), a Rabelais (1912), and a *Water Babies* (1915). He wrote and illustrated such humorous children's books as *The Adventures of Uncle Lubin* (1902) and *Bill the Minder* (1912).

Early in the twentieth century Robinson began advertising work for the Lamson Paragon Supply Company, and continued such activities all his life. But it was (Sir) Bruce Stirling Ingram who really launched him on his career by accepting some humorous drawings for the *Sketch*. He soon found his way into the *Bystander*, the *Strand Magazine*, the *Illustrated London News*, and other widely circulated periodicals. Before the outbreak of war in 1914 he had achieved world-wide fame as a humorist of infinite resource and the highest originality.

Although a quiet, shy, modest, and amiable man, who shunned all ostentation and liked best to live an equable family life, he was a celebrated person, chiefly because he made droll fun of the machine in an age which was enslaved by it. He caricatured machinery, just as an earlier artist might have caricatured human folly, by inventing absurd, complicated, jerry-built pieces of apparatus designed for such ridiculous purposes as shuffling bridge-hands, serving green peas to diners, or putting mites into cheese. The phrase 'a Heath Robinson contraption' gained general currency as a description of an unpractical, home-made piece of engineering, and remains part of the language. Robinson did not, however, confine himself to this type of humour. Everything he did was beautifully drawn and composed, and, whether in colour or black and white, had real decorative quality.

Robinson executed sundry theatrical commissions, notably for the old Empire and Alhambra theatres, which formerly stood in Leicester Square, London. He first broadcast in 1923, and was televised in 1938.

In 1903 he married Josephine Con-stance, daughter of John Latey [q.v.], art and literary editor of the *Penny Illustrated Paper*; there were four sons and one daughter of the marriage. He died at Highgate, London, 13 September 1944.

[*The Times*, 14 September 1944; W. Heath Robinson, *My Line of Life*, 1938; Langston Day, *The Life and Art of W. Heath Robinson*, 1947; private information.]

HERBERT B. GRIMSDITCH.

ROBISON, ROBERT (1883–1941), biochemist, was born at Newark-upon-Trent 29 December 1883, the only son of Robert Robison, grocer, by his wife, Jessie Thomson Clark. He obtained his early education at the Magnus Grammar School, Newark, and entered University College, Nottingham, in 1900. After obtaining his B.Sc. (London) in 1906 with second class honours in chemistry, he was awarded in 1907 an 1851 Exhibition scholarship for work carried out in collaboration with F. S. Kipping [q.v.] on derivatives of silicon. After two years' study in the laboratory of A. Hantzsch at Leipzig, where he gained his D.Phil. (*summa cum laude*), Robison returned to England in 1909 and in 1910 was appointed demonstrator in chemistry at University College, Galway. About a year later, however, he rejoined Kipping at Nottingham and remained there working on silicane-diols until he was appointed to the staff of the Lister Institute of Preventive Medicine, London, in 1913. He immediately engaged in the examination of the products of yeast fermentation and in collaboration with his new chief, (Sir) Arthur Harden [q.v.], soon announced the isolation of a hexosemonophosphoric ester which was later known as the 'Robison ester' and was destined to play an all-important part in the post-war development of biochemistry.

The war of 1914–18 caused a complete break in Robison's work and only after serving with the 29th division in Egypt, in Mudros during the Gallipoli campaign, in Egypt once more, and in Italy, did he again return in 1919 to the Lister Institute. His main problem at that time was the identification of the phosphoric esters formed during alcoholic fermentation and the care and skill with which this work was undertaken may be judged from the fact that six new hexosephosphoric esters were discovered within the next few years. While studying the action of emulsion on certain of these esters, Robison was led to consider whether a similar enzymic hydrolysis was involved in bone ossification and early in 1923 he announced the discovery of the enzyme, phosphatase, in aqueous extracts of bone of young, rapidly growing animals. From this time his more biological work included the experiments which led to the identification of a mechanism which played an important role in the deposition of the bone salts. His views on this subject were developed steadily and new ideas continually emerged up to the moment of his untimely death, and his work in this field is a rare example of beautifully planned research carried out with eminent skill.

Robison was elected F.R.S. in 1930 and appointed head of the biochemical department of the Lister Institute and professor of biochemistry in the university of London in 1931. He gave the Herter lectures on pathological chemistry in the university of New York in that year, published as *The Significance of Phosphoric Esters in Metabolism* (1932), and was awarded the Baly medal of the Royal College of Physicians, London, in 1933. Robison served as a member of the council of the Royal Society (1934–6) and of the Chemical Society (1936–9), and he was chairman of the Biochemical Society in 1935.

Robison married Ethel Ray, daughter of Samuel Walker, schoolmaster, of Newark, in 1910. They had one son and two daughters. The son and one daughter died in childhood. Robison died in London 18 June 1941.

[C. R. Harington in *Obituary Notices of Fellows of the Royal Society*, No. 10, December 1941; *Biochemical Journal*, vol. xxxv, No. 10, November 1941; personal knowledge.]

W. T. J. MORGAN.

RODD, JAMES RENNELL, first BARON RENNELL (1858–1941), diplomatist and scholar, was born in London 9 November 1858, the only son of a Cornishman, Major James Rennell Rodd, of the Duke of Cornwall's Light Infantry, by his wife, Elizabeth Anne, third daughter of Dr. Anthony Todd Thompson. He was a grandson of Vice-Admiral Sir John Tremayne Rodd, from whom he may have inherited his devotion to the sea, and James Rennell, the geographer [q.v.], was his great-grandfather. He was educated at Haileybury and at Balliol College, Oxford, where, as a commoner, he was awarded a third class in honour moderations (1878) and a second class in *literae humaniores* (1880). He won the Newdi-

gate prize for English verse in 1880 with a poem on Sir Walter Raleigh.

After a period of travel abroad, in France and Italy, Rodd much frequented the artistic and literary world of that time in London, and associated with men like (Sir) Edward Burne-Jones, who urged him to become a painter, Oscar Wilde, and J. A. McN. Whistler [qq.v.]. He eventually decided, however, in favour of diplomacy, in which, beyond a formal nomination for examination for the diplomatic service from Lord Granville, he had no sort of official or family influence to help him; yet his rise was rapid and at all important stages in his career he received approbation and expressions of confidence from successive secretaries of state. In 1884 he was sent as attaché to Berlin, being promoted third secretary in 1885, and during his service there he won the esteem of the Crown Prince and Princess. With the help of materials given to him by the Empress Frederick he published in 1888 *Frederick, Crown Prince and Emperor*, a biography which gave great offence in imperial circles at Berlin. That he might have said more than he did was apparent from his letters to *The Times* in 1928 which showed that the initiative in summoning (Sir) Morell Mackenzie [q.v.] to attend the Crown Prince came from German doctors rather than, as was freely alleged, from the Crown Princess.

From Berlin, Rodd was moved in 1888 to his first post in that area where his most important diplomatic and scholarly work was done, and became second secretary at Athens. Three years later he went to Rome, which he could remember in the days of the temporal power, and which he had visited in 1879 and 1880, and thence in 1892 to Paris. His stay was short, for in 1893 he was in charge of the British agency at Zanzibar and acting commissioner for British East Africa. As such he was in command of the expedition known as the second Witu campaign, and was present at the actions of Pumwani and Jongeni. From Zanzibar he was transferred in 1894 to Cairo where he worked with devotion and admiration under Lord Cromer [q.v.] in whose absences on leave he was in charge. His first important mission was in 1897 when he was sent to Abyssinia to negotiate a treaty with the Emperor Menelik. By it he secured permanent British representation at the Emperor's court, a most-favoured-nation arrangement in regard to commerce and to prevent munitions of war for the Mahdists passing through Abyssinia, and a definition of frontiers on the north and east of that country (but not on the south and west). He was rewarded by appointment as C.B. and in 1899 as K.C.M.G. for his management of the work in the agency at Cairo during the Fashoda crisis. Returning to Rome in 1902 as first secretary, he negotiated several treaties of delimitation of African territories with the Italian Government, and after promotion to the rank of counsellor of embassy he was transferred to Stockholm as minister, receiving the G.C.V.O. in 1905.

There now followed the most notable appointment in Rodd's career. During his tenure of the embassy at Rome from 1908 to 1919, not only did he prove to be *persona gratissima* in all circles but his judgement was invaluable to the British Government during the anxious days before Italy joined the Allies in 1915. Convinced that it was merely a matter of time and opportunity before Italy joined the Triple Entente, Rodd, acting in close understanding with his French colleague, refrained from exerting direct pressure and preferred, as a matter of psychological tactics, to allow the logic of events to weigh with the Italian Government in choosing the course of action felt to be in harmony with higher Italian interests as well as compatible with Italy's legal obligations under the Triple Alliance. The event justified his policy and he was rewarded with the G.C.M.G. He left the embassy in 1919, on being transferred to Lord Milner's special commission on the status of Egypt, and, having been promoted G.C.B. in 1920, he retired from the diplomatic service in 1921.

Retirement did not mean the close of Rodd's active work in foreign affairs. In 1921 and 1923 he was a representative of the British Government at the General Assembly of the League of Nations; in 1925 he was president of the court of conciliation between Austria and Switzerland; in 1928 he sat on the permanent commission of conciliation between Italy and Chile, and as a member of the permanent international commission for the advancement of peace between the United States and Venezuela. In that same year he turned to home politics and represented St. Marylebone as a Conservative from 1928 to 1932. In 1933 he was raised to the peerage as Baron Rennell, of Rodd, in the county of Hereford. He had been sworn of the Privy Council in 1908.

Considering what heavy claims were made on Rodd's time by his official work, his output of literary and scholarly work was remarkable. Between 1881 and 1940 he published some twenty volumes including a number of collections of poems, of which those to become the best known were *Ballads of the Fleet*, first published in 1897, and some renderings from the Greek Anthology (*Love, Worship and Death*, first published in 1916). His reminiscences (*Social and Diplomatic Memories*, 3 vols., 1922–5) give an authentic and pleasing account of the years of his official life. His classical and medieval studies bore fruit in *Customs and Lore of Modern Greece* (1892) and *The Princes of Achaia and the Chronicles of Morea* (2 vols., 1907). His detailed knowledge of the city of Rome is exhibited in what, outside learned circles, is his best-known work, *Rome of the Renaissance and Today* (1932); but his most important achievement may be held to be his *Homer's Ithaca* (1927), where his scholarship, local knowledge, seamanship, and common sense were all used to refute the theory propounded by Dörpfeld that the home of Odysseus was not in Ithaca but in Leucas (Santa Maura). His exposition led to excavations being carried out which have been held to confirm Rodd's thesis.

Courteous, unassuming, modest, but resolute, Rodd must be given a high place among the diplomats of his generation. He quickly won the devotion of his subordinates, the respect of the statesmen with whom he had to deal, and the affection of the learned men at Rome. His hobby was archaeology, and in pursuit of it, at the age of seventy-six, he narrowly escaped shipwreck. Whenever it was possible he owned or chartered a sailing yacht. Wherever he went he was greatly assisted by the talent and enterprise of his wife whom he married in 1894, Lilias Georgina (died 1951), fifth daughter of James Alexander Guthrie, of Craigie, Forfar. They had four sons and two daughters, and he was succeeded by his eldest son, Francis James Rennell (born 1895), a distinguished geographer and public servant. Rodd received numerous honours in foreign countries such as the Italian Order of St. Maurice and St. Lazarus and the Greek Order of the Redeemer, but none did he appreciate more than his election to the Accademia dei Lincei. He died at Ardath, Shamley Green, Surrey, 26 July 1941.

Of portraits of Lord Rennell in the possession of the family, one is by the younger Herkomer. There is also a pair of silver-points of Lady Rennell and himself by Violet, Duchess of Rutland. A cartoon by 'Spy' appeared in *Vanity Fair*, 7 January 1897.

[Sir J. R. Rodd, *Social and Diplomatic Memories*, 3 vols., 1922–5; *The Times*, 28 July 1941; private information; personal knowledge.]       PERCY LORAINE.

ROLLESTON, SIR HUMPHRY DAVY, baronet (1862–1944), physician, was born at Oxford 21 June 1862, the eldest son of George Rolleston, physician [q.v.], by his wife, Grace, daughter of John Davy and niece of Sir Humphry Davy [qq.v.]. He was educated at Marlborough, and at St. John's College, Cambridge, of which he became a scholar in 1885 and where he gained a first class in both parts of the natural sciences tripos in 1885 and 1886, and in 1889 was elected into a fellowship. He received his medical training at St. Bartholomew's Hospital, and he proceeded to his Cambridge M.D. in 1891. After acting as house-physician he was appointed demonstrator of anatomy at St. Bartholomew's, a post which he held for some years, at the same time gaining clinical experience as assistant physician to the Metropolitan Hospital. In 1890 he was elected curator of the museum, and in 1893 assistant physician, at St. George's Hospital. Soon afterwards he joined the staff of the Victoria Hospital for Children as assistant physician, and in due course he became physician and consulting physician to both hospitals. He took an active part in the meetings of the principal medical societies of London, and rapidly made a name for himself as a pathologist and as a most stimulating teacher. In 1894 he was admitted F.R.C.P. (London), and in the following year he delivered before the College a notable series of Goulstonian lectures on the suprarenal bodies. By this time he had carried out original work on the mechanism of the heart (with Charles Smart Roy) and on the anatomy of the appendicular region (with Charles Barrett Lockwood), and was regarded as one of the coming men in medicine.

In 1901 he went to South Africa as consulting physician to the Imperial Yeomanry Hospital at Pretoria during the latter part of the South African war, and this interlude had fortunate effects on his health, which had given some anxiety. Returning to London after the end of hostilities he became immersed in practice, teaching, and authorship. At the invitation of (Sir) T. C. Allbutt [q.v.], whom he had known at Cambridge, he became joint-editor of the second edition of Allbutt's great *System of Medicine* (1905–11). In 1905 he published the most substantial of his purely medical works, an exhaustive treatise on *Diseases of the Liver, Gall-bladder and Bile-ducts*. During the war of 1914–18 he served as consulting physician to the Royal Navy, with the temporary rank of surgeon rear-admiral, and was appointed C.B. in 1916 and K.C.B. in 1918. He wrote classical reports on cases of cerebrospinal fever in the navy and made this disease the subject of his Lumleian lectures in 1919. In 1916 he was called to attend Prince Albert (afterwards King George VI) who was suffering from an ulcer. By the end of the war he had attained a pre-eminent position in the profession and he held in succession the presidency of the Royal Society of Medicine (1918–20), the Royal College of Physicians (1922–6), and the Medical Society of London (1926–7). In 1925 he succeeded Allbutt as regius professor of physic at Cambridge and he filled this position with the greatest distinction until 1932, when he became emeritus. Although he now took a country-house at Haslemere, Rolleston could not retire; indeed, he added to his commitments and it may be doubted whether any medical man ever held so many offices or was engaged in such multifarious duties. He had long been regarded as the leading authority on the presentation of medical articles, and from 1928 to 1944 he undertook the main direction of the *Practitioner*; from 1936 onwards he was also editor-in-chief of the *British Encyclopaedia of Medical Practice*.

The services of Rolleston were widely called for and the offices which he filled and the Royal Commissions and boards on which he served were many. Nor were they confined to matters connected with his own profession, for his interests extended to local history and social experiments: witness his presidency of the London Cornish Association, of the Eugenics Society, and the Papworth Village Settlement. He was a trustee of the British Museum. His long and devoted services to the British Medical Association were recognized by the award of the Association's gold medal in 1926. He received almost every honour open to a British physician, including honorary degrees from the universities of Oxford, Durham, Glasgow, Bristol, Birmingham, Edinburgh, Padua, Paris, Bordeaux, Pennsylvania, and the National University of Ireland. In 1923 he was appointed physician-in-ordinary to King George V and from 1932 to 1936 he was physician-extraordinary. In 1924 he was created a baronet, and having been one of the team attending the King in his serious illness in 1928, he was appointed G.C.V.O. in 1929.

Rolleston himself confessed that he liked to write something every day, and the fruits of his almost incredible industry are to be seen in a score of books and some 600 papers and addresses which he wrote over a period of sixty years. His literary style, like his handwriting, was neat as an etching. The more important of his writings, in addition to those already mentioned, are a *Manual of Practical Morbid Anatomy* (with A. A. Kanthack, 1894); *Clinical Lectures and Essays on Abdominal and Other Subjects* (1904); *On Writing Theses for M.B. and M.D. Degrees* (1911); *Some Medical Aspects of Old Age* (1922); *Aspects of Age, Life, and Disease* (1928); the Harveian oration on *Cardiovascular Diseases since Harvey's Discovery* (1928); a memoir of Allbutt (1929); *The Cambridge Medical School: A Biographical History* (1932); and the Fitz-Patrick lectures on *The Endocrine Organs in Health and Disease* (1936). During his later years he paid increasing attention to the study of medical history, and the reputation which he acquired in this field tended to obscure his earlier achievements as a clinician and as a pathologist. One of the most modest and unassuming of men, he set an example of industry and achievement which few could follow. No medical man of his time had more friends both in and out of the profession which he adorned, and he had no enemies. He died at his home at Haslemere 23 September 1944.

He married in 1894 Lisette Eila, daughter of Francis Mackenzie Ogilvy, of London, and had two sons; the elder was killed in Flanders in 1915; and the younger in a riot in Zanzibar in 1936. The baronetcy therefore became extinct. A portrait of Rolleston by James Gunn is at St. George's Hospital, London.

[*British Medical Journal*, 30 September 1944; *Lancet*, 7 October 1944; *St. George's Hospital Gazette*, vol. xxxiv, December–January 1944–5; *St. Bartholomew's Hospital Journal*, January 1945; *Medical Press*, 4 October 1944.]          W. J. Bishop.

ROMER, MARK LEMON, Baron Romer (1866–1944), judge, was born at Crawley, Sussex, 9 August 1866, the second son of (Sir) Robert Romer, later lord justice of appeal, by his wife, Betty, daughter of Mark Lemon, the first editor of *Punch* [qq.v.]. Romer went up from Rugby to Trinity Hall, Cambridge, as an exhibitioner, where, like his father, he read mathematics, but without the same distinction, being among the junior optimes in 1888. Among his contemporaries were two future judicial colleagues—Frederic Herbert (afterwards Viscount) Maugham (who later married his sister Helen) and (Sir) Travers Humphreys.

Romer joined Lincoln's Inn (of which he became a bencher in 1910) and was called to the bar in 1890. Having built up a solid Chancery practice he took silk in 1906. In those days each Chancery silk attached himself to the court of a particular judge, in which no other leader could appear without a special fee marked on the brief—a custom more beneficial to the litigant than might appear—and Romer was so fortunate as to practise before 'the greatest master of equity of our generation'—Sir R. J. (later Lord) Parker [q.v.]. After Parker went to the House of Lords Romer appeared before Sir C. H. Sargant [q.v.]. Romer was a thoroughly sound lawyer, who inspired complete confidence in all, and although other Chancery silks of the day (a strong team) could present their arguments in a more distinctive manner, there was no surprise when in 1922 he succeeded Sir Arthur Frederick Peterson in the Chancery division and received the customary knighthood. The same year he was elected an honorary fellow of his college.

Chancery judges are seldom in the public eye, though a disappointed suitor once—unsuccessfully—flung handfuls of pebbles at Romer on the bench (the contempt was suitably punished); but in 1924 he considered a question of great importance to the City of London—the degree of care and skill required of company directors and auditors. The case (*In re City Equitable Fire Insurance Company Limited*, [1925] Ch. 407) was twenty-four days at hearing, and Romer's judgement, covering seventy-five pages of the reports and commended on appeal by a strong court, is a sensible and authoritative exposition of the law. In 1925 Parliament made sweeping reforms in the intricate structure of the law of real property. Some senior conveyancers and a few judges expressed the most gloomy apprehensions: they were not shared by Romer, and his judgements on several novel and difficult conveyancing questions showed a sane appreciation of the needs of a perplexed profession. Apart from their intrinsic merits, they gained authority from the fact (well known, though convention forbade any reference to it in the judgements) that Romer had done valuable work as chairman of a committee which considered the bills in draft. On the bench he was decisive, and though implacable if he suspected shabby conduct, always most careful to be fair. A man of great courtesy of manner, he enjoyed with the bar much of the popularity ¹ for which his father 'Bob' had been famous. He was not a talking judge.

In 1929, although not the senior Chancery judge, Romer was promoted to the Court of Appeal and, as is customary, sworn of the Privy Council. His robust good sense and knowledge of the world enabled him to tackle the unfamiliar common law business with noticeably greater success than many Chancery lords justices. (In the leading case of *Alexander* v. *Rayson*, [1936] 1 K.B. 169, the two common law members of the court were well content to acquiesce in his judgement.) In Romer, however, these qualities never concealed, as they have in others, a want of learning. Although he left nothing in the books displaying that power of subtle yet patient speculation characteristic of the greatest Chancery judges, he had a thorough mastery of some very different branches of the law. His judgements, admirably economical in their citation of authorities, often contain an illuminating turn of phrase. In 1934 he was appointed a member of the lord chancellor's Law Revision Committee; its report on the statutes of limitation owed much to his skill and labour.

In January 1938, on the resignation of Lord Roche, Romer was appointed a lord of appeal in ordinary, and created a life peer. The promotion was entirely justified. In the following years over a dozen appeals raising questions of unusual legal and social significance came before a House which could deploy an exceptionally distinguished array of talent, noticeably ready to expose and correct the errors of previous generations. Many of these great cases, so exhilarating to the lawyer, raised problems in the common

law, a field in which some members of the House moved with particular skill, but Romer's judgements, displaying an urbane command of principle, are often among the most helpful and authoritative. *Perrin* v. *Morgan*, [1943] A.C. 399, provided one of the rare opportunities of reviewing some of the more austere learning of the equity bar. An eighteenth-century rule required the word 'money' in a will to be construed in a strict sense which excluded, for example, stock exchange investments unless the context permitted a wider interpretation. The rule, described by Lord Greene in the Court of Appeal as 'a blot upon our jurisprudence', often led to unpalatable results, and the common law majority wished to abolish it. Romer could not agree. His reasons, framed in his customary compact and lucid style, are by no means unconvincing, and had the support of Lord Russell of Killowen [q.v.]. The fault lay not in the rule but in its misapplication. Certainty is of the greatest importance, so established rules of construction 'should be strictly observed, but they ought to be applied in a reasonable way'. The paramount object is to give effect to the testator's intentions. 'I have noticed in some of the reported cases on wills a tendency . . . to pay more attention to the rules of construction than to the language of the testator.' The tendency will hardly reappear. Romer sat often in the Judicial Committee of the Privy Council, where his talents were particularly helpful in dealing with the very variegated work of that tribunal. When he became a lord of appeal and so discarded the wig and robes of the Supreme Court, the observer noticed with admiration that he had preserved to the end of a long life the thick dark hair and fine manly presence of his youth.

In 1893 Romer married Anne Wilmot (died 1948), daughter of C. T. Ritchie, later Baron Ritchie of Dundee [q.v.], and by her had two sons. Her sister Mary married his lifelong friend at the equity bar, Lord Russell of Killowen. Romer died at Tadworth 19 August 1944, having resigned his position the previous April. Had he lived two months more, he would have had the pleasure of seeing his younger son, (Sir) Charles Robert Ritchie Romer, appointed a judge of the Chancery division; he became a lord justice of appeal in 1951. When Romer went to the bench there were three other judges whose fathers had sat before them, and when his son was appointed there were eight—but the family of Romer shares with that of Coleridge alone the remarkable distinction of having given three successive generations to the English judicial bench.

Two portraits of Romer by R. G. Eves remained in the possession of the artist. Another by John Crealock is in the possession of the family.

[*The Times*, 21 August 1944; private information.]                    R. F. V. HEUSTON.

ROSE, JOHN HOLLAND (1855–1942), historian, was born at Bedford 28 June 1855, the youngest son of Thomas Rose, draper, who died in 1861, by his second wife, Mary, daughter of Thomas Green, grocer, of Bedford. He was educated at Bedford Modern School, the Owens College, Manchester, where he came under the influence of (Sir) A. W. Ward [q.v.], and at Christ's College, Cambridge (1875–9), of which he became a scholar in classics in 1876. Although not distinguished in the tripos, then mainly linguistic, he retained throughout his life his love of the classics. On leaving Cambridge he became an assistant master at Dover College. Contemporary with him at Christ's was A. C. Haddon [q.v.], the anthropologist, and each married the other's sister. Rose's wife, Laura Kate, was the daughter of John Haddon, founder of the John Haddon printing works in Bouverie Square. On his marriage in 1880 Rose opened a school in Ventnor where his three children, a son and two daughters, were born, but after a few years he returned to London and took up university extension work for London and Cambridge universities.

Henceforth Rose's time was increasingly given to historical writing. Concentrating in particular on the Revolutionary and Napoleonic era, he produced in 1894 a textbook with that title remarkable for its breadth and authority. This was followed in 1902 by his most considerable work, the *Life of Napoleon I*, which went through eleven editions in his lifetime, and still remains the most comprehensive treatment of the subject in English, excelling both in its mastery of the general history and in its clear presentation of Napoleon. On this book Rose obtained the degree of Litt.D. at Cambridge in 1903 and established his reputation as a leading historian. In 1911 he was invited back to Cambridge to hold the

newly created readership in modern history and in this year he published a second important work, in two volumes, relating to the same period (*William Pitt and National Revival* and *William Pitt and the Great War*). His historical reputation rests primarily upon these two works, each based upon independent research in the archives, in which he was a pioneer, and illustrating his power of broad survey and clear, energetic, and honest narrative. Rose was a natural speaker, and long apprenticeship to local lecturing gave to his teaching a force and clarity which it never lost.

During the war of 1914–18 Rose lectured to popular audiences in the United Kingdom and to troops at the base camps on the western front; with such success that Lord Rothermere [q.v.], when he founded in 1919 the Vere Harmsworth professorship of naval history at Cambridge, reserving to himself the first appointment, nominated Rose to the chair. Rose accepted, after first offering to stand aside in favour of Sir Julian Corbett [q.v.], and turned his attention to a new field of history, in which he produced several works; of these the last, *Man and the Sea* (1935), was published in his eightieth year. He had been a contributor to two of the Cambridge co-operative histories, and in 1925 he became one of the editors of the *Cambridge History of the British Empire*, with A. P. Newton and E. A. Benians. At this he worked indefatigably, enjoying the contacts with Dominion scholars, until advancing years obliged him to retire. Intensely loyal to the British Empire, and with a strong faith in its historical and future significance to mankind, he founded in 1932 a studentship in his name to encourage the study of imperial history. He retired in the following year. After his return to Cambridge he had been elected a fellow of his college (1914), to which he was always closely attached, but he took little part in university business, for which he felt no aptitude. He died at Cambridge 3 March 1942.

Rose was a man of middle height and full figure, somewhat important in manner and speech, of independent spirit and great determination, a Congregationalist in religion, most kindhearted and friendly, fond of society and of children, and systematic in his habits of work and exercise. Music, walking, cycling, and his garden were his principal recreations. He liked travel and visited both the United

States (1921) and South Africa (1933) on lecturing tours. His life was devoted to his historical work, but, sound scholar though he was, his primary interest in history was as an instrument of popular education. He was happiest in writing for (as in addressing) the general public. As an historian he was a self-made man, who had the courage to attempt big things and the industry to carry them through to success. By his lectures and his writings he made a substantial contribution to the spread of historical knowledge. The universities of Manchester, Nebraska, and Warsaw, and Amherst College awarded him honorary degrees, and he was much gratified when, in 1933, the British Academy elected him a fellow.

A portrait painted by his daughter-in-law, Mrs. Charles Holland Rose, is in the possession of the family.

[*Cambridge Review*, 23 May 1942; *The Times*, 4 March 1942; private information; personal knowledge.]     E. A. BENIANS.

ROSE-INNES, SIR JAMES (1855–1942), chief justice of South Africa, was born at Grahamstown, Cape Colony, 8 January 1855, the eldest son of James Rose Innes, then provincial secretary to the lieutenant-governor and subsequently under-secretary for native affairs in the Civil Service of that colony, by his wife, Mary Ann, daughter of James Fleischer. Her sister married Sir J. G. Sprigg [q.v.]. Rose-Innes was educated at Bedford, Cape Colony, and at Gill College, Somerset East, and received the degrees of B.A. (1874) and LL.B. (1877) from the university of the Cape of Good Hope.

Rose-Innes was admitted to the bar at Cape Town in 1878 and practised there until 1902. He was a member of the Cape Parliament (legislative assembly) for Victoria East from 1884 to 1888, for the Cape division, 1888 to 1902, took silk in 1890, became attorney-general in Rhodes's first ministry in 1890, resigned in 1893, and subsequently held the same portfolio in the Sprigg ministry from 1900 to 1902. He was appointed K.C.M.G. in 1901. He was retained on behalf of the imperial Government during the trial which he attended at Pretoria of the members of the reform committee in 1896 following the collapse of the Jameson raid.

In 1902 Rose-Innes became chief justice of the Transvaal Colony. Upon the establishment of the Union in 1910, he accepted a seat on the Appeal Court and

in 1914, upon the death of Lord De Villiers [q.v.], became chief justice of South Africa. In the new year he was nominated a privy counsellor but was not sworn until 1919. While chief justice he acted on two occasions as officer administering the Government pending the arrival of the governor-general designate.

During his parliamentary career Rose-Innes was distinguished by his sincerity and moderation, being a powerful influence for justice and constitutionalism and a zealous champion of the rights of the native people. As a public speaker he was noted for his felicitous words on all occasions. As a judge he rendered great services. The confidence inspired, after the annexation of the Transvaal, by the Supreme Court, of which he was the head, was a potent factor in allaying the strong feeling caused by the South African war and its consequences.

As a jurist Rose-Innes by his learned judgements earned a high place among those who have expounded the Roman-Dutch system of jurisprudence and applied its principles to the decision of disputes in South Africa. When he joined the bench a controversy had arisen among the lawyers in South Africa as a result of judgements of De Villiers, in which it was held that the *justa causa* requisite in the Roman-Dutch law to make a promise enforceable was equivalent to 'valuable consideration' in the sense in which this expression is used in the English law of contract. The correctness of this view had been disputed as early as 1888 by (Sir) J. G. Kotzé [q.v.], then chief justice of the Transvaal. In a judgement given in 1904 the Transvaal Supreme Court, presided over by Rose-Innes, decided this question in favour of Kotzé's view, holding that *justa causa* (reasonable cause) is not the same thing as 'valuable consideration' and that the requisite of *justa causa* is satisfied when the undertaking sued upon was given by the defendant seriously and deliberately and with the intention that a lawful obligation should be established. Ultimately in 1919 the Court of Appeal confirmed this view and thus settled the law on the subject.

After retiring in 1927 Rose-Innes played a prominent part in the formation in 1929 of the Non-Racial Franchise Association, the purpose of which was to oppose the introduction in the Cape Province of a differentiation based solely on race or colour in regard to franchise rights. The association did its best (but without avail) to oppose the passing of Act 12 of 1936, a measure enacted by the Union Parliament which terminated the franchise rights to which Cape natives possessing the qualifications prescribed by the existing electoral law of the Cape Province were entitled, and which substituted a new Cape native voters' roll, voters on this roll to be entitled to elect three Europeans as members of the Union House of Assembly, and two Europeans as members of the Cape Provincial Council.

Rose-Innes married in 1881 Jessie Dods (died 1943), youngest daughter of William Dods Pringle, landowner and farmer, of Bedford, Cape Colony. They had a daughter, Dorothy, who married Count Helmuth von Moltke, of Kreisau, Silesia, and was the mother of the successor to that title whom the Nazis executed in Germany in January 1945. Rose-Innes died at Kenilworth, in the Cape Peninsula, 16 January 1942. There is a portrait of him by G. Crossland Robinson in the Houses of Parliament, Cape Town, and another, by Neville Lewis, at the Appeal Court building, Bloemfontein.

[*The Times*, 17 January 1942; *Law Reports* of the Transvaal Court and of the Union Court of Appeal, *passim*; Sir James Rose-Innes, *Autobiography*, edited by B. A. Tindall, 1949; private information; personal knowledge.]                         B. A. TINDALL.

ROTHENSTEIN, SIR WILLIAM (1872–1945), painter, and principal of the Royal College of Art, was born at Bradford, Yorkshire, 29 January 1872, the second son of Moritz Rothenstein, cloth merchant, who had emigrated to this country from Hanover in 1859 and was naturalized in 1867. The mother, Bertha, was a daughter of William Dux, of the Hildesheim banking family.

William, like his elder brother, Charles Lambert Rutherston, the collector, and his younger brother, Albert Daniel Rutherston, the artist, inherited his father's integrity of character, and the aesthetic tastes of his mother's family. She herself played with Frederick Delius [q.v.] while he was still a schoolboy. William was entirely unmusical, but showed signs as a small boy of his true gifts. He was educated at Bradford Grammar School where his talent for painting was encouraged. His spirit was tutored by the austere countryside of the West Riding, and a local artist, Ernest Sichel, a pupil of the Slade School of Fine Art under

Alphonse Legros [q.v.], was the means of persuading Moritz Rothenstein to allow his son to join this school of art in 1888 when he was sixteen. The next year the boy was attending the Académie Julian in Paris where he proved to be precociously brilliant. Later he came to be influenced by J. A. McN. Whistler [q.v.], but more lasting influences were through the friendly advice and example which the young Rothenstein won from Degas and Fantin-Latour after they had seen his work in public exhibition. Rothenstein's lifelong devotion to a form of ideal realism was strengthened also by his lasting admiration for the work of J. F. Millet.

Will Rothenstein, to use the name with which he signed the work of his early and middle periods, returned to England in 1893. Having been commissioned by John Lane [q.v.] to make lithographs of eminent Oxford characters, he astonished the university by his vital personality and unusually persuasive powers over older men. This adventure was the beginning of one of the greatest series of contemporary portraits, from Verlaine to Einstein and T. E. Lawrence, in the history of art. An iconography covering the years 1889 to 1925 records over 750 portrait drawings and 135 lithographs, and Rothenstein's work is to be found in all the principal galleries.

Rothenstein was essentially a thinker and teacher in life and work, and as his painting with the turn of the century became more serious and authoritative he was often invited to express in public his belief in the importance of the artist to the community and especially the need for powerful regional centres of the arts both in teaching and in creative practice. His visits to India in 1910 and America in 1912 increased his sense of social responsibility, and in 1917 he accepted an appointment as professor of civic art at the university of Sheffield, which he held until 1926.

During the war of 1914–18 Rothenstein as an official war artist recorded the battle front in France, and he also continued to do everything within his power to help younger painters. His interests moved from the work of his contemporaries of the New English Art Club to that of the post-war art student, and he was persuaded in 1920 to become principal of the Royal College of Art and so during the following fifteen years to sacrifice his personal desire for an uninterrupted life of painting. His reorganization was radical and his influence was soon to be seen in the work and teaching of his pupils throughout the British Isles and the Commonwealth. From 1927 to 1933 he was a trustee of the Tate Gallery, and from 1931 to 1938 a member of the Royal Fine Art Commission.

Although he retired from the College in 1935, the last ten years of Rothenstein's life were little given to quiet, for they were rather years in consolidation of, and farewell to, old friendships, the diversity of which is shown in his three volumes of memoirs: *Men & Memories* (2 vols., 1931–2) and *Since Fifty* (1939). His correspondence with his friends will be of the first importance to the historian. Although for years he suffered from cardiac asthma, he became an unofficial artist to the Royal Air Force during the war of 1939–45 and revived the vigour of his draughtsmanship in the cause of a new generation of heroic youth. He died 14 February 1945 at Far Oakridge, the Cotswold home which he made famous in many paintings throughout all seasons of the year.

In 1899 Rothenstein married a talented and beautiful young actress, Alice Kingsley, in private life Alice Mary (died 1957), daughter of Walter John Knewstub, a friend of Dante Gabriel Rossetti [q.v.]. Her sister married Sir William Orpen [q.v.]. There were two sons and two daughters of Rothenstein's marriage, the elder son, Sir John Rothenstein, becoming director of the Tate Gallery, the younger, Michael Rothenstein, a well-known painter.

Rothenstein was knighted in 1931, and in 1934, upon the occasion of his giving the Romanes lecture at Oxford, the university conferred upon him the honorary degree of D.Litt. He changed little in his later years from the lithe and gallantly liberal-minded protagonist of the artist in society which he had been in his youth and his vigorous middle age. As a draughtsman and painter he stood for a spirituality and standard of craftsmanship unfashionable in his period. It is probable that the future will more justly determine his great qualities. A number of his works are in the Tate Gallery, including portraits of James Stephens and Sir Rabindranath Tagore. Other portraits are in the National Portrait Gallery, including a self-portrait in chalk. There are self-portraits in oils in the city art galleries of Manchester, Sheffield, and Bradford, and one in pencil

at Leeds. A lithograph of Rothenstein by J. S. Sargent (1897) is in the British Museum; a portrait drawing (1904) by Augustus John is in the collection of Mrs. William Jessop; and an ink and wash drawing by Albert Rutherston is in the Manchester City Art Gallery.

[Rothenstein's own writings; John Rothenstein, *Portrait Drawings by William Rothenstein, 1889–1925*, 1926; H[ubert] W[ellington], *William Rothenstein* (Contemporary British Artists), 1923; *The Times*, 15 February 1945.]

KENNETH ROMNEY TOWNDROW.

ROUSE, WILLIAM HENRY DENHAM (1863–1950), schoolmaster and classical scholar, was born in Calcutta 30 May 1863, the son of the Rev. G. H. Rouse and his wife, Lydia, daughter of the Rev. W. H. R. Denham. His parents were strong Wesleyans, and worked as missionaries in India; both of them spoke and wrote Bengali. His mother was one of the first welfare workers among British soldiers in India. In later life Rouse became an Anglican and, in his own way, a very loyal one. He was educated at Haverfordwest Grammar School and Doveton College, Calcutta. In 1882 he was elected a scholar of Christ's College, Cambridge, and later a fellow (1888–94) and honorary fellow (1933). He was placed in the first class in both parts of the classical tripos (1885, 1886), and as a young man travelled extensively, especially in Crete and the Aegean Islands, where he found much to attract his interest, particularly with regard to folklore. His first-hand knowledge of India in his early years had given him a strong interest in the folk-lore of that country, and he edited and translated some of its literature. Later in life (1903–39) he was university teacher of Sanskrit at Cambridge, and he served as president of the Folklore Society (1904–6).

After holding assistant masterships at Bedford Grammar School, Cheltenham College, and Rugby School, he was in 1902 appointed headmaster of the Perse School, Cambridge, a post he held until he retired in 1928. During his headmastership the school became famous for the teaching of the classical languages by the 'direct method'; from the beginning of the course neither master nor pupils spoke any English during Greek and Latin lessons. Particular attention was given to clear and accurate enunciation, and Rouse, who took a full part in the teaching, taking the sixth form for the first half of every morning, himself set a striking example in this respect, not only in the reading of Greek and Latin in class, but also on more informal occasions at the School House, when he would read aloud from well-known English writers. Lively and topical comments and explanations, and conversations between master and boys—all in Greek or Latin—supplemented by pictures drawn by Rouse on the blackboard, provided an admirable way of acquiring familiarity with the literature and life of classical times. An incidental result was that for the more advanced pupils little formal instruction in verse and prose composition was needed: it had become almost second nature to them. Rouse's own two books, *Demonstrations in Latin Elegiac Verse* and *Demonstrations in Greek Iambic Verse* (both 1899), although typical of his attitude, do not adequately illustrate his own remarkable powers of verse composition.

He was no innovator for innovation's sake. All his reforms followed directly and inevitably from his belief that school work, and indeed all human activities, should be a natural and friendly business, instinct with living interest. Where old methods were good, he saw no need for alteration: he preferred the horse to the motor-car. Although a Tory of Tories, there was nothing stereotyped about him. He was a deliberate and insular patriot, but his interest in modern European languages and cultures was cosmopolitan; and he was proficient in several modern languages. To him the antiquity of the classical authors was an accident: his love for them was due not to their age but to their living qualities and universal human appeal. The same is true of his love for Greek folk-lore, and for the traditional songs and dances of England which his colleagues taught with his active encouragement. For, in his view, education was not merely an occupation for the classroom; he fully understood the value of manual as well as mental training, and established at the school a carpentry workshop and a printing press. Rouse knew the importance of getting—and retaining—a good staff in his school. He believed in men, not in organization; and the assistant masters, as his friends rather than as his subordinates, had freedom to exercise to the full their various gifts, thereby making the school justly famous. There was in Rouse no shade of envy or jealousy; he was a man filled with kindness, sincerity, and humour, and his laughter was an inspiration. Cant and pomposity were as abhorrent to him as jargon and slovenliness of speech. He was critical of the Board of Education and almost until the end of his headmastership refused to make provision for boys to take school examinations conducted by outside bodies.

The spirit of his teaching is admirably represented by two school books of his, both contrasting strikingly with the usual type of school textbook: *A Greek Boy at Home* (1909), and *Chanties in Greek and Latin* (original songs, set to well-known tunes, for singing in school, 1922). Perhaps the widest known of his books are his translations from Homer. His Cambridge doctorate was awarded after the publication of his work *Greek Votive Offerings* (1902), but before that he had written his books on verse composition, translated some Pali texts, and edited several volumes in the 'Temple Classics' series. He also edited a number of volumes of Blackie's plain texts. From 1907 to 1920 he was editor of the *Classical Review* (sole editor, 1907–10), and from its foundation until shortly before his death he was one of the editors of the Loeb Classical Library, to which he himself contributed three translations (Seneca's *Apocolocyntosis*, Lucretius, and Nonnus).

In stature he was short, and his dress and general appearance were at first sight unimpressive. He was never seen to wear an overcoat, or to be in a hurry; perhaps the slowness of his gait and the shortness of his steps were in some part due to the half-Wellingtons which he habitually wore. He was fond of good fare and good company, and in the later years of his retirement heartily enjoyed the society in the combination room of his old college to which his frequent visits, even during the difficulties of the black-out, brought a special touch of gaiety. He died, unmarried, at Hayling Island 10 February 1950. A portrait by H. W. G. Betteridge is in the hall of the Perse School; a bust in bronze by George Thomas (1928) is in the library of Christ's College, Cambridge.

[Private information; personal knowledge.]
A. L. PECK.

ROWLATT, Sir SIDNEY ARTHUR TAYLOR (1862–1945), judge, was born in Cairo 20 July 1862, the eldest son of Arthur Henry Rowlatt, manager of the Bank of Egypt, by his wife, Amelia Caroline, daughter of Sidney Terry, general merchant, of Bombay. He was educated at Fettes under the first head-master, Dr. A. W. Potts, and was one of a batch of his pupils who, going up to Cambridge in the 'eighties, won the annual Porson prize seven times in nine successive years. Entering King's College as a scholar in 1880, Rowlatt, apart from winning the Porson prize (1883), was Browne medallist (1883), honourably mentioned for the Chancellor's medal, and was placed in the first class in parts i and ii of the classical tripos in 1882 and 1884. For a short time after taking his degree he was a popular assistant master at Eton. In 1886 he was elected fellow of his college, awarded a Whewell scholar-ship, and called to the bar by the Inner Temple (of which he was to become a bencher in 1908 and treasurer in 1928). He was first a pupil of (Sir) F. A. Bosan-quet [q.v.] and afterwards of Abel John Ram. Recommended by A. T. Lawrence (later Lord Trevethin, q.v.), who knew Rowlatt as a promising member of the Oxford circuit, he became devil for R. B. (later Viscount) Finlay (whose notice Rowlatt contributed to this DICTIONARY), and thereby formed a friendship which lasted until Finlay's death and brought him many useful contacts in his career. In 1900 Finlay, as attorney-general, nominated Rowlatt for the appointment of junior counsel to the Board of Inland Revenue. The experience which Rowlatt thus gained was to prove very valuable when he sat on the bench, although the essentially judicial cast of his mind pre-served him from that prejudice in favour of the Crown which similar experience in other men is sometimes apt to create. In 1905 Rowlatt became junior counsel to the Treasury on the common law side. In 1912 Lord Haldane [q.v.] offered him a judgeship in place of Sir J. A. Hamilton (later Viscount Sumner, q.v.), who had been made a lord justice. He received the customary knighthood.

Rowlatt who, as recorder of Windsor, had already obtained some judicial ex-perience, soon showed his distinction as a judge. Although he often took the Com-mercial List and other non-jury cases in London and had his share of Old Bailey and circuit work, his scholarship, patience, impartiality, and good humour were seen to best advantage in revenue cases. His judgement in *Cape Brandy Syndicate* v. *Inland Revenue Commissioners*, [1921] 1 K.B. 64, is a good example of his clear reasoning and crisp style, as applied to the difficult question of the interpretation of a taxation statute. That his qualities as a judge were not recognized by promo-tion was perhaps in part due to the repu-tation which he won as an expert in the rather specialized field of revenue and to his own obvious enjoyment of the work, free, as he said on his retirement, from sensation and acute controversy. He retired from the King's Bench division in 1932.

His work as a judge did not, however, exhaust his public services. In 1917 he was appointed chairman of the committee on criminal conspiracies in India, which led to the passing of the Rowlatt Act in 1919, strengthening the hand of the Government in dealing with revolutionary crime. In recognition of his services in this connexion he was appointed K.C.S.I. in 1918. After his retirement from the bench, he was sworn a member of the Privy Council and sat on a number of appeals. He was also chairman of the Royal Commission on lotteries and betting (1932–3) and, in the war of 1939–45, of the general claims tribunal under the Compensation (Defence) Act of 1939. His ability as a lawyer, outside his own special subject of taxation, was shown by his book, first published in 1899, on *The Law of Principal and Surety*, which is clearly arranged, exhaustive in treat-ment, and has been recognized by the courts, on more than one occasion, as a work of great authority. As a man, Rowlatt was a witty and courteous com-panion, whose classical scholarship, al-though restrained by an essentially modest nature, could, when the occasion demand-ed, produce elegant, impromptu Latin verse. In court, he was from the point of view of counsel almost an ideal judge, quick to seize a point but loath to interrupt. When he spoke, it was with a cheerful almost boyish air, devoid of pomposity. He rarely reserved, and almost never wrote, a judgement. He died at Bagnor Manor, Newbury, Berkshire, 1 March 1945.

Rowlatt married in 1890 Elizabeth (died 1957), daughter of James Heming-way, railway contractor, of Macclesfield, and by her had four sons and two daughters. His third son, Sir John Row-latt, who became first parliamentary coun-sel to the Treasury in 1953, died in 1956.

There is a portrait by E. Matthew Hale in the possession of the family.

[*The Times*, 23 March 1932, 3, 7, 20, and 24 March 1945; *Solicitors' Journal, Law Journal*, and *Law Times*, 10 March 1945; private information.] NORMAN S. MARSH.

ROY, CAMILLE JOSEPH (1870–1943), French-Canadian man of letters, was born at Berthier-en-bas, Quebec, 22 October 1870, the sixteenth of at least twenty children of Benjamin Roy, a farmer, by his wife, Desanges Gosselin. Of this large family five became priests and one of them, Paul Eugène, archbishop of Quebec. Camille, who was ordained priest in 1894, was educated at the seminary at Quebec and at Laval University, where he was awarded the doctorate of philosophy in 1894. He also studied at the Catholic Institute and at the Sorbonne in Paris from 1898 to 1901 and came under the influence of Auguste Émile Faguet. He was well read in Greek and Latin as well as in French literature, a blend of teacher, novelist, historian, and keen observer of current affairs. He began teaching in the seminary in 1892 and in 1918 he was appointed professor of French literature at Laval, of which between 1924 and 1943 he was four times appointed rector. He became professor of Canadian literature in 1927. His influence on education in Quebec was notable. Under his rule, new faculties, including one of natural science, were introduced into the university; he founded the école normale supérieure, and for his services in the ecclesiastical sphere he was appointed by Pope Pius XI a protonotary apostolic in 1925.

It is not, however, for this administrative work that Roy will be remembered. From early days as a teacher, he had begun to lecture on French and French-Canadian literature. The two objects which he set before himself were stimulating the interest of his compatriots throughout North America in French-Canadian literature (he was one of the founders of the Société du Parler Français), and making it a national heritage. He found in it little to praise before 1840; but to him the significance of the Durham report was that 'c'est au lendemain du jour où Durham laissait entendre que nous n'étions pas un peuple parce que nous n'avions pas de littérature, que Garneau écrivit en pages ardentes l'épopée canadienne-française, et c'est à cette heure que s'élaborèrent, sous l'aiguillon de l'orgueil blessé, quelques-unes de nos meilleures œuvres intellectuelles' (Historiens de chez nous, p. 159). He urged his compatriots to bequeath to their descendants something of permanent value. If ever America lay in ruins and the Canadiens as a people were extinguished, 'nous voulons que de ces ruines mêmes surgisse encore la flamme de notre race' (Pour conserver notre héritage français, p. 151).

Although much wider in his sympathies than many Québecois, Roy distrusted certain tendencies in literature both in Europe and in America. He had no liking for the French romantics, and he considered the 'symbolist' school a non-French obscuration. But he did not therefore exaggerate the achievements of his compatriots. If he considered Nord–Sud the best native novel of the century, he would point out that it has not the art of Maria Chapdelaine, an objective novel by a Frenchman which had not been very cordially received by the French Canadians, and he thought that some native writers were too much preoccupied with the religious life of the Canadiens, and gave too little heed to their culture and their economic and social life. His praise of Pamphile LeMay as the equal of the French writers of sonnets showed his independence of thought no less than the qualified approval which he gave to L. H. Fréchette [q.v.]. If critics in Canada and abroad acclaimed the latter as a poetic genius, Roy, although considering him perhaps the best of the Canadian poets, regarded him as too much the orator, the imitator of Victor Hugo.

Among Roy's most important books are Essais sur la littérature canadienne (1907), Nos origines littéraires (1909), Manuel d'histoire de la littérature canadienne-française (1918), La critique littéraire au dix-neuvième siècle de Mme de Staël à Émile Faguet (1918), A l'ombre des érables (1924), and Études et croquis (1928). Although he had his detractors, Roy's more intelligent compatriots were proud of him for bringing Canadian literature to the notice of the world. He had what Matthew Arnold called the influence of an academy, and this was recognized both in Canada and in France. His style is terse and limpid; his sketches of nature and of scenes in Quebec are delightful. A rippling humour and deep humanism ran through his writings and in controversy kept him free from pettiness and intolerance, so that even on the things which he most disliked, professional sport and trashy newspapers, he never expended more than an urbane irony.

Roy had a full life, preaching, speaking on formal occasions, and lecturing to French audiences in many parts of Canada and the United States. In 1933 he made a tour of the principal universities of France, giving courses of lectures on French-Canadian literature. He received from the French Academy its gold medal in French literature in 1925, and honorary degrees from Ottawa and Toronto in 1927. He was elected a fellow of the Royal Society of Canada in 1904, and was president for 1928–9. He was appointed chevalier of the French Legion of Honour in 1925 and promoted officer in 1928. He died at Quebec 24 June 1943. A portrait of Roy, painted by G. Szoldatics in 1927, belongs to Laval University.

[*Proceedings* of the Royal Society of Canada, 1944; Frère Ludovic, *Bio-bibliographie* down to 1940, Quebec, 1941; *Queen's Quarterly*, Autumn 1928; *Revue canadienne*, July 1918; personal knowledge.]

CARLETON STANLEY.

ROYDEN, SIR THOMAS, second baronet, and BARON ROYDEN (1871–1950), shipowner, was born 22 May 1871, at Mossley Hill, Liverpool, the eldest son of (Sir) Thomas Bland Royden, later first baronet, by his wife, Alice Elizabeth, daughter of Thomas Dowdall, stockbroker, of Liverpool. His grandfather, Thomas Royden, began shipbuilding on the Mersey in 1820 and his father was the founder of the Indra Line of steamers.

He was educated at Winchester and Magdalen College, Oxford, where he was placed in the second class in classical honour moderations in 1892 and graduated in 1893. He began his business career at Liverpool in 1895 in his father's firm, Thomas Royden & Sons, shipowners, of which he became head when he succeeded his father as second baronet in 1917. His abilities and qualities of leadership brought him responsibility in a variety of commercial concerns. He was a director of many companies, among them the Anchor Line, Thos. and Jno. Brocklebank, Ltd., the Commonwealth and Dominion (which subsequently became the Port) Line, the Midland Bank, the Shell Transport and Trading Company, the Suez Canal Company, the Phoenix Assurance Company, and the Union Marine and General Insurance Company, and in 1941 he succeeded Lord Stamp [q.v.] as chairman of the London, Midland, and Scottish Railway. He was also chairman of Edmundsons' Electricity Corporation and the Imperial Continental Gas Association.

Royden became a director of the Cunard Steam-Ship Company in 1905 and of Cunard White Star, Ltd., on its inception in 1934, and he remained on the boards of both companies until his death. During his long connexion with the Cunard Line he served as deputy chairman from 1909 until 1922, and was chairman from 1922 until 1930. As chairman he successfully directed the company's affairs during a period of particular difficulty, and it was during this period that the project was formulated of building two liners of sufficient size and speed to maintain the Southampton to New York service in place of the three ships then required.

During the war of 1914–18 his extensive knowledge of shipping enabled him to render distinguished service to his country. In 1913 he shared in the preparation of a confidential plan for the transport of British troops and munitions across the Channel, a plan which was brought into operation on the outbreak of war in August 1914. He also served as chairman of the Admiralty transport advisory committee, as a member of the shipping control committee, and as a member of the Royal Commission on wheat supplies. When the United States entered the war in 1917, he visited that country to take part in arranging the transport of troops and war materials to Europe.

At the Paris peace conference in 1919 Royden represented the shipping controller, and in the same year was appointed C.H. for his public services. In 1944 he was created a baron. Recognition of his work for the Allies came also from the French Government, by whom he was made a commander of the Legion of Honour, and from the Government of Italy, who conferred on him the Order of St. Maurice and St. Lazarus. He also received the Afghan order, the Star of Afghaur.

Despite the heavy responsibilities of his commercial appointments, Royden found time and energy for many other activities. Among his public duties he was high sheriff of Cheshire in 1917, and was also deputy-lieutenant for the county, as well as a justice of the peace. From 1918 until 1922 he sat as Conservative member for Bootle, but he retired from politics soon after his appointment as chairman of the Cunard Steam-Ship Company. He was at one time president of the Chamber of Shipping of the United Kingdom, and chairman of the Liverpool Steamship Owners' Association, and from 1923 was a freeman of the Worshipful Company of Shipwrights. His lifelong interest in the sea and ships found additional expression in his work as secretary and treasurer of the training-ship *Indefatigable*, while his interest in Liverpool was reflected in the work he did for the David Lewis Northern Hospital, the Mersey Mission to Seamen, the Liverpool Shipbrokers' Benevolent Society, and the executive committee of Liverpool Cathedral. In 1940 he was made a fellow of Winchester College.

Royden travelled extensively in the United States and in the Far East, and throughout his life retained a great interest in sport. In his younger days he was a well-known rider to hounds, a polo player, a yachtsman, an oarsman, and as a point-to-point rider gained many victories; he was also a keen shot.

Royden died at his home at Alresford, Hampshire, 6 November 1950. In 1922 he married Quenelda Mary, widow of Charles James Williamson, of Liverpool, who gave Camp Hill to that city, and daughter of Harry Clegg, J.P., D.L., of Plas Llanfair, Anglesey. There were no children of the marriage and in consequence the barony lapsed upon Royden's death; his brother, Ernest Bland (born 1873), succeeded to the baronetcy.

A portrait of Royden by (Sir) Oswald Birley hangs in the board-room of the Cunard Steam-Ship Company in Cunard Building, Liverpool.

[Personal knowledge.]

FREDERIC A. BATES.

RUMBOLD, SIR HORACE GEORGE MONTAGU, ninth baronet (1869–1941), diplomatist, the eldest son of (Sir) Horace Rumbold, who became eighth baronet [q.v.], by his first wife, Caroline Barney, daughter of George Harrington, United States minister at Berne, was born 5 February 1869 at St. Petersburg, where his father was secretary of embassy.

Rumbold was educated at Eton, and in 1888 was appointed an honorary attaché in the diplomatic service, being posted to The Hague, where his father was then serving as minister. In February 1891 he passed a competitive examination for the diplomatic service, passing first of the three successful candidates out of an entry of thirteen. After a year at the Foreign Office he went to Cairo early in 1892 and became a third secretary in the following year. In 1895 he was transferred at his own request to Teheran, and

after promotion to second secretary in 1896 was posted in the following year to Vienna, where his father was then ambassador. On his father's retirement in 1900 Rumbold joined the staff of Lord Cromer [q.v.] in Cairo, where he remained for seven years, receiving promotion to first secretary in 1904. In 1907 he went to Madrid and in 1909, on promotion to counsellor of embassy, to Tokyo, where he served until 1913, when he was posted to the Berlin embassy. In the same year his father died and he succeeded to the baronetcy.

Rumbold had served under Sir (William) Edward Goschen at the Berlin embassy for less than nine months when war broke out in August 1914. He had been in charge of the embassy in July during Goschen's absence on leave. After two years at the Foreign Office, he went in 1916 as minister to Berne, where he 'acquired that reputation for sagacity which marked him out as one of the most discerning diplomatists of his age'. He was appointed K.C.M.G. in 1917. After the armistice he was sent in 1919 as the first British minister to the newly liberated Poland, and a year later, during the difficult negotiations with Turkey after the abortive Treaty of Sèvres, he was transferred to the still more arduous post of high commissioner and ambassador at Constantinople. This was perhaps the most exacting post of his whole career, for divided counsels among the Allies and intransigence on the part of the Turks culminated in the Chanak crisis of 1922. Rumbold served as deputy to Lord Curzon [q.v.] during the first Lausanne conference (November 1922 to February 1923) and acted as chief British delegate at the second Lausanne conference, finally signing the peace treaty with Turkey on 24 July 1923. It was a tribute to his tireless patience and masterly diplomatic skill. He was sworn of the Privy Council in 1921 and promoted G.C.M.G. in 1923.

In 1924 Rumbold went for four years to the less onerous post of the embassy in Madrid, and in the summer of 1928 was transferred to Berlin. He held that responsible post for five momentous years, during which Hitler rose from insignificance to be chancellor of the Reich. Rumbold was not an alarmist, but he was never in any doubt about the danger which Hitler represented. He had the gift of seeing facts and trends in their true perspective, and his dispatches from

Berlin fully bear this out in their clear and logical appraisement of the situation. But his warnings were not heeded. He retired from the diplomatic service in August 1933 and was appointed G.C.B. in 1934. In 1936 he went to Palestine as vice-chairman of the Royal Commission under Lord Peel [q.v.] on the rival Arab and Jewish claims to that country.

After the outbreak of war in 1939 Rumbold served in the Ministry of Economic Warfare until shortly before his death at Pythouse, Tisbury, Wiltshire, 24 May 1941. At this time he wrote a book, *The War Crisis in Berlin, July–August 1914* (1940), ably describing the events of which he had been an eye-witness during his first tour of duty at the Berlin embassy.

Rumbold married in 1905 Etheldred Constantia, younger daughter of the late Sir E. D. V. Fane [q.v.] of the diplomatic service. They had a son and two daughters, of whom the younger died in childhood. He was succeeded by his son, (Horace) Anthony (Claude) (born 1911), who followed his father and grandfather as a member of the diplomatic service. A portrait of Rumbold by P. A. de László (1926) is in the possession of the family.

[Sir Horace Rumbold, *The War Crisis in Berlin, July–August 1914*, second edition, 1944, with an introduction by Harold Nicolson; private information; personal knowledge.]      JAMES MARSHALL-CORNWALL.

RUNCIMAN, WALTER, first VISCOUNT RUNCIMAN OF DOXFORD (1870–1949), statesman, was born at South Shields 19 November 1870, the only child of Walter (later Baron) Runciman [q.v.]. He was educated at South Shields High School, privately, and at Trinity College, Cambridge, where he was placed in the third class of the history tripos in 1892. He then entered his father's shipping business and soon turned to politics, contesting Gravesend unsuccessfully as Liberal candidate in 1898. The next year he entered the House as Liberal member for Oldham defeating (Sir) Winston Churchill at the poll, but losing the seat to him in 1900. Runciman re-entered the House of Commons through a by-election in 1902 as member for Dewsbury and soon attracted the attention of the Liberal front bench by his forthright speeches—especially on financial and fiscal matters—which at once marked him as a rising force. In 1905 he was appointed parliamentary secretary to the Local Govern-

ment Board. Two years later he was promoted to the position of financial secretary to the Treasury, a stepping-stone to Cabinet rank.

When Asquith became prime minister in 1908 he singled out Runciman for the onerous post of president of the Board of Education which until then the Liberals had been notably unsuccessful in filling. Although he was a strong Methodist by heredity, and his religious opinions, like his views on temperance, were held with conviction, Runciman won the confidence of Church leaders, in particular Randall Davidson, the archbishop of Canterbury [q.v.]. When his education bill, which many held to be the best of the four which the Liberals unsuccessfully introduced, was withdrawn, the prime minister, in a vigorous protest, paid a special tribute to Runciman's 'patient, considerate and indomitable efforts'. Three years later, in a Cabinet reshuffle, Runciman was appointed president of the Board of Agriculture and Fisheries, where, although the choice appeared at first to many inappropriate, the modesty and sound business sense with which he handled agricultural affairs soon won him praise even from his political opponents.

In 1914, on the resignation of John Burns [q.v.], Runciman succeeded him as president of the Board of Trade where he became responsible for the unprecedented and arduous organization of shipping in war conditions. It was an admirable choice. Runciman rendered conspicuous service to the State as a master of both the strategy and the tactics of economic warfare and, in particular, by rescuing the shipping industry from the ruin with which it seemed threatened. Lord Grey of Fallodon [q.v.] was later to draw special attention to Runciman's work at the Board of Trade in the first two years of war, not only because it was 'efficient and valuable; but because it has received so little recognition'. After his resignation with Asquith in 1916 Runciman devoted himself to commerce. Like most of his Liberal colleagues he lost his seat in 1918, but he returned to the House in 1924 as member for Swansea West which he represented until 1929 when he transferred to St. Ives. From 1931 to 1937 he sat for that constituency as a Liberal National and again held office as president of the Board of Trade. He remained in the ministry when other Liberals withdrew, for unlike them he was a supporter of the Ottawa agreements. When

Chamberlain formed his Government on Baldwin's resignation in 1937, Runciman retired and accepted a peerage as Viscount Runciman of Doxford. On his father's death, two months later, the barony of Shoreston became merged in the viscountcy.

In July 1938 Runciman was invited by the foreign secretary, Lord Halifax, to go to Prague as 'independent mediator' between the Czechoslovak Government and the Sudeten German party. All that he and his small staff could 'hope for in the end', he reported on his arrival, was 'a little accommodation on some practical problems'. It was not forthcoming, despite his patience and the personal relationships which he established with both sides. Various concessions were reluctantly offered by the Czechoslovak Government at his instigation but these led only to increased demands and the artificial creation of 'outrages' by the Germans. Hitler's violent speech attacking the Czechs at Nuremberg, 12 September, ended all attempts at mediation and Runciman, who had confessed in a letter to Lord Halifax as early as 18 August that 'if by a miracle an agreement was reached, I would be astonished', returned home on 16 September, a tired man. Nevertheless, a month later he became lord president of the Council, but he failed to recover his spirits or his health, and resigned immediately after war was declared, feeling his strength no longer equal to the demands of office in such times. A long illness followed and he died at Doxford 13 November 1949.

Runciman had a remarkable capacity for understanding and marshalling economic facts which brought him great respect in the City where they particularly valued his long chairmanship (1920–31) of the United Kingdom Provident Institution. He was, however, always conscious of the claims of public service. The Liberal confusions and discords were, in the upshot, to deny him the highest political positions for which his promising start seemed to have marked him out. He never became chancellor of the Exchequer, an office for which, by 1914, many expected (and he himself perhaps hoped) that he would at length be chosen.

If Runciman lacked the popular appeal of a Lloyd George, he shared to a high degree with Asquith, his own leader, the art of expounding a complicated case in language which all could understand. His austerely handsome appearance and gifts of exposition obscured from sufficient public notice a capacity for fine and moving speech, but could not rob him of a reputation for integrity which was universally recognized. His rare personal charm was revealed only to his friends who knew him as a lively and delightful companion, with a zest for country pursuits and anything to do with the sea, who could talk or sing in perfect 'Northumbrian' or organize a midnight raid to the island of Milos, with an enthusiasm and geniality which his apparently cold manner would not have led the public to suspect in him. The arts, especially music, were his abiding pleasure and consolation. By the turn of politics, his very considerable ability, especially in administration, was never allowed sufficient opportunity. Not given his full chance, he was not given his full due.

Runciman received the honorary degrees of D.C.L. from the university of Oxford in 1934 and LL.D. from the universities of Manchester (1911) and Bristol (1929).

He married in 1898 Hilda (died 1956), daughter of James Cochran Stevenson, for a time member of Parliament for South Shields. Her election for St. Ives early in 1928 provided the first example of husband and wife sitting together in the House of Commons. They had two sons and three daughters, the elder son, Walter Leslie (born 1900), succeeding him in his titles. The younger son, Sir Steven Runciman, contributes to this SUPPLEMENT.

A portrait of Runciman by R. G. Eves hangs in the council-room of the Chamber of Shipping.

[*The Times*, 15 November 1949; Viscount Grey of Fallodon, *Twenty-Five Years*, vol. ii, 1925; Viscount Samuel, *Memoirs*, 1945; *Documents on British Foreign Policy 1919–1939*, third series, vol. ii, edited by E. L. Woodward and R. Butler, 1949; private information; personal knowledge.]

ARCHIBALD HURD.

RUSHBROOKE, JAMES HENRY (1870–1947), Baptist divine, was born in Bethnal Green 29 July 1870. He was the eldest child of James Rushbrooke, a railway worker, by his wife, Sarah. When the boy was two-and-a-half years old his father was transferred to Thorpe-le-Soken, Essex. Rushbrooke was fortunate that the village schoolmaster was a man of insight who, in spite of restricted opportunities, ably helped his promising pupil. At the age of fifteen Rushbrooke was sent to London into lodgings and became a clerk to the Willesden local authority. Introduced by an aunt to the Westbourne Park Baptist church, he passed under the spell of Dr. John Clifford (whose notice he later contributed to this DICTIONARY), then at the height of his power as a preacher and leader of militant nonconformity. The death in 1892, after only eleven months' married life, of his wife, Kate, daughter of James Partridge, of Thorpe-le-Soken, a deeply religious woman, and of their infant son, proved the turning-point in Rushbrooke's life. Clifford, who had already discerned his gifts, encouraged him to enter the Midland Baptist College to train for the Christian ministry. So successful did Rushbrooke prove as a student that without difficulty he secured the London M.A. degree and was given opportunity for further study abroad. In Berlin he attended Harnack's lectures.

On returning to England he became pastor first of the St. Mary's Gate Baptist church, Derby (1901–7), then of a church in Highgate (1907–10) and, in 1910, of the new Free Church in the Hampstead Garden Suburb. His marriage in 1902 to Dorothea Gertrud, daughter of Professor Anton Weber, a German portrait-painter, led to the maintenance of close links with the continent, and Rushbrooke threw himself with energy into the movements for peace. He became a member of the executive of the British section of the World Alliance for Promoting International Friendship through the Churches and was the first editor (1915–20) of its journal *Goodwill*. The contacts he thus made were of great assistance in his later work. He was on the continent when war broke out in 1914, and was for a time under arrest in Germany. At the close of the war Baptists turned to Rushbrooke to direct relief operations on the continent. He became Baptist commissioner for Europe, then eastern secretary of the Baptist World Alliance (1925–8), subsequently its general secretary (1928–39), finally, from 1939 until his death, its president. The growth of the Alliance was largely due to his statesmanlike qualities, his linguistic gifts, and the extensive journeyings which occupied the closing decades of his life. He travelled ceaselessly in Europe, paying several visits to Russia in the 'twenties, was frequently in North America and also visited South America, Asia, and Australasia, winning the confidence and regard of Baptists in every part of the world and becoming widely known as a vigilant and deter-

mined champion of religious liberty. He was president of the Baptist Union of Great Britain and Ireland in 1926, and of the National Free Church Council in 1934; and he received the honorary degrees of D.D. from McMaster University, Ontario (1921), and D.C.L. from Acadia University, Nova Scotia (1939). The war of 1939–45 caused him deep distress and his efforts on its conclusion to re-establish relations with Christians on the continent hastened his death which took place suddenly in Bristol 1 February 1947.

Rushbrooke had a keen and well-stored mind, and an unusual capacity for friendship with men and women of all classes and races. He served tirelessly the causes he had at heart. His wife, by whom he had one daughter, died in 1944. A portrait of Rushbrooke by L. D. M. Purser hangs in the Elders' Vestry of the Hampstead Garden Suburb Free Church.

[*The Times*, 3 February 1947; E. A. Payne, *James Henry Rushbrooke*, 1954; private information; personal knowledge.]

E. A. PAYNE.

RUSHCLIFFE, BARON (1872–1949), politician. [See BETTERTON, HENRY BUCKNALL.]

RUSSELL, FRANCIS XAVIER JOSEPH (FRANK), BARON RUSSELL OF KILLOWEN (1867–1946), judge, was born in London 2 July 1867, the fourth son of Charles Russell, afterwards Baron Russell of Killowen [q.v.], lord chief justice of England. At Beaumont College, where he was educated before proceeding to Oriel College, Oxford, Russell had as master of rhetoric an eminent scholar, Father Herbert Thurston, S.J., who became a lifelong friend. A brilliant speech in favour of Home Rule in the Oxford Union in 1887 impelled A. V. Dicey [q.v.], notwithstanding his disapproval of the proposed reform, to write a letter of congratulation to Russell's father who had lately been attorney-general in Gladstone's Government. In 1890 Russell's was one of three names listed in the first class in jurisprudence. In 1893 he was called to the bar by Lincoln's Inn and read in chambers with Henry Casson and (Sir) M. Ingle Joyce [q.v.]. As a junior counsel on the Chancery side he had an immediate success, due in some measure to family connexions, his elder brother (Sir) Charles Russell [q.v.] being already a partner in an eminent firm of solicitors who introduced him to practice in Privy Council cases.

In 1908 Russell took silk and attached himself to the court of Sir Charles Swinfen Eady (later Lord Swinfen, q.v.), on whose promotion he took his seat before Sir J. M. Astbury [q.v.]. In 1918 he joined the select band of Chancery 'specials' who were attached to no court, but went into all alike on payment of a special fee. In 1919, in the famous case of *Bourne* v. *Keane*, he appeared for the appellant in the House of Lords, and succeeded in persuading their lordships (Lord Birkenhead [q.v.] presiding) 'to take the greatest liberty the House of Lords has ever taken with established legal principles' and to declare that a bequest for Masses for the dead is a valid charitable bequest, and no longer void as a gift to superstitious uses.

Birkenhead offered the successful advocate the next vacancy on the bench, and in 1919 Russell, declining a knighthood, took his seat as a Chancery judge. By common accord he was a first-rate judge, patient, attentive, shrewd, courteous, and fair. In 1928 he was appointed to the Court of Appeal, and sworn of the Privy Council. In the next year he succeeded Lord Carson [q.v.] as a lord of appeal in ordinary, with a life peerage, taking the title of Baron Russell of Killowen. In the House of Lords and in the Privy Council, as in the Court of Appeal, he was as nearly as may be a perfect judge. His judgements are models of concise and lucid English. 'No judge in recent times had in a higher degree the art of saying in terse and clear language just what he meant and no more', wrote Lord Simonds. His dissenting judgements (which were rare) showed all his power and force of thought and character, as in *Banco de Portugal* v. *Waterlow & Sons, Ltd.*, [1932] A.C. 452, where his judgement, similar in view to that of Sir T. E. Scrutton [q.v.] in the Court of Appeal, was regarded in the City of London as superlative common sense; and in *Fender* v. *Mildmay*, [1938] A.C. at p. 34, where he reminded Lords and Commons that 'What was once a holy estate enduring for the joint lives of the spouses, is steadily assuming the characteristics of a contract for a tenancy at will.'

Always a loyal Irishman, Russell was aware that authority in England would have accepted him as arbitrator in the dispute with the Irish Free State concerning land annuities in the early 'thirties. He was a Catholic of great simplicity and strength of soul and the chapel in his home at Tadworth was a regular Mass centre for his family and all the neighbourhood. He was for many years president of the Beaumont Union and of the Thomas More Society from its inception in 1928 until 1946. In 1928 he was elected an honorary fellow of Oriel College.

As a lord of appeal Russell hesitated to join in political debates, but on the third reading of the matrimonial causes bill, 1937, he spoke strongly against the extension of grounds for divorce. He took a public part also in the Catholic opposition to the education bill of 1944. As a rule, however, he avoided publicity, and liked in the vacation to go on a long cruise with his family. At the Garrick Club, where he was for years chairman of trustees, he spoke on festive occasions with exquisite felicity and humour. The club possesses an excellent portrait of him by R. G. Eves.

At the beginning of 1946 Russell retired. On medical advice he gave up the golf he loved to play at Walton Heath, adjoining his home. On 20 December 1946 he died at Tadworth and was buried at Epsom. In 1900 Russell married Mary Emily (died 1956), fifth daughter of C. T. Ritchie, later Baron Ritchie of Dundee [q.v.]. They had one son and three daughters, one of whom died in infancy.

[*The Times*, 23 December 1946; *Law Times*, 4 January 1947; *Beaumont Review*, July 1947; private information; personal knowledge.]

RICHARD O'SULLIVAN.

RUSSELL, MARY ANNETTE, COUNTESS RUSSELL (1866–1941), writer, usually known as ELIZABETH, was born 31 August 1866 in Sydney, Australia, the daughter of Henry Herron Beauchamp and his wife, Elizabeth Weiss Lassetter. Her father was a member of a family which had left England to penetrate beyond the then recognized frontiers of Australia and New Zealand. His brother, Arthur, making his home in the latter country, was to become the grandfather of the writer known as Katherine Mansfield (Kathleen Murry, q.v.). Mary Beauchamp was twice married: first, in 1891 to Count Henning August von Arnim, a wealthy Prussian landowner, fifteen years her senior, whom she met while travelling in Italy. Count von Arnim died in 1910, and in 1916 his widow married, as his third wife, John Francis

Stanley, second Earl Russell. The marriage was not a success and in 1919 they separated.

The Count and Countess von Arnim had spent the greater part of their married life on the von Arnim estate which was situated at Nassenheide in Pomerania, not far from the Baltic shore. The estate, with its surroundings, and no less the owners and their three eldest daughters, presently became well known to English readers through the medium of her books of which the first, published in 1898, was *Elizabeth and her German Garden*. The feeling for the wild forest country around Nassenheide may well owe something to the author's pioneer forebears. The tale of the garden has charm for all horticulturists. The treatment of persons, not excluding the Count in his character as the Man of Wrath, is marked by brilliance and intense vivacity, salted with an impish wit which is always lively but can approach malice. In real life (Sir) Hugh Walpole [q.v.], coming to Nassenheide in 1907 as tutor to the two eldest daughters, suffered thus considerably at the hands of the Countess. He ended in later years by becoming not only her admirer but her friend. By then she had taken up her residence in England. She also acquired a chalet in Switzerland in the valley of the Rhône, known as the Chalet du Soleil. There and in England she became the centre of a circle into which many of the literary figures of the day were irresistibly drawn. The numerous allusions to her in contemporary memoirs emphasize her remarkable personality. Alice Meynell [q.v.] described her as one of the finest wits of her day. To Katherine Mansfield she was ever the 'dearest cousin'. Even the victims of her shafts usually found they could not keep away from her. She continued as an author. Before she left Pomerania she had already turned to the novel proper in *Princess Priscilla's Fortnight* (1905). Her later novels, including *Vera* (1921) and *Father* (1931), as well as the conversation piece *In the Mountains* (1920), which has the Swiss chalet for its background, are sombre in tone, reflecting the shadow of the war of 1914–18. Only in *The Enchanted April* (1922) did the Countess recapture something of the translucent quality, the gaiety, and the wit which had charmed readers of the books which told the story of the German garden and the Baltic shore. It is by these perhaps, reflecting as they do her own personality,

that she will be best remembered as an author.

There were four daughters and one son of her first marriage. She had no children by her second husband. She died 9 February 1941 at Charleston, South Carolina.

[*The Times*, 11 February 1941; *Annual Register*, 1941; private information.]

GLADYS SCOTT THOMSON.

[Leslie de Charms, *Elizabeth of the German Garden*, 1958.]

RUSSELL, SIR WALTER WESTLEY (1867–1949), painter and teacher, was born 31 May 1867 at Forest Gate, Essex, the son of William Henry Russell, a bookbinder, and his wife, Charlotte Emily Bradley. In his early twenties he studied painting at the Westminster School of Art under Frederick Brown [q.v.], from whom he gained, like Henry Tonks [q.v.] and other promising students of the period, a sound training in drawing and painting. Under Brown's guidance Russell was naturally led to the New English Art Club and the movement in British art which was influenced by the discoveries of the French Impressionists and was in revolt against the Royal Academy and Victorian prejudice.

Russell's early work consisted in illustrations and etchings reminiscent of the work of the illustrators of the 1860's and in portraits and interiors which he exhibited at the New English Art Club, of which he became a member in 1895. In the same year he joined the staff of the Slade School of Fine Art under Brown, who had been appointed Slade professor in 1893. With Tonks and P. Wilson Steer [q.v.] he became one of a team whose teaching had much influence on British painting at that time. He taught at the Slade School until 1927, apart from a period of war service (1916–19) when as a lieutenant in the Royal Engineers he was connected with camouflage work. He was mentioned in dispatches.

Russell first exhibited at the Royal Academy in 1898. In 1920 he was elected an associate, in 1926 a full member, and in 1927 he was elected keeper of the Royal Academy. Under the president and council he now became responsible for the Schools, at a time of important change in the teaching organization. This was the abolition of the visitor system, whereby members and associates taught on rota for two or three months at a time, and the substitution for it of a permanent teaching staff. Russell in his quiet way was no doubt instrumental in bringing this about, hoping thus to gain greater continuity in teaching and to carry on those principles of teaching learnt from Brown and developed so successfully at the Slade School. This is in fact what he was able to do, adding his individual contribution of sound, if somewhat laconic, criticism, which, together with the integrity of his own life and art, had a definite influence on his students. He retired from the keepership in 1942, on becoming a senior academician.

Meanwhile, working in his studio at 107 Cheyne Walk, Chelsea, he was steadily producing portraits, interiors, and landscapes. Among the earlier paintings 'Donkeys and Kites' (c. 1912), now in the Tate Gallery, was perhaps one of the most important landscapes. In 1926 he painted a series of Venetian scenes, evidently the prelude to an increasing interest in the effect of light on atmosphere. Among his earlier portraits 'Mr. Minney' (c. 1920, Tate Gallery) is outstanding, although not typical, for in it he came nearer than usual to a striking effect. In later years he was usually represented in the first room of the Royal Academy's summer exhibition by small paintings of female figures and portraits in domestic settings, such as 'The Amber Beads' in 1926 and 'Cordelia' in 1930, both of which are in the Tate Gallery. He also did many landscapes and seascapes in oil and water-colour, often painted at Blakeney, which he visited in the summer with Sir William Llewellyn [q.v.], then president of the Academy, and at Shoreham. These paintings are mostly very light in tone, the oils somewhat resembling water-colours, and reminiscent of Steer. Many of his best water-colours were shown at the exhibitions of the Royal Society of Painters in Water Colours of which he was made a member in 1930.

At first Russell was on the edge of, rather than inside, the circle which included George Moore, D. S. MacColl, J. S. Sargent, Henry Tonks, P. Wilson Steer [qq.v.], and Sir Augustus Daniel. Although Tonks and Steer remained his close friends throughout, latterly his ties with the Academy strengthened, and thus he became a link between it and those forces which had been so violently opposed to it. His position as keeper enabled him to observe and at times to influence the Academy's policy through the administration of succeeding councils,

and he was greatly respected by members for his sound judgement and quietly expressed good sense. He never went out of his way to create an impression, although he frequently succeeded in doing so with few words often humorous and always nicely timed.

In 1900 Russell married Lydia (died 1944), daughter of William Nelson Burton, of Wooburn Green, Buckinghamshire; there were no children. He was appointed a trustee of the National Gallery in 1927 and of the Tate Gallery in 1934; in 1931 he was appointed C.V.O. and in 1935 he was knighted. Five of his pictures in the Tate Gallery were purchased out of the Chantrey bequest, and he is represented in most of the important galleries in this country and in the Commonwealth. He died in London 16 April 1949. A water-colour drawing by Ambrose McEvoy is in the possession of the Royal Academy.

[*The Times*, 22 April 1949; Records of the Royal Academy of Arts; personal knowledge.]　　　W. T. MONNINGTON.

RYDER, CHARLES HENRY DUDLEY (1868-1945), geographer, was born at St. Servan, Brittany, 28 June 1868, the seventh son of Lieutenant-Colonel Spencer Charles Dudley Ryder by his wife, Julia, daughter of the Rev. William Money, chaplain at St. Servan. He was grandson of Henry Ryder, bishop of Lichfield and Coventry, and great-grandson of Nathaniel Ryder, first Baron Harrowby [qq.v.]. From Cheltenham College he was gazetted in 1886 to the Royal Engineers and in 1891 was appointed to the Survey of India as an assistant superintendent. In 1898-1900, now a captain, he was surveying with Henry Rodolph Davies in the Yunnan province of China, providing the first accurate maps of that region. Reaching Shanghai in July 1900 by descending the Yangtze he was in time to take part in the relief of Peking, and was mentioned in dispatches.

In the autumn of 1903 Ryder, who had returned to India, joined (Sir) Francis Younghusband [q.v.] across the frontier in Tibet and took charge of the surveying party which accompanied his force to Lhasa. For his services he was mentioned in dispatches and appointed to the D.S.O. On the suggestion of (Sir) Louis Dane [q.v.] Younghusband obtained the consent of the Tibetan Government to an expedition, under C. G. Rawling [q.v.] with

Ryder in charge of surveying, westwards from Gyantse to Gartok, which no European had ever visited and was now to be opened as a trade mart, and thence to India. It was a remarkable journey to undertake on the verge of winter in a country with which fighting had only just ceased. The small and practically unescorted party of some thirty people set out in October 1904 and travelled without hindrance over a thousand miles in Tibet. Ryder and his assistants surveyed about 40,000 square miles before Simla was reached in January 1905. They mapped the Tsangpo (Brahmaputra) from Shigatse to its source; established that no peaks rivalling Mount Everest exist in its vicinity; surveyed Lake Mansarowar and its neighbourhood and the Gartok branch of the Indus with adjoining territory; and completed the survey of the Sutlej from its source to the Indian frontier. Ryder received the Patron's medal of the Royal Geographical Society, the silver medal of the Royal Scottish Geographical Society, and the gold medal of the Paris Geographical Society. He was gazetted major in 1905, and from 1906 to 1913 was in charge of the re-survey of the North-West Frontier from Baluchistan to Chitral.

From December 1913 to October 1914 Ryder was in charge of the survey party of the British delegation under (Sir) Arnold Wilson [q.v.] on the Turco-Persian boundary commission. Most of the technical work fell to Ryder and his assistants. The commission demarcated the 1,180 miles of the frontier from the Persian Gulf to Mount Ararat; 227 boundary pillars were set up and new surveys were made of practically all the country concerned, resulting in thirty-five map sheets. The physical difficulties of the task were accentuated by political tension after the outbreak of war.

In 1916 Ryder was appointed a superintendent of the Survey of India and was in charge of the map publication office in Calcutta. In 1918–19, with the rank of colonel, he was deputy director of surveys in the Mesopotamia Expeditionary Force and was mentioned in dispatches. In 1919 he became surveyor-general of India and in 1924 he retired. He was appointed C.I.E. in 1915 and C.B. in 1922.

Ryder married in 1892 Ida Josephine, daughter of Lieutenant-Colonel Edward Evans Grigg, Indian Staff Corps, of Stevenage, Hertfordshire; they had three sons and three daughters. One son was killed in action in 1940; another, Commander (afterwards Captain) Robert Edward Dudley Ryder, R.N., became a polar explorer; he commanded the naval forces in the attack on St. Nazaire in March 1942, winning the Victoria Cross. Ryder died at Aldwick Bay, Bognor Regis, 13 July 1945.

[*The Times*, 16 July 1945; *Empire Survey Review*, vol. viii, 1945–6; *Geographical Journal*, vol. xxi, 1903, vol. xxvi, 1905, vol. lxvi, 1925; C. G. Rawling, *The Great Plateau*, 1905; H. R. Davies, *Yün-nan*, 1909; private information.]    R. N. RUDMOSE BROWN.

RYLE, JOHN ALFRED (1889–1950), physician, was born at Barnet 12 December 1889, the eldest son of Reginald John Ryle, medical practitioner, who later removed to Brighton, and his wife, Catherine Scott. He was a grandson of J. C. Ryle, bishop of Liverpool, and nephew of H. E. Ryle [qq.v.]. His younger brother, Gilbert, became Waynflete professor of metaphysical philosophy in the university of Oxford. Ryle was educated at Brighton College and Guy's Hospital, and almost immediately upon completing his training joined the Royal Army Medical Corps in the war of 1914–18, spending four years in France and Belgium. In 1919 he returned to Guy's as medical registrar, obtaining in that year his M.R.C.P. (London) and London M.D. with gold medal. In 1920 he became assistant physician and in 1924 was elected F.R.C.P. He achieved a high reputation at Guy's as clinical teacher and consulting physician. His main interest was in gastro-intestinal illness and he was responsible for the standardization of the fractional test meal and the invention of the tube which bears his name. Tall, fair, and handsome, he was popular alike with patients and students.

Fame and distinction in the clinical field, however, were not enough to satisfy Ryle who had for long been concerned with the social aspects of medicine. His life and thought were governed by a deep love of humanity. A rationalist like his father, his strong convictions on the nature of human rights (expressed in his *Fears may be Liars*, 1941) shone through all that he did. But for the war of 1914–18 he might have sought to fulfil what he felt to be his mission by working as a family doctor among the poor of the Borough. As it was, he changed his course to become in 1935 regius professor of physic at Cambridge and in 1936 a fellow of Gonville and Caius College. In the short time that remained before the outbreak of war he developed a strong research team, but he was not altogether happy, for college life did not appeal to him, and his views were becoming increasingly Socialist and pacifist.

When the war put an end to his activities by the dispersal of his colleagues, he joined the Emergency Medical Service with his headquarters in the Borough, first in a workman's flat, then when this was destroyed, in Guy's Hospital. He worked with unflagging zeal in organizing precautions against air attack and in the reception and sorting of casualties, and travelled widely as a consultant adviser for the Service. In 1943 he became professor of social medicine and director of the Institute at Oxford when it was created by the benefaction of Lord Nuffield. For the next six years he sought by research to enlarge the range of knowledge of social pathology and by his writing and teaching he did much to guide British medicine into these new fields in which so much of his heart had always lain. The change from clinical medicine was now complete and he had taken the difficult road of the pioneer. As he himself wrote in *Changing Disciplines* (1948):

'Thirty years of my life have been spent as a student and teacher of clinical medicine. In these thirty years I have watched disease in the ward being studied more and more thoroughly—if not always more thoughtfully—through the high power of the microscope; disease in man being investigated by more and more elaborate techniques and, on the whole, more and more mechanically. . . . The morbid "material" of the hospital ward consists very largely—if we exclude emergencies—of end-result conditions for which, as a rule, only a limited amount of relief repays the long stay, the patient investigation, and the anxious expectancy of the sick man or woman. With aetiology—the first essential for prevention—and with prevention itself the majority of physicians and surgeons have curiously little concern.'

Among Ryle's many contributions to medical literature were 135 published papers, the Goulstonian lectures published as *Gastric Function in Health and Disease* (1926), and *The Natural History of Disease* (1936). He was a frequent lecturer before learned societies and in addition to the M.A. of Oxford and Cam-

bridge also held the honorary degrees of M.D., Cambridge (1935), and D.Sc., McGill (1947). He was physician-extra-ordinary to the King from 1935, having previously been physician to the royal household; member of the Medical Research Council (1935–9); president of the Association of Physicians of Great Britain and Ireland (1942); member of the commission on higher education in the Colonies (1943–5), and of the double-day shift working committee of the Ministry of Labour and National Service (1945–6). In the summer of 1949 he fell ill and died 27 February 1950 at his home near Pulborough, Sussex.

Ryle married in 1914 Miriam Power, daughter of William Charles Scully, civil servant, of Cape Town; they had three sons and two daughters; the second son, Martin, a physicist, was elected F.R.S. in 1952.

[*British Medical Journal* and *Lancet*, 11 March 1950; private information; personal knowledge.]

FRASER BROCKINGTON.

SADLER, SIR MICHAEL ERNEST (1861–1943), educational pioneer and art patron, born at Barnsley 3 July 1861, was the eldest child of Michael Thomas Sadler, M.D., general practitioner, by his wife, Annie Eliza Adams, who came of Lincolnshire yeoman stock. Sadler was educated at Rugby, where he won a scholarship in 1876, and at Trinity College, Oxford, where he went as a classical scholar in 1880. He was placed in the first class in classical moderations in 1882 and in *literae humaniores* in 1884. In his second year he was elected president of the Union.

He inherited from his family, especially from his great-great-uncle, M. T. Sadler [q.v.], famous for factory reform, an inclination to public service. The form he selected was education, in which he evinced active interest from his earliest undergraduate days. In 1885 he succeeded (Sir) A. H. D. Acland [q.v.] as secretary of the extension lectures subcommittee of the Oxford University examinations delegacy. To this activity in 1886 he added that of steward of Christ Church and in 1890 he was elected student of Christ Church. The extension work grew so rapidly under his guidance that in 1892 its committee was converted into an independent delegacy; in 1885 it had been responsible for 27 courses of lectures, but by 1893 it was providing lecturers for nearly 400 courses in different parts of England, of which over 200 were arranged by various county councils. Innovations were rapidly introduced into the Oxford work which were adopted by other universities, such as travelling libraries for lecturers, and summer schools which brought extension lecture students to the older universities in the long vacations. Nothing new was added to the work after Sadler left; some activities disappeared and the number of courses dwindled. This was largely due to the growth of civic universities and university colleges which Sadler did much to promote, especially in Reading where his colleague (Sir) Halford Mackinder [q.v.] became first principal of the college in 1892.

Sadler gradually came to see that much of the value of extension work was lost because of the early age at which the students had left school. He therefore turned his attention to secondary education for which at that time the State made no systematic provision. He persuaded the university in 1893 to take the unprecedented step of summoning a conference to Oxford to discuss the matter. The conference, attended by notable people in church and state, with Sadler as its secretary, made so great an impression on the university that convocation addressed a memorial to the prime minister, W. E. Gladstone, urging him to appoint a Royal Commission on secondary education. Sadler was the most active member of the commission and its report, issued under the chairmanship of James (later Viscount) Bryce [q.v.], is still referred to as an authoritative and creative document on secondary education; it made legislation on the subject inevitable.

In 1895 Sadler left Oxford to become director of the office of special inquiries and reports in the government Department of Education, of which Acland was in charge. Unfortunately for Sadler the Liberal Government went out of office, and Acland with it, the same year. Sadler's department was responsible for building up a body of knowledge on educational policy and practice at home and abroad, and for supplying the Government with any information it required for the framing of its own policy. Under Sadler's directorship the office became a great research bureau. Between the years 1895 and 1903 eleven massive volumes appeared, the like of which had not been seen before in any country, containing carefully sifted infor-

mation, the most notable articles being contributed by the director who made a special study of German education. These volumes are said to have been the originators of the whole study of comparative education and to have set a standard never since surpassed. The French Government was so much impressed by the work of the office that it established one on similar lines.

Sadler also built up the library of the Education Department and made the office a centre in which all inquirers from home or abroad could find useful information and cordial welcome. In all his work he was helped by (Sir) Robert Morant [q.v.], the chief assistant in his office. But when Morant left to become private secretary to Sir John Gorst [q.v.] (who had succeeded Acland as head of the Education Department), and, later, secretary to the newly constituted Board of Education, Sadler ceased to be consulted on matters of educational policy. The research work of the office was starved by refusals to sanction the expenditure of trifling sums, while constant claims were made on it for day-to-day information. Sadler, feeling that no initiative was left to him, resigned in 1903. He was known by that time as the greatest living authority in England on educational matters and his advice was sought from all over the world. The consternation caused by his resignation compelled the Government to issue a blue book on the subject.

Shortly after his resignation from the Board Sadler accepted a part-time post as professor of education in the university of Manchester. He had also embarked on a series of investigations of the needs in secondary education of nine local education authorities. His recommendations, revolutionary though they were, were in all cases accepted. After 1906 he did much for the education of the adolescent, editing a volume on continuation education and working for the improvement of technical education. He also promoted national and international conferences on moral instruction and was responsible for issuing volumes on their discussions and findings. In 1908 he did much to secure harmony among those who disliked the provisions of the Act of 1902 which gave State aid to voluntary schools and he took a large share in drafting the education bill unsuccessfully introduced by Walter Runciman (later Viscount Runciman of Doxford, q.v.).

In 1911 Sadler became vice-chancellor

of the university of Leeds which had been created seven years earlier, and soon the whole district became throbbingly aware of the existence of the university. The number of faculties and students multiplied. Notable lecturers from all over the world attracted throngs to its halls. County authorities were wooed successfully, and increased or began to make grants to the university. Everything was done to bring town and gown together and to this day there is no university in the country which has a higher standing in its own city. Sadler made a great university of what had formerly been little more than an insignificant college. The challenge of the war of 1914–18 was met by intense activity in every department of the university, the vice-chancellor giving vigorous support to any project which would assist the war effort.

In 1917 Sadler went to India as president of a commission on the university of Calcutta, accompanied by J. W. Gregory, (Sir) Philip Hartog, and Ramsay Muir [qq.v.]. The revolution in Indian education brought about by the report which he and his colleagues produced is thought by some to have been the greatest of his achievements. He wrote about one-third of the contents of the five main volumes of the report which set the pattern for secondary as well as university education throughout India and also affected primary education. Local conditions prevented its chief recommendations from being put into effect in Calcutta until 1951, but in the meantime many other universities modelled on the report sprang into being. It was hailed not only as a document showing a profound understanding of Indian students and of Indian educational problems, but as a great essay on education.

Sadler returned to Leeds in 1919 to be met by numerous post-war problems, especially for the extension of the buildings and activities of the university, with which he coped with zeal and originality. In 1923 he accepted the mastership of University College, Oxford. His work for the college, in beautifying it and its chapel, where worship was a great reality to him, in the promotion of modern studies, in inducing former members to renew their associations with it, in making intimate and happy contacts with undergraduates and introducing them to the great world with which he was familiar, was accompanied by multitudinous activities outside. In Oxford he did much to obtain funds for the extension of the Bodleian Library, and brought into being the society of Friends of the Bodleian for the securing of manuscripts and rare books. The Oxford Preservation Trust owed much to him, and his work for it and other matters affecting the city won him its freedom (1931), an honour unique for a man in his position. He declined the mayoralty on the score of age. Outside Oxford his help was given to many overseas developments in education; he served on committees of the Colonial Office, doing doughty work for negro education and promoting the study and appreciation of negro art.

He retired from the mastership in 1934, partly in order to continue studies of the examination system in conjunction with his friend Sir Philip Hartog, and partly in the hope of completing a history of English education which he was never able to finish. The outbreak of war in 1939 put an end to outside activities, although he remained at the service of those who sought his advice.

By some Sadler was best known as a patron of the arts, for he was always glad to show, to lend, and frequently to give portions of his great collection of pictures which contained the works of old masters as well as the most audacious modern productions. Generosity, which was one of his most shining characteristics, led him to buy the works of unknown artists. The same generosity placed his eloquence at the service of small audiences as well as great ones. He was gay, witty, keenly sympathetic and almost incredibly kind, but not universally popular. Many were disconcerted by a buoyant manner which concealed a dogged faithfulness to the cause of education; and his modesty concealed his herculean labours. No other Englishman did so much for education in so many spheres, as investigator, scholar, adviser, administrator, pioneer at home and abroad. His creative enthusiasm was awakened more readily by the ideas of others than by his own. Many who have done great things in education in different parts of the world have declared that it was his inspiration and encouragement which made their work possible. As a man of action he rejoiced in the deeds of others; as a man of vision he was able to see their visions.

Sadler was twice married: first, in 1885 to Mary Ann (died 1931), daughter of Charles Harvey, linen-factor, of Barnsley, by whom he had one son, Michael Sadleir, author and publisher, who has contributed to this SUPPLEMENT; secondly, in 1934 to Eva Margaret (died 1940), daughter of Edmund Gilpin, stockbroker. He died at Old Headington, near Oxford, 14 October 1943.

In 1911 he was appointed C.B., and in 1919 after his work on the Calcutta University commission was created K.C.S.I. He received the honorary degrees of LL.D. from Cambridge, Columbia, Liverpool, and Toronto, and Litt.D. from Manchester, Sheffield, and Leeds. He was appointed Rede lecturer in 1928, and was elected an honorary student of Christ Church (1912) and an honorary fellow of University College, Oxford (1935).

There are portraits of Sadler in oil by Mark Gertler (1914); by Jacob Kramer (1917), the property of the Oxford delegacy for extra-mural studies; by Henry Lamb at the university of Leeds; by F. H. Shepherd in a group of the master and fellows at University College, Oxford. In the Brotherton library of the university of Leeds there is a bronze bust by Loris Rey (1933) of which there is a replica in the library of University College, Oxford.

[Michael Sadleir, *Michael Ernest Sadler, a Memoir*, 1949; *Papers Relating to the Resignation of the Director of Special Inquiries and Reports*, Cmd. 1602, 1903; Lynda Grier, *Achievement in Education*, 1952; private information; personal knowledge.]

LYNDA GRIER.

ST. JUST, first BARON (1870–1941), banker and politician. [See GRENFELL, EDWARD CHARLES.]

SALISBURY, fourth MARQUESS OF (1861–1947). [See CECIL, JAMES EDWARD HUBERT GASCOYNE-.]

SALMON, SIR ERIC CECIL HEYGATE (1896–1946), administrator, was born at Newcastle upon Tyne 3 July 1896, the eldest child and only son of Herbert John Salmon, sportsman and man of business, by his wife, Edith Juliet, daughter of Frederick Lambert, of Garratts Hall, Banstead. In 1910 he went to Malvern College where he was senior classical scholar and Faber exhibitioner, and in 1915 entered Corpus Christi College, Oxford, as a classical scholar. On account of the war he did not proceed to a degree, but in July 1916, his health having prevented

earlier enlistment, joined the Queen's Own Royal West Kent Regiment. The following April he was given command of the 41st divisional observation section, a group engaged in noting enemy movements, supplying information to commanders of fighting units, and guiding men into battle. In this work Salmon displayed great personal courage, cheerfulness, and a constant concern for the welfare of his men, whose devotion to him was unbounded. In September 1917 he was awarded the M.C. He maintained until death, by an annual reunion and many acts of kindness, the comradeship first forged in common danger.

In 1919 he entered the Ministry of Health in the administrative class. His war experience had bred in him a maturity and power of initiative beyond his years, and he soon displayed unusual independence of judgement. From 1925 to 1930 he dealt chiefly with local finance and legislation, work which taught him much about the ways of local authorities. He developed high forensic abilities, quickly gained the confidence of parliamentary committees, and held his own in argument with leading lights of the parliamentary bar. He was particularly successful as secretary to a series of departmental committees, including those on smoke abatement (1920), rent restriction (1930), and housing (1933).

In 1934 he secured in public competition the appointment of deputy clerk of the London County Council. In this new sphere he exchanged the civil servant's relative freedom from detailed direction for the daily contact with committees and their chairmen which characterizes local government administration. The newly elected Labour Council was anxious to show its prowess by an expansion of effort on all sides, and was apt to be impatient of any apparent tardiness in the official machine. The clerk and his deputy had thus a double task: to win the confidence of the new administration, and to ensure that some dozen separate departments, each under a professional head with views of his own, were harnessed with the minimum of friction to a common endeavour. In both these tasks Salmon's characteristic qualities were ably displayed. He won the confidence of members and colleagues alike, and was most warmly regarded throughout the service.

From 1935 onwards, and more especially after the passing of the Air-Raid Precautions Act, 1937, local authorities were preoccupied with civil defence. Salmon was made personally responsible for co-ordinating those services—rescue, ambulance, fire, and welfare—which were functions of the London County Council. When war came he succeeded Sir George Gater (then called to government service) as clerk of the Council. His immediate task was to resolve the many difficulties attending the embodiment of the civil defence services. In this he worked closely with the London regional commissioners and their staff, and established such cordial contacts, although unflagging in support of the Council's interests, that the relationship between the commissioners and the Council, in contrast to that prevailing in some regions, was one of friendly co-operation in a common effort.

As early as 1942 Salmon began to study the problems of reconstruction. Nor did he confine himself to his official concerns. He was one of a few who believed that administrators in central and local government on the one hand, and in industry and commerce on the other, needed a common forum for mutual understanding and the fruitful exchange of ideas, if the country was to adjust itself successfully to the changed conditions of the post-war world. Their enthusiasm gave birth to the Administrative Staff College, established with financial backing from industry and the co-operation of central and local government. In particular, Salmon's evidence, in 1943, to the chancellor of the Exchequer's committee on training for the Civil Service, did much to transform official scepticism into wholehearted support.

Salmon married in 1929 Hilda Marion, daughter of Canon Edward Ashurst Welch, and was for many years sustained and strengthened in his work by his domestic happiness. She and their two children (one son and one daughter) survived him. In 1942 he received the honorary degree of M.A. from Oxford University. He was knighted in 1943; and in 1944 became a member of the council of Malvern College, where his wisdom, tact, and insight greatly served his old school. He was appointed a deputy-lieutenant of the county of London in 1945. All his life he loved outdoor sports, particularly shooting and cricket, in both of which he excelled. An irresistible humour enhanced his great practical ability, and he retained in maturity an almost boyish gaiety. His death in London, 9 July 1946, at the height of his powers, was a noteworthy loss to the public service. His compelling personality brought out the best in others, and kindled in the public service of London a new spirit which will long survive him.

[*The Times*, 10 and 15 July 1946; Ministry of Health and War Office records; London County Council minutes, 1 August 1939 and 16 July 1946; private information; personal knowledge.]                    T. G. RANDALL.

SAMPSON, GEORGE (1873–1950), scholar, was born at Greenwich 6 April 1873, the youngest child of Thomas Sampson, mariner, and his wife, Sarah Ann Hows. In his earliest years, afterwards described in 'A Boy and His Books' (*Seven Essays*, 1947), he became an omnivorous reader and especially of poetry. Poor health prevented him from going to school until nearly eleven and circumstances compelled him to leave before he was sixteen. He was then set to work for London matriculation and was trained as an elementary schoolteacher at Southwark and Winchester. At thirty-seven he became headmaster of a higher-grade school and in 1925 he was appointed an inspector of schools by the London County Council.

As a schoolmaster, Sampson worked for the improved teaching of English in the spirit of a crusader. He was a member of the departmental committee on the teaching of English and served as general secretary of the English Association. In 1921 he published *English for the English*, a passionate plea for better teaching based on two principles: first, that 'it is the purpose of education not to prepare children *for* their occupations, but to prepare children *against* their occupations', and second, that 'a sound educational system must be based upon the great means of human intercourse—human speech in spoken and written word'. The book was a tract for the times, but became a minor classic; after many reprints, it appeared in a new edition in 1952.

With this pioneering work as a teacher Sampson combined a continuous activity as editor and critic. He edited Berkeley's works in 1897–8, and this was followed by editions of many authors, including Burke, Newman, Thomas More, George Herbert, Emerson, Keats, Bagehot, Coleridge, and Hazlitt. Some of these were specifically designed for use in schools and universities, but all of them bore the mark of an individual critical mind and this was recognized by the university of Cambridge which made him an honorary M.A. in 1920. The width and catholicity of Sampson's reading, supplemented by a pungent style, qualified him in a notable way as a literary historian. His supplement (1924) to Stopford Brooke's *Primer of English Literature* was a brilliant and epigrammatic survey. In 1941 he triumphed on a much larger scale. Twenty years before he had been invited to write a one-volume epitome of the *Cambridge History of English Literature*. Its completion was delayed by ill health, but when it was published it was rightly hailed as a *tour de force*. It was primarily designed as a handbook for students, but Sampson was one of nature's scholars and the book is as readable as it is informing. Throughout the long labour of condensation he retained an individual freshness and his supplementary chapter on the post-Victorians is a powerful piece of criticism. In music and the drama Sampson had a profound and scholarly interest. His 'Bach and Shakespeare' was chosen by the first Earl of Birkenhead as one of the *Hundred Best English Essays*, and Sampson in his *Seven Essays* included a spirited defence of Henry Irving. His opinions were strongly held and he did not aspire to be an essayist of gentle charm. But he was a warm-hearted friend and a good clubman. At the Reform, where he was a member of the library committee, he was a familiar figure in the group which gathered round T. E. Page, Arnold Bennett, H. G. Wells [qq.v.], and other literary men of his time.

In 1907 Sampson married Grace (died 1953), daughter of Frederick Lewis Alldis. There were no children. After his retirement he went to live at Hove where his later years were darkened by persistent insomnia. He died there 1 February 1950.

[Personal knowledge.]     S. C. ROBERTS.

SANKEY, JOHN, VISCOUNT SANKEY (1866–1948), lord chancellor, was born in Moreton-in-Marsh 26 October 1866, the son of Thomas Sankey, partner in the firm of Sankey and Norton, drapers and undertakers, by his second wife, Catalina, daughter of James Dewsbury, clerk, of Manchester. Sankey was educated at Lancing College and Jesus College, Oxford, where he was a scholar, and was placed in the second class in honour moderations (1887) and modern history (1889) and in the third class in the examination for the degree of bachelor of civil law in 1891. He was called to the bar by the Middle Temple in 1892. He began his practice in South Wales, and was soon busily engaged in workmen's compensa-

tion cases. He became a K.C. in 1909, and in 1914 was elevated to the bench with the customary knighthood. In 1915 he was chairman of the enemy aliens advisory committee and for his services was appointed G.B.E. in 1917.

In 1919 Sankey undertook the task with which his name will perhaps be chiefly associated, becoming chairman of the commission appointed under the Act of that year to inquire into the conditions of the coal industry. As a result of long and patient investigation, Sankey recommended nationalization of the coal-mines, and was much disappointed that his proposals were not implemented by legislation. His courage in standing by his convictions was unfortunately misconstrued by some of his old Conservative friends, but it was much appreciated by the Labour Party, and especially by Ramsay MacDonald. It was thought by many that Sankey was destined to be the first Labour lord chancellor, but in 1924 the claims of Lord Haldane [q.v.] could not be overlooked. In 1928 Sankey was promoted to the Court of Appeal and sworn of the Privy Council, and when Labour came into power for a second time in 1929 he was offered and accepted the Woolsack. He was created a baron and in 1932 a viscount. On the formation of the 'national' Government in 1931, he was one of the few ministers who elected to stay with MacDonald; he remained lord chancellor until 1935 when Baldwin became prime minister and preferred to recall Lord Hailsham [q.v.] who had served previously as Conservative lord chancellor.

During Sankey's chancellorship, his time was occupied far more with political than with judicial functions. The emphasis placed on the political side of a lord chancellor's work has steadily grown since he ceased to be chancellor, but he was himself faced with duties which made the most exacting demands on his time. Chief among these were his chairmanships of the inter-imperial relations committee of the Imperial Conference, and of the federal structure committee of the Indian Round Table Conference. But the fact that the claims of law reform were never absent from his mind was demonstrated by his appointment of the Law Revision Committee, composed partly of practising and partly of academic lawyers, to whom was entrusted the important task of suggesting improvements in certain indicated branches of English law. From their reports have sprung several valuable pieces of legislation, mutually linked by the common name of Law Reform Acts.

Although he could not be described as a great judge, Sankey's judicial work was by no means negligible. In *A.-G.* v. *Brown*, [1920] 1 K.B. 773, he made an important contribution to constitutional law, by applying the *eiusdem generis* rule of interpretation to Section 43 of the Customs Consolidation Act, 1876. This provided that 'the importation of arms, ammunition, gunpowder, *or any other goods*, may be prohibited by Proclamation or Order in Council'. A proclamation, which purported to be made under the section, forbade the importation of chemicals. Sankey held that this prohibition was invalid, for the words 'or any other goods' must be restricted to goods of like character with those specifically enumerated. He described the Customs Act of 1853, which was re-enacted by the Act of 1876, as 'the Magna Carta of free trade', and pointed out the unlikelihood that Parliament should have intended, at that very moment, to confer on the executive an unfettered power to forbid the importation of all articles indiscriminately. In *Henrietta Muir Edwards* v. *A.-G. for Canada*, [1930] A.C. 124, he delivered the judgement of the Privy Council which put upon Section 24 of the British North America Act an interpretation empowering the governor-general to summon women having the necessary qualifications to the Canadian Senate. During his short time at the Court of Appeal, he was a party to the decision in *Hardie and Lane* v. *Chilton*, [1928] 2 K.B. 306. A trader had paid a sum of money to an association as the price of its refraining from placing his name on its 'stop list' for breach of one of its regulations, a course which its constitution allowed it to take. It was held that he was not entitled to recover it as paid under duress. It had been decided in *R.* v. *Denyer*, [1926] 2 K.B. 258, that the secretary of such an association, demanding a money payment as the price of such restraint, brought himself within the definition of blackmail, and so the criminal and civil laws on the matter were in conflict, until the matter was resolved by a decision of the House of Lords in 1937 that a demand of money made for the protection of lawful business interests was outside the sphere of the law of larceny.

The judicial pronouncement by which Sankey will best be remembered is his speech in *Woolmington* v. *Director of Public Prosecutions*, [1935] A.C. 462. This disposed of a fallacy, originating in Foster's *Crown Law* and upheld by Sir William Blackstone [q.v.], that 'all homicide is presumed to be malicious, until the contrary appears upon the evidence'. Sankey referred to the fluid condition of the law of evidence in the eighteenth century, and laid down that there is no shifting of the burden on to the prisoner, after the Crown has proved that the deceased met his death at his hands, to prove in his turn that the killing did not amount to murder; but it rests with the Crown throughout to establish murder, and it is sufficient for the prisoner to raise a doubt as to his guilt. If the jury are satisfied with his explanation or are in reasonable doubt whether the act may not have been accidental or provoked, then the prisoner is entitled to acquittal or to a verdict of manslaughter, as the case may be.

Sankey was one of the kindliest of men, and this quality, together with his handsome figure and commanding presence, made him an excellent chairman, wherever he presided, in the House of Lords, or elsewhere. He was always much interested in matters religious and ecclesiastical. A high churchman, he was an active member of the governing bodies of Keble College and Pusey House. At the same time he did great work in framing the constitution of the disestablished Welsh Church.

He was a bencher of his Inn, an honorary fellow of Jesus College, Oxford, and high steward of the university from which he received the honorary degree of D.C.L. (1930), and he had also that of LL.D. from the universities of Wales (1929), Cambridge (1932), and Bristol (1933). He died unmarried in London, 6 February 1948, and the peerage accordingly became extinct. A portrait of Sankey by (Sir) Oswald Birley is at Jesus College and another by Evan Walters is in the National Museum of Wales.

[Personal knowledge.] H. G. HANBURY.

SARGANT, SIR CHARLES HENRY (1856–1942), judge, was born in London 20 April 1856, the son of Henry Sargant, a barrister and conveyancer of Lincoln's Inn. Henry Sargant and his wife, Catherine Emma, daughter of Samuel Beale, at one time member of Parliament for Derby, both came of families well known in the Midlands.

In a family record Charles Sargant is described as 'a precocious child, who taught himself to read at three'. Throughout life he remained a great reader, and he was endowed with a wonderful memory. On entering Rugby he was placed in the Lower Fifth, and then went straight ahead, being 'equally good at classics and mathematics'. In due course he became head of the school, won most of the open prizes, and gained a leaving exhibition and an open scholarship at New College, Oxford. There, in spite of indifferent health, he was placed in the first class of the honours list in classical moderations (1876), in the second class in mathematical moderations (1877), and the first class in *literae humaniores* (1879). His health prevented him from playing the more strenuous games, but he won the 'cue' at Oxford, and became a keen fisherman and a fairly reliable golfer.

On going down from Oxford he spent a year in the office of Beale & Co., solicitors, of Birmingham and London, who were afterwards very constant clients, and then read as a pupil in the chambers of the well-known conveyancer Edward Parker Wolstenholme. He was called to the bar by Lincoln's Inn in 1882, and after building up a conveyancing practice he began to engage in court work. Thereafter his success was assured. During his later years at the bar he would never take any conveyancing work; but he regarded it as an indispensable part of a Chancery barrister's training, and was, on occasion, a fine draftsman himself. It is probably no accident that two of his pupils, (Sir) Frederick Liddell and (Sir) William Graham-Harrison [q.v.], both attained the office of first parliamentary counsel to the Treasury.

In appearance Sargant was very far from a typical lawyer, with his large tawny moustache, full complexion, and benevolent blue eyes. In every other respect it would be difficult to imagine a man better qualified for the work he had chosen to do. For he had not only quickness and accuracy of mind, and a retentive memory, but common sense and breadth of view. 'Looking at the matter broadly' is a phrase which some will remember. In court, he often found the advantage to be gained by rapid mental arithmetic, and he had a great belief in the value of the first impressions of a trained mind. He never took silk—perhaps wisely. Not being particularly ambitious, nor particularly industrious, he never allowed his legal work to overwhelm him; there were other things in life for which a reasonable amount

of leisure was desirable. Although apparently rather shy, he was a sociable person, and at his best among intimate men friends; and his friendships were lifelong.

In 1900, somewhat late in life, he married Amelia Julia, eldest daughter of Dion Gambardella, civil engineer, by whom he had one son and two daughters.

In 1908 he was appointed junior counsel to the Treasury in equity matters. This made life more strenuous; but in the same year he had the great pleasure of being made a bencher of his Inn. Nor did he have to wait long for promotion, for in 1913 he was appointed a judge of the High Court. As was to be expected, he made an admirable Chancery judge for, in addition to the necessary learning, he had the rarer gifts of common sense and rapidity of mind. From the first his judgements stood the test of review in the Court of Appeal, to which he himself was promoted in 1923. He was knighted in 1913 and sworn a member of the Privy Council in 1923. In 1919 he received one of the most delightful of all honours, that of being elected an honorary fellow of his old college.

Soon after the war of 1914–18, Sargant was appointed chairman of a Royal Commission to allocate awards to inventors whose work had been useful in the war. This was breaking new ground, for no such body had ever existed before; and its chairman received great credit for the commission's first report, drafted by his own hand, which laid down the principles on which such awards should be made. He always looked back with pleasure on this piece of work, and regretted that his appointment to the Court of Appeal made it necessary for him to leave it.

In 1928 at the age of seventy-two, Sargant resigned his position as a lord justice of appeal. Afterwards he served for a while as chairman of the Board of Trade committee on patent law and practice, and sat occasionally on the Judicial Committee of the Privy Council. Towards the end of his life he became increasingly lame through arthritis, and, as in his earliest days, he found his chief resource in books. He died at Cambridge 23 July 1942: a brilliant lawyer, and a very lovable man. There is a chalk drawing by Sir William Rothenstein at New College, Oxford.

[*The Times*, 28 July 1942; private information; personal knowledge.]

PHILIP W. BAKER WILBRAHAM.

SASTRI, VALANGIMAN SANKARA-NARAYANA SRINIVASA (1869–1946), Indian social worker and politician, was born at Valangiman, Tanjore district, Madras, 22 September 1869, the son of a Brahmin priest, Sankaranarayana Sastri. He was educated at the Native High School and the Government College, Kumbakonam, and as a young man became a schoolmaster. In 1899 he was appointed headmaster of the Hindu High School, Triplicane, and while there came under the influence of Gopal Krishna Gokhale who in 1905 founded the Servants of India Society with the object of forming 'a select, compact and trustworthy corps of young men' prepared by study, observation, travel, and work of a probationary character to take a real part in public life. Sastri was appointed a member of that society in 1907 and on the death of Gokhale in 1915 became its president. Before that he had been elected a fellow of Madras University and nominated to the Madras legislative council, by which he was elected in 1916 to the viceroy's legislative council. From an early age Sastri had shown unusual proficiency in the English language and he was soon recognized in the legislative council as the most eloquent Indian of his time. Turning from social questions, such as marriage reform, to which he had first given his attention in the Servants of India Society, he became interested in two main problems: self-government for India and the rights of Indians within the Empire. During his active years he never turned away for long from those subjects, although his sense of duty led him to undertake work, such as serving on a committee on Indian railways, for which he had no special qualification.

Sastri was one of a group of nineteen legislators who in 1916 signed a memorandum proposing wider plans of constitutional reform than the British Government and Lord Chelmsford [q.v.], who had recently assumed office as viceroy, seemed prepared to sanction; and under the auspices of the Indian National Congress he took part in an active campaign for Indian home rule. He withdrew from the Congress when the report on constitutional reform signed by E. S. Montagu [q.v.] and Lord Chelmsford was published and, with other moderate reformers who disapproved of war on the established Government and of the civil disobedience preached by M. K. Gandhi [q.v.], helped to form the Indian Liberal Federation of which he became president in 1922. Though not a wholehearted admirer of the scheme of dyarchy introduced by the Government of India Act of 1919, he supported it and had been one of the three Indian members of the committee under Lord Southborough [q.v.] which devised the electoral scheme embodied in that Act. In 1921 he was elected a member of the Council of State and was in that year a representative of India at the Imperial Conference. That was his first great opportunity of pleading the cause he had most at heart. He contended that where Indians were lawfully settled they should be admitted into the general body of citizenship with no deductions made from the rights that other British subjects enjoyed; and the conference—South Africa dissenting in view of 'the exceptional circumstances of the greater part of the Union'—agreed to a resolution admitting in principle the claim of Indians to equality of citizenship. While in England for that conference, Sastri received the freedom of the City of London which, he said, he accepted not as a personal distinction, 'but in all sincerity and hopefulness as a symbol of, and prelude to, the conferment on India of the freedom of the British Empire'. Later in the year he represented India at the League of Nations Assembly and at the conference in Washington on the limitation of armaments.

To help in arriving at a practical interpretation of the resolution passed at the Imperial Conference, Sastri was sent by the Government of India in 1922 to Australia, New Zealand, and Canada, and in his report on that mission he urged the promotion of personal intercourse as the best solvent of prejudice. Nowhere was prejudice more firmly rooted than in South Africa. An Indian suggestion that a committee of inquiry should visit the Union was made in 1923 but both J. C. Smuts and J. B. M. Hertzog [qq.v.] were opposed to it, and it was not until 1926 that a proposal for a round table conference in South Africa on the status of the Indian population was accepted. Sastri was an obvious choice for that task. An agreement was reached in 1927 whereby the Union Government would seek to aid Indians domiciled in the Union to attain a European standard of life and to secure the help of the Government of India in repatriating Indians who could not be assimilated in the population. The agreement was much criticized in South Africa; but the appointment of Sastri in 1927 as the first 'agent' of the Government of India in South Africa, in order to secure effective co-operation, did much to allay resentment and was greeted with such satisfaction by the Union Government that it at once extended an amnesty to all Indians illegally present in its territory. Sastri was then at the height of his power, and the charm of his personality and his remarkable gifts as a speaker served him well in fighting his countrymen's battles. He had too the distinction of going to South Africa as a privy counsellor, the first Indian, apart from members of the Judicial Committee, to receive that honour (1921). That distinction was enhanced in 1930 when he was appointed a Companion of Honour: the only Indian to whom that honour had been granted.

On his return to India in 1929 he was asked to visit Malaya and to advise the Government of India on the conditions of labour there. In the same year he went to East Africa to help the Indian community in stating their views on proposals made for the closer union of Kenya, Tanganyika, and Uganda, and on his return he suggested in his report the lines on which Indian representation in the Kenya legislative council should be based. He was a member of the Royal Commission on labour in India appointed in 1929 and was a delegate to the first two of the three Round Table conferences held in London to consider the new constitution for India. His last work of importance—he had resigned the presidency of the Servants of India Society in 1927—was as vice-chancellor (1935–40) of the recently formed Annamalai University at Annamalainagar in the Madras presidency. He took little part in politics in his later years, feeling that events had moved too fast for him and his associates in the moderate party who had hoped to see a self-governing and undivided India enjoying 'full fraternity with other members of the Empire'.

Sastri, who died in the Madras presidency 17 April 1946, was twice married and had a son, V. S. Sankaran, by his first wife, and a daughter by his second wife. A portrait of Sastri in oils, by C. Nageswara Rao, hangs in the Sastri Hall of the Annamalai University.

[*Indian Year Book*; *Times of India*, 18 April 1946; *The Times*, 20 April 1946; personal knowledge.] S. T. SHEPPARD.

SAXL, FRIEDRICH ('FRITZ') (1890–1948), historian of art and, with Aby M. Warburg, founder of the Warburg Institute, was born in Vienna, 8 January 1890, the son of Ignaz Saxl, a distinguished lawyer who collaborated in the formation of the new Austrian civil code, and his wife, Wilhelmine Falk. Educated at the Maximilian Gymnasium in Vienna and at the universities of Vienna and Berlin, Saxl began his scholarly career with work on the authenticity and dating of Rembrandt's drawings (1912). In 1911 he had been awarded a scholarship at the Austrian Historical Institute in Rome, and he began there to compile his *Catalogue of Astrological and Mythological Illuminated Manuscripts of the Latin Middle Ages*, a work originally sponsored by the Heidelberg Academy (vol. i, 1915; vol. ii, 1927; vol. iii, 1953). This commission was the outcome of his acquaintance with Aby Warburg, whom he had met through their mutual interest in the imagery of pagan cults and myths, and its survival, during the Middle Ages in heterodox practices and learned disguises, and in the Renaissance as the prototype of a new style in life, literature, and the figurative arts. At that time Warburg had already made his most important contributions to the study of the Florentine fifteenth century, and had laid the foundations of his private library which Saxl was later to develop into the Warburg Institute. In 1913 Saxl became Warburg's assistant and settled in Hamburg.

From 1914 to 1918 Saxl served as a first lieutenant in the Austrian Army on the Italian front, and after the end of the war became an army education officer under the first Austrian Labour Government. In 1919 he was called back to Hamburg where Warburg had fallen dangerously ill, and he took charge of the library which he began to turn into a centre for research on the significance of the classical heritage in the history of European civilization. With the financial support of Warburg's brothers in Hamburg and New York, he made the library more widely accessible, invited scholars of international standing for lectures and research, and began to publish the series *Studien der Bibliothek Warburg*, later continued as *Studies of the Warburg Institute*. The newly founded university of Hamburg provided the academic background, and in 1927 it conferred the title of professor on Saxl; but fortunately the Institute remained a private undertaking which Saxl directed after Warburg's death in 1929. Saxl's writings, combined with the publications of the Institute issued under his stimulating editorship, focused attention on the classical tradition, and the Institute became a centre for research in this field. In 1933, when the rise of National Socialism seemed likely to put an end to the pursuit of liberal studies in Germany, Saxl found a new home for the Institute in England, assisted by a group of sponsors, and in particular by Samuel Courtauld and Lord Lee of Fareham [qq.v.]. It remained a private centre, continuing its lectures and publications, until in 1944 it was incorporated in the university of London. To the task of finding for the Institute its most useful place in English scholarship Saxl gave his single-minded devotion, whilst his great knowledge was always unassumingly and unstintingly at the disposal of anyone seeking his advice. He became a naturalized British subject in 1940 and was elected F.B.A. in 1944.

Coming to England gave to Saxl's work a fresh impetus and a new direction. To his earlier studies of English manuscript painting he now added the study of English medieval sculpture in which he stressed the features connecting it with classical and continental art. He helped to establish as an academic subject the history of art which had recently been introduced into English universities by the foundation of the Courtauld Institute. To the *Journal* of the Warburg and Courtauld Institutes he contributed articles on such subjects as pagan sacrifice in the Italian Renaissance, Aniello Falcone and his patrons, the classical inscription in Renaissance art and politics, and a spiritual encyclopaedia of the later Middle Ages. Among his other publications in English are *Classical Mythology in Mediaeval Art* (with E. Panofsky, Metropolitan Museum Studies, 4), *Classical Antiquity in Renaissance Painting* (National Gallery, London, 1938), *British Art and the Mediterranean* (with R. Wittkower, 1948), and *English Sculptures of the Twelfth Century* (ed. H. Swarzenski, 1954).

Saxl was a small, slightly built man who attracted and bewildered by the mercurial quality of his action. He had the great gift of communicating the excitement which he found in his own work. This was never more apparent than in the library of his Institute where he would not accept defeat in finding the precise information needed. If it fell outside the scope of his own field he usually knew to whom to turn, for he was alert to the work of others and in a seemingly casual way was often able to further the cause of scholarship by bringing together people

of like interests. His self-effacing manner and his dislike of anything resembling compulsion concealed great powers of will and endurance and high demands on others which he never thought it worth while to make explicit. For this reason he was often misinterpreted, but to those who understood him he set a sure standard of scholarly and personal behaviour and the example of an unusual charity.

In 1913 Saxl married Elise Bienenfeld, daughter of a Vienna cloth merchant. They had one son, a promising painter and architect who died young, and one daughter. Saxl died in Dulwich 22 March 1948.

[*Burlington Magazine*, July 1948; *Journal* of the Warburg and Courtauld Institutes, vol. x, 1947; Gertrud Bing, *A Memoir* in *Fritz Saxl, 1890–1948*, a volume of memorial essays edited by D. J. Gordon, 1957; personal knowledge.] GERTRUD BING.

SCHWABE, RANDOLPH (1885–1948), etcher, draughtsman, and teacher, was born in Manchester 9 May 1885, the son of Lawrence Schwabe, cotton merchant, whose father left Germany in 1820, and his wife, Octavie Henriette Ermen. He was educated privately in Hemel Hempstead and at fourteen went to the Royal College of Art. He transferred to the Slade School of Fine Art in 1900 where he remained until, in 1906, he went to the Académie Julian in Paris for eight months. He gradually became known as a draughtsman, etcher, and lithographer, and, during the war of 1914–18, made many drawings as an official war artist. After 1918 he taught in the Camberwell and Westminster schools of art and became a teacher of drawing at the Royal College of Art. In 1930 he succeeded Henry Tonks [q.v.] as Slade professor at University College, London, and principal of the Slade School, where he remained until his death. He was a member of the New English Art Club and the London Group. He collaborated with F. M. Kelly in *Historic Costume* (1925) and *A Short History of Costume and Armour* (1931), illustrated a number of other books, and made designs for some theatrical productions.

Schwabe had a remarkable amount of miscellaneous information on nearly all subjects and a scholarly knowledge of some—acquired by very wide reading. His slight stammer never hindered his flow of entertaining conversation; he had a quick and subtle sense of humour. He took the task of teaching very seriously and was much respected by all his students, though his gentle, kindly manner never inspired the terror commanded by his predecessor Henry Tonks. His drawings and prints are not remarkable for imagination but are beautifully precise and reasonable statements of fact.

In 1913 Schwabe married Gwendolen Rosamund, daughter of Herbert Jones, and one daughter was born. He died at Helensburgh, Dumbartonshire, 19 September 1948. A self-portrait pencil sketch is at the Slade School, and a chalk drawing by Francis Dodd is in the Manchester City Art Gallery.

[Introduction by Sir Charles Tennyson to the catalogue of the memorial exhibition, Arts Council, 1951; *The Times*, 21 September 1948; private information.]

STEPHEN BONE.

SCOTT, KATHLEEN (1878–1947), sculptor. [See KENNET, (EDITH AGNES) KATHLEEN, LADY KENNET.]

SCOTT, SIR LESLIE FREDERIC (1869–1950), judge, politician, and chairman of committees (always known to his contemporaries as Leslie Scott), was born 29 October 1869 at Hornsey, the eldest son of (Sir) John Scott [q.v.] who became judicial adviser to the Khedive. From Rugby he won a classical exhibition at New College, Oxford (of which he became an honorary fellow in 1939), and was placed in the second class both in honour moderations (1890) and in *literae humaniores* (1892). In 1894 he was called to the bar by the Inner Temple, of which he was afterwards a bencher, and read in chambers with his cousin (Sir) Maurice Hill [q.v.] and with Hugh Fenwick Boyd. He began his practice at Liverpool, chiefly in commercial and maritime cases, in which his industry and ability quickly won him a leading position as a junior. Amongst many pupils of his in Liverpool the most notable was F. E. Smith (later the Earl of Birkenhead, q.v.), a relationship which brought the comment that a hen had hatched out a very large duck. He moved his chambers to London in 1906, became a K.C. in 1909, and in the following year began his political career as Conservative member of Parliament for the Exchange division of Liverpool, a seat which he held until he resigned it in 1929. In 1922 he was, from March to October, solicitor-general, and was knighted. After the resignation of Lloyd George, Bonar Law was anxious to retain Scott in his Government as attorney-general or as home secretary; but Scott decided to

return to his private practice which *inter alia* took him to India in 1927 to prepare the case for the Indian princes before the statutory commission. In the same year he was sworn of the Privy Council. In 1935, at the age of sixty-six, he was appointed direct to the Court of Appeal, becoming in 1940 the senior lord justice. He retired in 1948.

Although some of Scott's judgements in commercial matters will continue to be cited as authoritative, it cannot be claimed that he made any important contribution to the common law. It has been said of him that he was inclined in seeking a solution of a legal problem to base himself upon over-wide generalizations: and some of his judgements were subsequently criticized, as in *Leachinsky* v. *Christie*, [1946] K.B. 124, criticized by Lord du Parcq [q.v.] in [1947] A.C. at pp. 604–5, and in *Bonnington Castings, Ltd.* v. *Wardlaw*, [1956] A.C. 613, where their lordships had to correct a dictum of Scott's.

In his extra-legal activities Scott's work deserves the highest commendation. He was full of public spirit and to use his own words (*Who's Who*, 1927) he was 'interested in all questions of social and industrial reform, particularly in connection with the development of agriculture and the improvement of the conditions of life affecting the rural population'.

He was a member, and frequently chairman, of many government and other committees. Amongst others, he was chairman of the Agricultural Organisation Society (1917–22); of the acquisition of land committee (1917–19); and of the committee on ministers' powers (1929–32) after the resignation in 1931 of Lord Donoughmore [q.v.]. The report of this committee, largely drafted by Scott himself, is a most important constitutional document. He was seconded from the Court of Appeal to sit upon the committee on land utilization in rural areas (1941–2), the report of which is usually called the Scott report. Those who worked with him unanimously pay tribute to his courtesy, his conscientiousness and his industry, qualities which he likewise showed as a judge.

Apart from this committee work, Scott was a founder-member and on the executive of the Council for the Preservation of Rural England, and was chairman of its Berkshire branch, in which capacity he helped to preserve the amenities of the village of Letcombe Basset. He was, in 1947, the first president of the National

Association of Parish Councils. He was also a zealous supporter of the welfare of mental defectives and from 1914 to 1947 was president and chairman of the Central Association for Mental Welfare. He was also profoundly interested in international maritime law and represented this country at four Brussels conferences on this subject.

In this energetic and many-sided life, Scott found time to write several books: *The Effect of War on Contracts* (1914), *British Agriculture, the Nation's Opportunity* (in collaboration, 1917), *The Case of Requisition* (with A. Hildesley, 1920), and *The New Law of Property Acts Explained* (with B. B. B. Benas, 1925). He was also a painter in oils and exhibited at the New English Art Club and at the Royal Scottish Academy.

He married in 1898 Ethel (died 1954), daughter of Henry A. James, of Suffolk Hall, Cheltenham; there were no children. He died at Oxford 19 May 1950. A riverside garden at Winchester was dedicated to him in 1952 in memory of his services to rural England.

A portrait by Mrs. Campbell Dodgson is privately owned.

[Family and personal information.]

P. A. LANDON.

SCOTT-ELLIS, THOMAS EVELYN, eighth BARON HOWARD DE WALDEN and fourth BARON SEAFORD (1880–1946), writer, sportsman, and patron and lover of the arts, was born in London 9 May 1880, the only son of Frederick George Ellis, seventh Baron Howard de Walden, whom he succeeded in 1899, by his wife, Blanche, daughter of William Holden, of Palace House, Lancashire, and grandson of the sixth baron, Charles Augustus Ellis [q.v.]. In 1917 he assumed the additional name and arms of Scott on succeeding to the Dean Castle estate in Kilmarnock. He was educated at Eton and the Royal Military College, Sandhurst, and was commissioned in the 10th Hussars in time to see two years' service in South Africa. After retiring from the regular army, he became a zealous and efficient territorial; in the war of 1914–18 he served in the Westminster Dragoons (of which he later became honorary colonel) and in the 9th battalion of the Royal Welch Fusiliers both in Gallipoli and in France.

On coming of age in 1901 Lord Howard de Walden succeeded to the control of his great estates in London and elsewhere. To this rich inheritance he brought great generosity and a rare variety of talents.

In 1906, within the space of a few days, he distinguished himself as spare man of the British Olympic fencing team at Athens and one of his horses won a good race at Newmarket. He was a consistent supporter of the turf, and a member of the Jockey Club from 1905 until 1924; perhaps his best season was in 1933 when he won a total of seventeen races. He was also a lover of sailing, a member of the Royal Yacht Squadron, and an early exponent (with the second Duke of Westminster) of motor-boat racing.

But if he paid these tributes to the contemporary world, Howard de Walden had also strong antiquarian tastes which included genealogy, heraldry, and armour. Of the last-named he formed an important collection at his Scottish home, including a number of classical specimens. In 1904 he produced the three volumes of the De Walden Library, of which perhaps *Some Feudal Lords and their Seals* is the most interesting. Furthermore, he played an important part in the production of *The Complete Peerage*: in addition to acting as one of the editors of volumes vi–x and xiii, he was a financial benefactor to the extent of at least £10,000. Throughout his life he was a keen medievalist, finding most interest perhaps in the fourteenth century, but often linking his scholarship to active life. Not only was he a good swordsman with either hand, but an exponent of falconry and hawking. Indeed it is probable that it was because of his love of medieval history and architecture that he gave up in 1912 the Tudor Audley End (the seat of the first Lord Howard de Walden), which for the preceding seven years he had rented from Lord Braybrooke, in favour of Chirk Castle, which he leased and made his home for thirty-four years.

In London he bought Seaford House in Belgrave Square, but the important urban property, which he had inherited through his grandmother from the Bentinck and Cavendish families, lay farther north in Marylebone and St. John's Wood. In this area he led the way as an enlightened landlord. Before he came of age there had been friction between his trustees and John Lewis, the founder of the well-known retail business. As a result of this, Lewis, who had already been to prison for contempt of court, in March 1911 goaded Howard de Walden into bringing a libel action, having for the past eighteen months posted placards abusing his landlord. Sir Edward (later Lord) Carson and F. E. Smith (later the Earl of Birkenhead) [qq.v.] appeared for the defence; Howard de Walden was represented by H. E. Duke (later Lord Merrivale, q.v.), and after a three-day hearing was awarded damages of one farthing. Reinforced in his earlier plans by the moral of this verdict, he announced in the autumn of that year that he was offering a new type of 999-year lease to his tenants, which made them virtually independent. Lewis, who had remained throughout on good terms with his landlord, acknowledged the virtue of this arrangement in a letter to *The Times* (14 November) and also admitted that his litigiousness had cost him over £40,000.

Lord Howard de Walden desired to spread his interests more widely and to take a share in colonial development. Accordingly in 1914 he sold sixty acres near Regent's Park for about £500,000, and in 1925 forty acres of land north-east of Oxford Circus were sold to the Audley Trust. Meanwhile the General Real Estates Investment and Trust, Ltd. (of which he himself was chairman), had acquired in 1922 a large portion of his west-end estate for a sum which was reported to exceed £4 million. He extended his interests by buying property and forest land on a large scale in Kenya, and also in Wales, whence the Ellis family originally stemmed. His concern in Cymric affairs was strong; he bred the native ponies, learned Welsh and fostered the study of that language.

Throughout his life Howard de Walden was keenly interested in the stage. He was himself the author of both dramas and librettos. With the composer Josef Holbrooke he produced (as T. E. Ellis) an operatic trilogy *The Cauldron of Annwn*. The first opera, *The Children of Don*, was presented by Oscar Hammerstein at the London Opera House in 1912; *Dylan* was conducted by (Sir) Thomas Beecham at Drury Lane in 1914 and marked the first use of cinematographic effects on the stage, which was another of Lord Howard de Walden's pursuits. The third opera, *Bronwen*, was played by the Carl Rosa Company at Huddersfield in 1929. Neither the unfamiliar Welsh mythological plots, nor the music of Holbrooke attracted the favourable notice of the critics. Using Byzantine themes, Howard de Walden was also the author of several plays. *Heraclius* was performed at the Holborn Empire in the autumn of 1924, but neither *Constantine* nor *Justinian II* has yet been published. He wrote in addition a charming series of pantomimes for children which were successively produced by his own family and their friends at Chirk.

Lord Howard de Walden married in 1912 Margherita Dorothy, daughter of Charles van Raalte, J.P., of Brownsea Island and Grosvenor Square. They had one son, John Osmael (born 1912), who succeeded to the titles, and five daughters. To the Tate Gallery, of which he was a trustee from 1938, he presented the bust of himself by Rodin, which is his best likeness. He was also a collector of modern paintings. In 1930 he embarked on a new field with his expedition to Uganda and the eastern Belgian Congo, the valuable botanical and zoological fruits of which were presented to the Natural History Museum.

The diverse talents of this versatile man were matched by his noble generosity to many branches of art and charity; hospitals, orchestras, and numerous individual artists, including the poet Dylan Thomas, benefited by his munificence and taste. In the breadth of his patronage and in his own widespread activity, he epitomized a splendid tradition of the English aristocracy, practising as well as stimulating the arts, sports, and learning which he loved. He died in London 5 November 1946, and was buried in the family vault at Dean Castle.

[*The Times*, 6 November 1946; private information.]  MICHAEL MACLAGAN.

**SEELY, JOHN EDWARD BERNARD**, first BARON MOTTISTONE (1868–1947), politician and soldier, was born at Brookhill Hall, between Derby and Nottingham, 31 May 1868. His family were wealthy colliery owners in the Midlands, and his grandfather, for many years member of Parliament for Lincoln, was a noted Radical, who won notoriety by entertaining Garibaldi at his home in the Isle of Wight. Seely was the fourth son and seventh child of (Sir) Charles Seely, who became first baronet, by his wife, Emily, daughter of William Evans, of Crumpsall Grange, Lancashire. He was brought up in Nottinghamshire but spent most of his holidays in the Isle of Wight for which he retained a constant affection. From his Tudor manor there he was eventually to take his title. He was educated at Harrow (where he fagged for Stanley Baldwin) and at Trinity College, Cambridge. He graduated in 1890 and was called to the bar by the Inner Temple in 1897. While an undergraduate he had joined the Hampshire Yeomanry. When the South African war broke out he succeeded in arranging private but immediate transport to South Africa for his squadron, through the good offices of his uncle, Sir Francis Evans, chairman of the Union Castle Line. He served against the Boers for eighteen months and his remarkable courage, although occasionally bringing him into conflict with authority, won him distinction and several decorations: he was appointed to the D.S.O. in 1900.

During his absence in South Africa Seely was elected Conservative member for the Isle of Wight (1900). In Parliament his handsome appearance, friendliness, incisive speech, and ebullient unorthodoxy quickly singled him out as a coming man. With some of the younger Conservatives, in particular (Sir) Winston Churchill and Lord Hugh Cecil (later Lord Quickswood), 'Jack' Seely maintained a sustained attack on the Balfour Government's administration of the army. He left the Conservative Party in 1904 on the combined issues of protection and 'Chinese slavery', and resigning his seat was re-elected without opposition at a by-election. In 1906 he was narrowly elected as a Liberal for the Abercromby division of Liverpool. When Campbell-Bannerman formed his Government, Seely was 'left outside', but when Asquith became prime minister in 1908 he was appointed under-secretary to the Colonial Office and in 1909 was sworn of the Privy Council. Since his chief, Lord Crewe [q.v.], was in the Lords, important work fell to the under-secretary, in particular the introduction of the measure which brought about the Union of South Africa. In 1911 Seely transferred to the War Office where in 1912 he succeeded Lord Haldane [q.v.] as secretary of state, an obvious choice having regard to his knowledge of army matters and his experience on the Committee of Imperial Defence. He worked in close accord with the chief of the imperial general staff, Sir John French (later the Earl of Ypres, q.v.), whom he always held in affectionate admiration. French and Seely were responsible for the invitation to Foch to attend the British manœuvres in 1912 and active in preparing the army for the war with Germany which Seely believed to be inevitable. The mobility of the proposed Expeditionary Force and in particular the development of a Flying Corps were his especial interests.

Seely and his advisers had some im-mediate anxieties nearer home. During the later months of 1913 there was some discussion in the army—and a great deal more outside—about the position of the armed forces should the Government be obliged to impose the policy of Home Rule for Ireland by force. In view of the speculation on this topic Seely wisely decided to confer in December with the general officers commanding in England, Scotland, and Ireland. At this conference, and after a discussion in which the secretary of state raised the whole question of the relations between the armed forces and the civil power, it was not disputed that officers who were domiciled in an area of disturbance—which in this case was Northern Ireland—should not be compelled to take part in any possible hostilities.

On 14 March 1914 a Cabinet committee of which Seely was a member decided to inform Sir Arthur Paget, commanding in Ireland, that there was reason to expect attempts to obtain arms and that certain depots in the north appeared to be insufficiently guarded. Paget replied that he was reluctant to move troops for fear of precipitating a crisis in the country. He was again summoned to London where by this time (Sir) Winston Churchill and Seely had persuaded themselves and the Cabinet that trouble was imminent; a view which the sudden departure of Sir Edward (later Lord) Carson [q.v.] for Belfast on the 19th did nothing to dispel. Certain movements of troops in Ireland were agreed. Paget was also instructed to talk to his officers in the sense of the discussions held in the previous December. The instructions which were given to him in writing provided that Ulster-domiciled officers might 'disappear' but stated that other officers who from conscientious reasons were not prepared to carry out their duty as ordered were to say so at once and be dismissed the Service. No doubt Seely is to be blamed for agreeing to instructions which gave officers the opportunity of pronouncing judgement on orders which might be issued to them, but the position was embittered by political pressure from outside and Seely was naturally anxious to meet the wishes of Paget and his own leading military advisers. But the results of these instructions were serious for, although no precise record has been kept of what Paget said when he got back to Dublin, his observations gave rise to the impression that immediate action against Ulster was contemplated and resulted in his reporting to London without further explanation that Brigadier-General (later General Sir) Hubert Gough and fifty-seven of his officers in the 3rd Cavalry brigade stationed at the Curragh 'preferred dismissal if ordered north'. Gough was accordingly relieved of his command and ordered to report to the War Office with his three colonels.

On Monday morning, 23 March, Seely, in the presence of Paget, French, and the adjutant-general, Sir Spencer Ewart [q.v.], reassured Gough about the Government's intentions, and agreed to provide written confirmation which Gough might show to his officers. Seely then went to a Cabinet meeting, which he had to leave before it concluded in order to attend the King to report on the situation. On his return, the Cabinet had broken up for luncheon and he failed to apprehend, from a few words with Asquith who was still in the room, that the document drafted for Gough by the adjutant-general and amended by the Cabinet was now inviolate. Seely, realizing that it did not entirely meet Gough's difficulties, accordingly added two paragraphs, one of which asserted that the Government had no intention of using the forces of the Crown 'to crush political opposition to the policy or principles of the Home Rule Bill'. In this he had the help of Lord Morley [q.v.] who was to answer for the Government in the Lords that afternoon. The revised memorandum, initialed by Seely himself, and by French and Ewart, was then handed to Gough. Later that day, on the prompting of (Sir) Henry Wilson [q.v.] who was in close touch with the Opposition, Gough sought additional clarification from French who, without informing Seely, gave Gough the further written assurance that his men would not be ordered to Ulster. Gough returned to his command, but the jubilation of his friends aroused strong feeling among the Liberal and Labour parties, many of whose members held that the Government had stooped to bargain with a troublesome group of officers. In the face of this it was out of the question for the Government to endorse the amended statement.

On 25 March in the House of Commons Seely took the entire blame, in an effort to avoid the resignations of the chief of the imperial general staff and the adjutant-general. Asquith, while repudiating the memorandum and making it clear that he thought the secretary of state had made an error of judgement, declined to accept Seely's resignation. During the next few days it became clear, however, that both French and Ewart felt that they must resign rather than dishonour their signatures. Strenuous efforts were made, between parliamentary storms, to retain French as chief of the imperial general staff. By 30 March, however, Asquith reluctantly concluded that the Government 'could not possibly survive any recognition, express or implied, of the Gough treaty, and it is equally clear that French will not remain except upon that footing. . . . I see no way out of the imbroglio but for Seely to go also and I propose myself, for a time, to take his place.'

The Curragh incident thus cost Seely his portfolio, although he remained a member of the Committee of Imperial Defence. Asquith's subsequent decision not to 'purge' the army (because this would have disorganized the Expeditionary Force) was noted by both sides in Ireland to his great disadvantage. And the strains and stresses which the episode had revealed in the army were noted too in Germany.

The question whether Seely would have speedily returned to office after taking part in what, in his own words, 'looked like a private bargain with a few rebellious officers', was engulfed by the outbreak of war. To one of his active disposition it was perhaps not unfortunate that he was no longer a member of the administration. He left London on 11 August 1914, and remained in France with scarcely a break until 1918, for the majority of the time in command of the Canadian Cavalry brigade. He and his horse Warrior (about which he later wrote an engaging book) were conspicuous in many actions in which 'the luckiest man in the army' seemed to reflect by his remarkable gallantry the more romantic exploits of an earlier tradition. Seely was appointed C.B. in 1916, C.M.G. in 1918, and was five times mentioned in dispatches. In 1918 he was gassed and retired from active service with the rank of major-general. He became parliamentary under-secretary and deputy minister of munitions, moving as under-secretary to the Air Ministry in January 1919. In November he resigned on the prime minister's refusal to give the Air Ministry a separate secretary of state.

Seely was member for the Ilkeston division of Derbyshire from a by-election in 1910 (after an earlier defeat in the same year at Abercromby) until 1922 when, in common with many coalition Liberals, he was defeated. He was elected as a Liberal for the Isle of Wight in 1923 but was defeated in the following year. He devoted the rest of his life to the savings movement—he was chairman of the national committee (1926–43), and an active vice-chairman till his death—and to country pursuits. From 1918 he was lord lieutenant of Hampshire and the Isle of Wight. Ships and the sea were always his principal recreation and for much of his life he was coxswain of the Brooke lifeboat. He was created a baron in 1933.

Throughout his strenuous life Seely was conspicuous for a gay and brave bearing, not commonly found at Westminster, and this won him a wide company of friends who, apart from his own political party, included Balfour, George Wyndham, Birkenhead, MacDonald, Henderson, and Snowden [qq.v.]. He was the author of two books of autobiography which, even in their titles, *Adventure* and *Fear, and be Slain*, faithfully revealed the tang of Seely's personality. Nor were his exciting experiences diminished in their telling.

Seely was twice married: first, in 1895 to Emily Florence (died 1913), daughter of the Hon. (Sir) Henry George Louis Crichton; secondly, in 1917 to the widow of his friend Captain George Crosfield Norris Nicholson, Evelyn Izmé, daughter of the tenth Baron and first Viscount Elibank. She survived him when he died in London 7 November 1947. There were three sons and four daughters of the first marriage and one son of the second. The eldest son was killed at Arras in 1917 and the second son, Henry John Alexander (born 1899), succeeded as second baron.

A portrait by Sir William Orpen is in the Imperial War Museum; another by Sir Alfred Munnings of Seely mounted on Warrior is in the National Art Gallery at Ottawa.

[*The Times*, 8 November 1947; J. E. B. Seely, *Adventure*, 1930, *Fear, and be Slain*, 1931, and (Lord Mottistone), *My Horse Warrior*, 1934; Sir C. E. Callwell, *Sir Henry Wilson*, 2 vols., 1927; Sir F. B. Maurice, *Haldane*, 2 vols., 1937–9; private information.]
ROGER FULFORD.

[Geoffrey Brooke, *Good Company*, 1954; A. P. Ryan, *Mutiny at the Curragh*, 1956.]

SELBIE, WILLIAM BOOTHBY (1862–1944), Congregational divine, was born at Chesterfield 24 December 1862, the eldest son of the Rev. Robert William Selbie, Congregational minister, of Salford, by his wife, Harriette Raine, daughter of William Boothby, surveyor of shipping, of Calcutta. He attended Manchester Grammar School and as a scholar of Brasenose College, Oxford, obtained a second class in classical moderations (1884) and in *literae humaniores* (1886). From 1886 to 1889 he was the first student at Mansfield College, Oxford, where he studied theology under A. M. Fairbairn whose notice he contributed to this DICTIONARY and whose life he wrote in 1914. In 1888 he was awarded the senior Septuagint prize. He remained at Mansfield a further year as tutor in Hebrew, and was then called to be minister of the Congregational church at Highgate (1890–1902). Thereafter for seven years he was minister of Emmanuel Congregational church in Cambridge and lecturer in pastoral theology at Cheshunt College (1907–9) until, on Fairbairn's retirement, he was called to Mansfield as principal (1909). He received the honorary degree of D.D. from Glasgow in 1911, and was admitted D.D. of Oxford by decree in 1920, one of the first of the non-Anglicans since the seventeenth century. From 1921 to 1924 he was Wilde lecturer in natural and comparative religion in Oxford, and in 1924 examiner in the honour school of theology. He was elected an honorary fellow of Brasenose in 1926.

Apart from the life of Fairbairn, Selbie's two most substantial writings were *Schleiermacher* (1913) and his Wilde lectures, *The Psychology of Religion* (1924). He was a faithful and diligent student and teacher, but his interest was pre-eminently in the work of preaching and the practical life of the churches. He edited the *Examiner* (after 1906 the *British Congregationalist*) from 1900 to 1909, was chairman of the Congregational Union of England and Wales from 1914 to 1915, and president of the National Free Church Council in 1917. He was a preacher of singular force and directness, and, more particularly in the years immediately following the war of 1914–18, he exercised great influence in Oxford by his preaching in Mansfield College chapel and by constant pastoral service of the many who from various churches came to seek his counsel. He retired in 1932, a sick man, but lived until 28 April 1944, when he died in Oxford. He married in 1890 Mildred Mary, daughter of Joseph Thompson, man of business, of Wilmslow, Cheshire. They had three sons, the eldest of whom was killed at Ypres in 1916, and one daughter. There is a portrait of Selbie by Ernest Moore at Mansfield College.

[*The Times*, 29 April 1944; *Oxford Magazine*, 1 June 1944; *Congregational Quarterly*, October 1944; private information; personal knowledge.]     NATHANIEL MICKLEM.

SELBORNE, second EARL OF (1859–1942), statesman. [See PALMER, WILLIAM WALDEGRAVE.]

SELFRIDGE, HARRY GORDON (1858–1947), man of business, was born 11 January 1858 at Ripon, Wisconsin, United States. He was the only son of Robert Oliver Selfridge, who owned a small dry goods business in Ripon, by his wife, Lois Frances Baxter. Robert O. Selfridge served from 1861 with the 3rd Michigan Cavalry until 1865 when he resigned, having risen to the rank of major and assistant adjutant-general. He did not return to his family, and died in an accident in 1873. In the meantime Harry was brought up by his mother at Jackson, Michigan, where she was a teacher. After attending the ordinary public schools he became a junior bank clerk at fourteen and about this time hoped to join the navy. He presented the necessary nomination for Annapolis, but was rejected as slightly under height.

In 1879 he joined the Chicago mail-order firm of Field, Leiter & Co. (later Marshall Field & Co.) as a clerk at ten dollars a week and in 1886 became manager of the retail department. He proved a most valuable lieutenant to Marshall Field, travelling to Boston, Philadelphia, and New York, and picking up new and fruitful ideas wherever he went. There followed trips to London, Paris, and other European centres, after which Selfridge thought of starting his own business. Rather than see that development Field made him a junior partner in 1890. But in 1904 Selfridge retired with a fortune of some £300,000 and bought the Chicago firm of Schlesinger and Mayer, quickly selling it again at a profit of £50,000. Travel, reading, club life, and the care of his collection of orchids failed to satisfy his needs; and in 1906 he arrived in London to survey the commercial scene. Despite the existence of a number of excellent general stores, he felt that there was room for another, which should have its own distinctive features. Scorning the mina-

tory advice of the pessimists, Selfridge secured a site on the north side of Oxford Street, and in 1908 building operations began.

In March 1909 the business of Selfridge & Co., Ltd., opened with 130 departments and a capital of £900,000. The shop aimed at covering all normal requirements, from groceries to a safe deposit. From the first Selfridge insisted that the staff should not badger the customer to buy. He provided a library, rest-rooms, a roof-garden, and (for many years) an information bureau which, without fee, would answer all kinds of difficult queries rapidly by telephone. All this was backed by masterly and persistent press advertising; and as the years went on the business prospered greatly. After the war of 1914–18 it acquired financial control of sundry London suburban and provincial stores, which were, however, allowed to retain their own character. In the months just before the war of 1939–45 the volume of business considerably decreased. Selfridge himself, through various personal follies which involved him in enormous expenditure, was heavily in debt to the company and in October 1939 he resigned from the board with the honorary title of president and a salary of £2,000 a year. The company was reorganized in 1941 and in 1951 its management passed into the hands of Lewis's, Ltd., of Liverpool.

From the outset of his career, Selfridge looked upon business as an exciting and glorious adventure. This point of view was emphasized in his book, *The Romance of Commerce* (1918), in many speeches, and in his staff relationships. It was well known that he himself had started from scratch without capital or influence. He gave his staff every incentive to progress, and was wont to say that if an employee was not promoted within three years 'there is something wrong with him— or with us'. He provided every recreative facility for his work-people, but avoided paternalism and saw to it that all clubs and societies were run by their own members. His imaginative qualities were shown by such things as the scheme whereby a customer pointing out any error of fact in one of the firm's advertisements was financially rewarded. He was a man of highly optimistic temperament and energetic character, accessible and of agreeable manner. Outside office hours he was an ardent theatregoer, and a devotee of orchids and bookbindings, assembling fine collections of both.

Selfridge remained an American citizen until 1937 when he was naturalized a British subject. He died at Putney Heath, London, 8 May 1947. He married in 1890 Rosalie Buckingham, of Chicago, who died in 1918. There were three daughters and a son of the marriage. A portrait by Sir William Orpen is at Selfridges.

[*The Times*, 9 May 1947 ; *Review of Reviews*, May 1910 ; T. C. Bridges and H. H. Tiltman, *Kings of Commerce*, 1928 ; *Current Biography*, March 1941 and June 1947 ; *Chicago Tribune*, 15 May 1904 ; J. W. Leonard, *The Book of Chicagoans*, 1905 ; private information.]

HERBERT B. GRIMSDITCH.

SELINCOURT, ERNEST DE (1870–1943), scholar and literary critic, was born at Streatham 24 September 1870, the third son of Charles Alexandre de Selincourt, merchant, by his wife, Theodora Bruce Bendall, sister of Cecil Bendall [q.v.]. He was educated at Dulwich College and University College, Oxford, where he was placed in the second class in *literae humaniores* in 1894, and was *proxime accessit* for the Chancellor's English essay prize.

After two years spent in lecturing at Bedford College, tutorial work in Oxford, and the study of Anglo-Saxon with Arthur Sampson Napier, de Selincourt was appointed lecturer in English language and literature at his own college, and in 1899 university lecturer. In 1908 he was elected professor of English language and literature at the university of Birmingham, where he served as dean of the faculty of arts from 1919 to 1931 and as vice-principal from 1931 to 1935.

De Selincourt made signal contribution to the growth of two newly founded academic institutions, the school of English language and literature at Oxford, and the university of Birmingham. At Oxford he supplied almost single-handed the literary teaching of the school in its early years, and by the fine quality of his lectures and by his scholarship, had much to do with establishing its reputation. At Birmingham, where the university was emerging from the Mason College, he put the full force of his mind into the struggle for the establishment of humane studies in the university and of the university itself as the centre of intellectual life in the city: as Professor Eric Robertson Dodds has written, 'he deserves to be remembered . . . as one of the men whose obstinate idealism and creative vision

transformed a group of unimportant provincial institutions . . . into the modern universities as we know them'.

Believing in learning and education in their broadest as well as highest interpretation, de Selincourt helped to strengthen the education department by bringing it into the main structure of the university ; linked the staff of the Workers' Educational Association with his own ; and made the local branch of the English Association a centre of English culture, drawing large audiences to the university. He did much also to bring good music and drama within reach of student and citizen.

An edition of the poems of Keats (1905) was de Selincourt's first important critical work. *Hyperion: A Facsimile of Keats's Autograph Manuscript* followed ; in 1906 appeared his scholarly reprint of Wordsworth's *Guide to the Lakes* ; and in 1912 his edition of Spenser with an admirable critical introduction. His most valuable service to English literature was given in definitive editions of William and Dorothy Wordsworth: *The Prelude*, edited from the manuscripts (1926), a masterpiece of scholarly technique and critical interpretation ; the *Letters of William and Dorothy Wordsworth* in six volumes (1935–9) ; Wordsworth's *Poetical Works*, vols. i and ii (1940–44) ; Dorothy Wordsworth's *George and Sarah Green* (1936), and *Journals* (2 vols., 1941). His life of Dorothy Wordsworth appeared in 1933, and a posthumous volume, *Wordsworthian and other Studies*, in 1947.

The function of criticism in de Selincourt's view was to make his author better understood—his editing was free from pedantry and dogmatism and a model of clarity and economy. Sensitive to literary form as to other forms of beauty, he valued literature as a vital expression of the spirit of man. He was professor of poetry at Oxford (1928–33) and his *Oxford Lectures on Poetry* (1934), ranging in subject from Chaucer to Bridges, gives the measure of his mature critical powers.

De Selincourt married in 1896 Ethel (died 1931), daughter of William Tuer Shawcross, mill-owner, of Rochdale, and had two sons and two daughters. He was elected F.B.A. in 1927 ; received the honorary degree of LL.D. from Edinburgh University in 1929 ; and became honorary fellow of University College, Oxford, in 1930. He was president of the English Association (1935–6). After his retirement from Birmingham in 1935 he lived at

Ladywood, his Grasmere home; he died at Kendal 22 May 1943.

The power and integrity of de Selincourt's character, his intolerance of the trivial and shoddy, made him formidable to the general, but to his family and friends he revealed delightful humour, generosity, and a singular power of affection. A portrait of him by Fred Yates hangs in the English department at Birmingham University; another by Gilbert Spencer, painted shortly before his death, is at Ladywood.

[*The Times*, 25 May 1943; Helen Darbishire in *Proceedings* of the British Academy, vol. xxix, 1943; private information; personal knowledge.]      HELEN DARBISHIRE.

SEQUEIRA, JAMES HARRY (1865–1948), dermatologist, was born in London 2 October 1865, the son of James Scott Sequeira, surgeon, by his wife, Maria Rosina Backwitz. Sequeira inherited a long tradition of medical service, going back through six generations. His great-grandfather had been physician to the Prince Regent of Portugal and to the Portuguese embassy in London, finally settling in this country. Sequeira was educated at King's College School and entered the London Hospital in 1884 with a scholarship. He took his M.B. in 1890 with honours in medicine and obstetrics, proceeded M.D. in 1891 and F.R.C.S. (England) in 1893, the year in which he won the Hutchinson prize. He was elected F.R.C.P. (London) in 1905.

In turn demonstrator in anatomy and medical tutor, Sequeira became first dermatologist to his hospital in 1902 after special study in Vienna and Copenhagen. He introduced 'Finsen Light' treatment into England in 1900 and in the following year translated Niels Finsen's book on phototherapy. By a remarkable demonstration of affected children he induced the president of the Local Government Board, Walter (later Viscount) Long [q.v.], in 1916 to issue regulations establishing clinics for venereal disease, of which Sequeira made a lifelong study. He was a pioneer worker in radiology and like many early workers in this field suffered from the effects of radiation. Recognized as an authority on radium he was asked to read a paper on its use at the International Congress of Surgery held in Stockholm in 1905.

A grandee in manner, Sequeira maintained the great clinical tradition of his hospital which was ever his first love. He was an inspiring and tireless teacher, whose textbook *Diseases of the Skin*, first published in 1911, was rewritten and republished in 1947. He was for some years editor of the *British Journal of Dermatology and Syphilis* and a prolific contributor to specialist journals.

In 1927 Sequeira retired and went to live in Kenya where he took an active interest in medical affairs and was able to make a study of leprosy. He was twice president of the Kenya branch of the British Medical Association and for ten years edited the *East African Medical Journal*.

Sequeira was a man of urbane distinction: a short square figure, a leonine head covered from an early age with thick white hair, wide full blue eyes, combining dignity with the greatest kindness. He was an accomplished pianist and delighted in the company of his family and friends and all who were in any way associated with his hospital.

In 1903 Sequeira married Nellie Adams; they adopted two children, a boy and a girl. He died at N'Dera, Kenya, 25 November 1948.

[*London Hospital Gazette*, March and April 1949; personal knowledge.]
W. J. O'DONOVAN.

SEWARD, SIR ALBERT CHARLES (1863–1941), botanist and geologist, was born at Lancaster 9 October 1863, the sixth child (and only son to survive childhood) of Abram Seward, who owned an ironmonger's business, but devoted much of his time to local administration and religious work, and was mayor of Lancaster in 1877, by his wife, Marian Smith. After education at Lancaster Grammar School Seward entered St. John's College, Cambridge, where he obtained a first class in each part of the natural sciences tripos (1885, 1886), and became a scholar of his college (1885). In 1886 he began to study palaeobotany, working for a year in Manchester under W. C. Williamson [q.v.], and afterwards visiting the principal museums of the continent to study the fossil plants in their collections. In 1888 he gained the Harkness scholarship and in 1890 was appointed university lecturer in botany at Cambridge. His essay on *Fossil Plants as Tests of Climate* won the Sedgwick prize, and was published in 1892; the books and papers on fossil plants which followed led to a fellowship of the Royal Society in 1898. His college awarded him a fellowship in 1899, which he resigned soon afterwards on appointment as fellow and tutor of Emmanuel College. In 1906 he succeeded H. Marshall Ward [q.v.] as professor of botany at Cambridge and relinquished his tutorship. He held the chair for thirty years and contributed greatly to the progress of the Cambridge Botany School as a place of study and research. Like his predecessor he possessed great ability as a lecturer to undergraduates, and attracted many students to the study of plants. He was assisted by an able staff of lecturers and demonstrators, among whom was his close friend F. F. Blackman [q.v.], the eminent plant physiologist. The number of students working in the Botany School considerably increased, and research students came from other universities at home and abroad, so that the building, which seemed so large when it was built in 1904, became much overcrowded until it was extended in 1934, with the financial help of the Rockefeller Trustees.

Throughout his scientific career Seward was an indefatigable research worker and encouraged original investigation in all branches of knowledge. Even when weighed down with administrative work he found time for the study of the collections of fossil plants which were sent to him from all parts of the world. He produced ten books and over a hundred original scientific papers. His textbook on *Fossil Plants for Students of Botany and Geology* was begun in 1897 and four volumes appeared at varying intervals from 1898 down to 1919. It gave a concise summary of the state of knowledge about the plants of past ages, covering all groups save the flowering plants. Its illustrations and long lists of references add to its permanent value. Another important book, published in 1931, was *Plant Life through the Ages* which dealt with the more general biological and geological problems arising from the study of fossil plants. These included a valuable study of the geographical distribution of plants in the world in former times, a subject in which the author had long been interested. The value of his contributions to science was recognized by the award of a Royal medal (1925) and the Darwin medal (1934) by the Royal Society, and Murchison (1908) and Wollaston medals (1930) by the Geological Society. His eminence as a botanist led to his appointment as president of the botany section of the British Association in 1903 and 1929. In 1930

he was president of the fifth International Botanical Congress; in the next year president of the International Union of Biological Sciences; and in 1939 president of the British Association.

In 1915 Seward accepted the invitation of the professors and fellows to become master of Downing College. The college had passed through many vicissitudes since its foundation in 1800; its endowments were small as compared with those of other colleges, and, owing to the war, its future seemed uncertain. During the twenty-one years of his mastership Downing attained a position and reputation higher than it had ever before possessed. Its numbers increased considerably, its buildings were improved by the addition of two handsome blocks designed by Sir Herbert Baker [q.v.], its members took a prominent part in the life of the university, and a corporate unity was established which had not before existed. In all of this the master took a leading part; his lodge became the centre of college life; he knew personally every undergraduate; he took an active interest in the college clubs and societies, and was very popular. He was interested in the improvement of the college amenities and of the college administration, but he always expected a high standard of intellectual endeavour from all resident members of the college. In 1924 he became vice-chancellor of the university. He had previously served on the council of the senate and on many boards and syndicates, and now again displayed the same administrative ability which he had shown in his laboratory and his college.

From 1922 to 1924 Seward was president of the Geological Society of London and helped to guide the affairs of the Society at a critical period. From his schooldays he had been intensely interested in geology, through the influence of his old friend J. E. Marr [q.v.], and he contributed many papers to the *Quarterly Journal* of the Geological Society. On the day before his death he completed a popular book on geology in which the fascination of this branch of knowledge is admirably displayed. Seward served on the council of the Royal Society for two periods and in 1934 became foreign secretary of the Society. In his later years he was the recipient of honorary degrees from the universities of Oxford, Dublin, Geneva, Manchester, Cape Town, Toronto, Edinburgh, Birmingham, Glasgow, and St. Andrews; and honorary memberships of many foreign learned societies including the Royal Swedish Academy, the American Academy of Arts and Sciences, the Norwegian Academy, the New York Academy of Sciences, the Geological Societies of South Africa and Belgium, and the Palaeontological Society of Russia. In 1936 he was knighted.

When the new statutes at Cambridge came into operation Seward chose to come under them, and consequently, on reaching the retiring age in 1936, he relinquished his professorship and mastership and removed to London. He maintained connexions with Cambridge, however, for he had been elected to honorary fellowships at each of his former colleges. He now devoted much of his time to the affairs of the Royal Society, the Advisory Council of the Department of Scientific and Industrial Research, and the standing commission on museums and art galleries. In 1938 he became a trustee of the British Museum. His free time was spent in research at the British Museum, where he was studying the early tertiary floras of Mull and the adjacent islands, a subject which formed the topic of his presidential address to the British Association in 1939. On the outbreak of war he returned to Cambridge for a time and then went to live in Oxford, where he died very suddenly 11 April 1941.

During a life of intense intellectual and administrative activity Seward regarded as a duty the work of making known to the public the discoveries of botanists and geologists. He wrote several popular books and many magazine articles on subjects which he found interesting, and was very generous in giving lectures to local scientific societies. He was joint-editor with (Sir) Francis Darwin [q.v.] of *More Letters of Charles Darwin* (1903), edited *Darwin and Modern Science* (1909), and *Science and the Nation* (1917), and was general editor of the Cambridge Botanical Handbooks.

Seward was twice married: first, in 1891 to Marion (died 1924), daughter of Robert Brewis, shipbuilder, of Hartlepool. To her he owed much when he was making his way in the scientific world, for she brought financial aid, and, in devotion to his interests, she relieved him of most of the duties which normally fall to the head of a family. She was an accomplished painter in water-colours and assisted him in the illustration of his books and papers. His second marriage, in 1927, was to Mary Adelia, daughter of James Henry Bogart,

of New York City. Both marriages were exceptionally happy in the common interest shown in his work, and in the assistance which he obtained in the social duties attaching to his position. By his first wife he had four daughters.

Of portraits of Seward, one, painted by James Gunn, is in Downing College; another, by Harold Knight, is in the Botany School at Cambridge.

[H. Hamshaw Thomas and F. O. Bower in *Obituary Notices of Fellows of the Royal Society*, No. 10, December 1941; *Quarterly Journal* of the Geological Society of London, vol. xcviii, 1942; private information; personal knowledge.]      H. HAMSHAW THOMAS.

SHAW, GEORGE BERNARD (1856–1950), playwright, was born 26 July 1856 at 3 Upper Synge Street, later renamed and renumbered 33 Synge Street, Dublin. His grandfather, Bernard Shaw, was 'a combination of solicitor, notary public, and stockbroker that prevailed at that time' in Dublin, who was ruined when his partner decamped with £50,000 of his money, together with large sums belonging to their clients. The shock was too much for him, and he collapsed and died, leaving his widow almost destitute. George Bernard Shaw's father, George Carr Shaw, was the eighth of her fifteen children, and was twelve at the time. He grew up to be a genial, ineffective man with a sardonic sense of humour and a keen appreciation of anticlimax: gifts which he transmitted to his son. He had no capacity to cope with the general traffic of existence. Through the influence of his kinsman, Sir Robert Shaw, the founder of the Royal Bank of Ireland, popularly known as Shaw's Bank, he was appointed to a sinecure in the Dublin Law Courts, which he held until it was abolished in 1850. He received a pension of £60 a year, which was immediately compounded for a lump sum and invested in a corn-mill in Dublin about which he knew nothing. His partner, a cloth merchant named Clibborn, was equally ignorant, with the result that the firm, Clibborn and Shaw, never flourished; nevertheless it maintained George Carr Shaw, although not Clibborn, until his death. He was still short of thirty-eight when he met Lucinda Elizabeth Gurly, a wilful young woman of twenty-one, who had a cold unloving heart, a ferocious chin, and no sense of humour whatsoever. She was the daughter of Walter Bagnall Gurly, an impoverished and unscrupulous country gentleman with an estate in county Carlow which was deeply embogged in debt, but she had been brought up by her aunt, Ellen Whitcroft, a hunchback with a pretty face and a severely puritanical temper. She sought refuge from her in marriage. It is improbable that George Carr Shaw married her: it seems certain that, although she bore him no love, it was she who married him. He was her senior by seventeen years, a feckless and unimpressive man with a squint, and a vice of which she was unaware. He was, he protested, 'a lifelong and bigoted teetotaller', a statement which he believed to be true because he tippled in secret and was morbidly ashamed of his habit when he was sober.

They rented a house in a lower-middle-class street in Dublin, and here were born two daughters and then George Bernard Shaw. It was loveless and genteelly poor: a place of 'downstarts', as Shaw was to call it. 'The adult who has been poor as a child', he once remarked, 'will never get the chill of poverty out of his bones.' This house was ruled by a disillusioned young woman of iron will who had no talent for domesticity, and was married to a drunkard whom she despised; a 'through-other' house, as the Irish say, where the meals were erratic and ill-cooked, and the children were brought up in an untidy kitchen by slatternly servants. Yet its gentility was overpowering. Catching him in conversation with the child of a retail ironmonger, Shaw's father rebuked him severely. The fact that the ironmonger was a richer and more efficient man than the corn miller merely aggravated his offence. It was subversive of all civilized society that a person who probably sold nails by the pennyworth across a counter should be better off than a descendant of Macduff, the thane of Fife, who slew Macbeth, and of Oliver Cromwell by way of his daughter Bridget and General Fleetwood, and was himself a wholesale merchant and second cousin to a baronet alive at that moment in Dublin.

His father's tippling seems not to have been noticed by the boy until he was past the age when it would have been observed by less remarkable infants. One evening George Carr Shaw took his son for a walk along a bank of a Dublin canal. Feeling jocular, he threatened to throw the boy into the water and, in a clumsy pretence at doing so, nearly did. This incident opened the boy's eyes, and he said to his mother, on his return, 'Mamma, I think Papa is drunk!', and was astounded to hear her

reply, 'Ah, when is he anything else?' In later life he wrote to (Dame) Ellen Terry [q.v.]: 'I have never believed in anything since: then the scoffer began. . . .' When he was accused of dishonouring his father by exposing his weakness, he retorted on his accusers with unaccustomed bitterness that neither his mother, his sisters, nor he himself had ever thought intoxication funny.

It was his father's tippling which turned Dublin into a desert for him and made a naturally romantic-minded lad with a vivid imagination a shy and nervous Ishmael. The father when drunk was impatient of contradiction. He lost his temper easily and was accustomed in his anger to smash anything breakable. Because he was excluded therefore from family parties, his wife and children were excluded too.

The characteristics of this singular household were, however, not totally disadvantageous. If the meals were casual, if the children were neglected by their mother and avoided their father, they were compelled to develop their own characters. And if there was no love or ordinary affection in the nearly graceless house, yet there was music in abundance. It was the music in the house, and the pictures in the National Gallery of Ireland, and the books in his father's attic, which saved Shaw from despair. His mother, who had a mezzo-soprano voice of unusual purity, had become acquainted with a lame musician in the next street. This was George John Vandaleur Lee who was the leader of an orchestra in Dublin and taught voice production by an unorthodox system which Shaw's mother reverentially named 'The Method'. In association with Lee, she filled her house with musicians, vocal and instrumental, and her son listened to them so well that he was able to boast that before he was fifteen he 'could sing and whistle from end to end leading works by Handel, Haydn, Mozart, Beethoven, Rossini, Bellini, Donizetti, and Verdi'.

Shaw's formal education, after some elementary instruction from a governess, and a grounding in Latin by his uncle, the Rev. William George Carroll, was, he declared in later life, entirely useless. In 1867 he entered the Wesley Connexional School (later Wesley College) where he was 'generally near or at the bottom of the class', and seemed to his masters to be an incorrigible dunce and 'a source of idleness in others, distracting them from their studies by interminable comic stories'. Despite these reports, he claimed with justice to be more cultured and widely read than any other person, teacher or pupil, in the school. Apart from his knowledge of music, he haunted the National Gallery of Ireland so persistently that he 'knew enough of a considerable number of painters to recognize their work at sight'. His reading ranged from the Bible and Bunyan to William Robertson's *History of Scotland*, Walter Scott, and Dickens.

His entrance to Wesley School had been preceded by a change greatly for the better in the economic circumstances of the Shaws. About the year 1866, Lee proposed that he and they should share a larger house in a more select street, and they removed to 1 Hatch Street. He also bought Torca Cottage, high on a hill at Dalkey, above Killiney Bay, and in full view of the Dublin and Wicklow mountains, where they lived during the summer months. It was here that Shaw first became aware of natural beauty, and the memory of happy days at Dalkey never faded.

After a few years of this felicity, Lee suddenly decided to remove to London; and the Shaws were faced with economic disaster, despite the fact that the father, sobered by a fit, had ceased to be a drunkard. Shaw's mother solved this problem abruptly and drastically. She broke up her home and virtually deserted her husband and son. Since her hopes of obtaining employment as a teacher of music, as well as the prospects of her elder daughter as a singer, depended upon Lee, she and the two girls would follow him to London. Her husband, tied to his mill, would remain in Ireland, and so would 'Sonny', who had now ended his formal education and had in 1871 become a junior clerk in the estate agency of two brothers, Charles Uniacke and Thomas Courtney Townshend, at a salary of eighteen shillings a month. A few months later, in 1872, his mother, with her daughters, departed from Dublin, to which she never returned. Except once, when he visited her in London, her husband never saw her again. If she wrote to her son, or showed the slightest interest in a boy who was now at the most difficult period of adolescence, no record of her letters or interest survives. Shaw's life with his father in dreary lodgings seems to have been largely one of isolation so complete that he was ignorant of elementary know-

ledge of social intercourse in the class from which he had sprung, and had to read a work entitled *Manners and Tone of Good Society, or Solecisms to be Avoided*. It was characteristic of him that he studied this work in the British Museum, and that his gratitude for its help forbade him to show any snobbery about acknowledging his debt to it.

His career in the estate office was spectacularly successful, despite his habit of training the premium apprentices to sing opera. The Townshends' cashier departed in haste, taking with him some of the rents which he had collected for his employers. Shaw, then sixteen, was appointed temporarily to his post, and filled it with such skill that he was confirmed in it; and within a year of entering the office his salary had risen to £48 a year. While he was in this employment he made his first appearance in print. In 1871 he had sent a letter to the *Vaudeville Magazine* which enraged the editor because he had to pay excess postage on it. The letter was not published. Four years later, in April 1875, he went to a revival meeting, conducted in Dublin by Dwight L. Moody and Ira D. Sankey, and was so repelled by what he saw that he wrote to *Public Opinion* to rebuke 'those members of the aristocracy' who participated in the services, which were suitable only for 'the rough' and 'the outcast of the streets'. Those who were redeemed became so 'highly objectionable' that 'their unconverted friends' longed for their relapse from grace! This letter, which appeared over the signature 'S', caused him to be regarded by his acquaintances as an atheist, although there is nothing in it to justify such a conclusion, nor, indeed, was Shaw at any time in his life an atheist or even an agnostic. It was a remarkable letter for a young man, not yet twenty, to have written, and it contained the germ of his creed. He was still saying when he was ninety substantially what he had written when he was nineteen. He had then no thought of authorship in his head. His ambition, so far as he had one, was to become a painter: a profession for which he had no talent whatsoever. He had, however, without perceiving the fact, qualified himself for criticism: the knowledge of pictures and music and drama which he gained in Dublin was to prove invaluable in London. But his mind was vague about his future, except in one respect: he knew that he did not intend to remain a clerk, despite the brightness of his prospects.

In 1876 Shaw's younger sister, who had suffered from consumption for several years, died at Ventnor, Isle of Wight. Her death brought her brother to a swift and definite decision. Dublin had become repulsive to him. He would join his mother and elder sister, now a popular singer, in London. He had already given a month's notice to the Townshends, who had offered him a higher salary to remain. Shaw now left Ireland, to which he did not return for twenty-nine years (and then only to please his wife). In a cul-de-sac, 13 Victoria (later Netherton) Grove, off the Fulham Road, began nine years of deep discouragement, amounting to desolation, which would have broken the spirit of a less resolute and courageous man.

His account of this period, which appeared in the 1905 edition of *The Irrational Knot*, exposed him to profound disapproval as a selfish son, who, 'callous as Comus to moral babble', lived on his aged parents when he should have striven manfully to keep himself. This myth does not survive examination. He took an impish delight in upsetting routine-minded people who like poor boys who rise to riches to be models of kindly consideration for all with whom they come in contact. He may have admired the genius who will not be dissuaded from his intention, no matter what suffering he may cause, but he did not behave like one. He had earned his livelihood at a time when other boys of his social class were at public schools and universities; he arrived in London when there was a deep trade depression and employment was not easy to obtain; in 1881 he was sick of the smallpox; nevertheless for about three of the nine years he engaged in several occupations; nor was he idling when he was out of employment, but was applying himself with great industry to writing novels. Moreover, his share, amounting to more than £1,000, of a bequest left by his maternal great-grandfather, to which he became entitled in 1877, far more than covered the cost of the very poor entertainment which his mother gave him. The whole of the bequest, about £4,000, with the consent of her children, was spent by their mother, as it became legally available, on the maintenance of her ramshackle home. Shaw, who was exceptionally generous to his relatives and had the rare habit of being continuously

grateful for any kindness he ever received, lived in the utmost discomfort with his mother until he married. For the greater part of the time he provided the means which kept her ill-managed house together; and he rewarded her well for the little she did for him, allowing her £400 a year at a time when that was a substantial sum, and buying the leases of the houses in which she lived.

Between the years 1878 and 1883, he wrote five novels: *Immaturity*, the best of the five, *The Irrational Knot*, *Love Among the Artists*, *Cashel Byron's Profession*, and *An Unsocial Socialist*, all of which were at that time refused by publishers in England and America. *Immaturity* was not published until fifty years after it was written. Shaw had little talent for narrative, and these novels, although they are interesting enough to read, are important only as scenarios for the plays he was eventually to write. He was economical: he did not waste his material. The end of *Love Among the Artists* is almost identical with the end of *Candida*; and some of the characters in the novels are sketches for characters in the plays. It is a singular fact that the thought of becoming a dramatist did not occur to him during these years, although it must have been plain to him that his efforts to make a living as a novelist were hopeless. His intellectual growth, however, was remarkable, and he was making important friendships which were to last until they were ended by death. He heard Henry George lecturing in London on the taxation of land values, and at once became a convert to land nationalization; but, soon afterwards, as a result of reading Karl Marx's *Das Kapital* in a French translation, he abandoned George's limited Socialism for the belief that all forms of capital should be nationalized.

The most important of Shaw's achievements at this time was his conquest of himself. Sensitive and shy and very nervous, he perceived that he could not hope to become effective unless he hardened his skin; and so, with astonishing persistence, he forced himself to speak on platforms, in public parks, and at street-corners, until he turned himself into one of the most effective orators and debaters in Great Britain. Few public speakers had so much power over an audience as Shaw, who could make it rock with laughter at one moment, and silence it at the next with a remark that went to the root of his matter. The shy young man, whose knees were almost knocking together as he addressed derisive or indifferent labourers in Victoria Park, held himself so tenaciously to his self-appointed task that Shaw who in 1884 could scarcely open his lips in public was, in 1888 with great confidence and assurance, addressing the British Association on economics for an hour. His industry was, he maintained, due to his superfluity of nervous energy caused by his conversion, when he was twenty-five, to vegetarian diet, but it was strengthened far more by the invincible will which refused to let him acknowledge defeat. His fertility and invention were as great as his application. From 1885, when he was twenty-nine, until 1926, when he was seventy, his record of great and diversified employment, which included the writing of thirty-six plays, most of them major works, as well as a vast amount of journalism and public service, was unsurpassed and not easily equalled.

Yet it was not until 1892 that he turned his thoughts to the theatre, and even then the impulse was not his, but a friend's. Oscar Wilde [q.v.] once stupidly remarked that Shaw had no enemies, but that his friends disliked him. In fact, like any man of distinctive character, Shaw had many enemies, some of whom were deeply embittered, and had numerous friends who were devoted to him. A man who could include among his close and faithful friends such diverse men and women as Beatrice Webb, William Morris, Annie Besant, Edward Carpenter, Ellen Terry, Mrs. Patrick Campbell, Harley Granville-Barker, T. E. Lawrence [qq.v.], Gilbert Murray, and Sir Barry Jackson, must have had unusual qualities of charm and personality.

Among the first of his friends were Sidney Webb and William Archer [qq.v.] who were not only very dissimilar from each other, but from Shaw himself. Webb was born a bureaucrat and planner, with one uncontrollable passion, for statistical surveys. Shaw joined the newly founded Fabian Society in 1884 and Webb followed in 1885, and they soon became its most powerful members. This society's influence not only on the Labour Party, but on all political parties in Great Britain, was out of all proportion to the size of its membership, and it was a main factor in preserving British Labour from domination by Marxist beliefs. Its effect on local government was profound. Archer, who was a dramatist as well as a dramatic critic, was a man of such

integrity and generous character that he could tell an author to his face how bad his play was without hurting his feelings. It was he who discovered Shaw studying *Das Kapital* and the score of *Tristan and Isolde* in the reading-room of the British Museum, and found the tall, red-headed young man—Shaw was over six feet in height—so much to his taste that he became his devoted friend for the rest of his life, although his conception of drama was so different from Shaw's that he once publicly appealed to him to abandon the theatre since he had no talent for writing plays. He was to recant that opinion handsomely. In 1885 Archer performed two great services. He persuaded the editor of the *Pall Mall Gazette* to employ Shaw as a reviewer of books at two guineas a thousand words, a task which Shaw performed until 1888, and he suggested that they should collaborate in writing a play. Archer could construct a plot, but was unable to write speakable dialogue: Shaw could write reams of fluent dialogue, but, he modestly asserted, could not construct plots. In this respect he underestimated himself. Archer supplied Shaw with his plot, and was dismayed to hear that it had been used up in two acts. The script revealed that Archer's work, except for the setting of the first act, had been entirely ignored, and that Shaw, now rampantly socialistic, had produced a singular comedy about slum landlords. Archer dissociated himself from the piece, and Shaw, feeling that he had failed as a dramatist, put his two acts away, and turned to other work. Archer, in no wise wounded by this abortive effort at collaboration, in refusing the post of art critic on the *World*, insisted that it should be given to Shaw, who held it from 1886 to 1889.

The years of poverty had ended, and the years of plenty now began. T. P. O'Connor [q.v.] founded a London evening paper, the *Star*, and Shaw, following failure as a leader-writer because he would propagand Socialism in Liberal columns, was appointed music critic at two guineas a week: a position he held from 1888 to 1890. Under the pen-name of Corno di Bassetto, he not only wrote the liveliest musical criticism then published, but innovated a custom, not yet fully adopted, of writing in excellent and understandable prose. There was none of the technical jargon which passed for profundity in Shaw's articles, which remain as readable after more than sixty years as they were on the day they were written. They have been collected under the title of *London Music in 1888–89* (1937). In 1889 *Fabian Essays in Socialism* was published, edited by Shaw, who contributed 'The Economic Basis of Socialism' and the text of his address to the British Association, 'The Transition to Social Democracy'. It immediately had an influential effect on current politics. In 1890 he retired from the *Star* and joined the *World* as its music critic at a salary of £5 a week. In the following year he published *The Quintessence of Ibsenism*.

Ibsen's effect on the world theatre was far greater than the popularity of his plays; and it was to be found not only in the work of advanced dramatists, such as Shaw was to become, but also in the work of conventional authors. A young Dutchman, J. T. Grein, in 1891 founded the Independent Theatre, the forerunner of the Stage Society, for the production of unusual and probably unprofitable plays. The first piece to be performed was Ibsen's *Ghosts*, which was received by an outburst of violent denunciation such as could have been displayed only by men with guilty consciences. *Ghosts*, however, seemed to deprive the Independent Theatre of its vitality, for Grein had no play with which to open his season in 1892. Shaw suggested that he should be announced as the author of the next piece, and, raking out the play he had abandoned, he hurriedly added a third act to it, gave it 'the far-fetched mock-scriptural title of *Widowers' Houses*', and had it performed at the Royalty Theatre, 9 December 1892. It was received with a howl which, although not so vulpine as that excited by Ibsen's tragedy, was sufficiently fierce. The play is ramshackle, and creates the impression of having been written while its author was descending from the plinth in Trafalgar Square and striding at great speed to a portable platform in Victoria Park. But it revealed the quality of its author, already renowned in a limited circle for the vigour of his criticism, and was the pioneer of a long series of exceptionally diversified plays, written with great rapidity, which had the utmost difficulty in obtaining performance in regular theatres, but most of which were eventually to be performed with great success all over the civilized world. It was followed, in 1893, by *The Philanderer*, which is Shaw's worst play, apart from pieces written in his extreme old age, and has seldom been performed. *Mrs. Warren's*

*Profession* came next, and was banned, until 1925, by the lord chamberlain because of a faint suggestion of incest in its theme. The piece proved that Shaw could, if he chose, write a 'well-made play'; a fact which was confirmed by the three succeeding plays, *Arms and the Man*, *Candida*, and *You Never Can Tell*. None of these plays, except the first, received public performance until some time later; and *Arms and the Man* (Avenue Theatre, 1894) lasted only a few weeks, taking about £20 at each performance.

It appeared, therefore, that Shaw was destined to failure as a dramatist no less than as a novelist; and, in 1895, he seemed to accept this as irrevocable, for he consented to become dramatic critic of the *Saturday Review*, which was then edited by J. T. (Frank) Harris [q.v.]. Shaw held the post for more than three years, at a salary of £6 a week, and enormously increased his prestige. In 1897 an American actor, Richard Mansfield, who had produced *Arms and the Man* in the United States in 1894, made a considerable success in New York of Shaw's next play, *The Devil's Disciple*. The royalties exceeded £2,000. Fortune now began to favour Shaw. Sir Henry Irving [q.v.] accepted a long one-act play, *The Man of Destiny*, and Cyril Maude accepted *You Never Can Tell*. It was during this period that Shaw and Ellen Terry conducted the brilliant correspondence which was eventually published in 1931. His luck did not, however, last long. Within a fortnight, in April 1897, disaster fell upon him: Irving refused to produce *The Man of Destiny*, and *You Never Can Tell* was withdrawn during its rehearsals because of the total inability of several members of the cast, two of whom threw up their parts, to perceive any point in the play. This blow might have discouraged some tough men for ever, but Shaw met misfortune with gay courage. He used it as a stimulant to write more plays. Nothing seemed able to daunt him from his purpose to capture the theatre, although he now realized that he had not only to attract an audience, but also to create actors. The single sign of discouragement detectable in his correspondence is to be found in a letter to Ellen Terry, who had deeply disappointed him by disliking *Captain Brassbound's Conversion*. He had written the part of Lady Cecily Waynflete for her, but she could not see herself in it: a singular defect in an actress of genius, as was plain to those who saw her in the part many years afterwards, when her powers were waning.

From 1897 until 1903 Shaw participated in municipal government as a vestryman and later borough councillor of St. Pancras, London, an experience which resulted in the publication of his small book, *The Common Sense of Municipal Trading* (1904). In 1898, as a result of overwork, he had a physical collapse, caused primarily through an injury to his foot. He had met, while staying with the Webbs, a wealthy Anglo-Irishwoman, Charlotte Frances, daughter of Horace Payne-Townshend, an Irish barrister, and Mary Susannah Kirby, an Englishwoman. On hearing of his illness, Miss Payne-Townshend went to nurse him in his mother's house, 29 Fitzroy Square, and was so horrified by the discomfort in which he was living that she proposed to remove him to a house in the country; but he, fearing that her generous impulse might bring scandal upon her, insisted that they should marry, which they did, 1 June 1898, in the register office of the Strand district. The bridegroom was not quite forty-two, and the bride his junior by six months. Their life together was entirely felicitous.

While Shaw was recovering from his illness, but still on crutches, *Caesar and Cleopatra* was completed, in 1899, and was produced in Newcastle upon Tyne with Mrs. Patrick Campbell [q.v.] as Cleopatra. From then onward, scarcely a year passed without the completion of a play. In 1901–3, his most brilliant comedy, *Man and Superman*, was written, but it was not until 1904, when he was forty-eight, that he began to gain authority in the west-end theatre, although he had for a number of years been recognized as a distinguished dramatist in the United States. In the autumn of that year, the famous seasons of plays, conducted by John E. Vedrenne, a business man, and Harley Granville-Barker [q.v.], an actor and producer of genius, began at the Royal Court Theatre, Sloane Square, London. The first of Shaw's plays to be performed was his latest piece, *John Bull's Other Island*, which attracted many members of the Cabinet and was seen by King Edward VII in 1905. *Man and Superman* followed, and was also produced in New York by Robert Loraine where it was an instantaneous success and earned large sums for its author and producer. In

November 1905 the first performance was given at the Court of *Major Barbara*, a play about armaments and the Salvation Army, in which a character called Cusins was plainly modelled on Professor Gilbert Murray. In 1906 *The Doctor's Dilemma*, with Sir Almroth Wright [q.v.] as the source of one of the characters, was produced, but in 1907 the productions at the Court ceased. There followed *Getting Married* (Haymarket Theatre, 1908), *The Shewing-Up of Blanco Posnet* (which was banned in Great Britain but produced at the Abbey Theatre, Dublin, 1909), *Misalliance* (Duke of York's Theatre, 1910), and *Fanny's First Play* (Little Theatre, 1911). This was written for Miss Lillah McCarthy (subsequently Lady Keeble) who had taken the leading part in several of Shaw's plays, and was performed 624 times.

It was in 1908 that Shaw's brilliant essay, *The Sanity of Art*, in which he made an overwhelming reply to Max Nordau's curious work, *Degeneration*, was published. Nordau had sought to prove that the rebel-artist was a decadent. In 1909 Shaw gave evidence before the joint select committee on dramatic censorship, but was less effective than he might have been because he used shock-tactics when he should have been indulgent to the weakness of other people's flesh. His meaning when he described himself as 'an immoral author' was plain enough to those who understood in what sense the word 'immoral' was used—that is, 'non-customary' —but the effect of the description on the general public was deplorable. His account of the proceedings is given in his preface to *The Shewing-Up of Blanco Posnet*. Shaw published his own plays, accompanied by prefaces, 'in a simple desire to give my customers good value for their money by eking out a pennorth of play with a pound of preface'. The prefaces were collected and published in a separate volume in 1934, as the plays had been in 1931.

In 1913 a charming play, *Androcles and the Lion*, was produced by Granville-Barker at the St. James's Theatre. In the following year, Sir Herbert Tree [q.v.] produced *Pygmalion* at His Majesty's Theatre with Mrs. Patrick Campbell as the flower-girl; Tree himself played the professor. It was surprisingly popular having regard to the fact that its main theme was concerned with phonetics, a subject which had occupied Shaw's mind from his young manhood, and was almost the last thought in his head, as his will

779

amply demonstrated. Yet he had no gift for languages. A minor element in the play's success was the flower-girl's remark, 'not bloody likely', which put the word 'bloody' almost into polite usage. The play had already been produced in Berlin in 1913.

The outbreak of war, however, cancelled all Shaw's popularity, and brought him great odium even among some of his friends. In November 1914 he published *Common Sense about the War* as a supplement to the *New Statesman* which he had helped to found in 1913. The general effect of the article, especially in the United States, was adverse to Great Britain, although its argument in some respect was identical with that used in a very popular work, *Ordeal by Battle*, by F. S. Oliver [q.v.]. The Germans were quick to exploit it, causing Shaw greater uneasiness than did his ostracism, although that was distressing enough, for there was a period when his arrival in a public place was a signal for those already there to leave it. But he was received into favour again after the end of the war, especially when it was observed how popular *Arms and the Man*, revived in London in 1919 by Robert Loraine, was with soldiers and ex-servicemen. In 1920 *Heartbreak House*, which had occupied him from 1913 until 1916, was performed for the first time in New York. It did not reach England until 1921. This impressive, Lear-like play, which contains his profoundest thoughts and many passages of sombre beauty, was considered by Shaw to be his best play, 'worth fifty *Candidas*', although this belief is challenged by many critics who give the premier place in his work to *Saint Joan*. His attitude to *Heartbreak House* was singularly reticent and reverential: he discussed it with reluctance and less often than any other play he wrote. It was followed by *Back to Methuselah*, 'a metabiological pentateuch', which received its first performance in New York (1922) and was first performed in England in 1923 at the Birmingham Repertory Theatre under the management of Sir Barry Jackson. This is a long, unequal, and difficult work, five plays rather than five acts, given on successive nights. It turns on Shaw's belief that the term of life is too short for us to profit by our experience, and that man must, therefore, will himself into greater longevity. It begins in Eden, passes through the first half of the twentieth century and ends 'as far as thought can reach', when everybody is all but immortal, no one dying except by accident or from discouragement. It is hard to understand why life should be wilfully extended when extended life is made by Shaw to seem so repulsive and dismal. But the play ends with a fine philosophic speech and a suggestion that time will not end except, perhaps, in an eternity of felicity when man, all passion spent, will live in a whirlpool of pure thought.

In 1923 Shaw translated a play by his Austrian translator, Siegfried Trebitsch, under the title of *Jitta's Atonement*, which Trebitsch had intended to be a tragedy: Shaw made a comedy of it. His major work in this year was *Saint Joan*, produced in New York in 1923, and in London (New Theatre) in 1924, with (Dame) Sybil Thorndike in the title-role. The play was an immense success in both cities, despite its length which was increased by a long and unnecessary epilogue in which, however, there are beautiful passages. The natural end of the play is the sixth scene, but Shaw was never able to convince himself that the audience brought any knowledge into the theatre or that any person who saw *Saint Joan* without the epilogue would realize that the Maid had been canonized.

Shaw was now beyond question the most famous living dramatist in the world. The single country which remained indifferent to his work was France, a country for which he himself, while he was still a music critic and unknown as a dramatist, had felt no affection. Its reputation as the citadel of the arts, he maintained, was spurious. Everywhere else, however, his works were frequently performed, and the dramatist who, until he was forty, could not obtain a regular public performance for any of his plays, was now in process of becoming the wealthiest author in history. He had always declined public honours, whether from the community or from universities, but he accepted the Nobel prize for 1925. (The money, more than £7,000, was used to establish the Anglo-Swedish Literary Foundation for the translation of Swedish literature into English, and it had issued four volumes of Strindberg's plays by 1939.) Shaw now resumed political writing. In 1928 he published *The Intelligent Woman's Guide to Socialism and Capitalism*, which had a wide sale, and in 1944 *Everybody's Political What's What?*. A remarkably popular short work, *The Adventures of the Black Girl in Her*

*Search for God*, finely illustrated by Mr. John Farleigh, was written in South Africa and published in 1932.

Shaw was now an old man, and his work, although it was still astonishingly vigorous and vivacious, showed unmistakable signs of his age. He became increasingly careless about form. The best of his work in this period, however, was full of wisdom and the beauty of mind often displayed by old men who keep their wits about them. *The Apple Cart* was unexpectedly popular, chiefly because of its avowal of anti-democratic doctrine and its acclamation of an able monarch. It was produced in Warsaw in June 1929, and was given in England in August at the first of the Malvern Festivals inaugurated by Sir Barry Jackson. *Too True to be Good* (Malvern, 1932) had a character, Private Meek, who was manifestly derived from T. E. Lawrence, for whom Shaw had great personal liking; *Geneva* (Malvern, 1938) included portraits of Mussolini and Hitler; in *In Good King Charles's Golden Days* (Malvern, 1939), Isaac Newton and George Fox are brilliantly portrayed. But Shaw's great work virtually ended with *Saint Joan*, which bears to him the same relationship that *The Tempest* bears to Shakespeare. The advent of the talking film, however, and in particular Gabriel Pascal's production of *Pygmalion*, followed by *Major Barbara* and *Caesar and Cleopatra*, brought Shaw new fame, and, incidentally, fortune.

Much of Shaw's time was spent in extensive travel to please his wife whose delight was in journeys abroad. His health, which was less robust than, in his advocacy of vegetable diet, he was accustomed to maintain, broke down seriously in 1938, when he suffered from pernicious anaemia; nor was the distress of his illness lessened by the fact that the injections by which it was eventually cured involved a violation of his beliefs about diet. His recovery was darkened by the decline in his wife's health. Her illness was long and painful and she died in 1943. There were no children of the marriage. In 1946 when Shaw reached his ninetieth year he was made an honorary freeman of Dublin and the first honorary freeman of the metropolitan borough of St. Pancras, London.

The rest of Shaw's life was quiet and solitary. The loss of his wife was more profoundly felt than he had ever imagined any loss could be: for he prided himself on a stoical fortitude in all loss and misfortune. All his friends who were his contemporaries, with a single exception, Edward R. Pease, first secretary of the Fabian Society, were dead. He had outlived his time. Music was still a comfort to him, and he kept his wireless set almost continuously in operation; but reading, which had been his chief resource, no longer satisfied him: his mind could not concentrate as it had been accustomed to do, nor could he remember anything as well as he once had. Yet his spirit was unbroken, although his body was frail, and he was unwilling to acknowledge decline. He fell frequently, but then he had always fallen, even as a young man. There were trees to be lopped and pruned in his garden at Ayot St. Lawrence where he had lived since 1906, and he would lop and prune them, although he had gardeners to do the work. In September 1950, while trimming his trees, he fell and fractured his thigh. He was removed to hospital where he remained until 4 October when his wish to return home was granted. The will to live was ebbing, and he wished to die where he had lived so long with Charlotte. On 2 November 1950 he died. The whole world paid tribute to him. In America the lights of Broadway were lowered; the Indian Government, under Pandit Nehru who had visited him the year before, adjourned a Cabinet meeting; and *The Times* gave him a first leader. There was a universal feeling of loss. His body was cremated, as his wife's had been, and their ashes were mingled and scattered in the garden of their house at Ayot which was left to the National Trust.

When Shaw's will was published, his fortune was found to be more than £300,000, the greater part of which was devoured by the State. The residue, after some bequests had been made, was left on trust to institute and finance inquiries for a 'Proposed British Alphabet' of at least forty letters. Subject to other directions regarding the alphabet, the ultimate residue was to be given in equal shares to the National Gallery of Ireland, the British Museum, and the Royal Academy of Dramatic Art. The bequests to the first two are significant of Shaw's unending gratitude for kindness or benefit received. In the National Gallery of Ireland he had learnt to understand pictures, and in the British Museum, when he was almost desperately poor, he had found the facilities for reading and study that he needed.

Shaw's general belief about life had its foundation in a religious faith; for Shaw was essentially a religious-minded man. But in religion, as in all else, he was heterodox—a heathen mystic, as G. K. Chesterton called him. His faith, so far as it can be put in a few words, was in creative evolution, based on Bergson, whose attraction to Roman Catholicism at the end of his life would have surprised Shaw had he known of it. The Life Force, an arid expression for Shaw's idea of God, is an imperfect spirit seeking to become perfect, using the method of trial and error, and scrapping its instruments when they are worn out or prove intractable. A cardinal point in his doctrine is that human beings, if they do not assist the Life Force to find perfection, may be scrapped as the mammoth beasts and other creatures now extinct have been. But the belief, although it was firmly held, was never adequately worked out and did not attain to the position of a philosophy. It may be found most simply expressed in *The Shewing-Up of Blanco Posnet.* His Socialism was no more than a desire for an orderly community. Poverty and ignorance and ill health were untidy conditions and must, therefore, be abolished. But no man was less democratic than Shaw, whose admiration was given largely to dictatorial people. He was essentially aristocratic and individualistic in temper. His purpose was to provoke thought, and he provoked it for more than half a century.

Of the many portraits and busts of Shaw, the house at Ayot has a portrait by Augustus John, a bust in bronze by Rodin, and a bronze statuette by Troubetzkoy, whose bust of Shaw is in the Tate Gallery. Another portrait by Augustus John entitled 'The Sleeping Philosopher' is in the possession of Queen Elizabeth the Queen Mother. There is a portrait by Feliks Topolski at Glasgow City Art Gallery. The National Gallery of Ireland has a portrait by John Collier and a life-size statue by Troubetzkoy. A bust by Epstein is in the National Portrait Gallery; busts by Rodin belong to the Royal Academy of Dramatic Art and the Municipal Gallery of Modern Art, Dublin; one by Strobl in the custody of the London County Council was bequeathed by Shaw to the future Shakespeare memorial national theatre.

[G. B. Shaw, prefaces to *The Irrational Knot,* 1905, *Immaturity,* 1930, and *London Music in 1888–89,* 1937; G. B. Shaw, *Sixteen Self Sketches,* 1949; Archibald Henderson, *Bernard Shaw: Playboy and Prophet,* 1911; Frank Harris, *Bernard Shaw,* with a postscript by Bernard Shaw, 1931; Hesketh Pearson, *Bernard Shaw,* 1942, followed by a *Postscript* by the same author, 1951; Blanche Patch, *Thirty Years with G.B.S.,* 1951; R. F. Rattray, *Bernard Shaw, a Chronicle,* 1951; St. John Ervine, *Bernard Shaw, His Life, Work and Friends,* 1956; private information; personal knowledge.]　　　St. John Ervine.

SHAW, HENRY SELBY HELE-(1854–1941), engineer. [See Hele-Shaw.]

SHAW, WILLIAM ARTHUR (1865–1943), archivist and historian, was born at Hooley Hill, Ashton-under-Lyne, 19 April 1865, the younger son of James Shaw, manufacturer, and his wife, Sarah Ann Hampshire. He was educated at the Owens College, Manchester, where he was awarded the Cobden Club prize and the Bradford history scholarship (1883), the Shuttleworth political economy scholarship (1884), and was appointed a Berkeley fellow (1886). He graduated B.A. in 1883, M.A. in 1886, and Litt.D. in 1892. He undertook editorial work for the Chetham Society and was already well known at the Public Record Office when in 1894 it was proposed to employ him on the continuation of the *Calendar of State Papers, Foreign, Elizabeth.* On the withdrawal of Treasury sanction for this work his services were utilized on the *Calendar of Treasury Papers,* already completed down to 1728. On Shaw's own representations the new volumes were not confined to the Treasury Board papers, but were to include other records of the department. In the introduction to Shaw's first volume will be found an explanation of the various classes of documents and the reasons for their inclusion or exclusion. As his calendars continued his introductions became more general, and he made full use of his exceptional knowledge of the political complexities of those days, approaching the subject with extraordinary liveliness and without any pretence of disguising his animosities which were usually well founded. Whereas in the five volumes of *Treasury Books and Papers* the introductions dealt with the nature of the records and the machinery of the Treasury and its control of expenditure, in the *Treasury Books* series which he also edited Shaw allowed himself wider latitude and his cogent array of facts and figures led in many cases to revisions, especially with regard to the policy and ability of Charles II.

Besides his official work Shaw wrote many articles and publications, chiefly on economics and on the history of the seventeenth century including *The History of Currency* (1895), *A History of the English Church during the Civil Wars and under the Commonwealth* (2 vols., 1900), *The Knights of England* (2 vols., 1906), and *Three Inventories of Pictures in the Collections of Henry VIII & Edward VI* (1937). He also wrote reports on the Sidney papers for the Historical Manuscripts Commission, many essays and other volumes for learned societies, and was a contributor to this DICTIONARY. In his own field he was essentially a pioneer. His masterly exposition of the breakdown of the medieval theory that 'the King should live of his own' and of the gradual change to more modern ideas of parliamentary control of expenditure explained much that had hitherto been obscured by reading into an earlier age nineteenth-century theories of public finance. A rapid and incessant worker, he retained to his last working day the figure, bearing, and quickness of speech and movement of a man of middle age.

Shaw was elected F.B.A. in 1940. He was twice married: first, to Clara Edith (died 1919), daughter of Thomas William John Goldsbrough, M.D., of London; and secondly, in 1924 to Mabel Elizabeth, daughter of Angus Grant, retired police officer, by whom he had one daughter. He died at Enfield 15 April 1943.

[*The Times*, 19 April 1943; Sir J. H. Clapham in *Proceedings* of the British Academy, vol. xxix, 1943; personal knowledge.]

F. HUGH SLINGSBY.

SHAW, SIR (WILLIAM) NAPIER (1854–1945), meteorologist, was born in Birmingham 4 March 1854, the third son of Charles Thomas Shaw, manufacturing goldsmith and jeweller, by his wife, Kezia, daughter of Thomas Lawden, gold-chain maker, of Birmingham. From King Edward VI's School at Birmingham he went as a scholar in mathematics to Emmanuel College, Cambridge, where in 1876 he was placed sixteenth wrangler and in the same year was awarded a first class in the natural sciences tripos. In the next year he was elected into a fellowship at his college, and was thereby involved in tutorial and official work in addition to his research in hygrometry, evaporation, and ventilation, an interest which he

never lost, and which later earned him the chairmanship of the atmospheric pollution committee. In 1900 he became secretary of the Meteorological Council. In practice this meant that he was director of the national meteorological organization, and his duties claimed so much of his time that, with the exception of his fellowship which he retained until 1906 (becoming thereafter an honorary fellow), he resigned all his Cambridge appointments including his assistant directorship of the Cavendish Laboratory, which he had held since 1898. In 1905 he was made director of the reorganized Meteorological Office, and in 1907 he became reader in meteorology in the university of London.

At the Meteorological Office, Shaw at once set about building up a staff possessed of the necessary training in physics, so that the office might become a centre of scientific meteorology, invigorated by his own enthusiasm, while he continued to encourage amateurs by personal advice, popular lectures, and papers. From his official researches two results proved to be of special value: the study of the upper atmosphere by means of instruments carried up by balloons and kites (in which W. H. Dines, whose notice Shaw contributed to this DICTIONARY, had long been interested), and, with the help of R. G. K. Lempfert, the determination of the paths of the air in and around the pressure systems of the North Atlantic by means of series of synoptic charts. The results were published in *The Life History of Surface Air Currents* (M.O. 174, 1906), and also formed an important feature of his *Forecasting Weather* (1911). They proved very fruitful for the elucidation of the structure of those systems, and were elaborated in the study of 'fronts', mainly by Norwegian meteorologists.

Shaw played a great part in the organization of the transmission of the observations made by ships at sea, and he devoted much energy to arranging conferences of meteorological services with a view to international co-operation. He was invited to preside over many of these between 1907 and 1924, and their success was very largely due to his personal popularity. In practical meteorology he introduced two valuable innovations: the replacement of the inch of mercury as a barometric unit by the 'millibar'; and the tephigram, with temperature and entropy as co-ordinates, which has remained in daily use for the analysis of the temperature and humidity up to the greatest heights that instruments can reach.

During the war of 1914–18 Shaw was relieved of routine administration by (Sir) H. G. Lyons [q.v.] so that his services might be available for government departments needing his advice. In 1920 he retired, having carried out the transfer of the Meteorological Office to the Air Ministry. None the less, until 1924 he occupied the new chair of meteorology at the Royal College of Science, and his crowning work was the completion in 1931 of his *Manual of Meteorology* (4 vols., 1926–31). This work, marked by nineteenth-century width of vision, was the most comprehensive treatment of the subject in English and is still an indispensable work of reference.

Shaw received many honours both at home and abroad. He was knighted in 1915, was president of the Royal Meteorological Society in 1918–19, of the mathematics and physics section of the British Association in 1908, and of the educational science section in 1919. He was elected F.R.S. in 1891 and awarded a Royal medal in 1923. He received honorary degrees from the universities of Aberdeen, Edinburgh, Manchester, Dublin, Athens, and Harvard, and was Halley lecturer at Oxford in 1918 and Rede lecturer at Cambridge in 1921. He was elected an honorary foreign member of the American Academy of Arts and Sciences, the Accademia dei Lincei, and of many other learned societies. A portrait in oils by Sir Walter Russell hangs in the Air Ministry in London and a copy in Emmanuel College. Shaw married in 1885 Sarah Jane Dugdale (died 1923), daughter of Thomas Harland, M.D., of Salford. She was a lecturer in mathematics at Newnham College, Cambridge. There were no children. Shaw died in London 23 March 1945.

[*The Times*, 26 March 1945; *Quarterly Journal* of the Royal Meteorological Society, vol. lx, No. 254, April 1934, vol. lxxi, Nos. 307–8, January–April 1945; E. Gold in *Obituary Notices of Fellows of the Royal Society*, No. 14, November 1945; *Selected Meteorological Papers of Sir Napier Shaw, F.R.S.*, 1955 (bibliography).]  W. G. KENDREW.

SHORT, SIR FRANCIS (FRANK) JOB (1857–1945), etcher and engraver, was born at Wollaston, Worcestershire, 19 June 1857, the only son of Job Till Short, engineer, by his wife, Emma, daughter of William Millward, also an engineer at Wollaston. Leaving school at the age of thirteen, Short was trained as an engineer, and was an associate member of the Institution of Civil Engineers from 1883 until his resignation in 1904. For a short time he attended evening classes in the Stourbridge School of Art and then, after a period of engineering work in London, abandoned his original profession and entered the National Art Training School (later the Royal College of Art), South Kensington, also attending a life class at the Westminster School of Art, under Frederick Brown [q.v.]. He was elected a member of the Royal Institute of Painters in Water Colours in 1917, but although he was interested in painting, and produced scholarly and poetic water-colours throughout his life, his main work lay in etching and engraving. Perhaps it was his early training in science and engineering which enabled him to make his own tools and invent new ones, to probe all known processes, and to discover new methods of technique. In a lecture he once said: 'An artist must be a workman; and an artist afterwards, if it please God.'

While still a student at South Kensington in 1885 Short won high approval from John Ruskin [q.v.] for some of his mezzotints after Turner's 'Liber Studiorum'. With Ruskin's encouragement he devoted much of his life to the reproduction of Turner's paintings, and mezzotinted forty plates of the 'Liber', including thirty based on unpublished plates or unengraved drawings. Such plates as the 'Via Mala' and 'Lucerne' are masterly renderings never equalled by the engravers who worked under Turner's own guidance. Their craft had died with them, but Short revived mezzotint and made it a new and living art in his translations not only of Turner, but of Reynolds, Constable, De Wint, Watts, and other painters. He showed new possibilities for the medium in using its qualities of tone and mass for his original landscapes, such as 'The Lifting Cloud' (1901), and 'When the Weary Moon was in the Wane' (1894). Entirely his own, too, was his work in aquatint, another method which he revived and developed. It might be claimed that no other aquatints ever made have surpassed his 'Sunrise o'er Whitby Scaur' (1899), or 'A Silver Tide' (1912) in technical accomplishment and atmospheric effect.

His early work as an etcher won praise from J. A. McN. Whistler [q.v.] who, from 1888 to 1900, frequently visited Short's studio for help with matters of technique or of printing. Short's etched work in bitten line, or dry-point, or soft-ground, was a direct interpretation of nature by means of straightforward, frequently outdoor, work upon the plate. Like Rembrandt and Whistler, he believed firmly in purity of line and clean printing, as may be seen in such plates as 'Sleeping till the Flood' (1887), 'Low Tide and the Evening Star and Rye's Long Pier Deserted' (1888), and 'A Wintry Blast on the Stourbridge Canal' (1890).

Short's outstanding powers led to his appointment in 1891 as teacher of etching at South Kensington; he later became professor of engraving, and retired in 1924. Many artists who were to gain high reputation owed much to his training, his high standards, and his constant advocacy of earnest and serious accomplishment in craft.

While he gave of his best in the service of others, his personal contribution to the art of engraving won deserved honour. He had been elected a fellow of the (Royal) Society of Painter-Etchers in 1885, and he succeeded Sir F. Seymour Haden [q.v.] as second president in 1910, retiring in 1938. He was elected A.R.A. in 1906 and R.A. (the first engraver to reach the higher rank) in 1911; and was treasurer of the Royal Academy from 1919 to 1932. He was awarded gold medals for engraving at Paris in 1889 and 1900; and was master of the Art-Workers' Guild in 1901. He was knighted in 1911.

Physically strong, with a powerful frame, a massive head, and large and benevolent eyes, Short was a man of quiet manner and kindly impulse, but of firm character and great strength of will. His qualities made him not only a remarkable teacher but a leader with a valuable influence in the art world of his day. Collections of his work are in the print rooms at the British Museum and the Victoria and Albert Museum.

Short married in 1889 Esther Rosamond (died 1925), daughter of Benjamin Barker, engineer, of London, and had one son, who died on active service in 1916, and one daughter. A tablet put up by the London County Council in 1951 at 56 Brook Green, Hammersmith, commemorates Short's residence there. He died at Ditchling, Sussex, 22 April 1945.

The Royal Academy owns a portrait of him by Arthur Hacker; oil portraits by Fred Roe and J. Souter, and a marble relief by T. Stirling Lee are in the possession of his daughter; a drypoint was made by Malcolm Osborne and a lithograph and a black-and-white drawing were made by Sir William Rothenstein. There is also a chalk drawing by A. W. Peters at the National Portrait Gallery, and the Art-Workers' Guild has an etching by C. J. Watson.

[Martin Hardie, *The Etched and Engraved Work of Sir Frank Short*, 3 vols., Print Collectors' Club, 1938–40; private information; personal knowledge.]      Martin Hardie.

SIBLY, Sir (THOMAS) FRANKLIN (1883–1948), geologist and university administrator, was the only son of Thomas Dix Sibly, solicitor, by his wife, Virginia, daughter of the Rev. Franklin Tonkin, vicar of Madron, Penzance. Born at Bristol 25 October 1883, he received his early education at Wycliffe College, Stonehouse, founded by his uncle, and later at St. Dunstan's, Burnham-on-Sea. He then entered University College, Bristol, whence he graduated with first class honours in experimental physics as an external candidate at London University in 1903. His interest turned to geology, and while studying at Birmingham he began research on the carboniferous limestones. A long series of careful articles, extending from 1905 to 1937, resulted from his continued interest in this field, which led to his becoming chairman of the Geological Survey Board from 1930 to 1943. In the autumn of 1908 he was appointed lecturer in geology at King's College, London, and shortly afterwards he became lecturer-in-charge, holding this post until 1913, when he was appointed professor of geology in University College, Cardiff. He proved a teacher of fine quality, clear and stimulating in exposition, and exercising over his students a firm control which they willingly accepted. He did much to develop the department, while continuing his researches assiduously. His next appointment was to the chair at Armstrong College, Newcastle upon Tyne, which he held from 1918 to 1920. Then his teaching ended when he was appointed first principal of University College, Swansea.

He had now found his true profession. Sibly was a most highly endowed administrator, who was able to combine very different traits in complete integration. He looked far ahead, whilst supervising daily matters of detail, and he had unlimited patience when working towards a distant end. He insisted on all things being done in formal order and with strict regard to the instruments of government, yet he disliked red-tape. He could be ruthless when circumstances required it, although he was of kindly and quite unselfish character. He bore a very formidable dignity when business was in hand: one saw him joyfully divest himself of it, as if taking off a garment, when the business was ended. He ruled firmly by strength of personality rather than by any display of authority, and the members of his staff, who felt some awe in public affairs, turned eagerly to him as a friend when they needed advice on either academic or personal problems, and his friendship never failed them.

He had become interested in university administration before he went to Swansea, and had acquired a considerable reputation for penetration and statesmanship. Now he had to establish a new institution, and to face all the problems, personal, financial, and political, which such an adventure entailed. He was thoroughly successful, and when he left in 1926 Swansea was already making a significant contribution to the Welsh university system. He increased his administrative experience by taking his turn as vice-chancellor of the university of Wales. In 1926 he became principal officer (later styled principal) of London University. This was not the happiest period of his life. In that great corporate institution he was necessarily remote from the teaching staff and the students, and Sibly was always avid for close personal relations with both bodies. In 1929 he accepted an invitation to become vice-chancellor of the university of Reading, where he remained to the end of his career, saying as he left that it had given him his happiest years. Reading had but recently obtained its charter, and was then the youngest, smallest, and probably the most financially insecure of the British universities, but it had two assets which appealed to him: a well-developed residential system, and a tradition of personal intimacy. He at once took in hand the university's finances, and by jealous husbandry and years of painstaking scrutiny they were restored. Sibly did not live to see the full fruits of his labours, but he knew that Reading was again in a position to advance.

Sibly's greatest work for Reading, however, was to bring it into the full stream of British university life by himself becoming in 1938 chairman of the Committee of Vice-Chancellors and Principals which soon had the duty of guiding the universities through the problems of the war. By common consent, it was due mainly to his statesmanship and skill in negotiation with government bodies that the universities emerged with enhanced strength and reputation. He was also a statutory commissioner for the university of Durham, a member of the Advisory Council of the Department of Scientific and Industrial Research, and chairman of the executive committee and council of the Universities Bureau of the British Empire (1929–34). His public services were recognized by a knighthood in 1938 and appointment as K.B.E. in 1943, and by a number of honorary degrees. He had accepted duties too heavy for one who had never been very robust, and his health gave way in the autumn of 1943. No full recovery was possible and he was obliged by medical advice to lay down his vice-chancellorship in 1946. He lived quietly in retirement in Reading where he died 13 April 1948.

In 1918 Sibly married Maude Evelyn, daughter of Charles L. Barfoot, of Newport; she had been his pupil. They had one son who became lecturer in geology in Reading University, where there is a portrait of Sibly by D. W. Dring.

[Private information; personal knowledge.]
A. W. WOLTERS.

SICKERT, WALTER RICHARD (1860–1942), painter, was born in Munich 31 May 1860, the eldest son of Oswald Adalbert Sickert, a Dane by birth who became German by the conquest of Schleswig in 1864 and later British by naturalization. His mother, Eleanor Louisa Moravia Henry, was of mixed Irish and English ancestry. The father was a painter by profession and was responsible for his son's early enthusiasm for the National Gallery and for Charles Keene [q.v.]. The family moved from Munich to London in 1868 and Sickert was educated at a private school in Bayswater, and, after 1875, at King's College, London, where he remained for two years. He had already the ambition to become a painter, but, having been advised by his father to look for a more lucrative profession, he tried first that of the stage, another early enthusiasm. He worked for a time with (Sir) Henry Irving, later with (Dame) Madge Kendal [qq.v.], and then at Sadler's Wells Theatre. But he never played more than very minor parts and soon gave up the experiment in favour of his true vocation.

Sickert went first (in 1881) to the Slade School of Fine Art and studied under Alphonse Legros [q.v.], but soon left to work with J. A. McN. Whistler [q.v.] at the latter's studio in Tite Street. Whistler influenced his pupil in three ways: by his independence of conventions, both social and artistic; technically, in his preference for dark tones and subdued colours; and through his affiliations with the French Impressionists, especially with Degas, who was later to become Sickert's favourite master and close friend and whom he first met in Paris in 1883. Sickert's summer holidays were spent at Dieppe where he met Degas, Renoir, Monet, Pissarro, together with many of the leading French writers of the day. This period is therefore important not only for the series of pictures of Dieppe but for the lasting impression made on Sickert's work by French culture. In 1885 he married Ellen, daughter of Richard Cobden [q.v.], but after a divorce in 1899, and a quarrel with Whistler, he lived for a period entirely on the continent, mainly in Dieppe; and in 1901 and 1903 two long visits to Venice, which he had already visited in 1895, proved fruitful. Apart from architecture and portraits his chief interest during this earlier period was in the theatre, especially the stage and the auditorium of the London music-halls.

Sickert had begun to show his pictures with the (Royal) Society of British Artists as early as 1884, but it was not long before he joined the New English Art Club, the founders of which were inspired by admiration for the French school and opposed to the Academy. A small group which, besides Sickert, included P. Wilson Steer and Frederick Brown [qq.v.] shortly afterwards became the leaders of this movement, holding an exhibition of their own under the title of the London Impressionists. The severe criticism which was meted out to the New English Art Club and the Impressionists was answered by such writers as George Moore, Roger Fry, and D. S. MacColl [qq.v.], as well as by Sickert, who wrote articles to the press on Whistler and J. F. Millet. Meanwhile, his name came to be known in Paris, but sales were few and prices small, and Sickert was hard pressed to make the barest living.

Sickert returned from the continent to London in 1905. That year showed marked changes in his technique, his subject-matter, and his whole relation to the artistic profession. Of the first he says:

'Under the influence of Pissarro . . . I have tried to recast my painting entirely and to observe colour in the shadows.' He also adopted Pissarro's method of laying on the paint in discrete patches and dots like mosaic. The subjects of this, the Camden Town, period were most often interiors with figures; they were not really illustrations, as many of the titles would suggest. The interest of the painter remained purely visual: the titles were added afterwards, and were constantly changed. At the same time he was making a new circle of friends. With Spencer Frederick Gore, he became the leader of a group of painters who had become dissatisfied with the New English Art Club. At first they used to exhibit their pictures at Sickert's studio in Fitzroy Street; later, from 1911, as the Camden Town Group, at the Carfax Gallery; and in 1913 they merged into the larger London Group. Sickert's chief contribution, however, was his sponsorship in 1908 of the Allied Artists' Association, holding an annual no-jury exhibition on the lines of the Salon des Indépendants in Paris, and several articles on the subject in the press, pleading for an equal chance for all to show what they were worth.

Sickert had always been interested in teaching, and many allusions are to be found in his writings to art schools and their methods. In 1908 he obtained a teaching appointment at the Westminster Technical Institute and two years later he opened a private school called Rowlandson House. Briefly, he advocated drawing on the scale of nature, the employment of clothed in preference to nude models, the welding of figure to background, and the use of studies for paintings rather than drawing for the sake of abstract study alone. One of his pupils was Christine Drummond, daughter of John Henry Angus, a Scottish leather merchant, and in 1911 he married her. They spent their summers near Dieppe until 1914 and, during the war, at Chagford (1915) and Bath (1916–17), places associated with a new departure in Sickert's work, that of pure landscape in subject and of a higher, brighter key in palette. In London he had rooms, first in Red Lion Square, afterwards at Whistler's old studio in Fitzroy Street. He exhibited pictures at the New English Art Club, the London Group, the Carfax Gallery, and the Royal Academy. He also showed etchings at Colnaghi's with the Society of Twelve. But etchings were never an important part of his work, although the number of his plates is very large. Indeed, he regarded the needle as an instrument of multiplication and had little sympathy with the modern vogue for 'states' and limited editions. After the war Sickert returned with his wife to Dieppe where she died in 1920. For a long time he was inconsolable; he remained at Dieppe for two years, painting portraits and baccarat scenes; then, suddenly recovering, he returned to London and took up his old enthusiasms, but again with certain changes in his practice. From 1923 onwards, with advancing age, he went out less often to draw at music-halls; he depended for his material on old notes, on photographs and, in the series of *Echoes*, on the black-and-white illustrations of the 'sixties. His paintings became looser in handling and brighter in key. His later pictures, unpopular though they are with many of his admirers as not wholly 'Sickert', display a decorative quality lacking in some of the earlier. In 1926 he married, as his third wife, Thérèse (died 1945), daughter of Jules Lessore, a water-colour draughtsman. She was herself well known as a painter and Sickert had long admired her work. After a time at Islington, where he opened a new school, and another period at Barnsbury Park, they moved first to Broadstairs and later to Bath where Sickert died, without issue, 22 January 1942.

Sickert occupies an important position in the history of English painting. Not only in his own practice but by his teaching and writing he led the fight for recognition of the new ideals in art which had first inspired the Impressionists of France. His writings cover the whole range of his experience in art and life. Written usually in response to a particular occasion (most often the exhibition of a contemporary's or an old master's pictures) they are topical in content, but the spirit of his approach is timeless. The style is witty, discursive, and conversational, but full of instruction and sound common sense. It is far more difficult to assess the value of his work as an artist. He would seem to be primarily a painter's painter. First and foremost it is his command of the medium of oil-paint, the skill of a great craftsman, that delights the eye. The darkness of his early work, combined with an uncompromising and passionless realism, prevented his becoming more generally popular. In some of his portraits and interiors there is a repellent, almost a brutal, feeling which, however fine the means, offends the spirit. But these are exceptions. As a whole, his work is infused by other qualities on which his real reputation depends; a robust virility, the antithesis of the aesthetic refinement of the 'nineties; a rejection of sham or the veneer of gentility; a sense of life and movement which can give a dramatic quality even to a still-life. His wit and charm were proverbial. Being free from professional jealousy he could be generous in praise of contemporaries of widely different aims from his own. For himself he desired less the fashionable advertisement of originality than a small but permanent niche in the line of the great tradition.

Examples of Sickert's work may be found in the Tate Gallery and many provincial galleries in England, also in Dieppe, Rouen, Boston, and throughout the Commonwealth.

Sickert was elected an associate of the Royal Society of Painter-Etchers and Engravers and was president of the London Group (1926) and of the Royal Society of British Artists (1928). He was elected A.R.A. in 1924 and R.A. in 1934 but resigned in the next year. In 1932 the university of Manchester conferred upon him the honorary degree of LL.D. and in 1938 he received the honorary degree of D.Litt. from the university of Reading.

The National Portrait Gallery has a painting of Sickert by P. Wilson Steer, a self-portrait, a pen-and-ink drawing by E. X. Kapp, and he is one of the figures in (Sir) William Orpen's 'Selecting Jury of the New English Art Club, 1909'; Sickert figures in Orpen's 'Hommage à Manet' in the Manchester City Art Gallery where there is also a water-colour drawing by Thérèse Lessore. The Tate Gallery has a portrait by Sylvia Gosse and a painting of Sickert and Steer by Henry Tonks. A portrait by J.-E. Blanche is in the possession of Sir John Rothenstein, another by J. A. McN. Whistler is in the Municipal Gallery of Modern Art, Dublin, and one by Henry Rayner was acquired by the Royal Society of British Artists.

[R. V. B. Emmons, *Life and Opinions of Walter Richard Sickert*, 1941; Lillian Browse, *Sickert*, 1943; *A Free House! the Writings of Walter Richard Sickert*, edited by Sir Osbert Sitwell, 1947; private information; personal knowledge.]     Robert V. B. Emmons.

SIDGREAVES, Sir ARTHUR FREDERICK (1882–1948), man of business, was born 12 June 1882 probably in the Straits Settlements where his father,

Sir Thomas Sidgreaves, was chief justice; his mother was Barbara Catharine, daughter of George Young, of Saverley House, Staffordshire. He was educated at Downside and in 1902 joined the commercial side of D. Napier & Son, Ltd., in which he acquired his first interest in motor-car development. In the war of 1914–18 he served in the Royal Naval Air Service and the Royal Air Force, and was latterly engaged in the Ministry of Munitions upon the production of aero-engines some of which were of Rolls-Royce design. He was appointed O.B.E. in 1918.

After returning for a time to D. Napier & Son, in 1920 Sidgreaves joined Rolls-Royce, Ltd., as export manager in the London offices. In 1926 he became general sales manager and in 1929 managing director. At this time the company was developing the 'R' engine and in 1931 the 'R'-engined Supermarine S.6 made aeronautical history by winning the Schneider Trophy for Great Britain. The experience gained in the development of this engine and the intensive team-work which lay behind its production enabled the company to provide the engines which sustained the Royal Air Force in the Battle of Britain ten years later.

When the Government introduced its shadow factory programme just before the outbreak of war in 1939, Sidgreaves with Mr. E. W. (subsequently Lord) Hives, the general manager, undertook on behalf of Rolls-Royce to build an entirely new factory at Crewe to augment production of the Merlin engine at Derby. Another factory was later built at Hillingdon, Glasgow, and went into production within six months of the commencement of building. In addition to these factories, the Merlin engine was also made by the Ford Motor Company in Manchester and Packards in America. This enormous production drive was supported by Sidgreaves's calm counsel and acceptance of the drain of effort and resources as a mortgage on the future. Disclaiming any technical ability he was able and quick to detect flaws in technical arguments with a gift of realistic appreciation. A man of kindly heart, simple, almost austere, he was a great reader, of discriminating yet catholic taste, interested in the arts, and, although by nature a recluse, a charming host and witty conversationalist. 'Sg.', his staff designation at Rolls-Royce, was president of the Society of British Aircraft Constructors, 1942–3, and in 1945 he was knighted for his services during the war.

He retired in 1946 and on 7 June 1948, his mind seemingly unbalanced through ill health, he threw himself under a train at Green Park underground station.

In 1938 he married Dorothy Jessica, daughter of the late Thomas Henry Bryant. An earlier marriage with Mabel Winifred Winter, by whom he had two sons, had been dissolved.

SIEPMANN, OTTO (1861–1947), teacher of modern languages, was born 9 May 1861 at Waldbröl, a village in the Rhineland, the eldest of the nine children of August Siepmann, a small landed proprietor, and his wife, Harriet Hasenbach. He went to a boarding-school at Colmar, and his early life in a frontier district, with a conflict of languages and a variety of local dialects, stamped him indelibly; he was made to be a teacher of languages. From the background of German educational standards of that period he derived the tradition of scholastic thoroughness, even to caricature. He taught for a time in Germany but in 1885 came to England and began his schoolmastering in Birchington. At periods between 1887 and 1890 he studied at Strasbourg University, and for a time he mingled with a number of young German teachers, writers, and artists in London. In 1888 he became a modern language master at Inverness College and in 1890 he went to Clifton College where he remained for the next thirty years, retiring in 1921. It was here that his influence first began to be felt in the educational world.

Siepmann had only elementary taste in literature, but he had a creative love for language. Unintelligible structures of German syntax acquired meaning, and the subtleties of French pronunciation justified their necessity, even to schoolboys who were more convinced of the value of classics or the reality of science. He produced his first version of phonetic script, and characteristically claimed that few Englishmen pronounced their own language on true principles. Although he became a naturalized British subject in 1905, had married an Englishwoman and had a family of children who gained distinction in scholarship and affairs, he never learnt to pronounce English as the English do.

He was convinced of the importance of modern language teaching and of due attention to pronunciation: 'There can be no doubt', he wrote, 'that greater attention to pronunciation, training of ear and tongue, is perfectly compatible with sound instruction and mental training.' The necessity of providing for his family, as well as his confident belief in his methods, led him to organize a mass-production of schoolbooks on French and German. These fell into three main groups: primers on French and German; a series of annotated French and German classics; and the well-known 'Word-and-Phrase' books. Later he produced courses for school certificate and matriculation, and later still, a series of tuition courses on gramophone records. But his distinctive contribution to class teaching lay in the original series. By modern standards they may appear primitive, but they made a sharp impact on teaching methods of the time. Any diligent user of the books emerged, not perhaps a scholar, but with a good foundation and a feel for the language.

The results of his methods were beyond dispute, and Clifton had cause to thank him for a notable series of scholarships in languages at the universities. In 1900 Siepmann became head of the newly founded modern languages department and, although he never gained the European reputation of others of the period who attacked the whole system of education, in his own field he achieved real distinction. He came to be the leading authority in this country on the teaching of modern languages and by his untiring propaganda raised it to a level which it had never attained before.

He had not the fastidiousness of the scholar; there were colleagues who were better scholars; but he knew this and respected them. Neither had he the scholar's diffidence; there was a jovial certainty about him, annoying at first but in the end warming. The schoolmaster whose memory endures is usually remembered as a whole, and often only upon later appreciation. Siepmann was sometimes a little ridiculous, but never dull; gradually in his classes he acquired a glow of liking round him, through which could be recognized the hard and lasting value of what he taught. He was a pioneer of methods which are now commonplace; a practising schoolmaster may rarely claim as much.

Siepmann married in 1889 Grace Florence (died 1938), daughter of John Baker, a naturalist, of Cambridge. There were three sons and three daughters of the marriage. He died at Crowthorne, Berkshire, 11 January 1947. A portrait by Fritz von Kamptz is at Clifton College.

[*Cliftonian*, March and July 1947; private information; personal knowledge.]

WILFRID EADY.

SINCLAIR, SIR EDWYN SINCLAIR ALEXANDER- (1865–1945), admiral. [See ALEXANDER-SINCLAIR.]

SITWELL, SIR GEORGE RERESBY, fourth baronet (1860–1943), antiquarian, was born in Green Street, Mayfair, 27 January 1860, the only son of Sir Sitwell Reresby Sitwell, third baronet, by his wife, Louisa Lucy, daughter of Colonel the Hon. Henry Hely-Hutchinson. He succeeded his father in 1862, thereby enjoying a long minority during which he was educated at Eton and at Christ Church, Oxford. He next contested Scarborough seven times as a Conservative and was a member of Parliament from 1885 to 1886 and from 1892 to 1895. Later (1908) he became a Liberal, but by then he had abandoned politics despite a talent for addressing large audiences.

Whilst at his preparatory school Sitwell had taught himself to read black-letter English from family documents, and in 1889, having bought the *Scarborough Post* and a private printing-press, he produced on this his first book, *The Barons of Pulford in the Eleventh and Twelfth Centuries and their Descendants*. The Sacheverell papers which he inherited led to the writing in 1894 of *The First Whig*, an account of the parliamentary career of William Sacheverell, to whom he was related collaterally and whose biography he contributed to this DICTIONARY. He also published *The Letters of the Sitwells and Sacheverells* (1900). His researches among family papers resulted in the clarification of many disputed points in the pedigrees of the older English families and he frequently worked in close co-operation with J. H. Round [q.v.], never relying on popularly accepted pedigrees but tracing them to their documented origins. He allowed himself the relaxation of writing a book in the form of fiction when he published in 1933 *Tales of My Native Village*, studies of medieval life, manners, art, minstrelsy, and religion. In addition to his studies of genealogical details, he paid considerable attention to heraldry on which he contributed articles to the *Ancestor*.

Sitwell spent much of his time at Renishaw Hall, the family seat in Derbyshire, where he filled seven sitting-rooms with memoranda on a multiplicity of subjects over which his active, inventive, but erratic mind continually ranged and upon which he expected to be consulted as an infallible authority: 'I must ask anyone entering the house never to contradict me or differ from me in any way, as it interferes with the functioning of the gastric juices and prevents my sleeping at night.' To his researches in genealogy and heraldry he added in particular the study of the construction and planning of formal gardens which was of genuine value and led to the publication *On the Making of Gardens* (1909, republished 1949). He redesigned the gardens at Renishaw on a formal plan, at the same time ornamenting the park with a large expanse of landscaped water, and to gain further information on the subject of garden planning he travelled extensively in Italy, a country to which he became progressively devoted. During his travels in the remoter parts of southern Italy between 1890 and 1910 he persisted in changing into full evening dress for dinner however small and primitive the inn.

In 1909 Sitwell purchased the Castello di Montegufoni, formerly the property of the Florentine family of Acciaiuoli and at that time the dwelling-place of nearly 300 peasants. 'The roof is in splendid order, and the drains can't be wrong, as there aren't any', he wrote to his elder son, ending with a characteristic warning against extravagance. The castle had undergone many alterations and Sitwell with the aid of the family documents set about the work of restoring the building to its original design. In 1925 he left England to make Montegufoni his residence, persuaded thereto by his three children, Osbert, Sacheverell, and Edith, who needed freedom to follow their own brilliant careers: 'The general atmosphere, which was always menacing, the interruptions, the scenes, the surprises, and the ambushes laid, the fussing, the necessity my father felt both for consulting and contradicting me, the economies, the extravagances, all put it beyond possibility to write a line when he was in the house.' (Sir Osbert Sitwell, *Laughter in the Next Room*, 1949.) Sitwell himself wrote to the archbishop of Canterbury and the chancellor of the Exchequer to explain that the newly imposed taxes obliged him to settle in Italy. He had never enjoyed the more obvious pleasures of social life and in Italy he retreated more and more into the seclusion of his scholarly investigations of Gothic life.

In 1886 Sitwell married Ida Emily Augusta Denison (died 1937), daughter of Baron (later the first Earl of) Londesborough. When Sitwell died at Porto Ronco, Locarno, Switzerland, 9 July 1943, he was proud of the fact that he had been lord of the manor of Eckington for eighty-one years—a longer period than any of his predecessors since the Conquest. He was succeeded by his elder son, (Francis) Osbert (born 1892), whose autobiography (5 vols., 1945–50) affectionately observes his difficult parent as 'one of the most singular characters of his epoch'.

There is a portrait of Sitwell (1898) by Henry Tonks. A family group (1900) by J. S. Sargent was designed to accompany two family groups of earlier Sitwells by J. S. Copley and John Partridge. All are in the possession of Sir Osbert Sitwell.

[Personal knowledge.]    DAVID HORNER.

SMITH, ARTHUR HAMILTON (1860–1941), archaeologist, was born in London 2 October 1860, the fourth son of the mathematician Archibald Smith [q.v.], by his wife, Susan Emma, daughter of Sir James Parker [q.v.]. His eldest brother was Sir James Parker Smith and a younger was Sir Henry Babington Smith [q.v.]. He was a scholar of Winchester College, and at the end of his time renounced a nomination to the Indian Civil Service, going instead to Trinity College, Cambridge, where he obtained a second class in part i of the classical tripos (1881) and a first class in part ii (1883), and was captain of the university shooting eight. After travelling in Asia Minor with (Sir) W. M. Ramsay [q.v.] he entered the department of Greek and Roman antiquities in the British Museum in 1886. He assisted the keeper, A. S. Murray [q.v.], in the rearrangement of the sculpture, and produced the official *Catalogue of Engraved Gems* (1888); the *Catalogue of Sculpture* (3 vols., 1892–1904); the *Guide* to the department, which ran through several editions; *White Athenian Vases* (1896) with reproductions by cyclograph, an invention of his own for the photographing of curved surfaces; and a complete edition of *The Sculptures of the Parthenon* (1910). He also published catalogues of the Lansdowne (1889), Yarborough (1897), and Woburn Abbey (1900) collections. In 1893–4 and again in 1896 he took part in expeditions to Cyprus, the results of which were published in *Excavations in Cyprus* (1900). In 1904 he became assistant keeper of his department and in 1909 keeper. As such he was responsible for the successful measures taken to protect the collections during the war of 1914–18.

Unofficially, Smith's principal activity was in connexion with the Society for the Promotion of Hellenic Studies, of which he was a member of council from 1887 onwards, joint-editor of the *Journal* from 1892 to 1898, librarian from 1896 to 1908, and president from 1924 to 1929. On the occasion of the centenary of the acquisition of the Elgin marbles he produced a fully documented history of the transaction ('Lord Elgin and his Collection', *Journal of Hellenic Studies*, vol. xxxvi, 1916), which vindicates Lord Elgin from the aspersions of Byron and others.

Smith retired from the museum in 1925, but on two occasions, in 1928–30 and in 1932, he undertook the directorship of the British School at Rome with which he had been connected since its foundation, and he did excellent service at a time of disciplinary difficulties. He was a good linguist, and established very friendly relations with foreign archaeologists.

His natural quietness of manner was intensified by deafness, caused by neglected mumps in 1876; but his thoroughness and conscientiousness, added to natural ability, made him a very efficient administrator. He was elected F.B.A. in 1924 and an honorary A.R.I.B.A. in 1925, and was a corresponding member of the German and Austrian Archaeological Institutes. In 1926 he was appointed C.B. He married in 1897 Gertrude, daughter of the Rev. Blomfield Jackson, prebendary of St. Paul's Cathedral; there was one daughter of the marriage. He died at Weybridge, whither he had retired, 28 September 1941.

[Sir F. G. Kenyon in *Proceedings* of the British Academy, vol. xxvii, 1941; private information; personal knowledge.]

F. G. KENYON.

SMITH, SIR CECIL HARCOURT- (1859–1944), archaeologist and director of the Victoria and Albert Museum. [See HARCOURT-SMITH.]

SMITH, SIR GEORGE ADAM (1856–1942), Old Testament scholar and theologian, was born at Calcutta 19 October 1856, the eldest child of George Smith, C.I.E., LL.D., principal of Doveton College, later editor of the *Calcutta Review* and

*Times* correspondent, by his wife, Janet Colquhoun, daughter of Robert Adam, of Sweethillocks, Morayshire, and great-niece of Alexander Adam [q.v.]. Brought home to Scotland at the age of two, Smith passed his boyhood with aunts at Leith, attending the Royal High School and afterwards the university of Edinburgh, where he graduated in arts in 1875. To the normal arts course he had added political economy, a subject destined to influence his later work as biblical expositor and friend of social reform.

In 1875 Smith entered New College, Edinburgh, for his divinity course, and came under the influence of the renowned Hebraist and Old Testament theologian, A. B. Davidson [q.v.]. Summer semesters were spent abroad, at Leipzig and Tübingen, studying theology, and in Berlin in 1878 he heard Harnack and Treitschke, recalling later the sinister note which characterized Treitschke's prelections on history. At the conclusion of his divinity studies, and before ordination, he passed some time in Cairo in the study of Arabic and travelled in Palestine, tramping the country on foot in the company of a single Arab muleteer. Shortly after his return to Scotland in 1880 he was called to undertake interim tutorial duty at the Free Church College, Aberdeen, in place of W. Robertson Smith [q.v.] who had been suspended from his chair. In 1882 Adam Smith was ordained by the presbytery of Aberdeen to the charge of Queen's Cross Free Church.

Smith's ministry at Aberdeen (1882–92) formed not the least remarkable episode in an eloquent and impassioned career of biblical teaching. Not a little of the force and appeal of his work as a preacher sprang from the clearness with which, in the period following the Robertson Smith trial, he discerned the spiritual issues of the conflict and set himself, as his wife subsequently wrote, 'to reconcile the outlook of an advanced scientific scholar with the spirit of devout reverence'. One remarkable fruit of this engagement was the series of lecture-sermons which, later published in the *Book of Isaiah* (2 vols., 1888–90), spread his influence far and wide. This book, with his work on the Holy Land, represents perhaps his finest literary achievement. If he gave the social and religious 'burden' of the Hebrew prophet a modernizing interpretation, it was in the justifiable sense that eternal truths, because they are eternal, relate themselves existentially to all ages. During this period, while on holiday at Zermatt (he was a keen mountaineer, and member of the Alpine Club), Smith met Alice Lilian, daughter of (Sir) George Buchanan [q.v.] of the medical department of the Local Government Board in London, and was married to her in 1889. With this gifted companion and other friends Smith, having now settled to write an historical geography of Palestine, undertook a tour of the country from the Negeb to Damascus, visiting the biblical sites, and accumulating rich stores of observation (1891).

In 1892 Smith was elected professor of Old Testament language, literature, and theology at the Free Church College, Glasgow. His duties gave enhanced opportunity to his influence as expositor, but they were also years of strenuous social activity centring in the college settlement in the Broomielaw district of Glasgow. As chairman of the Scottish Council for Women's Trades he assisted in the campaign against sweated labour. In the lecture-room spiritual insight and passion played as notable a part as literary and critical acumen. The movement of religious history which led from the prophets of Israel to Jesus Christ was for teacher and student not one episode of history merely, but the measure of all history, history in its climactic manifestation. During these years Smith visited America on four occasions: in 1896 as Percy Turnbull lecturer at the Johns Hopkins University; in 1899 as Lyman Beecher lecturer at Yale; in 1903 on another lecture tour; and in 1909 as visiting professor at the university of Chicago and Earle lecturer at Berkeley, California. He went to Palestine in 1901 and 1904, and wrote in succession his *Historical Geography of the Holy Land* (1894), his *Book of the Twelve Prophets* (2 vols., 1896–8), a *Life of Henry Drummond* (1898), *Modern Criticism and the Preaching of the Old Testament* (1901), and *Jerusalem* (2 vols., 1908). The Yale lectures on *Modern Criticism* aroused misgiving in certain conservative quarters in Scotland, and proceedings against him for heresy were pending, but were happily terminated by the confidence expressed in him by the General Assembly of his Church (1902).

The *Historical Geography of the Holy Land* was a remarkable revelation of Smith's insight into the interrelation of history, land, and religion, of his eye for colour, and of his plastic and poetic gift of English expression. He wished to furnish a description of Palestine in which the reader would everywhere detect 'the sound of running history'. The work took immediate rank as a classic of biblical exposition, and in 1931 it was completely revised for its twenty-fifth edition. Smith had given attention to the relation between the physiography of the country and the military campaignings of ancient and medieval conquerors, but could not foresee the excellent purpose to which the book would be put by Sir Edmund (later Viscount) Allenby [q.v.] in his Palestinian campaign in 1917. To the *Historical Geography* the volumes on *Jerusalem* provided an indispensable supplement.

In 1909 Smith was appointed by the Crown as principal of Aberdeen University, an office which he retained until his retirement in 1935. Amid the onerous public duties which now inevitably engaged his time, he wrote his Schweich lecture on *The Early Poetry of Israel* (1912, published 1913), his commentary on *Deuteronomy* in the Cambridge Bible (1918), his Baird lecture on *Jeremiah* (1922, published 1923), and prepared revisions of his *Isaiah* (1927) and *Twelve Prophets* (1928). Suffering came to him in these years, for of the three sons, who with four daughters composed his family, the two eldest, George and Dunlop, gave their lives in war, the one in France (1915), the other in East Africa (1917). Smith was knighted in 1916, and elected the same year moderator of the General Assembly of the United Free Church of Scotland. In 1918 with his eldest daughter he toured the United States under commission from the British Foreign Office and the American national committee on the Churches and the moral aims of the Allies, and delivered lectures published in the book *Our Common Conscience* (1919). The freedom of the city of Aberdeen was conferred upon him in 1931. In 1933 he was made a chaplain to the King in Scotland.

Smith received the honorary degree of D.D. from the universities of Edinburgh, Yale, Dublin, Oxford, Cambridge, Durham, and Glasgow; of LL.D. from Edinburgh, Aberdeen, and St. Andrews; and of Litt.D. from Cambridge and Sheffield. He was elected F.B.A. in 1916. On his retirement Sir George and Lady Adam Smith received striking tributes to the esteem in which their work was held, and Lady Adam Smith was accorded the honorary degree of LL.D. by the university of Aberdeen. They retired to Sweethillocks, Balerno, near Edinburgh, and there he died 3 March 1942, survived by his widow who died in 1949. Their daughter Janet Adam Smith became literary editor of the *New Statesman and Nation* in 1952.

Of painted portraits of Smith, that by Sir William Orpen (1927) is at King's College, Aberdeen; another, by J. B. Souter, in Trinity Hall, Aberdeen; a third, by John M. Aiken, is in the possession of the family.

S. A. Cook, in his valuable memoir in the *Proceedings* of the British Academy, hails Adam Smith as forming with A. B. Davidson and Robertson Smith a notable Scottish trio among those who established at a critical period the now prevailing position in Old Testament studies. In Adam Smith's work the interest of the preacher was predominant. Critical thought on technical matters has moved forward since his time, but the perennial value of the religious and ethical appeal of his writings remains undiminished. The interfusion of thought with emotion and feeling made his work in a peculiar sense an objectification of himself and very essentially a revelation of spirit.

[S. A. Cook in *Proceedings* of the British Academy, vol. xxviii, 1942; Lilian Adam Smith, *George Adam Smith: A Personal Memoir and Family Chronicle*, 1943; *Scotsman*, 9 March 1942; personal knowledge.]
W. MANSON.

SMITH, SIR HUBERT LLEWELLYN (1864–1945), civil servant and social investigator, was born at Bristol 17 April 1864, the youngest son of Samuel Wyatt Smith, grocer, by his wife, Louisa, daughter of James Scholefield, of Kingsholm, Gloucester. On both sides the family had been Quakers for many generations. Smith was educated at Bristol Grammar School and at Corpus Christi College, Oxford; he was a scholar of his college and obtained a first class in mathematical moderations (1884) and in the final school of mathematics (1886). He won the Cobden prize in 1886 and in 1934 was elected an honorary fellow of Corpus Christi.

After leaving Oxford Smith became a lecturer (1887–8) for the Oxford university extension delegacy and the Toynbee Trust, and secretary of the National Association for the Promotion of Technical and Secondary Education. He lived for some years at Toynbee Hall and elsewhere in the east end of London. He helped Ben Tillett [q.v.] at the time of the dock strike and with Vaughan Nash wrote *The Story of the Dockers' Strike* (1890). His early experience provided the background for his future work in the Board of Trade which he entered as the first commissioner of labour (1893) when he organized the system of information which prepared the way for the Trade Boards Act of 1909. He made a reputation as an industrial negotiator by a skilful settlement (1895) of an important dispute in the boot and shoe industry; and he served on the Royal Commission on secondary education (1894–5). From 1903 he was controller-general of the commercial, labour, and statistical department. In 1907 he became permanent secretary of the Board of Trade and both in that capacity and later, from 1919 to 1927, as chief economic adviser to the Government, was a dominant personality in economic policy. The extension of the social services initiated by Lloyd George brought new duties to the Board of Trade, for which Smith was specially qualified by his first-hand knowledge of conditions in the east end of London. Under (Sir) Winston Churchill as president, he planned the new system of unemployment insurance and, in most appropriate association with (Sir) William (subsequently Lord) Beveridge, set up the labour exchanges. Smith's responsibility for the commercial treaty work of his department brought him in contact with many other countries and their representatives; in 1905, for example, he negotiated a treaty with Romania and in 1911 a treaty with Japan. He was primarily responsible for the economic preparations for war; devised the valuable system of war risk insurance; and in 1915 organized, under Lloyd George, the new Ministry of Munitions.

After the war Smith headed the British economic section of the peace conference. In 1919 he also visited India as president of the viceregal committee on the reorganization of the government secretariat, and in the following year went to Persia as British member of the Anglo-Persian tariff commission.

From 1920 to 1927 Smith combined his duties as chief economic adviser with membership of the economic committee of the League of Nations; in this capacity and as British member of successive conferences (e.g. on communications and transit at Barcelona in 1921, on customs formalities at Geneva in 1923, and on industrial property at The Hague in 1925), and as substitute delegate to the League Assemblies of 1923 and 1924, he was for many years a principal personality in all negotiations affecting international trade.

In the meantime Smith found expression for the artistic side of his rich and varied nature. Sketching was always the favourite occupation of his leisure. *Through the High Pyrenees* (1898), written jointly with Edward Harold Spender, had been illustrated with his own drawings; and he retained a lifelong interest in the crafts and particularly in the training of craftsmen. He was chairman of the British Institute of Industrial Art throughout its fifteen years of existence, and published a short but illuminating study of *The Economic Laws of Art Production* (1924).

Retirement from official life in 1927, at the age of sixty-three, was only the starting-point for new and arduous work which reflected the interests which Smith had developed as a young man. He was for seven years (1928–35) director of the *New Survey of London Life and Labour*, a sequel after forty years to the monumental work of Charles Booth [q.v.] in which he had had a personal share. He then became chairman of the National Association of Boys' Clubs (1935–43), and in the same period wrote a history of *The Board of Trade* (1928) and completed a *History of East London* (1939), a labour of love for many years.

Smith married in 1901 Edith Maud Sophia, eldest daughter of George Mitchell Weekley, of Highgate, and had four sons and two daughters. He was appointed C.B. in 1903, K.C.B. in 1908, and G.C.B. in 1919. He died at Tytherington, Wiltshire, 19 September 1945.

This bare record of offices and achievements shows clearly the wide and varied range of Smith's interests and talents, and the unremitting industry that marked the whole of his long career. But in itself it does not reveal the personality and the remarkable qualities which could only be fully known by those who worked with him. He was beyond question one of the great civil servants of his time, one of those who not only administered policy but exercised a powerful influence in its formation. He had initiative combined with constructive and inventive genius, and his mind was powerful and massive. But his resolute and unyielding defence of the principles in which he believed was combined with both personal modesty and generous appreciation of others. He lived simply, and it is significant of his whole character and outlook that, as soon as he was released from the duties of his official career, he turned back to the social work and social studies of his youth. Though his work in later reigns he recalls the great Victorians.

[*Economic Journal*, March 1946; *The Times*, 21 and 25 September 1945; private information; personal knowledge.]    SALTER.

SMITH, (LLOYD) LOGAN PEARSALL (1865–1946), writer, was born of Quaker stock at Millville, New Jersey, 18 October 1865, the fourth child and second son of Robert Pearsall Smith, partner in a glass-bottle manufactory owned by John Mickle Whitall, whose daughter Hannah Tatum he had married. Pearsall Smith's paternal grandfather, John Jay Smith, editor and librarian, as a descendant of William Penn's secretary, James Logan [q.v.], was an hereditary trustee of the library bequeathed by Logan to the city of Philadelphia. It was there that the boy, originally intended to inherit the librarianship, first fell under the spell of books. Both his parents were famous as evangelical preachers and his mother, a gifted writer, was also widely known as the author of religious works under the initials 'H. W. S.' She encouraged the boy's faintly emerging talents as a writer, and his vocation received its deepest impulse when the family became closely acquainted with Walt Whitman.

Educated at the Quaker Penn Charter School, Haverford College, and Harvard University, Pearsall Smith, his earlier plans forsaken in favour of a business career, worked for a year in a branch of the family business in New York. He then resolved to devote himself to literature and obtained from his father an adequate sum to live on. With his family he settled in England and on the advice of his brother-in-law, B. F. C. Costelloe, a former member, went to Balliol College, Oxford. He obtained a second class in *literae humaniores* in 1891, was a favourite of Benjamin Jowett's, and was much influenced by the writing of Walter Pater [qq.v.]. He became a naturalized British subject in 1913 and only once returned to America, in 1921 for an operation.

His first book, *The Youth of Parnassus* (1895), short stories in decorous and conscientious imitation of Maupassant, although unsuccessful, brought him the friendship of Robert Bridges [q.v.]. In 1897–8, with his elder sister Mary Costelloe and Mr. Bernard Berenson, whom she was later to marry, he helped to produce a privately printed periodical, the *Golden Urn*. Among his contributions were four prose sketches and with these began the short pieces which he made into his masterpiece, *Trivia*. This first appeared in 1902. It was privately printed and attracted little attention. In 1907 he published an admirable biography in *The Life and Letters of Sir Henry Wotton*. He made himself a master of English; *The English Language* (1912) and *Words and Idioms* (1925) are models of entertaining and lucid erudition. These studies led him to assist Robert Bridges and others to inaugurate in 1913 the Society for Pure English which was eventually launched in 1919 and to which he contributed many important papers. A greatly enlarged and revised version of *Trivia* was published in 1918, to be followed by *More Trivia* (1922) and *Afterthoughts* (1931). In 1933 he rearranged the three in a single volume, *All Trivia*; until the end he was continually revising and polishing them. Other notable writings of his were *The Prospects of Literature* (1927), *On Reading Shakespeare* (1933), *Reperusals and Re-collections* (1936), his autobiographical *Unforgotten Years* (1938), *Milton and his Modern Critics* (1940), and several excellent and influential anthologies. His letters were of unusual merit.

Pearsall Smith travelled widely in Europe, North Africa, and the Near East. He never married. Sometimes he lived alone, but for most of the time he shared a house with his mother and, after her death, with his sister Alys, the first wife of Mr. Bertrand (subsequently Earl) Russell. Although his conversion at the age of four was recorded in a tract written by his father, he lost his faith when still young. But the moral structure determined his attitude to literature. He loved to implant a sometimes harassing conscience in the bosom of young writers. Always he preached and practised the difficult pursuit of perfection. 'What above all things I should like would be to make out of life . . . something delicate and durable. . . . To live on, in fact, after my funeral in a perfect phrase.' A certain spiritual timidity, however, almost always prevented him from pursuing subjects of depth or solemnity. Nevertheless he produced nothing not beautifully wrought, and, save for his fiction and verses, little which was not enduring. He retained a large residue of Quaker virtue; in spite of occasional divergences from commendable conduct, he often performed acts of thoughtful and unostentatious generosity. Less happily, he inherited a mild form of manic depression which shaped his existence with cycles of gloom and elevation. He composed only in times of elevation, when he might also amuse or startle his friends with curious practical jokes.

He was tall, and during much of his life was active in outdoor pursuits. Later he was mostly sedentary, and corpulence obscured an earlier comeliness. A portrait by Roger Fry is at Haverford College; a drawing by Sir William Rothenstein is in the possession of Mr. John Russell; there is a portrait in oils by Ethel Sands; a portrait in water-colour by Hilda Trevelyan belongs to the writer of this notice. Pearsall Smith died in the night 2 March 1946 at his home in Chelsea.

[L. L. Pearsall Smith, *A Religious Rebel*, 1949 (letters of Hannah Whitall Smith), and *Unforgotten Years*, 1938; John Russell, *A Portrait of Logan Pearsall Smith drawn from his Letters and Diaries*, 1950; R. Gathorne-Hardy, *Recollections of Logan Pearsall Smith*, 1949; Sir Desmond MacCarthy, *Memories*, 1953; Notices of John Jay Smith and Hannah Whitall Smith appear in the *Dictionary of American Biography*; unpublished family papers; private information; personal knowledge.]        ROBERT GATHORNE-HARDY.

SMITH, RODNEY (1860–1947), evangelist, known as 'Gipsy Smith', was born in a tent in the parish of Wanstead, near Epping Forest, 31 March 1860, the fourth child and second son of Cornelius Smith by his wife, Mary Welch. His gipsy parents travelled East Anglia making baskets, clothes-pegs, and tinware, and dealing in horses. The death of his mother from smallpox when he was still quite young greatly affected the boy, and he frequently referred to it in revivalist meetings throughout his life. Soon after the tragedy his father was converted at a meeting in a mission hall in London and with Rodney's two uncles began to hold open-air religious services. The boy himself was converted, 17 November 1876, after a service in the Primitive Methodist chapel in Fitzroy Street, Cambridge.

The next year he preached his first sermon and joined William Booth [q.v.] in the Christian Mission, soon to become the Salvation Army. Large crowds gathered to hear him. He had very little schooling, but when he moved to Bolton his fellow workers were an educated couple who helped him to lay 'the true foundations of all the educational equipment that I ever possessed'. After the formation of the Salvation Army he became a captain, but he felt 'rather uncomfortable and out of place', as he used to say, for 'being born in a field, I could not be crammed into a flowerpot'. He had few regrets when, in 1882, at Hanley, Staffordshire, he was dismissed for breaking a rule of the Army in allowing leading townsmen to present him with gifts, including a gold watch, in appreciation of his evangelistic services. A committee of local Free Church representatives at once engaged the large Imperial Circus Hall, and for four years he preached there to crowded congregations. In 1889 he made the first of many visits to the United States, and was helped by Dwight L. Moody and Ira D. Sankey, who became his friends. On returning to England he joined the Manchester Methodist Mission. He spent some time in Australia during a tour round the world in 1894, and in 1897 was appointed the first missioner for the National Free Church Council. He preached in most of the large towns in this country and also went to South Africa and America, resigning in 1912. During the war of 1914–18 he served with the Young Men's Christian Association in France and elsewhere, and was appointed M.B.E. in 1918 for his services. Later he toured the British Isles for the Methodist Church under the direction of the Home Mission Committee.

Gipsy Smith was an artist in the pulpit. Of medium height, thickset, swarthy, he had a melodious tenor voice, a lively imagination, a puckish sense of humour, and 'the wooing note' in preaching. Unconventional in his methods, he nevertheless avoided sensationalism. His love of flowers and trees and all living things in the countryside, and his intimate knowledge of gipsy lore, added to a lifelong study of the Bible, gave his addresses—many of which were published in book form—a touch of romantic originality. Perhaps only Sankey himself excelled him in the singing of simple Gospel solos.

In 1879 Smith married Annie E. Pennock (died 1937), the daughter of a merchant navy captain, of Whitby. In 1938 he married Mary Alice Shaw, of Los Angeles. There were two sons and one daughter of the first marriage. He died in the *Queen Mary* while travelling to New York 4 August 1947.

[*Gipsy Smith: His Life and Work*, by himself, revised edition, 1924; Harold Murray, *Sixty Years an Evangelist*, 1937; personal knowledge.]      R. G. BURNETT.

SMUTS, JAN CHRISTIAN (1870–1950), statesman, was born 24 May 1870 on the farm Bovenplaats, near Riebeek West in the Malmesbury district of the Cape Colony. His father, Jacobus Abraham Smuts, was a successful farmer and local notability who for many years represented Malmesbury in the colonial Parliament. His family and that of his wife, Catharina Petronella de Vries, were of Dutch origin, with a little Huguenot admixture, and both had settled at the Cape in the seventeenth century.

Jan was the second son, and physically a weak child. He had no formal education until, at the age of twelve, he was sent to school at Riebeek West. There he developed a passion for learning; four years later he entered the Victoria College, Stellenbosch, where he graduated in both science and literature in 1891. His academic record was brilliant. But both at school and at college he was a bookish recluse, taking no part in games or social life, and making few friends. His only significant friendship at Stellenbosch was with the fellow student whom he was later to marry.

In 1888 Cecil Rhodes [q.v.] visited Stellenbosch. Jan Smuts was chosen by the rector to reply, on behalf of the students, to Rhodes's address. The speech made a favourable impression on Rhodes and on John X. Merriman, and Rhodes advised the elder J. H. Hofmeyr [qq.v.] to 'keep an eye on that young fellow Smuts'. The political contacts thus made were to have an important influence on the young fellow in various ways.

Smuts won the Ebden scholarship, which enabled him to go to Christ's College, Cambridge. He had abandoned his original intention of taking orders, and now chose to study law. Again he was brilliantly successful in examinations; he wrote the two parts of the law tripos in 1894, and was placed first in the first class of each; F. W. Maitland [q.v.] regarded him as the best pupil he had ever taught. He was admitted to the Middle Temple, and was offered, but refused, a teaching appointment at Cambridge. As at Stellenbosch, he kept to himself, took no part in sport, and made few friends. In his spare time he wrote a treatise on Walt Whitman—'a study in the evolution of personality'—which expressed many of the ideas which were to guide his life; but he could not get it published.

In June 1895 Smuts returned home, was admitted to the Cape bar, and began what was intended to be an advocate's career. His lack of the social graces was a serious handicap, and few briefs came his way. He wrote articles for various papers, and occasionally reported parliamentary debates for them. This occupation brought him into contact with the political world at a decisive moment of South African history. The large views and limitless ambitions of Rhodes, who was now prime minister, appealed to Smuts whose own ideals, independently formed and less materialistic, in other respects closely resembled those of the Colossus.

Accusations made against Rhodes by Olive Schreiner and her husband [qq.v.] at Kimberley reminded the prime minister and Hofmeyr of the existence of the brilliant student of 1888. Hofmeyr invited Smuts to go to Kimberley to speak in defence of Rhodes. He did this with enthusiasm. Exactly two months later (Sir) L. S. Jameson [q.v.] crossed the Transvaal border on his disastrous raid. Rhodes, who was largely, if not directly, responsible, had done just what Smuts at Kimberley had said he was incapable of doing. Most of the disillusioned Cape Afrikaners turned bitterly against Rhodes whose co-operation with Hofmeyr came to an end. In 1896 Smuts, duped and humiliated, went to Johannesburg and was admitted to the Transvaal bar.

He was no more successful in his legal career in Johannesburg than he had been in Cape Town. But in 1898 his fortunes took an unexpected turn. The Volksraad had made a practice of legislating by simple resolution (*besluit*), passed at a single sitting, where the constitution required the longer process of an Act. The chief justice claimed the testing power, and pronounced a *besluit* unconstitutional. At the end of a long dispute on this matter, President Kruger dismissed the chief justice. Almost the whole of the legal profession, in the Transvaal and the rest of South Africa, took the judge's side in the dispute. Smuts defended the president —a course which led shortly to his appointment as state attorney of the republic. At the same time he abandoned his British nationality.

The work of ridding the police force of corruption and inefficiency had soon to give way to the more urgent business of foreign policy. Throughout the Anglo-Boer negotiations of 1899 Smuts worked for conciliation and peace. At the Bloemfontein conference in June he persuaded Kruger to make great concessions to meet the demands of Sir Alfred (later Viscount) Milner [q.v.] regarding the franchise;

but on this occasion Milner would accept nothing less than his pound of flesh. Negotiations between Smuts and Conyngham Greene, the British agent, likewise ended in failure, and war came in October.

Smuts had expounded the Boer case in a propaganda pamphlet, *A Century of Wrong*, which his later political opponents did not allow him to forget. While regular warfare lasted, he kept to his administrative duties, the last of which was the forcible removal of the Government's gold from a Pretoria bank, just as the British were about to enter the capital. Regular operations were then followed by two years of guerrilla warfare. Smuts left his desk and joined De la Rey in the field. In the winter of 1901 the Boer leaders decided to send a raiding commando into the Cape Colony to stir up rebellion; Smuts, with the rank of general, was given the command. He left the Transvaal with his small force at the end of July. After being hunted through the Free State for a month they crossed the Orange into the Cape Colony. There followed eight months of desperate struggle with the enemy and with rain, mud, cold, and hunger, of sharp encounters, tortuous marches, and hairbreadth escapes. Smuts went south nearly to Port Elizabeth, westward through the Little Karoo, north to Namaqualand, everywhere recruiting colonial rebels to build up his force. But no general rebellion was provoked.

From Namaqualand Smuts was summoned to a conference at Vereeniging, where terms of peace were to be discussed. Although he was not one of the elected Boer delegates, he was appointed by them to the commission they sent to negotiate in Pretoria. The discussions seemed to have reached deadlock when Lord Kitchener [q.v.] drew Smuts aside and gave his opinion that in two years' time the Liberals would come into power in England and would grant South Africa a constitution. The prospect decided Smuts for peace, and he was able to bring most of the 'bitter-enders' round to the same view. The wider union made a greater appeal to him than the narrower independence.

For a few years after the peace the Boer leaders remained in retirement from public life. But the death of Kruger in exile, his funeral at Pretoria, and above all the importation of Chinese labour for the Rand mines, stimulated them to new activity. A party, **Het Volk** (The People), was formed in the Transvaal. When the Liberals at last took office in England, Smuts was sent over by Het Volk to seek responsible government. He gave Campbell-Bannerman an undertaking that the Boers would not 'raise the question of the annexation of the new colonies or the British flag', and convinced him that the generous policy would be the right one. Campbell-Bannerman persuaded his Cabinet; responsible government was granted to the Transvaal in 1906 and to the Orange River Colony in 1907.

Smuts supported the claims of Louis Botha [q.v.] to the premiership of the Transvaal, and himself became colonial secretary and minister of education. To this partnership, which lasted until Botha's death, the prime minister contributed a winning personality and a capacity to handle men; Smuts was the tireless worker and master of the great ideas and of the administrative details.

The concession of responsible government to the new colonies made South African union a natural and practicable objective. This alone had reconciled Smuts and many others to the loss of independence. The question was publicly discussed in 1906, and supported by the colonial Parliaments in the following year. When the National Convention met in Durban in 1908, Smuts came to it as the only member with a detailed plan to offer, and accompanied by a larger staff of experts than all the other delegations together could muster. Smuts's plan, which for reasons of political tactics he had to put forward as his own, had in fact been elaborated in correspondence between himself and Merriman. It became the basis of the discussions. As befitted 'the Alexander Hamilton of the Convention', Smuts favoured strong government and the closest union; unlike his prototype, he was able to carry his main proposals against the advocates of a looser federation.

In 1910 the Botha–Smuts partnership moved on to the larger stage of the Union, Botha as premier and Smuts as minister of mines, defence, and the interior. Their party, Het Volk, merged with analogous parties in the other provinces to form the South African Party, embracing almost all the Afrikaners and a section of the English. The opposition parties, Unionist (the party of imperial sentiment) and Labour, were predominantly English. In 1913, however, the pattern was changed by the secession of J. B. M. Hertzog [q.v.] and his Nationalist followers from the South African Party.

It was changed further by Smuts's handling of industrial unrest. In 1907 he had used imperial troops to suppress a strike on the Rand mines. In 1913 a strike with small beginnings spread to all the gold-mines and led to riots, arson, and shooting in Johannesburg. The police were unable to keep order, the Colonial Office was unwilling to allow the use of British troops, and the South African Defence Force was only in the process of formation. Botha and Smuts drove to Johannesburg and under threats from armed strikers conceded their demands. The miners followed up this victory with a plan for a general strike in January 1914. Smuts, smarting from his previous humiliation, this time had his Defence Force ready, proclaimed martial law on the Rand, arrested the leaders, and had them on the high seas before the courts could order their release. For this he was indemnified by Parliament, but not by the Labour Party, which won control of the Transvaal provincial council at the next elections.

When war broke out in August the industrial dispute was temporarily suspended. So was the problem of the settlement and registration of Indians in the Transvaal, a question which for some years had involved Smuts in a conflict with M. K. Gandhi [q.v.], now for the first time evolving and applying his policy of passive resistance.

South Africa's first contribution to the imperial war effort was to take full responsibility for her own defence and to release the imperial troops still in the Union. At the urgent insistence of the British Government Botha agreed, further, to invade German South-West Africa. On 15 September a contingent of South African troops sailed for Lüderitzbucht; on the same day Beyers, commandant-general of the Defence Force, resigned his command, and the veteran guerrilla leader De la Rey was accidentally shot dead. Both were involved in the plotting of rebellion, which broke out in October. The bitterness of 1902, which Union was supposed to have exorcised, was revealed again in dangerous force. Botha and Smuts had to assume the tragic responsibility of suppressing with arms the revolt of their former comrades. Botha took command in the field, while Smuts in Pretoria handled the problems of administration. The rebellion was crushed quickly and so leniently that only one rebel suffered the death penalty for treason.

The campaign in South-West Africa followed in 1915, with Botha, in supreme command, advancing inland from Swakopmund and Smuts, in support, from Lüderitzbucht. Disregarding textbook methods, the raider of 1901 once again led his troops forward at reckless speed. The Germans, numerically inferior, were defeated on both fronts in a few months and surrendered. By July Botha and Smuts were back in the Union.

Their triumphal reception was followed by a bitterly fought general election, in which the Nationalists profited by the late domestic strife, and used the widows and orphans of the rebellion and the strikes as propaganda. At one violent meeting two shots were fired at Smuts. The South African Party lost its majority, but remained in office with Unionist support. Smuts, deeply hurt by the hostility of his own people, was glad to escape from 'this hell into which I have wandered' by accepting early in 1916 the command of all the imperial forces in East Africa, with the commission of lieutenant-general in the British Army.

His forces there were far more numerous than their opponents. Yet in East Africa the most formidable enemies were not the Germans but the land and climate. Smuts brought to bear his accustomed weapons of speed, surprise, and tenacity, and a sympathetic and inspiring leadership which he now displayed on this scale for the first time. Salaita Hill, the German outpost on the British side of Kilimanjaro, was outflanked on 8 March; by January 1917 the Germans under von Lettow-Vorbeck were eluding capture on the Rufiji river, and most of their great colony was in British hands. The triumph over natural obstacles was a notable achievement; but it was won at great cost in casualties from the climate and in the exhaustion of men and material. Dangerous risks had been taken, and the enemy, though decisively beaten, was still in the field.

In January 1917 Smuts was recalled to Cape Town, and was sent to London to represent the Union at the Imperial Conference and in the Imperial War Cabinet. From this followed an invitation by Lloyd George to join the British War Cabinet itself, which Smuts did in the unpaid capacity of what was described as a minister without portfolio. He remained, at the same time, a member of the South African Cabinet and Parliament. His tact put an end, in October 1917, to a critical strike in the Welsh coalfields.

Smuts began to assume the stature of a world statesman. His natural optimism, expressed in many speeches at this dark period of the war, helped to revive the spirits of the British people. The defence of the Empire by a man who had been one of its principal enemies fifteen years earlier gave a new moral force to the British cause. In 1917 he toured the western front, made a report, and later in the year gave his support to the plan which became the Passchendaele offensive. He was offered the Palestine command, but refused it on learning from Sir William Robertson [q.v.] that that theatre would not be given adequate forces and supplies. He was willing, however, to command the American Army in France in June 1918, but Lloyd George did not forward his suggestion to President Wilson. Smuts was mainly responsible for the organization of the Royal Air Force as an independent Service, and suggested the war priorities committee, of which he became the chairman.

At the same time Smuts was attending to the problems of the peace. He defined his ideal, which was later to be realized, of the British Commonwealth of Nations; and of the League of Nations, of which next to President Wilson he was the chief sponsor. In December 1918 he published a pamphlet called *The League of Nations: A Practical Suggestion* which helped to shape Wilson's ideas on the subject. He was the inventor of the mandates system, which, however, was never established in the form he proposed.

At the peace conference Smuts, who could remember Vereeniging, fought in vain for a magnanimous peace which would not provoke either social revolution or another war. His proposals on the subject of reparations, intended merely to secure a share of them to countries financially but not physically ruined, were carried far beyond what he had had in view, and were partly responsible for the reparations plan which was adopted. Yet Smuts so bitterly opposed the 'Carthaginian peace' that, almost till the last moment, he intended not to sign it. Botha agreed with him, yet he decided to sign in order to win for South Africa the international status of a signatory. Smuts signed only in order to preserve the unity of the delegation; he published a protest against the treaty on the following day, then left the stage of world affairs to return to the bitter politics of his own country.

In August 1919 Botha died and Smuts was called to the premiership. The hatreds of the war years were given full vent in the general election which he fought in 1920. The result was a bare majority for the South African Party, Unionists, and sympathetic Independents, together, over Nationalists and Labour. The only way out of the impasse was a simplification of the party system. Smuts approached Hertzog with a view to the co-operation or reunion of their parties. Hertzog's terms were similar to those which Smuts was to accept in 1933, but the atmosphere of 1920 was unfavourable to compromise. The Unionists then agreed to fuse with the South African Party, and another election in 1921 gave the enlarged party an absolute majority of twenty-four.

The four years following the armistice were a period of general unrest. Strikes and other disturbances by natives were frequent, and in three instances led to forcible police measures which gave Smuts the reputation, among his opponents, of a 'man of blood'. The violence culminated early in 1922 on the Rand. A reduction of the wages of some European coalminers started a chain of events which led by March to a general strike in that region. Although the new Communist Party helped to direct the movement, the sentiment of the strikers was as hostile to native workers as to the employers. Smuts, in his own words, allowed 'things to develop' before proclaiming martial law and calling up troops. Things had then developed so far that the red flag waved over the whole of the Rand except the central part of Johannesburg. Smuts, after a secret and adventurous journey from Cape Town, arrived there to direct operations. The rising was quickly suppressed; there had been nearly 700 casualties in all.

In 1921 the prime minister had been to London for an Imperial Conference. The King relied primarily on Smuts when he began to prepare the speech he was to deliver at the opening of the Ulster Parliament, and it was Smuts who mediated between the British Government and the Southern Irish leaders; the former state attorney of the South African republic persuaded some of the latter, as perhaps no other public man could have done, to enter into the negotiations which led to the Anglo-Irish Treaty.

In 1922, after the Rand rebellion, Smuts went to Rhodesia on another kind of mission. The British South Africa Company was about to relinquish its political responsibilities, and the electors of Southern Rhodesia were faced with the choice between eventual independent responsible government and annexation to the Union. In the latter case their votes would give the support which Smuts's tottering Government desperately needed, but in making the approach he looked less to this relief than to 'manifest destiny'. He offered terms so favourable that his opponents in the Union could use them as a weapon against him, but he failed to persuade the Rhodesians. In the referendum which followed they rejected his offer.

A succession of by-elections reduced the Government's majority, by 1924, to eight. Smuts made an election at Wakkerstroom a matter of confidence; defeated there, he decided, without consulting his colleagues, to go to the country. The Nationalist and Labour parties, each with its own scores to settle, had the previous year made an electoral pact which for the time being shelved both republicanism and Socialism. The Government was defeated and Smuts made way for Hertzog. Five years later *Rhodes redivivus*, as the Nationalists called him, spoke again of expansion to the north, of a great British African Dominion. His opponents interpreted this as a threat to engulf the white population in the mass of black Africa, and with that theme they won the elections of 1929.

In the long period of opposition Smuts had time, hitherto denied him, for his many avocations. He wrote *Holism and Evolution* (1926), his philosophy of the whole. In 1929 he delivered the Rhodes memorial lectures at Oxford, and lectured also in the United States. In 1931 he presided at the centenary meeting of the British Association for the Advancement of Science.

It was in 1931, too, that Britain abandoned the gold standard. Smuts strongly supported the same policy for South Africa. But the Union remained on gold, and, as Britain was her principal market, export prices fell and the consequences were acutely felt in 1932. At the end of that year Tielman Johannes de Villiers Roos, a former Nationalist minister and now a judge, resigned from the bench and returned to the political arena. He demanded an abandonment both of the gold standard and of racial bickering, and offered himself as the peacemaker. His dramatic intervention appears to have caused a panic in the Cabinet. The minister of finance spoke of a flight of currency abroad. The Reserve Bank reports afterwards showed that there had been little if any movement of this kind, but the Government went off gold on 27 December 1932, believing its hand to have been forced. Roos had expected this course to be taken by himself as prime minister, supported by Smuts, the South African Party, and some discontented Nationalists. Many of Smuts's followers favoured such a realignment. But after Hertzog had appropriated the essential part of Roos's policy, Roos found himself deserted.

The move to bring the parties together had, however, raised hopes which could not be immediately disappointed. The credit of the Government had been shaken; for months before going off gold, Hertzog had been saying that he would resign rather than do so. The South African Party had just won a sensational victory at a by-election. Smuts, after much heart-searching and consultation of friends, decided that the moment had come for a coalition which would end the twenty years' quarrel. His first offer of the olive branch made in the debate on a motion of no confidence was rejected by Hertzog; after negotiations behind the scenes it was offered a second time, and accepted.

The new Cabinet had six members from each party, with Hertzog as prime minister and Smuts as his deputy. The combined parties went to the country in a 'coupon' election and were solidly supported by it. Coalition was the prelude to a fusion of the parties in 1934 under the name of the United South African National Party. Hertzog remained the leader, and the new party was based on what were essentially Hertzog's principles, softened in their application now that the Statute of Westminster had given him the substance of his demand for independence. But a large section of the former Nationalists, under Dr. Daniel François Malan, and a small section of the South African Party, under Colonel Stallard, rejected fusion; they formed the 'purified' Nationalist and Dominion parties. Owing to the relative proportions of these defections, the followers of Smuts were a bigger force in the United Party than those of Hertzog. Yet the Hertzog policies were followed by the party. Its great preponderance enabled him in 1936 to pass his native bills by the requisite two-thirds majority.

As the ambitions of the Fascist powers unfolded, the unity of the United Party became harder to preserve. Hertzog's sympathies with Germany were unconcealed, and aroused alarm and indignation among Smuts's supporters; but Smuts continued to make concessions for the sake of racial peace.

The uneasy alliance could not survive the outbreak of war in 1939. When Parliament met on 4 September not only the United Party, but the Cabinet, was split. Hertzog proposed a policy of neutrality which Smuts rejected. After a tense debate the prime minister's motion was defeated by thirteen votes. He asked the governor-general, Sir Patrick Duncan [q.v.], for a dissolution. After a talk with Smuts, Duncan refused to dissolve, Hertzog resigned and Smuts was called once more to the premiership. His supporters retained the name and the organization of the United Party, but the Government was a coalition in which the Dominion Party and Labour Party also took part. The general election of 1943 gave it a substantial majority and a specific mandate from the electorate, which had been lacking in 1939.

Although the rebellion of 1914 was not repeated, the Opposition was again bitterly opposed to participation in the war. Sabotage, sympathy with the enemy, and, in country districts, ostracism and persecution of government supporters were common. Smuts, remembering the political martyrdoms of the earlier conflict, steadily refused to take the repressive measures which many of his followers demanded. He was rewarded by a schism in the Opposition ranks. There was a reunion of Hertzog's party with Malan's, but Hertzog himself and his closest associates were ejected from the new Herenigde Nasionale Party; there was bad blood also between this and the militant Ossewabrandwag.

The Government had nevertheless to make its contribution to the war in most unfavourable circumstances. In spite of these, South African troops were able to play an important part in the Abyssinian, North African, and Italian theatres; the contributions of the Air Force and the various technical services were especially notable. Smuts, who became a British field-marshal in 1941, paid frequent visits to Europe and North Africa, and steadily used his influence in allied counsels to support campaigns in the Middle East. (Sir) Winston Churchill, from his long friendship, 'always . . . found great comfort in feeling that our minds were in step' and consulted Smuts before many critical decisions, such as the changes in the Middle East command in 1942. In 1943 Smuts urged greater speed in the Mediterranean operations and in September even advocated the sacrifice of the future western front in favour of greater efforts in Italy and the Balkans. He was the first to call attention to the danger of uncoordinated operations in south-eastern Europe, a stimulus which led eventually to British intervention in Greece. He feared the post-war predominance of Russia which would result from its comparatively greater contribution to the victory. When the war ended, he resumed his old constructive labours by helping, at San Francisco, to create the United Nations.

Once again the conditions of peace were unfavourable to his tenure of office at home. The Opposition organized a united front for the general election of 1948, and won it by a narrow majority. Smuts was defeated in his own constituency, but later took over a safe seat from one of his supporters. To him there remained two years as leader of the Opposition. His lieutenant, the younger J. H. Hofmeyr [q.v.], was struck down by a coronary thrombosis. Soon after the public celebration of his eightieth birthday Smuts himself fell ill, and succumbed to the same disease 11 September 1950.

He died on his farm at Irene, near Pretoria, which had been his home since 1909. For nearly half a century he had been the dominant personality in South African affairs, and at times a great influence in the affairs of the world. The theme of his policies had been the sublimation of the part in the whole, and that in a greater whole: Union, a greater South Africa, British Commonwealth, League of Nations. In realizing his objects he had often been a lone figure, unable to suffer fools gladly or to make contact with the common man on the vulgar plane. 'The dogs may bark', he would say, 'but the caravan moves on.' In these traits lay his strength and his weakness. It was said by some that he was a great tree under which too little else could grow.

Of his personal appearance, the most striking characteristic was his 'haunting penetrative' grey-blue eyes. The tight lips and firm chin were concealed by a moustache and pointed beard. The complexion was fresh and ruddy. He was of medium height, slim and wiry; but the adjective 'slim' applied to him by his enemies was the Afrikaans adjective meaning 'clever' in the derogatory sense of 'cunning'.

His achievements were acknowledged by the conferment of many honours: he was sworn of the Privy Council in 1917 and made a Companion of Honour in the same year; in 1947 he was appointed to the Order of Merit. He became a K.C. in 1906, an honorary fellow of Christ's College, Cambridge, in 1915, F.R.S. in 1930, and an honorary bencher of the Middle Temple in 1947. He was president of the South African Association for the Advancement of Science (1925), rector of the university of St. Andrews (1931–4), chancellor of the universities of Cape Town (1936) and Cambridge (1948), where the Smuts professorship of the history of the British Commonwealth was founded in his memory in 1953. He received at least twenty-six honorary degrees and the freedom of eighteen towns and cities; there is reason to believe that these numbers (which were all he could recollect at the end of his life) were in fact exceeded. Many governments, South African, British, and foreign, had conferred military honours on him in three wars.

Smuts married in 1897 Sybella Margaretha (died 1954), daughter of Japie Krige, a farmer, of Stellenbosch. They had two sons and four daughters who survived infancy, and all but the elder son survived their father.

There are many portraits of Smuts; among them may be mentioned those by Simon Elwes in the National Art Gallery, Cape Town; by Sir William Orpen at the university of Cape Town; by Professor Arthur Pan at Christ's College, Cambridge, and South Africa House, London; by Frank O. Salisbury at St. Andrews; by Josselin Bodley at Rhodes House, Oxford; by Sir William Nicholson at the Fitzwilliam Museum, Cambridge, and the City of Johannesburg Art Gallery; and a drawing by Francis Dodd at the Imperial War Museum. A bronze bust by M. Kottler is in the National Portrait Gallery, where Smuts is also included in J. S. Sargent's group 'Some General Officers of the War of 1914–18'. A statue by Sir Jacob Epstein was unveiled by the Speaker of the House of Commons as a national memorial to Smuts in Parliament Square, London, in 1956.

[Sarah Gertrude Millin, General Smuts, 1936; F. S. Crafford, Jan Smuts, 1945; H. C. Armstrong, Grey Steel, a Study in Arrogance,

1937; J. C. Smuts, *Jan Christian Smuts*, 1952; Frank Owen, *Tempestuous Journey*, 1954; Sir Keith Hancock, *The Smuts Papers* (the Creighton lecture, 1955); John Ehrman, *Grand Strategy*, vol. v, 1956; private information.]

A. M. KEPPEL-JONES.

SMYTH, DAMF ETHEL MARY (1858–1944), composer, author, and feminist, was the daughter of Lieutenant-Colonel (later Major-General) John Hall Smyth, C.B., an artillery officer stationed at Woolwich, who had fought in the Indian Mutiny and was living at Sidcup, where Ethel Mary, the fourth of a family of six girls and two boys, was born 23 April 1858. Her mother was the daughter of a Norfolk Stracey who had married a Mr. Charles Struth and subsequently in Paris a Mr. Reece, from whom she was eventually separated. Emma, daughter of the first marriage, who became Mrs. Smyth, was thus subject to French education and to French ways, the effects of which she never quite lost even in the conventional atmosphere of an English officer's home. Her own background in the deliberate obscurity of her mother's life in Paris gave her some sympathy with her own rebellious daughter (whom she called 'the stormy petrel') when paternal opposition to a musical career for Ethel was at its height.

In the course of Ethel's education at home and at a boarding-school at Putney, musical talent showed itself early, although not with extraordinary precocity. It was taken in hand at a critical moment by the composer of the tune for the hymn 'Jerusalem the Golden', Alexander Ewing, then a captain in the Army Service Corps and a neighbour of the Smyths who had moved to Frimley. His wife (Juliana Horatia Ewing, q.v.) gave Ethel, then a girl of seventeen, some help in the writing of English, and prophetically declared that she would turn her into a writer some day. The battle for a musical career, which had begun at the age of twelve, was not decided until 1877 when after furious opposition from her father she got her way and went off to Leipzig to study at the Conservatorium. At Leipzig she obtained admission to the circle dominated by Brahms, studying with Heinrich von Herzogenberg, and forming a friendship with his wife Elisabeth which is the main theme of the autobiographical *Impressions that Remained*. Her first works, the product of her studies and couched as was natural enough in the idiom of German romanticism of the early 'eighties, were a Quintet for strings and a Sonata for violin and piano, which were obviously promising. She continued to compose assiduously, at first in the forms of chamber music, but in 1890 a Serenade in D in four movements for orchestra gained a performance at the Crystal Palace concerts and later in the same year an overture, 'Antony and Cleopatra', was performed there and in 1892 repeated by (Sir) George Henschel [q.v.] at one of his London concerts.

To the next year belongs the Mass in D, her most impressive work outside the category of opera. It is an oratorio setting in the style of the Viennese Masses which culminated in Beethoven's Mass in D, and although not a challenge to Beethoven on his own ground it is an assertion of the composer's ability to handle with confidence the largest forms on the highest themes. The work, although in the appropriate style, is not derivative, and when it was revived in 1924, thirty-one years after its original performance at the Royal Albert Hall under Sir Joseph Barnby [q.v.], the freshness of the invention and the mastery of its construction and its orchestration were noted as signs of its vitality. Sir Donald Tovey [q.v.] honoured it with one of his analytical notes, in the course of which he says that 'no choral work within modern times is more independent of all classical or modern antecedents except those of artistic commonsense'. Her other important oratorio 'The Prison', composed at the end of her long career—it was first performed in 1931 when she was seventy-three—was not successful, although it was based on a philosophical text by Henry B. Brewster, brother-in-law of Elisabeth von Herzogenberg, who figures largely in the composer's memoirs and certainly influenced her thought. Its intellectual sincerity is not matched by a similar imaginative intensity and its scrappiness suggests that the dissipation of her great energies and enthusiasms, however much they enriched her life, was not favourable to artistic creation.

For Ethel Smyth was an inveterate crusader. Her first battle was for her own career as a musician. Having got her training she fought for recognition not merely as a woman composer but as a composer without prefix or suffix. She actually secured performances of her operas in German theatres: *Fantasio* was produced at Weimar in 1898 and at Carlsruhe in 1901; the one-act *Der Wald* in Berlin and at Covent Garden in 1902, in New York in 1903, and at Strasbourg in 1904; *Der Strandrecht*, which became *The Wreckers*, at Leipzig and Prague in 1906. The first performance in England and in English was given at His Majesty's Theatre in 1909 under (Sir) Thomas Beecham and it had revivals at Covent Garden (1931) and Sadler's Wells (1939). *The Boatswain's Mate* (after the story by W. W. Jacobs, q.v.) would have been first given at Frankfurt but for the war and actually had its première in London in 1916. Her other operas were in one act: one, described as a dance dream, *Fête Galante*, produced at the Birmingham Repertory Theatre in 1923; the other, a farcical comedy, *Entente Cordiale*, produced at Bristol in 1926. This is a very considerable achievement in the notoriously hazardous and incalculable field of opera. *The Boatswain's Mate*, although suffering from a mixture of styles—it begins as a ballad opera with spoken dialogue and ends with continuous music—could safely take its place in a repertory of English comic opera along with the Savoy operas if ever the equivalent of an Opéra Comique were established in London. *The Wreckers*, of which the libretto was written by Henry B. Brewster, remains her greatest artistic achievement and her greatest success.

In the volume of her autobiography entitled *As Time Went On . . .* the conjunction of those two disparate ideas, achievement and success, forms the theme of some discussion on why she failed to obtain practical recognition in her own country by the performance of her works. (Incidentally there was not in her output a great deal of orchestral music, such as might have found its way into the programmes of the promenade concerts—the Concerto for violin and horn (1927) is her only large-scale symphonic work.) She did, however, win the recognition of an honorary doctorate of music from Durham in 1910, from Manchester University in 1930, and was the first woman recipient of the honorary degree at Oxford in 1926. She also received the honorary degree of LL.D. from St. Andrews in 1928. In 1922 she was appointed D.B.E.

Ethel Smyth was the first woman to compose music in the largest forms of opera, oratorio, and concerto, and to convince the sceptical world of music in England and in Germany that musical talent in a woman was not confined to salon music, such as Madame Chaminade

wrote gracefully, but could take its place beside that of the most serious-minded men. In battling for musical emancipation she was caught up into the larger movement for women's suffrage and found herself in 1912 marching through the streets with the militant suffragettes to her own 'March of the Women', composed for the movement, and subsequently conducting its strains with a toothbrush from the window of a cell in Holloway prison. The daughter of a soldier she was a fighter, and like many bonny fighters she fought too many battles, some of them unnecessary and none of them conducive to the frame of mind in which music can be composed.

About the reception of her literary work she could have no complaints. After the *Impressions that Remained* (2 vols., 1919) she maintained a succession of racily written sequels—*Streaks of Life* (1921), *A Final Burning of Boats* (1928), *Beecham and Pharaoh* (1935), *As Time Went On . . .* (1936), and *What Happened Next* (1940). In them the reader gets a true impression of the vigour and vitality of one who was full of high spirits, serious purpose, and English eccentricity. She had a charming singing voice with which she entertained the private circle of her friends, and a striking appearance, in tweeds and three-cornered hat, when she sometimes mounted the platform to conduct her own works in public. As an emancipated woman, an author, and a composer, she was a prominent figure who long outlived her Victorian origin and retained into extreme old age the vital qualities which made her all those things at once. She died, unmarried, at Woking 9 May 1944. A bust by Gilbert Bayes is at the Sadler's Wells Theatre. A portrait in oils, showing her in the robes of a D.Mus. of Oxford, was painted in 1936 by Neville (later the Earl of) Lytton and is now at the Royal College of Music.

[Her own writings; private information; personal knowledge.]     FRANK HOWES.

SMYTHE, FRANCIS SYDNEY (1900–1949), mountaineer, was born at Ivythorne, Maidstone, 6 July 1900, the son of Algernon Sydney Smythe, who owned a timber wharf and considerable property in and around Maidstone, by his second wife, Florence, daughter of Francis Reeves, of Wateringbury Hall, Wateringbury, Kent. His father died when Smythe was two years old.

After leaving Berkhamsted School

Smythe entered Faraday House Electrical Engineering College in 1919. In 1922 he was sent to Austria, and spent every week-end and holiday climbing and walking. In 1926 he joined the Royal Air Force and went to Egypt, but was invalided out the following year and cautioned to walk upstairs slowly for the rest of his life. For a year he worked with Kodak, Ltd.; and thereafter he supported himself by books, articles, and lectures on mountaineering, on which subject he contributed frequently to *The Times*.

In the Alps Smythe's finest climbs were the new routes which he and Professor Thomas Graham Brown forced up the Brenva face of Mont Blanc in 1927 and 1928. He took part in six expeditions in the Himalayas, and in 1931 led the expedition which conquered Kamet, the first peak over 25,000 feet to be climbed. He took part in the Everest expeditions of 1933, 1936, and 1938, and in 1933 equalled the height record (*c.* 28,000 feet) established by Edward Felix Norton in 1924. In 1946 and 1947 he visited the Rockies and in the latter year carried out some extremely successful explorations in the Lloyd George range of British Columbia. He was taken ill on the eve of a Himalayan expedition and flown back to England to die within a fortnight of his forty-ninth birthday, 27 June 1949, at Uxbridge.

Smythe learned to climb by climbing, for he never once employed a guide. He was not in the first flight as a rock climber, but he was one of the greatest mountaineers of the day, and his knowledge of the mountains was not confined to the summer, for he was a competent, although not a stylish, skier, and had a fine record of Alpine ski tours to his credit.

Dr. Raymond Greene, who joined him in his attack on Kamet, had the highest opinion of his qualities as a leader, and wrote of him: 'At great altitudes a new force seemed to enter into him. His body, still apparently frail as it had been in boyhood, was capable of astonishing feats of sudden strength and prolonged endurance and his mind, too, took on a different colour. At sea-level the mistaken sense of inferiority so unfairly implanted by his early experiences rendered him sometimes irritable, tactless, and easily offended. The self-confidence which flowed into his mind and body, the emanation as it were of the mountains whose strength he so greatly loved, changed him almost beyond recognition. It seemed impossible above 20,000 feet to disturb his composure

or his essential quietism.' The same writer also paid great tribute to his leadership on the approach to the North Col of Everest as 'the finest piece of ice-climbing I have ever seen'.

Smythe always rose to a great emergency. Surprised by a terrible storm high upon the Pétéret ridge of Mont Blanc, he led the first successful descent of the Rochers Grüber from the Col de Pétéret, and, to quote his companion, Dr. G. Graham Macphee, 'was never once at fault descending and crossing the complicated and difficult Fresnay glacier'.

Smythe's literary reputation suffered from the fact that he rather over-wrote himself, but the books by which he wished to be judged, notably *Climbs and Ski Runs* (1929), *Kamet Conquered* (1932), and *Camp Six* (1937), were favourably received by mountaineers. Most of his readers, however, were non-mountaineers, for it was his great merit to convey to those who had never climbed his own passion for the mountains. His books were always notable for their illustrations, for he was in the front rank of mountain photographers. He was at his best as an interpreter of mountain adventure, and at his weakest when he attempted to construct a religion from his mountain experiences. He matured late, and his interest in art and history was developing rapidly when he died. As a man he was modest and good-natured. He loved an argument about Alpine and other subjects, but was incapable of malice and found it difficult to understand malice in others.

In 1931 Smythe married Kathleen Mary, only daughter of Alexander Barks Johnson, marine consulting engineer. There were three sons of this marriage which was dissolved. Later he married Nona Isobel, daughter of David Richard Wilson Miller, owner of a sheep station in Canterbury, New Zealand, and formerly wife of Robert Macdonald Guthrie. This second marriage was very happy, and his second wife had a great influence in widening his mental horizons.

[*Alpine Journal*, November 1949; *British Ski Year Book*, 1950; private information; personal knowledge.]     ARNOLD LUNN.

SNELL, HENRY, BARON SNELL (1865–1944), politician and secularist, was born 1 April 1865 at Sutton-on-Trent, Nottinghamshire. His mother was Mary Snell, formerly Clark. The father's name was not registered, but the boy had a family upbringing in the cottage of his mother and stepfather. At the age of eight he was put to cattle-minding and bird-scaring, and the minute fragments of formal education which he picked up were gleaned from casual, seasonal attendance at the village school. At twelve he was sent to the hiring-fair at Newark, and engaged by a farmer as an indoor servant. From this employment he passed to several successive jobs in public houses (most of them in Nottingham), deriving from the experience a deep and lifelong distaste for alcohol and tobacco.

Despite this unpropitious start, Harry Snell painfully acquired a few books, and gradually learned to think for himself. Attendance at free-thought lectures caused him to join the secularist movement, and for a time the Unitarian Church. He progressed far enough in self-education to be able to draw benefit from evening classes which he attended at University College, Nottingham. For him Socialism was the sister of rationalism, and he joined first the Social Democratic Federation and then the Independent Labour Party.

In 1890, after a considerable experience of unemployment and a few years' clerical work, Snell went to London as assistant to the secretary of the Woolwich Charity Organization Society. In his spare time he greatly widened the scope of his reading, penetrating into economics, history, and philosophy; and by open-air work in the parks for the Ethical and Fabian movements he taught himself public speaking. In 1895 he became secretary to the first director of the London School of Economics and Political Science and later a lecturer under the Hutchinson Trust for the Fabian Society. In 1899 he was an organizer and lecturer in the Union of Ethical Societies of which he became secretary; he was also secretary of the Secular Education League from 1907 until 1931.

Snell stood unsuccessfully as Labour candidate for Huddersfield twice in 1910 and again in 1918. He was returned for East Woolwich for the London County Council in 1919 and in 1922; and in the latter year he was elected to Parliament for that division. He was one of the founders of a Labour Commonwealth group, and much of his parliamentary life was devoted to the affairs of the Commonwealth, which took him to South Africa, India, Palestine, and British Guiana.

In March 1931 Snell was created a baron, and until August was parliamentary under-secretary of state for India. Although he found the atmosphere of the Lords far less lively and stimulating than that of the lower House, he was soon at home there, acquitting himself with dignity and aplomb, earning much praise for his well-argued and well-expressed speeches. He did not stand for the London County Council in 1925, but in 1934, when Labour gained a majority on that body, he was recalled as chairman, serving until 1938. Much of his high reputation arises from his work in London municipal government. In 1940 Snell was appointed captain of the Honourable Corps of Gentlemen-at-Arms, and deputy leader of the House of Lords. He was appointed C.B.E. in 1930, sworn of the Privy Council in 1937, and made a C.H. in 1943. He received the honorary degree of LL.D. from London University in 1936.

Snell wrote *Daily Life in Parliament* (1930) and an autobiography *Men, Movements, and Myself* (1936). This last-named friendly, well-written, and modest book gives a vivid picture not only of the rise of a poor farm-boy to eminence, but of the rapid and far-reaching changes in English social life over a period of seventy years. He died in London 21 April 1944. He was unmarried and the peerage therefore became extinct.

Describing himself as 'passionately anti-clerical in outlook and temper', Snell spent a laborious and penurious life in devoted service to the rationalist and Socialist causes. He had no hobby but reading, and much of that was in subjects connected with his work. His sensitive conscience and keen sense of duty drove him so hard that from time to time his constitution rebelled and he was forced to rest. Although at times he could be witty and good company, he did not make friends easily, and his unremitting pre-occupation with ethics and sociology, unrelieved by any winning weaknesses, often made him seem bleak to more human mortals. A portrait of Snell by Francis Dodd is at County Hall, London.

[Lord Snell, *Men, Movements, and Myself*, 1936; *Current Biography*, May 1941; *The Times*, 22 April 1944; private information.]

HERBERT B. GRIMSDITCH.

SOMERS-COCKS, ARTHUR HERBERT TENNYSON, sixth BARON SOMERS (1887–1944), chief scout for Great Britain and the British Commonwealth and Empire, and governor of Victoria, Australia, was born at Freshwater, Isle of Wight, 20 March 1887, son of Herbert Haldane Somers-Cocks, late lieutenant of the

Coldstream Guards, and his wife, Blanche Margaret Standish, daughter of Major Herbert Clogstoun, V.C. He succeeded his great-uncle, the fifth baron, in the family honours in 1899 at the age of twelve.

Educated at Charterhouse, he joined the 1st Life Guards in 1906 after a year at New College, Oxford. An all-round athlete, he played cricket for Charterhouse, making a century in his first match against Westminster, helped to win the army rackets for his regiment in 1908, and played cricket for Worcestershire, occasionally captaining the side in 1923. His gift for athletics was supplemented by a natural appreciation of music and art, acquired in an artistic circle where Tennyson, Leighton, and G. F. Watts [qq.v.] were frequent visitors, and balanced by a strong sense of service.

After an accident at polo in 1911 he left the regiment and went to farm in Canada with his sister and her husband, then Lord Hyde. On the outbreak of war in 1914 he rejoined his regiment and served in France throughout the war, being promoted, 8 September 1918, to the command of the 6th battalion of the newly formed Tank Corps. For his services he was mentioned in dispatches, awarded the M.C., appointed to the D.S.O., and made a chevalier of the Legion of Honour.

Somers retired from the army in 1922 as a lieutenant-colonel, and devoted himself to a wide range of activities. When the Malvern Hills were once again threatened by industrial development he was one of the first landowners to offer to the National Trust for merely nominal compensation certain permanent rights over his (Eastnor Castle) property in the hills which ensured the preservation of their amenities and free public access to them in perpetuity. He was joint master of the Ledbury hounds in 1923–4; lord-in-waiting and one of the spokesmen of the Government in the House of Lords, 1924–6; and president of the Marylebone Cricket Club in 1936. He was appointed lord lieutenant of Herefordshire in 1933 and a director of the Great Western Railway Company in 1941.

From 1920 to the end of his life he took an active part in the Boy Scout movement for which his gift of leadership and youthful outlook eminently fitted him. In 1932 he became a chief's commissioner to Lord Baden-Powell [q.v.] who nominated him acting chief scout during his absence on a tour of South Africa in 1935; and deputy chief scout in 1936. After he had been designated by the founder to succeed him, he was duly appointed chief scout for Great Britain in January 1941, and for the British Commonwealth and Empire in March of the same year.

In 1926 Somers became governor of Victoria, and was appointed K.C.M.G. It was a popular choice and a successful governorship. His ease of manner, versatility, and unfeigned interest in all the activities of the state won the liking of all. His sincerity and shrewdness enabled him to exercise an influence where the experienced politician might not have ventured or the merely polished orator would have failed. His years of office are specially remembered for the interest which he and his wife took in the youth of the state. When the more formal duties of his office permitted him, he delighted to lead a party of scouts for a week's hike in the less-known hills, where his interest in natural history and especially in bird lore found happy scope. Inspired by the success of the Duke of York's camps in England, Somers initiated in 1929 a similar camp on the coast in Victoria for a hundred boys between sixteen and eighteen years of age selected from schools and commercial and industrial undertakings. Within two years the camp was equipped on a permanent basis by generous friends and its name was changed to Somers by the State of Victoria as a permanent memorial to the governor. He was acting governor-general of Australia for a few months before the appointment of Sir Isaac Isaacs [q.v.], and completed his term of office in 1931.

In 1940 Somers went to Egypt as commissioner for the Red Cross and St. John Ambulance in the Middle East. He returned home a sick man in the following year to continue his work as chief scout for a few months and then to face a long and fatal illness with characteristic courage. He died at Eastnor Castle 14 July 1944. He married in 1921 Daisy Finola, younger daughter of Captain Bertram Charles Christopher Spencer Meeking, 10th Hussars, by whom he had one daughter. He was succeeded in his titles by his uncle, Arthur Percy (1864–1953). A portrait of Somers by (Sir) Oswald Birley is at Boy Scout headquarters in London.

[*The Times*, 15 July 1944; private information; personal knowledge.]

ASTOR OF HEVER.

SOMERVILLE, EDITH ANNA ŒNONE (1858–1949), writer, was born 2 May 1858 in Corfu where her father,

Lieutenant-Colonel Thomas Henry Somerville, was commanding a battalion of the Buffs. Her mother was Adelaide Eliza, daughter of Vice-Admiral Sir Josiah Coghill, third baronet, by his second wife through whom she traced her descent from Chief Justice Charles Kendal Bushe [q.v.]. This eminent lawyer and wit was the great-grandfather both of Edith Somerville and of her cousin and co-author, Violet Florence Martin [q.v.], better known under her pen-name of Martin Ross. A cousin on her father's side was Charlotte Payne-Townshend who married G. B. Shaw [q.v.].

Her father retired in 1859 to his home at Drishane House, Skibbereen, county Cork, and there she spent most of her long life in a patriarchal atmosphere where the flavour of the eighteenth century still lingered. She was the eldest of a family of eight, having one sister and six brothers, of whom four had distinguished careers in the navy and army. Educated at home and for a short time at Alexandra College, Dublin, in her early years riding and drawing were her passion, which culminated later in the mastership of the West Carbery foxhounds and several one-man exhibitions of painting in London and New York. She had studied painting for a term in London and also in Düsseldorf, and in Paris at the studios of Colarossi and Delécluse.

On 17 January 1886 Edith Somerville first met Violet Martin and from that moment their literary partnership began, their first book, *An Irish Cousin*, appearing in 1889. Violet Martin died in 1915, by which time the cousins had published fourteen books, including *The Real Charlotte* (1894), *Some Experiences of an Irish R.M.* (1899), *Further Experiences of an Irish R.M.* (1908), and *In Mr. Knox's Country* (1915). Undaunted by the loss of her beloved partner, Edith Somerville continued to write on until the end of her life, sustained by the belief that the death of her cousin caused no break in their literary collaboration. The name of Martin Ross appeared as co-author in her further publications which included *Irish Memories* (1917), *Mount Music* (1919), and *The Big House of Inver* (1925).

Exactly five feet seven inches in height, Edith Somerville had an oval face with neat features, light-brown hair, which in her later years was snow-white, and grey-blue eyes. Slim of figure and usually dressed in a tweed coat and skirt, she looked and obviously felt her best on horseback, riding side-saddle, where her unshakeable nerve, beautiful hands and seat kept her in the first flight, and where as M.F.H. her great natural powers of command and leadership found their fullest scope. A portrait of her, at Drishane House, painted by John Crealock, shows her in her riding habit, with her hunting-horn in her hand.

She visited Denmark, France, and (with her great friend Dame Ethel Smyth, q.v.) Italy, also the United States; but apart from some travel essays and *The States Through Irish Eyes* (1931) all the Somerville and Ross books have their scenes laid in Ireland. They are alive with penetrating observation and wit, and in addition to enchanting their readers, they vividly depict many aspects of the Anglo-Irish way of life of the period. Many of them are illustrated by Edith Somerville herself.

Notable recognition of her contributions to literature were bestowed on her. In 1932 Trinity College, Dublin, conferred on her an honorary Litt.D., associating with hers the name of Violet Martin. In 1941 the Irish Academy of Letters, of which she was a founder-member, awarded her the Gregory gold medal, the principal literary honour in its gift; and in 1948 *The Real Charlotte* was published in the World's Classics series, a compliment which has only rarely been paid to a living author.

Edith Somerville was not content only to write and paint and ride to hounds. In 1875 she became the organist in the parish church of Castlehaven in which position for seventy-five years she exercised a benevolent autocracy over the choir and church music. Impelled by indomitable energy and unquenchable enthusiasm, she shared in the management of a farm; as an ardent feminist was the chairman of the Munster Women's Franchise League; and founded and directed the Castlehaven Nursing Association. Generous to a fault, a natural and inspiring leader, staunch friend and delightful companion, she died, unmarried, at her home, Drishane, in the parish of Castlehaven, 8 October 1949. A bibliography compiled and edited by Elizabeth Hudson, and containing explanatory notes by Edith Somerville, was published in a limited edition by The Sporting Gallery and Bookshop, Inc., New York (1942), and a study of her by her friend Geraldine Cummins, entitled *Dr. E. Œ. Somerville*, was published in 1952.

[Family papers and personal recollections.]

PATRICK COGHILL.

SOMERVILLE, SIR JAMES FOWNES (1882–1949), admiral of the fleet, was born at Weybridge, Surrey, 17 July 1882, the second son of Arthur Fownes Somerville, of Dinder House, Wells, Somerset, and his wife, Ellen, daughter of William Stanley Sharland, of New Norfolk, Tasmania. Descended from the Hood family through his paternal grandmother, the boy joined the *Britannia* as a naval cadet in 1897, went to sea the next year, and became a lieutenant in 1904. He qualified as a torpedo specialist three years later. Wireless telegraphy was then assimilated to the torpedo branch, and in 1912 Somerville was appointed to the torpedo school in the *Vernon*, where he was principally engaged in developing long-range, continuous-wave wireless, then an innovation. He became one of the foremost wireless specialists in the navy, and during the war of 1914–18 was successively fleet wireless officer to five different flag officers. For his services in this capacity in the Dardanelles in 1915 he was promoted to commander in December and appointed to the D.S.O. in 1916. Later he was employed in equipping ships of the Grand Fleet for the first time with wireless fire control. Although as a youngster his shipmates described him as shy and unassuming, 1918 found him a marked man likely to rise high in his profession. He showed signs of that confident resourcefulness, alertness, and quickness of mind which so characterized him in later years.

After service in a battleship in the Mediterranean, Somerville was promoted to captain in December 1921. He then became flag captain to (Sir) John Kelly [q.v.], and from 1925 to 1927 was director of the signal department at the Admiralty. He later returned to the Mediterranean, again as flag captain to his old chief, and from 1929 to 1931 was one of the directing staff at the Imperial Defence College. After further service afloat in command of the cruiser *Norfolk* in the Home Fleet, he was appointed in October 1932 commodore of the Royal Naval Barracks, Portsmouth, where he instituted many schemes for the benefit of the sailors and their wives. A rear-admiral in 1933, he became director of personal services at the Admiralty in May 1934, an appointment for which he was eminently suited. He insisted on the highest efficiency and each ship he commanded had been a happy one. His humanity, sympathy, and unfailing sense of humour greatly endeared him to the men. He knew their thoughts and could speak their language.

Somerville was appointed C.B. in 1935, and from 1936 until 1938 flew his flag in command of the Mediterranean destroyer flotillas. With the troubles in Palestine, the civil war in Spain, and the Italian war against Abyssinia, it was a period of great activity. He was promoted to vice-admiral in 1937. In July 1938 he took up his appointment as commander-in-chief, East Indies, with his flag in his old ship, the *Norfolk*, until, in the following April, he was invalided home for illness diagnosed as pulmonary tuberculosis. By the inflexible rule of the Service he was placed on the retired list. In spite of his complete recovery and the production of certificates from eminent civilian specialists stating that he had no traces of the disease, all his appeals for reinstatement were unavailing. He was promoted K.C.B. in 1939.

His services were not lost to the country. Recalled to the navy on the outbreak of war in 1939 he was engaged for a time with the development and production of the all-important radar. At the end of May 1940, during the evacuation from Dunkirk, he offered his services to (Sir) Bertram Ramsay [q.v.], the flag officer commanding at Dover. His fine work contributed materially to the success of this most difficult and sustained operation in which, as Ramsay wrote in his dispatch, Somerville's initiative and resource had never been put to better use.

Soon after the final fall of France, Somerville was selected to command Force H at Gibraltar, where his first and most disagreeable task was to ensure that the French fleet at Mers-el-Kebir (Oran) did not fall into the hands of the Germans. As the French admiral refused any of the various alternatives offered by the British Government, Somerville, after prolonged negotiations, was forced to bring the French ships to action on 3 July 1940. The tenor of his signals to the Admiralty during this unhappy period gave a clear indication of his intense personal repugnance for this drastic action. The composition of Force H varied from time to time, but thereafter, under his able and energetic direction, it provided the covering and escort force for some of the convoys to beleaguered Malta, during which his ships were in frequent action with Italian surface forces, submarines, and aircraft. Genoa was also bombarded from the sea and Leghorn attacked by his naval aircraft. Employed also in the North Atlantic, Force H and the aircraft from the *Ark Royal* played a decisive part in the chase and final destruction of the *Bismarck* in May 1941, and the conspicuous skill with which Somerville handled his force during this engagement was commended in dispatches. For his varied services Somerville was appointed K.B.E. in this same year.

In March 1942 after the entry of Japan into the war and the loss of the *Prince of Wales* and *Repulse* off Malaya, Somerville was appointed commander-in-chief, Eastern Fleet, with a hastily organized fleet greatly inferior to that of the Japanese, and was promoted to admiral on the retired list on 6 April. The overall strategy of the war necessitated a defensive policy to prevent a Japanese advance to the westward across the Indian Ocean. He relinquished this command in August 1944, and in the same month was reinstated on the active list and promoted to G.C.B.

In October 1944 Somerville was sent to Washington as head of the British Admiralty delegation, where his charm of manner, humour, and happy knack of putting his point of view with tactful forcefulness soon won him the regard and affection of his American colleagues. Always an entertaining companion with a gift for lightning repartee, he had few equals as a raconteur. Greatly loved by his many American friends, he did much for Britain at a time when the naval resources and strength of the United States were largely concentrated against Japan in the Pacific. Promoted to admiral of the fleet in the next vacancy in May 1945, Somerville remained in Washington until the following December.

On relinquishing this last appointment he lived at Dinder House in Somerset which he had inherited from his father in 1942, and was active in local and public affairs as lord lieutenant of the county and an alderman of the county council. He was promoted G.B.E. in 1946 and in the same year received the honorary degrees of D.C.L. from Oxford and LL.D. from Bristol.

An officer of great experience of the world and of men, a fine leader and a good seaman of great personal courage, Somerville gave exceptional service to the allied cause and to the Royal Navy. Modest and unassuming, he shunned publicity. Unafraid of responsibility, he was equally fearless in debate, even with his seniors, and would speak his mind frankly and forcefully, caring nothing for the con-

sequences. Yet those who knew him intimately said that he had no enemies, only hosts of friends who saw in him a lovable and stimulating personality.

He married in 1913 Mary Kerr (died 1945), daughter of Colonel Thomas Ryder Main, of Curdridge Croft, Botley, Hampshire. They had one daughter, and one son who also went into the Royal Navy. Somerville died at Dinder House 19 March 1949. A portrait of him by (Sir) Oswald Birley is in the Greenwich Collection.

[Private information; personal knowledge.]

TAPRELL DORLING.

SOUTHBOROUGH, first BARON (1860–1947), civil servant. [See HOPWOOD, FRANCIS JOHN STEPHENS.]

SOUTHWOOD, VISCOUNT (1873–1946), newspaper proprietor. [See ELIAS, JULIUS SALTER.]

SPEARMAN, CHARLES EDWARD (1863–1945), psychologist, was born in London 10 September 1863, the second son of Alexander Young Spearman by his second wife, Louisa Ann Caroline Amelia, daughter of Edward Pellew Mainwaring. He was educated at Leamington College and early became interested in philosophy, though he kept this interest largely to himself. Failing to find an adequate solution of the great problems of philosophy either in his own cogitations or in the works he consulted, and 'following the illustrious example of René Descartes', he entered the army in 1883, being gazetted to the Royal Munster Fusiliers and seeing active service in Burma (1883–4), where he gained a medal and two clasps. He passed the staff college examinations in 1896 and resigned his commission as captain in 1897, but had two further periods of military service, during the South African war (when he was deputy-assistant-adjutant-general in Guernsey) and the war of 1914–18 (when he was attached to the general staff, Tyne Defences). Before 1918 he returned to civilian life and directed various psychological researches for the Services, being twice thanked by the Admiralty in this connexion.

During his earlier army career Spearman became convinced that any genuine advance in philosophy would come mainly through psychology and transferred his allegiance to this discipline. Finding, however, little satisfaction in the British associationist writers to whom he first turned, he decided to study the new experimental developments in Germany, and from 1897 to 1907 (except during the South African war) he worked with Wilhelm Wundt at Leipzig (where he took his Ph.D.) and afterwards with Oswald Külpe at Würzburg and Georg Elias Müller at Göttingen. In 1907 he became reader in experimental psychology at University College, London, where he remained (except for his third period of military service) until his retirement as emeritus professor in 1931. In 1911 he had become Grote professor of philosophy of mind and logic and in 1928 professor of psychology. He enjoyed great success both as teacher and as a director of research, attracting a long series of distinguished students from many parts of the world.

Spearman's main contributions to psychology lay in two directions which, however, to his own great satisfaction, began to flow together as his work proceeded. The first stream consisted in the search for general laws in psychology, comparable to those which had been formulated in the physical sciences. Eventually in *The Nature of 'Intelligence' and the Principles of Cognition* (1923) he formulated eight such laws, three of them qualitative and 'noegenetic' (so called because they were concerned 'with the generating of items of knowledge not (necessarily) known before' and this knowledge seemed to be self-evident or 'noetic'), five of them quantitative, dealing with the conditions under which the noegenetic tendencies became actualized. In *Creative Mind* (1930) he applied these laws to aesthetics and other fields.

The other stream was concerned with the nature and interrelations of human abilities. Here Spearman took the great step of applying mathematical measures of correlation—already to some extent developed by Sir Francis Galton and Karl Pearson [qq.v.]—to the data obtained by tests and estimates. As a result of this work, which was given systematic form in *The Abilities of Man* (1927) and posthumously in *Human Ability* (with Ll. Wynn Jones, 1950), it appeared that there existed a single general factor of intelligence (or 'g', as Spearman called it) which enters to a varying extent into different kinds of ability and with which individuals are differently endowed. Further analysis showed that 'g' was exclusively concerned with mental processes of the 'noegenetic'

kind, as distinct from memory, sensory acuity, motor ability, &c., and it was here that the two lines of Spearman's work flowed together. The discovery of 'g' revealed the large degree of error in the earlier notion of independent 'faculties' and afforded a theoretical justification of Alfred Binet's practically very successful attempt at measuring intelligence by the application of tests of many different kinds. Entering into each test, however, there are, in addition to 'g', a number of more specific abilities (the 's' factor in Spearman's terminology). The whole modern school of 'factor analysis', with its attempt to apply modern statistical methods to the age-old problem of human faculties, owes its inception to this side of Spearman's work.

Spearman was elected F.R.S. in 1924, was president of the psychology section of the British Association in 1925, president of the British Psychological Society (1923–6), and an honorary member of this as also of a number of foreign societies. From 1931 to 1939 he travelled and taught in the United States and in India and Egypt; during the war of 1939–45 he was honorary psychological adviser to the local education authority at Chesterfield. In 1937 he published a great historical survey, *Psychology Down the Ages* (2 vols.).

In 1901 Spearman married Fanny, daughter of John Aikman, M.D., of Guernsey, by whom he had one son (who as a lieutenant in the Royal Navy was killed in Crete in 1941) and four daughters. He died in London 17 September 1945.

[Godfrey Thomson in *Obituary Notices of Fellows of the Royal Society*, No. 15, May 1947; *British Journal of Psychology*, vol. xxxvii, September 1946; *A History of Psychology in Autobiography*, edited by Carl Murchison, vol. i, 1930; personal knowledge.]

J. C. FLUGEL.

SPENDER, JOHN ALFRED (1862–1942), journalist and author, was born at Bath 23 December 1862, the eldest son of John Kent Spender, a well-known physician with literary connexions, by his wife, Lily Spender [q.v.]. Mrs. Spender attained some success as a novelist, and was enabled thereby to pay for the education of her eight children, two of whom, Harold and Hugh, in addition to their eldest brother, became journalists of some note. Alfred Spender was educated at Bath College, and in 1881 won an exhibition at Balliol College, Oxford. Jowett was then master, and among Spender's contemporaries were George Curzon (later Marquess Curzon of Kedleston), Cosmo Gordon Lang (later archbishop of Canterbury), and Sir Edward Grey (later Viscount Grey of Fallodon) [qq.v.]. Spender spoke at the Union, played Rugby and the violin, swam, obtained a first class in classical moderations (1882), and just missed a first in *literae humaniores* (1885) largely owing to illness during the examination.

For a man who became so commanding a figure in his profession Spender's entry into journalism was curiously fortuitous. When he left Oxford he had vague thoughts both of teaching and of the bar, but an uncle by marriage, William Saunders [q.v.], who was both owner of the *Eastern Morning News* of Hull and a Liberal candidate, engaged him at £2 a week as private secretary on the political side. This gave him a footing in a newspaper office, and he turned it to such good account that he was soon deputizing for the editor, and (after a brief and chequered interlude on the London *Echo*) became himself editor of the *Morning News* in 1886 at the age of twenty-three. After nearly five years in all at Hull he left as the result of differences with his uncle. Moving to London, he went to reside under Samuel Barnett [q.v.] at Toynbee Hall, became engaged to Mary (May), eldest daughter of William George Rawlinson [q.v.], the art-collector and writer on Turner, and wrote his first book, *The State and Pensions in Old Age* (1892); a letter from John (later Viscount) Morley [q.v.], warmly praising the volume, may be regarded as the starting-point of an intimacy which lasted until Morley's death.

Spender's career in London journalism did not begin until 1892. As an undergraduate he had occasionally had contributions accepted by the *Pall Mall Gazette* and he still wrote for it from time to time from Toynbee Hall. It thus happened that when the editor, (Sir) E. T. Cook [q.v.], needed an assistant he called on Spender; the appointment was unexpectedly confirmed, and in 1892 Spender became assistant editor of the *Pall Mall* and married. But disaster followed precipitately. Within a month the *Pall Mall* changed its owner and its politics (which were Liberal), and the whole staff, including Spender, resigned. Happily fortune took another rapid turn. (Sir) George Newnes [q.v.], the founder of *Tit-Bits* and the *Strand Magazine* and a strong Liberal, was willing to back his

convictions financially, with the result that less than four months after the *Pall Mall* crisis, on 31 January 1893, there appeared under Cook and Spender and the old staff the first issue of the *Westminster Gazette*, the fortunes of which Spender was to control for twenty-five of the best years of his life.

It was not, however, until 1896 that Spender became editor of the new journal. For three years before that date he was lieutenant to Cook, but when Cook accepted the editorship of the *Daily News*, Newnes without hesitation appointed Spender to the vacant post. So began one of the most remarkable editorships in British journalism, consisting as it did of the direction of a paper which never had a circulation greater than 27,000 and during most of its existence failed to touch 20,000; which regularly sustained a financial loss, though not more than its proprietors Newnes and later Lord Cowdray [q.v.] were content to meet; and which undoubtedly exerted a greater influence per copy than any other paper in the kingdom. That this achievement was due primarily to Spender, ably supported though he was by men like Sir F. C. Gould [q.v.] and Charles Geake, there can be no question. It was the front-page leader—nearly always from Spender's pen—which sold the *Westminster*; of no other paper, certainly of no other evening paper, could as much be said.

Day by day on that pea-green front page Spender preached a robust and reasoned Liberalism which sometimes left impetuous Radicals impatient but won high and constant commendation from such leaders as Rosebery, Campbell-Bannerman, Asquith, Haldane, and Morley. With all of them Spender stood on terms of confidential friendship. In his early days in the chair of the *Westminster* the Liberal Party was in the wilderness, and cleft by the South African war into Little Englanders and Liberal Imperialists. Through those years Spender's supreme and ceaseless endeavour was to prevent the split from becoming a final severance; although he never prevailed with the wayward Rosebery, in spite of a friendship which no political strains could jeopardize, it is not too much to say that but for his efforts at a critical moment in December 1905 Campbell-Bannerman's Cabinet might never have been formed. Once it was formed, and the sweeping Liberal victory of 1906 achieved, Spender found himself the most influential political journalist of his day. On terms of intimacy with half the Cabinet, described on occasions as an unofficial Cabinet minister, he enjoyed regularly confidences which he was too scrupulous to use as news, but which enabled him to write of the political problems of the moment with a background of knowledge unique in the journalism of the period. The range of his interests was limited only by the range of contemporary politics, but the cause of Anglo-German friendship stood especially high among them—the Emperor William II was a regular and frequently indignant reader of the *Westminster*—and in 1907 Spender formed one of a mission of friendship on the part of British editors to Germany, being the principal British speaker at a banquet which formed the climax of the visit. In spite of that, he was a convinced advocate of a strong navy, a subject on which he was constantly and vigorously stimulated by Lord Fisher [q.v.], who early realized what valuable allies the *Westminster* and its editor could be.

The best, and without doubt the happiest, years of Spender's life were those from 1896, when he became editor of the *Westminster*, to 1916, when the split between Asquith and Lloyd George dealt Liberalism a blow from which it never recovered. Spender supported Asquith without reserve, and his paper could no longer appeal to the whole party as in the past. It continued to lose money, and its chief proprietor, lending an ear to unwise advisers, decided to turn it into a morning paper. Spender could have continued in command, but he declined, and in October 1921 his long editorship really ended, although nominally he retained the position until February 1922. He regularly contributed special articles to the new *Westminster*, but in 1928 the paper finished a short and inglorious career. Thereafter he wrote, in not altogether happy conditions, for the *News Chronicle*, and later for the Westminster Press group of provincial papers controlled by Lord Cowdray's family.

Spender's severance from the *Westminster* had one fortunate effect, in that it left him free to write a series of notable books, for which his cultural background and familiarity with contemporary events admirably qualified him. He was the author of the official biography both of Campbell-Bannerman (2 vols., 1923) and, with Cyril Asquith (later Lord Asquith of Bishopstone), of Lord Oxford

and Asquith (2 vols., 1932). In addition he wrote the lives of the first Viscount Cowdray and Sir R. A. Hudson, secretary of the National Liberal Federation, both of which appeared in 1930. *The Public Life* (2 vols., 1925) and *Life, Journalism and Politics* (2 vols., 1927) are in part autobiographical, particularly the latter. Of his general works the most important are *Fifty Years of Europe* (1933) and *The Government of Mankind* (1938). *The Changing East* (1926) was the result of visits to Turkey, Egypt, and India in 1925–6. Two series of *The Comments of Bagshot* (1908, 1911), reprints of articles from the *Westminster*, had a considerable contemporary vogue.

Among Spender's public and political services were his membership of two Royal Commissions: on divorce and matrimonial causes (1909–12) and on the private manufacture of armaments (1935–6). Much more important was the part which he played as a member of Lord Milner's mission to Egypt in 1919–20 and in negotiations and discussions arising out of it. More important still were the efforts which he successfully exerted to get remedied without public exposure the scandalous inefficiency of the British army hospital arrangements in France in the early weeks of the war of 1914–18. In 1926 he was president of the National Liberal Federation. He was appointed C.H. in 1937.

In his later years Spender suffered from a painful illness, to which he succumbed at Bromley 21 June 1942. His widow died in 1947; there were no children. A portrait by Clive Gardiner, son of Spender's old friend A. G. Gardiner [q.v.], hangs in the Reform Club. A pencil drawing by Sir Muirhead Bone is in the Imperial War Museum.

[J. A. Spender, *The Public Life*, 1925, and *Life, Journalism and Politics*, 1927; Wilson Harris, *J. A. Spender*, 1946; private information; personal knowledge.]

WILSON HARRIS.

SPILSBURY, SIR BERNARD HENRY (1877–1947), pathologist, was born 16 May 1877 in Leamington, the elder son of James Spilsbury, analytical and manufacturing chemist, and his wife, Marion Elizabeth Joy. His father being of a restless disposition, Spilsbury was educated in turn at Leamington College, University College School, London, the Grammar School and the Owens College,

Manchester, and at Magdalen College, Oxford, where he graduated with a second class in natural science (physiology) in 1899. So far he showed no signs of exceptional ability. He entered the medical school of St. Mary's Hospital, Paddington, where he was fortunate to work under three of the founders of twentieth-century forensic medicine, Arthur Pearson Luff, (Sir) William Willcox [q.v.], and Augustus Joseph Pepper. Under their inspiration he specialized in the new science of pathology, and his early appointment as an assistant demonstrator delayed his full medical qualification until 1905. An injury to his right hand had made him train himself to be ambidextrous, and his immense patience, industry, and almost fanatical attention to detail soon marked him as a rising man. In appearance he was tall, dignified, and extremely good-looking. He was never interested in money for its own sake, and apart from being fastidious in dress spent little upon himself. He had a somewhat school-boy sense of humour, being addicted to practical jokes of a medical kind, but at an early age he developed the faculty of self-sufficiency and absorption in his profession which earned him the epithet aloof.

Spilsbury made his name at the trial of Crippen (1910), by which date he was already well known in the lecture-room, in coroners' courts, in criminal courts, and in the Medico-Legal Society, of which he was later a most popular president. His methodical habits led him to preserve the details of every post-mortem he conducted, and at his death his files contained some 25,000 entries. His memory was phenomenal, and he would sometimes enter up his records and write his reports days after the event, often while sitting in court waiting to give evidence. In the Crippen trial he was brought to assist the team from St. Mary's, and was called to corroborate Pepper's evidence as to the presence of a scar on a piece of skin. Cross-examined to the effect that he was merely echoing the opinion of his superior colleague Spilsbury replied, 'I am responsible for my own opinion, which has been formed on my own scientific knowledge . . .'. Those present describe his attitude in the witness-box as already detached, imperturbable, and serenely confident in the accuracy of his own judgement. This dispassionate concentration on exact answers to all questions within his province set the keynote of the man who for thirty-five years dominated English pathology. Soon after the Crippen trial Spilsbury was appointed junior honorary pathologist to the Home Office where he was associated with his old friend Willcox, and it was as such that he gave evidence in the trial of Seddon in 1912, where his characteristic brevity of answer was well displayed. In the 'Brides in the Bath' case (1915) Spilsbury for the first time became the principal witness for the Crown, for his evidence of the post-mortem findings on the bodies of the three women concerned preceded that of Willcox.

He was now established as the leading 'detective-pathologist' of the day, and is the obvious prototype of the doctor-detective in modern fiction. The cases of Voisin and Armstrong increased his stature as a witness, and in 1923 he was knighted. He had already left St. Mary's for St. Bartholomew's Hospital over an unfortunate affront by a colleague, but the change made little difference to the range or quality of his work. In the Mahon case (1924) Spilsbury achieved his greatest triumph in assembling the scattered remains of the murdered Emily Kaye. His autopsy on the body of Mahon was the first he performed on an executed man, and his research thereafter on such cases led to improvements in the 'drop'.

In the case of Thorne (1925) Spilsbury reached a crisis in his career as an expert witness when he was faced with a total of eight medical men for the defence on the issue whether Elsie Cameron had hanged herself or been murdered. The jury chose to believe Spilsbury, and a press campaign was launched to attack his alleged infallibility as a witness for the Crown. The attack was bitter, but in due course it died down and was never repeated. Spilsbury never claimed to be infallible, and was always ready to admit mistakes of fact or opinion. He had become, as someone called him, a professional cross-examinee, and if his method of giving evidence was at times didactic, this was a blemish soon removed. But he did speak from far greater experience of his subject than any other witness in the country, and his evidence was always dispassionately objective. Even if the answer to a question destroyed the case for the Crown he would give that answer with the same quiet certainty of considered opinion that he brought to his evidence in chief. It may be exasperating for defending counsel to be faced with a man whom the jury will almost certainly believe, but juries came to believe his evidence because in their opinion it was right.

To the dry precision of his work in court he added in private life an unfailing kindness to his junior colleagues, and to all who worked with him or needed his help. He lived for his work, and save for an occasional evening at a classical concert he had no other interests. For thirty-five years he gave evidence in nearly every murder trial in the south of England; and far into the night, often after a long day's travelling and work in court, he worked in his private laboratory on the poorly paid and routine work of a coroner's post-mortem.

In Fox (1930) and Rouse (1931), cases of murder with attempts to remove the evidence by fire; in Barney (1932) and Chaplin (1938), cases of death by shooting; in the numerous murders by strangulation by Cummins (1942); and in the second trial of Loughans (1944), where Spilsbury successfully gave evidence for the defence, he showed again his range of knowledge, passion for detail, and precision of opinion. In 1940 he had a slight stroke, and his son Peter was killed in an air raid on St. Thomas's Hospital where he was a house-surgeon. A year later a sister died, and in 1945 his son Alan, who was helping in his laboratory, died suddenly of consumption. Spilsbury's last big case was that of the murder of de Antiquis in Tottenham Court Road in April 1947; but he was failing rapidly. He knew that his coronary thrombosis was increasing, and arthritis was crippling his hands. In a mood of increasing depression he decided that his work was finished, and on 17 December 1947 he died by his own hand of carbon monoxide poisoning in his laboratory at University College. It is deeply to be regretted that he never wrote the memoirs which he had so long planned. He had raised the science of pathology to a level never before achieved, and proved himself in a hundred cases, in the words of a great English judge, 'the ideal scientific witness'.

In 1908 Spilsbury married Edith Caroline Mary, daughter of William Henry Horton, surgeon-dentist, of Moseley. She survived him with one son and one daughter.

[D. G. Browne and E. V. Tullett, *Bernard Spilsbury*, 1951; the writings and conversations of the Rt. Hon. Sir Travers Humphreys; personal knowledge.]

CHRISTMAS HUMPHREYS.

STALLYBRASS, WILLIAM TEULON SWAN (1883–1948), principal of Brasenose College and vice-chancellor of the university of Oxford, was born in Croydon 22 November 1883, the only son of William Swan Sonnenschein, a publisher (and brother of E. A. Sonnenschein, q.v.), and his wife, Helena, daughter of William Hensman Teulon, of Limpsfield, Surrey. Although in 1917, with his father, he assumed his paternal grandmother's maiden name of Stallybrass, he continued to be known, affectionately, as 'Sonners'. He was a scholar of Westminster and of Christ Church, Oxford, where he obtained a first class in classical moderations (1904) and a second class in *literae humaniores* (1906). He ran for Oxford in the cross-country race against Cambridge in 1905. He was called to the bar in 1909 by the Inner Temple but his career as a practising barrister was short, for he returned to Oxford in 1911 as fellow of Brasenose and tutor in jurisprudence. In 1914 he became vice-principal. The condition of his eyesight caused his rejection from any form of combatant service in the war of 1914–18, and he entered the Ministry of Munitions, where his work was recognized by the award of the O.B.E.

On his release in 1918 he was free to devote himself to the teaching of law in Brasenose and to the many other absorbing tasks which fall to the chief administrator of an Oxford college; for he speedily became the central figure therein. Rarely has any institution been so completely identified with one man. He made it his business as well as his supreme pleasure to know every Brasenose man, and countless undergraduates and old members were indebted to him for frank, wise, and friendly counsel. He was determined to fill the college with men of character, and proved most discerning in his selection. Among the ingredients of character athletic ability in his view took a high place. Some of his critics thought that he tended to place it too high, and certainly the success of Brasenose in every form of sport was remarkable. His own favourite game was cricket, and he was honorary treasurer and mentor of the Oxford University Cricket Club from 1914 to 1946. He was an admirable captain, and for many long vacations he managed three cricket tours, for which an invitation was greatly prized, for the Brasenose Wanderers, the Limpsfield Strollers, and the Authentics.

Despite impressions to the contrary, however, Stallybrass placed scholarship above athletics. Effort in either field he valued and commended, whether or not achievement followed. In addition to his work at Brasenose he lectured at Oriel College for many years and for a time at Lincoln College. In 1924 he became university lecturer, and from 1927 to 1939 reader, in criminal law and the law of evidence. He was never a great lecturer, for he had too pronounced a recourse to the method of dictation, but he was among the greatest of teachers of law. He also found repute as a writer. He prepared four editions of Salmond's *Law of Torts* which attracted growing attention in the courts, and established an ascendancy over all other textbooks on the subject. Perhaps his greatest, although not his best-known, work, was his D.C.L. dissertation (1930), a 'Comparison of the general principles of criminal law in England with the *Progetto definitivo di un nuovo codice penale italiano* of Alfredo Rocco': a masterly contribution to comparative law. Stallybrass was an honorary bencher of the Inner Temple, a member of the lord chancellor's Law Revision Committee, assessor in the vice-chancellor's court, and in the last year of his life president of the Society of Public Teachers of Law. His presidential address on 'Law in the Universities' was in his happiest vein. He became a chevalier of the Legion of Honour in 1947.

In 1936 Stallybrass became principal of Brasenose. The election was a foregone conclusion and gave general satisfaction. He was essentially a college man, but the university now claimed an ever-increasing share of his time. He had served in 1925–6 with great success as senior proctor and now, with some reluctance, joined the hebdomadal council. It was impossible for him to give other than of his best and he applied his informed common sense to all the intricacies of university administration. He soon had the details at his fingers' ends, and when in 1947 he became vice-chancellor he was able to supervise the complications of an overloaded post-war university with a remarkable understanding of the difficulties of those engaged in subjects to which he himself had not been trained. In a notable speech at the beginning of his second year in office he revealed a significant grasp of the changes involved. His relations with his brother vice-chancellors, with college heads, and with all the rank and file of the university were most happy. He quickly established the most cordial relations with the city of

Oxford and with government departments, especially with the Colonial Office. He was returning to Oxford from a conference in London by the midnight train when he inadvertently opened his carriage door and fell to his death, 28 October 1948. He was unmarried.

[*The Times*, 29 October 1948; private information; personal knowledge.]

H. G. HANBURY.

STAMP, JOSIAH CHARLES, first BARON STAMP (1880–1941), statistician and administrator, was born at Kilburn, London, 21 June 1880. Of the seven children of his father, Charles Stamp, he was the third but eldest son to survive infancy. His father had been manager of a railway bookstall at Wigan but at the time of Josiah's birth owned and managed a provision and general shop in London. His mother was Clara Jane, daughter of Richard Evans, a Welsh veterinary surgeon settled in Southwark. It was later said of Stamp by one of his colleagues— 'a Londoner of the middle class, he never sought to be anything else'. He was a delicate child and for this reason at the age of eleven was sent out of London to Bethany House, a private boarding-school at Goudhurst in Kent; there he received a deeply religious training and, gaining in health, he overcame his early nervousness and reserve. He made also a first acquaintance with political economy, writing home at the age of twelve to say that he was reading this subject because it seemed to him likely to be important.

Stamp's formal schooling ended before he was sixteen years old. A threatening illness of his father helped his decision to begin earning at once. In 1896 he entered the Civil Service by examination, as a boy clerk in the Inland Revenue Department, and, with a brief interval in the Board of Trade, spent the next twenty-three years and the whole of his official life in that department. He passed by examination into the next higher grade and went swiftly up the official ladder, becoming assistant inspector of taxes in Hereford at the age of twenty-three, first class inspector in London at twenty-nine, and assistant secretary to the Board of Inland Revenue at thirty-six. The first of these promotions coincided in time with his marriage in 1903 to Olive Jessie, daughter of Alfred Marsh, a builder, of Twickenham; she had been trained as a teacher at the university of Wales and this led to a lasting later association of both partners with Aberystwyth. This marriage decided also the religious community to which Stamp should belong. Brought up by a Baptist father and Church of England mother, he joined his wife in the Wesleyan connexion and became one of its pillars.

Long before this Stamp, having overcome his childish delicacy, had begun to show the inexhaustible energy which later was to become a legend. Neither his official work nor his marriage interfered with determined pursuit of academic studies. Steadily it became clear to one fresh circle after another how remarkable a brain and personality had come to the public service through the boy clerks' examination. He published his first paper in the *Economic Journal* in March 1910 on 'Wasting Assets and Income Tax'; this caught the attention of the editor, F. Y. Edgeworth [q.v.], who entered into correspondence with him. Stamp prepared himself at home, without teaching or guidance, for the external degree of B.Sc. in economics of the university of London, working late at night and amid the noise of a growing family; he was awarded in 1911 a first class so distinguished that Graham Wallas [q.v.], one of the examiners, asked to see him. He was drawn thus into the ambit of the London School of Economics and Political Science and helped and encouraged to write a thesis, by which he gained the degree of D.Sc. in economics in 1916. The thesis, published as *British Incomes and Property*, established forthwith his academic reputation. He had already, through the new fiscal problems of war, had the chance of impressing people more important than examiners; as he wrote in the preface to one of his later books, on *Taxation during the War* (1932), he was 'in constant contact with all the chancellors of the Exchequer and financial secretaries to the Treasury during the period from 1914 to 1920'. The end of the war gave him a yet more remarkable opportunity. He appeared in 1919 as one of the first witnesses before the Royal Commission on income-tax; the commissioners were so much impressed by his grasp and judgement that they asked to have him added to their number, and this was duly done by a special letter of appointment—perhaps unique among honours won by public service.

Before this, when just short of thirty-nine, Stamp had made a critical change of career, leaving the Civil Service for business, to join as secretary and director in March 1919 Nobel Industries, Ltd.,

from which Imperial Chemical Industries later developed. After seven years he made another change, becoming in 1926 president of the executive of the London, Midland, and Scottish Railway, recently constituted under the post-war amalgamation of the railways. In each case Stamp was sought out to give shape and direction to vast new organizations. In 1928 he was appointed a director of the Bank of England; this gave yet a fresh section of the business world the chance to appreciate his qualities and other tempting offers came his way. But the economic crisis of 1931 made it clear to him that he must make the railway his main task, and he did so to the end.

Nevertheless, Stamp combined this work by which he earned his living with an unbroken succession of public services of every kind. He was a member of the Northern Ireland special arbitration committee of 1923-5, of the committee on national debt and taxation in 1924-7, of the court of inquiry into the dispute in the coal-mining industry in 1925, of the statutory commission on the university of London constituted by an Act of 1926, and of the Economic Advisory Council established in 1930.

More important than any of these domestic tasks was the part played by Stamp in 1924 as British representative on the Dawes committee on German reparations, and its successor the Young committee of 1929. The first of these, in which Stamp played his full part and more, 'reinstated German economy and for five years kept the peace'. The Young report fell in more troublous times and exposed its authors to unfriendly criticism. But the two reports made and left him an outstanding international figure, and, followed as the first was by the marriage of his second son to a daughter of General Dawes, they set up in Stamp the practice of frequent visits to the United States; he was fond of saying that every British public man ought to go there every other year. At home, from the age of forty-five onwards he was established as a principal link between the academic world and business and Whitehall.

Less important possibly than his services to Governments, but even more characteristic of Stamp, was the service he gave to innumerable private organizations. He was, for more than twenty years in each case, president of the Abbey Road Permanent Building Society and chairman of the governors of the Leys School for boys and of Queenswood School for girls. He was an original member of the Pilgrim Trust, treasurer of the International Statistical Institute, joint secretary and editor of the Royal Statistical Society for ten years until he became its president (1930–32), and treasurer of the British Association from 1928 to 1935 until he was president (1936) of that also. He repaid his debt to the London School of Economics and Political Science by many years of service, as governor from 1925, vice-chairman from 1925 to 1935, and chairman thereafter until his death. In this last capacity he gave decisive help to the director of that day in introducing children's allowances as an addition to academic salaries; unheard of until then in any university of Britain, such allowances were familiar to Stamp in the Wesleyan ministry.

The good nature which led Stamp to undertake these and many other services was shown in other ways also—by his inexhaustible readiness to give addresses and by the number of prefaces which he contributed to books by others. And he was never content to be formal. He had always something to say which was worth saying and not expected by his audience. The preface to a book on building societies declared that 'a democracy that will not let its wealthy save and will not save for itself must slowly sink'. Eugenists were told that 'before every eugenic programme' they ought to 'pose the imminent question, What do I want to do in a stationary population?' Religious audiences and other audiences with eyes fixed on moral regeneration were reminded by this obviously religious man that 'so many of the problems of today are fundamentally intellectual or mental, and not moral'.

Once Stamp was known honours, official and academic, came thick and fast upon him. He was appointed C.B.E. in 1918, K.B.E. in 1920, G.B.E. in 1924, and G.C.B. in 1935. Three years later he was raised to the peerage as Baron Stamp, of Shortlands, in the county of Kent. His first honorary degrees were conferred upon him at the age of forty-six by the universities of Cambridge and Oxford; in the same year, 1926, he was elected F.B.A. and served as president of the economics section of the British Association. His first honorary degree from overseas was conferred by Harvard in 1927; thereafter the flow of such distinctions was unbroken. The final number of his honorary degrees

was twenty-three, six from the British Isles, ten from the United States, four from Canada, and three from other parts of the world. He was awarded the Guy medal of the Royal Statistical Society in 1919, and the grand cross with star of the Austrian Order of Merit in 1936. He was an honorary member of many foreign learned societies including the American Philosophical Society and the American Academy of Arts and Sciences.

Stamp's career illustrates three points in particular: the significance of religion, the conflict between scholarship and affairs, and the qualities which go to the handling of men. Religious feeling at home and in the school formed his character; as a lifelong friend said of him, religion pervaded his whole life. Pursuit of academic scholarship ranked next among his interests: he continued to read and to write throughout his life; he was never quite so happy as amongst academic people. But there is no doubt that his first book, in which he used his unrivalled direct knowledge of taxation to throw new light on *British Incomes and Property*, remained his best book, although his *Fundamental Principles of Taxation in the Light of Modern Developments* (1921) and his *Wealth and Taxable Capacity* (1922) are both important. As he became known, the claims of affairs upon him proved too absorbing to allow even his energy to equal his first original work. They were so insistent because it was for them that he was most highly gifted, by honesty and simplicity allied to intellect. It has been said of him that his handling of problems was so transparently honest and so sympathetic to all the different arguments presented to him that, however he decided any issue in dispute, those who were unsuccessful went away feeling little less happy than those who had succeeded. Many felt that if there was something affecting them which ought to be decided by someone other than themselves, they would sooner have Stamp decide it than anyone else of their acquaintance.

Stamp, with his wife and eldest son, Wilfrid Carlyle, was killed in an air raid in the shelter of his home at Shortlands 16 April 1941. The second of his four sons, Trevor Charles, became third baron. By this direct hit the Germans did more harm to their chief enemy than they could then have realized. In the difficult economic aftermath of war Stamp would have been an ideal negotiator between Britain and the United States which he knew so well.

Of three posthumous portraits by S. P. Kendrick, one is in the possession of the family, another at the Leys School, and the third at Queenswood School. A portrait by J. A. A. Berrie belongs to the Abbey National Building Society.

[J. H. Clapham in *Proceedings* of the British Academy, vol. xxvii, 1941; *Economic Journal*, June–September 1941; *The Times*, 18 April 1941; private information; personal knowledge.]          BEVERIDGE.

STANLEY, ALBERT HENRY, BARON ASHFIELD (1874–1948), chairman of the London Passenger Transport Board, was born at New Normanton, Derby, 8 August 1874, the son of Henry Knattriess, coach painter, and his wife, Elizabeth, daughter of George Twigg, of Derby. While still a child he was taken by his parents to the United States where his father had obtained a post in Detroit. Soon after his arrival there, his father changed his surname to Stanley.

Young Stanley received his education in Detroit, and was destined by his parents to enter the Church. He was himself, however, determined to become the manager of the Detroit Street Railway Company, and entering the service of the company as messenger and odd-job man he rose rapidly. Before he was twenty-eight he had fulfilled his first ambition and become the general superintendent of the company, which by that time had greatly expanded and had electrified its tramway system. During his time with the company there was an interval in 1898 when he served in the Spanish-American war as an ordinary seaman in the United States Navy.

Stanley left Detroit in October 1903 to take up the post of assistant general manager of the street railway department of the Public Service Corporation of New Jersey. In the following year he was promoted to take charge of the department, and in January 1907, when thirty-two, he became general manager of the Corporation. Only a few months later he accepted an invitation to return to England to be the general manager of the Underground Electric Railways Company of London, Ltd., and of its subsidiary companies, the Metropolitan District Railway and three tube railways. In 1910 Stanley was appointed managing director of the Underground Company and of its associated companies. In 1914 he received a knighthood for his services in connexion with London's passenger transport.

In December 1916 Stanley was selected to become president of the Board of Trade in Lloyd George's first Government, as one of the business men of proved capacity brought in at that time. He was sworn of the Privy Council and sat in the House of Commons as coalition Unionist member for Ashton-under-Lyne. In 1919 he retired from the Government and returned to the Underground group of companies, becoming chairman and managing director of the parent company and its subsidiaries. He was created a baron in 1920, and adopted the title of Baron Ashfield, of Southwell, in the county of Nottingham.

A stone panel, erected to the memory of Ashfield at one corner of the office building at St. James's Park Underground station, where for so many years he had presided, carries the inscription, 'Creator of London Transport'. There could be no more fitting summary of his career and achievement for, by the time he left it, London Transport was recognized as the finest urban transport system in the world. Although at one time Ashfield attained high office in the Government of the day, it was in transport, and in particular in the passenger transport problems of London, that his interest lay; and to him it was an almost passionate interest.

The idea of a single controlling authority over passenger transport in London was by no means a new one when Stanley first went to London in 1907. As early as 1863 a select committee of the House of Lords had recommended that every system of internal railway communication for London should be under one management. In 1905 the Royal Commission on London traffic had urged that 'railways and tramways dealing with urban and suburban traffic should be operated in large systems . . . competition, in such cases, is seldom effective, and may be wasteful, while the existence of a number of railways and tramways under separate management both adds to the working expenses and reduces the facilities for through communication'. Stanley was quick to accept the idea of a single passenger transport authority for London as the right ultimate solution, and set himself to the task.

The Underground Company had already obtained control of a substantial part of London's passenger transport when Stanley came to it. He had no particular theoretical approach in mind, but proceeded with characteristic energy towards his objective of the single authority by whatever means seemed appropriate and available at the time. At first it was by the acquisition of further transport companies, such as the London General Omnibus Company, taken over in 1912. In 1915 legislation was promoted to establish a 'common fund' within the Underground group, whereby the traffic receipts of the railway and bus companies were pooled. In this way the more profitable elements assisted those which were less profitable although equally necessary to the public. For Stanley kept the needs of the public ever before him. Further acquisitions took place after the war of 1914–18, and in 1928 Ashfield concluded negotiations with the London County Council whereby they and the Underground group promoted parallel bills in Parliament to confer authority upon each undertaking to make agreements for common management and common financial provisions for the Underground companies and the L.C.C. tramway system. The bills were hotly resisted by the Labour Party, then in opposition, on the ground that they would establish a virtual monopoly without a sufficient degree of public control. The Government fell, however, before the bills had become law, and was succeeded by a Labour Government in which Mr. Herbert Morrison, who had been the chief organizer of the opposition to the bills, became minister of transport. He, in common with Ashfield, was in sympathy with the basic idea of the single authority for London's passenger transport, but was convinced that this authority should be in the form of a public corporation. He therefore sponsored a bill to that end, which eventually became law in 1933, with only minor changes, under the succeeding 'national' Government, and established the London Passenger Transport Board. Although defeated over the bills which he had taken such a large part in promoting, Ashfield was sufficiently big-minded to be co-operative; a public corporation enabled his objective to be achieved, more quickly and completely, perhaps, than he had ever dared to hope.

It was almost inevitable that Ashfield should have been appointed chairman of the new Board, and, when in 1947 the next major expansion of single control in transport took place with the establishment of the British Transport Commission, that he should have been made a member.

Ashfield was a man with an immensely active mind, and a strong sense of public duty. He would never allow himself to be wholly satisfied, but would always seek further improvement. At the same time, he had great charm of manner and a sense of humour which concealed an almost ruthless determination to pursue whatever he felt, often intuitively rather than as a result of any close reasoning, to be the right course. He was in consequence a formidable negotiator. He did much for the welfare of his staff, and was regarded with respect and affection by all ranks. If, in the years between the wars, Ashfield was fortunate in having as his chief lieutenant Frank Pick [q.v.], who carried the main burden of daily administration, nevertheless much of the inspiration for public service and efficiency came from the chairman himself.

Stanley married in 1904 Grace Lowrey, daughter of Edward Lowrey Woodruff, of New York. They had two daughters but no son and the barony therefore became extinct on Ashfield's death in London 4 November 1948.

A portrait of Ashfield, by Sir William Orpen, hangs in the chairman's room at the head office of London Transport.

[Herbert Morrison, *Socialisation and Transport*, 1933; F. A. A. Menzler, 'Lord Ashfield' in *Public Administration*, vol. xxix, 1951; private information; personal knowledge.]

DAVID McKENNA.

STANLEY, SIR ARTHUR (1869–1947), philanthropist, was born at The Grove, Watford, 18 November 1869, the third son of Frederick Arthur Stanley, later sixteenth Earl of Derby [q.v.], and brother of the seventeenth Earl, a notice of whom appears below. Stanley, whose twin brother died in 1871, was educated at Wellington College, where he excelled at cricket and rackets, and entered the diplomatic service in 1891. For a few months in the following year he was private secretary to the first lord of the Treasury, A. J. Balfour, before returning to the Foreign Office as a clerk. In 1895, by this time a third secretary, he went to Cairo where he learnt some Arabic and was promoted second secretary in 1898. In that year he resigned, on the eve of his return, unopposed, as Conservative member for the Ormskirk division of Lancashire. He was not a frequent speaker in the House but was always ready to intervene in the interests of motoring for which he had much enthusiasm, although his technical knowledge was slight. He became a member of the (Royal) Automobile Club in 1901 and served as its chairman from 1905 until 1907 and again from 1912 to 1936. Throughout this vital period Stanley's services were indefatigably at the disposal of all who had to deal with the issues and legislation occasioned by the development of motoring.

The inevitable increase of accidents on the road was a source of much concern to Stanley with whom the suffering of the sick and the disabled, whatever the cause, had been a main preoccupation from the early 'nineties when an attack of rheumatic fever left him permanently disabled and frequently in pain. In later life his lameness confined him to an invalid chair but did little to lessen his philanthropic activities. In 1905 he was elected to the council, and in 1914 he became chairman of the executive committee, of the British Red Cross Society. As chairman of the joint war committee of the British Red Cross Society and the Order of St. John of Jerusalem in England throughout the whole of the war of 1914–18, he was concerned mainly with liaison work with the War Office and other government departments and with foreign societies; but visits to France and Italy maintained his contact with the vast work going on in the field. He was appointed C.B. for his services in 1916, and in 1917, on the inauguration of the Order of the British Empire, G.B.E. He was made a commander of the Legion of Honour in 1920.

In 1916 Stanley was elected first chairman of the (Royal) College of Nursing and in 1917 treasurer of St. Thomas's Hospital. Thereupon he decided to retire from Parliament and devote himself to hospital work. Living in the Treasurer's House he was always accessible and ever hospitable. His genuine, cheerful sympathy and eager interest in people soon made him a storehouse of information on the intricate workings of a great hospital. Nor were his activities confined to St. Thomas's, for he was prominent in the many movements for the cure and prevention of disease which gained impetus after the war. He was president, from 1920 until his death, of the British Hospitals Association, and in the field of voluntary hospitals he became a legendary figure of masterful charm. A benevolent autocrat, Stanley looked upon committees as bodies destined to ratify his decisions; they did so the more willingly for the selflessness with which he gave the whole of his considerable ability to the causes which he had so evidently and so deeply at heart.

In 1943 the Treasurer's House was bombed and, although the incident left Stanley quite unmoved, the difficulty of carrying on elsewhere in his disablement compelled his resignation. He relinquished also the chairmanship of the executive committee of the British Red Cross Society, and in 1944 he was promoted G.C.V.O. He had been appointed M.V.O. in 1905. He was also an honorary LL.D. of the university of Leeds (1925) and an honorary F.R.C.P. (Edinburgh). He died, unmarried, at Eastbourne 4 November 1947. St. Thomas's Hospital has a portrait by H. de T. Glazebrook which was presented in 1919 by the joint war committee of the British Red Cross Society and the Order of St. John. The Royal Automobile Club has a portrait by Solomon J. Solomon presented in 1923 by Canadian overseas officers who had accepted the hospitality of the club during the war.

[*Jubilee Book of the Royal Automobile Club, 1897–1947*, 1947; *British Red Cross Society and Order of St. John of Jerusalem, Reports on War Work, 1914–1919*, 1921; *St. Thomas's Hospital Gazette*, February 1948; *The Times*, 5 and 12 November 1947; private information.]

HELEN M. PALMER.

STANLEY, EDWARD GEORGE VILLIERS, seventeenth EARL OF DERBY (1865–1948), was born in London 4 April 1865, the eldest son of Frederick Arthur Stanley [q.v.] who became sixteenth Earl of Derby in 1893; his son then became known as Lord Stanley. Educated at Wellington College Stanley was gazetted from the militia to the Grenadier Guards in 1885. After spending two years in Canada (1889–91) as aide-de-camp to his father, the governor-general, Stanley returned to England and entered upon public life in 1892 as Conservative member for the West Houghton division of Lancashire.

In 1895 he became a junior lord of the Treasury. On the outbreak of the South African war in 1899 he was appointed chief press censor in Cape Town and later private secretary to the commander-in-chief, Lord Roberts [q.v.]; he was appointed C.B. in 1900, was twice mentioned in dispatches, and received the Queen's medal with six clasps. After the 'khaki election' of 1900 he became financial secretary to the War Office, entering on his duties immediately after his return to England in January

1901. In 1903 he became postmaster-general with a seat in the Cabinet and was sworn of the Privy Council. He was much concerned with wages policy and his brusque rejection of certain claims led to violent criticism in Parliament, the press, and among the workers who resented being described as 'bloodsuckers' and 'black-mailers' by their own minister in the House of Commons.

At the general election in 1906 Stanley, standing as a free trader, although with an open mind about colonial preference, shared in the general Conservative débâcle and lost his seat. In 1908 he succeeded to the earldom; he voted in the House of Lords for the rejection of the 1909 budget which resulted in the passing of the Parliament Act.

Derby's activities as a 'diehard peer' and his illiberal language about the Post Office workers were, however, soon forgotten. To him *noblesse oblige* was an instinct rather than an obligation; although after his defeat at West Houghton he held no ministerial office for ten years, by the devotion of his rank and wealth to the public service, by his genial disposition and benefactions, and by his popularity as a racing man, he built up for himself a unique position and prestige among all classes in the country. A member under Lord Esher [q.v.] of the committee on the Territorial Force (1906), he became chairman of the West Lancashire Territorial Association (1908–28) and its president (1928–48), and honorary colonel of several Lancashire units. He took a personal part in the municipal, commercial, academic, and masonic activities of Lancashire: he became lord mayor of Liverpool in 1911 and received the freedom of the city in 1912; he was president of the Liverpool Chamber of Commerce (1910–43), chairman of the Cotton Growing Association, and of the committee for the building of Liverpool Cathedral, and he succeeded his father as chancellor of the university. Equally at home with workers and leaders, he enjoyed the esteem of the Liverpool dockers and the close friendship of their leader (Sir) James Sexton [q.v.]. Later he was instrumental in bringing to an end the great cotton lock-out of 1931.

On the outbreak of war in 1914 Derby raised five battalions of the King's Regiment which were encamped in his park at Knowsley, and each original member received from him a solid silver cap badge, for by special permission they wore the Derby crest of the eagle and child. To promote the solidarity and mutual understanding of soldiers and workers he arranged for certain miners' leaders to visit the troops in France where they were also entertained by Sir Douglas (later Earl) Haig [q.v.] and other army commanders.

In 1915 the Government, alarmed by the shortage of recruits, were faced with the alternatives of introducing conscription or making the voluntary system more productive. Fearful that the former would disrupt the country they turned to Derby in an attempt to secure the latter, and in October he was appointed director of recruiting. Bluff, hearty, and always smiling, Derby was 'popular with all classes, including Labour and the Army'. Nor was the problem of national service new to him. Himself a conscriptionist, he had in 1902, when financial secretary to the War Office, written in a Bloemfontein newspaper an article advocating national service, although he explained later in Parliament that his views were not intended to be applied irrespective of other circumstances. There existed a strong body of Conservative conscriptionists led by Lord Curzon who looked with disfavour upon Derby's appointment on the basis of voluntary service, but at a meeting at Curzon's house Derby, in face of great pressure, successfully maintained that it was an inevitable first step. Curzon, Selborne, and (Sir) Austen Chamberlain [qq.v.] only agreed to remain in office after Asquith had promised in writing to propose conscription if the 'Derby scheme' failed.

Under this scheme, men were asked to attest voluntarily their willingness to serve and to await their call to the colours. The prime minister had pledged that if sufficient single men did not attest, they would be conscripted before married men were called up. Later in the House of Commons Asquith aptly recalled that 1915 was the five-hundredth anniversary of the battle of Agincourt and that, according to an old ballad, King Henry V had instructed the Lord Derby of the day:

'Go 'cruit me Cheshire and Lancashire,
And Derby hills that are so free;
No married man or widow's son,
No widow's curse shall go with me.'

By the end of December it was evident that the Derby scheme had not succeeded in its purpose, since insufficient single men had attested, and the first Military Service Act, limited to single men under forty-one, was passed within a month. The smoothness of the passage from voluntary to compulsory recruitment was a signal tribute to Derby's political instincts and perspicacity; only one under-secretary resigned because conscription was not introduced and only one Cabinet minister when it was. It was not, however, until after the disasters of March 1918 that the full Conscription Act was passed, when Derby, then secretary of state for war, saw the views which he had advocated in 1902 become the law of the land.

On the death in 1916 of Lord Kitchener [q.v.], whom he described as 'the best friend I ever had', Derby became under-secretary of state at the War Office. The end of the year saw grave dissatisfaction with the conduct of the war. Lloyd George, although willing that Asquith should remain prime minister, intended to withdraw from him the day-to-day direction of the war. Derby supported Lloyd George; Asquith, however, refused to accept the Merovingian role thus allotted to him and resigned. There were not wanting political observers who thought that if neither Bonar Law, to whom the premiership was first offered, nor Lloyd George could find sufficient support in Parliament, the choice might well fall on Derby himself. He had always been credited with two ambitions, to own a Derby winner and to be prime minister. He achieved the former, but the latter he publicly denied. He became secretary of state for war in the new administration. Lloyd George's first act was to create a small war committee of the Cabinet and it was at breakfast at Derby's house that he had discussed its constitution, although Derby himself did not become a member.

In February 1917 the War Cabinet agreed that the British Army in France should be placed under the French commander-in-chief, General Nivelle. The decision was taken, however, without Derby's knowledge, and was put, without warning, to Sir William Robertson [q.v.], the chief of the imperial general staff, and Sir Douglas Haig during allied conferences at Calais (26–27 February 1917) at which Lloyd George and Briand, the French prime minister, but not Derby, were present. The original scheme was firmly opposed by Robertson and Haig, but after much acrimony it was agreed that, for the forthcoming operations about Arras and the Aisne, Haig should conform to the orders of Nivelle. When Derby was informed of the full story of the Calais conference he was 'furious' and talked of resigning. 'If I had known', he wrote to Haig, 'there was to be any proposal to put you and our Army under the full control of the French, I should most vigorously have protested.' Difficulties arising out of the interpretation of the Calais agreement were eventually composed at a further conference in London in March.

Towards the end of the year further crises arose. Against the advice of the general staff, the prime minister wished to attack in the East and remain on the defensive in the West, and the War Cabinet refused to accept the general staff's expectation of a heavy German attack in France and the estimated requirements of an additional 615,000 men to bring the army up to strength. The British and French Governments agreed to set up an executive committee of the Supreme War Council with ultimate control over reserves and operations of both British and French armies. To this abrogation of the responsibilities of the chief of the imperial general staff, Robertson would not agree, and in February 1918 he was replaced by Sir Henry Wilson [q.v.]. Derby had already let it be known that, if Robertson went, he would go too, and Lloyd George records that at this stage Derby resigned three times in twenty-four hours. In his *War Memoirs* he accuses Derby of disloyalty to the War Cabinet and of conniving at military opposition to the prime minister's own policy of a unified command and an 'Eastern' as opposed to a 'Western' strategy, claiming that had he had Derby's full support, the 'carnage' of Passchendaele might have been averted and the battle of March 1918 might have been 'a smashing triumph'. That there was some liaison between the military and the parliamentary opposition cannot be doubted, but Lloyd George specifically acquits Derby of any complicity in this. Nor do the facts justify the other accusation. As secretary of state Derby was not responsible for strategical advice, a duty reserved to the chief of the imperial general staff. Yet both Haig and Robertson were Derby's subordinates. That Derby felt in an awkward position as between them and the prime minister is clear from what he wrote and said. To Lord Stamfordham [q.v.] he had written that he was in a weak position because he had accepted the decision to give supreme powers to the new executive committee at Versailles, yet proposed to resign because Robertson would not carry it out. In the House of Lords during the Robertson debate on 19 February 1918 he said that current newspaper controversies 'make one reluctant to do even what one thinks right, because one may fear that one may be involved in some intrigue'. Derby was involved in no intrigue; on the contrary, as Lord Esher had already assured him (29 December 1917) in counselling against resignation, 'You have done your best to hold the balance even between your civilian colleagues and the soldiers. What more can be asked of a secretary of state for war?' In Derby's natural loyalty to subordinates and vacillating reluctance to abandon Robertson, Lloyd George perceived only an intrigue against himself. Eventually Derby satisfied himself that Haig would work to the policy of the War Cabinet and that Robertson (whom he was finding difficult and ill-tempered) would not. He withdrew his resignation, but only as the result of a last-minute conversation with his under-secretary, Ian Macpherson (later Lord Strathcarron, q.v.), and after the offer of the War Office was in course of dispatch to (Sir) Austen Chamberlain.

Before the Robertson crisis had reached its final stages Derby had been offered a new appointment (January 1918); fearing that his removal from the War Office might be the first step towards the removal of Haig from G.H.Q., he sought an assurance that changes would not be made in the higher command on his departure. In April he was replaced by Lord Milner [q.v.] and Derby was appointed ambassador in Paris where, Lloyd George observed, 'it would not be obvious that his bluffness was only bluff', and where 'his powers of observation . . . were really serviceable to those who had to transact business amid the rapid and baffling fluctuations of French politics'. In Paris Derby had little share in the preparation of the Versailles Treaty, but as a member of the ambassadors' conference he took a leading part in supervising the execution of its provisions. He was a success alike with ministers and people. His interest in land, his aristocratic lineage, his wealth and generosity, the splendour of the Derby gold and silver plate, his devotion to horse-racing (his horses were as successful in France as they were in England) all endeared him to the Parisians who saw in him 'le type accompli d'un lord fermier'.

In 1920 he returned to England anxious to resume his Lancashire life in which he was always happiest. But it was not long before he was recalled to political life. In 1921 certain circles desired to open some form of personal negotiation with Sinn Fein leaders. Accordingly, one day in April, disguised in special glasses and answering to the name of Mr. Edwards, the Earl of Derby crossed to Dublin and had a two-hour interview with Mr. de Valera. This bizarre experiment in Irish politics, however, came to nothing. Early in 1922 Derby refused the India Office, but on the break-up of the Lloyd George coalition he returned to the War Office under the premiership of Bonar Law and remained there under Baldwin. After the Conservative defeat in 1924 Derby retired from national politics. He became lord lieutenant of Lancashire in 1928. For his services to art and commerce in the country he received the Albert medal of the Royal Society of Arts in 1936. He received honorary degrees from the universities of Liverpool, Birmingham, Oxford, and Cambridge, and the freedom of Bury, Manchester, and Douglas in the Isle of Man. He was also an honorary citizen of Cannes where he had a villa to which he was much attached. A firm believer in the necessity for the closest friendship with both France and the United States, he inaugurated the Franco-British Society on his return from Paris in 1920; and as president of the Pilgrims Society (1945–8), of the executive committee of which he had been chairman (1929–45), he initiated in 1946 the Roosevelt memorial in London.

Derby was fond of golf and shooting and was a member of the Royal Yacht Squadron (1909–35), as owner of the yawl *Onyx*. In his early days, as Lord Stanley, he had turned his attention to the traditional family interest, revived by his father, of horse-racing. At a house-party in 1893 at Knowsley (with its twenty-four gardeners, and stable of forty horses with twenty grooms) he told Lady Lytton that having just bought a valuable horse he had been unable to avert its untimely death, although he had caused it to be placed on a daily diet of a bottle of port, a bottle of brandy, and three dozen eggs. With other horses he was more successful, and he won the St. Leger six times and the Derby twice. He acted as steward of the Jockey Club five times between 1906 and 1911, and he often entertained King George V at Knowsley for the Grand National. He remained throughout his life one of the inner circle of the King's intimate friends, ever since in

1890 the future King had stayed in Canada with his father, the governor-general. Derby was appointed K.C.V.O. in 1905, G.C.V.O. in 1908, K.G. in 1915, G.C.B. in 1920, and in 1935 received from His Majesty the Royal Victorian Chain.

In appearance Derby was tall, moustached, with twinkling eyes, and in later life a very heavy man. He had not a creative or original mind, but his personality and devotion to duty provided a nucleus round which loyalties naturally grew. In affairs of business he was quick to seize a point and punctilious in answering private letters. A man of warm impulses, he was at times hesitant when faced with a dilemma. His amiability rendered him liable to the influence of whoever counselled him last, a weakness more apparent in Whitehall than to the country at large, and one which accounts for some denigratory opinions expressed of him by some of his political and military contemporaries. Derby possessed what Englishmen admire: geniality, generosity, public spirit, great wealth, and successful race-horses. 'If, by some unhappy catastrophe', Sir Joseph Davies once observed to J. H. Thomas [q.v.], 'our Royal Family was annihilated, and our people called for a new King I believe that their first choice would be Lord Derby.' On the occasion of his seventieth birthday in 1935, 82,000 people signed a testimonial to him which is preserved in twenty-two volumes at Knowsley. In the words of the public orator when he received the honorary degree of D.C.L. at Oxford, 'Indolis Anglicae specimen idem pacis erat mediusque belli'—Derby was a 'John Bull at the heart of things alike in peace and war'.

Portraits of him by Sir William Orpen are at the Masonic Temple, Manchester, at Knowsley (with a copy at the Liverpool Town Hall) and in the Walker Art Gallery; by Sir William Llewellyn at Knowsley (with a copy at the Liverpool Chamber of Commerce); at the university of Liverpool by Edward I. Halliday; at Wellington College by James Gunn; at the Liverpool Constitutional Club by F. T. Copnall; and at Knowsley by Sir John Lavery.

Derby married in 1889 Lady Alice Maude Olivia Montagu (died 1957), youngest daughter of the seventh Duke of Manchester. They had two sons, and a daughter whose death in 1927 in the hunting field saddened Derby's later years, as did that of his elder son Edward, Lord Stanley, in 1938 when secretary of state for the Dominions. The younger son was Oliver Stanley, a notice of whom appears below. Derby died 4 February 1948 at his home, Knowsley, where he was buried. He was succeeded as eighteenth earl by his grandson, Edward John (born 1918).

[*The Times*, 5 February 1948; *Liverpool Echo*, 4 February 1948; Viscount Esher, *Journals and Letters*, 4 vols., 1934–8; C. à C. Repington, *The First World War, 1914–1918*, 2 vols., 1920; *The Private Papers of Douglas Haig, 1914–1919*, edited by Robert Blake, 1952; Lloyd George, *War Memoirs*, 6 vols., 1933–6; Lord Beaverbrook, *Politicians and the War*, vol. ii, 1932; Sir Joseph Davies, *The Prime Minister's Secretariat*, 1951; Lady Emily Lutyens, *A Blessed Girl*, 1953; private information; personal knowledge.]

KENNETH LYON.

[Lord Beaverbrook, *Men and Power, 1917–1918*, 1956.]

STANLEY, OLIVER FREDERICK GEORGE (1896–1950), politician, was born in London 4 May 1896, the younger son of Edward George Villiers, Lord Stanley, who became the seventeenth Earl of Derby, a notice of whom appears above. Educated at Eton, he would have gone up to Oxford but for the outbreak of war in 1914. He received a commission in the Lancashire Hussars: in the early part of 1915 he was transferred to the Royal Field Artillery and to the division which his father had raised in Lancashire. The division went to France in November 1915 and Stanley had command of a battery when he was only nineteen years old. He knew his work, and his men had implicit confidence in him. He remained with the battery, by his own desire, throughout the war: he was awarded the M.C. in 1917, largely for his work during the fighting on the Somme, and later the croix de guerre.

In 1919 Stanley was called to the bar by Gray's Inn and read in the chambers of (Sir) Stephen Ogle Henn-Collins. There is no doubt that he would have done well at the bar had he not entered Parliament as Conservative member for Westmorland in 1924, after unsuccessfully fighting the Edge Hill division of Liverpool in 1923. His father had made over to him the Witherslack estate in 1922 and he and his wife entered upon an active life in the county. He was a member of the county council for some years. His parliamentary and other duties left him insufficient time to practise at the bar and he accordingly joined his uncle's firm of stockbrokers in the City. The experience which he gained of the City and of finance proved of great help to him in later years, as did his training in the law.

From 1924 until 1929 Stanley was parliamentary private secretary to the president of the Board of Education. In 1931 he became parliamentary under-secretary of state at the Home Office. He introduced the measure which became the Children and Young Persons Act of 1932, and during the consideration of the bill showed an understanding and ability which added to his growing reputation. Between 1933 and 1934 he was minister of transport and was largely responsible for the Road Traffic Act of 1934, which became law after he had ceased to be minister. This Act brought about the speed limit of thirty miles an hour in built-up areas, driving tests for new drivers, and a strengthening of the law in regard to insurance against third-party risks.

Stanley's term as minister of labour (1934–5) was considered by many to mark a set-back in his career. The position was unfortunate. The Unemployment Assistance Act of 1934 transferred the responsibility for relieving able-bodied unemployed to the newly constituted Unemployment Assistance Board, an independent body which had the right to decide the scales of relief subject to regulations which had been approved by Parliament. The allowances proved in some cases to be unsatisfactory and the Government introduced a measure suspending the regulations. Stanley accepted the responsibility although the minister and the Board were not in accord. Stanley, who was sworn of the Privy Council in 1934, went to the Board of Education in 1935 and did much to reawaken interest in education throughout the country. The Education Act of 1936 was ingeniously drafted to provide for an eventual raising of the school-leaving age by one year with exemptions for beneficial employment.

When Chamberlain became prime minister in 1937 Stanley was appointed president of the Board of Trade, an office which he held until 1940. He was responsible for the completion of a reciprocal trade agreement with the United States which was of great value in the years which followed: he was much concerned with plans for the Ministry of Food and with the raw materials department of the Ministry of Supply, as well as with various Acts dealing with trading with the enemy, war risks insurance, and control of exports

and imports. There followed a short spell as secretary of state for war during which the campaign in Norway took place, although he may scarcely be held responsible for its failure. When (Sir) Winston Churchill became prime minister in 1940 he appointed (Sir) Anthony Eden as secretary of state for war and Stanley rejoined the army in the belief that he should do so rather than accept some other office in the Government. His time was spent mostly in a branch known as the future operations planning staff which provided much of the groundwork for subsequent operations both in North Africa and on the continent. In November 1942 he became secretary of state for the Colonies, an office which gave him more pleasure than any he had filled, for it was entirely congenial to him. He was well liked, both at home and overseas, and initiated a policy of colonial development which met with general approval, showing, as it did, an appreciation of the help and guidance necessary in the changes which were taking place and a realization of the need for improved educational facilities to accompany them.

With the defeat of the Conservative Party in July 1945 Stanley, who had been elected member for Bristol West, went into opposition. He became chairman of the Conservative Party finance and imperial affairs committees in the House of Commons and until illness overtook him in the summer of 1950 was the chief spokesman of the party on finance.

The record of offices held by Stanley gives a wholly incomplete picture of a man whose ability grew and was increasingly recognized. His advice was sought on all matters of importance. Everyone liked and trusted him. He asked nothing for himself and his gift of friendship seemed to grow with the years. He became one of the foremost debaters in the House and members of all parties enjoyed his speeches, not only for their pungency and their sound approach to the matter under discussion, but also because of the touch of humour which he introduced into them—humour which was never misplaced and which left no rancour. After his death *The Times* said of him: 'Oliver Stanley had qualities which had won for him the affectionate esteem of men and women of all parties. . . . The House had long relished the brilliance and barbed gaiety of Mr. Stanley's speeches. . . .'

If Stanley's party had been returned to power during his lifetime his desire would have been to return to the Colonial Office, although many looked forward to seeing him as chancellor of the Exchequer, an office for which he seemed admirably fitted. But he had never been strong and a throat affection gave him much trouble for some time before he died at his home at Sulhamstead near Reading, 10 December 1950, less than three years after his father whom he had succeeded as chancellor of the university of Liverpool in 1948.

Stanley was a good shot and enjoyed a day's shooting, but perhaps he was happiest at his home and in his garden. He married in 1920 Lady Maureen Helen Vane-Tempest-Stewart, daughter of the seventh Marquess of Londonderry [q.v.]. She was a gifted speaker who greatly helped him in his election contests in Westmorland. Her death in 1942, following a long illness, was a severe blow to him. They had one son and one daughter.

[Private information; personal knowledge.]
JOHN E. SINGLETON.

STEBBING, (LIZZIE) SUSAN (1885–1943), philosopher, was born 2 December 1885 at Wimbledon, Surrey, the youngest of the six children of Alfred Charles Stebbing, barrister, by his wife, Elizabeth, daughter of William Elstob. She was educated privately before entering Girton College where she read history, being placed in the second class of part i of the tripos in 1906, of part ii in 1907, and of part i of the moral sciences tripos in 1908. In 1912 she obtained her M.A. (London) with distinction and in 1931 her D.Lit. (London). From 1913 to 1915 she lectured in philosophy at King's College, London; in 1915, became part-time, and in 1920 full-time, lecturer at Bedford College; and was reader in philosophy (1927) and professor (1933) in the university of London. She was visiting professor in Columbia University, New York, in 1931, president of the Aristotelian Society (1933) and of the Mind Association (1935). She was also from 1915 until her death a principal of the Kingsley Lodge School for Girls, Hampstead, now removed to Horley, Surrey.

Although she valued the humanities highly, Susan Stebbing's tastes were for the natural and abstract sciences, including mathematics. These led her naturally in philosophy to the new Cambridge analytic school which combined the empiricism of Hume with the sophisticated logic of *Principia Mathematica*. To Pro-

fessor G. E. Moore she always acknowledged a deep philosophical debt. To philosophical analysis she made notable contributions, clear, independent, critical; for she was never an orthodox disciple. Later, she welcomed the developments of Ludwig Wittgenstein and the 'Vienna circle' of logical positivists, many of whom she befriended when they were in exile after 1933. In logic, although not an originator, she was an admirable exponent and in *A Modern Introduction to Logic* (1930) first made generally accessible the revolutionary advance of this subject since 1900.

Perhaps her greatest gift was for teaching philosophy. Clear in exposition, fair and acute in criticism, she could analyse without destroying and illuminate without dogmatizing. Her passion for the subject was communicated to her listeners. She provoked discussion and stimulated her hearers to independent thought.

Susan Stebbing was no philosophical recluse. She combined rare intellectual quality with gaiety and warm-hearted concern for people and affairs. After the war of 1914–18 she lectured for the League of Nations Union and she kept the faith that reason can deliver men from evil, if they so choose. This view is expressed in *Ideals and Illusions* (1941). She died, unmarried, in London, 11 September 1943.

A full bibliography of her works appears in *Philosophical Studies* (Essays in memory of L. Susan Stebbing, 1948).

[*Mind*, July 1944; private information; personal knowledge.]
MARGARET MACDONALD.

STEER, PHILIP WILSON (1860–1942), painter, was born at Birkenhead 28 December 1860, the third child and second son of Philip Steer, portrait and landscape painter, by his wife, Emma, daughter of the Rev. William Harrison, perpetual curate of Woore, Shropshire. That the father was an excellent, straightforward painter is illustrated by his portrait of Mary Paige which is reproduced in the life of Steer by D. S. MacColl [q.v.].

In 1864 Steer's parents moved from Birkenhead to The Grange (subsequently called Apsley House) at Whitchurch near Ross-on-Wye. Together with his brother and sister he was educated at home by a governess, but on his father's death in 1871 he went to a preparatory school at Whitchurch and in 1875 to the Hereford

Cathedral School, where he remained until 1877. After this he was under a private tutor, Dr. Purcell, of Whitchurch, from whom Steer said he learned more in a few weeks than he ever did from anyone else. When he was three years old, his mother wrote that 'little Philly is busy doing a sketch in water colours under his Papa's direction. He says blue is his favourite colour.' The skill he had acquired by the age of fifteen may be gauged by his 'A Dead Bullfinch' belonging to Lieutenant-Colonel William Reed Hornby Steer. In 1878 he entered upon a course of study for the qualifying examination for entrance into the British Museum. If this project seems astonishing it must be remembered that Steer's father not only taught him drawing and painting, but also arranged a sort of museum for the children, and that, when yet a little boy, Steer began to collect coins, so that it appeared reasonable that he should seek nomination to a post in the numismatic department of the museum. But he found the preparatory work irksome and the project was abandoned. Nevertheless he never lost the interest in shells, fossils, and minerals inculcated by his father, and in the course of his life he gradually built up a valuable collection of Greek, Roman, and English coins.

Steer thenceforward followed his natural bent. He was entered as a student of the Gloucester School of Art where he worked under John Kemp. After unsuccessful application for admission to the Royal Academy Schools he went to Paris in 1882 where he studied at the Académie Julian under Bouguereau and afterwards in 1883 at the École des Beaux-Arts under Cabanel. His inability to speak French prevented him from taking much interest in the artistic life of Paris, and from passing the examination in French introduced at the Beaux-Arts. He had therefore to return to England, and by 1885 he was settled in a studio in Chelsea. In 1883–5 he had pictures accepted and hung in the Royal Academy. The first of these, a portrait of a man reading a newspaper, entitled 'What of the War?', is in the Tate Gallery. It is carefully executed, has little colour, and gives but slight indication of the direction soon to be taken by his talent.

In Paris Steer had seen paintings by J. A. McN. Whistler [q.v.] and in 1884 he saw there a posthumous exhibition of works by Manet, by both of whom, and especially by the latter, he was to be much influenced, even though, when he first saw these works, while admiring them he was also puzzled by them. When he returned to England he went to Walberswick in Suffolk and this, following, perhaps combined with, the 'delayed action' of Manet's work, which he had seen in Paris, was one of those fortunate accidents which have a decisive effect on a painter's career. The seascape at Walberswick, with its clean washed sky and the sweep of the sand where the river Blythe runs into the sea, the pebbly beaches, the bathers and paddling children, the pierhead and the humped wooden bridges over the dykes on which are seen figures silhouetted against the sea and sky, had an extraordinary effect on Steer. He suddenly burst out into colour: the child who said his favourite colour was blue found of a sudden that for which he must long have been subconsciously looking. Of the many beautiful pictures which he painted in the next few years, the loveliest are 'On the Pierhead' (Walberswick, 1888), and 'Children Paddling' (Swanage, 1894). In both (as well as in others of the same period) the horizon is high and the light blazes down on a blue sea. The pierhead in the former and the sand and pierside in the latter are simply-disposed large flat shapes diversified by the standing figures of the girls in the one and the paddling children in the other. Each gave Steer the chance to display his greatest gift: a clean, decisive, and exquisite sense of tone expressed in a high key in singing colour. It is a strange enough fact that, after his earlier successes at the Academy, the 'Pierhead' and an analogous work, now in the Tate Gallery, 'The Bridge, Étaples' (1887) were met at the Grosvenor Gallery exhibitions with a storm of abuse so violent that Steer even talked of giving up painting.

In the movement associated with the name of the New English Art Club, Steer was closely connected with Frederick Brown, Henry Tonks, and D. S. MacColl [qq.v.]. All his life he was a supporter and constant exhibitor at the club, and most of his best-known pictures were first shown there. After the appointment of Brown in 1893 to the Slade chair, Steer, in about 1895, began to teach at the Slade School of Fine Art. This he continued to do until Tonks, who succeeded Brown, retired in 1930. He used to go to the school, for the most part, once a week during term-time; he was much beloved by the students, even though, being extremely inarticulate, he was not in the conventional sense a good teacher; nevertheless his presence was invaluable. His comments, when extracted with difficulty from him, were of the simplest; if pressed for a criticism he would perhaps say: 'Why not try round brushes?' or, 'You might find cerulean blue was a better blue to use there'; but such remarks can be of the utmost help. Very often he would only say, 'I'd go on with that', or simply take the brush into his own hand. When the question arose of awarding a prize or appraising a student's worth, Tonks and Brown bowed to his judgement. Those who had the good fortune to be taught by him were proud that he should see their work and were conscious in him of that rare and inspiring quality, a complete unity between his personality and his painting. Affectionate fun has been poked—particularly in the portrait made by George Moore [q.v.] in *Conversations in Ebury Street*—at his many idiosyncrasies. Apart from his great height and his bulk, and the formal clothes—dark suit, stand-up collar, and black bow-tie—which never varied, the most striking characteristics were a monumental calm, and the fact that to him painting was a natural function. He was quite uninterested in theories of art, and if people began to argue, Steer would go to sleep; but there was none among his pupils who was unaware of his shrewdness and placid strength. It was his habit to spend the long summer vacation with several friends for company in painting landscape; his portrait and figure painting was chiefly done during the time when teaching kept him in London.

Steer's interest in water-colour began about 1900 and became as he grew older an increasingly important side of his work; indeed, although it may be too early yet to estimate truly the relative values of his work, there are some who believe that the water-colours, made towards the end of his life, may prove to be his greatest and most original contribution to modern art. His technical development is of exceptional interest. Of most good artists it is true to say that the handling in their earlier works is usually comparatively 'tight' and that it becomes 'looser' as they grow older. With Steer it was the reverse. In his earlier works he sometimes evaded difficulties of drawing and relied on beautiful quality of paint and his unfaltering sense of tone to see him through. As he grew older this partial solution no longer satisfied him and he strove continually for greater exactitude and clearer definition. This is well illustrated in what is perhaps his finest portrait, that of Mrs. Raynes, his old nurse and housekeeper, painted in 1922, and now in the Tate Gallery. The head in particular, although it gives such an impression of ease and largeness, is built up by a series of minute touches of a pointed sable, and each brush-stroke is an act of drawing.

The modesty and patience with which in this way Steer gradually achieved a greater intensity of expression in his painting is all the more noticeable since in his water-colours an ever-growing freedom and the certainty of an almost arbitrary calligraphy may be observed. But whether he sought in his paintings a greater degree of realization or in his water-colours a more emphatic arabesque, the quality which is never sacrificed is tone. It may be said that it is Steer's perception of the interdependence of the colour of things, and his ability to communicate the simple delight which he took in the discovery of a unifying principle which gives to his vision the quality of poetry.

Steer was admitted to the Order of Merit in 1931 and was elected an honorary member of the Liverpool Academy of Arts in 1906. He died, unmarried, at his home in Chelsea, 21 March 1942, of the bronchitis which had been his lifelong enemy.

Examples of Steer's work may be found in the British Museum, the Tate Gallery, the Imperial War Museum, the National Portrait Gallery, the Fitzwilliam Museum, the Ashmolean Museum, and many other art galleries.

A self-portrait at the age of eighteen is in the possession of Lieutenant-Colonel W. R. Hornby Steer; another (1906) is in the Uffizi Gallery at Florence; a third (1920) is in the Fitzwilliam Museum. A portrait by W. R. Sickert is in the National Portrait Gallery where there are also sketches by Henry Tonks and where Steer figures in (Sir) William Orpen's 'Selecting Jury of the New English Art Club, 1909' and D. G. MacLaren's 'Some Members of the New English Art Club'; he figures also in Orpen's 'Hommage à Manet' in the Manchester City Art Gallery; and there is a painting of Steer and Sickert by Henry Tonks in the Tate Gallery; a pencil drawing portrait-sketch by Ina Sheldon-Williams is in the British Museum; and a head and shoulders line-drawing by D. S. MacColl is in the possession of Miss Florence Hood.

[*The Times*, 23 March 1942; D. S. MacColl, *Life Work and Setting of Philip Wilson Steer*, 1945; Robin Ironside, *Wilson Steer*, 1943; private information; personal knowledge.]

ALLAN GWYNNE-JONES.

STEIN, SIR (MARK) AUREL (1862–1943), scholar, explorer, archaeologist, and geographer, was born in Budapest 26 November 1862, the second son of Nathan Stein, by his wife, Anna, daughter of Marc Hirschler and sister of Ignaz Hirschler, the Hungarian oculist, archaeologist, and member of the Hungarian Upper House. At his birth his mother was forty-five, his father older. Educated at public schools in Budapest and Dresden and at the universities of Vienna and Leipzig, he graduated Ph.D. at Tübingen in 1883 after studying Persian and Indian archaeology under Rudolf von Roth. He came to England in 1884, and until 1887 studied classical and oriental archaeology and languages at Oxford and the British Museum, with a year's interval in 1885 for military training in Hungary, where he completed a course of geography and surveying. In England he came into close contact with, amongst others, (Sir) Henry Yule and Sir H. C. Rawlinson [qq.v.], who greatly influenced his later work.

Stein's mother died in 1887 and his father in 1889; his home in Hungary was broken up and early in 1888 he went to India as principal of the Oriental College at Lahore and registrar of Punjab University, posts which he held until 1899. There he met P. S. Allen, (Sir) Thomas Arnold [qq.v.], (Sir) Edward Douglas Maclagan, then in the Punjab secretariat, and Fred Henry Andrews, principal of the School of Art at Lahore, all of whom remained close, lifelong friends. During this period he devoted his vacations to antiquarian and geographical research in Kashmir and on the North-West Frontier. In 1892 he published his Sanskrit edition of the *Rájataringiní* of Kalhana, the chronicle of the ancient Kashmir kings, and in 1900 appeared his great translation of this work, with notes and geographical memoir (also published separately in the *Journal* of the Asiatic Society of Bengal, vol. lxviii, 1899). He also wrote a paper on the Shahi kings of Kabul for the *Festgruß an Rudolf von Roth*, his old tutor at Tübingen, and in 1898 carried out a rapid archaeological survey of Buner while with the Malakand Field Force.

In 1899 Stein joined the Indian education service and became principal of the Calcutta Madrasah, but his plans for archaeological exploration in Central Asia were already far advanced, and with support from Lord Curzon [q.v.], his Punjab friends, and the Survey of India, he started in March 1900 at the age of thirty-seven his first great Central Asian expedition. Thereafter for forty-two years Stein was almost continuously engaged on archaeological exploration and in working on the results of his field-work. His chief explorations fall into four groups: (i) his four Central Asian expeditions, 1900–1, 1906–8, 1913–16, 1930; (ii) his 'reconnaissances' in Baluchistan and Persia connecting the earliest cultures of the Indus and Euphrates, carried out between 1927 and 1936; (iii) his elucidation of the routes and battlefields of Alexander's campaign from the battle of Arbela to the return to Babylon (331–323 B.C.); (iv) his examination of the Roman frontier with Parthia, chiefly in northern Iraq and the Jezira, undertaken towards the end of his life. Much other work, especially on Graeco-Buddhist remains in north-west India, occupied shorter expeditions.

In each Central Asian expedition Stein took different routes to and from Turkistan: by Gilgit and the Taghdumbash Pamir; by Peshawar, the Malakand, Swat, Chitral, and the Darkot and Baroghil passes; through unexplored Darel and Tangir; and through eastern Persia and Sistan. In his first expedition he examined the southern oases of the Taklamakan desert, concentrating chiefly on ancient settlements near Khotan, where among sand-buried ruins of riverain settlements he discovered numerous documents in Kharoshti, Chinese, ancient Tibetan, and other scripts. On his second expedition he carried out further intensive work in this Khotan region and extended his explorations of sites to the dried-up Lop Sea bed. At Miran, abandoned in the third century B.C., he discovered wall-paintings of classical design; at Lou-lan, a Chinese headquarters of the second century B.C., documents in Chinese and Kharoshti; and near the Lop Sea bed he traced the long-used caravan route between China and the West by the distribution of neolithic implements, metal objects and beads, and ancient coins of Han type. These discoveries led him on to explore Tun-huang, Su-chou, the Nan-shan, and the Etsin-gol basin and to trace for 400 miles the ancient frontier watch-towers, the Chinese *limes*, built to safeguard caravans. His greatest find was at 'the cave of the thousand Buddhas'—an enormous cache of documents, temple-banners, and paintings, which had been walled up since the eleventh century. During each of these expeditions he covered many thousands of miles and brought back to India and England hundreds of cases of valuable objects.

Stein's official position at this time was that of inspector-general of education in the North-West Frontier Province and Baluchistan. He became a naturalized British subject in 1904. In 1910 he transferred to the Archaeological Survey of India (from which he retired in 1929), and his third and longest Central Asian expedition was undertaken in that service. Again he went to Lop-Nor and the Etsin-gol, making new discoveries and collections on the way; thence he reached Kara-khoto, traversed 500 miles of the sterile, unexplored Pei-shan to Dzungaria, visited and surveyed the strange Turfan depression, at one point nearly 1,000 feet below sea-level, and followed the foot of the T'ien-shan to Kashgar, thus completing his circuit of the Taklamakan; thence he passed into Russian territory, crossed the Alai Pamir, traced the classical silk-route to Samarkand, and turned south through eastern Persia to Baluchistan, making on the way a detailed survey and archaeological reconnaissance of the Helmand basin in Sistan. Between the two wars political conditions for Central Asian travel were unfavourable, and Stein's fourth expedition in 1930, planned with the sanction of the central Chinese Government at Nanking, was foiled by local obstruction; some valuable additions, however, were made to his geographical surveys during a journey of some 2,000 miles round the Taklamakan desert. Throughout these expeditions Stein used as a basis of his exploration his profound knowledge of classical writings, a critical examination of Chinese annals, and of the travels of the Buddhist pilgrims (particularly Hsuien Tsang, his 'patron saint'), and of Marco Polo, gained from Yule, to whom he dedicated the results of his first journey. The scientific record of these discoveries was published in *Ancient Khotan* (2 vols., 1907), *Serindia* (5 vols., 1921), and *Innermost Asia* (4 vols., 1928), massive quarto tomes, profusely illustrated by plates and maps. His *Memoir on maps of Chinese Turkistan and Kansu*, with port-

folio of forty-seven maps and eleven triangulation charts, was published by the Survey of India in 1923, and narrative accounts of the first two journeys appeared in *Sand-buried Ruins of Khotan* (1903) and *Ruins of Desert Cathay* (2 vols., 1912). The art treasures brought back from Ch'ien-fo-tung were separately illustrated and described in a large portfolio, *The Thousand Buddhas* (1921).

Stein's second great task was prompted by Sir John Hubert Marshall's discoveries of the ancient Indus civilization during 1923–5, which led to a succession of arduous journeys in Baluchistan and Persia between 1927 and 1936 to connect this culture with that of the Euphrates. In 1927–8 in Waziristan, Baluchistan, and Makran he discovered abundant remains of the chalcolithic period; between 1930 and 1933 from Gwadar he travelled through Makran to Kerman, and made a detailed reconnaissance of south-western Persia from Minab through Laristan to Bushire, where most of the sites dated only from Mohammedan times; in 1933–4 he explored the province of Fars, discovering remains of chalcolithic and neolithic settlements; and in the following year he toured the Bakhtiari country and Luristan, and western Persia from Kermanshah to Lake Urmia (Rizaieh). The results of these investigations were published in *Archaeological Reconnaissances in North-Western India and South-Eastern Iran* (1937) and in *Old Routes of Western Iran* (1940).

Political difficulties which sometimes prevented Stein from working in Central Asia, Afghanistan, and Persia led him to an interest in the ancient sites of Babylonia. He had been impressed by the value of air reconnaissance in archaeology and by the researches of Father A. Poidebard along the Roman frontier posts of the Syrian desert. With the help of the Royal Air Force Stein carried out preliminary air reconnaissances of the Roman frontier in Iraq and the Jezira in 1929 and 1935, and supplemented these by a detailed examination on the ground in 1938 and 1939, discovering numerous remains of Roman occupation. His full report on this work was in typescript only at the time of his death, but short summaries appeared in the *Geographical Journal* (June 1940) and the *Journal* of the Royal Asiatic Society (October 1941).

Partly as a separate investigation and partly in connexion with these travels,

Stein was always looking for traces of Alexander's eastern campaign. During his work in Iraq he made a critical examination of the topographical features of Alexander's crossing of the Tigris and of the battle of Arbela. In 1934, when in south-west Persia, he examined Alexander's forcing of the 'Persian Gates' between Susiana and Persepolis, comparing the accounts of Arrian, Curtius, and Diodorus with the local topography and making a detailed survey of the ground. In 1926, when on an archaeological tour of Swat, primarily undertaken to examine Graeco-Buddhist remains, he picked up Alexander's trail and traced it to Pir Sar at a bend in the Indus, where he identified by exact topographical detail the 'Rock of Aornos'. In 1931 he made a thorough examination of the ground from Taxila through the Salt Range to the Jhelum, where he located the exact site of the defeat of Poros and interpreted Alexander's tactics; in his last expedition in 1943, he traced Alexander's retreat through Las Bela State and Baluchistan, the ancient Gedrosia.

From his earliest days Stein had tried to gain permission to explore Afghanistan, always to be thwarted. At last in 1943, when over eighty years of age, through the efforts of the United States minister at Kabul, he was granted permission. He reached Kabul on 19 October in great spirits. Two days later he caught a chill which developed into bronchitis; he had a stroke on the night of the 24th and died at the United States legation on the 26th. He was buried in the Christian cemetery at Kabul.

Short in stature, but well proportioned, wiry, and very hardy, Stein had indomitable determination and inexhaustible patience, energy, and endurance. He could walk Pathans and other hillmen much younger than himself off their legs, and at the end of a long march would write meticulous accounts of the day's work and long letters to his friends. He accepted 'no' as only a temporary negative, put into operation an alternative project elsewhere, and later returned to his original plan with invincible arguments. His brilliant intellect and wide knowledge of oriental languages, his simple tastes, his patience, and passion for accuracy, his astonishing memory for detail, his lavish acknowledgement of help and collaboration from friends, and his capacity for planning ahead and discovering the essentials of a problem in the shortest time, were all factors which enabled him to cover so large an area, and to solve so many problems. He rarely marched with European companions, but always took devoted Indian surveyors— Lal Singh and Ram Singh, the Sikhs of his earlier, Afraz Gul Khan and Mohammed Ayub Khan, Pathans of his later, travels. He was seldom ill and the loss of his toes from frostbite on the high K'un-lun in 1908 did not incapacitate him for long. Between his expeditions he pitched his tent on a high alpine meadow, Mohand Marg, above the Sind valley in Kashmir at 11,000 feet above sea-level, where he worked alone, sometimes in his sleeping bag, on the reports of his expeditions, occasionally visiting Srinagar to consult some book. On Mohand Marg a memorial stone inscribed in English and Hindustani has been erected by his friends. On his occasional visits to England he stayed with the Allens of Corpus Christi, Oxford. He began life with no private means, but by his frugality and in spite of his generosity —he did much for his relatives in Hungary after the war of 1914–18—he left a considerable sum to form the 'Stein–Arnold' fund, eventually to be used for geographical and antiquarian exploration in central and south-west Asia. Stein was a true nomad; he had no fixed abode and owned no roof. He never married, and in order to prove his will (P.P.R., 23 March 1944) the opinions of several learned counsel had to be sought before the judge in Chancery could rule that, although a British subject, Stein had never lost his Hungarian domicile of birth (Chancery proceedings 1946, S. 336, 21 March 1947).

Stein was appointed C.I.E. in 1910 and K.C.I.E. in 1912. He received the Back grant from the Royal Geographical Society in 1904 and the Founder's gold medal in 1909, the gold medal of the Royal Asiatic Society in 1932, and that of the Society of Antiquaries in 1935; other awards were the Flinders Petrie medal (1928), the Campbell memorial medal, the Huxley medallion, and medals from geographical and antiquarian societies of France, Sweden, Hungary, and the United States; from Hungary he received the croix de mérite and a special medallion struck in his honour. He was elected F.B.A. in 1921, was a fellow of the Institute of France, and received honorary degrees from the universities of Oxford, Cambridge, and St. Andrews. A chalk drawing by Sir William Rothenstein is in the National Portrait Gallery, and a sanguine drawing in the Manchester City Art Gallery.

[C. E. A. W. Oldham in *Proceedings* of the British Academy, vol. xxix, 1943; private information; personal knowledge.]

KENNETH MASON.

STEPHENS, JAMES (1880?–1950), writer, was by his own account born in Dublin on the same day and in the same year as James Joyce [q.v.]. It seems more probable, however, that he was the child born 9 February 1880 to Francis Stephens, at that time a vanman, and his wife, Charlotte Collins. In later life Stephens stated that his father was Frank Stephens, a bank clerk, but he chose always to surround his origins with mystery and probably knew little of them himself, for his father died when he was two and on his mother's remarriage he was placed in an orphanage. Here he received a firm grounding in the Protestant faith but little general education and at an early age he ran away. The fourth Earl Grey [q.v.], in sending a copy of the first edition of *The Crock of Gold* as a gift to a friend at Christmas in 1912, wrote that Stephens 'has been hungry for weeks as a boy, has slept in the parks, has fought with swans for a piece of bread, has tramped the roads, has lived on the kindness of poor people who liked the queer little boy, and yet he has grown up with the most independent spirit and with tireless energy, humour, inquisitiveness: he is a born Bohemian, small in stature, but quite big inside, large and roomy'.

It is said that Chaucer, Keats, Tom Moore, Byron, and Longfellow were short of stature; but surely James Stephens was shorter than these. Even with his high heels and elevators in his shoes he was scarcely four and a half feet high. His large eyes and full throat, due to a goitre, prevented anyone from thinking of him as a dwarf although they often thought of him as a leprechaun and sometimes as a changeling. His eyes were those of genius. In repose his face had the melancholy of a clown. At one time, it is said, he was an acrobat in a circus. His lack of inches gave him one advantage. He could cast off the conventions which bound ordinary people and become a gleeman, the most lyrical spirit of his time. Nobody had genius more on the surface. His body would sway to the rhythm of the poetry he recited, and this possession affected all around. His capacity for projecting himself into what he wrote was unprecedented.

He tells how he used to 'squat' beside the dog or the cat or beside a cow or a bird, 'and try to bring myself into the being of that creature. . . . I sat beside a small bush that day and tried to "bush" myself into it.' He not only used this power in his poems but in the *Reincarnations* (1918) of other poets. The best of these paraphrases—they cannot be called translations—is of the poems of Blind Raftery who flourished at the beginning of the nineteenth century. Raftery's praise of Mary Hynes, one of those rare beauties who grace castle or cottage once in a century or two, whom he calls 'The Blossom of the Branches', is wonderfully turned, and his paraphrase of 'The County Mayo' shows Stephens at his happiest.

He was the most cantative poet of his time and his genius was recognized early in his life so that he was able to give up his work as a scrivener in the office of a firm of attorneys. His first volume of poetry, *Insurrections* (1909), was dedicated to AE (G. W. Russell, q.v.) who recommended the publication of his first novel, *The Charwoman's Daughter* (1912). *The Crock of Gold*, published in the same year, and *The Demi-Gods* (1914) brought him into the first rank of prose writers. In 1912 he went to live in Paris but after the outbreak of war returned to Dublin where from 1915 to 1924 he was registrar of the National Portrait Gallery which has an excellent portrait of him by Patrick Tuohy. Later he left Ireland and divided his time between Paris and London. As he said of his lifelong friend, Arthur Griffith [q.v.], 'The hero, the man of goodwill, belongs to no nation. He is the international man and the world's currency.' These words apply too to the poet who was part of his country's inspiration. When Stephens received the honorary degree of Litt.D. in 1947 from Dublin University, the public orator, Sir Robert Tate, said that his 'genius is so varied that some critics compare him with Aeschylus, some with Milton, while others regard his gift as mainly if not entirely lyric. . . . But it may at least be safely said that he will always have a place among the muses' chief priests. In his presentation of the immensities— eternity, space, force—in his picture of the Lord walking in the deserted garden, in his account of what Thomas said in a pub about the anger of the Almighty, he passes beyond what is simply human and becomes a voice for the spirit of poetry; *Musas ipsas audire videaris.*'

Almost all Stephens's creative work was

done before 1914, but towards the end of his life he became widely known as a broadcaster of verse and stories. He was a founder-member of the Irish Academy of Letters and in 1942 he was awarded a Civil List pension. He married in 1919 Millicent Josephine (Cynthia), a widow, daughter of Thomas Howard Gardiner, a master upholsterer. They had one son who was killed when he stepped on a live rail at a railway station near London a few years before Stephens himself died at his home in London 26 December 1950. A portrait of Stephens by Sir William Rothenstein is in the Tate Gallery; a lithograph by Mary Duncan is in the National Portrait Gallery; and a bronze by E. Quinn is in the Municipal Gallery of Modern Art, Dublin.

[Private information; personal knowledge.]
OLIVER ST. JOHN GOGARTY.

STEPHENSON, MARJORY (1885–1948), biochemist, was born 24 January 1885 at Burwell, Cambridgeshire. She was the youngest of four children, the next in age being eight years older than herself. Her father, Robert Stephenson, was a farmer in a large way and something of a pioneer in scientific farming which was developing during his lifetime; her mother, Sarah Rogers, came from Newmarket.

Marjory Stephenson was educated at home until at the age of twelve she won a scholarship at Berkhamsted High School for Girls. She went to Newnham College, Cambridge, in 1903 and was placed in the second class of part i of the natural sciences tripos in 1906. She then wished to study medicine but economic pressure prevented this and she first studied and then taught domestic science for five years.

Her career as a biochemist began in 1911 when she joined R. H. A. Plimmer's laboratory at University College, London, where she assisted in the advanced teaching. It was here that she did her first research. Her earliest work dealt with animal lactase and with the esters of palmitic acid. Later she studied the metabolic aspect of experimental diabetes. This work was interrupted by the war of 1914–18 during which she worked with the Red Cross in France and in Salonika and was appointed M.B.E. in 1918 for her services.

After the war Marjory Stephenson returned to Cambridge and worked in the biochemical department under (Sir) Frederick Gowland Hopkins [q.v.]. She found her true direction in science when Hopkins encouraged her to leave the fields of animal metabolism and to initiate a comprehensive study of the biochemical activities of bacteria. She spent the rest of her life working on this line. The first edition of her book on *Bacterial Metabolism* appeared in 1930 and was of quite special importance. It was the first and for a long time the only book on the subject. It had a definite influence on the contemporary trend of research and translated Hopkins's ideas of dynamic biochemistry into the field of microbiology. There was a new edition in 1939 and she had prepared a third which was published in 1949 shortly after her death.

This new line of work at Cambridge was begun at a most exciting time. The Wieland–Thunberg theory of biological oxidation had been propounded. Hopkins had isolated what was thought to be an important hydrogen carrier, glutathione; and the Cambridge laboratory was turning to the study of intracellular enzymes with particular emphasis on oxidation mechanisms. This background had a profound and lasting effect on her approach to bacterial metabolism. She studied the problems of hydrogen donators in bacterial metabolism, and in collaboration with (Professor) Juda Hirsch Quastel made notable advances in the understanding of anaerobic growth. This led her to the investigation of the transfer of hydrogen. With Dr. L. H. Stickland she discovered an enzyme which activated molecular hydrogen in a mixed bacterial culture obtained from the river Ouse which was at that time polluted with waste from a sugar factory. The enzyme was named hydrogenase and it was found to have a wide distribution amongst coliform and other bacteria. Her original work ranged over a wide variety of problems. Her tools were washed cell-suspensions and, where possible, cell-free extracts.

As a teacher Marjory Stephenson had a very considerable influence in the biochemistry department in Cambridge and she became reader in chemical microbiology in the university in 1947. In 1945 she was one of the first two women scientists to be elected F.R.S. She took an active part in founding the Society for General Microbiology in 1945 and became the Society's second president in September 1947.

Marjory Stephenson was a vivid and attractive person who made many friends. She had wide interests outside her laboratory, delighted in travel, and also had a true countrywoman's happiness in her garden, notably in her fruit trees. She always maintained her connexion with Newnham, where there is a portrait drawing of her by Mrs. Campbell Dodgson. She died in Cambridge, unmarried, 12 December 1948.

[Muriel Robertson in *Obituary Notices of Fellows of the Royal Society*, No. 18, November 1949; *Journal of General Microbiology*, vol. iii, No. 3, 1949; personal knowledge.]

MURIEL ROBERTSON.

STEVENSON, SIR DANIEL MACAULAY, baronet (1851–1944), merchant, civic administrator, and philanthropist, was born in Glasgow 1 August 1851, the second of four sons and seven children of John Stevenson, engineer, by his wife, Jessie, daughter of Daniel E. Macaulay, editor of the *Liberator* and the *Free Trade Advocate*, also of Glasgow. He was educated at the Secular School and the Athenaeum, Glasgow, and, entering business, founded the firm of D. M. Stevenson & Co., coal exporters. During the war of 1914–18 he presided over the central executive committee on the supply of coal to France and Italy. In his twenty-two years' membership of Glasgow corporation, from 1892, Stevenson found outlet for a strong inherited impulse for social betterment. Some of the many reforms he initiated, such as the consolidation of the city debt, new methods of borrowing, and the provision of free municipal libraries, were widely copied. Under his lord-provostship (1911–14) the title of right honourable was first conferred upon the chief magistrate of Glasgow, and in 1929 Stevenson received the freedom of the city.

A great traveller, with a gift for languages, Stevenson was passionately devoted to the cause of international understanding. His many benefactions to this end included the endowment of two chairs of international history in the university of London, the one being a research professorship combined with the directorship of studies at the Royal Institute of International Affairs (Chatham House), the other being incorporated in the London School of Economics and Political Science. He also endowed the British Institute in Florence. He did much to further Franco-Scottish relations; and on the outbreak of the Spanish civil war in 1936 organized a Scottish ambulance unit for non-combatants. The Governments of France, Italy, Belgium, Spain, and Germany conferred honours upon him, and he enjoyed the friendship of many prominent persons abroad.

His munificence to Glasgow University, which conferred upon him its honorary LL.D. in 1914, ranks him among its greatest benefactors. It began, characteristically, with the endowment of a lectureship in citizenship (1921), followed, among many other gifts, by chairs of Italian and Spanish, exchange scholarships with German, French, and Spanish universities, and an extension of the department of engineering. In 1934 he was elected chancellor of the university. Music likewise commanded his generous support, notably in the foundation and endowment of the (Royal) Scottish Academy of Music.

Stevenson was possessed of great strength of character and tenacity of decision, and often found himself in consequence the centre of embittered controversy. In politics an ardent Liberal, he was for long prominent in the counsels of the party. He died, unmarried, in Glasgow 11 July 1944, and the baronetcy, created in 1914, became extinct. A portrait by D. S. Ewart and a bronze bust by A. Proudfoot are in Glasgow University, and a portrait by J. B. Anderson is in the Glasgow City Art Gallery.

[*The Times*, 12 July and 11 August 1944; *Glasgow Herald*, 12 July 1944; personal knowledge.]          WILLIAM C. ATKINSON.

STEWART, WILLIAM DOWNIE (1878–1949), New Zealand politician, was born in Dunedin 29 July 1878, the younger son of William Downie Stewart, barrister and solicitor and law reformer, and his wife, Rachel, daughter of George Hepburn, who died in November of the same year. Stewart was educated at the Otago Boys' High School and then entered his father's law office, also attending law classes at the university of Otago. His studies were temporarily interrupted by his father's death in 1898, but in 1900 he graduated LL.B. and was admitted as a solicitor. Although not distinguished at school or university, Stewart retained throughout life the temperament and interests of a student. Even as a young man he did not share the national interest in athletic sports. He visited England in 1904 and returned by way of Siberia and China. In December 1905 he contested the parliamentary constituency of Dunedin South. The high quality and light touch of his speeches attracted attention, but he was unsuccessful. In 1908 he visited the

United States. One outcome of this visit was the appearance in 1911 of *State Socialism in New Zealand*, a critical study written by Stewart in collaboration with Professor J. E. Le Rossignol, then professor of economics in the university of Denver. In 1913 Stewart, who had been elected to the Dunedin city council in 1907, was elected mayor of Dunedin. At the general election of December 1914 Stewart made his second attempt to enter Parliament and was elected, as a supporter of the Reform Party led by W. F. Massey [q.v.], for the constituency of Dunedin West, which from 1884 to 1890 had been represented by his father.

In 1915, with Massey's permission, Stewart arranged a pair in the House of Representatives and enlisted as a private soldier. His elder brother died on active service in November of that year and the following January Stewart left New Zealand as a second lieutenant in the ninth reinforcements, Otago Regiment. Whilst serving in France with the rank of captain, he contracted rheumatoid arthritis. In December 1916 he was invalided home and placed on the retired list. He continued to suffer from this disease for the rest of his life. He virtually retired from legal practice but, after a period of convalescence, resumed his political career. In March 1921 he joined Massey's Government as minister of internal affairs and minister of customs. He could then walk with crutches but later became unable to move about except in an invalid chair. He relinquished the internal affairs portfolio in 1923, becoming instead minister of industries and commerce. The portfolio of customs, which he found congenial, he held until 1928. He was associated with two revisions of the tariff, in 1921 and 1927, both based on the principle of moderate protection. He also negotiated trade agreements with Australia in 1922 and with Japan in 1928. In the ministry formed by J. G. Coates [q.v.] in May 1925 Stewart was at first minister of customs and of industries and commerce and for a few months attorney-general, but in May 1926 he became minister of finance, relinquishing all but the first of the other portfolios. From September 1926 to February 1927, during Coates's absence at the Imperial Conference, Stewart was acting prime minister. Stewart thought that the burden of public debt and the high rate of interest on the London money market made it advisable for New Zealand to 'taper off' borrowing for public works.

He also instituted a local government loans board to control local borrowing. In 1928, however, the electorate returned Sir Joseph Ward [q.v.] and his United Party in unexpected numbers, after a campaign in which Ward proposed to raise large loans for railways and land settlement; and Ward became prime minister with Labour support.

The economic and financial crisis which began in 1930 brought the United and Reform parties closer together, whilst Labour went into opposition. Stewart was the leading advocate in the Reform Party of the coalition which was formed, on the initiative of G. W. Forbes [q.v.], Ward's successor as prime minister and leader of the United Party, in September 1931. Stewart became minister of finance and of customs and attorney-general. The sole representative of city interests in a farmers' Government, he stood for the orthodox financial methods of retrenchment, increase of taxation, and return as soon as possible to balanced budgets. He resisted pressure from farming interests for compulsory reduction of interest rates and depreciation of the currency. He had, however, to impose exchange control from Christmas 1931 to July 1932. After the Ottawa conference, at which both Coates and Stewart were delegates, Coates, then minister of public works and of transport, was convinced by economists and organizations connected with farming of the necessity of 'raising the rate of exchange' and carried the Cabinet against Stewart. On 20 January 1933, under government pressure, the banks raised the rate for telegraphic transfers to London from £N.Z.110 to £N.Z.125 per £100 sterling, and Stewart resigned. His resignation confirmed his reputation as a man of principle. His unblemished integrity, breadth of outlook, and courage in face of disability rather than any lasting political achievements are his best claim to a place in New Zealand history.

Stewart remained in Parliament until December 1935, when his defeat by a Labour opponent ended his political career. He retained a number of directorships and published various historical works, the most important being *Sir Francis Bell: His Life and Times* (1937) and *William Rolleston* (1940). It was in conversation, however, rather than in his writings or speeches that Stewart was at his best. His knowledge of New Zealand politics was encyclopaedic. He was keenly interested in Commonwealth and international affairs and did much to promote their study in New Zealand. About two years before his death his health failed. He died, in the house in which he was born, 29 September 1949. He never married and lived most of his life with his younger sister. A portrait by R. N. Field is in her possession.

[*New Zealand Parliamentary Record, 1840–1949*, edited by G. H. Scholefield, 1950; *Otago Daily Times*, 1 October 1949 and *passim*; private information; personal knowledge.]

W. P. MORRELL.

STILES, SIR HAROLD JALLAND (1863–1946), surgeon, was born at Spalding 21 March 1863, the youngest son of Henry Tournay Stiles and his wife, Elizabeth Ellen, daughter of John Jalland, of Nottingham. Stiles's grandfather and father were country doctors in Lincolnshire, but the succession to the practice was with his brother, and Stiles had to make his own way in the profession. At sixteen he began to serve a modified apprenticeship to his father; but even at this early age his interest in surgery was plain, for all his spare time was used to make himself master of systematic human anatomy. When in 1880 Stiles went to Edinburgh to study medicine, the city captivated him and he determined to make his career there: and, as was so often to be apparent during his lifetime, when Stiles determined to do anything, it was as good as done. He graduated in 1885 with first class honours and was awarded the Ettles scholarship as the most distinguished student of his year. He prepared himself for surgery by working for ten years in the dissecting room and pathological laboratory, and by visits to European clinics. He was appointed to the staff of the Royal Infirmary of Edinburgh in 1895, but left in 1898 to become surgeon to the Royal Hospital for Sick Children and to Chalmers Hospital, where his great surgical attainments and exceptional powers of teaching rapidly brought him professional success and international reputation.

During the war of 1914–18, as a colonel in the Army Medical Service, he introduced and practised in conjunction with Sir Robert Jones [q.v.] methods which did much to raise the standard of orthopaedic surgery, and to establish it as a speciality; and his advice on matters of administration was highly valued. He was knighted in 1918 and appointed K.B.E. in 1919. In the latter year he returned to the Royal Infirmary as regius

professor of clinical surgery; his clinic attracted a constant stream of visitors from Europe and America where he had made many warm friendships and was an honorary member of a number of professional associations. He retired from the chair in 1925, while still in the fullness of his great powers. To the pursuits of his retirement Stiles devoted the same concentrated study which had characterized his professional work. In turn, as his physical strength lessened, he devoted himself to geology, to field botany, to the study of local lichens and sea-shells, and finally to pen-and-ink drawing: and was successful and happy in each.

During Stiles's professional career, his success in both consulting room and operating theatre, and his dominating and uncompromising personality, tended to obscure the much more significant influence which he exercised upon surgery throughout the British Isles and in particular in Scotland where he hastened the advent of scientific surgery by many years. It is true that the opportunity was his; but no one without great talents, prodigious industry, and unswerving sincerity of purpose could have made of it what he did. After a visit to Kocher in Berne (1893) he insisted on the substitution of sterilization of surgical materials by high-pressure steam for the more cumbersome method of sterilization by chemical solutions, and completed his crusade with a speed which has not since been equalled. He was thus a pioneer in linking the laboratory with the clinic. He was quick to master and to apply the principles of pathology and especially microscopic pathology to the management of disease; his notable researches into the spread of cancer brought him in 1895 the Walker prize of the Royal College of Surgeons, and he published a series of illuminating papers on the pathology of tuberculous disease of lymphatic glands, bones, and joints. His operation for diverting the urine to the large bowel was more than a technical triumph: it was the application of a comprehensive knowledge of biology.

Stiles served as president of the Association of Surgeons of Great Britain and Ireland (1921) and of the Royal College of Surgeons of Edinburgh (1923), and among other honours which came to him were the honorary degrees of D.Sc., Leeds (1922), and the LL.D. of St. Andrews (1922) and Edinburgh (1925).

In 1889 he married Cecilia Norton (died

1930), daughter of David Law, a civil engineer, of Glasgow, by whom he had one daughter; secondly, in 1931 he married Jean Morrison, daughter of James Bowser Thorburn, accountant, of Edinburgh, who survived him when he died at Gullane 19 April 1946. A portrait by Frederic Whiting hangs in the board-room of the Royal Hospital for Sick Children, Edinburgh.

[*British Medical Journal* and *Lancet*, 4 May 1946; private information; personal knowledge.]　　　　JAMES LEARMONTH.

STILL, SIR (GEORGE) FREDERIC (1868–1941), paediatrician, was born at Holloway, London, 27 February 1868, the son of George Still, customs clerk, by his wife, Eliza Andrew. He was educated at Merchant Taylors' School and at Gonville and Caius College, Cambridge, where he took a first class in the classical tripos (1888) and was Winchester prizeman (1889). His medical training was received at Guy's Hospital, where after qualification in 1893 he served as house-physician. Early in his career he decided to specialize in the diseases of childhood, and he was appointed assistant physician to the Hospital for Sick Children, Great Ormond Street. The thesis for which he was awarded the M.D. (Cambridge) in 1896 was on 'A Special Form of Joint Disease met with in Children', the substance of which appeared in the *Medico-Chirurgical Transactions* (1897, vol. lxxx) and in the first edition of Allbutt's *System of Medicine* (1897). In these publications Still established the entity of a chronic rheumatoid arthritis peculiar to childhood, a condition which became known as 'Still's disease'. Another important piece of work which he accomplished at this time was the identification of the organism responsible for the affection described by S. J. Gee and Sir Thomas Barlow [qq.v.] as posterior basic meningitis. In 1899 Still was appointed physician for diseases of children at King's College Hospital, the first hospital with a medical school to establish a special department for diseases of children, and in 1906 he was elected the first professor of diseases of children in King's College.

Still was an acute and accurate observer, and many of his articles and lectures on children's diseases have permanent value. He was co-editor with his former chief, Sir James Frederic Goodhart, of the 6th–12th editions (1899–1925) of the latter's *Diseases of Children*; in 1909 he published his own textbook, *Common Disorders and Diseases of Childhood*, which met with immediate success and reached a fifth edition in 1927. His Ingleby lectures at Birmingham in 1927 dealt with 'Place-in-family as a Factor of Disease'. In 1938 he published a small book entitled *Common Happenings in Childhood*, which gave further evidence of his vast experience and great clinical acumen. *Childhood and Other Poems* (1941) was a new edition, with additions, of poems which he had published privately for friends. He contributed to many textbooks, to the *Encyclopaedia Britannica*, and to this DICTIONARY. He kept up his interest in classics, and in 1931, on the centenary of King's College Medical School, wrote in Latin verse 'Carmen Scholae Medicinae', which was set to music and sung at the celebrations. Apart from his clinical writings he made several valuable contributions to the history of children's disease, and his *History of Paediatrics* (1931), an expansion of his FitzPatrick lectures before the Royal College of Physicians, is one of the best histories of any speciality.

At the summit of his career Still enjoyed an almost unique position as a children's consulting physician. In 1936 he was appointed physician-in-ordinary to the household of the Duke and Duchess of York, and in 1937 was made physician-extraordinary to His Majesty, and appointed K.C.V.O. When he retired from King's College in 1935 he was appointed consulting physician and emeritus professor; he had for many years been consulting physician to the Infants' Hospital, Vincent Square, to Dr. Barnardo's Homes, and to the Society for Waifs and Strays. He was the first president of the International Paediatric Association; was president of the International Paediatric Congress which met in London in 1933; and served as chairman of the National Association for the Prevention of Infant Mortality (1917–37). He was first president of the British Paediatric Society and an honorary member of many other learned bodies. At the Royal College of Physicians, of which he was elected a fellow in 1901, he was Murchison scholar in 1894, Goulstonian (1902), Lumleian (1918), and FitzPatrick (1928–9) lecturer; he was censor (1932–3). He was an honorary LL.D. of Edinburgh (1927) and an honorary fellow of the Royal Society of Medicine (1937), and was awarded the Dawson Williams memorial prize in 1934. On his retirement from King's College

Hospital he was presented with his portrait in oils painted by (Sir) Gerald Kelly, and a 'Dr. Still Cot' was endowed in his memory. Still, who was unmarried, died at Harnham Croft, Salisbury, 28 June 1941.

[*Archives of Disease in Childhood*, September 1941 (bibliography); *British Medical Journal* and *Lancet*, 12 July 1941.] W. J. BISHOP.

STOCKDALE, SIR FRANK ARTHUR (1883–1949), tropical agriculturist, was born at Honington, Lincolnshire, 24 June 1883, the eldest son of George Edmund Stockdale, of Wood House, Elm, Cambridgeshire. His ancestors had owned and farmed land in Lincolnshire, Cambridgeshire, and Norfolk for many generations. His mother, Eliza Rayson Farbon, was also of farming stock. By tradition and temperament and even in physical appearance Stockdale was a typical English farmer. His achievement was to carry his inherited love and understanding of the soil and its products into the wide field of tropical agriculture and to personify, so far as one man could, that application of scientific knowledge to the economic and social development of the colonial territories which was an outstanding feature of British colonial history between 1919 and 1939.

Stockdale was educated at Wisbech Grammar School and Magdalene College, Cambridge, where he was a Holmes exhibitioner. He graduated B.A. in 1904 with a first class in part i of the natural sciences tripos. In 1905 he was appointed mycologist and lecturer in agricultural science in the Imperial Department of Agriculture for the West Indies. In 1909 he was sent to British Guiana as assistant director of a new agricultural department, and in 1912 he went to Mauritius to form a similar department there. In 1916 he was promoted to be director of agriculture in Ceylon where, during thirteen years of office, he not only gave the agricultural department a permanent organization which made it a model for others, but also played a leading part in establishing rubber, tea, and coconut research institutions. From 1916 to 1928 he edited the *Tropical Agriculturist*.

Before 1914 there was virtually no central machinery for dealing with the scientific and economic problems of the colonies. After the war it was evident that social progress in these territories must depend upon their ability to better their economic position by increased agricultural production. It eventually became clear that this called for a central organization to provide advice, technical assistance, and trained agriculturists. It was not, however, until 1929 that a Colonial Agricultural Service was set up, with a colonial advisory council of agriculture and animal health, and a full-time agricultural adviser. By experience, qualifications, and personality, Stockdale was marked out for this important new post. For the ten years following his appointment he was the indefatigable promoter of agricultural development in the colonies. Much of his time was spent in touring, for he visited nearly all the territories, some more than once. His reports were 'models of clarity of exposition'. The value of his advice was largely due to his ability to view agricultural problems in relation to the general economy and social conditions of the territory concerned. He continued to preach the dangers of dependence upon a single crop, the essential virtues of mixed farming, and the disastrous effects of soil erosion. He could be depended upon to take the long-term view not only on matters of policy, but in assessing the potential ability and value of the officers of the Colonial Agricultural Service. These in their turn knew him as a kindly, approachable, and imperturbable leader who was always ready to hear the other man's point of view, although he would not give way on his own opinions unless he was satisfied that he had been mistaken. His early work showed that he might have made a considerable name as a pure scientist; but Stockdale was never able to regard the expansion of scientific knowledge as an end in itself, and he could be impatient with those who did. To him the achievements of science were means to an end—and that end the general welfare and improvement of the territories in which his work lay.

Stockdale was a natural choice for the post of comptroller for development and welfare in the West Indies which was established in 1940 on the recommendation of the West India Royal Commission. Assisted by a team of expert advisers, he was responsible for the administration of grants from the United Kingdom amounting to £1 million a year. He had no executive authority but co-operated with the colonial Governments concerned, in the formation and execution of their plans for development and improvement, and in determining how the grants might best be used. These duties were coupled, after 1942, with those of co-chairman of the Anglo-American Caribbean Commission.

By his own wish he retained the office of comptroller until the end of the war, instead of accepting preferment which he was offered in the administrative sphere. When, with the cessation of hostilities, it became possible to press on with the general policy of colonial development, he was invited to return to the Colonial Office as adviser on development planning. In 1948 he became vice-chairman of the new Colonial Development Corporation. His encyclopaedic knowledge of the colonies and their economic problems, and the immense fund of goodwill which stood to his credit throughout the colonial empire were invaluable assets to the Corporation in its early stages. In 1948 he also became chairman of the governing body of the Imperial College of Tropical Agriculture in Trinidad. The development and expansion of the College as a worthy academic institution to serve the colonies as a whole was an object to which Stockdale was strongly attached and which he pursued with characteristic faith and tenacity.

Stockdale was appointed C.B.E. in 1925, C.M.G. in 1932, and promoted K.C.M.G. in 1937 and G.C.M.G. in 1945. He died in London 3 August 1949. He married in 1908 Annie Dora (died 1948), daughter of Lewis Packer, sugar planter, of Warrens, Barbados; there were two sons of the marriage.

[*Nature*, 3 September 1949; official records; private information; personal knowledge.]
CHARLES JEFFRIES.

STOLL, SIR OSWALD (1866–1942), theatrical impresario, was born at Melbourne, Australia, 20 January 1866, the only child of Oswald James Alexander Gray, engineer and surveyor, originally of Enniskillen, by his wife, Adelaide, daughter of Patrick Macdonnell, surveyor, of Dublin. Mrs. Gray, widowed in 1869, married in 1879 John George Stoll, of Liverpool, owner of the Parthenon music-hall in that city, and changed her son's name to Stoll. Again widowed, she continued to operate the Parthenon, and Oswald was already at work there at the age of fourteen. Developing precociously, he began to write songs and successfully managed a theatrical agency while still a youth. In 1889 he acquired Leveno's music-hall at Cardiff, renamed it the Empire, and introduced twice-nightly programmes. During the 'nineties he opened

other 'Empires' at Swansea and Newport, and before long eight music-halls were under his control. His experiences of more than doubtful turns and rowdy audiences at Liverpool and Cardiff led him to aim at a better status for the music-hall, and throughout his career he strove to make all his houses places of inexpensive, wholesome entertainment to which a man might take his family.

In other areas the music-hall was being developed along similar lines by (Sir) Edward Moss, Richard Thornton, and Frank Allen. In 1900 these interests were merged with those of Stoll, in the firm of Moss Empires, Ltd., which opened the London Hippodrome in that year and the Coliseum on 24 December 1904, and came to control many of the largest houses in the country during the period up to the war of 1914–18 while this form of diversion remained immensely popular. Stoll's fine sense of entertainment value and first-rate business ability contributed greatly to the success of the company and brought him to the very head of the business of theatrical management.

On 31 December 1910 Stoll broke with the Moss Empires, retaining control of the Coliseum and a few provincial and suburban halls and soon afterwards acquiring the Alhambra. In March 1916, as chairman of the Opera House Syndicate, Ltd., he took over the London Opera House, soon turning it into a cinema. In 1919 it was sold to Stoll Picture Theatre (Kingsway), Ltd., of which company Stoll remained chairman for the rest of his life. During the war he initiated the War Seal Foundation for disabled officers. He contributed munificently and privately to this organization (which survives as the Sir Oswald Stoll Foundation) and to other good causes. He was knighted in 1919.

In its hey-day as a music-hall the Coliseum billed most of the famous variety turns of the time (including Vesta Tilley, Grock, Coram, Little Tich, and Wilkie Bard). But public taste was changing rapidly and in 1919 the house showed the Diaghilev ballet. The tendency was more and more towards large and lavish musical pieces. In April 1931 the Coliseum abandoned variety altogether and the Alhambra soon followed suit.

Apart from the wearing of a tall hat, Stoll had none of the characteristics of the impresario. He neither smoked nor drank and, outside business, his interests were in philosophy and economics on which he wrote several books. He would always attend the Coliseum and the Alhambra on Mondays and see the entire show. He was a man of firm character and absolute probity, popular alike with his staff and his artists. He was twice married: first, in 1892 to Harriet (died 1902), daughter of Samuel Lewis, manager at an ironworks, by whom he had a daughter; and secondly, in 1903 to Millicent, daughter of Joseph Shaw, architect and builder. They had three sons. Stoll died in London 9 January 1942. A portrait by Sir J. J. Shannon was lost in the bombing of Carlton House Terrace in November 1940.

[*The Times*, 10 January 1942; *Stage*, 2 April 1931 and 15 January 1942; H. C. Newton, *Idols of the 'Halls'*, 1928; private information.]    HERBERT B. GRIMSDITCH.

STONE, DARWELL (1859–1941), Anglo-Catholic theologian, was born at Rossett, Denbighshire, 15 September 1859, the youngest of the five children of the Rev. George Luther Stone, perpetual curate of that living, by his second wife, Elizabeth Darwell. His father died when he was four years old. He was educated at the Owens College, Manchester, and Merton College, Oxford, where he obtained second classes in classical moderations and *literae humaniores* (1880, 1882). He seems to have been a serious and retiring undergraduate of high church sympathies on whom sermons from the university pulpit by R. W. Church and H. P. Liddon [qq.v.] made a permanent impression. In 1883 he was ordained deacon, and after a spell of parish work at Ashbourne, Derbyshire, which he was soon compelled to give up through ill health, he was ordained priest and became vice-principal (1885), and later principal (1888), of the Dorchester Missionary College, Oxfordshire.

A strong sense of religious duty and vocation, aided by an innate love of learning, a judicial temper, uncommonly methodical habits, a retentive memory, and the relative leisure which his post offered him, inspired and helped him to amass in these years the vast theological knowledge on which he constantly drew in later life. At this period he also contributed extensively to the *Church Quarterly Review*, then an organ of the strictest high church orthodoxy, and his reviews did much to enhance the high quality of its anonymous scholarship. Its persistently critical attitude to the Christology of the *Lux Mundi* school was mainly due to Stone's influence with the editor. In 1903

V. S. S. Coles [q.v.] induced him to accept the vacant librarianship at Pusey House, Oxford, created by the election of F. E. Brightman [q.v.] to a fellowship at Magdalen, and on Coles's resignation (1909) Stone succeeded him in the principalship. During these years Stone published a steady stream of theological works, untechnical but weighty and learned, upholding the high church position. Besides two volumes, *Holy Baptism* (1899) and *The Holy Communion* (1904), in the 'Oxford Library of Practical Theology', of which, with W. C. E. Newbolt [q.v.], Stone was for many years editor, he wrote *Outlines of Christian Dogma* (1900), *The Christian Church* (1905), and his massive *History of the Doctrine of the Holy Eucharist* (2 vols., 1909).

Meanwhile Stone's devotion to high Anglican principles led Anglo-Catholics increasingly to seek his counsel, with the result that he was more and more drawn into ecclesiastical politics and almost automatically came to occupy the place of leader of the extreme Anglo-Catholic group in the Church. When it became clear that one of the primary objects of Prayer Book revision was to restrict supposedly Roman practices Stone, who had never concealed his strong attachment to much in the Roman system, was untiring in his efforts to safeguard their legitimacy in the Church of England. He strenuously defended the right of every parish priest to reserve the Sacrament, a practice which rapidly spread in the Church of England in the war of 1914–18, both for the purpose of communion and also for adoration; and when in 1917 the Federation of Catholic Priests was organized to defend Anglo-Catholic principles Stone accepted the chairmanship and became the leader of what was for several years an influential body. A fresh sphere of activities opened in 1921 by his election to the Convocation of Canterbury where in the Lower House he led the opposition to the new Prayer Book. Whilst stating the Anglo-Catholic difficulties he emphasized the diversity of objection to the revision and maintained that it offered no real prospect of settlement. In 1934 Stone resigned the principalship of Pusey House but continued to live in Oxford. He was still widely consulted on ecclesiastical matters and devoted himself largely to work on the projected Lexicon of Patristic Greek, of which he had been editor since 1915.

As an exponent of the view of the Church of England which looks wholly to the pre-Reformation Church (patristic and medieval) for its theological and devotional ideals, Stone has perhaps had no equal in learning, ability, or influence. He believed that the specifically Anglican elements in the Church of England were the fruit of the Protestant Reformation and that they had distorted the vision even of the Caroline divines of the seventeenth century to whom Anglo-Catholic apologists since the Oxford movement have constantly, but, as Stone believed, with inadequate historical justification, appealed. It was only as a fragment of the Church Universal that the true character of the Church of England was to be understood.

Stone's striking appearance made him a familiar figure in Oxford. His long beard which, until shortened in his later years, gave him a patriarchal appearance, in conjunction with his measured and exact mode of speech, made him the subject of many anecdotes. The intensity of his religious faith, which was one of the few things his natural reserve could not conceal, his loyalty to the cause to which he was committed, and his complete indifference to personal reward won for him the unlimited devotion and affection of his friends, while his patent fairness and sincerity in controversy made him a respected, and often loved, opponent. He died in Oxford, unmarried, 10 February 1941.

There is a portrait by James Gunn (1935) at Pusey House, Oxford, where a large collection of Stone's papers is preserved.

[F. L. Cross, *Darwell Stone, Churchman and Counsellor*, 1943 (bibliography); personal knowledge.]      F. L. Cross.

STONEY, GEORGE GERALD (1863–1942), engineer, was born in Dublin 28 November 1863, the eldest of the five children of George Johnstone Stoney [q.v.]. In early childhood Stoney lived in comfortable circumstances in Dublin, being educated at home. His father had a great reputation as a teacher as well as a scientist and had been entrusted by William Parsons, the third Earl of Rosse [q.v.] with the tuition of (Sir) Charles Parsons [q.v.] and his brothers. Although there was some nine years' difference in the ages of Parsons and Stoney, the connexion made them acquainted with one another. In June 1882 Stoney entered Trinity College, Dublin, where he was placed in the first class in mathematics and graduated in 1886 as second senior moderator and gold medallist in experimental science. In 1887 he qualified for the degree of B.A. in engineering, taking the first place in every group of subjects and gaining all three special certificates, the highest awards obtainable in the engineering school.

Stoney then entered the office of his uncle B. B. Stoney [q.v.], the chief engineer of the Dublin Port and Docks Board, with whom he had worked during the university vacations; but after a year he joined Parsons in the firm of Clarke, Chapman & Co., of which Parsons had become in 1884 a junior partner and chief electrical engineer. Thus began the long and fruitful period of their collaboration, and it was now that Stoney first became acquainted with the compound steam turbine, still in its infancy and mainly applied to small electric lighting plants for ships. The great step forward came, however, in 1889 when Parsons founded the firm of C. A. Parsons & Co. at Heaton, Newcastle upon Tyne. Stoney was one of the twelve employees who accompanied him from Gateshead, working at first as a fitter, but promoted in the following year to salary status at £2. 10s. a week. In 1893 the knowledge of the silvering of mirrors which he had gained from his father led to his appointment as manager of the searchlight reflector department, and he was also foreman of the test house, where completed turbo-generators were tested under steam before dispatch. More important than this was the able assistance which he gave to Parsons during the following years in establishing the reaction steam turbine, and the many patents which were taken out in his name in conjunction with Parsons are clear proof of his ability as an engineer. In 1895 he became chief designer of the steam turbine department. It was under his supervision that the turbine machinery of the *Turbinia* had been designed and built in 1894. When that famous little vessel revealed to the Admiralty the potentialities of the steam turbine as a marine engine at the diamond jubilee review at Spithead in 1897, Stoney was a member of her crew.

Stoney played a large part in the design and construction of the many turbo-alternators which mark the stages in the growth of the Parsons company. By 1910 he had become technical manager of the entire Heaton works, and in 1911 he was elected F.R.S. His father, uncle, and cousin were also fellows. It seemed as though his future was assured, but differences of opinion arose between him and Parsons and eventually he resigned in June 1912, having seen in these twenty-four years steam-turbine installations develop in size from 32 kW. to 25,000 kW. on land, and from 2,300 s.h.p. to 74,000 s.h.p. at sea.

After his resignation, Stoney took up consulting work, but on the outbreak of war in 1914 he gave his services as joint secretary of the Tyneside Irish battalions, four of which were raised in the district. He also served on the Admiralty board of inventions and research and later on the anti-submarine scientific research committee in Lancashire. In 1915 he joined the Newcastle upon Tyne education committee, and in 1917 he accepted the chair of mechanical engineering in the College of Technology at Manchester. In those years he published several papers, mainly on steam turbines, and was a member of the original committee appointed by the Institution of Mechanical Engineers to report on what experiments relating to the subject of 'the action of steam passing through nozzles and steam turbines' could with advantage be undertaken. The subsequent research was carried out at Manchester and in 1920 Stoney was appointed reporter for this work. In the same year he was given the honorary degree of D.Sc. by the university of Durham.

While he was at Manchester Stoney was reconciled with Parsons and in 1926 he relinquished his chair and returned to Heaton as director of research, a post which he occupied until his retirement in 1930. He died at Newcastle upon Tyne 15 May 1942. A portrait of him by T. B. Garvie hangs in the Heaton works. In 1906 Stoney received the Watt medal of the Institution of Civil Engineers, in 1914 the gold medal of the North East Coast Institution of Engineers and Shipbuilders, and in 1937 the Parsons memorial medal for the second Parsons memorial lecture read before the Institution of Electrical Engineers.

Stoney married in 1894 Isabella Mary (died 1930), second daughter of Michael Lowes, farmer, of Corbridge-on-Tyne. She is commemorated by the 'Isabella Stoney prize' endowed by her husband at the Manchester College of Technology. There were no children.

[R. Dowson in *Obituary Notices of Fellows of the Royal Society*, No. 11, November 1942; personal knowledge.]        CLAUDE GIBB.

STOUT, GEORGE FREDERICK (1860–1944), philosopher, was born in South Shields 6 January 1860, the elder son of George Stout, shipbroker, by his wife, Eliza, daughter of Richard Frankland, whitesmith, of Whitby. He was educated in South Shields at the school of Charles Addison who was eccentric, of violent temper, but a brilliant classic who persuaded Stout to go to Cambridge, where the latter was the first from South Shields ever to matriculate. Admitted to St. John's College in 1879, he became a scholar in 1881 after gaining a first class in part i of the classical tripos; in 1882 he gained a first class in part ii, adding, in 1883, a first in the moral sciences tripos; he was elected fellow of St. John's in 1884. Although in the classical tripos he had gained special distinction in ancient philosophy and in the moral sciences tripos in metaphysics, it was to psychology that he turned his attention. James Ward [q.v.] was then in Cambridge and had recently published his article in the ninth edition of the *Encyclopaedia Britannica* on Herbart as well as the now famous article on psychology, and it was Ward who directed Stout's interest. In July 1888 Stout published in *Mind* the first of the series of articles entitled 'The Herbartian Psychology'. Further articles quickly followed, all showing Stout's main interest and one which never left him, namely the nature of consciousness, of our knowledge of the material world, and the relation between mind and matter.

In 1891 Stout became editor of *Mind* and during a distinguished editorship (1891–1920) it became Britain's leading philosophical journal. After the renewal of his fellowship in 1893 he was appointed university lecturer in the moral sciences in 1894. At St. John's on the top floor of the New Court overlooking the Cam he occupied rooms where he lectured chiefly on the history of philosophy. Capable of great absorption in his work, he impressed his pupils by his width of learning and a gift, never lost, of going to the heart of a problem and unravelling its intricacies. Stout was then an extremely busy man living in a society of great intellectual distinction which included colleagues like Henry Sidgwick, Ward, W. E. Johnson, and J. M'T. E. M'Taggart [qq.v.]; the Moral Sciences Club was very active and he took a lively part in its discussions; he had, also, in successive years, two pupils of great distinction, (Professor) G. E. Moore and Mr. Bertrand (subsequently

Earl) Russell. Yet he found time to publish his *Analytic Psychology* (1896) which placed him among the best British psychological authors, past or present. Packed with skilful detailed introspection, close argument, and wide scholarship, the book is remarkable for the fruitful way in which he relates noesis to sentience, the repudiation of psychological atomism, the doctrine of the apprehension of form which later attracted Kurt Koffka, and the account of mental activity. But it was a work of analysis, the precursor of a promised work on topics which could best be treated genetically.

In 1896 Stout became the first Anderson lecturer in comparative psychology at Aberdeen where he had the opportunity of fulfilling the programme outlined in the *Analytic*. His class consisted of honours students in mental philosophy and he had what he most desired, complete freedom of method. His lecture syllabus revealed the pattern of his *Manual of Psychology* (2 vols., 1898–9). This became a well-known textbook, running into five editions, the last (1938) in conjunction with (Professor) Cecil Alec Mace, but it is also an original contribution, with a distinctive treatment of perception, of animal consciousness, and the psychology of the higher-thought processes, lacking, however, any account of moral sentiments.

In 1898 Stout went to Oxford as the first Wilde reader in mental philosophy until 1903 when he was elected professor of logic and metaphysics at St. Andrews. Here he turned his attention to the problems to which his psychological studies were preparatory, namely epistemology and the relation of mind and matter in the universe. His articles, many afterwards published collectively in *Studies in Philosophy and Psychology* (1930), show the change in interest. From 1919 to 1921, as Gifford lecturer in Edinburgh, he delivered lectures entitled 'Mind and Matter in Man and the Universe'. The lectures were idealistic in standpoint, but afterwards he began to change his views and publication was long delayed. The first volume, entitled *Mind and Matter*, appeared in 1931. Although written with very great care, the work has not been considered of outstanding philosophical importance. His account of the perception of ourselves as body-minds and of striving as a pervasive feature in the universe is interesting, but his system as a whole, which could only be understood after the publication, posthumously, of the second volume, *God and*

*Nature* (1952), in part is sketchy and, in part, breaks down under detailed examination. In any case, the interests and method of British philosophers had entirely changed in the thirty years which elapsed between the delivery and final publication of the lectures.

Stout was elected F.B.A. in 1903 and honorary fellow of St. John's College in 1927, and received honorary doctorates from the universities of Aberdeen, Durham, and St. Andrews. In stature, diminutive but well proportioned; absent-minded but sharp in repartee; in manner, dignified and courteous; a Liberal in politics; theistic but non-Christian; he gained the affection and loyalty of both colleagues and pupils, who recognized in him a man endowed with outstanding intellectual powers and possessed of wide learning and culture.

In 1899 Stout married Ella (died 1935), second daughter of the Rev. William Turnbull Ker, Free Church minister, of Deskford, Banffshire, and had one son. He relinquished his chair in 1936 and went to live with his son in Edinburgh. On the latter's appointment as professor of moral and political philosophy in Sydney, he accompanied him to Australia and died in Sydney 18 August 1944. A crayon drawing (1921) by James Paterson is in the possession of his son; there is a copy in pencil in the university of St. Andrews.

[G. F. Stout, *God and Nature*, 1952, edited by his son, A. K. Stout, with a memoir by J. A. Passmore, and a bibliography; C. A. Mace in *Proceedings of the British Academy*, vol. xxxi, 1945; *Australasian Journal of Psychology and Philosophy*, vol. xxii, 1944 (bibliography); *Mind*, July 1945; *British Journal of Psychology*, vol. xxxvi, part 2, 1946; private information; personal knowledge.]      J. N. WRIGHT.

STRACHAN, DOUGLAS (1875–1950), artist in stained glass, was born 26 May 1875 at Aberdeen, the eldest son of Hercules Strachan, a solicitor, by his wife, Isabella Davidson. He was educated at Robert Gordon's College and Gray's School of Art, Aberdeen, and then served an apprenticeship as lithographer in the office of the *Aberdeen Free Press*. Completing a year's study in the life school of the Royal Scottish Academy, he went to Manchester to become a black-and-white artist for several newspapers and political cartoonist on the *Manchester Chronicle* (1895–7). Thereafter he pursued his art studies in France and Italy, Spain and

Morocco, Holland, Vienna, Egypt, Palestine, Greece, and Constantinople. Returning to Aberdeen in 1898, he devoted himself to the mural decoration of the Trades and Music halls of that city, and to portraiture which shortly took him to London. But he could not express himself with entire satisfaction in portrait painting, and early in the century, back in Aberdeen, he found his true medium in stained-glass art which was to be his life's work and to win him an international reputation.

Among the earliest examples of this work are memorial windows in King's College chapel, Aberdeen. In 1908 he removed to Edinburgh where, from 1909 to 1911, he was head of the craft section in the Edinburgh College of Art. A great opportunity came his way when Sir Schomberg K. McDonnell [q.v.], secretary to the Office of Works, selected Strachan to execute the window group which Great Britain contributed to the Palace of Peace at The Hague. This was completed in 1913 and made Strachan's work known to a wider public. Later his fame was completely established with the seven glorious windows for the shrine of the Scottish National War Memorial in Edinburgh Castle (1927). These, like his other best work, have been compared with the windows of Chartres, Canterbury, York, King's College at Cambridge, and Fairford. His mastery is also to be seen in the memorial windows for the church of St. Thomas at Winchelsea (1929–33), and windows in Glasgow Cathedral and University chapel; in St. Giles' Cathedral, and in St. Margaret's chapel at the Castle, Edinburgh; and in St. John's church, Perth. Strachan himself considered that his finest work was the window in St. Paul's Cathedral, London, made for the Goldsmiths' Company in 1932 but subsequently destroyed by enemy action.

Strachan was elected an honorary member of the Royal Scottish Academy in 1920, received the honorary degree of LL.D. from Aberdeen University in 1923, and served on the Royal Fine Art Commission for Scotland, 1933–47. In later life he moved from Edinburgh to Pittendriech, Lasswade, Midlothian, where he combined a residence with a studio.

A keen reader, a lover of music, and an enthusiastic traveller, Strachan was, to quote Sir John Stirling-Maxwell, 'a man of great kindness and modesty and courage, with all the pride proper in a great artist, but without a trace of the vanity which in some artists is a besetting sin. As a companion he was interesting and stimulating, completely reliable, appreciative of the work of other artists, and a great lover of children.' Strachan's advent in stained-glass painting coincided with the Scottish renaissance in that art, on which his influence was profound and far-reaching. He never identified himself wholly with any art movement. Owing to the impress of a strongly personal style on all he achieved, his work is easily distinguishable. Instead of the obvious or the conventional, there is original conception and treatment. He often surmounted difficult technical problems, employed heavy leadwork in an unusual way, stressed the relationship between lighting, colour, and detail, and combined effectively colour design with mental appeal and human feeling. Suffused with poetic vision, his rich colour schemes always harmonize with the grey masonry of the best church architecture. In his many religious themes he seldom introduced a halo, rather favouring sometimes a symbol of modern import. His views on art are expressed in two lectures on 'Design and Craft' (1910) and 'Modern Art and the Future' (1918).

In 1909 Strachan married Elsie Isobel, daughter of John Cromar, dental surgeon, of Aberdeen; they had two daughters. He died at Pittendriech 20 November 1950. A self-portrait, executed when Strachan was a comparatively young man, is in the possession of the family.

[*The Times* and *Scotsman*, 21 November 1950; *Scotland's S.M.T. Magazine*, December 1948; *123rd Annual Report* of the Council of the Royal Scottish Academy, 1950; *Life and Work*, March 1951; *Catalogue* of the memorial exhibition of Strachan's works held in the Scottish Lyceum Gallery, Edinburgh, 1951; *Journal* of the British Society of Master Glass-Painters, vol. xi, No. 1, 1951–2; private information.]                           W. M. PARKER.

STRAKOSCH, SIR HENRY (1871–1943), financier, was born at Hohenau, Austria, 9 May 1871, the second son of Edward Strakosch, an Austrian sugar manufacturer, by his wife, Mathilde Winterburg. He was educated at the Wasa Gymnasium, Vienna, and privately in England, after which, in 1891, he entered upon a career in banking in London. A group of bankers in 1895 sent him to South Africa to wind up the affairs of a syndicate in which they were interested, and Strakosch next joined the staff of A. Goerz & Co., a South African mining finance house, later renamed the Union Corporation, Ltd. On the death of Adolf Goerz in 1900, Strakosch returned to London as manager and later as managing director (1902) and chairman (1924) of the company which during his leadership financed and developed some of the richest gold-mines on the Rand and paid dividends totalling twelve times its issued capital.

In public service the name of Strakosch, who was naturalized in 1907, is associated in the main with South Africa, the League of Nations, and notably with India. His advice was sought in 1919 by the Government of South Africa on currency and banking, and his recommendations, which were published in a pamphlet, *The South African Currency and Exchange Problem* (1920), were accepted in full by the Union Parliament and led to the establishment of the South African Reserve Bank, the first of its kind in the Empire outside the United Kingdom. Thereafter Strakosch was the representative of the Union of South Africa at successive congresses and conferences, including the Brussels conference of 1920, the Genoa conference of 1922, and the Imperial Conference of 1923. He was for seventeen years (1920–37) a member of the financial committee of the League of Nations and its first chairman (1920–21). He was thus closely connected with the reorganization of the currency of many states, notably of Austria, Hungary, Danzig, Estonia, Bulgaria, Greece, and, in 1928, of Portugal.

In the problems of Indian finance Strakosch had long been interested when he was appointed a member of the Royal Commission on Indian currency and finance in 1925. In this he played an influential part: the section of its report which recommended the creation of the Reserve Bank came from his pen and marked an advance towards Indian financial autonomy. In 1930 he was appointed a member of the Council of India, and on the dissolution of that body in 1937 he became adviser to the secretary of state for India until the breakdown of his health in 1942. Moreover he was delegate for India at the Ottawa conference in 1932 and at the world economic conference in London in 1933. Strakosch never lost sight in this work of the interests and aspirations of India, and Indian economists highly valued his advice.

In addition to this immense amount of committee work, Strakosch published a number of pamphlets and memoranda,

chiefly on gold and monetary policy. In one of them, 'Gold and the Price Level' (a supplement to *The Economist*, 5 July 1930), the evidence which he gave before the Macmillan committee was embodied. In 1929 he became chairman of the Economist Newspaper, Ltd., a position which he held until his death which took place, after an unsuccessful operation, at Walton-on-the-Hill 30 October 1943.

In 1941 Strakosch married Mabel Elizabeth Vincent (née Millett), widow of Joseph Temperley, shipowner, of Lower Kingswood, Surrey. He had been knighted in 1921 after the publication of his report on South African finance. In 1924 he was appointed K.B.E., and he was promoted G.B.E. in 1927 after the publication of the report on Indian currency. The university of Manchester conferred upon him the honorary degree of LL.D. in 1938.

[*The Economist*, 6 November 1943; *The Times*, 1 and 2 November 1943; private information; personal knowledge.] C. E. T.

**STRANGWAYS, ARTHUR HENRY FOX** (1859–1948), schoolmaster, music critic, and founder-editor of *Music and Letters*, was born 14 September 1859 at Norwich, the eldest son of Captain (later Colonel) Walter Aston Fox Strangways of the Royal Artillery, and his wife, Harriet Elizabeth, second daughter of John Edward Buller, of Enfield. In the paternal line he was descended from Sir Stephen Fox [q.v.].

Fox Strangways was educated at Wellington College and Balliol College, Oxford, where he was placed in the third class in *literae humaniores* in 1882. For the next two years he studied music, especially the piano, at the Hochschule in Berlin, but he did not at once enter the musical profession. He was a schoolmaster first at Dulwich College (1884–6), then at Wellington (1887–1910). In 1893 he also became organist but relinquished this on becoming a tutor in 1901. On his retirement from Wellington he visited India, where his field-work and researches resulted in *The Music of Hindostan* (1914) which still holds its place as an authoritative work. On his return in 1911 he wrote occasional criticisms of concerts for *The Times* and shortly afterwards joined the staff, writing regularly in the absence on war service of his senior colleague, but by far his junior in years, H. C. Colles [q.v.]. In 1925 he joined the staff of the *Observer* as music critic, where he remained until the outbreak of war in 1939. A selection from his weekly articles edited by (Sir) Steuart Wilson was published in 1936 under the title *Music Observed*. He was a considerable contributor to the third edition of *Grove's Dictionary of Music and Musicians* (1927) which Colles edited. In 1933 he wrote in collaboration with Miss Maud Karpeles the life of his friend and colleague, founder of the English Folk-Dance Society, Cecil Sharp [q.v.].

His main contribution to musical journalism was the establishment of *Music and Letters*, a quarterly review appearing first in January 1920, of which he was sole proprietor as well as editor. The avowed objects were expressed in a manner wholly characteristic of the editor who wrote that music was 'a subject of rational enquiry like any other' and that it was not needful to be 'so busy with ideas as to be careless of words'. In this spirit he continued the journal until the end of 1936, when it was rescued from disappearance by the transfer of its responsibilities to Mr. Richard Capell. In the earlier years of the journal Fox Strangways had interested himself in printing translations into English of German *lieder*, most of which were his own versions. In 1924 a volume called *Schubert's Songs Translated* and in 1928 a similar volume of Schumann, and later a small album of Brahms, were issued, all in conjunction with (Sir) Steuart Wilson. After his retirement to Devon in 1939 in his eightieth year, Fox Strangways completed single-handed the translation of all the songs of Brahms, Hugo Wolf, and Richard Strauss, and most of the songs of Liszt. These versions in typescript were deposited in the music library of the British Broadcasting Corporation in 1947. As well as this not inconsiderable task he planned and partly completed an anthology of English verse never set to music, but of suitable quality, as a useful time-saver for students without literary experience. He died, unmarried, 2 May 1948 at Dinton, near Salisbury, the birthplace of Henry Lawes [q.v.].

Fox Strangways brought into the field of musical journalism an intellect trained to exactitude of observation and of subsequent expression. His twenty-five years of schoolmastering had not narrowed his interests; he had contrived to combine with his duties the pleasure of riding to hounds. Although he lacked sympathy with all forms of fiction, he had a strong vein of poetry and romanticism in his nature and a deep appreciation of the profounder emotions which music could arouse. This was well expressed in the final sentences of his article on Indian music in *Grove's Dictionary*: this music, he wrote, 'reveals man in the presence of God. We do not and we shall not make much out of it without patience and practice, but it is worth both. We say no less, but we can say no more, of our own.'

Two pencil drawings of Fox Strangways were made by Sir William Rothenstein.

[*Grove's Dictionary of Music and Musicians*; *Music and Letters*, July 1948; private information; personal knowledge.]

STEUART WILSON.

STRATHMORE AND KINGHORNE, fourteenth EARL OF (1855–1944). [See BOWES-LYON, CLAUDE GEORGE.]

STRONG, EUGÉNIE (1860–1943), classical archaeologist and historian of art, was born in London 25 March 1860, the elder daughter of Frederick William Sellers by his wife, Anna, daughter of Charles Oates, British consul-general at Naples. Her maternal great-grandfather was the Baron du Cluseau, of the Château de Clérant in the Périgord (Dordogne). She had a cosmopolitan education, first at Valladolid in Spain, then in France, at the convent of the Sisters of St. Paul at Dourdan, and finally at Girton College, Cambridge, where she obtained a third class in the classical tripos of 1882. Deciding to make archaeology her career, she went to London to study and was soon invited to give university extension lectures and demonstrations on Greek art at the British Museum. After a short period in Greece as a student of the British School at Athens, she worked for some years in Germany with Adolf Furtwängler, whose *Meisterwerke der griechischen Plastik* she translated into English in 1895. This was the most notable of her early publications on Greek subjects. But her historical introduction and commentary to *The Elder Pliny's Chapters on the History of Art*, published in 1896 with a translation by Katharine Jex-Blake, formed a link between Greece and Rome; and in 1900 her translation, with preface, under the title of *Roman Art*, of Franz Wickhoff's study of the miniatures in the Vienna codex of the book of Genesis marked her final choice of Roman archaeology as the major field of her activities.

In 1897 Eugénie Sellers married Sandford Arthur Strong [q.v.], the distinguished orientalist and historian of art, librarian to the Duke of Devonshire and keeper of the collections at Chatsworth; they had no children. After her husband's death in 1904 she carried on his work at Chatsworth, and also published, in 1907, her most significant and enduring contribution to scholarship, *Roman Sculpture from Augustus to Constantine*. This remarkable piece of pioneer work may be said to have secured recognition for Roman art as a subject worthy of attention on its own merits, not as a mere appendix to Greek art. It also secured for its author her appointment, in 1909, as assistant director of the British School at Rome; and in Rome she lived until her death.

In Rome, as an apostle of 'Romanità', Mrs. Strong was increasingly inclined to trace the secret of imperial art to a native Italic quality, which, as it were, resisted, and maintained itself against, the tide of Hellenic influence. This tendency, which sometimes led her to underestimate Rome's continuity with Greece and to underrate the services rendered by contemporary Greek artists to the imperial idea, runs through all her most important writings— the revised and enlarged edition, in Italian, of *Roman Sculpture* (1923–6), *Art in Ancient Rome from the Earliest Times to Justinian* (2 vols., 1929), and the two chapters entitled 'The Art of the Roman Republic' and 'The Art of the Augustan Age' which she contributed to volumes ix (1932) and x (1934), respectively, of the *Cambridge Ancient History*. Her *Apotheosis and After Life* (1915) is of especial interest as revealing that deep sensitiveness to the symbolic and religious aspects of Roman art which made her so attractive an interpreter, in particular, of the stucco reliefs in the underground basilica near the Porta Maggiore in Rome, which came to light in 1917. She was a frequent contributor to the *Journal of Roman Studies* and to other learned periodicals; and her reports on archaeological discoveries in Italy became a valuable feature of the *Times Literary Supplement*.

Mrs. Strong's interest in post-classical art is illustrated by her *La Chiesa Nuova* (S. Maria in Vallicella), published in 1923, and by a history of the Vatican Palace, upon which she had embarked, but which she did not live to complete.

In 1920 Mrs. Strong delivered the Rhind lectures in Edinburgh on Roman painting. She was a life fellow of Girton College, was appointed C.B.E. in 1927, and was awarded the Serena gold medal for Italian studies by the British Academy and the

gold medal of the city of Rome in 1938. She received honorary degrees from the universities of St. Andrews and Manchester and was a member of a number of British and foreign learned societies.

Mrs. Strong retired from the British School at Rome in 1925; but she continued, at her flat in the Via Balbo, that life of unremitting study and hospitality which made her rooms an intellectual and social centre for scholars, students, and distinguished persons of all types and nationalities. She died in Rome 16 September 1943.

[*The Times*, 21 September 1943; *Antiquaries Journal*, vol. xxiii, 1943; *Cambridge Review*, 20 November 1943; *Bibliography of Eugénie Strong*, 1938; Gladys Scott Thomson, *Mrs. Arthur Strong: A Memoir*, 1949; personal knowledge.]     J. M. C. TOYNBEE.

STRONG, THOMAS BANKS (1861–1944), bishop successively of Ripon and Oxford, was born in Brompton, London, 24 October 1861, the eldest of the family of three sons and one daughter of Thomas Banks Strong, a clerk in the War Office, by his wife, Anna Lawson. Strong's mother was a learned Hebraist; Eugénie Strong (above) was the wife of his brother S. A. Strong the orientalist [q.v.]. He went to Westminster School in 1873, when only eleven years old, and gained an exhibition there in the following year. In 1879 he matriculated at Christ Church, Oxford, as a junior student, and was awarded a first class in classical moderations in 1881 and a second class in *literae humaniores* in 1883. In 1884 he was appointed lecturer at Christ Church, and in 1888 he was elected to a studentship, having been ordained deacon in 1885 and priest in 1886. In 1892 he was promoted to be censor and held that office for nearly twice the usual period until 1901, when he was nominated to be dean on the recommendation of his predecessor, Francis Paget [q.v.], who that year became bishop of Oxford.

Strong began his work at Christ Church as tutor of candidates for the honour school of theology as well as of many pass-men. That he was a good scholar and a skilled theologian is shown by his *Manual of Theology* (1892), a blend of the old orthodoxy and the new learning; by his Bampton lectures for 1895 on *Christian Ethics* (1896), in spite of their obvious limitations; and by his thesis for the B.D. degree (*The Doctrine of the Real Presence,*

1899). But it was in his strong pastoral instinct that he revealed his true self. Those who knew Christ Church well and were intimate with him between the years 1888 and 1920 would say that there was a distinction about him which escaped the notice of the casual observer. Retiring and shy, sometimes even awkward in company, neither fluent as an orator, eloquent as a preacher, nor lively and attractive as a writer, nevertheless he had a quality which made members of the House feel that, when he left, the place would never be the same again. The link between him and them was one of real affection, and that was one reason why, in spite of a casualness, almost a flippancy, of manner, he came through a most difficult and trying period as censor of Christ Church with a reputation greatly enhanced, and why, after nearly twenty years as dean, he found his fullest happiness among the junior members of the university. Of their mutual affection his correspondence with all sorts of younger men during the war of 1914-18 was abundant evidence.

Outside the House Strong had long been prominent. He was intimate with the *Lux Mundi* fellowship, and he regularly joined them at Longworth while Dr. John Richardson Illingworth was rector there. He received but did not accept an invitation to succeed Robert Lawrence Ottley as principal of Pusey House, and from 1906 he was actively engaged in the Lower House of the Convocation of Canterbury on the revision of the Prayer Book. As examining chaplain to Bishops Lightfoot and Westcott [qq.v.] and as an intimate friend of Bishop Harold Ernest Bilbrough and Henry Edwin Savage, dean of Lichfield, he had gained acquaintance with the north of England and its parochial problems. But it was his vice-chancellorship of Oxford (1913-17) which made him well known to the outside world. That heavy office was made many times more exacting by the outbreak of war in August 1914. He then presided over a small committee to deal with applicants for commissions. His most remarkable skill as a chairman and his shrewd judgement of men enabled the committee to interview 2,000 candidates before term began in October. He seemed to have an uncanny insight into the men before him, and in many cases he kept up his interest in them during their time in the forces. His excellence as an administrator became widely known, and appointment as G.B.E.

for his services followed in 1918. It was not therefore surprising to those who knew him that he was offered the bishopric of Ripon in 1920.

If Ripon was not Christ Church, at any rate he was happy there. Much of the work appealed to him, especially in the great urban area of Leeds where he was always welcome and where he was able to make some contribution to the university in its earlier days. The change, however, to the bishopric of Oxford in 1925 was another matter. He was sixty-four years old; health and eyesight were impaired; the diocese was agricultural, and he was a Londoner. The connexion with the university of Oxford had been snapped, although he was still an active and trusted delegate of the Press. There his skill was long remembered in the reading of musical proofs, for he was no mean performer and composer, and he had a surprising gift of musical appreciation. When he became dean, he found among the deanery papers a letter from Sir John Stainer recommending him to Dean H. G. Liddell as cathedral organist in the place of C. W. Corfe [qq.v.]. It may well be that his greatest happiness at the end of his life was at Cuddesdon, where his close touch with the college enabled him to renew the love for the young which was one of his chief titles to remembrance at Christ Church. He retired in 1937 and died, unmarried, in London 8 June 1944.

Strong's gifts were too variegated and his character was too elusive for him to be placed in any category. As a conversationalist among intimates he was supreme, for his mind was as rapid as quicksilver, whimsical and unexpected, taking up the conversation as it came, and making it sparkle with felicitous anecdote. Perhaps posterity may learn more about him from the portrait by Sir William Orpen which hangs in the Hall at Christ Church than from any words. There is also a drawing by Sir William Rothenstein in the senior common-room.

Honorary degrees were conferred upon Strong by the universities of Durham (D.D., 1913), Oxford (D.Mus., 1917), and Leeds (Litt.D., 1922).

[Harold Anson, *T. B. Strong*, 1949; private information; personal knowledge.]

C. M. BLAGDEN.

STRUTT, ROBERT JOHN, fourth BARON RAYLEIGH (1875-1947), experimental physicist, was born 28 August 1875 at the family home, Terling Place, Essex.

He was the eldest son of the renowned physicist John William Strutt, third Baron Rayleigh [q.v.]. His mother was Evelyn Georgiana Mary, daughter of James Maitland Balfour, of Whittinghame, East Lothian, and sister of the first and second Earls of Balfour, F. M. Balfour, and Eleanor Mildred Sidgwick [qq.v.]. As a boy Strutt was somewhat aloof, a form of shyness produced perhaps through the workings of a mind of fine quality striving to show its own individuality in a brilliant milieu and perplexed by innumerable questions which might be amenable to scientific attack. This characteristic never quite left him even when he had won renown by his discoveries. It was not such as led to self-effacement, for he had self-assurance and a kindly humour. Although his temperament might have led him to withdraw from the world of affairs, he fulfilled his part as to both scientific responsibilities and those of his estate.

Strutt was at Eton from 1889 to 1894; he won the college science prize and entered Trinity College, Cambridge, in October 1894, graduating with a first class in both parts of the natural sciences tripos in 1897 and 1898 respectively. He shared with (Sir) Henry Dale the award of a Coutts Trotter studentship in 1898. Soon after graduating he began to publish results of experimental work carried out under the influence of (Sir) J. J. Thomson [q.v.] in the Cavendish Laboratory. He was a fellow of Trinity, 1900–6. In 1908 he was appointed professor of physics at the Imperial College of Science and Technology, South Kensington, remaining until he succeeded to the title on the death of his father in 1919, and being appointed emeritus professor in 1920. He was chairman of the governing body of the College from 1936 until his death.

Rayleigh was an experimental philosopher who, like Henry Cavendish [q.v.], worked independently out of pure curiosity, inquiring zealously into the ways of nature. His work was carried out entirely by himself (he had one laboratory assistant, R. Thompson, who came to him as a boy in 1908 and remained with him throughout); much of it was done in his private laboratory at Terling Place. He was a prolific and skilful investigator. His papers number over 300, of which 113 were published in the *Proceedings* of the Royal Society: far more than those of any other fellow in the same period. His inquiries ranged wide. His most important contributions were his investigations into

the age of minerals and rocks by measurements of their radioactivity and helium content, his discovery of active nitrogen, and his studies of the resonance and fluorescence of metallic vapours excited by electric discharges. But a number of other subjects came under his investigation: electrical discharges *in vacuo*, the Becquerel rays, ozone in the atmosphere, the light of the night sky, optical contact, the green flash at sunset, the glow of phosphorus, iridescent colours in nature, the bending of marble and glass, and the formation of pebbles, pallasites, and red sandstones. His work on the helium content of rocks was pioneering research and led to a great extension of the estimate of Lord Kelvin [q.v.] of the age of the earth, and a closer accord with geological evidence.

Rayleigh was very methodical in his ways, and in keeping with this characteristic his papers are a model of lucid presentation. He was author of one of the earliest books on radioactivity—*The Becquerel Rays and the Properties of Radium* (1904). He also wrote two admirable biographies, one of his father (1924) and the other of Sir J. J. Thomson (1942), and a number of other authoritative notices in memory of distinguished men of science.

Rayleigh was elected F.R.S. in 1905; he served twice on the council before becoming the Society's foreign secretary (1929–34). He received the Rumford medal in 1920. He was chairman of the executive committee of the National Physical Laboratory (1932–9), president of the Physical Society of London (1934–6), and joint president of the International Congress of Physics held in London in 1934. He went to South Africa in 1929 as president of the mathematics and physics section of the British Association and was president of the Association in 1938 at the meeting in Cambridge. He made clear in his presidential address that science could not be held responsible for the way the results of scientific investigations were applied. He was president of the Royal Institution from 1945 until his death, and during the course of his life he delivered in the Institution eight Friday evening discourses on different subjects. He gave a lecture for the Royal Society on 'Newton as an experimenter' on the occasion of the tercentenary of Newton's birth.

Honorary degrees were awarded to Rayleigh by the universities of Dublin (Sc.D., 1913), Durham (D.Sc., 1929), and Edinburgh (LL.D., 1933). He served on the Advisory Council of the Department of Scientific and Industrial Research (1929–34). For many years he was a member of the committee of the Radium Institute and served as chairman of the civil research committee on radium requirements (1928). He was also a member of Royal Commissions on awards to inventors and on nitrogen requirements. Amongst other public duties he was a trustee of the Beit memorial fellowships (1928–46), a fellow of Eton College (1935–45), and a justice of the peace for Essex. He was president of the Central Council of Milk Recording Societies (1939). He took active interest in the debates in the House of Lords and spoke on several occasions on matters relating to science. Like his father, he was interested in the physical aspects of psychical phenomena. His outlook was consistently that of a man of science on all matters, his work imbued with something of the spirit of experimental philosophers of bygone times, and his character noble and kindly. He died at his home in Essex 13 December 1947.

In 1905 Strutt married Lady Mary Hilda Clements, second daughter of the fourth Earl of Leitrim. By this marriage he had three sons and two daughters, and he was succeeded as fifth baron by his eldest son, John Arthur (born 1908). His first wife died in 1919, only a few weeks before the death of his father. In 1920 he married Kathleen Alice, O.B.E., widow of Captain James Harold Cuthbert, D.S.O., Scots Guards, of Beaufront Castle, Northumberland, and eldest daughter of John Coppin Straker, of Stagshaw House, Northumberland. Lady Rayleigh had three sons and one daughter by her first marriage and one son by the second. The family circle was therefore a large one. There is an oil portrait of Rayleigh by Melton Fisher at Terling Place and a drawing by Augustus John is in the possession of the family.

[Sir Alfred Egerton in *Obituary Notices of Fellows of the Royal Society*, No. 18, November 1949.]    A. C. EGERTON.

STUBBS, SIR REGINALD EDWARD (1876–1947), colonial governor, was born in Oxford 13 October 1876, the youngest of the five sons of the Rev. William Stubbs [q.v.], the eminent constitutional historian who became bishop successively of Chester and Oxford. From Radley he won an exhibition to Corpus Christi College, Oxford, and, having inherited his father's scholastic ability, took a first class in classical moderations (1897) and in *literae humaniores* (1899). In 1900 he passed into the Civil Service and was posted to the Colonial Office, where he served for thirteen years.

In those days there was little if any interchange between the staff of the Colonial Office and the Colonial Service overseas, but to this practice Stubbs became one of the early exceptions. In his relatively short service in an Office where promotion was not rapid, he had already made his mark as a forceful, determined man who knew his mind and was prepared to speak it. In 1910–11 he was on a special mission to Malaya and Hong Kong which proved the prelude to his appointment in 1913 as colonial secretary of Ceylon. There he remained throughout the war of 1914–18 and so consolidated his reputation that in 1919 he received unprecedentedly quick promotion to the important governorship of Hong Kong. Despite boycotts and troubles on the mainland affecting Hong Kong, he served with success for the full term of six years. In 1926 he was transferred as captain-general and governor-in-chief to Jamaica, where again he remained six years. Jamaica, largest of the British Antillean colonies, was already in the throes of the constitutional growing pains which preceded the grant of the 1944 constitution based on universal adult suffrage. Stubbs, with his lack of illusions, caustic tongue, and disinclination to suffer fools gladly, was well fitted to keep those strivings within the bounds of realism.

On the expiry of his term of office, there fell vacant the governorship of Cyprus, a post of lesser financial importance than either Hong Kong or Jamaica. Nevertheless Stubbs accepted the post, partly because he wanted to be nearer home, partly perhaps because he had read two masterly lectures on 'The Medieval Kingdoms of Cyprus and Armenia' delivered by his father as regius professor of modern history at Oxford some months after the British occupation of Cyprus in 1878. It was a good appointment, for Cyprus was still smarting from the effects of the disturbances of 1931 and required the direction of an experienced hand.

Stubbs was not left there for more than a year. In 1933 he complied with the request of the Colonial Office to return, as governor, to Ceylon; and he remained there until 1937 when he retired on pension after the unusual experience of having held three first-class governorships and one other. He undertook one more colonial duty in 1938–9 when he revisited the Caribbean as vice-chairman of the important West India Royal Commission under Lord Moyne [q.v.] which led to the setting up, among other things, of the West Indian department of development and welfare, of which Sir Frank Stockdale [q.v.] became comptroller.

Stubbs was a lover of animals, especially of Siamese cats, and was a fellow of the Zoological Society. He did not emulate his father's literary and historical pursuits except to the extent of editing a volume of Sir Charles Lucas's *Historical Geography of the British Colonies*; but he inherited more than his share of his father's directness of speech.

On retirement Stubbs settled eventually at Bearsted in Kent where he died suddenly of heart failure 7 December 1947. For the six years preceding his death he was chairman of the northern division appellate tribunal for conscientious objectors. He was appointed C.M.G. in 1914, K.C.M.G. in 1919, and G.C.M.G. in 1928, and had received the first class of the Japanese Order of the Rising Sun. He was elected an honorary fellow of Corpus Christi College in 1926.

In 1909 Stubbs married Winefrid Marjory, daughter of a London doctor, Frederick Womack. She received the C.B.E. in 1919 and survived her husband. They had two sons and one daughter. A portrait by Mrs. Alabaster is in the possession of the family.

[*The Times*, 9 December 1947; personal knowledge.]                H. C. LUKE.

STUDD, SIR (JOHN EDWARD) KYNASTON, first baronet (1858–1944), philanthropist, was the eldest of three well-known cricketing brothers, the sons of Edward Studd, of Tidworth House, Marlborough, Wiltshire, an indigo planter in Bihar, by his second wife, Dorothy Sophia, daughter of John Thomas, a Calcutta merchant, of Bletsoe, Bedfordshire. He was born at Netheravon, Wiltshire, 26 July 1858, and was educated at Eton and Trinity College, Cambridge, taking his degree in 1884. He was in the cricket eleven at both Eton and Cambridge. With his brothers he played in 1882 in the university side which beat the Australians by six wickets, and in 1884 he was captain of the Cambridge eleven. In 1930 he was elected president of the Marylebone Cricket Club.

It had been intended that Kynaston Studd should join the family firm of J. Thomas & Co., but Dwight L. Moody, the evangelist, was a friend of his father and invited Kynaston, who had given up all his prospects in the City in order to train as a medical missionary, to conduct evangelistic work. Nothing came of this project, but when Quintin Hogg [q.v.] asked him to join in pioneering the Regent Street Polytechnic, Studd accepted, and thenceforward became Hogg's lieutenant. He was honorary secretary from 1885, vice-president in 1901, and, on Hogg's death in 1903, president of the Polytechnic. He held the office until his death.

Studd was also a keen freemason, being junior grand warden in 1929, president of the board of benevolence, and provincial grand master for Cambridgeshire from 1934. As a volunteer, he was commandant of the West London Volunteer Corps, and, with the rank of major, a member of the general purposes committee of the Territorial Forces Association from its inception until 1936. For his services during the war of 1914–18 he was appointed O.B.E. in 1919.

It is remarkable that one who had deliberately turned his back on a business career should have become lord mayor of London. He entered upon civic life at the instance of members of the Polytechnic, and it was not until he was well advanced in middle age that he joined a City company, the Fruiterers, and later the Merchant Taylors. He stood as a candidate for the shrievalty, and was elected senior sheriff in 1922. During his year of office he succeeded Sir William Treloar [q.v.] as alderman of Farringdon Without. In 1928 he was elected lord mayor, and entered on a mayoralty marked by his splendid entertainment of King Fuad II of Egypt, an official visit to Amsterdam where he received the gold medal of the city, and, to the great delight of the cricketing world, a dinner at the Mansion House to many of the leading cricketers of the day. Studd was knighted in 1923 and created a baronet in 1929. In the same year he received the honorary degree of LL.D. from the university of Cambridge.

Studd was twice married: first, in 1884 to Hilda (died 1921), daughter of Sir Thomas William Brograve Proctor-Beauchamp, fourth baronet, of Langley Park, Norwich, by whom he had four sons and one daughter; and secondly, in 1924 to Princess Alexandra, daughter of Prince Paul Lieven, grand master of the ceremonies at the imperial court of Russia.

One of his sons was killed at Ypres in 1915. Studd died in London 14 January 1944, and was succeeded in the baronetcy by his eldest son Eric (born 1887). His career is a conspicuous example of how a man, devoid of personal ambition, can be raised by his fellow citizens to the highest post they have to bestow, by their esteem for generosity in judgement as well as in gifts, high Christian example, great modesty, and unobtrusive but constant devotion to the service of mankind. A portrait of Studd as lord mayor by Alice Burton is in the possession of the Regent Street Polytechnic.

[*The Times*, 15 January 1944; private information; personal knowledge.]

B. STUDD.

SUTTON, SIR BERTINE ENTWISLE (1886–1946), air marshal, was born in Kensington 17 December 1886, the son of the Rev. Alfred Sutton, vicar of Bridekirk, Cockermouth, by his wife, Bertha Frances Entwisle, daughter of John Edward Walker. He was educated at Eton and University College, Oxford, and while an undergraduate became one of the original members of the Oxford University Mounted Infantry. He graduated B.A. in 1908 and worked for a time in a solicitor's office in London, but before long he joined the publishing firm of Hutchinson.

Soon after the outbreak of war in 1914 Sutton became a private in the Inns of Court Officers' Training Corps. In the autumn of that year he was commissioned as second lieutenant in the Westmorland and Cumberland Yeomanry and went to France. At the beginning of 1916 he was seconded to the Royal Flying Corps as an observer, and towards the end of that year gained his 'wings' as a pilot. During his service in France with the Army Co-operation squadrons, one of which he commanded, he distinguished himself by carrying out many valuable reconnaissances and patrols at low altitudes, particularly during the third battle of Ypres. For this fine work, during which he was wounded, he was awarded the M.C. in 1917 and later in the same year was appointed to the D.S.O. for conspicuous gallantry and devotion to duty. The citation added that 'by his energy, skill, and courage he set a magnificent example to his squadron'.

Sutton ended the war as an acting lieutenant-colonel in the newly formed Royal Air Force, and in 1919 was granted a permanent commission in that Service as a squadron leader (flying). In 1921 he attended the Army Staff College, and the following year had the distinction of being selected as one of the five original instructors on the formation of the Royal Air Force Staff College, where he proved himself a born teacher. He displayed there on one occasion the same example of courage as in the war. Practice parachute jumps from the air were being carried out and one parachute failed to open. The commanding officer of the station ordered the practices to stop, but Sutton, who was among those who saw the accident, asked for an aircraft to be kept in action, immediately put on parachute harness and proceeded to make a successful jump. In 1929 he was appointed Royal Air Force instructor at the Imperial Defence College. Two and a half years later he was posted to India where he commanded No. 1 Group near the frontier, and then served as senior air staff officer at air headquarters before returning to England in 1936 to command No. 22 Army Co-operation Group. By 1937 he had attained the rank of air vice-marshal.

On the outbreak of war in 1939 he was commanding No. 21 Group, and two years later returned to the Royal Air Force Staff College as commandant. Between 1942 and 1945, as an air marshal, he was a member of the Air Council, in the responsible post of air member for personnel. In June 1945 he retired from the Royal Air Force. He was appointed O.B.E. in 1919, C.B. in 1939, and promoted K.B.E. in 1942.

Sutton used to say that he was more interested in people than in anything else, and it was this characteristic, combined with his other gifts, which made him so fine a leader and so wise an administrator. Moreover, his innate friendliness which did not diminish as he rose in rank made him most popular with both officers and men. A penetrating mind lay behind his gaiety and keen sense of humour, and the easy charm which delighted his friends cloaked real firmness and determination which could, if the interests of the Service demanded, turn even to ruthlessness.

It was sometimes said of him that he would have been equally successful as a don; and undoubtedly his love of literature and the drama coloured his whole life. His fine critical faculties were ever on the alert in his scholarly explorations of literary highways and by-ways in verse and prose. Although not interested in

854

ordinary games, he took pleasure in many open-air activities, and he shared with his father, who became an honorary canon of Carlisle, a deep affection for his native Cumberland, and was always happy walking the fells, hunting or riding, and fishing in the Derwent.

In 1928 Sutton married Margaret Griselda, daughter of Alexander Dundas Ogilvy Wedderburn, C.B.E., K.C., and widow of Stuart Andros de la Rue, third son of Sir Thomas Andros de la Rue, first baronet [q.v.]. There were two sons of the marriage. Sutton was not destined to enjoy for long his retirement in his happy home near Newbury with his library, pictures, and garden. Never robust, the strain of his arduous war-time duties had undermined his health, and he died there 28 September 1946.

[Air Ministry records; private information; personal knowledge.]

E. BENTLEY BEAUMAN.

SWANN, SIR OLIVER (1878–1948), air vice-marshal, was born in Wimbledon 18 November 1878, the son of John Frederick Schwann, merchant, and his wife, Margaret Anne Holland. He was educated at a private school and then passed into the *Britannia* as a naval cadet. Whilst carrying out the normal duties of a naval officer he began to take an interest in flying; by the time he had reached the rank of commander he was selected, in 1910, to assist (Sir) Murray Sueter, who may well be called the father of naval aviation, in the construction and development of the naval airship which, in 1909, had been ordered from Vickers Sons & Maxim. This airship was built at Barrow in Furness but owing to structural weakness the vessel broke its back before it could be tested in flight. Meanwhile Schwann had changed his allegiance from the lighter- to the heavier-than-air vessel. From his own pocket he bought an Avro landplane, fitted floats to it, and although he had not yet qualified as a pilot succeeded in flying it off the water. Not surprisingly the aircraft crashed, but by Schwann's initiative and courage the seaplane was born.

In 1912 Schwann took his international aviator's licence and, becoming deputy to (Sir) Murray Sueter, director of the newly formed air department at the Admiralty, with him was largely instrumental in creating the Royal Naval Air Service. Shortly after the outbreak of war in 1914, Schwann, by then promoted captain, was given command of one of the first seaplane carriers, the *Campania*. He had not the good fortune to take part with his ship in any important naval action, but on the formation of the Royal Air Force in 1918 he was transferred with several other senior naval officers to high appointments in the new Service. He had by this time simplified the spelling of his name. In the course of his successful career in the Royal Air Force Swann became, as air member for personnel (1922–3), a very important member of the Air Council at a time when the future of the Service was in balance. Later he commanded the air force in the Middle East (1923–6) where his administrative ability and his charm of manner made him an efficient and popular A.O.C. It was somewhat ironical that one who was in the air department at the Admiralty when the Government's decision that there should be a unified air service—the Royal Flying Corps, naval and military wings—was flouted by the Admiralty, should end his career in the reconstituted and unified flying service, the Royal Air Force. It is to his credit that once he had cast in his lot with the Royal Air Force he gave it his undivided loyalty. He retired in 1929 but was re-employed during the war of 1939–45, although past the normal age for recall, and continued to devote himself to his country's service until he was sixty-five. He died at Guildford 7 March 1948. He was appointed C.B. and C.B.E. in 1919 and promoted K.C.B. in 1924.

In 1913 Swann married Elizabeth, daughter of William Laidlaw-Purves, aural surgeon, of London; they had one son and two daughters.

[*The Times*, 8 March 1948; personal knowledge.]

P. B. JOUBERT.

SWETTENHAM, SIR FRANK ATHELSTAN(E) (1850–1946), colonial administrator, was born 28 March 1850 at Belper, Derbyshire, the youngest son of James Oldham Swettenham, attorney-at-law, by his wife, Charlotte Elizabeth, daughter of Charles Carr. He was educated mainly by his mother until her death in 1861 when, the family being then in Scotland, he went as a day boy to a preparatory school. In 1866, while his two elder brothers were at Cambridge, he went for two years as a boarder to St. Peter's School, York. On the suggestion of his brother Alexander, already in the Ceylon Civil Service and later governor of Jamaica, he tried for a cadetship in the Straits

Settlements, passing out second of some twenty competitors.

Swettenham arrived in Singapore in January 1871, and being attached to the secretariat was set to learn Malay, in which he attained a proficiency that was to start his successful career. His education had not been such as to qualify him for research, as is shown by the obsolete history in his *British Malaya* (1906), and by the fragment of a Malay–English dictionary which he started to publish in 1886 in collaboration with (Sir) Hugh Clifford [q.v.]; but few cadets of the Straits Settlements, except Sir W. E. Maxwell [q.v.], had been distinguished for scholarship, and Swettenham's attainments in colloquial Malay were exceptional. In 1872 he was put in charge of the land offices at Penang and in Province Wellesley, where he came into daily contact with the Malay peasant. But now the young cadet's career was about to be made by a change in British policy. The humiliating Naning wars of 1830 and 1832, and the Siamese invasion and occupation of Kedah (1821–42), after that state had leased to the British the island of Penang and Province Wellesley, had made the home Government averse from intervention in the Malay States, however anarchic they might be. Under the East India Company and its successor the India Office (1858–67), even the colony of the Straits Settlements was regarded as a distant and burdensome residency. Soon after its transfer to the Colonial Office, it was decided, although reluctantly, to listen to the protests of Chinese merchants in the colony on the disorder in the adjacent states and to try to get the rulers to accept British advisers. Owing to his knowledge of Malay, Swettenham was sent to Larut in Perak to summon leading Chinese miners (whose followers had disturbed even sea traffic and Penang by faction fights) and also any Malay chiefs he could find to meet the governor of the colony, Sir Andrew Clarke [q.v.], on 15 January 1874, at Pangkor in the Dindings.

Swettenham's account of the Pangkor treaty, which led to Perak receiving a British resident, is not quite in accord with what came to be known later of Malay government; for in strict legality three claimants to the Perak throne and all the major chiefs should have been present. Only one claimant, Raja 'Abdullah attended, with those chiefs who favoured him. 'Abdullah was glad to sign any treaty that won him a throne. At the same time the heads of the rival Chinese mining factions undertook to destroy stockades, surrender war-boats, and restore ravished Chinese women. As one of a commission of three Swettenham spent an arduous month in seeing that the promise of the Chinese was kept. In August 1874 he was sent to live at Langat and give informal advice to the Sultan of Selangor. That ruler wrote to the governor that his young adviser 'is very able; he is also very clever in the customs of Malay government and at gaining the hearts of Rajas with soft words, delicate and sweet, so that all men rejoice in him as in the perfume of an open flower'. Malays always responded to the tact and tolerant cynicism which distinguished Swettenham, for these were characteristics they had in common. His youthful tact led to Selangor's acceptance of a British resident, Swettenham remaining as assistant resident.

In 1875 he was sent several times to Perak to help its resident, James Wheeler Woodford Birch, who was ignorant of Malay, in interviews with Sultan 'Abdullah. In October 1875, with Swettenham as interpreter, the new governor of the Straits Settlements, Sir W. F. D. Jervois [q.v.], interviewed the Perak ruler and decided to increase the powers of the British resident. The posting of the consequent proclamation was entrusted to Birch and Swettenham. Birch was killed by the Malays; Swettenham, who was up-river, escaped with Malay help past the scene of the murder. He was then appointed deputy commissioner with the expedition (1875–6) sent to arrest the murderers and pacify the state, receiving mention in dispatches and the governor's thanks for his 'courage, ability, energy, and zeal'.

After his first furlough in 1877 Swettenham spent the next four years in the Singapore secretariat in charge of Malay affairs, until in 1882 he became resident of Selangor and lived in the then village of Kuala Lumpur. He was now able to begin the work of inspiring and directing the material development of the Malay States in the shape of roads, railways, and government buildings. Social services, other than the provision of schools and hospitals, were not then within the purview of administrators. Just as Malaya's land system will always recall the work of Sir W. E. Maxwell, so Swettenham's name is linked with its material development. Courage was needed to embark on long-term expenditure before rubber had begun to produce large revenues, and when even government servants were officially invited to invest in Malaya to assist its tardy progress. In 1884–5 Swettenham acted as resident of Perak, and walked over the main range from Slim in Perak to Pahang on a diplomatic mission to its Sultan. From April 1887–9 he remained resident of Selangor, and from 1889 until 1895 he was resident of Perak.

In 1895 the four states of Perak, Selangor, Negri Sembilan, and Pahang were federated, and Swettenham became their chief federal officer, styled resident-general. Whether the idea of a federation was first mooted by him or by the governor of the colony, Sir Cecil Clementi Smith, was a matter of dispute between them. It was, in any event, an obvious course, and Swettenham deserves credit for gaining the acceptance of the several states and for initiating the change.

In 1900 he was instructed to visit and report on the naval station at Wei-Hai-Wei. In 1901 he was appointed high commissioner for the Malay States and governor of the Straits Settlements, when he introduced legislation putting a prohibitive duty on the export of tin-ore to save the local smelting industry from American competition. In 1904 he retired after more than thirty years of 'exceptionally trying service', refusing the offer of the governorship of Kenya. In 1909 Swettenham was appointed chairman of a Royal Commission to report on the finances of Mauritius. On the outbreak of war he became first an assistant director of the Press Bureau under F. E. Smith (later the Earl of Birkenhead, q.v.), and from 1915 joint director. He was appointed K.C.M.G. in 1897, G.C.M.G. in 1909 and C.H. in 1917.

A keen hunter, a good shot, and a witty raconteur, Swettenham found a niche in British society not generally attained by a colonial civil servant. For a decade he was a yearly visitor to many country-houses. After his retirement a number of directorships were offered him by rubber companies eager to benefit by his knowledge and acute practical brain. At the very end of his long life he played an active part in condemning Whitehall's policy and method of creating a Malayan union.

In 1878 Swettenham married Constance Sydney, daughter of Carlyle Frederick Holmes, J.P., of Druries, Harrow, whom he divorced sixty years later under the Matrimonial Causes Act of 1937, for she had long been of unsound mind; in 1939 he married Vera Seton, widow of Captain Neil Guthrie of the Irish Guards, and daughter of John Gordon. There were no children of either marriage. He died in London 11 June 1946. His portrait by J. S. Sargent hangs in the Victoria Memorial Hall, Singapore.

Swettenham's *Malay Sketches* (1895) and *The Real Malay* (1899) give impressionist pictures of the Malay of the last century. His best-known book was *Unaddressed Letters* (1898). After retirement he wrote *Also and Perhaps* (1912), *Arabella in Africa* (1925), and, at the age of ninety-one, his autobiography.

[Sir Frank Swettenham, *Footprints in Malaya*, 1942, and *British Malaya*, 1906; personal knowledge.]

R. O. WINSTEDT.

SYKES, SIR PERCY MOLESWORTH (1867–1945), soldier and administrator, was born at Canterbury 28 February 1867, the only son of the Rev. William Sykes, chaplain to the forces, by his wife, Mary, daughter of Anthony Oliver Molesworth, captain, Royal Artillery. He was educated at Rugby and the Royal Military College, Sandhurst, and was gazetted in 1888 to the 16th Lancers, transferring the same year to the 2nd Dragoon Guards. In 1893, when his regiment was in India, he made his first Persian journey, from the Caspian Sea to Kerman. Next year he travelled through Baluchistan and was appointed the first British consul for Kerman and Persian Baluchistan. After working with (Sir) Thomas Holdich [q.v.] on the Persia–Baluchistan boundary commission (1896), he founded in 1898 the consulate of Seistan and Kain. He was promoted captain in 1897.

Sykes served in the South African war in the intelligence department and commanded the Montgomery Imperial Yeomanry. He was wounded, mentioned in dispatches, and awarded the Queen's medal with three clasps. He transferred to the Indian Army in 1902, was promoted major in 1906 and lieutenant-colonel in 1914. Returning to Persia after the South African war he made another long expedition extending over several years. After some time in charge of the consulate-general he was appointed consul-general for Khorasan in 1906 and remained there until 1913. In 1915 he served as substitute to Sir George Macartney [q.v.], consul-general at Kashgar, in Chinese Turkestan.

Towards the end of 1915 most of South Persia was under German influence; German agents had organized a large body of Persian irregulars which threatened the flanks of the Mesopotamia Expeditionary Force. The greater part of the Persian gendarmerie had either gone over to the enemy, under the influence of their Swedish officers, or dispersed for lack of pay, and the country was approaching a state of anarchy. With the agreement of the Persian Government, Sykes, with the temporary rank of brigadier-general, was sent at the head of a mission to South Persia to raise a Persian force 11,000 strong to replace the gendarmerie. He arrived in Bandar Abbas in March 1916 with a handful of officers and a small escort, and at once began recruiting. In April he was reinforced by a section of mountain guns, 500 infantry, and a squadron of cavalry and in the next month he left for Kerman where in a friendly atmosphere he continued recruiting. On 14 August he reached Yezd whence he proceeded by forced marches to Isfahan to join the Russians who were threatened by the advancing Turks. He arrived on 11 September to find that the enemy had retreated. When it was clear that they would advance no farther and the Russian position had been strengthened, Sykes turned south to Shiraz (11 November) where he made the bold decision to absorb a mutinous gendarmerie of some 3,000 men in the South Persia Rifles. In this he was successful and gradually some semblance of order was restored to the country, a fact which was not without influence on the situation in Afghanistan and on the North-West Frontier of India. Sykes's achievement was due mainly to his unrivalled knowledge of the country and his high reputation and personal influence among the Persians.

In March 1917 the South Persia Rifles, never more than 8,000 strong, received recognition from the Persian Government only to have it withdrawn in June when a new Government took office. Anti-British propaganda increased and the situation had so far deteriorated by April 1918 that, in reply to a British note, the Persian Government denounced the South Persia Rifles as a foreign force. The publication of this reply deliberately encouraged local hostility to the presence of the British and gave rise to serious disaffection in the force. There was a rising under the Kashgai chief, Solat, and Shiraz was invested. An attack planned to coincide with a rising in Shiraz was forestalled by Sykes (16 June) who struck first at the tribesmen on the outskirts of the town and then seized the key-points in Shiraz itself. He next persuaded the governor-general to appoint a new chief in place of Solat whose supporters gradually deserted him and who was finally defeated in October. The war ended, Sykes left Persia, and in 1920 retired from the army.

Sykes was a scholar as well as a soldier, his literary output being considerable; in addition to describing his travels, he wrote historical, geographical, and biographical works, amongst them his *History of Persia* (2 vols., 1915), which was translated into Persian by order of the Persian Government, and his *History of Afghanistan* (2 vols., 1940). From 1932 until his death Sykes was honorary secretary of the Royal Central Asian Society; and for his journeys in Persia he was awarded the Back grant (1899) and the Patron's gold medal (1902) of the Royal Geographical Society. He was appointed C.M.G. in 1902, C.I.E. in 1911, K.C.I.E. in 1915, and C.B. in 1919.

He married in 1902 Evelyn, eldest daughter of Colonel Bruce Outram Seton, R.E., and had four sons and two daughters. He died in London 11 June 1945.

[Sir Percy Sykes, *Ten Thousand Miles in Persia*, 1902, and *Through Deserts and Oases of Central Asia*, with Ella Sykes, 1920; *The Times*, 13 June 1945; *Journal of the Royal Central Asian Society*, vol. xxxii, July–October, 1945; private information; personal knowledge.]          C. DALRYMPLE BELGRAVE.


SYMONS, ARTHUR WILLIAM (1865–1945), poet, translator, critic, and editor, was born at Milford Haven 28 February 1865, the second child and only son of the Rev. Mark Symons, Wesleyan Methodist minister, by his wife, Lydia Pascoe, both of old Cornish stock. Mark Symons's nephew and great-nephew were the artists William Christian Symons [q.v.] and Mark Lancelot Symons. Between 1865 and 1885 Arthur Symons's father was in charge of nine different circuits. 'I have never known', wrote Arthur Symons, 'what it is to have a home, as most children know it; a home that has been warmed through and through by the same flesh. . . . If I have been a vagabond and have never been able to root myself in any one place in the world, it is because I have no early memories of any one sky or soil. It has freed me from many prejudices in giving me its own unresting kind of freedom.'

Educated until he was sixteen in various

Devonshire schools, Symons was by nature introspective and self-absorbed and he determined from a very early age to devote his life to literature. He read much and as an adolescent composed a great number of poems. In 1884 he was introduced to Richard Garnett [q.v.] and in the same year F. J. Furnivall [q.v.] commissioned him to edit and preface certain volumes of the 'Shakspere Quarto Facsimiles'. When he was twenty-one his first article, which was on French literature, and his first critical work, *An Introduction to the Study of Browning*, were published. The latter was given an extremely good review in the *Guardian* by Walter Pater [q.v.], and from that time dated the friendship of the Oxford master for the young man who was to be so influenced by him. Symons became friendly, too, with John Addington Symonds, Ernest Rhys, Havelock Ellis [qq.v.], and Dykes Campbell. He edited several volumes for the 'Mermaid' series, the 'Camelot Classics', and the 'Henry Irving Shakespeare'. His first book of verse, *Days and Nights*, appeared in 1889.

From 1889 onwards Symons went frequently to France and rapidly became versed in its literature and art. There he knew Paul Verlaine, Stéphane Mallarmé, Rodin, and many others. He contributed regularly to the *Athenaeum*, the *Saturday Review*, and the *Fortnightly Review*. The part he played amongst the young writers of the 'nineties increased steadily in importance. He was a member of the Rhymers' Club with his friend W. B. Yeats [q.v.], and in 1896 with Aubrey Beardsley [q.v.] produced the *Savoy*. He published several books of poetry and criticism, not the least of them being his *Symbolist Movement in Literature* (1899) which proved him to be the finest observer of contemporary French literature. His tastes developed and he was soon 'one of the subtlest critics now writing, here or abroad . . . remarkable for wide sensibilities, for connoisseurship in music and painting and acting, as well as in literature, and for his willingness to judge a particular work of art on its own lines. . . . He can also transmit the emotions which a work of art has stirred in him, and he writes of these things like one possessed with the idea that the beauty which artists create and discover is as important as anything in the world.' ((Sir) Desmond MacCarthy in the *Albany Review*, May 1907.) In addition to his work as a critic Symons gave unparalleled evocations of many of the European cities which he loved; he wrote plays and had some of them performed; he edited anthologies and a number of other works, and made translations from authors in six languages.

A life so full wore down his health and in 1908 in Italy he broke down. For about two years he knew what he himself had once termed 'the fatal initiation of madness' when he was confined in mental hospitals suffering probably from manic depressive psychosis. Many years later he published an account of his experiences in *Confessions: A Study in Pathology* (1930). Only gradually did he return to normal, and he never completely found his former self. Although he continued writing, much of what he produced remained unpublished. Between 1919 and 1930 he seemed to recover his usual working rhythm, but his work, on the whole, attained less frequently its former quality. Without entirely ignoring the times, he yet shut himself apart with those artists and writers he had admired between 1890 and 1908.

Symons was an artist, contemptuous of success, perceptive, and scrupulous. His work was constructed on his own exacting faith in the eternal value of art and his epicureanism took the form of a quest for 'the universal science of Beauty'. He wrote an exquisitely sensitive prose which perfectly conveyed his personal impressions and aesthetic judgements on an eclectic field of art. In 1901 he brought out in two volumes poems published up till that date and in 1924 almost all his poems appeared again in the first three volumes of his collected works, together with two volumes of his tragedies and several of his critical works. The edition remained unfinished.

Symons married in 1901 Rhoda (died 1936), daughter of John Edward Bowser, a shipowner and shipbuilder of Newcastle upon Tyne. In 1906 he bought a beautiful twelfth-century dwelling, Island Cottage, at Wittersham in Kent where he died 22 January 1945. There are many portraits of him: one by J.-E. Blanche (1895) is in the Tate Gallery, where there are also two drawings by Augustus John; a portrait by John is now in the United States.

[Arthur Symons's own publications; *Times Literary Supplement*, 3 February 1945; A. B. Sklare, 'Arthur Symons: an Appreciation of the Critic of Literature' in *Journal of Aesthetics and Art Criticism*, June 1951; private information; private collection.]

ROGER A. LHOMBREAUD.

TAGORE, Sir RABINDRANATH (1861–1941), Indian writer, was born at Jorasanko, Calcutta, 6 May 1861, the youngest of the seven sons of Debendranath Tagore, the Maharshi, or 'great sage', a leader of a sect of strictly monotheistic beliefs based on the teachings of the Upanishads. His father was seldom at home and in his earlier years Tagore was left to the care of servants, tutors, and schoolmasters, but as he grew older he resisted further formal education and moved into the orbit of his highly intellectual family. The vast mansion, which in Hindu fashion housed his brothers with their wives and children, teemed with creative activity: 'we wrote, we sang, we acted, we poured ourselves out on every side'. It was not until late in life that Tagore turned seriously to painting, but his musical talent developed early—his songs became very popular in Bengal—and verse he wrote from the age of eight, when a relative introduced him to the *payar* metre of fourteen syllables. Through the three languages in which he was educated Tagore's formation as a writer may be traced to the Sanskrit classics, the English romantics, notably Shelley, and the poets of Bengal; in the Vaishnava lyrics which he began to study when he was fifteen he found 'lyrical movement; and images startling and new'. It was not long before he was writing poems, essays, reviews, and short stories for the periodical *Bharati*, produced by his brothers, and for other journals. His early work was imitative, but with the experimental poems published in book form as *Evening Songs* Tagore broke with tradition, 'found his genius', and established himself as a poet in his own right.

In 1883 Tagore married, and for some years afterwards he managed the family estate at Shileida on the banks of the Ganges. Here his talent matured; the Bengali landscape and the life of the country people were to be an enduring source of inspiration to him—in the abundant wealth of natural imagery in his verse, and not least in his short stories. At the turn of the century he 'found his language', but aroused criticism, by adopting the colloquial *hasanta*, the omission of the final vowel; this gave his verse greater variety and, when he wished, 'a ruggedness and craggy strength'. At about the same time his themes which had hitherto been secular became more spiritual. It was the most creative period of his life: a second edition

of his collected poems published in 1903 ran to thirteen volumes. There was in addition much journalism, for some years mainly in *Sadhana*, the writing of dramas, and the regular appearance of short stories.

Of Tagore's novels, several of which were written between 1901 and 1907, the best known and most influential was *Gora*, of which an English translation was published in 1924. It dealt with social problems among educated young Bengalis who had become westernized and had broken with their own traditions. In it, he defined his own attitude to the conflict between progress and tradition; a conflict to which he had sought to offer a solution, in a synthesis of Asian and European cultures such as he had achieved in his own writing, by founding (1901) a school at Santiniketan, Bolpur. Based on the old pattern of the *ashram*, the school nevertheless incorporated a number of Western ideas on education and discipline; in 1914 an agricultural school was added. From the first Santiniketan was envisaged as much more than a school; it was to be 'a home for the spirit of India'. Tagore was intensely patriotic, but after a spell of political activity at the time of the partition of Bengal he came increasingly to believe that the cultural and social regeneration of his people (the removal, for instance, of such abuses as child marriage and untouchability) was of greater importance for his country than political freedom as an end in itself. As a consequence his incursions into politics were rare.

It was not until 1912 that Tagore began to be known outside India. Within a year his reputation was world-wide and in November 1913 he was awarded the Nobel prize for literature. During a visit to England he had shown his own English translations of some of his poems to (Sir) William Rothenstein [q.v.] whom he had met in India. Rothenstein in turn showed them to W. B. Yeats and A. C. Bradley [qq.v.]; as a result *Gitanjali* ('Song Offerings') was published with an introduction by Yeats, in 1912 by the India Society for its members, and in 1913 for the general public. There followed a lecture tour in the United States (1912–13) and in England in the summer of 1913. Tagore made a deep impression. The fascination which the East has for the West was enhanced by his appearance—tall, stately, and serene, with flowing beard and curling hair, dark but already silvering—by his fluency of expression and melodious voice. Translations of his works—poems, symbolical dramas, short stories—and reprints of his lectures, his 'message to the western world', followed with more rapidity than discrimination. The drawing-room cult of the 'poet-seer' was encouraged at the expense of his more virile work and was not altogether beneficial to his serious reputation which, as Edward Thompson [q.v.] pointed out in 1921, 'began to decline, almost as soon as it reached its height'.

In 1919, after Amritsar, Tagore 'in giving voice to the protest of the millions of my countrymen' sought to renounce the knighthood which he had received four years earlier. Yet he was no supporter of the passive resistance urged by M. K. Gandhi [q.v.], for he believed that non-violence was for those who sought their spiritual perfection and that it was not safe to impose it upon all sorts and conditions of men for the attainment of a political end. In refraining from speech or conduct likely to provoke violence in others, Tagore exemplified his own conception of the creed, but at a time of rising nationalist feeling inevitably lost some popularity with his fellow countrymen. Far from wishing to isolate India from the West he now (1921) extended his ideas from India to the world by adding to his school an international university, Visvabharati: a centre to which scholars might come from any nation to exchange ideas and study the civilizations of the East with a view to a closer understanding between East and West. It was for the West in particular that in his own philosophical writings Tagore sought to interpret the main Indian tradition of the Upanishads and the *Bhagavad Gita*. He made no claim to originality as a philosopher. His aim was not to analyse or to speculate about this tradition but, by expressing it in his own vivid phrases and homely analogies, to show its relevance to life in the modern world. Although he drew his inspiration from the ancient wisdom of India he yet found much to admire in the practical achievements of the West, and in Christianity much that reminded him of his own faith. Indeed, to a European mind, he was perhaps too free an interpreter of both traditions, reading the one into the other and reconciling them too readily. Yet in this, too, he was the authentic representative of Indian thought which has frequently created through interpretation and made of interpretation a mode of creation.

Although he continued to write with remarkable freshness until the end of his life, Tagore was much occupied in his later years with his university and with travel abroad in the service of his ideal of a universal human culture and world unity; an ideal which met with diminishing response as the international situation deteriorated. Yet in Britain, as throughout the world, although critical judgement of his work varied and popular interest in him had to some extent declined, Tagore increasingly came to be respected as one of the most distinguished Indians of his day; a recognition which in turn added to his reputation in his own country. He was a man of great sincerity and nobility of character; an aristocrat of gentleness and courage, of grace and wit; a thinker, a dreamer; and above all else a lyrical poet inspired for over sixty years by the wonder of the created world. To the West his qualities as a writer are not, and cannot be, fully known, for much of his best work remains untranslated and much has suffered even in his own translation. Nevertheless he was a product of Western influence whose greatest achievement as a writer was perhaps 'to have cut a channel in which the three by no means easily reconcilable influences of ancient Indian, modern European, and popular Bengali origin could happily mingle'. Certainly, as *The Times* recorded after his death, he was 'the most notable Indian writer . . . of the whole period of British administration in India'.

In 1930 Tagore delivered the Hibbert lectures at Oxford, published in the next year as *The Religion of Man*. At a special convocation of the university of Oxford held at Santiniketan in 1940 the honorary degree of D.Litt. was conferred upon him. A year later, 7 August 1941, he died at Calcutta. His wife died in 1902; a son survived him.

A self-portrait by Tagore sent from Visvabharati was in the Indian Exhibition in London in 1948. Among other portraits may be mentioned the *Six Portraits* (1915) by Rothenstein. A pencil drawing by the same artist is in the Tate Gallery and two more are in the Manchester City Art Gallery.

[Sir Rabindranath Tagore, *My Reminiscences*, 1917; E. J. Thompson, *Rabindranath Tagore, his Life and Work*, 1921, and *Rabindranath Tagore, Poet and Dramatist*, revised ed. 1948; V. Lesný, *Rabindranath Tagore, his Personality and Work*, translated by G. M. Phillips, 1939; *The Times*, 8 August

1941; *Times Literary Supplement*, 16 August 1941; J. C. Ghosh, *Bengali Literature*, 1948; private information.]

HELEN M. PALMER.

TAIT, JAMES (1863–1944), historian, was born at Broughton, Salford, 19 June 1863, the second son and third child in a family of twelve children of Robert Ramsay Tait, a seed merchant, who came from Jedburgh. His mother was Annie Case, a member of a well-known academic family: James Tait was proud of this connexion. At the age of sixteen, after attending a private school, he entered the Owens College, Manchester, just before it became a college in the new Victoria University. Tait was in fact one of the first history graduates (1883) of the new university with which, except for the years (1884–7) at Balliol College, Oxford (where he won an exhibition), his whole life was to be so closely associated. Returning to Manchester after obtaining a first class in modern history (1887), he served successively as assistant lecturer in English history and literature (1887), as lecturer in ancient history (1896), and as professor of ancient and medieval history (1902–19). From 1890 to 1897 he held a non-resident prize fellowship at Pembroke College, Oxford. After his retirement from the chair, for more than twenty years he lived quietly in Fallowfield and later at Wilmslow working indefatigably at his research, yet keeping in close social touch with the university. During these years he served (1925–35) as chairman of the Manchester University Press. His closest friend was Edward Fiddes, the former registrar, and their wise counsel was of great service to the university.

The keynote of Tait's life was his consuming interest in historical research, and it is by his reputation as a scholar that he will be chiefly remembered. None the less, he was a successful and painstaking teacher, and played a great part in the development of the Manchester history school. The foundations had already been well laid by R. C. Christie and (Sir) A. W. Ward [qq.v.] when in 1890 T. F. Tout [q.v.] succeeded Ward as professor of medieval and modern history, and thus began a thirty years' partnership which was deeply to influence the development of historical studies in Great Britain. Alike in nothing but their common devotion to research, Tout and Tait imparted to their school a new quality of exact scholarship, which slowly but surely won for it an in-

fluence out of all proportion to its size. The introduction of an undergraduate thesis, closely connected with the special subject, was their chief innovation, and the weight of the experiment was largely borne by Tait. The object was to make the undergraduate course a better bridge than heretofore to advanced study, and in this aim they achieved considerable success. There was a new insistence upon research which led in turn to the foundation of the Manchester University Press. Tait's *Mediaeval Manchester and the Beginnings of Lancashire* (1904), perhaps his best book, was the first volume in the historical series. Yet the broad lines were not forgotten and the Manchester course was almost alone in including the outlines of both ancient and European history. The continuous, obscure toil of undergraduate teaching, which this ambitious scheme involved, although it hampered, never crippled, Tait's own steady output of learned work; and retirement when it came was simply an opportunity for further undistracted research.

Apart from his teaching the events of Tait's life must be sought in his writings. A man of studied moderation in speech, reticent, and disliking any display of emotion, he did what is duly demanded in university politics and no more. His real life lay in his study. From 1891 to 1900 he contributed a great many articles to this DICTIONARY, a useful apprenticeship: and in the same period he began a long connexion with the *English Historical Review*, especially as a reviewer, a role for which his critical temper suited him to perfection. It was, in fact, a review (October 1897) of *Domesday Book and Beyond* by F. W. Maitland [q.v.] which first brought him to the front, and showed him to be as much a master of the early as of the later Middle Ages. Already he was drawn to municipal history, but the beginning made by his *Mediaeval Manchester* was not at once followed up. For the next fifteen years his energy was chiefly devoted to the volumes of the *Victoria County History* dealing with Lancashire, and to the Chetham Society, which flourished anew under his presidency (1915–25). After his retirement he returned to the borough, on which, in addition to editing the second volume of Adolphus Ballard's unfinished *British Borough Charters, 1216–1307* (1923), he published his definitive *Medieval English Borough* (1936). His last years showed no slackening of energy or loss of grip, and shortly before his death he completed an elaborate genealogical commentary on the Herefordshire Domesday.

The outstanding characteristics of Tait's work are its immense range and the exacting standards of his scholarship. He saw his medieval history as a whole, but with a temperamental caution confined himself severely to what could be demonstrated by exact proof. His influence, exercised chiefly through his reviews and an extensive private correspondence, was very great, and brought, although slowly, growing recognition with the years. In 1920 he was made an honorary professor and received the honorary degree of Litt.D. of Manchester University. The following year he was elected a fellow of the British Academy, from which in 1943 he generously resigned in order to make way for some younger scholar. From 1923 to 1932 he was first president of the English Place-Name Society, to which he made notable contributions, and in 1933 he was elected an honorary fellow of Pembroke, and received the honorary degree of D.Litt. from Oxford. The presentation, on his seventieth birthday (1933), of *Historical Essays in Honour of James Tait* marked him out as the most revered figure in English medieval studies.

Tait's whole life, it has been well said, was given to Manchester and to its university. He was unmarried and his tastes were of the simplest. A traveller and a great walker, he ordered his life so as to achieve the maximum of continuous, unflagging study. A lover too of literature, music, and painting, he could find relaxation in the reading of novels and more particularly in detective fiction. His friendships were firm, if rarely intimate, and lasting; and since he took children seriously he was a coveted visitor in the homes of his married friends. He died suddenly at Wilmslow 4 July 1944.

A drawing of Tait by Ronald Allan is in the possession of the Manchester University Press.

[F. M. Powicke in *Proceedings* of the British Academy, vol. xxx (bibliography from 1934 to 1944), 1944; *English Historical Review*, vol. lx, May 1945; *Historical Essays in Honour of James Tait* (bibliography to 1933), 1933; personal knowledge.]    V. H. GALBRAITH.

TAIT, SIR (WILLIAM ERIC) CAMPBELL (1886–1946), admiral, was born at Morice Town, Devonport, 12 August 1886, the eldest son of Surgeon, later deputy Surgeon-General, William Tait, R.N., by his wife, Emma, daughter of John Green-way, solicitor, of Ford Park, Compton Gifford, near Plymouth.

Entering the *Britannia* in 1902, Tait next served in the cruiser *Grafton* in the Pacific and then in the *Drake* in the Atlantic. He was promoted sub-lieutenant in August 1906 and after taking gunnery and navigation courses at Portsmouth joined the battleship *Prince of Wales* in the Mediterranean in May 1907, but transferred to the cruiser *Flora* on the China station in August. He returned home in the autumn of 1909 having been promoted lieutenant in April. Between 1910 and 1912 he was watchkeeper successively in the battleship *Irresistible*, the cruiser *Furious*, the battleship *Hindustan*, and the destroyer *Staunch*, all in home waters. He went next to the *Collingwood* in which he saw active service after the outbreak of war and was present at the battle of Jutland. In 1917 he was promoted lieutenant-commander, transferring to the *Malaya*, and during the last half of the year he was acting equerry to Prince Albert (later King George VI), being appointed M.V.O. In June 1919 he joined the royal yacht *Victoria and Albert* and in August 1921 was promoted commander. In January 1922 he took up an appointment for duty with naval officers under training at the university of Cambridge. Returning to sea in September 1922 he spent two years as executive officer of the light cruiser *Hawkins*, flagship of the commander-in-chief, China station. For the next two years he was training commander at Chatham and was promoted captain at the end of 1926.

After a senior officers' war course at Greenwich he returned to sea in February 1928 and commanded four cruisers in succession, an unusual occurrence in peacetime: the *Dragon* in the Mediterranean and the *Capetown*, *Delhi*, and *Despatch* on the America and West Indies station. Following a senior officers' course at Sheerness he became deputy director of the intelligence division of the naval staff at the Admiralty in April 1932. In November 1933 he joined the staff of the commander-in-chief, China station; and from 1934 to 1937 he commanded the cruiser *Shropshire* in the Mediterranean. In August 1937 he became commodore, and a year later rear-admiral, of the Royal Naval Barracks, Portsmouth. Here he greatly contributed to the smooth mobilization of the fleet in 1939 and was appointed C.B. in 1940. From May 1940 to his promotion to vice-admiral in October

1941 he was director of personal services at the Admiralty and in January and February 1942 flew his flag in the *Resolution* as vice-admiral commanding third battle squadron and second-in-command, Eastern Fleet. Then, until May 1944, he held the most important appointment of his naval career, that of commander-in-chief, South Atlantic, first at Freetown, Sierra Leone, and from March 1942 at Simonstown. In 1942 he played a notable part in the establishment of a combined headquarters at Cape Town. This was a striking example of Commonwealth co-operation. It owed its success to Tait and to Major-General I. P. de Villiers, then G.O.C. Coastal Command in South Africa. From the first, thanks to the skill and tact of these two men, the experiment was fully justified by its results. The existence of a combined headquarters meant much at a critical period of the war, when the U-boat peril was a menace to shipping in African waters. The Royal Navy and the South African Army and Air Force worked in the most complete and cordial co-operation. Tait was promoted K.C.B. in 1943 and retired in December 1944 on his appointment as governor and commander-in-chief of Southern Rhodesia, a post to which he brought all his outstanding gifts of judgement and tact. He was promoted admiral in May 1945 and died in Rhodesia 17 July 1946, having been in bad health for some time. Tait was a man of good physique and striking appearance, with a ruddy complexion, very pronounced bushy eyebrows, and red hair. He possessed a dry sense of humour but was a man of considerable reserve.

In 1919 Tait married Katie Cynthia, daughter of the late Captain Hubert H. Grenfell, R.N. [q.v.], inventor of illuminated night sights for naval guns and one-time naval attaché for Europe. They had two daughters.

[*The Times*, 18 July 1946; private information; personal knowledge.]

J. H. LHOYD-OWEN.

TAYLOR, ALFRED EDWARD (1869–1945), philosopher, was born at Oundle 22 December 1869, the elder son of the Rev. Alfred Taylor, a Wesleyan minister, and formerly a missionary on the Gold Coast, and his wife, Caroline Esther Fax. He was educated at Kingswood School, Bath, and at New College, Oxford, of which he was elected a scholar and, in 1931, an honorary fellow. He obtained first classes

in honour moderations (1889) and *literae humaniores* (1891). His career was entirely academic, beginning with a prize fellowship at Merton College, Oxford (1891–8), and after service as assistant lecturer in Greek and philosophy at the Owens College, Manchester (1896–1903), as Frothingham professor of philosophy at McGill University, Montreal (1903–8), as professor of moral philosophy in the university of St. Andrews (1908–24), it ended with the professorship of moral philosophy at the university of Edinburgh, from which he retired in 1941, while continuing to do the work of the chair until 1944.

Taylor was a man of very remarkable learning. On Plato he was an authority of international repute. With John Burnet [q.v.], who was his colleague at St. Andrews, he adhered steadfastly to the theory that most of what Plato in his dialogues attributes to Socrates comes from Socrates' own teaching; but this did not prevent him from learning from other Platonic scholars who did not share his views in this matter, notably in his later years from Professor Werner W. Jaeger, whose *Paideia* he wholeheartedly admired.

Men have said that Taylor was too learned ever to be a real philosopher, and that his knowledge, classical, historical, literary, scientific, and mathematical, interfered with sustained metaphysical analysis and construction. Certainly his scholarly work occupied much of his time, and he was incapable of writing without a wealth of learned allusion. Yet in the end, Taylor was a philosopher. His contribution was threefold. First, owing to his intimate friendship with F. H. Bradley [q.v.] when he was at Merton, his early work on conduct and metaphysical issues showed the influence of the Oxford brand of Hegelian idealism; but from this he emancipated himself, partly as a result of a study of the writings of Ernst Mach, partly as a result of association with Samuel Alexander [q.v.] at Manchester, and with G. F. Stout [q.v.] at St. Andrews, partly as a result of sustained study of Galileo, Leibniz, and Descartes. Gradually a revised conception of the task of metaphysical philosophy formed in his mind, and the fruits of it may be seen not only in his Gifford lectures delivered at St. Andrews in 1926–8 on *The Faith of a Moralist* (published in 1930) but in the earlier study of 'Theism' contributed to Hastings's *Encyclopaedia of Religion and Ethics*. This latter work is one of the most valuable introductions to theistic metaphysics in the English language, and is a noteworthy combination of scholarly and analytical acumen. It is perhaps of more lasting worth than his last book *Does God Exist?* (1945) where possibly too much weight is placed on the argument from design.

Secondly, Taylor's deep interest in the problems of religion drove him inevitably to a study of the medieval schoolmen. The fruits of this are to be seen in all the writings of his post-Bradleian period, and he is always remarkable for the discriminating freedom with which he handles scholastic concepts. His contribution to the development of neo-scholasticism is important because it is indirect. But, thirdly, it is as a moralist that his work is perhaps most important. His Edinburgh lectures have not been published; perhaps his handwriting will make it impossible; but in scattered articles on such problems as freedom, the nature of goodness, the relation of the right and the good, he showed something of the depth of his reflection. He was of course a profound student of Plato and Aristotle, as his works, including *Plato, the Man and his Work* (1926) and *A Commentary on Plato's Timaeus* (1927), show; but he had also mastered Kant's ethics, considering them of far greater importance than their author's theory of knowledge. To his students he conveyed the sense of standing in a great tradition of reflection on the problems of conduct, which he was concerned to expound and develop. With many of the moderns (for example, the Oxford deontological school) he was impatient; and by the time one had heard him out, the grounds of his impatience were clear.

Taylor was a strong Anglo-Catholic and on occasion spoke at Anglo-Catholic congresses as well as contributing to the well-known symposium *Essays Catholic and Critical* (edited by the Rev. Edward Gordon Selwyn, 1926). None who heard him speak on religion will easily forget the depth of his faith; none who knew him at all will forget the great kindness and generosity of which he was capable, shown not least to his assistants and to the very weakest members of his classes.

Honours bestowed on Taylor, besides his honorary fellowship, included the fellowship of the British Academy (1911), membership of the Accademia dei Lincei (1929), and of the Prussian Academy of Sciences (1936), together with honorary degrees from the universities of St. Andrews (D.Litt. and LL.D.), Manchester (Litt.D.), and Aberdeen (LL.D.).

In 1900 Taylor married Lydia Jutsum (died 1938), an authoress, second daughter of Edmund Passmore, of Ruggs, Somerset; there was one son. Taylor died in Edinburgh 31 October 1945.

[Sir W. D. Ross in *Proceedings* of the British Academy, vol. xxxi, 1945 (bibliography); *Guardian*, 16 November 1945.]

D. M. MacKINNON.

TEGART, SIR CHARLES AUGUSTUS (1881–1946), Indian police officer, was born in Londonderry 5 October 1881, the second son of the Rev. Joseph Poulter Tegart, priest-in-charge of the chapel-of-ease, and later rector of Dunboyne, county Meath, by his wife, Georgina Johnston. Educated at Portora Royal School, Enniskillen, and Trinity College, Dublin, Tegart entered the Indian Police in 1901 and was assigned to Bengal as a probationary assistant superintendent. In 1906 he was posted to Calcutta as acting deputy commissioner and found there the dominant interest of his life. The partition of Bengal in the previous year, although justified administratively, had deeply offended Bengali national feeling. The emotional Bengali character proved a ready soil for extreme political movements and a numerous student element largely ignorant and undisciplined was soon inflamed into anti-British and revolutionary violence which did not cease when partition was annulled in 1911. Murders, attempted murders, robberies by violence, derailments, thefts of arms, soon had a marked effect on both the administration and the general populace. Prosecutions failed because witnesses were intimidated, but the full fury of the terrorists turned upon those police officers employed in countering their plots. Several of the ablest lost their lives and the native police were subjected to a social ostracism peculiarly cruel in a caste-regulated society.

The Government had no option but to intern by regulation the more dangerous of the leaders and this temporarily checked a state of affairs which, after 1914, was worsening beyond control. The unrest in India had attracted the attention of Germany, whose officials and nationals in the United States joined with certain Indians in a plot to ship weapons to India for the use of revolutionaries. The scheme had serious possibilities but was fortunately soon discovered and defeated, an important base of operations being unearthed in Calcutta.

In the anti-terrorist campaign the services of Tegart, who became deputy commissioner in 1913, were outstanding, whether in respect of intelligence or of leadership. He had able lieutenants, British and Indian, but throughout he did more, knew more, and risked more than any of them. He had sources of information known only to himself, and had trained a band of watchers to a high degree of efficiency. Always he lived dangerously in the most literal sense and worked under the constant shadow of death. Numerous plots were laid against him, as well he knew, but they left him completely fearless and unperturbed. It was this stoutness of heart as well as patent mastery of his job which animated and sustained his officers in the face of a common duty and common danger, binding them to him in ties of real friendship. Although Tegart could show a grim face to terrorism it could never conceal a warmhearted, intensely human, and magnetic personality. Even some who had sought his life became, after passing through his hands, his allies and helpers. By 1917 an improved situation enabled Tegart to take leave, although he was soon recalled to place his wide knowledge of Indian unrest before the Indian sedition committee under Sir Sidney Rowlatt [q.v.]. Early in 1918 Tegart served in France and he remained with the army of occupation, afterwards undertaking special duties in England.

Tegart returned to Calcutta in 1923 as commissioner of police, a post for which his unrivalled knowledge of terrorism had well equipped him. The release of internees after the war led to a fresh outbreak of even greater violence. In 1924 an Englishman was shot in mistake for Tegart in Calcutta's main street. Internment again brought some relief but the campaign was renewed on the temporary relinquishment of the Government's special powers in 1930. The inspector-generals of prisons and of police were murdered, the one in Calcutta and the other in Dacca. In Chittagong an armed rising looted the armoury and only by mischance failed to kill most of the Europeans. Tegart himself had a miraculous escape in Calcutta when two bombs damaged his car and wounded his driver;

he received public congratulations from friends and Indian nationalists alike.

Tegart was a strong and successful commissioner, reducing crime and securing respect for law and order by matching his words with his actions. He was greatly trusted by the large, influential European community as by the law-abiding classes generally. In the city's social and sporting life he was a prominent and immensely popular figure. In 1931 he retired, having become something of a legendary figure, bearing a charmed life. The talk on 'Terrorism in India' which he gave to the Royal Empire Society in 1932 was a singularly unembittered account of a movement which had endangered his life for a quarter of a century.

It was significant of both the gravity of the situation in India and Tegart's own repute that on his return to England he became the first police officer to be appointed to the Council of India, on which he served until 1936. In the following year he was deputed to advise the Palestine administration on attacks by Arabs on Jews and he carried through various protective measures, although the outbreak of war in 1939 prevented a full test of their efficiency. There too he narrowly escaped death in an ambush, when his staff officer was murdered at his side. In the war he gave valuable service to the Ministry of Food in countering black market operations, and so continued until laid aside by the illness which caused his death at Warminster 6 April 1946.

Tegart was awarded the King's police medal in 1911 and was appointed M.V.O. in 1912 during the royal visit. He received the C.I.E. in 1917, the C.S.I. in 1931, and was knighted in 1926. He was advanced to K.C.I.E. in 1937. In 1933 he received the honorary LL.D. of Trinity College, Dublin. In 1922 he married Kathleen Frances, daughter of the Rev. James Lloyd Herbert, rector of Disserth, Llandrindod Wells. There were no children. A portrait of Tegart by an anonymous artist was shown in the 'Men and Women of Empire' exhibition at the Hans Galleries, London, in 1950.

[The Times, 8 and 23 April 1946; Sir Charles Tegart, 'Terrorism in India', a speech published by the Royal Empire Society, 1932; personal knowledge.]                D. PETRIE.

TEICHMAN, SIR ERIC (1884–1944), diplomatist and traveller, whose original name was Erik Teichmann, changed by deed poll in 1906, was born at Eltham,

Kent, 16 January 1884, the youngest of the six children of Emil Teichmann by his wife, Mary Lydia, daughter of Frederick Augustus Schroeter, a London fur merchant. His ancestors were for many generations master foresters to the court of the principality of Ansbach. His father settled in England in the 'sixties and became senior partner in a fur trading company. Eric Teichman was educated at Charterhouse and at Gonville and Caius College, Cambridge, and represented the university against Oxford in the point-to-point steeplechase of 1903. After taking an ordinary degree by way of the medieval and modern languages tripos in 1904, he spent nearly two years studying on the continent and travelling extensively in Russia. In 1907 he went to Peking as a student interpreter in the consular service. Although he was already suffering severely from arthritis and a few years later became almost a cripple as the result of a riding accident, he never allowed this to interfere with his love for riding, shooting, and exploration. He travelled much in Central Asia and spent most of the early part of his career on special service on the Tibetan border and in the loess highlands of the north-west, regions upon which he became the acknowledged authority.

After 1919 he was almost continuously in Peking where he was Chinese secretary from 1924 and was given the local rank of counsellor of embassy in 1927. Between September 1935 and January 1936 he journeyed home through Central Asia in order to carry out a special mission to Urumchi on the way. He travelled from Suiyuan to Kashgar by motor-truck, crossed the Pamir and the Karakoram ranges to Gilgit by pony and on foot, thence by air to Delhi. He then wrote *Journey to Turkistan* (1937), his 'swan song of Asiatic travel', since ill health compelled him to retire. He had previously published *Travels of a Consular Officer in North-West China* (1921) and *Travels of a Consular Officer in Eastern Tibet* (1922), and in 1938 he published *Affairs of China*. All these books are of the utmost value to students of the Far East. In 1942 he agreed to go out again for one year as adviser to the British embassy at Chungking. He again travelled home through Central Asia but published no record of this journey. He was appointed C.I.E. in 1919, C.M.G. in 1927, and K.C.M.G. in 1933, and was awarded the Murchison grant by the Royal Geographical Society in 1925. On his re-turn for the last time from China he was appointed G.C.M.G. in 1944, and on 3 December of the same year he was shot dead by an American soldier whom he disturbed poaching in the grounds of his Norfolk home at Honingham Hall. In 1921 Teichman married Ellen Cecilia, widow of Major Douglas Scott Niven, and daughter of Marmaduke John Teesdale, of Walton-on-the-Hill. There were no children.

A coloured crayon drawing of Teichman, done by Miss Jacobs at Peking, hangs at Honingham Hall, Norfolk.

[*The Times*, 5 December 1944; private information; personal knowledge.]

J. T. PRATT.

TEMPEST, DAME MARIE (1864–1942), actress, whose legal name before her first marriage was MARY SUSAN ETHERINGTON, was born 15 July 1864 in the Marylebone Road, London, the daughter of Edwin Etherington, a stationer, and his wife, Sarah Mary, daughter of Henry Castle, a draper. Edwin Etherington was the illegitimate son of Sarah Etherington (daughter of Thomas Etherington, a blacksmith, and his wife, Hannah). The Etheringtons had been settled in the district of Midhurst, Sussex, for several generations, and both Edwin and his mother, Sarah, were baptized at Fernhurst. Edwin's father is reputed to have been a soldier of family, but his identity has not transpired. He seems, according to the standards of his time, to have behaved well, and to have made ample provision for Sarah's son; he may have been the 'tall blond soldier' (mentioned by Marie Tempest's biographer), the mysterious 'guardian' who lived in bachelor rooms in Wigmore Street and was sometimes visited by the little girl who may have been his granddaughter. Edwin Etherington was described to Mr. Hector Bolitho by Marie Tempest as 'an improvident, charming soldier who was often tipsy'; even so, he carried on business as Edwin Etherington & Co., booksellers and stationers, first at 9 and then at 28 Wigmore Street, between the years 1860 and 1873. He died at 84 Mount Street in 1880 at the age of forty-two. His marriage appears not to have been a success and his wife had departed for Canada, taking two of her children with her but leaving Mary Susan in the care of his mother.

The tale at this point becomes such a mixture of romance and mystery that it is difficult, if not impossible, to disentangle fact from fiction. 'Grandmamma Etherington' now becomes a domineering old lady, a woman of wealth and great respectability, living in 'a grand house' in Whitehall and on terms of some familiarity with Mr. and Mrs. Gladstone. But she was neither wealthy nor highly placed in society. She could hardly have taken her granddaughter to luncheon parties to be petted by Mrs. Charles Tennant, Sir Charles Dilke, and Joseph Chamberlain; nor was she accustomed to drop in on the Gladstones. Solid ground is reached only when we learn that Mary Susan's grandmother had married William Marriage, a servant, at St. George's, Hanover Square, in 1852. Marriage eventually became the yeoman or caretaker of the Chapel Royal, Whitehall, in 1869, and it was there that his wife died in 1884. Her knowledge of notabilities was presumably the result of her employment in service and at the Chapel Royal.

The distinguished soldier in the background was probably responsible for Mary Susan's expensive education. She was sent, first to school at Midhurst, then to the Ursuline convent at Thildonck, Belgium, finally to a private school in Paris, where she learnt to speak French with fluency and a good accent. It is not certain that Lady Susan Vane-Tempest, from whom Mary Susan took her stage-name, was her godmother, as Marie Tempest claimed, since there are no known facts about the child's baptism. The consultation with the Gladstones about her ambition to become an actress, an ambition which horrified her grandmother, is very likely to have taken place as Marie Tempest related, the sort of visit that a caretaker's wife might easily make to a distinguished member of the congregation at the Chapel Royal. It might well be that Mr. Gladstone tried to dissuade the young girl from her deplorable ambition. He addressed her, it is said, at great length, mentioning the Greek dramatists and the morality plays with easy, if irrelevant, erudition, and ended by assuring her that if she persisted in her desire to join the theatrical profession, she would damn herself irretrievably and perish in what he clearly believed to be the purlieus of hell. The lecture amused Mary Susan as little as his oratory is said to have amused Queen Victoria; and she kept to her determination. By the time she was sixteen it was already plain that she had a fine soprano voice, and after her return

from Paris she was sent to the Royal Academy of Music to study singing under Manuel Garcia [q.v.]. These studies, enforced by rough treatment from Garcia, were so successful that she won bronze, silver, and gold medals; and it was almost inevitable, therefore, that she should appear on the operatic stage. In May 1885 she made her début in Suppé's *Boccaccio* at the Comedy Theatre.

She became a leading lady immediately, and remained one for the rest of her life, although her interest in the theatre was not deep, nor did she cultivate friendships on the stage. After she had sung the principal parts in light operas by Edward Jones, Hervé, and Messager, she sealed her popularity by her performance in *Dorothy* when she succeeded to the eponymous part in 1887. Her fine voice was not her only, or even her chief, attraction. She was a comedienne, as her nose proclaimed her. Like Lynette's,

Lightly was her slender nose
Tip-tilted like the petal of a flower.

All comediennes bear this badge. Her face was highly intelligent, but not pretty, yet it seemed winsome. She was small, but her figure was superb, and she had very beautiful hands. It was her personality that won her the favour she enjoyed for the whole of her stage career, and her grace and great distinction of manner. Her curtsey was almost world-renowned, and her fine taste in clothes made women everywhere willing to follow her lead. There had seldom, if ever, before been seen on the English stage an actress who combined so many charms and accomplishments. But her unique position in the theatre was not won or maintained by chance. Few actresses worked as hard as she did, or took so much trouble to improve their performance. In rehearsal she was the first to arrive at the theatre and the last to leave. She would not make a move on the stage without instruction from the producer, although she was likely to modify the instruction. Her passion for elegance belonged to the eighteenth century, a period in which she would have been very happy. Her habits were regular. She ate well, but carefully, and she was temperate. She slept for two hours every afternoon, and avoided late parties. At the age of seventy she had the figure of a girl of seventeen. She achieved this youthful look by what may be called an intellectual process: she shed all that reminded her of the past; and insisted that her surroundings should be new, changing a dinner service as often as she changed a hat.

For five years, 1890–95, she was as popular in New York as she had been in London. On her return to England in 1895, George Edwardes engaged her to play the principal parts in a series of musical comedies at Daly's Theatre, such as *An Artist's Model*, *The Geisha*, *A Greek Slave*, and *San Toy*; and she remained with him until 1900 when she wisely decided to test herself in straight plays. In 1901 she made her first decided success in straight comedy when she played the principal part in *Becky Sharp*, adapted from Thackeray's *Vanity Fair* by Robert Hichens [q.v.] and Cosmo Gordon-Lennox; and this success was followed by one in a completely contrasting part, that of Polly Eccles in *Caste*. The critics, who had been cold to her before the production of these two plays, now capitulated and accepted her as a comedienne of the rank of Réjane. Her title was never disputed. In a great variety of plays by authors who included Arnold Bennett, H. A. Jones, Sir James Barrie [qq.v.], Robert Marshall, A. A. Milne, John Hastings Turner, Mr. Somerset Maugham, Mr. Noël Coward, Mr. H. M. Harwood, and Mr. St. John Ervine, she delighted playgoers at home and abroad. In October 1914 she began a world tour which took her through North America, Australia, New Zealand, South Africa, India, the Straits Settlements, China, Japan, and the Philippines. She returned to London in 1923 in a play which was a disastrous failure, and there was a fear that she might have lost her audience at home; but a revival of *The Marriage of Kitty* removed it.

In 1935 Marie Tempest celebrated her golden jubilee on the stage at a testimonial matinée at Drury Lane Theatre, attended by King George V and Queen Mary. The money raised, £5,000, was used to endow a Marie Tempest ward at St. George's Hospital, London, for the benefit of actors and actresses. In 1937 she was appointed D.B.E.

In 1885 she married Alfred Edward Izard; this marriage, a student romance with a pianist whom she had met at the Royal Academy of Music, was a failure and was dissolved in 1889. She did not marry again until she met Cosmo Charles Gordon-Lennox (died 1921), a grandson of the fifth Duke of Richmond [q.v.], whom she married in 1898. He was the author of one of her most popular comedies, *The Marriage of Kitty*. Despite

their liking for each other they were incompatible and the marriage collapsed. After his death she found felicity in her marriage in 1921 to William Graham Browne, an actor from Ulster, whose taste and talent were similar to hers. This identity of likes and dislikes made him her ideal producer; and their union was entirely happy. He died in 1937 and his death was a disaster to her. The outbreak of war in 1939 made her solitude almost unbearable; she became a lonely old woman in a world where she felt herself an alien. She was not reluctant to go when she died in London 14 October 1942. Her age was seventy-eight, but she still had the grace of a young, enchanting girl. Her only child, a son, was born in 1888.

Marie Tempest was painted on several occasions by (Sir) William Nicholson: 'Marie Tempest with a Blenheim spaniel' (1903) is owned by Roland, Browse and Delbanco; 'Marie Tempest being fitted' (1908) by Mr. Gareth Maufe; 'Souvenir de Marie' (1908) is in the Municipal Gallery of Modern Art, Dublin; she also figures, with the Nicholson children, in 'The Tree' (*c.* 1912) owned by Miss Marguerite Steen. A portrait by J.-E. Blanche (1903) is at the Garrick Club.

[Hector Bolitho, *Marie Tempest*, 1936; *Who's Who in the Theatre*; private information; personal knowledge.]

St. John Ervine.

TEMPLE, WILLIAM (1881–1944), archbishop of Canterbury, younger son of Frederick Temple [q.v.] by his wife Beatrice Blanche, daughter of William Saunders Sebright Lascelles, son of the second Earl of Harewood [q.v.], was born at The Palace, Exeter, 15 October 1881. He was educated at Rugby (1894–1900) where he became a scholar in 1895 and at Balliol College, Oxford, of which he was an exhibitioner. He was placed in the first class in honour moderations (1902) and *literae humaniores* (1904). His undergraduate years foreshowed several of the special characteristics, interests, and aims which were to mark his whole career. He already had the gift of expressing himself clearly and persuasively in writing and speech (in the Hilary term of his last year he was president of the Union), formed aesthetic tastes which stood unchanged—for forty years Browning remained his favourite poet and Botticelli his favourite painter—and took a personal interest in the lives of the poor, which he showed by visiting the university settlements in Bethnal Green and Bermondsey. The dominating influence of Edward Caird [q.v.] left an enduring stamp on his thought and outlook: alike in small issues and great Temple learned to search for a synthesis in apparently conflicting theories or ideals; and in the last year of his life he wrote to a friend of 'my habitual tendency to discover that everybody is quite right—but I was brought up by Caird and I can never get out of that habit'.

Of the thirty posts offered to him after taking his degree, he chose a fellowship at the Queen's College, Oxford, where he went into residence in October 1904. He was elected an honorary fellow in 1925, and by virtue of his position as archbishop of York he later became its visitor. At first his tutorial duties were light, so that he was able to visit the continent of Europe and sit at the feet of Eucken, Wendt, Harnack, and Simmel. With characteristic enthusiasm he identified himself, on his return, with the aims of the Workers' Educational Association, a body in which he saw a great brotherhood in pursuit of a culture and knowledge as yet within the reach only of a few: from 1908 to 1924 he was its president, and his loyalty to the Association was lifelong. In 1908 came the great crisis of Temple's life. As long as he could remember, he had determined to be ordained, and in January 1906 he had approached the bishop of Oxford, Francis Paget [q.v.], with a request to be admitted to the diaconate; but Paget, with the utmost courtesy, had expressed regret that he could not ordain one who could not go farther than say that he was 'inclined, very tentatively, to accept the doctrine of the Virgin Birth, and with rather more confidence, that of the Bodily Resurrection of Our Lord'. The blow fell even more heavily on his mother than on Temple himself, but his closest friends begged him to regard neither the application nor the refusal as final, and he continued his study of the Christian faith and took an active part in practical Christian work. B. H. Streeter and H. Scott Holland [qq.v.], each in his own way, helped him to overcome the difficulties he had once felt in the declaration required from ordinands; and in March 1908 he asked the archbishop of Canterbury, Randall Davidson [q.v.], for an interview. This was readily granted and, after an exchange of letters between Davidson and Paget, the archbishop (in Canterbury Cathedral) made Temple a deacon on 20 December 1908 and ordained him priest on 19 December 1909. The last part of the long vacation in 1910 was spent in a tour of Australian universities, and during the voyage out he decided to accept the headmastership of Repton School. For two and a half years he enjoyed a pleasant interlude. He contributed to *Foundations* (1912), a composite volume by seven Oxford men, described as 'A Statement of Christian Belief in Terms of Modern Thought'; and he became increasingly immersed in the wider activities of the Church. 'I doubt', he wrote during his first term at Repton, 'whether headmastering is really my line'—although *Repton School Sermons* (1913) remains to show the power of his spiritual appeal to the young—and there was little surprise when in 1914 he accepted the benefice of St. James's, Piccadilly, offered by Lord Chancellor Haldane. Here he set himself to 'vindicate the ways of God to man', preaching frequently on the judgement and the love of God at a time when the faith of many Christians was being severely tested, in their effort to reconcile the existence of a God of Love with the horrors of war. *Papers for Wartime* (1914–15) to which he contributed and the Bishop Paddock lectures on *Church and Nation* (1915, delivered in the United States) followed; and in 1915 he was appointed honorary chaplain to the King. But the most important event in these years was his marriage in 1916 to Frances Gertrude Acland, daughter of Frederick Henry Anson, and granddaughter of Sir T. D. Acland (died 1898, q.v.). Temple sat late into the night before his wedding to finish off *Mens Creatrix* (1917)—the earliest of his larger works, in which were laid down the foundations of his philosophical argument for Christian theism.

The years of the war of 1914–18 were a time of severe testing for the national Church; and Temple took the lead in more than one effort to revitalize it and give it the sense of direction which, at a time of grave crisis, it appeared to lack. He was one of the secretaries of the National Mission of Repentance and Hope (1916); for two and a half years (1915–18) he edited the *Challenge*; he was the chosen leader of the Life and Liberty Movement (1917); and none worked more effectively than he for the passage of the enabling bill through Parliament (1919). Temple was convinced that, in spite of its limited effect, the National Mission achieved at least one notable result in bringing together the various parties of the Church for a common effort; to deepen this unity was his aim as the editor of the *Challenge*, and at the same time to widen the sphere of the Church's activities, especially in the nation's social and industrial life. His success was less marked as editor than as leader of the Life and Liberty Movement—founded by H. R. L. Sheppard [q.v.] to secure for the Church a measure of independence in the conduct of its affairs—and the popular imagination was struck by Temple's resignation of the living of St. James's so that he might devote himself entirely to the work of the movement. His election as a proctor in Convocation for the diocese of London in 1917, and his appointment as canon of Westminster two years later, gave him the centres of influence which he needed. The abbey was crowded whenever he preached, and among his spare-time duties was the editorship of the *Pilgrim*, which he held until the journal ceased publication in 1927.

In November 1920 Lloyd George offered him the bishopric of Manchester. For eight years Temple did faithful and effective work as teacher, pastor, evangelist, and administrator, while taking an active part in the central life of the Church and writing (1921) the life of his old headmaster John Percival [q.v.], *Christus Veritas* (1924), *Personal Religion and the Life of Fellowship* (1926), and *Christ in His Church* (1925)—the charge given at his primary visitation of the diocese in 1924. This charge had the same enthusiastic reception as all his addresses to the Manchester diocesan conference, each of which was printed after delivery. In 1925 he took his seat in the House of Lords. He carried through the creation of the new diocese of Blackburn (1927), took the chair in 1924 at the inter-denominational Conference on Christian Politics, Economics and Citizenship ('Copec'), and intervened—after not too sound a briefing—in an attempt to mediate between the contending groups in the coal stoppage of 1926. Temple was widely criticized for this 'interference', as he was for his concurrence with Randall Davidson's policy when in June 1928 the House of Commons rejected the revised Prayer Book for the second time. On Christmas Day 1927 Temple had written after the first rejection that, if the Book did not pass at the second attempt, 'some sort of disestablishment is (I suppose) the necessary result'; but by adroitness of manœuvre and delay Randall Davidson won the bishops over to the view that any such attempt at severance was unwise and would be widely misinterpreted. During his last two years at Manchester Temple took a leading part in the Œcumenical Movement, both at Lausanne (1927) and Jerusalem (1928). In each branch of its work—Evangelism, 'Faith and Order', and 'Life and Work'—his influence was progressively felt. He was elected chairman of the Edinburgh conference of 1937; and it was largely due to the trust placed in his judgement that in June 1940 the Church Assembly passed a resolution welcoming the establishment of the World Council of Churches, and that on 23 September 1942 he was able to inaugurate the British Council of Churches at a great service in St. Paul's Cathedral.

On 10 January 1929 Temple was enthroned as primate of England in York Minster. During his two primacies three particular motives were to be discerned at the heart of his greatest efforts and achievements. Of these the first was the desire for social and national righteousness. This dominant passion possessed him from his earliest years; it had led him into the Workers' Educational Association and later into the Labour Party which he joined in 1918; and for the seven years of his membership he found in the Labour movement an outlet for his social idealism. To discover and apply the Christian social gospel remained his set purpose. At the Malvern conference (1941), in the greatest of his smaller books *Christianity and Social Order* (1942, of which 139,000 copies were quickly sold), in *Men Without Work* (1938, a scientific and human investigation into unemployment conducted by a committee led by Temple under the sponsorship of the Pilgrim Trust, and approved even in Whitehall), in speeches throughout the country for the 'Religion and Life' campaign, in letters to *The Times*—here even his most loyal friends felt that he might have shown a more selective restraint—he developed his plea for justice and righteousness. It should be remembered that for the last five years of his life every plan and every utterance was set against the dark background of war; and his sermons and talks through the microphone attracted the wide notice of men serving in the forces. The British Broadcasting Corporation (of whose general advisory council he was made chairman in 1935) wisely used Temple to the full. Yet the tone of his broadcasts was maintained at a consistently high level; it was never anything but the specifically Christian social gospel that he preached, which was not necessarily that of some ephemeral left-wing party. 'The whole business', he wrote in 1943, 'of applying Christian principles to social questions is secondary to the fundamental truths of the Gospel, and to present the matter in any other way would seem to me to be complete apostasy.'

His second motive was the union of the Churches, and for promoting this his own churchmanship made him peculiarly fitted. In his early days it was for a broad church movement founded on the Scriptures that he had hoped, but from 1905 onwards the emphasis is seen to shift; it is now the authority of the Church ('which is alive') to which he looks rather than to that of the Bible; and his movement in a 'catholic' direction was accelerated by the influence of Charles Gore [q.v.] and H. Scott Holland. But he retained a sympathetic understanding of all schools of thought, in both the established and the Free Churches. He was chairman of the committee on unity of the Lambeth Conference of 1930, at which the discussions with the Free Church representatives were badly mismanaged; and when the 'Lambeth conversations' were resumed it was largely due to Temple's frank apology for the blunder that they were carried forward in a friendly atmosphere. At the same conference he drafted the report on the proposed Church of South India and presented it to the bishops; and seventeen years later, when the Church of South India was inaugurated in Madras, it was recognized that Temple's early advocacy at the Lambeth Conference was among the factors which had been decisive in bringing the scheme to fruition.

Temple's third motive was to present, in any way (and to whatever audience) possible, a reasoned exposition of the Christian faith. Especially brilliant as a teacher of youth, he kept contact with the Student Christian Movement all his life, until, at the end, none of its conferences was considered complete unless Temple was a chief speaker. His missions to the universities, especially the Oxford mission in 1931, were unique in their influence on young men and women, and the Oxford addresses were printed in one of his most deservedly popular books,

*Christian Faith and Life* (1931), of which eleven impressions were printed in fourteen years. In his *Readings in St. John's Gospel* (first series 1939, second series 1940) he gave to the Christian world what has been called the greatest devotional treatise written by an Anglican since William Law's *Serious Call*: the first series was described by Dr. Reinhold Niebuhr as 'tremendously stimulating . . . it represents a new medium in its combination of devotional and scholarly treatment'; and when he published his Gifford lectures (1934), *Nature, Man, and God*—a plea for dialectical realism as against the dialectical materialism of Marx—astonishment was general that an archbishop, burdened with routine and all the problems of administration, could produce a contribution of such permanent value to the philosophy of Christian theism. It was notable (a sober critic testified) for 'the range of the argument, the logical cogency of the reasoning, the grandeur of the synthesis, and the intellectual integrity it displays'. In one conference after another his leadership was sought—of these the Malvern conference in 1941, the Oxford conference on 'Church, Community and State' (1937), and the Edinburgh conference (1937) were among the most outstanding—and it was Temple who was chosen to preach at the service with which the disarmament conference at Geneva was opened in 1932.

When Cosmo Gordon Lang [q.v.] resigned the primacy of all England, there was only one reason for doubting whether Temple would succeed him: 'some of my recent utterances', he confessed to his brother, 'have not been liked in political circles'. But the strong desire of his predecessor; Temple's reputation at home, in the Anglican communion overseas, and in the continental Churches; his prophetic leadership; his wide and massive knowledge ('to a man of my generation', G. B. Shaw [q.v.] wrote, 'an archbishop of Temple's enlightenment was a realized impossibility'); his immense powers of concentration; the personal devotion of his life—such a combination of distinctive gifts and graces made it impossible for him to be passed over, and on 23 April 1942 he was enthroned in Canterbury Cathedral. In the short two and a half years of his primacy much creative work stood to his credit, not least the prominent part which he took in a complete overhaul of the nation's educational system. It was the obvious moment for a settlement. Mr. Richard Austen Butler—patient, diplomatic, and enthusiastic for reform—was president of the Board of Education; Parliament and the nation were alike distressed at many signs of the inadequacy of the existing system; and the old sectarian bitterness had died down. But no factor proved more potent in securing a settlement than the trust which the nonconformist leaders placed in Temple's honesty and sense of justice: so it was that in 1944 the new Education Act was placed on the statute book. Temple's forceful activity was thrust out in many other directions—in some more successfully than in others. He roused much criticism by a reference to the British banking system in a speech at the Royal Albert Hall in September 1942; but the summing up of the *Spectator* was roughly true, that 'support for Dr. Temple and his Albert Hall speech far outweighs the criticism it has evoked . . . the Primate is a man of great knowledge and brilliant intellect, as well as of abundant moral courage'. If during the two and a half years of his primacy—handicapped as he was by recurring, and often crippling, attacks of gout—he put out his full strength, he showed also a weakness to which he himself had pleaded guilty, the inclination 'to expound what I think to be the truth to anybody who has asked me and is willing to listen'. It was difficult for him, as Randall Davidson once remarked, ever to say 'no'. The last of his books, *The Church Looks Forward* (1944), was his legacy to all who would follow the quest for Christian truth in its relevance to the personal and social problems of community life.

Towards the end he began to doubt whether he was capable of leading the younger Christian thinkers—although he 'might do a little in steering them'. He was a philosopher before he was a theologian, and it was commonly said that he was too much of a theologian for the philosophers and too much of a philosopher for the theologians. His approach to theology, derived from the liberal outlook common in the universities in the early years of the twentieth century, stressed a theology of Incarnation rather than of Redemption, and his Christo-centric metaphysic was out of line with the dogmatic theology to which the younger thinkers were calling their contemporaries to return. Yet it was one of these whose tribute should be recorded in any assessment of Temple's character: 'it was not his great intellect, or his astonishing gifts of understanding, or the wideness of the theological rift, that made the deepest impression, but the fact of his holiness'. Many qualities raised Temple high above the level of his contemporaries in Church and State, but witness was world-wide that the true secret of his great influence lay in the fact that he combined, in a rare blend, the virtues of the friendly, simple, humorous, and approachable person. He died without issue at Westgate-on-Sea, Kent, 26 October 1944; his ashes were buried in the cloister garth at Canterbury, next to his father's grave.

Temple received a Cambridge doctorate (1933) which was the first honorary degree of D.D. given by the university under its new statutes; he received the honorary degree of D.C.L. from Oxford University (1934); the honorary degree of D.D. from the universities of Manchester (1929), Durham (1929), and Dublin (1934); of D.Litt. from Sheffield (1931); and LL.D. from Leeds (1930) and Princeton (1936). A portrait by J. W. Nichol is at Repton School and a copy at the Queen's College, Oxford; by T. C. Dugdale at Lambeth Palace and another in the Manchester City Art Gallery; by P. A. de László at Church House, Westminster, and 'a study' at Balliol College, Oxford; by (Sir) Oswald Birley at Bishopthorpe.

[*The Times*, 27 October 1944; F. A. Iremonger, *William Temple, his Life and Letters*, 1948; A. E. Baker, *William Temple and his Message* (with a memoir by G. K. A. Bell, bishop of Chichester), Penguin Books, 1946; G. K. A. Bell, *Life of Archbishop Davidson*, 2 vols., 1935 (for the general problems of the Church in Temple's day); private information, including letters written to his elder brother, Colonel F. C. Temple; personal knowledge.]

F. A. IREMONGER.

TENNANT, MARGARET MARY EDITH (usually known as MAY) (1869–1946), pioneer in public social work, was born at Rathgar, county Dublin, 5 April 1869, the only daughter of George Whitley Abraham, registrar in lunacy, and his wife, Margaret, daughter of Cornelius Curtin. She was privately educated, mainly by her father. After his death, she sought fortune in London at the age of eighteen, and found employment as secretary to Lady Dilke [q.v.], scholar, and promoter of trade unions among women, whose influence was decisive on a young and enthusiastic mind.

May Abraham learnt rapidly to handle

labour problems, especially those concerned with the employment of women in sweated and dangerous trades. She became treasurer of the Women's Trade Union League, and was prominent in the struggle for State inspection of laundries. Her work as an assistant commissioner on the Royal Commission on Labour (1891) led to her appointment by Asquith, then home secretary, in 1893 as the first woman factory inspector in England. Her inquiries and reports had appreciable influence on the provisions of the 1895 Factory and Workshop Act. She concerned herself particularly with the three evils of illegal overtime, bad sanitation, and dangerous trades. In 1895 she was a member of a departmental committee on dangerous trades of which the chairman was Harold John Tennant, a Liberal member of Parliament and son of Sir Charles Tennant, first baronet [q.v.]. He subsequently became secretary of state for Scotland. They were married in 1896 when she resigned her post as superintending inspector.

Unofficially May Tennant remained in close touch with her old activities, and her advice and counsel were sought in many directions. She was chairman of the Industrial Law Committee and in 1909 was appointed a member of the Royal Commission on divorce. She was a member of the Central Committee on Women's Employment from 1914 until 1939; during the war of 1914–18 she was chief adviser on women's welfare in the Ministry of Munitions, and among other posts was director of the women's section of the National Service Department, 1917. In that year she was appointed C.H.

In the post-war years she developed new interests in connexion with maternal mortality, the provision of nurses, and other medical questions. During the war of 1939–45 she worked indefatigably, despite failing health, for the Royal Air Force Benevolent Fund. A woman of great charm and personality, she was an expert gardener and a skilled angler. She died at Cornhill, Rolvenden, 11 July 1946. Her husband had died in 1935 and her eldest son was killed on active service in 1917. Three sons and one daughter survived her.

[Violet Markham, *May Tennant*, 1949; personal knowledge.]

VIOLET MARKHAM.

THANKERTON, BARON (1873–1948), judge. [See WATSON, WILLIAM.]

THOMAS, BERTRAM SIDNEY (1892–1950), explorer, was born 13 June 1892 at Avon Villa, Pill, Bristol, the son of William Henry Thomas, master mariner, and his wife, Eliza Ann, *née* Thomas. His education was confined to a normal course at the village school of Pill and private tuition, until he secured employment in the Post Office in 1908 and was seemingly destined to the humdrum life of a civil servant in England for the rest of his days. There is no record of his prowess in any form of sport; but a natural, although untutored, talent for music, maintained and developed throughout his life, provided a satisfying outlet for a sensitive mind both in the conventional atmosphere of his early career and in the more romantic setting of Arabian scenes, in which most of his life was spent.

Opportunity knocked at his door with the outbreak of war in 1914 when he joined the North Somersetshire Yeomanry and served with it in Belgium. Two years later he transferred to the Somerset Light Infantry to go to Mesopotamia, where he spent six years: the first two with his regiment, and the rest in the political department, for which he was recruited by (Sir) Arnold Wilson [q.v.] as one of his promising 'young men'. In various civil posts, and notably as political officer at Shatra during the Iraq rebellion of 1920, he fully justified the choice. On Wilson's replacement by Sir Percy Cox [q.v.], Thomas was retained as a member of the much reduced British staff required to act as advisers to Arab administrative officials serving under the provisional Government which took office at the end of 1920.

Thomas was appointed O.B.E. for his services and two years later was transferred to Trans-Jordan as assistant to the chief British representative at the court of the Amir Abdullah. In 1924 he was offered and accepted the post of financial adviser (afterwards prime minister) in the Sultanate of Muscat. His official activities in this post were interspersed with exploratory journeys in the little-known hinterlands of his charge, during which he did much valuable geographical and ethnological work. These journeys were but a prelude to the remarkable feat of exploration on which his claim to fame may be said to rest. The Rub'al Khali, or Great Southern Desert of Arabia, had never been crossed by any European explorer and it was, indeed, believed that the journey was impossible. Nevertheless

Thomas not only attempted the crossing but triumphantly achieved it in 1930–31, when he travelled by camel from Dhufar on the Indian Ocean to Dauha on the Persian Gulf in fifty-eight days. His exploit was greeted with world-wide admiration, and learned societies hastened to honour him with their highest awards, among them the Royal Geographical Society which awarded him the Founder's medal (1931).

Thomas had now reached the peak of his career, and his subsequent activities were, perhaps inevitably, something of an anticlimax. He retired from Muscat and produced a number of literary works including *Alarms and Excursions in Arabia* (1931), *Arabia Felix* (1932), a history of *The Arabs* (1937), and also some linguistic studies. He delivered the Lowell lectures at Boston in 1934 and obtained the degree of Ph.D. from Cambridge University in 1935. He also received the honorary degrees of D.Sc. from Acadia University, Nova Scotia, and D.Litt. from Bristol (1934). After the outbreak of war in 1939 he served for a time as public relations officer at Bahrain (1942–3) and in 1944 became director of the Middle East Centre of Arabic Studies, first in Palestine and later at Shamlan in the Lebanon, of which he was the effective founder. He retired from this post in 1948 and was appointed C.M.G. in the following year.

In 1933 Thomas married Bessie Mary, daughter of the late Surgeon-Major Edmond Hoile, and had one daughter. He died in the house where he was born 27 December 1950. A portrait by (Sir) Walter Russell was exhibited at the Academy in 1933.

[Private information; personal knowledge.]
H. St. J. B. Philby.

THOMAS, FREEMAN FREEMAN-, first MARQUESS OF WILLINGDON (1866–1941), governor-general of Canada and viceroy of India. [See FREEMAN-THOMAS.]

THOMAS, JAMES HENRY (1874–1949), trade-union leader and politician, was born at Newport, Monmouthshire, 3 October 1874, the son of a domestic servant, Elizabeth Mary Thomas. He was brought up by his grandmother, a woman of strong character who lived by taking in washing and endured poverty with a courage which deeply impressed her grandson. The child was sent at five to the Newport national schools and at nine years old he started working, outside school hours, at a chemist's shop for 4s. a week. At twelve he left school and in 1889, having passed through a few blind-alley jobs, he was accepted by the Great Western Railway as an engine-cleaner, the first rung on the ladder towards becoming an engine-driver. As a call-boy, he had at first much spare time, which he spent in the public library. A little later he organized among his fellow cleaners a successful strike against a reduction of their tallow ration. In 1894 he was promoted to fireman and four years later first attended as a delegate the annual congress of the Amalgamated Society of Railway Servants. In the same year (1898) he was transferred to Swindon where in 1901 he was elected to the borough council in preference to his own superintendent. He took his municipal work seriously, served on a number of committees, and was chairman (1904–5) of the finance and law committee and (1905–6) of the electricity and tramways committee. His earnings at this time, as an engine-turner, were no more than 33s. a week.

Thereafter his career ran in two main channels—trade-unionism and politics. He was president of his union in 1905 and in the course of a second term of office in 1906 was elected organizing secretary. Thereupon he gave up his work on the railway and removed first to Manchester, then to Cardiff, and finally to London. In 1910 he was elected assistant secretary and in the following year played a leading part in the first nation-wide British railway strike which brought railway trade-unionism into the forefront of the Labour movement. When his union merged with two others in 1913 to form the National Union of Railwaymen Thomas was at first assistant secretary, then, from the beginning of 1917, general secretary, and from 1919 (save for an interlude of nine months in 1924) until 1931 parliamentary general secretary.

Meanwhile Thomas had been returned to Parliament for Derby as early as January 1910. After the outbreak of war in 1914 he was a strong supporter of the war effort and of voluntary enlistment; but steadfastly opposed conscription, which he nevertheless loyally accepted when it came. In 1917 he went to America and Canada with the Balfour mission, and in the same year he was sworn of the Privy Council. Although he voted in favour of Labour participation in the

Lloyd George coalition (he had opposed the former coalition) he himself declined office more than once, feeling that he could best serve Labour by getting nothing out of the war for himself. After an unofficial strike which had started among the railwaymen of South Wales and spread to London in 1918 Thomas resigned from his secretaryship in protest at an action 'as wicked as it is dangerous'. Pressed to withdraw his resignation he found his position immeasurably strengthened and the seven years between 1919 and 1926 saw his greatest trade-union prominence.

The end of the war brought a period of abnormal social unrest, with strikes in many industries. The railway strike of 1919 which was directed by Thomas was perhaps the most successful: not merely because it was well organized but because in negotiating the settlement Thomas sought and obtained, not the maximum terms which might have been wrung at the moment, but the maximum which his men could hope to retain when the slump came. For this moderation he was much criticized by the hotheads at the time; but the ensuing years soon justified his wisdom, which was set in relief by the results accruing to the Miners' Federation from an opposite policy.

The next phase saw the end of the 'Triple Industrial Alliance' which the three great trade unions—those of the miners, transport workers, and railwaymen—had agreed upon shortly before the outbreak of war and ratified in 1915. The strike action of these unions affected each other; moreover, they had it in common that their strikes hit primarily not their employers but the public. If, it was argued, they concerted their demands, the threat of a simultaneous strike would be such a blow to the public that employers would be compelled to surrender. The aim of the Alliance was concerted action on matters 'of a national character or vitally affecting a principle' and the fact that no very definite provision was made for 'sympathetic' strikes was to prove its downfall. The railwaymen did not ask for the support of the Alliance in 1919 but in the spring of 1921 the Alliance agreed upon a strike following upon the termination of the State control of the mines, an issue which was soon to confront the railwaymen as well. The movement was wrecked by the extremism of the miners' leaders who threw over their own general secretary (who had shown himself prepared to discuss a temporary wages settlement), and claimed the support of the other two unions in a refusal to meet the Government. Both the railway and the transport leaders declined it, foreseeing a loss of public sympathy at this intransigence and an incomplete stoppage owing to the confusion of the situation. The Triple Alliance collapsed and the date (15 April) long figured in the calendar of the extreme Left as 'Black Friday'. Thomas, who had played a leading part, secured the approval of his own members; but extremists everywhere made him their chief target. In self-defence he brought a libel action against a Communist newspaper, and was awarded £2,000 damages with costs.

The last big conflict in Thomas's trade-union story was the general strike of 1926. Although far too sagacious to desire, he could not prevent, it; but at the end he played a valuable part in winding it up. By this time Thomas had had his first experience of government responsibility as colonial secretary in Ramsay MacDonald's administration of 1924. A suggestion that, as a close associate of MacDonald, he might go to the Foreign Office had not found favour even with his friends. The Colonial Office suited him well, for he had a strong patriotic feeling for the country and for the Empire, and his brief term of office included the British Empire Exhibition at Wembley and a visit to South Africa. After the downfall of the Government *The Times* remarked that Thomas, who had 'long shown himself possessed of tact, imagination, and courage', had 'done more than any man to support the thesis that "Labour is fit to govern"'. He again obtained office in MacDonald's second Cabinet of 1929, this time retaining the post of general secretary to his union, although not, of course, discharging its routine duties. He was again suggested for, and would have liked, the Foreign Office, did not want the Dominions Office, and finally agreed to become lord privy seal with a special mandate to deal with unemployment. But the onset of the world economic crisis made his task impossible; he received much criticism for his over-optimism. Although his resignation was not accepted when he offered it after coming into conflict with Sir Oswald Mosley, who subsequently left the Government, he was nevertheless transferred to the Dominions Office in June 1930 to prepare for the forthcoming Imperial Conference. Meanwhile the crisis went on and in August 1931 MacDonald formed his 'national' Government in which Labour would not join. Only four of his Cabinet colleagues stayed by his side, but Thomas was one. He was returned as a National Labour candidate for Derby and remained at the Dominions Office, where he was not a success, until Baldwin transferred him to the Colonial Office in November 1935. Thomas's union censured his support of MacDonald with exceptional bitterness. He was deprived not only of his office as general secretary, but of his membership and even of his earned pension. Utterly devoted as he had been to his union, he felt these blows intensely.

In 1932 it fell to Thomas to deal with the action of Mr. de Valera in withholding from Great Britain the proceeds of the Irish land annuities. In this he proved ineffective since it was not the Cabinet's policy to apply any adequate degree of pressure. His last five years in office were sorrowful and did not fulfil his earlier promise. MacDonald insisted upon his retention; but the liking of his Conservative colleagues did not compensate for his ostracism by Labour, and in his unhappiness he developed a proneness to intemperance.

In 1936 such large insurances were effected at Lloyd's in advance of the budget as pointed to a leakage of its secrets. The heaviest insurances were taken out by two close friends of Thomas. With special parliamentary sanction the Government set up a judicial tribunal consisting of Mr. Justice (later Lord) Porter and two King's Counsel. Before it both Thomas and his friends denied leakage, but the tribunal found that 'unauthorized disclosure' had been made by Thomas to two of his friends separately, and Thomas's public career ended. There was no finding that the disclosure had been deliberate or made for Thomas's enrichment. 'I don't think', said Baldwin privately, 'Jim deliberately gave anything away. What he most likely did was to let his tongue wag when he was in his cups.' In a moving farewell to the House of much dignity Thomas repeated that he had never consciously revealed a budget secret and the general feeling towards him in Parliament and elsewhere was one of sympathy and deep regret.

'Thank God your old Dad is not alive to see this', Thomas remarked amid his distress when he surrendered his seal of office to King Edward VIII. He had enjoyed the friendship of King George V to a marked degree, and indeed had friends in many walks of life. For almost a quarter of a century he was undoubtedly one of the chief figures in British trade-unionism. His strong hold down to 1931 over his own great union had been won by unremitting devotion to its affairs—in his office during the week, and at week-ends on personal visits to the branches all over the country. But he had also no common endowment of eloquence, insight, humour, joviality, and an engaging common sense —qualities which were emphasized in his speech by a peculiarly pungent working-class accent, a defiant avoidance of the aspirate, and an occasional Rabelaisian turn. He was equally effective, whether on platforms addressing mass meetings, or round a table persuading a knot of negotiators. The House of Commons always heard him with marked attention.

In 1919 Thomas became chairman of the parliamentary committee of the Trades Union Congress and in 1920 presided over the annual congress at Portsmouth. In 1920–24 he was president of the International Federation of Trade Unions. He received doctorates from the universities of Cambridge (1920) and Oxford (1926). He died in London 21 January 1949. He was survived by his wife, Agnes (daughter of Joseph Hill, a boilermaker journeyman) whom he had known since childhood and married in 1898. They had three sons, one of whom, Leslie Montagu Thomas, became a Conservative member of Parliament, and three daughters. Two portraits of Thomas, both by Ernest Townsend, are in the possession of his family. A chalk drawing by S. Morse Brown has been lent by the artist to the National Museum of Wales.

[J. H. Thomas, *My Story*, 1937; biographies by H. R. S. Phillpott, 1932, and Basil Fuller, 1933; G. W. Alcock, *Fifty Years of Railway Trade-Unionism*, 1922; Viscount Snowden, *An Autobiography*, 2 vols., 1934; *Budget Disclosure Inquiry*, Cmd. 5184, 1936; H.R.H. the Duke of Windsor, *A King's Story*, 1951; Thomas Jones, *A Diary with Letters, 1931–50*, 1954; private information.]

R. C. K. Ensor.

THOMPSON, Sir D'ARCY WENTWORTH (1860–1948), zoologist and classical scholar, was born in Edinburgh 2 May 1860, the only son by his first wife of D'Arcy Wentworth Thompson [q.v.] who at that time was a classical master at the Edinburgh Academy. His mother,

Fanny, who was a daughter of Joseph Gamgee, the veterinary surgeon, and sister of J. S. and Arthur Gamgee [qq.v.], died when he was born. In 1863 the father was appointed professor of Greek at Queen's College, Galway, and the child was left in charge of an aunt in the home of his maternal grandfather. He was accustomed to attribute the first awakening of his interest in biology to his grandfather, just as he owed to his father his abiding love for the classics. He was educated at the Edinburgh Academy and after three years (1877–80) as a medical student at Edinburgh University, where he came under the influence of Sir C. Wyville Thomson [q.v.], then just returned from the *Challenger* expedition, he went to Trinity College, Cambridge, in 1880 as a sub-sizar, and became a scholar the following year. He speedily joined the brilliant group of young men gathered round (Sir) Michael Foster and F. M. Balfour [qq.v.] who were then laying the foundations of the modern Cambridge school of biology. He was awarded firsts in both parts of the natural sciences tripos (1882, 1883), and spent a year as demonstrator in physiology under Foster. In 1884 he was appointed professor of biology (later altered to natural history) in the recently founded University College in Dundee. When, in 1897, the college was incorporated in the university of St. Andrews, he became a member of the senate in the university in which he was to spend the rest of his life.

While at Dundee Thompson devoted much attention to building up a teaching museum of zoology which, with the help of the last of the Dundee whalers, became very rich in specimens from the Arctic seas. In 1896 and again in 1897 he visited the Pribylov Islands as a member of the British-American commission of inquiry on the fur-seal fishery in the Bering Sea, and in the latter year he represented the British Government at the international conference on the subject at Washington. For his services on these occasions he was appointed C.B. in 1898. In that year he was also made a member of the Fishery Board for Scotland, a position which he held until the supersession of the Board in 1939. He was one of the British representatives on the International Council for the Exploration of the Sea from its beginning in 1902. To the official publications of all these bodies he contributed many reports and papers on fishery statistics, on oceanography, and so on.

In 1917, on the retirement of W. C. M'Intosh [q.v.], he was translated to the senior chair of natural history in the United College of the university, and thenceforward made his home in St. Andrews. It was in 1917 also that his most important biological work, the volume *On Growth and Form*, was published. This remarkable book at once attracted attention. It came at a time when the trend of biological thought was turning away from the historical (or phylogenetic) methods that had become traditional, towards an interpretation of the structure of living things in terms of the physical forces acting within the lifetime of the individual organism. Just how far this mode of interpretation takes us came as a surprise to many readers who were attracted to the book by the perfect lucidity of its style and the wealth of illustrative material it brought together from writers ancient and modern, most of whom the average biologist had never even heard of. Thompson, however, was too experienced and too wise a naturalist to imagine that such an interpretation would take us all the way, and in his second edition (1942) he has to add a caution. In the end, he says, 'the twofold problem of accumulated inheritance, and of perfect structural adaptation, confronts us once again and passes all our understanding'. Evidence of the influence of this book on a younger generation is given by the volume of *Essays on Growth and Form presented to D'Arcy Wentworth Thompson* by a group of British and American biologists on the occasion of his completing sixty years as a professor (1945). The volume includes an exhaustive bibliography of his writings.

Apart from publications bearing directly upon the science of zoology, Thompson wrote much on matters of classical scholarship, especially on the natural history of ancient writers. His major works in this department were *A Glossary of Greek Birds* (1895), an annotated translation of Aristotle's *Historia Animalium* (1910), *A Glossary of Greek Fishes* (1945), besides many contributions to the latest Liddell and Scott, and other collective works.

In the later years of his long life Thompson received many honours from universities and other learned bodies ranging from Aberdeen to Johannesburg, and from Boston (U.S.A.) to Delhi. He was elected F.R.S. in 1916, was a vice-president in 1931–3, and received the Darwin medal in 1946. The Linnean Society awarded him the Linnean gold medal in 1938. He was president of the Royal Society of Edinburgh, 1934–9, and of the Classical Association in 1929. He was knighted in 1937.

At the end of 1946 Thompson flew to India as one of the delegates from the Royal Society to the Indian Science Congress at Delhi, but the strain of the journey by air proved too much for one of his age, and he never quite recovered his health. He died at St. Andrews 21 June 1948. He married in 1901 Ada Maureen (died 1949), daughter of William B. Drury, solicitor, of Dublin; there were three daughters of the marriage.

Thompson was a man of very distinguished presence, a ready and polished speaker, whose lectures and addresses displayed a range of interests and of knowledge that would have been remarkable at any time but seemed doubly so in our age of specialists. He loved teaching and he taught to the very last, for even in his final illness he gathered his honours students in his sick-room for talks that none of them will forget. A full-length portrait of Thompson in academic robes, painted by D. S. Ewart, is in the rooms of the Royal Society of Edinburgh. A three-quarter length portrait by the same artist is in the zoological department of the university of St. Andrews. A bronze head, modelled by Alfred Forrest, is in the library of the university.

[Clifford Dobell in *Obituary Notices of Fellows of the Royal Society*, No. 18, October 1949; *Year Book of the Royal Society of Edinburgh, 1948 and 1949*, 1950; private information; personal knowledge.]
W. T. CALMAN.
[Ruth D'Arcy Thompson, *D'Arcy Wentworth Thompson, the Scholar-Naturalist, 1860–1948*, with a postscript by P. B. Medawar, 1958.]

THOMPSON, EDWARD JOHN (1886–1946), writer, was born at Hazel Grove, Stockport, 9 April 1886, the eldest son of the Rev. John Moses Thompson, the son of a farmer near Penrith, and his wife, Elizabeth Penney. Thompson's earliest memories were of South India where both his parents were Wesleyan missionaries. His father died in 1894 and his mother with six children struggled against poverty, first at Stockport and then at Walthamstow. From Kingswood School, Bath, Edward would have gained a university scholarship, but he was sent to

work in a bank in Bethnal Green. From Richmond College, having graduated B.A. at London University in 1909, he was ordained and went in 1910 to the Wesleyan College at Bankura, Bengal. *Introducing the Arnisons* (1935) and *John Arnison* (1939) are modified autobiography, as is, in part, *An Indian Day* (1927).

Already a poet, he taught English literature at Bankura, studied Bengali, and sought mental experience outside the college, meeting (Sir) Rabindranath Tagore [q.v.] in 1913 and eventually coming to understand Bengali poetry better than any other Englishman. He became chaplain in 1916 with the 7th division, went through the Mesopotamian and Palestine campaigns, and was awarded the M.C. *These Men Thy Friends* (1927) and *In Araby Orion* (1930) resulted from these experiences. In 1920 he returned to Bankura as acting principal. Hitherto uninterested in Indian politics he, with other missionaries, opposed the widespread approval of the action of General R. E. H. Dyer [q.v.] at Amritsar in 1919. Thompson now became convinced that Indians and British would be fundamentally irreconcilable until India had self-government. *The Other Side of the Medal* (1925) explains the Mutiny's legacy of bitterness among Indians.

Remaining predominantly a poet, although all his novels and historical works were written after forty, he returned to England in 1923 to devote himself to literature, resigning from the Wesleyan ministry. He was lecturer in Bengali at Oxford to Indian Civil Service probationers (1923–33), Leverhulme research fellow (1934–6), and research fellow in Indian history at Oriel College (1936–46), the funds being provided by Henry Norman Spalding. He worked hard by public and private writing and speaking for Indian self-determination and for the changed outlook in England which made possible the handing over of power in 1947. A friend of Mr. Nehru, and friendly with M. K. Gandhi [q.v.] and other Indian politicians and literary men, he at the same time did all he could to strengthen the 'ties of the spirit' which he hoped would always unite the two countries. He objected to unscrupulous propaganda, and so, while lecturing in America, found himself speaking up for 'the constantly criticized British Empire'. Of the force inherent in the sudden emergence of the Pakistan idea he was hardly aware. He revisited India in 1932, 1937, and, with the aid of the Rhodes Trustees, in late 1939.

Although he wrote much, he maintained throughout his imaginative grasp, in such books as *The Youngest Disciple* (1938), about Gautama; *Sir Walter Ralegh* (1935); *Lord Metcalfe* (1937), his best work on Indian history; *Burmese Silver* (1937), geographically unrealistic but magnificent in atmosphere and description. As a poet he sought vision, not psychological subtleties. After youthful romance came such religious poems as 'The Eternal Comrade', 'Christus Immanens', 'The Cricket Pitch'. He is the only notable English poet of Indian scenery or of the Mesopotamian and Palestine campaigns. After *Collected Poems* (1930) he went on until *New Recessional* (1942), which shows the effect of the war of 1939–45 in changes of technique and a rock-bottom concern with human life as it is. His *100 Poems* (1944) ends with the lyric masterpiece 'Harbour Music'. Characteristically he neither founded nor followed any poetic school.

In 1919 Thompson married Theodosia, daughter of the Rev. William Jessup, D.D., an American Presbyterian missionary in the Lebanon. Gay in his home life, Thompson was outspoken, uncompromising but fair in controversy. He was no respecter of prejudices. Horrified by the Munich agreement in 1938, his forecast was as accurate as Cassandra's. He talked much of his work and interests, little of himself, as one 'heartily sick of my own personality which ceases to interest as one grows older'. He died 28 April 1946 at Bledlow, Buckinghamshire. He had two sons; the elder, William Frank Thompson, died heroically in Bulgaria in 1944 and his father assisted in the preparation of his memoir, *There is a Spirit in Europe* . . ., but did not live to see it published in 1947.

[Private information; personal knowledge.]
H. M. MARGOLIOUTH.

THOMPSON, SIR (HENRY FRANCIS) HERBERT, second baronet (1859–1944), Egyptologist, was born in London 2 April 1859, the only son of (Sir) Henry Thompson [q.v.], surgeon, and later first baronet, by his wife, Kate Fanny, daughter of George Loder, of Bath. She was a well-known pianist, who transmitted to her son an early knowledge and love of music which throughout his life remained a chief source of delight. He especially liked to recall that he had spoken with three men who had known Beethoven.

At Marlborough, although he was head of the school at the age of sixteen, a total lack of interest in athletic sport deprived him of the happiness which, conjoined with the influence of his precocious brains, he might have derived from the companionship of his schoolfellows. But it came at last on the day of his leaving school, when his house-master gave him a book, the inscription in which made it the most precious item in his fine library. From Marlborough he went to Germany in order to study the language, and thence to a short course of training in the City of London, before entering Trinity College, Cambridge. There, chiefly because of over-scrupulous attention, springing from parental zeal, scholastic distinctions evaded him. From Cambridge, at his father's wish, he went to the bar. The life was uncongenial, but the experience gained in drafting statutes in the chambers of William Otto Danckwerts was valuable, and not least that which came from attending at the case of *Crawford* v. *Crawford and Dilke*, in which Danckwerts appeared for the petitioner in 1886.

Seven years after being called to the bar by the Inner Temple, Thompson, when travelling with his father in 1889, met T. H. Huxley [q.v.] whose reference to him in a letter to (Sir) Michael Foster [q.v.] shows that Thompson's intellectual powers had impressed the great scientist. Although past the age of thirty he had not yet found his vocation in life. Once more at his father's wish, he turned to natural science, but biological work in London brought on serious trouble with his eyes, and even when work could be resumed use of the microscope was forbidden. But now fortune began to smile. The proximity of the Egyptological department of University College, London, and Thompson's examination of some skeletal remains for (Sir) Flinders Petrie [q.v.], the head of the department, led to his taking up at the age of forty what was to become his real life-work, Egyptology. In the department there were also F. Ll. Griffith and W. E. Crum [qq.v.]. Both were teaching and it was natural that, after some general work on the whole field, he should specialize in the two branches of the subject, demotic and Coptic, in which these scholars, who came to be among Thompson's greatest friends, were respectively the acknowledged leaders in this country.

The first-fruits of this new association with Griffith appeared in the labours of four years when the first volume of *The Demotic Magical Papyrus of London and Leiden* was published in 1904. During the next ten years, Thompson's publications included an account of a number of demotic papyri found by Petrie at Rifeh in the latter's *Gizeh and Rifeh* (1907), *The Coptic (Sahidic) Version of Certain Books of the Old Testament* (1908), 'The Coptic Inscriptions', in Quibell's *Excavations at Saqqara*, vols. iii–iv (Cairo, 1909–12), and the demotic and Coptic texts in *Theban Ostraca* (1913).

The end of the war of 1914–18, during which Thompson had spent his nights at a London terminus on duty as a special constable, found him ready to withdraw to the country, intending to abandon Egyptology and return to the classics. He did in fact retire to Aspley Guise, where he shared a house with George Herbert Fowler; but J. L. Starkey's discovery in Egypt of a papyrus manuscript of St. John's Gospel was followed by an appeal from Petrie for his skill as an editor, and this earliest copy of that gospel which we possess appeared in 1924. Shortly afterwards he was invited by the keeper of Egyptian and Assyrian antiquities in the British Museum to compile a handlist of the long and important series of demotic papyri in the museum, to serve as a basis for a full-length catalogue which the trustees intended to publish. Only when this was completed did he turn to intensive work on a group of papyri which he published as *A Family Archive from Siût* (2 vols., 1934), a major task for Thompson's scholarship, and also a monument of his generosity, for he enabled the British Museum to purchase the papyri and thereby made a most notable contribution to demotic studies and to our knowledge of law in ancient Egypt. This work is now coming to be recognized as a classic second only to Griffith's *Catalogue of the Demotic Papyri in the John Rylands Library, Manchester*. But leisure still eluded Thompson. He moved to Bath, his mother's old home, where he could be near his friend Crum, and help him in the final stages of his Coptic dictionary and work also at another batch of demotic papyri (which he had helped the British Museum to acquire), to say nothing of making a preliminary study of the extremely important Coptic papyri, discovered in 1930, and containing the largest body of Manichean texts which have survived (later edited by Charles Robert C. Allberry). At the outbreak of war in 1939, by which time he had reached the age of eighty, he placed his house at the disposal of the Admiralty and moved to the edge of the city into smaller quarters, where it was impossible to house his books. Then at last his intention to cease publication prevailed; but it was not until his health failed in 1944 that he found it impossible to take his full share of duty as a fire-watcher.

By 1904, the year in which he succeeded his father in the baronetcy, Thompson had established himself as a demotic scholar, and on the death of Griffith in 1934 he was left head and shoulders above any other living student of that branch of Egyptology. When he died at Bath, 26 May 1944, he was among the first three or four Copticists of his day. If his output was comparatively small when his pre-eminence in his own field is taken into account, this should be attributed to the lateness of his entry into that field, made as it was at an age when most men must have either established their reputations or come to be regarded as failures. This may also perhaps explain why honours came to him but sparsely. He received the honorary degree of D.Litt. from the university of Oxford in 1926, became a fellow of University College, London, in 1930, and was elected F.B.A. in 1933. It is worth observing, as characteristic of his overwhelming modesty, as well as of his generosity, that three years later he resigned in order to make way for a younger man. If his reserve prevented him from making many friends, once friendship was made, it became a close and lasting bond, and he had a wide circle of acquaintances. He never married, and on his death the baronetcy became extinct.

[*The Times*, 29 May 1944; private information; personal knowledge.]

S. R. K. GLANVILLE.

THOMPSON, REGINALD CAMPBELL (1876–1941), Assyriologist, was born in London 21 August 1876, the eldest of the four sons of Reginald Edward Thompson, physician, by his wife, Anne Isabella, daughter of Augustus De Morgan [q.v.]. From St. Paul's School, where he had already displayed a private interest in cuneiform, he went up with an exhibition to Gonville and Caius College, Cambridge, in 1895, winning a scholarship in Hebrew and a first class in the oriental languages tripos (1898). The paramount interest of his life carried him almost at once (1899) into the Egyptian and Assyrian department of the British Museum, and although he remained there only a few years, resigning in 1905, his term of service was of extraordinary fertility in published work, and he even acquired some objects for the museum. He produced in six years no fewer than eight, and had a share in two more, parts of the *Cuneiform Texts in the British Museum*, covering a wide field of matter, Assyrian lexicography, incantations, omens, and late Babylonian letters. His copies of these were as accurate as they were neat, and not only provided a wealth of material for other scholars, but were the basis of translations and studies of his own, written simultaneously.

The first visit to the Near East made by Thompson as an orientalist was in 1904, when he accompanied Leonard William King on a mission to obtain a more complete and accurate version of the great rock-inscription of Darius at Bisitun, following and imitating the famous pioneer exploit of Sir H. C. Rawlinson [q.v.]. The result of their labours was afterwards published (in 1907), and has since been universally accepted as the standard text. Much later, at the end of the war of 1914–18, he undertook some soundings at Ur and a more thorough examination at Eridu in southern Babylonia. But his greatest contribution to the material of his science was made by four seasons of excavation, between 1927 and 1932, upon the mound of Nineveh, where his discoveries not only added considerably to the stock of remains, literary, architectural, and artistic, of the Assyrian empire, but revealed that on the site of this latest capital there had been a flourishing population since the earliest ages before history. Other expeditions which he shared or directed were at Carchemish (1911) and Wadi Sargah in Upper Egypt (1913).

After two years (1907–9) as assistant professor of Semitic languages at the university of Chicago, and on his return from Carchemish, and not long after his marriage, he settled near Oxford, whence he went to serve in the Mesopotamian campaign. His election to a fellowship at Merton College in 1923 enabled him to turn from the general writings which had marked the years of war to a steady preoccupation with the material of Assyrian natural science, in the knowledge of which

he rapidly established himself as the leading authority. The texts which he had published earlier in life had been largely devoted to this branch of ancient learning, and he now succeeded, by a long series of books and articles, in demonstrating the factual content and elucidating the processes of Assyrian science, as preserved in a mass of literature concerning medicine, botany, chemistry, and technology; his work upon this material is partly summed up in his twin dictionaries of Assyrian chemistry and geology (1936) and of Assyrian botany (published posthumously in 1949). Before this he had contributed six chapters to the *Cambridge Ancient History*, and in 1930 he brought out a new and exhaustive edition of *The Epic of Gilgamish*, presenting a completer text than had ever before been achieved, which at once became the canon of that celebrated poem. It had been foreshadowed by a verse translation very characteristic of the author, who in his life had turned his hand with no small success to the literature of travel, verse both serious and gay, and even to fiction. His distinction was recognized by the British Academy which elected him a fellow in 1934, and he succeeded to the Shillito readership in Assyriology at Oxford in 1937. For five years he edited the scientific journal *Iraq*.

On the formation of the Home Guard during the war of 1939–45, in accordance with the manly ideals and active habits which had marked his whole life, Thompson sought military service, and overstrain led to his sudden death when on duty at Moulsford 23 May 1941.

Thompson married in 1911 Barbara Brodrick, daughter of (Sir) Richard Atkinson Robinson, of Whitby. They had two sons, of whom the elder was killed on active service in the Royal Air Force in 1941, and one daughter.

[G. R. Driver in *Proceedings* of the British Academy, vol. xxx, 1944; *Nature*, 28 June 1941; *Archiv für Orientforschung*, vol. xiv, 1942; personal knowledge.]    C. J. GADD.

THORNE, WILLIAM JAMES (1857–1946), Labour leader, known as Will Thorne, was born in Birmingham 8 October 1857, the son of Thomas Thorne and his second wife, Emma Everiss. Both his parents worked in the brickyards, as their parents had done before them. Thomas Thorne also worked as a gas-stoker at Saltley gas works during the winter months. He had a family by his first wife and four children by his second—Will, the eldest, and three girls. He was a heavy drinker, and much given to fighting. He died when Will was seven years old, as the result of a blow from a horse-dealer who was sent to prison for nine months for manslaughter. After his death the family was very poor. Mrs. Thorne got home work sewing hooks and eyes on cards at $1\frac{1}{2}d.$ a gross of cards, and was also given an allowance of 4s. a week and four loaves of bread by the Birmingham guardians. Will went to work for $10\frac{1}{2}$ hours a day at the age of six, turning a wheel for a rope-maker for half a crown a week, and also working for his uncle, a barber, at the week-ends. His next jobs were at brick and tile works. At the age of nine he was getting 8s. a week. He then held a succession of labouring jobs as plumber's mate, metal-roller's assistant in an ammunition factory, nut and bolt tapper in a wagon works, builder's labourer, and brick-maker's assistant.

In 1875 his mother married again—a carpenter and joiner named George Thompson, of a more violent temper and an even heavier drinker than her first husband. Consequently Will went on tramp and became for a time a navvy on the construction of the Burton and Derby Railway. Returning to Birmingham he was again employed in the brickfields and then went to the Saltley gas works which belonged to the Birmingham corporation. He was still working there when in 1879 he married Harriet, daughter of John Hallam, a fellow worker at Saltley and an active Radical. Thorne achieved the abolition of Sunday work, but dissatisfied with the conditions at Saltley he left and in November 1881 tramped to London with two friends to seek work at the Old Kent Road gas works, belonging to the South Metropolitan Gas Company of which (Sir) George Livesey [q.v.] was then engineer and secretary. By this time his wife had had twins—boy and girl; but the boy died at six months. Mother and daughter joined him in south London; but presently Thorne was dismissed because work was slack, returned with his family to Birmingham and again found work at Saltley gas works. Again he left owing to a dispute about conditions and, tramping once more to London, got a job at Beckton gas works, lodging in Canning Town and soon bringing his wife, now with three children, to join him. About this time (1884) he joined the Social Democratic Federation of H. M. Hyndman [q.v.] for which he became an active propagandist. He had already tried to lead several strikes at his places of employment, although there were no trade unions among the less skilled workers. At Beckton, attempts had been made in 1884 and 1885 to form a union; but these had failed. At length on 31 March 1889, aided by Ben Tillett [q.v.], Thorne succeeded in establishing the National Union of Gasworkers and General Labourers out of which grew the huge National Union of General and Municipal Workers. The gas works then worked a shift of twelve hours; and Thorne's first task was to persuade his fellow members to make their first objective not a rise in wages but the eight-hour day. A petition was drawn up and sent to the London gas companies; and the Gas Light and Coke Company, which owned the Beckton and other works, was the first to concede the eight-hour day, without the need for a strike. Other companies followed suit; and the movement, and with it the union, spread rapidly to other parts of the country. In London it helped to prepare the ground for the great dock strike and for the establishment of the Dockers' Union with Ben Tillett as secretary. Thorne was the main speaker at the meeting at which the dock strike was begun.

In June 1889 Thorne had been elected general secretary of his union—the first of the 'new unions'—and occupied the position until he retired in 1934. Having received no formal education—at the time of his first marriage he could not sign his own name—he had a difficult time in adapting himself to the unfamiliar tasks of office and financial administration. But, as the union grew, he was able to get skilled office assistants and to spend most of his time in organizing and negotiating work. After the concession of the eight-hour day, the union put forward a demand for double pay for Sunday work. While the negotiations were in progress Livesey launched a profit-sharing scheme at the South Metropolitan Gas Company's works in the hope of breaking the union. This led to a strike which lasted more than two months, cost the union £20,000, and was not successful.

In 1890 Thorne was a delegate to the Trades Union Congress at Liverpool, where he helped to carry a resolution in favour of the legal eight-hour day. From 1894 to 1933 he was a member of the parliamentary committee (from 1921 the general council) of the Congress. He was its chairman in 1896–7 and 1911–12, presiding over the annual congress of 1912. In 1891 he was elected as a Socialist to the West Ham town council on which he remained, as an alderman from 1910, for the rest of his life. He was mayor in 1917–18 and was made a freeman of the borough in 1931. In 1898 he went as a fraternal delegate to the American Federation of Labor convention at Kansas City, and in 1913 as first fraternal delegate from Great Britain to the Canadian Trades and Labour Congress at St. John, New Brunswick. He stood as parliamentary candidate for West Ham (South) in 1900 but was defeated. In 1906 he won the seat and held it until he retired in 1945. On the outbreak of war in 1914 he took the side of the majority in supporting it and was made lieutenant-colonel in the West Ham Volunteer Force. In 1917, as a Labour delegate, with (Sir) James O'Grady and William Stephen Sanders, he went to Russia during the period between the two revolutions. He was appointed C.B.E. in 1930 and sworn of the Privy Council in 1945. His only book, an autobiography, *My Life's Battles*, appeared in 1925.

Thorne was a big man, very strongly built, and capable in his younger days of great feats of physical endurance. Such education as he acquired came to him in manhood, through his friendship with fellow Socialists, especially Ben Tillett, Edward Aveling and his wife, Eleanor Marx Aveling, who gave him much help in building up his union, and his close friends Pete Curran and J. R. Clynes [q.v.]. In Parliament he was no great figure; he gave his life to the affairs of his union and to West Ham. His mind was straightforward and without subtlety: he was an effective speaker at open-air meetings and had a great hold on the less skilled workers whom he had taught the value of combination. He owed his influence to his entire, single-minded honesty and devotion and to his immense capacity for hard work. Politically he remained faithful to the Social Democratic Federation, of which he was chairman in 1930, but he did not play an active part in it after the early years. His union came first in his thoughts and he did not aspire to political leadership. He died in London 2 January 1946.

Not long after his first wife's death, Thorne married in 1894 Emily, daughter of his friend William Byford, treasurer of the Gasworkers' Union. After her death he married in 1925 Rebecca Cecilia,

daughter of the late Thomas Sinclair, chief marine draughtsman. She died in the following year and in 1930 he married Beatrice Nellie, daughter of the late George Collins. By his first wife he had four sons and three daughters, and by his second, three sons and three daughters. His eldest surviving son, Will, was killed at Ypres in 1917; Karl, his favourite son, died in 1924. He was survived by his fourth wife, two sons and six daughters. A portrait by Margaretta Hicks is in the possession of the National Union of General and Municipal Workers.

[Will Thorne, *My Life's Battles*, 1925; Anon., *Sixty Years of the National Union of General and Municipal Workers, 1889–1949*, 1949; H. W. Lee and E. Archbold, *Social Democracy in Britain*, 1935; *Stratford Express*, 4 and 11 January 1946; personal knowledge.]

G. D. H. COLE.

TILLETT, BENJAMIN (1860–1943), Labour leader, known as Ben Tillett, was born at Easton, Bristol, 11 September 1860, the eighth child of Benjamin Tillett, a railway labourer, by his first wife, Elizabeth Lane, who died when Benjamin was in his third year. He left home at the age of eight in circumstances which foreshadowed the life which was to follow, for, when he was not allowed to keep a dog which he had found injured, Ben took the dog, ran away, and joined a circus. He entered the Royal Navy at thirteen years of age, served in the *Ganges*, *Sealark*, and *Resistance*, and earned some repute as a boxer. Health compelled him to quit the navy for the mercantile marine, and shortly afterwards in his early twenties he became a tea-porter at the London docks.

Tillett was greatly shocked by the conditions in which the dockers were employed and at a meeting in 1887 suggested the formation of the Tea Operatives' and General Labourers' Association of which he was appointed secretary. The union made headway and in August 1889, after a meeting at which Will Thorne (a notice of whom appears above) was the principal speaker, the great London dock strike began. The dockers demanded 6d. an hour and 8d. for overtime; work for not less than four hours at a stretch with calls at stated times, and the abolition of contract and piece work. Tillett was described by his contemporaries as 'the man of the period with a spark of genius and imagination'; it was a new and significant departure in trade-union history to enlist, as he did, the help of skilled craftsmen such as Tom Mann and John Burns [qq.v.], both of them trained engineers. Processions, picketing, and relief were organized with a remarkable maintenance of order. The last was made possible by contributions from many sources, not least from overseas—notably Australia—whence came over £30,000.

After five weeks the strike was brought to an end by the influence of Cardinal Manning [q.v.] and the dock workers secured substantial improvements in their conditions, gaining a minimum payment of 6d. an hour. Tillett's union now shouldered greater responsibilities and had won a stable membership. Its name was changed to the Dock, Wharf, Riverside and General Workers' Union, commonly known as the Dockers' Union, with branches in most of the important ports. Several similar organizations, mostly regional, were formed, and Tillett, realizing the weakness which this involved, campaigned in the early 'nineties for federation, but although some groupings took place, they were short-lived owing to the reluctance of the affiliated organizations to concede authority.

Efforts to strengthen the trade-union organization of transport workers finally achieved success in 1910 when the executive of Tillett's union invited all kindred bodies to a conference in London. From this the National Transport Workers' Federation was formed, and, typical of Tillett's generosity and imaginative approach to the problem, he nominated Harry Gosling [q.v.], the leader of the small but powerful union of Thames lightermen, as president. With Gosling he began a tour of all the ports, popularizing the idea of federation and declaring the need for discipline within its ranks. In 1911 another great strike of dockers occurred, originating in support of the seamen who were in conflict with the shipowners. The strike was noteworthy for the solidarity of all those involved in it, although it has been estimated that only half the transport workers were organized. Lastly, not satisfied with national organization, Tillett worked also for the International Federation of Ship, Dock and River Workers which he helped to found in 1896. Visits to strikers led to his ejection from both Antwerp and Hamburg.

In the 'nineties and again in 1908 Tillett visited Australia, where the system of compulsory arbitration for the settlement of trade disputes greatly impressed him; and he made many efforts to convert the British Trades Union Congress to this policy. On his initiative the matter was for a number of years the principal subject of debate at the annual congress. He often declared that he hated strikes, knowing too well the hardship which they inflicted on the women and children of the strikers, and he said that he had never fomented a strike for its own sake.

In the political aspects of the Labour movement Tillett was always interested. He became an alderman in 1892 of the London County Council; was a member of the parliamentary committee of the Trades Union Congress from 1892 to 1894, a member of the Social Democratic Federation, and one of the founders of the Independent Labour Party and of the Labour Party. After contesting West Bradford in 1892 and 1895, Eccles in 1906, and Swansea Town in January 1910, he sat for North Salford from 1917 to 1924 and again from 1929 to 1931.

Tillett was wholehearted in his support of the war of 1914–18 and gave many lectures and appeals for unstinted service, touring some 3,000 miles of the battle fronts; 'by his knowledge of men and methods', said the commander-in-chief Sir John French (later the Earl of Ypres, q.v.), he 'reached a class who would not generally attend meetings or lectures'.

From 1921 until 1931 Tillett was a member of the general council of the Trades Union Congress, and its chairman in 1928–9, presiding over the annual congress of 1929. In 1922 his union amalgamated in the Transport and General Workers' Union in which he became secretary to the political and international department until he retired on pension in 1931. He belonged to the evangelistic days of trade-unionism, when men spoke with natural oratory. In him the new union of organized unskilled labourers, in whose well-being the craft unions had shown but little interest, found its principal inspiration.

In 1882 Tillett married Jane Tomkins; they had two daughters who survived infancy. He died at Golders Green 27 January 1943. A bronze bust by J. A. Stevenson is in the City Art Gallery, Bristol, and portraits by Eric Kennington and T. A. West are in the possession of the family.

[Ben Tillett, *Memories and Reflections*, 1931, *A Brief History of the Dockers' Union*,

1910, and *History of the London Transport Workers' Strike 1911*, 1912; H. Llewellyn Smith and Vaughan Nash, *The Story of the Dockers' Strike*, 1890; private information; personal knowledge.] J. J. TAYLOR.

TIWANA, NAWAB SIR (MUHAMMAD) UMAR HAYAT (1874–1944), statesman, was born at Kalra, Punjab, 1 October 1874. He was the only son of Sahib Khan, C.S.I., head of the Tiwana clan and one of the largest landowners in the Punjab. His father died in 1878 and he was brought up in the traditions of a family which had raised the 18th Tiwana Lancers and was steadfast in loyalty to the British Government as the deliverer of the Moslems of the Punjab from Sikh tyranny and the inaugurator of a régime of peace and law in India.

After education at the Aitchison Chiefs' College, Lahore, he received an honorary commission (1901) as a lieutenant in the 18th Tiwana Lancers. He saw active service in Somaliland (1903) and Tibet (1904) and on the staff with the Indian Expeditionary Force in France (1914–15) and in Mesopotamia where his intelligence work and advice on soldiers' welfare was of great value, and in the Afghan war (1919). Appointed K.C.I.E. (1916), he served on the army in India committee (1919–20).

While a member of the Council of State (1921–8) he was an active supporter of Government in measures concerned with the maintenance of law and order. He took part in all debates about the Indian Army, its composition and recruitment, pay and pensions, and the welfare of its troops. He vigorously opposed the campaign of the Congress Party which in his view threatened a too-rapid devolution of power into the hands of a narrow oligarchy, mainly Hindu and drawn from the banking and trading communities to the detriment of the agricultural classes—especially the Moslems—who although backward in education paid the bulk of the taxes and in the case of the martial people of the north-west bore the burden of the defence of the country. He advocated gradual political advance, waiting for its consummation until the Indian peoples had become more united and better equipped for wider responsibilities.

As a member of the Council of India (1929–34) he was at the India Office during the period of the Round Table conferences and the joint parliamentary committee preceding the Government of India Act of 1935. His knowledge was of value to the secretary of state for India and his military adviser. He was appointed G.B.E. in 1934 and an honorary major-general in 1935. He was made honorary aide-de-camp to the King in 1930 and reappointed in 1936, and in 1935 he became an honorary colonel of the 19th King George's Own Lancers. During his last decade he left the stage of public affairs to his son (Sir) Khizar Hayat Tiwana (born 1900), living to see him become prime minister of the Punjab in 1942. He died at Kalra 24 March 1944.

[Official papers; family records; personal knowledge.] GEOFFREY DE MONTMORENCY.

TOPLEY, WILLIAM WHITEMAN CARLTON (1886–1944), bacteriologist, was born at Lewisham, London, 19 January 1886, the eldest of the three sons of Ebenezer Topley, wholesale grocer, by his wife, Elizabeth Whiteman. William Topley [q.v.] was his uncle. He was educated at the City of London School and at St. John's College, Cambridge, of which he became a scholar in 1906 and where he gained a first class in the natural sciences tripos of 1907. His medical training was received at St. Thomas's Hospital, and he qualified in 1909. After serving as house-physician, demonstrator of morbid anatomy, and assistant director of the pathological laboratory at St. Thomas's Hospital in 1910, he was appointed bacteriologist to the Samaritan Free Hospital for Women, director of the clinical pathological department and lecturer on bacteriology at Charing Cross Hospital from 1911 to 1922, and professor of bacteriology, university of Manchester, from 1922 to 1927. During the war of 1914–18 he served as a captain, Royal Army Medical Corps, and in 1915 was bacteriologist to the British sanitary commission in Serbia. From 1927 to 1941 he was professor of bacteriology and immunology at London University and director of the division of bacteriology and immunology at the London School of Hygiene and Tropical Medicine. He was a member of the Medical Research Council from 1938 until 1941, and early in 1939 he took a leading part in the organization of emergency laboratory services to meet the needs of impending war.

At the Royal College of Physicians Topley was Murchison scholar in 1910; was admitted a fellow in 1918; he delivered the Goulstonian lectures in 1919 and the Milroy lectures in 1926. In 1930 he was elected F.R.S., served on the council of the Royal Society from 1936–7 and 1938–40, was Croonian lecturer in 1941, and received a Royal medal in 1942 for his work on experimental epidemiology and immunology. In 1942 he was elected an honorary fellow of St. John's College, Cambridge. In 1941 he was appointed secretary of the Agricultural Research Council, and he was also a member of the War Cabinet scientific advisory committee and of the colonial research advisory committee.

Topley was not only a brilliant investigator but also a great administrator. As an inspirer of young men he had no superior and for more than twenty years he was a conspicuous figure in British medicine. His own investigations were mainly concerned with the spread of bacterial infection, and he was one of the first to use experimental methods in the study of epidemics. The most important of his numerous published papers were those dealing with his researches on experimental epidemiology (1925–39); much of this work was summarized in the Special Report No. 209 issued by the Medical Research Council in 1936. *The Principles of Bacteriology and Immunity* which he wrote with Dr. Graham Selby Wilson (2 vols., 1929) rapidly established itself as the standard work of reference in the English language. His *Outline of Immunity* (1933) was a masterly review of the then state of knowledge in this subject.

Topley married in 1912 Kate, daughter of Frederick William Amsden, of Sevenoaks, Kent; they had twin daughters. He died suddenly in London 21 January 1944.

[M. Greenwood in *Obituary Notices of Fellows of the Royal Society*, No. 13, November 1944; *Journal of Pathology and Bacteriology*, vol. lvi, July 1944; *The Times*, 22 January 1944; *British Medical Journal* and *Lancet*, 5 February 1944; *Nature*, 19 February 1944.]
W. J. BISHOP.

TOWSE, SIR (ERNEST) BEACHCROFT (BECKWITH) (1864–1948), soldier and pioneer of blind welfare, was born in London 23 April 1864, the elder of the two sons of Robert Beckwith Towse, solicitor, and his wife, an Irish girl, Julia Ann Corcoran. High-spirited and adventurous, Towse was educated at Stubbington House and Wellington College, and in 1883 joined the 3rd Seaforth Highlanders. In 1886 he transferred to the Gordon Highlanders; he served with the Chitral relief force, was present at the

storming of the Malakand pass, was promoted captain in 1896, and took part in the North-West Frontier and Tirah campaigns. In October 1899 he went with the 1st battalion of his regiment to South Africa and was present at the advance on Kimberley and the battle of Magersfontein. On 30 April 1900, when rallying his force of twelve men to attack some 150 Boers, he received the serious injury which cost him his sight. For his gallantry on this occasion and for an earlier attempt at Magersfontein to carry his mortally wounded commanding officer to safety, he was awarded the Victoria Cross.

His brilliant military career behind him, Towse turned all his vigorous powers of body and mind to the service of the blind community. In 1901 he joined the council of the National Institute for the Blind, then known as the British and Foreign Blind Association, and became vice-chairman the same year. He was also a member of the committee of the Incorporated Association for Promoting the General Welfare of the Blind. In the years which followed he travelled the length and breadth of the country to help the work of the Institute and foster public interest in the welfare of the blind. When war broke out in 1914 Towse was soon in uniform again as a staff captain for base hospitals in France and Belgium. He brought comfort to many as they lay wounded, writing letters home from his braille notes; in this work he was probably one of the first of the now familiar welfare officers, and was mentioned in dispatches.

Before going to the war himself he suggested to the National Institute for the Blind that they should set up a sub-committee to look after the blinded ex-servicemen. This, under the inspiration of Sir C. Arthur Pearson [q.v.], developed into St. Dunstan's, but Towse realized that there was still no help available for ex-servicemen who went blind through causes other than the war, or for the blind dependants of servicemen. In 1923, therefore, he inaugurated a Special Fund for Blind Ex-Servicemen which continued in existence as the Sir Beachcroft Towse Ex-Service Fund.

His concern for all who returned from the war led him to help in launching in 1917 the organization of the Comrades of the Great War and as chairman he travelled during two years over 12,000 miles in the British Isles. This organization subsequently merged with others to form the British Legion of which he became a vice-president in 1927, remaining in office until his death.

Captain Towse's striking figure with its soldierly bearing and immaculate attire, including a fascinating tartan waistcoat, was also often to be seen at great functions. In 1900 he was made a sergeant-at-arms in ordinary, and from 1903 to 1939 he was a member of the Honourable Corps of Gentlemen-at-Arms. In 1920 he was appointed C.B.E. and in 1927 K.C.V.O. in recognition of his valuable services to the blind and to ex-servicemen. In 1916 he became a knight of grace of the Order of St. John of Jerusalem.

The war of 1939–45 brought Towse into yet another field of service when he made his home at Long Meadow, Goring-on-Thames, available for civilians blinded through air raids. It thus became the first Queen Elizabeth Home of Recovery and he remained there in charge of this important work of rehabilitation. In 1944, on account of continuous ill health and advancing years, he resigned from the chairmanship of the National Institute for the Blind which he had assumed in 1923. His resignation was received 'with a sense of personal loss and poignancy of regret almost too deep for words', and he was elected president, an office which had been vacant since the death of Pearson in 1921.

Towse was also a member of the livery of the Fishmongers' Company and of the court of the Clothworkers' Company, health alone preventing him from taking up the mastership of the latter, to which he was elected in 1941. He was also vice-president of Worcester College for the Blind, of the Greater London Fund for the Blind, of the Hepburn Starey Blind Aid Society, and chairman of the British Wireless for the Blind Fund. In early life his chief interests, apart from his Service career, had been polo, hunting, and big game shooting. After he was blinded he became a very fine fisherman and a skilful carpenter and joiner.

Towse married in 1892 Gertrude (died 1935), daughter of John Christie, a stockbroker. There were no children of the marriage and in his later years he was cared for by a niece. He died at his home at Goring 21 June 1948.

[Private information; personal knowledge.]
BASIL CURTIS.

TRITTON, SIR WILLIAM ASHBEE (1875–1946), engineer, was born in Islington 19 June 1875, the son of William Birch Tritton, a stockbroker and a member of a Hythe family, and his wife, Ellen Hannah Ashbee. Tritton was educated at Christ's College, Finchley, and King's College, London. In 1891 he was apprenticed with J. & H. Gwynne, of Hammersmith, hydraulic engineers. After completing his apprenticeship and serving with an assay company, he became an inspector of steel rails. He next joined J. I. Thornycroft & Co. at their Chiswick works and was responsible for the building of circulating pumps in torpedo boats. He gained further experience as a shift engineer with the Metropolitan Electric Supply Company and in 1899 entered the toolroom of the Linotype Company, Ltd. In this post he seems to have visited Germany and gained the experience which enabled him in 1904 to go out on behalf of R. Garrett & Sons, Ltd., of Leiston, Suffolk, to clear up difficulties which had arisen in their German works.

In 1905 he accepted the position of general manager of William Foster & Co., Ltd., of Lincoln. The firm's affairs were then in a poor condition, but Tritton's energy and ability effected a recovery; in the process he was in touch with agents all over the world, especially in Russia and the Argentine. In 1911 he became managing director.

Tritton came into prominence in the war of 1914–18 through the part he played in the design and production of tanks. At the beginning of the war he was invited to discuss the problem of transporting 15-inch howitzers with Rear-Admiral (Sir) Reginald Bacon [q.v.], managing director of the Coventry Ordnance Works. Their proposals were laid before (Sir) Winston Churchill, first lord of the Admiralty, and the first sea lord, and an order for tractors was placed with Tritton's company. During the trials, which proved satisfactory, a large ditch was crossed by a tractor, and (Sir) Winston Churchill asked whether a machine could be constructed which would cross trenches. Tritton then designed a tractor which could cross a trench eight feet wide by means of its wheels and an automatic portable bridge. The machine was not used, however, because of its weight, and because in the meantime the whole conception had caught the imagination of (Sir) Winston Churchill who, with his customary energy, appointed a landships committee, 20 February 1915, under the chairmanship of (Sir) Eustace Tennyson-D'Eyncourt, to investigate the project more fully. Meanwhile, (Sir) Ernest

Swinton was urging similar proposals upon the War Office. In June a joint naval and military committee was formed to co-ordinate experiments which had been based on alternative proposals of a large wheel tractor or a caterpillar tractor. Tritton had been in close consultation from the beginning and at the end of July was told more exactly what the machine was required to do. The first design, 'Little Willie', with an endless chain track, was ready to move by 19 September 1915. It was not successful but was re-designed and first operated on 3 December. Meanwhile Lieutenant (later Major) Walter Gordon Wilson, who was working with Tritton on the problem, had suggested that the track should be carried all round the machine rather than on two side girders. A new, much bigger, and more complex machine, known as 'Big Willie' and later as 'Mother', designed by Tritton and Wilson, was ready to move under its own power on 6 January 1916. Swathed in tarpaulins, it was taken by rail to Hatfield for trials at which Lloyd George, Balfour, McKenna, Kitchener, Robertson and many other soldiers, and engineers were present. The trials were adjudged successful and orders were placed with Fosters and other firms. To preserve secrecy the new machines were described as 'tanks', an inoffensive term which took on a new meaning when the machines first went into action in France, 15 September 1916. Although their first appearance was somewhat disappointing, improvements were soon made. Tritton, who was knighted in 1917, was appointed director of construction of the mechanical warfare supply department (tanks) and he devised a modified tank, lighter, smaller, and faster, known as the Whippet, which was used successfully at Cambrai and in the campaigns of 1918 under the command of (Sir) H. J. Elles [q.v.].

In 1919 the Royal Commission on awards to inventors had the difficult task of assessing the claims of those who had helped in the evolution of the tank. To Tritton and Wilson the commission accorded by far the highest award and the credit of designing and producing the tank 'in a concrete practical shape'.

In 1927 Tritton formed Gwynnes Pumps, Ltd., to take over the business of Gwynnes, of Hammersmith, and transferred its activities to Lincoln. He took a leading part in the maintenance of essential services during the general strike in 1926 and he became chairman of Fosters in 1939. A cautious and pains-taking man, he was a pleasant and hospitable companion and a good employer. He was of even temper, although strong views, strongly expressed, sometimes gave the impression that he was hasty. He took little part in public life, although he gave valuable expert help to the Lincoln County Hospital extension schemes. He became a justice of the peace in 1934 and was for a time chairman of his bench.

In 1916 Tritton married Isabella Johnstone White (died 1950), daughter of Grahame Gillies, of Perth; there were no children. Tritton died at Lincoln 24 September 1946.

[Sir W. A. Tritton, *The Tank: its Birth and Development*, privately printed for William Foster & Co., Ltd.; J. F. C. Fuller, *Tanks in the Great War, 1914–18*, 1920; *A Short History of the Royal Tank Corps*, 1930; Sir Albert G. Stern, *Tanks 1914–1918*, 1919; Sir Ernest D. Swinton, *Eyewitness*, 1932; Winston S. Churchill, *The World Crisis*, vol. ii, 1923; private information; personal knowledge.]

J. W. F. HILL.

TROUBRIDGE, SIR THOMAS HOPE (1895–1949), vice-admiral, was born at Southsea 1 February 1895, the only son of Lieutenant (later Admiral Sir) Ernest Charles Thomas Troubridge [q.v.] by his first wife, Edith Duffus. He came of a long line which gave distinguished service to Britain, chiefly in the Royal Navy, and was a direct descendant of Rear-Admiral Sir Thomas Troubridge [q.v.] who led the line at the battle of Cape St. Vincent. Troubridge entered the Royal Navy as a cadet in 1908, and, passing through Osborne and Dartmouth, was gazetted midshipman in September 1912. In the war of 1914–18 he saw action off the Dogger Bank and at Jutland, became a lieutenant in 1916, and in the following year was appointed to coastal motor-boats in which he remained until the armistice.

He then served for a time as staff officer to his father who was at Budapest as president of the International Danube Commission. There Troubridge learnt German and laid the foundations of a knowledge of foreign countries and of diplomatic usage which became far wider than is usually possessed by a naval officer. On returning to England he took a course in gunnery and then served as a gunnery officer in the *Queen Elizabeth* (1922–4). Specialization in a technical branch was not, perhaps, his true vocation and he soon abandoned a gunnery career to take the naval staff course (1924) after which he served in the Atlantic Fleet as staff officer operations. In 1928 he was appointed to the royal yacht *Victoria and Albert* and was promoted to commander at the end of 1929. He was next selected for the army staff course at Camberley. The friendships which he there made were to stand him in good stead later when, in the war of 1939–45, he came to take a prominent part in combined operations; for many of the senior army officers concerned in them had been at Camberley with him. From the Staff College he returned to destroyers with command of the *Voyager* in the Mediterranean Fleet. He remained in destroyers, except for a break for courses, until promoted captain in 1934 at the age of thirty-nine. In that rank his first appointment was in 1936 as naval attaché, Berlin, at a time when it was still hoped that, by the Anglo-German naval agreement of 1935, a new German challenge to British supremacy at sea might be held off and a *modus vivendi* reached with Hitler. Troubridge remained in Berlin until the end of July 1939.

On New Year's Day, 1940, Troubridge was appointed to command the aircraft carrier *Furious* in the Home Fleet. The most important operations in which she took part were those off Norway in April and May 1940 when a few dozen naval aircraft working from carriers tried to remedy our lack of air power on land. Their effort, although inevitably unsuccessful, was a glorious chapter in the story of British naval aviation. In June 1941 Troubridge was appointed to command the battleship *Nelson*, then flying the flag of Sir James Somerville [q.v.] in Force H at Gibraltar. It was a period of intense activity, chiefly for the supply of the besieged island of Malta. During one of the many convoy operations to carry stores and men to that island the *Nelson* was torpedoed by an aircraft and damaged, 27 September 1941. Troubridge next returned to aircraft carriers with command of the *Indomitable*, which was serving in the recently reconstituted Eastern Fleet. In her he took part in the assault and capture of the base of Diego Suarez in Madagascar in May 1942. In August of that year Troubridge returned to the task of relieving Malta. The *Indomitable* formed part of a powerful force assembled to fight through a convoy of fourteen ships at a critical time. She was severely damaged by German dive-bombers in the process and only five of

the fourteen merchant ships in the convoy reached their destination. Troubridge was appointed to the D.S.O. for his services in this operation.

The damage to the *Indomitable* released Troubridge at a time when preparations were being made in Britain and the United States for the invasion of North Africa. This was the first major combined operation of the war and marked the resumption by the Allies of the strategic offensive. Troubridge was appointed, with the rank of commodore, to command the Central Task Force, the duty of which was to attack and seize the great French naval base at Oran. His force, which consisted of thirty-four transports and seventy warships, struck in the small hours of 8 November 1942. Stiff French resistance had to be overcome, but Oran was captured on 10 November and the first major enemy base in North Africa passed into allied hands. Troubridge received the American D.S.M. and a bar to the D.S.O. He returned to England early in 1943 and was promoted to rear-admiral. His successful service in the invasion of North Africa made it inevitable that his experience would be used in the other great combined operations now being prepared. With his flag in the headquarters ship *Bulolo* he was next appointed to command, under Sir Bertram Ramsay [q.v.], one of the four great naval forces organized for the invasion of Sicily. Troubridge's force, consisting of some seventy-five warships, was responsible for transporting the 5th and 50th divisions and the 231st brigade from ports in the Middle East to the rendezvous off the enemy coast, and thereafter for landing and protecting the troops assigned to the two northern sectors of the assault area on the east coast of Sicily. The landings took place early on 10 July and by 10 a.m. Troubridge was able to report 'all beaches captured'.

The campaign for the liberation of Europe now moved to the mainland of Italy. Troubridge's force did not take part in the landing at Salerno in September, but in January 1944 he was responsible for landing the 1st British division to the north of Anzio. The landings were wholly successful although the operation encountered serious, even critical, difficulties after the troops were ashore.

In July 1944 Troubridge was appointed to command the force of nine British and American escort carriers organized to give air escort and cover to the forces invading the south of France. The carrier force arrived off the assault area early on 15 August and remained until the 27th, by which time the success of the landings was beyond doubt. For his 'distinguished service and zeal' on this occasion Troubridge was appointed C.B. The seven British carriers which he commanded now went back to the eastern Mediterranean. His next duty was to hamper the German withdrawal from Greece, Crete, and the Aegean Islands with his carrier aircraft and light surface forces. During the latter part of September many successful minor actions were fought. Early in October Troubridge was relieved and returned to England shortly afterwards.

On 1 May 1945 he joined the Board of Admiralty as fifth sea lord, whose particular responsibility was for the naval air service. In December he was promoted K.C.B. 'for distinguished service throughout the war in Europe'. In September 1946 he hoisted his flag again, this time ashore, as admiral (air) in command of all naval air stations in Britain. In January 1947 he was promoted vice-admiral and a year later took up what was to prove his last active appointment— that of flag officer (air) and second-in-command of the Mediterranean Fleet. He thus returned to the station in which he had served with such distinction during the war. Unhappily his health gave way and he returned home in November 1948. His sudden death followed 29 September 1949 at Hawkley, Hampshire.

Troubridge was an officer of commanding presence, possessed of great gifts of mind and of personality. He played most games and excelled especially at cricket, and rackets at which he won the navy championship. To those who knew him well it was no surprise that war service rapidly proved him one of the outstanding fighting leaders of his Service. Although he had no experience of naval aviation until early in the war, he may justly be regarded as one of the pioneers in the use of carrier-borne aircraft, particularly in combined operations. But for his early death he would probably have risen to the highest posts which the Royal Navy can offer.

In 1925 Troubridge married Lilly, daughter of Herman Greverus Kleinwort, banker, by whom he had three sons and one daughter. His eldest son entered the Royal Navy and his second son the Royal Marines. A portrait by Richard Marientreu is in the possession of the family.

[Private information; Admiralty records.]

S. W. ROSKILL.

TURNER, SIR BEN (1863–1942), Labour pioneer, was born at Holmfirth, Yorkshire, 25 August 1863, the second son of Jonathan Turner, by his wife, Emma Moorhouse. They were hand-loom weavers, with Luddite and Chartist ancestry. Such education as Turner received from dame and church schools was subsequently widened by a scholarship (together with work as secretary) in the Secular Sunday School at Huddersfield, and by attendance at a Mechanics' Institute. Beginning at the age of nine and a half in helping domestic hand-loom weaving at $3\frac{1}{2}d.$ a day, he gradually rose through various stages of employment, and in 1882 joined the recently formed weavers' association which eventually became the General Union of Weavers and Textile Workers. This led to his coming under one of the great influences in his career, his association with Allen Gee, a friendship which lasted until Gee's death, and whereby Turner became one of the pioneers of the Labour movement in Yorkshire. He was appointed an officer in his union in 1889, and was its president from 1902 until 1922 when it amalgamated with two other unions to form the National Union of Textile Workers over which he presided until 1933. He was also president of the National Association of Unions in the Textile Trade from 1917 until 1929.

Turner's keen support of the orthodox Radical doctrines of the day, from republicanism to voluntary (as opposed to compulsory) vaccination, developed into Socialism, and he joined successively the Social Democratic Federation, the Fabian Society, and, on its foundation at Bradford in 1893, the Independent Labour Party. He supported the resolution of the Trades Union Congress in 1899 which brought the Labour Party into being and he served for seventeen years on the national executive. In his parliamentary ambitions he was handicapped by phases of unpopularity. He had twice contested Dewsbury and, after the redistribution of seats in 1918, had once contested Batley and Morley before he succeeded in gaining that seat in 1922 and 1923; but he lost it in 1924, regained it in 1929, and was heavily defeated in 1931. The only political office which he held was the parliamentary secretaryship for mines in 1929, but he resigned the following year.

In the local politics of Batley, of which he was later elected an honorary freeman, he served the borough for forty-eight years as councillor, as alderman, and four times as mayor; he was elected a councillor (1910) and later an alderman of the West Riding of Yorkshire. In trade-union politics his most vigorous doctrine was that overtime aggravated the evil of unemployment. In 1910 he attended the American Federation of Labor convention; in 1920 he was a Labour Party delegate of the first official delegation to Russia of the Labour Party and Trades Union Congress. He served on the general council of the Trades Union Congress from 1921 until 1928, was its chairman, 1927–8, and presided over the annual congress of 1928. Tenure of this high office marked the zenith of Turner's career for in conjunction with Sir Alfred Mond (later Lord Melchett, q.v.) he entered into the negotiations which bear their names for establishing a method of conciliation between employers and employed in industrial disputes. Like similar attempts, these proved abortive.

Turner's public services were recognized by his appointment as O.B.E. in 1917, C.B.E. in 1930, and by a knighthood in 1931. In periods of unemployment during his youth he had eked out a living by journalism and in authorship. He showed some merit in his handling of Yorkshire dialect, and with justifiable pride could show that his fellow Fabian, G. B. Shaw [q.v.], had consulted him on dialect in the early drafts of St. Joan. A volume of Collected Rhymes and Verse was published in 1934.

In 1884 Turner married a cotton spinner, Elizabeth (died 1939), daughter of Joash Hopkinson, and was survived by five daughters. A portrait painted in 1917 by R. H. Blackham is in the Batley Council Chambers. Turner died at Batley 30 September 1942.

[Ben Turner, About Myself, 1930; The Times, 2 October 1942; personal knowledge.]
　　　　　　　　　　J. S. MIDDLETON.

TURNER, WALTER JAMES REDFERN (1889–1946), poet, musical critic, journalist, and playwright, was born 13 October 1889 at Melbourne, Australia, where his father, Walter James Turner, was a well-known figure and organist of the pro-cathedral. His mother, Alice Watson, was also a capable musician; Noel Mewton-Wood, the pianist, was his nephew. The death of his younger brother in boyhood caused a violent shock which

afterwards gave rise to a personal mythology which emerges in several of his books and poems, including the famous 'Romance'. He was educated at Scotch College, Melbourne, and afterwards had a single year at the School of Mines. Coming to England in about 1907 he soon escaped to a more congenial life in Germany; during this period he travelled in France, Italy, Austria, and South Africa.

Although during the war he served with the Royal Garrison Artillery and, to his lasting surprise, rose to the rank of captain, he had published two volumes of poetry by 1918 and emerged from the war a recognized poet and member of the Georgian group. Among his closest friends at this time were Mr. Siegfried Sassoon and Mr. Ralph Hodgson. He now launched the journalistic career which he was never ashamed of enjoying. He was an influential musical critic of the New Statesman from 1916 until 1940 and dramatic critic of the London Mercury from 1919 to 1923; he served as literary editor of the Daily Herald from 1920 to 1923 when it was under the idealistic management of George Lansbury [q.v.], and was literary editor of the Spectator from 1942 until his death.

All through the inter-war years he was immensely prolific, publishing a volume of poems every two or three years, several minor works of musical criticism, studies of Beethoven, Mozart, Wagner, and Berlioz, and his satirical comedy The Man who Ate the Popomack (1922). He was one of a group of friends much addicted to conversation which included Mark Gertler [q.v.] and Professor John Nicolas Mavrogordato; during the 'thirties, too, his friendship with W. B. Yeats [q.v.] ripened, and Yeats, who delighted in his poetry, included a large selection in the Oxford Book of Modern Verse. Through Yeats, Turner met Dorothy Wellesley and with her was associated in the wartime launching of the successful 'Britain in Pictures' series of which he was the general editor. In 1935 and 1936 there appeared the autobiographical Blow for Balloons and Henry Airbubble: with their wit, poetic penetration, fantasy, and occasional cussedness they perfectly reflect the author's own nature; it only remains to add that Turner had a knowledge of the world, even a kind of ruthlessness, which was yet in perfect harmony with the innocence of a true artist. His poetry is as idiosyncratic as was his nature; although by experimenting with free metrical forms and colloquial idiom he made concessions to the spirit of the time, his poetry was too rich in imagery and sound, too lyrical, sensuous, and unintellectual to belong to the fashionable trends of the inter-war period. Although no believer in the careful polishing of verses, he wrote a few lyrics which may justly be called perfect. The poetic gift never left him; his last volume, *Fossils of a Future Time?* (1946), was in the press when he died after a cerebral haemorrhage, 18 November 1946, in his house at Hammersmith Terrace, Chiswick. In 1918 he married Delphine Marguerite (died 1951), daughter of the late Gabriel Dubuis, a scientific and medical inventor; they had no children. Portraits by Gilbert Spencer and Sir William Nicholson and a drawing by Eric Kennington are privately owned. A drawing by (Sir) William Rothenstein is reproduced in *Twenty-Four Portraits* (2nd series, 1923).

[Private information; personal knowledge.]
JACQUETTA HAWKES.

TYNDALE-BISCOE, CECIL EARLE (1863–1949), missionary and educationist in Kashmir, was born 9 February 1863 at Holton, Oxfordshire, the son of William Earle Tyndale by his wife, Elizabeth Carey, daughter of George Glas Sandeman, of Westfield, South Hayling, Hampshire. His father changed his surname to Biscoe on inheriting Holton Park, but the son later added Tyndale to his name. He was the fourth child in a family of eight, seven of them sons.

Tyndale-Biscoe was educated at Bradfield, and went up to Jesus College, Cambridge, in 1882. There he quickly made his mark, particularly on the river. He coxed the college boat which was head of the river for three years in succession and won the Grand Challenge Cup at Henley in 1886; and he coxed the winning Cambridge boat in 1884. Graduating B.A. in 1886, he was ordained deacon in 1887 and priest in 1890. After serving curacies at Bradfield, Berkshire, and in Whitechapel, he went to Kashmir in 1890 as head of the school recently established by the Church Missionary Society at Srinagar. Here he worked for fifty-seven years, accomplishing one of the most remarkable pieces of work ever done in the mission field. The school grew until it contained some 1,800 pupils in six schools, one of them being a girls' school, perhaps the most remarkable of all his achievements. He resigned in 1947 and went to Southern

Rhodesia where he died at Salisbury 1 August 1949. His work was recognized by the award of the Kaisar-i-Hind gold medal in 1912, to which was added a bar in 1929. He was appointed honorary canon in Lahore Cathedral in 1932, becoming canon emeritus in 1942. He was elected an honorary fellow of Jesus College, Cambridge, in 1945.

Tyndale-Biscoe was in many ways unique. His book *Fifty Years against the Stream* (1931) and his autobiography, *Tyndale-Biscoe of Kashmir* (1951), give the picture of a man of unconventional methods, of amazing moral courage, and complete disregard of public opinion. Compromise was a word unknown to him. He found himself surrounded by social abuses and corrupt practices, but carried through reform after reform in the face of bitter opposition. Profoundly influenced by his own experiences at school, he held character to be the most important matter in education. All his work was to this end and all he did was founded on the example of Christ. That he made an impression on the youth of Kashmir may be judged from the fact that it was frequently considered a better qualification for an appointment to be a 'Biscoe boy' and all that that meant than to have a university degree. His rowing experience in Cambridge stood him in good stead among the lakes and rivers of Kashmir. His school crest was a pair of paddles, crossed, bearing the motto 'In all things be men'. The greatest honour that a boy could achieve was to save life. A unique honour board with names of boys who have done this occupies the central place in the hall of his first school.

In 1891 he married Blanche Violet (died 1947), daughter of the Rev. Richard Bennett Burges, formerly vicar of St. Paul's, Birmingham. There were three sons and one daughter of the marriage.

[Private information; personal knowledge.]
GEORGE BARNE.

TYRRELL, WILLIAM GEORGE, BARON TYRRELL (1866–1947), diplomatist, was born at Naini Tal, India, 17 August 1866, the son of William Henry Tyrrell, who became judge of the High Court of Judicature, North-Western Provinces of India, and his wife, Julia, daughter of Lieutenant-Colonel John Howard Wakefield, of the East India Company. Her sister married Prince Radolin who was German ambassador in Paris at the outbreak of war in 1914. R. Y. Tyrrell [q.v.] was William Tyrrell's uncle and farther back in his pedigree there was oriental blood which had its influence perhaps in his seemingly oblique approaches to problems and personalities, and in his uncanny nimbleness of thought and intuition. A Roman Catholic, he was educated in Germany under the auspices of Prince Radolin and came to know the country and the people as well as any Englishman of his time. Then in 1885 he went up to Balliol, in the great days of Benjamin Jowett [q.v.], and in 1889 he entered the Foreign Office. He was private secretary (1896–1903) to the permanent under-secretary of state, Sir T. H. (later Lord) Sanderson [q.v.], a position of some importance; was secretary to the Committee of Imperial Defence (1903–4) early in its history; and then became acting second secretary at Rome, his only foreign post until he went to Paris as ambassador in 1928.

At the end of 1905 when the Liberals came into power, Sir Edward Grey (later Viscount Grey of Fallodon, q.v.) appointed Tyrrell to be his 'précis-writer'. In 1907 Tyrrell became Grey's principal private secretary, a key position which he held for eight critical years. Grey recorded that Tyrrell's power of understanding the point of view of foreigners was 'of the greatest value in making the British position both more intelligible and more acceptable to them'. By 1911 every statesman in Europe dealing with foreign affairs knew the reputation and influence of Grey's private secretary, and in that year, when the Germans dispatched the *Panther* to Agadir, Clemenceau is reported to have said, 'Je voudrais savoir ce qu'en pense le petit Japonais au bord de la Tamise.' For Tyrrell, neat and dapper, was short in stature, although well proportioned; his complexion was sallow; under his broad forehead his humorous eyes twinkled half-closed; he had expressive hands and gestures. In later years his abundant hair was iron-grey, and he wore a grey moustache. In 1913 Walter H. Page wrote home of Tyrrell: 'He of course has Sir Edward's complete confidence, but he's also a man on his own account. . . . It's a good head and a good place to put good ideas.'

The war, which to the last he had hoped would be averted, proved a tragedy to Tyrrell whose younger son was killed in 1915 and the elder early in 1918. It reacted upon a nervous, sensitive, and affectionate nature already overstrained by years of intensely exacting work, and there was a period of breakdown when it seemed that his brilliant career had burned itself out. But he recovered, worked for the Government during the war, and was a member of the committee set up under Sir Walter (later Lord) Phillimore [q.v.] to study the question of a League of Nations. In 1918 Tyrrell became head of the political intelligence department of the Foreign Office, and in October assistant under-secretary. In 1919 he went to the peace conference in Paris where he showed himself a fierce critic of Lloyd George. In subsequent years Tyrrell left no stone unturned in order to secure a reversal of what he held to be the dangerous pro-German drift in British foreign policy begun under that prime minister's influence. In 1919 he accompanied his old chief, Lord Grey, to Washington on a special mission which contributed towards preserving Anglo-American friendship after America's withdrawal from Europe. Lord Curzon [q.v.] was by then foreign secretary and in 1922–3 Tyrrell was his principal adviser at the Lausanne conference with the new Turkey of Mustapha Kemal. In 1924 Ramsay MacDonald, by his direct approach to the French premier, Poincaré, initiated the restoration of friendship and co-operation between Britain and France, and in this shifting of policy Tyrrell, who was firmly established in MacDonald's confidence, played an important part. It was his lifelong belief that British policy in Europe must be based upon agreement with France. In 1925 on the death of Sir Eyre Crowe [q.v.] Tyrrell became permanent under-secretary of state and in the same year the new policy reached its culmination in the Locarno Treaties. In the midst of this halcyon period Tyrrell asked to be relieved of the toil of the Foreign Office and to be given a post abroad, a request to which his chief, Sir Austen Chamberlain [q.v.], replied: 'You have given me stomach-ache indeed!' However, in 1928 Tyrrell was appointed ambassador in Paris, still the most illustrious of all diplomatic posts.

Tyrrell made a great and powerful position for himself in the French capital, where famous Frenchmen who knew and trusted him would come for his advice in matters both official and private. Soon, however, in the confusion which followed after 1931, Britain and France alike lost all sense of policy. The warnings of Tyrrell, as of many others, especially with regard to the danger of concessions to German clamour, were ignored. Tyrrell's policy was to deal with Germany only after agreement with France had been secured, a line which had produced valuable results in the years before 1914 and after 1924.

In 1934 Tyrrell retired from Paris and from the foreign service at the age of nearly sixty-eight, a record for British diplomatists of that period. He had been appointed C.B. (1909), K.C.M.G. (1913), K.C.V.O. (1919), G.C.M.G. (1925), K.C.B. (1927), and G.C.B. (1934). He had been raised to the peerage as Baron Tyrrell, of Avon, in the county of Southampton, in 1929, was sworn of the Privy Council in 1928, and received the grand cross of the Legion of Honour in 1934. He was elected an honorary fellow of Balliol College in 1930 and received the honorary degrees of D.C.L. of Oxford (1934) and LL.D. of Dublin (1935).

Tyrrell lived out his last years in a flat in Chesham House, once the London residence of the Tsars' ambassadors. Here he was ever ready to join in discussion and to give advice, to welcome visitors from home and from abroad, newspapermen, and representatives of all political parties. From 1935 he held the office of president of the British Board of Film Censors which made his clear schoolboy signature familiar throughout the length and breadth of the land.

In the foreign service Tyrrell's name will always be coupled with that of Sir Eyre Crowe, his colleague and lifelong friend. 'It is difficult', wrote (Sir) Harold Nicolson in *Lord Carnock* (1930), 'to conceive of two men more diverse from each other in temperament and attainments. Sir William Tyrrell was intuitive, conciliatory, elastic, and possessed a remarkable instinct for avoiding diplomatic difficulties. . . . [He] did more than any man to increase the prestige of the Foreign Office in circles which had hitherto regarded British diplomacy as mysterious and aloof: he was on excellent terms with journalists and Members of Parliament. . . . Sir Eyre Crowe believed in facts; Sir William Tyrrell believed in personal relations; the former relied upon lucidity; the latter upon atmosphere; the minutes of Sir Eyre Crowe were precise and forcible; the conversations of Sir William Tyrrell were intangible but suggestive; the former concentrated his energies upon penetrating the matter in hand without regard to collateral contingencies; the latter, who

kept aloof from the machinery of office life, excelled in examining the outer radius of international problems . . . it was by pliant and adaptable gaiety that Sir William Tyrrell conquered so many hearts.'

In his *Avenues of History* (1952) Sir Lewis Namier, rejecting von Kühlmann's claim to have been in close understanding with Tyrrell in the years before the outbreak of war in 1914, points out that Tyrrell was not the man 'unreservedly to show his hand'. 'Complex, versatile, talkative, but exceedingly secretive, he was amiable, and even yielding on the surface, but a stubborn fighter underneath. He avoided, if he could, personal collisions, and professed a preference for "long-range artillery"; yet he disliked writing—active and restless, he shunned the drudgery of office drafts, and . . . was selective even in his reading of office files. . . . Tyrrell's curious, occasionally even impish ways gave rise to doubts among some people; in reality he was a loyal friend, who fought the battles of his chiefs, colleagues, and subordinates, often with complete disregard for his own person.'

Tyrrell left little on record either in private correspondence or in minutes on official documents, which in later years used generally to return to the departments with only the initials 'W. T.' and the date. Some interesting messages from him, when ambassador in Paris, may be found in the second series of the *Documents on British Foreign Policy, 1919–1939* (notably in volumes iii and iv). He conducted the affairs of his office, most astutely, by personal contact and conversation. His influence with Cabinet ministers was very great. For intuition, skill, adroitness, and persuasive power Tyrrell stands perhaps first among British diplomatists. He had an unrivalled flair for detecting the essential and for finding solutions for what appeared insoluble. References to him will be found in the principal diplomatic memoirs and historical studies of the period; but Tyrrell left nothing himself, neither memoirs nor letters, by which posterity may obtain an adequate idea of the influence, the methods, the intelligence or the charm of his remarkable character.

In 1890 he married Margaret Ann (died 1939), daughter of David Urquhart [q.v.] and like himself a Roman Catholic. They had two daughters, but since both sons were killed the title became extinct when Tyrrell died at his home in London

14 March 1947. A portrait by P. A. de László is in the possession of the family.

[Personal knowledge; private information.]
F. ASHTON-GWATKIN.

TYRWHITT-WILSON, SIR GERALD HUGH, fifth baronet, and fourteenth BARON BERNERS (1883–1950), musician, artist, and author, was born at Apley Park, Bridgnorth, 18 September 1883, the only child of Lieutenant (later Commodore) Hugh Tyrwhitt (third son of Baroness Berners, who had married Sir Henry Thomas Tyrwhitt) and his wife, Julia Mary, daughter of William Orme Foster, M.P., of Apley Park. Berners's two volumes of autobiography, First Childhood (1934) and A Distant Prospect (1945), give an account of his life until he left Eton. From these two books which are written in a delightful and deceptively simple style, we may gather that he did not take willingly to the sporting country life for which his parents and grandmother intended him, but he retained a knowledge of animal life, particularly birds and plants. Eventually he entered the diplomatic service as an honorary attaché in the embassies at Constantinople (1909–11) and Rome (1911–19). In 1918 he inherited from his uncle the barony of Berners, and the Tyrwhitt baronetcy, in the next year taking the additional name of Wilson. He sold much of the Berners property and bought Faringdon House in Berkshire where he lived for the remainder of his life, entertaining his many friends and occasionally visiting London and Rome where he owned a house overlooking the Forum.

Berners's chief delight in life was music, and the second volume of his autobiography movingly describes how at Eton his appreciation developed and his mind opened to pleasure in the arts generally. The book is probably the best of his prose works. He did not live to finish the third volume which has not been published. He wrote in addition five humorous light novels, satirizing various aspects of English social life: The Camel (1936), Far from the Madding War, Count Omega, Percy Wallingford and Mr. Pidger, and The Romance of a Nose (all published in 1941). He also wrote a prose lampoon The Girls of Radcliff Hall (1937) which was published locally in Faringdon.

In the world of music Berners will be remembered chiefly for his contributions to ballet music between 1926 and 1946 but earlier works by which he first became well known as a composer should not be forgotten. Berners received much of his musical education abroad and studied for a short time with Stravinsky and Casella. Among his earliest published works are 'Trois petites marches funèbres' of 1914 ('Pour un homme d'état', 'Pour un canari', 'Pour une tante à héritage') which at once demonstrated his skill in portraying humour and satire. These pieces were followed by others including 'Fragments psychologiques' and 'Valses bourgeoises'. Berners's sense of parody inspired several songs set to German, English, and French words, and his parodies of national styles are also seen in two orchestral works 'Three Pieces for Orchestra' of 1916 ('Chinoiserie', 'Valse sentimentale', and 'Kasatchok') and 'Fantaisie Espagnole' of 1918. Later Berners turned to opera and set to music Mérimée's one-act comedy Le Carrosse du Saint-Sacrament which was produced in Paris in 1924 in a triple bill which included works by Stravinsky and Sauguet.

In 1926 appeared 'The Triumph of Neptune', the first of the series of ballets for which Berners supplied the music. This score was written for the Diaghilev ballet. Another, 'Luna Park', was included in (Sir) C. B. Cochran's 1930 revue. These were followed by three scores composed for the Sadler's Wells Ballet Company. The first, 'A Wedding Bouquet', for which Berners also designed the costumes and which employs a chorus with words by Gertrude Stein, was produced at Sadler's Wells Theatre in 1937. The second, 'Cupid and Psyche', followed in 1939, while 'Les Sirènes' was produced at Covent Garden in 1946. Although Berners achieved early in his career a reputation as a specialist in musical humour and parody, these are not by any means the principal characteristics of all his compositions. Everywhere considerable technical skill and originality are evident, and it is a matter of regret that his music is so rarely heard today.

Berners was also a talented landscape painter in oil and held exhibitions at the Lefevre Galleries, London, in 1931 and 1936. He painted mostly in the manner of early Corot, of whose early paintings he had a fine collection. Another manner he employed for slightly satiric paintings was that of the Douanier Rousseau. He also collected works by Derain, Sisley, Matisse, Dufy, and Constable.

In Who's Who Berners recorded 're-creation: none'. This was quite true, for there was hardly a moment of the day when he was not either composing, painting, or writing. He was extremely self-critical and destroyed much that he did. Personally he was shy and quiet, but he had a remarkable gift for making friends and a loyalty to them which no reverses in their fortunes would shake. He was a man of few words and nearly all of those were extremely amusing. His wit was barbed and mischievous, but never harmful. He delighted in making jokes, whether practical or verbal, which exposed pretentiousness or hypocrisy. He was no respecter of persons nor the upholder of any political creed. He never made a public speech in his life, except for the three short sentences with which he opened the Faringdon cinema. He died unmarried at Faringdon House, 19 April 1950, when the barony passed to his cousin, Vera Ruby, wife of Harold Williams. The baronetcy became extinct. A caricature by Sir Max Beerbohm and a portrait by Gregorio Prieto are at Faringdon House.

[*Miniature Essays: Lord Berners*, published by J. & W. Chester, Ltd., 1922; *Catalogue of Paintings by Lord Berners*, with a foreword by Clive Bell, 1931; *Catalogue of Three Exhibitions*, Alex. Reid and Lefevre, Ltd., 1936; private information; personal knowledge.]

J. BETJEMAN.

ULLSWATER, first VISCOUNT (1855–1949), Speaker of the House of Commons. [See LOWTHER, JAMES WILLIAM.]

UNDERHILL, EVELYN, afterwards MRS. STUART MOORE (1875–1941), religious writer, was born at Wolverhampton 6 December 1875, the only child of (Sir) Arthur Underhill, barrister, and a bencher of Lincoln's Inn, by his wife, Alice Lucy, younger daughter of Moses Ironmonger, justice of the peace, of Wolverhampton. She was educated at home, save for three years at a private school in Folkestone, and later went to King's College for Women, London, where she read history and botany. She also became a first-class bookbinder. During her girlhood and the greater part of her married life her holidays were spent yachting, both her father and her husband being enthusiastic yachtsmen. From 1898 to 1913 she went abroad every spring and came to know and love the artistic treasures of France and Italy.

Evelyn Underhill began writing before she was sixteen and her first publication, *A Bar-Lamb's Ballad Book*, of humorous verse concerned with the law, appeared in 1902. In 1907 she married Hubert Stuart Moore, a barrister, whom she had known

since childhood. They had many interests in common in country life and country lore, and in a love of cats. She shared her husband's interest in wood and metal work and made many of the designs which he carried out.

The year of her marriage witnessed her final conversion to the Christian faith, although not to Anglicanism, for her attraction was then towards Rome. But the outbreak of the modernist storm in the same year made it seem to her that the demands of Rome postulated a surrender of her intellectual honour. Through her first important book, *Mysticism* (1911), she made the acquaintance of Baron Friedrich von Hügel [q.v.] to whom 'under God', she wrote, 'I owe . . . my whole spiritual life'. Ten years later she formally put herself under his spiritual direction and she remained his pupil until his death in 1925.

From the time of her conversion Evelyn Underhill's life consisted of various forms of religious work. She was fond of quoting St. Teresa's saying that 'to give Our Lord a perfect service Martha and Mary must combine'. Her mornings were given to writing and her afternoons to visiting the poor and to the direction of souls. As she grew older the work of direction increased until it finally became her chief interest, but it was not until 1921 that she solved her own problem and became a practising member of the Anglican communion. In 1924 she began to conduct retreats, and a number of her books consist of these conferences. Her other publications include three novels, two books of verse, a number of works on philosophy and religion, and various editions of, and critical essays on, mystics such as Ruysbroeck and Walter Hilton. She also wrote reviews and special articles for the *Spectator* (of which she was for some years the theological editor), and later for *Time and Tide*. In 1921 she gave the Upton lectures on religion at Manchester College, Oxford, later published under the title *The Life of the Spirit and the Life of To-day* (1922). While working on *Worship* (1936), written for the Library of Constructive Theology, she became deeply interested in the Greek Orthodox Church and joined the Fellowship of St. Alban and St. Sergius.

During the war of 1914–18 Evelyn Underhill worked at the Admiralty in the naval intelligence (Africa) department, but her views changed and in 1939 she found herself a Christian pacifist. She joined the Anglican Pacifist Fellowship and wrote for it an uncompromising pamphlet *The Church and War* (1940).

In 1913 Evelyn Underhill became an honorary fellow of King's College for Women and in 1927 fellow of King's College; in 1939 she received the honorary degree of D.D. from the university of Aberdeen. She had a vivid, lively personality with a keen sense of humour and great lightness of touch. As befitted a good Incarnationalist she was interested in every side of life and had a passion for efficiency in everything she undertook. In her dealings with people, and especially with her pupils, she was always a little shy, having a great hatred, as she said, of 'pushing souls about'. This love of souls coupled with the determination to help them to grow at God's pace and not at their own or hers, won her the love and trust of all who went to her for help.

Evelyn Underhill died at Hampstead 15 June 1941. She had no children.

[*The Times*, 18 June 1941; *The Letters of Evelyn Underhill*, edited by Charles Williams, 1943; personal knowledge.]

MARJORIE VERNON.

[Margaret Cropper, *Evelyn Underhill*, 1958.]

UTHWATT, AUGUSTUS AN-DREWES, BARON UTHWATT (1879–1949), judge, was born 25 April 1879 at Ballarat, Victoria, Australia, the third of the six sons of Thomas Andrewes Uthwatt by his wife, Annie, daughter of William O'Don-nell Hazlitt, of Dunmow, county Donegal. He came of an old English family and in 1916 his father, on the death of a cousin, became lord of the manor of Maids More-ton, Buckinghamshire. He was educated at Ballarat College and at Melbourne University where he graduated B.A. in 1899 with first class honours and pro-ceeded LL.B. He then entered Balliol College, Oxford, took his degree of B.C.L. with second class honours in 1903 and was Vinerian scholar in 1905. In 1947 he was elected an honorary fellow of Balliol.

Uthwatt was called to the bar in 1904 by Gray's Inn, of which he subsequently became a bencher (1927) and treasurer (1939). He read in chambers as the pupil of the great equity lawyer R. J. (later Lord) Parker [q.v.]. In 1916 he was appointed legal adviser to the newly formed Ministry of Food, where he did notable work in developing the technique, essential to food control but then relatively new, of legislation by Order in Council. At the end of the war he was offered, but declined, a knighthood.

He returned to practice after the war and in 1934 became junior counsel on the Chancery side to the Treasury and the Board of Trade, and to the attorney-general in charity matters. He was ap-pointed a judge of the High Court, and knighted, in 1941 and a lord of appeal in ordinary, with a life peerage, in 1946 when he was sworn of the Privy Council.

Although never engaged in politics, Uthwatt maintained a keen interest in the development of social ideas and was probably best known to the public as chairman of the committee on compensa-tion and betterment (1941), for its report was commonly known as the Uthwatt report. This recommended and devised a scheme for transferring to the State the increase in value of land arising from development; it was carried into effect, although with considerable differences, by the Town and Country Planning Act, 1947. An earlier committee of which Uthwatt was chairman originated the Landlord and Tenant (War Damage) Acts for distributing fairly between landlord and tenant the loss arising from war damage in the war of 1939–45. He was also at his death chairman of a committee on leasehold property.

Uthwatt's private practice as a barrister comprised many of the larger commercial and revenue cases both in and out of court. In court work, although he had not, and perhaps rather disdained, the arts of the great advocate, he had the ability to grasp and state in a few sentences the essential point of a complicated matter. To an observer he gave the first impression of a genial man, with gown usually askew, saying much less than the other barristers in the case; later came the realization that his brief words were always listened to and often conclusive. He once said that all true legal argument consisted of clearing away irrelevance and asserting the point; when that was done the rest would be false analogy or obscuring an opponent's issues. He had also the capacity, characteristic of the fine lawyer, of seeming to know by instinct what the law was. He was quite as much interested in his work out of court as in litigation and brought to it a very practical approach, regarding the law less as an obstacle than as a means of carrying out safely any reasonable business arrangement which his clients desired.

A judge, especially in the lower courts, deals with a diversity of matters which happen to come before him. Uthwatt's judicial career was perhaps too short for it to be said that the development of any particular branch of the law will be specially associated with his decisions. He has, however, on individual points left judgements which reflect his qualities of mind, as concise and illuminating statements on difficult issues of law. Examples are his judgement in the Chancery division in *Re Anstead*, [1943] Ch. 161, which deals with the tangled issues that arise on the administration of estates, and the judgement of the Judicial Committee of the Privy Council delivered by him in *Perera (M.G.)* v. *Peiris*, [1949] A.C. 1. This case deals with the question of privilege in libel actions, a matter outside Uthwatt's previous legal experience, and is an interesting example of the light which a fresh mind can bring to an old problem. He died at Sandwich 24 April 1949 during the hearing of an appeal to the Privy Council on the validity of a law nationalizing Australian banks, a case in which, because of his Australian connexion, his opinion would have been especially valuable.

Personally Uthwatt was a man of warm heart and notable sincerity, with many friends in all branches of life. He married in 1927 Mary Baxter (died 1951), daughter of the Rev. Charles Edwin Meeres, vicar of Eastry, Kent, formerly the wife of John Lewis James Bonhote from whom she obtained a divorce. They had no children.

[Private information; personal knowledge.]
J. W. BRUNYATE.

VANBRUGH, DAME IRENE (1872–1949), actress, whose original name was IRENE BARNES, was born at Exeter 2 December 1872, the fourth and youngest daughter of the Rev. Reginald Henry Barnes, prebendary of Exeter Cathedral and vicar of Heavitree, by his wife, Frances Mary Emily, daughter of William Nation, barrister. The Nations were an old Exeter family, members of which had given great support to the theatre and had helped in the discovery of Edmund Kean [q.v.]. Irene was the fifth child in a family of six, Violet Vanbrugh, a notice of whom appears below, being the eldest. The stage-name of Vanbrugh was first adopted by Violet at the suggestion of (Dame) Ellen Terry [q.v.] who remained throughout her life an invaluable friend. Violet's successful entry upon a stage career under J. L. Toole [q.v.] in 1886 set Irene an example rare in those days among strictly brought-up daughters of professional men.

Irene was educated at Exeter High School and by prolonged trips to the continent with her father, and at a school near Earl's Court, recommended by Ellen Terry, when the family removed to London. Like Violet, Irene had a spell of training under Sarah Thorne at the Theatre Royal, Margate, where she made her first stage appearance in August 1888, as Phoebe in *As You Like It*. On Boxing Day of the same year she made her London début, on the recommendation of Lewis Carroll [q.v.], as the White Queen and Jack of Hearts in a revival of *Alice in Wonderland* at the Globe Theatre in Newcastle Street, Strand. She then again followed Violet's lead by joining Toole's company. She played a big round of parts in already popular plays like *Dot* and *Uncle Dick's Darling*. With Toole she toured Australia in 1890. On her return, still with Toole, she made her first original creations as Thea Tesman in the first play by (Sir) James Barrie [q.v.], his burlesque, *Ibsen's Ghost* (1891), and as Bell Golightly in his *Walker, London* (1892). She then joined (Sir) Herbert Tree [q.v.] at the Haymarket Theatre as Lettice in *The Tempter* (1893) by H. A. Jones [q.v.]. In the following year she passed to the St. James's Theatre and played a number of secondary parts under the management of (Sir) George Alexander [q.v.], afterwards joining the company of her brother-in-law, Arthur Bourchier [q.v.], at the Royalty Theatre and on an American visit. On her return, at the Court Theatre (1898) she created the part of Rose in *Trelawny of the 'Wells'* by (Sir) Arthur Pinero [q.v.], and, during the same season, of Stella in Robert Marshall's *His Excellency the Governor*.

Then came Irene Vanbrugh's first great triumph, her Sophy Fullgarney in the production by (Sir) John Hare [q.v.] at the Globe Theatre of Pinero's *The Gay Lord Quex* (1899). As with many of her creations, Irene Vanbrugh's intelligence, sympathy, and alertness avoided extravagance in a subtle expression of class-contrast. This gave the character an intensity of appeal which was at the time something quite new. Her Letty in Pinero's play of that name at the Duke of York's Theatre (1903) was a less memorable success. It was at the St. James's Theatre as Nina Jesson in Pinero's *His House in Order* (1906)—a delicately temperamental study of the second wife of a pompous member of Parliament—that Irene Vanbrugh touched the heights once more. She also scored notably as Marise in *The Thief*, adapted from Henry Bernstein, at the St. James's Theatre (1907),

Her Zoe Blundell, too, in Pinero's *Mid-Channel* at the same theatre (1909) was specially worthy of remembrance. She gave another poignant performance in the title-part of Mr. Somerset Maugham's play *Grace*, at the Duke of York's Theatre (1910). She created many other attractive characters of a quite different order, such as Lady Mary Lasenby in Barrie's *The Admirable Crichton* at the Duke of York's Theatre (1902), Kate, in his one-act play *The Twelve-Pound Look* at the Hippodrome (1911), and Rosalind in his one-act play of that name also produced at the Duke of York's Theatre (1912). In this she was commanded to appear before the King at Queen Alexandra's birthday-party at Sandringham. Norah Marsh in Mr. Maugham's *The Land of Promise* at the Duke of York's Theatre (1914) was an achievement of high merit; but its deserved success suffered from the outbreak of war. She was more fortunate with her Olivia in A. A. Milne's *Mr. Pim Passes By* at the New Theatre (1920). Even so, she never excelled her early Pinero creations.

One of her latest and most appreciated successes was in Mr. Norman Ginsbury's *Viceroy Sarah* in which she succeeded (Dame) Edith Evans as the Duchess of Marlborough for the run at the Whitehall Theatre (1935). She appeared three times in plays by G. B. Shaw [q.v.], the last being as Catherine of Braganza in *In Good King Charles's Golden Days* when it was produced at the Malvern Festival (1939) and afterwards presented in London at the New Theatre (1940) only to be stopped by the war. During the Battle of Britain she carried out a characteristic piece of war work by giving, with Violet Vanbrugh and (Sir) Donald Wolfit, extracts from *The Merry Wives of Windsor* at the Strand Theatre during lunch-time.

Irene Vanbrugh, who was appointed D.B.E. in 1941, celebrated her golden jubilee at a testimonial matinée in His Majesty's Theatre, 20 June 1938. At this she appeared in an act from *The Gay Lord Quex* and one from A. A. Milne's *Belinda* in which she had been seen at the New Theatre in 1918, and also in the title-part of Barrie's *Rosalind*. The performance was attended by Queen Elizabeth and realized over £2,000 which was divided between the Elizabeth Garrett Anderson Hospital and the Theatrical Ladies' Guild. Irene Vanbrugh was constant in her promotion of every theatrical good cause. She was a particularly keen supporter of the Royal Academy of Dramatic Art, both because her brother, Sir Kenneth Barnes, was its first principal and because she was deeply conscious of its value to the art and welfare of the theatre. Notable among her performances for charities was her appearance as Lady Gay Spanker in an 'all-star' revival at the St. James's Theatre of her father-in-law's famous comedy, *London Assurance* (1913), given in aid of King George's Pension Fund for Actors and Actresses. In 1919, to avert selling the (Royal) Academy of Dramatic Art theatre, then partly completed, she had the old film *Masks and Faces* remade with a star-cast, as well as Shaw, Pinero, Barrie, and Sir Squire Bancroft [qq.v.] sitting round at a council meeting.

Although Irene Vanbrugh allowed nothing to deter her main interest from the living theatre, which she loved and in the future of which she believed with her whole heart, she found time from 1933 to appear in a number of films, including *Head of the Family*, *Catherine the Great*, *The Way of Youth*, *Escape Me Never*, *Wings of the Morning*, and *Knight Without Armour*. Towards the close of her life she wrote a delightful autobiography entitled *To Tell My Story* (1948). It contains some characteristically well-informed character-sketches of the dramatists, actors, actresses, and others with whom it was her lot to work; letters from Pinero, Barrie, Shaw, and others; and vivid glimpses of life in America, Australia, and other parts of the world visited during her tours. In her writings, and otherwise, she gave the impression of having enjoyed a career of manifold opportunity and fulfilment.

Irene Vanbrugh married in 1901 Dion Boucicault the younger [q.v.], who became her manager (1915) and with whom she acted until his death in 1929. There were no children. She died in London after a short illness 30 November 1949.

Among the portraits of Irene Vanbrugh may be numbered a painting of her as Rose Trelawny by Sir William Rothenstein, in the possession of Mr. George Spiegleberg; as herself by Solomon J. Solomon, the property of Sir Colin Anderson; as Lady Mary Lasenby in Act I of *The Admirable Crichton* by Charles Buchel, which was the property of Sir Kenneth Barnes, and in Act II, by the same, at the Royal Academy of Dramatic Art; as herself by (Sir) Oswald Birley, in the possession of the Melbourne Art Gallery; as Rosalind in Barrie's *Rosalind* by Sir John Lavery, the property of Mr. Michael Barnes; at her jubilee matinée by Ursula

Bradley, at the Royal Academy of Dramatic Art; and as herself by Joseph Oppenheimer, the property of the artist.

[Dame Irene Vanbrugh, *To Tell My Story*, 1948; private information; personal knowledge.]       S. R. LITTLEWOOD.

VANBRUGH, VIOLET (1867–1942), actress, whose original name was VIOLET AUGUSTA MARY BARNES, was born at Exeter 11 June 1867, the eldest sister of Irene Vanbrugh, a notice of whom appears above. After schooling in Exeter, France, and Germany, Violet determined to go on the stage at a time when this was by no means usual with girls of her education and social standing, and when there were no dramatic schools outside the theatre itself. Remembering the advice of General Gordon [q.v.] a friend of the family, to allow his children to follow their bent, her father permitted her to make the attempt. With fifty pounds to spend and a nurse as companion she journeyed to London and after three months succeeded in interesting (Dame) Ellen Terry, on whose recommendation J. L. Toole [qq.v.] gave her her first engagement: at Toole's Theatre in February 1886 she walked on in fantastic male costume as one of the crowd in the burlesque, *Faust and Loose*. From there she went to the Criterion Theatre and had her first speaking part in London as Ellen in *The Little Pilgrim*. She then joined Sarah Thorne's repertory company at the Theatre Royal, Margate, where she had an invaluable training, learning a new part every week. In the autumn of the same year she rejoined Toole, playing Lady Anne in *The Butler* both on tour and afterwards in London. Among other parts in which she appeared with Toole were May Fielding in *Dot* and Kitty Maitland in *The Don*. She then returned to Margate and gained valuable experience in a variety of parts. After returning to London in 1888, she joined W. H. and (Dame) Madge Kendal [qq.v.] whom she accompanied on their first two American tours, having the supreme benefit of Madge Kendal's advice and example. Violet Vanbrugh played Baronne de Préfont in *The Ironmaster*, Lady Ingram in *A Scrap of Paper*, and other leading parts which fell to her quite unexpectedly when she was called upon to replace Olga Brandon, who at the last moment was unable to go.

After two years in America, Violet Vanbrugh returned to London, intending to take the rest of which she felt in need.

Shortly after, an extraordinary and unexpected piece of good luck came, when (Sir) Henry Irving [q.v.], with whom she had then a slight acquaintance, stopped a hansom-cab in which she was driving and offered her there and then the part of Ann Boleyn in his production of *King Henry VIII* at the Lyceum Theatre. In this she duly appeared (5 January 1892) at the same time understudying Ellen Terry as Cordelia in *King Lear* and as Rosamund in *Becket*.

In the following year Violet Vanbrugh was engaged by Augustin Daly, the American manager, to join his company at Daly's Theatre, headed by Ada Rehan, whom she understudied. Among the parts she played at Daly's in 1893–4 were Lady Sneerwell in *The School for Scandal*, Alithea in *The Country Girl*, and Olivia in *Twelfth Night*. In 1894 she married Arthur Bourchier [q.v.], who had been a member of Daly's company. She joined him, taking the title-part in *The Chili Widow*, when he went into management at the Royalty Theatre, afterwards appearing as Stella in *The Queen's Proctor*—a version of *Divorçons*. With Bourchier she went to America, and on her return (1898) created the part of Lady Beauvedere in *The Ambassador* with (Sir) George Alexander [q.v.] at the St. James's Theatre. She took the leading part in a succession of plays, most of them by contemporary authors, and many of them produced by Bourchier during his lease of the Garrick Theatre. In 1906 at Stratford on Avon she played Lady Macbeth to her husband's Macbeth, the play being revived the same year at the Garrick Theatre. At Stratford also in 1910 she played Beatrice in *Much Ado About Nothing*. Both she and Arthur Bourchier were then engaged by Sir Herbert Tree [q.v.] at His Majesty's Theatre, where, in September of that year, she made a great success as Queen Katherine in *King Henry VIII*. In the following year she appeared in Tree's revival of *The Merry Wives of Windsor* as Mistress Ford to Ellen Terry's Mistress Page. At His Majesty's again in 1915 she played Queen Katherine in an 'all-star' revival of *King Henry VIII*, given in aid of King George's Pension Fund for Actors and Actresses.

From then onward she played many other parts, but Mistress Ford and Queen Katherine remained the characters for which she was chiefly remembered. She reappeared as Mistress Ford at the Hippodrome, Manchester, in 1934, with her sister

Irene as Mistress Page, and again in a notable performance at the Ring Theatre, Blackfriars, in March 1937. In June following both sisters took the same parts in a revival at the open-air theatre in Regent's Park. In the same year her golden jubilee as an actress was celebrated with a luncheon in her honour. She appeared in one or two films towards the close of her life, including the film-version of *Pygmalion* by G. B. Shaw [q.v.] in 1938; but she allowed nothing to interfere with her devotion to the living theatre. She endowed every part she took with an appealing dignity and charm. As a pioneer, alike of her family and her generation, in taking up the stage as a calling for serious-minded well-brought-up girls, and as one who never forfeited her pride in high ideals on or off the stage, Violet Vanbrugh deserved all the honours which came to her. She wrote a delightful book of reminiscences with, for title, the family motto, *Dare To Be Wise* (1925), in which is to be found much valuable advice to young actresses.

Violet Vanbrugh divorced her husband in 1917. Her daughter, Prudence, has done excellent work on the stage. Violet Vanbrugh died in London 11 November 1942.

There is a portrait of Violet Vanbrugh by Charles Buchel at the Stratford on Avon Memorial Theatre, showing her as Lady Macbeth, and one of her as Katherine of Aragon by the same painter at the Royal Academy of Dramatic Art. The Vanbrugh Theatre, the new private theatre of the Royal Academy of Dramatic Art, was opened in 1954 in commemoration of both sisters.

[Violet Vanbrugh, *Dare To Be Wise*, 1925; *The Times*, 12 November, 1942; *Who's Who in the Theatre*; private information; personal knowledge.]                    S. R. LITTLEWOOD.

VANE-TEMPEST-STEWART, CHARLES STEWART HENRY, seventh MARQUESS OF LONDONDERRY (1878–1949), politician, was born at 76 Eaton Place, London, 13 May 1878, the eldest son of Charles Stewart Vane-Tempest(-Stewart), Viscount Castlereagh, later the sixth Marquess of Londonderry [q.v.]. Educated at Eton and the Royal Military College, Sandhurst, he obtained a commission in the Royal Horse Guards in 1897, but left the army in 1906 when, as Viscount Castlereagh, he was elected to the House of Commons as Conservative member for Maidstone which he continued to repre-

sent, despite an immediate petition to unseat him, until he succeeded his father in 1915.

On the outbreak of war in 1914 he served in France first as aide-de-camp to Lieutenant-General Sir William Pulteney and later as second-in-command of his old regiment. He was twice mentioned in dispatches. In 1917, however, he was recalled to attend the Irish convention as a member of the Ulster delegation. Whereas he refused to yield to the nationalist demand for an all-Ireland Parliament, his approach to the problems was nevertheless conciliatory. In 1919 he was appointed finance member of the Air Council, with the duty of answering for air matters in the House of Lords, his kinsman, (Sir) Winston Churchill, being then secretary of state for air as well as war. In that year Londonderry was appointed K.G. and in 1920 he became under-secretary of state for air, but resigned this post in 1921 in order to become leader of the Senate of Northern Ireland and minister of education in the Government then being formed in Belfast under the premiership of his friend, Sir James Craig (later Viscount Craigavon, q.v.). By common consent he filled these posts with much tact and skill during the next five years, and the measure establishing Ulster's educational system was popularly known as the Londonderry Act.

Besides Mount Stewart, the family property in county Down, Londonderry owned extensive English estates, which included Wynyard Park in county Durham as well as valuable coal-mines in the neighbourhood of Seaham Harbour. The mounting crisis in the mines in 1926 impelled him to return to England where he exerted his influence to bring owners and miners together in friendly co-operation. A generous employer himself, he was resolutely opposed to nationalization.

In 1928 Londonderry became first commissioner of works, and although he went out of office with the rest of the Baldwin ministry in the following year, he returned to this post for a few months on the formation of the 'national' Government under Ramsay MacDonald in 1931. Later in that year he went back to the Air Ministry as secretary of state, a position he had declined in 1922. From 1931 to 1935 he proved himself an able and active minister, bringing to his task a spirit of initiative and enterprise which made him well liked. It was largely due to his encouragement that the Royal Air Force was equipped with the Hurricanes and Spitfires which were later employed in the Battle of Britain. An enthusiastic aviator himself, Londonderry flew his own aircraft and held a certificate for 'blind flying' as well as the ordinary pilot's 'A' licence for which he qualified at the age of fifty-five. He made frequent inspections, on one occasion undertaking a 16,000-mile tour in the Middle East and India. Through his lead Northern Ireland obtained its first civil aerodrome, at Newtownards near Mount Stewart.

In 1932 and 1933 Londonderry attended the disarmament conference at Geneva, for much of the time as head of the British delegation, and he played a prominent and afterwards much criticized part in the discussions on the abolition by international agreement of bombing aircraft and indeed air forces altogether. At home he was bitterly assailed by Labour and pacifist opinion which accused him of raising every possible obstacle to abolition. Whereas he was never opposed to the principle of abolition, he considered an international convention useless unless civil aviation were also controlled, since it was readily adaptable to bombing. In the absence of any measure of agreement on this point, Londonderry felt bound to keep a nucleus of the Royal Air Force intact as a military weapon. A phrase which he subsequently used in the House of Lords (22 May 1935) to the effect that at Geneva he had had the utmost difficulty in preserving the use of bomber aircraft even for police work in the outlying districts of the Middle East and India was widely employed against him.

While foreign air forces continued to grow, his pleas in the Cabinet for additional British squadrons were largely unavailing, and during his first two years of office the air estimates were reduced. With the breakdown of the disarmament conference and the knowledge that Germany was secretly rearming in the air, this reduction was halted, and it was officially conceded that the British aim must at least be parity with other air forces. In 1935 Hitler claimed that the German air force was equal in strength to the British, and although this claim was incorrect, it was widely accepted, and Londonderry, who had previously been criticized for wanting to do too much, was now assailed for having done too little, and certain sections of the press campaigned for his removal from the Air Ministry. This came about when Baldwin became prime minister in 1935.

For a short time Londonderry was lord privy seal and leader of the House of Lords, but following the general election later in the year his ministerial career came to an abrupt close. He afterwards defended his air policy in an autobiographical work, *Wings of Destiny* (1943).

Londonderry was now free to realize his desire to visit Germany and meet the Nazi leaders, in particular Goering. This he did in 1936 and again in 1937, when he was the guest of Goering and von Papen, and he published an account of his conversations, including an interview with Hitler, in a book *Ourselves and Germany* (1938). He returned this hospitality by entertaining Ribbentrop, Hitler's ambassador, in London, and also at Mount Stewart and Wynyard. An invitation to Goering to stay at Londonderry House should he attend the coronation in 1937 was not accepted. Well intentioned no doubt as Londonderry was in constituting himself an amateur ambassador of good will, it is not surprising that, as the aggressive aims of the Nazis were revealed, his stock fell heavily in popular estimation. After the outbreak of a war which he had finally come to accept as inevitable, he became, in 1942, first regional commissioner of the Northern Ireland Air Training Corps. He inspired the formation of numerous squadrons and frequently flew gliders with cadets. He retained his interest in gliding after the war and it was as the result of an accident in 1947, when the tow rope of his glider broke, that he died at Mount Stewart 11 February 1949.

Londonderry married in 1899 Edith Helen, daughter of Henry (later Viscount) Chaplin [q.v.]. Their only son, Edward Charles Stewart Robert (1902–55), succeeded to the titles, and the eldest of their four daughters, Maureen Helen, married Oliver Stanley [q.v.]. His wife, who founded the Women's Legion and was appointed D.B.E. in 1917 and who survived him, supported him fully in his numerous public activities. Together they maintained the tradition of political entertaining for the Conservative Party established by his parents, particularly at Londonderry House. In 1946 the greater part of this house was handed over to the Royal Aero Club as a national aviation centre. Burdened by taxation, he had already made various charitable dispositions of his property: in 1945 he presented his Welsh mansion and grounds, Plas Machynlleth, to the people of Machynlleth. He also equipped Dene House which he owned at

Seaham Harbour as a sanatorium for sick miners. He was a privy counsellor of Ireland (1918), Northern Ireland (1922), and Great Britain (1925). He was lord lieutenant of county Durham and lieutenant of county Down, and chancellor of the university of Durham as well as of the Queen's University, Belfast. His many interests included race-horse breeding—his most successful horse Polemarch won the St. Leger in 1921; and he was a member of the Jockey Club. He also liked sailing and raced his own yacht regularly in the regattas on Strangford Lough. The gross value of the estate left by his will exceeded a million pounds.

As a public speaker Londonderry was fluent and attractive, if his observations were not always very profound. He never lacked courage. Always friendly and courteous in his manner, he had a distinguished personal appearance which seemed to derive not a little from his illustrious ancestor, the second Marquess, generally known as Lord Castlereagh [q.v.]. There are three portraits of Londonderry by Sir John Lavery. The first (1923) is in Londonderry House where there is also a full-length portrait of him in Garter robes by Glyn Philpot (1921). The second (1924) shows him in his robes as chancellor of the Queen's University, Belfast, and is in the Belfast City Museum and Art Gallery. The third (1924), in evening dress with his Garter order, is at Mount Stewart, where there is also a portrait of him in military uniform (1914) by P. A. de László. A portrait in flying kit, by Cuthbert Orde (1936), is in the possession of the Royal Aero Club.

[*Belfast Telegraph*, 11 February 1949; *Belfast News-Letter*, 12 and 16 February 1949; *The Times*, 12 and 17 February 1949; Marquess of Londonderry, *Ourselves and Germany*, 1938, and *Wings of Destiny*, 1943; Marchioness of Londonderry, *Retrospect*, 1938; H. Montgomery Hyde, *Londonderry House and its Pictures*, 1937; private information; personal knowledge.]

H. MONTGOMERY HYDE.

VEREKER, JOHN STANDISH SURTEES PRENDERGAST, in the peerage of Ireland sixth and in the peerage of the United Kingdom first VISCOUNT GORT (1886–1946), field-marshal, was born in London 10 July 1886, the elder son of John Gage Prendergast Vereker, later fifth Viscount Gort, by his wife, Eleanor, daughter and coheiress of Robert Smith Surtees [q.v.], the famous novelist, of Hamsterley Hall, county Durham. He was educated at Harrow, being a schoolboy when he succeeded to the family honours in 1902, and at the Royal Military College, Sandhurst. He was gazetted ensign in the Grenadier Guards in 1905.

On the outbreak of war with Germany in August 1914, the month of his promotion to captain, Gort went to France as aide-de-camp to the commander of the I Corps, Sir Douglas (later Earl) Haig [q.v.]. In 1915 he was appointed G.S.O. 3 to the I Corps, and later brigade-major of the 4th (Guards) brigade, which became the 1st Guards brigade. He was present at the battles of Festubert and Loos. In July 1916 he was appointed G.S.O. 2 to the operations branch at G.H.Q. In January 1917 a special sub-section of the operations branch was formed, with Gort as assistant to its chief, to work out details of the campaign for that year, which it was then hoped would include a landing from the sea behind the German front near Middelkerke. This was a landmark in staff organization: the conception of a planning staff without other duties was a novelty. This sub-section of the operations branch was the embryo of the modern planning staff.

Gort was a competent staff officer, but his greatest gift was for leadership. In April 1917 he was appointed to command the 4th battalion, Grenadier Guards, shortly before the arduous offensive in Flanders. On the first day of that offensive, 31 July, in the battle of Pilckem Ridge, he was wounded, but, despite great pain, remained until the captured ground had been consolidated. For his exploits on that occasion he received a bar to the D.S.O. to which he had been appointed earlier in the year. He returned to lead his battalion in a later phase of the offensive. In November he was wounded again in the battle of Cambrai. In March 1918, now commanding the 1st battalion of his regiment, he played a part in stemming the German offensive at Arras. He was awarded a second bar to the D.S.O. Already he had acquired a reputation for the rarest gallantry, complete disregard of personal danger, and the power to keep alive in troops under his command a spirit of endeavour, untamed by loss and strain.

The great day of Gort's career was 27 September 1918. The occasion was an episode in the victorious British offensive, the passage of the Canal du Nord and storm of the Hindenburg line near the village of Flesquières, in which he found himself temporarily in command of the 3rd Guards brigade. The situation with which he was confronted was all too familiar: the brigade was to pass through and capture the third objective, but found that the second had not been fully attained. Gort first led his own battalion up under very heavy fire to its starting line. He was then wounded, but personally directed a tank against an obstacle holding up the advance. The brigade's left flank was completely exposed, but he covered it with one of his battalions, the 1st Welsh Guards. Severely wounded for the second time, he struggled up from the stretcher on which he had been lying and continued to direct the attack. Later on he collapsed, but recovering partially, insisted on waiting until the success signals were seen. It was an extraordinary feat of physical courage and of will, which was fittingly rewarded by the Victoria Cross. In the course of the war he was also awarded the M.C. and was eight times mentioned in dispatches.

Gort attended the Staff College on its reopening in 1919. In 1921, a brevet lieutenant-colonel, he returned as instructor. He then reverted to regimental duty. In 1926 he became chief instructor at the Senior Officers' School at Sheerness, and his promotion to the rank of colonel was antedated to January 1925. He went on to command the Grenadier Guards and regimental district in 1930, became director of military training in India in 1932, and in 1936 went to the Staff College, Camberley, for the third time, now as commandant.

The secretary of state for war, Leslie (later Lord) Hore-Belisha, desired to rejuvenate the higher appointments at the War Office. His eye fell upon Gort, who early in 1937 was still only fifty years of age. He was appointed military secretary to the secretary of state and later in the year chief of the imperial general staff. He was promoted full general, skipping the intermediate rank of lieutenant-general. He was also appointed C.B., and promoted K.C.B. in 1938. Apart from his desire to introduce younger blood into the general staff, Hore-Belisha was attracted by the almost legendary prestige and reputation for bravery attaching to Gort's name, which he knew would create favourable public interest in the army. Yet it must be borne in mind that up to this point Gort had won every step by attainments as well as character. His staff record was excel-

lent. The appointment of commandant of the Staff College was one of the most important which could come the way of an officer of his seniority in view of its influence on the future career of the most promising officers.

This does not necessarily imply that his appointment to chief of the imperial general staff was ideal. Gort might possibly have been better placed in a home command in peace and at the head of an army corps in war than as chief of the imperial general staff in peace with reversion of the post of commander-in-chief of an expeditionary force in the event of war. In fact, this reversion was not immediately settled. Even after Gort's appointment it was not at once decided that the precedent of 1914 should be followed and that on the outbreak of war he should assume the command of the expeditionary force. Sir John Dill [q.v.] had been nominated for this post, and it was only at short notice that the appointment was given to Gort and that Dill became one of his corps commanders.

The force which Gort took to France in September 1939 on the outbreak of war with Germany was stationed on the neutral Belgian frontier and thus out of contact with the enemy. Beginning at a strength of four divisions, it finally reached that of ten (without counting several sent out without artillery for pioneer work). The winter, generally bad, was occupied with training and construction of defences. Meanwhile plans were devised for action in the event of a German invasion of Belgium. The question of an allied advance into Belgium in such a case was one of high policy, which passed over Gort's head in view of his subordination to the French command. 'It was therefore not for me to comment on it', he writes in his dispatches—a phrase hardly to be justified in the circumstances. Either in person or through his chief of the general staff, Gort had actually participated in the discussions. Yet the plan adopted, that of a rapid advance followed by the formation of a front on the Dyle and the Meuse, caused him anxiety. When the time came the advance was carried out with little difficulty. The trouble was to follow.

The main interest of the operations resulting from the German invasion on 10 May 1940 does not attach to the British Expeditionary Force. It was outflanked on its right by the German break-through on the Meuse, and in the last phase on its left also by the collapse of Belgian resistance. It carried out successive withdrawals, while covering the long right flank. The severance of communications with the base ports in Normandy and Brittany made it necessary to switch supplies from Britain to the northern ports, but by 22 May Boulogne and Calais were no longer available. Ostend was inadequate, so supplies had to be concentrated on Dunkirk, but after the 26th could be landed only on the beach because the cranes had been put out of action. Attempts, by combined thrusts from north and south, to break the German corridor which extended to the coast and had split the allied armies in two were ill co-ordinated and ineffective. A temporary and limited success was gained by a British attack south of Arras on 21 May, carried out in small strength. Gort clearly had little faith in this operation and less in the ability of the French to cut through from the south. On the 19th he had felt that 'there might be no other course open' but withdrawal to the Channel ports. Sir Edmund (subsequently Lord) Ironside, chief of the imperial general staff, had on the 20th brought instructions for the whole British force to break through towards Amiens and take station on the left of the French Army. Gort had replied that it could not disengage itself for this operation, and Ironside had agreed to the limited action taken.

Henceforward Gort insisted that the principal effort must come from the south, although again not believing that anything serious would be effected. There he proved right; but the French case was that he should have attacked simultaneously from the north. On 24 May the Government told him that, while it still believed a French break-through possible, he was authorized to withdraw to the coast if he could not co-operate. On 25 May he abandoned preparations to attack southwards and moved the two divisions involved to fill a gap between the British and Belgian armies. 'By doing so', says the official historian, 'he saved the British Expeditionary Force.' On the 26th the Government informed him that a French break-through was no longer likely and he was again authorized to operate towards the coast. By the 30th the force had withdrawn to a perimeter between Nieuport and Dunkirk, and rapid evacuation was in progress. Late on the 31st, under orders which left him no discretion, Gort handed over command of the rear-guard to Major-General Alexander (subsequently Earl Alexander of Tunis) and went aboard a ship for England. So ended tragic events which have been the subject of fierce controversy. Gort had realized that a Belgian collapse was impending. His appreciation of French capabilities was less favourable than that of the British Government, and he felt assured that the line he consistently followed was the only one that could save his troops from destruction. It is now virtually certain that he was correct. In the course of the campaign he was promoted G.C.B. and received the grand cross of the French Legion of Honour.

Although he had not failed, it was decided that the task of reorganizing the army and preparing for apparently inevitable invasion should go to another hand. He was appointed inspector-general to the forces, a disappointing post for a former commander-in-chief. In 1941 he went to Gibraltar as governor and commander-in-chief. British fortunes were low, and the fortress appeared to be in grave danger. Three great achievements stand to the credit of his governorship: hurrying on the work of putting everything vital into the shelter of vast new excavations in the rock; construction on nominally neutral ground of the air landing strip which proved of immense value in subsequent campaigns; and by sheer personal charm and character so improving local Anglo-Spanish relations that all unfriendly incidents ceased, although there had as yet been no amelioration of the British strategic position.

On transfer to Malta in May 1942, Gort took over without repining a task which might have sent his name down into history under a stigma, however unjust that would have been. He was informed that in all probability the island could not hold out for more than six weeks; it might even have to be surrendered without being invaded, a still more pitiful end to the defence. In April, before his arrival, Spitfire aircraft, flown in from carriers, had been destroyed on the ground. Now another flight was due. Gort, aware that the bowsers from which fuel was pumped into the tanks had been destroyed, had experimented at Gibraltar in filling them from cans. At the Maltese airfields the estimated time for getting the aircraft into the air again was forty minutes. He suggested that, carried out as a drill, it could be done much faster and promised the aid of as many troops as could be employed. The army in the main did the refuelling, while the Royal Air Force attended to rearming, as aircraft had to be flown in without cannon. The Spitfires were in the air before hostile dive-bombers, warned by radar, arrived from Sicily; and there was no loss. It was a first step to the salvation of Malta. Almost immediately afterwards the minelayer *Welshman*, with ammunition, was due. Convinced that a determined attack would be made on her and fearing that like some of her predecessors she would be sunk in dock with her cargo, Gort concentrated all available artillery about the Grand Harbour. He set no limit to expenditure of shell, although stocks were perilously low. Spitfires and guns between them played havoc with the attacking aircraft, and the last dive-bombing attack on Malta was routed. Gort also organized the discharging at top speed and the dispersal of the cargoes of merchant shipping. His methods produced remarkable results, but were not fully tested by heavy bombing.

His other great achievement was in rationing. He made, from improvised equipment, kitchens which served a free daily meal to any who needed it. At first 10,000 meals a day were served, but when store cupboards emptied the number rose to some 200,000 out of a population of 270,000. It is not often given to one man, however great his power, to accomplish so much in the survival of a beleaguered fortress of priceless worth. On the lifting of the siege he turned his energies successfully to preparing the island for use as a base for the invasion of Sicily. The Maltese fully realized the debt they owed him. His popularity became extraordinary. Young children habitually recognized him in the streets of Valetta and gave him a military salute. When he left Malta in 1944 it took him several hours to make his way through the throng which had assembled to bid him farewell. The islanders bestowed upon him a sword of honour and his achievement was rewarded by promotion to the rank of field-marshal in 1943.

Gort's next appointment was that of high commissioner and commander-in-chief of Palestine and high commissioner of Trans-Jordan. He ardently looked forward to this experience, although it was expected to be almost as trying as the last. In fact, the bloodshed and confusion which afflicted Palestine were not renewed in his time. A serious illness compelled him to resign in 1945, and he died in London 31 March 1946. It was during this last illness that in 1945 the viscountcy in

the peerage of the United Kingdom was conferred upon him.

The outstanding achievement of his service in the war of 1939–45 was his organization of the defence of Malta. It was widely held that in France he hampered himself by undue concern with detail. The criticism may well be valid, yet the same critics might have put the experiments in refuelling aircraft under the same heading. With the garrison and people of Malta he made his gallant and invincible personality felt as strongly as when in command of a unit in the war of 1914–18. As a staff officer he was thorough and capable. In character he was upright and honourable. He regulated his conduct by a strict code of duty. Although somewhat shy in manner, he possessed a personal charm and magnetism which made him a welcome companion.

Gort married in 1911 his cousin, Corinna Katherine, only daughter of George Medlicott Vereker, formerly a captain in the Royal Dublin Fusiliers. The marriage was dissolved in 1925. His only son, Charles Standish, Grenadier Guards, died in 1941, and the elder of his two daughters died in childhood. The United Kingdom viscountcy became extinct with Gort's death and he was succeeded in his Irish titles by his brother, Standish Robert Gage Prendergast (born 1888).

There are portraits of Gort, in the Guards' Club by (Sir) Oswald Birley and White's Club by Henry Carr; and three in the Imperial War Museum, two by R. G. Eves and one by Edward Seago.

[Sir J. E. Edmonds and others, (Official) *History of the Great War. Military Operations, France and Belgium, 1917*, vol. ii, 1948, *1918*, vol. v, 1947; Viscount Gort, *Dispatches, 1939–40*, 1941; L. F. Ellis, (Official) *History of the Second World War. France and Flanders, 1939–40*, 1953; private information; personal knowledge.]     CYRIL FALLS.

VILLIERS, MARGARET ELIZABETH CHILD-, COUNTESS OF JERSEY (1849–1945), was born 29 October 1849 at Stoneleigh Abbey, Warwickshire, the eldest daughter of William Henry Leigh, who became second Baron Leigh in the next year, by his wife, Lady Caroline Amelia Grosvenor, daughter of the second Marquess of Westminster, and sister of the first Duke of Westminster [qq.v.]. In 1872 she left this beautiful old home to marry Victor Albert George Child-Villiers, seventh Earl of Jersey [q.v.]. They had two sons and four daughters, of whom the eldest daughter died in infancy and the elder son and third daughter both predeceased their mother. Their life was mainly spent at Middleton Park, near Bicester, and at Osterley Park, near Isleworth: the latter, with its architecture, furniture, and pictures, is one of the most beautiful houses of the Georgian period, and probably the finest piece of work by the Adam brothers. The garden-parties which Lord and Lady Jersey used to give there every summer were a prominent feature of the London season. Lady Jersey also travelled a great deal in far countries, and she lived in New South Wales from 1891 to 1893 when Lord Jersey was governor there. Having seen so much of the British Empire in what was perhaps its grandest period, she easily absorbed the imperial idea, and, by showing much hospitality at Osterley to many visitors from the ends of the earth, and by helping in 1901 to found the Victoria League, of which she was president for twenty-six years, she contributed towards making the words 'the bonds that link the Empire' something more than a mere phrase. Although Lady Jersey had seen so many lands in five continents, her principal interest was always people, and there were probably not many rulers and statesmen visiting London from different parts of the Empire who were not at some time received at Osterley. Adding as she did to her wide knowledge of people and places a keen interest in contemporary affairs, which never deserted her even in old age, she might well have said with Aeneas the long period through which she lived, 'quorum pars magna fui', or, with Tennyson's Ulysses, 'I am a part of all that I have met'.

In politics Lady Jersey was a Unionist, but a free trader; she was opposed to women's suffrage, believing that for women there is far more important work than politics. She was also profoundly sceptical of the efficacy of the [League of Nations. She was a good speaker and spoke much in public, at a time when few women did. She took an active interest in the welfare of children, great numbers of whom from the London schools she used to entertain at Osterley, and she was president of the Children's Happy Evenings Association from its foundation in 1894 until the war of 1914–18. After Lord Jersey's death in 1915 she went to live in Montagu Square; she became a magistrate at the children's court,

which she used to attend regularly, and also a governor of Charterhouse.

Details of Lady Jersey's long life up to the year 1900 may be found in her autobiography, *Fifty-One Years of Victorian Life* (1922): she also wrote many articles on travel for the *Nineteenth Century* and other reviews, and children's plays and stories which were much acted and read.

Lady Jersey was made C.B.E. in 1920 for work with the Red Cross, and D.B.E. in 1927. She died at Middleton Park 22 May 1945 in her ninety-sixth year. Her days extended through so long a period of English history that she remembered the first Duke of Wellington, as well as the Prince Consort when Queen Victoria and he came to stay at Stoneleigh in her childhood, and she lived to hear the news of the defeat of Hitler. There were not many interesting personalities in England whom she did not know in the long period which lay between.

A portrait of Lady Jersey in a group at a private view of an exhibition of old masters in 1888 by H. Jamyn Brooks is in the National Portrait Gallery. Other portraits by Des Anges, Smiechen, and Ellis Roberts are in private possession.

[*The Times*, 23 May 1945 ; Countess of Jersey, *Fifty-One Years of Victorian Life*, 1922; personal knowledge.]          DUNSANY.

VINCENT, SIR EDGAR, sixteenth baronet, VISCOUNT D'ABERNON (1857–1941), financier and diplomatist, was born at Slinfold, Sussex, 19 August 1857, the seventh and youngest son of the Rev. (Sir) Frederick Vincent who became the eleventh baronet, rector of Slinfold, and prebendary of Chichester Cathedral, and the fifth son by his second wife, Maria Copley, daughter of Robert Herries Young, of Auchenskeoch, Dumfriesshire. Sir C. E. H. Vincent [q.v.] was an elder brother. From Eton Vincent qualified as a student dragoman at Constantinople but chose an army career and was gazetted to the Coldstream Guards in 1877. In 1879, with T. G. Dickson, he published a *Handbook to Modern Greek* which has remained a textbook. While still in the army he was appointed in 1880 private secretary to Lord Edmond Petty-Fitzmaurice (later Lord Fitzmaurice, q.v.) then commissioner for Eastern Roumelia, and in 1881 assistant to Her Majesty's commissioner for the evacuation of the territory ceded to Greece by Turkey.

This episode clearly showed that Vincent's real gifts were administrative rather than military and in 1882 he resigned his commission in the army and was appointed British, Belgian, and Dutch representative on the council of the Ottoman public debt at Constantinople. This was followed the next year by his promotion in March to the post of president of the council of the Ottoman public debt, and by his transfer in November to Egypt as financial adviser to the Egyptian Government. In 1887 he was appointed K.C.M.G. and in 1889 he returned to Constantinople as governor of the Imperial Ottoman Bank.

To a man thus gifted and favoured at so early an age every road to further success was open; but during Vincent's tenure of the governorship, smooth progress to further distinction was checked. His was a bold, speculative mind, and the success of his financial operations tempted others to imitate him, but with far less success, and the bank was involved in serious loss. Vincent accordingly left Constantinople in 1897, returned to England, bought Esher Place, and shortly afterwards entered politics. In 1899 he was elected Conservative member for Exeter but lost the seat in 1906. In December 1910 he stood as a Liberal for Colchester, but defeat caused him to abandon all hope of a parliamentary career, for which indeed he was not well fitted, for his rapidity of perception made him see every side of a question and stood in the way of a wholehearted acceptance of general principles. This period of political and social activity, however, which included a connexion with the turf, brought him into close contact with all the leading men of the day. In 1914 he was raised to the peerage as Baron D'Abernon, of Esher, in the county of Surrey, taking his title from the old family seat of Stoke D'Abernon. He had already in 1912 been appointed chairman of the Royal Commission on imperial trade, but, more important, in 1915 he became chairman of the Central Control Board (Liquor Traffic). In that office, he urged the heavy taxation of all forms of alcoholic refreshment, both because he was convinced of the deleterious effects of alcohol on the human body, and because he argued that no loss would be caused to the revenue, as consumption did not decrease *pari passu* with increase in taxation. He was promoted G.C.M.G. in 1917.

In June 1920 D'Abernon was selected by Lloyd George to be the first ambassador to the new German republic and sworn of the Privy Council. The appointment caused surprise and even criticism, but Lloyd George adhered to his decision, and Lord Curzon [q.v.], then foreign secretary, explained to D'Abernon himself that the special qualifications required for the post at that juncture were 'a close familiarity with economic and financial subjects and wide experience in dealing on friendly terms with various classes of men'. On presenting his letters of credence on 2 July D'Abernon conveyed the broad outlines of British policy and indicated his own attitude in the phrase that 'in the execution of my mission I shall constantly remember that peace has been signed'. Shortly afterwards, during the closing stages of the Spa conference, an appeal was received from the Polish Government for allied support against the Bolshevik advance on Warsaw. D'Abernon, who was at the conference, was appointed a special delegate on the Anglo-French mission to Warsaw, which was sent as an indication of 'moral and technical support'. He arrived in Warsaw on 25 July. Thanks to the vigorous and prompt action of General Weygand, but also to the calm and determined support of D'Abernon, the mission succeeded in its task and the Russians were driven back in great disorder.

D'Abernon remained at Berlin until October 1926. During those six years, the questions of reparations, disarmament, occupation of German territory, French security, and the gradual admission of Germany to equal partnership with her former enemies were discussed, analysed, and finally settled in an atmosphere of bickerings and quarrels resulting from past antagonisms and mutual fear. Reasonable compromise and frank solution were impeded and delayed by extraneous considerations. Finance, political rancour, an exacerbated public opinion encouraged rash action and hindered calm consideration. It was a period of innumerable conferences from which emerged, with the advent of Stresemann to power, the Treaty of Locarno and the admission of Germany into the League of Nations.

D'Abernon was too well acquainted with human nature to imagine that a swift remedy could be found through reason, logic, or experience to problems so complex. He realized that time was an essential factor, and he therefore, as an enlightened arbitrator, contented himself with giving advice in homœopathic doses. Like others, he was aware that the payment of enormous sums, whether in cash or in kind, was not only impossible of accomplishment but directly contrary to the best interests of the claimants. He had to fight on two fronts. On the one side was a series of bewildered and pedantically obstinate German Governments without the skill to understand the healing value of time and compromise; on the other were the British and allied Governments. But the need for time and patience was not to be an excuse for doing nothing. In 1924 at his instigation an Anglo-German treaty of commerce on lines which he had suggested was concluded. The triumph of his career was the conclusion of the Treaty of Locarno in 1925. He was on terms of close friendship with Stresemann, of whose abilities and character he had the highest opinion, and the plan for a pact of mutual guarantee, as the only appropriate method of settling the question of French security, was suggested by D'Abernon, adopted and sponsored by Stresemann, and finally brought to completion by D'Abernon's persistence and energy.

With the conclusion of the treaty, D'Abernon rightly conceived that he had accomplished his mission as 'an ambassador of peace'. He therefore resigned his appointment and left Berlin in October 1926. His departure was accompanied by almost embarrassing demonstrations of friendship, and the German Government presented him with a valuable collection of old German silver, which His Majesty's Government authorized him to accept. He was advanced to a viscountcy and appointed G.C.B. in the same year. Whatever may originally have been the reasons which impelled Lloyd George to insist on the appointment, the issue showed that the prime minister's action had been right.

In person, D'Abernon was tall, handsome, and imposing, with a clear resonant voice and powers of felicitous speech which ensured the attention of the listener. His conversation abounded in aphorisms and pungent comments on men and things, but he never sought to impose his views on his company, and he always listened carefully to the suggestions of his staff. Among those who distrusted rapidity of thought and confused it with superficiality the rapid course of his very agile mind aroused antagonism. That the mediatorial position which he took up at Berlin should expose him to the charge of being pro-German, whereas personally he was if anything pro-French, was inevitable; but in the main time has shown that his judgement during his embassy at Berlin was correct, and that his main object, the restoration of peace,

with the end of Franco-German rivalry as the first step thereto, had been achieved.

Retirement from so eminent a position did not mean inactivity to D'Abernon. The mere recital of posts which he held after 1926 shows the variety of his interests and the demands made upon his time. He was a trustee of the National Gallery and of the Tate Gallery; chairman of the Royal Commission on national museums and public galleries and subsequently of the standing commission. He served also as chairman of the Medical Research Council, the Industrial Fatigue Research Board, and as president of the National Institute of Industrial Psychology. He was a member of the Royal Mint advisory committee, president of the Royal Statistical Society, and in 1929 he led a British economic mission to South America. He was chairman (and later president) of the Lawn Tennis Association and of the Thoroughbred Horse Breeders' Association and a member of the Racecourse Betting Control Board.

In 1934 D'Abernon was elected F.R.S. He succeeded his brother as sixteenth baronet in 1936 and died at Hove, heirless, after a long illness 1 November 1941. In 1890 he married one of the reigning beauties of London, Lady Helen Venetia Duncombe (died 1954), daughter of the first Earl of Feversham, of Ryedale. There were no children.

A full-length portrait of D'Abernon in the robes of a G.C.B. by Augustus John hangs in the Tate Gallery. A pencil drawing by Francis Dodd is in the National Portrait Gallery. A cartoon by 'Spy' appeared in *Vanity Fair*, 20 April 1899.

[*The Times*, 3 November 1941; Sir Henry Dale in *Obituary Notices of Fellows of the Royal Society*, No. 11, November 1942; Viscount D'Abernon, *An Ambassador of Peace*, 3 vols., 1929–30.]

JOSEPH ADDISON.

VOYSEY, CHARLES FRANCIS ANNESLEY (1857–1941), architect, was born at Hessle, near Hull, 28 May 1857, the eldest son of the Rev. Charles Voysey [q.v.], who was expelled from the Church of England in 1871 for heretical doctrines and then founded the Theistic Church. The young Voysey thus grew up in an unorthodox atmosphere and was proud of his connexion with John Wesley [q.v.] whose sister was his great-great-great-grandmother. In later life Voysey resembled Wesley so closely that he once sat as a model for a portrait of him. Something of his dissenting ancestry appears in his attitude to architecture, for he was always a puritan and a rebel against the established order. Except for a period of less than two years at Dulwich College, where he was regarded as an unsatisfactory pupil, his education was meagre and was confined to study at home. He stated in his old age that he went into architecture because it was then the only profession which he could enter without passing any examination; but heredity may have influenced him, for his grandfather, Annesley Voysey, was an architect. From 1874 to 1879 he was a pupil of John Pollard Seddon, an architect of the Gothic revival, and then became an assistant to George Devey [q.v.], whose practice consisted mainly of large country-houses.

Some time between 1881 and 1884, Voysey commenced practice on his own account in London. His first commission, for a house, is said to have been due to the publication of an imaginary design in a technical journal. Throughout his career, his work was made known by the technical press and also by such magazines as the *Studio*, which contained articles on his buildings at intervals between 1897 and 1905. He was a regular exhibitor at the Royal Academy. He designed various buildings while still serving his articles, but his earliest commission of any size seems to have been the erection of the South Devon Sanatorium at Teignmouth and the alteration of the adjoining Royal Hotel, from 1882 to 1884. During the next five years he was partly engaged in designing stained glass, fabrics, wallpaper, furniture, and other decorative accessories; and several of his early architectural works were houses or studios for artists and manufacturers encountered in this way. A house and studio at Bedford Park, Chiswick (1888), marked his progress towards the intensely individual style which was soon to make him famous. Hitherto his work had resembled that of R. Norman Shaw [q.v.] and Devey, with half-timbered gables and many other features then fashionable, but from 1890 the characteristic 'Voysey style' became manifest. His standard prescription for domestic design resulted in long, low houses with plain roughcast walls, buttresses at the angles, grey or green slate roofs of steep pitch with gables, small low leaded windows with square stone mullions and dressings, black chimney-pots, rooms only eight feet high, and specially designed furniture and accessories of every kind. In his designs for fabrics, wallpapers, and so on, the influence of William Morris [q.v.] is evident. His houses were extremely simple but not particularly cheap, for they were well built. He deliberately avoided the classical or neo-Georgian fashions which were popular about the turn of the century, regarding them as un-English. In his rejection of the elaborate quasi-Elizabethan style affected by Devey, Shaw, and Sir Ernest George [q.v.], he may certainly be described as the originator of a new movement; moreover, he was the mentor of C. R. Mackintosh [q.v.], usually acclaimed as a pioneer.

Between 1890 and 1914 Voysey enjoyed an extensive domestic practice, and his methods of design had a considerable vogue abroad, enhanced by the publication between 1900 and 1905 of books by Hermann Muthesius in German. Among the large number of country-houses built by him during this period are those at Castle Morton near Malvern, Colwall in Herefordshire, Ockham Park, 'Lowick' near Frensham, Studland Bay, Puttenham, Shackleford, Windermere (two large houses), Glassonby, Oxshott, Sandgate ('Spade House' for H. G. Wells), Chorleywood ('The Orchard', Voysey's own house), North Luffenham in Rutland, 'Vodin' on Pyrford Common, 'Wilverley' on Holtye Common, Frinton, Kendal, Henley-in-Arden; also designs for houses in Egypt and Massachusetts. In Chelsea he erected town-houses in Swan Walk and Hans Road, and numerous studios for artists. Other work included inns at Elmesthorpe and at Stetchworth near Newmarket, a cottage hospital at Beaworthy in Devon, and Sanderson's factory at Chiswick. Occasionally he submitted designs in competition for public buildings, but none was successful. All through his active career he was a hard worker and a confirmed individualist. He conducted his practice on somewhat old-fashioned lines, doing most of the work himself and relying for the rest mainly upon pupils. He published only one book, *Individuality* (1915), and a pamphlet, *Reason as a Basis of Art* (1906).

The outbreak of war in 1914 virtually extinguished Voysey's practice but it had already begun to decline. His rather mannered and very English style had little in common with the cosmopolitan architecture which penetrated England between the two world wars. Possibly a factor contributing to his eclipse was his obstinacy in refusing to comply with the wishes of his patrons if they conflicted with his own ideals. Whatever the cause, he ceased to figure prominently in English architecture, although he executed a few war memorials. He was out of harmony with the general body of his profession until his last years, being opposed to the registration of architects and to the system of education favoured by the Royal Institute of British Architects, but was elected a fellow of that body in 1929 and was awarded the Royal gold medal for architecture in 1940. For many years he was a zealous member of the Art-Workers' Guild of which he was master in 1924. Late in life he was granted a Civil List pension. From about 1917 onwards, he chose to live alone in a service flat in St. James's Street, spending most of his days at the Arts Club not far away where he had many friends. Somewhat below the middle height, he never played games but was fond of company and enjoyed an argument. Intellectually he was an artist rather than a scholar.

In 1885 Voysey married Mary Maria, daughter of Henry Evans, of Torquay; they had two sons, one of whom became an architect, and one daughter. Voysey died at Winchester 12 February 1941. A portrait (1924) by Meredith Frampton belongs to the Art-Workers' Guild, and another by W. Lee Hankey to the Arts Club.

[*The Times*, 13 February 1941; *Journal of the Royal Institute of British Architects*, 17 March 1941; *Architectural Review*, May 1941 and *passim*; *Builder*, 21 February 1941; *Architects' Journal*, 20 March 1941; articles in the *Studio*; private information; personal knowledge.]                    MARTIN S. BRIGGS.

WADSWORTH, EDWARD ALEXANDER (1889–1949), painter, was born at Cleckheaton, Yorkshire, 29 October 1889, the only son of Fred Wadsworth, worsted spinner, and his wife, Hannah Smith, of Peterhead, who died at his birth. He was educated at Fettes College, leaving at the age of sixteen to study engineering in Munich. There he attended the Knirr School of Art, and his chief recreation was the opera. He then decided to take up painting as a profession, and returning to England studied at the Bradford School of Art until a scholarship took him to the Slade School of Fine Art, where he worked from 1910 to 1912.

He exhibited in London with the Vorticists and other advanced independent groups of artists until the outbreak of war in 1914 when he served with the Royal Naval Volunteer Reserve as an intelligence officer in Mudros, and was later employed on dazzle camouflage at English home ports. After the war his 'Black Country' drawings were exhibited in London and published in 1920 with an introduction by Arnold Bennett. A number of wood-engravings also belong to this earlier period, but thenceforward, apart from the copper-engravings for a book published in 1926, *Sailing Ships and Barges of the Western Mediterranean and Adriatic Seas*, he worked entirely in tempera. This medium was indeed the great influence on his painting. He made several journeys to Italy where he saw the early masterpieces in tempera. Although essentially of the twentieth century Wadsworth painted in the strict tradition of the early Italian painters in tempera using the technique according to the teaching of Cennino Cennini. He had a passion for the sea and although his subjects covered a wide range he resorted always to the symbolism of the sea. His engineering skill and creative talent combined to make him an artist of unusual qualities with a highly individual style.

In 1927 a collection of his work was shown in Paris, and there were subsequent one-man shows in London. His pictures were purchased by continental and American museums as well as by the larger public galleries in this country, including the British Museum and the Tate Gallery where there was a memorial exhibition in 1951. His commissioned work ranged from designing the initial letters used by T. E. Lawrence in his *Seven Pillars of Wisdom* to large-scale panels in the *Queen Mary*, the De La Warr pavilion, Bexhill, and the Canadian War Museum. He was elected A.R.A. in 1943, was a member of the Society of Mural Painters, and sat on the selection committee of the Chantrey bequest (1945–6).

An accomplished linguist, his artistic and human discernment was deepened by his many travels in France, Italy, and Germany. He favoured the simple life coupled with powerful motor-cars which he drove with great skill and no less speed. He had more than his share of physical and moral courage and was, for an artist, unusually businesslike, answering letters by return of post and punctiliously fulfilling his commissions. He was a combative yet sympathetic conversationalist. In appearance he was dark, clean-shaven, with rather shaggy eyebrows. A self-portrait in oils (1911) is in the possession of his family. He married in 1912 Fanny

Mary, daughter of George Eveleigh, banker, of Horncastle, Lincolnshire. His wife, a professional violinist, survived him when he died in London 21 June 1949. He was extremely happy in his marriage, a devoted father to his two daughters, and a very good friend.

[Private information; personal knowledge.]
SIDNEY ROGERSON.

WAKE-WALKER, SIR WILLIAM FREDERIC (1888–1945), admiral, was born at Watford 24 March 1888, the younger son of Frederic George Arthur Wake-Walker, solicitor, by his wife, Mary Eleanor, daughter of William Forster, barrister, of London, and grandson of Admiral Sir Baldwin Wake Walker [q.v.], first baronet. He was educated for a short time at Haileybury but left to become a naval cadet in the *Britannia* in January 1903. He went to sea as a midshipman in May 1904 and for three years served in the *Good Hope*, flagship of Sir Wilmot Fawkes, commander of the first cruiser squadron. He spent some months as sub-lieutenant in the battleship *Illustrious* and after passing first class in all his examinations at Greenwich and winning a prize, received rapid promotion to the rank of lieutenant. After short spells in the *Eclipse* and the *Warrior*, he joined the *Invincible*, one of the three original battle cruisers, as a watchkeeper in March 1909. He transferred to the *Vernon*, torpedo school, in August 1910 and by 1912 had qualified as a torpedo specialist.

In January 1913 Wake-Walker joined the *Cochrane*, second cruiser squadron, as torpedo lieutenant and was still serving in her at the outbreak of war in August 1914. At the end of September 1915 he rejoined the *Vernon* and in July 1916, the month of his promotion to lieutenant-commander, he was transferred to the new battleship *Ramillies*, which was so severely damaged during her launching on the Clyde in September 1916 that she was unable to join the Grand Fleet until November 1917. He was appointed O.B.E. for his war services in 1919.

In April 1919 Wake-Walker was appointed to the *Coventry* and though promoted commander in June 1920 remained in her until August 1921. From September 1921 to December 1925 he was employed ashore, first at the Royal Naval College, Greenwich, then on the naval staff at the Admiralty, and finally at the Tactical School, Portsmouth. He returned to sea at the end of 1925 as executive officer of the *Royal Oak*, and was promoted captain at the end of 1927 at the early age of thirty-nine. After taking the senior officers' technical and war courses he commanded the *Castor*, third cruiser squadron, on the Mediterranean and China stations until July 1930, when he became deputy director of the training and staff duties division of the naval staff at the Admiralty. From September 1932 until July 1935 he was again at sea, in command of the *Dragon* on the America and West Indies station, but in October 1935 returned to the Admiralty as director of torpedoes and mining. In January 1938 he took over the command of the *Revenge* in the Home Fleet and remained in command until he reached flag rank on 10 January 1939.

After a senior officers' war course Wake-Walker became in September 1939 rear-admiral commanding the twelfth cruiser squadron, in the Northern Patrol. He returned to the Admiralty at the end of October as rear-admiral in charge of mine-laying, but at the end of November he became responsible for co-ordinating all technical measures for dealing with the German magnetic mine, a task he discharged with conspicuous success. On 29 May 1940, during the evacuation from Dunkirk, he was sent to Dover 'for command of sea-going ships and vessels off the Belgian coast'. He spent six days and nights under almost constant attack off the beaches and was chiefly responsible for the control of the 'little ships' which helped to bring the allied armies safely back to the United Kingdom. For this service he was appointed C.B.

Wake-Walker then commanded successively: the newly formed first mine-laying squadron, from June 1940, flying his flag in the *Southern Prince*; Force K, from December 1940, with his flag in the aircraft carrier *Formidable*; and, from January 1941, the first cruiser squadron, with his flag in the *Norfolk*. It was he who on 23 May 1941 first reported the German battleship *Bismarck* and the cruiser *Prinz Eugen* in the Denmark Strait. He played a leading role in the subsequent operations and took part in the final attack which led to the destruction of the enemy battleship on 27 May. For this he was appointed C.B.E.

In February 1942 Wake-Walker hauled down his flag and in April was promoted vice-admiral. In May he became third sea lord and controller of the navy, and was appointed K.C.B. in 1943. As controller he was largely responsible for the great development of landing craft which made possible the victorious allied invasions of northern and southern Europe. He reached admiral's rank on VE-Day 8 May 1945, but the strain of his services had proved too great and on 24 September 1945 he died suddenly in London, only a few hours after formally accepting the appointment of commander-in-chief, Mediterranean.

In 1916 Wake-Walker married Muriel, daughter of Sir Collingwood Hughes, tenth baronet, whose ancestor, Admiral Sir Richard Hughes [q.v.], had been Howe's second-in-command at the relief of Gibraltar in 1782. They had two sons, both of whom entered the Royal Navy, and two daughters. Throughout his long and distinguished naval career Wake-Walker proved himself a conspicuous and inspiring leader who rapidly gained the confidence of those whose privilege it was to serve under him. His appreciation of the needs of his subordinates and his unfailing interest in their welfare endeared him to all. A portrait of Wake-Walker by A. D. Wales Smith is in the possession of the family.

[*The Times*, 26 September 1945; *Annual Register*, 1945; private information; personal knowledge.]                    J. H. LHOYD-OWEN.

WAKEFIELD, CHARLES CHEERS, VISCOUNT WAKEFIELD (1859–1941), man of business and philanthropist, was born in Liverpool 12 December 1859, the youngest son of John Wakefield, a customs official, by his wife, Mary, daughter of William Cheers, of Manchester. After schooling at Liverpool Institute he became the employee of an oil-broker, and made several journeys round the world. Moving to London in 1891, he founded in 1899 his own firm, C. C. Wakefield & Co., dealing in lubricating oils and appliances. In those days the petrol-driven motor was in the experimental stage, and the firm of Wakefield made its early reputation in locomotive lubricants. This reputation was to endure, but Wakefield had the foresight to plan for a rapid expansion of the motor industry. He stuck to his speciality, making no excursions into the wider field of propulsive oils; and he invariably ploughed back a large proportion of his profits into the concern. These factors, combined with a faculty for choosing the right technical experts and an appreciation of the value of advertising, rapidly brought him great wealth. The trade name, 'Castrol', which he adopted for his products, arose from the fact that the early motor lubricants contained a considerable proportion of castor oil.

Established at Cannon Street, in the City of London, Wakefield became a zealous worker for the City and a warm enthusiast for its dignities and traditions. He was elected to the Court of Common Council in 1904, and served as sheriff in 1907 and 1908, being knighted in the latter year. He became alderman of the Bread Street ward in 1908, and during the session of 1915–16 was lord mayor. Holding office during a most critical period of the war, he took a very energetic part in the recruiting movement, and paid visits in 1916 both to the western front and to the Grand Fleet at Scapa Flow. He received a baronetcy in 1917 and was appointed C.B.E. in 1919.

Wakefield's interest in the City always remained deep and warm, and he showed himself a ready benefactor to its causes. He gave generous aid to Guildhall Library and Art Gallery. He was president of the City of London branch of the League of Mercy and of the Tower Hill improvement fund to which he also gave generously. He was deputy-lieutenant of the City, served at various times as master of the Haberdashers', Cordwainers', Gardeners', and Spectacle Makers' companies, and was especially proud to be the first member of the corporation to be made an honorary freeman of the City, in 1935. In 1920 he deputized for the lord mayor as head of a civic deputation to the seventh congress of the Sokols at Prague where he had a great personal success. Two years later he went to the United States as head of a delegation from the Sulgrave Institution, and presented a statue of Burke to Washington and busts of Pitt and Lord Bryce to Pittsburgh and New York.

Interested in fostering imperial strength and friendship, Wakefield actively supported the Imperial Cadet movement, served as honorary colonel of the Imperial Cadet Yeomanry, and in 1932 gave £25,000 to the Imperial Institute. As early as 1910 he had foreseen the future importance of air communications as an imperial link. He financed Sir Alan Cobham's return flight to Australia and his flight round Africa, and gave monetary aid to Amy Johnson [q.v.] for her Australian flight. He provided Wakefield scholarships for Royal Air Force cadets at Cranwell; and as a vice-president of the Institution of Aeronautical Engineers he presented an annual medal for the designer of the best safety device in aviation. He was chairman of the Royal Air Force Benevolent Fund, on behalf of which in 1940, at the age of eighty, he went to see Lord Nuffield and returned with a cheque for £250,000.

Motoring, too, was very naturally a pursuit near to his heart. He financed Sir Henry Segrave's speed trials at Daytona and Miami and presented the Wakefield gold trophy for maximum speed on land. He presented the Golden Arrow car to the nation; and he owned the three Miss England speed-boats which set up world water-speed records. He was twice president of the Motor and Cycle Trades Benevolent Fund.

Among Wakefield's other benevolent interests, one cause which moved him very deeply was the work of the Bethlem Royal Hospital. He was president, and a generous benefactor, of both this and the Bridewell Hospital and of the Mental Aftercare Association. A governor of St. Thomas's and St. Bartholomew's hospitals, and treasurer of the National Children's Home and Orphanage, he gave lavishly to all in both time and money.

Wakefield's books, *America To-day and To-morrow* (1924), and *On Leaving School and the Choice of a Career* (1927), were practical and forward-looking, and the latter brought him a voluminous correspondence, all of which was answered with care. Although he was primarily a man of business, he was far from blind to the need for cultural advancement. He endowed a series of lectures for the Raleigh tercentenary under the aegis of the British Academy; the Dickens Fellowship benefited by books and relics; and the British Museum by an anonymous guarantee of £50,000 towards the purchase of the *Codex Sinaiticus*. He purchased for the nation the Howard Grace (otherwise the Thomas à Becket) Cup, the Armada Jewel, the papers of Sir Isaac Newton, Nelson's personal log-book, and the Mint collection.

Wakefield was elected a fellow of King's College, London, was an honorary LL.D. of Colgate University, Hamilton, New York, and was made an honorary F.B.A. in 1938. He was raised to the peerage as Baron Wakefield, of Hythe, in the county of Kent, in 1930, and advanced to a viscountcy, also of Hythe, in 1934. He was appointed G.C.V.O. in 1936.

Wakefield owed his business success to his qualities of foresight, courage, and energy. He attached good men to him by probity and fair dealing, and was content to leave detail to them. Rigorously prompt and thorough himself, he could sternly discount a lame excuse, but was patient and kindly, and as solicitous for the well-being of friends and associates as he was for that of the multitudinous beneficiaries of his public acts. Courteous and wise in his dealings, he had an unusually strong sense of obligation to the State for its protection. This particularly expressed itself in a very full and prompt settlement of taxation. He even disapproved of perfectly legitimate covenants for partial remission of income-tax on charitable donations, whether donor or recipient benefited thereby; and on one occasion, irked by suggestions that such a saving could be made, he sent a cheque overnight for the full amount of £25,000 which had been under discussion.

In 1887 Wakefield married Sarah Frances (died 1950), daughter of William Graham, book-keeper, of Wavertree, Liverpool. She became a dame of grace of the Order of St. John of Jerusalem. They had no children. Wakefield remained active in business until a month before his death which took place at Beaconsfield, Buckinghamshire, 15 January 1941. The peerage became extinct.

Portraits of Wakefield by (Sir) Oswald Birley are at the Bethlem Royal Hospital and at the Royal Aero Club, Piccadilly; another, by Frank E. Beresford, is the property of the Worshipful Company of Haberdashers; another, by Sir John Lavery, belongs to the mayor and corporation of Hythe where he is commemorated by an annual Wakefield Day.

[*The Times*, 16 January 1941; private information.]      HERBERT B. GRIMSDITCH.

**WALCOT, WILLIAM** (1874–1943), architect and graphic artist, was born at Lustdorf, near Odessa, 10 March 1874, son of Frank Walcot, merchant, and Catherine, daughter of Gottlieb Reichert, landowner. He went to school at Amiens and Paris, and at the age of seventeen began architectural studies at St. Petersburg under Louis Benois at the Imperial Academy of Art. After further study at the École des Beaux-Arts and the Atelier Redon, in Paris, he set up as an architect in Moscow. He visited Rome and London, where he settled early in the twentieth century.

Though he continued architecture for some time, Walcot now turned more to water-colours and etchings, but it was still buildings which chiefly called forth his enthusiasm. Indeed Walcot's high reputation is likely to rest chiefly on his reconstructions of the buildings of antiquity. He was deeply learned in the architectural history of ancient Rome; and his original and special contribution to art was the re-creation of classical scenes in the etched medium, not as cold studies but as visualizations of the life of antiquity, with people moving about their business in temples and palaces to which his superb (but often unorthodox) technique gave a renewed life.

The Fine Art Society, art dealers, sent Walcot to Venice and Rome, and successfully exhibited the resultant water-colours in 1909. An exhibition at Edinburgh in 1913 also drew favourable attention; the London firm, H. C. Dickins, became his publishers, sponsored a river series, 'The Arteries of Great Britain', and in 1919 issued a folio of his architectural water-colours and etchings. Walcot's activities ranged from the illustrations to Flaubert's *Salammbô* to the making of elevations for fellow architects, to whose drawings he gave animation which they themselves were unable to impart. He became a member of the Royal Society of British Artists in 1913 and an associate of the Royal Society of Painter-Etchers and Engravers in 1916. He was also an associate of the British School at Rome, and in 1922 was elected a fellow of the Royal Institute of British Architects. In the 'thirties of the century he was at the height of his success, running studios in Rome, London, and Oxford and leading a lavish and generous life. But the war of 1939–45 resulted in the cancellation of several valuable contracts and virtually ruined him. Nevertheless he played a worthy part in the team which produced the County of London Plan in 1943. He had noble and grandiose ideas on town planning and was the artist-architect *par excellence*.

Anxious, frustrated, and in despair with a time that was out of joint, Walcot ended his own life, dying at Hurstpierpoint 21 May 1943. He married, first, at St. Petersburg, in his early twenties, an Irish lady-in-waiting at the imperial court. All records disappeared in the revolution of October 1917, but it is known that she contracted tuberculosis, and died, before 1900, within two or three years of marriage. Secondly he married in 1911, Alice Maria, daughter of the late William Wheelan, painter; she bore him two daughters and survived him.

[*Architectural Water-Colours & Etchings of W. Walcot*, with an introduction by Sir Reginald Blomfield, R.A., 1919; M. C. Salaman, *William Walcot R.E.* (Modern Masters of Etching), 1927; *The Times*, 15 June 1943; private information.]

HERBERT B. GRIMSDITCH.

WALKER, ERNEST (1870–1949), musician, was born in Bombay 15 July 1870, the son of Edward Walker, partner in a firm of East India merchants, by his wife, Caroline Cooper. His parents brought him to England in 1871 and later settled at Anerley, near the Crystal Palace, where he frequented the concerts, then under the direction of (Sir) August Manns [q.v.]. Educated at private schools, at the age of seventeen he was admitted to Balliol College, Oxford, where the master, Benjamin Jowett [q.v.], took a special interest in him. He was placed in the second class of the honours list in classical moderations (1889) and *literae humaniores* (1891). Philosophy was his chief interest in his work for the schools and he was deeply influenced by R. L. Nettleship [q.v.]. He became intimate with the college organist, John Farmer [q.v.], and helped him in the Balliol Sunday evening concerts. He proceeded to take the degrees of B.Mus. (1893) and D.Mus. (1898), and was assistant organist at Balliol from 1891 until on Farmer's death in 1901 he succeeded him as organist and director of music, greatly raising the standard of the concerts. In 1913 he resigned the organistship, thinking participation in chapel services inconsistent with his views on religion, but held the directorship until 1925, when he retired in order to devote himself to composition. He was elected an honorary fellow of the college in 1926.

Walker took a large part in all the musical activities of the university, and was for many years a teacher and examiner. He did much to improve the standard of the musical degrees and, with Sir Hugh Allen [q.v.], to raise the status of music in the university; in 1944 it was constituted an independent faculty.

He was a fine pianist with a catholic taste, and as an accompanist had an almost unique reputation. His compositions were scholarly, restrained, and sensitive; they fall naturally into two groups. The earlier consisted mostly of vocal music and followed the German diatonic tradition; the best known are the 'Five songs for four voices from "England's Helicon"' (1900). About 1914 diatonics gave place to harmonics and his style became more terse and enigmatic. The bulk of the music was now instrumental. Typical of this period is the 'cello and piano Sonata (composed in 1914); the passion of the first movement is unique in Walker's work.

Walker was much in request for reviews and critical articles and analytical notes to concert programmes. But his reputation as a writer rests mainly on *A History of Music in England* (1907), which has remained a classic. He also wrote *Beethoven* in the 'Music of the Masters' series (1905), and in 1946 collected some of his articles under the title *Free Thought and the Musician*; the essay which gives the title discusses the effect of rationalist views on the professional musician's life. In all his writings his scrupulous accuracy and sincerity are conspicuous.

Naturally a retiring, even shy, man, Walker was gentle and quiet in his ways, but always strong in his protest against anything false or shoddy. He was unmarried, but made many friends, especially among his pupils and fellow musicians. Early in life he tended to high church Anglicanism, but that gave way to agnosticism and ultimately to atheistic rationalism. Yet there was always something of the mystic in him, which found expression both in his music and in his lasting love of nature. He continued to live in Oxford after his retirement and died there 21 February 1949.

A drawing of Walker by Francis Dodd (1934) is at Balliol College, and another by Sir Muirhead Bone (1946) is in the possession of the Misses Deneke.

[Margaret Deneke, *Ernest Walker*, 1951, with a chapter on Walker's compositions by Ivor Keys; personal knowledge.]

CYRIL BAILEY.

WALKER, FREDERIC JOHN (1896–1944), captain, Royal Navy, was born at Plymouth 3 June 1896, a son of Lieutenant (later Captain) Frederic Murray Walker, R.N., by his wife, Lucy Selina, daughter of Major Horace William Scriven. He was a grandson of Colonel Sir George Walker, K.C.B., of Crawfordton, Dumfries. Entering Osborne in 1909 and Dartmouth in 1911, he quickly showed conspicuous qualities and was awarded the King's medal for his term. He went to sea as a cadet in the training cruiser *Cornwall* in 1913 and joined the *Ajax*, second battle squadron, as a midshipman in 1914. Promoted sub-lieutenant in 1916 and lieutenant in 1918, he served successively in the

destroyers *Mermaid* and *Sarpedon*. After the war of 1914–18 he served two years as a watchkeeper in the battleship *Valiant* before starting technical courses in 1921 to become one of the navy's first anti-submarine specialists. After serving in the *Osprey*, the anti-submarine school at Portland, he was anti-submarine officer of the Atlantic Fleet from 1926 to 1928 and of the Mediterranean Fleet from 1928 until promoted commander in 1931. Between 1931 and 1937 he commanded successively the destroyer *Shikari*, which controlled the target battleship *Centurion*, and the sloop *Falmouth* on the China station. From 1937 to 1940 he was again in the *Osprey*, and was responsible for development in anti-submarine material and methods at the outbreak of the war. He joined the staff of (Sir) Bertram Ramsay [q.v.] at Dover in January 1940 and was mentioned in dispatches in August for his services at Dunkirk. In October 1941 he joined the sloop *Stork* as senior officer, thirty-sixth escort group.

Walker rapidly proved a veritable giant among U-boat killers. In December 1941 his group escorting a convoy destroyed four within five days. Then, in April 1942, it sank another. In June Walker was promoted captain and in 1943, after temporarily commanding the escort base in Liverpool, became senior officer of the famous second escort group. Success followed success. Between June 1943 and his untimely death, 9 July 1944, at the naval hospital, Liverpool, from a stroke due to overwork, his frigates and sloops destroyed another sixteen submarines. For his dazzling exploits Walker was appointed C.B. and D.S.O. with three bars, and in addition received the unusual reward of two years' seniority as captain. Even after his death his gallant spirit lived on in the second escort group, which by the end of the war had destroyed seven more enemy submarines.

In 1919 Walker married Jessica Eileen Ryder, daughter of William Ryder Stobart, a man of business, of Etherley Lodge, Bishop Auckland, and had three sons and one daughter. In August 1943 his eldest son, Lieutenant John Timothy Ryder Walker, R.N.V.R., was lost in the British submarine *Parthian*. A portrait of Walker by A. R. Sims is in the Anti-Submarine School war memorial room.

[*The Times*, 11 July 1944; Terence Robertson, *Walker, R.N.*, 1956; private information; personal knowledge.]

J. H. LHOYD-OWEN.

WALKER, Sir NORMAN PURVIS (1862–1942), dermatologist and president of the General Medical Council, was born at Dysart, Fife, 2 August 1862, only son of the Rev. Dr. Norman Lockhart Walker, for many years editor of the magazine of the Free Church of Scotland, and his wife, Christian Normand. He was educated at the Edinburgh Academy and graduated M.B., C.M. (Edinburgh, 1884), and M.D. (1888). His first post was that of resident physician at the Edinburgh Royal Infirmary in 1885. During the next five years he was in general practice in Dalston, a suburb of Carlisle, being president of the Carlisle Medical Society in 1890. Having decided to devote himself to dermatology he went abroad and studied at Vienna and Prague. On returning to Edinburgh he was appointed assistant physician to the skin department of the Royal Infirmary (1892–1906); full physician (1906–24); and consulting physician (1925–42); he was also lecturer in dermatology in the university. In 1895 he translated from the Norwegian Hansen and Looft's *Leprosy in its Clinical and Pathological Aspects*, and in 1896 he followed this up with a translation of *The Histopathology of Diseases of the Skin* by Paul Gerson Unna of Hamburg, who was his former teacher and close friend. His own *Introduction to Dermatology* first appeared in 1899. He was for some years co-editor of the *Scottish Medical and Surgical Journal* and the *Edinburgh Medical Journal*.

Walker had a natural aptitude for university administration and, as time went on, he became closely identified with academic affairs. He became a member of the university court and a curator of patronage, and was inspector of anatomy for Scotland. At the Royal College of Physicians of Edinburgh he was elected a fellow (1892), was treasurer (1908–29), and president (1929–31). In 1906 he was president of the Fife Medical Association. He was an honorary member of the American and a corresponding member of the New York, French, and Danish dermatological societies, an honorary fellow of the American Medical Association and an honorary member of the Association of Military Surgeons of the United States. He took a conspicuous part in the organization of medical services in Scotland during and after the war of 1914–18, and was especially interested in the work of the Highlands and Islands Medical Service Board.

Walker was the direct representative for Scotland on the General Medical Council from 1906 to 1941. After serving his apprenticeship as chairman of business he was in 1931 elected president of the Council in succession to Sir Donald MacAlister [q.v.], and he held the office until 1939. Although he had not the brilliant qualities of his predecessor he had an encyclopaedic knowledge of the Council's history and procedure, and he proved an able, business-like president. In 1922 and 1927 he visited India at the instance of the secretary of state to examine and report on the state of medical education in general and of midwifery practice in particular. For this onerous task he was admirably equipped not only by his knowledge and experience but also by reason of his great tact and judgement. His reports shaped the policy of the General Medical Council in regard to the recognition of Indian qualifications and contributed greatly to the improvement of medical education in India.

Walker was knighted in 1923 and his other distinctions included the honorary degrees of LL.D., St. Andrews (1920), Edinburgh (1926), and Bristol (1933), and M.D. of Dublin (1935). He married in 1887 Annie, only daughter of Edward Trimble, of Dalston; they had three sons and one daughter. He died at Balerno 7 November 1942. A portrait by John Bowie is in the council chamber of the General Medical Council.

[*British Medical Journal* and *Lancet*, 21 November 1942; *The Times*, 10 November 1942; *Edinburgh Medical Journal*, December 1942; *British Journal of Dermatology and Syphilis*, April 1943.]

W. J. Bishop.

WALKER, Sir WILLIAM FREDERIC WAKE- (1888–1945), admiral. [See Wake-Walker.]

WALLACE, Sir CUTHBERT SIDNEY, baronet (1867–1944), surgeon, was born at Surbiton, Surrey, 20 June 1867, the fourth son of the Rev. John Wallace, of Haslemere by his wife, Marion K. J. Agnes, daughter of Francis Howard Greenway, of Sydney, New South Wales. He was educated at Haileybury and at St. Thomas's Hospital and qualified in medicine in 1891. He became F.R.C.S. (England) in 1893 and graduated M.B., B.S. (London), obtaining the gold medal in obstetric medicine and qualifying for the gold medal in surgery in 1894. He was appointed resident assistant surgeon at

St. Thomas's in 1897 at a time when the principles of antisepsis were beginning to give way to those of asepsis in surgical work. It was mainly owing to Wallace's enthusiasm and his grasp of the practical problems involved that the operating theatres and wards were successfully remodelled on the aseptic basis. While these changes were in progress the South African war broke out and Wallace went to South Africa as surgeon to the Portland Hospital. He collaborated with (Sir) Anthony Bowlby [q.v.] and other colleagues in writing an account of their experiences under the title of *A Civilian War Hospital* (1901). Wallace's early experience of gunshot wounds was greatly enlarged during the war of 1914–18 in which he served as consulting surgeon to the First Army of the British Expeditionary Force and eventually became major-general, Army Medical Service. When King George V was inspecting the Royal Flying Corps at Hesdigneul aerodrome in October 1915, His Majesty's horse reared and threw its rider, and Wallace was one of the doctors called in to attend him. Wallace's books on *War Surgery of the Abdomen* (1918) and *Surgery at a Casualty Clearing Station* (in collaboration with (Sir) John Fraser, 1918) were important contributions to the abdominal surgery of war.

At St. Thomas's Hospital Wallace was assistant surgeon (1900–13), dean of the medical school (1907–9 and 1918–28), and full surgeon (1913–30). He was also surgeon to the East London Hospital for Children, dean of the medical faculty of London University, director of medical services and research at Mount Vernon Hospital, member of the Medical Research Council, of the Radium Commission, and of the Army Medical Advisory Board. In June 1940 he was appointed chairman of the Medical Research Council's committee on war wounds, and he was for five years consultant adviser in surgery to the Emergency Medical Service. He was closely associated with the work of the Royal College of Surgeons, being for many years a member of the board of examiners and of council, Bradshaw lecturer (1927), Hunterian orator (1934), and president (1935–8).

Apart from the books mentioned above he was the author of *Prostatic Enlargement* (1907), and of many papers in the *St. Thomas's Hospital Reports* and elsewhere. He was one of the editors and contributors to the (Official) *History of the Great War. Medical Services, Surgery of the War* (2

vols., 1922). He was in the front rank as an operator and was an inspiring teacher. For his military services he was appointed C.M.G. (1916), C.B. (1918), and promoted K.C.M.G. (1919). He was also awarded the American D.S.M. and was an officer of the Legion of Honour. He received the honorary degrees of D.Sc., Oxford (1936), D.C.L., Durham (1937), and LL.D., Birmingham (1938). He was created a baronet in 1937. In 1912 he married Florence Mildred, youngest daughter of Herbert Jackson, of Sussex Place, Regent's Park, London. They had no children and the baronetcy became extinct when he died in London 24 May 1944. A portrait by George Harcourt is at St. Thomas's Hospital Medical School.

[*British Medical Journal*, 10 June and 1 July 1944; *Lancet*, 10 June 1944; *The Times*, 31 May 1944; *St. Thomas's Hospital Gazette*, October 1944; *Royal College of Surgeons of England. A record of the years 1901 to 1950*, 1951.]                    W. J. BISHOP.

WALLS, TOM KIRBY (1883–1949), actor-producer, was born 18 February 1883 at Kingsthorpe, Northampton, the son of a plumber, John William Walls, by his wife, Ellen Brewer, and was educated at Northampton County School. Best-favoured among his earliest ambitions was the job of engine-driver and, his father thinking this altogether worthy, he presently became a cleaner. This seemed insufficiently advanced to Walls; he drove a locomotive without permission (or, indeed, any skill) and was thereupon dismissed. He went to Canada for a year, liked it little, and returned to London, there joining C Division of the Metropolitan Police. This still was not what he wanted. He was (rightly) convinced that the stage called him so he joined a pierrot troupe on the Brighton front and considered himself well paid at 45s. a week. He proved himself a real man of the theatre in his début in pantomime in Glasgow in 1905. Thence he graduated slowly and carefully into musical comedy, touring the United Kingdom, North America, and Australia. In England he made his first London appearance (1907) at the Empire Theatre, Leicester Square, in Edwardian revue. From 1912 onward he found a really firm footing in the west end, his forte being portrayals of eccentric old gentlemen. At the Gaiety Theatre he was in *The Sunshine Girl*, *The Beauty Spot*, and *Faust on Toast*; at Daly's Theatre in *The Marriage Market*, a revival of *A*

*Country Girl*, and *Betty*, and at the Winter Garden Theatre in *Kissing Time*.

In 1922 there came a tremendous stroke of luck. In partnership with Leslie Henson he produced, at the Shaftesbury Theatre, a farce by Will Evans and 'Valentine' (Mr. A. T. Pechey) called *Tons of Money*. It proved a phenomenal success and ran for two years. On the strength of its handsome profits the Aldwych Theatre was taken over with *It Pays to Advertise*, an American farce. This was followed by *A Cuckoo in the Nest* by Mr. Ben Travers whose pieces from then on became an institution in London theatreland. Farce had known no such boom since Sir Arthur Pinero [q.v.]; Travers had the wit and ability to write for an established company headed by the bold, racy, amorous Walls and the fluttering asinine Mr. Ralph Lynn —perfect foils for each other—with Mary Brough and Mr. Robertson Hare in support. Over a period of six years some £1,500,000 was taken at the box-office with *Rookery Nook*, *Thark*, *Plunder*, *A Cup of Kindness*, *A Night Like This*, and *Turkey Time*.

When talking-films arrived these shows proved profitable subjects to satisfy the big new demand for British screen comedy all over the Empire and for seven years Walls deserted the theatre for the film studio. A steady and mounting prosperity led him to finance touring companies and to take over the Fortune Theatre. Above all it enabled him to maintain a racing stable adjoining his lovely house at Ewell, Surrey. Horses had always been a passion with him. His early childhood was spent in the Pytchley country, he had ridden to hounds before he was ten years old, and much later was given to arriving at the theatre for a performance still dressed in hunting pink. He set up as a trainer in 1927 with sometimes twenty-five and more animals in his care. Success on the turf was intermittent, but he brought off a most spectacular triumph by winning the Derby in 1932 with April the Fifth which he had bought as a yearling for £200, and thus became the first actor-owner to lead in a Derby winner.

Walls returned to the stage as suddenly as he had left it. He turned producer with some success, and as an actor again he played principally in revivals of comedies by Frederick Lonsdale. There were some less irresponsible roles: even a film Duke of Wellington. A serious hunting accident interrupted his activities for several months and a little later his fortune and fortunes began slowly to decline—partly because of ill-fated ventures, partly because he saw no reason to reduce his high scale of living. He was always a bon viveur, a princely host, and a confident gambler. He was impulsively generous in all money matters. This, and the cost of maintaining his lavish establishment, put too great a strain upon his financial resources. In 1948 his few remaining horses were sold and he gave up training. Both were hard blows for him and now deafness much hampered him in his acting. His last stage appearance (1948) was as Edward Moulton-Barrett in a revival of *The Barretts of Wimpole Street*. It was not well received.

In the hey-day of his career Walls earned immense sums of money: at the peak of his film success more than £30,000 a year. But when he died at his home, 27 November 1949, he was not solvent. Within a few months his house with many of his effects and his stables had to be sold by his executors. By his wish his ashes were scattered over the Derby course at Epsom.

Although Walls, because of his limited and specialized range, might not be classed as a great actor, his methods qualified him to be remembered as a first-rank character comedian in the peculiarly exacting field of farce where the need for perfect timing is paramount; here his real talent lay. In private life he was a strenuous-living sportsman of almost Regency vintage, occasionally disputatious but with a vast circle of friends and acquaintances.

He married in 1912 Hilda Edwardes, of the musical comedy stage, and had one son, Tom, a fine steeplechase rider. A bronze head of Walls as master of the Sussex draghounds was executed by Alec Dearnley.

[*The Times*, 29 November 1949; private information; personal knowledge.]

SEAN FIELDING.

WALPOLE, SIR HUGH SEYMOUR (1884–1941), novelist and man of letters, was born in Auckland, New Zealand, 13 March 1884, the eldest of the three children of the Rev. George Henry Somerset Walpole, incumbent of St. Mary's Cathedral, Auckland, and later bishop of Edinburgh, by his wife, Mildred Helen, daughter of Charles Barham, physician, of Truro. He was collaterally descended on his father's side from the family of Sir Robert Walpole, on his mother's from the author of *The Ingoldsby Legends*.

He was educated at the King's School, Canterbury, and at Durham School, and in 1903 went up to Emmanuel College, Cambridge. That he should take orders had been since adolescence an understood thing, and on coming down from Cambridge in 1906 after taking honours in the historical tripos, he joined the staff of the Mersey Mission to Seamen. Six months' experience of his inability to perform uncongenial and (to him) frightening work convinced him that he had neither the vocation nor capacity for the priesthood. He spent a year travelling in France and Germany and another year as an assistant master at Epsom College. In 1909 he went to London, published his first novel (*The Wooden Horse*) and made the acquaintance of a number of writers, among whom Arnold Bennett and Henry James [qq.v.] became lasting friends. With James, Walpole's relations were especially close—almost those of a son with a father—and the affectionate admiration felt by the younger for the older man persisted throughout their half-dozen years of intimacy, despite James's habit of treating his ardent disciple with gentle raillery.

Walpole had a wide knowledge of English fiction, and of the eighteenth and nineteenth centuries as well as of his own time. He was an especial devotee of Anthony Trollope, whom he resembled in that, as Trollope said of himself, he was 'impregnated with his own creations'. But, in one of his queer flashes of self-admiration masquerading as candour, he threw light on a fundamental difference between them, when he wrote: 'I am far too twisted and fantastic a novelist ever to succeed in catching Trollope's marvellous normality.'

From the start of his writing career Walpole displayed the fertility, the industry, and the almost reckless self-exposure to unkind depreciation which were characteristic of him throughout his life. As a youngster, he learnt his craft in public, rushing into print, at least annually, with a blend of defiant courage and readiness to take offence at once praiseworthy and illogical. He dreaded hostile criticism, yet courted it, and that he received much more than he deserved was largely due to his pathetic urgency in publishing whatsoever a prolific talent might produce.

Between 1909 and the outbreak of war in 1914 Walpole published six novels. Of these, *Mr. Perrin and Mr. Traill* (1911) deserves to be remembered for its own sake. *Maradick at Forty* (1910), *Fortitude* (1913), and *The Duchess of Wrexe* (1914) are of interest as demonstrating what

became permanent tendencies in his more mature work. He would over-labour a single character as a somewhat nebulous symbol: he would strive to portray a mortal presentation of evil; he could catch the décors of life with instinctive precision: and, being a genuine lover of books for their own sake and a voracious reader, he never failed to make apt use of recollected reading.

As an established and popular writer, he continued to cherish a touching faith in his latest work, but if that faith proved misplaced, he would take a melancholy pride in admitting disillusionment. During the mid-nineteen-thirties, and in the Jamesian manner, he appended to the Cumberland edition of his works a series of prefaces. These prefaces, in conjunction with three little volumes of personal confession (*The Crystal Box*, 1924, *The Apple Trees*, 1932, and *Roman Fountain*, 1940), constitute a literary autobiography of the most revealing kind. Their self-absorption, their acute intelligence when adjudging his own or other people's novels, their alternations of complacency and regretful acceptance of public indifference or critical dispraise show us the essential Walpole.

During the war of 1914–18 Walpole served with the Russian Red Cross in Galicia and later was in charge of the Anglo-Russian propaganda bureau in Petrograd. He witnessed the first, and only just missed witnessing the second, of the two revolutions of 1917, deriving from his experiences in Russia material for two novels—*The Dark Forest* (1916) and *The Secret City* (1919). These books take a high place among his works, on account of their intuitive understanding of an alien mentality and the vigour of their narrative power.

All this firmly established Walpole as a successful writer and a prominent figure in London literary and artistic circles. In 1919 he undertook the first of a series of lecture tours in the United States, where he became immediately popular. His genial and attractive appearance, his complete lack of aloofness, his exciting fluency as a speaker, his obvious and genuine liking for his hosts, all provoked the warm friendliness eagerly bestowed by Americans on any foreigner whom they find acceptable. His books (their number steadily increased) sold in large numbers on both sides of the Atlantic: his lectures became more and more profitable, and he was henceforth in a position to give rein to what may fairly be described as three hobbies—generous help, financial and otherwise, to individuals in distress or disappointment, the collecting of books and manuscripts, and the collecting of pictures. His method, as kindly benefactor, as bibliophile, and as patron of art, was wholly characteristic. It was lavish, zealous, unflagging in energy; but its standards were unpredictable. As a picture-buyer he was shrewd, if tempestuous; and the posthumous exhibition of his treasures showed him to have bought 'names' and bought them skilfully, rather than to have speculated in struggling talent. His book-purchases were less disciplined; but considering the extent of his library, it contained a higher proportion of worthwhile and well-selected items than might have been the case.

In his personal relationships Walpole was equally erratic. Whereas many of his contemporaries found him a warm and enthusiastic friend, others declared him self-pitying, absurdly resentful of criticism, and at times recklessly malicious. The first judgement was the more reliable. Walpole wished above all things to be *liked*, and only when he felt himself mocked or denigrated did the fundamental self-distrust and timidity which underlay that robust and confident exterior turn to rancour.

As a novelist Walpole was underrated by the majority of his fellow writers. His flow of words, his exuberant romanticism, and his taste for highly coloured descriptions were in direct conflict with the tough American school, headed by Hemingway and others, which became dominant between the wars and disconcerted Walpole by inviting comparisons he was powerless to evade. It is true that he fell short of the greatness to which his consuming ambition aspired. But he had the inventiveness, the mastery of narrative, the feeling for language, the realistic power combined with a command alike of fantasy and terror which are granted only to a born novelist. He rightly took pride in his brilliance as a raconteur, and those privileged to listen to his verbal descriptions of writers he had known felt that, if only he would write these down, they would come to be regarded as his best work.

Walpole's extensive output (during his lifetime and after his death were published forty-two novels and volumes of stories, books about Trollope and Conrad, and the three books about himself already mentioned) is so varied that individual works are approved or otherwise according to the taste of the reader. His personal preference was for *John Cornelius* (1937); literary critics favoured *Mr. Perrin and Mr. Traill*, a story of common-room life at a boys' school; those addicted to imaginative symbolism fancied *The Cathedral* (1922) or *Harmer John* (1926); and a high proportion of his vast public regarded as the finest fruit of his genius the four instalments of the Herries saga (*Rogue Herries*, 1930, *Judith Paris*, 1931, *The Fortress*, 1932, *Vanessa*, 1933) into which—maybe in excessive volume—he poured all that he had of love for Cumberland, of sentimental idolization of traditional English jollity, of fondness for period trappings in skilfully expurgated form.

Excursions into the macabre, which showed Walpole uneasily subject to the fascination of cruelty and fear, constituted a class apart. The best of them is *The Old Ladies* (1924), with *Portrait of a Man with Red Hair* (1925) a respectable second. Similarly distinct from the main body of his work are the stories of childhood. He had a tenderness toward boyhood and, when writing of it, found release from his own inhibitions, defiances, and apprehensions. For this reason posterity may decide that the most real Walpole of all—because the most unselfconscious, kindly, and understanding friend—is the Walpole of the Jeremy trilogy (*Jeremy*, 1919, *Jeremy and Hamlet*, 1923, *Jeremy at Crale*, 1927).

Walpole's benefactions to the Tate Gallery and to the Fitzwilliam Museum, as well as his important bequests of manuscripts and books to the National Library of Scotland, to the Bodleian Library and to the King's School, Canterbury, were fully recorded after his death.

Uncelebrated, because purposely concealed during his lifetime, were other aspects of his passionate devotion to the cause of letters; his generous kindness to literary aspirants and to writers fallen on evil days took many forms. By immediate financial assistance, by prefaces freely supplied or by collaboration volunteered, by introductions and recommendations to likely publishers, Walpole relieved the distresses of authorship to a degree which will never be fully known. In several cases he undertook the entire cost of educating the children of necessitous writers, because he respected their work and because he loved books.

As the first chairman of the selection committee of the Book Society (a body formed in 1929), he so influenced the monthly 'choice' of a new book that its selling value was predominantly to the advantage of unknown authors. He was also the first chairman of the Society of Bookmen (the precursor of the National Book League) and, by unstinting expenditure of personal time and effort, nursed that now impressive organization through its early conflicts between the obstinate individualisms of the various branches of the book trade.

Appointed C.B.E. in 1918 and knighted in 1937, Walpole was the Rede lecturer at Cambridge in 1925 and a prominent member of the Royal Society of Literature and of the English Association. He was unmarried, and died at his home near Keswick, 1 June 1941.

Three portraits of Walpole in oil were painted by Sir Gerald Kelly (one has disappeared, a second is in the Antipodes, the third is in the possession of the artist); a portrait by Augustus John is at the King's School, Canterbury, and a red chalk drawing by the same artist is in the Fitzwilliam Museum, Cambridge; there are two portraits by W. R. Sickert (one in the Fitzwilliam Museum, the other in the Glasgow City Art Gallery); the National Portrait Gallery has a portrait by Stephen Bone. A bronze by (Sir) Jacob Epstein is in the Fitz Park Museum, Keswick, and another, by Benno Schotz, is in the Scottish National Portrait Gallery.

[R. Hart-Davis, *Hugh Walpole*, 1952; private information; personal knowledge.]

MICHAEL SADLEIR.

WALTON, FREDERICK PARKER (1858–1948), academic jurist, was born in Nottingham 28 November 1858, the son of Isaac Walton, banker's clerk, and his wife, Mary Ann Parker. He was educated at Lincoln College, Oxford, where he gained a first class in classical moderations (1881) and a second class in *literae humaniores* (1883). From Oxford he went to Edinburgh where he took the LL.B. degree in 1886 with distinction, and in the same year was called to the Scottish bar. He lectured in Roman law at Glasgow University, and also acquired some practical experience as legal secretary to the lord advocate, J. B. Balfour (later Lord Kinross, q.v.). But it was in the academic field that his career was destined to lie. In 1897 he became dean of the law faculty of McGill University, relinquishing the position in order to become director of the Khedivial School of Law at Cairo in 1915. He returned to England in 1923 and settled in Oxford where his old college

elected him an honorary fellow in 1933. He continued to study and to write and acted for some years as secretary of the Law Club, in the exercise of which function he came much into contact with the members of the Oxford faculty.

Walton's innate modesty alone prevented him from taking his due place among the foremost academic jurists of his time. He was a pioneer of the study of comparative law, versed in the legal systems of England and of Scotland, and of many other countries. The width of his learning was remarkable and extended far beyond the confines of law. His *Historical Introduction to the Roman Law* (1903, 4th ed. 1920) contains a vast amount of information on the archaeological origins of Rome and the ethnological background of her people. He insisted always on the vital importance of historical treatment of legal surveys. Law, shepherded into isolation from history, was to him meaningless, and he may be said to have followed Sohm, and forestalled Sir Paul Vinogradoff [q.v.] in the realization of the importance of the continuity of Roman law.

A learned Romanist, he showed himself also a profound canonist. This quality appears in his *Handbook of Husband and Wife, according to the Law of Scotland* (1893, 3rd ed. 1951), a contribution to legal literature the very substantial nature of which is belied by the modesty of its title, and in his edition, in the Stair Society publications, of Lord Hermand's *Consistorial Decisions*. To the same series he also contributed a chapter on 'Courts of the Officials and the Commissary Courts, 1512–1830'. His preoccupation with the marriage law was further shown by his publication of a book written for laymen in a light vein, and yet replete with valuable information, entitled *Scotch Marriages, Regular and Irregular* (1893).

His longest, and possibly his best-known, work was his exhaustive treatise, *The Egyptian Law of Obligations* (1920, 2nd ed. 1923). This is a commentary on the Egyptian code which must necessarily be, in effect, also a commentary on the French code. His avowed aim in writing it was to create a mutual understanding between the students and practitioners of the civil law and the common law. To this end he packed the treatise with references to the English and to the German law, most prominent among which are the chapters on mistake and misrepresentation in contract. Especially interesting to modern jurists is his long chapter on stipulation *pur autrui*, and the whole part devoted to quasi-contracts. He expressed the intention of following up this great work with a treatise on 'Responsibility for Torts', an intention which was realized to a certain extent by articles on 'Motive as an element in torts in the common and in the civil law', 'Responsibility for breach of duty to neighbours, in making use of an immoveable', 'Delictual responsibility in civil law', and 'The French law as to the right of privacy', all of which reveal the hand of a master. If there is one subject which, more than any other, may be named as Walton's speciality, it is the doctrine of abuse of rights. Although constrained to admit that this doctrine, in its more general form, is unknown to English law, he yet claimed that the standpoint of the English cases is not really so far from that of the countries whose jurisprudence has admitted it, as would at first sight have appeared to be the case.

Walton started to write a treatise on French law, but finding that his old friend Sir Maurice Amos [q.v.] was engaged on the same enterprise, arranged to collaborate with him, and the valuable *Introduction to French Law* (1935) was the result. Although Walton's output was enormous, neither his style nor the content of what he wrote ever sank from the high level he always contrived to maintain. He never wrote anything which was not first-rate. The keynote of his entire exposition is thoroughness, and yet his writings are always most attractive to the student. His place among the greatest legal scholars of his age is secure. He was the most charming of men, who gained and held the affection of all who knew him. He was a K.C. of the Quebec bar, and an honorary LL.D. of the university of Aberdeen (1906) and of McGill (1915).

In 1892 Walton married Mary Victoria Hamilton, daughter of the Rev. Duncan Taylor, of Edinburgh, a minister of the established Church of Scotland. Upon the death of his wife in 1932 Walton left Oxford and went to live in Edinburgh where he died 21 March 1948. There were no children.

[Private information; personal knowledge.]
H. G. HANBURY.

WARBURTON, ADRIAN (1918–1944), photographic reconnaissance pilot, born at Middlesbrough, 10 March 1918, was the younger child of Commander Geoffrey Warburton, R.N., D.S.O., O.B.E., by his wife, Muriel, daughter of Barnard Hankey Davidson, of the Burmese Police Force. He was educated at St. Edward's School, Oxford, and in 1936 was articled to a chartered accountant in London. Living at home at Enfield, in 1937 he joined an armoured territorial unit which he left after little more than a year when he began to learn to fly. Shortly before his twenty-first birthday in 1939 he joined the R.A.F. Volunteer Reserve with a short-service commission. Although at first his progress as a pilot was not above the average, he was given a permanent commission before the end of the year.

In September 1940, while still a pilot officer, Warburton made his first operational photographic reconnaissance flight, from Malta, where he had been posted with No. 431 Flight (then operating with Martin Marylands). From then on his flying career was one of spectacular success. A great individualist, with an exceptional talent for both high-altitude and low-level photography, 'nothing could keep him on the ground'. Soon he was awarded the D.F.C. for his steady record of daring and successful sorties. He was especially notable for his aggressive persistence in the face of danger and for his resourcefulness, as well as for his brilliant flying and accurate photography, and he first became famous as 'the man who had photographed the Italian fleet at Taranto from fifty feet'. Although it was no part of his duties he often attacked the enemy when flying types of aircraft equipped with guns for defence.

During 1941 and 1942, at six-monthly intervals, he was appointed to the D.S.O. and awarded two bars to his D.F.C. For eight months of this time he was attached to No. 2 Photographic Reconnaissance Unit at Heliopolis, but most of his photographic flights were made from Malta which was ideally placed for tracking the Axis convoys between Naples and North Africa.

In August 1942 Warburton attained the acting rank of squadron leader and was put in command of No. 69 Squadron which had succeeded No. 431 Flight at Malta. Before the end of the year he was given the acting rank of wing commander. This promotion coincided with one of his most remarkable adventures: on 15 November he set off from Malta to photograph Bizerta, but did not return and was reported missing. Several days later he reported back to base, when it proved that during the reconnaissance his Spitfire had been hit, but after crash-landing at the allied-held airfield at Bone he had managed to make his way back to Malta, via Algiers and Gibraltar, flying in three different kinds of aircraft.

In 1943 when the Americans of the United States Air Force's 3rd Reconnaissance Group began to operate from Malta, Warburton befriended them and became their great hero. Fair, slight, and good-looking, he had an impish, inquisitive, and friendly personality, but his normal manner was almost shy—in marked contrast to the ruthless daring in the air which had made him a legendary figure. In October 1943 he was attached to the allied headquarters of photographic reconnaissance in the Mediterranean Area (the Northwest African Photographic Reconnaissance Wing) commanded by Colonel Elliott Roosevelt, and then based at Tunis. He was awarded the American D.F.C. for a particularly daring low-level reconnaissance of the heavily defended coastline of Pantelleria. This was his sixth decoration—he had already received a bar to his D.S.O.—hence the legend of 'six-medal Warburton', although he was more usually known as 'Warby'.

As the result of a serious motor accident near Tunis Warburton was grounded, but after a few weeks in hospital he went to Italy to take command of the newly formed British reconnaissance wing (No. 336). Early in 1944, however, he returned to England and was posted to the special duties list. On 12 April 1944 he took off from Mount Farm, the American photographic reconnaissance base in Oxfordshire, in a Lightning, allegedly to fly to San Severo in Italy. He never arrived, and no information has subsequently come to light to show what happened.

In October 1939 Warburton married Eileen Adelaide Mary, daughter of William Henry Mitchell, chargeman of shipwrights, H.M. dockyard, Portsmouth.

[Air Ministry and U.S. Air Force records; private information; Constance Babington Smith, *Evidence in Camera*, 1958.]

CONSTANCE BABINGTON SMITH.

WARD, IDA CAROLINE (1880–1949), phonetician and West African language scholar, was born at Bradford, Yorkshire, 4 October 1880, the eighth child of Samson Ward, a wool merchant, by his wife, Hannah, daughter of Charles Tempest, also of Bradford. She went to school in Bradford and then to Darlington Training College and Durham University where she graduated B.Litt. in 1902.

After sixteen years of secondary school-teaching she joined the phonetics department of University College, London, in 1919, and became an authority in the phonetics of the main European languages, and on speech defects. Her interest turned to African languages and in 1932 she joined the staff of what later became the School of Oriental and African Studies of London University, and in 1933 was awarded the D.Lit. for her *Phonetic and Tonal Structure of Efik* which opened a new chapter in the study of African languages by analysing scientifically the element of tone which plays a vital part in them. There followed her important *Introduction to the Ibo Language* (1936) with its elucidation of Ibo vowel harmony as well as of tone.

In 1937 she became head of the new department of African languages and cultures at the School and in 1944 was made professor of West African languages. She gradually built up the department from small beginnings into an institution of international standing for research, teaching, and consultation. Missionary and educational bodies sought her help, and after the war of 1939–45 the Colonial Office called for courses in about eleven African languages for some hundred colonial officials annually. She also trained Africans in the scientific study of their own mother tongues. The importance of this contribution became increasingly evident with the development of the African university colleges, such as Ibadan. Working at a crucial time in African history she matched her opportunity by her achievement which received official recognition in 1948 when she was appointed C.B.E., and after her death when the secretary of state for the Colonies paid tribute to the immense amount of time and work which she had devoted to the interests of colonial peoples.

After her third visit to West Africa she published her report on Gold Coast language problems (1945) and her *Introduction to the Yoruba Language* appeared posthumously in 1952. In 1948 she visited universities and learned societies in the United States and in that year retired from her chair, although continuing as adviser in African studies. She also gave unstinted help to the International African Institute whose *Handbook of African Languages* she helped to plan. Her own *Practical Phonetics for Students of African*

*Languages* (with Professor D. H. Westermann, 1933) was widely influential.

Ida Ward's achievements were due not only to scholarship but to her warm human qualities. Her Christianity was a living force and her large-hearted generosity, her zest, wisdom, and courage made working with her a continuous and fruitful adventure. Her genial common sense, sound judgement, and adaptability helped her in dealing with official bodies and difficult situations. Friendly, unpretentious, accessible, but with natural dignity, she was 'a great and good woman' who was regarded with affectionate respect by white and black alike and communicated to them her own enjoyment of life. She was unmarried, but the happy home life which she shared with her widowed sister and the keen interest she took in her great-nephews and nieces were as real to her as her work. She died at Guildford 10 October 1949.

[*Bulletin* of the School of Oriental and African Studies, vol. xiii, part 2, 1950; private information; personal knowledge.]

M. M. GREEN.

WARD, ROBERT McGOWAN BARRINGTON- (1891–1948), journalist. [See BARRINGTON-WARD.]

WARE, SIR FABIAN ARTHUR GOULSTONE (1869–1949), editor, and originator of the Imperial War Graves Commission, was born at Clifton, Bristol, 17 June 1869, the son of Charles Ware, chartered accountant, by his wife, Amy Carew Goulstone. He had a strict upbringing from his father who in middle life had become a Plymouth Brother, and was educated privately, going on to the universities of London and of Paris, obtaining from the latter the degree of B.Sc. in 1894. Ware himself became a member of the Church of England. He taught in secondary schools for several years, four of them at Bradford, and was an occasional examiner for the Board of Education. In 1901, encouraged by Lord Milner [q.v.], he became assistant director of education for the Transvaal, and by 1903 was director of education, and a member of the Transvaal legislative council.

Ware was already writing for the *Morning Post* and in 1905 Lord Glenesk [q.v.] invited him to become its editor. He was now thirty-five, 'erratic but brilliant, often mistaken but dogged, courageous, persistent and brimful of ideas'. The *Morning Post* was an old-fashioned concern and, as Ware remarked in a letter to Glenesk, he 'found it necessary to master a regular mythology of minor divinities created by the old traditions'. The fortunes of the Unionist Party were at their lowest ebb, social reform was in the air, and Ware exerted himself to prevent the Conservatives from missing the tide. A sympathetic welcome was given to the emergence of the Labour Party and social subjects were not neglected amid the burning political questions of the day on which the paper gave guidance, not always orthodox, to Conservative thought. Among those writing for the *Morning Post* at this time were (Sir) William (subsequently Lord) Beveridge and Mr. R. H. Tawney, as well as Maurice Baring, Spenser Wilkinson [qq.v.], Richard Jebb, and Hilaire Belloc. Ware's position, aided by his natural charm, greatly extended his acquaintanceship, particularly with political leaders at home and throughout the Empire. Although his vision of imperial greatness kept him within the Conservative fold, his reformer's mind rejected the idea of imperial federation in favour of imperial co-operation.

After the death of Glenesk difficulties arose and Ware left the *Morning Post* in 1911. In the following year he was appointed special commissioner to the board of the Rio Tinto Company and, while negotiating with the French Government on their behalf, he was able to renew old friendships and make new contacts in France. He was thus well equipped for his next task: the commemoration of the Empire's dead whose graves are for the most part in British war cemeteries in France, marking the line of battle from the Channel to the Marne. While in command of a mobile unit of the British Red Cross Society with the French Army in 1914, he foresaw the need for a service to register and mark British military graves in France and Flanders. Such a service he created and inspired, with the encouragement of Sir Nevil Macready [q.v.], at first under the Red Cross and later under Macready's department when Ware became, in 1916, director of graves registration and inquiries with the temporary rank of brigadier-general.

Profoundly moved by the comradeship of the forces from the various parts of the Empire, he saw in the creation of a permanent body, composed of representatives of Britain and the Dominions and entrusted with the task of commemorating the dead and maintaining their graves, a living testimony to the principles of imperial co-operation in which he believed. His work led to the constitution of the Imperial War Graves Commission by royal charter in 1917 when he was appointed to the principal executive post of vice-chairman. In 1918 he was promoted major-general, but relinquished the post of director-general of graves registration and inquiries in 1919 in order to devote his whole time to the Commission. Due to his imagination, persistence, and diplomacy, the Commission became and remained the sole permanent imperial executive organization responsible to all the Commonwealth Governments represented upon it.

Ware was also successful in gaining the confidence and ready assistance of the French, Belgian, and other foreign Governments in whose territories British war graves were to be found. In 1915 he instigated the passing of a French law granting perpetual rights in the land on which allied graves were situated and in 1918, encouraged in particular by Clemenceau and Lord Derby [q.v.], he negotiated the Anglo-French war graves agreement which became the model for many similar agreements.

The work of the Commission satisfied Ware in yet another sphere, for in it he found scope for the creative imagination of the artist which by temperament he was, and for the expression of a profound human sympathy. He bent all his considerable powers to the task of commemorating permanently the individual sacrifice of each soldier and to giving to British war cemeteries all over the world the quiet and familiar beauty of an English garden.

In 1939 Ware again became director-general of graves registration and inquiries but he resigned in 1944, finding that the expansion of the Commission's work claimed all his time and energies. With failing health, he relinquished the vice-chairmanship of the Commission in 1948.

Ware also concerned himself with rural activities in Gloucestershire, was chairman of the executive of the Parents' National Educational Union, a director of the *Nineteenth Century and After*, and an honorary associate of the Royal Institute of British Architects. He was appointed C.M.G. in 1917, C.B. in 1919, K.B.E. in 1920, and K.C.V.O. in 1922. He was a chevalier and later a grand officer of the Legion of Honour, and held the croix de guerre; he was also a commander of the Order of the Crown of Belgium, and an honorary LL.D. (1929) of the university of Aberdeen.

Ware was tall and lean, of handsome and intellectual aspect, with black hair and moustache, and artistic hands. His very deep-set brown eyes were almost hooded and gave the impression that he was thinking rather than observing. Nevertheless, he had the valuable gift of making every visitor feel that he was the most important person Ware had ever met. There is a portrait of him by his son, Harry Fabian Ware, who became a painter and who owns the portrait. In 1895 Ware married Anna Margaret (died 1952), daughter of E. W. Phibbs, of Clifton, by whom he had one son and one daughter. He died 28 April 1949 at Amberley, Gloucestershire, and his name is commemorated in St. George's chapel, Westminster Abbey.

[Sir Fabian Ware, *The Immortal Heritage*, 1937; *Westminster Gazette*, 14 June 1911; *The Times*, 29 April 1949; Lord Beveridge, *Power and Influence*, 1953; private information; personal knowledge.]

F. C. Sillar.

WATSON, Sir DAVID MILNE MILNE-, first baronet (1869–1945), man of business. [See Milne-Watson.]

WATSON, JOHN CHRISTIAN (1867–1941), first Labour prime minister of Australia, was born at Valparaiso, Chile, 9 April 1867, the son of George Thomas Watson. He was taken to New Zealand as a child and attended the State school at Oamaru. On leaving school he was apprenticed as a printer to the *North Otago Times*, and at the age of nineteen he went to Sydney, New South Wales, and worked as a compositor on the *Star*. He was a keen trade-unionist and soon became prominent in his own union. At the age of twenty-six he was elected president of the Sydney trades and labour council. In July 1894, at the age of twenty-seven, he was elected to the legislative assembly of New South Wales as a Labour member, representing the constituency of Young. He was chosen to be the leader of his party in the legislative assembly, and he led it with skill, firmness, and moderation, although it was always in opposition.

Upon the inauguration of the Commonwealth of Australia in 1901, Watson retired from the legislative assembly of New South Wales and stood for election to the Australian House of Representatives. He was returned for the constituency of

Bland, New South Wales, and became the leader of the substantial and influential group of sixteen Labour members in the House, and eight in the Senate. In the early years of the Commonwealth no party had an absolute majority, and minority Governments held office. There were three parties in a House of Representatives which itself contained only seventy-five members and in a Senate of thirty-six. (Sir) Edmund Barton [q.v.] became prime minister, as the leader of a party which favoured protection, and he held office through the support of Watson and his Labour followers. (Sir) George Reid [q.v.] led the Opposition, his party standing for a tariff for revenue purposes only. Watson made the most of his strategic position and in the first Parliament his support and pressure secured the passage of two important Acts which laid the statutory foundation of the White Australia policy —an Immigration Restriction Act designed to prevent the entry of Japanese and Chinese immigrants, and an Act abolishing the employment of Pacific Islanders in Queensland.

In the second general election for the Commonwealth Parliament, held on 16 December 1903, the Labour Party increased its numbers to twenty-four in the House and fifteen in the Senate, and its support was more important than ever to Alfred Deakin [q.v.] who had succeeded Barton in the prime-ministership in September 1903 upon the latter's appointment to be one of the first three judges of the High Court of Australia. In March 1904, however, Watson withdrew his party's support from the Government over a dispute about an arbitration bill and Deakin was defeated on 27 April. Watson was invited to form a Government, and, as-sured of Deakin's benevolent intentions, accepted. At the age of thirty-seven he became the first Labour prime minister not only of Australia, but, it is said, of any country having a system of parliamentary government. In his Cabinet of eight were seven 'working men', two of whom, Andrew Fisher [q.v.] and William Morris Hughes, were later to become prime ministers of the Commonwealth.

Watson's tenure of office was short. After scarcely four months he too fell, in consequence of the carrying on 12 August 1904 of an amendment against him on the same arbitration bill. He asked the governor-general for a dissolution, but it was refused, and he resigned on 17 August 1904. He was succeeded by Reid, but

within ten months, more than half of which were spent in recess, Reid had been defeated, and when he, in his turn, was refused a dissolution on 5 July 1905, he resigned and Deakin returned to office with Watson's support. The Deakin ministry, confirmed in office by a general election in December 1906, was to hold office for three and a half years, until November 1908. Before that time, however, on 30 October 1907, Watson, only forty years of age, resigned the leadership of his party, declaring that his health had deteriorated, and that he felt unable to stand the strain. Perhaps, too, he felt out of sympathy with some of his followers, and restless at the control exercised upon its leaders by the Labour caucus. Although he did not retire from the House of Representatives until the end of the Parliament in December 1909, he remained a private member and did not seek office in the Labour Government, under the prime-ministership of Andrew Fisher, which came to power upon the defeat of Deakin in November 1908.

Watson lived for another thirty years and more, but apart from declaring his support for conscription in 1916—a step which led to his expulsion from the Political Labour League—he took no part in political matters. He continued to live in Sydney, and entered business where he became director of a number of companies. He visited Britain in 1915.

Watson's influence upon the Australian Labour Party and upon Australian politics clearly cannot be measured by his short term of office as prime minister. He was an excellent leader of his party in its early days. Although moderate and responsible, he perfected the discipline of the party and enforced the rule by which members were bound by decisions taken by the party in caucus, and were free only on matters where such decisions had not been taken. Although, as has been suggested, he may have come to regret the effects upon its leadership of this discipline in his party, there is no doubt that it brought considerable advantages. He was the right man for his party at that time, making it a constitutional party, yet exploiting to the full all the advantages he could get for it in a delicate political situation. Although by no means lacking in force and incisiveness, he conducted his campaigns with tact and courtesy, and his opponents respected his character and integrity.

Watson was twice married: first, in 1889 to Ada Jane Low who predeceased him; and secondly, in 1925 to Antonia Lane, who survived him and by whom he had one daughter. He died in Sydney 18 November 1941. A portrait by Sir John Longstaff hangs in Parliament House, Canberra.

[*The Times*, *Sydney Morning Herald*, and the *Age*, Melbourne, 19 November 1941; H. G. Turner, *The First Decade of the Australian Commonwealth*, 1911; Sir G. H. Reid, *My Reminiscences*, 1917; Walter Murdoch, *Alfred Deakin*, 1923; private information.]

K. C. WHEARE.

WATSON, WILLIAM, BARON THANKERTON (1873–1948), judge, was born in Edinburgh 8 December 1873, the third son of William (later Baron) Watson, of Thankerton [q.v.]. He was educated at Winchester, and at Jesus College, Cambridge, where he was placed in the third class in both parts of the law tripos in 1894 and 1895. In 1899 he was admitted to the Faculty of Advocates and achieved considerable success, for he was a man of tireless industry. He became a K.C. in 1914, procurator of the Church of Scotland in 1918, and an advocate depute in 1919. In the meantime he had taken to politics, and was Unionist member for South Lanarkshire from 1913 until 1918. In 1922, not being then in the House, he was appointed solicitor-general for Scotland, and, later in the year, lord advocate, and was sworn of the Privy Council. In October 1924 he was elected Conservative member for Carlisle, defeating the Labour candidate by more than 2,000 votes and gaining the first Conservative success in the constituency for some fifty years.

In 1929 Watson became a lord of appeal in ordinary, in succession to Lord Shaw (later Lord Craigmyle, q.v.), taking the title of Baron Thankerton, of Thankerton, in the county of Lanark, his grandfather having been minister of the parish of Covington and Thankerton. He explained, in all good humour, that he refrained from taking the title assumed by his father 'lest haply he should besmirch it'. Like his father, and Lord Macnaghten [q.v.], he went straight from the bar to the House of Lords. There were those who thought that his lack of experience might stand in his way; but they were soon to be undeceived. In what Theobald Mathew [q.v.] once described as the 'most eminent and least taciturn of tribunals' Thankerton soon made his mark. His industry was such that he would generally get up a case beforehand, and come into the chamber much better prepared than most of his colleagues. He was always kind and considerate to youthful counsel, going out of his way to help them in their difficulties. At the sitting of the appellate committee of the House of Lords, 14 June 1948, Lord Porter said: 'Perhaps his most characteristic quality was the devotion which he gave to his work, and the eagerness with which he sought a true solution of the problems presented to him. He always took a broad and comprehensive view of the matters which came up for consideration, and never spared himself.'

Thankerton's opinions were masterpieces of concise and lucid statement. Every now and then he would coin a phrase, or sum up his view of the matter in a pithy sentence, well calculated to abide in the memory of those whose task it is to discover the law in the annals of the past. In the case of *Fender* v. *Mildmay*, [1938] A.C. at p. 23, Thankerton said: 'There can be little question as to the proper function of the Courts in questions of public policy. Their duty is to expound, and not to expand, such policy.' Again, in *Franklin and Others* v. *Minister of Town & Country Planning*, [1948] A.C. at p. 103, the question was whether the decision of a minister could be impugned on the ground of 'bias'. The proper significance of the word, said Thankerton, 'is to denote a departure from the standard of even-handed justice which the law requires from those who occupy judicial office, . . . such as an arbitrator'. And here is a rule for the guidance of those who have to interpret a statute. 'The intention of Parliament', said he, 'is not to be judged of by what is in its mind, but by its expression of that mind in the statute itself' (*Wicks* v. *Director of Public Prosecutions*, [1947] A.C. at p. 367).

Towards the end of his life it fell to Thankerton to preside in two of the heaviest appeals to come before the House of Lords in recent years. One, in July 1946, was the case of an Indian who had been seen apparently to be burnt on a funeral pyre in 1909 and who in 1930 'returned' to life and successfully claimed his wife and property. The other was the series of 'whisky appeals' (*Ross & Coulter* v. *Inland Revenue*, 1948 S. C. (H.L.) 1).

Thankerton was tall and in later years developed a slight stoop, but he never looked an old man; his black hair became just tinged with grey, and he was very active to the last, walking long distances, even in town. He had a ready smile, enjoyed a good story, and had a considerable fund of after-dinner anecdotes with which he would delight the lawyers of Gray's Inn of which he became an honorary bencher in 1928. In 1929 he was made an honorary fellow of his college, and received the honorary degree of LL.D. from Edinburgh University. In 1936 he and Lady Thankerton visited Canada and the United States as guests of the American and Canadian bar associations. In Canada he received an honorary degree from Acadia University. Thankerton was a member of the Royal Company of Archers, took a keen interest in golf and shooting, and spent many an hour at the cinema. Indoors, his hobby was knitting, at which he was very skilful. He died in London 13 June 1948. He married in 1902 Sophia Marjorie, daughter of John James Cowan, of Bavelaw Castle, Balerno; there were two sons and one daughter of the marriage.

[*The Times*, 14 June et seq. 1948; *Scotsman*, 14 June 1948; private information.]

W. Valentine Ball.

WATT, MARGARET ROSE (1868–1948), who introduced Women's Institutes into England and Wales, was born 4 June 1868 at Collingwood, Ontario, the daughter of Henry Robertson, Q.C., and his wife, Margaret, *née* Rose. She graduated B.A. at Toronto University in 1889 and proceeded M.A. in the following year. For a time she did journalistic work in New York, and in 1893 married Alfred Tennyson Watt, medical officer of health for British Columbia. Her interest in Women's Institutes began when she joined the Metchosin Women's Institute, Vancouver Island, on its formation in 1909 and helped to develop the movement in British Columbia as secretary, from 1911, to the British Columbia government's women's advisory board.

After her husband's death in 1913 Mrs. Watt came to England with her two boys in order to give them an English education. The outbreak of war in 1914 brought the need for a combined effort of countrywomen to produce and preserve food. Mrs. Watt was quick to perceive this need, and to apply the experience she had gained in Canada to the formation of a similar movement in this country. At first her efforts to interest government departments and individuals led to nothing, but in 1915 she aroused the enthusiasm of Nugent Harris of the Agricultural Organisation Society, and very soon afterwards the first institute was started in Wales, and some months later the first English institute at Singleton, west Sussex. Sponsored at the outset by the Agricultural Organisation Society, and then in 1917 by the Board of Agriculture, the movement spread rapidly and by 1927 had become a free and independent voluntary organization, with an ever-increasing scope.

Mrs. Watt then grasped an even wider opportunity; she conceived a plan for linking together the whole world in an association of rural women, whose interchange of knowledge and experience would be of mutual advantage. It was at her instigation that the Associated Country Women of the World came into being in 1930, first as an off-shoot of the International Council of Women, then as an independent organization.

The outbreak of war in 1939 caught Mrs. Watt in Canada where she remained for the duration, speaking and working for the Associated Country Women of the World, which she served as president until September 1947. It is given to few people to see the result of their labours in such abundant measure. In 1951 the Women's Institute members in England and Wales alone numbered 450,000, and the Associated Country Women of the World had a membership of over five million. Mrs. Watt was appointed M.B.E. in 1919 and received the Belgian médaille de mérite agricole in 1923 and the French médaille d'Agriculture in 1935. She died in Montreal 29 November 1948. A portrait by her son, Robin Watt, is at Denman College, another is in his possession, and a third belongs to his brother.

[*Montreal Gazette*, 30 November 1948; Inez Jenkins, *The History of the Women's Institute Movement of England and Wales*, 1953; private information; personal knowledge.]

Frances Farrer.

WAUCHOPE, Sir ARTHUR GRENFELL (1874–1947), soldier and administrator, was born in Edinburgh 1 March 1874, the second son of David Baird Wauchope, wine merchant in Leith and cadet of the old family of Wauchope of Niddrie Marischal, and his wife, Helen Anne Mure, of Caldwell. Wauchope was educated at Repton and in 1893 was commissioned into the Renfrew militia battalion of the Argyll and Sutherland Highlanders. In January 1896 he was gazetted a regular second lieutenant in the Black Watch, joining the 2nd battalion in Edinburgh of which for the first twenty months the commanding officer was his second cousin and head of his family, the redoubtable Andrew Gilbert Wauchope [q.v.]. The 2nd Black Watch was one of the first units to embark for South Africa on the outbreak of war and the elder Wauchope, now major-general commanding the Highland brigade, made his young kinsman his galloper. At Magersfontein (11 December 1899) where General Wauchope and most of his commanding officers were killed, young Wauchope was severely wounded. When dawn broke he was lying out in the open and although he was partly protected by an ant-hill a bright new pair of gaiters made him a target throughout the day for a Boer sniper who several times hit him in the legs. From these injuries Wauchope never fully recovered. He was appointed to the D.S.O. (1900) and served as an extra aide-de-camp to the governor of Cape Colony (1902–3) until fit to return to his battalion stationed at Ambala in India. Serving in it was A. P. (later Earl) Wavell [q.v.] who, although nine years his junior, became his lifelong friend.

When war broke out in 1914 the battalion was at Bareilly as part of the Meerut division, with which it sailed immediately for France. Wauchope, now a major, was wounded in December. After a short spell in Scotland he returned to the trenches near Neuve Chapelle and took charge of the battalion scouts. He was present at the Aubers Ridge fighting in May 1915 and commanded his battalion on 25 September at Loos, when it overran four lines of enemy trenches. In November the battalion left for Mesopotamia, with Wauchope confirmed in command. In January 1916 at Shaikh Sa'ad, during the first attempt to relieve (Sir) Charles Townshend [q.v.] at Kut, he was severely wounded in the chest by a shell fragment at the beginning of the battle; but he continued to command until the battalion was digging in on its objective. Whilst recovering in India he made representations which brought about an improvement of rations for the troops in Mesopotamia. Wauchope returned to take command of the composite Highland battalion formed of the remnants of the 2nd Black Watch and 1st Seaforth and then of his own battalion when it had been reinforced. He commanded it at Sannaiyat in February 1917, at the fall of Baghdad in March, and at Mushahida later in the same month. He subsequently commanded the 8th and 34th Indian brigades, continuing with the latter until after the Turkish armistice.

In 1920 Wauchope resumed his interrupted command of his old battalion, now in Upper Silesia, becoming commander of the 2nd brigade, which included it, in May 1921, during the insurrection which followed the plebiscite. In September 1922 he took command of the Londonderry brigade, but was promoted major-general in January 1923. In that rank he held four appointments: military member of the overseas settlement delegation to Australia and New Zealand (1923); chief of the British section of the military inter-allied commission of control in Berlin (1924–7); general officer commanding the 44th Home Counties division (1927–9); and in Northern Ireland (1929–31).

In 1931 Wauchope's appointment as high commissioner and commander-in-chief of Palestine and high commissioner of Trans-Jordan in succession to Sir John Chancellor aroused some surprise, for he was little known outside the army. Ramsay MacDonald had said that he wanted to appoint a general 'but one who does it with his head, not his feet'. Wauchope entered upon his task with application and devotion. He was a man of high ideals, cultivated tastes, tireless energy and considerable personal fortune. Hospitable and generous, and without heirs, he expended the greater part of his fortune in munificence in Palestine; many projects and institutions, Jewish and Arab, owed as much to his purse as to his eager interest in agriculture, education, public health, Arab villages and Jewish colonies. He travelled continuously to watch their growth. He encouraged both the native arts of the indigenous Arabs and the imported European cultures of the Jews. Passionately fond of music, he did much to encourage such ventures as the Palestine Symphony Orchestra; he continued to take the same interest in the town planning of Jerusalem as had characterized the governorship of Sir Ronald Storrs.

As the flood of Jewish immigration increased the Arabs clamoured for its restriction and for the prohibition of the sale of any more land to the immigrants, who often had funds at their disposal great enough to tempt impoverished Arab landowners to sell. To this agitation Wauchope refused to yield. Other considerations apart, the immigrants were a source of considerable financial gain to Palestine as a whole, and Wauchope had a deep-seated belief that generous loans and country-wide prosperity might reconcile the Arabs. He made and retained many friends in both camps, but it seemed to the Arabs and the Jews alike that, in the incompatible terms of the mandate, his warmer sympathies were with the Jews, although he favoured the idea of a legislative council which was not acceptable to them. The early years of Wauchope's administration were generally adjudged successful and there was little criticism when his term of office was renewed for a further five years. During the Arab insurrection of 1936, however, Wauchope's support for local officials who took stern measures seemed to many to be half-hearted. In some cases he relieved them of their posts. He appeared convinced that the situation would improve with time; but had he shown more strictness in the early stages it would perhaps not have become so serious. As the troubles developed, so did criticism of his handling of the situation. Strong reinforcements had to be sent to the country; the supreme command was transferred from the air officer commanding to General Sir John Dill [q.v.] and the 1st division at Aldershot was mobilized, made up to strength with reservists, and dispatched at short notice to Palestine. A Royal Commission under Lord Peel [q.v.] arrived in the country in November to investigate the situation and make recommendations. When in 1937 Wavell succeeded Dill the hand of the military was strengthened at the expense of the high commissioner. Although the worst excesses of the Arabs were curbed, the troubles continued. Wauchope, whose health, already frail, had been greatly worn down, relinquished his office in February 1938. He took no further part in public life, beyond serving as colonel of the Black Watch from 1940 until succeeded by Wavell in 1946, but lived quietly in London and Hampshire until his death in London 14 September 1947. He was unmarried and was buried among his forebears at Niddrie Marischal.

Wauchope was small in stature and most unmilitary in appearance; he resembled rather one of the many musicians or artists in whose company he took so much delight. He was, nevertheless, a most stalwart soldier, who had spent the whole of the war of 1914–18 commanding troops in the line, except when recovering from his wounds. Until these restricted him in later life, he was a keen shot, shikari, and games-player; he had travelled widely in little-known parts of India and Burma in pursuit of game. There was almost no limit to his interests or to his inquisitive

mind; his searching catechisms, with the answers to which he had usually provided himself, were all too familiar to his subordinates. Although widely read, he wrote nothing himself except a short history of his regiment, published in 1908. He also edited a three-volume account of its activities in the war of 1914–18.

He was appointed C.I.E. (1919), C.B. (1923), K.C.B. (1931), G.C.M.G. (1933), and G.C.B. (1938). He was made a general in 1936. The only portrait known to exist is a crayon drawing by an unknown Palestinian artist in the possession of the Black Watch.

[The Times, 15 September 1947; Appreciation by the first Earl Wavell in the Red Hackle (chronicle of the Black Watch), January 1948; Chaim Weizmann, Trial and Error, 1949; personal knowledge.]

BERNARD FERGUSSON.


WAVELL, ARCHIBALD PERCIVAL, first EARL WAVELL (1883–1950), field-marshal, was born 5 May 1883 at Colchester, the only son and second of the three children of Major, afterwards Major-General, Archibald Graham Wavell by his wife, Lillie, daughter of Richard N. Percival, of Springfields, Bradwall, Cheshire. Although the family had for some generations been soldiers (A. J. B. Wavell [q.v.] was his cousin), it derived from a stock of which traces have been found for four or more centuries in and around the city of Winchester.

Wavell received his education at Winchester, where he was in College, and passed fourth into the Royal Military College, Sandhurst, in 1900. After a six-months' course he was gazetted to the Black Watch in time to see service in South Africa. In 1903 he went to India where his early childhood had been spent, and he took part in the Bazar Valley campaign of 1908. At his first attempt he headed the list of entrants to the Staff College and in 1911, on completing his course, he was sent for a year to the Russian Army. When war broke out in 1914, he was in the War Office, but managed to get overseas. At Ypres in June 1915 he had the misfortune to lose an eye, and was awarded the M.C. In October 1916 he was sent as liaison officer to the army of the Grand Duke Nicholas, which was fighting in Turkey before Erzerum. In June 1917 he went as liaison officer to Palestine and in March 1918, as a brigadier-general, joined the staff of Sir Edmund (later Viscount) Allenby [q.v.] for whom he conceived a great admiration.

The next ten years were divided between the War Office and the staff. During this period Wavell, already well known within the army, became known outside it as an officer untrammelled by convention; and the general public came to associate him with a phrase he used in a lecture: that his ideal infantryman was a cross between a poacher, a gunman, and a cat-burglar. In 1930 he received command of the 6th brigade at Blackdown which had been chosen for experimental purposes; and five years later, after a short period on half-pay (which he spent in writing a report on the Middle East and in re-writing Field Service Regulations), he was appointed to the command of the 2nd division at Aldershot.

By this time his influence in the army had imperceptibly become considerable. He was recognized as an exceptional trainer of troops. Among the younger generals there was a feeling that the older ones had grown lethargic; public interest in the army was at a low ebb. Wavell's views were sought with respect by both old guard and new. Before he had completed his term with the 2nd division, he was appointed in July 1937 to command in Palestine and Trans-Jordan. Soon after his arrival Arab troubles, which had died down since the outbreak of 1936, broke out with fresh ferocity, and were at their height when he was brought home in April 1938 to take over the Southern Command, one of the two most important commands in the country. He had been there little more than a year when he was sent, at the end of July 1939, to form the new command of the Middle East.

When war broke out in September, the forces at his disposal were small; when Italy came into the war in June 1940 his command had been reinforced by Dominion and Indian troops, but was menaced by superior forces on several fronts. Bold patrolling by light covering troops in the Western Desert imposed upon Graziani's Italians a caution quite out of proportion to the relative strengths of the two armies. Wavell was able also to delay the Italian advances into the Sudan from Ethiopia; but upon the Somaliland front, where the defection of the French in Jibuti prejudiced the defence, the local commander was forced to give ground. During Wavell's temporary absence in London the decision was taken to evacuate the protectorate rather than lose its small but valuable garrison. The prime minister disapproved of this decision, Wavell defended it, and relations between (Sir) Winston Churchill and Wavell were never very happy thereafter. But Wavell's stock never sank either with his troops or with the public, and it rose with the authorities during and after his remarkable run of success in the winter of 1940–41. He had been keeping a careful eye on the gingerly advance of the Italians in the west, and he detected unsoundness in their dispositions. Containing the threat to the Sudan with an elaborate bluff, he switched the 4th Indian division from that front for use in the Western Desert, and caught the Italians napping at Sidi Barrani on 9 and 10 December. The 4th Indian division returned to the Sudan, while the remainder of the Western Desert army swept up Bardia and Tobruk. By mid-February, the whole of Cyrenaica was in British hands, with 130,000 prisoners, more than 800 field guns, and 400 tanks.

Meanwhile (Sir) Alan Gordon Cunningham's army from Kenya and (Sir) William Platt's in the Sudan were forcing the Italians from Ethiopia back into their remotest mountains; they capitulated in the north in May and in the south some weeks later. Elsewhere, however, the odds against Wavell had mounted. He had been urged to send help on a larger scale to Greece, which since the end of October 1940 had been fighting stoutly and successfully against greatly superior Italian forces in Epirus. Hitherto Britain had contributed only air support with ground defence, anti-aircraft, and medical units; but on 9 January 1941 he was told that the support of Greece must now take precedence of all operations in the Middle East. His first reaction was sharply adverse; but throughout January and February mounting pressure was brought to bear on him to reinforce the Greeks with fighting formations and units. After conversations with the Greeks, in which both the Cabinet and the chiefs of staff were represented by (Sir) Anthony Eden and Sir John Dill [q.v.], and during which various stipulations which he made were accepted by the Greeks, Wavell agreed to intervention at a moment when the enthusiasm of the Cabinet and chiefs of staff was cooling.

In two respects he had been misled: the Greeks had accepted in the conversations that they would withdraw from their exposed positions to a line on the River Aliakmon more in keeping with the weakness of the joint armies; and Wavell's intelligence had assured him that the German ground forces in North Africa, whose arrival was known to be imminent, would not be able to take the field until mid-April at the earliest. But the Greeks did not shorten their line; and the Germans appeared in strength on the frontiers of Cyrenaica before the end of March. By that time a high proportion of Wavell's army, and much of the best of it, was irrevocably committed in Greece; by the middle of April, both Greece and Cyrenaica had been lost, Tobruk was invested, and vast quantities of fighting troops, military technicians, tanks, and material were in enemy hands.

Stout efforts were made to defend Crete, but it was invaded from the air on 20 May and lost after desperate fighting before the month ended. The Royal Navy and the Royal Air Force in the Middle East had both crippled themselves in these operations. New anxieties had developed; Rashid Ali in Iraq had thrown in his lot with the enemy, and Syria, occupied by Vichy forces, was harbouring Germans and seemed likely to follow the example of Iraq. Wavell was urged to undertake three almost simultaneous operations against Iraq, against Syria, and against Rommel in the desert. He protested that he had not the resources for all three, but was overruled. Although the operation against Iraq was successful by early June, a series of operations against Rommel proved a costly failure by 17 June; in Syria, however, the French asked for an armistice early in July. But at the beginning of the month Wavell had been superseded by Sir Claude Auchinleck, whose place he took as commander-in-chief in India.

At first India was by comparison almost a sinecure; but when, in December 1941, Japan came into the war, Wavell, whose reputation stood high in the United States, was nominated supreme commander of the ill-fated command of the South-West Pacific. The speed, preparedness, and overwhelming strength of the Japanese were in inverse ratio to those of the defence. Wavell was criticized for the loss of the British 18th division in Singapore, which was landed only two days before the capitulation; but he still enjoyed the confidence of his troops, and his resilience as a commander was exemplified by the fact that he gave orders for the eventual recapture of Burma to be studied by his planning staff before its evacuation was complete. Policy dictated that the German war should be won before the Japanese, and Wavell had to fight the Burma war with the minimum of help from home. He had little success, and in June 1943 he was appointed viceroy of India in succession to the Marquess of Linlithgow and in July was raised to the peerage as Viscount Wavell, of Cyrenaica and of Winchester. He had been promoted field-marshal in January of that year.

Wavell entered upon his last public service with his usual willingness to shoulder an unpopular task, although, as he wrote to a friend, 'I fear I have no talent for persuasion'. Hindus and Moslems were at loggerheads and had somehow to be reconciled before India might be granted self-government. Wavell's first act was administrative and characteristic. Bengal was in the grip of famine and the new viceroy relieved a critical situation by an immediate personal reconnaissance followed by extensive military aid. Thereafter he was immersed in politics. In the summer of 1945 he took the initiative in releasing the Congress leaders who had been in jail since the rebellion of 1942. He then set to work with limitless patience to seek some way of securing agreement on the future of India. When the first series of talks broke down in July 1945 he issued a public statement taking the blame on himself. His task was not made easier by the fact that after the general election of 1945 the Labour Government, although desiring to endow India with self-government, did not lay down a clear-cut policy. A delegation of three Cabinet ministers conferred with the viceroy and with the party leaders for months in Delhi during 1946, but the parties could not agree. Wavell urged the Government to make up its mind what it would do in the absence of Indian agreement. A definite statement of policy was not made until February 1947, when Wavell's replacement by Lord Mountbatten of Burma was simultaneously announced with some abruptness. Wavell was created an earl with the additional title of Viscount Keren, of Eritrea and Winchester, and returned to London untrammelled by heavy responsibility for the first time for ten years.

The last three years of his life were spent in London and in travel. He was able to indulge at leisure the taste in letters which had long been among his most precious relaxations. He became president of the Royal Society of Literature, and of the Kipling, Browning, Poetry, and Virgil societies; he had been chancellor of Aberdeen University since 1945. He was colonel of the Black Watch; and he steeped himself in regimental matters, visiting its allied regiments in Canada and South Africa. He received honorary degrees from the universities of Aberdeen, St. Andrews, Cambridge, London, Oxford, and McGill. He was a commander of the Legion of Honour and received decorations from many countries including Greece, Ethiopia, Poland, Czechoslovakia, Holland, China, Russia, and the United States. He was appointed C.M.G. (1919), C.B. (1935), K.C.B. (1939), G.C.B. (1941), and G.C.S.I. and G.C.I.E. in 1943, in which year he was sworn of the Privy Council.

In 1950 Wavell showed signs of illness, culminating in jaundice; in May he underwent a severe operation, from which he seemed to be recovering, when he relapsed and died in London 24 May. His body lay in the chapel of St. John at the Tower, of which he had been constable since 1948; on 7 June it was carried up-river in a barge to Westminster, where a service was held; and he was buried that evening by the men of his regiment in the chantry close of his old school at Winchester.

In appearance Wavell was broad and thickset, sturdy and physically tough, with a deep ridge on either side of his mouth. His silences were proverbial, but among intimates he was the most congenial and jovial of company. He delighted in horses and horsemanship, in golf and shooting. He had a prodigious memory and would quote poetry with gusto and at length. His widely popular anthology, *Other Men's Flowers* (1944), consisted entirely of pieces which he had by heart, and showed how catholic was his taste. His *The Palestine Campaigns* (1928) and his biography of his former chief Allenby (produced during years of high pressure and published in two volumes, 1940 and 1943, and in one volume in 1946) were masterly and easy to read. He had delivered the Lees Knowles lectures at Cambridge on 'Generals and Generalship' in 1939; these were published in 1941. He also published essays and lectures on military subjects, which were collected during his lifetime under the title *The Good Soldier* (1948).

As a soldier, for all his misfortunes in the war of 1939–45, his reputation at its end stood as high as those of any of his contemporaries. In none of the eleven campaigns which he fought did he have preponderance in men or in weapons. He left the Middle East, he was relieved of command in Asia, before the arrival of the material and reinforcements with which his successors were to win their country's battles and their own renown. Yet at no time, in public or in private, in print or by the spoken word, did he ever complain or repine.

Wavell married in 1915 Eugénie Marie, daughter of Colonel John Owen Quirk, and had three daughters and one son, Archibald John Arthur (1916–53) who succeeded his father in his titles, which became extinct when he was killed in Kenya, 24 December 1953, in an attack on Mau-Mau terrorists.

A portrait of Wavell by Simon Elwes was in India.

[Lord Wavell, Dispatches from the Somaliland Protectorate, the Middle East, and the Western Desert, the Middle East, and the Eastern Theatre based on India (Supplements to the *London Gazette*, 5, 13, 26 June, 3 July, and 18 September 1946); R. J. Collins, *Lord Wavell*, 1947; Winston S. Churchill, *The Second World War*, vols. iii–v, 1950–52; I. S. O. Playfair and others, (Official) *History of the Second World War. The Mediterranean and Middle East*, vols. i and ii, 1954–6; Sir John Kennedy, *The Business of War*, edited by Bernard Fergusson, 1957; private information; personal knowledge.]

BERNARD FERGUSSON.

[V. P. Menon, *The Transfer of Power in India*, 1957.]

WEBB, (MARTHA) BEATRICE (1858–1943). [See under WEBB, SIDNEY JAMES.]

WEBB, SIDNEY JAMES, BARON PASSFIELD (1859–1947), social reformer and historian, was born in London 13 July 1859, the younger son of Charles Webb, of Cranbourn Street, Leicester Square, a public accountant in a very modest way, by his wife, Elizabeth Mary, daughter of Benjamin Stacey. The family income was mainly derived from the hairdressing business carried on by Mrs. Webb. Sidney Webb was educated in Switzerland and Mecklenburg-Schwerin, at the Birkbeck Institute, and the City of London College, and by his own intensive reading. His first employment was a clerkship (1875–8) in the City office of a firm of colonial brokers. In 1878 he entered the Civil Service by open competition, obtaining a place as a second division clerk in the War Office. A year later, again by open competition, he gained a place in the Surveyor of Taxes' Office, which was followed in 1881 by a first division clerk-ship in the Colonial Office. In 1885 he was called to the bar by Gray's Inn and in the next year obtained his LL.B. from London University with third class honours.

About 1879 Webb had met G. B. Shaw [q.v.] at the Zetetical Society and the two formed a lifelong friendship. Shaw intro-duced Webb to the Fabian Society which he joined in 1885. With Sydney (later Lord) Olivier and Graham Wallas [qq.v.], they dominated the counsels of the Society for many years. Here, too, Webb displayed his marked gift for organization and for effective propaganda by both the spoken and the written word, and also an encyclopaedic knowledge. He wrote, as Fabian tracts, *Facts for Socialists* (1887) and *Facts for Londoners* (1889), and in the latter year made a striking contribution to *Fabian Essays in Socialism*, a book which has been described by G. D. H. Cole as 'the most important single publication in the history of British Socialism'. In 1891 Webb resigned from the Civil Service in order to take a leading part in the Progressive campaign for the London County Council, to which, in 1892, he was returned as member for Deptford by a large majority. He held the seat until 1910.

In 1892 Webb married (MARTHA) BEATRICE POTTER (1858–1943), born at Standish House, near Gloucester, 22 January 1858, the eighth of the nine daughters of Richard Potter, railway and industrial magnate, by his wife, Lauren-cina, daughter of Lawrence Heyworth, a Liverpool merchant. Lawrence Hey-worth, like Beatrice's paternal grand-father, Richard Potter [q.v.], was a Liberal member of Parliament and a follower of John Bright. Beatrice Potter grew up mainly at Standish House. She was educated at home by governesses; by extensive travel on the continent; and by a wide and serious range of reading. She came out at the age of eighteen and for six years followed the social round. In 1882 her mother died, and she became not only the manager of her father's houses, in London and in the country, but his close associate in his multifarious busi-ness enterprises, travelling frequently with him. Stimulated to a lively concern in philosophic and social problems by her intimate friendship with Herbert Spencer [q.v.] she took over the rent collecting which her sister Catherine (Kate) gave up on her marriage in 1883 to L. H. Courtney (later Lord Courtney of Penwith, q.v.). Of

her other sisters, one married Lord Parmoor and another Henry Hobhouse [qq.v.]. Rent collecting led on to investigations in con-nexion with the survey of *Life and Labour of the People in London* directed by her cousin's husband Charles Booth [q.v.]. Some results of the inquiry into 'The Dock Life of East London' which she made for the survey were published in the *Nineteenth Century* for October 1887; this was followed by other articles, including one on sweated labour, a subject on which she gave evidence in 1888 before the inquiry committee of the House of Lords. This led her to embark upon a study of the co-operative movement; the small book entitled *The Co-operative Movement in Great Britain* which she published in 1891 was original in approach and treat-ment. She had read *Fabian Essays* with admiration for Sidney Webb's contribu-tion, and, in the course of her work on the co-operative movement, they met. He was a convinced collectivist; she was moving fast in that direction. Soon, they were privately engaged: six months after the death of her father, they married.

From the day of their marriage, the establishment of what Beatrice called 'the firm of Webb' represented so com-plete a fusion of husband and wife, for public service and for private happiness, that it is impossible to treat their lives separately. At the time, to many of her friends and of his, there was something strange in the alliance of the tall, hand-some, brilliantly gifted woman, who was pre-eminently a member of the governing class, and the undersized little man who, although purely English, looked, with his beard and eyeglasses, like a foreigner, and spoke like a cockney. Those who saw it so, saw the surface only. She, a year before their marriage, had written with charac-teristic candour in the diary which she kept throughout her life: 'We are both of us second-rate minds; but we are curiously combined. I am the investigator and he the executant; between us we have a wide and varied experience of men and affairs. We have also an unearned salary. These are unique circumstances. A considerable work should be the result if we use our combined talents with a deliberate and persistent purpose.' Deliberate and per-sistent purpose dominated their lives; the motto, *pro bono publico*, inscribed within the rings which they exchanged, was loyally maintained.

After spending their honeymoon in inspecting trade societies in Ireland and attending the Trades Union Congress in Glasgow, the Webbs set up house at 41 Grosvenor Road (afterwards Millbank). This, with its view over the Thames and its convenient distance from Westminster, became home and workshop; here they organized the life 'according to plan' and performed the works of research and social direction which made them a dominant force in British life and British social thinking. To plain living they were dedicated and from it they never varied. Travel and secretaries were their only luxuries. In 1894 appeared the first-fruits of their devoted labours, *The History of Trade Unionism*. Hailed as 'masterly' by *The Times*, it has since been widely translated and has become an indispensable textbook. In treating trade unions seriously the Webbs were pioneers; their historical study was backed by intimate acquaintance with the actual movement. It was Sidney who drafted the minority report of the Royal Commission on Labour signed in 1894 by Tom Mann [q.v.] and three others. Having laid their foundation in fact, the Webbs dealt with theory in *Industrial Democracy*, published in two volumes in 1897. On their books, they worked together; to these the mornings were rigorously devoted: Sidney's afternoons were mainly claimed by the London County Council. Caring everything for results and nothing for credit in achieving them, he was unrivalled as a committee man and unsurpassed as a draftsman. For the planned organization of the work of the Council and for the progressive extension of its services he was largely responsible. His chief concern, however, was education. As chairman of the Council's technical education board, he brought about the raising of the level of higher education in London. He then turned to the wretched state of elementary schools in the metropolis, at this time the concern of the school boards. He became convinced of the necessity of a plan of uniform control if reform was to be accomplished, and set out a scheme in a Fabian tract entitled *The Education Muddle and the Way Out* (1901). The mind of A. J. Balfour who was mainly responsible for the passage through Parliament of the Education Acts of 1902 and 1903 had been subjected to steady permeation at 41 Grosvenor Road. Many other minds, Liberal as well as Conservative, were subjected to the same process. In close association with R. B. (later Viscount) Haldane [q.v.] a

teaching university for London was brought into being. Moreover, in 1895 the Webbs launched the idea which issued in the London School of Economics and Political Science. To this institution they both gave unwearying service, and from 1912 until 1927 Sidney was honorary professor of public administration there.

In 1898, with two important books to their credit and their position both as writers and as public characters fully established, the Webbs went on a tour of the Dominions and the United States. They had already made plans and set in train research for the monumental task of writing the history and anatomizing the functions of 'local collective activity' in England. The first of the nine massive volumes of the comprehensive history of *English Local Government* appeared in 1906; the last in 1929.

The rights and wrongs of the South African war divided the Fabian Society, as they did opinion in Great Britain as a whole. The Webbs were on the side of the majority; they had small sympathy with the pacifism of the Independent Labour Party and its leaders J. Keir Hardie and Ramsay MacDonald [qq.v.], and not much, at this stage, with their political aims. They expected social progress in general, and the advance of collectivization in particular, to come from the influence exerted by an '*élite* of unassuming experts' upon persons in power rather than from political action by a labelled party. They were in close touch, both social and professional, with Conservative and Liberal leaders, and with key persons in the Government, the Civil Service, the press, and the universities; they 'went out' a great deal and gave many 'little parties'; but the object of it all was never left out of mind.

Up to 1906 Sidney rather than Beatrice carried on the outside and public activities of 'the firm'. He served on the Royal Commission appointed in 1903 to review trade-union law in the light of the Taff Vale judgement, and on a number of departmental committees. At the end of 1905, however, Balfour, on the eve of his resignation of office, appointed Beatrice one of the members of the Royal Commission on the Poor Laws and relief of distress; it was indeed generally believed that pressure by the Webbs had caused him to appoint a body which was bound to produce a general inquest into poverty and, with Beatrice Webb on it, collectivization. The lengthy deliberations of this commission were indeed dominated by her, although, in the end, only George Lansbury [q.v.] and two others besides herself signed in 1909 the famous minority report which the partners drafted; their old friend (and enemy) John Burns [q.v.] defeated them from the stronghold of the Local Government Board. The report, however, published at a very modest price in a special Fabian edition, had a spectacular sale: in support of its recommendations for the prevention of destitution by the break-up of the Poor Law, a great propaganda campaign was organized by 'the firm', which now appeared in a wholly new role. A national committee, including a long list of imposing names, was formed; conferences, regional and national, and summer schools were organized; branches, local committees, a research department, and a weekly paper were set up; the partners spoke, night after night, at enthusiastic meetings up and down the country: a veritable crusade was carried on. In the upshot it was a failure, and they knew it. Later they said: 'The Royal Commission of 1906–9 was in fact from a constructive standpoint as big a failure as the Royal Commission of 1834 was a success.' This is an exaggeration; in the years which followed, the fabric of the old Poor Law was gradually dismantled and the new system of social insurances took its place.

A significant legacy of the crusade was the transformation in April 1913 of its magazine into an independent weekly, the *New Statesman*. By an ingenious, and then novel, scheme, foundation subscribers received this at the reduced rate of a guinea per annum. Sidney was the original chairman of its board, and Beatrice a member; both of them wrote regularly for it in its early days, but there was never any interference with the freedom of the editor. By 1931 the paper was so strongly established that it absorbed the Liberal *Nation*.

The crusade marks a turning-point in the activities of the Webbs; they discovered that it was only within narrow limits possible to move the older parties in the direction of the far-reaching social reforms on which their hearts were set. Solid support for collectivist ideals could come only from a party which fully shared them, and that was the rising Labour Party, upon which, hitherto, they had looked with something of suspicion. The Webbs always accepted facts, and they accepted this fact, although, at the time,

the circumstances were peculiarly difficult. From a journey to the Far East which they made in 1911–12 they returned to a scene agitated by forces which they disliked and did not wholly understand. It was the epoch of industrial strife, marked by serious strikes in important industries; of the militant suffrage movement; of the rise, as sudden as its later fall, of syndicalism. Within the Fabian Society itself, the Webbs were under attack; H. G. Wells [q.v.] had resigned abruptly in 1908 and wrote maliciously of them in his novel *The New Machiavelli* (1911); later (1915), the young Guild Socialists, led by William Mellor and G. D. H. Cole, were also hot against them.

As was invariably the case, the Webbs met these attacks with equanimity. They continued to admire Wells as a writer and Cole as a thinker: the latter in fact afterwards became a close associate. No two persons ever showed less resentment or more generosity; they never 'answered back' or became involved, at any stage, in personal feuds. The cause was what mattered; they went on with their work. They consolidated their relations with the Labour Party. With Arthur Henderson [q.v.], its secretary, these relations were warmly friendly, with MacDonald less than that; but personal feeling never limited their loyal co-operativeness. On the outbreak of war Sidney was called in to serve upon the committee, covering all sections of the party, set up to watch over the home front; here, those divided on the war itself nevertheless combined effectively, a task to which he made a major contribution. In 1915 he became a member of the party executive, upon which he served for the next ten years. Working closely with Henderson, he took a large part in the reorganization of the party on the basis of the admission of 'workers by hand and by brain'. He also drafted the statement of policy adopted in 1918, *Labour and the New Social Order*, which did much to attract to the party recruits from all classes. Another memorable war-time document was *The Wages of Men and Women—Should They Be Equal?*, drafted by Beatrice as a minority report of a government committee on the vexed question of the pay of women war workers. In this classic statement of the 'rate for the job' she made handsome amends for her one-time opposition to women's suffrage. *A Constitution for the Socialist Commonwealth of Great Britain*, issued in

1920, marked at once their absorption into the Labour Party and their hospitality to the new ideas; there is a good deal of Guild Socialism in the book, as well as much 'gradualism'.

One upshot of the Webbs' now established absorption in the party was Sidney's decision to stand for Parliament. Both of them had often been approached to this end and in 1918 he had offered himself without success to the electors of London University. In 1920, however, at a time when the problem of the coal-mines was uppermost (he had served on the coal industry commission of 1919) he undertook to contest the Seaham division of Durham, then held by a Liberal. The partners, who did nothing by half, threw themselves with immense energy into organizing the constituency as it had never been organized before; Sidney's small *Story of the Durham Miners (1662–1921)* (1921) was one aspect of their thoroughness. He was returned in 1922 by a majority of nearly 12,000 and subsequent contests proved that he had created a safe seat. In 1924 in the first Labour Government he was sworn of the Privy Council as president of the Board of Trade, a congenial post, for, although not a House of Commons man, he was an excellent administrator. After the general election in October, he told his constituents that he did not mean to stand again. In 1923 the Webbs had acquired Passfield Corner, near Liphook in Hampshire; thither they now planned to retire and write. This, however, was not to be. When in 1929 MacDonald formed his second administration he appealed to Sidney; inevitably duty prevailed, although it took the disagreeable form of a peerage (under the title of Baron Passfield) and a most difficult assignment as secretary of state first for Dominion affairs and for the Colonies (1929–30), then for the Colonies (1930–31) at a time when the Colonial Office was heavily under fire on the Palestinian question. Moreover, although Beatrice, who refused to be known as Lady Passfield, played a gallant part in the social duties of a minister's wife, and went beyond them in order to help colleagues and their wives, neither was happy about the approach or performance of the Government. When the crisis of 1931 came, there was never any question of where they stood. Both accepted release with relief.

The opportunity was at once used for a long-planned visit to Russia. In 1929 the Webbs had talked with Trotsky; at that stage they were by no means in sympathy with revolution in Russia. From their own sojourn in 1932, for which they undertook the most intensive preparation that reading could afford, they returned profoundly impressed and conveyed that impression to vast numbers of readers of their *Soviet Communism: a New Civilisation?* (2 vols., 1935). Those who were, at the time, shocked by this abandonment of 'gradualism' by its chief exponents had not studied with sufficient care the basic attitude of the partners, or allowed enough either for their consistent desire to see a professional *élite* in charge of affairs or for their profound belief in deliberate planning. From the mid-'thirties onwards, Russian events and problems continued to be their main interest; the pain of the war was, for them, to some extent redeemed by alliance with Russia in 1941.

The long partnership was broken on 30 April 1943 when Beatrice died at Passfield Corner. On 13 October 1947, Sidney also died there. They had no children and the title became extinct. In December of that year the ashes of the Webbs were buried in Westminster Abbey. Sidney was appointed to the Order of Merit in 1944 and received honorary degrees from the universities of London, Wales, and Munich. Beatrice was elected F.B.A. in 1931 and received honorary degrees from the universities of Manchester, Edinburgh, and Munich.

Judgement on the large body of the Webbs' written work is not now as favourable as when it was first published. The combined literary style is heavy, and, despite enlivening passages, the books are as a whole hard reading. But they broke fresh ground and set new standards; their influence on social study and social method has been immense. Fortunately for those who come after, the portraits of Sidney and of Beatrice have been drawn, fully and fairly, in their habit as they lived, in Beatrice Webb's *My Apprenticeship* (1926) which tells the story of her life and of its background up to her marriage, and *Our Partnership* (published posthumously in 1948), which carries the story down to June 1911, and closes with passages connecting its events with the Webbs' outlook on Russia. In each case the book consists of extracts from Beatrice's daily diary, skilfully woven into a narrative texture. Two further volumes of the diaries, down to 1932, have been edited by Margaret Cole. The picture gallery includes a high proportion of notable people, in all fields save the purely artistic, of the period; its supreme achievement, however, lies in the faithful and candid presentation of two great servants of the public weal and in the complete conviction conveyed to the reader of the reality and happiness of their union.

A portrait of the Webbs, by Sir William Nicholson, is at the London School of Economics and Political Science. The National Portrait Gallery has a portrait of Beatrice Webb by Edward S. Swinson.

[*The Times*, 1 May 1943 and 14 October 1947; *Times Literary Supplement*, 20 October 1945; Beatrice Webb, *My Apprenticeship*, 1926, and *Our Partnership* (edited by Barbara Drake and Margaret I. Cole), 1948; *Beatrice Webb's Diaries, 1912–1924*, 1952, and *1924–1932*, 1956 (edited by Margaret I. Cole); M. A. Hamilton, *Sidney and Beatrice Webb*, 1933; Margaret I. Cole, *Beatrice Webb*, 1945; E. R. Pease, *History of the Fabian Society*, revised ed. 1925; R. H. Tawney in *Proceedings* of the British Academy, vol. xxix, 1943; *The Webbs and their Work* (edited by Margaret I. Cole), 1949; personal knowledge.]     MARY AGNES HAMILTON.

WEBSTER, BENJAMIN (1864–1947), actor, was born in London 2 June 1864, the son of William Shakespeare Webster and his wife, Anne Sarah Johnson. He was a grandson of Benjamin Nottingham Webster [q.v.] the famous manager under whom, at the Haymarket and Adelphi theatres, served all the great early Victorian stars including W. C. Macready [q.v.]. Ben's father was a solicitor, and after leaving King's College School Ben was trained for the law and called to the bar by the Inner Temple in 1885. But soon afterwards, through his sister, he met May Whitty (see below) then a junior member of the company of (Sir) John Hare and W. H. Kendal [qq.v.], joined the company (1887) to be near her, and so became an actor. Then a golden-haired youth with classical features and immense charm, he soon won his way as an accomplished juvenile lead. In 1888 he joined (Sir) Henry Irving [q.v.] to play Malcolm in *Macbeth*, then with (Sir) George Alexander [q.v.] from 1890 he was in the original casts of *The Second Mrs. Tanqueray*, *Liberty Hall*, and *Lady Windermere's Fan*. In 1892, after a seven years' courtship, he married May, and with her returned to Irving at the Lyceum Theatre in 1895 and remained with him there and in America until Irving's last season at the Lyceum in 1898. At the age of forty, in 1904, he was still young and played the youthful Hippolytus brilliantly for Harley Granville-Barker [q.v.]. In the Royal Court Theatre season which followed he played a number of parts including the original Ridgeon of *The Doctor's Dilemma* by G. B. Shaw [q.v.]. In 1905 and 1907 he was in America again playing leads for Mrs. Patrick Campbell [q.v.] and others. In later years his skill and distinction of style always earned him a position in London, but he was too well balanced to excel as a tragedian and perhaps too grave to reach the heights as a comedian. In 1936 he shared in his wife's great success in *Night Must Fall* in New York, and when the play was filmed in 1937 he went to Hollywood and remained there with her until his death 26 February 1947.

WEBSTER, DAME MARY LOUISE (MAY) (1865–1948), actress, was born in Liverpool 19 June 1865, the daughter of Alfred Whitty, journalist, and his wife, Mary Ashton. Her grandfather was Michael James Whitty [q.v.], founder and editor of the *Liverpool Daily Post* and chief constable of Liverpool. She made her début there in 1881 and after an appearance in London in 1882 at the Comedy Theatre she joined the company of Hare and the Kendals. Her work always bore the impress of Mrs. Kendal's training. As a charming ingénue she appeared with all the leading actor-managers of the day, including the Bancrofts, Wyndham, and Forbes-Robertson [qq.v.], and made her first big personal success in *Our Flat* in 1889. With her husband she joined Irving's company (1895–8) but was still cast for rather colourless parts which somewhat belied her own character. Her Susan Throssell in the original run of *Quality Street* in 1903 was the climax of this part of her career. But she played Countess Cathleen in Dublin in 1899 in the play of that name by W. B. Yeats [q.v.] and in America in 1905–7 she was given stronger work. Her daughter, Margaret Webster, who became an eminent producer, was born in New York at this time.

Back in London in 1910 May gave a series of clever character studies in Charles Frohman's repertory season in plays by Meredith, Barker, and Pinero [qq.v.] and in other engagements until the outbreak of war in 1914 changed the current of her life. She had always been a public-spirited woman and about 1900 she had taken up the cause of women's suffrage, becoming chairman of the Actresses' Franchise League. Although a convinced pacifist, she now switched the whole organization over to beneficent war work. A Women's Emergency Corps was formed, pioneering in such causes as women's land work, camp shows for the troops, and workrooms for out-of-work actresses. She was chairman of the Three Arts Women's Employment Fund and the British Women's Hospitals Committee which eventually created the Star and Garter Home for disabled servicemen at Richmond; for the great organizing ability which she showed in this and other similar causes she was appointed D.B.E. in 1918. Practical charity, based on self-help, and a keen eye for humbug were characteristic of all her work.

After the war she returned to the theatre with a much more assured and dominant style. In her youth she was a tiny delicate figure with a small round face, dark hair, Irish blue-grey eyes, and an air of impudent innocence. In mature age her face and figure expressed a downright common-sense motherliness. She played in Pinero's *The Enchanted Cottage*, Frederick Lonsdale's *The Last of Mrs. Cheyney*, made a hit in both London and New York as the old Nanny in John van Druten's *There's Always Juliet*, and was with (Sir) John Gielgud in *The Maitlands*. In 1935 at the age of seventy she made the greatest success of her life in Mr. Emlyn Williams's *Night Must Fall*, a terrifying performance of a terrified woman. She repeated the success in New York in 1936 and again when the play was filmed in Hollywood in 1937. From this followed a completely new and successful career in films of which *The Thirteenth Chair*, *The Lady Vanishes*, and *Mrs. Miniver* will be the best remembered. She made one or two notable appearances again on the stage in New York including Madame Raquin, and the nurse in (Sir) Laurence Olivier's production of *Romeo and Juliet*. She and Ben never returned to England but made their home in Hollywood, drawing round them there a circle of friends almost as close as that in England. Their home in Covent Garden from the 'nineties onwards had always been both a meeting-place of the famous English and American actors and a refuge for all in trouble. They were both deeply interested in actors' organization. British Actors' Equity, the actors' trade union, was founded at their home and they

did active work for all the theatrical charities. Almost continuously through the changing period from Hare and the Kendals, through Irving, Pinero, Wilde, Barrie, Barker, and van Druten; from the first silent English film to modern Hollywood, Ben and May Webster served the theatre with integrity and distinction, retaining throughout the affection and respect of the whole profession. Perhaps Ben missed London more than May did, especially his beloved Garrick, of which he had once been the youngest member the club had ever had. But Ben and May were inseparable from their marriage in 1892 to their golden wedding in 1942; Ben was proud of May's late-lark success, and he continued, they say, almost to his death the loving nightly custom of brushing his wife's hair. She did not long survive him, dying in Hollywood 29 May 1948. Margaret Webster was their only child except for a son who died at birth.

[*Who's Who in the Theatre*; private information; personal knowledge.]

LEWIS CASSON.

WEDGWOOD, JOSIAH CLEMENT, first BARON WEDGWOOD (1872–1943), politician, was born at Barlaston, north Staffordshire, 16 March 1872. He was the second surviving son of Clement Francis Wedgwood by his wife, Emily Catherine, daughter of James Meadows Rendel [q.v.], and on his father's side a direct descendant of Josiah Wedgwood [q.v.], founder of the famous pottery manufacture. Educated at Clifton, he at first hoped for a military career, but could not pass the necessary medical tests. After studying in Germany he started work as an apprentice in Elswick shipyard in 1890, but in 1892 won a scholarship at the Royal Naval College, Greenwich. After passing out of Greenwich he worked for a year in the drawing offices at Portsmouth dockyard before returning in 1896 to Elswick as a naval architect. The South African war, in which he served as a captain in the Elswick battery attached to the 2nd Cavalry brigade, gave him his first military experience. He joined Milner's 'kindergarten' and was resident magistrate at Ermelo, Transvaal (1902–4). Compelled by his wife's ill health to return to England, he immersed himself at once in local and national politics, becoming an ardent advocate of the taxation of land values as preached by Henry George. He was returned in the election of 1906 as Liberal member for

Newcastle under Lyme, a borough which he represented without a break until 1942. In the House of Commons he very soon made his mark as a vigorous speaker, in and out of season an advocate of the taxation of land values, and a vehement defender of the liberties of the individual. His speech condemning the 'Syndicalist' prosecutions of 1912 attracted considerable attention.

In the war of 1914–18 Wedgwood served first in Belgium in command of armoured cars attached to the Naval Reserve, and in April 1915 was in the Gallipoli expedition where he played a prominent part in the famous landing from the *River Clyde* on V beach, for which he was afterwards appointed to the D.S.O. Badly wounded on 6 May, he was invalided home and was for a short time in the Ministry of Munitions. Later he served under General Smuts in East Africa. Appointed in 1916 to the Royal Commission on Mesopotamia he submitted a somewhat controversial minority report emphasizing the need to gratify Indian aspirations towards independence. Late in 1916 he visited the United States on a mission of good will, and, after the October revolution of 1917, was sent to investigate the situation in Russia.

Immediately after the war his divorce received considerable publicity. Wedgwood had married in 1894 his first cousin, Ethel Kate (died 1952), daughter of Baron Bowen [q.v.]. His marriage was at first happy, and there were two sons and five daughters, but his wife left him in 1913. In order to obtain a divorce in the state of the law as it was then, he went through the usual sordid formality of signing a hotel visitors' book for himself and another woman as man and wife, so that his wife could divorce him. When the case came up he was made the object of violent attack by certain religious bodies in his constituency. Unable to defend himself until the decree was made absolute, he felt it his duty, as soon as it was possible, to reveal the true facts of the case for the satisfaction of his loyal constituents. This was the first open revelation of the state of the divorce laws by a public man. It caused a considerable stir at the time and was partly responsible for the gradual alteration of the law which has since taken place.

Wedgwood abandoned the Liberal Party for the Independent Labour Party in April 1919 and in August joined the Labour Party, being for a time a member of the executive and vice-chairman of the parliamentary Labour party (1921–4). In the first Labour Cabinet he was chancellor of the Duchy of Lancaster, and was sworn of the Privy Council, but owing to disagreement with his colleagues about the rigidity of party discipline he became, during the later 'twenties and the 'thirties, steadily more independent of the party, although he never wholly severed his connexion with it.

During the last twenty years of his life he devoted himself to various causes, of which the taxation of land values, the independence of India, and the Jewish question were the most important. He elaborated his views on the British Empire as a free association of democratic peoples in such books as *The Future of the Indo-British Commonwealth* (1921) and *The Seventh Dominion* (1928) which dealt respectively with the future of India as a Dominion and with the possibility of giving Dominion status to the Jewish national home in Palestine. In 1920–21 he toured India and attended a meeting of the Indian National Congress. Later he toured America, the Balkans, and South Africa speaking on Zionism. With the advent of Hitler in 1933 he threw himself wholeheartedly into the work of helping refugees from Nazism, strongly condemned appeasement, and early advocated rearmament to meet the menace of the dictators. His interest in foreign questions did not, however, interfere with his attachment to his native potteries and his constituents found him well informed and consistently helpful in local affairs. He was twice (1930–32) mayor of Newcastle under Lyme.

During the war of 1939–45 Wedgwood made another tour of the United States, but this was interrupted by illness and darkened by attacks from the isolationist press. He was raised to the peerage as Baron Wedgwood, of Barlaston, in 1942. During his year in the House of Lords he suffered increasingly from heart trouble but intervened none the less vigorously in debate, especially on the Palestine question. He died in London, 26 July 1943, and was buried at Barlaston. His son, Francis Charles Bowen (born 1898), succeeded him as second baron.

Outside politics Wedgwood's chief interests were local and family history. He was for many years treasurer of the English Place-Name Society and it was largely as a result of his endeavours, as chairman of the committee on House of

Commons records from 1929 to 1942, that the scheme for compiling the *History of Parliament* was set in motion. Disagreements on methods of work and the war caused the work to be interrupted shortly before his death, but it was resumed in 1951. His publications include *The Road to Freedom and What Lies Beyond* (in collaboration with his first wife, 1913), *Staffordshire Pottery and its History* (1913), *Essays and Adventures of a Labour M.P.* (1924), *Forever Freedom* (an anthology, with Allan Nevins, 1940), *Memoirs of a Fighting Life* (foreword by (Sir) Winston Churchill, 1940), as well as two works on family history and his contributions to the *History of Parliament*.

After the dissolution of his first marriage Wedgwood married in 1919 Florence Ethel, daughter of Edward Guy Willett, of London, whose quiet and congenial help and companionship were of great value to him.

Wedgwood's vigorous opinions and combative temperament did not always make him an easy colleague, but his sincerity, generosity, and wit won him friends in all parties and in every walk of life. He summarized his guiding ideas in his last book, *Testament to Democracy* (1942); many of them ran against the general current of progressive thought in his time. Briefly, he believed in justice, self-reliance, and respect for the individual, and he remained from first to last vehemently true to his ideals.

[C. V. Wedgwood, *The Last of the Radicals*, 1951; J. C. Wedgwood, *Memoirs of a Fighting Life*, 1940; private information; personal knowledge.]      C. V. WEDGWOOD.

WELCH, ADAM CLEGHORN (1864–1943), Scottish divine, was born 14 May 1864 at Goshen, Jamaica, the sixth child of the Rev. John Welch, missionary, and his wife, Flora, daughter of Robert Hogg, a member of a well-known Border farming family. On the death of both parents when he was six years old, he was brought to Scotland by his mother's family. Educated at Galashiels Academy, George Watson's College, and the university, Edinburgh, he graduated M.A. in 1883 and entered the ministry of the United Presbyterian Church. The loss of his three brothers in early manhood, and later of his only son in childhood, gave his ministry that unusual sensitiveness to the sorrows of men and women which characterized it to the end.

Welch exercised ministries at Water-beck in Dumfriesshire, Helensburgh, and Glasgow from 1887 to 1913, and was recognized as one of the most powerful expository preachers of his time. His writing dates from the beginning of his ministry, and his first scholarly interests were in systematic theology and church history. His first book, on *Anselm and his Work* (1901), is still vivid and reliable. It was his only published work when in 1909, on the occasion of the Calvin quatercentenary, the university of Halle conferred on him the honorary degree of doctor of theology, Welch being one of only three persons in the United Kingdom to receive it at that time. He had already turned to Old Testament studies, his great life-work, and his second main work, in 1912, was *The Religion of Israel under the Kingdom* (the Kerr lectures). Edinburgh University enrolled him as an honorary D.D. in 1913 and in the same year he was appointed professor of Hebrew and Old Testament exegesis at New College, Edinburgh.

A teaching career of twenty-one years made Welch one of the greatest Old Testament scholars Scotland has produced. His interest in all Old Testament problems was specifically theological, and he was unrivalled in his knowledge of the needs and the eccentricities of students. His biblical and historical studies had made him very uneasy about the accepted Wellhausen hypothesis, and for many years he was convinced of the need for a radical recasting of it. It was a notable day in his career and in the sphere of biblical criticism when, in October 1921, he gave a lecture on 'The present position of Old Testament criticism', presenting a threefold challenge to the dominant critical theories of the Pentateuch. Nearly all his subsequent books are given to the development of the positions adumbrated in this lecture: *The Code of Deuteronomy* (1924), *Deuteronomy, the Framework to the Code* (1932), *Post-Exilic Judaism* (1935), *Prophet and Priest in old Israel* (1936), and *The Work of the Chronicler* (1939). Other volumes of rare quality were published on the Psalms, Jeremiah, and Daniel. A far-reaching ferment of discussion was created by all these works, and Old Testament criticism will never return to the easy acceptance of the position before 1921.

Welch retired in 1934. His portrait by David Alison was presented to New College, Edinburgh. The two crowning honours of his life were his election in

1934 as president of the Society for Old Testament Study, in the founding of which he had shared, and his appointment as Schweich lecturer in 1938. He married in 1903 Grace Marion, daughter of Thomas Steven, of Helensburgh; they had one son and two daughters. Welch was an able and trusted churchman, who brought incisive wisdom and pungent candour to every discussion. His sure, unprejudiced judgement and his sharp humour assisted him in playing a leading part in the reunion of the Scottish Church. He died at Helensburgh 19 February 1943.

[A memorial volume, *Kings and Prophets of Israel*, edited by N. W. Porteous, with a memoir by G. S. Gunn, was published in 1952.]      GEORGE S. GUNN.

WELLS, HERBERT GEORGE (1866–1946), author, was born at 47 High Street, Bromley, Kent, 21 September 1866. His father, Joseph Wells, was the son of a Kentish gardener and his mother, Sarah, the daughter of George Neal, a Sussex innkeeper. She had been a lady's maid and was nearly forty-four when Herbert was born to her as her fourth child and third son; her daughter had already died. Joseph Wells had begun as a gardener but became a cricketer who, playing for Kent on 26 June 1862, bowled four Sussex batsmen in successive balls. His seasonal earnings as a cricket professional supplemented the slender takings of the shop in Bromley where he tried to sell china-ware, lamp-wicks, paraffin, and cricket accessories. He was an unsuccessful tradesman and the Wells household was continually overhung by the threat of insolvency.

The family circumstances into which Herbert George ('Bertie' in his family circle) was born and grew up were penurious to the verge of squalor. In that 'gaunt and impossible home' the prim little lady's maid became an incompetent and discouraged drudge whose anxieties about present poverty and future salvation were not assuaged by the likeable but easy-going traits of her husband.

Wells's origins and upbringing, like his adolescent vicissitudes and frustrations, profoundly influenced not only his novels but his social attitudes and explained much which seemed contradictory in his public character: the Socialist-individualist; the republican who repudiated titles but inherited from his mother a deference towards those who held them; the atheist who invoked God in *Mr. Britling Sees It Through*; the supranationalist who remained to the end so obviously English and cockney English at that; the pansophist with a snook-cocking disrespect for pedagogy; the philosopher who despaired of the wisdom of *Homo sapiens*, but gave a lifetime to the pursuit of a more perfect world; the hedonist, reacting against drudgery; the sensualist, revolting against piety.

By the standards of his later knowledge Wells was virtually self-taught. 'Mr. Morley's Commercial Academy' which he first attended was a school, in a single room built over a scullery, for tradesmen's sons themselves destined for trade. To that end, it specialized in long-addition sums, book-keeping, and copper-plate flourishes which Wells retained to the last in his signature. Part boarding-, part day-school, its pupils were prepared for the examinations of the College of Preceptors from which body Wells at the age of thirteen was granted a certificate bracketing him, with another boy, first 'in all England' in book-keeping.

Wells, however, by an accident had been self-liberated from these narrow frontiers. He had been dropped at the age of seven by the son of the landlord of the Bell Inn and his leg was broken. The contrite landlady kept the victim supplied not only with delicacies unknown in his indigent home but also with books supplementing those which his father borrowed from the Literary Institute. He discovered books of travel and Wood's *Natural History* and 'that quite a number of things had happened and quite a number of interesting things existed outside the world of English affairs'.

When Wells was eleven his father broke his leg and the resultant limp put an end to his career as cricket coach. The chronic insolvency of the china-shop now became acute and after three years' struggle to make ends meet the home was broken up. Mrs. Wells returned as housekeeper to Miss Featherstonhaugh at Up Park, Sussex, where she had been lady's maid. The two elder brothers, Frank and Fred, were already journeymen drapers and Bertie became probationary apprentice with Rodgers and Denyer at Windsor. His book-keeping certificate did not compensate for his inattention and both he and his employers agreed that he was unfitted to be a draper. A courtesy 'uncle', headmaster of a national school at Wookey, Somerset, offered the fourteen-year-old the role of student teacher. He had to teach, with his fists, boys as big as himself, but he learned scepticism, an irreverence for religion, and something of sex before the authorities discovered that the headmaster had obtained his post by false pretences.

After an interlude at Up Park in which he made the most of a library which introduced him, then or later, to Voltaire, Tom Paine, and Plato, he went to a pharmaceutical chemist in Midhurst to attempt a new career. He found, however, that the cost of qualifying was well beyond his family means, and he knew no Latin. For Latin lessons he went to the headmaster of the local grammar school, Horace Byatt, for whom he formed a liking which was mutual.

Apprenticeship to pharmacy, however, still proving too expensive, Wells had to make a fourth start in life at the age of fifteen. Again it was drapery, this time at Hyde's Emporium, Southsea. For two years he rebelliously rolled blankets, huckaback, Turkey twill, and lace-curtains, ran errands, and kept the pin-bowls replenished. Yet 'living-in' included a library of several hundred books and even in the thirteen-hour working day there were opportunities—behind a pile of cotton goods—to study Latin.

With more than two years of his indentures to go he appealed desperately to Byatt and received the offer of a student assistantship starting at £20 a year. His mother, who had already paid £40 of his £50 apprenticeship premium, refused to release him. Waylaying her as she was returning to Up Park with the procession of servants from church he persuaded his mother under threat of suicide to forfeit his indentures.

Midhurst (1883–4) changed the course of Wells's life. Under Byatt's eye he did some classroom teaching but he was also an earnest pupil. Since it was an endowed school, he had to be confirmed in order to retain his job. Having no faith he fiercely resented the hypocrisy thrust upon him. Byatt was entitled, under the science scheme of the Education Department, to organize evening classes and qualify for a grant. Wells was accordingly enrolled as a night student in the bogus science class designed to earn the headmaster £4 if his pupil gained an advanced first class in the examinations. To this end Wells crammed himself with elementary science, for the first time, and passed the examination with such success that he was offered a free studentship, with a maintenance grant of £1 a week, at the Normal School (later Royal College) of Science, South Kensington.

He was enrolled under T. H. Huxley [q.v.] who remained, for him, the greatest of all teachers. In his first year's study of biology, Wells distinguished himself, but continuing with physics and geology under other teachers he became lax and failed his third year examinations. He had hoped to become a research scientist: another false start due, in this instance, to truancy into literature and politics. He had spent more of his time in the library than in the laboratory and his evenings had been devoted to the pursuit of his new-found Socialism at meetings addressed by William Morris, Graham Wallas, and G. B. Shaw [qq.v.].

Wells next taught at Holt Academy, Wrexham, where he permanently damaged a kidney in a game of football and developed the symptoms of tuberculosis with haemorrhages which were to recur. This meant retirement to Up Park and fresh opportunity for reading. In 1889 he obtained a more congenial teaching post at Henley House School, Kilburn, kept by the father of A. A. Milne and where the future Lord Northcliffe [q.v.] had been a pupil. In 1890 he took his B.Sc. with a first class in zoology and a second in geology. A year later, as a full-time tutor on fees of £4 a week, at the University Tutorial College, he married his cousin Isabel Mary Wells in whose home he had lodged in London. He was already trying his hand at journalism on scientific subjects but his reading of (Sir) James Barrie's *When A Man's Single*, during a breakdown in health in 1893, encouraged him to attempt a more popular approach which was well received by editors.

In 1893 he left his wife for Amy Catherine Robbins (died 1927), one of his students at the Tutorial College whom he married when his divorce was completed in 1895. They had two sons, George Philip (who was to collaborate with his father and (Sir) Julian Huxley in producing *The Science of Life*) and Frank Richard.

Wells's writing period now began in earnest. He found a ready market for his short stories (such as *The Stolen Bacillus*, 1895) and proved himself a master of the technique. *The Time Machine* which in the hindsight of later years he regarded as one of his 'social fables' was received by the public in 1895 as a diverting extravaganza. It was the beginning of that long series of fantastic and imaginative romances which ranged from *The Invisible Man* (1897) to *The Shape of Things to Come* (1933): a series for which the adjective 'Wellsian' was coined (to become his private bugbear) and which gained him the reputation of prophet, a role he was willing to assume in such publications as *Anticipations* (1901). His foresight of the war in the air, of tanks, of the atomic bomb and 'the war of 1940' were to be remembered when his misses (like his discarding of the idea of a submarine) were forgotten. His ingenious knack was to seize upon some emerging scientific fact, such as the significance of radium, and fictionally to predict results like the artificial splitting of the atom: in that instance, in *The World Set Free* (1914), with a margin of error of a year. Although he might have to ignore gravity by inventing a substance like 'cavorite', there was usually a basis of scientific fact even in his most 'Wellsian' romances.

Alternating with such scientific excursions and, later, with his social tracts, were his 'real' novels beginning with *The Wheels of Chance* (1896), followed by *Love and Mr. Lewisham* (1900), *Kipps* (1905), *Tono-Bungay* (1909), *Ann Veronica* (1909), *The History of Mr. Polly* (1910), and continuing for the next thirty years. In popular esteem *Kipps*, *Tono-Bungay*, and *Mr. Polly* were the most successful and enduring of this genre of Wells's novels. They were rich in characterization and borrowed heavily from Wells's impressionable years: the running-down shop at Bromley, the drapers, the chemist's shop at Midhurst, or Up Park. Wells himself always had an attachment to *Mr. Lewisham* with the almost autobiographical account of Midhurst Grammar School, South Kensington college life, and Wells's drab little romance and first marriage. Nor did he understand the lack of popular appreciation of *The Bulpington of Blup* (1932) which, he thought, equalled *Kipps* in characterization.

*Ann Veronica* was notorious in its day and led to scandalized reviews and pulpit denunciations of its 'youthful heroine' who 'was allowed a frankness of desire and sexual enterprise, hitherto unknown in English popular fiction'. Wells was taken aback by the outburst because he was recording his times—and his experience. He pursued the topic of freer love, defiantly, in *The New Machiavelli* (1911) and *Marriage* (1912). He had already become the 'satyr-cupid' of Socialism by his Fabian address 'Socialism and the Middle Classes' (1906) in which he had argued the impermanence of the institution of marriage and advocated the endowment of motherhood as a service to the State. This was made a political issue in Manchester in 1906 when W. Joynson-Hicks (later Viscount Brentford, q.v.) alleged that Socialists (e.g. Wells) advocated that wives should be held in common, a suggestion which Wells repudiated. Nevertheless, his frank behaviour offended many who regarded themselves as advanced thinkers, socially and politically, of whom Wells might otherwise have been the leader.

By now he had developed a 'drill' in his writing. He was producing argument-by-narrative books and following them up by fiction romanticizing his social theses. He called his novels 'social fables' and would point out that *Ann Veronica* was merely a version of some of his arguments in *A Modern Utopia* (1905). Sometimes the two genres became superimposed. His characters were liable to talk too much and his novels to become shapeless. By 1910 he had acquired a 'mission'. He was preoccupied with the future of mankind and with ideas of his 'New Republic' and 'The World State' and the political philosophy he was later to call 'The Open Conspiracy'. He moved restlessly from one movement to another seeking the means of realizing his ideal. Despite his repeated and savage disappointments he maintained his optimistic belief in the perfectibility of the human race through scientific progress. He was searching for an instrument, an *élite* of leadership—the Fabian Society, the Samurai of *A Modern Utopia*; captains of industry in *The World of William Clissold* (3 vols., 1926); or the aviators in *The Shape of Things to Come*—which would rescue people from their own stupidities. And each time it was possible to note 'the same phases in the recurrent cycle of his questing mind, hope, disillusionment, bitter enmity'.

The outbreak of war in 1914 threw him into confusion. He found himself as emotionally involved as most people and professionally involved during an interlude at Crewe House preparing propaganda for Germany. It was to him *The War That Will End War* (1914), the prelude to his World State, and it entangled him in other ways. *Mr. Britling Sees It Through* (1916) was a powerful but conventional novel in which Wells returned to God and, when challenged by the rationalists, he went farther in *God The Invisible King* (1917). He was, subsequently, to recant his theism as he was to recant his vituperative attacks on those who had not wholeheartedly endorsed 'his' war. He took up the idea of the League of Nations but was presently assailing it as an institution which was thwarting him in his pursuit of the World State.

After the war he began his assault on education: to its failures he ascribed much of the misery of mankind. He entered upon his encyclopaedic phase with *The Outline of History* (1920), followed by *The Science of Life* (1931), and *The Work, Wealth and Happiness of Mankind* (1932). Despite many defects into which his desire for unification led him, these works were substantial and influential achievements on which Wells's reputation might have rested had he never written his scientific romances or his novels. 'If he had done nothing else, this great trilogy alone would have justified his title to be the greatest public teacher of our time.' (Sir Arthur (subsequently Lord) Salter, *Personality in Politics*, 1947). Nor did Wells expect them to achieve the worldwide success—and royalties—which they produced. They were his public-spirited attempt to transform history into 'human ecology' and to derive education for world citizenship from the common origins, problems, and purposes of mankind: an argument he elaborated in *World Brain* (1938) in which he maintained, on the eve of war, that civilization was a 'race between education and catastrophe'.

In politics, as in his social relationships, Wells was impatient, irascible, and unpredictable. He flounced in and out of party Socialism. He was the *enfant terrible* of the early Fabians who were nevertheless stimulated, if exasperated, by his clash with Shaw and the Webbs. Realizing that the leadership would not come his way, he resigned in 1908. He twice fought London University as Labour parliamentary candidate (1922, 1923) and he voted Labour in the last year of his life, but in the intervals he conducted violent guerrilla campaigns. He would subscribe to principles but was impatient both of personalities and of the slowness of the democratic processes. As a politician he had short use for details or programmes: his was the broad sweep. 'I can say bright things', he wrote, 'but I cannot manage stupid people.' With the

disadvantage of a small piping voice which made him sound querulous he was a poor public speaker and had neither the tact nor patience to handle a committee. His recognition of his own inadequacy in political organization led him into his abortive search for chosen instruments which he discarded one after another, before they could fulfil his purpose. He was once described as a world optimist but a local pessimist. Politically he was naïve, as his two visits to Russia revealed. His interviews with Lenin and Stalin were a tribute to his world-wide acceptance as a major thinker, but his handling of them did not add to his reputation. The interviews were an anticlimax, as Shaw pointed out in a controversy which followed Wells's account of the second visit.

In the same year, 1934, there appeared his *Experiment in Autobiography* in two absorbing volumes written as if he were 'an observer rather than a participant' and with a self-critical freedom from vanity which did not conceal the fact that the writer was not entirely dissatisfied with H. G. Wells. But the book represented, especially in the first volume, a remarkable contribution to social history.

Towards the end of his life he turned to films as a medium and in 1936 wrote the script of *The Man Who Could Work Miracles* and the epic *Things To Come*. He also tried the radio in the hope that the microphone would compensate for the oratorical weakness of his voice, but he remained rather a broadcasting 'event' than a personality. His published works grew pessimistic and repetitive. He clamoured, urgently, for the world to listen, but his preoccupation with wide issues seemed too remote from the day-to-day problems of humanity to shape the action for which he pressed. His *The Fate of Homo Sapiens* (1939) was recriminatory, but he repented his despair and in 1940 called for a 'great debate' in *The New World Order, The Rights of Man*, and *The Commonsense of War and Peace*. The debate was launched on a world scale but was overtaken by the *Blitzkrieg*. A committee under Lord Sankey [q.v.] drafted the British version of a proposed declaration of human rights which to the last months of his life Wells was trying to universalize in correspondence with philosophers throughout the world. The episode of the human rights debate was characteristic of the contradictory personality of Wells. He despaired of individual reason but insisted on individual liberty. He defended free speech but tried, unsuccessfully, to impose the letter of his version of 'rights' on his distinguished colleagues. What seemed like embittered truculence would suddenly melt into chuckling acquiescence. His four-years' efforts to universalize it arose from the shock to his English reasoning of the pallid reception which the draft received in the Far East, due, as he discovered, to the inflexion of the rights being in the idiom of Western parliamentary democracy. So he turned from oriental translators to the Eastern philosophers. He did not live to see most of the declaration embodied in the United Nations' Convention of Human Rights but he would probably have resented the result as falling short of his own prescriptions.

Wells, with his injured kidney, his incipient tuberculosis, and, later, his diabetes, lived to be almost eighty, after a lifetime of intense productivity. His was an emotionally and intellectually turbulent life, at the end of which he felt the frustrations more than he realized the achievements. He underestimated his influence on the thinking of three decades because he could not recognize the mutations from the seeds which he had scattered and which had sprouted all over the world. And he was frustrated by never recognizing the reapers he sought so impatiently. It was his genius to stimulate imagination and to set people thinking about the possibilities of the world in which they lived. His own outlook was dictated by his materialistic interpretation of life, and thwarted by the inadequacies of the human material from which he wanted to shape his higher species. Protesting his belief in the common man, he found the clay too common for his purposes. He thought instead of mankind in terms abstracted from his own experience; yet even this depersonalized version proved reluctant to conform to his requirements. He came nearest to flesh-and-blood men in his earlier novels such as *Kipps* when he wrote of what he knew. His remarkable talent as a novelist was increasingly subordinated to his theories of scientific progress and education. Of Wells as a writer, it has been suggested, the tragedy was that 'having the power to become a great comic genius, fit for the company of Dickens, he declined the potentiality, preferring rather to become a minor prophet'. That may be an underestimate of his influence on his times and

on events but it was a risk he took deliberately.

Wells's reputation for impatience, querulousness, petulance, and 'spoiled-childishness' set his public character. Maybe he even capitalized it, by calculated aggressiveness. Its origins were in his health, particularly in his diabetes, and those who knew him well knew his capacity (and craving) for friendship. He was always surprised and hurt when people took umbrage, or felt they had offended him, because of a fit of temper which he had quickly forgotten. He was indiscriminate in his kindnesses-by-stealth, encouraging do-gooders or sponsoring young authors or supporting movements which could only be an embarrassment to him. In his permanent relationships, with those who ignored his moods or his impishness, he inspired real affection. If he could on occasion be spiteful, he also suffered from spite.

He was appalled by the war of 1939–45 which he had himself predicted and through which he lived at 13 Hanover Terrace, Regent's Park, defying the high explosives and putting out incendiary bombs with the help of two women servants. There were personal frustrations too. He had received an honorary D.Lit. from London University (1936) and was an honorary fellow of the Imperial College of Science and Technology, but he desperately wanted to be a fellow of the Royal Society, somehow to redress that failure at South Kensington and to escape the gibe of 'Wellsian' and 'pseudo-scientist'. At seventy-eight he submitted a doctoral thesis on *The Quality of Illusion in the Continuity of Individual Life in the Higher Metazoa with particular reference to the Species Homo Sapiens* to the university of London and became D.Sc. He believed, wrongly, that this would prevail upon the Royal Society to give him the one honour which he really wanted. The books of his last years were postscripts to his once-vigorous thinking: the pathetic *Mind at the End of its Tether* (1945) and the more benign *The Happy Turning* (1945). He produced over a hundred books, and persisted in writing almost to the end which came in his sleep at his home in London 13 August 1946.

In appearance Wells was unimpressive: short, compact, and inclined to plumpness. His hands and feet were small, his arms short and ill-placed. His hair and moustache were light brown, skimpy and untidy, his grey eyes meditative or with an impish twinkle, his brow broad. He moved and spoke rapidly and, save on the platform, was a fascinating talker, especially in a small circle: at the corner table in the Reform Club or at the Savile; or with guests at his villa at Malagnou near Grasse on the Riviera where he wrote many of his books; and particularly with the young for whom he had a warm appeal and a patience which belied his public *persona*. Even so, like his own William Clissold, he could maintain that 'I have never given myself to anyone', and at the end he fulfilled the claim in his autobiography: 'I shall die, as I have lived, the responsible centre of my world.' He knew his limitations but resented being reminded of them. Yet he himself acknowledged in 1938, in one of his periodic moods of disgruntlement, that his epitaph would be: 'He was clever but he was not clever enough.'

Wells's literary remains were purchased by the university of Illinois. A sketch of Wells by Feliks Topolski is in the possession of Baroness Budberg. The National Portrait Gallery has a small plasticine medallion by Theodore Spicer-Simson. Of several drawings by (Sir) William Rothenstein one is reproduced in *Twenty-Four Portraits* (1920). A lithograph by Rothenstein is in the Bradford City Art Gallery.

[*The Times*, 14 August 1946; *Times Literary Supplement*, 19 July 1947 and 23 February 1951; J. D. Beresford, *H. G. Wells*, 1915; E. R. Pease, *History of the Fabian Society*, 1916; Ivor Brown, *H. G. Wells*, 1923; *The Book of Catherine Wells*, 1928; Geoffrey West, *H. G. Wells*, 1930; H. G. Wells, *Experiment in Autobiography*, 2 vols., 1934, and 'My Obituary' in the *Coronet Magazine*, 1937; G. B. Shaw, 'Wells' in the *New Statesman and Nation*, 17 August 1946; Beatrice Webb, *Our Partnership*, 1948; Vincent Brome, *H. G. Wells*, 1951; Wilson Harris, *Life So Far*, 1954.]　　　　RITCHIE CALDER.

WHEELER, SIR WILLIAM IRELAND DE COURCY (1879–1943), surgeon, was born in Dublin 8 May 1879. His father, also William Ireland (later de Courcy-) Wheeler, was president of the Royal College of Surgeons in Ireland in 1883–4. His mother was Frances Victoria, daughter of Henry Shaw, of Tullamain, county Dublin, granddaughter of Bernard Shaw, and thus a cousin of G. B. Shaw [q.v.]. Wheeler graduated as a junior moderator in natural science at Trinity College, Dublin, in 1899, and took the M.D. degree in 1902. He was a demon-

strator and assistant to the professor of anatomy there, and for his researches into deaths under chloroform the Dublin Biological Association, of which he was later to become president, awarded him its medal in 1903. In 1904 he joined the staff of Mercer's Hospital and he was also attached to the Rotunda and to the National Children's Hospital. He became F.R.C.S. (Ireland) in 1905. While he was still in his twenties his whole career was threatened by an accident which caused the loss of an eye, but he overcame this handicap and in after years few suspected its existence. During the war of 1914–18 he served in France with the rank of lieutenant-colonel, was mentioned twice in dispatches, and in 1919 he was knighted. He was honorary surgeon to the forces in Ireland, donor and surgeon to the Dublin Hospital for Wounded Officers, and consulting surgeon to the Ministry of Pensions. His work as head of the military surgical centre at Blackrock, near Dublin, led to a close friendship with Sir Robert Jones [q.v.].

After the war Wheeler became known as a leading surgeon not only in Dublin but throughout Great Britain and America. He was appointed surgeon-in-ordinary to the lord lieutenant (1922), and was president of the Royal College of Surgeons in Ireland (1923–5), of the surgical section of the Royal Academy of Medicine in Ireland, of the Irish Medical Schools and Graduates Association, and of the Leinster branch of the British Medical Association (1925–6). Wheeler was a close friend and visitor of George Washington Crile, the brothers Mayo, and other leading surgeons of the United States. He was an honorary fellow of the American College of Surgeons and president of the Post Graduate Assembly of North America. His versatility and wide contacts made him a valued member of the editorial staffs of the leading surgical journals both British and American.

In 1932 Wheeler was persuaded by Lord Iveagh to migrate to England and to accept a position on the visiting staff of the newly constructed Southend General Hospital. He also joined in London the staffs of All Saints' Hospital for Genito-Urinary Diseases and the Metropolitan Ear, Nose and Throat Hospital. He took an active part in the medical life of London, frequenting the medical societies, and becoming chairman of the Marylebone division of the British Medical Association and a year or two later president of the metropolitan counties branch. On the outbreak of war in 1939 he was appointed consulting surgeon to the Royal Navy in Scotland, with the rank of surgeon rear-admiral.

Wheeler was the author of a *Handbook of Operative Surgery* (1918); *Injuries and Diseases of Bone* (1928); *Pillars of Surgery* (the John B. Murphy oration, 1933); and a large number of papers and addresses on almost every branch of surgery. Apart from his clinical wisdom and his brilliance as an operating surgeon, Wheeler had a genius for friendship and few surgeons of his time were so well known both at home and abroad. He died suddenly in Aberdeen 11 September 1943. He married in 1909 Elsie, eldest daughter of Baron Shaw, of Dunfermline (later Baron Craigmyle, q.v.), and they had a son and a daughter.

[*British Medical Journal*, 25 September and 2 October 1943; *Lancet*, 25 September 1943; *The Times*, 14 September 1943.]

W. J. BISHOP.

WHIBLEY, LEONARD (1863–1941), classical scholar, was born at Gravesend 20 April 1863, the second son of Ambrose Whibley, linen draper, of Gravesend and Bristol, by his second wife, Mary Jenn, daughter of the late John Davey, iron merchant. He was educated at Bristol Grammar School and entered Pembroke College, Cambridge, as a scholar in 1882. In 1885 he was classed with A. E. Brooke and R. S. Conway [qq.v.] in the first division of the first class of the classical tripos, part i, and in the following year gained a distinguished first in part ii. In 1888 he was the first winner of the recently established Prince Consort prize for historical studies, his subject being 'Political Parties in Athens during the Peloponnesian War' and in 1889 he was elected into a fellowship at Pembroke.

He did not immediately settle into the academic groove. For a time he was associated with the publishing firm of Methuen and shared a house at Fernhurst with his brother Charles, W. E. Henley, and G. W. Steevens [qq.v.]; he was also for a short period assistant secretary of the University Press, but decided to be a teacher and an historian rather than a publisher. In 1893 he won the Hare prize with an essay on Greek oligarchies, which was published in book form three years later. From 1899 to 1910 he was university lecturer in ancient history and in 1905 edited the *Companion to Greek Studies* for the University Press, of which body he was a syndic for some years. The *Companion* was recognized as a standard book of reference for students and was revised more than once during its editor's lifetime. In college Whibley served as classical lecturer, assistant tutor, and domestic bursar. He had a shrewd business sense and a fine, though not extravagant, taste in food and wine. To the friends and pupils whom he entertained in his rooms he seemed to embody all the qualities of the bachelor don. But in 1920, after serving for a time in the Foreign Office, he quietly astonished his colleagues by announcing his forthcoming marriage to Henriette Leiningen (Rhita), daughter of Major-General William Brown Barwell and Elise, Countess of Leiningen-Westerburg. After his marriage he went to live first at Wrecclesham and afterwards at Frensham, Surrey; but he remained senior fellow of Pembroke and kept close touch with the college. He also developed a keen interest in eighteenth-century literature and especially in Thomas Gray. From 1925 he collaborated with P. J. Toynbee [q.v.] in the preparation of a new edition of Gray's letters and on Toynbee's death in 1932 he revised the whole work, sparing no pains to secure textual accuracy and factual comment. The three volumes, published in 1935, are a model of editorial scholarship.

Whibley was a good clubman. With A. D. Godley [q.v.] he was a co-founder, in 1900, of the Arcades, an Oxford and Cambridge dining-club, and he was happy in his membership of the Johnson Club. To undergraduates he was friend as well as teacher. His literary discipline was strict and he would prick any bubble of pretentiousness with a dry economy of wit; but, once he believed in a pupil, he would take infinite trouble on his behalf. In 1939 he celebrated the jubilee of his Pembroke fellowship and on 8 November 1941 he died at Frensham, leaving no issue. There is a pencil drawing by Miss D. W. Hawksley at Pembroke College.

[Personal knowledge.]      S. C. ROBERTS.

WHISTLER, REGINALD JOHN, (REX) (1905–1944), artist, was born at Eltham, Kent, 24 June 1905, the second of three sons of Henry Whistler, architect and estate agent, and his wife, Helen Frances Mary, daughter of the Rev. Charles Slegg Ward, vicar of Wootton-St.-Lawrence, Basingstoke. His maternal great-great-grandfather was

Paul Storr the silversmith. He was educated at Haileybury and although he made little formal progress there he was already known as a wit, and continued to pour out sketches and drawings, on which he had engaged since early childhood. Between 1912 and 1923 he won a prize every year at the exhibition of the Royal Drawing Society. Leaving Haileybury in 1922, he went to the Royal Academy Schools, but stayed there only one term, being considered 'unpromising' by Charles Sims [q.v.]. At the Slade School of Fine Art, to which he then applied, he was at once accepted by Henry Tonks [q.v.] who in later years told Sir Osbert Sitwell that in the whole course of his own career as artist and teacher he had only met three or four people with a natural gift for drawing, and that Rex Whistler was one of them.

Tonks perceived that Whistler's talent lay in imaginative decoration and encouraged him to follow his bent. He began to paint seriously in oils. In 1924, with Miss Mary Adshead (later Mrs. Stephen Bone), Whistler decorated the walls of the Highways Club, Shadwell, London. When, in 1926, Sir Joseph (later Lord) Duveen [q.v.] offered a new refreshment room to the Tate Gallery, Tonks recommended Whistler as mural decorator. The room was opened in November 1927; and the young artist's murals, on the fanciful theme of 'The Pursuit of Rare Meats', were at once acclaimed by critics and public alike for their decorative skill, their wit and resourcefulness.

From that moment, at the early age of twenty-two, Whistler was launched on a promising career. His style was quite out of key with the rather rash experimentalism of the 'twenties—having more than a touch of the rococo, and finding its inspiration in the seventeenth and eighteenth and later in the nineteenth centuries—but it made an instant appeal to the taste of the day. Connoisseurs like Captain David Euan Wallace and Sir Philip Sassoon [q.v.] were quick to commission murals from him; but his most impressive wall-decorations were done in 1937 for the Marquess of Anglesey at Plâs Newydd, Anglesey, and for Lady Louis Mountbatten (later Countess Mountbatten of Burma) at Brook House, Park Lane, London.

While still at school Whistler had begun to discover the delights of poetry, and in his first year at the Slade School had compiled his own private anthology, pro-fusely illustrated in the margins. The decade after the war of 1914–18 saw a healthy and brilliant revival of British book production, and in this movement Whistler naturally enough took part. Some of his most delightful work was done in the ephemeral medium of the dust-wrapper, but fortunately some examples have been reproduced for posterity in the *Life and Drawings* by his younger brother Laurence. More enduring by their very nature are his book-illustrations, which virtually began with Edith Olivier's *Mildred* (1926). Among his finest productions were illustrations for a limited edition of Swift's *Gulliver's Travels* in two volumes (1930), a Hans Andersen (1935), and a series for A. E. W. Mason's *Königsmark*, done in 1940–41 and published in 1952. The originals of the last are in the Tate Gallery. A favourite method was to construct a highly decorative rococo marginal frame, in which the illustration was set; and in this, as in so much else, Whistler showed the influence of the seventeenth and eighteenth centuries.

The stage also proved a fruitful field for his high imagination and decorative talent. Work in this kind included scenery and costume for ballets such as *The Rake's Progress*, 1935, and *Le Spectre de la Rose*, 1944, both for Sadler's Wells Company; for plays, including Laurence Housman's *Victoria Regina* in New York in 1935 and London in 1937, and Oscar Wilde's *An Ideal Husband*, 1943; scenery for the operas *Fidelio* and *The Marriage of Figaro* (both 1934), and contributions to half a dozen of (Sir) C. B. Cochran's revues.

Apart from these three main lines of work, Whistler showed an astonishing versatility and adaptability in such varied fields as designs for textiles, china, carpets, bookplates, letter-headings, and even luggage labels for Imperial Airways. Although he took a commission in the Welsh Guards in the winter of 1939, he still kept up a vigorous flow of work until he went overseas with the Guards armoured division at Arromanches, Normandy, at the end of June 1944. He left on the walls of the officers' mess at Brighton a mural painting which is now in the Art Gallery of that town. He could easily have sought employment in camouflage or as an official war artist, but he preferred to carry out the infinitely more dangerous task of an active tank troop leader. In an attack across the Orne, east of Caen, 18 July 1944, he was killed by a shellburst near the village of Le Mesnil, during his first hours in action.

In spite of the echoes from Patinir, Watteau, Canaletto, Boucher, and others which appear in his work, Whistler had a freshness, a graceful wit, and a linear resource which were all his own. That he should have made his way so instantly and so certainly in a period devoted in such large measure to 'the cube, the cone, and the cylinder' is a tribute not only to his artistic personality but to the perception of the connoisseurs, publishers, and theatre managers who employed him.

There was no trace of the intellectual in Whistler, yet he has been described as one of the most sensitively cultured and intelligent of men. Well built and of medium height, agile in such pursuits as dancing, skating, and ski-ing, he won a quick popularity with everyone by his warmth, his wit, his enthusiastic and persuasive conversation, his charm of manner, and the modest distinction of his bearing. He himself was not married; but children took to him instantly, and he loved them wholeheartedly, spending hours making drawings for their entertainment. A self-portrait in oils is in the Tate Gallery; others are in the possession of Mr. Laurence Whistler. A small full-length figure of himself is also included in his mural decoration at Plâs Newydd.

[*The Times*, 28 and 31 July, 7 August, and 23 September 1944; Laurence Whistler, *Rex Whistler, 1905–1944: His Life and His Drawings*, 1948.] HERBERT B. GRIMSDITCH.

WHITE, SIR WILLIAM HALE- (1857–1949), physician. [See HALE-WHITE.]

WHITEHEAD, ALFRED NORTH (1861–1947), mathematician and philosopher, was born at Ramsgate 15 February 1861, the son of the Rev. Alfred Whitehead, at that time headmaster of a private school in Ramsgate, and later vicar of St. Peter's, Isle of Thanet, and honorary canon of Canterbury, by his wife, Maria Sarah Buckmaster. His elder brother, Henry, became ultimately bishop of Madras.

At Sherborne School, Whitehead won the Digby prize for mathematics and science three years in succession and in his last year was head of the school and captain of football and cricket. He proceeded in 1880 to Trinity College, Cambridge, where he was a scholar, and where he remained for the next thirty years. In the mathematical tripos of 1883 he was bracketed fourth wrangler: in 1884 he was elected a fellow of his college, and a few months afterwards was put on the staff as an assistant lecturer.

Whitehead's first considerable work was published in 1898 under the title of *A Treatise on Universal Algebra, with Applications*. Its purpose was to investigate systems of symbolic reasoning allied to ordinary algebra, such as the quaternions of Sir W. R. Hamilton [q.v.], Hermann Grassmann's calculus of extension, and symbolic logic: the latter subject was treated very fully, the system described being that devised by George Boole [q.v.] in 1854. The book was highly original, and the reputation based on it led to the election of Whitehead as F.R.S. in 1903.

Of his pupils among the scholars of Trinity during the last decade of the nineteenth century, there was one, Mr. Bertrand (subsequently Earl) Russell, who became a specially attached disciple. In 1900 Whitehead and Russell went together to Paris to attend congresses on mathematics and philosophy, and there they heard an account of the work of Giuseppe Peano of Turin, who in the years immediately preceding had invented a new ideography for use in symbolic logic. Boole had used only the ordinary algebraic symbols: but Peano introduced symbols to represent logical notions such as 'is contained in', 'the aggregate of all $x$'s such that', 'there exists', 'is a', 'the only'. Peano's ideograms represent constitutive elements of all the other notions in logic, just as the chemical atoms are the constitutive elements of all substances in chemistry; and they are capable of replacing ordinary language for the purposes of any deductive theory. Whitehead and Russell immediately saw that this ideography was vastly superior to anything previously known, and they resolved to devote themselves to its development, and in particular to attempt thereby to settle the vexed question of the foundations of mathematics. They arrived at the position that 'mathematics is a part of logic': so that a separate 'philosophy of mathematics' does not exist; this of course contradicts the Kantian doctrine that mathematical proofs depend on *a priori* forms of intuition. The investigation was published in the three colossal volumes of *Principia Mathematica* which appeared in 1910–13, and which undoubtedly form the greatest single contribution to logic that has appeared in the two thousand years since Aristotle.

While *Principia Mathematica* was Whitehead's main occupation during the first decade of the twentieth century, he wrote a remarkable paper 'On Mathematical Concepts of the Material World' which occupied sixty-one pages of the *Philosophical Transactions* of the Royal Society (1906). In this he was feeling his way to a general philosophy of nature: as the ultimate existents, he rejected particles of matter and points of space (thereby severing himself completely from classical physics), and in their stead postulated what he called *linear objective reals*, which were something like Faraday's lines of force. Some of the principles of his later philosophy first appear here.

In 1910 Whitehead resigned from Trinity College where he was now senior lecturer in mathematics, and removed to London. At first he had no teaching appointment, then in 1911–14 he was on the staff of University College, and from 1914 to 1924 he held a chair of applied mathematics in the Imperial College of Science and Technology.

There was to have been a fourth volume of the *Principia*, written chiefly by Whitehead, and treating of geometry. But he now became more and more involved in questions which really belonged to epistemology and metaphysics. The discovery of the special theory of relativity in 1904 had opened up new prospects in the philosophy of nature. In 1915–17 he published several papers of a definitely philosophical character, which were followed by two books, *An Enquiry Concerning the Principles of Natural Knowledge* (1919) and *The Concept of Nature* (1920). He now gave his adhesion definitely to the general standpoint of the process philosophies associated with the names of Bergson, Samuel Alexander [q.v.], and C. L. Morgan [q.v.] and put forward the doctrine that the ultimate components of reality are *events*. An event is never instantaneous, it always lasts over a certain (although perhaps very short) duration of time: the notions of an *instant* of time and a *point* of space were not, in his scheme, accepted as primitive, but were obtained by a limiting process which he called the 'method of extensive abstraction'.

While Whitehead was engaged in his development of process metaphysics in 1914–19, a cosmological discovery of profound philosophical importance was given to the world, namely the theory of general relativity, in which the physical phenomenon of gravitation was expressed by a curvature of space-time, varying according to the physical situation from point to point over the whole universe. Whitehead criticized it, and devised an alternative theory which he set forth in a book, *The Principle of Relativity*, in 1922; his work has not, however, won general acceptance.

In 1924 he resigned his chair at the Imperial College in order to accept a professorship in the philosophical department of Harvard University, which he occupied until his final retirement in 1937. In the session 1927–8 he returned to this country in order to deliver the Gifford lectures at Edinburgh University. These, which were published in 1929 under the title *Process and Reality, an Essay in Cosmology*, may be regarded as the definitive exposition of his mature philosophy, to which he gave the name 'Philosophy of Organism'.

In this, as in the earlier works, the beginning is made with *events*. Those events which are 'the final real things of which the world is made up' were now called 'actual entities'. Thus the category of 'actual entities' plays the same fundamental part in the philosophy of organism as the category of 'substance' plays in many older philosophies; but whereas the term 'substance' is associated with the notion of something that endures, an 'actual entity' according to Whitehead has no permanence. In order to emphasize the difference between his philosophy and the philosophies of substance, Whitehead described an actual entity not as a 'subject' but as a 'superject', a term designed to suggest its emergence *from* antecedent entities *to* itself. He accounted for the permanence that is discovered amidst the flux of events by postulating what he called 'eternal objects', which have some resemblance to the 'forms' or 'ideas' of Plato; they have a potentiality of *ingression* into the becoming of actual entities, thereby contributing definiteness of character to them. He also introduced a concept which he called 'creativity', corresponding more or less to Plato's χώρα, or Aristotle's πρώτη ὕλη, or to the 'neutral stuff' of the modern 'neutral monists'. It is an ultimate, behind all forms, without a character of its own: but particular eternal objects can infuse their own character into it, thereby constituting actual entities. Thus it is by creativity that the actual world has its character of passage into novelty. It will be seen that Whitehead's writing abounded in new words, and new senses of old words; he had indeed the conviction that ordinary speech, which, as he had shown in *Principia Mathematica*, is inadequate for the purposes of logic, is still more inadequate for the purposes of metaphysics. A new term 'prehension' signified that one actual entity grasps other actual entities into a unity. This word made it possible to express the nature of an actual entity very simply: 'The essence of an actual entity consists solely in the fact that it is a prehending thing.' The word 'concretion' or 'concrescence' is another novelty: it means that togetherness or unity that comes to exist as a result of the prehension. Every event originates as a unity of concrescent prehensions: the process of concrescence *is* Being.

Metaphysical principles, in Whitehead's view, are truths about the nature of God. His God, however, is not omnipotent, and cannot be identified with the God of the Christian religion: he is a non-temporal 'actual entity'.

In his later years, Whitehead was acknowledged as one of the greatest living philosophers, and was the recipient of many distinctions. In 1922 he was the first recipient of the James Scott prize of the Royal Society of Edinburgh; in 1925 he received the Sylvester medal of the Royal Society; and in 1930 the Butler medal of Columbia University. In 1931 he attained the honour of combining fellowship of the British Academy with fellowship of the Royal Society; and in 1945 he was appointed to the Order of Merit.

In 1890 Whitehead married Evelyn Ada Maud Rice, daughter of Captain Arthur Robert Willoughby-Wade, of the Seaforth Highlanders, and niece of the Chinese scholar and diplomat Sir T. F. Wade [q.v.]. They had one daughter and two sons, the younger of whom died in action in 1918. Whitehead died at Cambridge, Massachusetts, 30 December 1947.

[Sir Edmund Whittaker in *Obituary Notices of Fellows of the Royal Society*, No. 17, November 1948; A. N. Whitehead, *Essays in Science and Philosophy*, 1948; private information; personal knowledge.]
EDMUND T. WHITTAKER.

WHITLEY, WILLIAM THOMAS (1858–1942), historian of art, was born in Kensington 27 January 1858, son of William Whitley, dyer and cleaner, by his wife, Mary, daughter of Patrick Gilder, labourer, of Marylebone. He was educated privately and later with reluctance entered his father's business; but his ambition was to be a painter and he devoted in early life considerable time to that art, exhibiting landscapes and figure subjects at the Royal Academy and elsewhere. Later, he devoted his whole time to research in connexion with British art and artists. He was the original representative and principal writer for the article which appeared twice a week in the *Morning Post* on 'Art and Artists'. He also contributed to most of the important art periodicals, such as the *Burlington Magazine*, the *Connoisseur*, the *Studio*, and to the annual publications of the Walpole Society.

A modest and unassuming man, Whitley was an indefatigable worker, and a conscientious scholar. One of the main sources of his information was the files of eighteenth- and nineteenth-century country newspapers, and few men would have faced, as he did, the laborious task of searching through this mass of material, preserved not only in London, but in many of the towns where the artists worked. He was, however, well rewarded, and was able to explode many legends which had long been current. His chief publications were *Thomas Gainsborough* (1915), *Artists and their Friends in England, 1700–1799* (2 vols., 1928), *Art in England, 1800–1820* (1928), *Art in England, 1821–1837* (1930), *Gilbert Stuart* (1932), and *Thomas Heaphy* (1933). His books are full of amusing anecdotes and telling comments on the ideas of the time as well as records of the life and work of the artists, and are indispensable to any serious student of British painting.

In 1888 Whitley married Mary, daughter of William Alford; she was a journalist who helped him in his work. She died in 1931, leaving one son. In that year Whitley was awarded a Civil List pension for his services to the history of art. He died at Farnborough 17 November 1942.

[Private information; personal knowledge.]
MARY WOODALL.

WHITTEN BROWN, SIR ARTHUR (1886–1948), air navigator and engineer. [See BROWN.]

WHITTY, DAME MARY LOUISE (MAY) (1865–1948), actress. [See under WEBSTER, BENJAMIN.]

WILKINSON, ELLEN CICELY (1891–1947), trade-unionist and politician, was born in Chorlton upon Medlock, Manchester, 8 October 1891, the third of the four children of Richard Wilkinson, a cotton operative and insurance agent, by his wife, Ellen Wood. Richard Wilkinson, whose mother was Irish, had a keen sense of justice and a quick temper. Ellen Wood, like her mother and her daughter, was a member of the Manchester and Salford Co-operative Society. Ellen Wilkinson grew up with a sturdy Lancashire sense of economy, a deep loyalty to people and movements, a hatred of injustice, coupled with a liveliness of temperament amounting at times to impishness, and a gift for cajolery. It may well be that from her father she also inherited the tendencies to the asthma and bronchitis which eventually killed her.

Educated at elementary and secondary schools in Manchester, Ellen Wilkinson in 1910 won the Jones history entrance scholarship to the university, where in 1913 she was placed in the second class of the honours list in history. In 1946 she received from the university the honorary degree of LL.D.

In 1913 Ellen Wilkinson became an organizer of the National Union of Women's Suffrage Societies in Manchester. In 1915 she was appointed a national woman organizer for the Amalgamated Union of Co-operative Employees (later the Union of Shop, Distributive and Allied Workers). From 1919 until 1925 she represented the union on four trade boards, and her work, particularly on behalf of the laundry workers, had a very rich effect on the policy of the union. In 1912 she joined the Independent Labour Party and proved herself a confident, effective speaker, and a vivid, fluent writer. She joined the Communist Party on its formation in Great Britain in 1920, was elected to her union's panel of parliamentary candidates, and while still a member of the Communist Party stood unsuccessfully in 1923 as official Labour candidate for Ashton-under-Lyne. In that year she was elected a member of the Manchester city council and remained a member until 1926. In 1924 she resigned from the Communist Party, although remaining very left-wing in her outlook, and became Labour member for Middlesbrough East, a seat which she held until 1931. In 1929 she became parliamentary private secretary to Susan Lawrence [q.v.] who was parliamentary secretary at the Ministry of Health.

As a Communist Ellen Wilkinson visited Russia in 1921, and in the same decade she visited most of the Labour and Socialist parties in Europe. During the general strike of 1926 she worked energetically on behalf of the miners and went to the United States to collect funds for their dependants. From 1931 to 1935 she was out of Parliament, but her trade-union work continued, and she wrote, agitated, and was prominent in debate in the Labour Party executive and conferences. In 1932 she visited India at the head of a delegation from the India League, and she again visited America. She spoke at the last democratic election in Germany before Hitler came to power, realized the growing menace of Nazism, and did much to help German refugees. She also published a number of books: *Clash* (1929), *Peeps at Politicians* (1930), *Division Bell Mystery* (1932), and *Why Fascism?* (with Edward Conze, 1934).

In 1935 Ellen Wilkinson became Labour member for Jarrow and was immediately immersed in work, both in and out of Parliament, for the depressed areas in the north-east. In 1936 she led the march of the workers of Jarrow to London, herself walking the greater part of the way. Three years later she wrote Jarrow's story in her most important book, *The Town that was Murdered*. The year 1937 found her fighting passionately against the policy of 'non-intervention' in Spain. Her visits to that country were the foundation of her influence on this issue in Great Britain—in universities, the Labour Party, and throughout the country. In 1938, stirred by the abuses of the hire-purchase system, she carried the hire purchase bill through the House of Commons with the support of all parties.

At the outbreak of war in 1939 Ellen Wilkinson at last found herself completely in line with official Labour Party policy, and she subsequently supported the coalition Government of 1940. In that year she became parliamentary secretary to the Ministry of Pensions and then to the Ministry of Home Security. Her experience in fighting Communism within her union, once she had realized where its policy was leading, was of great value to her in counteracting Communist attempts to sow disaffection in the air-raid shelters. As usual she had to be in the heat of the battle, and she spent days and nights in the shelters when conditions were at their worst. Her administrative ability was growing, and she used it to the utmost in playing a full part in the reorganization of civil defence and the fire service. During this period she had a succession of accidents but she refused to allow them to interrupt her work.

In 1945 she went to San Francisco for the preliminary meetings of the United Nations, and when the Labour Party came into office she was appointed minister of education with Cabinet rank, and was sworn of the Privy Council. Her last great battle was fought and won to ensure that the Education Act of 1944 would be implemented. When at last she held a position in which her talents, courage, and conviction would seem, through her war-time experience in office, about to mature into statesmanship, she died, worn out, in London 6 February 1947.

Ellen Wilkinson was small in stature, and this, with her vivid colouring, seemed to add to the force of her personality, both on the platform and in private discussion. Her intense loyalty to people, her integrity, directness, courage, and the strength of her emotions gave her a great influence. But the effect of her work, felt in her trade union, the House of Commons, the Labour Party, and amongst countless people in many parts of the world, was rather the sum of a long series of isolated efforts than the working out of any sustained policy. Her political speeches were based primarily on personal emotion not unassisted by platform art and sheer vitality. She was stirred by individual events and by her love of people. If she heard of oppression, wherever it might be, she had to go and see for herself, and take action. She was a tough and hard fighter who always won the respect of her opponent.

In many ways she remained a child, loving fun, and making mystery and excitement of simple events. Although she loved beautiful things she was not extravagant in the use of money. The warmth and vitality of her personality will remain long in the memory of the women of Jarrow to whose dull existence she brought colour and renewed hope. A portrait of Ellen Wilkinson by Norman Hepple is in the possession of the family.

[*The Times*, 7 February 1947; private information; personal knowledge.]

DOROTHY M. ELLIOTT.

WILLCOX, SIR WILLIAM HENRY (1870–1941), physician and toxicologist, was born at Thorpe End, Melton Mowbray, 18 January 1870, the son of William Willcox, master draper, and his wife, Mary Elizabeth Barnes. He was educated at Wymondham Grammar School, Oakham, at the Wyggeston School, Leicester, and at University College, London. After taking the degree of B.Sc. at London University in 1892, he was for a short time a science master in a boys' school. In 1895 he entered St. Mary's Hospital medical school with a scholarship, and he qualified as L.S.A. (1899), M.B. (London, 1900, winning a gold medal), D.P.H. (1900), and M.D. (1901). At St. Mary's he was awarded the Cheadle gold medal and a scholarship in forensic medicine, and was lecturer on chemical pathology (1900–30), medical registrar (1904–6), lecturer on forensic medicine (1906–35), physician to out-patients (1907–13), and physician (1913–35). He was admitted F.I.C. (1901), M.R.C.P. (London, 1905), and F.R.C.P. (1910).

Willcox's connexion with St. Mary's Hospital—the home of modern forensic medicine—his double qualification as a medical man and as a chemist, and his temperament fitted him admirably for the role of medico-legal expert. He was junior analyst to the Home Office (1904–8), senior analyst (1908–19), and medical adviser from 1919 until his death. One of his most brilliant achievements was the identification of hyoscine in the Crippen case (1910). In this and in other famous cases he was associated with (Sir) Bernard Spilsbury [q.v.]. His work in the Seddon case (1912), the first in which the Marsh-Berzelius test for arsenic was applied quantitatively for forensic purposes, also made history. He gave evidence for the Crown at the trials of Smith (the 'Brides in the Bath' case, 1915), and Armstrong (1922). He was described as the most deliberate and painstaking expert witness who ever stepped into the box; his testimony was rarely shaken.

In the war of 1914–18 he served in Gallipoli and Mesopotamia as consulting physician to the forces, and his work was said by Sir Stanley Maude [q.v.] to be equal to two divisions. After the war he devoted more time to clinical medicine and built up a large consulting practice. In addition to his work at St. Mary's Hospital he was senior physician to the London Fever Hospital and to St. Luke's Hostel for the Clergy. He took a special interest in the rheumatic diseases and gave untiring assistance to the Empire

Rheumatism Council. Industrial toxicology also engaged his attention and the results of his war-time studies of cases of poisoning in munition workers and those engaged in the manufacture of aeroplanes were summarized in his Lettsomian (1919) and Lumleian (1931) lectures. He was for many years visitor for the Privy Council to the examinations of the Pharmaceutical Society of Great Britain. He was president of the Harveian Society (1922), West London Medico-Chirurgical Society (1923), Society for the Study of Inebriety (1924–7), Medico-Legal Society (1928–9), Medical Society of London (1936–7), and the section of pharmacology and therapeutics of the Royal Society of Medicine (1940–41). In 1932 he was president of the section of forensic medicine of the British Medical Association and in 1935, when the Association's annual meeting was held at Melbourne, he was president of the section of pharmacology, therapeutics, and anaesthetics. On that occasion the university of Melbourne conferred on him the honorary degree of M.D. He was master of the Society of Apothecaries in 1935–6.

Willcox was a physician of wide interests and exceptional industry. The fact that he was often working at his desk long after midnight did not prevent him from riding in the park before breakfast. He took a great interest in the Royal Academy of Dancing and did much to further its interests, particularly on the educational side. He was appointed C.M.G. (1916), C.B. (1917), and K.C.I.E. (1921). He was a knight of grace of the Order of St. John of Jerusalem. In 1901 he married Mildred (died 1953), daughter of W. Griffin, of Clapton, Northamptonshire; there were three sons and one daughter of the marriage. He died at his house in Welbeck Street, London, 8 July 1941.

[*The Times*, 9 July 1941; *St. Mary's Hospital Gazette*, vol. xlvii, 1941; *British Medical Journal* and *Lancet*, 19 July 1941; D. G. Browne and E. V. Tullett, *Bernard Spilsbury*, 1951; Sir Arnold Wilson, *Loyalties —Mesopotamia, 1914–17*, 1930.]

W. J. BISHOP.

WILLIAMS, (ARTHUR FREDERIC) BASIL (1867–1950), historian, was born in London 4 April 1867, the only son of Frederick George Adolphus Williams, barrister-at-law, and his wife, Mary Katharine Lemon. Although born a Londoner, he attached great importance to his Somerset ancestry, and occupied his old age with genealogical researches. He was educated at Marlborough and New College, Oxford, where he was a scholar and was placed in the first class in classical moderations (1888) and the second class in *literae humaniores* (1890). He obtained a clerkship in the House of Commons where it was his duty to attend the parliamentary committee of inquiry into the responsibility for the Jameson raid; the appearance of Cecil Rhodes [q.v.] made a deep impression on him, and perhaps this accounts for his decision, many years later, to write Rhodes's biography. Williams volunteered for service in the South African war, and spent a year's campaign in the same unit with Erskine Childers [q.v.]. The friendship thus confirmed meant much to him later: he co-operated with Childers in attempts to work out a solution of the Home Rule question, wrote a memoir of him after his execution in 1922, and also contributed a notice of him to this DICTIONARY.

After a brief return to England, Williams went out again to South Africa as a civilian, and put his services at the disposal of Lord Milner [q.v.]. He assisted Lionel Curtis, then town clerk at Johannesburg, and worked later in the education department. He frequently insisted that these military and administrative experiences proved valuable to him in his career as an historian, to which he now gave himself in earnest after his second return to England.

He had already chosen the eighteenth century as his field of study, and had distinguished himself by a series of articles on Sir Robert Walpole's foreign policy in the *English Historical Review* (1900–1). Much of his best work was biographical at least in form: his lives of William Pitt, Earl of Chatham (1913), and Stanhope (1932) are likely to remain for a long time the most satisfactory treatment of their subjects. His later book on *Carteret and Newcastle* (1943) is similar though less exhaustive and less well balanced. He also wrote a general work on British history under the early Hanoverians, with the title *The Whig Supremacy 1714–60* (1939). All these books were written from a British point of view, with a certain unaffected patriotism, but showed remarkable comprehension of the relation between Great Britain and Europe. At the same time he did not lose sight of South Africa which became for him a secondary sphere of historical interest; in 1921 he published his life of Cecil Rhodes and as late as 1946 he brought out a little book on *Botha, Smuts and South Africa*.

In the earlier part of his career as an historian, Williams had no professional post, but lived on his private income. At one time he thought of a political career, and stood for Parliament twice unsuccessfully as a Liberal in 1910. In the war of 1914–18 he served as an education officer in the Royal Field Artillery and in 1919 was appointed O.B.E. for his services. He was Kingsford professor of history at McGill University (1921–5), and then held the chair of history at Edinburgh until 1937 when he retired under the age limit. He was elected F.B.A. in 1935. He died at Chelsea 5 January 1950.

In 1905 Williams married Dorothy (died 1948), daughter of Francis William Caulfeild, a descendant of William Caulfeild, first Viscount Charlemont [q.v.]. There were two sons of the marriage.

[Williams's unpublished 'Family Memoir' written in 1939; Richard Pares in *Proceedings of the British Academy*, vol. xxxvi, 1950; private information; personal knowledge.]

RICHARD PARES.

WILLIAMS, CHARLES WALTER STANSBY (1886–1945), author and scholar, was born in London 20 September 1886, the only son of Richard Walter Stansby Williams, clerk, of Islington, by his wife, Mary, daughter of Thomas Wall, cabinet-maker, of London. He was educated at St. Albans School and at University College, London. In 1908 Williams joined the Oxford University Press as a reader, and remained a member of the staff, increasingly valued and much beloved, until his death. His duties, however, as literary adviser in a publisher's office, although carried out with enthusiasm and wisdom, occupied a relatively small place in his life. In 1912 he published his first book of verse, *The Silver Stair*, and, for the next thirty-three years, wrote, lectured, and conversed with a tireless and brilliant energy. In that time he produced, apart from anthologies, a number of prefaces and a rarely interrupted series of reviews, over thirty volumes of poetry, plays, literary criticism, fiction, biography, and theological argument.

Williams was an unswerving and devoted member of the Church of England with a refreshing tolerance for the scep-

ticism of others, and a firm belief in the necessity of a 'doubting Thomas' in any apostolic body. More and more in his writings he devoted himself to the propagation and elaboration of two main doctrines—romantic love, and the co-inherence of all human creatures. These themes formed the substance of all his later volumes, and found their fullest expression in the novels (which he described as 'psychological thrillers'), in his Arthurian poems, and in many books of literary and theological exegesis. His early verse was written in traditional form, but this he later abandoned in favour of a stressed prosody built upon a framework of loosely organized interior rhymes.

Many of Williams's contemporaries found him difficult and obscure. Although the charge angered him, it was not altogether unjustified, for he used the word 'romantic' in a sense that was highly personal and never fully defined. Its basis in his mind was Wordsworth's 'feeling intellect', and what he chiefly meant by it was the exploratory action of the mind working on the primary impact of an emotional experience. It was his view that the romantic approach could reveal objective truth, and this conviction, at variance with the normal implication of the word, led to much misunderstanding and doubt among his readers. In order to be fully equipped for the task of following the thought of any one of his volumes, it was not only necessary to have read the majority of its fellows, but to have spent many talkative hours in his company. The art of conversation and the craft of lecturing were his two most brilliant, provocative, and fruitful methods of communication. His influence on the minds of the young was salutary and inspiring, for he set his face against all vagueness of thought and pretentiousness of expression, and insisted, in all matters of literary commentary, upon a close and first-hand study of the texts. His favourite words of tutorial criticism were—'but that's not what he *says*'. The honorary degree of M.A. bestowed upon him by the university of Oxford in 1943 was a well-deserved recognition of two successive courses of lectures which brought brilliance and a climate of intellectual excitement into the atmosphere of Oxford in wartime.

About the relative importance of Williams's many books opinion must always differ. It is safe to say that the fullest expression of his mature views is to be found in criticism in *The English Poetic Mind* (1932), *Reason and Beauty in the Poetic Mind* (1933), and *The Figure of Beatrice* (1943): in poetry and drama in *Taliessin through Logres* (1938), *The Region of the Summer Stars* (1944), and *Thomas Cranmer of Canterbury* (the Canterbury Festival play for 1936): and in theology in *He Came Down from Heaven* (1938) and *The Descent of the Dove* (1939). Among his biographical works the most notable are *Bacon* (1933), *James I* (1934), *Rochester* (1935), and *Queen Elizabeth* (1936); and among his novels *War in Heaven* (1930), *The Place of the Lion* (1931), *Many Dimensions* (1931), *Descent into Hell* (1937), and *All Hallows' Eve* (1945).

In 1917 Williams married Florence, youngest daughter of James Edward Worrall Conway, ironmonger, of St. Albans, and had one son. He died at Oxford 15 May 1945.

[C. S. Lewis, Preface to *Essays presented to Charles Williams*, 1947; private information; personal knowledge.]

G. W. S. HOPKINS.

WILLIAMS, SIR JOHN FISCHER (1870–1947), international lawyer, was born in London 26 February 1870, the only son of John Williams, a member of a firm trading in China, by his wife, Augusta Elizabeth, daughter of Maximilian Fischer, of Liverpool and later of Macao, China. He was educated at Harrow and, when only sixteen, was elected to a scholarship at New College, Oxford, but being too young to matriculate spent a year on the continent studying modern languages. He was placed in the first class in *literae humaniores* and elected a fellow of his college in 1892, and was awarded the Arnold essay prize in 1893. He then read for the bar in the chambers of (Sir) Henry Studdy Theobald, and was called by Lincoln's Inn in 1894. He practised for some years at the Chancery bar and took silk in 1921. He unsuccessfully contested Oxford City as a Liberal at the general election of December 1910, and, although he did not again seek to enter Parliament, he remained a staunch Liberal throughout his life. He was a strong believer in proportional representation and for many years was treasurer of the Proportional Representation Society.

During the war of 1914–18 Williams served in the aliens branch of the Home Office, and it was at this time that he began to be specially interested in inter-national law. From 1920 to 1930 he was legal adviser to the British delegation on the Reparation Commission set up in Paris by the Treaty of Versailles, and he represented the delegation in several arbitrations which took place at The Hague between the Commission and the German Government under the Dawes plan in 1926 and the years following.

After his retirement in 1930 Williams settled in Oxford and was employed by the Foreign Office on commissions and conferences. He took part as counsel or as arbitrator in several international arbitrations, and in 1936 he was made a member of the British panel on the Permanent Court of Arbitration at The Hague. He also acted as chairman of the Royal Commission on tithe, the report of which led to the passing of the Tithe Act, 1936. Besides this public work he devoted himself by lecturing and writing to promoting the study of international law, and he collaborated actively in the work of the Institut de Droit International to which he had been elected in 1929. Most of his published work consisted of monographs and articles in learned journals and a number of these were collected in his *Chapters on Current International Law and the League of Nations* (1929). All his work combined the clearness and the realism of a first-class legal mind with the forward-looking outlook of the idealist. His last years were saddened by the failure of the League, from which he had hoped much, and by the outbreak of war in 1939.

In person Williams was tall and handsome, in manner invariably courteous, modest in his estimate of his own work and generous in his appreciation of others. He was twice married: first, in 1896 to Florence, daughter of Richard Keown-Boyd, by whom he had one daughter; the marriage was dissolved; in 1911 he married Eleanor Marjorie, daughter of Robert Evelyn Hay Murray, of Hascombe, Surrey, by whom he had four daughters, one of whom, Jenifer, married in 1941 Mr. H. L. A. Hart who became in 1952 professor of jurisprudence at Oxford. Fischer Williams was appointed C.B.E. in 1917 and knighted in 1923. He died in Oxford 17 May 1947.

[Private information; personal knowledge.]
J. L. BRIERLY.

WILLIAMS, NORMAN POWELL (1883–1943), divine, was born at Durham 5 September 1883, the eldest son of the

Rev. Thomas Powell Williams, for many years vicar of St. Mary's church, Tyne Dock, South Shields, by his wife and first cousin, Jane, daughter of Edward Williams, farmer, of Radnorshire. Williams, who was the third of six children but the only one to survive, was educated at the Royal Grammar School, Newcastle upon Tyne, and Durham School and in 1902 he was elected scholar of Christ Church, Oxford. After taking a first class in honour moderations (1904) and in *literae humaniores* (1906) he held a prize fellowship at Magdalen College from 1906 to 1909, and during part of that time studied at the universities of Strasbourg and Berlin where he made the acquaintance of Harnack and Dr. Albert Schweitzer. He was ordained deacon in 1908, on the title of his Magdalen fellowship; and priest in 1909, having in the meantime been elected chaplain fellow of Exeter College.

Williams was a brilliant tutor and lecturer, and was fortunate in having some able pupils, among whom were Geoffrey Francis Fisher (later archbishop of Canterbury) and (the Rev.) Philip Thomas Byard Clayton. His initial discourse to a new pupil is summarized in his chapter 'What is Theology?' in the book *The Study of Theology* (1939), edited by Kenneth Escott Kirk, bishop of Oxford. During the war Williams held three appointments as schoolmaster, at Eton (1916–17), Malvern (1917), and the Royal Naval College, Dartmouth (1918–19).

Williams was Bampton lecturer for 1924, taking as his subject *The Ideas of the Fall and of Original Sin*. These lectures rank among the most important of the series. The historical part, which occupies the first six lectures, is a contribution of permanent value, but the last two lectures in which he turned from history to reconstruction, and in which he made great use of the new study of psychology, have won less approval. These lectures formed the thesis with which Williams took the degree of doctor of divinity, and in the year in which they were published (1927) he was elected to the Lady Margaret professorship of divinity with a canonry of Christ Church.

Williams devoted much of his time to the improvement of the services and furniture of the cathedral. He was made treasurer of the chapter, and for the last four years of his life was sub-dean. He was also active in regard to the affairs of the Church at large, being intimately concerned with the establishment of communion between the Church of England and the Old Catholic Churches in 1932, and with the work of the Westminster Group and the Church Self-Government League. He was one of the first two proctors for Oxford University in the Convocation of Canterbury (1936).

Theologically Williams belonged to what is sometimes called the Liberal Catholic school in the Church of England. In his early life he engaged in some controversy in defence of the traditional belief in the Resurrection and in defence of the use of the Athanasian creed. Throughout his life he was particularly concerned with the problem of authority in matters of belief and in public worship. His principal writings in this connexion were: *Form and Content in the Christian Tradition*, a correspondence with William Sanday [q.v.], published in 1916; an article 'Tradition' in Hastings's *Encyclopaedia of Religion and Ethics*; and 'The Theology of the Catholic Revival' in *Northern Catholicism* (edited by him in conjunction with Charles Harris in 1933). At the time of his death he was engaged upon a commentary on the Epistle to the Romans.

In manner Williams generally appeared cold and reserved. He was shy and did not make friends easily, while his concise and emphatic manner of speech, combined with a certain impatience of stupid people, made approach to him difficult. In his sermons he was able to give expression more easily to his feelings. He was a most eloquent preacher, admirably lucid, impressive, and stimulating. His writings are marked by an equal lucidity and great power of logic.

In 1927 Williams married Muriel de Lérisson, daughter of Arthur Philip Cazenove, stockbroker. They had two sons, and three daughters of whom the youngest died in infancy. Williams died at Christ Church 11 May 1943.

[E. W. Kemp, *N. P. Williams*, 1954; *The Times*, 12 and 14 May 1943; private information; personal knowledge.]    E. W. KEMP.

**WILLIAMS-FREEMAN, JOHN PEERE** (1858–1943), archaeologist, was born at Hamble Cliff near Southampton 13 April 1858, the youngest son of Frederick Peere Williams-Freeman, of Greatham, Sussex, by his wife, Augusta Sarah, daughter of Captain Henry Edward Napier, R.N., F.R.S. [q.v.]. He was educated at Haileybury and at the Royal Military Academy, Woolwich (1876–8). He obtained a commission in the Royal Artillery, but resigned it soon afterwards for family reasons and studied medicine, first in London at University College Hospital and then at Durham University, taking the degree of M.B. in 1885 and M.D. in 1888. From 1889 until 1928 he practised at Weyhill, Hampshire, holding besides several clinical appointments. On retirement he went to live at Botley, Hampshire, but eventually returned to his former region, living at Thruxton.

Although of no mean standing in the medical profession, it was as an archaeologist that he earned his chief claims to recognition. From youth onwards his interests were widespread, and he was a clear and original thinker and an accurate observer. In 1901 he met Percy Farrer, a near neighbour, who stimulated his growing interest in the prehistoric earthworks around. Other contacts followed and in 1915 he published his book *Field Archaeology as illustrated by Hampshire*, a model of its kind. It was the first book to attempt to set prehistoric man in his original natural environment of vegetation, a method now become part of the normal procedure. He did no excavation but was first and foremost a field-archaeologist, having himself invented that term. In the course of his practice he was able to observe the countryside and its natural features. He noted the reaction of the crops to silted-up prehistoric ditches and the like, and realized, before air-photography, how informative air-photographs would be to the prehistorian. He often discussed these matters with O. G. S. Crawford, and when eventually chance put before him a set of air-photographs of his own region, he showed them to the latter to whom it fell to develop an important new technique. Williams-Freeman was essentially an alert-minded countryman, bringing to bear upon archaeology a good brain well disciplined by professional training. Although one of the last and best of the amateur, that is, part-time, archaeologists of the nineteenth century, he belonged rather to the twentieth in his methods and outlook, which were those of modern professional archaeologists.

In 1897 Williams-Freeman married his cousin, Mabel Christiana, daughter of Charles George Napier; they had one son and five daughters, the son and one daughter dying in infancy. Williams-

Freeman died at Thruxton 20 December 1943.

[*Proceedings* of the Hampshire Field Club and Archaeological Society, 1944; *Burke's Landed Gentry*, 1952; personal knowledge.]

O. G. S. Crawford.

WILLINGDON, first Marquess of (1866–1941), governor-general of Canada and viceroy of India. [See Freeman-Thomas, Freeman.]

WILSON, Sir GERALD HUGH TYRWHITT-, fifth baronet, and fourteenth Baron Berners (1883–1950), musician, artist, and author. [See Tyrwhitt-Wilson.]

WILSON, Sir SAMUEL HERBERT (1873–1950), colonial administrator, was born in Dublin 31 October 1873, the third son of James Wilson, LL.D., barrister-at-law, and his wife, Elizabeth, daughter of Joseph Holmes, landowner, of county Sligo. Wilson was educated privately and at the Royal Military Academy, Woolwich, from which he passed into the Royal Engineers in 1893. As a subaltern he saw active service in the South African war until the middle of 1900 when a severe attack of enteric fever brought him home. He received his captaincy in 1904 and two years later was posted to the general staff at the War Office, where he served until 1910.

The turning-point of his career was his appointment in 1911 as assistant secretary of the Committee of Imperial Defence and secretary of the Oversea Defence Committee. During the war of 1914–18 he served with the general staff on the western front, earning promotion to the rank of brigadier-general, the C.B., seven mentions in dispatches, and several foreign decorations; but at the end of the war he returned to his committee work and continued with it until 1921. In this work he was brought into close contact with government departments, especially the Colonial Office, and gained an insight into imperial and world affairs and into the working of the government machine.

In 1921 Wilson accepted the governorship of Trinidad and Tobago, and three years later he was appointed captain-general and governor-in-chief of Jamaica. In 1925 he returned to London as permanent under-secretary of state at the Colonial Office. Until that year, the Colonial Office had dealt with the affairs of all parts of the British Empire overseas except those handled in the India Office. After the war it became increasingly clear that a single government department could not satisfactorily combine the conduct of what were essentially diplomatic relations with the self-governing Dominions, and the direct administration of dependent territories. Accordingly, in 1925 the Dominions Office was formally separated from the Colonial Office, although the two secretaryships of state were held by a single minister until 1930.

The choice of Wilson as the first permanent head of the separate Colonial Office—a post which he held until his retirement in 1933—was due to the conviction of the secretary of state, L. S. Amery, that it was urgently necessary to bring the ministers and civil servants of the London office into closer relationship and sympathy with the 'men on the spot'. Wilson was considered to be particularly suited for this task both by personality and by reason of his special combination of experience at home and overseas.

The period of his administration (in the course of which he paid short official visits to Africa and Malaya) was marked by several important developments. Two conferences of colonial governors were held (1927, 1930). A policy of unification of the Colonial Service was adopted and a personnel division established in the Colonial Office (1930). The internal organization of the Office, which had previously been arranged almost entirely on a geographical basis, was remodelled and expanded so as to provide for the handling on a subject basis of matters relating to the colonial territories as a whole. A regular scheme was instituted for the interchange of administrative staff between the Office and the Colonies. A system of expert advisory services covering a wide field was built up to help the Office and the colonial Governments in dealing with the growing complexity of their work.

To accomplish these measures, breaking away as they did from established tradition, called for a combination of good humour, patience, and firmness which Wilson was well qualified to exhibit. The essence of his character was single-mindedness. He knew what he wanted; and although he was not always able to formulate his aims with civil service precision or to support them by argument in such terms as to secure their immediate acceptance by some colleagues possessed of more subtle minds and greater intellectual brilliance, yet his simplicity, sincerity, and modesty gained him the respect and affection even of those who did not wholly sympathize with his reforms. He had the good military commander's quality of being content to outline his general objective and of trusting his subordinates to find out the best way of executing his policy in detail. He preferred the practical and empirical to the academic approach, the spoken to the written word, the enthusiasm of youth to the caution of seniority. His manner and appearance were those of the soldier rather than of the civil servant.

His advice and influence did much to establish a new conception of colonial administration and development as a combined operation, in which the Colonial Office at the centre and the Colonial Service in the oversea territories should work together in genuine partnership, and thus to promote the remarkable economic, political, and social advance of the colonial territories in the two decades which followed his retirement.

Wilson was appointed C.M.G. (1914), K.C.M.G. (1923), G.C.M.G. (1929), C.B. (1918), K.C.B. (1927), and K.B.E. (1921). He died in London, after having been for some time in failing health, 5 August 1950. He married in 1902 Marie Ida Gabarino, daughter of Francis Henry Alexander Theodore Gervers, a London diamond merchant of Dutch origin. There was one son, who was killed on active service in 1943, and one daughter. A portrait of Wilson (1920) by John St. Helier Lander is in the possession of the family.

[The Times, 7 August 1950; official records; private information; personal knowledge.]

CHARLES JEFFRIES.

WINGATE, ORDE CHARLES (1903–1944), major-general, was born at Naini Tal, India, 26 February 1903, the third child and eldest son in a family of seven. Both the Bible and the sword were strongly in the family tradition, as also was service in Eastern lands. His grandfather, William Wingate, who came of a Scottish family long settled in Stirlingshire, had been for ten years a missionary to the Jews in Hungary. His father, Colonel George Wingate, who served for more than thirty years in the Indian Army, taking part in three frontier expeditions, had established the Central Asian Mission to the tribes on the North-West Frontier and in Baltistan. His mother, Mary Ethel Stanley, daughter of Captain Charles Orde Browne, Royal Horse Artillery, came of a

Gloucestershire family, which had a tradition of military service but had produced also in the preceding generation a distinguished Persian scholar. Her ancestors included Granville Sharp, the philanthropist [q.v.].

Both Orde Wingate's father and mother were Plymouth Brethren, and he was brought up in a strictly puritan household, which was shown by his deep knowledge and study of the Bible. He was a day boy at Charterhouse, near which his father had settled on retirement. He went on to the Royal Military Academy, Woolwich, and was gazetted to a commission in the Royal Artillery in August 1923. As a boy Wingate had shown proficiency in swimming, boxing, and rifle-shooting rather than in organized games. He was keenly interested in observation of wild birds and beasts, and was fond of music. On joining his battery he became an enthusiastic horseman, riding boldly and well to hounds, and competing with success in point-to-point races and show-jumping. In 1926 he qualified as an instructor in equitation at the army school at Weedon, an exacting test of horsemanship. But he kept his brain active as well as his body, and with the encouragement of his father's cousin, General Sir Reginald Wingate, he began to learn Arabic at the School of Oriental Studies in London. In the autumn of 1927 he went to the Sudan to continue his study of that language. His method of reaching the Sudan was typical. He had practically no means except his pay. He had financed his hunting by his success at races and horse-shows. He now bought a pedal bicycle, rode it to Brindisi, where he sold it and with the proceeds took passage in an Italian boat to Port Sudan. He obtained an appointment in the Sudan Defence Force, in which he spent five years (1928–33) serving mainly on the Abyssinian frontier.

Wingate next made an expedition in the Libyan desert in search of the legendary oasis of Zerzura. He spent five weeks in the desert from the beginning of February 1933 until early in March. Exploration of the desert by motor-car was just beginning at this period, but Wingate went on foot, with camels to carry his gear. His journey produced no results but gave him valuable experience.

During the voyage home Wingate met his future wife, Lorna Elizabeth Margaret, daughter of Walter Moncrieff Paterson, of Tilliefoure, Monymusk, Aberdeenshire, whom he married in January 1935. From 1933 to 1936 he served with artillery units in England. Towards the end of 1936 he applied for and obtained a post on the intelligence staff in Palestine, then in the throes of an Arab rebellion against Jewish immigration. Influenced by the family tradition, Wingate soon became sympathetic to the Jewish cause and he was impressed by the organization and efficiency of the Jewish settlements. He spent his spare time and leave in visiting these settlements and in learning Hebrew, and became a convinced Zionist. He and his wife became friends of the Jewish leader, Chaim Weizmann. The rebellion dragged on; and presently Wingate obtained permission to organize night squads, mainly of youths from the Jewish settlements, to combat Arab sabotage and terrorism. He showed that such work could be more efficiently carried out by local teams than by the orthodox procedure of regular soldiers. The work was exacting and dangerous but productive of results. Wingate's methods had great success and did much to bring the rebellion to an end. He was appointed to the D.S.O. for his services and was wounded in a skirmish in July 1938. His pro-Jewish sympathies and his uncompromising way of expressing his opinions were not always acceptable to some of his superiors and led to controversy with them. Wingate was never an easy subordinate.

The outbreak of war in 1939 found Wingate serving as a brigade-major with an anti-aircraft unit. He was about to attend a course at the Camberley Staff College in 1940, when he was summoned to the Middle East. Sir Archibald (later Earl) Wavell [q.v.], under whom he had served for some months in Palestine, had asked for him to organize assistance to the rebels in Abyssinia, as a means of embarrassing the Italians, who had now entered the war. Wingate arrived in Khartoum in the late autumn of 1940. He set to work with restless energy and driving power to collect troops, arms, and camels to make an entry into central Abyssinia. One of his first acts was to fly in at great risk to an improvised landing ground and to contact Colonel Daniel Arthur Sandford (a British officer with a long knowledge of Abyssinia who had gone in previously on foot) and some of the principal rebels. In January 1941 Wingate crossed the frontier with the exiled Emperor Haile Selassie, a small mixed force of Sudanese and Ethiopians, and a handful of British officers and N.C.O.s,

Less than four months later, on 5 May 1941, he entered Addis Ababa with the Emperor. By a combination of daring and bluff his small force of under 2,000 men had made its way through the rough mountains of western Abyssinia, capturing or putting to flight many Italian garrisons which greatly outnumbered the force. It was a remarkable achievement, the strain of which told on even Wingate's iron nerve and constitution; and he was in hospital in Cairo for some months.

On recovery, Wingate returned home but was soon recalled East again by Wavell, now commander-in-chief in India, to help in stemming the Japanese invasion of Burma. When Wingate arrived the retreat from Burma had been ordered. There was just time before the complete withdrawal for him to visit the front. He quickly grasped the lie of the country and the enemy's tactics and mentality. He put forward proposals for the formation and training of a 'long range penetration group' to operate behind the Japanese lines in the reconquest of Burma. His theory was based on two new factors in war: the power to supply forces for a long period by air, and the use of portable wireless sets to maintain touch between scattered columns. Wingate's ideas were accepted, and in June 1942 he was made a brigadier and given a mixed force of British, Gurkha, and Burmese (Karens, Kachins, and Chins) to organize and train. His preparations were complete by February 1943; and about the middle of that month his eight columns crossed the Chindwin river and struck against the Japanese rear. For some six weeks the force moved and fought behind the enemy front; and although in the end some of the columns had great difficulty in extricating themselves and returning to the base, Wingate's theories had fully justified themselves. He had received a bar to his D.S.O. for his work in Abyssinia and was now given a second bar.

In August 1943 Wingate accompanied (Sir) Winston Churchill to Quebec where he explained his theories to the war leaders, including Roosevelt and Churchill, both of whom he greatly impressed. He was given a force equivalent to a division to train for the operations for the reconquest of Burma under Admiral Lord Louis Mountbatten (later Earl Mountbatten of Burma), and was promoted major-general. The training of the new force was carried out during the winter of 1943–4, and operations began early in March 1944. A new feature of the operations was that the greater part of the force was landed behind the enemy lines by glider and transport aircraft, only one brigade entering on foot. Three weeks after the original landings Wingate's forces commanded a wide area some 200 miles inside the enemy lines. On 24 March during a tropical storm Wingate was flying over the Naga jungles of north Assam in a bomber on a visit to one of his units. From some cause never ascertained the plane crashed into the jungle and all the occupants were killed. He was buried in the Arlington cemetery, United States.

Orde Wingate was cast in the same mould as Thomas Cochrane (Earl of Dundonald), Charles George ('Chinese') Gordon, T. E. Lawrence (with whom on his mother's side he could claim kinship) [qq.v.], and others, who have had a genius for novel and unorthodox methods of warfare and the opportunity and energy to put them into practice. Such men are seldom very tractable subordinates, nor are they always easy to serve. Wingate's dynamic personality won acceptance for his ideas. At a time when Japanese tactics of infiltration had produced a feeling of helplessness in some quarters, he showed that similar tactics could be applied even more effectively and on a wider scale against the Japanese themselves. He was no haphazard marauder; his operations were always most carefully planned, his training thorough, and his administrative preparations as complete as possible. He had undoubtedly a high degree of military genius.

Apart from military affairs, Wingate had read widely and thought deeply on many subjects, on which he had very definite views. He could express himself clearly in speech or on paper. He had a strong personal faith in religion and a real belief in prayer.

Wingate had one son, born in 1944 after his father's death.

[*Geographical Journal*, vol. lxxxiii, 1934; private information; personal knowledge.]
WAVELL.

WINNINGTON-INGRAM, ARTHUR FOLEY (1858–1946), bishop of London, was born at the rectory, Stanford-on-Teme, Worcestershire, 26 January 1858, the fourth of the ten children of the rector, the Rev. Edward Winnington-Ingram, who was also lord of the manor of Ribbesford, by his wife, Maria Louisa, daughter of Henry Pepys [q.v.], bishop of Worcester. He was connected through both parents with leading county families, and possessed, as an unselfconscious inheritance, an easy approach to all sorts and conditions of people.

Winnington-Ingram was educated at Marlborough for which he retained a firm loyalty, spending a Sunday there every year. At Keble College, Oxford, he took first class honours in classical moderations (1879) and a second class in *literae humaniores* (1881). In his last years at school and at Oxford he suffered a period of doubt about the Christian faith, and he deferred his intended ordination to the ministry of the Church of England. After three years in a travelling tutorship on the continent, having been challenged by events to think more deeply and to read more widely, he recaptured intellectually the faith which he had never ceased to practise, and held it with untroubled serenity for the rest of his life. He was ordained deacon by the bishop of Lichfield (W. D. Maclagan, afterwards archbishop of York, q.v.) in 1884 and priest in the same year. After serving as assistant curate in the parish of St. Mary's, Shrewsbury, he was appointed domestic chaplain to the bishop of Lichfield and in three useful years learned method and administration under a good master. Maclagan declined to release him to Bishop Webber of Brisbane, but in 1888 the call to go to Bethnal Green as head of the Oxford House in succession to Hensley Henson [q.v.] was irresistible.

Winnington-Ingram's days in east London were the happiest, and perhaps the most fruitful, of his life. He at once understood the character of its inhabitants, and relished cockney humour. His personal magnetism and sincere evangelical zeal brought many of the best young men from Oxford to share with him in a religious and social adventure which caught the spirit of the times. A new house was opened and thirty residents joined Ingram in organizing clubs for men and boys, provident and housing schemes, and the Children's Country Holiday Fund. The day's work was mapped out for himself and his residents with a mastery of method which stood him in good stead then and afterwards. He also spent much time and thought on Christian apologetics, and was a successful speaker on Sunday afternoons in Victoria Park. Here his fairmindedness, lucid exposition, ready repartee, and fiery zeal for the Gospel won more than a hear-

ing. He did not at first attempt to build up the life of the worshipping Church in an area where, according to him, only one per cent. went to church or chapel. He made human contacts, and took every likely or unlikely opportunity to exercise his own pastoral ministry. When he became rector of Bethnal Green, however, in 1895, he quickly gathered a great congregation. By 1897, when Mandell Creighton, bishop of London [q.v.], nominated him as suffragan bishop of Stepney and canon of St. Paul's Cathedral, Ingram's work had turned the tide in Bethnal Green, and made the Church a real influence in the life of the people. At this period also he was developing his gifts as a mission preacher.

Winnington-Ingram was consecrated bishop of Stepney at St. Paul's Cathedral, on St. Andrew's Day, 30 November 1897. In addition to the personal work among the clergy and church people of his district, he began an exhausting but highly successful campaign of money-raising for the East London Church Fund. On the death of Mandell Creighton in 1901 he was appointed bishop of London, at the instance of King Edward VII. He held the see for thirty-eight years. There have been critics of Ingram's faulty or optimistic administration of his diocese. It is true that in his later years he made mistakes in ecclesiastical discipline and in his judgement of men. He once remarked that he found it difficult to say 'no', and that a bishop should be made of sterner stuff. If history does not accord greatness to him as bishop of London, he was nevertheless creative in the lives of others. He ordained no fewer than 2,205 men to the ministry, many of whom owed their vocation, under God, to him. In the early years of his episcopate he was undoubtedly among the foremost Christian leaders in the country. Although burdened with the administration of a huge and unwieldy diocese, he took every opportunity of preaching the Gospel, in the same simple and cogent terms, to rich and poor, old and young, in all parts of London, and at the universities and public schools. The most exacting part of his ministry was personal and pastoral. He gave undivided attention to all he encountered and reaped in return the grateful affection of a multitude of men and women of all conditions. Fulham Palace was a centre of constant hospitality, and if some imposed on his kindness many genuine needs were assuaged by his practical generosity and spiritual counsel.

Winnington-Ingram's intellectual equipment was solid, but dated. He gave the same answers to doubters in 1944 as he had given in 1884. He never moved from the orthodox position he had always held; nor was he ever in any sense a party man, although unmerited labels were attached to his name. He was a churchman, *tout court*, and in his prime an unrivalled preacher of the everlasting Gospel.

His capacity for work was immense; but he insisted on due recreation. A number of hobbies and interests were retained from his country upbringing—particularly fishing; he played tennis and hockey until past seventy and golf until the end of his days. He enjoyed the inestimable gift of sound health and practised a simple, frugal, nearly ascetic, way of life.

He made a number of visits to Canada and the United States. There is no doubt that his visits to Canada had a lasting effect, both in Church life and in strengthening ties of friendship between Canada and the home country. He laid the foundation stone of Victoria Cathedral in Vancouver Island in 1926. The northwestern tower, rebuilt and completed in 1953, is named after him in commemoration of his diligent work as chairman of the British Columbia and Yukon Church Aid Society. A patriot and an imperialist, he was entirely fearless, to the point of naïvety, in advocating the cause of the Allies in two world wars. As chaplain to the London Rifle Brigade he seldom missed a camp. His visits to France and Salonika in the war of 1914-18 were a marked contribution to the morale of a citizen army. He was appointed K.C.V.O. in 1915. In 1939 he resigned his see. He died at Upton-on-Severn, Worcestershire, 26 May 1946 and was buried in St. Paul's Cathedral on 7 June. He was unmarried.

There is a portrait by Sir Hubert von Herkomer at Fulham Palace and a replica at Keble College, Oxford; another by George Hall Neale is at the London Diocesan Office; a portrait head by Erica White is in her possession and a replica is in the possession of the Rev. G. E. Reindorp.

[A. F. Winnington-Ingram, *Fifty Years' Work in London, 1889-1939*, 1940; S. C. Carpenter, *Winnington-Ingram*, 1949; Percy Colson, *Life of the Bishop of London*, 1935; personal knowledge.]

CUTHBERT THICKNESSE.

WINSTANLEY, DENYS ARTHUR (1877-1947), historian, was born 5 December 1877 at 31 Woburn Square, Bloomsbury, the son of Howard Winstanley, auctioneer, by his wife, Katharine Skilbeck. He was educated at Merchant Taylors' School and went up to Trinity College, Cambridge, as a sub-sizar in 1897. He was placed in the first class of the honours list in the history tripos in 1899 and 1900, and in 1901 was Lightfoot scholar. From 1903 to 1906 he was in the north of England as a school inspector, and then returned to Trinity as fellow and lecturer. In the war of 1914-18 he did intelligence work in Egypt. In 1919 he became tutor and in 1925 senior tutor of Trinity. In 1935 he became vice-master. As lecturer and as tutor he won the affection of successive generations of undergraduates. As a teacher of history he had an extraordinary power of interesting young men in the subject, and filling them with his own enthusiasm.

The affection with which Winstanley was regarded by both dons and undergraduates was due to the entirely unselfish kindness of his disposition, his wide-ranging interest in other people (in their manners and characters rather than in their opinions or fortunes), and his shrewd insight into friends, colleagues, and pupils expressed in terms of humane and witty epigram. He was not a loud or continuous talker, but in the combination room or by his own fireside he kept the ball of conversation moving with skill, and his own incursions into the talk were the best part of it.

His historical writings fall into two groups: his studies of the politics of the early years of George III, and his histories of Cambridge University. *Personal and Party Government, 1760-6* (1910), and *Lord Chatham and the Whig Opposition* (1912) were followed by *The University of Cambridge in the Eighteenth Century* (1922), the story of the Duke of Newcastle's political exploitation of the university. That book led Winstanley on to his history of the university, the principal work of his life. It consists of a series of volumes, each with a separate title: *Unreformed Cambridge* (1935), *Early Victorian Cambridge* (1940), and *Later Victorian Cambridge* (1947), taking the story down to the new statutes of 1882, beyond which he had no intention of going. He had, in fact, completed his life's work. It is based on profound and accurate scholarship, enlightened by insight into the men of the past, Whewell and Adam Sedgwick for example, as shrewd and humorous as his insight into his own contemporaries. It is true that his wit came out more strongly in his conversation than in his writings. The history of the university must, to a large extent, be a record of institutions and statutes; but whenever there is a story to be told of personal controversy he always tells it most interestingly, most fully, and most fairly, as in the cases of the Peterhouse mastership in his first volume, Christopher Wordsworth and Thirlwall in his second, and Robinson's vote in the last volume. Happy is the university that has such an historian.

Winstanley was never married. He died in his rooms in Trinity Great Court, 20 March 1947, and was buried at Cambridge. There is a drawing of him by Francis Dodd in the library at Trinity College.

[Personal knowledge.] G. M. TREVELYAN.

WITHERS, HARTLEY (1867–1950), financial editor and author, was born at Aigburth, Liverpool, 15 July 1867, the fourth son of Henry Hartley Withers, gentleman, and his wife, Jane Livingston, daughter of Matthew Dobson Lowndes, also of Liverpool. He was educated at Westminster where he was a Queen's scholar and captain of the school, and at Christ Church, Oxford, where he was a junior student and took a first class in classical moderations (1888) and a third in *literae humaniores* (1890). For a short time he was a temporary assistant master at Clifton College, and then became a clerk in a firm of stockbrokers in the City, contributing meanwhile occasional articles to the *Pall Mall Gazette*, the *Westminster Gazette*, *The Economist* and the *Spectator*.

In 1894 Withers joined the staff of the City office of *The Times*. From 1905 to 1910 he was in charge of that office, as City editor, although Wynnard Hooper at Printing House Square retained a general responsibility for financial matters. In 1910–11 Withers was City editor of the *Morning Post*, but he then returned to the City with Seligman Brothers, the merchant bankers. During 1915–16 he was at the Treasury as director of financial inquiries, a post which created a precedent and foreshadowed the shape of things to come.

In 1916 Withers became editor of *The Economist* where he remained until 1921 when he became editor of the financial supplement of the *Saturday Review*. He held this post until 1923 after which he took no further part in active journalism.

Withers was a man with a keen mind and a sardonic sense of humour. He was intolerant of slipshod thinking, and was always zealous to verify a point of detail. He may hardly be described as a great editor. Where he made his mark was in his series of books, particularly his earlier works, of which the first, *The Meaning of Money*, was published in 1909. His great merit was that he was most readable. He could see the world's economic and financial system as a whole, and explain it in words intelligible to the ordinary man who, by reason of the war of 1914–18 and its aftermath, had perforce to seek an understanding of economic affairs. Withers's real legacy, however, was to the generation of financial journalists who came after him. How great this was may be seen by contrasting the arid, technical City article of fifty years earlier with the broad view taken by those writing at the time of his death, which took place at Colchester 21 March 1950.

Withers was twice married: first, in 1896, to the mother of a schoolfriend, Letitia, daughter of Robert James Tennent, M.P., of Rush Park, Belfast, and widow of Henry Harrison, of Holywood House, Ardkeen; and secondly, in 1921, to Alice, daughter of J. R. Elliott, by whom he had one daughter.

[*The Times*, 22 March 1950; private information; personal knowledge.]
NORMAN CRUMP.

WOOD, SIR HENRY JOSEPH (1869–1944), musical conductor, was born in London 3 March 1869, the only child of Henry Joseph Wood, an optician and model engineer who was a keen amateur 'cellist and for twenty-five years tenor soloist at St. Sepulchre's church, Holborn. His mother Martha, daughter of Evan Morris, a Welsh farmer, possessed a natural soprano voice, and it was she who awakened her son's interest in music and provided him with his early tuition. Otherwise the child was self-taught, and it is remarkable evidence of his gifts that at the age of ten he often acted as deputy organist at St. Mary Aldermanbury. It was as an organist that he first came before the public, the recitals of 'Master Henry J. Wood' being a feature of the Fisheries and Inventions exhibitions of 1883 and 1885. From 1878 until he was fifteen Wood was educated at a school in Argyll Street, where he carried off all the prizes for painting, drawing, and music. At this time painting was nearly as strong an interest as music and for some years he continued to study in his spare time at the Slade School of Fine Art and the St. John's Wood School of Art. In 1911 he gave an exhibition of fifty sketches in oil at the Piccadilly Arcade Gallery in aid of the Queen's Hall Orchestra Endowment Fund.

After a short period of private tuition from Ebenezer Prout [q.v.] and his son Louis, Wood studied for two years at the Royal Academy of Music, where his professors were W. C. Macfarren for piano, Charles Steggall for organ, Ebenezer Prout for composition, and Manuel Garcia [qq.v.] for singing. The association with Garcia determined his ambition to become a singing teacher, and he gained valuable experience by accompanying at the lessons given by Garcia and other eminent professors of the time. After leaving the Academy and during the period in which he was attempting to secure a foothold in the musical profession, Wood published a number of songs and wrote several works on a more ambitious scale, but soon realized that his vocation did not lie in composition. His ability as an accompanist and his knowledge of singing led him inevitably to the musical stage and to conducting.

His first professional experience as a conductor was gained with the Arthur Rousbey Opera Company in 1889, and in the following year he was engaged by R. D'Oyly Carte [q.v.] to superintend the rehearsals of *Ivanhoe* for Sir Arthur Sullivan [q.v.]. This led to his appointment as assistant conductor at the Savoy Theatre, and further operatic experience included a season with the Carl Rosa Opera Company in 1891, with Leslie Crotty's Georgina Burns Light Opera Company in 1892, and Signor Lago's Italian opera season later in the same year when Tchaikovsky's opera *Eugene Onegin* was produced for the first time in England on 17 October at the Olympic Theatre, London. In between these conducting engagements he continued his work both as an accompanist and teacher of singing, in partnership with Gustav Garcia in his operatic school in Berners Street.

In 1894 Wood paid a visit to the Wagner Festival at Bayreuth, and there became acquainted with Felix Mottl. This meeting resulted in his being engaged as musical adviser to Schulz-Curtius for the Wagner concerts given at the newly built Queen's Hall. The manager of the hall, Robert Newman, had decided to run a series of promenade concerts, and saw in the twenty-five-year-old conductor the ideal musical director for the series. The financial backing for the concerts was assisted by a music lover and throat specialist, George Clark Cathcart, who provided £2,000, on condition that the existing high pitch, ruinous to singers' voices, should be abandoned and the lower French pitch introduced. So came into being, in August 1895, the most remarkable and influential series of concerts in the history of British music. Newman was to be associated with them for over thirty years, Wood for fifty. Although tribute must surely be paid to the manager, the series will always be associated, and rightly so, with the name of its founder-conductor.

The direction of a nightly series of promenade concerts, taking place over a period of anything from eight to ten weeks, both established Wood's reputation and encouraged Newman to embark on an ambitious and comprehensive scheme for his new hall. In 1896 a short series of symphony concerts was inaugurated, and in the following year the schedule at Queen's Hall included promenade concerts, symphony concerts, Sunday orchestral concerts, and concerts by the Queen's Hall Choral Society. As a recognition of these achievements, Queen Victoria commanded a performance of the Queen's Hall Orchestra under Wood at Windsor Castle 24 November 1898. In 1899 came the first London Musical Festival, shared by Lamoureux with his Paris Orchestra and Wood with his Queen's Hall Orchestra, the two joining forces for the final concert.

Despite this heavy schedule of London concerts, Wood found time in the following years to train and conduct an increasing number of choral societies and orchestras in the provinces. In 1898 he accepted the post of director of the Nottingham Sacred Harmonic Society and later founded the Nottingham City Orchestra. In 1900 he was appointed conductor of the Wolverhampton Festival Choral Society, in 1902 of the Sheffield, in 1904 of the Westmorland, and in 1908 of the Norwich, festivals. Such activities could only have been undertaken by a man of phenomenal energy who possessed also the most detailed technical knowledge of his work, a man who prepared everything minutely in advance, not only for himself, but for all those with whom he was associated. A mere clockwork precision, however, was far from his ideal. Wood was one of the earliest British conductors to insist on the importance of interpretation, and his scores were invariably marked with a wealth of expressive detail. It was characteristic that when he was about to conduct Bach's B minor Mass at the Sheffield Festival of 1911, he sent each member of the choir 168 pages of notes on details of interpretation.

In 1898 Wood married his first wife, Olga, daughter of Princess Sofie Ouroussoff, of Podolia, Russia. She had been his singing pupil, and to her he owed a broadening and refining of his musical outlook and an increased interest and enthusiasm for Russian music. This artistically fruitful marriage was unhappily short. His wife died in 1909. Meanwhile a critical situation had arisen at Queen's Hall owing to the bankruptcy of Robert Newman in 1901. After some negotiation a syndicate was formed by (Sir) Edgar Speyer [q.v.] and activities were again carried on under Newman's management. This successful régime was responsible for such important musical events as the visits of Strauss, Debussy, Sibelius, and Grieg to conduct their own compositions at Queen's Hall. During this period also, Wood received international recognition, being invited in 1904 to conduct the New York Philharmonic-Symphony Orchestra, an invitation never previously extended to a British-born conductor.

Wood was knighted in 1911 and in the same year married Muriel Ellen, daughter of Major Ferdinand William Greatrex of the 1st (Royal) Dragoons, by whom he had two daughters. His provincial activities at this time had reached a peak, and included the Sheffield, Norwich, Birmingham, Wolverhampton, and Westmorland festivals, the Cardiff orchestral concerts, the Gentlemen's concerts and later Brand Lane's concerts at Manchester, the Liverpool Philharmonic, and concerts at Leicester and Hull. Meanwhile his Queen's Hall concerts continued to reflect the most important trends in contemporary music. As a single instance, Schönberg's revolutionary 'Five Orchestral Pieces' were played at a promenade concert in 1912, the year of their first world performance.

In the war years of 1914–18 Wood and Newman carried on at Queen's Hall, and when in 1915 public opinion forced Speyer to leave the country, the Queen's Hall orchestral concerts were taken over by the publishing firm of Chappell, the lessees of the hall, and the orchestra was renamed the New Queen's Hall Orchestra. Three years after the end of hostilities Wood was chosen, together with Arthur Nikisch and Gabriel Pierné, to conduct at the international festival at Zürich, and in the same year he was awarded the gold medal of the Royal Philharmonic Society. In 1926 he conducted the Handel Festival at the Crystal Palace. Two years earlier he had enlarged his important work as a teacher by taking over the orchestral classes at the Royal Academy of Music, and interesting himself in the conducting students there. It was characteristic of Wood that the dates of these classes were always the first to be entered into his bulky engagement diary, and nothing was allowed to disturb them. The debt of orchestral players to Wood is indeed immense, and all who came into contact with him admit how much he taught them. Their sobriquet 'Old Timber' was not merely a play on words, but a symbol of solid admiration and heartfelt respect.

Academic recognition of his services to the cause of music was given by Manchester University in 1924 by the conferring of an honorary D.Mus. Oxford followed suit in 1926, Cambridge in 1935, and London in 1939, and Birmingham awarded him the honorary degree of M.Mus. in 1927. In 1924 he was elected a fellow of the Royal College of Music and in 1928 he became an honorary freeman of the Worshipful Company of Musicians. He was appointed an officer of the Legion of Honour (1926) and received the Order of the Crown of Belgium (1920). Tempting offers were made from America and in 1926 Wood conducted at the Hollywood Bowl, choosing his programmes from the music of living British composers. Realizing the importance of the work still to be done in England, he had declined in 1918 the offer of an appointment for six months in every year with the Boston Symphony Orchestra.

In 1926 the death of Robert Newman severed an association which had lasted for over thirty years, and in the same year Chappells announced that they were unable to continue financing the promenade concerts. Negotiations between Wood and the British Broadcasting Corporation resulted in the Corporation's sponsoring the 1927 season, and the historic series of concerts became not only financially secure but were also broadcast for the first time. Programmes were freed from previous commercial considerations, and with the formation of the B.B.C. Symphony Orchestra in 1930 rehearsals became increasingly satisfactory. At a press interview Wood declared that he was on the threshold of realizing his lifelong ambition 'of truly democratizing the message of music and making its beneficial effect universal'.

On 5 October 1938, the occasion of his jubilee as a conductor, a concert was held at the Royal Albert Hall, the proceeds of which, together with a Jubilee Fund, were devoted to the endowment of nine beds for orchestral musicians in London hospitals. A fund was also founded within the British Musicians' Pension Society for the benefit of orchestral players' dependants. At the same time Wood presented to the Royal Academy of Music his library of 2,800 orchestral scores and 1,920 sets of parts, and also established a Henry Wood Fund to assist necessitous students.

Wood now awaited the consummation of his life-work, the jubilee of the promenade concerts, but on the outbreak of hostilities in 1939 the season was abruptly cut short, and early in 1940 the fate of the series appeared to be in the balance. Eventually a season was sponsored by the Royal Philharmonic Society, Wood conducting the London Symphony Orchestra, until continuous air raids brought the season to a close in September. The Queen's Hall was destroyed by enemy action 10 May 1941, but the promenade concerts that year were given without interruption at the Royal Albert Hall, and in the following year the B.B.C. was once more able to undertake their management.

In 1944 Wood was appointed C.H. and shortly before his jubilee promenade season he formally handed over the trusteeship of the concerts to the B.B.C., it being mutually agreed between Wood and the Corporation that these should in future be known as 'The Henry Wood Promenade Concerts' in order that their aims and ideals should be perpetuated. Wood was able to achieve his ambition of conducting on the opening night of his fiftieth promenade season, but his health had for some time been failing and he died 19 August 1944 in hospital at Hitchin. His ashes were laid to rest in St. Sepulchre's church, Holborn, where a St. Cecilia window was dedicated to his memory in 1946.

Of Wood, Sir Hugh Allen [q.v.] wrote: 'No one has had greater influence on the music of his time and generation, nor given himself so unsparingly to its service.' By his thoroughness, integrity, enthusiasm, and human understanding Wood did more than any other man to spread the love of orchestral music and raise its level of performance. He was the first British conductor to found a stable and permanent orchestra and to train it fully at rehearsal. As early as 1904 he had refused to allow the system by which deputies could be provided, and in 1913 he was the first conductor to introduce women into a British orchestra. His meticulous insistence on tuning, his innovation of sectional rehearsals for each department of the orchestra, and his careful marking of orchestral parts so as to secure unanimity of bowing, phrasing, and dynamics provided a basis for the present high standard of British orchestral playing. As a teacher of orchestras, choirs, and singers he influenced and developed almost every sphere of British music, while his constant encouragement of British composers was one of the greatest contributory factors in this country's musical renaissance. His selfless devotion to music was equalled only by the thoroughness which he brought to every aspect of his art.

A portrait of Wood by Frank O. Salisbury is in the National Portrait Gallery, which also possesses a pencil drawing by Madame H. E. Wiener. A portrait by Flora Lion, is in the Savage Club, which has also in its keeping a portrait by Meredith Frampton. In a memorial room at the Royal Academy of Music is a bust by Donald Gilbert, together with eight oil-paintings by Wood and other mementoes of him. These are the gift of Lady (Jessie) Wood, and it is a condition of the gift that the bust will occupy every year its dominant position on the platform at the Henry Wood Promenade Concerts.

Wood's publications include *The Gentle Art of Singing* (4 vols., 1927–8, and abridged in 1 vol., 1930) and *About Conducting* (1945).

[Sir Henry Wood, *My Life of Music*, 1938; Rosa Newmarch, *Henry J. Wood*, 1904, and *A Quarter of a Century of Promenade Concerts*, 1920; Bernard Shore, *The Orchestra Speaks*, 1938; Symposium, *Sir Henry Wood: Fifty Years of Proms*, 1944; Robert Elkin, *Queen's Hall*, 1944; Thomas Russell, *The Proms*, 1949; Jessie Wood, *The Last Years of Henry J. Wood*, 1954; *Musical Times*, September 1944; *Grove's Dictionary of Music and Musicians*; *The Times*, 21 August 1944; personal knowledge.]     JULIAN HERBAGE.

WOOD, SIR (HOWARD) KINGSLEY (1881–1943), politician, was born in West Sculcoates, Hull, 19 August 1881, the eldest of the three children of the Rev. Arthur Wood, Wesleyan minister, by his wife, Harriett Siddons Howard, a connexion of Sarah Siddons [q.v.]. He was educated at the Central Foundation Boys' School in Cowper Street, off the City Road, London, where his father was for nine years minister of Wesley's chapel with which Wood himself retained a life-long connexion, serving for many years as treasurer. He was articled to a solicitor and admitted in 1903, having taken honours in his law finals and won the John Mackrell prize. He devoted his energies to the practice which he set up in the City until in 1911 he was elected to the London County Council on which he remained until 1919 as Municipal Reform member for Woolwich, serving on committees on old-age pensions, housing, and insurance.

In the discussions which preceded the national health insurance scheme of 1911 Wood was retained by the industrial insurance companies and as their principal adviser was largely responsible for bringing them into the scheme. When he was knighted in January 1918 he was deputy chairman of the London Pension Authority and chairman of the London Insurance Committee. He was also a member of the National Insurance Advisory Committee and (1917–19) chairman of the council of the Faculty of Insurance (of which he was president, 1919–20 and 1922–3–4). He thus played a considerable part in the negotiations which preceded the establishment of the Ministry of Health, the government proposal for which he wholeheartedly and influentially supported among the Approved Societies once the case had been clearly put forward.

In December 1918 Wood was elected Conservative member of Parliament for West Woolwich, a constituency which he continued to represent until his death. In 1919 he became parliamentary private secretary to the first minister of health, Christopher (later Viscount) Addison, and remained at the ministry until the break-up of the coalition in 1922. He returned in November 1924 as parliamentary secretary under Neville Chamberlain in the second Baldwin administration. In the course of an effective partnership which lasted four and a half years and enhanced the reputation of both, Chamberlain came to regard him as a trusted colleague and friend. During the general strike of 1926 Wood was civil commissioner in the northern division; in 1928 he was sworn of the Privy Council.

In the following year he fought a hard election and during the period in opposition proved himself a valuable party man, maintaining with pleasant good humour a persistent and astute criticism of the Labour Government. In 1930 he was unanimously elected chairman of the executive committee of the National Union of Conservative and Unionist Associations. On the formation of the 'national' Government in 1931 he became parliamentary secretary to the Board of Education until after the general election when he became the fourth postmaster-general of that year. For some time the Post Office had been under criticism, it being widely held that what was in fact mainly a vast commercial undertaking should cease to be a government department. A committee on Post Office reform, appointed by Wood in 1932 at the request of no fewer than 320 government supporters, did not recommend this step. Nor, under Wood, was it necessary; his approach was essentially that of a business man. He carried out the changes recommended by the committee which included the appointment, in 1934, of a director-general—almost equivalent to a managing director—in place of the secretary to the Post Office, and the formation of the Post Office Board. The commercial conception of the department was further underlined by a new financial relationship with the Treasury which allowed the Post Office to pay a fixed annual contribution to the Exchequer and use any surplus profit for the improvement of its services. Wood concentrated especially upon the weakest service—the telephone. To the attractions of increased efficiency and lower charges he added the weight of full-scale publicity including advertisements, posters, exhibitions, 'national telephone weeks', and films. The film unit and library of the Empire Marketing Board was taken over in 1933, and as the G.P.O. Film Unit made a reputation for the quality of its productions. In the same year a new Advisory Council was set up as a link between the Post Office and the public, and a public relations officer was appointed. Although in 1935 it became necessary to make it punishable to use offensive language to telephone operators, this was no more than a sign of growth in a service which in five years had seen a greater numerical increase in subscribers than in any other country. During Wood's term of office his department was more often a source of national pride than of irritation. His standing in the country and the Government was recognized when in December 1933, at Chamberlain's suggestion, he was given a seat in the Cabinet; and it was natural that in the election year of 1935 he should become chairman of the government committee set up to deal with propaganda.

When Baldwin became prime minister in June 1935 Wood was transferred to the Ministry of Health where his predecessor had not been popular and where Wood's particular gifts as an administrator and publicist were needed to carry out the Government's policy of slum clearance. In February 1938 his prestige was confirmed when he was unanimously elected grand master of the Primrose League in succession to Baldwin who had held the office since 1925.

In May 1938 Chamberlain, who gave Wood his confidence to an unwonted degree, moved him to the Air Ministry in circumstances similar to, but much more critical than those which had attended his earlier appointment to the Post Office. The air estimates had provided the occasion for severe criticism of the Ministry's administration and the demand for an inquiry. Wood's appointment was unexpected since he had no previous experience of a Service ministry, but he had shown himself highly efficient, had made no unpopular mistakes, and enjoyed the confidence not only of his chief but of the party, the House, and the public. *The Times* expressed the general hope that he would 'increase the output of aeroplanes with the same bright suavity as that with which he increased the number of telephone subscribers'. To this eleventh-hour task Wood brought all his customary assiduity; the Empire Air Training Scheme took shape, production was stepped up, and in March 1940 he was able to report that in the preceding twelve months the fighting strength of the Royal Air Force had increased by at least 100 per cent. In April, exhausted by his efforts, he changed places with Sir Samuel Hoare (subsequently Viscount Templewood), becoming lord privy seal. A month later Wood had the unhappy task of fortifying Chamberlain, his admired friend, in his decision to relinquish the premiership. It was wiser counsel than his earlier recommendation of a dissolution after Munich.

Under (Sir) Winston Churchill, Wood went to the Treasury. In July 1940 he introduced a supplementary budget on disappointingly orthodox lines with the exception of a modified imposition of the purchase tax proposed by his predecessor and the compulsory deduction of income-tax at source from wages and salaries. He did not live to see in operation the scheme devised in 1943 (P.A.Y.E.) by which the tax so deducted was calculated on current, not past, earnings. The autumn of 1940 was an anxious time at the Treasury: vast orders were being placed in the United States for which, with dollar reserves rapidly running out, there was no apparent means of payment. Fortunately the belief that American opinion was changing proved justified. The air raids were also at their height and at the request of the prime minister Wood produced a compulsory insurance scheme against war damage which became a claim upon the State.

On becoming chancellor of the Exchequer Wood had at once called in a consultative council of eminent authorities to advise him on policy. Among them was J. M. (later Lord) Keynes [q.v.] who was soon given a room in the Treasury and whose influence was to be noted in Wood's budget of 1941. Whilst the standard rate of income-tax was increased to 10s. in the pound and allowances were reduced so that over two million more persons became liable for tax, the reductions in allowances were offset by post-war credits, thus introducing the compulsory savings for which Keynes had been pressing. Twenty per cent. of the excess profits tax was also to be refunded after the war; and control of the cost of living was to be continued and extended by means of subsidies. This new conception of the budget as an instrument of economic policy was accompanied by the welcome innovation of a white paper on the sources of war finance and the size and distribution of the national income. Although not so intended, this became the first of an annual series. The budget was greeted as the first real war budget, by which country 'crossed into the land of promise where the nation's real resources, and not its money, become the basis of public economics' (*The Economist*, 25 September 1943). Wood's budget of 1942 continued the new orthodoxy. In 1943 he balanced his budget at the unprecedented figure of

£5,756 million of which half was raised by taxation. The rate of borrowing averaged only 2% and the cost of living had not risen more than 30% over the pre-war level. It was a remarkable achievement; but a few months later, 21 September 1943, Wood died suddenly at his home in London on the morning of the day on which he was to announce in Parliament his proposals for P.A.Y.E.

Although he lacked the traditional Conservative background and had not the advantage of oratorical gifts (his voice was thin and high and he often spoke from notes) Wood rose high in the counsels of his party. Moved more than once into the line of fire, his ability to turn away wrath was due as much to his acknowledged competence as to his agreeable personality. Men liked working for him, for he was amiable and accessible: of rather less than middle height he was a brisk, plump, and genial man to whom success apparently came easily, for he bore his burdens lightly. To any task he nevertheless brought great thoroughness and energy of mind, shrewd judgement, and an unusual willingness to seek and accept advice from all quarters. This was the more readily forthcoming since it was known that Wood could be relied upon to take the necessary decision and maintain it, not only in the Cabinet where his influence was considerable, but also in Parliament where he was adept at handling criticism or opposition. To some extent he had the good fortune to reap where others had sown—his most personal achievement may be said to have been at the Post Office—but it was to his credit, and greatly to the advantage of the country, especially perhaps at the Air Ministry and hardly less so at the Treasury, that the harvest was gathered with speed, efficiency, and good will.

In 1905 Wood married Agnes Lilian (died 1955), daughter of Henry Frederick Fawcett, an artist; there were no children. A portrait (1928) by A. T. Nowell is with the firm which Wood founded, Kingsley Wood, Williams, Murphy and Ross.

[*The Times, passim*, and 22 and 23 September 1943; *Lloyd George's Ambulance Wagon*, the memoirs of W. J. Braithwaite, edited by Sir Henry N. Bunbury, 1957; private information.]     HELEN M. PALMER.

WOOD, THOMAS (1892–1950), composer, was born 28 November 1892 at Chorley, Lancashire, the only child of Thomas Wood, a master mariner, and his wife, Hannah Lee. As a child he accompanied his father on many voyages and he always regarded this experience as an education of the most effective kind. It was supplemented, in his case, however, by other schooling, both general and musical; and Wood had already completed an external degree in music at Oxford before he arrived there in 1913 to work for the degree of B.A. which he obtained in 1918. In 1916 he migrated from Christ Church to Exeter College, with which he was to be associated for the rest of his life, and in 1917 his studies were interrupted by a period at the Admiralty. After the war, at the Royal College of Music, he studied under the direction of Sir Charles Stanford [q.v.] to whom Wood's music owes much. He became D.Mus. in 1920.

After a spell as director of music at Tonbridge School, where in a short time he made a great mark, Wood returned to Exeter College as lecturer (1924–7) and there began the compositions for which he soon became known. During the next thirty years he produced a series of works, both choral and orchestral, of which the most successful were 'Forty Singing Seamen' (1925), 'A Seaman's Overture' (1927), 'Daniel and the Lions' (1938), 'Chanticleer' (1947), and 'The Rainbow' (1951).

Apart from music the prevailing passions of Wood's life were the sea, foreign travel, and the British Empire. For the Empire he had the romantic idealist's love which partly derived from and partly created a rare talent for understanding the ways of men in countries far from his own, and interpreting them at home. He undertook extensive journeys, sometimes for musical activities, sometimes for personal interests, and at least once (1944) for the Government. These journeys provided material for a number of books of which *Cobbers* (1934) has been widely acclaimed as a penetrating account of the Australian scene and character. Wood's music was naturally influenced by these interests. English life, in the country or at sea, and the ways of ordinary men and women are the constant themes to which its sturdy plain-spoken individuality is well suited. After 1945, having come to feel that his wide interests were dissipating his talent, Wood prepared to devote himself wholly to musical composition. His sudden and untimely death frustrated an intention upon which his friends had based high hopes.

Perhaps the most remarkable aspect of Wood's achievement was the way in which he overcame the lifelong handicap of eyesight so defective as to be near blindness. To read a music-score was at all times a terrible burden, and it was impossible to understand how he could write one. He overcame this disability with courage, energy, and gaiety, and no doubt the discipline was a factor which added distinction to his character. The cost was heavy, and after his death it was realized how great had been the strain which this misfortune had imposed.

Wood married in 1924 St. Osyth Mahala Eustace, daughter of Thomas Eustace Smith. She survived him when he died at Bures, Suffolk, 19 November 1950. He had been elected an honorary fellow of his college, and made a member of the Arts Council, in the previous year.

[Thomas Wood, *True Thomas*, 1936; private information; personal knowledge.]

THOMAS ARMSTRONG.

WOODWARD, SIR ARTHUR SMITH (1864–1944), palaeontologist, born 23 May 1864 at Macclesfield, was the elder son of Edward Woodward, silk-dyer, and his wife, Margaret Smith. Both families had long been silk traders in Macclesfield. Woodward's parents were musical; and his father had studied chemistry and was a keen photographer. As a child Woodward collected wild flowers, beetles, and seaweeds, and while he was on holiday at Llandudno a workman gave him a Carboniferous brachiopod from a copper-mine on the Great Orme. This made him wonder how fossils came to be where they were found and so led him to study geology.

He attended Macclesfield Grammar School which awarded him a scholarship to the Owens College, Manchester. In addition to studying chemistry he was taught by (Sir) William Boyd Dawkins, the archaeologist and geologist, who became his lifelong friend and whose notice Woodward contributed to this DICTIONARY. In 1882, and before graduation, he successfully competed, although the youngest of the fourteen candidates, for a vacancy in the department of geology of the British Museum, then recently transferred to South Kensington. The keeper, Henry Woodward (one of the family of geologists, but unrelated to Smith Woodward), set him to work under the direction of William Davies [q.v.] arranging the collections of fossil vertebrates for exhibi-

tion. The beauty and perfection of the fishes in the famous collections of the Earl of Enniskillen and his friend Sir Philip Egerton [q.v.], which the museum had just acquired, turned Woodward to the special study of fossil fishes. He attended the Swiney lectures given by Ramsay Heatley Traquair, then the great authority on the subject, and evening classes in comparative anatomy and general biology at King's College. At the suggestion of the keeper, Woodward began to make a catalogue of all the fossil fishes in the department and thus entered upon his life-work which was to make him the greatest palaeo-ichthyologist of his time.

The first of the four volumes of the catalogue appeared in 1889, the last in 1901. This great work stands out from among more than 600 publications by Woodward, most of them papers communicated to scientific journals, not only as a monument of meticulous accuracy, of intense research, and of complete mastery of all that had previously been published; but also as the source of many other ichthyological publications. It became the mainspring of his multifarious activities: he acquired a speaking knowledge of several European languages; travelled widely in quest of new material, both in the field and in public and private collections; made contact with palaeontologists of many nationalities, and entertained them at home; and sought further to enrich the collections until, by the wealth of its material, his department drew researchers from all parts of the world.

In 1892 Woodward became assistant keeper and in 1901 he succeeded to the keepership. Delegating to the assistant keeper the supervision of invertebrata, he was able to give his whole attention, outside his administrative duties, to vertebrates generally, and to fossil fishes in particular. To this study, and to furthering the efficiency and reputation of the geological department, he devoted his life; and his successes brought him world-wide recognition and fame, attested both by the important positions which he was called upon to fill and by the many honours which came to him. The Royal Society elected him a fellow in 1901 and awarded him a Royal medal (1917); he served as president of a number of scientific societies and received several other medals, including the Lyell (1896) and Wollaston (1924) medals of the Geological Society, the Prix Cuvier of the

French Academy of Sciences (1918), and the Mary Clark Thompson medal of the National Academy of Sciences, Washington (1942). He also held honorary doctorates from the universities of Glasgow, St. Andrews, Tartu, and Athens. He was knighted in 1924 after his retirement from the British Museum which he never again entered, but he continued to work and travel until blindness overtook him a few years before his death at his home at Haywards Heath 2 September 1944. His library of nearly 10,000 works was purchased by University College, London.

In the light of the Piltdown disclosures made in 1953 it would be superfluous to enlarge upon the amount of time and thought which Woodward spent upon the famous skull which was the subject of much controversy from the announcement in 1912 of its discovery by Charles Dawson, a Sussex solicitor and fellow of the Geological Society. It should be said, however, that long before the fraud was revealed, it seemed to some a pity that Woodward should have allowed himself to be turned, even temporarily, from his life-work by pursuing a research for which he had no special training and to which it was unlikely that his genius would be most usefully applied.

Woodward has been described as a strict disciplinarian; although perhaps not easily approachable by the diffident, he could certainly be most kind and considerate to his junior staff, and tolerant of their youthful crudities. During his forty-two years at the museum he was absent through sickness for only one half-day—with a broken arm. His outside interests were few and this perhaps made it difficult for him to understand the wider outlook of his colleagues, to whom his single-minded zeal and devotion to duty were nevertheless an inspiration. Yet he appreciated music, and, surprisingly, enjoyed taking his children to the pantomime. He married in 1894 Maud Leonora Ida, daughter of the geologist Harry Govier Seeley [q.v.]; they had one son who entered the Colonial Service and died in 1924, and one daughter.

Woodward is one of a group examining the Piltdown skull, painted by John Cooke, in the possession of the Geological Society.

[C. Forster-Cooper in *Obituary Notices of Fellows of the Royal Society*, No. 14, November 1945; *Proceedings* of the Linnean Society of London, Session 156 (1943–4), part 3, 1945; *Quarterly Journal* of the Geological Society of London, vol. ci, 1945; *Proceedings Volume of the Geological Society of America for 1945*, 1946; J. S. Weiner, *The Piltdown Forgery*, 1955; personal knowledge.]

W. D. LANG.

WOOLF, (ADELINE) VIRGINIA (1882–1941), novelist and critic, was born 25 January 1882 in Kensington, the second daughter of (Sir) Leslie Stephen [q.v.] and his second wife, Julia Prinsep, the widow of Herbert Duckworth. From early childhood, Virginia Stephen was distinguished by two characteristics which were to determine the course of her history: on the one hand a brilliant and imaginative creative intelligence, and on the other a nervous system of extreme fragility, which, under any severe intellectual or emotional strain, was liable to break down and throw her open to fits of suicidal manic depression. Too delicate for the rigours of regular school, she spent her childhood at her family's London house in Hyde Park Gate and country home at St. Ives in Cornwall. Her father taught her, talked to her, and gave her the run of his library. By the time she grew up, she was already one of the most richly cultured minds of her day. Her mother died in 1895; after this, she was looked after by her elder half-sister Stella Duckworth. Her half-brother, George Duckworth, attempted to launch her, at the age of nineteen, and her sister Vanessa in formal London society. With small success: although too aesthetically sensitive not to find food for her imagination in the world of fashion, Virginia was at once too intellectual and too unconventional to feel at home there. Meanwhile she had started writing and was soon contributing to the *Times Literary Supplement*. Her father's death in 1904 was followed by her nervous breakdown. After this Virginia, together with her sister Vanessa and her brother Adrian, settled in Gordon Square where they collected round them a group of brilliant young men whom their elder brother Thoby had got to know at Cambridge; notably Roger Fry, J. M. (later Lord) Keynes, Lytton Strachey [qq.v.], Dr. Edward Morgan Forster, Mr. Leonard Woolf, and Mr. Clive Bell. Thus was inaugurated the celebrated Bloomsbury circle, which stood for a point of view combining a rich and refined culture with declared opposition to the religious and moral standards of Victorian orthodoxy. Thoby's death in 1906 came as a blow which threatened

Virginia Stephen's mental stability for four years. She continued, however, to live in Bloomsbury, first in Fitzroy Square, and after 1911 in Brunswick Square, devoting herself to the study and perfection of her art.

In 1912 she married Leonard Sidney Woolf with whom she lived partly in London and partly in Sussex. In 1914 she had another serious breakdown, and although after a year she recovered, for the rest of her life her husband saw to it that she lived very quietly. Her condition was never secure: for literary work and the society of her friends, the two things in which she found most satisfaction, were, if over-indulged in, both liable to upset it. Finishing a book, in particular, always left her exhausted. Leonard Woolf's devoted care, however, was successful in preserving her for many years. It was during this period that her chief work was done and her fame established. Of her novels, *Voyage Out* appeared in 1915, *Night and Day* in 1919. They were in a relatively traditional form. *Jacob's Room*, in which Virginia Woolf's characteristic manner first fully revealed itself, came out in 1922, *Mrs. Dalloway* in 1925, *To the Lighthouse* in 1927, *The Waves* in 1931, *The Years* in 1937. She also published two fantasies: *Orlando* (1928) and *Flush* (1933); two books of critical and biographical essays, *The Common Reader* (first series, 1925, second series, 1932); a biography of Roger Fry (1940), and two gracefully written feminist pamphlets, *A Room of One's Own* (1929) and *Three Guineas* (1938). She also took an active part in the management of the Hogarth Press which was founded by her and her husband in 1917. During these years she lived partly in London, in Tavistock Square, and partly at Rodmell in Sussex. In 1939 the Woolfs moved to Mecklenburgh Square where they remained until the bombing of 1940, after which they retired to Rodmell. There in 1941 Virginia Woolf's nervous system suffered its final collapse under the strain of the war, and she drowned herself, 28 March. The following books were published posthumously: *Between the Acts*, a novel (1941); and *A Haunted House*, short stories (1943); four volumes of essays, *The Death of the Moth* (1942), *The Moment* (1947), *The Captain's Death Bed* (1950), and *Granite and Rainbow* (1958); and extracts from her diary, *A Writer's Diary* (1953).

In spite of her disabilities, Virginia Woolf contrived to make a strong and influential personal impression on some of the most distinguished minds of her time. Her closest literary friends were her oldest, notably Dr. Forster and Lytton Strachey; but she was also intimate with others, Lady Ottoline Morrell [q.v.], Miss V. Sackville-West, and in later years Miss Elizabeth Bowen. She was shy in general society; and, even in congenial company, her personality could be formidable from its uncompromising fastidiousness. But it was also fascinating both for her ethereal beauty and for her conversation which combined fresh naturalness and an inexhaustible interest in other people with flights of whimsical fancy and a glinting satirical humour. As a writer she is in the first rank of English women. Her critical essays, at once so charming in form and so just and penetrating in judgement, are perhaps her securest achievement. But her most individual contribution to letters lies in her fiction. This shows the limitations of its author's personality: dramatic force and elemental human sentiment lie outside its scope. But it is distinguished by a subtle power to convey the processes of unspoken thought and feeling; by an extraordinary sensibility to the beautiful in nature and art; and by an original mastery of form that reveals itself alike in the intricate and musical design of her novels and in the shimmering felicities of her style. In Virginia Woolf the English aesthetic movement brought forth its most exquisite flower.

A small sketch in oil of Virginia Woolf by her sister, Vanessa Bell, is in the possession of the artist, who has also a small sketch in oil by Roger Fry, and a portrait and an ink drawing by Duncan Grant. The National Portrait Gallery has a chalk drawing by Francis Dodd and a lead bust by Stephen Tomlin. A portrait by J.-E. Blanche is believed to be in France.

[Personal knowledge.]

DAVID CECIL.

[B. J. Kirkpatrick, *A Bibliography of Virginia Woolf*, 1957.]

WRIGHT, SIR ALMROTH EDWARD (1861–1947), bacteriologist, was born at Middleton Tyas, near Richmond, Yorkshire, 10 August 1861, the second son of the Rev. Charles Henry Hamilton Wright [q.v.], an eminent authority on the Old Testament and a champion of Protestantism, by his wife, Ebba Johanna Dorothea, daughter of Nils Wilhelm Almroth, governor of the Royal Mint, Stockholm. Sir C. T. H. Wright [q.v.] was a younger brother.

Wright was educated privately by his parents and tutors (his father held chaplaincies at that time in Dresden and Boulogne), and later at the Royal Academical Institution, Belfast. At the age of seventeen he entered Trinity College, Dublin, and took his degree in modern literature in 1882, and his medical degree a year later. With a travelling scholarship he spent a year in Germany studying under Cohnheim, Weigert, and Ludwig, three of the leaders in pathology and physiological chemistry. On his return to London he read law for a time, and later took a clerkship at the Admiralty 'because that gave him plenty of leisure' to spend in medical research at the Brown Institution (University of London) under Charles Scot Roy, Leonard Charles Wooldridge, and (Sir) V. A. H. Horsley [q.v.]. Between 1887 and 1892 he held junior posts in the universities of Cambridge and Sydney, and also worked for a further term in Germany.

His first important appointment, that of professor of pathology at the Army Medical School at Netley (1892–1902), turned Wright's mind away from physiological chemistry and towards bacteriology, and during these years he achieved one of his notable successes by the introduction of anti-typhoid inoculation, a process believed to have saved thousands of lives. He also served on the first Indian plague commission from 1898 to 1900. In 1902, owing to some difference of opinion with the War Office about the employment of anti-typhoid vaccine in the army, he resigned his professorship and took up a similar appointment at St. Mary's Hospital in London, which he retained until 1946.

During the first ten years of this period he developed an entirely new school in medicine, that of 'therapeutic immunization' by vaccines, not for the prevention of microbic infections, but for their treatment. His small laboratory of 1902 had by 1908 expanded into a considerable research institute. In 1911 he went to South Africa to study pneumonia among the natives of the Rand gold-mines, and he introduced there a system of prophylactic inoculation somewhat similar to that against typhoid fever.

On his return to England Wright gave up his large private practice in order to devote more time to research work, and he was soon appointed director of the bacteriological department of the newly founded Medical Research Committee (later Council). But the outbreak of war in 1914 interfered with that project and Wright was soon in France as a temporary colonel in the Army Medical Service, setting up a laboratory for research on wound infections. He remained there until 1919, carrying out valuable scientific work. This led to the extensive trial of salt solution as an osmotic agent to 'draw' lymph into the wounds; and also provided the scientific basis for the early closure of such wounds. For this work he was awarded the Buchanan medal of the Royal Society (1917), the first gold medal by the Royal Society of Medicine (1920), and the Leconte prize by the Paris Académie des Sciences (1915).

After the war Wright returned to St. Mary's Hospital, and for a further twenty-five years continued to work on the problems of immunization, in particular on the changes induced in blood in response to 'vaccination' by bacterial products. Throughout his fifty years of concentration upon medical science he was continually devising new and ingenious techniques. These were described in his *Technique of the Teat and Capillary Glass Tube* (1912). In addition to this his scientific publications amounted to more than 130 papers, which he wrote always with the most scrupulous regard to literary quality. Few writers can have introduced so many new words. By the philosophical outlook displayed in all these writings, by his tireless practice of the experimental method, and by his technical achievements, Wright takes rank, with Pasteur, Ehrlich, and Metchnikoff, among the founders of modern immunology.

His labours were not confined to medical science. The operations of the human mind were never far from his thoughts, and he strove incessantly to build up what he called 'a system of Logic which searches for Truth'. The greater part of his writings on this theme survived only in manuscript, but were published posthumously (*Alethetropic Logic*, 1953) under the direction of his grandson, Dr. G. J. Romanes. Wright also published in 1913 *The Unexpurgated Case Against Woman Suffrage*.

Wright was knighted in 1906; appointed C.B. in 1915 and K.B.E. in 1919. He was elected F.R.S. in 1906; became a corresponding member of the Institut de

France and was an officer of the Order of the Crown of Belgium, and a member of the Order of St. Sava, Serbia. He received the freedom of the city of Belfast (1912) and was made an honorary fellow of Trinity College, Dublin, in 1931. He received honorary degrees from the universities of Dublin, Edinburgh, Belfast, Leeds, Paris, and Buenos Aires.

Wright married in 1889 Jane Georgina (died 1926), daughter of Robert Mackay Wilson, J.P., of Coolcarrigan, county Kildare, by whom he had two sons and one daughter. He died at his home, Southernwood, Farnham Common, Buckinghamshire, 30 April 1947. A notable portrait of Wright seated at his laboratory bench, by Sir Gerald Kelly, hangs in the Wright–Fleming Institute at St. Mary's Hospital; a drawing was made by Francis Dodd for the Medical Research Club.

[Leonard Colebrook in *Obituary Notices of Fellows of the Royal Society*, No. 17, November 1948; *St. Mary's Hospital Gazette*, vol. xlv, 1939; Leonard Colebrook, *Almroth Wright*, 1954; private information; personal knowledge.]                    LEONARD COLEBROOK.

WRIGHT, SIR (WILLIAM) CHARLES, second baronet (1876–1950), ironmaster and steelmaker, was born in Birmingham 13 January 1876, the only son of (Sir) John Roper Wright, who became first baronet, by his first wife, Jane Eliza, daughter of Charles Wilson, of Birmingham. Wright was educated privately and had begun to study for his army entrance examination when he decided to join his father in the steelmaking business of Wright, Butler & Co., Ltd. This he did in 1893 not long after the introduction of the new American (McKinley) tariffs which had greatly depressed many trades, especially the tinplate trade in South Wales. He at once applied himself zealously to learning the business, passing through all the production departments of the company's works in Glamorganshire and Monmouthshire.

On the merging of his firm and other companies into Baldwins, Ltd., in 1902, Wright continued in the business and within a year was elected to the board. His responsibilities increased with the rapid development of the company and he soon became a leading figure in the iron and steel industry and in the public life of South Wales. He was a justice of the peace for Glamorgan and, in 1912, high sheriff of the county. In 1907 he took command of the Glamorgan Royal Garrison Artillery (militia) and on the outbreak of war in 1914 he was mobilized from the reserve of officers. In 1917 he was appointed controller of iron and steel production in the Ministry of Munitions where he remained until the end of the war. For his services he was appointed C.B. in 1918 and K.B.E. in 1920; he was also made an officer of the Legion of Honour and a knight commander of the Order of the Crown of Italy.

In 1925 Wright became chairman and managing director of Baldwins, Ltd. He was president of the Iron and Steel Institute (1931–3) and of the British Iron and Steel Federation (1937–8). He went to the iron and steel control, Ministry of Supply, on its formation in 1939, as deputy controller, and succeeded Sir Andrew Duncan as controller in January 1940. He resigned on account of illness towards the end of 1942, and for his services was promoted G.B.E. in 1943.

His father had been associated with Sir William Siemens [q.v.] in the Siemens open-hearth process of steelmaking, and his firm was one of the first to produce steel by that process on a commercial scale at its Landore Works, South Wales. The process was a revolutionary one, but Charles Wright himself saw its possibilities and took a leading part in its development with far-reaching results. He was also active in the reconstruction of the iron and steel works at Port Talbot about 1912, the building of the adjacent Margam Iron and Steel Works four years later and of the modern iron and steel works of Guest, Keen, Baldwins Iron and Steel Co., Ltd., at Cardiff in 1934–5. This last project was to a great extent his own conception. Credit is also due to him in the initial stages for help in planning the new plants later built by the Steel Company of Wales, Ltd.

Throughout his busy life Wright kept himself abreast of the times by frequent visits to overseas iron and steel companies, in particular those in the United States. His relations with leaders of the steel industry in that country were most cordial, and these contacts, coupled with his great knowledge of the industry, proved of inestimable value when he acted as steel controller in the two wars. He was also on the board and chairman of many companies other than steel concerns.

Wright had great human qualities, not the least among them generosity, kindness, and consideration for others, whatever their station in life. His relations with all grades of employees were eminently friendly and he inspired affection to a high degree in those with whom he came in contact. He was a hard worker himself and expected and got willing cooperation from others, for he was a born leader with the faculty of getting all who served him to work together as a happy team. A man of action, to whom order and method came naturally, when there was work to be done he tackled it eagerly and gave quick decisions with a sure touch. He was a tall man with a fine presence. His portrait, painted by (Sir) Oswald Birley, was presented to him by the industry and is in the possession of the family. A copy hangs in the council-room of the British Iron and Steel Federation in Steel House, London.

In 1898 Wright married Maud, daughter of Isaac Butler, J.P., of Panteg House, Monmouthshire, who was also a director of Wright, Butler & Co., Ltd. There were no children of the marriage, and the baronetcy, to which Wright succeeded in 1926, became extinct when he died at his home, Englemere Hill, Ascot, 14 August 1950.

[Private information; personal knowledge.]
J. B. NEILSON.

WRONG, GEORGE MACKINNON (1860–1948), Canadian historian, was the descendant of English and Scottish families whose efforts to re-create British rural gentry in the unfavourable environments of Barbados, New York, New Brunswick, or Upper Canada petered out just after his birth, 25 June 1860, on his grandfather's pioneer farm at Grovesend, Canada, near Lake Erie. His bookish, fanciful father (Gilbert), his mother (Christian Mackinnon), and their many dependants moved a few miles eastward to Vienna, a village which was dwindling (with the forest industries) but possessed a good grammar school. 'We were very poor.'

At nineteen, although of Methodist family, Wrong escaped from commercial employment in Toronto through the support of the Rev. J. P. Sheraton, principal of the newly incorporated Wycliffe College, a low-church divinity school. By 1883 his energies and abilities had enabled him concurrently to complete his studies in divinity and to graduate from the university of Toronto with first class honours in mental and moral philosophy. Although he entered holy orders and

occasionally thereafter served and preached, he now preferred to follow his scholarly bent as lecturer in ecclesiastical history and liturgics at Wycliffe and by vacation study in England and on the continent. When Sir Daniel Wilson [q.v.], president of the university and its professor of history and ethnology, died in 1892, Wrong applied for the chair, but was made lecturer only. Two years later he was promoted to the higher place. This appointment was attributed by some to nepotism of Edward Blake [q.v.], chancellor of the university and since 1886 Wrong's father-in-law. A professor who made the charge in the press was dismissed and his removal provoked a 'students' strike' in which W. L. Mackenzie King and Hamar (later Viscount) Greenwood [qq.v.] took a leading part. This and other university matters were investigated by Royal Commission in 1895. Wrong was cleared of the grievous, if stimulating, accusation, just as he was ready to exhibit his matured qualities.

His chosen role was to prod Canadians into realization and emulation of the new historical scholarship of Germany, Great Britain, and the United States. He laid the foundations of national enterprises along such lines by founding the *Review of Historical Publications relating to Canada* which from 1897 to 1919 (and since 1920 as part of the quarterly *Canadian Historical Review*) annually listed or reviewed exactingly every discoverable cogent item. It caused a prodigious ado for several years and made it unwise to publish uncritical history. Wrong managed to combine extensive study, writing, editorial work, public and academic responsibilities, and social activity in Canada, Great Britain, and the United States, perhaps because he rose daily at 5 a.m. A great teacher, he built up a group of associates in history at Toronto who sustained a partially tutorial instruction.

More than any other person of his day, he made English-speaking Canadians aware of sound history, an achievement which was signalized by honours at home and abroad. Shortly after 1900, he and others whom he had influenced directly or indirectly began to furnish good, readable textbooks of British and Canadian history which secured recognition in the primary and secondary schools. Cooperative scholarship provided higher education and serious readers with large series of biographical and historical monographs which incorporated the best available scholarship. Wrong's editorial assistance to the Canadian publisher Robert Glasgow in the *Chronicles of Canada* (32 vols., Toronto, 1914–16) laid the foundations for Glasgow's later *Chronicles of America* (50 vols., New Haven, 1918–21) to which Wrong contributed *The Conquest of New France* (1918) and *Washington and his Comrades in Arms* (1921). In 1905 he played a leading role in founding the Champlain Society, whose admirable editions of original or rare historical materials reflected his editorial hand for at least twenty years. He used his retirement after 1927 for writing some long-planned books until health and eyesight began to fail him about 1940. In particular *The Rise and Fall of New France* (2 vols., 1928) and *Canada and the American Revolution* (New York, 1935) are very attractive examples of his matured scholarship and expository art. *A Canadian Manor and Its Seigneurs* (Toronto, 1908), a charming product of research into the records of Murray Bay, was reprinted in 1926.

Wrong's personal charm and his unconcealed admiration of the best wherever he found it won him a great circle of loyal friends, both lowly and exalted, in North America and Europe. He and his first wife, Sophia Hume Blake (died 1931), and their children formed an unusual Anglo-Canadian group whose interests and hospitalities were happily interlaced. Margaret Christian (1887–1948) became a leader in African education; Edward Murray (1889–1928) was fellow and tutor of Magdalen College, Oxford; Harold Verschoyle (1891–1916) was killed in action; Humphrey Hume (1894–1954), after teaching history at the university of Toronto, entered the Canadian Department of External Affairs in 1927 and subsequently held its highest posts at home and abroad; and Agnes Honoria (born 1903) married C. H. A. Armstrong, Q.C., of Toronto. In 1933 Wrong married Elizabeth Burgwynne. She survived him when he died about midnight 28 June 1948 in Toronto. A portrait by Lois Swann is in the possession of the family; another by Sir E. Wyly Grier is at the university of Toronto.

[G. M. Wrong, *The Chronicle of a Family*, privately circulated, 1938; W. S. Wallace, 'The Life and Work of George M. Wrong' (bibliography) in the *Canadian Historical Review*, September 1948; Chester Martin, 'Professor G. M. Wrong and History in Canada' in *Essays in Canadian History presented to George Mackinnon Wrong*, edited by R. Flenley, Toronto, 1939; private information; personal knowledge.]

J. B. BREBNER.

WROTTESLEY, SIR FREDERIC JOHN (1880–1948), judge, was born in Hampstead 20 March 1880, the third son of the Rev. Francis John Wrottesley, then a curate in Hampstead and later vicar of Denstone, Staffordshire, a great-nephew of the first Baron Wrottesley [q.v.], by his wife Agnes Mabel Stilwell, daughter of Frederic John Freeland. He was a kinsman of George Wrottesley [q.v.]. Educated at Tonbridge and at Lincoln College, Oxford, where he was a classical scholar, Wrottesley gave to both institutions a wholehearted devotion while within their walls and in after-life. He obtained a second class in classical moderations in 1901 and a third in *literae humaniores* in 1903, and was called to the bar by the Inner Temple in 1907. He won rapid success in the charmed circle of the parliamentary bar, but his career was interrupted by the war of 1914–18 when he was commissioned in the Royal Field Artillery, serving in France, attaining the rank of major and being mentioned in dispatches. His war record like all other activities of his life showed that everything he handled he handled well. He became a K.C. in 1926 and in 1930 was made recorder of Wolverhampton. In 1931 he was chairman of the gas legislation committee appointed by the Board of Trade to inquire into the working of the basic price system for gas companies, and in 1936 he conducted an inquiry into the marketing of sugar-beet. His experience of the parliamentary bar familiarized him closely with many matters of local government. He was a good friend to the teachers of law and much interested in his subject from the academic angle, and he was no stranger to legal authorship, for his works *The Examination of Witnesses in Court* (1910) and *Letters to a Young Barrister* (1930) won golden opinions from the profession.

It was on the bench that his career came to its full maturity. He was appointed a judge of the King's Bench division and knighted in 1937. There were those who speculated with some uneasiness how well one who, however replete with learning and common sense, had practised exclusively in the parliamentary bar, would acquit himself when confronted with problems of ordinary criminal and civil law. Their apprehensions were soon shown to be groundless. At the very outset of his judicial career a supreme test awaited him in the shape of a case involving that very difficult piece of legislation, the Truck Act of 1831, and incidentally also a matter connected with the statute of limitation then in force. The case was *Pratt* v. *Cook*, [1938] 2 K.B. 51. His judgement on the point of the operation of the Truck Act was reversed by a divided Court of Appeal which was, however, unanimous in approving his view on the period of limitation. Then in 1940 his entire judgement was restored by the House of Lords. This achievement set the seal on his judicial reputation, and he was ever afterwards regarded as a learned, careful, and just judge, possessed of that undefinable quality, the true judicial temperament.

His success on the civil side inspired professional optimism about his success on the criminal side; nor was it disappointed. His lack of previous experience of crime and criminals seemed to constitute no bar to his understanding of the problems involved. He took the trouble to study criminology, together with the history and practice of the prison system, and to get acquainted with those concerned in the daily administration of the multiplicity of matters affecting punishment and probation. By characteristic efforts he acquired a profound knowledge of the ramifications of criminal law itself, and rapidly took his place in the foremost rank of criminal judges. Perhaps the most interesting of his decisions, from a legal point of view, was *R.* v. *Jarmain*, [1946] K.B. 74, where he applied what might be called the doctrine of 'follow-through'. It was in a sense an extension of the doctrine of constructive crime, whereby a person who causes the death of another person in the course of committing a felony involving violence is guilty of murder; for here the felony, larceny, had been committed after the death. Wrottesley, delivering the judgement of the Court of Criminal Appeal affirming Jarmain's conviction for murder, ruled that a person who uses violent measures in the commission of a felony does so at his own risk, and is guilty of murder even though the death of the victim were caused by inadvertence and were interposed, in point of time, between the attempt at the felony and its ultimate consummation.

In 1947 he was raised to the Court of Appeal and sworn of the Privy Council, a promotion which gave rise to widespread satisfaction. But he was destined to enjoy only a short tenure of his seat, for in 1948 growing ill health forced his resignation. He had, however, occupied it long enough to complete what many would regard as the crowning achievements of his career in the fields of equity and constitutional law, for he was a member of the court which prepared the elaborate judgement in *Re Diplock*, [1948] Ch. 465. Trustees of a will had, in obedience to its provisions, distributed the testator's property among charities. This action turned out to have been premature, since one of the next-of-kin succeeded in convincing the House of Lords that the will did not create a valid charitable bequest. The Court of Appeal in a long and learned judgement held that the next-of-kin were entitled to recover from the recipients the money thus wrongly paid away. In *R.* v. *Chancellor of St. Edmundsbury and Ipswich Diocese*, [1948] 1 K.B. 195, Wrottesley read the judgement of the court, which laid down that while the King's Bench division can issue an order for prohibition, it cannot issue an order for certiorari to an ecclesiastical court.

Wrottesley was a bencher of his Inn and was an honorary fellow of Lincoln College, Oxford, which was always one of the main interests of his life, and which he was always more than ready to help with his wise advice. He was the most prudent of counsellors and the truest of friends. He married in 1915 Marion Cecil (died 1955), daughter of Lieutenant-Colonel William Patterson of the Duke of Cornwall's Light Infantry. There was no issue of the marriage. He died 14 November 1948 at his home near Basingstoke. A pastel by Eric Kennington is in Skinners' Hall (Wrottesley was master of the Company, 1940–41); a portrait by M. Grixoni is in the possession of the family.

[Personal knowledge.] H. G. HANBURY.

WYLD, HENRY CECIL KENNEDY (1870–1945), English philologist and lexicographer, was born in London 27 March 1870, the only son of Henry Wyld, commander in the service of the East India Company, and grandson of a Fifeshire landowner, James Wyld. His mother was Louise, daughter of Benjamin Kennedy, a Scottish gentleman living in the county of Fife.

After a year at Charterhouse Wyld was educated privately at Lausanne (1885–8) and then at the universities of Bonn and Heidelberg, and at Corpus Christi College, Oxford. He studied philology, phonetics, and linguistics with Henry Sweet [q.v.] and took his B.Litt. in 1899. On Sweet's recommendation he was in the same year appointed independent lecturer in the English language at University College, Liverpool. In 1904 the newly chartered university of Liverpool elected him its first Baines professor of English language and philology. From 1902 to 1910 he also acted as special inspector in the teaching of phonetics in the training colleges of Scotland. He remained at Liverpool until 1920, active in university administration, and by his teaching, lecturing, and writing established himself among the foremost philologists in the country. Most of his books and articles were written during this period, including his excellent *Historical Study of the Mother Tongue, an Introduction to Philological Method* (1906) and *A Short History of English* (1914) which, reissued in a third edition in 1927, enlarged considerably and revised mainly in the light of the researches of himself and his pupils, remains unsurpassed in its field. In *A History of Modern Colloquial English* (1920, 3rd ed., with six short appendixes, 1936) he developed with obvious personal satisfaction, as well as with remarkable success, the new technique, first evolved by his friend, Robert Eugen Zachrisson of the Royal University of Upsala, Sweden, for investigating the chronological problems of the New English period.

In 1920 Wyld was elected Merton professor of English language and literature in the university of Oxford and held his professorial fellowship at Merton College for the rest of his life. Here he completed his *Studies in English Rhymes* (1923), another (short) pioneer book designed mainly for students of literature. In 1932 appeared his excellent one-volume *Universal Dictionary of the English Language*, a dictionary of contemporary usage, both literary and colloquial, which, although it imposed a 'long and laborious' task and sometimes tried his patience, offered him a challenge which in its final results stirred many to think of him as a *Johnsonius redivivus*. Its size and comprehensiveness, its methodical arrangement, its unusually full treatment of etymologies, its clear and precise definitions, together with its brief and racy illustrative sentences mostly of his own coining, give it real and permanent value.

Wyld greatly enjoyed his lecturing at Oxford, and his pupils invariably found his exposition clear and intensely invigorating. Despite the grievous affliction of bad eyesight, he continued his philological researches and added to the number of his learned articles.

In 1932 he was awarded the British Academy's Sir Israel Gollancz biennial prize for his contributions to the study of English philology, and the Royal University of Upsala conferred upon him the honorary degree of Ph.D. He was also an honorary member of the Modern Language Association and of the Linguistic Society of America.

He was a tallish, well-built, broad-shouldered man and in his youth was fond of outdoor pursuits, especially riding and hunting. His pleasant reverberating voice enhanced his excellent pronunciation of English; and his easy flow of resounding words, his ready wit, his extensive knowledge of men, affairs, languages, and literatures and, not least, his forceful personality, made him a lively conversationalist and friend. His Johnsonian literary style reflected the man.

In 1890 Wyld married Grace Muriel (died 1954), daughter of John Proctor, an Irish landowner of Ballina, county Mayo. They had two sons and two daughters. He died at Alvescot, Oxfordshire, 26 January 1945. A portrait of him when young by John Mackie is in the possession of the family. He is also included in a group painted by Albert Lipczinski (1915) of some of the staff of Liverpool University where the painting hangs in the common-room of the faculty of arts.

[Private information; personal knowledge.]
HAROLD ORTON.

YORKE, WARRINGTON (1883–1943), physician, was born at Lancaster 11 April 1883, the eldest of the six children of the Rev. Henry Lefroy Yorke, a Wesleyan Methodist minister, and his wife, Margaret Warrington. He attended University School, Southport, and Epworth College, Rhyl, and studied medicine at Liverpool University, qualifying as M.B., Ch.B. (Liverpool) in 1905. He proceeded to the M.D. in 1907, became M.R.C.P. (London) (1929), and was elected F.R.C.P. (1934). In 1906 he was elected to the Holt fellowship in physiology and worked under (Sir) Charles Scott Sherrington, at whose suggestion he joined the Liverpool School of Tropical Medicine in 1907. Almost immediately he was sent with Wakelin Barratt to Nyasaland to study blackwater fever. On his return in 1909 he was appointed research assistant, then director of the Liverpool School research laboratory at Runcorn. During 1911–12 he was in Northern Rhodesia on the British South Africa Company's sleeping sickness commission. He proved that the tsetse fly, *Glossina morsitans*, was the transmitter of Rhodesian sleeping sickness, and that wild animals formed a reservoir of the infection. This work was carried out almost simultaneously with the researches of Sir David Bruce [q.v.] in Nyasaland. From 1914 until 1929 Yorke was Walter Myers professor of parasitology and from 1929 until his death Alfred Jones professor of tropical medicine at Liverpool. He was assistant physician for tropical diseases in the Liverpool Royal Infirmary (1920–29) and full physician (1929–43).

Yorke's work on the trypanosomes and nematodes earned for him an international reputation, and his later work on the chemotherapy of parasitic diseases, especially that on the aromatic diamidines, was of equal value. In 1927 he served on the chemotherapy committee of the Medical Research Council; in 1935 on the malaria commission of the League of Nations; and in 1936 he became a member of the tropical medical research committee of the Medical Research Council. He was awarded the Chalmers memorial gold medal of the Royal Society of Tropical Medicine in 1925 and was elected F.R.S. in 1932. After the outbreak of war in 1939 he was in frequent consultation with the Government and his knowledge and experience proved of the greatest value in connexion with the dispatch of large forces to Africa and the Middle East. Yorke was the author of a monograph on *The Nematode Parasites of Vertebrates* (1926) in collaboration with Dr. Philip Alan Maplestone, and of some 160 reports and papers, the majority of which appeared in the *Annals of Tropical Medicine and Parasitology*. His researches added greatly to the fuller understanding of many tropical diseases. He died at his home in Birkenhead 24 April 1943. He married in 1916 Elizabeth Annie Greening, and had a son and a daughter. A Warrington Yorke memorial fund was established in 1944 to endow the chemotherapeutic research department of the Liverpool School of Tropical Medicine.

[*British Medical Journal* and *Lancet*, 8 May 1943; C. M. Wenyon in *Obituary Notices of Fellows of the Royal Society*, No. 13, November 1944; *The Times*, 26 April 1943.]

W. J. BISHOP.

YOUNG, SIR HUBERT WINTHROP (1885–1950), soldier and administrator, the second of the four distinguished sons of (Sir) W. Mackworth Young [q.v.] of the Indian Civil Service, by his second wife, was born at Wrexham 6 July 1885. His father and his maternal grandfather both held office as lieutenant-governor of the Punjab. Educated at Eton where he was a scholar, and the Royal Military Academy, Woolwich, he was commissioned in 1904 in the Royal Garrison Artillery. Stationed at Aden he studied Arabic for the army interpretership. In 1908 he transferred to the 116th Mahrattas, Indian Army. Returning from leave in 1913 he travelled via Syria and Iraq and at Carchemish stayed with T. E. Lawrence [q.v.]. The meeting made a deep impression on both men and had an important influence on Young's career.

Appointed adjutant of the 116th Mahrattas in 1913, Young was given by the colonel full scope for his extraordinary abilities. He completely transformed the battalion, increasing its efficiency and raising its morale beyond recognition by his energy, organizing ability, and personal knowledge of the men, by his invention of a smart *pagri*, and by the composition, with the Indian officers, of several marching songs celebrating the great exploits of Mahratta history (one of these, *Ek sau solah mahrataja*, became very popular). When war came in 1914 Young worked at army headquarters for a while, but he reverted to his regiment and served on the North-West Frontier. In 1915 he was sent to Mesopotamia where he served as assistant political officer and was chiefly responsible for the construction of the Shaiba *bund*. Transferred to the local resources department in 1917 as deputy director, he earned a mention in dispatches for speeding up grain deliveries.

At the request of Lawrence, Young was transferred to the Hejaz operations in March 1918. He organized all transport and supplies for the composite force which cut the railway behind the Turkish army just before the final attack by Sir Edmund (later Viscount) Allenby [q.v.]. He was mentioned in dispatches, appointed to the D.S.O., and received the Order of the Nahdha, third class. After a short period as president of the local resources board in Damascus, he took leave to England.

He was soon appointed to the newly formed Eastern department of the Foreign Office, where his experience of both aspects of the Arab question helped to form the policy eventually adopted in Iraq. He served in the Middle East department of the Colonial Office as assistant secretary from its formation in 1921 until the end of 1926. He then became colonial secretary, Gibraltar, until 1929; was counsellor to the high commissioner for Iraq, 1929–32; and envoy extraordinary and minister plenipotentiary in Baghdad, October and November 1932. He then became governor and commander-in-chief of Nyasaland until 1934; of Northern Rhodesia (1934–8); and of Trinidad and Tobago (1938–42). His health prevented him from accepting another post: in fact much of his heavy war-time work in Trinidad was done in spite of a warning heart attack.

In the Colonial Service, where his duties lay chiefly in Africa, he was noted for energy and foresight in helping to develop air communications, and for his sympathy with native interests, which did not, however, cause him to neglect those of the European community. In Northern Rhodesia he identified himself with provisions for the constant review of labour conditions and with the development of social services and the establishment of trust lands for the native population. In Trinidad, labour, hospitals, and housing occupied his special attention. He was knighted in 1932 and promoted K.C.M.G. in 1934, having been appointed C.M.G. in 1923. After retirement he engaged in relief work, in particular as European regional officer for the United Nations Relief and Rehabilitation Administration (1944–5). In 1945 he unsuccessfully contested Harrow West as a Liberal, and in 1947 Edge Hill, Liverpool. He served on the board of the Royal Free Hospital from 1945 and was chairman from 1946 until his death.

Young had many talents. He wrote well, as may be seen from his book *The Independent Arab* (1933); he talked well; he was an excellent linguist and a gifted amateur pianist and organist. An unusual combination of intellectual and man of action, he was fertile in ideas and determined in putting them into effect. This made him appear formidable at first, and he was sometimes considered overbearing; but his moral courage made him at least as stiff with his superiors, if he thought their policy mistaken, as he ever was with anyone else, and he had the kindest heart,

his sympathy for the underdog being equalled only by his devotion to the public service.

In 1924 Young married Margaret Rose Mary, daughter of Colonel Frank Romilly Reynolds, R.E.; they had three sons. He died at Evora, Portugal, 20 April 1950. The original of the portrait of Young reproduced in *Seven Pillars of Wisdom*, painted by Lady Young, is in the possession of the family.

[Sir Hubert Young, *The Independent Arab*, 1933; private information; personal knowledge.]                                              R. W. BULLARD.

YOUNG, WILLIAM HENRY (1863–1942), mathematician, was born in London 20 October 1863, the eldest son of Henry Young, a grocer and a member of the Turners' and the Fishmongers' companies, by his wife, Hephzibah, daughter of John Jeal. He went to the City of London School and in 1881 to Cambridge as a scholar of Peterhouse. He took his degree as fourth wrangler in 1884, his friends having expected him to be higher in the list. In later years he related that he would not restrict the width of his interests (intellectual and athletic) by the intensive preparation necessary to become senior wrangler. Instead of sending in an essay for a Smith's prize as most young mathematicians do, he competed for and won a prize for theology.

Young was a fellow of Peterhouse from 1886 to 1892, but he held no permanent office either in the college or the university. He established himself as a very successful tripos coach. In 1896 he married Grace Emily (died 1944) daughter of Henry Williams Chisholm, warden of the Standards. Grace Chisholm Young, as she liked thenceforth to be called, was a woman of conspicuous ability and determination. At Cambridge, as a scholar of Girton, she had taken both parts of the tripos and ranked as equal to a wrangler. At Oxford she was placed in the first class in the final mathematical school. At Göttingen she had broken down the imperial ban on women in the universities, studied for three years under Klein and in 1895 won the Ph.D. degree, *magna cum laude*, with full official sanction. She came to be one of the very few women know internationally as mathematicians.

In 1897 Klein came to Cambridge for an honorary degree and his visit set the seal on a resolution which the Youngs had taken to work at Göttingen. After some months there, they (with their first child) lived in Italy for more than a year, returning in September 1899 to Göttingen, where they made their home until 1908. For some years Young went to Cambridge during term-time to teach and examine. In 1908 the family moved to Geneva, and from 1915 their permanent home was in or near Lausanne. Young mastered many languages, and he twice travelled round the world.

Young did hardly any research until he was in his late thirties, but between 1900 and 1924 his activity was intense and he wrote three books and more than 200 papers. His wife collaborated in two of the books and a number of the papers, and did independent work as well. Towards the close of the last century, it was broadly true that the processes of mathematical analysis could be carried out provided that only continuous functions were encountered. Artificial and unaesthetic restrictions had repeatedly to be made to keep discontinuities out. The time was ripe for new ideas which should transform the subject. The English schools of pure mathematics then lacked the vitality of the continental, and the first steps were taken in Paris in 1898 by Baire and Borel. In the ensuing development Lebesgue, by general consent, stands first; but there is no one else who contributed more than Young. Young's first work was independent of Lebesgue; he had found definitions of measure and integration different in form from Lebesgue's, but equivalent in essentials. He was anticipated by some two years, and the disappointment was a blow; but he recognized the anticipation magnanimously—'the Lebesgue integral' is his own phrase—and set himself wholeheartedly to develop the theory of integration. There are several aspects of it which Young made his own, notably his treatment of the Stieltjes integral and his method of monotone sequences.

There are two other fields in which Young's powers are shown at their highest. In the first of these, the theory of Fourier series and other orthogonal series, he proved theorems of striking simplicity and beauty. Moreover, he initiated many lines of thought which were worked out more fully by younger men, notably G. H. Hardy [q.v.] and Professor J. E. Littlewood. The second field—and therein lay what was probably his most fundamental work—was the differential calculus of functions of more than one variable.

This is well expounded in his Cambridge tract (1910), but perhaps the best tribute to it is that de la Vallée Poussin rewrote part of his *Cours d'Analyse Infinitésimale* in accordance with Young's treatment.

The immediate and abiding impression which Young gave was one of restless vitality; it was shown in his gait, his gestures, and his words. His appearance was striking; in early married life he grew a beard, red in contrast with his dark hair, and he wore it very long in later years. Many stories were current about him, all turning on his energy, mental and physical. He had three sons and three daughters, of whom Dr. Rosalind Cecily Young and Professor Laurence Chisholm Young have continued their parents' work in pure mathematics. The eldest son was killed as an airman in France in 1917.

Young held special part-time chairs at Calcutta (1913–16) and Liverpool (1913–19). He was professor at Aberystwyth from 1919 to 1923. He did not meet the recognition he deserved. This was due in part to his late start, and in part to a certain conservative hostility to the modern theory of real functions—a theory which few Englishmen in the early years of this century understood. Even when his profundity and originality were better appreciated, he was passed over in elections to chairs in favour of men who might be expected to be less exacting colleagues.

He was an honorary doctor of the universities of Calcutta, Geneva, and Strasbourg, an honorary fellow of Peterhouse (1939), fellow (1907) and Sylvester medallist (1928) of the Royal Society, De Morgan medallist (1917) and president (1922–4) of the London Mathematical Society, and president of the International Union of Mathematicians (1929–36). The fall of France in 1940 found him at Lausanne, where he had to remain, unhappy and restive, until his sudden death 7 July 1942.

[G. H. Hardy in *Obituary Notices of Fellows of the Royal Society*, No. 12, November 1943; *Nature*, 22 August 1942; private information; personal knowledge.]      J. C. BURKILL.

YOUNGER, ROBERT, BARON BLANESBURGH (1861–1946), judge, was the fifth son of James Younger, of Alloa, Clackmannanshire, of the well-known family of brewers, by his wife, Janet, daughter of John McEwan, also of Alloa, where Robert Younger was born 12 September 1861. His eldest brother was the first Viscount Younger of Leckie [q.v.]. He was educated at the Edinburgh Academy and at Balliol College, Oxford, being placed in the third class of the honours list in classical moderations in 1881 and in the second class in jurisprudence in 1883. In 1884 he was called to the bar by the Inner Temple and entered as a pupil the chambers of J. G. Barnes (later Lord Gorell, q.v.). Later he transferred to Lincoln's Inn where he devilled for some years for H. B. Buckley (later Lord Wrenbury, q.v.).

Thus nurtured in the law and aided by his natural aptitudes and buoyant disposition, Younger early entered upon a career of successful advocacy in which enthusiasm was happily blended with learning and efficiency. In 1900 he took silk and in senior practice enhanced his reputation and his popularity. He became a bencher of Lincoln's Inn in 1907 and was elected treasurer of the Inn in 1932. In 1915 he was appointed a judge of the Chancery division in succession to Sir T. R. Warrington (later Lord Warrington of Clyffe, q.v.), and was knighted. His next move was to the Court of Appeal of which he became a lord justice in 1919 in succession to Sir H. E. Duke (later Lord Merrivale, q.v.), and was sworn of the Privy Council. Finally, after the promotion of Lord Cave [q.v.] to the Woolsack in 1922, Younger succeeded him in 1923 as a lord of appeal in ordinary, when a life peerage was conferred upon him with the title of Baron Blanesburgh, of Alloa, in the county of Clackmannan.

This brief summary of Younger's successive steps up the ladder of professional promotion records the conventional progress of a successful lawyer, but 'conventional' is the last epithet which might be appropriately applied to him. Indeed, his career was largely a tribute to his personality which, in the charm it radiated, displayed few of the qualities commonly, if unkindly, regarded as typical of the legal mind. In disposition generous and genial, he attracted affection in every quarter, while preserving a sensitive privacy in his intimate life within which he cultivated his love of literature and the arts. He possessed a large library and a well-selected collection of modern paintings, and he was an honorary member of the Royal Society of Painters in Water Colours. In music he found his prevailing delight, and he was a fellow and vice-president of the Royal College of Music.

As a judge, the motto on his crest—

*Celer et Audax*—not inaptly described him. He was certainly quick in discerning and emphatically indicating what he conceived to be the essential points at issue, and when he dissented from his colleagues, as not infrequently occurred, he did so with the boldness of conviction, yet always with courtesy and good temper. The strain of emotionalism which was the accompaniment of his sensitiveness disposed him to sympathize with those on whom the law seemed to bear hardly. His retirement from judicial work in 1937 was hastened by failing eyesight.

Apart from the law, Younger rendered notable public service in various capacities, chiefly in connexion with matters arising out of the war of 1914–18. In May 1915 he was appointed a member of an advisory committee set up by the Government to deal with claims by enemy subjects in this country for exemption from internment or deportation. The sub-committee on deportation of which he was chairman dealt with over 16,000 cases. In September 1915 the Home Office appointed him chairman of a committee on the treatment by the enemy of British prisoners of war. He was also chairman of a committee established in 1920 to advise on applications from ex-enemy nationals for release of their property. Probably his most arduous public service was rendered from 1925 to 1930 as principal British representative on the Reparation Commission under the treaty of peace with Germany. The chancellor of the Exchequer in conveying to him the thanks of the Government for his work in this capacity wrote that 'your legal experience and your resources of judgement, tact and persuasiveness have enabled you to safeguard British interests without losing the esteem and sympathy of your colleagues and you have filled the position of British delegate with the highest distinction'.

Younger was also concerned with questions relating to trading with the enemy, broadcasting, unemployment relief, and mining subsidence. The Goldsmiths' Company, of which he was prime warden, 1931–2, and the Royal Caledonian Schools of which he was chairman, were among his other interests.

The ample means which he enjoyed enabled Younger to gratify his generous instincts by many benefactions. To Dunblane Cathedral he gave its beautiful west window in 1906 in memory of his mother, and later four other windows on the south side of the choir. His title of Blanesburgh was chosen to mark his association with Dunblane, and St. Blane was one of the supporters in his coat of arms. Balliol College, of which he was an honorary fellow (1916) and from 1934 visitor, has special reason to cherish his memory gratefully, for he presented to the college hall new panelling and a new organ case, and also, besides other gifts, bore the cost of redecorating and reseating the chapel. The college law society bears his name. At Winchelsea, where he had a country-house in which he lived after his retirement, he adorned the church with memorial windows by Douglas Strachan [q.v.].

For his public services Younger was appointed G.B.E. in 1917. The university of Oxford conferred on him the honorary degree of D.C.L. (1928), and from the universities of Edinburgh (1919) and St. Andrews (1929) he received the honorary degree of LL.D. He was also chairman of the delegates of King's College, London (1929–44).

Younger was unmarried. He died at Winchelsea 17 August 1946. There is a portrait of him by H. G. Riviere at Balliol College.

[*The Times*, 20 August 1946; *Law Times*, 31 August 1946; personal knowledge.]

MACMILLAN.

YOUNGHUSBAND, SIR FRANCIS EDWARD (1863–1942), soldier, diplomatist, explorer, geographer, and mystic, was born at Murree, India, 31 May 1863, the second son of Major (later Major-General) John William Younghusband, by his wife, Clara Jane, daughter of Robert Grant Shaw. He was educated at Clifton and the Royal Military College, Sandhurst, and commissioned in the 1st (King's) Dragoon Guards in 1882, then stationed at Meerut. At Dharmsala in 1884 he met men who had accompanied his uncle, R. B. Shaw [q.v.], the first Englishman to cross the Himalaya to Yarkand and Kashgar. After a first Himalayan journey in Kangra and Kulu he was sent on a reconnaissance of the Indus and Afghan border and then attached to the intelligence department to revise the gazetteer of Kashmir. In 1886 he joined (Sir) Henry Evan Murchison James, of the Indian Civil Service, on a seven-months' expedition to Manchuria, then little known, rediscovering 'the Long White Mountain' (unvisited by Europeans since its discovery by a Jesuit

nearly 200 years earlier) and exploring the Sungari source (see H. E. M. James, *The Long White Mountain*, 1888). To Peking came Colonel Mark Sever Bell, V.C., intent upon returning to India overland and Younghusband obtained leave to do likewise. The two took different routes to Hami, Younghusband the more direct by the Gobi desert which had never then been crossed by a European. Leaving Peking 4 April 1887 he reached Hami in seventy days, and finding Bell had gone ahead travelled by the southern foot of the T'ien Shan, passing through Turfan, Aksu, and Kashgar; thence to Yarkand and by the unknown Aghil and Karakoram ranges and the hazardous Muztagh pass he reached Baltistan and Kashmir; this intrepid journey ended at Rawalpindi seven months after he left Peking.

In 1889 Younghusband, now a captain, returned to the Karakoram to investigate the attacks on trade-caravans by Kanjut raiders from Hunza, and to explore the passes between Yarkand and Hunza. Reaching Shahidulla by the Karakoram pass he descended the Yarkand river and by his route of 1887 crossed the Aghil pass into the Shaksgam valley, explored the Urdok and 'Crevasse' glaciers, and followed the Shaksgam down to its junction with the Yarkand river. Thence he explored the Shimshal pass, crossed the Ilisu pass to the Taghdumbash Pamir, having encountered Captain Grombchevski, an officer in the Russian army, who was exploring the northern approaches to India. After a number of interviews with the Hunza chief Younghusband returned to India.

In 1889 Younghusband was appointed to the Indian foreign department and in 1890 with (Sir) George Macartney [q.v.] he traversed the Little and Great Pamirs as far west as Yashil Kul, a lake at the head of the Alichur Pamir, crossed the Rang Kul Pamir, and by the Kizil Su valley reached Kashgar. In the summer of 1891 he set out on the return journey, reaching the Pamirs by the Gez defile, and carried out further explorations until he met a Cossack patrol under Colonel Yonoff, who informed him of the large area which Russia proposed to annex, the boundary between Russia, China, and Afghanistan not having then been demarcated. Yonoff received orders to escort Younghusband from 'Russian territory' and Younghusband returned by new passes to Gilgit. A sharp protest from

Lord Salisbury brought an apology from the Russians and eventual agreement upon the boundary.

These journeys, fully recorded in *The Heart of a Continent* (1896), established Younghusband's reputation as a Central Asian explorer of the first rank. Early accounts were given before the Royal Geographical Society (*Proceedings*, new series, August 1888 and April 1892) and he was awarded the Founder's medal in 1890. In the following year he was appointed C.I.E. On his return from the third expedition he became political officer in Hunza, and in 1893–4 political agent in Chitral where he was visited by George Curzon (later Marquess Curzon of Kedleston, q.v.) with whom he formed a firm friendship. Younghusband accompanied the Chitral relief force in 1895 as *Times* correspondent, and afterwards wrote an account of the campaign with his brother. His travels in these parts appeared first in the *Geographical Journal* (May 1895). Long leave in 1895–7 was spent as *Times* correspondent in the Transvaal and Rhodesia and he was in Johannesburg at the time of the Jameson raid. *South Africa of To-Day* was published in 1898. In that year he became political agent of Haraoti and Tonk and in 1901 he received the Kaisar-i-Hind medal. In the following year Curzon appointed him resident in Indore and in 1903 asked him to head a mission to Tibet whose hostility had long been a source of trouble on the frontier. Preliminary negotiations met with strong opposition and in 1903–4 Younghusband advanced on Lhasa with a military escort commanded by (Sir) J. R. L. Macdonald [q.v.]. Supremely fitted for his task, Younghusband's fine qualities brought his mission to a successful conclusion with a minimum of strife and he secured a treaty in time to withdraw his troops before the onset of winter. He was thought, however, to have exceeded his instructions over the terms of the treaty. He received a K.C.I.E.; it was not until 1917 that he was appointed K.C.S.I.

From 1906 until 1909 Younghusband was resident in Kashmir. He retired in 1910 and published his book *India and Tibet*. In England he became an active councillor of the Royal Geographical Society and president in 1919. During his three-years' term of office he revived the project of conquering Mount Everest and became first chairman of the Mount Everest Committee, formed jointly by the Society and the Alpine Club. His was the enthusiastic spirit which dominated the first three expeditions, and he never surrendered that interest. In addition to his own works, *The Epic of Mount Everest* (1926) and *Everest: the Challenge* (1936), he contributed forewords or prefaces to books such as *Everest, 1933* by Mr. Hugh Ruttledge (1934) and *Himalayan Quest* edited by Herr Paul Bauer (1938). He was one of the founders of the Himalayan Club in 1928 and Himalayan explorers consulted him freely before setting out.

Younghusband was a mystic, a devout Christian who had long pondered upon the mysteries of life and explored the religions and philosophies of the East, particularly Hinduism and Buddhism. His religious philosophy may be found in *Life in the Stars* (1927) and *The Living Universe* (1933). His faculty of understanding the Eastern mind contributed much to his success as an explorer, political officer, and as a commander of men's hearts, for he inspired devotion in all who served with him. Wise and imperturbable, he had great physical and moral courage, as was exemplified when he rode unarmed with two companions into a Tibetan armed camp to interview the commander. In his retirement he helped in the organization of the Conference of Religions of the Empire held in London in 1924 and founded the World Congress of Faiths in 1936.

Younghusband received honorary degrees from the universities of Cambridge (D.Sc., 1905), Edinburgh (LL.D., 1905), and Bristol (LL.D., 1912). In 1897 he married Helen Augusta, eldest daughter of Charles Magniac, M.P., of Colworth, Bedfordshire; they had a son who died in infancy and a daughter. He died at Lytchett Minster, near Poole, 31 July 1942. A portrait by Harold Speed is in the possession of the family. Another by (Sir) W. Q. Orchardson (1906) is in the National Portrait Gallery.

[*The Times*, 3, 4, and 26 August 1942; *Times Literary Supplement*, 8 August 1942; *Geographical Journal*, vol. c, 1942; *Alpine Journal*, May 1943; George Seaver, *Francis Younghusband*, 1952; personal knowledge.]

KENNETH MASON.

# CUMULATIVE INDEX

## TO THE BIOGRAPHIES CONTAINED IN THE SUPPLEMENTS OF THE DICTIONARY OF NATIONAL BIOGRAPHY 1901–1950

| | |
|---|---|
| Broadbent, Sir William Henry . | 1835–1907 |
| Broadhurst, Henry . . . | 1840–1911 |
| Brock, Sir Osmond de Beauvoir . | 1869–1947 |
| Brock, Sir Thomas . . . | 1847–1922 |
| Brodribb, Charles William . | 1878–1945 |
| Brodribb, William Jackson . | 1829–1905 |
| Brodrick, George Charles . . | 1831–1903 |
| Brodrick, (William) St. John (Fremantle), Earl of Midleton | 1856–1942 |
| Bromby, Charles Hamilton. See under Bromby, Charles Henry. | |
| Bromby, Charles Henry . . | 1814–1907 |
| Broodbank, Sir Joseph Guinness | 1857–1944 |
| Brooke, Alan England . . | 1863–1939 |
| Brooke, Sir Charles Anthony Johnson . . . . | 1829–1917 |
| Brooke, Rupert . . . | 1887–1915 |
| Brooke, Stopford Augustus . | 1832–1916 |
| Brooke, Zachary Nugent . . | 1883–1946 |
| Brooking Rowe, Joshua. See Rowe . . . . . | 1837–1908 |
| Brotherhood, Peter . . . | 1838–1902 |
| Brough, Bennett Hooper . . | 1860–1908 |
| Brough, Lionel . . . | 1836–1909 |
| Brough, Robert . . . | 1872–1905 |
| Broughton, Rhoda . . . | 1840–1920 |
| Brown, Sir Arthur Whitten . | 1886–1948 |
| Brown, Ernest William . . | 1866–1938 |
| Brown, Frederick . . . | 1851–1941 |
| Brown, George Douglas, 'George Douglas' . . . . | 1869–1902 |
| Brown, Sir George Thomas . | 1827–1906 |
| Brown, Gerard Baldwin . . | 1849–1932 |
| Brown, Horatio Robert Forbes . | 1854–1926 |
| Brown, Joseph . . . | 1809–1902 |
| Brown, Peter Hume . . | 1849–1918 |
| Brown, Sir Walter Langdon Langdon-. See Langdon-Brown . | 1870–1946 |
| Brown, William Haig. See Haig Brown . . . . | 1823–1907 |
| Browne, Edward Granville . | 1862–1926 |
| Browne, George Forrest . | 1833–1930 |
| Browne, Sir James Crichton- . | 1840–1938 |
| Browne, Sir James Frankfort Manners . . . . | 1823–1910 |
| Browne, Sir Samuel James . | 1824–1901 |
| Browne, Thomas . . . | 1870–1910 |
| Browning, Sir Montague Edward | 1863–1947 |
| Browning, Oscar . . . | 1837–1923 |
| Bruce, Alexander Hugh, Baron Balfour of Burleigh . . | 1849–1921 |
| Bruce, Charles Granville . | 1866–1939 |
| Bruce, Sir David . . . | 1855–1931 |
| Bruce, Sir George Barclay . | 1821–1908 |
| Bruce, Sir Henry Harvey . | 1862–1948 |
| Bruce, Victor Alexander, Earl of Elgin . . . . . | 1849–1917 |
| Bruce, William Speirs . . | 1867–1921 |
| Brunton, Sir Thomas Lauder . | 1844–1916 |
| Brushfield, Thomas Nadauld . | 1828–1910 |
| Bryce, James, Viscount . | 1838–1922 |
| Brydon, John McKean . | 1840–1901 |
| Buchan, Alexander . . . | 1829–1907 |
| Buchan, John, Baron Tweedsmuir . . . . . | 1875–1940 |
| Buchanan, George . . . | 1827–1905 |
| Buchanan, Sir George Cunningham . . . . . | 1865–1940 |
| Buchanan, Sir George Seaton . | 1869–1936 |

| | |
|---|---|
| Buchanan, Sir George William . | 1854–1924 |
| Buchanan, James, Baron Woolavington . . . | 1849–1935 |
| Buchanan, Robert Williams . | 1841–1901 |
| Buckland, William Warwick . | 1859–1946 |
| Buckle, George Earle . . | 1854–1935 |
| Buckley, Henry Burton, Baron Wrenbury . . . . | 1845–1935 |
| Buckmaster, Stanley Owen, Viscount . . . . | 1861–1934 |
| Buckton, George Bowdler. . | 1818–1905 |
| Budge, Sir Ernest Alfred Thompson Wallis . . . | 1857–1934 |
| Bulfin, Sir Edward Stanislaus . | 1862–1939 |
| Bullen, Arthur Henry . . | 1857–1920 |
| Buller, Arthur Henry Reginald . | 1874–1944 |
| Buller, Sir Redvers Henry . | 1839–1908 |
| Buller, Sir Walter Lawry . | 1838–1906 |
| Bulloch, William . . . | 1868–1941 |
| Bulwer, Sir Edward Earle Gascoyne . . . . | 1829–1910 |
| Bulwer-Lytton, Victor Alexander George Robert, Earl of Lytton | 1876–1947 |
| Bunsen, Ernest de . . . | 1819–1903 |
| Bunsen, Sir Maurice William Ernest de. See De Bunsen . | 1852–1932 |
| Bunting, Sir Percy William . | 1836–1911 |
| Burbidge, Edward . . . | 1839–1903 |
| Burbidge, Frederick William . | 1847–1905 |
| Burbury, Samuel Hawksley . | 1831–1911 |
| Burdett-Coutts, Angela Georgina, Baroness . . . | 1814–1906 |
| Burdon, John Shaw . . | 1826–1907 |
| Burdon-Sanderson, Sir John Scott . . . . . | 1828–1905 |
| Burge, Hubert Murray . . | 1862–1925 |
| Burgh Canning, Hubert George De, Marquess of Clanricarde . | 1832–1916 |
| Burkitt, Francis Crawford . | 1864–1935 |
| Burn, Robert . . . | 1829–1904 |
| Burn-Murdoch, John . . | 1852–1909 |
| Burnand, Sir Francis Cowley . | 1836–1917 |
| Burne, Sir Owen Tudor . . | 1837–1909 |
| Burnet, John . . . . | 1863–1928 |
| Burnet, Sir John James . | 1857–1938 |
| Burnett, Sir Charles Stuart . | 1882–1945 |
| Burney, Sir Cecil . . . | 1858–1929 |
| Burnham, Baron. See Levy-Lawson, Edward . . . | 1833–1916 |
| Burnham, Viscount. See Lawson, Harry Lawson Webster Levy- | 1862–1933 |
| Burns, Dawson . . . | 1828–1909 |
| Burns, John Elliot . . . | 1858–1943 |
| Burnside, William . . . | 1852–1927 |
| Burroughs (afterwards Traill-Burroughs), Sir Frederick William . . . . | 1831–1905 |
| Burrows, Montagu . . . | 1819–1905 |
| Burt, Thomas . . . | 1837–1922 |
| Burton, Baron. See Bass, Michael Arthur . . . . | 1837–1909 |
| Bury, John Bagnell . . | 1861–1927 |
| Bushell, Stephen Wootton . | 1844–1908 |
| Busk, Rachel Harriette . | 1831–1907 |
| Butcher, Samuel Henry . | 1850–1910 |
| Butler, Arthur Gray . . | 1831–1909 |
| Butler, Arthur John . . | 1844–1910 |
| Butler, Edward Joseph Aloysius (Dom Cuthbert) . . . | 1858–1934 |

| | |
|---|---|
| Cecil, Robert Arthur Talbot Gas- | |
| coyne-, Marquess of Salisbury . | 1830–1903 |
| Chads, Sir Henry . . . | 1819–1906 |
| Chadwick, Hector Munro . . | 1870–1947 |
| Chadwick, Roy . . . | 1893–1947 |
| Chalmers, James . . . | 1841–1901 |
| Chalmers, Sir Mackenzie Dalzell . | 1847–1927 |
| Chalmers, Robert, Baron . . | 1858–1938 |
| Chamberlain, (Arthur) Neville . | 1869–1940 |
| Chamberlain, Sir Crawford Trotter | 1821–1902 |
| Chamberlain, Houston Stewart . | 1855–1927 |
| Chamberlain, Joseph . . | 1836–1914 |
| Chamberlain, Sir (Joseph) Austen | 1863–1937 |
| Chamberlain, Sir Neville Bowles | 1820–1902 |
| Chambers, Raymond Wilson . | 1874–1942 |
| Chamier, Stephen Henry Edward | 1834–1910 |
| Champneys, Basil . . . | 1842–1935 |
| Champneys, Sir Francis Henry . | 1848–1930 |
| Chance, Sir James Timmins . | 1814–1902 |
| Channell, Sir Arthur Moseley . | 1838–1928 |
| Channer, George Nicholas . . | 1842–1905 |
| Chaplin, Henry, Viscount . . | 1840–1923 |
| Chapman, Edward John . | 1821–1904 |
| Charles, James . . . | 1851–1906 |
| Charles, Robert Henry . . | 1855–1931 |
| Charlesworth, Martin Percival . | 1895–1950 |
| Charley, Sir William Thomas . | 1833–1904 |
| Charnwood, Baron. See Benson, | |
| Godfrey Rathbone . . | 1864–1945 |
| Charrington, Frederick Nicholas | 1850–1936 |
| Charteris, Archibald Hamilton . | 1835–1908 |
| Chase, Drummond Percy . . | 1820–1902 |
| Chase, Frederic Henry . | 1853–1925 |
| Chase, Marian Emma . . | 1844–1905 |
| Chase, William St. Lucian . | 1856–1908 |
| Chauvel, Sir Henry George . | 1865–1945 |
| Chavasse, Francis James . | 1846–1928 |
| Cheadle, Walter Butler . | 1835–1910 |
| Cheatle, Arthur Henry . | 1866–1929 |
| Cheetham, Samuel . . . | 1827–1908 |
| Chelmsford, Baron. See Thesiger, | |
| Frederic Augustus . . | 1827–1905 |
| Chelmsford, Viscount. See Thesi- | |
| ger, Frederic John Napier . | 1868–1933 |
| Chermside, Sir Herbert Charles . | 1850–1929 |
| Chesterton, Gilbert Keith . . | 1874–1936 |
| Chetwode, Sir Philip Walhouse, | |
| Baron . . . . . | 1869–1950 |
| Chevalier, Albert . . . | 1861–1923 |
| Cheylesmore, Baron. See Eaton, | |
| Herbert Francis . . | 1848–1925 |
| Cheylesmore, Baron. See Eaton, | |
| William Meriton . . . | 1843–1902 |
| Cheyne, Thomas Kelly . . | 1841–1915 |
| Cheyne, Sir (William) Watson . | 1852–1932 |
| Child, Harold Hannyngton . | 1869–1945 |
| Child, Thomas . . . | 1839–1906 |
| Child-Villiers, Margaret Eliza- | |
| beth, Countess of Jersey. See | |
| Villiers . . . . | 1849–1945 |
| Child-Villiers, Victor Albert | |
| George, Earl of Jersey. See | |
| Villiers . . . . | 1845–1915 |
| Childers, Robert Erskine . | 1870–1922 |
| Childs, William Macbride . | 1869–1939 |
| Chilston, Viscount. See Akers- | |
| Douglas, Aretas . . | 1851–1926 |
| Chilston, Viscount. See Akers- | |
| Douglas, Aretas . . . | 1876–1947 |
| Chirol, Sir (Ignatius) Valentine . | 1852–1929 |
| Chisholm, Hugh . . . | 1866–1924 |
| Cholmondeley, Hugh, Baron | |
| Delamere . . . . | 1870–1931 |
| Christie, Sir William Henry Ma- | |
| honey . . . . . | 1845–1922 |
| Chrystal, George . . . | 1851–1911 |
| Chubb, Sir Lawrence Wensley . | 1873–1948 |
| Church, Sir William Selby . | 1837–1928 |
| Clanricarde, Marquess of. See | |
| Burgh Canning, Hubert George | |
| De . . . . . | 1832–1916 |
| Clanwilliam, Earl of. See Meade, | |
| Richard James . . . | 1832–1907 |
| Clapham, Sir Alfred William . | 1883–1950 |
| Clapham, Sir John Harold . | 1873–1946 |
| Clark, Albert Curtis . . | 1859–1937 |
| Clark, John Willis . . | 1833–1910 |
| Clarke, Sir Andrew . . | 1824–1902 |
| Clarke, Sir Caspar Purdon . | 1846–1911 |
| Clarke, Charles Baron . | 1832–1906 |
| Clarke, Sir Edward George . | 1841–1931 |
| Clarke, George Sydenham, Baron | |
| Sydenham of Combe . | 1848–1933 |
| Clarke, Henry Butler . | 1863–1904 |
| Clarke, Sir Marshal James . | 1841–1909 |
| Clarke, Maude Violet . | 1892–1935 |
| Clasper, John Hawks . . | 1836–1908 |
| Clausen, Sir George . . | 1852–1944 |
| Clauson, Albert Charles, Baron . | 1870–1946 |
| Clayden, Peter William . | 1827–1902 |
| Clayton, Sir Gilbert Falkingham | 1875–1929 |
| Clementi, Sir Cecil . . | 1875–1947 |
| Clerk, Sir Dugald . . | 1854–1932 |
| Clerke, Agnes Mary . . | 1842–1907 |
| Clerke, Ellen Mary. See under | |
| Clerke, Agnes Mary. | |
| Clery, Sir Cornelius Francis . | 1838–1926 |
| Cleworth, Thomas Ebenezer . | 1854–1909 |
| Clifford, Frederick . . | 1828–1904 |
| Clifford, Sir Hugh Charles . | 1866–1941 |
| Clifford, John . . . | 1836–1923 |
| Clive, Sir Robert Henry . | 1877–1948 |
| Clodd, Edward . . . | 1840–1930 |
| Close, Maxwell Henry . | 1822–1903 |
| Clowes, Sir William Laird . | 1856–1905 |
| Clunies-Ross, George . . | 1842–1910 |
| Clutton, Henry Hugh . | 1850–1909 |
| Clutton-Brock, Arthur . | 1868–1924 |
| Clyde, James Avon, Lord . | 1863–1944 |
| Clynes, John Robert . . | 1869–1949 |
| Coates, Joseph Gordon . | 1878–1943 |
| Cobb, Gerard Francis . | 1838–1904 |
| Cobbe, Sir Alexander Stanhope . | 1870–1931 |
| Cobbe, Frances Power . | 1822–1904 |
| Cobden-Sanderson, Thomas James | 1840–1922 |
| Cochrane, Douglas Mackinnon | |
| Baillie Hamilton, Earl of | |
| Dundonald . . . | 1852–1935 |
| Cochrane-Baillie, Charles Wallace | |
| Alexander Napier Ross, Baron | |
| Lamington. See Baillie . | 1860–1940 |
| Cockerell, Douglas Bennett . | 1870–1945 |
| Cocks, Arthur Herbert Tennyson | |
| Somers-, Baron Somers. See | |
| Somers-Cocks . . | 1887–1944 |
| Coghlan, Sir Charles Patrick John | 1863–1927 |
| Cohen, Arthur . . . | 1829–1914 |
| Coillard, François . . | 1834–1904 |

# Cumulative Index 1901–1950

| | | |
|---|---|---|
| Cokayne, George Edward . | . | 1825–**1911** |
| Coke, Thomas William, Earl of | | |
| Leicester . . . . | | 1822–**1909** |
| Coker, Ernest George . | . | 1869–**1946** |
| Coleman, William Stephen | . | 1829–**1904** |
| Coleridge, Bernard John Seymour, Baron . . . | | 1851–**1927** |
| Coleridge, Mary Elizabeth | . | 1861–**1907** |
| Coleridge, Stephen William Buchanan . . . | . | 1854–**1936** |
| Coleridge-Taylor, Samuel . | . | 1875–**1912** |
| Coles, Charles Edward, (Pasha). | | 1853–**1926** |
| Coles, Vincent Stuckey Stratton. | | 1845–**1929** |
| Collen, Sir Edwin Henry Hayter. | | 1843–**1911** |
| Colles, Henry Cope . | . | 1879–**1943** |
| Collett, Sir Henry . | . | 1836–**1901** |
| Collie, John Norman | . | 1859–**1942** |
| Collier, John . . | . | 1850–**1934** |
| Collings, Jesse . . | . | 1831–**1920** |
| Collingwood, Cuthbert | . | 1826–**1908** |
| Collingwood, Robin George | | 1889–**1943** |
| Collins, John Churton | . | 1848–**1908** |
| Collins, Michael . | . | 1890–**1922** |
| Collins, Richard Henn, Baron | . | 1842–**1911** |
| Collins, William Edward . | . | 1867–**1911** |
| Colnaghi, Martin Henry . | . | 1821–**1908** |
| Colomb, Sir John Charles Ready | | 1838–**1909** |
| Colton, Sir John . | . | 1823–**1902** |
| Colvile, Sir Henry Edward | . | 1852–**1907** |
| Colville, Sir Stanley Cecil James | | 1861–**1939** |
| Colvin, Sir Auckland . | . | 1838–**1908** |
| Colvin, Ian Duncan . | . | 1877–**1938** |
| Colvin, Sir Sidney . | . | 1845–**1927** |
| Colvin, Sir Walter Mytton. See under Colvin, Sir Auckland. | | |
| Commerell, Sir John Edmund | . | 1829–**1901** |
| Common, Andrew Ainslie . | . | 1841–**1903** |
| Compton, Lord Alwyne Frederick | | 1825–**1906** |
| Comrie, Leslie John . | . | 1893–**1950** |
| Conder, Charles . | . | 1868–**1909** |
| Conder, Claude Reignier . | . | 1848–**1910** |
| Congreve, Sir Walter Norris | . | 1862–**1927** |
| Coningham, Sir Arthur . | . | 1895–**1948** |
| Connaught and Strathearn, Duke of. See Arthur William Patrick Albert. . . . . | | 1850–**1942** |
| Connemara, Baron. See Bourke, Robert . . . . | | 1827–**1902** |
| Connor, Ralph, *pseudonym.* See Gordon, Charles William | | 1860–**1937** |
| Conquest, George Augustus | . | 1837–**1901** |
| Conrad, Joseph . . | . | 1857–**1924** |
| Conway, Robert Seymour . | . | 1864–**1933** |
| Conway, William Martin, Baron Conway of Allington . | . | 1856–**1937** |
| Conybeare, Frederick Cornwallis | | 1856–**1924** |
| Cook, Arthur James . | . | 1883–**1931** |
| Cook, Sir Basil Alfred Kemball-. See Kemball-Cook . | . | 1876–**1949** |
| Cook, Sir Edward Tyas . | . | 1857–**1919** |
| Cook, Sir Francis . | . | 1817–**1901** |
| Cook, Sir Joseph . | . | 1860–**1947** |
| Cook, Stanley Arthur | . | 1873–**1949** |
| Cooke, George Albert . | . | 1865–**1939** |
| Coolidge, William Augustus Brevoort . . . . | . | 1850–**1926** |
| Cooper, Sir Alfred . | . | 1838–**1908** |
| Cooper, Sir Daniel . | . | 1821–**1902** |
| Cooper, Edward Herbert . | . | 1867–**1910** |

| | | |
|---|---|---|
| Cooper, Sir (Francis) D'Arcy | . | 1882–**1941** |
| Cooper, James . . | . | 1846–**1922** |
| Cooper, James Davis . | . | 1823–**1904** |
| Cooper, Sir (Thomas) Edwin | . | 1874–**1942** |
| Cooper, Thomas Sidney . | . | 1803–**1902** |
| Cooper, Thompson . . | . | 1837–**1904** |
| Copeland, Ralph . . | . | 1837–**1905** |
| Copinger, Walter Arthur . | . | 1847–**1910** |
| Coppin, George Selth . | . | 1819–**1906** |
| Coppinger, Richard William | . | 1847–**1910** |
| Corbet, Matthew Ridley . | . | 1850–**1902** |
| Corbett, John . . . | . | 1817–**1901** |
| Corbett, Sir Julian Stafford | . | 1854–**1922** |
| Corbould, Edward Henry . | . | 1815–**1905** |
| Corelli, Marie, *pseudonym.* See Mackay, Mary . . | | 1855–**1924** |
| Corfield, William Henry . | . | 1843–**1903** |
| Cornford, Francis Macdonald | . | 1874–**1943** |
| Cornish, Charles John . | . | 1858–**1906** |
| Cornish, Francis Warre Warre-. See Warre-Cornish . | . | 1839–**1916** |
| Cornish, Vaughan . . | . | 1862–**1948** |
| Cornwell, James . . | . | 1812–**1902** |
| Corry, Montagu William Lowry, Baron Rowton . . | . | 1838–**1903** |
| Cory, John . . . | . | 1828–**1910** |
| Coryndon, Sir Robert Thorne | . | 1870–**1925** |
| Couch, Sir Arthur Thomas Quiller- ('Q'). See Quiller-Couch . | | 1863–**1944** |
| Couch, Sir Richard . . | . | 1817–**1905** |
| Coulton, George Gordon . | . | 1858–**1947** |
| Couper, Sir George Ebenezer Wilson . . . . . | | 1824–**1908** |
| Courtauld, Samuel . . | . | 1876–**1947** |
| Courthope, William John . | . | 1842–**1917** |
| Courtney, Leonard Henry, Baron | | 1832–**1918** |
| Courtney, William Leonard | . | 1850–**1928** |
| Cousin, Anne Ross . . | . | 1824–**1906** |
| Cowans, Sir John Steven . | . | 1862–**1921** |
| Coward, Sir Henry . . | . | 1849–**1944** |
| Cowdray, Viscount. See Pearson, Weetman Dickinson | . | 1856–**1927** |
| Cowell, Edward Byles . | . | 1826–**1903** |
| Cowen, Sir Frederic Hymen | . | 1852–**1935** |
| Cowie, William Garden . | . | 1831–**1902** |
| Cowley, Sir Arthur Ernest | . | 1861–**1931** |
| Cowper, Francis Thomas De Grey, Earl . . . | . | 1834–**1905** |
| Cox, George (called Sir George) William . . . | . | 1827–**1902** |
| Cox, Harold . . . | . | 1859–**1936** |
| Cox, Sir Percy Zachariah . | . | 1864–**1937** |
| Cozens-Hardy, Herbert Hardy, Baron . . . . | . | 1838–**1920** |
| Craddock, Sir Reginald Henry . | | 1864–**1937** |
| Cradock, Sir Christopher George Francis Maurice . . | . | 1862–**1914** |
| Craig, Isa. See Knox. . | . | 1831–**1903** |
| Craig, James, Viscount Craigavon | | 1871–**1940** |
| Craig, William James . | . | 1843–**1906** |
| Craigavon, Viscount. See Craig, James. | | |
| Craigie, Pearl Mary Teresa, 'John Oliver Hobbes' . | . | 1867–**1906** |
| Craigmyle, Baron. See Shaw, Thomas . . . | . | 1850–**1937** |
| Craik, Sir Henry . . | . | 1846–**1927** |
| Cranbrook, Earl of. See Gathorne-Hardy, Gathorne . . | . | 1814–**1906** |

| | | |
|---|---|---|
| Crane, Walter . . . | 1845–1915 | Curtis, Edmund . . . 1881–1943 |
| Craven, Hawes . . . | 1837–1910 | Curzon, George Nathaniel, Mar- |
| Craven, Henry Thornton . | 1818–1905 | quess Curzon of Kedleston . 1859–1925 |
| Crawford, Earl of. See Lindsay, | | Curzon-Howe, Sir Assheton Gore 1850–1911 |
| David Alexander Edward . | 1871–1940 | Cushendun, Baron. See McNeill, |
| Crawford, Earl of. See Lindsay, | | Ronald John . . . 1861–1934 |
| James Ludovic . . . | 1847–1913 | Cushny, Arthur Robertson . 1866–1926 |
| Crawfurd, Oswald John Frede- | | Cust, Henry John Cockayne . 1861–1917 |
| rick . . . . | 1834–1909 | Cust, Sir Lionel Henry . 1859–1929 |
| Crawfurd, Sir Raymond Henry | | Cust, Robert Needham . 1821–1909 |
| Payne. . . . . | 1865–1938 | Custance, Henry . . 1842–1908 |
| Creagh, Sir Garrett O'Moore . | 1848–1923 | Custance, Sir Reginald Neville . 1847–1935 |
| Creagh, William . . . | 1828–1901 | Cutts, Edward Lewes . . 1824–1901 |
| Creed, John Martin . | 1889–1940 | |
| Cremer, Sir William Randal . | 1838–1908 | D'Abernon, Viscount. See Vin- |
| Crewe-Milnes, Robert Offley Ash- | | cent, Sir Edgar . . . 1857–1941 |
| burton, Marquess of Crewe . | 1858–1945 | Dafoe, John Wesley. . . 1866–1944 |
| Crichton-Browne, Sir James. See | | Dale, Sir David . . . 1829–1906 |
| Browne . . . . | 1840–1938 | Dallinger, William Henry . 1842–1909 |
| Cripps, Charles Alfred, Baron | | Dalrymple-Hay, Sir Harley |
| Parmoor . . . . | 1852–1941 | Hugh. See Hay . . . 1861–1940 |
| Cripps, Wilfred Joseph . | 1841–1903 | Dalton, Ormonde Maddock . 1866-1945 |
| Crocker, Henry Radcliffe-. See | | Dalziel, Davison Alexander, |
| Radcliffe-Crocker . . | 1845–1909 | Baron. . . . . 1854–1928 |
| Crockett, Samuel Rutherford . | 1860–1914 | Dalziel, Edward . . . 1817–1905 |
| Croft, Henry Page, Baron. . | 1881–1947 | Dalziel, George . . . 1815–1902 |
| Croft, John . . . | 1833–1905 | Dalziel, James Henry, Baron |
| Crofts, Ernest . . . | 1847–1911 | Dalziel of Kirkcaldy . . 1868–1935 |
| Croke, Thomas William . | 1824–1902 | Dalziel, Thomas Bolton Gilchrist |
| Cromer, Earl of. See Baring, | | Septimus . . . . 1823–1906 |
| Evelyn . . . . | 1841–1917 | Dane, Sir Louis William . 1856–1946 |
| Crompton, Henry . . | 1836–1904 | Daniel, Charles Henry Olive . 1836–1919 |
| Crompton, Rookes Evelyn Bell . | 1845–1940 | Daniel, Evan . . . . 1837–1904 |
| Crookes, Sir William . | 1832–1919 | Danvers, Frederic Charles . 1833–1906 |
| Crooks, William . | 1852–1921 | Darbyshire, Alfred . . 1839–1908 |
| Cross, Charles Frederick . | 1855–1935 | D'Arcy, Charles Frederick . 1859–1938 |
| Cross, Richard Assheton, Vis- | | Darling, Charles John, Baron . 1849–1936 |
| count . . . . | 1823–1914 | Darwin, Sir Francis . . 1848–1925 |
| Crossman, Sir William . | 1830–1901 | Darwin, Sir George Howard . 1845–1912 |
| Crosthwaite, Sir Charles Haukes | | Darwin, Sir Horace . . 1851–1928 |
| Todd . . . . | 1835–1915 | Dashwood, Edmée Elizabeth |
| Crowe, Eyre . . . | 1824–1910 | Monica, 'E. M. Delafield' . 1890–1943 |
| Crowe, Sir Eyre Alexander Barby | | Daubeney, Sir Henry Charles |
| Wichart . . . | 1864–1925 | Barnston . . . . 1810–1903 |
| Crozier, William Percival . | 1879–1944 | Davenport-Hill, Rosamond. See |
| Crum, Walter Ewing . | 1865–1944 | Hill . . . . . 1825–1902 |
| Crump, Charles George . | 1862–1935 | Davey, Horace, Baron . . 1833–1907 |
| Cruttwell, Charles Robert Mow- | | David, Albert Augustus . 1867–1950 |
| bray Fraser . . . | 1887–1941 | David, Sir (Tannatt William) |
| Cruttwell, Charles Thomas . | 1847–1911 | Edgeworth . . . . 1858–1934 |
| Cubitt, William George . | 1835–1903 | Davids, Thomas William Rhys . 1843–1922 |
| Cullen, William . | 1867–1948 | Davidson, Andrew Bruce . 1831–1902 |
| Cullingworth, Charles James . | 1841–1908 | Davidson, Charles . . 1824–1902 |
| Cummings, Bruce Frederick, | | Davidson, James Leigh Strachan-. |
| 'W. N. P. Barbellion' . . | 1889–1919 | See Strachan-Davidson . . 1843–1916 |
| Cuningham, James McNabb . | 1829–1905 | Davidson, John . . . 1857–1909 |
| Cunningham, Daniel John . | 1850–1909 | Davidson, John Thain . . 1833–1904 |
| Cunningham, William . | 1849–1919 | Davidson, Randall Thomas, |
| Cunninghame Graham, Robert | | Baron Davidson of Lambeth . 1848–1930 |
| Bontine. See Graham . . | 1852–1936 | Davies, Charles Maurice . 1828–1910 |
| Currie, Sir Arthur William . | 1875–1933 | Davies, David, Baron . . 1880–1944 |
| Currie, Sir Donald . . | 1825–1909 | Davies, Sir (Henry) Walford . 1869–1941 |
| Currie, Sir James . | 1868–1937 | Davies, John Llewelyn . 1826–1916 |
| Currie (formerly Singleton), | | Davies, Robert . . . 1816–1905 |
| Mary Montgomerie, Lady, | | Davies, (Sarah) Emily . . 1830–1921 |
| 'Violet Fane' . . . | 1843–1905 | Davies, William Henry . 1871–1940 |
| Currie, Philip Henry Wodehouse, | | Davis, Charles Edward . . 1827–1902 |
| Baron. . . . . | 1834–1906 | Davis, Henry William Carless . 1874–1928 |
| Curtin, John . . . | 1885–1945 | Davitt, Michael . . 1846–1906 |

| | | | | |
|---|---|---|---|---|
| Douglas, Sir Charles Whittingham Horsley | 1850–1914 | Dunphie, Charles James | 1820–1908 |
| Douglas, George, *pseudonym*. See Brown, George Douglas | 1869–1902 | Dunraven and Mount-Earl, Earl of. See Quin, Windham Thomas Wyndham- | 1841–1926 |
| Douglas, George Cunninghame Monteath | 1826–1904 | Dunstan, Sir Wyndham Rowland | 1861–1949 |
| Douglas, Sir (Henry) Percy | 1876–1939 | Du Parcq, Herbert, Baron | 1880–1949 |
| Douglas-Pennant, George Sholto Gordon, Baron Penrhyn | 1836–1907 | Dupré, August | 1835–1907 |
| | | Durand, Sir Henry Mortimer | 1850–1924 |
| Douglas-Scott-Montagu, John Walter Edward, Baron Montagu of Beaulieu | 1866–1929 | Durnford, Sir Walter | 1847–1926 |
| | | Dutt, Romesh Chunder | 1848–1909 |
| Dove, Dame (Jane) Frances | 1847–1942 | Dutton, Joseph Everett | 1874–1905 |
| Dove, John | 1872–1934 | Duveen, Joseph, Baron | 1869–1939 |
| Dowden, Edward | 1843–1913 | Duveen, Sir Joseph Joel | 1843–1908 |
| Dowden, John | 1840–1910 | Dyer, Reginald Edward Harry | 1864–1927 |
| Dowie, John Alexander | 1847–1907 | Dyer, Sir William Turner Thiselton-. See Thiselton-Dyer | 1843–1928 |
| Doyle, Sir Arthur Conan | 1859–1930 | | |
| Doyle, John Andrew | 1844–1907 | Dyke, Sir William Hart | 1837–1931 |
| Dredge, James | 1840–1906 | Dyson, Sir Frank Watson | 1868–1939 |
| Dreschfeld, Julius | 1846–1907 | Dyson, William Henry (Will) | 1880–1938 |
| Drew, Sir Thomas | 1838–1910 | | |
| Dreyer, Georges | 1873–1934 | Eady, Charles Swinfen, Baron Swinfen | 1851–1919 |
| Dreyer, John Louis Emil | 1852–1926 | Eardley-Wilmot, Sir Sainthill. See Wilmot | 1852–1929 |
| Drinkwater, John | 1882–1937 | | |
| Driver, Samuel Rolles | 1846–1914 | Earle, John | 1824–1903 |
| Druce, George Claridge | 1850–1932 | Earle, Sir Lionel | 1866–1948 |
| Drummond, Sir George Alexander | 1829–1910 | East, Sir Alfred | 1849–1913 |
| | | East, Sir Cecil James | 1837–1908 |
| Drummond, James | 1835–1918 | Eastlake, Charles Locke | 1836–1906 |
| Drummond, Sir Peter Roy Maxwell | 1894–1945 | Eaton, Herbert Francis, Baron Cheylesmore | 1848–1925 |
| Drummond, William Henry | 1854–1907 | Eaton, William Meriton, Baron Cheylesmore | 1843–1902 |
| Drury, (Edward) Alfred (Briscoe) | 1856–1944 | Ebsworth, Joseph Woodfall | 1824–1908 |
| Drury-Lowe, Sir Drury Curzon | 1830–1908 | Eddington, Sir Arthur Stanley | 1882–1944 |
| Dryland, Alfred | 1865–1946 | Eddis, Eden Upton | 1812–1901 |
| Drysdale, Learmont | 1866–1909 | Edge, Sir John | 1841–1926 |
| Du Cane, Sir Edmund Frederick | 1830–1903 | Edge, Selwyn Francis | 1868–1940 |
| Duckett, Sir George Floyd | 1811–1902 | Edgeworth, Francis Ysidro | 1845–1926 |
| Duckworth, Sir Dyce | 1840–1928 | Edouin, Willie | 1846–1908 |
| Dudgeon, Leonard Stanley | 1876–1938 | Edward VII, King | 1841–1910 |
| Dudgeon, Robert Ellis | 1820–1904 | Edward of Saxe-Weimar, Prince | 1823–1902 |
| Dudley, Earl of. See Ward, William Humble | 1867–1932 | Edwards, Alfred George | 1848–1937 |
| | | Edwards, Sir Fleetwood Isham | 1842–1910 |
| Duff, Sir Alexander Ludovic | 1862–1933 | Edwards, Henry Sutherland | 1828–1906 |
| Duff, Sir Beauchamp | 1855–1918 | Edwards, John Passmore | 1823–1911 |
| Duff, Sir Mountstuart Elphinstone Grant. See Grant Duff | 1829–1906 | Edwards, Matilda Barbara Betham- | 1836–1919 |
| Dufferin and Ava, Marquess of. See Blackwood, Frederick Temple Hamilton-Temple | 1826–1902 | Edwards, Sir Owen Morgan | 1858–1920 |
| | | Egerton, Sir Charles Comyn | 1848–1921 |
| Duffy, Sir Charles Gavan | 1816–1903 | Egerton, Hugh Edward | 1855–1927 |
| Duffy, Sir Frank Gavan | 1852–1936 | Elgar, Sir Edward William | 1857–1934 |
| Duffy, Patrick Vincent | 1836–1909 | Elgar, Francis | 1845–1909 |
| Duke, Sir Frederick William | 1863–1924 | Elgin, Earl of. See Bruce, Victor Alexander | 1849–1917 |
| Duke, Henry Edward, Baron Merrivale | 1855–1939 | Elias, Julius Salter, Viscount Southwood | 1873–1946 |
| Du Maurier, Sir Gerald Hubert Edward Busson | 1873–1934 | Eliot, Sir Charles Norton Edgecumbe | 1862–1931 |
| Duncan, Sir Patrick | 1870–1943 | Eliot, Sir John | 1839–1908 |
| Dundonald, Earl of. See Cochrane, Douglas Mackinnon Baillie Hamilton | 1852–1935 | Ellerman, Sir John Reeves | 1862–1933 |
| | | Ellery, Robert Lewis John | 1827–1908 |
| | | Elles, Sir Hugh Jamieson | 1880–1945 |
| Dunedin, Viscount. See Murray, Andrew Graham | 1849–1942 | Ellicott, Charles John | 1819–1905 |
| Dunhill, Thomas Frederick | 1877–1946 | Elliot, Arthur Ralph Douglas | 1846–1923 |
| Dunlop, John Boyd | 1840–1921 | Elliot, Sir George Augustus | 1813–1901 |
| Dunmore, Earl of. See Murray, Charles Adolphus | 1841–1907 | Elliot, Gilbert John Murray Kynynmond, Earl of Minto | 1845–1914 |
| | | Elliot, Sir Henry George | 1817–1907 |

| | | | | |
|---|---|---|---|---|
| FitzAlan-Howard, Henry, Duke of Norfolk. See Howard | 1847–1917 | | Fowler, Ellen Thorneycroft. See Felkin | 1860–1929 |
| Fitzclarence, Charles | 1865–1914 | | Fowler, Henry Hartley, Viscount Wolverhampton | 1830–1911 |
| FitzGerald, George Francis | 1851–1901 | | Fowler, Henry Watson | 1858–1933 |
| FitzGerald, Sir Thomas Naghten | 1838–1908 | | Fowler, Sir James Kingston | 1852–1934 |
| FitzGibbon, Gerald | 1837–1909 | | Fowler, Sir Ralph Howard | 1889–1944 |
| Fitzmaurice, Baron. See Petty-Fitzmaurice, Edmond George | 1846–1935 | | Fowler, Thomas | 1832–1904 |
| Fitzmaurice, Sir Maurice | 1861–1924 | | Fowler, William Warde | 1847–1921 |
| Fitzmaurice-Kelly, James | 1857–1923 | | Fox, Sir Francis | 1844–1927 |
| Fitzpatrick, Sir Dennis | 1837–1920 | | Fox, Samson | 1838–1903 |
| FitzPatrick, Sir (James) Percy | 1862–1931 | | Fox Bourne, Henry Richard. See Bourne | 1837–1909 |
| FitzRoy, Edward Algernon | 1869–1943 | | Fox Strangways, Arthur Henry. See Strangways | 1859–1948 |
| Fleay, Frederick Gard | 1831–1909 | | Foxwell, Arthur | 1853–1909 |
| Flecker, Herman Elroy (James Elroy) | 1884–1915 | | Foxwell, Herbert Somerton | 1849–1936 |
| Fleming, David Hay | 1849–1931 | | Frampton, Sir George James | 1860–1928 |
| Fleming, David Pinkerton, Lord | 1877–1944 | | Frankfort de Montmorency, Viscount. See De Montmorency, Raymond Harvey | 1835–1902 |
| Fleming, George | 1833–1901 | | Frankland, Percy Faraday | 1858–1946 |
| Fleming, James | 1830–1908 | | Fraser, Alexander Campbell | 1819–1914 |
| Fleming, Sir (John) Ambrose | 1849–1945 | | Fraser, Sir Andrew Henderson Leith | 1848–1919 |
| Fleming, Sir Sandford | 1827–1915 | | Fraser, Claud Lovat | 1890–1921 |
| Fletcher, Charles Robert Leslie | 1857–1934 | | Fraser, Donald | 1870–1933 |
| Fletcher, James | 1852–1908 | | Fraser, Peter | 1884–1950 |
| Fletcher, Sir Walter Morley | 1873–1933 | | Fraser, Simon Joseph, Baron Lovat | 1871–1933 |
| Flett, Sir John Smith | 1869–1947 | | Fraser, Sir Thomas Richard | 1841–1920 |
| Flint, Robert | 1838–1910 | | Frazer, Sir James George | 1854–1941 |
| Flower, Robin Ernest William | 1881–1946 | | Fream, William | 1854–1906 |
| Floyer, Ernest Ayscoghe | 1852–1903 | | Fréchette, Louis Honoré | 1839–1908 |
| Flux, Sir Alfred William | 1867–1942 | | Freeman, Gage Earle | 1820–1903 |
| Foakes Jackson, Frederick John. See Jackson | 1855–1941 | | Freeman, John | 1880–1929 |
| Fogerty, Elsie | 1865–1945 | | Freeman, John Peere Williams-. See Williams-Freeman | 1858–1943 |
| Forbes, George William | 1869–1947 | | Freeman, Sir Ralph | 1880–1950 |
| Forbes, James Staats | 1823–1904 | | Freeman-Mitford, Algernon Bertram, Baron Redesdale. See Mitford | 1837–1916 |
| Forbes, Stanhope Alexander | 1857–1947 | | Freeman-Thomas, Freeman, Marquess of Willingdon | 1866–1941 |
| Forbes-Robertson, Sir Johnston. See Robertson | 1853–1937 | | Fremantle, Sir Edmund Robert | 1836–1929 |
| Ford, Edward Onslow | 1852–1901 | | French, John Denton Pinkstone, Earl of Ypres | 1852–1925 |
| Ford, Ford Madox (formerly Ford Hermann Hueffer) | 1873–1939 | | Frere, Mary Eliza Isabella | 1845–1911 |
| Ford, Patrick | 1837–1913 | | Frere, Walter Howard | 1863–1938 |
| Ford, William Justice | 1853–1904 | | Freshfield, Douglas William | 1845–1934 |
| Fordham, Sir Herbert George | 1854–1929 | | Freyer, Sir Peter Johnston | 1851–1921 |
| Forestier-Walker, Sir Frederick William Edward Forestier | 1844–1910 | | Friese-Greene, William. See Greene | 1855–1921 |
| Forman, Alfred William. See Forman, Henry Buxton. | | | Frith, William Powell | 1819–1909 |
| Forman, Henry Buxton | 1842–1917 | | Frowde, Henry | 1841–1927 |
| Forrest, Sir George William David Starck | 1845–1926 | | Fry, Danby Palmer | 1818–1903 |
| Forrest, John, Baron | 1847–1918 | | Fry, Sir Edward | 1827–1918 |
| Forster, Hugh Oakeley Arnold-. See Arnold-Forster | 1855–1909 | | Fry, Joseph Storrs | 1826–1913 |
| Forster, Sir Martin Onslow | 1872–1945 | | Fry, Roger Eliot | 1866–1934 |
| Forsyth, Andrew Russell | 1858–1942 | | Fry, Thomas Charles | 1846–1930 |
| Fortescue, George Knottesford | 1847–1912 | | Fryatt, Charles Algernon | 1872–1916 |
| Fortescue, Hugh, Earl | 1818–1905 | | Fuller, Sir Cyril Thomas Moulden | 1874–1942 |
| Fortescue, Sir John William | 1859–1933 | | Fuller, Sir (Joseph) Bampfylde | 1854–1935 |
| Foster, Sir Clement Le Neve | 1841–1904 | | Fuller, Sir Thomas Ekins | 1831–1910 |
| Foster, Sir George Eulas | 1847–1931 | | Fuller-Maitland, John Alexander. See Maitland | 1856–1936 |
| Foster, Joseph | 1844–1905 | | Fulleylove, John | 1845–1908 |
| Foster, Sir Michael | 1836–1907 | | Furneaux, William Mordaunt | 1848–1928 |
| Foster, Sir (Thomas) Gregory | 1866–1931 | | Furness, Christopher, Baron | 1852–1912 |
| Fotheringham, John Knight | 1874–1936 | | | |
| Foulkes, Isaac | 1836–1904 | | | |
| Fowle, Thomas Welbank | 1835–1903 | | | |
| Fowler, Alfred | 1868–1940 | | | |

| | | |
|---|---|---|
| Goldsmid, Sir Frederick John . | 1818–1908 | |
| Goldsmid-Montefiore, Claude Joseph. See Montefiore . . | 1858–1938 | |
| Gollancz, Sir Hermann . . | 1852–1930 | |
| Gollancz, Sir Israel . . | 1863–1930 | |
| Goodall, Frederick . . . | 1822–1904 | |
| Goode, Sir William Athelstane Meredith . . . | 1875–1944 | |
| Goodenough, Frederick Craufurd | 1866–1934 | |
| Goodenough, Sir William Edmund . . . . . | 1867–1945 | |
| Goodman (formerly Salaman), Julia . . . . . | 1812–1906 | |
| Goodrich, Edwin Stephen . . | 1868–1946 | |
| Gordon, Arthur Charles Hamilton-, Baron Stanmore . . | 1829–1912 | |
| Gordon, Charles William, 'Ralph Connor' . . . . | 1860–1937 | |
| Gordon, George Stuart . . | 1881–1942 | |
| Gordon (formerly Marjoribanks), Ishbel Maria, Marchioness of Aberdeen and Temair. See under Gordon, John Campbell. | | |
| Gordon, James Frederick Skinner | 1821–1904 | |
| Gordon, John Campbell, Marquess of Aberdeen and Temair | 1847–1934 | |
| Gordon, Sir John James Hood . | 1832–1908 | |
| Gordon, Sir Thomas Edward . | 1832–1914 | |
| Gordon-Lennox, Charles Henry, Duke of Richmond . . | 1818–1903 | |
| Gore, Albert Augustus . . | 1840–1901 | |
| Gore, Charles . . . . | 1853–1932 | |
| Gore, George . . . | 1826–1908 | |
| Gore, John Ellard . . . | 1845–1910 | |
| Gorell, Baron. See Barnes, John Gorell . . . . . | 1848–1913 | |
| Gorst, Sir John Eldon . . | 1835–1916 | |
| Gorst, Sir (John) Eldon . . | 1861–1911 | |
| Gort, Viscount. See Vereker, John Standish Surtees Prendergast . . . . | 1886–1946 | |
| Goschen, George Joachim, Viscount . . . . . | 1831–1907 | |
| Gosling, Harry . . . | 1861–1930 | |
| Gossage, Sir (Ernest) Leslie . | 1891–1949 | |
| Gosse, Sir Edmund William . | 1849–1928 | |
| Gosselin, Sir Martin le Marchant Hadsley . . . . | 1847–1905 | |
| Gosset, William Sealy, 'Student' . | 1876–1937 | |
| Gotch, John Alfred . . . | 1852–1942 | |
| Gott, John . . . . | 1830–1906 | |
| Gott, William Henry Ewart . | 1897–1942 | |
| Gough, Sir Charles John Stanley | 1832–1912 | |
| Gough, Sir Hugh Henry . . | 1833–1909 | |
| Gough, John Edmond . . | 1871–1915 | |
| Gough-Calthorpe, Augustus Cholmondeley, Baron Calthorpe . | 1829–1910 | |
| Gough-Calthorpe, Sir Somerset Arthur. See Calthorpe . . | 1864–1937 | |
| Gould, Sir Francis Carruthers . | 1844–1925 | |
| Gould, Nathaniel . . . | 1857–1919 | |
| Goulding, Frederick . . . | 1842–1909 | |
| Gower, (Edward) Frederick Leveson-. See Leveson-Gower . | 1819–1907 | |
| Gowers, Sir William Richard . | 1845–1915 | |
| Grace, Edward Mills . . | 1841–1911 | |
| Grace, William Gilbert . . | 1848–1915 | |
| Graham, Henry Grey . . | 1842–1906 | |
| Graham, Hugh, Baron Atholstan | 1848–1938 | |
| Graham, John Anderson . . | 1861–1942 | |
| Graham, Robert Bontine Cunninghame . . . . | 1852–1936 | |
| Graham, Sir Ronald William . | 1870–1949 | |
| Graham, Thomas Alexander Ferguson . . . . . | 1840–1906 | |
| Graham, William . . . | 1839–1911 | |
| Graham, William . . . | 1887–1932 | |
| Graham-Harrison, Sir William Montagu . . . . | 1871–1949 | |
| Graham-Little, Sir Ernest Gordon Graham . . . | 1867–1950 | |
| Grahame, Kenneth . . . | 1859–1932 | |
| Granet, Sir (William) Guy . . | 1867–1943 | |
| Grant, Sir (Alfred) Hamilton . | 1872–1937 | |
| Grant, Sir Charles. See under Grant, Sir Robert. | | |
| Grant, George Monro . . | 1835–1902 | |
| Grant, Sir Robert . . . | 1837–1904 | |
| Grant Duff, Sir Mountstuart Elphinstone . . . . | 1829–1906 | |
| Grantham, Sir William . . | 1835–1911 | |
| Granville-Barker, Harley Granville . . . . . | 1877–1946 | |
| Graves, Alfred Perceval . . | 1846–1931 | |
| Graves, George Windsor . . | 1873 ?–1949 | |
| Gray, Benjamin Kirkman . . | 1862–1907 | |
| Gray, George Buchanan . . | 1865–1922 | |
| Gray, George Edward Kruger . | 1880–1943 | |
| Gray, Herbert Branston . . | 1851–1929 | |
| Greaves, Walter . . . | 1846–1930 | |
| Green, Alice Sophia Amelia (Mrs. Stopford Green) . . . | 1847–1929 | |
| Green, Charles Alfred Howell . | 1864–1944 | |
| Green, Samuel Gosnell . . | 1822–1905 | |
| Greenaway, Catherine (Kate) . | 1846–1901 | |
| Greene, Harry Plunket . . | 1865–1936 | |
| Greene, William Friese- . . | 1855–1921 | |
| Greene, Sir (William) Graham . | 1857–1950 | |
| Greenidge, Abel Hendy Jones . | 1865–1906 | |
| Greenwell, William . . . | 1820–1918 | |
| Greenwood, Frederick . . | 1830–1909 | |
| Greenwood, Hamar, Viscount . | 1870–1948 | |
| Greenwood, Thomas . . | 1851–1908 | |
| Greer, (Frederick) Arthur, Baron Fairfield . . . . | 1863–1945 | |
| Greet, Sir Phillip Barling Ben . | 1857–1936 | |
| Grego, Joseph . . . . | 1843–1908 | |
| Gregory, Sir Augustus Charles . | 1819–1905 | |
| Gregory, Edward John . . | 1850–1909 | |
| Gregory, Isabella Augusta, Lady | 1852–1932 | |
| Gregory, John Walter . . | 1864–1932 | |
| Gregory, Robert . . . | 1819–1911 | |
| Greiffenhagen, Maurice William | 1862–1931 | |
| Grenfell, Bernard Pyne . . | 1869–1926 | |
| Grenfell, Edward Charles, Baron St. Just . . . . | 1870–1941 | |
| Grenfell, Francis Wallace, Baron | 1841–1925 | |
| Grenfell, George . . . | 1849–1906 | |
| Grenfell, Hubert Henry . . | 1845–1906 | |
| Grenfell, Julian Henry Francis . | 1888–1915 | |
| Grenfell, Sir Wilfred Thomason . | 1865–1940 | |
| Grenfell, William Henry, Baron Desborough . . . . | 1855–1945 | |
| Greville, Frances Evelyn, Countess of Warwick . . . | 1861–1938 | |
| Grey, Albert Henry George, Earl | 1851–1917 | |
| Grey, Sir Edward, Viscount Grey of Fallodon . . . . | 1862–1933 | |

| | | | |
|---|---|---|---|
| Hardie, William Ross | 1862–1916 | Hawke, Sir (John) Anthony | 1869–1941 |
| Hardiman, Alfred Frank | 1891–1949 | Hawke, Martin Bladen, Baron | |
| Hardinge, Charles, Baron Hardinge of Penshurst | 1858–1944 | Hawke of Towton | 1860–1938 |
| Hardwicke, Earl of. See Yorke, | | Hawker, Mary Elizabeth, 'Lanoe Falconer' | 1848–1908 |
| Albert Edward Philip Henry | 1867–1904 | Hawkins, Sir Anthony Hope, | |
| Hardy, Frederic Daniel | 1827–1911 | 'Anthony Hope' | 1863–1933 |
| Hardy, Gathorne Gathorne-, Earl of Cranbrook. See Gathorne-Hardy | 1814–1906 | Hawkins, Henry, Baron Brampton | 1817–1907 |
| Hardy, Godfrey Harold | 1877–1947 | Haworth, Sir (Walter) Norman | 1883–1950 |
| Hardy, Herbert Hardy Cozens-, Baron Cozens-Hardy. See Cozens-Hardy | 1838–1920 | Hawtrey, Sir Charles Henry | 1858–1923 |
| | | Hay, Sir Harley Hugh Dalrymple- | 1861–1940 |
| | | Hayes, Edwin | 1819–1904 |
| Hardy, Thomas | 1840–1928 | Hayman, Henry | 1823–1904 |
| Hardy, Sir William Bate | 1864–1934 | Hayne, Charles Hayne Seale-. See Seale-Hayne | 1833–1903 |
| Hare, Augustus John Cuthbert | 1834–1903 | Hayward, Robert Baldwin | 1829–1903 |
| Hare, Sir John | 1844–1921 | Hazlitt, William Carew | 1834–1913 |
| Harewood, Earl of. See Lascelles, Henry George Charles | 1882–1947 | Head, Barclay Vincent | 1844–1914 |
| | | Head, Sir Henry | 1861–1940 |
| Harington, Sir Charles ('Tim') | 1872–1940 | Headlam, Arthur Cayley | 1862–1947 |
| Harker, Alfred | 1859–1939 | Headlam, Walter George | 1866–1908 |
| Harland, Henry | 1861–1905 | Headlam-Morley, Sir James Wycliffe | 1863–1929 |
| Harley, Robert | 1828–1910 | | |
| Harmsworth, Alfred Charles William, Viscount Northcliffe | 1865–1922 | Healy, John Edward | 1872–1934 |
| | | Healy, Timothy Michael | 1855–1931 |
| Harmsworth, Harold Sidney, Viscount Rothermere | 1868–1940 | Hearn, Mary Anne, 'Marianne Farningham' | 1834–1909 |
| Harper, Sir George Montague | 1865–1922 | Heath, Christopher | 1835–1905 |
| Harraden, Beatrice | 1864–1936 | Heath, Sir (Henry) Frank | 1863–1946 |
| Harrel, Sir David | 1841–1939 | Heath, Sir Leopold George | 1817–1907 |
| Harrington, Timothy Charles | 1851–1910 | Heath, Sir Thomas Little | 1861–1940 |
| Harris, Frederick Leverton | 1864–1926 | Heath Robinson, William. See Robinson | 1872–1944 |
| Harris, George Robert Canning, Baron | 1851–1932 | | |
| | | Heathcote, John Moyer | 1834–1912 |
| Harris, James Rendel | 1852–1941 | Heaton, Sir John Henniker | 1848–1914 |
| Harris, James Thomas ('Frank') | 1856–1931 | Heaviside, Oliver | 1850–1925 |
| Harris, Thomas Lake | 1823–1906 | Hector, Annie French, 'Mrs. Alexander' | 1825–1902 |
| Harrison, Frederic | 1831–1923 | | |
| Harrison, Jane Ellen | 1850–1928 | Hector, Sir James | 1834–1907 |
| Harrison, Mary St. Leger, 'Lucas Malet'. | 1852–1931 | Heinemann, William | 1863–1920 |
| | | Hele-Shaw, Henry Selby | 1854–1941 |
| Harrison, Reginald | 1837–1908 | Helena Victoria, Princess | 1870–1948 |
| Harrison, Sir William Montagu Graham-. See Graham-Harrison | 1871–1949 | Hellmuth, Isaac | 1817–1901 |
| | | Hely-Hutchinson, Richard Walter John, Earl of Donoughmore | 1875–1948 |
| Hart, Sir Robert | 1835–1911 | Hemming, George Wirgman | 1821–1905 |
| Hartington, Marquess of. See Cavendish, Spencer Compton | 1833–1908 | Hemphill, Charles Hare, Baron | 1822–1908 |
| | | Henderson, Arthur | 1863–1935 |
| Hartley, Sir Charles Augustus | 1825–1915 | Henderson, Sir David | 1862–1921 |
| Hartog, Sir Philip(pe) Joseph | 1864–1947 | Henderson, George Francis Robert | 1854–1903 |
| Hartshorn, Vernon | 1872–1931 | | |
| Hartshorne, Albert | 1839–1910 | Henderson, George Gerald | 1862–1942 |
| Harty, Sir (Herbert) Hamilton | 1879–1941 | Henderson, Joseph | 1832–1908 |
| Harvey, Sir John Martin Martin-. See Martin-Harvey | 1863–1944 | Henderson, Sir Nevile Meyrick | 1882–1942 |
| | | Henderson, Sir Reginald Guy Hannam | 1881–1939 |
| Harwood, Basil | 1859–1949 | | |
| Harwood, Sir Henry Harwood | 1888–1950 | Henderson, William George | 1819–1905 |
| Hassall, John | 1868–1948 | Henley, William Ernest | 1849–1903 |
| Hastie, William | 1842–1903 | Hennell, Sara (1812–1899). See under Bray, Caroline | 1814–1905 |
| Hastings, James | 1852–1922 | | |
| Hatton, Harold Heneage Finch-. See Finch-Hatton | 1856–1904 | Hennessey, John Bobanau Nickerlieu | 1829–1910 |
| | | Hennessy, Henry | 1826–1901 |
| Hatton, Joseph | 1841–1907 | Henry, Sir Edward Richard | 1850–1931 |
| Havelock, Sir Arthur Elibank | 1844–1908 | Henry, Mitchell | 1826–1910 |
| Haverfield, Francis John | 1860–1919 | Henschel, Sir George | 1850–1934 |
| Haweis, Hugh Reginald | 1838–1901 | Henson, Herbert Hensley | 1863–1947 |
| Haweis, Mary. See under Haweis, Hugh Reginald. | | Henty, George Alfred | 1832–1902 |

| | | | | |
|---|---|---|---|---|
| Keetley, Charles Robert Bell | 1848–1909 | Kingscote, Sir Robert Nigel Fitzhardinge | 1830–1908 | |
| Keith, Arthur Berriedale | 1879–1944 | Kingsford, Charles Lethbridge | 1862–1926 | |
| Keith, Sir William John | 1873–1937 | Kingston, Charles Cameron | 1850–1908 | |
| Kekewich, Sir Arthur | 1832–1907 | Kinnear, Alexander Smith, Baron | 1833–1917 | |
| Kekewich, Robert George | 1854–1914 | Kinns, Samuel | 1826–1903 | |
| Kelly, Frederick Septimus | 1881–1916 | Kinross, Baron. See Balfour, John Blair | 1837–1905 | |
| Kelly, James Fitzmaurice-. See Fitzmaurice-Kelly | 1857–1923 | Kipling, (Joseph) Rudyard | 1865–1936 | |
| Kelly, Sir John Donald | 1871–1936 | Kipping, Frederic Stanley | 1863–1949 | |
| Kelly, Mary Anne, 'Eva' (1826–1910). See under O'Doherty, Kevin Izod | 1823–1905 | Kirk, Sir John | 1832–1922 | |
| | | Kirk, Sir John | 1847–1922 | |
| Kelly, William | 1821–1906 | Kitchener, Horatio Herbert, Earl | 1850–1916 | |
| Kelly-Kenny, Sir Thomas | 1840–1914 | Kitchin, George William | 1827–1912 | |
| Keltie, Sir John Scott | 1840–1927 | Kitson, James, Baron Airedale | 1835–1911 | |
| Kelvin, Baron. See Thomson, William | 1824–1907 | Kitton, Frederick George | 1856–1904 | |
| | | Knight, Joseph | 1829–1907 | |
| Kemball, Sir Arnold Burrowes | 1820–1908 | Knight, Joseph | 1837–1909 | |
| Kemball-Cook, Sir Basil Alfred | 1876–1949 | Knollys, Francis, Viscount | 1837–1924 | |
| Kemble, Henry | 1848–1907 | Knott, Ralph | 1878–1929 | |
| Kemp, Stanley Wells | 1882–1945 | Knowles, Sir James Thomas | 1831–1908 | |
| Kendal, Dame Margaret Shafto (Madge) | 1848–1935 | Knox, Edmund Arbuthnott | 1847–1937 | |
| | | Knox, Sir George Edward | 1845–1922 | |
| Kendal, William Hunter | 1843–1917 | Knox (formerly Craig), Isa | 1831–1903 | |
| Kennedy, Sir Alexander Blackie William | 1847–1928 | Knox, Wilfred Lawrence | 1886–1950 | |
| | | Knox-Little, William John | 1839–1918 | |
| Kennedy, Harry Angus Alexander | 1866–1934 | Knutsford, Viscount. See Holland, Sir Henry Thurstan | 1825–1914 | |
| Kennedy, Sir William Rann | 1846–1915 | Knutsford, Viscount. See Holland, Sydney George | 1855–1931 | |
| Kennet, (Edith Agnes) Kathleen, Lady | 1878–1947 | Kotzé, Sir John Gilbert | 1849–1940 | |
| Kennett, Robert Hatch | 1864–1932 | Kruger Gray, George Edward. See Gray | 1880–1943 | |
| Kenny, Courtney Stanhope | 1847–1930 | Kuczynski, Robert Rene | 1876–1947 | |
| Kensit, John | 1853–1902 | Kylsant, Baron. See Philipps, Owen Cosby | 1863–1937 | |
| Kent, Duke of. See George Edward Alexander Edmund | 1902–1942 | Kynaston (formerly Snow), Herbert | 1835–1910 | |
| Kent, (William) Charles (Mark) | 1823–1902 | | | |
| Kenyon, George Thomas | 1840–1908 | Labouchere, Henrietta. See Hodson | 1841–1910 | |
| Kenyon-Slaney, William Slaney | 1847–1908 | Labouchere, Henry Du Pré | 1831–1912 | |
| Keogh, Sir Alfred | 1857–1936 | Lacey, Thomas Alexander | 1853–1931 | |
| Keppel, Sir George Olof Roos-. See Roos-Keppel | 1866–1921 | Lafont, Eugène | 1837–1908 | |
| | | Laidlaw, Anna Robena | 1819–1901 | |
| Keppel, Sir Henry | 1809–1904 | Laidlaw, John | 1832–1906 | |
| Ker, William Paton | 1855–1923 | Laidlaw, Sir Patrick Playfair | 1881–1940 | |
| Kerr, John | 1824–1907 | Laird, John | 1887–1946 | |
| Kerr, Philip Henry, Marquess of Lothian | 1882–1940 | Lake, Kirsopp | 1872–1946 | |
| | | Lake, Sir Percy Henry Noel | 1855–1940 | |
| Kerr, Robert | 1823–1904 | Lamb, Sir Horace | 1849–1934 | |
| Kerr, Lord Walter Talbot | 1839–1927 | Lambart, Frederick Rudolph, Earl of Cavan | 1865–1946 | |
| Kettle, Edgar Hartley | 1882–1936 | Lambert, Brooke | 1834–1901 | |
| Keyes, Roger John Brownlow, Baron | 1872–1945 | Lambert, George | 1842–1915 | |
| Keynes, John Maynard, Baron | 1883–1946 | Lambourne, Baron. See Lockwood, Amelius Mark Richard | 1847–1928 | |
| Kidd, Benjamin | 1858–1916 | Lamington, Baron. See Baillie, Charles Wallace Alexander Napier Ross Cochrane- | 1860–1940 | |
| Kilbracken, Baron. See Godley, (John) Arthur | 1847–1932 | | | |
| Killen, William Dool | 1806–1902 | Lanchester, Frederick William | 1868–1946 | |
| Kimberley, Earl of. See Wodehouse, John | 1826–1902 | Lane, Sir Hugh Percy | 1875–1915 | |
| Kinahan, George Henry | 1829–1908 | Lane, John | 1854–1925 | |
| Kincairney, Lord. See Gloag, William Ellis | 1828–1909 | Lane, Sir (William) Arbuthnot | 1856–1943 | |
| | | Lane Poole, Reginald. See Poole | 1857–1939 | |
| King, Edward | 1829–1910 | Lane-Poole, Stanley Edward. See Poole | 1854–1931 | |
| King, Sir (Frederic) Truby | 1858–1938 | | | |
| King, Sir George | 1840–1909 | Lang, (Alexander) Matheson | 1877–1948 | |
| King, Haynes | 1831–1904 | Lang, Andrew | 1844–1912 | |
| King, William Lyon Mackenzie | 1874–1950 | | | |
| Kingsburgh, Lord. See Macdonald, John Hay Athole | 1836–1919 | | | |

| | | |
|---|---|---|
| Lindsay, David . . . | 1856–1922 | Lopes, Sir Lopes Massey . . 1818–1908 |
| Lindsay, David Alexander Edward, Earl of Crawford . . | 1871–1940 | Lord, Thomas . . . . 1808–1908 |
| Lindsay, James Gavin . | 1835–1903 | Loreburn, Earl. See Reid, Robert Threshie . . . 1846–1923 |
| Lindsay, James Ludovic, Earl of Crawford . . . . | 1847–1913 | Lorimer, Sir Robert Stodart . 1864–1929 |
| Lindsay (afterwards Loyd-Lindsay), Robert James, Baron Wantage . . . . | 1832–1901 | Lotbinière, Sir Henry Gustave Joly de. See Joly de Lotbinière . . . . . 1829–1908 |
| Lindsay, Sir Ronald Charles . | 1877–1945 | Lothian, Marquess of. See Kerr, Philip Henry . . . 1882–1940 |
| Lindsay, Thomas Martin . | 1843–1914 | Louise Caroline Alberta, princess |
| Lindsay, Wallace Martin . | 1858–1937 | of Great Britain . . . 1848–1939 |
| Lingen, Ralph Robert Wheeler, Baron . . . . . | 1819–1905 | Louise Victoria Alexandra Dagmar, Princess Royal of Great |
| Linlithgow, Marquess of. See Hope, John Adrian Louis . | 1860–1908 | Britain . . . . 1867–1931 |
| Lipton, Sir Thomas Johnstone . | 1850–1931 | Lovat, Baron. See Fraser, Simon Joseph . . . . 1871–1933 |
| Lister, Arthur . . . . | 1830–1908 | Love, Augustus Edward Hough 1863–1940 |
| Lister, Joseph, Baron . . | 1827–1912 | Lovelace, Earl of. See Milbanke, |
| Lister, Samuel Cunliffe, Baron Masham . . . . | 1815–1906 | Ralph Gordon Noel King . 1839–1906 |
| Little, Andrew George . | 1863–1945 | Lovett, Richard . . . 1851–1904 |
| Little, Sir Ernest Gordon Graham Graham-. See Graham-Little . | 1867–1950 | Low, Alexander, Lord . . 1845–1910 |
| Little, William John Knox-. See Knox-Little . . . . | 1839–1918 | Low, Sir Robert Cunliffe . . 1838–1911 |
| | | Low, Sir Sidney James Mark . 1857–1932 |
| Littler, Sir Ralph Daniel Makinson . . . . . | 1835–1908 | Lowe, Sir Drury Curzon Drury-. See Drury-Lowe . . . 1830–1908 |
| Liveing, George Downing . | 1827–1924 | Lowry, Henry Dawson . . 1869–1906 |
| Livesey, Sir George Thomas . | 1834–1908 | Lowry, Thomas Martin . . 1874–1936 |
| Llandaff, Viscount. See Matthews, Henry . . | 1826–1913 | Lowther, Hugh Cecil, Earl of Lonsdale . . . . 1857–1944 |
| Llewellyn, Sir (Samuel Henry) William . . . . | 1858–1941 | Lowther, James . . . 1840–1904 |
| Lloyd, Dorothy Jordan . | 1889–1946 | Lowther, James William, Viscount Ullswater . . . 1855–1949 |
| Lloyd, George Ambrose, Baron . | 1879–1941 | Löwy, Albert or Abraham . 1816–1908 |
| Lloyd, Sir John Edward . | 1861–1947 | Loyd-Lindsay. See Lindsay, Robert James, Baron Wantage . 1832–1901 |
| Lloyd, Marie, pseudonym. See Wood, Matilda Alice Victoria . | 1870–1922 | Luard, Sir William Garnham . 1820–1910 |
| Lloyd George, David, Earl Lloyd-George of Dwyfor . . . | 1863–1945 | Lubbock, Sir John, Baron Avebury . . . . . 1834–1913 |
| Lloyd James, Arthur. See James | 1884–1943 | Luby, Thomas Clarke . . 1821–1901 |
| Loates, Thomas . . . | 1867–1910 | Lucas, Baron. See Herbert, Auberon Thomas . . 1876–1916 |
| Loch, Sir Charles Stewart . . | 1849–1923 | Lucas, Sir Charles Prestwood . 1853–1931 |
| Lock, Walter . . . . | 1846–1933 | Lucas, Edward Verrall . . 1868–1938 |
| Locke, William John . . | 1863–1930 | Lucas, Keith . . . 1879–1916 |
| Lockey, Charles . . . | 1820–1901 | Luckock, Herbert Mortimer . 1833–1909 |
| Lockwood, Amelius Mark Richard, Baron Lambourne . | 1847–1928 | Lucy, Sir Henry William . . 1843–1924 |
| Lockyer, Sir (Joseph) Norman . | 1836–1920 | Ludlow, John Malcolm Forbes . 1821–1911 |
| Lodge, Eleanor Constance . | 1869–1936 | Lugard, Frederick John Dealtry, Baron . . . . . 1858–1945 |
| Lodge, Sir Oliver Joseph . . | 1851–1940 | Luke, Baron. See Johnston, George Lawson . . . 1873–1943 |
| Lodge, Sir Richard . . | 1855–1936 | Luke, Jemima . . . 1813–1906 |
| Loftie, William John . . | 1839–1911 | Lukin, Sir Henry Timson . . 1860–1925 |
| Loftus, Lord Augustus William Frederick Spencer . . | 1817–1904 | Lunn, Sir Henry Simpson . . 1859–1939 |
| Logue, Michael . . . | 1840–1924 | Lupton, Joseph Hirst . . 1836–1905 |
| Lohmann, George Alfred . . | 1865–1901 | Lush, Sir Charles Montague . 1853–1930 |
| Londonderry, Marquess of. See Vane-Tempest-Stewart, Charles Stewart . . . . . | 1852–1915 | Lusk, Sir Andrew . . . 1810–1909 |
| | | Lutyens, Sir Edwin Landseer . 1869–1944 |
| | | Lutz, (Wilhelm) Meyer . . 1829–1903 |
| Londonderry, Marquess of. See Vane-Tempest-Stewart, Charles Stewart Henry . . . | 1878–1949 | Luxmoore, Sir (Arthur) Fairfax (Charles Coryndon) . . 1876–1944 |
| | | Lyall, Sir Alfred Comyn . . 1835–1911 |
| Long, Walter Hume, Viscount Long of Wraxall . . . | 1854–1924 | Lyall, Sir Charles James . . 1845–1920 |
| | | Lyall, Edna, pseudonym. See Bayly, Ada Ellen . . 1857–1903 |
| Longhurst, William Henry . | 1819–1904 | Lygon, William, Earl Beauchamp 1872–1938 |
| Lonsdale, Earl of. See Lowther, Hugh Cecil . . . . | 1857–1944 | Lynch, Arthur Alfred . . 1861–1934 |
| | | Lynd, Robert Wilson . . 1879–1949 |

| | |
|---|---|
| Pollen, John Hungerford . . | 1820–1902 |
| Pollock, Bertram . . . | 1863–1943 |
| Pollock, Ernest Murray, Viscount Hanworth . . . . | 1861–1936 |
| Pollock, Sir Frederick . . | 1845–1937 |
| Pollock, Hugh McDowell . . | 1852–1937 |
| Ponsonby, Arthur Augustus William Harry, Baron Ponsonby of Shulbrede . . . | 1871–1946 |
| Poole, Reginald Lane . . | 1857–1939 |
| Poole, Stanley Edward Lane- . | 1854–1931 |
| Poore, George Vivian . . | 1843–1904 |
| Pope, George Uglow . . | 1820–1908 |
| Pope, Samuel . . . . | 1826–1901 |
| Pope, William Burt . . . | 1822–1903 |
| Pope, Sir William Jackson . | 1870–1939 |
| Portal, Melville . . . | 1819–1904 |
| Portal, Sir Wyndham Raymond, Viscount . . . | 1885–1949 |
| Porter, Sir Andrew Marshall . | 1837–1919 |
| Postan (formerly Power), Eileen Edna le Poer . . . | 1889–1940 |
| Postgate, John Percival . | 1853–1926 |
| Pott, Alfred . . . . | 1822–1908 |
| Potter, (Helen) Beatrix (Mrs. Heelis) . . . . | 1866–1943 |
| Poulton, Sir Edward Bagnall . | 1856–1943 |
| Pound, Sir (Alfred) Dudley (Pickman Rogers) . . | 1877–1943 |
| Powell, Frederick York . . | 1850–1904 |
| Powell, Sir (George) Allan . | 1876–1948 |
| Powell, Sir Richard Douglas . | 1842–1925 |
| Powell, Robert Stephenson Smyth Baden-, Baron Baden-Powell. See Baden-Powell . | 1857–1941 |
| Power, Sir D'Arcy . . . | 1855–1941 |
| Power, Eileen Edna le Poer. See Postan . . . | 1889–1940 |
| Power, Sir John Cecil . . | 1870–1950 |
| Power, Sir William Henry . | 1842–1916 |
| Poynder, Sir John Poynder Dickson-, Baron Islington . . | 1866–1936 |
| Poynter, Sir Edward John . | 1836–1919 |
| Poynting, John Henry . . | 1852–1914 |
| Prain, Sir David . . . | 1857–1944 |
| Pratt, Hodgson . . . | 1824–1907 |
| Pratt, Joseph Bishop . . | 1854–1910 |
| Preece, Sir William Henry . | 1834–1913 |
| Prendergast, Sir Harry North Dalrymple . . . . | 1834–1913 |
| Previté-Orton, Charles William . | 1877–1947 |
| Price, Frederick George Hilton . | 1842–1909 |
| Price, Thomas . . . . | 1852–1909 |
| Prichard, Harold Arthur . . | 1871–1947 |
| Primrose, Archibald Philip, Earl of Rosebery . . . | 1847–1929 |
| Primrose, Sir Henry William . | 1846–1923 |
| Pringle, William Mather Rutherford . . . . . | 1874–1928 |
| Pringle-Pattison, Andrew Seth. See Pattison . . . | 1856–1931 |
| Prinsep, Valentine Cameron (Val) | 1838–1904 |
| Prior, Melton . . . . | 1845–1910 |
| Pritchard, Sir Charles Bradley . | 1837–1903 |
| Pritchett, Robert Taylor . . | 1828–1907 |
| Probert, Lewis . . . | 1841–1908 |
| Procter, Francis . . . | 1812–1905 |
| Proctor, Robert George Collier . | 1868–1903 |
| Propert, John Lumsden . . | 1834–1902 |

| | |
|---|---|
| Prothero, Sir George Walter . | 1848–1922 |
| Prothero, Rowland Edmund, Baron Ernle . . . | 1851–1937 |
| Prout, Ebenezer . . . | 1835–1909 |
| Pryde, James Ferrier . . | 1866–1941 |
| Prynne, George Rundle . . | 1818–1903 |
| Puddicombe, Anne Adalisa, 'Allen Raine' . . . . | 1836–1908 |
| Pullen, Henry William . . | 1836–1903 |
| Purcell, Albert Arthur William . | 1872–1935 |
| Purse, Benjamin Ormond . . | 1874–1950 |
| Purser, Louis Claude . . | 1854–1932 |
| Purvis, Arthur Blaikie . . | 1890–1941 |
| Pyne, Louisa Fanny Bodda. See Bodda Pyne . . . | 1832–1904 |
| Quarrier, William . . . | 1829–1903 |
| Quick, Sir John . . . | 1852–1932 |
| Quick, Oliver Chase . . . | 1885–1944 |
| Quiller-Couch, Sir Arthur Thomas ('Q') . . . . | 1863–1944 |
| Quilter, Harry . . . | 1851–1907 |
| Quilter, Sir William Cuthbert . | 1841–1911 |
| Quin, Windham Thomas Wyndham-, Earl of Dunraven and Mount-Earl . . . . | 1841–1926 |
| Rackham, Arthur . . . | 1867–1939 |
| Radcliffe-Crocker, Henry . . | 1845–1909 |
| Rae, William Fraser . . | 1835–1905 |
| Raggi, Mario . . . . | 1821–1907 |
| Railton, Herbert . . . | 1858–1910 |
| Raine, Allen, pseudonym. See Puddicombe, Anne Adalisa . | 1836–1908 |
| Raines, Sir Julius Augustus Robert . . . . | 1827–1909 |
| Rainy, Adam Rolland. See under Rainy, Robert. | |
| Rainy, Robert . . . | 1826–1906 |
| Rait, Sir Robert Sangster . . | 1874–1936 |
| Raleigh, Sir Walter Alexander . | 1861–1922 |
| Ralston, James Layton . . | 1881–1948 |
| Ramé, Marie Louise, 'Ouida'. See De la Ramée . . . | 1839–1908 |
| Ramsay, Alexander . . . | 1822–1909 |
| Ramsay, Sir Bertram Home . | 1883–1945 |
| Ramsay, Sir James Henry . | 1832–1925 |
| Ramsay, Sir William . . | 1852–1916 |
| Ramsay, Sir William Mitchell . | 1851–1939 |
| Ramsay-Steel-Maitland, Sir Arthur Herbert Drummond. See Steel-Maitland . . . | 1876–1935 |
| Ramsden, Omar . . . | 1873–1939 |
| Randall, Richard William . . | 1824–1906 |
| Randall-MacIver, David . . | 1873–1945 |
| Randegger, Alberto . . . | 1832–1911 |
| Randles, Marshall . . . | 1826–1904 |
| Randolph, Francis Charles Hingeston-. See Hingeston-Randolph . . . . . | 1833–1910 |
| Randolph, Sir George Granville | 1818–1907 |
| Ranjitsinhji, Maharaja Jam Saheb of Nawanagar. See Nawanagar . . . . | 1872–1933 |
| Rankeillour, Baron. See Hope, James Fitzalan . . . | 1870–1949 |
| Rankin, Sir George Claus . . | 1877–1946 |
| Ransom, William Henry . . | 1824–1907 |
| Raper, Robert William . . | 1842–1915 |

| | |
|---|---|
| Robinson, Vincent Joseph . | 1829–1910 |
| Robinson, Sir (William) Arthur . | 1874–1950 |
| Robinson, William Heath . . | 1872–1944 |
| Robinson, William Leefe . . | 1895–1918 |
| Robison, Robert . . . | 1883–1941 |
| Robson, William Snowdon, Baron . . . . | 1852–1918 |
| Roby, Henry John . . | 1830–1915 |
| Rodd, James Rennell, Baron Rennell . . . . | 1858–1941 |
| Rogers, Annie Mary Anne Henley | 1856–1937 |
| Rogers, Benjamin Bickley . | 1828–1919 |
| Rogers, Edmund Dawson . | 1823–1910 |
| Rogers, James Guinness . | 1822–1911 |
| Rogers, Leonard James . | 1862–1933 |
| Rolleston, Sir Humphry Davy . | 1862–1944 |
| Rolls, Charles Stewart . | 1877–1910 |
| Romer, Mark Lemon, Baron . | 1866–1944 |
| Romer, Sir Robert . . . | 1840–1918 |
| Ronald, Sir Landon . . . | 1873–1938 |
| Ronan, Stephen . . . | 1848–1925 |
| Rookwood, Baron. See Selwin-Ibbetson, Henry John . . | 1826–1902 |
| Rooper, Thomas Godolphin . | 1847–1903 |
| Roos-Keppel, Sir George Olof . | 1866–1921 |
| Roose, Edward Charles Robson . | 1848–1905 |
| Ropes, Arthur Reed, 'Adrian Ross' . . . . | 1859–1933 |
| Roscoe, Sir Henry Enfield . | 1833–1915 |
| Rose, John Holland . . | 1855–1942 |
| Rose-Innes, Sir James . . | 1855–1942 |
| Rosebery, Earl of. See Primrose, Archibald Philip . . . | 1847–1929 |
| Rosenhain, Walter . . . | 1875–1934 |
| Ross, Adrian, *pseudonym*. See Ropes, Arthur Reed. | |
| Ross, Sir Alexander George . | 1840–1910 |
| Ross, Sir (Edward) Denison . | 1871–1940 |
| Ross, Sir John . . . | 1829–1905 |
| Ross, Sir John . . . | 1853–1935 |
| Ross, Joseph Thorburn . | 1849–1903 |
| Ross, Martin, *pseudonym*. See Martin, Violet Florence . . | 1862–1915 |
| Ross, Sir Ronald . . . | 1857–1932 |
| Ross, William Stewart, 'Saladin' | 1844–1906 |
| Rosse, Earl of. See Parsons, Laurence . . . . | 1840–1908 |
| Rossetti, William Michael . . | 1829–1919 |
| Rothenstein, Sir William . . | 1872–1945 |
| Rothermere, Viscount. See Harmsworth, Harold Sidney . | 1868–1940 |
| Rothschild, Lionel Walter, Baron | 1868–1937 |
| Rothschild, Sir Nathan Meyer, Baron . . . . . | 1840–1915 |
| Round, John Horace . . | 1854–1928 |
| Rousby, William Wybert . . | 1835–1907 |
| Rouse, William Henry Denham | 1863–1950 |
| Routh, Edward John . . . | 1831–1907 |
| Rowe, Joshua Brooking . . | 1837–1908 |
| Rowlands, David, 'Dewi Môn' . | 1836–1907 |
| Rowlatt, Sir Sidney Arthur Taylor . . . . . | 1862–1945 |
| Rowntree, Joseph . . | 1836–1925 |
| Rowton, Baron. See Corry, Montagu William Lowry . | 1838–1903 |
| Roy, Camille Joseph . . | 1870–1943 |
| Royce, Sir (Frederick) Henry . | 1863–1933 |
| Royden, Sir Thomas, Baron . | 1871–1950 |
| Rudolf, Edward de Montjoie . | 1852–1933 |
| Ruggles-Brise, Sir Evelyn John . | 1857–1935 |
| Rumbold, Sir Horace . . | 1829–1913 |
| Rumbold, Sir Horace George Montagu . . . . | 1869–1941 |
| Runciman, Walter, Baron . | 1847–1937 |
| Runciman, Walter, Viscount Runciman of Doxford . . | 1870–1949 |
| Rundall, Francis Hornblow . | 1823–1908 |
| Rundle, Sir (Henry Macleod) Leslie . . . . . | 1856–1934 |
| Rusden, George William . . | 1819–1903 |
| Rushbrooke, James Henry . | 1870–1947 |
| Rushcliffe, Baron. See Betterton, Henry Bucknall . . | 1872–1949 |
| Russell, Arthur Oliver Villiers, Baron Ampthill . . . | 1869–1935 |
| Russell, Sir Charles . . . | 1863–1928 |
| Russell, Francis Xavier Joseph (Frank), Baron Russell of Killowen . . . . | 1867–1946 |
| Russell, George William, 'AE' . | 1867–1935 |
| Russell, Henry Chamberlaine . | 1836–1907 |
| Russell, Herbrand Arthur, Duke of Bedford . . . . | 1858–1940 |
| Russell, Mary Annette, Countess | 1866–1941 |
| Russell, Mary du Caurroy, Duchess of Bedford. See under Russell, Herbrand Arthur. | |
| Russell, Thomas O'Neill . . | 1828–1908 |
| Russell, Sir Walter Westley . | 1867–1949 |
| Russell, William Clark . . | 1844–1911 |
| Russell, Sir William Howard . | 1820–1907 |
| Russell, William James . . | 1830–1909 |
| Rutherford, Ernest, Baron Rutherford of Nelson . . | 1871–1937 |
| Rutherford, Mark, *pseudonym*. See White, William Hale . | 1831–1913 |
| Rutherford, William Gunion . | 1853–1907 |
| Rutland, Duke of. See Manners, (Lord) John James Robert . | 1818–1906 |
| Ryder, Charles Henry Dudley . | 1868–1945 |
| Rye, Maria Susan . . . | 1829–1903 |
| Rye, William Brenchley . . | 1818–1901 |
| Ryle, Herbert Edward . . | 1856–1925 |
| Ryle, John Alfred . . . | 1889–1950 |
| Ryrie, Sir Granville de Laune . | 1865–1937 |
| Sackville-West, Lionel Sackville, Baron Sackville . . | 1827–1908 |
| Sadler, Sir Michael Ernest . | 1861–1943 |
| St. Aldwyn, Earl. See Hicks Beach, Sir Michael Edward . | 1837–1916 |
| St. Davids, Viscount. See Philipps, Sir John Wynford . | 1860–1938 |
| St. Helier, Baron. See Jeune, Francis Henry . . . | 1843–1905 |
| St. John, Sir Spenser Buckingham . . . . . | 1825–1910 |
| St. John, Vane Ireton Shaftesbury. See under St. John, Sir Spenser Buckingham. | |
| St. Just, Baron. See Grenfell, Edward Charles . . . | 1870–1941 |
| Saintsbury, George Edward Bateman . . . . | 1845–1933 |
| Saklatvala, Shapurji . . | 1874–1936 |
| Saladin, *pseudonym*. See Ross, William Stewart . . . | 1844–1906 |
| Salaman, Charles Kensington . | 1814–1901 |

| | | | | |
|---|---|---|---|---|
| Stewart, Charles | . . . | 1840–1907 | Strutt, Robert John, Baron Ray- | |
| Stewart, Sir Halley . | . . | 1838–1937 | leigh . . . . . | 1875–1947 |
| Stewart, Isla . | . . . | 1855–1910 | Stuart-Jones, Sir Henry. See | |
| Stewart, James | . . . | 1831–1905 | Jones . . . . | 1867–1939 |
| Stewart, John Alexander . | . | 1846–1933 | Stubbs, Sir Reginald Edward . | 1876–1947 |
| Stewart, William Downie . | . | 1878–1949 | Stubbs, William . . . | 1825–1901 |
| Stewart, Sir William Houston . | 1822–1901 | Studd, Sir (John Edward) Kyn- | |
| Stiles, Sir Harold Jalland . | . | 1863–1946 | aston . . . . . | 1858–1944 |
| Still, Sir (George) Frederic | . | 1868–1941 | Sturdee, Sir Frederick Charles | |
| Stirling, Sir James . | . | 1836–1916 | Doveton . . . . | 1859–1925 |
| Stirling, James Hutchison | . | 1820–1909 | Sturgis, Julian Russell . . | 1848–1904 |
| Stockdale, Sir Frank Arthur | . | 1883–1949 | Sturt, George . . . . | 1863–1927 |
| Stocks, John Leofric | . | 1882–1937 | Sturt, Henry Gerard, Baron | |
| Stoddart, Andrew Ernest . | . | 1863–1915 | Alington . . . . | 1825–1904 |
| Stokes, Adrian | . . . | 1887–1927 | Sumner, Viscount. See Hamil- | |
| Stokes, Sir Frederick Wilfrid | | ton, John Andrew . . | 1859–1934 |
| Scott . . . . . | 1860–1927 | Sutherland, Alexander . . | 1852–1902 |
| Stokes, Sir George Gabriel | . | 1819–1903 | Sutherland, Sir Thomas . . | 1834–1922 |
| Stokes, Sir John | . . | 1825–1902 | Sutro, Alfred . . . . | 1863–1933 |
| Stokes, Whitley | . . . | 1830–1909 | Sutton, Sir Bertine Entwisle . | 1886–1946 |
| Stoll, Sir Oswald | . . | 1866–1942 | Sutton, Henry Septimus . . | 1825–1901 |
| Stone, Darwell | . . . | 1859–1941 | Sutton, Sir John Bland- . . | 1855–1936 |
| Stoney, Bindon Blood | . | 1828–1909 | Sutton, Martin John . . | 1850–1913 |
| Stoney, George Gerald | . | 1863–1942 | Swain, Joseph. . . . | 1820–1909 |
| Stoney, George Johnstone | . | 1826–1911 | Swan, John Macallan . . | 1847–1910 |
| Stopford, Sir Frederick William . | 1854–1929 | Swan, Sir Joseph Wilson . | 1828–1914 |
| Story, Robert Herbert . | . | 1835–1907 | Swann, Sir Oliver . . . | 1878–1948 |
| Story-Maskelyne, Mervyn Her- | | Swayne, Joseph Griffiths . . | 1819–1903 |
| bert Nevil . . . . | 1823–1911 | Swaythling, Baron. See Mon- | |
| Stout, George Frederick . . | 1860–1944 | tagu, Samuel . . . | 1832–1911 |
| Stout, Sir Robert . . | 1844–1930 | Sweet, Henry . . . . | 1845–1912 |
| Strachan, Douglas . . . | 1875–1950 | Swete, Henry Barclay . . | 1835–1917 |
| Strachan, John . . . | 1862–1907 | Swettenham, Sir Frank Athel- | |
| Strachan-Davidson, James Leigh | 1843–1916 | stan(e) . . . . | 1850–1946 |
| Strachey, Sir Arthur. See under | | Swift, Sir Rigby Philip Watson . | 1874–1937 |
| Strachey, Sir John. | | Swinburne, Algernon Charles . | 1837–1909 |
| Strachey, Sir Edward . . | 1812–1901 | Swinfen, Baron. See Eady, | |
| Strachey, Sir Edward, Baron | | Charles Swinfen . . . | 1851–1919 |
| Strachie . . . . | 1858–1936 | Swinton, Alan Archibald Camp- | |
| Strachey, (Giles) Lytton . . | 1880–1932 | bell . . . . . | 1863–1930 |
| Strachey, Sir John . . | 1823–1907 | Sydenham of Combe, Baron. See | |
| Strachey, John St. Loe . . | 1860–1927 | Clarke, George Sydenham . | 1848–1933 |
| Strachey, Sir Richard . . | 1817–1908 | Sykes, Sir Mark . . | 1879–1919 |
| Strachie, Baron. See Strachey, | | Sykes, Sir Percy Molesworth . | 1867–1945 |
| Sir Edward. | | Syme, David . . . . | 1827–1908 |
| Strakosch, Sir Henry . | 1871–1943 | Symes-Thompson, Edmund . | 1837–1906 |
| Strang, William . . . | 1859–1921 | Symonds, Sir Charters James . | 1852–1932 |
| Strangways, Arthur Henry Fox . | 1859–1948 | Symons, Arthur William . | 1865–1945 |
| Strathcarron, Baron. See Mac- | | Symons, William Christian . | 1845–1911 |
| pherson, (James) Ian . . | 1880–1937 | Synge, John Millington . . | 1871–1909 |
| Strathclyde, Baron. See Ure, | | | |
| Alexander . . . . | 1853–1928 | Tadema, Sir Lawrence Alma-. | |
| Strathcona, Baron. See Smith, | | See Alma-Tadema . . | 1836–1912 |
| Donald Alexander . . | 1820–1914 | Tagore, Sir Rabindranath. . | 1861–1941 |
| Strathmore and Kinghorne, Earl | | Tait, Frederick Guthrie. See | |
| of. See Bowes-Lyon, Claude | | under Tait, Peter Guthrie. | |
| George . . . . | 1855–1944 | Tait, James . . . . | 1863–1944 |
| Streeter, Burnett Hillman . | 1874–1937 | Tait, Peter Guthrie . . | 1831–1901 |
| Stretton, Hesba, *pseudonym*. See | | Tait, Sir (William Eric) Campbell | 1886–1946 |
| Smith, Sarah . . . | 1832–1911 | Talbot, Edward Stuart . . | 1844–1934 |
| Strickland, Gerald, Baron . | 1861–1940 | Talbot, Sir George John . | 1861–1938 |
| Strong, Eugénie . . | 1860–1943 | Tallack, William . . | 1831–1908 |
| Strong, Sir Samuel Henry. . | 1825–1909 | Tangye, Sir Richard . . | 1833–1906 |
| Strong, Sandford Arthur . | 1863–1904 | Tanner, Joseph Robson . | 1860–1931 |
| Strong, Thomas Banks . | 1861–1944 | Tarte, Joseph Israel. . | 1848–1907 |
| Struthers, Sir John . . | 1857–1925 | Taschereau, Sir Henri Elzéar . | 1836–1911 |
| Strutt, Edward Gerald . | 1854–1930 | Taschereau, Sir Henri Thomas . | 1841–1909 |
| Strutt, John William, Baron | | Tata, Sir Dorabji Jamsetji . | 1859–1932 |
| Rayleigh . . . . | 1842–1919 | Tata, Jamsetji Nasarwanji . | 1839–1904 |

| | | |
|---|---|---|
| Trotter, Wilfred Batten Lewis . | 1872–1939 | |
| Troubridge, Sir Ernest Charles Thomas | . . | 1862–1926 |
| Troubridge, Sir Thomas Hope . | 1895–1949 | |
| Troup, Robert Scott | . . | 1874–1939 |
| Truman, Edwin Thomas . | . | 1818–1905 |
| Tucker, Alfred Robert | . | 1849–1914 |
| Tucker, Sir Charles . | . | 1838–1935 |
| Tucker, Henry William | . | 1830–1902 |
| Tuke, Henry Scott . | . . | 1858–1929 |
| Tupper, Sir Charles . | . . | 1821–1915 |
| Tupper, Sir Charles Lewis. | . | 1848–1910 |
| Turner, Sir Ben | . . | 1863–1942 |
| Turner, Charles Edward . | . | 1831–1903 |
| Turner, Cuthbert Hamilton | . | 1860–1930 |
| Turner, Herbert Hall | . | 1861–1930 |
| Turner, James Smith | . | 1832–1904 |
| Turner, Walter James Redfern . | 1889–1946 | |
| Turner, Sir William . | . | 1832–1916 |
| Turnor, Christopher Hatton | . | 1873–1940 |
| Turpin, Edmund Hart | . | 1835–1907 |
| Tutton, Alfred Edwin Howard . | 1864–1938 | |
| Tweed, John | . . . | 1869–1933 |
| Tweedmouth, Baron. See Marjoribanks, Edward | . | 1849–1909 |
| Tweedsmuir, Baron. See Buchan, John . | . . . | 1875–1940 |
| Tyabji, Badruddin | . . | 1844–1906 |
| Tyler, Thomas | . . | 1826–1902 |
| Tylor, Sir Edward Burnett | . | 1832–1917 |
| Tylor, Joseph John . | . | 1851–1901 |
| Tynan, Katharine. See Hinkson | | 1861–1931 |
| Tyndale-Biscoe, Cecil Earle | . | 1863–1949 |
| Tyrrell, George | . . | 1861–1909 |
| Tyrrell, Robert Yelverton. | . | 1844–1914 |
| Tyrrell, William George, Baron . | | 1866–1947 |
| Tyrwhitt-Wilson, Sir Gerald Hugh, Baron Berners . | . | 1883–1950 |
| | | |
| Ullswater, Viscount. See Lowther, James William | . . | 1855–1949 |
| Underhill, Edward Bean . | . | 1813–1901 |
| Underhill, Evelyn (Mrs. Stuart Moore) | . . . | 1875–1941 |
| Unwin, Sir Raymond | . . | 1863–1940 |
| Unwin, William Cawthorne | . | 1838–1933 |
| Ure, Alexander, Baron Strathclyde . | . . . | 1853–1928 |
| Urwick, William | . . | 1826–1905 |
| Uthwatt, Augustus Andrewes, Baron . | . . . | 1879–1949 |
| | | |
| Vallance, William Fleming | . | 1827–1904 |
| Vanbrugh, Dame Irene | . | 1872–1949 |
| Vanbrugh, Violet . | . | 1867–1942 |
| Vandam, Albert Dresden . | . | 1843–1903 |
| Vane-Tempest-Stewart, Charles Stewart, Marquess of Londonderry . | . . . | 1852–1915 |
| Vane-Tempest-Stewart, Charles Stewart Henry, Marquess of Londonderry | . | 1878–1949 |
| Van Horne, Sir William Cornelius | | 1843–1915 |
| Vansittart, Edward Westby | . | 1818–1904 |
| Vaughan, Bernard John . | . | 1847–1922 |
| Vaughan, David James . | . | 1825–1905 |
| Vaughan, Herbert Alfred . | . | 1832–1903 |
| Vaughan, Kate | . . | 1852 ?–1903 |
| Vaughan, William Wyamar | . | 1865–1938 |

| | | |
|---|---|---|
| Veitch, Sir Harry James . | . | 1840–1924 |
| Veitch, James Herbert | . . | 1868–1907 |
| Venn, John . . . | . | 1834–1923 |
| Vereker, John Standish Surtees Prendergast, Viscount Gort . | 1886–1946 | |
| Verney, Margaret Maria, Lady . | 1844–1930 | |
| Vernon-Harcourt, Leveson Francis | . | 1839–1907 |
| Verrall, Arthur Woollgar . | . | 1851–1912 |
| Vestey, William, Baron . | . | 1859–1940 |
| Vezin, Hermann . | . | 1829–1910 |
| Vezin (formerly Mrs. Charles Young), Jane Elizabeth | . | 1827–1902 |
| Victoria Adelaide Mary Louise, Princess Royal of Great Britain and German Empress | . . | 1840–1901 |
| Victoria Alexandra Olga Mary, princess of Great Britain | . | 1868–1935 |
| Villiers, John Henry De, Baron. See De Villiers | . . . | 1842–1914 |
| Villiers, Margaret Elizabeth Child-, Countess of Jersey | . | 1849–1945 |
| Villiers, Victor Albert George Child-, Earl of Jersey | . | 1845–1915 |
| Vincent, Sir (Charles Edward) Howard | . . . | 1849–1908 |
| Vincent, Sir Edgar, Viscount D'Abernon . | . . | 1857–1941 |
| Vincent, James Edmund . | . | 1857–1909 |
| Vines, Sydney Howard | . | 1849–1934 |
| Vinogradoff, Sir Paul Gavrilovitch . | . . . | 1854–1925 |
| Von Hügel, Friedrich, Baron of the Holy Roman Empire | . | 1852–1925 |
| Voysey, Charles | . . | 1828–1912 |
| Voysey, Charles Francis Annesley | . . . . | 1857–1941 |
| | | |
| Wace, Henry . | . . . | 1836–1924 |
| Waddell, Lawrence Augustine (later Austine) | . . | 1854–1938 |
| Wade, Sir Willoughby Francis . | 1827–1906 | |
| Wadsworth, Edward Alexander | | 1889–1949 |
| Waggett, Philip Napier | . | 1862–1939 |
| Wain, Louis William | . | 1860–1939 |
| Wake-Walker, Sir William Frederic | . . . | 1888–1945 |
| Wakefield, Charles Cheers, Viscount . | . . . | 1859–1941 |
| Wakley, Thomas. See under Wakley, Thomas Henry. | | |
| Wakley, Thomas Henry . | . | 1821–1907 |
| Walcot, William | . . | 1874–1943 |
| Walker, Sir Byron Edmund | . | 1848–1924 |
| Walker, Sir Emery . | . | 1851–1933 |
| Walker, Ernest | . . | 1870–1949 |
| Walker, Frederic John | . | 1896–1944 |
| Walker, Frederick William | . | 1830–1910 |
| Walker, Sir Frederick William Edward Forestier-. See Forestier-Walker . | . . | 1844–1910 |
| Walker, Sir James . | . | 1863–1935 |
| Walker, Sir Mark | . . | 1827–1902 |
| Walker, Sir Norman Purvis . | 1862–1942 | |
| Walker, Sir Samuel . | . | 1832–1911 |
| Walker, Vyell Edward . | . | 1837–1906 |
| Walker, Sir William Frederic Wake-. See Wake-Walker . | 1888–1945 | |
| Walkley, Arthur Bingham | . | 1855–1926 |

| | |
|---|---|
| Westcott, Brooke Foss . . | 1825–1901 |
| Wester Wemyss, Baron. See | |
| Wemyss, Rosslyn Erskine . | 1864–1933 |
| Westlake, John . . . | 1828–1913 |
| Westland, Sir James . . | 1842–1903 |
| Weston, Agnes Elizabeth . . | 1840–1918 |
| Weston, Sir Aylmer Gould Hunter- . . . . | 1864–1940 |
| Weston, Frank . . . | 1871–1924 |
| Wet, Christiaan Rudolph De. See De Wet . . . . | 1854–1922 |
| Weyman, Stanley John . . | 1855–1928 |
| Weymouth, Richard Francis . | 1822–1902 |
| Wharton, Sir William James Lloyd . . . . . | 1843–1905 |
| Wheatley, John . . . | 1869–1930 |
| Wheeler, Sir William Ireland de Courcy . . . . | 1879–1943 |
| Wheelhouse, Claudius Galen . | 1826–1909 |
| Whibley, Charles . . . | 1859–1930 |
| Whibley, Leonard . . . | 1863–1941 |
| Whistler, James Abbott McNeill | 1834–1903 |
| Whistler, Reginald John (Rex) | 1905–1944 |
| White, Sir (Cyril) Brudenell (Bingham) . . . . | 1876–1940 |
| White, Sir George Stuart . . | 1835–1912 |
| White, Henry Julian . . | 1859–1934 |
| White, John Campbell, Baron Overtoun . . . . | 1843–1908 |
| White, William Hale, novelist under the pseudonym of Mark Rutherford . . . . | 1831–1913 |
| White, Sir William Hale-. See Hale-White . . . . | 1857–1949 |
| White, Sir William Henry . | 1845–1913 |
| Whitehead, Alfred North . . | 1861–1947 |
| Whitehead, Robert . . . | 1823–1905 |
| Whiteing, Richard . . . | 1840–1928 |
| Whiteley, William . . . | 1831–1907 |
| Whiteway, Sir William Vallance | 1828–1908 |
| Whitla, Sir William . . . | 1851–1933 |
| Whitley, John Henry . . | 1866–1935 |
| Whitley, William Thomas. . | 1858–1942 |
| Whitman, Alfred Charles . . | 1860–1910 |
| Whitmore, Sir George Stoddart . | 1830–1903 |
| Whitney, James Pounder . . | 1857–1939 |
| Whitten Brown, Sir Arthur. See Brown . . . . | 1886–1948 |
| Whitty, Dame Mary Louise (May) (1865–1948). See under Webster, Benjamin . . | 1864–1947 |
| Whitworth, William Allen . | 1840–1905 |
| Whymper, Edward . . . | 1840–1911 |
| Whymper, Josiah Wood . . | 1813–1903 |
| Whyte, Alexander . . . | 1836–1921 |
| Wickham, Edward Charles . | 1834–1910 |
| Wiggins, Joseph . . . | 1832–1905 |
| Wigham, John Richardson . | 1829–1906 |
| Wigram, Woolmore . . . | 1831–1907 |
| Wilberforce, Ernest Roland . | 1840–1907 |
| Wild, (John Robert) Francis . | 1873–1939 |
| Wilding, Anthony Frederick . | 1883–1915 |
| Wilkie, Sir David Percival Dalbreck . . . . . | 1882–1938 |
| Wilkins, Augustus Samuel . | 1843–1905 |
| Wilkins, William Henry . | 1860–1905 |
| Wilkins, Ellen Cicely . . | 1891–1947 |
| Wilkinson, George Howard . | 1833–1907 |
| Wilkinson, (Henry) Spenser . | 1853–1937 |

| | |
|---|---|
| Wilkinson, Sir Nevile Rodwell . | 1869–1940 |
| Wilkinson, Norman . . . | 1882–1934 |
| Wilks, Sir Samuel . . . | 1824–1911 |
| Will, John Shiress . . . | 1840–1910 |
| Willcocks, Sir James . . | 1857–1926 |
| Willcox, Sir William Henry . | 1870–1941 |
| Willes, Sir George Ommanney . | 1823–1901 |
| Willett, William . . . | 1856–1915 |
| Williams, Alfred . . . | 1832–1905 |
| Williams, (Arthur Frederic) Basil | 1867–1950 |
| Williams, Charles . . . | 1838–1904 |
| Williams, Charles Hanson Greville . . . . . | 1829–1910 |
| Williams, Charles Walter Stansby | 1886–1945 |
| Williams, Sir Edward Leader . | 1828–1910 |
| Williams, Sir George . . | 1821–1905 |
| Williams, Hugh . . . | 1843–1911 |
| Williams, John Carvell . . | 1821–1907 |
| Williams, Sir John Fischer . | 1870–1947 |
| Williams, Norman Powell . . | 1883–1943 |
| Williams, Sir Roland Bowdler Vaughan . . . . | 1838–1916 |
| Williams, Rowland, 'Hwfa Môn' | 1823–1905 |
| Williams, Watkin Hezekiah, 'Watcyn Wyn' . . . | 1844–1905 |
| Williams-Freeman, John Peere . | 1858–1943 |
| Williamson, Alexander William . | 1824–1904 |
| Willingdon, Marquess of. See Freeman-Thomas, Freeman . | 1866–1941 |
| Willis, Henry . . . . | 1821–1901 |
| Willis, William . . . | 1835–1911 |
| Willock, Henry Davis . . | 1830–1903 |
| Willoughby, Digby . . . | 1845–1901 |
| Wills, Sir George Alfred . . | 1854–1928 |
| Wills, William Henry, Baron Winterstoke. . . . | 1830–1911 |
| Wilmot, Sir Sainthill Eardley- . . | 1852–1929 |
| Wilson, Sir Arnold Talbot . | 1884–1940 |
| Wilson, Arthur. See under Wilson, Charles Henry, Baron Nunburnholme. . . . | |
| Wilson, Sir Arthur Knyvet . | 1842–1921 |
| Wilson, Charles Henry, Baron Nunburnholme . . . | 1833–1907 |
| Wilson, Sir Charles Rivers . | 1831–1916 |
| Wilson, Sir Charles Robert . | 1863–1904 |
| Wilson, Sir Charles William . | 1836–1905 |
| Wilson, Edward Adrian . | 1872–1912 |
| Wilson, George Fergusson. . | 1822–1902 |
| Wilson, Sir Gerald Hugh Tyrwhitt-, Baron Berners. See Tyrwhitt-Wilson . . . | 1883–1950 |
| Wilson, Sir Henry Hughes . | 1864–1922 |
| Wilson, Henry Schütz . . | 1824–1902 |
| Wilson, Herbert Wrigley . | 1866–1940 |
| Wilson, Sir Jacob . . . | 1836–1905 |
| Wilson, James Maurice . . | 1836–1931 |
| Wilson, John Cook . . . | 1849–1915 |
| Wilson, John Dove . . . | 1833–1908 |
| Wilson, Joseph Havelock . . | 1858–1929 |
| Wilson, Samuel Alexander Kinnier . . . . . | 1874–1937 |
| Wilson, Sir Samuel Herbert . | 1873–1950 |
| Wilson, William Edward . . | 1851–1908 |
| Wimborne, Viscount. See Guest, Ivor Churchill . . . | 1873–1939 |
| Wimshurst, James . . . | 1832–1903 |
| Windus, William Lindsay . . | 1822–1907 |
| Wingate, Orde Charles . . | 1903–1944 |

PRINTED IN GREAT BRITAIN
AT THE UNIVERSITY PRESS, OXFORD
BY VIVIAN RIDLER
PRINTER TO THE UNIVERSITY